Official 1994
National Football League

# Record & Fact Book

PARTRIDGE PRESS

LONDON · NEW YORK · TORONTO · SYDNEY · AUCKLAND

A National Football League Book.

# NATIONAL FOOTBALL LEAGUE, 1994

410 Park Avenue, New York, N.Y. 10022 (212) 758-1500

**Commissioner:** Paul Tagliabue
**President:** Neil Austrian

## LEAGUE OFFICE

**Executive Vice President and League Counsel:** Jay Moyer
**Vice President-Communications & Government Affairs:** Joe Browne
**Vice President-Business Development:** Roger Goodell
**Vice President-Broadcasting & Productions:** Val Pinchbeck, Jr.
**Chief Financial Officer:** Tom Spock
**Executive Director of Special Events:** Jim Steeg
**Vice President-Internal Audit:** Tom Sullivan

### COMMUNICATIONS

**Director of Communications:** Greg Aiello
**Director of International Public Relations:** Pete Abitante
**Director of Information, AFC:** Leslie Hammond
**Director of Information, NFC:** Reggie Roberts

### BROADCASTING

**Director of Broadcasting Services:** Dick Maxwell
**Director of Broadcasting Research:** Joe Ferreira
**Assistant Director of Broadcasting/Productions:** Nancy Behar

### OPERATIONS

**Director of Club Relations/Stadium Operations:** Joe Ellis
**Director of Game Operations/League Secretary:** Jan Van Duser
**Director of Football Development:** Gene Washington
**Assistant Director of Game Operations:** Tim Davey

### OFFICIATING

**Director of Officiating:** Jerry Seeman
**Assistant Director of Officiating:** Jack Reader
**Supervisor of Officials:** Leo Miles
**Supervisor of Officials:** Ron DeSouza

### ADMINISTRATION

**Director of Administration:** John Buzzeo
**Comptroller:** Joe Siclare

### SECURITY

**Director of Security:** Warren Welsh
**Assistant Director of Security:** Charles Jackson, Jr.

## NFL ENTERPRISES

**President:** Ron Bernard
**Vice President-Marketing & Sales:** Tola Murphy-Baran
**Vice President-Worldwide Distribution:** Bill Moses

## NFL FILMS

**President:** Steve Sabol
**Vice President-Television Sponsorships:** John Collins
**Vice President-In Charge of Production:** Jay Gerber
**Vice President-Video Operations:** Jeff Howard
**Vice President-Editor-in-Chief:** Bob Ryan
**Vice President-Special Projects:** Phil Tuckett
**Vice President-Finance and Administration:** Barry Wolper

## NFL MANAGEMENT COUNCIL

**Executive Vice President-Labor Relations/Chairman NFLMC:** Harold Henderson
**Vice President-General Counsel:** Dennis Curran
**Vice President-Operations & Compliance:** Peter Ruocco
**Director of Player Programs:** Lem Burnham
**Director of Player Personnel/Football Operations:** Joel Bussert
**Director of Compliance:** William Duffy
**Director of Labor Operations:** Peter Hadhazy

## NFL PROPERTIES

**Vice President-Worldwide Retail Licensing:** Jim Connelly
**Vice President-Business Development/Special Events:** Don Garber
**Vice President-Marketing/Sales:** Jim Schwebel
**Vice President-Creative Services:** John Wiebusch

**Vice President-Sales:** Roger Atkin
**Vice President-Creative Director:** Bruce Burke
**Vice President-Legal/Business Affairs and General Counsel:** Gary Gertzog
**Vice President and Chief Financial Officer:** Ken Hall
**Vice President-Player Relations and Retail/Club Marketing:** Mark Holtzman

**Cover Photograph by James D. Smith.**


Printed in the United States of America.

A National Football League Book.
Compiled by the NFL Communications Department and Seymour Siwoff, Elias Sports Bureau.
Edited by Chris Hardart, NFL Communications Department and Chuck Garrity, Jr., NFLP Creative Services.

Statistics by Elias Sports Bureau.
Produced by NFL Properties, Inc., Creative Services Division.

Published in the U.K. 1994 by Partridge Press
a division of Transworld Publishers Ltd.
61-63 Uxbridge Road, London, W5 5SA



Published in the U.S.A. by Workman Publishing Company, New York.

A catalogue record of this book is available from the British Library.

# INDEX

# 1994 SCHEDULE AND NOTE CALENDAR

(All times local except Barcelona, Berlin, Mexico City, and Tokyo which are EDT.)
Nationally televised games in parentheses.

| | | | |
|---|---|---|---|
| **PRESEASON/FIRST WEEK** | **Saturday, July 30** | Pro Football Hall of Fame Game at Canton, Ohio | |
| | | Atlanta ____ vs. San Diego ____ | (ABC) 12:00 |
| | | Miami ____ at New York Giants ____ | 8:00 |
| | **Sunday, July 31** | American Bowl at Barcelona | |
| | | Denver ____ vs. Los Angeles Raiders ____ | (NBC) 1:00 * |
| | | Houston ____ at Kansas City ____ | 8:00 |
| | | Minnesota ____ at Dallas ____ | 8:00 |
| | **Friday, August 5** | New Orleans ____ at New England ____ | 8:00 |
| | | New York Jets ____ at Detroit ____ | 7:30 |
| | | Philadelphia ____ at Chicago ____ | 7:00 |
| | | San Francisco ____ at Arizona ____ | 6:30 |
| | | Seattle ____ at Indianapolis ____ | 7:30 |
| | **Saturday, August 6** | American Bowl at Tokyo (August 7) | |
| | | Kansas City ____ vs. Minnesota ____ | (ESPN) 10:00 ** |
| | | Atlanta ____ at Denver ____ | 7:00 |
| | | Cincinnati ____ at Tampa Bay ____ | 7:30 |
| | | Cleveland ____ at New York Giants ____ | 8:00 |
| | | Houston ____ vs. San Diego ____ at San Antonio, Tex. | 7:00 |
| | | Los Angeles Rams ____ vs. Green Bay ____ at Madison, Wis. | 12:00 |
| | | Pittsburgh ____ at Miami ____ | 8:00 |
| | **Sunday, August 7** | Los Angeles Raiders ____ at Dallas ____ | 8:00 |
| | **Monday, August 8** | Washington ____ at Buffalo ____ | (ABC) 8:00 |

* Barcelona game actual kickoff 7:00 P.M., July 31.
** Tokyo game actual kickoff 11:00 A.M., August 7.

| | | | |
|---|---|---|---|
| **PRESEASON/SECOND WEEK** | **Friday, August 12** | Denver ____ at San Francisco ____ | (FOX) 5:00 |
| | | Buffalo ____ at Atlanta ____ | 7:00 |
| | | Kansas City ____ at Washington ____ | 8:00 |
| | **Saturday, August 13** | American Bowl at Berlin | |
| | | New York Giants ____ vs. San Diego ____ | (NBC) 1:30 † |
| | | Chicago ____ at Arizona ____ | 6:00 |
| | | Detroit ____ at Cleveland ____ | 7:30 |
| | | Indianapolis ____ at Cincinnati ____ | 7:30 |
| | | Los Angeles Raiders ____ at Pittsburgh ____ | 6:00 |
| | | Miami ____ vs. Green Bay ____ at Milwaukee | 7:00 |
| | | New England ____ at Los Angeles Rams ____ | 7:00 |
| | | New Orleans ____ at Minnesota ____ | 7:00 |
| | | New York Jets ____ at Philadelphia ____ | 7:30 |
| | | Tampa Bay ____ at Seattle ____ | 6:00 |
| | **Monday, August 15** | American Bowl at Mexico City | |
| | | Dallas ____ vs. Houston ____ | (ABC) 9:00 †† |

† Berlin game actual kickoff 7:30 P.M., August 13.
†† Mexico City game actual kickoff 7:00 P.M., August 15.

| | | | |
|---|---|---|---|
| **PRESEASON/THIRD WEEK** | **Thursday, August 18** | San Francisco ____ at San Diego ____ | (TNT) 5:00 |
| | | Washington ____ at New England ____ | 7:00 |
| | **Friday, August 19** | Arizona ____ at Detroit ____ | 7:30 |
| | | Atlanta ____ at Cleveland ____ | 7:30 |
| | | Green Bay ____ at New Orleans ____ | (FOX) 7:00 |
| | **Saturday, August 20** | Buffalo ____ vs. Houston ____ at San Antonio, Tex. | (ESPN) 7:00 |
| | | Cincinnati ____ at Philadelphia ____ | 7:30 |
| | | Indianapolis ____ at Pittsburgh ____ | 6:00 |
| | | Los Angeles Raiders ____ at Los Angeles Rams ____ | 7:00 |
| | | Minnesota ____ at Seattle ____ | 7:00 |
| | | New York Giants ____ at New York Jets ____ | 8:00 |
| | | Tampa Bay ____ at Miami ____ | 8:00 |
| | **Sunday, August 21** | Denver ____ at Dallas ____ | (TNT) 7:00 |
| | **Monday, August 22** | Chicago ____ at Kansas City ____ | (ABC) 7:00 |

| | | | |
|---|---|---|---|
| **PRESEASON/FOURTH WEEK** | **Thursday, August 25** | Arizona ____ at Denver ____ | 7:00 |
| | | Cleveland ____ at Indianapolis ____ | 7:30 |
| | | Dallas ____ at New Orleans ____ | (ESPN) 7:00 |
| | | Los Angeles Rams ____ at San Diego ____ | 7:00 |
| | **Friday, August 26** | Detroit ____ at Cincinnati ____ | 7:30 |
| | | Kansas City ____ at Buffalo ____ | (TNT) 8:00 |
| | | Miami ____ at Minnesota ____ | 7:00 |
| | | New England ____ at Green Bay ____ | 7:00 |
| | | New York Jets ____ at Tampa Bay ____ | 7:30 |
| | | Philadelphia ____ at Atlanta ____ | 7:00 |
| | | Pittsburgh ____ at Washington ____ | 8:00 |
| | | Seattle ____ at San Francisco ____ | 6:00 |
| | **Saturday, August 27** | Los Angeles Raiders ____ at Houston ____ | (NBC) 1:00 |
| | | New York Giants ____ at Chicago ____ | (FOX) 7:00 |
| **FIRST WEEK** | **Sunday, September 4 (FOX-TV National Weekend)** | Arizona 12 at Los Angeles Rams 14 | 1:00 |
| | | Atlanta 28 at Detroit 31 (OT) | 1:00 |
| | | Cleveland 28 at Cincinnati 20 | 1:00 |
| | | Dallas 26 at Pittsburgh 9 | 4:00 |
| | | Houston 21 at Indianapolis 45 | 12:00 |
| | | Kansas City 30 at New Orleans 17 | 12:00 |
| | | Minnesota 10 at Green Bay 16 | 12:00 |
| | | New England 35 at Miami 39 | 4:00 |
| | | New York Jets 23 at Buffalo 3 | 4:00 |
| | | Philadelphia 23 at New York Giants 28 | 1:00 |
| | | Seattle 28 at Washington 7 | 1:00 |
| | | Tampa Bay 9 at Chicago 21 | 12:00 |
| | **Sunday Night** | San Diego 37 at Denver 34 | (TNT) 6:00 |
| | **Monday, September 5** | Los Angeles Raiders 14 at San Francisco 44 | (ABC) 6:00 |
| **SECOND WEEK** | **Sunday, September 11 (NBC-TV National Weekend)** | Buffalo 38 at New England 35 | 1:00 |
| | | Cincinnati 10 at San Diego 27 | 1:00 |
| | | Denver 22 at New York Jets 25 (OT) | 4:00 |
| | | Detroit 3 at Minnesota 10 | 12:00 |
| | | Houston 17 at Dallas 20 | 3:00 |
| | | Indianapolis 10 at Tampa Bay 24 | 1:00 |
| | | Los Angeles Rams 13 at Atlanta 31 | 1:00 |
| | | Miami 24 vs. Green Bay 14 at Milwaukee | 12:00 |
| | | Pittsburgh 17 at Cleveland 10 | 1:00 |
| | | San Francisco 17 at Kansas City 24 | 12:00 |
| | | Seattle 38 at Los Angeles Raiders 9 | 1:00 |
| | | Washington 38 at New Orleans 24 | 3:00 |
| | **Sunday Night** | New York Giants 20 at Arizona 17 | (TNT) 5:00 |
| | **Monday, September 12** | Chicago 22 at Philadelphia 30 | (ABC) 9:00 |
| **THIRD WEEK** | **Sunday, September 18 (FOX-TV National Weekend)** | Arizona 0 at Cleveland 32 | 1:00 |
| | | Buffalo 15 at Houston 7 | 12:00 |
| | | Green Bay 7 at Philadelphia 13 | 1:00 |
| | | Indianapolis 21 at Pittsburgh 31 | 1:00 |
| | | Los Angeles Raiders 48 at Denver 16 | 2:00 |
| | | Minnesota 42 at Chicago 14 | 12:00 |
| | | New England 31 at Cincinnati 28 | 1:00 |
| | | New Orleans 9 at Tampa Bay 7 | 1:00 |
| | | New York Jets 14 at Miami 28 | 1:00 |
| | | San Diego 24 at Seattle 10 | 1:00 |
| | | San Francisco 34 at Los Angeles Rams 19 | 1:00 |
| | | Washington 23 at New York Giants 31 | 4:00 |
| | **Sunday Night** | Kansas City 30 at Atlanta 10 | (TNT) 8:00 |
| | **Monday, September 19** | Detroit 20 at Dallas 17 | (ABC) 8:00 |

## 1994 SCHEDULE AND NOTE CALENDAR

**FOURTH WEEK**
**Open Dates: Arizona, Dallas, New York Giants, Philadelphia**

| | | |
|---|---|---|
| **Sunday, September 25 (NBC-TV National Weekend)** | Atlanta 27 at Washington 20 | 1:00 |
| | Cincinnati 13 at Houston 20 | 3:00 |
| | Cleveland 21 at Indianapolis 14 | 12:00 |
| | Los Angeles Rams 16 at Kansas City 0 | 12:00 |
| | Miami 35 at Minnesota 38 | 12:00 |
| | New England 23 at Detroit 17 | 4:00 |
| | New Orleans 13 at San Francisco 24 | 1:00 |
| | Pittsburgh 13 at Seattle 30 | 1:00 |
| | San Diego 26 at Los Angeles Raiders 24 | 1:00 |
| | Tampa Bay 3 at Green Bay 30 | 12:00 |
| **Sunday Night** | Chicago 19 at New York Jets 7 | (TNT) 8:00 |
| **Monday, September 26** | Denver 20 at Buffalo 27 | (ABC) 9:00 |

**FIFTH WEEK**
**Open Dates: Denver, Kansas City, Los Angeles Raiders, San Diego**

| | | |
|---|---|---|
| **Sunday, October 2 (FOX-TV National Weekend)** | Atlanta 8 at Los Angeles Rams 5 | 1:00 |
| | Buffalo 13 at Chicago 20 | 3:00 |
| | Dallas 34 at Washington 7 | 1:00 |
| | Detroit 14 at Tampa Bay 24 | 1:00 |
| | Green Bay 16 at New England 17 | 1:00 |
| | Minnesota 7 at Arizona 17 | 1:00 |
| | New York Giants 22 at New Orleans 27 | 3:00 |
| | New York Jets 7 at Cleveland 27 | 1:00 |
| | Philadelphia 40 at San Francisco 8 | 1:00 |
| | Seattle 15 at Indianapolis 17 | 12:00 |
| **Sunday Night** | Miami 23 at Cincinnati 7 | (TNT) 8:00 |
| **Monday, October 3** | Houston 14 at Pittsburgh 30 | (ABC) 9:00 |

**SIXTH WEEK**
**Open Dates: Cincinnati, Cleveland, Houston, Pittsburgh**

| | | |
|---|---|---|
| **Sunday, October 9 (NBC-TV National Weekend)** | Arizona 3 at Dallas 38 | 3:00 |
| | Denver 16 at Seattle 9 | 1:00 |
| | Indianapolis 6 at New York Jets 16 | 1:00 |
| | Kansas City 6 at San Diego 20 | 1:00 |
| | Los Angeles Raiders 21 at New England 17 | 4:00 |
| | Los Angeles Rams 17 at Green Bay 24 | 12:00 |
| | Miami 11 at Buffalo 21 | 1:00 |
| | New Orleans 7 at Chicago 17 | 12:00 |
| | San Francisco 27 at Detroit 21 | 1:00 |
| | Tampa Bay 13 at Atlanta 34 | 1:00 |
| **Sunday Night** | Washington 17 at Philadelphia 21 | (TNT) 8:00 |
| **Monday, October 10** | Minnesota 27 at New York Giants 10 | (ABC) 9:00 |

**SEVENTH WEEK**
**Open Dates: Chicago, Detroit, Green Bay, Minnesota, Seattle, Tampa Bay**

| | | |
|---|---|---|
| **Thursday, October 13** | Cleveland 11 at Houston 8 | (TNT) 7:00 |
| **Sunday, October 16 (FOX-TV National Weekend)** | Arizona 19 at Washington 16 (OT) | 1:00 |
| | Cincinnati 10 at Pittsburgh 14 | 1:00 |
| | Indianapolis 27 at Buffalo 17 | 1:00 |
| | Los Angeles Raiders 17 at Miami 20 (OT) | 1:00 |
| | New England 17 at New York Jets 24 | 1:00 |
| | New York Giants 10 at Los Angeles Rams 17 | 1:00 |
| | Philadelphia 13 at Dallas 24 | 3:00 |
| | San Diego 36 at New Orleans 22 | 3:00 |
| | San Francisco 42 at Atlanta 3 | 1:00 |
| **Monday, October 17** | Kansas City 31 at Denver 28 | (ABC) 7:00 |

**EIGHTH WEEK**
**Open Dates: Buffalo, Miami, New England, New York Jets**

| | | |
|---|---|---|
| **Thursday, October 20** | Green Bay 10 at Minnesota 13 (OT) | (TNT) 7:00 |
| **Sunday, October 23 (FOX-TV National Weekend)** | Atlanta 17 at Los Angeles Raiders 30 | 1:00 |
| | Chicago 16 at Detroit 21 | 1:00 |
| | Cincinnati 13 at Cleveland 37 | 1:00 |
| | Dallas 28 at Arizona 21 | 1:00 |
| | Denver 20 at San Diego 15 | 1:00 |
| | Los Angeles Rams 34 at New Orleans 37 | 12:00 |
| | Pittsburgh 10 at New York Giants 6 | 1:00 |
| | Seattle 23 at Kansas City 38 | 12:00 |
| | Tampa Bay 16 at San Francisco 41 | 1:00 |
| | Washington 41 at Indianapolis 27 | 12:00 |
| **Monday, October 24** | Houston 6 at Philadelphia 21 | (ABC) 9:00 |

| | | |
|---|---|---|
| **NINTH WEEK** Open Dates: Atlanta, Los Angeles Rams, New Orleans, San Francisco | | |
| **Sunday, October 30** (NBC-TV National Weekend) | Cleveland 14 at Denver 26 | 2:00 |
| | Dallas 23 at Cincinnati 20 | 1:00 |
| | Detroit 28 at New York Giants 25 (OT) | 1:00 |
| | Houston 14 at Los Angeles Raiders 17 | 1:00 |
| | Kansas City 10 at Buffalo 44 | 1:00 |
| | Miami 23 at New England 3 | 1:00 |
| | Minnesota 36 at Tampa Bay 13 | 4:00 |
| | New York Jets 25 at Indianapolis 28 | 4:00 |
| | Philadelphia 31 at Washington 29 | 1:00 |
| | Seattle 15 at San Diego 35 | 1:00 |
| **Sunday Night** | Pittsburgh 17 at Arizona 20 (OT) | (TNT) 6:00 |
| **Monday, October 31** | Green Bay 33 at Chicago 6 | (ABC) 8:00 |

| | | |
|---|---|---|
| **TENTH WEEK** | | |
| **Sunday, November 6** (NBC-TV National Weekend) | Arizona 7 at Philadelphia 17 | 4:00 |
| | Buffalo 17 at New York Jets 22 | 4:00 |
| | Chicago 20 at Tampa Bay 6 | 1:00 |
| | Cincinnati 20 at Seattle 17 (OT) | 1:00 |
| | Denver 20 at Los Angeles Rams 27 | 1:00 |
| | Detroit 30 vs. Green Bay 38 at Milwaukee | 12:00 |
| | Indianapolis 21 at Miami 22 | 1:00 |
| | New England 6 at Cleveland 13 | 1:00 |
| | New Orleans 20 at Minnesota 21 | 12:00 |
| | Pittsburgh 12 at Houston 9 | 12:00 |
| | San Diego 9 at Atlanta 10 | 1:00 |
| | San Francisco 37 at Washington 22 | 1:00 |
| **Sunday Night** | Los Angeles Raiders 3 at Kansas City 13 | (ESPN) 7:00 |
| **Monday, November 7** | New York Giants 10 at Dallas 38 | (ABC) 8:00 |

| | | |
|---|---|---|
| **ELEVENTH WEEK** Open Dates: Indianapolis, Washington | | |
| **Sunday, November 13** (FOX-TV National Weekend) | Arizona 10 at New York Giants 9 | 1:00 |
| | Atlanta 32 at New Orleans 33 | 12:00 |
| | Chicago 17 at Miami 14 | 1:00 |
| | Cleveland 26 at Philadelphia 7 | 1:00 |
| | Dallas 14 at San Francisco 21 | 1:00 |
| | Houston 31 at Cincinnati 34 | 1:00 |
| | Los Angeles Raiders 20 at Los Angeles Rams 17 | 1:00 |
| | Minnesota 20 at New England 26 (OT) | 1:00 |
| | New York Jets 10 at Green Bay 17 | 3:00 |
| | San Diego 14 at Kansas City 13 | 12:00 |
| | Seattle 10 at Denver 17 | 2:00 |
| **Sunday Night** | Tampa Bay 9 at Detroit 14 | (ESPN) 8:00 |
| **Monday, November 14** | Buffalo 10 at Pittsburgh 23 | (ABC) 9:00 |

| | | |
|---|---|---|
| **TWELFTH WEEK** | | |
| **Sunday, November 20** (FOX-TV National Weekend) | Atlanta 28 at Denver 32 | 2:00 |
| | Cleveland 13 at Kansas City 20 | 12:00 |
| | Detroit 10 at Chicago 20 | 12:00 |
| | Green Bay 20 at Buffalo 29 | 1:00 |
| | Indianapolis 17 at Cincinnati 13 | 1:00 |
| | Miami 13 at Pittsburgh 16 (OT) | 1:00 |
| | New Orleans 19 at Los Angeles Raiders 24 | 1:00 |
| | New York Jets 31 at Minnesota 21 | 3:00 |
| | Philadelphia 6 at Arizona 12 | 2:00 |
| | San Diego 17 at New England 23 | 1:00 |
| | Tampa Bay 21 at Seattle 22 | 1:00 |
| | Washington 7 at Dallas 31 | 12:00 |
| **Sunday Night** | Los Angeles Rams 27 at San Francisco 31 | (ESPN) 5:00 |
| **Monday, November 21** | New York Giants 13 at Houston 10 | (ABC) 8:00 |

# 1994 SCHEDULE AND NOTE CALENDAR

| | | | |
|---|---|---|---|
| **THIRTEENTH WEEK** | **Thursday, November 24** | Buffalo 21 at Detroit 35 | (NBC) 12:30 |
| | | Green Bay 31 at Dallas 42 | (FOX) 3:00 |
| | **Sunday, November 27** | Chicago 19 at Arizona 16 (OT) | 2:00 |
| | **(NBC-TV National Weekend)** | Cincinnati 13 at Denver 15 | 2:00 |
| | | Houston 10 at Cleveland 34 | 1:00 |
| | | Kansas City 9 at Seattle 10 | 1:00 |
| | | Los Angeles Rams 17 at San Diego 31 | 1:00 |
| | | Miami 28 at New York Jets 24 | 1:00 |
| | | New York Giants 21 at Washington 19 | 4:00 |
| | | Philadelphia 21 at Atlanta 28 | 1:00 |
| | | Pittsburgh 21 at Los Angeles Raiders 3 | 1:00 |
| | | Tampa Bay 20 at Minnesota 17 (OT) | 12:00 |
| | **Sunday Night** | New England 12 at Indianapolis 10 | (ESPN) 8:00 |
| | **Monday, November 28** | San Francisco 35 at New Orleans 14 | (ABC) 8:00 |
| **FOURTEENTH WEEKEND** | **Thursday, December 1** | Chicago 27 at Minnesota 33 (OT) | (ESPN) 7:00 |
| | **Sunday, December 4** | Arizona 30 at Houston 12 | 3:00 |
| | **(FOX-TV National Weekend)** | Atlanta 14 at San Francisco 50 | 1:00 |
| | | Dallas 31 at Philadelphia 19 | 1:00 |
| | | Denver 20 at Kansas City 17 (OT) | 3:00 |
| | | Green Bay 31 at Detroit 34 | 1:00 |
| | | Indianapolis 31 at Seattle 19 | 1:00 |
| | | New Orleans 31 at Los Angeles Rams 15 | 1:00 |
| | | New York Giants 16 at Cleveland 13 | 4:00 |
| | | New York Jets 13 at New England 24 | 1:00 |
| | | Pittsburgh 38 at Cincinnati 15 | 1:00 |
| | | Washington 21 at Tampa Bay 26 | 1:00 |
| | **Sunday Night** | Buffalo 42 at Miami 31 | (ESPN) 8:00 |
| | **Monday, December 5** | Los Angeles Raiders 24 at San Diego 17 | (ABC) 6:00 |
| **FIFTEENTH WEEK** | **Saturday, December 10** | Cleveland 19 at Dallas 14 | (NBC) 3:00 |
| | | Detroit 18 at New York Jets 7 | (FOX) 12:30 |
| | **Sunday, December 11** | Chicago 3 at Green Bay 40 | 12:00 |
| | **(FOX-TV National Weekend)** | Cincinnati 20 at New York Giants 27 | 1:00 |
| | | Denver 13 at Los Angeles Raiders 23 | 1:00 |
| | | Indianapolis 13 at New England 28 | 1:00 |
| | | Los Angeles Rams 14 at Tampa Bay 24 | 1:00 |
| | | Minnesota 21 at Buffalo 17 | 1:00 |
| | | Philadelphia 3 at Pittsburgh 14 | 1:00 |
| | | San Francisco 38 at San Diego 15 | 1:00 |
| | | Seattle 16 at Houston 14 | 3:00 |
| | | Washington 15 at Arizona 17 | 2:00 |
| | **Sunday Night** | New Orleans 29 at Atlanta 20 | (ESPN) 8:00 |
| | **Monday, December 12** | Kansas City 28 at Miami 45 | (ABC) 9:00 |
| **SIXTEENTH WEEK** | **Saturday, December 17** | Denver 19 at San Francisco 42 | (NBC) 1:00 |
| | | Minnesota 19 at Detroit 41 | (FOX) 12:30 |
| | **Sunday, December 18** | Atlanta 17 vs. Green Bay 21 at Milwaukee | 12:00 |
| | **(NBC-TV National Weekend)** | Cincinnati 7 at Arizona 28 | 2:00 |
| | | Cleveland 7 at Pittsburgh 17 | 1:00 |
| | | Houston 9 at Kansas City 31 | 3:00 |
| | | Los Angeles Rams 13 at Chicago 27 | 12:00 |
| | | Miami 6 at Indianapolis 10 | 1:00 |
| | | New England 41 at Buffalo 17 | 1:00 |
| | | New York Giants 16 at Philadelphia 13 | 4:00 |
| | | San Diego 21 at New York Jets 6 | 1:00 |
| | | Tampa Bay 17 at Washington 14 | 1:00 |
| | **Sunday Night** | Los Angeles Raiders 17 at Seattle 16 | (ESPN) 5:00 |
| | **Monday, December 19** | Dallas 24 at New Orleans 16 | (ABC) 8:00 |

**SEVENTEENTH WEEK**

**Saturday, December 24**
**(NBC-TV National Weekend)**

Arizona 10 at Atlanta 6 — 1:00
Buffalo 9 at Indianapolis 10 — 1:00
Dallas 10 at New York Giants 15 — 1:00
Green Bay 34 at Tampa Bay 19 — 1:00
Kansas City 19 at Los Angeles Raiders 9 — 1:00
New England 13 at Chicago 3 — 12:00
New Orleans 30 at Denver 28 — 2:00
New York Jets 10 at Houston 24 — 3:00
Philadelphia 30 at Cincinnati 33 — 1:00
Pittsburgh 34 at San Diego 37 — 1:00
Seattle 9 at Cleveland 35 — 1:00
Washington 24 at Los Angeles Rams 21 — 1:00

**Sunday Night, December 25**
Detroit 20 at Miami 27 — (ESPN) 8:00

**Monday, December 26**
San Francisco 14 at Minnesota 21 — (ABC ) 8:00

**Wild Card Playoff Games**
**Site Priorities**
Three Wild Card teams (division non-champions with best three records) from each conference and the division champion with the third-best record in each conference will enter the first round of the playoffs. The division champion with the third-best record will play host to the Wild Card team with the third-best record. The Wild Card team with the best record will play host to the Wild Card team with the second-best record. There are no restrictions on intra-division games.

**Saturday, December 31, 1994**
American Football Conference
Kansas City at Miami (ABC)
17-27
National Football Conference
Green Bay at Detroit (ABC)
16-12

**Sunday, January 1, 1995**
American Football Conference
New England at Cleveland (NBC)
13-20
National Football Conference
Chicago at Minnesota (FOX)
35-18

**Divisional Playoff Games**
**Site Priorities**
In each conference, the two division champions with the highest won-lost-tied percentage during the regular season will play host to the Wild Card winners. The division champion with the best record in each conference is assured of playing the Wild Card survivor with the poorest record. There are no restrictions on intra-division games.

**Saturday, January 7, 1995**
American Football Conference
Cleveland at Pittsburgh (NBC)
9-29
National Football Conference
Chicago at SanFransisco (FOX)
15-44

**Sunday, January 8, 1995**
American Football Conference
Miami at San Diego (NBC)
21-22
National Football Conference
Green Bay at Dallas. (FOX)
9-35

**Championship Games**
**Site Priorities**
**for Championship Games**
The home teams will be the surviving playoff winners with the best won-lost-tied percentage during the regular season. A Wild Card team cannot play host unless two Wild Card teams are in the game, in which case the Wild Card team with the best record will play host.

**Sunday, January 15, 1995**
American Football Conference
San Diego at Pittsburgh (NBC)
17-13
National Football Conference
Dallas. at San Fransisco (FOX)
28-38

**Super Bowl XXIX**

**Sunday, January 29, 1995**
Super Bowl XXIX at Joe Robbie Stadium, Miami, Florida
San Diego at San Fransisco (ABC)
26-49

**AFC-NFC Pro Bowl**

**Sunday, February 5, 1995**
AFC-NFC Pro Bowl at Honolulu, Hawaii
AFC ______ at NFC ______ (ABC)

# POSTSEASON, NATIONALLY TELEVISED, AND INTERCONFERENCE GAMES

## POSTSEASON GAMES

| | |
|---|---|
| Saturday, Dec. 31 | AFC and NFC Wild Card Playoffs (ABC) |
| Sunday, January 1 | AFC and NFC Wild Card Playoffs (NBC and FOX) |
| Saturday, January 7 | AFC and NFC Divisional Playoffs (NBC and FOX) |
| Sunday, January 8 | AFC and NFC Divisional Playoffs (NBC and FOX) |
| Sunday, January 15 | AFC and NFC Championship Games (NBC and FOX) |
| Sunday, January 29 | Super Bowl XXIX at Joe Robbie Stadium, Miami, Florida (ABC) |
| Sunday, February 5 | AFC-NFC Pro Bowl at Honolulu, Hawaii (ABC) |

## 1994 NATIONALLY TELEVISED GAMES

**Regular Season**

| | |
|---|---|
| Sunday, September 4 | Dallas at Pittsburgh (day, FOX) |
| | San Diego at Denver (night, TNT) |
| Monday, September 5 | Los Angeles Raiders at San Francisco (night, ABC) |
| Sunday, September 11 | Houston at Dallas (day, NBC) |
| | New York Giants at Arizona (night, TNT) |
| Monday, September 12 | Chicago at Philadelphia (night, ABC) |
| Sunday, September 18 | San Francisco at Los Angeles Rams (day, FOX) |
| | Kansas City at Atlanta (night, TNT) |
| Monday, September 19 | Detroit at Dallas (night, ABC) |
| Sunday, September 25 | San Diego at Los Angeles Raiders (day, NBC) |
| | Chicago at New York Jets (night, TNT) |
| Monday, September 26 | Denver at Buffalo (night, ABC) |
| Sunday, October 2 | Philadelphia at San Francisco (day, FOX) |
| | Miami at Cincinnati (night, TNT) |
| Monday, October 3 | Houston at Pittsburgh (night, ABC) |
| Sunday, October 9 | Kansas City at San Diego (day, NBC) |
| | Washington at Philadelphia (night, TNT) |
| Monday, October 10 | Minnesota at New York Giants (night, ABC) |
| Thursday, October 13 | Cleveland at Houston (night, TNT) |
| Sunday, October 16 | Philadelphia at Dallas (day, FOX) |
| Monday, October 17 | Kansas City at Denver (night, ABC) |
| Thursday, October 20 | Green Bay at Minnesota (night, TNT) |
| Sunday, October 23 | Dallas at Arizona (day, FOX) |
| Monday, October 24 | Houston at Philadelphia (night, ABC) |
| Sunday, October 30 | Houston at Los Angeles Raiders (day, NBC) |
| | Pittsburgh at Arizona (night, TNT) |
| Monday, October 31 | Green Bay at Chicago (night, ABC) |
| Sunday, November 6 | Buffalo at New York Jets (day, NBC) |
| | Los Angeles Raiders at Kansas City (night, ESPN) |
| Monday, November 7 | New York Giants at Dallas (night, ABC) |
| Sunday, November 13 | Dallas at San Francisco (day, FOX) |
| | Tampa Bay at Detroit (night, ESPN) |
| Monday, November 14 | Buffalo at Pittsburgh (night, ABC) |
| Sunday, November 20 | New Orleans at Los Angeles Raiders(day, FOX) |
| | Los Angeles Rams at San Francisco (night, ESPN) |
| Monday, November 21 | New York Giants at Houston (night, ABC) |
| Thursday, November 24 | Buffalo at Detroit (day, NBC) |
| | Green Bay at Dallas (day, FOX) |
| Sunday, November 27 | Pittsburgh at Los Angeles Raiders (day, NBC) |
| | New England at Indianapolis (night, ESPN) |
| Monday, November 28 | San Francisco at New Orleans (night, ABC) |
| Thursday, December 1 | Chicago at Minnesota (night, ESPN) |
| Sunday, December 4 | Arizona at Houston (day, FOX) |
| | Buffalo at Miami (night, ESPN) |
| Monday, December 5 | Los Angeles Raiders at San Diego (night, ABC) |
| Saturday, December 10 | Cleveland at Dallas (day, NBC) |
| | Detroit at New York Jets (day, FOX) |
| Sunday, December 11 | San Francisco at San Diego (day, FOX) |
| | New Orleans at Atlanta (night, ESPN) |
| Monday, December 12 | Kansas City at Miami (night, ABC) |
| Saturday, December 17 | Denver at San Francisco (day, NBC) |
| | Minnesota at Detroit (day, FOX) |
| Sunday, December 18 | Houston at Kansas City (day, NBC) |
| | Los Angeles Raiders at Seattle (night, ESPN) |
| Monday, December 19 | Dallas at New Orleans (night, ABC) |
| Saturday, December 24 | Kansas City at Los Angeles Raiders (day, NBC) |
| Sunday, December 25 | Detroit at Miami (night, ESPN) |
| Monday, December 26 | San Francisco at Minnesota (night, ABC) |

## 1994 AFC-NFC INTERCONFERENCE GAMES

(All Times Local)

| | | |
|---|---|---|
| September 4 | Dallas at Pittsburgh | 4:00 |
| | Kansas City at New Orleans | 12:00 |
| | Seattle at Washington | 1:00 |
| September 5 | Los Angeles Raiders at San Francisco | 6:00 |
| September 11 | Houston at Dallas | 3:00 |
| | Indianapolis at Tampa Bay | 1:00 |
| | Miami vs. Green Bay at Milwaukee | 12:00 |
| | San Francisco at Kansas City | 12:00 |
| September 18 | Arizona at Cleveland | 1:00 |
| | Kansas City at Atlanta | 8:00 |
| September 25 | Los Angeles Rams at Kansas City | 12:00 |
| | Miami at Minnesota | 12:00 |
| | New England at Detroit | 4:00 |
| | Chicago at New York Jets | 8:00 |
| October 2 | Buffalo at Chicago | 3:00 |
| | Green Bay at New England | 1:00 |
| October 16 | San Diego at New Orleans | 3:00 |
| October 23 | Atlanta at Los Angeles Raiders | 1:00 |
| | Pittsburgh at New York Giants | 1:00 |
| | Washington at Indianapolis | 12:00 |
| October 24 | Houston at Philadelphia | 9:00 |
| October 30 | Dallas at Cincinnati | 1:00 |
| | Pittsburgh at Arizona | 6:00 |
| November 6 | Denver at Los Angeles Rams | 1:00 |
| | San Diego at Atlanta | 1:00 |
| November 13 | Chicago at Miami | 1:00 |
| | Cleveland at Philadelphia | 1:00 |
| | Los Angeles Raiders at Los Angeles Rams | 1:00 |
| | Minnesota at New England | 1:00 |
| | New York Jets at Green Bay | 3:00 |
| November 20 | Atlanta at Denver | 2:00 |
| | Green Bay at Buffalo | 1:00 |
| | New Orleans at Los Angeles Raiders | 1:00 |
| | New York Jets at Minnesota | 3:00 |
| | Tampa Bay at Seattle | 1:00 |
| November 21 | New York Giants at Houston | 8:00 |
| November 24 | Buffalo at Detroit | 12:30 |
| November 27 | Los Angeles Rams at San Diego | 1:00 |
| December 4 | Arizona at Houston | 3:00 |
| | New York Giants at Cleveland | 4:00 |
| December 10 | Cleveland at Dallas | 3:00 |
| | Detroit at New York Jets | 12:30 |
| December 11 | Cincinnati at New York Giants | 1:00 |
| | Minnesota at Buffalo | 1:00 |
| | Philadelphia at Pittsburgh | 1:00 |
| | San Francisco at San Diego | 1:00 |
| December 17 | Denver at San Francisco | 1:00 |
| December 18 | Cincinnati at Arizona | 2:00 |
| December 24 | New England at Chicago | 12:00 |
| | New Orleans at Denver | 2:00 |
| | Philadelphia at Cincinnati | 1:00 |
| December 25 | Detroit at Miami | 8:00 |

**1994**

| | |
|---|---|
| July 5 | Claiming period of 24 hours begins in waiver system. All waiver requests for the rest of the year are no-recall and no-withdrawal. |
| July 10 | Los Angeles Raiders are first team to open training camp. Veteran players cannot be required to report earlier than 15 days prior to club's first preseason game or July 15, whichever is later. |
| July 15 | Signing periods ends at 4 P.M., Eastern Daylight Time, for Unrestricted Free Agents to whom June 1 tender (or June 14 tender to Transition Player) was made by Old Club. After this date and through 4 P.M., Eastern Daylight Time, on November 8, Old Club has exclusive negotiating rights with its unsigned Unrestricted Free Agents. |
| July 30 | Hall of Fame Game, Canton, Ohio: Atlanta vs. San Diego. |
| July 31 | American Bowl, Barcelona, Spain: Denver vs. Los Angeles Raiders. |
| August 5 | If a drafted rookie has not signed with his club by this date, he may not be traded to any other club in 1994. |
| August 6 | American Bowl, Tokyo, Japan: Kansas City vs. Minnesota. |
| August 13 | American Bowl, Berlin, Germany: New York Giants vs. San Diego. |
| August 15 | American Bowl, Mexico City, Mexico: Dallas vs. Houston. |
| August 23 | Roster cutdown to maximum of 60 players on Active List by 4 P.M., Eastern Daylight Time. |
| August 28 | Roster cutdown to maximum of 53 players on Active/Inactive List by 4 P.M., Eastern Daylight Time. Clubs may dress minimum of 42 and maximum of 45 players and third quarterback for each regular season and postseason game. |
| August 29 | After 4 P.M., Eastern Daylight Time, clubs may establish a Practice Squad of five players by signing free agents who do not have a season of free-agency credit, unless that season was achieved by spending an entire regular season on Reserve/Injured or Reserve/Physically Unable to Perform. |
| September 2 | All clubs are required to identify their 49-player Active List by 7:00 P.M., Eastern Daylight Time, on this Friday and thereafter on each Friday before a regular-season Sunday game. No later than one hour and 15 minutes prior to kickoff, clubs must identify their 45-player Active List and third quarterback, if any. |
| September 4-5 | Regular season opens. |
| September 20 | Priority on multiple waiver claims is now based on the current season's standing. |
| September 28-29 | Special League meeting on realignment and player-stocking for expansion teams, Dallas, Texas. |
| October 11 | All trading ends at 4 P.M., Eastern Daylight Time. |
| October 12 | Players with at least four previous pension credits are subject to the waiver system for the remainder of the regular season and post-season. |
| November 1-2 | NFL Fall Meeting, Chicago, Illinois. |
| November 8 | Deadline for clubs to sign by 4 P.M., Eastern Time, their Unrestricted Free Agents to whom June 1 tender was made. If still unsigned after this date, such players are prohibited from playing in NFL in 1994. |
| November 8 | Deadline for clubs to sign by 4 P.M., Eastern Time, their Restricted Free Agents to whom June 1 tender was made. If such players remain unsigned, they are prohibited from playing in NFL in 1994. |
| November 8 | Deadline for clubs to sign Drafted players by 4 P.M., Eastern Time. If such players remain unsigned, they are prohibited from playing in NFL in 1994. |
| November 26 | Deadline for reinstatement of players in Reserve List categories of Retired and Did Not Report. |
| December 23 | Deadline for waiver requests in 1994, except for "special waiver requests" by teams participating in playoffs. |
| December 27 | Clubs may begin signing free-agent players for the 1995 season. |
| December 31 | Wild Card Playoff Games. |

**1995**

| | |
|---|---|
| January 1 | Wild Card Playoff Games. |
| January 7-8 | Divisional Playoff Games. |
| January 15 | AFC and NFC Championship Games. |
| January 29 | Super Bowl XXIX at Joe Robbie Stadium, Miami, Florida. |
| February 5 | AFC-NFC Pro Bowl, Honolulu, Hawaii. |
| February 9-13 | Combine Timing and Testing, Hoosier Dome, Indianapolis, Indiana. |
| March 12-17 | NFL Annual Meeting, Phoenix, Arizona. |
| Late April | Annual player selection meeting, New York, New York. |
| July 29 | Hall of Fame Game, Canton, Ohio. |
| September 3-4 | Regular season opens. |
| *December 30-31 | Wild Card Playoff Games. |

***1996**

| | |
|---|---|
| *January 6-7 | Divisional Playoff Games. |
| *January 14 | AFC and NFC Championship Games. |
| *January 28 | Super Bowl XXX, Sun Devil Stadium, Tempe, Arizona |
| *February 4 | AFC-NFC Pro Bowl, Honolulu, Hawaii. |

**Tentatively scheduled.*

# WAIVERS

## WAIVERS

The waiver system is a procedure by which player contracts or NFL rights to players are made available by a club to other clubs in the League. During the procedure, the 27 other clubs either file claims to obtain the players or waive the opportunity to do so—thus the term "waiver." Claiming clubs are assigned players on a priority based on the inverse of won-and-lost standing. The claiming period normally is 10 days during the offseason and 24 hours from early July through December. In some circumstances, another 24 hours is added on to allow the original club to rescind its action (known as a recall of a waiver request) and/or the claiming club to do the same (known as withdrawal of a claim). If a player passes through waivers unclaimed and is not recalled by the original club, he becomes a free agent. All waivers from July through December are no recall and no withdrawal. Under the Collective Bargaining Agreement, from the beginning of the waiver system each year through the trading deadline (October 11, 1994), any veteran who has acquired four years of pension credit is not subject to the waiver system if the club desires to release him. After the trading deadline, such players are subject to the waiver system.

## ACTIVE/INACTIVE LIST

The Active/Inactive List is the principal status for players participating for a club. It consists of all players under contract who are eligible for preseason, regular-season, and postseason games. In 1994, teams will be permitted to open training camp with no more than 80 players under contract and thereafter must meet two mandatory roster reductions prior to the season opener. Teams will be permitted an Active List of 45 players and an Inactive List of eight players for each regular-season and postseason game during the 1994 season. Provided that a club has two quarterbacks on its 45-player Active List, a third quarterback from its Inactive List is permitted to dress for the game, but if he participates in the game, the other two quarterbacks are thereafter prohibited from playing. Teams also are permitted to establish Practice Squads of up to five players who are eligible to participate in practice, but these players remain free agents and are eligible to sign with any other team in the league.

August 23.............Roster reduction to 60 players
August 28.............Roster reduction to 53 players
August 29.............Teams establish a Practice Squad of up to five players

In addition to the squad limits described above, there also is an overall roster limit of 80 players that is applicable to players on a team's Active, Inactive, and Exempt Lists, and any players on the Practice Squad and on the Reserve List as Injured, Physically Unable to Perform, Non-Football Illness/Injury, and Suspended.

## RESERVE LIST

The Reserve List is a status for players who, for reasons of injury, retirement, military service, or other circumstances, are not immediately available for participation with a club. Players on Reserve/Injured are not eligible to practice or return to the Active/Inactive List in the same season that they are placed on Reserve.

Players in the category of Reserve/Retired or Reserve/Did Not Report may not be reinstated during the period from 30 days before the end of the regular season through the postseason.

## TRADES

Unrestricted trading between the AFC and NFC is allowed in 1994 through October 11, after which trading will end until 1995.

## ANNUAL ACTIVE PLAYER LIMITS

**NFL**

| Year(s) | Limit |
|---|---|
| 1991-94 | 45** |
| 1985-90 | 45 |
| 1983-84 | 49 |
| 1982 | 45†-49 |
| 1978-81 | 45 |
| 1975-77 | 43 |
| 1974 | 47 |
| 1964-73 | 40 |
| 1963 | 37 |
| 1961-62 | 36 |
| 1960 | 38 |
| 1959 | 36 |
| 1957-58 | 35 |
| 1951-56 | 33 |
| 1949-50 | 32 |
| 1948 | 35 |
| 1947 | 35*-34 |
| 1945-46 | 33 |
| 1943-44 | 28 |
| 1940-42 | 33 |
| 1938-39 | 30 |
| 1936-37 | 25 |
| 1935 | 24 |
| 1930-34 | 20 |
| 1926-29 | 18 |
| 1925 | 16 |

**45 plus a third quarterback
† 45 for first two games
* 35 for first three games

**AFL**

| Year(s) | Limit |
|---|---|
| 1966-69 | 40 |
| 1965 | 38 |
| 1964 | 34 |
| 1962-63 | 33 |
| 1960-61 | 35 |

The following procedures will be used to break standings ties for postseason playoffs and to determine regular-season schedules.

## TO BREAK A TIE WITHIN A DIVISION

If, at the end of the regular season, two or more clubs in the same division finish with identical won-lost-tied percentages, the following steps will be taken until a champion is determined.

**TWO CLUBS**

1. Head-to-head (best won-lost-tied percentage in games between the clubs).
2. Best won-lost-tied percentage in games played within the division.
3. Best won-lost-tied percentage in games played within the conference.
4. Best won-lost-tied percentage in common games, if applicable.
5. Best net points in division games.
6. Best net points in all games.
7. Strength of schedule.
8. Best net touchdowns in all games.
9. Coin toss.

**THREE OR MORE CLUBS**

(Note: If two clubs remain tied after third or other clubs are eliminated during any step, tiebreaker reverts to step 1 of the two-club format).

1. Head-to-head (best won-lost-tied percentage in games among the clubs).
2. Best won-lost-tied percentage in games played within the division.
3. Best won-lost-tied percentage in games played within the conference.
4. Best won-lost-tied percentage in common games.
5. Best net points in division games.
6. Best net points in all games.
7. Strength of schedule.
8. Best net touchdowns in all games.
9. Coin toss.

## TO BREAK A TIE FOR THE WILD CARD TEAM

If it is necessary to break ties to determine the three Wild Card clubs from each conference, the following steps will be taken.

1. If the tied clubs are from the same division, apply division tiebreaker.
2. If the tied clubs are from different divisions, apply the following steps.

**TWO CLUBS**

1. Head-to-head, if applicable.
2. Best won-lost-tied percentage in games played within the conference.
3. Best won-lost-tied percentage in common games, minimum of four.
4. Best average net points in conference games.
5. Best net points in all games.
6. Strength of schedule.
7. Best net touchdowns in all games.
8. Coin toss.

**THREE OR MORE CLUBS**

(Note: If two clubs remain tied after third or other clubs are eliminated, tiebreaker reverts to step 1 of applicable two-club format.)

1. Apply division tiebreaker to eliminate all but the highest ranked club in each division prior to proceeding to step 2. The original seeding within a division upon application of the division tiebreaker remains the same for all subsequent applications of the procedure that are necessary to identify the three Wild Card participants.
2. Head-to-head sweep. (Applicable only if one club has defeated each of the others or if one club has lost to each of the others).
3. Best won-lost-tied percentage in games played within the conference.
4. Best won-lost-tied percentage in common games, minimum of four.
5. Best average net points in conference games.
6. Best net points in all games.
7. Strength of schedule.
8. Best net touchdowns in all games.
9. Coin toss.

When the first Wild Card team has been identified, the procedure is repeated to name the second Wild Card, i.e., eliminate all but the highest-ranked club in each division prior to proceeding to step 2, and repeated a third time, if necessary, to identify the third Wild Card. In situations where three or more teams from the same division are involved in the procedure, the original seeding of the teams remains the same for subsequent applications of the tiebreaker if the top-ranked team in that division qualifies for a Wild Card berth.

## OTHER TIE-BREAKING PROCEDURES

1. Only one club advances to the playoffs in any tie-breaking step. Remaining tied clubs revert to the first step of the applicable division or Wild Card tiebreakers. As an example, if two clubs remain tied in any tie-breaker step after all other clubs have been eliminated, the procedure reverts to step one of the two-club format to determine the winner. When one club wins the tie-breaker, all other clubs revert to step 1 of the applicable two-club or three-club format.
2. In comparing division and conference records or records against common opponents among tied teams, the best won-lost-tied percentage is the deciding factor since teams may have played an unequal number of games.
3. To determine home-field priority among division titlists, apply Wild Card tiebreakers.
4. To determine home-field priority for Wild Card qualifiers, apply division tiebreakers (if teams are from the same division) or Wild Card tiebreakers (if teams are from different divisions).

## TIE-BREAKING PROCEDURE FOR SELECTION MEETING

If two or more clubs are tied in the selection order, the strength-of-schedule tie-breaker is applied, subject to the following exceptions for playoff clubs:

1. The Super Bowl winner is last and the Super Bowl loser next-to-last.
2. Any non-Super Bowl playoff club involved in a tie shall be assigned priority within its segment below that of non-playoff clubs and in the order that the playoff clubs exited from the playoffs. Thus, within a tied segment a playoff club that loses in the Wild Card game will have priority over a playoff club that loses in the Divisional playoff game, which in turn will have priority over a club that loses in the Conference Championship game. If two tied clubs exited the playoffs in the same round, the tie is broken by strength-of-schedule.

If any ties cannot be broken by strength-of-schedule, the divisional or conference tie-breakers, whichever are applicable, are applied. Any ties that still exist are broken by a coin flip.

## NFL PASSER RATING SYSTEM

The NFL rates its passers for statistical purposes against a fixed performance standard based on statistical achievements of all qualified pro passers since 1960. The current system replaced one that rated passers in relation to their position in a total group based on various criteria. The current system, which was adopted in 1973, removes inequities that existed in the former method and, at the same time, provides a means of comparing passing performances from one season to the next.

It is important to remember that the system is used to rate **passers,** not **quarterbacks.** Statistics do not reflect leadership, play-calling, and other intangible factors that go into making a successful professional quarterback. Four categories are used as a basis for compiling a rating:

—Percentage of touchdown passes per attempt
—Percentage of completions per attempt
—Percentage of interceptions per attempt
—Average yards gained per attempt

The **average** standard is 1.000. The bottom is .000. To earn a 2.000 rating, a passer must perform at exceptional levels, i.e., 70 percent in completions, 10 percent in touchdowns, 1.5 percent in interceptions, and 11 yards average gain per pass attempt. The **maximum** a passer can receive in any category is 2.375.

For example, to gain a 2.375 in completion percentage, a passer would have to complete 77.5 percent of his passes. The NFL record is 70.55 by Ken Anderson (Cincinnati, 1982). To earn a 2.375 in percentage of touchdowns, a passer would have to achieve a percentage of 11.9. The record is 13.9 percent by Sid Luckman (Chicago, 1943). To gain 2.375 in percentage of interceptions, a passer would have to go the entire season without an interception. The 2.375 figure in average yards is 12.50, compared with the NFL record of 11.17 by Tommy O'Connell (Cleveland, 1957).

In order to make the rating more understandable, the point rating is then converted into a scale of 100. For instance, if a passer completes 11 of 23 passes for 114 yards, with 1 touchdown and no interceptions, the four components would be:

—**Percentage of Completions**—11 of 23 is 47.8 percent. The point rating is 0.890.

—**Percentage of Touchdown Passes**—1 touchdown in 23 attempts works out to 4.3 percent for a rating of 0.860.

—**Percentage of Interceptions**—You can't do better than zero, so the passer receives a maximum rating of 2.375.

—**Average Yards Gained Per Attempt**—114 yards divided by 23 attempts equals 4.96 yards per attempt for a corresponding rating of 0.490.

The sum of the four components is 4.615, which converts to a rating of 76.9. In order for a passer to achieve 100, his points would have to total 6.000. In rare cases, where statistical performance has been superior, it is possible for a passer to surpass 100.

The following is a list of qualifying passers who had a single-season passer rating of 100 or higher:

| Player, Team | Season | Rating | Att. | Comp. | Pct. | Yds. | Avg. | TD | TD Pct. | Int. | Int. Pct. |
|---|---|---|---|---|---|---|---|---|---|---|---|
| Joe Montana, San Francisco | 1989 | 112.4 | 386 | 271 | 70.2 | 3,521 | 9.12 | 26 | 6.7 | 8 | 2.1 |
| Milt Plum, Cleveland | 1960 | 110.4 | 250 | 151 | 60.4 | 2,297 | 9.19 | 21 | 8.4 | 5 | 2.0 |
| Sammy Baugh, Washington | 1945 | 109.9 | 182 | 128 | 70.3 | 1,669 | 9.17 | 11 | 6.0 | 4 | 2.2 |
| Dan Marino, Miami | 1984 | 108.9 | 564 | 362 | 64.2 | 5,084 | 9.01 | 48 | 8.5 | 17 | 3.0 |
| Sid Luckman, Chicago Bears | 1943 | 107.5 | 202 | 110 | 54.5 | 2,194 | 10.86 | 28 | 13.9 | 12 | 5.9 |
| Steve Young, San Francisco | 1992 | 107.0 | 402 | 268 | 66.7 | 3,465 | 8.62 | 25 | 6.2 | 7 | 1.7 |
| Bart Starr, Green Bay | 1966 | 105.0 | 251 | 156 | 62.2 | 2,257 | 8.99 | 14 | 5.6 | 3 | 1.2 |
| Roger Staubach, Dallas | 1971 | 104.8 | 211 | 126 | 59.7 | 1,882 | 8.92 | 15 | 7.1 | 4 | 1.9 |
| Y.A. Tittle, N.Y. Giants | 1963 | 104.8 | 367 | 221 | 60.2 | 3,145 | 8.57 | 36 | 9.8 | 14 | 3.8 |
| Bart Starr, Green Bay | 1968 | 104.3 | 171 | 109 | 63.7 | 1,617 | 9.46 | 15 | 8.8 | 8 | 4.7 |
| Ken Stabler, Oakland | 1976 | 103.4 | 291 | 194 | 66.7 | 2,737 | 9.41 | 27 | 9.3 | 17 | 5.8 |
| Joe Montana, San Francisco | 1984 | 102.9 | 432 | 279 | 64.6 | 3,630 | 8.40 | 28 | 6.5 | 10 | 2.3 |
| Charlie Conerly, N.Y. Giants | 1959 | 102.7 | 194 | 113 | 58.2 | 1,706 | 8.79 | 14 | 7.2 | 4 | 2.1 |
| Bert Jones, Baltimore | 1976 | 102.5 | 343 | 207 | 60.3 | 3,104 | 9.05 | 24 | 7.0 | 9 | 2.6 |
| Joe Montana, San Francisco | 1987 | 102.1 | 398 | 266 | 66.8 | 3,054 | 7.67 | 31 | 7.8 | 13 | 3.3 |
| Steve Young, San Francisco | 1991 | 101.8 | 279 | 180 | 64.5 | 2,517 | 9.02 | 17 | 6.1 | 8 | 2.9 |
| Len Dawson, Kansas City | 1966 | 101.7 | 284 | 159 | 56.0 | 2,527 | 8.90 | 26 | 9.2 | 10 | 3.5 |
| Steve Young, San Francisco | 1993 | 101.5 | 462 | 314 | 68.0 | 4,023 | 8.71 | 29 | 6.3 | 16 | 3.5 |
| Jim Kelly, Buffalo | 1990 | 101.2 | 346 | 219 | 63.3 | 2,829 | 8.18 | 24 | 6.9 | 9 | 2.6 |

## ACTIVE COACHES' CAREER RECORDS (Order Based on Career Victories)

Start of 1994 Season

| Coach | Team(s) | Yrs. | Regular Season Won | Lost | Tied | Pct. | Postseason Won | Lost | Tied | Pct. | Career Won | Lost | Tied | Pct. |
|---|---|---|---|---|---|---|---|---|---|---|---|---|---|---|
| Don Shula | Baltimore Colts, Miami Dolphins | 31 | 309 | 143 | 6 | .681 | 18 | 15 | 0 | .545 | 327 | 158 | 6 | .672 |
| Chuck Knox | Los Angeles Rams, Buffalo Bills, Seattle Seahawks | 21 | 182 | 135 | 1 | .574 | 7 | 11 | 0 | .389 | 189 | 146 | 1 | .564 |
| Dan Reeves | Denver Broncos, New York Giants | 13 | 121 | 78 | 1 | .608 | 8 | 7 | 0 | .533 | 129 | 85 | 1 | .602 |
| Marv Levy | Kansas City Chiefs, Buffalo Bills | 13 | 110 | 81 | 0 | .576 | 10 | 6 | 0 | .625 | 120 | 87 | 0 | .580 |
| Tom Flores | Oakland-Los Angeles Raiders, Seattle Seahawks | 11 | 91 | 77 | 0 | .542 | 8 | 3 | 0 | .727 | 99 | 80 | 0 | .553 |
| Marty Schottenheimer | Cleveland Browns, Kansas City Chiefs | 10 | 94 | 56 | 1 | .626 | 5 | 8 | 0 | .385 | 99 | 64 | 1 | .607 |
| Bill Parcells | New York Giants, New England Patriots | 9 | 82 | 60 | 1 | .577 | 8 | 3 | 0 | .727 | 90 | 63 | 1 | .588 |
| Jack Pardee | Chicago Bears, Washington Redskins, Houston Oilers | 10 | 86 | 68 | 0 | .558 | 1 | 5 | 0 | .167 | 87 | 73 | 0 | .544 |
| Jim Mora | New Orleans Saints | 8 | 77 | 50 | 0 | .606 | 0 | 4 | 0 | .000 | 77 | 54 | 0 | .588 |
| Sam Wyche | Cincinnati Bengals, Tampa Bay Buccaneers | 10 | 71 | 88 | 0 | .447 | 3 | 2 | 0 | .600 | 74 | 90 | 0 | .451 |
| George Seifert | San Francisco 49ers | 5 | 62 | 18 | 0 | .775 | 6 | 3 | 0 | .667 | 68 | 21 | 0 | .764 |
| Ted Marchibroda | Baltimore-Indianapolis Colts | 7 | 54 | 52 | 0 | .509 | 0 | 3 | 0 | .000 | 54 | 55 | 0 | .495 |
| Art Shell | Los Angeles Raiders | 5 | 45 | 31 | 0 | .592 | 2 | 3 | 0 | .400 | 47 | 34 | 0 | .580 |
| Wayne Fontes | Detroit Lions | 5 | 42 | 43 | 0 | .494 | 1 | 2 | 0 | .333 | 43 | 45 | 0 | .489 |
| Buddy Ryan | Philadelphia Eagles, Arizona Cardinals | 5 | 43 | 35 | 1 | .551 | 0 | 3 | 0 | .000 | 43 | 38 | 1 | .530 |
| Rich Kotite | Philadelphia Eagles | 3 | 29 | 19 | 0 | .604 | 1 | 1 | 0 | .500 | 30 | 20 | 0 | .600 |
| Bill Belichick | Cleveland Browns | 3 | 20 | 28 | 0 | .417 | 0 | 0 | 0 | .000 | 20 | 28 | 0 | .417 |
| Bill Cowher | Pittsburgh Steelers | 2 | 20 | 12 | 0 | .625 | 0 | 2 | 0 | .000 | 20 | 14 | 0 | .588 |
| Dennis Green | Minnesota Vikings | 2 | 20 | 12 | 0 | .625 | 0 | 2 | 0 | .000 | 20 | 14 | 0 | .588 |
| Bobby Ross | San Diego Chargers | 2 | 19 | 13 | 0 | .594 | 1 | 1 | 0 | .500 | 20 | 14 | 0 | .588 |
| Mike Holmgren | Green Bay Packers | 2 | 18 | 14 | 0 | .563 | 1 | 1 | 0 | .500 | 19 | 15 | 0 | .559 |
| Wade Phillips | New Orleans Saints, Denver Broncos | 2 | 10 | 10 | 0 | .500 | 0 | 1 | 0 | .000 | 10 | 11 | 0 | .476 |
| Dave Shula | Cincinnati Bengals | 2 | 8 | 24 | 0 | .250 | 0 | 0 | 0 | .000 | 8 | 24 | 0 | .250 |
| Dave Wannstedt | Chicago Bears | 1 | 7 | 9 | 0 | .438 | 0 | 0 | 0 | .000 | 7 | 9 | 0 | .438 |
| Pete Carroll | New York Jets | 0 | 0 | 0 | 0 | .000 | 0 | 0 | 0 | .000 | 0 | 0 | 0 | .000 |
| June Jones | Atlanta Falcons | 0 | 0 | 0 | 0 | .000 | 0 | 0 | 0 | .000 | 0 | 0 | 0 | .000 |
| Barry Switzer | Dallas Cowboys | 0 | 0 | 0 | 0 | .000 | 0 | 0 | 0 | .000 | 0 | 0 | 0 | .000 |
| Norv Turner | Washington Redskins | 0 | 0 | 0 | 0 | .000 | 0 | 0 | 0 | .000 | 0 | 0 | 0 | .000 |

## COACHES WITH 100 CAREER VICTORIES (Order Based on Career Victories)

Start of 1994 Season

| Coach | Team(s) | Yrs. | Regular Season Won | Lost | Tied | Pct. | Postseason Won | Lost | Tied | Pct. | Career Won | Lost | Tied | Pct. |
|---|---|---|---|---|---|---|---|---|---|---|---|---|---|---|
| **Don Shula** | Baltimore Colts, Miami Dolphins | 31 | 309 | 143 | 6 | .681 | 18 | 15 | 0 | .545 | 327 | 158 | 6 | .672 |
| George Halas | Chicago Bears | 40 | 318 | 148 | 31 | .671 | 6 | 3 | 0 | .667 | 324 | 151 | 31 | .671 |
| Tom Landry | Dallas Cowboys | 29 | 250 | 162 | 6 | .605 | 20 | 16 | 0 | .556 | 270 | 178 | 6 | .601 |
| Earl (Curly) Lambeau | Green Bay Packers, Chicago Cardinals, Washington Redskins | 33 | 226 | 132 | 22 | .624 | 3 | 2 | 0 | .600 | 229 | 134 | 22 | .623 |
| Chuck Noll | Pittsburgh Steelers | 23 | 193 | 148 | 1 | .566 | 16 | 8 | 0 | .667 | 209 | 156 | 1 | .572 |
| **Chuck Knox** | Los Angeles Rams, Buffalo Bills, Seattle Seahawks | 21 | 182 | 135 | 1 | .574 | 7 | 11 | 0 | .389 | 189 | 146 | 1 | .564 |
| Paul Brown | Cleveland Browns, Cincinnati Bengals | 21 | 166 | 100 | 6 | .621 | 4 | 8 | 0 | .333 | 170 | 108 | 6 | .609 |
| Bud Grant | Minnesota Vikings | 18 | 158 | 96 | 5 | .620 | 10 | 12 | 0 | .455 | 168 | 108 | 5 | .607 |
| Steve Owen | New York Giants | 23 | 151 | 100 | 17 | .595 | 2 | 8 | 0 | .200 | 153 | 108 | 17 | .581 |
| Joe Gibbs | Washington Redskins | 12 | 124 | 60 | 0 | .674 | 16 | 5 | 0 | .762 | 140 | 65 | 0 | .683 |
| Hank Stram | Kansas City Chiefs, New Orleans Saints | 17 | 131 | 97 | 10 | .571 | 5 | 3 | 0 | .625 | 136 | 100 | 10 | .573 |
| Weeb Ewbank | Baltimore Colts, New York Jets | 20 | 130 | 129 | 7 | .502 | 4 | 1 | 0 | .800 | 134 | 130 | 7 | .507 |
| **Dan Reeves** | Denver Broncos, New York Giants | 13 | 121 | 78 | 1 | .608 | 8 | 7 | 0 | .553 | 129 | 85 | 1 | .602 |
| Sid Gillman | Los Angeles Rams, Los Angeles-San Diego Chargers, Houston Oilers | 18 | 122 | 99 | 7 | .550 | 1 | 5 | 0 | .167 | 123 | 104 | 7 | .541 |
| **Marv Levy** | Kansas City Chiefs, Buffalo Bills | 13 | 110 | 81 | 0 | .576 | 10 | 6 | 0 | .625 | 120 | 87 | 0 | .580 |
| George Allen | Los Angeles Rams, Washington Redskins | 12 | 116 | 47 | 5 | .705 | 2 | 7 | 0 | .222 | 118 | 54 | 5 | .681 |
| Don Coryell | St. Louis Cardinals, San Diego Chargers | 14 | 111 | 83 | 1 | .572 | 3 | 6 | 0 | .333 | 114 | 89 | 1 | .561 |
| Mike Ditka | Chicago Bears | 11 | 106 | 62 | 0 | .631 | 6 | 6 | 0 | .500 | 112 | 68 | 0 | .622 |
| John Madden | Oakland Raiders | 10 | 103 | 32 | 7 | .750 | 9 | 7 | 0 | .563 | 112 | 39 | 7 | .731 |
| Ray (Buddy) Parker | Chicago Cardinals, Detroit Lions, Pittsburgh Steelers | 15 | 104 | 75 | 9 | .577 | 3 | 1 | 0 | .750 | 107 | 76 | 9 | .581 |
| Vince Lombardi | Green Bay Packers, Washington Redskins | 10 | 96 | 34 | 6 | .728 | 9 | 1 | 0 | .900 | 105 | 35 | 6 | .740 |
| Bill Walsh | San Francisco 49ers | 10 | 92 | 59 | 1 | .609 | 10 | 4 | 0 | .714 | 102 | 63 | 1 | .617 |

*Active coaches in bold.*

## DRAFT LIST FOR 1994

59th Annual NFL Draft, April 24-25, 1994

### ARIZONA CARDINALS
**(Drafted alternately 10-9-11)**
1. Jamir Miller—10, LB, UCLA
2. Chuck Levy—38, RB, Arizona
   *Choice to Miami
3. Rich Braham—76, G, West Virginia
   Eric England—89, DE, Texas A&M, from Green Bay through Miami
4. Perry Carter—107, DB, Southern Mississippi, from New England
   John Reece—113, DB, Nebraska
   Terry Irving—115, LB, McNeese State, from San Diego through Miami
5. Anthony Redmon—139, G, Auburn
6. Terry Samuels—172, TE, Kentucky
7. Frank Harvey—204, RB, Georgia

### ATLANTA FALCONS
**(Drafted alternately 7-8)**
1. Choice to San Francisco through Indianapolis and Los Angeles Rams
2. Choice to Philadelphia
   *Bert Emanuel—45, WR, Rice, from Minnesota
3. Anthony Phillips—72, DB, Texas A&M-Kingsville
   *Choice to Los Angeles Rams through Indianapolis
   Alai Kalaniuvalu—99, G, Oregon State, from Dallas through San Francisco and Denver
4. Perry Klein—111, QB, C.W. Post
   Mitch Davis—118, LB, Georgia, from Philadelphia
5. Harrison Houston—138, WR, Florida
6. Choice to Green Bay through Los Angeles Raiders
7. Jamal Anderson—201, RB, Utah

### BUFFALO BILLS
**(Drafted 27)**
1. Jeff Burris—27, DB, Notre Dame
2.*Bucky Brooks—48, WR, North Carolina
   Lonnie Johnson—61, TE, Florida State
   *Sam Rogers—64, LB, Colorado
3.*Marlo Perry—81, LB, Jackson State
   Corey Louchiey—98, T, South Carolina
4. Sean Crocker—130, DB, North Carolina
5. A.J. Ofodile—158, TE, Missouri
6. Anthony Abrams—188, DE, Clark, Ga.
   *Kevin Knox—192, WR, Florida State
7. Filmel Johnson—221, DB, Illinois

### CHICAGO BEARS
**(Drafted alternately 11-10-9)**
1. John Thierry—11, DE, Alcorn State
2. Marcus Spears—39, T, N.W. Louisiana
3. Jim Flanigan—74, DT, Notre Dame
4. Raymont Harris—114, RB, Ohio State
5. Choice to Pittsburgh
6. Lloyd Hill—170, WR, Texas Tech
7. Dennis Collier—205, DB, Colorado

### CINCINNATI BENGALS
**(Drafted 1)**
1. Dan Wilkinson—1, DT, Ohio State
2. Darnay Scott—30, WR, San Diego State
3. Jeff Cothran—66, RB, Ohio State
   *Steve Shine—86, LB, Northwestern
4. Corey Sawyer—104, DB, Florida State
5. Trent Pollard—132, T, Eastern Washington
6. Kimo Von Oelhoffen—162, DT, Boise State
   Jerry Reynolds—184, T, Nevada-Las Vegas, from Los Angeles Raiders
7. Ramondo Stallings—195, DE, San Diego State

### CLEVELAND BROWNS
**(Drafted alternately 9-11-10)**
1. Antonio Langham—9, DB, Alabama
   *Derrick Alexander—29, WR, Michigan, from Philadelphia
2. Choice to Minnesota through Philadelphia and Atlanta
3. Romeo Bandison—75, DT, Oregon
4. Choice to Miami
5. Issac Booth—141, DB, California
6. Robert Strait—171, RB, Baylor
7. Andre Hewitt—203, T, Clemson

### DALLAS COWBOYS
**(Drafted 28)**
1. Shante Carver—23, DE, Arizona State, from San Francisco
   Choice to San Francisco
2.*Larry Allen—46, G, Sonoma State
   Choice to San Francisco
3. Choice to Atlanta through San Francisco and Denver
   *George Hegamin—102, T, North Carolina State
4. Willie Jackson—109, WR, Florida, from Tampa Bay
   DeWayne Dotson—131, LB, Mississippi
5. Choice to Los Angeles Raiders
6. Choice to Los Angeles Rams
   *Darren Studstill—191, DB, West Virginia, from Los Angeles Rams
7. Toddrick McIntosh—216, DT, Florida State, from Los Angeles Raiders
   Choice to New England

### DENVER BRONCOS
**(Drafted alternately 18-17-16-20-19)**
1. Choice to Minnesota
2. Allen Aldridge—51, LB, Houston
3. Choice to San Francisco
4. Randy Fuller—123, DB, Tennessee State
5. Choice to Green Bay through San Francisco
6. Choice to Minnesota
7. Keith Burns—210, LB, Oklahoma State
   Butler By'not'e—212, RB, Ohio State, from Green Bay
   Tom Nalen—218, C, Boston College, from New York Giants

### DETROIT LIONS
**(Drafted alternately 21-23-22)**
1. Johnnie Morton—21, WR, Southern California
2. Van Malone—57, DB, Texas
3. Shane Bonham—93, DT, Tennessee
4. Vaughn Bryant—124, DB, Stanford
5. Tony Semple—154, G, Memphis State
6. Jocelyn Borgella—183, DB, Cincinnati
7. Tom Beer—215, LB, Wayne State, Mich.

### GREEN BAY PACKERS
**(Drafted alternately 20-19-18-17-16)**
1. Aaron Taylor—16, T, Notre Dame, from Miami
   Choice to Miami
2. Choice to San Francisco
3.*Le Shon Johnson—84, RB, Northern Illinois, from San Francisco
   Choice to Arizona through Miami
4. Choice to Los Angeles Raiders
   Gabe Wilkins—126, DE, Gardner-Webb, from San Francisco through Los Angeles Raiders
5. Terry Mickens—146, WR, Florida A&M
   Dorsey Levens—149, RB, Georgia Tech, from Denver through San Francisco
6. Jay Kearney—169, WR, West Virginia, from Atlanta through Los Angeles Raiders
   Ruffin Hamilton—175, LB, Tulane, from San Diego through San Francisco
   Bill Schroeder—181, WR, Wisconsin-LaCrosse
   *Paul Duckworth—190, LB, Connecticut, from Philadelphia through San Francisco
7. Choice to Denver

### HOUSTON OILERS
**(Drafted 26)**
1. Henry Ford—26, DE, Arkansas
2. Jeremy Nunley—60, DE, Alabama
3. Choice to Washington
   *Malcolm Seabron—101, WR, Fresno State
4. Michael Davis—119, DB, Cincinnati, from Minnesota
   Sean Jackson—129, RB, Florida State
5. Roderick Lewis—157, TE, Arizona
   *Jim Reid—161, T, Virginia
6. Lee Gissendaner—187, WR, Northwestern
   *Barron Wortham—194, LB, Texas-El Paso
7. Lemanski Hall—220, LB, Alabama

### INDIANAPOLIS COLTS
**(Drafted alternately 2-3)**
1. Marshall Faulk—2, RB, San Diego State
   Trev Alberts—5, LB, Nebraska, from Los Angeles Rams
2. Eric Mahlum—32, G, California
3. Jason Mathews—67, T, Texas A&M
4. Brad Banta—106, TE, Southern California
5. John Covington—133, DB, Notre Dame
6. Lamont Warren —164, RB, Colorado
7. Lance Teichelman—196, DT, Texas A&M

### KANSAS CITY CHIEFS
**(Drafted alternately 25-24)**
1. Greg Hill—25, RB, Texas A&M
2. Donnell Bennett—58, RB, Miami
3. Lake Dawson—92, WR, Notre Dame, from San Francisco
   Chris Penn—96, WR, Tulsa
4. Bracey Walker—127, DB, North Carolina
5. James Burton—151, DB, Fresno State, from Minnesota
   Rob Waldrop—156, DT, Arizona
6. Anthony Daigle—185, RB, Fresno State
7. Steve Matthews—199, QB, Memphis State, from Los Angeles Rams
   Tracy Greene—219, TE, Grambling

### LOS ANGELES RAIDERS
**(Drafted alternately 22-21-23)**
1. Rob Fredrickson—22, LB, Michigan State
2. James Folston—52, DE, N.E. Louisiana, from Minnesota
   Choice to Minnesota
3. Calvin Jones—80, RB, Nebraska, from New York Jets
   Choice to New York Jets
4. Austin Robbins—120, DT, North Carolina, from Green Bay
   Choice to Minnesota
5. Choice to New York Jets
   Roosevelt Patterson—159, G, Alabama, from Dallas
6. Choice to Cincinnati
7. Choice to Dallas
   Rob Holmberg—217, LB, Penn State, from San Francisco through Dallas

### LOS ANGELES RAMS
**(Drafted alternately 5-4-6)**
1. Choice to Indianapolis
   Wayne Gandy—15, T, Auburn, from San Diego through San Francisco
2. Isaac Bruce—33, WR, Memphis State
   *Toby Wright—49, DB, Nebraska
   Brad Ottis—56, DT, Wayne State, Neb., from San Francisco
3. Keith Lyle—71, DB, Virginia
   *James Bostic—83, RB, Auburn, from Atlanta through Indianapolis
   *Ernest Jones—100, LB, Oregon, from Philadelphia through San Francisco
4. Chris Brantley—108, WR, Rutgers
5. Choice to New England through Arizona
6. Rickey Brady—167, TE, Oklahoma
   Ronald Edwards—189, T, North Carolina A&T, from Dallas
   *Choice to Dallas
7. Choice to Kansas City

### MIAMI DOLPHINS
**(Drafted alternately 16-20-19-18-17)**
1. Choice to Green Bay
   Tim Bowens—20, DT, Mississippi, from Green Bay
2. Aubrey Beavers—54, LB, Oklahoma
   *Tim Ruddy—65, C, Notre Dame, from Arizona
3. Choice to New England
4. Ronnie Woolfork—112, LB, Colorado, from Cleveland
   Choice to New England through Arizona

5. William Gaines—147, DT, Florida
6. Brant Boyer—177, LB, Arizona
7. Sean Hill—214, DB, Montana State

**MINNESOTA VIKINGS**
**(Drafted alternately 19-18-17-16-20)**
1. DeWayne Washington—18, DB, North Carolina State, from Denver
   Todd Steussie—19, T, California
2. David Palmer—40, WR, Alabama, from Cleveland through Philadelphia and Atlanta
   *Choice to Atlanta
   Choice to Los Angeles Raiders
   Fernando Smith—55, DE, Jackson State, from Los Angeles Raiders
3. Choice to Pittsburgh
4. Choice to Houston
   Mike Wells—125, DT, Iowa, from Los Angeles Raiders
5. Shelly Hammonds—134, DB, Penn State, from Washington
   Choice to Kansas City
6. Andrew Jordan—179, TE, Western Carolina, from Denver
   Choice to Pittsburgh
7. Pete Bercich—211, LB, Notre Dame

**NEW ENGLAND PATRIOTS**
**(Drafted alternately 4-6-5)**
1. Willie McGinest—4, DE, Southern California
2. Kevin Lee—35, WR, Alabama
3. Choice to San Diego
   Ervin Collier—78, NT, Florida A&M, from San Diego
   Joe Burch—90, C, Texas Southern, from Miami
4. Choice to Arizona
   John Burke—121, TE, Virginia Tech, from Miami through Arizona
5. Pat O'Neill—135, P, Syracuse, from Los Angeles Rams through Arizona
   Choice to San Diego
6. Steve Hawkins—166, WR, Western Michigan
   Max Lane —168, T, Navy, from Seattle
7. Jay Walker—198, QB, Howard
   Marty Moore—222, LB, Kentucky, from Dallas

**NEW ORLEANS SAINTS**
**(Drafted alternately 12-15-14-13)**
1. Choice to New York Jets
   Joe Johnson—13, DE, Louisville, from New York Jets
2. Mario Bates—44, RB, Arizona State
3. Winfred Tubbs—79, LB, Texas
4. Doug Nussmeier—116, QB, Idaho
5. Herman Carroll—142, DE, Mississippi State
   Craig Novitsky—143, G, UCLA, from New York Jets
6. Derrell Mitchell—176, WR, Texas Tech
7. Lance Lundberg—213, T, Nebraska

**NEW YORK GIANTS**
**(Drafted alternately 24-25)**
1. Thomas Lewis—24, WR, Indiana
2. *Thomas Randolph—47, DB, Kansas State
   Jason Sehorn—59, DB, Southern California
3. Gary Downs—95, RB, North Carolina State
4. Chris Maumalanga—128, DT, Kansas
5. Chad Bratzke—155, DE, Eastern Kentucky
6. Jason Winrow—186, G, Ohio State
7. Choice to Denver

**NEW YORK JETS**
**(Drafted alternately 13-12-15-14)**
1. Aaron Glenn—12, DB, Texas A&M, from New Orleans
   Choice to New Orleans
2. Ryan Yarborough—41, WR, Wyoming
3. Choice to Los Angeles Raiders
   Lou Benfatti—94, DT, Penn State, from Los Angeles Raiders
4. Orlando Parker—117, WR, Troy State
5. Choice to New Orleans
   Horace Morris—152, LB, Tennessee from Los Angeles Raiders
6. Fred Lester—173, RB, Alabama A&M
7. Glenn Foley—208, QB, Boston College

**PHILADELPHIA EAGLES**
**(Drafted alternately 14-13-12-15)**
1. Bernard Williams—14, T, Georgia
   *Choice to Cleveland
2. Bruce Walker—37, DT, UCLA, from Atlanta
   Charlie Garner—42, RB, Tennessee
3. Joe Panos—77, G, Wisconsin
   *Choice to Los Angeles Rams through San Francisco
   *Eric Zomalt—103, DB, California
4. Choice to Atlanta
5. Marvin Goodwin—144, DB, UCLA
6. Ryan McCoy—174, LB, Houston
   *Choice to Green Bay through San Francisco
   *Mitch Berger—193, P, Colorado
7. Mark Montgomery—206, RB, Wisconsin

**PITTSBURGH STEELERS**
**(Drafted alternately 17-16-20-19-18)**
1. Charles Johnson—17, WR, Colorado
2. Brentson Buckner—50, DE, Clemson
3. Jason Gildon—88, LB, Oklahoma State, from Minnesota
   Bam Morris—91, RB, Texas Tech
4. Taase Faumui—122, DE, Hawaii
5. Myron Bell—140, DB, Michigan State, from Chicago
   Gary Brown—148, T, Georgia Tech
6. Jim Miller—178, QB, Michigan State
   Eric Ravotti—180, LB, Penn State, from Minnesota
7. Brice Abrams—209, RB, Michigan State

**SAN DIEGO CHARGERS**
**(Drafted alternately 15-14-13-12)**
1. Choice to L.A. Rams through San Francisco
2. Isaac Davis—43, G, Arkansas
   *Vaughn Parker—63, G, UCLA
3. Andre Coleman—70, WR, Kansas State, from New England
   Choice to New England
   *Willie Clark—82, DB, Notre Dame
4. Choice to Arizona through Miami
5. Aaron Laing—137, TE, New Mexico State, from New England
   Rodney Harrison—145, DB, Western Illinois
   Darren Krein—150, DE, Miami, from Seattle
   *Tony Vinson—160, RB, Towson State
6. Choice to Green Bay through San Francisco
7. Zane Beehn—207, LB, Kentucky

**SAN FRANCISCO 49ERS**
**(Drafted alternately 23-22-21)**
1. Bryant Young—7, DT, Notre Dame, from Atlanta through Indianapolis and Los Angeles Rams
   Choice to Dallas
   William Floyd—28, RB, Florida State, from Dallas
2. Kevin Mitchell—53, LB, Syracuse, from Green Bay
   Choice to Los Angeles Rams
   Tyronne Drakeford—62, DB, Virginia Tech, from Dallas
3. *Choice to Green Bay
   *Doug Brien—85, K, California
   Cory Fleming—87, WR, Tennessee, from Denver
   Choice to Kansas City
4. Choice to Green Bay through Los Angeles Raiders
5. Tony Peterson—153, LB, Notre Dame
6. Lee Woodall—182, LB, West Chester, Pa.
7. Choice to Los Angeles Raiders through Dallas

**SEATTLE SEAHAWKS**
**(Drafted alternately 8-7)**
1. Sam Adams—8, DT, Texas A&M
2. Kevin Mawae—36, C, Louisiana State
3. Lamar Smith—73, RB, Houston
4. Larry Whigham —110, DB, N.E. Louisiana
5. Choice to San Diego
6. Choice to New England
7. Carlester Crumpler—202, TE, East Carolina

**TAMPA BAY BUCCANEERS**
**(Drafted alternately 6-5-4)**
1. Trent Dilfer—6, QB, Fresno State
2. Errict Rhett—34, RB, Florida
3. Harold Bishop—69, TE, Louisiana State
4. Choice to Dallas
5. Pete Pierson—136, T, Washington
6. Bernard Carter —165, LB, East Carolina
7. Jim Pyne—200, C, Virginia Tech

**WASHINGTON REDSKINS**
**(Drafted alternately 3-2)**
1. Heath Shuler—3, QB, Tennessee
2. Tre Johnson—31, T, Temple
3. Tydus Winans—68, WR, Fresno State
   Joseph Patton—97, G, Alabama A&M, from Houston
4. Kurt Haws—105, TE, Utah
5. Choice to Minnesota
6. Dexter Nottage—163, DE, Florida A&M
7. Gus Frerotte—197, QB, Tulsa

*Compensatory pick

**NUMBER OF PLAYERS DRAFTED**

**BY POSITION:**

| | |
|---|---|
| Defensive Backs | 34 |
| Linebackers | 33 |
| Wide Receivers | 29 |
| Running Backs | 28 |
| Defensive Ends | 18 |
| Defensive Tackles | 18 |
| Tackles | 18 |
| Guards | 13 |
| Tight Ends | 13 |
| Quarterbacks | 9 |
| Centers | 5 |
| Punters | 2 |
| Kickers | 1 |
| Nose Tackles | 1 |
| Kick Returners | 0 |

**BY COLLEGE (3 or more players):**

| | |
|---|---|
| Notre Dame | 10 |
| Alabama | 6 |
| Colorado | 6 |
| Florida State | 6 |
| Texas A&M | 6 |
| California | 5 |
| Fresno State | 5 |
| Nebraska | 5 |
| Ohio State | 5 |
| Tennessee | 5 |
| UCLA | 5 |
| Arizona | 4 |
| Florida | 4 |
| Michigan State | 4 |
| North Carolina | 4 |
| Penn State | 4 |
| Southern California | 4 |
| Auburn | 3 |
| Florida A&M | 3 |
| Georgia | 3 |
| Houston | 3 |
| Kentucky | 3 |
| Memphis State | 3 |
| North Carolina State | 3 |
| San Diego State | 3 |
| Texas Tech | 3 |
| Virginia Tech | 3 |
| West Virginia | 3 |

# AFC ACTIVE STATISTICAL LEADERS

## TOP ACTIVE PASSERS, AMERICAN FOOTBALL CONFERENCE

1,000 or more attempts

| | Yrs. | Att. | Comp. | Pct. Comp. | Yards | Avg. Gain | TD | Pct. TD | Had Int. | Pct. Int. | Rating Pts. |
|---|---|---|---|---|---|---|---|---|---|---|---|
| Joe Montana, K.C. | 14 | 4898 | 3110 | 63.5 | 37268 | 7.61 | 257 | 5.2 | 130 | 2.7 | 93.1 |
| Dan Marino, Mia. | 11 | 5434 | 3219 | 59.2 | 40720 | 7.49 | 298 | 5.5 | 168 | 3.1 | 88.1 |
| Jim Kelly, Buff. | 8 | 3494 | 2112 | 60.4 | 26413 | 7.56 | 179 | 5.1 | 126 | 3.6 | 86.0 |
| Boomer Esiason, N.Y.J. | 10 | 3851 | 2185 | 56.7 | 29092 | 7.55 | 190 | 4.9 | 140 | 3.6 | 82.1 |
| Jeff Hostetler, Raiders | 8 | 1051 | 601 | 57.2 | 7651 | 7.28 | 34 | 3.2 | 22 | 2.1 | 82.1 |
| Bernie Kosar, Mia. | 11 | 3213 | 1889 | 58.8 | 22314 | 6.94 | 119 | 3.7 | 81 | 2.5 | 81.9 |
| Neil O'Donnell, Pitt. | 3 | 1085 | 611 | 56.3 | 7454 | 6.87 | 38 | 3.5 | 23 | 2.1 | 80.5 |
| Mark Rypien, Clev. | 6 | 2207 | 1244 | 56.4 | 15928 | 7.22 | 101 | 4.6 | 75 | 3.4 | 80.2 |
| John Elway, Den. | 11 | 4890 | 2723 | 55.7 | 34246 | 7.00 | 183 | 3.7 | 167 | 3.4 | 75.9 |
| Steve DeBerg, Mia. | 18 | 4965 | 2844 | 57.3 | 33872 | 6.82 | 193 | 3.9 | 203 | 4.1 | 74.2 |
| Jim Harbaugh, Ind. | 7 | 1759 | 1023 | 58.2 | 11567 | 6.58 | 50 | 2.8 | 56 | 3.2 | 74.2 |
| Don Majkowski, Ind. | 7 | 1631 | 902 | 55.3 | 10975 | 6.73 | 56 | 3.4 | 57 | 3.5 | 73.1 |
| Jay Schroeder, Cin. | 9 | 2570 | 1293 | 50.3 | 18553 | 7.22 | 110 | 4.3 | 101 | 3.9 | 72.0 |
| Vinny Testaverde, Clev. | 7 | 2390 | 1256 | 52.6 | 16617 | 6.95 | 91 | 3.8 | 121 | 5.1 | 66.4 |
| Mike Tomczak, Pitt. | 9 | 1418 | 731 | 51.6 | 9828 | 6.93 | 53 | 3.7 | 68 | 4.8 | 66.4 |
| Jack Trudeau, N.Y.J. | 8 | 1536 | 812 | 52.9 | 9647 | 6.28 | 41 | 2.7 | 62 | 4.0 | 64.4 |
| Vince Evans, Raiders | 13 | 1182 | 586 | 49.6 | 8027 | 6.79 | 44 | 3.7 | 66 | 5.6 | 60.8 |

## TOP ACTIVE RUSHERS, AFC

2,000 or more yards

| | Yrs. | Att. | Yards | TD |
|---|---|---|---|---|
| 1. Marcus Allen, K.C. | 12 | 2296 | 9309 | 91 |
| 2. Thurman Thomas, Buff. | 6 | 1731 | 7631 | 41 |
| 3. Earnest Byner, Clev. | 10 | 1662 | 6663 | 48 |
| 4. John L. Williams, Pitt. | 8 | 1148 | 4579 | 17 |
| 5. Marion Butts, N.E. | 5 | 1031 | 4297 | 31 |
| 6. Lorenzo White, Hou. | 6 | 809 | 3322 | 26 |
| 7. Johnny Johnson, N.Y.J. | 4 | 806 | 3147 | 18 |
| 8. Kenneth Davis, Buff. | 8 | 732 | 3132 | 25 |
| 9. Barry Foster, Pitt. | 4 | 699 | 3092 | 21 |
| 10. Keith Byars, Mia. | 8 | 814 | 2941 | 20 |
| **Other Leading Rushers** | | | | |
| Bobby Humphrey | 4 | 695 | 2857 | 15 |
| Harold Green, Cin. | 4 | 721 | 2843 | 5 |
| Rod Bernstine, Den. | 7 | 630 | 2823 | 21 |
| Mark Higgs, Mia. | 6 | 732 | 2764 | 14 |
| Brad Baxter, N.Y.J. | 5 | 634 | 2462 | 30 |
| Leonard Russell, N.E. | 3 | 689 | 2437 | 13 |
| John Elway, Den. | 11 | 538 | 2435 | 22 |
| Ronnie Harmon, S.D. | 8 | 500 | 2326 | 7 |
| Derrick Fenner, Cin. | 5 | 550 | 2149 | 27 |
| Chris Warren, Sea. | 4 | 513 | 2113 | 11 |
| Blair Thomas, N.E. | 4 | 468 | 2009 | 5 |

## TOP ACTIVE PASS RECEIVERS, AFC

275 or more receptions

| | Yrs. | No. | Yards | TD |
|---|---|---|---|---|
| 1. Art Monk, N.Y.J. | 14 | 888 | 12026 | 65 |
| 2. Andre Reed, Buff. | 9 | 586 | 8233 | 58 |
| 3. Ernest Givins, Hou. | 8 | 506 | 7414 | 45 |
| 4. Marcus Allen, K.C. | 12 | 480 | 4496 | 21 |
| 5. Bill Brooks, Buff. | 8 | 471 | 6532 | 33 |
| John L. Williams, Pitt. | 8 | 471 | 4151 | 16 |
| 7. Keith Byars, Mia. | 8 | 432 | 4145 | 16 |
| 8. Irving Fryar, Mia. | 10 | 427 | 6736 | 43 |
| 9. Webster Slaughter, Hou. | 8 | 421 | 6224 | 36 |
| 10. Reggie Langhorne | 9 | 411 | 5446 | 19 |
| **Other Leading Receivers** | | | | |
| Vance Johnson, S.D. | 9 | 403 | 5525 | 37 |
| Ronnie Harmon, S.D. | 8 | 401 | 4103 | 16 |
| Earnest Byner, Clev. | 10 | 389 | 3611 | 12 |
| Haywood Jeffires, Hou. | 7 | 386 | 4652 | 33 |
| Anthony Miller, Den. | 6 | 374 | 5582 | 37 |
| Mark Carrier, Clev. | 7 | 364 | 5764 | 30 |
| Brian Blades, Sea. | 6 | 335 | 4474 | 22 |
| Willie Gault, Raiders | 11 | 333 | 6635 | 44 |
| Keith Jackson, Mia. | 6 | 329 | 3963 | 31 |
| Curtis Duncan, Hou. | 7 | 322 | 3935 | 20 |
| Tim McGee, Cin. | 8 | 308 | 5028 | 27 |
| Thurman Thomas, Buff. | 6 | 295 | 3053 | 16 |
| Pete Metzelaars, Buff. | 12 | 280 | 2797 | 21 |

## TOP ACTIVE SCORERS, AFC

250 or more points

| | Yrs. | TD | FG | PAT | TP |
|---|---|---|---|---|---|
| 1. Nick Lowery | 15 | 0 | 329 | 486 | 1473 |
| 2. Gary Anderson, Pitt. | 12 | 0 | 285 | 384 | 1239 |
| 3. Matt Bahr, N.E. | 19 | 0 | 250 | 459 | 1209 |
| 4. Al Del Greco, Hou. | 12 | 0 | 161 | 317 | 800 |
| 5. Dean Biasucci, Ind. | 9 | 0 | 160 | 218 | 698 |
| 6. Marcus Allen, K.C. | 12 | 113 | 0 | 0 | 678 |
| 7. Jeff Jaeger, Raiders | 6 | 0 | 131 | 191 | 584 |
| 8. Pete Stoyanovich, Mia. | 5 | 0 | 125 | 174 | 549 |
| 9. John Carney, S.D. | 8 | 0 | 97 | 130 | 421 |
| 10. Art Monk, N.Y.J. | 14 | 65 | 0 | 0 | 390 |
| **Other Leading Scorers** | | | | | |
| Steve Christie, Buff. | 4 | 0 | 85 | 128 | 383 |
| Earnest Byner, Clev. | 10 | 61 | 0 | 0 | 366 |
| Andre Reed, Buff. | 9 | 59 | 0 | 0 | 354 |
| Thurman Thomas, Buff. | 6 | 57 | 0 | 0 | 342 |
| Irving Fryar, Mia. | 10 | 47 | 0 | 0 | 282 |
| Ernest Givins, Hou. | 8 | 46 | 0 | 0 | 276 |
| Willie Gault, Raiders | 11 | 45 | 0 | 0 | 270 |
| Matt Stover, Clev. | 3 | 0 | 53 | 98 | 257 |
| John Kasay, Sea. | 3 | 0 | 62 | 70 | 256 |

## TOP ACTIVE INTERCEPTORS, AFC

20 or more interceptions

| | Yrs. | No. | Yards | TD |
|---|---|---|---|---|
| 1. Ronnie Lott, N.Y.J. | 13 | 63 | 730 | 5 |
| 2. Gill Byrd, S.D. | 10 | 42 | 546 | 2 |
| 3. Eugene Robinson, Sea. | 9 | 38 | 536 | 0 |
| Albert Lewis, Raiders | 11 | 38 | 329 | 0 |
| 5. David Fulcher, Raiders | 8 | 31 | 246 | 2 |
| 6. Dennis Smith, Den. | 13 | 30 | 431 | 0 |
| Mark Kelso | 8 | 30 | 327 | 1 |
| Lionel Washington, Raiders | 11 | 30 | 292 | 2 |
| 9. Felix Wright | 8 | 29 | 492 | 2 |
| 10. Rod Woodson, Pitt. | 7 | 28 | 549 | 2 |
| **Other Leading Interceptors** | | | | |
| Eugene Daniel, Ind. | 10 | 27 | 240 | 1 |
| Nate Odomes, Sea. | 7 | 26 | 224 | 1 |
| Cris Dishman, Hou. | 6 | 23 | 250 | 0 |
| Don Griffin, Clev. | 8 | 22 | 49 | 0 |
| Louis Oliver, Cin. | 5 | 21 | 459 | 2 |
| Gene Atkins, Mia. | 7 | 21 | 324 | 0 |
| Wilber Marshall, Hou. | 10 | 21 | 271 | 3 |

## TOP ACTIVE QUARTERBACK SACKERS, AFC (since 1982)

50 or more sacks

| | Yrs. | No. |
|---|---|---|
| 1. Greg Townsend, Raiders | 11 | 107.5 |
| 2. Bruce Smith, Buff. | 9 | 106.0 |
| 3. Simon Fletcher, Den. | 9 | 85.5 |
| 4. Kevin Greene, Pitt. | 9 | 85.0 |
| 5. Lee Williams, Hou. | 10 | 82.5 |
| 6. Leonard Marshall | 11 | 81.5 |
| 7. Leslie O'Neal, S.D. | 7 | 80.5 |
| 8. Karl Mecklenburg, Den. | 11 | 77.5 |
| 9. Ray Childress, Hou. | 9 | 68.5 |
| 10. Derrick Thomas, K.C. | 5 | 66.0 |
| **Other Leading Sackers** | | |
| Jeff Bryant, Sea. | 12 | 63.0 |
| Clay Matthews, Clev. | 16 | 62.0 |
| Keith Willis, N.Y.J. | 12 | 59.0 |
| Bill Pickel, N.Y.J. | 11 | 56.0 |
| Neil Smith, K.C. | 6 | 56.0 |
| Duane Bickett | 9 | 50.0 |

## TOP ACTIVE PUNT RETURNERS, AFC

40 or more punt returns

| | Yrs. | No. | Yards | Avg. | TD |
|---|---|---|---|---|---|
| 1. Eric Metcalf, Clev. | 5 | 92 | 993 | 10.8 | 3 |
| 2. Glyn Milburn, Den. | 1 | 40 | 425 | 10.6 | 0 |
| 3. Tim Brown, Raiders | 6 | 193 | 1960 | 10.2 | 2 |
| 4. Kelvin Martin, Sea. | 7 | 170 | 1700 | 10.0 | 3 |
| 5. Irving Fryar, Mia. | 10 | 206 | 2055 | 10.0 | 3 |
| 6. Dale Carter, K.C. | 2 | 65 | 645 | 9.9 | 2 |
| 7. Rod Woodson, Pitt. | 7 | 218 | 2043 | 9.4 | 2 |
| 8. Jeff Query, Cin. | 5 | 76 | 712 | 9.4 | 0 |
| 9. Don Griffin, Clev. | 8 | 74 | 667 | 9.0 | 1 |
| 10. Kitrick Taylor, Den. | 6 | 63 | 568 | 9.0 | 1 |
| **Other Leading Punt Returners** | | | | | |
| Chris Warren, Sea. | 4 | 94 | 819 | 8.7 | 1 |
| Vance Johnson, S.D. | 9 | 81 | 689 | 8.5 | 0 |
| Willie Drewrey, Hou. | 9 | 192 | 1597 | 8.3 | 0 |
| Scott Miller, Mia. | 3 | 52 | 423 | 8.1 | 0 |
| Patrick Robinson, Cin. | 1 | 43 | 305 | 7.1 | 0 |
| Bill Brooks, Buff. | 8 | 44 | 295 | 6.7 | 0 |

## TOP ACTIVE KICKOFF RETURNERS, AFC

40 or more kick returns

| | Yrs. | No. | Yards | Avg. | TD |
|---|---|---|---|---|---|
| 1. Tim Brown, Raiders | 6 | 47 | 1204 | 25.6 | 1 |
| 2. Anthony Miller, Den. | 6 | 50 | 1269 | 25.4 | 2 |
| 3. Willie Gault, Raiders | 11 | 45 | 1088 | 24.2 | 1 |
| 4. Vance Johnson, S.D. | 9 | 45 | 1027 | 22.8 | 0 |
| 5. Jon Vaughn, Sea. | 3 | 70 | 1561 | 22.3 | 2 |
| 6. Rod Woodson, Pitt. | 7 | 205 | 4529 | 22.1 | 2 |
| 7. Tim McGee, Cin. | 8 | 58 | 1249 | 21.5 | 0 |
| 8. Eric Ball, Cin. | 5 | 73 | 1559 | 21.4 | 0 |
| 9. Steve Tasker, Buff. | 11 | 42 | 896 | 21.3 | 0 |
| 10. Gene Atkins, Mia. | 7 | 71 | 1508 | 21.2 | 0 |
| **Other Leading Kickoff Returners** | | | | | |
| Leonard Harris, Hou. | 8 | 57 | 1193 | 20.9 | 0 |
| Chris Warren, Sea. | 4 | 86 | 1794 | 20.9 | 0 |
| Randy Baldwin, Clev. | 4 | 55 | 1133 | 20.6 | 0 |
| Willie Drewrey, Hou. | 9 | 102 | 2097 | 20.6 | 0 |
| Harvey Williams, Raiders | 3 | 48 | 982 | 20.5 | 0 |
| Alexander Wright, Raiders | 6 | 69 | 1399 | 20.3 | 2 |
| Eric Metcalf, Clev. | 5 | 130 | 2596 | 20.0 | 2 |
| Ronnie Harmon, S.D. | 8 | 58 | 1148 | 19.8 | 0 |
| Aaron Craver, Mia. | 2 | 40 | 789 | 19.7 | 0 |
| Robert Delpino, Den. | 6 | 68 | 1339 | 19.7 | 0 |
| Dwight Stone, Pitt. | 7 | 98 | 1904 | 19.4 | 1 |
| Kelvin Martin, Sea. | 7 | 54 | 1035 | 19.2 | 0 |
| Kenneth Davis, Buff. | 8 | 41 | 707 | 17.2 | 0 |
| Mark Ingram, Mia. | 7 | 47 | 742 | 15.8 | 0 |

## TOP ACTIVE PUNTERS, AFC

50 or more punts

| | Yrs. | No. | Avg. | LG |
|---|---|---|---|---|
| 1. Tom Rouen, Den. | 1 | 67 | 45.0 | 62 |
| 2. Rohn Stark, Ind. | 12 | 912 | 43.9 | 72 |
| 3. Rick Tuten, Sea. | 5 | 307 | 43.1 | 65 |
| 4. Rich Camarillo, Hou. | 13 | 854 | 42.9 | 76 |
| 5. Jim Arnold, Mia. | 11 | 820 | 42.5 | 71 |
| 6. Brian Hansen, N.Y.J. | 9 | 689 | 42.3 | 73 |
| 7. Lee Johnson, Cin. | 13 | 607 | 41.8 | 70 |
| 8. Mike Saxon, N.E. | 9 | 664 | 41.6 | 64 |
| 9. Mark Royals, Pitt. | 7 | 329 | 41.4 | 62 |
| 10. Jeff Gossett, Raiders | 14 | 773 | 41.2 | 64 |
| **Other Leading Punters** | | | | |
| John Kidd, S.D. | 10 | 708 | 40.8 | 67 |
| Chris Mohr, Buff. | 5 | 272 | 40.1 | 61 |
| Louie Aguiar, K.C. | 4 | 210 | 39.6 | 71 |

## TOP ACTIVE PASSERS, NATIONAL FOOTBALL CONFERENCE

1,000 or more attempts

| | Yrs. | Att. | Comp. | Pct. Comp. | Yards | Avg. Gain | TD | Pct. TD | Had Int. | Pct. Int. | Rating Pts. |
|---|---|---|---|---|---|---|---|---|---|---|---|
| Steve Young, S.F. | 9 | 1968 | 1222 | 62.1 | 15900 | 8.08 | 105 | 5.3 | 58 | 2.9 | 93.0 |
| Dave Krieg, Det. | 14 | 4178 | 2431 | 58-2 | 30485 | 7.30 | 217 | 5.2 | 163 | 3.9 | 82.0 |
| Troy Aikman, Dall. | 5 | 1920 | 1191 | 62.0 | 13627 | 7.10 | 69 | 3.6 | 66 | 3.4 | 81.0 |
| Ken O'Brien | 10 | 3602 | 2110 | 58.6 | 25094 | 6.97 | 128 | 3.6 | 98 | 2.7 | 80.4 |
| Warren Moon, Minn. | 10 | 4546 | 2632 | 57.9 | 33685 | 7.41 | 196 | 4.3 | 166 | 3.7 | 80.4 |
| Randall Cunningham, Phil. | 9 | 2751 | 1540 | 56.0 | 19043 | 6.92 | 131 | 4.8 | 87 | 3.2 | 80.3 |
| Bobby Hebert, Atl. | 8 | 2485 | 1465 | 59.0 | 17608 | 7.09 | 109 | 4.4 | 92 | 3.7 | 79.9 |
| Jim McMahon, Ariz. | 12 | 2525 | 1465 | 58.0 | 17884 | 7.08 | 99 | 3.9 | 87 | 3.4 | 78.7 |
| Phil Simms, N.Y.G. | 14 | 4647 | 2576 | 55.4 | 33462 | 7.20 | 199 | 4.3 | 157 | 3.4 | 78.5 |
| Jim Everett, N.O. | 8 | 3277 | 1847 | 56.4 | 23758 | 7.25 | 142 | 4.3 | 123 | 3.8 | 78.1 |
| Steve Beuerlein, Ariz. | 5 | 1028 | 551 | 53.6 | 7545 | 7.34 | 44 | 4.3 | 36 | 3.5 | 77.0 |
| Wade Wilson, N.O. | 12 | 2216 | 1261 | 56.9 | 15958 | 7.20 | 91 | 4.1 | 94 | 4.2 | 75.5 |
| Chris Miller, Rams | 7 | 2089 | 1129 | 54.0 | 14066 | 6.73 | 87 | 4.2 | 72 | 3.4 | 74.7 |
| Rodney Peete, Dall. | 5 | 1125 | 641 | 57.0 | 8164 | 7.26 | 38 | 3.4 | 49 | 4.4 | 72.9 |
| Bubby Brister, Phil. | 8 | 1786 | 957 | 53.6 | 12009 | 6.72 | 65 | 3.6 | 62 | 3.5 | 72.4 |
| Rich Gannon, Wash. | 6 | 1128 | 635 | 56.3 | 7161 | 6.35 | 43 | 3.8 | 43 | 3.8 | 72.3 |
| Jeff George, Atl. | 4 | 1532 | 874 | 57.0 | 9551 | 6.23 | 41 | 2.7 | 46 | 3.0 | 72.0 |
| Chris Chandler, Rams | 8 | 1066 | 585 | 54.9 | 6769 | 6.35 | 34 | 3.2 | 48 | 4.5 | 66.1 |

## TOP ACTIVE QUARTERBACK SACKERS, NFC (since 1982)

50 or more sacks

| | Yrs. | No. |
|---|---|---|
| 1. Reggie White, G.B. | 9 | 137.0 |
| 2. Richard Dent, S.F. | 11 | 124.5 |
| 3. Rickey Jackson, N.O. | 13 | 115.0 |
| 4. Steve McMichael, G.B. | 14 | 92.5 |
| 5. Chris Doleman, Atl. | 9 | 88.5 |
| Sean Jones, G.B. | 10 | 88.5 |
| 7. Jim Jeffcoat, Dall. | 11 | 86.5 |
| 8. Pat Swilling, Det. | 8 | 83.0 |
| 9. Charles Mann | 11 | 82.0 |
| 10. Clyde Simmons, Ariz. | 8 | 76.0 |
| **Other Leading Sackers** | | |
| Tim Harris, Phil. | 8 | 75.0 |
| Charles Haley, Dall. | 8 | 73.5 |
| Freddie Joe Nunn, Ariz. | 9 | 66.5 |
| Michael Cofer, Det. | 10 | 62.5 |
| William Fuller, Phil. | 8 | 59.0 |
| Keith Millard | 10 | 58.0 |

## TOP ACTIVE RUSHERS, NFC

2,000 or more yards

| | Yrs. | Att. | Yards | TD |
|---|---|---|---|---|
| 1. Roger Craig, Minn. | 11 | 1991 | 8189 | 56 |
| 2. Herschel Walker, Phil. | 9 | 1794 | 7468 | 55 |
| 3. Barry Sanders, Det. | 5 | 1432 | 6789 | 55 |
| 4. Neal Anderson | 8 | 1515 | 6166 | 51 |
| 5. Emmitt Smith, Dall. | 4 | 1262 | 5699 | 50 |
| 6. Dalton Hilliard, N.O. | 8 | 1126 | 4164 | 39 |
| 7. Randall Cunningham, Phil. | 9 | 591 | 4096 | 29 |
| 8. Rodney Hampton, N.Y.G. | 4 | 914 | 3732 | 31 |
| 9. Gary Anderson, Det. | 10 | 869 | 3409 | 16 |
| 10. Merril Hoge, Chi. | 7 | 819 | 3115 | 21 |
| **Other Leading Rushers** | | | | |
| Reggie Cobb, G.B. | 4 | 878 | 3061 | 21 |
| Barry Word, Minn. | 6 | 705 | 2897 | 16 |
| Steve Young, S.F. | 9 | 431 | 2676 | 20 |
| Cleveland Gary, Rams | 5 | 667 | 2634 | 24 |
| Brad Muster, N.O. | 6 | 519 | 2228 | 23 |
| Heath Sherman, Phil. | 5 | 537 | 2130 | 10 |
| Craig Heyward | 6 | 500 | 2019 | 13 |

## TOP ACTIVE PASS RECEIVERS, NFC

275 or more receptions

| | Yrs. | No. | Yards | TD |
|---|---|---|---|---|
| 1. Jerry Rice, S.F. | 9 | 708 | 11776 | 118 |
| 2. Gary Clark, Ariz. | 9 | 612 | 9560 | 62 |
| 3. Henry Ellard, Wash. | 11 | 593 | 9761 | 48 |
| 4. Roger Craig, Minn. | 11 | 566 | 4911 | 17 |
| 5. Eric Martin, N.O. | 9 | 532 | 7854 | 48 |
| 6. Sterling Sharpe, G.B. | 6 | 501 | 7015 | 47 |
| 7. Steve Jordan, Minn. | 12 | 495 | 6284 | 28 |
| 8. Anthony Carter, Det. | 9 | 478 | 7636 | 52 |
| 9. Ricky Sanders | 8 | 414 | 5854 | 36 |
| 10. Herschel Walker, Phil. | 9 | 410 | 3887 | 16 |
| **Other Leading Receivers** | | | | |
| Andre Rison, Atl. | 5 | 394 | 5365 | 52 |
| Rodney Holman, Det. | 12 | 343 | 4573 | 36 |
| Michael Irvin, Dall. | 6 | 337 | 5694 | 34 |
| Mark Jackson, N.Y.G. | 8 | 334 | 5454 | 28 |
| Mark Bavaro, Phil. | 8 | 334 | 4518 | 36 |
| Cris Carter, Minn. | 7 | 327 | 4577 | 42 |
| Jay Novacek, Dall. | 9 | 313 | 3450 | 23 |
| Gary Anderson, Det. | 10 | 302 | 2999 | 15 |
| Neal Anderson | 8 | 302 | 2763 | 20 |
| Jessie Hester, Rams | 8 | 298 | 4807 | 23 |
| Tom Rathman, S.F. | 8 | 294 | 2490 | 8 |
| John Taylor, S.F. | 7 | 277 | 4680 | 36 |

## TOP ACTIVE SCORERS, NFC

250 or more points

| | Yrs. | TD | FG | PAT | TP |
|---|---|---|---|---|---|
| 1. Eddie Murray, Phil. | 16 | 0 | 277 | 432 | 1263 |
| 2. Morten Andersen, N.O. | 12 | 0 | 274 | 380 | 1202 |
| 3. Norm Johnson, Atl. | 12 | 0 | 222 | 444 | 1110 |
| 4. Kevin Butler, Chi. | 9 | 0 | 199 | 318 | 915 |
| 5. Tony Zendejas, Rams | 9 | 0 | 165 | 283 | 778 |
| 6. Jerry Rice, S.F. | 9 | 124 | 0 | 0 | 744 |
| 7. Chip Lohmiller, Wash. | 6 | 0 | 155 | 232 | 697 |
| 8. Mike Cofer, S.F. | 7 | 0 | 129 | 294 | 681 |
| 9. Fuad Reveiz, Minn. | 10 | 0 | 128 | 293 | 677 |
| 10. Greg Davis, Ariz. | 9 | 0 | 122 | 180 | 546 |
| **Other Leading Scorers** | | | | | |
| David Treadwell | 5 | 0 | 124 | 160 | 532 |
| Chris Jacke, G.B. | 5 | 0 | 116 | 166 | 514 |
| Roger Craig, Minn. | 11 | 73 | 0 | 0 | 438 |
| Herschel Walker, Phil. | 9 | 72 | 0 | 0 | 432 |
| Neal Anderson | 8 | 71 | 0 | 0 | 426 |
| Gary Clark, Ariz. | 9 | 62 | 0 | 0 | 372 |
| Barry Sanders, Det. | 5 | 60 | 0 | 0 | 360 |
| Anthony Carter, Det. | 9 | 54 | 0 | 0 | 324 |
| Dalton Hilliard, N.O. | 8 | 53 | 0 | 0 | 318 |
| Emmitt Smith, Dall. | 4 | 53 | 0 | 0 | 318 |
| Henry Ellard, Wash. | 11 | 52 | 0 | 0 | 312 |
| Andre Rison, Atl. | 5 | 52 | 0 | 0 | 312 |
| Eric Martin, N.O. | 9 | 48 | 0 | 0 | 288 |
| Sterling Sharpe, G.B. | 6 | 48 | 0 | 0 | 288 |
| Cris Carter, Minn. | 7 | 43 | 0 | 0 | 258 |

## TOP ACTIVE INTERCEPTORS, NFC

20 or more interceptions

| | Yrs. | No. | Yards | TD |
|---|---|---|---|---|
| 1. Darrell Green, Wash. | 11 | 34 | 276 | 2 |
| 2. Eric Allen, Phil. | 6 | 31 | 421 | 5 |
| 3. Kevin Ross, Atl. | 10 | 30 | 551 | 2 |
| Wes Hopkins | 10 | 30 | 241 | 1 |
| 5. Carl Lee | 11 | 29 | 349 | 2 |
| Tim McKyer, Det. | 8 | 29 | 136 | 1 |
| 6. Jerry Gray, T.B. | 9 | 28 | 374 | 3 |
| Mike Prior, G.B. | 8 | 28 | 352 | 1 |
| Scott Case, Atl. | 10 | 28 | 255 | 1 |
| 9. Vencie Glenn, Minn. | 10 | 26 | 398 | 1 |
| 10. Deion Sanders, Atl. | 5 | 24 | 520 | 3 |
| **Other Leading Interceptors** | | | | |
| Tim McDonald, S.F. | 7 | 23 | 338 | 1 |
| Terry Taylor, Rams | 10 | 21 | 228 | 2 |
| Thomas Everett, T.B. | 7 | 20 | 229 | 0 |

## TOP ACTIVE PUNT RETURNERS, NFC

40 or more punt returns

| | Yrs. | No. | Yards | Avg. | TD |
|---|---|---|---|---|---|
| 1. Mel Gray, Det. | 8 | 160 | 1851 | 11.6 | 3 |
| 2. Henry Ellard, Wash. | 11 | 135 | 1527 | 11.3 | 4 |
| Darrell Green, Wash. | 11 | 51 | 576 | 11.3 | 0 |
| 4. David Meggett, N.Y.G. | 5 | 176 | 1907 | 10.8 | 4 |
| 5. John Taylor, S.F. | 7 | 138 | 1461 | 10.6 | 2 |
| 6. Mitchell Price, Rams | 9 | 50 | 513 | 10.3 | 2 |
| 7. Brian Mitchell, Wash. | 4 | 115 | 1171 | 10.2 | 3 |
| 8. Johnny Bailey, Ariz. | 4 | 127 | 1225 | 9.6 | 2 |
| 9. Anthony Parker, Minn. | 5 | 42 | 400 | 9.5 | 0 |
| 10. Clifford Hicks, Rams | 9 | 100 | 942 | 9.4 | 0 |
| **Other Leading Punt Returners** | | | | | |
| Terance Mathis, Atl. | 4 | 50 | 445 | 8.9 | 1 |
| Tony Smith, Atl. | 2 | 48 | 410 | 8.5 | 0 |
| Deion Sanders, Atl. | 5 | 93 | 789 | 8.5 | 2 |

## TOP ACTIVE KICKOFF RETURNERS, NFC

40 or more kick returns

| | Yrs. | No. | Yards | Avg. | TD |
|---|---|---|---|---|---|
| 1. Tony Smith, Atl. | 2 | 45 | 1120 | 24.9 | 1 |
| 2. Mel Gray, Det. | 8 | 264 | 6374 | 24.1 | 3 |
| 3. Corey Harris, G.B. | 4 | 49 | 1173 | 23.9 | 0 |
| 4. Robert Brooks, G.B. | 2 | 41 | 949 | 23.1 | 1 |
| 5. Deion Sanders, Atl. | 5 | 147 | 3388 | 23.0 | 3 |
| 6. Nate Lewis, Rams | 4 | 92 | 2047 | 22.3 | 1 |
| 7. Herschel Walker, Phil. | 9 | 76 | 1676 | 22.1 | 1 |
| 8. Charles Wilson, T.B. | 4 | 82 | 1797 | 21.9 | 1 |
| 9. Qadry Ismail, Minn. | 1 | 42 | 902 | 21.5 | 0 |
| 10. Johnny Bailey, Ariz. | 4 | 98 | 2063 | 21.1 | 0 |
| **Other Leading Kickoff Returners** | | | | | |
| David Meggett, N.Y.G. | 5 | 117 | 2441 | 20.9 | 1 |
| Marc Logan, S.F. | 7 | 85 | 1760 | 20.7 | 1 |
| Dexter Carter, S.F. | 4 | 105 | 2171 | 20.7 | 1 |
| Brian Mitchell, Wash. | 4 | 103 | 2118 | 20.6 | 0 |

## TOP ACTIVE PUNTERS, NFC

50 or more punts

| | Yrs. | No. | Avg. | LG |
|---|---|---|---|---|
| 1. Greg Montgomery, Det. | 6 | 310 | 43.6 | 77 |
| 2. Reggie Roby, Wash. | 11 | 633 | 43.4 | 77 |
| Sean Landeta, Rams | 9 | 568 | 43.4 | 71 |
| 4. Harold Alexander, Atl. | 1 | 72 | 43.3 | 75 |
| 5. Tommy Barnhardt, N.O. | 9 | 387 | 42.8 | 65 |
| 6. Harry Newsome | 9 | 683 | 42.5 | 84 |
| 7. Mike Horan, N.Y.G. | 11 | 601 | 42.3 | 75 |
| 8. John Jett, Dall. | 1 | 56 | 41.8 | 59 |
| 9. Scott Fulhage, Atl. | 6 | 399 | 41.4 | 65 |
| 10. Chris Gardocki, Chi. | 3 | 159 | 40.7 | 61 |
| **Other Leading Punters** | | | | |
| Bryan Wagner, G.B. | 7 | 404 | 40.6 | 71 |
| Jeff Feagles, Ariz. | 6 | 478 | 40.4 | 77 |
| Dan Stryzinski, T.B. | 4 | 306 | 40.0 | 63 |
| Klaus Wilmsmeyer, S.F. | 2 | 91 | 40.0 | 61 |

## WHAT TO LOOK FOR IN 1994

**Don Shula**, celebrating his twenty-fifth season in Miami, enters his thirty-second overall season as an NFL head coach. Shula, the all-time winningest coach in NFL history with 327 career victories (including postseason), needs 10 regular-season wins to record the most regular-season victories in history, surpassing George Halas, who amassed 318 in 40 years as head coach of the Chicago Bears.
**Tom Flores**, Seattle, and **Marty Schottenheimer**, Kansas City, each need just 1 win to reach 100 career victories. Flores has recorded his 99 wins in 11 NFL seasons and Schottenheimer has 99 in 10.
**Wayne Fontes**, Detroit, needs 13 wins to become the Lions' all-time winningest coach, surpassing Buddy Parker (50), Potsy Clark (54), and George Wilson (55). Fontes has recorded 43 victories in six seasons as Lions head coach.
**Jerry Rice**, San Francisco, needs 3 touchdowns to become the NFL's all-time touchdown scoring leader, surpassing Jim Brown who tallied 126 in his nine-year NFL career, and Walter Payton, with 125 in 13 seasons. Rice has totaled 124 touchdowns (118 receiving, 6 rushing) during his nine-year NFL career.

Rice is the 49ers' all-time leader with 11,776 receiving yards and needs 224 yards to become the fifth receiver in NFL history to reach 12,000 career yards.
**Dan Marino**, Miami, needs 2,321 yards to move past Dan Fouts (43,040) into second place on the NFL's all-time passing yardage chart behind Fran Tarkenton (47,003). Marino has passed for 40,720 yards during his 11 NFL seasons. Marino (3,219 completions and 5,434 attempts) needs just 79 completions and 171 attempts to surpass Fouts in both categories and move into second place behind Tarkenton (3,686 completions and 6,467 attempts). Marino (298) also needs 2 touchdown passes to become only the second player in NFL history to reach 300 touchdown passes during a career. Tarkenton threw 342 scoring passes during his 18-year NFL career.

Marino (17) needs just one more game with at least 4 touchdown passes to break a tie for the NFL record with Johnny Unitas.
**Emmitt Smith**, Dallas, can become only the second player in history to win four consecutive rushing titles. Smith, who led the league with 1,486 yards in 1993, 1,713 yards in 1992, and 1,563 yards in 1991, would join Jim Brown, who won five consecutive rushing titles from 1957-61.
**Steve Jordan**, Minnesota, needs 47 receptions to pass Kellen Winslow (541) and move into second place on the NFL's all-time receiving list for tight ends. Jordan has 495 receptions in 12 NFL seasons. Ozzie Newsome is the NFL's all-time tight end leader with 662 receptions.
**Joe Montana**, Kansas City, needs 2,732 passing yards to become the fifth player in history to throw for 40,000 career yards, joining Fran Tarkenton (47,003), Dan Fouts (43,040), Dan Marino (40,720), and Johnny Unitas (40,239). Montana has passed for 37,268 yards in 15 NFL seasons.
**Sterling Sharpe**, Green Bay, enters 1994 with 501 receptions in his six seasons with the Packers and needs 30 more to pass James Lofton, the Packers' career leader with 530 catches. Sharpe became the first receiver in history to accumulate 100 receptions in two consecutive seasons (108 in 1992, 112 in 1993).
**Marcus Allen**, Kansas City, has scored 113 touchdowns (91 rushing, 21 receiving, and 1 return) in 12 NFL seasons to tie Lenny Moore for fifth on the all-time chart. With 14 touchdowns, Allen could become the all-time touchdown scorer in NFL history, surpassing Jim Brown (126), Walter Payton (125), Jerry Rice (124, active), and John Riggins (116).
**John Elway**, Denver, can tie Dan Marino's NFL record nine seasons passing for 3,000-or-more yards. Elway has posted eight 3,000-yard passing seasons in 11 years with the Broncos. Elway also has passed for 34,246 yards and needs 754 more to become the sixth quarterback to reach 35,000 career yards. Elway (183) also needs 17 touchdown passes to become the sixteenth quarterback to throw for 200 touchdowns.
**Mel Gray**, Detroit, needs 549 yards to surpass Ron Smith (6,922) as the NFL's all-time kickoff return yardage leader. Gray has amassed 6,374 kickoff return yards in eight NFL seasons. Gray (264) also needs 12 kickoff returns to pass Smith, who is the league's all-time leader with 275 career kickoff returns.
**Andre Rison**, Atlanta, needs 18 catches to surpass Alfred Jenkins (359 receptions) as the club's all-time reception leader . Rison has 342 receptions for 4,547 yards in four seasons with Atlanta.
**Steve Young**, San Francisco, can extend his NFL-record streak of three consecutive seasons with a passer rating of more than 100. Young, who achieved passer ratings of 101.8 in 1991 and 107.0 in 1992, completed 314 of 462 for a club single-season record 4,023 yards with 29 touchdowns and 16 interceptions for a passer rating of 101.5 in 1993.
**Phil Simms**, New York Giants, needs just 1 touchdown pass to become the sixteenth quarterback in history to throw for 200 scores. Simms has tallied his 199 touchdown passes in 15 NFL seasons.
**Ernest Givins**, Houston, needs 64 receiving yards to break Drew Hill's club-record 7,477. Givins has 7,414 receiving yards in eight seasons with the Oilers. Givins is the team's all-time pass-catcher with 506 receptions.
**Troy Aikman**, Dallas, has thrown for at least 3,000 yards in each of the past two seasons (3,445 in 1992 and 3,100 in 1993). With at least 3,000 yards in 1994, he would become the first quarterback in club history to throw for over 3,000 yards in 3 consecutive seasons.
**Thurman Thomas**, Buffalo, needs six more 100-yard rushing performances to exceed Hall of Fame running back O.J. Simpson's club-record 41. Thomas has rushed for more than 100 yards in 36 career games.
**Warren Moon**, Minnesota, needs 4 more touchdown passes to reach 200 in his career. Moon threw 196 touchdown passes in 10 seasons with the Houston Oilers.

Moon has passed for 33,685 yards and needs 1,315 to become the sixth quarterback in history to reach 35,000 passing yards.
**Darrell Green**, Washington, has 34 career interceptions in 11 seasons with the Redskins, 3 from surpassing the club's all-time leader, Brig Owens, who had 36 career interceptions.
**Jim Kelly**, Buffalo, needs 3 touchdown passes to become the Bills' all-time leader, surpassing Joe Ferguson (181). Kelly has thrown 179 touchdowns in his eight-year career with the Bills. Kelly (26,413 yards and 2,112 completions) also needs 1,178 yards and 77 completions to surpass club-leader Ferguson in those two categories.
**Monte Coleman**, Washington, needs to play in just six more games to pass Art Monk (205) in first place on the club's all-time list for games played. Coleman has played in 200 games during his 15-year career with the Redskins. In addition, Coleman will play his sixteenth season with the team, equaling Sammy Baugh's record of service with the Redskins.
**Eric Green**, Pittsburgh, needs 1 touchdown reception to break a tie with Bennie Cunningham (20) and move into first place on the club's all-time list for touchdowns by a tight end. Green (152 receptions and 2,063 yards) also needs 51 receptions and 817 yards to pass Cunningham in those two tight end categories.
**Boomer Esiason**, New York Jets, needs 908 yards to become the eighteenth quarterback in history to throw for 30,000 career passing yards. Esiason has passed for 29,092 yards in 10 NFL seasons.
**Reggie Brooks**, Washington, gained 1,063 rushing yards in his rookie season. Brooks can become the first Redskins' rusher to gain over 1,000 yards in each of his first two NFL seasons.
**Chris Jacke**, Green Bay, has made 116 field goals in five seasons with the Packers and needs 5 more to break Chester Marcol's club record of 120.
**Paul Gruber**, Tampa Bay, has started all 90 games in which he has played since being drafted in 1988. With 10 consecutive starts, Gruber would become the first Buccaneers player to start his first 100 games.

# EXPANSION TEAMS TO BEGIN PLAY IN 1995

## CAROLINA PANTHERS

**Team Colors:** Black, Panther Blue, and Silver
**Suite 1600**
**227 West Trade Street**
**Charlotte, North Carolina 28202**
**Telephone: (704) 358-7000**

### CLUB OFFICIALS

Founder/Owner: Jerry Richardson
President: Mike McCormack
General Manager: Bill Polian
Director of Business Operations: Mark Richardson
Assistant Director of Business Operations: Charles Waddell
Counsel: Richard Thigpen
Chief Financial Officer: Dave Olsen
Controller: Lisa Garber
Director of Stadium Operations: Jon Richardson
Assistant General Manager: Joe Mack
Director Player Personnel: Dom Anile
Pro Scout: Mike Murphy
Scouts: Edwin Bailey, Boyd Dowler, Ralph Hawkins
Director of Marketing/Communications: Charlie Dayton
Director of Ticket Sales: Phil Youtsey
Director of Community Affairs/Player Relations: Donnie Shell
Director of Family Programs: B.J. Waymer
Director of Information Systems: Roger Goss
Video Director: Dave Sutherby
Trainer: John Kasik
**1995 Stadium Site:** Clemson Stadium • **Capacity:** 82,000
Clemson, South Carolina
**Stadium Beginning 1996:**
Carolinas Stadium • **Capacity:** 73,000
Charlotte, North Carolina 28202
**Training Camp:** Wofford College
Spartanburg, SC 29303

CAROLINAS STADIUM

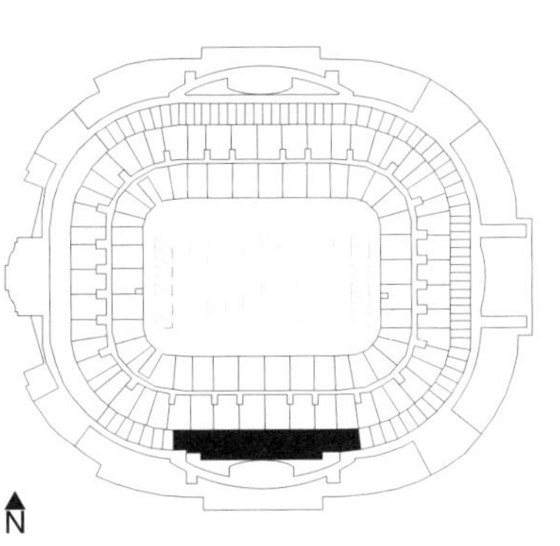


## JACKSONVILLE JAGUARS

**Team Colors:** Teal, Gold, and Black
**One Stadium Place**
**Jacksonville, Florida 32202**
**Telephone: (904) 633-6000**

### CLUB OFFICIALS

Chairman and Chief Executive Officer: Wayne Weaver
President and Chief Operating Officer: David Seldin
Head Coach: Tom Coughlin
Vice President-Football Operations: Michael Huyghue
Senior Vice President-Marketing: Dan Connell
Vice President-Ticket Operations: Judy Seldin
Vice President-Broadcasting and Creative Services: Peter Scheurmier
Executive Director of Communications: Dan Edwards
Executive Director of Administration: John Jones
Defensive Assistant Coach: Randy Edsall
Defensive Assistant Coach: Steve Szabo
Offensive Assistant Coach: Pete Carmichael
Offensive Assistant Coach: Jerald Ingram
Offensive Assistant Coach: Mike Maser
Director of College Scouting: Richard Reiprish
Director of Pro Personnel: Ron Hill
Assistant Director of Pro Personnel: Fran Foley
Scouts: Tim Mingey, Rick Mueller, Gene Smith
Video Director: Mike Perkins
Head Trainer: Michael Ryan
Equipment Manager: Bob Monica
Director of Finance: David Blasic
Director of Special Events and Promotions: Ann Carroll
Director of Corporate Sponsorship: David Rowan
Manager of Contract Information: Daren Anderson
Manager of Football Operations: Joe Baker
Manager of Football Projects: Ron Williams
Manager of Office Services: Karen Battle
Manager of Ticketholder Services: Steve Greenfield
Manager of Stadium Club Programs: Melissa Scott
Corporate Sponsorship Representative: Macky Weaver

GATOR BOWL

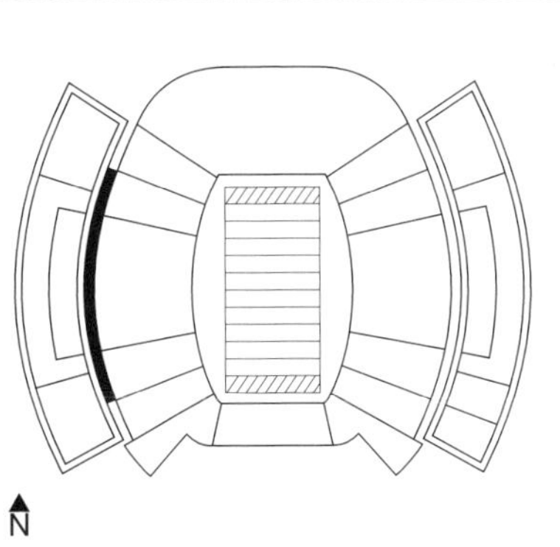


Public Relations Representative: David Auchter
Production Assistant: Joe Bailey
Executive Assistant, Office of the President: Sandy Dodd
Executive Assistant, Head Coach: Joanna Raney
Executive Assistant, Vice President-Football Operations: Pam Yonge
**Stadium:** Gator Bowl • **Capacity:** 73,000
One Stadium Place
Jacksonville, Florida 32202
**Playing Surface:** Grass
**Training Camp:** TBA

# The AFC

# BUFFALO BILLS

**American Football Conference**
**Eastern Division**
**Team Colors:** Royal Blue, Scarlet Red, and White
**One Bills Drive**
**Orchard Park, New York 14127-2296**
**Telephone: (716) 648-1800**

## CLUB OFFICIALS

President: Ralph C. Wilson
Exec. V.P./General Manager: John Butler
V.P./Administration: Jerry Foran
Corporate V.P.: Linda Bogdan
V.P./Head Coach: Marv Levy
Treasurer: Jeffrey C. Littmann
Asst. G.M./Business Operations: Bill Munson
Director of Business Operations: Jim Overdorf
Director of Marketing and Sales: John Livsey
Director of Merchandising: Christy Wilson Hofmann
Director of Player Personnel: Dwight Adams
Director of Pro Personnel: A.J. Smith
Director of Player/Alumni Relations: Jerry Butler
Director of Public/Community Relations: Denny Lynch
Director of Media Relations: Scott Berchtold
Director of Stadium Operations: George Koch
Stadium Operations Supervisor: Pete Reidy
Director of Security: Bill Bambach
Ticket Director: June Foran
Equipment Manager: Dave Hojnowski
Strength/Conditioning Coordinator: Rusty Jones
Trainers: Ed Abramoski, Bud Carpenter, Bill Ford
Video Director: Henry Kunttu
**Stadium:** Rich Stadium • **Capacity:** 80,437
One Bills Drive
Orchard Park, New York 14127-2296
**Playing Surface:** AstroTurf
**Training Camp:** Fredonia State University
Fredonia, New York 14063

## 1994 SCHEDULE

### PRESEASON

| | | |
|---|---|---|
| Aug. 8 | **Washington** | 8:00 |
| Aug. 12 | at Atlanta | 7:00 |
| Aug. 20 | vs. Houston at San Antonio, Tex. | 7:00 |
| Aug. 26 | **Kansas City** | 8:00 |

### REGULAR SEASON

| | | |
|---|---|---|
| Sept. 4 | **New York Jets** | 4:00 |
| Sept. 11 | at New England | 1:00 |
| Sept. 18 | at Houston | 12:00 |
| Sept. 26 | **Denver** (Monday) | 9:00 |
| Oct. 2 | at Chicago | 3:00 |
| Oct. 9 | **Miami** | 1:00 |
| Oct. 16 | **Indianapolis** | 1:00 |
| Oct. 23 | Open Date | |
| Oct. 30 | **Kansas City** | 1:00 |
| Nov. 6 | at New York Jets | 4:00 |
| Nov. 14 | at Pittsburgh (Monday) | 9:00 |
| Nov. 20 | **Green Bay** | 1:00 |
| Nov. 24 | at Detroit (Thanksgiving) | 12:30 |
| Dec. 4 | at Miami | 8:00 |
| Dec. 11 | **Minnesota** | 1:00 |
| Dec. 18 | **New England** | 1:00 |
| Dec. 24 | at Indianapolis | 1:00 |

## RECORD HOLDERS

### INDIVIDUAL RECORDS—CAREER

| Category | Name | Performance |
|---|---|---|
| Rushing (Yds.) | O.J. Simpson, 1969-1977 | 10,183 |
| Passing (Yds.) | Joe Ferguson, 1973-1984 | 27,590 |
| Passing (TDs) | Joe Ferguson, 1973-1984 | 181 |
| Receiving (No.) | Andre Reed, 1985-1993 | 586 |
| Receiving (Yds.) | Andre Reed, 1985-1993 | 8,233 |
| Interceptions | George (Butch) Byrd, 1964-1970 | 40 |
| Punting (Avg.) | Paul Maguire, 1964-1970 | 42.1 |
| Punt Return (Avg.) | Keith Moody, 1976-79 | 10.5 |
| Kickoff Return (Avg.) | Wallace Francis, 1973-74 | 27.2 |
| Field Goals | Scott Norwood, 1985-1991 | 133 |
| Touchdowns (Tot.) | O.J. Simpson, 1969-1977 | 70 |
| Points | Scott Norwood, 1985-1991 | 670 |

### INDIVIDUAL RECORDS—SINGLE SEASON

| Category | Name | Performance |
|---|---|---|
| Rushing (Yds.) | O.J. Simpson, 1973 | 2,003 |
| Passing (Yds.) | Jim Kelly, 1991 | 3,844 |
| Passing (TDs) | Jim Kelly, 1991 | 33 |
| Receiving (No.) | Andre Reed, 1989 | 88 |
| Receiving (Yds.) | Andre Reed, 1989 | 1,312 |
| Interceptions | Billy Atkins, 1961 | 10 |
| | Tom Janik, 1967 | 10 |
| Punting (Avg.) | Billy Atkins, 1961 | 44.5 |
| Punt Return (Avg.) | Keith Moody, 1977 | 13.1 |
| Kickoff Return (Avg.) | Ed Rutkowski, 1963 | 30.2 |
| Field Goals | Scott Norwood, 1988 | 32 |
| Touchdowns (Tot.) | O.J. Simpson, 1975 | 23 |
| Points | O.J. Simpson, 1975 | 138 |

### INDIVIDUAL RECORDS—SINGLE GAME

| Category | Name | Performance |
|---|---|---|
| Rushing (Yds.) | O.J. Simpson, 11-25-76 | 273 |
| Passing (Yds.) | Joe Ferguson, 10-9-83 | 419 |
| Passing (TDs) | Jim Kelly, 9-8-91 | 6 |
| Receiving (No.) | Greg Bell, 9-8-85 | 13 |
| | Andre Reed, 9-18-89 | 13 |
| | Thurman Thomas, 9-15-91 | 13 |
| Receiving (Yds.) | Jerry Butler, 9-23-79 | 255 |
| Interceptions | Many Times | 3 |
| | Last time by Jeff Nixon, 9-7-80 | |
| Field Goals | Pete Gogolak, 12-5-65 | 5 |
| | Scott Norwood, 9-25-88 | 5 |
| Touchdowns (Tot.) | Cookie Gilchrist, 12-8-63 | 5 |
| Points | Cookie Gilchrist, 12-8-63 | 30 |

## COACHING HISTORY

**(247-269-8)**

| | | |
|---|---|---|
| 1960-61 | Buster Ramsey | 11-16-1 |
| 1962-65 | Lou Saban | 38-18-3 |
| 1966-68 | Joe Collier* | 13-17-1 |
| 1968 | Harvey Johnson | 1-10-1 |
| 1969-70 | John Rauch | 7-20-1 |
| 1971 | Harvey Johnson | 1-13-0 |
| 1972-76 | Lou Saban** | 32-29-1 |
| 1976-77 | Jim Ringo | 3-20-0 |
| 1978-82 | Chuck Knox | 38-38-0 |
| 1983-85 | Kay Stephenson*** | 10-26-0 |
| 1985-86 | Hank Bullough**** | 4-17-0 |
| 1986-93 | Marv Levy | 89-45-0 |

*Released after two games in 1968
**Resigned after five games in 1976
***Released after four games in 1985
****Released after nine games in 1986

## RICH STADIUM

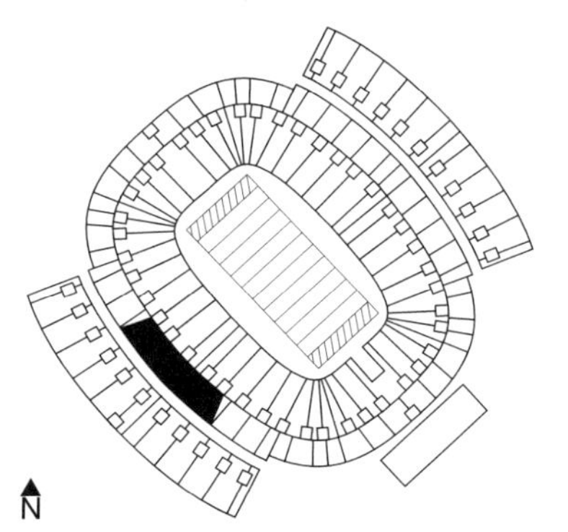

## 1993 TEAM RECORD

**PRESEASON (2-3)**

| Date | Result | | Opponents |
|---|---|---|---|
| 7/30 | L | 7-14 | at Detroit |
| 8/7 | L | 6-20 | vs. Minnesota at Berlin |
| 8/12 | W | 30-7 | at Kansas City |
| 8/21 | L | 12-32 | vs. Tampa Bay at Orlando |
| 8/27 | W | 17-16 | Atlanta |

**REGULAR SEASON (12-4)**

| Date | Result | | Opponents | Att. |
|---|---|---|---|---|
| 9/5 | W | 38-14 | New England | 79,751 |
| 9/12 | W | 13-10 | at Dallas | 63,226 |
| 9/26 | L | 13-22 | Miami | 79,635 |
| 10/3 | W | 17-14 | N.Y. Giants | 79,283 |
| 10/11 | W | 35-7 | Houston | 79,613 |
| 10/24 | W | 19-10 | at N.Y. Jets | 71,541 |
| 11/1 | W | 24-10 | Washington | 79,106 |
| 11/7 | W | 13-10 | at New England (OT) | 54,326 |
| 11/15 | L | 0-23 | at Pittsburgh | 60,265 |
| 11/21 | W | 23-9 | Indianapolis | 79,101 |
| 11/28 | L | 7-23 | at Kansas City | 74,452 |
| 12/5 | L | 24-25 | L.A. Raiders | 79,478 |
| 12/12 | W | 10-7 | at Philadelphia | 60,769 |
| 12/19 | W | 47-34 | at Miami | 71,597 |
| 12/26 | W | 16-14 | N.Y. Jets | 70,817 |
| 1/2 | W | 30-10 | at Indianapolis | 43,028 |

**POSTSEASON (2-1)**

| | | | | |
|---|---|---|---|---|
| 1/15 | W | 29-23 | L.A. Raiders | 61,923 |
| 1/23 | W | 30-13 | Kansas City | 76,642 |
| 1/30 | L | 13-30 | Dallas | 72,817 |

(OT) Overtime

**SCORE BY PERIODS**

| | | | | | | | |
|---|---|---|---|---|---|---|---|
| Bills | 64 | 113 | 51 | 98 | 3 | — | 329 |
| Opponents | 71 | 62 | 67 | 42 | 0 | — | 242 |

**ATTENDANCE**

Home 626,784 Away 499,204 Total 1,125,988
Single-game home record, 80,366 (9-29-91)
Single-season home record, 635,899 (1991)*
*NFL record

## 1993 TEAM STATISTICS

| | Bills | Opp. |
|---|---|---|
| Total First Downs | 316 | 331 |
| Rushing | 117 | 114 |
| Passing | 176 | 199 |
| Penalty | 23 | 18 |
| Third Down: Made/Att | 98/225 | 107/235 |
| Third Down Pct. | 43.6 | 45.5 |
| Fourth Down: Made/Att | 5/8 | 6/18 |
| Fourth Down Pct. | 62.5 | 33.3 |
| Total Net Yards | 5260 | 5554 |
| Avg. Per Game | 328.8 | 347.1 |
| Total Plays | 1078 | 1119 |
| Avg. Per Play | 4.9 | 5.0 |
| Net Yards Rushing | 1943 | 1921 |
| Avg. Per Game | 121.4 | 120.1 |
| Total Rushes | 550 | 500 |
| Net Yards Passing | 3317 | 3633 |
| Avg. Per Game | 207.3 | 227.1 |
| Sacked/Yards Lost | 31/218 | 37/256 |
| Gross Yards | 3535 | 3889 |
| Att./Completions | 497/304 | 582/323 |
| Completion Pct. | 61.2 | 55.5 |
| Had Intercepted | 18 | 23 |
| Punts/Avg. | 74/40.4 | 65/41.8 |
| Net Punting Avg. | 74/36.0 | 65/35.1 |
| Penalties/Yards Lost | 94/630 | 99/681 |
| Fumbles/Ball Lost | 26/17 | 35/24 |
| Touchdowns | 37 | 25 |
| Rushing | 12 | 7 |
| Passing | 20 | 18 |
| Returns | 5 | 0 |
| Avg. Time of Possession | 27:30 | 32:30 |

## 1993 INDIVIDUAL STATISTICS

| PASSING | Att | Cmp | Yds. | Pct. | TD | Int | Tkld. | Rate |
|---|---|---|---|---|---|---|---|---|
| Kelly | 470 | 288 | 3382 | 61.3 | 18 | 18 | 25/171 | 79.9 |
| Reich | 26 | 16 | 153 | 61.5 | 2 | 0 | 6/47 | 103.5 |
| Thomas | 1 | 0 | 0 | 0.0 | 0 | 0 | 0/0 | 39.6 |
| Bills | 497 | 304 | 3535 | 61.2 | 20 | 18 | 31/218 | 81.0 |
| Opponents | 582 | 323 | 3889 | 55.5 | 18 | 23 | 37/256 | 70.0 |

| SCORING | TD R | TD P | TD Rt | PAT | FG | Saf | PTS |
|---|---|---|---|---|---|---|---|
| Christie | 0 | 0 | 0 | 36/37 | 23/32 | 0 | 105 |
| K. Davis | 6 | 0 | 0 | 0/0 | 0/0 | 0 | 36 |
| Reed | 0 | 6 | 0 | 0/0 | 0/0 | 0 | 36 |
| Thomas | 6 | 0 | 0 | 0/0 | 0/0 | 0 | 36 |
| Brooks | 0 | 5 | 0 | 0/0 | 0/0 | 0 | 30 |
| Metzelaars | 0 | 4 | 0 | 0/0 | 0/0 | 0 | 24 |
| Beebe | 0 | 3 | 0 | 0/0 | 0/0 | 0 | 18 |
| Jones | 0 | 0 | 1 | 0/0 | 0/0 | 1 | 8 |
| Copeland | 0 | 0 | 1 | 0/0 | 0/0 | 0 | 6 |
| Gardner | 0 | 1 | 0 | 0/0 | 0/0 | 0 | 6 |
| McKeller | 0 | 1 | 0 | 0/0 | 0/0 | 0 | 6 |
| Odomes | 0 | 0 | 1 | 0/0 | 0/0 | 0 | 6 |
| Talley | 0 | 0 | 1 | 0/0 | 0/0 | 0 | 6 |
| Washington | 0 | 0 | 1 | 0/0 | 0/0 | 0 | 6 |
| Bills | 12 | 20 | 5 | 36/37 | 23/32 | 1 | 329 |
| Opponents | 7 | 18 | 0 | 23/25 | 23/35 | 0 | 242 |

| RUSHING | No. | Yds. | Avg. | LG | TD |
|---|---|---|---|---|---|
| Thomas | 355 | 1315 | 3.7 | 27 | 6 |
| K. Davis | 109 | 391 | 3.6 | 19 | 6 |
| Kelly | 36 | 102 | 2.8 | 17 | 0 |
| Gardner | 20 | 56 | 2.8 | 8 | 0 |
| Turner | 11 | 36 | 3.3 | 10 | 0 |
| Brooks | 3 | 30 | 10.0 | 15 | 0 |
| Reed | 9 | 21 | 2.3 | 15 | 0 |
| Fina | 1 | -2 | -2.0 | -2 | 0 |
| Reich | 6 | -6 | -1.0 | -1 | 0 |
| Bills | 550 | 1943 | 3.5 | 27 | 12 |
| Opponents | 500 | 1921 | 3.8 | 35 | 7 |

| RECEIVING | No. | Yds. | Avg. | LG | TD |
|---|---|---|---|---|---|
| Metzelaars | 68 | 609 | 9.0 | 51 | 4 |
| Brooks | 60 | 714 | 11.9 | 32 | 5 |
| Reed | 52 | 854 | 16.4 | 65t | 6 |
| Thomas | 48 | 387 | 8.1 | 37 | 0 |
| Beebe | 31 | 504 | 16.3 | 65t | 3 |
| K. Davis | 21 | 95 | 4.5 | 28 | 0 |
| Copeland | 13 | 242 | 18.6 | 60 | 0 |
| Gardner | 4 | 50 | 12.5 | 22 | 1 |
| McKeller | 3 | 35 | 11.7 | 13t | 1 |
| Tasker | 2 | 26 | 13.0 | 22 | 0 |
| Awalt | 2 | 19 | 9.5 | 10 | 0 |
| Bills | 304 | 3535 | 11.6 | 65t | 20 |
| Opponents | 323 | 3889 | 12.0 | 54t | 18 |

| INTERCEPTIONS | No. | Yds. | Avg. | LG | TD |
|---|---|---|---|---|---|
| Odomes | 9 | 65 | 7.2 | 25 | 0 |
| Talley | 3 | 74 | 24.7 | 61t | 1 |
| Jones | 2 | 92 | 46.0 | 85t | 1 |
| Darby | 2 | 32 | 16.0 | 32 | 0 |
| Williams | 2 | 11 | 5.5 | 6 | 0 |
| M. Patton | 2 | 0 | 0.0 | 0 | 0 |
| Washington | 1 | 27 | 27.0 | 27t | 1 |
| Bennett | 1 | 5 | 5.0 | 5 | 0 |
| B. Smith | 1 | 0 | 0.0 | 0 | 0 |
| Bills | 23 | 306 | 13.3 | 85t | 3 |
| Opponents | 18 | 174 | 9.7 | 35 | 0 |

| PUNTING | No. | Yds. | Avg. | In 20 | LG |
|---|---|---|---|---|---|
| Mohr | 74 | 2991 | 40.4 | 19 | 58 |
| Bills | 74 | 2991 | 40.4 | 19 | 58 |
| Opponents | 65 | 2719 | 41.8 | 20 | 58 |

| PUNT RETURNS | No. | FC | Yds. | Avg. | LG | TD |
|---|---|---|---|---|---|---|
| Copeland | 31 | 7 | 274 | 8.8 | 47t | 1 |
| Brooks | 1 | 0 | 3 | 3.0 | 3 | 0 |
| Tasker | 1 | 0 | 0 | 0.0 | 0 | 0 |
| Bills | 33 | 7 | 277 | 8.4 | 47t | 1 |
| Opponents | 29 | 24 | 247 | 8.5 | 27 | 0 |

| KICKOFF RETURNS | No. | Yds. | Avg. | LG | TD |
|---|---|---|---|---|---|
| Copeland | 24 | 436 | 18.2 | 28 | 0 |
| Beebe | 10 | 160 | 16.0 | 22 | 0 |
| K. Davis | 8 | 100 | 12.5 | 18 | 0 |
| Lamb | 2 | 40 | 20.0 | 23 | 0 |
| Turner | 1 | 10 | 10.0 | 10 | 0 |
| Bills | 45 | 746 | 16.6 | 28 | 0 |
| Opponents | 43 | 850 | 19.8 | 49 | 0 |

| SACKS | No. |
|---|---|
| B. Smith | 14.0 |
| Bennett | 5.0 |
| Wright | 4.5 |
| Hansen | 3.5 |
| Barnett | 2.0 |
| Jones | 2.0 |
| Talley | 2.0 |
| Goganious | 1.0 |
| Parrella | 1.0 |
| M. Patton | 1.0 |
| Lodish | 0.5 |
| Washington | 0.5 |
| Bills | 37.0 |
| Opponents | 31.0 |

## 1994 DRAFT CHOICES

| Round | Name | Pos. | College |
|---|---|---|---|
| 1 | Jeff Burris | DB | Notre Dame |
| 2 | Bucky Brooks | WR | North Carolina |
| | Lonnie Johnson | TE | Florida State |
| | Sam Rogers | LB | Colorado |
| 3 | Marlo Perry | LB | Jackson State |
| | Corey Louchiey | T | South Carolina |
| 4 | Sean Crocker | DB | North Carolina |
| 5 | A.J. Ofodile | TE | Missouri |
| 6 | Anthony Abrams | DT | Clark, Ga. |
| | Kevin Knox | WR | Florida State |
| 7 | Filmel Johnson | DB | Illinois |

# BUFFALO BILLS

## 1994 VETERAN ROSTER

| No. | Name | Pos. | Ht. | Wt. | Birthdate | NFL Exp. | College | Hometown | How Acq. | '93 Games/ Starts |
|---|---|---|---|---|---|---|---|---|---|---|
| 86 | # Awalt, Rob | TE | 6-5 | 242 | 4/9/64 | 8 | San Diego State | Sacramento, Calif. | FA-'92 | 12/1 |
| 77 | Barnett, Oliver | DE | 6-3 | 292 | 4/9/66 | 5 | Kentucky | Louisville, Ky. | RFA(Atl)-'93 | 16/6 |
| 82 | Beebe, Don | WR | 5-11 | 180 | 12/18/64 | 6 | Chadron State | Sugar Grove, Ill. | D3-'89 | 14/14 |
| 97 | Bennett, Cornelius | LB | 6-2 | 238 | 8/25/65 | 8 | Alabama | Birmingham, Ala. | T(Ind)-'87 | 16/16 |
| 80 | Brooks, Bill | WR | 6-0 | 189 | 4/6/64 | 9 | Boston University | Framingham, Mass. | UFA(Ind)-'93 | 16/13 |
| 96 | Brown, Monty | LB | 6-0 | 228 | 4/13/70 | 2 | Ferris State | Bridgeport, Mich. | FA-'93 | 13/0 |
| 2 | Christie, Steve | K | 6-0 | 185 | 11/13/67 | 5 | William & Mary | Oakville, Canada | PB(TB)-'92 | 16/0 |
| 85 | Copeland, Russell | WR | 6-0 | 200 | 11/4/71 | 2 | Memphis State | Tupelo, Miss. | D4-'93 | 16/2 |
| 66 | Crafts, Jerry | T | 6-6 | 351 | 1/6/68 | 3 | Louisville | Tulsa, Okla. | FA-'92 | 16/0 |
| 43 | Darby, Matt | S | 6-1 | 200 | 11/19/68 | 3 | UCLA | Virginia Beach, Va. | D5-'92 | 16/3 |
| 65 | Davis, John | G | 6-4 | 310 | 8/22/65 | 8 | Georgia Tech | Ellijay, Ga. | PB(Hou)-'89 | 16/16 |
| 23 | Davis, Kenneth | RB | 5-10 | 208 | 4/16/62 | 9 | Texas Christian | Temple, Tex. | PB(GB)-'89 | 16/0 |
| 62 | Devlin, Mike | C | 6-1 | 293 | 11/16/69 | 2 | Iowa | Marlton, N.J. | D5a-'93 | 12/0 |
| 70 | Fina, John | T-G | 6-4 | 285 | 3/11/69 | 3 | Arizona | Tucson, Ariz. | D1-'92 | 16/16 |
| 33 | Fuller, Eddie | RB | 5-9 | 198 | 6/22/68 | 5 | Louisiana State | Leesville, La. | D4-'90 | 7/0 |
| 35 | Gardner, Carwell | RB | 6-2 | 244 | 11/27/66 | 5 | Louisville | Louisville, Ky. | D2-'90 | 13/2 |
| 50 | Goganious, Keith | LB | 6-2 | 239 | 12/7/68 | 3 | Penn State | Virginia Beach, Va. | D3-'92 | 16/7 |
| 26 | Gulledge, David | S | 6-1 | 203 | 10/26/67 | 2 | Jacksonville State | Pell City, Ala. | FA-'94 | 0* |
| 90 | Hansen, Phil | DE | 6-5 | 278 | 5/20/68 | 4 | North Dakota State | Ellendale, N.D. | D2-'91 | 11/9 |
| 36 | † Henderson, Jerome | CB-S | 5-10 | 189 | 8/8/69 | 4 | Clemson | Statesville, N.C. | FA-'93 | 3/0* |
| 67 | Hull, Kent | C | 6-5 | 284 | 1/13/61 | 9 | Mississippi State | Greenwood, Miss. | FA-'86 | 14/13 |
| 20 | Jones, Henry | S | 5-11 | 197 | 12/29/67 | 4 | Illinois | St. Louis, Mo. | D1-'91 | 16/16 |
| 12 | Kelly, Jim | QB | 6-3 | 226 | 2/14/60 | 9 | Miami | East Brady, Pa. | D1b-'83 | 16/16 |
| 63 | Lingner, Adam | C | 6-4 | 268 | 11/2/60 | 12 | Illinois | Rock Island, Ill. | PB(KC)-'89 | 16/0 |
| 73 | Lodish, Mike | NT | 6-3 | 280 | 8/11/67 | 5 | UCLA | Birmingham, Mich. | D10-'90 | 15/1 |
| 55 | Maddox, Mark | LB | 6-1 | 233 | 3/23/68 | 4 | Northern Michigan | Milwaukee, Wis. | D9-'91 | 11/8 |
| 84 | # McKeller, Keith | TE | 6-4 | 242 | 7/9/64 | 8 | Jacksonville State | Fairfield, Ala. | D9-'87 | 8/1 |
| 88 | Metzelaars, Pete | TE | 6-7 | 254 | 5/24/60 | 13 | Wabash | Portage, Mich. | T(Sea)-'85 | 16/16 |
| 9 | Mohr, Chris | P | 6-5 | 215 | 5/11/66 | 5 | Alabama | Thomson, Ga. | FA-'91 | 16/0 |
| 74 | † Parker, Glenn | G-T | 6-5 | 305 | 4/22/66 | 5 | Arizona | Huntington Beach, Calif. | D3-'90 | 16/9 |
| 92 | Parrella, John | DE-NT | 6-3 | 296 | 11/22/69 | 2 | Nebraska | Topeka, Kan. | D2-'93 | 10/0 |
| 44 | Paterra, Greg | RB | 5-11 | 224 | 5/11/67 | 3 | Slippery Rock | McKeesport, Pa. | FA-'94 | 0* |
| 99 | Patton, James | DE-NT | 6-3 | 287 | 1/5/70 | 3 | Texas | Houston, Tex. | D2-'92 | 2/0 |
| 53 | Patton, Marvcus | LB | 6-2 | 243 | 5/1/67 | 5 | UCLA | Lawndale, Calif. | D8-'90 | 16/16 |
| 94 | Pike, Mark | DE | 6-4 | 272 | 12/27/63 | 9 | Georgia Tech | Villa Hills, Ky. | D7b-'86 | 14/0 |
| 83 | Reed, Andre | WR | 6-2 | 190 | 1/29/64 | 10 | Kutztown | Allentown, Pa. | D4a-'85 | 15/15 |
| 14 | Reich, Frank | QB | 6-4 | 205 | 12/4/61 | 10 | Maryland | Lebanon, Pa. | D3a-'85 | 15/0 |
| 24 | Schulz, Kurt | S | 6-1 | 208 | 12/12/68 | 3 | Eastern Washington | Yakima, Wash. | D7-'92 | 12/0 |
| 78 | Smith, Bruce | DE | 6-4 | 273 | 6/18/63 | 10 | Virginia Tech | Norfolk, Va. | D1a-'85 | 16/16 |
| 28 | Smith, Thomas | CB | 5-11 | 188 | 12/5/70 | 2 | North Carolina | Gates, N.C. | D1-'93 | 16/1 |
| 11 | Strom, Rick | QB | 6-2 | 197 | 3/11/65 | 6 | Georgia Tech | Pittsburgh, Pa. | UFA(Pitt)-'94 | 0* |
| 56 | Talley, Darryl | LB | 6-4 | 235 | 7/10/60 | 12 | West Virginia | Cleveland, Ohio | D2-'83 | 16/16 |
| 89 | Tasker, Steve | WR | 5-9 | 181 | 4/10/62 | 10 | Northwestern | Leoti, Kan. | W(Hou)-'86 | 15/0 |
| 34 | Thomas, Thurman | RB | 5-10 | 198 | 5/16/66 | 7 | Oklahoma State | Missouri City, Tex. | D2-'88 | 16/16 |
| 21 | Turner, Nate | RB | 6-1 | 255 | 5/28/69 | 3 | Nebraska | Chicago, Ill. | D6-'92 | 13/0 |
| 25 | Washington, Mickey | CB | 5-9 | 191 | 7/8/68 | 4 | Texas A&M | Beaumont, Tex. | FA-'93 | 16/6 |
| 91 | Wright, Jeff | NT | 6-3 | 274 | 6/13/63 | 7 | Central Missouri State | Lawrence, Kan. | D8b-'88 | 15/15 |

* Gulledge last active with Washington in '92; Henderson played 1 game with New England, 2 games with Buffalo in '93; Paterra on injured reserve with Buffalo in '91; Strom inactive for 16 games with Pittsburgh.

# Unrestricted free agent; subject to developments.

† Restricted free agent; subject to developments.

Traded—CB-S James Williams to Arizona.

Players lost through free agency (4): T Howard Ballard (Sea; 16 games in '93), QB Gale Gilbert (SD; 1), LB Richard Harvey (Den; 15), CB Nate Odomes (Sea; 16).

Also played with Bills in '93—S Mark Kelso (14 games), WR Brad Lamb (1), G Tom Myslinski (1), CB David Pool (2), G Jim Ritcher (12), WR Chris Walsh (3), CB-S James Williams (15).

## COACHING STAFF

**Head Coach,**
**Marv Levy**

**Pro Career:** Begins his eighth full season as Bills head coach. Led the Bills to their fourth consecutive AFC championship in 1993. Under Levy, the Bills recorded 13-3 records in 1990 and 1991, the best regular-season marks in club history. He guided the Bills to their second consecutive AFC East title with a 9-7 record in 1989. Finished 1988 season with a 12-4 record and a berth in the AFC Championship Game. In his first full year with Bills in 1987, he led team to a 7-8 record. Replaced Hank Bullough on November 3, 1986, and compiled a 2-5 record over the final seven weeks of the season. Previously served as head coach of the Kansas City Chiefs from 1978-1982 and produced a 31-42 mark. Levy began his pro coaching career in 1969 as an assistant with the Philadelphia Eagles. He joined George Allen and the Los Angeles Rams as an assistant one year later and followed Allen to Washington, where he remained with the Redskins through the 1972 season when Washington played in Super Bowl VII. He was named head coach of the Montreal Alouettes (CFL) in 1973 and posted a 50-34-4 record and two Grey Cup victories (1974, 1977) in five seasons in Canada. After two seasons away from football, he became head coach of the Chicago Blitz of the USFL in 1984. No pro playing experience. Career NFL record: 120-87.
**Background:** Running back at Coe College 1948-50. Coached at high school level for two years before returning to alma mater from 1953-55. Joined New Mexico staff in 1956 and served as head coach there in 1958-59. Head coach at California from 1960-63 before becoming head coach at William & Mary from 1964-68.
**Personal:** Born August 3, 1928, Chicago, Ill. Levy was Phi Beta Kappa at Coe College and earned master's degree in English history from Harvard. He lives with his wife Mary Frances in Hamburg, N.Y.

### ASSISTANT COACHES

**Tom Bresnahan,** offensive coordinator-offensive line; born January 21, 1935, Springfield, Mass., lives in Hamburg, N.Y. Tackle Holy Cross 1953-55. No pro playing experience. College coach: Williams 1963-67, Columbia 1968-72, Navy 1973-80. Pro coach: Kansas City Chiefs 1981-82, New York Giants 1983-84, St. Louis/Phoenix Cardinals 1986-88, joined Bills in 1989.
**Walt Corey,** defensive coordinator-linebackers; born May 9, 1938, Latrobe, Pa., lives in West Seneca, N.Y. Defensive end Miami 1957-59. Pro linebacker Kansas City Chiefs 1960-66. College coach: Utah State 1967-69, Miami 1970-71. Pro coach: Kansas City Chiefs 1972-74, 1978-86, Cleveland Browns 1975-77, joined Bills in 1987.
**Bruce DeHaven,** special teams; born September 6, 1952, Trousdale, Kan., lives in East Aurora, N.Y. No college or pro playing experience. College coach: Kansas 1979-81, New Mexico State 1982. Pro coach: New Jersey Generals (USFL) 1983, Pittsburgh Maulers (USFL) 1984, Orlando Renegades (USFL) 1985, joined Bills in 1987.
**Charlie Joiner,** receivers; born October 14, 1947, Many, La., lives in Orchard Park, N.Y. Wide receiver Grambling 1965-68. Defensive back-wide receiver Houston Oilers 1969-72, Cincinnati Bengals 1972-75, San Diego Chargers 1976-86. Pro coach: San Diego Chargers 1987-91, joined Bills in 1992.
**Rusty Jones,** strength and conditioning; born August 14, 1953, Berwick, Maine, lives in Lakeview, N.Y. No college or pro playing experience. College coach: Springfield 1978-79. Pro coach: Pittsburgh Maulers (USFL) 1983-84, joined Bills in 1985.
**Don Lawrence,** offensive quality control-tight ends; born June 4, 1937, Cleveland, Ohio, lives in Orchard Park, N.Y. Offensive-defensive lineman Notre Dame 1957-58. Pro offensive-defensive lineman Washington Redskins 1959-61. College coach: Notre Dame 1961-63, Kansas State 1964-65, Cincinnati 1966, Virginia 1970-73 (head coach 1971-73), Texas Christian 1974-75, Missouri 1976-77. Pro coach: British Columbia Lions (CFL) 1978-79, Kansas City Chiefs 1980-82, 1987-88, Buffalo Bills 1983-84, Tampa Bay Buccaneers 1985-86, Winnipeg Blue Bombers (CFL) 1989, rejoined Bills in 1990.
**Chuck Lester,** administrative assistant to head coach, assistant linebackers coach; born May 18, 1955, Chicago, Ill., lives in Orchard Park, N.Y. Linebacker Oklahoma 1974. No pro playing experience. College coach: Iowa State 1980-81, Oklahoma 1982-84. Pro coach: Kansas City Chiefs 1984-86 (scout), joined Bills in 1987.
**Elijah Pitts,** assistant head coach-running backs; born February 3, 1938, Mayflower, Ark., lives in Orchard Park, N.Y. Running back Philander Smith 1957-60. Pro running back Green Bay Packers 1961-69, 1971, Los Angeles Rams 1970, Chicago Bears 1970, New Orleans Saints 1970. Pro coach: Los Angeles Rams 1974-77, Buffalo Bills 1978-80, Houston Oilers 1981-83, Hamilton Tiger-Cats (CFL) 1984, rejoined Bills in 1985.
**Dick Roach,** defensive backs; born August 23, 1937, Rapid City, S.D., lives in West Seneca, N.Y. Defensive back Black Hills State 1952-55. No pro playing experience. College coach: Montana State 1966-69, Oregon State 1970, Wyoming 1971-72, Fresno State 1973, Washington State 1974-75. Pro coach: Montreal Alouettes (CFL) 1976-77, Kansas City Chiefs 1978-80, New England Patriots 1981, Michigan Panthers (USFL) 1983-84, Tampa Bay Buccaneers 1985-86, joined Bills in 1987.
**Dan Sekanovich,** defensive line; born July 27, 1933, West Hazelton, Pa., lives in Orchard Park, N.Y. End Tennessee 1951-53. Pro defensive end Montreal Alouettes (CFL) 1954. College coach: Susquehanna 1961-63, Connecticut 1964-67, Pittsburgh 1968, Navy 1969-70, Kentucky 1971-72. Pro coach: Montreal Alouettes (CFL) 1973-76, New York Jets 1977-82, Atlanta Falcons 1983-85, Miami Dolphins 1986-91, joined Bills in 1992.
**Jim Shofner,** quarterbacks; born December 18, 1935, Grapevine, Tex., lives in Orchard Park, N.Y. Running back Texas Christian 1955-57. Pro defensive back Cleveland Browns 1958-63. College coach: Texas Christian 1964-66, 1974-76 (head coach). Pro coach: San Francisco 49ers 1967-73, 1977, Cleveland Browns 1978-80, 1990-91 (head coach last 7 games in 1990, director of player personnel in 1991), Houston Oilers 1981-82, Dallas Cowboys 1983-85, St. Louis/Phoenix Cardinals 1986-89, joined Bills in 1992.

## 1994 FIRST-YEAR ROSTER

| Name | Pos. | Ht. | Wt. | Birthdate | College | Hometown | How Acq. |
|---|---|---|---|---|---|---|---|
| Abrams, Anthony | DT | 6-3 | 298 | 2/16/71 | Clark, Ga. | Warner Robins, Ga. | D6a |
| Bock, John | G | 6-3 | 286 | 2/11/71 | Indiana State | Berwyn, Ill. | FA |
| Branch, Darrick (1) | WR | 5-11 | 195 | 2/10/70 | Hawaii | Dallas, Tex. | FA |
| Brooks, Bucky | WR | 6-0 | 190 | 1/22/71 | North Carolina | Raleigh, N.C. | D2a |
| Bryant, Phil (1) | RB | 5-10 | 208 | 3/27/70 | Virginia Tech | Landover, Md. | FA |
| Burris, Jeff | CB-S | 6-0 | 204 | 6/7/72 | Notre Dame | Rock Hill, S.C. | D1 |
| Collins, Mike | CB-S | 5-11 | 195 | 4/25/71 | West Virginia | Huntington, W. Va. | FA |
| Crocker, Sean | CB-S | 5-9 | 191 | 6/14/71 | North Carolina | Wakefield, Va. | D4 |
| Evans, Greg | S | 6-1 | 217 | 6/28/71 | Texas Christian | Daingerfield, Tex. | FA |
| Feexico, Sonny | F | 6-2 | 240 | 11/29/68 | E. Central Oklahoma | Norman, Okla. | FA |
| Fieldings, Anthony (1) | LB | 6-1 | 237 | 7/9/71 | Morningside | Eustis, Fla. | FA |
| Hendrickson, Craig (1) | T | 6-3 | 290 | 5/5/68 | Minnesota | Tucson, Ariz. | FA |
| Herget, Todd | LB | 6-2 | 226 | 8/9/69 | Brigham Young | Lethbridge, Ala. | FA |
| Hoyem, Steve | T | 6-7 | 287 | 11/12/70 | Stanford | Boise, Idaho | FA |
| Johnson, Filmel | CB-S | 5-10 | 187 | 12/24/70 | Illinois | Detroit, Mich. | D7 |
| Johnson, Lonnie | TE | 6-3 | 230 | 2/14/71 | Florida State | Miami, Fla. | D2b |
| Jourdain, Yonel(1) | RB | 5-11 | 204 | 4/20/71 | Southern Illinois | Evanston, Ill. | FA |
| Knox, Kevin | WR | 6-3 | 195 | 1/30/71 | Florida State | Miami, Fla. | D6b |
| Lacina, Corbin (1) | T | 6-4 | 297 | 11/2/70 | Augustana, S.D. | Woodbury, Minn. | D6-'93 |
| Lawson, Shawn (1) | CB | 5-11 | 176 | 9/27/70 | Baylor | Longview, Tex. | FA |
| Louchiey, Corey | T | 6-8 | 305 | 10/10/71 | South Carolina | Greenville, S.C. | D3b |
| Marrow, Vince (1) | TE | 6-3 | 251 | 8/17/68 | Toledo | Youngstown, Ohio | D11-'92 |
| McKay, Orlando (1) | WR | 5-10 | 176 | 10/2/69 | Washington | Mesa, Ariz. | FA |
| Ofodile, A.J. | TE | 6-7 | 260 | 10/9/73 | Missouri | Detroit, Mich. | D5 |
| Ostroski, Jerry (1) | G | 6-4 | 310 | 7/12/70 | Tulsa | Collegeville, Pa. | FA |
| Perry, Mario | LB | 6-4 | 250 | 8/25/72 | Jackson State | Forest, Miss. | D3a |
| Philion, Ed | DT | 6-2 | 273 | 3/27/70 | Ferris State | Essex, Canada | FA |
| Rodgers, Matt (1) | QB | 6-3 | 205 | !/8/69 | Iowa | Walpole, Mass. | D12-'92 |
| Rogers, Sam | LB | 6-3 | 245 | 5/30/70 | Colorado | Pontiac, Mich. | D2c |
| Silvestri, Don (1) | K | 6-4 | 210 | 12/25/68 | Pittsburgh | Perkasie, Pa. | FA |
| Thomas, Damon | WR | 6-2 | 215 | 12/15/70 | Wayne State | Clovis, Calif. | FA |
| Tindale, Tim | RB | 5-10 | 220 | 4/15/71 | Western Ontario | London, Canada | FA |
| Young, Glenn (1) | LB | 6-3 | 240 | 5/2/69 | Syracuse | Scarborough, Canada | FA |

The term NFL Rookie is defined as a player who is in his first season of professional football and has not been on the roster of another professional football team for any regular-season or postseason games. A Rookie is designated by an "R" on NFL rosters. Players who have been active in another professional football league or players who have NFL experience, including either preseason training camp or being on an Active List or Inactive List, or on Reserve/Injured or Reserve/Physically Unable to Perform for fewer than six regular-season games, are termed NFL First-Year Players. An NFL First-Year Player is designated by a "1" on NFL rosters. Thereafter, a player is credited with an additional year of experience for each season in which he accumulates six games on the Active List or Inactive List, or on Reserve/Injured or Reserve/Physically Unable to Perform.

## NOTES

# CINCINNATI BENGALS

**American Football Conference**
**Central Division**
**Team Colors:** Black, Orange, and White
**200 Riverfront Stadium**
**Cincinnati, Ohio 45202**
**Telephone: (513) 621-3550**

## CLUB OFFICIALS

President/General Manager: Michael Brown
Vice President: John Sawyer
Assistant General Manager/Director of Player Personnel: Pete Brown
Secretary/Treasurer:Katherine Blackburn
Assistant Secretary/Assistant Treasurer, Scouting: Paul Brown
Assistant Director of Player Personnel: Frank Smouse
Scouting/Personnel: Jim Lippincott
Business Manager: Bill Connelly
Public Relations Directors: Allan Heim, Jack Brennan
Accountant: Jay Reis
Ticket Manager: Paul Kelly
Consultant: John Murdough, Bill Johnson
Trainer: Paul Sparling
Assistant Trainer: Rob Recker
Equipment Manager: Tom Gray
Video Director: Al Davis
**Stadium:** Riverfront Stadium • **Capacity:** 60,389
200 Riverfront Stadium
Cincinnati, Ohio 45202
**Playing Surface:** AstroTurf-8
**Training Camp:** Wilmington College
Wilmington, Ohio 45177

## 1994 SCHEDULE

**PRESEASON**

| | | |
|---|---|---|
| Aug. 6 | at Tampa Bay | 7:30 |
| Aug. 13 | **Indianapolis** | 7:30 |
| Aug. 20 | at Philadelphia | 7:30 |
| Aug. 26 | **Detroit** | 7:30 |

**REGULAR SEASON**

| | | |
|---|---|---|
| Sept. 4 | **Cleveland** | 1:00 |
| Sept. 11 | at San Diego | 1:00 |
| Sept. 18 | **New England** | 1:00 |
| Sept. 25 | at Houston | 3:00 |
| Oct. 2 | **Miami** | 8:00 |
| Oct. 9 | Open Date | |
| Oct. 16 | at Pittsburgh | 1:00 |
| Oct. 23 | at Cleveland | 1:00 |
| Oct. 30 | **Dallas** | 1:00 |
| Nov. 6 | at Seattle | 1:00 |
| Nov. 13 | **Houston** | 1:00 |
| Nov. 20 | **Indianapolis** | 1:00 |
| Nov. 27 | at Denver | 2:00 |
| Dec. 4 | **Pittsburgh** | 1:00 |
| Dec. 11 | at New York Giants | 1:00 |
| Dec. 18 | at Arizona | 2:00 |
| Dec. 24 | **Philadelphia** | 1:00 |

## RECORD HOLDERS

**INDIVIDUAL RECORDS—CAREER**

| Category | Name | Performance |
|---|---|---|
| Rushing (Yds.) | James Brooks, 1984-1991 | 6,447 |
| Passing (Yds.) | Ken Anderson, 1971-1986 | 32,838 |
| Passing (TDs) | Ken Anderson, 1971-1986 | 197 |
| Receiving (No.) | Isaac Curtis, 1973-1984 | 420 |
| Receiving (Yds.) | Isaac Curtis, 1973-1984 | 7,106 |
| Interceptions | Ken Riley, 1969-1983 | 63 |
| Punting (Avg.) | Dave Lewis, 1970-73 | 43.9 |
| Punt Return (Avg.) | Mitchell Price, 1990-92 | 10.4 |
| Kickoff Return (Avg.) | Lemar Parrish, 1970-78 | 24.7 |
| Field Goals | Jim Breech, 1980-1992 | 225 |
| Touchdowns (Tot.) | Pete Johnson, 1977-1983 | 70 |
| Points | Jim Breech, 1980-1992 | 1,246 |

**INDIVIDUAL RECORDS—SINGLE SEASON**

| Category | Name | Performance |
|---|---|---|
| Rushing (Yds.) | James Brooks, 1989 | 1,239 |
| Passing (Yds.) | Boomer Esiason, 1986 | 3,959 |
| Passing (TDs) | Ken Anderson, 1981 | 29 |
| Receiving (No.) | Dan Ross, 1981 | 71 |
| Receiving (Yds.) | Eddie Brown, 1988 | 1,273 |
| Interceptions | Ken Riley, 1976 | 9 |
| Punting (Avg.) | Dave Lewis, 1970 | 46.2 |
| Punt Return (Avg.) | Mike Martin, 1984 | 15.7 |
| Kickoff Return (Avg.) | Lemar Parrish, 1970 | 30.2 |
| Field Goals | Horst Muhlmann, 1972 | 27 |
| Touchdowns (Tot.) | Pete Johnson, 1981 | 16 |
| Points | Jim Breech, 1985 | 120 |

**INDIVIDUAL RECORDS—SINGLE GAME**

| Category | Name | Performance |
|---|---|---|
| Rushing (Yds.) | James Brooks, 12-23-90 | 201 |
| Passing (Yds.) | Boomer Esiason, 10-7-90 | 490 |
| Passing (TDs) | Boomer Esiason, 12-21-86 | 5 |
| | Boomer Esiason, 10-29-89 | 5 |
| Receiving (No.) | James Brooks, 12-25-89 | 12 |
| Receiving (Yds.) | Eddie Brown, 11-6-88 | 216 |
| Interceptions | Many times | 3 |
| | Last time by David Fulcher, 12-16-89 | |
| Field Goals | Many times | 3 |
| | Last time by Doug Pelfrey, 10-10-93 | |
| Touchdowns (Tot.) | Larry Kinnebrew, 10-28-84 | 4 |
| Points | Larry Kinnebrew, 10-28-84 | 24 |

## COACHING HISTORY

**(187-212-1)**

| | | |
|---|---|---|
| 1968-75 | Paul Brown | 55-59-1 |
| 1976-78 | Bill Johnson* | 18-15-0 |
| 1978-79 | Homer Rice | 8-19-0 |
| 1980-83 | Forrest Gregg | 34-27-0 |
| 1984-91 | Sam Wyche | 64-68-0 |
| 1992-93 | Dave Shula | 8-24-0 |

*Resigned after five games in 1978

**RIVERFRONT STADIUM**

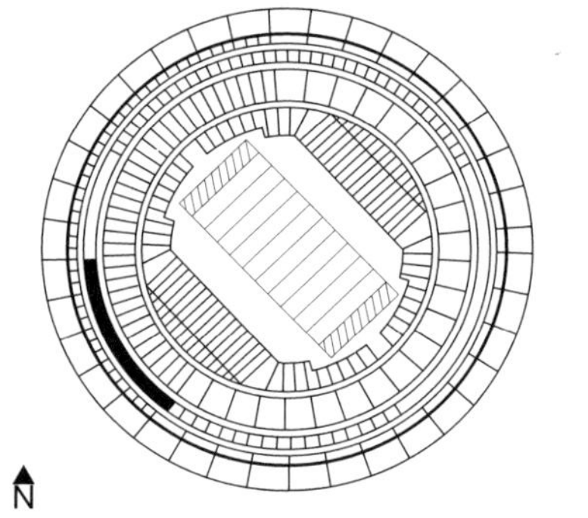

## 1993 TEAM RECORD

**PRESEASON (2-2)**

| Date | Result | | Opponents |
|---|---|---|---|
| 8/7 | L | 16-27 | N.Y. Giants |
| 8/14 | W | 24-7 | at Indianapolis |
| 8/20 | L | 7-30 | at Detroit |
| 8/27 | W | 23-3 | Philadelphia |

**REGULAR SEASON (3-13)**

| Date | Result | | Opponents | Att. |
|---|---|---|---|---|
| 9/5 | L | 14-27 | at Cleveland | 75,508 |
| 9/12 | L | 6-9 | Indianapolis | 50,299 |
| 9/19 | L | 7-34 | at Pittsburgh | 53,682 |
| 9/26 | L | 10-19 | Seattle | 46,880 |
| 10/10 | L | 15-17 | at Kansas City | 75,394 |
| 10/17 | L | 17-28 | Cleveland | 55,647 |
| 10/24 | L | 12-28 | at Houston | 50,039 |
| 11/7 | L | 16-24 | Pittsburgh | 51,202 |
| 11/14 | L | 3-38 | Houston | 42,347 |
| 11/21 | L | 12-17 | at N.Y. Jets | 64,264 |
| 11/28 | W | 16-10 | L.A. Raiders | 43,272 |
| 12/5 | L | 8-21 | at San Francisco | 60,039 |
| 12/12 | L | 2-7 | at New England | 29,794 |
| 12/19 | W | 15-3 | L.A. Rams | 36,612 |
| 12/26 | W | 21-17 | Atlanta | 27,014 |
| 1/2 | L | 13-20 | at New Orleans | 58,036 |

**SCORE BY PERIODS**

| | | | | | | | |
|---|---|---|---|---|---|---|---|
| Bengals | 41 | 74 | 18 | 54 | 0 | — | 187 |
| Opponents | 42 | 119 | 63 | 95 | 0 | — | 319 |

**ATTENDANCE**

Home 353,273 Away 466,756 Total 820,029
Single-game home record, 60,284 (10-17-71)
Single-season home record, 473,288 (1990)

## 1993 TEAM STATISTICS

| | Bengals | Opp. |
|---|---|---|
| Total First Downs | 239 | 306 |
| Rushing | 89 | 134 |
| Passing | 133 | 159 |
| Penalty | 17 | 13 |
| Third Down: Made/Att | 80/232 | 85/212 |
| Third Down Pct. | 34.5 | 40.1 |
| Fourth Down: Made/Att | 10/26 | 7/11 |
| Fourth Down Pct. | 38.5 | 63.6 |
| Total Net Yards | 4052 | 5018 |
| Avg. Per Game | 253.3 | 313.6 |
| Total Plays | 986 | 1000 |
| Avg. Per Play | 4.1 | 5.0 |
| Net Yards Rushing | 1511 | 2220 |
| Avg. Per Game | 94.4 | 138.8 |
| Total Rushes | 423 | 521 |
| Net Yards Passing | 2541 | 2798 |
| Avg. Per Game | 158.8 | 174.9 |
| Sacked/Yards Lost | 53/289 | 22/154 |
| Gross Yards | 2830 | 2952 |
| Att./Completions | 510/272 | 457/251 |
| Completion Pct. | 53.3 | 54.9 |
| Had Intercepted | 11 | 12 |
| Punts/Avg. | 90/43.9 | 74/42.2 |
| Net Punting Avg. | 90/36.6 | 74/36.2 |
| Penalties/Yards Lost | 105/773 | 73/567 |
| Fumbles/Ball Lost | 24/9 | 22/14 |
| Touchdowns | 16 | 37 |
| Rushing | 3 | 15 |
| Passing | 11 | 20 |
| Returns | 2 | 2 |
| Avg. Time of Possession | 28:58 | 31:02 |

## 1993 INDIVIDUAL STATISTICS

| PASSING | Att | Cmp | Yds. | Pct. | TD | Int | Tkld. | Rate |
|---|---|---|---|---|---|---|---|---|
| Klingler | 343 | 190 | 1935 | 55.4 | 6 | 9 | 40/202 | 66.6 |
| Schroeder | 159 | 78 | 832 | 49.1 | 5 | 2 | 13/87 | 70.0 |
| Wilhelm | 6 | 4 | 63 | 66.7 | 0 | 0 | 0/0 | 101.4 |
| L. Johnson | 1 | 0 | 0 | 0.0 | 0 | 0 | 0/0 | 39.6 |
| Pickens | 1 | 0 | 0 | 0.0 | 0 | 0 | 0/0 | 39.6 |
| Bengals | 510 | 272 | 2830 | 53.3 | 11 | 11 | 53/289 | 67.9 |
| Opponents | 457 | 251 | 2952 | 54.9 | 20 | 12 | 22/154 | 78.4 |

| SCORING | TD R | TD P | TD Rt | PAT | FG | Saf | PTS |
|---|---|---|---|---|---|---|---|
| Pelfrey | 0 | 0 | 0 | 13/16 | 24/31 | 0 | 85 |
| Pickens | 0 | 6 | 0 | 0/0 | 0/0 | 0 | 36 |
| Query | 0 | 4 | 0 | 0/0 | 0/0 | 0 | 24 |
| Ball | 1 | 0 | 0 | 0/0 | 0/0 | 0 | 6 |
| Brim | 0 | 0 | 1 | 0/0 | 0/0 | 0 | 6 |
| Fenner | 1 | 0 | 0 | 0/0 | 0/0 | 0 | 6 |
| Miles | 1 | 0 | 0 | 0/0 | 0/0 | 0 | 6 |
| Thompson | 0 | 1 | 0 | 0/0 | 0/0 | 0 | 6 |
| D. Williams | 0 | 0 | 1 | 0/0 | 0/0 | 0 | 6 |
| A. Williams | 0 | 0 | 0 | 0/0 | 0/0 | 1 | 2 |
| Bengals | 3 | 11 | 2 | 13/16 | 24/31 | 3 | 187 |
| Opponents | 15 | 20 | 2 | 37/37 | 20/28 | 0 | 319 |

| RUSHING | Att. | Yds. | Avg. | LG | TD |
|---|---|---|---|---|---|
| Green | 215 | 589 | 2.7 | 25 | 0 |
| Fenner | 121 | 482 | 4.0 | 26 | 1 |
| Klingler | 41 | 282 | 6.9 | 29 | 0 |
| Miles | 22 | 56 | 2.5 | 15 | 1 |
| Schroeder | 10 | 41 | 4.1 | 20 | 0 |
| Ball | 8 | 37 | 4.6 | 18 | 1 |
| Query | 2 | 13 | 6.5 | 8 | 0 |
| Robinson | 1 | 6 | 6.0 | 6 | 0 |
| Benjamin | 3 | 5 | 1.7 | 2 | 0 |
| Bengals | 423 | 1511 | 3.6 | 29 | 3 |
| Opponents | 521 | 2220 | 4.3 | 38t | 15 |

| RECEIVING | No. | Yds. | Avg. | LG | TD |
|---|---|---|---|---|---|
| Query | 56 | 654 | 11.7 | 51 | 4 |
| Fenner | 48 | 427 | 8.9 | 40 | 0 |
| McGee | 44 | 525 | 11.9 | 37 | 0 |
| Pickens | 43 | 565 | 13.1 | 36 | 6 |
| Green | 22 | 115 | 5.2 | 16 | 0 |
| Thompson | 17 | 87 | 5.1 | 10 | 1 |
| Rembert | 8 | 101 | 12.6 | 21 | 0 |
| Robinson | 8 | 72 | 9.0 | 14 | 0 |
| Miles | 6 | 89 | 14.8 | 27 | 0 |
| Carroll | 6 | 81 | 13.5 | 28 | 0 |
| Frisch | 6 | 43 | 7.2 | 12 | 0 |
| Ball | 4 | 39 | 9.8 | 24 | 0 |
| Thomason | 2 | 8 | 4.0 | 5 | 0 |
| Benjamin | 1 | 16 | 16.0 | 16 | 0 |
| Stegall | 1 | 8 | 8.0 | 8 | 0 |
| Bengals | 272 | 2830 | 10.4 | 51 | 11 |
| Opponents | 251 | 2952 | 11.8 | 71t | 20 |

| INTERCEPTIONS | No. | Yds. | Avg. | LG | TD |
|---|---|---|---|---|---|
| Brim | 3 | 74 | 24.7 | 30 | 1 |
| D. Williams | 2 | 126 | 63.0 | 97t | 1 |
| White | 2 | 19 | 9.5 | 14 | 0 |
| Francis | 2 | 12 | 6.0 | 12 | 0 |
| Grant | 1 | 17 | 17.0 | 17 | 0 |
| R. Jones | 1 | 0 | 0.0 | 0 | 0 |
| Tovar | 1 | 0 | 0.0 | 0 | 0 |
| Wheeler | 0 | 24 | — | 24 | 0 |
| Bengals | 12 | 272 | 22.7 | 97t | 2 |
| Opponents | 11 | 49 | 4.5 | 30 | 0 |

| PUNTING | No. | Yds. | Avg. | In 20 | LG |
|---|---|---|---|---|---|
| L. Johnson | 90 | 3954 | 43.9 | 24 | 60 |
| Bengals | 90 | 3954 | 43.9 | 24 | 60 |
| Opponents | 74 | 3123 | 42.2 | 20 | 72 |

| PUNT RETURNS | No. | FC | Yds. | Avg. | LG | TD |
|---|---|---|---|---|---|---|
| Robinson | 43 | 6 | 305 | 7.1 | 36 | 0 |
| Pickens | 4 | 2 | 16 | 4.0 | 9 | 0 |
| Simmons | 1 | 0 | 0 | 0.0 | 0 | 0 |
| Bengals | 48 | 8 | 321 | 6.7 | 36 | 0 |
| Opponents | 47 | 13 | 416 | 8.9 | 39 | 0 |

| KICKOFF RETURNS | No. | Yds. | Avg. | LG | TD |
|---|---|---|---|---|---|
| Robinson | 30 | 567 | 18.9 | 42 | 0 |
| Ball | 23 | 501 | 21.8 | 45 | 0 |
| Benjamin | 4 | 78 | 19.5 | 24 | 0 |
| Miles | 4 | 65 | 16.3 | 24 | 0 |
| Shaw | 0 | 0 | — | — | 0 |
| Bengals | 61 | 1211 | 19.9 | 45 | 0 |
| Opponents | 38 | 831 | 21.9 | 66 | 0 |

| SACKS | No. |
|---|---|
| Stubbs | 5.0 |
| A. Williams | 4.0 |
| Copeland | 3.0 |
| Krumrie | 3.0 |
| Francis | 2.0 |
| D. Williams | 2.0 |
| Frier | 1.0 |
| Hinkle | 1.0 |
| McDonald | 1.0 |
| Bengals | 22.0 |
| Opponents | 53.0 |

## 1994 DRAFT CHOICES

| Round | Name | Pos. | College |
|---|---|---|---|
| 1 | Dan Wilkinson | DT | Ohio State |
| 2 | Darnay Scott | WR | San Diego State |
| 3 | Jeff Cothran | RB | Ohio State |
| | Steve Shine | LB | Northwestern |
| 4 | Corey Sawyer | DB | Florida State |
| 5 | Trent Pollard | T | Eastern Washington |
| 6 | Kimo von Oelhoffen | DT | Boise State |
| | Jerry Reynolds | T | Nevada-Las Vegas |
| 7 | Ramondo Stallings | DE | San Diego State |

## CINCINNATI BENGALS

### 1994 VETERAN ROSTER

| No. | Name | Pos. | Ht. | Wt. | Birthdate | NFL Exp. | College | Hometown | How Acq. | '93 Games/ Starts |
|---|---|---|---|---|---|---|---|---|---|---|
| 42 | Ball, Eric | RB | 6-2 | 220 | 7/1/66 | 6 | UCLA | Ypsilanti, Mich. | D2-'89 | 15/1 |
| 21 | Benjamin, Ryan | RB | 5-7 | 183 | 4/23/70 | 2 | Pacific | Pixley, Calif. | FA-'93 | 1/0 |
| 60 | Bradley, Chuck | T | 6-5 | 296 | 4/9/70 | 2 | Kentucky | Fern Creek, Ky. | W(Hou)-'93 | 1/0 |
| 65 | Brilz, Darrick | G | 6-3 | 287 | 2/14/64 | 8 | Oregon | Pinole Valley, Calif. | UFA(Sea)-'94 | 0* |
| 43 | Brim, Mike | CB | 6-0 | 192 | 1/23/66 | 7 | Virginia Union | Danville, Va. | UFA(NYJ)-'93 | 16/16 |
| 33 | Broussard, Steve | RB | 5-7 | 201 | 2/22/67 | 5 | Washington State | Los Angeles, Calif. | FA-'94 | 8/0* |
| 72 | Brumfield, Scott | T | 6-8 | 320 | 8/19/70 | 2 | Brigham Young | Spanish Fork, Utah | FA-'93 | 16/7 |
| 32 | Carpenter, Ron | S | 6-1 | 188 | 1/20/70 | 2 | Miami, Ohio | Cincinnati, Ohio | W(Minn)-'93 | 13/0* |
| 92 | Copeland, John | DE | 6-3 | 286 | 9/20/70 | 2 | Alabama | Lanett, Ala. | D1-'93 | 14/14 |
| 44 | Fenner, Derrick | RB | 6-3 | 228 | 4/6/67 | 6 | North Carolina | Oxon Hill, Md. | PB(Sea)-'92 | 15/14 |
| 50 | Francis, James | LB | 6-5 | 252 | 8/4/68 | 5 | Baylor | Houston, Tex. | D1-'90 | 14/12 |
| 97 | Frier, Mike | DE | 6-5 | 299 | 3/20/69 | 3 | Appalachian State | Jacksonville, N.C. | W(Sea)-'92 | 16/6 |
| 47 | Frisch, David | TE | 6-7 | 260 | 6/22/70 | 2 | Colorado | House Springs, Mo. | FA-'93 | 11/2 |
| 58 | Gordon, Alex | LB | 6-5 | 245 | 9/14/64 | 8 | Cincinnati | Jacksonville, Fla. | PB(Raid)-'91 | 16/3 |
| 24 | Grant, Alan | CB | 5-10 | 187 | 10/1/66 | 5 | Stanford | Pasadena, Calif. | W(SF)-'93 | 12/1* |
| 28 | Green, Harold | RB | 6-2 | 222 | 1/29/68 | 5 | South Carolina | Ladson, S.C. | D2-'90 | 15/15 |
| 27 | Gunn, Lance | S | 6-3 | 222 | 1/9/70 | 2 | Texas | Houston, Tex. | D7-'93 | 8/8 |
| 98 | Hinkle, George | DE | 6-5 | 288 | 3/17/65 | 7 | Arizona | St. Louis, Mo. | FA-'93 | 13/9 |
| 12 | Hollas, Donald | QB | 6-3 | 215 | 11/22/67 | 3 | Rice | Kingsville, Tex. | D4-'91 | 0* |
| 71 | Howe, Garry | NT | 6-1 | 298 | 6/20/68 | 2 | Colorado | Spencer, Iowa | FA-'93 | 1/0 |
| 68 | Johnson, Donnell | T | 6-7 | 310 | 12/24/69 | 2 | Johnson C. Smith | Miami, Fla. | FA-'93 | 7/0 |
| 11 | Johnson, Lee | P-K | 6-2 | 200 | 11/27/61 | 10 | Brigham Young | Conroe, Tex. | W(Clev)-'88 | 16/0 |
| 66 | Jones, Dan | T | 6-7 | 304 | 7/22/70 | 2 | Maine | Malden, Mass. | FA-'93 | 15/5 |
| 25 | Jones, Rod | CB | 6-0 | 185 | 3/31/64 | 9 | Southern Methodist | Dallas, Tex. | T(TB)-'90 | 16/16 |
| 7 | Klingler, David | QB | 6-2 | 205 | 2/17/69 | 3 | Houston | Stratford, Tex. | D1a-'92 | 14/13 |
| 64 | Kozerski, Bruce | G-C | 6-4 | 287 | 4/2/62 | 11 | Holy Cross | Plains, Pa. | D9-'84 | 15/15 |
| 69 | Krumrie, Tim | NT | 6-2 | 274 | 5/20/60 | 12 | Wisconsin | Eau Claire, Wis. | D10-'83 | 16/16 |
| 56 | McDonald, Ricardo | LB | 6-2 | 235 | 11/8/69 | 3 | Pittsburgh | Kingston, Jamaica | D4-'92 | 14/12 |
| 85 | McGee, Tim | WR | 5-10 | 183 | 8/7/64 | 9 | Tennessee | Cleveland, Ohio | FA-'94 | 13/12* |
| 82 | McGee, Tony | TE | 6-3 | 246 | 4/21/71 | 2 | Michigan | Terre Haute, Ind. | D2-'93 | 15/15 |
| 59 | McGill, Karmeeleyah | LB | 6-3 | 224 | 1/11/71 | 2 | Notre Dame | Clearwater, Fla. | FA-'93 | 4/0 |
| 36 | Miles, Ostell | RB | 6-0 | 236 | 8/6/71 | 3 | Houston | Pueblo, Colo. | D9-'92 | 15/2 |
| 62 | Moore, Eric | G | 6-5 | 290 | 1/21/65 | 7 | Indiana | Berkeley, Mo. | UFA(NYG)-'94 | 7/5* |
| 73 | Moyer, Ken | T | 6-7 | 297 | 11/19/66 | 5 | Toledo | Temperance, Mich. | FA-'89 | 16/14 |
| 29 | Oliver, Louis | S | 6-2 | 224 | 3/9/66 | 6 | Florida | Belle Glade, Fla. | UFA(Mia)-'94 | 11/11* |
| 93 | Parten, Ty | NT | 6-4 | 272 | 10/13/69 | 2 | Arizona | Washington, D.C. | D3a-'93 | 11/1 |
| 9 | Pelfrey, Doug | K | 5-11 | 185 | 9/25/70 | 2 | Kentucky | Ft. Thomas, Ky. | D8-'93 | 15/0 |
| 80 | Pickens, Carl | WR | 6-2 | 206 | 3/23/70 | 3 | Tennessee | Murphy, N.C. | D2-'92 | 13/12 |
| 89 | Query, Jeff | WR | 6-0 | 165 | 3/7/67 | 6 | Millikin | Maroa, Ill. | W(Hou)-'92 | 16/16 |
| 88 | Rembert, Reggie | WR | 6-5 | 200 | 12/25/66 | 4 | West Virginia | Okeechobee, Fla. | FA-'94 | 3/0* |
| 81 | Robinson, Patrick | WR | 5-8 | 176 | 10/3/69 | 2 | Tennessee State | Memphis, Tenn. | W(Hou)-'93 | 15/3 |
| 87 | Sadowski, Troy | TE | 6-5 | 250 | 12/8/65 | 5 | Georgia | Chamblee, Ga. | UFA(NYJ)-'94 | 13/1* |
| 77 | Sargent, Kevin | T | 6-6 | 284 | 3/31/69 | 3 | Eastern Washington | Bremerton, Wash. | FA-'92 | 1/1 |
| 10 | Schroeder, Jay | QB | 6-4 | 215 | 6/28/61 | 11 | UCLA | Pacific Palisades, Calif. | UFA(Raid)0-'93 | 9/3 |
| 74 | Scott, Tom | T | 6-6 | 330 | 6/25/70 | 2 | East Carolina | Burke County, N.C. | D6-'93 | 13/13 |
| 90 | Shaw, Eric | LB | 6-3 | 248 | 9/17/71 | 3 | Louisiana Tech | Pensacola, Fla. | D12-'92 | 14/9 |
| 22 | Simmons, Marcello | CB | 6-1 | 180 | 8/8/71 | 2 | Southern Methodist | Tomball, Tex. | D4-'93 | 16/2 |
| 91 | Smith, Brad | LB | 6-2 | 228 | 9/5/69 | 2 | Texas Christian | Houston, Tex. | FA-'93 | 7/0 |
| 84 | Stegall, Milt | WR | 6-0 | 184 | 1/25/70 | 3 | Miami, Ohio | Cincinnati, Ohio | FA-'92 | 4/0 |
| 53 | Stephens, Santo | LB | 6-4 | 232 | 6/16/69 | 2 | Temple | Capital Heights, Md. | W(KC)-'94 | 16/0* |
| 96 | # Stubbs, Daniel | LB | 6-4 | 264 | 1/3/65 | 7 | Miami | Red Bank, N.J. | W(Dall)-'91 | 16/0 |
| 49 | Thomason, Jeff | TE | 6-4 | 233 | 12/30/69 | 3 | Oregon | Newport Beach, Calif. | FA-'92 | 3/0 |
| 48 | Thompson, Craig | TE | 6-2 | 244 | 1/13/69 | 3 | North Carolina A&T | Hartsville, S.C. | D5-'92 | 13/0 |
| 51 | Tovar, Steve | LB | 6-3 | 244 | 4/25/70 | 2 | Ohio State | Elyria, Ohio | D3-'93 | 16/9 |
| 34 | Vinson, Fernandus | S | 5-10 | 197 | 11/3/68 | 4 | North Carolina State | Montgomery, Ala. | D7-'91 | 16/7 |
| 63 | Walter, Joe | T | 6-7 | 292 | 6/18/63 | 10 | Texas Tech | Dallas, Tex. | D7a-'85 | 16/16 |
| 37 | Wheeler, Leonard | CB | 5-11 | 189 | 1/15/69 | 3 | Troy State | Toccoa, Ga. | D3-'92 | 16/2 |
| 4 | Wilhelm, Erik | QB | 6-3 | 217 | 11/19/65 | 5 | Oregon State | Lake Oswego, Ore. | FA-'93 | 1/0 |
| 94 | † Williams, Alfred | LB | 6-6 | 240 | 11/6/68 | 4 | Colorado | Houston, Tex. | D1-'91 | 16/16 |
| 31 | Williams, Darryl | S | 6-0 | 191 | 1/7/70 | 3 | Miami | Miami, Fla. | D1a-'92 | 16/16 |

* Brilz played 16 games with Seattle in '93; Broussard played 8 games with Atlanta; Carpenter played 7 games with Minnesota; Grant played 3 games with San Francisco; Hollas missed '93 season due to injury; Tim McGee played 13 games with Washington; Moore played 7 games with N.Y. Giants; Oliver played 11 games with Miami; Rembert played 3 games with Cincinnati; Sadowski played 13 games with N.Y. Jets; Stephens played 16 games with Kansas City.

\# Unrestricted free agent; subject to developments.

† Restricted free agent; subject to developments.

Players lost through free agency (1): LB Randy Kirk (Ariz; 16 games in '93).

Also played with Bengals in '93—WR Wesley Carroll (12 games), WR Allen Degraffenreid (2), CB-S R.J. Kors (7), G Jack Linn (3), DE Roosevelt Nix (10), CB Mitchell Price (1), G Tom Rayam (10), WR Reggie Thornton (1), CB Sheldon White (8).

## COACHING STAFF

**Head Coach,**
**Dave Shula**

**Pro Career:** Shula is in his third year as head coach of the Cincinnati Bengals. He became the sixth head coach in Bengals history on December 27, 1991. Shula was offensive coordinator and quarterbacks coach for Dallas in 1989-90 before joining Cincinnati in 1991 as receivers coach. Shula began his coaching career with the Miami Dolphins in 1982. In 1988, Shula was named assistant head coach with the Dolphins. He was a wide receiver and kick return specialist with the Baltimore Colts in 1981. Career record: 8-24.

**Background:** Outstanding wide receiver at Dartmouth where he was a two-time All-Ivy League selection.

**Personal:** Born May 28, 1959, Lexington, Ky. Dave and his wife, Leslie, live in Cincinnati, and have three sons—Daniel, Christopher, and Matthew.

### ASSISTANT COACHES

**Paul Alexander,** tight ends; born February 12, 1960, Rochester, N.Y., lives in Cincinnati. Tackle Cortland State 1978-81. No pro playing experience. College coach: Penn State 1982-84, Michigan 1985-86, Central Michigan 1987-91. Pro coach: New York Jets 1992-93, joined Bengals in 1994.

**Jim Anderson,** running backs; born March 27, 1948, Harrisburg, Pa., lives in Cincinnati. Linebacker-defensive end Cal Western (U.S. International) 1967-70. No pro playing experience. College coach: Cal Western 1970-71, Scottsdale, Ariz., Community College 1973, Nevada-Las Vegas 1974-75, Southern Methodist 1976-80, Stanford 1981-83. Pro coach: Joined Bengals in 1984.

**Ken Anderson,** quarterbacks; born February 15, 1949, Batavia, Ill., lives in Lakeside Park, Ky. Quarterback Augustana (Ill.) 1967-70. Pro quarterback Cincinnati Bengals 1971-86. Pro coach: Joined Bengals in 1992.

**Marv Braden,** special teams; born January 25, 1938, Kansas City, Mo., lives in Cincinnati. Linebacker Southwest Missouri State 1956-59. No pro playing experience. College coach: Parsons 1963-66, Northeast Missouri State 1967-68 (head coach), Cal Western (U.S. International) 1969-72, Iowa State 1973, Southern Methodist 1974-75, Michigan State 1976. Pro coach: Denver Broncos 1977-80, San Diego Chargers 1981-85, St. Louis/Phoenix Cardinals 1986-89, joined Bengals in 1990.

**Bruce Coslet,** offensive coordinator; born August 5, 1946, Oakdale, Calif., lives in Cincinnati. Tight end University of Pacific 1965-67. Pro tight end Cincinnati Bengals 1969-76. Pro coach: San Francisco 49ers 1980, Cincinnati Bengals 1981-89, New York Jets (head coach) 1990-93, rejoined Bengals in 1994.

**Bobby DePaul,** defensive assistant; born January 29, 1963, Cheverly, Md., lives in Cincinnati. Linebacker Maryland 1982-83. No pro playing experience. College coach: Catholic University 1986-88. Pro coach: Washington Redskins 1989-93, joined Bengals in 1994.

**Jim McNally,** offensive line; born December 13, 1943, Buffalo, N.Y., lives in Cincinnati. Guard Buffalo 1961-65. No pro playing experience. College coach: Buffalo 1966-69, Marshall 1973-75, Boston College 1976-78, Wake Forest 1979. Pro coach: Joined Bengals in 1980.

**Ron Meeks,** defensive backfield; born August 27, 1954, Jacksonville, Fla., lives in Cincinnati. Defensive back Arkansas State 1975-76. Pro defensive back Hamilton Tiger-Cats (CFL) 1977-79, Ottawa Roughriders (CFL) 1979, Toronto Argonauts (CFL) 1980-81. College coach: Arkansas State 1984-85, Miami 1986-87, New Mexico State 1988, Fresno State 1989-90. Pro coach: Dallas Cowboys 1991, joined Bengals in 1992.

**Joe Pascale,** linebackers; born April 4, 1946, New York, N.Y., lives in Cincinnati. Linebacker Connecticut 1963-66. No pro playing experience. College coach: Connecticut 1967-68, Rhode Island 1969-73, Idaho State 1974-76 (head coach 1976), Princeton 1977-79. Pro coach: Montreal Alouettes (CFL) 1980-81. Ottawa Rough Riders (CFL) 1982-83, New Jersey Generals (USFL) 1984-85, St. Louis/Phoenix Cardinals 1986-93, joined Bengals in 1994.

**Larry Peccatiello,** defensive coordinator; born December 21, 1935, Newark, N.J., lives in Cincinnati. Receiver William & Mary 1955-58. No pro playing experience. College coach: William & Mary 1961-68, Navy 1969-70, Rice 1971. Pro coach: Houston Oilers 1972-75, Seattle Seahawks 1976-80, Washington Redskins 1981-93, joined Bengals in 1994.

**Joe Wessel,** defensive line; born January 5, 1962, Miami, Fla., lives in Cincinnati. Quarterback-safety Florida State 1981-84. No pro playing experience. College coach: Louisiana State 1985-90, Notre Dame 1991-93. Pro coach: Joined Bengals in 1994.

**Richard Williamson,** wide receivers, born April 13, 1941, Ft. Deposit, Ala., lives in Cincinnati. Receiver Alabama 1961-62. No pro playing experience. College coach: Alabama 1963-67, 1970-71, Arkansas 1968-69, 1972-74, Memphis State 1975-80 (head coach). Pro coach: Kansas City Chiefs 1983-86, Tampa Bay Buccaneers 1987-91 (interim head coach final three games of 1990 season, head coach 1991), joined Bengals in 1992.

**Kim Wood,** strength; born July 12, 1945, Barrington, Ill., lives in Cincinnati. Running back Wisconsin 1965-68. No pro playing experience. Pro coach: Joined Bengals in 1975.

## 1994 FIRST-YEAR ROSTER

| Name | Pos. | Ht. | Wt. | Birthdate | College | Hometown | How Acq. |
|---|---|---|---|---|---|---|---|
| Beckett, Andrew | DE | 6-4 | 265 | 3/15/72 | Rutgers | Barrington, N.J. | FA |
| Cothran, Jeff | RB | 6-2 | 231 | 6/28/71 | Ohio State | Middletown, Ohio | D3 |
| Dickey, Troy | WR | 6-3 | 226 | 4/8/71 | Arizona | Houston, Tex. | FA |
| Duckett, Forey (1) | CB | 6-3 | 195 | 2/5/70 | Nevada-Reno | Pinole, Calif. | D5 |
| Ford, Artis (1) | DE | 6-3 | 275 | 9/30/71 | Mississippi | Pahokee, Fla. | FA |
| Hill, Jeff | WR | 5-11 | 178 | 9/24/72 | Purdue | Cincinnati, Ohio | FA |
| Jefferson, Kevin | LB | 6-2 | 232 | 1/14/74 | Lehigh | Greensburg, Pa. | FA |
| Johnson, Lance | C | 6-1 | 265 | 11/27/70 | Notre Dame | Charlotte, N.C. | FA |
| Phillips, Jey | CB | 6-2 | 183 | 12/21/71 | Arizona | El Paso, Tex. | FA |
| Pollard, Trent | G-T | 6-4 | 325 | 11/20/72 | Eastern Washington | Seattle, Wash. | D5 |
| Reynolds, Jerry | G-T | 6-6 | 300 | 4/2/70 | Nevada-Las Vegas | Ft. Thomas, Ky. | D6a |
| Richardson, Terry | RB | 6-1 | 205 | 10/8/71 | Syracuse | Ft. Lauderdale, Fla. | FA |
| Sawyer, Corey | CB | 5-11 | 171 | 10/4/71 | Florida State | Key West, Fla. | D4 |
| Scott, Darnay | WR | 6-1 | 180 | 7/7/72 | San Diego State | St. Louis, Mo. | D2 |
| Shine, Steve | LB | 6-6 | 232 | 11/28/70 | Northwestern | Kokomo, Ind. | D3a |
| Stallings, Ramondo | DE | 6-7 | 285 | 11/21/71 | San Diego State | Winston-Salem, N.C. | D7 |
| Truitt, Gregg (1) | RB | 6-0 | 235 | 12/8/65 | Penn State | Sarasota, Fla. | FA |
| Turner, Elbert (1) | WR | 5-11 | 165 | 3/19/68 | Illinois | Gary, Ind. | FA |
| von Oelhoffen, Kimo | DT | 6-4 | 300 | 1/30/71 | Boise State | Molokai, Hawaii | D6 |
| Wilkinson, Dan | DT | 6-5 | 300 | 3/13/73 | Ohio State | Dayton, Ohio | D1 |
| Williams, Ronald (1) | RB | 6-1 | 203 | 5/19/72 | Clemson | Ninety Six, S.C. | FA |
| Woodside, Ray | G | 6-4 | 280 | 8/22/72 | Cincinnati | Oberlin, Ohio | FA |

The term NFL Rookie is defined as a player who is in his first season of professional football and has not been on the roster of another professional football team for any regular-season or postseason games. A Rookie is designated by an "R" on NFL rosters. Players who have been active in another professional football league or players who have NFL experience, including either preseason training camp or being on an Active List or Inactive List, or on Reserve/Injured or Reserve/Physically Unable to Perform for fewer than six regular-season games, are termed NFL First-Year Players. An NFL First-Year Player is designated by a "1" on NFL rosters. Thereafter, a player is credited with an additional year of experience for each season in which he accumulates six games on the Active List or Inactive List, or on Reserve/Injured or Reserve/Physically Unable to Perform.

## NOTES

# CLEVELAND BROWNS

**American Football Conference**
**Central Division**
**Team Colors:** Seal Brown, Orange, and White
**80 First Avenue**
**Berea, Ohio 44017**
**Telephone: (216) 891-5000**

## CLUB OFFICIALS

President and Owner: Arthur B. Modell
Executive Vice President/Legal and Administration: Jim Bailey
Vice President/Assistant to President: David Modell
Vice President/Public Relations: Kevin Byrne
Director of Player Personnel: Michael Lombardi
Director of Pro Personnel: Ozzie Newsome
Treasurer: Mike Srsen
Director of Operations/Information: Bob Eller
Director of Business Operations: Pat Moriarty
Assistant Director of Public Relations: Francine Lubera
Player Relations/Media Services: Dino Lucarelli
Scouts: Tom Dimitroff, Ron Marciniak, Terry McDonough, Vince Newsome, Scott Pioli, Ernie Plank, Ellis Rainsberger, Phil Savage, Bill Shunkwiler, Lionel Vital
Head Trainer: Bill Tessendorf
Facilities Manager: Charley Cusick
Equipment Manager: Ed Carroll
**Stadium:** Cleveland Stadium •**Capacity:** 78,512
West 3rd Street
Cleveland, Ohio 44114
**Playing Surface:** Grass
**Training Camp:** 80 First Avenue
Berea, Ohio 44017

## 1994 SCHEDULE

**PRESEASON**

| | | |
|---|---|---|
| Aug. 6 | at New York Giants | 8:00 |
| Aug. 13 | **Detroit** | 7:30 |
| Aug. 19 | **Atlanta** | 7:30 |
| Aug. 25 | at Indianapolis | 7:30 |

**REGULAR SEASON**

| | | |
|---|---|---|
| Sept. 4 | at Cincinnati | 1:00 |
| Sept. 11 | **Pittsburgh** | 1:00 |
| Sept. 18 | **Arizona** | 1:00 |
| Sept. 25 | at Indianapolis | 12:00 |
| Oct. 2 | **New York Jets** | 1:00 |
| Oct. 9 | Open Date | |
| Oct. 13 | at Houston (Thursday) | 7:00 |
| Oct. 23 | **Cincinnati** | 1:00 |
| Oct. 30 | at Denver | 2:00 |
| Nov. 6 | **New England** | 1:00 |
| Nov. 13 | at Philadelphia | 1:00 |
| Nov. 20 | at Kansas City | 12:00 |
| Nov. 27 | **Houston** | 1:00 |
| Dec. 4 | **New York Giants** | 4:00 |
| Dec. 10 | at Dallas (Saturday) | 3:00 |
| Dec. 18 | at Pittsburgh | 1:00 |
| Dec. 24 | **Seattle** | 1:00 |

## RECORD HOLDERS

**INDIVIDUAL RECORDS—CAREER**

| Category | Name | Performance |
|---|---|---|
| Rushing (Yds.) | Jim Brown, 1957-1965 | 12,312 |
| Passing (Yds.) | Brian Sipe, 1974-1983 | 23,713 |
| Passing (TDs) | Brian Sipe, 1974-1983 | 154 |
| Receiving (No.) | Ozzie Newsome, 1978-1990 | 662 |
| Receiving (Yds.) | Ozzie Newsome, 1978-1990 | 7,980 |
| Interceptions | Thom Darden, 1972-74, 1976-1981 | 45 |
| Punting (Avg.) | Horace Gillom, 1950-56 | 43.8 |
| Punt Return (Avg.) | Greg Pruitt, 1973-1981 | 11.8 |
| Kickoff Return (Avg.) | Greg Pruitt, 1973-1981 | 26.3 |
| Field Goals | Lou Groza, 1950-59, 1961-67 | 234 |
| Touchdowns (Tot.) | Jim Brown, 1957-1965 | *126 |
| Points | Lou Groza, 1950-59, 1961-67 | 1,349 |

**INDIVIDUAL RECORDS—SINGLE SEASON**

| Category | Name | Performance |
|---|---|---|
| Rushing (Yds.) | Jim Brown, 1963 | 1,863 |
| Passing (Yds.) | Brian Sipe, 1980 | 4,132 |
| Passing (TDs) | Brian Sipe, 1980 | 30 |
| Receiving (No.) | Ozzie Newsome, 1983 | 89 |
| | Ozzie Newsome, 1984 | 89 |
| Receiving (Yds.) | Webster Slaughter, 1989 | 1,236 |
| Interceptions | Thom Darden, 1978 | 10 |
| Punting (Avg.) | Gary Collins, 1965 | 46.7 |
| Punt Return (Avg.) | Leroy Kelly, 1965 | 15.6 |
| Kickoff Return (Avg.) | Billy Reynolds, 1954 | 29.5 |
| Field Goals | Matt Bahr, 1984 | 24 |
| | Matt Bahr, 1988 | 24 |
| Touchdowns (Tot.) | Jim Brown, 1965 | 21 |
| Points | Jim Brown, 1965 | 126 |

**INDIVIDUAL RECORDS—SINGLE GAME**

| Category | Name | Performance |
|---|---|---|
| Rushing (Yds.) | Jim Brown, 11-24-57 | 237 |
| | Jim Brown, 11-19-61 | 237 |
| Passing (Yds.) | Bernie Kosar, 1-3-87 | 489 |
| Passing (TDs) | Frank Ryan, 12-12-64 | 5 |
| | Bill Nelsen, 11-2-69 | 5 |
| | Brian Sipe, 10-7-79 | 5 |
| Receiving (No.) | Ozzie Newsome, 10-14-84 | 14 |
| Receiving (Yds.) | Ozzie Newsome, 10-14-84 | 191 |
| Interceptions | Many times | 3 |
| | Last time by Frank Minnifield, 11-22-87 | |
| Field Goals | Don Cockroft, 10-19-75 | 5 |
| Touchdowns (Tot.) | Dub Jones, 11-25-51 | *6 |
| Points | Dub Jones, 11-25-51 | 36 |

*NFL Record

## COACHING HISTORY

**(368-268-10)**

| | | |
|---|---|---|
| 1950-62 | Paul Brown | 115-49-5 |
| 1963-70 | Blanton Collier | 79-38-2 |
| 1971-74 | Nick Skorich | 30-26-2 |
| 1975-77 | Forrest Gregg* | 18-23-0 |
| 1977 | Dick Modzelewski | 0-1-0 |
| 1978-84 | Sam Rutigliano** | 47-52-0 |
| 1984-88 | Marty Schottenheimer | 46-31-0 |
| 1989-90 | Bud Carson*** | 12-14-1 |
| 1990 | Jim Shofner | 1-6-0 |
| 1991-93 | Bill Belichick | 20-28-0 |

*Resigned after 13 games in 1977
**Released after eight games in 1984
***Released after nine games in 1990

**CLEVELAND STADIUM**

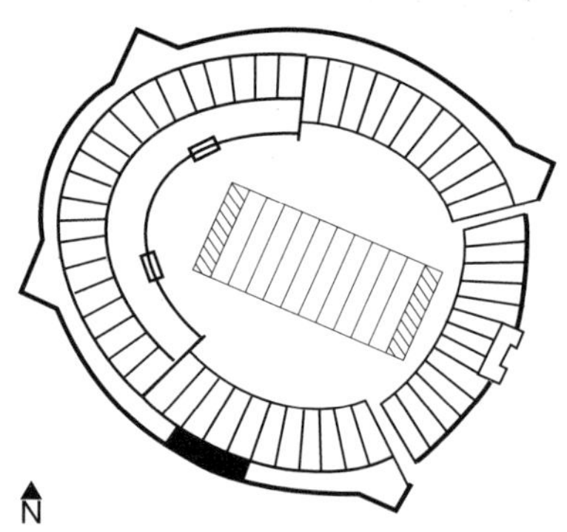

## 1993 TEAM RECORD

**PRESEASON (2-2)**

| Date | Result | | Opponents |
|---|---|---|---|
| 8/9 | L | 12-41 | at Washington |
| 8/14 | W | 12-9 | vs. New England at Toronto |
| 8/21 | W | 21-10 | L.A. Rams |
| 8/27 | L | 20-23 | at Tampa Bay |

**REGULAR SEASON (7-9)**

| Date | Result | | Opponents | Att. |
|---|---|---|---|---|
| 9/5 | W | 27-14 | Cincinnati | 75,508 |
| 9/13 | W | 23-13 | San Francisco | 78,218 |
| 9/19 | W | 19-16 | at L.A. Raiders | 48,617 |
| 9/26 | L | 10-23 | at Indianapolis | 59,654 |
| 10/10 | L | 14-24 | Miami | 78,138 |
| 10/17 | W | 28-17 | at Cincinnati | 55,647 |
| 10/24 | W | 28-23 | Pittsburgh | 78,118 |
| 11/7 | L | 14-29 | Denver | 77,818 |
| 11/14 | L | 5-22 | at Seattle | 54,622 |
| 11/21 | L | 20-27 | Houston | 71,668 |
| 11/28 | L | 14-17 | at Atlanta | 54,510 |
| 12/5 | W | 17-13 | New Orleans | 60,388 |
| 12/12 | L | 17-19 | at Houston | 58,720 |
| 12/19 | L | 17-20 | New England | 48,618 |
| 12/26 | W | 42-14 | at L.A. Rams | 34,155 |
| 1/2 | L | 9-16 | at Pittsburgh | 49,208 |

**SCORE BY PERIODS**

| | | | | | | | |
|---|---|---|---|---|---|---|---|
| Browns | 56 | 99 | 58 | 91 | 0 | — | 304 |
| Opponents | 64 | 110 | 52 | 81 | 0 | — | 307 |

**ATTENDANCE**

Home 568,474 Away 415,133 Total 983,607
Single-game home record, 85,073 (9-21-70)
Single-season home record, 620,496 (1980)

## 1993 TEAM STATISTICS

| | Browns | Opp. |
|---|---|---|
| Total First Downs | 264 | 290 |
| Rushing | 91 | 94 |
| Passing | 152 | 170 |
| Penalty | 21 | 26 |
| Third Down: Made/Att | 66/201 | 88/231 |
| Third Down Pct. | 32.8 | 38.1 |
| Fourth Down: Made/Att | 11/14 | 6/13 |
| Fourth Down Pct. | 78.6 | 46.2 |
| Total Net Yards | 4740 | 4778 |
| Avg. Per Game | 296.3 | 298.6 |
| Total Plays | 948 | 1040 |
| Avg. Per Play | 5.0 | 4.6 |
| Net Yards Rushing | 1701 | 1654 |
| Avg. Per Game | 106.3 | 103.4 |
| Total Rushes | 425 | 451 |
| Net Yards Passing | 3039 | 3124 |
| Avg. Per Game | 189.9 | 195.3 |
| Sacked/Yards Lost | 45/289 | 48/342 |
| Gross Yards | 3328 | 3466 |
| Att./Completions | 478/262 | 541/306 |
| Completion Pct. | 54.8 | 56.6 |
| Had Intercepted | 19 | 13 |
| Punts/Avg. | 84/43.2 | 85/42.4 |
| Net Punting Avg. | 84/35.6 | 85/34.1 |
| Penalties/Yards Lost | 121/842 | 105/821 |
| Fumbles/Ball Lost | 27/17 | 29/9 |
| Touchdowns | 36 | 30 |
| Rushing | 8 | 9 |
| Passing | 23 | 19 |
| Returns | 5 | 2 |
| Avg. Time of Possession | 29:32 | 30:28 |

## 1993 INDIVIDUAL STATISTICS

| PASSING | Att | Cmp | Yds. | Pct. | TD | Int | Tkld. | Rate |
|---|---|---|---|---|---|---|---|---|
| Testaverde | 230 | 130 | 1797 | 56.5 | 14 | 9 | 17/101 | 85.7 |
| Kosar | 138 | 79 | 807 | 57.2 | 5 | 3 | 21/128 | 77.2 |
| Philcox | 108 | 52 | 699 | 48.1 | 4 | 7 | 7/60 | 54.5 |
| Hoard | 1 | 0 | 0 | 0.0 | 0 | 0 | 0/0 | 39.6 |
| Jackson | 1 | 1 | 25 | 100.0 | 0 | 0 | 0/0 | 118.8 |
| Browns | 478 | 262 | 3328 | 54.8 | 23 | 19 | 45/289 | 76.2 |
| Opponents | 541 | 306 | 3466 | 56.6 | 19 | 13 | 48/342 | 77.6 |

| SCORING | TD R | TD P | TD Rt | PAT | FG | Saf | PTS |
|---|---|---|---|---|---|---|---|
| Stover | 0 | 0 | 0 | 36/36 | 16/22 | 0 | 84 |
| Jackson | 0 | 8 | 0 | 0/0 | 0/0 | 0 | 48 |
| Carrier | 1 | 3 | 1 | 0/0 | 0/0 | 0 | 30 |
| Metcalf | 1 | 2 | 2 | 0/0 | 0/0 | 0 | 30 |
| McCardell | 0 | 4 | 0 | 0/0 | 0/0 | 0 | 24 |
| Vardell | 3 | 1 | 0 | 0/0 | 0/0 | 0 | 24 |
| Kinchen | 0 | 2 | 0 | 0/0 | 0/0 | 0 | 12 |
| Baldwin | 0 | 1 | 0 | 0/0 | 0/0 | 0 | 6 |
| J. Jones | 1 | 0 | 0 | 0/0 | 0/0 | 0 | 6 |
| Mack | 1 | 0 | 0 | 0/0 | 0/0 | 0 | 6 |
| Moore | 0 | 0 | 1 | 0/0 | 0/0 | 0 | 6 |
| Mustafaa | 0 | 0 | 1 | 0/0 | 0/0 | 0 | 6 |
| Philcox | 1 | 0 | 0 | 0/0 | 0/0 | 0 | 6 |
| Tillman | 0 | 1 | 0 | 0/0 | 0/0 | 0 | 6 |
| Wolfley | 0 | 1 | 0 | 0/0 | 0/0 | 0 | 6 |
| Pleasant | 0 | 0 | 0 | 0/0 | 0/0 | 1 | 2 |
| Riddick | 0 | 0 | 0 | 0/0 | 0/0 | 1 | 2 |
| Browns | 8 | 23 | 5 | 36/36 | 16/22 | 2 | 304 |
| Opponents | 9 | 19 | 2 | 30/30 | 31/38 | 2 | 307 |

| RUSHING | Att. | Yds. | Avg. | LG | TD |
|---|---|---|---|---|---|
| Vardell | 171 | 644 | 3.8 | 54 | 3 |
| Metcalf | 129 | 611 | 4.7 | 55 | 1 |
| Hoard | 56 | 227 | 4.1 | 30 | 0 |
| Testaverde | 18 | 74 | 4.1 | 14 | 0 |
| Baldwin | 18 | 61 | 3.4 | 11 | 0 |
| Mack | 10 | 33 | 3.3 | 7 | 1 |
| Carrier | 4 | 26 | 6.5 | 15t | 1 |
| Kosar | 14 | 19 | 1.4 | 10 | 0 |
| Philcox | 2 | 3 | 1.5 | 3t | 1 |
| J. Jones | 2 | 2 | 1.0 | 1t | 1 |
| Jackson | 1 | 1 | 1.0 | 1 | 0 |
| Browns | 425 | 1701 | 4.0 | 55 | 8 |
| Opponents | 451 | 1654 | 3.7 | 49 | 9 |

| RECEIVING | No. | Yds. | Avg. | LG | TD |
|---|---|---|---|---|---|
| Metcalf | 63 | 539 | 8.6 | 49t | 2 |
| Carrier | 43 | 746 | 17.3 | 55 | 3 |
| Jackson | 41 | 756 | 18.4 | 62t | 8 |
| Hoard | 35 | 351 | 10.0 | 41 | 0 |
| Kinchen | 29 | 347 | 12.0 | 40 | 2 |
| Vardell | 19 | 151 | 7.9 | 28t | 1 |
| McCardell | 13 | 234 | 18.0 | 43 | 4 |
| Tillman | 5 | 68 | 13.6 | 18 | 1 |
| Wolfley | 5 | 25 | 5.0 | 9 | 1 |
| Smith | 4 | 55 | 13.8 | 17 | 0 |
| Rowe | 3 | 37 | 12.3 | 16 | 0 |
| C. Williams | 1 | 14 | 14.0 | 14 | 0 |
| Baldwin | 1 | 5 | 5.0 | 5t | 1 |
| Browns | 262 | 3328 | 12.7 | 62t | 23 |
| Opponents | 306 | 3466 | 11.3 | 56 | 19 |

| INTERCEPTIONS | No. | Yds. | Avg. | LG | TD |
|---|---|---|---|---|---|
| Turner | 5 | 25 | 5.0 | 19 | 0 |
| S. Jones | 3 | 0 | 0.0 | 0 | 0 |
| Mustafaa | 1 | 97 | 97.0 | 97t | 1 |
| Hilliard | 1 | 54 | 54.0 | 54 | 0 |
| Speer | 1 | 22 | 22.0 | 22 | 0 |
| Matthews | 1 | 10 | 10.0 | 10 | 0 |
| M. Johnson | 1 | 0 | 0.0 | 0 | 0 |
| Browns | 13 | 208 | 16.0 | 97t | 1 |
| Opponents | 19 | 246 | 12.9 | 69 | 0 |

| PUNTING | No. | Yds. | Avg. | In 20 | LG |
|---|---|---|---|---|---|
| Hansen | 82 | 3632 | 44.3 | 15 | 72 |
| Browns | 84 | 3632 | 43.2 | 15 | 72 |
| Opponents | 85 | 3603 | 42.4 | 24 | 61 |

| PUNT RETURNS | No. | FC | Yds. | Avg. | LG | TD |
|---|---|---|---|---|---|---|
| Metcalf | 36 | 11 | 464 | 12.9 | 91t | 2 |
| Carrier | 6 | 1 | 92 | 15.3 | 56t | 1 |
| Turner | 0 | 0 | 7 | — | 7 | 0 |
| Browns | 42 | 12 | 563 | 13.4 | 91t | 3 |
| Opponents | 49 | 14 | 438 | 8.9 | 36 | 0 |

| KICKOFF RETURNS | No. | Yds. | Avg. | LG | TD |
|---|---|---|---|---|---|
| Baldwin | 24 | 444 | 18.5 | 31 | 0 |
| Metcalf | 15 | 318 | 21.2 | 47 | 0 |
| Hoard | 13 | 286 | 22.0 | 39 | 0 |
| Vardell | 4 | 58 | 14.5 | 16 | 0 |
| Kinchen | 1 | 0 | 0.0 | 0 | 0 |
| Smith | 1 | 13 | 13.0 | 13 | 0 |
| Browns | 58 | 1119 | 19.3 | 47 | 0 |
| Opponents | 46 | 814 | 17.7 | 49 | 0 |

| SACKS | No. |
|---|---|
| Pleasant | 11.0 |
| Burnett | 9.0 |
| Perry | 6.0 |
| J. Jones | 5.5 |
| Matthews | 5.5 |
| M. Johnson | 4.0 |
| Ball | 3.0 |
| Footman | 1.0 |
| P. Johnson | 1.0 |
| W. Johnson | 1.0 |
| Walls | 1.0 |
| Browns | 48.0 |
| Opponents | 45.0 |

## 1994 DRAFT CHOICES

| Round | Name | Pos. | College |
|---|---|---|---|
| 1 | Antonio Langham | CB | Alabama |
| | Derrick Alexander | WR | Michigan |
| 3 | Romeo Bandison | DT | Oregon |
| 5 | Issac Booth | CB | California |
| 6 | Robert Strait | RB | Baylor |
| 7 | Andre Hewitt | T | Clemson |

## CLEVELAND BROWNS

### 1994 VETERAN ROSTER

| No. | Name | Pos. | Ht. | Wt. | Birthdate | NFL Exp. | College | Hometown | How Acq. | '93 Games/ Starts |
|---|---|---|---|---|---|---|---|---|---|---|
| 73 | Arvie, Herman | T | 6-4 | 305 | 10/12/70 | 2 | Grambling | Opelousas, La. | D5-'93 | 16/0 |
| 25 | Briggs, Greg | S | 6-3 | 210 | 10/19/68 | 2 | Texas Southern | Meadville, Miss. | FA-'93 | 0* |
| 77 | Brown, Orlando | T | 6-7 | 325 | 12/12/70 | 2 | South Carolina State | Washington D.C. | FA-'93 | 0* |
| 52 | Brown, Richard | LB | 6-3 | 240 | 9/21/65 | 7 | San Diego State | Westminster, Calif. | PB(SD)-'91 | 0* |
| 90 | Burnett, Rob | DE | 6-4 | 280 | 8/27/67 | 5 | Syracuse | Coram, N.Y. | D5-'90 | 16/16 |
| 23 | Byner, Earnest | RB | 5-10 | 215 | 9/15/62 | 11 | East Carolina | Milledgeville, Ga. | UFA(Wash)-'94 | 16/3* |
| 56 | Caldwell, Mike | LB | 6-2 | 235 | 8/31/71 | 2 | Middle Tennessee State | Oak Ridge, Tenn. | D3-'93 | 15/1 |
| 83 | Carrier, Mark | WR | 6-0 | 185 | 10/28/65 | 8 | Nicholls State | Lafayette, La. | UFA(TB)-'93 | 16/16 |
| 72 | Dahl, Bob | G | 6-5 | 300 | 11/5/68 | 3 | Notre Dame | Chagrin Falls, Ohio | FA-'92 | 16/16 |
| 51 | Dixon, Gerald | LB | 6-3 | 250 | 6/20/69 | 3 | South Carolina | Rock Hill, S.C. | D3b-'92 | 11/0 |
| 61 | Everitt, Steve | C | 6-5 | 290 | 8/21/70 | 2 | Michigan | Miami, Fla. | D1-'93 | 16/16 |
| 78 | Footman, Dan | DE | 6-5 | 290 | 1/13/69 | 2 | Florida State | Tampa, Fla. | D2-'93 | 8/0 |
| 37 | t- Frank, Donald | CB | 6-0 | 192 | 10/24/65 | 5 | Winston-Salem State | Tarboro, N.C. | T(SD)-'94 | 16/16* |
| 8 | Goebel, Brad | QB | 6-3 | 198 | 10/13/67 | 4 | Baylor | Cuero, Tex. | FA-'93 | 0* |
| 28 | Griffin, Don | CB | 6-0 | 176 | 3/17/64 | 9 | Middle Tennessee State | Camilla, Ga. | UFA(SF)-'94 | 12/12* |
| 31 | Hairston, Stacey | CB | 5-9 | 180 | 8/16/67 | 2 | Ohio Northern | Columbus, Ohio | FA-'93 | 16/0 |
| 55 | Hill, Travis | LB | 6-2 | 240 | 10/3/69 | 2 | Nebraska | Houston, Tex. | D7-'93 | 0* |
| 33 | Hoard, Leroy | RB | 5-11 | 225 | 5/15/68 | 5 | Michigan | New Orleans, La. | D2-'90 | 16/7 |
| 64 | Hoover, Houston | G | 6-2 | 300 | 2/6/65 | 7 | Jackson State | Yazoo City, Miss. | UFA(Atl)-'93 | 16/16 |
| 81 | † Jackson, Michael | WR | 6-4 | 195 | 4/12/69 | 4 | Southern Mississippi | Kentwood, La. | D6-'91 | 15/11 |
| 94 | Johnson, Bill | DE-DT | 6-4 | 290 | 12/9/68 | 3 | Michigan State | Chicago, Ill. | D3a-'92 | 10/0 |
| 53 | # Johnson, Pepper | LB | 6-3 | 248 | 7/29/64 | 9 | Ohio State | Detroit, Mich. | FA-'93 | 16/11 |
| 47 | Jones, David | TE | 6-3 | 255 | 11/9/68 | 3 | Delaware State | Hillside, N.J. | FA-'94 | 0* |
| 96 | † Jones, James | DT | 6-2 | 290 | 2/6/69 | 4 | Northern Iowa | Davenport, Iowa | D3-'91 | 16/12 |
| 22 | Jones, Selwyn | CB | 6-0 | 185 | 5/13/70 | 3 | Colorado State | Missouri City, Tex. | D7-'92 | 11/2 |
| 66 | Jones, Tony | T | 6-5 | 295 | 5/24/66 | 7 | Western Carolina | Cannesville, Ga. | FA-'88 | 16/16 |
| 88 | Kinchen, Brian | TE | 6-2 | 240 | 8/6/65 | 7 | Louisiana State | Baton Rouge, La. | FA-'91 | 16/15 |
| 34 | # Mack, Kevin | RB | 6-0 | 225 | 8/9/62 | 9 | Clemson | Kings Mountain, N.C. | SD1a-'84 | 4/0 |
| 57 | # Matthews, Clay | LB | 6-2 | 245 | 3/15/56 | 17 | Southern California | New Trier, Ill. | D1a-'78 | 16/15 |
| 87 | McCardell, Keenan | WR | 6-1 | 175 | 1/6/70 | 3 | Nevada-Las Vegas | Houston, Tex. | FA-'92 | 6/3 |
| 80 | McLemore, Tom | TE | 6-5 | 250 | 3/14/70 | 3 | Southern | Shreveport, La. | W(Det)-'93 | 4/0 |
| 21 | Metcalf, Eric | RB | 5-10 | 190 | 1/23/68 | 6 | Texas | Arlington, Va. | D1-'89 | 16/9 |
| 65 | Milstead, Rod | G | 6-2 | 290 | 11/10/69 | 3 | Delaware State | Bryans Road, Md. | T(Dall)-'92 | 0* |
| 27 | Moore, Stevon | S | 5-11 | 210 | 2/9/67 | 6 | Mississippi | Wiggins, Miss. | FA-'92 | 16/16 |
| 48 | Mustafaa, Najee | CB | 6-1 | 190 | 6/20/64 | 8 | Georgia Tech | East Point, Ga. | UFA(Minn)-'93 | 14/14 |
| 92 | Perry, Michael Dean | DT | 6-1 | 285 | 8/27/65 | 7 | Clemson | Aiken, S.C. | D2-'88 | 16/13 |
| 17 | # Philcox, Todd | QB | 6-4 | 225 | 9/25/66 | 5 | Syracuse | Norwalk, Conn. | PB(Cin)-'91 | 5/4 |
| 98 | Pleasant, Anthony | DE | 6-5 | 280 | 1/27/68 | 5 | Tennessee State | Century, Fla. | D3-'90 | 16/13 |
| 49 | Reeves, Walter | TE | 6-4 | 270 | 12/16/65 | 6 | Auburn | Eugaula, Ala. | UFA(Ariz)-'94 | 16/15* |
| 42 | Riddick, Louis | S | 6-2 | 215 | 3/15/69 | 3 | Pittsburgh | Quakertown, Pa. | FA-'93 | 15/0 |
| 86 | Rowe, Patrick | WR | 6-1 | 195 | 2/17/69 | 3 | San Diego State | San Diego, Calif. | D2-'92 | 5/0 |
| 11 | Rypien, Mark | QB | 6-4 | 234 | 10/2/62 | 8 | Washington State | Spokane, Wash. | FA-'94 | 12/10* |
| 75 | † Sagapolutele, Pio | DE | 6-6 | 297 | 11/28/69 | 4 | San Diego State | Honolulu, Hawaii | D4-'91 | 8/0 |
| 84 | Smith, Rico | WR | 6-0 | 185 | 1/14/69 | 3 | Colorado | Paramount, Calif. | D6a-'92 | 10/1 |
| 43 | Speer, Del | S | 6-0 | 200 | 2/1/70 | 2 | Florida | Miami, Fla. | FA-'93 | 16/2 |
| 50 | Stams, Frank | LB | 6-2 | 230 | 7/17/66 | 6 | Notre Dame | Akron, Ohio | T(Rams)-'92 | 14/0 |
| 3 | Stover, Matt | K | 5-11 | 178 | 1/27/68 | 5 | Louisiana Tech | Dallas, Tex. | PB(NYG)-'91 | 16/0 |
| 54 | Sutter, Ed | LB | 6-3 | 235 | 10/3/69 | 2 | Northwestern | Peoria, Ill. | W(NE)-'93 | 15/0 |
| 12 | Testaverde, Vinny | QB | 6-5 | 215 | 11/13/63 | 8 | Miami | Floral Park, N.Y. | UFA(TB)-'93 | 10/6 |
| 85 | # Tillman, Lawyer | WR | 6-5 | 230 | 5/20/66 | 6 | Auburn | Mobile, Ala. | D2-'89 | 7/0 |
| 7 | Tupa, Tom | P-QB | 6-4 | 230 | 2/6/66 | 6 | Ohio State | Brecksville, Ohio | FA-'94 | 0* |
| 29 | Turner, Eric | S | 6-1 | 207 | 9/20/68 | 4 | UCLA | Ventura, Calif. | D1-'91 | 16/16 |
| 44 | Vardell, Tommy | RB | 6-2 | 230 | 2/20/69 | 3 | Stanford | El Cajon, Calif. | D1-'92 | 16/12 |
| 62 | † Williams, Gene | T-G | 6-2 | 305 | 10/14/68 | 4 | Iowa State | Omaha, Neb. | T(Mia)-'93 | 16/14 |
| 63 | Williams, Wally | C | 6-2 | 300 | 2/19/71 | 2 | Florida A&M | Tallahassee, Fla. | FA-'93 | 2/0 |
| 60 | Withycombe, Mike | G | 6-5 | 300 | 11/18/64 | 6 | Fresno State | Lemoore, Calif. | UFA(SD)-'94 | 0* |

* Briggs last on injured list with Dallas in '92; O. Brown, R. Brown, and Hill missed '93 season due to injury; Byner played 16 games with Washington; Frank played 16 games with San Diego in '93; Goebel active for 3 games but did not play; Griffin played 12 games with San Francisco; D. Jones last active with L.A. Raiders in '92; Milstead inacitve for 11 games; Reeves played 16 games with Arizona; Rypien played 12 games with Washington; Tupa inactive for 2 games; Withycombe active for 3 games with San Diego but did not play.

\# Unrestricted free agent; subject to developments.

† Restricted free agent; subject to developments.

t- Browns traded for Frank (San Diego).

Players lost through free agency (3): P Brian Hansen (NYJ; 16 games in '93), CB Randy Hilliard (Den; 12), LB Mike Johnson (Det; 16).

Also played with Browns in '93—RB Randy Baldwin (14 games), DT Jerry Ball (16), LB David Brandon (6), CB Tim Jacobs (2), T-G Ed King (6), QB Bernie Kosar (7), S Erik McMillan (3), CB Terry Taylor (10), CB Everson Walls (7), TE Clarence Williams (7), RB Ron Wolfley (16), C Lance Zeno (2).

## COACHING STAFF

**Head Coach,**
**Bill Belichick**

**Pro Career:** Became the Browns' tenth head coach on February 5, 1991. Belichick formerly was defensive coordinator of the New York Giants, who defeated the Buffalo Bills 20-19 in Super Bowl XXV. He also coordinated the Giants' defense that won Super Bowl XXI in 1986. Began coaching career at 23 as a special assistant to Ted Marchibroda with the Baltimore Colts in 1975. He tutored the Detroit Lions' tight ends, wide receivers, and special teams in 1976-77, before joining the Denver Broncos in 1978. He joined the Giants in 1979 as a defensive assistant and special teams coach, moved to linebackers in 1981-82, and became defensive coordinator in 1983. Career record: 20-28.

**Background:** Attended Annapolis (Maryland) High School and Phillips Academy in Andover, Mass. Played football and lacrosse at Wesleyan (Conn.) University. Earned a bachelor's degree in economics from Wesleyan in 1975.

**Personal:** Born April 16, 1952, in Nashville, Tenn. Bill and his wife, Debby, live in Brecksville, Ohio, and have three children—Amanda, Stephen, and Brian.

### ASSISTANT COACHES

**Ernie Adams,** special assignments; born March 31, 1953, Waltham, Mass., lives in Lakewood, Ohio. No college or pro playing experience. College coach: Northwestern 1971-74. Pro coach: New England Patriots 1975-78, New York Giants 1979-81 (Pro Personnel Director 1982-85), joined Browns in 1991.

**Jacob Burney,** defensive line; born January 24, 1959, Chattanooga, Tenn., lives in Berea, Ohio. Defensive tackle Tennessee-Chattanooga 1977-80. No pro playing experience. College coach: New Mexico 1983-86, Tulsa 1987, Mississippi State 1988, Wisconsin 1989, UCLA 1990-92, Tennessee 1993. Pro coach: Joined Browns in 1994.

**Steve Crosby,** offensive coordinator; born July 3, 1950, Great Bend, Kan., lives in Strongsville, Ohio. Running back Fort Hays State 1969-72. Pro running back New York Giants 1974-76. Pro coach: Miami Dolphins 1979-82, Atlanta Falcons 1983-84, 1986-89, Cleveland Browns 1985, New England Patriots 1990, rejoined Browns in 1991.

**Rod Dowhower,** quarterbacks; born April 15, 1943, Ord, Neb., lives in Berea, Ohio. Quarterback San Diego State 1963-65. No pro playing experience. College coach: San Diego State 1966-72, UCLA 1974-75, Boise State 1976, Stanford 1977-79 (head coach 1979). Pro coach: St. Louis Cardinals 1973, 1982-84, Denver Broncos 1980-81, Indianapolis Colts 1985-86 (head coach), Atlanta Falcons 1987-89, Washington Redskins 1990-93, joined Browns in 1994.

**Kirk Ferentz,** offensive line; born August 1, 1955, Royal Oak, Mich., lives in North Royalton, Ohio. Linebacker Connecticut 1973-76. No pro playing experience. College coach: Connecticut 1977, Pittsburgh 1980, Iowa 1981-89, Maine 1990-92 (head coach). Pro coach: Joined Browns in 1993.

**Pat Hill,** tight ends-assistant offensive line; born December 17, 1951, Los Angeles, Calif., lives in Berea, Ohio. Center California-Riverside 1971-73. No pro playing experience. College coach: Los Angeles Valley Junior College 1974-76, Utah 1977-80, Nevada-Las Vegas 1981-82, Fresno State 1985-89, Arizona 1990-91. Pro coach: Calgary Stampeders (CFL) 1983-84, joined Browns in 1992.

**Scott O'Brien,** special teams; born June 25, 1957, Superior, Wis., lives in Strongsville, Ohio. Defensive end Wisconsin-Superior 1975-78. Pro defensive end Green Bay Packers 1979, Toronto Argonauts (CFL) 1979. College coach: Wisconsin-Superior 1980-82, Nevada-Las Vegas 1983-85, Rice 1986, Pittsburgh 1987-90. Pro coach: Joined Browns in 1991.

**Nick Saban,** defensive coordinator; born October 31, 1951, Fairmont, W. Va., lives in Medina, Ohio. Defensive back Kent State 1969-72. No pro playing experience. College coach: Kent State 1973-76, Syracuse 1977, West Virginia 1978-79, Ohio State 1980-81, Navy 1982, Michigan State 1983-87, Toledo 1990 (head coach). Pro coach: Houston Oilers 1988-89, joined Browns in 1991.

**Mike Sheppard,** receivers; born October 29, 1951, Tulsa, Okla., lives in Strongsville, Ohio. Wide receiver Cal Lutheran 1969-72. No pro playing experience. College coach: Cal Lutheran 1974-76, Brigham Young 1977-78, U.S. International 1979, Idaho State 1980-81, Long Beach State 1982, 1984-86 (head coach), Kansas 1983, New Mexico 1987-91 (head coach), California 1992. Pro coach: Joined Browns in 1993.

**Jerry Simmons,** strength and conditioning; born June 15, 1954, Elkhart, Kan., lives in Strongsville, Ohio. Linebacker Fort Hays State 1976-77. No pro playing experience. College coach: Fort Hays State 1978, Clemson 1980, Rice 1981-82, Southern California 1983-87. Pro coach: New England Patriots 1988-90, joined Browns in 1991.

**Kevin Spencer,** offensive assistant; born November 2, 1953, Queens, N.Y., lives in Bay Village, Ohio. No college or pro playing experience. College coach: State University of New York 1975-76, Cornell 1979-80, Ithaca 1981-86, Wesleyan 1987-91 (head coach). Pro coach: Joined Browns in 1991.

**Rick Venturi,** defensive backs; born February 23, 1946, Taylorville, Ill., lives in Strongsville, Ohio. Quarterback-defensive back Northwestern 1965-67. No pro playing experience. College coach: Northwestern 1968-72, 1978-80 (head coach), Purdue 1973-76, Illinois 1977. Pro coach: Hamilton Tiger-Cats (CFL) 1981, Indianapolis Colts 1982-93 (interim head coach 1991), joined Browns in 1994.

**Woody Widenhofer,** linebackers; born January 20, 1943, Butler, Pa., lives in Berea, Ohio. Linebacker Missouri 1961-64. No pro playing experience. College coach: Michigan State 1969-70, Eastern Michigan 1971, Minnesota 1972, Missouri 1985-88 (head coach). Pro coach: Pittsburgh Steelers 1973-83, Oklahoma Outlaws (USFL) 1984 (head coach), Detroit Lions 1989-92, joined Browns in 1993.

## 1994 FIRST-YEAR ROSTER

| Name | Pos. | Ht. | Wt. | Birthdate | College | Hometown | How Acq. |
|---|---|---|---|---|---|---|---|
| Alexander, Derrick | WR | 6-2 | 195 | 11/6/71 | Michigan | Detroit, Mich. | D1b |
| Bandison, Romeo | DT | 6-5 | 290 | 2/12/71 | Oregon | Mill Valley, Calif. | D3 |
| Bomba, Matt (1) | DE-DT | 6-5 | 275 | 5/22/68 | Indiana | Bloomington, Ind. | FA |
| Booth, Isaac | CB-S | 6-3 | 190 | 5/23/71 | California | Indianapolis, Ind. | D5 |
| Cobb, Robert | QB | 6-2 | 217 | 2/7/71 | Northeast Louisiana | Monroe, La. | FA |
| Derby, John (1) | LB | 6-0 | 232 | 3/24/68 | Iowa | Pittsburgh, Pa. | FA |
| Eichloff, Dan | K | 6-0 | 215 | 6/3/72 | Kansas | Ft. Lauderdale, Fla. | FA |
| Ferrell, Kerry (1) | WR | 5-11 | 173 | 7/8/70 | Syracuse | Piscataway, N.J. | FA |
| Gray, Jim (1) | DT | 6-2 | 285 | 7/5/69 | West Virginia | West Mifflin, Pa. | FA |
| Hartley, Frank (1) | TE | 6-2 | 268 | 12/15/67 | Illinois | Chicago, Ill. | FA |
| Hewitt, Andre | T | 6-6 | 285 | 4/26/71 | Clemson | Pittsburgh, Pa. | D7 |
| Jacobs, Tim (1) | CB | 5-10 | 185 | 4/5/70 | Delaware | Landover, Md. | FA |
| Kalal, Tim (1) | P | 6-3 | 205 | 9/13/67 | Miami | Longview, Wash. | FA |
| Killian, P.J. | LB | 6-2 | 242 | 5/19/71 | Virginia | Pittsburgh, Pa. | FA |
| Langham, Antonio | CB | 6-0 | 180 | 7/31/72 | Alabama | Town Creek, Ala. | D1a |
| Lee, Marcus | RB | 5-10 | 227 | 5/21/71 | Syracuse | Springfield, Mass. | FA |
| Leomiti, Carlson | T-G | 6-3 | 384 | 1/10/71 | San Diego State | Carson, Calif. | FA |
| Lyle, Rick | DE-DT | 6-5 | 275 | 2/26/71 | Missouri | Kansas City, Mo. | FA |
| McKenzie, Rich (1) | LB | 6-2 | 240 | 4/15/71 | Penn State | Ft. Lauderdale, Fla. | D6-'93 |
| Montford, Joe | LB | 6-0 | 210 | 7/30/70 | South Carolina State | Columbia, S.C. | FA |
| Myles, Tim | DE-DT | 6-1 | 280 | 6/22/70 | Vermillion J.C. | Duluth, Minn. | FA |
| Strait, Robert | RB | 6-1 | 255 | 11/14/69 | Baylor | Cuero, Tex. | D6 |
| Toney, Eudean | S | 6-1 | 208 | 4/13/72 | Grambling | Monroe, La. | FA |
| Tremble, Greg | S | 5-11 | 188 | 4/16/72 | Georgia | Atlanta, Ga. | FA |
| Werdel, John | P | 6-2 | 205 | 3/16/71 | Washington | Bakersfield, Calif. | FA |

The term NFL Rookie is defined as a player who is in his first season of professional football and has not been on the roster of another professional football team for any regular-season or postseason games. A Rookie is designated by an "R" on NFL rosters. Players who have been active in another professional football league or players who have NFL experience, including either preseason training camp or being on an Active List or Inactive List, or on Reserve/Injured or Reserve/Physically Unable to Perform for fewer than six regular-season games, are termed NFL First-Year Players. An NFL First-Year Player is designated by a "1" on NFL rosters. Thereafter, a player is credited with an additional year of experience for each season in which he accumulates six games on the Active List or Inactive List, or on Reserve/Injured or Reserve/Physically Unable to Perform.

## NOTES

# DENVER BRONCOS

**American Football Conference**
**Western Division**
**Team Colors:** Orange, Royal Blue, and White
**13655 Broncos Parkway**
**Englewood, Colorado 80112**
**Telephone: (303) 649-9000**

## CLUB OFFICIALS

President-Chief Executive Officer: Pat Bowlen
General Manager: John Beake
Head Coach: Wade Phillips
Chief Financial Officer-Treasurer: Robert M. Hurley
Director of Football Operations/Player Personnel: Bob Ferguson
Director of Media Relations: Jim Saccomano
Assistant to the General Manager/Community Relations: Fred Fleming
Ticket Manager: Gail Stuckey
Director of Operations: Bill Harpole
Director of Marketing: Rosemary Manratty
Director of Player Relations: Bill Thompson
Trainer: Steve Antonopulos
Equipment Manager: Doug West
Video Director: Kent Erickson
**Stadium:** Denver Mile High Stadium
•**Capacity:** 76,273
1900 West Eliot
Denver, Colorado 80204
**Playing Surface:** Grass (PAT)
**Training Camp:** University of Northern Colorado
Greeley, Colorado 80639

## 1994 SCHEDULE

**PRESEASON**

| | | |
|---|---|---|
| July 31 | vs. L.A. Raiders at Barcelona | 1:00 |
| Aug. 6 | **Atlanta** | 7:00 |
| Aug. 12 | at San Francisco | 5:00 |
| Aug. 21 | at Dallas | 7:00 |
| Aug. 25 | **Arizona** | 7:00 |

**REGULAR SEASON**

| | | |
|---|---|---|
| Sept. 4 | **San Diego** | 6:00 |
| Sept. 11 | at New York Jets | 4:00 |
| Sept. 18 | **Los Angeles Raiders** | 2:00 |
| Sept. 26 | at Buffalo (Monday) | 9:00 |
| Oct. 2 | Open Date | |
| Oct. 9 | at Seattle | 1:00 |
| Oct. 17 | **Kansas City** (Monday) | 7:00 |
| Oct. 23 | at San Diego | 1:00 |
| Oct. 30 | **Cleveland** | 2:00 |
| Nov. 6 | at Los Angeles Rams | 1:00 |
| Nov. 13 | **Seattle** | 2:00 |
| Nov. 20 | **Atlanta** | 2:00 |
| Nov. 27 | **Cincinnati** | 2:00 |
| Dec. 4 | at Kansas City | 3:00 |
| Dec. 11 | at Los Angeles Raiders | 1:00 |
| Dec. 17 | at San Francisco (Saturday) | 1:00 |
| Dec. 24 | **New Orleans** | 2:00 |

## RECORD HOLDERS

### INDIVIDUAL RECORDS—CAREER

| Category | Name | Performance |
|---|---|---|
| Rushing (Yds.) | Floyd Little, 1967-1975 | 6,323 |
| Passing (Yds.) | John Elway, 1983-1993 | 34,246 |
| Passing (TDs) | John Elway, 1983-1993 | 183 |
| Receiving (No.) | Lionel Taylor, 1960-66 | 543 |
| Receiving (Yds.) | Lionel Taylor, 1960-66 | 6,872 |
| Interceptions | Steve Foley, 1976-1986 | 44 |
| Punting (Avg.) | Jim Fraser, 1962-64 | 45.2 |
| Punt Return (Avg.) | Rick Upchurch, 1975-1983 | 12.1 |
| Kickoff Return (Avg.) | Abner Haynes, 1965-66 | 26.3 |
| Field Goals | Jim Turner, 1971-79 | 151 |
| Touchdowns (Tot.) | Floyd Little, 1967-1975 | 54 |
| Points | Jim Turner, 1971-79 | 742 |

### INDIVIDUAL RECORDS—SINGLE SEASON

| Category | Name | Performance |
|---|---|---|
| Rushing (Yds.) | Otis Armstrong, 1974 | 1,407 |
| Passing (Yds.) | John Elway, 1993 | 4,030 |
| Passing (TDs) | John Elway, 1993 | 25 |
| Receiving (No.) | Lionel Taylor, 1961 | 100 |
| Receiving (Yds.) | Steve Watson, 1981 | 1,244 |
| Interceptions | Goose Gonsoulin, 1960 | 11 |
| Punting (Avg.) | Jim Fraser, 1963 | 46.1 |
| Punt Return (Avg.) | Floyd Little, 1967 | 16.9 |
| Kickoff Return (Avg.) | Bill Thompson, 1969 | 28.5 |
| Field Goals | Gene Mingo, 1962 | 27 |
| | David Treadwell, 1989, 1991 | 27 |
| Touchdowns (Tot.) | Sammy Winder, 1986 | 14 |
| Points | Gene Mingo, 1962 | 137 |

### INDIVIDUAL RECORDS—SINGLE GAME

| Category | Name | Performance |
|---|---|---|
| Rushing (Yds.) | Otis Armstrong, 12-8-74 | 183 |
| Passing (Yds.) | Frank Tripucka, 9-15-62 | 447 |
| Passing (TDs) | Frank Tripucka, 10-28-62 | 5 |
| | John Elway, 11-18-84 | 5 |
| Receiving (No.) | Lionel Taylor, 11-29-64 | 13 |
| | Bobby Anderson, 9-30-73 | 13 |
| Receiving (Yds.) | Lionel Taylor, 11-27-60 | 199 |
| Interceptions | Goose Gonsoulin, 9-18-60 | *4 |
| | Willie Brown, 11-15-64 | *4 |
| Field Goals | Gene Mingo, 10-6-63 | 5 |
| | Rich Karlis, 11-20-83 | 5 |
| Touchdowns (Tot.) | Many times | 3 |
| | Last time by Shannon Sharpe, 12-12-93 | |
| Points | Gene Mingo, 12-10-60 | 21 |

*NFL Record

## COACHING HISTORY

**(250-259-10)**

| | | |
|---|---|---|
| 1960-61 | Frank Filchock | 7-20-1 |
| 1962-64 | Jack Faulkner* | 9-22-1 |
| 1964-66 | Mac Speedie** | 6-19-1 |
| 1966 | Ray Malavasi | 4-8-0 |
| 1967-71 | Lou Saban*** | 20-42-3 |
| 1971 | Jerry Smith | 2-3-0 |
| 1972-76 | John Ralston | 34-33-3 |
| 1977-80 | Robert (Red) Miller | 42-25-0 |
| 1981-92 | Dan Reeves | 117-79-1 |
| 1993 | Wade Phillips | 9-8-0 |

*Released after four games in 1964
**Resigned after two games in 1966
***Resigned after nine games in 1971

**DENVER MILE HIGH STADIUM**

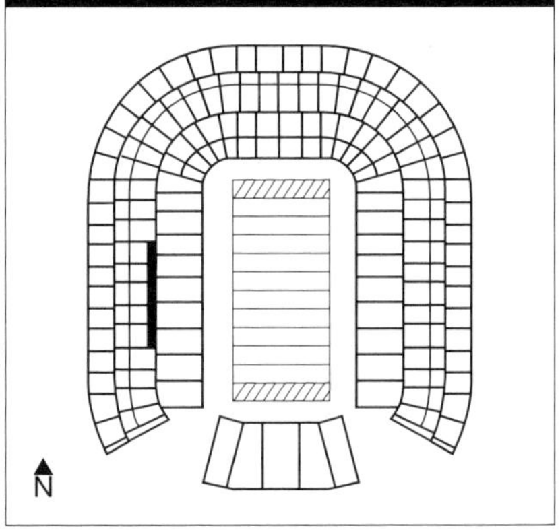

# DENVER BRONCOS

## 1993 TEAM RECORD

**PRESEASON (2-2)**

| Date | Result | | Opponents |
|---|---|---|---|
| 8/7 | W | 23-7 | at Tampa Bay |
| 8/16 | L | 13-16 | San Francisco |
| 8/20 | W | 34-24 | Miami |
| 8/27 | L | 9-34 | at Phoenix |

**REGULAR SEASON (9-7)**

| Date | Result | | Opponents | Att. |
|---|---|---|---|---|
| 9/5 | W | 26-20 | at N.Y. Jets | 68,130 |
| 9/12 | W | 34-17 | San Diego | 75,074 |
| 9/20 | L | 7-15 | at Kansas City | 78,453 |
| 10/3 | W | 35-13 | Indianapolis | 74,953 |
| 10/10 | L | 27-30 | at Green Bay | 58,943 |
| 10/18 | L | 20-23 | L.A. Raiders | 75,712 |
| 10/31 | W | 28-17 | Seattle | 73,644 |
| 11/7 | W | 29-14 | at Cleveland | 77,818 |
| 11/14 | L | 23-26 | Minnesota | 67,329 |
| 11/21 | W | 37-13 | Pittsburgh | 74,840 |
| 11/28 | W | 17-9 | at Seattle | 57,812 |
| 12/5 | L | 10-13 | at San Diego | 60,233 |
| 12/12 | W | 27-21 | Kansas City | 75,822 |
| 12/18 | W | 13-3 | at Chicago | 53,056 |
| 12/26 | L | 10-17 | Tampa Bay | 73,434 |
| 1/2 | L | 30-33 | at L.A. Raiders (OT) | 66,904 |

**POSTSEASON (0-1)**

| | | | | |
|---|---|---|---|---|
| 1/9 | L | 24-42 | at L.A. Raiders | 65,314 |

**SCORE BY PERIODS**

| | | | | | | | |
|---|---|---|---|---|---|---|---|
| Broncos | 66 | 147 | 91 | 69 | 0 | — | 373 |
| Opponents | 53 | 82 | 62 | 84 | 3 | — | 284 |

**ATTENDANCE**

Home 590,808 Away 521,349 Total 1,112,157
Single-game home record, 76,105 (1-4-87)
Single-season home record, 598,224 (1981)

## 1993 TEAM STATISTICS

| | Broncos | Opp. |
|---|---|---|
| Total First Downs | 327 | 280 |
| Rushing | 105 | 86 |
| Passing | 187 | 181 |
| Penalty | 35 | 13 |
| Third Down: Made/Att | 98/225 | 71/215 |
| Third Down Pct. | 43.6 | 33.0 |
| Fourth Down: Made/Att | 2/11 | 8/17 |
| Fourth Down Pct. | 18.2 | 47.1 |
| Total Net Yards | 5461 | 5149 |
| Avg. Per Game | 341.3 | 321.8 |
| Total Plays | 1060 | 1005 |
| Avg. Per Play | 5.2 | 5.1 |
| Net Yards Rushing | 1693 | 1418 |
| Avg. Per Game | 105.8 | 88.6 |
| Total Rushes | 468 | 397 |
| Net Yards Passing | 3768 | 3731 |
| Avg. Per Game | 235.5 | 233.2 |
| Sacked/Yards Lost | 39/293 | 46/238 |
| Gross Yards | 4061 | 3969 |
| Att./Completions | 553/350 | 562/314 |
| Completion Pct. | 63.3 | 55.9 |
| Had Intercepted | 10 | 18 |
| Punts/Avg. | 68/44.4 | 81/43.7 |
| Net Punting Avg. | 68/37.1 | 81/36.0 |
| Penalties/Yards Lost | 112/822 | 128/1019 |
| Fumbles/Ball Lost | 29/18 | 27/13 |
| Touchdowns | 42 | 27 |
| Rushing | 13 | 6 |
| Passing | 27 | 21 |
| Returns | 2 | 0 |
| Avg. Time of Possession | 31:35 | 28:25 |

## 1993 INDIVIDUAL STATISTICS

| PASSING | Att. | Comp. | Yds. | Pct. | TD | Int. | Tkld. | Rate |
|---|---|---|---|---|---|---|---|---|
| Elway | 551 | 348 | 4030 | 63.2 | 25 | 10 | 39/293 | 92.8 |
| Maddox | 1 | 1 | 1 | 100.0 | 1 | 0 | 0/0 | 118.8 |
| Marshall | 1 | 1 | 30 | 100.0 | 1 | 0 | 0/0 | 158.3 |
| Broncos | 553 | 350 | 4061 | 63.3 | 27 | 10 | 39/293 | 94.2 |
| Opponents | 562 | 314 | 3969 | 55.9 | 21 | 18 | 46/238 | 77.2 |

| SCORING | TD R | TD P | TD Rt | PAT | FG | Saf | PTS |
|---|---|---|---|---|---|---|---|
| Elam | 0 | 0 | 0 | 41/42 | 26/35 | 0 | 119 |
| Sharpe | 0 | 9 | 0 | 0/0 | 0/0 | 0 | 54 |
| Delpino | 8 | 0 | 0 | 0/0 | 0/0 | 0 | 48 |
| V. Johnson | 0 | 5 | 0 | 0/0 | 0/0 | 0 | 30 |
| Bernstine | 4 | 0 | 0 | 0/0 | 0/0 | 0 | 24 |
| Russell | 0 | 3 | 1 | 0/0 | 0/0 | 0 | 24 |
| Milburn | 0 | 3 | 0 | 0/0 | 0/0 | 0 | 18 |
| Rivers | 1 | 1 | 0 | 0/0 | 0/0 | 1 | 14 |
| Marshall | 0 | 2 | 0 | 0/0 | 0/0 | 0 | 12 |
| Tillman | 0 | 2 | 0 | 0/0 | 0/0 | 0 | 12 |
| Croel | 0 | 0 | 1 | 0/0 | 0/0 | 0 | 6 |
| R. Johnson | 0 | 1 | 0 | 0/0 | 0/0 | 0 | 6 |
| Wyman | 0 | 1 | 0 | 0/0 | 0/0 | 0 | 6 |
| Broncos | 13 | 27 | 2 | 41/42 | 26/35 | 1 | 373 |
| Opponents | 6 | 21 | 0 | 27/27 | 31/36 | 1 | 284 |

| RUSHING | Att. | Yds. | Avg. | LG | TD |
|---|---|---|---|---|---|
| Bernstine | 223 | 816 | 3.7 | 24 | 4 |
| Delpino | 131 | 445 | 3.4 | 18 | 8 |
| Milburn | 52 | 231 | 4.4 | 26 | 0 |
| Elway | 44 | 153 | 3.5 | 18 | 0 |
| Rivers | 15 | 50 | 3.3 | 14 | 1 |
| Rouen | 1 | 0 | 0.0 | 0 | 0 |
| Maddox | 2 | -2 | -1.0 | -1 | 0 |
| Broncos | 468 | 1693 | 3.6 | 26 | 13 |
| Opponents | 397 | 1418 | 3.6 | 28 | 6 |

| RECEIVING | No. | Yds. | Avg. | LG | TD |
|---|---|---|---|---|---|
| Sharpe | 81 | 995 | 12.3 | 63 | 9 |
| Russell | 44 | 719 | 16.3 | 43 | 3 |
| Bernstine | 44 | 372 | 8.5 | 41 | 0 |
| Milburn | 38 | 300 | 7.9 | 50 | 3 |
| V. Johnson | 36 | 517 | 14.4 | 56 | 5 |
| Marshall | 28 | 360 | 12.9 | 40 | 2 |
| Delpino | 26 | 195 | 7.5 | 25 | 0 |
| R. Johnson | 20 | 243 | 12.2 | 38 | 1 |
| Tillman | 17 | 193 | 11.4 | 30 | 2 |
| Kimbrough | 8 | 79 | 9.9 | 16 | 0 |
| Rivers | 6 | 59 | 9.8 | 17 | 1 |
| K. Taylor | 1 | 28 | 28.0 | 28 | 0 |
| Wyman | 1 | 1 | 1.0 | 1t | 1 |
| Broncos | 350 | 4061 | 11.6 | 63 | 27 |
| Opponents | 314 | 3969 | 12.6 | 74t | 21 |

| INTERCEPTIONS | No. | Yds. | Avg. | LG | TD |
|---|---|---|---|---|---|
| Smith | 3 | 57 | 19.0 | 36 | 0 |
| Braxton | 3 | 37 | 12.3 | 25 | 0 |
| Atwater | 2 | 81 | 40.5 | 68 | 0 |
| Dronett | 2 | 13 | 6.5 | 7 | 0 |
| Lang | 2 | 4 | 2.0 | 4 | 0 |
| Croel | 1 | 22 | 22.0 | 22t | 1 |
| F. Robinson | 1 | 13 | 13.0 | 13 | 0 |
| Wyman | 1 | 9 | 9.0 | 9 | 0 |
| Bradford | 1 | 0 | 0.0 | 0 | 0 |
| Dimry | 1 | 0 | 0.0 | 0 | 0 |
| Hall | 1 | 0 | 0.0 | 0 | 0 |
| Broncos | 18 | 236 | 13.1 | 68 | 1 |
| Opponents | 10 | 79 | 7.9 | 19 | 0 |

| PUNTING | No. | Yds. | Avg. | In 20 | LG |
|---|---|---|---|---|---|
| Rouen | 67 | 3017 | 45.0 | 17 | 62 |
| Broncos | 68 | 3017 | 44.4 | 17 | 62 |
| Opponents | 81 | 3541 | 43.7 | 22 | 61 |

| PUNT RETURNS | No. | FC | Yds. | Avg. | LG | TD |
|---|---|---|---|---|---|---|
| Milburn | 40 | 1 | 425 | 10.6 | 54 | 0 |
| Bradford | 1 | 0 | 0 | 0.0 | 0 | 0 |
| Broncos | 41 | 11 | 425 | 10.4 | 54 | 0 |
| Opponents | 33 | 8 | 337 | 10.2 | 37 | 0 |

| KICKOFF RETURNS | No. | Yds. | Avg. | LG | TD |
|---|---|---|---|---|---|
| Russell | 18 | 374 | 20.8 | 49 | 0 |
| Milburn | 12 | 188 | 15.7 | 26 | 0 |
| Delpino | 7 | 146 | 20.9 | 49 | 0 |
| Meeks | 1 | 9 | 9.0 | 9 | 0 |
| Sharpe | 1 | 0 | 0.0 | 0 | 0 |
| Broncos | 39 | 717 | 18.4 | 49 | 0 |
| Opponents | 63 | 1119 | 17.8 | 68 | 0 |

| SACKS | No. |
|---|---|
| Fletcher | 13.5 |
| Mecklenburg | 9.0 |
| Dronett | 7.0 |
| Croel | 5.0 |
| J. Robinson | 3.5 |
| Kragen | 3.0 |
| Wyman | 2.0 |
| Atwater | 1.0 |
| Oshodin | 1.0 |
| Williams | 1.0 |
| Broncos | 46.0 |
| Opponents | 39.0 |

## 1994 DRAFT CHOICES

| Round | Name | Pos. | College |
|---|---|---|---|
| 2 | Allen Aldridge | LB | Houston |
| 4 | Randy Fuller | DB | Tennessee State |
| 7 | Keith Burns | LB | Oklahoma State |
| | Butler By'not'e | RB | Ohio State |
| | Tom Nalen | C | Boston College |

# DENVER BRONCOS

## 1994 VETERAN ROSTER

| No. | | Name | Pos. | Ht. | Wt. | Birthdate | NFL Exp. | College | Hometown | How Acq. | '93 Games/ Starts |
|---|---|---|---|---|---|---|---|---|---|---|---|
| 58 | | Alexander, Elijah | LB | 6-2 | 230 | 8/8/70 | 3 | Kansas State | Ft. Worth, Tex. | W(TB)-'93 | 16/0 |
| 27 | | Atwater, Steve | S | 6-3 | 217 | 10/28/66 | 6 | Arkansas | Chicago, Ill. | D1-'89 | 16/16 |
| 11 | | Ball, Michael | CB-S | 6-1 | 215 | 8/5/64 | 7 | Southern | New Orleans, La. | FA-'94 | 0* |
| 33 | | Bernstine, Rod | RB | 6-3 | 238 | 2/8/65 | 8 | Texas A&M | Bryan, Tex. | UFA(SD)-'93 | 15/14 |
| 83 | | Bonner, Melvin | WR | 6-3 | 207 | 2/18/70 | 2 | Baylor | Hempstead, Tex. | D6-'93 | 3/0 |
| 23 | | Bradford, Ronnie | CB | 5-10 | 188 | 10/1/70 | 2 | Colorado | Commerce City, Colo. | FA-'93 | 10/3 |
| 10 | | Campbell, Jeff | WR | 5-8 | 167 | 3/26/68 | 5 | Colorado | Vail, Colo. | UFA(Det)-'94 | 10/0* |
| 15 | | Carlson, Jeff | QB | 6-3 | 212 | 5/23/66 | 4 | Weber State | Long Beach, Calif. | FA-'94 | 0* |
| 20 | | Crockett, Ray | CB | 5-10 | 185 | 1/5/67 | 6 | Baylor | Dallas, Tex. | UFA(Det)-'94 | 16/16* |
| 51 | | Croel, Mike | LB | 6-3 | 231 | 6/6/69 | 4 | Nebraska | Detroit, Mich. | D1-'91 | 16/16 |
| 39 | | Delpino, Robert | RB | 6-0 | 205 | 11/2/65 | 7 | Missouri | Dodge City, Kan. | UFA(Rams)-'93 | 16/4 |
| 29 | # | Dimry, Charles | CB | 6-0 | 175 | 1/31/66 | 7 | Nevada-Las Vegas | San Diego, Calif. | PB(Atl)-'91 | 12/11 |
| 54 | | Donahue, Mitch | LB | 6-2 | 254 | 2/4/68 | 4 | Wyoming | Billings, Mont. | W(SF)-'93 | 13/0 |
| 99 | | Dronett, Shane | DE | 6-6 | 275 | 1/12/71 | 3 | Texas | Orange, Tex. | D2-'92 | 16/16 |
| 97 | | Drozdov, Darren | NT | 6-3 | 280 | 4/7/69 | 2 | Maryland | Wilmington, Del. | FA-'93 | 6/2 |
| 1 | | Elam, Jason | K | 5-11 | 192 | 3/8/70 | 2 | Hawaii | Ft. Walton Beach, Fla. | D3b-'93 | 16/0 |
| 7 | | Elway, John | QB | 6-3 | 215 | 6/28/60 | 12 | Stanford | Port Angeles, Wash. | T(Balt)-'83 | 16/16 |
| 88 | | Evans, Jerry | TE | 6-4 | 250 | 9/28/68 | 2 | Toledo | Lorain, Ohio | FA-'93 | 14/2 |
| 73 | | Fletcher, Simon | LB | 6-5 | 240 | 2/18/62 | 10 | Houston | Bay City, Tex. | D2b-'85 | 16/16 |
| 68 | | Freeman, Russell | T | 6-7 | 290 | 9/2/69 | 3 | Georgia Tech | Homestead, Pa. | FA-'92 | 14/14 |
| 75 | | Habib, Brian | G | 6-7 | 292 | 12/2/64 | 7 | Washington | Ellensburg, Wash. | UFA(Minn)-'93 | 16/16 |
| 40 | | Hall, Darryl | S | 6-2 | 210 | 8/1/66 | 2 | Washington | Oscoda, Mich. | FA-'93 | 16/2 |
| 52 | | Harvey, Richard | LB | 6-1 | 242 | 9/11/66 | 5 | Tulane | Pascagoula, Miss. | UFA(Buff)-'94 | 15/0* |
| 89 | † | Johnson, Reggie | TE | 6-2 | 256 | 1/27/68 | 4 | Florida State | Pensacola, Fla. | D2-'91 | 13/12 |
| 31 | | Jones, Rondell | S | 6-2 | 210 | 5/7/71 | 2 | North Carolina | Sunderland, Mass. | D3a-'93 | 16/0 |
| 72 | | Kartz, Keith | C | 6-4 | 270 | 5/5/63 | 8 | California | Las Vegas, Nev. | FA-'87 | 12/10 |
| 80 | | Kimbrough, Tony | WR | 6-2 | 192 | 9/17/70 | 2 | Jackson State | Weir, Miss. | D7b-'93 | 15/0 |
| 21 | # | Lang, Le-Lo | CB | 5-11 | 185 | 1/23/67 | 5 | Washington | Los Angeles, Calif. | D5b-'90 | 16/0 |
| 59 | # | Lucas, Tim | LB | 6-3 | 230 | 4/3/61 | 8 | California | Stockton, Calif. | FA-'87 | 7/0 |
| 37 | | Lynn, Anthony | RB | 6-3 | 230 | 12/21/68 | 2 | Texas Tech | McKinney, Tex. | FA'-93 | 13/0 |
| 8 | | Maddox, Tommy | QB | 6-4 | 195 | 9/2/71 | 3 | UCLA | Shreveport, La. | D1-'92 | 16/0 |
| 78 | | Maggs, Don | T | 6-5 | 290 | 11/1/61 | 9 | Tulane | Youngstown, Ohio | UFA(Hou)-'93 | 7/2 |
| 77 | # | Mecklenburg, Karl | LB | 6-3 | 235 | 9/1/60 | 12 | Minnesota | Edina, Minn. | D12-'83 | 16/16 |
| 61 | | Meeks, Bob | G | 6-2 | 279 | 5/28/69 | 3 | Auburn | Andulusia, Ala. | D10-'92 | 8/0 |
| 64 | # | Melander, Jon | G | 6-7 | 280 | 12/27/66 | 5 | Minnesota | Fridley, Minn. | W(Cin)-'93 | 14/7 |
| 22 | | Milburn, Glyn | RB | 5-8 | 177 | 2/19/71 | 2 | Stanford | Santa Monica, Calif. | D2-'93 | 16/2 |
| 83 | | Miller, Anthony | WR | 5-11 | 190 | 4/15/65 | 7 | Tennessee | Pasadena, Calif. | RFA(SD)-'94 | 16/16* |
| 52 | # | Mills, Jeff | LB | 6-3 | 238 | 10/8/68 | 5 | Nebraska | Montclair, N.J. | W(SD)-'90 | 13/0 |
| 12 | | Moore, Shawn | QB | 6-2 | 213 | 4/4/68 | 3 | Virginia | Martinsville, Va. | D11-'91 | 0* |
| 91 | | Oshodin, Willie | DE | 6-4 | 260 | 9/16/69 | 4 | Villanova | Benn City, Nigeria | FA-'92 | 15/5 |
| 81 | t- | Pritchard, Mike | WR | 5-10 | 190 | 10/26/69 | 4 | Colorado | Las Vegas, Nev. | T(Atl)-'94 | 15/14* |
| 38 | | Rivers, Reggie | RB | 6-1 | 215 | 2/22/68 | 4 | Southwest Texas State | Dayton, Ohio | FA-'91 | 16/2 |
| 36 | | Robinson, Frank | CB | 5-11 | 174 | 1/11/69 | 3 | Boise State | Newark, N.J. | D5-'92 | 16/2 |
| 94 | | Robinson, Jeff | DE | 6-4 | 265 | 2/20/70 | 2 | Idaho | Kennewick, Wash. | D4-'93 | 16/0 |
| 16 | | Rouen, Tom | P | 6-3 | 215 | 6/9/68 | 2 | Colorado | Hindsdale, Ill. | FA-'93 | 16/0 |
| 85 | | Russell, Derek | WR | 6-0 | 179 | 6/22/69 | 4 | Arkansas | Little Rock, Ark. | D4-'91 | 13/12 |
| 55 | | Sanders, Glenell | LB | 6-1 | 237 | 11/4/66 | 2 | Louisiana Tech | Clinton, La. | FA-'94 | 0* |
| 76 | # | Scrafford, Kirk | T | 6-6 | 265 | 3/13/67 | 5 | Montana | Billings, Mont. | W(Cin)-'93 | 16/0 |
| 84 | | Sharpe, Shannon | TE | 6-2 | 230 | 6/26/68 | 5 | Savannah State | Glennville, Ga. | D7-'90 | 16/12 |
| 26 | t- | Smith, Ben | CB | 5-11 | 185 | 5/14/67 | 5 | Georgia | Warner Robins, Ga. | T(Phil)-'94 | 13/3* |
| 49 | # | Smith, Dennis | S | 6-3 | 200 | 2/3/59 | 14 | Southern California | Santa Monica, Calif. | D1-'81 | 14/14 |
| 95 | | Taylor, Alphonso | DT | 6-3 | 350 | 9/7/69 | 2 | Temple | Trenton, N.J. | W(Phx)-'93 | 3/0 |
| 81 | # | Taylor, Kitrick | WR | 5-11 | 189 | 7/22/64 | 6 | Washington State | Pomona, Calif. | FA-'93 | 2/0 |
| 87 | | Tillman, Cedric | WR | 6-2 | 204 | 7/22/70 | 3 | Alcorn State | Gulfport, Miss. | D11-'92 | 14/3 |
| 98 | t- | Washington, Ted | NT | 6-4 | 295 | 4/13/68 | 4 | Louisville | Tampa, Fla. | T(SF)-'94 | 12/12* |
| 79 | | Widell, Dave | G-C | 6-6 | 292 | 5/14/65 | 7 | Boston College | Hartford, Conn. | T(Dall)-'91 | 15/15 |
| 90 | | Williams, Dan | DE | 6-4 | 290 | 12/15/69 | 2 | Toledo | Ypsilanti, Mich. | D1-'93 | 13/11 |
| 92 | | Wyman, Dave | LB | 6-2 | 248 | 3/31/64 | 8 | Stanford | San Diego, Calif. | UFA(Sea)-'93 | 16/16 |
| 65 | | Zimmerman, Gary | T | 6-6 | 294 | 12/13/61 | 9 | Oregon | Walnut, Calif. | T(Minn)-'94 | 16/16 |

* Ball last active with Indianapolis in '92; Campbell played 10 games with Detroit in '93; Carlson last active with New England in '92; Crockett played 16 games with Detroit; Harvey played 15 games with Buffalo; Miller played 16 games with San Diego; Moore inactive for 16 games; Pritchard played 15 games with Atlanta; Sanders last active with L.A. Rams in '92; B. Smith played 13 games with Philadelphia; Washington played 12 games with San Francisco.

\# Unrestricted free agent; subject to developments.

† Restricted free agent; subject to developments.

Traded—WR Arthur Marshall to N.Y. Giants.

t- Broncos traded for Pritchard (Atlanta), Smith (Philadelphia), Washington (San Francisco).

Players lost through free agency (3): CB Tyrone Braxton (Mia; 16 games in '93), WR Vance Johnson (SD; 10), CB David Pool (Minn; 0).

Also played with Broncos in '93—NT Greg Kragen (14 games), WR Arthur Marshall (16), WR Barry Rose (3).

## COACHING STAFF

**Head Coach,**
**Wade Phillips**

**Pro Career:** Became the tenth head coach in Broncos history on January 25, 1993, moving into the head-coaching slot from his previous position as defensive coordinator. In his first year as the Broncos' head coach, Phillips had the youngest team in the NFL and still led Denver back into the playoffs with a 9-7 regular-season record. Under Phillips's leadership, the Broncos' defense led the American Football Conference in fewest points allowed in two of the past five seasons (1989 and 1991), and the 1991 Denver team was paced by a defensive unit that led the AFC in 12 different categories. In addition to his role as defensive coordinator with the Broncos, Phillips assumed the capacity of interim head coach during the 1990 preseason posting a win over Indianapolis. Going into his sixth season with Denver, Phillips came to the Broncos from Philadelphia, where he was the defensive coordinator and linebackers coach from 1986-88. He served as defensive coordinator at New Orleans from 1981-85 and was the interim head coach for the final four games of the 1985 season (1-3 record). Prior to joining the Saints, Phillips spent five seasons at Houston, coaching the linebackers (1976) and defensive line (1977-80). Career record: 10-11.

**Background:** Phillips began his coaching career at his alma mater, the University of Houston, in 1969, and then coached at Orange (Texas) High School for three years (1970-72) before moving to Oklahoma State (1973-74) and Kansas (1975).

**Personal:** The son of former NFL head coach Bum Phillips, Phillips was born in Orange, Texas on June 21, 1947. He attended Port Neches-Groves High School. He went on to be a three-year starter at linebacker at Houston under head coach Bill Yeoman. Wade and his wife, Laurie, live in Denver and have two children—Tracy and Wesley.

### ASSISTANT COACHES

**Vernon Banks,** strength and conditioning; born May 24, 1956, Alvin, Tex., lives in Denver. Defensive back-running back Blinn Junior College 1976-77, Texas A&M 1978-79. No pro playing experience. College coach: Texas A&M 1981-83, Houston 1985, Wyoming 1986-87, 1992, Stanford 1987-89, Colorado 1990-91. Pro coach: Joined Broncos in 1993.

**Barney Chavous,** defensive assistant; born March 22, 1951, Aiken, S.C., lives in Englewood, Colo. Defensive end South Carolina State 1969-72. Pro defensive end Denver Broncos 1973-85. Pro coach: Joined Broncos in 1989.

**Jim Fassel,** assistant head coach-offensive coordinator; born August 31, 1949, Anaheim, Calif., lives in Greenwood Village, Colo. Quarterback Southern California 1969-70, Long Beach State 1971. Pro quarterback Chicago Bears 1972, Houston Oilers 1972, San Diego Chargers 1972. College coach: Fullerton (Calif.) Junior College 1973, Utah 1976, 1985-89 (head coach), Weber State 1977-78, Stanford 1979-83. Pro coach: Hawaii (WFL) 1974, Portland Breakers (USFL) 1984, New York Giants 1990-92, joined Broncos in 1993.

**Mo Forte,** wide receivers; born March 1, 1947, Hannibal, Mo., lives in Littleton, Colo. Running back Minnesota 1965-68. No pro playing experience. College coach: Minnesota 1970-75, Duke 1976-77, Michigan State 1978-79, Arizona State 1980-81, North Carolina A&T 1982-87 (head coach). Pro coach: Joined Broncos in 1988.

**Leon Fuller,** defensive backs; born July 28, 1938, Nederland, Tex., lives in Denver. Linebacker Alabama 1957-60. No pro playing experience. College coach: Alabama 1962, Oklahoma State 1963-66, Kentucky 1967-68, New Mexico 1969-73, West Texas State 1974, Wyoming 1975-76, Texas 1977-81, 1989-93, Colorado State 1982-88 (head coach). Pro coach: Joined Broncos in 1994.

**Bishop Harris,** running backs; born November 23, 1941, Phoenix City, Ala., lives in Denver. Defensive back North Carolina College 1960-64. No pro playing experience. College coach: Duke 1972-75, North Carolina State 1977-79, Louisiana State 1980-83, Notre Dame 1984-85, Minnesota 1986-90, North Carolina Central 1991-92 (head coach). Pro coach: Joined Broncos in 1993.

**John Levra,** offensive line; born October 2, 1937, Arma, Kan., lives in Englewood, Colo. Guard-linebacker Pittsburg (Kan.) State 1963-65. No pro playing experience. College coach: Stephen F. Austin 1971-74, Kansas 1975-78, North Texas State 1979. Pro coach: British Columbia Lions (CFL) 1980, New Orleans Saints 1981-85, Chicago Bears 1986-92, joined Broncos in 1993.

**Rex Norris,** defensive line; born December 10, 1939, Tipton, Ind., lives in Denver. Linebacker San Angelo (Texas) Junior College 1959-60, East Texas State 1961-62. No pro playing experience. College coach: Navarro (Texas) Junior College 1970-71, Texas A&M 1972, Oklahoma 1973-83, Arizona State 1984, Florida 1988-89, Tennessee 1990-91, Texas 1992-93. Pro coach: Detroit Lions 1985-87, joined Broncos in 1994.

**Alvin Reynolds,** assistant defensive backs/quality control; born June 24, 1959, Pineville, La., lives in Aurora, Colo. Safety Indiana State 1978-81. No pro playing experience. College coach: Indiana State 1982-92. Pro coach: Joined Broncos in 1993.

**Harold Richardson,** special assistant to head coach/offense; born September 27, 1944, Houston, Tex., lives in Englewood, Colo. Tight end Southern Methodist 1964-67. No pro playing experience. College coach: Southern Methodist 1971-72, Oklahoma State 1973-76, Texas Christian 1977-78, North Texas State 1979-80, Colorado State 1986-88. Pro coach: New Orleans Saints 1981-85, joined Broncos in 1989.

**Richard Smith,** special teams/linebackers; born October 17, 1955, Los Angeles, Calif., lives in Denver. Offensive lineman Rio Hondo (Calif.) Junior College 1975-76, Fresno State 1977-78. No pro playing experience. College coach: Rio Hondo (Calif.) Junior College 1979-80, Cal State-Fullerton 1981-83, California 1984-86, Arizona 1987. Pro coach: Houston Oilers 1988-92, joined Broncos in 1993.

**Les Steckel,** H-backs-tight ends; born July 1, 1946, North Hampton, Pa., lives in Louisville, Colo. Running back Kansas 1964-68. No pro playing experience. College coach: Colorado 1972-76, 1991-92, Navy 1977, Brown 1989. Pro coach: San Francisco 49ers 1978, Minnesota Vikings 1979-84 (head coach, 1984), New England Patriots 1985-88, joined Broncos in 1993.

**Charlie Waters,** defensive coordinator; born September 10, 1948, Miami, Fla., lives in Greenwood Village, Colo. Safety Clemson 1967-69. Pro safety Dallas Cowboys 1970-81. Pro coach: Joined Broncos in 1988.

**John Paul Young,** linebackers; born December 31, 1939, Dallas, Tex., lives in Denver. Linebacker Texas-El Paso 1959-61. No pro playing experience. College coach: Texas El-Paso 1962-63, Southern Methodist 1967-68, Oklahoma State 1969, Texas A&M 1970-77, Texas Tech 1989-91. Pro coach: Houston Oilers 1978-80, New Orleans Saints 1981-85, Kansas City Chiefs 1986-88, Dallas Texans (Arena League, head coach) 1992, joined Broncos in 1993.

## 1994 FIRST-YEAR ROSTER

| Name | Pos. | Ht. | Wt. | Birthdate | College | Hometown | How Acq. |
|---|---|---|---|---|---|---|---|
| Aldridge, Allen | LB | 6-1 | 245 | 5/30/72 | Houston | Houston, Tex. | D2 |
| Bell, Trumane | TE | 6-3 | 235 | 11/26/71 | Nebraska | Chicago, Ill. | FA |
| Burns, Keith | LB | 6-2 | 245 | 5/16/72 | Oklahoma State | Greeleyville, S.C. | D7a |
| By'not'e, Butler | RB | 5-9 | 190 | 9/29/72 | Ohio State | Louis, Miss. | D7b |
| Carswell, Dwayne | TE | 6-3 | 261 | 1/18/72 | Liberty | Jacksonville, Fla. | FA |
| Dyet, Brian | DE | 6-4 | 257 | 12/12/70 | Colorado | Denver, Colo. | FA |
| Farkas, Kevin | T | 6-9 | 360 | 2/4/71 | Appalachian State | Richmond, Va. | FA |
| Fowler, Carlos | DT | 6-2 | 278 | 8/30/72 | Wisconsin | Cleveland, Ohio | FA |
| Fuller, Randy | CB | 5-9 | 173 | 6/2/70 | Tennessee State | Columbus, Ga. | D4 |
| Geter, Eric (1) | CB | 5-11 | 190 | 6/24/70 | Clemson | Gay, Ga. | FA |
| Hall, Kenny | G-T | 6-4 | 315 | 7/15/71 | Fresno State | Wallugan, Ill. | FA |
| Hampel, Olaf (1) | G | 6-6 | 305 | 6/24/67 | No College | Essen, Germany | FA |
| Hasselbach, Harald (1) | DT | 6-6 | 280 | 9/22/67 | Washington | Amsterdam, Holland | FA |
| Jacobs, Ray | LB | 6-2 | 244 | 8/18/72 | North Carolina | Hampstead, N.C. | FA |
| Lofton, Billy | DE | 6-2 | 290 | 10/28/71 | Kentucky | Wilmington, N.C. | FA |
| Mosley, Tim | WR | 6-3 | 187 | 1/19/71 | Northern Iowa | Ft. Dodge, Iowa | FA |
| Nalen, Tom | C | 6-2 | 280 | 5/13/71 | Boston College | Foxboro, Mass. | D7c |
| Redmond, Jamie (1) | CB | 5-9 | 185 | 10/1/69 | Middle Tennessee St. | Savannah, Ga. | FA |
| Rose, Barry | WR | 6-0 | 185 | 7/28/68 | Wis.-Stevens Point | Hudson, Wis. | FA |
| Savage, Sebastian (1) | CB | 5-11 | 196 | 12/12/69 | North Carolina State | Union, S.C. | FA |
| Smith, Rod | WR | 6-0 | 183 | 5/15/70 | Missouri Southern | Texarkana, Ark. | FA |
| Snowden, Chuck | RB | 6-0 | 209 | 4/21/71 | Northern Colorado | Washington, D.C. | FA |
| Strother, Deon | RB | 5-11 | 213 | 4/12/72 | Southern California | Saginaw, Mich. | FA |
| Swann, Charles (1) | WR | 6-1 | 188 | 10/29/70 | Indiana State | Memphis, Tenn. | FA |
| Vaughn, Scott | T | 6-5 | 319 | 4/9/71 | Rutgers | Easton, Pa. | FA |

The term NFL Rookie is defined as a player who is in his first season of professional football and has not been on the roster of another professional football team for any regular-season or postseason games. A Rookie is designated by an "R" on NFL rosters. Players who have been active in another professional football league or players who have NFL experience, including either preseason training camp or being on an Active List or Inactive List, or on Reserve/Injured or Reserve/Physically Unable to Perform for fewer than six regular-season games, are termed NFL First-Year Players. An NFL First-Year Player is designated by a "1" on NFL rosters. Thereafter, a player is credited with an additional year of experience for each season in which he accumulates six games on the Active List or Inactive List, or on Reserve/Injured or Reserve/Physically Unable to Perform.

## NOTES

# HOUSTON OILERS

**American Football Conference**
**Central Division**
**Team Colors:** Columbia Blue, Scarlet, and White
**6910 Fannin Street**
**Houston, Texas 77030**
**Telephone: (713) 797-9111**

## CLUB OFFICIALS

President: K.S. (Bud) Adams, Jr.
Exec. V.P./General Manager: Floyd Reese
Exec. V.P./Administration: Mike McClure
Exec. V.P./Finance: Scott Thompson
Exec. Assistant to President: Thomas S. Smith
Vice President/General Counsel: Steve Underwood
Vice President/Player Personnel and Scouting: Mike Holovak
Senior Vice President//Marketing and Broadcasting: Don MacLachlan
Director of Business Operations: Lewis Mangum
Director of Media Services: TBA
Director of Accounting Services: Marilan Logan
Controller: Jackie Curley
Director of Ticket Administration Services: Mike Mullis
Assistant Ticket Manager: Ralph Stolarski
Director of Security: Grady Sessums
Director of Computer Services: Steve Reese
Director of Player Relations: Willie Alexander
Head Trainer: Brad Brown
Assistant Trainer: Don Moseley
Equipment Manager: Dan Murray
Video Coordinator: Ken Sparacino
**Stadium:** Astrodome • **Capacity:** 59,905
8400 Kirby Drive
Houston, Texas 77054
**Playing Surface:** AstroTurf-8
**Training Camp:** Prassel Residence Hall
Trinity University
San Antonio, Texas 78212

## 1994 SCHEDULE

### PRESEASON

| | | |
|---|---|---|
| July 31 | at Kansas City | 8:00 |
| Aug. 6 | vs. San Diego at San Antonio, Tex. | 7:00 |
| Aug. 15 | vs. Dallas at Mexico City | 9:00 |
| Aug. 20 | vs. Buffalo at San Antonio, Tex. | 7:00 |
| Aug. 27 | **Los Angeles Raiders** | 1:00 |

### REGULAR SEASON

| | | |
|---|---|---|
| Sept. 4 | at Indianapolis | 12:00 |
| Sept. 11 | at Dallas | 3:00 |
| Sept. 18 | **Buffalo** | 12:00 |
| Sept. 25 | **Cincinnati** | 3:00 |
| Oct. 3 | at Pittsburgh (Monday) | 9:00 |
| Oct. 9 | Open Date | |
| Oct. 13 | **Cleveland** (Thursday) | 7:00 |
| Oct. 24 | at Philadelphia (Monday) | 9:00 |
| Oct. 30 | at Los Angeles Raiders | 1:00 |
| Nov. 6 | **Pittsburgh** | 12:00 |
| Nov. 13 | at Cincinnati | 1:00 |
| Nov. 21 | **New York Giants** (Monday) | 8:00 |
| Nov. 27 | at Cleveland | 1:00 |
| Dec. 4 | **Arizona** | 3:00 |
| Dec. 11 | **Seattle** | 3:00 |
| Dec. 18 | at Kansas City | 3:00 |
| Dec. 24 | **New York Jets** | 3:00 |

## RECORD HOLDERS

### INDIVIDUAL RECORDS—CAREER

| Category | Name | Performance |
|---|---|---|
| Rushing (Yds.) | Earl Campbell, 1978-1984 | 8,574 |
| Passing (Yds.) | Warren Moon, 1984-1993 | 33,685 |
| Passing (TDs) | Warren Moon, 1984-1993 | 196 |
| Receiving (No.) | Ernest Givins, 1986-1993 | 506 |
| Receiving (Yds.) | Drew Hill, 1985-1991 | 7,477 |
| Interceptions | Jim Norton, 1960-68 | 45 |
| Punting (Avg.) | Greg Montgomery, 1988-1993 | 43.6 |
| Punt Return (Avg.) | Billy Johnson, 1974-1980 | 13.2 |
| Kickoff Return (Avg.) | Bobby Jancik, 1962-67 | 26.4 |
| Field Goals | Tony Zendejas, 1985-1990 | 117 |
| Touchdowns (Tot.) | Earl Campbell, 1978-1984 | 73 |
| Points | George Blanda, 1960-66 | 596 |

### INDIVIDUAL RECORDS—SINGLE SEASON

| Category | Name | Performance |
|---|---|---|
| Rushing (Yds.) | Earl Campbell, 1980 | 1,934 |
| Passing (Yds.) | Warren Moon, 1991 | 4,690 |
| Passing (TDs) | George Blanda, 1961 | 36 |
| Receiving (No.) | Charlie Hennigan, 1964 | 101 |
| Receiving (Yds.) | Charlie Hennigan, 1961 | *1,746 |
| Interceptions | Fred Glick, 1963 | 12 |
| | Mike Reinfeldt, 1979 | 12 |
| Punting (Avg.) | Greg Montgomery, 1992 | 46.9 |
| Punt Return (Avg.) | Billy Johnson, 1977 | 15.4 |
| Kickoff Return (Avg.) | Ken Hall, 1960 | 31.2 |
| Field Goals | Al Del Greco, 1993 | 29 |
| Touchdowns (Tot.) | Earl Campbell, 1979 | 19 |
| Points | Al Del Greco, 1993 | 126 |

### INDIVIDUAL RECORDS—SINGLE GAME

| Category | Name | Performance |
|---|---|---|
| Rushing (Yds.) | Billy Cannon, 12-10-61 | 216 |
| Passing (Yds.) | Warren Moon, 12-16-90 | 527 |
| Passing (TDs) | George Blanda, 11-19-61 | *7 |
| Receiving (No.) | Charlie Hennigan, 10-13-61 | 13 |
| | Haywood Jeffires, 10-13-91 | 13 |
| Receiving (Yds.) | Charlie Hennigan, 10-13-61 | 272 |
| Interceptions | Many times | 3 |
| | Last time by Marcus Robertson, 11-21-93 | |
| Field Goals | Skip Butler, 10-12-75 | 6 |
| Touchdowns (Tot.) | Billy Cannon, 12-10-61 | 5 |
| Points | Billy Cannon, 12-10-61 | 30 |

*NFL Record

## COACHING HISTORY

**(243-273-6)**

| | | |
|---|---|---|
| 1960-61 | Lou Rymkus* | 12-7-1 |
| 1961 | Wally Lemm | 10-0-0 |
| 1962-63 | Frank (Pop) Ivy | 17-12-0 |
| 1964 | Sammy Baugh | 4-10-0 |
| 1965 | Hugh Taylor | 4-10-0 |
| 1966-70 | Wally Lemm | 28-40-4 |
| 1971 | Ed Hughes | 4-9-1 |
| 1972-73 | Bill Peterson** | 1-18-0 |
| 1973-74 | Sid Gillman | 8-15-0 |
| 1975-80 | O.A. (Bum) Phillips | 59-38-0 |
| 1981-83 | Ed Biles*** | 8-23-0 |
| 1983 | Chuck Studley | 2-8-0 |
| 1984-85 | Hugh Campbell**** | 8-22-0 |
| 1985-89 | Jerry Glanville | 35-35-0 |
| 1990-93 | Jack Pardee | 43-26-0 |

*Released after five games in 1961
**Released after five games in 1973
***Resigned after six games in 1983
****Released after 14 games in 1985

**ASTRODOME**

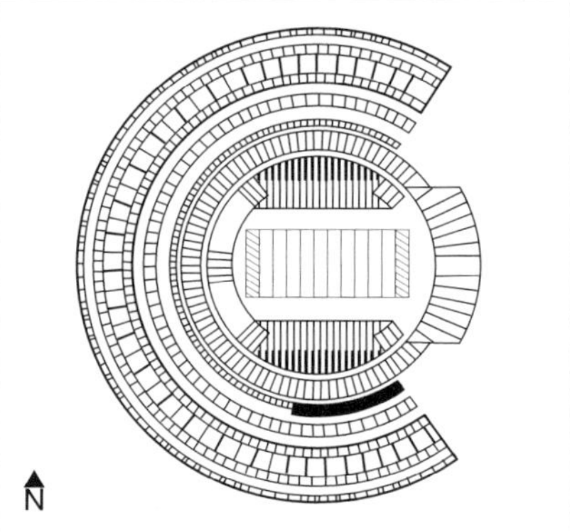

## 1993 TEAM RECORD

**PRESEASON (1-3)**

| Date | Result | | Opponents |
|---|---|---|---|
| 8/7 | L | 28-37 | vs. New Orleans at San Antonio |
| 8/16 | L | 20-24 | Detroit |
| 8/21 | W | 23-20 | vs. Dallas at San Antonio |
| 8/28 | L | 10-20 | Seattle |

**REGULAR SEASON (12-4)**

| Date | Result | | Opponents | Att. |
|---|---|---|---|---|
| 9/5 | L | 21-33 | at New Orleans | 69,029 |
| 9/12 | W | 30-0 | Kansas City | 59,780 |
| 9/19 | L | 17-18 | at San Diego | 58,519 |
| 9/26 | L | 13-28 | L.A. Rams | 53,072 |
| 10/11 | L | 7-35 | at Buffalo | 79,613 |
| 10/17 | W | 28-14 | at New England | 51,037 |
| 10/24 | W | 28-12 | Cincinnati | 50,039 |
| 11/7 | W | 24-14 | Seattle | 50,447 |
| 11/14 | W | 38-3 | at Cincinnati | 42,347 |
| 11/21 | W | 27-20 | at Cleveland | 71,668 |
| 11/28 | W | 23-3 | Pittsburgh | 61,238 |
| 12/5 | W | 33-17 | Atlanta | 58,186 |
| 12/12 | W | 19-17 | Cleveland | 58,720 |
| 12/19 | W | 26-17 | at Pittsburgh | 57,592 |
| 12/25 | W | 10-7 | at San Francisco | 61,744 |
| 1/2 | W | 24-0 | N.Y. Jets | 61,040 |

**POSTSEASON (0-1)**

| | | | | |
|---|---|---|---|---|
| 1/16 | L | 20-28 | Kansas City | 64,011 |

**SCORE BY PERIODS**

| | | | | | | | |
|---|---|---|---|---|---|---|---|
| Oilers | 68 | 131 | 75 | 94 | 0 | — | 368 |
| Opponents | 40 | 73 | 50 | 75 | 0 | — | 238 |

**ATTENDANCE**

Home 452,522 Away 491,549 Total 944,071
Single-game home record, 63,705 (9-6-92)
Single-season home record, 494,447 (1992)

## 1993 TEAM STATISTICS

| | Oilers | Opp. |
|---|---|---|
| Total First Downs | 330 | 289 |
| Rushing | 101 | 73 |
| Passing | 208 | 184 |
| Penalty | 21 | 32 |
| Third Down: Made/Att | 94/211 | 64/208 |
| Third Down Pct. | 44.5 | 30.8 |
| Fourth Down: Made/Att | 3/12 | 12/24 |
| Fourth Down Pct. | 25.0 | 50.0 |
| Total Net Yards | 5658 | 4874 |
| Avg. Per Game | 353.6 | 304.6 |
| Total Plays | 1066 | 1003 |
| Avg. Per Play | 5.3 | 4.9 |
| Net Yards Rushing | 1792 | 1273 |
| Avg. Per Game | 112.0 | 79.6 |
| Total Rushes | 409 | 369 |
| Net Yards Passing | 3866 | 3601 |
| Avg. Per Game | 241.6 | 225.1 |
| Sacked/Yards Lost | 43/279 | 52/313 |
| Gross Yards | 4145 | 3914 |
| Att./Completions | 614/357 | 582/302 |
| Completion Pct. | 58.1 | 51.9 |
| Had Intercepted | 25 | 26 |
| Punts/Avg. | 56/45.3 | 79/43.7 |
| Net Punting Avg. | 56/38.7 | 79/36.9 |
| Penalties/Yards Lost | 132/1005 | 103/791 |
| Fumbles/Ball Lost | 37/20 | 32/17 |
| Touchdowns | 40 | 26 |
| Rushing | 11 | 9 |
| Passing | 23 | 16 |
| Returns | 6 | 1 |
| Avg. Time of Possession | 31:48 | 28:12 |

## 1993 INDIVIDUAL STATISTICS

| PASSING | Att. | Cmp. | Yds. | Pct. | TD | Int | Tkld. | Rate |
|---|---|---|---|---|---|---|---|---|
| Moon | 520 | 303 | 3485 | 58.3 | 21 | 21 | 34/218 | 75.2 |
| Carlson | 90 | 51 | 605 | 56.7 | 2 | 4 | 8/53 | 66.2 |
| Richardson | 4 | 3 | 55 | 75.0 | 0 | 0 | 1/8 | 116.7 |
| Oilers | 614 | 357 | 4145 | 58.1 | 23 | 25 | 43/279 | 74.2 |
| Opponents | 582 | 302 | 3914 | 51.9 | 16 | 26 | 52/313 | 63.9 |

| SCORING | TD R | TD P | TD Rt | PAT | FG | Saf | PTS |
|---|---|---|---|---|---|---|---|
| Del Greco | 0 | 0 | 0 | 39/40 | 29/34 | 0 | 126 |
| G. Brown | 6 | 2 | 0 | 0/0 | 0/0 | 0 | 48 |
| Jeffires | 0 | 6 | 0 | 0/0 | 0/0 | 0 | 36 |
| Slaughter | 0 | 5 | 0 | 0/0 | 0/0 | 0 | 30 |
| Givins | 0 | 4 | 0 | 0/0 | 0/0 | 0 | 24 |
| Duncan | 0 | 3 | 0 | 0/0 | 0/0 | 0 | 18 |
| Carlson | 2 | 0 | 0 | 0/0 | 0/0 | 0 | 12 |
| White | 2 | 0 | 0 | 0/0 | 0/0 | 0 | 12 |
| Childress | 0 | 0 | 1 | 0/0 | 0/0 | 0 | 6 |
| Dishman | 0 | 0 | 1 | 0/0 | 0/0 | 0 | 6 |
| Harris | 0 | 1 | 0 | 0/0 | 0/0 | 0 | 6 |
| Jackson | 0 | 0 | 1 | 0/0 | 0/0 | 0 | 6 |
| Lewis | 0 | 0 | 1 | 0/0 | 0/0 | 0 | 6 |
| Moon | 1 | 0 | 0 | 0/0 | 0/0 | 0 | 6 |
| Orlando | 0 | 0 | 1 | 0/0 | 0/0 | 0 | 6 |
| Robertson | 0 | 0 | 1 | 0/0 | 0/0 | 0 | 6 |
| Tillman | 0 | 1 | 0 | 0/0 | 0/0 | 0 | 6 |
| Wellman | 0 | 1 | 0 | 0/0 | 0/0 | 0 | 6 |
| Oilers | 11 | 23 | 6 | 39/40 | 29/34 | 1 | 368 |
| Opponents | 9 | 16 | 1 | 25/26 | 19/28 | 0 | 238 |

| RUSHING | Att. | Yds. | Avg. | LG | TD |
|---|---|---|---|---|---|
| G. Brown | 195 | 1002 | 5.1 | 26 | 6 |
| White | 131 | 465 | 3.5 | 14 | 2 |
| Moon | 48 | 145 | 3.0 | 35 | 1 |
| Tillman | 9 | 94 | 10.4 | 34 | 0 |
| Carlson | 14 | 41 | 2.9 | 10t | 2 |
| Givins | 6 | 19 | 3.2 | 16 | 0 |
| Maston | 1 | 10 | 10.0 | 10 | 0 |
| Richardson | 2 | 9 | 4.5 | 11 | 0 |
| Wellman | 2 | 6 | 3.0 | 4 | 0 |
| Coleman | 1 | 1 | 1.0 | 1 | 0 |
| Oilers | 409 | 1792 | 4.4 | 35 | 11 |
| Opponents | 369 | 1273 | 3.4 | 29 | 9 |

| RECEIVING | No. | Yds. | Avg. | LG | TD |
|---|---|---|---|---|---|
| Slaughter | 77 | 904 | 11.7 | 41 | 5 |
| Givins | 68 | 887 | 13.0 | 80t | 4 |
| Jeffires | 66 | 753 | 11.4 | 66t | 6 |
| Duncan | 41 | 456 | 11.1 | 47 | 3 |
| White | 34 | 229 | 6.7 | 20 | 0 |
| Wellman | 31 | 430 | 13.9 | 44 | 1 |
| G. Brown | 21 | 240 | 11.4 | 38t | 2 |
| Coleman | 9 | 129 | 14.3 | 25 | 0 |
| Harris | 4 | 53 | 13.3 | 17t | 1 |
| R. Brown | 2 | 30 | 15.0 | 26 | 0 |
| Maston | 1 | 14 | 14.0 | 14 | 0 |
| Norgard | 1 | 13 | 13.0 | 13 | 0 |
| Tillman | 1 | 4 | 4.0 | 4t | 1 |
| Drewrey | 1 | 3 | 3.0 | 3 | 0 |
| Oilers | 357 | 4145 | 11.6 | 80t | 23 |
| Opponents | 302 | 3914 | 13.0 | 53t | 16 |

| INTERCEPTIONS | No. | Yds. | Avg. | Long | TD |
|---|---|---|---|---|---|
| Robertson | 7 | 137 | 19.6 | 69 | 0 |
| Dishman | 6 | 74 | 12.3 | 30 | 0 |
| Jackson | 5 | 54 | 10.8 | 22t | 1 |
| Orlando | 3 | 68 | 22.7 | 38t | 1 |
| McDowell | 3 | 31 | 10.3 | 13 | 0 |
| Lewis | 1 | 47 | 47.0 | 47t | 1 |
| Bishop | 1 | 1 | 1.0 | 1 | 0 |
| Oilers | 26 | 412 | 15.8 | 69 | 3 |
| Opponents | 25 | 309 | 12.4 | 42 | 0 |

| PUNTING | No. | Yds. | Avg. | In 20 | LG |
|---|---|---|---|---|---|
| Gr. Montgomery | 54 | 2462 | 45.6 | 13 | 77 |
| Sullivan | 2 | 73 | 36.5 | 1 | 37 |
| Oilers | 56 | 2535 | 45.3 | 14 | 77 |
| Opponents | 79 | 3454 | 43.7 | 15 | 71 |

| PUNT RETURNS | No. | FC | Yds. | Avg. | LG | TD |
|---|---|---|---|---|---|---|
| Drewrey | 41 | 19 | 275 | 6.7 | 18 | 0 |
| Oilers | 41 | 19 | 275 | 6.7 | 18 | 0 |
| Opponents | 28 | 5 | 249 | 8.9 | 30 | 0 |

| KICKOFF RETURNS | No. | Yds. | Avg. | LG | TD |
|---|---|---|---|---|---|
| Drewrey | 15 | 293 | 19.5 | 34 | 0 |
| Mills | 11 | 230 | 20.9 | 37 | 0 |
| Coleman | 3 | 37 | 12.3 | 16 | 0 |
| Gl. Brown | 2 | 29 | 14.5 | 16 | 0 |
| Oilers | 31 | 589 | 19.0 | 37 | 0 |
| Opponents | 60 | 1062 | 17.7 | 36 | 0 |

| SACKS | No. |
|---|---|
| S. Jones | 13.0 |
| Fuller | 10.0 |
| Childress | 9.0 |
| Gl. Montgomery | 6.0 |
| L. Williams | 3.0 |
| Lathon | 2.0 |
| Marshall | 2.0 |
| Barrow | 1.0 |
| Bishop | 1.0 |
| Bowden | 1.0 |
| McDowell | 1.0 |
| Robinson | 1.0 |
| Teeter | 1.0 |
| Oilers | 52.0 |
| Opponents | 43.0 |

## 1994 DRAFT CHOICES

| Round | Name | Pos. | College |
|---|---|---|---|
| 1 | Henry Ford | DE | Arkansas |
| 2 | Jeremy Nunley | DE | Alabama |
| 3 | Malcolm Seabron | WR | Fresno State |
| 4 | Mike Davis | DB | Cincinnati |
| | Sean Jackson | RB | Florida State |
| 5 | Roderick Lewis | TE | Arizona |
| | Jim Reid | T | Virginia |
| 6 | Lee Gissendaner | WR | Northwestern |
| | Barron Wortham | LB | Texas-El Paso |
| 7 | Lemanski Hall | LB | Alabama |

# HOUSTON OILERS

## 1994 VETERAN ROSTER

| No. | | Name | Pos. | Ht. | Wt. | Birthdate | NFL Exp. | College | Hometown | How Acq. | '93 Games/ Starts |
|---|---|---|---|---|---|---|---|---|---|---|---|
| 51 | | Barrow, Micheal | LB | 6-1 | 236 | 4/19/70 | 2 | Miami | Homestead, Fla. | D2-'93 | 16/0 |
| 23 | | Bishop, Blaine | S-CB | 5-8 | 197 | 7/24/70 | 2 | Ball State | Indianapolis, Ind. | D8-'93 | 16/2 |
| 59 | † | Bowden, Joe | LB | 5-11 | 230 | 2/25/70 | 3 | Oklahoma | Mesquite, Tex. | D5a-'92 | 16/6 |
| 33 | † | Brown, Gary | RB | 5-11 | 233 | 7/1/69 | 4 | Penn State | Williamsport, Pa. | D8-'91 | 16/8 |
| 17 | | Brown, Reggie | WR | 6-1 | 195 | 5/5/70 | 2 | Alabama State | Miami, Fla. | FA-'93 | 4/0 |
| 22 | | Brown, Tony | CB | 5-9 | 183 | 5/15/70 | 3 | Fresno State | Granada Hills, Calif. | D5b-'92 | 16/0 |
| 16 | | Camarillo, Rich | P | 5-11 | 195 | 11/29/59 | 14 | Washington | Pico Rivera, Calif. | UFA(Ariz)-'94 | 16/0* |
| 14 | | Carlson, Cody | QB | 6-3 | 202 | 11/5/63 | 8 | Baylor | San Antonio, Tex. | D3-'87 | 8/2 |
| 46 | | Carter, Pat | TE | 6-4 | 258 | 8/1/66 | 7 | Florida State | Sarasota, Fla. | UFA(Rams)-'94 | 11/10* |
| 79 | | Childress, Ray | DT | 6-6 | 272 | 10/20/62 | 10 | Texas A&M | Richardson, Tex. | D1a-'85 | 16/16 |
| 87 | | Coleman, Pat | WR | 5-7 | 176 | 4/8/67 | 4 | Mississippi | Cleveland, Miss. | FA-'91 | 13/1 |
| 66 | # | Dawson, Doug | G | 6-3 | 288 | 12/27/61 | 8 | Texas | Houston, Tex. | FA-'90 | 16/16 |
| 3 | | Del Greco, Al | K | 5-10 | 202 | 3/2/62 | 11 | Auburn | Coral Gables, Fla. | FA-'91 | 16/0 |
| 28 | † | Dishman, Cris | CB | 6-0 | 188 | 8/13/65 | 7 | Purdue | Louisville, Ky. | D5a-'88 | 16/16 |
| 77 | | Donnalley, Kevin | T | 6-5 | 305 | 6/10/68 | 4 | North Carolina | Raleigh, N.C. | D3b-'91 | 16/6 |
| 38 | † | Dumas, Mike | S | 5-11 | 181 | 3/18/69 | 4 | Indiana | Lowell, Mich. | D2a-'91 | 0* |
| 80 | | Duncan, Curtis | WR | 5-11 | 184 | 1/26/65 | 8 | Northwestern | Detroit, Mich. | D10-'87 | 12/12 |
| 55 | † | Flannery, John | G-C | 6-3 | 304 | 1/13/69 | 4 | Syracuse | Pottsville, Pa. | D2c-'91 | 0* |
| 81 | | Givins, Ernest | WR | 5-9 | 178 | 9/3/64 | 9 | Louisville | St. Petersburg, Fla. | D2-'86 | 16/16 |
| 82 | | Hannah, Travis | WR | 5-7 | 161 | 1/31/70 | 2 | Southern California | Hawthorne, Calif. | D4-'93 | 12/0 |
| 27 | # | Hoage, Terry | S | 6-2 | 201 | 4/11/62 | 11 | Georgia | Huntsville, Tex. | FA-'93 | 7/0* |
| 72 | | Hopkins, Brad | T | 6-3 | 306 | 9/5/70 | 2 | Illinois | Moline, Ill. | D1-'93 | 16/11 |
| 24 | † | Jackson, Steve | CB | 5-8 | 182 | 4/8/69 | 4 | Purdue | Houston, Tex. | D3a-'91 | 16/12 |
| 84 | # | Jeffires, Haywood | WR | 6-2 | 201 | 12/12/64 | 8 | North Carolina State | Greensboro, N.C. | D1b-'87 | 16/16 |
| 56 | | Kozak, Scott | LB | 6-3 | 222 | 11/28/65 | 6 | Oregon | Colton, Ore. | D2-'89 | 16/0 |
| 57 | | Lathon, Lamar | LB | 6-3 | 252 | 12/23/67 | 5 | Houston | Wharton, Tex. | D1-'90 | 13/1 |
| 29 | † | Lewis, Darryll | CB | 5-9 | 183 | 12/16/68 | 4 | Arizona | La Puente, Calif. | D2b-'91 | 4/4 |
| 58 | # | Marshall, Wilber | LB | 6-1 | 240 | 4/18/62 | 11 | Florida | Titusville, Fla. | T(Wash)-'93 | 10/10 |
| 47 | | Maston, Le'Shai | RB | 6-1 | 215 | 10/7/70 | 2 | Baylor | Dallas, Tex. | FA-'93 | 10/0 |
| 74 | | Matthews, Bruce | C | 6-5 | 298 | 8/8/61 | 12 | Southern California | Arcadia, Calif. | D1-'83 | 16/16 |
| 78 | # | McCants, Keith | DE | 6-3 | 265 | 4/19/68 | 5 | Alabama | Mobile, Ala. | FA-'93 | 13/0 |
| 25 | | McDowell, Bubba | S | 6-1 | 198 | 11/4/66 | 6 | Miami | Merritt Island, Fla. | D3-'89 | 14/14 |
| 48 | | Mills, John Henry | TE | 6-0 | 222 | 10/31/69 | 2 | Wake Forest | Tallahassee, Fla. | D5-'93 | 16/0 |
| 94 | | Montgomery, Glenn | DT | 6-0 | 282 | 3/31/67 | 6 | Houston | Gretna, La. | D5-'89 | 16/11 |
| 63 | # | Munchak, Mike | G | 6-3 | 284 | 3/5/60 | 13 | Penn State | Scranton, Pa. | D1-'82 | 13/12 |
| 64 | | Norgard, Erik | C-G | 6-1 | 282 | 11/4/65 | 5 | Colorado | Arlington, Wash. | FA-'90 | 16/4 |
| 26 | | Orlando, Bo | S | 5-10 | 180 | 4/3/66 | 5 | West Virginia | Berwick, Pa. | FA-'90 | 16/3 |
| 7 | | Richardson, Bucky | QB | 6-1 | 228 | 2/7/69 | 3 | Texas A&M | Baton Rouge, La. | D8-'92 | 2/0 |
| 68 | | Roberts, Tim | DT | 6-6 | 318 | 4/14/69 | 3 | Southern Mississippi | Atlanta, Ga. | D5c-'92 | 6/0 |
| 31 | † | Robertson, Marcus | S | 5-11 | 197 | 10/2/69 | 4 | Iowa State | Pasadena, Calif. | D4b-'91 | 13/13 |
| 50 | | Robinson, Eddie | LB | 6-1 | 245 | 4/13/70 | 3 | Alabama State | New Orleans, La. | D2-'92 | 16/15 |
| 12 | | Salisbury, Sean | QB | 6-5 | 217 | 3/9/63 | 6 | Southern California | Escondido, Calif. | UFA(Minn)-'94 | 11/4* |
| 89 | # | Slaughter, Webster | WR | 6-1 | 175 | 10/19/64 | 9 | San Diego State | Stockton, Calif. | FA-'92 | 14/14 |
| 54 | | Smith, Al | LB | 6-1 | 244 | 11/26/64 | 8 | Utah State | Los Angeles, Calif. | D6a-'87 | 16/16 |
| 71 | | Teeter, Mike | DE | 6-2 | 260 | 10/4/67 | 3 | Michigan | Fruitport, Mich. | FA-'93 | 14/0 |
| 70 | | Thomas, Stan | T | 6-5 | 295 | 10/28/68 | 4 | Texas | San Diego, Calif. | FA-'93 | 14/0 |
| 32 | | Tillman, Spencer | RB | 5-11 | 206 | 4/21/64 | 8 | Oklahoma | Tulsa, Okla. | PB(SF)-'92 | 15/0 |
| 88 | | Wellman, Gary | WR | 5-9 | 173 | 8/9/67 | 3 | Southern California | Westlake Hills, Calif. | D5-'91 | 11/3 |
| 44 | # | White, Lorenzo | RB | 5-11 | 222 | 4/12/66 | 7 | Michigan State | Ft. Lauderdale, Fla. | D1-'88 | 8/8 |
| 73 | | Williams, David | T | 6-5 | 292 | 6/21/66 | 6 | Florida | Lakeland, Fla. | D1-'89 | 15/15 |
| 97 | | Williams, Lee | DT-DE | 6-6 | 275 | 10/15/62 | 11 | Bethune-Cookman | Ft. Lauderdale, Fla. | T(SD)-'91 | 14/5 |

* Camarillo played 16 games with Phoenix in '93; Carter played 11 games with L.A. Rams; Dumas and Flannery missed '93 season due to injury; Hoage played 4 games with San Francisco, 3 games with Houston; Salisbury played 11 games with Minnesota.

# Unrestricted free agent; subject to developments.

† Restricted free agent; subject to developments.

Traded—QB Warren Moon to Minnesota.

Players lost through free agency (3): DE William Fuller (Phil; 16 games in '93), DE Sean Jones (GB; 16), P Greg Montgomery (Det; 15).

Also played with Oilers in '93—S Melvin Aldridge (1 game), DT Jeff Alm (2), WR Willie Drewrey (16), WR Leonard Harris (4), WR Tony Jones (2), CB Emanuel Martin (1), WR Damon Mays (1), QB Warren Moon (15), P Kent Sullivan (1), DE-DT Craig Veasey (1).

## COACHING STAFF

**Head Coach,**
**Jack Pardee**

**Pro Career:** Named the Oilers' fourteenth head coach on January 9, 1990. Houston has qualified for playoffs in each of his four seasons with the Oilers. Accepted post after serving three years (1987-89) as head coach at University of Houston. While at Houston, Cougars set more than 100 NCAA/Southwest Conference records in 1988 and 1989. In 1986, was a scout for the Green Bay Packers. Prior to that, was head coach of successful Houston Gamblers of the USFL from 1984-85 as team led league in total offense and scoring in both seasons. Spent 1982 in private business after serving as defensive coordinator for San Diego Chargers in 1981. That season, Chargers won AFC's Western Division and advanced to AFC Championship Game. From 1978-80, was head coach of the Washington Redskins, earning NFL coach of the year honors in 1979. Was head coach of the Chicago Bears from 1975-77, earning NFC coach of the year accolades in 1976 and leading the club in 1977 to its first playoff berth in 14 years. Was general manager/head coach for Florida Blazers of the World Football League in 1974, winning division title and advancing to WFL title game. Began coaching career as Washington Redskins' assistant in 1973. Drafted by Los Angeles Rams in second round in 1957 and played 15 seasons at linebacker for Rams (1957-64, 1966-70) and Washington Redskins (1971-72). Was an all-pro selection in 1963 and 1971, and is a member of Rams' fortieth anniversary team. Career record: 87-73.
**Background:** Played linebacker and fullback in All-America and Academic All-America career for coach Paul (Bear) Bryant at Texas A&M (1953-56). Is a member of the Texas A&M Hall of Fame, National Football Foundation Hall of Fame, College Football Hall of Fame, Texas Sports Hall of Fame, and Senior Bowl Hall of Fame.
**Personal:** Born April 19, 1936, Exira, Iowa. Jack and his wife, Phyllis, live in Missouri City, Tex., and have two sons, Steven and Ted, and three daughters—Judee, Anne, and Susan.

### ASSISTANT COACHES

**Charlie Baggett,** receivers; born January 21, 1953, Fayetteville, N.C., lives in Houston. Quarterback Michigan State 1972-75. No pro playing experience. College coach: Bowling Green 1977-80, Minnesota 1981-82, Michigan State 1983-92. Pro coach: Joined Oilers in 1993.
**Tom Bettis,** defensive backs; born March 17, 1933, Chicago, Ill., lives in Pearland, Tex. Linebacker-guard Purdue 1952-54. Pro linebacker Green Bay Packers 1955-61, Pittsburgh Steelers 1962, Chicago Bears 1963. Pro coach: Chicago Bears 1964-65 (scout), Kansas City Chiefs 1966-77 (interim head coach 1977), 1988, St. Louis Cardinals 1978-84, Cleveland Browns 1985, Houston Oilers 1986-87, Philadelphia Eagles 1989-90, Los Angeles Rams 1991, rejoined Oilers in 1993.
**Frank Bush,** quality control; born January 10, 1963, Athens, Ga., lives in Houston. Linebacker North Carolina State 1981-84. Pro linebacker Houston Oilers 1985-86. Pro coach: Joined Oilers in 1987 as scout, named assistant coach in 1992.
**Dick Coury,** offensive coordinator; born September 29, 1929, Athens, Ohio, lives in Missouri City, Tex. Quarterback Notre Dame 1950-54. No pro playing experience. College coach: Southern California 1967-69, Cal State-Fullerton 1970-71 (head coach). Pro coach: Denver Broncos 1972-73, Portland Storm (WFL) 1974 (head coach), San Diego Chargers 1975, Philadelphia Eagles 1976-81, Boston/New Orleans/Portland Breakers (USFL) 1983-85 (head coach), Los Angeles Rams 1986-90, New England Patriots 1991-92, Minnesota Vikings 1993, joined Oilers in 1994.
**Jeff Fisher,** defensive coordinator; born February 25, 1958, Culver City, Calif., lives in Sugar Land, Tex. Defensive back Southern California 1977-80. Pro defensive back Chicago Bears 1981-85. Pro coach: Philadelphia Eagles 1986-90, Los Angeles Rams 1991, San Francisco 49ers 1992-93, joined Oilers in 1994.
**Kevin Gilbride,** assistant head coach-offense; born August 27, 1951, New Haven, Conn., lives in Missouri City, Tex. Quarterback-tight end Southern Connecticut State 1970-73. No pro playing experience. College coach: Idaho State 1974-75, Tufts 1976-77, American International 1978-79, Southern Connecticut State 1980-84 (head coach), East Carolina 1987-88. Pro coach: Ottawa Rough Riders (CFL) 1985-86, joined Oilers in 1989.
**Frank Novak,** special teams-running backs; born May 18, 1938, Worcester, Mass., lives in Missouri City, Tex. Quarterback Northern Michigan 1959-61. No pro playing experience. College coach: Northern Michigan 1966-72, East Carolina 1973, Virginia 1974-75, Western Illinois 1976-77, Holy Cross 1978-83, Massachusetts 1986, Missouri 1988. Pro coach: Oklahoma Outlaws (USFL) 1984, Birmingham Stallions (USFL) 1985, joined Oilers in 1989.
**Jim Stanley,** defensive line; born June 22, 1934, Dunham, Ky., lives in Pearland, Tex. Guard-defensive tackle Texas A&M 1954-57. No pro playing experience. College coach: Southern Methodist 1961, Texas-El Paso 1962, Oklahoma State 1963-68, 1972-78 (head coach 1973-78), Navy 1969-70. Pro coach: Winnipeg Blue Bombers (CFL) 1971, New York Giants 1979, Atlanta Falcons 1980-82, Michigan Panthers (USFL) 1983-84 (head coach), Tampa Bay Buccaneers 1986, joined Oilers in 1990.
**Steve Watterson,** strength and rehabilitation; born November 27, 1956, Newport, R.I., lives in Sugar Land, Tex. Attended Rhode Island. No college or pro playing experience. Pro coach: Philadelphia Eagles 1984-85 (assistant trainer), joined Oilers in 1986 (elevated to assistant coach in 1988).
**Gregg Williams,** linebackers; born July 15, 1958, Excelsior Springs, Mo., lives in Katy, Tex. Quarterback Northeast Missouri State 1976-79. No pro playing experience. College coach: Houston 1988-89. Pro coach: Houston Oilers 1990-92 (quality control coordinator), named assistant coach in 1993.
**Bob Young,** offensive line; born September 3, 1942, Marshall, Tex., lives in Missouri City, Tex. Guard Texas 1960-61, Howard Payne 1962-63. Pro guard Denver Broncos 1966-70, Houston Oilers 1971, 1980, St. Louis Cardinals 1972-79, New Orleans Saints 1981. College coach: Houston 1987-89. Pro coach: Houston Gamblers (USFL) 1984-85, joined Oilers in 1990.

## 1994 FIRST-YEAR ROSTER

| Name | Pos. | Ht. | Wt. | Birthdate | College | Hometown | How Acq. |
|---|---|---|---|---|---|---|---|
| Aldridge, Melvin (1) | S | 6-2 | 195 | 7/22/70 | Murray State | Pittsburg, Tex. | FA |
| Davis, Mike | CB | 6-1 | 192 | 1/14/72 | Cincinnati | Springfield, Ohio | D4a |
| Ford, Henry | DE | 6-3 | 284 | 10/30/71 | Arkansas | Ft. Worth, Tex. | D1 |
| Gissendaner, Lee | WR | 5-9 | 175 | 10/25/71 | Northwestern | Stow, Ohio | D6a |
| Hall, Lemanski | LB | 6-0 | 229 | 11/24/70 | Alabama | Valley, Ala. | D7 |
| Jackson, Sean | RB | 6-1 | 222 | 2/6/71 | Florida State | New Orleans, La. | D4b |
| Lewis, Roderick | TE | 6-5 | 254 | 6/9/71 | Arizona | Dallas, Tex. | D5a |
| Nunley, Jeremy | DE | 6-5 | 278 | 9/19/71 | Alabama | Winchester, Tenn. | D2 |
| Reid, Jim | T | 6-6 | 306 | 2/13/71 | Virginia | Newport News, Va. | D5b |
| Seabron, Malcolm | WR | 6-0 | 194 | 12/29/72 | Fresno State | Sacramento, Calif. | D3 |
| Wortham, Barron | LB | 5-11 | 244 | 11/1/69 | Texas-El Paso | Everman, Tex. | D6b |

The term NFL Rookie is defined as a player who is in his first season of professional football and has not been on the roster of another professional football team for any regular-season or postseason games. A Rookie is designated by an "R" on NFL rosters. Players who have been active in another professional football league or players who have NFL experience, including either preseason training camp or being on an Active List or Inactive List, or on Reserve/Injured or Reserve/Physically Unable to Perform for fewer than six regular-season games, are termed NFL First-Year Players. An NFL First-Year Player is designated by a "1" on NFL rosters. Thereafter, a player is credited with an additional year of experience for each season in which he accumulates six games on the Active List or Inactive List, or on Reserve/Injured or Reserve/Physically Unable to Perform.

## NOTES

# INDIANAPOLIS COLTS

**American Football Conference**
**Eastern Division**
**Team Colors:** Royal Blue and White
**P.O. Box 535000**
**Indianapolis, Indiana 46253**
**Telephone: (317) 297-2658**

## CLUB OFFICIALS

President-Treasurer: Robert Irsay
Vice President-General Manager: James Irsay
Vice President-Director of Football Operations: Bill Tobin
Vice President-General Counsel: Michael G. Chernoff
Assistant General Manager: Bob Terpening
Director of Pro Personnel: Clyde Powers
Director of College Player Personnel: George Boone
Controller: Kurt Humphrey
Director of Operations: Pete Ward
Director of Public Relations: Craig Kelley
Ticket Manager: Larry Hall
Director of Sales: Rene Longoria
Assistant Directors of Public Relations: Rod St. Clair, Todd Stewart
Purchasing Administrator: David Filar
Administrative Assistant: Nicole Kucharski
Equipment Manager: Jon Scott
Assistant Equipment Manager: Mike Mays
Video Director: Marty Heckscher
Assistant Video Director: John Starliper
Head Trainer: Hunter Smith
Assistant Trainer: Dave Hammer
Team Physician and Orthopedic Surgeon: K. Donald Shelbourne
Orthopedic Surgeon: Arthur C. Rettig
Physician: Douglas Robertson
**Stadium:** Hoosier Dome • **Capacity:** 60,273
100 South Capitol Avenue
Indianapolis, Indiana 46225
**Playing Surface:** AstroTurf
**Training Camp:** Anderson University
Anderson, Indiana 46011

## 1994 SCHEDULE

### PRESEASON

| | | |
|---|---|---|
| Aug. 5 | **Seattle** | 7:30 |
| Aug. 13 | at Cincinnati | 7:30 |
| Aug. 20 | at Pittsburgh | 6:00 |
| Aug. 25 | **Cleveland** | 7:30 |

### REGULAR SEASON

| | | |
|---|---|---|
| Sept. 4 | **Houston** | 12:00 |
| Sept. 11 | at Tampa Bay | 1:00 |
| Sept. 18 | at Pittsburgh | 1:00 |
| Sept. 25 | **Cleveland** | 12:00 |
| Oct. 2 | **Seattle** | 12:00 |
| Oct. 9 | at New York Jets | 1:00 |
| Oct. 16 | at Buffalo | 1:00 |
| Oct. 23 | **Washington** | 12:00 |
| Oct. 30 | **New York Jets** | 4:00 |
| Nov. 6 | at Miami | 1:00 |
| Nov. 13 | Open Date | |
| Nov. 20 | at Cincinnati | 1:00 |
| Nov. 27 | **New England** | 8:00 |
| Dec. 4 | at Seattle | 1:00 |
| Dec. 11 | at New England | 1:00 |
| Dec. 18 | **Miami** | 1:00 |
| Dec. 24 | **Buffalo** | 1:00 |

## RECORD HOLDERS

### INDIVIDUAL RECORDS—CAREER

| Category | Name | Performance |
|---|---|---|
| Rushing (Yds.) | Lydell Mitchell, 1972-77 | 5,487 |
| Passing (Yds.) | Johnny Unitas, 1956-1972 | 39,768 |
| Passing (TDs) | Johnny Unitas, 1956-1972 | 287 |
| Receiving (No.) | Raymond Berry, 1955-1967 | 631 |
| Receiving (Yds.) | Raymond Berry, 1955-1967 | 9,275 |
| Interceptions | Bob Boyd, 1960-68 | 57 |
| Punting (Avg.) | Rohn Stark, 1982-1993 | 43.9 |
| Punt Return (Avg.) | Wendell Harris, 1964 | 12.6 |
| Kickoff Return (Avg.) | Jim Duncan, 1969-1971 | 32.5 |
| Field Goals | Dean Biasucci 1984, 1986-1993 | 160 |
| Touchdowns (Tot.) | Lenny Moore, 1956-1967 | 113 |
| Points | Dean Biasucci, 1984, 1986-1993 | 698 |

### INDIVIDUAL RECORDS—SINGLE SEASON

| Category | Name | Performance |
|---|---|---|
| Rushing (Yds.) | Eric Dickerson, 1988 | 1,659 |
| Passing (Yds.) | Johnny Unitas, 1963 | 3,481 |
| Passing (TDs) | Johnny Unitas, 1959 | 32 |
| Receiving (No.) | Reggie Langhorne, 1993 | 85 |
| Receiving (Yds.) | Raymond Berry, 1960 | 1,298 |
| Interceptions | Tom Keane, 1953 | 11 |
| Punting (Avg.) | Rohn Stark, 1985 | 45.9 |
| Punt Return (Avg.) | Clarence Verdin, 1989 | 12.9 |
| Kickoff Return (Avg.) | Jim Duncan, 1970 | 35.4 |
| Field Goals | Raul Allegre, 1983 | 30 |
| Touchdowns (Tot.) | Lenny Moore, 1964 | 20 |
| Points | Lenny Moore, 1964 | 120 |

### INDIVIDUAL RECORDS—SINGLE GAME

| Category | Name | Performance |
|---|---|---|
| Rushing (Yds.) | Norm Bulaich, 9-19-71 | 198 |
| Passing (Yds.) | Johnny Unitas, 9-17-67 | 401 |
| Passing (TDs) | Gary Cuozzo, 11-14-65 | 5 |
| | Gary Hogeboom, 10-4-87 | 5 |
| Receiving (No.) | Lydell Mitchell, 12-15-74 | 13 |
| | Joe Washington, 9-2-79 | 13 |
| Receiving (Yds.) | Raymond Berry, 11-10-57 | 224 |
| Interceptions | Many times | 3 |
| | Last time by Mike Prior, 12-20-92 | |
| Field Goals | Many times | 5 |
| | Last time by Dean Biasucci, 9-25-88 | |
| Touchdowns (Tot.) | Many times | 4 |
| | Last time by Eric Dickerson, 10-31-88 | |
| Points | Many times | 24 |
| | Last time by Eric Dickerson, 10-31-88 | |

## COACHING HISTORY

### BALTIMORE 1953-1983
**(289-302-7)**

| | | |
|---|---|---|
| 1953 | Keith Molesworth | 3-9-0 |
| 1954-62 | Weeb Ewbank | 61-52-1 |
| 1963-69 | Don Shula | 73-26-4 |
| 1970-72 | Don McCafferty* | 26-11-1 |
| 1972 | John Sandusky | 4-5-0 |
| 1973-74 | Howard Schnellenberger** | 4-13-0 |
| 1974 | Joe Thomas | 2-9-0 |
| 1975-79 | Ted Marchibroda | 41-36-0 |
| 1980-81 | Mike McCormack | 9-23-0 |
| 1982-84 | Frank Kush*** | 11-28-1 |
| 1984 | Hal Hunter | 0-1-0 |
| 1985-86 | Rod Dowhower**** | 5-24-0 |
| 1986-91 | Ron Meyer# | 36-36-0 |
| 1991 | Rick Venturi | 1-10-0 |
| 1992-93 | Ted Marchibroda | 13-19-0 |

*Released after five games in 1972
**Released after three games in 1974
***Resigned after 15 games in 1984
****Released after 13 games in 1986
#Released after five games in 1991

### HOOSIER DOME

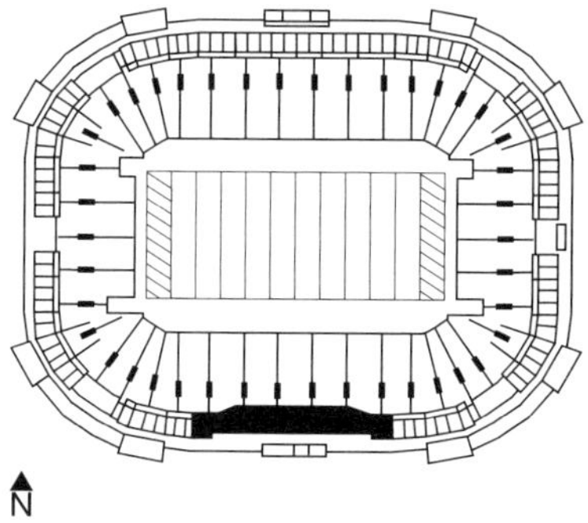

## 1993 TEAM RECORD

**PRESEASON (2-2)**

| Date | Result | | Opponents |
|---|---|---|---|
| 8/7 | W | 16-13 | at Seattle |
| 8/14 | L | 7-24 | Cincinnati |
| 8/20 | W | 18-7 | L.A. Raiders |
| 8/27 | L | 10-41 | at Green Bay |

**REGULAR SEASON (4-12)**

| Date | Result | | Opponents | Att. |
|---|---|---|---|---|
| 9/5 | L | 20-24 | Miami | 51,858 |
| 9/12 | W | 9-6 | at Cincinnati | 50,299 |
| 9/26 | W | 23-10 | Cleveland | 59,654 |
| 10/3 | L | 13-35 | at Denver | 74,953 |
| 10/10 | L | 3-27 | Dallas | 60,453 |
| 10/24 | L | 27-41 | at Miami | 57,301 |
| 10/31 | W | 9-6 | New England | 46,522 |
| 11/7 | L | 24-30 | at Washington | 50,523 |
| 11/14 | L | 17-31 | N.Y. Jets | 47,351 |
| 11/21 | L | 9-23 | at Buffalo | 79,101 |
| 11/29 | L | 0-31 | San Diego | 54,110 |
| 12/5 | W | 9-6 | at N.Y. Jets | 45,799 |
| 12/12 | L | 6-20 | at N.Y. Giants | 70,411 |
| 12/19 | L | 10-20 | Philadelphia | 44,952 |
| 12/26 | L | 0-38 | at New England | 26,571 |
| 1/2 | L | 10-30 | Buffalo | 43,028 |

**SCORE BY PERIODS**

| | | | | | | | |
|---|---|---|---|---|---|---|---|
| Colts | 19 | 60 | 29 | 81 | 0 | — | 189 |
| Opponents | 96 | 96 | 98 | 88 | 0 | — | 378 |

**ATTENDANCE**

Home 407,928 Away 454,958 Total 862,886
Single-game home record, 61,479 (11-13-83)
Single-season home record, 481,305 (1984)

## 1993 TEAM STATISTICS

| | Colts | Opp. |
|---|---|---|
| Total First Downs | 269 | 334 |
| Rushing | 71 | 151 |
| Passing | 180 | 166 |
| Penalty | 18 | 17 |
| Third Down: Made/Att | 61/209 | 85/206 |
| Third Down Pct. | 29.2 | 41.3 |
| Fourth Down: Made/Att | 9/22 | 8/12 |
| Fourth Down Pct. | 40.9 | 66.7 |
| Total Net Yards | 4705 | 5638 |
| Avg. Per Game | 294.1 | 352.4 |
| Total Plays | 988 | 1050 |
| Avg. Per Play | 4.8 | 5.4 |
| Net Yards Rushing | 1288 | 2521 |
| Avg. Per Game | 80.5 | 157.6 |
| Total Rushes | 365 | 575 |
| Net Yards Passing | 3417 | 3117 |
| Avg. Per Game | 213.6 | 194.8 |
| Sacked/Yards Lost | 29/206 | 21/121 |
| Gross Yards | 3623 | 3238 |
| Att./Completions | 594/332 | 454/270 |
| Completion Pct. | 55.9 | 59.5 |
| Had Intercepted | 15 | 10 |
| Punts/Avg. | 83/43.3 | 71/40.2 |
| Net Punting Avg. | 83/35.9 | 71/36.1 |
| Penalties/Yards Lost | 94/685 | 87/610 |
| Fumbles/Ball Lost | 34/20 | 25/11 |
| Touchdowns | 16 | 45 |
| Rushing | 4 | 20 |
| Passing | 10 | 22 |
| Returns | 2 | 3 |
| Avg. Time of Possession | 27:55 | 32:05 |

## 1993 INDIVIDUAL STATISTICS

| PASSING | Att. | Cmp. | Yds. | Pct. | TD | Int. | Tkld. | Rate |
|---|---|---|---|---|---|---|---|---|
| George | 407 | 234 | 2526 | 57.5 | 8 | 6 | 26/190 | 76.3 |
| Trudeau | 162 | 85 | 992 | 52.5 | 2 | 7 | 2/11 | 57.4 |
| Majkowski | 24 | 13 | 105 | 54.2 | 0 | 1 | 1/5 | 48.1 |
| Johnson | 1 | 0 | 0 | 0.0 | 0 | 1 | 0/0 | 0.0 |
| Colts | 594 | 332 | 3623 | 55.9 | 10 | 15 | 29/206 | 69.2 |
| Opponents | 454 | 270 | 3238 | 59.5 | 22 | 10 | 21/121 | 88.3 |

| SCORING | TD R | TD P | TD Rt | PAT | FG | Saf | PTS |
|---|---|---|---|---|---|---|---|
| Biasucci | 0 | 0 | 0 | 15/16 | 26/31 | 0 | 93 |
| Culver | 3 | 1 | 1 | 0/0 | 0/0 | 0 | 30 |
| Cash | 0 | 3 | 0 | 0/0 | 0/0 | 0 | 18 |
| Langhorne | 0 | 3 | 0 | 0/0 | 0/0 | 0 | 18 |
| Dawkins | 0 | 1 | 0 | 0/0 | 0/0 | 0 | 6 |
| Herrod | 0 | 0 | 1 | 0/0 | 0/0 | 0 | 6 |
| Hester | 0 | 1 | 0 | 0/0 | 0/0 | 0 | 6 |
| Johnson | 1 | 0 | 0 | 0/0 | 0/0 | 0 | 6 |
| Verdin | 0 | 1 | 0 | 0/0 | 0/0 | 0 | 6 |
| Colts | 4 | 10 | 2 | 15/16 | 26/31 | 0 | 189 |
| Opponents | 20 | 22 | 3 | 43/45 | 21/30 | 1 | 378 |

| RUSHING | Att. | Yds. | Avg. | LG | TD |
|---|---|---|---|---|---|
| Potts | 179 | 711 | 4.0 | 34 | 0 |
| Johnson | 95 | 331 | 3.5 | 14 | 1 |
| Culver | 65 | 150 | 2.3 | 9 | 3 |
| George | 13 | 39 | 3.0 | 14 | 0 |
| Verdin | 3 | 33 | 11.0 | 29 | 0 |
| Stark | 1 | 11 | 11.0 | 11 | 0 |
| Toner | 2 | 6 | 3.0 | 6 | 0 |
| Majkowski | 2 | 4 | 2.0 | 4 | 0 |
| Trudeau | 5 | 3 | 0.6 | 2 | 0 |
| Colts | 365 | 1288 | 3.5 | 34 | 4 |
| Opponents | 575 | 2521 | 4.4 | 57t | 20 |

| RECEIVING | No. | Yds. | Avg. | LG | TD |
|---|---|---|---|---|---|
| Langhorne | 85 | 1038 | 12.2 | 72t | 3 |
| Hester | 64 | 835 | 13.0 | 58 | 1 |
| Johnson | 55 | 443 | 8.1 | 36 | 0 |
| Cash | 43 | 402 | 9.3 | 37 | 3 |
| Dawkins | 26 | 430 | 16.5 | 68 | 1 |
| Potts | 26 | 189 | 7.3 | 24 | 0 |
| Arbuckle | 15 | 90 | 6.0 | 23 | 0 |
| Culver | 11 | 112 | 10.2 | 26 | 1 |
| Cox | 4 | 59 | 14.8 | 24 | 0 |
| Verdin | 2 | 20 | 10.0 | 19 | 1 |
| Toner | 1 | 5 | 5.0 | 5 | 0 |
| Colts | 332 | 3623 | 10.9 | 72t | 10 |
| Opponents | 270 | 3238 | 12.0 | 77 | 22 |

| INTERCEPTIONS | No. | Yds. | Avg. | LG | TD |
|---|---|---|---|---|---|
| Buchanan | 4 | 45 | 11.3 | 28 | 0 |
| Baylor | 3 | 11 | 3.7 | 7 | 0 |
| Herrod | 1 | 29 | 29.0 | 29 | 0 |
| Daniel | 1 | 17 | 17.0 | 17 | 0 |
| Belser | 1 | 14 | 14.0 | 11 | 0 |
| Colts | 10 | 116 | 11.6 | 29 | 0 |
| Opponents | 15 | 247 | 16.5 | 56t | 1 |

| PUNTING | No. | Yds. | Avg. | In 20 | LG |
|---|---|---|---|---|---|
| Stark | 83 | 3595 | 43.3 | 18 | 65 |
| Colts | 83 | 3595 | 43.3 | 18 | 65 |
| Opponents | 71 | 2855 | 40.2 | 30 | 59 |

| PUNT RETURNS | No. | FC | Yds. | Avg. | LG | TD |
|---|---|---|---|---|---|---|
| Verdin | 30 | 17 | 173 | 5.8 | 24 | 0 |
| Colts | 30 | 17 | 173 | 5.8 | 24 | 0 |
| Opponents | 41 | 12 | 352 | 8.6 | 71t | 1 |

| KICKOFF RETURNS | No. | Yds. | Avg. | LG | TD |
|---|---|---|---|---|---|
| Verdin | 50 | 1050 | 21.0 | 38 | 0 |
| Culver | 3 | 51 | 17.0 | 20 | 0 |
| Butcher | 2 | 2 | 1.0 | 2 | 0 |
| Cash | 1 | 11 | 11.0 | 11 | 0 |
| Radecic | 1 | 10 | 10.0 | 10 | 0 |
| Colts | 57 | 1124 | 19.7 | 38 | 0 |
| Opponents | 37 | 551 | 14.9 | 37 | 0 |

| SACKS | No. |
|---|---|
| Hand | 5.5 |
| Bickett | 3.5 |
| Herrod | 2.0 |
| Peguese | 2.0 |
| McClendon | 1.5 |
| Siragusa | 1.5 |
| Clancy | 1.0 |
| Coryatt | 1.0 |
| Emtman | 1.0 |
| Sims | 1.0 |
| Stargell | 1.0 |
| Colts | 21.0 |
| Opponents | 29.0 |

## 1994 DRAFT CHOICES

| Round | Name | Pos. | College |
|---|---|---|---|
| 1 | Marshall Faulk | RB | San Diego State |
| | Trev Alberts | LB | Nebraska |
| 2 | Eric Mahlum | G | California |
| 3 | Jason Mathews | T | Texas A&M |
| 4 | Brad Banta | TE | Southern California |
| 5 | John Covington | DB | Notre Dame |
| 6 | Lamont Warren | RB | Colorado |
| 7 | Lance Teichelman | DT | Texas A&M |

## INDIANAPOLIS COLTS

### 1994 VETERAN ROSTER

| No. | | Name | Pos. | Ht. | Wt. | Birthdate | NFL Exp. | College | Hometown | How Acq. | '93 Games/ Starts |
|---|---|---|---|---|---|---|---|---|---|---|---|
| 33 | | Ambrose, Ashley | CB-S | 5-10 | 177 | 9/17/70 | 3 | Mississippi Valley State | New Orleans, La. | D2-'92 | 14/6 |
| 81 | | Arbuckle, Charles | TE | 6-3 | 248 | 9/13/68 | 4 | UCLA | Beaumont, Tex. | FA-'92 | 16/2 |
| 86 | | Baker, Shannon | WR | 5-9 | 185 | 7/20/71 | 2 | Florida State | Lakeland, Fla. | FA-'93 | 0* |
| 36 | # | Baylor, John | CB-S | 6-0 | 208 | 3/5/65 | 7 | Southern Mississippi | Meridian, Miss. | D5-'88 | 16/11 |
| 29 | | Belser, Jason | CB-S | 5-9 | 187 | 5/28/70 | 3 | Oklahoma | Kansas City, Mo. | D8a-'92 | 16/16 |
| 56 | | Bennett, Tony | LB | 6-2 | 243 | 7/1/67 | 5 | Mississippi | Clarksdale, Miss. | UFA(GB)-'94 | 10/7* |
| 4 | | Biasucci, Dean | K | 6-0 | 190 | 7/25/62 | 10 | Western Carolina | Niagara Falls, N.Y. | FA-'86 | 16/0 |
| 99 | | Brandon, Michael | DE | 6-4 | 290 | 7/30/68 | 2 | Florida | Berry, Fla. | FA-'93 | 15/0 |
| 34 | | Buchanan, Ray | CB-S | 5-9 | 193 | 9/29/71 | 2 | Louisville | Chicago, Ill. | D3-'93 | 16/5 |
| 53 | # | Butcher, Paul | LB | 6-0 | 230 | 11/8/63 | 8 | Wayne State | Dearborn, Mich. | FA-'93 | 16/0 |
| 71 | | Call, Kevin | T | 6-7 | 308 | 11/13/61 | 11 | Colorado State | Boulder, Colo. | D5b-'84 | 10/0 |
| 88 | † | Cash, Kerry | TE | 6-4 | 252 | 8/7/69 | 4 | Texas | San Antonio, Tex. | D5-'91 | 16/14 |
| 55 | | Coryatt, Quentin | LB | 6-3 | 250 | 8/1/70 | 3 | Texas A&M | St. Croix, Virgin Islands | D1b-'92 | 16/16 |
| 80 | | Cox, Aaron | WR | 5-10 | 178 | 3/13/65 | 7 | Arizona State | Los Angeles, Calif. | UFA(Rams)-'92 | 11/0 |
| 35 | | Culver, Rodney | RB | 5-9 | 224 | 12/23/69 | 3 | Notre Dame | Detroit, Mich. | D4a-'92 | 16/1 |
| 38 | | Daniel, Eugene | CB-S | 5-11 | 188 | 5/4/61 | 11 | Louisiana State | Baton Rouge, La. | D8-'84 | 16/16 |
| 87 | | Dawkins, Sean | WR | 6-4 | 213 | 2/3/71 | 2 | California | Red Bank, N.J. | D1-'93 | 16/7 |
| 69 | | Dixon, Randy | G | 6-3 | 305 | 3/12/65 | 8 | Pittsburgh | Clewiston, Fla. | D4-'87 | 15/15 |
| 90 | | Emtman, Steve | DT | 6-4 | 300 | 4/16/70 | 3 | Washington | Spokane, Wash. | D1a-'92 | 5/5 |
| 48 | | Etheredge, Carlos | TE | 6-5 | 236 | 8/10/70 | 2 | Miami | Albuquerque, N.M. | D6-'93 | 0* |
| 37 | # | Goode, Chris | CB-S | 6-0 | 199 | 9/17/63 | 8 | Alabama | Town Creek, Ala. | D10-'87 | 14/10 |
| 59 | | Grant, Stephen | LB | 6-0 | 231 | 12/23/69 | 3 | West Virginia | Miami, Fla. | D10-'92 | 16/0 |
| 75 | | Gray, Cecil | T | 6-4 | 292 | 2/16/68 | 5 | North Carolina | Norfolk, Va. | FA-'93 | 6/2 |
| 30 | | Gray, Derwin | CB-S | 5-10 | 190 | 4/9/71 | 2 | Brigham Young | San Antonio, Tex. | D4a-'93 | 11/0 |
| 78 | | Hand, Jon | DE | 6-7 | 301 | 11/13/63 | 9 | Alabama | Sylacauga, Ala. | D1-'86 | 15/14 |
| 12 | | Harbaugh, Jim | QB | 6-3 | 215 | 12/23/63 | 8 | Michigan | Ann Arbor, Mich. | FA-'94 | 15/15 |
| 54 | | Herrod, Jeff | LB | 6-0 | 249 | 7/29/66 | 7 | Mississippi | Birmingham, Ala. | D9-'88 | 14/14 |
| 25 | | Humphrey, Ronald | RB | 5-10 | 201 | 3/3/69 | 2 | Mississippi Valley State | Marland, Tex. | FA-'93 | 0* |
| 23 | # | Johnson, Anthony | RB | 6-0 | 222 | 10/25/67 | 5 | Notre Dame | Indianapolis, Ind. | D2-'90 | 13/8 |
| 63 | | Lowdermilk, Kirk | C | 6-4 | 280 | 4/10/63 | 10 | Ohio State | Canton, Ohio | UFA(Minn)-'93 | 16/16 |
| 7 | | Majkowski, Don | QB | 6-3 | 203 | 2/25/64 | 8 | Virginia | Depew, N.Y. | FA-'93 | 3/0 |
| 61 | | McCoy, Tony | NT | 6-0 | 279 | 6/10/69 | 3 | Florida | Orlando, Fla. | D4b-'92 | 6/0 |
| 57 | | McDonald, Devon | LB | 6-4 | 240 | 11/8/69 | 2 | Notre Dame | Kingston, Jamaica | D4b-'93 | 16/0 |
| 73 | | Moss, Zefross | T | 6-6 | 338 | 8/17/66 | 6 | Alabama State | Tuscaloosa, Ala. | T(Dall)-'89 | 16/16 |
| 32 | | O'Neal, Robert | CB-S | 6-1 | 194 | 1/2/71 | 2 | Clemson | Atlanta, Ga. | FA-'93 | 0* |
| 96 | # | Peguese, Willis | DE | 6-4 | 273 | 12/18/66 | 5 | Miami | Miami, Fla. | FA-'93 | 13/4 |
| 42 | | Potts, Roosevelt | RB | 6-0 | 258 | 1/8/71 | 2 | Northeast Louisiana | Rayville, La. | D2-'93 | 16/15 |
| 52 | | Ratigan, Brian | LB | 6-4 | 226 | 12/27/70 | 2 | Notre Dame | Council Bluffs, Iowa | FA-'93 | 0* |
| 74 | | Schultz, William | T | 6-5 | 305 | 5/1/67 | 5 | Southern California | Granada Hills, Calif. | D4b-'90 | 14/14 |
| 92 | | Sims, Thomas | NT | 6-2 | 291 | 4/18/67 | 5 | Pittsburgh | Detroit, Mich. | FA-'93 | 5/3 |
| 98 | | Siragusa, Tony | NT | 6-3 | 303 | 5/14/67 | 5 | Pittsburgh | Kenilworth, N.J. | FA-'90 | 14/14 |
| 3 | | Stark, Rohn | P | 6-3 | 203 | 5/4/59 | 13 | Florida State | Minneapolis, Minn. | D2b-'82 | 16/0 |
| 79 | † | Staysniak, Joe | T | 6-4 | 296 | 12/8/66 | 4 | Ohio State | Elyria, Ohio | FA-'92 | 14/1 |
| 94 | | Thomas, Marquise | LB | 6-4 | 255 | 5/25/71 | 2 | Mississippi | Fresno, Calif. | D8-'93 | 0* |
| 28 | | Toner, Ed | RB | 6-0 | 240 | 3/22/68 | 3 | Boston College | Lynn, Mass. | FA-'92 | 16/1 |
| 85 | | Turner, Floyd | WR | 5-11 | 198 | 5/29/66 | 6 | Northwestern Louisiana | Mansfield, La. | UFA(NO)-'94 | 10/2* |
| 72 | | Vander Poel, Mark | T | 6-7 | 303 | 3/5/68 | 3 | Colorado | Upland, Calif. | D4-'91 | 0* |
| 67 | | Wolford, Will | T | 6-5 | 300 | 5/18/64 | 9 | Vanderbilt | Louisville, Ky. | RFA(Buff)-'93 | 12/12 |

* Baker active for 14 games but did not play; Bennett played 10 games with Green Bay in '93; Etheredge, Humphrey, Radigan, and Vander Poel missed '93 season due to injury; O'Neal active for 10 games but did not play; Thomas active for 1 game but did not play; Turner played 10 games with New Orleans.

\# Unrestricted free agent; subject to developments.

† Restricted free agent; subject to developments.

Traded—QB Jeff George to Atlanta.

Players lost through free agency (2): C Trevor Matich (Wash; 16 games in '93); CB Tony Stargell (TB; 16).

Also played with Colts in '93—CB-S Michael Ball (5 games), LB Duane Bickett (15), DE Sam Clancy (16), QB Jeff George (13), WR Jessie Hester (16), WR Reggie Langhorne (16), DE-DT Skip McClendon (16), WR Eddie Miller (1), LB Scott Radecic (16), QB Jack Trudeau (5), WR Clarence Verdin (16), RB Warren Williams (5).

## COACHING STAFF

**Head Coach,**
**Ted Marchibroda**

**Pro Career:** Marchibroda ranks as the third-winningest head coach in Colts history with a 54-55 record. He returned to the Colts on January 28, 1992, after serving as head coach with the team from 1975-79. Marchibroda's first tenure produced a 41-36 overall record and three AFC Eastern Divisional titles (1975, 10-4; 1976, 11-3; and 1977, 10-4). He took over a Colts team that was 2-12 in 1974 and produced an eight-game improvement, then the best one-season turnaround in NFL history. It marked the first time a coach had taken a team from last to first place in one season. Marchibroda authored a 9-7 record two years ago, thus his 1975 and 1992 Colts squads posted two of the four eight-game seasonal turnarounds in NFL history. The Colts were 4-12 in 1993. His three divisional championships represent the most titles won by a Colts head coach. Prior to returning to the Colts, Marchibroda served five years as an assistant with the Buffalo Bills, the last three as offensive coordinator. Marchibroda began his career as backfield coach with the Washington Redskins in 1961. He joined George Allen's staff with the Los Angeles Rams in 1966. He moved with Allen to the Redskins in 1971, where he served as offensive coordinator through the 1974 season. After his stint with the Colts, Marchibroda served as quarterback coach with Chicago in 1981, then moved on to Detroit as offensive coordinator from 1982-83. He served that same role in Philadelphia from 1984-85 before joining Buffalo in 1987. Marchibroda was the first draft pick of the Pittsburgh Steelers in 1953 and played one year before serving in the Army. He returned to Pittsburgh for the 1955-56 seasons. His top year was 1956, completing 124 of 275 passes for 1,585 yards and 12 touchdowns. Marchibroda's playing career ended with the Chicago Cardinals in 1957. Career record: 54-55.

**Background:** Quarterback at St. Bonaventure 1950-51 and University of Detroit 1952. Led nation in total offense at Detroit. He was a football, basketball (all-state selection), and baseball player at Franklin (Pa.) High School.

**Personal:** Born March 15, 1931, Franklin, Pa. Ted and his wife, Ann, reside in Indianapolis. They have two daughters, Jodi and Lonni, and two sons, Ted Jr. and Robert.

### ASSISTANT COACHES

**Tom Batta,** special teams; born October 6, 1942, Youngstown, Ohio, lives in Indianapolis. Offensive-defensive line Kent State 1961-63. No pro playing experience. College coach: Akron 1973, Colorado 1974-78, Kansas 1979-82, North Carolina State 1983. Pro coach: Minnesota Vikings 1984-93, joined Colts in 1994.

**Greg Blache,** defensive line; born March 9, 1949, New Orleans, La., lives in Indianapolis. No college or pro playing experience. College coach: Notre Dame 1973-75, 1981-83, Tulane 1976-80, Southern University 1986, Kansas 1987. Pro coach: Jacksonville Bulls (USFL) 1984-85, Green Bay Packers 1988-93, joined Colts in 1994.

**Ron Blackledge,** offensive line; born April 15, 1938, Canton, Ohio, lives in Indianapolis. Tight end-defensive end Bowling Green 1957-59. No pro playing experience. College coach: Ashland 1968-69, Cincinnati 1970-72, Kentucky 1973-75, Princeton 1976, Kent State 1977-81 (head coach 1979-81). Pro coach: Pittsburgh Steelers 1982-91, joined Colts in 1992.

**Fred Bruney,** defensive assistant; born December 30, 1931, Martins Ferry, Ohio, lives in Indianapolis. Running back-defensive back Ohio State 1950-52. Pro defensive back San Francisco 49ers 1953-56, Pittsburgh Steelers 1957, Los Angeles Rams 1958, Boston Patriots 1960-62. College coach: Ohio State 1959. Pro coach: Boston Patriots 1962-63, Philadelphia Eagles 1964-68, 1977-85, Atlanta Falcons 1969-76, 1986-89, Tampa Bay Buccaneers 1990, New York Giants 1991-92, joined Colts in 1993.

## 1994 FIRST-YEAR ROSTER

| Name | Pos. | Ht. | Wt. | Birthdate | College | Hometown | How Acq. |
|---|---|---|---|---|---|---|---|
| Alberts, Trev | LB | 6-4 | 243 | 8/8/70 | Nebraska | Cedar Falls, Iowa | D1b |
| Allen, Russell | DE | 6-6 | 296 | 4/8/71 | Oklahoma | Oklahoma City, Okla. | FA |
| Bailey, Aaron | WR | 5-10 | 184 | 10/24/71 | Louisville | Ann Arbor, Mich. | FA |
| Banta, Brad | TE | 6-6 | 254 | 12/14/70 | Southern California | Baton Rouge, La. | D4 |
| Borrelli, Marc | T | 6-5 | 286 | 4/30/71 | Boston College | Philadelphia, Pa. | FA |
| Campbell, Darnell | RB | 6-1 | 224 | 4/2/70 | Boston College | Brockton, Mass. | FA |
| Cook, Mike (1) | WR | 6-4 | 205 | 3/20/71 | Stanford | Fountain Valley, Calif. | FA |
| Courtney, Marvin | RB | 6-0 | 204 | 1/15/71 | Mississippi | Greenville, Miss. | FA |
| Covington, John | CB-S | 6-0 | 198 | 4/22/72 | Notre Dame | Winter Haven, Fla. | D5 |
| Ericson, Todd | CB-S | 6-3 | 205 | 6/28/71 | Montana | Butte, Mont. | FA |
| Faulk, Marshall | RB | 5-10 | 200 | 2/26/73 | San Diego State | New Orleans, La. | D1a |
| Houston, William | RB | 6-1 | 260 | 3/18/71 | Ohio State | Trotwood, Ohio | FA |
| Jordan, Todd | QB-P | 6-2 | 231 | 6/18/70 | Mississippi State | Tupelo, Miss. | FA |
| Justin, Paul (1) | QB | 6-4 | 202 | 5/19/68 | Arizona State | Schaumberg, Ill. | FA |
| Mahlum, Eric | G | 6-4 | 285 | 12/6/70 | California | San Diego, Calif. | D2 |
| Mathews, Jason | T | 6-5 | 284 | 2/9/71 | Texas A&M | Orange, Tex. | D3 |
| McEntyre, Kenny | CB-S | 5-9 | 181 | 12/7/70 | Kansas State | Dallas, Tex. | FA |
| Orton, Jason | CB-S | 5-11 | 175 | 4/25/71 | Indiana | Terre Haute, Ind. | FA |
| Pointer, Deron | WR | 5-11 | 175 | 9/9/71 | Washington State | Tacoma, Wash. | FA |
| Ray, John (1) | T | 6-8 | 350 | 4/26/69 | West Virginia | South Charleston, W.Va. | FA |
| Simon, Jose | DT | 6-3 | 291 | 6/24/72 | Texas A&I | Middletown, Calif. | FA |
| Smith, Terry | WR | 6-0 | 200 | 4/20/71 | Clemson | Clemson, S.C. | FA |
| Stablein, Brian (1) | WR | 6-1 | 185 | 4/14/70 | Ohio State | Erie, Pa. | FA |
| Starks, Glenn | RB | 6-1 | 205 | 2/14/72 | Central Oklahoma St. | Covington, Tenn. | FA |
| Teichelman, Lance | DE-DT | 6-4 | 274 | 10/21/70 | Texas A&M | San Antonio, Tex. | D7 |
| Vickers, Kipp (1) | G-T | 6-2 | 275 | 8/27/69 | Miami | Holiday, Fla. | FA |
| Ware, Cassius | LB | 5-11 | 243 | 6/8/71 | Mississippi | Batesville, Miss. | FA |
| Warren, Lamont | RB | 5-11 | 194 | 1/4/73 | Colorado | Indianapolis, Ind. | D6 |
| Whittington, Bernard | DE | 6-6 | 257 | 7/20/71 | Indiana | St. Louis, Mo. | FA |

The term NFL Rookie is defined as a player who is in his first season of professional football and has not been on the roster of another professional football team for any regular-season or postseason games. A Rookie is designated by an "R" on NFL rosters. Players who have been active in another professional football league or players who have NFL experience, including either preseason training camp or being on an Active List or Inactive List, or on Reserve/Injured or Reserve/Physically Unable to Perform for fewer than six regular-season games, are termed NFL First-Year Players. An NFL First-Year Player is designated by a "1" on NFL rosters. Thereafter, a player is credited with an additional year of experience for each season in which he accumulates six games on the Active List or Inactive List, or on Reserve/Injured or Reserve/Physically Unable to Perform.

## NOTES

**Gene Huey,** running backs; born July 20, 1947, Uniontown, Pa., lives in Indianapolis. Defensive back-wide receiver Wyoming 1966-69. No pro playing experience. College coach: Wyoming 1970-74, New Mexico 1975-77, Nebraska 1978-87, Ohio State 1988-91. Pro coach: Joined Colts in 1992.

**Jim Johnson,** linebackers; born May 26, 1941, Maywood, Ill., lives in Indianapolis. Quarterback Missouri 1959-62. Pro tight end Buffalo Bills 1963-64. College coach: Missouri Southern 1967-68 (head coach), Drake 1969-72, Indiana 1973-76, Notre Dame 1977-80. Pro coach: Oklahoma Outlaws (USFL) 1984, Jacksonville Bulls (USFL) 1985, Phoenix Cardinals 1986-93, joined Colts in 1994.

**Hank Kuhlman,** tight ends; born October 6, 1937, Webster Groves, Mo., lives in Indianapolis. Running back Missouri 1956-59. No pro playing experience. College coach: Missouri 1962-71, Notre Dame 1975-77. Pro coach: Green Bay Packers 1972-74, Chicago Bears 1978-82, Birmingham Stallions (USFL) 1983-85, Phoenix Cardinals 1986-90 (scout, 1990), Tampa Bay Buccaneers 1991, joined Colts in 1994.

**Nick Nicolau,** offensive coordinator; born May 5, 1933, New York, N.Y., lives in Indianapolis. Running back Southern Connecticut 1957-59. No pro playing experience. College coach: Southern Connecticut 1960, Springfield 1961, Bridgeport 1962-69 (head coach 1965-69), Massachusetts 1970, Connecticut 1971-72, Kentucky 1973-75, Kent State 1976. Pro coach: Hamilton Tiger-Cats (CFL) 1977, Montreal Alouettes (CFL) 1978-79, New Orleans Saints 1980, Denver Broncos 1981-87, Los Angeles Raiders 1988, Buffalo Bills 1989-91, joined Colts in 1992.

**Jimmy Robinson,** wide receivers; born January 3, 1953, Atlanta, Ga., lives in Indianapolis. Wide receiver Georgia Tech 1972-74. Pro wide receiver Atlanta Falcons 1975, New York Giants 1976-79, San Francisco 49ers 1980, Denver Broncos 1981. College coach: Georgia Tech 1986-89. Pro coach: Memphis Showboats (USFL) 1984-85, Atlanta Falcons 1990-93, joined Colts in 1994.

**Pat Thomas,** secondary; born September 1, 1954, Plano, Tex., lives in Indianapolis. Cornerback Texas A&M 1972-75. Pro cornerback Los Angeles Rams 1976-82. College coach: Houston 1987-89. Pro coach Houston Gamblers (USFL) 1984-85, Houston Oilers 1990-92, joined Colts in 1994.

**Vince Tobin,** defensive coordinator; born September 29, 1943, Burlington Junction, Mo., lives in Indianapolis. Defensive back-running back Missouri 1961-64. No pro playing experience. College coach: Missouri 1967-76. Pro coach: British Columbia Lions (CFL) 1977-82, Philadelphia/Baltimore Stars (USFL) 1983-85, Chicago Bears 1986-92, joined Colts in 1994.

**Tom Zupancic,** strength and conditioning; born September 14, 1955, Indianapolis, lives in Indianapolis. Defensive tackle-offensive tackle Indiana Central 1975-78. No pro playing experience. Pro coach: Joined Colts in 1984.

# KANSAS CITY CHIEFS

**American Football Conference**
**Western Division**
**Team Colors:** Red, Gold, and White
**One Arrowhead Drive**
**Kansas City, Missouri 64129**
**Telephone: (816) 924-9300**

## CLUB OFFICIALS

Founder: Lamar Hunt
Chairman of the Board: Jack Steadman
President/General Manager and Chief Operating Officer: Carl Peterson
Executive Vice President: Tim Connolly
Vice President/Player Personnel: Lynn Stiles
Assistant General Manager: Dennis Thum
Secretary: Jim Seigfreid
Director of Finance/Treasurer: Dale Young
Director of Public Relations: Bob Moore
Director of Operations: Jeff Klein
Director of Marketing & Sales: Dennis Watley
Director of Development: Ken Blume
Assistant Director of Public Relations: Jim Carr
Director of Promotions: Phil Thomas
Community Relations Manager: Brenda Sniezek
Ticket Manager: Dave Hopkins
Equipment Manager: Mike Davidson
Asst. Equipment Managers: Allen Wright, Darin Kerns
Trainer: Dave Kendall
Assistant Trainer: Bud Epps
Video Coordinator: Mike Dennis
Assistant Video Coordinator: Mike Kirk
**Stadium:** Arrowhead Stadium • **Capacity:** 78,067
One Arrowhead Drive
Kansas City, Missouri 64129
**Playing Surface:** Grass
**Training Camp:** University of Wisconsin-River Falls
River Falls, Wisconsin 54022

## 1994 SCHEDULE

**PRESEASON**

| | | |
|---|---|---|
| July 31 | **Houston** | 8:00 |
| Aug. 6 | vs. Minnesota at Tokyo | 10:00 |
| Aug. 12 | at Washington | 8:00 |
| Aug. 22 | **Chicago** | 7:00 |
| Aug. 26 | at Buffalo | 8:00 |

**REGULAR SEASON**

| | | |
|---|---|---|
| Sept. 4 | at New Orleans | 12:00 |
| Sept. 11 | **San Francisco** | 12:00 |
| Sept. 18 | at Atlanta | 8:00 |
| Sept. 25 | **Los Angeles Rams** | 12:00 |
| Oct. 2 | Open Date | |
| Oct. 9 | at San Diego | 1:00 |
| Oct. 17 | at Denver (Monday) | 7:00 |
| Oct. 23 | **Seattle** | 12:00 |
| Oct. 30 | at Buffalo | 1:00 |
| Nov. 6 | **Los Angeles Raiders** | 7:00 |
| Nov. 13 | **San Diego** | 12:00 |
| Nov. 20 | **Cleveland** | 12:00 |
| Nov. 27 | at Seattle | 1:00 |
| Dec. 4 | **Denver** | 3:00 |
| Dec. 12 | at Miami (Monday) | 9:00 |
| Dec. 18 | **Houston** | 3:00 |
| Dec. 24 | at Los Angeles Raiders | 1:00 |

## RECORD HOLDERS

**INDIVIDUAL RECORDS—CAREER**

| Category | Name | Performance |
|---|---|---|
| Rushing (Yds.) | Christian Okoye, 1987-1992 | 4,897 |
| Passing (Yds.) | Len Dawson, 1962-1975 | 28,507 |
| Passing (TDs) | Len Dawson, 1962-1975 | 237 |
| Receiving (No.) | Henry Marshall, 1976-1987 | 416 |
| Receiving (Yds.) | Otis Taylor, 1965-1975 | 7,306 |
| Interceptions | Emmitt Thomas, 1966-1978 | 58 |
| Punting (Avg.) | Jerrel Wilson, 1963-1977 | 43.5 |
| Punt Return (Avg.) | J.T. Smith, 1979-1984 | 10.6 |
| Kickoff Return (Avg.) | Noland Smith, 1967-69 | 26.8 |
| Field Goals | Nick Lowery, 1980-1993 | 329 |
| Touchdowns (Tot.) | Otis Taylor, 1965-1975 | 60 |
| Points | Nick Lowery, 1980-1993 | 1,466 |

**INDIVIDUAL RECORDS—SINGLE SEASON**

| Category | Name | Performance |
|---|---|---|
| Rushing (Yds.) | Christian Okoye, 1989 | 1,480 |
| Passing (Yds.) | Bill Kenney, 1983 | 4,348 |
| Passing (TDs) | Len Dawson, 1964 | 30 |
| Receiving (No.) | Carlos Carson, 1983 | 80 |
| Receiving (Yds.) | Carlos Carson, 1983 | 1,351 |
| Interceptions | Emmitt Thomas, 1974 | 12 |
| Punting (Avg.) | Jerrel Wilson, 1965 | 46.0 |
| Punt Return (Avg.) | Abner Haynes, 1960 | 15.4 |
| Kickoff Return (Avg.) | Dave Grayson, 1962 | 29.7 |
| Field Goals | Nick Lowery, 1990 | 34 |
| Touchdowns (Tot.) | Abner Haynes, 1962 | 19 |
| Points | Nick Lowery, 1990 | 139 |

**INDIVIDUAL RECORDS—SINGLE GAME**

| Category | Name | Performance |
|---|---|---|
| Rushing (Yds.) | Barry Word, 10-14-90 | 200 |
| Passing (Yds.) | Len Dawson, 11-1-64 | 435 |
| Passing (TDs) | Len Dawson, 11-1-64 | 6 |
| Receiving (No.) | Ed Podolak, 10-7-73 | 12 |
| Receiving (Yds.) | Stephone Paige, 12-22-85 | 309 |
| Interceptions | Bobby Ply, 12-16-62 | *4 |
| | Bobby Hunt, 12-4-64 | *4 |
| | Deron Cherry, 9-29-85 | *4 |
| Field Goals | Many times | 5 |
| | Last time by Nick Lowery, 9-20-93 | |
| Touchdowns (Tot.) | Abner Haynes, 11-26-61 | 5 |
| Points | Abner Haynes, 11-26-61 | 30 |

*NFL Record

## COACHING HISTORY

**DALLAS TEXANS 1960-62**
**(263-241-12)**

| | | |
|---|---|---|
| 1960-74 | Hank Stram | 129-79-10 |
| 1975-77 | Paul Wiggin* | 11-24-0 |
| 1977 | Tom Bettis | 1-6-0 |
| 1978-82 | Marv Levy | 31-42-0 |
| 1983-86 | John Mackovic | 30-35-0 |
| 1987-88 | Frank Gansz | 8-22-1 |
| 1989-93 | Marty Schottenheimer | 53-33-1 |

*Released after seven games in 1977

**ARROWHEAD STADIUM**

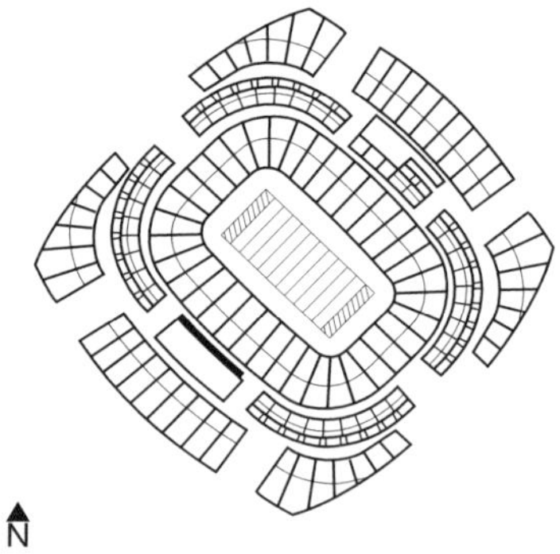

## 1993 TEAM RECORD

**PRESEASON (3-1)**

| Date | Result | | Opponents |
|---|---|---|---|
| 8/7 | W | 29-21 | vs. Green Bay at Milw. |
| 8/12 | L | 7-30 | Buffalo |
| 8/21 | W | 27-20 | Minnesota |
| 8/27 | W | 27-20 | at New England |

**REGULAR SEASON (11-5)**

| Date | Result | | Opponents | Att. |
|---|---|---|---|---|
| 9/5 | W | 27-3 | at Tampa Bay | 63,378 |
| 9/12 | L | 0-30 | at Houston | 59,780 |
| 9/20 | W | 15-7 | Denver | 78,453 |
| 10/3 | W | 24-9 | L.A. Raiders | 77,395 |
| 10/10 | W | 17-15 | Cincinnati | 75,394 |
| 10/17 | W | 17-14 | at San Diego | 60,729 |
| 10/31 | L | 10-30 | at Miami | 67,765 |
| 11/8 | W | 23-16 | Green Bay | 76,742 |
| 11/14 | W | 31-20 | at L.A. Raiders | 66,553 |
| 11/21 | L | 17-19 | Chicago | 76,872 |
| 11/28 | W | 23-7 | Buffalo | 74,452 |
| 12/5 | W | 31-16 | at Seattle | 58,551 |
| 12/12 | L | 21-27 | at Denver | 75,822 |
| 12/19 | W | 28-24 | San Diego | 74,778 |
| 12/26 | L | 10-30 | at Minnesota | 59,236 |
| 1/2 | W | 34-24 | Seattle | 72,136 |

**POSTSEASON (2-1)**

| | | | | |
|---|---|---|---|---|
| 1/8 | W | 27-24 | Pittsburgh (OT) | 74,515 |
| 1/16 | W | 28-20 | at Houston | 64,011 |
| 1/23 | L | 13-30 | at Buffalo | 76,642 |

(OT) Overtime

**SCORE BY PERIODS**

| | | | | | | | |
|---|---|---|---|---|---|---|---|
| Chiefs | 71 | 108 | 82 | 67 | 0 | — | 328 |
| Opponents | 51 | 86 | 50 | 104 | 0 | — | 291 |

**ATTENDANCE**

Home 606,222 Away 511,814 Total 1,118,036
Single-game home record, 82,094 (11-5-72)
Single-season home record, 612,773 (1992)

## 1993 TEAM STATISTICS

| | Chiefs | Opp. |
|---|---|---|
| Total First Downs | 300 | 300 |
| Rushing | 94 | 103 |
| Passing | 180 | 161 |
| Penalty | 26 | 36 |
| Third Down: Made/Att | 82/203 | 86/210 |
| Third Down Pct. | 40.4 | 41.0 |
| Fourth Down: Made/Att | 4/9 | 3/13 |
| Fourth Down Pct. | 44.4 | 23.1 |
| Total Net Yards | 4835 | 4771 |
| Avg. Per Game | 302.2 | 298.2 |
| Total Plays | 970 | 1013 |
| Avg. Per Play | 5.0 | 4.7 |
| Net Yards Rushing | 1655 | 1620 |
| Avg. Per Game | 103.4 | 101.3 |
| Total Rushes | 445 | 453 |
| Net Yards Passing | 3180 | 3151 |
| Avg. Per Game | 198.8 | 196.9 |
| Sacked/Yards Lost | 35/204 | 35/228 |
| Gross Yards | 3384 | 3379 |
| Att./Completions | 490/287 | 525/312 |
| Completion Pct. | 58.6 | 59.4 |
| Had Intercepted | 10 | 21 |
| Punts/Avg. | 77/42.1 | 68/44.6 |
| Net Punting Avg. | 77/35.4 | 68/37.8 |
| Penalties/Yards Lost | 121/969 | 127/1015 |
| Fumbles/Ball Lost | 28/18 | 30/17 |
| Touchdowns | 37 | 30 |
| Rushing | 14 | 11 |
| Passing | 20 | 18 |
| Returns | 3 | 1 |
| Avg. Time of Possession | 29:28 | 30:32 |

## 1993 INDIVIDUAL STATISTICS

| PASSING | Att. | Cmp. | Yds. | Pct. | TD | Int. | Tkld. | Rate |
|---|---|---|---|---|---|---|---|---|
| Montana | 298 | 181 | 2144 | 60.7 | 13 | 7 | 12/61 | 87.4 |
| Krieg | 189 | 105 | 1238 | 55.6 | 7 | 3 | 22/138 | 81.4 |
| Blundin | 3 | 1 | 2 | 33.3 | 0 | 0 | 0/0 | 42.4 |
| Anders | 0 | 0 | 0 | — | 0 | 0 | 1/5 | -1.0 |
| Chiefs | 490 | 287 | 3384 | 58.6 | 20 | 10 | 35/204 | 84.8 |
| Opponents | 525 | 312 | 3379 | 59.4 | 18 | 21 | 35/228 | 73.2 |

| SCORING | TD R | TD P | TD Rt | PAT | FG | Saf | PTS |
|---|---|---|---|---|---|---|---|
| Lowery | 0 | 0 | 0 | 37/37 | 23/29 | 0 | 106 |
| Allen | 12 | 3 | 0 | 0/0 | 0/0 | 0 | 90 |
| Davis | 0 | 7 | 0 | 0/0 | 0/0 | 0 | 42 |
| Cash | 0 | 4 | 0 | 0/0 | 0/0 | 0 | 24 |
| Birden | 0 | 2 | 0 | 0/0 | 0/0 | 0 | 12 |
| McNair | 2 | 0 | 0 | 0/0 | 0/0 | 0 | 12 |
| Anders | 0 | 1 | 0 | 0/0 | 0/0 | 0 | 6 |
| Barnett | 0 | 1 | 0 | 0/0 | 0/0 | 0 | 6 |
| Hayes | 0 | 1 | 0 | 0/0 | 0/0 | 0 | 6 |
| A. Lewis | 0 | 0 | 1 | 0/0 | 0/0 | 0 | 6 |
| Saleaumua | 0 | 0 | 1 | 0/0 | 0/0 | 0 | 6 |
| Thomas | 0 | 0 | 1 | 0/0 | 0/0 | 0 | 6 |
| Valerio | 0 | 1 | 0 | 0/0 | 0/0 | 0 | 6 |
| Chiefs | 14 | 20 | 3 | 37/37 | 23/29 | 0 | 328 |
| Opponents | 11 | 18 | 1 | 27/30 | 28/32 | 0 | 291 |

| RUSHING | Att. | Yds. | Avg. | LG | TD |
|---|---|---|---|---|---|
| Allen | 206 | 764 | 3.7 | 39 | 12 |
| Anders | 75 | 291 | 3.9 | 18 | 0 |
| McNair | 51 | 278 | 5.5 | 47 | 2 |
| J. Stephens | 6 | 18 | 3.0 | 7 | 0 |
| H. Williams | 42 | 149 | 3.5 | 19 | 0 |
| Montana | 25 | 64 | 2.6 | 17 | 0 |
| F. Jones | 5 | 34 | 6.8 | 13 | 0 |
| E. Thompson | 11 | 28 | 2.5 | 14 | 0 |
| Krieg | 21 | 24 | 1.1 | 20 | 0 |
| Barnett | 1 | 3 | 3.0 | 3 | 0 |
| Carter | 1 | 2 | 2.0 | 2 | 0 |
| Cash | 1 | 0 | 0.0 | 0 | 0 |
| Chiefs | 445 | 1655 | 3.7 | 47 | 14 |
| Opponents | 453 | 1620 | 3.6 | 38 | 11 |

| RECEIVING | No. | Yds. | Avg. | LG | TD |
|---|---|---|---|---|---|
| Davis | 52 | 909 | 17.5 | 66t | 7 |
| Birden | 51 | 721 | 14.1 | 50t | 2 |
| Anders | 40 | 326 | 8.2 | 27 | 1 |
| Allen | 34 | 238 | 7.0 | 18t | 3 |
| Hayes | 24 | 331 | 13.8 | 49 | 1 |
| Cash | 24 | 242 | 10.1 | 24 | 4 |
| Barnett | 17 | 182 | 10.7 | 25 | 1 |
| McNair | 10 | 74 | 7.4 | 24 | 0 |
| F. Jones | 9 | 111 | 12.3 | 19 | 0 |
| H. Jones | 7 | 91 | 13.0 | 22 | 0 |
| Dyal | 7 | 83 | 11.9 | 31 | 0 |
| H. Williams | 7 | 42 | 6.0 | 14 | 0 |
| E. Thompson | 4 | 33 | 8.3 | 13 | 0 |
| Valerio | 1 | 1 | 1.0 | 1t | 1 |
| Chiefs | 287 | 3384 | 11.8 | 66t | 20 |
| Opponents | 312 | 3379 | 10.8 | 77t | 18 |

| INTERCEPTIONS | No. | Yds. | Avg. | LG | TD |
|---|---|---|---|---|---|
| A. Lewis | 6 | 61 | 10.2 | 24 | 0 |
| Mincy | 5 | 44 | 8.8 | 20 | 0 |
| Ross | 2 | 49 | 24.5 | 48 | 0 |
| Bayless | 2 | 14 | 7.0 | 16 | 0 |
| Terry | 1 | 21 | 21.0 | 21 | 0 |
| Marts | 1 | 20 | 20.0 | 20 | 0 |
| Saleaumua | 1 | 13 | 13.0 | 13 | 0 |
| Smith | 1 | 3 | 3.0 | 3 | 0 |
| Carter | 1 | 0 | 0.0 | 0 | 0 |
| Taylor | 1 | 0 | 0.0 | 0 | 0 |
| Chiefs | 21 | 225 | 10.7 | 48 | 0 |
| Opponents | 10 | 111 | 11.1 | 48 | 0 |

| PUNTING | No. | Yds. | Avg. | In 20 | LG |
|---|---|---|---|---|---|
| Barker | 76 | 3240 | 42.6 | 19 | 59 |
| Chiefs | 77 | 3240 | 42.1 | 19 | 59 |
| Opponents | 68 | 3035 | 44.6 | 23 | 67 |

| PUNT RETURNS | No. | FC | Yds. | Avg. | LG | TD |
|---|---|---|---|---|---|---|
| Carter | 27 | 4 | 247 | 9.1 | 30 | 0 |
| Birden | 5 | 3 | 43 | 8.6 | 12 | 0 |
| Hughes | 3 | 0 | 49 | 16.3 | 29 | 0 |
| Mincy | 2 | 0 | 9 | 4.5 | 9 | 0 |
| Chiefs | 37 | 7 | 348 | 9.4 | 30 | 0 |
| Opponents | 43 | 15 | 352 | 8.2 | 54 | 0 |

| KICKOFF RETURNS | No. | Yds. | Avg. | LG | TD |
|---|---|---|---|---|---|
| Hughes | 14 | 266 | 19.0 | 30 | 0 |
| Dickerson | 11 | 237 | 21.5 | 44 | 0 |
| F. Jones | 9 | 156 | 17.3 | 29 | 0 |
| J. Stephens | 5 | 88 | 17.6 | 25 | 0 |
| H. Williams | 3 | 53 | 17.7 | 26 | 0 |
| Anders | 1 | 47 | 47.0 | 47 | 0 |
| Marts | 1 | 0 | 0.0 | 0 | 0 |
| McNair | 1 | 28 | 28.0 | 28 | 0 |
| Birden | 0 | 0 | — | — | 0 |
| Chiefs | 45 | 875 | 19.4 | 47 | 0 |
| Opponents | 49 | 1007 | 20.6 | 60 | 0 |

| SACKS | No. |
|---|---|
| Smith | 15.0 |
| Thomas | 8.0 |
| Saleaumua | 3.5 |
| Marts | 2.0 |
| Phillips | 1.5 |
| Bayless | 1.0 |
| Mickell | 1.0 |
| Newton | 1.0 |
| Terry | 1.0 |
| Ross | 0.5 |
| B.Thompson | 0.5 |
| Chiefs | 35.0 |
| Opponents | 35.0 |

## 1994 DRAFT CHOICES

| Round | Name | Pos. | College |
|---|---|---|---|
| 1 | Greg Hill | RB | Texas A&M |
| 2 | Donnell Bennett | RB | Miami |
| 3 | Lake Dawson | WR | Notre Dame |
| | Chris Penn | WR | Tulsa |
| 4 | Bracey Walker | DB | North Carolina |
| 5 | James Burton | DB | Fresno State |
| | Rob Waldrop | DT | Arizona |
| 6 | Anthony Daigle | RB | Fresno State |
| 7 | Steve Matthews | QB | Memphis State |
| | Tracy Greene | TE | Grambling |

## KANSAS CITY CHIEFS

### 1994 VETERAN ROSTER

| No. | | Name | Pos. | Ht. | Wt. | Birthdate | NFL Exp. | College | Hometown | How Acq. | '93 Games/ Starts |
|---|---|---|---|---|---|---|---|---|---|---|---|
| 5 | | Aguiar, Louie | P | 6-2 | 215 | 6/30/66 | 4 | Utah State | Livermore, Calif. | FA-'94 | 16/0* |
| 32 | | Allen, Marcus | RB | 6-2 | 210 | 3/26/60 | 13 | Southern California | San Diego, Calif. | UFA(Raid)-'93 | 16/10 |
| 76 | † | Alt, John | T | 6-8 | 307 | 5/30/62 | 11 | Iowa | Columbia Heights, Minn. | D1b-'84 | 16/16 |
| 38 | | Anders, Kimble | RB | 5-11 | 221 | 9/10/66 | 4 | Houston | Galveston, Tex. | FA-'91 | 16/13 |
| 50 | | Anderson, Erick | LB | 6-1 | 235 | 10/7/68 | 3 | Michigan | Glenbrook, Ill. | D7-'92 | 16/0 |
| 82 | | Barnett, Tim | WR | 6-1 | 200 | 4/19/68 | 4 | Jackson State | Rosedale, Miss. | D3-'91 | 8/1 |
| 87 | | Bartrum, Mike | TE | 6-4 | 234 | 6/23/70 | 2 | Marshall | Pomeroy, Ohio | FA-'93 | 3/0 |
| 30 | # | Bayless, Martin | S | 6-2 | 219 | 10/11/62 | 11 | Bowling Green | Dayton, Ohio | PB(SD)-'92 | 16/10 |
| 88 | | Birden, J.J. | WR | 5-9 | 165 | 5/16/65 | 6 | Oregon | Portland, Ore. | FA-'90 | 16/16 |
| 14 | | Blundin, Matt | QB | 6-5 | 233 | 3/7/69 | 3 | Virginia | Ridley, Pa. | D2-'92 | 1/0 |
| 13 | t- | Bono, Steve | QB | 6-4 | 215 | 5/11/62 | 10 | UCLA | Norristown, Pa. | T(SF)-'94 | 8/0* |
| 34 | | Carter, Dale | CB-KR | 6-1 | 188 | 11/28/69 | 3 | Tennessee | Covington, Ga. | D1-'92 | 15/11 |
| 89 | | Cash, Keith | TE | 6-4 | 240 | 8/7/69 | 3 | Texas | San Antonio, Tex. | PB(Pitt)-'92 | 15/0 |
| 99 | | Casillas, Tony | DT | 6-3 | 273 | 10/26/63 | 9 | Oklahoma | Tulsa, Okla. | UFA(Dall)-'94 | 15/14* |
| 22 | | Cobb, Trevor | RB | 5-9 | 190 | 11/20/70 | 2 | Rice | Pasadena, Tex. | FA-'93 | 0* |
| 24 | | Collins, Mark | CB | 5-10 | 190 | 1/16/64 | 9 | Cal State-Fullerton | San Bernardino, Calif. | UFA(NYG)-'94 | 16/16* |
| 84 | | Davis, Willie | WR | 6-0 | 172 | 10/10/67 | 3 | Central Arkansas | Altheimer, Ark. | FA-'92 | 16/15 |
| 23 | | Dickerson, Ron | RB | 6-0 | 211 | 8/31/71 | 2 | Arkansas | State College, Pa. | FA-'93 | 6/0 |
| 2 | | Elliot, Lin | K | 6-0 | 182 | 11/11/68 | 2 | Texas Tech | Waco, Tex. | FA-'94 | 2/0* |
| 59 | | Fields, Jaime | LB | 5-11 | 230 | 8/28/70 | 2 | Washington | Lynwood, Calif. | D4-'93 | 6/0 |
| 74 | | Graham, Derrick | T | 6-4 | 306 | 3/18/67 | 5 | Appalachian State | Groveland, Fla. | D5a-'90 | 11/2 |
| 61 | | Grunhard, Tim | C | 6-2 | 299 | 5/17/68 | 5 | Notre Dame | Chicago, Ill. | D2-'90 | 16/16 |
| 83 | | Hughes, Danan | WR | 6-1 | 201 | 12/11/70 | 2 | Iowa | Bayonne, N.J. | D7-'93 | 6/0 |
| 91 | | Johnson, Jimmie | TE | 6-2 | 248 | 10/6/66 | 6 | Howard | Augusta, Ga. | FA-'94 | 6/4* |
| 65 | | Knapp, Lindsay | G-T | 6-5 | 280 | 2/25/70 | 2 | Notre Dame | Deerfield, Ill. | D5-'93 | 0* |
| 8 | | Lowery, Nick | K | 6-4 | 207 | 5/27/56 | 15 | Dartmouth | Washington, D.C. | FA-'80 | 16/0 |
| 77 | | McDaniels, Pellom | DE | 6-3 | 278 | 2/21/68 | 2 | Oregon State | San Jose, Calif. | FA-'93 | 10/0 |
| 92 | | Mickell, Darren | DT | 6-4 | 280 | 8/3/70 | 3 | Florida | Miami, Fla. | SD2-'92 | 16/1 |
| 42 | † | Mincy, Charles | S | 5-11 | 197 | 12/16/69 | 4 | Washington | Los Angeles, Calif. | D5-'91 | 16/4 |
| 19 | | Montana, Joe | QB | 6-2 | 205 | 6/11/56 | 16 | Notre Dame | Monongahela, Pa. | T(SF)-'93 | 11/11 |
| 96 | | Newton, Tim | DT | 6-0 | 269 | 3/23/63 | 9 | Florida | Orlando, Fla. | FA-'93 | 16/0 |
| 75 | | Phillips, Joe | DT | 6-5 | 300 | 7/15/63 | 8 | Southern Methodist | Vancouver, Wash. | FA-'92 | 16/16 |
| 39 | | Pickens, Bruce | CB | 5-11 | 190 | 5/9/68 | 4 | Nebraska | Kansas City, Mo. | FA-'93 | 7/4* |
| 52 | # | Rogers, Tracy | LB | 6-2 | 241 | 8/13/67 | 5 | Fresno State | Taft, Calif. | FA-'90 | 14/14 |
| 97 | † | Saleaumua, Dan | DT | 6-0 | 300 | 11/25/64 | 8 | Arizona State | San Diego, Calif. | PB(Det)-'89 | 16/16 |
| 68 | | Shields, Will | G | 6-2 | 296 | 9/15/71 | 2 | Nebraska | Lawton, Okla. | D3-'93 | 16/15 |
| 66 | | Siglar, Ricky | T | 6-7 | 304 | 6/14/66 | 3 | San Jose State | Manzano, N.M. | FA-'93 | 14/14 |
| 54 | | Simien, Tracy | LB | 6-1 | 250 | 5/21/67 | 4 | Texas Christian | Bay City, Tex. | FA-'91 | 16/14 |
| 90 | | Smith, Neil | DE | 6-4 | 273 | 4/10/66 | 7 | Nebraska | New Orleans, La. | D1-'88 | 16/15 |
| 21 | | Stephens, John | RB | 6-1 | 215 | 2/23/66 | 7 | Northwestern Louisiana | Springhill, La. | FA-'93 | 12/5* |
| 79 | | Szott, Dave | G | 6-4 | 290 | 12/12/67 | 5 | Penn State | Clifton, N.J. | D7-'90 | 14/13 |
| 27 | | Taylor, Jay | CB | 5-10 | 170 | 11/8/67 | 6 | San Jose State | San Diego, Calif. | T(Phx)-'93 | 15/1 |
| 25 | | Terry, Doug | S | 5-11 | 197 | 12/12/69 | 3 | Kansas | Liberal, Kan. | FA-'92 | 15/8 |
| 58 | | Thomas, Derrick | LB | 6-3 | 242 | 1/1/67 | 6 | Alabama | Miami, Fla. | D1-'89 | 16/15 |
| 45 | | Thompson, Ernie | RB | 5-11 | 257 | 10/25/69 | 2 | Indiana | Terre Haute, Ind. | FA-'93 | 16/2 |
| 94 | | Traylor, Keith | DE | 6-2 | 290 | 9/3/69 | 3 | Central Oklahoma | Malvern, Ark. | FA-'94 | 5/0* |
| 73 | | Valerio, Joe | G-C | 6-5 | 295 | 2/11/69 | 4 | Pennsylvania | Ridley, Pa. | D2-'91 | 13/0 |
| 72 | | Villa, Danny | G | 6-5 | 300 | 9/21/64 | 8 | Arizona State | Nogales, Ariz. | UFA(Phx)-'93 | 13/3 |
| 26 | | Watson, Tim | S | 6-1 | 213 | 8/13/70 | 2 | Howard | Ft. Valley, Ga. | FA-'93 | 4/0 |
| 41 | | Whitmore, David | S | 6-0 | 232 | 7/6/67 | 5 | Stephen F. Austin | Daingerfield, Tex. | T(SF)-'93 | 6/6 |
| 47 | | Wilburn, Barry | CB | 6-3 | 186 | 12/9/63 | 7 | Mississippi | Memphis, Tenn. | FA-'94 | 0* |

* Aguiar played 16 games with N.Y. Jets in '93; Bono played 8 games with San Francisco; Casillas played 15 games with Dallas; Cobb missed '93 season due to injury; Collins played 16 games with N.Y. Giants; Elliott played 2 games with Dallas; Johnson played 6 games with Detroit; Knapp inactive for 16 games; Pickens played 4 games with Atlanta, 3 games with Kansas City; Stephens played 5 games with Green Bay, 7 games with Kansas City; Traylor played 5 games with Green Bay; Wilburn last active with Cleveland in '92.

# Unrestricted free agent; subject to developments.

† Restricted free agent; subject to developments.

t- Chiefs trade for Bono (San Francisco).

Players lost through free agency (4): QB Dave Krieg (Det; 12 games in '93), CB Albert Lewis (Raid; 14), LB Lonnie Marts (TB; 16), CB Kevin Ross (Atl; 15).

Also played with Chiefs in '93—P Bryan Barker (16 games), TE Mike Dyal (6), DE Leonard Griffin (4), TE Jonathan Hayes (16), WR Fred Jones (10), WR Hassan Jones (8), CB Garry Lewis (1), G Reggie McElroy (8), S Erik McMillan (1), RB Todd McNair (15), CB-S Muhammed Oliver (2), G Tom Ricketts (3), LB Santo Stephens (16), S Bennie Thompson (16), RB Harvey Williams (7).

## COACHING STAFF

**Head Coach,**
**Marty Schottenheimer**

**Pro Career:** In five seasons as head coach of the Kansas City Chiefs, Schottenheimer has established the highest winning percentage in franchise history (.632). Moreover, his .626 regular-season winning percentage is third highest among active NFL coaches. He has directed the Chiefs to five of their seven winning seasons since 1974 and has taken Kansas City to the playoffs four consecutive years, a team record. He is the only coach that has taken his team to the playoffs eight times since 1985 and has missed the playoffs only once as an NFL head coach. As head coach of the Cleveland Browns from midseason in 1984 through 1988, he led the club to four playoff berths, three AFC Central Division titles, two AFC Championship Game appearances, and captured AFC coach of the years honors (1986). He first joined the Browns in 1980 as defensive coordinator after serving as linebackers coach of the Detroit Lions in 1978-79. His first NFL coaching job came with the New York Giants, where he was linebackers coach and later defensive coordinator from 1975-77. He also served as an assistant coach with the Portland Storm (WFL) in 1974. A seventh-round draft choice of the Buffalo Bills in 1965, he played linebacker with the Bills until 1968 and finished his pro playing career with the Boston Patriots in 1969-70. Career record: 99-64-1.

**Background:** Schottenheimer was an All-America linebacker at the University of Pittsburgh 1962-64. Following his retirement from pro football, he worked as a real estate developer in both Miami and Denver from 1971-74.

**Personal:** Born September 23, 1943, Canonsburg, Pa. Marty and his wife, Patricia, live in Overland Park, Kan., and have one daughter, Kristen, and one son, Brian.

### ASSISTANT COACHES

**Dave Adolph,** defensive coordinator-linebackers; born June 6, 1937, Akron, Ohio, lives in Overland Park, Kan. Guard-linebacker Akron 1955-58. No pro playing experience. College coach: Akron 1963-64, Connecticut 1965-68, Kentucky 1969-72, Illinois 1973-76, Ohio State 1977-78. Pro coach: Cleveland Browns 1979-84, 1986-88, San Diego Chargers 1985, Los Angeles Raiders 1989-91, joined Chiefs in 1992.

**Russ Ball,** assistant strength and conditioning; born August 28, 1959, Moberly, Mo., lives in Kansas City. Center Central Missouri State 1977-80. No pro playing experience. College coach: Missouri 1981-88. Pro coach: Joined Chiefs in 1989.

**John Bunting,** defensive assistant; born July 15, 1950, Portland, Me., lives in Kansas City. Linebacker North Carolina 1968-71. Pro linebacker Philadelphia Eagles 1972-82, Philadelphia Stars (USFL) 1983-84. College coach: Brown 1986, Rowan College 1987-92 (head coach 1988-92). Pro coach: Baltimore Stars (USFL) 1985, joined Chiefs in 1993.

**Herman Edwards,** defensive backs; born April 27, 1954, Ft. Monmouth, N.J., lives in Blue Springs, Mo. Defensive back California 1972-75, San Diego State 1976. Pro cornerback Philadelphia Eagles 1977-85, Los Angeles Rams 1986, Atlanta Falcons 1986. Pro scout: Kansas City Chiefs 1989-91. Pro coach: Joined Chiefs in 1992.

**Alex Gibbs,** offensive line; born February 11, 1941, Morganton, N.C., lives in Kansas City. Running back-defensive back Davidson College 1959-63. No pro playing experience. College coach: Duke 1969-70, Kentucky 1971-72, West Virginia 1973-74, Ohio State 1975-78, Auburn 1979-81, Georgia 1982-83. Pro coach: Denver Broncos 1984-87, Los Angeles Raiders 1988-89, San Diego Chargers 1990-91, Indianapolis Colts 1992, joined Chiefs in 1993.

**Paul Hackett,** offensive coordinator-quarterbacks; born July 5, 1947, Burlington, Vt., lives in Overland Park, Kan. Quarterback Cal-Davis 1965-68. No pro playing experience. College coach: Cal-Davis 1970-71, California 1972-75, Southern California 1976-80, Pittsburgh 1989-92 (head coach 1990-92). Pro coach: Cleveland Browns 1981-82, San Francisco 49ers 1983-85, Dallas Cowboys 1986-88, joined Chiefs in 1993.

**Mike McCarthy,** offensive assistant-quality control; born November 10, 1963, Pittsburgh, Pa., lives in Overland Park, Kan. Tight end Baker University 1985-86. No pro playing experience. College coach: Fort Hays State 1987-88, Pittsburgh 1989-92. Pro coach: Joined Chiefs in 1993.

**Tom Pratt,** defensive line; born June 21, 1935, Edgerton, Wis., lives in Overland Park, Kan. Linebacker Miami 1953-56. No pro playing experience. College coach: Miami 1957-59, Southern Mississippi 1960-62. Pro coach: Kansas City Chiefs 1963-77, New Orleans Saints 1978-80, Cleveland Browns 1981-88, rejoined Chiefs in 1989.

**Jimmy Raye,** running backs; born March 26, 1946, Fayetteville, N.C., lives in Kansas City. Quarterback Michigan State 1965-67. Pro defensive back Philadelphia Eagles 1969. College coach: Michigan State 1971-75, Wyoming 1976. Pro coach: San Francisco 49ers 1977, Detroit Lions 1978-79, Atlanta Falcons 1980-82, 1987-89, Los Angeles Rams 1983-84, 1991, Tampa Bay Buccaneers 1985-86, New England Patriots 1990, joined Chiefs in 1992.

**Dave Redding,** strength and conditioning; born June 14, 1952, North Platte, Neb., lives in Kansas City. Defensive end Nebraska 1972-75. No pro playing experience. College coach: Nebraska 1976, Washington State 1977, Missouri 1978-81. Pro coach: Cleveland Browns 1982-88, joined Chiefs in 1989.

**Al Saunders,** assistant head coach-receivers; born February 1, 1947, London, England, lives in Kansas City. Defensive back San Jose State 1966-68. No pro playing experience. College coach: Southern California 1970-71, Missouri 1972, Utah State 1973-75, California 1976-81, Tennessee 1982. Pro coach: San Diego Chargers 1983-88 (head coach 1986-88), joined Chiefs in 1989.

**Kurt Schottenheimer,** special teams; born October 1, 1949, McDonald, Pa., lives in Kansas City. Defensive back Miami 1969-70. No pro playing experience. College coach: William Patterson 1974, Michigan State 1978-82, Tulane 1983, Louisiana State 1984-85, Notre Dame 1986. Pro coach: Cleveland Browns 1987-88, joined Chiefs in 1989.

**Darvin Wallis,** special assistant-quality control; born February 14, 1949, Ft. Branch, Ind., lives in Overland Park, Kan. Defensive end Arizona 1970-71. No pro playing experience. College coach: Adams State 1976-77, Tulane 1978-79, Mississippi 1980-81. Pro coach: Cleveland Browns 1982-88, joined Chiefs in 1989.

## 1994 FIRST-YEAR ROSTER

| Name | Pos. | Ht. | Wt. | Birthdate | College | Hometown | How Acq. |
|---|---|---|---|---|---|---|---|
| Ale, Arnold (1) | LB | 6-2 | 230 | 6/17/70 | UCLA | Carson, Calif. | FA |
| Alexander, Ken | LB | 6-3 | 254 | 12/15/71 | Florida State | Austin, Tex. | FA |
| Anderson, Dunstan | DE | 6-4 | 260 | 12/31/70 | Tulsa | Ft. Worth, Tex. | FA |
| Bennett, Donnell | RB | 5-11 | 241 | 9/14/72 | Miami | Ft. Lauderdale, Fla. | D2 |
| Booker, Vaughn (1) | DE | 6-5 | 290 | 2/24/68 | Cincinnati | Cincinnati, Ohio | FA |
| Boyd, Larry | DE | 6-2 | 285 | 1/3/71 | Arizona State | Glimer, Tex. | FA |
| Burton, James | CB | 5-9 | 185 | 4/22/71 | Fresno State | Long Beach, Calif. | D5a |
| Daigle, Anthony | RB | 5-10 | 198 | 4/5/70 | Fresno State | Benicia, Calif. | D6 |
| Dawson, Lake | WR | 6-1 | 204 | 1/2/72 | Notre Dame | Federal Way, Wash. | D3a |
| DeGraffenreid, Allen (1) | WR | 6-3 | 200 | 5/1/70 | Ohio State | Cincinnati, Ohio | FA |
| Freese, Jerry | LB | 6-2 | 221 | 5/25/70 | N.E. Oklahoma | Melbourne, Fla. | FA |
| Gaddy, Robert | T | 6-4 | 295 | 6/22/71 | Alcorn State | Coila, Miss. | FA |
| Gay, Matt (1) | S | 5-11 | 180 | 4/3/70 | Kansas | Chicago, Ill. | FA |
| Greene, Tracy | TE-T | 6-4 | 276 | 11/5/72 | Grambling | Grambling, La. | D7b |
| Grow, Monty | S | 6-3 | 214 | 9/4/71 | Florida | Inverness, Fla. | FA |
| Hill, Greg | RB | 5-11 | 207 | 2/23/72 | Texas A&M | Dallas, Tex. | D1 |
| Kwarta, Bret | G | 6-2 | 290 | 1/28/71 | California-Davis | Mullica, N.J. | FA |
| Ma'afala, Nick (1) | DT | 6-2 | 295 | 4/13/67 | Hawaii | Honolulu, Hawaii | FA |
| Martin, Emerson | G | 6-2 | 293 | 5/6/71 | Hampton | Elizabethtown, N.C. | FA |
| Matthews, Steve | QB | 6-2 | 217 | 10/13/70 | Memphis State | Tullahoma, Tenn. | D7a |
| McCullough, Russ (1) | T | 6-10 | 315 | 10/31/68 | Missouri | Olathe, Kan. | FA |
| Montgomery, Fred (1) | WR | 6-0 | 183 | 8/30/71 | New Mexico State | Greenville, Miss. | FA |
| Penn, Chris | WR | 6-0 | 195 | 4/20/71 | Tulsa | Lenapah, Okla. | D3b |
| Randall, Brian | CB | 6-0 | 185 | 1/28/71 | Delaware State | Swedesboro, N.J. | FA |
| Shufelt, Pete (1) | LB | 6-2 | 241 | 10/28/69 | Texas-El Paso | Tucson, Ariz. | FA |
| Stephens, Michael | WR | 6-1 | 195 | 10/9/72 | Nevada | Gardena, Calif. | FA |
| Van Pelt, Alex (1) | QB | 6-1 | 219 | 5/1/70 | Pittsburgh | San Antonio, Tex. | FA |
| Waldrop, Rob | DT | 6-1 | 276 | 12/1/71 | Arizona | Scottsdale, Ariz. | D5b |
| Walker, Bracey | S | 5-10 | 200 | 10/28/70 | North Carolina | Pine Forest, N.C. | D4 |

The term NFL Rookie is defined as a player who is in his first season of professional football and has not been on the roster of another professional football team for any regular-season or postseason games. A Rookie is designated by an "R" on NFL rosters. Players who have been active in another professional football league or players who have NFL experience, including either preseason training camp or being on an Active List or Inactive List, or on Reserve/Injured or Reserve/Physically Unable to Perform for fewer than six regular-season games, are termed NFL First-Year Players. An NFL First-Year Player is designated by a "1" on NFL rosters. Thereafter, a player is credited with an additional year of experience for each season in which he accumulates six games on the Active List or Inactive List, or on Reserve/Injured or Reserve/Physically Unable to Perform.

## NOTES

# LOS ANGELES RAIDERS

**American Football Conference**
**Western Division**
**Team Colors:** Silver and Black
**332 Center Street**
**El Segundo, California 90245**
**Telephone: (310) 322-3451**

## CLUB OFFICIALS

President of the Managing General Partner:
Al Davis
Executive Assistant: Al LoCasale
Pro Football Scout: George Karras
Legal Affairs: Jeff Birren, Amy Trask
Finance: Klaus Leitenbauer
Senior Administrator: Morris Bradshaw
Business Manager: John Novak
Senior Executive: John Herrera
Publications: Mike Taylor
Community Relations: Gil Lafferty-Hernandez
Administrative Assistants: Mario Perez,
Marc McKinney
Ticket Operations: Peter Eiges
Trainers: George Anderson, H. Rod Martin,
Jonathan Jones
Equipment Manager: Richard Romanski
Assistant Equipment Manager: Bob Romanski
**Stadium:** Los Angeles Memorial Coliseum
•**Capacity:** 67,800
3911 South Figueroa Street
Los Angeles, California 90037
**Playing Surface:** Grass
**Training Camp:** Radisson Hotel
Oxnard, California 93030

## 1994 SCHEDULE

**PRESEASON**

| | | |
|---|---|---|
| July 31 | vs. Denver at Barcelona | 1:00 |
| Aug. 7 | at Dallas | 8:00 |
| Aug. 13 | at Pittsburgh | 6:00 |
| Aug. 20 | at Los Angeles Rams | 7:00 |
| Aug. 27 | at Houston | 1:00 |

**REGULAR SEASON**

| | | |
|---|---|---|
| Sept. 5 | at San Francisco (Monday) | 6:00 |
| Sept. 11 | **Seattle** | 1:00 |
| Sept. 18 | at Denver | 2:00 |
| Sept. 25 | **San Diego** | 1:00 |
| Oct. 2 | Open Date | |
| Oct. 9 | at New England | 4:00 |
| Oct. 16 | at Miami | 1:00 |
| Oct. 23 | **Atlanta** | 1:00 |
| Oct. 30 | **Houston** | 1:00 |
| Nov. 6 | at Kansas City | 7:00 |
| Nov. 13 | at Los Angeles Rams | 1:00 |
| Nov. 20 | **New Orleans** | 1:00 |
| Nov. 27 | **Pittsburgh** | 1:00 |
| Dec. 5 | at San Diego (Monday) | 6:00 |
| Dec. 11 | **Denver** | 1:00 |
| Dec. 18 | at Seattle | 5:00 |
| Dec. 24 | **Kansas City** | 1:00 |

## RECORD HOLDERS

**INDIVIDUAL RECORDS—CAREER**

| Category | Name | Performance |
|---|---|---|
| Rushing (Yds.) | Marcus Allen, 1982-1992 | 8,545 |
| Passing (Yds.) | Ken Stabler, 1970-79 | 19,078 |
| Passing (TDs) | Ken Stabler, 1970-79 | 150 |
| Receiving (No.) | Fred Biletnikoff, 1965-1978 | 589 |
| Receiving (Yds.) | Fred Biletnikoff, 1965-1978 | 8,974 |
| Interceptions | Willie Brown, 1967-1978 | 39 |
| | Lester Hayes, 1977-1986 | 39 |
| Punting (Avg.) | Ray Guy, 1973-1986 | 42.5 |
| Punt Return (Avg.) | Claude Gibson, 1963-65 | 12.6 |
| Kickoff Return (Avg.) | Jack Larscheid, 1960-61 | 28.4 |
| Field Goals | George Blanda, 1967-1975 | 156 |
| Touchdowns (Tot.) | Marcus Allen, 1982-1992 | 98 |
| Points | George Blanda, 1967-1975 | 863 |

**INDIVIDUAL RECORDS—SINGLE SEASON**

| Category | Name | Performance |
|---|---|---|
| Rushing (Yds.) | Marcus Allen, 1985 | 1,759 |
| Passing (Yds.) | Ken Stabler, 1979 | 3,615 |
| Passing (TDs) | Daryle Lamonica, 1969 | 34 |
| Receiving (No.) | Todd Christensen, 1986 | 95 |
| Receiving (Yds.) | Art Powell, 1964 | 1,361 |
| Interceptions | Lester Hayes, 1980 | 13 |
| Punting (Avg.) | Ray Guy, 1973 | 45.3 |
| Punt Return (Avg.) | Claude Gibson, 1964 | 14.4 |
| Kickoff Return (Avg.) | Harold Hart, 1975 | 30.5 |
| Field Goals | Jeff Jaeger, 1993 | *35 |
| Touchdowns (Tot.) | Marcus Allen, 1984 | 18 |
| Points | Jeff Jaeger, 1993 | 132 |

**INDIVIDUAL RECORDS—SINGLE GAME**

| Category | Name | Performance |
|---|---|---|
| Rushing (Yds.) | Bo Jackson, 11-30-87 | 221 |
| Passing (Yds.) | Jeff Hostetler, 10-31-93 | 424 |
| Passing (TDs) | Tom Flores, 12-22-63 | 6 |
| | Daryle Lamonica, 10-19-69 | 6 |
| Receiving (No.) | Dave Casper, 10-3-76 | 12 |
| Receiving (Yds.) | Art Powell, 12-22-63 | 247 |
| Interceptions | Many times | 3 |
| | Last time by Charles Phillips, 12-8-75 | |
| Field Goals | Many times | 4 |
| | Last time by Jeff Jaeger, 1-2-94 | |
| Touchdowns (Tot.) | Art Powell, 12-22-63 | 4 |
| | Marcus Allen, 9-24-84 | 4 |
| Points | Art Powell, 12-22-63 | 24 |
| | Marcus Allen, 9-24-84 | 24 |

*NFL Record

## COACHING HISTORY

**OAKLAND 1960-1981**
**(325-200-11)**

| | | |
|---|---|---|
| 1960-61 | Eddie Erdelatz* | 6-10-0 |
| 1961-62 | Marty Feldman** | 2-15-0 |
| 1962 | Red Conkright | 1-8-0 |
| 1963-65 | Al Davis | 23-16-3 |
| 1966-68 | John Rauch | 35-10-1 |
| 1969-78 | John Madden | 112-39-7 |
| 1979-87 | Tom Flores | 91-56-0 |
| 1988-89 | Mike Shanahan*** | 8-12-0 |
| 1989-93 | Art Shell | 47-34-0 |

*Released after two games in 1961
**Released after five games in 1962
***Released after four games in 1989

**LOS ANGELES MEMORIAL COLISEUM**

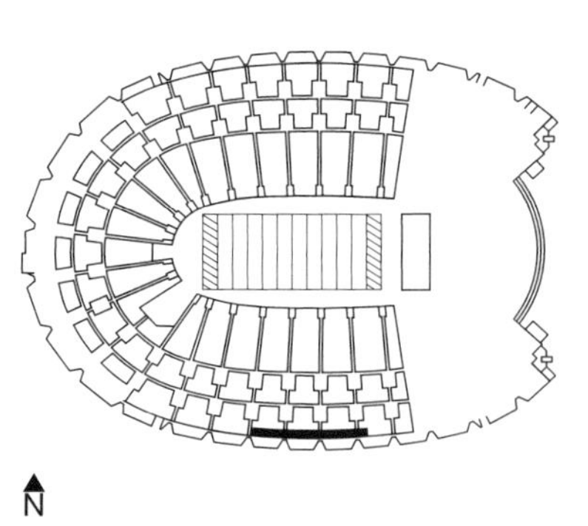

## 1993 TEAM RECORD

**PRESEASON (2-3)**

| Date | Result | | Opponents |
|---|---|---|---|
| 7/31 | W | 19-3 | vs. Green Bay at Canton |
| 8/8 | L | 0-27 | vs. San Francisco at Stanford Stadium |
| 8/14 | L | 7-13 | at Dallas |
| 8/20 | L | 7-18 | at Indianapolis |
| 8/28 | W | 20-19 | at L.A. Rams |

**REGULAR SEASON (10-6)**

| Date | Result | | Opponents | Att. |
|---|---|---|---|---|
| 9/5 | W | 24-7 | Minnesota | 44,120 |
| 9/12 | W | 17-13 | at Seattle | 58,836 |
| 9/19 | L | 16-19 | Cleveland | 48,617 |
| 10/3 | L | 9-24 | at Kansas City | 77,395 |
| 10/10 | W | 24-20 | N.Y. Jets | 41,627 |
| 10/18 | W | 23-20 | at Denver | 75,712 |
| 10/31 | L | 23-30 | San Diego | 45,122 |
| 11/7 | W | 16-14 | at Chicago | 59,750 |
| 11/14 | L | 20-31 | Kansas City | 66,553 |
| 11/21 | W | 12-7 | at San Diego | 60,615 |
| 11/28 | L | 10-16 | at Cincinnati | 43,272 |
| 12/5 | W | 25-24 | at Buffalo | 79,478 |
| 12/12 | W | 27-23 | Seattle | 38,161 |
| 12/19 | W | 27-20 | Tampa Bay | 40,532 |
| 12/26 | L | 0-28 | at Green Bay | 54,482 |
| 1/2 | W | 33-30 | Denver (OT) | 66,904 |

**POSTSEASON (1-1)**

| | | | | |
|---|---|---|---|---|
| 1/9 | W | 42-24 | Denver | 65,314 |
| 1/15 | L | 23-29 | at Buffalo | 61,923 |

(OT) Overtime

**SCORE BY PERIODS**

| | | | | | | | |
|---|---|---|---|---|---|---|---|
| Raiders | 77 | 93 | 50 | 83 | 3 | — | 306 |
| Opponents | 34 | 108 | 57 | 127 | 0 | — | 326 |

**ATTENDANCE**

Home 391,636 Away 509,540 Total 901,176
Single-game home record, 91,494 (9-29-91)
Single-season home record, 516,205 (1986)

## 1993 TEAM STATISTICS

| | Raiders | Opp. |
|---|---|---|
| Total First Downs | 292 | 302 |
| Rushing | 95 | 111 |
| Passing | 168 | 154 |
| Penalty | 29 | 37 |
| Third Down: Made/Att | 74/202 | 74/204 |
| Third Down Pct. | 36.6 | 36.3 |
| Fourth Down: Made/Att | 1/8 | 5/9 |
| Fourth Down Pct. | 12.5 | 55.6 |
| Total Net Yards | 5014 | 4723 |
| Avg. Per Game | 313.4 | 295.2 |
| Total Plays | 978 | 996 |
| Avg. Per Play | 5.1 | 4.7 |
| Net Yards Rushing | 1425 | 1865 |
| Avg. Per Game | 89.1 | 116.6 |
| Total Rushes | 433 | 494 |
| Net Yards Passing | 3589 | 2858 |
| Avg. Per Game | 224.3 | 178.6 |
| Sacked/Yards Lost | 50/293 | 45/283 |
| Gross Yards | 3882 | 3141 |
| Att./Completions | 495/281 | 457/258 |
| Completion Pct. | 56.8 | 56.5 |
| Had Intercepted | 14 | 14 |
| Punts/Avg. | 71/41.8 | 80/42.1 |
| Net Punting Avg. | 71/35.1 | 80/34.3 |
| Penalties/Yards Lost | 148/1181 | 105/801 |
| Fumbles/Ball Lost | 23/11 | 23/9 |
| Touchdowns | 29 | 37 |
| Rushing | 10 | 17 |
| Passing | 17 | 17 |
| Returns | 2 | 3 |
| Avg. Time of Possession | 30:21 | 29:39 |

## 1993 INDIVIDUAL STATISTICS

| PASSING | Att. | Cmp. | Yds. | Pct. | TD | Int. | Tkld. | Rate |
|---|---|---|---|---|---|---|---|---|
| Hostetler | 419 | 236 | 3242 | 56.3 | 14 | 10 | 38/206 | 82.5 |
| Evans | 76 | 45 | 640 | 59.2 | 3 | 4 | 12/87 | 77.7 |
| Raiders | 495 | 281 | 3882 | 56.8 | 17 | 14 | 50/293 | 81.7 |
| Opponents | 457 | 258 | 3141 | 56.5 | 17 | 14 | 45/283 | 77.4 |

| SCORING | TD R | TD P | TD Rt | PAT | FG | Saf | PTS |
|---|---|---|---|---|---|---|---|
| Jaeger | 0 | 0 | 0 | 27/29 | 35/44 | 0 | 132 |
| Brown | 0 | 7 | 1 | 0/0 | 0/0 | 0 | 48 |
| Hostetler | 5 | 0 | 0 | 0/0 | 0/0 | 0 | 30 |
| A. Wright | 0 | 4 | 0 | 0/0 | 0/0 | 0 | 24 |
| Jett | 0 | 3 | 0 | 0/0 | 0/0 | 0 | 18 |
| McCallum | 3 | 0 | 0 | 0/0 | 0/0 | 0 | 18 |
| Bell | 1 | 0 | 0 | 0/0 | 0/0 | 0 | 6 |
| Glover | 0 | 1 | 0 | 0/0 | 0/0 | 0 | 6 |
| Horton | 0 | 1 | 0 | 0/0 | 0/0 | 0 | 6 |
| Ismail | 0 | 1 | 0 | 0/0 | 0/0 | 0 | 6 |
| McDaniel | 0 | 0 | 1 | 0/0 | 0/0 | 0 | 6 |
| Robinson | 1 | 0 | 0 | 0/0 | 0/0 | 0 | 6 |
| Raiders | 10 | 17 | 2 | 27/29 | 35/44 | 0 | 306 |
| Opponents | 17 | 17 | 3 | 37/37 | 21/33 | 2 | 326 |

| RUSHING | Att. | Yds. | Avg. | LG | TD |
|---|---|---|---|---|---|
| Robinson | 156 | 591 | 3.8 | 16 | 1 |
| Hostetler | 55 | 202 | 3.7 | 19 | 5 |
| Bell | 67 | 180 | 2.7 | 12 | 1 |
| S. Smith | 47 | 156 | 3.3 | 13 | 0 |
| McCallum | 37 | 114 | 3.1 | 14 | 3 |
| Montgomery | 37 | 106 | 2.9 | 15 | 0 |
| Evans | 14 | 51 | 3.6 | 17 | 0 |
| R. Jordan | 12 | 33 | 2.8 | 12 | 0 |
| Brown | 2 | 7 | 3.5 | 14 | 0 |
| Jett | 1 | 0 | 0.0 | 0 | 0 |
| Ismail | 4 | -5 | -1.2 | 10 | 0 |
| Gossett | 1 | -10 | -10.0 | -10 | 0 |
| Raiders | 433 | 1425 | 3.3 | 19 | 10 |
| Opponents | 494 | 1865 | 3.8 | 60t | 17 |

| RECEIVING | No. | Yds. | Avg. | LG | TD |
|---|---|---|---|---|---|
| Brown | 80 | 1180 | 14.8 | 71t | 7 |
| Horton | 43 | 467 | 10.9 | 32 | 1 |
| Jett | 33 | 771 | 23.4 | 74t | 3 |
| A. Wright | 27 | 462 | 17.1 | 68t | 4 |
| Ismail | 26 | 353 | 13.6 | 43t | 1 |
| S. Smith | 18 | 187 | 10.4 | 22 | 0 |
| Robinson | 15 | 142 | 9.5 | 58 | 0 |
| Bell | 11 | 111 | 10.1 | 18 | 0 |
| Montgomery | 10 | 43 | 4.3 | 9 | 0 |
| Gault | 8 | 64 | 8.0 | 12 | 0 |
| Glover | 4 | 55 | 13.8 | 26 | 1 |
| R. Jordan | 4 | 42 | 10.5 | 33 | 0 |
| McCallum | 2 | 5 | 2.5 | 3 | 0 |
| Raiders | 281 | 3882 | 13.8 | 74t | 17 |
| Opponents | 258 | 3141 | 12.2 | 66t | 17 |

| INTERCEPTIONS | No. | Yds. | Avg. | LG | TD |
|---|---|---|---|---|---|
| McDaniel | 5 | 87 | 17.4 | 36t | 1 |
| Anderson | 2 | 52 | 26.0 | 27 | 0 |
| Hoskins | 2 | 34 | 17.0 | 20 | 0 |
| Washington | 2 | 0 | 0.0 | 0 | 0 |
| McGlockton | 1 | 19 | 19.0 | 19 | 0 |
| Trapp | 1 | 7 | 7.0 | 7 | 0 |
| Bates | 1 | 0 | 0.0 | 0 | 0 |
| Raiders | 14 | 199 | 14.2 | 36t | 1 |
| Opponents | 14 | 289 | 20.6 | 102t | 2 |

| PUNTING | No. | Yds. | Avg. | In 20 | LG |
|---|---|---|---|---|---|
| Gossett | 71 | 2971 | 41.8 | 19 | 61 |
| Raiders | 71 | 2971 | 41.8 | 19 | 61 |
| Opponents | 80 | 3369 | 42.1 | 13 | 56 |

| PUNT RETURNS | No. | FC | Yds. | Avg. | LG | TD |
|---|---|---|---|---|---|---|
| Brown | 40 | 20 | 465 | 11.6 | 74t | 1 |
| Raiders | 40 | 20 | 465 | 11.6 | 74t | 1 |
| Opponents | 35 | 7 | 301 | 8.6 | 28 | 0 |

| KICKOFF RETURNS | No. | Yds. | Avg. | LG | TD |
|---|---|---|---|---|---|
| Ismail | 25 | 605 | 24.2 | 66 | 0 |
| A. Wright | 10 | 167 | 16.7 | 28 | 0 |
| Gault | 7 | 187 | 26.7 | 60 | 0 |
| Robinson | 4 | 57 | 14.3 | 33 | 0 |
| Peat | 2 | 18 | 9.0 | 10 | 0 |
| K. Smith | 2 | 15 | 7.5 | 8 | 0 |
| McCallum | 1 | 12 | 12.0 | 12 | 0 |
| Turk | 1 | 0 | 0.0 | 0 | 0 |
| Raiders | 52 | 1061 | 20.4 | 66 | 0 |
| Opponents | 45 | 783 | 17.4 | 49 | 0 |

| SACKS | No. |
|---|---|
| A. Smith | 12.5 |
| Townsend | 7.5 |
| McGlockton | 7.0 |
| Long | 6.0 |
| Harrison | 3.0 |
| Bruce | 2.0 |
| Wallace | 2.0 |
| Anderson | 1.0 |
| Broughton | 1.0 |
| Kelly | 1.0 |
| Washington | 1.0 |
| Raiders | 45.0 |
| Opponents | 50.0 |

## 1994 DRAFT CHOICES

| Round | Name | Pos. | College |
|---|---|---|---|
| 1 | Rob Fredrickson | LB | Michigan State |
| 2 | James Folston | DE | N.E. Louisiana |
| 3 | Calvin Jones | RB | Nebraska |
| 4 | Austin Robbins | DT | North Carolina |
| 5 | Roosevelt Patterson | G | Alabama |
| 7 | Rob Holmberg | LB | Penn State |

## LOS ANGELES RAIDERS

### 1994 VETERAN ROSTER

| No. | | Name | Pos. | Ht. | Wt. | Birthdate | NFL Exp. | College | Hometown | How Acq. | '93 Games/ Starts |
|---|---|---|---|---|---|---|---|---|---|---|---|
| 33 | | Anderson, Eddie | S | 6-1 | 210 | 7/22/63 | 9 | Fort Valley State | Warner Robins, Ga. | FA-'87 | 16/16 |
| 29 | | Bates, Patrick | S | 6-3 | 220 | 11/27/70 | 2 | Texas A&M | Galveston, Tex. | D1-'93 | 13/0 |
| 43 | † | Bell, Nick | RB | 6-2 | 255 | 8/19/68 | 4 | Iowa | Las Vegas, Nev. | D2-'91 | 10/3 |
| 54 | | Biekert, Greg | LB | 6-2 | 240 | 3/14/69 | 2 | Colorado | Longmont, Colo. | D7-'93 | 16/0 |
| 97 | | Broughton, Willie | DT | 6-5 | 285 | 9/9/64 | 8 | Miami | Ft. Pierce, Fla. | FA-'92 | 15/0 |
| 81 | | Brown, Tim | WR | 6-0 | 195 | 7/22/66 | 7 | Notre Dame | Dallas, Tex. | D1-'88 | 16/16 |
| 56 | | Bruce, Aundray | DE | 6-5 | 260 | 1/30/66 | 7 | Auburn | Montgomery, Ala. | PB(Atl)-'92 | 16/0 |
| 92 | | Collons, Ferric | DT | 6-6 | 295 | 12/4/69 | 2 | California | Sacramento, Calif. | FA-'92 | 0* |
| 31 | | Dixon, Rickey | S | 5-11 | 185 | 12/26/66 | 7 | Oklahoma | Dallas, Tex. | T(Cin)-'93 | 9/0 |
| 46 | | Dorn, Torin | CB | 6-0 | 190 | 2/28/68 | 5 | North Carolina | Southfield, Mich. | D4-'90 | 15/0 |
| 11 | | Evans, Vince | QB | 6-2 | 215 | 6/19/55 | 14 | Southern California | Greensboro, N.C. | FA-'92 | 8/1 |
| 45 | # | Fulcher, David | LB | 6-3 | 245 | 9/28/64 | 9 | Arizona State | Los Angeles, Calif. | FA-'93 | 3/0 |
| 34 | t- | Gainer, Derrick | RB | 5-11 | 240 | 8/15/66 | 4 | Florida A&M | Plant City, Fla. | T(Dall)-'94 | 11/0* |
| 83 | | Gault, Willie | WR | 6-1 | 175 | 9/5/60 | 12 | Tennessee | Griffin, Ga. | T(Chi)-'91 | 15/0 |
| 87 | | Glover, Andrew | TE | 6-6 | 245 | 8/12/67 | 4 | Grambling | Geismar, La. | D10-'91 | 15/0 |
| 66 | | Gogan, Kevin | G | 6-7 | 325 | 11/2/64 | 8 | Washington | Pacifica, Calif. | UFA(Dall)-'94 | 16/16* |
| 7 | | Gossett, Jeff | P | 6-2 | 195 | 1/25/57 | 13 | Eastern Illinois | Charleston, Ill. | T(Hou)-'88 | 16/0 |
| 74 | | Harrison, Nolan | DT | 6-5 | 285 | 1/25/69 | 4 | Indiana | Flossmoor, Ill. | D6-'91 | 16/14 |
| 80 | | Hobbs, Daryl | WR | 6-2 | 175 | 5/23/68 | 2 | Pacific | Los Angeles, Calif. | FA-'93 | 3/0 |
| 12 | | Hobert, Billy Joe | QB | 6-3 | 230 | 1/8/71 | 2 | Washington | Puyallup, Wash. | D3-'93 | 0* |
| 20 | | Hoskins, Derrick | S | 6-2 | 205 | 11/16/70 | 3 | Southern Mississippi | Philadelphia, Miss. | D5-'92 | 16/16 |
| 15 | | Hostetler, Jeff | QB | 6-3 | 220 | 4/22/61 | 11 | West Virginia | Davidsville, Pa. | UFA(NYG)-'93 | 15/15 |
| 86 | | Ismail, Raghib | WR | 5-10 | 180 | 11/16/69 | 2 | Notre Dame | Wilkes-Barre, Pa. | D4-'90 | 13/0 |
| 18 | | Jaeger, Jeff | K | 5-11 | 190 | 11/28/64 | 8 | Washington | Kent, Wash. | PB(Clev)-'89 | 16/0 |
| 82 | | Jett, James | WR | 5-10 | 165 | 12/28/70 | 2 | West Virginia | Charlestown, W. Va. | FA-'93 | 16/1 |
| 52 | | Jones, Mike | LB | 6-1 | 230 | 4/15/69 | 4 | Missouri | Kansas City, Mo. | FA-'91 | 16/2 |
| 85 | | Jordan, Charles | WR | 5-10 | 175 | 10/9/69 | 2 | Long Beach City College | Inglewood, Calif. | FA-'93 | 0* |
| 23 | | Jordan, Randy | RB | 5-10 | 210 | 6/6/70 | 2 | North Carolina | Manson, N.C. | FA-'93 | 10/2 |
| 25 | | Land, Dan | CB | 6-0 | 195 | 7/3/65 | 6 | Albany State | Donalsonville, Ga. | FA-'89 | 15/0 |
| 79 | # | Lanier, Ken | T | 6-3 | 290 | 7/8/59 | 14 | Florida State | Columbus, Ohio | UFA(Den)-'93 | 2/2 |
| 24 | | Lewis, Albert | CB | 6-2 | 195 | 10/6/60 | 12 | Grambling | Mansfield, La. | UFA(KC)-'94 | 14/13* |
| 41 | | McCallum, Napoleon | RB | 6-2 | 225 | 10/6/63 | 6 | Navy | Milford, Ohio | FA-'92 | 13/1 |
| 36 | | McDaniel, Terry | CB | 5-10 | 180 | 2/8/65 | 7 | Tennessee | Saginaw, Mich. | D1-'88 | 16/16 |
| 91 | | McGlockton, Chester | DT | 6-4 | 315 | 9/16/69 | 3 | Clemson | Whiteville, Miss. | D1-'92 | 16/16 |
| 21 | | Montgomery, Tyrone | RB | 6-0 | 190 | 8/3/70 | 2 | Mississippi | Greenville, Miss. | FA-'93 | 12/0 |
| 65 | # | Montoya, Max | G | 6-5 | 295 | 5/2/56 | 16 | UCLA | La Puente, Calif. | PB(Cin)-'90 | 16/16 |
| 72 | | Mosebar, Don | C | 6-6 | 300 | 9/11/61 | 12 | Southern California | Visalia, Calif. | D1-'83 | 16/16 |
| 99 | | Moss, Winston | LB | 6-3 | 240 | 12/24/65 | 8 | Miami | Miami, Fla. | T(TB)-'91 | 16/16 |
| 64 | # | Peat, Todd | G | 6-2 | 305 | 5/20/64 | 6 | Northern Illinois | Champaign, Ill. | FA-'92 | 16/0 |
| 71 | | Perry, Gerald | T | 6-6 | 300 | 11/12/64 | 7 | Southern | Columbia, S.C. | UFA(Rams)-'93 | 15/15 |
| 96 | # | Powers, Warren | DT | 6-7 | 285 | 2/1/65 | 5 | Maryland | Baltimore, Md. | FA-'93 | 0* |
| 28 | | Robinson, Greg | RB | 5-10 | 200 | 8/7/69 | 2 | Northeast Louisiana | Grenada, Miss. | D8-'93 | 12/12 |
| 78 | | Skrepenak, Greg | G | 6-6 | 310 | 1/31/70 | 3 | Michigan | Wilkes-Barre, Pa. | D2-'92 | 0* |
| 94 | | Smith, Anthony | DE | 6-3 | 260 | 6/28/67 | 5 | Arizona | Elizabeth City, N.C. | D1-'90 | 16/2 |
| 39 | | Smith, Kevin | TE | 6-4 | 255 | 7/25/69 | 2 | UCLA | Oakland, Calif. | D7-'91 | 10/1 |
| 77 | | Stephens, Rich | T | 6-7 | 300 | 11/1/65 | 2 | Tulsa | St. Louis, Mo. | FA-'92 | 16/1 |
| 93 | | Townsend, Greg | DE | 6-3 | 275 | 11/3/61 | 12 | Texas Christian | Compton, Calif. | D4-'83 | 16/16 |
| 37 | | Trapp, James | CB | 6-0 | 180 | 12/28/69 | 2 | Clemson | Lawton, Okla. | D3-'93 | 14/2 |
| 67 | | Turk, Dan | C | 6-4 | 290 | 8/25/62 | 10 | Wisconsin | Milwaukee, Wis. | FA-'89 | 16/0 |
| 51 | | Wallace, Aaron | LB | 6-3 | 240 | 4/17/67 | 5 | Texas A&M | Dallas, Tex. | D2-'90 | 16/14 |
| 48 | | Washington, Lionel | CB | 6-0 | 185 | 10/21/60 | 12 | Tulane | New Orleans, La. | T(StL)-'87 | 16/16 |
| 68 | | Wilkerson, Bruce | T | 6-5 | 295 | 7/28/64 | 8 | Tennessee | Philadelphia, Tenn. | D2-'87 | 14/14 |
| 22 | | Williams, Harvey | RB | 6-2 | 220 | 4/22/67 | 4 | Louisiana State | Hempstead, Tex. | UFA(KC)-'94 | 7/6* |
| 88 | | Williams, Jamie | TE | 6-4 | 240 | 4/25/60 | 12 | Nebraska | Davenport, Iowa | UFA(SF)-'94 | 16/0* |
| 76 | | Wisniewski, Steve | G | 6-4 | 285 | 4/7/67 | 6 | Penn State | Houston, Tex. | D2-'89 | 16/16 |
| 89 | | Wright, Alexander | WR | 6-0 | 190 | 7/19/67 | 5 | Auburn | Albany, Ga. | T(Dall)-'92 | 15/15 |

* Collons inactive for 16 games in '93; Gogan played 16 games with Dallas; Gainer played 11 games with Dallas; Hobert active for 1 game but did not play; C. Jordan inactive for 16 games; Lewis played 14 games with Kansas City; Powers last active with L.A. Rams in '92; Skrepenak inactive for 16 games; H. Williams played 7 games with Kansas City; J. Williams played 16 games with San Francisco.

# Unrestricted free agent; subject to developments.

† Restricted free agent; subject to developments.

Retired—Howie Long, 13-year defensive end, 16 games in '93; Steve Wright, 11-year tackle, 0 games in '93.

Traded—CB-S Elvis Patterson to Dallas.

t- Raiders traded for Gainer.

Players lost through free agency (2): TE Ethan Horton (Wash; 16 games in '93), LB Joe Kelly (Rams; 16).

Also played with Raiders in '93—TE John Duff (1 game), S Elvis Patterson (3), RB Steve Smith (16).

## COACHING STAFF

**Head Coach,**
**Art Shell**

**Pro Career:** Named ninth head coach in Raiders' history on October 3, 1989. Had been Raiders' offensive line coach for seven years, including 1983 world championship season. He first joined the coaching staff in 1983 after 15 seasons as one of the greatest offensive tackles in pro football history. Came to Raiders in 1968 as a third-round draft choice out of Maryland State (now Maryland-Eastern Shore). Went on to play in 207 league games, including first 156 in a row, and 24 playoff games for the Raiders. Starting left tackle in Super Bowl XI and XV victories. Selected to Pro Bowl eight times—most by any Raiders player. Inducted into Pro Football Hall of Fame on August 5, 1989. Also named to state of South Carolina Sports Hall of Fame. Career record: 47-34.
**Background:** All-America tackle as junior and senior and three-year All-Conference on both offense and defense at Maryland State 1965-67. Also lettered in basketball.
**Personal:** Born November 26, 1946, Charleston, S.C. Art and wife, Janice, live in Palos Verdes, California, with their sons—Arthur III and Christopher.

### ASSISTANT COACHES

**Fred Biletnikoff,** wide receivers; born February 23, 1943, Erie, Pa., lives in El Segundo, Calif. Wide receiver Florida State 1962-64. Pro wide receiver Oakland Raiders 1965-78, Montreal Alouettes (CFL) 1980. College coach: Palomar, Calif., J.C. 1983, Diablo Valley, Calif., J.C. 1984, 1986. Pro coach: Oakland Invaders (USFL) 1985, Calgary Stampeders (CFL) 1987-88, joined Raiders in 1989.
**Gunther Cunningham,** defensive line; born June 19, 1946, Munich, Germany, lives in Palos Verdes, Calif. Linebacker Oregon 1965-67. No pro playing experience. College coach: Oregon 1969-71, Arkansas 1972, Stanford 1973-76, California 1977-80. Pro coach: Hamilton Tiger-Cats (CFL) 1981, Baltimore/Indianapolis Colts 1982-84, San Diego Chargers 1985-90, joined Raiders in 1991.
**John Fox,** defensive coordinator; born February 8, 1955, Virginia Beach, Va., lives in Palos Verdes, Calif. Defensive back San Diego State 1975-77. No pro playing experience. College coach: U.S. International 1979, Boise State 1980, Long Beach State 1981, Utah 1982, Kansas 1983, 1985, Iowa State 1984, Pittsburgh 1986-88. Pro coach: Los Angeles Express (USFL) 1985, Pittsburgh Steelers 1989-91, San Diego Chargers 1992-93, joined Raiders in 1994.
**Ray Hamilton,** defensive line; born January 20, 1951, Omaha, Neb., lives in Culver City, Calif. Nose tackle Oklahoma 1969-72. Pro nose tackle-defensive end New England Patriots 1973-81. College coach: Tennessee 1992. Pro coach: New England Patriots 1985-89, Tampa Bay Buccaneers 1991, joined Raiders in 1993.
**Jim Haslett,** linebackers; born December 9, 1955, Pittsburgh, Pa., lives in Palos Verdes, Calif. Defensive end Indiana University (Pa.) 1975-78. Linebacker Buffalo Bills 1979-86, New York Jets 1987. College coach: Buffalo 1988-90. Pro coach: Sacramento Surge (World League) 1991-92, joined Raiders in 1993.
**Odis McKinney,** defensive backs; born May 19, 1957, Detroit, Mich., lives in Manhattan Beach, Calif. Defensive back Colorado 1976-77. Pro defensive back New York Giants 1978-79, Oakland/Los Angeles Raiders 1980-85, Kansas City Chiefs 1985, Los Angeles Raiders 1986. Pro coach: Joined Raiders in 1990.
**Bill Meyers,** offensive line-tight ends; born October 8, 1946, Chippewa Falls, Wis., lives in Surfside, Calif. Tackle Stanford 1970-71. No pro playing experience. College coach: California 1972-73, 1977-78, Santa Clara 1974-76, Notre Dame 1979-81, Missouri 1985-86, Pittsburgh 1987-92. Pro coach: Green Bay Packers 1982-83, Pittsburgh Steelers 1984, joined Raiders in 1993.
**Steve Ortmayer,** football operations-special teams; born February 13, 1944, Painesville, Ohio, lives in Palos Verdes Estates, Calif. La Verne College 1966. No college or pro playing experience. College coach: Colorado 1967-73, Georgia Tech 1974. Pro coach: Kansas City Chiefs 1975-77,Oakland/Los Angeles Raiders 1978-86, San Diego Chargers 1987-89 (Director of Football Operations), rejoined Raiders in 1990.
**Jack Reilly,** offensive backfield; born May 22, 1945, Boston, Mass., lives in El Segundo, Calif. Quarterback Washington State 1963, Santa Monica, Calif., J.C. 1964, Long Beach State 1965-66. No pro playing experience. College coach: El Camino, Calif., J.C. 1980-84 (head coach 1981-84), Utah 1985-89. Pro coach: San Diego Chargers 1990-93, joined Raiders in 1994.
**Jack Stanton,** defensive backs; born June 6, 1938, Bridgeville, Pa., lives in El Segundo, Calif. Running back North Carolina State 1959-60. Pro running back Pittsburgh Steelers 1961, Toronto Argonauts (CFL) 1962-63. College coach: George Washington 1966, North Carolina State 1968-72, Florida State 1973, 1976-83, North Carolina 1974-75, Purdue 1986, New Mexico 1987-88. Pro coach: Atlanta Falcons 1984-85, joined Raiders in 1989.
**Tom Walsh,** offense; born April 16, 1949, Vallejo, Calif., lives in Manhattan Beach, Calif. UC-Santa Barbara 1971. No college or pro playing experience. College coach: University of San Diego 1972-76, U.S. International 1979 (head coach), Murray State 1980, Cincinnati 1981. Pro coach: Joined Raiders in 1982.
**Mike White,** offensive line; born January 4, 1936, Berkeley, Calif., lives in Newport Beach, Calif. Offensive end California 1955-57. No pro playing experience. College coach: California 1958-63, 1972-77 (head coach), Stanford 1964-71, Illinois 1980-87 (head coach). Pro coach: San Francisco 49ers 1978-79, joined Raiders in 1990.
**Arthur Whittington,** assistant; born September 4, 1955, Cuero, Tex; lives in El Segundo, Calif. Running back Southern Methodist 1974-77. Pro running back Oakland Raiders 1978-81, Oakland Invaders (USFL) 1983-85. College coach: Southern Methodist 1986. Pro coach: Joined Raiders in 1994.

## 1994 FIRST-YEAR ROSTER

| Name | Pos. | Ht. | Wt. | Birthdate | College | Hometown | How Acq. |
|---|---|---|---|---|---|---|---|
| Brabham, Cary (1) | S | 6-0 | 195 | 8/11/70 | Southern Methodist | Hughes Springs, Tex. | FA |
| Butler, Darren (1) | CB | 5-10 | 175 | 1/19/70 | Alcorn State | Tylertown, Miss. | FA |
| Duff, John (1) | TE | 6-7 | 250 | 7/31/67 | New Mexico | Tustin, Calif. | FA |
| Elliott, Matt | G | 6-4 | 285 | 5/27/71 | Northern Arizona | Yorba Linda, Calif. | FA |
| Folston, James | LB | 6-3 | 240 | 8//14/71 | Northeast Louisiana | Cocoa, Fla. | D2 |
| Fredrickson, Rob | LB | 6-4 | 235 | 5/13/71 | Michigan State | St. Joseph, Mich. | D1 |
| Gallatin, Donovan | S | 6-1 | 210 | 2/16/71 | UCLA | El Segundo, Calif. | FA |
| Hill, James | RB | 5-11 | 215 | 2/20/70 | Colorado | Colorado Springs, Colo. | FA |
| Holmberg, Rob | LB | 6-3 | 225 | 5/6/71 | Penn State | Mt. Pleasant, Pa. | D7 |
| Johnson, Billy | RB | 5-10 | 200 | 9/21/70 | Arizona | San Jose, Calif. | FA |
| Jones, Brian (1) | LB | 6-3 | 245 | 1/22/68 | Texas | Lubbock, Tex. | FA |
| Jones, Calvin | RB | 5-11 | 215 | 11/27/70 | Nebraska | Omaha, Neb. | D3 |
| Kralik, Joe | WR | 5-11 | 185 | 12/14/70 | Washington | Puyallup, Wash. | FA |
| Morris, Cree | QB | 6-7 | 235 | 12/17/70 | St. Mary's | Escondido, Calif. | FA |
| Morton, John (1) | WR | 6-0 | 185 | 9/24/69 | Western Michigan | Auburn Hills, Mich. | FA |
| Neujahr, Quentin | C | 6-4 | 285 | 1/30/71 | Kansas State | Ulysses, Neb. | FA |
| Patterson, Roosevelt | G | 6-3 | 310 | 7/12/70 | Alabama | Prichard, Ala. | D5 |
| Ridley, Lester (1) | CB | 6-1 | 180 | 11/15/70 | Iowa State | Omaha, Neb. | FA |
| Robbins, Austin | DT | 6-6 | 300 | 3/1/71 | North Carolina | Washington, D.C. | D4 |
| Skartvedt, Doug | T | 6-3 | 305 | 7/2/71 | Iowa State | Hubbard, Iowa | FA |
| Stubbins, Willie | T | 6-5 | 290 | 5/23/67 | Texas Southern | Tifton, Ga. | FA |
| White, Alberto (1) | DE | 6-3 | 240 | 4/3/71 | Texas Southern | Miami, Fla. | FA |

The term NFL Rookie is defined as a player who is in his first season of professional football and has not been on the roster of another professional football team for any regular-season or postseason games. A Rookie is designated by an "R" on NFL rosters. Players who have been active in another professional football league or players who have NFL experience, including either preseason training camp or being on an Active List or Inactive List, or on Reserve/Injured or Reserve/Physically Unable to Perform for fewer than six regular-season games, are termed NFL First-Year Players. An NFL First-Year Player is designated by a "1" on NFL rosters. Thereafter, a player is credited with an additional year of experience for each season in which he accumulates six games on the Active List or Inactive List, or on Reserve/Injured or Reserve/Physically Unable to Perform.

## NOTES

# MIAMI DOLPHINS

**American Football Conference**
**Eastern Division**
**Team Colors:** Aqua, Coral, and White
**Joe Robbie Stadium**
**2269 N.W. 199th Street**
**Miami, Florida 33056**
**Telephone: (305) 620-5000**

## CLUB OFFICIALS

President: Timothy J. Robbie
Executive Vice President: Daniel T. Robbie
Executive Vice President: Janet Robbie
Executive VP/General Manager: Eddie J. Jones
General Counsel: Jann M. Iliff
Treasurer: Jill R. Strafaci
Assistant General Manager: Bryan Wiedmeier
Head Coach: Don Shula
Director of Player Personnel: Tom Heckert
Director of College Scouting: Tom Braatz
Director of Facility Operations: John Glode
Director of Media Relations: Harvey Greene
Media Relations Assistant: Scott Stone
Marketing Director: David Evans
Community Relations Director: Fudge Browne
Ticket Director: Lamar Vernon
Sales Director: Lynn Abramson
Trainer: Ryan Vermillion
Equipment Manager: Bob Monica
**Stadium:** Joe Robbie Stadium • **Capacity:** 74,916
2269 N.W. 199th Street
Miami, Florida 33056
**Playing Surface:** Grass (PAT)
**Training Camp:** Nova University
7500 S.W. 30th Street
Davie, Florida 33314

## 1994 SCHEDULE

**PRESEASON**

| | | |
|---|---|---|
| July 30 | at New York Giants | 8:00 |
| Aug. 6 | **Pittsburgh** | 8:00 |
| Aug. 13 | vs. Green Bay at Milwaukee | 7:00 |
| Aug. 20 | **Tampa Bay** | 8:00 |
| Aug. 26 | at Minnesota | 7:00 |

**REGULAR SEASON**

| | | |
|---|---|---|
| Sept. 4 | **New England** | 4:00 |
| Sept. 11 | vs. Green Bay at Milwaukee | 12:00 |
| Sept. 18 | **New York Jets** | 1:00 |
| Sept. 25 | at Minnesota | 12:00 |
| Oct. 2 | at Cincinnati | 8:00 |
| Oct. 9 | at Buffalo | 1:00 |
| Oct. 16 | **Los Angeles Raiders** | 1:00 |
| Oct. 23 | Open Date | |
| Oct. 30 | at New England | 1:00 |
| Nov. 6 | **Indianapolis** | 1:00 |
| Nov. 13 | **Chicago** | 1:00 |
| Nov. 20 | at Pittsburgh | 1:00 |
| Nov. 27 | at New York Jets | 1:00 |
| Dec. 4 | **Buffalo** | 8:00 |
| Dec. 12 | **Kansas City** (Monday) | 9:00 |
| Dec. 18 | at Indianapolis | 1:00 |
| Dec. 25 | **Detroit** | 8:00 |

## RECORD HOLDERS

**INDIVIDUAL RECORDS—CAREER**

| Category | Name | Performance |
|---|---|---|
| Rushing (Yds.) | Larry Csonka, 1968-1974, 1979 | 6,737 |
| Passing (Yds.) | Dan Marino, 1983-1993 | 40,720 |
| Passing (TDs) | Dan Marino, 1983-1993 | 298 |
| Receiving (No.) | Mark Clayton, 1983-1992 | 550 |
| Receiving (Yds.) | Mark Duper, 1982-1992 | 8,869 |
| Interceptions | Jake Scott, 1970-75 | 35 |
| Punting (Avg.) | Reggie Roby, 1983-1992 | 43.3 |
| Punt Return (Avg.) | Freddie Solomon, 1975-77 | 11.4 |
| Kickoff Return (Avg.) | Mercury Morris, 1969-1975 | 26.5 |
| Field Goals | Garo Yepremian, 1970-78 | 165 |
| Touchdowns (Tot.) | Mark Clayton, 1983-1992 | 82 |
| Points | Garo Yepremian, 1970-78 | 830 |

**INDIVIDUAL RECORDS—SINGLE SEASON**

| Category | Name | Performance |
|---|---|---|
| Rushing (Yds.) | Delvin Williams, 1978 | 1,258 |
| Passing (Yds.) | Dan Marino, 1984 | *5,084 |
| Passing (TDs) | Dan Marino, 1984 | *48 |
| Receiving (No.) | Mark Clayton, 1988 | 86 |
| Receiving (Yds.) | Mark Clayton, 1984 | 1,389 |
| Interceptions | Dick Westmoreland, 1967 | 10 |
| Punting (Avg.) | Reggie Roby, 1991 | 45.7 |
| Punt Return (Avg.) | Freddie Solomon, 1975 | 12.3 |
| Kickoff Return (Avg.) | Duriel Harris, 1976 | 32.9 |
| Field Goals | Pete Stoyanovich, 1991 | 31 |
| Touchdowns (Tot.) | Mark Clayton, 1984 | 18 |
| Points | Pete Stoyanovich, 1992 | 124 |

**INDIVIDUAL RECORDS—SINGLE GAME**

| Category | Name | Performance |
|---|---|---|
| Rushing (Yds.) | Mercury Morris, 9-30-73 | 197 |
| Passing (Yds.) | Dan Marino, 10-23-88 | 521 |
| Passing (TDs) | Bob Griese, 11-24-77 | 6 |
| | Dan Marino, 9-21-86 | 6 |
| Receiving (No.) | Jim Jensen, 11-6-88 | 12 |
| Receiving (Yds.) | Mark Duper, 11-10-85 | 217 |
| Interceptions | Dick Anderson, 12-3-73 | *4 |
| Field Goals | Garo Yepremian, 9-26-71 | 5 |
| Touchdowns (Tot.) | Paul Warfield, 12-15-73 | 4 |
| Points | Paul Warfield, 12-15-73 | 24 |

*NFL Record

## COACHING HISTORY

**(269-171-4)**

| | | |
|---|---|---|
| 1966-69 | George Wilson | 15-39-2 |
| 1970-93 | Don Shula | 254-132-2 |

**JOE ROBBIE STADIUM**

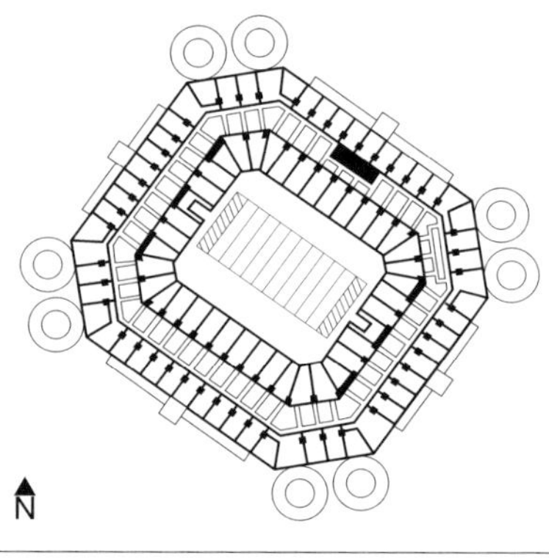

## 1993 TEAM RECORD

**PRESEASON (3-1)**

| Date | Result | | Opponents |
|---|---|---|---|
| 8/6 | W | 28-27 | at Atlanta |
| 8/14 | W | 19-10 | Washington |
| 8/20 | L | 24-34 | at Denver |
| 8/28 | W | 23-17 | N.Y. Giants |

**REGULAR SEASON (9-7)**

| Date | Result | | Opponents | Att. |
|---|---|---|---|---|
| 9/5 | W | 24-20 | at Indianapolis | 51,858 |
| 9/12 | L | 14-24 | N.Y. Jets | 70,314 |
| 9/26 | W | 22-13 | at Buffalo | 79,635 |
| 10/4 | W | 17-10 | Washington | 68,568 |
| 10/10 | W | 24-14 | at Cleveland | 78,138 |
| 10/24 | W | 41-27 | Indianapolis | 57,301 |
| 10/31 | W | 30-10 | Kansas City | 67,765 |
| 11/7 | L | 10-27 | at N.Y. Jets | 71,306 |
| 11/14 | W | 19-14 | at Philadelphia | 64,213 |
| 11/21 | W | 17-13 | New England | 59,982 |
| 11/25 | W | 16-14 | at Dallas | 60,198 |
| 12/5 | L | 14-19 | N.Y. Giants | 72,161 |
| 12/13 | L | 20-21 | Pittsburgh | 70,232 |
| 12/19 | L | 34-47 | Buffalo | 71,597 |
| 12/27 | L | 20-45 | at San Diego | 60,311 |
| 1/2 | L | 27-33 | at New England (OT) | 53,883 |

(OT) Overtime

**SCORE BY PERIODS**

| | | | | | | | |
|---|---|---|---|---|---|---|---|
| Dolphins | 100 | 76 | 85 | 88 | 0 | — | 349 |
| Opponents | 56 | 126 | 71 | 92 | 6 | — | 351 |

**ATTENDANCE**

Home 537,920 Away 519,542 Total 1,057,462
Single-game home record, 72,161 (12-5-93)
Single-season home record, 537,920 (1993)

## 1993 TEAM STATISTICS

| | Dolphins | Opp. |
|---|---|---|
| Total First Downs | 309 | 332 |
| Rushing | 85 | 103 |
| Passing | 207 | 205 |
| Penalty | 17 | 24 |
| Third Down: Made/Att | 100/218 | 103/229 |
| Third Down Pct. | 45.9 | 45.0 |
| Fourth Down: Made/Att | 8/17 | 3/10 |
| Fourth Down Pct. | 47.1 | 30.0 |
| Total Net Yards | 5812 | 5150 |
| Avg. Per Game | 363.3 | 321.9 |
| Total Plays | 1030 | 1061 |
| Avg. Per Play | 5.6 | 4.9 |
| Net Yards Rushing | 1459 | 1665 |
| Avg. Per Game | 91.2 | 104.1 |
| Total Rushes | 419 | 460 |
| Net Yards Passing | 4353 | 3485 |
| Avg. Per Game | 272.1 | 217.8 |
| Sacked/Yards Lost | 30/211 | 29/197 |
| Gross Yards | 4564 | 3682 |
| Att./Completions | 581/342 | 572/350 |
| Completion Pct. | 58.9 | 61.2 |
| Had Intercepted | 18 | 13 |
| Punts/Avg. | 58/39.7 | 76/41.3 |
| Net Punting Avg. | 58/32.2 | 76/34.9 |
| Penalties/Yards Lost | 81/663 | 92/650 |
| Fumbles/Ball Lost | 32/16 | 30/14 |
| Touchdowns | 40 | 43 |
| Rushing | 10 | 12 |
| Passing | 27 | 26 |
| Returns | 3 | 5 |
| Avg. Time of Possession | 28:59 | 31:01 |

## 1993 INDIVIDUAL STATISTICS

| PASSING | Att. | Cmp. | Yds. | Pct. | TD | Int. | Tkld. | Rate |
|---|---|---|---|---|---|---|---|---|
| Mitchell | 233 | 133 | 1773 | 57.1 | 12 | 8 | 7/49 | 84.2 |
| DeBerg | 188 | 113 | 1521 | 60.1 | 6 | 7 | 15/116 | 81.0 |
| Marino | 150 | 91 | 1218 | 60.7 | 8 | 3 | 7/42 | 95.9 |
| Pederson | 8 | 4 | 41 | 50.0 | 0 | 0 | 1/4 | 65.1 |
| Byars | 2 | 1 | 11 | 50.0 | 1 | 0 | 0/0 | 106.3 |
| Dolphins | 581 | 342 | 4564 | 58.9 | 27 | 18 | 30/211 | 86.4 |
| Opponents | 572 | 350 | 3682 | 61.2 | 26 | 13 | 29/197 | 85.6 |

| SCORING | TD R | TD P | TD Rt | PAT | FG | Saf | PTS |
|---|---|---|---|---|---|---|---|
| Stoyanovich | 0 | 0 | 0 | 37/37 | 24/32 | 0 | 109 |
| Byars | 3 | 3 | 0 | 0/0 | 0/0 | 0 | 36 |
| Ingram | 0 | 6 | 0 | 0/0 | 0/0 | 0 | 36 |
| K. Jackson | 0 | 6 | 0 | 0/0 | 0/0 | 0 | 36 |
| Kirby | 3 | 3 | 0 | 0/0 | 0/0 | 0 | 36 |
| Fryar | 0 | 5 | 0 | 0/0 | 0/0 | 0 | 30 |
| Higgs | 3 | 0 | 0 | 0/0 | 0/0 | 0 | 18 |
| Martin | 0 | 3 | 0 | 0/0 | 0/0 | 0 | 18 |
| McDuffie | 0 | 0 | 2 | 0/0 | 0/0 | 0 | 12 |
| Baty | 0 | 1 | 0 | 0/0 | 0/0 | 0 | 6 |
| Marino | 1 | 0 | 0 | 0/0 | 0/0 | 0 | 6 |
| L. Oliver | 0 | 0 | 1 | 0/0 | 0/0 | 0 | 6 |
| Dolphins | 10 | 27 | 3 | 37/40 | 24/32 | 0 | 349 |
| Opponents | 12 | 26 | 5 | 40/42 | 17/27 | 1 | 351 |

| RUSHING | Att. | Yds. | Avg. | LG | TD |
|---|---|---|---|---|---|
| Higgs | 186 | 693 | 3.7 | 31 | 3 |
| Kirby | 119 | 390 | 3.3 | 20 | 3 |
| Byars | 64 | 269 | 4.2 | 77t | 3 |
| Mitchell | 21 | 89 | 4.2 | 32 | 0 |
| Parmalee | 4 | 16 | 4.0 | 12 | 0 |
| Saxon | 5 | 13 | 2.6 | 9 | 0 |
| Martin | 1 | 6 | 6.0 | 6 | 0 |
| Pederson | 2 | -1 | -0.5 | 0 | 0 |
| DeBerg | 4 | -4 | -1.0 | -1 | 0 |
| Fryar | 3 | -4 | -1.3 | 2 | 0 |
| Marino | 9 | -4 | -0.4 | 4t | 1 |
| McDuffie | 1 | -4 | -4.0 | -4 | 0 |
| Dolphins | 419 | 1459 | 3.5 | 77t | 10 |
| Opponents | 460 | 1665 | 3.6 | 65t | 12 |

| RECEIVING | No. | Yds. | Avg. | LG | TD |
|---|---|---|---|---|---|
| Kirby | 75 | 874 | 11.7 | 47 | 3 |
| Fryar | 64 | 1010 | 15.8 | 65t | 5 |
| Byars | 61 | 613 | 10.0 | 27 | 3 |
| Ingram | 44 | 707 | 16.1 | 77t | 6 |
| K. Jackson | 39 | 613 | 15.7 | 57t | 6 |
| Martin | 20 | 347 | 17.4 | 80t | 3 |
| McDuffie | 19 | 197 | 10.4 | 18 | 0 |
| Higgs | 10 | 72 | 7.2 | 15 | 0 |
| Baty | 5 | 78 | 15.6 | 32 | 1 |
| Miller | 2 | 15 | 7.5 | 8 | 0 |
| Banks | 1 | 26 | 26.0 | 26 | 0 |
| M. Williams | 1 | 11 | 11.0 | 11 | 0 |
| Parmalee | 1 | 1 | 1.0 | 1 | 0 |
| Dolphins | 342 | 4564 | 13.3 | 80t | 27 |
| Opponents | 350 | 3682 | 10.5 | 54 | 26 |

| INTERCEPTIONS | No. | Yds. | Avg. | LG | TD |
|---|---|---|---|---|---|
| Brown | 5 | 43 | 8.6 | 29 | 0 |
| L. Oliver | 2 | 60 | 30.0 | 56t | 1 |
| Vincent | 2 | 29 | 14.5 | 23 | 0 |
| Green | 2 | 0 | 0.0 | 0 | 0 |
| Cox | 1 | 26 | 26.0 | 26 | 0 |
| Hobley | 1 | 17 | 17.0 | 17 | 0 |
| Dolphins | 13 | 175 | 13.5 | 56t | 1 |
| Opponents | 18 | 329 | 18.3 | 97t | 2 |

| PUNTING | No. | Yds. | Avg. | In 20 | LG |
|---|---|---|---|---|---|
| Hatcher | 58 | 2304 | 39.7 | 13 | 56 |
| Dolphins | 58 | 2304 | 39.7 | 13 | 56 |
| Opponents | 76 | 3135 | 41.3 | 19 | 60 |

| PUNT RETURNS | No. | FC | Yds. | Avg. | LG | TD |
|---|---|---|---|---|---|---|
| McDuffie | 28 | 22 | 317 | 11.3 | 72t | 2 |
| Vincent | 0 | 0 | 9 | — | 9 | 0 |
| Dolphins | 28 | 22 | 326 | 11.6 | 72t | 2 |
| Opponents | 32 | 12 | 359 | 11.2 | 64t | 1 |

| KICKOFF RETURNS | No. | Yds. | Avg. | LG | TD |
|---|---|---|---|---|---|
| McDuffie | 32 | 755 | 23.6 | 48 | 0 |
| M. Williams | 8 | 180 | 22.5 | 39 | 0 |
| Kirby | 4 | 85 | 21.3 | 26 | 0 |
| Miller | 2 | 22 | 11.0 | 16 | 0 |
| Baty | 1 | 7 | 7.0 | 7 | 0 |
| Fryar | 1 | 10 | 10.0 | 10 | 0 |
| Saxon | 1 | 7 | 7.0 | 7 | 0 |
| Vincent | 0 | 2 | — | 2 | 0 |
| Dolphins | 49 | 1068 | 21.8 | 48 | 0 |
| Opponents | 62 | 1239 | 20.0 | 40 | 0 |

| SACKS | No. |
|---|---|
| Cross | 10.5 |
| Coleman | 5.5 |
| Cox | 5.0 |
| Hunter | 3.0 |
| Veasey | 2.0 |
| Klingbeil | 1.5 |
| Alexander | 1.0 |
| Griggs | 0.5 |
| Dolphins | 29.0 |
| Opponents | 30.0 |

## 1994 DRAFT CHOICES

| Round | Name | Pos. | College |
|---|---|---|---|
| 1 | Tim Bowens | DT | Mississippi |
| 2 | Aubrey Beavers | LB | Oklahoma |
| | Tim Ruddy | C | Notre Dame |
| 4 | Ronnie Woolfork | LB | Colorado |
| 5 | William Gaines | DT | Florida |
| 6 | Brant Boyer | LB | Arizona |
| 7 | Sean Hill | DB | Montana State |

# MIAMI DOLPHINS

## 1994 VETERAN ROSTER

| No. | | Name | Pos. | Ht. | Wt. | Birthdate | NFL Exp. | College | Hometown | How Acq. | '93 Games/ Starts |
|---|---|---|---|---|---|---|---|---|---|---|---|
| 32 | # | Alexander, Bruce | CB | 5-8 | 178 | 9/17/65 | 6 | Stephen F. Austin | Lufkin, Tex. | PB(Det)-'92 | 14/0 |
| 6 | | Arnold, Jim | P | 6-3 | 211 | 1/31/61 | 12 | Vanderbilt | Dalton, Ga. | UFA(Det)-'94 | 16/0* |
| 28 | | Atkins, Gene | S | 5-11 | 200 | 11/22/64 | 8 | Florida A&M | Tallahassee, Fla. | UFA(NO)-'94 | 16/16* |
| 84 | # | Baty, Greg | TE | 6-6 | 240 | 8/28/64 | 8 | Stanford | Sparta, N.J. | FA-'90 | 16/1 |
| 66 | | Blake, Eddie | G | 6-3 | 315 | 12/18/68 | 2 | Auburn | Fayetteville, Tenn. | D2-'92 | 0* |
| 34 | | Braxton, Tyrone | CB | 5-11 | 185 | 12/17/64 | 8 | North Dakota State | Madison, Wis. | UFA(Den)-'94 | 16/16* |
| 37 | | Brown, J.B. | CB | 6-0 | 190 | 1/5/67 | 6 | Maryland | Washington, D.C. | D12-'89 | 16/16 |
| 41 | | Byars, Keith | RB | 6-1 | 256 | 10/14/63 | 9 | Ohio State | Dayton, Ohio | UFA(Phil)-'93 | 16/16 |
| 90 | | Coleman, Marco | DE | 6-3 | 262 | 12/18/69 | 3 | Georgia Tech | Dayton, Ohio | D1b-'92 | 15/15 |
| 51 | | Cox, Bryan | LB | 6-4 | 242 | 2/17/68 | 4 | Western Illinois | East St. Louis, Ill. | D5a-'91 | 16/16 |
| 49 | | Craver, Aaron | RB | 6-0 | 220 | 12/18/68 | 4 | Fresno State | Compton, Calif. | D3-'91 | 0* |
| 91 | | Cross, Jeff | DE | 6-4 | 273 | 3/25/66 | 7 | Missouri | Blythe, Calif. | D9-'88 | 16/16 |
| 17 | # | DeBerg, Steve | QB | 6-3 | 220 | 1/19/54 | 18 | San Jose State | Anaheim, Calif. | FA-'93 | 8/5* |
| 65 | | Dellenbach, Jeff | T-C | 6-5 | 290 | 2/14/63 | 10 | Wisconsin | Wausau, Wis. | D4b-'85 | 16/16 |
| 74 | # | Dennis, Mark | T | 6-6 | 296 | 4/15/65 | 8 | Illinois | Washington, Ill. | D8b-'87 | 16/0 |
| 80 | | Fryar, Irving | WR | 6-0 | 200 | 9/28/62 | 11 | Nebraska | Mount Holly, N.J. | T(NE)-'93 | 16/16 |
| 62 | | Gray, Chris | G-T | 6-4 | 289 | 6/19/70 | 2 | Auburn | Birmingham, Ala. | D5-'93 | 5/0 |
| 42 | | Green, Chris | S-CB | 5-11 | 192 | 2/26/68 | 4 | Illinois | Lawrenceburg, Ind. | D7-'91 | 14/0 |
| 59 | # | Grimsley, John | LB | 6-2 | 236 | 2/25/62 | 11 | Kentucky | Canton, Ohio | T(Hou)-'91 | 13/9 |
| 45 | # | Harden, Bobby | S | 6-0 | 205 | 2/8/67 | 5 | Miami | Fort Lauderdale, Fla. | D12-'90 | 8/0 |
| 73 | | Heller, Ron | T | 6-6 | 293 | 8/25/62 | 11 | Penn State | Farmingdale, N.Y. | UFA(Phil)-'93 | 16/16 |
| 21 | | Higgs, Mark | RB | 5-7 | 196 | 4/11/66 | 7 | Kentucky | Owensboro, Ky. | PB(Phil)-'90 | 16/8 |
| 50 | | Hollier, Dwight | LB | 6-2 | 250 | 4/21/69 | 3 | North Carolina | Hampton, Va. | D4-'92 | 16/10 |
| 82 | | Ingram, Mark | WR | 5-11 | 190 | 8/23/68 | 8 | Michigan State | Flint, Mich. | UFA(NYG)-'93 | 16/16 |
| 88 | | Jackson, Keith | TE | 6-2 | 254 | 4/19/65 | 7 | Oklahoma | Little Rock, Ark. | UFA(Phil)-'92 | 15/15 |
| 24 | # | Jackson, Vestee | CB | 6-0 | 186 | 8/14/63 | 9 | Washington | Fresno, Calif. | T(Chi)-'91 | 16/5 |
| 43 | | Kirby, Terry | RB | 6-1 | 219 | 1/20/70 | 2 | Virginia | Tabb, Va. | D3-'93 | 16/8 |
| 99 | † | Klingbeil, Chuck | NT | 6-1 | 289 | 11/2/65 | 4 | Northern Michigan | Houghton, Mich. | FA-'91 | 16/16 |
| 19 | | Kosar, Bernie | QB | 6-5 | 215 | 11/25/63 | 10 | Miami | Boardman, Ohio | UFA(Dall)-'94 | 11/7* |
| 47 | | Malone, Darrell | CB | 5-10 | 182 | 11/23/67 | 3 | Jacksonville State | Jacksonville, Ala. | FA-'92 | 16/1 |
| 13 | | Marino, Dan | QB | 6-4 | 224 | 9/15/61 | 12 | Pittsburgh | Pittsburgh, Pa. | D1-'83 | 5/5 |
| 81 | | McDuffie, O.J. | WR | 5-10 | 185 | 12/2/69 | 2 | Penn State | Gates Mills, Ohio | D1-'93 | 16/0 |
| 15 | # | Millen, Hugh | QB | 6-5 | 216 | 11/22/63 | 9 | Washington | Seattle, Wash. | FA-'93 | 0* |
| 93 | # | Odom, Cliff | LB | 6-2 | 236 | 8/15/58 | 14 | Texas-Arlington | Beaumont, Tex. | PB(Ind)-'90 | 14/1 |
| 56 | # | Offerdahl, John | LB | 6-3 | 238 | 8/17/64 | 9 | Western Michigan | Fort Atkinson, Wis. | D2-'86 | 9/8 |
| 20 | | Oliver, Muhammad | CB-S | 5-11 | 180 | 3/12/69 | 3 | Oregon | Brooklyn, N.Y. | FA-'93 | 4/0* |
| 30 | | Parmalee, Bernie | RB | 5-11 | 204 | 9/16/67 | 3 | Ball State | Jersey City, N.J. | FA-'92 | 16/0 |
| 14 | | Pederson, Doug | QB | 6-3 | 209 | 1/31/68 | 2 | Northeast Louisiana | Ferndale, Wash. | FA-'93 | 7/0 |
| 22 | | Saxon, James | RB | 5-11 | 237 | 3/23/66 | 7 | San Jose State | Burton, S.C. | PB(KC)-'92 | 16/0 |
| 69 | | Sims, Keith | G | 6-3 | 303 | 6/17/67 | 5 | Iowa State | Watchung, N.J. | D2-'90 | 16/16 |
| 55 | | Singleton, Chris | LB | 6-2 | 242 | 2/2/67 | 5 | Arizona | Parsippany, N.J. | FA-'93 | 17/4* |
| 29 | | Smith, Frankie | CB | 5-9 | 186 | 10/8/68 | 2 | Baylor | Groesbeck, Tex. | FA-'93 | 5/1 |
| 33 | | Stewart, Michael | S | 6-0 | 199 | 7/12/65 | 8 | Fresno State | Bakersfield, Calif. | UFA(Rams)-'94 | 16/14* |
| 11 | | Stouffer, Kelly | QB | 6-3 | 214 | 7/6/64 | 6 | Colorado State | Rushville, Neb. | FA-'94 | 0* |
| 10 | | Stoyanovich, Pete | K | 5-11 | 195 | 4/28/67 | 6 | Indiana | Dearborn Heights, Mich. | D8-'89 | 16/0 |
| 57 | | Thayer, Tom | C-G | 6-4 | 284 | 8/16/61 | 10 | Notre Dame | Catholic, Ill. | FA-'93 | 3/0 |
| 94 | | Veasey, Craig | NT | 6-2 | 300 | 12/25/66 | 5 | Houston | Houston, Tex. | FA-'93 | 14/0 |
| 23 | | Vincent, Troy | CB | 6-0 | 192 | 6/8/70 | 3 | Wisconsin | Trenton, N.J. | D1a-'92 | 13/13 |
| 78 | | Webb, Richmond | T | 6-6 | 302 | 1/11/67 | 5 | Texas A&M | Dallas, Tex. | D1-'90 | 16/16 |
| 79 | | Webster, Larry | DT | 6-5 | 288 | 1/18/69 | 3 | Maryland | Elkton, Md. | D3-'92 | 13/9 |
| 60 | # | Weidner, Bert | G-C | 6-2 | 290 | 1/20/66 | 5 | Kent State | Eden, N.Y. | D11-'89 | 16/11 |
| 26 | # | Williams, Jarvis | S | 5-11 | 200 | 5/16/65 | 7 | Florida | Palatka, Fla. | D2-'88 | 16/14 |
| 87 | | Williams, Mike | WR | 5-11 | 187 | 10/9/66 | 3 | Northeastern | Katonah, N.Y. | FA-'91 | 13/0 |
| 85 | | Williams, Ronnie | TE | 6-3 | 259 | 1/19/66 | 3 | Oklahoma State | North Natchez, Miss. | FA-'93 | 11/0 |

* Arnold played 16 games with Detroit in '93; Atkins played 16 games with New Orleans; Blake inactive for 16 games; Braxton played 16 games with Denver; Craver missed '93 season due to injury; DeBerg played 3 games with Tampa Bay, 5 games with Miami; Kosar played 7 games with Cleveland, 4 games with Dallas; Millen was inactive for 8 games with Dallas, 7 games with Miami; Oliver played 2 games with Kansas City, 2 games with Green Bay; Singleton played 8 games with New England, 9 games with Miami; Stewart played 16 games with L.A. Rams; Stouffer last active with Seattle in '92.

# Unrestricted free agent; subject to developments.

† Restricted free agent; subject to developments.

Traded—WR Tony Martin to San Diego.

Players lost through free agency (5): DE-LB David Griggs (SD; 9 games in '93), DE Jeffrey Hunter (TB; 5), QB Scott Mitchell (Det; 13), S Louis Oliver (Cin; 11), C Jeff Uhlenhake (NO; 5).

Also played with Dolphins in '93—WR Fred Banks (2 games), S-CB Stephen Braggs (11), LB Chuck Bullough (3), NT Mike Golic (15), P Dale Hatcher (16), S Liffort Hobley (4), WR Tony Martin (12), LB David Merritt (4), WR Scott Miller (3), DT Karl Wilson (2).

## COACHING STAFF

**Head Coach,**
**Don Shula**

**Pro Career:** Begins his thirty-second season as an NFL head coach, and twenty-fifth with the Dolphins. Miami has won or shared first place in the AFC East in 14 of his 24 years and has earned 14 playoff berths in that span. Has most wins (327) in NFL history, surpassing George Halas's 324 in 1993. Captured back-to-back NFL championships, defeating Washington 14-7 in Super Bowl VII and Minnesota 24-7 in Super Bowl VIII. Lost to Dallas 24-3 in Super Bowl VI, to Washington 27-17 in Super Bowl XVII, and to San Francisco 38-16 in Super Bowl XIX. His 17-0 team in 1972 is the only team in NFL history to go undefeated throughout the regular season and postseason. Started his pro playing career with Cleveland Browns as defensive back in 1951. After two seasons with Browns, spent 1953-56 with Baltimore Colts and 1957 with Washington Redskins. Joined Detroit Lions as defensive coach in 1960 and was named head coach of the Colts in 1963. Baltimore had a 13-1 record in 1968 and captured NFL championship before losing to New York Jets in Super Bowl III. Career record: 327-158-6.

**Background:** Outstanding offensive player at John Carroll University in Cleveland before becoming defensive specialist as a pro. His alma mater awarded him a doctorate in humanities in May, 1973. Served as assistant coach at Virginia in 1958 and at Kentucky in 1959.

**Personal:** Born January 4, 1930, in Painesville, Ohio. Don and his wife, Mary Anne, live in Miami. He has five children—Dave, Donna, Sharon, Annie, and Mike. Dave is Cincinnati's head coach and Mike is tight ends coach with Chicago.

### ASSISTANT COACHES

**Joel Collier,** staff assistant; born December 25, 1963, Buffalo, N.Y., lives in Miami. Linebacker Northern Colorado 1984-87. No pro playing experience. College coach: Syracuse 1988-89. Pro coach: Tampa Bay Buccaneers 1990, New England Patriots 1991-93, joined Dolphins in 1994.

**John Gamble,** strength; born June 26, 1957, Richmond, Va., lives in Miami. Linebacker Hampton Institute 1975-78. No pro playing experience. College coach: Virginia 1982-93. Pro coach: Joined Dolphins in 1994.

**Joe Greene,** defensive line; born September 24, 1946, Temple, Tex., lives in Miami. Defensive tackle North Texas State 1966-68. Pro defensive tackle Pittsburgh Steelers 1969-81. Inducted into Pro Football Hall of Fame in 1987. Pro coach: Pittsburgh Steelers 1987-91, joined Dolphins in 1992.

**George Hill,** linebackers; born April 28, 1933, Bay Village, Ohio, lives in Miami. Tackle-fullback Denison 1954-57. No pro playing experience. College coach: Findlay 1959, Denison 1960-64, Cornell 1965, Duke 1966-70, Ohio State 1971-78. Pro coach: Philadelphia Eagles 1979-84, Indianapolis Colts 1985-88, joined Dolphins in 1989.

**Rich McGeorge,** assistant offensive line-tight ends; born September 14, 1948, Roanoke, Va., lives in Miami. Tight end Elon College 1966-69. Pro tight end Green Bay Packers 1970-78. College coach: Duke 1981-82, 1987-89, Florida 1990-92. Pro coach: Birmingham Stallions (USFL) 1983-84, Tampa Bay Bandits (USFL) 1985, joined Dolphins in 1993.

**Tony Nathan,** offensive backs; born December 14, 1956, Birmingham, Ala., lives in Miami. Running back Alabama 1975-78. Pro running back Miami Dolphins 1979-87. Pro coach: Joined Dolphins in 1988.

**Tom Olivadotti,** defense; born September 22, 1945, Long Branch, N.J., lives in Cooper City, Fla. Defensive back-wide receiver Upsala 1963-66. No pro playing experience. College coach: Princeton 1975-77, Boston College 1978-79, Miami 1980-83. Pro coach: Cleveland Browns 1985-86, joined Dolphins in 1987.

**Mel Phillips,** defensive backs; born January 6, 1942, Shelby, N.C., lives in Miami Lakes, Fla. Defensive back-running back North Carolina A&T 1964-65. Pro defensive back San Francisco 49ers 1966-77. Pro coach: Detroit Lions 1980-84, joined Dolphins in 1985.

**John Sandusky,** assistant head coach-offensive line; born December 28, 1925, Philadelphia, Pa., lives in Hollywood, Fla. Tackle Villanova 1946-49. Pro tackle Cleveland Browns 1950-55, Green Bay Packers 1956. College coach: Villanova 1957-58. Pro coach: Baltimore Colts 1959-72 (head coach 1972), Philadelphia Eagles 1973-75, joined Dolphins in 1976.

**Larry Seiple,** wide receivers; born February 14, 1945, Allentown, Pa., lives in Miami Lakes, Fla. Running back-receiver-punter Kentucky 1964-66. Pro punter-tight end-receiver-running back Miami Dolphins 1967-77. College coach: Miami 1978-79. Pro coach: Detroit Lions 1980-84, Tampa Bay Buccaneers 1985-86, joined Dolphins in 1988.

**Gary Stevens,** offense-quarterbacks; born March 19, 1943, Cleveland, Ohio, lives in Kendall, Fla. Running back John Carroll 1963-65. No pro playing experience. College coach: Louisville 1971-74, Kent State 1975, West Virginia 1976-79, Miami 1980-88. Pro coach: Joined Dolphins in 1989.

**Junior Wade,** strength and conditioning; born February 2, 1947, Bath, S.C., lives in Miami. South Carolina State 1969. No college or pro playing experience. Pro coach: Joined Dolphins in 1975, coach since 1983.

**Mike Westhoff,** special teams; born January 10, 1948, Pittsburgh, Pa., lives in Ft. Lauderdale, Fla. Center-linebacker Wichita State 1967-69. No pro playing experience. College coach: Indiana 1974-75, Dayton 1976, Indiana State 1977, Northwestern 1978-80, Texas Christian 1981. Pro coach: Baltimore/Indianapolis Colts 1982-84, Arizona Outlaws (USFL) 1985, joined Dolphins in 1986.

## 1994 FIRST-YEAR ROSTER

| Name | Pos. | Ht. | Wt. | Birthdate | College | Hometown | How Acq. |
|---|---|---|---|---|---|---|---|
| Albright, Ethan | T | 6-5 | 285 | 5/1/71 | North Carolina | Greensboro, N.C. | FA |
| Araguz, Leo | P | 6-0 | 185 | 1/18/70 | Stephen F. Austin | Harlingen, Tex. | FA |
| Ballard, Jim | QB | 6-3 | 223 | 4/16/72 | Mount Union | Cuyahoga Falls, Ohio | FA |
| Barnett, Ja'Karl | LB | 6-0 | 235 | 11/16/70 | Jacksonville State | Opelika, Ala. | FA |
| Beavers, Aubrey | LB | 6-3 | 233 | 8/30/71 | Oklahoma | Houston, Tex. | D2a |
| Borgognone, Dirk (1) | K | 6-2 | 220 | 1/9/68 | Pacific | Reno, Nev. | FA |
| Bowens, Tim | DT | 6-4 | 317 | 2/7/73 | Mississippi | Okolona, Miss. | D1 |
| Boyer, Brant | LB | 6-0 | 233 | 6/27/71 | Arizona | Ogden, Utah | D6 |
| Brothen, Kevin (1) | C | 6-1 | 284 | 11/16/69 | Vanderbilt | Chicago, Ill. | FA |
| Brown, Reggie (1) | WR | 5-11 | 175 | 6/1/68 | Mesa, Colo. | Denver, Colo. | FA |
| Bullough, Chuck (1) | LB | 6-1 | 234 | 3/3/69 | Michigan State | Orchard Park, N.Y. | FA |
| Caesar, Mark (1) | DT | 6-2 | 295 | 1/12/70 | Miami | Newark, N.J. | FA |
| Cartwright, Ricardo (1) | CB | 5-10 | 185 | 5/27/65 | Florida A&M | Freeport, Bahamas | FA |
| Coons, Rob (1) | TE | 6-5 | 245 | 9/18/69 | Pittsburgh | Brea, Calif. | FA |
| Covington, Leevary | LB | 6-0 | 246 | 6/10/71 | North Carolina A&T | Rockingham, N.C. | FA |
| Davis, Dwayne | S | 6-1 | 203 | 9/27/70 | Colorado | Gulfport, Miss. | FA |
| Davis, Robert | CB | 5-9 | 188 | 8/6/72 | Vanderbilt | Nashville, Tenn. | FA |
| Dixon, Johnny | S | 5-11 | 204 | 2/13/71 | Mississippi | Harvey, La. | FA |
| Foxx, Dion | LB | 6-3 | 249 | 6/11/71 | James Madison | Richmond, Va. | FA |
| Francisco, Paul | TE | 6-6 | 236 | 10/14/69 | Boston University | Dorchester, Mass. | FA |
| Gaines, William | DT | 6-5 | 300 | 6/20/71 | Florida | Jackson, Miss. | D5 |
| Hill, Sean | CB | 5-10 | 176 | 8/14/71 | Montana State | Ft. Carson, Colo. | D7 |
| Hopkins, Jimmie | DE | 6-5 | 255 | 1/5/71 | Arizona | Brawley, Calif. | FA |
| Johnson, Demeris (1) | WR | 6-0 | 183 | 8/26/69 | Western Illinois | Detroit, Mich. | FA |
| Letcher, Morris | WR | 5-9 | 167 | 11/8/70 | East Carolina | Kansas City, Kan. | FA |
| Mash, Alex | LB | 6-0 | 256 | 12/16/70 | Georgia Southern | Thomasville, Ga. | FA |
| McGuire, Stephen (1) | RB | 5-10 | 236 | 11/20/69 | Miami | Brooklyn, N.Y. | FA |
| Middleton, Mike (1) | S | 5-11 | 224 | 12/4/69 | Indiana | Cincinnati, Ohio | FA |
| Novak, Jeff (1) | T | 6-5 | 295 | 7/27/67 | Southwest Texas State | Cook County, Ill. | FA |
| Quarles, Shelton | LB | 6-1 | 234 | 9/11/71 | Vanderbilt | Whites Creek, Tenn. | FA |
| Richardson, Sean | RB | 5-10 | 248 | 6/10/71 | Jacksonville State | Auburn, Ala. | FA |
| Rooks, George (1) | DT | 6-3 | 298 | 8/9/70 | Syracuse | White Plains, N.Y. | FA |
| Rowell, Tony (1) | G | 6-4 | 293 | 7/24/69 | Florida | Melbourne, Fla. | FA |
| Rowley, Bryan | WR | 5-10 | 176 | 11/2/70 | Utah | Orem, Utah | FA |
| Ruddy, Tim | C | 6-3 | 286 | 4/27/72 | Notre Dame | Scranton, Pa. | D2b |
| Schulte, Scott | RB | 5-10 | 200 | 11/13/71 | Hillsdale College | Delphos, Ohio | FA |
| Seigler, Dexter | CB | 5-9 | 178 | 1/11/72 | Miami | Avon Park, Fla. | FA |
| Spikes, Irving | RB | 5-8 | 215 | 12/20/70 | Northeast Louisiana | Ocean Springs, Miss. | FA |
| Spralding, Melvin | LB | 6-1 | 235 | 10/9/69 | South Carolina State | Alachua, Fla. | FA |
| Sturdivant, Mark | DE | 6-3 | 274 | 7/2/71 | Maryland | Silver Spring, Md. | FA |
| Williams, Jay | DE | 6-3 | 266 | 10/13/71 | Wake Forest | Washington, D.C. | FA |
| Woolfork, Ronnie | LB | 6-3 | 256 | 12/21/70 | Colorado | Detroit, Mich. | D4 |

The term NFL Rookie is defined as a player who is in his first season of professional football and has not been on the roster of another professional football team for any regular-season or postseason games. A Rookie is designated by an "R" on NFL rosters. Players who have been active in another professional football league or players who have NFL experience, including either preseason training camp or being on an Active List or Inactive List, or on Reserve/Injured or Reserve/Physically Unable to Perform for fewer than six regular-season games, are termed NFL First-Year Players. An NFL First-Year Player is designated by a "1" on NFL rosters. Thereafter, a player is credited with an additional year of experience for each season in which he accumulates six games on the Active List or Inactive List, or on Reserve/Injured or Reserve/Physically Unable to Perform.

## NOTES

# NEW ENGLAND PATRIOTS

**American Football Conference**
**Eastern Division**
**Team Colors:** Blue, Red, Silver, and White
**Foxboro Stadium**
**60 Washington Street**
**Foxboro, Massachusetts 02035**
**Telephone: (508) 543-8200**

## CLUB OFFICIALS

President/Chief Executive Officer: Robert K. Kraft
Vice President-Owner's Repesentative: Jonathan A. Kraft
Vice President-Business Operations: Andrew Wasynczuk
Vice President-Football Operations: Patrick Forté
Vice President-Finance: James Hausmann
Vice President-Event Management: Brian O'Donovan
Corporate Marketing and Sales: Daniel A. Kraft
Director of Public and Community Relations: Donald Lowery
Assistant Director of Public Relations: Stacey James
Director of Player Resources: Andre Tippett
Controller: Virginia Widman
Director of Pro Scouting: Bobby Grier
Director of College Scouting: Charles Armey
Director of Data Processing: Peg Myers
Director of Ticketing: Ken Sternfeld
Marketing Manager: Mitch Hardin
National Accounts Manager: Richard Doucette
Assistant General Manager Foxboro Stadium: Raymond J. Cantwell
Head Trainer: Ron O'Neil
Equipment Manager: Don Brocher
Video Director: Ken Deininger
**Stadium:** Foxboro Stadium • **Capacity:** 60,290
60 Washington Street
Foxboro, Massachusetts 02035
**Playing Surface:** Grass
**Training Camp:** Bryant College
Route 7
Smithfield, Rhode Island 02917

## 1994 SCHEDULE

### PRESEASON

| | | |
|---|---|---|
| Aug. 5 | **New Orleans** | 8:00 |
| Aug. 13 | at Los Angeles Rams | 7:00 |
| Aug. 18 | **Washington** | 7:00 |
| Aug. 26 | at Green Bay | 7:00 |

### REGULAR SEASON

| | | |
|---|---|---|
| Sept. 4 | at Miami | 4:00 |
| Sept. 11 | **Buffalo** | 1:00 |
| Sept. 18 | at Cincinnati | 1:00 |
| Sept. 25 | at Detroit | 4:00 |
| Oct. 2 | **Green Bay** | 1:00 |
| Oct. 9 | **Los Angeles Raiders** | 4:00 |
| Oct. 16 | at New York Jets | 1:00 |
| Oct. 23 | Open Date | |
| Oct. 30 | **Miami** | 1:00 |
| Nov. 6 | at Cleveland | 1:00 |
| Nov. 13 | **Minnesota** | 1:00 |
| Nov. 20 | **San Diego** | 1:00 |
| Nov. 27 | at Indianapolis | 8:00 |
| Dec. 4 | **New York Jets** | 1:00 |
| Dec. 11 | **Indianapolis** | 1:00 |
| Dec. 18 | at Buffalo | 1:00 |
| Dec. 24 | at Chicago | 12:00 |

## RECORD HOLDERS

### INDIVIDUAL RECORDS—CAREER

| Category | Name | Performance |
|---|---|---|
| Rushing (Yds.) | Sam Cunningham, 1973-79, 1981-82 | 5,453 |
| Passing (Yds.) | Steve Grogan, 1975-1990 | 26,886 |
| Passing (TDs) | Steve Grogan, 1975-1990 | 182 |
| Receiving (No.) | Stanley Morgan, 1977-1989 | 534 |
| Receiving (Yds.) | Stanley Morgan, 1977-1989 | 10,352 |
| Interceptions | Raymond Clayborn, 1977-1989 | 36 |
| Punting (Avg.) | Rich Camarillo, 1981-87 | 42.6 |
| Punt Return (Avg.) | Mack Herron, 1973-75 | 12.0 |
| Kickoff Return (Avg.) | Horace Ivory, 1977-1981 | 27.6 |
| Field Goals | Gino Cappelletti, 1960-1970 | 176 |
| Touchdowns (Tot.) | Stanley Morgan, 1977-1989 | 68 |
| Points | Gino Cappelletti, 1960-1970 | 1,130 |

### INDIVIDUAL RECORDS—SINGLE SEASON

| Category | Name | Performance |
|---|---|---|
| Rushing (Yds.) | Jim Nance, 1966 | 1,458 |
| Passing (Yds.) | Vito (Babe) Parilli, 1964 | 3,465 |
| Passing (TDs) | Vito (Babe) Parilli, 1964 | 31 |
| Receiving (No.) | Stanley Morgan, 1986 | 84 |
| Receiving (Yds.) | Stanley Morgan, 1986 | 1,491 |
| Interceptions | Ron Hall, 1964 | 11 |
| Punting (Avg.) | Rich Camarillo, 1983 | 44.6 |
| Punt Return (Avg.) | Mack Herron, 1974 | 14.8 |
| Kickoff Return (Avg.) | Raymond Clayborn, 1977 | 31.0 |
| Field Goals | Tony Franklin, 1986 | 32 |
| Touchdowns (Tot.) | Steve Grogan, 1976 | 13 |
| | Stanley Morgan, 1979 | 13 |
| Points | Gino Cappelletti, 1964 | 155 |

### INDIVIDUAL RECORDS—SINGLE GAME

| Category | Name | Performance |
|---|---|---|
| Rushing (Yds.) | Tony Collins, 9-18-83 | 212 |
| Passing (Yds.) | Tony Eason, 9-21-86 | 414 |
| Passing (TDs) | Vito (Babe) Parilli, 11-15-64 | 5 |
| | Vito (Babe) Parilli, 10-15-67 | 5 |
| | Steve Grogan, 9-9-79 | 5 |
| Receiving (No.) | Art Graham, 11-20-66 | 11 |
| | Tony Collins, 11-29-87 | 11 |
| Receiving (Yds.) | Stanley Morgan, 11-8-81 | 182 |
| Interceptions | Many times | 3 |
| | Last time by Roland James, 10-23-83 | |
| Field Goals | Gino Cappelletti, 10-4-64 | 6 |
| Touchdowns (Tot.) | Many times | 3 |
| | Last time by Stanley Morgan, 9-21-86 | |
| Points | Gino Cappelletti, 12-18-65 | 28 |

*NFL Record

## COACHING HISTORY

**BOSTON 1960-1970**
**(225-276-9)**

| | | |
|---|---|---|
| 1960-61 | Lou Saban* | 7-12-0 |
| 1961-68 | Mike Holovak | 53-47-9 |
| 1969-70 | Clive Rush** | 5-16-0 |
| 1970-72 | John Mazur*** | 9-21-0 |
| 1972 | Phil Bengtson | 1-4-0 |
| 1973-78 | Chuck Fairbanks**** | 46-41-0 |
| 1978 | Hank Bullough-Ron Erhardt# | 0-1-0 |
| 1979-81 | Ron Erhardt | 21-27-0 |
| 1982-84 | Ron Meyer## | 18-16-0 |
| 1984-89 | Raymond Berry | 51-41-0 |
| 1990 | Rod Rust | 1-15-0 |
| 1991-92 | Dick MacPherson | 8-24-0 |
| 1993 | Bill Parcells | 5-11-0 |

*Released after five games in 1961
**Released after seven games in 1970
***Resigned after nine games in 1972
****Suspended for final regular-season game in 1978
#Co-coaches
##Released after eight games in 1984

### FOXBORO STADIUM

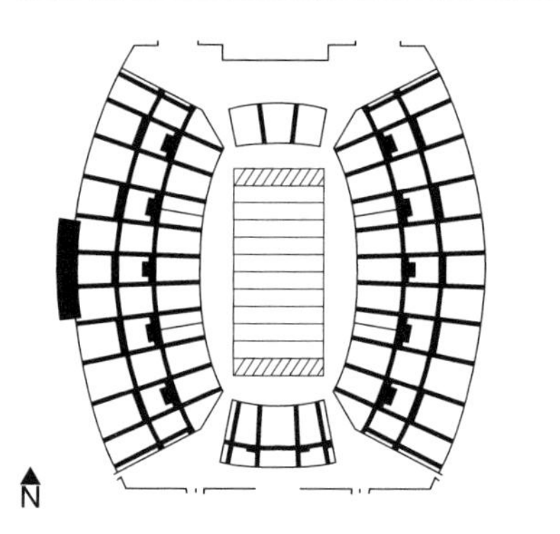

## 1993 TEAM RECORD

**PRESEASON (1-3)**

| Date | Result | | Opponents |
|---|---|---|---|
| 8/7 | L | 7-13 | at San Diego |
| 8/14 | L | 9-12 | vs. Cleveland at Toronto |
| 8/20 | W | 21-17 | Green Bay |
| 8/27 | L | 20-27 | Kansas City |

**REGULAR SEASON (5-11)**

| Date | Result | | Opponents | Att. |
|---|---|---|---|---|
| 9/5 | L | 14-38 | at Buffalo | 79,751 |
| 9/12 | L | 16-19 | Detroit (OT) | 54,151 |
| 9/19 | L | 14-17 | Seattle | 50,392 |
| 9/26 | L | 7-45 | at New York Jets | 64,836 |
| 10/10 | W | 23-21 | at Phoenix | 36,115 |
| 10/17 | L | 14-28 | Houston | 51,037 |
| 10/24 | L | 9-10 | at Seattle | 56,526 |
| 10/31 | L | 6-9 | at Indianapolis | 46,522 |
| 11/7 | L | 10-13 | Buffalo (OT) | 54,326 |
| 11/21 | L | 13-17 | at Miami | 59,982 |
| 11/28 | L | 0-6 | New York Jets | 42,810 |
| 12/5 | L | 14-17 | at Pittsburgh | 51,358 |
| 12/12 | W | 7-2 | Cincinnati | 29,794 |
| 12/19 | W | 20-17 | at Cleveland | 48,618 |
| 12/26 | W | 38-0 | Indianapolis | 26,571 |
| 1/2 | W | 33-27 | Miami (OT) | 53,883 |

(OT) Overtime

**SCORE BY PERIODS**

| | | | | | | | |
|---|---|---|---|---|---|---|---|
| Patriots | 33 | 60 | 54 | 85 | 6 | — | 238 |
| Opponents | 41 | 103 | 26 | 110 | 6 | — | 286 |

**ATTENDANCE**

Home 362,964 Away 443,708 Total 806,672
Single-game home record, 61,457 (12-5-71)
Single-season home record, 482,572 (1986)

## 1993 TEAM STATISTICS

| | Patriots | Opp. |
|---|---|---|
| Total First Downs | 315 | 269 |
| Rushing | 116 | 97 |
| Passing | 169 | 161 |
| Penalty | 30 | 11 |
| Third Down: Made/Att | 92/237 | 96/231 |
| Third Down Pct. | 38.8 | 41.6 |
| Fourth Down: Made/Att | 13/27 | 5/13 |
| Fourth Down Pct. | 48.1 | 38.5 |
| Total Net Yards | 5065 | 4796 |
| Avg. Per Game | 316.6 | 299.8 |
| Total Plays | 1091 | 1013 |
| Avg. Per Play | 4.6 | 4.7 |
| Net Yards Rushing | 1780 | 1951 |
| Avg. Per Game | 111.3 | 121.9 |
| Total Rushes | 502 | 505 |
| Net Yards Passing | 3285 | 2845 |
| Avg. Per Game | 205.3 | 177.8 |
| Sacked/Yards Lost | 23/127 | 34/242 |
| Gross Yards | 3412 | 3087 |
| Att./Completions | 566/289 | 474/280 |
| Completion Pct. | 51.1 | 59.1 |
| Had Intercepted | 24 | 13 |
| Punts/Avg. | 76/40.7 | 90/41.2 |
| Net Punting Avg. | 76/34.8 | 90/34.7 |
| Penalties/Yards Lost | 64/468 | 111/803 |
| Fumbles/Ball Lost | 30/10 | 20/9 |
| Touchdowns | 26 | 32 |
| Rushing | 9 | 9 |
| Passing | 17 | 20 |
| Returns | 0 | 3 |
| Avg. Time of Possession | 29:43 | 30:17 |

## 1993 INDIVIDUAL STATISTICS

| PASSING | Att. | Cmp. | Yds. | Pct. | TD | Int. | Tkld. | Rate |
|---|---|---|---|---|---|---|---|---|
| Bledsoe | 429 | 214 | 2494 | 49.9 | 15 | 15 | 16/99 | 65.0 |
| Secules | 134 | 75 | 918 | 56.0 | 2 | 9 | 7/28 | 54.3 |
| Zolak | 2 | 0 | 0 | 0.0 | 0 | 0 | 0/0 | 39.6 |
| Turner | 1 | 0 | 0 | 0.0 | 0 | 0 | 0/0 | 39.6 |
| Patriots | 566 | 289 | 3412 | 51.1 | 17 | 24 | 23/127 | 62.1 |
| Opponents | 474 | 280 | 3087 | 59.1 | 20 | 13 | 34/242 | 81.1 |

| SCORING | TD R | TD P | TD Rt | PAT | FG | Saf | PTS |
|---|---|---|---|---|---|---|---|
| Sisson | 0 | 0 | 0 | 15/15 | 14/26 | 0 | 57 |
| Coates | 0 | 8 | 0 | 0/0 | 0/0 | 0 | 48 |
| Russell | 7 | 0 | 0 | 0/0 | 0/0 | 0 | 42 |
| Bahr | 0 | 0 | 0 | 10/10 | 5/5 | 0 | 25 |
| Brisby | 0 | 2 | 0 | 0/0 | 0/0 | 0 | 12 |
| Timpson | 0 | 2 | 0 | 0/0 | 0/0 | 0 | 12 |
| Turner | 0 | 2 | 0 | 0/0 | 0/0 | 0 | 12 |
| Cook | 0 | 1 | 0 | 0/0 | 0/0 | 0 | 6 |
| Crittenden | 0 | 1 | 0 | 0/0 | 0/0 | 0 | 6 |
| Croom | 1 | 0 | 0 | 0/0 | 0/0 | 0 | 6 |
| Gash | 1 | 0 | 0 | 0/0 | 0/0 | 0 | 6 |
| McMurtry | 0 | 1 | 0 | 0/0 | 0/0 | 0 | 6 |
| Patriots | 9 | 17 | 0 | 25/25 | 19/31 | 0 | 238 |
| Opponents | 9 | 20 | 3 | 32/32 | 20/24 | 1 | 286 |

| RUSHING | Att. | Yds. | Avg. | LG | TD |
|---|---|---|---|---|---|
| Russell | 300 | 1088 | 3.6 | 21 | 7 |
| Turner | 50 | 231 | 4.6 | 49 | 0 |
| Croom | 60 | 198 | 3.3 | 22 | 1 |
| Gash | 48 | 149 | 3.1 | 14 | 1 |
| Bledsoe | 32 | 82 | 2.6 | 15 | 0 |
| Secules | 8 | 33 | 4.1 | 13 | 0 |
| Saxon | 2 | 2 | 1.0 | 2 | 0 |
| Zolak | 1 | 0 | 0.0 | 0 | 0 |
| Crittenden | 1 | -3 | -3.0 | -3 | 0 |
| Patriots | 502 | 1780 | 3.5 | 49 | 9 |
| Opponents | 505 | 1951 | 3.9 | 57 | 9 |

| RECEIVING | No. | Yds. | Avg. | LG | TD |
|---|---|---|---|---|---|
| Coates | 53 | 659 | 12.4 | 54t | 8 |
| Brisby | 45 | 626 | 13.9 | 39 | 2 |
| Timpson | 42 | 654 | 15.6 | 48 | 2 |
| Turner | 39 | 333 | 8.5 | 26 | 2 |
| Russell | 26 | 245 | 9.4 | 69 | 0 |
| McMurtry | 22 | 241 | 11.0 | 20 | 1 |
| Cook | 22 | 154 | 7.0 | 17 | 1 |
| Crittenden | 16 | 293 | 18.3 | 44 | 1 |
| Gash | 14 | 93 | 6.6 | 15 | 0 |
| Croom | 8 | 92 | 11.5 | 21 | 0 |
| T. Brown | 2 | 22 | 11.0 | 14 | 0 |
| Patriots | 289 | 3412 | 11.8 | 82 | 17 |
| Opponents | 280 | 3087 | 11.0 | 56 | 20 |

| INTERCEPTIONS | No. | Yds. | Avg. | LG | TD |
|---|---|---|---|---|---|
| Hurst | 4 | 53 | 13.3 | 24 | 0 |
| Wren | 3 | -7 | -2.3 | 2 | 0 |
| Barnett | 1 | 40 | 40.0 | 40 | 0 |
| V. Brown | 1 | 24 | 24.0 | 24 | 0 |
| Collins | 1 | 8 | 8.0 | 8 | 0 |
| Thompson | 1 | 4 | 4.0 | 4 | 0 |
| Lambert | 1 | 0 | 0.0 | 0 | 0 |
| Ray | 1 | 0 | 0.0 | 0 | 0 |
| Patriots | 13 | 122 | 9.4 | 40 | 0 |
| Opponents | 24 | 201 | 8.4 | 34 | 1 |

| PUNTING | No. | Yds. | Avg. | In 20 | LG |
|---|---|---|---|---|---|
| Saxon | 73 | 3096 | 42.4 | 25 | 59 |
| Patriots | 76 | 3096 | 40.7 | 25 | 59 |
| Opponents | 90 | 3709 | 41.2 | 19 | 58 |

| PUNT RETURNS | No. | FC | Yds. | Avg. | LG | TD |
|---|---|---|---|---|---|---|
| T. Brown | 25 | 9 | 224 | 9.0 | 19 | 0 |
| Harris | 23 | 4 | 201 | 8.7 | 21 | 0 |
| Crittenden | 2 | 1 | 37 | 18.5 | 30 | 0 |
| Smith | 1 | 0 | 0 | 0.0 | 0 | 0 |
| Patriots | 51 | 14 | 462 | 9.1 | 30 | 0 |
| Opponents | 34 | 6 | 313 | 9.2 | 47t | 1 |

| KICKOFF RETURNS | No. | Yds. | Avg. | LG | TD |
|---|---|---|---|---|---|
| Crittenden | 23 | 478 | 20.8 | 44 | 0 |
| T. Brown | 15 | 243 | 16.2 | 29 | 0 |
| Harris | 6 | 90 | 15.0 | 19 | 0 |
| Sabb | 2 | 0 | 0.0 | 0 | 0 |
| Cook | 1 | 8 | 8.0 | 8 | 0 |
| Coates | 0 | 0 | — | — | 0 |
| Patriots | 47 | 819 | 17.4 | 44 | 0 |
| Opponents | 44 | 921 | 20.9 | 42 | 0 |

| SACKS | No. |
|---|---|
| Slade | 9.0 |
| Tippett | 8.5 |
| A. Jones | 3.5 |
| Pitts | 3.0 |
| Sabb | 2.0 |
| Williams | 2.0 |
| Agnew | 1.5 |
| V. Brown | 1.0 |
| Collins | 1.0 |
| Hurst | 1.0 |
| Thompson | 1.0 |
| Goad | 0.5 |
| Patriots | 34.0 |
| Opponent | 23.0 |

## 1994 DRAFT CHOICES

| Round | Name | Pos. | College |
|---|---|---|---|
| 1 | Willie McGinest | DE | Southern California |
| 2 | Kevin Lee | WR | Alabama |
| 3 | Ervin Collier | NT | Florida A&M |
| | Joe Burch | C | Texas Southern |
| 4 | John Burke | TE | Virginia Tech |
| 5 | Pat O'Neill | P | Syracuse |
| 6 | Steve Hawkins | WR | Western Michigan |
| | Max Lane | T | Navy |
| 7 | Jay Walker | QB | Howard |
| | Marty Moore | LB | Kentucky |

# NEW ENGLAND PATRIOTS

## 1994 VETERAN ROSTER

| No. | Name | Pos. | Ht. | Wt. | Birthdate | NFL Exp. | College | Hometown | How Acq. | '93 Games/ Starts |
|---|---|---|---|---|---|---|---|---|---|---|
| 92 | Agnew, Ray | DE | 6-3 | 272 | 12/9/67 | 5 | North Carolina State | Winston-Salem, N.C. | D1b-'90 | 16/1 |
| 78 | Armstrong, Bruce | T | 6-4 | 284 | 9/7/65 | 8 | Louisville | Miami, Fla. | D1-'87 | 16/16 |
| 65 | Arthur, Mike | C | 6-3 | 280 | 5/7/68 | 4 | Texas A&M | Houston, Tex. | W(Cin)-'93 | 13/11 |
| 3 | Bahr, Matt | K | 5-10 | 175 | 7/6/56 | 16 | Penn State | Langhorne, Pa. | W(Phil)-'93 | 14/0* |
| 42 | Barnett, Harlon | S | 5-11 | 200 | 1/2/67 | 5 | Michigan State | Cincinnati, Ohio | W(Clev)-'93 | 14/12 |
| 52 | Bavaro, David | LB | 6-1 | 228 | 3/27/67 | 3 | Syracuse | Danvers, Mass. | FA-'93 | 12/0 |
| 11 | Bledsoe, Drew | QB | 6-5 | 233 | 2/14/72 | 2 | Washington State | Walla Walla, Wash. | D1-'93 | 13/12 |
| 82 | Brisby, Vincent | WR | 6-1 | 186 | 1/25/71 | 2 | Northeast Louisiana | Lake Charles, La. | D2c-'93 | 16/12 |
| 30 | Brown, Corwin | S | 6-1 | 192 | 4/25/70 | 2 | Michigan | Chicago, Ill. | D4b-'93 | 15/12 |
| 80 | Brown, Troy | WR-KR | 5-9 | 183 | 7/2/71 | 2 | Marshall | Blackville, S.C. | D8-'93 | 12/0 |
| 59 | Brown, Vincent | LB | 6-2 | 245 | 1/9/65 | 7 | Mississippi Valley State | Decatur, Ga. | D2-'88 | 16/16 |
| 44 | t- Butts, Marion | RB | 6-1 | 248 | 8/1/66 | 6 | Florida State | Sylvester, Ga. | T(SD)-'94 | 16/16* |
| 99 | Carthen Jason | LB | 6-3 | 255 | 11/16/70 | 2 | Ohio University | Toledo, Ohio | W(Buff)-'93 | 5/0 |
| 69 | Chung, Eugene | G | 6-4 | 295 | 6/14/69 | 3 | Virginia Tech | Oakton, Va. | D1-'92 | 16/16 |
| 87 | Coates, Ben | TE | 6-5 | 245 | 8/16/69 | 4 | Livingstone College | Greenwood, S.C. | D5b-'91 | 16/10 |
| 54 | Collins, Todd | LB | 6-2 | 242 | 5/27/70 | 3 | Carson-Newman | New Market, Tenn. | D3a-'92 | 16/12 |
| 81 | Crittenden, Ray | WR | 6-1 | 188 | 3/1/70 | 2 | Virginia Tech | Washington, D.C. | FA-'93 | 16/2 |
| 26 | Croom, Corey | RB | 5-11 | 212 | 5/22/71 | 2 | Ball State | Sandusky, Ohio | FA-'93 | 14/1 |
| 50 | DeOssie, Steve | LB | 6-2 | 248 | 11/22/62 | 11 | Boston College | Roslindale, Mass. | UFA(NYJ)-'94 | 15/0* |
| 33 | Gash, Sam | RB | 5-11 | 224 | 3/7/69 | 3 | Penn State | Hendersonville, N.C. | D8b-'92 | 15/4 |
| 67 | Gisler, Mike | G | 6-4 | 300 | 8/26/69 | 2 | Houston | Range, Tex. | FA-'93 | 12/0 |
| 72 | Goad, Tim | NT | 6-3 | 280 | 2/28/66 | 7 | North Carolina | Stuart, Va. | D4a-'88 | 16/15 |
| 88 | Griffith, Richard | TE | 6-5 | 256 | 7/31/69 | 2 | Arizona | Tucson, Ariz. | D5b-'93 | 3/0 |
| 29 | Guyton, Myron | S | 6-1 | 205 | 8/26/67 | 6 | Eastern Kentucky | Thomasville, Ga. | UFA(NYG)-'94 | 16/16* |
| 77 | Harlow, Pat | T | 6-6 | 290 | 3/16/69 | 4 | Southern California | Norco, Calif. | D1a-'91 | 16/16 |
| 37 | Hurst, Maurice | CB | 5-10 | 185 | 9/17/67 | 6 | Southern | New Orleans, La. | D4a-'89 | 16/16 |
| 98 | Johnson, Mario | NT | 6-3 | 288 | 1/30/70 | 3 | Missouri | Florissant, Mo. | W(NYJ)-'93 | 6/0 |
| 97 | Jones, Aaron | DE | 6-5 | 267 | 12/18/66 | 7 | Eastern Kentucky | Orlando, Fla. | UFA(Pitt)-'93 | 11/1 |
| 61 | Kratch, Bob | G | 6-3 | 288 | 1/6/66 | 6 | Iowa | Mahwah, N.J. | UFA(NYG)-'94 | 16/16* |
| 28 | Lambert, Dion | S | 6-1 | 185 | 2/12/69 | 3 | UCLA | Lake View Terrace, Calif. | D4a-'92 | 14/4 |
| 35 | Legette, Burnie | RB | 6-1 | 243 | 12/5/70 | 2 | Michigan | Colorado Springs, Colo. | FA-'93 | 7/0 |
| 75 | Lewis, Bill | C | 6-6 | 290 | 7/12/63 | 9 | Nebraska | Sioux City, Iowa | UFA(Phx)-'93 | 7/5 |
| 43 | Lewis, Vernon | CB | 5-10 | 192 | 10/27/70 | 2 | Pittsburgh | Houston, Tex. | FA-'93 | 10/0 |
| 70 | Moore, Brandon | T | 6-6 | 290 | 6/21/70 | 2 | Duke | Bowling Springs, Pa. | FA-'93 | 16/0 |
| 93 | Pitts, Mike | DE | 6-5 | 277 | 9/25/60 | 12 | Alabama | Baltimore, Md. | UFA(Phil)-'93 | 16/15 |
| 23 | Ray, Terry | S | 6-1 | 205 | 10/12/69 | 3 | Oklahoma | Killeen, Tex. | W(Atl)-'93 | 15/1 |
| | Reynolds, Ricky | CB | 5-11 | 190 | 1/19/65 | 8 | Washington State | Sacramento, Calif. | UFA(TB)-'94 | 14/13* |
| 71 | Rucci, Todd | G | 6-5 | 291 | 7/14/70 | 2 | Penn State | Upper Darby, Pa. | D2b-'93 | 2/1 |
| 32 | † Russell, Leonard | RB | 6-2 | 235 | 11/17/69 | 4 | Arizona State | Long Beach, Calif. | D1b-'91 | 16/15 |
| 95 | Sabb, Dwayne | LB | 6-4 | 248 | 10/9/69 | 3 | New Hampshire | Union, N.J. | D5-'92 | 14/7 |
| 7 | Saxon, Mike | P | 6-3 | 202 | 7/10/62 | 10 | San Diego State | Whittier, Calif | FA-'93 | 16/0 |
| 9 | Sisson, Scott | K | 6-1 | 197 | 7/21/71 | 2 | Georgia Tech | Marietta, Ga. | D5-'93 | 13/0 |
| 68 | Skene, Doug | G | 6-6 | 295 | 6/17/70 | 2 | Michigan | Fairview, Tex. | FA-'93 | 0* |
| 53 | Slade, Chris | LB | 6-4 | 232 | 1/30/71 | 2 | Virginia | Newport News, Va. | D2a-'93 | 16/5 |
| 22 | Smith, Rod | CB | 5-11 | 187 | 3/12/70 | 3 | Notre Dame | Roseville, Minn. | D2-'92 | 16/9 |
| 66 | Staten, Mark | G | 6-6 | 308 | 10/8/70 | 2 | Miami, Ohio | Dowagiac, Mich. | FA-'93 | 0* |
| 31 | Thomas, Blair | RB | 5-10 | 202 | 10/7/67 | 5 | Penn State | Philadelphia, Pa. | UFA(NYJ)-'94 | 11/5* |
| 83 | # Timpson, Michael | WR | 5-10 | 175 | 6/6/67 | 6 | Penn State | Hialeah, Fla. | D4-'89 | 16/7 |
| 34 | Turner, Kevin | RB | 6-1 | 224 | 6/12/69 | 3 | Alabama | Prattville, Ala. | D3b-'92 | 16/9 |
| 76 | Washington, John | DE | 6-4 | 290 | 2/20/63 | 9 | Oklahoma State | Houston, Tex. | UFA(Atl)-'93 | 16/13 |
| 51 | White, David | LB | 6-2 | 235 | 2/27/70 | 2 | Nebraska | New Orleans, La. | W(Buff)-'93 | 6/0 |
| 27 | Wren, Darryl | CB | 6-1 | 188 | 1/25/67 | 4 | Pittsburg State, Kan. | Tulsa, Okla. | W(Buff)-'93 | 12/5 |
| 16 | Zolak, Scott | QB | 6-5 | 222 | 12/13/67 | 4 | Maryland | Monongahela, Pa. | D4-'91 | 3/0 |

* Bahr played 11 games with Philadelphia, 3 games with New England in '93; Butts played 16 games with San Diego; DeOssie played 8 games with N.Y. Giants, 7 games with N.Y. Jets; Guyton played 16 games with N.Y. Giants; Kratch played 16 games with N.Y. Giants; Reynolds played 14 games with Tampa Bay; Skene inactive for 8 games; Staten inactive for 9 games; Thomas played 11 games with N.Y. Jets.

\# Unrestricted free agent; subject to developments.

† Restricted free agent; subject to developments.

t- Patriots traded for Butts (San Diego).

Retired—Andre Tippett, 12-year linebacker, 16 games in '93.

Players lost through free agency (2): WR Greg McMurtry (Rams; 16 games in '93), DE Brent Williams (Sea; 13).

Also played with Patriots in '93—G Rich Baldinger (15 games), TE Marv Cook (16), DE Chris Gannon (4), CB Jerome Henderson (1), C Todd Jones (4), RB Scott Lockwood (2), QB Scott Secules (12), LB Chris Singleton (8), CB Reyna Thompson (15), CB-S Adrian White (5).

## COACHING STAFF

**Head Coach,**
**Bill Parcells**

**Pro Career:** On January 21, 1993, Parcells became the franchise's thirteenth head coach since the Patriots' inception in 1960. He enters the 1994 season on a four-game winning streak. Season-ending victory knocked the Miami Dolphins out of the playoffs and gave the Patriots a fourth-place finish in the AFC East. Parcells made his NFL coaching debut with the New England Patriots as the linebackers coach on Ron Erhardt's staff in 1980. He accepted the same position on the New York Giants staff in 1981 and was named the Giants head coach in 1983. In eight seasons at the helm of the Giants, Parcells led his teams to two Super Bowl championships. His first title came in 1986, with a 39-20 victory over the Denver Broncos. Four years later, the Giants claimed another championship with a 20-19 victory over the Buffalo Bills. On May 15, 1991, health concerns caused Parcells to resign from the Giants. During his two seasons away from coaching, Parcells entertained football audiences from the broadcast booth, in 1991 as a studio analyst and in 1992 as a color commentator for NBC Sports. Career record: 90-63-1.

**Background:** Linebacker at Wichita State 1961-63. College assistant Hastings (Neb.) 1964, Wichita State 1965, Army 1966-69, Florida State 1970-72, Vanderbilt 1973-74, Texas Tech 1975-77, Air Force 1978 (head coach).

**Personal:** Born August 22, 1941, Englewood, N.J. Bill and his wife, Judy, live in Foxboro, Mass., and have three daughters—Suzy, Jill, and Dallas.

### ASSISTANT COACHES

**Maurice Carthon,** offensive assistant; born April 24, 1961, Chicago, Ill., lives in Foxboro, Mass. Running back Arkansas State 1979-82. Pro running back New Jersey Generals (USFL) 1983-85, New York Giants 1985-91, Indianapolis Colts 1992. Pro coach: Joined Patriots in 1994.

**Romeo Crennel,** defensive line; born June 18, 1947, Lynchburg, Va., lives in Foxboro, Mass. Defensive tackle, linebacker Western Kentucky 1966-69. No pro playing experience. College coach: Western Kentucky 1970-74, Texas Tech 1975-77, Mississippi 1978-79, Georgia Tech 1980. Pro coach: New York Giants 1981-92, joined Patriots in 1993.

**Al Groh,** defensive coordinator; born July 13, 1944, New York City, lives in Foxboro, Mass. Defensive end Virginia 1964-67. No pro playing experience. College coach: Army 1968-69, Virginia 1970-72, North Carolina 1973-77, Air Force 1978-79, Texas Tech 1980, Wake Forest 1981-86 (head coach), South Carolina 1988. Pro coach: Atlanta Falcons 1987, New York Giants 1989-91, Cleveland Browns 1992, joined Patriots in 1993.

**Fred Hoaglin,** offensive line; born January 28, 1944, Alliance, Ohio, lives in Cumberland, R.I. Center Pittsburgh 1962-65. Pro center Cleveland Browns 1966-72, Baltimore Colts 1973, Houston Oilers 1974-75, Seattle Seahawks 1976. Pro coach: Detroit Lions 1978-84, New York Giants 1985-92, joined Patriots in 1993.

**Chris Palmer,** wide receivers; born September 23, 1949, Mt. Kisco, N.Y., lives in Foxboro, Mass. Quarterback Southern Connecticut State 1968-71. No pro playing experience. College coach: Connecticut 1972-74, Lehigh 1975, Colgate 1976-82, New Haven 1986-87 (head coach), Boston University 1988-89 (head coach). Pro coach: Montreal Concordes (CFL) 1983, New Jersey Generals (USFL) 1984-85, Houston Oilers 1990-92, joined Patriots in 1993.

**Johnny Parker,** strength and conditioning; born February 1, 1947, Greenville, S.C., lives in Foxboro, Mass. Graduate of Mississippi, master's degree from Delta State University. No college or pro playing experience. College coach: South Carolina 1974-76, Indiana 1977-79, Louisiana State 1980, Mississippi 1981-83. Pro coach: New York Giants 1984-92, joined Patriots in 1993.

**Ray Perkins,** offensive coordinator, born November 6, 1941, Mount Olive, Miss., lives in Foxboro, Mass. Wide receiver Alabama 1964-66. Pro receiver Baltimore Colts 1967-71. College coach: Mississippi State 1973, Alabama 1983-86 (head coach), Arkansas State 1992 (head coach). Pro coach: New England Patriots 1974-77, San Diego Chargers 1978, New York Giants 1979-82 (head coach), Tampa Bay Buccaneers 1987-90 (head coach), rejoined Patriots in 1993.

**Michael Pope,** running backs; born March 15, 1942, Monroe, N.C., lives in Foxboro, Mass. Quarterback Lenoir Rhyne 1962-64. No pro playing experience. College coach: Florida State 1970-74, Texas Tech 1975-77, Mississippi 1978-82. Pro coach: New York Giants 1983-91, Cincinnati Bengals 1992-93, joined Patriots in 1994.

**Dante Scarnecchia,** special assistant, born February 15, 1948, Los Angeles, Calif., lives in Wrentham, Mass. Center-guard California Western 1968-70. No pro playing experience. College coach: California Western (now U.S. International) 1970-72, Iowa State 1973, Southern Methodist 1975-76, 1980-81, Pacific 1977-78, Northern Arizona 1979. Pro coach: New England Patriots 1982-89, Indianapolis Colts 1990, rejoined Patriots in 1991.

**Mike Sweatman,** special teams, born October 23, 1947, Kansas City, Mo., lives in Foxboro, Mass. Linebacker Kansas 1964-67. No pro playing experience. College coach: Kansas 1973-74, 1979-82, Tulsa 1977-78, Tennessee 1983. Pro coach: Minnesota Vikings 1984, New York Giants 1985-92, joined Patriots in 1993.

**Bob Trott,** defensive backs, born March 19, 1954, Kannapolis, N.C., lives in Franklin, Mass. Defensive back North Carolina 1973-75. No pro playing experience. College coach: North Carolina 1976-77, Air Force 1978-83, Arkansas 1984-89, Clemson 1990. Pro coach: New York Giants 1990-92, joined Patriots in 1993.

**Charlie Weis,** tight ends, born March 30, 1956, Trenton, N.J., lives in Foxboro, Mass. Graduate of Notre Dame. No college or pro playing experience. College coach: South Carolina 1985-88. Pro coach: New York Giants 1990-92, joined Patriots in 1993.

## 1994 FIRST-YEAR ROSTER

| Name | Pos. | Ht. | Wt. | Birthdate | College | Hometown | How Acq. |
|---|---|---|---|---|---|---|---|
| Ballard, Gregory | WR | 6-3 | 190 | 5/5/71 | Kansas | Lawrence, Kan. | FA |
| Barnett, Troy | DE | 6-4 | 282 | 5/24/71 | North Carolina | Jacksonville, N.C. | FA |
| Basham, Bernard | DE | 6-6 | 281 | 6/23/71 | Virginia Tech | Roanoke, Va. | FA |
| Botkin, Kirk | TE | 6-2 | 233 | 3/19/71 | Arkansas | Baytown, Tex. | FA |
| Boyd, Jean | S | 5-11 | 185 | 6/12/71 | Arizona State | Paramount, Calif. | FA |
| Burch, Joe | C | 6-2 | 278 | 8/8/71 | Texas Southern | Dallas, Tex. | D3b |
| Burke, John | TE | 6-3 | 258 | 9/7/71 | Virginia Tech | Holmdel, N.J. | D4 |
| Collier, Ervin | NT | 6-3 | 287 | 5/12/71 | Florida A&M | Jacksonville, Fla. | D3a |
| Dixon, Todd | WR | 5-10 | 175 | 6/8/71 | Wake Forest | Billerica, Mass. | FA |
| Durkin, Bill | G | 6-5 | 281 | 3/18/71 | Massachusetts | Stratford, Conn. | FA |
| Glenn, Kevin | WR | 6-1 | 166 | 10/5/71 | Illinois State | Brandon, Fla. | FA |
| Green, Damacio | CB | 5-10 | 183 | 2/1/71 | Virginia State | Miami, Fla. | FA |
| Hawkins, Steve | WR | 6-5 | 207 | 3/16/71 | Western Michigan | Detroit, Mich. | D6a |
| Harris, Ronnie (1) | WR | 5-10 | 170 | 6/4/70 | Oregon | San Jose, Calif. | FA |
| Henry, Mario | WR | 6-1 | 184 | 9/14/71 | Rutgers | Medford, N.J. | FA |
| Hooks, Bryan (1) | DE | 6-3 | 286 | 9/15/70 | Arizona State | Tempe, Ariz. | FA |
| Kerr, Mike (1) | LB | 6-5 | 236 | 10/10/69 | Florida | Miami, Fla. | FA |
| Lane, Max | T | 6-6 | 295 | 2/22/71 | Navy | Norborne, Mo. | D6b |
| Lee, Kevin | WR | 6-1 | 194 | 1/1/71 | Alabama | Mobile, Ala. | D2 |
| McGinest, Willie | LB | 6-4 | 255 | 12/11/71 | Southern California | Long Beach, Calif. | D1 |
| Moore, Marty | LB | 6-1 | 242 | 3/19/71 | Kentucky | Ft. Thomas, Ky. | D7b |
| O'Neill, Pat | P-K | 6-1 | 195 | 2/9/71 | Syracuse | Harrisburg, Pa. | D5 |
| Reynolds, Don (1) | DE | 6-3 | 278 | 11/25/69 | Virginia | Axton, Va. | FA |
| Stanley, Sylvester | NT | 6-2 | 283 | 5/14/70 | Michigan | Youngstown, Ohio | FA |
| Stephens, Eric | CB | 5-10 | 170 | 12/19/70 | Jacksonville State | Walterboro, S.C. | FA |
| Tylski, Rich | G | 6-4 | 287 | 2/27/71 | Utah State | San Diego, Calif. | FA |
| Walker, Jay | QB | 6-3 | 230 | 1/24/72 | Howard | Los Angeles, Calif. | D7a |
| Washington, Jerrod | RB | 6-1 | 205 | 3/10/72 | Virginia | Philadelphia, Pa. | FA |
| Witherspoon, Derrick | RB | 5-10 | 198 | 2/14/71 | Clemson | Sumter, S.C. | FA |

The term NFL Rookie is defined as a player who is in his first season of professional football and has not been on the roster of another professional football team for any regular-season or postseason games. A Rookie is designated by an "R" on NFL rosters. Players who have been active in another professional football league or players who have NFL experience, including either preseason training camp or being on an Active List or Inactive List, or on Reserve/Injured or Reserve/Physically Unable to Perform for fewer than six regular-season games, are termed NFL First-Year Players. An NFL First-Year Player is designated by a "1" on NFL rosters. Thereafter, a player is credited with an additional year of experience for each season in which he accumulates six games on the Active List or Inactive List, or on Reserve/Injured or Reserve/Physically Unable to Perform.

## NOTES

# NEW YORK JETS

**American Football Conference**
**Eastern Division**
**Team Colors:** Kelly Green and White
**1000 Fulton Avenue**
**Hempstead, New York 11550**
**Telephone: (516) 538-6600**

## CLUB OFFICIALS

Chairman of the Board: Leon Hess
President: Steve Gutman
V.P./General Manager: Dick Steinberg
Director of Player Personnel: Dick Haley
Assistant General Manager: James Harris
Pro Personnel Director: Jim Royer
Assistant Pro Personnel Director: Pat Kirwan
Talent Scouts: Joe Collins, Don Grammer, Sid Hall, Ron Nay, Marv Sunderland
College Scouting Coordinator: John Griffin
Director of Public Relations: Frank Ramos
Asst. Director of Public Relations: Brooks Thomas
Public Relations Assistants: Ken Ilchuk, Sharon Kelleher, Doug Miller
Travel Coordinator: Kevin Coyle
Treasurer & C.F.O.: Mike Gerstle
Controller: Mike Minarczyk
Director of Operations: Mike Kensil
Exec. Director of Business Operations: Bob Parente
Marketing Manager: Bruce Popko
Ticket Manager: Gerry Parravano
Video Director: Jim Pons
Assistant Video Director: John Seiter
Trainer: Bob Reese
Assistant Trainers: Joe Patten, Darryl Conway
Equipment Manager: Bill Hampton
Assistant Equipment Manager: Clay Hampton
**Stadium:** Giants Stadium •**Capacity:** 77,121
East Rutherford, New Jersey 07073
**Playing Surface:** AstroTurf
**Training Center:** 1000 Fulton Avenue
Hempstead, New York 11550

## 1994 SCHEDULE

**PRESEASON**

| | | |
|---|---|---|
| Aug. 5 | at Detroit | 7:30 |
| Aug. 13 | at Philadelphia | 7:30 |
| Aug. 20 | **New York Giants** | 8:00 |
| Aug. 26 | at Tampa Bay | 7:30 |

**REGULAR SEASON**

| | | |
|---|---|---|
| Sept. 4 | at Buffalo | 4:00 |
| Sept. 11 | **Denver** | 4:00 |
| Sept. 18 | at Miami | 1:00 |
| Sept. 25 | **Chicago** | 8:00 |
| Oct. 2 | at Cleveland | 1:00 |
| Oct. 9 | **Indianapolis** | 1:00 |
| Oct. 16 | **New England** | 1:00 |
| Oct. 23 | Open Date | |
| Oct. 30 | at Indianapolis | 4:00 |
| Nov. 6 | **Buffalo** | 4:00 |
| Nov. 13 | at Green Bay | 3:00 |
| Nov. 20 | at Minnesota | 3:00 |
| Nov. 27 | **Miami** | 1:00 |
| Dec. 4 | at New England | 1:00 |
| Dec. 10 | **Detroit** (Saturday) | 12:30 |
| Dec. 18 | **San Diego** | 1:00 |
| Dec. 24 | at Houston | 3:00 |

## RECORD HOLDERS

**INDIVIDUAL RECORDS—CAREER**

| Category | Name | Performance |
|---|---|---|
| Rushing (Yds.) | Freeman McNeil, 1981-1992 | 8,074 |
| Passing (Yds.) | Joe Namath, 1965-1976 | 27,057 |
| Passing (TDs) | Joe Namath, 1965-1976 | 170 |
| Receiving (No.) | Don Maynard, 1960-1972 | 627 |
| Receiving (Yds.) | Don Maynard, 1960-1972 | 11,732 |
| Interceptions | Bill Baird, 1963-69 | 34 |
| Punting (Avg.) | Curley Johnson, 1961-68 | 42.8 |
| Punt Return (Avg.) | Dick Christy, 1961-63 | 16.2 |
| Kickoff Return (Avg.) | Bobby Humphery, 1984-89 | 22.8 |
| Field Goals | Pat Leahy, 1974-1991 | 304 |
| Touchdowns (Tot.) | Don Maynard, 1960-1972 | 88 |
| Points | Pat Leahy, 1974-1991 | 1,470 |

**INDIVIDUAL RECORDS—SINGLE SEASON**

| Category | Name | Performance |
|---|---|---|
| Rushing (Yds.) | Freeman McNeil, 1985 | 1,331 |
| Passing (Yds.) | Joe Namath, 1967 | 4,007 |
| Passing (TDs) | Al Dorow, 1960 | 26 |
| | Joe Namath, 1967 | 26 |
| Receiving (No.) | Al Toon, 1988 | 93 |
| Receiving (Yds.) | Don Maynard, 1967 | 1,434 |
| Interceptions | Dainard Paulson, 1964 | 12 |
| Punting (Avg.) | Curley Johnson, 1965 | 45.3 |
| Punt Return (Avg.) | Dick Christy, 1961 | 21.3 |
| Kickoff Return (Avg.) | Bobby Humphery, 1984 | 30.7 |
| Field Goals | Jim Turner, 1968 | 34 |
| Touchdowns (Tot.) | Art Powell, 1960 | 14 |
| | Don Maynard, 1965 | 14 |
| | Emerson Boozer, 1972 | 14 |
| Points | Jim Turner, 1968 | 145 |

**INDIVIDUAL RECORDS—SINGLE GAME**

| Category | Name | Performance |
|---|---|---|
| Rushing (Yds.) | Freeman McNeil, 9-15-85 | 192 |
| Passing (Yds.) | Joe Namath, 9-24-72 | 496 |
| Passing (TDs) | Joe Namath, 9-24-72 | 6 |
| Receiving (No.) | Clark Gaines, 9-21-80 | 17 |
| Receiving (Yds.) | Don Maynard, 11-17-68 | 228 |
| Interceptions | Many times | 3 |
| | Last time by Erik McMillan, 10-23-88 | |
| Field Goals | Jim Turner, 11-3-68 | 6 |
| | Bobby Howfield, 12-3-72 | 6 |
| Touchdowns (Tot.) | Wesley Walker, 9-21-86 | 4 |
| Points | Wesley Walker, 9-21-86 | 24 |

## COACHING HISTORY

**New York Titans 1960-62**
**(226-277-8)**

| | | |
|---|---|---|
| 1960-61 | Sammy Baugh | 14-14-0 |
| 1962 | Clyde (Bulldog) Turner | 5-9-0 |
| 1963-73 | Weeb Ewbank | 73-78-6 |
| 1974-75 | Charley Winner* | 9-14-0 |
| 1975 | Ken Shipp | 1-4-0 |
| 1976 | Lou Holtz** | 3-10-0 |
| 1976 | Mike Holovak | 0-1-0 |
| 1977-82 | Walt Michaels | 41-49-1 |
| 1983-89 | Joe Walton | 54-59-1 |
| 1990-93 | Bruce Coslet | 26-39-0 |

*Released after nine games in 1975
**Resigned after 13 games in 1976

**GIANTS STADIUM**

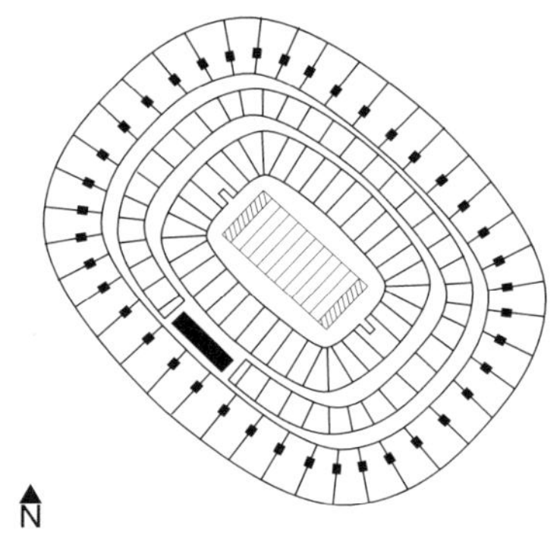

## 1993 TEAM RECORD

**PRESEASON (0-4)**

| Date | Result | | Opponents |
|---|---|---|---|
| 8/7 | L | 13-17 | at Pittsburgh |
| 8/13 | L | 13-24 | Philadelphia |
| 8/21 | L | 13-14 | at N.Y. Giants |
| 8/27 | L | 3-17 | at Washington |

**REGULAR SEASON (8-8)**

| Date | Result | | Opponents | Att. |
|---|---|---|---|---|
| 9/5 | L | 20-26 | Denver | 68,130 |
| 9/12 | W | 24-14 | at Miami | 70,314 |
| 9/26 | W | 45-7 | New England | 64,836 |
| 10/3 | L | 30-35 | Philadelphia | 72,593 |
| 10/10 | L | 20-24 | at L.A. Raiders | 41,627 |
| 10/24 | L | 10-19 | Buffalo | 71,541 |
| 10/31 | W | 10-6 | at N.Y. Giants | 71,659 |
| 11/7 | W | 27-10 | Miami | 71,306 |
| 11/14 | W | 31-17 | at Indianapolis | 47,351 |
| 11/21 | W | 17-12 | Cincinnati | 64,264 |
| 11/28 | W | 6-0 | at New England | 42,810 |
| 12/5 | L | 6-9 | Indianapolis | 45,799 |
| 12/11 | W | 3-0 | at Washington | 47,970 |
| 12/18 | L | 7-28 | Dallas | 73,233 |
| 12/26 | L | 14-16 | at Buffalo | 70,817 |
| 1/2 | L | 0-24 | at Houston | 61,040 |

**SCORE BY PERIODS**

| | | | | | | | |
|---|---|---|---|---|---|---|---|
| Jets | 65 | 105 | 37 | 63 | 0 | — | 270 |
| Opponents | 36 | 77 | 68 | 66 | 0 | — | 247 |

**ATTENDANCE**

Home 531,702 Away 453,588 Total 985,290
Single-game home record, 75,945 (9-20-92)
Single-season home record, 603,619 (1992)

## 1993 TEAM STATISTICS

| | Jets | Opp. |
|---|---|---|
| Total First Downs | 304 | 266 |
| Rushing | 106 | 93 |
| Passing | 173 | 161 |
| Penalty | 25 | 12 |
| Third Down: Made/Att | 92/220 | 81/200 |
| Third Down Pct. | 41.8 | 40.5 |
| Fourth Down: Made/Att | 10/21 | 9/19 |
| Fourth Down Pct. | 47.6 | 47.4 |
| Total Net Yards | 5212 | 4712 |
| Avg. Per Game | 325.8 | 294.5 |
| Total Plays | 1031 | 949 |
| Avg. Per Play | 5.1 | 5.0 |
| Net Yards Rushing | 1880 | 1473 |
| Avg. Per Game | 117.5 | 92.1 |
| Total Rushes | 521 | 420 |
| Net Yards Passing | 3332 | 3239 |
| Avg. Per Game | 208.3 | 202.4 |
| Sacked/Yards Lost | 21/160 | 32/195 |
| Gross Yards | 3492 | 3434 |
| Att./Completions | 489/294 | 497/296 |
| Completion Pct. | 60.1 | 59.6 |
| Had Intercepted | 12 | 19 |
| Punts/Avg. | 73/38.4 | 66/43.3 |
| Net Punting Avg. | 73/34.4 | 66/37.6 |
| Penalties/Yards Lost | 86/555 | 86/661 |
| Fumbles/Ball Lost | 38/16 | 30/18 |
| Touchdowns | 31 | 26 |
| Rushing | 14 | 8 |
| Passing | 16 | 15 |
| Returns | 1 | 3 |
| Avg. Time of Possession | 32:16 | 27:44 |

## 1993 INDIVIDUAL STATISTICS

| PASSING | Att. | Cmp. | Yds. | Pct. | TD | Int. | Tkld. | Rate |
|---|---|---|---|---|---|---|---|---|
| Esiason | 473 | 288 | 3421 | 60.9 | 16 | 11 | 18/139 | 84.5 |
| Nagle | 14 | 6 | 71 | 42.9 | 0 | 0 | 3/21 | 58.9 |
| Aguiar | 2 | 0 | 0 | 0.0 | 0 | 1 | 0/0 | 0.0 |
| Jets | 489 | 294 | 3492 | 60.1 | 16 | 12 | 21/160 | 82.6 |
| Opponents | 497 | 296 | 3434 | 59.6 | 15 | 19 | 32/195 | 74.6 |

| SCORING | TD R | TD P | TD Rt | PAT | FG | Saf | PTS |
|---|---|---|---|---|---|---|---|
| Blanchard | 0 | 0 | 0 | 31/31 | 17/26 | 0 | 82 |
| B. Baxter | 7 | 0 | 0 | 0/0 | 0/0 | 0 | 42 |
| Mitchell | 0 | 6 | 0 | 0/0 | 0/0 | 0 | 36 |
| Burkett | 0 | 4 | 0 | 0/0 | 0/0 | 0 | 24 |
| J. Johnson | 3 | 1 | 0 | 0/0 | 0/0 | 0 | 24 |
| Thornton | 0 | 2 | 0 | 0/0 | 0/0 | 0 | 12 |
| F. Baxter | 0 | 1 | 0 | 0/0 | 0/0 | 0 | 6 |
| Chaffey | 0 | 1 | 0 | 0/0 | 0/0 | 0 | 6 |
| Esiason | 1 | 0 | 0 | 0/0 | 0/0 | 0 | 6 |
| Mathis | 1 | 0 | 0 | 0/0 | 0/0 | 0 | 6 |
| Moore | 0 | 1 | 0 | 0/0 | 0/0 | 0 | 6 |
| Murrell | 1 | 0 | 0 | 0/0 | 0/0 | 0 | 6 |
| B. Thomas | 1 | 0 | 0 | 0/0 | 0/0 | 0 | 6 |
| B. Washington | 0 | 0 | 1 | 0/0 | 0/0 | 0 | 6 |
| Jets | 14 | 16 | 1 | 31/31 | 17/26 | 1 | 270 |
| Opponents | 8 | 15 | 3 | 26/26 | 21/26 | 1 | 247 |

| Rushing | Att. | Yds. | Avg. | LG | TD |
|---|---|---|---|---|---|
| J. Johnson | 198 | 821 | 4.1 | 57t | 3 |
| B. Baxter | 174 | 559 | 3.2 | 16 | 7 |
| B. Thomas | 59 | 221 | 3.7 | 24 | 1 |
| Murrell | 34 | 157 | 4.6 | 37t | 1 |
| Esiason | 45 | 118 | 2.6 | 17 | 1 |
| Mathis | 2 | 20 | 10.0 | 17t | 1 |
| Chaffey | 5 | 17 | 3.4 | 7 | 0 |
| Moore | 1 | -6 | -6.0 | -6 | 0 |
| Aguiar | 3 | -27 | -9.0 | 5 | 0 |
| Jets | 521 | 1880 | 3.6 | 57t | 14 |
| Opponents | 420 | 1473 | 3.5 | 29 | 8 |

| RECEIVING | No. | Yds. | Avg. | LG | TD |
|---|---|---|---|---|---|
| J. Johnson | 67 | 641 | 9.6 | 48 | 1 |
| Moore | 64 | 843 | 13.2 | 51 | 1 |
| Burkett | 40 | 531 | 13.3 | 77 | 4 |
| Mitchell | 39 | 630 | 16.2 | 65t | 6 |
| Mathis | 24 | 352 | 14.7 | 46 | 0 |
| B. Baxter | 20 | 158 | 7.9 | 24 | 0 |
| Thornton | 12 | 108 | 9.0 | 22 | 2 |
| B. Thomas | 7 | 25 | 3.6 | 7 | 0 |
| Carpenter | 6 | 83 | 13.8 | 18 | 0 |
| Murrell | 5 | 12 | 2.4 | 8 | 0 |
| Chaffey | 4 | 55 | 13.8 | 20t | 1 |
| F. Baxter | 3 | 48 | 16.0 | 25 | 1 |
| Sadowski | 2 | 14 | 7.0 | 11 | 0 |
| Esiason | 1 | -8 | -8.0 | -8 | 0 |
| Jets | 294 | 3492 | 11.9 | 77 | 16 |
| Opponents | 296 | 3434 | 11.6 | 68t | 15 |

| INTERCEPTIONS | No. | Yds. | Avg. | LG | TD |
|---|---|---|---|---|---|
| B. Washington | 6 | 128 | 21.3 | 62t | 1 |
| Lott | 3 | 35 | 11.7 | 29 | 0 |
| Hasty | 2 | 22 | 11.0 | 22 | 0 |
| E. Thomas | 2 | 20 | 10.0 | 20 | 0 |
| Lewis | 2 | 4 | 2.0 | 3 | 0 |
| Lageman | 1 | 15 | 15.0 | 15 | 0 |
| Young | 1 | 6 | 6.0 | 6 | 0 |
| Clifton | 1 | 3 | 3.0 | 3 | 0 |
| Houston | 1 | 0 | 0.0 | 0 | 0 |
| Jets | 19 | 233 | 12.3 | 62t | 1 |
| Opponents | 12 | 310 | 25.8 | 94t | 3 |

| PUNTING | No. | Yds. | Avg. | In 20 | LG |
|---|---|---|---|---|---|
| Aguiar | 73 | 2806 | 38.4 | 21 | 71 |
| Jets | 73 | 2806 | 38.4 | 21 | 71 |
| Opponents | 66 | 2859 | 43.3 | 17 | 68 |

| PUNT RETURNS | No. | FC | Yds. | Avg. | LG | TD |
|---|---|---|---|---|---|---|
| Hicks | 17 | 4 | 157 | 9.2 | 20 | 0 |
| Mathis | 14 | 8 | 99 | 7.1 | 16 | 0 |
| Jets | 31 | 12 | 256 | 8.3 | 20 | 0 |
| Opponents | 26 | 12 | 156 | 6.0 | 36 | 0 |

| KICKOFF RETURNS | No. | Yds. | Avg. | LG | TD |
|---|---|---|---|---|---|
| Murrell | 23 | 342 | 14.9 | 23 | 0 |
| Prior | 9 | 126 | 14.0 | 27 | 0 |
| Mathis | 7 | 102 | 14.6 | 28 | 0 |
| R. Anderson | 4 | 66 | 16.5 | 22 | 0 |
| B. Thomas | 2 | 39 | 19.5 | 28 | 0 |
| Sadowski | 1 | 0 | 0.0 | 0 | 0 |
| Jets | 46 | 675 | 14.7 | 28 | 0 |
| Opponents | 47 | 911 | 19.4 | 45 | 0 |

| SACKS | No. |
|---|---|
| Lageman | 8.5 |
| M. Washington | 5.5 |
| Lewis | 4.0 |
| Houston | 3.0 |
| Marshall | 2.0 |
| Clifton | 1.0 |
| Frase | 1.0 |
| D. Jones | 1.0 |
| Lott | 1.0 |
| Mersereau | 1.0 |
| Turner | 1.0 |
| Young | 1.0 |
| Team | 2.0 |
| Jets | 32.0 |
| Opponents | 21.0 |

## 1994 DRAFT CHOICES

| Round | Name | Pos. | College |
|---|---|---|---|
| 1 | Aaron Glenn | DB | Texas A&M |
| 2 | Ryan Yarborough | WR | Wyoming |
| 3 | Lou Benfatti | DT | Penn State |
| 4 | Orlando Parker | WR | Troy State |
| 5 | Horace Morris | LB | Tennessee |
| 6 | Fred Lester | RB | Alabama A&M |
| 7 | Glenn Foley | QB | Boston College |

## NEW YORK JETS

### 1994 VETERAN ROSTER

| No. | | Name | Pos. | Ht. | Wt. | Birthdate | NFL Exp. | College | Hometown | How Acq. | '93 Games/ Starts |
|---|---|---|---|---|---|---|---|---|---|---|---|
| 20 | | Anderson, Richie | RB | 6-2 | 215 | 9/13/71 | 2 | Penn State | Sandy Spring, Md. | D6-'93 | 7/0 |
| 98 | | Barber, Kurt | LB | 6-4 | 241 | 1/5/69 | 3 | Southern California | Paducah, Ky. | D2-'92 | 13/0 |
| 6 | | Baumann, Charlie | K | 6-1 | 200 | 8/25/67 | 3 | West Virginia | Erie, Pa. | FA-'94 | 0* |
| 30 | | Baxter, Brad | RB | 6-1 | 235 | 5/5/67 | 5 | Alabama State | Slocomb, Ala. | FA-'89 | 16/13 |
| 84 | | Baxter, Fred | TE | 6-3 | 250 | 6/14/71 | 2 | Auburn | Brundidge, Ala. | D5a-'93 | 7/0 |
| 9 | | Blake, Jeff | QB | 6-0 | 202 | 12/4/70 | 3 | East Carolina | Sanford, Fla. | D6b-'92 | 0* |
| 10 | | Blanchard, Cary | K | 6-1 | 225 | 11/5/68 | 3 | Oklahoma State | Hurst, Tex. | W(NO)-'92 | 16/0 |
| 76 | | Brown, James | T | 6-6 | 321 | 1/3/70 | 2 | Virginia State | Philadelphia, Pa. | W(Ind)-'92 | 14/1 |
| 66 | # | Cadigan, Dave | G | 6-4 | 285 | 4/6/65 | 7 | Southern California | Newport Beach, Calif. | D1-'88 | 16/16 |
| 50 | | Cadrez, Glenn | LB | 6-3 | 240 | 1/2/70 | 3 | Houston | El Centro, Calif. | D6a-'92 | 16/0 |
| 82 | | Carpenter, Rob | WR | 6-2 | 190 | 8/1/68 | 4 | Syracuse | Amityville, N.Y. | PB(NE)-'92 | 16/0 |
| 28 | | Chaffey, Pat | RB | 6-1 | 220 | 4/19/67 | 4 | Oregon State | Aurora, Ore. | PB(Atl)-'92 | 3/0 |
| 59 | | Clifton, Kyle | LB | 6-4 | 236 | 8/23/62 | 11 | Texas Christian | Bridgeport, Tex. | D3-'84 | 16/16 |
| 69 | | Criswell, Jeff | T | 6-7 | 291 | 3/7/64 | 7 | Graceland, Iowa | Searsboro, Iowa | FA-'88 | 16/16 |
| 52 | | Dixon, Cal | C | 6-4 | 284 | 10/11/69 | 3 | Florida | Merritt Island, Fla. | D5-'92 | 16/0 |
| 62 | | Duffy, Roger | G-C | 6-3 | 285 | 7/16/67 | 5 | Penn State | Canton, Ohio | D8-'90 | 16/1 |
| 7 | | Esiason, Boomer | QB | 6-5 | 220 | 4/17/61 | 11 | Maryland | East Islip, N.Y. | T(Cin)-'93 | 16/16 |
| 60 | | Evans, Donald | DT-DE | 6-2 | 282 | 3/14/64 | 7 | Winston-Salem State | Raleigh, N.C. | UFA(Pitt)-'94 | 16/16* |
| 91 | | Frase, Paul | DT-DE | 6-5 | 270 | 5/5/65 | 6 | Syracuse | Barrington, N.H. | D6-'88 | 16/4 |
| 21 | | Green, Victor | CB | 5-9 | 195 | 12/8/69 | 2 | Akron | Americus, Ga. | FA-'93 | 11/0 |
| 96 | † | Gunn, Mark | DT-DE | 6-5 | 279 | 7/24/68 | 4 | Pittsburgh | Cleveland, Ohio | D4-'91 | 12/0 |
| 11 | | Hansen, Brian | P | 6-4 | 215 | 10/26/60 | 10 | Sioux Falls | Hawarden, Iowa | UFA(Clev)-'94 | 16/0* |
| 40 | | Hasty, James | CB | 6-0 | 201 | 5/23/65 | 7 | Washington State | Seattle, Wash. | D3b-'88 | 16/16 |
| 55 | | Houston, Bobby | LB | 6-2 | 239 | 10/26/67 | 4 | North Carolina State | Hyattsville, Md. | PB(Atl)-'91 | 16/14 |
| 39 | | Johnson, Johnny | RB | 6-3 | 220 | 6/11/68 | 5 | San Jose State | Santa Cruz, Calif. | T(Phx)-'93 | 15/9 |
| 49 | | Johnson, Troy | LB | 6-2 | 236 | 11/10/64 | 6 | Oklahoma | Houston, Tex. | FA-'94 | 0* |
| 54 | | Jones, Marvin | LB | 6-2 | 240 | 6/28/72 | 2 | Florida State | Miami, Fla. | D1-'93 | 9/0 |
| 56 | | Lageman, Jeff | DE | 6-5 | 266 | 7/18/67 | 6 | Virginia | Great Falls, Va. | D1-'89 | 16/16 |
| 57 | | Lewis, Mo | LB | 6-3 | 250 | 10/21/69 | 4 | Georgia | Peachtree, Ga. | D3-'91 | 16/16 |
| 42 | | Lott, Ronnie | S | 6-1 | 203 | 5/8/59 | 14 | Southern California | Rialto, Calif. | UFA(Raid)-'93 | 16/16 |
| 75 | | Malamala, Siupeli | T | 6-5 | 308 | 1/15/69 | 3 | Washington | Kalaheo, Hawaii | D3-'92 | 15/15 |
| 70 | | Marshall, Leonard | DT | 6-4 | 288 | 10/22/61 | 12 | Louisiana State | Franklin, La. | UFA(NYG)-'93 | 12/12 |
| 86 | | Mitchell, Johnny | TE | 6-3 | 237 | 1/20/71 | 3 | Nebraska | Chicago, Ill. | D1-'92 | 14/14 |
| 81 | | Monk, Art | WR | 6-3 | 210 | 12/5/57 | 15 | Syracuse | White Plains, N.Y. | FA-'94 | 16/5* |
| 85 | † | Moore, Rob | WR | 6-3 | 205 | 9/27/68 | 5 | Syracuse | Hempstead, N.Y. | SD1-'90 | 13/13 |
| 29 | | Murrell, Adrian | RB | 5-11 | 205 | 10/16/70 | 2 | West Virginia | Wahiawa, Hawaii | D5b-'93 | 16/0 |
| 95 | | Oglesby, Alfred | DT | 6-4 | 276 | 1/27/67 | 4 | Houston | Weimer, Tex. | FA-'94 | 0* |
| 71 | # | Pickel, Bill | DT | 6-5 | 265 | 11/5/59 | 12 | Rutgers | Maspeth, N.Y. | PB(Raid)-'91 | 16/3 |
| 37 | | Prior, Anthony | CB-S | 5-11 | 185 | 3/27/70 | 2 | Washington State | Riverside, Calif. | FA-'93 | 16/0 |
| 92 | | Rudolph, Coleman | DE-DT | 6-4 | 270 | 10/22/70 | 2 | Georgia Tech | Valdosta, Ga. | D2-'93 | 4/0 |
| 53 | | Sweeney, Jim | C-G | 6-4 | 286 | 8/8/62 | 11 | Pittsburgh | Pittsburgh, Pa. | D2a-'84 | 16/16 |
| 27 | | Terrell, Pat | S | 6-2 | 210 | 3/18/68 | 5 | Notre Dame | St. Petersburg, Fla. | UFA(Rams)-'94 | 13/3* |
| 80 | | Thornton, James | TE | 6-2 | 242 | 2/8/65 | 7 | Cal State-Fullerton | Santa Rosa, Calif. | UFA(Chi)-'93 | 13/6 |
| 16 | | Trudeau, Jack | QB | 6-3 | 227 | 9/9/62 | 9 | Illinois | Livermore, Calif. | FA-'94 | 5/5* |
| 23 | | Turner, Marcus | CB-S | 6-0 | 190 | 1/13/66 | 6 | UCLA | Long Beach, Calif. | PB(Phx)-'92 | 16/0 |
| 68 | | Ware, David | G-T | 6-6 | 285 | 2/21/70 | 2 | Virginia | Roanoke, Va. | D4-'93 | 0* |
| 48 | | Washington, Brian | S | 6-1 | 206 | 9/10/65 | 6 | Nebraska | Richmond, Va. | W(Clev)-'89 | 16/16 |
| 97 | | Washington, Marvin | DE | 6-6 | 272 | 10/22/65 | 6 | Idaho | Dallas, Tex. | D6a-'89 | 16/16 |
| 67 | | White, Dwayne | G | 6-2 | 315 | 2/10/67 | 5 | Alcorn State | Philadelphia, Pa. | D7a-'90 | 15/15 |
| 22 | | Williams, Perry | CB | 6-2 | 203 | 5/12/61 | 12 | North Carolina State | Rockingham, N.C. | UFA(NYG)-'94 | 8/6* |
| 77 | | Willig, Matt | T | 6-8 | 305 | 1/21/69 | 2 | Southern California | Santa Fe Springs, Calif. | FA-'92 | 3/0 |
| 31 | # | Young, Lonnie | S-CB | 6-1 | 196 | 7/18/63 | 10 | Michigan State | Flint, Mich. | T(Phx)-'91 | 9/2 |

* Baumann last active with New England in '92; Blake and Ware inactive for 16 games; Evans played 16 games with Pittsburgh in '93; Hansen played 16 games with Cleveland; T. Johnson last active with Detroit in '92; Monk played 16 games with Washington; Ogelsby inactive for 1 game; Terrell played 13 games with L.A. Rams; Trudeau played 5 games with Indianapolis; Williams played 8 games with N.Y. Giants.

\# Unrestricted free agent; subject to developments.

† Restricted free agent; subject to developments.

Retired—Chris Burkett, 9-year veteran wide receiver, 16 games in '93.

Players lost through free agency (4): LB Steve DeOssie (NE; 7 games in '93), WR-KR Terance Mathis (Atl; 16), TE Troy Sadowski (Cin; 13), RB Blair Thomas (NE; 11).

Also played with Jets in '93—P Louie Aguiar (16 games), WR Dale Dawkins (4), CB-KR Clifford Hicks (10), LB Don Jones (6), LB Mike Merriweather (1), DT Scott Mersereau (13), QB Browning Nagle (3), S Damon Pieri (5), CB Eric Thomas (16), DT-DE Karl Wilson (5).

## COACHING STAFF

**Head Coach,**
**Pete Carroll**

**Pro Career:** Became New York's ninth head coach on January 7, 1994. Carroll, one of the most respected young coaches in the NFL, spent the past four seasons as the Jets' defensive coordinator. His aggressive, attacking schemes helped turn the Jets' defense into one of the NFL's finest units. Carroll entered the pro ranks as defensive backs coach with the Buffalo Bills in 1984. He coached the Minnesota Vikings defensive backs from 1985-89. Carroll joined the Jets in 1990.

**Background:** Defensive back at the University of the Pacific from 1969-72. No pro playing experience. College coach: Arkansas 1977, Iowa State 1978, Ohio State 1979, North Carolina State 1980-82, Pacific 1983.

**Personal:** Born September 15, 1951, in San Francisco. Pete and his wife, Glena, live on Long Island, and have three children—Brennan, Nathan, and Jaime.

### ASSISTANT COACHES

**Larry Beightol,** offensive line; born November 21, 1942, Morrisdale, Pa., lives on Long Island. Guard-linebacker Catawba College 1961-63. No pro playing experience. College coach: William & Mary 1968-71, North Carolina State 1972-75, Auburn 1976, Arkansas 1977-78, 1980-82, Louisiana Tech 1979 (head coach), Missouri 1983-84. Pro coach: Atlanta Falcons 1985-86, Tampa Bay Buccaneers 1987-88, San Diego Chargers 1989, joined Jets in 1990.

**Don Breaux,** tight ends; born August 3, 1940, Jennings, La., lives on Long Island. Quarterback McNeese State 1959-61. Pro quarterback Denver Broncos 1963, San Diego Chargers 1964-65. College coach: Florida State 1966-67, Arkansas 1968-71, 1977-80, Florida 1973-74, Texas 1975-76. Pro coach: Washington Redskins 1981-1993, joined Jets in 1994.

**Larry Coyer,** defensive line; born April 19, 1943, Huntington, W. Va., lives on Long Island. Quarterback-defensive back Marshall 1961-65. No pro playing experience. College coach: Marshall 1965-67, Bowling Green 1973, Iowa 1974-77, Oklahoma State 1978, Iowa State 1979-83, UCLA 1987-89, Houston 1990, Ohio State 1991-92, East Carolina 1993. Pro coach: Michigan Panthers (USFL) 1984-85, Memphis Showboats (USFL) 1986, joined Jets in 1994.

**Ed Donatell,** defensive backs; born February 4, 1957, Akron, Ohio, lives on Long Island. Safety Glenville State 1975-78. No pro playing experience. College coach: Kent State 1979-80, Washington 1981-82, Pacific 1983-85, Idaho 1986-88, Cal State-Fullerton 1989. Pro coach: Joined Jets in 1990.

**Foge Fazio,** linebackers; born February 28, 1939, Dawmont, W.Va., lives on Long Island. Linebacker-center Pittsburgh 1957-60. No pro playing experience. College coach: Boston University 1967, Harvard 1968, Pittsburgh 1969-72, 1977-81, 1982-85 (head coach), Cincinnati 1973-76, Notre Dame 1986-87. Pro coach: Atlanta Falcons 1988-89, joined Jets in 1990.

**Walt Harris,** quarterbacks; born November 9, 1946, Modesto, Calif., lives on Long Island. Defensive back Pacific 1966-67. No pro playing experience. College coach: Pacific 1970-73, 1989-91 (head coach), California 1974-77, Michigan State 1978-79, Illinois 1980-82, Tennessee 1983-88. Pro coach: Joined Jets in 1992.

**Greg Mackrides,** strength and conditioning; born July 9, 1954, Philadelphia, Pa., lives on Long Island. No college or pro playing experience. College coach: Villanova 1984-85, Fairfield 1986-88. U.S. Olympic Wrestling team 1988, U.S. Pan American and World touring teams 1986-88. Pro coach: New York Knicks (NBA) 1987-90, joined Jets in 1990.

**Richard Mann,** receivers; born April 20, 1947, Aliquippa, Pa., lives on Long Island. Wide receiver Arizona State 1966-68. No pro playing experience. College coach: Arizona State 1974-79, Louisville 1980-81. Pro coach: Baltimore/Indianapolis Colts 1982-84, Cleveland Browns 1985-93, joined Jets in 1994.

**Greg Robinson,** defensive coordinator; born October 9, 1951, Los Angeles, Calif., lives on Long Island. Linebacker-tight end Pacific 1972-73. No pro playing experience. College coach: Cal State-Fullerton 1977-79, North Carolina State 1980-81, UCLA 1982-89. Pro coach: Joined Jets in 1990.

**Johnny Roland,** running backs; born May 21, 1943, Corpus Christi, Tex., lives on Long Island. Running back Missouri 1963-65. Pro running back St. Louis Cardinals 1966-72, New York Giants 1973. College coach: Notre Dame 1975. Pro coach: Green Bay Packers 1974, Philadelphia Eagles 1976-78, Chicago Bears 1983-92, joined Jets in 1993.

**Brad Seely,** special teams; born September 6, 1956, Vinton, Iowa, lives on Long Island. Tackle-guard South Dakota State 1974-77. No pro playing experience. College coach: Colorado State 1980, Southern Methodist 1981, North Carolina State 1982, Pacific 1983, Oklahoma State 1984-88. Pro coach: Indianapolis Colts 1989-93, joined Jets in 1994.

**Ray Sherman,** offensive coordinator; born November 27, 1951, Berkeley, Calif., lives on Long Island. Wide receiver Laney, Calif., J.C. 1969-70, Fresno State 1971-72. Pro defensive back Green Bay Packers 1973. College coach: San Jose State 1974, California 1975, 1981, Michigan State 1976-77, Wake Forest 1978-80, Purdue 1982-85, Georgia 1986-87. Pro coach: Houston Oilers 1988-89, Atlanta Falcons 1990, San Francisco 49ers 1991-93, joined Jets in 1994.

**Steve Trimble,** defensive assistant-quality control; born May 11, 1958, Cumberland, Md., lives on Long Island. Defensive back Maryland 1976-80. Pro defensive back Denver Broncos 1981-1983, Denver Gold (USFL) 1984-85, Chicago Bears 1987. College coach: New Mexico Highlands 1986-87, Colorado 1988-90, Howard 1991-92. Pro coach: Detroit Drive (Arena League) 1988-89, Cincinnati Rockers (Arena League) 1993, joined Jets in 1994.

**Sparky Woods,** offensive assistant; born December 20, 1953, Oneida, Tenn., lives on Long Island. Quarterback-defensive back Carson-Newman 1972-75. No pro playing experience. College coach: Tennessee 1976, Kansas 1977, North Alabama 1978, Iowa State 1979-82, Appalachian State 1983, 1984-88, South Carolina 1989-93 (head coach). Pro coach: Joined Jets in 1994.

## 1994 FIRST-YEAR ROSTER

| Name | Pos. | Ht. | Wt. | Birthdate | College | Hometown | How Acq. |
|---|---|---|---|---|---|---|---|
| Adams, Kyle | G | 6-4 | 290 | 5/7/71 | Syracuse | Webster, N.Y. | FA |
| Alipate, Tuineau (1) | LB | 6-1 | 234 | 8/21/67 | Washington State | Union City, Calif. | FA |
| Allen, Alan | WR | 6-1 | 191 | 8/9/71 | Idaho | Tacoma, Wash. | FA |
| Anderson, Mike | LB | 6-0 | 235 | 10/5/70 | Nebraska | Grand Island, Neb. | FA |
| Anderson, Stevie (1) | WR | 6-5 | 205 | 5/12/70 | Grambling | Jonesboro, La. | FA |
| Ball, LaVar | TE | 6-5 | 273 | 10/23/68 | Cal State-Los Angeles | Canoga Park, Calif. | FA |
| Beckford, Gary | CB-S | 5-11 | 200 | 10/18/72 | Bowie State | Wheaton, Md. | FA |
| Benfatti, Lou | DT | 6-4 | 280 | 3/9/71 | Penn State | Green Pond, N.J. | D3 |
| Burke, Paul | TE | 6-3 | 248 | 2/16/67 | Idaho | Detroit, Mich. | FA |
| Chapman, Lindsey | RB | 5-8 | 197 | 1/1/71 | California | Marrero, La. | FA |
| Cooke, Jeff | DT | 6-1 | 271 | 6/3/71 | East Carolina | Sanford, N.C. | FA |
| Crisp, Jackie | T | 6-7 | 296 | 7/18/72 | Colorado Mines | Cheyenne, Wyo. | FA |
| Davis, Rob (1) | DT | 6-3 | 275 | 12/10/68 | Shippensburg State | District Heights, Md. | FA |
| Doggette, Cecil (1) | CB-S | 5-8 | 185 | 11/15/70 | West Virginia | Queens, N.Y. | FA |
| Fisher, Bill | DT | 6-2 | 278 | 7/30/70 | Rowan | Cherry Hill, N.J. | FA |
| Foley, Glenn | QB | 6-2 | 205 | 10/10/70 | Boston College | Cherry Hill, N.J. | D7 |
| Glenn, Aaron | CB-S | 5-9 | 185 | 9/16/72 | Texas A&M | Aldine, Tex. | D1 |
| Hales, Ross | TE | 6-6 | 262 | 10/20/70 | Indiana | Elkhart, Ind. | FA |
| Lester, Fred | RB | 6-0 | 241 | 8/1/71 | Alabama A&M | Miami, Fla. | D6 |
| McIver, Everett (1) | T | 6-6 | 309 | 8/5/70 | Elizabeth City State | Fayetteville, N.C. | FA |
| Mitter, Craig (1) | RB | 5-9 | 200 | 1/25/70 | Rutgers | Matawan, N.J. | FA |
| Morris, Horace | LB | 6-2 | 230 | 5/29/71 | Tennessee | Miami, Fla. | D5 |
| Nelson, Chico | CB-S | 6-0 | 200 | 12/25/69 | Ohio State | Sarasota, Fla. | FA |
| Papasedero, Fran | DT | 6-2 | 275 | 3/2/69 | Springfield | Boston, Mass. | FA |
| Parker, Orlando | WR | 5-11 | 183 | 3/7/72 | Troy State | Montgomery, Ala. | D4 |
| Pieri, Damon (1) | S | 6-0 | 186 | 9/25/70 | San Diego State | Phoenix, Ariz. | FA |
| Shale, Cris (1) | P | 6-0 | 200 | 6/27/68 | Bowling Green | Beaver Creek, Ohio | FA |
| Shedd, Kenny (1) | WR-KR | 5-9 | 166 | 2/14/71 | Northern Iowa | Davenport, Iowa | D5c-'93 |
| Solari, Steve | LB | 6-0 | 235 | 2/25/71 | Texas A&M | Houston, Tex. | FA |
| Trice, Robert | RB | 5-10 | 204 | 5/21/70 | Cal State-Northridge | Burgaw, N.C. | FA |
| Wisdom, Terrence (1) | G | 6-4 | 305 | 12/4/71 | Syracuse | Roosevelt, N.Y. | FA |
| Yarborough, Ryan | WR | 6-2 | 195 | 4/26/71 | Wyoming | Park Forest, Ill. | D2 |
| Yatkowski, Paul | DT | 6-2 | 278 | 11/18/70 | Tennessee | Winnipeg, Canada | FA |

The term NFL Rookie is defined as a player who is in his first season of professional football and has not been on the roster of another professional football team for any regular-season or postseason games. A Rookie is designated by an "R" on NFL rosters. Players who have been active in another professional football league or players who have NFL experience, including either preseason training camp or being on an Active List or Inactive List, or on Reserve/Injured or Reserve/Physically Unable to Perform for fewer than six regular-season games, are termed NFL First-Year Players. An NFL First-Year Player is designated by a "1" on NFL rosters. Thereafter, a player is credited with an additional year of experience for each season in which he accumulates six games on the Active List or Inactive List, or on Reserve/Injured or Reserve/Physically Unable to Perform.

## NOTES

# PITTSBURGH STEELERS

**American Football Conference**
**Central Division**
**Team Colors:** Black and Gold
**Three Rivers Stadium**
**300 Stadium Circle**
**Pittsburgh, Pennsylvania 15212**
**Telephone: (412) 323-1200**

## CLUB OFFICIALS

President: Daniel M. Rooney
Vice President: John R. McGinley
Vice President: Arthur J. Rooney, Jr.
Secretary and Counsel: Arthur J. Rooney II
Administration Advisor: Charles H. Noll
Director of Communications: Joe Gordon
Public Relations Coordinator: Rob Boulware
P.R. Assistant/Community Relations: Ron Miller
Controller: Michael J. Hagan
Assistant Controller: Dan Ferens
Assistant Controller: Jim Ellenberger
Director of Football Operations: Tom Donahoe
Football Business Manager: James A. Boston
College Personnel Coordinator: Tom Modrak
Pro Personnel Coordinator: Charles Bailey
College Scouts: Phil Kreidler, Bob Lane, Max McCartney, Bob Schmitz
Ticket Sales Manager: Geraldine R. Glenn
Player Development Coordinator: Anthony Griggs
Trainers: John Norwig, Rick Burkholder
Equipment Manager: Anthony Parisi
Field Manager: Rodgers Freyvogel
**Stadium:** Three Rivers Stadium
•**Capacity:** 59,600
300 Stadium Circle
Pittsburgh, Pennsylvania 15212
**Playing Surface:** AstroTurf
**Training Camp:** St. Vincent College
Latrobe, Pennsylvania 15650

## 1994 SCHEDULE

**PRESEASON**

| | | |
|---|---|---|
| Aug. 6 | at Miami | 8:00 |
| Aug. 13 | **Los Angeles Raiders** | 6:00 |
| Aug. 20 | **Indianapolis** | 6:00 |
| Aug. 26 | at Washington | 8:00 |

**REGULAR SEASON**

| | | |
|---|---|---|
| Sept. 4 | **Dallas** | 4:00 |
| Sept. 11 | at Cleveland | 1:00 |
| Sept. 18 | **Indianapolis** | 1:00 |
| Sept. 25 | at Seattle | 1:00 |
| Oct. 3 | **Houston** (Monday) | 9:00 |
| Oct. 9 | Open Date | |
| Oct. 16 | **Cincinnati** | 1:00 |
| Oct. 23 | at New York Giants | 1:00 |
| Oct. 30 | at Arizona | 6:00 |
| Nov. 6 | at Houston | 12:00 |
| Nov. 14 | **Buffalo** (Monday) | 9:00 |
| Nov. 20 | **Miami** | 1:00 |
| Nov. 27 | at Los Angeles Raiders | 1:00 |
| Dec. 4 | at Cincinnati | 1:00 |
| Dec. 11 | **Philadelphia** | 1:00 |
| Dec. 18 | **Cleveland** | 1:00 |
| Dec. 24 | at San Diego | 1:00 |

## RECORD HOLDERS

**INDIVIDUAL RECORDS—CAREER**

| Category | Name | Performance |
|---|---|---|
| Rushing (Yds.) | Franco Harris, 1972-1983 | 11,950 |
| Passing (Yds.) | Terry Bradshaw, 1970-1983 | 27,989 |
| Passing (TDs) | Terry Bradshaw, 1970-1983 | 212 |
| Receiving (No.) | John Stallworth, 1974-1987 | 537 |
| Receiving (Yds.) | John Stallworth, 1974-1987 | 8,723 |
| Interceptions | Mel Blount, 1970-1983 | 57 |
| Punting (Avg.) | Bobby Joe Green, 1960-61 | 45.7 |
| Punt Return (Avg.) | Bobby Gage, 1949-1950 | 14.9 |
| Kickoff Return (Avg.) | Lynn Chandnois, 1950-56 | 29.6 |
| Field Goals | Gary Anderson, 1982-1993 | 285 |
| Touchdowns (Tot.) | Franco Harris, 1972-1983 | 100 |
| Points | Gary Anderson, 1982-1993 | 1,239 |

**INDIVIDUAL RECORDS—SINGLE SEASON**

| Category | Name | Performance |
|---|---|---|
| Rushing (Yds.) | Barry Foster, 1992 | 1,690 |
| Passing (Yds.) | Terry Bradshaw, 1979 | 3,724 |
| Passing (TDs) | Terry Bradshaw, 1978 | 28 |
| Receiving (No.) | John Stallworth, 1984 | 80 |
| Receiving (Yds.) | John Stallworth, 1984 | 1,395 |
| Interceptions | Mel Blount, 1975 | 11 |
| Punting (Avg.) | Bobby Joe Green, 1961 | 47.0 |
| Punt Return (Avg.) | Bobby Gage, 1949 | 16.0 |
| Kickoff Return (Avg.) | Lynn Chandnois, 1952 | 35.2 |
| Field Goals | Gary Anderson, 1985 | 33 |
| Touchdowns (Tot.) | Louis Lipps, 1985 | 15 |
| Points | Gary Anderson, 1985 | 139 |

**INDIVIDUAL RECORDS—SINGLE GAME**

| Category | Name | Performance |
|---|---|---|
| Rushing (Yds.) | John Fuqua, 12-20-70 | 218 |
| Passing (Yds.) | Bobby Layne, 12-3-58 | 409 |
| Passing (TDs) | Terry Bradshaw, 11-15-81 | 5 |
| | Mark Malone, 9-8-85 | 5 |
| Receiving (No.) | J.R. Wilburn, 10-22-67 | 12 |
| Receiving (Yds.) | Buddy Dial, 10-22-61 | 235 |
| Interceptions | Jack Butler, 12-13-53 | *4 |
| Field Goals | Gary Anderson, 10-23-88 | 6 |
| Touchdowns (Tot.) | Ray Mathews, 10-17-54 | 4 |
| | Roy Jefferson, 11-3-68 | 4 |
| Points | Ray Mathews, 10-17-54 | 24 |
| | Roy Jefferson, 11-3-68 | 24 |

*NFL Record

## COACHING HISTORY

**Pittsburgh Pirates 1933-1940**
**(390-426-20)**

| | | |
|---|---|---|
| 1933 | Forrest (Jap) Douds | 3-6-2 |
| 1934 | Luby DiMelio | 2-10-0 |
| 1935-36 | Joe Bach | 10-14-0 |
| 1937-39 | Johnny Blood (McNally)* | 6-19-0 |
| 1939-40 | Walt Kiesling | 3-13-3 |
| 1941 | Bert Bell** | 0-2-0 |
| | Aldo (Buff) Donelli*** | 0-5-0 |
| 1941-44 | Walt Kiesling**** | 13-20-2 |
| 1945 | Jim Leonard | 2-8-0 |
| 1946-47 | Jock Sutherland | 13-10-1 |
| 1948-51 | Johnny Michelosen | 20-26-2 |
| 1952-53 | Joe Bach | 11-13-0 |
| 1954-56 | Walt Kiesling | 14-22-0 |
| 1957-64 | Raymond (Buddy) Parker | 51-48-6 |
| 1965 | Mike Nixon | 2-12-0 |
| 1966-68 | Bill Austin | 11-28-3 |
| 1969-91 | Chuck Noll | 209-156-1 |
| 1992-93 | Bill Cowher | 20-14-0 |

*Released after three games in 1939
**Resigned after two games in 1941
***Released after five games in 1941
****Co-coach with Earle (Greasy) Neale in Philadelphia-Pittsburgh merger in 1943 and with Phil Handler in Chicago Cardinals-Pittsburgh merger in 1944

### THREE RIVERS STADIUM

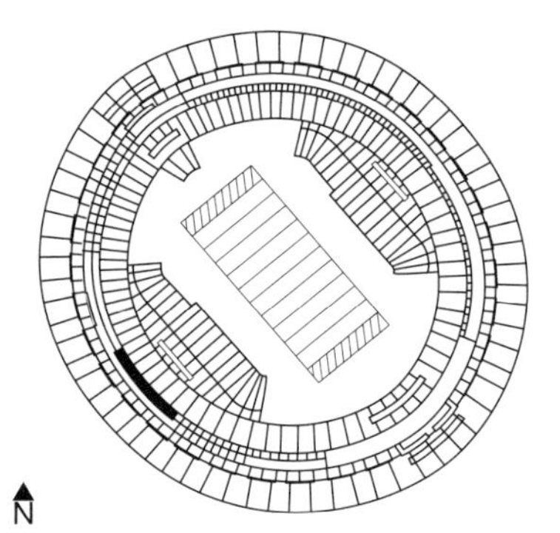

## 1993 TEAM RECORD

**PRESEASON (2-3)**

| Date | Result | | Opponents |
|---|---|---|---|
| 8/1 | L | 14-21 | vs. San Francisco at Barcelona |
| 8/7 | W | 17-13 | N.Y. Jets |
| 8/14 | W | 23-17 | at N.Y. Giants |
| 8/22 | L | 3-10 | Washington |
| 8/26 | L | 13-30 | at Minnesota |

**REGULAR SEASON (9-7)**

| Date | Result | | Opponents | Att. |
|---|---|---|---|---|
| 9/5 | L | 13-24 | San Francisco | 57,502 |
| 9/12 | L | 0-27 | at L.A. Rams | 50,588 |
| 9/19 | W | 34-7 | Cincinnati | 53,682 |
| 9/27 | W | 45-17 | at Atlanta | 65,477 |
| 10/10 | W | 16-3 | San Diego | 55,264 |
| 10/17 | W | 37-14 | New Orleans | 56,056 |
| 10/24 | L | 23-28 | at Cleveland | 78,118 |
| 11/7 | W | 24-16 | at Cincinnati | 51,202 |
| 11/15 | W | 23-0 | Buffalo | 60,265 |
| 11/21 | L | 13-37 | at Denver | 74,840 |
| 11/28 | L | 3-23 | at Houston | 61,238 |
| 12/5 | W | 17-14 | New England | 51,358 |
| 12/13 | W | 21-20 | at Miami | 70,232 |
| 12/19 | L | 17-26 | Houston | 57,592 |
| 12/26 | L | 6-16 | at Seattle | 51,814 |
| 1/2 | W | 16-9 | Cleveland | 49,208 |

**POSTSEASON (0-1)**

| | | | | |
|---|---|---|---|---|
| 1/8 | L | 24-27 | at Kansas City (OT) | 74,515 |

(OT) Overtime

**SCORE BY PERIOD**

| | | | | | | | |
|---|---|---|---|---|---|---|---|
| Steelers | 38 | 110 | 79 | 81 | 0 | — | 308 |
| Opponents | 75 | 102 | 40 | 64 | 0 | — | 281 |

**ATTENDANCE**

Home 440,927 Away 503,509 Total 944,436
Single-game home record, 60,265 (11-15-93)
Single-season home record, 471,306 (1992)

## 1993 TEAM STATISTICS

| | Steelers | Opp. |
|---|---|---|
| Total First Downs | 307 | 267 |
| Rushing | 116 | 74 |
| Passing | 180 | 163 |
| Penalty | 11 | 30 |
| Third Down: Made/Att | 92/235 | 68/201 |
| Third Down Pct. | 39.1 | 33.8 |
| Fourth Down: Made/Att | 8/16 | 4/10 |
| Fourth Down Pct. | 50.0 | 40.0 |
| Total Net Yards | 5235 | 4531 |
| Avg. Per Game | 327.2 | 283.2 |
| Total Plays | 1079 | 962 |
| Avg. Per Play | 4.9 | 4.7 |
| Net Yards Rushing | 2003 | 1368 |
| Avg. Per Game | 125.2 | 85.5 |
| Total Rushes | 491 | 399 |
| Net Yards Passing | 3232 | 3163 |
| Avg. Per Game | 202.0 | 197.7 |
| Sacked/Yards Lost | 48/374 | 42/277 |
| Gross Yards | 3606 | 3440 |
| Att./Completions | 540/299 | 521/277 |
| Completion Pct. | 55.4 | 53.2 |
| Had Intercepted | 12 | 24 |
| Punts/Avg. | 89/42.5 | 82/43.9 |
| Net Punting Avg. | 89/34.2 | 82/38.1 |
| Penalties/Yards Lost | 100/861 | 77/652 |
| Fumbles/Ball Lost | 28/15 | 37/14 |
| Touchdowns | 32 | 30 |
| Rushing | 13 | 6 |
| Passing | 16 | 16 |
| Returns | 3 | 8 |
| Avg. Time of Possession | 32:15 | 27:45 |

## 1993 INDIVIDUAL STATISTICS

| PASSING | Att. | Cmp. | Yds. | Pct. | TD | Int. | Tkld. | Rate |
|---|---|---|---|---|---|---|---|---|
| O'Donnell | 486 | 270 | 3208 | 55.6 | 14 | 7 | 41/331 | 79.5 |
| Tomczak | 54 | 29 | 398 | 53.7 | 2 | 5 | 7/43 | 51.3 |
| Steelers | 540 | 299 | 3606 | 55.4 | 16 | 12 | 48/374 | 76.7 |
| Opponents | 521 | 277 | 3440 | 53.2 | 16 | 24 | 42/277 | 64.9 |

| SCORING | TD R | TD P | TD Rt | PAT | FG | Saf | PTS |
|---|---|---|---|---|---|---|---|
| Anderson | 0 | 0 | 0 | 32/32 | 28/30 | 0 | 116 |
| Foster | 8 | 1 | 0 | 0/0 | 0/0 | 0 | 54 |
| Green | 0 | 5 | 0 | 0/0 | 0/0 | 0 | 30 |
| Hoge | 1 | 4 | 0 | 0/0 | 0/0 | 0 | 30 |
| Stone | 1 | 2 | 0 | 0/0 | 0/0 | 0 | 18 |
| Thigpen | 0 | 3 | 0 | 0/0 | 0/0 | 0 | 18 |
| Thompson | 3 | 0 | 0 | 0/0 | 0/0 | 0 | 18 |
| Davidson | 0 | 0 | 1 | 0/0 | 0/0 | 0 | 6 |
| Kirkland | 0 | 0 | 1 | 0/0 | 0/0 | 0 | 6 |
| Mills | 0 | 1 | 0 | 0/0 | 0/0 | 0 | 6 |
| Woodson | 0 | 0 | 1 | 0/0 | 0/0 | 0 | 6 |
| Steelers | 13 | 16 | 3 | 32/32 | 28/30 | 0 | 308 |
| Opponents | 6 | 16 | 8 | 29/30 | 24/29 | 0 | 281 |

| RUSHING | Att. | Yds. | Avg. | LG | TD |
|---|---|---|---|---|---|
| Thompson | 205 | 763 | 3.7 | 36 | 3 |
| Foster | 177 | 711 | 4.0 | 38 | 8 |
| Hoge | 51 | 249 | 4.9 | 30 | 1 |
| Stone | 12 | 121 | 10.1 | 38t | 1 |
| O'Donnell | 26 | 111 | 4.3 | 27 | 0 |
| Worley | 10 | 33 | 3.3 | 8 | 0 |
| Mills | 3 | 12 | 4.0 | 19 | 0 |
| Cuthbert | 1 | 7 | 7.0 | 7 | 0 |
| Woodson | 1 | 0 | 0.0 | 0 | 0 |
| Tomczak | 5 | -4 | -0.8 | 2 | 0 |
| Steelers | 491 | 2003 | 4.1 | 38t | 13 |
| Opponents | 399 | 1368 | 3.4 | 37 | 6 |

| RECEIVING | No. | Yds. | Avg. | LG | TD |
|---|---|---|---|---|---|
| Green | 63 | 942 | 15.0 | 71t | 5 |
| Stone | 41 | 587 | 14.3 | 44 | 2 |
| Graham | 38 | 579 | 15.2 | 51 | 0 |
| Thompson | 38 | 259 | 6.8 | 28 | 0 |
| Hoge | 33 | 247 | 7.5 | 18 | 4 |
| Mills | 29 | 386 | 13.3 | 30 | 1 |
| Foster | 27 | 217 | 8.0 | 21 | 1 |
| Thigpen | 9 | 154 | 17.1 | 39t | 3 |
| Cooper | 9 | 112 | 12.4 | 38 | 0 |
| Davenport | 4 | 51 | 12.8 | 19 | 0 |
| Hastings | 3 | 44 | 14.7 | 18 | 0 |
| Worley | 3 | 13 | 4.3 | 9 | 0 |
| Jorden | 1 | 12 | 12.0 | 12 | 0 |
| Cuthbert | 1 | 3 | 3.0 | 3 | 0 |
| Steelers | 299 | 3606 | 12.1 | 71t | 16 |
| Opponents | 277 | 3440 | 12.4 | 66t | 16 |

| INTERCEPTIONS | No. | Yds. | Avg. | LG | TD |
|---|---|---|---|---|---|
| Woodson | 8 | 138 | 17.3 | 63t | 1 |
| Perry | 4 | 61 | 15.3 | 30 | 0 |
| Lake | 4 | 31 | 7.8 | 26 | 0 |
| Johnson | 3 | 51 | 17.0 | 26 | 0 |
| G. Jones | 2 | 11 | 5.5 | 11 | 0 |
| Figures | 1 | 78 | 78.0 | 78 | 0 |
| Henry | 1 | 10 | 10.0 | 10 | 0 |
| Davidson | 1 | 6 | 6.0 | 6 | 0 |
| Steelers | 24 | 386 | 16.1 | 78 | 1 |
| Opponents | 12 | 216 | 18.0 | 97t | 2 |

| PUNTING | No. | Yds. | Avg. | In 20 | LG |
|---|---|---|---|---|---|
| Royals | 89 | 3781 | 42.5 | 28 | 61 |
| Steelers | 89 | 3781 | 42.5 | 28 | 61 |
| Opponents | 82 | 3600 | 43.9 | 23 | 58 |

| PUNT RETURNS | No. | FC | Yds. | Avg. | LG | TD |
|---|---|---|---|---|---|---|
| Woodson | 42 | 10 | 338 | 8.0 | 39 | 0 |
| Figures | 5 | 2 | 15 | 3.0 | 6 | 0 |
| Steelers | 47 | 12 | 353 | 7.5 | 39 | 0 |
| Opponents | 50 | 16 | 678 | 13.6 | 91t | 3 |

| KICKOFF RETURNS | No. | Yds. | Avg. | LG | TD |
|---|---|---|---|---|---|
| Woodson | 15 | 294 | 19.6 | 44 | 0 |
| Hastings | 12 | 177 | 14.8 | 22 | 0 |
| Stone | 11 | 168 | 15.3 | 30 | 0 |
| Thompson | 4 | 77 | 19.3 | 27 | 0 |
| Worley | 4 | 85 | 21.3 | 26 | 0 |
| Hoge | 3 | 33 | 11.0 | 15 | 0 |
| Cooper | 1 | 2 | 2.0 | 2 | 0 |
| Thigpen | 1 | 23 | 23.0 | 23 | 0 |
| W. Williams | 1 | 19 | 19.0 | 19 | 0 |
| Steelers | 52 | 878 | 16.9 | 44 | 0 |
| Opponents | 54 | 1165 | 21.6 | 97t | 1 |

| SACKS | No. |
|---|---|
| Greene | 12.5 |
| Evans | 6.5 |
| Lloyd | 6.0 |
| Lake | 5.0 |
| Brown | 3.0 |
| Davidson | 2.5 |
| Woodson | 2.0 |
| Steed | 1.5 |
| Henry | 1.0 |
| Kirkland | 1.0 |
| G. Williams | 1.0 |
| Steelers | 42.0 |
| Opponents | 48.0 |

## 1994 DRAFT CHOICES

| Round | Name | Pos. | College |
|---|---|---|---|
| 1 | Charles Johnson | WR | Colorado |
| 2 | Brentson Buckner | DE | Clemson |
| 3 | Jason Gildon | LB | Oklahoma State |
| | Bam Morris | RB | Texas Tech |
| 4 | Taase Faumui | DE | Hawaii |
| 5 | Myron Bell | DB | Michigan State |
| | Gary Brown | T | Georgia Tech |
| 6 | Jim Miller | QB | Michigan State |
| | Eric Ravotti | LB | Penn State |
| 7 | Brice Abrams | RB | Michigan State |

## PITTSBURGH STEELERS

### 1994 VETERAN ROSTER

| No. | Name | Pos. | Ht. | Wt. | Birthdate | NFL Exp. | College | Hometown | How Acq. | '93 Games/ Starts |
|---|---|---|---|---|---|---|---|---|---|---|
| 1 | Anderson, Gary | K | 5-11 | 179 | 7/16/59 | 13 | Syracuse | Durban, South Africa | W(Buff)-'82 | 16/0 |
| 50 | Barnes, Reggie | LB | 6-1 | 235 | 10/23/69 | 2 | Oklahoma | Grand Prairie, Tex. | FA-'93 | 16/0 |
| 94 | Brown, Chad | LB | 6-2 | 240 | 7/12/70 | 2 | Colorado | Pasadena, Calif. | D2-'93 | 16/9 |
| 42 | Cuthbert, Randy | RB | 6-2 | 225 | 1/16/70 | 2 | Duke | Chalfont, Pa. | FA-'93 | 10/0 |
| 80 | Davenport, Charles | WR | 6-3 | 210 | 11/22/68 | 3 | North Carolina State | Fayetteville, N.C. | D4-'92 | 16/0 |
| 64 | # Davidson, Kenny | DE | 6-5 | 275 | 8/17/67 | 5 | Louisiana State | Shreveport, La. | D2-'90 | 16/9 |
| 63 | Dawson, Dermontti | C | 6-2 | 286 | 6/17/65 | 7 | Kentucky | Lexington, Ky. | D2-'88 | 16/16 |
| 21 | Figures, Deon | CB | 6-0 | 200 | 1/10/70 | 2 | Colorado | Compton, Calif. | D1-'93 | 15/4 |
| 79 | Finn, Mike | T | 6-4 | 290 | 9/26/67 | 2 | Arkansas-Pine Bluff | Texarkana, Tex. | FA-'92 | 0* |
| 29 | Foster, Barry | RB | 5-10 | 218 | 12/8/68 | 5 | Arkansas | Duncanville, Tex. | D5-'90 | 9/9 |
| 60 | Gammon, Kendall | C-G | 6-4 | 286 | 10/23/68 | 3 | Pittsburg State | Wichita, Kan. | D11-'92 | 16/0 |
| 86 | Green, Eric | TE | 6-5 | 280 | 6/22/67 | 5 | Liberty | Savannah, Ga. | D1-'90 | 16/16 |
| 91 | Greene, Kevin | LB | 6-3 | 247 | 7/31/62 | 10 | Auburn | Oxford, Ala. | UFA(Rams)-'93 | 16/16 |
| 28 | Haller, Alan | CB | 5-11 | 185 | 8/9/70 | 2 | Michigan State | Lansing, Mich. | FA-'93 | 4/0 |
| 77 | Haselrig, Carlton | G | 6-1 | 295 | 1/22/66 | 5 | Pittsburgh-Johnstown | Johnstown, Pa. | D12-'89 | 9/4 |
| 88 | Hastings, Andre | WR | 6-0 | 188 | 11/7/70 | 2 | Georgia | Atlanta, Ga. | D3-'93 | 6/0 |
| 76 | Henry, Kevin | DE | 6-4 | 275 | 10/23/68 | 2 | Mississippi State | Mound Bayou, Miss. | D4-'93 | 12/1 |
| 65 | Jackson, John | T | 6-6 | 297 | 1/4/65 | 7 | Eastern Kentucky | Cincinnati, Ohio | D10-'88 | 16/16 |
| 25 | Jones, Gary | S | 6-1 | 214 | 11/30/67 | 5 | Texas A&M | Tyler, Tex. | D9-'90 | 13/2 |
| 30 | Jones, Victor | RB | 5-8 | 215 | 12/5/67 | 5 | Louisiana State | Zachary, La. | FA-'93 | 16/0 |
| 84 | Jorden, Tim | TE | 6-3 | 240 | 10/30/66 | 5 | Indiana | Middletown, Ohio | FA-'92 | 16/1 |
| 62 | Kalis, Todd | G | 6-5 | 296 | 5/10/65 | 7 | Arizona State | Phoenix, Ariz. | UFA(Minn)-'94 | 16/7* |
| 87 | Keith, Craig | TE | 6-3 | 262 | 4/27/71 | 2 | Lenoir-Rhyne | Raleigh, N.C. | D7b-'93 | 1/0 |
| 99 | Kirkland, Levon | LB | 6-1 | 252 | 2/17/69 | 3 | Clemson | Lamar, S.C. | D2-'92 | 16/13 |
| 37 | Lake, Carnell | S | 6-1 | 210 | 7/15/67 | 6 | UCLA | Inglewood, Calif. | D2-'89 | 14/14 |
| 95 | Lloyd, Greg | LB | 6-2 | 226 | 5/26/65 | 8 | Ft. Valley State | Ft. Valley, Ga. | D6b-'87 | 15/15 |
| 67 | Love, Duval | G | 6-3 | 288 | 6/24/63 | 10 | UCLA | Fountain Valley, Calif. | PB(Rams)-'92 | 16/16 |
| 56 | Mack, Rico | LB | 6-4 | 239 | 2/22/71 | 2 | Appalachian State | Statham, Ga. | FA-'93 | 8/0 |
| 89 | † Mills, Ernie | WR | 5-11 | 192 | 10/28/68 | 4 | Florida | Dunnellon, Fla. | D3-'91 | 14/5 |
| 14 | O'Donnell, Neil | QB | 6-3 | 230 | 7/3/66 | 5 | Maryland | Madison, N.J. | D3a-'90 | 16/15 |
| 55 | # Olsavsky, Jerry | LB | 6-1 | 224 | 3/29/67 | 6 | Pittsburgh | Youngstown, Ohio | D10-'89 | 7/7 |
| 66 | Palelei, Siulagi | G | 6-3 | 322 | 10/15/70 | 2 | Nevada-Las Vegas | American Samoa | D5a-'93 | 3/0 |
| 39 | Perry, Darren | S | 5-11 | 196 | 12/29/68 | 3 | Penn State | Deep Creek, Va. | D8a-'92 | 16/16 |
| 3 | Royals, Mark | P | 6-5 | 215 | 6/22/65 | 5 | Appalachian State | Mathews, Va. | PB(TB)-'92 | 16/0 |
| 97 | Seals, Ray | DE | 6-3 | 290 | 6/17/65 | 7 | No College | Syracuse, N.Y. | UFA(TB)-'94 | 16/11* |
| 72 | Searcy, Leon | T | 6-3 | 304 | 12/21/69 | 3 | Miami | Orlando, Fla. | D1-'92 | 16/16 |
| 24 | Shelton, Richard | S | 5-10 | 202 | 1/2/66 | 5 | Liberty | Marietta, Ga. | FA-'91 | 9/2 |
| 69 | Solomon, Ariel | C-G | 6-5 | 290 | 7/16/68 | 4 | Colorado | Boulder, Colo. | D10-'91 | 16/0 |
| 93 | Steed, Joel | NT | 6-2 | 295 | 2/17/69 | 3 | Colorado | Denver, Colo. | D3-'92 | 14/12 |
| 20 | Stone, Dwight | WR-RB | 6-0 | 180 | 1/28/64 | 8 | Middle Tennessee State | Florala, Ala. | FA-'87 | 16/15 |
| 73 | Strzelczyk, Justin | T | 6-5 | 295 | 8/18/68 | 5 | Maine | Seneca, N.Y. | D11-'90 | 16/12 |
| 96 | Sutton, Ricky | DE | 6-2 | 281 | 4/27/71 | 2 | Auburn | Tucker, Ga. | FA-'93 | 7/0 |
| 82 | Thigpen, Yancey | WR | 6-1 | 207 | 8/15/69 | 3 | Winston-Salem State | Pinetops, N.C. | FA-'92 | 12/0 |
| 34 | † Thompson, Leroy | RB | 5-11 | 217 | 2/3/69 | 4 | Penn State | Knoxville, Tenn. | D6-'91 | 15/6 |
| 18 | Tomczak, Mike | QB | 6-1 | 195 | 10/23/62 | 10 | Ohio State | Calumet City, Ill. | UFA(Clev)-'93 | 7/1 |
| 98 | Williams, Gerald | DE | 6-3 | 288 | 9/8/63 | 9 | Auburn | Lanett, Ala. | D2-'86 | 10/8 |
| 22 | Williams, John L. | RB | 5-11 | 231 | 11/23/64 | 9 | Florida | Palatka, Fla. | UFA(Sea)-'94 | 16/9* |
| 27 | Williams, Willie | CB | 5-9 | 188 | 12/26/70 | 2 | Western Carolina | Columbia, S.C. | D6-'93 | 16/0 |
| 26 | Woodson, Rod | CB | 6-0 | 200 | 3/10/65 | 8 | Purdue | Fort Wayne, Ind. | D1-'87 | 16/16 |
| 90 | Zgonina, Jeff | DT | 6-1 | 284 | 5/24/70 | 2 | Purdue | Lake Grove, Ill. | D7a-'93 | 5/0 |

* Finn active with Steelers for 9 games in '93 but did not play; Kalis played 16 games with Minnesota; Seals played 16 games with Tampa Bay; J.L. Williams played 16 games with Seattle.

\# Unrestricted free agent; subject to developments.

† Restricted free agent; subject to developments.

Traded—TE Adrian Cooper to Minnesota, RB Tim Worley to Chicago, WR Jeff Graham to Chicago.

Retired—LB Bryan Hinkle, 13-year veteran, 12 games in '93.

Players lost through free agency (4): DE Donald Evans (NYJ; 16 games in '93), RB Merril Hoge (Chi; 16), CB D.J. Johnson (Atl; 16), QB Rick Strom (Buff; 0).

Also played with Steelers in '93—TE Adrian Cooper (14 games), G-T Dan Fike (3), WR Jeff Graham (15), S Larry Griffin (12), LB Dave Hoffmann (1), RB Tim Worley (5).

## COACHING STAFF

**Head Coach,**
**Bill Cowher**

**Pro Career:** Became the fifteenth head coach in Steelers' history on January 21, 1992, succeeding the retired Chuck Noll. Cowher is the second-youngest head coach in the NFL. Named *AP* NFL Coach of the Year in 1992, after becoming one of only 12 coaches in NFL history to win 11 games in his first season. Began his NFL career as a free agent linebacker with the Philadelphia Eagles in 1979, and then signed with the Cleveland Browns the following year. Cowher played three seasons (1980-82) in Cleveland before being traded back to the Eagles, where he played two more years (1983-84). Cowher began his coaching career in 1985 at age 28 under Marty Schottenheimer with the Cleveland Browns. He was the Browns' special teams coach in 1985-86 and secondary coach in 1987-88 before following Schottenheimer to the Kansas City Chiefs in 1989 as defensive coordinator. Career record: 20-14.

**Background:** Excelled in football, basketball, and track for Carlynton High in Crafton, Pa. Was a three-year starter at linebacker for North Carolina State, serving as captain and earning team MVP honors as senior. Graduated in 1979 with education degree.

**Personal:** Born in Pittsburgh, Pa., on May 8, 1957. His wife Kaye, also a North Carolina State graduate, played professional basketball for the New York Stars of the Women's Professional Basketball League with twin sister Faye. Bill and Kaye live in Pittsburgh and have three daughters—Meagan Lyn, Lauren Marie, and Lindsay Morgan.

### ASSISTANT COACHES

**Bobby April, Jr.,** special teams; born April 15, 1953, New Orleans, La., lives in Pittsburgh. Defensive end/linebacker Nicholls State 1972-75. No pro playing experience. College coach: Tulane 1979, Arizona 1980-86, Southern California 1987-90. Pro coach: Atlanta Falcons 1991-93, joined Steelers in 1994.

**Dom Capers,** defensive coordinator; born August 7, 1950, Cambridge, Ohio, lives in Pittsburgh. Defensive back Mount Union College 1968-71. No pro playing experience. College coach: Hawaii 1975-76, San Jose State 1977, California 1978-79, Tennessee 1980-81, Ohio State 1982-83. Pro coach: Philadelphia/Baltimore Stars (USFL) 1984-85, New Orleans Saints 1986-91, joined Steelers in 1992.

**Ron Erhardt,** offensive coordinator; born February 27, 1931, Mandan, N.D., lives in Pittsburgh. Quarterback Jamestown (N.D.) College 1951-54. No pro playing experience. College coach: North Dakota State 1963-72 (head coach 1966-72). Pro coach: New England Patriots 1973-81 (head coach 1979-81), New York Giants 1982-91, joined Steelers in 1992.

**Chan Gailey,** wide receivers; born January 5, 1952, Gainesville, Ga., lives in Pittsburgh. Quarterback Florida 1970-73. No pro playing experience. College coach: Troy State 1976-78, 1983-84, Air Force 1979-82, Samford (head coach) 1992. Pro coach: Denver Broncos 1985-90, Birmingham Fire (WL) 1991-92, joined Steelers in 1994.

**Dick Hoak,** running backs; born December 8, 1939, Jeannette, Pa., lives in Greensburg, Pa. Halfback-quarterback Penn State 1958-60. Pro running back Pittsburgh Steelers 1961-70. Pro coach: Joined Steelers in 1972.

**Pat Hodgson,** tight ends; born January 30, 1944, Columbus, Ga., lives in Pittsburgh. Tight end Georgia 1963-65. Pro tight end Washington Redskins 1966, Minnesota Vikings 1967. College coach: Georgia 1968-70, 1972-77, Florida State 1971, Texas Tech 1978. Pro coach: San Diego Chargers 1978, New York Giants 1979-87, joined Steelers in 1992.

**Dick LeBeau,** defensive backs; born September 9, 1937, London, Ohio, lives in Pittsburgh. Defensive back-offensive back Ohio State 1954-57. Pro cornerback Detroit Lions 1959-72. Pro coach: Philadelphia Eagles 1972-75, Green Bay Packers 1976-79, Cincinnati Bengals 1980-91, joined Steelers in 1992.

**Marvin Lewis,** linebackers; born September 23, 1958, McDonald, Pa., lives in Pittsburgh. Linebacker Idaho State 1977-80. No pro playing experience. College coach: Idaho State 1981-84, Long Beach State 1985-86, New Mexico 1987-89, Pittsburgh 1990-91. Pro coach: Joined Steelers in 1992.

**John Mitchell,** defensive line; born October 15, 1951, Mobile, Ala., lives in Pittsburgh. Defensive end Eastern Arizona J.C. 1969-70, Alabama 1971-72. No pro playing experience. College coach: Alabama 1973-76, Arkansas 1977-82, Temple 1986, Louisiana State 1987-90. Pro coach: Birmingham Stallions (USFL) 1983-85, Cleveland Browns 1991-1993, joined Steelers in 1994.

**Kent Stephenson,** offensive line; born February 4, 1942, Anita, Iowa, lives in Pittsburgh. Guard-nose tackle Northern Iowa 1962-64. No pro playing experience. College coach: Wayne State 1965-68, North Dakota 1969-71, Southern Methodist 1972-73, Iowa 1974-76, Oklahoma State 1977-78, Kansas 1979-82. Pro coach: Michigan Panthers (USFL) 1983-84, Seattle Seahawks 1985-91, joined Steelers in 1992.

## 1994 FIRST-YEAR ROSTER

| Name | Pos. | Ht. | Wt. | Birthdate | College | Hometown | How Acq. |
|---|---|---|---|---|---|---|---|
| Abrams, Brice | RB | 6-1 | 258 | 8/10/71 | Michigan State | Detroit, Mich. | FA |
| Adams, Frank | CB | 5-8 | 176 | 11/7/70 | South Carolina | Gastonia, N.C. | FA |
| Allen, Andre | C-G | 6-0 | 310 | 2/28/71 | Jacksonville State | Oxford, Ala. | FA |
| Avery, Steve (1) | RB | 6-2 | 226 | 8/18/66 | Northern Michigan | Brookfield, Wis. | FA |
| Baker, Mike | WR | 6-0 | 188 | 1/9/69 | West Virginia | Waverly, Ga. | FA |
| Bell, Myron | S | 5-11 | 203 | 9/15/71 | Michigan State | Toledo, Ohio | D5a |
| Brown, Gary | T | 6-4 | 288 | 6/25/71 | Georgia Tech | Brentwood, N.Y. | D5b |
| Buckner, Brentson | DE | 6-2 | 305 | 9/30/71 | Clemson | Columbus, Ga. | D2 |
| Calloway, Dominic | CB | 6-0 | 182 | 4/24/72 | Memphis State | Anniston, Ala. | FA |
| Dukes, Chuckie (1) | RB | 5-9 | 202 | 5/16/70 | Boston College | Albany, N.Y. | FA |
| Edwards, Pheathur | DE | 6-2 | 281 | 1/3/71 | Jackson State | Boligee, Ala. | FA |
| Faumui, Taase | DE | 6-3 | 278 | 3/19/71 | Hawaii | Honolulu, Hawaii | D4 |
| Foggie, Fred (1) | CB-S | 6-0 | 200 | 6/10/69 | Minnesota | Laurens, S.C. | FA |
| Gildon, Jason | LB | 6-3 | 237 | 7/31/72 | Oklahoma State | Altus, Okla. | D3a |
| Hoffmann, Dave (1) | LB | 6-2 | 233 | 7/24/70 | Washington | San Jose, Calif. | FA |
| Holliday, Corey | WR | 6-2 | 208 | 1/31/71 | North Carolina | Richmond, Va. | FA |
| Johnson, Charles | WR | 6-0 | 189 | 1/3/72 | Colorado | San Bernardino, Calif. | D1 |
| Kelly, Andy (1) | QB | 6-3 | 212 | 5/6/68 | Tennessee | Dayton, Tenn. | FA |
| Kinsler, Latish | S | 6-2 | 193 | 8/16/71 | Cincinnati | Montclair, N.J. | FA |
| Miller, Jim | QB | 6-2 | 226 | 2/9/71 | Michigan State | Waterford, Mich. | D6a |
| Morris, Byron "Bam" | RB | 6-0 | 235 | 1/13/72 | Texas Tech | Cooper, Tex. | D3b |
| Parker, Curtis | T | 6-3 | 312 | 3/8/71 | North Carolina | Wingate, N.C. | FA |
| Rasby, Walter | TE | 6-3 | 247 | 9/7/72 | Wake Forest | Washington, N.C. | FA |
| Ravotti, Eric | LB | 6-3 | 254 | 3/16/71 | Penn State | Freeport, Pa. | D6b |
| Robinson, Ed | LB | 6-0 | 228 | 12/7/70 | Florida | DeFuniak Springs, Fla. | FA |
| Scott, Patrick | LB | 6-4 | 229 | 6/4/71 | South Carolina State | Durham, N.C. | FA |
| Shepherd, Leslie (1) | WR | 5-11 | 189 | 11/3/69 | Temple | Forestville, Md. | FA |
| Simpson, Tim (1) | G-C | 6-2 | 296 | 3/5/69 | Illinois | Peoria, Ill. | FA |
| Volpe, Jon (1) | RB | 5-7 | 201 | 4/17/68 | Stanford | Kincheloe, Mich. | FA |
| Williams, Chris | DE | 6-3 | 281 | 8/8/70 | Hampton | Houston, Tex. | FA |

The term NFL Rookie is defined as a player who is in his first season of professional football and has not been on the roster of another professional football team for any regular-season or postseason games. A Rookie is designated by an "R" on NFL rosters. Players who have been active in another professional football league or players who have NFL experience, including either preseason training camp or being on an Active List or Inactive List, or on Reserve/Injured or Reserve/Physically Unable to Perform for fewer than six regular-season games, are termed NFL First-Year Players. An NFL First-Year Player is designated by a "1" on NFL rosters. Thereafter, a player is credited with an additional year of experience for each season in which he accumulates six games on the Active List or Inactive List, or on Reserve/Injured or Reserve/Physically Unable to Perform.

## NOTES

# SAN DIEGO CHARGERS

**American Football Conference**
**Western Division**
**Team Colors:** Navy Blue, White, and Gold
**San Diego Jack Murphy Stadium**
**P.O. Box 609609**
**San Diego, California 92160-9609**
**Telephone: (619) 280-2111**

## CLUB OFFICIALS

Chairman of the Board/President: Alex G. Spanos
Vice Chairman: Dean A. Spanos
General Manager: Bobby Beathard
Vice President-Finance: Jeremiah T. Murphy
Assistant General Manager: Dick Daniels
Director of Player Personnel: Billy Devaney
Director of Pro Personnel: Rudy Feldman
Director of College Scouting: John Hinek
Coordinator of Football Operations: Marty Hurney
Director of Public Relations: Bill Johnston
Chief Financial Officer: Jeanne Bonk
Business Manager: Pat Curran
Director of Marketing: Rich Israel
Director of Ticket Operations: Joe Scott
Video Director: Gene Leff
Head Trainer: Keoki Kamau
Equipment Manager: Sid Brooks
**Stadium:** San Diego Jack Murphy Stadium
**Capacity:** 60,789
9449 Friars Road
San Diego, California 92108
**Playing Surface:** Grass
**Training Camp:** University of California-San Diego
Third College
La Jolla, California 92037

## 1994 SCHEDULE

**PRESEASON**

| | | |
|---|---|---|
| July 30 | vs. Atlanta at Canton, Ohio | 12:00 |
| Aug. 6 | vs. Houston at San Antonio, Tex. | 7:00 |
| Aug. 13 | vs. N.Y. Giants at Berlin | 1:30 |
| Aug. 18 | **San Francisco** | 5:00 |
| Aug. 25 | **Los Angeles Rams** | 7:00 |

**REGULAR SEASON**

| | | |
|---|---|---|
| Sept. 4 | at Denver | 6:00 |
| Sept. 11 | **Cincinnati** | 1:00 |
| Sept. 18 | at Seattle | 1:00 |
| Sept. 25 | at Los Angeles Raiders | 1:00 |
| Oct. 2 | Open Date | |
| Oct. 9 | **Kansas City** | 1:00 |
| Oct. 16 | at New Orleans | 3:00 |
| Oct. 23 | **Denver** | 1:00 |
| Oct. 30 | **Seattle** | 1:00 |
| Nov. 6 | at Atlanta | 1:00 |
| Nov. 13 | at Kansas City | 12:00 |
| Nov. 20 | at New England | 1:00 |
| Nov. 27 | **Los Angeles Rams** | 1:00 |
| Dec. 5 | **Los Angeles Raiders** (Monday) | 6:00 |
| Dec. 11 | **San Francisco** | 1:00 |
| Dec. 18 | at New York Jets | 1:00 |
| Dec. 24 | **Pittsburgh** | 1:00 |

## RECORD HOLDERS

**INDIVIDUAL RECORDS—CAREER**

| Category | Name | Performance |
|---|---|---|
| Rushing (Yds.) | Paul Lowe, 1960-67 | 4,963 |
| Passing (Yds.) | Dan Fouts, 1973-1987 | 43,040 |
| Passing (TDs) | Dan Fouts, 1973-1987 | 254 |
| Receiving (No.) | Charlie Joiner, 1976-1986 | 586 |
| Receiving (Yds.) | Lance Alworth, 1962-1970 | 9,585 |
| Interceptions | Gill Byrd, 1983-1992 | 42 |
| Punting (Avg.) | Ralf Mojsiejenko, 1985-88 | 42.9 |
| Punt Return (Avg.) | Leslie (Speedy) Duncan, 1964-1970 | 12.3 |
| Kickoff Return (Avg.) | Leslie (Speedy) Duncan, 1964-1970 | 25.2 |
| Field Goals | Rolf Benirschke, 1977-1986 | 146 |
| Touchdowns (Tot.) | Lance Alworth, 1962-1970 | 83 |
| Points | Rolf Benirschke, 1977-1986 | 766 |

**INDIVIDUAL RECORDS—SINGLE SEASON**

| Category | Name | Performance |
|---|---|---|
| Rushing (Yds.) | Marion Butts, 1990 | 1,225 |
| Passing (Yds.) | Dan Fouts, 1981 | 4,802 |
| Passing (TDs) | Dan Fouts, 1981 | 33 |
| Receiving (No.) | Kellen Winslow, 1980 | 89 |
| Receiving (Yds.) | Lance Alworth, 1965 | 1,602 |
| Interceptions | Charlie McNeil, 1961 | 9 |
| Punting (Avg.) | Dennis Partee, 1969 | 44.6 |
| Punt Return (Avg.) | Leslie (Speedy) Duncan, 1965 | 15.5 |
| Kickoff Return (Avg.) | Keith Lincoln, 1962 | 28.4 |
| Field Goals | John Carney, 1993 | 31 |
| Touchdowns (Tot.) | Chuck Muncie, 1981 | 19 |
| Points | John Carney, 1993 | 124 |

**INDIVIDUAL RECORDS—SINGLE GAME**

| Category | Name | Performance |
|---|---|---|
| Rushing (Yds.) | Gary Anderson, 12-18-88 | 217 |
| Passing (Yds.) | Dan Fouts, 10-19-80 | 444 |
| | Dan Fouts, 12-11-82 | 444 |
| Passing (TDs) | Dan Fouts, 11-22-81 | 6 |
| Receiving (No.) | Kellen Winslow, 10-7-84 | 15 |
| Receiving (Yds.) | Wes Chandler, 12-20-82 | 260 |
| Interceptions | Many times | 3 |
| | Last time by Pete Shaw, 11-2-80 | |
| Field Goals | John Carney, 9-5-93 | 6 |
| | John Carney, 9-18-93 | 6 |
| Touchdowns (Tot.) | Kellen Winslow, 11-22-81 | 5 |
| Points | Kellen Winslow, 11-22-81 | 30 |

## COACHING HISTORY

**(250-253-11)**

| | | |
|---|---|---|
| 1960-69 | Sid Gillman* | 83-51-6 |
| 1969-70 | Charlie Waller | 9-7-3 |
| 1971 | Sid Gillman** | 4-6-0 |
| 1971-73 | Harland Svare*** | 7-17-2 |
| 1973 | Ron Waller | 1-5-0 |
| 1974-78 | Tommy Prothro**** | 21-39-0 |
| 1978-86 | Don Coryell# | 72-60-0 |
| 1986-88 | Al Saunders | 17-22-0 |
| 1989-91 | Dan Henning | 16-32-0 |
| 1992-93 | Bobby Ross | 20-14-0 |

*Retired after nine games in 1969
**Resigned after 10 games in 1971
***Resigned after eight games in 1973
****Resigned after four games in 1978
#Resigned after eight games in 1986

**SAN DIEGO JACK MURPHY STADIUM**

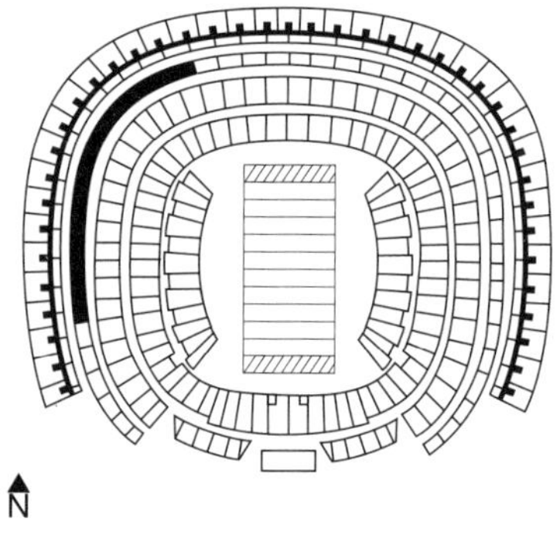

## 1993 TEAM RECORD,

**PRESEASON (3-1)**

| Date | Result | | Opponents |
|---|---|---|---|
| 8/7 | W | 13-7 | New England |
| 8/14 | W | 23-17 | at L.A. Rams |
| 8/21 | W | 10-3 | Phoenix |
| 8/28 | L | 14-30 | at San Francisco |

**REGULAR SEASON (8-8)**

| Date | Result | | Opponents | Att. |
|---|---|---|---|---|
| 9/5 | W | 18-12 | Seattle | 58,039 |
| 9/12 | L | 17-34 | at Denver | 75,074 |
| 9/19 | W | 18-17 | Houston | 58,519 |
| 10/3 | L | 14-31 | at Seattle | 54,778 |
| 10/10 | L | 3-16 | at Pittsburgh | 55,264 |
| 10/17 | L | 14-17 | Kansas City | 60,729 |
| 10/31 | W | 30-23 | at L.A. Raiders | 45,122 |
| 11/7 | W | 30-17 | at Minnesota | 55,527 |
| 11/14 | L | 13-16 | Chicago | 58,459 |
| 11/21 | L | 7-12 | L.A. Raiders | 60,615 |
| 11/29 | W | 31-0 | at Indianapolis | 54,110 |
| 12/5 | W | 13-10 | Denver | 60,233 |
| 12/12 | L | 13-20 | Green Bay | 57,930 |
| 12/19 | L | 24-28 | at Kansas City | 74,778 |
| 12/27 | W | 45-20 | Miami | 60,311 |
| 1/2 | W | 32-17 | at Tampa Bay | 35,587 |

**SCORE BY PERIODS**

| | | | | | | | |
|---|---|---|---|---|---|---|---|
| Chargers | 66 | 76 | 67 | 113 | 0 | — | 322 |
| Opponents | 50 | 102 | 83 | 55 | 0 | — | 290 |

**ATTENDANCE**

Home 474,835 Away 450,240 Total 925,075

Single-game home record, 64,411 (12-15-84)

Single-season home record, 494,103 (1988)

## 1993 TEAM STATISTICS

| | Chargers | Opp. |
|---|---|---|
| Total First Downs | 313 | 299 |
| Rushing | 120 | 86 |
| Passing | 171 | 192 |
| Penalty | 22 | 21 |
| Third Down: Made/Att | 89/224 | 83/210 |
| Third Down Pct. | 39.7 | 39.5 |
| Fourth Down: Made/Att | 6/15 | 4/8 |
| Fourth Down Pct. | 40.0 | 50.0 |
| Total Net Yards | 4967 | 5066 |
| Avg. Per Game | 310.4 | 316.6 |
| Total Plays | 1050 | 1002 |
| Avg. Per Play | 4.7 | 5.1 |
| Net Yards Rushing | 1824 | 1314 |
| Avg. Per Game | 114.0 | 82.1 |
| Total Rushes | 455 | 414 |
| Net Yards Passing | 3143 | 3752 |
| Avg. Per Game | 196.4 | 234.5 |
| Sacked/Yards Lost | 32/240 | 32/206 |
| Gross Yards | 3383 | 3958 |
| Att./Completions | 563/301 | 556/329 |
| Completion Pct. | 53.5 | 59.2 |
| Had Intercepted | 14 | 22 |
| Punts/Avg. | 74/42.3 | 72/42.1 |
| Net Punting Avg. | 74/36.4 | 72/35.5 |
| Penalties/Yards Lost | 87/699 | 94/724 |
| Fumbles/Ball Lost | 13/5 | 19/12 |
| Touchdowns | 33 | 30 |
| Rushing | 14 | 10 |
| Passing | 18 | 17 |
| Returns | 1 | 3 |
| Average Time of Possession | 29:52 | 30:08 |

## 1993 INDIVIDUAL STATISTICS

| PASSING | Att. | Cmp. | Yds. | Pct. | TD | Int. | Tkld. | Rate |
|---|---|---|---|---|---|---|---|---|
| Humphries | 324 | 173 | 1981 | 53.4 | 12 | 10 | 18/142 | 71.5 |
| Friesz | 238 | 128 | 1402 | 53.8 | 6 | 4 | 14/98 | 72.8 |
| Means | 1 | 0 | 0 | 0.0 | 0 | 0 | 0/0 | 39.6 |
| Chargers | 563 | 301 | 3383 | 53.5 | 18 | 14 | 32/240 | 72.0 |
| Opponents | 556 | 329 | 3958 | 59.2 | 17 | 22 | 32/206 | 74.8 |

| SCORING | TD R | TD P | TD Rt | PAT | FG | Saf | PTS |
|---|---|---|---|---|---|---|---|
| Carney | 0 | 0 | 0 | 31/33 | 31/40 | 0 | 124 |
| Means | 8 | 0 | 0 | 0/0 | 0/0 | 0 | 48 |
| A. Miller | 0 | 7 | 0 | 0/0 | 0/0 | 0 | 42 |
| Butts | 4 | 0 | 0 | 0/0 | 0/0 | 0 | 24 |
| Lewis | 0 | 4 | 0 | 0/0 | 0/0 | 0 | 24 |
| Harmon | 0 | 2 | 0 | 0/0 | 0/0 | 0 | 12 |
| Jefferson | 0 | 2 | 0 | 0/0 | 0/0 | 0 | 12 |
| Young | 0 | 2 | 0 | 0/0 | 0/0 | 0 | 12 |
| Bieniemy | 1 | 0 | 0 | 0/0 | 0/0 | 0 | 6 |
| Frank | 0 | 0 | 1 | 0/0 | 0/0 | 0 | 6 |
| Kidd | 1 | 0 | 0 | 0/0 | 0/0 | 0 | 6 |
| Walker | 0 | 1 | 0 | 0/0 | 0/0 | 0 | 6 |
| Chargers | 14 | 18 | 1 | 31/33 | 31/40 | 0 | 322 |
| Opponents | 10 | 17 | 3 | 30/30 | 26/33 | 1 | 290 |

| RUSHING | Att. | Yds. | Avg. | LG | TD |
|---|---|---|---|---|---|
| Butts | 185 | 746 | 4.0 | 27 | 4 |
| Means | 160 | 645 | 4.0 | 65t | 8 |
| Harmon | 46 | 216 | 4.7 | 19 | 0 |
| Bieniemy | 33 | 135 | 4.1 | 12 | 1 |
| Jefferson | 5 | 53 | 10.6 | 33 | 0 |
| Humphries | 8 | 37 | 4.6 | 27 | 0 |
| Friesz | 10 | 3 | 0.3 | 2 | 0 |
| Lewis | 3 | 2 | 0.7 | 7 | 0 |
| Hendrickson | 1 | 0 | 0.0 | 0 | 0 |
| A. Miller | 1 | 0 | 0.0 | 0 | 0 |
| Kidd | 3 | -13 | -4.3 | 2t | 1 |
| Chargers | 455 | 1824 | 4.0 | 65t | 14 |
| Opponents | 414 | 1314 | 3.2 | 19 | 10 |

| RECEIVING | No. | Yds. | Avg. | LG | TD |
|---|---|---|---|---|---|
| A. Miller | 84 | 1162 | 13.8 | 66t | 7 |
| Harmon | 73 | 671 | 9.2 | 37 | 2 |
| Lewis | 38 | 463 | 12.2 | 47 | 4 |
| Jefferson | 30 | 391 | 13.0 | 39t | 2 |
| Walker | 21 | 212 | 10.1 | 25t | 1 |
| Butts | 15 | 105 | 7.0 | 23 | 0 |
| Pupunu | 13 | 142 | 10.9 | 28 | 0 |
| Barnes | 10 | 137 | 13.7 | 21 | 0 |
| Means | 10 | 59 | 5.9 | 11 | 0 |
| Young | 6 | 41 | 6.8 | 12t | 2 |
| Bieniemy | 1 | 0 | 0.0 | 0 | 0 |
| Chargers | 301 | 3383 | 11.2 | 66t | 18 |
| Opponents | 329 | 3958 | 12.0 | 71t | 17 |

| INTERCEPTIONS | No. | Yds. | Avg. | LG | TD |
|---|---|---|---|---|---|
| Carrington | 7 | 104 | 14.9 | 28 | 0 |
| Frank | 3 | 119 | 39.7 | 102t | 1 |
| Seau | 2 | 58 | 29.0 | 42 | 0 |
| Pope | 2 | 14 | 7.0 | 12 | 0 |
| Plummer | 2 | 7 | 3.5 | 6 | 0 |
| Vanhorse | 2 | 0 | 0.0 | 0 | 0 |
| Hendrickson | 1 | 16 | 16.0 | 16 | 0 |
| Gordon | 1 | 3 | 3.0 | 3 | 0 |
| Davis | 1 | 0 | 0.0 | 0 | 0 |
| Richard | 1 | -2 | -2.0 | -2 | 0 |
| Chargers | 22 | 319 | 14.5 | 102t | 1 |
| Opponents | 14 | 271 | 19.4 | 68 | 2 |

| PUNTING | No. | Yds. | Avg. | In 20 | LG |
|---|---|---|---|---|---|
| Kidd | 57 | 2431 | 42.6 | 16 | 67 |
| Sullivan | 13 | 541 | 41.6 | 3 | 50 |
| Carney | 4 | 155 | 38.8 | 1 | 46 |
| Chargers | 74 | 3127 | 42.3 | 20 | 67 |
| Opponents | 72 | 3031 | 42.1 | 23 | 77 |

| PUNT RETURNS | No. | FC | Yds. | Avg. | LG | TD |
|---|---|---|---|---|---|---|
| Gordon | 31 | 15 | 395 | 12.7 | 54 | 0 |
| Lewis | 3 | 2 | 17 | 5.7 | 7 | 0 |
| Chargers | 34 | 17 | 412 | 12.1 | 54 | 0 |
| Opponents | 36 | 21 | 292 | 8.1 | 30 | 0 |

| KICKOFF RETURNS | No. | Yds. | Avg. | LG | TD |
|---|---|---|---|---|---|
| Lewis | 33 | 684 | 20.7 | 60 | 0 |
| Bieniemy | 7 | 110 | 15.7 | 18 | 0 |
| Hendrickson | 2 | 25 | 12.5 | 13 | 0 |
| Means | 2 | 22 | 11.0 | 14 | 0 |
| A. Miller | 2 | 42 | 21.0 | 29 | 0 |
| Harmon | 1 | 18 | 18.0 | 18 | 0 |
| Chargers | 47 | 901 | 19.2 | 60 | 0 |
| Opponents | 64 | 1063 | 16.6 | 48 | 0 |

| SACKS | No. |
|---|---|
| O'Neal | 12.0 |
| Mims | 7.0 |
| Grossman | 4.5 |
| Lee | 3.0 |
| Richard | 2.0 |
| Winter | 2.0 |
| Carrington | 1.0 |
| Pope | 0.5 |
| Chargers | 32.0 |
| Opponents | 32.0 |

## 1994 DRAFT CHOICES

| Round | Name | Pos. | College |
|---|---|---|---|
| 2 | Isaac Davis | G | Arkansas |
| | Vaughn Parker | G | UCLA |
| 3 | Andre Coleman | WR | Kansas State |
| | Willie Clark | DB | Notre Dame |
| 5 | Aaron Laing | TE | New Mexico State |
| | Rodney Harrison | DB | Western Illinois |
| | Darren Krein | DE | Miami |
| | Tony Vinson | RB | Towson State |
| 7 | Zane Beehn | LB | Kentucky |

# SAN DIEGO CHARGERS

## 1994 VETERAN ROSTER

| No. | Name | Pos. | Ht. | Wt. | Birthdate | NFL Exp. | College | Hometown | How Acq. | '93 Games/ Starts |
|---|---|---|---|---|---|---|---|---|---|---|
| 52 | # Anno, Sam | LB | 6-3 | 240 | 1/26/65 | 8 | Southern California | Santa Monica, Calif. | PB(TB)-'92 | 16/0 |
| 85 | Barnes, Johnnie | WR | 6-1 | 180 | 7/21/68 | 3 | Hampton | Suffolk, Va. | FA-'92 | 14/0 |
| 37 | Boles, Eric | TE | 6-3 | 210 | 4/29/70 | 2 | Central Washington | Tacoma, Wash. | FA-'94 | 0* |
| 67 | Brock, Stan | T | 6-6 | 295 | 6/8/58 | 15 | Colorado | Portland, Ore. | UFA(NO)-'93 | 16/16 |
| 58 | Bush, Lewis | LB | 6-2 | 245 | 12/2/69 | 2 | Washington State | Tacoma, Wash. | D4b-'93 | 16/0 |
| 22 | # Byrd, Gill | CB-S | 5-11 | 198 | 2/20/61 | 12 | San Jose State | San Francisco, Calif. | D1c-'83 | 0* |
| 3 | Carney, John | K | 5-11 | 170 | 4/20/64 | 5 | Notre Dame | West Palm Beach, Fla. | FA-'90 | 16/0 |
| 29 | Carrington, Darren | S | 6-2 | 200 | 10/10/66 | 6 | Northern Arizona | Bronx, N.Y. | FA-'91 | 16/14 |
| 44 | Castle, Eric | S | 6-3 | 212 | 3/15/70 | 2 | Oregon | Lebanon, Ore. | D6-'93 | 5/0 |
| 68 | Cocozzo, Joe | G | 6-4 | 300 | 8/7/70 | 2 | Michigan | Mechanicville, N.Y. | D3-'93 | 16/5 |
| 51 | Crews, Terry | LB | 6-2 | 245 | 7/30/68 | 3 | Western Michigan | Flint, Mich. | FA-'94 | 10/0* |
| 93 | Davis, Reuben | DT | 6-5 | 340 | 5/7/65 | 7 | North Carolina | Greensboro, N.C. | UFA(Ariz)-'94 | 16/15* |
| 23 | Dunson, Walter | WR | 5-9 | 173 | 10/24/70 | 2 | Middle Tennessee State | Carrollton, Ga. | D5-'93 | 0* |
| 84 | Dyal, Mike | TE | 6-2 | 240 | 5/20/66 | 7 | Texas A&I | Kerrville, Tex. | FA-'93 | 10/0* |
| 40 | Fuller, James | S | 6-0 | 208 | 8/5/69 | 3 | Portland State | Tacoma, Wash. | D8-'92 | 10/0 |
| 56 | Gibson, Dennis | LB | 6-2 | 240 | 2/8/64 | 8 | Iowa State | Ankeny, Iowa | UFA(Det)-'94 | 15/15* |
| 5 | Gilbert, Gale | QB | 6-3 | 210 | 12/20/61 | 9 | California | Red Bluff, Calif. | UFA(Buff)-'94 | 1/0* |
| 21 | Gordon, Darrien | CB | 5-11 | 182 | 11/14/70 | 2 | Stanford | Shawnee, Okla. | D1-'93 | 16/7 |
| 7 | Green, Trent | QB | 6-3 | 211 | 7/9/70 | 2 | Indiana | St. Louis, Mo. | D8-'93 | 0* |
| 92 | Griggs, David | LB | 6-3 | 250 | 2/5/67 | 5 | Virginia | Miami Beach, Fla. | UFA(Mia)-'94 | 9/0* |
| 53 | Hall, Courtney | C-G | 6-1 | 281 | 8/26/68 | 6 | Rice | Wilmington, Calif. | D2a-'89 | 16/16 |
| 33 | Harmon, Ronnie | RB | 5-11 | 207 | 5/7/64 | 9 | Iowa | Queens, N.Y. | PB(Buff)-'90 | 16/1 |
| 28 | Harper, Dwayne | CB | 5-11 | 175 | 3/29/66 | 7 | South Carolina State | Orangeburg, S.C. | UFA(Sea)-'94 | 14/14* |
| 34 | # Hendrickson, Steve | RB-LB | 6-0 | 250 | 8/30/66 | 6 | California | Napa, Calif. | FA-'90 | 16/10 |
| 12 | Humphries, Stan | QB | 6-2 | 223 | 4/14/65 | 6 | Northeast Louisiana | Shreveport, La. | T(Wash)-'92 | 12/10 |
| 80 | Jefferson, Shawn | WR | 5-11 | 172 | 2/22/69 | 4 | Central Florida | Jacksonville, Fla. | T(Hou)-'91 | 16/4 |
| 99 | Johnson, Raylee | DE | 6-3 | 245 | 6/1/70 | 2 | Arkansas | Fordyce, Ark. | D4a-'93 | 9/0 |
| 89 | Johnson, Vance | WR | 5-11 | 180 | 3/13/63 | 10 | Arizona | Tucson, Ariz. | UFA(Den)-'94 | 10/8* |
| 74 | Jonassen, Eric | T | 6-5 | 310 | 8/16/68 | 3 | Bloomsburg, Pa. | Glen Burnie, Md. | D5c-'92 | 16/2 |
| 10 | # Kidd, John | P | 6-3 | 208 | 8/22/61 | 11 | Northwestern | Findlay, Ohio | PB(Buff)-'90 | 14/0 |
| 98 | Lee, Shawn | DT | 6-2 | 300 | 10/24/66 | 7 | North Alabama | Brooklyn, N.Y. | FA-'92 | 16/15 |
| 81 | t- Martin, Tony | WR | 6-0 | 181 | 9/5/65 | 5 | Mesa, Colo. | Miami, Fla. | T(Mia)-'94 | 12/0* |
| 88 | May, Deems | TE | 6-4 | 263 | 3/6/69 | 3 | North Carolina | Lexington, N.C. | D7-'92 | 15/1 |
| 20 | Means, Natrone | RB | 5-10 | 245 | 4/26/72 | 2 | North Carolina | Harrisburg, N.C. | D2-'93 | 16/0 |
| 71 | Milinichik, Joe | G | 6-5 | 300 | 3/30/63 | 9 | North Carolina State | Emmaus, Pa. | UFA(Rams)-'93 | 10/10 |
| 54 | Miller, Doug | LB | 6-3 | 232 | 10/29/69 | 2 | South Dakota State | Sturgis, S.D. | D7-'93 | 8/0 |
| 94 | Mims, Chris | DE-DT | 6-5 | 290 | 9/29/70 | 3 | Tennessee | Los Angeles, Calif. | D1-'92 | 16/7 |
| 77 | † Moten, Eric | G-T | 6-2 | 306 | 4/11/68 | 4 | Michigan State | Cleveland Heights, Ohio | D2c-'91 | 4/4 |
| 91 | O'Neal, Leslie | DE | 6-4 | 265 | 5/7/64 | 9 | Oklahoma State | Little Rock, Ark. | D1a-'86 | 16/16 |
| 86 | Pupunu, Alfred | TE | 6-2 | 255 | 10/17/69 | 3 | Weber State | Salt Lake City, Utah | W(KC)-'92 | 16/7 |
| 24 | Richard, Stanley | S | 6-2 | 197 | 10/21/67 | 4 | Texas | Hawkins, Tex. | D1-'91 | 16/16 |
| 55 | Seau, Junior | LB | 6-3 | 250 | 1/19/69 | 5 | Southern California | Oceanside, Calif. | D1-'90 | 16/16 |
| 82 | Seay, Mark | WR | 6-0 | 175 | 4/11/67 | 2 | Long Beach State | San Bernardino, Calif. | W(SF)-'93 | 1/0 |
| 72 | Swayne, Harry | T | 6-5 | 295 | 2/2/65 | 8 | Rutgers | Philadelphia, Pa. | PB(TB)-'91 | 11/11 |
| 25 | Vanhorse, Sean | CB | 5-10 | 180 | 7/22/68 | 5 | Howard | Baltimore, Md. | PB(Det)-'92 | 15/10 |
| 90 | White, Reggie | DT | 6-4 | 300 | 3/22/70 | 3 | North Carolina A&T | Mulford Mills, Md. | D6-'92 | 8/0 |
| 64 | Whitley, Curtis | C | 6-1 | 285 | 5/10/69 | 3 | Clemson | Smithfield, N.C. | D5a-'92 | 15/0 |
| 57 | # Williams, Jerrol | LB | 6-4 | 240 | 7/5/67 | 6 | Purdue | Las Vegas, Nev. | RFA(Pitt)-'93 | 6/5 |
| 87 | Young, Duane | TE | 6-1 | 270 | 5/29/68 | 4 | Michigan State | Kalamazoo, Mich. | D5-'91 | 16/15 |

* Boles on injured reserve for 16 games with Jets in '93; Byrd and Dunson missed '93 season due to injury; Crews played 10 games with San Diego; Davis played 16 games with Phoenix; Dyal played 6 games with Kansas City, 4 games with San Diego; Gibson played 15 games with Detroit; Gilbert played 1 game with Buffalo; Green inactive for 16 games; Griggs played 9 games with Miami; Harper played 14 games with Seattle; Johnson played 10 games with Denver; Martin played 12 games with Miami.

\# Unrestricted free agent; subject to developments.

† Restricted free agent; subject to developments.

Traded—RB Marion Butts to New England, CB Donald Frank to Cleveland, DE Burt Grossman to Philadelphia, WR Nate Lewis to L.A. Rams, CB Marquez Pope to L.A. Rams.

t- Chargers traded for Martin (Miami).

Players lost through free agency (5): QB John Friesz (Wash; 12 games in '93), WR Anthony Miller (Den; 16), LB Gary Plummer (SF; 16), T Mike Withycombe (Clev; 0), G Mike Zandofsky (Atl; 16).

Also played with Chargers in '93—RB Eric Bieniemy (16 games), LB Jeff Brady (3), RB Marion Butts (16), CB Brian Davis (11), S Floyd Fields (13), CB Donald Frank (16), DE Burt Grossman (10), WR Nate Lewis (15), T Mike Mooney (1), CB Marquez Pope (16), G-T Raymond Smoot (2), P Kent Sullivan (2), TE Derrick Walker (12), DT Blaise Winter (16).

## COACHING STAFF

**Head Coach,**
**Bobby Ross**

**Pro Career:** Begins third season as San Diego's head coach. In 1992, led the Chargers to an 11-5 regular-season record and the team's first AFC Western Division title since 1981. Named ninth head coach in Chargers' history on January 2, 1992. Ross began his pro coaching career in 1978 as an assistant with the Kansas City Chiefs, where he coached special teams and defense in 1978-79 and offensive backs in 1980-81. No pro playing experience. Career record: 20-14.

**Background:** Played quarterback and defensive back for Virginia Military Institute. Began coaching career in 1965 at VMI. Moved on as an assistant at William & Mary 1967-70, Rice 1971, and Maryland 1972. Head coach at The Citadel 1973-77. Compiled 39-19-1 (.672) record as he led Maryland (1982-86) to three Atlantic Coast Conference titles and made four bowl game appearances in five seasons. Guided Georgia Tech (1987-91) to first ACC title in school history. Under Ross, the Yellow Jackets won first national championship as country's only undefeated team (11-0-1) in 1990. Named consensus national coach of the year in 1990. Career collegiate head coaching record: 94-76-2.

**Personal:** Born December 23, 1936, Richmond, Va. Bobby and wife, Alice, live in San Diego and have five children—Chris, Kevin, Robbie, Mary, and Teresa.

### ASSISTANT COACHES

**Bill Arnsparger,** defensive coordinator; born December 16, 1926, Paris, Ky., lives in San Diego. Tackle Miami (Ohio) 1946-49. No pro playing experience. College coach: Miami (Ohio) 1950, Ohio State 1951-53, Kentucky 1954-61, Tulane 1962-63, Louisiana State 1984-86, Florida 1987-91 (athletic director). Pro coach: Baltimore Colts 1964-69, Miami Dolphins 1970-73, 1976-83, New York Giants 1974-76 (head coach), joined Chargers in 1992.

**Sylvester Croom,** offensive backs; born September 25, 1954, Tuscaloosa, Ala., lives in San Diego. Center Alabama 1971-74. Pro center New Orleans Saints 1975. College coach: Alabama 1976-86. Pro coach: Tampa Bay Buccaneers 1987-90, Indianapolis Colts 1991, joined Chargers in 1992.

**John Dunn,** strength and conditioning; born July 22, 1956, Hillsdale, N.Y., lives in San Diego. Guard Penn State 1974-77. No pro playing experience. College coach: Penn State 1978. Pro coach: Washington Redskins 1984-86, Los Angeles Raiders 1987-89, joined Chargers in 1990.

**Frank Falks,** H-Backs-tight ends; born March 9, 1943, Tampa, Fla., lives in San Diego. Linebacker Joplin (Missouri) J.C. 1963-64, Parsons College 1965-66. No pro playing experience. College coach: Parsons College 1967-69, Kansas State 1970-72, Arkansas 1973-77, Wyoming 1978-79, San Diego State 1980, Oklahoma State 1981-82, Southern California 1983-86, Arizona State 1987-91, Ohio State 1992-93. Pro coach: Joined Chargers in 1994.

**Ralph Friedgen,** offensive coordinator; born April 4, 1947, Harrison, N.Y., lives in San Diego. Guard Maryland 1967-68. No pro playing experience. College coach: The Citadel 1973-79, William & Mary 1980, Murray State 1981, Maryland 1982-86, Georgia Tech 1987-91. Pro coach: Joined Chargers in 1992.

**Dale Lindsey,** linebackers; born January 18, 1943, Bedford, Ind., lives in San Diego. Linebacker Western Kentucky 1961-64. Pro linebacker Cleveland Browns 1965-73. College coach: Southern Methodist 1988-89. Pro coach: Cleveland Browns 1974, Portland Storm (WFL) 1975, Toronto Argonauts (CFL) 1979-82, Boston Breakers (USFL) 1983, New Jersey Generals (USFL) 1984-85, Green Bay Packers 1986-87, New England Patriots 1990, Tampa Bay Buccaneers 1991, joined Chargers in 1992.

**Carl Mauck,** offensive line; born July 7, 1947, McLeansboro, Ill., lives in San Diego. Linebacker-center Southern Illinois 1966-68. Pro center Baltimore Colts 1969, Miami Dolphins 1970, San Diego Chargers 1971-74, Houston Oilers 1975-81. Pro coach: New Orleans Saints 1982-85, Kansas City Chiefs 1986-88, Tampa Bay Buccaneers 1991, joined Chargers in 1992.

**John Misciagna,** quality control; born December 11, 1954, Brooklyn, N.Y., lives in San Diego. Guard Dickinson College 1973-76. No pro playing experience. College coach: Indiana (Pa.) University 1977, Columbia 1978-79, Maryland 1980-88, Georgia Tech 1989-91. Pro coach: Joined Chargers in 1992.

**Dennis Murphy,** defensive line; born October 22, 1940, Endicott, N.Y., lives in San Diego. Tight end-defensive lineman Notre Dame 1959-61. No pro playing experience. College coach: Notre Dame 1968-74, Colgate 1975, Holy Cross 1976-77, Eastern Michigan 1978-81, Maryland 1982-91, Navy 1992-93. Pro coach: Joined Chargers in 1994.

**Chuck Priefer,** special teams; born July 26, 1941, Cleveland, Ohio, lives in San Diego. No college or pro playing experience. College coach: Miami (Ohio) 1977, North Carolina 1978-83, Kent State 1986, Georgia Tech 1987-91. Pro coach: Green Bay Packers 1984-85, joined Chargers in 1992.

**Dwain Painter,** quarterbacks; born February 13, 1942, Monroeville, Pa., lives in San Diego. Quarterback-defensive back Rutgers 1961-64. No pro playing experience. College coach: San Jose State 1971-72, UCLA 1976-78, Northern Arizona 1979-81 (head coach), Georgia Tech 1982-85, Texas 1986, Illinois 1987. Pro coach: Pittsburgh Steelers 1988-91, Indianapolis Colts 1992-93, joined Chargers in 1994.

**Willie Shaw,** defensive backs; born January 11, 1944, San Diego, Calif., lives in San Diego. Cornerback New Mexico 1966-68. No pro playing experience. College coach: San Diego City College 1970-73, Stanford 1974-76, 1989-91, Long Beach State 1977-78, Oregon 1979, Arizona State 1980-84. Pro coach: Detroit Lions 1985-88, Minnesota Vikings 1992-93, joined Chargers in 1994.

**Jerry Sullivan,** wide receivers; born July 13, 1944, Miami, Fla., lives in San Diego. Quarterback Florida State 1963-64. No pro playing experience. College coach: Kansas State 1971-72, Texas Tech 1973-75, South Carolina 1976-82, Indiana 1983, Louisiana State 1984-90, Ohio State 1991. Pro coach: Joined Chargers in 1992.

## 1994 FIRST-YEAR ROSTER

| Name | Pos. | Ht. | Wt. | Birthdate | College | Hometown | How Acq. |
|---|---|---|---|---|---|---|---|
| Beeching, Todd | T | 6-7 | 305 | 3/15/71 | Southern Mississippi | Stockbridge, Ga. | FA |
| Beehn, Zane | LB | 6-4 | 252 | 9/28/71 | Kentucky | Owensboro, Ky. | D7 |
| Bennett, Darren (1) | P | 6-5 | 235 | 1/9/65 | No College | Western Australia | FA |
| Berger, Blaine | DE | 6-5 | 285 | 12/28/70 | Utah | Idaho Falls, Idaho | FA |
| Binn, David | TE | 6-3 | 234 | 2/6/72 | California | San Mateo, Calif. | FA |
| Breedlove, Brad | WR | 5-10 | 175 | 10/30/69 | Duke | Lecanto, Fla. | FA |
| Brohm, Jeff | QB | 6-1 | 200 | 4/24/71 | Louisville | Louisville, Ky. | FA |
| Caldwell, Henry | RB | 5-10 | 216 | 8/7/71 | Central Missouri State | Daytona Beach, Fla. | FA |
| Carter, Grant | LB | 6-2 | 222 | 12/30/70 | Pacific | Lake Oswego, Ore. | FA |
| Clark, Willie | CB | 5-10 | 186 | 1/6/72 | Notre Dame | Wheatland, Calif. | D3b |
| Coleman, Andre | WR-KR | 5-9 | 165 | 1/18/71 | Kansas State | Hermitage, Pa. | D3a |
| Currie, Herschel | CB | 6-1 | 190 | 9/8/65 | Oregon State | San Jose, Calif. | FA |
| Davis, Isaac | G | 6-3 | 325 | 4/8/72 | Arkansas | Malvern, Ark. | D2a |
| Engel, Greg | C | 6-3 | 293 | 1/18/71 | Illinois | Bloomington, Ill. | FA |
| Greene, Ernest | T | 6-5 | 294 | 2/25/71 | Savannah State | Savannah, Ga. | FA |
| Gregory, James | DT | 6-3 | 283 | 7/26/71 | Alabama | St. Louis, Mo. | FA |
| Harrison, Rodney | S | 6-0 | 201 | 12/15/72 | Western Illinois | Marion, Ill. | D5b |
| Hocker, Shawn | G | 6-4 | 288 | 7/27/71 | North Carolina | Sarasota, Fla. | FA |
| Hollis, Mike | K | 5-7 | 164 | 5/22/72 | Idaho | Spokane, Wash. | FA |
| Johnson, Chris | S | 6-0 | 205 | 8/7/71 | San Diego State | San Diego, Calif. | FA |
| Johnson, Tom | LB | 6-4 | 245 | 12/28/70 | Georgia Tech | Huntsville, Ala. | FA |
| Krein, Darren | DE | 6-4 | 258 | 7/7/71 | Miami | Aurora, Colo. | D5c |
| Laing, Aaron | TE | 6-3 | 264 | 7/19/71 | New Mexico State | Houston, Tex. | D5a |
| Lane, Greg | CB | 5-9 | 181 | 10/31/71 | Notre Dame | Austin, Tex. | FA |
| Long, Juan | LB | 6-2 | 245 | 11/21/71 | Mississippi State | Tupelo, Miss. | FA |
| McAlister, Scott (1) | P | 6-3 | 210 | 3/30/69 | North Carolina | Greensboro, N.C. | FA |
| Mitchell, Shannon | TE | 6-2 | 245 | 3/28/72 | Georgia | Alcoa, Tenn. | FA |
| Munoz, Jose | G | 6-3 | 280 | 5/7/71 | Ball State | Merrillville, Ind. | FA |
| Parker, Vaughn | G-T | 6-3 | 296 | 6/5/71 | UCLA | Buffalo, N.Y. | D2b |
| Ramaekers, Kevin | DT | 6-4 | 278 | 12/18/69 | Nebraska | Norfolk, Neb. | FA |
| Rivers, Ron | RB | 5-8 | 200 | 11/13/71 | Fresno State | Highland, Calif. | FA |
| Rodahaffer, Chris | T | 6-5 | 295 | 4/30/71 | San Diego State | Lodi, Calif. | FA |
| Smoot, Raymond (1) | G-T | 6-4 | 305 | 7/24/70 | Louisiana State | Leesville, La. | FA |
| Snyder, Sean (1) | P | 6-2 | 190 | 9/21/69 | Kansas State | Greenville, Tex. | FA |
| Stanley, Israel (1) | DE | 6-2 | 250 | 4/21/70 | Arizona State | San Diego, Calif. | FA |
| Sullivan, Kent (1) | P | 6-0 | 202 | 5/15/67 | California-Lutheran | Middlebury, Ind. | FA |
| Thomas, Chris (1) | WR | 6-1 | 180 | 7/16/71 | Cal Poly-SLO | Ventura, Calif. | FA |
| Thomas, Cornell | DE | 6-3 | 250 | 11/11/72 | West Georgia State | Norcross, Ga. | FA |
| Thomas, Sean | CB | 6-1 | 189 | 1/22/72 | Duke | Westerville, Ohio | FA |
| Thompson, Chris | LB | 6-0 | 253 | 6/17/69 | Bowie State | Adelphi, Md. | FA |
| Vinson, Tony | RB | 6-1 | 229 | 3/13/71 | Towson State | Denbigh, Va. | D5d |
| Ward, Jim | DT | 6-3 | 288 | 9/2/71 | Slippery Rock | Munhall, Pa. | FA |
| Watson, Darrius | S | 6-0 | 193 | 6/11/71 | Louisville | Torrance, Calif. | FA |
| Wilbert, Patrick | DT | 6-4 | 330 | 8/24/71 | Angelo State | Big Spring, Tex. | FA |
| Williams, Michael (1) | CB-S | 5-10 | 185 | 5/28/70 | UCLA | Los Angeles, Calif. | FA |
| Wyatt, Earnest | WR | 5-8 | 175 | 4/9/70 | Northeast Louisiana | Monroe, La. | FA |

The term NFL Rookie is defined as a player who is in his first season of professional football and has not been on the roster of another professional football team for any regular-season or postseason games. A Rookie is designated by an "R" on NFL rosters. Players who have been active in another professional football league or players who have NFL experience, including either preseason training camp or being on an Active List or Inactive List, or on Reserve/Injured or Reserve/Physically Unable to Perform for fewer than six regular-season games, are termed NFL First-Year Players. An NFL First-Year Player is designated by a "1" on NFL rosters. Thereafter, a player is credited with an additional year of experience for each season in which he accumulates six games on the Active List or Inactive List, or on Reserve/Injured or Reserve/Physically Unable to Perform.

## NOTES

# SEATTLE SEAHAWKS

**American Football Conference**
**Western Division**
**Team Colors:** Blue, Green, and Silver
**11220 N.E. 53rd Street**
**Kirkland, Washington 98033**
**Telephone: (206) 827-9777**

## CLUB OFFICIALS

Owner: Ken Behring
President: David Behring
General Manager/Head Coach: Tom Flores
Executive Vice President: Mickey Loomis
Vice President/Football Operations: Chuck Allen
Vice President/Administration and Public Relations: Gary Wright
Player Personnel Director: Mike Allman
Publicity Director: Dave Neubert
Community Relations Director: Sandy Gregory
Sales and Marketing Director: Reggie McKenzie
Data Processing Director: Sterling Monroe
Ticket Manager: James Nagaoka
Trainer: Jim Whitesel
Equipment Manager: Terry Sinclair
Team Physicians: Dr. Kevin Auld, Dr. Pierce Scranton, Dr. James Trombold, Dr. Pete Van Patten
**Stadium:** Kingdome • **Capacity:** 66,400
201 South King Street
Seattle, Washington 98104
**Playing Surface:** AstroTurf
**Training Camp:** 11220 N.E. 53rd Street
Kirkland, Washington 98033

## 1994 SCHEDULE

**PRESEASON**

| | | |
|---|---|---|
| Aug. 5 | at Indianapolis | 7:30 |
| Aug. 13 | **Tampa Bay** | 6:00 |
| Aug. 20 | **Minnesota** | 7:00 |
| Aug. 26 | at San Francisco | 6:00 |

**REGULAR SEASON**

| | | |
|---|---|---|
| Sept. 4 | at Washington | 1:00 |
| Sept. 11 | at Los Angeles Raiders | 1:00 |
| Sept. 18 | **San Diego** | 1:00 |
| Sept. 25 | **Pittsburgh** | 1:00 |
| Oct. 2 | at Indianapolis | 12:00 |
| Oct. 9 | **Denver** | 1:00 |
| Oct. 16 | Open Date | |
| Oct. 23 | at Kansas City | 12:00 |
| Oct. 30 | at San Diego | 1:00 |
| Nov. 6 | **Cincinnati** | 1:00 |
| Nov. 13 | at Denver | 2:00 |
| Nov. 20 | **Tampa Bay** | 1:00 |
| Nov. 27 | **Kansas City** | 1:00 |
| Dec. 4 | **Indianapolis** | 1:00 |
| Dec. 11 | at Houston | 3:00 |
| Dec. 18 | **Los Angeles Raiders** | 5:00 |
| Dec. 24 | at Cleveland | 1:00 |

## RECORD HOLDERS

**INDIVIDUAL RECORDS—CAREER**

| Category | Name | Performance |
|---|---|---|
| Rushing (Yds.) | Curt Warner, 1983-89 | 6,705 |
| Passing (Yds.) | Dave Krieg, 1980-1991 | 26,132 |
| Passing (TDs) | Dave Krieg, 1980-1991 | 195 |
| Receiving (No.) | Steve Largent, 1976-1989 | 819 |
| Receiving (Yds.) | Steve Largent, 1976-1989 | 13,089 |
| Interceptions | Dave Brown, 1976-1986 | 50 |
| Punting (Avg.) | Rick Tuten, 1991-93 | 44.0 |
| Punt Return (Avg.) | Paul Johns, 1981-84 | 11.4 |
| Kickoff Return (Avg.) | Bobby Joe Edmonds, 1986-88 | 22.1 |
| Field Goals | Norm Johnson, 1982-1990 | 159 |
| Touchdowns (Tot.) | Steve Largent, 1976-1989 | 101 |
| Points | Norm Johnson, 1982-1990 | 810 |

**INDIVIDUAL RECORDS—SINGLE SEASON**

| Category | Name | Performance |
|---|---|---|
| Rushing (Yds.) | Curt Warner, 1986 | 1,481 |
| Passing (Yds.) | Dave Krieg, 1984 | 3,671 |
| Passing (TDs) | Dave Krieg, 1984 | 32 |
| Receiving (No.) | Brian Blades, 1993 | 80 |
| Receiving (Yds.) | Steve Largent, 1985 | 1,287 |
| Interceptions | John Harris, 1981 | 10 |
| | Kenny Easley, 1984 | 10 |
| Punting (Avg.) | Rick Tuten, 1993 | 44.5 |
| Punt Return (Avg.) | Bobby Joe Edmonds, 1987 | 12.6 |
| Kickoff Return (Avg.) | Al Hunter, 1978 | 24.1 |
| Field Goals | John Kasay, 1991 | 25 |
| Touchdowns (Tot.) | David Sims, 1978 | 15 |
| | Sherman Smith, 1979 | 15 |
| | Derrick Fenner, 1990 | 15 |
| Points | Norm Johnson, 1984 | 110 |

**INDIVIDUAL RECORDS—SINGLE GAME**

| Category | Name | Performance |
|---|---|---|
| Rushing (Yds.) | Curt Warner, 11-27-83 | 207 |
| Passing (Yds.) | Dave Krieg, 11-20-83 | 418 |
| Passing (TDs) | Dave Krieg, 12-2-84 | 5 |
| | Dave Krieg, 9-15-85 | 5 |
| | Dave Krieg, 11-28-88 | 5 |
| Receiving (No.) | Steve Largent, 10-18-87 | 15 |
| Receiving (Yds.) | Steve Largent, 10-18-87 | 261 |
| Interceptions | Kenny Easley, 9-3-84 | 3 |
| | Eugene Robinson, 12-6-92 | 3 |
| Field Goals | Norm Johnson, 9-20-87 | 5 |
| | Norm Johnson, 12-18-88 | 5 |
| Touchdowns (Tot.) | Daryl Turner, 9-15-85 | 4 |
| | Curt Warner, 12-11-88 | 4 |
| Points | Daryl Turner, 9-15-85 | 24 |
| | Curt Warner, 12-11-88 | 24 |

*NFL Record

## COACHING HISTORY

**(130-153-0)**

| | | |
|---|---|---|
| 1976-82 | Jack Patera* | 35-59-0 |
| 1982 | Mike McCormack | 4-3-0 |
| 1983-91 | Chuck Knox | 83-67-0 |
| 1992-93 | Tom Flores | 8-24-0 |

*Released after two games in 1982

## KINGDOME

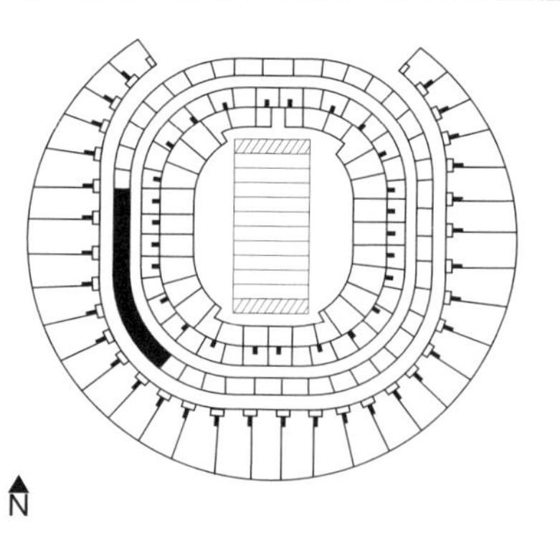

## 1993 TEAM RECORD,

**PRESEASON (2-2)**

| Date | Result | | Opponents |
|---|---|---|---|
| 8/7 | L | 13-16 | Indianapolis |
| 8/14 | L | 10-23 | at Minnesota |
| 8/21 | W | 30-0 | San Francisco |
| 8/28 | W | 20-10 | at Houston |

**REGULAR SEASON (6-10)**

| Date | Result | | Opponents | Att. |
|---|---|---|---|---|
| 9/5 | L | 12-18 | at San Diego | 58,039 |
| 9/12 | L | 13-17 | L.A. Raiders | 58,836 |
| 9/19 | W | 17-14 | at New England | 50,392 |
| 9/26 | W | 19-10 | at Cincinnati | 46,880 |
| 10/3 | W | 31-14 | San Diego | 54,778 |
| 10/17 | L | 10-30 | at Detroit | 60,801 |
| 10/24 | W | 10-9 | New England | 56,526 |
| 10/31 | L | 17-28 | at Denver | 73,644 |
| 11/7 | L | 14-24 | at Houston | 50,447 |
| 11/14 | W | 22-5 | Cleveland | 54,622 |
| 11/28 | L | 9-17 | Denver | 57,812 |
| 12/5 | L | 16-31 | Kansas City | 58,551 |
| 12/12 | L | 23-27 | at L.A. Raiders | 38,161 |
| 12/19 | L | 27-30 | Phoenix (OT) | 45,737 |
| 12/26 | W | 16-6 | Pittsburgh | 51,814 |
| 1/2 | L | 24-34 | at Kansas City | 72,136 |

(OT) Overtime

**SCORE BY PERIODS**

| | | | | | | | |
|---|---|---|---|---|---|---|---|
| Seahawks | 72 | 64 | 45 | 99 | 0 | — | 280 |
| Opponents | 65 | 104 | 66 | 76 | 3 | — | 314 |

**ATTENDANCE**

Home 438,676 Away 450,500 Total 889,176
Single-game home record, 64,673 (11-8-92)
Single-season home record, 514,984 (1992)

## 1993 TEAM STATISTICS

| | Seahawks | Opp. |
|---|---|---|
| Total First Downs | 279 | 322 |
| Rushing | 114 | 106 |
| Passing | 144 | 193 |
| Penalty | 21 | 23 |
| Third Down: Made/Att | 80/224 | 91/229 |
| Third Down Pct. | 35.7 | 39.7 |
| Fourth Down: Made/Att | 6/14 | 6/13 |
| Fourth Down Pct. | 42.9 | 46.2 |
| Total Net Yards | 4669 | 5313 |
| Avg. Per Game | 291.8 | 332.1 |
| Total Plays | 1019 | 1085 |
| Avg. Per Play | 4.6 | 4.9 |
| Net Yards Rushing | 2015 | 1660 |
| Avg. Per Game | 125.9 | 103.8 |
| Total Rushes | 473 | 452 |
| Net Yards Passing | 2654 | 3653 |
| Avg. Per Game | 165.9 | 228.3 |
| Sacked/Yards Lost | 48/242 | 38/244 |
| Gross Yards | 2896 | 3897 |
| Att./Completions | 498/280 | 595/333 |
| Completion Pct. | 56.2 | 56.0 |
| Had Intercepted | 18 | 22 |
| Punts/Avg. | 91/44.0 | 73/42.4 |
| Net Punting Avg. | 91/37.3 | 73/35.6 |
| Penalties/Yards Lost | 99/745 | 109/818 |
| Fumbles/Ball Lost | 25/13 | 23/15 |
| Touchdowns | 29 | 32 |
| Rushing | 13 | 12 |
| Passing | 13 | 16 |
| Returns | 3 | 4 |
| Avg. Time of Possession | 29:03 | 30:57 |

## 1993 INDIVIDUAL STATISTICS

| PASSING | Att. | Cmp. | Yds. | Pct. | TD | Int. | Tkld. | Rate |
|---|---|---|---|---|---|---|---|---|
| Mirer | 486 | 274 | 2833 | 56.4 | 12 | 17 | 47/235 | 67.0 |
| Gelbaugh | 5 | 3 | 39 | 60.0 | 0 | 1 | 1/7 | 45.0 |
| McGwire | 5 | 3 | 24 | 60.0 | 1 | 0 | 0/0 | 111.7 |
| Tuten | 1 | 0 | 0 | 0.0 | 0 | 0 | 0/0 | 39.6 |
| Williams | 1 | 0 | 0 | 0.0 | 0 | 0 | 0/0 | 39.6 |
| Seahawks | 498 | 280 | 2896 | 56.2 | 13 | 18 | 48/242 | 66.8 |
| Opponents | 595 | 333 | 3897 | 56.0 | 16 | 22 | 38/244 | 69.6 |

| SCORING | TD R | TD P | TD Rt | PAT | FG | Saf | PTS |
|---|---|---|---|---|---|---|---|
| Kasay | 0 | 0 | 0 | 29/29 | 23/28 | 0 | 98 |
| C. Warren | 7 | 0 | 0 | 0/0 | 0/0 | 0 | 42 |
| Martin | 0 | 5 | 0 | 0/0 | 0/0 | 0 | 30 |
| Williams | 3 | 1 | 0 | 0/0 | 0/0 | 0 | 24 |
| Blades | 0 | 3 | 0 | 0/0 | 0/0 | 0 | 18 |
| Mirer | 3 | 0 | 0 | 0/0 | 0/0 | 0 | 18 |
| Edmunds | 0 | 2 | 0 | 0/0 | 0/0 | 0 | 12 |
| Stephens | 0 | 0 | 1 | 0/0 | 0/0 | 2 | 10 |
| Blackmon | 0 | 0 | 1 | 0/0 | 0/0 | 0 | 6 |
| Green | 0 | 1 | 0 | 0/0 | 0/0 | 0 | 6 |
| Johnson | 0 | 1 | 0 | 0/0 | 0/0 | 0 | 6 |
| Nash | 0 | 0 | 1 | 0/0 | 0/0 | 0 | 6 |
| Edwards | 0 | 0 | 0 | 0/0 | 0/0 | 1 | 2 |
| Seahawks | 13 | 13 | 3 | 29/29 | 23/28 | 4 | 280 |
| Opponents | 12 | 16 | 4 | 31/32 | 29/39 | 2 | 314 |

| RUSHING | Att. | Yds. | Avg. | LG | TD |
|---|---|---|---|---|---|
| C. Warren | 273 | 1072 | 3.9 | 45t | 7 |
| Williams | 82 | 371 | 4.5 | 38 | 3 |
| Mirer | 68 | 343 | 5.0 | 33 | 3 |
| Vaughn | 36 | 153 | 4.3 | 37 | 0 |
| Blades | 5 | 52 | 10.4 | 26 | 0 |
| Bates | 2 | 12 | 6.0 | 6 | 0 |
| Johnson | 2 | 8 | 4.0 | 5 | 0 |
| D. Thomas | 1 | 4 | 4.0 | 4 | 0 |
| Mayes | 1 | 2 | 2.0 | 2 | 0 |
| Martin | 1 | 0 | 0.0 | 0 | 0 |
| Gelbaugh | 1 | -1 | -1.0 | -1 | 0 |
| McGwire | 1 | -1 | -1.0 | -1 | 0 |
| Seahawks | 473 | 2015 | 4.3 | 45t | 13 |
| Opponents | 452 | 1660 | 3.7 | 30t | 12 |

| RECEIVING | No. | Yds. | Avg. | LG | TD |
|---|---|---|---|---|---|
| Blades | 80 | 945 | 11.8 | 41 | 3 |
| Williams | 58 | 450 | 7.8 | 25 | 1 |
| Martin | 57 | 798 | 14.0 | 53t | 5 |
| Edmunds | 24 | 239 | 10.0 | 32 | 2 |
| Green | 23 | 178 | 7.7 | 20 | 1 |
| C. Warren | 15 | 99 | 6.6 | 21 | 0 |
| D. Thomas | 11 | 95 | 8.6 | 20 | 0 |
| R. Thomas | 7 | 67 | 9.6 | 16 | 0 |
| Johnson | 3 | 15 | 5.0 | 8 | 1 |
| Bates | 1 | 6 | 6.0 | 6 | 0 |
| Roberts | 1 | 4 | 4.0 | 4 | 0 |
| Seahawks | 280 | 2896 | 10.3 | 53t | 13 |
| Opponents | 333 | 3897 | 11.7 | 58t | 16 |

| INTERCEPTIONS | No. | Yds. | Avg. | LG | TD |
|---|---|---|---|---|---|
| E. Robinson | 9 | 80 | 8.9 | 28 | 0 |
| Hunter | 4 | 54 | 13.5 | 34 | 0 |
| Gray | 3 | 33 | 11.0 | 16 | 0 |
| Blackmon | 2 | 0 | 0.0 | 0 | 0 |
| Nash | 1 | 13 | 13.0 | 13t | 1 |
| Jefferson | 1 | 12 | 12.0 | 12 | 0 |
| Porter | 1 | 4 | 4.0 | 4 | 0 |
| Harper | 1 | 0 | 0.0 | 0 | 0 |
| Seahawks | 22 | 196 | 8.9 | 34 | 1 |
| Opponents | 18 | 159 | 8.8 | 40 | 0 |

| PUNTING | No. | Yds. | Avg. | In 20 | LG |
|---|---|---|---|---|---|
| Tuten | 90 | 4007 | 44.5 | 21 | 64 |
| Seahawks | 91 | 4007 | 44.0 | 21 | 64 |
| Opponents | 73 | 3097 | 42.4 | 19 | 60 |

| PUNT RETURNS | No. | FC | Yds. | Avg. | LG | TD |
|---|---|---|---|---|---|---|
| Martin | 32 | 15 | 270 | 8.4 | 33 | 0 |
| McCloughan | 1 | 0 | 10 | 10.0 | 10 | 0 |
| Seahawks | 33 | 15 | 280 | 8.5 | 33 | 0 |
| Opponents | 47 | 21 | 475 | 10.1 | 74t | 1 |

| KICKOFF RETURNS | No. | Yds. | Avg. | LG | TD |
|---|---|---|---|---|---|
| Bates | 30 | 603 | 20.1 | 46 | 0 |
| Vaughn | 16 | 280 | 17.5 | 31 | 0 |
| Martin | 3 | 38 | 12.7 | 15 | 0 |
| Tuatagaloa | 1 | 10 | 10.0 | 10 | 0 |
| Seahawks | 50 | 931 | 18.6 | 46 | 0 |
| Opponents | 52 | 967 | 18.6 | 95t | 1 |

| SACKS | No. |
|---|---|
| Sinclair | 8.0 |
| Kennedy | 6.5 |
| McCrary | 4.0 |
| Tuatagaloa | 3.5 |
| Edwards | 3.0 |
| Stephens | 2.5 |
| Wooden | 2.5 |
| E. Robinson | 2.0 |
| R. Robinson | 1.5 |
| Bryant | 1.0 |
| Gray | 1.0 |
| Porter | 1.0 |
| Rodgers | 1.0 |
| Nash | 0.5 |
| Seahawks | 38.0 |
| Opponents | 48.0 |

## 1994 DRAFT CHOICES

| Round | Name | Pos. | College |
|---|---|---|---|
| 1 | Sam Adams | DT | Texas A&M |
| 2 | Kevin Mawae | C | Louisiana State |
| 3 | Lamar Smith | RB | Houston |
| 4 | Larry Whigham | DB | N.E. Louisiana |
| 7 | Carlester Crumpler | TE | East Carolina |

## SEATTLE SEAHAWKS

### 1994 VETERAN ROSTER

| No. | | Name | Pos. | Ht. | Wt. | Birthdate | NFL Exp. | College | Hometown | How Acq. | '93 Games/ Starts |
|---|---|---|---|---|---|---|---|---|---|---|---|
| 39 | | Allred, Brian | CB | 5-10 | 175 | 3/16/69 | 2 | Sacramento State | Columbia Md. | FA-'93 | 4/0 |
| 75 | | Ballard, Howard | T | 6-6 | 336 | 11/3/63 | 7 | Alabama A&M | Ashland, Ala. | UFA(Buff)-'94 | 16/16* |
| 15 | t- | Barrett, Reggie | WR | 6-3 | 215 | 8/14/69 | 4 | Texas-El Paso | Corpus Christi, Tex. | T(Det)-'94 | 13/2* |
| 81 | | Bates, Michael | WR | 5-10 | 189 | 12/19/69 | 2 | Arizona | Tucson, Ariz. | D6-'92 | 16/1 |
| 25 | | Blackmon, Robert | S | 6-0 | 197 | 5/12/67 | 5 | Baylor | Van Vleck, Tex. | D2b-'90 | 16/16 |
| 69 | | Blackshear, Jeff | G | 6-6 | 315 | 3/29/69 | 2 | Northeast Louisiana | Ft. Pierce, Fla. | D8a-'93 | 15/2 |
| 89 | † | Blades, Brian | WR | 5-11 | 189 | 7/24/66 | 7 | Miami | Ft. Lauderdale, Fla. | D2-'88 | 16/16 |
| 51 | | Brandon, David | LB | 6-4 | 230 | 2/9/65 | 8 | Memphis State | Memphis, Tenn. | FA-'93 | 13/0* |
| 77 | # | Bryant, Jeff | DE | 6-5 | 281 | 5/22/60 | 13 | Clemson | Decatur, Ga. | D1-'82 | 16/15 |
| 79 | | Childs, Jason | T | 6-4 | 285 | 1/6/69 | 2 | North Dakota | Plymouth, Minn. | W(SF)-'93 | 0* |
| 50 | | Davis, Anthony | LB | 6-0 | 231 | 3/7/69 | 2 | Utah | Pasco, Wash. | FA-'92 | 10/0 |
| 53 | | Donaldson, Ray | C | 6-3 | 300 | 5/18/58 | 15 | Georgia | Rome, Ga. | FA-'93 | 16/16 |
| 82 | | Edmunds, Ferrell | TE | 6-6 | 254 | 4/16/65 | 7 | Maryland | Danville, Va. | UFA(Mia)-'93 | 16/16 |
| 67 | | Edwards, Antonio | DE | 6-3 | 270 | 3/10/70 | 2 | Valdosta State | Moultrie, Ga. | D8b-'93 | 9/0 |
| 59 | | Frerotte, Mitch | G | 6-3 | 286 | 3/30/65 | 7 | Penn State | Kittanning, Pa. | UFA(Buff)-'93 | 0* |
| 18 | | Gelbaugh, Stan | QB | 6-3 | 207 | 12/4/62 | 6 | Maryland | Mechanicsburg, Pa. | PB(Phx)-'92 | 1/0 |
| 7 | | Graham, Jeff | QB | 6-5 | 220 | 2/5/66 | 3 | Long Beach State | Costa Mesa, Calif. | FA-'92 | 0* |
| 26 | | Gray, Carlton | CB | 6-0 | 191 | 6/26/71 | 2 | UCLA | Cincinnati, Ohio | D2-'93 | 10/2 |
| 87 | | Green, Paul | TE | 6-3 | 230 | 10/8/66 | 3 | Southern California | Clovis, Calif. | FA-'92 | 15/8 |
| 76 | | Hitchcock, Bill | G | 6-6 | 291 | 8/26/65 | 4 | Purdue | Kirkland, Canada | FA-'91 | 14/14 |
| 27 | | Hunter, Patrick | CB | 5-11 | 186 | 10/24/64 | 9 | Nevada | San Francisco, Calif. | D3-'86 | 15/15 |
| 43 | | Johnson, Tracy | RB | 6-0 | 230 | 11/29/66 | 6 | Clemson | Kannapolis, N.C. | PB(Atl)-'92 | 16/1 |
| 93 | # | Junior, E.J. | LB | 6-3 | 242 | 12/8/59 | 14 | Alabama | Nashville, Tenn. | FA-'92 | 4/0 |
| 83 | # | Junkin, Trey | TE | 6-2 | 237 | 1/23/61 | 12 | Louisiana Tech | Winfield, La. | FA-'90 | 16/1 |
| 4 | † | Kasay, John | K | 5-10 | 189 | 10/27/69 | 4 | Georgia | Athens, Ga. | D4-'91 | 16/0 |
| 78 | | Keim, Mike | T | 6-7 | 301 | 11/12/65 | 2 | Brigham Young | Springerville, Ariz. | FA-'92 | 3/0 |
| 96 | | Kennedy, Cortez | DT | 6-3 | 293 | 8/23/68 | 5 | Miami | Rivercrest, Ark. | D1-'90 | 16/16 |
| 84 | | Martin, Kelvin | WR | 5-9 | 162 | 5/14/65 | 8 | Boston College | Jacksonville, Fla. | UFA(Dall)-'93 | 16/14 |
| 44 | † | McCloughan, Dave | S | 6-1 | 185 | 11/20/66 | 4 | Colorado | Loveland, Colo. | T(GB)-'93 | 15/1 |
| 92 | | McCrary, Michael | DE | 6-4 | 250 | 7/7/70 | 2 | Wake Forest | Vienna, Va. | D7-'93 | 15/0 |
| 10 | | McGwire, Dan | QB | 6-8 | 239 | 12/18/67 | 4 | San Diego State | Claremont, Calif. | D1-'91 | 2/0 |
| 3 | | Mirer, Rick | QB | 6-2 | 216 | 3/19/70 | 2 | Notre Dame | Goshen, Ind. | D1-'93 | 16/16 |
| 98 | | Murphy, Kevin | LB | 6-2 | 235 | 9/8/63 | 9 | Oklahoma | Richardson, Tex. | UFA(SD)-'93 | 14/10 |
| 72 | # | Nash, Joe | DT | 6-3 | 278 | 10/11/60 | 13 | Boston College | Dorchester, Mass. | FA-'82 | 16/16 |
| 37 | | Odomes, Nate | CB | 5-10 | 188 | 8/25/65 | 8 | Wisconsin | Columbus, Ga. | UFA(Buff)-'94 | 16/15* |
| 97 | | Porter, Rufus | LB | 6-1 | 227 | 5/18/65 | 7 | Southern | Baton Rouge, La. | FA-'88 | 7/6 |
| 73 | | Roberts, Ray | T | 6-6 | 304 | 6/3/69 | 3 | Virginia | Asheville, N.C. | D1-'92 | 16/16 |
| 41 | | Robinson, Eugene | S | 6-0 | 191 | 5/28/63 | 10 | Colgate | Hartford, Conn. | FA-'85 | 16/16 |
| 37 | | Robinson, Rafael | S | 5-11 | 200 | 6/19/69 | 3 | Wisconsin | Jefferson, Tex. | FA-'92 | 16/1 |
| 91 | | Rodgers, Tyrone | DT | 6-3 | 266 | 4/27/69 | 3 | Washington | Wilmington, Calif. | FA-'92 | 16/0 |
| 71 | | Shaw, Rickie | T | 6-4 | 294 | 12/26/69 | 2 | North Crolina | Whiteville, N.C. | W(NO)-'93 | 0* |
| 70 | | Sinclair, Michael | DE | 6-4 | 271 | 1/31/68 | 3 | Eastern New Mexico | Beaumont, Tex. | D6-'91 | 9/1 |
| 58 | | Spitulski, Bob | LB | 6-3 | 235 | 9/10/69 | 3 | Central Florida | Orlando, Fla. | D3-'92 | 6/0 |
| 94 | | Stephens, Rod | LB | 6-1 | 237 | 6/14/66 | 5 | Georgia Tech | Atlanta, Ga. | FA-'90 | 13/13 |
| 86 | # | Thomas, Robb | WR | 5-11 | 175 | 3/29/66 | 6 | Oregon State | Corvallis, Ore. | FA-'92 | 16/0 |
| 56 | | Tofflemire, Joe | C | 6-3 | 273 | 7/7/65 | 6 | Arizona | Post Falls, Idaho | D2-'89 | 0* |
| 99 | # | Tuatagaloa, Natu | DE | 6-4 | 274 | 5/25/66 | 6 | California | San Rafael, Calif. | FA-'92 | 16/15 |
| 14 | | Tuten, Rick | P | 6-2 | 218 | 1/5/65 | 5 | Florida State | Ocala, Fla. | FA-'91 | 16/0 |
| 22 | † | Vaughn, Jon | RB | 5-9 | 203 | 3/12/70 | 4 | Michigan | Florissant, Mo. | T(NE)-'93 | 16/2 |
| 42 | | Warren, Chris | RB | 6-2 | 225 | 1/24/67 | 5 | Ferrum | Burke, Va. | D4-'90 | 14/14 |
| 88 | | Warren, Terrence | WR | 6-1 | 200 | 8/2/69 | 2 | Hampton | Suffolk, Va. | D5-'93 | 2/0 |
| 95 | | Wells, Dean | LB | 6-3 | 238 | 7/20/70 | 2 | Kentucky | Louisville, Ky. | D4-'93 | 14/1 |
| 64 | | Williams, Brent | DE | 6-4 | 285 | 10/23/64 | 9 | Toledo | Flint, Mich. | UFA(NE)-'94 | 13/2* |
| 90 | | Wooden, Terry | LB | 6-3 | 239 | 1/14/67 | 5 | Syracuse | Farmington, Conn. | D2a-'90 | 16/16 |

* Ballard played 16 games with Buffalo in '93; Barrett active for 16 games with Detroit; Brandon played 6 games with Cleveland, 7 games with Seattle; Childs active for 2 games but did not play; Frerotte inactive for 5 games; Graham inactive for 16 games; Odomes played 16 games with Buffalo; Shaw active for 2 games but did not play; Tofflemire active for 13 games but did not play; Williams played 13 games with New England.

\# Unrestricted free agent; subject to developments.

† Restricted free agent; subject to developments.

t- Seahawks traded for Barrett (Detroit).

Retired—C Grant Feasel, 11-year veteran, 0 games in '93; RB Rueben Mayes, 8-year veteran, 1 game in '93.

Players lost through free agency (4): G Darrick Brilz (Cin; 16 games in '93), CB Dwayne Harper (SD; 14), T Andy Heck (Chi; 16), RB John L. Williams (Pitt; 16).

Also played with Seahawks in '93—LB Ray Berry (7 games), LB Dino Hackett (3), CB James Jefferson (10), WR Doug Thomas (16).

## COACHING STAFF

**Head Coach,**
**Tom Flores**

**Pro Career:** Named the fourth head coach in the history of the Seahawks on January 6, 1992. Had served as president and general manager from February 22, 1989. Flores previously served as the head coach of the Oakland/Los Angeles Raiders from 1979 through 1987. He won two Super Bowl titles with the Raiders, 27-10 over the Philadelphia Eagles in Super Bowl XV after the 1980 season, and 38-9 over the Washington Redskins in Super Bowl XVIII in 1983. Those are the only Super Bowl triumphs by an AFC team in the 1980s. The 1980 Raiders are the only Wild Card team to win the Super Bowl. Flores was a member of the Raiders' organization for 22 seasons, as a quarterback (1960-61, 1963-66), assistant coach (1972-78), and head coach (1979-87). Also played for the Buffalo Bills (1967-68) and Kansas City Chiefs (1969-70), and coached with the Bills (1971) before returning to the Raiders as a coach. Is one of two players in league history to have Super Bowl rings as a player (Kansas City, Super Bowl IV), assistant coach (Raiders, Super Bowl XI) and head coach (Raiders, Super Bowls XV and XVIII). Still holds the Raiders' record with six touchdown passes in a 1963 game. Career record: 99-80-0.
**Background:** Quarterback at Fresno, California, Junior College 1954-55 and the College of the Pacific 1956-57. Coached at his alma mater in 1959 before joining the Raiders as a quarterback in 1960.
**Personal:** Born March 21, 1937, in Fresno, California. Tom and his wife, Barbara, live in Kirkland, Washington, and have twin sons, Mark and Scott, and a daughter, Kim.

### ASSISTANT COACHES

**Tommy Brasher,** defensive line; born December 30, 1940, El Dorado, Ark., lives in Redmond, Wash. Linebacker Arkansas 1962-63. No pro playing experience. College coach: Arkansas 1970, Virginia Tech 1971, Northeast Louisiana 1974, 1976, Southern Methodist 1977-81. Pro coach: Shreveport Steamer (WFL) 1975, New England Patriots 1982-84, Philadelphia Eagles 1985, Atlanta Falcons 1986-89, Tampa Bay Buccaneers 1990, joined Seahawks in 1992.
**Bob Bratkowski,** wide receivers; born December 2, 1955, San Angelo, Tex., lives in Redmond, Wash. Wide receiver Washington State 1974, 1976-77. No pro playing experience. College coach: Missouri 1978-80, Weber State 1981-85, Wyoming 1986, Washington State 1987-88, Miami 1989-91. Pro coach: Joined Seahawks in 1992.
**Dave Brown,** defensive assistant; born January 16, 1953, Akron, Ohio, lives in Woodinville, Wash. Defensive back Michigan 1972-74. Pro defensive back Pittsburgh Steelers 1975, Seattle Seahawks 1976-86, Green Bay Packers 1987-90. Pro coach: Joined Seahawks in 1992.
**Tom Catlin,** quality control; born September 8, 1931, Ponca City, Okla., lives in Redmond, Wash. Center-linebacker Oklahoma 1950-52. Pro linebacker Cleveland Browns 1953-54, 1957-58, Philadelphia Eagles 1959. College coach: Army 1956. Pro coach: Dallas Texans-Kansas City Chiefs 1960-65, Los Angeles Rams 1966-77, Buffalo Bills 1978-82, joined Seahawks in 1983.
**Larry Kennan,** offensive coordinator-quarterbacks; born June 13, 1944, Pomona, Calif., lives in Kirkland, Wash. Quarterback La Verne College 1962-65. No pro playing experience. College coach: Colorado 1969-71, Nevada-Las Vegas 1973-75, Southern Methodist 1976-78, Lamar 1979-81 (head coach). Pro coach: Los Angeles Raiders 1982-87, Denver Broncos 1988, Indianapolis Colts 1989-90, London Monarchs (World League) 1991 (head coach), joined Seahawks in 1992.
**Arnie Matsumoto,** staff assistant; born December 18, 1962, Isesaki, Gumma, Japan, lives in Kirkland, Wash. No college or pro playing experience. Pro coach: Joined Seahawks in 1989.
**Paul Moyer,** defensive backfield; born July 26, 1961, Villa Park, Calif., lives in Renton, Wash. Safety Fullerton, Calif., J.C. 1979-80, Arizona State 1981-82. Pro safety Seattle Seahawks 1983-89. Pro coach: Joined Seahawks in 1990
**Howard Mudd,** offensive line; born February 10, 1942, Midland, Mich., lives in Kirkland, Wash. Guard Hillsdale College 1961-63. Pro guard San Francisco 49ers 1964-69, Chicago Bears 1969-71. College coach: California 1972-73. Pro coach: San Diego Chargers 1974-76, San Francisco 49ers 1977, Seattle Seahawks 1978-82, Cleveland Browns 1983-88, Kansas City Chiefs 1989-92, rejoined Seahawks in 1993.
**Russ Purnell,** special teams-tight ends; born June 12, 1948, Chicago, Ill., lives in Bellevue, Wash. Center Orange Coast, Calif., J.C. 1966-67, Whittier College 1968-69. No pro playing experience. College coach: Whittier 1970-71, Southern California 1982-85. Pro coach: Joined Seahawks in 1986.
**Frank Raines,** strength and conditioning; born November 29, 1960, Portsmouth, Va., lives in Renton, Wash. No college or pro playing experience. Pro coach: Washington Redskins 1986-89, joined Seahawks in 1990.
**Clarence Shelmon,** running backs; born September 17, 1952, Bossier, La., lives in Kirkland, Wash. Running back Houston 1971-75. No pro playing experience. College coach: Army 1978-80, Indiana 1981-83, Arizona 1984-86, Southern California 1987-90. Pro coach: Los Angeles Rams 1991, joined Seahawks in 1992.
**Rusty Tillman,** defensive coordinator-linebackers; born February 27, 1948, Beloit, Wis., lives in Redmond, Wash. Linebacker Northern Arizona 1967-69. Pro linebacker Washington Redskins 1970-77. Pro coach: Joined Seahawks in 1979.

## 1994 FIRST-YEAR ROSTER

| Name | Pos. | Ht. | Wt. | Birthdate | College | Hometown | How Acq. |
|---|---|---|---|---|---|---|---|
| Adams, Sam | DT | 6-3 | 285 | 6/13/73 | Texas A&M | Houston, Tex. | D1 |
| Atkins, James (1) | G | 6-6 | 291 | 1/28/70 | S.W. Louisiana | Amite, La. | FA |
| Atkinson, Jason | LB | 6-3 | 230 | 10/11/70 | Texas A&M | Houston, Tex. | FA |
| Bellamy, Jay | S | 5-11 | 177 | 7/8/72 | Rutgers | Matawan, N.J. | FA |
| Bryant, Steve | LB | 6-3 | 240 | 7/2/71 | Nevada | Sparks, Nev. | FA |
| Butler, Hillary | LB | 6-2 | 240 | 1/5/71 | Washington | Tacoma, Wash. | FA |
| Carter, Marcus | WR | 5-11 | 205 | 8/18/71 | S.W. Louisiana | Mansfield, La. | FA |
| Crumpler, Carlester | TE | 6-6 | 255 | 9/5/71 | East Carolina | Greenville, N.C. | D7 |
| DeVries, Jed | T | 6-5 | 282 | 1/6/71 | Utah State | Plain City, Utah | FA |
| Gordon, Steve (1) | C | 6-3 | 279 | 4/15/69 | California | Nevada City, Calif. | FA |
| Hamilton, Bobby | DE | 6-4 | 266 | 7/1/71 | Southern Mississippi | East Marion, Miss. | FA |
| Kegarise, Mike | T | 6-5 | 310 | 6/19/71 | Edinboro | Milan, Ohio | FA |
| Mawae, Kevin | C | 6-4 | 288 | 1/23/71 | Louisiana State | Savannah, Ga. | D2 |
| McDaniel, Curtis | DT | 6-3 | 283 | 2/12/70 | Jacksonville State | Ft. Payne, Ala. | FA |
| McKnight, James | WR | 6-0 | 181 | 6/17/72 | Liberty | Apopka, Fla. | FA |
| Seegars, Stacy | G | 6-3 | 337 | 4/26/71 | Clemson | Kershaw, N.C. | FA |
| Shamsid-Deen, M. (1) | RB | 5-11 | 200 | 11/16/69 | Tenn.-Chattanooga | Decatur, Ga. | D8-'92 |
| Smith, Lamar | RB | 5-11 | 230 | 11/29/70 | Houston | Ft. Wayne, Ind. | D3 |
| Strong, Mack (1) | RB | 6-0 | 211 | 9/11/71 | Georgia | Columbus, Ga. | FA |
| Tinner, Glenn | G | 6-5 | 292 | 3/3/70 | Temple | Hanover, Pa. | FA |
| Watters, Orlando | CB | 5-11 | 177 | 10/26/71 | Arkansas | Anniston, Ala. | FA |
| Werner, Matt | DT | 6-3 | 265 | 6/14/71 | UCLA | Anaheim, Calif. | FA |
| Whigham, Larry | S | 6-2 | 202 | 6/23/72 | Southeast Louisiana | Hattiesburg, Miss. | D4 |
| Wood, Rick | RB | 6-2 | 242 | 7/19/71 | Norfolk State | Washington, D.C. | FA |

The term NFL Rookie is defined as a player who is in his first season of professional football and has not been on the roster of another professional football team for any regular-season or postseason games. A Rookie is designated by an "R" on NFL rosters. Players who have been active in another professional football league or players who have NFL experience, including either preseason training camp or being on an Active List or Inactive List, or on Reserve/Injured or Reserve/Physically Unable to Perform for fewer than six regular-season games, are termed NFL First-Year Players. An NFL First-Year Player is designated by a "1" on NFL rosters. Thereafter, a player is credited with an additional year of experience for each season in which he accumulates six games on the Active List or Inactive List, or on Reserve/Injured or Reserve/Physically Unable to Perform.

## NOTES

# The NFC

# ARIZONA CARDINALS

**National Football Conference**
**Eastern Division**
**Team Colors:** Cardinal Red, Black, and White
**P.O. Box 888**
**Phoenix, Arizona 85001-0888**
**Telephone: (602) 379-0101**

## CLUB OFFICIALS

President: William V. Bidwill
Head Coach and General Manager: Buddy Ryan
Executive Vice President: Joe Rhein
Vice President: Larry Wilson
Secretary and General Counsel:
Thomas J. Guilfoil
Treasurer and Chief Financial Officer:
Charley Schlegel
Assistant General Manager: Bob Ackles
Director of Broadcast Sales: John Shean
Public Relations Director: Paul Jensen
Media Coordinator: Greg Gladysiewski
Director of Community Relations: Adele Harris
Director of Marketing: Joe Castor
Ticket Manager: Steve Walsh
Trainer: John Omohundro
Assistant Trainers: Jim Shearer, Jeff Herndon
Equipment Manager: Mark Ahlemeier
Assistant Equipment Manager: Steve Christensen
**Stadium:** Sun Devil Stadium • **Capacity:** 73,377
Fifth Street
Tempe, Arizona 85287
**Playing Surface:** Grass
**Training Camp:** Northern Arizona University
Flagstaff, Arizona 86011

## 1994 SCHEDULE

**PRESEASON**

| | | |
|---|---|---|
| Aug. 5 | **San Francisco** | 6:30 |
| Aug. 13 | **Chicago** | 6:00 |
| Aug. 19 | at Detroit | 7:30 |
| Aug. 25 | at Denver | 7:00 |

**REGULAR SEASON**

| | | |
|---|---|---|
| Sept. 4 | at Los Angeles Rams | 1:00 |
| Sept. 11 | **New York Giants** | 5:00 |
| Sept. 18 | at Cleveland | 1:00 |
| Sept. 25 | Open Date | |
| Oct. 2 | **Minnesota** | 1:00 |
| Oct. 9 | at Dallas | 3:00 |
| Oct. 16 | at Washington | 1:00 |
| Oct. 23 | **Dallas** | 1:00 |
| Oct. 30 | **Pittsburgh** | 6:00 |
| Nov. 6 | at Philadelphia | 4:00 |
| Nov. 13 | at New York Giants | 1:00 |
| Nov. 20 | **Philadelphia** | 2:00 |
| Nov. 27 | **Chicago** | 2:00 |
| Dec. 4 | at Houston | 3:00 |
| Dec. 11 | **Washington** | 2:00 |
| Dec. 18 | **Cincinnati** | 2:00 |
| Dec. 24 | at Atlanta | 1:00 |

## RECORD HOLDERS

**INDIVIDUAL RECORDS—CAREER**

| Category | Name | Performance |
|---|---|---|
| Rushing (Yds.) | Ottis Anderson, 1979-1986 | 7,999 |
| Passing (Yds.) | Jim Hart, 1966-1983 | 34,639 |
| Passing (TDs) | Jim Hart, 1966-1983 | 209 |
| Receiving (No.) | Roy Green, 1979-1990 | 522 |
| Receiving (Yds.) | Roy Green, 1979-1990 | 8,497 |
| Interceptions | Larry Wilson, 1960-1972 | 52 |
| Punting (Avg.) | Jerry Norton, 1959-1961 | 44.9 |
| Punt Return (Avg.) | Charley Trippi, 1947-1955 | 13.7 |
| Kickoff Return (Avg.) | Ollie Matson, 1952, 1954-58 | 28.5 |
| Field Goals | Jim Bakken, 1962-1978 | 282 |
| Touchdowns (Tot.) | Roy Green, 1979-1990 | 70 |
| Points | Jim Bakken, 1962-1978 | 1,380 |

**INDIVIDUAL RECORDS—SINGLE SEASON**

| Category | Name | Performance |
|---|---|---|
| Rushing (Yds.) | Ottis Anderson, 1979 | 1,605 |
| Passing (Yds.) | Neil Lomax, 1984 | 4,614 |
| Passing (TDs) | Charley Johnson, 1963 | 28 |
| | Neil Lomax, 1984 | 28 |
| Receiving (No.) | J.T. Smith, 1987 | 91 |
| Receiving (Yds.) | Roy Green, 1984 | 1,555 |
| Interceptions | Bob Nussbaumer, 1949 | 12 |
| Punting (Avg.) | Jerry Norton, 1960 | 45.6 |
| Punt Return (Avg.) | John (Red) Cochran, 1949 | 20.9 |
| Kickoff Return (Avg.) | Ollie Matson, 1958 | 35.5 |
| Field Goals | Jim Bakken, 1967 | 27 |
| Touchdowns (Tot.) | John David Crow, 1962 | 17 |
| Points | Jim Bakken, 1967 | 117 |
| | Neil O'Donoghue, 1984 | 117 |

**INDIVIDUAL RECORDS—SINGLE GAME**

| Category | Name | Performance |
|---|---|---|
| Rushing (Yds.) | John David Crow, 12-18-60 | 203 |
| Passing (Yds.) | Neil Lomax, 12-16-84 | 468 |
| Passing (TDs) | Jim Hardy, 10-2-50 | 6 |
| | Charley Johnson, 9-26-65 | 6 |
| | Charley Johnson, 11-2-69 | 6 |
| Receiving (No.) | Sonny Randle, 11-4-62 | 16 |
| Receiving (Yds.) | Sonny Randle, 11-4-62 | 256 |
| Interceptions | Bob Nussbaumer, 11-13-49 | *4 |
| | Jerry Norton, 11-20-60 | *4 |
| Field Goals | Jim Bakken, 9-24-67 | *7 |
| Touchdowns (Tot.) | Ernie Nevers, 11-28-29 | *6 |
| Points | Ernie Nevers, 11-28-29 | *40 |

*NFL Record

## COACHING HISTORY

**Chicago 1920-1959, St. Louis 1960-1987, Phoenix 1988-1993**
**(386-526-39)**

| | | |
|---|---|---|
| 1920-22 | John (Paddy) Driscoll | 17-8-4 |
| 1923-24 | Arnold Horween | 13-8-1 |
| 1925-26 | Norman Barry | 16-8-2 |
| 1927 | Guy Chamberlin | 3-7-1 |
| 1928 | Fred Gillies | 1-5-0 |
| 1929 | Dewey Scanlon | 6-6-1 |
| 1930 | Ernie Nevers | 5-6-2 |
| 1931 | LeRoy Andrews* | 0-1-0 |
| 1931 | Ernie Nevers | 5-3-0 |
| 1932 | Jack Chevigny | 2-6-2 |
| 1933-34 | Paul Schissler | 6-15-1 |
| 1935-38 | Milan Creighton | 16-26-4 |
| 1939 | Ernie Nevers | 1-10-0 |
| 1940-42 | Jimmy Conzelman | 8-22-3 |
| 1943-45 | Phil Handler** | 1-29-0 |
| 1946-48 | Jimmy Conzelman | 27-10-0 |
| 1949 | Phil Handler-Buddy Parker*** | 2-4-0 |
| 1949 | Raymond (Buddy) Parker | 4-1-1 |
| 1950-51 | Earl (Curly) Lambeau**** | 7-15-0 |
| 1951 | Phil Handler-Cecil Isbell# | 1-1-0 |
| 1952 | Joe Kuharich | 4-8-0 |
| 1953-54 | Joe Stydahar | 3-20-1 |
| 1955-57 | Ray Richards | 14-21-1 |
| 1958-61 | Frank (Pop) Ivy## | 17-29-2 |
| 1961 | Chuck Drulis-Ray Prochaska-Ray Willsey### | 2-0-0 |
| 1962-65 | Wally Lemm | 27-26-3 |
| 1966-70 | Charley Winner | 35-30-5 |
| 1971-72 | Bob Hollway | 8-18-2 |
| 1973-77 | Don Coryell | 42-29-1 |
| 1978-79 | Bud Wilkinson#### | 9-20-0 |
| 1979 | Larry Wilson | 2-1-0 |
| 1980-85 | Jim Hanifan | 39-50-1 |
| 1986-89 | Gene Stallings@ | 23-34-1 |
| 1989 | Hank Kuhlmann | 0-5-0 |
| 1990-93 | Joe Bugel | 20-44-0 |

* Resigned after one game in 1931
** Co-coach with Walt Kiesling in Chicago Cardinals-Pittsburgh merger in 1944
*** Co-coaches for first six games in 1949
**** Resigned after 10 games in 1951
\# Co-coaches
\## Resigned after 12 games in 1961
\### Co-coaches
\#### Released after 13 games in 1979
@ Released after 11 games in 1989

**SUN DEVIL STADIUM**

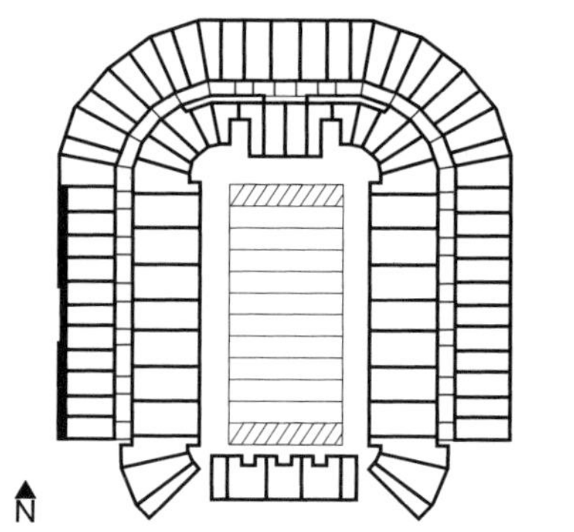

## 1993 TEAM RECORD

**PRESEASON (3-1)**

| Date | Result | | Opponents |
|---|---|---|---|
| 8/7 | W | 24-13 | L.A. Rams |
| 8/14 | W | 11-10 | at Chicago |
| 8/21 | L | 3-10 | at San Diego |
| 8/27 | W | 34-9 | Denver |

**REGULAR SEASON (7-9)**

| Date | Result | | Opponents | Att. |
|---|---|---|---|---|
| 9/5 | L | 17-23 | at Philadelphia | 59,831 |
| 9/12 | W | 17-10 | at Washington | 53,525 |
| 9/19 | L | 10-17 | Dallas | 73,025 |
| 9/26 | L | 20-26 | at Detroit | 57,180 |
| 10/10 | L | 21-23 | New England | 36,115 |
| 10/17 | W | 36-6 | Washington | 48,143 |
| 10/24 | L | 14-28 | at San Francisco | 62,020 |
| 10/31 | L | 17-20 | New Orleans | 36,778 |
| 11/7 | W | 16-3 | Philadelphia | 41,634 |
| 11/14 | L | 15-20 | at Dallas | 64,224 |
| 11/28 | L | 17-19 | at N.Y. Giants | 59,979 |
| 12/5 | W | 38-10 | L.A. Rams | 33,964 |
| 12/12 | L | 14-21 | Detroit | 39,393 |
| 12/19 | W | 30-27 | at Seattle (OT) | 45,737 |
| 12/26 | W | 17-6 | N.Y. Giants | 53,414 |
| 1/2 | W | 27-10 | at Atlanta | 44,360 |

(OT) Overtime

**SCORE BY PERIODS**

| | | | | | | | |
|---|---|---|---|---|---|---|---|
| Cardinals | 54 | 98 | 79 | 92 | 3 | — | 326 |
| Opponents | 58 | 84 | 53 | 74 | 0 | — | 269 |

**ATTENDANCE**

Home 362,466 Away 446,856 Total 809,322
Single-game home record, 71,628 (11-22-92)
Single-season home record, 472,937 (1988)

## 1993 TEAM STATISTICS

| | Cardinals | Opp. |
|---|---|---|
| Total First Downs | 295 | 278 |
| Rushing | 107 | 106 |
| Passing | 173 | 158 |
| Penalty | 15 | 14 |
| Third Down: Made/Att | 102/221 | 76/206 |
| Third Down Pct. | 46.2 | 36.9 |
| Fourth Down: Made/Att | 7/14 | 1/5 |
| Fourth Down Pct. | 50.0 | 20.0 |
| Total Net Yards | 5213 | 5167 |
| Avg. Per Game | 325.8 | 322.9 |
| Total Plays | 1007 | 962 |
| Avg. Per Play | 5.2 | 5.4 |
| Net Yards Rushing | 1809 | 1861 |
| Avg. Per Game | 113.1 | 116.3 |
| Total Rushes | 452 | 433 |
| Net Yards Passing | 3404 | 3306 |
| Avg. Per Game | 212.8 | 206.6 |
| Sacked/Yards Lost | 33/231 | 34/205 |
| Gross Yards | 3635 | 3511 |
| Att./Completions | 522/310 | 495/281 |
| Completion Pct. | 59.4 | 56.8 |
| Had Intercepted | 20 | 9 |
| Punts/Avg. | 73/43.7 | 78/42.7 |
| Net Punting Avg. | 73/37.8 | 78/36.8 |
| Penalties/Yards Lost | 77/644 | 95/730 |
| Fumbles/Ball Lost | 23/11 | 27/17 |
| Touchdowns | 37 | 27 |
| Rushing | 12 | 13 |
| Passing | 21 | 14 |
| Returns | 4 | 0 |
| Avg. Time of Possession | 31:54 | 28:06 |

## 1993 INDIVIDUAL STATISTICS

| PASSING | Att | Cmp | Yds. | Pct. | TD | Int | Tkld. | Rate |
|---|---|---|---|---|---|---|---|---|
| Beuerlein | 418 | 258 | 3164 | 61.7 | 18 | 17 | 29/206 | 82.5 |
| Chandler | 103 | 52 | 471 | 50.5 | 3 | 2 | 4/25 | 64.8 |
| Hearst | 1 | 0 | 0 | 0.0 | 0 | 1 | 0/0 | 0.0 |
| Cardinals | 522 | 310 | 3635 | 59.4 | 21 | 20 | 33/231 | 78.0 |
| Opponents | 495 | 281 | 3511 | 56.8 | 14 | 9 | 34/205 | 80.8 |

| SCORING | TD R | TD P | TD Rt | PAT | FG | Saf | PTS |
|---|---|---|---|---|---|---|---|
| G. Davis | 0 | 0 | 0 | 37/37 | 21/28 | 0 | 100 |
| Moore | 9 | 0 | 0 | 0/0 | 0/0 | 0 | 54 |
| Proehl | 0 | 7 | 0 | 0/0 | 0/0 | 0 | 42 |
| Clark | 0 | 4 | 0 | 0/0 | 0/0 | 0 | 24 |
| R. Hill | 0 | 4 | 0 | 0/0 | 0/0 | 0 | 24 |
| Centers | 0 | 3 | 0 | 0/0 | 0/0 | 0 | 18 |
| Bailey | 1 | 0 | 1 | 0/0 | 0/0 | 0 | 12 |
| Williams | 0 | 0 | 2 | 0/0 | 0/0 | 0 | 12 |
| Blount | 1 | 0 | 0 | 0/0 | 0/0 | 0 | 6 |
| Edwards | 0 | 1 | 0 | 0/0 | 0/0 | 0 | 6 |
| Hearst | 1 | 0 | 0 | 0/0 | 0/0 | 0 | 6 |
| Lynch | 0 | 0 | 1 | 0/0 | 0/0 | 0 | 6 |
| Reeves | 0 | 1 | 0 | 0/0 | 0/0 | 0 | 6 |
| Rolle | 0 | 1 | 0 | 0/0 | 0/0 | 0 | 6 |
| Swann | 0 | 0 | 0 | 0/0 | 0/0 | 1 | 2 |
| Cardinals | 12 | 21 | 4 | 37/37 | 21/28 | 2 | 326 |
| Opponents | 13 | 14 | 0 | 27/27 | 26/35 | 1 | 269 |

| RUSHING | Att. | Yds. | Avg. | LG | TD |
|---|---|---|---|---|---|
| Moore | 263 | 1018 | 3.9 | 20 | 9 |
| Hearst | 76 | 264 | 3.5 | 57 | 1 |
| Bailey | 49 | 253 | 5.2 | 31 | 1 |
| Centers | 25 | 152 | 6.1 | 33 | 0 |
| Proehl | 8 | 47 | 5.9 | 17 | 0 |
| Beuerlein | 22 | 45 | 2.0 | 20 | 0 |
| Blount | 5 | 28 | 5.6 | 7 | 1 |
| Chandler | 3 | 2 | 0.7 | 1 | 0 |
| Camarillo | 1 | 0 | 0.0 | 0 | 0 |
| Cardinals | 452 | 1809 | 4.0 | 57 | 12 |
| Opponents | 433 | 1861 | 4.3 | 48 | 13 |

| RECEIVING | No. | Yds. | Avg. | LG | TD |
|---|---|---|---|---|---|
| Centers | 66 | 603 | 9.1 | 29 | 3 |
| Proehl | 65 | 877 | 13.5 | 51t | 7 |
| Clark | 63 | 818 | 13.0 | 55 | 4 |
| R. Hill | 35 | 519 | 14.8 | 58t | 4 |
| Bailey | 32 | 243 | 7.6 | 30 | 0 |
| Edwards | 13 | 326 | 25.1 | 65t | 1 |
| Rolle | 10 | 67 | 6.7 | 22 | 1 |
| Reeves | 9 | 67 | 7.4 | 18 | 1 |
| Hearst | 6 | 18 | 3.0 | 9 | 0 |
| Blount | 5 | 36 | 7.2 | 9 | 0 |
| Ware | 3 | 45 | 15.0 | 27 | 0 |
| Moore | 3 | 16 | 5.3 | 6 | 0 |
| Cardinals | 310 | 3635 | 11.7 | 65t | 21 |
| Opponents | 281 | 3511 | 12.5 | 86 | 14 |

| INTERCEPTIONS | No. | Yds. | Avg. | LG | TD |
|---|---|---|---|---|---|
| Lynch | 3 | 13 | 4.3 | 13 | 0 |
| Williams | 2 | 87 | 43.5 | 46t | 1 |
| Booty | 2 | 24 | 12.0 | 19 | 0 |
| Oldham | 1 | 0 | 0.0 | 0 | 0 |
| Zordich | 1 | 0 | 0.0 | 0 | 0 |
| Cardinals | 9 | 124 | 13.8 | 46t | 1 |
| Opponents | 20 | 143 | 7.2 | 37 | 0 |

| PUNTING | No. | Yds. | Avg. | In 20 | LG |
|---|---|---|---|---|---|
| Camarillo | 73 | 3189 | 43.7 | 23 | 61 |
| Cardinals | 73 | 3189 | 43.7 | 23 | 61 |
| Opponents | 78 | 3333 | 42.7 | 23 | 62 |

| PUNT RETURNS | No. | FC | Yds. | Avg. | LG | TD |
|---|---|---|---|---|---|---|
| Bailey | 35 | 5 | 282 | 8.1 | 58t | 1 |
| Blount | 9 | 3 | 90 | 10.0 | 25 | 0 |
| Edwards | 3 | 3 | 12 | 4.0 | 11 | 0 |
| Cardinals | 47 | 11 | 384 | 8.2 | 58t | 1 |
| Opponents | 30 | 19 | 267 | 8.9 | 33 | 0 |

| KICKOFF RETURNS | No. | Yds. | Avg. | LG | TD |
|---|---|---|---|---|---|
| Bailey | 31 | 699 | 22.5 | 48 | 0 |
| Blount | 8 | 163 | 20.4 | 27 | 0 |
| Edwards | 3 | 51 | 17.0 | 20 | 0 |
| Lofton | 1 | 18 | 18.0 | 18 | 0 |
| Moore | 1 | 9 | 9.0 | 9 | 0 |
| Smith | 1 | 11 | 11.0 | 11 | 0 |
| Cardinals | 45 | 951 | 21.1 | 48 | 0 |
| Opponents | 51 | 994 | 19.5 | 61 | 0 |

| SACKS | No. |
|---|---|
| Harvey | 9.5 |
| Nunn | 6.5 |
| Swann | 3.5 |
| Bankston | 3.0 |
| Booty | 3.0 |
| M. Jones | 3.0 |
| Stowe | 1.5 |
| R. Davis | 1.0 |
| E. Hill | 1.0 |
| Lynch | 1.0 |
| Oldham | 1.0 |
| Cardinals | 34.0 |
| Opponents | 33.0 |

## 1994 DRAFT CHOICES

| Round | Name | Pos. | College |
|---|---|---|---|
| 1 | Jamir Miller | LB | UCLA |
| 2 | Chuck Levy | RB | Arizona |
| 3 | Rich Braham | G | West Virginia |
| | Eric England | DE | Texas A&M |
| 4 | Perry Carter | DB | Southern Mississippi |
| | John Reece | DB | Nebraska |
| | Terry Irving | LB | McNeese State |
| 5 | Anthony Redmon | G | Auburn |
| 6 | Terry Samuels | TE | Kentucky |
| 7 | Frank Harvey | RB | Georgia |

## ARIZONA CARDINALS

### 1994 VETERAN ROSTER

| No. | | Name | Pos. | Ht. | Wt. | Birthdate | NFL Exp. | College | Hometown | How Acq. | '93 Games/ Starts |
|---|---|---|---|---|---|---|---|---|---|---|---|
| 63 | | Bankston, Michael | DE-DT | 6-2 | 290 | 3/12/70 | 3 | Sam Houston State | East Bernard, Tex. | D4b-'92 | 16/12 |
| 7 | | Beuerlein, Steve | QB | 6-2 | 209 | 3/7/65 | 8 | Notre Dame | Hollywood, Calif. | UFA(Dall)-'93 | 16/14 |
| 25 | | Blount, Eric | RB-KR | 5-9 | 190 | 9/22/70 | 3 | North Carolina | Ayden, N.C. | D8-'92 | 6/0 |
| 42 | | Booty, John | S | 6-0 | 180 | 10/9/65 | 7 | Texas Christian | Carthage, Tex. | UFA(Phil)-'93 | 12/12 |
| 54 | # | Braxton, David | LB | 6-2 | 230 | 5/26/65 | 6 | Wake Forest | Jacksonville, N.C. | FA-'90 | 16/0 |
| 78 | | Brown, Chad | DE | 6-7 | 265 | 7/9/71 | 2 | Mississippi | Thomasville, Ga. | D8a-'93 | 5/0 |
| 26 | | Cecil, Chuck | S | 6-0 | 190 | 11/8/64 | 7 | Arizona | San Diego, Calif. | UFA(GB)-'93 | 15/7 |
| 37 | | Centers, Larry | RB | 6-0 | 200 | 6/1/68 | 5 | Stephen F. Austin | Tatum, Tex. | D5-'90 | 16/9 |
| 84 | | Clark, Gary | WR | 5-9 | 173 | 5/1/62 | 10 | James Madison | Dublin, Va. | UFA(Wash)-'93 | 14/10 |
| 62 | | Coleman, Ben | G | 6-6 | 335 | 5/18/71 | 2 | Wake Forest | South Hill, Va. | D2-'93 | 12/0 |
| 59 | | Cunningham, Ed | C | 6-3 | 290 | 8/17/69 | 3 | Washington | Alexandria, Va. | D3-'92 | 15/15 |
| 64 | | Cunningham, Rick | T | 6-6 | 307 | 1/4/67 | 4 | Texas A&M | Los Angeles, Calif. | FA-'92 | 16/16 |
| 5 | | Davis, Greg | K | 6-0 | 200 | 10/29/65 | 7 | Citadel | Atlanta, Ga. | PB(Atl)-'91 | 16/0 |
| 65 | | Dye, Ernest | G | 6-6 | 325 | 7/15/71 | 2 | South Carolina | Greenwood, S.C. | D1b-'93 | 7/1 |
| 83 | | Edwards, Anthony | WR | 5-9 | 190 | 5/26/66 | 6 | New Mexico Highlands | Casa Grande, Ariz. | FA-'91 | 16/0 |
| 80 | | Fann, Chad | TE | 6-3 | 250 | 6/7/70 | 2 | Florida A&M | Jacksonville, Fla. | FA-'93 | 1/0 |
| 10 | | Feagles, Jeff | P | 6-1 | 205 | 3/7/66 | 7 | Miami | Scottsdale, Ariz. | UFA(Phil)-'94 | 16/0* |
| 2 | | Furrer, Will | QB | 6-3 | 210 | 2/5/68 | 3 | Virginia Tech | Pullman, Wash. | W(Chi)-'93 | 0* |
| 31 | # | Harris, Odie | S | 6-0 | 190 | 4/1/66 | 7 | Sam Houston State | Bryan, Tex. | W(Clev)-'92 | 16/0 |
| 23 | | Hearst, Garrison | RB | 5-11 | 215 | 1/4/71 | 2 | Georgia | Lincolnton, Ga. | D1a-'93 | 6/5 |
| 58 | | Hill, Eric | LB | 6-2 | 250 | 11/14/66 | 6 | Louisiana State | Galveston, Tex. | D1-'89 | 13/12 |
| 81 | † | Hill, Randal | WR | 5-10 | 177 | 9/21/69 | 4 | Miami | Miami, Fla. | T(Mia)-'91 | 16/8 |
| 97 | | Hyche, Steve | LB | 6-2 | 226 | 6/12/63 | 5 | Livingston | Cordova, Ala. | FA-'91 | 2/0 |
| 53 | # | Jax, Garth | LB | 6-3 | 240 | 9/16/63 | 9 | Florida State | Houston, Tex. | PB(Dall)-'89 | 16/0 |
| 72 | | Johnson, Chuckie | DT | 6-4 | 310 | 3/5/69 | 2 | Auburn | Fayetteville, N.C. | FA-'93 | 5/0 |
| 75 | † | Jones, Mike | DE-DT | 6-4 | 285 | 8/25/69 | 4 | North Carolina State | Columbia, S.C. | D2-'91 | 16/2 |
| 59 | | Joyner, Seth | LB | 6-2 | 235 | 11/18/64 | 9 | Texas-El Paso | Spring Valley, N.Y. | UFA(Phil)-'94 | 16/16* |
| 57 | | Kirk, Randy | LB | 6-2 | 231 | 12/27/64 | 7 | San Diego State | San Diego, Calif. | UFA(Cin)-'94 | 16/0* |
| 28 | | Lofton, Steve | CB | 5-9 | 180 | 11/26/68 | 4 | Texas A&M | Jacksonville, Miss. | FA-'91 | 13/0 |
| 29 | # | Lynch, Lorenzo | CB | 5-10 | 200 | 4/6/63 | 8 | Cal State-Sacramento | Oakland, Calif. | PB(Chi)-'90 | 16/15 |
| 9 | | McMahon, Jim | QB | 6-1 | 195 | 8/21/59 | 13 | Brigham Young | Jersey City, N.J. | FA-'94 | 12/12* |
| 94 | | Merritt, David | LB | 6-1 | 237 | 9/8/71 | 2 | North Carolina State | Raleigh, N.C. | FA-'93 | 3/0 |
| 30 | | Moore, Ron | RB | 5-10 | 220 | 11/26/70 | 2 | Pittsburg State | Spencer, Okla. | D4-'93 | 16/11 |
| 27 | † | Oldham, Chris | CB | 5-9 | 183 | 10/28/68 | 4 | Oregon | Sacramento, Calif. | FA-'92 | 16/6 |
| 87 | | Proehl, Ricky | WR | 6-0 | 190 | 3/7/68 | 5 | Wake Forest | Hillsborough, N.J. | D3-'90 | 16/16 |
| 79 | | Rucker, Keith | DE-DT | 6-3 | 325 | 11/20/68 | 3 | Ohio Wesleyan | University Park, Ill. | FA-'92 | 16/15 |
| 67 | | Sharpe, Luis | T | 6-5 | 295 | 6/16/60 | 13 | UCLA | Detroit, Mich. | D1-'82 | 16/16 |
| 96 | | Simmons, Clyde | DE | 6-6 | 280 | 6/16/60 | 9 | Western Carolina | Wilmington, N.C. | UFA(Phil)-'94 | 16/16* |
| 90 | | Stowe, Tyronne | LB | 6-1 | 249 | 5/30/65 | 8 | Rutgers | Passaic, N.J. | PB(Pitt)-'91 | 15/15 |
| 98 | | Swann, Eric | DE-DT | 6-4 | 310 | 8/16/70 | 4 | No College | Swann Station, N.C. | D1-'91 | 9/9 |
| 71 | | Tucker, Mark | C | 6-3 | 290 | 4/29/68 | 2 | Southern California | Los Angeles, Calif. | FA-'93 | 0* |
| 52 | | Wallerstedt, Brett | LB | 6-1 | 240 | 11/24/70 | 2 | Arizona State | Manhattan, Kan. | D6-'93 | 7/0 |
| 85 | | Ware, Derek | RB-TE | 6-2 | 255 | 9/17/67 | 3 | Central State, Ohio | Sacramento, Calif. | D7-'92 | 16/1 |
| 35 | † | Williams, Aeneas | CB | 5-10 | 187 | 1/29/69 | 4 | Southern | New Orleans, La. | D3-'91 | 16/16 |
| 21 | t- | Williams, James | CB | 5-10 | 185 | 3/30/67 | 5 | Fresno State | Coalinga, Calif. | T(Buff)-'94 | 15/11* |
| 68 | | Wolf, Joe | G | 6-6 | 295 | 12/28/66 | 6 | Boston College | Allentown, Pa. | D1b-'89 | 8/5 |
| 38 | # | Zordich, Michael | S | 6-1 | 200 | 10/12/63 | 8 | Penn State | Youngstown, Ohio | PB(NYJ)-'89 | 16/9 |

* Feagles played 16 games with Philadelphia in '93; Furrer active for 1 game but did not play; Joyner played 16 games with Philadelphia; Kirk played 16 games with Cincinnati; McMahon played 12 games with Minnesota; Simmons played 16 games with Philadelphia; Tucker active for 4 games but did not play; Williams played 15 games with Buffalo.

# Unrestricted free agent; subject to developments.

† Restricted free agent; subject to developments.

t- Cardinals traded for J. Williams (Buffalo).

Players lost through free agency (7): P Rich Camarillo (Hou; 16 games in '93), QB Chris Chandler (Rams; 4), DE Reuben Davis (SD; 16), LB Ken Harvey (Wash; 16), CB Robert Massey (Det; 10), TE Walter Reeves (Clev; 16), G Lance Smith (NYG; 16).

Also played with Cardinals in '93—RB Johnny Bailey (13 games), TE Pat Beach (15), CB Dexter Davis (6), S Dave Duerson (16), LB Jock Jones (7), C Kani Kauahi (1), G Mark May (11), LB Freddie Joe Nunn (16), TE Butch Rolle (16).

## COACHING STAFF

**Head Coach,**
**Buddy Ryan**

**Pro Career:** Named head coach and general manager on February 3, 1994. Became thirty-second head coach in the history of the franchise dating back to 1920. Known as one of the game's top defensive minds, he devised the "46 defense" with its multiple variations of alignments and coverages. Served as defensive coordinator for Houston Oilers' in 1993. Defense set a club record with 52 quarterback sacks and ranked first in the league in both rushing defense (79.6 yards per game) and interceptions (26). Posted 43-35-1 record as head coach for Philadelphia Eagles from 1986-1990, a span which included consecutive playoff berths his final three seasons with records of 10-6, 11-5, and 10-6, highlighted by the NFC East title in 1988, the Eagles' first divisional crown since 1980. Defensive coordinator of the Chicago Bears from 1978-1985 as the Bears' defense set an NFL record with 72 quarterback sacks in 1984, then a year later led the league in nine defensive categories. In Chicago's Super Bowl XX victory over New England, Chicago held the Patriots to a Super Bowl record fewest first downs (7) and fewest rushing first downs (1), while allowing just 123 total yards. En route to the Super Bowl, Chicago posted playoff shutouts against the Los Angeles Rams and New York Giants, an unprecedented accomplishment in NFL postseason annals. Served as defensive line coach for Bud Grant's Minnesota Vikings in 1976-77 as the "Purple People Eaters" line of Carl Eller, Alan Page, and Jim Marshall helped the Vikings reach Super Bowl XI. Ryan was a member of the New York Jets defensive staff from 1968-1975 under Hall of Fame coach Weeb Ewbank, when Jets upset heavily-favored Baltimore Colts in Super Bowl III. Career record: 43-35-1.

**Background:** Ryan was a four-year letterman at Oklahoma State from 1952-55 as a guard. While serving in the U.S. Army in Korea, Ryan played on the Fourth Army championship team in Japan. He began his coaching career at the high school level in Texas at Gainesville (1957-59) and Marshall (1960), then was a college assistant at Buffalo (1961-65), Vanderbilt (1966), and Pacific (1967). Has a master's degree in education from Middle Tennessee State.

**Personal:** Born February 17, 1934, in Frederick, Oklahoma. Buddy and his wife, Joan, live in Phoenix and have three sons—twins Rex and Rob, and Jim.

### ASSISTANT COACHES

**David Atkins,** offensive coordinator-running backs; born May 18, 1949, Victoria, Tex., lives in Phoenix. Running back Texas-El Paso 1970-72. Pro running back San Francisco 49ers 1973, Honolulu (WFL) 1974, San Diego Chargers 1975. College coach: Texas-El Paso 1979-80, San Diego State 1981-85. Pro coach: Philadelphia Eagles 1986-92, New England Patriots 1993, joined Cardinals in 1994.

**Matt Cavanaugh,** quarterbacks; born October 27, 1956, Youngstown, Ohio, lives in Phoenix. Quarterback Pittsburgh 1974-77. Pro quarterback New England Patriots 1978-82, San Francisco 49ers 1983-85, Philadelphia Eagles 1986-89, New York Giants 1990-91. College coach: Pittsburgh 1993. Pro coach: Joined Cardinals in 1994.

**Ted Cottrell,** linebackers; born June 13, 1947, Chester, Pa., lives in Phoenix. Linebacker Delaware Valley College 1966-68. Pro linebacker Atlanta Falcons 1969-70, Winnipeg Blue Bombers (CFL) 1971. College coach: Rutgers 1973-80, 1983. Pro coach: Kansas City Chiefs 1981-82, New Jersey Generals (USFL) 1983-84, Buffalo Bills 1986-89, joined Cardinals in 1990.

**Ronnie Jones,** defensive coordinator; born October 17, 1955, Dumas, Tex., lives in Phoenix. Running back Northwestern Oklahoma, State 1974-77. No pro playing experience. College coach: Northeastern Oklahoma State 1979-83, Tulsa 1984, Arizona State 1985-86. Pro coach: Philadelphia Eagles 1987-90, Los Angeles Rams 1991, Los Angeles Raiders 1992, Houston Oilers 1993, joined Cardinals in 1994.

**George Martinez,** quality control; born August 5, 1961, Fort Bragg, N.C., lives in Phoenix. Quarterback Northwestern Oklahoma State 1969-72. No pro playing experience. College coach: East Central Oklahoma 1981-87, Panhandle State 1988, New Mexico Highlands 1989-91 (head coach). Pro coach: Joined Cardinals in 1994.

**Guy Morriss,** offensive line assistant; born May 13, 1951, Colorado City, Tex., lives in Phoenix. Guard Texas Christian 1969-72. Pro guard Philadelphia Eagles 1973-83, New England Patriots 1984-87. College coach: Valdosta State 1992-93. Pro coach: New England Patriots 1988-89, joined Cardinals in 1994.

**Dan Neal,** offensive line; born August 30, 1949, Corbin, Ky., lives in Phoenix. Center Kentucky 1970-72. Pro center Baltimore Colts 1973-74, Chicago Bears 1975-83. Pro coach: Philadelphia Eagles 1986-91, joined Cardinals in 1994.

**Ted Plumb,** receivers-tight ends; born August 20, 1939, Reno, Nev., lives in Phoenix. Wide receiver Baylor 1960-61. Pro wide receiver Buffalo Bills 1962. College coach: Cerritos, Calif., J.C. 1966-67, Texas Christian 1968-70, Tulsa 1971, Kansas 1972-73. Pro coach: New York Giants 1974-76, Atlanta Falcons 1977-79, Chicago Bears 1980-85, Philadelphia Eagles 1986-89, joined Cardinals in 1990.

**Al Roberts,** special teams; born January 6, 1944, Fresno, Calif., lives in Phoenix. Running back Washington 1964-65, Puget Sound 1967-68. No pro playing experience. College coach: Washington 1977-82, Purdue 1986, Wyoming 1987. Pro coach: Los Angeles Express (USFL) 1983-84, Houston Oilers 1984-85, Philadelphia Eagles 1988-90, New York Jets 1991-93, joined Cardinals in 1994.

**Bob Rogucki,** strength and conditioning; born September 27, 1953, Clarksburg, W. Va., lives in Phoenix. No college or pro playing experience. College coach: Penn State 1981, Weber State 1982, Army 1983-89. Pro coach: Joined Cardinals in 1990.

**Rex Ryan,** defensive line; born December 13, 1962, Ardmore, Okla., lives in Phoenix. Defensive end Southwest Oklahoma State 1983-86. No pro playing experience. College coach: Eastern Kentucky 1987-88, New Mexico Highlands 1989, Morehead State 1990-93. Pro coach: Joined Cardinals in 1994.

**Robert Ryan,** defensive backs; born December 13, 1962, Ardmore, Okla., lives in Phoenix. Defensive end-linebacker Southwest Oklahoma State 1983-86. No pro playing experience. College coach: Western Kentucky 1987, Ohio State 1988, Tennessee State 1989-93. Pro coach: Joined Cardinals in 1994.

## 1994 FIRST-YEAR ROSTER

| Name | Pos. | Ht. | Wt. | Birthdate | College | Hometown | How Acq. |
|---|---|---|---|---|---|---|---|
| Alexander, Brent | S | 5-10 | 184 | 7/10/71 | Tennessee State | Gallatin, Tenn. | FA |
| Braham, Rich | G | 6-4 | 290 | 11/6/70 | West Virginia | Morgantown, W. Va. | D3a |
| Bruere, Carl | WR | 6-2 | 185 | 11/14/68 | New Mexico Highlands | Albuquerque, N.M. | FA |
| Carter, Perry | CB | 5-11 | 194 | 8/15/71 | Southern Mississippi | McComb, Miss. | D4a |
| Ciaccio, Tom | QB | 6-1 | 190 | 8/28/69 | Holy Cross | Gloversville, N.Y. | FA |
| England, Eric | DE | 6-2 | 283 | 3/25/71 | Texas A&M | Sugar Land, Tex. | D3b |
| Faulkner, Greg | T | 6-4 | 305 | 4/29/72 | Millersville, Pa. | Royersford, Pa. | FA |
| Gardner, Gerome | DT | 6-0 | 260 | 3/31/72 | Tennessee State | Columbus, Ga. | FA |
| Harvey, Frank | RB | 6-0 | 245 | 1/19/71 | Georgia | Dawson, Ga. | D7 |
| Henesey, Brian | RB | 5-10 | 215 | 12/10/69 | Bucknell | Radnor, Pa. | FA |
| Irving, Terry | LB | 6-0 | 224 | 7/3/71 | McNeese State | Galveston, Tex. | D4c |
| Jenkins, Lennie | DT | 6-2 | 257 | 10/4/71 | Northeast Louisiana | Media, Pa. | FA |
| Kurinsky, York | T | 6-3 | 286 | 11/11/71 | Valdosta State | St. Charles, Ill. | FA |
| Levy, Chuck | QB-RB | 6-0 | 197 | 1/7/72 | Arizona | Torrance, Calif. | D2 |
| Lopez, Kenny | DE | 6-2 | 275 | 1/10/70 | Miami | Key West, Fla. | FA |
| McLeod, David | WR | 5-11 | 172 | 8/15/71 | James Madison | Richmond, Va. | FA |
| Miller, Jamir | LB | 6-4 | 242 | 11/19/73 | UCLA | Oakland, Calif. | D1 |
| Moody, Mike (1) | T | 6-5 | 285 | 5/9/69 | Southern California | San Francisco, Calif. | FA |
| Owens, Anthony (1) | WR | 6-0 | 194 | 3/8/69 | Tennessee State | Nashville, Tenn. | FA |
| Pinckney, Jon (1) | WR | 6-0 | 189 | 5/6/69 | Stanford | Bethlehem, Pa. | FA |
| Redmon, Anthony | G | 6-4 | 308 | 4/6/71 | Auburn | Brewton, Ala. | D5 |
| Reece, John | CB | 6-0 | 203 | 1/24/71 | Nebraska | Crowell, Tex. | D4b |
| Reeves, Bryan | WR | 5-11 | 195 | 7/10/70 | Nevada | Los Angeles, Calif. | FA |
| Richardson, Mose | CB | 6-2 | 180 | 11/22/71 | Indiana | Dayton, Ohio | FA |
| Samuels, Terry | TE | 6-2 | 254 | 9/27/70 | Kentucky | Louisville, Ky. | D6 |
| Shadwick, Richard | DE | 6-4 | 255 | 7/20/70 | Morehead State | Nicholasville, Ky. | FA |
| Tate, Will | WR | 5-10 | 170 | 2/5/71 | San Diego State | San Diego, Calif. | FA |
| Wallace, Sean | S | 5-8 | 185 | 11/13/72 | Southern | New Orleans, La. | FA |

The term NFL Rookie is defined as a player who is in his first season of professional football and has not been on the roster of another professional football team for any regular-season or postseason games. A Rookie is designated by an "R" on NFL rosters. Players who have been active in another professional football league or players who have NFL experience, including either preseason training camp or being on an Active List or Inactive List, or on Reserve/Injured or Reserve/Physically Unable to Perform for fewer than six regular-season games, are termed NFL First-Year Players. An NFL First-Year Player is designated by a "1" on NFL rosters. Thereafter, a player is credited with an additional year of experience for each season in which he accumulates six games on the Active List or Inactive List, or on Reserve/Injured or Reserve/Physically Unable to Perform.

## NOTES

# ATLANTA FALCONS

**National Football Conference**
**Western Division**
**Team Colors:** Black, Red, Silver, and White
**2745 Burnette Road**
**Suwanee, Georgia 30174**
**Telephone: (404) 945-1111**

## CLUB OFFICIALS

Chairman of the Board: Rankin M. Smith, Sr.
President: Taylor Smith
Vice President & Chief Financial Officer: Jim Hay
Vice President of Player Personnel: Ken Herock
Director of Player Development: Tommy Nobis
Director of Public Relations: Charlie Taylor
Director of Administration: Rob Jackson
Asst. Director of Public Relations: Frank Kleha
Public Relations Assistant: Gary Glenn
Marketing Reps: Todd Marble, John Knox
Director of Community Relations: Carol Breeding
Director of Ticket Operations: Jack Ragsdale
Asst. Director of Ticket Operations: Mike Jennings
Administrative Asst./Finance: Kevin Anthony
Administrative Asst./Player Personnel: Danny Mock
Scouts: Bill Baker, Scott Campbell, Dick Corrick, Elbert Dubenion, Bill Groman
Director of Pro Personnel: Chuck Connor
Controller: Wallace Norman
Trainer: Ron Medlin
Assistant Trainer: Arnold Gamber
Equipment Manager: Whitey Zimmerman
Assistant Equipment Manager: Horace Daniel
Equipment Assistant: Craig Campanozzi
Video Director: Tom Atcheson
Assistant Video Director: Lou Crocker
**Stadium:** Georgia Dome • **Capacity:** 71,594
One Georgia Dome Drive
Atlanta, Georgia 30313
**Playing Surface:** Artificial turf
**Training Camp:** 2745 Burnette Road
Suwanee, Georgia 30174

## 1994 SCHEDULE

**PRESEASON**

| | | |
|---|---|---|
| July 30 | vs. San Diego at Canton, Ohio | 12:00 |
| Aug. 6 | at Denver | 7:00 |
| Aug. 12 | **Buffalo** | 7:00 |
| Aug. 19 | at Cleveland | 7:30 |
| Aug. 26 | **Philadelphia** | 7:00 |

**REGULAR SEASON**

| | | |
|---|---|---|
| Sept. 4 | at Detroit | 1:00 |
| Sept. 11 | **Los Angeles Rams** | 1:00 |
| Sept. 18 | **Kansas City** | 8:00 |
| Sept. 25 | at Washington | 1:00 |
| Oct. 2 | at Los Angeles Rams | 1:00 |
| Oct. 9 | **Tampa Bay** | 1:00 |
| Oct. 16 | **San Francisco** | 1:00 |
| Oct. 23 | at Los Angeles Raiders | 1:00 |
| Oct. 30 | Open Date | |
| Nov. 6 | **San Diego** | 1:00 |
| Nov. 13 | at New Orleans | 12:00 |
| Nov. 20 | at Denver | 2:00 |
| Nov. 27 | **Philadelphia** | 1:00 |
| Dec. 4 | at San Francisco | 1:00 |
| Dec. 11 | **New Orleans** | 8:00 |
| Dec. 18 | vs. Green Bay at Milwaukee | 12:00 |
| Dec. 24 | **Arizona** | 1:00 |

## RECORD HOLDERS

**INDIVIDUAL RECORDS—CAREER**

| Category | Name | Performance |
|---|---|---|
| Rushing (Yds.) | Gerald Riggs, 1982-88 | 6,631 |
| Passing (Yds.) | Steve Bartkowski, 1975-1985 | 23,468 |
| Passing (TDs) | Steve Bartkowski, 1975-1985 | 154 |
| Receiving (No.) | Alfred Jenkins, 1975-1983 | 359 |
| Receiving (Yds.) | Alfred Jenkins, 1975-1983 | 6,257 |
| Interceptions | Rolland Lawrence, 1973-1980 | 39 |
| Punting (Avg.) | Rick Donnelly, 1985-89 | 42.6 |
| Punt Return (Avg.) | Al Dodd, 1973-74 | 11.8 |
| Kickoff Return (Avg.) | Ron Smith, 1966-67 | 24.3 |
| Field Goals | Mick Luckhurst, 1981-87 | 115 |
| Touchdowns (Tot.) | Gerald Riggs, 1982-88 | 48 |
| | Andre Rison, 1990-93 | 48 |
| Points | Mick Luckhurst, 1981-87 | 558 |

**INDIVIDUAL RECORDS—SINGLE SEASON**

| Category | Name | Performance |
|---|---|---|
| Rushing (Yds.) | Gerald Riggs, 1985 | 1,719 |
| Passing (Yds.) | Steve Bartkowski, 1981 | 3,830 |
| Passing (TDs) | Steve Bartkowski, 1980 | 31 |
| Receiving (No.) | Andre Rison, 1992 | 93 |
| Receiving (Yds.) | Alfred Jenkins, 1981 | 1,358 |
| Interceptions | Scott Case, 1988 | 10 |
| Punting (Avg.) | Billy Lothridge, 1968 | 44.3 |
| Punt Return (Avg.) | Gerald Tinker, 1974 | 13.9 |
| Kickoff Return (Avg.) | Sylvester Stamps, 1987 | 27.5 |
| Field Goals | Nick Mike-Mayer, 1973 | 26 |
| | Norm Johnson, 1993 | 26 |
| Touchdowns (Tot.) | Andre Rison, 1993 | 15 |
| Points | Mick Luckhurst, 1981 | 114 |

**INDIVIDUAL RECORDS—SINGLE GAME**

| Category | Name | Performance |
|---|---|---|
| Rushing (Yds.) | Gerald Riggs, 9-2-84 | 202 |
| Passing (Yds.) | Steve Bartkowski, 11-15-81 | 416 |
| Passing (TDs) | Wade Wilson, 12-13-92 | 5 |
| Receiving (No.) | William Andrews, 11-15-81 | 15 |
| Receiving (Yds.) | Alfred Jackson, 12-2-84 | 193 |
| Interceptions | Many times | 2 |
| | Last time by Deion Sanders, 12-11-93 | |
| Field Goals | Nick Mike-Mayer, 11-4-73 | 5 |
| | Tim Mazzetti, 10-30-78 | 5 |
| Touchdowns (Tot.) | Many times | 3 |
| | Last time by Andre Rison, 9-19-93 | |
| Points | Many times | 18 |
| | Last time by Andre Rison, 9-19-93 | |

## COACHING HISTORY

**(158-259-5)**

| | | |
|---|---|---|
| 1966-68 | Norb Hecker* | 4-26-1 |
| 1968-74 | Norm Van Brocklin** | 37-49-3 |
| 1974-76 | Marion Campbell*** | 6-19-0 |
| 1976 | Pat Peppler | 3-6-0 |
| 1977-82 | Leeman Bennett | 47-44-0 |
| 1983-86 | Dan Henning | 22-41-1 |
| 1987-89 | Marion Campbell**** | 11-32-0 |
| 1989 | Jim Hanifan | 0-4-0 |
| 1990-93 | Jerry Glanville | 28-38-0 |

*Released after three games in 1968
**Released after eight games in 1974
***Released after five games in 1976
****Retired after 12 games in 1989

**GEORGIA DOME**

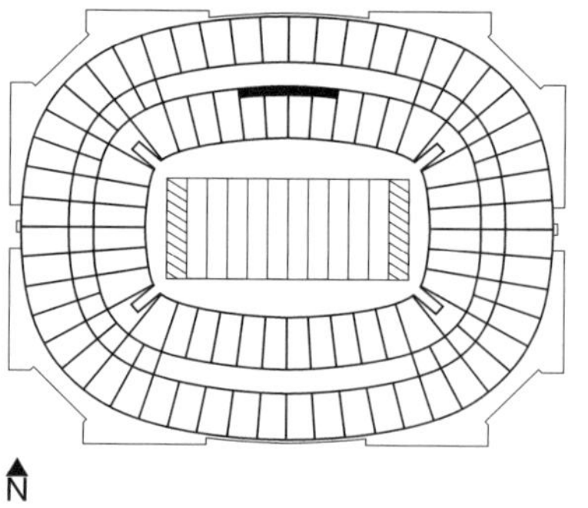

## 1993 TEAM RECORD

**PRESEASON (1-3)**

| Date | Result | | Opponents |
|---|---|---|---|
| 8/6 | L | 27-28 | Miami |
| 8/14 | W | 20-10 | Tampa Bay |
| 8/21 | L | 20-37 | at Philadelphia |
| 8/27 | L | 16-17 | at Buffalo |

**REGULAR SEASON (6-10)**

| Date | Result | | Opponents | Att. |
|---|---|---|---|---|
| 9/5 | L | 13-30 | at Detroit | 56,216 |
| 9/12 | L | 31-34 | New Orleans | 64,287 |
| 9/19 | L | 30-37 | at San Francisco | 63,032 |
| 9/27 | L | 17-45 | Pittsburgh | 65,477 |
| 10/3 | L | 0-6 | at Chicago | 57,441 |
| 10/14 | W | 30-24 | L.A. Rams | 45,231 |
| 10/24 | W | 26-15 | at New Orleans | 69,043 |
| 10/31 | L | 24-31 | Tampa Bay | 50,647 |
| 11/14 | W | 13-0 | at L.A. Rams | 37,073 |
| 11/21 | W | 27-14 | Dallas | 67,337 |
| 11/28 | W | 17-14 | Cleveland | 54,510 |
| 12/5 | L | 17-33 | at Houston | 58,186 |
| 12/11 | W | 27-24 | San Francisco | 64,688 |
| 12/19 | L | 17-30 | at Washington | 50,192 |
| 12/26 | L | 17-21 | at Cincinnati | 27,014 |
| 1/2 | L | 10-27 | Phoenix | 44,360 |

**SCORE BY PERIODS**

| | | | | | | | |
|---|---|---|---|---|---|---|---|
| Falcons | 60 | 77 | 68 | 111 | 0 | — | 316 |
| Opponents | 78 | 116 | 100 | 91 | 0 | — | 385 |

**ATTENDANCE**

Home 456,537 Away 418,197 Total 874,734

Single-game home record, 69,898 (11-9-92)

Single-season home record, 553,979 (1992)

## 1993 TEAM STATISTICS

| | Falcons | Opp. |
|---|---|---|
| Total First Downs | 292 | 278 |
| Rushing | 91 | 79 |
| Passing | 185 | 180 |
| Penalty | 16 | 19 |
| Third Down: Made/Att. | 80/209 | 73/200 |
| Third Down: Pct | 38.3 | 36.5 |
| Fourth Down: Made/Att. | 10/18 | 7/16 |
| Fourth Down: Pct | 55.6 | 43.8 |
| Total Net Yards | 5110 | 5421 |
| Avg. Per Game | 319.4 | 338.8 |
| Total Plays | 1008 | 951 |
| Avg. Per Play | 5.1 | 5.7 |
| Net Yards Rushing | 1590 | 1784 |
| Avg. Per Game | 99.4 | 111.5 |
| Total Rushes | 395 | 419 |
| Net Yards Passing | 3520 | 3637 |
| Avg. Per Game | 220.0 | 227.3 |
| Sacked/Yards Lost | 40/267 | 27/149 |
| Gross Yards | 3787 | 3786 |
| Att./Completions | 573/334 | 505/308 |
| Completion Pct. | 58.3 | 61.0 |
| Had Intercepted | 25 | 13 |
| Punts/Avg. | 72/43.3 | 74/40.9 |
| Net Punting Avg. | 72/37.6 | 74/35.9 |
| Penalties/Yards Lost | 111/838 | 100/874 |
| Fumbles/Ball Lost | 31/17 | 25/11 |
| Touchdowns | 34 | 46 |
| Rushing | 4 | 14 |
| Passing | 28 | 27 |
| Returns | 2 | 5 |
| Avg. Time of Possession | 31:23 | 28:37 |

## 1993 INDIVIDUAL STATISTICS

| Passing | Att. | Comp. | Yds. | Pct. | TD | Int. | Tkld. | Rate |
|---|---|---|---|---|---|---|---|---|
| Hebert | 430 | 263 | 2978 | 61.2 | 24 | 17 | 29/190 | 84.0 |
| Tolliver | 76 | 39 | 464 | 51.3 | 3 | 5 | 3/15 | 56.0 |
| Miller | 66 | 32 | 345 | 48.5 | 1 | 3 | 8/62 | 50.4 |
| Sanders | 1 | 0 | 0 | 0.0 | 0 | 0 | 0/0 | 39.6 |
| Falcons | 573 | 334 | 3787 | 58.3 | 28 | 25 | 40/267 | 76.3 |
| Opponents | 505 | 308 | 3786 | 61.0 | 27 | 13 | 27/149 | 91.2 |

| SCORING | TD R | TD P | TD Rt | PAT | FG | Saf | PTS |
|---|---|---|---|---|---|---|---|
| Johnson | 0 | 0 | 0 | 34/34 | 26/27 | 0 | 112 |
| Rison | 0 | 15 | 0 | 0/0 | 0/0 | 0 | 90 |
| Pritchard | 0 | 7 | 0 | 0/0 | 0/0 | 0 | 42 |
| Haynes | 0 | 4 | 0 | 0/0 | 0/0 | 0 | 24 |
| Pegram | 3 | 0 | 0 | 0/0 | 0/0 | 0 | 18 |
| Broussard | 1 | 0 | 0 | 0/0 | 0/0 | 0 | 6 |
| Clark | 0 | 0 | 1 | 0/0 | 0/0 | 0 | 6 |
| Mims | 0 | 1 | 0 | 0/0 | 0/0 | 0 | 6 |
| Sanders | 0 | 1 | 0 | 0/0 | 0/0 | 0 | 6 |
| T. Smith | 0 | 0 | 1 | 0/0 | 0/0 | 0 | 6 |
| Falcons | 4 | 28 | 2 | 34/34 | 26/27 | 0 | 316 |
| Opponents | 14 | 27 | 5 | 45/46 | 20/31 | 2 | 385 |

| RUSHING | Att. | Yds. | Avg. | LG | TD |
|---|---|---|---|---|---|
| Pegram | 292 | 1185 | 4.1 | 29 | 3 |
| Broussard | 39 | 206 | 5.3 | 26 | 1 |
| Dickerson | 26 | 91 | 3.5 | 10 | 0 |
| Hebert | 24 | 49 | 2.0 | 14 | 0 |
| Tolliver | 7 | 48 | 6.9 | 24 | 0 |
| Miller | 2 | 11 | 5.5 | 6 | 0 |
| Pritchard | 2 | 4 | 2.0 | 4 | 0 |
| Mims | 1 | 3 | 3.0 | 3 | 0 |
| Alexander | 2 | -7 | -3.5 | 0 | 0 |
| Falcons | 395 | 1590 | 4.0 | 29 | 4 |
| Opponents | 419 | 1784 | 4.3 | 74t | 14 |

| RECEIVING | No. | Yds. | Avg. | LG | TD |
|---|---|---|---|---|---|
| Rison | 86 | 1242 | 14.4 | 53t | 15 |
| Pritchard | 74 | 736 | 9.9 | 34 | 7 |
| Haynes | 72 | 778 | 10.8 | 98t | 4 |
| Hill | 34 | 384 | 11.3 | 30 | 0 |
| Pegram | 33 | 302 | 9.2 | 30 | 0 |
| Mims | 12 | 107 | 8.9 | 19 | 1 |
| Lyons | 8 | 63 | 7.9 | 14 | 0 |
| Sanders | 6 | 106 | 17.7 | 70t | 1 |
| Dickerson | 6 | 58 | 9.7 | 30 | 0 |
| Phillips | 1 | 15 | 15.0 | 15 | 0 |
| Broussard | 1 | 4 | 4.0 | 4 | 0 |
| Hinton | 1 | -8 | -8.0 | -8 | 0 |
| Falcons | 334 | 3787 | 11.3 | 98t | 28 |
| Opponents | 308 | 3786 | 12.3 | 72 | 27 |

| INTERCEPTIONS | No. | Yds. | Avg. | LG | TD |
|---|---|---|---|---|---|
| Sanders | 7 | 91 | 13.0 | 41 | 0 |
| Walker | 3 | 7 | 2.3 | 7 | 0 |
| Clark | 2 | 59 | 29.5 | 38 | 0 |
| Eaton | 1 | 0 | 0.0 | 0 | 0 |
| Case | 0 | 3 | — | 3 | 0 |
| Falcons | 13 | 160 | 12.3 | 44 | 0 |
| Opponents | 25 | 345 | 13.8 | 78 | 2 |

| PUNTING | No. | Yds. | Avg. | In 20 | LG |
|---|---|---|---|---|---|
| Alexander | 72 | 3114 | 43.3 | 21 | 75 |
| Falcons | 72 | 3114 | 43.3 | 21 | 75 |
| Opponents | 74 | 3029 | 40.9 | 23 | 66 |

| PUNT RETURNS | No. | FC | Yds. | Avg. | LG | TD |
|---|---|---|---|---|---|---|
| T. Smith | 32 | 17 | 255 | 8.0 | 51 | 0 |
| Sanders | 2 | 1 | 21 | 10.5 | 16 | 0 |
| Clark | 1 | 0 | 0 | 0.0 | 0 | 0 |
| Falcons | 35 | 18 | 276 | 7.9 | 51 | 0 |
| Opponents | 41 | 17 | 350 | 8.5 | 30 | 0 |

| KICKOFF RETURNS | No. | Yds. | Avg. | LG | TD |
|---|---|---|---|---|---|
| T. Smith | 38 | 948 | 24.9 | 97t | 1 |
| Sanders | 7 | 169 | 24.1 | 31 | 0 |
| Pegram | 4 | 63 | 15.8 | 28 | 0 |
| Montgomery | 2 | 53 | 26.5 | 33 | 0 |
| Phillips | 2 | 38 | 19.0 | 29 | 0 |
| Mims | 1 | 22 | 22.0 | 22 | 0 |
| Ruether | 1 | 7 | 7.0 | 7 | 0 |
| Falcons | 55 | 1300 | 23.6 | 97t | 1 |
| Opponents | 55 | 1064 | 19.3 | 65 | 0 |

| SACKS | No. |
|---|---|
| Holt | 6.5 |
| Geathers | 3.5 |
| C. Smith | 3.5 |
| Agee | 2.5 |
| Gardner | 2.0 |
| Tuggle | 2.0 |
| Case | 1.5 |
| Conner | 1.5 |
| Gann | 1.0 |
| George | 1.0 |
| Logan | 1.0 |
| Falcons | 26.0 |
| Opponents | 40.0 |

## 1994 DRAFT CHOICES

| Round | Name | Pos. | College |
|---|---|---|---|
| 2 | Bert Emanuel | WR | Rice |
| 3 | Anthony Phillips | DB | Texas A&M-Kingsville |
| | Alai Kalaniuvalu | G | Oregon State |
| 4 | Perry Klein | QB | C.W. Post |
| | Mitch Davis | LB | Georgia |
| 5 | Harrison Houston | WR | Florida |
| 7 | Jamal Anderson | RB | Utah |

# ATLANTA FALCONS

### 1994 VETERAN ROSTER

| No. | | Name | Pos. | Ht. | Wt. | Birthdate | NFL Exp. | College | Hometown | How Acq. | '93 Games/ Starts |
|---|---|---|---|---|---|---|---|---|---|---|---|
| 98 | | Age, Louis | T | 6-7 | 360 | 2/1/70 | 2 | Southwest Louisiana | New Orleans. La. | FA-'94 | 0* |
| 68 | | Agee, Mel | DE-DT | 6-5 | 298 | 11/22/68 | 3 | Illinois | Chicago, Ill. | FA-'92 | 11/7 |
| 5 | | Alexander, Harold | P | 6-2 | 224 | 10/20/70 | 2 | Appalachian State | Pickens, S.C. | D3-'93 | 16/0 |
| 92 | | Archambeau, Lester | DE | 6-5 | 275 | 6/27/67 | 5 | Stanford | Montville, N.J. | T(GB)-'93 | 15/11 |
| 25 | # | Case, Scott | S | 6-1 | 188 | 5/17/62 | 11 | Oklahoma | Edmond, Okla. | D2-'84 | 16/16 |
| 27 | | Clark, Vinnie | CB | 6-0 | 194 | 1/22/69 | 4 | Ohio State | Cincinnati, Ohio | T(GB)-'93 | 15/9 |
| 56 | # | Conner, Darion | LB | 6-2 | 245 | 9/28/67 | 5 | Jackson State | Prairie Point, Miss. | D2-'90 | 14/10 |
| 51 | | Dinkins, Howard | LB | 6-1 | 230 | 4/26/69 | 3 | Florida State | Jacksonville, Fla. | D3-'92 | 3/0 |
| 59 | t- | Doleman, Chris | DE | 6-5 | 275 | 10/16/61 | 10 | Pittsburgh | York, Pa. | T(Minn)-'94 | 16/16* |
| 49 | | Figaro, Cedric | LB | 6-3 | 255 | 8/17/66 | 6 | Notre Dame | Lafayette, La. | FA-'94 | 0* |
| 48 | | Ford, Darryl | LB | 6-1 | 225 | 6/22/66 | 3 | New Mexico State | Dallas, Tex. | FA-'94 | 11/0* |
| 65 | | Fortin, Roman | G-C | 6-5 | 295 | 2/26/67 | 5 | San Diego State | Ventura, Calif. | PB(Det)-'92 | 16/1 |
| 14 | # | Gagliano, Bob | QB | 6-3 | 205 | 9/5/58 | 10 | Utah State | Los Angeles, Calif. | FA-'93 | 0* |
| 76 | | Gann, Mike | DE | 6-5 | 270 | 10/19/63 | 10 | Notre Dame | Lakewood, Colo. | D2-'85 | 8/8 |
| 67 | | Gardner, Moe | NT | 6-2 | 261 | 8/10/68 | 4 | Illinois | Indianapolis, Ind. | D4-'91 | 16/16 |
| 97 | | Geathers, Jumpy | DT | 6-7 | 290 | 6/26/60 | 11 | Wichita State | Lafayette Hills, Pa. | UFA(Wash)-'93 | 14/0 |
| 1 | t- | George, Jeff | QB | 6-4 | 218 | 12/8/67 | 5 | Illinois | Indianapolis, Ind. | T(Ind)-'94 | 13/11* |
| 50 | | George, Ron | LB | 6-2 | 225 | 3/20/70 | 2 | Stanford | Heidelberg, Germany | D5-'93 | 12/4 |
| 53 | | Gordon, Dwayne | LB | 6-1 | 231 | 11/2/69 | 2 | New Hampshire | LaGrangeville, N.Y. | FA-'93 | 5/0 |
| 47 | | Harper, Roger | S | 6-2 | 223 | 10/26/70 | 2 | Ohio State | Columbus, Ohio | D2-'93 | 16/12 |
| 83 | | Harris, Leonard | WR | 5-8 | 166 | 11/27/60 | 9 | Texas Tech | McKinney, Tex. | FA-'94 | 4/2* |
| 3 | | Hebert, Bobby | QB | 6-4 | 215 | 8/19/60 | 9 | Northwestern Louisiana | Mandeville, La. | UFA(NO)-'93 | 14/12 |
| 95 | | Holt, Pierce | DE | 6-4 | 275 | 1/1/62 | 7 | Angelo State | Marlin, Tex. | RFA(SF)-'93 | 16/15 |
| 44 | | Johnson, D.J. | CB | 6-0 | 183 | 7/14/66 | 6 | Kentucky | Louisville, Ky. | UFA(Pitt)-'94 | 16/15* |
| 9 | | Johnson, Norm | K | 6-2 | 203 | 5/31/60 | 13 | UCLA | Garden Grove, Calif. | FA-'91 | 15/0 |
| 85 | | Jones, Tony | WR | 5-7 | 145 | 12/30/65 | 5 | Texas | Grapeland, Tex. | FA-'94 | 2/0* |
| 78 | | Kenn, Mike | T | 6-7 | 286 | 2/9/56 | 17 | Michigan | Evanston, Ill. | D1-'78 | 16/16 |
| 66 | | Kennedy, Lincoln | G-T | 6-6 | 335 | 2/12/71 | 2 | Washington | San Diego, Calif. | D1-'93 | 16/16 |
| 88 | | Le Bel, Harper | TE | 6-4 | 248 | 7/14/63 | 6 | Colorado State | Sherman Oaks, Calif. | PB(Phil)-'91 | 16/0 |
| 73 | | Logan, Ernie | DE | 6-3 | 285 | 5/18/68 | 4 | East Carolina | Fayetteville, N.C. | FA-'93 | 8/1 |
| 86 | | Lyons, Mitch | TE | 6-4 | 255 | 5/13/70 | 2 | Michigan State | Grand Rapids, Mich. | D6-'93 | 16/8 |
| 81 | | Mathis, Terance | WR | 5-10 | 177 | 6/7/67 | 5 | New Mexico | Stone Mountain, Ga. | UFA(NYJ)-'94 | 16/3* |
| 22 | | Montgomery, Alton | S | 6-0 | 202 | 6/16/68 | 5 | Houston | Griffin, Ga. | T(Den)-'93 | 8/0 |
| 33 | | Pegram, Erric | RB | 5-9 | 188 | 1/7/69 | 4 | North Texas State | Dallas, Tex. | D6-'91 | 16/14 |
| 82 | # | Phillips, Jason | WR | 5-7 | 166 | 10/11/66 | 6 | Houston | Houston, Tex. | PB(Det)-'91 | 6/0 |
| 96 | | Richardson, Huey | DE | 6-4 | 243 | 2/3/68 | 3 | Florida | Atlanta, Ga. | FA-'94 | 0* |
| 80 | | Rison, Andre | WR | 6-1 | 188 | 3/18/67 | 6 | Michigan State | Flint, Mich. | T(Ind)-'90 | 16/16 |
| 35 | | Ross, Kevin | S | 5-9 | 182 | 1/16/62 | 11 | Temple | Paulsboro, N.J. | UFA(KC)-'94 | 15/15* |
| 55 | # | Ruether, Mike | G-C | 6-4 | 286 | 9/20/62 | 9 | Texas | Shawnee Mission, Kan. | FA-'90 | 16/0 |
| 21 | † | Sanders, Deion | CB | 6-1 | 185 | 8/9/67 | 6 | Florida State | Ft. Myers, Fla. | D1-'89 | 11/10 |
| 83 | | Sanders, Ricky | WR | 5-11 | 178 | 8/30/62 | 9 | Southwest Texas State | Temple, Tex. | FA-'94 | 16/11* |
| 37 | # | Shelley, Elbert | CB | 5-11 | 185 | 12/24/64 | 8 | Arkansas State | Tyronza, Ark. | D11-'87 | 16/0 |
| 90 | | Smith, Chuck | LB-DE | 6-2 | 254 | 12/21/69 | 3 | Tennessee | Athens, Ga. | D2-'92 | 15/1 |
| 28 | | Smith, Tony | RB | 6-1 | 224 | 6/29/70 | 3 | Southern Mississippi | Vicksburg, Miss. | D1b-'92 | 15/0 |
| 32 | # | Stinson, Lemuel | CB | 5-9 | 180 | 5/10/66 | 7 | Texas Tech | Houston, Tex. | FA-'93 | 0* |
| 52 | # | Tippins, Ken | LB | 6-1 | 235 | 7/22/66 | 6 | Middle Tennessee State | Adel, Ga. | FA-'90 | 14/1 |
| 11 | # | Tolliver, Billy Joe | QB | 6-1 | 218 | 2/7/66 | 6 | Texas Tech | Boyd, Tex. | T(SD)-'91 | 7/2 |
| 58 | | Tuggle, Jessie | LB | 5-11 | 230 | 2/14/65 | 8 | Valdosta State | Spalding, Ga. | FA-'87 | 16/16 |
| 45 | | Walker, Darnell | CB | 5-8 | 164 | 1/17/70 | 2 | Oklahoma | St. Louis, Mo. | D7-'93 | 15/8 |
| 48 | | Washington, Charles | S | 6-1 | 217 | 10/8/66 | 5 | Cameron | Dallas, Tex. | FA-'93 | 6/0 |
| 70 | | Whitfield, Bob | T | 6-5 | 308 | 10/18/71 | 3 | Stanford | Carson, Calif. | D1a-'92 | 16/16 |
| 94 | | Wilkins, David | DE-LB | 6-4 | 240 | 2/24/69 | 2 | Eastern Kentucky | Cincinnati, Ohio | FA-'94 | 0* |
| 72 | | Zandofsky, Mike | C-G | 6-2 | 305 | 11/30/65 | 6 | Washington | Corvallis, Ore. | UFA(SD)-'94 | 16/16* |

* Age last active with Chicago in '92; Doleman played 16 games with Minnesota in '93; Figaro last active with Cleveland in '92; Ford played 11 games with Detroit; Gagliano active for 2 games but did not play; J. George played 13 games with Indianapolis; Harris played 4 games with Houston; D. Johnson played 16 games with Pittsburgh; Jones played 2 games with Houston; Mathis played 16 games with N.Y. Jets; Richardson last active with Washington in '92; Ross played 15 games with Kansas City; R. Sanders played 16 games with Washington; Stinson inactive for 10 games; Wilkins last active with San Francisco in '92; Zandofsky played 16 games with San Diego.

\# Unrestricted free agent; subject to developments.

† Restricted free agent; subject to developments.

Retired—RB Eric Dickerson, 11-year veteran, 4 games in '93.

Traded—CB Bruce Pickens to Green Bay, WR Mike Pritchard to Denver.

t- Falcons traded for Doleman (Minnesota), J. George (Indianapolis).

Players lost through free agency (3): WR Michael Haynes (NO; 16 games in '93), T Chris Hinton (Minn; 16), QB Chris Miller (Rams; 3).

Also played with Falcons in '93—G Keith Alex (14 games), RB Steve Broussard (8), DE Rick Bryan (2), S Jeff Donaldson (13), C Jamie Dukes (16), S Tracey Eaton (16), NT Tory Epps (2), NT Bill Goldberg (5), DE Tim Green (9), WR Drew Hill (16), CB Melvin Jenkins (14), WR David Mims (15), CB Brian Mitchell (5), CB Bruce Pickens (4), WR Mike Pritchard (15), LB Jesse Solomon (16).

## COACHING STAFF

**Head Coach,**
**June Jones**

**Pro Career:** Became the eighth head coach in Falcons history on January 24, 1994, succeeding Jerry Glanville. Most recently was Falcons' assistant head coach-offense since 1991. He played four seasons (1977-79, 1981) in NFL mainly as a backup quarterback to Falcons' all-time leading passer Steve Bartkowski. He was a member of the Falcons' first-ever playoff team in 1978. Jones began his coaching career as wide receivers coach of Houston Gamblers of the USFL in 1984. He became the offensive coordinator of the Denver Gold (USFL) in 1985 and then moved on to Ottawa Roughriders of the CFL in 1986. He was quarterbacks coach of the Houston Oilers in 1987-89. Was the quarterbacks and receivers coach for Detroit Lions in 1989-90.
**Background:** Guided Portland State to back-to-back 8-3 seasons, serving as team captain during his senior year, after also playing at Hawaii and Oregon. Jones and new Redskins head coach, Norv Turner, were backups to Hall of Famer quarterback Dan Fouts at Oregon. Jones has been a winning member of a Grey Cup team, a division titlist with Jim Kelly in the USFL, and has advanced to the postseason in both NFL conferences.
**Personal:** Born on February 19, 1953, in Portland, Oregon. June and his wife, Diane, live in Lake Lanier, Ga., and have three daughters—Jennifer, Kellie, Nicole, and son June, IV.

### ASSISTANT COACHES

**Keith Armstrong,** outside linebackers; born December 15, 1963, Philadelphia, Pa., lives in Atlanta. Running back Temple 1983-86. No pro playing experience. College coach: Akron 1989, Oklahoma State 1990-92, Notre Dame 1993. Pro coach: Joined Falcons in 1994.
**Jim Bates,** defensive coordinator; born May 31, 1946, Pontiac, Mich., lives in Atlanta. Linebacker Tennessee 1964-67. No pro playing experience. College coach: Tennessee 1968, 1989, Southern Mississippi 1972, Villanova 1973-74, Kansas State 1975-76, West Virginia 1977, Texas Tech 1978-83, Florida 1990. Pro coach: San Antonio Gunslingers (USFL) 1984-85 (head coach 1985), Detroit Drive (Arena Football) 1988, Cleveland Browns 1991-93, joined Falcons in 1994.
**Greg Brown,** secondary; born October 10, 1957, Denver, Colo., lives in Atlanta. No college or pro playing experience. College coach: Wyoming 1987-88, Purdue 1989-90, Colorado 1991-93. Pro coach: Denver Gold (USFL) 1983-84, Tampa Bay Buccaneers 1984-86, joined Falcons in 1994.
**Darrell "Mouse" Davis,** quarterbacks; born September 6, 1932, Palouse, Wash., lives in Atlanta. Quarterback Western Oregon State 1952-55. No pro playing experience. College coach: Portland State 1974-80 (head coach 1975-80). Pro coach: Toronto Argonauts (CFL) 1982-83, Houston Gamblers (USFL) 1984, Denver Gold (USFL) 1985, Detroit Lions 1989-90, NY/NJ Knights (WL) 1991-92, joined Falcons in 1994.
**Frank Gansz,** assistant head coach-offense; born November 22, 1938, Altoona, Pa., lives in Atlanta. Center-linebacker Navy 1957-59. No pro playing experience. College coach: Air Force 1964, Colgate 1968, Navy 1969, Oklahoma State 1973, 1975, Army 1974, UCLA 1976-77. Pro coach: San Francisco 49ers 1978, Cincinnati Bengals 1979-80, Kansas City Chiefs 1981-82, 1986-88 (head coach 1987-88), Philadelphia Eagles 1983-85, Detroit Lions 1989-93, joined Falcons in 1994.
**Joe Haering,** linebackers; born February 1, 1946, Pittsburgh, Pa., lives in Atlanta. Linebacker Bucknell 1961-65. No pro playing experience. College coach: Bucknell 1969, Kentucky 1970-72, Boston University 1973-74, Kent State 1975-77. Pro coach: New York Jets 1978-79, Hamilton Tiger-Cats (CFL) 1980, Chicago Blitz (USFL) 1982-83, Pittsburgh Maulers (USFL) 1984, Denver Gold (USFL) 1985, NY/NJ Knights (WL) 1992, joined Falcons in 1994.
**Milt Jackson,** receivers; born October 16, 1943, Groesbeck, Tex., lives in Atlanta. Defensive back Tulsa 1965-66. Pro defensive back San Francisco 49ers 1967. College coach: Oregon State 1973, Rice 1974, California 1975-76, Oregon 1977-78, UCLA 1979. Pro coach: San Francisco 49ers 1980-82, Buffalo Bills 1983-84, Philadelphia Eagles 1985, Houston Oilers 1986-88, Indianapolis Colts 1989-91, Los Angeles Rams 1992-93, joined Falcons in 1994.
**Tim Jorgensen,** strength and conditioning; born April 21, 1955, St. Louis, Mo., lives in Snellville, Ga. Guard Southwest Missouri State 1974-76. No pro playing experience. College coach: Southwest Missouri State 1977-78, Alabama 1979, Louisiana State 1980-83. Pro coach: Philadelphia Eagles 1984-86, joined Falcons in 1987.
**Bill Kollar,** defensive line; born November 12, 1952, Warren, Ohio, lives in Atlanta. Defensive end Montana State 1971-74. Pro defensive end Cincinnati Bengals 1974-76, Tampa Bay Buccaneers 1977-81. College coach: Illinois 1985-87, Purdue 1988-89. Pro coach: Tampa Bay Buccaneers 1984, joined Falcons in 1990.
**Bob Palcic,** offensive line; born July 2, 1948, Dunkirk, N.Y., lives in Atlanta. Linebacker Dayton 1968-70. No pro playing experience. College coach: Dayton 1974-75, Ball State 1976-77, Wisconsin 1978-81, Arizona 1984-85, Ohio State 1986-91, Southern California 1992, UCLA 1993. Pro coach: Joined Falcons in 1994.
**Ollie Wilson,** running backs; born March 31, 1951, Worcester, Mass., lives in Atlanta. Wide receiver Springfield 1971-73. No pro playing experience. College coach: Springfield 1975, Northeastern 1976-82, California 1983-90. Pro coach: Joined Falcons in 1991.

## 1994 FIRST-YEAR ROSTER

| Name | Pos. | Ht. | Wt. | Birthdate | College | Hometown | How Acq. |
|---|---|---|---|---|---|---|---|
| Addison, Bryan (1) | S | 6-0 | 200 | 4/13/70 | Hawaii | Los Angeles, Calif. | FA |
| Alex, Keith (1) | G | 6-4 | 307 | 6/9/69 | Texas A&M | Beaumont, Tex. | FA |
| Anderson, Jamal | RB | 5-10 | 246 | 3/6/72 | Utah | El Camino, Calif. | D7 |
| Barber, Rudy | G | 6-2 | 286 | 9/21/71 | Miami | Miami, Fla. | FA |
| Bedosky, Mike | G | 6-4 | 289 | 2/13/71 | Missouri | Jefferson City, Mo. | FA |
| Davis, Mitch | LB | 6-3 | 238 | 7/7/71 | Georgia | Mobile, Ala. | D4 |
| Dixon, Corey | WR | 5-7 | 155 | 2/16/72 | Nebraska | Dallas, Tex. | FA |
| Earle, John (1) | G | 6-4 | 290 | 7/3/69 | Western Illinois | Blue Springs, Mo. | FA |
| Emanuel, Bert | WR | 5-10 | 171 | 10/27/70 | Rice | Houston, Tex. | D2 |
| Ferguson, Reggie | WR | 5-9 | 180 | 10/7/71 | Louisville | Jacksonville, Fla. | FA |
| Goldberg, Bill (1) | DT | 6-2 | 266 | 12/29/69 | Georgia | Tulsa, Okla. | FA |
| Guiles, Jonathan | DE | 6-4 | 270 | 7/27/71 | South Carolina State | Georgetown, S.C. | FA |
| Harrison, Tony | WR | 5-10 | 188 | 9/25/71 | Texas A&M | Houston, Tex. | FA |
| Hatch, Lawrence (1) | CB | 5-11 | 194 | 5/22/71 | Florida | Tucker, Ga. | FA |
| Heidenreich, Jon (1) | G | 6-5 | 285 | 6/28/69 | Northeast Louisiana | Duluth, Ga. | FA |
| Houston, Harrison | WR | 5-9 | 174 | 1/26/72 | Florida | Pensacola, Fla. | D5 |
| Jack, Eric | CB | 5-10 | 177 | 4/19/72 | New Mexico | El Paso, Tex. | FA |
| Jack, Keith | WR | 5-9 | 177 | 5/11/71 | Houston | Daly City, Calif. | FA |
| Jackson, Tyoka | DE | 6-1 | 266 | 11/22/71 | Penn State | Forestville, Md. | FA |
| James, John (1) | T-G | 6-3 | 294 | 3/28/70 | Mississippi State | Atlanta, Ga. | FA |
| Johnson, Clint | WR | 5-7 | 178 | 1/6/72 | Notre Dame | Altamonte Springs, Fla. | FA |
| Johnson, Pat | S | 6-1 | 201 | 6/10/72 | Purdue | Mineral Point, Mo. | FA |
| Kalaniuvalu, Alal | G | 6-3 | 302 | 10/23/71 | Oregon State | Seattle, Wash. | D3 |
| Klein, Perry | QB | 6-2 | 218 | 3/25/71 | C.W. Post | Santa Monica, Calif. | D4 |
| Lowery, Tim (1) | RB | 5-11 | 247 | 11/29/70 | Clark, Ga. | Effingham, Calif. | FA |
| Mims, David (1) | WR | 5-8 | 191 | 7/7/70 | Baylor | Daingerfield, Tex. | FA |
| Paulk, Tim (1) | LB | 6-0 | 232 | 4/3/68 | Florida | Miami, Fla. | FA |
| Peterson, Todd (1) | K | 5-10 | 176 | 2/4/70 | Georgia | Valdosta, Ga. | FA |
| Phillips, Anthony | CB | 6-0 | 217 | 10/5/70 | Texas A&M-Kingsville | Galveston, Tex. | D3 |
| Rogers, Joe | WR | 5-7 | 161 | 5/23/71 | Texas Southern | Miami, Fla. | FA |
| Sally, Lamar (1) | DE | 6-5 | 281 | 8/11/70 | Central Michigan | Detroit, Mich. | FA |
| Spencer, Darryl (1) | WR | 5-8 | 172 | 3/21/70 | Miami | Merritt Island, Fla. | FA |
| Tobeck, Robbie (1) | C | 6-4 | 275 | 3/6/70 | Washington State | Tarpon Springs, Fla. | FA |
| Tyner, Scott | P-K | 6-1 | 189 | 4/11/72 | Oklahoma State | Edgewood, Tex. | FA |
| Wallace, Anthony (1) | RB | 6-0 | 191 | 7/8/69 | California | Pasadena, Calif. | FA |
| Walton, Tim | CB | 5-11 | 180 | 3/11/71 | Ohio State | Columbus, Ga. | FA |
| White, Stan | QB | 6-2 | 202 | 8/14/71 | Auburn | Birmingham, Ala. | FA |
| Williams, Thomas | DT | 6-3 | 274 | 12/19/70 | Wyoming | Pueblo, Colo. | FA |

The term NFL Rookie is defined as a player who is in his first season of professional football and has not been on the roster of another professional football team for any regular-season or postseason games. A Rookie is designated by an "R" on NFL rosters. Players who have been active in another professional football league or players who have NFL experience, including either preseason training camp or being on an Active List or Inactive List, or on Reserve/Injured or Reserve/Physically Unable to Perform for fewer than six regular-season games, are termed NFL First-Year Players. An NFL First-Year Player is designated by a "1" on NFL rosters. Thereafter, a player is credited with an additional year of experience for each season in which he accumulates six games on the Active List or Inactive List, or on Reserve/Injured or Reserve/Physically Unable to Perform.

## NOTES

# CHICAGO BEARS

**National Football Conference**
**Central Division**
**Team Colors:** Navy Blue, Orange, and White
**Halas Hall, 250 North Washington**
**Lake Forest, Illinois 60045**
**Telephone: (708) 295-6600**

## CLUB OFFICIALS

Chairman of the Board: Edward W. McCaskey
President and CEO: Michael B. McCaskey
Secretary: Virginia H. McCaskey
Vice President: Tim McCaskey
Vice President of Operations: Ted Phillips
Director of Player Personnel: Rod Graves
Director of Administration: Tim LeFevour
Director of Community Relations: Pat McCaskey
Player Liaison: Brian McCaskey
Director of Marketing/Communications: Ken Valdiserri
Manager of Promotions: John Bostrom
Manager of Sales: Jack Trompeter
Director of Public Relations: Bryan Harlan
Asst. Director of Public Relations: Doug Green
Ticket Manager: George McCaskey
Computer Systems: Greg Gershuny
Video Director: Dean Pope
Trainer: Fred Caito
Strength Coordinator: Clyde Emrich
Physical Dev. Coordinator: Russ Reiderer
Equipment Manager: Gary Haeger
Assistant Equipment Manager: Tony Medlin
Scouts: Gary Smith, Jeff Shiver, Charlie Mackey, Bobby Riggle, Mike McCartney
**Stadium:** Soldier Field • **Capacity:** 66,950
425 McFetridge Place
Chicago, Illinois 60605
**Playing Surface:** Grass
**Training Camp:** University of Wisconsin-Platteville
Platteville, Wisconsin 53818

## 1994 SCHEDULE

**PRESEASON**

| | | |
|---|---|---|
| Aug. 5 | **Philadelphia** | 7:00 |
| Aug. 13 | at Arizona | 6:00 |
| Aug. 22 | at Kansas City | 7:00 |
| Aug. 27 | **New York Giants** | 7:00 |

**REGULAR SEASON**

| | | |
|---|---|---|
| Sept. 4 | **Tampa Bay** | 12:00 |
| Sept. 12 | at Philadelphia (Monday) | 9:00 |
| Sept. 18 | **Minnesota** | 12:00 |
| Sept. 25 | at New York Jets | 8:00 |
| Oct. 2 | **Buffalo** | 3:00 |
| Oct. 9 | **New Orleans** | 12:00 |
| Oct. 16 | Open Date | |
| Oct. 23 | at Detroit | 1:00 |
| Oct. 31 | **Green Bay** (Monday) | 8:00 |
| Nov. 6 | at Tampa Bay | 1:00 |
| Nov. 13 | at Miami | 1:00 |
| Nov. 20 | **Detroit** | 12:00 |
| Nov. 27 | at Arizona | 2:00 |
| Dec. 1 | at Minnesota (Thursday) | 7:00 |
| Dec. 11 | at Green Bay | 12:00 |
| Dec. 18 | **Los Angeles Rams** | 12:00 |
| Dec. 24 | **New England** | 12:00 |

## RECORD HOLDERS

**INDIVIDUAL RECORDS—CAREER**

| Category | Name | Performance |
|---|---|---|
| Rushing (Yds.) | Walter Payton, 1975-1987 | *16,726 |
| Passing (Yds.) | Sid Luckman, 1939-1950 | 14,686 |
| Passing (TDs) | Sid Luckman, 1939-1950 | 137 |
| Receiving (No.) | Walter Payton, 1975-1987 | 492 |
| Receiving (Yds.) | Johnny Morris, 1958-1967 | 5,059 |
| Interceptions | Gary Fencik, 1976-1987 | 38 |
| Punting (Avg.) | George Gulyanics, 1947-1952 | 44.5 |
| Punt Return (Avg.) | Ray (Scooter) McLean, 1940-47 | 14.8 |
| Kickoff Return (Avg.) | Gale Sayers, 1965-1971 | 30.6 |
| Field Goals | Kevin Butler, 1985-1993 | 197 |
| Touchdowns (Tot.) | Walter Payton, 1975-1987 | 125 |
| Points | Kevin Butler, 1985-1993 | 915 |

**INDIVIDUAL RECORDS—SINGLE SEASON**

| Category | Name | Performance |
|---|---|---|
| Rushing (Yds.) | Walter Payton, 1977 | 1,852 |
| Passing (Yds.) | Bill Wade, 1962 | 3,172 |
| Passing (TDs) | Sid Luckman, 1943 | 28 |
| Receiving (No.) | Johnny Morris, 1964 | 93 |
| Receiving (Yds.) | Johnny Morris, 1964 | 1,200 |
| Interceptions | Mark Carrier, 1990 | 10 |
| Punting (Avg.) | Bobby Joe Green, 1963 | 46.5 |
| Punt Return (Avg.) | Harry Clark, 1943 | 15.8 |
| Kickoff Return (Avg.) | Gale Sayers, 1967 | 37.7 |
| Field Goals | Kevin Butler, 1985 | 31 |
| Touchdowns (Tot.) | Gale Sayers, 1965 | **22 |
| Points | Kevin Butler, 1985 | **144 |

**INDIVIDUAL RECORDS—SINGLE GAME**

| Category | Name | Performance |
|---|---|---|
| Rushing (Yds.) | Walter Payton, 11-20-77 | *275 |
| Passing (Yds.) | Johnny Lujack, 12-11-49 | 468 |
| Passing (TDs) | Sid Luckman, 11-14-43 | *7 |
| Receiving (No.) | Jim Keane, 10-23-49 | 14 |
| Receiving (Yds.) | Harlon Hill, 10-31-54 | 214 |
| Interceptions | Many times | 3 |
| | Last time by Mark Carrier, 12-9-90 | |
| Field Goals | Roger LeClerc, 12-3-61 | 5 |
| | Mac Percival, 10-20-68 | 5 |
| Touchdowns (Tot.) | Gale Sayers, 12-12-65 | *6 |
| Points | Gale Sayers, 12-12-65 | 36 |

*NFL Record
**NFL Rookie Record

## COACHING HISTORY

**Decatur Staleys 1920,**
**Chicago Staleys 1921**
**(586-384-42)**

| | | |
|---|---|---|
| 1920-29 | George Halas | 84-31-19 |
| 1930-32 | Ralph Jones | 24-10-7 |
| 1933-42 | George Halas* | 88-24-4 |
| 1942-45 | Hunk Anderson-Luke Johnsos** | 24-12-2 |
| 1946-55 | George Halas | 76-43-2 |
| 1956-57 | John (Paddy) Driscoll | 14-10-1 |
| 1958-67 | George Halas | 76-53-6 |
| 1968-71 | Jim Dooley | 20-36-0 |
| 1972-74 | Abe Gibron | 11-30-1 |
| 1975-77 | Jack Pardee | 20-23-0 |
| 1978-81 | Neill Armstrong | 30-35-0 |
| 1982-92 | Mike Ditka | 112-68-0 |
| 1993 | Dave Wannstedt | 7-9-0 |

*Retired after five games to enter U.S. Navy
**Co-coaches

**SOLDIER FIELD**

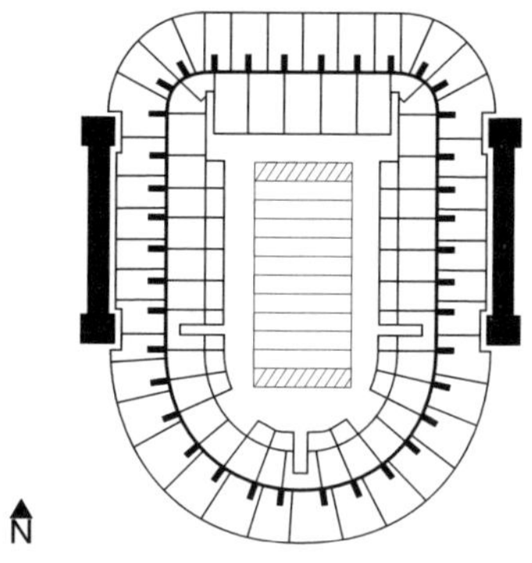

## 1993 TEAM RECORD

**PRESEASON (1-3)**

| Date | Result | | Opponents |
|---|---|---|---|
| 8/8 | L | 9-13 | at Philadelphia |
| 8/14 | L | 10-11 | Phoenix |
| 8/23 | L | 14-20 | at New Orleans |
| 8/27 | W | 23-21 | Dallas |

**REGULAR SEASON (7-9)**

| Date | Result | | Opponents | Att. |
|---|---|---|---|---|
| 9/5 | L | 20-26 | N.Y. Giants | 66,900 |
| 9/12 | L | 7-10 | at Minnesota | 57,921 |
| 9/26 | W | 47-17 | Tampa Bay | 58,329 |
| 10/3 | W | 6-0 | Atlanta | 57,441 |
| 10/10 | W | 17-6 | at Philadelphia | 63,601 |
| 10/25 | L | 12-19 | Minnesota | 64,677 |
| 10/31 | L | 3-17 | at Green Bay | 58,945 |
| 11/7 | L | 14-16 | L.A. Raiders | 59,750 |
| 11/14 | W | 16-13 | at San Diego | 58,459 |
| 11/21 | W | 19-17 | at Kansas City | 76,872 |
| 11/25 | W | 10-6 | at Detroit | 76,699 |
| 12/5 | W | 30-17 | Green Bay | 62,236 |
| 12/12 | L | 10-13 | at Tampa Bay | 56,667 |
| 12/18 | L | 3-13 | Denver | 53,056 |
| 12/26 | L | 14-20 | Detroit | 43,443 |
| 1/2 | L | 6-20 | at L.A. Rams | 39,147 |

**SCORE BY PERIODS**

| | | | | | | |
|---|---|---|---|---|---|---|
| Bears | 37 | 85 | 56 | 56 | 0 | — 234 |
| Opponents | 45 | 83 | 38 | 64 | 0 | — 230 |

**ATTENDANCE**

Home 465,832 Away 488,311 Total 954,143
Single-game home record, 66,900 (9-5-93)
Single-season home record, 528,465 (1992)

## 1993 TEAM STATISTICS

| | Bears | Opp. |
|---|---|---|
| Total First Downs | 226 | 289 |
| Rushing | 98 | 112 |
| Passing | 113 | 163 |
| Penalty | 15 | 14 |
| Third Down: Made/Att | 73/211 | 80/214 |
| Third Down Pct. | 34.6 | 37.4 |
| Fourth Down: Made/Att | 4/14 | 6/15 |
| Fourth Down Pct. | 28.6 | 40.0 |
| Total Net Yards | 3717 | 4653 |
| Avg. Per Game | 232.3 | 290.8 |
| Total Plays | 913 | 1026 |
| Avg. Per Play | 4.1 | 4.5 |
| Net Yards Rushing | 1677 | 1835 |
| Avg. Per Game | 104.8 | 114.7 |
| Total Rushes | 477 | 476 |
| Net Yards Passing | 2040 | 2818 |
| Avg. Per Game | 127.5 | 176.1 |
| Sacked/Yards Lost | 48/230 | 46/287 |
| Gross Yards | 2270 | 3105 |
| Att./Completions | 388/230 | 504/306 |
| Completion Pct. | 59.3 | 60.7 |
| Had Intercepted | 16 | 18 |
| Punts/Avg. | 80/38.5 | 78/41.4 |
| Net Punting Avg. | 80/36.6 | 78/36.2 |
| Penalties/Yards Lost | 68/587 | 91/783 |
| Fumbles/Ball Lost | 29/14 | 24/12 |
| Touchdowns | 22 | 22 |
| Rushing | 10 | 9 |
| Passing | 7 | 12 |
| Returns | 5 | 1 |
| Avg. Time of Possession | 28:36 | 31:24 |

## 1993 INDIVIDUAL STATISTICS

| PASSING | Att | Cmp | Yds. | Pct. | TD | Int | Tkld. | Rate |
|---|---|---|---|---|---|---|---|---|
| Harbaugh | 325 | 200 | 2002 | 61.5 | 7 | 11 | 43/210 | 72.1 |
| Willis | 60 | 30 | 268 | 50.0 | 0 | 5 | 5/20 | 27.6 |
| Gardocki | 2 | 0 | 0 | 0.0 | 0 | 0 | 0/0 | 39.6 |
| Anderson | 1 | 0 | 0 | 0.0 | 0 | 0 | 0/0 | 39.6 |
| Bears | 388 | 230 | 2270 | 59.3 | 7 | 16 | 48/230 | 64.7 |
| Opponents | 504 | 306 | 3105 | 60.7 | 12 | 18 | 46/287 | 71.4 |

| SCORING | TD R | TD P | TD Rt | PAT | FG | Saf | PTS |
|---|---|---|---|---|---|---|---|
| Butler | 0 | 0 | 0 | 21/22 | 27/36 | 0 | 102 |
| Anderson | 4 | 0 | 0 | 0/0 | 0/0 | 0 | 24 |
| Harbaugh | 4 | 0 | 0 | 0/0 | 0/0 | 0 | 24 |
| Obee | 0 | 3 | 0 | 0/0 | 0/0 | 0 | 18 |
| Baker | 0 | 0 | 2 | 0/0 | 0/0 | 0 | 12 |
| Conway | 0 | 2 | 0 | 0/0 | 0/0 | 0 | 12 |
| Worley | 2 | 0 | 0 | 0/0 | 0/0 | 0 | 12 |
| Carrier | 0 | 0 | 1 | 0/0 | 0/0 | 0 | 6 |
| Jones | 0 | 0 | 1 | 0/0 | 0/0 | 0 | 6 |
| Lincoln | 0 | 0 | 1 | 0/0 | 0/0 | 0 | 6 |
| Waddle | 0 | 1 | 0 | 0/0 | 0/0 | 0 | 6 |
| Wetnight | 0 | 1 | 0 | 0/0 | 0/0 | 0 | 6 |
| Bears | 10 | 7 | 5 | 21/22 | 27/36 | 0 | 234 |
| Opponents | 9 | 12 | 1 | 20/22 | 26/34 | 0 | 230 |

| RUSHING | Att. | Yds. | Avg. | LG | TD |
|---|---|---|---|---|---|
| Anderson | 202 | 646 | 3.2 | 45 | 4 |
| Worley | 110 | 437 | 4.0 | 28 | 2 |
| Harbaugh | 60 | 277 | 4.6 | 25 | 4 |
| Heyward | 68 | 206 | 3.0 | 11 | 0 |
| Conway | 5 | 44 | 8.8 | 18 | 0 |
| Green | 15 | 29 | 1.9 | 10 | 0 |
| Christian | 8 | 19 | 2.4 | 12 | 0 |
| Lewis | 7 | 13 | 1.9 | 3 | 0 |
| Willis | 2 | 6 | 3.0 | 6 | 0 |
| Bears | 477 | 1677 | 3.5 | 45 | 10 |
| Opponents | 476 | 1835 | 3.9 | 26t | 9 |

| RECEIVING | No. | Yds. | Avg. | LG | TD |
|---|---|---|---|---|---|
| Waddle | 44 | 552 | 12.5 | 38 | 1 |
| Anderson | 31 | 160 | 5.2 | 35 | 0 |
| Obee | 26 | 351 | 13.5 | 48 | 3 |
| Conway | 19 | 231 | 12.2 | 38t | 2 |
| Christian | 16 | 160 | 10.0 | 36 | 0 |
| Heyward | 16 | 132 | 8.3 | 20 | 0 |
| Jennings | 14 | 150 | 10.7 | 29 | 0 |
| Green | 13 | 63 | 4.8 | 9 | 0 |
| Davis | 12 | 132 | 11.0 | 17 | 0 |
| Gedney | 10 | 98 | 9.8 | 24 | 0 |
| Wetnight | 9 | 93 | 10.3 | 25t | 1 |
| Worley | 8 | 49 | 6.1 | 15 | 0 |
| Whitaker | 6 | 53 | 8.8 | 18 | 0 |
| Lewis | 4 | 26 | 6.5 | 18 | 0 |
| Banks | 1 | 19 | 19.0 | 19 | 0 |
| Harbaugh | 1 | 1 | 1.0 | 1 | 0 |
| Bears | 230 | 2270 | 9.9 | 48 | 7 |
| Opponents | 306 | 3105 | 10.1 | 67 | 12 |

| INTERCEPTIONS | No. | Yds. | Avg. | Long | TD |
|---|---|---|---|---|---|
| Carrier | 4 | 94 | 23.5 | 34t | 1 |
| Jones | 4 | 52 | 13.0 | 22 | 0 |
| Lincoln | 3 | 109 | 36.3 | 80t | 1 |
| Woolford | 2 | 18 | 9.0 | 18 | 0 |
| Blaylock | 2 | 3 | 1.5 | 3 | 0 |
| Dent | 1 | 24 | 24.0 | 24 | 0 |
| Mangum | 1 | 0 | 0.0 | 0 | 0 |
| McMichael | 1 | 0 | 0.0 | 0 | 0 |
| Bears | 18 | 300 | 16.7 | 86t | 2 |
| Opponents | 16 | 105 | 6.6 | 25 | 1 |

| PUNTING | No. | Yds. | Avg. | In | LG |
|---|---|---|---|---|---|
| Gardocki | 80 | 3080 | 38.5 | 28 | 58 |
| Bears | 80 | 3080 | 38.5 | 28 | 58 |
| Opponents | 78 | 3231 | 41.4 | 22 | 75 |

| PUNT RETURNS | No. | FC | Yds. | Avg. | LG | TD |
|---|---|---|---|---|---|---|
| Obee | 35 | 20 | 289 | 8.3 | 28 | 0 |
| Bears | 35 | 20 | 289 | 8.3 | 28 | 0 |
| Opponents | 22 | 38 | 115 | 5.2 | 34 | 0 |

| KICKOFF RETURNS | No. | Yds. | Avg. | LG | TD |
|---|---|---|---|---|---|
| Conway | 21 | 450 | 21.4 | 55 | 0 |
| Green | 9 | 141 | 15.7 | 30 | 0 |
| Obee | 9 | 159 | 17.7 | 34 | 0 |
| Worley | 2 | 36 | 18.0 | 24 | 0 |
| A. Fontenot | 1 | 8 | 8.0 | 8 | 0 |
| Heyward | 1 | 12 | 12.0 | 12 | 0 |
| Mangum | 1 | 0 | 0.0 | 0 | 0 |
| Ryan | 1 | 5 | 5.0 | 5 | 0 |
| Bears | 45 | 811 | 18.0 | 55 | 0 |
| Opponents | 53 | 918 | 17.3 | 35 | 0 |

| SACKS | No. |
|---|---|
| Dent | 12.5 |
| Armstrong | 11.5 |
| Zorich | 7.0 |
| McMichael | 6.0 |
| Spellman | 2.5 |
| Cox | 2.0 |
| A. Fontenot | 1.0 |
| Gayle | 1.0 |
| Jones | 1.0 |
| Simpson | 0.5 |
| Bears | 46.0 |
| Opponents | 48.0 |

## 1994 DRAFT CHOICES

| Round | Name | Pos. | College |
|---|---|---|---|
| 1 | John Thierry | DE | Alcorn State |
| 2 | Marcus Spears | T | N.W. Louisiana |
| 3 | Jim Flanigan | DT | Notre Dame |
| 4 | Raymont Harris | RB | Ohio State |
| 6 | Lloyd Hill | WR | Texas Tech |
| 7 | Dennis Collier | DB | Colorado |

## CHICAGO BEARS

### 1994 VETERAN ROSTER

| No. | | Name | Pos. | Ht. | Wt. | Birthdate | NFL Exp. | College | Hometown | How Acq. | '93 Games/ Starts |
|---|---|---|---|---|---|---|---|---|---|---|---|
| 35 | # | Anderson, Neal | RB | 5-11 | 215 | 8/14/64 | 9 | Florida | Graceville, Fla. | D1-'86 | 15/11 |
| 93 | | Armstrong, Trace | DE | 6-4 | 265 | 10/5/65 | 6 | Florida | Birmingham, Ala. | D1b-'89 | 16/16 |
| 70 | | Auzenne, Troy | T | 6-7 | 290 | 6/26/69 | 3 | California | Baldwin Park, Calif. | D2-'92 | 11/11 |
| 91 | | Baker, Myron | LB | 6-1 | 228 | 1/6/71 | 2 | Louisiana Tech | Haughton, La. | D4b-'93 | 16/0 |
| 47 | | Blaylock, Anthony | CB | 5-10 | 185 | 2/21/65 | 7 | Winston-Salem State | Raleigh, N.C. | UFA(SD)-'93 | 9/9 |
| 62 | | Bortz, Mark | G | 6-6 | 282 | 2/12/61 | 12 | Iowa | Pardeeville, Wis. | D8-'83 | 16/16 |
| 6 | # | Butler, Kevin | K | 6-1 | 204 | 7/24/62 | 10 | Georgia | Redan, Ga. | D4-'85 | 16/0 |
| 59 | | Cain, Joe | LB | 6-1 | 233 | 6/11/65 | 6 | Oregon Tech | Compton, Calif. | RFA(Sea)-'93 | 15/15 |
| 20 | | Carrier, Mark | S | 6-1 | 192 | 4/28/68 | 5 | Southern California | Long Beach, Calif. | D1-'90 | 16/16 |
| 44 | | Christian, Bob | RB | 5-10 | 225 | 11/14/68 | 2 | Northwestern | St. Louis, Mo. | FA-'92 | 14/1 |
| 80 | | Conway, Curtis | WR-KR | 6-0 | 185 | 3/13/71 | 2 | Southern California | Hawthorne, Calif. | D1-'93 | 16/7 |
| 86 | | Cook, Marv | TE | 6-4 | 234 | 2/24/66 | 6 | Iowa | West Branch, Iowa | FA-'94 | 16/12* |
| 54 | # | Cox, Ron | LB | 6-2 | 235 | 2/27/68 | 5 | Fresno State | Fresno, Calif. | D2b-'90 | 16/2 |
| 82 | # | Davis, Wendell | WR | 6-0 | 188 | 1/3/66 | 7 | Louisiana State | Shreveport, La. | D1-'88 | 5/4 |
| 95 | # | Dent, Richard | DE | 6-5 | 265 | 12/13/60 | 12 | Tennessee State | Atlanta, Ga. | D8-'83 | 16/16 |
| 37 | | Douglass, Maurice | CB | 5-11 | 202 | 2/12/64 | 8 | Kentucky | Dayton, Ohio | D8-'86 | 16/1 |
| 65 | | Epps, Tory | DT | 6-1 | 280 | 5/28/67 | 5 | Memphis State | Uniontown, Pa. | FA-'93 | 5/0* |
| 74 | | Fontenot, Albert | DE | 6-4 | 265 | 9/17/70 | 2 | Baylor | Houston, Tex. | D4c-'93 | 16/0 |
| 67 | | Fontenot, Jerry | G-C | 6-3 | 287 | 11/21/66 | 6 | Texas A&M | Lafayette, La. | D3-'89 | 16/16 |
| 17 | | Gardocki, Chris | P-K | 6-1 | 188 | 2/7/70 | 4 | Clemson | Stone Mountain, Calif. | D3-'91 | 16/0 |
| 23 | # | Gayle, Shaun | S | 5-11 | 202 | 3/8/62 | 11 | Ohio State | Bethel, Va. | D10-'84 | 16/16 |
| 84 | | Gedney, Chris | TE | 6-5 | 262 | 8/9/70 | 2 | Syracuse | Liverpool, N.Y. | D3-'93 | 7/4 |
| 81 | t- | Graham, Jeff | WR | 6-1 | 193 | 2/14/69 | 4 | Ohio State | Dayton, Ohio | T(Pitt)-'94 | 15/12* |
| 22 | | Green, Robert | RB | 5-8 | 209 | 9/10/70 | 3 | William & Mary | Ft. Washington, Md. | W(Wash)-'93 | 16/0 |
| 64 | | Heck, Andy | T | 6-6 | 298 | 1/1/67 | 6 | Notre Dame | Fairfax, Va. | RFA(Sea)-'94 | 16/16* |
| 33 | | Hoge, Merril | RB | 6-2 | 230 | 1/26/65 | 8 | Idaho State | Pocatello, Idaho | UFA(Pitt)-'94 | 16/13* |
| 85 | | Jennings, Keith | TE | 6-4 | 265 | 5/19/66 | 5 | Clemson | Summerville, S.C. | FA-'91 | 13/10 |
| 25 | | Johnson, Keshon | CB | 5-10 | 179 | 7/17/70 | 2 | Arizona | Fresno, Calif. | D7-'93 | 15/0 |
| 53 | | Jones, Dante | LB | 6-2 | 230 | 3/23/65 | 7 | Oklahoma | Dallas, Tex. | D2-'88 | 16/16 |
| 12 | | Kramer, Erik | QB | 6-1 | 199 | 11/6/64 | 5 | North Carolina State | Burbank, Calif. | UFA(Det)-'94 | 5/4* |
| 58 | | Leeuwenburg, Jay | G-C | 6-2 | 288 | 6/18/69 | 3 | Colorado | Kirkwood, Mo. | W(KC)-'92 | 16/16 |
| 39 | | Lincoln, Jeremy | CB | 5-10 | 180 | 4/7/69 | 3 | Tennessee | Toledo, Ohio | D3-'92 | 16/7 |
| 26 | | Mangum, John | S | 5-10 | 182 | 3/16/67 | 5 | Alabama | Magee, Miss. | D7-'90 | 12/1 |
| 9 | | Matthews, Shane | QB | 6-3 | 197 | 6/1/70 | 2 | Florida | Pascagoula, Miss. | FA-'93 | 0* |
| 60 | | McGuire, Gene | C | 6-2 | 286 | 7/17/70 | 3 | Notre Dame | Lynn Haven, Fla. | W(NO)-'93 | 9/0 |
| 24 | | Miniefield, Kevin | CB | 5-9 | 178 | 3/2/70 | 2 | Arizona State | Phoenix, Ariz. | FA-'93 | 8/0 |
| 92 | | Minter, Barry | LB | 6-2 | 242 | 1/28/70 | 2 | Tulsa | Mt. Pleasant, Tex. | T(Dall)-'93 | 2/0 |
| 69 | | Myslinski, Tom | G | 6-2 | 293 | 12/7/68 | 2 | Tennessee | Rome, N.Y. | FA-'93 | 1/0 |
| 83 | | Obee, Terry | WR | 5-10 | 180 | 6/15/68 | 2 | Oregon | Richmond, Calif. | UFA(Minn)-'93 | 16/5 |
| 75 | | Perry, Todd | G | 6-5 | 298 | 11/28/70 | 2 | Kentucky | Elizabethtown, Ky. | D4a-'93 | 13/3 |
| 99 | | Ryan, Tim | DT | 6-4 | 265 | 9/8/67 | 5 | Southern California | San Jose, Calif. | D3a-'90 | 11/0 |
| 98 | | Simpson, Carl | DT | 6-2 | 282 | 4/18/70 | 2 | Florida State | Appling County, Ga. | D2-'93 | 11/0 |
| 55 | | Smith, Vinson | LB | 6-2 | 236 | 7/3/65 | 7 | East Carolina | Statesville, N.C. | T(Dall)-'93 | 16/13 |
| 96 | | Snow, Percy | LB | 6-2 | 245 | 11/5/67 | 5 | Michigan State | Canton, Ohio | W(KC)-'93 | 10/0 |
| 90 | | Spellman, Alonzo | DE | 6-4 | 282 | 9/27/71 | 3 | Ohio State | Rancocas, N.J. | D1-'92 | 16/0 |
| 27 | | Tillman, Lewis | RB | 6-0 | 195 | 4/16/66 | 6 | Jackson State | Oklahoma City, Okla. | UFA(NYG)-'94 | 16/7* |
| 78 | # | Van Horne, Keith | T | 6-6 | 290 | 11/6/57 | 14 | Southern California | Fullerton, Calif. | D1-'81 | 13/3 |
| 87 | | Waddle, Tom | WR | 6-0 | 185 | 2/20/67 | 5 | Boston College | Cincinnati, Ohio | FA-'89 | 15/15 |
| 4 | | Walsh, Steve | QB | 6-3 | 210 | 12/1/66 | 6 | Miami | St. Paul, Minn. | FA-'94 | 2/1* |
| 89 | | Wetnight, Ryan | TE | 6-2 | 228 | 11/5/70 | 2 | Stanford | Fresno, Calif. | FA-'93 | 10/1 |
| 71 | | Williams, James | T | 6-7 | 330 | 3/29/68 | 4 | Cheyney State | Allderdice, Pa. | FA-'91 | 3/0 |
| 21 | | Woolford, Donnell | CB | 5-9 | 188 | 1/6/66 | 6 | Clemson | Byrd, N.C. | D1a-'89 | 16/16 |
| 38 | t- | Worley, Tim | RB | 6-2 | 226 | 9/24/66 | 5 | Georgia | Lumberton, N.C. | T(Pitt)-'93 | 15/3* |
| 97 | | Zorich, Chris | DT | 6-1 | 275 | 3/13/69 | 4 | Notre Dame | Chicago, Ill. | D2-'91 | 16/16 |

* Cook played 16 games with New England in '93; Epps played 2 games with Atlanta, 3 games with Chicago; Graham played 15 games with Pittsburgh; Heck played 16 games with Seattle; Hoge played 16 games with Pittsburgh; Kramer played 5 games with Detroit; Matthews inactive for 12 games; Tillman played 16 games with N.Y. Giants; Walsh played 2 games with New Orleans; Worley played 5 games with Pittsburgh, 10 games with Chicago.

\# Unrestricted free agent; subject to developments.

† Restricted free agent; subject to developments.

t- Bears traded for Graham (Pittsburgh), Worley (Pittsburgh).

Also played with Bears in '93—WR Fred Banks (8 games), QB Jim Harbaugh (15), RB Craig Heyward (16), RB John Ivlow (2), RB Darren Lewis (2), DT Steve McMichael (16), WR Anthony Morgan (1), LB Jim Morrissey (2), S Markus Paul (8), DT William Perry (7), G Vernice Smith (6), TE Danta Whitaker (5), QB Peter Tom Willis (5), G John Wojciechowski (14).

## COACHING STAFF

**Head Coach,**
**Dave Wannstedt**

**Pro Career:** Led Bears to a 7-9 record in rookie season. Named Chicago's head coach on January 19, 1993. He was an integral part of one of the most successful turnarounds in NFL history, helping to turn the 1989 Dallas Cowboys, which finished the season 1-15, into Super Bowl champions four years later. In January, 1992, he was named Dallas's assistant head coach and defensive coordinator. He was the defensive coordinator for the Cowboys in 1989. Selected by the Green Bay Packers in the fifteenth round of the 1974 draft, but spent the entire season on injured reserve. Career record: 7-9.
**Background:** Played offensive tackle at the University of Pittsburgh from 1970-73. Began coaching career at Pittsburgh in 1975 and was part of the staff that led the Panthers to a 12-0 record and the NCAA championship in 1976. In 1979, he took a job with Jimmy Johnson at Oklahoma State as defensive line coach. After two seasons, he was promoted to defensive coordinator. In 1983, Wannstedt was the defensive line coach for Southern California before rejoining Johnson at the University of Miami as the Hurricanes' defensive coordinator. In his first year (1986), Miami went 11-0 before losing to Penn State in the Fiesta Bowl. The following season Miami was crowned NCAA champion with a perfect 12-0 record.
**Personal:** Born May 21, 1952, Pittsburgh, Pa. Dave and his wife, Jan, live in Lake Forest, Ill. and have two children—Keri and Jami.

### ASSISTANT COACHES

**Danny Abramowicz,** special teams; born July 13, 1945, Steubenville, Ohio, lives in Lake Forest, Ill. Wide receiver Xavier 1964-66. Pro wide receiver New Orleans Saints 1967-73, San Francisco 49ers 1973-74. Pro coach: Joined Bears in 1992.
**Clarence Brooks,** defensive line; born May 20, 1951, New York, N.Y., lives in Lake Forest, Ill. Guard Massachusetts 1970-73. No pro playing experience. College coach: Massachusetts 1976-80,Syracuse 1981-89, Arizona 1990-92. Pro coach: Joined Bears in 1993.
**Ivan Fears,** wide receivers; born November 15, 1954, Portsmouth, Va., lives in Lake Forest, Ill. Running back William and Mary 1973-75. No pro playing experience. College coach: William and Mary 1977-80, Syracuse 1981-90. Pro coach: New England Patriots 1991-92, joined Bears in 1993.
**Carlos Mainord,** defensive assistant; born August 26, 1944, Greenville, Tex., lives in Lake Forest, Ill. Linebacker Navarro (Tex.) Junior College 1962-63, McMurry College 1964-65. No pro playing experience. College coach: McMurry College 1966-68, Texas Tech 1969, 1983-85, 1987-92, Ranger (Tex.) Junior College 1970-71, 1972-77 (head coach), Rice 1978-82, Miami 1986. Pro coach: Joined Bears in 1993.
**David McGinnis,** linebackers; born August 7, 1951, Independence, Kan., lives in Lake Forest, Ill. Defensive back Texas Christian 1970-72. No pro playing experience. College coach: Texas Christian 1973-74, 1982, Missouri 1975-77, Indiana State 1978-81, Kansas State 1983-85. Pro coach: Joined Bears in 1986.
**Joe Pendry,** running backs; born August 5, 1947, Matheny, W. Va., lives in Lake Forest, Ill. Tight end West Virginia 1966-67. No pro playing experience. College coach: West Virginia 1967-74, 1976-77, Kansas State 1975, Pittsburgh 1978-79, Michigan State 1980-81. Pro coach: Philadelphia Stars (USFL) 1983, Pittsburgh Maulers (USFL) 1984 (head coach), Cleveland Browns 1985-88, Kansas City Chiefs 1989-92, joined Bears in 1993.
**Mike Shula,** tight ends; born June 23, 1965, Baltimore, Md., lives in Lake Forest, Ill. Quarterback Alabama 1984-87. Pro quarterback Tampa Bay Buccaneers 1987. Pro coach: Tampa Bay Buccaneers 1988-90, Miami Dolphins 1991-92, joined Bears in 1993.
**Bob Slowik,** defensive coordinator-defensive backs; born May 16, 1954, Pittsburgh, Pa., lives in Lake Forest, Ill. Cornerback Delaware 1973-76. No pro playing experience. College coach: Delaware 1977, Florida 1978-81, Drake 1982, Rutgers 1983, East Carolina 1984-91. Pro coach: Dallas Cowboys 1992, joined Bears in 1993.
**Ron Turner,** offensive coordinator-quarterbacks; born December 5, 1953, Martinez, Calif., lives in Lake Forest, Ill. Running back-defensive back Pacific 1973-76. No pro playing experience. College coach: Pacific 1977, Arizona 1978-80, Northwestern 1981-82, Pittsburgh 1983-84, Southern California 1985-87, Texas A&M 1988, Stanford 1989-91, San Jose State 1992 (head coach). Pro coach: Joined Bears in 1993.
**Tony Wise,** offensive line; born December 28, 1951, Albany, N.Y., lives in Lake Forest, Ill. Offensive lineman Ithaca College 1971-72. No pro playing experience. College coach: Albany State 1973, Bridgeport 1974, Central Connecticut State 1975, Washington State 1976, Pittsburgh 1977-78, Oklahoma State 1979-83, Syracuse 1984, Miami 1985-88. Pro coach: Dallas Cowboys 1989-92, joined Bears in 1993.

## 1994 FIRST-YEAR ROSTER

| Name | Pos. | Ht. | Wt. | Birthdate | College | Hometown | How Acq. |
|---|---|---|---|---|---|---|---|
| Acorn, Daron (1) | K | 6-2 | 235 | 5/12/71 | Akron | Vancouver, Wash. | FA |
| Bass, Robert | LB | 6-1 | 239 | 11/10/70 | Miami | Tilden, N.Y. | FA |
| Brooks, Anthony (1) | WR | 5-11 | 193 | 8/3/68 | East Texas State | Irving, Tex. | FA |
| Brooks, Donny | CB | 5-11 | 188 | 1/26/70 | Texas Tech | Rockdale, Tex. | FA |
| Burger, Todd (1) | G | 6-3 | 296 | 3/20/70 | Penn State | Clark, N.J. | FA |
| Bussie, Arthur | DE | 6-4 | 258 | 2/25/70 | Northeast Louisiana | Camden, N.J. | FA |
| Carter, Antonio | RB | 5-11 | 216 | 8/23/72 | Minnesota | Columbus, Ohio | FA |
| Collier, Dennis | S | 5-9 | 187 | 5/17/71 | Colorado | San Bernardino, Calif. | D7 |
| Dunning, Josh | G | 6-3 | 302 | 12/5/71 | Washington State | Eatonville, Wash. | FA |
| Durgin, Marcus | CB | 6-1 | 191 | 7/29/72 | Samford, Ala. | Prichard, Ala. | FA |
| Flanigan, Jim | DT | 6-2 | 280 | 8/27/71 | Notre Dame | Green Bay, Wis. | D3 |
| Frier, Matt | WR | 5-11 | 190 | 9/1/71 | Florida State | Live Oak, Fla. | FA |
| Givens, Reggie (1) | LB | 6-1 | 220 | 10/3/71 | Penn State | Sussex, Va. | FA |
| Harris, Raymont | RB | 6-1 | 225 | 12/23/70 | Ohio State | Lorain, Ohio | D4 |
| Hawkins, Garland (1) | DE | 6-3 | 253 | 2/19/70 | Syracuse | Washington, D.C. | FA |
| Hightower, Mike | RB | 5-9 | 191 | 8/17/71 | East Texas State | Paris, Tex. | FA |
| Hill, Lloyd | WR | 6-1 | 189 | 1/16/72 | Texas Tech | Hobbs, N.M. | D6 |
| Ireland, Darwin | LB | 5-11 | 240 | 5/26/71 | Arkansas | Pine Bluff, Tex. | FA |
| Kmet, Frank (1) | G | 6-3 | 294 | 3/13/70 | Purdue | Arlington Heights, Ill. | FA |
| Marshall, Anthony | S | 6-1 | 205 | 9/16/70 | Louisiana State | Mobile, Ala. | FA |
| Martin, John | RB | 5-7 | 185 | 8/31/71 | Memphis State | Homestead, Fla. | FA |
| Norman, Todd | T | 6-5 | 300 | 9/11/71 | Notre Dame | Huntington Beach, Calif. | FA |
| Primus, Greg (1) | WR | 5-11 | 190 | 10/20/70 | Colorado State | Denver, Colo. | FA |
| Sanders, Steven | WR | 5-8 | 161 | 9/26/72 | Virginia Tech | Virginia Beach, Fla. | FA |
| Schwantz, Jim (1) | LB | 6-2 | 232 | 1/23/70 | Purdue | Palatine, Ill. | FA |
| Shorten, Oscar | DT | 6-3 | 285 | 1/27/71 | Abilene Christian | Tascosa, Tex. | FA |
| Spears, Marcus | T | 6-4 | 300 | 9/28/71 | N.W. Louisiana | Baton Rouge, La. | D2 |
| Thierry, John | DE | 6-4 | 260 | 9/4/71 | Alcorn State | Opelousas, La. | D1 |
| Thompson, Aubrey | TE | 6-1 | 230 | 2/19/71 | Utah State | Atlanta, Ga. | FA |
| Walker, Cedric | S | 6-1 | 205 | 2/16/71 | Stephen F. Austin | Lufkin, Tex. | FA |

The term NFL Rookie is defined as a player who is in his first season of professional football and has not been on the roster of another professional football team for any regular-season or postseason games. A Rookie is designated by an "R" on NFL rosters. Players who have been active in another professional football league or players who have NFL experience, including either preseason training camp or being on an Active List or Inactive List, or on Reserve/Injured or Reserve/Physically Unable to Perform for fewer than six regular-season games, are termed NFL First-Year Players. An NFL First-Year Player is designated by a "1" on NFL rosters. Thereafter, a player is credited with an additional year of experience for each season in which he accumulates six games on the Active List or Inactive List, or on Reserve/Injured or Reserve/Physically Unable to Perform.

## NOTES

# DALLAS COWBOYS

**National Football Conference**
**Eastern Division**
**Team Colors:** Royal Blue, Metallic Silver Blue, and White
**Cowboys Center**
**One Cowboys Parkway**
**Irving, Texas 75063**
**Telephone: (214) 556-9900**

## CLUB OFFICIALS

Owner/President/General Manager: Jerry Jones
Vice President: Stephen Jones
Vice President: Mike McCoy
Vice President/Marketing: George Hays
Treasurer: Jack Dixon
Marketing and Special Events Coordinator: Charlotte Anderson
Public Relations Director: Rich Dalrymple
Assistant Director of Public Relations: Brett Daniels
Director of College Scouting: Larry Lacewell
Director of Operations: Bruce Mays
Trainer: Kevin O'Neill
Equipment Manager: Mike McCord
Video Director: Robert Blackwell
Cheerleader Director: Kelli McGonagill
**Stadium:** Texas Stadium •**Capacity:** 65,846 Irving, Texas 75062
**Playing Surface:** Texas Turf
**Training Camp:** St. Edward's University Austin, Texas 78704

## 1994 SCHEDULE

### PRESEASON

| | | |
|---|---|---|
| July 31 | **Minnesota** | 8:00 |
| Aug. 7 | **Los Angeles Raiders** | 8:00 |
| Aug. 15 | vs. Houston at Mexico City | 9:00 |
| Aug. 21 | **Denver** | 7:00 |
| Aug. 25 | at New Orleans | 7:00 |

### REGULAR SEASON

| | | |
|---|---|---|
| Sept. 4 | at Pittsburgh | 4:00 |
| Sept. 11 | **Houston** | 3:00 |
| Sept. 19 | **Detroit** (Monday) | 8:00 |
| Sept. 25 | Open Date | |
| Oct. 2 | at Washington | 1:00 |
| Oct. 9 | **Arizona** | 3:00 |
| Oct. 16 | **Philadelphia** | 3:00 |
| Oct. 23 | at Arizona | 1:00 |
| Oct. 30 | at Cincinnati | 1:00 |
| Nov. 7 | **New York Giants** (Monday) | 8:00 |
| Nov. 13 | at San Francisco | 1:00 |
| Nov. 20 | **Washington** | 12:00 |
| Nov. 24 | **Green Bay** (Thanksgiving) | 3:00 |
| Dec. 4 | at Philadelphia | 1:00 |
| Dec. 10 | **Cleveland** (Saturday) | 3:00 |
| Dec. 19 | at New Orleans (Monday) | 8:00 |
| Dec. 24 | at New York Giants | 1:00 |

## RECORD HOLDERS

### INDIVIDUAL RECORDS—CAREER

| Category | Name | Performance |
|---|---|---|
| Rushing (Yds.) | Tony Dorsett, 1977-1987 | 12,036 |
| Passing (Yds.) | Roger Staubach, 1969-1979 | 22,700 |
| Passing (TDs) | Danny White, 1976-1988 | 155 |
| Receiving (No.) | Drew Pearson, 1973-1983 | 489 |
| Receiving (Yds.) | Tony Hill, 1977-1986 | 7,988 |
| Interceptions | Mel Renfro, 1964-1977 | 52 |
| Punting (Avg.) | Mike Saxon, 1985-1992 | 41.5 |
| Punt Return (Avg.) | Bob Hayes, 1965-1974 | 11.1 |
| Kickoff Return (Avg.) | Mel Renfro, 1964-1977 | 26.4 |
| Field Goals | Rafael Septien, 1978-1986 | 162 |
| Touchdowns (Tot.) | Tony Dorsett, 1977-1987 | 86 |
| Points | Rafael Septien, 1978-1986 | 874 |

### INDIVIDUAL RECORDS—SINGLE SEASON

| Category | Name | Performance |
|---|---|---|
| Rushing (Yds.) | Emmitt Smith, 1992 | 1,713 |
| Passing (Yds.) | Danny White, 1983 | 3,980 |
| Passing (TDs) | Danny White, 1983 | 29 |
| Receiving (No.) | Michael Irvin, 1991 | 93 |
| Receiving (Yds.) | Michael Irvin, 1991 | 1,523 |
| Interceptions | Everson Walls, 1981 | 11 |
| Punting (Avg.) | Sam Baker, 1962 | 45.4 |
| Punt Return (Avg.) | Bob Hayes, 1968 | 20.8 |
| Kickoff Return (Avg.) | Mel Renfro, 1965 | 30.0 |
| Field Goals | Eddie Murray, 1993 | 28 |
| Touchdowns (Tot.) | Emmitt Smith, 1992 | 19 |
| Points | Rafael Septien, 1983 | 123 |

### INDIVIDUAL RECORDS—SINGLE GAME

| Category | Name | Performance |
|---|---|---|
| Rushing (Yds.) | Emmitt Smith, 10-31-93 | 237 |
| Passing (Yds.) | Don Meredith, 11-10-63 | 460 |
| Passing (TDs) | Many times | 5 |
| | Last time by Danny White, 10-30-83 | |
| Receiving (No.) | Lance Rentzel, 11-19-67 | 13 |
| Receiving (Yds.) | Bob Hayes, 11-13-66 | 246 |
| Interceptions | Herb Adderley, 9-26-71 | 3 |
| | Lee Roy Jordan, 11-4-73 | 3 |
| | Dennis Thurman, 12-13-81 | 3 |
| Field Goals | Roger Ruzek, 12-21-87 | 5 |
| | Eddie Murray, 10-3-93 | 5 |
| Touchdowns (Tot.) | Many times | 4 |
| | Last time by Emmitt Smith, 11-18-90 | |
| Points | Many times | 24 |
| | Last time by Emmitt Smith, 11-18-90 | |

## COACHING HISTORY

**(321-215-6)**

| | | |
|---|---|---|
| 1960-88 | Tom Landry | 270-178-6 |
| 1989-93 | Jimmy Johnson | 51-37-0 |

### TEXAS STADIUM

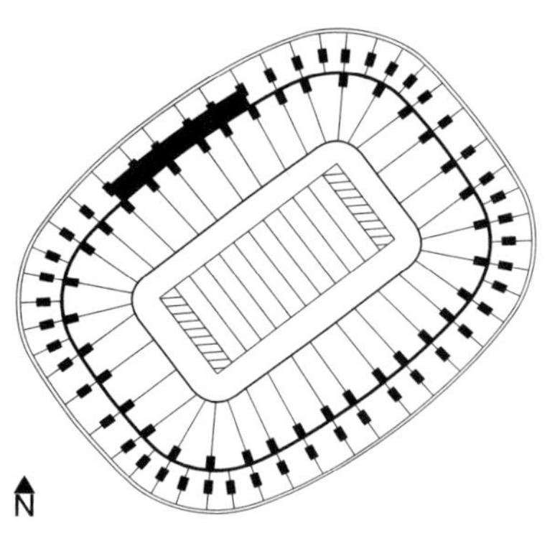

## 1993 TEAM RECORD

**PRESEASON (1-3-1)**

| Date | Result | | Opponents |
|---|---|---|---|
| 8/1 | L | 7-13 | Minnesota |
| 8/8 | T | 13-13 | vs. Detroit at London (OT) |
| 8/14 | W | 13-7 | L.A. Raiders |
| 8/21 | L | 20-23 | vs. Houston at San Antonio |
| 8/27 | L | 21-23 | at Chicago |

**REGULAR SEASON (12-4)**

| Date | Result | | Opponents | Att. |
|---|---|---|---|---|
| 9/6 | L | 16-35 | at Washington | 56,345 |
| 9/12 | L | 10-13 | Buffalo | 63,226 |
| 9/19 | W | 17-10 | at Phoenix | 73,025 |
| 10/3 | W | 36-14 | Green Bay | 63,568 |
| 10/10 | W | 27-3 | at Indianapolis | 60,453 |
| 10/17 | W | 26-17 | San Francisco | 65,099 |
| 10/31 | W | 23-10 | at Philadelphia | 61,912 |
| 11/7 | W | 31-9 | N.Y. Giants | 64,735 |
| 11/14 | W | 20-15 | Phoenix | 64,224 |
| 11/21 | L | 14-27 | at Atlanta | 67,337 |
| 11/25 | L | 14-16 | Miami | 60,198 |
| 12/6 | W | 23-17 | Philadelphia | 64,521 |
| 12/12 | W | 37-20 | at Minnesota | 63,321 |
| 12/18 | W | 28-7 | at N.Y. Jets | 73,233 |
| 12/26 | W | 38-3 | Washington | 64,497 |
| 1/2 | W | 16-13 | at N.Y. Giants (OT) | 77,356 |

**POSTSEASON (3-0)**

| Date | Result | | Opponents | Att. |
|---|---|---|---|---|
| 1/16 | W | 27-17 | Green Bay | 64,790 |
| 1/23 | W | 38-21 | San Francisco | 64,902 |
| 1/30 | W | 30-13 | Buffalo | 72,817 |

(OT) Overtime

**SCORE BY PERIODS**

| | | | | | | | |
|---|---|---|---|---|---|---|---|
| Cowboys | 76 | 124 | 86 | 87 | 3 | — | 376 |
| Opponents | 43 | 46 | 79 | 61 | 0 | — | 229 |

**ATTENDANCE**

Home 510,068 Away 532,982 Total 1,043,050
Single-game home record, 80,259 (11-24-66)
Single-season home record, 511,541 (1981)

## 1993 TEAM STATISTICS

| | Cowboys | Opp. |
|---|---|---|
| Total First Downs | 322 | 297 |
| Rushing | 120 | 94 |
| Passing | 172 | 176 |
| Penalty | 30 | 27 |
| Third Down: Made/Att | 83/198 | 87/219 |
| Third Down Pct. | 41.9 | 39.7 |
| Fourth Down: Made/Att | 7/12 | 6/17 |
| Fourth Down Pct. | 58.3 | 35.3 |
| Total Net Yards | 5615 | 4767 |
| Avg. Per Game | 350.9 | 297.9 |
| Total Plays | 994 | 1012 |
| Avg. Per Play | 5.6 | 4.7 |
| Net Yards Rushing | 2161 | 1651 |
| Avg. Per Game | 135.1 | 103.2 |
| Total Rushes | 490 | 423 |
| Net Yards Passing | 3454 | 3116 |
| Avg. Per Game | 215.9 | 194.8 |
| Sacked/Yards Lost | 29/163 | 34/231 |
| Gross Yards | 3617 | 3347 |
| Att./Completions | 475/317 | 555/334 |
| Completion Pct. | 66.7 | 60.2 |
| Had Intercepted | 6 | 14 |
| Punts/Avg. | 56/41.8 | 78/41.3 |
| Net Punting Avg. | 56/37.7 | 78/34.8 |
| Penalties/Yards Lost | 94/744 | 87/653 |
| Fumbles/Ball Lost | 33/16 | 22/14 |
| Touchdowns | 41 | 23 |
| Rushing | 20 | 7 |
| Passing | 18 | 14 |
| Returns | 3 | 2 |
| Avg. Time of Possession | 30:56 | 29:04 |

## 1993 INDIVIDUAL STATISTICS

| PASSING | Att. | Comp. | Yds. | Pct. | TD | Int. | Tkld. | Rate |
|---|---|---|---|---|---|---|---|---|
| Aikman | 392 | 271 | 3100 | 69.1 | 15 | 6 | 26/153 | 99.0 |
| Kosar | 63 | 36 | 410 | 57.1 | 3 | 0 | 2/4 | 92.7 |
| Garrett | 19 | 9 | 61 | 47.4 | 0 | 0 | 1/6 | 54.9 |
| Harper | 1 | 1 | 46 | 100.0 | 0 | 0 | 0/0 | 118.8 |
| Cowboys | 475 | 317 | 3617 | 66.7 | 18 | 6 | 29/163 | 96.8 |
| Opponents | 555 | 334 | 3347 | 60.2 | 14 | 14 | 34/231 | 75.3 |

| SCORING | TD R | TD P | TD Rt | PAT | FG | Saf | PTS |
|---|---|---|---|---|---|---|---|
| Murray | 0 | 0 | 0 | 38/38 | 28/33 | 0 | 122 |
| E. Smith | 9 | 1 | 0 | 0/0 | 0/0 | 0 | 60 |
| Irvin | 0 | 7 | 0 | 0/0 | 0/0 | 0 | 42 |
| K. Williams | 2 | 2 | 2 | 0/0 | 0/0 | 0 | 36 |
| Harper | 0 | 5 | 0 | 0/0 | 0/0 | 0 | 30 |
| Johnston | 3 | 1 | 0 | 0/0 | 0/0 | 0 | 24 |
| Lassic | 3 | 0 | 0 | 0/0 | 0/0 | 0 | 18 |
| Coleman | 2 | 0 | 0 | 0/0 | 0/0 | 0 | 12 |
| Novacek | 1 | 1 | 0 | 0/0 | 0/0 | 0 | 12 |
| Elliott | 0 | 0 | 0 | 2/3 | 2/4 | 0 | 8 |
| Galbraith | 0 | 1 | 0 | 0/0 | 0/0 | 0 | 6 |
| K. Smith | 0 | 0 | 1 | 0/0 | 0/0 | 0 | 6 |
| Cowboys | 20 | 18 | 3 | 40/41 | 30/37 | 0 | 376 |
| Opponents | 7 | 14 | 2 | 23/23 | 22/27 | 1 | 229 |

| RUSHING | Att. | Yds. | Avg. | LG | TD |
|---|---|---|---|---|---|
| E. Smith | 283 | 1486 | 5.3 | 62t | 9 |
| Lassic | 75 | 269 | 3.6 | 15 | 3 |
| Coleman | 34 | 132 | 3.9 | 16 | 2 |
| Aikman | 32 | 125 | 3.9 | 20 | 0 |
| Johnston | 24 | 74 | 3.1 | 11 | 3 |
| Gainer | 9 | 29 | 3.2 | 8 | 0 |
| K. Williams | 7 | 26 | 3.7 | 12 | 2 |
| Agee | 6 | 13 | 2.2 | 6 | 0 |
| Kosar | 9 | 7 | 0.8 | 4 | 0 |
| Irvin | 2 | 6 | 3.0 | 9 | 0 |
| Novacek | 1 | 2 | 2.0 | 2t | 1 |
| Garrett | 8 | -8 | -1.0 | 0 | 0 |
| Cowboys | 490 | 2161 | 4.4 | 62t | 20 |
| Opponents | 423 | 1651 | 3.9 | 77t | 7 |

| RECEIVING | No. | Yds. | Avg. | LG | TD |
|---|---|---|---|---|---|
| Irvin | 88 | 1330 | 15.1 | 61t | 7 |
| E. Smith | 57 | 414 | 7.3 | 86 | 1 |
| Johnston | 50 | 372 | 7.4 | 20 | 1 |
| Novacek | 44 | 445 | 10.1 | 30 | 1 |
| Harper | 36 | 777 | 21.6 | 80t | 5 |
| K. Williams | 20 | 151 | 7.6 | 33 | 2 |
| Lassic | 9 | 37 | 4.1 | 9 | 0 |
| Gainer | 6 | 37 | 6.2 | 8 | 0 |
| Coleman | 4 | 24 | 6.0 | 10 | 0 |
| T. Williams | 1 | 25 | 25.0 | 25 | 0 |
| Price | 1 | 4 | 4.0 | 4 | 0 |
| Galbraith | 1 | 1 | 1.0 | 1t | 1 |
| Cowboys | 317 | 3617 | 11.4 | 86 | 18 |
| Opponents | 334 | 3347 | 10.0 | 70t | 14 |

| INTERCEPTIONS | No. | Yds. | Avg. | LG | TD |
|---|---|---|---|---|---|
| K. Smith | 6 | 56 | 9.3 | 32t | 1 |
| Bates | 2 | 25 | 12.5 | 22 | 0 |
| Everett | 2 | 25 | 12.5 | 17 | 0 |
| Washington | 1 | 38 | 38.0 | 24 | 0 |
| Norton | 1 | 25 | 25.0 | 25 | 0 |
| Marion | 1 | 2 | 2.0 | 2 | 0 |
| Gant | 1 | 0 | 0.0 | 0 | 0 |
| Cowboys | 14 | 171 | 12.2 | 32t | 1 |
| Opponents | 6 | 47 | 7.8 | 26 | 0 |

| PUNTING | No. | Yds. | Avg. | In 20 | LG |
|---|---|---|---|---|---|
| Jett | 56 | 2342 | 41.8 | 22 | 59 |
| Cowboys | 56 | 2342 | 41.8 | 22 | 59 |
| Opponents | 78 | 3219 | 41.3 | 21 | 60 |

| PUNT RETURNS | No. | FC | Yds. | Avg. | LG | TD |
|---|---|---|---|---|---|---|
| K. Williams | 36 | 14 | 381 | 10.6 | 64t | 2 |
| Washington | 1 | 0 | 0 | 0.0 | 0 | 0 |
| Cowboys | 37 | 14 | 381 | 10.3 | 64t | 2 |
| Opponents | 32 | 12 | 169 | 5.3 | 20 | 0 |

| KICKOFF RETURNS | No. | Yds. | Avg. | LG | TD |
|---|---|---|---|---|---|
| K. Williams | 31 | 689 | 22.2 | 49 | 0 |
| Gant | 1 | 18 | 18.0 | 18 | 0 |
| Hennings | 1 | 7 | 7.0 | 7 | 0 |
| R. Jones | 1 | 12 | 12.0 | 12 | 0 |
| Novacek | 1 | -1 | -1.0 | -1 | 0 |
| K. Smith | 1 | 33 | 33.0 | 33 | 0 |
| Vanderbeek | 0 | 0 | — | 0 | 0 |
| Cowboys | 36 | 758 | 21.1 | 49 | 0 |
| Opponents | 66 | 1225 | 18.6 | 95t | 1 |

| SACKS | No. |
|---|---|
| Tolbert | 7.5 |
| Jeffcoat | 6.0 |
| J. Jones | 5.5 |
| Haley | 4.0 |
| Maryland | 2.5 |
| Casillas | 2.0 |
| Norton | 2.0 |
| Roper | 2.0 |
| Edwards | 1.5 |
| D. Smith | 1.0 |
| Cowboys | 34.0 |
| Opponents | 29.0 |

## 1994 DRAFT CHOICES

| Round | Name | Pos. | College |
|---|---|---|---|
| 1 | Shante Carver | DE | Arizona State |
| 2 | Larry Allen | G | Sonoma State |
| 3 | George Hegamin | T | North Carolina State |
| 4 | Willie Jackson | WR | Florida |
| | DeWayne Dotson | LB | Mississippi |
| 6 | Darren Studstill | DB | West Virginia |
| 7 | Toddrick McIntosh | DT | Florida State |

# DALLAS COWBOYS

## 1994 VETERAN ROSTER

| No. | | Name | Pos. | Ht. | Wt. | Birthdate | NFL Exp. | College | Hometown | How Acq. | '93 Games/ Starts |
|---|---|---|---|---|---|---|---|---|---|---|---|
| 34 | # | Agee, Tommie | RB | 6-0 | 235 | 2/22/64 | 8 | Auburn | Maplesville, Ala. | FA-'93 | 12/0 |
| 8 | | Aikman, Troy | QB | 6-4 | 228 | 11/21/66 | 6 | UCLA | Henryetta, Okla. | D1-'89 | 14/14 |
| 40 | # | Bates, Bill | S | 6-1 | 205 | 6/6/61 | 12 | Tennessee | Knoxville, Tenn. | FA-'83 | 16/0 |
| 24 | | Brown, Larry | CB | 5-11 | 182 | 11/30/69 | 4 | Texas Christian | Los Angeles, Calif. | D12-'91 | 16/16 |
| 44 | | Coleman, Lincoln | RB | 6-1 | 249 | 8/12/69 | 2 | Baylor | Dallas, Tex. | FA-'93 | 7/0 |
| 56 | | Collins, Roosevelt | LB | 6-4 | 244 | 1/25/68 | 2 | Texas Christian | Shreveport, La. | FA-'94 | 0* |
| 68 | # | Cornish, Frank | C-G | 6-4 | 287 | 9/24/67 | 5 | UCLA | Chicago, Ill. | PB(SD)-'92 | 14/3 |
| 81 | | Daniel, Tim | WR | 5-11 | 192 | 9/14/69 | 3 | Florida A&M | Atlanta, Ga. | D11-'92 | 0* |
| 58 | | Edwards, Dixon | LB | 6-1 | 222 | 3/25/68 | 4 | Michigan State | Cincinnati, Ohio | D2-'91 | 16/15 |
| 46 | | Fishback, Joe | S | 6-0 | 212 | 11/29/67 | 5 | Carson-Newman | Knoxville, Tenn. | FA-'93 | 6/0 |
| 89 | # | Galbraith, Scott | TE | 6-2 | 255 | 1/7/67 | 5 | Southern California | Sacramento, Calif. | FA-'93 | 7/0 |
| 29 | | Gant, Kenneth | S | 5-11 | 189 | 4/18/67 | 5 | Albany State | Lakeland, Fla. | D9-'90 | 12/1 |
| 17 | | Garrett, Jason | QB | 6-2 | 195 | 3/28/66 | 2 | Princeton | Chagrin, Ohio | FA-'93 | 5/1 |
| 94 | | Haley, Charles | DE | 6-5 | 250 | 1/6/64 | 9 | James Madison | Campbell County, Va. | T(SF)-'92 | 14/11 |
| 80 | | Harper, Alvin | WR | 6-3 | 208 | 7/6/67 | 4 | Tennessee | Frostproof, Fla. | D1b-'91 | 16/15 |
| 70 | # | Hellestrae, Dale | G-C | 6-5 | 275 | 7/11/62 | 10 | Southern Methodist | Scottsdale, Ariz. | T(Raid)-'90 | 16/0 |
| 95 | | Hennings, Chad | DT | 6-6 | 286 | 10/20/65 | 3 | Air Force | Elberon, Iowa | D11-'88 | 13/0 |
| 47 | | Holmes, Clayton | CB | 5-10 | 181 | 8/23/69 | 3 | Carson-Newman | Florence, S.C. | D3a-'92 | 0* |
| 88 | | Irvin, Michael | WR | 6-2 | 205 | 3/5/66 | 7 | Miami | Ft. Lauderdale, Fla. | D1-'88 | 16/16 |
| 77 | | Jeffcoat, Jim | DE | 6-5 | 280 | 4/1/61 | 12 | Arizona State | Cliffwood, N.J. | D1-'83 | 16/3 |
| 19 | | Jett, John | P | 6-0 | 184 | 11/11/68 | 2 | East Carolina | Reedville, Va. | FA-'93 | 16/0 |
| 48 | | Johnston, Daryl | RB | 6-2 | 238 | 2/10/66 | 6 | Syracuse | Youngstown, N.Y. | D2-'89 | 16/16 |
| 55 | | Jones, Robert | LB | 6-2 | 237 | 9/27/69 | 3 | East Carolina | Nottoway, Va. | D1b-'92 | 13/3 |
| 60 | | Kennard, Derek | G | 6-3 | 300 | 9/9/62 | 9 | Nevada-Reno | Stockton, Calif. | UFA(NO)-'94 | 16/16* |
| 25 | | Lassic, Derrick | RB | 5-10 | 188 | 1/26/70 | 2 | Alabama | North Rockland, N.Y. | D4a-'93 | 10/3 |
| 78 | | Lett, Leon | DE-DT | 6-6 | 285 | 10/12/68 | 4 | Emporia State | Fair Hope, Ala. | D7-'91 | 11/6 |
| 31 | | Marion, Brock | S | 5-11 | 189 | 6/11/70 | 2 | Nevada-Reno | Bakersfield, Calif. | D7-'93 | 15/0 |
| 67 | | Maryland, Russell | DT | 6-1 | 279 | 3/22/69 | 4 | Miami | Chicago, Ill. | D1a-'91 | 16/12 |
| 98 | | Myles, Godfrey | LB | 6-1 | 242 | 9/22/68 | 4 | Florida | Miami, Fla. | D3a-'91 | 10/0 |
| 61 | | Newton, Nate | G | 6-3 | 325 | 12/20/61 | 9 | Florida A&M | Orlando, Fla. | FA-'86 | 16/16 |
| 84 | | Novacek, Jay | TE | 6-4 | 232 | 10/24/62 | 10 | Wyoming | Gothenburg, Neb. | PB(Phx)-'90 | 16/16 |
| 43 | t- | Patterson, Elvis | CB-S | 5-11 | 195 | 10/21/60 | 11 | Kansas | Houston, Tex. | T(Raid)-'93 | 11/0 |
| 9 | | Peete, Rodney | QB | 6-0 | 193 | 3/16/66 | 6 | Southern California | Shawnee Mission, Kan. | UFA(Det)-'94 | 10/10* |
| 89 | t- | Price, Jim | TE | 6-4 | 247 | 10/2/66 | 4 | Stanford | Pine Brook, N.J. | T(Rams)-'93 | 8/0* |
| 74 | | Rentie, Caesar | T-G | 6-3 | 323 | 11/10/64 | 2 | Oklahoma | Hartshorne, Okla. | FA-'94 | 0* |
| 59 | | Smith, Darrin | LB | 6-1 | 227 | 4/15/70 | 2 | Miami | Miami, Fla. | D2b-'93 | 16/13 |
| 22 | | Smith, Emmitt | RB | 5-9 | 209 | 5/15/69 | 5 | Florida | Escambia, Fla. | D1-'90 | 14/13 |
| 82 | | Smith, Jimmy | WR | 6-1 | 205 | 2/9/69 | 3 | Jackson State | Jackson, Miss. | D2a-'92 | 0* |
| 26 | | Smith, Kevin | CB | 5-11 | 180 | 4/7/70 | 3 | Texas A&M | Orange, Tex. | D1a-'92 | 16/16 |
| 53 | # | Stepnoski, Mark | C | 6-2 | 264 | 1/20/67 | 6 | Pittsburgh | Erie, Pa. | D3a-'89 | 13/13 |
| 65 | | Stone, Ron | T | 6-5 | 309 | 7/20/71 | 2 | Boston College | West Roxbury, Mass. | D4b-'93 | 0* |
| 41 | | Thomas, Dave | CB | 6-2 | 208 | 8/25/68 | 2 | Tennessee | Miami, Fla. | D8a-'93 | 12/0 |
| 92 | | Tolbert, Tony | DE | 6-6 | 263 | 12/29/67 | 6 | Texas-El Paso | Englewood, N.J. | D4-'89 | 16/16 |
| 71 | | Tuinei, Mark | T | 6-5 | 305 | 3/31/60 | 12 | Hawaii | Honolulu, Hawaii | FA-'83 | 16/16 |
| 91 | # | Vanderbeek, Matt | LB-DE | 6-3 | 243 | 8/16/67 | 5 | Michigan State | Upland, Calif. | W(Ind)-'93 | 16/0 |
| 37 | | Washington, James | S | 6-1 | 209 | 1/10/65 | 7 | UCLA | Los Angeles, Calif. | PB(Rams)-'90 | 14/1 |
| 79 | | Williams, Erik | T | 6-6 | 324 | 9/7/68 | 4 | Central State, Ohio | Philadelphia, Pa. | D3c-'91 | 16/16 |
| 85 | | Williams, Kevin | WR | 5-9 | 192 | 1/25/71 | 2 | Miami | Dallas, Tex. | D2a-'93 | 16/1 |
| 86 | | Williams, Tyrone | WR | 6-5 | 220 | 3/26/70 | 2 | Western Ontario | Halifax, Nova Scotia | FA-'92 | 5/0 |
| 42 | | Wilson, Robert | RB | 6-0 | 258 | 1/13/69 | 2 | Texas A&M | Houston, Tex. | FA-'94 | 0* |
| 28 | | Woodson, Darren | S | 6-1 | 215 | 4/25/69 | 3 | Arizona State | Phoenix, Ariz. | D2b-'92 | 16/15 |

* Collins inactive for 2 games with Miami in '93; Daniel active for 16 games; Holmes, J. Smith, and Wilson missed '93 season due to injury; Kennard played 16 games with New Orleans in '93; Price played 5 games with L.A. Rams, 3 games with Dallas; Rentie last active with Chicago in '88; Stone active for 4 games but did not play.

\# Unrestricted free agent; subject to developments.

† Restricted free agent; subject to developments.

Traded—S Thomas Everett to Tampa Bay, RB Derrick Gainer to L.A. Raiders.

t- Cowboys traded for Patterson (L.A. Raiders), Price (L.A. Rams).

Players lost through free agency (7): DT Tony Casillas (KC; 15 games in '93), G John Gesek (Wash; 14), G-T Kevin Gogan (Raid; 16), DT Jimmie Jones (Rams; 15), QB Bernie Kosar (Mia; 8 with Cleveland, 4 with Dallas), K Eddie Murray (Phil; 14), LB Ken Norton (SF; 16).

Also played with Cowboys in '93—LB Bobby Abrams (5 games), TE Kelly Blackwell (2), K Lin Elliot (2), S Thomas Everett (16), S Chris Hall (1), Hugh Millen (0), LB John Roper (3), S Robert Williams (4).

## COACHING STAFF

**Head Coach,**
**Barry Switzer**

**Pro Career:** Named the third head coach in Cowboys history on March 30, 1994. No pro playing experience.

**Background:** Played at Arkansas from 1955-59 before beginning his assistant coaching career at his alma mater in 1962. Moved on to Oklahoma in 1966, and was named the Sooners' offensive coordinator in 1967. As head coach at Oklahoma from 1973-88, Switzer registered a career record of 157-29-4. His .837 winning percentage at Oklahoma is the fourth highest mark in college history, behind only Notre Dame's Knute Rockne (.881) and Frank Leahy (.864) and Carlisle's George Woodruff (.846). He guided the Sooners to 28 consecutive wins from 1973-75 and went 37 straight games without a defeat. Switzer's Oklahoma teams won national championships (1974, 1975, and 1985) and 12 Big Eight Conference championships.

**Personal:** Born October 5, 1937, Crossett, Arkansas. Switzer lives in Irving, Texas. He has two sons—Greg and Doug and one daughter Kathy.

### ASSISTANT COACHES

**Hubbard Alexander,** wide receivers; born February 14, 1939, Winston-Salem, N.C., lives in Coppell, Tex. Center Tennessee State 1958-61. No pro playing experience. College coach: Tennessee State 1962-63, Vanderbilt 1974-78, Miami 1979-88. Pro coach: Joined Cowboys in 1989.

**Joe Avezzano,** special teams; born November 17, 1943, Yonkers, N.Y., lives in Coppell, Tex. Guard Florida State 1961-65. Pro center Boston Patriots 1966. College coach: Florida State 1968, Iowa State 1969-72, Pittsburgh 1973-76, Tennessee 1977-79, Oregon State 1980-84 (head coach), Texas 1985-88. Pro coach: Joined Cowboys in 1990.

**John Blake,** defensive line; born March 6, 1961, Sand Springs, Okla., lives in Irving, Tex. Nose tackle Oklahoma 1980-83. No pro playing experience. College coach: Oklahoma 1986-87, 1989-92, Tulsa 1988. Pro coach: Joined Cowboys in 1993.

**Joe Brodsky,** running backs; born June 9, 1934, Miami, Fla., lives in Coppell, Tex. Fullback-linebacker Florida 1953-56. No pro playing experience. College coach: Miami 1978-88. Pro coach: Joined Cowboys in 1989.

**Dave Campo,** defensive backs; born July 18, 1947, New London, Conn., lives in Coppell, Tex. Defensive back Central Connecticut State 1967-70. No pro playing experience. College coach: Central Connecticut State 1971-72, Albany State 1973, Bridgeport 1974, Pittsburgh 1975, Washington State 1976, Boise State 1977-79, Oregon State 1980, Weber State 1981-82, Iowa State 1983, Syracuse 1984-86, Miami 1987-88. Pro coach: Joined Cowboys in 1989.

**Butch Davis,** defensive coordinator; born November 17, 1951, Tahlequah, Okla., lives in Coppell, Tex. Defensive end Arkansas 1971-74. No pro playing experience. College coach: Oklahoma State 1979-83, Miami 1984-88. Pro coach: Joined Cowboys in 1989.

**Jim Eddy,** linebackers; born May 2, 1939, Checotah, Okla., lives in Irving, Tex. Defensive back-running back New Mexico State 1956-59. No pro playing experience. College coach: New Mexico State 1965-70, Texas El-Paso 1971-72, Houston 1987-89. Pro coach: Saskatchewan Rough Riders (CFL) 1974-78 (head coach 1977-78), Hamilton Tiger Cats (CFL) 1979-80, Montreal Alouettes (CFL) 1981 (head coach), Toronto Argonauts (CFL) 1982-83, Houston Gamblers (USFL) 1984-85, Houston Oilers 1990-92, joined Cowboys in 1993.

**Robert Ford,** tight ends; born June 21, 1951, Belton, Tex., lives in Coppell, Tex. Wide receiver Houston 1970-72. No pro playing experience. College coach: Western Illinois 1974-76, New Mexico 1977-79, Oregon State 1980-81, Mississippi State 1982-83, Kansas 1986, Texas Tech 1987-88, Texas A&M 1989-90. Pro coach: Houston Gamblers (USFL) 1985, joined Cowboys in 1991.

**Steve Hoffman,** kickers-research and development; born September 8, 1958, Camden, N.J., lives in Coppell, Tex. Quarterback-running back-wide receiver Dickinson College 1979-82. Pro punter Washington Federals (USFL) 1983. College coach: Miami 1985-87. Pro coach: Joined Cowboys in 1989.

**Hudson Houck,** offensive line; born January 7, 1943, Los Angeles, Calif., lives in Irving, Tex. Center Southern California 1962-64. No pro playing experience. College coach: Southern California 1970-72, 1976-82, Stanford 1973-75. Pro coach: Los Angeles Rams 1983-91, Seattle Seahawks 1992, joined Cowboys in 1993.

**Mike Woicik,** strength and conditioning; born September 26, 1956, Westwood, Mass., lives in Coppell, Tex. Boston College 1974-78. No college or pro playing experience. College coach: Springfield 1978-80, Syracuse 1980-89. Pro coach: Joined Cowboys in 1990.

**Ernie Zampese,** offensive coordinator; born March 12, 1936, Santa Barbara, Calif., lives in Mission Viejo, Calif. Halfback Southern California 1956-58. No pro playing experience. College coach: Hancock, Calif., J.C. 1962-65, Cal Poly-SLO 1966, San Diego State 1967-75. Pro coach: San Diego Chargers 1976, 1979-86, New York Jets 1977-78 (scout), Los Angeles Rams 1987-93, joined Cowboys in 1994.

**Mike Zimmer,** defensive assistant; born June 5, 1956, Peoria, Ill., lives in Irving, Tex. Quarterback-linebacker Illinois State 1974-76. No pro playing experience. College coach: Missouri 1979-80, Weber State 1981-88, Washington State 1989-93. Pro coach: Joined Cowboys in 1994.

## 1994 FIRST-YEAR ROSTER

| Name | Pos. | Ht. | Wt. | Birthdate | College | Hometown | How Acq. |
|---|---|---|---|---|---|---|---|
| Allen, Larry | G | 6-3 | 325 | 11/27/71 | Sonoma State | Napa, Calif. | D2 |
| Batiste, Michael | DT | 6-3 | 301 | 12/24/70 | Tulane | Beaumont, Tex. | FA |
| Bell, Coleman (1) | TE | 6-2 | 232 | 4/22/70 | Miami | Tampa, Fla. | FA |
| Boniol, Chris | K | 5-11 | 159 | 12/9/71 | Louisiana Tech | Alexandria, La. | FA |
| Bretz, Brad (1) | QB | 6-4 | 208 | 8/17/70 | Cal State-Hayward | San Jose, Calif. | FA |
| Burch, Alfie | CB | 6-0 | 196 | 3/24/71 | Michigan | Warren, Ohio | FA |
| Carver, Shante | DE | 6-5 | 240 | 2/12/71 | Arizona State | Stockton, Calif. | D1 |
| Cunningham, Richie | K | 5-10 | 165 | 8/18/70 | Southwest Louisiana | Houma, La. | FA |
| Dotson, Dewayne | LB | 6-1 | 250 | 6/10/71 | Mississippi | Hendersonville, Tenn. | D4b |
| Fayak, Craig | K | 6-1 | 188 | 7/22/72 | Penn State | Belle Vernon, Pa. | FA |
| Garrett, Judd (1) | RB | 6-2 | 214 | 6/25/67 | Princeton | Monmouth Beach, N.J. | FA |
| Hegamin, George | T | 6-7 | 355 | 2/14/73 | North Carolina State | Camden, N.J. | D3 |
| Hill, Shelby | WR | 6-0 | 207 | 8/29/71 | Syracuse | Phoenix, Ariz. | FA |
| Jackson, Willie | WR | 6-1 | 205 | 8/16/71 | Florida | Gainesville, Fla. | D4a |
| Jones, Tommy | CB | 5-8 | 167 | 1/21/71 | Fresno State | Lemoore, Calif. | FA |
| Joyce, Matt | T-G | 6-7 | 283 | 3/30/72 | Richmond | St. Petersburg, Fla. | FA |
| Mason, Mark | RB | 5-7 | 189 | 4/25/72 | Maryland | Potomac, Md. | FA |
| Mays, Marvin | DE | 6-3 | 262 | 9/16/69 | S.E. Oklahoma | Senatobia, Miss. | FA |
| McClanahan, Anthony | LB | 6-1 | 238 | 4/3/71 | Washington State | Bakersfield, Calif. | FA |
| McCormack, Hurvin | DT | 6-5 | 271 | 4/6/72 | Indiana | Brooklyn, N.Y. | FA |
| McIntosh, Toddrick | DT | 6-3 | 277 | 1/22/72 | Florida State | Richardson, Tex. | D7 |
| Mills, Toby | C | 6-0 | 270 | 12/29/71 | Arizona State | Henderson, Tex. | FA |
| Mundy, Aaron | TE | 6-5 | 252 | 11/9/71 | Virginia | Hampton, Va. | FA |
| Parrish, James (1) | T | 6-6 | 310 | 5/19/68 | Temple | Baltimore, Md. | FA |
| Powe, Keith (1) | DE | 6-4 | 265 | 6/5/69 | Texas-El Paso | Houston, Tex. | FA |
| Richardson, Tony | RB | 6-1 | 224 | 12/17/71 | Auburn | Daleville, Ala. | FA |
| Schorp, Greg | TE | 6-3 | 242 | 9/6/71 | Texas A&M | San Antonio, Tex. | FA |
| Studstill, Darren | CB-S | 6-1 | 186 | 8/9/70 | West Virginia | Palm Beach Garden, Fla. | D6 |
| Wagner, Keith | T | 6-4 | 302 | 1/22/70 | Abilene Christian | Corpus Christi, Tex. | FA |
| Wilkins, Jeff | K | 6-1 | 180 | 4/19/72 | Youngstown State | Austintown, Ohio | FA |
| Younger, Jermaine | LB | 6-0 | 262 | 6/1/71 | Utah State | Hayward, Calif. | FA |

The term NFL Rookie is defined as a player who is in his first season of professional football and has not been on the roster of another professional football team for any regular-season or postseason games. A Rookie is designated by an "R" on NFL rosters. Players who have been active in another professional football league or players who have NFL experience, including either preseason training camp or being on an Active List or Inactive List, or on Reserve/Injured or Reserve/Physically Unable to Perform for fewer than six regular-season games, are termed NFL First-Year Players. An NFL First-Year Player is designated by a "1" on NFL rosters. Thereafter, a player is credited with an additional year of experience for each season in which he accumulates six games on the Active List or Inactive List, or on Reserve/Injured or Reserve/Physically Unable to Perform.

## NOTES

# DETROIT LIONS

**National Football Conference**
**Central Division**
**Team Colors:** Honolulu Blue and Silver
**Pontiac Silverdome**
**1200 Featherstone Road**
**Pontiac, Michigan 48342**
**Telephone: (313) 335-4131**

## CLUB OFFICIALS

President-Owner: William Clay Ford
Executive Vice President-COO: Chuck Schmidt
Vice President Administration/Communications: Bill Keenist
Director of Player Personnel: Ron Hughes
Director of Pro Personnel: Kevin Colbert
Scouts: Milt Davis, Dirk Dierking, Tom Dimitroff, Allen Hughes, Scott McEwen, Jim Owens, Rick Spielman, John Trump
Director of Player Programs/Pro Scouting Assistant: Larry Lee
Controller/Travel Coordinator: Tom Lesnau
Director of Marketing, Sales, and Ticket Operations: Fred Otto
Director of Marketing: Steve Harms
Director of Community Relations and Detroit Lions Charities: Tim Pendell
Media Relations Coordinator: Mike Murray
Media Relations Assistant: James Petrylka
Strength and Conditioning: Bert Hill
Trainer: Kent Falb
Equipment Manager: Dan Jaroshewich
Video Director: Steve Hermans
**Stadium:** Pontiac Silverdome • **Capacity:** 80,368
1200 Featherstone Road
Pontiac, Michigan 48342
**Playing Surface:** AstroTurf
**Training Camp:** Pontiac Silverdome
1200 Featherstone Road
Pontiac, Michigan 48342

## 1994 SCHEDULE

**PRESEASON**

| | | |
|---|---|---|
| Aug. 5 | **New York Jets** | 7:30 |
| Aug. 13 | at Cleveland | 7:30 |
| Aug. 19 | **Arizona** | 7:30 |
| Aug. 26 | at Cincinnati | 7:30 |

**REGULAR SEASON**

| | | |
|---|---|---|
| Sept. 4 | **Atlanta** | 1:00 |
| Sept. 11 | at Minnesota | 12:00 |
| Sept. 19 | at Dallas (Monday) | 8:00 |
| Sept. 25 | **New England** | 4:00 |
| Oct. 2 | at Tampa Bay | 1:00 |
| Oct. 9 | **San Francisco** | 1:00 |
| Oct. 16 | Open Date | |
| Oct. 23 | **Chicago** | 1:00 |
| Oct. 30 | at New York Giants | 1:00 |
| Nov. 6 | vs. Green Bay at Milwaukee | 12:00 |
| Nov. 13 | **Tampa Bay** | 8:00 |
| Nov. 20 | at Chicago | 12:00 |
| Nov. 24 | **Buffalo** (Thanksgiving) | 12:30 |
| Dec. 4 | **Green Bay** | 1:00 |
| Dec. 10 | at New York Jets (Saturday) | 12:30 |
| Dec. 17 | **Minnesota** (Saturday) | 12:30 |
| Dec. 25 | at Miami | 8:00 |

## RECORD HOLDERS

### INDIVIDUAL RECORDS—CAREER

| Category | Name | Performance |
|---|---|---|
| Rushing (Yds.) | Barry Sanders, 1989-1993 | 6,789 |
| Passing (Yds.) | Bobby Layne, 1950-58 | 15,710 |
| Passing (TDs) | Bobby Layne, 1950-58 | 118 |
| Receiving (No.) | Charlie Sanders, 1968-1977 | 336 |
| Receiving (Yds.) | Gail Cogdill, 1960-68 | 5,220 |
| Interceptions | Dick LeBeau, 1959-1972 | 62 |
| Punting (Avg.) | Yale Lary, 1952-53, 1956-1964 | 44.3 |
| Punt Return (Avg.) | Jack Christiansen, 1951-58 | 12.8 |
| Kickoff Return (Avg.) | Pat Studstill, 1961-67 | 25.7 |
| Field Goals | Eddie Murray, 1980-1991 | 243 |
| Touchdowns (Tot.) | Barry Sanders, 1989-1993 | 60 |
| Points | Eddie Murray, 1980-1991 | 1,113 |

### INDIVIDUAL RECORDS—SINGLE SEASON

| Category | Name | Performance |
|---|---|---|
| Rushing (Yds.) | Barry Sanders, 1991 | 1,548 |
| Passing (Yds.) | Gary Danielson, 1980 | 3,223 |
| Passing (TDs) | Bobby Layne, 1951 | 26 |
| Receiving (No.) | James Jones, 1984 | 77 |
| Receiving (Yds.) | Pat Studstill, 1966 | 1,266 |
| Interceptions | Don Doll, 1950 | 12 |
| | Jack Christiansen, 1953 | 12 |
| Punting (Avg.) | Yale Lary, 1963 | 48.9 |
| Punt Return (Avg.) | Jack Christiansen, 1952 | 21.5 |
| Kickoff Return (Avg.) | Tom Watkins, 1965 | 34.4 |
| Field Goals | Jason Hanson, 1993 | 34 |
| Touchdowns (Tot.) | Barry Sanders, 1991 | 17 |
| Points | Jason Hanson, 1993 | 130 |

### INDIVIDUAL RECORDS—SINGLE GAME

| Category | Name | Performance |
|---|---|---|
| Rushing (Yds.) | Barry Sanders, 11-24-91 | 220 |
| Passing (Yds.) | Bobby Layne, 11-5-50 | 374 |
| Passing (TDs) | Gary Danielson, 12-9-78 | 5 |
| Receiving (No.) | Cloyce Box, 12-3-50 | 12 |
| | James Jones, 9-28-86 | 12 |
| Receiving (Yds.) | Cloyce Box, 12-3-50 | 302 |
| Interceptions | Don Doll, 10-23-49 | *4 |
| Field Goals | Garo Yepremian, 11-13-66 | 6 |
| Touchdowns (Tot.) | Cloyce Box, 12-3-50 | 4 |
| Points | Cloyce Box, 12-3-50 | 24 |

*NFL Record

## COACHING HISTORY

**Portsmouth Spartans 1930-33**
**(409-421-32)**

| | | |
|---|---|---|
| 1930 | Hal (Tubby) Griffen | 5-6-3 |
| 1931-36 | George (Potsy) Clark | 49-20-6 |
| 1937-38 | Earl (Dutch) Clark | 14-8-0 |
| 1939 | Elmer (Gus) Henderson | 6-5-0 |
| 1940 | George (Potsy) Clark | 5-5-1 |
| 1941-42 | Bill Edwards* | 4-9-1 |
| 1942 | John Karcis | 0-8-0 |
| 1943-47 | Charles (Gus) Dorais | 20-31-2 |
| 1948-50 | Alvin (Bo) McMillin | 12-24-0 |
| 1951-56 | Raymond (Buddy) Parker | 50-24-2 |
| 1957-64 | George Wilson | 55-45-6 |
| 1965-66 | Harry Gilmer | 10-16-2 |
| 1967-72 | Joe Schmidt | 43-35-7 |
| 1973 | Don McCafferty | 6-7-1 |
| 1974-76 | Rick Forzano** | 15-17-0 |
| 1976-77 | Tommy Hudspeth | 11-13-0 |
| 1978-84 | Monte Clark | 43-63-1 |
| 1985-88 | Darryl Rogers*** | 18-40-0 |
| 1988-93 | Wayne Fontes | 43-45-0 |

*Released after three games in 1942
**Resigned after four games in 1976
***Released after 11 games in 1988

**PONTIAC SILVERDOME**

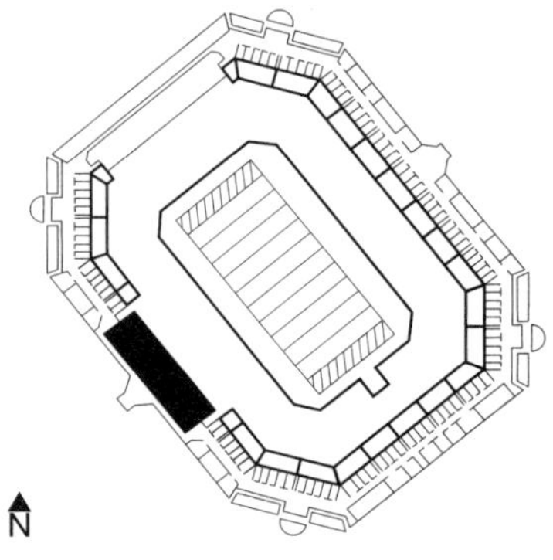

## 1993 TEAM RECORD

**PRESEASON (4-0-1)**

| Date | Result | | Opponents |
|---|---|---|---|
| 7/30 | W | 14-7 | Buffalo |
| 8/8 | T | 13-13 | vs. Dallas at London (OT) |
| 8/16 | W | 24-20 | at Houston |
| 8/20 | W | 30-7 | Cincinnati |
| 8/27 | W | 17-16 | at New Orleans |

**REGULAR SEASON (10-6)**

| Date | Result | | Opponents | Att. |
|---|---|---|---|---|
| 9/5 | W | 30-13 | Atlanta | 56,216 |
| 9/12 | W | 19-16 | at New England (OT) | 54,151 |
| 9/19 | L | 3-14 | at New Orleans | 69,039 |
| 9/26 | W | 26-20 | Phoenix | 57,180 |
| 10/3 | L | 10-27 | at Tampa Bay | 40,794 |
| 10/17 | W | 30-10 | Seattle | 60,801 |
| 10/24 | W | 16-13 | at L.A. Rams | 43,850 |
| 10/31 | W | 30-27 | at Minnesota | 53,428 |
| 11/7 | W | 23-0 | Tampa Bay | 65,295 |
| 11/21 | L | 17-26 | at Green Bay | 55,119 |
| 11/25 | L | 6-10 | Chicago | 76,699 |
| 12/5 | L | 0-13 | Minnesota | 63,216 |
| 12/12 | W | 21-14 | at Phoenix | 39,393 |
| 12/19 | L | 17-55 | San Francisco | 77,052 |
| 12/26 | W | 20-14 | at Chicago | 43,443 |
| 1/2 | W | 30-20 | Green Bay | 77,510 |

**POSTSEASON (0-1)**

| | | | | |
|---|---|---|---|---|
| 1/8 | L | 24-28 | Green Bay | 68,479 |

(OT) Overtime

**SCORE BY PERIODS**

| | | | | | | | |
|---|---|---|---|---|---|---|---|
| Lions | 44 | 102 | 62 | 87 | 3 | — | 298 |
| Opponents | 61 | 86 | 78 | 67 | 0 | — | 292 |

**ATTENDANCE**

Home 533,969 Away 399,217 Total 933,186

Single-game home record, 80,444 (12-20-81)

Single-season home record, 622,593 (1980)

## 1993 TEAM STATISTICS

| | Lions | Opp. |
|---|---|---|
| Total First Downs | 248 | 279 |
| Rushing | 101 | 108 |
| Passing | 139 | 154 |
| Penalty | 8 | 17 |
| Third Down: Made/Att | 73/211 | 92/225 |
| Third Down Pct. | 34.6 | 40.9 |
| Fourth Down: Made/Att | 5/12 | 7/11 |
| Fourth Down Pct. | 41.7 | 63.6 |
| Total Net Yards | 4658 | 4669 |
| Avg. Per Game | 291.1 | 291.8 |
| Total Plays | 937 | 990 |
| Avg. Per Play | 5.0 | 4.7 |
| Net Yards Rushing | 1944 | 1649 |
| Avg. Per Game | 121.5 | 103.1 |
| Total Rushes | 456 | 433 |
| Net Yards Passing | 2714 | 3020 |
| Avg. Per Game | 169.6 | 188.8 |
| Sacked/Yards Lost | 46/229 | 43/253 |
| Gross Yards | 2943 | 3273 |
| Att./Completions | 435/264 | 514/309 |
| Completion Pct. | 60.7 | 60.1 |
| Had Intercepted | 19 | 19 |
| Punts/Avg. | 72/44.5 | 81/43.1 |
| Net Punting Avg. | 72/36.8 | 81/37.0 |
| Penalties/Yards Lost | 93/665 | 73/500 |
| Fumbles/Ball Lost | 29/13 | 34/16 |
| Touchdowns | 28 | 32 |
| Rushing | 9 | 12 |
| Passing | 15 | 19 |
| Returns | 4 | 1 |
| Avg. Time of Possession | 29:27 | 30:33 |

## 1993 INDIVIDUAL STATISTICS

| PASSING | Att | Cmp | Yds. | Pct. | TD | Int | Tkld. | Rate |
|---|---|---|---|---|---|---|---|---|
| Peete | 252 | 157 | 1670 | 62.3 | 6 | 14 | 34/174 | 66.4 |
| Kramer | 138 | 87 | 1002 | 63.0 | 8 | 3 | 5/35 | 95.1 |
| Ware | 45 | 20 | 271 | 44.4 | 1 | 2 | 7/20 | 53.1 |
| Lions | 435 | 264 | 2943 | 60.7 | 15 | 19 | 46/229 | 74.1 |
| Opponents | 514 | 309 | 3273 | 60.1 | 19 | 19 | 43/253 | 75.6 |

| SCORING | TD R | TD P | TD Rt | PAT | FG | Saf | PTS |
|---|---|---|---|---|---|---|---|
| Hanson | 0 | 0 | 0 | 28/28 | 34/43 | 0 | 130 |
| H. Moore | 0 | 6 | 0 | 0/0 | 0/0 | 0 | 36 |
| D. Moore | 3 | 1 | 0 | 0/0 | 0/0 | 0 | 24 |
| Sanders | 3 | 0 | 0 | 0/0 | 0/0 | 0 | 18 |
| Clay | 0 | 0 | 2 | 0/0 | 0/0 | 0 | 12 |
| Green | 0 | 2 | 0 | 0/0 | 0/0 | 0 | 12 |
| Hallock | 0 | 2 | 0 | 0/0 | 0/0 | 0 | 12 |
| Holman | 0 | 2 | 0 | 0/0 | 0/0 | 0 | 12 |
| Lynch | 2 | 0 | 0 | 0/0 | 0/0 | 0 | 12 |
| Perriman | 0 | 2 | 0 | 0/0 | 0/0 | 0 | 12 |
| Gray | 0 | 0 | 1 | 0/0 | 0/0 | 0 | 6 |
| Jamison | 0 | 0 | 1 | 0/0 | 0/0 | 0 | 6 |
| Peete | 1 | 0 | 0 | 0/0 | 0/0 | 0 | 6 |
| Lions | 9 | 15 | 4 | 28/28 | 34/43 | 0 | 298 |
| Opponents | 12 | 19 | 1 | 31/32 | 23/30 | 0 | 292 |

| RUSHING | Att. | Yds. | Avg. | LG | TD |
|---|---|---|---|---|---|
| Sanders | 243 | 1115 | 4.6 | 42 | 3 |
| D. Moore | 88 | 405 | 4.6 | 48 | 3 |
| Lynch | 53 | 207 | 3.9 | 15 | 2 |
| Peete | 45 | 165 | 3.7 | 28 | 1 |
| Ware | 7 | 23 | 3.3 | 8 | 0 |
| Perriman | 4 | 16 | 4.0 | 16 | 0 |
| Matthews | 2 | 7 | 3.5 | 9 | 0 |
| Kramer | 10 | 5 | 0.5 | 4 | 0 |
| C. Richards | 4 | 1 | 0.3 | 1 | 0 |
| Lions | 456 | 1944 | 4.3 | 48 | 9 |
| Opponents | 433 | 1649 | 3.8 | 50t | 12 |

| RECEIVING | No. | Yds. | Avg. | LG | TD |
|---|---|---|---|---|---|
| H. Moore | 61 | 935 | 15.3 | 93t | 6 |
| Perriman | 49 | 496 | 10.1 | 34 | 2 |
| Sanders | 36 | 205 | 5.7 | 17 | 0 |
| Green | 28 | 462 | 16.5 | 47 | 2 |
| Holman | 25 | 244 | 9.8 | 28t | 2 |
| D. Moore | 21 | 169 | 8.0 | 20 | 1 |
| Lynch | 13 | 82 | 6.3 | 11 | 0 |
| Matthews | 11 | 171 | 15.5 | 40 | 0 |
| Hallock | 8 | 88 | 11.0 | 24 | 2 |
| Campbell | 7 | 55 | 7.9 | 12 | 0 |
| Johnson | 2 | 18 | 9.0 | 9 | 0 |
| Thompson | 1 | 15 | 15.0 | 15 | 0 |
| Turner | 1 | 7 | 7.0 | 7 | 0 |
| Fralic | 1 | -4 | -4.0 | -4 | 0 |
| Lions | 264 | 2943 | 11.1 | 93t | 15 |
| Opponents | 309 | 3273 | 10.6 | 80t | 19 |

| INTERCEPTIONS | No. | Yds. | Avg. | LG | TD |
|---|---|---|---|---|---|
| Swilling | 3 | 16 | 5.3 | 14 | 0 |
| Jamison | 2 | 48 | 24.0 | 35t | 1 |
| Crockett | 2 | 31 | 15.5 | 31 | 0 |
| Colon | 2 | 28 | 14.0 | 27 | 0 |
| McNeil | 2 | 19 | 9.5 | 16 | 0 |
| McKyer | 2 | 10 | 5.0 | 10 | 0 |
| Spielman | 2 | -2 | -1.0 | 0 | 0 |
| White | 1 | 5 | 5.0 | 5 | 0 |
| Owens | 1 | 1 | 1.0 | 1 | 0 |
| Gibson | 1 | 0 | 0.0 | 0 | 0 |
| Scroggins | 1 | 0 | 0.0 | 0 | 0 |
| Lions | 19 | 156 | 8.2 | 35t | 1 |
| Opponents | 19 | 177 | 9.3 | 63t | 1 |

| PUNTING | No. | Yds. | Avg. | In 20 | LG |
|---|---|---|---|---|---|
| Arnold | 72 | 3207 | 44.5 | 15 | 68 |
| Lions | 72 | 3207 | 44.5 | 15 | 68 |
| Opponents | 81 | 3489 | 43.1 | 25 | 57 |

| PUNT RETURNS | No. | FC | Yds. | Avg. | LG | TD |
|---|---|---|---|---|---|---|
| Gray | 23 | 14 | 197 | 8.6 | 35 | 0 |
| Turner | 17 | 4 | 152 | 8.9 | 53 | 0 |
| Lions | 40 | 18 | 349 | 8.7 | 53 | 0 |
| Opponents | 45 | 5 | 377 | 8.4 | 21 | 0 |

| KICKOFF RETURNS | No. | Yds. | Avg. | LG | TD |
|---|---|---|---|---|---|
| Gray | 28 | 688 | 24.6 | 95t | 1 |
| Anderson | 3 | 51 | 17.0 | 24 | 0 |
| Turner | 15 | 330 | 22.0 | 46 | 0 |
| Clay | 2 | 34 | 17.0 | 20 | 0 |
| Hallock | 1 | 11 | 11.0 | 11 | 0 |
| Jamison | 1 | 0 | 0.0 | 0 | 0 |
| Lynch | 1 | 22 | 22.0 | 22 | 0 |
| D. Moore | 1 | 68 | 68.0 | 68 | 0 |
| V. Jones | 0 | 0 | — | — | 0 |
| Lions | 52 | 1204 | 23.2 | 95t | 1 |
| Opponents | 30 | 609 | 20.3 | 64 | 0 |

| SACKS | No. |
|---|---|
| Porcher | 8.5 |
| Scroggins | 8.0 |
| Swilling | 6.5 |
| Pritchett | 4.0 |
| Owens | 3.0 |
| Hayworth | 2.0 |
| Jamison | 2.0 |
| Spindler | 2.0 |
| White | 1.5 |
| Clay | 1.0 |
| Colon | 1.0 |
| Crockett | 1.0 |
| Gibson | 1.0 |
| London | 1.0 |
| Spielman | 0.5 |
| Lions | 43.0 |
| Opponents | 46.0 |

## 1994 DRAFT CHOICES

| Round | Name | Pos. | College |
|---|---|---|---|
| 1 | Johnnie Morton | WR | Southern California |
| 2 | Van Malone | DB | Texas |
| 3 | Shane Bonham | DT | Tennessee |
| 4 | Vaughn Bryant | DB | Stanford |
| 5 | Tony Semple | G | Memphis State |
| 6 | Jocelyn Borgella | DB | Cincinnati |
| 7 | Thomas Beer | LB | Wayne State, Mich. |

# DETROIT LIONS

## 1994 VETERAN ROSTER

| No. | | Name | Pos. | Ht. | Wt. | Birthdate | NFL Exp. | College | Hometown | How Acq. | '93 Games/ Starts |
|---|---|---|---|---|---|---|---|---|---|---|---|
| 43 | # | Anderson, Gary | RB | 6-1 | 190 | 4/18/61 | 9 | Arkansas | Columbia, Mo. | FA-'93 | 10/1* |
| 36 | | Blades, Bennie | S | 6-1 | 221 | 9/3/66 | 7 | Miami | Ft. Lauderdale, Fla. | D1-'88 | 4/4 |
| 66 | | Bouwens, Shawn | G | 6-4 | 290 | 5/25/68 | 4 | Nebraska-Wesleyan | Lincoln, Neb. | FA-'91 | 15/1 |
| 75 | | Brown, Lomas | T | 6-4 | 287 | 3/30/63 | 10 | Florida | Miami, Fla. | D1-'85 | 11/11 |
| 68 | | Burton, Leonard | C | 6-3 | 275 | 6/18/64 | 8 | South Carolina | Memphis, Tenn. | FA-'94 | 0* |
| 50 | # | Caston, Toby | LB | 6-1 | 243 | 7/17/65 | 8 | Louisiana State | Monroe, La. | FA-'93 | 9/0 |
| 32 | | Clay, Willie | CB | 5-9 | 184 | 9/5/70 | 3 | Georgia Tech | Pittsburgh, Pa. | D8-'92 | 16/1 |
| 21 | † | Colon, Harry | S | 6-0 | 203 | 2/14/69 | 4 | Missouri | Kansas City, Kan. | FA-'92 | 15/11 |
| 77 | | Compton, Mike | C-G | 6-6 | 297 | 9/18/70 | 2 | West Virginia | Glenwood, Iowa | D3b-'93 | 8/0 |
| 76 | | Conover, Scott | T | 6-4 | 285 | 9/27/68 | 4 | Purdue | Freehold, N.J. | D5-'91 | 1/0 |
| 53 | | Glover, Kevin | C | 6-2 | 282 | 6/17/63 | 10 | Maryland | Upper Marlboro, Md. | D2-'85 | 16/16 |
| 23 | | Gray, Mel | WR-KR | 5-9 | 171 | 3/16/61 | 9 | Purdue | Williamsburg, Va. | FA-'89 | 11/0 |
| 86 | | Green, Willie | WR | 6-2 | 181 | 4/2/66 | 5 | Mississippi | Athens, Ga. | D8a-'90 | 16/6 |
| 89 | | Hall, Ron | TE | 6-4 | 245 | 3/15/64 | 8 | Hawaii | Escondido, Calif. | UFA(TB)-'94 | 16/16* |
| 49 | | Hallock, Ty | TE | 6-3 | 249 | 4/30/71 | 2 | Michigan State | Greenville, Mich. | D7-'93 | 16/4 |
| 4 | | Hanson, Jason | K | 5-11 | 183 | 6/17/70 | 3 | Washington State | Spokane, Wash. | D2b-'92 | 16/0 |
| 99 | | Hayworth, Tracy | LB | 6-3 | 260 | 12/18/67 | 5 | Tennessee | Franklin, Tenn. | D7-'90 | 11/2 |
| 81 | # | Holman, Rodney | TE | 6-3 | 238 | 4/20/60 | 13 | Tulane | Ypsilanti, Mich. | UFA(Cin)-'93 | 16/16 |
| 58 | # | Jamison, George | LB | 6-1 | 235 | 9/30/62 | 9 | Cincinnati | Bridgeton, N.J. | SD2-'84 | 16/16 |
| 25 | | Jeffries, Greg | CB | 5-9 | 184 | 10/16/71 | 2 | Virginia | High Point, N.C. | D6-'93 | 7/0 |
| 51 | | Johnson, Mike | LB | 6-1 | 230 | 11/26/62 | 9 | Virginia Tech | Hyattsville, Md. | UFA(Clev)-'94 | 16/16* |
| 57 | # | Jones, Victor | LB | 6-2 | 250 | 10/19/66 | 7 | Virginia Tech | Rockville, Md. | FA-'89 | 16/1 |
| 52 | | Kowalkowski, Scott | LB | 6-2 | 228 | 8/23/68 | 4 | Notre Dame | Orchard Lake, Mich. | FA-'94 | 0* |
| 17 | | Krieg, Dave | QB | 6-1 | 202 | 10/20/58 | 15 | Milton | Schofield, Wis. | UFA(KC)-'94 | 12/5* |
| 55 | | London, Antonio | LB | 6-2 | 234 | 4/14/71 | 2 | Alabama | Tullahoma, Tenn. | D3a-'93 | 14/0 |
| 16 | | Long, Chuck | QB | 6-4 | 217 | 2/18/63 | 8 | Iowa | Wheaton, Ill. | FA-'94 | 0* |
| 73 | | Lutz, Dave | G-T | 6-6 | 305 | 12/20/59 | 12 | Georgia Tech | Peachland, N.C. | UFA(KC)-'93 | 16/16 |
| 40 | | Massey, Robert | CB | 5-11 | 195 | 2/16/67 | 6 | North Carolina Central | Charlotte, N.C. | UFA(Ariz)-'94 | 10/10* |
| 83 | # | Matthews, Aubrey | WR | 5-7 | 165 | 9/15/62 | 9 | Delta State | Pascaguola, Miss. | FA-'90 | 14/2 |
| 33 | # | McKyer, Tim | CB | 6-0 | 174 | 9/5/63 | 9 | Texas-Arlington | Port Arthur, Tex. | UFA(Atl)-'93 | 15/4 |
| 47 | | McNeil, Ryan | CB | 6-0 | 175 | 10/4/70 | 2 | Miami | Ft. Pierce, Fla. | D2-'93 | 16/2 |
| 19 | | Mitchell, Scott | QB | 6-6 | 230 | 1/2/68 | 5 | Utah | Springville, Utah | UFA(Mia)-'94 | 13/7* |
| 9 | | Montgomery, Greg | P | 6-4 | 215 | 10/29/64 | 6 | Michigan State | Red Bank, N.J. | UFA(Hou)-'94 | 15/0* |
| 31 | | Moore, Derrick | RB | 6-1 | 227 | 10/13/67 | 3 | Northeast Oklahoma St. | Albany, Ga. | W(Atl)-'93 | 13/3 |
| 84 | | Moore, Herman | WR | 6-3 | 210 | 10/20/69 | 4 | Virginia | Danville, Va. | D1-'91 | 15/15 |
| 90 | † | Owens, Dan | DE | 6-3 | 280 | 3/16/67 | 5 | Southern California | Whittier, Calif. | D2-'90 | 15/11 |
| 80 | | Perriman, Brett | WR | 5-9 | 180 | 10/10/65 | 7 | Miami | Miami, Fla. | T(NO)-'91 | 15/15 |
| 91 | | Porcher, Robert | DE | 6-3 | 283 | 7/30/69 | 3 | South Carolina State | Wendo, S.C. | D1-'92 | 16/4 |
| 94 | † | Pritchett, Kelvin | DE | 6-2 | 281 | 10/24/69 | 2 | Mississippi | Atlanta, Ga. | T(Dall)-'91 | 16/5 |
| 67 | | Richards, Dave | G | 6-5 | 310 | 4/11/66 | 7 | UCLA | Dallas, Tex. | UFA(SD)-'93 | 15/15 |
| 63 | # | Rodenhauser, Mark | C | 6-5 | 280 | 6/1/61 | 7 | Illinois State | Addison, Ill. | FA-'93 | 16/0 |
| 20 | | Sanders, Barry | RB | 5-8 | 203 | 7/16/68 | 6 | Oklahoma State | Wichita, Kan. | D1-'89 | 11/11 |
| 38 | † | Scott, Kevin | CB | 5-9 | 175 | 5/19/69 | 4 | Stanford | Phoenix, Ariz. | D4-'91 | 12/10 |
| 59 | | Scroggins, Tracy | LB | 6-2 | 255 | 9/11/69 | 3 | Tulsa | Chectah, Okla. | D2a-'92 | 16/0 |
| 54 | | Spielman, Chris | LB | 6-0 | 247 | 10/11/65 | 7 | Ohio State | Massilon, Ohio | D2b-'88 | 16/16 |
| 93 | | Spindler, Marc | DE | 6-5 | 290 | 11/28/69 | 5 | Pittsburgh | West Scranton, Pa. | D3-'90 | 16/16 |
| 56 | | Swilling, Pat | LB | 6-3 | 242 | 10/25/64 | 9 | Georgia Tech | Toccoa, Ga. | T(NO)-'93 | 14/14 |
| 71 | | Tharpe, Larry | T | 6-4 | 299 | 11/19/70 | 3 | Tennessee State | Macon, Ga. | D6-'92 | 5/3 |
| 81 | | Thompson, Marty | TE | 6-3 | 243 | 12/9/69 | 2 | Fresno State | Mammoth Lakes, Calif. | FA-'93 | 6/2 |
| 35 | | White, William | S | 5-10 | 191 | 2/19/66 | 7 | Ohio State | Lima, Ohio | D4-'88 | 16/16 |

* Anderson played 6 games with Tampa Bay, 4 games with Detroit in '93; Burton last active with Detroit in '92; Hall played 16 games with Tampa Bay; Johnson played 16 games with Cleveland; Kowalkowski missed '93 season due to injury; Krieg played 12 games with Kansas City; Long on injured reserve with Detroit in '92; Massey played 10 games with Arizona; Mitchell played 13 games with Miami; Montgomery played 15 games with Houston.

# Unrestricted free agent; subject to developments.

† Restricted free agent; subject to developments.

Traded—WR Reggie Barnett to Seattle.

Retired—Lawrence Pete, 6-year nose tackle, 12 games in '93.

Players lost through free agency (7): P Jim Arnold (Mia; 16 games in '93), WR Jeff Campbell (Den; 10), CB Ray Crockett (Den; 16), LB Dennis Gibson (SD; 15), QB Erik Kramer (Chi; 5), QB Rodney Peete (Dall; 10), QB Andre Ware (Minn; 5).

Also played with Lions in '93—LB Darryl Ford (11 games in '93), G Bill Fralic (16), CB Melvin Jenkins (1), TE Jimmy Johnson (6), T Jack Linn (3), RB Eric Lynch (4), (6), RB Curvin Richards (1), NT Mack Travis (4), WR Vernon Turner (7).

## COACHING STAFF

**Head Coach,**
**Wayne Fontes**

**Pro Career:** Became the Lions' seventeenth head coach on December, 22, 1988, after serving five weeks as interim head coach (2-3 record). Has led the Lions to two Central Division championships in the last three seasons. The Lions captured the NFC Central title with a 10-6 record in 1993, but were eliminated in the first round of the playoffs. Detroit finished 5-11 in 1992. In 1991, Fontes led the Lions to a 12-4 record and the team's first NFC Central Division title since 1983. The Lions notched their first playoff victory since 1957 and reached the NFC Championship Game in 1991. The Lions were 6-10 in 1990. In 1989, Fontes's first full season, the Lions finished 7-9, including five consecutive season-ending wins. He began the 1988 season as Detroit's defensive coordinator and secondary coach, following a nine-year stint with the Tampa Bay Buccaneers. A former defensive back with the New York Jets, Fontes advanced from secondary coach to defensive coordinator to assistant head coach of the Buccaneers during his years with Tampa Bay. As a player with the Jets, his brief pro career was cut short by a broken leg after two seasons (1963-64). However, his 83-yard interception return against Houston (12-15-63) did stand as the Jets' team record until it was broken in 1989 by Erik McMillan's 93-yard return. Career record: 43-45.

**Background:** A former two-sport star (football and baseball) at Michigan State, Fontes earned all-Big Ten honors at defensive back for the Spartans. He earned his bachelor's degree in education and biological science and later earned his master's degree in administration, all from Michigan State. Fontes became defensive backfield coach at Dayton in 1968. He also served in the same capacity at Iowa (1969-71) and Southern California (1972-75).

**Personal:** Born February 17, 1939, New Bedford, Mass. Fontes and his wife, Evelyn, live in Rochester Hills, Mich., and have three children—Mike, Scott, and Kim.

### ASSISTANT COACHES

**Paul Boudreau,** offensive line; born December 30, 1949, Somerville, Mass., lives in Rochester Hills, Mich. Guard Boston College 1971-73. No pro playing experience. College coach: Boston College 1974-76, Maine 1977-78, Dartmouth 1979-81, Navy 1983. Pro coach: Edmonton Eskimos (CFL) 1983-86, New Orleans Saints 1987-93, joined Lions in 1994.

**Don Clemons,** outside linebackers; born February 15, 1954, Newark, N.J., lives in Rochester, Mich. Defensive end Muehlenberg College 1973-76. No pro playing experience. College coach: Kutztown State 1977-78, New Mexico 1979, Arizona State 1980-84. Pro coach: Joined Lions in 1985.

**John Fontes,** defensive backs; born June 24, 1949, New Bedford, Mass., lives in Rochester Hills, Mich. Defensive back Iowa 1969-70. No pro playing experience. College coach: Iowa 1971-72, Oregon State 1976-80, Northwestern 1985, Miami 1986, Louisiana State 1987-89. Pro coach: Tampa Bay Storm (Arena League) 1991, Sacramento Surge (World League) 1992, joined Lions in 1992.

**Steve Kazor,** special teams; born February 24, 1948, New Kensington, Pa., lives in Oxford, Mich. Nose tackle Westminster College 1967-70. No pro playing experience. College coach: Emporia State 1973 (head coach), Texas Arlington 1974, Colorado State 1975, Wyoming 1976, Texas 1977-78, Texas-El Paso 1979-80, Iowa Wesleyan 1993 (head coach). Pro coach: Chicago Bears 1982-92, joined Lions in 1994.

**Lamar Leachman,** defensive line; born August 7, 1934, Cartersville, Ga., lives in Pontiac, Mich. Center-linebacker Tennessee 1952-55. No pro playing experience. College coach: Richmond 1966-67, Georgia Tech 1968-71, Memphis State 1972, South Carolina 1973. Pro coach: New York Stars (WFL) 1974, Toronto Argonauts (CFL) 1975-77, Montreal Alouettes (CFL) 1978-79, New York Giants 1980-89, joined Lions in 1990.

**Dave Levy,** assistant head coach-offensive coordinator; born October 25, 1932, Carrollton, Mo., lives in Southfield, Mich. Guard UCLA 1952-53. No pro playing experience. College coach: UCLA 1954, Long Beach City College 1955, Southern California 1960-75. Pro coach: San Diego Chargers 1980-88, joined Lions in 1989.

**Billie Matthews,** running backs; born March 15, 1930, Houston, Tex., lives in Rochester, Mich. Quarterback Southern University 1948-51. No pro playing experience. College coach: Kansas 1970, UCLA 1971-78. Pro coach: San Francisco 49ers 1979-82, Philadelphia Eagles 1983-84, Indianapolis Colts 1985-86, Kansas City Chiefs 1987-88, joined Lions in 1989.

**Tom Moore,** quarterbacks; born November 7, 1938, Owatanna, Minn., lives in Rochester Hills, Mich. Quarterback Iowa 1957-60. No pro playing experience. College coach: Iowa 1961-62, Dayton 1965-68, Wake Forest 1969, Georgia Tech 1970-71, Minnesota 1972-73, 1975-76. Pro coach: New York Stars (WFL) 1974, Pittsburgh Steelers 1977-89, Minnesota Vikings 1990-93, joined Lions in 1994.

**Herb Paterra,** defensive coordinator; born November 8, 1940, Glassport, Pa., lives in Rochester Hills, Mich. Offensive guard-linebacker Michigan State 1960-62. Pro linebacker Buffalo Bills 1963-64, Hamilton Tiger-Cats (CFL) 1965-68. College coach: Michigan State 1969-71, Wyoming 1972-74. Pro coach: Charlotte Hornets (WFL) 1975, Hamilton Tiger-Cats (CFL) 1978-79, Los Angeles Rams 1980-82, Edmonton Eskimos (CFL) 1983, Green Bay Packers 1984-85, Buffalo Bills 1986, Tampa Bay Buccaneers 1987-88, joined Lions in 1989.

**Charlie Sanders,** receivers; born August 25, 1946, Greensboro, N.C., lives in Rochester, Mich. Tight end Minnesota 1966-67. Pro tight end Detroit Lions 1968-77. Pro coach: Joined Lions in 1989.

**Howard Tippett,** linebackers; born September 23, 1938, Tallassee, Ala., lives in Rochester Hills, Mich. Quarterback-safety East Tennessee State 1956-58. No pro playing experience. College coach: Tulane 1963-65, West Virginia 1966, 1970-71, Houston 1967-69, Wake Forest 1972, Mississippi State 1973, 1979, Washington State 1976, Oregon 1977-78, UCLA 1980, Illinois 1987. Pro coach: Jacksonville Express (WFL) 1974-75, Tampa Bay Buccaneers 1981-86, Green Bay Packers 1988-91, Los Angeles Rams 1992-93, joined Lions in 1994.

## 1994 FIRST-YEAR ROSTER

| Name | Pos. | Ht. | Wt. | Birthdate | College | Hometown | How Acq. |
|---|---|---|---|---|---|---|---|
| Batiste, Raymond | G | 6-4 | 305 | 11/3/71 | N.E. Louisiana | New Orleans, La. | FA |
| Beer, Tom | LB | 6-1 | 237 | 3/27/69 | Wayne State | Bay Port, Mich. | D7 |
| Bonham, Shane | DE | 6-4 | 260 | 10/18/70 | Tennessee | Fairbanks, Alaska | D3 |
| Borgella, Jocelyn | CB | 5-10 | 180 | 8/26/71 | Cincinnati | Miami, Fla. | D6 |
| Brown, Ernie | DE | 6-2 | 280 | 3/14/71 | Syracuse | Pittsburgh, Pa. | FA |
| Bryant, Vaughn | CB | 5-9 | 187 | 3/20/72 | Stanford | Detroit, Mich. | D4 |
| Butland, Josh | P | 6-5 | 240 | 5/6/69 | Michigan State | Troy, Mich. | FA |
| Green, Eric | WR-KR | 5-10 | 170 | 4/7/71 | Illinois-Benedictine | Plainfield, N.J. | FA |
| Jones, Jason | G | 6-3 | 282 | 5/16/70 | Hampton | Williamsburg, Va. | FA |
| Kaplan, Scott (1) | K | 6-0 | 190 | 2/17/70 | Pittsburgh | Coral Springs, Fla. | FA |
| Lynch, Eric (1) | RB | 5-10 | 224 | 5/16/70 | Grand Valley State | Woodhaven, Mich. | FA |
| Mack, Travis (1) | NT | 6-1 | 280 | 7/3/70 | California | Las Vegas, Nev. | FA |
| Malone, Van | S | 5-11 | 188 | 7/1/70 | Texas | Houston, Tex. | D2 |
| Moore, Kyle (1) | DE | 6-3 | 250 | 2/27/71 | Kansas State | Newark, N.J. | FA |
| Morton, Johnnie | WR | 5-9 | 190 | 10/7/71 | Southern California | Torrance, Calif. | D1 |
| Oglesby, John | RB | 6-0 | 230 | 12/31/70 | Texas Christian | Detroit, Mich. | FA |
| Powers, Ricky | RB | 6-0 | 205 | 11/30/71 | Michigan | Akron, Ohio | FA |
| Roberts, Ray | TE | 6-2 | 251 | 3/6/71 | Northern Illinois | Chicago, Ill. | FA |
| Ryans, Larry (1) | WR | 5-11 | 182 | 7/28/71 | Clemson | Greenwood, S.C. | FA |
| Semple, Tony | G | 6-4 | 286 | 12/20/70 | Memphis State | Lincoln, Ill. | D5 |
| Wilson, James | DE | 6-3 | 253 | 1/10/70 | Tennessee | Hampton, Va. | FA |
| Woodley, Richard | WR | 5-9 | 180 | 1/13/72 | Texas Christian | Texas City, Tex. | FA |

The term NFL Rookie is defined as a player who is in his first season of professional football and has not been on the roster of another professional football team for any regular-season or postseason games. A Rookie is designated by an "R" on NFL rosters. Players who have been active in another professional football league or players who have NFL experience, including either preseason training camp or being on an Active List or Inactive List, or on Reserve/Injured or Reserve/Physically Unable to Perform for fewer than six regular-season games, are termed NFL First-Year Players. An NFL First-Year Player is designated by a "1" on NFL rosters. Thereafter, a player is credited with an additional year of experience for each season in which he accumulates six games on the Active List or Inactive List, or on Reserve/Injured or Reserve/Physically Unable to Perform.

## NOTES

**National Football Conference**
**Central Division**
**Team Colors:** Dark Green, Gold, and White
**1265 Lombardi Avenue**
**Green Bay, Wisconsin 54304**
**Telephone: (414) 496-5700**

## CLUB OFFICIALS

President, CEO: Robert E. Harlan
Vice President: John Fabry
Secretary: Peter M. Platten III
Treasurer: John R. Underwood
Vice President-Administration: Michael R. Reinfeldt
Exec. V.P. and General Manager: Ron Wolf
Exec. Assistant to the President: Phil Pionek
Exec. Director of Public Relations: Lee Remmel
Director of Marketing: Jeff Cieply
Asst. Director of Public Relations: Jeff Blumb
Dir. of Community Relations: Mark Schiefelbein
General Legal Counsel: Lance Lopes
Director of Pro Personnel: Ted Thompson
Director of College Scouting: John Math
Green Bay Ticket Director: Mark Wagner
Milwaukee Ticket Director: Marge Paget
Controller: Dick Blasczyk
Dir. of Computer Operations: Wayne A. Wichlacz
Video Director: Al Treml
Trainer: Pepper Burruss
Equipment Manager: Gordon Batty
Corporate Security Officer: Jerry Parins
Stadium Supervisor: Ted Eisenreich
**Stadium:** Lambeau Field • **Capacity:** 59,543
1265 Lombardi Avenue
Green Bay, Wisconsin 54304
Milwaukee County Stadium
• **Capacity:** 56,051
201 South 46th Street
Milwaukee, Wisconsin 53214
**Playing Surfaces:** Grass
**Training Camp:** St. Norbert College
West De Pere, Wisconsin 54115

## 1994 SCHEDULE

**PRESEASON**

| | | |
|---|---|---|
| Aug. 6 | vs. L.A. Rams at Madison, Wis. | 12:00 |
| Aug. 13 | vs. Miami at Milwaukee | 7:00 |
| Aug. 19 | at New Orleans | 7:00 |
| Aug. 26 | **New England** | 7:00 |

**REGULAR SEASON**

| | | |
|---|---|---|
| Sept. 4 | **Minnesota** | 12:00 |
| Sept. 11 | **Miami** at Milwaukee | 12:00 |
| Sept. 18 | at Philadelphia | 1:00 |
| Sept. 25 | **Tampa Bay** | 12:00 |
| Oct. 2 | at New England | 1:00 |
| Oct. 9 | **Los Angeles Rams** | 12:00 |
| Oct. 16 | Open Date | |
| Oct. 20 | at Minnesota (Thursday) | 7:00 |
| Oct. 31 | at Chicago (Monday) | 8:00 |
| Nov. 6 | **Detroit** at Milwaukee | 12:00 |
| Nov. 13 | **New York Jets** | 3:00 |
| Nov. 20 | at Buffalo | 1:00 |
| Nov. 24 | at Dallas (Thanksgiving) | 3:00 |
| Dec. 4 | at Detroit | 1:00 |
| Dec. 11 | **Chicago** | 12:00 |
| Dec. 18 | **Atlanta** at Milwaukee | 12:00 |
| Dec. 24 | at Tampa Bay | 1:00 |

## RECORD HOLDERS

**INDIVIDUAL RECORDS—CAREER**

| Category | Name | Performance |
|---|---|---|
| Rushing (Yds.) | Jim Taylor, 1958-1966 | 8,207 |
| Passing (Yds.) | Bart Starr, 1956-1971 | 23,718 |
| Passing (TDs) | Bart Starr, 1956-1971 | 152 |
| Receiving (No.) | James Lofton, 1978-1986 | 530 |
| Receiving (Yds.) | James Lofton, 1978-1986 | 9,656 |
| Interceptions | Bobby Dillon, 1952-59 | 52 |
| Punting (Avg.) | Dick Deschaine, 1955-57 | 42.6 |
| Punt Return (Avg.) | Billy Grimes, 1950-52 | 13.2 |
| Kickoff Return (Avg.) | Travis Williams, 1967-1970 | 26.7 |
| Field Goals | Chester Marcol, 1972-1980 | 120 |
| Touchdowns (Tot.) | Don Hutson, 1935-1945 | 105 |
| Points | Don Hutson, 1935-1945 | 823 |

**INDIVIDUAL RECORDS—SINGLE SEASON**

| Category | Name | Performance |
|---|---|---|
| Rushing (Yds.) | Jim Taylor, 1962 | 1,474 |
| Passing (Yds.) | Lynn Dickey, 1983 | 4,458 |
| Passing (TDs) | Lynn Dickey, 1983 | 32 |
| Receiving (No.) | Sterling Sharpe, 1993 | *112 |
| Receiving (Yds.) | Sterling Sharpe, 1992 | 1,461 |
| Interceptions | Irv Comp, 1943 | 10 |
| Punting (Avg.) | Jerry Norton, 1963 | 44.7 |
| Punt Return (Avg.) | Billy Grimes, 1950 | 19.1 |
| Kickoff Return (Avg.) | Travis Williams, 1967 | *41.1 |
| Field Goals | Chester Marcol, 1972 | 33 |
| Touchdowns (Tot.) | Jim Taylor, 1962 | 19 |
| Points | Paul Hornung, 1960 | *176 |

**INDIVIDUAL RECORDS—SINGLE GAME**

| Category | Name | Performance |
|---|---|---|
| Rushing (Yds.) | Jim Taylor, 12-3-61 | 186 |
| Passing (Yds.) | Lynn Dickey, 10-12-80 | 418 |
| Passing (TDs) | Many times<br>Last time by Lynn Dickey, 9-4-83 | 5 |
| Receiving (No.) | Don Hutson, 11-22-42 | 14 |
| Receiving (Yds.) | Bill Howton, 10-21-56 | 257 |
| Interceptions | Bobby Dillon, 11-26-53 | *4 |
| | Willie Buchanon, 9-24-78 | *4 |
| Field Goals | Chris Jacke, 11-11-90 | 5 |
| Touchdowns (Tot.) | Paul Hornung, 12-12-65 | 5 |
| Points | Paul Hornung, 10-8-61 | 33 |

*NFL Record

## COACHING HISTORY

**(508-428-36)**

| | | |
|---|---|---|
| 1921-49 | Earl (Curly) Lambeau | 212-106-21 |
| 1950-53 | Gene Ronzani* | 14-31-1 |
| 1953 | Hugh Devore-<br>Ray (Scooter) McLean** | 0-2-0 |
| 1954-57 | Lisle Blackbourn | 17-31-0 |
| 1958 | Ray (Scooter) McLean | 1-10-1 |
| 1959-67 | Vince Lombardi | 98-30-4 |
| 1968-70 | Phil Bengtson | 20-21-1 |
| 1971-74 | Dan Devine | 25-28-4 |
| 1975-83 | Bart Starr | 53-77-3 |
| 1984-87 | Forrest Gregg | 25-37-1 |
| 1988-91 | Lindy Infante | 24-40-0 |
| 1992-93 | Mike Holmgren | 19-15-0 |

*Released after 10 games in 1953
**Co-coaches

**MILWAUKEE/LAMBEAU FIELD**

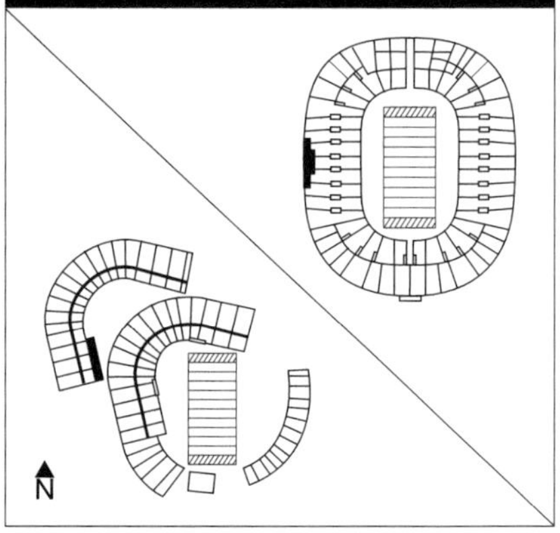

## 1993 TEAM RECORD

**PRESEASON (1-4)**

| Date | Result | | Opponents |
|---|---|---|---|
| 7/31 | L | 3-19 | vs. L.A. Raiders at Canton |
| 8/7 | L | 21-29 | Kansas City at Milw. |
| 8/14 | L | 17-26 | vs. New Orleans at Madison |
| 8/21 | L | 17-21 | at New England |
| 8/27 | W | 41-10 | Indianapolis |

**REGULAR SEASON (9-7)**

| Date | Result | | Opponents | Att. |
|---|---|---|---|---|
| 9/5 | W | 36-6 | L.A. Rams | 54,648 |
| 9/12 | L | 17-20 | Philadelphia | 59,061 |
| 9/26 | L | 13-15 | at Minnesota | 61,746 |
| 10/3 | L | 14-36 | at Dallas | 63,568 |
| 10/10 | W | 30-27 | Denver | 58,943 |
| 10/24 | W | 37-14 | at Tampa Bay | 47,354 |
| 10/31 | W | 17-3 | Chicago | 58,945 |
| 11/8 | L | 16-23 | at Kansas City | 76,742 |
| 11/14 | W | 19-17 | at New Orleans | 69,043 |
| 11/21 | W | 26-17 | Detroit | 55,119 |
| 11/28 | W | 13-10 | Tampa Bay | 56,995 |
| 12/5 | L | 17-30 | at Chicago | 62,236 |
| 12/12 | W | 20-13 | at San Diego | 57,930 |
| 12/19 | L | 17-21 | Minnesota | 54,773 |
| 12/26 | W | 28-0 | L.A. Raiders | 54,482 |
| 1/2 | L | 20-30 | at Detroit | 77,510 |

**POSTSEASON (1-1)**

| | | | | |
|---|---|---|---|---|
| 1/8 | W | 28-24 | at Detroit | 68,479 |
| 1/16 | L | 17-27 | at Dallas | 64,790 |

**SCORE BY PERIODS**

| | | | | | | | |
|---|---|---|---|---|---|---|---|
| Packers | 97 | 95 | 77 | 71 | 0 | — | 340 |
| Opponents | 29 | 76 | 90 | 87 | 0 | — | 282 |

**ATTENDANCE**

Home 452,966 Away 516,129 Total 969,095
Single-game home record, 59,061 (9-12-93, Lambeau Field), 56,258 (9-28-80, Milwaukee County Stadium)
Single-season home record, 456,944 (1992)

## 1993 TEAM STATISTICS

| | Packers | Opp. |
|---|---|---|
| Total First Downs | 282 | 261 |
| Rushing | 98 | 88 |
| Passing | 166 | 157 |
| Penalty | 18 | 16 |
| Third Down: Made/Att | 81/218 | 70/217 |
| Third Down Pct. | 37.2 | 32.3 |
| Fourth Down: Made/Att | 9/16 | 3/19 |
| Fourth Down Pct. | 56.3 | 15.8 |
| Total Net Yards | 4750 | 4482 |
| Avg. Per Game | 296.9 | 280.1 |
| Total Plays | 1006 | 999 |
| Avg. Per Play | 4.7 | 4.5 |
| Net Yards Rushing | 1619 | 1582 |
| Avg. Per Game | 101.2 | 98.9 |
| Total Rushes | 448 | 424 |
| Net Yards Passing | 3131 | 2900 |
| Avg. Per Game | 195.7 | 181.3 |
| Sacked/Yards Lost | 30/199 | 46/301 |
| Gross Yards | 3330 | 3201 |
| Att./Completions | 528/322 | 529/290 |
| Completion Pct. | 61.0 | 54.8 |
| Had Intercepted | 24 | 18 |
| Punts/Avg. | 74/42.9 | 79/40.2 |
| Net Punting Avg. | 74/36.3 | 79/34.3 |
| Penalties/Yards Lost | 85/734 | 85/712 |
| Fumbles/Ball Lost | 26/10 | 33/15 |
| Touchdowns | 35 | 27 |
| Rushing | 14 | 6 |
| Passing | 19 | 16 |
| Returns | 2 | 5 |
| Avg. Time of Possession | 30:53 | 29:07 |

## 1993 INDIVIDUAL STATISTICS

| PASSING | Att | Cmp | Yds. | Pct. | TD | Int | Tkld. | Rate |
|---|---|---|---|---|---|---|---|---|
| Favre | 522 | 318 | 3303 | 60.9 | 19 | 24 | 30/199 | 72.2 |
| Detmer | 5 | 3 | 26 | 60.0 | 0 | 0 | 0/0 | 73.8 |
| Sharpe | 1 | 1 | 1 | 100.0 | 0 | 0 | 0/0 | 79.2 |
| Packers | 528 | 322 | 3330 | 61.0 | 19 | 24 | 30/199 | 72.2 |
| Opponents | 529 | 290 | 3201 | 54.8 | 16 | 18 | 46/301 | 68.9 |

| SCORING | TD R | TD P | TD Rt | PAT | FG | Saf | PTS |
|---|---|---|---|---|---|---|---|
| Jacke | 0 | 0 | 0 | 35/35 | 31/37 | 0 | 128 |
| Sharpe | 0 | 11 | 0 | 0/0 | 0/0 | 0 | 66 |
| E. Bennett | 9 | 1 | 0 | 0/0 | 0/0 | 0 | 60 |
| J. Harris | 0 | 4 | 0 | 0/0 | 0/0 | 0 | 24 |
| Clayton | 0 | 3 | 0 | 0/0 | 0/0 | 0 | 18 |
| Thompson | 3 | 0 | 0 | 0/0 | 0/0 | 0 | 18 |
| Brooks | 0 | 0 | 1 | 0/0 | 0/0 | 0 | 6 |
| Butler | 0 | 0 | 1 | 0/0 | 0/0 | 0 | 6 |
| Favre | 1 | 0 | 0 | 0/0 | 0/0 | 0 | 6 |
| Stephens | 1 | 0 | 0 | 0/0 | 0/0 | 0 | 6 |
| Packers | 14 | 19 | 2 | 35/35 | 31/37 | 1 | 340 |
| Opponents | 6 | 16 | 5 | 27/27 | 31/40 | 0 | 282 |

| RUSHING | Att. | Yds. | Avg. | LG | TD |
|---|---|---|---|---|---|
| Thompson | 169 | 654 | 3.9 | 60t | 3 |
| E. Bennett | 159 | 550 | 3.5 | 19 | 9 |
| Favre | 58 | 216 | 3.7 | 27 | 1 |
| Stephens | 48 | 173 | 3.6 | 22 | 1 |
| Brooks | 3 | 17 | 5.7 | 21 | 0 |
| Sharpe | 4 | 8 | 2.0 | 5 | 0 |
| Wilson | 6 | 3 | 0.5 | 5 | 0 |
| Detmer | 1 | -2 | -2.0 | -2 | 0 |
| Packers | 448 | 1619 | 3.6 | 60t | 14 |
| Opponents | 424 | 1582 | 3.7 | 60 | 6 |

| RECEIVING | No. | Yds. | Avg. | LG | TD |
|---|---|---|---|---|---|
| Sharpe | 112 | 1274 | 11.4 | 54 | 11 |
| E. Bennett | 59 | 457 | 7.7 | 39t | 1 |
| J. Harris | 42 | 604 | 14.4 | 66t | 4 |
| Clayton | 32 | 331 | 10.3 | 32 | 3 |
| West | 25 | 253 | 10.1 | 24 | 0 |
| Brooks | 20 | 180 | 9.0 | 25 | 0 |
| Thompson | 18 | 129 | 7.2 | 34 | 0 |
| Stephens | 5 | 31 | 6.2 | 10 | 0 |
| Lewis | 2 | 21 | 10.5 | 17 | 0 |
| Wilson | 2 | 18 | 9.0 | 11 | 0 |
| Chmura | 2 | 13 | 6.5 | 7 | 0 |
| C. Harris | 2 | 11 | 5.5 | 6 | 0 |
| Morgan | 1 | 8 | 8.0 | 8 | 0 |
| Packers | 322 | 3330 | 10.3 | 66t | 19 |
| Opponents | 290 | 3201 | 11.0 | 67t | 16 |

| INTERCEPTIONS | No. | Yds. | Avg. | LG | TD |
|---|---|---|---|---|---|
| Butler | 6 | 131 | 21.8 | 39 | 0 |
| Holland | 2 | 41 | 20.5 | 30 | 0 |
| Buckley | 2 | 31 | 15.5 | 31 | 0 |
| Simmons | 2 | 21 | 10.5 | 19 | 0 |
| Teague | 1 | 22 | 22.0 | 22 | 0 |
| Paup | 1 | 8 | 8.0 | 8 | 0 |
| Prior | 1 | 1 | 1.0 | 1 | 0 |
| Brock | 1 | 0 | 0.0 | 0 | 0 |
| Evans | 1 | 0 | 0.0 | 0 | 0 |
| Mitchell | 1 | 0 | 0.0 | 0 | 0 |
| Packers | 18 | 255 | 14.2 | 39 | 0 |
| Opponents | 24 | 437 | 18.2 | 86t | 3 |

| PUNTING | No. | Yds. | Avg. | In 20 | LG |
|---|---|---|---|---|---|
| Wagner | 74 | 3174 | 42.9 | 19 | 60 |
| Packers | 74 | 3174 | 42.9 | 19 | 60 |
| Opponents | 79 | 3176 | 40.2 | 20 | 58 |

| PUNT RETURNS | No. | FC | Yds. | Avg. | LG | TD |
|---|---|---|---|---|---|---|
| Prior | 17 | 3 | 194 | 11.4 | 24 | 0 |
| Brooks | 16 | 4 | 135 | 8.4 | 35 | 0 |
| Buckley | 11 | 5 | 76 | 6.9 | 39 | 0 |
| Teague | 1 | 0 | -1 | -1.0 | -1 | 0 |
| Packers | 45 | 12 | 404 | 9.0 | 39 | 0 |
| Opponents | 38 | 12 | 350 | 9.2 | 35 | 0 |

| KICKOFF RETURNS | No. | Yds. | Avg. | LG | TD |
|---|---|---|---|---|---|
| Brooks | 23 | 611 | 26.6 | 95t | 1 |
| C. Harris | 16 | 482 | 30.1 | 65 | 0 |
| Thompson | 9 | 171 | 19.0 | 42 | 0 |
| Wilson | 9 | 197 | 21.9 | 37 | 0 |
| Jurkovic | 2 | 22 | 11.0 | 13 | 0 |
| Chmura | 1 | 0 | 0.0 | 0 | 0 |
| Packers | 60 | 1483 | 24.7 | 95t | 1 |
| Opponents | 70 | 1407 | 20.1 | 68 | 0 |

| SACKS | No. |
|---|---|
| White | 13.0 |
| Paup | 11.0 |
| T. Bennett | 6.5 |
| Jurkovic | 5.5 |
| Koonce | 3.0 |
| Brock | 2.0 |
| Holland | 2.0 |
| Butler | 1.0 |
| Patterson | 1.0 |
| Simmons | 1.0 |
| Packers | 46.0 |
| Opponents | 30.0 |

## 1994 DRAFT CHOICES

| Round | Name | Pos. | College |
|---|---|---|---|
| 1 | Aaron Taylor | G | Notre Dame |
| 3 | LeShon Johnson | RB | Northern Illinois |
| 4 | Gabe Wilkins | DE | Gardner-Webb |
| 5 | Terry Mickens | WR | Florida A&M |
| | Dorsey Levens | RB | Georgia Tech |
| 6 | Jay Kearney | WR | West Virginia |
| | Ruffin Hamilton | LB | Tulane |
| | Bill Schroeder | WR | Wisconsin-LaCrosse |
| | Paul Duckworth | LB | Connecticut |

## GREEN BAY PACKERS

### 1994 VETERAN ROSTER

| No. | | Name | Pos. | Ht. | Wt. | Birthdate | NFL Exp. | College | Hometown | How Acq. | '93 Games/ Starts |
|---|---|---|---|---|---|---|---|---|---|---|---|
| 51 | | Barker, Tony | LB | 6-2 | 235 | 9/7/68 | 2 | Rice | Wichita, Kan. | FA-'94 | 0* |
| 34 | | Bennett, Edgar | RB | 6-0 | 216 | 2/15/69 | 3 | Florida State | Jacksonville, Fla. | D4-'92 | 16/14 |
| 62 | # | Brock, Matt | DE | 6-5 | 280 | 1/14/66 | 6 | Oregon | San Diego, Calif. | D3a-'89 | 16/13 |
| 87 | | Brooks, Robert | WR | 6-0 | 174 | 6/23/70 | 3 | South Carolina | Greenwood, S.C. | D3-'92 | 14/0 |
| 71 | | Brown, Gilbert | NT | 6-2 | 330 | 2/22/71 | 2 | Kansas | Detroit, Mich. | W(Minn)-'93 | 2/0 |
| 8 | | Brunnell, Mark | QB | 6-1 | 208 | 9/17/70 | 2 | Washington | Santa Maria, Calif. | D5a-'93 | 0* |
| 27 | | Buckley, Terrell | CB | 5-9 | 174 | 6/7/71 | 3 | Florida State | Pascagoula, Miss. | D1-'92 | 16/16 |
| 36 | | Butler, LeRoy | S | 6-0 | 193 | 7/19/68 | 5 | Florida State | Jacksonville, Fla. | D2-'90 | 16/16 |
| 63 | | Campen, James | C | 6-2 | 280 | 6/11/64 | 8 | Tulane | Shingle Springs, Calif. | PB(NO)-'89 | 4/4 |
| 89 | | Chmura, Mark | TE | 6-5 | 242 | 2/22/69 | 3 | Boston College | South Deerfield, Mass. | D6-'92 | 14/0 |
| 32 | | Cobb, Reggie | RB | 6-0 | 215 | 7/7/68 | 5 | Tennessee | Knoxville, Tenn. | UFA(TB)-'94 | 12/10* |
| 54 | | Coleman, Keo | LB | 6-1 | 255 | 5/1/70 | 3 | Mississippi State | Milwaukee, Wis. | FA-'93 | 12/2 |
| 99 | | Davey, Don | DE | 6-4 | 270 | 4/8/68 | 4 | Wisconsin | Manitowoc, Wis. | FA-'92 | 9/0 |
| 11 | | Detmer, Ty | QB | 6-0 | 190 | 10/30/67 | 3 | Brigham Young | San Antonio, Tex. | D9a-'92 | 3/0 |
| 32 | | Dingle, Mike | RB | 6-2 | 240 | 1/30/69 | 3 | South Carolina | Moncks Corner, S.C. | FA-'94 | 0* |
| 58 | | D'Onofrio, Mark | LB | 6-2 | 235 | 3/17/69 | 2 | Penn State | North Bergen, N.J. | D2-'92 | 0* |
| 72 | | Dotson, Earl | T | 6-3 | 315 | 12/17/70 | 2 | Texas A&I | Beaumont, Tex. | D3-'93 | 13/0 |
| 33 | | Evans, Doug | CB | 6-0 | 188 | 5/13/70 | 2 | Louisiana Tech | Haynesville, La. | D6a-'93 | 16/0 |
| 93 | | Evans, Mike | DE | 6-3 | 270 | 6/2/67 | 2 | Michigan | Ashburnham, Mass. | FA-'94 | 0* |
| 4 | † | Favre, Brett | QB | 6-2 | 218 | 10/10/69 | 4 | Southern Mississippi | Kiln, Miss. | T(Atl)-'92 | 16/16 |
| 76 | | Galbreath, Harry | G | 6-1 | 275 | 1/1/65 | 7 | Tennessee | Clarksville, Tenn. | UFA(Mia)-'93 | 16/16 |
| 30 | | Harris, Corey | CB | 5-11 | 195 | 10/25/69 | 3 | Vanderbilt | Indianapolis, Ind. | W(Hou)-'92 | 11/0 |
| 80 | † | Harris, Jackie | TE | 6-3 | 243 | 1/4/68 | 5 | Northeast Louisiana | Pine Bluff, Ark. | D4-'90 | 12/12 |
| 24 | # | Hauck, Tim | S | 5-10 | 185 | 12/20/66 | 5 | Montana | Big Timber, Mont. | PB(NE)-'91 | 13/0 |
| 67 | | Hutchins, Paul | T | 6-4 | 335 | 2/11/70 | 2 | Western Michigan | Chicago, Ill. | FA-'93 | 1/0 |
| 13 | | Jacke, Chris | K | 6-0 | 200 | 3/12/66 | 6 | Texas-El Paso | Richardson, Tex. | D6-'89 | 16/0 |
| 96 | | Jones, Sean | DE | 6-7 | 268 | 12/19/62 | 11 | Northeastern | Montclair, N.J. | UFA(Hou)-'94 | 16/16* |
| 64 | | Jurkovic, John | NT | 6-2 | 285 | 8/18/67 | 3 | Eastern Illinois | Calumet City, Ill. | FA-'91 | 16/12 |
| 77 | | Jurkovic, Mirko | T | 6-3 | 290 | 5/19/70 | 2 | Notre Dame | Calumet City, Ill. | FA-'94 | 0* |
| 53 | | Koonce, George | LB | 6-1 | 238 | 10/15/68 | 3 | Eastern Carolina | Vanceboro, N.C. | FA-'92 | 15/15 |
| 78 | | LaBounty, Matt | DE | 6-3 | 254 | 1/3/69 | 2 | Oregon | San Marin, Calif. | W(SF)-'93 | 6/0* |
| 85 | # | Lewis, Ron | WR | 5-11 | 189 | 3/25/68 | 5 | Florida State | Jacksonville, Fla. | FA-'93 | 9/0 |
| | | McMichael, Steve | DT | 6-2 | 268 | 10/17/57 | 15 | Texas | Frees, Tex. | FA-'94 | 16/16* |
| 44 | | McNabb, Dexter | RB | 6-1 | 245 | 7/9/69 | 3 | Florida State | DeFuniak Springs, Fla. | D5a-'92 | 16/0 |
| 97 | | Merriweather, Mike | LB | 6-2 | 228 | 11/26/60 | 12 | Pacific | Vallejo, Calif. | FA-'93 | 1/0* |
| 94 | | Mersereau, Scott | NT | 6-3 | 275 | 4/8/65 | 8 | Southern Connecticut | Riverhead, N.Y. | FA-'94 | 13/13* |
| 47 | | Mitchell, Roland | CB | 5-11 | 195 | 3/15/64 | 7 | Texas Tech | Bay City, Tex. | PB(Atl)-'91 | 16/16 |
| 81 | | Morgan, Anthony | WR | 6-1 | 195 | 11/15/67 | 4 | Tennessee | Cleveland, Ohio | W(Chi)-'93 | 3/0* |
| 95 | | Paup, Bryce | LB | 6-5 | 247 | 2/29/68 | 5 | Northern Iowa | Scranton, Iowa | D6-'90 | 15/14 |
| 45 | | Prior, Mike | S | 6-0 | 215 | 11/14/63 | 9 | Illinois State | Chicago Heights, Ill. | UFA(Ind)-'93 | 16/4 |
| 73 | # | Robbins, Tootie | T | 6-5 | 315 | 6/2/58 | 13 | Eastern Carolina | Windsor, N.C. | FA-'93 | 12/11 |
| 75 | | Ruettgers, Ken | T | 6-6 | 290 | 8/20/62 | 10 | Southern California | Bakersfield, Calif. | D1-'85 | 16/16 |
| 84 | | Sharpe, Sterling | WR | 6-1 | 210 | 4/6/65 | 7 | South Carolina | Glennville, Ga. | D1-'88 | 16/16 |
| 59 | | Simmons, Wayne | LB | 6-2 | 240 | 12/15/69 | 2 | Clemson | Hilton Head, S.C. | D1a-'93 | 14/8 |
| 68 | | Sims, Joe | T | 6-3 | 310 | 3/1/69 | 4 | Nebraska | Sudbury, Mass. | FA-'92 | 13/5 |
| 31 | | Teague, George | S | 6-1 | 187 | 2/18/71 | 2 | Alabama | Montgomery, Ala. | D1b-'93 | 16/12 |
| 39 | # | Thompson, Darrell | RB | 6-0 | 217 | 11/23/67 | 5 | Minnesota | Rochester, Minn. | D1b-'90 | 16/11 |
| 9 | | Wagner, Bryan | P | 6-2 | 200 | 3/28/62 | 7 | Cal State-Northridge | Chula Vista, Calif. | FA-'92 | 16/0 |
| 23 | | Walker, Sammy | CB | 5-11 | 203 | 1/20/69 | 4 | Texas Tech | McKinney, Tex. | FA-'93 | 8/1 |
| 86 | # | West, Ed | TE | 6-1 | 245 | 8/2/61 | 11 | Auburn | Leighton, Ala. | FA-'93 | 16/7 |
| 92 | | White, Reggie | DE | 6-5 | 290 | 12/19/61 | 10 | Tennessee | Chattanooga, Tenn. | UFA(Phil)-'93 | 16/16 |
| 74 | # | Widell, Doug | G | 6-4 | 280 | 9/23/66 | 6 | Boston College | Hartford, Conn. | T(Den)-'93 | 16/9 |
| 20 | | Williams, Kevin | RB | 6-1 | 215 | 2/17/70 | 2 | UCLA | Spring, Tex. | FA-'93 | 3/0 |
| 56 | | Willis, James | LB | 6-1 | 235 | 9/2/72 | 2 | Auburn | Huntsville, Ga. | D5b-'93 | 13/0 |
| 29 | | Wilson, Marcus | RB | 6-1 | 210 | 4/16/68 | 3 | Virginia | Rochester, N.Y. | FA-'92 | 16/0 |
| 52 | | Winters, Frank | C-G | 6-3 | 285 | 1/23/64 | 8 | Western Illinois | Union City, N.J. | PB(KC)-'92 | 16/16 |
| 60 | | Zeno, Lance | C | 6-4 | 279 | 4/15/67 | 3 | UCLA | Fountain Valley, Calif. | W(TB)-'93 | 5/0 |

* Barker last active with Washington in '92; Brunell active for 1 game in '93 but did not play; Cobb played 12 games with Tampa Bay; Dingle on injured reserve with Cincinnati in '92; D'Onofrio missed '93 season due to injury; Evans last active with Kansas City in '92; Jones played 16 games with Houston; M. Jurkovic last active with Chicago in '92; LaBounty played 6 games with San Francisco; McMichael played 16 games with Chicago; Merriweather played 1 game with N.Y. Jets; Mersereau played 13 games with N.Y. Jets; Morgan played 1 game with Chicago.

\# Unrestricted free agent; subject to developments.

† Restricted free agent; subject to developments.

Retired: Johnny Holland, 7-year linebacker, 16 games in '93; Brian Noble, 9-year linebacker, 2 games in '93.

Traded—DE Lester Archambeau to Atlanta, RB John Stephens to Atlanta.

Players lost through free agency (1)—LB Tony Bennett (Ind; 10 games in '93).

Also played with the Packers in '93—WR Mark Clayton (16 games), WR Brett Collins (4), WR Shawn Collins (4), DE David Grant (7), T Tunch Ilkin (1), TE Darryl Ingram (2), NT Bill Maas (14), G Rich Moran (3), LB Jim Morrissey (6), LB Joe Mott (2), CB Muhammed Oliver (2), DE Shawn Patterson (5), CB Bruce Pickens (2), RB John Stephens (5), LB Keith Traylor (5).

## COACHING STAFF

**Head Coach,**
**Mike Holmgren**

**Pro Career:** Became Packers' eleventh head coach on January 11, 1992. He led team to first back-to-back winning seasons (identical 9-7 records) since 1966-67 and first playoff berth (1993). Holmgren was offensive coordinator for the San Francisco 49ers under George Seifert (1989-91) after spending three previous seasons (1986-88) as quarterbacks coach under Bill Walsh. During his six-year tenure with San Francisco, the 49ers won five consecutive NFC Western Division championships (1986-1990) and back-to-back Super Bowls (XXIII and XXIV). In that span, San Francisco compiled the NFL's best overall record (71-23-1, a .753 percentage). The 49ers never ranked lower than third overall in his three years as offensive coordinator. Career record: 19-15.
**Background:** Quarterback at Southern California (1966-69) and was drafted by the St. Louis Cardinals in the eighth round of the 1970 NFL draft. He served as an assistant coach at San Francisco State (1981) and Brigham Young (1982-85) before his tenure with the 49ers. Earned his bachelor of science degree in business finance at Southern California (1970).
**Personal:** Born June 15, 1948, in San Francisco. He and his wife, Kathy, live in Green Bay and have four daughters—Calla, Jenny, Emily, and Gretchen.

### ASSISTANT COACHES

**Larry Brooks,** defensive line; born June 10, 1950, Prince George, Va., lives in Green Bay. Defensive lineman Virginia State 1968-71. Pro defensive tackle Los Angeles Rams 1972-82. College coach: Virginia State 1992-93. Pro coach: Los Angeles Rams 1983-90, joined Packers in 1994.
**Nolan Cromwell,** special teams; born January 30, 1955, Smith Center, Kan., lives in Green Bay. Quarterback-safety Kansas 1973-76. Pro defensive back Los Angeles Rams 1977-87. Pro coach: Los Angeles Rams 1991, joined Packers in 1992.
**Jon Gruden,** wide receivers; born August 17, 1963, Sandusky, Ohio, lives in Green Bay. Quarterback Dayton 1983-85. No pro playing experience. College coach: Tennessee 1986-87, Southeast Missouri 1988, Pacific 1989, Pittsburgh 1991. Pro coach: San Francisco 49ers 1990, joined Packers in 1992.
**Gil Haskell,** running backs; born September 24, 1943, San Francisco, Calif., lives in Green Bay. Defensive back San Francisco State 1961, 1963-65. No pro playing exprience. College coach: Southern California 1978-82. Pro coach: Los Angeles Rams 1983-91, joined Packers in 1992.
**Dick Jauron,** defensive backs; born October 7, 1950, Peoria, Ill., lives in Green Bay. Defensive back Yale 1970-72. Pro defensive back Detroit Lions 1973-77, Cincinnati Bengals 1978-80. Pro coach: Buffalo Bills 1985, joined Packers in 1986.
**Kent Johnston,** strength and conditioning; born February 21, 1956, Mexia, Tex., lives in Green Bay. Defensive back Stephen F. Austin 1974-77. No pro playing experience. College coach: Northeast Louisiana 1979, Northwestern Louisiana 1980-81, Alabama 1983-86. Pro coach: Tampa Bay Buccaneers 1987-91, joined Packers in 1992.
**Sherman Lewis,** offensive coordinator; born June 29, 1942, Louisville, Ky., lives in Green Bay. Running back Michigan State 1961-63. Pro running back Toronto Argonauts (CFL) 1964-65, New York Jets 1966. College coach: Michigan State 1969-82. Pro coach: San Francisco 49ers 1983-91, joined Packers in 1992.
**Jim Lind,** defensive assistant-quality control; born November 11, 1947, Isle, Minn., lives in Green Bay. Linebacker Bethel College 1965-66; defensive back Bemidji State 1971-72. No pro playing experience. College coach: St. Cloud State 1977-78, St. John's (Minn.) 1979-80, Brigham Young 1981-82, Minnesota-Morris 1983-86 (head coach), Wisconsin-Eau Claire 1987-91 (head coach). Pro coach: Joined Packers in 1992.
**Tom Lovat,** offensive line; born December 28, 1938, Bingham, Utah, lives in Green Bay. Guard-linebacker Utah 1958-60. No pro playing experience. College coach: Utah 1967, 1972-76 (head coach 1974-76), Idaho State 1968-70, Stanford 1977-79, Wyoming 1989. Pro coach: Saskatchewan Roughriders (CFL) 1971, Green Bay Packers 1980, St. Louis-Phoenix Cardinals 1981-84, 1990-91, Indianapolis Colts 1985-88, rejoined Packers in 1992.
**Steve Mariucci,** quarterbacks; born November 4, 1955, Iron Mountain, Mich., lives in Green Bay. Quarterback Northern Michigan 1974-77. No pro playing experience. College coach: Northern Michigan 1978-79, Cal State-Fullerton 1980-82, Louisville 1983-84, Southern California 1986, California 1987-91. Pro coach: Orlando Renegades (USFL) 1985, Los Angeles Rams 1985, joined Packers in 1992.
**Andy Reid,** tight ends-offensive line assistant; born March 19, 1958, Los Angeles, Calif., lives in Green Bay. Offensive tackle-guard Brigham Young 1978-80. No pro playing experience. College coach: San Francisco State 1983-85, Northern Arizona 1986, Texas-El Paso 1987, Missouri 1988-91. Pro coach: Joined Packers in 1992.
**Fritz Shurmur,** defensive coordinator; born July 15, 1932, Riverview, Mich., lives in Green Bay. No pro playing experience. College coach: Albion 1956-61, Wyoming 1962-74 (head coach 1971-74). Pro coach: Detroit Lions 1975-77, New England Patriots 1978-81, Los Angeles Rams 1982-90, Phoenix Cardinals 1991-93, joined Packers in 1994.
**Harry Sydney,** general assistant, born June 26, 1959, Fayetteville, N.C., lives in Green Bay. Quarterback/running back Kansas 1978-81. Pro running back San Francisco 49ers 1987-91, Green Bay Packers 1992. Pro coach: Joined Packers in 1994.
**Bob Valesente,** linebackers; born July 19, 1940, Seneca Falls, N.Y., lives in Green Bay. Halfback Ithaca College 1958-61. No pro playing experience. College coach: Cornell 1964-74, Cincinnati 1975-76, Arizona 1977-79, Mississippi State 1980-81, Kansas 1984-87 (head coach, 1986-87), Maryland 1988, Pittsburgh 1989. Pro coach: Baltimore Colts 1982-83, Pittsburgh Steelers 1990-91, joined Packers in 1992.

## 1994 FIRST-YEAR ROSTER

| Name | Pos. | Ht. | Wt. | Birthdate | College | Hometown | How Acq. |
|---|---|---|---|---|---|---|---|
| Bierman, Randy | T | 6-5 | 298 | 4/30/71 | Illinois | Waukegan, Ill. | FA |
| Brown, Victor | S | 6-1 | 208 | 4/21/70 | Tennessee | Junction City, Kan. | FA |
| Cotton, Curtis (1) | S | 6-0 | 212 | 10/15/69 | Nebraska | Omaha, Neb. | FA |
| Crawford, Lionel (1) | WR | 5-10 | 185 | 12/24/69 | Wisconsin | Houston, Tex. | FA |
| Dean, Charlie | TE | 6-2 | 246 | 7/12/70 | Florida | Inverness, Fla. | FA |
| Duckworth, Paul | LB | 6-1 | 245 | 3/12/71 | Connecticut | Danbury, Conn. | D6d |
| Eller, Matt (1) | DE | 6-5 | 275 | 1/30/70 | Bethel College, Minn. | Radcliffe, Iowa | FA |
| Fisher, John (1) | C | 6-3 | 270 | 9/4/69 | Tennessee | Milan, Tex. | FA |
| Frazier, Daryl | WR | 6-1 | 181 | 1/23/71 | Florida | Winter Haven, Fla. | FA |
| Hamilton, Ruffin | LB | 6-1 | 230 | 3/2/71 | Tulane | Zachary, La. | D6b |
| Harris, Willie (1) | WR | 6-1 | 194 | 11/8/70 | Mississippi State | Moss Point, Miss. | FA |
| Hentrich, Craig (1) | P-K | 6-3 | 200 | 5/18/71 | Notre Dame | Alton, Ill. | FA |
| Holt, Reggie | S | 5-11 | 201 | 2/18/71 | Wisconsin | Miami, Fla. | FA |
| Hope, Charles (1) | G-T | 6-3 | 308 | 3/12/70 | Central State, Ohio | New Castle, Del. | FA |
| Johnson, LeShon | RB | 5-11 | 204 | 1/15/71 | Northern Illinois | Haskell, Okla. | D3 |
| Kearney, Jay | WR | 6-1 | 194 | 9/29/71 | West Virginia | Piscataway, N.J. | D6a |
| Levens, Dorsey | RB | 6-1 | 231 | 5/21/70 | Georgia Tech | Syracuse, N.Y. | D5b |
| McGill, Lenny | CB | 6-1 | 194 | 5/31/71 | Arizona State | Escondido, Calif. | FA |
| Mickens, Terry | WR | 6-0 | 203 | 2/21/71 | Florida A&M | Tallahassee, Fla. | D5a |
| Perez, Chris (1) | T | 6-6 | 295 | 6/21/69 | Kansas | Palatine, Ill. | FA |
| Schroeder, Bill | WR | 6-1 | 195 | 1/9/71 | Wisconsin-LaCrosse | Sheboygan, Wis. | D6c |
| Shackerford, Lamark | NT | 6-0 | 255 | 3/12/72 | Wisconsin | Gary, Ind. | FA |
| Showell, Malcolm (1) | DE | 6-6 | 275 | 10/1/68 | Delaware State | Baltimore, Md. | FA |
| Smith, LeRoy (1) | LB | 6-0 | 230 | 1/6/69 | Iowa | Atco, N.J. | FA |
| Taylor, Aaron | G | 6-4 | 307 | 11/14/72 | Notre Dame | Concord, Calif. | D1 |
| Warner, Kurt | QB | 6-2 | 198 | 6/22/71 | Northern Iowa | Cedar Rapids, Iowa | FA |
| Wilkins, Gabe | DE | 6-4 | 292 | 9/1/71 | Gardner-Webb | Cowpens, S.C. | D4 |
| Williams, Mark | LB | 6-3 | 229 | 5/17/71 | Ohio State | Upper Marlboro, Md. | FA |
| Wilner, Jeff | TE | 6-4 | 253 | 12/31/71 | Wesleyan, Conn. | Exeter, N.H. | FA |

The term NFL Rookie is defined as a player who is in his first season of professional football and has not been on the roster of another professional football team for any regular-season or postseason games. A Rookie is designated by an "R" on NFL rosters. Players who have been active in another professional football league or players who have NFL experience, including either preseason training camp or being on an Active List or Inactive List, or on Reserve/Injured or Reserve/Physically Unable to Perform for fewer than six regular-season games, are termed NFL First-Year Players. An NFL First-Year Player is designated by a "1" on NFL rosters. Thereafter, a player is credited with an additional year of experience for each season in which he accumulates six games on the Active List or Inactive List, or on Reserve/Injured or Reserve/Physically Unable to Perform.

## NOTES

# LOS ANGELES RAMS

**National Football Conference**
**Western Division**
**Team Colors:** Royal Blue, Gold, and White
**Business Address:**
**2327 West Lincoln Avenue**
**Anaheim, California 92801**
**Telephone: (714) 535-7267**
**Ticket Office:**
**Anaheim Stadium**
**1900 State College Boulevard**
**Anaheim, California 92806**
**Telephone: (714) 937-6767**

## CLUB OFFICIALS

Owner/President: Georgia Frontiere
Executive Vice President: John Shaw
Senior Vice President: Jay Zygmunt
Vice President-Head Coach: Chuck Knox
Vice President-Media and Community Relations: Marshall Klein
Director of Player Personel: John Becker
Administrator of Pro Personnel: Jack Faulkner
Executive Director: Mary Olson-Kromolowski
Treasurer: Jeff Brewer
Director of Player Relations: Paul (Tank) Younger
Director of Operations: John Oswald
Director of Public Relations: Rick Smith
Director of Ticket Operations: Don Nims
Trainer: Jim Anderson
Equipment Manager: Todd Hewitt
Video Director: Mickey Dukich
Scouts: Lawrence McCutcheon, David Razzano, Pete Russell, Harley Sewell, Frank Trump, Ron Waller
**Stadium:** Anaheim Stadium • **Capacity:** 69,008
Anaheim, California 92806
**Playing Surface:** Grass
**Training Camp:** University of California-Irvine
Irvine, California 92715

## 1994 SCHEDULE

**PRESEASON**

| | | |
|---|---|---|
| Aug. 6 | vs. Green Bay at Madison, Wis. | 12:00 |
| Aug. 13 | **New England** | 7:00 |
| Aug. 20 | **Los Angeles Raiders** | 7:00 |
| Aug. 25 | at San Diego | 7:00 |

**REGULAR SEASON**

| | | |
|---|---|---|
| Sept. 4 | **Arizona** | 1:00 |
| Sept. 11 | at Atlanta | 1:00 |
| Sept. 18 | **San Francisco** | 1:00 |
| Sept. 25 | at Kansas City | 12:00 |
| Oct. 2 | **Atlanta** | 1:00 |
| Oct. 9 | at Green Bay | 12:00 |
| Oct. 16 | **New York Giants** | 1:00 |
| Oct. 23 | at New Orleans | 12:00 |
| Oct. 30 | Open Date | |
| Nov. 6 | **Denver** | 1:00 |
| Nov. 13 | **Los Angeles Raiders** | 1:00 |
| Nov. 20 | at San Francisco | 5:00 |
| Nov. 27 | at San Diego | 1:00 |
| Dec. 4 | **New Orleans** | 1:00 |
| Dec. 11 | at Tampa Bay | 1:00 |
| Dec. 18 | at Chicago | 12:00 |
| Dec. 24 | **Washington** | 1:00 |

## RECORD HOLDERS

**INDIVIDUAL RECORDS—CAREER**

| Category | Name | Performance |
|---|---|---|
| Rushing (Yds.) | Eric Dickerson, 1983-87 | 7,245 |
| Passing (Yds.) | Jim Everett, 1986-1993 | 23,758 |
| Passing (TDs) | Roman Gabriel, 1962-1972 | 154 |
| Receiving (No.) | Henry Ellard, 1983-1993 | 593 |
| Receiving (Yds.) | Henry Ellard, 1983-1993 | 9,761 |
| Interceptions | Ed Meador, 1959-1970 | 46 |
| Punting (Avg.) | Danny Villanueva, 1960-64 | 44.2 |
| Punt Return (Avg.) | Henry Ellard, 1983-1992 | 11.3 |
| Kickoff Return (Avg.) | Tom Wilson, 1956-1961 | 27.1 |
| Field Goals | Mike Lansford, 1982-1990 | 158 |
| Touchdowns (Tot.) | Eric Dickerson, 1983-87 | 58 |
| Points | Mike Lansford, 1982-1990 | 789 |

**INDIVIDUAL RECORDS—SINGLE SEASON**

| Category | Name | Performance |
|---|---|---|
| Rushing (Yds.) | Eric Dickerson, 1984 | *2,105 |
| Passing (Yds.) | Jim Everett, 1989 | 4,310 |
| Passing (TDs) | Jim Everett, 1988 | 31 |
| Receiving (No.) | Henry Ellard, 1988 | 86 |
| Receiving (Yds.) | Elroy (Crazylegs) Hirsch, 1951 | 1,425 |
| Interceptions | Dick (Night Train) Lane, 1952 | *14 |
| Punting (Avg.) | Danny Villanueva, 1962 | 45.5 |
| Punt Return (Avg.) | Woodley Lewis, 1952 | 18.5 |
| Kickoff Return (Avg.) | Verda (Vitamin T) Smith, 1950 | 33.7 |
| Field Goals | David Ray, 1973 | 30 |
| Touchdowns (Tot.) | Eric Dickerson, 1983 | 20 |
| Points | David Ray, 1973 | 130 |

**INDIVIDUAL RECORDS—SINGLE GAME**

| Category | Name | Performance |
|---|---|---|
| Rushing (Yds.) | Eric Dickerson, 1-4-86 | 248 |
| Passing (Yds.) | Norm Van Brocklin, 9-28-51 | *554 |
| Passing (TDs) | Many times | 5 |
| | Last time by Jim Everett, 9-25-88 | |
| Receiving (No.) | Tom Fears, 12-3-50 | *18 |
| Receiving (Yds.) | Willie Anderson, 11-26-89 | *336 |
| Interceptions | Many times | 3 |
| | Last time by Pat Thomas, 10-7-79 | |
| Field Goals | Bob Waterfield, 12-9-51 | 5 |
| Touchdowns (Tot.) | Bob Shaw, 12-11-49 | 4 |
| | Elroy (Crazylegs) Hirsch, 9-28-51 | 4 |
| | Harold Jackson, 10-14-73 | 4 |
| Points | Bob Shaw, 12-11-49 | 24 |
| | Elroy (Crazylegs) Hirsch, 9-28-51 | 24 |
| | Harold Jackson, 10-14-73 | 24 |

*NFL Record

## COACHING HISTORY

**Cleveland 1937-1945**
**(407-357-20)**

| | | |
|---|---|---|
| 1937-38 | Hugo Bezdek* | 1-13-0 |
| 1938 | Art Lewis | 4-4-0 |
| 1939-42 | Earl (Dutch) Clark | 16-26-2 |
| 1944 | Aldo (Buff) Donelli | 4-6-0 |
| 1945-46 | Adam Walsh | 16-5-1 |
| 1947 | Bob Snyder | 6-6-0 |
| 1948-49 | Clark Shaughnessy | 14-8-3 |
| 1950-52 | Joe Stydahar** | 19-9-0 |
| 1952-54 | Hamp Pool | 23-11-2 |
| 1955-59 | Sid Gillman | 28-32-1 |
| 1960-62 | Bob Waterfield*** | 9-24-1 |
| 1962-65 | Harland Svare | 14-31-3 |
| 1966-70 | George Allen | 49-19-4 |
| 1971-72 | Tommy Prothro | 14-12-2 |
| 1973-77 | Chuck Knox | 57-20-1 |
| 1978-82 | Ray Malavasi | 43-36-0 |
| 1983-91 | John Robinson | 79-74-0 |
| 1992-93 | Chuck Knox | 11-21-0 |

*Released after three games in 1938
**Resigned after one game in 1952
***Resigned after eight games in 1962

**ANAHEIM STADIUM**

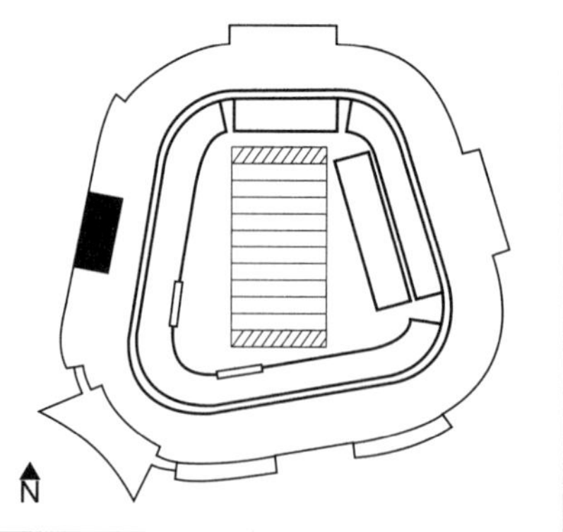

## 1993 TEAM RECORD

**PRESEASON (0-4)**

| Date | Result | | Opponents |
|---|---|---|---|
| 8/7 | L | 13-24 | at Phoenix |
| 8/14 | L | 17-23 | San Diego |
| 8/21 | L | 10-21 | at Cleveland |
| 8/28 | L | 19-20 | L.A. Raiders |

**REGULAR SEASON (5-11)**

| Date | Result | | Opponents | Att. |
|---|---|---|---|---|
| 9/5 | L | 6-36 | at Green Bay | 54,648 |
| 9/12 | W | 27-0 | Pittsburgh | 50,588 |
| 9/19 | L | 10-20 | at N.Y. Giants | 76,213 |
| 9/26 | W | 28-13 | at Houston | 53,072 |
| 10/3 | L | 6-37 | New Orleans | 50,709 |
| 10/14 | L | 24-30 | at Atlanta | 45,231 |
| 10/24 | L | 13-16 | Detroit | 43,850 |
| 10/31 | L | 17-40 | at San Francisco | 63,417 |
| 11/14 | L | 0-13 | Atlanta | 37,073 |
| 11/21 | W | 10-6 | Washington | 45,546 |
| 11/28 | L | 10-35 | San Francisco | 62,143 |
| 12/5 | L | 10-38 | at Phoenix | 33,964 |
| 12/12 | W | 23-20 | at New Orleans | 69,033 |
| 12/19 | L | 3-15 | at Cincinnati | 36,612 |
| 12/26 | L | 14-42 | Cleveland | 34,155 |
| 1/2 | W | 20-6 | Chicago | 39,147 |

**SCORE BY PERIODS**

| | | | | | | | |
|---|---|---|---|---|---|---|---|
| Rams | 52 | 40 | 40 | 89 | 0 | — | 221 |
| Opponents | 72 | 95 | 92 | 108 | 0 | — | 367 |

**ATTENDANCE**

Home 363,211 Away 432,190 Total 795,401
Single-game home record, 69,898 (11-9-92)
Single-season home record, 553,979 (1992)

## 1993 TEAM STATISTICS

| | Rams | Opp. |
|---|---|---|
| Total First Downs | 278 | 304 |
| Rushing | 117 | 117 |
| Passing | 147 | 179 |
| Penalty | 14 | 8 |
| Third Down: Made/Att | 79/202 | 102/218 |
| Third Down Pct. | 39.1 | 46.8 |
| Fourth Down: Made/Att | 5/11 | 10/17 |
| Fourth Down Pct. | 45.5 | 58.8 |
| Total Net Yards | 4804 | 5411 |
| Avg. Per Game | 300.3 | 338.2 |
| Total Plays | 953 | 1003 |
| Avg. Per Play | 5.0 | 5.4 |
| Net Yards Rushing | 2014 | 1851 |
| Avg. Per Game | 125.9 | 115.7 |
| Total Rushes | 449 | 480 |
| Net Yards Passing | 2790 | 3560 |
| Avg. Per Game | 174.4 | 222.5 |
| Sacked/Yards Lost | 31/231 | 35/203 |
| Gross Yards | 3021 | 3763 |
| Att./Completions | 473/247 | 488/299 |
| Completion Pct. | 52.2 | 61.3 |
| Had Intercepted | 19 | 11 |
| Punts/Avg. | 80/40.9 | 58/42.3 |
| Net Punting Avg. | 80/31.7 | 58/37.4 |
| Penalties/Yards Lost | 71/526 | 80/542 |
| Fumbles/Ball Lost | 20/11 | 26/9 |
| Touchdowns | 25 | 40 |
| Rushing | 8 | 18 |
| Passing | 16 | 17 |
| Returns | 1 | 5 |
| Avg. Time of Possession | 28:18 | 31:42 |

## 1993 INDIVIDUAL STATISTICS

| PASSING | Att | Cmp | Yds. | Pct. | TD | Int | Tkld. | Rate |
|---|---|---|---|---|---|---|---|---|
| Everett | 274 | 135 | 1652 | 49.3 | 8 | 12 | 18/125 | 59.7 |
| Rubley | 189 | 108 | 1338 | 57.1 | 8 | 6 | 13/106 | 80.1 |
| Pagel | 9 | 3 | 23 | 33.3 | 0 | 1 | 0/0 | 2.8 |
| Gary | 1 | 1 | 8 | 100.0 | 0 | 0 | 0/0 | 100.0 |
| Rams | 473 | 247 | 3021 | 52.2 | 16 | 19 | 31/231 | 66.8 |
| Opponents | 488 | 299 | 3763 | 61.3 | 17 | 11 | 35/203 | 87.5 |

| SCORING | TD R | TD P | TD Rt | PAT | FG | Saf | PTS |
|---|---|---|---|---|---|---|---|
| Zendejas | 0 | 0 | 0 | 23/25 | 16/23 | 0 | 71 |
| Bettis | 7 | 0 | 0 | 0/0 | 0/0 | 0 | 42 |
| Anderson | 0 | 4 | 0 | 0/0 | 0/0 | 0 | 24 |
| Drayton | 0 | 4 | 0 | 0/0 | 0/0 | 0 | 24 |
| Ellard | 0 | 2 | 0 | 0/0 | 0/0 | 0 | 12 |
| Gary | 1 | 1 | 0 | 0/0 | 0/0 | 0 | 12 |
| Jones | 0 | 2 | 0 | 0/0 | 0/0 | 0 | 12 |
| Boykin | 0 | 0 | 1 | 0/0 | 0/0 | 0 | 6 |
| Carter | 0 | 1 | 0 | 0/0 | 0/0 | 0 | 6 |
| Kinchen | 0 | 1 | 0 | 0/0 | 0/0 | 0 | 6 |
| McNeal | 0 | 1 | 0 | 0/0 | 0/0 | 0 | 6 |
| Rams | 8 | 16 | 1 | 23/25 | 16/23 | 0 | 221 |
| Opponents | 18 | 17 | 5 | 38/40 | 29/37 | 1 | 367 |

| RUSHING | Att. | Yds. | Avg. | LG | TD |
|---|---|---|---|---|---|
| Bettis | 294 | 1429 | 4.9 | 71t | 7 |
| Gary | 79 | 293 | 3.7 | 15 | 1 |
| Rubley | 29 | 102 | 3.5 | 13 | 0 |
| Lester | 11 | 74 | 6.7 | 26 | 0 |
| Everett | 19 | 38 | 2.0 | 14 | 0 |
| Lang | 9 | 29 | 3.2 | 28 | 0 |
| Ellard | 2 | 18 | 9.0 | 15 | 0 |
| Kinchen | 2 | 10 | 5.0 | 8 | 0 |
| R. White | 2 | 10 | 5.0 | 5 | 0 |
| Drayton | 1 | 7 | 7.0 | 7 | 0 |
| Jones | 1 | 4 | 4.0 | 4 | 0 |
| Rams | 449 | 2014 | 4.5 | 71t | 8 |
| Opponents | 480 | 1851 | 3.9 | 35t | 18 |

| RECEIVING | No. | Yds. | Avg. | LG | TD |
|---|---|---|---|---|---|
| Ellard | 61 | 945 | 15.5 | 54 | 2 |
| Anderson | 37 | 552 | 14.9 | 56t | 4 |
| Gary | 36 | 289 | 8.0 | 60t | 1 |
| Drayton | 27 | 319 | 11.8 | 27 | 4 |
| Bettis | 26 | 244 | 9.4 | 28 | 0 |
| Lester | 18 | 154 | 8.6 | 21 | 0 |
| Carter | 14 | 166 | 11.9 | 38 | 1 |
| Kinchen | 8 | 137 | 17.1 | 35t | 1 |
| McNeal | 8 | 75 | 9.4 | 22t | 1 |
| Jones | 5 | 56 | 11.2 | 21t | 2 |
| Lang | 4 | 45 | 11.3 | 21 | 0 |
| LaChapelle | 2 | 23 | 11.5 | 14 | 0 |
| Lofton | 1 | 16 | 16.0 | 16 | 0 |
| Rams | 247 | 3021 | 12.2 | 60t | 16 |
| Opponents | 299 | 3763 | 12.6 | 80t | 17 |

| INTERCEPTIONS | No. | Yds. | Avg. | LG | TD |
|---|---|---|---|---|---|
| Bailey | 2 | 41 | 20.5 | 41 | 0 |
| Rolling | 2 | 21 | 10.5 | 12 | 0 |
| Terrell | 2 | 1 | 0.5 | 1 | 0 |
| Lyght | 2 | 0 | 0.0 | 0 | 0 |
| Stewart | 1 | 30 | 30.0 | 30 | 0 |
| Conlan | 1 | 28 | 28.0 | 28 | 0 |
| Homco | 1 | 6 | 6.0 | 6 | 0 |
| Rams | 11 | 127 | 11.5 | 41 | 0 |
| Opponents | 19 | 347 | 18.3 | 54 | 2 |

| PUNTING | No. | Yds. | Avg. | In 20 | LG |
|---|---|---|---|---|---|
| Landeta | 42 | 1825 | 43.5 | 7 | 66 |
| McJulien | 21 | 795 | 37.9 | 5 | 56 |
| Bracken | 17 | 651 | 38.3 | 3 | 51 |
| Rams | 80 | 3271 | 40.9 | 15 | 66 |
| Opponents | 58 | 2451 | 42.3 | 18 | 68 |

| PUNT RETURNS | No. | FC | Yds. | Avg. | LG | TD |
|---|---|---|---|---|---|---|
| Buchanan | 8 | 1 | 41 | 5.1 | 12 | 0 |
| Kinchen | 7 | 4 | 32 | 4.6 | 8 | 0 |
| Ellard | 2 | 8 | 18 | 9.0 | 13 | 0 |
| Henley | 1 | 0 | 8 | 8.0 | 8 | 0 |
| M. Price | 1 | 2 | 3 | 3.0 | 3 | 0 |
| Rams | 19 | 15 | 102 | 5.4 | 13 | 0 |
| Opponents | 43 | 16 | 533 | 12.4 | 74t | 2 |

| KICKOFF RETURNS | No. | Yds. | Avg. | LG | TD |
|---|---|---|---|---|---|
| Boykin | 13 | 216 | 16.6 | 29 | 0 |
| Griffith | 8 | 169 | 21.1 | 29 | 0 |
| M. Price | 8 | 144 | 18.0 | 23 | 0 |
| R. White | 8 | 122 | 15.3 | 35 | 0 |
| Kinchen | 6 | 96 | 16.0 | 22 | 0 |
| Israel | 5 | 92 | 18.4 | 23 | 0 |
| Drayton | 1 | -15 | -15.0 | -15 | 0 |
| Rams | 49 | 824 | 16.8 | 35 | 0 |
| Opponents | 47 | 984 | 20.9 | 45 | 0 |

| SACKS | No. |
|---|---|
| Gilbert | 10.5 |
| Stokes | 9.5 |
| Young | 7.0 |
| Robinson | 3.0 |
| Boutte | 1.0 |
| Henderson | 1.0 |
| Rocker | 1.0 |
| Stewart | 1.0 |
| Woods | 1.0 |
| Rams | 35.0 |
| Opponents | 31.0 |

## 1994 DRAFT CHOICES

| Round | Name | Pos. | College |
|---|---|---|---|
| 1 | Wayne Gandy | T | Auburn |
| 2 | Isaac Bruce | WR | Memphis State |
| | Toby Wright | DB | Nebraska |
| | Brad Ottis | DE | Wayne State, Neb. |
| 3 | Keith Lyle | DB | Virginia |
| | James Bostic | RB | Auburn |
| | Ernest Jones | LB | Oregon |
| 4 | Chris Brantley | WR | Rutgers |
| 6 | Rickey Brady | TE | Oklahoma |
| | Ronald Edwards | T | North Carolina A&T |

# LOS ANGELES RAMS

## 1994 VETERAN ROSTER

| No. | | Name | Pos. | Ht. | Wt. | Birthdate | NFL Exp. | College | Hometown | How Acq. | '93 Games/ Starts |
|---|---|---|---|---|---|---|---|---|---|---|---|
| 83 | | Anderson, Willie | WR | 6-0 | 172 | 3/7/65 | 7 | UCLA | Paulsboro, N.J. | D2b-'88 | 15/15 |
| 77 | | Ashmore, Darryl | T | 6-7 | 300 | 11/1/69 | 3 | Northwestern | Peoria, Ill. | D7-'92 | 9/7 |
| 28 | † | Bailey, Robert | CB | 5-9 | 176 | 9/3/68 | 4 | Miami | Miami, Fla. | D4-'91 | 9/3 |
| 71 | | Belin, Chuck | G | 6-2 | 312 | 10/27/70 | 2 | Wisconsin | Milwaukee, Wis. | D5b-'93 | 0* |
| 36 | | Bettis, Jerome | RB | 5-11 | 243 | 2/16/72 | 2 | Notre Dame | Detroit, Mich. | D1-'93 | 16/12 |
| 96 | | Boutte, Marc | DT | 6-4 | 296 | 7/26/69 | 3 | Louisiana State | Lake Charles, La. | D3a-'92 | 16/16 |
| 21 | | Boykin, Deral | S | 5-11 | 196 | 9/2/70 | 2 | Louisville | Kent, Ohio | D6-'93 | 16/0 |
| 61 | | Brostek, Bern | C | 6-3 | 300 | 9/11/66 | 5 | Washington | Honolulu, Hawaii | D1-'90 | 16/16 |
| 89 | | Buchanan, Richard | WR | 5-10 | 178 | 5/8/69 | 2 | Northwestern | Maywood, Ill. | FA-'93 | 5/0 |
| 51 | # | Bush, Blair | C | 6-3 | 275 | 11/25/56 | 17 | Washington | Palos Verdes, Calif. | PB(GB)-'92 | 16/0 |
| 17 | | Chandler, Chris | QB | 6-4 | 225 | 10/12/65 | 7 | Washington | Everett, Wash. | UFA(Ariz)-'94 | 4/2* |
| 54 | | Collins, Brett | LB | 6-1 | 234 | 10/8/68 | 3 | Washington | Portland, Ore. | W(GB)-'93 | 14/0* |
| 56 | | Conlan, Shane | LB | 6-3 | 235 | 3/4/64 | 8 | Penn State | Frewsburg, N.Y. | UFA(Buff)-'93 | 12/11 |
| 29 | † | Davis, Dexter | CB | 5-10 | 185 | 3/20/70 | 5 | Clemson | Sumter, S.C. | FA-'93 | 12/4* |
| 84 | | Drayton, Troy | TE | 6-3 | 255 | 6/29/70 | 2 | Penn State | Steelton, Pa. | D2-'93 | 16/2 |
| 43 | | Gary, Cleveland | RB | 6-0 | 226 | 5/4/66 | 6 | Miami | Indiantown, Fla. | D1b-'89 | 15/4 |
| 90 | | Gilbert, Sean | DT | 6-4 | 315 | 4/10/70 | 3 | Pittsburgh | Aliquippa, Pa. | D1-'92 | 16/16 |
| 79 | | Goeas, Leo | G-T | 6-4 | 292 | 8/15/66 | 5 | Hawaii | Honolulu, Hawaii | T(SD)-'93 | 16/16 |
| 42 | | Griffin, Courtney | CB | 5-10 | 180 | 12/19/66 | 2 | Fresno State | Fresno, Calif. | FA-'92 | 7/1 |
| 30 | | Griffith, Howard | RB | 6-0 | 226 | 11/17/67 | 2 | Illinois | Chicago, Ill. | FA-'93 | 15/0 |
| 24 | # | Henderson, Wymon | CB | 5-10 | 188 | 12/15/61 | 9 | Nevada-Las Vegas | N. Miami Beach, Fla. | FA-'93 | 9/4 |
| 20 | # | Henley, Darryl | CB | 5-9 | 172 | 10/30/66 | 5 | UCLA | La Verne, Calif. | D2c-'89 | 5/4 |
| 23 | | Hicks, Clifford | S-CB | 5-10 | 187 | 8/18/64 | 8 | Oregon | San Diego, Calif. | UFA(NYJ)-'94 | 10/0* |
| 57 | | Homco, Thomas | LB | 6-0 | 245 | 1/8/70 | 2 | Northwestern | Highland, Ind. | FA-'92 | 16/3 |
| 31 | | Israel, Steve | CB | 5-11 | 186 | 3/16/69 | 3 | Pittsburgh | Lawnside, N.J. | D2-'92 | 16/12 |
| 72 | | Jones, Clarence | T | 6-6 | 280 | 5/6/68 | 4 | Maryland | Brooklyn, N.Y. | FA-'94 | 4/0* |
| 98 | | Jones, Jimmie | DT | 6-4 | 276 | 1/9/66 | 5 | Miami | Lake Okeechobee, Fla. | UFA(Dall)-'94 | 15/2* |
| 52 | | Kelly, Joe | LB | 6-2 | 235 | 12/11/64 | 9 | Washington | Los Angeles, Calif. | FA-'94 | 16/14* |
| 81 | | Kinchen, Todd | WR | 6-0 | 187 | 1/7/69 | 3 | Louisiana State | Baton Rouge, La. | D3b-'92 | 6/1 |
| 88 | | LaChapelle, Sean | WR | 6-3 | 205 | 7/29/70 | 2 | UCLA | Napa, Calif. | D5a-'93 | 10/0 |
| 5 | | Landeta, Sean | P | 6-0 | 210 | 1/6/62 | 10 | Towson State | Baltimore, Md. | FA-'93 | 16/0* |
| 38 | | Lang, David | RB | 5-11 | 213 | 3/28/67 | 4 | Northern Arizona | San Bernardino, Calif. | D12-'90 | 6/0 |
| 34 | | Lester, Tim | RB | 5-9 | 215 | 6/5/68 | 3 | Eastern Kentucky | Miami, Fla. | D10-'92 | 16/14 |
| 87 | t- | Lewis, Nate | WR | 5-11 | 198 | 10/19/66 | 5 | Oregon Tech | Moultrie, Ga. | T(SD)-'94 | 15/9* |
| 64 | | Loneker, Keith | G | 6-3 | 330 | 6/21/71 | 2 | Kansas | Roselle Park, N.J. | FA-'93 | 4/2 |
| 41 | | Lyght, Todd | CB | 6-0 | 186 | 2/9/69 | 4 | Notre Dame | Flint, Mich. | D1-'91 | 9/9 |
| 53 | # | Martin, Chris | LB | 6-2 | 241 | 12/19/60 | 12 | Auburn | Huntsville, Ala. | T(KC)-'93 | 16/4 |
| 86 | | McMurtry, Greg | WR | 6-2 | 207 | 10/15/67 | 5 | Michigan | Brockton, Mass. | UFA(NE)-'94 | 14/8* |
| 82 | # | McNeal, Travis | TE | 6-3 | 244 | 1/10/67 | 6 | Tennessee-Chattanooga | Birmingham, Ala. | FA-'92 | 16/6 |
| 13 | | Miller, Chris | QB | 6-2 | 212 | 8/9/65 | 8 | Oregon | Eugene, Ore. | UFA(Atl)-'94 | 3/2* |
| 66 | | Newberry, Tom | G | 6-2 | 285 | 12/20/62 | 9 | Wisconsin-LaCrosse | Onalaska, Wis. | D2-'86 | 9/9 |
| 26 | | Newman, Anthony | S | 6-0 | 199 | 11/25/65 | 7 | Oregon | Beaverton, Ore. | D2a-'88 | 16/16 |
| 69 | | Pahukoa, Jeff | G-T | 6-2 | 298 | 2/9/69 | 4 | Washington | Marysville, Wash. | D12a-'91 | 16/5 |
| 58 | † | Phifer, Roman | LB | 6-2 | 230 | 3/5/68 | 4 | UCLA | Pineville, N.C. | D2-'91 | 16/16 |
| 22 | t- | Pope, Marquez | S-CB | 5-10 | 193 | 10/29/70 | 3 | Fresno State | Nashville, Tenn. | T(SD)-'94 | 16/1* |
| 27 | | Price, Mitchell | CB | 5-9 | 181 | 5/10/67 | 5 | Tulane | San Antonio, Tex. | FA-'93 | 6/0* |
| 72 | | Robbins, Kevin | T | 6-4 | 286 | 12/12/67 | 3 | Michigan State | Washington, D.C. | FA-'93 | 1/0 |
| 97 | | Robinson, Gerald | DE | 6-3 | 262 | 5/4/63 | 8 | Auburn | Notasulga, Ala. | PB(SD)-'91 | 16/3 |
| 92 | | Rocker, David | DT | 6-4 | 267 | 3/12/69 | 4 | Auburn | Atlanta, Ga. | FA-'91 | 14/0 |
| 59 | | Rolling, Henry | LB | 6-2 | 225 | 9/8/65 | 8 | Nevada-Reno | Henderson, Nev. | UFA(SD)-'93 | 12/9 |
| 12 | | Rubley, T.J. | QB | 6-3 | 205 | 11/29/68 | 3 | Tulsa | Davenport, Iowa | D9-'92 | 9/7 |
| 78 | | Slater, Jackie | T | 6-4 | 285 | 5/27/54 | 19 | Jackson State | Jackson, Miss. | D3-'76 | 8/8 |
| 60 | | Stokes, Fred | DE | 6-3 | 274 | 3/14/64 | 8 | Georgia Southern | Vidalia, Ga. | UFA(Wash)-'93 | 15/15 |
| 99 | | Tanuvasa, Maa | DT | 6-2 | 277 | 11/6/70 | 2 | Hawaii | Mililani, Hawaii | D8b-'93 | 0* |
| 37 | | Taylor, Terry | CB | 5-10 | 185 | 7/18/61 | 10 | Southern Illinois | Warren, Ohio | FA-'94 | 10/7* |
| 55 | | White, Leon | LB | 6-3 | 242 | 10/4/63 | 9 | Brigham Young | La Mesa, Calif. | FA-'92 | 14/0 |
| 44 | | White, Russell | RB | 5-11 | 216 | 12/15/70 | 2 | California | Encino, Calif. | D3-'93 | 5/0 |
| 76 | | Young, Robert | DE | 6-6 | 273 | 1/29/69 | 4 | Mississippi State | Jackson, Miss. | D5-'91 | 6/6 |
| 10 | | Zendejas, Tony | K | 5-8 | 165 | 5/15/60 | 10 | Nevada-Reno | Chino, Calif. | PB(Hou)-'91 | 16/0 |

* Belin active for 5 games in '93 but did not play; Chandler played 4 games with Phoenix; Collins played 4 games with Green Bay, 10 games with L.A. Rams; Davis played 6 games with Phoenix, 6 games with L.A. Rams; Hicks played 10 games with N.Y. Jets; C. Jones played 4 games with N.Y. Jets; J. Jones played 15 games with Dallas; Kelly played 16 games with L.A. Raiders; Landeta played 8 games with N.Y. Giants, 8 games with L.A. Rams; Lewis played 15 games with San Diego; Miller played 3 games with Atlanta; McMurtry played 14 games with New England; Pope played 16 games with San Diego; Price played 1 game with Cincinnati; Taylor played 10 games with Cleveland; Tanuvasa missed '93 season due to injury.

\# Unrestricted free agent; subject to developments.

† Restricted free agent; subject to developments.

Traded—QB Jim Everett to New Orleans, TE Jim Price to Dallas.

t- Rams traded for Lewis (San Diego), Pope (San Diego).

Players lost through free agency (5): TE Pat Carter (Hou; 11 games in '93), WR Henry Ellard (Wash; 16), S Michael Stewart (Mia; 16), S Pat Terrell (NYJ; 13), DE Tony Woods (Wash; 14).

Also played with Rams in '93—P Don Bracken (3 games), LB Jeff Brady (6), T Irv Eatman (16), QB Jim Everett (10), T Robert Jenkins (8), WR Ernie Jones (10), WR James Lofton (1), P Paul McJulien (5), QB Mike Pagel (7), CB Sam Seale (1), LB Leon White (14).

## COACHING STAFF

**Head Coach,**
**Chuck Knox**

**Pro Career:** Started his second tour of duty as Rams head coach on January 8, 1992, after serving as Seattle's head coach from 1983-91 and leading the Seahawks into the playoffs four times, including the AFC Western Division title in 1988. Previously served as head coach of Buffalo Bills 1978-82, leading them to the AFC East title in 1980. Led the Rams to five consecutive NFC West titles (1973-77) before taking over Bills. Pro assistant with New York Jets 1963-66, coaching offensive line, before moving to Detroit in 1967. Served Lions as offensive line coach until named head coach of Rams in 1973. No pro playing experience. Career record: 189-146-1.

**Background:** Played tackle for Juniata College in Huntingdon, Pa., 1950-53. Was an assistant coach at his alma mater in 1954, then spent 1955 season at Tyrone High in Tyrone, Pa. Was head coach at Ellwood City (Pa.) High School from 1956-58. Moved to Wake Forest as an assistant coach in 1959-60, then Kentucky in 1961-62.

**Personal:** Born April 27, 1932, in Sewickley, Pa. Chuck and his wife, Shirley live in Villa Park, Calif., and have four children—Chris, Kathy, Colleen, and Chuck.

### ASSISTANT COACHES

**Chris Clausen,** strength and conditioning coordinator; born February 21, 1958, Evergreen Park, Ill., lives in Huntington Beach, Calif. Cornerback Indiana 1976-79. No pro playing experience. College coach: San Diego State 1987-88. Pro coach: San Diego Chargers 1989-91, joined Rams in 1992.

**George Dyer,** defensive coordinator; born May 4, 1940, Alhambra, Calif., lives in Villa Park, Calif. Center-linebacker U.C. Santa Barbara 1961-63. No pro playing experience. College coach: Humboldt State 1964-66, Coalinga (Calif.) J.C. 1967 (head coach), Portland State 1968-71, Idaho 1972, San Jose State 1973, Michigan State 1977-79, Arizona State 1980-81. Pro coach: Winnipeg Blue Bombers (CFL) 1974-76, Buffalo Bills 1982, Seattle Seahawks 1983-91, joined Rams in 1992.

**Jim Erkenbeck,** offensive line; born September 10, 1929, Los Angeles, Calif., lives in Anaheim Hills, Calif. Linebacker-end San Diego State 1949-52. No pro playing experience. College coach: San Diego State 1960-63, Grossmont (Calif.) J.C. 1964-67, Utah State 1968, Washington State 1969-71, California 1972-76. Pro coach: Winnipeg Blue Bombers (CFL) 1977, Montreal Alouettes (CFL) 1978-81, Calgary Stampeders (CFL) 1982, Philadelphia/Baltimore Stars (USFL) 1983-85, New Orleans Saints 1986, Dallas Cowboys 1987-88, Kansas City Chiefs 1989-91, joined Rams in 1992.

**Greg Gaines,** defensive assistant; born October 16, 1958, Martinsville, Va., lives in Mission Viejo, Calif. Linebacker Tennessee 1976-80. Pro linebacker Seattle Seahawks 1981-88, Kansas City Chiefs 1989. Pro coach: Joined Rams in 1992.

**Chick Harris,** offensive coordinator; born September 21, 1945, Durham, N.C., lives in Irvine, Calif. Running back Northern Arizona 1966-69. No pro playing experience. College coach: Colorado State 1970-72, Long Beach State 1973-74, Washington 1975-80. Pro coach: Buffalo Bills 1981-82, Seattle Seahawks 1983-91, joined Rams in 1992.

**Chuck Knox, Jr.,** offensive assistant-running backs; born June 19, 1965, Englewood, N.J., lives in Villa Park, Calif. Running back Arizona 1984-88. No pro playing experience. Pro coach: Joined Rams in 1993.

**Mike Martz,** quarterbacks; born May 13, 1951, Sioux Falls, S.D., lives in Huntington Beach, Calif. Tight end San Diego Mesa (Calif.) Junior College 1969-70, U.C. Santa Barbara 1971, Fresno State 1972. No pro playing experience. College coach: San Diego Mesa (Calif.) Junior College 1974, 1976-77, San Jose State 1975, Santa Ana (Calif.) Junior College 1978-79, Fresno State 1979, Pacific 1980-81, Minnesota 1982-83, Arizona State 1984-91. Pro coach: Joined Rams in 1992.

**Steve Moore,** receivers; born August 19, 1947, Los Angeles, lives in Huntington Beach, Calif. Wide receiver U.C. Santa Barbara 1968-69. No pro playing experience. College coach: U.C. Santa Barbara 1970-71, Army 1975, Rice 1976-77. Pro coach: Buffalo Bills 1978-82, Seattle Seahawks 1983-88, joined Rams in 1994.

**Rod Perry,** defensive backfield; born September 11, 1953, Fresno, Calif., lives in Anaheim Hills, Calif. Defensive back Colorado 1972-74. Pro cornerback Los Angeles Rams 1975-82, Cleveland Browns 1983-84. College coach: Columbia 1985, Fresno City College 1986, Fresno State 1987-88. Pro coach: Seattle Seahawks 1989-91, joined Rams in 1992.

**Dick Selcer,** linebackers; born August 22, 1937, Cincinnati, Ohio, lives in Anaheim Hills, Calif. Running back Notre Dame 1955-58. No pro playing experience. College coach: Xavier, Ohio 1962-64, 1970-71 (head coach), Cincinnati, 1965-66, Brown 1967-69, Wisconsin 1972-74, Kansas State 1975-77, Southwestern Louisiana 1978-80. Pro coach: Houston Oilers 1981-83, Cincinnati Bengals 1984-91, joined Rams in 1992.

**Wayne Sevier,** special teams; born July 3, 1941, San Diego, Calif., lives in Newport Beach, Calif. Quarterback Chaffey, Calif., J.C. 1960, San Diego State 1961-62. No pro playing experience. College coach: California Western 1968-69. Pro coach: St. Louis Cardinals 1974-75, Atlanta Falcons 1976, San Diego Chargers 1979-80, 1987-88, Washington Redskins 1981-86, 1989-93, joined Rams in 1994.

**Rennie Simmons,** tight ends; born February 25, 1942, Poughkeepsie, N.Y., lives in Anaheim, Calif. Center San Diego State 1963-65. No pro playing experience. College coach: Cal State-Fullerton 1972-75, Cerritos, Calif., J.C. 1976-80. Pro coach: Washington Redskins 1981-93, joined Rams in 1994.

**Joe Vitt,** assistant head coach-safeties; born August 23, 1954, Camden, N.J., lives in Mission Viejo, Calif. Linebacker Towson State 1973-75. No pro playing experience. Pro coach: Baltimore Colts 1979-81, Seattle Seahawks 1982-91, joined Rams in 1992.

## 1994 FIRST-YEAR ROSTER

| Name | Pos. | Ht. | Wt. | Birthdate | College | Hometown | How Acq. |
|---|---|---|---|---|---|---|---|
| Bostic, James | RB | 5-11 | 230 | 3/13/72 | Auburn | Ft. Lauderdale, Fla. | D3b |
| Brady, Rickey | TE | 6-4 | 246 | 11/19/71 | Oklahoma | Oklahoma City, Okla. | D6a |
| Brantley, Chris | WR | 5-10 | 180 | 12/12/70 | Rutgers | Teaneck, N.J. | D4 |
| Brasher, Bob (1) | TE | 6-5 | 244 | 4/30/70 | Arizona State | San Diego, Calif. | FA |
| Bruce, Isaac | WR | 6-0 | 178 | 11/10/72 | Memphis State | Ft. Lauderdale, Fla. | D2a |
| Bryant, Beno | RB | 5-9 | 170 | 1/1/71 | Washington | Los Angeles, Calif. | FA |
| Buffaloe, Jeff (1) | P | 6-1 | 194 | 9/18/70 | Memphis State | Memphis, Tenn. | FA |
| Edwards, Ronald | T | 6-5 | 311 | 9/18/71 | North Carolina A&T | Temple Hill, Md. | D6b |
| Farmer, Willie (1) | WR | 6-2 | 190 | 12/12/68 | Virginia Union | Tampa, Fla. | FA |
| Farr, D'Marco | DT | 6-1 | 270 | 6/9/71 | Washington | Richmond, Calif. | FA |
| Gandy, Wayne | T | 6-4 | 289 | 2/10/71 | Auburn | Haines City, Fla. | D1 |
| Jones, Ernest | LB | 6-2 | 239 | 4/1/71 | Oregon | Utica, N.Y. | D3c |
| Jones, Jeff (1) | WR | 5-10 | 185 | 10/19/70 | California | Irvine, Calif. | FA |
| Kirchoff, Jay (1) | K | 6-4 | 198 | 5/28/70 | Arizona | Plymouth, Minn. | FA |
| Lyle, Keith | S | 6-2 | 204 | 4/17/72 | Virginia | Vienna, Va. | D3a |
| Mason, Andy | LB | 6-2 | 228 | 8/31/71 | Washington | Longview, Wash. | FA |
| McDougal, Kevin | QB | 6-2 | 182 | 5/29/72 | Notre Dame | Pompano Beach, Fla. | FA |
| O'Bannon, Turhon | WR | 6-0 | 195 | 3/23/70 | New Mexico | Reseda, Calif. | FA |
| Ottis, Brad | DE | 6-4 | 272 | 8/2/72 | Wayne State, Neb. | Wahoo, Neb. | D2c |
| Patrick, Kevin | DE | 6-3 | 255 | 7/30/71 | Miami | West Palm Beach, Fla. | FA |
| Ross, Jermaine | WR | 5-11 | 192 | 4/27/71 | Purdue | Jeffersonville, Ind. | FA |
| Setzer, Rusty | RB | 5-7 | 184 | 12/16/69 | Grand Valley State | Gary, Ind. | FA |
| Starck, Justin | T | 6-6 | 310 | 11/4/71 | Oregon | Salem,Ore. | FA |
| Turk, Matt (1) | P | 6-5 | 230 | 6/16/68 | Wis.-Whitewater | Greenfield, Wis. | FA |
| Wilson, David (1) | S | 5-10 | 192 | 6/10/70 | California | Reseda, Calif. | FA |
| Wright, Toby | S | 5-11 | 203 | 11/19/70 | Nebraska | Phoenix, Ariz. | D2b |

The term NFL Rookie is defined as a player who is in his first season of professional football and has not been on the roster of another professional football team for any regular-season or postseason games. A Rookie is designated by an "R" on NFL rosters. Players who have been active in another professional football league or players who have NFL experience, including either preseason training camp or being on an Active List or Inactive List, or on Reserve/Injured or Reserve/Physically Unable to Perform for fewer than six regular-season games, are termed NFL First-Year Players. An NFL First-Year Player is designated by a "1" on NFL rosters. Thereafter, a player is credited with an additional year of experience for each season in which he accumulates six games on the Active List or Inactive List, or on Reserve/Injured or Reserve/Physically Unable to Perform.

## NOTES

# MINNESOTA VIKINGS

**National Football Conference**
**Central Division**
**Team Colors:** Purple, Gold, and White
**9520 Viking Drive**
**Eden Prairie, Minnesota 55344**
**Telephone: (612) 828-6500**

## CLUB OFFICERS

Chairman of the Board: John C. Skoglund
Vice Chairmen: Jaye F. Dyer, Philip S. Maas
Directors: N. Bud Grossman, Roger L. Headrick, James R. Jundt, Elizabeth MacMillan, Carol S. Sperry, Wheelock Whitney

## CLUB OFFICIALS

President/CEO: Roger L. Headrick
Vice President Administration/Team Operations: Jeff Diamond
Vice President Player Personnel: Frank Gilliam
Assistant General Manager/College Scouting: Jerry Reichow
Assistant General Manager/Pro Personnel: Paul Wiggin
Director of Finance: Nick Valentine
Director of Research and Dev.: Mike Eayrs
Director of Marketing: Kernal Buhler
Director of Public Relations: David Pelletier
Director of Team Operations: Breck Spinner
Ticket Manager: Harry Randolph
Director of Security: Steve Rollins
Player Personnel Coordinator: Scott Studwell
Equipment Manager: Dennis Ryan
Trainer: Fred Zamberletti
Video Director: Larry Kohout
**Stadium:** Hubert H. Humphrey Metrodome
• **Capacity:** 63,000
500 11th Avenue South
Minneapolis, Minnesota 55415
**Playing Surface:** AstroTurf
**Training Camp:** Mankato State University
Mankato, Minnesota 56001

## 1994 SCHEDULE

**PRESEASON**

| | | |
|---|---|---|
| July 31 | at Dallas | 8:00 |
| Aug. 6 | vs. Kansas City at Tokyo | 10:00 |
| Aug. 13 | **New Orleans** | 7:00 |
| Aug. 20 | at Seattle | 7:00 |
| Aug. 26 | **Miami** | 7:00 |

**REGULAR SEASON**

| | | |
|---|---|---|
| Sept. 4 | at Green Bay | 12:00 |
| Sept. 11 | **Detroit** | 12:00 |
| Sept. 18 | at Chicago | 12:00 |
| Sept. 25 | **Miami** | 12:00 |
| Oct. 2 | at Arizona | 1:00 |
| Oct. 10 | at New York Giants (Monday) | 9:00 |
| Oct. 16 | Open Date | |
| Oct. 20 | **Green Bay** (Thursday) | 7:00 |
| Oct. 30 | at Tampa Bay | 4:00 |
| Nov. 6 | **New Orleans** | 12:00 |
| Nov. 13 | at New England | 1:00 |
| Nov. 20 | **New York Jets** | 3:00 |
| Nov. 27 | **Tampa Bay** | 12:00 |
| Dec. 1 | **Chicago** (Thursday) | 7:00 |
| Dec. 11 | at Buffalo | 1:00 |
| Dec. 17 | at Detroit (Saturday) | 12:30 |
| Dec. 26 | **San Francisco** (Monday) | 8:00 |

## RECORD HOLDERS

**INDIVIDUAL RECORDS—CAREER**

| Category | Name | Performance |
|---|---|---|
| Rushing (Yds.) | Chuck Foreman, 1973-79 | 5,879 |
| Passing (Yds.) | Fran Tarkenton, 1961-66, 1972-78 | 33,098 |
| Passing (TDs) | Fran Tarkenton, 1961-66, 1972-78 | 239 |
| Receiving (No.) | Steve Jordan, 1982-1993 | 495 |
| Receiving (Yds.) | Anthony Carter, 1985-1993 | 7,636 |
| Interceptions | Paul Krause, 1968-1979 | 53 |
| Punting (Avg.) | Harry Newsome, 1990-93 | 43.8 |
| Punt Return (Avg.) | Tommy Mason, 1961-66 | 10.4 |
| Kickoff Return (Avg.) | Bob Reed, 1962-63 | 27.1 |
| Field Goals | Fred Cox, 1963-1977 | 282 |
| Touchdowns (Tot.) | Bill Brown, 1962-1974 | 76 |
| Points | Fred Cox, 1963-1977 | 1,365 |

**INDIVIDUAL RECORDS—SINGLE SEASON**

| Category | Name | Performance |
|---|---|---|
| Rushing (Yds.) | Terry Allen, 1992 | 1,201 |
| Passing (Yds.) | Tommy Kramer, 1981 | 3,912 |
| Passing (TDs) | Tommy Kramer, 1981 | 26 |
| Receiving (No.) | Rickey Young, 1978 | 88 |
| Receiving (Yds.) | Anthony Carter, 1988 | 1,225 |
| Interceptions | Paul Krause, 1975 | 10 |
| Punting (Avg.) | Bobby Walden, 1964 | 46.4 |
| Punt Return (Avg.) | Leo Lewis, 1987 | 12.5 |
| Kickoff Return (Avg.) | John Gilliam, 1972 | 26.3 |
| Field Goals | Rich Karlis, 1989 | 31 |
| Touchdowns (Tot.) | Chuck Foreman, 1975 | 22 |
| Points | Chuck Foreman, 1975 | 132 |

**INDIVIDUAL RECORDS—SINGLE GAME**

| Category | Name | Performance |
|---|---|---|
| Rushing (Yds.) | Chuck Foreman, 10-24-76 | 200 |
| Passing (Yds.) | Tommy Kramer, 11-2-86 | 490 |
| Passing (TDs) | Joe Kapp, 9-28-69 | *7 |
| Receiving (No.) | Rickey Young, 12-16-79 | 15 |
| Receiving (Yds.) | Sammy White, 11-7-76 | 210 |
| Interceptions | Many times | 3 |
| | Last time by Jack Del Rio, 12-5-93 | |
| Field Goals | Rich Karlis, 11-5-89 | *7 |
| Touchdowns (Tot.) | Chuck Foreman, 12-20-75 | 4 |
| | Ahmad Rashad, 9-2-79 | 4 |
| Points | Chuck Foreman, 12-20-75 | 24 |
| | Ahmad Rashad, 9-2-79 | 24 |

*NFL Record

## VIKINGS COACHING HISTORY

**(275-232-9)**

| | | |
|---|---|---|
| 1961-66 | Norm Van Brocklin | 29-51-4 |
| 1967-83 | Bud Grant | 161-99-5 |
| 1984 | Les Steckel | 3-13-0 |
| 1985 | Bud Grant | 7-9-0 |
| 1986-91 | Jerry Burns | 55-46-0 |
| 1992-93 | Dennis Green | 20-14-0 |

**HUBERT H. HUMPHREY METRODOME**

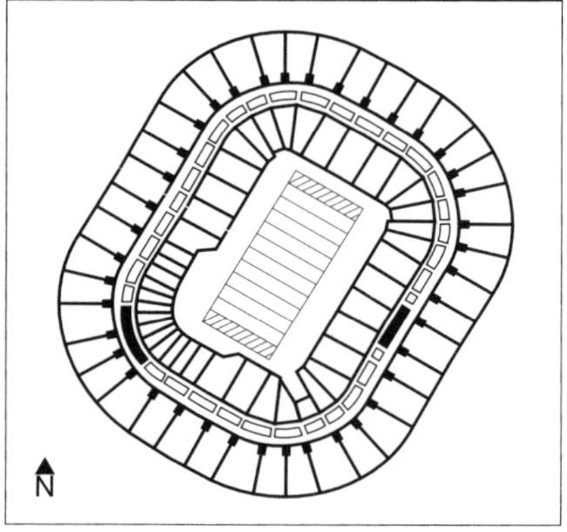

## 1993 TEAM RECORD

**PRESEASON (4-1)**

| Date | Result | | Opponents |
|---|---|---|---|
| 8/1 | W | 13-7 | at Dallas |
| 8/7 | W | 20-6 | vs. Buffalo at Berlin |
| 8/14 | W | 23-10 | Seattle |
| 8/21 | L | 20-27 | at Kansas City |
| 8/26 | W | 30-13 | Pittsburgh |

**REGULAR SEASON (9-7)**

| Date | Result | | Opponents | Att. |
|---|---|---|---|---|
| 9/5 | L | 7-24 | at L.A. Raiders | 44,120 |
| 9/12 | W | 10-7 | Chicago | 57,921 |
| 9/26 | W | 15-13 | Green Bay | 61,746 |
| 10/3 | L | 19-38 | at San Francisco | 63,071 |
| 10/10 | W | 15-0 | Tampa Bay | 54,215 |
| 10/25 | W | 19-12 | at Chicago | 64,677 |
| 10/31 | L | 27-30 | Detroit | 53,428 |
| 11/7 | L | 17-30 | San Diego | 55,527 |
| 11/14 | W | 26-23 | at Denver | 67,329 |
| 11/21 | L | 10-23 | at Tampa Bay | 40,848 |
| 11/28 | L | 14-17 | New Orleans | 53,030 |
| 12/5 | W | 13-0 | at Detroit | 63,216 |
| 12/12 | L | 20-37 | Dallas | 63,321 |
| 12/19 | W | 21-17 | at Green Bay | 54,773 |
| 12/26 | W | 30-10 | Kansas City | 59,236 |
| 12/31 | W | 14-9 | at Washington | 42,836 |

**POSTSEASON (0-1)**

| Date | Result | | Opponents | Att. |
|---|---|---|---|---|
| 1/9 | L | 10-17 | at N.Y. Giants | 75,089 |

**SCORE BY PERIODS**

| | | | | | | | |
|---|---|---|---|---|---|---|---|
| Vikings | 49 | 81 | 83 | 64 | 0 | — | 277 |
| Opponents | 67 | 93 | 36 | 94 | 0 | — | 290 |

**ATTENDANCE**

Home 458,424 Away 440,870 Total 899,294
Single-game home record, 63,321 (12-12-93)
Single-season home record, 485,616 (1992)

## 1993 TEAM STATISTICS

| | Vikings | Opp. |
|---|---|---|
| Total First Downs | 283 | 259 |
| Rushing | 85 | 98 |
| Passing | 182 | 139 |
| Penalty | 16 | 22 |
| Third Down: Made/Att | 72/212 | 81/207 |
| Third Down Pct. | 34.0 | 39.1 |
| Fourth Down: Made/Att | 4/7 | 3/6 |
| Fourth Down Pct. | 57.1 | 50.0 |
| Total Net Yards | 4824 | 4406 |
| Avg. Per Game | 301.5 | 275.4 |
| Total Plays | 1008 | 938 |
| Avg. Per Play | 4.8 | 4.7 |
| Net Yards Rushing | 1624 | 1536 |
| Avg. Per Game | 101.5 | 96.0 |
| Total Rushes | 447 | 415 |
| Net Yards Passing | 3200 | 2870 |
| Avg. Per Game | 200.0 | 179.4 |
| Sacked/Yards Lost | 35/181 | 45/276 |
| Gross Yards | 3381 | 3146 |
| Att./Completions | 526/315 | 478/310 |
| Completion Pct. | 59.9 | 64.9 |
| Had Intercepted | 14 | 24 |
| Punts/Avg. | 90/42.9 | 78/42.4 |
| Net Punting Avg. | 90/35.4 | 78/37.8 |
| Penalties/Yards Lost | 109/806 | 97/768 |
| Fumbles/Ball Lost | 15/10 | 24/10 |
| Touchdowns | 28 | 31 |
| Rushing | 8 | 14 |
| Passing | 18 | 11 |
| Returns | 2 | 6 |
| Avg. Time of Possession | 30:28 | 29:33 |

## 1993 INDIVIDUAL STATISTICS

| PASSING | Att | Cmp | Yds. | Pct. | TD | Int | Tkld. | Rate |
|---|---|---|---|---|---|---|---|---|
| McMahon | 331 | 200 | 1968 | 60.4 | 9 | 8 | 23/104 | 76.2 |
| Salisbury | 195 | 115 | 1413 | 59.0 | 9 | 6 | 12/77 | 84.0 |
| Vikings | 526 | 315 | 3381 | 59.9 | 18 | 14 | 35/181 | 79.1 |
| Opponents | 478 | 310 | 3146 | 64.9 | 11 | 24 | 45/276 | 70.3 |

| SCORING | TD R | TD P | TD Rt | PAT | FG | Saf | PTS |
|---|---|---|---|---|---|---|---|
| Reveiz | 0 | 0 | 0 | 27/28 | 26/35 | 0 | 105 |
| C. Carter | 0 | 9 | 0 | 0/0 | 0/0 | 0 | 54 |
| A. Carter | 0 | 5 | 0 | 0/0 | 0/0 | 0 | 30 |
| Graham | 3 | 0 | 0 | 0/0 | 0/0 | 0 | 18 |
| Craig | 1 | 1 | 0 | 0/0 | 0/0 | 0 | 12 |
| Smith | 2 | 0 | 0 | 0/0 | 0/0 | 0 | 12 |
| Word | 2 | 0 | 0 | 0/0 | 0/0 | 0 | 12 |
| Ismail | 0 | 1 | 0 | 0/0 | 0/0 | 0 | 6 |
| Jordan | 0 | 1 | 0 | 0/0 | 0/0 | 0 | 6 |
| McGriggs | 0 | 0 | 1 | 0/0 | 0/0 | 0 | 6 |
| McMillian | 0 | 0 | 1 | 0/0 | 0/0 | 0 | 6 |
| Tice | 0 | 1 | 0 | 0/0 | 0/0 | 0 | 6 |
| Thomas | 0 | 0 | 0 | 0/0 | 0/0 | 1 | 2 |
| Vikings | 8 | 18 | 2 | 27/28 | 26/35 | 2 | 277 |
| Opponents | 14 | 11 | 6 | 29/31 | 25/33 | 0 | 290 |

| RUSHING | Att. | Yds. | Avg. | LG | TD |
|---|---|---|---|---|---|
| Graham | 118 | 488 | 4.1 | 31 | 3 |
| Word | 142 | 458 | 3.2 | 14 | 2 |
| Smith | 82 | 399 | 4.9 | 26t | 2 |
| Craig | 38 | 119 | 3.1 | 11 | 1 |
| McMahon | 33 | 96 | 2.9 | 16 | 0 |
| Evans | 14 | 32 | 2.3 | 5 | 0 |
| A. Carter | 7 | 19 | 2.7 | 9 | 0 |
| Ismail | 3 | 14 | 4.7 | 6 | 0 |
| Salisbury | 10 | -1 | -0.1 | 6 | 0 |
| Vikings | 447 | 1624 | 3.6 | 31 | 8 |
| Opponents | 415 | 1536 | 3.7 | 45 | 14 |

| RECEIVING | No. | Yds. | Avg. | LG | TD |
|---|---|---|---|---|---|
| C. Carter | 86 | 1071 | 12.5 | 58 | 9 |
| A. Carter | 60 | 775 | 12.9 | 39 | 5 |
| Jordan | 56 | 542 | 9.7 | 53 | 1 |
| Smith | 24 | 111 | 4.6 | 12 | 0 |
| Ismail | 19 | 212 | 11.2 | 37 | 1 |
| Craig | 19 | 169 | 8.9 | 31 | 1 |
| Tennell | 15 | 122 | 8.1 | 17 | 0 |
| Word | 9 | 105 | 11.7 | 27 | 0 |
| Graham | 7 | 46 | 6.6 | 11 | 0 |
| Tice | 6 | 39 | 6.5 | 21 | 1 |
| Reed | 5 | 65 | 13.0 | 18 | 0 |
| Truitt | 4 | 40 | 10.0 | 13 | 0 |
| Evans | 4 | 39 | 9.8 | 21 | 0 |
| Guliford | 1 | 45 | 45.0 | 45 | 0 |
| Vikings | 315 | 3381 | 10.7 | 58 | 18 |
| Opponents | 310 | 3146 | 10.1 | 93t | 11 |

| INTERCEPTIONS | No. | Yds. | Avg. | LG | TD |
|---|---|---|---|---|---|
| Glenn | 5 | 49 | 9.8 | 23 | 0 |
| McMillian | 4 | 45 | 11.3 | 22t | 1 |
| Del Rio | 4 | 3 | 0.8 | 3 | 0 |
| Lee | 3 | 20 | 6.7 | 19 | 0 |
| Scott | 2 | 26 | 13.0 | 26 | 0 |
| C. Jenkins | 2 | 7 | 3.5 | 4 | 0 |
| McGriggs | 1 | 63 | 63.0 | 63t | 1 |
| Parker | 1 | 1 | 1.0 | 1 | 0 |
| Pearson | 1 | 0 | 0.0 | 0 | 0 |
| Doleman | 1 | -3 | -3.0 | -3 | 0 |
| Vikings | 24 | 211 | 8.8 | 63t | 2 |
| Opponents | 14 | 166 | 11.9 | 41t | 3 |

| PUNTING | No. | Yds. | Avg. | In 20 | LG |
|---|---|---|---|---|---|
| Newsome | 90 | 3862 | 42.9 | 25 | 64 |
| Vikings | 90 | 3862 | 42.9 | 25 | 64 |
| Opponents | 78 | 3307 | 42.4 | 23 | 59 |

| PUNT RETURNS | No. | FC | Yds. | Avg. | LG | TD |
|---|---|---|---|---|---|---|
| Guliford | 29 | 15 | 212 | 7.3 | 50 | 0 |
| Parker | 9 | 6 | 64 | 7.1 | 20 | 0 |
| Smith | 1 | 2 | 4 | 4.0 | 4 | 0 |
| Vikings | 39 | 23 | 280 | 7.2 | 50 | 0 |
| Opponents | 46 | 22 | 560 | 12.2 | 72t | 1 |

| KICKOFF RETURNS | No. | Yds. | Avg. | LG | TD |
|---|---|---|---|---|---|
| Ismail | 42 | 902 | 21.5 | 47 | 0 |
| Guliford | 5 | 101 | 20.2 | 29 | 0 |
| Smith | 3 | 41 | 13.7 | 16 | 0 |
| Craig | 1 | 11 | 11.0 | 11 | 0 |
| Del Rio | 1 | 4 | 4.0 | 4 | 0 |
| Evans | 1 | 11 | 11.0 | 11 | 0 |
| Graham | 1 | 16 | 16.0 | 16 | 0 |
| McMillian | 1 | 0 | 0.0 | 0 | 0 |
| Vikings | 55 | 1086 | 19.7 | 47 | 0 |
| Opponents | 58 | 1420 | 24.5 | 99t | 1 |

| SACKS | No. |
|---|---|
| Doleman | 12.5 |
| Randle | 12.5 |
| Thomas | 9.0 |
| Barker | 6.0 |
| C. Jenkins | 2.5 |
| R. Harris | 1.0 |
| Sheppard | 1.0 |
| Del Rio | 0.5 |
| Vikings | 45.0 |
| Opponents | 35.0 |

## 1994 DRAFT CHOICES

| Round | Name | Pos. | College |
|---|---|---|---|
| 1 | DeWayne Washington | DB | North Carolina State |
| | Todd Steussie | T | California |
| 2 | David Palmer | RB | Alabama |
| | Fernando Smith | DE | Jackson State |
| 4 | Mike Wells | DT | Iowa |
| 5 | Shelly Hammonds | DB | Penn State |
| 6 | Andrew Jordan | TE | Western Carolina |
| 7 | Pete Bercich | LB | Notre Dame |

## MINNESOTA VIKINGS

### 1994 VETERAN ROSTER

| No. | Name | Pos. | Ht. | Wt. | Birthdate | NFL Exp. | College | Hometown | How Acq. | '93 Games/ Starts |
|---|---|---|---|---|---|---|---|---|---|---|
| 50 | Abrams, Bobby | LB | 6-3 | 230 | 4/12/67 | 5 | Michigan | Detroit, Mich. | FA-'93 | 4/0 |
| 72 | Adams, Scott | G-T | 6-5 | 293 | 9/28/66 | 3 | Georgia | Lake City, Fla. | FA-'91 | 15/9 |
| 21 | Allen, Terry | RB | 5-10 | 197 | 2/21/68 | 5 | Clemson | Commerce, Ga. | D9-'90 | 0* |
| 4 | Barker, Bryan | P | 6-1 | 187 | 6/28/64 | 5 | Santa Clara | Orinda, Calif. | FA-'94 | 16/0* |
| 92 | Barker, Roy | DT | 6-4 | 280 | 2/14/69 | 3 | North Carolina | New York, N.Y. | D4-'92 | 16/16 |
| 80 | Carter, Cris | WR | 6-3 | 197 | 11/25/65 | 8 | Ohio State | Middletown, Ohio | W(Phil)-'90 | 16/16 |
| 62 | Christy, Jeff | C | 6-3 | 277 | 2/2/69 | 2 | Pittsburgh | Freeport, Pa. | FA-'93 | 9/0 |
| 87 | t- Cooper, Adrian | TE | 6-5 | 263 | 4/27/68 | 4 | Oklahoma | Denver, Colo. | T(Pitt)-'94 | 14/3* |
| 33 | # Craig, Roger | RB | 6-0 | 211 | 7/10/60 | 12 | Nebraska | Davenport, Iowa | PB(Raid)-'92 | 14/3 |
| 77 | Culpepper, Brad | DT | 6-1 | 260 | 5/8/68 | 3 | Florida | Tallahassee, Fla. | D10-'92 | 15/0 |
| 75 | Dafney, Bernard | T | 6-5 | 331 | 11/1/69 | 3 | Tennessee | Los Angeles, Calif. | FA-'92 | 16/4 |
| 55 | Del Rio, Jack | LB | 6-4 | 243 | 4/4/63 | 10 | Southern California | Hayward, Calif. | PB(Dall)-'92 | 16/16 |
| 29 | Evans, Charles | RB | 6-1 | 226 | 4/16/67 | 2 | Clark, Ga. | Augusta, Ga. | FA-'93 | 3/0 |
| 54 | Garnett, Dave | LB | 6-2 | 225 | 12/6/70 | 2 | Stanford | Naperville, Ill. | FA-'93 | 16/0 |
| 66 | Gerak, John | G | 6-3 | 285 | 1/6/70 | 2 | Penn State | Struthers, Ohio | D3a-'93 | 4/0 |
| 25 | Glenn, Vencie | S | 6-0 | 201 | 10/26/64 | 9 | Indiana State | Silver Spring, Md. | PB(NO)-'92 | 16/16 |
| 31 | Graham, Scottie | RB | 5-9 | 215 | 3/28/69 | 2 | Ohio State | Long Island, N.Y. | FA-'93 | 7/3 |
| 84 | Guliford, Eric | WR | 5-8 | 165 | 10/25/69 | 2 | Arizona State | Peoria, Ariz. | FA-'93 | 10/0 |
| 99 | Harris, James | DE | 6-4 | 270 | 5/13/68 | 2 | Temple | East St. Louis, Ill. | FA-'93 | 6/0 |
| 90 | Harris, Robert | DE | 6-4 | 285 | 6/13/69 | 2 | Southern | Riviera Beach, Fla. | D2-'92 | 16/0 |
| 78 | Hinton, Chris | T | 6-4 | 305 | 7/31/61 | 12 | Northwestern | Chicago, Ill. | FA-'94 | 16/16* |
| 82 | Ismail, Qadry | WR | 6-0 | 192 | 11/8/70 | 2 | Syracuse | Wilkes-Barre, Pa. | D2-'93 | 15/3 |
| 51 | Jenkins, Carlos | LB | 6-3 | 217 | 7/12/68 | 4 | Michigan State | Lantana, Fla. | D3a-'91 | 16/16 |
| 14 | Johnson, Brad | QB | 6-5 | 221 | 9/13/68 | 2 | Florida State | Black Mountain, N.C. | D9a-'92 | 0* |
| 83 | # Jordan, Steve | TE | 6-3 | 242 | 1/10/61 | 13 | Brown | Phoenix, Ariz. | D7-'82 | 14/12 |
| 32 | Lee, Amp | RB | 5-11 | 200 | 10/1/71 | 3 | Florida State | Chipley, Fla. | FA-'94 | 15/3* |
| 61 | Lindsay, Everett | G | 6-4 | 290 | 9/18/70 | 2 | Mississippi | Raleigh, N.C. | D5-'93 | 12/12 |
| 91 | Manusky, Greg | LB | 6-1 | 233 | 8/12/66 | 7 | Colgate | Wilkes-Barre, Pa. | FA-'91 | 16/0* |
| 58 | McDaniel, Ed | LB | 5-11 | 230 | 2/2/69 | 3 | Clemson | Leesville, S.C. | D5-'92 | 7/1 |
| 64 | McDaniel, Randall | G | 6-3 | 280 | 12/19/64 | 7 | Arizona State | Avondale, Ariz. | D1-'88 | 16/16 |
| 37 | † McGriggs, Lamar | S | 6-3 | 210 | 5/9/68 | 4 | Western Illinois | Harvey, Ill. | FA-'93 | 9/4 |
| 1 | t- Moon, Warren | QB | 6-3 | 212 | 11/18/56 | 11 | Washington | Los Angeles, Calif. | T(Hou)-'94 | 15/14* |
| 68 | Morris, Mike | C | 6-5 | 284 | 2/22/61 | 7 | Northeast Missouri State | Centerville, Iowa | FA-'91 | 16/0 |
| 85 | # Novoselsky, Brent | TE | 6-2 | 237 | 1/8/66 | 7 | Pennsylvania | Niles, Ill. | FA-'89 | 15/0 |
| 27 | Parker, Anthony | CB | 5-10 | 181 | 2/11/66 | 4 | Arizona State | Tempe, Ariz. | PB(Ind)-'92 | 14/0 |
| 28 | Pool, David | CB | 5-9 | 182 | 12/20/66 | 5 | Carson-Newman | Cincinnati, Ohio | UFA(Den)-'94 | 0* |
| 93 | Randle, John | DT | 6-1 | 275 | 12/12/67 | 5 | Texas A&I | Hearne, Tex. | FA-'90 | 16/16 |
| 86 | Reed, Jake | WR | 6-3 | 212 | 9/28/67 | 3 | Grambling | Covington, Ga. | D3b-'91 | 10/1 |
| 7 | # Reveiz, Fuad | K | 5-11 | 223 | 2/24/63 | 10 | Tennessee | Miami, Fla. | FA-'90 | 16/0 |
| 60 | Schreiber, Adam | C-G | 6-4 | 288 | 2/20/62 | 11 | Texas | Huntsville, Ala. | PB(NYJ)-'90 | 16/16 |
| 38 | Scott, Todd | S | 5-10 | 207 | 1/23/68 | 4 | Southwestern Louisiana | Galveston, Tex. | D6-'91 | 13/12 |
| 59 | Sheppard, Ashley | LB | 6-3 | 243 | 1/21/69 | 2 | Clemson | North Pitt, N.C. | D4-'93 | 10/0 |
| 26 | Smith, Robert | RB | 6-0 | 195 | 3/4/72 | 2 | Ohio State | Euclid, Ohio | D1-'93 | 10/2 |
| 53 | # Strickland, Fred | LB | 6-2 | 245 | 8/15/64 | 7 | Purdue | Wanaque, N.J. | UFA(Rams)-'93 | 16/15 |
| 46 | Tennell, Derek | TE | 6-2 | 251 | 2/12/64 | 6 | UCLA | West Covina, Calif. | FA-'93 | 16/6 |
| 97 | Thomas, Henry | DT | 6-2 | 277 | 1/12/65 | 8 | Louisiana State | Houston, Tex. | D3-'87 | 13/13 |
| 94 | Thornton, John | DT | 6-0 | 303 | 6/28/69 | 2 | Cincinnati | Flint, Mich. | FA-'94 | 0* |
| 89 | Truitt, Olanda | WR | 6-0 | 186 | 1/4/71 | 2 | Mississippi State | Birmingham, Ala. | W(Raid)-'93 | 8/0 |
| 95 | † Tuaolo, Esera | DT | 6-2 | 274 | 7/11/68 | 4 | Oregon State | Honolulu, Hawaii | FA-'92 | 11/3 |
| 15 | Walsh, Chris | WR | 6-1 | 185 | 12/12/68 | 2 | Stanford | Concord, Calif. | FA-'94 | 3/0* |
| 11 | Ware, Andre | QB | 6-2 | 205 | 7/31/68 | 5 | Houston | Dickinson, Tex. | UFA(Det)-'94 | 5/2* |
| 35 | West, Ronnie | WR | 6-2 | 215 | 6/23/68 | 3 | Pittsburg State, Kan. | Wilcox, Ga. | D9b-'92 | 0* |
| 23 | # Word, Barry | RB | 6-2 | 242 | 1/17/63 | 6 | Virginia | Long Island, Va. | T(KC)-'93 | 13/8 |

* Allen and West missed '93 season due to injury; B. Barker played 16 games with Kansas City in '93; Cooper played 14 games with Pittsburgh; Hinton played 16 games with Atlanta; Johnson inactive for 16 games; A. Lee played 15 games with San Francisco; Manusky played 16 games with Minnesota; Pool active for 2 games but did not play; Moon played 15 games with Houston; Thornton inactive for 2 games; Walsh played 3 games with Buffalo; Ware played 5 games with Detroit.

\# Unrestricted free agent; subject to developments.

† Restricted free agent; subject to developments.

Traded—DE Chris Doleman to Atlanta.

t- Vikings traded for Cooper (Pittsburgh), Moon (Houston).

Players lost through free agency (4): WR Anthony Carter (Det; 15 games in '93), T Tim Irwin (TB; 16), G Todd Kalis (Pitt; 16), QB Sean Salisbury (Hou; 11).

Also played with Vikings in '93—S Ron Carpenter (7 games), DE Chris Doleman (16), LB Bruce Holmes (1), CB Izel Jenkins (4), S Shawn Jones (1), CB Carl Lee (16), QB Jim McMahon (12), CB Audray McMillian (16), P Harry Newsome (16), CB Jayice Pearson (13), TE Mike Tice (16), QB Gino Torretta (1).

## COACHING STAFF

**Head Coach,**
**Dennis Green**

**Pro Career:** Named the fifth head coach in Vikings history on January 10, 1992. In 1993 Green became only the eleventh head coach in the history of the NFL to lead his team to the playoffs in each of his first two seasons as a head coach in the league. Last year, he led the Vikings through a season of adversity to a 9-7 record and a postseason berth. In December, Minnesota compiled a 4-1 record despite playing four playoff teams, including three division winners. In his first season with the Vikings in 1992, Green became one of only eight coaches since the NFL merger in 1970 to lead a team to a division title in his first year as a head coach. He earned NFL coach of the year recognition from the Washington Touchdown Club and NFC coach of the year honors from *United Press International* and *College & Pro Football Newsweekly.* Coached special teams and receivers for the San Francisco 49ers in 1979. Returned to San Francisco from 1986-88 as receivers coach. Credited with the development of two of the game's premier wide receivers—Jerry Rice and John Taylor. Coached with 49ers in Super Bowl XXIII. Played one season for British Columbia Lions (CFL). Career record: 20-14.

**Background:** Running back at Iowa 1968-70. Began coaching career at Iowa as a graduate assistant in 1972. Moved to Dayton in 1973 as running backs and receivers coach before returning to Iowa from 1974-76 to coach receivers and quarterbacks. Running backs coach at Stanford from 1977-78. Returned to Stanford in 1980 as offensive coordinator. Head coach at Northwestern from 1981-85. Green earned Big Ten coach-of-the-year honors in 1982. In 1989, Green was named head coach at Stanford where he led the Cardinal to the 1991 Aloha Bowl, its first postseason appearance since 1986.

**Personal:** Born February 17, 1949, in Harrisburg, Pa. Graduated from Iowa with bachelor of science degree in recreation. Dennis, and his wife, Margie, live in Eden Prairie, Minn., and have two children—Patti and Jeremy.

### ASSISTANT COACHES

**Brian Billick,** offensive coordinator/quarterbacks; born February 28, 1954, Redlands, Calif., lives in Eden Prairie, Minn. Tight end Brigham Young 1974-76. Pro tight end Dallas Cowboys 1977. College coach: Brigham Young 1978, Redlands 1979, San Diego State 1981-85, Utah State 1986-88, Stanford 1989-91. Pro coach: Joined Vikings in 1992.

**Tony Dungy,** defensive coordinator; born October 6, 1955, Jackson, Mich., lives in Eden Prairie, Minn. Quarterback Minnesota 1973-76. Pro safety Pittsburgh Steelers 1977-78, San Francisco 49ers 1979. College coach: Minnesota 1980. Pro coach: Pittsburgh Steelers 1981-88, Kansas City Chiefs 1989-91, joined Vikings in 1992.

**Chris Foerster,** offensive line assistant; born October 12, 1961, Milwaukee, Wis., lives in Maple Grove, Minn. Center Colorado State 1979-82. No pro playing experience. College coach: Colorado State 1983-87, Stanford 1988-91, Minnesota 1992. Pro coach: Joined Vikings in 1993.

**Carl Hargrave,** offensive assistant; born November 8, 1954, Frankfurt, Germany, lives in Eden Prairie, Minn. Defensive back Upper Iowa 1972-75. No pro playing experience. College coach: Upper Iowa 1977-80, Northwestern 1981-85, Pittsburgh 1986, Houston 1987-91, Iowa 1992-93. Pro coach: Joined Vikings in 1994.

**Monte Kiffin,** inside linebackers; born February 29, 1940, Lexington, Ky., lives in Bloomington, Minn. Offensive-defensive tackle Nebraska 1958-61. Pro defensive end Winnipeg Blue Bombers (CFL) 1965. College coach: Nebraska 1966-76, Arkansas 1977-79, North Carolina State 1980-82 (head coach). Pro coach: Green Bay Packers 1983, Buffalo Bills 1984-85, Minnesota Vikings 1986-89, New York Jets 1990, rejoined Vikings in 1991.

**Jerry Rhome,** receivers; born March 6, 1942, Dallas Tex., lives in Eden Prairie, Minn. Quarterback Southern Methodist 1960-61, Tulsa 1963-64. Pro quarterback Dallas Cowboys 1965-68, Cleveland Browns 1969, Houston Oilers 1970, Los Angeles Rams 1971-72. College coach: Tulsa 1973-75. Pro coach: Seattle Seahawks 1976-82, Washington Redskins 1983-87, San Diego Chargers 1988, Dallas Cowboys 1989, Phoenix Cardinals 1990-93, joined Vikings in 1994.

**Keith Rowen,** offensive line; born September 2, 1952, New York, N.Y., lives in Eden Prairie, Minn. Offensive tackle Stanford 1972-74. No pro playing experience. College coach: Stanford 1975-76, Long Beach State 1977-78, Arizona 1979-82. Pro coach: Boston/New Orleans Breakers (USFL) 1983-84, Cleveland Browns 1984, Indianapolis Colts 1985-88, New England Patriots 1989, Atlanta Falcons 1990-93, joined Vikings in 1994.

**Richard Solomon,** defensive backs; born December 8, 1949, New Orleans, La., lives in Eden Prairie, Minn. Running back-defensive back Iowa 1970-73. No pro playing experience. College coach: Dubuque 1973-75, Southern Illinois 1976, Iowa 1977-78, Syracuse 1979, Illinois 1980-86. Pro coach: New York Giants 1987-91 (scout), joined Vikings in 1992.

**John Teerlinck,** defensive line; born April 9, 1951, Rochester, N.Y., lives in Eden Prairie, Minn. Defensive lineman Western Illinois 1970-73. Pro defensive tackle San Diego Chargers 1974-76. College coach: Iowa Lakes J.C. 1977, Eastern Illinois 1978-79, Illinois 1980-82. Pro coach: Chicago Blitz (USFL) 1983, Arizona Wranglers/Outlaws (USFL) 1984-85, Cleveland Browns 1989-90, Los Angeles Rams 1991, joined Vikings in 1992.

**Trent Walters,** outside linebackers; born November 20, 1943, Knoxville, Tenn., lives in Eden Prairie, Minn. Defensive back Indiana 1963-65. Pro defensive back Edmonton Eskimos (CFL) 1966-67. College coach: Indiana 1968-71, Louisville 1972, Indiana 1973-80, Washington 1981-83, Pittsburgh 1985, Louisville 1986-90, Texas A&M 1991-93. Pro coach: Cincinnati Bengals 1984, joined Vikings in 1994.

**Steve Wetzel,** strength and conditioning; born May 11, 1963, Washington D.C., lives in Eden Prairie, Minn. No college or pro playing experience. College coach: Maryland 1985-89, George Mason 1990. Pro coach: Washington Redskins 1990-91, joined Vikings in 1992.

**Tyrone Willingham,** running backs; born December 30, 1953, Jacksonville, N.C., lives in Deephaven, Minn. Quarterback Michigan State 1974-77. No pro playing experience. College coach: Michigan State 1977, 1980-82, Central Michigan 1978-79, North Carolina State 1983-85, Rice 1986-88, Stanford 1989-91. Pro coach: Joined Vikings in 1992.

**Mike Wolf,** assistant strength and conditioning; born May 15, 1965, Allentown, Pa., lives in Eden Prairie, Minn. Center Penn State 1983-87. No pro playing experience. College coach: Vanderbilt 1988-89, Lehigh 1990, Penn State 1991. Pro coach: Joined Vikings in 1992.

**Gary Zauner,** special teams; born November 2, 1950, Milwaukee, Wis., lives in Eden Prairie, Minn. Kicker Wisconsin-LaCrosse 1968-72. No pro playing experience. College coach: Brigham Young 1979-80, San Diego State 1981-86, New Mexico 1987-88, Long Beach State 1990-91. Pro coach: Joined Vikings in 1994.

## 1994 FIRST-YEAR ROSTER

| Name | Pos. | Ht. | Wt. | Birthdate | College | Hometown | How Acq. |
|---|---|---|---|---|---|---|---|
| Bercich, Pete | LB | 6-1 | 240 | 12/23/71 | Notre Dame | Joliet, Ill. | D7 |
| Boudreaux, Frank (1) | DT | 6-5 | 273 | 6/20/70 | Northwestern | Honolulu, Hawaii | FA |
| Boyd, Malik | CB | 5-10 | 175 | 11/5/70 | Southern | Houston, Tex. | FA |
| Boyd, Tracy (1) | T | 6-4 | 296 | 8/27/67 | Elizabeth City State | Crowley, La. | FA |
| Brown, Phil | RB | 5-10 | 210 | 12/30/70 | Texas | Commerce, Tex. | FA |
| Buck, Edward | S | 5-11 | 175 | 2/6/71 | Alcorn State | Brandon, Miss. | FA |
| Gray, Lance | RB | 6-1 | 220 | 6/14/70 | Nebraska | Owego, N.Y. | FA |
| Griffith, Robert (1) | CB-S | 5-11 | 200 | 11/30/70 | San Diego State | San Diego, Calif. | FA |
| Hammonds, Shelly | CB | 5-10 | 187 | 2/13/71 | Penn State | Barnwell, S.C. | D5 |
| Harrison, Todd (1) | TE | 6-4 | 260 | 3/20/69 | North Carolina State | Gainesville, Fla. | FA |
| Jones, Richard (1) | P | 6-3 | 198 | 3/25/65 | Arizona State | Scottsdale, Ariz. | FA |
| Jordan, Andrew | TE | 6-4 | 268 | 6/21/72 | Western Carolina | Charlotte, N.C. | D6 |
| Lasley, J.J. (1) | RB | 6-0 | 220 | 2/9/70 | Stanford | Encino, Calif. | FA |
| Lenseigne, Tony (1) | TE | 6-4 | 235 | 8/7/69 | Eastern Washington | Yakima, Wash. | FA |
| Palmer, David | RB | 5-8 | 167 | 11/19/72 | Alabama | Birmingham, Ala. | D2a |
| Riemer, Troy | T | 6-5 | 287 | 12/1/70 | Texas | Austin, Tex. | FA |
| Sims, William (1) | LB | 6-3 | 265 | 12/30/70 | S.W. Louisiana | Brooks County, Ga. | FA |
| Smith, Fernando | DE | 6-6 | 270 | 8/2/71 | Jackson State | Flint, Mich. | D2b |
| Staten, Robert (1) | RB | 5-11 | 235 | 1/23/69 | Jackson State | Shubuta, Miss. | FA |
| Steussie, Todd | T | 6-5 | 298 | 12/1/70 | California | Canoga Park, Calif. | D1b |
| Washington, DeWayne | CB | 5-11 | 192 | 12/1/72 | North Carolina State | Burham, N.C. | D1a |
| Wells, Mike | DT | 6-3 | 287 | 1/6/71 | Iowa | Arnold, Mo. | D4 |

The term NFL Rookie is defined as a player who is in his first season of professional football and has not been on the roster of another professional football team for any regular-season or postseason games. A Rookie is designated by an "R" on NFL rosters. Players who have been active in another professional football league or players who have NFL experience, including either preseason training camp or being on an Active List or Inactive List, or on Reserve/Injured or Reserve/Physically Unable to Perform for fewer than six regular-season games, are termed NFL First-Year Players. An NFL First-Year Player is designated by a "1" on NFL rosters. Thereafter, a player is credited with an additional year of experience for each season in which he accumulates six games on the Active List or Inactive List, or on Reserve/Injured or Reserve/Physically Unable to Perform.

## NOTES

# NEW ORLEANS SAINTS

**National Football Conference**
**Western Division**
**Team Colors:** Old Gold, Black, and White
**6928 Saints Drive**
**Metairie, Louisiana 70003**
**Telephone: (504) 733-0255**

## CLUB OFFICIALS

Owner: Tom Benson
Executive Vice President/Administration: Jim Miller
Vice President/Football Operations: Bill Kuharich
Vice President/Head Coach: Jim Mora
Vice President/Marketing: Greg Suit
Director of Pro Personnel: Chet Franklin
Treasurer: Bruce Broussard
Administrative Coordinator: Austin Dejan
Comptroller: Charleen Sharpe
Director of Corporate Sales: Bill Ferrante
Director of Media Relations: Rusty Kasmiersky
Assistant Director of Media Relations: Neal Gulkis
Data Processing Manager: Jay Romig
Director of Travel/Entertainment/Special Projects: Barra Birrcher
Director of Community Relations: Chanel Lagarde
Player Personnel Scouts: Bill Baker, Hamp Cook, Hokie Gajan, Tom Marino, Carmen Piccone
Ticket Manager: Sandy King
Trainer: Dean Kleinschmidt
Equipment Manager: Dan Simmons
Video Director: Albert Aucoin
**Stadium:** Louisiana Superdome
• **Capacity:** 69,056
1500 Poydras Street
New Orleans, Louisiana 70112
**Playing Surface:** AstroTurf
**Training Camp:** University of Wisconsin-La Crosse
La Crosse, Wisconsin 54601

## 1994 SCHEDULE

### PRESEASON

| | | |
|---|---|---|
| Aug. 5 | at New England | 8:00 |
| Aug. 13 | at Minnesota | 7:00 |
| Aug. 19 | **Green Bay** | 7:00 |
| Aug. 25 | **Dallas** | 7:00 |

### REGULAR SEASON

| | | |
|---|---|---|
| Sept. 4 | **Kansas City** | 12:00 |
| Sept. 11 | **Washington** | 3:00 |
| Sept. 18 | at Tampa Bay | 1:00 |
| Sept. 25 | at San Francisco | 1:00 |
| Oct. 2 | **New York Giants** | 3:00 |
| Oct. 9 | at Chicago | 12:00 |
| Oct. 16 | **San Diego** | 3:00 |
| Oct. 23 | **Los Angeles Rams** | 12:00 |
| Oct. 30 | Open Date | |
| Nov. 6 | at Minnesota | 12:00 |
| Nov. 13 | **Atlanta** | 12:00 |
| Nov. 20 | at Los Angeles Raiders | 1:00 |
| Nov. 28 | **San Francisco** (Monday) | 8:00 |
| Dec. 4 | at Los Angeles Rams | 1:00 |
| Dec. 11 | at Atlanta | 8:00 |
| Dec. 19 | **Dallas** (Monday) | 8:00 |
| Dec. 24 | at Denver | 2:00 |

## RECORD HOLDERS

### INDIVIDUAL RECORDS—CAREER

| Category | Name | Performance |
|---|---|---|
| Rushing (Yds.) | George Rogers, 1981-84 | 4,267 |
| Passing (Yds.) | Archie Manning, 1971-1982 | 21,734 |
| Passing (TDs) | Archie Manning, 1971-1982 | 115 |
| Receiving (No.) | Eric Martin, 1985-1993 | 532 |
| Receiving (Yds.) | Eric Martin, 1985-1993 | 7,854 |
| Interceptions | Dave Waymer, 1980-89 | 37 |
| Punting (Avg.) | Tommy Barnhardt, 1987, 1989-1993 | 42.9 |
| Punt Return (Avg.) | Tyrone Hughes, 1993 | 13.6 |
| Kickoff Return (Avg.) | Walter Roberts, 1967 | 26.3 |
| Field Goals | Morten Andersen, 1982-1993 | 274 |
| Touchdowns (Tot.) | Dalton Hilliard, 1986-1993 | 53 |
| Points | Morten Andersen, 1982-1993 | 1,202 |

### INDIVIDUAL RECORDS—SINGLE SEASON

| Category | Name | Performance |
|---|---|---|
| Rushing (Yds.) | George Rogers, 1981 | 1,674 |
| Passing (Yds.) | Archie Manning, 1980 | 3,716 |
| Passing (TDs) | Archie Manning, 1980 | 23 |
| Receiving (No.) | Eric Martin, 1988 | 85 |
| Receiving (Yds.) | Eric Martin, 1989 | 1,090 |
| Interceptions | Dave Whitsell, 1967 | 10 |
| Punting (Avg.) | Tommy Barnhardt, 1992 | 44.0 |
| Punt Return (Avg.) | Mel Gray, 1987 | 14.7 |
| Kickoff Return (Avg.) | Don Shy, 1969 | 27.9 |
| Field Goals | Morten Andersen, 1985 | 31 |
| Touchdowns (Tot.) | Dalton Hilliard, 1989 | 18 |
| Points | Morten Andersen, 1987 | 121 |

### INDIVIDUAL RECORDS—SINGLE GAME

| Category | Name | Performance |
|---|---|---|
| Rushing (Yds.) | George Rogers, 9-4-83 | 206 |
| Passing (Yds.) | Archie Manning, 12-7-80 | 377 |
| Passing (TDs) | Billy Kilmer, 11-2-69 | 6 |
| Receiving (No.) | Tony Galbreath, 9-10-78 | 14 |
| Receiving (Yds.) | Wes Chandler, 9-2-79 | 205 |
| Interceptions | Tommy Myers, 9-3-78 | 3 |
| | Dave Waymer, 10-6-85 | 3 |
| | Reggie Sutton, 10-18-87 | 3 |
| | Gene Atkins, 12-22-91 | 3 |
| Field Goals | Morten Andersen, 12-1-85 | 5 |
| | Morten Andersen, 11-15-87 | 5 |
| | Morten Andersen, 12-3-92 | 5 |
| Touchdowns (Tot.) | Many times | 3 |
| | Last time by Rueben Mayes, 9-23-90 | |
| Points | Many times | 18 |
| | Last time by Rueben Mayes, 9-23-90 | |

## COACHING HISTORY

**(160-241-5)**

| | | |
|---|---|---|
| 1967-70 | Tom Fears* | 13-34-2 |
| 1970-72 | J.D. Roberts | 7-25-3 |
| 1973-75 | John North** | 11-23-0 |
| 1975 | Ernie Hefferle | 1-7-0 |
| 1976-77 | Hank Stram | 7-21-0 |
| 1978-80 | Dick Nolan*** | 15-29-0 |
| 1980 | Dick Stanfel | 1-3-0 |
| 1981-85 | O.A. (Bum) Phillips**** | 27-42-0 |
| 1985 | Wade Phillips | 1-3-0 |
| 1986-93 | Jim Mora | 77-54-0 |

*Released after seven games in 1970
**Released after six games in 1975
***Released after 12 games in 1980
****Resigned after 12 games in 1985

### LOUISIANA SUPERDOME

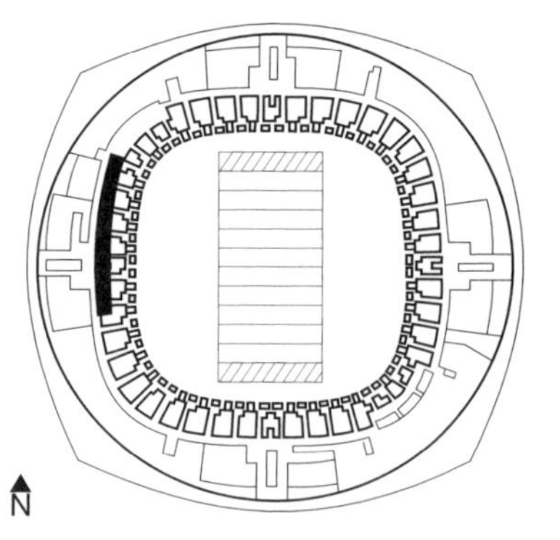

## 1993 TEAM RECORD

**PRESEASON (4-1)**

| Date | Result | | Opponents |
|---|---|---|---|
| 7/31 | W | 28-16 | vs. Philadelphia at Tokyo |
| 8/7 | W | 37-28 | vs. Houston at San Antonio |
| 8/14 | W | 26-17 | vs. Green Bay at Madison |
| 8/23 | W | 20-14 | Chicago |
| 8/27 | L | 16-17 | Detroit |

**REGULAR SEASON (8-8)**

| Date | Result | | Opponents | Att. |
|---|---|---|---|---|
| 9/5 | W | 33-21 | Houston | 69,029 |
| 9/12 | W | 34-31 | at Atlanta | 64,287 |
| 9/19 | W | 14-3 | Detroit | 69,039 |
| 9/26 | W | 16-13 | San Francisco | 69,041 |
| 10/3 | W | 37-6 | at L.A. Rams | 50,709 |
| 10/17 | L | 14-37 | at Pittsburgh | 56,056 |
| 10/24 | L | 15-26 | Atlanta | 69,043 |
| 10/31 | W | 20-17 | at Phoenix | 36,778 |
| 11/14 | L | 17-19 | Green Bay | 69,043 |
| 11/22 | L | 7-42 | at San Francisco | 66,500 |
| 11/28 | W | 17-14 | at Minnesota | 53,030 |
| 12/5 | L | 13-17 | at Cleveland | 60,388 |
| 12/12 | L | 20-23 | L.A. Rams | 69,033 |
| 12/20 | L | 14-24 | N.Y. Giants | 69,036 |
| 12/26 | L | 26-37 | at Philadelphia | 50,085 |
| 1/2 | W | 20-13 | Cincinnati | 58,036 |

**SCORE BY PERIODS**

| | | | | | | | |
|---|---|---|---|---|---|---|---|
| Saints | 66 | 80 | 60 | 111 | 0 | — | 317 |
| Opponents | 78 | 106 | 72 | 87 | 0 | — | 343 |

**ATTENDANCE**

Home 541,300 Away 437,833 Total 979,133
Single-game home record, 70,940 (11-4-79)
Single-season home record, 548,655 (1991)

## 1993 TEAM STATISTICS

| | Saints | Opp. |
|---|---|---|
| Total First Downs | 264 | 273 |
| Rushing | 94 | 116 |
| Passing | 158 | 145 |
| Penalty | 12 | 12 |
| Third Down: Made/Att | 72/203 | 92/227 |
| Third Down Pct. | 35.5 | 40.5 |
| Fourth Down: Made/Att | 7/11 | 9/16 |
| Fourth Down Pct. | 63.6 | 56.3 |
| Total Net Yards | 4707 | 4696 |
| Avg. Per Game | 294.2 | 293.5 |
| Total Plays | 935 | 1008 |
| Avg. Per Play | 5.0 | 4.7 |
| Net Yards Rushing | 1766 | 2090 |
| Avg. Per Game | 110.4 | 130.6 |
| Total Rushes | 414 | 513 |
| Net Yards Passing | 2941 | 2606 |
| Avg. Per Game | 183.8 | 162.9 |
| Sacked/Yards Lost | 40/242 | 51/318 |
| Gross Yards | 3183 | 2924 |
| Att./Completions | 481/274 | 444/259 |
| Completion Pct. | 57.0 | 58.3 |
| Had Intercepted | 21 | 10 |
| Punts/Avg. | 77/43.6 | 80/42.3 |
| Net Punting Avg. | 77/37.5 | 80/34.8 |
| Penalties/Yards Lost | 81/663 | 86/590 |
| Fumbles/Ball Lost | 24/13 | 30/20 |
| Touchdowns | 33 | 39 |
| Rushing | 10 | 7 |
| Passing | 18 | 22 |
| Returns | 5 | 10 |
| Avg. Time of Possession | 28:32 | 31:28 |

## 1993 INDIVIDUAL STATISTICS

| PASSING | Att | Cmp | Yds. | Pct. | TD | Int | Tkld. | Rate |
|---|---|---|---|---|---|---|---|---|
| Wilson | 388 | 221 | 2457 | 57.0 | 12 | 15 | 37/225 | 70.1 |
| M. Buck | 54 | 32 | 448 | 59.3 | 4 | 3 | 3/17 | 87.6 |
| Walsh | 38 | 20 | 271 | 52.6 | 2 | 3 | 0/0 | 60.3 |
| Barnhardt | 1 | 1 | 7 | 100.0 | 0 | 0 | 0/0 | 95.8 |
| Saints | 481 | 274 | 3183 | 57.0 | 18 | 21 | 40/242 | 71.4 |
| Opponents | 444 | 259 | 2924 | 58.3 | 22 | 10 | 51/318 | 85.3 |

| SCORING | TD R | TD P | TD Rt | PAT | FG | Saf | PTS |
|---|---|---|---|---|---|---|---|
| Andersen | 0 | 0 | 0 | 33/33 | 28/35 | 0 | 117 |
| Early | 0 | 6 | 0 | 0/0 | 0/0 | 0 | 36 |
| Brown | 2 | 1 | 0 | 0/0 | 0/0 | 0 | 18 |
| Hilliard | 2 | 1 | 0 | 0/0 | 0/0 | 0 | 18 |
| Hughes | 0 | 0 | 3 | 0/0 | 0/0 | 0 | 18 |
| E. Martin | 0 | 3 | 0 | 0/0 | 0/0 | 0 | 18 |
| Muster | 3 | 0 | 0 | 0/0 | 0/0 | 0 | 18 |
| Smith | 0 | 2 | 0 | 0/0 | 0/0 | 0 | 12 |
| Brenner | 0 | 1 | 0 | 0/0 | 0/0 | 0 | 6 |
| Dowdell | 0 | 1 | 0 | 0/0 | 0/0 | 0 | 6 |
| McAfee | 1 | 0 | 0 | 0/0 | 0/0 | 0 | 6 |
| Mills | 0 | 0 | 1 | 0/0 | 0/0 | 0 | 6 |
| Neal | 1 | 0 | 0 | 0/0 | 0/0 | 0 | 6 |
| Ned | 1 | 0 | 0 | 0/0 | 0/0 | 0 | 6 |
| Newman | 0 | 1 | 0 | 0/0 | 0/0 | 0 | 6 |
| Small | 0 | 1 | 0 | 0/0 | 0/0 | 0 | 6 |
| Turner | 0 | 1 | 0 | 0/0 | 0/0 | 0 | 6 |
| Warren | 0 | 0 | 1 | 0/0 | 0/0 | 0 | 6 |
| Stowers | 0 | 0 | 0 | 0/0 | 0/0 | 1 | 2 |
| Saints | 10 | 18 | 5 | 33/33 | 28/35 | 1 | 317 |
| Opponents | 7 | 22 | 10 | 35/39 | 24/30 | 1 | 343 |

| RUSHING | Att. | Yds. | Avg. | LG | TD |
|---|---|---|---|---|---|
| Brown | 180 | 705 | 3.9 | 60 | 2 |
| Wilson | 31 | 230 | 7.4 | 44 | 0 |
| Muster | 64 | 214 | 3.3 | 18 | 3 |
| Neal | 21 | 175 | 8.3 | 74t | 1 |
| Hilliard | 50 | 165 | 3.3 | 16 | 2 |
| McAfee | 51 | 160 | 3.1 | 27 | 1 |
| Ned | 9 | 71 | 7.9 | 35t | 1 |
| Early | 2 | 32 | 16.0 | 26 | 0 |
| Barnhardt | 1 | 18 | 18.0 | 18 | 0 |
| M. Buck | 1 | 0 | 0.0 | 0 | 0 |
| Walsh | 4 | -4 | -1.0 | -1 | 0 |
| Saints | 414 | 1766 | 4.3 | 74t | 10 |
| Opponents | 513 | 2090 | 4.1 | 71t | 7 |

| RECEIVING | No. | Yds. | Avg. | LG | TD |
|---|---|---|---|---|---|
| E. Martin | 66 | 950 | 14.4 | 54t | 3 |
| Early | 45 | 670 | 14.9 | 63t | 6 |
| Hilliard | 40 | 296 | 7.4 | 34 | 1 |
| Muster | 23 | 195 | 8.5 | 31 | 0 |
| Brown | 21 | 170 | 8.1 | 19 | 1 |
| Smith | 16 | 180 | 11.3 | 23 | 2 |
| Small | 16 | 164 | 10.3 | 17 | 1 |
| Turner | 12 | 163 | 13.6 | 52 | 1 |
| Brenner | 11 | 171 | 15.5 | 27 | 1 |
| Ned | 9 | 54 | 6.0 | 14 | 0 |
| Newman | 8 | 121 | 15.1 | 32 | 1 |
| Dowdell | 6 | 46 | 7.7 | 11t | 1 |
| McAfee | 1 | 3 | 3.0 | 3 | 0 |
| Saints | 274 | 3183 | 11.6 | 63t | 18 |
| Opponents | 259 | 2924 | 11.3 | 98t | 22 |

| INTERCEPTIONS | No. | Yds. | Avg. | LG | TD |
|---|---|---|---|---|---|
| Atkins | 3 | 59 | 19.7 | 37 | 0 |
| Taylor | 2 | 32 | 16.0 | 30 | 0 |
| V. Buck | 2 | 28 | 14.0 | 28 | 0 |
| Jones | 1 | 12 | 12.0 | 12 | 0 |
| Turnbull | 1 | 2 | 2.0 | 2 | 0 |
| Cook | 1 | 0 | 0.0 | 0 | 0 |
| Saints | 10 | 133 | 13.3 | 37 | 0 |
| Opponents | 21 | 444 | 21.1 | 67t | 6 |

| PUNTING | No. | Yds. | Avg. | In 20 | LG |
|---|---|---|---|---|---|
| Barnhardt | 77 | 3356 | 43.6 | 26 | 58 |
| Saints | 77 | 3356 | 43.6 | 26 | 58 |
| Opponents | 80 | 3384 | 42.3 | 20 | 60 |

| PUNT RETURNS | No. | FC | Yds. | Avg. | LG | TD |
|---|---|---|---|---|---|---|
| Hughes | 37 | 21 | 503 | 13.6 | 83t | 2 |
| Newman | 1 | 0 | 14 | 14.0 | 14 | 0 |
| Saints | 38 | 21 | 517 | 13.6 | 83t | 2 |
| Opponents | 36 | 18 | 348 | 9.7 | 75t | 1 |

| KICKOFF RETURNS | No. | Yds. | Avg. | LG | TD |
|---|---|---|---|---|---|
| Hughes | 30 | 753 | 25.1 | 99t | 1 |
| McAfee | 28 | 580 | 20.7 | 55 | 0 |
| Brown | 3 | 58 | 19.3 | 23 | 0 |
| Hilliard | 1 | 17 | 17.0 | 17 | 0 |
| Dowdell | 0 | 52 | — | 52 | 0 |
| Saints | 62 | 1460 | 23.5 | 99t | 1 |
| Opponents | 40 | 788 | 19.7 | 47 | 0 |

| SACKS | No. |
|---|---|
| Turnbull | 13.0 |
| Jackson | 11.5 |
| Johnson | 5.0 |
| W. Martin | 5.0 |
| V. Buck | 3.0 |
| Miller | 2.5 |
| Goff | 2.0 |
| Mills | 2.0 |
| Williams | 2.0 |
| Atkins | 1.0 |
| Cook | 1.0 |
| Jones | 1.0 |
| Smeenge | 1.0 |
| Warren | 1.0 |
| Saints | 51.0 |
| Opponents | 40.0 |

## 1994 DRAFT CHOICES

| Round | Name | Pos. | College |
|---|---|---|---|
| 1 | Joe Johnson | DE | Louisville |
| 2 | Mario Bates | RB | Arizona State |
| 3 | Winfred Tubbs | LB | Texas |
| 4 | Doug Nussmeier | QB | Idaho |
| 5 | Herman Carroll | DE | Mississippi State |
| | Craig Novitsky | G | UCLA |
| 6 | Derrell Mitchell | WR | Texas Tech |
| 7 | Lance Lundberg | T | Nebraska |

# NEW ORLEANS SAINTS

## 1994 VETERAN ROSTER

| No. | Name | Pos. | Ht. | Wt. | Birthdate | NFL Exp. | College | Hometown | How Acq. | '93 Games/ Starts |
|---|---|---|---|---|---|---|---|---|---|---|
| 7 | Andersen, Morten | K | 6-2 | 221 | 8/19/60 | 13 | Michigan State | Indianapolis, Ind. | D4-'82 | 16/0 |
| 6 | Barnhardt, Tommy | P | 6-2 | 207 | 6/11/63 | 8 | North Carolina | China Grove, N.C. | FA-'89 | 16/0 |
| 24 | Brown, Derek | RB | 5-9 | 186 | 4/15/71 | 2 | Nebraska | Anaheim, Calif. | D4b-'93 | 13/12 |
| 16 | Buck, Mike | QB | 6-3 | 227 | 4/22/67 | 5 | Maine | Sayville, N.Y. | D6a-'90 | 4/1 |
| 26 | Buck, Vince | CB | 6-0 | 198 | 1/12/68 | 5 | Central State, Ohio | Owensboro, Ky. | D2-'90 | 16/16 |
| 40 | Coghill, George | S | 6-2 | 196 | 3/30/70 | 2 | Wake Forest | Fredericksburg, Va. | FA-'93 | 0* |
| 41 | # Cook, Toi | CB | 5-11 | 188 | 12/3/64 | 8 | Stanford | Van Nuys, Calif. | D8-'87 | 16/16 |
| 71 | Cooper, Richard | T | 6-5 | 290 | 11/1/64 | 5 | Tennessee | Memphis, Tenn. | FA-'89 | 16/16 |
| 63 | Davidson, Jeff | G | 6-5 | 305 | 10/3/67 | 4 | Ohio State | Akron, Ohio | FA-'94 | 0* |
| 95 | Dixon, Ronnie | NT | 6-2 | 292 | 5/10/71 | 2 | Cincinnati | Clinton, N.C. | D6-'93 | 2/0 |
| 72 | Dombrowski, Jim | G | 6-5 | 298 | 10/19/63 | 9 | Virginia | Williamsville, N.Y. | D1-'86 | 16/2 |
| 80 | Dowdell, Marcus | WR | 5-10 | 179 | 5/22/70 | 2 | Tennessee State | Birmingham, Ala. | D10-'92 | 9/1 |
| 63 | Dunbar, Karl | DE | 6-4 | 275 | 5/18/67 | 3 | Louisiana State | Opelousas, La. | FA-'92 | 13/1 |
| 32 | Dunbar, Vaughn | RB | 5-10 | 204 | 9/4/68 | 3 | Indiana | Ft. Wayne, Ind. | D1-'92 | 0* |
| 89 | Early, Quinn | WR | 6-0 | 188 | 4/13/65 | 7 | Iowa | South Great Neck, N.Y. | PB(SD)-'91 | 16/15 |
| 17 | t- Everett, Jim | QB | 6-5 | 212 | 1/3/63 | 9 | Purdue | Albuquerque, N.M. | T(Rams)-'94 | 10/9* |
| 55 | Freeman, Reggie | LB | 6-1 | 233 | 5/8/70 | 2 | Florida State | Clewiston, Fla. | D2-'93 | 10/0 |
| 66 | Garten, Joe | C-G | 6-2 | 290 | 8/13/68 | 3 | Colorado | Valencia, Calif. | FA-'94 | 0* |
| 91 | Goff, Robert | NT | 6-3 | 270 | 10/2/65 | 7 | Auburn | Bradenton, Fla. | T(TB)-'90 | 16/9 |
| 81 | Haynes, Michael | WR | 6-0 | 184 | 12/24/65 | 7 | Northern Arizona | New Orleans, La. | FA-'94 | 16/16* |
| 38 | Henderson, Othello | S | 6-0 | 192 | 8/23/72 | 2 | UCLA | Killeen, Tex. | D7-'93 | 5/1 |
| 61 | # Hilgenberg, Joel | C-G | 6-2 | 252 | 7/10/62 | 11 | Iowa | Iowa City, Iowa | D4-'84 | 9/9 |
| 21 | # Hilliard, Dalton | RB | 5-8 | 204 | 1/21/64 | 9 | Louisiana State | Patterson, La. | D2-'86 | 16/0 |
| 33 | Hughes, Tyrone | CB | 5-9 | 175 | 1/14/70 | 2 | Nebraska | New Orleans, La. | D5-'93 | 16/0 |
| 57 | # Jackson, Rickey | LB | 6-2 | 243 | 3/20/58 | 14 | Pittsburgh | Pahokee, Fla. | D2-'81 | 16/16 |
| 53 | Johnson, Vaughan | LB | 6-3 | 235 | 3/24/62 | 9 | North Carolina State | Morehead City, N.C. | SD1-'84 | 15/13 |
| 27 | Jones, Reginald | CB | 6-1 | 202 | 1/11/69 | 4 | Memphis State | West Memphis, Ark. | D5-'91 | 12/2 |
| 43 | Legette, Tyrone | CB | 5-9 | 177 | 2/15/70 | 3 | Nebraska | Columbia, S.C. | D3-'92 | 14/1 |
| 46 | Lumpkin, Sean | S | 6-0 | 206 | 1/4/70 | 3 | Minnesota | St. Louis Park, Minn. | D4b-'92 | 12/0 |
| 84 | Martin, Eric | WR | 6-1 | 207 | 11/8/61 | 10 | Louisiana State | Van Vleck, Tex. | D7-'85 | 16/13 |
| 93 | Martin, Wayne | DE | 6-5 | 275 | 10/26/65 | 6 | Arkansas | Cherry Valley, Ark. | D1-'89 | 16/16 |
| 39 | # Maxie, Brett | S | 6-2 | 194 | 1/13/62 | 10 | Texas Southern | Dallas, Tex. | FA-'85 | 1/1 |
| 96 | Mayfield, Corey | NT | 6-3 | 290 | 2/25/70 | 2 | Oklahoma | Tyler, Tex. | FA-'94 | 0* |
| 69 | Miller, Les | DE | 6-7 | 285 | 3/1/65 | 8 | Fort Hays State | Arkansas City, Kan. | PB(SD)-'91 | 13/11 |
| 51 | # Mills, Sam | LB | 5-9 | 225 | 6/3/59 | 9 | Montclair State | Long Branch, N.J. | FA-'86 | 9/7 |
| 22 | Muster, Brad | RB | 6-4 | 235 | 4/11/65 | 7 | Stanford | Santa Rosa, Calif. | FA-'93 | 13/11 |
| 23 | Neal, Lorenzo | RB | 5-11 | 240 | 12/27/70 | 2 | Fresno State | Lemoore, Calif. | D4a-'93 | 2/2 |
| 36 | Ned, Derrick | RB | 6-1 | 210 | 1/5/69 | 2 | Grambling State | Eunice, La. | FA-'92 | 14/1 |
| 79 | Nelson, Royce | G | 6-4 | 315 | 8/9/70 | 2 | Nicholls State | New Orleans, La. | FA-'93 | 0* |
| 70 | Port, Chris | G-T | 6-5 | 290 | 11/2/67 | 4 | Duke | Wanaque, N.J. | FA-'90 | 15/15 |
| 64 | Ricketts, Tom | G | 6-5 | 305 | 11/21/65 | 6 | Pittsburgh | Murrysville, Pa. | FA-'94 | 3/0* |
| 77 | Roaf, William | T | 6-5 | 300 | 4/18/70 | 2 | Louisiana Tech | Pine Bluff, Ark. | D1a-'93 | 16/16 |
| 83 | Small, Torrance | WR | 6-3 | 201 | 9/6/70 | 3 | Alcorn State | Tampa, Fla. | D5-'92 | 11/0 |
| 99 | Smeenge, Joel | DE | 6-5 | 250 | 4/1/68 | 4 | Western Michigan | Grand Rapids, Mich. | D3-'90 | 16/2 |
| 82 | Smith, Irv | TE | 6-3 | 246 | 10/13/71 | 2 | Notre Dame | Pemberton, N.J. | D1b-'93 | 16/8 |
| 37 | Spencer, Jimmy | CB | 5-9 | 180 | 3/29/69 | 3 | Florida | South Bay, Fla. | FA-'92 | 16/3 |
| 52 | Stonebreaker, Michael | LB | 6-0 | 235 | 1/14/67 | 2 | Notre Dame | Glencoe, Ill. | FA-'94 | 0* |
| 34 | Tillison, Ed | RB | 5-10 | 229 | 12/12/69 | 3 | N.W. Missouri State | Pearl River, La. | FA-'94 | 0* |
| 97 | Turnbull, Renaldo | DE | 6-4 | 255 | 1/5/66 | 5 | West Virginia | St. Thomas, Virgin Islands | D1-'90 | 15/14 |
| 62 | Uhlenhake, Jeff | C | 6-3 | 284 | 1/28/66 | 6 | Ohio State | Newark, Ohio | UFA(Mia)-'94 | 5/5* |
| 87 | Wainright, Frank | TE | 6-3 | 236 | 10/10/67 | 4 | Northern Colorado | Arvada, Colo. | D8-'91 | 16/2 |
| 85 | Walls, Wesley | TE | 6-5 | 250 | 2/26/66 | 6 | Mississippi | Pontotic, Miss. | UFA(SF)-'94 | 6/0* |
| 73 | # Warren, Frank | DE | 6-4 | 290 | 9/14/59 | 13 | Auburn | Birmingham, Ala. | D3a-'81 | 8/7 |
| 94 | # Wilks, Jim | NT | 6-5 | 275 | 3/12/58 | 14 | San Diego State | Pasadena, Calif. | D12-'81 | 8/1 |
| 90 | Williams, James | LB | 6-0 | 230 | 10/10/68 | 5 | Mississippi State | North Natchez, Miss. | D6b-'90 | 16/9 |
| 65 | Williams, Willie | T | 6-6 | 295 | 8/6/67 | 3 | Louisiana State | Houston, Tex. | FA-'94 | 0* |
| 18 | Wilson, Wade | QB | 6-3 | 206 | 2/1/59 | 14 | East Texas State | Commerce, Tex. | FA-'93 | 14/14 |
| 92 | # Winston, DeMond | LB | 6-2 | 239 | 9/14/68 | 5 | Vanderbilt | Lansing, Mich. | D4-'90 | 16/0 |

* Coghill, V. Dunbar, Nelson, and Tillison missed '93 season due to injury; Davidson last active with Denver in '92; Everett played 10 games with L.A. Rams in '93; Garten on injured reserve with Green Bay in '92; Haynes played 16 games with Atlanta; Mayfield last active with Tampa Bay in '92; Ricketts played 3 games with Kansas City; Stonebreaker last active with Chicago in '91; Uhlenhake played 5 games with Miami; Walls played 6 games with San Francisco; Williams last active with Arizona in '91.

\# Unrestricted free agent; subject to developments.

† Restricted free agent; subject to developments.

t- Saints traded for Everett (L.A. Rams).

Players lost through free agency (4): S Gene Atkins (Mia; 16 games in '93), G Derek Kennard (Dall; 16) S Keith Taylor (Wash; 16), WR Floyd Turner (Ind; 10).

Also played with Saints in '93—TE Jesse Anderson (1 game), TE Hoby Brenner (10), DE Jeff Faulkner (1), C Jay Hilgenberg (9), CB Cedric Mack (1), RB Fred McAfee (15), WR Patrick Newman (16), TE Tommie Stowers (4).

## COACHING STAFF

**Vice President-Head Coach, Jim Mora**

**Pro Career:** Begins ninth year as an NFL head coach. Led Saints to a 12-4 record and their third straight playoff appearance in 1992. Guided Saints to an 11-5 mark and the club's first-ever NFC West title in 1991. Was named 1987 NFL coach of the year after leading Saints to a 12-3 record and the team's first playoff appearance. Came to New Orleans following a three-year career as the winningest coach in USFL history as head coach of the Philadelphia/Baltimore Stars. Directed Stars to championship game in each of his three seasons and won league championship in 1984 and 1985. He won USFL coach of the year honors following the 1984 season. Mora began his pro coaching career in 1978 as defensive line coach of the Seattle Seahawks. In 1982, he became defensive coordinator of the New England Patriots and played a vital role in the Patriots' march to the playoffs that year. No pro playing experience. Career record: 77-54.

**Background:** Played tight end and defensive end at Occidental College. Assistant coach at Occidental from 1960-63 and head coach from 1964-66. Linebacker coach at Stanford (1967) on a staff that included former Eagles head coach Dick Vermeil. Defensive assistant at Colorado 1968-73. Linebacker coach under Vermeil at UCLA 1974. Defensive coordinator at Washington 1975-77. Received bachelor's degree in physical education from Occidental in 1957. Also holds master's degree in education from Southern California.

**Personal:** Born May 24, 1935, in Glendale, Calif. Jim and his wife, Connie, live in Metairie, La., and have three sons—Michael, Stephen, and Jim (defensive backs coach for the Saints).

### ASSISTANT COACHES

**Vic Fangio,** linebackers; born August 22, 1958, Dunmore, Pa., lives in Destrehan, La. Defensive back East Stroudsburg 1976-78. No pro playing experience. College coach: North Carolina 1983. Pro coach: Philadelphia/Baltimore Stars (USFL) 1984-85, joined Saints in 1986.

**Joe Marciano,** tight ends-special teams; born February 10, 1954, Scranton, Pa., lives in Kenner, La. Quarterback Temple 1972-75. No pro playing experience. College coach: East Stroudsburg 1977, Rhode Island 1978-79, Villanova 1980, Penn State 1981, Temple 1982. Pro coach: Philadelphia/Baltimore Stars (USFL) 1983-85, joined Saints in 1986.

**John Matsko,** offensive line; born February 2, 1951, Cleveland, Ohio, lives in Mandeville, La. Fullback Kent State 1970-73. No pro playing experience. College coach: Kent State 1973, Miami, Ohio 1974-75, 1977, North Carolina 1978-84, Navy 1985, Arizona 1986, Southern California 1987-91. Pro coach: Phoenix Cardinals 1992-93, joined Saints in 1994.

**Jim Mora,** defensive backs; born November 19, 1961, Los Angeles, Calif., lives in New Orleans. Defensive back Washington 1980-83. No pro playing experience. College coach: Washington 1984. Pro coach: San Diego Chargers 1985-91, joined Saints in 1992.

**Chip Myers,** offensive assistant; born July 9, 1945, Panama City, Fla., lives in Mandeville, La. Receiver Northwestern Oklahoma 1964-66. Pro receiver San Francisco 49ers 1967, Cincinnati Bengals 1969-76. College coach: Illinois 1980-82. Pro coach: Tampa Bay Buccaneers 1983-84, Indianapolis Colts 1985-88, New York Jets 1990-93, joined Saints in 1994.

**Russell Paternostro,** strength and conditioning; born July 21, 1940, New Orleans, La., lives in Covington, La. San Diego State. No college or pro playing experience. Pro coach: Joined Saints in 1981.

**John Pease,** defensive line; born October 14, 1943, Pittsburgh, Pa., lives in Kenner, La. Wingback Utah 1963-64. No pro playing experience. College coach: Fullerton, Calif., J.C. 1970-73, Long Beach State 1974-76, Utah 1977, Washington 1978-83. Pro coach: Philadelphia/Baltimore Stars (USFL) 1983-85, joined Saints in 1986.

**Steve Sidwell,** defensive coordinator; born August 30, 1944, Winfield, Kan., lives in New Orleans. Linebacker Colorado 1962-65. No pro playing experience. College coach: Colorado 1966-73, Nevada-Las Vegas 1974-75, Southern Methodist 1976-81. Pro coach: New England Patriots 1982-84, Indianapolis Colts 1985, joined Saints in 1986.

**Jim Skipper,** running backs; born January 23, 1949, Breaux Bridge, La., lives in Kenner, La. Defensive back Whittier College 1971-72. No proplaying experience. College coach: Cal Poly-Pomona 1974-76, San Jose State 1977-78, Pacific 1979, Oregon 1980-82. Pro coach: Philadelphia/Baltimore Stars (USFL) 1983-85, joined Saints in 1986.

**Carl Smith,** offensive coordinator-quarterbacks; born April 26, 1948, Wasco, Calif., lives in Kenner, La. Defensive back Cal Poly-SLO 1968-70. No pro playing experience. College coach: Cal Poly-SLO 1971, Colorado 1972-73, Southwestern Louisiana 1974-78, Lamar 1979-81, North Carolina State 1982. Pro coach: Philadelphia/Baltimore Stars (USFL) 1983-85, joined Saints in 1986.

**Steve Walters,** wide receivers; born June 16, 1948, Jonesboro, Ark., lives in Destrehan, La. Quarterback-defensive back Arkansas 1967-70. No pro playing experience. College coach: Tampa 1973, Northeast Louisiana 1974-75, Morehead State 1976, Tulsa 1977-78, Memphis State 1979, Southern Methodist 1980-81, Alabama 1985. Pro coach: New England Patriots 1982-84, joined Saints in 1986.

**Everett Withers,** defensive assistant; born June 15, 1963, Charlotte, N.C., lives in Kenner, La. Defensive back Appalachian State 1983-86. No pro playing experience. College coach: Appalachian State 1987, Austin Peay 1988-90, Tulane 1991, Southern Mississippi 1992-93. Pro coach: Joined Saints in 1994.

## 1994 FIRST-YEAR ROSTER

| Name | Pos. | Ht. | Wt. | Birthdate | College | Hometown | How Acq. |
|---|---|---|---|---|---|---|---|
| Backes, Tom (1) | T | 6-4 | 273 | 3/19/68 | Oklahoma | El Paso, Tex. | FA |
| Bates, Mario | RB | 6-1 | 217 | 1/16/73 | Arizona State | Tucson, Ariz. | D2 |
| Bowden, Andre (1) | LB | 6-3 | 240 | 4/4/68 | Fayetteville State | Fuquay-Varina, N.C. | FA |
| Brown, Tim | LB | 6-0 | 222 | 1/20/71 | West Virginia | McKeesport, Pa. | FA |
| Byrd, Israel (1) | CB | 5-11 | 184 | 2/1/71 | Utah State | St. Louis, Mo. | FA |
| Caldwell, Mike | WR | 6-0 | 200 | 3/28/71 | California | San Ramon, Calif. | FA |
| Campbell, Matt | TE | 6-5 | 256 | 7/14/72 | South Carolina | North Augusta, S.C. | FA |
| Carroll, Herman | DE | 6-4 | 265 | 6/20/71 | Mississippi State | North Natchez, Miss. | D5a |
| Cooper, Hunkie (1) | WR | 5-8 | 185 | 5/17/69 | Nevada-Las Vegas | Palestine, Tex. | FA |
| Dawkins, Ralph | RB | 5-8 | 195 | 10/20/70 | Louisville | Jacksonville, Fla. | FA |
| Dixon, Ernest | LB | 6-1 | 250 | 10/17/71 | South Carolina | Ft. Mill, S.C. | FA |
| Hamilton, Brandon | CB | 5-9 | 173 | 3/5/72 | Tulane | Baton Rouge, La. | FA |
| Hanna, Jim | NT | 6-4 | 255 | 8/10/71 | Louisville | W. Palm Beach, Fla. | FA |
| Henry, Adam | WR | 6-1 | 184 | 4/27/72 | McNeese State | Beaumont, Tex. | FA |
| Jeffcoat, Jerold (1) | NT | 6-2 | 285 | 8/30/69 | Temple | Matawan, N.J. | FA |
| Johnson, Joe | DE | 6-4 | 285 | 7/11/72 | Louisville | St. Louis, Mo. | D1 |
| Johnson, Tyrone | WR | 5-11 | 171 | 9/4/71 | Western State, Colo. | Aurora, Colo. | FA |
| Kline, Alan | T | 6-5 | 277 | 5/25/71 | Ohio State | Tiffin, Ohio | FA |
| Knight, Kelvin | S | 6-0 | 203 | 1/7/71 | Mississippi State | North Natchez, Miss. | FA |
| Lundberg, Lance | T | 6-4 | 308 | 8/15/70 | Nebraska | Wausa, Neb. | D7 |
| McCleskey, J.J. (1) | WR | 5-7 | 177 | 4/10/70 | Tennessee | Knoxville, Tenn. | FA |
| McDaniels, Terry | T | 6-3 | 287 | 4/24/71 | Southern California | Pasadena, Calif. | FA |
| Milburn, Darryl (1) | DE | 6-3 | 245 | 10/25/68 | Grambling | Baton Rouge, La. | FA |
| Mitchell, Darrell | WR | 5-9 | 190 | 9/16/71 | Texas Tech | Miami, Fla. | D6 |
| Novitsky, Craig | G | 6-5 | 295 | 5/12/71 | UCLA | Dumfries, Va. | D5b |
| Nussmeier, Doug | QB | 6-3 | 211 | 12/11/70 | Idaho | Lake Oswego, Ore. | D4 |
| Orr, Thomas | CB | 5-10 | 197 | 8/14/72 | West Virginia | Elizabeth, N.J. | FA |
| Pahukoa, Shane (1) | S | 6-2 | 202 | 11/25/70 | Washington | Marysville, Calif. | FA |
| Rhem, Steve | WR | 6-2 | 212 | 11/9/71 | Minnesota | Ocala, Fla. | FA |
| Rollins, Baron (1) | G | 6-4 | 335 | 7/23/70 | Louisiana Tech | Winnsboro, La. | FA |
| Roth, Tom (1) | G | 6-5 | 285 | 9/19/68 | Southern Illinois | Godfrey, Ill. | FA |
| Thomas, Franklin (1) | TE | 6-3 | 262 | 4/22/68 | Grambling | New Orleans, La. | FA |
| Tubbs, Winfred | LB | 6-4 | 250 | 9/24/70 | Texas | Fairfield, Tex. | D3 |
| Washington, Sean | CB | 5-10 | 182 | 5/25/71 | Rice | Houston, Tex. | FA |
| Wilson, Ray | S | 6-2 | 202 | 8/26/71 | New Mexico | Panama City, Fla. | FA |
| Young, Jim | CB | 5-11 | 188 | 2/16/71 | Purdue | Union, N.J. | FA |

The term NFL Rookie is defined as a player who is in his first season of professional football and has not been on the roster of another professional football team for any regular-season or postseason games. A Rookie is designated by an "R" on NFL rosters. Players who have been active in another professional football league or players who have NFL experience, including either preseason training camp or being on an Active List or Inactive List, or on Reserve/Injured or Reserve/Physically Unable to Perform for fewer than six regular-season games, are termed NFL First-Year Players. An NFL First-Year Player is designated by a "1" on NFL rosters. Thereafter, a player is credited with an additional year of experience for each season in which he accumulates six games on the Active List or Inactive List, or on Reserve/Injured or Reserve/Physically Unable to Perform.

## NOTES

# NEW YORK GIANTS

**National Football Conference**
**Eastern Division**
**Team Colors:** Blue, Red, and White
**Giants Stadium**
**East Rutherford, New Jersey 07073**
**Telephone: (201) 935-8111**

## CLUB OFFICIALS

President/Co-CEO: Wellington T. Mara
Chairman/Co-CEO: Preston Robert Tisch
Executive Vice President/General Counsel: John K. Mara, Esq.
Treasurer: Jonathan Tisch
Vice President-General Manager: George Young
Assistant General Manager: Harry Hulmes
Controller: John Pasquali
Director of Player Personnel: Tom Boisture
Director of Pro Personnel: Tim Rooney
Assistant Director of Player Personnel: Rick Donohue
Director of Administration: Tom Power
Senior Director of Marketing: Rusty Hawley
Director of Promotion: Frank Mara
Ticket Manager: John Gorman
Director of Public Relations: Pat Hanlon
Assistant Controller: Christine Prokops
Assistant Director of Public Relations: Aaron Salkin
Assistant Director of Marketing: Bill Smith
Head Trainer: Ronnie Barnes
Assistant Trainers: John Johnson, Michael Colello, Steve Kennelly
Equipment Manager: Ed Wagner, Jr.
**Stadium:** Giants Stadium • **Capacity:** 77,553
East Rutherford, New Jersey 07073
**Playing Surface:** AstroTurf
**Training Camp:** Fairleigh Dickinson-Madison
Florham Park, N.J. 07932

## 1994 SCHEDULE

### PRESEASON

| | | |
|---|---|---|
| July 30 | **Miami** | 8:00 |
| Aug. 6 | **Cleveland** | 8:00 |
| Aug. 13 | vs. San Diego at Berlin | 1:30 |
| Aug. 20 | at New York Jets | 8:00 |
| Aug. 27 | at Chicago | 7:00 |

### REGULAR SEASON

| | | |
|---|---|---|
| Sept. 4 | **Philadelphia** | 1:00 |
| Sept. 11 | at Arizona | 5:00 |
| Sept. 18 | **Washington** | 4:00 |
| Sept. 25 | Open Date | |
| Oct. 2 | at New Orleans | 3:00 |
| Oct. 10 | **Minnesota** (Monday) | 9:00 |
| Oct. 16 | at Los Angeles Rams | 1:00 |
| Oct. 23 | **Pittsburgh** | 1:00 |
| Oct. 30 | **Detroit** | 1:00 |
| Nov. 7 | at Dallas (Monday) | 8:00 |
| Nov. 13 | **Arizona** | 1:00 |
| Nov. 21 | at Houston (Monday) | 8:00 |
| Nov. 27 | at Washington | 4:00 |
| Dec. 4 | at Cleveland | 4:00 |
| Dec. 11 | **Cincinnati** | 1:00 |
| Dec. 18 | at Philadelphia | 4:00 |
| Dec. 24 | **Dallas** | 1:00 |

## RECORD HOLDERS

### INDIVIDUAL RECORDS—CAREER

| Category | Name | Performance |
|---|---|---|
| Rushing (Yds.) | Joe Morris, 1982-88 | 5,296 |
| Passing (Yds.) | Phil Simms, 1979-1993 | 33,462 |
| Passing (TDs) | Phil Simms, 1979-1993 | 199 |
| Receiving (No.) | Joe Morrison, 1959-1972 | 395 |
| Receiving (Yds.) | Frank Gifford, 1952-1960, 1962-64 | 5,434 |
| Interceptions | Emlen Tunnell, 1948-1958 | 74 |
| Punting (Avg.) | Don Chandler, 1956-1964 | 43.8 |
| Punt Return (Avg.) | David Meggett, 1989-1993 | 10.8 |
| Kickoff Return (Avg.) | Rocky Thompson, 1971-72 | 27.2 |
| Field Goals | Pete Gogolak, 1966-1974 | 126 |
| Touchdowns (Tot.) | Frank Gifford, 1952-1960, 1962-64 | 78 |
| Points | Pete Gogolak, 1966-1974 | 646 |

### INDIVIDUAL RECORDS—SINGLE SEASON

| Category | Name | Performance |
|---|---|---|
| Rushing (Yds.) | Joe Morris, 1986 | 1,516 |
| Passing (Yds.) | Phil Simms, 1984 | 4,044 |
| Passing (TDs) | Y.A. Tittle, 1963 | 36 |
| Receiving (No.) | Earnest Gray, 1983 | 78 |
| Receiving (Yds.) | Homer Jones, 1967 | 1,209 |
| Interceptions | Otto Schnellbacher, 1951 | 11 |
| | Jim Patton, 1958 | 11 |
| Punting (Avg.) | Don Chandler, 1959 | 46.6 |
| Punt Return (Avg.) | Merle Hapes, 1942 | 15.5 |
| Kickoff Return (Avg.) | John Salscheider, 1949 | 31.6 |
| Field Goals | Ali Haji-Sheikh, 1983 | 35 |
| Touchdowns (Tot.) | Joe Morris, 1985 | 21 |
| Points | Ali Haji-Sheikh, 1983 | 127 |

### INDIVIDUAL RECORDS—SINGLE GAME

| Category | Name | Performance |
|---|---|---|
| Rushing (Yds.) | Gene Roberts, 11-12-50 | 218 |
| Passing (Yds.) | Phil Simms, 10-13-85 | 513 |
| Passing (TDs) | Y.A. Tittle, 10-28-62 | *7 |
| Receiving (No.) | Mark Bavaro, 10-13-85 | 12 |
| Receiving (Yds.) | Del Shofner, 10-28-62 | 269 |
| Interceptions | Many times | 3 |
| | Last time by Terry Kinard, 9-27-87 | |
| Field Goals | Joe Danelo, 10-18-81 | 6 |
| Touchdowns (Tot.) | Ron Johnson, 10-2-72 | 4 |
| | Earnest Gray, 9-7-80 | 4 |
| Points | Ron Johnson, 10-2-72 | 24 |
| | Earnest Gray, 9-7-80 | 24 |

*NFL Record

## COACHING HISTORY

**(507-414-32)**

| | | |
|---|---|---|
| 1925 | Bob Folwell | 8-4-0 |
| 1926 | Joe Alexander | 8-4-1 |
| 1927-28 | Earl Potteiger | 15-8-3 |
| 1929-30 | LeRoy Andrews* | 24-5-1 |
| 1930 | Benny Friedman | 2-0-0 |
| 1930-53 | Steve Owen | 155-108-17 |
| 1954-60 | Jim Lee Howell | 55-29-4 |
| 1961-68 | Allie Sherman | 57-54-4 |
| 1969-73 | Alex Webster | 29-40-1 |
| 1974-76 | Bill Arnsparger** | 7-28-0 |
| 1976-78 | John McVay | 14-23-0 |
| 1979-82 | Ray Perkins | 24-35-0 |
| 1983-90 | Bill Parcells | 85-52-1 |
| 1991-92 | Ray Handley | 14-18-0 |
| 1993 | Dan Reeves | 12-6-0 |

*Released after 15 games in 1930
**Released after seven games in 1976

## GIANTS STADIUM

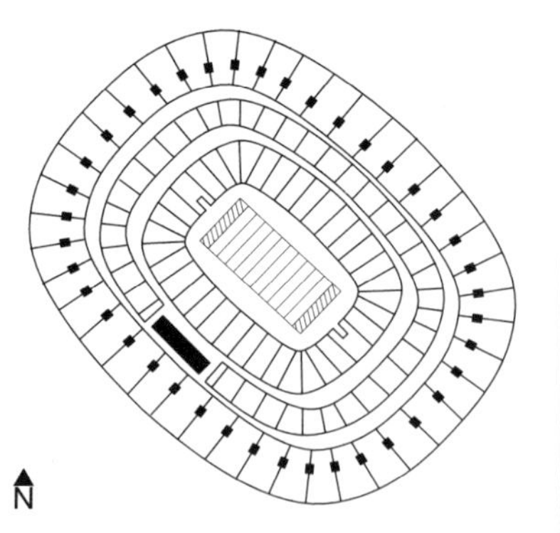

## 1993 TEAM RECORD

**PRESEASON (2-2)**

| Date | Result | | Opponents |
|---|---|---|---|
| 8/7 | W | 27-16 | at Cincinnati |
| 8/14 | L | 17-23 | Pittsburgh |
| 8/21 | W | 14-13 | N.Y. Jets |
| 8/28 | L | 17-23 | at Miami |

**REGULAR SEASON (11-5)**

| Date | Result | | Opponents | Att. |
|---|---|---|---|---|
| 9/5 | W | 26-20 | at Chicago | 66,900 |
| 9/12 | W | 23-7 | Tampa Bay | 75,891 |
| 9/19 | W | 20-10 | L.A. Rams | 76,213 |
| 10/3 | L | 14-17 | at Buffalo | 79,283 |
| 10/10 | W | 41-7 | at Washington | 53,715 |
| 10/17 | W | 21-10 | Philadelphia | 76,050 |
| 10/31 | L | 6-10 | N.Y. Jets | 71,659 |
| 11/7 | L | 9-31 | at Dallas | 64,735 |
| 11/14 | W | 20-6 | Washington | 76,606 |
| 11/21 | W | 7-3 | at Philadelphia | 62,928 |
| 11/28 | W | 19-17 | Phoenix | 59,979 |
| 12/5 | W | 19-14 | at Miami | 72,161 |
| 12/12 | W | 20-6 | Indianapolis | 70,411 |
| 12/20 | W | 24-14 | at New Orleans | 69,036 |
| 12/26 | L | 6-17 | at Phoenix | 53,414 |
| 1/2 | L | 13-16 | Dallas (OT) | 77,356 |

**POSTSEASON (1-1)**

| | | | | |
|---|---|---|---|---|
| 1/9 | W | 17-10 | Minnesota | 75,089 |
| 1/15 | L | 3-44 | at San Francisco | 67,143 |

(OT) Overtime

**SCORE BY PERIODS**

| | | | | | | |
|---|---|---|---|---|---|---|
| Giants | 61 | 112 | 43 | 72 | 0 | — 288 |
| Opponents | 40 | 60 | 40 | 62 | 3 | — 205 |

**ATTENDANCE**

Home 584,165 Away 522,172 Total 1,106,337
Single-game home record, 77,356 (1-2-94)
Single-season home record, 608,706 (1992)

## 1993 TEAM STATISTICS

| | Giants | Opp. |
|---|---|---|
| Total First Downs | 300 | 268 |
| Rushing | 127 | 89 |
| Passing | 153 | 161 |
| Penalty | 20 | 18 |
| Third Down: Made/Att | 90/221 | 67/196 |
| Third Down Pct. | 40.7 | 34.2 |
| Fourth Down: Made/Att | 5/11 | 12/23 |
| Fourth Down Pct. | 45.5 | 52.2 |
| Total Net Yards | 5145 | 4663 |
| Avg. Per Game | 321.6 | 291.4 |
| Total Plays | 1024 | 950 |
| Avg. Per Play | 5.0 | 4.9 |
| Net Yards Rushing | 2210 | 1547 |
| Avg. Per Game | 138.1 | 96.7 |
| Total Rushes | 560 | 395 |
| Net Yards Passing | 2935 | 3116 |
| Avg. Per Game | 183.4 | 194.8 |
| Sacked/Yards Lost | 40/245 | 41/238 |
| Gross Yards | 3180 | 3354 |
| Att./Completions | 424/257 | 514/298 |
| Completion Pct. | 60.6 | 58.0 |
| Had Intercepted | 9 | 18 |
| Punts/Avg. | 78/41.9 | 80/40.3 |
| Net Punting Avg. | 78/37.8 | 80/34.7 |
| Penalties/Yards Lost | 90/596 | 98/820 |
| Fumbles/Ball Lost | 19/8 | 27/10 |
| Touchdowns | 30 | 22 |
| Rushing | 11 | 7 |
| Passing | 17 | 13 |
| Returns | 2 | 2 |
| Avg. Time of Possession | 32:18 | 27:42 |

## 1993 INDIVIDUAL STATISTICS

| PASSING | Att | Cmp | Yds. | Pct. | TD | Int | Tkld. | Rate |
|---|---|---|---|---|---|---|---|---|
| Simms | 400 | 247 | 3038 | 61.8 | 15 | 9 | 37/217 | 88.3 |
| Graham | 22 | 8 | 79 | 36.4 | 0 | 0 | 3/28 | 47.3 |
| Meggett | 2 | 2 | 63 | 100.0 | 2 | 0 | 0/0 | 158.3 |
| Giants | 424 | 257 | 3180 | 60.6 | 17 | 9 | 40/245 | 88.4 |
| Opponents | 514 | 298 | 3354 | 58.0 | 13 | 18 | 41/238 | 71.4 |

| SCORING | TD R | TD P | TD Rt | PAT | FG | Saf | PTS |
|---|---|---|---|---|---|---|---|
| Treadwell | 0 | 0 | 0 | 28/29 | 25/31 | 0 | 103 |
| Cross | 0 | 5 | 0 | 0/0 | 0/0 | 0 | 30 |
| Hampton | 5 | 0 | 0 | 0/0 | 0/0 | 0 | 30 |
| M. Jackson | 0 | 4 | 0 | 0/0 | 0/0 | 0 | 24 |
| Bunch | 2 | 1 | 0 | 0/0 | 0/0 | 0 | 18 |
| Calloway | 0 | 3 | 0 | 0/0 | 0/0 | 0 | 18 |
| Tillman | 3 | 0 | 0 | 0/0 | 0/0 | 0 | 18 |
| McCaffrey | 0 | 2 | 0 | 0/0 | 0/0 | 0 | 12 |
| Sherrard | 0 | 2 | 0 | 0/0 | 0/0 | 0 | 12 |
| Collins | 0 | 0 | 1 | 0/0 | 0/0 | 0 | 6 |
| Meggett | 0 | 0 | 1 | 0/0 | 0/0 | 0 | 6 |
| Rasheed | 1 | 0 | 0 | 0/0 | 0/0 | 0 | 6 |
| Daluiso | 0 | 0 | 0 | 0/0 | 1/3 | 0 | 3 |
| Hamilton | 0 | 0 | 0 | 0/0 | 0/0 | 1 | 2 |
| Giants | 11 | 17 | 2 | 28/30 | 26/34 | 1 | 288 |
| Opponents | 7 | 13 | 2 | 22/22 | 17/23 | 0 | 205 |

| RUSHING | Att. | Yds. | Avg. | LG | TD |
|---|---|---|---|---|---|
| Hampton | 292 | 1077 | 3.7 | 20 | 5 |
| Tillman | 121 | 585 | 4.8 | 58 | 3 |
| Meggett | 69 | 329 | 4.8 | 23 | 0 |
| Bunch | 33 | 128 | 3.9 | 13 | 2 |
| Rasheed | 9 | 42 | 4.7 | 23t | 1 |
| Simms | 28 | 31 | 1.1 | 9 | 0 |
| M. Jackson | 3 | 25 | 8.3 | 20 | 0 |
| Graham | 2 | -3 | -1.5 | -1 | 0 |
| Da. Brown | 3 | -4 | -1.3 | -1 | 0 |
| Giants | 560 | 2210 | 3.9 | 58 | 11 |
| Opponents | 395 | 1547 | 3.9 | 46 | 7 |

| RECEIVING | No. | Yds. | Avg. | LG | TD |
|---|---|---|---|---|---|
| M. Jackson | 58 | 708 | 12.2 | 40t | 4 |
| Meggett | 38 | 319 | 8.4 | 50 | 0 |
| Calloway | 35 | 513 | 14.7 | 47 | 3 |
| McCaffrey | 27 | 335 | 12.4 | 31 | 2 |
| Sherrard | 24 | 433 | 18.0 | 55t | 2 |
| Cross | 21 | 272 | 13.0 | 32 | 5 |
| Hampton | 18 | 210 | 11.7 | 62 | 0 |
| Bunch | 13 | 98 | 7.5 | 15 | 1 |
| Pierce | 12 | 212 | 17.7 | 54 | 0 |
| De. Brown | 7 | 56 | 8.0 | 14 | 0 |
| Tillman | 1 | 21 | 21.0 | 21 | 0 |
| Crawford | 1 | 6 | 6.0 | 6 | 0 |
| Rasheed | 1 | 3 | 3.0 | 3 | 0 |
| Simms | 1 | -6 | -6.0 | -6 | 0 |
| Giants | 257 | 3180 | 12.4 | 62 | 17 |
| Opponents | 298 | 3354 | 11.3 | 58 | 13 |

| INTERCEPTIONS | No. | Yds. | Avg. | LG | TD |
|---|---|---|---|---|---|
| Collins | 4 | 77 | 19.3 | 50t | 1 |
| G. Jackson | 4 | 32 | 8.0 | 29 | 0 |
| Guyton | 2 | 34 | 17.0 | 19 | 0 |
| Miller | 2 | 18 | 9.0 | 11 | 0 |
| Raymond | 2 | 11 | 5.5 | 11 | 0 |
| Tate | 1 | 12 | 12.0 | 12 | 0 |
| Armstead | 1 | 0 | 0.0 | 0 | 0 |
| Beamon | 1 | 0 | 0.0 | 0 | 0 |
| Campbell | 1 | 0 | 0.0 | 0 | 0 |
| Giants | 18 | 184 | 10.2 | 50t | 1 |
| Opponents | 9 | 175 | 19.4 | 85t | 1 |

| PUNTING | No. | Yds. | Avg. | In 20 | LG |
|---|---|---|---|---|---|
| Horan | 44 | 1882 | 42.8 | 13 | 60 |
| Landeta | 33 | 1390 | 42.1 | 11 | 57 |
| Giants | 78 | 3272 | 41.9 | 24 | 60 |
| Opponents | 80 | 3224 | 40.3 | 23 | 54 |

| PUNT RETURNS | No. | FC | Yds. | Avg. | LG | TD |
|---|---|---|---|---|---|---|
| Meggett | 32 | 20 | 331 | 10.3 | 75t | 1 |
| Giants | 32 | 20 | 331 | 10.3 | 75t | 1 |
| Opponents | 44 | 10 | 247 | 5.6 | 28 | 0 |

| KICKOFF RETURNS | No. | Yds. | Avg. | LG | TD |
|---|---|---|---|---|---|
| Meggett | 24 | 403 | 16.8 | 35 | 0 |
| Calloway | 6 | 89 | 14.8 | 21 | 0 |
| Cross | 2 | 15 | 7.5 | 13 | 0 |
| Giants | 32 | 507 | 15.8 | 35 | 0 |
| Opponents | 29 | 646 | 22.3 | 68 | 0 |

| SACKS | No. |
|---|---|
| Hamilton | 11.5 |
| Miller | 6.5 |
| Taylor | 6.0 |
| Fox | 4.5 |
| Howard | 3.5 |
| Dillard | 3.0 |
| Bailey | 1.5 |
| McGhee | 1.5 |
| Brooks | 1.0 |
| Collins | 1.0 |
| Strahan | 1.0 |
| Giants | 41.0 |
| Opponents | 40.0 |

## 1994 DRAFT CHOICES

| Round | Name | Pos. | College |
|---|---|---|---|
| 1 | Thomas Lewis | WR | Indiana |
| 2 | Thomas Randolph | DB | Kansas State |
| | Jason Sehorn | DB | Southern California |
| 3 | Gary Downs | RB | North Carolina State |
| 4 | Chris Maumalanga | DT | Kansas |
| 5 | Chad Bratzke | DE | Eastern Kentucky |
| 6 | Jason Winrow | G | Ohio State |

## NEW YORK GIANTS

### 1994 VETERAN ROSTER

| No. | Name | Pos. | Ht. | Wt. | Birthdate | NFL Exp. | College | Hometown | How Acq. | '93 Games/ Starts |
|---|---|---|---|---|---|---|---|---|---|---|
| 98 | Armstead, Jessie | LB | 6-1 | 238 | 10/26/70 | 2 | Miami | Dallas, Tex. | D8-'93 | 16/0 |
| 54 | Bailey, Carlton | LB | 6-3 | 235 | 12/15/64 | 7 | North Carolina | Baltimore, Md. | UFA(Buff)-'93 | 16/16 |
| 21 | Beamon, Willie | CB | 5-11 | 170 | 6/14/70 | 2 | Northern Iowa | Riviera Beach, Fla. | FA-'93 | 13/0 |
| 78 | Bishop, Greg | T | 6-5 | 298 | 5/2/71 | 2 | Pacific | Lodi, Calif. | D4-'93 | 8/0 |
| 94 | Brooks, Michael | LB | 6-1 | 235 | 3/2/64 | 8 | Louisiana State | Ruston, La. | UFA(Den)-'93 | 13/13 |
| 17 | Brown, Dave | QB | 6-5 | 215 | 2/25/70 | 3 | Duke | Westfield, N.J. | SD1-'92 | 1/0 |
| 86 | Brown, Derek | TE | 6-6 | 252 | 3/31/70 | 3 | Notre Dame | Fairfax, Va. | D1-'92 | 16/0 |
| 55 | Buckley, Marcus | LB | 6-3 | 235 | 2/3/71 | 2 | Texas A&M | Ft. Worth, Tex. | D3-'93 | 16/2 |
| 33 | † Bunch, Jarrod | RB | 6-2 | 248 | 8/9/68 | 4 | Michigan | Ashtabula, Ohio | D1-'91 | 13/8 |
| 80 | # Calloway, Chris | WR | 5-10 | 185 | 3/29/68 | 5 | Michigan | Chicago, Ill. | FA-'92 | 16/9 |
| 37 | † Campbell, Jesse | S | 6-1 | 215 | 4/11/69 | 4 | North Carolina State | Vanceboro, N.C. | FA-'92 | 16/0 |
| 85 | Crawford, Keith | WR | 6-2 | 180 | 11/21/70 | 2 | Howard Payne | Palestine, Tex. | FA-'93 | 7/0 |
| 87 | Cross, Howard | TE | 6-5 | 245 | 8/8/67 | 6 | Alabama | Huntsville, Ala. | D6-'89 | 16/16 |
| 3 | † Daluiso, Brad | K | 6-2 | 207 | 12/31/67 | 4 | UCLA | San Diego, Calif. | FA-'93 | 15/0 |
| 62 | Davis, Scott | G | 6-3 | 289 | 1/29/70 | 2 | Iowa | Glenwood, Iowa | D6-'93 | 4/0 |
| 58 | # Dent, Burnell | LB | 6-2 | 235 | 3/16/63 | 8 | Tulane | New Orleans, La. | FA-'93 | 0* |
| 71 | Dillard, Stacey | NT | 6-5 | 288 | 9/17/68 | 3 | Oklahoma | Clarksville, Tex. | D6-'92 | 16/16 |
| 76 | Elliott, John | T | 6-7 | 305 | 4/1/65 | 7 | Michigan | Lake Ronkonkoma, N.Y. | D2-'88 | 11/11 |
| 95 | Flythe, Mark | DE | 6-7 | 290 | 10/4/68 | 2 | Penn State | Philadelphia, Pa. | FA-'93 | 2/0 |
| 93 | Fox, Mike | DE | 6-6 | 275 | 8/5/67 | 5 | West Virginia | Akron, Ohio | D2-'90 | 16/16 |
| 10 | Graham, Kent | QB | 6-5 | 220 | 11/1/68 | 3 | Ohio State | Wheaton, Ill. | D8-'92 | 9/0 |
| 75 | Hamilton, Keith | DE | 6-6 | 280 | 5/25/71 | 3 | Pittsburgh | Lynchburg, Va. | D4-'92 | 16/16 |
| 27 | Hampton, Rodney | RB | 5-11 | 215 | 4/3/69 | 5 | Georgia | Houston, Tex. | D1-'90 | 12/10 |
| 2 | # Horan, Mike | P | 5-11 | 190 | 2/1/59 | 10 | Long Beach State | Orange, Calif. | FA-'93 | 8/0 |
| 74 | Howard, Erik | NT | 6-4 | 268 | 11/12/64 | 9 | Washington State | San Jose, Calif. | D2a-'86 | 16/0 |
| 47 | # Jackson, Greg | S | 6-1 | 200 | 8/20/66 | 6 | Louisiana State | Hialeah, Fla. | D3a-'89 | 16/16 |
| 24 | # Jenkins, Izel | CB | 5-10 | 190 | 5/27/64 | 7 | North Carolina State | Wilson, N.C. | FA-'93 | 9/0* |
| 69 | Johnson, Chuck | T | 6-3 | 280 | 5/22/69 | 2 | Texas | Freeport, Tex. | FA-'94 | 0* |
| 81 | † McCaffrey, Ed | WR | 6-5 | 215 | 8/17/68 | 4 | Stanford | Allentown, Pa. | D3-'91 | 16/1 |
| 30 | Meggett, David | RB | 5-7 | 180 | 4/30/66 | 6 | Towson State | Charleston, S.C. | D5-'89 | 16/1 |
| 57 | † Miller, Corey | LB | 6-2 | 255 | 10/25/68 | 4 | South Carolina | Pageland, S.C. | D6-'91 | 16/14 |
| 65 | # Oates, Bart | C | 6-3 | 265 | 12/16/58 | 10 | Brigham Young | Albany, Ga. | FA-'85 | 16/15 |
| 84 | Pierce, Aaron | TE | 6-5 | 246 | 9/6/69 | 3 | Washington | Seattle, Wash. | D3-'92 | 13/6 |
| 51 | Powell, Andre | LB | 6-1 | 226 | 6/5/69 | 2 | Penn State | York, Pa. | FA-'93 | 15/1 |
| 44 | Rasheed, Kenyon | RB | 5-10 | 245 | 8/23/70 | 2 | Oklahoma | Kansas City, Mo. | FA-'93 | 5/3 |
| 39 | Raymond, Corey | CB | 5-11 | 180 | 7/28/69 | 3 | Louisiana State | New Iberia, La. | FA-'92 | 16/8 |
| 72 | Riesenberg, Doug | T | 6-5 | 275 | 7/22/65 | 8 | California | Moscow, Idaho | D6a-'87 | 16/16 |
| 66 | # Roberts, William | G | 6-5 | 280 | 8/5/62 | 10 | Ohio State | Miami, Fla. | D1b-'84 | 16/16 |
| 88 | Sherrard, Mike | WR | 6-2 | 187 | 6/21/63 | 9 | UCLA | Los Angeles, Calif. | UFA(SF)-'93 | 6/5 |
| 11 | Simms, Phil | QB | 6-3 | 214 | 11/3/55 | 16 | Morehead State | Louisville, Ky. | D1-'79 | 16/16 |
| 28 | Smith, Joey | CB-S | 5-10 | 190 | 5/30/69 | 2 | Louisville | Knoxville, Tenn. | FA-'94 | 0* |
| 61 | Smith, Lance | G | 6-3 | 285 | 1/1/63 | 10 | Louisiana State | Kannapolis, N.C. | UFA(Ariz)-'94 | 16/16* |
| 22 | Sparks, Phillippi | CB | 5-11 | 186 | 4/15/69 | 3 | Arizona State | Glendale, Calif. | D2-'92 | 5/3 |
| 92 | Strahan, Michael | DE | 6-4 | 253 | 11/21/71 | 2 | Texas Southern | Westbury, Tex. | D2-'93 | 9/0 |
| 49 | # Tate, David | S | 6-1 | 200 | 11/22/64 | 7 | Colorado | Buffalo Grove, Ill. | FA-'93 | 14/1 |
| 97 | Thigpen, Tommy | LB | 6-2 | 242 | 3/17/71 | 2 | North Carolina | Dumfries, Va. | D5-'93 | 0* |
| 90 | Widmer, Corey | LB | 6-3 | 276 | 12/25/68 | 3 | Montana State | Bozeman, Mont. | D7-'92 | 11/0 |
| 59 | Williams, Brian | C | 6-5 | 300 | 6/8/66 | 6 | Minnesota | Mt. Lebanon, Pa. | D1-'89 | 16/1 |

* Dent inactive for 6 games in '93; Jenkins played 4 games with Minnesota, 5 games with N.Y. Giants; Johnson inactive for 1 game with Denver; Marshall played 16 games with Denver; J. Smith last active with N.Y. Giants in '92; L. Smith played 16 games with Phoenix in '93; Thigpen missed '93 season due to injury.

\# Unrestricted free agent; subject to developments.

† Restricted free agent; subject to developments.

t- Giants traded for Marshall (Denver).

Retired—LB Lawrence Taylor, 13-year veteran, 16 games in '93.

Players lost through free agency (6): CB Mark Collins (KC; 16 games in '93), S Myron Guyton (NE; 16), G Bob Kratch (NE; 16), T Eric Moore (Cin; 7), RB Lewis Tillman (Chi; 16), CB Perry Williams (NYJ; 8).

Also played with Giants in '93—LB Steve DeOssie (8 games), WR Mark Jackson (16), T Clarence Jones (4), P Sean Landeta (8), LB Kanavis McGhee (10), DE George Thornton (5), K David Treadwell (16).

## COACHING STAFF

**Head Coach,**
**Dan Reeves**

**Pro Career:** After being named the fourteenth head coach in New York Giants history on January 27, 1993, Reeves led his squad to an 11-5 record and a berth in the playoffs as a Wild Card team in his first season with the Giants. Reeves's regular-season record of 11-5 is the best-ever for a first-year Giants coach. He became just the second head coach in Giants history to lead his team to the playoffs in his first season with the Giants. Reeves was named the *Associated Press* coach of the year after helping the Giants improve from a 6-10 record in 1992. Reeves came to the Giants after spending 12 years as head coach of the Denver Broncos. His 129 career victories going into the 1994 season gives him the thirteenth-most victories in NFL history and gives him the third-best among active head coaches in the NFL, behind Miami's Don Shula (327) and the Rams' Chuck Knox (190). He has participated in 45 NFL postseason games, 15 games as a head coach, 16 as an assistant, 6 as a player-coach, and 8 as a player. Reeves has played or coached in a record eight Super Bowls, including leading Denver to three Super Bowl appearances. He was the only AFC coach in the decade of the 1980s to lead his team to consecutive Super Bowl appearances, and he led Denver to seven 10-victory seasons in his 12 years there. Until taking the Denver post, Reeves had been a member of the Dallas coaching staff since 1970 when he spent two seasons as a player-coach. In 1972, he was a full-time assistant coach in charge of the offensive backfield. Reeves was in private business in 1973 before returning to the coaching ranks in 1974 as the backfield coach for the Cowboys. He remained in that position until 1977 when he was named offensive coordinator on Tom Landry's staff. Reeves's record of success dates back to his playing days with the Dallas Cowboys. Reeves began his professional football career as a free-agent running back for Dallas in 1965. Reeves was an all-purpose player during his eight seasons (1965-72) with Dallas (1,900 yards rushing with 25 touchdowns and 129 pass receptions for 1,693 yards and 17 touchdowns) and he finished his playing career as the fifth all-time rusher in Dallas history. In addition, he completed 30 passes, including two for touchdowns, and he also returned punts and kickoffs at various times as he played in the 1966, 1967, and 1970 NFL Championship Games. Career record: 129-85-1.

**Background:** Quarterback at South Carolina from 1962-64. He was inducted into the school's Hall of Fame in 1978.

**Personal:** Born January 19, 1944, Americus, Ga. Dan and his wife, Pam, live in East Rutherford, N.J., and have three children—Dana, Laura, and Lee. They also have two grandchildren-Caitlin and Ashley.

### ASSISTANT COACHES

**Don Blackmon,** linebackers; born March 14, 1958, Pompano Beach, Fla., lives in Morristown, N.J. Linebacker Tulsa 1977-80. Pro linebacker New England Patriots 1981-87. Pro coach: New England Patriots 1988-90, Cleveland Browns 1991-92, joined Giants in 1993.

**Dave Brazil,** defensive quality control; born March 25, 1936, Detroit, Mich., lives in East Rutherford, N.J. No college or pro playing experience. College coach: Holy Cross 1968, Tulsa 1969-70, Eastern Michigan 1971-73, Boston College 1980, Kent State 1981-82. Pro coach: Detroit Wheels (WFL) 1974, Chicago Fire (WFL) 1975, Kansas City Chiefs 1984-88, Pittsburgh Steelers 1989-91, joined Giants in 1992.

**James Daniel,** tight ends; born January 17, 1953, Wetumpka, Ala., lives in Clifton, N.J. Offensive guard Alabama State 1970-73. No pro playing experience. College coach: Auburn 1981-92. Pro coach: Joined Giants in 1993.

**Joe DeCamillis,** special teams; born June 29, 1965, Arvada, Colo., lives in Morris Township, N.J. Wrestler Wyoming 1983-87. No pro playing experience. College coach: Wyoming 1988. Pro coach: Denver Broncos 1989-92, joined Giants 1993.

**Kerry Goode,** assistant strength and conditioning; born July 28, 1965, Town Creek, Ala., lives in Mahwah, N.J. Tailback Alabama 1983-87. Pro running back Tampa Bay Buccaneers 1988, Denver Broncos 1989, Miami Dolphins 1990. Pro coach: Joined Giants in 1993.

**George Henshaw,** offensive coordinator-quarterbacks; born January 22, 1948, Midlothian, Va., lives in Smoke Rise, N.J. Defensive tackle West Virginia 1967-69. No pro playing experience. College coach: West Virginia 1970-75, Florida State 1976-82, Alabama 1983-86, Tulsa 1987 (head coach). Pro coach: Denver Broncos 1988-92, joined Giants in 1993.

**Earl Leggett,** defensive line, born March 5, 1935, Jacksonville, Fla., lives in Randolph, N.J. Tackle Hinds J.C. 1953-54, Louisiana State 1955-56. Pro defensive tackle Chicago Bears 1957-65, Los Angeles Rams 1966, New Orleans Saints 1967-68. College coach: Nicholls State 1971, Texas Christian 1972-73. Pro coach: Southern California Sun (WFL) 1974-75, Seattle Seahawks 1976-77, San Francisco 49ers 1978, Oakland/Los Angeles Raiders 1980-88, Denver Broncos 1989-92, joined Giants in 1993.

**Pete Mangurian,** offensive line; born June 17, 1955, Los Angeles, Calif., lives in Denville, N.J. Defensive lineman Louisiana State 1975-78. No pro playing experience. College coach: Southern Methodist 1979-80, New Mexico State 1981, Stanford 1982-83, Louisiana State 1984-87. Pro coach: Denver Broncos 1988-92, joined Giants in 1993.

**Al Miller,** strength and conditioning; born August 29, 1947, El Dorado, Ark., lives in Randolph, N.J. Wide receiver Northeast Louisiana 1965-69. No pro playing experience. College coach: Northwestern Louisiana 1974-78, Mississippi State 1980. Northeast Louisiana 1981, Alabama 1982-84. Pro coach: Denver Broncos 1987-92, joined Giants in 1993.

**Mike Nolan,** defensive coordinator, born March 7, 1959, Baltimore, Md., lives in Chatham, N.J. Safety Oregon 1977-80. No pro playing experience. College coach: Stanford 1982-83, Rice 1984-85, Louisiana State 1986. Pro coach: Denver Broncos 1987-92, joined Giants in 1993.

**Dick Rehbein,** wide receivers; born November 22, 1955, Green Bay, Wis., lives in Wayne, N.J. Center Ripon 1973-77. No pro playing experience. Pro coach: Green Bay Packers 1979-83, Los Angeles Express (USFL) 1984, Minnesota Vikings 1984-91, joined Giants in 1992.

**George Sefcik,** running backs, born December 27, 1939, Cleveland, Ohio, lives in Cranford, N.J. Halfback Notre Dame 1959-61. No pro playing experience. College coach: Notre Dame 1963-68, Kentucky 1969-72. Pro coach: Baltimore Colts 1973-74, Cleveland Browns 1975-77, 1989-90, Cincinnati Bengals 1978-83, Green Bay Packers 1984-87, Kansas City Chiefs 1988, joined Giants in 1991.

**Zaven Yaralian,** defensive backs, born February 5, 1952, Syria, lives in Mountain Lakes, N.J. Defensive back Nebraska 1972-73. Pro defensive back Green Bay Packers 1974, Philadelphia Bell (WFL) 1975. College coach: Nebraska 1975, Washington State 1976-77, Missouri 1978-83, Florida 1984-87, Colorado 1988-89. Pro coach: Chicago Bears 1990-92, joined Giants in 1993.

## 1994 FIRST-YEAR ROSTER

| Name | Pos. | Ht. | Wt. | Birthdate | College | Hometown | How Acq. |
|---|---|---|---|---|---|---|---|
| Alexander, Mike | C | 6-3 | 260 | 12/19/69 | San Diego State | Wilmington, Calif. | FA |
| Bloedorn, Kurt (1) | P | 6-5 | 207 | 10/20/67 | Cal State-Fullerton | Brea, Calif. | FA |
| Brannon, Steve (1) | DE | 6-3 | 265 | 11/27/68 | Hampton | Georgetown, S.C. | FA |
| Bratzke, Chad | DE | 6-4 | 262 | 9/15/71 | Eastern Kentucky | Brandon, Fla. | D5 |
| Brown, John | CB-S | 5-9 | 183 | 9/2/70 | Houston | Palo Duro, Tex. | FA |
| Brown, Leon | RB | 5-10 | 190 | 5/16/70 | Louisville | Jacksonville, Fla. | FA |
| Dillard, Ivory | G-T | 6-3 | 299 | 8/15/71 | Florida A&M | Dallas, Tex. | FA |
| Douglas, Donald | S | 6-2 | 203 | 12/9/70 | Houston | Liberty, Tex. | FA |
| Douglas, Omar | WR | 5-10 | 170 | 6/3/72 | Minnesota | New Orleans, La. | FA |
| Downs, Gary | RB | 6-0 | 212 | 6/28/71 | North Carolina State | Columbus, Ga. | D3 |
| Elias, Keith | RB | 5-9 | 191 | 2/3/72 | Princeton | Lacey Township, N.J. | FA |
| Fox, Brian (1) | QB | 6-4 | 214 | 12/23/70 | Florida | Orlando, Fla. | FA |
| Gant, Eric | RB | 6-2 | 245 | 10/13/70 | Grambling | Lakeland, Fla. | FA |
| Jones, Milton | DE | 6-5 | 270 | 3/24/71 | Central State, Ohio | Detroit, Mich. | FA |
| Kozlowski, Brian (1) | TE | 6-3 | 245 | 10/4/70 | Connecticut | Rochester, N.Y. | FA |
| Lewis, Thomas | WR | 6-1 | 185 | 1/10/72 | Indiana | Akron, Ohio | D1 |
| Marks, Duane | LB | 6-4 | 238 | 11/19/70 | Duke | Missouri City, Tex. | FA |
| Maumalanga, Chris | DT | 6-2 | 288 | 12/15/71 | Kansas | Redwood City, Calif. | D4 |
| Pyne, Dave | C | 6-4 | 292 | 10/25/70 | Lafayette | Milford, Mass. | FA |
| Randolph, Thomas | CB | 5-9 | 176 | 10/5/70 | Kansas State | Norfolk, Va. | D2a |
| Ray, Leonard | DT | 6-3 | 295 | 1/21/69 | Louisville | Port St. Joe, Fla. | FA |
| Reese, Darren | G | 6-4 | 285 | 10/25/70 | Ohio | Elida, Ohio | FA |
| Sehorn, Jason | S | 6-2 | 212 | 4/15/71 | Southern California | Mt. Shasta, Calif. | D2b |
| Smith, Shawn | LB | 6-2 | 236 | 7/5/71 | San Diego State | Buena, N.J. | FA |
| Townes, William | DT | 6-5 | 270 | 8/1/72 | Nevada-Las Vegas | Dallas, Tex. | FA |
| Weir, Eric (1) | WR | 6-2 | 175 | 7/15/70 | Vanderbilt | Houston, Tex. | FA |
| Winrow, Jason | G | 6-4 | 321 | 1/16/71 | Ohio State | Bridgeton, N.J. | D6 |

The term NFL Rookie is defined as a player who is in his first season of professional football and has not been on the roster of another professional football team for any regular-season or postseason games. A Rookie is designated by an "R" on NFL rosters. Players who have been active in another professional football league or players who have NFL experience, including either preseason training camp or being on an Active List or Inactive List, or on Reserve/Injured or Reserve/Physically Unable to Perform for fewer than six regular-season games, are termed NFL First-Year Players. An NFL First-Year Player is designated by a "1" on NFL rosters. Thereafter, a player is credited with an additional year of experience for each season in which he accumulates six games on the Active List or Inactive List, or on Reserve/Injured or Reserve/Physically Unable to Perform.

## NOTES

# PHILADELPHIA EAGLES

**National Football Conference**
**Eastern Division**
**Team Colors:** Kelly Green, Silver, and White
**Veterans Stadium**
**Broad Street and Pattison Avenue**
**Philadelphia, Pennsylvania 19148**
**Telephone: (215) 463-2500**

## CLUB OFFICIALS

Owner: Jeffrey Lurie
President-Chief Operating Officer: Harry Gamble
Vice President: Suzi Braman
V.P.-Chief Financial Officer: Mimi Box
V.P.-Sales and Development: Decker Uhlhorn
Vice President-Player Personnel/Operations: John Wooten
Asst. to Pres.: George Azar
Asst. to Pres.-General Counsel: Bob Wallace
Director of Pro Scouting: Tom Gamble
Director of Public Relations: Ron Howard
Asst. Director of Public Relations: Michael Gilbert
Director of Marketing: Leslie Stephenson-Matz
Dir. of Alumni Relations/Traveling Sec.: Jim Gallagher
Director of Administration: Vicki Chatley
Ticket Manager: Leo Carlin
Penthouse Suites Sales: Andrea Minassian
Asst. Director of Penthouse Sales: Ken Iman
Dir. Penthouse Operations: Christiana Noyalas
Trainer: Otho Davis
Asst. Trainer: David Price
Equipment Manager: Rusty Sweeney
Video Director: Mike Dougherty
**Stadium:** Veterans Stadium • **Capacity:** 65,178
3501 South Broad Street
Philadelphia, Pennsylvania 19148
**Playing Surface:** AstroTurf-8
**Training Camp:** West Chester University
West Chester, Pennsylvania 19382

## 1994 SCHEDULE

**PRESEASON**

| | | |
|---|---|---|
| Aug. 5 | at Chicago | 7:00 |
| Aug. 13 | **New York Jets** | 7:30 |
| Aug. 20 | **Cincinnati** | 7:30 |
| Aug. 26 | at Atlanta | 7:00 |

**REGULAR SEASON**

| | | |
|---|---|---|
| Sept. 4 | at New York Giants | 1:00 |
| Sept. 12 | **Chicago** (Monday) | 9:00 |
| Sept. 18 | **Green Bay** | 1:00 |
| Sept. 25 | Open Date | |
| Oct. 2 | at San Francisco | 1:00 |
| Oct. 9 | **Washington** | 8:00 |
| Oct. 16 | at Dallas | 3:00 |
| Oct. 24 | **Houston** (Monday) | 9:00 |
| Oct. 30 | at Washington | 1:00 |
| Nov. 6 | **Arizona** | 4:00 |
| Nov. 13 | **Cleveland** | 1:00 |
| Nov. 20 | at Arizona | 2:00 |
| Nov. 27 | at Atlanta | 1:00 |
| Dec. 4 | **Dallas** | 1:00 |
| Dec. 11 | at Pittsburgh | 1:00 |
| Dec. 18 | **New York Giants** | 4:00 |
| Dec. 24 | at Cincinnati | 4:00 |

## RECORD HOLDERS

### INDIVIDUAL RECORDS—CAREER

| Category | Name | Performance |
|---|---|---|
| Rushing (Yds.) | Wilbert Montgomery, 1977-1984 | 6,538 |
| Passing (Yds.) | Ron Jaworski, 1977-1986 | 26,963 |
| Passing (TDs) | Ron Jaworski, 1977-1986 | 175 |
| Receiving (No.) | Harold Carmichael, 1971-1983 | 589 |
| Receiving (Yds.) | Harold Carmichael, 1971-1983 | 8,978 |
| Interceptions | Bill Bradley, 1969-1976 | 34 |
| Punting (Avg.) | Joe Muha, 1946-1950 | 42.9 |
| Punt Return (Avg.) | Steve Van Buren, 1944-1951 | 13.9 |
| Kickoff Return (Avg.) | Steve Van Buren, 1944-1951 | 26.7 |
| Field Goals | Paul McFadden, 1984-87 | 91 |
| Touchdowns (Tot.) | Harold Carmichael, 1971-1983 | 79 |
| Points | Bobby Walston, 1951-1962 | 881 |

### INDIVIDUAL RECORDS—SINGLE SEASON

| Category | Name | Performance |
|---|---|---|
| Rushing (Yds.) | Wilbert Montgomery, 1979 | 1,512 |
| Passing (Yds.) | Randall Cunningham, 1988 | 3,808 |
| Passing (TDs) | Sonny Jurgensen, 1961 | 32 |
| Receiving (No.) | Keith Jackson, 1988 | 81 |
| | Keith Byars, 1990 | 81 |
| Receiving (Yds.) | Mike Quick, 1983 | 1,409 |
| Interceptions | Bill Bradley, 1971 | 11 |
| Punting (Avg.) | Joe Muha, 1948 | 47.2 |
| Punt Return (Avg.) | Steve Van Buren, 1944 | 15.3 |
| Kickoff Return (Avg.) | Al Nelson, 1972 | 29.1 |
| Field Goals | Paul McFadden, 1984 | 30 |
| Touchdowns (Tot.) | Steve Van Buren, 1945 | 18 |
| Points | Paul McFadden, 1984 | 116 |

### INDIVIDUAL RECORDS—SINGLE GAME

| Category | Name | Performance |
|---|---|---|
| Rushing (Yds.) | Steve Van Buren, 11-27-49 | 205 |
| Passing (Yds.) | Bobby Thomason, 11-18-53 | 437 |
| Passing (TDs) | Adrian Burk, 10-17-54 | *7 |
| Receiving (No.) | Don Looney, 12-1-40 | 14 |
| Receiving (Yds.) | Tommy McDonald, 12-10-60 | 237 |
| Interceptions | Russ Craft, 9-24-50 | *4 |
| Field Goals | Tom Dempsey, 11-12-72 | 6 |
| Touchdowns (Tot.) | Many times | 4 |
| | Last time by Wilbert Montgomery, 10-7-79 | |
| Points | Bobby Walston, 10-17-54 | 25 |

*NFL Record

## COACHING HISTORY

**(363-434-24)**

| | | |
|---|---|---|
| 1933-35 | Lud Wray | 9-21-1 |
| 1936-40 | Bert Bell | 10-44-2 |
| 1941-50 | Earle (Greasy) Neale* | 66-44-5 |
| 1951 | Alvin (Bo) McMillin** | 2-0-0 |
| 1951 | Wayne Millner | 2-8-0 |
| 1952-55 | Jim Trimble | 25-20-3 |
| 1956-57 | Hugh Devore | 7-16-1 |
| 1958-60 | Lawrence (Buck) Shaw | 20-16-1 |
| 1961-63 | Nick Skorich | 15-24-3 |
| 1964-68 | Joe Kuharich | 28-41-1 |
| 1969-71 | Jerry Williams*** | 7-22-2 |
| 1971-72 | Ed Khayat | 8-15-2 |
| 1973-75 | Mike McCormack | 16-25-1 |
| 1976-82 | Dick Vermeil | 57-51-0 |
| 1983-85 | Marion Campbell**** | 17-29-1 |
| 1985 | Fred Bruney | 1-0-0 |
| 1986-90 | Buddy Ryan | 43-38-1 |
| 1991-93 | Rich Kotite | 30-20-0 |

*Co-coach with Walt Kiesling in Philadelphia-Pittsburgh merger in 1943
**Retired after two games in 1951
***Released after three games in 1971
****Released after 15 games in 1985

**VETERANS STADIUM**

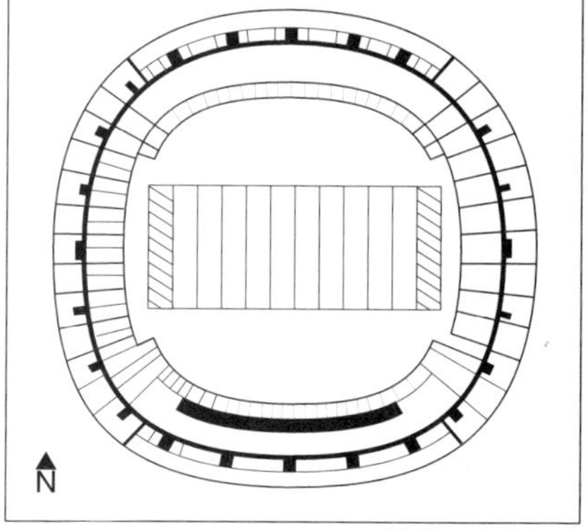

## 1993 TEAM RECORD

**PRESEASON (3-2)**

| Date | Result | | Opponents |
|---|---|---|---|
| 7/31 | L | 16-28 | vs. New Orleans at Tokyo |
| 8/8 | W | 13-9 | Chicago |
| 8/13 | W | 24-13 | at N.Y. Jets |
| 8/21 | W | 37-20 | Atlanta |
| 8/27 | L | 3-23 | at Cincinnati |

**REGULAR SEASON (8-8)**

| Date | Result | | Opponents | Att. |
|---|---|---|---|---|
| 9/5 | W | 23-17 | Phoenix | 59,831 |
| 9/12 | W | 20-17 | at Green Bay | 59,061 |
| 9/19 | W | 34-31 | Washington | 65,435 |
| 10/3 | W | 35-30 | at N.Y. Jets | 72,593 |
| 10/10 | L | 6-17 | Chicago | 63,601 |
| 10/17 | L | 10-21 | at N.Y. Giants | 76,050 |
| 10/31 | L | 10-23 | Dallas | 61,912 |
| 11/7 | L | 3-16 | at Phoenix | 41,634 |
| 11/14 | L | 14-19 | Miami | 64,213 |
| 11/21 | L | 3-7 | N.Y. Giants | 62,928 |
| 11/28 | W | 17-14 | at Washington | 46,663 |
| 12/6 | L | 17-23 | at Dallas | 64,521 |
| 12/12 | L | 7-10 | Buffalo | 60,769 |
| 12/19 | W | 20-10 | at Indianapolis | 44,952 |
| 12/26 | W | 37-26 | New Orleans | 50,085 |
| 1/3 | W | 37-34 | at San Francisco (OT) | 61,653 |

(OT) Overtime

**SCORE BY PERIODS**

| | | | | | | | |
|---|---|---|---|---|---|---|---|
| Eagles | 36 | 101 | 56 | 97 | 3 | — | 293 |
| Opponents | 65 | 94 | 55 | 101 | 0 | — | 315 |

**ATTENDANCE**

Home 488,774 Away 467,127 Total 955,901
Single-game home record, 72,111 (11-1-81)
Single-season home record, 557,325 (1980)

## 1993 TEAM STATISTICS

| | Eagles | Opp. |
|---|---|---|
| Total First Downs | 303 | 271 |
| Rushing | 104 | 91 |
| Passing | 184 | 155 |
| Penalty | 15 | 25 |
| Third Down: Made/Att | 92/224 | 66/205 |
| Third Down Pct. | 41.1 | 32.2 |
| Fourth Down: Made/Att | 7/16 | 15/20 |
| Fourth Down Pct. | 43.8 | 75.0 |
| Total Net Yards | 4922 | 5019 |
| Avg. Per Game | 307.6 | 313.7 |
| Total Plays | 1054 | 966 |
| Avg. Per Play | 4.7 | 5.2 |
| Net Yards Rushing | 1761 | 2080 |
| Avg. Per Game | 110.1 | 130.0 |
| Total Rushes | 456 | 467 |
| Net Yards Passing | 3161 | 2939 |
| Avg. Per Game | 197.6 | 183.7 |
| Sacked/Yards Lost | 42/302 | 36/214 |
| Gross Yards | 3463 | 3153 |
| Att./Completions | 556/328 | 463/251 |
| Completion Pct. | 59.0 | 54.2 |
| Had Intercepted | 13 | 20 |
| Punts/Avg. | 83/40.0 | 75/41.8 |
| Net Punting Avg. | 83/35.3 | 75/36.2 |
| Penalties/Yards Lost | 101/770 | 85/610 |
| Fumbles/Ball Lost | 32/21 | 33/15 |
| Touchdowns | 35 | 35 |
| Rushing | 7 | 11 |
| Passing | 23 | 22 |
| Returns | 5 | 2 |
| Avg. Time of Possession | 31:00 | 29:00 |

## 1993 INDIVIDUAL STATISTICS

| PASSING | Att | Cmp | Yds. | Pct. | TD | Int | Tkld. | Rate |
|---|---|---|---|---|---|---|---|---|
| Brister | 309 | 181 | 1905 | 58.6 | 14 | 5 | 19/148 | 84.9 |
| O'Brien | 137 | 71 | 708 | 51.8 | 4 | 3 | 15/116 | 67.4 |
| Cunningham | 110 | 76 | 850 | 69.1 | 5 | 5 | 7/33 | 88.1 |
| Walker | 0 | 0 | 0 | — | 0 | 0 | 1/5 | -1.0 |
| Eagles | 556 | 328 | 3463 | 59.0 | 23 | 13 | 42/302 | 81.2 |
| Opponents | 463 | 251 | 3153 | 54.2 | 22 | 20 | 36/214 | 73.5 |

| SCORING | TD R | TD P | TD Rt | PAT | FG | Saf | PTS |
|---|---|---|---|---|---|---|---|
| Williams | 0 | 10 | 0 | 0/0 | 0/0 | 0 | 60 |
| Bahr | 0 | 0 | 0 | 18/19 | 8/13 | 0 | 42 |
| Ruzek | 0 | 0 | 0 | 13/16 | 8/10 | 0 | 37 |
| Bavaro | 0 | 6 | 0 | 0/0 | 0/0 | 0 | 36 |
| Allen | 0 | 0 | 4 | 0/0 | 0/0 | 0 | 24 |
| Walker | 1 | 3 | 0 | 0/0 | 0/0 | 0 | 24 |
| Hebron | 3 | 0 | 0 | 0/0 | 0/0 | 0 | 18 |
| Sherman | 2 | 0 | 0 | 0/0 | 0/0 | 0 | 12 |
| Young | 0 | 2 | 0 | 0/0 | 0/0 | 0 | 12 |
| Bailey | 0 | 1 | 0 | 0/0 | 0/0 | 0 | 6 |
| Cunningham | 1 | 0 | 0 | 0/0 | 0/0 | 0 | 6 |
| Evans | 0 | 0 | 1 | 0/0 | 0/0 | 0 | 6 |
| Joseph | 0 | 1 | 0 | 0/0 | 0/0 | 0 | 6 |
| Flores | 0 | 0 | 0 | 0/0 | 0/0 | 1 | 2 |
| Eagles | 7 | 23 | 5 | 31/35 | 16/23 | 2 | 293 |
| Opponents | 11 | 22 | 2 | 34/35 | 23/34 | 1 | 315 |

| RUSHING | Att. | Yds. | Avg. | LG | TD |
|---|---|---|---|---|---|
| Walker | 174 | 746 | 4.3 | 35 | 1 |
| Sherman | 115 | 406 | 3.5 | 19 | 2 |
| Hebron | 84 | 297 | 3.5 | 33 | 3 |
| Joseph | 39 | 140 | 3.6 | 12 | 0 |
| Cunningham | 18 | 110 | 6.1 | 26 | 1 |
| Brister | 20 | 39 | 2.0 | 13 | 0 |
| O'Brien | 4 | 17 | 4.3 | 11 | 0 |
| Feagles | 2 | 6 | 3.0 | 6 | 0 |
| Eagles | 456 | 1761 | 3.9 | 35 | 7 |
| Opponents | 467 | 2080 | 4.5 | 85t | 11 |

| RECEIVING | No. | Yds. | Avg. | LG | TD |
|---|---|---|---|---|---|
| Walker | 75 | 610 | 8.1 | 55 | 3 |
| Williams | 60 | 725 | 12.1 | 80t | 10 |
| Bavaro | 43 | 481 | 11.2 | 27 | 6 |
| Bailey | 41 | 545 | 13.3 | 58 | 1 |
| Joseph | 29 | 291 | 10.0 | 48 | 1 |
| Barnett | 17 | 170 | 10.0 | 21 | 0 |
| Young | 14 | 186 | 13.3 | 49t | 2 |
| Lofton | 13 | 167 | 12.8 | 32 | 0 |
| Sherman | 12 | 78 | 6.5 | 21 | 0 |
| Hebron | 11 | 82 | 7.5 | 12 | 0 |
| Johnson | 10 | 81 | 8.1 | 17 | 0 |
| Sydner | 2 | 42 | 21.0 | 31 | 0 |
| Lawrence | 1 | 5 | 5.0 | 5 | 0 |
| Eagles | 328 | 3463 | 10.6 | 80t | 23 |
| Opponents | 251 | 3153 | 12.6 | 69 | 22 |

| INTERCEPTIONS | No. | Yds. | Avg. | LG | TD |
|---|---|---|---|---|---|
| Allen | 6 | 201 | 33.5 | 94t | 4 |
| Miano | 4 | 26 | 6.5 | 16 | 0 |
| W. Thomas | 2 | 39 | 19.5 | 21 | 0 |
| McMillian | 2 | 25 | 12.5 | 17 | 0 |
| Hager | 1 | 19 | 19.0 | 19 | 0 |
| Evans | 1 | 8 | 8.0 | 7 | 0 |
| Joyner | 1 | 6 | 6.0 | 6 | 0 |
| Hopkins | 1 | 0 | 0.0 | 0 | 0 |
| Simmons | 1 | 0 | 0.0 | 0 | 0 |
| O. Smith | 1 | 0 | 0.0 | 0 | 0 |
| Eagles | 20 | 324 | 16.2 | 94t | 4 |
| Opponents | 13 | 107 | 8.2 | 41 | 0 |

| PUNTING | No. | Yds. | Avg. | In 20 | LG |
|---|---|---|---|---|---|
| Feagles | 83 | 3323 | 40.0 | 31 | 60 |
| Eagles | 83 | 3323 | 40.0 | 31 | 60 |
| Opponents | 75 | 3137 | 41.8 | 28 | 59 |

| PUNT RETURNS | No. | FC | Yds. | Avg. | LG | TD |
|---|---|---|---|---|---|---|
| Sikahema | 33 | 20 | 275 | 8.3 | 25 | 0 |
| O. Smith | 0 | 0 | 9 | — | 9 | 0 |
| Eagles | 33 | 20 | 284 | 8.6 | 25 | 0 |
| Opponents | 35 | 19 | 311 | 8.9 | 83t | 1 |

| KICKOFF RETURNS | No. | Yds. | Avg. | LG | TD |
|---|---|---|---|---|---|
| Sikahema | 30 | 579 | 19.3 | 35 | 0 |
| Walker | 11 | 184 | 16.7 | 30 | 0 |
| Sydner | 9 | 158 | 17.6 | 36 | 0 |
| Hebron | 3 | 35 | 11.7 | 18 | 0 |
| Johnson | 1 | 7 | 7.0 | 7 | 0 |
| O. Smith | 0 | 24 | — | 24 | 0 |
| Eagles | 54 | 987 | 18.3 | 36 | 0 |
| Opponents | 53 | 1133 | 21.4 | 60 | 0 |

| SACKS | No. |
|---|---|
| Harmon | 11.5 |
| W. Thomas | 6.5 |
| Simmons | 5.0 |
| Millard | 4.0 |
| Flores | 3.0 |
| Allen | 2.0 |
| Joyner | 2.0 |
| Hager | 1.0 |
| Perry | 1.0 |
| Eagles | 36.0 |
| Opponents | 42.0 |

## 1994 DRAFT CHOICES

| Round | Name | Pos. | College |
|---|---|---|---|
| 1 | Bernard Williams | T | Georgia |
| 2 | Bruce Walker | DT | UCLA |
| | Charlie Garner | RB | Tennessee |
| 3 | Joe Panos | G | Wisconsin |
| | Eric Zomalt | DB | California |
| 5 | Marvin Goodwin | DB | UCLA |
| 6 | Ryan McCoy | LB | Houston |
| | Mitch Berger | P | Colorado |
| 7 | Mark Montgomery | RB | Wisconsin |

# PHILADELPHIA EAGLES

## 1994 VETERAN ROSTER

| No. | Name | Pos. | Ht. | Wt. | Birthdate | NFL Exp. | College | Hometown | How Acq. | '93 Games/ Starts |
|---|---|---|---|---|---|---|---|---|---|---|
| 72 | Alexander, David | C | 6-3 | 275 | 7/28/64 | 8 | Tulsa | Broken Arrow, Okla. | D5-'87 | 16/16 |
| 21 | Allen, Eric | CB | 5-10 | 180 | 11/22/65 | 7 | Arizona State | San Diego, Calif. | D2-'88 | 16/16 |
| 82 | Bailey, Victor | WR | 6-2 | 196 | 7/3/70 | 2 | Missouri | Ft. Worth, Tex. | D2-'93 | 16/10 |
| 62 | # Baldinger, Brian | G-T | 6-4 | 278 | 1/7/60 | 13 | Duke | Indianapolis, Ind. | FA-'92 | 12/4 |
| 24 | Barlow, Corey | CB | 5-9 | 182 | 11/1/70 | 2 | Auburn | Atlanta, Ga. | D5-'91 | 10/0 |
| 86 | Barnett, Fred | WR | 6-0 | 199 | 6/17/66 | 5 | Arkansas State | Gunnison, Miss. | D3-'90 | 4/4 |
| 84 | Bavaro, Mark | TE | 6-4 | 245 | 4/28/63 | 9 | Notre Dame | Danvers, Mass. | UFA(Clev)-'93 | 16/16 |
| 6 | Brister, Bubby | QB | 6-3 | 207 | 8/15/62 | 9 | Northeast Louisiana | Alexandria, La. | FA-'93 | 10/8 |
| 39 | Brooks, Tony | RB | 6-0 | 230 | 8/17/69 | 2 | Notre Dame | Tulsa, Okla. | D4a-'92 | 0* |
| 71 | Chalenski, Mike | DE-DT | 6-5 | 288 | 1/28/70 | 2 | UCLA | Elizabeth, N.J. | FA-'93 | 15/0 |
| 12 | Cunningham, Randall | QB | 6-4 | 205 | 3/27/63 | 10 | Nevada-Las Vegas | Santa Barbara, Calif. | D2-'85 | 4/4 |
| 78 | Davis, Antone | T | 6-4 | 325 | 2/28/67 | 4 | Tennessee | Ft. Valley, Ga. | D1-'91 | 16/16 |
| 56 | Evans, Byron | LB | 6-2 | 235 | 2/23/64 | 8 | Arizona | Phoenix, Ariz. | D4-'87 | 11/10 |
| 95 | † Flores, Mike | DE | 6-3 | 256 | 12/1/66 | 4 | Louisville | Youngstown, Ohio | D11-'91 | 16/11 |
| 61 | # Floyd, Eric | G | 6-5 | 310 | 10/28/65 | 5 | Auburn | Rome, Ga. | PB(SD)-'92 | 3/3 |
| 33 | # Frizzell, William | S | 6-3 | 206 | 9/8/62 | 11 | North Carolina Central | Rose, N.C. | FA-'92 | 16/2 |
| 93 | Fuller, William | DE | 6-3 | 274 | 3/8/62 | 9 | North Carolina | Chesapeake, Va. | UFA(Hou)-'94 | 16/16* |
| 69 | t- Grossman, Burt | DE | 6-4 | 275 | 4/10/67 | 6 | Pittsburgh | Bala-Cynwyd, Pa. | T(SD)-'94 | 10/10* |
| 54 | Hager, Britt | LB | 6-1 | 225 | 2/20/66 | 6 | Texas | Odessa, Tex. | D3b-'89 | 16/7 |
| 65 | # Hallstrom, Ron | G | 6-6 | 315 | 6/11/59 | 13 | Iowa | Moline, Ill. | FA-'93 | 12/8 |
| 91 | Harmon, Andy | DT | 6-4 | 265 | 4/6/69 | 4 | Kent State | Centerville, Ohio | D6-'91 | 16/15 |
| 97 | Harris, Tim | DE | 6-6 | 258 | 9/10/64 | 9 | Memphis State | Memphis, Tenn. | UFA(SF)-'93 | 4/3 |
| 45 | Hebron, Vaughn | RB | 5-8 | 196 | 10/7/70 | 2 | Virginia Tech | Baltimore, Md. | FA-'93 | 16/4 |
| 73 | Holmes, Lester | G | 6-3 | 301 | 9/27/69 | 2 | Jackson State | Tylertown, Miss. | D1a-'93 | 12/6 |
| 76 | Hudson, John | G-C | 6-2 | 275 | 1/29/68 | 5 | Auburn | Memphis, Tenn. | D11-'90 | 16/0 |
| 98 | Jeter, Tommy | DT | 6-5 | 282 | 9/20/69 | 3 | Texas | Nacogdoches, Tex. | D3-'92 | 7/0 |
| 87 | Johnson, Maurice | TE | 6-2 | 243 | 1/9/67 | 4 | Temple | Washington, D.C. | FA-'91 | 16/2 |
| 8 | Jones, Preston | QB | 6-3 | 223 | 7/3/70 | 2 | Georgia | Anderson, S.C. | FA-'93 | 0* |
| 32 | Joseph, James | RB | 6-2 | 222 | 10/28/67 | 4 | Auburn | Phenix City, Ala. | D7-'91 | 16/5 |
| 68 | # McHale, Tom | G | 6-4 | 290 | 2/25/63 | 8 | Cornell | Gaithersburg, Md. | FA-'93 | 8/4 |
| 29 | McMillian, Mark | CB | 5-7 | 162 | 4/29/70 | 3 | Alabama | Los Angeles, Calif. | D10-'92 | 16/12 |
| 38 | # Miano, Rich | S | 6-1 | 200 | 9/3/62 | 10 | Hawaii | Honolulu, Hawaii | FA-'91 | 16/14 |
| 3 | Murray, Eddie | K | 5-11 | 195 | 8/29/56 | 15 | Tulane | Victoria, Canada | FA-'94 | 14/0* |
| 58 | Oden, Derrick | LB | 5-11 | 230 | 9/29/70 | 2 | Alabama | Hillcrest, Ala. | D6-'93 | 12/0 |
| 90 | Perry, William | DT | 6-2 | 335 | 12/16/62 | 10 | Clemson | Aiken, S.C. | W(Chi)-'93 | 15/8* |
| 42 | Reid, Mike | S | 6-1 | 218 | 11/24/70 | 2 | North Carolina State | Spartanburg, S.C. | D3b-'93 | 9/0 |
| 94 | Renfro, Leonard | DT | 6-2 | 291 | 6/29/70 | 2 | Colorado | Detroit, Mich. | D1b-'93 | 14/2 |
| 53 | t- Romanowski, Bill | LB | 6-4 | 231 | 4/2/66 | 7 | Boston College | Vernon, Conn. | T(SF)-'94 | 16/16* |
| 55 | Rose, Ken | LB | 6-1 | 215 | 6/9/62 | 8 | Nevada-Las Vegas | Sacramento, Calif. | FA-'90 | 5/0 |
| 79 | # Schad, Mike | G | 6-5 | 290 | 10/2/63 | 9 | Queens College, Canada | Bellville, Canada | PB(Rams)-'89 | 13/13 |
| 23 | Sherman, Heath | RB | 6-0 | 205 | 3/27/67 | 6 | Texas A&I | El Campo, Tex. | D6-'89 | 15/7 |
| 30 | Smith, Otis | CB | 5-11 | 184 | 10/22/65 | 5 | Missouri | Metairie, La. | FA-'90 | 15/0 |
| 85 | Sydner, Jeff | WR-KR | 5-6 | 170 | 11/11/69 | 3 | Hawaii | Columbus, Ohio | D6-'92 | 4/0 |
| 46 | Thomas, Markus | RB | 5-10 | 192 | 7/12/70 | 2 | Eastern Kentucky | Cincinnati, Ohio | FA-'93 | 0* |
| 51 | † Thomas, William | LB | 6-2 | 218 | 8/13/68 | 4 | Texas A&M | Amarillo, Tex. | D4-'91 | 16/16 |
| 76 | Thompson, Broderick | T | 6-5 | 295 | 8/14/60 | 9 | Kansas | Cerritos, Calif. | T(SD)-'93 | 10/10 |
| 34 | Walker, Herschel | RB | 6-1 | 225 | 3/3/62 | 9 | Georgia | Wrightsville, Ga. | FA-'92 | 16/16 |
| 20 | # Waters, Andre | S | 5-11 | 200 | 3/10/62 | 11 | Cheyney State | Pahokee, Fla. | FA-'84 | 9/8 |
| 89 | Williams, Calvin | WR | 5-11 | 190 | 3/3/67 | 5 | Purdue | Baltimore, Md. | D5-'90 | 16/14 |
| 83 | # Young, Michael | WR | 6-1 | 183 | 2/21/62 | 10 | UCLA | Hanford, Calif. | FA-'93 | 10/0 |

* Brooks missed '93 season due to injury; Fuller played 16 games with Houston in '93; Grossman played 10 games with San Diego; Jones active for 1 game but did not play; Murray played 14 games with Dallas; Perry played 7 games with Chicago, 8 games with Philadelphia; Romanowski played 16 games with San Francisco; M. Thomas inactive for 16 games.

# Unrestricted free agent; subject to developments.

† Restricted free agent; subject to developments.

Traded—CB-S Ben Smith to Denver.

t- Eagles traded for Grossman (San Diego), Romanowski (San Francisco).

Players lost through free agency (3): P Jeff Feagles (Ariz; 16 games in '93), LB Seth Joyner (Ariz; 16), DE Clyde Simmons (Ariz; 16).

Also played with Eagles in '93—K Matt Bahr (11 games), LB Louis Cooper (11), S Wes Hopkins (15), WR Reggie Lawrence (1), WR James Lofton (9), S Erik McMillan (6), DT Keith Millard (14), DT Gerald Nichols (7), QB Ken O'Brien (5), WR Paul Richardson (1), LB John Roper (3), K Roger Ruzek (5), G Rob Selby (1), CB-S Ben Smith (13).

## COACHING STAFF

**Head Coach,**
**Rich Kotite**

**Pro Career:** Became the eighteenth head coach in Eagles' history on January 8, 1991. After a 3-5 start in his rookie year as head coach, marked by a season-ending injury to quarterback Randall Cunningham on opening day and subsequent injuries to backup Jim McMahon, Kotite rallied the Eagles. Philadelphia narrowly missed the playoffs after winning seven of their last eight games on the strength of the league's best defense. In his second season, the Eagles returned to the playoffs for the fourth time in five years, recording an 11-5 mark along the way to give the club five consecutive seasons of 10-or-more wins. A year ago, Kotite led the Eagles to a blistering 4-0 start before a series of season-ending injuries to starters—including Pro Bowlers Cunningham and wide receiver Fred Barnett—brought on a skid. Kotite, however, nearly guided the club into the playoffs again by rallying the depleted Eagles to a three-game winning streak at season's end and an 8-8 finish that narrowly missed a playoff berth. Kotite originally served as the team's offensive coordinator in 1990 when the club led the NFL in rushing and topped the NFC in scoring and touchdown passes. Kotite had served previously as the New York Jets' offensive coordinator and receivers coach from 1985-89 after originally joining the club as receivers coach in 1983. In each of Kotite's years at the helm of the New York offense, the Jets finished near the top in the AFC in total offense, including a third-place ranking in 1985. Kotite began his pro coaching career with New Orleans in 1977 before joining Cleveland as receiver's coach from 1978-1982 and aiding in the development of perennial all-pro tight end Ozzie Newsome. During his playing career, he was known as a scrappy tight end and outstanding special teams performer with the New York Giants (1967, 1969-72) and Steelers (1968). Career record: 30-20.
**Background:** Attended Poly Prep in Brooklyn, N.Y. After a brief boxing career at the University of Miami where he was the school's heavyweight champ, he served as a sparring partner for Cassius Clay, later known as Muhammad Ali. Kotite became a Little All-America tight end at Wagner College in Staten Island, N.Y.
**Personal:** Born in Brooklyn on October 13, 1942. He and his wife, Elizabeth, live in Mt. Laurel, N.J. and have one daughter—Alexandra.

### ASSISTANT COACHES

**Zeke Bratkowski,** offensive coordinator-quarterbacks; born October 20, 1931, Danville, Ill., lives in Mt. Laurel, N.J. Quarterback Georgia 1951-53. Pro quarterback Chicago Bears 1954, 1957-60, Los Angeles Rams 1961-63, Green Bay Packers 1963-68, 1971. Pro coach: Green Bay Packers 1969-70, 1975-81, Chicago Bears 1972-74, Baltimore-Indianapolis Colts 1982-84, New York Jets 1985-89, Cleveland Browns 1990, joined Eagles in 1991.
**Lew Carpenter,** receivers-tight ends; born January 12, 1932, Hayti, Mo., lives in Mt. Laurel, N.J. Running backend Arkansas 1950-52. Pro running back-defensive back-end Detroit Lions 1953-55, Cleveland Browns 1957-58, Green Bay Packers 1959-63. College coach: Southwest Texas State 1989. Pro coach: Minnesota Vikings 1964-66, Atlanta Falcons 1967-68, Washington Redskins 1969-70, St. Louis Cardinals 1971-72, Houston Oilers 1973-74, Green Bay Packers 1975-85, Detroit Lions 1986-88, joined Eagles in 1990.
**Bud Carson,** defensive coordinator-secondary; born April 28, 1931, Freeport, Pa., lives in Mt. Laurel, N.J. Defensive back North Carolina 1950-52. No pro playing experience. College coach: North Carolina 1957-64, South Carolina 1965, Georgia Tech 1966-71 (head coach 1967-71), Kansas 1984. Pro coach: Pittsburgh Steelers 1972-77, Los Angeles Rams 1978-81, Baltimore Colts 1982, Kansas City Chiefs 1983, New York Jets 1985-88, Cleveland Browns 1989-90 (head coach), joined Eagles in 1991.
**Peter Giunta,** defensive assistant; born August 11, 1956, Salem, Mass., lives in Bensalem, Pa. Running back-defensive back Northeastern 1974-77. No pro playing experience. College coach: Penn State 1981-83, Brown 1984-87, Lehigh 1988-90. Pro coach: Joined Eagles in 1991.
**Dale Haupt,** defensive line; born April 12, 1929, Manitowoc, Wis., lives in Cherry Hill, N.J. Defensive lineman-linebacker Wyoming 1950-53. No pro playing experience. College coach: Tennessee 1960-63, Iowa State 1964-65, Richmond 1966-71, North Carolina State 1972-76, Duke 1977. Pro coach: Chicago Bears 1978-85, joined Eagles in 1986.
**Bill Muir,** offensive line; born October 26, 1942, Pittsburgh, Pa., lives in Mt. Laurel, N.J. Tackle Susquehanna 1962-64. No pro playing experience. College coach: Susquehanna 1965, Delaware Valley 1966-67, Rhode Island 1970-71, Idaho State 1972-73, Southern Methodist 1976-77. Pro coach: Orlando (Continental Football League) 1968-69, Houston-Shreveport Steamer (WFL) 1975, New England Patriots 1982-84, Detroit Lions 1985-88, Indianapolis Colts 1989-91, joined Eagles in 1992.
**Larry Pasquale,** special teams coordinator; born April 21, 1941, Brooklyn, N.Y., lives in Mt. Laurel, N.J. Quarterback Bridgeport 1961-63. No pro playing experience. College coach: Slippery Rock State 1967, Boston University 1968, Navy 1969-70, Massachusetts 1971-75, Idaho State 1976. Pro coach: Montreal Alouettes (CFL) 1977-78, Detroit Lions 1979, New York Jets 1980-89, San Diego Chargers 1990-91, joined Eagles in 1992.
**Jim Vechiarella,** linebackers; born February 20, 1937, Youngstown, Ohio, lives in Mt. Laurel, N.J. Linebacker Youngstown State 1955-57. No pro playing experience. College coach: Youngstown State 1964-74, Southern Illinois 1976-77, Tulane 1978-80. Pro coach: Charlotte (WFL) 1975, Los Angeles Rams 1981-82, Kansas City Chiefs 1983-85, New York Jets 1986-89, Cleveland Browns 1990, joined Eagles in 1991.
**Jim Williams,** strength and conditioning; born March 29, 1948, Kingston, Pa., lives in Mt. Laurel, N.J. No college or pro playing experience. College coach: Nebraska 1972-74, Arkansas 1974-77, Wyoming 1977-79. Pro coach: New York Giants 1979-81, New York Jets 1982-89, joined Eagles in 1991.
**Richard Wood,** running backs; born February 2, 1936, Lanett, Ala., lives in Mt. Laurel, N.J. Quarterback Auburn 1956-59. Pro quarterback Baltimore Colts 1960-61, San Diego Chargers 1962, Denver Broncos 1962, New York Jets 1963-64, Oakland Raiders 1965, Miami Dolphins 1966. College coach: Georgia 1967-68, Mississippi 1971-73, Auburn 1986. Pro coach: Oakland Raiders 1969-70, Cleveland Browns 1974, New Orleans Saints 1976-77, Atlanta Falcons 1978-82, Philadelphia Eagles 1983, Kansas City Chiefs 1987-88, New England Patriots 1989-90, rejoined Eagles in 1991.

## 1994 FIRST-YEAR ROSTER

| Name | Pos. | Ht. | Wt. | Birthdate | College | Hometown | How Acq. |
|---|---|---|---|---|---|---|---|
| Barnett, Alonza | CB | 6-2 | 210 | 7/17/70 | North Carolina A&T | Jacksonville, N.C. | FA |
| Berger, Mitch | P | 6-2 | 231 | 6/24/72 | Colorado | Kamloops, Canada | D6b |
| Brown, Curt (1) | DT | 6-5 | 260 | 4/5/70 | North Carolina | Virginia Beach, Va. | FA |
| Clapp, Darrell | G-T | 6-5 | 300 | 10/13/70 | Houston | Corpus Christi, Tex. | FA |
| Cummins, Jeff (1) | DE | 6-6 | 270 | 5/25/69 | Oregon | Torrance, Calif. | FA |
| Dausin, Chris | C | 6-4 | 285 | 12/18/69 | Texas A&M | San Antonio, Tex. | FA |
| Dixon, Mark | G | 6-4 | 290 | 11/26/70 | Virginia | Jamestown, N.C. | FA |
| Fiedler, Jay | QB | 6-1 | 215 | 12/29/71 | Dartmouth | Oceanside, N.Y. | FA |
| Frazier, Derrick (1) | CB | 5-10 | 178 | 4/29/70 | Texas A&M | Sugar Land, Tex. | D3a-'93 |
| Gamble, David | WR | 6-1 | 193 | 6/14/71 | New Hampshire | Albany, N.Y. | FA |
| Garlick, Tom | WR | 5-11 | 180 | 9/22/71 | Fordham | Philadelphia, Pa. | FA |
| Garner, Charlie | RB | 5-9 | 181 | 2/13/72 | Tennessee | Falls Church, Va. | D2b |
| Goodwin, Marvin | S | 6-0 | 199 | 9/21/72 | UCLA | Camden, N.J. | D5 |
| Hall, Ray | DT | 6-4 | 267 | 3/2/71 | Washington State | Seattle, Wash. | FA |
| Jackson, Al | CB | 6-0 | 182 | 9/7/71 | Georgia | Pensacola, Fla. | FA |
| Knight, Dewayne | S | 6-2 | 206 | 10/8/70 | Virginia Tech | Newport News, Va. | FA |
| Lawrence, Reggie (1) | WR | 6-0 | 178 | 4/12/70 | North Carolina State | Camden, N.J. | FA |
| Lewis, Darrell | S | 6-0 | 205 | 3/24/71 | San Diego State | San Diego, Calif. | FA |
| McCoy, Ryan | LB | 6-2 | 237 | 3/13/72 | Houston | Beaumont, Tex. | D6a |
| McGill, Jason (1) | WR | 6-0 | 192 | 1/12/72 | Georgia Tech | Miami, Fla. | FA |
| McKenzie, Mike | TE | 6-2 | 247 | 9/18/70 | Baylor | San Antonio, Tex. | FA |
| Mendez, Jaime | S | 5-11 | 194 | 2/20/71 | Kansas State | Youngstown, Ohio | FA |
| Miller, Derrick | WR | 5-10 | 170 | 12/7/70 | Virginia State | Steelton, Pa. | FA |
| Morrill, Matt | DE | 6-3 | 261 | 8/13/71 | Delaware | Neshanic, N.J. | FA |
| Montgomery, Mark | RB | 5-11 | 220 | 2/19/72 | Wisconsin | St. Paul, Minn. | D7 |
| O'Neal, Brian | RB | 6-0 | 233 | 2/25/70 | Penn State | Cincinnati, Ohio | FA |
| Pale, Peter | G | 6-3 | 279 | 12/30/71 | Hawaii | Molokai, Hawaii | FA |
| Panos, Joe | G-C | 6-2 | 296 | 1/24/71 | Wisconsin | Brookfield, Wis. | D3a |
| Richardson, Paul (1) | WR | 6-3 | 204 | 2/25/69 | UCLA | Los Angeles, Calif. | FA |
| Schrock, Chris (1) | P | 6-2 | 225 | 10/18/70 | Boston University | Hamilton, Mass. | FA |
| Shankle, William | CB | 5-10 | 195 | 4/28/70 | Oklahoma | Houston, Tex. | FA |
| Simien, Erik | LB | 6-2 | 233 | 12/31/70 | Nevada-Las Vegas | Los Angeles, Calif. | FA |
| Smith, Herman | DE | 6-5 | 242 | 1/25/71 | Portland State | Portland, Ore. | FA |
| Smith, Jemone | WR | 6-5 | 200 | 7/22/71 | Indiana, Pa. | Harrisburg, Pa. | FA |
| Starcevich, Steve (1) | K | 6-4 | 225 | 10/21/66 | Philadelphia Textile | Northville, Mich. | FA |
| Walker, Bruce | DT | 6-3 | 326 | 7/18/72 | UCLA | Compton, Calif. | D2a |
| Williams, Bernard | T | 6-8 | 317 | 7/18/72 | Georgia | Memphis, Tenn. | D1 |
| Woodard, Marc | LB | 6-0 | 234 | 2/21/70 | Mississippi State | Kosciusko, Miss. | FA |
| Wooten, Al | RB | 5-11 | 232 | 9/9/70 | Syracuse | Niagara Falls, N.Y. | FA |
| Zomalt, Eric | S | 5-11 | 197 | 8/9/72 | California | Los Angeles, Calif. | D3b |

The term NFL Rookie is defined as a player who is in his first season of professional football and has not been on the roster of another professional football team for any regular-season or postseason games. A Rookie is designated by an "R" on NFL rosters. Players who have been active in another professional football league or players who have NFL experience, including either preseason training camp or being on an Active List or Inactive List, or on Reserve/Injured or Reserve/Physically Unable to Perform for fewer than six regular-season games, are termed NFL First-Year Players. An NFL First-Year Player is designated by a "1" on NFL rosters. Thereafter, a player is credited with an additional year of experience for each season in which he accumulates six games on the Active List or Inactive List, or on Reserve/Injured or Reserve/Physically Unable to Perform.

## NOTES

# SAN FRANCISCO 49ERS

**National Football Conference**
**Western Division**
**Team Colors:** Forty Niners Gold and Scarlet
**4949 Centennial Boulevard**
**Santa Clara, California 95054**
**Telephone: (408) 562-4949**

## CLUB OFFICIALS

Owner: Edward J. DeBartolo, Jr.
President: Carmen Policy
Vice President-Football Administration: John McVay
Vice President-Business Operations & C.F.O.: Keith Simon
Coordinator of Football Operations/Player Personnel: Dwight Clark
Director of Pro Personnel: Allan Webb
Director of College Scouting: Vinny Cerrato
Director of Public/Community Relations: Rodney Knox
Director of Marketing/Promotions: Laurie Albrecht
Coordinator of Football Operations: Neal Dahlen
Ticket Manager: Lynn Carrozzi
Director of Stadium Operations: Murlan (Mo) Fowell
Video Director: Robert Yanagi
Trainer: Lindsy McLean
Equipment Manager: Bronco Hinek
**Stadium:** Candlestick Park • **Capacity:** 69,423
San Francisco, California 94124
**Playing Surface:** Grass
**Training Camp:** Sierra Community College
Rocklin, California 95677

## 1994 SCHEDULE

**PRESEASON**

| | | |
|---|---|---|
| Aug. 5 | at Arizona | 6:30 |
| Aug. 12 | **Denver** | 5:00 |
| Aug. 18 | at San Diego | 5:00 |
| Aug. 26 | **Seattle** | 6:00 |

**REGULAR SEASON**

| | | |
|---|---|---|
| Sept. 5 | **Los Angeles Raiders** (Monday) | 6:00 |
| Sept. 11 | at Kansas City | 12:00 |
| Sept. 18 | at Los Angeles Rams | 1:00 |
| Sept. 25 | **New Orleans** | 1:00 |
| Oct. 2 | **Philadelphia** | 1:00 |
| Oct. 9 | at Detroit | 1:00 |
| Oct. 16 | at Atlanta | 1:00 |
| Oct. 23 | **Tampa Bay** | 1:00 |
| Oct. 30 | Open Date | |
| Nov. 6 | at Washington | 1:00 |
| Nov. 13 | **Dallas** | 1:00 |
| Nov. 20 | **Los Angeles Rams** | 5:00 |
| Nov. 28 | at New Orleans (Monday) | 8:00 |
| Dec. 4 | **Atlanta** | 1:00 |
| Dec. 11 | at San Diego | 1:00 |
| Dec. 17 | **Denver** (Saturday) | 1:00 |
| Dec. 26 | at Minnesota (Monday) | 8:00 |

## RECORD HOLDERS

**INDIVIDUAL RECORDS—CAREER**

| Category | Name | Performance |
|---|---|---|
| Rushing (Yds.) | Joe Perry, 1950-1960, 1963 | 7,344 |
| Passing (Yds.) | Joe Montana, 1979-1992 | 35,124 |
| Passing (TDs) | Joe Montana, 1979-1992 | 244 |
| Receiving (No.) | Jerry Rice, 1985-1993 | 708 |
| Receiving (Yds.) | Jerry Rice, 1985-1993 | 11,776 |
| Interceptions | Ronnie Lott, 1981-1990 | 51 |
| Punting (Avg.) | Tommy Davis, 1959-1969 | 44.7 |
| Punt Return (Avg.) | Manfred Moore, 1974-75 | 14.7 |
| Kickoff Return (Avg.) | Abe Woodson, 1958-1964 | 29.4 |
| Field Goals | Ray Wersching, 1977-1987 | 190 |
| Touchdowns (Tot.) | Jerry Rice, 1985-1993 | 124 |
| Points | Ray Wersching, 1977-1987 | 979 |

**INDIVIDUAL RECORDS—SINGLE SEASON**

| Category | Name | Performance |
|---|---|---|
| Rushing (Yds.) | Roger Craig, 1988 | 1,502 |
| Passing (Yds.) | Steve Young, 1993 | 4,023 |
| Passing (TDs) | Joe Montana, 1987 | 31 |
| Receiving (No.) | Jerry Rice, 1990 | 100 |
| Receiving (Yds.) | Jerry Rice, 1986 | 1,570 |
| Interceptions | Dave Baker, 1960 | 10 |
| | Ronnie Lott, 1986 | 10 |
| Punting (Avg.) | Tommy Davis, 1965 | 45.8 |
| Punt Return (Avg.) | Dana McLemore, 1982 | 22.3 |
| Kickoff Return (Avg.) | Joe Arenas, 1953 | 34.4 |
| Field Goals | Mike Cofer, 1989 | 29 |
| Touchdowns (Tot.) | Jerry Rice, 1987 | 23 |
| Points | Jerry Rice, 1987 | 138 |

**INDIVIDUAL RECORDS—SINGLE GAME**

| Category | Name | Performance |
|---|---|---|
| Rushing (Yds.) | Delvin Williams, 10-31-76 | 194 |
| Passing (Yds.) | Joe Montana, 10-14-90 | 476 |
| Passing (TDs) | Joe Montana, 10-14-90 | 6 |
| Receiving (No.) | Jerry Rice, 10-14-90 | 13 |
| Receiving (Yds.) | John Taylor, 12-11-89 | 286 |
| Interceptions | Dave Baker, 12-4-60 | *4 |
| Field Goals | Ray Wersching, 10-16-83 | 6 |
| Touchdowns (Tot.) | Jerry Rice, 10-14-90 | 5 |
| Points | Jerry Rice, 10-14-90 | 30 |

*NFL Record

## COACHING HISTORY

**(350-284-13)**

| | | |
|---|---|---|
| 1950-54 | Lawrence (Buck) Shaw | 33-25-2 |
| 1955 | Norman (Red) Strader | 4-8-0 |
| 1956-58 | Frankie Albert | 19-17-1 |
| 1959-63 | Howard (Red) Hickey* | 27-27-1 |
| 1963-67 | Jack Christiansen | 26-38-3 |
| 1968-75 | Dick Nolan | 56-56-5 |
| 1976 | Monte Clark | 8-6-0 |
| 1977 | Ken Meyer | 5-9-0 |
| 1978 | Pete McCulley** | 1-8-0 |
| 1978 | Fred O'Connor | 1-6-0 |
| 1979-88 | Bill Walsh | 102-63-1 |
| 1989-93 | George Seifert | 68-21-0 |

*Resigned after three games in 1963
**Released after nine games in 1978

**CANDLESTICK PARK**

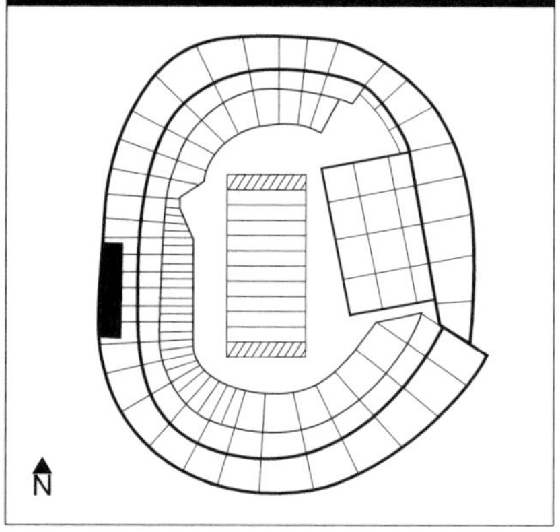

## 1993 TEAM RECORD

**PRESEASON (4-1)**

| Date | Result | | Opponents |
|---|---|---|---|
| 8/1 | W | 21-14 | vs. Pittsburgh at Barcelona |
| 8/8 | W | 27-0 | vs. L.A. Raiders at Stanford Stadium |
| 8/16 | W | 16-13 | at Denver |
| 8/21 | L | 0-30 | at Seattle |
| 8/28 | W | 30-14 | San Diego |

**REGULAR SEASON (10-6)**

| Date | Result | | Opponents | Att. |
|---|---|---|---|---|
| 9/5 | W | 24-13 | at Pittsburgh | 57,502 |
| 9/13 | L | 13-23 | at Cleveland | 78,218 |
| 9/19 | W | 37-30 | Atlanta | 63,032 |
| 9/26 | L | 13-16 | at New Orleans | 69,041 |
| 10/3 | W | 38-19 | Minnesota | 63,071 |
| 10/17 | L | 17-26 | at Dallas | 65,099 |
| 10/24 | W | 28-14 | Phoenix | 62,020 |
| 10/31 | W | 40-17 | L.A. Rams | 63,417 |
| 11/14 | W | 45-21 | at Tampa Bay | 43,835 |
| 11/22 | W | 42-7 | New Orleans | 66,500 |
| 11/28 | W | 35-10 | at L.A. Rams | 62,143 |
| 12/5 | W | 21-8 | Cincinnati | 60,039 |
| 12/11 | L | 24-27 | at Atlanta | 64,688 |
| 12/19 | W | 55-17 | at Detroit | 77,052 |
| 12/25 | L | 7-10 | Houston | 61,744 |
| 1/3 | L | 34-37 | Philadelphia (OT) | 61,653 |

**POSTSEASON (1-1)**

| | | | | |
|---|---|---|---|---|
| 1/15 | W | 44-3 | N.Y. Giants | 67,143 |
| 1/23 | L | 21-38 | at Dallas | 64,902 |

(OT) Overtime

**SCORE BY PERIODS**

| | | | | | | | |
|---|---|---|---|---|---|---|---|
| 49ers | 97 | 158 | 108 | 110 | 0 | — | 473 |
| Opponents | 44 | 106 | 57 | 85 | 3 | — | 295 |

**ATTENDANCE**

Home 501,476 Away 517,578 Total 1,019,054
Single-game home record, 66,500 (11-22-93)
Single-season home record, 523,355 (1992)

## 1993 TEAM STATISTICS

| | 49ers | Opp. |
|---|---|---|
| Total First Downs | 372 | 297 |
| Rushing | 134 | 109 |
| Passing | 212 | 171 |
| Penalty | 26 | 17 |
| Third Down: Made/Att | 89/186 | 87/214 |
| Third Down Pct. | 47.8 | 40.7 |
| Fourth Down: Made/Att | 10/16 | 9/20 |
| Fourth Down Pct. | 62.5 | 45.0 |
| Total Net Yards | 6435 | 4997 |
| Avg. Per Game | 402.2 | 312.3 |
| Total Plays | 1022 | 1012 |
| Avg. Per Play | 6.3 | 4.9 |
| Net Yards Rushing | 2133 | 1800 |
| Avg. Per Game | 133.3 | 112.5 |
| Total Rushes | 463 | 404 |
| Net Yards Passing | 4302 | 3197 |
| Avg. Per Game | 268.9 | 199.8 |
| Sacked/Yards Lost | 35/178 | 44/316 |
| Gross Yards | 4480 | 3513 |
| Att./Completions | 524/354 | 564/314 |
| Completion Pct. | 67.6 | 55.7 |
| Had Intercepted | 17 | 19 |
| Punts/Avg. | 42/40.9 | 68/43.9 |
| Net Punting Avg. | 42/34.5 | 68/36.4 |
| Penalties/Yards Lost | 95/800 | 99/743 |
| Fumbles/Ball Lost | 32/13 | 20/11 |
| Touchdowns | 61 | 30 |
| Rushing | 26 | 6 |
| Passing | 29 | 23 |
| Returns | 6 | 1 |
| Avg. Time of Possession | 30:24 | 29:36 |

## 1993 INDIVIDUAL STATISTICS

| PASSING | Att | Cmp | Yds. | Pct. | TD | Int | Tkld. | Rate |
|---|---|---|---|---|---|---|---|---|
| Young | 462 | 314 | 4023 | 68.0 | 29 | 16 | 31/160 | 101.5 |
| Bono | 61 | 39 | 416 | 63.9 | 0 | 1 | 4/18 | 76.9 |
| J. Taylor | 1 | 1 | 41 | 100.0 | 0 | 0 | 0/0 | 118.8 |
| 49ers | 524 | 354 | 4480 | 67.6 | 29 | 17 | 35/178 | 98.9 |
| Opponents | 564 | 314 | 3513 | 55.7 | 23 | 19 | 44/316 | 74.0 |

| SCORING | TD R | TD P | TD Rt | PAT | FG | Saf | PTS |
|---|---|---|---|---|---|---|---|
| Cofer | 0 | 0 | 0 | 59/61 | 16/26 | 0 | 107 |
| Rice | 1 | 15 | 0 | 0/0 | 0/0 | 0 | 96 |
| Watters | 10 | 1 | 0 | 0/0 | 0/0 | 0 | 66 |
| Logan | 7 | 0 | 0 | 0/0 | 0/0 | 0 | 42 |
| J. Taylor | 0 | 5 | 0 | 0/0 | 0/0 | 0 | 30 |
| Jones | 0 | 3 | 0 | 0/0 | 0/0 | 0 | 18 |
| Lee | 1 | 2 | 0 | 0/0 | 0/0 | 0 | 18 |
| Rathman | 3 | 0 | 0 | 0/0 | 0/0 | 0 | 18 |
| Carter | 1 | 0 | 1 | 0/0 | 0/0 | 0 | 12 |
| Davis | 0 | 0 | 2 | 0/0 | 0/0 | 0 | 12 |
| Young | 2 | 0 | 0 | 0/0 | 0/0 | 0 | 12 |
| Beach | 0 | 1 | 0 | 0/0 | 0/0 | 0 | 6 |
| Bono | 1 | 0 | 0 | 0/0 | 0/0 | 0 | 6 |
| Hanks | 0 | 0 | 1 | 0/0 | 0/0 | 0 | 6 |
| McGruder | 0 | 0 | 1 | 0/0 | 0/0 | 0 | 6 |
| Singleton | 0 | 1 | 0 | 0/0 | 0/0 | 0 | 6 |
| Tamm | 0 | 0 | 1 | 0/0 | 0/0 | 0 | 6 |
| Williams | 0 | 1 | 0 | 0/0 | 0/0 | 0 | 6 |
| 49ers | 26 | 29 | 6 | 59/61 | 16/26 | 0 | 473 |
| Opponents | 6 | 23 | 1 | 30/30 | 27/30 | 2 | 295 |

| RUSHING | Att. | Yds. | Avg. | LG | TD |
|---|---|---|---|---|---|
| Watters | 208 | 950 | 4.6 | 39 | 10 |
| Young | 69 | 407 | 5.9 | 35 | 2 |
| Logan | 58 | 280 | 4.8 | 45 | 7 |
| Lee | 72 | 230 | 3.2 | 13 | 1 |
| Rathman | 19 | 80 | 4.2 | 19 | 3 |
| Carter | 10 | 72 | 7.2 | 50t | 1 |
| Rice | 3 | 69 | 23.0 | 43t | 1 |
| J. Taylor | 2 | 17 | 8.5 | 12 | 0 |
| Walker | 5 | 17 | 3.4 | 11 | 0 |
| Bono | 12 | 14 | 1.2 | 10 | 1 |
| Wilmsmeyer | 2 | 0 | 0.0 | 0 | 0 |
| Musgrave | 3 | -3 | -1.0 | -1 | 0 |
| 49ers | 463 | 2133 | 4.6 | 50t | 26 |
| Opponents | 404 | 1800 | 4.5 | 41 | 6 |

| RECEIVING | No. | Yds. | Avg. | LG | TD |
|---|---|---|---|---|---|
| Rice | 98 | 1503 | 15.3 | 80t | 15 |
| Jones | 68 | 735 | 10.8 | 29 | 3 |
| J. Taylor | 56 | 940 | 16.8 | 76t | 5 |
| Logan | 37 | 348 | 9.4 | 24 | 0 |
| Watters | 31 | 326 | 10.5 | 48t | 1 |
| Williams | 16 | 132 | 8.3 | 15 | 1 |
| Lee | 16 | 115 | 7.2 | 22 | 2 |
| Rathman | 10 | 86 | 8.6 | 17 | 0 |
| Singleton | 8 | 126 | 15.8 | 33 | 1 |
| Beach | 5 | 59 | 11.8 | 20t | 1 |
| Turner | 3 | 64 | 21.3 | 32 | 0 |
| Carter | 3 | 40 | 13.3 | 14 | 0 |
| Young | 2 | 2 | 1.0 | 6 | 0 |
| Walker | 1 | 4 | 4.0 | 4 | 0 |
| 49ers | 354 | 4480 | 12.7 | 80t | 29 |
| Opponents | 314 | 3513 | 11.2 | 65t | 23 |

| INTERCEPTIONS | No. | Yds. | Avg. | LG | TD |
|---|---|---|---|---|---|
| McGruder | 5 | 89 | 17.8 | 37 | 1 |
| Davis | 4 | 45 | 11.3 | 41t | 1 |
| Hanks | 3 | 104 | 34.7 | 67t | 1 |
| McDonald | 3 | 23 | 7.7 | 21 | 0 |
| Griffin | 3 | 6 | 2.0 | 3 | 0 |
| Johnson | 1 | 0 | 0.0 | 0 | 0 |
| 49ers | 19 | 267 | 14.1 | 67t | 3 |
| Opponents | 17 | 157 | 9.2 | 30 | 0 |

| PUNTING | No. | Yds. | Avg. | In 20 | LG |
|---|---|---|---|---|---|
| Wilmsmeyer | 42 | 1718 | 40.9 | 11 | 61 |
| 49ers | 42 | 1718 | 40.9 | 11 | 61 |
| Opponents | 68 | 2985 | 43.9 | 12 | 57 |

| PUNT RETURNS | No. | FC | Yds. | Avg. | LG | TD |
|---|---|---|---|---|---|---|
| Carter | 34 | 20 | 411 | 12.1 | 72t | 1 |
| Kelm | 1 | 0 | 0 | 0.0 | 0 | 0 |
| 49ers | 35 | 20 | 411 | 11.7 | 72t | 1 |
| Opponents | 15 | 8 | 171 | 11.4 | 50 | 0 |

| KICKOFF RETURNS | No. | Yds. | Avg. | LG | TD |
|---|---|---|---|---|---|
| Carter | 25 | 494 | 19.8 | 60 | 0 |
| Lee | 10 | 160 | 16.0 | 28 | 0 |
| Walker | 3 | 51 | 17.0 | 30 | 0 |
| Brandes | 1 | 10 | 10.0 | 10 | 0 |
| Kelm | 1 | 0 | 0.0 | 0 | 0 |
| Walls | 0 | 0 | — | — | 0 |
| Williams | 0 | 0 | — | — | 0 |
| 49ers | 40 | 715 | 17.9 | 60 | 0 |
| Opponents | 61 | 1196 | 19.6 | 50 | 0 |

| SACKS | No. |
|---|---|
| Stubblefield | 10.5 |
| Harrison | 6.0 |
| Brown | 5.5 |
| T. Wilson | 5.5 |
| Romanowski | 3.0 |
| Washington | 3.0 |
| K. Wilson | 3.0 |
| Johnson | 2.0 |
| Roberts | 1.5 |
| Smith | 1.5 |
| Fagan | 1.0 |
| Kelly | 1.0 |
| Thomas | 0.5 |
| 49ers | 44.0 |
| Opponents | 35.0 |

## 1994 DRAFT CHOICES

| Round | Name | Pos. | College |
|---|---|---|---|
| 1 | Bryant Young | DT | Notre Dame |
| | William Floyd | RB | Florida State |
| 2 | Kevin Mitchell | LB | Syracuse |
| | Tyronne Drakeford | DB | Virginia Tech |
| 3 | Doug Brien | K | California |
| | Cory Fleming | WR | Tennessee |
| 5 | Tony Peterson | LB | Notre Dame |
| 6 | Lee Woodall | LB | West Chester, Pa. |

# SAN FRANCISCO 49ERS

## 1994 VETERAN ROSTER

| No. | Name | Pos. | Ht. | Wt. | Birthdate | NFL Exp. | College | Hometown | How Acq. | '93 Games/ Starts |
|---|---|---|---|---|---|---|---|---|---|---|
| 79 | Barton, Harris | G | 6-4 | 286 | 4/19/64 | 8 | North Carolina | Atlanta, Ga. | D1a-'87 | 15/15 |
| 83 | Beach, Sanjay | WR | 6-1 | 194 | 2/21/66 | 4 | Colorado State | Chandler, Ariz. | FA-'94 | 9/0 |
| 65 | Boatswain, Harry | T | 6-4 | 295 | 6/26/69 | 4 | New Haven | Brooklyn, N.Y. | D5b-'91 | 16/2 |
| 71 | Bollinger, Brian | G | 6-5 | 285 | 11/21/68 | 3 | North Carolina | Indialantic, Fla. | D3-'92 | 16/0 |
| 85 | # Brandes, John | TE | 6-2 | 249 | 4/2/64 | 8 | Cameron | Arlington, Tex. | FA-'93 | 9/0 |
| 96 | Brown, Dennis | DE | 6-4 | 290 | 11/6/67 | 5 | Washington | Long Beach, Calif. | D2a-'90 | 16/16 |
| 54 | # Caldwell, Ravin | LB | 6-3 | 240 | 8/4/63 | 8 | Arkansas | Ft. Smith, Ark. | FA-'93 | 0* |
| 35 | Carter, Dexter | RB | 5-9 | 174 | 9/15/67 | 5 | Florida State | Baxley, Ga. | D1-'90 | 16/0 |
| 6 | # Cofer, Mike | K | 6-1 | 190 | 2/19/64 | 7 | North Carolina State | Charlotte, N.C. | FA-'88 | 16/0 |
| 50 | Dalman, Chris | G-C | 6-3 | 285 | 3/15/70 | 2 | Stanford | Salinas, Calif. | D6-'93 | 15/0 |
| 25 | Davis, Eric | CB | 5-11 | 178 | 1/26/68 | 5 | Jacksonville State | Anniston, Ala. | D2b-'90 | 16/16 |
| 63 | Deese, Derrick | G | 6-3 | 270 | 5/17/70 | 3 | Southern California | Culver City, Calif. | FA-'92 | 0* |
| 75 | # Fagan, Kevin | DE | 6-3 | 254 | 4/25/63 | 8 | Miami | Lake Worth, Fla. | D4c-'86 | 7/7 |
| 67 | # Foster, Roy | G | 6-4 | 290 | 5/24/60 | 13 | Southern California | Los Angeles, Calif. | PB(Mia)-'91 | 1/0 |
| 18 | Grbac, Elvis | QB | 6-5 | 232 | 8/13/70 | 2 | Michigan | Willoughby Hills, Ohio | D8-'93 | 0* |
| 28 | Hall, Dana | S | 6-2 | 206 | 7/8/69 | 3 | Washington | Diamond Bar, Calif. | D1-'92 | 13/7 |
| 36 | Hanks, Merton | CB | 6-2 | 185 | 3/12/68 | 4 | Iowa | Dallas, Tex. | D5a-'91 | 16/14 |
| 45 | Hardy, Adrian | CB | 5-11 | 194 | 8/16/70 | 2 | Northwestern Louisiana | New Orleans, La. | D2-'93 | 10/0 |
| 55 | Johnson, John | LB | 6-3 | 230 | 5/8/68 | 4 | Clemson | La Grange, Ga. | D2c-'91 | 15/12 |
| 84 | Jones, Brent | TE | 6-4 | 230 | 2/12/63 | 8 | Santa Clara | San Jose, Calif. | FA-'87 | 16/16 |
| 90 | # Jordan, Darin | LB | 6-2 | 245 | 12/4/64 | 5 | Northeastern | Stoughton, Mass. | PB(Raid)-'91 | 14/0 |
| 58 | Kelly, Todd | LB | 6-2 | 259 | 11/27/70 | 2 | Tennessee | Hampton, Va. | D1b-'93 | 14/5 |
| 52 | # Kelm, Larry | LB | 6-4 | 240 | 11/29/64 | 8 | Texas A&M | Corpus Christi, Tex. | FA-'93 | 10/1 |
| 43 | Logan, Marc | RB | 6-0 | 212 | 5/9/65 | 7 | Kentucky | Lexington, Ky. | PB(Mia)-'92 | 14/12 |
| 46 | McDonald, Tim | S | 6-2 | 215 | 1/26/65 | 8 | Southern California | Fresno, Calif. | FA-'93 | 16/16 |
| 26 | # McGruder, Michael | CB | 5-10 | 190 | 5/6/64 | 5 | Kent State | Cleveland, Ohio | FA-'92 | 16/5 |
| 62 | # McIntyre, Guy | G | 6-3 | 276 | 2/17/61 | 11 | Georgia | Thomasville, Ga. | D3-'84 | 16/16 |
| 14 | Musgrave, Bill | QB | 6-2 | 205 | 11/11/67 | 4 | Oregon | Grand Junction, Colo. | FA-'91 | 1/0 |
| 51 | Norton, Ken | LB | 6-2 | 241 | 9/29/66 | 7 | UCLA | Los Angeles, Calif. | UFA(Dall)-'94 | 16/16* |
| 50 | Plummer, Gary | LB | 6-2 | 247 | 1/26/60 | 9 | California | Fremont, Calif. | UFA(SD)-'94 | 16/15* |
| 44 | # Rathman, Tom | RB | 6-1 | 232 | 10/7/62 | 9 | Nebraska | Grand Island, Neb. | D3a-'86 | 8/4 |
| 80 | Rice, Jerry | WR | 6-2 | 200 | 10/13/62 | 10 | Mississippi Valley State | Crawford, Miss. | D1-'85 | 16/16 |
| 91 | # Roberts, Larry | DE | 6-3 | 275 | 6/2/63 | 9 | Alabama | Dothan, Ala. | D2-'86 | 6/0 |
| 38 | Russell, Damien | S | 6-1 | 204 | 8/20/70 | 2 | Virginia Tech | Washington, D.C. | D6-'92 | 16/0 |
| 61 | Sapolu, Jesse | C | 6-4 | 278 | 3/10/61 | 12 | Hawaii | Honolulu, Hawaii | D11-'83 | 16/16 |
| 88 | Singleton, Nate | WR | 5-11 | 190 | 7/5/68 | 2 | Grambling | Marrero, La. | FA-'93 | 16/0 |
| 95 | Smith, Artie | DE | 6-4 | 303 | 5/15/70 | 2 | Louisiana Tech | Stillwater, Okla. | D5-'93 | 16/6 |
| 94 | Stubblefield, Dana | DT | 6-2 | 302 | 11/14/70 | 2 | Kansas | Cleves, Ohio | Dla-'93 | 16/14 |
| 64 | Tamm, Ralph | G-C | 6-4 | 280 | 3/11/66 | 7 | West Chester, Pa. | Philadelphia, Pa. | PB(Cin)-'92 | 16/16 |
| 82 | Taylor, John | WR | 6-1 | 185 | 3/31/62 | 9 | Delaware State | Pennsauken, N.J. | D3c-'86 | 16/16 |
| 72 | Thomas, Mark | DE | 6-5 | 273 | 5/6/69 | 3 | North Carolina State | Lilburn, Ga. | D4a-'92 | 11/1 |
| 74 | Wallace, Steve | T | 6-5 | 280 | 12/27/64 | 9 | Auburn | Atlanta, Ga. | D4b-'86 | 15/15 |
| 99 | # Walter, Mike | LB | 6-3 | 246 | 11/30/60 | 12 | Oregon | Eugene, Ore. | FA-'84 | 15/9 |
| 32 | Watters, Ricky | RB | 6-1 | 212 | 4/7/69 | 4 | Notre Dame | Harrisburg, Pa. | D2a-'91 | 13/13 |
| 10 | Wilmsmeyer, Klaus | P | 6-1 | 210 | 12/4/67 | 3 | Louisville | Mississauga, Canada | FA-'92 | 15/0 |
| 77 | Wilson, Karl | DE | 6-5 | 277 | 9/10/64 | 7 | Louisiana State | Amite, La. | FA-'93 | 12/2* |
| 92 | Wilson, Troy | DE | 6-4 | 235 | 11/20/70 | 2 | Pittsburg State, Kan. | Topeka, Kan. | D7-'93 | 10/0 |
| 8 | Young, Steve | QB | 6-2 | 205 | 10/11/61 | 10 | Brigham Young | Greenwich, Conn. | T(TB)-'87 | 16/16 |

* Caldwell last active with Washington in '92; Deese inactive for 6 games in '93; Grbac inactive for 16 games; Norton played 16 games with Dallas; Plummer played 16 games with San Diego; Wilson played 5 games with N.Y. Jets, 2 games with Miami, 5 games with San Francisco.

\# Unrestricted free agent; subject to developments.

† Restricted free agent; subject to developments.

Traded—QB Steve Bono to Kansas City, LB Bill Romanowski to Philadelphia, NT Ted Washington to Denver.

Players lost through free agency (3): CB Don Griffin (Clev; 12 games in '93), TE Wesley Walls (NO; 6), TE Jamie Williams (Raid; 16).

Also played with 49ers in '93—QB Steve Bono (8 games), LB Keith DeLong (4), LB Brett Faryniarz (2), LB Antonio Goss (14), CB Alan Grant (3), DE Martin Harrison (11), S Terry Hoage (4), DE Matt LaBounty (6), T James Parrish (1), LB Bill Romanowski (16), WR Odessa Turner (7), RB Adam Walker (10), NT Ted Washington (12).

## COACHING STAFF

**Head Coach,**
**George Seifert**

**Pro Career:** Named 49ers' head coach on January 26, 1989, after serving as the team's defensive coordinator since 1983. Immediately earned a place in league history, winning a record 17 games his first year and becoming only the second rookie head coach to lead his team to a Super Bowl title (Don McCafferty of Baltimore in 1970 was the first). Recorded the NFL's best won-loss mark in 1990, posting a 14-2 record and guided San Francisco to its fifth consecutive NFC West title. In 1991, the 49ers recorded a 10-6 mark, missing the playoffs for the first time since 1982. Again earned a trip to the NFC Championship Game in 1993, posting a 10-6 record mark and winning the NFC West. Joined 49ers as secondary coach in 1980. In only his second season in the pro ranks, San Francisco had the second best defense in the league and won a Super Bowl (XVI) title, despite starting three rookies in the defensive backfield. Appointed the team's defensive coordinator in 1983. Finished 1987 with the top defense in the NFL and a 13-2 record. No pro playing experience. Career record: 68-21.

**Background:** Linebacker at University of Utah (1960-62). Served a six-month tour of duty with the U.S. Army following graduation. Returned to Utah as a graduate assistant in 1964. Named head coach at Westminster College in Salt Lake City in 1965. Assistant at Iowa (1966), Oregon (1967-71), and Stanford (1972-74). Left Stanford to become head coach at Cornell (1975-76). Joined Bill Walsh's staff at Stanford in 1977 and helped the Cardinal to a two-year mark of 17-7, including victories in the Sun and Bluebonnet Bowls. Received bachelor's degree in zoology (1963) and master's degree in physical education (1966) from Utah.

**Personal:** Born January 22, 1940, in San Francisco. He and his wife, Linda, have two children—Eve and Jason—and live in Los Altos, Calif.

### ASSISTANT COACHES

**Jerry Attaway,** conditioning; born January 3, 1946, Susanville, Calif., lives in San Jose, Calif. Defensive back Yuba, Calif., J.C. 1964-65, Cal-Davis 1967. No pro playing experience. College coach: Cal-Davis 1970-71, Idaho 1972-74, Utah State 1975-77, Southern California 1978-82. Pro coach: Joined 49ers in 1983.

**Mike Barnes,** conditioning assistant; born March 13, 1966, Rochester N.Y., lives in Walnut Creek, Calif. No college or pro playing experience. College coach: Texas A&M 1990, California 1991-93. Pro coach: Joined 49ers in 1994.

**Dwaine Board,** defensive line; born November 29, 1956, Rocky Mount, Va., lives in Redwood City, Calif. Defensive lineman North Carolina A&T 1974-77. Pro defensive lineman San Francisco 49ers 1979-87, New Orleans Saints 1988. Pro coach: Joined 49ers in 1991.

**Tom Holmoe,** defensive backs; born March 7, 1960, Glendale, Calif., lives in Foster City, Calif. Defensive back Brigham Young 1979-82. Pro defensive back San Francisco 49ers 1983-89. College coach: Brigham Young 1990-91, Stanford 1992-93. Pro coach: Joined 49ers in 1994.

**Carl Jackson,** running backs; born August 16, 1940, Bay City, Tex., lives in San Jose, Calif. Quarterback Prairie View A&M 1959-62. No pro playing experience. College coach: North Texas State 1976-78, Iowa 1979-91. Pro coach: Joined 49ers in 1992.

**Larry Kirksey,** wide receivers; born January 6, 1951, Harlan, Ky., lives in Pleasanton, Calif. Wide receiver Eastern Kentucky 1970-72. No pro playing experience. College coach: Miami, Ohio 1974-76, Kentucky 1977-81, Kansas 1982, Kentucky State 1983 (head coach), Florida 1984-88, Pittsburgh 1989, Alabama 1990-93. Pro coach: Joined 49ers in 1994.

**Gary Kubiak,** quarterbacks; born August 15, 1961, Houston, Tex., lives in Santa Clara, Calif. Quarterback Texas A&M 1979-82. Pro quarterback Denver Broncos 1983-91. College coach: Texas A&M 1992-93. Pro coach: Joined 49ers in 1994.

**Alan Lowry,** special teams; born November 21, 1950, Irving, Tex., lives in Danville, Calif. Defensive back-quarterback Texas 1970-72. No pro playing experience. College coach: Virginia Tech 1974, Wyoming 1975, Texas 1976-81. Pro coach: Dallas Cowboys 1982-90, Tampa Bay Buccaneers 1991, joined 49ers in 1992.

**John Marshall,** linebackers; born October 2, 1945, Arroyo Grande, Calif., lives in Pleasanton, Calif. Linebacker Washington State 1964. No pro playing experience. College coach: Oregon 1970-76, Southern California 1977-79. Pro coach: Green Bay Packers 1980-82, Atlanta Falcons 1983-85, Indianapolis Colts 1986-88, joined 49ers in 1989.

**Bobb McKittrick,** offensive line; born December 29, 1935, Baker, Ore., lives in San Mateo, Calif. Guard Oregon State 1955-57. No pro playing experience. College coach: Oregon State 1961-64, UCLA 1965-70. Pro coach: Los Angeles Rams 1971-72, San Diego Chargers 1974-78, joined 49ers in 1979.

**Bill McPherson,** assistant head coach; born October 24, 1931, Santa Clara, Calif., lives in San Jose, Calif. Tackle Santa Clara 1950-52. No pro playing experience. College coach: Santa Clara 1963-74, UCLA 1975-77. Pro coach: Philadelphia Eagles 1978, joined 49ers in 1979.

**Brian Pariani,** offensive coaches assistant; born July 2, 1965, San Francisco, Calif., lives in Menlo Park, Calif. No college or pro playing experience. College coach: UCLA 1989. Pro coach: Joined 49ers in 1991.

**Ray Rhodes,** defensive coordinator; born October 20, 1950, Mexia, Tex., lives in Pleasanton, Calif. Running back-wide receiver Texas Christian 1969-70, Tulsa 1972-73. Pro defensive back New York Giants 1974-79, San Francisco 49ers 1980. Pro coach: San Francisco 49ers 1980-91, Green Bay Packers 1992-93, rejoined 49ers in 1994.

**Mike Shanahan,** offensive coordinator; born August 24, 1952, Oak Park, Ill., lives in Saratoga, Calif. Quarterback Eastern Illinois 1970-73. No pro playing experience. College coach: Oklahoma 1975-76, Northern Arizona 1977, Eastern Illinois 1978, Minnesota 1979, Florida 1980-83. Pro coach: Denver Broncos 1984-87, 1989-91, Los Angeles Raiders 1988-89 (head coach), joined 49ers in 1992.

**Mike Solari,** tight ends-offensive line assistant; born January 16, 1955, Daly City, Calif., lives in Pleasanton, Calif. Offensive lineman San Diego State 1975-76. No pro playing experience. College coach: Mira Vista (Calif.) Junior College 1977-78, U.S. International 1979, Boise State 1980, Cincinnati 1981-82, Kansas 1983-85, Pittsburgh 1986, Alabama 1990-91. Pro coach: Dallas Cowboys 1987-88, Phoenix Cardinals 1989, joined 49ers in 1992.

## 1994 FIRST-YEAR ROSTER

| Name | Pos. | Ht. | Wt. | Birthdate | College | Hometown | How Acq. |
|---|---|---|---|---|---|---|---|
| Barnes, Tomur (1) | CB | 5-10 | 188 | 9/8/70 | North Texas State | Baytown, Tex. | FA |
| Bridewell, Jeff (1) | QB | 6-5 | 220 | 5/13/67 | California-Davis | Napa, Calif. | FA |
| Brien, Doug | K | 5-11 | 177 | 11/24/70 | California | Concord, Calif. | D3a |
| Browning, Alfonzo | WR | 6-2 | 203 | 7/27/72 | Kentucky | San Francisco, Calif. | FA |
| Bryant, Junior (1) | DE | 6-4 | 275 | 1/16/71 | Notre Dame | Omaha, Neb. | FA |
| Burnett, Bryce (1) | TE | 6-3 | 225 | 3/9/69 | San Jose State | Flossmoor, Ill. | FA |
| Carolan, Brett | TE | 6-3 | 241 | 3/10/71 | Washington State | Novato, Calif. | FA |
| Collins, Ron | G | 6-5 | 289 | 9/30/71 | Fresno State | San Bernardino, Calif. | FA |
| Drakeford, Tyronne | CB | 5-9 | 185 | 6/21/71 | Virginia Tech | Camden, S.C. | D2b |
| Fleming, Cory | WR | 6-1 | 207 | 3/19/71 | Tennessee | Nashville, Tenn. | D3b |
| Floyd, William | RB | 6-1 | 242 | 2/17/72 | Florida State | St. Petersburg, Fla. | D1b |
| Fountaine, Jamal | DE | 6-3 | 240 | 1/29/71 | Washington | San Francisco, Calif. | FA |
| Hillman, Jay (1) | RB | 6-0 | 230 | 3/10/68 | Boston University | Oxford, Conn. | FA |
| Ivlow, John (1) | RB | 5-11 | 226 | 1/26/70 | Colorado State | Joliet, Ill. | FA |
| Jefferson, Anthony | CB | 5-11 | 197 | 3/11/70 | Sonoma State | Hawthorne, Calif. | FA |
| Kellogg, Jackie | CB | 6-1 | 188 | 3/29/71 | Eastern Washington | Tacoma, Wash. | FA |
| Millen, Alec (1) | T | 6-7 | 285 | 9/25/70 | Georgia | Atlanta, Ga. | FA |
| Mitchell, Kevin | LB | 6-1 | 260 | 1/1/71 | Syracuse | Harrisburg, Pa. | D2a |
| Owens, Darrick (1) | WR | 6-2 | 216 | 11/5/70 | Mississippi | Tallahassee, Fla. | FA |
| Pay, Gary (1) | C | 6-4 | 285 | 1/20/68 | Brigham Young | Glendale, Ariz. | FA |
| Popson, Ted (1) | TE | 6-4 | 250 | 9/10/66 | Portland State | Lake Tahoe, Calif. | FA |
| Peterson, Anthony | LB | 6-0 | 223 | 1/23/72 | Notre Dame | Monongahela, Pa. | D5 |
| Preston, P.J. | LB | 6-2 | 221 | 11/9/71 | Virginia Tech | Martinsville, Va. | FA |
| Thompson, Tom | P | 5-10 | 192 | 4/27/72 | Oregon | Lompoc, Calif. | FA |
| Woodall, Lee | S | 6-0 | 220 | 10/31/69 | West Chester, Pa. | Carlisle, Pa. | D6 |
| Young, Alan | DE | 6-3 | 253 | 1/20/71 | Vanderbilt | Woodstock, N.Y. | FA |
| Young, Bryant | DT | 6-2 | 276 | 1/27/72 | Notre Dame | Chicago Heights, Ill. | D1a |

The term NFL Rookie is defined as a player who is in his first season of professional football and has not been on the roster of another professional football team for any regular-season or postseason games. A Rookie is designated by an "R" on NFL rosters. Players who have been active in another professional football league or players who have NFL experience, including either preseason training camp or being on an Active List or Inactive List, or on Reserve/Injured or Reserve/Physically Unable to Perform for fewer than six regular-season games, are termed NFL First-Year Players. An NFL First-Year Player is designated by a "1" on NFL rosters. Thereafter, a player is credited with an additional year of experience for each season in which he accumulates six games on the Active List or Inactive List, or on Reserve/Injured or Reserve/Physically Unable to Perform.

## NOTES

# TAMPA BAY BUCCANEERS

**National Football Conference**
**Central Division**
**Team Colors:** Florida Orange, White, and Red
**One Buccaneer Place**
**Tampa, Florida 33607**
**Telephone: (813) 870-2700**

## CLUB OFFICIALS

Owner: Hugh F. Culverhouse
V.P.-Football Administration: Rich McKay
Director of Player Personnel: Jerry Angelo
Director of College Scouting: Tim Ruskell
Director of Ticket Sales and Operations: Rick Odioso
Director of Public Relations: Chip Namias
Director of Corporate Sales/Broadcasting: Jim Overton
Director of Advertising & Sales: Paul Sickmon
Controller: Patrick Smith
College Scouts: Mike Ackerley, Brian Gardner Ruston Webster, Mike Yowarsky
Pro Personnel Asst.: John Garrett, John Idzik
Office Manager: Deb Matzke
Asst. Director/Ticket Operations: Lori Grimm
Asst. Director/Media Relations: Scott Smith
Computer Services Coordinator: Terri Kimbell
Assistant Director/Community Relations: Sherry Gruden
Media Relations Assistant: Jearl Lett
Assistant Director of Sales/Advertising: Jayne Portnoy
Corporate Sales Assistant: Heidi Soderholm
Trainer: Chris Smith
Assistant Trainer: Joe Joe Petrone
Equipment Manager: Frank Pupello
Video Director: Davy Levy
Assistant Video Director: Pat Brazil
**Stadium:** Tampa Stadium • **Capacity:** 74,321
Tampa, Florida 33607
**Playing Surface:** Grass
**Training Camp:** University of Tampa
Tampa, Florida 33606

## 1994 SCHEDULE

**PRESEASON**

| | | |
|---|---|---|
| Aug. 6 | **Cincinnati** | 7:30 |
| Aug. 13 | at Seattle | 6:00 |
| Aug. 20 | at Miami | 8:00 |
| Aug. 26 | **New York Jets** | 7:30 |

**REGULAR SEASON**

| | | |
|---|---|---|
| Sept. 4 | at Chicago | 12:00 |
| Sept. 11 | **Indianapolis** | 1:00 |
| Sept. 18 | **New Orleans** | 1:00 |
| Sept. 25 | at Green Bay | 12:00 |
| Oct. 2 | **Detroit** | 1:00 |
| Oct. 9 | at Atlanta | 1:00 |
| Oct. 16 | Open Date | |
| Oct. 23 | at San Francisco | 1:00 |
| Oct. 30 | **Minnesota** | 4:00 |
| Nov. 6 | **Chicago** | 1:00 |
| Nov. 13 | at Detroit | 8:00 |
| Nov. 20 | at Seattle | 1:00 |
| Nov. 27 | at Minnesota | 12:00 |
| Dec. 4 | **Washington** | 1:00 |
| Dec. 11 | **Los Angeles Rams** | 1:00 |
| Dec. 18 | at Washington | 1:00 |
| Dec. 24 | **Green Bay** | 1:00 |

## RECORD HOLDERS

**INDIVIDUAL RECORDS—CAREER**

| Category | Name | Performance |
|---|---|---|
| Rushing (Yds.) | James Wilder, 1981-89 | 5,957 |
| Passing (Yds.) | Vinny Testaverde, 1987-1992 | 14,820 |
| Passing (TDs) | Vinny Testaverde, 1987-1992 | 77 |
| Receiving (No.) | James Wilder, 1981-89 | 430 |
| Receiving (Yds.) | Mark Carrier, 1987-1992 | 5,018 |
| Interceptions | Cedric Brown, 1977-1984 | 29 |
| Punting (Avg.) | Frank Garcia, 1983-87 | 41.1 |
| Punt Return (Avg.) | Willie Drewrey, 1989-1992 | 9.4 |
| Kickoff Return (Avg.) | Isaac Hagins, 1976-1980 | 21.9 |
| Field Goals | Donald Igwebuike, 1985-89 | 94 |
| Touchdowns (Tot.) | James Wilder, 1981-89 | 46 |
| Points | Donald Igwebuike, 1985-89 | 416 |

**INDIVIDUAL RECORDS—SINGLE SEASON**

| Category | Name | Performance |
|---|---|---|
| Rushing (Yds.) | James Wilder, 1984 | 1,544 |
| Passing (Yds.) | Doug Williams, 1981 | 3,563 |
| Passing (TDs) | Doug Williams, 1980 | 20 |
| | Vinny Testaverde, 1989 | 20 |
| Receiving (No.) | Mark Carrier, 1989 | 86 |
| Receiving (Yds.) | Mark Carrier, 1989 | 1,422 |
| Interceptions | Cedric Brown, 1981 | 9 |
| Punting (Avg.) | Larry Swider, 1981 | 42.7 |
| Punt Return (Avg.) | Courtney Hawkins, 1993 | 11.1 |
| Kickoff Return (Avg.) | Isaac Hagins, 1977 | 23.5 |
| Field Goals | Steve Christie, 1990 | 23 |
| Touchdowns (Tot.) | James Wilder, 1984 | 13 |
| Points | Donald Igwebuike, 1989 | 99 |

**INDIVIDUAL RECORDS—SINGLE GAME**

| Category | Name | Performance |
|---|---|---|
| Rushing (Yds.) | James Wilder, 11-6-83 | 219 |
| Passing (Yds.) | Doug Williams, 11-16-80 | 486 |
| Passing (TDs) | Steve DeBerg, 9-13-87 | 5 |
| Receiving (No.) | James Wilder, 9-15-85 | 13 |
| Receiving (Yds.) | Mark Carrier, 12-6-87 | 212 |
| Interceptions | Many times | 2 |
| | Last time by Joe King and Milton Mack, 12-27-92 | |
| Field Goals | Many times | 4 |
| | Last time by Steve Christie, 12-16-90 | 4 |
| Touchdowns (Tot.) | Jimmie Giles, 10-20-85 | 4 |
| Points | Jimmie Giles, 10-20-85 | 24 |

## COACHING HISTORY

**(82-197-1)**

| | | |
|---|---|---|
| 1976-84 | John McKay | 45-91-1 |
| 1985-86 | Leeman Bennett | 4-28-0 |
| 1987-90 | Ray Perkins* | 19-41-0 |
| 1990-91 | Richard Williamson | 4-15-0 |
| 1992-93 | Sam Wyche | 10-22-0 |

*Released after 13 games in 1990

**TAMPA STADIUM**

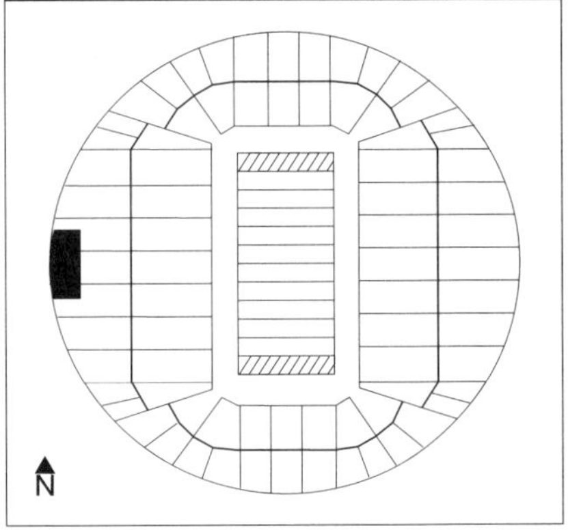

## 1993 TEAM RECORD

**PRESEASON (2-2)**

| Date | Result | | Opponents |
|---|---|---|---|
| 8/7 | L | 7-23 | Denver |
| 8/14 | L | 10-20 | at Atlanta |
| 8/21 | W | 32-12 | vs. Buffalo at Orlando |
| 8/27 | W | 23-20 | Cleveland |

**REGULAR SEASON (5-11)**

| Date | Result | | Opponents | Att. |
|---|---|---|---|---|
| 9/5 | L | 3-27 | Kansas City | 63,378 |
| 9/12 | L | 7-23 | at N.Y. Giants | 75,891 |
| 9/26 | L | 17-47 | at Chicago | 58,329 |
| 10/3 | W | 27-10 | Detroit | 40,794 |
| 10/10 | L | 0-15 | at Minnesota | 54,215 |
| 10/24 | L | 14-37 | Green Bay | 47,354 |
| 10/31 | W | 31-24 | at Atlanta | 50,647 |
| 11/7 | L | 0-23 | at Detroit | 65,295 |
| 11/14 | L | 21-45 | San Francisco | 43,835 |
| 11/21 | W | 23-10 | Minnesota | 40,848 |
| 11/28 | L | 10-13 | at Green Bay | 56,995 |
| 12/5 | L | 17-23 | Washington | 49,035 |
| 12/12 | W | 13-10 | Chicago | 56,667 |
| 12/19 | L | 20-27 | at L.A. Raiders | 40,532 |
| 12/26 | W | 17-10 | at Denver | 73,434 |
| 1/2 | L | 17-32 | San Diego | 35,587 |

(OT) Overtime

**SCORE BY PERIODS**

| | | | | | | | |
|---|---|---|---|---|---|---|---|
| Buccaneers | 19 | 74 | 89 | 55 | 0 | — | 237 |
| Opponents | 72 | 133 | 75 | 96 | 0 | — | 376 |

**ATTENDANCE**

Home 377,498 Away 475,338 Total 852,836

Single-game home record, 72,077 (10-8-89)

Single-season home record, 545,980 (1979)

## 1993 TEAM STATISTICS

| | Buccaneers | Opp. |
|---|---|---|
| Total First Downs | 241 | 280 |
| Rushing | 80 | 109 |
| Passing | 141 | 152 |
| Penalty | 20 | 19 |
| Third Down: Made/Att | 74/213 | 85/224 |
| Third Down Pct. | 34.7 | 37.9 |
| Fourth Down: Made/Att | 3/12 | 5/16 |
| Fourth Down Pct. | 25.0 | 31.3 |
| Total Net Yards | 4311 | 5246 |
| Avg. Per Game | 269.4 | 327.9 |
| Total Plays | 949 | 1011 |
| Avg. Per Play | 4.5 | 5.2 |
| Net Yards Rushing | 1290 | 1994 |
| Avg. Per Game | 80.6 | 124.6 |
| Total Rushes | 402 | 479 |
| Net Yards Passing | 3021 | 3252 |
| Avg. Per Game | 188.8 | 203.3 |
| Sacked/Yards Lost | 39/274 | 29/132 |
| Gross Yards | 3295 | 3384 |
| Att./Completions | 508/262 | 503/300 |
| Completion Pct. | 51.6 | 59.6 |
| Had Intercepted | 25 | 9 |
| Punts/Avg. | 94/40.1 | 76/43.3 |
| Net Punting Avg. | 94/35.3 | 76/36.3 |
| Penalties/Yards Lost | 89/765 | 126/913 |
| Fumbles/Ball Lost | 28/11 | 27/13 |
| Touchdowns | 27 | 40 |
| Rushing | 6 | 15 |
| Passing | 19 | 22 |
| Returns | 2 | 3 |
| Avg. Time of Possession | 28:38 | 31:22 |

## 1993 INDIVIDUAL STATISTICS

| PASSING | Att | Cmp | Yds. | Pct. | TD | Int | Tkld. | Rate |
|---|---|---|---|---|---|---|---|---|
| Erickson | 457 | 233 | 3054 | 51.0 | 18 | 21 | 35/236 | 66.4 |
| DeBerg | 39 | 23 | 186 | 59.0 | 1 | 3 | 3/27 | 47.6 |
| Weldon | 11 | 6 | 55 | 54.5 | 0 | 1 | 1/11 | 30.5 |
| Moore | 1 | 0 | 0 | 0.0 | 0 | 0 | 0/0 | 39.6 |
| Buccaneers | 508 | 262 | 3295 | 51.6 | 19 | 25 | 39/274 | 64.1 |
| Opponents | 503 | 300 | 3384 | 59.6 | 22 | 9 | 29/132 | 86.9 |

| SCORING | TD R | TD P | TD Rt | PAT | FG | Saf | PTS |
|---|---|---|---|---|---|---|---|
| Husted | 0 | 0 | 0 | 27/27 | 16/22 | 0 | 75 |
| Hawkins | 0 | 5 | 0 | 0/0 | 0/0 | 0 | 30 |
| Cobb | 3 | 1 | 0 | 0/0 | 0/0 | 0 | 24 |
| Copeland | 0 | 4 | 0 | 0/0 | 0/0 | 0 | 24 |
| Workman | 2 | 2 | 0 | 0/0 | 0/0 | 0 | 24 |
| L. Thomas | 0 | 2 | 0 | 0/0 | 0/0 | 0 | 12 |
| G. Anderson | 0 | 1 | 0 | 0/0 | 0/0 | 0 | 6 |
| Armstrong | 0 | 1 | 0 | 0/0 | 0/0 | 0 | 6 |
| Ro. Hall | 0 | 1 | 0 | 0/0 | 0/0 | 0 | 6 |
| Mack | 0 | 0 | 1 | 0/0 | 0/0 | 0 | 6 |
| McDowell | 0 | 1 | 0 | 0/0 | 0/0 | 0 | 6 |
| Moore | 0 | 1 | 0 | 0/0 | 0/0 | 0 | 6 |
| Royster | 1 | 0 | 0 | 0/0 | 0/0 | 0 | 6 |
| Seals | 0 | 0 | 1 | 0/0 | 0/0 | 0 | 6 |
| Buccaneers | 6 | 19 | 2 | 27/27 | 16/22 | 0 | 237 |
| Opponents | 15 | 22 | 3 | 38/40 | 32/35 | 1 | 376 |

| RUSHING | Att. | Yds. | Avg. | LG | TD |
|---|---|---|---|---|---|
| Cobb | 221 | 658 | 3.0 | 16 | 3 |
| Workman | 78 | 284 | 3.6 | 21 | 2 |
| Royster | 33 | 115 | 3.5 | 19 | 1 |
| Erickson | 26 | 96 | 3.7 | 15 | 0 |
| G. Anderson | 28 | 56 | 2.0 | 13 | 0 |
| Copeland | 3 | 34 | 11.3 | 22 | 0 |
| Harris | 7 | 29 | 4.1 | 12 | 0 |
| C. Wilson | 2 | 7 | 3.5 | 4 | 0 |
| McDowell | 2 | 6 | 3.0 | 3 | 0 |
| Armstrong | 2 | 5 | 2.5 | 4 | 0 |
| Buccaneers | 402 | 1290 | 3.2 | 22 | 6 |
| Opponents | 479 | 1994 | 4.2 | 78t | 15 |

| RECEIVING | No. | Yds. | Avg. | LG | TD |
|---|---|---|---|---|---|
| Hawkins | 62 | 933 | 15.0 | 67 | 5 |
| Workman | 54 | 411 | 7.6 | 42t | 2 |
| Copeland | 30 | 633 | 21.1 | 67t | 4 |
| Ro. Hall | 23 | 268 | 11.7 | 37t | 1 |
| C. Wilson | 15 | 225 | 15.0 | 24 | 0 |
| Dawsey | 15 | 203 | 13.5 | 24 | 0 |
| G. Anderson | 11 | 89 | 8.1 | 28 | 1 |
| Armstrong | 9 | 86 | 9.6 | 29 | 1 |
| Cobb | 9 | 61 | 6.8 | 19 | 1 |
| L. Thomas | 8 | 186 | 23.3 | 62t | 2 |
| McDowell | 8 | 26 | 3.3 | 9 | 1 |
| Claiborne | 5 | 61 | 12.2 | 16 | 0 |
| Royster | 5 | 18 | 3.6 | 10 | 0 |
| Harris | 4 | 48 | 12.0 | 25 | 0 |
| Moore | 4 | 47 | 11.8 | 19t | 1 |
| Buccaneers | 262 | 3295 | 12.6 | 67t | 19 |
| Opponents | 300 | 3384 | 11.3 | 53t | 22 |

| INTERCEPTIONS | No. | Yds. | Avg. | LG | TD |
|---|---|---|---|---|---|
| King | 3 | 29 | 9.7 | 28 | 0 |
| Mack | 1 | 27 | 27.0 | 27t | 1 |
| D. Anderson | 1 | 6 | 6.0 | 6 | 0 |
| Nickerson | 1 | 6 | 6.0 | 6 | 0 |
| Reynolds | 1 | 3 | 3.0 | 3 | 0 |
| Carter | 1 | 0 | 0.0 | 0 | 0 |
| Seals | 1 | 0 | 0.0 | 0t | 1 |
| Buccaneers | 9 | 71 | 7.9 | 28 | 2 |
| Opponents | 25 | 280 | 11.2 | 59t | 1 |

| PUNTING | No. | Yds. | Avg. | In 20 | LG |
|---|---|---|---|---|---|
| Stryzinski | 93 | 3772 | 40.6 | 24 | 57 |
| Buccaneers | 94 | 3772 | 40.1 | 24 | 57 |
| Opponents | 76 | 3290 | 43.3 | 20 | 64 |

| PUNT RETURNS | No. | FC | Yds. | Avg. | LG | TD |
|---|---|---|---|---|---|---|
| G. Anderson | 17 | 1 | 113 | 6.6 | 15 | 0 |
| Hawkins | 15 | 8 | 166 | 11.1 | 35 | 0 |
| Claiborne | 6 | 6 | 32 | 5.3 | 13 | 0 |
| Buccaneers | 38 | 15 | 311 | 8.2 | 35 | 0 |
| Opponents | 53 | 23 | 394 | 7.4 | 54 | 0 |

| KICKOFF RETURNS | No. | Yds. | Avg. | LG | TD |
|---|---|---|---|---|---|
| C. Wilson | 23 | 454 | 19.7 | 42 | 0 |
| Turner | 6 | 61 | 10.2 | 19 | 0 |
| G. Anderson | 12 | 181 | 15.1 | 24 | 0 |
| Royster | 8 | 102 | 12.8 | 26 | 0 |
| Workman | 5 | 67 | 13.4 | 19 | 0 |
| Claiborne | 4 | 57 | 14.3 | 33 | 0 |
| Buccaneers | 58 | 922 | 15.9 | 42 | 0 |
| Opponents | 28 | 499 | 17.8 | 46 | 0 |

| SACKS | No. |
|---|---|
| Seals | 8.5 |
| Curry | 5.0 |
| Dotson | 5.0 |
| Price | 3.0 |
| Wheeler | 2.0 |
| Ahanotu | 1.5 |
| Jones | 1.0 |
| Nickerson | 1.0 |
| Reynolds | 1.0 |
| B. Thomas | 1.0 |
| Buccaneers | 29.0 |
| Opponents | 39.0 |

## 1994 DRAFT CHOICES

| Round | Name | Pos. | College |
|---|---|---|---|
| 1 | Trent Dilfer | QB | Fresno State |
| 2 | Errict Rhett | RB | Florida |
| 3 | Harold Bishop | TE | Louisiana State |
| 5 | Pete Pierson | T | Washington |
| 6 | Bernard Carter | LB | East Carolina |
| 7 | Jim Pyne | C | Virginia Tech |

# TAMPA BAY BUCCANEERS

## 1994 VETERAN ROSTER

| No. | | Name | Pos. | Ht. | Wt. | Birthdate | NFL Exp. | College | Hometown | How Acq. | '93 Games/ Starts |
|---|---|---|---|---|---|---|---|---|---|---|---|
| 72 | | Ahanotu, Chidi | DE-DT | 6-2 | 280 | 10/11/70 | 2 | California | Berkeley, Calif. | D6-'93 | 16/10 |
| 44 | | Anderson, Darren | CB | 5-10 | 180 | 1/11/69 | 2 | Toledo | Cincinnati, Ohio | FA-'92 | 14/1 |
| 86 | | Armstong, Tyji | TE | 6-4 | 250 | 10/3/70 | 3 | Mississippi | Inkster, Mich. | D3b-'92 | 12/7 |
| 62 | | Beckles, Ian | G | 6-1 | 295 | 7/20/67 | 5 | Indiana | Montreal, Canada | D5-'90 | 14/14 |
| 53 | | Brady, Ed | LB | 6-2 | 235 | 6/17/62 | 11 | Illinois | Morris, Ill. | PB(Cin)-'92 | 16/0 |
| 28 | | Buckley, Curtis | CB-S | 6-0 | 185 | 9/25/70 | 2 | East Texas State | Silsbee, Tex. | FA-'93 | 10/2 |
| 27 | | Bussey, Barney | S | 6-0 | 210 | 5/20/62 | 9 | South Carolina State | Lincolnton, Ga. | UFA(Cin)-'93 | 16/7 |
| 23 | | Carter, Marty | S | 6-1 | 200 | 12/17/69 | 4 | Middle Tennessee State | La Grange, Ga. | D8-'91 | 16/14 |
| 89 | | Collins, Shawn | WR | 6-2 | 205 | 2/20/67 | 6 | Northern Arizona | San Diego, Calif. | FA-'93 | 4/0* |
| 88 | | Copeland, Horace | WR | 6-2 | 195 | 1/1/71 | 2 | Miami | Orlando, Fla. | D4b-'93 | 14/8 |
| 25 | | Covington, Tony | S | 5-11 | 195 | 12/26/67 | 4 | Virginia | Winston-Salem, N.C. | D4-'91 | 0* |
| 75 | | Curry, Eric | DE | 6-5 | 270 | 2/3/70 | 2 | Alabama | Thomasville, Ga. | D1-'93 | 10/10 |
| 80 | | Dawsey, Lawrence | WR | 6-0 | 195 | 11/16/67 | 4 | Florida State | Dothan, Ala. | D3-'91 | 4/4 |
| 76 | | Dill, Scott | T | 6-5 | 290 | 4/5/66 | 7 | Memphis State | Birmingham, Ala. | PB(Phx)-'90 | 16/16 |
| 71 | | Dotson, Santana | DE | 6-5 | 270 | 12/19/69 | 3 | Baylor | Houston, Tex. | D5b-'92 | 16/13 |
| 93 | | DuBose, Demetrius | LB | 6-1 | 240 | 3/23/71 | 2 | Notre Dame | Seattle, Wash. | D2-'93 | 15/4 |
| 7 | | Erickson, Craig | QB | 6-2 | 205 | 5/17/69 | 3 | Miami | West Palm Beach, Fla. | D4-'92 | 16/15 |
| 22 | t- | Everett, Thomas | S | 5-9 | 185 | 11/21/64 | 8 | Baylor | Daingerfield, Tex. | T(Dall)-'94 | 16/16* |
| 20 | # | Gray, Jerry | S | 6-0 | 195 | 12/16/62 | 10 | Texas | Lubbock, Tex. | UFA(Hou)-'93 | 14/5 |
| 26 | | Green, Rogerick | CB | 5-10 | 185 | 12/14/69 | 3 | Kansas State | San Antonio, Tex. | D5-'92 | 0* |
| 74 | | Gruber, Paul | T | 6-5 | 290 | 2/24/65 | 7 | Wisconsin | Prairie du Sac, Wis. | D1-'88 | 10/10 |
| 43 | | Harris, Rudy | RB | 6-1 | 255 | 9/18/71 | 2 | Clemson | Brockton, Mass. | D4a-'93 | 10/2 |
| 85 | | Hawkins, Courtney | WR | 5-9 | 180 | 12/12/69 | 3 | Michigan State | Flint, Mich. | D2-'92 | 16/12 |
| 95 | | Hill, Tony | DE | 6-6 | 255 | 10/23/68 | 3 | Tennessee-Chattanooga | Camak, Ga. | FA-'94 | 0* |
| 5 | | Husted, Michael | K | 6-0 | 190 | 6/16/70 | 2 | Virginia | Hampton, Va. | FA-'93 | 16/0 |
| 78 | | Irwin, Tim | T | 6-7 | 300 | 12/13/58 | 14 | Tennessee | Knoxville, Tenn. | UFA(Minn)-'94 | 16/16* |
| 24 | † | Jones, Roger | CB | 5-9 | 175 | 4/22/69 | 4 | Tennessee State | Nashville, Tenn. | FA-'92 | 16/5 |
| 41 | | King, Joe | S | 6-2 | 195 | 5/7/68 | 4 | Oklahoma State | Dallas, Tex. | PB(Clev)-'92 | 15/10 |
| 79 | | Love, Sean | G | 6-3 | 290 | 9/6/68 | 2 | Penn State | Tamaqua, Pa. | FA-'93 | 2/0 |
| 47 | | Lynch, John | S | 6-2 | 220 | 9/25/71 | 2 | Stanford | Solana Beach, Calif. | D3b-'93 | 15/4 |
| 21 | | Mack, Milton | CB | 5-11 | 195 | 9/20/63 | 8 | Alcorn State | Jackson, Miss. | PB(NO)-'92 | 12/3 |
| 97 | | Marts, Lonnie | LB | 6-1 | 230 | 11/10/68 | 5 | Tulane | New Orleans, La. | UFA(KC)-'94 | 16/15* |
| 61 | | Mayberry, Tony | C | 6-4 | 290 | 12/8/67 | 5 | Wake Forest | Springfield, Va. | D4-'90 | 16/16 |
| 35 | | Mayhew, Martin | CB | 5-8 | 175 | 10/8/65 | 7 | Florida State | Tallahassee, Fla. | UFA(Wash)-'93 | 15/14 |
| 33 | | McDowell, Anthony | RB | 5-11 | 235 | 11/12/68 | 3 | Texas Tech | Killeen, Tex. | D8-'92 | 4/3 |
| 70 | | McRae, Charles | T | 6-7 | 300 | 9/16/68 | 4 | Tennessee | Clinton, Tenn. | D1-'91 | 13/4 |
| 83 | | Moore, Dave | TE | 6-2 | 245 | 11/11/69 | 2 | Pittsburgh | Roxbury, N.J. | FA-'92 | 15/1 |
| 56 | | Nickerson, Hardy | LB | 6-2 | 230 | 9/1/65 | 8 | California | Los Angeles, Calif. | UFA(Pitt)-'93 | 16/16 |
| 36 | | Paul, Markus | S | 6-2 | 200 | 4/1/66 | 6 | Syracuse | Osceola, Fla. | FA-'93 | 9/0* |
| 92 | | Price, Shawn | DE-DT | 6-5 | 260 | 3/28/70 | 2 | Pacific | North Tahoe, Nev. | FA-'93 | 9/6 |
| 66 | | Reimers, Bruce | G | 6-7 | 300 | 9/28/60 | 11 | Iowa State | Humboldt, Iowa | PB(Cin)-'92 | 11/10 |
| 31 | | Royster, Mazio | RB | 6-1 | 200 | 8/3/70 | 3 | Southern California | Pomona, Calif. | D11-'92 | 14/0 |
| 64 | | Ryan, Tim | G | 6-2 | 280 | 9/2/68 | 4 | Notre Dame | Kansas City, Mo. | D5-'91 | 6/0 |
| 29 | | Stargell, Tony | CB-S | 5-11 | 190 | 8/7/66 | 5 | Tennessee State | La Grange, Ga. | UFA(Ind)-'94 | 16/1* |
| 4 | | Stryzinski, Dan | P | 6-1 | 195 | 5/15/65 | 5 | Indiana | Indianapolis, Ind. | PB(Pitt)-'92 | 16/0 |
| 67 | | Sullivan, Mike | G | 6-3 | 290 | 12/22/67 | 3 | Miami | Chicago, Ill. | FA-'92 | 11/3 |
| 51 | | Thomas, Broderick | LB | 6-4 | 250 | 2/20/67 | 6 | Nebraska | Houston, Tex. | D1-'89 | 16/8 |
| 87 | | Thomas, Lamar | WR | 6-1 | 170 | 2/12/70 | 2 | Miami | Gainesville, Fla. | D3a-'93 | 14/2 |
| 30 | | Turner, Vernon | KR-WR | 5-8 | 185 | 1/6/67 | 4 | Carson-Newman | Staten Island, N.Y. | FA-'93 | 8/0* |
| 13 | | Vlasic, Mark | QB | 6-3 | 205 | 10/25/63 | 8 | Iowa | Center Township, Pa. | UFA(KC)-'93 | 0* |
| 11 | | Weldon, Casey | QB | 6-1 | 200 | 2/3/68 | 3 | Florida State | Tallahassee, Fla. | FA-'93 | 3/0 |
| 77 | | Wheeler, Mark | NT | 6-2 | 280 | 4/1/70 | 3 | Texas A&M | San Marcos, Tex. | D3a-'92 | 10/10 |
| 54 | # | Williams, Jimmy | LB | 6-3 | 230 | 11/15/60 | 13 | Nebraska | Washington, D.C. | T(Minn)-'92 | 11/8 |
| 96 | | Wilson, Bernard | NT | 6-2 | 295 | 8/17/70 | 2 | Tennessee State | Nashville, Tenn. | FA-'93 | 13/2 |
| 84 | | Wilson, Charles | WR | 5-10 | 185 | 7/1/68 | 4 | Memphis State | Tallahassee, Fla. | FA-'92 | 15/1 |
| 99 | | Winter, Blaise | DT | 6-4 | 295 | 1/31/62 | 10 | Syracuse | Blauvelt, N.Y. | FA-'94 | 16/16* |
| 46 | | Workman, Vince | RB | 5-10 | 205 | 5/9/68 | 6 | Ohio State | Dublin, Ohio | RFA(GB)-'93 | 16/11 |

* Collins played 4 games with Green Bay in '93; Covington and Green missed '93 season due to injury; Everett played 16 games with Dallas; HIll last active with Dallas in '92; Irwin played 16 games with Minnesota; Marts played 16 games with Kansas City; Paul played 8 games with Chicago, 1 game with Tampa Bay; Stargell played 16 games with Indianapolis; Turner played 7 games with Detroit, 1 game with Tampa Bay; Vlasic inactive for 9 games; Winter played 16 games with San Diego.

\# Unrestricted free agent; subject to developments.

† Restricted free agent; subject to developments.

t- Buccaneers traded for Everett (Dallas).

Players lost through free agency (4): RB Reggie Cobb (GB; 12 games in '93), TE Ron Hall (Det; 16), CB Ricky Reynolds (NE; 14), DE Ray Seals (Pitt; 16).

Also played with Buccaneers in '93—T Theo Adams (7 games in '93), RB Gary Anderson (6), LB Darrick Brownlow (15), LB Reggie Burnette (5), WR Robert Claiborne (5), QB Steve DeBerg (3), DE-NT Eric Hayes (2), T Rob Taylor (16), G-T Pat Tomberlin (2).

## COACHING STAFF

**Head Coach,**
**Sam Wyche**

**Pro Career:** Became the Buccaneers' fifth head coach on January 10, 1992, after eight seasons with the Cincinnati Bengals. Led the Bengals to the AFC championship in 1988 and Super Bowl XXIII against the San Francisco 49ers. Played quarterback with the Bengals 1968-70, Washington Redskins 1971-73, Detroit Lions 1974-75, St. Louis Cardinals 1976, and Buffalo Bills 1977. Quarterback coach with the San Francisco 49ers 1979-82. Career record: 74-90.

**Background:** Attended North Fulton High School in Atlanta. Quarterback at Furman University from 1963-65. Assistant coach at South Carolina in 1967. Head coach at Indiana in 1983.

**Personal:** Born January 5, 1945, in Atlanta, Georgia. Sam and wife, Jane, live in Tampa, and have two children—Zak and Kerry.

### ASSISTANT COACHES

**Maxie Baughan,** linebackers; born August 3, 1938, Forkland, Ala., lives in Tampa. Center-linebacker Georgia Tech 1956-60. Pro linebacker Philadelphia Eagles 1960-65, Los Angeles Rams 1966-70, Washington Redskins 1971, 1974. College coach: Georgia Tech 1972-73, Cornell 1983-88 (head coach). Pro coach: Baltimore Colts 1975-79, Detroit Lions 1980-82, Minnesota Vikings 1990-91, joined Buccaneers in 1992.

**Ken Clarke,** defensive line; born August 28, 1956, Savannah, Ga., lives in Tampa. Defensive tackle Syracuse 1974-77. Pro defensive tackle Philadelphia Eagles 1978-87, Seattle Seahawks 1988, Minnesota Vikings 1989-91. Pro coach: Joined Buccaneers in 1994.

**David Culley,** receivers; born September 17, 1955, Sparta, Tenn., lives in Tampa. Quarterback Vanderbilt 1973, 1975-77. No pro playing experience. College coach: Austin Peay 1978, Vanderbilt 1979-81, Middle Tennessee State 1982, Tennessee-Chattanooga 1983, Western Kentucky 1984, Southwestern Louisiana 1985-89, Texas-El Paso 1989-90, Texas A&M 1991-93. Pro coach: Joined Buccaneers in 1994.

**Johnny Lynn,** defensive backs; born December 19, 1956, Los Angeles, Calif., lives in Tampa. Defensive back UCLA 1975-78. Pro defensive back New York Jets 1979-86. College coach: Arizona 1988-93. Pro coach: Joined Buccaneers in 1994.

**Mike Mularkey,** offensive assistant; born November 19, 1961, Ft. Lauderdale, Fla., lives in Tampa. Tight end Florida 1979-82. Pro tight end Minnesota 1983-88, Pittsburgh 1989-91. Pro coach: Joined Buccaneers in 1994.

**Willie Peete,** running backs; born July 14, 1937, Mesa, Ariz., lives in Tampa. Fullback Arizona 1956-59. No pro playing experience. College coach: Arizona 1960-62, 1971-82. Pro coach: Kansas City Chiefs 1983-86, Green Bay Packers 1987-91, joined Buccaneers in 1992.

**Floyd Peters,** defensive coordinator; born May 21, 1936, Council Bluffs, Iowa; lives in Tampa. Defensive lineman San Francisco State 1954-57. Defensive tackle Baltimore Colts 1958, Cleveland Browns 1959-62, Detroit Lions 1963, Philadelphia Eagles 1964-69, Washington Redskins 1970. Pro coach: Miami Dolphins 1971-73 (scout), New York Giants 1974-75, San Francisco 49ers 1976-77, Detroit Lions 1978-81, St. Louis Cardinals 1982-85, Minnesota Vikings 1986-90, joined Buccaneers in 1991.

**Turk Schonert,** quarterbacks; born January 15, 1957, Placentia, Calif., lives in Tampa. Quarterback Stanford 1976-79. Pro quarterback Cincinnati Bengals 1981-85, 1988-89, Atlanta Falcons 1986. Pro coach: Joined Buccaneers in 1992.

**George Stewart,** special teams; born December 29, 1958, Little Rock, Ark., lives in Tampa. Guard Arkansas 1977-80. No pro playing experience. College coach: Minnesota 1984-85, Notre Dame 1986-88. Pro coach: Pittsburgh Steelers 1989-91, joined Buccaneers in 1992.

**Bob Wylie,** offensive line; born February 16, 1951, Providence, R.I., lives in Tampa. Linebacker Colorado 1969-71. No pro playing experience. College coach: Brown 1980-82, Holy Cross 1983-84, Ohio University 1985-87, Colorado State 1988-89. Pro coach: New York Jets 1990-91, joined Buccaneers in 1992.

## 1994 FIRST-YEAR ROSTER

| Name | Pos. | Ht. | Wt. | Birthdate | College | Hometown | How Acq. |
|---|---|---|---|---|---|---|---|
| Allison, Joe | K | 6-0 | 185 | 1/20/71 | Memphis State | Miami, Fla. | FA |
| Bishop, Harold | TE | 6-4 | 250 | 4/8/70 | Louisiana State | Tuscaloosa, Ala. | D3 |
| Carter, Bernard | LB | 6-3 | 245 | 8/22/71 | East Carolina | Tallahassee, Fla. | D6 |
| Crisman, Joel | G | 6-5 | 290 | 2/3/71 | Southern California | Grundy Center, Iowa | FA |
| Davis, Tyree (1) | WR | 5-9 | 165 | 9/23/70 | Central Arkansas | Altheimer, Ark. | D7-'93 |
| Dilfer, Trent | QB | 6-4 | 230 | 3/13/72 | Fresno State | Aptos, Calif. | D1 |
| Ellison, Jerry | RB | 5-11 | 195 | 12/20/71 | Tenn.-Chatanooga | Augusta, Ga. | FA |
| Hadnot, Butch (1) | RB | 6-1 | 230 | 3/31/70 | Texas | Kirbyville, Tex. | FA |
| Holliday, Tommy | G | 6-3 | 280 | 11/16/69 | Southern | Baton Rouge, La. | FA |
| Holstein, Scott | P | 6-5 | 210 | 6/6/71 | Louisiana State | Baton Rouge, La. | FA |
| Mills, Vidal | S | 5-11 | 190 | 7/21/72 | Bethune-Cookman | Tampa, Fla. | FA |
| Pierson, Pete | T | 6-5 | 285 | 2/4/71 | Washington | Portland, Ore. | D5 |
| Pyne, Jim | C | 6-2 | 280 | 11/23/71 | Virginia Tech | Milford, Mass. | D7 |
| Rhett, Errict | RB | 5-11 | 210 | 12/11/70 | Florida | Pembroke Pines, Fla. | D2 |
| Saunders, Cedric | TE | 6-3 | 240 | 9/30/72 | Ohio State | Sarasota, Fla. | FA |
| Small, Eddie | WR | 6-1 | 200 | 12/9/72 | Mississippi | Jacksonville, Fla. | FA |
| Smith, Dedric | WR | 5-7 | 170 | 9/16/71 | Savannah State | Atlanta, Ga. | FA |
| Warren, Corey | WR | 5-10 | 195 | 11/9/71 | Oklahoma | Houston, Tex. | FA |
| White, Paul | CB-S | 5-9 | 185 | 11/8/71 | Miami | Tampa, Fla. | FA |
| Williams, Germaine | RB | 5-10 | 230 | 2/4/71 | Louisiana State | Donaldsonville, La. | FA |

The term NFL Rookie is defined as a player who is in his first season of professional football and has not been on the roster of another professional football team for any regular-season or postseason games. A Rookie is designated by an "R" on NFL rosters. Players who have been active in another professional football league or players who have NFL experience, including either preseason training camp or being on an Active List or Inactive List, or on Reserve/Injured or Reserve/Physically Unable to Perform for fewer than six regular-season games, are termed NFL First-Year Players. An NFL First-Year Player is designated by a "1" on NFL rosters. Thereafter, a player is credited with an additional year of experience for each season in which he accumulates six games on the Active List or Inactive List, or on Reserve/Injured or Reserve/Physically Unable to Perform.

## NOTES

# WASHINGTON REDSKINS

**National Football Conference**
**Eastern Division**
**Team Colors:** Burgundy and Gold
**Redskin Park**
**P.O. Box 17247**
**Washington, D.C. 20041**
**Telephone: (703) 478-8900**

## CLUB OFFICIALS

Chairman of the Board-CEO: Jack Kent Cooke
Executive Vice President: John Kent Cooke
House Counsel: Stuart Haney
Controller: Gregory Dillon
Board of Directors: Jack Kent Cooke, John Kent Cooke, Ralph Kent Cooke, James Lacher
General Manager: Charley Casserly
Assistant General Manager: Bobby Mitchell
Director of Pro Player Personnel: Kirk Mee
Director of College Scouting: George Saimes
Scouts: Chuck Banker, Gene Bates, Larry Bryan, Scott Cohen, Mike Hagen, Reed Johnson, Mel Kaufman, Miller McCalmon, Joe Mendes
Director of Communications: Rick Vaughn
Director of Media Relations: Mike McCall
Director of Information: John Autry
Director of Stadium Operations/Club Promotions: John Kent Cooke, Jr.
Assistant Promotions/Advertising Director: John Wagner
Video Director: Donnie Schoenmann
Asst. Video Director: Hugh McPhillips
Ticket Manager: Jeff Ritter
Head Trainer: Bubba Tyer
Assistant Trainers: Al Bellamy, Kevin Bastin
Equipment Manager: Jay Brunetti
Asst. Equipment Manager: Jeff Parsons
**Stadium:** RFK Stadium • **Capacity:** 56,454
Washington, D.C. 20003
**Playing Surface:** Grass
**Training Camp:** Dickinson College
Carlisle, Pennsylvania 17013

## 1994 SCHEDULE

**PRESEASON**

| | | |
|---|---|---|
| Aug. 8 | at Buffalo | 8:00 |
| Aug. 12 | **Kansas City** | 8:00 |
| Aug. 18 | at New England | 7:00 |
| Aug. 26 | **Pittsburgh** | 8:00 |

**REGULAR SEASON**

| | | |
|---|---|---|
| Sept. 4 | **Seattle** | 1:00 |
| Sept. 11 | at New Orleans | 3:00 |
| Sept. 18 | at New York Giants | 4:00 |
| Sept. 25 | **Atlanta** | 1:00 |
| Oct. 2 | **Dallas** | 1:00 |
| Oct. 9 | at Philadelphia | 8:00 |
| Oct. 16 | **Arizona** | 1:00 |
| Oct. 23 | at Indianapolis | 12:00 |
| Oct. 30 | **Philadelphia** | 1:00 |
| Nov. 6 | **San Francisco** | 1:00 |
| Nov. 13 | Open Date | |
| Nov. 20 | at Dallas | 12:00 |
| Nov. 27 | **New York Giants** | 4:00 |
| Dec. 4 | at Tampa Bay | 1:00 |
| Dec. 11 | at Arizona | 2:00 |
| Dec. 18 | **Tampa Bay** | 1:00 |
| Dec. 24 | at Los Angeles Rams | 1:00 |

## RECORD HOLDERS

**INDIVIDUAL RECORDS—CAREER**

| Category | Name | Performance |
|---|---|---|
| Rushing (Yds.) | John Riggins, 1976-79, 1981-85 | 7,472 |
| Passing (Yds.) | Joe Theismann, 1974-1985 | 25,206 |
| Passing (TDs) | Sammy Baugh, 1937-1952 | 187 |
| Receiving (No.) | Art Monk, 1980-1993 | *888 |
| Receiving (Yds.) | Art Monk, 1980-1993 | 12,028 |
| Interceptions | Brig Owens, 1966-1977 | 36 |
| Punting (Avg.) | Sammy Baugh, 1937-1952 | *45.1 |
| Punt Return (Avg.) | Johnny Williams, 1952-53 | 12.8 |
| Kickoff Return (Avg.) | Bobby Mitchell, 1962-68 | 28.5 |
| Field Goals | Mark Moseley, 1974-1986 | 263 |
| Touchdowns (Tot.) | Charley Taylor, 1964-1977 | 90 |
| Points | Mark Moseley, 1974-1986 | 1,206 |

**INDIVIDUAL RECORDS—SINGLE SEASON**

| Category | Name | Performance |
|---|---|---|
| Rushing (Yds.) | John Riggins, 1983 | 1,347 |
| Passing (Yds.) | Jay Schroeder, 1986 | 4,109 |
| Passing (TDs) | Sonny Jurgensen, 1967 | 31 |
| Receiving (No.) | Art Monk, 1984 | 106 |
| Receiving (Yds.) | Bobby Mitchell, 1963 | 1,436 |
| Interceptions | Dan Sandifer, 1948 | 13 |
| Punting (Avg.) | Sammy Baugh, 1940 | *51.4 |
| Punt Return (Avg.) | Johnny Williams, 1952 | 15.3 |
| Kickoff Return (Avg.) | Mike Nelms, 1981 | 29.7 |
| Field Goals | Mark Moseley, 1983 | 33 |
| Touchdowns (Tot.) | John Riggins, 1983 | *24 |
| Points | Mark Moseley, 1983 | 161 |

**INDIVIDUAL RECORDS—SINGLE GAME**

| Category | Name | Performance |
|---|---|---|
| Rushing (Yds.) | Gerald Riggs, 9-17-89 | 221 |
| Passing (Yds.) | Sammy Baugh, 10-31-43 | 446 |
| Passing (TDs) | Sammy Baugh, 10-31-43, 11-23-47 | 6 |
| | Mark Rypien, 11-10-91 | 6 |
| Receiving (No.) | Art Monk, 12-15-85 | 13 |
| | Kelvin Bryant, 12-7-86 | 13 |
| | Art Monk, 11-4-90 | 13 |
| Receiving (Yds.) | Anthony Allen, 10-4-87 | 255 |
| Interceptions | Sammy Baugh, 11-14-43 | *4 |
| | Dan Sandifer, 10-31-48 | *4 |
| Field Goals | Many times | 5 |
| | Last time by Chip Lohmiller, 10-25-92 | |
| Touchdowns (Tot.) | Dick James, 12-17-61 | 4 |
| | Larry Brown, 12-4-73 | 4 |
| Points | Dick James, 12-17-61 | 24 |
| | Larry Brown, 12-4-73 | 24 |

*NFL Record

## COACHING HISTORY

**Boston 1932-36**
**(450-377-26)**

| | | |
|---|---|---|
| 1932 | Lud Wray | 4-4-2 |
| 1933-34 | William (Lone Star) Dietz | 11-11-2 |
| 1935 | Eddie Casey | 2-8-1 |
| 1936-42 | Ray Flaherty | 56-23-3 |
| 1943 | Arthur (Dutch) Bergman | 7-4-1 |
| 1944-45 | Dudley DeGroot | 14-6-1 |
| 1946-48 | Glen (Turk) Edwards | 16-18-1 |
| 1949 | John Whelchel* | 3-3-1 |
| 1949-51 | Herman Ball** | 4-16-0 |
| 1951 | Dick Todd | 5-4-0 |
| 1952-53 | Earl (Curly) Lambeau | 10-13-1 |
| 1954-58 | Joe Kuharich | 26-32-2 |
| 1959-60 | Mike Nixon | 4-18-2 |
| 1961-65 | Bill McPeak | 21-46-3 |
| 1966-68 | Otto Graham | 17-22-3 |
| 1969 | Vince Lombardi | 7-5-2 |
| 1970 | Bill Austin | 6-8-0 |
| 1971-77 | George Allen | 69-35-1 |
| 1978-80 | Jack Pardee | 24-24-0 |
| 1981-92 | Joe Gibbs | 140-65-0 |
| 1993 | Richie Petitbon | 4-12 |

*Released after seven games in 1949
**Released after three games in 1951

**ROBERT F. KENNEDY STADIUM**

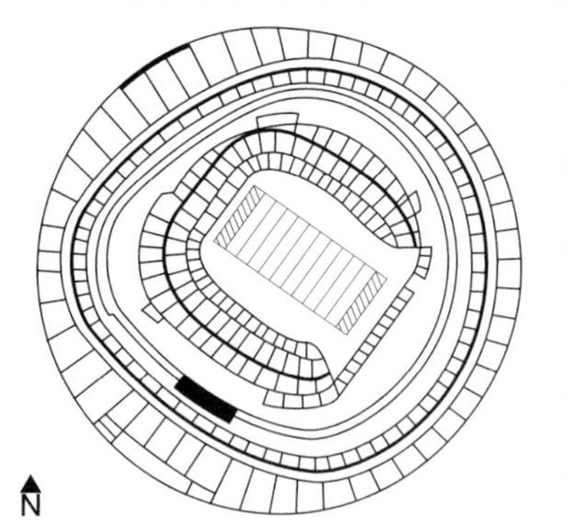

## 1993 TEAM RECORD

**PRESEASON (3-1)**

| Date | Result | | Opponents |
|---|---|---|---|
| 8/9 | W | 41-12 | Cleveland |
| 8/14 | L | 10-19 | at Miami |
| 8/22 | W | 10-3 | at Pittsburgh |
| 8/27 | W | 17-3 | N.Y. Jets |

**REGULAR SEASON (4-12)**

| Date | Result | | Opponents | Att. |
|---|---|---|---|---|
| 9/6 | W | 35-16 | Dallas | 56,345 |
| 9/12 | L | 10-17 | Phoenix | 53,525 |
| 9/19 | L | 31-34 | at Philadelphia | 65,435 |
| 10/4 | L | 10-17 | at Miami | 68,568 |
| 10/10 | L | 7-41 | N.Y. Giants | 53,715 |
| 10/17 | L | 6-36 | at Phoenix | 48,143 |
| 11/1 | L | 10-24 | at Buffalo | 79,106 |
| 11/7 | W | 30-24 | Indianapolis | 50,523 |
| 11/14 | L | 6-20 | at N.Y. Giants | 76,606 |
| 11/21 | L | 6-10 | at L.A. Rams | 45,546 |
| 11/28 | L | 14-17 | Philadelphia | 46,663 |
| 12/5 | W | 23-17 | at Tampa Bay | 49,035 |
| 12/11 | L | 0-3 | N.Y. Jets | 47,970 |
| 12/19 | W | 30-17 | Atlanta | 50,192 |
| 12/26 | L | 3-38 | at Dallas | 64,497 |
| 12/31 | L | 9-14 | Minnesota | 42,836 |

**SCORE BY PERIODS**

| | | | | | | | |
|---|---|---|---|---|---|---|---|
| Redskins | 23 | 77 | 59 | 71 | 0 | — | 230 |
| Opponents | 81 | 92 | 69 | 103 | 0 | — | 345 |

**ATTENDANCE**

Home 401,769 Away 496,936 Total 898,705
Single-game home record, 56,345 (9-6-93)
Single-season home record, 443,678 (1992)

## 1993 TEAM STATISTICS

| | Redskins | Opp. |
|---|---|---|
| Total First Downs | 255 | 304 |
| Rushing | 92 | 127 |
| Passing | 143 | 157 |
| Penalty | 20 | 20 |
| Third Down: Made/Att. | 74/213 | 92/215 |
| Third Down: Pct | 34.7 | 42.8 |
| Fourth Down: Made/Att. | 5/16 | 5/15 |
| Fourth Down: Pct | 31.3 | 33.3 |
| Total Net Yards | 4273 | 5499 |
| Avg. Per Game | 267.1 | 343.7 |
| Total Plays | 969 | 1027 |
| Avg. Per Play | 4.4 | 5.4 |
| Net Yards Rushing | 1728 | 2112 |
| Avg. Per Game | 108.0 | 132.0 |
| Total Rushes | 396 | 513 |
| Net Yards Passing | 2545 | 3387 |
| Avg. Per Game | 159.1 | 211.7 |
| Sacked/Yards Lost | 40/219 | 31/197 |
| Gross Yards | 2764 | 3584 |
| Att./Completions | 533/287 | 483/291 |
| Completion Pct. | 53.8 | 60.2 |
| Had Intercepted | 21 | 17 |
| Punts/Avg. | 83/43.9 | 73/41.0 |
| Net Punting Avg/ | 83/37.4 | 73/36.6 |
| Penalties/Yards Lost | 90/597 | 100/782 |
| Fumbles/Ball Lost | 24/10 | 25/14 |
| Touchdowns | 26 | 42 |
| Rushing | 11 | 14 |
| Passing | 11 | 24 |
| Returns | 4 | 4 |
| Avg. Time of Possession | 27:58 | 32:02 |

## 1993 INDIVIDUAL STATISTICS

| PASSING | Att. | Comp. | Yds. | Pct. | TD | Int. | Tkld. | Rate |
|---|---|---|---|---|---|---|---|---|
| Rypien | 319 | 166 | 1514 | 52.0 | 4 | 10 | 16/87 | 56.3 |
| Gannon | 125 | 74 | 704 | 59.2 | 3 | 7 | 16/87 | 59.6 |
| Conklin | 87 | 46 | 496 | 52.9 | 4 | 3 | 8/45 | 70.9 |
| Mitchell | 2 | 1 | 50 | 50.0 | 0 | 1 | 0/0 | 56.3 |
| Redskins | 533 | 287 | 2764 | 53.8 | 11 | 21 | 40/219 | 59.0 |
| Opponents | 483 | 291 | 3584 | 60.2 | 24 | 17 | 31/197 | 85.1 |

| SCORING | TD R | TD P | TD Rt | PAT | FG | Saf | PTS |
|---|---|---|---|---|---|---|---|
| Lohmiller | 0 | 0 | 0 | 24/26 | 16/28 | 0 | 72 |
| Sanders | 0 | 4 | 0 | 0/0 | 0/0 | 0 | 24 |
| Brooks | 3 | 0 | 0 | 0/0 | 0/0 | 0 | 18 |
| McGee | 0 | 3 | 0 | 0/0 | 0/0 | 0 | 18 |
| Mitchell | 3 | 0 | 0 | 0/0 | 0/0 | 0 | 18 |
| Rypien | 3 | 0 | 0 | 0/0 | 0/0 | 0 | 18 |
| Middleton | 0 | 2 | 0 | 0/0 | 0/0 | 0 | 12 |
| Monk | 0 | 2 | 0 | 0/0 | 0/0 | 0 | 12 |
| Byner | 1 | 0 | 0 | 0/0 | 0/0 | 0 | 6 |
| Coleman | 0 | 0 | 1 | 0/0 | 0/0 | 0 | 6 |
| Gannon | 1 | 0 | 0 | 0/0 | 0/0 | 0 | 6 |
| Gouveia | 0 | 0 | 1 | 0/0 | 0/0 | 0 | 6 |
| Green | 0 | 0 | 1 | 0/0 | 0/0 | 0 | 6 |
| A. Johnson | 0 | 0 | 1 | 0/0 | 0/0 | 0 | 6 |
| Redskins | 11 | 11 | 4 | 24/26 | 16/28 | 1 | 230 |
| Opponents | 14 | 24 | 4 | 40/42 | 17/22 | 1 | 345 |

| RUSHING | Att. | Yds. | Avg. | LG | TD |
|---|---|---|---|---|---|
| Brooks | 223 | 1063 | 4.8 | 85t | 3 |
| Mitchell | 63 | 246 | 3.9 | 29t | 3 |
| Ervins | 50 | 201 | 4.0 | 18 | 0 |
| Byner | 23 | 105 | 4.6 | 16 | 1 |
| Gannon | 21 | 88 | 4.2 | 12 | 1 |
| Howard | 2 | 17 | 8.5 | 9 | 0 |
| Sanders | 1 | 7 | 7.0 | 7 | 0 |
| Rypien | 9 | 4 | 0.4 | 5 | 3 |
| Roby | 1 | 0 | 0.0 | 0 | 0 |
| Monk | 1 | -1 | -1.0 | -1 | 0 |
| Conklin | 2 | -2 | -1.0 | -1 | 0 |
| Redskins | 396 | 1728 | 4.4 | 85t | 11 |
| Opponents | 513 | 2112 | 4.1 | 35 | 14 |

| RECEIVING | No. | Yds. | Avg. | LG | TD |
|---|---|---|---|---|---|
| Sanders | 58 | 638 | 11.0 | 50 | 4 |
| Monk | 41 | 398 | 9.7 | 29 | 2 |
| McGee | 39 | 500 | 12.8 | 54 | 3 |
| Byner | 27 | 194 | 7.2 | 20 | 0 |
| Middleton | 24 | 154 | 6.4 | 18 | 2 |
| Howard | 23 | 286 | 12.4 | 27 | 0 |
| Brooks | 21 | 186 | 8.9 | 43 | 0 |
| Mitchell | 20 | 157 | 7.9 | 18 | 0 |
| Ervins | 16 | 123 | 7.7 | 20 | 0 |
| Wycheck | 16 | 113 | 7.1 | 20 | 0 |
| Clifton | 2 | 15 | 7.5 | 10 | 0 |
| Redskins | 287 | 2764 | 9.6 | 54 | 11 |
| Opponents | 291 | 3584 | 12.3 | 80t | 24 |

| INTERCEPTIONS | No. | Yds. | Avg. | LG | TD |
|---|---|---|---|---|---|
| Carter | 6 | 54 | 9.0 | 29 | 0 |
| Green | 4 | 10 | 2.5 | 6 | 0 |
| Coleman | 2 | 27 | 13.5 | 14 | 0 |
| A. Johnson | 1 | 69 | 69.0 | 69t | 1 |
| Gouveia | 1 | 59 | 59.0 | 59t | 1 |
| Edwards | 1 | 17 | 17.0 | 17 | 0 |
| A. Collins | 1 | 5 | 5.0 | 5 | 0 |
| Copeland | 1 | 0 | 0.0 | 0 | 0 |
| Redskins | 17 | 241 | 14.2 | 69t | 2 |
| Opponents | 21 | 209 | 10.0 | 30 | 2 |

| PUNTING | No. | Yds. | Avg. | In 20 | LG |
|---|---|---|---|---|---|
| Roby | 78 | 3447 | 44.2 | 25 | 60 |
| Goodburn | 5 | 197 | 39.4 | 3 | 49 |
| Redskins | 83 | 3644 | 43.9 | 28 | 60 |
| Opponents | 73 | 2995 | 41.0 | 20 | 65 |

| PUNT RETURNS | No. | FC | Yds. | Avg. | LG | TD |
|---|---|---|---|---|---|---|
| Mitchell | 29 | 7 | 193 | 6.7 | 48 | 0 |
| Howard | 4 | 0 | 25 | 6.3 | 13 | 0 |
| Green | 1 | 1 | 27 | 27.0 | 24 | 0 |
| Mays | 1 | 0 | 0 | 0.0 | 0 | 0 |
| Redskins | 35 | 8 | 245 | 7.0 | 48 | 0 |
| Opponents | 34 | 23 | 343 | 10.1 | 62t | 2 |

| KICKOFF RETURNS | No. | Yds. | Avg. | LG | TD |
|---|---|---|---|---|---|
| Mitchell | 33 | 678 | 20.5 | 68 | 0 |
| Howard | 21 | 405 | 19.3 | 33 | 0 |
| Ervins | 2 | 29 | 14.5 | 18 | 0 |
| Bowles | 1 | 27 | 27.0 | 27 | 0 |
| Brooks | 1 | 12 | 12.0 | 12 | 0 |
| Buck | 1 | 15 | 15.0 | 15 | 0 |
| Redskins | 59 | 1166 | 19.8 | 68 | 0 |
| Opponents | 36 | 722 | 20.1 | 43 | 0 |

| SACKS | No. |
|---|---|
| Coleman | 6.0 |
| A. Collins | 6.0 |
| Palmer | 4.5 |
| T. Johnson | 4.0 |
| Noga | 4.0 |
| Wilson | 2.0 |
| Gouveia | 1.5 |
| Banks | 1.0 |
| Faulkner | 1.0 |
| Mann | 1.0 |
| Redskins | 31.0 |
| Opponents | 40.0 |

## 1994 DRAFT CHOICES

| Round | Name | Pos. | College |
|---|---|---|---|
| 1 | Heath Shuler | QB | Tennessee |
| 2 | Tre Johnson | T | Temple |
| 3 | Tydus Winans | WR | Fresno State |
| | Joe Patton | G | Alabama A&M |
| 4 | Kurt Haws | TE | Utah |
| 6 | Dexter Nottage | DE | Florida A&M |
| 7 | Gus Frerotte | QB | Tulsa |

# WASHINGTON REDSKINS

## 1994 VETERAN ROSTER

| No. | | Name | Pos. | Ht. | Wt. | Birthdate | NFL Exp. | College | Hometown | How Acq. | '93 Games/ Starts |
|---|---|---|---|---|---|---|---|---|---|---|---|
| 40 | | Brooks, Reggie | RB | 5-8 | 202 | 1/19/71 | 2 | Notre Dame | Tulsa, Okla. | D2-'93 | 16/11 |
| 67 | | Brown, Ray | T | 6-5 | 312 | 12/12/62 | 9 | Arkansas State | Marion, Ark. | PB(Phx)-'89 | 16/14 |
| 99 | # | Buck, Jason | DE | 6-4 | 274 | 7/27/63 | 8 | Brigham Young | St. Anthony, Idaho | FA-'91 | 13/3 |
| 25 | | Carter, Tom | CB | 5-11 | 181 | 9/5/72 | 2 | Notre Dame | St. Petersburg, Fla. | D1-'93 | 14/11 |
| 51 | # | Coleman, Monte | LB | 6-2 | 242 | 11/4/57 | 16 | Central Arkansas | Pine Bluff, Ark. | D11-'79 | 14/4 |
| 55 | | Collins, Andre | LB | 6-1 | 231 | 5/4/68 | 5 | Penn State | Cinnaminson, N.J. | D2-'90 | 13/13 |
| 91 | | Collins, Shane | DE | 6-3 | 267 | 4/11/69 | 3 | Arizona State | Bozeman, Mont. | D2-'92 | 7/5 |
| 12 | # | Conklin, Cary | QB | 6-4 | 225 | 2/29/68 | 5 | Washington | Yakima, Wash. | D4-'90 | 4/2 |
| 26 | | Copeland, Danny | S | 6-2 | 210 | 1/24/66 | 7 | Eastern Kentucky | Thomasville, Ga. | PB(KC)-'91 | 14/14 |
| 27 | | Edwards, Brad | S | 6-2 | 207 | 3/22/66 | 7 | South Carolina | Fayetteville, N.C. | PB(Minn)-'90 | 16/16 |
| 24 | | Eilers, Pat | S | 5-11 | 197 | 9/3/66 | 4 | Notre Dame | St. Paul, Minn. | FA-'93 | 11/0 |
| 64 | | Elewonibi, Moe | T | 6-4 | 286 | 12/16/65 | 5 | Brigham Young | British Columbia, Canada | D3-'90 | 15/15 |
| 85 | | Ellard, Henry | WR | 5-11 | 182 | 7/21/61 | 12 | Fresno State | Fresno, Calif. | UFA(Rams)-'94 | 16/16* |
| 52 | | Elliott, Matt | C | 6-1 | 265 | 10/1/68 | 3 | Michigan | Carmel, Ind. | D12-'92 | 0* |
| 32 | † | Ervins, Ricky | RB | 5-7 | 195 | 12/7/68 | 4 | Southern California | Pasadena, Calif. | D3-'91 | 15/1 |
| 92 | | Faulkner, Jeff | DE | 6-4 | 305 | 4/4/64 | 5 | Southern | Miami, Fla. | FA-'93 | 5/3 |
| 17 | | Friesz, John | QB | 6-4 | 218 | 5/19/67 | 5 | Idaho | Coeur D'Alene, Idaho | UFA(SD)-'94 | 12/6* |
| 16 | # | Gannon, Rich | QB | 6-3 | 208 | 12/20/65 | 8 | Delaware | Philadelphia, Pa. | T(Minn)-'93 | 8/4 |
| 75 | | Gesek, John | C | 6-5 | 282 | 2/18/63 | 8 | Cal State-Sacramento | Danville, Calif. | UFA(Dall)-'94 | 14/0* |
| 54 | | Gouveia, Kurt | LB | 6-1 | 233 | 9/14/64 | 9 | Brigham Young | Honolulu, Hawaii | D8-'86 | 16/16 |
| 90 | | Graf, Rick | LB | 6-5 | 244 | 8/29/64 | 8 | Wisconsin | Madison, Wis. | UFA(Hou)-'93 | 5/0 |
| 28 | | Green, Darrell | CB | 5-8 | 170 | 2/15/60 | 12 | Texas A&I | Houston, Tex. | D1-'83 | 16/16 |
| 56 | | Hamilton, Rick | LB | 6-2 | 241 | 4/19/70 | 2 | Central Florida | Inverness, Fla. | D3a-'93 | 16/0 |
| 57 | | Harvey, Ken | LB | 6-2 | 245 | 5/6/65 | 7 | California | Austin, Tex. | UFA(Ariz)-'94 | 16/6* |
| 86 | | Hobbs, Stephen | WR | 5-11 | 200 | 11/14/65 | 7 | North Alabama | Mendenhall, Miss. | PB(KC)-'89 | 0* |
| 96 | | Hollinquest, Lamont | LB | 6-3 | 245 | 10/24/70 | 2 | Southern California | Downey, Calif. | D8-'93 | 16/0 |
| 89 | | Horton, Ethan | TE | 6-4 | 240 | 12/19/62 | 8 | North Carolina | Kannapolis, N.C. | UFA(Raid)-'94 | 16/16* |
| 80 | | Howard, Desmond | WR | 5-9 | 180 | 5/15/70 | 3 | Michigan | Cleveland, Ohio | D1-'92 | 16/5 |
| 60 | | Huntington, Greg | C | 6-3 | 287 | 9/22/70 | 2 | Penn State | Birmingham, Ala. | D5-'93 | 9/0 |
| 88 | | Jenkins, James | TE | 6-2 | 241 | 8/17/67 | 3 | Rutgers | Staten Island, N.Y. | FA-'91 | 15/5 |
| 47 | | Johnson, AJ | CB | 5-8 | 175 | 6/22/67 | 5 | Southwest Texas State | San Antonio, Tex. | D6-'89 | 13/3 |
| 78 | | Johnson, Tim | DT | 6-3 | 275 | 1/29/65 | 8 | Penn State | Sarasota, Fla. | T(Pitt)-'90 | 15/15 |
| 79 | | Lachey, Jim | T | 6-6 | 294 | 6/4/63 | 10 | Ohio State | St. Henry, Ohio | T(Raid)-'88 | 0* |
| 8 | | Lohmiller, Chip | K | 6-3 | 215 | 7/16/66 | 7 | Minnesota | Woodbury, Minn. | D2-'88 | 16/0 |
| 59 | | Matich, Trevor | C | 6-4 | 297 | 10/9/61 | 10 | Brigham Young | Sacramento, Calif. | UFA(Ind)-'94 | 16/4* |
| 20 | | Mays, Alvoid | CB-S | 5-9 | 172 | 7/10/66 | 5 | West Virginia | Bradenton, Fla. | FA-'90 | 15/2 |
| 63 | | McKenzie, Raleigh | C-G | 6-2 | 279 | 2/8/63 | 10 | Tennessee | Knoxville, Tenn. | D11-'85 | 16/16 |
| 87 | | Middleton, Ron | TE | 6-2 | 262 | 7/17/65 | 8 | Auburn | Atmore, Ala. | PB(Clev)-'90 | 16/16 |
| 30 | # | Mitchell, Brian | RB | 5-10 | 203 | 8/18/68 | 5 | Southwestern Louisiana | Plaquemine, La. | D5-'90 | 16/4 |
| 62 | | Moore, Darryl | G | 6-2 | 292 | 1/27/69 | 3 | Texas-El Paso | Minden, La. | D8-'92 | 12/0 |
| 4 | | O'Hara, Pat | QB | 6-3 | 205 | 9/27/68 | 3 | Southern California | Santa Monica, Calif. | FA-'94 | 0* |
| 89 | # | Orr, Terry | TE | 6-2 | 235 | 9/27/61 | 10 | Texas | Savannah, Ga. | FA-'91 | 4/0 |
| 97 | | Palmer, Sterling | DE | 6-5 | 256 | 2/4/71 | 2 | Florida State | Ft. Lauderdale, Fla. | D4-'93 | 14/10 |
| 1 | | Roby, Reggie | P | 6-2 | 258 | 7/30/61 | 12 | Iowa | East Waterloo, Iowa | FA-'93 | 15/0 |
| 69 | | Schlereth, Mark | G | 6-3 | 278 | 1/25/66 | 6 | Idaho | Anchorage, Alaska | D10-'89 | 9/8 |
| 74 | | Siever, Paul | G | 6-5 | 294 | 8/10/69 | 3 | Penn State | Coatesville, Pa. | FA-'93 | 0* |
| 76 | | Simmons, Ed | T | 6-5 | 300 | 12/31/63 | 8 | Eastern Washington | Seattle, Wash. | D6-'87 | 13/13 |
| 61 | | Smith, Vernice | G | 6-3 | 298 | 10/24/65 | 5 | Florida A&M | Orlando, Fla. | FA-'93 | 14/8* |
| 84 | | Stock, Mark | WR | 6-0 | 180 | 4/27/66 | 4 | Virginia Military Institute | Atlanta, Ga. | FA-'92 | 3/0 |
| 41 | | Thomas, Johnny | CB | 5-9 | 191 | 8/3/64 | 7 | Baylor | Houston, Tex. | FA-'92 | 16/0 |
| 77 | # | Wahler, Jim | DT | 6-4 | 275 | 7/29/66 | 6 | UCLA | San Jose, Calif. | FA-'92 | 8/0 |
| 94 | † | Wilson, Bobby | DT | 6-2 | 297 | 3/4/68 | 4 | Michigan State | Chicago, Ill. | D1-'91 | 12/9 |
| 98 | | Woods, Tony | DE | 6-4 | 269 | 9/11/65 | 8 | Pittsburgh | South Orange, N.J. | UFA(Rams)-'94 | 13/7* |
| 22 | | Wycheck, Frank | RB | 6-3 | 235 | 10/14/71 | 2 | Maryland | Philadelphia, Pa. | D6b-'93 | 9/7 |

* Ellard played 16 games with L.A. Rams in '93; Elliott, Hobbs, and Lachey missed '93 season due to injury; Friesz played 12 games with San Diego; Gesek played 14 games with Dallas; Harvey played 16 games with Phoenix; Horton played 16 games with L.A. Raiders; Matich played 16 games with Indianapolis; O'Hara last active with San Diego in '92; Siever active for 1 game but did not play; V. Smith played 6 games with Chicago, 8 games with Washington; Woods played 13 games with L.A. Rams.

\# Unrestricted free agent; subject to developments.

† Restricted free agent; subject to developments.

Players lost through free agency (1): RB Earnest Byner (Clev; 16 games in '93).

Also played with Redskins in '93—LB Carl Banks (15 games), C Guy Bingham (14), C Jeff Bostic (16), S Todd Bowles (10), P Kelly Goodburn (1), G-T Joe Jacoby (5), DE Charles Mann (12), WR Tim McGee (13), WR Art Monk (16), DT Gerald Nichols (2), DE Al Noga (16), C Marc Raab (2), TE Jim Riggs (3), QB Mark Rypien (12), WR Ricky Sanders (16), DT Eric Williams (4), DE Keith Willis (1).

## COACHING STAFF

**Head Coach,**
**Norv Turner**

**Pro Career:** Enters his first seaon as head coach of the Washington Redskins after serving three years as the Dallas Cowboys' offensive coordinator. Turner guided the Cowboys' prolific offense during back-to-back Super Bowl championship seasons. He inherited a Cowboys offense that finished twenty-eighth in total offense in 1990, and a year later improved to ninth. The Cowboys finished fourth in the league offensively the past two seasons. In three seasons under Turner, quarterback Troy Aikman compiled a 91.7 rating, and running back Emmitt Smith won three consecutive NFL rushing titles. Prior to joining the Cowboys, Turner coached six seasons (1985-1990) with the Los Angeles Rams where he oversaw the passing game. Quarterback Jim Everett enjoyed his best seasons under Turner, while Willie Anderson led the NFL in yards per catch in 1989 and 1990, and Henry Ellard was the league's leading receiver in 1988.

**Background:** Turner played quarterback for three seasons at the University of Oregon (1972-74). He began his coaching career as a graduate assistant at Oregon in 1975. A year later, he moved to the University of Southern California, where he coached from 1976-1984.

**Personal:** Born May 17, 1952, in LeJeune, N.C. Turner and his wife, Nancy, live in Oakton, Va., and have three children—Scott, Stephanie, and Drew.

### ASSISTANT COACHES

**Jason Arapoff,** assistant conditioning; born July 8, 1965, Weymouth, Mass., lives in Centreville,Va. Defensive back Springfield College 1985-88. No pro playing experience. Pro coach: Joined Redskins in 1992.

**Cam Cameron,** quarterbacks; born February 6, 1961, Chapel Hill, N.C., lives in Ashburn, Va. Quarterback Indiana 1980-83. No pro playing experience. College coach: Michigan 1984-93. Pro coach: Joined Redskins in 1994.

**Russ Grimm,** tight ends; born May 2, 1959, Scottdale, Pa., lives in Fairfax, Va. Guard-center Pittsburgh 1977-80. Pro guard Washington Redskins 1981-91. Pro coach: Joined Redskins in 1992.

**Mike Haluchak,** linebackers; born November 28, 1949, Concord, Calif., lives in Ashburn, Va. Linebacker Southern California 1967-70. No pro playing experience. College coach: Southern California 1976-77, Cal State-Fullerton 1978, Pacific 1979-80, California 1981, North Carolina State 1982. Pro coach: Oakland Invaders (USFL) 1983-85, San Diego Chargers 1986-91, Cincinnati Bengals 1992-93, joined Redskins in 1994.

**Jim Hanifan,** offensive line; born September 21, 1933, Compton, Calif., lives in Ashburn, Va. Tight end California 1952-54. Pro tight end Toronto Argonauts (CFL) 1955. College coach: Glendale, Calif., J.C. 1964-66, Utah 1967-70, California 1971-72, San Diego State 1972-73. Pro coach: St. Louis Cardinals 1974-85 (head coach 1980-85), Atlanta Falcons 1987-89 (interim head coach last four games of 1989), joined Redskins in 1990.

**Ray Horton,** defensive assistant; born April 12, 1960, Tacoma, Wash., lives in Ashburn, Va. Defensive back Washington 1979-82. Pro defensive back Cincinnati Bengals 1983-88, Dallas Cowboys 1989-92. Pro coach: Joined Redskins in 1994.

**Bobby Jackson,** running backs; born February 16, 1940, Forsyth, Ga., lives in Sterling, Va. Linebacker-running back Samford (Ga.) 1959-62. No pro playing experience. College coach: Florida State 1965-69, Kansas State 1970-74, Louisville 1975-76, Tennessee 1977-82. Pro coach: Atlanta Falcons 1983-86, San Diego Chargers 1987-91, Phoenix Cardinals 1992-93, joined Redskins in 1994.

**Bob Karmelowicz,** defensive line; born July 22, 1949, New Britain, Conn., lives in Ashburn, Va. Nose tackle Bridgeport 1972. No pro playing experience. College coach: Arizona State 1974-79, Massachusetts 1979-80, Texas-El Paso 1980-81, Illinois 1982-87, Washington State 1987-89, Miami 1990-91. Pro coach: Cincinnati Bengals 1992-93, joined Redskins in 1994.

**Ron Lynn,** defensive coordinator, born December 6, 1944, Youngstown, Ohio, lives in Sterling, Va. Quarterback-defensive back Mt. Union (Ohio) 1963-65. No pro playing experience. College coach: Toledo 1966, Mt. Union (Ohio) 1967-73, Kent State 1974-76, San Jose State 1977-78, Pacific 1979, California 1980-82. Pro coach: Oakland Invaders (USFL) 1983-85, San Diego Chargers 1986-91, Cincinnati Bengals 1992-93, joined Redskins in 1994.

**Dan Riley,** conditioning; born October 19, 1949, Syracuse, N.Y., lives in Ashburn, Va. No college or pro playing experience. College coach: Army 1973-76, Penn State 1977-81. Pro coach: Joined Redskins in 1982.

**Terry Robiskie,** receivers; born November 12, 1954, New Orleans, La., lives in Clifton, Va. Running back Louisiana State 1973-76. Pro running back Oakland Raiders 1977-79, Miami Dolphins 1980-81. Pro coach: Oakland/Los Angeles Raiders 1982-1993, joined Redskins in 1994.

**Pete Rodriguez,** special teams; born July 25, 1940, Chicago, Ill., lives in Sterling, Va. Guard-linebacker Denver University 1959-60, Western State, Colo. 1961-63. No pro playing experience. College coach: Western State, Colo. 1964, Arizona 1968-69, Western Illinois 1970-73, 1979-82 (head coach), Florida State 1974-75, Iowa State 1976-78, Northern Iowa 1986. Pro coach: Michigan Panthers (USFL) 1983-84, Denver Gold (USFL) 1985, Jacksonville Bulls (USFL) 1986, Ottawa Rough Riders (CFL) 1987, Los Angeles Raiders 1988-89, Phoenix Cardinals 1990-93, joined Redskins in 1994.

**Emmitt Thomas,** defensive backs; born June 4, 1943, Angleton,Tex., lives in Reston, Va. Quarterback-wide receiver Bishop (Tex.) College 1963-65. Pro defensive back Kansas City Chiefs 1966-78. College coach: Central Missouri State 1979-80. Pro coach: St. Louis Cardinals 1981-85, joined Redskins in 1986.

## 1994 FIRST-YEAR ROSTER

| Name | Pos. | Ht. | Wt. | Birthdate | College | Hometown | How Acq. |
|---|---|---|---|---|---|---|---|
| Bell, William | RB | 5-11 | 203 | 7/22/71 | Georgia Tech | Miami, Fla. | FA |
| Clifton, Gregory (1) | WR | 5-11 | 175 | 2/6/68 | Johnson C. Smith | Charlotte, N.C. | FA |
| Cruz, Rick | LB | 6-4 | 250 | 10/16/69 | Portland State | Bakersfield, Calif. | FA |
| Dingle, Nate | LB | 6-3 | 254 | 7/23/71 | Cincinnati | Well, Maine | FA |
| Domingos, Steven | P-K | 6-4 | 205 | 4/15/67 | San Francisco State | Visalia, Calif. | FA |
| Duckett, Tico (1) | RB | 5-10 | 195 | 2/4/70 | Michigan State | Kalamazoo, Mich. | FA |
| Earle, Guy (1) | T | 6-4 | 290 | 4/1/68 | Chadron State | Keyport, N.J. | FA |
| Floyd, Gonzalo | LB | 6-3 | 233 | 9/2/71 | Texas-El Paso | Orange Park, Fla. | FA |
| Frerotte, Gus | QB | 6-2 | 221 | 7/31/71 | Tulsa | Ford Cliff, Pa. | D7 |
| Hall, Chris (1) | S | 6-2 | 184 | 4/25/70 | East Carolina | Pemberton, N.J. | FA |
| Haws, Kurt | TE | 6-5 | 248 | 9/25/69 | Utah | Mesa, Ariz. | D4 |
| Hinchcliff, Willie (1) | WR | 6-0 | 195 | 9/13/69 | Auckland Institute | Auckland, New Zealand | FA |
| Hochertz, Martin (1) | DE | 6-5 | 269 | 10/21/68 | Southern Illinois | Cary, Ill. | FA |
| Johnson, Tre | T | 6-2 | 315 | 8/30/71 | Temple | Peekskill, N.Y. | D2 |
| Lawrence, Tyler | LB | 6-4 | 248 | 2/7/70 | North Carolina State | Greensboro, N.C. | FA |
| Mills, Lamar | DE | 6-5 | 270 | 1/26/71 | Indiana | Detroit, Mich. | FA |
| Morrison, Darryl (1) | CB | 5-11 | 185 | 5/19/71 | Arizona | Phoenix, Ariz. | D6a-'93 |
| Nottage, Dexter | DE | 6-4 | 273 | 11/14/70 | Florida A&M | Miami, Fla. | D6 |
| Olobia, Austin (1) | WR | 5-11 | 195 | 7/18/69 | Washington State | Belgin, Nigeria | FA |
| Owens, Dondre | CB | 5-9 | 170 | 7/10/72 | Howard | Lanham, Md. | FA |
| Patton, Joe | G | 6-5 | 288 | 1/5/72 | Alabama A&M | Birmingham, Ala. | D3b |
| Rowe, Ray (1) | TE | 6-2 | 256 | 7/28/69 | San Diego State | San Diego, Calif. | D6-'92 |
| Rush, Tyrone | RB | 5-11 | 196 | 2/5/71 | North Alabama | Philadelphia, Miss. | FA |
| Satterfield, Brian | RB | 6-0 | 204 | 12/22/69 | North Alabama | Blue Ridge, Ga. | FA |
| Shuler, Heath | QB | 6-2 | 221 | 12/31/71 | Tennessee | Bryson City, N.C. | D1 |
| Simmons, Jason | DE | 6-5 | 250 | 12/20/70 | Ohio State | Akron, Ohio | FA |
| Williams, Keith | WR | 5-10 | 177 | 6/18/71 | San Diego State | Lodi, Calif. | FA |
| Wilson, Pierre | DT | 6-4 | 310 | 5/5/71 | Clemson | Jackson, Miss. | FA |
| Winans, Tydus | WR | 5-11 | 180 | 7/26/72 | Fresno State | Los Angeles, Calif. | D6b |
| Wright, Damon | WR | 5-9 | 159 | 10/30/71 | Carson-Newman | High Springs, Fla. | FA |

The term NFL Rookie is defined as a player who is in his first season of professional football and has not been on the roster of another professional football team for any regular-season or postseason games. A Rookie is designated by an "R" on NFL rosters. Players who have been active in another professional football league or players who have NFL experience, including either preseason training camp or being on an Active List or Inactive List, or on Reserve/Injured or Reserve/Physically Unable to Perform for fewer than six regular-season games, are termed NFL First-Year Players. An NFL First-Year Player is designated by a "1" on NFL rosters. Thereafter, a player is credited with an additional year of experience for each season in which he accumulates six games on the Active List or Inactive List, or on Reserve/Injured or Reserve/Physically Unable to Perform.

## NOTES

# 1993 Season in Review

## TRADES

### 1993 INTERCONFERENCE TRADES

San Francisco's eighth-round selection in 1993 from San Francisco to San Diego for the Chargers' sixth-round selection in 1994. (4/26)

Quarterback **Hugh Millen** from New England to Dallas for the Cowboys' seventh-round selection in 1994. (4/28)

Linebacker **Chris Martin** from Kansas City to the Los Angeles Rams for the Rams' seventh-round selection in 1994. (5/7)

Wide receiver **Mervyn Fernandez** from the Los Angeles Raiders to San Francisco for the 49ers' fourth-round selection in 1994. (5/10)

Tackle **Rick Trumbull** from Cleveland to Tampa Bay for past consideration. (6/1)

Running back **Eric Dickerson** from the Los Angeles Raiders to Atlanta for the Falcons' sixth-round selection in 1994. (7/9)

Guard **Gene Williams** from Miami to Cleveland for the Browns' fifth-round selection in 1994. (7/14)

Defensive back **Rickey Dixon** from Cincinnati to the Los Angeles Raiders for the Raiders' seventh-round selection in 1994. (7/16)

Guard **Dan Fike** from Cleveland to Green Bay for the Packers' seventh-round selection in 1994. (8/5)

Guard **Doug Widell** from Denver to Green Bay for the Packers' seventh-round selection in 1994. (8/24)

Tackle **Gary Zimmerman** from Minnesota to Denver for the Broncos' first- and sixth-round selections in 1994 and the Broncos' second-round selection in 1995. (8/24)

Wide receiver **Vance Johnson** from Denver to Minnesota for the Vikings' seventh-round selection in 1994. (8/24)

Wide receiver **Sam Graddy** from the Los Angeles Raiders to the Los Angeles Rams for the Rams' sixth-round selection in 1995. (8/24)

Running back **Barry Word** from Kansas City to Minnesota for the Vikings' fifth-round selection in 1994. (8/30)

Defensive back **Elvis Patterson** and the Raiders' seventh-round selection in 1994 from the Los Angeles Raiders to Dallas for the Cowboys' fifth-round selection in 1994. (10/13)

Running back **Tim Worley** from Pittsburgh to Chicago for the Bears' fifth-round selection in 1994 and the Dallas Cowboys' sixth-round selection in 1995. (10/19)

### 1994 INTERCONFERENCE TRADES

Defensive back **James Williams** from Buffalo to Phoenix for the Cardinals' best fourth-round selection in 1995. (3/9)

Wide receiver **Nate Lewis** from San Diego to the Los Angeles Rams for the Rams' fourth-round selection in 1995. (3/18)

Tight end **Adrian Cooper** from Pittsburgh to Minnesota for the Vikings' third- and sixth-round selections in 1994. (3/21)

Quarterback **Jeff George** from Indianapolis to Atlanta for the Falcons' first- (seventh selection in round one) and third-round (seventh selection in round three) selections in 1994 and the Falcons' second-round selection in 1996. (3/24)

Defensive end **Burt Grossman** from San Diego to Philadelphia for the Eagles' sixth-round selection in 1995. (4/7)

Defensive back **Marquez Pope** from San Diego to the Los Angeles Rams for the Rams' sixth-round selection in 1995. (4/11)

Quarterback **Warren Moon** from Houston to Minnesota for the Vikings' fourth-round selection in 1994. (4/18)

Defensive back **Ben Smith** from Philadelphia to Denver for the Broncos' third-round selection in 1995. (4/18)

Defensive tackle **Ted Washington** and Dallas's third-round selection in 1994 from San Francisco to Denver for the Broncos' third-and fifth-round selections in 1994. (4/20)

Los Angeles Rams' first-round selection in 1994 to Indianapolis for the Colts' first-round choice from Atlanta and third-round compensatory selection from Atlanta in 1994. Indianapolis selected linebacker **Trev Alberts** (Nebraska). The Los Angeles Rams selected running back **James Bostic** (Auburn). (4/24)

New Orleans' first-round selection in 1994 to the New York Jets for the Jets' first- and fifth-round selections in 1994. New York selected defensive back **Aaron Glenn** (Texas A&M). New Orleans selected defensive end **Joe Johnson** (Louisville) and guard **Craig Novitsky** (UCLA). (4/24)

Miami's first-round selection in 1994 to Green Bay for the Packers' first- and third-round selections in 1994. Green Bay selected tackle **Aaron Taylor** (Notre Dame). Miami selected defensive tackle **Tim Bowens** (Mississippi). (4/24)

Philadelphia's compensatory first-round selection in 1994 to Cleveland for the Browns' second-round selection in 1994 and second-round selection in 1995. Cleveland selected wide receiver **Derrick Alexander** (Michigan). (4/24)

The Los Angeles Raiders' second- and fourth-round selections in 1994 to Minnesota for the Vikings' second-round selection in 1994. Los Angeles selected defensive end **James Folston** (Northeast Louisiana). Minnesota selected defensive end **Fernando Smith** (Jackson State) and defensive tackle **Mike Wells** (Iowa). (4/24)

Denver's third-round selection from Dallas in 1994 and first-round selection in 1995 to Atlanta for Falcons' wide receiver **Mike Pritchard** and Atlanta's seventh-round selection in 1995. Atlanta selected guard **Alai Kalaniuvalu** (Oregon State). (4/24)

Arizona's second-round compensatory selection in 1994 to Miami for the Dolphins' third-round selection from Green Bay, fourth-round selection from San Diego, and Miami's fourth-round selection in 1994. Miami selected center **Tim Ruddy** (Notre Dame). Arizona selected defensive end **Eric England** (Texas A&M), linebacker **Terry Irving** (McNeese State), and defensive back **Perry Carter** (Southern Mississippi). (4/24)

New England's fourth-round selection in 1994 to Arizona for the Cardinals' fourth-round selection from Miami and fifth-round selection from the Los Angeles Rams in 1994. Arizona selected defensive back **Perry Carter** (Southern Mississippi). New England selected tight end **John Burke** (Virginia Tech) and punter **Pat O'Neill** (Syracuse). (4/25)

Green Bay's fourth-round selection in 1994 to the Los Angeles Raiders for the Raiders' fourth-round selection from San Francisco and sixth-round selection from Atlanta. The Raiders selected defensive tackle **Austin Robbins** (North Carolina). Green Bay selected defensive end **Gabe Wilkins** (Gardner-Webb) and wide receiver **Jay Kearney** (West Virginia). (4/25)

The New York Giants' seventh-round selection in 1994 to Denver for Broncos' wide receiver **Arthur Marshall**. The Broncos selected center **Tom Nalen** (Boston College). (4/25)

San Francisco's seventh-round selection through Dallas in 1994 to the Los Angeles Raiders for past consideration. The Raiders selected linebacker **Rob Holmberg** (Penn State). (4/25)

### 1993 AFC TRADES

Defensive tackle **George Williams** from Cleveland to New England for linebacker **Rob McGovern**. (8/16)

Wide receiver **David Daniels** from Seattle to the New York Jets for the Jets' seventh-round selection in 1994. (8/23)

Tight end **David Jones** from the Los Angeles Raiders to Cleveland for past consideration. (8/24)

Running back **Jon Vaughn** from New England to Seattle for the Seahawks' sixth-round selection in 1994. (8/26)

Guard **Rich Baldinger** from Kansas City to New England for Dallas' seventh-round selection in 1994. (8/30)

### 1994 AFC TRADES

Defensive back **Donald Frank** from San Diego to Cleveland for the Browns' sixth-round selection in 1995. (3/4)

Wide receiver **Tony Martin** from Miami to San Diego for the Chargers' fourth-round selection in 1994. (3/24)

New England's third- and fifth-round selections in 1994 to San Diego for the Chargers' third-round selection and running back **Marion Butts**. San Diego selected wide receiver **Andre Coleman** (Kansas State) and tight end **Aaron Laing** (New Mexico State). New England selected defensive tackle **Ervin Collier** (Florida A&M). (4/25)

The New York Jets' third-round selection in 1994 to the Los Angeles Raiders for the Raiders' third- and fifth-round selections in 1994. The Raiders selected running back **Calvin Jones** (Nebraska). The Jets selected defensive tackle **Lou Benfatti** (Penn State) and linebacker **Horace Morris** (Tennessee). (4/25)

Seattle's fifth-round selection in 1994 to San Diego for the Chargers' fourth-round selection in 1995. The Chargers selected defensive end **Darren Krein** (Miami). (4/25)

### 1993 NFC TRADES

Defensive end **Lester Archambeau** from Green Bay to Atlanta for wide receiver **James Milling**. (6/3)

Defensive back **Chris Crooms** from the Los Angeles Rams to Green Bay for the Packers' fifth-round selection in 1994. (8/11)

Tackle **Stan Thomas** from Chicago to Atlanta for the Falcons' fifth-round selection in 1994. (8/17)

Tight end **Kelly Blackwell**, defensive back **Markus Paul**, and linebacker **John Roper** from Chicago to Dallas for linebackers **Barry Minter** and **Vinson Smith** and the Cowboys' sixth-round selection in 1995. (8/17)

Quarterback **Rich Gannon** from Minnesota to Washington for the Redskins' fifth-round selection in 1994. (8/20)

Wide receiver **Ernie Jones** from Phoenix to the Los Angeles Rams for the Rams' fifth-round selection in 1994. (8/26)

Punter **Tim Kalal** from Atlanta to Green Bay for New England's seventh-round selection in 1994, if available. (8/30)

Tight end **Jim Price** from the Los Angeles Rams to Dallas for the Cowboys' sixth-round pick in 1994. (10/5)

Defensive back **Bruce Pickens** from Atlanta to Green Bay for New England's seventh-round pick in 1994, if available. (10/12)

Running back **Eric Dickerson** from Atlanta to Green Bay for running back **John Stephens**. (10/12)

### 1994 NFC TRADES

Quarterback **Jim Everett** from the Los Angeles Rams to New Orleans for the Saints' seventh-round selection in 1995. (3/18)

Defensive back **Thomas Everett** from Dallas to Tampa Bay for the Buccaneers' fourth-round selection in 1994. (4/5)

Linebacker **Bill Romanowski** from San Francisco to Philadelphia for the Eagles' third-round compensatory selection and sixth-round compensatory selection in 1994. (4/24)

The Los Angeles Rams' first-round selection from Atlanta in 1994 to San Francisco for the 49ers' first-round selection from San Diego, second-round selection, and third-round compensatory selection from Philadelphia in 1994. San Francisco selected defensive tackle **Bryant Young** (Notre Dame). Los Angeles selected tackle **Wayne Gandy** (Auburn), defensive tackle **Brad Ottis** (Wayne State), and linebacker **Ernest Jones** (Oregon). (4/24)

San Francisco's first- and seventh-round selections in 1994 to Dallas for the Cowboys' first- and second-round selections in 1994. Dallas selected defensive end **Shante Carver** (Arizona State). San Francisco selected running back **William Floyd** (Florida State) and defensive back **Tyronne Drakeford** (Virginia Tech). (4/24)

Green Bay's second-round selection in 1994 to San Francisco for the 49ers' third-round compensatory selection, fifth-round selection from Denver, sixth-round selection from San Diego, and sixth-round compensatory selection from Philadelphia in 1994. San Francisco selected linebacker **Kevin Mitchell** (Syracuse). Green Bay selected running back **LeShon Johnson** (Northern Illinois), running back **Dorsey Levens** (Georgia Tech), linebacker **Ruffin Hamilton** (Tulane), and linebacker **Paul Duckworth** (Connecticut). (4/24)

Philadelphia's second-round selection from Cleveland and fourth-round selection in 1994 to Atlanta for the Falcons' second-round selection in 1994. Philadelphia selected defensive tackle **Bruce Walker** (UCLA). Atlanta selected linebacker **Mitch Davis** (Georgia). (4/24)

Defensive end **Chris Doleman** from Minnesota with the Vikings' second-round compensatory selection in 1994 to Atlanta for the Falcons' second-round selection from Cleveland in 1994 and first-round selection in 1995. Minnesota selected wide receiver **David Palmer** (Alabama). Atlanta selected wide receiver **Bert Emanuel** (Rice). (4/24)

The Los Angeles Rams' sixth-round compensatory selection in 1994 to Dallas for the Cowboys' fourth-round selection in 1995. The Cowboys selected defensive back **Darren Studstill** (West Virginia). (4/25)

## FINAL STANDINGS

### AMERICAN FOOTBALL CONFERENCE

| Eastern Division | W | L | T | Pct. | Pts. | OP |
|---|---|---|---|---|---|---|
| Miami | 3 | 1 | 0 | .750 | 94 | 88 |
| Indianapolis | 2 | 2 | 0 | .500 | 51 | 85 |
| Buffalo*** | 2 | 3 | 0 | .400 | 72 | 89 |
| New England | 1 | 3 | 0 | .250 | 57 | 69 |
| N.Y. Jets | 0 | 4 | 0 | .000 | 42 | 72 |
| **Central Division** | | | | | | |
| Cincinnati | 2 | 2 | 0 | .500 | 70 | 67 |
| Cleveland | 2 | 2 | 0 | .500 | 65 | 83 |
| Pittsburgh++ | 2 | 3 | 0 | .400 | 70 | 91 |
| Houston | 1 | 3 | 0 | .250 | 81 | 101 |
| **Western Division** | | | | | | |
| Kansas City | 3 | 1 | 0 | .750 | 90 | 91 |
| San Diego | 3 | 1 | 0 | .750 | 60 | 57 |
| Denver | 2 | 2 | 0 | .500 | 79 | 81 |
| Seattle | 2 | 2 | 0 | .500 | 73 | 49 |
| L.A. Raiders* | 2 | 3 | 0 | .400 | 53 | 80 |

### NATIONAL FOOTBALL CONFERENCE

| Eastern Division | W | L | T | Pct. | Pts. | OP |
|---|---|---|---|---|---|---|
| Phoenix | 3 | 1 | 0 | .750 | 72 | 42 |
| Washington | 3 | 1 | 0 | .750 | 78 | 37 |
| Philadelphia+ | 3 | 2 | 0 | .600 | 93 | 93 |
| N.Y. Giants | 2 | 2 | 0 | .500 | 75 | 75 |
| Dallas** | 1 | 3 | 1 | .300 | 74 | 79 |
| **Central Division** | | | | | | |
| Detroit** | 4 | 0 | 1 | .900 | 98 | 63 |
| Minnesota*** | 4 | 1 | 0 | .800 | 106 | 63 |
| Tampa Bay | 2 | 2 | 0 | .500 | 72 | 75 |
| Chicago | 1 | 3 | 0 | .250 | 56 | 65 |
| Green Bay* | 1 | 4 | 0 | .200 | 99 | 106 |
| **Western Division** | | | | | | |
| New Orleans+ | 4 | 1 | 0 | .800 | 127 | 92 |
| San Francisco++ | 4 | 1 | 0 | .800 | 94 | 71 |
| Atlanta | 1 | 3 | 0 | .250 | 83 | 92 |
| L.A. Rams | 0 | 4 | 0 | .000 | 59 | 88 |

** includes Hall of Fame Game*
*** includes American Bowl '93 in London*
**** includes American Bowl '93 in Berlin*
*+ includes American Bowl '93 in Tokyo*
*++ includes American Bowl '93 in Barcelona*

## AFC PRESEASON RECORDS—TEAM BY TEAM

**BUFFALO (2-3)**

| | | |
|---|---|---|
| 16 | *N.Y. Giants | 27 |
| 7 | Detroit | 14 |
| 6 | Minnesota (ABBe) | 20 |
| 30 | Kansas City | 7 |
| 12 | Tampa Bay (ORL) | 32 |
| 17 | *Atlanta | 16 |
| **72** | | **89** |

**CINCINNATI (2-2)**

| | | |
|---|---|---|
| 16 | *N.Y. Giants | 27 |
| 24 | Indianapolis | 7 |
| 7 | Detroit | 30 |
| 23 | *Philadelphia | 3 |
| **70** | | **67** |

**CLEVELAND (2-2)**

| | | |
|---|---|---|
| 12 | Washington | 41 |
| 12 | New England (TOR) | 9 |
| 21 | *L.A. Rams | 10 |
| 20 | Tampa Bay | 23 |
| **65** | | **83** |

**DENVER (2-2)**

| | | |
|---|---|---|
| 23 | Tampa Bay | 7 |
| 13 | *San Francisco | 16 |
| 34 | *Miami | 24 |
| 9 | Phoenix | 34 |
| **79** | | **81** |

**HOUSTON (1-3)**

| | | |
|---|---|---|
| 28 | New Orleans (SA) | 37 |
| 20 | *Detroit | 24 |
| 23 | Dallas (SA) | 20 |
| 10 | *Seattle | 20 |
| **81** | | **101** |

**INDIANAPOLIS (2-2)**

| | | |
|---|---|---|
| 16 | Seattle | 13 |
| 7 | *Cincinnati | 24 |
| 18 | *L.A. Raiders | 7 |
| 10 | Green Bay | 41 |
| **51** | | **85** |

**KANSAS CITY (3-1)**

| | | |
|---|---|---|
| 29 | Green Bay (MIL) | 21 |
| 7 | *Buffalo | 30 |
| 27 | *Minnesota | 20 |
| 27 | New England | 20 |
| **90** | | **91** |

**L.A. RAIDERS (2-3)**

| | | |
|---|---|---|
| 19 | Green Bay (HOF) | 3 |
| 0 | San Fran. (PAL) | 27 |
| 7 | Dallas | 13 |
| 7 | Indianapolis | 18 |
| 20 | L.A. Rams | 19 |
| **53** | | **80** |

**MIAMI (3-1)**

| | | |
|---|---|---|
| 28 | Atlanta | 27 |
| 19 | *Washington | 10 |
| 24 | Denver | 34 |
| 23 | *N.Y. Giants | 17 |
| **94** | | **88** |

**NEW ENGLAND (1-3)**

| | | |
|---|---|---|
| 7 | San Diego | 13 |
| 9 | Cleveland (TOR) | 12 |
| 21 | *Green Bay | 17 |
| 20 | *Kansas City | 27 |
| **57** | | **69** |

**N.Y. JETS (0-4)**

| | | |
|---|---|---|
| 13 | Pittsburgh | 17 |
| 13 | *Philadelphia | 24 |
| 13 | N.Y. Giants | 14 |
| 3 | Washington | 17 |
| **42** | | **72** |

**PITTSBURGH (2-3)**

| | | |
|---|---|---|
| 14 | San Fran. (ABBa) | 21 |
| 17 | *N.Y. Jets | 13 |
| 23 | N.Y. Giants | 17 |
| 3 | *Washington | 10 |
| 13 | Minnesota | 30 |
| **70** | | **91** |

**SAN DIEGO (3-1)**

| | | |
|---|---|---|
| 13 | *New England | 7 |
| 23 | L.A. Rams | 17 |
| 10 | *Phoenix | 3 |
| 14 | San Francisco | 30 |
| **60** | | **57** |

**SEATTLE (2-2)**

| | | |
|---|---|---|
| 13 | *Indianapolis | 16 |
| 10 | Minnesota | 23 |
| 30 | *San Francisco | 0 |
| 20 | Houston | 10 |
| **73** | | **49** |

## NFC PRESEASON RECORDS—TEAM BY TEAM

**ATLANTA (1-3)**

| | | |
|---|---|---|
| 27 | *Miami | 28 |
| 20 | *Tampa Bay | 10 |
| 20 | Philadelphia | 37 |
| 16 | Buffalo | 17 |
| **83** | | **92** |

**CHICAGO (1-3)**

| | | |
|---|---|---|
| 9 | Philadelphia | 13 |
| 10 | *Phoenix | 11 |
| 14 | New Orleans | 20 |
| 23 | *Dallas | 21 |
| **56** | | **65** |

**DALLAS (1-3-1)**

| | | |
|---|---|---|
| 7 | *Minnesota | 13 |
| 13 | Detroit (ABL)(OT) | 13 |
| 13 | *L.A. Raiders | 7 |
| 20 | Houston (SA) | 23 |
| 21 | Chicago | 23 |
| **74** | | **79** |

**DETROIT (4-0-1)**

| | | |
|---|---|---|
| 14 | *Buffalo | 7 |
| 13 | Dallas (ABL)(OT) | 13 |
| 24 | Houston | 20 |
| 30 | *Cincinnati | 7 |
| 17 | New Orleans | 16 |
| **98** | | **63** |

**GREEN BAY (1-4)**

| | | |
|---|---|---|
| 3 | L.A. Raid. (HOF) | 19 |
| 21 | Kansas City (MIL) | 29 |
| 17 | N.O. (MAD) | 26 |
| 17 | New England | 21 |
| 41 | *Indianapolis | 10 |
| **99** | | **106** |

**L.A. RAMS (0-4)**

| | | |
|---|---|---|
| 13 | Phoenix | 24 |
| 17 | *San Diego | 23 |
| 10 | Cleveland | 21 |
| 19 | *L.A. Raiders | 20 |
| **59** | | **88** |

**MINNESOTA (4-1)**

| | | |
|---|---|---|
| 13 | Dallas | 7 |
| 20 | Buffalo (ABBe) | 6 |
| 23 | *Seattle | 10 |
| 20 | Kansas City | 27 |
| 30 | *Pittsburgh | 13 |
| **106** | | **63** |

**NEW ORLEANS (4-1)**

| | | |
|---|---|---|
| 28 | Phil. (ABT) | 16 |
| 37 | Houston (SA) | 28 |
| 26 | Green Bay (MAD) | 17 |
| 20 | *Chicago | 14 |
| 16 | *Detroit | 17 |
| **127** | | **92** |

**N.Y. GIANTS (2-2)**

| | | |
|---|---|---|
| 27 | Cincinnati | 16 |
| 17 | *Pittsburgh | 23 |
| 14 | *N.Y. Jets | 13 |
| 17 | Miami | 23 |
| **75** | | **75** |

**PHILADELPHIA (3-2)**

| | | |
|---|---|---|
| 16 | N.O. (ABT) | 28 |
| 13 | *Chicago | 9 |
| 24 | N.Y. Jets | 13 |
| 37 | *Atlanta | 20 |
| 3 | Cincinnati | 23 |
| **93** | | **93** |

**PHOENIX (3-1)**

| | | |
|---|---|---|
| 24 | *L.A. Rams | 13 |
| 11 | Chicago | 10 |
| 3 | San Diego | 10 |
| 34 | *Denver | 9 |
| **72** | | **42** |

**SAN FRANCISCO (4-1)**

| | | |
|---|---|---|
| 21 | Pitts. (ABBa) | 14 |
| 27 | Raiders (PAL) | 0 |
| 16 | Denver | 13 |
| 0 | Seattle | 30 |
| 30 | *San Diego | 14 |
| **94** | | **71** |

**TAMPA BAY (2-2)**

| | | |
|---|---|---|
| 7 | *Denver | 23 |
| 10 | Atlanta | 20 |
| 32 | Buffalo (ORL) | 12 |
| 23 | *Cleveland | 20 |
| **72** | | **75** |

**WASHINGTON (3-1)**

| | | |
|---|---|---|
| 41 | *Cleveland | 12 |
| 10 | Miami | 19 |
| 10 | Pittsburgh | 3 |
| 17 | *N.Y. Jets | 3 |
| **78** | | **37** |

*denotes home game
(OT) denotes overtime
(HOF) denotes Hall of Fame Game
(ABBa) denotes American Bowl '93 in Barcelona
(ABBe) denotes American Bowl '93 in Berlin
(ABL) denotes American Bowl '93 in London
(ABT) denotes American Bowl '93 in Tokyo
(MAD) denotes game played in Madison, Wis.
(MIL) denotes game played in Milwaukee, Wis.
(ORL) denotes game played in Orlando, Fla.
(PAL) denotes game played in Palo Alto, Calif.
(SA) denotes game played in San Antonio, Tex.
(TOR) denotes game played in Toronto, Canada

# 1993 NFL STANDINGS/RESULTS

## FINAL STANDINGS

### AMERICAN FOOTBALL CONFERENCE

| Eastern Division | W | L | T | Pct. | Pts. | OP |
|---|---|---|---|---|---|---|
| Buffalo | 12 | 4 | 0 | .750 | 329 | 242 |
| Miami | 9 | 7 | 0 | .563 | 349 | 351 |
| N.Y Jets | 8 | 8 | 0 | .500 | 270 | 247 |
| New England | 5 | 11 | 0 | .313 | 238 | 286 |
| Indianapolis | 4 | 12 | 0 | .250 | 189 | 378 |
| **Central Division** | | | | | | |
| Houston | 12 | 4 | 0 | .750 | 368 | 238 |
| *Pittsburgh | 9 | 7 | 0 | .563 | 308 | 281 |
| Cleveland | 7 | 9 | 0 | .438 | 304 | 307 |
| Cincinnati | 3 | 13 | 0 | .188 | 187 | 319 |
| **Western Division** | | | | | | |
| Kansas City | 11 | 5 | 0 | .688 | 328 | 291 |
| *L.A. Raiders | 10 | 6 | 0 | .625 | 306 | 326 |
| *Denver | 9 | 7 | 0 | .563 | 373 | 284 |
| San Diego | 8 | 8 | 0 | .500 | 322 | 290 |
| Seattle | 6 | 10 | 0 | .375 | 280 | 314 |

### NATIONAL FOOTBALL CONFERENCE

| Eastern Division | W | L | T | Pct. | Pts. | OP |
|---|---|---|---|---|---|---|
| Dallas | 12 | 4 | 0 | .750 | 376 | 229 |
| *N.Y. Giants | 11 | 5 | 0 | .688 | 288 | 205 |
| Philadelphia | 8 | 8 | 0 | .500 | 293 | 315 |
| Phoenix | 7 | 9 | 0 | .438 | 326 | 269 |
| Washington | 4 | 12 | 0 | .250 | 230 | 345 |
| **Central Division** | | | | | | |
| Detroit | 10 | 6 | 0 | .625 | 298 | 292 |
| *Minnesota | 9 | 7 | 0 | .563 | 277 | 290 |
| *Green Bay | 9 | 7 | 0 | .563 | 340 | 282 |
| Chicago | 7 | 9 | 0 | .438 | 234 | 230 |
| Tampa Bay | 5 | 11 | 0 | .313 | 237 | 376 |
| **Western Division** | | | | | | |
| San Francisco | 10 | 6 | 0 | .625 | 473 | 295 |
| New Orleans | 8 | 8 | 0 | .500 | 317 | 343 |
| Atlanta | 6 | 10 | 0 | .375 | 316 | 385 |
| L.A. Rams | 5 | 11 | 0 | .313 | 221 | 367 |

**Wild-Card qualifier for playoffs*
*Minnesota finished ahead of Green Bay based on a head-to-head sweep (2-0)*

**WILD CARD PLAYOFFS**
**AFC**
Kansas City 27, Pittsburgh 24 (OT), January 8, at Kansas City
Los Angeles Raiders 42, Denver 24, January 9, at Los Angeles
**NFC**
Green Bay 28, Detroit 24, January 8, at Detroit
New York Giants 17, Minnesota 10, January 9, at New York

**DIVISIONAL PLAYOFFS**
**AFC**
Buffalo 29, Los Angeles Raiders 23, January 15, at Buffalo
Kansas City 28, Houston 20, January 16, at Houston
**NFC**
San Francisco 44, New York Giants 3, January 15, at San Francisco
Dallas 27, Green Bay 17, January 16, at Dallas

**CHAMPIONSHIP GAMES**
**AFC**
Buffalo 30, Kansas City 13, January 23, at Buffalo
**NFC**
Dallas 38, San Francisco 21, January 23, at Dallas

**SUPER BOWL XXVIII**
Dallas 30, Buffalo 13, January 30, at Georgia Dome, Atlanta, Georgia

**AFC-NFC PRO BOWL**
NFC 17, AFC 3, February 6, at Aloha Stadium, Honolulu, Hawaii

## AFC SEASON RECORDS—TEAM BY TEAM

**BUFFALO (12-4)**

| | | |
|---|---|---|
| 38 | * New England | 14 |
| 13 | at Dallas | 10 |
| | OPEN DATE | |
| 13 | * Miami | 22 |
| 17 | * N.Y. Giants | 14 |
| 35 | * Houston | 7 |
| | OPEN DATE | |
| 19 | at N.Y. Jets | 10 |
| 24 | * Washington | 10 |
| 13 | at New Eng. (OT) | 10 |
| 0 | at Pittsburgh | 23 |
| 23 | * Indianapolis | 9 |
| 7 | at Kansas City | 23 |
| 24 | * L.A. Raiders | 25 |
| 10 | at Philadelphia | 7 |
| 47 | at Miami | 34 |
| 16 | * N.Y. Jets | 14 |
| 30 | at Indianapolis | 10 |
| 329 | | 242 |

**HOUSTON (12-4)**

| | | |
|---|---|---|
| 21 | at New Orleans | 33 |
| 30 | * Kansas City | 0 |
| 17 | at San Diego | 18 |
| 13 | * L.A. Rams | 28 |
| | OPEN DATE | |
| 7 | at Buffalo | 35 |
| 28 | at New England | 14 |
| 28 | * Cincinnati | 12 |
| | OPEN DATE | |
| 24 | * Seattle | 14 |
| 38 | at Cincinnati | 3 |
| 27 | at Cleveland | 20 |
| 23 | * Pittsburgh | 3 |
| 33 | * Atlanta | 17 |
| 19 | * Cleveland | 17 |
| 26 | at Pittsburgh | 17 |
| 10 | at San Francisco | 7 |
| 24 | * N.Y. Jets | 0 |
| 368 | | 238 |

**MIAMI (9-7)**

| | | |
|---|---|---|
| 24 | at Indianapolis | 20 |
| 14 | * N.Y. Jets | 24 |
| | OPEN DATE | |
| 22 | at Buffalo | 13 |
| 17 | * Washington | 10 |
| 24 | at Cleveland | 14 |
| | OPEN DATE | |
| 41 | * Indianapolis | 27 |
| 30 | * Kansas City | 10 |
| 10 | at N.Y. Jets | 27 |
| 19 | at Philadelphia | 14 |
| 17 | * New England | 13 |
| 16 | at Dallas | 14 |
| 14 | * N.Y. Giants | 19 |
| 20 | * Pittsburgh | 21 |
| 34 | * Buffalo | 47 |
| 20 | at San Diego | 45 |
| 27 | at New Eng. (OT) | 33 |
| 349 | | 351 |

**SAN DIEGO (8-8)**

| | | |
|---|---|---|
| 18 | * Seattle | 12 |
| 17 | at Denver | 34 |
| 18 | * Houston | 17 |
| | OPEN DATE | |
| 14 | at Seattle | 31 |
| 3 | at Pittsburgh | 16 |
| | OPEN DATE | |
| 14 | * Kansas City | 17 |
| 30 | at L.A. Raiders | 23 |
| 30 | at Minnesota | 17 |
| 13 | * Chicago | 16 |
| 7 | * L.A. Raiders | 12 |
| 31 | at Indianapolis | 0 |
| 13 | * Denver | 10 |
| 13 | * Green Bay | 20 |
| 24 | at Kansas City | 28 |
| 45 | * Miami | 20 |
| 32 | at Tampa Bay | 17 |
| 322 | | 290 |

**CINCINNATI (3-13)**

| | | |
|---|---|---|
| 14 | at Cleveland | 27 |
| 6 | * Indianapolis | 9 |
| 7 | at Pittsburgh | 34 |
| 10 | * Seattle | 19 |
| 15 | at Kansas City | 17 |
| | OPEN DATE | |
| 17 | * Cleveland | 28 |
| 12 | at Houston | 28 |
| | OPEN DATE | |
| 16 | * Pittsburgh | 24 |
| 3 | * Houston | 38 |
| 12 | at N.Y. Jets | 17 |
| 16 | * L.A. Raiders | 10 |
| 8 | at San Francisco | 21 |
| 2 | at New England | 7 |
| 15 | * L.A. Rams | 3 |
| 21 | * Atlanta | 17 |
| 13 | at New Orleans | 20 |
| 187 | | 319 |

**INDIANAPOLIS (4-12)**

| | | |
|---|---|---|
| 20 | * Miami | 24 |
| 9 | at Cincinnati | 6 |
| | OPEN DATE | |
| 23 | * Cleveland | 10 |
| 13 | at Denver | 35 |
| 3 | * Dallas | 27 |
| | OPEN DATE | |
| 27 | at Miami | 41 |
| 9 | * New England | 6 |
| 24 | at Washington | 30 |
| 17 | * N.Y. Jets | 31 |
| 9 | at Buffalo | 23 |
| 0 | * San Diego | 31 |
| 9 | at N.Y. Jets | 6 |
| 6 | at N.Y. Giants | 20 |
| 10 | * Philadelphia | 20 |
| 0 | at New England | 38 |
| 10 | * Buffalo | 30 |
| 189 | | 378 |

**NEW ENGLAND (5-11)**

| | | |
|---|---|---|
| 14 | at Buffalo | 38 |
| 16 | * Detroit (OT) | 19 |
| 14 | * Seattle | 17 |
| 7 | at N.Y. Jets | 45 |
| | OPEN DATE | |
| 23 | at Phoenix | 21 |
| 14 | * Houston | 28 |
| 9 | at Seattle | 10 |
| 6 | at Indianapolis | 9 |
| 10 | * Buffalo (OT) | 13 |
| | OPEN DATE | |
| 13 | at Miami | 17 |
| 0 | * N.Y. Jets | 6 |
| 14 | at Pittsburgh | 17 |
| 7 | * Cincinnati | 2 |
| 20 | at Cleveland | 17 |
| 38 | * Indianapolis | 0 |
| 33 | * Miami (OT) | 27 |
| 238 | | 286 |

**SEATTLE (6-10)**

| | | |
|---|---|---|
| 12 | at San Diego | 18 |
| 13 | * L.A. Raiders | 17 |
| 17 | at New England | 14 |
| 19 | at Cincinnati | 10 |
| 31 | * San Diego | 14 |
| | OPEN DATE | |
| 10 | at Detroit | 30 |
| 10 | * New England | 9 |
| 17 | at Denver | 28 |
| 14 | at Houston | 24 |
| 22 | * Cleveland | 5 |
| | OPEN DATE | |
| 9 | * Denver | 17 |
| 16 | * Kansas City | 31 |
| 23 | at L.A. Raiders | 27 |
| 27 | * Phoenix (OT) | 30 |
| 16 | * Pittsburgh | 6 |
| 24 | at Kansas City | 34 |
| 280 | | 314 |

**CLEVELAND (7-9)**

| | | |
|---|---|---|
| 27 | * Cincinnati | 14 |
| 23 | * San Francisco | 13 |
| 19 | at L.A. Raiders | 16 |
| 10 | at Indianapolis | 23 |
| | OPEN DATE | |
| 14 | * Miami | 24 |
| 28 | at Cincinnati | 17 |
| 28 | * Pittsburgh | 23 |
| | OPEN DATE | |
| 14 | * Denver | 29 |
| 5 | at Seattle | 22 |
| 20 | * Houston | 27 |
| 14 | at Atlanta | 17 |
| 17 | * New Orleans | 13 |
| 17 | at Houston | 19 |
| 17 | * New England | 20 |
| 42 | at L.A. Rams | 14 |
| 9 | at Pittsburgh | 16 |
| 304 | | 307 |

**KANSAS CITY (11-5)**

| | | |
|---|---|---|
| 27 | at Tampa Bay | 3 |
| 0 | at Houston | 30 |
| 15 | * Denver | 7 |
| | OPEN DATE | |
| 24 | * L.A. Raiders | 9 |
| 17 | * Cincinnati | 15 |
| 17 | at San Diego | 14 |
| | OPEN DATE | |
| 10 | at Miami | 30 |
| 23 | * Green Bay | 16 |
| 31 | at L.A. Raiders | 20 |
| 17 | * Chicago | 19 |
| 23 | * Buffalo | 7 |
| 31 | at Seattle | 16 |
| 21 | at Denver | 27 |
| 28 | * San Diego | 24 |
| 10 | at Minnesota | 30 |
| 34 | * Seattle | 24 |
| 328 | | 291 |

**N.Y. JETS (8-8)**

| | | |
|---|---|---|
| 20 | * Denver | 26 |
| 24 | at Miami | 14 |
| | OPEN DATE | |
| 45 | * New England | 7 |
| 30 | * Philadelphia | 35 |
| 20 | at L.A. Raiders | 24 |
| | OPEN DATE | |
| 10 | * Buffalo | 19 |
| 10 | at N.Y. Giants | 6 |
| 27 | * Miami | 10 |
| 31 | at Indianapolis | 17 |
| 17 | * Cincinnati | 12 |
| 6 | at New England | 0 |
| 6 | * Indianapolis | 9 |
| 3 | at Washington | 0 |
| 7 | * Dallas | 28 |
| 14 | at Buffalo | 16 |
| 0 | at Houston | 24 |
| 270 | | 247 |

**DENVER (9-7)**

| | | |
|---|---|---|
| 26 | at N.Y. Jets | 20 |
| 34 | * San Diego | 17 |
| 7 | at Kansas City | 15 |
| | OPEN DATE | |
| 35 | * Indianapolis | 13 |
| 27 | at Green Bay | 30 |
| 20 | * L.A. Raiders | 23 |
| | OPEN DATE | |
| 28 | * Seattle | 17 |
| 29 | at Cleveland | 14 |
| 23 | * Minnesota | 26 |
| 37 | * Pittsburgh | 13 |
| 17 | at Seattle | 9 |
| 10 | at San Diego | 13 |
| 27 | * Kansas City | 21 |
| 13 | at Chicago | 3 |
| 10 | * Tampa Bay | 17 |
| 30 | at L.A. Raiders (OT) | 33 |
| 373 | | 284 |

**L.A. RAIDERS (10-6)**

| | | |
|---|---|---|
| 24 | * Minnesota | 7 |
| 17 | at Seattle | 13 |
| 16 | * Cleveland | 19 |
| | OPEN DATE | |
| 9 | at Kansas City | 24 |
| 24 | * N.Y. Jets | 20 |
| 23 | at Denver | 20 |
| | OPEN DATE | |
| 23 | * San Diego | 30 |
| 16 | at Chicago | 14 |
| 20 | * Kansas City | 31 |
| 12 | at San Diego | 7 |
| 10 | at Cincinnati | 16 |
| 25 | at Buffalo | 24 |
| 27 | * Seattle | 23 |
| 27 | * Tampa Bay | 20 |
| 0 | at Green Bay | 28 |
| 33 | * Denver (OT) | 30 |
| 306 | | 326 |

**PITTSBURGH (9-7)**

| | | |
|---|---|---|
| 13 | * San Francisco | 24 |
| 0 | at L.A. Rams | 27 |
| 34 | * Cincinnati | 7 |
| 45 | at Atlanta | 17 |
| | OPEN DATE | |
| 16 | * San Diego | 3 |
| 37 | * New Orleans | 14 |
| 23 | at Cleveland | 28 |
| | OPEN DATE | |
| 24 | at Cincinnati | 16 |
| 23 | * Buffalo | 0 |
| 13 | at Denver | 37 |
| 3 | at Houston | 23 |
| 17 | * New England | 14 |
| 21 | at Miami | 20 |
| 17 | * Houston | 26 |
| 6 | at Seattle | 16 |
| 16 | * Cleveland | 9 |
| 308 | | 281 |

## NFC SEASON RECORDS—TEAM BY TEAM

### ATLANTA (6-10)

| | | |
|---|---|---|
| 13 | at Detroit | 30 |
| 31 | *New Orleans | 34 |
| 30 | at San Francisco | 37 |
| 17 | *Pittsburgh | 45 |
| 0 | at Chicago | 6 |
| | OPEN DATE | |
| 30 | *L.A. Rams | 24 |
| 26 | at New Orleans | 15 |
| 24 | *Tampa Bay | 31 |
| | OPEN DATE | |
| 13 | at L.A. Rams | 0 |
| 27 | *Dallas | 14 |
| 17 | *Cleveland | 14 |
| 17 | at Houston | 33 |
| 27 | *San Francisco | 24 |
| 17 | at Washington | 30 |
| 17 | at Cincinnati | 21 |
| 10 | *Phoenix | 27 |
| 316 | | 385 |

### CHICAGO (7-9)

| | | |
|---|---|---|
| 20 | *N.Y. Giants | 26 |
| 7 | at Minnesota | 10 |
| | OPEN DATE | |
| 47 | *Tampa Bay | 17 |
| 6 | *Atlanta | 0 |
| 17 | at Philadelphia | 6 |
| | OPEN DATE | |
| 12 | *Minnesota | 19 |
| 3 | at Green Bay | 17 |
| 14 | *L.A. Raiders | 16 |
| 16 | at San Diego | 13 |
| 19 | at Kansas City | 17 |
| 10 | at Detroit | 6 |
| 30 | *Green Bay | 17 |
| 10 | at Tampa Bay | 13 |
| 3 | *Denver | 13 |
| 14 | *Detroit | 20 |
| 6 | at L.A. Rams | 20 |
| 234 | | 230 |

### DALLAS (12-4)

| | | |
|---|---|---|
| 16 | at Washington | 35 |
| 10 | *Buffalo | 13 |
| 17 | at Phoenix | 10 |
| | OPEN DATE | |
| 36 | *Green Bay | 14 |
| 27 | at Indianapolis | 3 |
| 26 | *San Francisco | 17 |
| | OPEN DATE | |
| 23 | at Philadelphia | 10 |
| 31 | *N.Y. Giants | 9 |
| 20 | *Phoenix | 15 |
| 14 | at Atlanta | 27 |
| 14 | *Miami | 16 |
| 23 | *Philadelphia | 17 |
| 37 | at Minnesota | 20 |
| 28 | at N.Y. Jets | 7 |
| 38 | *Washington | 3 |
| 16 | at N.Y. Giants (OT) | 13 |
| 376 | | 229 |

### DETROIT (10-6)

| | | |
|---|---|---|
| 30 | *Atlanta | 13 |
| 19 | at New Eng. (OT) | 16 |
| 3 | at New Orleans | 14 |
| 26 | *Phoenix | 20 |
| 10 | at Tampa Bay | 27 |
| | OPEN DATE | |
| 30 | *Seattle | 10 |
| 16 | at L.A. Rams | 13 |
| 30 | at Minnesota | 27 |
| 23 | *Tampa Bay | 0 |
| | OPEN DATE | |
| 17 | at Green Bay | 26 |
| 6 | *Chicago | 10 |
| 0 | *Minnesota | 13 |
| 21 | at Phoenix | 14 |
| 17 | *San Francisco | 55 |
| 20 | at Chicago | 14 |
| 30 | *Green Bay | 20 |
| 298 | | 292 |

*denotes home games
(OT) denotes overtime

### GREEN BAY (9-7)

| | | |
|---|---|---|
| 36 | *L.A. Rams | 6 |
| 17 | *Philadelphia | 20 |
| | OPEN DATE | |
| 13 | at Minnesota | 15 |
| 14 | at Dallas | 36 |
| 30 | *Denver | 27 |
| | OPEN DATE | |
| 37 | at Tampa Bay | 14 |
| 17 | *Chicago | 3 |
| 16 | at Kansas City | 23 |
| 19 | at New Orleans | 17 |
| 26 | *Detroit | 17 |
| 13 | *Tampa Bay | 10 |
| 17 | at Chicago | 30 |
| 20 | at San Diego | 13 |
| 17 | *Minnesota | 21 |
| 28 | *L.A. Raiders | 0 |
| 20 | at Detroit | 30 |
| 340 | | 282 |

### L.A. RAMS (5-11)

| | | |
|---|---|---|
| 6 | at Green Bay | 36 |
| 27 | *Pittsburgh | 0 |
| 10 | at N.Y. Giants | 20 |
| 28 | at Houston | 13 |
| 6 | *New Orleans | 37 |
| | OPEN DATE | |
| 24 | at Atlanta | 30 |
| 13 | *Detroit | 16 |
| 17 | at San Francisco | 40 |
| | OPEN DATE | |
| 0 | *Atlanta | 13 |
| 10 | *Washington | 6 |
| 10 | *San Francisco | 35 |
| 10 | at Phoenix | 38 |
| 23 | at New Orleans | 20 |
| 3 | at Cincinnati | 15 |
| 14 | *Cleveland | 42 |
| 20 | *Chicago | 6 |
| 221 | | 367 |

### MINNESOTA (9-7)

| | | |
|---|---|---|
| 7 | at L.A. Raiders | 24 |
| 10 | *Chicago | 7 |
| | OPEN DATE | |
| 15 | *Green Bay | 13 |
| 19 | at San Francisco | 38 |
| 15 | *Tampa Bay | 0 |
| | OPEN DATE | |
| 19 | at Chicago | 12 |
| 27 | *Detroit | 30 |
| 17 | *San Diego | 30 |
| 26 | at Denver | 23 |
| 10 | at Tampa Bay | 23 |
| 14 | *New Orleans | 17 |
| 13 | at Detroit | 0 |
| 20 | *Dallas | 37 |
| 21 | at Green Bay | 17 |
| 30 | *Kansas City | 10 |
| 14 | at Washington | 9 |
| 277 | | 290 |

### NEW ORLEANS (8-8)

| | | |
|---|---|---|
| 33 | *Houston | 21 |
| 34 | at Atlanta | 31 |
| 14 | *Detroit | 3 |
| 16 | *San Francisco | 13 |
| 37 | at L.A. Rams | 6 |
| | OPEN DATE | |
| 14 | at Pittsburgh | 37 |
| 15 | *Atlanta | 26 |
| 20 | at Phoenix | 17 |
| | OPEN DATE | |
| 17 | *Green Bay | 19 |
| 7 | at San Francisco | 42 |
| 17 | at Minnesota | 14 |
| 13 | at Cleveland | 17 |
| 20 | *L.A. Rams | 23 |
| 14 | *N.Y. Giants | 24 |
| 26 | at Philadelphia | 37 |
| 20 | *Cincinnati | 13 |
| 317 | | 343 |

### N.Y. GIANTS (11-5)

| | | |
|---|---|---|
| 26 | at Chicago | 20 |
| 23 | *Tampa Bay | 7 |
| 20 | *L.A. Rams | 10 |
| | OPEN DATE | |
| 14 | at Buffalo | 17 |
| 41 | at Washington | 7 |
| 21 | *Philadelphia | 10 |
| | OPEN DATE | |
| 6 | *N.Y. Jets | 10 |
| 9 | at Dallas | 31 |
| 20 | *Washington | 6 |
| 7 | at Philadelphia | 3 |
| 19 | *Phoenix | 17 |
| 19 | at Miami | 14 |
| 20 | *Indianapolis | 6 |
| 24 | at New Orleans | 14 |
| 6 | at Phoenix | 17 |
| 13 | *Dallas (OT) | 16 |
| 288 | | 205 |

### PHILADELPHIA (8-8)

| | | |
|---|---|---|
| 23 | *Phoenix | 17 |
| 20 | at Green Bay | 17 |
| 34 | *Washington | 31 |
| | OPEN DATE | |
| 35 | at N.Y. Jets | 30 |
| 6 | *Chicago | 17 |
| 10 | at N.Y. Giants | 21 |
| | OPEN DATE | |
| 10 | *Dallas | 23 |
| 3 | at Phoenix | 16 |
| 14 | *Miami | 19 |
| 3 | *N.Y. Giants | 7 |
| 17 | at Washington | 14 |
| 17 | at Dallas | 23 |
| 7 | *Buffalo | 10 |
| 20 | at Indianapolis | 10 |
| 37 | *New Orleans | 26 |
| 37 | at San Fran. (OT) | 34 |
| 293 | | 315 |

### PHOENIX (7-9)

| | | |
|---|---|---|
| 17 | at Philadelphia | 23 |
| 17 | at Washington | 10 |
| 10 | *Dallas | 17 |
| 20 | at Detroit | 26 |
| | OPEN DATE | |
| 21 | *New England | 23 |
| 36 | *Washington | 6 |
| 14 | at San Francisco | 28 |
| 17 | *New Orleans | 20 |
| 16 | *Philadelphia | 3 |
| 15 | at Dallas | 20 |
| | OPEN DATE | |
| 17 | at N.Y. Giants | 19 |
| 38 | *L.A. Rams | 10 |
| 14 | *Detroit | 21 |
| 30 | at Seattle (OT) | 27 |
| 17 | *N.Y. Giants | 6 |
| 27 | at Atlanta | 10 |
| 326 | | 269 |

### SAN FRANCISCO (10-6)

| | | |
|---|---|---|
| 24 | at Pittsburgh | 13 |
| 13 | at Cleveland | 23 |
| 37 | *Atlanta | 30 |
| 13 | at New Orleans | 16 |
| 38 | *Minnesota | 19 |
| | OPEN DATE | |
| 17 | at Dallas | 26 |
| 28 | *Phoenix | 14 |
| 40 | *L.A. Rams | 17 |
| | OPEN DATE | |
| 45 | at Tampa Bay | 21 |
| 42 | *New Orleans | 7 |
| 35 | at L.A. Rams | 10 |
| 21 | *Cincinnati | 8 |
| 24 | at Atlanta | 27 |
| 55 | at Detroit | 17 |
| 7 | *Houston | 10 |
| 34 | *Philadelphia (OT) | 37 |
| 473 | | 295 |

### TAMPA BAY (5-11)

| | | |
|---|---|---|
| 3 | *Kansas City | 27 |
| 7 | at N.Y. Giants | 23 |
| | OPEN DATE | |
| 17 | at Chicago | 47 |
| 27 | *Detroit | 10 |
| 0 | at Minnesota | 15 |
| | OPEN DATE | |
| 14 | *Green Bay | 37 |
| 31 | at Atlanta | 24 |
| 0 | at Detroit | 23 |
| 21 | *San Francisco | 45 |
| 23 | *Minnesota | 10 |
| 10 | at Green Bay | 13 |
| 17 | *Washington | 23 |
| 13 | *Chicago | 10 |
| 20 | at L.A. Raiders | 27 |
| 17 | at Denver | 10 |
| 17 | *San Diego | 32 |
| 237 | | 376 |

### WASHINGTON (4-12)

| | | |
|---|---|---|
| 35 | *Dallas | 16 |
| 10 | *Phoenix | 17 |
| 31 | at Philadelphia | 34 |
| | OPEN DATE | |
| 10 | at Miami | 17 |
| 7 | *N.Y. Giants | 41 |
| 6 | at Phoenix | 36 |
| | OPEN DATE | |
| 10 | at Buffalo | 24 |
| 30 | *Indianapolis | 24 |
| 6 | at N.Y. Giants | 20 |
| 6 | at L.A. Rams | 10 |
| 14 | *Philadelphia | 17 |
| 23 | at Tampa Bay | 17 |
| 0 | *N.Y. Jets | 3 |
| 30 | *Atlanta | 17 |
| 3 | at Dallas | 38 |
| 9 | *Minnesota | 14 |
| 230 | | 345 |

Attendance figures as they appear in the following, and in the club-by-club sections starting on page 24, are turnstile counts and not paid attendance. Paid attendance totals are on page 217.

## FIRST WEEK SUMMARIES

AMERICAN FOOTBALL CONFERENCE

| Eastern Division | W | L | T | Pct. | Pts. | OP |
|---|---|---|---|---|---|---|
| Buffalo | 1 | 0 | 0 | 1.000 | 38 | 14 |
| Miami | 1 | 0 | 0 | 1.000 | 24 | 20 |
| Indianapolis | 0 | 1 | 0 | .000 | 20 | 24 |
| New England | 0 | 1 | 0 | .000 | 14 | 38 |
| N.Y. Jets | 0 | 1 | 0 | .000 | 20 | 26 |
| **Central Division** | | | | | | |
| Cleveland | 1 | 0 | 0 | 1.000 | 27 | 14 |
| Cincinnati | 0 | 1 | 0 | .000 | 14 | 27 |
| Houston | 0 | 1 | 0 | .000 | 21 | 33 |
| Pittsburgh | 0 | 1 | 0 | .000 | 13 | 24 |
| **Western Division** | | | | | | |
| Denver | 1 | 0 | 0 | 1.000 | 26 | 20 |
| Kansas City | 1 | 0 | 0 | 1.000 | 27 | 3 |
| L.A. Raiders | 1 | 0 | 0 | 1.000 | 24 | 7 |
| San Diego | 1 | 0 | 0 | 1.000 | 18 | 12 |
| Seattle | 0 | 1 | 0 | .000 | 12 | 18 |

NATIONAL FOOTBALL CONFERENCE

| Eastern Division | W | L | T | Pct. | Pts. | OP |
|---|---|---|---|---|---|---|
| N.Y. Giants | 1 | 0 | 0 | 1.000 | 26 | 20 |
| Philadelphia | 1 | 0 | 0 | 1.000 | 23 | 17 |
| Washington | 1 | 0 | 0 | 1.000 | 35 | 16 |
| Dallas | 0 | 1 | 0 | .000 | 16 | 35 |
| Phoenix | 0 | 1 | 0 | .000 | 17 | 23 |
| **Central Division** | | | | | | |
| Detroit | 1 | 0 | 0 | 1.000 | 30 | 13 |
| Green Bay | 1 | 0 | 0 | 1.000 | 36 | 6 |
| Chicago | 0 | 1 | 0 | .000 | 20 | 26 |
| Minnesota | 0 | 1 | 0 | .000 | 7 | 24 |
| Tampa Bay | 0 | 1 | 0 | .000 | 3 | 27 |
| **Western Division** | | | | | | |
| New Orleans | 1 | 0 | 0 | 1.000 | 33 | 21 |
| San Francisco | 1 | 0 | 0 | 1.000 | 24 | 13 |
| Atlanta | 0 | 1 | 0 | .000 | 13 | 30 |
| L.A. Rams | 0 | 1 | 0 | .000 | 6 | 36 |

## SUNDAY, SEPTEMBER 5

**DETROIT 30, ATLANTA 13**—at Silverdome, attendance 56,216. The Lions raced to a 24-3 halftime lead and coasted to the victory over the Falcons. Detroit took a 7-0 advantage just 3:05 into the game on a 26-yard touchdown run by Barry Sanders, which capped a 61-yard drive on the Lions' first possession. Linebacker George Jamison returned an interception 35 yards for a touchdown late in the first quarter, and Rodney Peete tossed a 21-yard touchdown pass to Herman Moore in the second period as the Lions turned the game into a rout. Forced to play catch-up, Falcons quarterback Chris Miller attempted 50 passes and completed 26 for 260 yards, including a 32-yard touchdown to Andre Rison. But Miller also was intercepted twice and sacked 6 times. Wide receiver Mike Pritchard caught 10 passes for Atlanta, and Rison finished with 106 yards on 6 receptions. Moore caught 4 passes for 113 yards for the Lions.

| | | | | | | |
|---|---|---|---|---|---|---|
| **Atlanta** | 0 | 3 | 3 | 7 | — | 13 |
| **Detroit** | 14 | 10 | 3 | 3 | — | 30 |

Det — Sanders 26 run (Hanson kick)
Det — Jamison 35 interception return (Hanson kick)
Det — FG Hanson 44
Det — Moore 21 pass from Peete (Hanson kick)
Atl — FG Johnson 54
Atl — FG Johnson 20
Det — FG Hanson 37
Atl — Rison 32 pass from Miller (Johnson kick)
Det — FG Hanson 37

**CLEVELAND 27, CINCINNATI 14**—at Cleveland Stadium, attendance 75,508. The Browns spotted the Bengals a 14-point first-quarter lead, then rallied behind their defense to win. Cleveland sacked Cincinnati quarterback David Klingler 6 times, intercepted 2 passes, and returned a fumble for the clinching score in the fourth quarter. The Browns also executed a goal-line stand late in the game, keeping the Bengals out of the end zone after facing first-and-goal from the 1-yard line. Cleveland, which fell behind 14-0 in the game's initial 12 minutes, tied it by halftime on a 13-yard touchdown pass from Bernie Kosar to Michael Jackson and a 1-yard touchdown run by Tommy Vardell, the latter coming just 28 seconds before intermission. Matt Stover kicked a pair of field goals in the third quarter to put the Browns ahead 20-14, and cornerback Everson Walls made the key play of the game one minute into the final period. Walls sacked Klingler, forcing the fumble that safety Steven Moore recovered and returned 22 yards for a touchdown.

| | | | | | | |
|---|---|---|---|---|---|---|
| **Cincinnati** | 14 | 0 | 0 | 0 | — | 14 |
| **Cleveland** | 0 | 14 | 6 | 7 | — | 27 |

Cin — Miles 4 run (Pelfrey kick)
Cin — Pickens 5 pass from Klingler (Pelfrey kick)
Cle — Jackson 13 pass from Kosar (Stover kick)
Cle — Vardell 1 run (Stover kick)
Cle — FG Stover 28
Cle — FG Stover 34
Cle — Moore 22 fumble recovery return (Stover kick)

**DENVER 26, N.Y. JETS 20**—at Giants Stadium, attendance 68,130. John Elway passed for 269 yards and 2 touchdowns and rookies Glyn Milburn and Jason Elam played key roles as the Broncos beat the Jets. Elway, who completed 20 of 29 passes, broke a 6-6 tie with a 3-yard touchdown pass to Cedric Tillman 27 seconds before halftime. He then marched his team 80 yards following the second-half kickoff to another touchdown, a 25-yard pass to Milburn. That score was set up when Milburn, a running back who was Denver's second-round draft choice, went 50 yards with a catch on third-and-19. Elam, a third-round pick, kicked 4 field goals in as many tries as the Broncos built a 26-6 advantage and withstood a pair of touchdown passes by New York's Boomer Esiason in the fourth quarter. Esiason, the veteran quarterback who was acquired from the Bengals in the offseason, completed 29 of 40 passes for 371 yards. Wide receiver Rob Moore had 9 receptions for 140 yards.

| | | | | | | |
|---|---|---|---|---|---|---|
| **Denver** | 6 | 7 | 13 | 0 | — | 26 |
| **N.Y. Jets** | 0 | 6 | 0 | 14 | — | 20 |

Den — FG Elam 28
Den — FG Elam 30
Jets — FG Blanchard 22
Jets — FG Blanchard 43
Den — Tillman 3 pass from Elway (Elam kick)
Den — Milburn 25 pass from Elway (Elam kick)
Den — FG Elam 30
Den — FG Elam 41
Jets — Mitchell 5 pass from Esiason (Blanchard kick)
Jets — Moore 6 pass from Esiason (Blanchard kick)

**KANSAS CITY 27, TAMPA BAY 3**—at Tampa Stadium, attendance 63,378. Joe Montana threw 3 touchdown passes in his debut with Kansas City, leading the Chiefs to an easy victory over the Buccaneers. Montana, acquired from the 49ers in the offseason after missing most of the last two years with an elbow injury, completed his first 8 passes. He finished 14 of 21 for 246 yards before leaving the game with a sprained right wrist late in the third quarter. He gave Kansas City the lead for good with a 19-yard touchdown pass to Willie Davis 39 seconds into the second period. Later in the quarter, he threw a 50-yard touchdown pass to J.J. Birden, and he finished his day with a 12-yard scoring toss to running back Marcus Allen with 5:08 to go in the third quarter. Allen, the former Raiders running back who signed with the Chiefs as a free agent, also ran for 79 yards on 13 carries. Kansas City amassed 400 total yards while allowing Tampa Bay only 157.

| | | | | | | |
|---|---|---|---|---|---|---|
| **Kansas City** | 0 | 17 | 7 | 3 | — | 27 |
| **Tampa Bay** | 3 | 0 | 0 | 0 | — | 3 |

TB — FG Husted 35
KC — W. Davis 19 pass from Montana (Lowery kick)
KC — FG Lowery 21
KC — Birden 50 pass from Montana (Lowery kick)
KC — Allen 12 pass from Montana (Lowery kick)
KC — FG Lowery 23

**GREEN BAY 36, L.A. RAMS 6**—at Milwaukee County Stadium, attendance 54,648. Brett Favre passed for 264 yards and 2 touchdowns and wide receiver Sterling Sharpe caught 7 passes for 120 yards and a touchdown as the Packers easily handled the Rams. Sharpe, who set an NFL record with 108 receptions in 1992, gave Green Bay a 9-3 lead with a 50-yard touchdown catch midway through the first quarter, and the Packers were not challenged after that. Favre's second touchdown pass, a 4-yard toss to Mark Clayton, came with 40 seconds remaining in the first half and made it 19-6. Edgar Bennett rushed for 2 touchdowns in the third quarter.

| | | | | | | |
|---|---|---|---|---|---|---|
| **L.A. Rams** | 3 | 3 | 0 | 0 | — | 6 |
| **Green Bay** | 9 | 10 | 14 | 3 | — | 36 |

Rams — FG Zendejas 31
GB — Safety, Noble tackled Gary in end zone
GB — Sharpe 50 pass from Favre (Jacke kick)
GB — FG Jacke 51
Rams — FG Zendejas 32
GB — Clayton 3 pass from Favre (Jacke kick)
GB — Bennett 11 run (Jacke kick)
GB — Bennett 1 run (Jacke kick)
GB — FG Jacke 33

**MIAMI 24, INDIANAPOLIS 20**—at Hoosier Dome, attendance 51,858. Dan Marino's 1-yard touchdown pass to tight end Greg Baty with 35 seconds left lifted the Dolphins past the Colts. Indianapolis had rallied from a 17-10 deficit to take a 20-17 lead on a 25-yard touchdown pass from Jack Trudeau to rookie wide receiver Sean Dawkins and a 33-yard field goal by Dean Biasucci with 5:04 left in the game. Marino then marched Miami 80 yards in 13 plays, completing all 8 of his pass attempts on the drive. The winning pass came on third down. Cornerback Troy Vincent secured the victory by intercepting Trudeau's pass with 10 seconds remaining.

| | | | | | | |
|---|---|---|---|---|---|---|
| **Miami** | 7 | 3 | 7 | 7 | — | 24 |
| **Indianapolis** | 7 | 0 | 3 | 10 | — | 20 |

Ind — Culver 56 fumble recovery return (Biasucci kick)
Mia — Jackson 40 pass from Marino (Stoyanovich kick)
Mia — FG Stoyanovich 20
Ind — FG Biasucci 26
Mia — Jackson 27 pass from Marino (Stoyanovich kick)
Ind — Dawkins 25 pass from Trudeau (Biasucci kick)
Ind — FG Biasucci 33
Mia — Baty 1 pass from Marino (Stoyanovich kick)

**L.A. RAIDERS 24, MINNESOTA 7**—at Los Angeles Memorial Coliseum, attendance 45,136. Jeff Hostetler completed 23 of 27 passes for 225 yards and 1 touchdown to lead the Raiders past the defending NFC Central Division champions. Los Angeles dominated the game from the opening kickoff, when rookie safety Patrick Bates recovered a fumble on his first play as a professional. Hostetler, who signed with the Raiders as a free agent in the offseason, took only three plays to get his new team in the end zone, completing his first pass attempt for 17 yards and a touchdown to Tim Brown. Los Angeles led 21-0 at the half and coasted to the victory. The Raiders outgained the Vikings 312-205 and maintained possession for more than 39 minutes. Minnesota's lone touchdown came in the final minute on a 1-yard run by Roger Craig.

| | | | | | | |
|---|---|---|---|---|---|---|
| **Minnesota** | 0 | 0 | 0 | 7 | — | 7 |
| **L.A. Raiders** | 7 | 14 | 0 | 3 | — | 24 |

Raid — Brown 17 pass from Hostetler (Jaeger kick)
Raid — Robinson 1 run (Jaeger kick)
Raid — McDaniel 36 interception return (Jaeger kick)
Raid — FG Jaeger 21
Minn — Craig 1 run (Reveiz kick)

**BUFFALO 38, NEW ENGLAND 14**—at Rich Stadium, attendance 79,751. Jim Kelly threw 4 touchdown passes, 3 of them to wide receiver Andre Reed, and the Bills broke open a close game by scoring 3 times in a span of 6:26 of the fourth quarter. Buffalo led just 17-14 until Kelly teamed with Reed on a 22-yard touchdown pass on the first play of the fourth quarter. After safety Matt Darby recovered a fumble, Kelly found Reed for 14 yards and another touchdown, and rookie Russell Copeland finished the scoring spree by returning a punt 47 yards for a touchdown with 8:30 left in the game. Reed finished with 6 catches for 110 yards, while Bills running back Thurman Thomas ran for 114 yards on 24 carries. Patriots quarterback Drew Bledsoe, the top pick in the 1993 NFL draft, completed 14 of 30 passes for 148 yards and 2 scores, including a 54-yard touchdown to tight end Ben Coates. Buffalo won on opening day for the sixth consecutive year.

| | | | | | | |
|---|---|---|---|---|---|---|
| **New England** | 0 | 7 | 7 | 0 | — | 14 |
| **Buffalo** | 0 | 17 | 0 | 21 | — | 38 |

Buff — FG Christie 28
Buff — Brooks 4 pass from Kelly (Christie kick)

| | | |
|---|---|---|
| NE | — | Coates 54 pass from Bledsoe (Sisson kick) |
| Buff | — | Reed 41 pass from Kelly (Christie kick) |
| NE | — | McMurtry 2 pass from Bledsoe (Sisson kick) |
| Buff | — | Reed 22 pass from Kelly (Christie kick) |
| Buff | — | Reed 14 pass from Kelly (Christie kick) |
| Buff | — | Copeland 47 punt return (Christie kick) |

**N.Y. GIANTS 26, CHICAGO 20**—at Soldier Field, attendance 66,900. Phil Simms's 1-yard touchdown pass to running back Jarrod Bunch with 1:07 remaining gave the Giants the victory in a see-saw game in which the lead changed hands three times in the final quarter. Three of David Treadwell's four field goals staked New York to a 9-7 first-half advantage, before the Bears rallied to go ahead 17-9 midway through the third quarter. The Giants closed the deficit to 17-16 on Simms's 40-yard touchdown pass to Mark Jackson with 19 seconds to go in the third quarter, then went ahead on Treadwell's 36-yard field goal with 9:44 left in the game. Kevin Butler's 34-yard field goal gave Chicago its last lead at 20-19 with 3:07 left. But New York drove 80 yards in 8 plays to the winning touchdown. Simms passed 38 yards to Mike Sherrard to convert a third-and-18, and had a 24-yard completion to Chris Calloway on the march. The Giants also were aided by a pass interference penalty that positioned the ball on the 1. Simms finished with 24 completions in 34 attempts for 277 yards. Another veteran, linebacker Lawrence Taylor, made a successful return from the Achilles tendon injury that kept him out of the final seven games of 1992. Taylor had 2 sacks and forced and recovered a fumble to quell any hopes of a Bears' comeback in the final minute. Chicago had its NFL-best nine-game winning streak on opening day snapped.

| | | | | | | |
|---|---|---|---|---|---|---|
| **N.Y. Giants** | 3 | 6 | 7 | 10 | — | 26 |
| **Chicago** | 0 | 7 | 10 | 3 | — | 20 |

| | | |
|---|---|---|
| Giants | — | FG Treadwell 19 |
| Giants | — | FG Treadwell 35 |
| Giants | — | FG Treadwell 23 |
| Chi | — | Obee 2 pass from Harbaugh (Butler kick) |
| Chi | — | Baker 5 blocked punt return (Butler kick) |
| Chi | — | FG Butler 20 |
| Giants | — | M. Jackson 40 pass from Simms (Treadwell kick) |
| Giants | — | FG Treadwell 36 |
| Chi | — | FG Butler 34 |
| Giants | — | Bunch 1 pass from Simms (Treadwell kick) |

**PHILADELPHIA 23, PHOENIX 17**—at Veterans Stadium, attendance 59,831. Randall Cunningham passed for 192 yards and ran for 49, and the Eagles held off the Cardinals to win. Cunningham completed 18 of 29 passes and also scored on a 9-yard bootleg to give Philadelphia a 14-0 lead in the second quarter. Phoenix rallied in the second half on a 27-yard touchdown pass from Chris Chandler to running back Larry Centers and cornerback Lorenzo Lynch's 55-yard touchdown return of a fumble recovery, but it wasn't enough to overcome a slow start. The Eagles had 359 total yards and limited the Cardinals to 231. Chandler and starting quarterback Steve Beuerlein combined to complete only 15 of 39 passes for Phoenix.

| | | | | | | |
|---|---|---|---|---|---|---|
| **Phoenix** | 0 | 3 | 7 | 7 | — | 17 |
| **Philadelphia** | 7 | 7 | 2 | 7 | — | 23 |

| | | |
|---|---|---|
| Phil | — | Sherman 1 run (Ruzek kick) |
| Phil | — | Cunningham 9 run (Ruzek kick) |
| Phx | — | FG Davis 24 |
| Phil | — | Safety, Camarillo ran out of end zone |
| Phx | — | Centers 27 pass from Chandler (Davis kick) |
| Phil | — | Hebron 5 run (Ruzek kick) |
| Phx | — | Lynch 55 fumble recovery return (Davis kick) |

**SAN FRANCISCO 24, PITTSBURGH 13**—at Three Rivers Stadium, attendance 57,502. Steve Young shook off the effects of a broken thumb on his throwing hand to throw 3 touchdown passes in the 49ers' victory. Young, who suffered the injury in a preseason game against the Raiders one month earlier and was questionable for this game until midweek, completed 24 of 36 passes for 240 yards with 3 interceptions. He helped stake San Francisco to a 17-0 lead in the first half with 2 short touchdown passes to Jerry Rice, then put the game away with a 5-yard touchdown pass to tight end Brent Jones early in the fourth quarter. The latter came after Pittsburgh's ailing Neil O'Donnell, normally the starting quarterback but sidelined the first half with tendinitis in his elbow, relieved an ineffective Mike Tomczak and led the Steelers to 10 third-quarter points that trimmed the 49ers' advantage to 17-13. San Francisco sacked the Pittsburgh quarterbacks 5 times, including 2 by rookie defensive end Dana Stubblefield. Steelers cornerback Rod Woodson intercepted 2 passes.

| | | | | | | |
|---|---|---|---|---|---|---|
| **San Francisco** | 10 | 7 | 0 | 7 | — | 24 |
| **Pittsburgh** | 0 | 3 | 10 | 0 | — | 13 |

| | | |
|---|---|---|
| SF | — | FG Cofer 37 |
| SF | — | Rice 5 pass from Young (Cofer kick) |
| SF | — | Rice 6 pass from Young (Cofer kick) |
| Pitt | — | FG Anderson 29 |
| Pitt | — | Foster 5 run (Anderson kick) |
| Pitt | — | FG Anderson 39 |
| SF | — | B. Jones 5 pass from Young (Cofer kick) |

**SAN DIEGO 18, SEATTLE 12**—at San Diego Jack Murphy Stadium, attendance 58,039. John Carney's club-record 6 field goals provided the Chargers with all their points in a victory over the Seahawks. It was San Diego's first opening-day win in seven years. Carney's fourth field goal of the game, a 32-yard kick 3:21 before halftime, gave the defending AFC Western Division champions the lead for good at 12-10. He added kicks of 51 and 19 yards in the fourth quarter before the Chargers gave up a concession safety on the final play of the game. Seattle had taken a 7-0 advantage only 53 seconds into the game when defensive tackle Joe Nash intercepted a Stan Humphries pass that was tipped by Cortez Kennedy and ran 13 yards for a touchdown. But the Seahawks could muster little offense, totaling just 240 yards. Rookie quarterback Rick Mirer completed 20 of 27 passes, but for only 154 yards.

| | | | | | | |
|---|---|---|---|---|---|---|
| **Seattle** | 7 | 3 | 0 | 2 | — | 12 |
| **San Diego** | 6 | 6 | 0 | 6 | — | 18 |

| | | |
|---|---|---|
| Sea | — | Nash 13 interception return (Kasay kick) |
| SD | — | FG Carney 26 |
| SD | — | FG Carney 44 |
| Sea | — | FG Kasay 27 |
| SD | — | FG Carney 50 |
| SD | — | FG Carney 32 |
| SD | — | FG Carney 51 |
| SD | — | FG Carney 19 |
| Sea | — | Safety, Kidd downed ball in end zone |

## SUNDAY NIGHT, SEPTEMBER 5

**NEW ORLEANS 33, HOUSTON 21**—at Louisiana Superdome, attendance 69,029. The Saints fell behind on the game's first possession, then dominated the Oilers to win easily. Wade Wilson passed for 206 yards, rookie Lorenzo Neal rushed for 89 yards, and Morten Andersen kicked 4 field goals for New Orleans. The Saints raced to a 33-7 advantage after Warren Moon's 6-yard touchdown pass to Haywood Jeffires 6:13 into the game. Dalton Hilliard's 2-yard touchdown run early in the second quarter put the Saints ahead for good, and Andersen's 47-yard field goal 11 seconds before halftime gave New Orleans a 13-7 lead. The Saints then marched 82 yards with the second-half kickoff, consuming 8:09 en route to another field goal by Andersen. They put the game out of reach when defensive end Frank Warren returned a fumble 47 yards for a touchdown early in the fourth quarter to make it 26-7. Moon completed 21 of 32 passes for 241 yards for Oilers, but he was sacked 3 times and intercepted once. Houston also lost 4 fumbles. Saints cornerback Toi Cook had 7 tackles, a sack, a fumble recovery, and an interception.

| | | | | | | |
|---|---|---|---|---|---|---|
| **Houston** | 7 | 0 | 0 | 14 | — | 21 |
| **New Orleans** | 3 | 10 | 6 | 14 | — | 33 |

| | | |
|---|---|---|
| Hou | — | Jeffires 6 pass from Moon (Del Greco kick) |
| NO | — | FG Andersen 28 |
| NO | — | Hilliard 2 run (Andersen kick) |
| NO | — | FG Andersen 37 |
| NO | — | FG Andersen 18 |
| NO | — | FG Andersen 47 |
| NO | — | Warren 47 fumble recovery return (Andersen kick) |
| NO | — | D. Brown 2 run (Andersen kick) |
| Hou | — | Carlson 1 run (Del Greco kick) |
| Hou | — | Robertson 80 fumble recovery return (Del Greco kick) |

## MONDAY, SEPTEMBER 6

**WASHINGTON 35, DALLAS 16**—at RFK Stadium, attendance 56,345. Brian Mitchell ran for 116 yards and 2 touchdowns, and the Redskins stunned the defending Super Bowl champions with a lopsided victory. Washington put the game away with a back-breaking 99-yard touchdown drive in the third quarter, after Dallas had pulled within 21-13 on a 32-yard touchdown pass from Troy Aikman to Alvin Harper. Mitchell inadvertently downed the ensuing kickoff at the Redskins' 1-yard line, but Washington took 13 plays and more than seven minutes to march the length of the field. Mark Rypien capped the drive by throwing a 15-yard touchdown pass to Art Monk with six seconds left in the third quarter. Rypien directed a ball-control passing attack and completed 22 of 34 passes for 161 yards. The Cowboys' Troy Aikman passed for 267 yards but Dallas, playing without Emmitt Smith, the NFL's leading rusher in 1991 and 1992, managed only 91 rushing yards. The Cowboys also lost 4 fumbles, 2 on punts, that enabled the Redskins to build a 14-6 halftime lead.

| | | | | | | |
|---|---|---|---|---|---|---|
| **Dallas** | 6 | 0 | 7 | 3 | — | 16 |
| **Washington** | 0 | 14 | 14 | 7 | — | 35 |

| | | |
|---|---|---|
| Dall | — | Harper 80 pass from Aikman (kick failed) |
| Wash | — | Sanders 15 pass from Rypien (Lohmiller kick) |
| Wash | — | Mitchell 1 run (Lohmiller kick) |
| Wash | — | Middleton 1 pass from Rypien (Lohmiller kick) |
| Dall | — | Harper 32 pass from Aikman (Elliott kick) |
| Wash | — | Monk 15 pass from Rypien (Lohmiller kick) |
| Dall | — | FG Elliott 22 |
| Wash | — | Mitchell 29 run (Lohmiller kick) |

## SECOND WEEK SUMMARIES

### AMERICAN FOOTBALL CONFERENCE

| Eastern Division | W | L | T | Pct. | Pts. | OP |
|---|---|---|---|---|---|---|
| Buffalo | 2 | 0 | 0 | 1.000 | 51 | 24 |
| Indianapolis | 1 | 1 | 0 | .500 | 29 | 30 |
| Miami | 1 | 1 | 0 | .500 | 38 | 44 |
| N.Y. Jets | 1 | 1 | 0 | .500 | 44 | 40 |
| New England | 0 | 2 | 0 | .000 | 30 | 57 |
| **Central Division** | | | | | | |
| Cleveland | 2 | 0 | 0 | 1.000 | 50 | 27 |
| Houston | 1 | 1 | 0 | .500 | 51 | 33 |
| Cincinnati | 0 | 2 | 0 | .000 | 20 | 36 |
| Pittsburgh | 0 | 2 | 0 | .000 | 13 | 51 |
| **Western Division** | | | | | | |
| Denver | 2 | 0 | 0 | 1.000 | 60 | 37 |
| L.A. Raiders | 2 | 0 | 0 | 1.000 | 41 | 20 |
| Kansas City | 1 | 1 | 0 | .500 | 27 | 33 |
| San Diego | 1 | 1 | 0 | .500 | 35 | 46 |
| Seattle | 0 | 2 | 0 | .000 | 25 | 35 |

### NATIONAL FOOTBALL CONFERENCE

| Eastern Division | W | L | T | Pct. | Pts. | OP |
|---|---|---|---|---|---|---|
| N.Y. Giants | 2 | 0 | 0 | 1.000 | 49 | 27 |
| Philadelphia | 2 | 0 | 0 | 1.000 | 43 | 34 |
| Phoenix | 1 | 1 | 0 | .500 | 34 | 33 |
| Washington | 1 | 1 | 0 | .500 | 45 | 33 |
| Dallas | 0 | 2 | 0 | .000 | 26 | 48 |
| **Central Division** | | | | | | |
| Detroit | 2 | 0 | 0 | 1.000 | 49 | 29 |
| Green Bay | 1 | 1 | 0 | .500 | 53 | 26 |
| Minnesota | 1 | 1 | 0 | .500 | 17 | 31 |
| Chicago | 0 | 2 | 0 | .000 | 27 | 36 |
| Tampa Bay | 0 | 2 | 0 | .000 | 10 | 50 |
| **Western Division** | | | | | | |
| New Orleans | 2 | 0 | 0 | 1.000 | 67 | 52 |
| L.A. Rams | 1 | 1 | 0 | .500 | 33 | 36 |
| San Francisco | 1 | 1 | 0 | .500 | 37 | 36 |
| Atlanta | 0 | 2 | 0 | .000 | 44 | 64 |

## SUNDAY, SEPTEMBER 12

**BUFFALO 13, DALLAS 10**—at Texas Stadium, attendance 63,226. Safety Matt Darby intercepted a pass at the goal line in the closing seconds to preserve the Bills' victory, handing the defending Super Bowl champions their second consecutive defeat. It was a dramatic reversal for Buffalo, which turned over the ball 9 times while being routed by the Cowboys 52-17 in Super Bowl XXVII eight months earlier. After the Bills' Steve Tasker recovered rookie Kevin Williams's fumbled punt return at Dallas's 34-yard line, Steve Christie kicked a 35-yard field goal to break a 10-10 tie with 2:49 left in the game. The Cowboys took over on their 20 and marched 69 yards to Buffalo's 11. But Troy Aikman's pass over the middle bounced off the shoulder pads of tight end Jay Novacek, who collided with Darby. The ball deflected in the air and Darby made a lunging interception at the 1. Dallas outgained the Bills 393-229 but was intercepted twice and lost a pair of fumbles. Aikman finished with 28 completions in a career-high 45 attempts for 297 yards. Cowboys wide receiver Michael Irvin caught 8 passes for 115 yards, while Novacek had 8 receptions for 106 yards.

| | | | | | | |
|---|---|---|---|---|---|---|
| **Buffalo** | 7 | 3 | 0 | 3 | — | 13 |
| **Dallas** | 0 | 3 | 0 | 7 | — | 10 |

Buff — Gardner 10 pass from Kelly (Christie kick)
Buff — FG Christie 48
Dall — FG Elliott 43
Dall — K. Williams 5 run (Elliott kick)
Buff — FG Christie 35

**MINNESOTA 10, CHICAGO 7**—at Metrodome, attendance 56,285. Jim McMahon's 16-yard touchdown pass to Cris Carter midway through the fourth quarter lifted the Vikings over the Bears. Playing for the first time against the team that traded him five years earlier, McMahon completed 23 of 29 passes for 173 yards and was not intercepted. Running back Barry Word, acquired from the Chiefs to replace injured Terry Allen, supplied most of the rest of the offense, gaining 94 yards on 24 carries and catching 5 passes for 58 yards. But it was the Vikings' defense that made the difference, limiting Chicago to only 7 first downs and 140 total yards. Minnesota maintained possession for more than 37 of the game's 60 minutes.

| | | | | | | |
|---|---|---|---|---|---|---|
| **Chicago** | 7 | 0 | 0 | 0 | — | 7 |
| **Minnesota** | 0 | 3 | 0 | 7 | — | 10 |

Chi — Harbaugh 1 run (Butler kick)
Minn — FG Reveiz 22
Minn — C. Carter 16 pass from McMahon (Reveiz kick)

**DETROIT 19, NEW ENGLAND 16**—at Foxboro Stadium, attendance 54,151. Jason Hanson's 38-yard field goal with 3:56 left in overtime won it for the Lions. The Patriots had forced the extra session when Drew Bledsoe threw a 2-yard touchdown pass to wide receiver Vincent Brisby with 12 seconds remaining in the fourth quarter. In the overtime, Detroit quarterback Rodney Peete marched his team 60 yards in 11 plays to the winning kick. Peete, who had thrown 3 interceptions, lost a fumble, and suffered 3 sacks earlier in the game, completed passes of 14 yards to Barry Sanders, 13 yards to Herman Moore, and 17 yards to Brett Perriman to position Hanson for his fourth field goal of the game. The Lions' only touchdown came 11 seconds into the game when cornerback Willie Clay returned a fumble on the opening kickoff 15 yards for a score. Bledsoe completed 28 of 49 passes for 239 yards for New England. Rookie linebacker Chris Slade had all 3 of the Patriots' sacks. Sanders ran for 148 yards on 32 carries for Detroit.

| | | | | | | | |
|---|---|---|---|---|---|---|---|
| **Detroit** | 7 | 0 | 3 | 6 | 3 | — | 19 |
| **New England** | 6 | 3 | 0 | 7 | 0 | — | 16 |

Det — Clay 15 fumble recovery return (Hanson kick)
NE — FG Sisson 26
NE — FG Sisson 21
NE — FG Sisson 32
Det — FG Hanson 22
Det — FG Hanson 26
Det — FG Hanson 23
NE — Brisby 2 pass from Bledsoe (Sisson kick)
Det — FG Hanson 38

**INDIANAPOLIS 9, CINCINNATI 6**—at Riverfront Stadium, attendance 50,299. Dean Biasucci kicked 3 field goals, including the winning 42-yard kick with three seconds remaining, as the Colts edged the Bengals. The decisive kick came four plays after Indianapolis linebacker Quentin Coryatt hit Cincinnati quarterback David Klingler as he threw, forcing a pass that cornerback John Baylor intercepted at midfield. Baylor returned the theft 7 yards, and the Bengals were penalized 15 yards for a facemask penalty that moved the ball to the 28-yard line to set up Biasucci's winning kick. Doug Pelfrey kicked a pair of field goals for Cincinnati, but also missed a 35-yard attempt with 2:18 to go in the game when the ball was tipped by Colts linebacker Scott Radecic.

| | | | | | | |
|---|---|---|---|---|---|---|
| **Indianapolis** | 0 | 3 | 3 | 3 | — | 9 |
| **Cincinnati** | 3 | 0 | 3 | 0 | — | 6 |

Cin — FG Pelfrey 35
Ind — FG Biasucci 53
Cin — FG Pelfrey 23
Ind — FG Biasucci 31
Ind — FG Biasucci 42

**HOUSTON 30, KANSAS CITY 0**—at Astrodome, attendance 59,780. The Oilers rebounded from an opening-game loss to the Saints by blanking the Chiefs. Kansas City played without starting quarterback Joe Montana, who was nursing an injured wrist. Houston struggled offensively, accumulating only 57 rushing yards and 247 total yards, but used 3 field goals by Al Del Greco and an opportunistic defense to hand the Chiefs their first shutout loss since 1987. Leading 16-0 in the fourth quarter, the Oilers put the game out of reach when cornerback Cris Dishman stripped the ball from Kansas City tight end Mike Dyal and raced 58 yards for a touchdown with 5:34 left to play. Safety Marcus Robertson set up the final touchdown, a 1-yard run by Lorenzo White, with his second interception of the game. He returned his first theft 48 yards to set up a field goal late in the first half. Houston forced 5 turnovers and sacked the Chiefs' Dave Krieg 4 times. Kansas City managed only 10 first downs, 46 rushing yards, and 206 total yards. Warren Moon completed 22 of 35 passes for 204 yards and a touchdown for the Oilers.

| | | | | | | |
|---|---|---|---|---|---|---|
| **Kansas City** | 0 | 0 | 0 | 0 | — | 0 |
| **Houston** | 0 | 7 | 6 | 17 | — | 30 |

Hou — Duncan 2 pass from Moon (Del Greco kick)
Hou — FG Del Greco 25
Hou — FG Del Greco 22
Hou — FG Del Greco 50
Hou — Dishman 58 fumble recovery return (Del Greco kick)
Hou — White 1 run (Del Greco kick)

**NEW ORLEANS 34, ATLANTA 31**—at Georgia Dome, attendance 64,287. Morten Andersen kicked a 44-yard field goal as time expired and the Saints survived a 21-point fourth-quarter barrage to beat the Falcons. Wade Wilson threw 3 touchdown passes as New Orleans built a seemingly insurmountable 31-10 advantage through three quarters. But Atlanta rallied behind free-agent quarterback Bobby Hebert, who spent his first seven seasons with the Saints and was on the field for the first time with his new team. Hebert threw a 4-yard touchdown pass to Michael Haynes 2:34 into the fourth quarter, then tossed a club-record 98-yard scoring pass to the speedster 1:35 later to trim the Falcons' deficit to 31-24. His 3-yard touchdown pass to Mike Pritchard with 2:40 remaining in the game tied the score at 31-31. But after Atlanta got the ball back again, New Orleans linebacker Renaldo Turnbull stripped Hebert of the ball and recovered it on the Falcons' 32-yard line with 22 seconds left. Andersen's winning kick came three plays later. The usually conservative Saints amassed a club-record 557 yards, including a 74-yard run by rookie Lorenzo Neal on their first play from scrimmage. But Neal later broke his ankle and was lost for the season. Wilson, who played with the Falcons in 1992, completed 22 of 34 passes for 341 yards. Hebert was 14 of 18 for 243 yards for Atlanta, which had 380 total yards. Haynes caught 7 passes for 182 yards. Andersen kicked a 27-yard field goal in the first quarter to extend his consecutive streak to an NFL-record 25 in a row. But he missed his next two attempts, from 42 and 50 yards, before converting on the last play.

| | | | | | | |
|---|---|---|---|---|---|---|
| **New Orleans** | 10 | 14 | 7 | 3 | — | 34 |
| **Atlanta** | 0 | 10 | 0 | 21 | — | 31 |

NO — Neal 74 run (Andersen kick)
NO — FG Andersen 27
Atl — Pegram 1 run (Johnson kick)
NO — Early 42 pass from Wilson (Andersen kick)
Atl — FG Johnson 20
NO — Early 18 pass from Wilson (Andersen kick)
NO — I. Smith 1 pass from Wilson (Andersen kick)
Atl — Haynes 4 pass from Hebert (Johnson kick)
Atl — Haynes 98 pass from Hebert (Johnson kick)
Atl — Pritchard 3 pass from Hebert (Johnson kick)
NO — FG Andersen 44

**N.Y. JETS 24, MIAMI 14**—at Joe Robbie Stadium, attendance 70,314. Boomer Esiason threw 2 touchdown passes and ran for another as the Jets upset the Dolphins. Esiason, who threw for more than 300 yards for the second consecutive week, set up Cary Blanchard's tie-breaking 39-yard field goal late in the third quarter with a 46-yard, flea-flicker pass to Terance Mathis. His 20-yard scoring toss to running back Pat Chaffey capped a 73-yard fourth-quarter drive and gave New York a 10-point advantage with 4:14 left. Dan Marino passed for 286 yards for Miami but had little help as the Dolphins could manage only 27 rushing yards. Marino became only the fourth player in NFL history to pass for more than 40,000 yards in his career, finishing the game at 40,024. Esiason completed 22 of 33 attempts for 323 yards.

| | | | | | | |
|---|---|---|---|---|---|---|
| **N.Y. Jets** | 0 | 14 | 3 | 7 | — | 24 |
| **Miami** | 7 | 7 | 0 | 0 | — | 14 |

Mia — K. Jackson 57 pass from Marino (Stoyanovich kick)
Jets — Esiason 4 run (Blanchard kick)
Jets — Baxter 3 pass from Esiason (Blanchard kick)
Mia — Ingram 25 pass from Marino (Stoyanovich kick)
Jets — FG Blanchard 39
Jets — Chaffey 20 pass from Esiason (Blanchard kick)

**PHILADELPHIA 20, GREEN BAY 17**—at Lambeau Field, attendance 59,061. Roger Ruzek's 30-yard field goal with five seconds left lifted the Eagles to victory in a game that featured Packers defensive end Reggie White playing against his old teammates for the first time. White, the seven-time Pro Bowl defensive end who signed with Green Bay as a free agent in the offseason, had 2 sacks and forced a pair of fumbles in the first quarter. But Philadelphia stole the spotlight by rallying from a 10-point deficit in the fourth quarter. Ruzek's 27-yard field goal and Randall Cunningham's 40-yard touchdown pass to rookie wide receiver Victor Bailey with 4:14 left in the game tied the score at 17-17. After the Packers failed to make a first down, Vai Sikahema's 13-yard punt return positioned the Eagles at the Green Bay 45-yard line. Philadelphia then consumed most of the time remaining on the clock by marching 32 yards on the ground to the winning field goal. The game was played before a crowd of 59,061, the second largest ever at historic Lambeau Field.

| | | | | | | |
|---|---|---|---|---|---|---|
| **Philadelphia** | 0 | 7 | 0 | 13 | — | 20 |
| **Green Bay** | 7 | 3 | 7 | 0 | — | 17 |

GB — Sharpe 2 pass from Favre (Jacke kick)
GB — FG Jacke 23
Phil — Bavaro 2 pass from Cunningham (Ruzek kick)
GB — J. Harris 15 pass from Favre (Jacke kick)
Phil — FG Ruzek 27
Phil — Bailey 40 pass from Cunningham (Ruzek kick)
Phil — FG Ruzek 30

**PHOENIX 17, WASHINGTON 10**—at RFK Stadium, attendance 53,525. The Cardinals built a 17-0 halftime lead and hung on to stun the Redskins. It was Phoenix's first victory at RFK Stadium in 15 years. Washington suffered a blow when quarterback Mark Rypien injured his knee while scrambling in the second quarter. He was expected to miss three to six weeks. Cary Conklin, who spent his first two NFL seasons on injured reserve and threw only 2 passes in 1992, replaced Rypien and threw a 9-yard touchdown pass to Ricky Sanders in the third quarter, but it wasn't enough. Johnny Bailey returned a punt 58 yards for a touchdown in the first quarter and rookie Garrison Hearst, the Cardinals' first-round draft choice, had 76 of his team's 152 rushing yards as the Cardinals controlled the ball on the ground. Phoenix outgained the Redskins 303-233 and maintained possession for 35:54.

| | | | | | | |
|---|---|---|---|---|---|---|
| **Phoenix** | 10 | 7 | 0 | 0 | — | 17 |
| **Washington** | 0 | 0 | 7 | 3 | — | 10 |

Phx — Bailey 58 punt return (Davis kick)
Phx — FG Davis 53
Phx — Moore 18 run (Davis kick)
Wash — Sanders 9 pass from Conklin (Lohmiller kick)
Wash — FG Lohmiller 23

**L.A. RAMS 27, PITTSBURGH 0**—at Anaheim Stadium, attendance 50,588. The Rams rebounded from a lopsided loss to the Packers on opening day by blanking the defending AFC Central Division champions. Jim Everett passed for 221 yards and rookies Troy Drayton and Jerome Bettis scored their first NFL touchdowns. Tony Zendejas added a pair of long-range field goals, including a club-record 54-yard kick. Los Angeles amassed 314 total yards while limiting the Steelers to 175. Rams defensive tackle Sean Gilbert had 4 sacks. Wide receiver Henry Ellard caught 9 passes for 127 yards.

| | | | | | | |
|---|---|---|---|---|---|---|
| **Pittsburgh** | 0 | 0 | 0 | 0 | — | 0 |
| **L.A. Rams** | 0 | 14 | 3 | 10 | — | 27 |

Rams — Drayton 22 pass from Everett (Zendejas kick)
Rams — Gary 6 run (Zendejas kick)
Rams — FG Zendejas 54
Rams — FG Zendejas 50
Rams — Bettis 29 run (Zendejas kick)

**DENVER 34, SAN DIEGO 17**—at Mile High Stadium, attendance 75,074. John Elway completed 24 of 34 passes for 294 yards and 2 touchdowns to lead the Broncos past the Chargers. The game was scoreless until Denver went to the No-Huddle offense at the outset of the second quarter. Two minutes into the period, Elway capped an 87-yard drive with a 34-yard touchdown pass to Arthur Marshall. San Diego fumbled two plays later and Broncos linebacker Karl Mecklenburg recovered at the Chargers' 25-yard line. A penalty moved the ball to the 12, and Elway's touchdown pass to Reggie Rivers made it 14-0. San Diego closed to 17-14 midway through the third quarter, turning an interception and a fumble recovery into touchdowns just 2:19 apart. Denver countered with a 12-play, 80-yard drive, capped by a 1-yard touchdown run by former Chargers running back Rod Bernstine. Elway made the key play on the march, scrambling on third-and-19 before finding Vance Johnson for a 46-yard gain to the 1. Stan Humphries passed for 298 yards for San Diego, which amassed 26 first downs and 390 total yards. Chargers wide receiver Nate Lewis caught 10 passes for 119 yards. Running back Ronnie Harmon had 10 catches for 81 yards.

| | | | | | | |
|---|---|---|---|---|---|---|
| **San Diego** | 0 | 0 | 14 | 3 | — | 17 |
| **Denver** | 0 | 17 | 7 | 10 | — | 34 |

Den — Marshall 34 pass from Elway (Elam kick)
Den — Rivers 12 pass from Elway (Elam kick)
Den — FG Elam 20
SD — Walker 25 pass from Humphries (Carney kick)
SD — Lewis 24 pass from Humphries (Carney kick)
Den — Bernstine 1 run (Elam kick)
SD — FG Carney 30
Den — FG Elam 54
Den — Delpino 1 run (Elam kick)

**N.Y. GIANTS 23, TAMPA BAY 7**—at Giants Stadium, attendance 75,891. Rodney Hampton gained 134 yards on 29 carries and scored a touchdown as the Giants ground out a methodical victory over the Buccaneers. New York ran the football 41 times for 181 yards and maintained possession for 35:04 of the game's 60 minutes. The Giants led 17-7 at halftime and increased the lead to 20-7 early in the third quarter before Tampa Bay threatened to get back in the game. The Buccaneers drove 79 yards to New York's 1-yard line before Reggie Cobb was stopped short of the goal line on fourth down. David Treadwell added his third field goal of the game in the fourth quarter. Craig Erickson started his first game for Tampa Bay and completed 16 of 28 passes for 174 yards.

| | | | | | | |
|---|---|---|---|---|---|---|
| **Tampa Bay** | 0 | 7 | 0 | 0 | — | 7 |
| **N.Y. Giants** | 7 | 10 | 3 | 3 | — | 23 |

Giants— Cross 18 pass from Simms (Treadwell kick)
Giants— Hampton 2 run (Treadwell kick)
TB — Armstrong 17 pass from Erickson (Husted kick)
Giants— FG Treadwell 33
Giants— FG Treadwell 22
Giants— FG Treadwell 46

## SUNDAY NIGHT, SEPTEMBER 12

**L.A. RAIDERS 17, SEATTLE 13**—at Kingdome, attendance 58,836. Jeff Hostetler's 33-yard touchdown pass to Tim Brown broke a 10-10 tie 1:13 before halftime and the Raiders went on to beat the Seahawks. The decisive touchdown came three plays after Los Angeles linebacker Aaron Wallace recovered rookie quarterback Rick Mirer's fumble at the Raiders' 48-yard line. In the second half, Seattle managed only a 53-yard field goal by John Kasay with 7:49 left in the game. Los Angeles's defense limited the Seahawks to 232 total yards and harassed Mirer, sacking him 5 times, 4 of them by end Anthony Smith. Brown finished with 9 catches for 97 yards.

| | | | | | | |
|---|---|---|---|---|---|---|
| **L.A. Raiders** | 7 | 10 | 0 | 0 | — | 17 |
| **Seattle** | 0 | 10 | 0 | 3 | — | 13 |

Raid — Hostetler 2 run (Jaeger kick)
Sea — Warren 6 run (Kasay kick)
Sea — FG Kasay 39
Raid — FG Jaeger 36
Raid — Brown 33 pass from Hostetler (Jaeger kick)
Sea — FG Kasay 53

## MONDAY, SEPTEMBER 13

**CLEVELAND 23, SAN FRANCISCO 13**—at Cleveland Stadium, attendance 78,512. Bernie Kosar threw a 30-yard touchdown pass to Michael Jackson with 35 seconds left in the first half, and the Browns' defense shut out the 49ers in the second half to preserve the victory. San Francisco had 396 total yards but was stifled by 3 interceptions, a lost fumble, a blocked field-goal attempt, and a fumbled snap on another field-goal try. The loss snapped the 49ers' nine-game regular-season winning streak. Jackson finished with 5 catches for a career-high 105 yards for the Browns. Defensive tackle James Jones scored a touchdown on a 1-yard run after lining up as a blocking back in the second quarter.

| | | | | | | |
|---|---|---|---|---|---|---|
| **San Francisco** | 6 | 7 | 0 | 0 | — | 13 |
| **Cleveland** | 3 | 17 | 3 | 0 | — | 23 |

SF — FG Cofer 46
Cle — FG Stover 47
SF — FG Cofer 28
Cle — J. Jones 1 run (Stover kick)
Cle — FG Stover 41
SF — Logan 4 run (Cofer kick)
Cle — Jackson 30 pass from Kosar (Stover kick)
Cle — FG Stover 33

## THIRD WEEK SUMMARIES

**AMERICAN FOOTBALL CONFERENCE**

| **Eastern Division** | **W** | **L** | **T** | **Pct.** | **Pts.** | **OP** |
|---|---|---|---|---|---|---|
| Buffalo | 2 | 0 | 0 | 1.000 | 51 | 24 |
| Indianapolis | 1 | 1 | 0 | .500 | 29 | 30 |
| Miami | 1 | 1 | 0 | .500 | 38 | 44 |
| N.Y. Jets | 1 | 1 | 0 | .500 | 44 | 40 |
| New England | 0 | 3 | 0 | .000 | 44 | 74 |
| **Central Division** | | | | | | |
| Cleveland | 3 | 0 | 0 | 1.000 | 69 | 43 |
| Houston | 1 | 2 | 0 | .333 | 68 | 51 |
| Pittsburgh | 1 | 2 | 0 | .333 | 47 | 58 |
| Cincinnati | 0 | 3 | 0 | .000 | 27 | 70 |
| **Western Division** | | | | | | |
| Denver | 2 | 1 | 0 | .667 | 67 | 52 |
| Kansas City | 2 | 1 | 0 | .667 | 42 | 40 |
| L.A. Raiders | 2 | 1 | 0 | .667 | 57 | 39 |
| San Diego | 2 | 1 | 0 | .667 | 53 | 63 |
| Seattle | 1 | 2 | 0 | .333 | 42 | 49 |

**NATIONAL FOOTBALL CONFERENCE**

| **Eastern Division** | **W** | **L** | **T** | **Pct.** | **Pts.** | **OP** |
|---|---|---|---|---|---|---|
| N.Y. Giants | 3 | 0 | 0 | 1.000 | 69 | 37 |
| Philadelphia | 3 | 0 | 0 | 1.000 | 77 | 65 |
| Dallas | 1 | 2 | 0 | .333 | 43 | 58 |
| Phoenix | 1 | 2 | 0 | .333 | 44 | 50 |
| Washington | 1 | 2 | 0 | .333 | 76 | 67 |
| **Central Division** | | | | | | |
| Detroit | 2 | 1 | 0 | .667 | 52 | 43 |
| Green Bay | 1 | 1 | 0 | .500 | 53 | 26 |
| Minnesota | 1 | 1 | 0 | .500 | 17 | 31 |
| Chicago | 0 | 2 | 0 | .000 | 27 | 36 |
| Tampa Bay | 0 | 2 | 0 | .000 | 10 | 50 |
| **Western Division** | | | | | | |
| New Orleans | 3 | 0 | 0 | 1.000 | 81 | 55 |
| San Francisco | 2 | 1 | 0 | .667 | 74 | 66 |
| L.A. Rams | 1 | 2 | 0 | .333 | 43 | 56 |
| Atlanta | 0 | 3 | 0 | .000 | 74 | 101 |

## SUNDAY, SEPTEMBER 19

**SAN FRANCISCO 37, ATLANTA 30**—at Candlestick Park, attendance 63,032. Steve Young threw 3 touchdown pass and completed a key pass to himself as the 49ers beat Atlanta in a wild game. San Francisco trailed 20-16 late in the third quarter but had moved the ball to the Falcons' 8-yard line when Young, scrambling to avoid a sack, threw a pass that was batted in the air near the goal line. The ball bounced back to Young, who caught it and was tackled at the 2 after a 6-yard gain. Ricky Watters then ran for a touchdown on the next play to give San Francisco the lead for good. The two teams accounted for 859 total yards, including 478 by the 49ers, who never punted. San Francisco had 268 rushing yards, including 43 by wide receiver Jerry Rice on a fourth-quarter reverse for the clinching touchdown. Young completed 18 of 22 passes for 210 yards and Watters ran for 112 yards on 19 carries. Atlanta running back Erric Pegram, starting in place of injured Eric Dickerson, rushed for 192 yards on 27 carries. Quarterback Bobby Hebert, a free-agent signee making his first start for the Falcons, completed 23 of 38 passes for 199 yards and 3 touchdowns, all of them to Andre Rison.

| | | | | | | |
|---|---|---|---|---|---|---|
| **Atlanta** | 3 | 10 | 7 | 10 | — | 30 |
| **San Francisco** | 3 | 6 | 14 | 14 | — | 37 |

Atl — FG Johnson 42
SF — FG Cofer 46
Atl — Rison 12 pass from Hebert (Johnson kick)
SF — Williams 9 pass from Young (kick failed)
Atl — FG Johnson 38
SF — Jones 20 pass from Young (Cofer kick)
Atl — Rison 3 pass from Hebert (Johnson kick)
SF — Watters 2 run (Cofer kick)
SF — Singleton 6 pass from Young (Cofer kick)
Atl — FG Johnson 27
SF — Rice 43 run (Cofer kick)
Atl — Rison 16 pass from Hebert (Johnson kick)

**PITTSBURGH 34, CINCINNATI 7**—at Three Rivers Stadium, attendance 53,682. The Steelers amassed 404 total yards and breezed to victory. It was the first win of the year for the defending AFC Central Division champions. Quarterback Neil O'Donnell, playing with tendinitis in his right elbow, completed 21 of 25 passes for 189 yards and 3 touchdowns. His 18-yard touchdown pass to Yancey Thigpen with 36 seconds left in the first half gave Pittsburgh a 17-7 lead. His 9-yard scoring toss to Dwight Stone late in the third quarter made it 27-7. Stone also ran 38 yards on a reverse for a touchdown. Cincinnati's David Klingler completed 17 of 21 passes, but the Bengals managed only 170 total yards. Klingler was 11 of 12 in the first half, including a 15-yard touchdown pass to Carl Pickens.

| | | | | | | |
|---|---|---|---|---|---|---|
| **Cincinnati** | 0 | 7 | 0 | 0 | — | 7 |
| **Pittsburgh** | 7 | 10 | 10 | 7 | — | 34 |

Pitt — Mills 3 pass from O'Donnell (Anderson kick)
Pitt — FG Anderson 33
Cin — Pickens 15 pass from Klingler (Pelfrey kick)
Pitt — Thigpen 18 pass from O'Donnell (Anderson kick)
Pitt — FG Anderson 34
Pitt — Stone 9 pass from O'Donnell (Anderson kick)
Pitt — Stone 38 run (Anderson kick)

**CLEVELAND 19, L.A. RAIDERS 16**—at Los Angeles Memorial Coliseum, attendance 48,617. Eric Metcalf ran 1 yard for a touchdown with 2 seconds left, capping a 19-point fourth quarter and lifting the Browns to a dramatic come-from-behind victory. Los Angeles led 13-0 at halftime behind the strength of its defense, which limited Cleveland to only 37 total yards in the first half and did not permit the Browns to cross midfield. But the Raiders could not put Cleveland away, settling for short field goals by Jeff Jaeger after interceptions had positioned them in first-and-goal situations. Then in the second half, Los Angeles managed only 17 total yards and 1 first down, which came via penalty. Still, the Raiders led 16-3 until backup quarterback Vinny Testaverde, who replaced an ineffective Bernie Kosar in the fourth quarter, marched the Browns 90 yards in 12 plays, the last a 12-yard touchdown pass to Lawyer Tillman to trim the deficit to 16-10 with 2:26 remaining. After failing to make a first down on their next possession, the Raiders elected to give up a safety rather than punt from their own end zone. But Metcalf returned the ensuing free kick 37 yards, and Cleveland began its winning drive from Los Angeles's 45-yard line. Testaverde completed passes of 17 and 16 yards to Mark Carrier, his former teammate at Tampa Bay, and Metcalf took a pitchout and ran for the winning score on second down, even though the Browns had no timeouts left. Metcalf, who scored 4 touchdowns in a victory over the Raiders at the Coliseum last year, had minus-3 yards rushing until his winning run.

| | | | | | | |
|---|---|---|---|---|---|---|
| **Cleveland** | 0 | 0 | 0 | 19 | — | 19 |
| **L.A. Raiders** | 10 | 3 | 0 | 3 | — | 16 |

Raid — Glover 2 pass from Hostetler (Jaeger kick)
Raid — FG Jaeger 24
Raid — FG Jaeger 27
Cle — FG Stover 32
Raid — FG Jaeger 53
Cle — Tillman 12 pass from Testaverde (Stover kick)
Cle — Safety, Gossett ran out of end zone
Cle — Metcalf 1 run (Stover kick)

**NEW ORLEANS 14, DETROIT 3**—at Louisiana Superdome, attendance 69,039. Wade Wilson threw 2 touchdown passes, but it was the Saints' defense that keyed the victory over the Lions. New Orleans allowed Detroit only 9 first downs and 165 total yards, and sacked Lions quarterback Rodney Peete 5 times, knocking him out of the game with a knee sprain in the fourth quarter. Renaldo Turnbull, who took over for Pro Bowl linebacker Pat Swilling after Swilling was traded to the Lions, had 3 sacks, 2 of which forced fumbles that teammate Rickey Jackson recovered. One set up an 18-yard drive for the clinching touchdown in the third quarter. Detroit took a 3-0 lead on a 41-yard field goal by Jason Hanson in the second quarter, but the Saints countered with a 73-yard touchdown drive over the next 6:17 to take the lead for good on a 17-yard pass from Wilson to tight end Hoby Brenner. New Orleans got 121 rushing yards from rookie Derek Brown while limiting the Lions' Barry Sanders to 76.

| | | | | | | |
|---|---|---|---|---|---|---|
| **Detroit** | 0 | 3 | 0 | 0 | — | 3 |
| **New Orleans** | 0 | 7 | 7 | 0 | — | 14 |

Det — FG Hanson 41
NO — Brenner 17 pass from Wilson (Andersen kick)
NO — Martin 12 pass from Wilson (Andersen kick)

**SAN DIEGO 18, HOUSTON 17**—at San Diego Jack Murphy Stadium, attendance 58,519. John Carney equaled his club record set two weeks earlier by kicking 6 field goals in as many attempts, including the game-winner from 27 yards with three seconds left. Carney, already 13-for-13 on the season, also ran his string of field goals to an NFL-record 29, dating back to the 1992 season. The previous mark was 25, which the Saints' Morten Andersen held for just one week. The Oilers trailed 15-14 until backup quarterback Cody Carlson rallied his team with an apparent go-ahead 8-yard touchdown pass to Haywood Jeffires. But officials ruled that Jeffires had caught the ball out of bounds, and Houston had to settle for a 27-yard field goal by Al Del Greco with 4:59 remaining. The Chargers took the ensuing kickoff and marched 75 yards in 13 plays to Carney's winning kick. Carney was the hero for the second time in three weeks. He also scored all of San Diego's points in an 18-12 victory over Seattle on opening day.

| | | | | | | |
|---|---|---|---|---|---|---|
| **Houston** | 0 | 14 | 0 | 3 | — | 17 |
| **San Diego** | 3 | 6 | 3 | 6 | — | 18 |

SD — FG Carney 34
SD — FG Carney 34
SD — FG Carney 27
Hou — Slaughter 2 pass from Moon (Del Greco kick)
Hou — D. Lewis 47 interception return (Del Greco kick)
SD — FG Carney 27
SD — FG Carney 36
Hou — FG Del Greco 27
SD — FG Carney 27

**N.Y. GIANTS 20, L.A. RAMS 10**—at Giants Stadium, attendance 76,213. Rodney Hampton rushed for 134 yards on a career-high 41 carries to power the Giants past the Rams. Hampton capped a 60-yard drive on the first possession of the game when he ran 1 yard for a touchdown to give New York a lead it would never relinquish. The Giants led 13-3 at halftime. Cornerback Mark Collins helped seal the outcome with a 50-yard interception return for a touchdown with 4:32 left in the third quarter. The Giants iced the game by eating up large amounts of time on the strength of Hampton's running. New York finished with 146 rushing yards to only 45 for the Rams, ran 79 plays to only 41 for Los Angeles, and maintained possession for 43:29 of the game's 60 minutes. Phil Simms completed 21 of 27 passes for 217 yards for the Giants. The Rams' Jim Everett was just 11 of 28 for 135 yards, but did have a 51-yard touchdown pass to Willie Anderson early in the fourth quarter.

| | | | | | | |
|---|---|---|---|---|---|---|
| **L.A. Rams** | 0 | 3 | 0 | 7 | — | 10 |
| **N.Y. Giants** | 7 | 6 | 7 | 0 | — | 20 |

Giants— Hampton 1 run (Treadwell kick)
Giants— FG Treadwell 34
Rams — FG Zendejas 52
Giants— FG Treadwell 19
Giants— Collins 50 interception return (Treadwell kick)
Rams — Anderson 51 pass from Everett (Zendejas kick)

**SEATTLE 17, NEW ENGLAND 14**—at Foxboro Stadium, attendance 50,392. The Seahawks built a 17-0 advantage through three quarters then held on to win when Scott Sisson's 54-yard field goal try in the final minute bounced off the crossbar. With the victory, Seattle snapped a six-game losing streak dating back to the 1992 season; the Patriots dropped their eighth in a row. Rick Mirer threw a 4-yard touchdown pass to Brian Blades to cap the opening drive of the game, and Chris Warren ran 15 yards for a touchdown late in the third quarter as the Seahawks built their 17-point advantage. But New England quarterback Drew Bledsoe, who passed for 240 yards, rallied his team to a pair of fourth-quarter touchdowns before Sisson's attempt to send the game into overtime. Warren rushed for 174 yards on a club-record 36 carries for Seattle.

| | | | | | | |
|---|---|---|---|---|---|---|
| **Seattle** | 7 | 0 | 10 | 0 | — | 17 |
| **New England** | 0 | 0 | 0 | 14 | — | 14 |

Sea — Blades 4 pass from Mirer (Kasay kick)
Sea — FG Kasay 24
Sea — Warren 15 run (Kasay kick)
NE — Coates 25 pass from Bledsoe (Sisson kick)
NE — Gash 4 run (Sisson kick)

**PHILADELPHIA 34, WASHINGTON 31**—at Veterans Stadium, attendance 65,435. Randall Cunningham threw 3 touchdown passes to Calvin Williams, including the game-winner with 10 seconds left, as the Eagles remained undefeated by rallying from an 11-point second-half deficit. Philadelphia trailed 21-10 late in the third quarter, but cornerback Eric Allen's 29-yard interception return for a touchdown and Cunningham's 9-yard touchdown pass to Williams with 8:23 left helped tie the score at 24-24. That tie lasted only 21 seconds, however, because rookie running back Reggie Brooks raced 85 yards for a touchdown on the next play from scrimmage to put the Redskins back in front 31-24. The Eagles closed to within four points when Matt Bahr, signed two days earlier to replace injured Roger Ruzek, kicked a 42-yard field goal with 3:57 to go in the game. Philadelphia forced Washington to punt, then took over at its 17-yard line with 1:54 remaining. Cunningham accounted for all 83 yards on the winning drive, completing 6 of 9 passes for 74 yards and scrambling for 9 yards. He finished with a team-high 49 rushing yards and completed 25 of 39 passes for 360 yards. Williams had career highs with 8 catches and 181 yards. The Redskins' Cary Conklin, filling in for injured Mark Rypien, completed 17 of 36 passes for 218 yards and 3 touchdowns in his first career start. Brooks gained 154 yards on 22 carries.

| | | | | | | |
|---|---|---|---|---|---|---|
| **Washington** | 0 | 14 | 7 | 10 | — | 31 |
| **Philadelphia** | 3 | 7 | 7 | 17 | — | 34 |

Phil — FG Bahr 27
Wash — McGee 11 pass from Conklin (Lohmiller kick)
Wash — Sanders 34 pass from Conklin (Lohmiller kick)
Phil — Williams 80 pass from Cunningham (Bahr kick)
Wash — Middleton 1 pass from Conklin (Lohmiller kick)
Phil — Allen 29 interception return (Bahr kick)
Wash — FG Lohmiller 38
Phil — Williams 9 pass from Cunningham (Bahr kick)
Wash — Brooks 85 run (Lohmiller kick)
Phil — FG Bahr 42
Phil — Williams 10 pass from Cunningham (Bahr kick)

## SUNDAY NIGHT, SEPTEMBER 19

**DALLAS 17, PHOENIX 10**—at Sun Devil Stadium, attendance 73,025. Derrick Lassic ran for 2 touchdowns, Troy Aikman passed for 281 yards, and the Cowboys notched their first victory of the season. Running back Emmitt Smith also made his 1993 debut and rushed for 45 yards in less than one half of action. Lassic, starting in place of Smith, ran 8 yards for a touchdown in the first quarter and 2 yards for a score in the third quarter as Dallas built a 17-0 advantage and held on for the victory. Aikman completed 21 of 27 passes with no interceptions and no sacks. Wide receiver Alvin Harper caught 6 passes for 136 yards. Phoenix's Steve Beuerlein completed 20 of 27 passes for 218 yards and 1 touchdown against his former teammates. The crowd of more than 73,000 was the largest ever to see the Cardinals play in Sun Devil Stadium. There were only 90 no-shows.

| | | | | | | |
|---|---|---|---|---|---|---|
| **Dallas** | 7 | 3 | 7 | 0 | — | 17 |
| **Phoenix** | 0 | 0 | 7 | 3 | — | 10 |

Dall — Lassic 8 run (Murray kick)
Dall — FG Murray 23
Dall — Lassic 2 run (Murray kick)
Phx — Proehl 12 pass from Beuerlein (G. Davis kick)
Phx — FG G. Davis 20

## MONDAY, SEPTEMBER 20

**KANSAS CITY 15, DENVER 7**—at Arrowhead Stadium, attendance 78,453. Nick Lowery kicked 5 field goals to give the Chiefs the victory and upstage the quarterback duel between Kansas City's Joe Montana and the Broncos' John Elway. Lowery had 4 field goals by halftime as the Chiefs built a 12-0 advantage. It was 15-0 before Denver drove 91 yards to the game's lone touchdown, Elway's 2-yard pass to Vance Johnson with 1:24 left in the fourth quarter. Montana, back in the lineup after sitting out one week with an injured wrist, completed 21 of 36 passes for 273 yards. Kansas City's Willie Davis caught 6 passes for 139 yards, and Marcus Allen ran for 91 yards. Elway was 28 of 45 for 300 yards. But the Broncos managed only 35 rushing yards, turned over the ball 3 times, and were whistled for 14 penalties.

| | | | | | | |
|---|---|---|---|---|---|---|
| **Denver** | 0 | 0 | 0 | 7 | — | 7 |
| **Kansas City** | 6 | 6 | 0 | 3 | — | 15 |

KC — FG Lowery 34
KC — FG Lowery 41
KC — FG Lowery 52
KC — FG Lowery 44
KC — FG Lowery 20
Den — V. Johnson 2 pass from Elway (Elam kick)

## FOURTH WEEK SUMMARIES

**AMERICAN FOOTBALL CONFERENCE**

| Eastern Division | W | L | T | Pct. | Pts. | OP |
|---|---|---|---|---|---|---|
| Buffalo | 2 | 1 | 0 | .667 | 64 | 46 |
| Indianapolis | 2 | 1 | 0 | .667 | 52 | 40 |
| Miami | 2 | 1 | 0 | .667 | 60 | 57 |
| N.Y. Jets | 2 | 1 | 0 | .667 | 89 | 47 |
| New England | 0 | 4 | 0 | .000 | 51 | 119 |
| **Central Division** | | | | | | |
| Cleveland | 3 | 1 | 0 | .750 | 79 | 66 |
| Pittsburgh | 2 | 2 | 0 | .500 | 92 | 75 |
| Houston | 1 | 3 | 0 | .250 | 81 | 79 |
| Cincinnati | 0 | 4 | 0 | .000 | 37 | 89 |
| **Western Division** | | | | | | |
| Denver | 2 | 1 | 0 | .667 | 67 | 52 |
| Kansas City | 2 | 1 | 0 | .667 | 42 | 40 |
| L.A. Raiders | 2 | 1 | 0 | .667 | 57 | 39 |
| San Diego | 2 | 1 | 0 | .667 | 53 | 63 |
| Seattle | 2 | 2 | 0 | .500 | 61 | 59 |

**NATIONAL FOOTBALL CONFERENCE**

| Eastern Division | W | L | T | Pct. | Pts. | OP |
|---|---|---|---|---|---|---|
| N.Y. Giants | 3 | 0 | 0 | 1.000 | 69 | 37 |
| Philadelphia | 3 | 0 | 0 | 1.000 | 77 | 65 |
| Dallas | 1 | 2 | 0 | .333 | 43 | 58 |
| Washington | 1 | 2 | 0 | .333 | 76 | 67 |
| Phoenix | 1 | 3 | 0 | .250 | 64 | 76 |
| **Central Division** | | | | | | |
| Detroit | 3 | 1 | 0 | .750 | 78 | 63 |
| Minnesota | 2 | 1 | 0 | .667 | 32 | 44 |
| Chicago | 1 | 2 | 0 | .333 | 74 | 53 |
| Green Bay | 1 | 2 | 0 | .333 | 66 | 41 |
| Tampa Bay | 0 | 3 | 0 | .000 | 27 | 97 |
| **Western Division** | | | | | | |
| New Orleans | 4 | 0 | 0 | 1.000 | 97 | 68 |
| L.A. Rams | 2 | 2 | 0 | .500 | 71 | 69 |
| San Francisco | 2 | 2 | 0 | .500 | 87 | 82 |
| Atlanta | 0 | 4 | 0 | .000 | 91 | 146 |

## SUNDAY, SEPTEMBER 26

**INDIANAPOLIS 23, CLEVELAND 10**—at Hoosier Dome, attendance 59,654. The Colts scored 2 touchdowns in the closing minutes to hand the Browns their first loss of the season. Cleveland led 10-9 until Indianapolis embarked on a 65-yard drive that was capped by Anthony Johnson's 6-yard touchdown run with 3:14 left in the game. The Browns still had time to rally, but quarterback Vinny Testaverde, who replaced an ineffective Bernie Kosar for the second consecutive week, threw an interception and fumbled on Cleveland's next two possessions. The latter was recovered in the end zone by Colts linebacker Jeff Herrod for an insurance touchdown with 1:09 left. The fumble came after 1 of 5 Indianapolis sacks, and the third by linebacker Duane Bickett. Jack Trudeau passed for 260 yards and wide receiver Jessie Hester caught 7 passes for 110 yards for Indianapolis. The Colts improved to 2-1 and completed the month of September with a winning record for the first time since 1977.

| | | | | | | |
|---|---|---|---|---|---|---|
| **Cleveland** | 0 | 0 | 7 | 3 | — | 10 |
| **Indianapolis** | 0 | 6 | 3 | 14 | — | 23 |

Ind — FG Biasucci 27
Ind — FG Biasucci 19
Cle — Kinchen 10 pass from Testaverde (Stover kick)
Ind — FG Biasucci 26
Cle — FG Stover 32
Ind — Johnson 6 run (Biasucci kick)
Ind — Herrod fumble recovery in end zone (Biasucci kick)

**MINNESOTA 15, GREEN BAY 13**—at Metrodome, attendance 61,077. Fuad Reveiz kicked 5 field goals, including the game-winner from 22 yards with four seconds left, to give the Vikings the victory. The winning kick was set up when Jim McMahon completed a 45-yard pass to wide receiver Eric Guliford on the previous play. It was the first down from scrimmage that Guliford, a rookie free agent, had played in his NFL career. Earlier, Reveiz's 49-yard field-goal attempt with 2:40 to go in the game bounced off the crossbar. He got another chance after Minnesota got the ball back at its 17-yard line with 1:53 remaining. McMahon had a key 19-yard completion to Cris Carter on fourth-and-8 on the winning drive. It was the second tough loss in a row for the Packers, who previously had fallen to the Eagles on a field goal with 10 seconds to go.

| | | | | | | |
|---|---|---|---|---|---|---|
| **Green Bay** | 7 | 3 | 0 | 3 | — | 13 |
| **Minnesota** | 3 | 3 | 6 | 3 | — | 15 |

GB — Favre 2 run (Jacke kick)
Minn — FG Reveiz 35
Minn — FG Reveiz 19
GB — FG Jacke 49
Minn — FG Reveiz 29
Minn — FG Reveiz 51
GB — FG Jacke 20
Minn — FG Reveiz 22

**L.A. RAMS 28, HOUSTON 13**—at Astrodome, attendance 53,072. Jim Everett passed for 316 yards and 3 touchdowns as the Rams stunned the Oilers. Everett, who completed 19 of 28 passes, became the first quarterback in 31 games to throw for more than 300 yards against Houston's defense. He threw a 4-yard touchdown pass to Willie Anderson to open the scoring midway through the first quarter, then put the game out of reach with a pair of second-half scoring tosses. After the Oilers had trimmed a 14-0 deficit to 14-13 on a pair of field goals by Al Del Greco and an 80-yard bomb from Warren Moon to Ernest Givins, Los Angeles responded with a 9-play, 66-yard drive that ended with Everett's 22-yard touchdown pass to tight end Travis McNeal with 1:21 left in the third quarter. Two minutes and 21 seconds later, Everett teamed with wide receiver Henry Ellard on a 48-yard touchdown pass. Ellard finished with 6 catches for 132 yards. Moon passed for 310 yards, but completed only 19 of 42 attempts, was intercepted twice, and suffered 4 sacks.

| | | | | | | |
|---|---|---|---|---|---|---|
| **L.A. Rams** | 7 | 7 | 7 | 7 | — | 28 |
| **Houston** | 0 | 3 | 10 | 0 | — | 13 |

Rams — Anderson 4 pass from Everett (Zendejas kick)
Rams — Bettis 1 run (Zendejas kick)
Hou — FG Del Greco 52
Hou — FG Del Greco 25
Hou — Givins 80 pass from Moon (Del Greco kick)
Rams — McNeal 22 pass from Everett (Zendejas kick)
Rams — Ellard 48 pass from Everett (Zendejas kick)

**MIAMI 22, BUFFALO 13**—at Rich Stadium, attendance 79,635. Dan Marino passed for 1 touchdown and ran for another as the Dolphins handled the Bills with ease. Miami built a 19-6 first-half advantage and never was seriously threatened. After Buffalo's Steve Christie had narrowed the margin to 19-6 with a 59-yard field goal on the final play of the first half, the Dolphins put the game away with a time-consuming drive that led to a field goal following the second-half kickoff. Miami held the ball for more than 12 minutes in the third quarter, including 8:23 on the opening march. Marino completed 20 of 32 passes for 282 yards and moved past Johnny Unitas into third place on the NFL's all-time list with 40,306 yards.

| | | | | | | |
|---|---|---|---|---|---|---|
| **Miami** | 16 | 3 | 3 | 0 | — | 22 |
| **Buffalo** | 0 | 6 | 0 | 7 | — | 13 |

Mia — FG Stoyanovich 30
Mia — Fryar 36 pass from Marino (kick failed)
Mia — Marino 4 run (Stoyanovich kick)
Mia — FG Stoyanovich 23
Buff — FG Christie 40
Buff — FG Christie 59
Mia — FG Stoyanovich 24
Buff — Brooks 27 pass from Kelly (Christie kick)

**DETROIT 26, PHOENIX 20**—at Silverdome, attendance 57,180. Quarterback Andre Ware made his first start of the season and threw the go-ahead touchdown pass to Brett Perriman in the third quarter of the Lions' victory. Ware, given the starting nod over Rodney Peete, completed 11 of 24 passes for 194 yards. He directed a 66-yard, 4-play drive to open the third quarter, capped by his scoring toss to Perriman, to give Detroit the lead for good at 23-17 three minutes into the second half. Derrick Moore, who ran 1 yard for a touchdown in the second quarter, set up the touchdown pass with a 48-yard run. Jason Hanson kicked 4 field goals for Lions. He also missed a 43-yard try in the third quarter, his first miss in 31 attempts from inside 45 yards in his career. Steve Beuerlein completed 23 of 31 passes for 288 yards and 2 touchdowns for the Cardinals, who hurt themselves by losing 3 fumbles.

| | | | | | | |
|---|---|---|---|---|---|---|
| **Phoenix** | 0 | 17 | 0 | 3 | — | 20 |
| **Detroit** | 6 | 10 | 7 | 3 | — | 26 |

Det — FG Hanson 44
Det — FG Hanson 22
Phx — Proehl 51 pass from Beuerlein (Davis kick)
Det — FG Hanson 33
Det — D. Moore 1 run (Hanson kick)
Phx — Reeves 2 pass from Beuerlein (Davis kick)
Phx — FG Davis 54
Det — Perriman 9 pass from Ware (Hanson kick)
Phx — FG Davis 30
Det — FG Hanson 38

**NEW ORLEANS 16, SAN FRANCISCO 13**—at Louisiana Superdome, attendance 69,041. Morten Andersen's 49-yard field goal with five seconds remaining lifted the Saints to their fourth consecutive victory. The 49ers' Mike Cofer tied the game at 13-13 on a 30-yard field goal with 1:14 left. That capped a 15-play, 68-yard drive that took 7:23. But New Orleans started its next possession on its 23-yard line and marched 45 yards to Andersen's winning kick. Wade Wilson passed for 37 yards and scrambled for 8 more on the drive. San Francisco accumulated 339 yards to the Saints' 264, but New Orleans's defense harassed 49ers quarterback Steve Young most of the day, sacking him 6 times and intercepting a pass. Saints linebacker Rickey Jackson had 3 sacks. San Francisco's Ricky Watters rushed for 135 yards on 25 carries.

| | | | | | | |
|---|---|---|---|---|---|---|
| **San Francisco** | 0 | 3 | 7 | 3 | — | 13 |
| **New Orleans** | 3 | 7 | 3 | 3 | — | 16 |

NO — FG Andersen 33
NO — Brown 1 run (Andersen kick)
SF — FG Cofer 34
SF — Logan 23 run (Cofer kick)
NO — FG Andersen 39
SF — FG Cofer 30
NO — FG Andersen 39

**SEATTLE 19, CINCINNATI 10**—at Riverfront Stadium, attendance 46,880. Linebacker Rod Stephens recovered a fumble in the end zone with 4:38 remaining to give the Seahawks the victory. It was Seattle's second win of the season, matching its total for all of 1992. Cincinnati had rallied from a 9-0 deficit to take a 10-9 fourth-quarter advantage on Doug Pelfrey's 23-yard field goal and a 21-yard touchdown pass from Jay Schroeder to Carl Pickens with 8:21 to go. But on their next possession, the Bengals coughed up the football at their 4-yard line when linebacker Kevin Murphy hit running back Harold Green, and Stephens recovered for the winning score. John Kasay added his fourth field goal of the game, from 35 yards, with 2:27 left, after Cincinnati turned over the ball on downs.

| | | | | | | |
|---|---|---|---|---|---|---|
| **Seattle** | 0 | 6 | 3 | 10 | — | 19 |
| **Cincinnati** | 0 | 0 | 0 | 10 | — | 10 |

Sea — FG Kasay 32
Sea — FG Kasay 35
Sea — FG Kasay 23
Cin — FG Pelfrey 23
Cin — Pickens 21 pass from Schroeder (Pelfrey kick)
Sea — Stephens fumble recovery in end zone (Kasay kick)
Sea — FG Kasay 35

**CHICAGO 47, TAMPA BAY 17**—at Soldier Field, attendance 58,329. The Bears forced 7 turnovers and routed the Buccaneers, giving rookie head coach Dave Wannstedt his first victory. Tampa Bay led 3-0 until Chicago broke the game open with 4 second-quarter touchdowns, 3 of them within a span of 4:04. Bears quarterback Jim Harbaugh ran 1 yard for a touchdown with 4:51 left in the first half, then threw a 25-yard touchdown pass to tight end Ryan Wetnight at the 1:10 mark. Defensive tackle Chris Zorich sacked Buccaneers quarterback Craig Erickson on the next play from scrimmage and end Trace Armstrong recovered at the Tampa Bay 17-yard line. Harbaugh then teamed with Tom Waddle on another touchdown pass 47 seconds before intermission. Tampa Bay countered with a 62-yard touchdown on a desperation pass to end the first half and close within 28-10, but the Buccaneers were not able to mount a serious challenge. Erickson passed for 240 yards but completed only 13 of 32 passes and was intercepted twice. Backups Steve DeBerg and Casey Weldon also threw interceptions, and Tampa Bay lost 3 fumbles, 1 of which was returned 8 yards for a touchdown by Chicago linebacker Myron Baker. Harbaugh completed 17 of 22 passes for 192 yards, and Bears running back Neal Anderson gained 104 yards on 23 carries.

| | | | | | | |
|---|---|---|---|---|---|---|
| **Tampa Bay** | 3 | 7 | 0 | 7 | — | 17 |
| **Chicago** | 0 | 28 | 3 | 16 | — | 47 |

TB — FG Husted 20
Chi — Anderson 1 run (Butler kick)
Chi — Harbaugh 1 run (Butler kick)
Chi — Wetnight 25 pass from Harbaugh (Butler kick)
Chi — Waddle 17 pass from Harbaugh (Butler kick)
TB — L. Thomas 62 pass from Erickson (Husted kick)
Chi — FG Butler 33
Chi — FG Butler 40
Chi — Baker 8 fumble return (Butler kick)
Chi — FG Butler 32
TB — McDowell 3 pass from DeBerg (Husted kick)
Chi — FG Butler 31

## SUNDAY NIGHT, SEPTEMBER 26

**N.Y. JETS 45, NEW ENGLAND 7**—at Giants Stadium, attendance 64,836. The Jets scored on all five of their first-half possessions and blasted the Patriots, spoiling the return of Bill Parcells to Giants Stadium. Parcells, who led the New York Giants to two Super Bowl titles in his eight seasons as that club's head coach, remained winless in his first year as New England's head coach. The Jets marched 73 yards in 10 plays the first time they had the ball, capping the drive with a 1-yard touchdown run by Brad Baxter 6:40 into the first quarter. Baxter had 2 of New York's 5 rushing touchdowns. Jets quarterback Boomer Esiason completed his first 13 passes and set a club record with 18 consecutive completions over a two-game span. He finished the night with 17 completions in 21 attempts for 217 yards and 1 touchdown, with no interceptions or sacks. New York amassed 388 total yards, and limited the Patriots to 211. With the victory, the Jets moved into a four-way tie for first place in the AFC East.

| | | | | | | |
|---|---|---|---|---|---|---|
| **New England** | 0 | 0 | 0 | 7 | — | 7 |
| **N.Y. Jets** | 14 | 21 | 0 | 10 | — | 45 |

Jets — B. Baxter 1 run (Blanchard kick)
Jets — Johnson 6 run (Blanchard kick)
Jets — B. Baxter 4 run (Blanchard kick)
Jets — Thornton 13 pass from Esiason (Blanchard kick)
Jets — Mathis 17 run (Blanchard kick)
Jets — FG Blanchard 42
Jets — Murrell 37 run (Blanchard kick)
NE — Russell 5 run (Sisson kick)

## MONDAY, SEPTEMBER 27

**PITTSBURGH 45, ATLANTA 17**—at Georgia Dome, attendance 65,477. Barry Foster ran for 3 touchdowns and Neil O'Donnell passed for 2 as the Steelers kept the Falcons winless. Atlanta led 17-10 five minutes into the second quarter, thanks to touchdowns by the special teams (Tony Smith's 97-yard kickoff return) and defense (cornerback Vinnie Clark's 46-yard fumble return). But Pittsburgh rallied to go up 24-17 at halftime on Foster's 7-yard touchdown run and O'Donnell's 4-yard scoring pass to Dwight Stone. The latter was set up when rookie cornerback Deon Figures returned an interception 78 yards to the 1-yard line. O'Donnell's 7-yard touchdown pass to Yancey Thigpen and Foster's third touchdown run, from 1 yard early in the fourth quarter, turned the game into a rout. O'Donnell finished with 19 completions in 25 attempts for 259 yards. Cornerback Rod Woodson had 2 interceptions for the Steelers, who forced 6 turnovers.

| | | | | | | |
|---|---|---|---|---|---|---|
| **Pittsburgh** | 7 | 17 | 7 | 14 | — | 45 |
| **Atlanta** | 14 | 3 | 0 | 0 | — | 17 |

Pitt — Foster 30 run (Anderson kick)
Atl — T. Smith 97 kickoff return (N. Johnson kick)
Atl — Clark 46 fumble return (N. Johnson kick)
Pitt — FG Anderson 21

Atl — FG N. Johnson 49
Pitt — Foster 7 run (Anderson kick)
Pitt — Stone 4 pass from O'Donnell (Anderson kick)
Pitt — Thigpen 7 pass from O'Donnell (Anderson kick)
Pitt — Foster 1 run (Anderson kick)
Pitt — Davidson 18 fumble return (Anderson kick)

## FIFTH WEEK SUMMARIES

**AMERICAN FOOTBALL CONFERENCE**

| Eastern Division | W | L | T | Pct. | Pts. | OP |
|---|---|---|---|---|---|---|
| Buffalo | 3 | 1 | 0 | .750 | 81 | 60 |
| Miami | 3 | 1 | 0 | .750 | 77 | 67 |
| Indianapolis | 2 | 2 | 0 | .500 | 65 | 75 |
| N.Y. Jets | 2 | 2 | 0 | .500 | 119 | 82 |
| New England | 0 | 4 | 0 | .000 | 51 | 119 |
| **Central Division** | | | | | | |
| Cleveland | 3 | 1 | 0 | .750 | 79 | 66 |
| Pittsburgh | 2 | 2 | 0 | .500 | 92 | 75 |
| Houston | 1 | 3 | 0 | .250 | 81 | 79 |
| Cincinnati | 0 | 4 | 0 | .000 | 37 | 89 |
| **Western Division** | | | | | | |
| Denver | 3 | 1 | 0 | .750 | 102 | 65 |
| Kansas City | 3 | 1 | 0 | .750 | 66 | 49 |
| Seattle | 3 | 2 | 0 | .600 | 92 | 73 |
| L.A. Raiders | 2 | 2 | 0 | .500 | 66 | 63 |
| San Diego | 2 | 2 | 0 | .500 | 67 | 94 |

**NATIONAL FOOTBALL CONFERENCE**

| Eastern Division | W | L | T | Pct. | Pts. | OP |
|---|---|---|---|---|---|---|
| Philadelphia | 4 | 0 | 0 | 1.000 | 112 | 95 |
| N.Y. Giants | 3 | 1 | 0 | .750 | 83 | 54 |
| Dallas | 2 | 2 | 0 | .500 | 79 | 72 |
| Phoenix | 1 | 3 | 0 | .250 | 64 | 76 |
| Washington | 1 | 3 | 0 | .250 | 86 | 84 |
| **Central Division** | | | | | | |
| Detroit | 3 | 2 | 0 | .600 | 88 | 90 |
| Chicago | 2 | 2 | 0 | .500 | 80 | 53 |
| Minnesota | 2 | 2 | 0 | .500 | 51 | 82 |
| Green Bay | 1 | 3 | 0 | .250 | 80 | 77 |
| Tampa Bay | 1 | 3 | 0 | .250 | 54 | 107 |
| **Western Division** | | | | | | |
| New Orleans | 5 | 0 | 0 | 1.000 | 134 | 74 |
| San Francisco | 3 | 2 | 0 | .600 | 125 | 101 |
| L.A. Rams | 2 | 3 | 0 | .400 | 77 | 106 |
| Atlanta | 0 | 5 | 0 | .000 | 91 | 152 |

## SUNDAY, OCTOBER 3

**CHICAGO 6, ATLANTA 0**—at Soldier Field, attendance 57,441. Kevin Butler kicked 2 field goals and the Bears thwarted the Falcons' in the closing minutes to win. Butler's field goals included a 52-yard kick in the third quarter, matching his career high. Late in the game, Atlanta drove to Chicago's 8-yard line, but turned over the ball on downs with 1:25 to play. The Falcons outgained the Bears 271-220, but suffered 3 turnovers and were whistled for 11 penalties. Atlanta quarterback Bobby Hebert left the game after three quarters with an elbow injury.

| | | | | | | |
|---|---|---|---|---|---|---|
| **Atlanta** | 0 | 0 | 0 | 0 | — | 0 |
| **Chicago** | 0 | 3 | 3 | 0 | — | 6 |

Chi — FG Butler 48
Chi — FG Butler 52

**TAMPA BAY 27, DETROIT 10**—at Tampa Stadium, attendance 40,794. The Buccaneers spotted the Lions a 10-point first-half lead, then rallied to win. Detroit wasted little time getting on the scoreboard, taking the opening kickoff and marching 80 yards in only 5 plays, the last a 20-yard touchdown run by Barry Sanders 2:06 into the game. Jason Hanson's 30-yard field goal early in the second quarter made it 10-0, but Tampa Bay closed to 10-3 on Michael Husted's 52-yard field goal as time ran out in the first half. In the third quarter, the Buccaneers erupted for touchdowns on three consecutive possessions. Craig Erickson capped an 80-yard drive with a 15-yard touchdown pass to Courtney Hawkins to tie the score, and cornerback Darren Anderson intercepted an Andre Ware pass to set up Reggie Cobb's 3-yard touchdown run. Erik Kramer relieved Ware at quarterback for the Lions but was intercepted by safety Joe King, setting up Erickson's 37-yard touchdown pass to tight end Ron Hall. Erickson, making only his third NFL start, completed 14 of 25 passes for 210 yards, and Cobb rushed for 113 yards on 25 carries. Sanders, who had 50 yards on Detroit's opening drive, finished with 130 yards on 22 carries.

| | | | | | | |
|---|---|---|---|---|---|---|
| **Detroit** | 7 | 3 | 0 | 0 | — | 10 |
| **Tampa Bay** | 0 | 3 | 21 | 3 | — | 27 |

Det — Sanders 20 run (Hanson kick)
Det — FG Hanson 30
TB — FG Husted 52
TB — Hawkins 15 pass from Erickson (Husted kick)
TB — Cobb 3 run (Husted kick)
TB — Hall 37 pass from Erickson (Husted kick)
TB — FG Husted 46

**DALLAS 36, GREEN BAY 14**—at Texas Stadium, attendance 63,568. Troy Aikman passed for 317 yards and Eddie Murray kicked 5 field goals as the Cowboys easily handled the Packers. After Dallas fell behind 7-0, Aikman brought his team even with a 61-yard touchdown pass to Michael Irvin midway through the first quarter. The Cowboys then relied on Murray to build a 19-7 advantage, and put the game out of reach on Emmitt Smith's 22-yard touchdown run 7:11 into the second half. Aikman completed 18 of 23 passes and was not intercepted. Irvin caught 7 passes for 155 yards, and Smith rushed for 71 yards in his first start of the season. Robert Brooks returned a kickoff 95 yards for a touchdown for the Packers, who lost their third straight game.

| | | | | | | |
|---|---|---|---|---|---|---|
| **Green Bay** | 7 | 0 | 7 | 0 | — | 14 |
| **Dallas** | 10 | 6 | 13 | 7 | — | 36 |

GB — Bennett 1 run (Jacke kick)
Dall — Irvin 61 pass from Aikman (Murray kick)
Dall — FG Murray 33
Dall — FG Murray 19
Dall — FG Murray 19
Dall — FG Murray 50
Dall — E. Smith 22 run (Murray kick)
GB — Brooks 95 kickoff return (Jacke kick)
Dall — FG Murray 48
Dall — Lassic 1 run (Murray kick)

**DENVER 35, INDIANAPOLIS 13**—at Mile High Stadium, attendance 74,953. The Broncos scored on their first four possessions and routed the Colts. With John Elway completing 13 of 17 passes for 156 yards, including touchdowns of 3 yards to Glyn Milburn and 22 yards to Shannon Sharpe, Denver built a 28-0 advantage midway through the second quarter. Indianapolis tried to rally, pulling within 28-13 on a pair of Dean Biasucci field goals and Jack Trudeau's 4-yard touchdown pass to tight end Kerry Cash 10 seconds before halftime. But the Broncos used a trick play to score the clinching touchdown with nine seconds left in the third quarter. Wide receiver Arthur Marshall tossed a 30-yard touchdown pass to Derek Russell on a fake reverse to make it 35-13. Robert Delpino rushed for 83 yards and a touchdown and Rod Bernstine added 60 yards and a score as Denver amassed 196 rushing yards en route to 454 total yards. Elway finished with 20 completions in 30 attempts for 230 yards.

| | | | | | | |
|---|---|---|---|---|---|---|
| **Indianapolis** | 0 | 10 | 3 | 0 | — | 13 |
| **Denver** | 21 | 7 | 7 | 0 | — | 35 |

Den — Delpino 2 run (Elam kick)
Den — Bernstine 9 run (Elam kick)
Den — Milburn 3 pass from Elway (Elam kick)
Den — Sharpe 22 pass from Elway (Elam kick)
Ind — FG Biasucci 28
Ind — Cash 4 pass from Trudeau (Biasucci kick)
Ind — FG Biasucci 28
Den — Russell 30 pass from Marshall (Elam kick)

**KANSAS CITY 24, L.A. RAIDERS 9**—at Arrowhead Stadium, attendance 77,395. Joe Montana threw 2 touchdown passes before injuring a hamstring in the Chiefs' victory. Montana capped Kansas City's first drive with a 1-yard touchdown pass to tackle-eligible Joe Valerio, and threw a 15-yard scoring pass to Willie Davis on the next series. The veteran quarterback completed 7 of 9 passes for 68 yards, but had to leave the game in the second quarter when he was injured while scrambling out of bounds. Raiders linebacker Aaron Wallace was assessed a late-hit penalty on the play, 1 of 16 infractions for 168 yards whistled against Los Angeles. Marcus Allen, playing against his former teammates for the first time, capped that same drive with a 4-yard touchdown run for a 21-3 lead. Allen became only the tenth player in NFL history to score 100 touchdowns. Former Notre Dame and Canadian Football League star Raghib (Rocket) Ismail made his NFL debut for the Raiders and caught 4 passes for 75 yards, including a 43-yard touchdown in the fourth quarter. Los Angeles played without injured starting quarterback Jeff Hostetler. Backup Vince Evans completed 15 of 26 passes for 192 yards and was not intercepted. But he was sacked 6 times, 4 by defensive end Neil Smith and 2 by linebacker Derrick Thomas.

| | | | | | | |
|---|---|---|---|---|---|---|
| **L.A. Raiders** | 0 | 3 | 0 | 6 | — | 9 |
| **Kansas City** | 14 | 7 | 3 | 0 | — | 24 |

KC — Valerio 1 pass from Montana (Lowery kick)
KC — Davis 15 pass from Montana (Lowery kick)
Raid — FG Jaeger 27
KC — Allen 4 run (Lowery kick)
KC — FG Lowery 29
Raid — Ismail 43 pass from Evans (kick blocked)

**SAN FRANCISCO 38, MINNESOTA 19**—at Candlestick Park, attendance 63,071. Defense and special teams made the key plays in the 49ers' victory over the Vikings. San Francisco led 14-7 in the second quarter when cornerback Eric Davis increased the advantage to 14 points with a 41-yard interception return for a touchdown. After Minnesota closed to within 24-19 early in the fourth quarter, the 49ers' Dexter Carter returned a punt 22 yards. That led to a 56-yard touchdown drive, capped by Ricky Watters' 3-yard run with 5:54 to play. Carter put the game away just 68 seconds later with a 72-yard punt return for a touchdown. San Francisco managed only 254 total yards, but Carter added 131 yards on 5 punt returns. The Vikings' Jim McMahon completed 25 of 45 passes for 223 yards and 2 touchdowns.

| | | | | | | |
|---|---|---|---|---|---|---|
| **Minnesota** | 7 | 2 | 3 | 7 | — | 19 |
| **San Francisco** | 7 | 14 | 3 | 14 | — | 38 |

Minn — Tice 3 pass from McMahon (Reveiz kick)
SF — Rice 39 pass from Young (Cofer kick)
SF — Logan 1 run (Cofer kick)
SF — Davis 41 interception return (Cofer kick)
Minn — Safety, H. Thomas tackled Young in end zone
SF — FG Cofer 22
Minn — FG Reveiz 21
Minn — C. Carter 9 pass from McMahon (Reveiz kick)
SF — Watters 3 run (Cofer kick)
SF — D. Carter 72 punt return (Cofer kick)

**NEW ORLEANS 37, L.A. RAMS 6**—at Anaheim Stadium, attendance 50,709. The Saints broke open a close game with 3 fourth-quarter touchdowns and raised their record to 5-0. New Orleans led just 16-6 early in the final period when the Rams marched to the Saints' 34-yard line. But New Orleans linebacker Rickey Jackson sacked Los Angeles quarterback Jim Everett, forcing a fumble that defensive end Wayne Martin recovered at the 45. Five plays later, Wade Wilson threw a 30-yard touchdown pass to Patrick Newman to give the Saints a 17-point cushion with 13:51 left. Less than three minutes later, Tyrone Hughes returned a punt 74 yards for a touchdown to break open the game. Wilson completed 15 of 25 passes for 205 yards and also had a 15-yard scoring toss to Derek Brown in the first quarter. Everett, who had directed an upset of Houston one week earlier, completed only 10 of 26 passes for 126 yards with 1 interception. Rams rookie running back Jerome Bettis gained 102 yards on 22 carries. Kicker Tony Zendejas converted a 53-yard field goal late in the first quarter, his ninth successful kick in a row from 50 yards or more.

| | | | | | | |
|---|---|---|---|---|---|---|
| **New Orleans** | 10 | 3 | 3 | 21 | — | 37 |
| **L.A. Rams** | 3 | 0 | 3 | 0 | — | 6 |

NO — Brown 15 pass from Wilson (Andersen kick)
NO — FG Andersen 48
Rams — FG Zendejas 53
NO — FG Andersen 25
Rams — FG Zendejas 37
NO — FG Andersen 43
NO — Newman 30 pass from Wilson (Andersen kick)
NO — Hughes 74 punt return (Andersen kick)
NO — Ned 35 run (Andersen kick)

**PHILADELPHIA 35, N.Y. JETS 30**—at Giants Stadium, attendance 72,593. Cornerback Eric Allen returned a fourth-quarter interception 94 yards for the winning touchdown as the Eagles rallied from a 21-point deficit to defeat the Jets and remain unbeaten. It was a costly victory for Philadelphia, however, which was hit hard by injuries, most notably a broken leg suffered by starting quarterback Randall Cunningham, who was expected to miss at least two months. Wide receiver Fred Barnett, the team's leading pass catcher in 1992, and Jeff Sydner, a special teams star, were lost for the season with knee injuries. Nevertheless, the Eagles rallied to win for the third consecutive game. Quarterback Boomer Esiason staked New York to a 21-0 first-half advantage with 3 touchdown passes, 2 to tight end Johnny Mitchell. Philadelphia closed to 21-14 by intermission, but Esiason and Mitchell teamed for another touchdown, a 65-yard pass, on the Jets' first play of the second half. Bubby Brister, Cunningham's replacement, threw his second touchdown pass and rookie Vaughn Hebron ran 1 yard for a touchdown to tie the game at 28-28 early in the fourth quarter. After New York regained the lead with a safety, Allen won the game with his interception with 8:43 to go. Brister finished with 11 completions in 16 attempts for 108 yards. Mitchell caught 7 passes for 146 yards and Chris Burkett had 4 receptions for 103 yards for the Jets, who amassed 417 total yards but turned over the ball 3 times. Esiason completed 19 of 33 attempts for 297 yards and 4 touchdowns.

| | | | | | | |
|---|---|---|---|---|---|---|
| **Philadelphia** | 0 | 14 | 7 | 14 | — | 35 |
| **N.Y. Jets** | 14 | 7 | 7 | 2 | — | 30 |

Jets — Thornton 7 pass from Esiason (Blanchard kick)
Jets — Mitchell 14 pass from Esiason (Blanchard kick)
Jets — Mitchell 12 pass from Esiason (Blanchard kick)
Phil — Walker 8 run (Bahr kick)
Phil — Bavaro 10 pass from Brister (Bahr kick)
Jets — Mitchell 65 pass from Esiason (Blanchard kick)
Phil — Williams 11 pass from Brister (Bahr kick)
Phil — Hebron 1 run (Bahr kick)
Jets — Safety, Brister intentionally grounded ball in end zone
Phil — Allen 94 interception return (Bahr kick)

**SEATTLE 31, SAN DIEGO 14**—at Kingdome, attendance 54,778. Rookie quarterback Rick Mirer passed for 282 yards as the Seahawks upset the Chargers. Seattle, which won only two games in 1992, won its third in a row and improved to 3-2. Defending AFC Western Division champion San Diego fell to 2-2. Mirer, the second overall selection in the 1993 draft, completed 25 of 40 passes. But one of the key plays of the game was made by backup quarterback Dan McGwire in the closing seconds of the first half. After Mirer sprained his ankle when hit by Chargers linebacker Junior Seau 21 seconds before intermission, McGwire tossed a 17-yard touchdown pass to Brian Blades with 10 seconds left in the first half, giving the Seahawks a 17-7 lead. Chris Warren's 1-yard run and Kelvin Martin's 18-yard touchdown catch made it 31-7 before reserve quarterback John Friesz led San Diego to a touchdown late in the game. Chargers wide receiver Anthony Miller caught 10 passes for 123 yards. Blades had 10 receptions for 132 yards for Seattle. Defensive end Michael Sinclair had 3 sacks.

| | | | | | | |
|---|---|---|---|---|---|---|
| **San Diego** | 7 | 0 | 0 | 7 | — | 14 |
| **Seattle** | 7 | 10 | 7 | 7 | — | 31 |

Sea — Mirer 2 run (Kasay kick)
SD — Butts 2 run (Carney kick)
Sea — FG Kasay 33
Sea — Blades 17 pass from McGwire (Kasay kick)
Sea — C. Warren 1 run (Kasay kick)
Sea — Martin 18 pass from Mirer (Kasay kick)
SD — Miller 11 pass from Friesz (Carney kick)

## SUNDAY NIGHT, OCTOBER 3

**BUFFALO 17, N.Y. GIANTS 14**—at Rich Stadium, attendance 79,813. Jim Kelly's 8-yard touchdown pass to tight end Pete Metzelaars lifted the Bills past the Giants. It was the first time the two teams had met since New York beat Buffalo in Super Bowl XXV. The Bills jumped out to a 10-point lead in the first quarter, but the Giants rallied to take a 14-10 halftime advantage behind a pair of short touchdown passes by Phil Simms. It remained that way until Buffalo marched 73 yards in 11 plays to the winning score. Thurman Thomas rushed for 122 yards on 26 carries for Buffalo. The Bills intercepted 3 of Simms's passes, including an 85-yard touchdown return by safety Henry Jones.

| | | | | | | |
|---|---|---|---|---|---|---|
| **N.Y. Giants** | 0 | 14 | 0 | 0 | — | 14 |
| **Buffalo** | 10 | 0 | 0 | 7 | — | 17 |

Buff — FG Christie 24
Buff — Jones 85 interception return (Christie kick)
Giants — Calloway 5 pass from Simms (Treadwell kick)
Giants — M. Jackson 3 pass from Simms (Treadwell kick)
Buff — Metzelaars 8 pass from Kelly (Christie kick)

## MONDAY, OCTOBER 4

**MIAMI 17, WASHINGTON 10**—at Joe Robbie Stadium, attendance 68,568. Dan Marino passed for 253 yards and a touchdown as the Dolphins handed the Redskins their third consecutive defeat. Marino teamed with Tony Martin on the third play of the game for an 80-yard touchdown pass, then directed a 73-yard drive to Mark Higgs's 1-yard run for a 14-0 lead just 7:39 into the game. Washington closed within 4 points on a 28-yard field goal by Chip Lohmiller and backup quarterback Rich Gannon's 12-yard touchdown pass to Ricky Sanders with 11:08 left in the game. But the Redskins never got a chance to take the lead, because Miami held the ball for the next 13 plays and 7:10 before Pete Stoyanovich kicked a 37-yard field goal with 3:58 remaining. Washington's last chance ended when Troy Vincent intercepted a pass from Gannon in the final minute. The Dolphins outgained an ineffective Redskins' offense 354-232. Rookie running back Terry Kirby gained 94 yards on 16 carries and had 3 catches for 36 yards in his first NFL start. He had an 18-yard run and a 34-yard reception on the second touchdown drive. The Redskins, who had not won since beating defending Super Bowl-champion Dallas in the opener, lost three in a row for the first time since 1988.

| | | | | | | |
|---|---|---|---|---|---|---|
| **Washington** | 0 | 3 | 0 | 7 | — | 10 |
| **Miami** | 14 | 0 | 0 | 3 | — | 17 |

Mia — Martin 80 pass from Marino (Stoyanovich kick)
Mia — Higgs 1 run (Stoyanovich kick)
Wash — FG Lohmiller 28
Wash — Sanders 12 pass from Gannon (Lohmiller kick)
Mia — FG Stoyanovich 37

## SIXTH WEEK SUMMARIES

**AMERICAN FOOTBALL CONFERENCE**

| Eastern Division | W | L | T | Pct. | Pts. | OP |
|---|---|---|---|---|---|---|
| Buffalo | 4 | 1 | 0 | .800 | 116 | 67 |
| Miami | 4 | 1 | 0 | .800 | 101 | 81 |
| Indianapolis | 2 | 3 | 0 | .400 | 68 | 102 |
| N.Y. Jets | 2 | 3 | 0 | .400 | 139 | 106 |
| New England | 1 | 4 | 0 | .200 | 74 | 140 |
| **Central Division** | | | | | | |
| Cleveland | 3 | 2 | 0 | .600 | 93 | 90 |
| Pittsburgh | 3 | 2 | 0 | .600 | 108 | 78 |
| Houston | 1 | 4 | 0 | .200 | 88 | 114 |
| Cincinnati | 0 | 5 | 0 | .000 | 52 | 106 |
| **Western Division** | | | | | | |
| Kansas City | 4 | 1 | 0 | .800 | 83 | 64 |
| Denver | 3 | 2 | 0 | .600 | 129 | 95 |
| L.A. Raiders | 3 | 2 | 0 | .600 | 90 | 83 |
| Seattle | 3 | 2 | 0 | .600 | 92 | 73 |
| San Diego | 2 | 3 | 0 | .400 | 70 | 110 |

**NATIONAL FOOTBALL CONFERENCE**

| Eastern Division | W | L | T | Pct. | Pts. | OP |
|---|---|---|---|---|---|---|
| N.Y. Giants | 4 | 1 | 0 | .800 | 124 | 61 |
| Philadelphia | 4 | 1 | 0 | .800 | 118 | 112 |
| Dallas | 3 | 2 | 0 | .600 | 106 | 75 |
| Phoenix | 1 | 4 | 0 | .200 | 85 | 99 |
| Washington | 1 | 4 | 0 | .200 | 93 | 125 |
| **Central Division** | | | | | | |
| Chicago | 3 | 2 | 0 | .600 | 97 | 59 |
| Detroit | 3 | 2 | 0 | .600 | 88 | 90 |
| Minnesota | 3 | 2 | 0 | .600 | 66 | 82 |
| Green Bay | 2 | 3 | 0 | .400 | 110 | 104 |
| Tampa Bay | 1 | 4 | 0 | .200 | 54 | 122 |
| **Western Division** | | | | | | |
| New Orleans | 5 | 0 | 0 | 1.000 | 134 | 74 |
| San Francisco | 3 | 2 | 0 | .600 | 125 | 101 |
| L.A. Rams | 2 | 3 | 0 | .400 | 77 | 106 |
| Atlanta | 0 | 5 | 0 | .000 | 91 | 152 |

## SUNDAY, OCTOBER 10

**CHICAGO 17, PHILADELPHIA 6**—at Veterans Stadium, attendance 63,601. Defensive end Richard Dent had 2 sacks and an interception as the Bears moved into a tie for first place in the NFC Central by winning their third consecutive game and handing the Eagles their first defeat. Dent's interception came midway through the first quarter of a scoreless tie. He returned the ball 24 yards to Philadelphia's 30-yard line, setting up Kevin Butler's 37-yard field goal. On the Eagles' next possession, Chicago defensive end Trace Armstrong forced a fumble that linebacker Dante Jones recovered, and three plays later Jim Harbaugh teamed with rookie wide receiver Curtis Conway on a 32-yard touchdown pass. Philadelphia, which started the season 4-0, averted a shutout when Bubby Brister threw a 7-yard touchdown pass to Calvin Williams with 23 seconds left. It was not a productive day for Brister, who was replacing injured Randall Cunningham as the Eagles' quarterback. Brister completed 18 of 33 passes for 209 yards, but was intercepted twice, lost 2 fumbles, and was sacked 7 times. Philadelphia had its 11-game winning streak at Veterans Stadium snapped.

| | | | | | | |
|---|---|---|---|---|---|---|
| **Chicago** | 10 | 7 | 0 | 0 | — | 17 |
| **Philadelphia** | 0 | 0 | 0 | 6 | — | 6 |

Chi — FG Butler 37
Chi — Conway 32 pass from Harbaugh (Butler kick)
Chi — Harbaugh 1 run (Butler kick)
Phil — Williams 7 pass from Brister (kick failed)

**KANSAS CITY 17, CINCINNATI 15**—at Arrowhead Stadium, attendance 75,394. Nick Lowery's 37-yard field goal with 2:43 remaining lifted the Chiefs to victory over the winless Bengals. Cincinnati had taken a 15-14 lead on the last of rookie Doug Pelfrey's club-record tying 5 field goals, from 34 yards with 5:59 to play. But Kansas City quarterback Dave Krieg, playing in place of injured Joe Montana, moved his team into Bengals territory with a 28-yard completion to J.J. Birden, and Lowery converted the winning kick moments later. The Chiefs managed only 203 total yards (Cincinnati had 277), but won their third consecutive game and moved into sole possession of first place in the AFC Western Division.

| | | | | | | |
|---|---|---|---|---|---|---|
| **Cincinnati** | 3 | 9 | 0 | 3 | — | 15 |
| **Kansas City** | 0 | 7 | 7 | 3 | — | 17 |

Cin — FG Pelfrey 23
Cin — FG Pelfrey 24
Cin — FG Pelfrey 42
KC — Barnett 8 pass from Krieg (Lowery kick)
Cin — FG Pelfrey 47
KC — Allen 9 run (Lowery kick)
Cin — FG Pelfrey 34
KC — FG Lowery 37

**DALLAS 27, INDIANAPOLIS 3**—at Hoosier Dome, attendance 60,453. Emmitt Smith rushed for 104 yards and 1 touchdown, and Troy Aikman passed for 245 yards and another score to lead the Cowboys to their third consecutive victory. Leading 14-3 in the third quarter, Dallas put the game out of reach when tight end Jay Novacek, the holder on field-goal attempts, took the snap in field-goal formation and ran 2 yards for a touchdown. Eddie Murray added a pair of field goals in the fourth quarter. The Colts amassed 361 total yards, including 113 rushing yards by rookie Roosevelt Potts, but were victimized by 4 turnovers. Indianapolis also suffered a severe blow when defensive tackle Steve Emtman suffered a season-ending injury to his right knee in the second quarter. Emtman, the top overall pick in the 1992 draft, missed the final seven games of his rookie year when he injured his left knee.

| | | | | | | |
|---|---|---|---|---|---|---|
| **Dallas** | 14 | 0 | 7 | 6 | — | 27 |
| **Indianapolis** | 0 | 3 | 0 | 0 | — | 3 |

Dall — Johnston 1 pass from Aikman (Murray kick)
Dall — E. Smith 20 run (Murray kick)
Ind — FG Biasucci 27
Dall — Novacek 2 run (Murray kick)
Dall — FG Murray 30
Dall — FG Murray 32

**MIAMI 24, CLEVELAND 14**—at Cleveland Stadium, attendance 78,138. Scott Mitchell replaced injured Dan Marino and threw a pair of third-quarter touchdown passes to rally the Dolphins past the Browns. Marino, who started his 145th consecutive game for Miami, tore his Achilles tendon in the second quarter and was lost for the season. Mitchell's first pass was intercepted by Cleveland cornerback Najee Mustafaa, who returned it a club-record 97 yards for a touchdown to give the Browns a 14-10 halftime advantage. In the third quarter, Mitchell teamed with wide receiver Tony Martin (19 yards) and tight end Keith Jackson (3 yards) for touchdowns. Marino completed 14 of 19 passes for 161 yards and a touchdown before being injured, while Mitchell was 10 of 16 for 118 yards. The Browns could muster only 202 total yards, and for the third consecutive game, starting quarterback Bernie Kosar was relieved by backup Vinny Testaverde. Kosar completed 15 of 19 passes, but for only 82 yards, and was sacked 5 times. Testaverde did not fare any better, completing only 6 of 13 for 44 yards, but was sacked only once and earned the starting assignment against Cincinnati the following week.

| | | | | | | |
|---|---|---|---|---|---|---|
| **Miami** | 0 | 10 | 14 | 0 | — | 24 |
| **Cleveland** | 7 | 7 | 0 | 0 | — | 14 |

Cle — M. Jackson 14 pass from Kosar (Stover kick)
Mia — FG Stoyanovich 52
Mia — Ingram 13 pass from Marino (Stoyanovich kick)
Cle — Mustafaa 97 interception return (Stover kick)
Mia — Martin 19 pass from Mitchell (Stoyanovich kick)
Mia — K. Jackson 3 pass from Mitchell (Stoyanovich kick)

**NEW ENGLAND 23, PHOENIX 21**—at Sun Devil Stadium, attendance 36,115. Backup quarterback Scott Secules threw a 2-yard touchdown pass to tight end Ben Coates with 3:56 remaining, lifting the Patriots past the Cardinals. It was New England's first victory of the season and snapped a nine-game losing streak dating back to 1992. Phoenix lost its third in a row. The Cardinals took a 21-16 lead on Steve Beuerlein's third touchdown pass of the game, a 30-yard toss to Randal Hill with 7:35 to go. But the Patriots won by marching 84 yards in just 3 plays for the winning score. The key blow was running back Leonard Russell's 69-yard run with a lateral from running back Kevin Turner, after Turner had caught a 13-yard pass from Secules. Russell was tackled at the 2-yard line, but Secules teamed with Coates for the winning score on the next play. Secules, who entered the game in the closing seconds of the first half after starter Drew Bledsoe sprained his knee, completed 12 of 20 passes for 214 yards. Russell ran for 116 yards on 28 carries. New England, which entered the game ranked twenty-third in the league in total offense, finished with 432 yards.

| | | | | | | |
|---|---|---|---|---|---|---|
| **New England** | 0 | 13 | 3 | 7 | — | 23 |
| **Phoenix** | 0 | 14 | 0 | 7 | — | 21 |

NE — Coates 4 pass from Bledsoe (Sisson kick)
Phx — Proehl 6 pass from Beuerlein (Davis kick)
Phx — Proehl 15 pass from Beuerlein (Davis kick)
NE — FG Sisson 29
NE — FG Sisson 23
NE — FG Sisson 31
Phx — R. Hill 30 pass from Beuerlein (Davis kick)
NE — Coates 2 pass from Secules (Sisson kick)

**N.Y. GIANTS 41, WASHINGTON 7**—at RFK Stadium, attendance 53,715. Phil Simms threw 3 touchdown passes and the Giants built a 27-0 first-half lead en route to handing the Redskins their worst defeat at home in 45 years. Simms, who completed his first 10 passes, finished 14 of 17 for 182 yards. Tight end Howard Cross and wide receiver Mike Sherrard each caught 2 touchdown passes, David Meggett threw a touchdown pass on a halfback option play, and Lewis Tillman and rookie Kenyon Rasheed ran for scores. Tillman, who replaced injured Rodney Hampton in the lineup, gained a career-high 104 yards on 29 carries. He got New York rolling with a 3-yard touchdown run to cap the Giants' first possession, a 13-play, 89-yard drive. New York then scored on each of its next three possessions to turn the game into a rout. Washington's lone score came on a 12-yard touchdown pass from Mark Rypien to Tim McGee with 53 seconds left in the first half. Rypien, playing for the first time since injuring his knee in week 2, completed 21 of 35 passes for 220 yards but could not prevent the Redskins' fourth consecutive defeat.

| | | | | | | |
|---|---|---|---|---|---|---|
| **N.Y. Giants** | 7 | 20 | 0 | 14 | — | 41 |
| **Washington** | 0 | 7 | 0 | 0 | — | 7 |

Giants— Tillman 3 run (Treadwell kick)
Giants— Cross 7 pass from Simms (kick failed)
Giants— Sherrard 42 pass from Meggett (Treadwell kick)
Giants— Cross 17 pass from Simms (Treadwell kick)
Wash — McGee 12 pass from Rypien (Lohmiller kick)
Giants— Sherrard 55 pass from Simms (Treadwell kick)
Giants— Rasheed 23 run (Treadwell kick)

**L.A. RAIDERS 24, N.Y. JETS 20**—at Los Angeles Memorial Coliseum, attendance 41,627. Nick Bell ran 1 yard for a touchdown with four seconds left to give the Raiders a dramatic come-from-behind victory. After rallying from a 17-0 first-half deficit to tie the game, Los Angeles fell behind again when the Jets' Cary Blanchard kicked a 20-yard field goal with 4:29 remaining. But the Raiders responded by marching 72 yards in 11 plays to the winning score. Quarterback Vince Evans passed for 57 yards on the drive, including a 6-yard completion to Tim Brown to position the ball on the 1-yard line. With no timeouts left, Raiders coaches were signaling for a pass into the ground to stop the clock and set up a game-tying field goal, but Evans did not see them. Instead, he handed off to Bell, who scored behind a block by tackle Gerald Perry. The Jets built their first-half lead on a 6-yard run by Blair Thomas, a 62-yard interception return by Brian Washington, and Blanchard's 25-yard field goal. After Washington's interception return, which came 3:51 into the second quarter, Raiders quarterback Jeff Hostetler, still not fully recovered from the sprained ankle that kept him out of the previous game, was replaced by Evans. The 38-year-old quarterback completed 14 of 22 passes for 247 yards, including touchdowns of 42 yards to James Jett and 68 yards to Alexander Wright.

| | | | | | | |
|---|---|---|---|---|---|---|
| **N.Y. Jets** | 0 | 17 | 0 | 3 | — | 20 |
| **L.A. Raiders** | 0 | 7 | 10 | 7 | — | 24 |

Jets — B. Thomas 6 run (Blanchard kick)
Jets — B. Washington 62 interception return (Blanchard kick)
Jets — FG Blanchard 25
Raid — Jett 42 pass from Evans (Jaeger kick)
Raid — Wright 68 pass from Evans (Jaeger kick)
Raid — FG Jaeger 42
Jets — FG Blanchard 20
Raid — Bell 1 run (Jaeger kick)

**PITTSBURGH 16, SAN DIEGO 3**—at Three Rivers Stadium, attendance 55,264. Linebacker Levon Kirkland returned a fumble 16 yards for the only touchdown of the game as the Steelers won their third straight game. Pittsburgh's offense accumulated 304 total yards, but could manage only 3 field goals by Gary Anderson. So the Steelers relied on their defense, which limited the Chargers to 138 total yards, including just 19 on the ground in 20 attempts. San Diego's only score came on John Carney's 33-yard field goal three seconds before halftime, and their best chance for a touchdown was thwarted by safety Darren Perry's goal-line interception in the third quarter. On that play, Chargers quarterback John Friesz was knocked out of the game when hit by Pittsburgh linebacker Kevin Greene. Stan Humphries replaced Friesz, and on his first series was sacked by linebacker Greg Lloyd. The ball came loose, and Kirkland converted the fumble into the clinching score. Barry Foster led the Steelers with 110 yards on 23 carries.

| | | | | | | |
|---|---|---|---|---|---|---|
| **San Diego** | 0 | 3 | 0 | 0 | — | 3 |
| **Pittsburgh** | 3 | 3 | 7 | 3 | — | 16 |

Pitt — FG Anderson 37
Pitt — FG Anderson 34
SD — FG Carney 33
Pitt — Kirkland 16 fumble return (Anderson kick)
Pitt — FG Anderson 35

**MINNESOTA 15, TAMPA BAY 0**—at Metrodome, attendance 53,562. The Vikings' defense dominated this one, limiting the Buccaneers to 169 total yards and forcing 5 turnovers. Safety Vencie Glenn had 2 of Minnesota's 4 interceptions, and defensive tackle Roy Barker pressured Tampa Bay quarterback Craig Erickson into an intentional grounding call in the end zone for a safety that gave the Vikings a 5-0 lead with 6:19 to go in the second quarter. Barry Word ran 1 yard for a touchdown 4:24 later to increase the advantage to 12-0. Minnesota was not threatened after that. The Vikings won for the ninth consecutive time against an NFC Central opponent and moved into a three-way tie for first place in the division.

| | | | | | | |
|---|---|---|---|---|---|---|
| **Tampa Bay** | 0 | 0 | 0 | 0 | — | 0 |
| **Minnesota** | 0 | 12 | 0 | 3 | — | 15 |

Minn — FG Reveiz 26
Minn — Safety, Erickson called for intentional grounding in end zone
Minn — Word 1 run (Reveiz kick)
Minn — FG Reveiz 25

## SUNDAY NIGHT, OCTOBER 10

**GREEN BAY 30, DENVER 27**—at Lambeau Field, attendance 58,943. The Packers snapped their three-game losing streak by building a 30-7 halftime lead, then holding on to win. Green Bay manufactured its big advantage by scoring on all six of its first-half possessions. The Broncos' lone score of the half came on a 14-yard pass from John Elway to Vance Johnson 3:27 into the second quarter, trimming the Packers' lead to 17-7. But Green Bay quarterback Brett Favre countered just 24 seconds later with a 66-yard touchdown pass to tight end Jackie Harris. Denver chipped away at its deficit in the second half, and pulled within three points on Jason Elam's 37-yard field goal with 8:31 left in the game. The Broncos had a chance to win or tie after cornerback Le-Lo Lang's interception gave them the ball at the Packers' 43-yard line with 2:05 to go. But Green Bay defensive end Reggie White had sacks of Elway on consecutive plays to secure the victory. Favre finished with 20 completions in 32 attempts for 235 yards, with 3 interceptions. The Packers' Sterling Sharpe caught 10 passes for 70 yards and Harris had 5 receptions for 128 yards. Denver's Elway completed 33 of 59 passes for 367 yards. Vance Johnson had 10 catches for 148 yards.

| | | | | | | |
|---|---|---|---|---|---|---|
| **Denver** | 0 | 7 | 14 | 6 | — | 27 |
| **Green Bay** | 17 | 13 | 0 | 0 | — | 30 |

GB — FG Jacke 28
GB — Stephens 1 run (Jacke kick)
GB — Bennett 1 run (Jacke kick)
Den — V. Johnson 14 pass from Elway (Elam kick)
GB — Harris 66 pass from Favre (Jacke kick)
GB — FG Jacke 32
GB — FG Jacke 21
Den — Croel 22 interception return (Elam kick)
Den — Bernstine 2 run (Elam kick)
Den — FG Elam 47
Den — FG Elam 37

## MONDAY, OCTOBER 11

**BUFFALO 35, HOUSTON 7**—at Rich Stadium, attendance 79,928. Jim Kelly broke a 7-7 tie with a pair of touchdown passes to Andre Reed, and the Bills went on to hand the Oilers their third consecutive defeat. Kelly, who also threw a 34-yard touchdown pass to Don Beebe in the first quarter, teamed with Reed on scoring tosses of 24 and 39 yards just 3:51 apart in the second quarter. Thurman Thomas's 7-yard run 3:34 before halftime turned the game into a rout. Buffalo's defense took over after that and finished the night with 7 turnovers. Kelly had 15 completions in 25 attempts for 247 yards, while Thomas rushed for 92 yards, including 90 before intermission. Houston managed 329 total yards, but stymied itself with the turnovers, 12 penalties, and 4 sacks. The game was a rematch of the 1992 AFC Wild Card Game, in which Buffalo rallied from a 35-3 third-quarter deficit to win 41-38 in overtime.

| | | | | | | |
|---|---|---|---|---|---|---|
| **Houston** | 7 | 0 | 0 | 0 | — | 7 |
| **Buffalo** | 7 | 21 | 0 | 7 | — | 35 |

Buff — Beebe 34 pass from Kelly (Christie kick)
Hou — L. Harris 17 pass from Moon (Del Greco kick)
Buff — Reed 24 pass from Kelly (Christie kick)
Buff — Reed 39 pass from Kelly (Christie kick)
Buff — Thomas 7 run (Christie kick)
Buff — K. Davis 3 run (Christie kick)

## SEVENTH WEEK SUMMARIES

**AMERICAN FOOTBALL CONFERENCE**

| **Eastern Division** | **W** | **L** | **T** | **Pct.** | **Pts.** | **OP** |
|---|---|---|---|---|---|---|
| Buffalo | 4 | 1 | 0 | .800 | 116 | 67 |
| Miami | 4 | 1 | 0 | .800 | 101 | 81 |
| Indianapolis | 2 | 3 | 0 | .400 | 68 | 102 |
| N.Y. Jets | 2 | 3 | 0 | .400 | 139 | 106 |
| New England | 1 | 5 | 0 | .167 | 88 | 168 |
| **Central Division** | | | | | | |
| Cleveland | 4 | 2 | 0 | .667 | 121 | 107 |
| Pittsburgh | 4 | 2 | 0 | .667 | 145 | 92 |
| Houston | 2 | 4 | 0 | .333 | 116 | 128 |
| Cincinnati | 0 | 6 | 0 | .000 | 69 | 134 |
| **Western Division** | | | | | | |
| Kansas City | 5 | 1 | 0 | .833 | 100 | 78 |
| L.A. Raiders | 4 | 2 | 0 | .667 | 113 | 103 |
| Denver | 3 | 3 | 0 | .500 | 149 | 118 |
| Seattle | 3 | 3 | 0 | .500 | 102 | 103 |
| San Diego | 2 | 4 | 0 | .333 | 84 | 127 |

**NATIONAL FOOTBALL CONFERENCE**

| **Eastern Division** | **W** | **L** | **T** | **Pct.** | **Pts.** | **OP** |
|---|---|---|---|---|---|---|
| N.Y. Giants | 5 | 1 | 0 | .833 | 145 | 71 |
| Dallas | 4 | 2 | 0 | .667 | 132 | 92 |
| Philadelphia | 4 | 2 | 0 | .667 | 128 | 133 |
| Phoenix | 2 | 4 | 0 | .333 | 121 | 105 |
| Washington | 1 | 5 | 0 | .167 | 99 | 161 |

| | | | | | | |
|---|---|---|---|---|---|---|
| **Central Division** | | | | | | |
| Detroit | 4 | 2 | 0 | .667 | 118 | 100 |
| Chicago | 3 | 2 | 0 | .600 | 97 | 59 |
| Minnesota | 3 | 2 | 0 | .600 | 66 | 82 |
| Green Bay | 2 | 3 | 0 | .400 | 110 | 104 |
| Tampa Bay | 1 | 4 | 0 | .200 | 54 | 122 |
| **Western Division** | | | | | | |
| New Orleans | 5 | 1 | 0 | .833 | 148 | 111 |
| San Francisco | 3 | 3 | 0 | .500 | 142 | 127 |
| L.A. Rams | 2 | 4 | 0 | .333 | 101 | 136 |
| Atlanta | 1 | 5 | 0 | .167 | 121 | 176 |

## THURSDAY, OCTOBER 14

**ATLANTA 30, L.A. RAMS 24**—at Georgia Dome, attendance 45,231. Billy Joe Tolliver threw a career-high 3 touchdown passes and the Falcons rallied from a 14-point deficit to win their first game of the season. A 56-yard touchdown pass from Jim Everett and a 2-yard run by Jerome Bettis helped stake the Rams to a 17-3 lead late in the first half. But Tolliver, Atlanta's third-string quarterback who was starting because of injuries to Bobby Hebert and Chris Miller, threw a 21-yard touchdown pass to Andre Rison 1:50 before intermission to trim the Falcons' deficit to 17-10. Los Angeles led 24-20 until Tolliver and Rison teamed again, this time on a 42-yard touchdown pass that gave Atlanta the lead for the first time with 4:40 remaining in the game. The Falcons added a field goal 1:11 later after recovering a fumble on the ensuing kickoff. Everett passed for 294 yards, but also threw 2 interceptions that led to Atlanta's second-half touchdowns. He marched the Rams from their 20-yard line to the Falcons' 27 with less than a minute to go, but threw 4 consecutive incompletions from there. Bettis ran for 85 yards for Los Angeles, which averaged nearly 7 yards per play and piled up 456 total yards. Tolliver completed 18 of 34 passes for 213 yards.

| | | | | | | |
|---|---|---|---|---|---|---|
| **L.A. Rams** | 10 | 7 | 7 | 0 | — | 24 |
| **Atlanta** | 3 | 7 | 7 | 13 | — | 30 |

Rams — Anderson 56 pass from Everett (Zendejas kick)
Atl — FG Johnson 28
Rams — FG Zendejas 52
Rams — Bettis 2 run (Zendejas kick)
Atl — Rison 21 pass from Tolliver (Johnson kick)
Atl — Mims 3 pass from Tolliver (Johnson kick)
Rams — Gary 60 pass from Everett (Zendejas kick)
Atl — FG Johnson 32
Atl — Rison 42 pass from Tolliver (Johnson kick)
Atl — FG Johnson 34

## SUNDAY, OCTOBER 17

**CLEVELAND 28, CINCINNATI 17**—at Riverfront Stadium, attendance 55,647. Vinny Testaverde led the Browns to the victory by throwing 3 touchdown passes in his first start of the season. Testaverde, who had come off the bench to replace Bernie Kosar each of the past three games, completed only 11 of 24 passes for 127 yards, but he staked his team to a 21-0 lead by throwing all of his scoring passes in the game's first 21 minutes. Wide receiver Mark Carrier's 15-yard run on a reverse put the game out of reach after the Bengals had closed within 21-10. Tommy Vardell led Cleveland with 98 rushing yards. Cincinnati managed only 34 rushing yards and 194 total yards.

| | | | | | | |
|---|---|---|---|---|---|---|
| **Cleveland** | 7 | 14 | 0 | 7 | — | 28 |
| **Cincinnati** | 0 | 7 | 3 | 7 | — | 17 |

Cle — Vardell 28 pass from Testaverde (Stover kick)
Cle — Baldwin 5 pass from Testaverde (Stover kick)
Cle — Kinchen 1 pass from Testaverde (Stover kick)
Cin — Query 11 pass from Schroeder (Pelfrey kick)
Cin — FG Pelfrey 49
Cle — Carrier 15 run (Stover kick)
Cin — Pickens 24 pass from Schroeder (Pelfrey kick)

**HOUSTON 28, NEW ENGLAND 14**—at Foxboro Stadium, attendance 51,037. Warren Moon came off the bench to throw 2 touchdown passes as the Oilers snapped a three-game losing streak. The game was scoreless until Houston quarterback Cody Carlson, making his first start of the season, scrambled 10 yards for a touchdown midway through the second quarter. But Carlson pulled a groin muscle on the run and was replaced by Moon during the Oilers' next drive. That 57-yard march ended when Moon threw a 7-yard touchdown pass to Webster Slaughter to make it 14-0 15 seconds before halftime. After the Patriots closed the deficit to 7 points early in the second half, Moon directed an 85-yard drive that took nearly 10 minutes and culminated in his second scoring toss to Slaughter, this one from 2 yards. Cornerback Steve Jackson returned an interception 22 yards for the clinching touchdown with 9:58 left in the game. Moon completed 16 of 21 passes for 102 yards. New England quarterback Scott Secules, starting in place of injured Drew Bledsoe, completed 23 of 40 attempts for 280 yards and a touchdown, but was intercepted 3 times.

| | | | | | | |
|---|---|---|---|---|---|---|
| **Houston** | 0 | 14 | 7 | 7 | — | 28 |
| **New England** | 0 | 0 | 7 | 7 | — | 14 |

Hou — Carlson 10 run (Del Greco kick)
Hou — Slaughter 7 pass from Moon (Del Greco kick)
NE — Turner 7 pass from Secules (Sisson kick)
Hou — Slaughter 2 pass from Moon (Del Greco kick)
Hou — Jackson 22 interception return (Del Greco kick)
NE — Russell 1 run (Sisson kick)

**KANSAS CITY 17, SAN DIEGO 14**—at San Diego Jack Murphy Stadium, attendance 60,729. Marcus Allen's 1-yard touchdown run with 1:57 remaining capped an 80-yard drive and gave the Chiefs the victory. The Chargers had taken a 14-10 early in the fourth quarter on John Friesz's 4-yard touchdown pass to Anthony Miller. But later in the quarter, Chiefs defensive end Neil Smith blocked John Carney's 31-yard field goal try (Smith also swatted away Carney's 46-yard attempt in the third quarter), and Kansas City took over at its 20-yard line with 3:27 left. Montana completed a 22-yard pass to tight end Keith Cash, and a 15-yard penalty for roughing the passer on the same play put the ball at the Chargers' 43. Still there on fourth-and-10, Montana threw 12 yards to Willie Davis to keep the drive alive. Later, Allen's 18-yard run on a draw play moved the ball to the 1 and set up the winning score. Montana, questionable for the game because of a hamstring injury suffered two weeks earlier against the Raiders, completed 21 of 39 passes for 284 yards. Kansas City won for the fifth time in six games, its best start in 22 years.

| | | | | | | |
|---|---|---|---|---|---|---|
| **Kansas City** | 7 | 3 | 0 | 7 | — | 17 |
| **San Diego** | 0 | 7 | 0 | 7 | — | 14 |

KC — Allen 15 pass from Montana (Lowery kick)
SD — Means 7 run (Carney kick)
KC — FG Lowery 37
SD — Miller 4 pass from Friesz (Carney kick)
KC — Allen 1 run (Lowery kick)

**PITTSBURGH 37, NEW ORLEANS 14**—at Three Rivers Stadium, attendance 56,056. Cornerback Rod Woodson returned an interception 63 yards for a touchdown just 1:39 into the game, and the Steelers went on to hand the Saints, the league's last unbeaten team, their first loss of the season. Woodson intercepted his second pass of the game later in the first quarter, setting up Neil O'Donnell's 20-yard touchdown pass to Barry Foster. Foster ran 1 yard for a touchdown to make it 24-0 with 2:29 left in the first half, and to that point New Orleans had yet to record a first down. Pittsburgh went on to build a 37-0 advantage before backup quarterback Mike Buck threw 2 touchdown passes in the last 4:15 for the Saints. New Orleans's starting quarterback, Wade Wilson, entered the game with a string of 107 pass attempts without an interception, but was picked off 3 times while completing only 6 of 26 passes for 85 yards. Leroy Thompson ran for 101 yards, and Barry Foster had 75 for the Steelers. Pittsburgh's defense forced 5 turnovers.

| | | | | | | |
|---|---|---|---|---|---|---|
| **New Orleans** | 0 | 0 | 0 | 14 | — | 14 |
| **Pittsburgh** | 14 | 10 | 6 | 7 | — | 37 |

Pitt — Woodson 63 interception return (Anderson kick)
Pitt — Foster 20 pass from O'Donnell (Anderson kick)
Pitt — FG Anderson 40
Pitt — Foster 1 run (Anderson kick)
Pitt — FG Anderson 22
Pitt — FG Anderson 29
Pitt — Green 26 pass from Tomczak (Anderson kick)
NO — Small 3 pass from Buck (Andersen kick)
NO — Early 63 pass from Buck (Andersen kick)

**N.Y. GIANTS 21, PHILADELPHIA 10**—at Giants Stadium, attendance 76,050. Lewis Tillman ran for a career-high 169 yards and 2 touchdowns, and the Giants moved into sole possession of first place in the NFC Eastern Division by beating the Eagles. Philadelphia led 3-0 until Phil Simms's 17-yard touchdown pass to Ed McCaffrey 4:53 into the second quarter gave New York the lead for good. Tillman, who ran for more than 100 yards for the second consecutive week while replacing injured starter Rodney Hampton, scored on a 1-yard run 3:53 before halftime. He put the game out of reach by running 10 yards for another touchdown with 10:07 left in the game. The Giants amassed 210 of their 347 total yards on the ground. Tillman averaged nearly 8.5 yards on his 20 carries.

| | | | | | | |
|---|---|---|---|---|---|---|
| **Philadelphia** | 0 | 3 | 0 | 7 | — | 10 |
| **N.Y. Giants** | 0 | 14 | 0 | 7 | — | 21 |

Phil — FG Bahr 47
Giants — McCaffrey 17 pass from Simms (Treadwell kick)
Giants — Tillman 1 run (Treadwell kick)
Giants — Tillman 10 run (Treadwell kick)
Phil — Bavaro 13 pass from O'Brien (Bahr kick)

**DALLAS 26, SAN FRANCISCO 17**—at Texas Stadium, attendance 65,099. Michael Irvin caught 12 passes for 168 yards and a touchdown to lead the Cowboys past the 49ers in a rematch of the 1992 NFC Championship Game, also won by Dallas. Irvin made the key play of the game as time ran out in the third quarter, making a juggling 36-yard touchdown catch with San Francisco cornerback Michael McGruder in close pursuit, giving the Cowboys the lead for good. Trailing 23-17, the 49ers marched to Dallas's 6-yard line, but could not score when the drive stalled and the snap on a short field-goal attempt went awry. Eddie Murray's 18-yard field goal, his fourth of the game, clinched it with 4:21 to go. San Francisco quarterback Steve Young completed 24 of 33 passes for 267 yards, and the 49ers rolled up 25 first downs and 403 total yards, but managed only 1 offensive touchdown. Troy Aikman completed 21 of 35 passes for 243 yards for the Cowboys, who won their fourth straight game.

| | | | | | | |
|---|---|---|---|---|---|---|
| **San Francisco** | 10 | 0 | 7 | 0 | — | 17 |
| **Dallas** | 3 | 13 | 7 | 3 | — | 26 |

SF — Davis 47 fumble return (Cofer kick)
Dall — FG Murray 48
SF — FG Cofer 25
Dall — FG Murray 39
Dall — E. Smith 1 run (Murray kick)
Dall — FG Murray 29
SF — B. Jones 12 pass from Young (Cofer kick)
Dall — Irvin 36 pass from Aikman (Murray kick)
Dall — FG Murray 18

**DETROIT 30, SEATTLE 10**—at Silverdome, attendance 60,801. Mel Gray's 95-yard kickoff return for a touchdown broke open a close game and helped the Lions take over first place in the NFC Central Division. John Kasay's 19-yard field goal 4:56 into the second half had pulled the Seahawks within 14-10. But Gray, whose fumble on the opening kickoff led to Seattle's first score, countered with his big return. Jason Hanson added 3 field goals to keep the game out of reach. Rodney Peete, back in as Detroit's starting quarterback, threw second-quarter touchdown passes of 13 and 11 yards to Herman Moore, and Barry Sanders rushed for 101 yards on 22 carries.

| | | | | | | |
|---|---|---|---|---|---|---|
| **Seattle** | 7 | 0 | 3 | 0 | — | 10 |
| **Detroit** | 0 | 14 | 13 | 3 | — | 30 |

Sea — Martin 6 pass from Mirer (Kasay kick)
Det — Moore 13 pass from Peete (Hanson kick)
Det — Moore 11 pass from Peete (Hanson kick)
Sea — FG Kasay 19
Det — Gray 95 kickoff return (Hanson kick)
Det — FG Hanson 34
Det — FG Hanson 32
Det — FG Hanson 35

**PHOENIX 36, WASHINGTON 6**—at Sun Devil Stadium, attendance 48,143. The Cardinals swept the season series from Washington for the first time since 1974 and handed the Redskins their fifth consecutive defeat. Steve Beuerlein passed for 250 yards, including a 42-yard touchdown to Ricky Proehl that put Phoenix ahead 20-3 early in the second half. Defensive end Eric Swann and linebacker Freddie Joe Nunn each had 2 sacks as the Cardinals' defense limited Washington to 2 field goals. Swann also recorded a safety, tackling Redskins running back Reggie Brooks in the end zone one minute into the fourth quarter.

| | | | | | | |
|---|---|---|---|---|---|---|
| **Washington** | 3 | 0 | 3 | 0 | — | 6 |
| **Phoenix** | 0 | 13 | 7 | 16 | — | 36 |

Wash — FG Lohmiller 43
Phx — FG Davis 23
Phx — FG Davis 45
Phx — Hearst 1 run (Davis kick)
Phx — Proehl 42 pass from Beuerlein (Davis kick)
Wash — FG Lohmiller 38
Phx — Safety, Swann tackled Brooks in end zone
Phx — Bailey 14 run (Davis kick)
Phx — Moore 1 run (Davis kick)

## MONDAY, OCTOBER 18

**L.A. RAIDERS 23, DENVER 20**—at Mile High Stadium, attendance 75,712. Jeff Jaeger's 53-yard field goal with 16 seconds left gave the Raiders the victory and spoiled another of John Elway's comeback efforts. The Broncos trailed 13-3 early in the fourth quarter until Elway threw a 27-yard touchdown pass to Arthur Marshall to trim the deficit to 3 points with 11:47 remaining. Raiders quarterback Jeff Hostetler fumbled the snap on the next play from scrimmage, and nose tackle Greg Kragen's recovery at the 5-yard line set up Elway's 2-yard touchdown pass to tight end Reggie Johnson, giving Denver its first lead at 17-13 with 10:48 to go. But the Broncos' advantage lasted only 23 seconds because Hostetler teamed with rookie James Jett on a 74-yard touchdown pass that put Los Angeles back in front. Jason Elam kicked a 37-yard field goal on Denver's next possession to tie the game, but the Raiders held the Broncos the next time they had the ball, then used a 20-yard completion from Hostetler to Tim Brown to set up Jaeger's winning kick. Hostetler completed 15 of 24 passes for 264 yards and 2 touchdowns, while Brown caught 6 passes for 116 yards. Russell had 5 catches for 111 yards for the Broncos, and Rod Bernstine ran for 101 yards on 23 carries.

| | | | | | | |
|---|---|---|---|---|---|---|
| **L.A. Raiders** | 10 | 3 | 0 | 10 | — | 23 |
| **Denver** | 0 | 0 | 3 | 17 | — | 20 |

Raid — Wright 11 pass from Hostetler (Jaeger kick)
Raid — FG Jaeger 32
Raid — FG Jaeger 49
Den — FG Elam 40
Den — Marshall 27 pass from Elway (Elam kick)
Den — R. Johnson 2 pass from Elway (Elam kick)
Raid — Jett 74 pass from Hostetler (Jaeger kick)
Den — FG Elam 37
Raid — FG Jaeger 53

## EIGHTH WEEK SUMMARIES

### AMERICAN FOOTBALL CONFERENCE

| Eastern Division | W | L | T | Pct. | Pts. | OP |
|---|---|---|---|---|---|---|
| Buffalo | 4 | 1 | 0 | .800 | 116 | 67 |
| Miami | 4 | 1 | 0 | .800 | 101 | 81 |
| Indianapolis | 2 | 3 | 0 | .400 | 68 | 102 |
| N.Y. Jets | 2 | 3 | 0 | .400 | 139 | 106 |
| New England | 1 | 5 | 0 | .167 | 88 | 168 |
| **Central Division** | | | | | | |
| Cleveland | 4 | 2 | 0 | .667 | 121 | 107 |
| Pittsburgh | 4 | 2 | 0 | .667 | 145 | 92 |
| Houston | 2 | 4 | 0 | .333 | 116 | 128 |
| Cincinnati | 0 | 6 | 0 | .000 | 69 | 134 |
| **Western Division** | | | | | | |
| Kansas City | 5 | 1 | 0 | .833 | 100 | 78 |
| L.A. Raiders | 4 | 2 | 0 | .667 | 113 | 103 |
| Denver | 3 | 3 | 0 | .500 | 149 | 118 |
| Seattle | 3 | 3 | 0 | .500 | 102 | 103 |
| San Diego | 2 | 4 | 0 | .333 | 84 | 127 |

### NATIONAL FOOTBALL CONFERENCE

| Eastern Division | W | L | T | Pct. | Pts. | OP |
|---|---|---|---|---|---|---|
| N.Y. Giants | 5 | 1 | 0 | .833 | 145 | 71 |
| Dallas | 4 | 2 | 0 | .667 | 132 | 92 |
| Philadelphia | 4 | 2 | 0 | .667 | 128 | 133 |
| Phoenix | 2 | 4 | 0 | .333 | 121 | 105 |
| Washington | 1 | 5 | 0 | .167 | 99 | 161 |
| **Central Division** | | | | | | |
| Detroit | 4 | 2 | 0 | .667 | 118 | 100 |
| Chicago | 3 | 2 | 0 | .600 | 97 | 59 |
| Minnesota | 3 | 2 | 0 | .600 | 66 | 82 |
| Green Bay | 2 | 3 | 0 | .400 | 110 | 104 |
| Tampa Bay | 1 | 4 | 0 | .200 | 54 | 122 |
| **WESTERN DIVISION** | | | | | | |
| New Orleans | 5 | 1 | 0 | .833 | 148 | 111 |
| San Francisco | 3 | 3 | 0 | .500 | 142 | 127 |
| L.A. Rams | 2 | 4 | 0 | .333 | 101 | 136 |
| Atlanta | 1 | 5 | 0 | .167 | 121 | 176 |

## SUNDAY, OCTOBER 24

**ATLANTA 26, NEW ORLEANS 15**—at Louisiana Superdome, attendance 69,043. Ailing Bobby Hebert completed 13 of 16 passes, 2 for touchdowns, to lead the Falcons' upset of the Saints. Hebert, who threw for 163 yards, was not expected to play against his former teammates because of an elbow injury. But with Chris Miller sidelined by injury and Billy Joe Tolliver suffering a sprained shoulder less than five minutes into the game, Hebert was pressed into duty. He responded by throwing short touchdown passes to Andre Rison and Michael Haynes in the second quarter as Atlanta built a 17-6 halftime lead. Running back Erric Pegram helped keep New Orleans at a distance by rushing for 132 yards on 34 carries as the Falcons maintained possession for more than 36 of the game's 60 minutes. That was uncharacteristic of the Saints, who were forced to take to the air to play catchup. New Orleans quarterback Wade Wilson completed 27 of 45 passes for 277 yards, but was intercepted twice.

| | | | | | | |
|---|---|---|---|---|---|---|
| **Atlanta** | 0 | 17 | 3 | 6 | — | 26 |
| **New Orleans** | 3 | 3 | 7 | 2 | — | 15 |

NO — FG Andersen 40
Atl — FG Johnson 19
Atl — Rison 5 pass from Hebert (Johnson kick)
Atl — Haynes 9 pass from Hebert (Johnson kick)
NO — FG Andersen 27
Atl — FG Johnson 32
NO — Early 23 pass from Wilson (Andersen kick)
Atl — FG Johnson 38
Atl — FG Johnson 30
NO — Safety, Alexander ran out of end zone

**BUFFALO 19, N.Y. JETS 10**—at Giants Stadium, attendance 71,541. Linebacker Darryl Talley made the key play, returning an interception 61 yards for a touchdown in the third quarter, as the Bills won their third in a row. The Jets took the opening kickoff and held the ball for 7:58, marching 80 yards in 16 plays, the last a 1-yard touchdown run by Brad Baxter. New York led 7-6 midway through the third quarter and had the ball at Buffalo's 39-yard line after an interception and 22-yard return by cornerback James Hasty. But on the first play following the turnover, Talley intercepted Boomer Esiason's pass and gave the Bills the lead for good. Steve Christie kicked 4 field goals, including the clincher from 30 yards with 3:37 remaining. That came 6 plays after the first interception of defensive end Bruce Smith's nine-year career. Despite failing to score an offensive touchdown, Buffalo held substantial advantages over the Jets in first downs (27-15), total yards (413-237), plays (81-49), and time of possession (37:16-22:44). Bills quarterback Jim Kelly passed for 224 yards, and Thurman Thomas rushed for 117 yards and caught 7 passes for 67 yards.

| | | | | | | |
|---|---|---|---|---|---|---|
| **Buffalo** | 0 | 6 | 7 | 6 | — | 19 |
| **N.Y. Jets** | 7 | 0 | 0 | 3 | — | 10 |

Jets — B. Baxter 1 run (Blanchard kick)
Buff — FG Christie 37
Buff — FG Christie 33
Buff — Talley 61 interception return (Christie kick)
Buff — FG Christie 22
Jets — FG Blanchard 33
Buff — FG Christie 30

**HOUSTON 28, CINCINNATI 12**—at Astrodome, attendance 50,039. Warren Moon passed for 253 yards and 2 touchdowns and the Oilers handed the Bengals their seventh consecutive defeat of 1993 and thirteenth in 14 games dating to 1992. Moon completed 24 of 34 passes as Houston amassed 369 total yards. Still, the Oilers struggled against winless Cincinnati and trailed 12-7 late in the third quarter until Lorenzo White capped a 71-yard drive with a 4-yard touchdown run. Houston put the game out of reach with a pair of fourth-quarter touchdowns.

| | | | | | | |
|---|---|---|---|---|---|---|
| **Cincinnati** | 0 | 9 | 3 | 0 | — | 12 |
| **Houston** | 7 | 0 | 7 | 14 | — | 28 |

Hou — Wellman 9 pass from Moon (Del Greco kick)
Cin — Query 8 pass from Schroeder (kick failed)
Cin — FG Pelfrey 53
Cin — FG Pelfrey 50
Hou — White 4 run (Del Greco kick)
Hou — Jeffires 11 pass from Moon (Del Greco kick)
Hou — Brown 25 run (Del Greco kick)

**DETROIT 16, L.A. RAMS 13**—at Anaheim Stadium, attendance 43,850. Jason Hanson's 18-yard field goal with four seconds left gave the Lions the victory and spoiled a fourth-quarter comeback by the Rams that was engineered by backup quarterback T.J. Rubley. Detroit built a 13-0 lead midway through the fourth quarter on 2 field goals by Hanson and a 5-yard touchdown run by Barry Sanders. But Rubley, who replaced an ineffective Jim Everett in the third quarter, threw a 4-yard touchdown pass to Ernie Jones with 4:19 to go in the game, then capped a 68-yard drive with a 21-yard touchdown pass to Jones with 1:52 left. Tony Zendejas's extra-point try following the second touchdown bounced off the left upright, leaving the game tied at 13-13. Ex-Rams player Vernon Turner, in the game because Pro Bowl kick returner Mel Gray was injured, returned the ensuing kickoff 45 yards to give the Lions possession at Los Angeles's 44-yard line. Rodney Peete sandwiched passes of 13 yards to Sanders and 25 yards to tight end Rodney Holman around a 5-yard run by Sanders, positioning Hanson for his winning kick. Peete completed 15 of 25 passes for 249 yards, and Detroit wide receiver Herman Moore caught 6 passes for 120 yards. Rubley was 12 of 17 for 151 yards and scrambled 3 times for 24 yards in his NFL debut. Rams rookie Jerome Bettis ran for 113 yards on 23 carries. Los Angeles tackle Jackie Slater played in his 245th NFL game, equaling the all-time record for offensive linemen held by Jeff Van Note and Mike Webster. But Slater left the game in the first half with a torn shoulder muscle.

| | | | | | | |
|---|---|---|---|---|---|---|
| **Detroit** | 0 | 3 | 3 | 10 | — | 16 |
| **L.A. Rams** | 0 | 0 | 0 | 13 | — | 13 |

Det — FG Hanson 25
Det — FG Hanson 24
Det — Sanders 5 run (Hanson kick)
Rams — Jones 4 pass from Rubley (Zendejas kick)
Rams — Jones 21 pass from Rubley (kick failed)
Det — FG Hanson 18

**GREEN BAY 37, TAMPA BAY 14**—at Tampa Stadium, attendance 47,354. Sterling Sharpe caught 4 touchdown passes to lead the Packers' rout of the Buccaneers. Sharpe had 3 of his scoring catches in the first half as Green Bay built a 24-0 lead at intermission. He was instrumental on the Packers' third touchdown drive, catching 3 passes for 41 yards, including a 10-yard touchdown, and lining up at quarterback for two plays that resulted in a 5-yard gain on a keeper and his 1-yard completion to Mark Clayton. Brett Favre completed 20 of 35 passes for 268 yards and Darrell Thompson rushed for 105 yards for Green Bay, which accumulated 421 yards of total offense. Sharpe finished with 10 catches for 147 yards. Tampa Bay's Craig Erickson teamed with rookie wide receiver Horace Copeland on touchdowns of 26 and 67 yards in the second half.

| | | | | | | |
|---|---|---|---|---|---|---|
| **Green Bay** | 7 | 17 | 6 | 7 | — | 37 |
| **Tampa Bay** | 0 | 0 | 7 | 7 | — | 14 |

GB — Sharpe 7 pass from Favre (Jacke kick)
GB — Sharpe 30 pass from Favre (Jacke kick)
GB — Sharpe 10 pass from Favre (Jacke kick)
GB — FG Jacke 50
GB — FG Jacke 44
GB — FG Jacke 24
TB — Copeland 26 pass from Erickson (Husted kick)
GB — Sharpe 32 pass from Favre (Jacke kick)
TB — Copeland 67 pass from Erickson (Husted kick)

**SEATTLE 10, NEW ENGLAND 9**—at Kingdome, attendance 56,526. Rick Mirer threw a 1-yard touchdown pass to Brian Blades with 25 seconds remaining to lift the Seahawks past the Patriots. New England, behind 3 field goals by Scott Sisson, led 9-3 when Seattle took possession at its 46-yard line with 3:30 to play. Mirer completed 7 of 10 passes for 39 yards on the ensuing march to the winning touchdown. He finished with 22 completions in 43 attempts for 203 yards. Blades caught 9 passes for 70 yards. The Patriots' Leonard Russell rushed for 97 yards on 21 carries.

| | | | | | | |
|---|---|---|---|---|---|---|
| **New England** | 0 | 0 | 3 | 6 | — | 9 |
| **Seattle** | 0 | 3 | 0 | 7 | — | 10 |

Sea — FG Kasay 30

| | | |
|---|---|---|
| NE | — | FG Sisson 36 |
| NE | — | FG Sisson 25 |
| NE | — | FG Sisson 19 |
| Sea | — | Blades 1 pass from Mirer (Kasay kick) |

**SAN FRANCISCO 28, PHOENIX 14**—at Candlestick Park, attendance 62,020. Steve Young passed for 247 yards and 2 touchdowns to lead the 49ers to a methodical victory over the Cardinals. San Francisco pulled within one game of the lead in the NFC Western Division by building a 28-0 advantage before Phoenix's Steve Beuerlein threw a pair of scoring passes in the final quarter. Young teamed with Jerry Rice on both of his touchdown throws. Rice, who caught 9 passes for 155 yards, moved past Lenny Moore and into fourth place on the NFL's all-time list with 114 career touchdowns. Ricky Watters ran for 95 yards as San Francisco rolled up 428 total yards. Phoenix actually outgained the 49ers, rushing for 107 yards and passing for 322, but was victimized by 3 interceptions, including 1 by San Francisco cornerback Eric Davis at the 1-yard line. Beuerlein completed 26 of 50 passes for 334 yards.

| | | | | | | |
|---|---|---|---|---|---|---|
| **Phoenix** | 0 | 0 | 0 | 14 | — | 14 |
| **San Francisco** | 0 | 14 | 0 | 14 | — | 28 |

| | | |
|---|---|---|
| SF | — | Logan 1 run (Cofer kick) |
| SF | — | Rice 8 pass from Young (Cofer kick) |
| SF | — | Rice 7 pass from Young (Cofer kick) |
| SF | — | Watters 19 run (Cofer kick) |
| Phx | — | Edwards 65 pass from Beuerlein (G. Davis kick) |
| Phx | — | Proehl 4 pass from Beuerlein (G. Davis kick) |

**CLEVELAND 28, PITTSBURGH 23**—at Cleveland Stadium, attendance 78,118. The Browns' Eric Metcalf stunned the Steelers with a 75-yard punt return for the winning touchdown with 2:05 remaining. Metcalf, who returned a punt 91 yards for a score in the second quarter, became the seventh player in NFL history to return 2 punts for touchdowns in the same game. After a scoreless first quarter, things heated up in the battle for first place in the AFC Central Division. Two big plays—Vinny Testaverde's 62-yard touchdown pass to Michael Jackson and Metcalf's long punt return—staked Cleveland to a 14-0 lead, but the Steelers countered with a pair of long scoring drives, capped by short touchdown runs by Barry Foster, to tie the score at 14-14. Pittsburgh, which dominated much of the game, drove to 3 field goals in the second half, the last of which put the Steelers ahead 23-21 with 7:51 remaining. The Browns began to move the ball on their next possession, but Testaverde suffered a slightly separated shoulder when scrambling for a first down with 7:27 to play. Bernie Kosar replaced Testaverde, but the drive stalled and Cleveland was forced to punt. The Browns' defense then held Pittsburgh without a first down, setting the stage for Metcalf's heroics. Neil O'Donnell completed 25 of 39 passes for a career-high 355 yards for the Steelers, who amassed 444 total yards to just 245 for Cleveland.

| | | | | | | |
|---|---|---|---|---|---|---|
| **Pittsburgh** | 0 | 14 | 6 | 3 | — | 23 |
| **Cleveland** | 0 | 14 | 7 | 7 | — | 28 |

| | | |
|---|---|---|
| Cle | — | Jackson 62 pass from Testaverde (Stover kick) |
| Cle | — | Metcalf 91 punt return (Stover kick) |
| Pitt | — | Foster 4 run (Anderson kick) |
| Pitt | — | Foster 1 run (Anderson kick) |
| Pitt | — | FG Anderson 30 |
| Cle | — | Wolfley 4 pass from Testaverde (Stover kick) |
| Pitt | — | FG Anderson 46 |
| Pitt | — | FG Anderson 30 |
| Cle | — | Metcalf 75 punt return (Stover kick) |

## SUNDAY NIGHT, OCTOBER 24

**MIAMI 41, INDIANAPOLIS 27**—at Joe Robbie Stadium, attendance 57,301. Quarterback Scott Mitchell was impressive in his starting debut, and rookies Terry Kirby and O.J. McDuffie scored their first career touchdowns as the Dolphins won their fourth consecutive game and handed the Colts their third straight defeat. Mitchell, starting because Dan Marino was lost for the season with an Achilles tendon injury one week earlier, completed 12 of 19 passes for 190 yards and 1 touchdown, with no interceptions. His 44-yard touchdown pass to Kirby gave Miami a 17-0 first-quarter lead. Earlier in the period, McDuffie raced 71 yards with a punt return for a touchdown. Kirby also had a 14-yard touchdown run late in the third quarter as the Dolphins built a 34-13 advantage. Still, Indianapolis battled, closing to within 34-20 on Jeff George's 6-yard touchdown pass to Reggie Langhorne with 9:56 left. But Miami safety Louis Oliver put the game out of reach by returning an interception 56 yards for a touchdown 2:48 later. George completed 27 of 44 passes for 260 yards and 2 touchdowns, but was intercepted 3 times. The Dolphins' Mark Higgs ran for 114 yards on 17 carries to help Miami head coach Don Shula record his 323rd career victory, just 1 short of the NFL record held by the legendary George Halas.

| | | | | | | |
|---|---|---|---|---|---|---|
| **Indianapolis** | 0 | 6 | 7 | 14 | — | 27 |
| **Miami** | 17 | 3 | 14 | 7 | — | 41 |

| | | |
|---|---|---|
| Mia | — | FG Stoyanovich 23 |
| Mia | — | McDuffie 71 punt return (Stoyanovich kick) |
| Mia | — | Kirby 44 pass from Mitchell (Stoyanovich kick) |
| Ind | — | Culver 3 pass from George (kick failed) |
| Mia | — | FG Stoyanovich 39 |
| Ind | — | Culver 1 run (Biasucci kick) |
| Mia | — | Fryar 11 pass from Byars (Stoyanovich kick) |
| Mia | — | Kirby 14 run (Stoyanovich kick) |
| Ind | — | Langhorne 6 pass from George (Biasucci kick) |
| Mia | — | Oliver 56 interception return (Stoyanovich kick) |
| Ind | — | Culver 3 run (Biasucci kick) |

## MONDAY, OCTOBER 25

**MINNESOTA 19, CHICAGO 12**—at Soldier Field, attendance 64,677. Cornerback Audray McMillian returned an interception 22 yards for a touchdown, and linebacker Jack Del Rio picked off a pass at the goal line with three seconds remaining to preserve the Vikings' victory. The Bears did little offensively until taking over at their 4-yard line and advancing to Minnesota's 25 late in the game. But Del Rio's interception was the last in a series of big plays by the Vikings' top-ranked defense, which also forced a fumble to set up Robert Smith's 26-yard touchdown run in the first quarter. Minnesota harassed Chicago quarterback Jim Harbaugh all night, sacking him 8 times, including 3½ by defensive tackle John Randle. Smith, the Vikings' first-round pick in the 1993 draft, ran for 80 yards while Barry Word added 78. Kevin Butler kicked 4 field goals, including a career-best 55-yard boot, to account for all of the Bears' points.

| | | | | | | |
|---|---|---|---|---|---|---|
| **Minnesota** | 10 | 3 | 6 | 0 | — | 19 |
| **Chicago** | 3 | 6 | 0 | 3 | — | 12 |

| | | |
|---|---|---|
| Chi | — | FG Butler 37 |
| Minn | — | FG Reveiz 39 |
| Minn | — | R. Smith 26 run (Reveiz kick) |
| Chi | — | FG Butler 39 |
| Chi | — | FG Butler 55 |
| Minn | — | FG Reveiz 26 |
| Minn | — | McMillian 22 interception return (kick failed) |
| Chi | — | FG Butler 35 |

## NINTH WEEK SUMMARIES

### AMERICAN FOOTBALL CONFERENCE

| Eastern Division | W | L | T | Pct. | Pts. | OP |
|---|---|---|---|---|---|---|
| Buffalo | 6 | 1 | 0 | .857 | 159 | 87 |
| Miami | 6 | 1 | 0 | .857 | 172 | 118 |
| Indianapolis | 3 | 4 | 0 | .429 | 104 | 149 |
| N.Y. Jets | 3 | 4 | 0 | .429 | 159 | 131 |
| New England | 1 | 7 | 0 | .125 | 103 | 187 |
| **Central Division** | | | | | | |
| Cleveland | 5 | 2 | 0 | .714 | 149 | 130 |
| Pittsburgh | 4 | 3 | 0 | .571 | 168 | 120 |
| Houston | 3 | 4 | 0 | .429 | 144 | 140 |
| Cincinnati | 0 | 7 | 0 | .000 | 81 | 162 |
| **Western Division** | | | | | | |
| Kansas City | 5 | 2 | 0 | .714 | 110 | 108 |
| Denver | 4 | 3 | 0 | .571 | 177 | 135 |
| L.A. Raiders | 4 | 3 | 0 | .571 | 136 | 133 |
| Seattle | 4 | 4 | 0 | .500 | 129 | 140 |
| San Diego | 3 | 4 | 0 | .429 | 114 | 150 |

### NATIONAL FOOTBALL CONFERENCE

| Eastern Division | W | L | T | Pct. | Pts. | OP |
|---|---|---|---|---|---|---|
| Dallas | 5 | 2 | 0 | .714 | 155 | 102 |
| N.Y. Giants | 5 | 2 | 0 | .714 | 151 | 81 |
| Philadelphia | 4 | 3 | 0 | .571 | 138 | 156 |
| Phoenix | 2 | 6 | 0 | .250 | 152 | 153 |
| Washington | 1 | 6 | 0 | .143 | 109 | 185 |
| **Central Division** | | | | | | |
| Detroit | 6 | 2 | 0 | .750 | 164 | 140 |
| Green Bay | 4 | 3 | 0 | .571 | 164 | 121 |
| Minnesota | 4 | 3 | 0 | .571 | 112 | 124 |
| Chicago | 3 | 4 | 0 | .429 | 112 | 95 |
| Tampa Bay | 2 | 5 | 0 | .286 | 99 | 183 |
| **Western Division** | | | | | | |
| New Orleans | 6 | 2 | 0 | .750 | 183 | 154 |
| San Francisco | 5 | 3 | 0 | .625 | 210 | 158 |
| Atlanta | 2 | 6 | 0 | .250 | 171 | 222 |
| L.A. Rams | 2 | 6 | 0 | .250 | 131 | 192 |

## SUNDAY, OCTOBER 31

**GREEN BAY 17, CHICAGO 3**—at Lambeau Field, attendance 58,945. Defensive end Reggie White became the NFL's all-time sack leader by recording 2 of the Packers' 7 sacks in a victory over the Bears. White, who joined Green Bay as a free agent in 1993 after eight seasons with Philadelphia, improved his career total to 130½ sacks, 1 better than Giants linebacker Lawrence Taylor. But it was a fourth-quarter sack by the Packers' LeRoy Butler that was the key play against Chicago. The Bears trailed 10-3 while driving to Green Bay's 12-yard line early in the period. Butler blitzed and sacked Bears quarterback Jim Harbaugh, forcing a fumble that the Packers' safety recovered. Later in the quarter, Darrell Thompson ran 17 yards for the clinching touchdown. Green Bay's offense managed only 261 total yards against Chicago's stingy defense. But the Bears continued to struggle offensively, and extended a dubious string of 10 quarters without a touchdown. Harbaugh completed 15 of his 19 passes, but for only 149 yards. Chicago had just 230 total yards.

| | | | | | | |
|---|---|---|---|---|---|---|
| **Chicago** | 0 | 3 | 0 | 0 | — | 3 |
| **Green Bay** | 3 | 7 | 0 | 7 | — | 17 |

| | | |
|---|---|---|
| GB | — | FG Jacke 40 |
| GB | — | Sharpe 21 pass from Favre (Jacke kick) |
| Chi | — | FG Butler 33 |
| GB | — | Thompson 17 run (Jacke kick) |

**DALLAS 23, PHILADELPHIA 10**—at Veterans Stadium, attendance 61,912. Emmitt Smith rushed for a club-record 237 yards, including a clinching 62-yard touchdown run in the fourth quarter, to power the Cowboys past the Eagles in a driving rain. Smith, who averaged 7.9 yards on his 30 carries, broke Dallas's single-game mark of 206 yards, set by Tony Dorsett in 1977, also against the Eagles. Smith's performance was the sixth best in league history. The Cowboys built a 10-0 lead in the second quarter on a field goal by Eddie Murray and wide receiver Kevin Williams's 11-yard touchdown run on a reverse. Philadelphia closed within 10-7 on a 3-yard touchdown pass from Ken O'Brien to Herschel Walker 1:25 before halftime. Murray kicked 2 more field goals in the second half to give Dallas a 16-10 edge, and Smith's touchdown run put the game out of reach with 3:45 remaining. The Cowboys won their fifth in a row to pull into a tie for first place in the NFC East, while the Eagles dropped their third straight after beginning the season 4-0.

| | | | | | | |
|---|---|---|---|---|---|---|
| **Dallas** | 3 | 7 | 3 | 10 | — | 23 |
| **Philadelphia** | 0 | 7 | 0 | 3 | — | 10 |

| | | |
|---|---|---|
| Dall | — | FG Murray 35 |
| Dall | — | K. Williams 11 run (Murray kick) |
| Phil | — | Walker 3 pass from O'Brien (Bahr kick) |
| Dall | — | FG Murray 23 |
| Phil | — | FG Bahr 33 |
| Dall | — | FG Murray 40 |
| Dall | — | E. Smith 62 run (Murray kick) |

**MIAMI 30, KANSAS CITY 10**—at Joe Robbie Stadium, attendance 67,765. Scott Mitchell threw 3 touchdown passes to help Dolphins coach Don Shula record his 324th career victory, equaling the legendary George Halas's NFL record. Mitchell, who completed 22 of 33 passes for 344 yards, threw touchdown passes of 27 yards to Irving Fryar and 8 yards to Keith Byars as Miami built a 13-3 halftime lead. The Dolphins put the game out of reach when Mitchell teamed with Mark Ingram on a 77-yard touchdown pass just 28 seconds into the second half. Miami controlled the clock after that, finishing with 139 rushing yards while maintaining possession for nearly 37 of the game's 60 minutes. The Chiefs, who had their four-game winning streak snapped, managed 305 total yards but lost 3 fumbles. Quarterback Joe Montana completed the 3,000th pass of his career, but left the game in the second quarter with a hamstring injury. Shula's career record improved to 324-152-6 (a .678 winning percentage) in 31 seasons with the Dolphins and Baltimore Colts. Halas was 324-151-31 (.671) in 40 years with the Bears.

| | | | | | | |
|---|---|---|---|---|---|---|
| **Kansas City** | 0 | 3 | 0 | 7 | — | 10 |
| **Miami** | 6 | 7 | 14 | 3 | — | 30 |

Mia — Fryar 27 pass from Mitchell (pass failed)
Mia — Byars 8 pass from Mitchell (Stoyanovich kick)
KC — FG Lowery 47
Mia — Ingram 77 pass from Mitchell (Stoyanovich kick)
Mia — Kirby 1 run (Stoyanovich kick)
Mia — FG Stoyanovich 34
KC — Cash 6 pass from Krieg (Lowery kick)

**SAN FRANCISCO 40, L.A. RAMS 17**—at Candlestick Park, attendance 63,417. Steve Young passed for 245 yards and the 49ers' defense harassed Rams quarterback T.J. Rubley in his first NFL start. Young completed 22 of 34 passes and tossed a 15-yard touchdown pass to John Taylor on the game's pivotal play in the second quarter. San Francisco led just 6-3 when Young's pass bounced off the hands of Rams cornerback Steve Israel, who had an open field ahead of him. Taylor made a juggling catch and gave the 49ers a 13-3 lead. Meanwhile, San Francisco's defense exerted heavy pressure on Rubley, who got the starting nod over veteran Jim Everett. Rubley was sacked 7 times, pressured on numerous occasions, and intercepted twice. He completed only 2 of 6 passes for 20 while the 49ers built a commanding 23-3 lead at halftime. Rubley fared better in the second half and finished 15 of 26 for 158 yards, including a 35-yard touchdown pass to Todd Kinchen in the third quarter. Mark Logan had 2 short touchdown runs for San Francisco.

| | | | | | | |
|---|---|---|---|---|---|---|
| **L.A. Rams** | 3 | 0 | 7 | 7 | — | 17 |
| **San Francisco** | 6 | 17 | 7 | 10 | — | 40 |

Rams — FG Zendejas 50
SF — Watters 1 run (kick failed)
SF — Taylor 15 pass from Young (Cofer kick)
SF — Logan 1 run (Cofer kick)
SF — FG Cofer 25
Rams — Kinchen 35 pass from Rubley (Zendejas kick)
SF — Logan 1 run (Cofer kick)
Rams — Bettis 1 run (Zendejas kick)
SF — FG Cofer 28
SF — McGruder 32 interception return (Cofer kick)

**INDIANAPOLIS 9, NEW ENGLAND 6**—at Hoosier Dome, attendance 46,522. Dean Biasucci kicked 3 field goals, including the winner from 37 yards with 2:42 left, as Indianapolis snapped a three-game losing streak. The Patriots, who fell to 1-7, lost their fourth game by 3 points or fewer. New England managed 363 total yards against Indianapolis, but had three drives stalled by turnovers. Its last threat ended when Colts rookie defensive back Ray Buchanan intercepted a pass with 1:55 to go. Jeff George completed 18 of 26 passes for 200 yards for the Colts. The Patriots' Scott Secules was 23 of 37 for 279 yards. Tight end Ben Coates caught 6 passes for 108 yards. This was the second consecutive game between these teams that failed to produce a touchdown. Biasucci accounted for all the points with 2 field goals in Indianapolis's 6-0 victory over New England late in the 1992 season.

| | | | | | | |
|---|---|---|---|---|---|---|
| **New England** | 0 | 3 | 0 | 3 | — | 6 |
| **Indianapolis** | 3 | 0 | 0 | 6 | — | 9 |

Ind — FG Biasucci 27
NE — FG Sisson 40
Ind — FG Biasucci 38
NE — FG Sisson 26
Ind — FG Biasucci 37

**NEW ORLEANS 20, PHOENIX 17**—at Sun Devil Stadium, attendance 36,778. The Saints rallied from a 10-point halftime deficit to beat the Cardinals and maintain their hold on first place in the NFC West. Phoenix managed only 143 total yards—just 38 in the second half—against the Saints, but took a 17-7 lead on the strength of its defense. Cornerback Aeneas Williams scooped up a fumble and ran 20 yards for a touchdown late in the first quarter, then intercepted a pass and returned it 46 yards for another touchdown in the second. But Morten Andersen's 48-yard field goal and Wade Wilson's 25-yard touchdown pass to Quinn Early 3:10 into the fourth quarter tied the game at 17-17. Moments later, safety Gene Atkins intercepted a pass at the Cardinals' 24-yard line to position Andersen for the decisive field goal with 7:34 remaining. Linebacker Renaldo Turnbull had 3 of New Orleans's 6 sacks.

| | | | | | | |
|---|---|---|---|---|---|---|
| **New Orleans** | 7 | 0 | 3 | 10 | — | 20 |
| **Phoenix** | 10 | 7 | 0 | 0 | — | 17 |

NO — Muster 1 run (Andersen kick)
Phx — FG Davis 28
Phx — Williams 20 fumble return (Davis kick)
Phx — Williams 46 interception return (Davis kick)
NO — FG Andersen 48
NO — Early 25 pass from Wilson (Andersen kick)
NO — FG Andersen 38

**N.Y. JETS 10, N.Y. GIANTS 6**—at Giants Stadium, attendance 71,659. Brad Baxter ran 2 yards for a touchdown late in the third quarter and the Jets held on to beat the Giants. The Giants led 6-3 at halftime, but the Jets put together an 18-play, 79-yard touchdown drive that consumed 11:15 of the third quarter. Along the way, they converted 3 third-down opportunities and a fourth-down try. Baxter's score came with 2:04 left in the quarter and was the first touchdown run against the Giants' defense all season. The Jets, who snapped a three-game losing streak, had failed to hold second-half leads in all three of the defeats. The Giants threatened to extend that string, moving from their 33-yard line to a first-and-goal at the Jets' 6 with 1:05 to go. But on fourth down from the 11, Phil Simms's end-zone pass fell incomplete. The loss dropped the Giants into a tie for first place in the NFC East.

| | | | | | | |
|---|---|---|---|---|---|---|
| **N.Y. Jets** | 0 | 3 | 7 | 0 | — | 10 |
| **N.Y. Giants** | 3 | 3 | 0 | 0 | — | 6 |

Giants— FG Treadwell 28
Jets — FG Blanchard 21
Giants— FG Treadwell 23
Jets — B. Baxter 2 run (Blanchard kick)

**SAN DIEGO 30, L.A. RAIDERS 23**—at Los Angeles Memorial Coliseum, attendance 45,122. Defensive back Donald Frank returned an interception 102 yards for a touchdown, breaking a 17-17 tie in the third quarter and lifting the Chargers past the Raiders. Los Angeles quarterback Jeff Hostetler, who passed for a club-record 424 yards, had just teamed with James Jett on a 55-yard pass play that gave the Raiders a first-and-goal at San Diego's 5-yard line. After a running play moved the ball to the 3, Hostetler tried to find Tim Brown on a slant pattern in the end zone. But Frank stepped in front of the pass and returned it untouched for the go-ahead score with 3:24 left in the third period. Moments later, linebacker Gary Plummer intercepted Hostetler's pass in Chargers' territory, setting up a 47-yard drive to a 36-yard field goal by John Carney 1:22 into the fourth quarter. Los Angeles could not get closer than seven points after that. Hostetler, who finished with 20 completions in 32 attempts, broke the Raiders' record of 419 yards held by Cotton Davidson. Brown caught 5 passes for 156 yards and 2 touchdowns, including a 71-yard bomb on the Raiders' first play from scrimmage. But Los Angeles was ineffective rushing the ball, gaining only 65 yards on the ground. Meanwhile, San Diego's Natrone Means (68 yards) and Marion Butts (64) combined for 132 of their team's 177 rushing yards.

| | | | | | | |
|---|---|---|---|---|---|---|
| **San Diego** | 7 | 3 | 14 | 6 | — | 30 |
| **L.A. Raiders** | 10 | 0 | 7 | 6 | — | 23 |

Raid — Brown 71 pass from Hostetler (Jaeger kick)
SD — A. Miller 29 pass from Friesz (Carney kick)
Raid — FG Jaeger 38
SD — FG Carney 45
Raid — Brown 38 pass from Hostetler (Jaeger kick)
SD — Butts 12 run (Carney kick)
SD — Frank 102 interception return (Carney kick)
SD — FG Carney 36
Raid — FG Jaeger 21
SD — FG Carney 38
Raid — FG Jaeger 31

**DENVER 28, SEATTLE 17**—at Mile High Stadium, attendance 73,644. John Elway threw 2 touchdown passes and Robert Delpino ran for 2 to lead the Broncos to their twentieth victory in the last 23 games at Mile High Stadium. Seattle converted an interception on Denver's first play into an early touchdown, but the Broncos responded by scoring touchdowns on three consecutive drives in the second quarter. Elway, who completed 23 of 36 passes for 255 yards, capped an 80-yard drive with a 20-yard touchdown pass to Vance Johnson, Delpino ran 2 yards for a score, and Elway tossed a 5-yard touchdown pass to Shannon Sharpe. The latter came 44 seconds before halftime and came 9 plays after cornerback Tyrone Braxton's interception and 12-yard return to Denver's 35-yard line.

| | | | | | | |
|---|---|---|---|---|---|---|
| **Seattle** | 7 | 0 | 3 | 7 | — | 17 |
| **Denver** | 0 | 21 | 7 | 0 | — | 28 |

Sea — J. Williams 10 run (Kasay kick)
Den — V. Johnson 20 pass from Elway (Elam kick)
Den — Delpino 2 run (Elam kick)
Den — Sharpe 5 pass from Elway (Elam kick)
Sea — FG Kasay 53
Den — Delpino 1 run (Elam kick)
Sea — J. Williams 2 run (Kasay kick)

**TAMPA BAY 31, ATLANTA 24**—at Georgia Dome, attendance 50,647. Craig Erickson threw 4 touchdown passes as the Buccaneers built a 31-3 lead, then withstood a furious rally by the Falcons to win. Erickson completed 18 of 28 passes for 318 yards. His 44-yard touchdown pass to rookie Horace Copeland with 2:21 left in the third quarter gave Tampa Bay its 28-point advantage. But Atlanta's Tony Smith returned the ensuing kickoff 46 yards, and on the next play, Bobby Hebert threw a 53-yard touchdown pass to Andre Rison to make it 31-10. Smith's 51-yard punt return set up Hebert's 9-yard touchdown pass to Rison 10 seconds into the fourth quarter, and when Hebert teamed with Mike Pritchard on a 5-yard touchdown pass with 9:37 to go, the Falcons trailed by only 7 points. Atlanta had a chance to tie the game, moving to the Buccaneers' 9-yard line in the closing minute, but Hebert's fourth-down pass was tipped away by Tampa Bay defensive lineman Chidi Ahanotu. Hebert finished with 25 completions in 47 attempts for 277 yards. Rison caught 11 passes for 147 yards. The Buccaneers' Copeland caught 2 touchdown passes for the second consecutive week.

| | | | | | | |
|---|---|---|---|---|---|---|
| **Tampa Bay** | 7 | 10 | 14 | 0 | — | 31 |
| **Atlanta** | 0 | 0 | 10 | 14 | — | 24 |

TB — Workman 42 pass from Erickson (Husted kick)
TB — Cobb 5 pass from Erickson (Husted kick)
TB — FG Husted 24
Atl — FG Johnson 34
TB — Copeland 60 pass from Erickson (Husted kick)
TB — Copeland 44 pass from Erickson (Husted kick)
Atl — Rison 53 pass from Hebert (Johnson kick)
Atl — Rison 9 pass from Hebert (Johnson kick)
Atl — Pritchard 5 pass from Hebert (Johnson kick)

## SUNDAY NIGHT, OCTOBER 31

**DETROIT 30, MINNESOTA 27**—at Metrodome, attendance 53,739. Derrick Moore's 1-yard touchdown run with 40 seconds remaining gave the Lions the come-from-behind victory in a battle for first place in the NFC Central Division. Vikings quarterback Sean Salisbury, who entered the game in the first quarter after starter Jim McMahon suffered a shoulder injury, threw 2 touchdown passes to help Minnesota take a 27-13 lead into the fourth quarter. But on the first play of the period, Detroit quarterback Rodney Peete took advantage of a breakdown in coverage to find Herman Moore all alone for a 93-yard touchdown pass. Jason Hanson's third field goal of the game, from 32 yards with 5:20 to go, trimmed the Lions' deficit to 27-23, and after holding the Vikings without a first down, Detroit marched 61 yards to the winning score. It appeared Minnesota had stopped the drive on fourth-and-8 from the 12-yard line, when Peete's pass for Brett Perriman was tipped away by Anthony Parker at the goal line. But Parker was whistled for pass interference, and Moore scored on the next play. Peete finished with 20 completions in 28 attempts for 273 yards. Salisbury was 25 of 37 for 234 yards and ignited the Vikings' offense, which had not scored more than 19 points in a game all season.

| | | | | | | |
|---|---|---|---|---|---|---|
| **Detroit** | 7 | 6 | 0 | 17 | — | 30 |
| **Minnesota** | 7 | 10 | 10 | 0 | — | 27 |

Minn — A. Carter 10 pass from Salisbury (Reveiz kick)
Det — Clay 39 fumble return (Hanson kick)
Det — FG Hanson 34
Minn — C. Carter 5 pass from Salisbury (Reveiz kick)
Det — FG Hanson 44
Minn — FG Reveiz 48
Minn — R. Smith 1 run (Reveiz kick)
Minn — FG Reveiz 37
Det — H. Moore 93 pass from Peete (Hanson kick)

| | | |
|---|---|---|
| Det | — | FG Hanson 32 |
| Det | — | D. Moore 1 run (Hanson kick) |

**MONDAY, NOVEMBER 1**

**BUFFALO 24, WASHINGTON 10**—at Rich Stadium, attendance 79,106. Jim Kelly threw 2 touchdown passes and the Bills intercepted 4 passes while completing a season sweep of the teams that defeated them in the last three Super Bowls. Kelly completed 18 of 24 passes for 238 yards and got Buffalo off to a good start by throwing a 65-yard touchdown pass to Andre Reed six minutes into the game. Kelly's 11-yard touchdown pass to Bill Brooks with 10 seconds left in the first quarter broke a 7-7 tie and gave the Bills the lead for good. Thurman Thomas helped put the game out of reach with a 1-yard touchdown run in the third quarter. Thomas ran for 129 yards on 28 carries, and Reed finished with 7 receptions for 159 yards as Buffalo amassed 402 total yards. Cornerback Nate Odomes intercepted 2 of Mark Rypien's passes, and the Bills stopped four consecutive drives with interceptions to keep the Redskins from closing their deficit. The game was the first between these two teams since Washington's 37-24 victory in Super Bowl XXVI following the 1991 season. Earlier this year, Buffalo avenged its losses to the Giants and Cowboys in Super Bowl XXV and XXVII.

| | | | | | | |
|---|---|---|---|---|---|---|
| **Washington** | 7 | 3 | 0 | 0 | — | 10 |
| **Buffalo** | 14 | 0 | 7 | 3 | — | 24 |

| | | |
|---|---|---|
| Buff | — | Reed 65 pass from Kelly (Christie kick) |
| Wash | — | R. Brooks 7 run (Lohmiller kick) |
| Buff | — | B. Brooks 11 pass from Kelly (Christie kick) |
| Wash | — | FG Lohmiller 19 |
| Buff | — | Thomas 1 run (Christie kick) |
| Buff | — | FG Christie 45 |

**TENTH WEEK SUMMARIES**

**AMERICAN FOOTBALL CONFERENCE**

| Eastern Division | W | L | T | Pct. | Pts. | OP |
|---|---|---|---|---|---|---|
| Buffalo | 7 | 1 | 0 | .875 | 172 | 97 |
| Miami | 6 | 2 | 0 | .750 | 182 | 145 |
| N.Y. Jets | 4 | 4 | 0 | .500 | 186 | 141 |
| Indianapolis | 3 | 5 | 0 | .375 | 128 | 179 |
| New England | 1 | 8 | 0 | .111 | 113 | 200 |
| **Central Division** | | | | | | |
| Cleveland | 5 | 3 | 0 | .625 | 163 | 159 |
| Pittsburgh | 5 | 3 | 0 | .625 | 192 | 136 |
| Houston | 4 | 4 | 0 | .500 | 168 | 154 |
| Cincinnati | 0 | 8 | 0 | .000 | 97 | 186 |
| **Western Division** | | | | | | |
| Kansas City | 6 | 2 | 0 | .750 | 133 | 124 |
| Denver | 5 | 3 | 0 | .625 | 206 | 149 |
| L.A. Raiders | 5 | 3 | 0 | .625 | 152 | 147 |
| San Diego | 4 | 4 | 0 | .500 | 144 | 167 |
| Seattle | 4 | 5 | 0 | .444 | 143 | 164 |

**NATIONAL FOOTBALL CONFERENCE**

| Eastern Division | W | L | T | Pct. | Pts. | OP |
|---|---|---|---|---|---|---|
| Dallas | 6 | 2 | 0 | .750 | 186 | 111 |
| N.Y. Giants | 5 | 3 | 0 | .625 | 160 | 112 |
| Philadelphia | 4 | 4 | 0 | .500 | 141 | 172 |
| Phoenix | 3 | 6 | 0 | .333 | 168 | 156 |
| Washington | 2 | 6 | 0 | .250 | 139 | 209 |
| **Central Division** | | | | | | |
| Detroit | 7 | 2 | 0 | .778 | 187 | 140 |
| Green Bay | 4 | 4 | 0 | .500 | 180 | 144 |
| Minnesota | 4 | 4 | 0 | .500 | 129 | 154 |
| Chicago | 3 | 5 | 0 | .375 | 126 | 111 |
| Tampa Bay | 2 | 6 | 0 | .250 | 99 | 206 |
| **Western Division** | | | | | | |
| New Orleans | 6 | 2 | 0 | .750 | 183 | 154 |
| San Francisco | 5 | 3 | 0 | .625 | 210 | 158 |
| Atlanta | 2 | 6 | 0 | .250 | 171 | 222 |
| L.A. Rams | 2 | 6 | 0 | .250 | 131 | 192 |

**SUNDAY, NOVEMBER 7**

**BUFFALO 13, NEW ENGLAND 10**—at Foxboro Stadium, attendance 54,326. Steve Christie tied the game by kicking a 27-yard field goal with 14 seconds left in regulation, then won it with a 30-yard field goal 9:22 into overtime. The Bills rallied from a 10-point deficit in the fourth quarter to post their fifth consecutive victory. First, Jim Kelly capped an 80-yard drive with a 9-yard touchdown pass to tight end Pete Metzelaars with 7:48 remaining. After moving into field-goal range on its next possession only to lose a fumble, Buffalo got the ball back at its 13-yard line with 1:04 remaining. In 50 seconds, the Bills moved 78 yards to the tying field goal, the big play a 56-yard pass from Kelly to Russell Copeland. Another long pass, Kelly's 46-yard completion to Andre Reed, set up the winning kick in overtime. Kelly completed 29 of 46 passes for 317 yards, and Thurman Thomas ran for 111 yards for Buffalo, which outgained the Patriots 432-284 but stymied itself with 3 lost fumbles. New England dropped its fourth in a row to fall to 1-8, but five of the eight losses have come by 3 points or less.

| | | | | | | | |
|---|---|---|---|---|---|---|---|
| **Buffalo** | 0 | 0 | 0 | 10 | 3 | — | 13 |
| **New England** | 0 | 0 | 7 | 3 | 0 | — | 10 |

| | | |
|---|---|---|
| NE | — | Russell 2 run (Sisson kick) |
| NE | — | FG Sisson 27 |
| Buff | — | Metzelaars 9 pass from Kelly (Christie kick) |
| Buff | — | FG Christie 27 |
| Buff | — | FG Christie 30 |

**DENVER 29, CLEVELAND 14**—at Cleveland Stadium, attendance 77,818. John Elway threw for 244 yards and 3 touchdowns to lead the Broncos past the Browns. After a scoreless first quarter, Denver broke the game open with 16 points in a span of less than five minutes in the second quarter. First, Elway's 56-yard completion to Vance Johnson set up a 2-yard touchdown pass to running back Glyn Milburn 3:54 into the period. On Cleveland's next possession, reserve running back Reggie Rivers broke through to block a punt out of the end zone for a safety and a 9-0 lead. Moments later, Elway capped the scoring spree with a 38-yard touchdown pass to Derek Russell 6:07 before halftime. After the Browns pulled within 16-7 early in the second half, Elway teamed with tight end Shannon Sharpe on a 33-yard touchdown pass. Rookie Jason Elam added a pair of field goals in the fourth quarter. Elway finished with 17 completions in 23 attempts while beating the Browns for the ninth time in 11 tries in his career. The Broncos' balanced offense also produced 159 rushing yards, including 82 from Rod Bernstine. Bernie Kosar threw a pair of touchdown passes to Michael Jackson in what would be his last game with the Browns. Kosar, whose final pass was a 38-yard touchdown to Jackson with 12 seconds remaining, completed 16 of 30 passes for 226 yards but was sacked 6 times.

| | | | | | | |
|---|---|---|---|---|---|---|
| **Denver** | 0 | 16 | 7 | 6 | — | 29 |
| **Cleveland** | 0 | 0 | 7 | 7 | — | 14 |

| | | |
|---|---|---|
| Den | — | Milburn 2 pass from Elway (Elam kick) |
| Den | — | Safety, Rivers blocked punt out of end zone |
| Den | — | Russell 38 pass from Elway (Elam kick) |
| Cle | — | Jackson 8 pass from Kosar (Stover kick) |
| Den | — | Sharpe 33 pass from Elway (Elam kick) |
| Den | — | FG Elam 22 |
| Den | — | FG Elam 38 |
| Cle | — | Jackson 38 pass from Kosar (Stover kick) |

**L.A. RAIDERS 16, CHICAGO 14**—at Soldier Field, attendance 59,750. The Raiders escaped with the victory when Kevin Butler's 30-yard field-goal try as time expired hooked wide left. Los Angeles appeared comfortably ahead 16-7 late in the game. But Chicago, the third-period touchdown of which was its first in 13 quarters, pulled within 2 points by marching 66 yards to Jim Harbaugh's 13-yard touchdown pass to Terry Obee with 1:13 to go. After the Bears recovered the ensuing onside kick, quarterback Jim Harbaugh scrambled 25 yards. When the Raiders were penalized for a late hit on the same play, Chicago was in position for the go-ahead field goal. But Butler, who entered the game 10-for-10 inside 40 yards this season before misfiring on a 21-yard try early in the fourth quarter, failed to convert the kick. Cold weather and swirling winds limited the effectiveness of both teams' passing offenses, but Los Angeles, which entered the game ranked twenty-sixth in the NFL in rushing, ran for 179 yards. Three backs had 50 yards or more, topped by Greg Robinson's 70 yards on 12 carries. Neal Anderson ran for 75 yards and a touchdown on 28 carries for the Bears.

| | | | | | | |
|---|---|---|---|---|---|---|
| **L.A. Raiders** | 3 | 10 | 0 | 3 | — | 16 |
| **Chicago** | 0 | 0 | 7 | 7 | — | 14 |

| | | |
|---|---|---|
| Raid | — | FG Jaeger 31 |
| Raid | — | McCallum 1 run (Jaeger kick) |
| Raid | — | FG Jaeger 21 |
| Chi | — | Anderson 3 run (Butler kick) |
| Raid | — | FG Jaeger 21 |
| Chi | — | Obee 13 pass from Harbaugh (Butler kick) |

**N.Y. JETS 27, MIAMI 10**—at Giants Stadium, attendance 71,306. Boomer Esiason threw 3 touchdown passes and the Jets beat the Dolphins for the second time this season. New York took the opening kickoff and scored on Esiason's 17-yard touchdown pass to tight end Johnny Mitchell 4:51 into the game. Moments later, Lonnie Young intercepted Scott Mitchell's pass, setting up Cary Blanchard for a 37-yard field goal and a 10-0 Jets' lead. Esiason's second touchdown pass to Mitchell (2 yards) came 19 seconds before halftime and made it 17-3. After Scott Mitchell threw a 65-yard touchdown pass to Irving Fryar to pull Miami within 20-10 late in the third quarter, New York countered with a 13-play, 70-yard drive to the clinching touchdown, Esiason's 12-yard pass to Chris Burkett with 8:43 left in the game. Esiason finished with 23 completions in 32 attempts for 256 yards. The Dolphins managed only 48 rushing yards, taking to the air after falling behind early. Mitchell completed 23 of 44 passes for 297 yards. Fryar caught 7 passes for 111 yards. Miami's Don Shula remained tied with George Halas for the most coaching wins in NFL history.

| | | | | | | |
|---|---|---|---|---|---|---|
| **Miami** | 0 | 3 | 7 | 0 | — | 10 |
| **N.Y. Jets** | 10 | 7 | 3 | 7 | — | 27 |

| | | |
|---|---|---|
| Jets | — | Mitchell 17 pass from Esiason (Blanchard kick) |
| Jets | — | FG Blanchard 37 |
| Mia | — | FG Stoyanovich 48 |
| Jets | — | Mitchell 2 pass from Esiason (Blanchard kick) |
| Jets | — | FG Blanchard 43 |
| Mia | — | Fryar 65 pass from Mitchell (Stoyanovich kick) |
| Jets | — | Burkett 12 pass from Esiason (Blanchard kick) |

**DALLAS 31, N.Y. GIANTS 9**—at Texas Stadium, attendance 64,735. The Cowboys rolled to their sixth consecutive victory in impressive fashion and took over sole possession of first place in the NFC Eastern Division. Troy Aikman completed his first 10 passes, including 28- and 50-yard scoring strikes to Alvin Harper, as Dallas built a 17-6 halftime advantage. But Aikman, who finished 11 of 13 for 162 yards, was forced to leave the game after straining a hamstring while scrambling with 9:30 remaining in the third quarter. Reserve quarterback Jason Garrett took over and directed a pair of scoring drives, each of which ended in short touchdown runs by Emmitt Smith. Garrett was 5 of 6 for 34 yards, while Smith ran for 117 yards on 24 carries. Harper positioned the Cowboys for Smith's 2-yard touchdown run with 9:02 left when he took a handoff and then completed a 46-yard pass to Michael Irvin.

| | | | | | | |
|---|---|---|---|---|---|---|
| **N.Y. Giants** | 0 | 6 | 0 | 3 | — | 9 |
| **Dallas** | 10 | 7 | 0 | 14 | — | 31 |

| | | |
|---|---|---|
| Dall | — | FG Murray 34 |
| Dall | — | Harper 28 pass from Aikman (Murray kick) |
| Giants | — | FG Treadwell 22 |
| Dall | — | Harper 50 pass from Aikman (Murray kick) |
| Giants | — | FG Treadwell 45 |
| Dall | — | E. Smith 1 run (Murray kick) |
| Dall | — | E. Smith 2 run (Murray kick) |
| Giants | — | FG Treadwell 29 |

**PHOENIX 16, PHILADELPHIA 3**—at Sun Devil Stadium, attendance 41,634. Rookie Ron Moore rushed for 160 yards as the Cardinals handed the Eagles their fourth consecutive defeat. Phoenix dominated on the ground, rushing for 243 of their 359 total yards. Moore, playing in place of injured starter and 1993 first-round draft choice Garrison Hearst, equaled a club record with 36 carries. The game's lone touchdown came 7 plays after Cardinals cornerback Aeneas Williams returned an interception 41 yards to Philadelphia's 34-yard line midway through the second quarter. Moore ran 4 yards on fourth-and-1 and also had a 10-yard run on the short drive, which was capped by Chris Chandler's 10-yard touchdown pass to Gary Clark. Larry Centers ran for 59 yards and caught 4 passes for 46 yards for Phoenix, which controlled the ball for more than 38 minutes. The Eagles managed only 65 yards on the ground and 205 yards in all.

| | | | | | | |
|---|---|---|---|---|---|---|
| **Philadelphia** | 3 | 0 | 0 | 0 | — | 3 |
| **Phoenix** | 3 | 13 | 0 | 0 | — | 16 |

| | | |
|---|---|---|
| Phil | — | FG Bahr 27 |
| Phx | — | FG Davis 23 |
| Phx | — | FG Davis 20 |
| Phx | — | Clark 10 pass from Chandler (Davis kick) |
| Phx | — | FG Davis 29 |

**PITTSBURGH 24, CINCINNATI 16**—at Riverfront Stadium, attendance 51,202. The Steelers spotted the winless Bengals 16 points, then roared back to the victory to move into a tie for first place in the AFC Central Division. Safety Darryl Williams returned an interception 97 yards for a touchdown and Cincinnati recovered a fumbled snap to help build its 16-0 lead 3:50 before halftime. But Pittsburgh quarterback Neil O'Donnell shook off the mistakes and completed a 71-yard touchdown pass to tight end Eric Green 2:49 before halftime. After three straight incomplete passes, the Bengals punted, and the Steelers marched 60 yards to pull within 16-14 on O'Donnell's 9-yard touchdown pass to Merril Hoge with eight seconds remaining in the half. Barry Foster ran 1 yard for a touchdown 1:22 into the fourth quarter to put Pittsburgh ahead for the first time. Foster finished with 120 yards on 25 carries. The Steelers had 390 total yards, Cincinnati just 199.

| | | | | | | |
|---|---|---|---|---|---|---|
| **Pittsburgh** | 0 | 14 | 0 | 10 | — | 24 |
| **Cincinnati** | 3 | 13 | 0 | 0 | — | 16 |

Cin — FG Pelfrey 32
Cin — Williams 97 interception return (kick failed)
Cin — Query 7 pass from Schroeder (Pelfrey kick)
Pitt — Green 71 pass from O'Donnell (Anderson kick)
Pitt — Hoge 9 pass from O'Donnell (Anderson kick)
Pitt — Foster 1 run (Anderson kick)
Pitt — FG Anderson 23

**SAN DIEGO 30, MINNESOTA 17**—at Metrodome, attendance 54,960. John Friesz threw 2 touchdown passes and rookie Natrone Means ran for 105 yards to lead the Chargers past the Vikings. Minnesota rallied from a 16-3 deficit to take a 17-16 lead on Barry Word's 1-yard touchdown run late in the third quarter. But on the Vikings' next possession, San Diego cornerback Sean Vanhorse intercepted Sean Salisbury's pass at the Chargers' 39-yard line. San Diego then marched 61 yards in 7 plays, taking the lead on a 7-yard touchdown run by Means with 10:12 left in the game. Minnesota rookie Qadry Ismail fumbled the ensuing kickoff, and it took the Chargers just three plays to capitalize, the touchdown coming when Friesz threw 18 yards to Shawn Jefferson. Friesz completed 20 of 32 passes for 268 yards for San Diego. Anthony Miller caught 7 passes for 142 yards, including a 66-yard touchdown. Salisbury completed 29 of 47 passes for 347 yards for the Vikings, but Minnesota was hurt by the lack of a running game. The Vikings gained only 20 yards on the ground, the lowest single-game total in franchise history. Anthony Carter caught 10 passes for 164 yards.

| | | | | | | |
|---|---|---|---|---|---|---|
| **San Diego** | 7 | 3 | 6 | 14 | — | 30 |
| **Minnesota** | 0 | 3 | 14 | 0 | — | 17 |

SD — Butts 3 run (Carney kick)
SD — FG Carney 36
Minn — FG Reveiz 20
SD — Miller 66 pass from Friesz (kick failed)
Minn — A. Carter 9 pass from Salisbury (Reveiz kick)
Minn — Word 1 run (Reveiz kick)
SD — Means 7 run (Carney kick)
SD — Jefferson 18 pass from Friesz (Carney kick)

**HOUSTON 24, SEATTLE 14**—at Astrodome, attendance 50,447. Warren Moon completed 36 of 55 passes for 369 yards and 2 touchdowns, and the Oilers won their third consecutive game. Moon completed all 7 of his attempts on the game's opening drive, a 79-yard march capped by his 3-yard touchdown pass to Webster Slaughter 6:55 into the first quarter. After a 53-yard touchdown pass from Rick Mirer to Kelvin Martin tied the game, Houston took the lead for good when Moon teamed with Ernest Givins on a 14-yard scoring toss with 20 seconds left in the period. Al Del Greco added 3 field goals in the second quarter. The Oilers rolled up 26 first downs and 458 total yards while maintaining possession for more than 40 of the game's 60 minutes. Slaughter caught 9 passes for 135 yards.

| | | | | | | |
|---|---|---|---|---|---|---|
| **Seattle** | 7 | 0 | 0 | 7 | — | 14 |
| **Houston** | 13 | 9 | 2 | 0 | — | 24 |

Hou — Slaughter 3 pass from Moon (Del Greco kick)
Sea — Martin 53 pass from Mirer (Kasay kick)
Hou — Givins 14 pass from Moon (kick failed)
Hou — FG Del Greco 33
Hou — FG Del Greco 51
Hou — FG Del Greco 39
Hou — Safety, Mirer called for intentionally grounding in the end zone
Sea — Warren 10 run (Kasay kick)

**DETROIT 23, TAMPA BAY 0**—at Pontiac Silverdome, attendance 65,295. Barry Sanders ran for 187 yards on 29 carries to lead the Lions to their seventh victory in nine games this season, their best start in 31 years. Detroit's defense was dominant, limiting the Buccaneers to only 6 first downs and 146 total yards while posting its first shutout since 1983. Quarterback Rodney Peete completed 16 of 22 passes for 134 yards without an interception. He completed all 4 of his attempts for 54 yards and ran 9 yards for a touchdown on the decisive drive of the game early in the third quarter. Leading just 6-0, the Lions marched 81 yards in 10 plays the first time they had the ball in the second half to open up a 13-point advantage.

| | | | | | | |
|---|---|---|---|---|---|---|
| **Tampa Bay** | 0 | 0 | 0 | 0 | — | 0 |
| **Detroit** | 3 | 3 | 7 | 10 | — | 23 |

Det — FG Hanson 29
Det — FG Hanson 49
Det — Peete 9 run (Hanson kick)
Det — Moore 1 run (Hanson kick)
Det — FG Hanson 37

## SUNDAY NIGHT, NOVEMBER 7

**WASHINGTON 30, INDIANAPOLIS 24**—at RFK Stadium, attendance 50,523. The Redskins used takeaways and big plays to halt their losing streak at six. The game was scoreless until Washington safety Darrell Green scooped up a loose ball and returned it 79 yards for a touchdown 2:03 into the second quarter. The fumble was forced when linebacker Kurt Gouveia tackled Colts running back Roosevelt Potts, who had caught a short pass from Jeff George. Moments later, linebacker Andre Collins intercepted George's pass. Though forced to punt following that turnover, the Redskins got a break when Indianapolis's Clarence Verdin muffed the kick. Washington's Rick Hamilton recovered the ball at the Colts' 6-yard line, and two plays later, quarterback Mark Rypien ran 1 yard for a touchdown and a 14-0 lead. Rypien set up his 1-yard touchdown run in the third quarter with a 42-yard pass to Tim McGee, then positioned the Redskins for a field goal in the fourth quarter with a 43-yard completion to Reggie Brooks. Brooks also ran for 105 yards on 21 carries. George completed 37 of 59 passes for 376 yards and 3 touchdowns as Indianapolis had sizable advantages in plays (78-60) and total yards (405-275). But 2 of his scoring passes came in the final 1:50 with the game out of reach.

| | | | | | | |
|---|---|---|---|---|---|---|
| **Indianapolis** | 0 | 10 | 0 | 14 | — | 24 |
| **Washington** | 0 | 14 | 6 | 10 | — | 30 |

Wash — Green 79 fumble return (Lohmiller kick)
Wash — Rypien 1 run (Lohmiller kick)
Ind — Langhorne 72 pass from George (Biasucci kick)
Ind — FG Biasucci 22
Wash — Rypien 1 run (kick failed)
Wash — FG Lohmiller 24
Wash — Mitchell 2 run (Lohmiller kick)
Ind — Cash 9 pass from George (Biasucci kick)
Ind — Verdin 1 pass from George (Biasucci kick)

## MONDAY, NOVEMBER 8

**KANSAS CITY 23, GREEN BAY 16**—at Arrowhead Stadium, attendance 76,742. Defensive tackle Dan Saleaumua returned a fumble for a touchdown, then forced a key fumble in the fourth quarter as the Chiefs ended the Packers' three-game winning streak. Kansas City trailed 9-3 until linebacker Derrick Thomas stripped the ball from Green Bay quarterback Brett Favre on the Packers' first play from scrimmage in the second half. Saleaumua picked up the loose ball and ran 16 yards for the touchdown that put the Chiefs ahead for good. Nick Lowery's field goal and a 1-yard touchdown run by Marcus Allen extended Kansas City's advantage to 20-9 1:06 into the fourth quarter. But Green Bay countered just 55 seconds after Allen's score with a 35-yard touchdown pass from Favre to tight end Jackie Harris. The Packers appeared to be on the verge of taking the lead the next time they had the ball. But Saleaumua's jarring hit on running back Darrell Thompson forced a fumble at the Chiefs' 2-yard line, and Kansas City linebacker Tracy Rogers recovered in the end zone to end the threat. After Lowery added another field goal with 3:26 to go, Green Bay's last chance was foiled when safety Martin Bayless intercepted a pass with 1:40 to play. It was the sixth turnover of the game for Packers, who did not force any. Favre completed 20 of 34 passes for 213 yards, but was intercepted 3 times. Dave Krieg, starting while Joe Montana nursed an injured hamstring, completed 17 of 30 passes for 170 yards for the Chiefs. He was sacked 4 times, 3 times by Bryce Paup.

| | | | | | | |
|---|---|---|---|---|---|---|
| **Green Bay** | 3 | 6 | 0 | 7 | — | 16 |
| **Kansas City** | 3 | 0 | 10 | 10 | — | 23 |

KC — FG Lowery 23
GB — FG Jacke 23
GB — FG Jacke 51
GB — FG Jacke 19
KC — Saleaumua 16 fumble return (Lowery kick)
KC — FG Lowery 34
KC — Allen 1 run (Lowery kick)
GB — Harris 35 pass from Favre (Jacke kick)
KC — FG Lowery 40

## ELEVENTH WEEK SUMMARIES

**AMERICAN FOOTBALL CONFERENCE**

| Eastern Division | W | L | T | Pct. | Pts. | OP |
|---|---|---|---|---|---|---|
| Buffalo | 7 | 2 | 0 | .778 | 172 | 120 |
| Miami | 7 | 2 | 0 | .778 | 201 | 159 |
| N.Y. Jets | 5 | 4 | 0 | .556 | 217 | 158 |
| Indianapolis | 3 | 6 | 0 | .333 | 145 | 210 |
| New England | 1 | 8 | 0 | .111 | 113 | 200 |
| **Central Division** | | | | | | |
| Pittsburgh | 6 | 3 | 0 | .667 | 215 | 136 |
| Cleveland | 5 | 4 | 0 | .556 | 168 | 181 |
| Houston | 5 | 4 | 0 | .556 | 206 | 157 |
| Cincinnati | 0 | 9 | 0 | .000 | 100 | 224 |
| **Western Division** | | | | | | |
| Kansas City | 7 | 2 | 0 | .778 | 164 | 144 |
| Denver | 5 | 4 | 0 | .556 | 229 | 175 |
| L.A. Raiders | 5 | 4 | 0 | .556 | 172 | 178 |
| Seattle | 5 | 5 | 0 | .500 | 165 | 169 |
| San Diego | 4 | 5 | 0 | .444 | 157 | 183 |

**NATIONAL FOOTBALL CONFERENCE**

| Eastern Division | W | L | T | Pct. | Pts. | OP |
|---|---|---|---|---|---|---|
| Dallas | 7 | 2 | 0 | .778 | 206 | 126 |
| N.Y. Giants | 6 | 3 | 0 | .667 | 180 | 118 |
| Philadelphia | 4 | 5 | 0 | .444 | 155 | 191 |
| Phoenix | 3 | 7 | 0 | .300 | 183 | 176 |
| Washington | 2 | 7 | 0 | .222 | 145 | 229 |
| **Central Division** | | | | | | |
| Detroit | 7 | 2 | 0 | .778 | 187 | 140 |
| Green Bay | 5 | 4 | 0 | .556 | 199 | 161 |
| Minnesota | 5 | 4 | 0 | .556 | 155 | 177 |
| Chicago | 4 | 5 | 0 | .444 | 142 | 124 |
| Tampa Bay | 2 | 7 | 0 | .222 | 120 | 251 |
| **Western Division** | | | | | | |
| New Orleans | 6 | 3 | 0 | .667 | 200 | 173 |
| San Francisco | 6 | 3 | 0 | .667 | 255 | 179 |
| Atlanta | 3 | 6 | 0 | .333 | 184 | 222 |
| L.A. Rams | 2 | 7 | 0 | .222 | 131 | 205 |

## SUNDAY, NOVEMBER 14

**ATLANTA 13, L.A. RAMS 0**—at Anaheim Stadium, attendance 37,073. Six Falcons recorded 1 sack each as Atlanta posted its first shutout on the road in 16 years, handing the Rams their fifth consecutive defeat. Eric Pegram rushed for 128 yards on 27 carries and Bobby Hebert threw a 31-yard touchdown pass to Andre Rison in the third quarter, but it was the Falcons' defense that made the difference, limiting Los Angeles to 260 total yards. Rams quarterback Jim Everett completed 20 of 41 passes for 203 yards but was intercepted twice, lost a fumble, and was sacked for 38 yards in losses. Atlanta entered the game with the league's lowest-rated defense and had allowed more points than any other team in the NFL. The Falcons had just 10 sacks in their first eight games. The Rams were shut out for the first time since 1987.

| | | | | | | |
|---|---|---|---|---|---|---|
| **Atlanta** | 3 | 3 | 7 | 0 | — | 13 |
| **L.A. Rams** | 0 | 0 | 0 | 0 | — | 0 |

Atl — FG Johnson 46
Atl — FG Johnson 44
Atl — Rison 31 pass from Hebert (Johnson kick)

**SEATTLE 22, CLEVELAND 5**—at Kingdome, attendance 54,622. The Seahawks recovered 5 fumbles and intercepted 2 passes en route to knocking the Browns out of first place in the AFC Central Division. Cleveland was playing its first game without long-time quarterback Bernie Kosar, who was waived earlier in the week. The Browns turned to Todd Philcox, who was making only the second start of his four-year career. Philcox completed just 9 of 20 passes for 85 yards, with 2 interceptions. He also fumbled twice, including 1 on the game's first play from scrimmage. Seattle safety Robert Blackmon picked up the loose ball and returned it 5 yards for a touchdown just 14 seconds into the first quarter, giving the Seahawks all the points they would need. Cleveland dominated the first half, maintaining possession for nearly 22 minutes and limiting Seattle to 2 first downs and 38 total yards, but still trailed 7-5. Two more fumbles and an interception, all in the shadow of the Seahawks' goal line, stymied Browns' scoring opportunities. In the second half, Seattle's offense came to life and put the game out of reach. Chris Warren finished the game with 112 rushing yards, all but 5 coming after intermission. Safety Eugene Robinson had both of the Seahawks' interceptions and recovered a fumble.

| | | | | | | |
|---|---|---|---|---|---|---|
| **Cleveland** | 2 | 3 | 0 | 0 | — | 5 |
| **Seattle** | 7 | 0 | 7 | 8 | — | 22 |

Sea — Blackmon 5 fumble return (Kasay kick)
Cle — Safety, Pleasant tackled Mirer in end zone
Cle — FG Stover 25
Sea — J. Williams 23 pass from Mirer (Kasay kick)
Sea — FG Kasay 42
Sea — FG Kasay 47
Sea — Safety, Edwards tackled Philcox in end zone

**GREEN BAY 19, NEW ORLEANS 17**—at Louisiana Superdome, attendance 69,043. Chris Jacke's fourth field goal of the game, from 36 yards with three seconds left, gave the Packers their fourth victory in the last five games. Jacke's winning kick was set up by wide receiver Sterling Sharpe, who caught a 54-yard pass from Brett Favre to position the ball on the Saints' 19-yard line. Up to that point, Green Bay had done little offensively. The Packers managed only 13 first downs and 194 total yards, and Favre was sacked 6 times, including 3 by New Orleans linebacker Rickey Jackson. But Green Bay stayed close by converting 3 of the Saints' 5 turnovers into 13 points. Linebacker Johnny Holland's interception and 11-yard return early in the fourth quarter positioned Jacke for a 44-yard field goal that gave the Packers a 16-14 lead with 8:01 remaining. But New Orleans's Fred McAfee returned the ensuing kickoff 55 yards, and seven plays later, Morten Andersen's 27-yard field goal put the Saints back in front with 3:38 to go. After an exchange of punts, Green Bay drove to the winning field goal. New Orleans rookie Derek Brown led all rushers with 106 yards on 21 carries.

| | | | | | | |
|---|---|---|---|---|---|---|
| **Green Bay** | 3 | 7 | 3 | 6 | — | 19 |
| **New Orleans** | 0 | 14 | 0 | 3 | — | 17 |

GB — FG Jacke 38
NO — Early 24 pass from Wilson (Andersen kick)
GB — Harris 1 pass from Favre (Jacke kick)
NO — Dowdell 11 pass from Wilson (Andersen kick)
GB — FG Jacke 20
GB — FG Jacke 44
NO — FG Andersen 27
GB — FG Jacke 36

**HOUSTON 38, CINCINNATI 3**—at Riverfront Stadium, attendance 42,347. Warren Moon threw 4 touchdown passes, Gary Brown rushed for 166 yards, and the Oilers dominated the Bengals while winning their fourth in a row. Moon, who completed 23 of 31 passes for 225 yards, threw 3 of his touchdown passes to Haywood Jeffires, the last of which was a 12-yard collaboration that put Houston ahead 35-0 6:04 into the second half. With Lorenzo White nursing a pulled hamstring, Brown got the first start of his three-year career and carried 26 times. His 4-yard touchdown run in the second quarter capped a 7-play, 70-yard drive. The Oilers had 32 first downs to just 9 for Cincinnati, and amassed 462 total yards to 165. Houston's balanced attack produced 240 rushing yards and 222 passing yards. Bengals quarterbacks David Klingler and Jay Schroeder combined to complete only 8 of 28 passes for 80 yards. Cincinnati fell to 0-9, the worst start in franchise history.

| | | | | | | |
|---|---|---|---|---|---|---|
| **Houston** | 7 | 21 | 10 | 0 | — | 38 |
| **Cincinnati** | 0 | 0 | 3 | 0 | — | 3 |

Hou — Duncan 3 pass from Moon (Del Greco kick)
Hou — Brown 4 run (Del Greco kick)
Hou — Jeffires 21 pass from Moon (Del Greco kick)
Hou — Jeffires 6 pass from Moon (Del Greco kick)
Hou — Jeffires 12 pass from Moon (Del Greco kick)
Hou — FG Del Greco 39
Cin — FG Pelfrey 46

**KANSAS CITY 31, L.A. RAIDERS 20**—at Los Angeles Memorial Coliseum, attendance 66,553. Dave Krieg threw 3 touchdown passes, and Marcus Allen ran for a key touchdown in his return to Los Angeles, spurring the Chiefs to the victory. Krieg, playing in place of injured Joe Montana, completed just 12 of 27 passes for 178 yards. But his 66-yard touchdown pass to Willie Davis late in the third quarter put Kansas City ahead for good, and his 4-yard scoring toss to tight end Keith Cash with 2:52 remaining in the game clinched the victory. He also had a 15-yard touchdown pass to running back Kimble Anders in the second quarter. That capped a 13-play, 80-yard drive and trimmed the Raiders' lead to 14-7. It was 17-7 at halftime, before Allen's 39-yard run in the third quarter set up his own score from 4 yards to make it 17-14. Allen, appearing for the first time in a Chiefs' uniform in the stadium in which he played four years at USC and 11 with the Raiders, rushed for 85 yards on 17 carries. Kansas City outgained Los Angeles 338-280, but the margin was 218-65 after intermission. Davis caught 5 passes for 115 yards. Krieg became the seventeenth quarterback in NFL history to surpass 30,000 career passing yards.

| | | | | | | |
|---|---|---|---|---|---|---|
| **Kansas City** | 0 | 7 | 14 | 10 | — | 31 |
| **L.A. Raiders** | 7 | 10 | 0 | 3 | — | 20 |

Raid — McCallum 4 run (Jaeger kick)
Raid — Horton 8 pass from Hostetler (Jaeger kick)
KC — Anders 15 pass from Krieg (Lowery kick)
Raid — FG Jaeger 35
KC — Allen 4 run (Lowery kick)
KC — Davis 66 pass from Krieg (Lowery kick)
Raid — FG Jaeger 30
KC — FG Lowery 29
KC — Cash 4 pass from Krieg (Lowery kick)

**MIAMI 19, PHILADELPHIA 14**—at Veterans Stadium, attendance 64,213. Don Shula became the winningest head coach in NFL history by guiding the Dolphins past the Eagles. The victory was the 325th of Shula's 31-year coaching career. George Halas had 324 wins in his 40 years as coach of the Chicago Bears. To get Shula his milestone victory, Miami had to overcome a 14-13 halftime deficit with a reserve quarterback who never had thrown an NFL pass before. Doug Pederson, a former World League player, took over when Scott Mitchell separated his shoulder with the Dolphins trailing by a point. Mitchell was starting in place of Dan Marino, who was lost for the season with an Achilles tendon injury suffered five weeks earlier. With Pederson at the helm, Miami played conservatively, settling for a pair of second-half field goals by Pete Stoyanovich to win. Pederson completed 3 of 6 passes for 34 yards, including 11-yard strikes to O.J. McDuffie and Terry Kirby on a 45-yard march to Stoyanovich's fourth-quarter field goal. The victory was not secured, however, until Eagles quarterback Ken O'Brien lost his grip on the football while attempting to pass, and the Dolphins recovered with just over two minutes left. That stymied a drive that had reached Miami's 22-yard line. Shula, who coached seven years with the Baltimore Colts before joining the Dolphins in 1970, raised his career record to 325-153-6. Halas was 324-151-31 in four separate 10-year stints with the Bears.

| | | | | | | |
|---|---|---|---|---|---|---|
| **Miami** | 6 | 7 | 3 | 3 | — | 19 |
| **Philadelphia** | 0 | 14 | 0 | 0 | — | 14 |

Mia — Kirby 8 pass from Mitchell (kick failed)
Phil — Williams 11 pass from O'Brien (Bahr kick)
Mia — Higgs 1 run (Stoyanovich kick)
Phil — Williams 8 pass from O'Brien (Bahr kick)
Mia — FG Stoyanovich 46
Mia — FG Stoyanovich 45

**MINNESOTA 26, DENVER 23**—at Mile High Stadium, attendance 67,329. Sean Salisbury passed for a career-high 366 yards and 2 touchdowns as the Vikings erased a 17-point deficit to beat the Broncos. John Elway's 2 touchdown passes helped Denver to a 20-3 lead midway through the second quarter. But Salisbury countered with scoring strikes of 9 yards to Cris Carter and 17 yards to Roger Craig just 3:08 apart to pull Minnesota within 20-17 at halftime. Fuad Reveiz kicked 3 field goals in the second half, including a 43-yard kick with 2:49 left in the game, to complete the comeback. The victory was sealed in the final minute when the Vikings recovered Glyn Milburn's fumble to thwart a Broncos' drive that had reached Minnesota's 21-yard line. Salisbury finished with 19 completions in 37 attempts, and Cris Carter caught 6 passes for 134 yards. Anthony Carter had 111 yards on his 4 receptions. Tackle Tim Irwin blocked 2 kicks, an extra point attempt and a 26-yard field-goal try in the third quarter. Elway completed 30 of 40 passes for 290 yards for Denver. Tight end Shannon Sharpe caught 7 passes for 104 yards. The two teams were whistled for 23 penalties, including 13 on the Vikings.

| | | | | | | |
|---|---|---|---|---|---|---|
| **Minnesota** | 3 | 14 | 3 | 6 | — | 26 |
| **Denver** | 6 | 14 | 0 | 3 | — | 23 |

Den — Russell 4 pass from Elway (kick blocked)
Minn — FG Reveiz 25
Den — Delpino 3 run (Elam kick)
Den — V. Johnson 15 pass from Elway (Elam kick)
Minn — C. Carter 9 pass from Salisbury (Reveiz kick)
Minn — Craig 17 pass from Salisbury (Reveiz kick)
Minn — FG Reveiz 19
Minn — FG Reveiz 35
Den — FG Elam 53
Minn — FG Reveiz 43

**N.Y. JETS 31, INDIANAPOLIS 17**—at Hoosier Dome, attendance 47,351. Johnny Johnson rushed for 141 yards, including the game-clinching 57-yard touchdown run late in the fourth quarter, to lead the Jets to their third consecutive victory. Johnson averaged nearly 7 yards on his 21 carries and keyed a rushing attack that produced 202 yards. New York had 458 total yards, including 256 passing from Boomer Esiason. Indianapolis, meanwhile, mustered only 215 total yards, most of it coming on Reggie Langhorne's 8 catches for 112 yards. Still, the Colts trailed only 24-17 and had the Jets pinned at their 2-yard line after Rohn Stark's punt midway through the fourth quarter. But New York covered 98 yards on a 9-play drive capped by Johnson's touchdown with 2:22 remaining.

| | | | | | | |
|---|---|---|---|---|---|---|
| **N.Y. Jets** | 7 | 10 | 7 | 7 | — | 31 |
| **Indianapolis** | 3 | 7 | 7 | 0 | — | 17 |

Ind — FG Biasucci 41
Jets — B. Baxter 1 run (Blanchard kick)
Jets — Burkett 15 pass from Esiason (Blanchard kick)
Ind — Cash 3 pass from George (Biasucci kick)
Jets — FG Blanchard 22
Jets — Burkett 4 pass from Esiason (Blanchard kick)
Ind — Culver 1 run (Biasucci kick)
Jets — Johnson 57 run (Blanchard kick)

**DALLAS 20, PHOENIX 15**—at Texas Stadium, attendance 64,224. Bernie Kosar, released earlier in the week by the Browns, came off the bench to throw for 199 yards and a touchdown in the Cowboys' seventh consecutive victory. With Troy Aikman nursing a hamstring injury, Kosar took over for Jason Garrett 10:11 into the game with Dallas leading 3-0. By halftime, he had completed 7 of 8 passes for 152 yards and directed touchdown drives of 65 and 86 yards. His 1-yard touchdown pass to tight end Jay Novacek gave the Cowboys a 17-0 lead at intermission. The Cardinals rallied in the second half, but could pull no closer than the final score. Dallas safety Kenneth Gant's interception with 57 seconds left sealed the victory. Cowboys running back Emmitt Smith rushed for 80 yards on 24 carries and caught 4 passes for 102 yards. Kosar finished with 13 completions in 21 attempts. His 86-yard completion to Smith, who took a short pass and turned it into a big gain, was the fifth-longest in franchise history. Chris Chandler completed 27 of 46 passes for 214 yards and a touchdown for Phoenix.

| | | | | | | |
|---|---|---|---|---|---|---|
| **Phoenix** | 0 | 0 | 10 | 5 | — | 15 |
| **Dallas** | 3 | 14 | 0 | 3 | — | 20 |

Dall — FG Murray 44
Dall — Smith 4 run (Murray kick)
Dall — Novacek 1 pass from Kosar (Murray kick)
Phx — FG Davis 19
Phx — Centers 17 pass from Chandler (Davis kick)
Dall — FG Murray 43
Phx — Safety, Kosar called for intentionally grounding in the end zone
Phx — FG Davis 47

**SAN FRANCISCO 45, TAMPA BAY 21**—at Tampa Stadium, attendance 43,835. Jerry Rice caught 8 passes for 172 yards and 4 touchdowns in the 49ers' rout of the Buccaneers. Rice's 12-yard touchdown grab 5:16 into the game gave San Francisco a lead it would never relinquish, and his 2 second-period touchdowns put the game out of reach. The 49ers led 17-0 until Tampa Bay quarterback Craig Erickson threw 2 touchdown passes in a 14-second span to trim the Buccaneers' deficit to 3 points. But San Francisco took just two plays to counter, with quarterback Steve Young and Rice teaming on a 51-yard touchdown pass 6:19 before halftime. Rice's third touchdown, on a 9-yard reception, came in the final minute of the second quarter and made it 31-14 at the half. That gave him 117 career touchdowns, moving him past John Riggins and into third place on the NFL's all-time list. Number 118 came on a 26-yard scoring catch late in the third quarter. Young completed 23 of 29 passes for 311 yards while directing 8 possessions, 6 of which resulted in touchdowns. Ricky Watters ran for 88 yards and caught 5 passes for 35 yards as San Francisco rolled up 448 total yards. Erickson completed 17 of 27 passes for 239 yards for the Buccaneers.

| | | | | | | |
|---|---|---|---|---|---|---|
| **San Francisco** | 10 | 21 | 7 | 7 | — | 45 |
| **Tampa Bay** | 0 | 14 | 7 | 0 | — | 21 |

SF — Rice 12 pass from Young (Cofer kick)
SF — FG Cofer 44
SF — Tamm 1 run (Cofer kick)
TB — G. Anderson 14 pass from Erickson (Husted kick)
TB — Workman 18 pass from Erickson (Husted kick)
SF — Rice 51 pass from Young (Cofer kick)
SF — Rice 9 pass from Young (Cofer kick)
TB — Workman 3 run (Husted kick)
SF — Rice 26 pass from Young (Cofer kick)
SF — Watters 1 run (Cofer kick)

**N.Y. GIANTS 20, WASHINGTON 6**—at Giants Stadium, attendance 76,606. Rodney Hampton, back in the lineup for the first time in more than a month, ran for 78 yards and a touchdown as the Giants ground out a victory over the Redskins. New York took the opening kickoff and held the ball for 7:44, marching 80 yards in 12 plays, the last of which was Hampton's 1-yard touchdown run. The Giants never trailed and kept the ball mostly on the ground; 38 of their 57 plays were rushes, and 152 of their 262 total yards came via the running game. Quarterback Phil Simms attempted only 15 passes, completing 9 for 100 yards. Running back David Meggett, who threw a 42-yard touchdown pass on a halfback-option play in a 41-7 victory over Washington earlier in the year, tossed a 21-yard scoring strike to Chris Calloway on a similar play in this one. Mark Rypien threw for 239 yards, and Reggie Brooks ran for 91 for the Redskins, who fell to 2-7, their worst start in 30 years.

| | | | | | | |
|---|---|---|---|---|---|---|
| **Washington** | 0 | 0 | 3 | 3 | — | 6 |
| **N.Y. Giants** | 7 | 7 | 3 | 3 | — | 20 |

Giants— Hampton 1 run (Treadwell kick)
Giants— Calloway 21 pass from Meggett (Treadwell kick)
Giants— FG Treadwell 43
Wash — FG Lohmiller 27
Giants— FG Treadwell 39
Wash — FG Lohmiller 33

## SUNDAY NIGHT, NOVEMBER 14

**CHICAGO 16, SAN DIEGO 13**—at San Diego Jack Murphy Stadium, attendance 58,459. Jim Harbaugh threw a 38-yard touchdown pass to Curtis Conway, and the Bears hung on to upset the Chargers. The decisive scoring pass came with 4:08 remaining in the third quarter and San Diego leading 10-9. It came one play after Chicago's Terry Obee returned a punt 25 yards. The Chargers then held the ball for more than eight minutes on a 19-play drive, but managed only a 26-yard field goal by John Carney to pull within three points 3:55 into the fourth quarter. San Diego had a chance to tie the game with 71 seconds remaining, but Carney's 41-yard field-goal try was wide left.

| | | | | | | |
|---|---|---|---|---|---|---|
| **Chicago** | 0 | 6 | 10 | 0 | — | 16 |
| **San Diego** | 3 | 7 | 0 | 3 | — | 13 |

SD — FG Carney 28
SD — Kidd 2 run (Carney kick)
Chi — FG Butler 33
Chi — FG Butler 54
Chi — FG Butler 20
Chi — Conway 38 pass from Harbaugh (Butler kick)
SD — FG Carney 26

## MONDAY, NOVEMBER 15

**PITTSBURGH 23, BUFFALO 0**—at Three Rivers Stadium, attendance 60,265. Leroy Thompson rushed for 108 yards and a touchdown as the Steelers ended the Bills' five-game winning streak with surprising ease. Thompson, who replaced Barry Foster at running back after Foster sprained an ankle on Pittsburgh's first possession, carried 30 times and gave the Steelers all the points they would need on a 9-yard touchdown run 9:24 into the game. Neil O'Donnell threw a 1-yard touchdown pass to tight end Eric Green in the third quarter, and Gary Anderson kicked 3 field goals. A stifling defense did the rest, limiting Buffalo to 9 first downs and 157 total yards while knocking quarterback Jim Kelly (concussion) and wide receivers Andre Reed (broken bone in his wrist) and Don Beebe (concussion) out of the game. Pittsburgh had 400 total yards and maintained possession for 44:51 of the game's 60 minutes.

| | | | | | | |
|---|---|---|---|---|---|---|
| **Buffalo** | 0 | 0 | 0 | 0 | — | 0 |
| **Pittsburgh** | 7 | 3 | 10 | 3 | — | 23 |

Pitt — Thompson 9 run (Anderson kick)
Pitt — FG Anderson 37
Pitt — Green 1 pass from O'Donnell (Anderson kick)
Pitt — FG Anderson 19
Pitt — FG Anderson 31

## TWELFTH WEEK SUMMARIES

| AMERICAN FOOTBALL CONFERENCE | | | | | | |
|---|---|---|---|---|---|---|
| **Eastern Division** | **W** | **L** | **T** | **Pct.** | **Pts.** | **OP** |
| Buffalo | 8 | 2 | 0 | .800 | 195 | 129 |
| Miami | 8 | 2 | 0 | .800 | 218 | 172 |
| N.Y. Jets | 6 | 4 | 0 | .600 | 234 | 170 |
| Indianapolis | 3 | 7 | 0 | .300 | 154 | 233 |
| New England | 1 | 9 | 0 | .100 | 126 | 217 |
| **Central Division** | | | | | | |
| Houston | 6 | 4 | 0 | .600 | 233 | 177 |
| Pittsburgh | 6 | 4 | 0 | .600 | 228 | 173 |
| Cleveland | 5 | 5 | 0 | .500 | 188 | 208 |
| Cincinnati | 0 | 10 | 0 | .000 | 112 | 241 |
| **Western Division** | | | | | | |
| Kansas City | 7 | 3 | 0 | .700 | 181 | 163 |
| Denver | 6 | 4 | 0 | .600 | 266 | 188 |
| L.A. Raiders | 6 | 4 | 0 | .600 | 184 | 185 |
| Seattle | 5 | 5 | 0 | .500 | 165 | 169 |
| San Diego | 4 | 6 | 0 | .400 | 164 | 195 |

| NATIONAL FOOTBALL CONFERENCE | | | | | | |
|---|---|---|---|---|---|---|
| **Eastern Division** | **W** | **L** | **T** | **Pct.** | **Pts.** | **OP** |
| Dallas | 7 | 3 | 0 | .700 | 220 | 153 |
| N.Y. Giants | 7 | 3 | 0 | .700 | 187 | 121 |
| Philadelphia | 4 | 6 | 0 | .400 | 158 | 198 |
| Phoenix | 3 | 7 | 0 | .300 | 183 | 176 |
| Washington | 2 | 8 | 0 | .200 | 151 | 239 |
| **Central Division** | | | | | | |
| Detroit | 7 | 3 | 0 | .700 | 204 | 166 |
| Green Bay | 6 | 4 | 0 | .600 | 225 | 178 |
| Chicago | 5 | 5 | 0 | .500 | 161 | 141 |
| Minnesota | 5 | 5 | 0 | .500 | 165 | 200 |
| Tampa Bay | 3 | 7 | 0 | .300 | 143 | 261 |
| **Western Division** | | | | | | |
| San Francisco | 7 | 3 | 0 | .700 | 297 | 186 |
| New Orleans | 6 | 4 | 0 | .600 | 207 | 215 |
| Atlanta | 4 | 6 | 0 | .400 | 211 | 236 |
| L.A. Rams | 3 | 7 | 0 | .300 | 141 | 211 |

## SUNDAY, NOVEMBER 21

**CHICAGO 19, KANSAS CITY 17**—at Arrowhead Stadium, attendance 76,872. Neal Anderson ran 1 yard for a touchdown with 3:09 remaining as the Bears snapped the Chiefs' 10-game winning streak at home. Kansas City jumped out to a 14-0 lead on the strength of 2 rushing touchdowns by Marcus Allen. But Chicago pulled within 17-12, and Bears cornerback Jeremy Lincoln made the key play of the game late in the fourth quarter. From his 2-yard line, Chiefs quarterback Dave Krieg threw a pass to Jonathan Hayes. Kansas City's tight end bobbled the low throw, and Lincoln picked it off at the 12. He returned the theft 8 yards, and three plays later Anderson ran for the winning score. Allen, who rushed for 78 yards, became the ninth player in NFL history to run for 9,000 yards in his career. His 2 touchdowns raised his career total to 107, sixth on the league's all-time chart.

| | | | | | | |
|---|---|---|---|---|---|---|
| **Chicago** | 0 | 6 | 6 | 7 | — | 19 |
| **Kansas City** | 7 | 7 | 3 | 0 | — | 17 |

KC — Allen 2 run (Lowery kick)
KC — Allen 8 run (Lowery kick)
Chi — FG Butler 32
Chi — FG Butler 45
Chi — Worley 25 run (kick blocked)
KC — FG Lowery 20
Chi — Anderson 1 run (Butler kick)

**N.Y. JETS 17, CINCINNATI 12**—at Giants Stadium, attendance 64,264. Brad Baxter and Johnny Johnson capped long drives with touchdown runs in the second quarter, and the Jets went on to record their fourth consecutive victory. The winless Bengals led 3-0 until New York embarked on a 19-play, 94-yard drive that culminated in Baxter's 5-yard touchdown run 4:13 before halftime. Quarterback Boomer Esiason got the drive going by completing a 12-yard pass to Johnson on third-and-6 from the Jets' 12-yard line, then had a 26-yard completion to Johnson later in the drive and converted a fourth-and-1 by sneaking 2 yards for a first down. He teamed with Johnson again the next time New York had the ball, completing a 48-yard pass to the running back to key an 80-yard drive. Johnson's 6-yard touchdown run with 57 seconds left in the second quarter capped that march and made it 14-3. Cincinnati closed within 17-10 on David Klingler's 4-yard touchdown pass to Jeff Query with 2:09 remaining in the game, but the Jets ran all but one second off the clock before giving up a concession safety.

| | | | | | | |
|---|---|---|---|---|---|---|
| **Cincinnati** | 3 | 0 | 0 | 9 | — | 12 |
| **N.Y. Jets** | 0 | 14 | 0 | 3 | — | 17 |

Cin — FG Pelfrey 28
Jets — B. Baxter 5 run (Blanchard kick)
Jets — Johnson 6 run (Blanchard kick)
Jets — FG Blanchard 42
Cin — Query 4 pass from Klingler (Pelfrey kick)
Cin — Safety, Aguiar threw ball out of back of end zone

**ATLANTA 27, DALLAS 14**—at Georgia Dome, attendance 71,253. Bobby Hebert threw 3 touchdown passes and the Falcons stunned the Cowboys, snapping the defending Super Bowl champions' seven-game winning streak. Atlanta dominated from the outset, taking the opening kickoff and marching 73 yards to Norm Johnson's 26-yard field goal. The 14-play drive consumed 8:48. After forcing a punt, the Falcons drove to another field goal by Johnson the next time they had the ball. At that point, Atlanta had amassed 133 total yards to 1 for Dallas, and had run 29 plays to 3. The Falcons didn't let up, driving 87 yards to Hebert's 13-yard touchdown pass to Mike Pritchard 4:37 before halftime, then opening up a 20-0 advantage when the pair teamed again on an 11-yard touchdown pass midway through the third quarter. The Cowboys, already playing without injured starting quarterback Troy Aikman, lost running back Emmitt Smith for the rest of the game with a bruised right quadriceps suffered shortly before halftime. Smith left having gained only 1 yard on 1 carry and 9 yards on 4 receptions. Bernie Kosar, making his first start for Dallas, completed 22 of 39 passes for 186 yards. Hebert was 24 of 32 for 315 yards as Atlanta outgained the Cowboys 400-230. Cornerback Deion Sanders lined up at wide receiver late in the game and turned a short pass from Hebert into a 70-yard touchdown.

| | | | | | | |
|---|---|---|---|---|---|---|
| **Dallas** | 0 | 0 | 7 | 7 | — | 14 |
| **Atlanta** | 3 | 10 | 7 | 7 | — | 27 |

Atl — FG Johnson 26
Atl — FG Johnson 24
Atl — Pritchard 13 pass from Hebert (Johnson kick)
Atl — Pritchard 11 pass from Hebert (Johnson kick)
Dall — Galbraith 1 pass from Kosar (Murray kick)
Atl — Sanders 70 pass from Hebert (Johnson kick)
Dall — K. Williams 28 pass from Kosar (Murray kick)

**GREEN BAY 26, DETROIT 17**—at Milwaukee County Stadium, attendance 55,119. Edgar Bennett scored 2 touchdowns and Chris Jacke kicked 4 field goals as the Packers pulled within one game of the first-place Lions in the NFC Central Division. Trailing 17-16 early in the fourth quarter, Green Bay drove to Jacke's fourth field goal, from 34 yards, to take a 19-17 advantage with 9:03 left in the game. Later in the period, Packers safety LeRoy Butler intercepted Rodney Peete's pass at Detroit's 36-yard line and returned it 22 yards to the 14. That set up the game-clinching 2-yard touchdown run by Bennett with 1:51 to go. Bennett also had a 1-yard touchdown run to open the scoring 3:37 into the game. Brett Favre completed 24 of 33 passes for 259 yards for the Packers, who rolled up 404 total yards while limiting the Lions to just 205. Detroit's Barry Sanders ran for 75 yards and joined Eric Dickerson and Tony Dorsett as the only players in NFL history to rush for more than 1,000 yards in each of their first five seasons.

| | | | | | | |
|---|---|---|---|---|---|---|
| **Detroit** | 0 | 10 | 7 | 0 | — | 17 |
| **Green Bay** | 10 | 3 | 3 | 10 | — | 26 |

GB — E. Bennett 1 run (Jacke kick)
GB — FG Jacke 27
Det — Green 17 pass from Peete (Hanson kick)
Det — FG Hanson 50
GB — FG Jacke 52
Det — Hallock 1 pass from Peete (Hanson kick)

GB — FG Jacke 20
GB — FG Jacke 34
GB — E. Bennett 2 run (Jacke kick)

**HOUSTON 27, CLEVELAND 20**—at Cleveland Stadium, attendance 71,668. Gary Brown rushed for 194 yards on 34 carries to lead the Oilers to their fifth consecutive victory. Brown, making his second consecutive start in place of injured Lorenzo White, followed his 166-yard effort against Cincinnati one week earlier with the best single-game performance by a Houston runner in 13 years. He capped a 76-yard drive 3:07 into the second quarter with an 11-yard touchdown run to give the Oilers a lead they would never relinquish. Warren Moon threw a 4-yard touchdown pass to Curtis Duncan and ran 4 yards for another touchdown to help Houston build a 27-10 advantage in the fourth quarter. Browns quarterback Todd Philcox completed 22 of 47 passes for a career-high 316 yards, but was intercepted 4 times. Cleveland also had a punt blocked, which led to a field goal. Marcus Robertson equaled a club record with 3 interceptions for the Oilers.

| | | | | | | |
|---|---|---|---|---|---|---|
| **Houston** | 0 | 14 | 3 | 10 | — | 27 |
| **Cleveland** | 3 | 7 | 0 | 10 | — | 20 |

Cle — FG Stover 21
Hou — Brown 11 run (Del Greco kick)
Hou — Duncan 4 pass from Moon (Del Greco kick)
Cle — Metcalf 13 pass from Philcox (Stover kick)
Hou — FG Del Greco 28
Hou — Moon 4 run (Del Greco kick)
Hou — FG Del Greco 30
Cle — Carrier 24 pass from Philcox (Stover kick)
Cle — FG Stover 44

**BUFFALO 23, INDIANAPOLIS 9**—at Rich Stadium, attendance 79,101. A second-quarter safety led to the deciding touchdowns in the Bills' victory. Indianapolis led 6-0 after 2 lengthy drives that stalled inside Buffalo's 10-yard line resulted in field goals by Dean Biasucci. But midway through the second quarter, the Bills' Henry Jones sacked Colts quarterback Jeff George in the end zone for a safety. After the ensuing free kick, Buffalo drove 55 yards and took a 9-6 lead on Kenneth Davis's 1-yard run 2:35 before halftime. Then the Bills' Richard Harvey stripped the ball from Indianapolis's Clarence Verdin on the following kickoff and Keith Goganious recovered for Buffalo at the Colts' 26. It took the Bills only 2 plays to convert that into Jim Kelly's 23-yard touchdown pass to Bill Brooks with 1:55 remaining in the second quarter. After Biasucci's third field goal pulled Indianapolis within 16-9 midway through the third period, Kelly capped an 80-yard drive with a 13-yard touchdown pass to tight end Keith McKeller for the game's final points. The Colts, who failed to score a touchdown for the fourth time in 10 games this season, had two drives thwarted in the end zone in the fourth quarter, one on a fourth-down incompletion and one on cornerback Nate Odomes's interception. Kelly passed for 274 yards and Thurman Thomas rushed for 116 for Buffalo. George threw for 262 yards for Indianapolis.

| | | | | | | |
|---|---|---|---|---|---|---|
| **Indianapolis** | 3 | 3 | 3 | 0 | — | 9 |
| **Buffalo** | 0 | 16 | 7 | 0 | — | 23 |

Ind — FG Biasucci 26
Ind — FG Biasucci 22
Buff — Safety, Jones tackled George in end zone
Buff — Davis 1 run (Christie kick)
Buff — Brooks 23 pass from Kelly (Christie kick)
Ind — FG Biasucci 37
Buff — McKeller 13 pass from Kelly (Christie kick)

**L.A. RAIDERS 12, SAN DIEGO 7**—at San Diego Jack Murphy Stadium, attendance 60,615. Jeff Jaeger's 4 field goals kept the Raiders within a game of first place in the AFC West. Los Angeles dominated from the outset, taking the opening kickoff and marching 86 yards on a 19-play drive that chewed up 11:22. That drive stalled at the Chargers' 2-yard line, and Jaeger kicked a 20-yard field goal. A 13-play, 89-yard drive stalled at the 3 late in the second quarter, and Jaeger kicked another 20-yard field goal. It was 12-0 before Stan Humphries got San Diego on the board by completing 6 consecutive passes on a 73-yard drive that culminated in his 9-yard touchdown toss to Nate Lewis with 1:53 left in the game. But an onside kick attempt failed, and the Chargers did not get the ball back until only 14 seconds remained. The Raiders finished the game with substantial advantages in total yards (421-154) and time of possession (41:48-18:12). Jeff Hostetler passed for 270 yards and Greg Robinson rushed for 89. James Jett caught 7 passes for 138 yards.

| | | | | | | |
|---|---|---|---|---|---|---|
| **L.A. Raiders** | 3 | 3 | 3 | 3 | — | 12 |
| **San Diego** | 0 | 0 | 0 | 7 | — | 7 |

Raid — FG Jaeger 20
Raid — FG Jaeger 20
Raid — FG Jaeger 37
Raid — FG Jaeger 27
SD — Lewis 9 pass from Humphries (Carney kick)

**MIAMI 17, NEW ENGLAND 13**—at Joe Robbie Stadium, attendance 59,982. Seventeen-year veteran Steve DeBerg rallied the Dolphins past the Patriots by throwing 2 touchdown passes in the fourth quarter. New England led 6-3 until DeBerg gave Miami the lead for the first time by teaming with running back Keith Byars on an 11-yard touchdown pass with 9:28 left in the game. He threw a 44-yard scoring strike to Irving Fryar for the clinching points with 2:49 to go. Drew Bledsoe's 40-yard touchdown pass to Ray Crittenden with 71 seconds left made it close, but the Dolphins recovered the ensuing onside kickoff. DeBerg, at 39 the oldest player in the NFL, started for the fifth different team in his career. He was acquired less than two weeks earlier as a free agent and finished with 16 completions in 27 attempts for 252 yards. Mark Higgs complemented DeBerg's passing by rushing for 108 yards. Bledsoe threw for 275 yards for the Patriots, who lost their fifth straight game.

| | | | | | | |
|---|---|---|---|---|---|---|
| **New England** | 3 | 0 | 3 | 7 | — | 13 |
| **Miami** | 0 | 0 | 3 | 14 | — | 17 |

NE — FG Sisson 28
Mia — FG Stoyanovich 23
NE — FG Sisson 40
Mia — Byars 11 pass from DeBerg (Stoyanovich kick)
Mia — Fryar 44 pass from DeBerg (Stoyanovich kick)
NE — Crittenden 40 pass from Bledsoe (Sisson kick)

**N.Y. GIANTS 7, PHILADELPHIA 3**—at Veterans Stadium, attendance 62,928. Phil Simms's 26-yard touchdown pass to Mark Jackson on the first play of the fourth quarter lifted the Giants to their first victory at Veterans Stadium since 1987. New York, which pulled into a tie with Dallas for first place in the NFC East, managed only 292 total yards but struck quickly for the game's lone touchdown, moving 80 yards in only 3 plays. Simms's 50-yard completion to running back David Meggett was the big blow. The veteran quarterback completed 13 of 22 passes for 187 yards. Rodney Hampton rushed for 101 yards on 24 carries. Eagles quarterbacks Ken O'Brien and Bubby Brister combined to complete only 13 of 32 passes for 130 yards.

| | | | | | | |
|---|---|---|---|---|---|---|
| **N.Y. Giants** | 0 | 0 | 0 | 7 | — | 7 |
| **Philadelphia** | 0 | 0 | 3 | 0 | — | 3 |

Phil — FG Bahr 35
Giants — M. Jackson 26 pass from Simms (Treadwell kick)

**DENVER 37, PITTSBURGH 13**—at Mile High Stadium, attendance 74,840. John Elway passed for 276 yards to lead the Broncos' rout of the Steelers. Pittsburgh entered the game with the league's leading defense, but Elway had 230 passing yards by halftime as Denver scored on four of its first five possessions to build a comfortable 20-0 lead. The key blow was a 95-yard touchdown drive after Steelers running back Leroy Thompson lost a fumble at the Broncos' 5-yard line with his team trailing only 3-0. Elway completed passes of 31 yards to Reggie Johnson and 27 yards to Leonard Russell on the 9-play march, which was capped by the first of Robert Delpino's two 1-yard touchdown runs. Elway added a 13-yard touchdown pass to Vance Johnson midway through the third quarter.

| | | | | | | |
|---|---|---|---|---|---|---|
| **Pittsburgh** | 0 | 0 | 6 | 7 | — | 13 |
| **Denver** | 10 | 10 | 14 | 3 | — | 37 |

Den — FG Elam 48
Den — Delpino 1 run (Elam kick)
Den — Russell recovered fumble in end zone (Elam kick)
Den — FG Elam 27
Pitt — FG Anderson 37
Den — Delpino 1 run (Elam kick)
Den — V. Johnson 13 pass from Elway (Elam kick)
Pitt — FG Anderson 38
Den — FG Elam 28
Pitt — Thigpen 39 pass from Tomczak (Anderson kick)

**L.A. RAMS 10, WASHINGTON 6**—at Anaheim Stadium, attendance 45,546. T.J. Rubley came off the bench to lead the Rams to 10 fourth-quarter points and the victory over the Redskins. With Los Angeles trailing 6-0 and starting quarterback Jim Everett ineffective, Rubley entered the game on the last play of the third quarter. He took only four plays to get the Rams in the end zone, completing a 38-yard pass to tight end Pat Carter on third-and-17 and a 25-yard pass to rookie tight end Troy Drayton for the touchdown with 13:31 left in the game. Rubley's 29-yard pass to Willie Anderson set up Tony Zendejas's 23-yard field goal with 3:10 to go. Washington tried to rally, driving to Los Angeles's 27-yard line in the closing moments, but safety Michael Stewart preserved the win for the Rams by intercepting Rich Gannon's pass. Rubley completed 5 of 6 passes for 112 yards in his short stint. Gannon was 25 of 40 for the Redskins, but for only 172 yards.

| | | | | | | |
|---|---|---|---|---|---|---|
| **Washington** | 3 | 0 | 3 | 0 | — | 6 |
| **L.A. Rams** | 0 | 0 | 0 | 10 | — | 10 |

Wash — FG Lohmiller 19
Wash — FG Lohmiller 34
Rams — Drayton 25 pass from Rubley (Zendejas kick)
Rams — FG Zendejas 23

## SUNDAY NIGHT, NOVEMBER 21

**TAMPA BAY 23, MINNESOTA 10**—at Tampa Stadium, attendance 40,848. Vince Workman gained 123 yards from scrimmage and scored on a 1-yard run in the fourth quarter to lead the Buccaneers' upset of the Vikings. Minnesota led 7-6 at halftime, but 52 seconds into the third quarter, Tampa Bay cornerback Milton Mack intercepted Sean Salisbury's pass and returned it 27 yards for the touchdown that gave the Buccaneers the lead for good. Workman, who rushed for 58 yards and caught 7 passes for 65 yards, scored the clinching touchdown 4:40 into the fourth quarter after Craig Erickson completed a 27-yard pass to Horace Copeland. Erickson was 19 of 32 for 239 yards. Wide receiver Anthony Carter supplied most of Minnesota's offense by catching 9 passes for 104 yards.

| | | | | | | |
|---|---|---|---|---|---|---|
| **Minnesota** | 0 | 7 | 3 | 0 | — | 10 |
| **Tampa Bay** | 3 | 3 | 10 | 7 | — | 23 |

TB — FG Husted 26
TB — FG Husted 54
Minn — A. Carter 2 pass from Salisbury (Reveiz kick)
TB — Mack 27 interception return (Husted kick)
TB — FG Husted 21
Minn — FG Reveiz 43
TB — Workman 1 run (Husted kick)

## MONDAY, NOVEMBER 22

**SAN FRANCISCO 42, NEW ORLEANS 7**—at Candlestick Park, attendance 66,500. Steve Young threw 3 touchdown passes and ran for another as the 49ers blasted the Saints to take over first place in the NFC West. Safety Merton Hanks returned an interception 67 yards for a touchdown 6:54 into the game, and San Francisco turned the game into a rout by scoring touchdowns on five consecutive possessions in the second and third quarters. Two of Young's scoring tosses went to Jerry Rice, including 1 of 14 yards that gave the 49ers a 42-0 lead with 5:54 to go in the third quarter. Young completed 14 of 21 passes for 205 yards. Ricky Watters ran for 116 yards on 16 carries. San Francisco amassed 25 first downs and 455 total yards, while intercepting 4 passes and sending New Orleans to its fourth loss in five games.

| | | | | | | |
|---|---|---|---|---|---|---|
| **New Orleans** | 0 | 0 | 0 | 7 | — | 7 |
| **San Francisco** | 7 | 21 | 14 | 0 | — | 42 |

SF — Hanks 67 interception return (Cofer kick)
SF — J. Taylor 26 pass from Young (Cofer kick)
SF — Rice 11 pass from Young (Cofer kick)
SF — Young 7 run (Cofer kick)
SF — Logan 5 run (Cofer kick)
SF — Rice 14 pass from Young (Cofer kick)
NO — F. Turner 6 pass from M. Buck (Andersen kick)

## THIRTEENTH WEEK SUMMARIES

### AMERICAN FOOTBALL CONFERENCE

| Eastern Division | W | L | T | Pct. | Pts. | OP |
|---|---|---|---|---|---|---|
| Miami | 9 | 2 | 0 | .818 | 234 | 186 |
| Buffalo | 8 | 3 | 0 | .727 | 202 | 152 |
| N.Y. Jets | 7 | 4 | 0 | .636 | 240 | 170 |
| Indianapolis | 3 | 8 | 0 | .273 | 154 | 264 |
| New England | 1 | 10 | 0 | .091 | 126 | 223 |
| **Central Division** | | | | | | |
| Houston | 7 | 4 | 0 | .636 | 256 | 180 |
| Pittsburgh | 6 | 5 | 0 | .545 | 231 | 196 |
| Cleveland | 5 | 6 | 0 | .455 | 202 | 225 |
| Cincinnati | 1 | 10 | 0 | .091 | 128 | 251 |
| **Western Division** | | | | | | |
| Kansas City | 8 | 3 | 0 | .727 | 204 | 170 |
| Denver | 7 | 4 | 0 | .636 | 283 | 197 |
| L.A. Raiders | 6 | 5 | 0 | .545 | 194 | 201 |
| San Diego | 5 | 6 | 0 | .455 | 195 | 195 |
| Seattle | 5 | 6 | 0 | .455 | 174 | 186 |

### NATIONAL FOOTBALL CONFERENCE

| Eastern Division | W | L | T | Pct. | Pts. | OP |
|---|---|---|---|---|---|---|
| N.Y. Giants | 8 | 3 | 0 | .727 | 206 | 138 |
| Dallas | 7 | 4 | 0 | .636 | 234 | 169 |
| Philadelphia | 5 | 6 | 0 | .455 | 175 | 212 |
| Phoenix | 3 | 8 | 0 | .273 | 200 | 195 |
| Washington | 2 | 9 | 0 | .182 | 165 | 256 |
| **Central Division** | | | | | | |
| Detroit | 7 | 4 | 0 | .636 | 210 | 176 |
| Green Bay | 7 | 4 | 0 | .636 | 238 | 188 |
| Chicago | 6 | 5 | 0 | .545 | 171 | 147 |
| Minnesota | 5 | 6 | 0 | .455 | 179 | 217 |
| Tampa Bay | 3 | 8 | 0 | .273 | 153 | 274 |
| **Western Division** | | | | | | |
| San Francisco | 8 | 3 | 0 | .727 | 332 | 196 |
| New Orleans | 7 | 4 | 0 | .636 | 224 | 229 |
| Atlanta | 5 | 6 | 0 | .455 | 228 | 250 |
| L.A. Rams | 3 | 8 | 0 | .273 | 151 | 246 |

## THURSDAY, NOVEMBER 25

**CHICAGO 10, DETROIT 6**—at Pontiac Silverdome, attendance 76,699. Jim Harbaugh's 42-yard pass to Terry Obee provided the game's only touchdown, but it was a key play by punter Chris Gardocki that helped preserve the Bears' win. Ahead 10-6 late in the third quarter, Chicago lined up to punt at its 35-yard line, and but the snap sailed over Gardocki's head and toward the end zone. Gardocki scooped up the loose ball and kicked it while off balance and being chased behind his own goal line. The result was only a 4-yard punt from the original line of scrimmage, but instead of a safety, touchdown, or field position deep inside Bears' territory, the Lions took over at the 39. Cornerback Jeremy Lincoln snuffed that threat with an interception, and Chicago went on to win its third in succession on the road. Defensive end Trace Armstrong set up all of the Bears' points by recovering 2 fumbles.

| | | | | | | |
|---|---|---|---|---|---|---|
| **Chicago** | 0 | 10 | 0 | 0 | — | 10 |
| **Detroit** | 0 | 3 | 3 | 0 | — | 6 |

Chi — FG Butler 27
Det — FG Hanson 39
Chi — Obee 42 pass from Harbaugh (Butler kick)
Det — FG Hanson 27

**MIAMI 16, DALLAS 14**—at Texas Stadium, attendance 60,198. Pete Stoyanovich kicked a 19-yard field goal as time ran out to cap a wild finish and give the Dolphins an improbable victory. The Cowboys appeared to have won the game when Stoyanovich's 41-yard field goal try in the final seconds was blocked by defensive end Jimmie Jones. But defensive tackle Leon Lett muffed the ball while trying to recover it at the 7-yard line and Miami center Jeff Dellenbach fell on it at the 1 with three seconds remaining. Had no Dallas player touched the loose football, the Cowboys would have taken over possession. Instead, the Dolphins made the most of their reprieve by kicking the winning field goal on the next play. The game was played in freezing temperatures, and an unexpected snowstorm in Dallas covered the field with sleet and made footing treacherous and tackling difficult. Miami's Keith Byars equaled a club record for the longest touchdown run from scrimmage when he rambled 77 yards in the first quarter. Cowboys rookie Kevin Williams scored both of his team's touchdown. The victory, coupled with Buffalo's loss to Kansas City later in the weekend, gave the Dolphins sole possession of first in the AFC East.

| | | | | | | |
|---|---|---|---|---|---|---|
| **Miami** | 7 | 0 | 3 | 6 | — | 16 |
| **Dallas** | 0 | 14 | 0 | 0 | — | 14 |

Mia — Byars 77 run (Stoyanovich kick)
Dall — K. Williams 4 pass from Aikman (Murray kick)
Dall — K. Williams 64 punt return (Murray kick)
Mia — FG Stoyanovich 20
Mia — FG Stoyanovich 31
Mia — FG Stoyanovich 19

## SUNDAY, NOVEMBER 28

**KANSAS CITY 23, BUFFALO 7**—at Arrowhead Stadium, attendance 74,452. Joe Montana, starting for the first time in four weeks, threw 2 touchdown passes to lead the Chiefs over the Bills. After spotting Buffalo a 7-0 lead in the first quarter, Kansas City dominated the rest of the way. Montana, apparently recovered from a nagging hamstring injury, completed 18 of 32 passes for 208 yards, including touchdowns of 18 yards to running back Marcus Allen and 1 yard to tight end Keith Cash. Allen rushed for 74 yards on 22 carries, and caught 2 passes for 28 yards. The Chiefs' defense took care of the rest, forcing 4 turnovers and limiting the Bills to 43 rushing yards. Buffalo quarterback Jim Kelly completed 23 of 36 passes for 214 yards but was intercepted 3 times, while Thurman Thomas was held to a season-low 25 yards on 15 carries.

| | | | | | | |
|---|---|---|---|---|---|---|
| **Buffalo** | 7 | 0 | 0 | 0 | — | 7 |
| **Kansas City** | 7 | 3 | 10 | 3 | — | 23 |

Buff — Davis 9 run (Christie kick)
KC — Allen 18 pass from Montana (Lowery kick)
KC — FG Lowery 30
KC — Cash 1 pass from Montana (Lowery kick)
KC — FG Lowery 22
KC — FG Lowery 34

**ATLANTA 17, CLEVELAND 14**—at Georgia Dome, attendance 54,510. Bobby Hebert threw 2 touchdown passes in the first half as the Falcons built a 17-point lead, then hung on to win. The victory was the fifth in six games for Atlanta, which started the season 0-5. The Browns, who lost their fourth in a row, managed only 42 total yards while falling behind 17-0 at halftime. But Cleveland rallied in the second half, getting on the scoreboard when Todd Philcox threw a 35-yard touchdown pass to Mark Carrier on the final play of the third quarter. Philcox's 3-yard touchdown run on a quarterback draw with 3:31 left in the game pulled his team within 3 points, but the next time the Browns got the ball back, it was on their 34-yard line with no timeouts and just 53 seconds remaining. Falcons defensive end Chuck Smith sacked Philcox on the first play to end Cleveland's hopes. Hebert, who completed 13 of 18 passes for 144 yards in the first half, finished 21 of 29 for 214 yards. Philcox was 14 of 26 for 206 yards.

| | | | | | | |
|---|---|---|---|---|---|---|
| **Cleveland** | 0 | 0 | 7 | 7 | — | 14 |
| **Atlanta** | 10 | 7 | 0 | 0 | — | 17 |

Atl — FG Johnson 51
Atl — Rison 14 pass from Hebert (Johnson kick)
Atl — Pritchard 8 pass from Hebert (Johnson kick)
Cle — Carrier 35 pass from Philcox (Stover kick)
Cle — Philcox 3 run (Stover kick)

**DENVER 17, SEATTLE 9**—at Kingdome, attendance 57,812. The Broncos kept pace with first-place Kansas City in the AFC West by beating the Seahawks in Seattle for the first time since 1989. Denver quarterback John Elway made the key play of the game, ducking underneath blitzing linebacker David Brandon and completing a 50-yard touchdown pass to Shannon Sharpe on the first play of the second quarter. That put the Broncos ahead 7-0 and they never trailed. The Seahawks managed to pull within 1 point in the fourth quarter when Rick Mirer completed a 10-yard touchdown pass to Kelvin Martin with 7:55 remaining. But Denver countered with an 80-yard drive that culminated in Rod Bernstine's clinching 2-yard touchdown run with 4:06 left. The victory was not without cost for the Broncos, however, who lost wide receiver Vance Johnson for the remainder of the season when he fractured his ankle. The defense-oriented game featured 20 punts, including a club-record 12 by Seattle's Rick Tuten.

| | | | | | | |
|---|---|---|---|---|---|---|
| **Denver** | 0 | 7 | 3 | 7 | — | 17 |
| **Seattle** | 0 | 0 | 2 | 7 | — | 9 |

Den — Sharpe 50 pass from Elway (Elam kick)
Sea — Safety, Stephens tackled Elway in end zone
Den — FG Elam 25
Sea — Martin 10 pass from Mirer (Kasay kick)
Den — Bernstine 2 run (Elam kick)

**CINCINNATI 16, L.A. RAIDERS 10**—at Riverfront Stadium, attendance 43,272. Eric Ball ran 1 yard for a touchdown and rookie Doug Pelfrey kicked 3 field goals as the Bengals stunned the Raiders for their first victory after opening the season with 10 consecutive losses. The defeat was costly for the 6-5 Raiders, who fell two games behind first-place Kansas City in the AFC West and into a battle for a wild-card playoff berth. The game began amid snow flurries and a swirling wind, and the icy conditions contributed to Los Angeles's 4 missed field goals, a lost fumble, and an interception. Quarterback Jeff Hostetler completed only 12 of 32 passes for 220 yards, but was victimized by numerous dropped balls. Cincinnati quarterback David Klingler, meanwhile, was efficient and error-free, completing 14 of 20 attempts for 157 yards. The Bengals also ran for 131 yards and did not commit a turnover.

| | | | | | | |
|---|---|---|---|---|---|---|
| **L.A. Raiders** | 0 | 0 | 0 | 10 | — | 10 |
| **Cincinnati** | 3 | 7 | 3 | 3 | — | 16 |

Cin — FG Pelfrey 45
Cin — Ball 1 run (Pelfrey kick)
Cin — FG Pelfrey 34
Raid — Hostetler 4 run (Jaeger kick)
Cin — FG Pelfrey 44
Raid — FG Jaeger 34

**NEW ORLEANS 17, MINNESOTA 14**—at Metrodome, attendance 53,030. Saints rookie Tyrone Hughes tied the game by returning a kickoff 99 yards for a touchdown on the last play of the third quarter and Morten Andersen won it with a 24-yard field goal five minutes into the fourth quarter. New Orleans marched 76 yards to a touchdown following the game's opening kickoff, and the Vikings countered with an 80-yard drive to tie the score. It remained 7-7 until Minnesota quarterback Sean Salisbury threw his second touchdown pass of the game, a 7-yard toss to Cris Carter with six seconds left in the third quarter. But Hughes, a reserve cornerback, tied it again by becoming the first New Orleans player since 1989 to return a kickoff for a touchdown. The Saints then drove 73 yards to Andersen's winning kick the next time they had the ball. The key play of the drive was quarterback Wade Wilson's 28-yard run. Wilson, who also scrambled 13 yards for a first down on New Orleans's opening drive, was playing in the Metrodome for the first time since being released by the Vikings in 1992. Minnesota drove to an apparent game-tying 41-yard field goal by Fuad Reveiz in the final minute, but the Vikings' Fred Strickland was cited for holding. Reveiz's subsequent 51-yard try was blocked by Jim Wilks.

| | | | | | | |
|---|---|---|---|---|---|---|
| **New Orleans** | 7 | 0 | 7 | 3 | — | 17 |
| **Minnesota** | 7 | 0 | 7 | 0 | — | 14 |

NO — McAfee 3 run (Andersen kick)
Minn — Jordan 14 pass from Salisbury(Reveiz kick)
Minn — C. Carter 7 pass from Salisbury (Reveiz kick)
NO — Hughes 99 kickoff return (Andersen kick)
NO — FG Andersen 24

**N.Y. JETS 6, NEW ENGLAND 0**—at Foxboro Stadium, attendance 42,810. Cary Blanchard kicked a pair of field goals, and the Jets won their fifth in a row by recording their first shutout in 11 years. Scoring was kept low by torrential rains and winds that gusted up to 68 miles per hour. Still, the Patriots had chances to win, driving inside New York's 20-yard line twice in the fourth quarter. But Scott Sisson's 28-yard field goal attempt with 5:25 remaining was blocked, and wide receiver Michael Timpson fumbled at the 7 when hit by free safety Lonnie Young after catching a pass with 1:28 to play. Strong safety Brian Washington recovered to secure the victory for the Jets. Hard-luck New England fell to 1-10 but lost for the seventh time by 6 points or less. Patriots running back Leonard Russell accounted for the majority of his team's 289 total yards by rushing 27 times for 147 yards.

| | | | | | | |
|---|---|---|---|---|---|---|
| **N.Y. Jets** | 3 | 3 | 0 | 0 | — | 6 |
| **New England** | 0 | 0 | 0 | 0 | — | 0 |

Jets — FG Blanchard 33
Jets — FG Blanchard 23

**PHILADELPHIA 17, WASHINGTON 14**—at RFK Stadium, attendance 46,663. The Eagles snapped their six-game losing streak when running back James Joseph caught a 2-yard touchdown pass from Bubby Brister with 46 seconds remaining. The winning play negated a fourth-quarter rally by the Redskins. Washington entered the fourth period trailing 10-0, but scored 2 touchdowns in a span of 5:36 to take a 14-10 lead. Tim McGee sparked the comeback by catching a 17-yard touchdown pass from

Rich Gannon 3:40 into the final quarter, and then turning a short pass into a 54-yard gain on Washington's next possession, a 77-yard march that ended with Gannon's 6-yard touchdown pass to Art Monk with 5:44 to go. But Philadelphia drove 75 yards in 12 plays to the winning score, completing its first season sweep of the Redskins in 13 years.

| | | | | | | |
|---|---|---|---|---|---|---|
| **Philadelphia** | 3 | 7 | 0 | 7 | — | 17 |
| **Washington** | 0 | 0 | 0 | 14 | — | 14 |

Phil — FG Bahr 22
Phil — Hebron 1 run (Bahr kick)
Wash — McGee 17 pass from Gannon (Lohmiller kick)
Wash — Monk 6 pass from Gannon (Lohmiller kick)
Phil — Joseph 2 pass from Brister (Bahr kick)

**N.Y. GIANTS 19, PHOENIX 17**—at Giants Stadium, attendance 59,979. Brad Daluiso's 54-yard field goal with 32 seconds remaining lifted the Giants to the victory and into first place in the NFC's Eastern Division. It was another heartbreaking defeat for the Cardinals, who got 2 touchdown passes from Steve Beuerlein and limited New York's top-ranked rushing offense to 46 yards, but could not prevent their tenth consecutive loss at Giants Stadium. Beuerlein's second touchdown pass, a 17-yard toss to Ricky Proehl late in the third quarter, gave Phoenix a 17-13 lead. But David Treadwell, New York's primary kicker, booted a 22-yard field-goal 2:04 into the fourth quarter to trim the Giants' deficit to 17-16. Later in the quarter, New York drove 30 yards, converting a second-and-29 situation along the way. On fourth-and-10 from the Cardinals' 37-yard line, New York elected to go with Daluiso, whose strong leg earned him a spot on the roster as a kickoff and long field-goal specialist.

| | | | | | | |
|---|---|---|---|---|---|---|
| **Phoenix** | 10 | 0 | 7 | 0 | — | 17 |
| **N.Y. Giants** | 3 | 3 | 7 | 6 | — | 19 |

Phx — FG G. Davis 47
Phx — Rolle 1 pass from Beuerlein (G. Davis kick)
Giants— FG Treadwell 22
Giants— FG Treadwell 37
Giants— McCaffrey 20 pass from Simms (Treadwell kick)
Phx — Proehl 17 pass from Beuerlein (G. Davis kick)
Giants— FG Treadwell 22
Giants— FG Daluiso 54

**SAN FRANCISCO 35, L.A. RAMS 10**—at Anaheim Stadium, attendance 62,143. Steve Young passed for a career-high 462 yards and 4 touchdowns to lead the 49ers to their fifth consecutive victory. Young completed 26 of 32 passes, most of them to wide receivers Jerry Rice (8 catches for 166 yards and 2 touchdowns) and John Taylor (6 for 150 yards and 1 touchdown). Running back Ricky Watters scored 2 touchdowns, 1 on a 48-yard catch 1:50 before halftime to give San Francisco a 21-3 advantage at intermission. The 49ers then put the game out of reach when Young threw a 76-yard touchdown pass to Taylor on the second play of the third quarter. San Francisco amassed 539 total yards and averaged 8.2 yards per play while beating the Rams in Anaheim Stadium for the seventh consecutive time and twelfth time in the last 13 years. Rice upped his league-leading total to 1,048 receiving yards, and broke the NFL record for consecutive 1,000-yard seasons with eight. Rams tackle Jackie Slater played in his 246th career game, the most ever by an offensive lineman. He helped lead the way for rookie Jerome Bettis, who gained a career-high 133 yards on 18 carries.

| | | | | | | |
|---|---|---|---|---|---|---|
| **San Francisco** | 7 | 14 | 7 | 7 | — | 35 |
| **L.A. Rams** | 3 | 0 | 0 | 7 | — | 10 |

SF — Watters 6 run (Cofer kick)
Rams — FG Zendejas 25
SF — Rice 39 pass from Young (Cofer kick)
SF — Watters 48 pass from Young (Cofer kick)
SF — Taylor 76 pass from Young (Cofer kick)
SF — Rice 7 pass from Young (Cofer kick)
Rams — Ellard 14 pass from Rubley (Zendejas kick)

**GREEN BAY 13, TAMPA BAY 10**—at Lambeau Field, attendance 56,995. Brett Favre's 2-yard touchdown pass to Sterling Sharpe with 1:16 remaining lifted the Packers to the victory. Green Bay won for the sixth time in the last seven games and moved into a tie for first place in the NFC Central Division. The Buccaneers appeared on the verge of an upset when quarterback Craig Erickson and wide receiver Courtney Hawkins teamed on a 9-yard touchdown pass with 7:33 to go, giving Tampa Bay a 10-6 advantage. But the Packers, who had managed fewer than 200 total yards and only a pair of field goals to that point, marched 75 yards in 15 plays to the winning score. Sharpe caught 3 passes on the drive, and Mark Clayton converted a second-and-20 with a 28-yard reception.

| | | | | | | |
|---|---|---|---|---|---|---|
| **Tampa Bay** | 0 | 0 | 3 | 7 | — | 10 |
| **Green Bay** | 0 | 3 | 3 | 7 | — | 13 |

GB — FG Jacke 24
TB — FG Husted 30
GB — FG Jacke 36
TB — Hawkins 9 pass from Erickson (Husted kick)
GB — Sharpe 2 pass from Favre (Jacke kick)

## SUNDAY NIGHT, NOVEMBER 28

**HOUSTON 23, PITTSBURGH 3**—at Astrodome, attendance 61,238. Houston won its sixth in a row and moved into sole possession of first place in the AFC Central by beating the division-rival Steelers. The Oilers began the season 1-4 but the victory over Pittsburgh gave them their longest winning streak in 31 years. Warren Moon completed 21 of 34 passes for 295 yards and a touchdown. After Pittsburgh's Gary Anderson tied the game at 3-3 on a 42-yard field goal with 2:23 remaining in the first half, Houston marched 79 yards in seven plays to take the lead for good. Moon completed passes of 25, 24, and 18 yards to Ernest Givins on the 93-second drive, which was capped by Gary Brown's 3-yard touchdown run 50 seconds before intermission. Moon's 66-yard touchdown pass to Haywood Jeffires came only five plays into the second half and helped break the game open. Jeffires finished with 7 catches for 139 yards. Givins had 5 receptions to raise his career total to 484, surpassing Drew Hill (480) for the most in Oilers' history.

| | | | | | | |
|---|---|---|---|---|---|---|
| **Pittsburgh** | 0 | 3 | 0 | 0 | — | 3 |
| **Houston** | 0 | 10 | 10 | 3 | — | 23 |

Hou — FG Del Greco 43
Pitt — FG Anderson 42
Hou — Brown 3 run (Del Greco kick)
Hou — Jeffires 66 pass from Moon (Del Greco kick)
Hou — FG Del Greco 21
Hou — FG Del Greco 28

## MONDAY, NOVEMBER 29

**SAN DIEGO 31, INDIANAPOLIS 0**—at Hoosier Dome, attendance 54,110. Stan Humphries passed for 216 yards and 2 touchdowns to lead a balanced attack as the Chargers blanked the Colts. Humphries, who backed up John Friesz the previous six weeks because of a shoulder injury suffered in the preseason, regained his starting job and completed passes to eight different receivers, finishing with 16 completions in 25 attempts. He sparked San Diego's sluggish offense by throwing second-quarter touchdown passes to Shawn Jefferson and Nate Lewis. The Chargers' 14 points before intermission was the most they had scored in the first half of any game this year. San Diego's rushing attack also was effective, amassing 247 yards. Marion Butts ran for 80 yards, Natrone Means had 74, and Eric Bieniemy 64. Butts and Bieniemy put the game out of reach with short fourth-quarter touchdown runs. The Chargers outgained the Colts 474-262.

| | | | | | | |
|---|---|---|---|---|---|---|
| **San Diego** | 0 | 14 | 3 | 14 | — | 31 |
| **Indianapolis** | 0 | 0 | 0 | 0 | — | 0 |

SD — Jefferson 39 pass from Humphries (Carney kick)
SD — Lewis 8 pass from Humphries (Carney kick)
SD — FG Carney 36
SD — Butts 1 run (Carney kick)
SD — Bieniemy 4 run (Carney kick)

## FOURTEENTH WEEK SUMMARIES

**AMERICAN FOOTBALL CONFERENCE**

| **Eastern Division** | **W** | **L** | **T** | **Pct.** | **Pts.** | **OP** |
|---|---|---|---|---|---|---|
| Miami | 9 | 3 | 0 | .750 | 248 | 205 |
| Buffalo | 8 | 4 | 0 | .667 | 226 | 177 |
| N.Y. Jets | 7 | 5 | 0 | .583 | 246 | 179 |
| Indianapolis | 4 | 8 | 0 | .333 | 163 | 270 |
| New England | 1 | 11 | 0 | .083 | 140 | 240 |
| **Central Division** | | | | | | |
| Houston | 8 | 4 | 0 | .667 | 289 | 197 |
| Pittsburgh | 7 | 5 | 0 | .583 | 248 | 210 |
| Cleveland | 6 | 6 | 0 | .500 | 219 | 238 |
| Cincinnati | 1 | 11 | 0 | .083 | 136 | 272 |
| **Western Division** | | | | | | |
| Kansas City | 9 | 3 | 0 | .750 | 235 | 186 |
| Denver | 7 | 5 | 0 | .583 | 293 | 210 |
| L.A. Raiders | 7 | 5 | 0 | .583 | 219 | 225 |
| San Diego | 6 | 6 | 0 | .500 | 208 | 205 |
| Seattle | 5 | 7 | 0 | .417 | 190 | 217 |

**NATIONAL FOOTBALL CONFERENCE**

| **Eastern Division** | **W** | **L** | **T** | **Pct.** | **Pts.** | **OP** |
|---|---|---|---|---|---|---|
| N.Y. Giants | 9 | 3 | 0 | .750 | 225 | 152 |
| Dallas | 8 | 4 | 0 | .667 | 257 | 186 |
| Philadelphia | 5 | 7 | 0 | .417 | 192 | 235 |
| Phoenix | 4 | 8 | 0 | .333 | 238 | 205 |
| Washington | 3 | 9 | 0 | .250 | 188 | 273 |
| **Central Division** | | | | | | |
| Chicago | 7 | 5 | 0 | .583 | 201 | 164 |
| Detroit | 7 | 5 | 0 | .583 | 210 | 189 |
| Green Bay | 7 | 5 | 0 | .583 | 255 | 218 |
| Minnesota | 6 | 6 | 0 | .500 | 192 | 217 |
| Tampa Bay | 3 | 9 | 0 | .250 | 170 | 297 |
| **Western Division** | | | | | | |
| San Francisco | 9 | 3 | 0 | .750 | 353 | 204 |
| New Orleans | 7 | 5 | 0 | .583 | 237 | 246 |
| Atlanta | 5 | 7 | 0 | .417 | 245 | 283 |
| L.A. Rams | 3 | 9 | 0 | .250 | 161 | 284 |

## SUNDAY, DECEMBER 5

**HOUSTON 33, ATLANTA 17**—at Astrodome, attendance 58,186. Warren Moon threw for 342 yards and 1 touchdown, and the Oilers forced 7 turnovers while rallying to their seventh consecutive victory. The Falcons took a 14-6 advantage when Bobby Hebert threw touchdown passes on their last possession of the first half and first possession of the second. But it took Houston only four plays to drive 80 yards and close within 14-13 on Moon's 25-yard touchdown pass to Webster Slaughter, and Atlanta self-destructed after that. First, Oilers defensive end William Fuller sacked Hebert, forcing a fumble that tackle Ray Childress recovered in the end zone for the go-ahead touchdown 25 seconds before the end of the third quarter. Moments later, cornerback Steve Jackson intercepted Hebert's pass and returned it 16 yards to the Falcons' 9-yard line, setting up Al Del Greco's field goal to put Houston ahead 23-14 2:44 into the fourth quarter. Three plays after that, cornerback Cris Dishman intercepted a pass and returned it 20 yards to Atlanta's 22. It took the Oilers six plays to score from there, with Gary Brown's 1-yard touchdown run with 9:09 left putting the game out of reach. Moon finished with 24 completions in 42 attempts, while Slaughter caught 8 passes for 108 yards. Hebert completed 30 of 52 passes for 317 yards, but the Falcons could not overcome his 6 interceptions. Jackson had 2 of the thefts for Houston.

| | | | | | | |
|---|---|---|---|---|---|---|
| **Atlanta** | 0 | 7 | 7 | 3 | — | 17 |
| **Houston** | 3 | 3 | 14 | 13 | — | 33 |

Hou — FG Del Greco 52
Hou — FG Del Greco 43
Atl — Pritchard 9 pass from Hebert (Johnson kick)
Atl — Rison 6 pass from Hebert (Johnson kick)
Hou — Slaughter 25 pass from Moon (Del Greco kick)
Hou — Childress recovered fumble in end zone (Del Greco kick)
Hou — FG Del Greco 21
Hou — G. Brown 1 run (Del Greco kick)
Atl — FG Johnson 30
Hou — FG Del Greco 36

**SAN DIEGO 13, DENVER 10**—at San Diego Jack Murphy Stadium, attendance 60,233. John Carney kicked a 34-yard field goal with three seconds left and the Chargers overcame a 10-point halftime deficit to beat the Broncos and keep their playoff hopes alive. Denver forged a 10-0 lead at intermission on a 30-yard field goal by Jason Elam and a 1-yard touchdown pass from holder Tommy Maddox to linebacker David Wyman on a fake field goal attempt. It was the first touchdown of the seven-year veteran's NFL career. But San Diego rallied to tie the game on Carney's 27-yard field goal and Natrone Means's 1-yard touchdown run with 11:32 remaining in the game. The Broncos countered with a 56-yard drive that took more than six minutes, but Jason Elam missed a 42-yard field-goal attempt. The Chargers started their winning drive from their 5-yard line with 2:57 to go. Stan Humphries completed 7 of 10 passes for 72 yards on the 12-play, 79-yard march. He was 22 of 39 for 229 yards in all. Denver quarterback John Elway completed only 14 of 32 passes for 171 yards and failed to throw a touchdown pass for the first time in 1993.

| | | | | | | |
|---|---|---|---|---|---|---|
| **Denver** | 3 | 7 | 0 | 0 | — | 10 |
| **San Diego** | 0 | 0 | 3 | 10 | — | 13 |

Den — FG Elam 30
Den — Wyman 1 pass from Maddox (Elam kick)
SD — FG Carney 27
SD — Means 1 run (Carney kick)
SD — FG Carney 34

**CHICAGO 30, GREEN BAY 17**—at Soldier Field, attendance 62,236. Linebacker Dante Jones returned a fumble for 1 touchdown and intercepted a pass that resulted in another as the Bears climbed into a three-way tie for first place in the NFC Central Division by winning their fourth consecutive game. Chicago was outgained 466-210, and the Bears' offense failed to produce a touchdown. But the defense, led by Jones, put the ball in the end zone three times. The first time came 7:04 into the game, when Jones intercepted Brett Favre's pass and returned it 6 yards before lateraling to cornerback Jeremy Lincoln, who raced 80 yards for a touchdown. Early in the second half, Jones picked up a fumble by Favre and returned it 32 yards for a touchdown and a 17-7 lead. The Packers quickly rallied to tie on Chris Jacke's 26-yard field goal and Favre's 22-yard touchdown pass to Mark Clayton after Keo Coleman recovered Curtis Conway's fumble on the ensuing kickoff. The Bears' offense didn't get on the field in the second half until less than five minutes remained in the third quarter, but they marched to Kevin Butler's 24-yard field goal on that initial possession to regain the lead at 20-17. After Butler's 29-yard field goal made it 23-17 with 5:19 remaining, Chicago's defense came up with two more big plays, stopping Green Bay on fourth-and-1 from the the Bears' 26, and then forcing an interception that Mark Carrier returned 34 yards for the clinching touchdown with 1:41 to play. The Packers' Favre completed 36 of 54 passes for 402 yards and 2 touchdowns, but also threw 3 interceptions. Sterling Sharpe caught 10 passes for 114 yards and 1 touchdown.

| | | | | | | |
|---|---|---|---|---|---|---|
| **Green Bay** | 7 | 0 | 10 | 0 | — | 17 |
| **Chicago** | 7 | 3 | 10 | 10 | — | 30 |

Chi — Lincoln 80 interception return on lateral from D. Jones (Butler kick)
GB — Sharpe 18 pass from Favre (Jacke kick)
Chi — FG Butler 29
Chi — D. Jones 32 fumble return (Butler kick)
GB — FG Jacke 26
GB — Clayton 22 pass from Favre (Jacke kick)
Chi — FG Butler 24
Chi — FG Butler 29
Chi — Carrier 34 interception return (Butler kick)

**INDIANAPOLIS 9, N.Y. JETS 6**—at Giants Stadium, attendance 45,799. Dean Biasucci kicked 3 field goals, including the game-winner from 38 yards with one second left, and the Colts snapped the Jets' five-game winning streak. Indianapolis was 1 of 13 on third-down conversions and managed only 7 first downs and 169 total yards. But following interceptions, the Colts had to drive a total of only 1 yard to their 2 fourth-quarter field goals. The first theft came late in the third period with Indianapolis trailing 6-3, when defensive back Ray Buchanan picked off Boomer Esiason's pass and returned it 28 yards to the Jets' 6-yard line. Three plays netted only 1 yard, but Biasucci kicked a 24-yard field goal six seconds into the fourth quarter to tie the score. Late in the game, the Colts drove to New York's 31-yard line, only to be stopped on downs. But cornerback Eugene Daniel intercepted Esiason on the next play, and returned the ball 17 yards to the Jets' 36 with 61 seconds remaining. A personal foul penalty moved the ball to the 21, and from there Biasucci converted the kick that gave Indianapolis its third 9-6 victory of the season and its fifth consecutive win over the Jets in New York. With his 3 field goals, Biasucci moved past Pro Football Hall of Fame running back Lenny Moore and into first place on the Colts' all-time scoring list.

| | | | | | | |
|---|---|---|---|---|---|---|
| **Indianapolis** | 0 | 3 | 0 | 6 | — | 9 |
| **N.Y. Jets** | 0 | 3 | 3 | 0 | — | 6 |

Jets — FG Blanchard 28
Ind — FG Biasucci 42
Jets — FG Blanchard 19
Ind — FG Biasucci 24
Ind — FG Biasucci 38

**KANSAS CITY 31, SEATTLE 16**—at Kingdome, attendance 58,551. Marcus Allen ran for 3 touchdowns and linebacker Derrick Thomas returned a fumble for a score to help the Chiefs open up a two-game lead in the AFC West. Kansas City led just 10-3 and the Seahawks were driving early in the second quarter when Chiefs defensive end Darren Mickell sacked quarterback Rick Mirer, forcing a fumble. Thomas scooped up the loose ball and raced 86 yards for a touchdown. Kansas City, which led 17-6 at halftime, broke open the game when Allen scored 2 third-quarter touchdowns following turnovers. First, cornerback Albert Lewis intercepted Rick Mirer's pass and returned it 24 yards to Seattle's 13-yard line. Kimble Anders ran 12 yards to the 1, and Allen scored on the next play to make it 24-6 3:07 into the second half. On the Seahawks' next possession, Lewis recovered Kelvin Martin's fumble at Seattle's 47, and two plays later Allen ran 30 yards for the touchdown that put the game out of reach. The Chiefs won for the sixth time in the seven games that Joe Montana had started at quarterback. Montana completed 20 of 30 passes for 239 yards. Rick Mirer was 18 of 30 for 287 yards for the Seahawks, who produced a season-high 365 total yards. Brian Blades caught 7 passes for 134 yards.

| | | | | | | |
|---|---|---|---|---|---|---|
| **Kansas City** | 10 | 7 | 14 | 0 | — | 31 |
| **Seattle** | 3 | 3 | 7 | 3 | — | 16 |

Sea — FG Kasay 22
KC — Allen 1 run (Lowery kick)
KC — FG Lowery 47
KC — Thomas 86 fumble return (Lowery kick)
Sea — FG Kasay 26
KC — Allen 1 run (Lowery kick)
KC — Allen 30 run (Lowery kick)
Sea — Warren 1 run (Kasay kick)
Sea — FG Kasay 37

**L.A. RAIDERS 25, BUFFALO 24**—at Rich Stadium, attendance 79,478. Jeff Hostetler passed for 289 yards, including the game-winning touchdown on a 29-yard pass to Tim Brown with 4:58 remaining, as the Raiders bounced back from a dismal loss to the Bengals to beat the Bills. Buffalo led 24-16 until Los Angeles scored 10 points in the final nine minutes. First, Raiders cornerback Terry McDaniel intercepted a Jim Kelly pass and returned it 35 yards to Buffalo's 12-yard line. Though Los Angeles moved backwards to the 30, Jeff Jaeger kicked a 47-yard field goal to trim the Raiders' deficit to 24-19 with 8:47 to go. Then, after a punt, the Raiders took over at their 43. On successive plays, Hostetler completed passes of 18 yards to Nick Bell and 10 yards to James Jett before teaming with Brown on the winning touchdown pass. Brown caught 10 passes for 183 yards and helped the Raiders, who had been struggling offensively, amass 399 total yards. Greg Robinson (56 yards), Bell (44), and Hostetler (39, including an 11-yard touchdown) combined to rush for 138 yards. Buffalo wide receiver Don Beebe caught 4 passes for 115 yards, including a 65-yard touchdown in the final minute of the first half. Thomas ran for 74 yards and became the eighth player in NFL history to rush for more than 1,000 yards in five consecutive seasons.

| | | | | | | |
|---|---|---|---|---|---|---|
| **L.A. Raiders** | 3 | 7 | 6 | 9 | — | 25 |
| **Buffalo** | 0 | 14 | 3 | 7 | — | 24 |

Raid — FG Jaeger 37
Buff — Thomas 3 run (Christie kick)
Raid — Hostetler 11 run (Jaeger kick)
Buff — Beebe 65 pass from Kelly (Christie kick)
Raid — FG Jaeger 34
Buff — FG Christie 35
Raid — FG Jaeger 26
Buff — Thomas 1 run (Christie kick)
Raid — FG Jaeger 47
Raid — Brown 29 pass from Hostetler (kick blocked)

**PHOENIX 38, L.A. RAMS 10**—at Sun Devil Stadium, attendance 33,964. Ron Moore rushed for 126 yards and a club-record 4 touchdowns on 29 carries to power the Cardinals past the Rams. Phoenix started the rout early, taking the opening kickoff and marching 78 yards to a touchdown, Moore's 1-yard run 5:26 into the game. It was 14-3 at halftime, and the rookie running back broke open the game with 19- and 1-yard touchdown runs in the third quarter. His final touchdown, another 1-yard run in the fourth quarter, made it 38-3. Steve Beuerlein complemented Moore's running by completing 14 of 25 passes for 250 yards and 1 touchdown, a 22-yarder to Gary Clark in the second quarter. Clark caught 8 passes for 159 yards. Rams rookie Jerome Bettis rushed for 115 yards on 16 carries.

| | | | | | | |
|---|---|---|---|---|---|---|
| **L.A. Rams** | 3 | 0 | 0 | 7 | — | 10 |
| **Phoenix** | 7 | 7 | 14 | 10 | — | 38 |

Phx — Moore 1 run (G. Davis kick)
Rams — FG Zendejas 22
Phx — Clark 22 pass from Beuerlein (G. Davis kick)
Phx — Moore 19 run (G. Davis kick)
Phx — Moore 1 run (G. Davis kick)
Phx — FG G. Davis 27
Phx — Moore 1 run (G. Davis kick)
Rams — Drayton 4 pass from Everett (Zendejas kick)

**MINNESOTA 13, DETROIT 0**—at Pontiac Silverdome, attendance 63,216. Quarterback Jim McMahon returned to the Vikings' lineup, but it was Minnesota's defense that made the difference in this one, creating a logjam atop the NFC Central. The Lions' loss, coupled with the Bears' victory over the Packers, left Detroit, Chicago, and Green Bay tied for first place, with the Vikings just one game behind. Against the Lions, Minnesota relied on its defense, which limited Detroit to 219 total yards and intercepted 5 passes. Safety Lamar McGriggs returned 1 of them 63 yards for the clinching touchdown with 2:19 left in the game. Linebacker Jack Del Rio, who entered the 1993 season with 5 interceptions in eight years in the league, picked off 3. Lions quarterback Rodney Peete completed 18 of 30 passes, but for only 138 yards. He suffered 4 of the interceptions and was lifted in favor of Andre Ware after McGriggs' touchdown. McMahon, out more than a month with a dislocated shoulder, completed just 15 of 32 passes for 145 yards, but set up Minnesota's 2 first-half field goals with completions of 26 yards to Anthony Carter and 31 yards to Roger Craig.

| | | | | | | |
|---|---|---|---|---|---|---|
| **Minnesota** | 3 | 3 | 0 | 7 | — | 13 |
| **Detroit** | 0 | 0 | 0 | 0 | — | 0 |

Minn — FG Reveiz 37
Minn — FG Reveiz 29
Minn — McGriggs 63 interception return (Reveiz kick)

**PITTSBURGH 17, NEW ENGLAND 14**—at Three Rivers Stadium, attendance 51,358. Linebacker Levon Kirkland stopped quarterback Drew Bledsoe on fourth-and-goal from inside the 1-yard line in the closing seconds to preserve the Steelers' victory. Bledsoe, who completed 18 of 48 passes for 296 yards, was intercepted 5 times in the second half to thwart drives inside Pittsburgh territory, and also lost a fumble late in the first half that led to the Steelers' go-ahead touchdown. But in the closing 3:47, he drove the Patriots from their 5-yard line to within a foot of the goal line on a lengthy, 16-play drive. But with 17 seconds remaining, his sneak attempt was stopped by Kirkland inches short of the end zone. Bledsoe's 3-yard touchdown pass to tight end Ben Coates and Leonard Russell's 3-yard run staked New England to a 14-0 first-quarter lead. But Pittsburgh countered Russell's touchdown with an 80-yard march capped by Neil O'Donnell's 5-yard touchdown pass to Merril Hoge 3:13 into the second quarter. Gary Anderson's 35-yard field goal and O'Donnell's 1-yard touchdown pass to Hoge 10 seconds before halftime completed the scoring. The latter touchdown came seven plays after defensive lineman Jeff Zgonina recovered Bledsoe's fumble at the Patriots' 18.

| | | | | | | |
|---|---|---|---|---|---|---|
| **New England** | 14 | 0 | 0 | 0 | — | 14 |
| **Pittsburgh** | 0 | 17 | 0 | 0 | — | 17 |

NE — Coates 3 pass from Bledsoe (Sisson kick)
NE — Russell 3 run (Sisson kick)
Pitt — Hoge 5 pass from O'Donnell (Anderson kick)
Pitt — FG Anderson 35
Pitt — Hoge 1 pass from O'Donnell (Anderson kick)

**CLEVELAND 17, NEW ORLEANS 13**—at Municipal Stadium, attendance 60,388. The Browns recorded a club-record 9 sacks and shut down the Saints' offense in the second half to snap a four-game losing streak. Todd Philcox started the game at quarterback for Cleveland, but was replaced in the second quarter by Vinny Testaverde, who played for the first time since separating his shoulder against the Steelers six weeks earlier. Each threw a touchdown pass to Michael Jackson, with Testaverde's 4-yard toss breaking a 10-10 tie late in the third quarter and providing the winning points. The Browns relied primarily on their defense, however, which held New Orleans to only 22 yards in the second half, including minus-6 in the fourth quarter. Saints quarterback Wade Wilson completed 15 of 29 passes for 119 yards, but the 9 sacks dropped New Orleans's net-passing total to just 48 yards. The Saints could muster only 79 yards on the ground. Defensive ends Anthony Pleasant and Rob Burnett each had 2 sacks for Cleveland.

| | | | | | | |
|---|---|---|---|---|---|---|
| **New Orleans** | 7 | 0 | 3 | 3 | — | 13 |
| **Cleveland** | 10 | 0 | 7 | 0 | — | 17 |

Cle — Jackson 8 pass from Philcox (Stover kick)
NO — Martin 10 pass from Wilson (Andersen kick)
Cle — FG Stover 43
NO — FG Andersen 41
Cle — Jackson 4 pass from Testaverde (Stover kick)
NO — FG Andersen 27

**N.Y. GIANTS 19, MIAMI 14**—at Joe Robbie Stadium, attendance 72,161. Phil Simms passed for 257 yards to lead the Giants to the victory in a battle of division leaders. Simms completed 17 of 24 passes and directed an 86-yard touchdown march shortly before halftime that put New York ahead for good. He accounted for all but 3 of the yards on the drive by completing 5 of 6 passes, including a 20-yard touchdown to tight end Howard Cross to break a 7-7 tie 1:12 before intermission. David Treadwell's 42-yard field goal and a safety gave the Giants a 12-point cushion that rendered meaningless Steve DeBerg's 25-yard touchdown pass to Tony Martin with 61 seconds left in the game. The Dolphins amassed 408 total yards but suffered 3 sacks, 2 interceptions, a lost fumble, and a blocked field goal. DeBerg completed 26 of 41 passes for 365 yards. New York's victory was the first during the regular season by an NFC team at Joe Robbie Stadium, which opened in 1987.

| | | | | | | |
|---|---|---|---|---|---|---|
| **N.Y. Giants** | 7 | 7 | 3 | 2 | — | 19 |
| **Miami** | 7 | 0 | 0 | 7 | — | 14 |

Giants— Hampton 14 run (Treadwell kick)
Mia — Byars 6 run (Stoyanovich kick)
Giants— H. Cross 20 pass from Simms (Treadwell kick)
Giants— FG Treadwell 42
Giants— Safety, Hamilton sacked DeBerg in end zone
Mia — Martin 25 pass from DeBerg (Stoyanovich kick)

**WASHINGTON 23, TAMPA BAY 17**—at Tampa Stadium, attendance 49,035. Reggie Brooks rushed for 128 yards, including a 78-yard touchdown, to spark the Redskins to the victory. Washington led 10-0 at halftime, then Brooks helped break open the game with his long scoring run on the first play of the second half. The Buccaneers tried to rally, scoring 10 points within an 88-second span of the third quarter to pull within 17-10, but Redskins linebacker Kurt Gouveia intercepted Craig Erickson's pass and returned it 59 yards for the clinching touchdown with 1:43 left in the third quarter. Washington cornerback Darrell Green had 2 interceptions, 1 of which set up Chip Lohmiller's 51-yard field goal as time expired in the first half.

| | | | | | | |
|---|---|---|---|---|---|---|
| **Washington** | 7 | 3 | 13 | 0 | — | 23 |
| **Tampa Bay** | 0 | 0 | 10 | 7 | — | 17 |

Wash — Gannon 1 run (Lohmiller kick)
Wash — FG Lohmiller 51
Wash — Brooks 78 run (Lohmiller kick)
TB — FG Husted 31
TB — Seals interception in end zone (Husted kick)
Wash — Gouveia 59 interception return (kick failed)
TB — Hawkins 4 pass from Erickson (Husted kick)

## SUNDAY NIGHT, DECEMBER 5

**SAN FRANCISCO 21, CINCINNATI 8**—at Candlestick Park, attendance 60,039. Ricky Watters ran for 3 touchdowns and the 49ers won their sixth in a row despite struggling against the 1-11 Bengals. Cincinnati entered the game ranked last in the league in total offense, while San Francisco ranked first. But the Bengals outgained the 49ers 339-284 and maintained possession for more than 36 of the game's 60 minutes. San Francisco struck quickly, driving 55 yards following the opening kickoff to a touchdown 2:01 into the game. Steve Young completed a 43-yard pass to Jerry Rice on the first play, and Watters eventually scored from 2 yards out. Cincinnati rallied to take an 8-7 lead at halftime on a safety and 2 field goals by Doug Pelfrey. But the key play of the game came early in the fourth quarter, when the Bengals faked a punt near midfield. Punter Lee Johnson's pass was batted down by Amp Lee, and the 49ers took over possession at Cincinnati's 44-yard line. Seven plays later, Watters ran 2 yards for the touchdown that put San Francisco ahead for good. After holding the Bengals without a first down and forcing a punt, the 49ers then marched 56 yards in 11 plays to an insurance touchdown, Watters's 4-yard run on the first play of the fourth quarter.

| | | | | | | |
|---|---|---|---|---|---|---|
| **Cincinnati** | 2 | 6 | 0 | 0 | — | 8 |
| **San Francisco** | 7 | 0 | 7 | 7 | — | 21 |

SF — Watters 2 run (Cofer kick)
Cin — Safety, A. Williams tackled Young in end zone
Cin — FG Pelfrey 38
Cin — FG Pelfrey 29
SF — Watters 2 run (Cofer kick)
SF — Watters 4 run (Cofer kick)

## MONDAY, DECEMBER 6

**DALLAS 23, PHILADELPHIA 17**—at Texas Stadium, attendance 64,521. Emmitt Smith rushed for 172 yards on 23 carries to pace the Cowboys past the Eagles. Troy Aikman threw an 11-yard touchdown pass to Michael Irvin, and Eddie Murray kicked 3 field goals to help Dallas forge a 16-0 first-half lead. But the Eagles pulled within 6 points on Matt Bahr's 25-yard field goal on the last play of the first half, and Bubby Brister's 2-yard touchdown pass to tight end Mark Bavaro. Then Smith, who ran for a club-record 237 yards in a 23-10 victory over the Eagles five weeks earlier, broke off a 57-yard run to set up Daryl Johnston for the game-clinching, 2-yard touchdown run 5:44 into the fourth quarter. Brister added another touchdown pass late in the fourth quarter for the Eagles, and finished with 27 completions in 45 attempts for 248 yards.

| | | | | | | |
|---|---|---|---|---|---|---|
| **Philadelphia** | 0 | 3 | 7 | 7 | — | 17 |
| **Dallas** | 7 | 9 | 0 | 7 | — | 23 |

Dall — Irvin 11 pass from Aikman (Murray kick)
Dall — FG Murray 23
Dall — FG Murray 19
Dall — FG Murray 47
Phil — FG Bahr 25
Phil — Bavaro 2 pass from Brister (Bahr kick)
Dall — Johnston 2 run (Murray kick)
Phil — Bavaro 8 pass from Brister (Bahr kick)

## FIFTEENTH WEEK SUMMARIES

**AMERICAN FOOTBALL CONFERENCE**

| Eastern Division | W | L | T | Pct. | Pts. | OP |
|---|---|---|---|---|---|---|
| Buffalo | 9 | 4 | 0 | .692 | 236 | 184 |
| Miami | 9 | 4 | 0 | .692 | 268 | 226 |
| N.Y. Jets | 8 | 5 | 0 | .615 | 249 | 179 |
| Indianapolis | 4 | 9 | 0 | .308 | 169 | 290 |
| New England | 2 | 11 | 0 | .154 | 147 | 242 |
| **Central Division** | | | | | | |
| Houston | 9 | 4 | 0 | .692 | 308 | 214 |
| Pittsburgh | 8 | 5 | 0 | .615 | 269 | 230 |
| Cleveland | 6 | 7 | 0 | .462 | 236 | 257 |
| Cincinnati | 1 | 12 | 0 | .077 | 138 | 279 |
| **Western Division** | | | | | | |
| Kansas City | 9 | 4 | 0 | .692 | 256 | 213 |
| Denver | 8 | 5 | 0 | .615 | 320 | 231 |
| L.A. Raiders | 8 | 5 | 0 | .615 | 246 | 248 |
| San Diego | 6 | 7 | 0 | .462 | 221 | 225 |
| Seattle | 5 | 8 | 0 | .385 | 213 | 244 |

**NATIONAL FOOTBALL CONFERENCE**

| Eastern Division | W | L | T | Pct. | Pts. | OP |
|---|---|---|---|---|---|---|
| N.Y. Giants | 10 | 3 | 0 | .769 | 245 | 158 |
| Dallas | 9 | 4 | 0 | .692 | 294 | 206 |
| Philadelphia | 5 | 8 | 0 | .385 | 199 | 245 |
| Phoenix | 4 | 9 | 0 | .308 | 252 | 226 |
| Washington | 3 | 10 | 0 | .231 | 188 | 276 |
| **Central Division** | | | | | | |
| Detroit | 8 | 5 | 0 | .615 | 231 | 203 |
| Green Bay | 8 | 5 | 0 | .615 | 275 | 231 |
| Chicago | 7 | 6 | 0 | .538 | 211 | 177 |
| Minnesota | 6 | 7 | 0 | .462 | 212 | 254 |
| Tampa Bay | 4 | 9 | 0 | .308 | 183 | 307 |
| **Western Division** | | | | | | |
| San Francisco | 9 | 4 | 0 | .692 | 377 | 231 |
| New Orleans | 7 | 6 | 0 | .538 | 257 | 269 |
| Atlanta | 6 | 7 | 0 | .462 | 272 | 307 |
| L.A. Rams | 4 | 9 | 0 | .308 | 184 | 304 |

## SATURDAY, DECEMBER 11

**N.Y. JETS 3, WASHINGTON 0**—at RFK Stadium, attendance 47,970. Cary Blanchard's 45-yard field goal late in the first quarter accounted for the only points in the Jets' victory. New York failed to score a touchdown for the third consecutive week, but won for the second time in that span. The drought started with a 6-0 victory over the Patriots, followed by a 9-6 loss to the Colts. Blanchard accounted for all the points in the stretch with 5 field goals. Still, the Jets remained in the thick of the playoff hunt and pulled within one game of first place in the AFC East. They limited the Redskins to only 7 first downs while outgaining them 308-150, and maintained possession for 41 minutes. Johnny Johnson rushed for 155 yards on 32 carries. Washington quarterbacks Rich Gannon and Mark Rypien combined to complete only 9 of 23 passes for 79 yards.

| | | | | | | |
|---|---|---|---|---|---|---|
| **N.Y. Jets** | 3 | 0 | 0 | 0 | — | 3 |
| **Washington** | 0 | 0 | 0 | 0 | — | 0 |

Jets — FG Blanchard 45

**ATLANTA 27, SAN FRANCISCO 24**—at Georgia Dome, attendance 64,688. The Falcons stayed alive in the race for a wild-card playoff berth by rallying for 20 points in the fourth quarter to beat the 49ers. San Francisco appeared on the verge of its seventh consecutive victory when quarterback Steve Young, who passed for 268 yards and a touchdown, increased his team's lead to 24-7 by running 10 yards for a touchdown with 2:22 left in the third quarter. But Atlanta took the ensuing kickoff and marched 80 yards in 9 plays, the last a 1-yard touchdown pass from Bobby Hebert to Michael Haynes 1:23 into the fourth quarter. Midway through the period, 49ers return specialist Dexter Carter muffed a punt, giving Atlanta possession on San Francisco's 6-yard line. Three plays later, Hebert's 6-yard touchdown pass to Andre Rison pulled the Falcons within 24-21 with 6:48 to go. Norm Johnson's 47-yard field goal tied the game at 2:12 mark, and when Carter lost a fumble on the subsequent kickoff, Johnson was positioned for the winning field goal from 37 yards with 28 seconds left. Hebert completed 24 of 39 passes for 290 yards and 3 touchdowns. Two of his scoring tosses went to Andre Rison, who caught 6 passes for 107 yards. The 49ers' Jerry Rice caught 6 passes for 105 yards. Atlanta's Deion Sanders intercepted Young on San Francisco's first and last possessions of the game. The Falcons won for the sixth time in their last eight games.

| | | | | | | |
|---|---|---|---|---|---|---|
| **San Francisco** | 7 | 10 | 7 | 0 | — | 24 |
| **Atlanta** | 7 | 0 | 0 | 20 | — | 27 |

SF — Lee 6 pass from Young (Cofer kick)
Atl — Rison 5 pass from Hebert (Johnson kick)
SF — Rathman 2 run (Cofer kick)
SF — FG Cofer 32
SF — Young 10 run (Cofer kick)
Atl — Haynes 1 pass from Hebert (Johnson kick)
Atl — Rison 6 pass from Hebert (Johnson kick)
Atl — FG Johnson 47
Atl — FG Johnson 37

## SUNDAY, DECEMBER 12

**BUFFALO 10, PHILADELPHIA 7**—at Veterans Stadium, attendance 60,769. Steve Christie's 34-yard field goal with 2:18 remaining lifted the Bills past the Eagles. Buffalo's victory, coupled with Miami's loss to the Steelers the next night, left the Bills and Dolphins tied atop the AFC East. Philadelphia, which lost for the eighth time in its past nine games, led 7-0 and was driving toward another score in the fourth quarter when running back Heath Sherman fumbled at Buffalo's 29-yard line. Bills cornerback Mickey Washington recovered, and Buffalo marched 71 yards to the tying score, Frank Reich's 2-yard touchdown pass to tight end Pete Metzelaars with 3:44 remaining. Vai Sikahema fumbled on the ensuing kickoff, and Jerome Henderson recovered for the Bills at the Eagles' 22-yard line. Christie, who had missed 3 field-goal tries earlier in the game, converted his winning kick three plays later. Buffalo made its fourth-quarter rally without starting quarterback Jim Kelly and running back Thurman Thomas. Kelly, who completed 17 of 27 passes for 210 yards, sprained an ankle and left the game early in the final period. Thomas bruised his left forearm in the first quarter and gave way to Kenneth Davis, who ran for 70 yards on 18 carries. Wide receiver Bill Brooks had 10 receptions for 90 yards. Bubby Brister completed 28 of 48 passes for 299 yards and a touchdown for the Eagles, who had 366 total yards but were stymied by 4 lost fumbles. Running back Herschel Walker caught a career-high 11 passes for 109 yards.

| | | | | | | |
|---|---|---|---|---|---|---|
| **Buffalo** | 0 | 0 | 0 | 10 | — | 10 |
| **Philadelphia** | 0 | 0 | 7 | 0 | — | 7 |

Phil — C. Williams 19 pass from Brister (Bahr kick)
Buff — Metzelaars 2 pass from Reich (Christie kick)
Buff — FG Christie 34

**TAMPA BAY 13, CHICAGO 10**—at Tampa Stadium, attendance 56,667. The Buccaneers snapped Chicago's four-game winning streak, knocking the Bears out of a first-place tie in the NFC Central Division. Tampa Bay's Courtney Hawkins returned a punt 34 yards to set up Mazio Royster's 4-yard touchdown run in the second quarter, and Michael Husted kicked 2 field goals, including the decisive 42-yard kick late in the third quarter. The Bears' best chance after that was thwarted when running back Tim Worley was stopped on fourth-and-1 at the Buccaneers' 36-yard line with 9:26 left in the game. Chicago's only touchdown came after a 39-yard pass interference penalty positioned Neal Anderson for a 1-yard touchdown run. Kevin Butler had a 55-yard field goal to equal his career long. Bears starting quarterback Jim Harbaugh sat out the second half after bruising his throwing hand in the second quarter. He completed 11 of 18 passes for 81 yards in his abbreviated appearance. Backup Peter Tom Willis completed 11 of 18 for 86 yards.

| | | | | | | |
|---|---|---|---|---|---|---|
| **Chicago** | 0 | 3 | 7 | 0 | — | 10 |
| **Tampa Bay** | 3 | 7 | 3 | 0 | — | 13 |

TB — FG Husted 38
TB — Royster 4 run (Husted kick)
Chi — FG Butler 55
Chi — Anderson 1 run (Butler kick)
TB — FG Husted 42

**NEW ENGLAND 7, CINCINNATI 2**—at Foxboro Stadium, attendance 29,794. Drew Bledsoe's 8-yard pass to tight end Ben Coates 44 seconds before halftime accounted for the game's only touchdown and was enough for the Patriots to edge the Bengals. Cincinnati managed only 11 first downs and 165 total yards, but still had a chance to tie the score late in the game after New England punter Mike Saxon mishandled a snap from center. His hurried kick was blocked and the Bengals recovered at the Patriots' 30-yard line. They marched to the 1, but on fourth-and-goal with 1:21 remaining, running back Eric Ball was stopped for a 1-yard loss. Moments later, Saxon lined up to punt again, but Marv Cook intentionally snapped the ball out of the end zone for a safety with 19 seconds left.

| | | | | | | |
|---|---|---|---|---|---|---|
| **Cincinnati** | 0 | 0 | 0 | 2 | — | 2 |
| **New England** | 0 | 7 | 0 | 0 | — | 7 |

NE — Coates 8 pass from Bledsoe (Sisson kick)
Cin — Safety, ball snapped out of end zone

**HOUSTON 19, CLEVELAND 17**—at Astrodome, attendance 63,016. Al Del Greco kicked 4 field goals and the Oilers overcame an early 10-point deficit to win their eighth consecutive game. The Browns fell to 6-7 and clung only to slim wild-card playoff hopes. Cleveland scored on its first play from scrimmage, a 49-yard touchdown pass from Vinny Testaverde to running back Eric Metcalf, then added a 53-yard field goal by Matt Stover to take a 10-0 lead just 5:50 into the game. Houston rallied to go on top 16-10 at halftime, but Testaverde's second touchdown pass, a 28-yard toss to Mark Carrier 3:36 into the third quarter, put the Browns back on top 17-16. It still was a one-point game early in the fourth quarter when cornerback Cris Dishman intercepted Testaverde's pass at Cleveland's 39-yard line with 13:08 to go. A 20-yard pass interference penalty accounted for most of the yards on the Oilers' 32-yard march to Del Greco's 25-yard field goal with 10:39 remaining. Stover had a chance to win the game with a long field goal, but his 56-yard try in the final minutes was wide right. Houston won despite sputtering on offense in the second half. The Oilers managed only 257 total yards for the game, just 56 after intermission. Gary Brown rushed for 109 yards on 23 carries. The Browns, meanwhile, amassed 410 total yards, but turned the ball over 3 times. Testaverde, making his first start since separating his shoulder seven weeks earlier, completed 19 of 37 passes for 319 yards. Metcalf ran for 82 yards on 18 carries and caught 5 passes for 101 yards.

| | | | | | | |
|---|---|---|---|---|---|---|
| **Cleveland** | 10 | 0 | 7 | 0 | — | 17 |
| **Houston** | 3 | 13 | 0 | 3 | — | 19 |

Cle — Metcalf 49 pass from Testaverde (Stover kick)
Cle — FG Stover 53
Hou — FG Del Greco 27
Hou — FG Del Greco 48
Hou — Tillman 4 pass from Moon (Del Greco kick)
Hou — FG Del Greco 49
Cle — Carrier 28 pass from Testaverde (Stover kick)
Hou — FG Del Greco 25

**DALLAS 37, MINNESOTA 20**—at Metrodome, attendance 63,321. Emmitt Smith rushed for 104 yards and a touchdown, and Michael Irvin caught 8 passes for 125 yards and a score to power the Cowboys past the Vikings. Dallas scored on seven of its first eight possessions to build a 37-13 lead 5:30 into the fourth quarter. Minnesota led 6-3 until Irvin caught a 10-yard touchdown pass from Troy Aikman early in the second quarter to give the Cowboys the lead for good. That capped a 5-play, 74-yard drive on which Irvin had the key gain, a 37-yard reception. He had a 22-yard catch on Dallas's next series, another 74-yard march that culminated in Smith's 4-yard touchdown run with 5:15 left in the first half. Eddie Murray kicked a 52-yard field goal as time expired for a 20-6 lead at intermission. Daryl Johnston capped another lengthy drive, a 12-play, 73-yard march, with a 1-yard touchdown run midway through the third quarter to put the game out of reach. Aikman finished with 19 completions in 29 attempts for 208 yards, with no interceptions and no sacks. Minnesota quarterbacks Jim McMahon and Sean Salisbury combined to complete 20 of 25 passes for 178 yards. But the Vikings squandered their best chances early in the game, driving inside the Cowboys' 5-yard line on each of their first two possessions, but coming away with only 6 points on a pair of field goals by Fuad Reveiz.

| | | | | | | |
|---|---|---|---|---|---|---|
| **Dallas** | 3 | 17 | 7 | 10 | — | 37 |
| **Minnesota** | 6 | 0 | 7 | 7 | — | 20 |

Minn — FG Reveiz 19
Dall — FG Murray 51
Minn — FG Reveiz 21
Dall — Irvin 10 pass from Aikman (Murray kick)
Dall — E. Smith 4 run (Murray kick)
Dall — FG Murray 52
Dall — Johnston 1 run (Murray kick)
Minn — Graham 1 run (Reveiz kick)
Dall — FG Murray 46
Dall — Coleman 1 run (Murray kick)
Minn — A. Carter 9 pass from Salisbury (Reveiz kick)

**DETROIT 21, PHOENIX 14**—at Sun Devil Stadium, attendance 39,393. Erik Kramer, making his first start of the season, completed 19 of 25 passes for 257 yards and 3 touchdowns as the Lions remained tied with the Packers for first place in the NFC Central. Kramer, elevated to starter over Rodney Peete and Andre Ware earlier in the week, threw scoring passes of 6 yards to Herman Moore, 28 yards to tight end Rodney Holman, and 43 yards to Willie Green. The scoring pass to Green came 49 seconds into the fourth quarter and proved to be the decisive points. Late in the game, the Cardinals drove from their 9-yard to Detroit's 1, but failed to score. Defensive end Kelvin Pritchett threw Ron Moore for a 3-yard loss on second down, and cornerback Ryan McNeil intercepted Steve Beuerlein's pass at the goal line on fourth down. Beuerlein completed 23 of 35 passes for 219 yards, but was intercepted 3 times and sacked 4 times. Pritchett and end Robert Porcher each had 2 sacks. Dexter Moore rushed for 107 yards on 20 carries and caught 7 passes for 54 yards for the Lions.

| | | | | | | |
|---|---|---|---|---|---|---|
| **Detroit** | 0 | 7 | 7 | 7 | — | 21 |
| **Phoenix** | 0 | 7 | 7 | 0 | — | 14 |

Phx — Blount 6 run (Davis kick)
Det — H. Moore 6 pass from Kramer (Hanson kick)
Phx — R. Moore 1 run (Davis kick)
Det — Holman 28 pass from Kramer (Hanson kick)
Det — Green 43 pass from Kramer (Hanson kick)

**N.Y. GIANTS 20, INDIANAPOLIS 6**—at Giants Stadium, attendance 70,411. The Giants became the first team to clinch a playoff berth by methodically pounding the Colts. Rodney Hampton ran for a career-high 173 yards on 33 carries as New York garnered 205 of its 290 total yards on the ground, exploiting the NFL's lowest-rated rushing defense. The Giants marched 70 and 67 yards, most of it on the ground, to touchdowns the first two times they had the ball. Hampton had 116 yards on 16 carries as New York built a 13-6 advantage at halftime. The Giants then maintained possession for nearly 12 minutes of the third quarter, and finished the scoring on Jarrod Bunch's 2-yard touchdown run on the first play of the fourth quarter. Jeff George completed 22 of 38 passes for 254 yards for the Colts, but could not get his team into the end zone. New York qualified for the playoffs for the first time since 1990, when they went on to win Super Bowl XXV.

| | | | | | | |
|---|---|---|---|---|---|---|
| **Indianapolis** | 0 | 6 | 0 | 0 | — | 6 |
| **N.Y. Giants** | 7 | 6 | 0 | 7 | — | 20 |

Giants— Hampton 1 run (Treadwell kick)
Giants— Calloway 17 pass from Simms (kick failed)
Ind — FG Biasucci 21
Ind — FG Biasucci 26
Giants— Bunch 2 run (Treadwell kick)

**DENVER 27, KANSAS CITY 21**—at Mile High Stadium, attendance 75,822. John Elway's 3 touchdown passes to tight end Shannon Sharpe helped the Broncos pull within one game of the first-place Chiefs in the AFC West. Kansas City, trying to avoid its eleventh consecutive defeat at Mile High Stadium, jumped out to a 14-3 lead in the second quarter and still led 21-17 after Joe Montana teamed with Willie Davis on a 29-yard touchdown pass with 2:59 left in the third quarter. But early in the fourth period, Denver's Reggie Rivers blocked Bryan Barker's punt from the Chiefs' 42-yard line, and the Broncos took over on the 11. Three plays later, Elway's 6-yard touchdown pass to Sharpe gave the Broncos the lead for good. Jason Elam added a 53-yard field goal with 2:26 to go, and Kansas City could not get past its 46 on its final possession. Elway completed 20 of 30 passes for 221 yards and Rod Bernstine rushed for 90 yards on 23 carries for Denver. Sharpe caught 10 passes for 65 yards. Montana was 17 of 30 for 237 yards and 2 touchdowns for the Chiefs.

| | | | | | | |
|---|---|---|---|---|---|---|
| **Kansas City** | 7 | 7 | 7 | 0 | — | 21 |
| **Denver** | 3 | 7 | 7 | 10 | — | 27 |

KC — Hayes 11 pass from Montana (Lowery kick)
Den — FG Elam 36
KC — Allen 4 run (Lowery kick)
Den — Sharpe 9 pass from Elway (Elam kick)
Den — Sharpe 14 pass from Elway (Elam kick)
KC — Davis 29 pass from Montana (Lowery kick)
Den — Sharpe 6 pass from Elway (Elam kick)
Den — FG Elam 53

**L.A. RAMS 23, NEW ORLEANS 20**—at Louisiana Superdome, attendance 69,033. Rookie Jerome Bettis ran for 212 yards and a touchdown as the Rams stunned the Saints. Bettis averaged 7.6 yards on his 28 attempts while becoming the eighth rookie in NFL history to rush for more than 200 yards in a game. Among the previous seven, only Jim Brown (237 yards), Tom Wilson (223), and Bo Jackson (221) had more productive days. Remarkably, Bettis compiled his big numbers in only three quarters of play. He ran for 125 yards in the first quarter, including a 71-yard touchdown, but suffered a bruised abdomen and sat out the second period. While he was on the bench, New Orleans got a pair of field goals from Morten Andersen to take a 13-10 lead at halftime. But Fred McAfee fumbled the second-half kickoff and Rams rookie Deral Boykin picked up the loose ball and ran 6 yards for the go-ahead touchdown. Later in the quarter, Bettis carried 10 times for 51 yards on an 80-yard touchdown drive that gave Los Angeles a 23-13 advantage. Rams quarterback T.J. Rubley completed only 5 of 13 passes for 47 yards, but capped that march with an 11-yard touchdown pass to tight end Pat Carter. The Saints pulled within 3 points on Dalton Hilliard's 2-yard run 4:37 into the fourth quarter but could get no closer. The victory snapped Los Angeles's seven-game losing streak to the Saints. New Orleans dropped its sixth decision in eight games since starting the season 5-0.

| | | | | | | |
|---|---|---|---|---|---|---|
| **L.A. Rams** | 10 | 0 | 13 | 0 | — | 23 |
| **New Orleans** | 7 | 6 | 0 | 7 | — | 20 |

NO — Mills 30 fumble return (Andersen kick)
Rams — FG Zendejas 22
Rams — Bettis 71 run (Zendejas kick)
NO — FG Andersen 18
NO — FG Andersen 32
Rams — Boykin 6 fumble return (Zendejas kick)
Rams — Carter 11 pass from Rubley (kick failed)
NO — Hilliard 2 run (Andersen kick)

**L.A. RAIDERS 27, SEATTLE 23**—at Los Angeles Memorial Coliseum, attendance 38,161. Jeff Hostetler passed for 278 yards and a touchdown and the Raiders built a 27-9 lead in the third quarter, then withstood the Seahawks' comeback attempt. Los Angeles trailed 9-3 until taking the lead for good on Hostetler's 4-yard run with 32 seconds left in the first half. Just 1:45 into the second half, Tim Brown returned a punt 74 yards for a touchdown. Jeff Jaeger's 48-yard field goal and a 56-yard bomb from Hostetler to James Jett came just 98 seconds apart and gave the Raiders a seemingly insurmountable 18-point lead. But after Jaeger missed a 50-yard field-goal try early in the fourth quarter, Seattle quarterback Rick Mirer rallied his team, capping a 13-play, 68-yard drive by running 2 yards for a touchdown with 6:24 remaining. Cornerback James Jefferson intercepted a pass on Los Angeles's next possession, and the Seahawks launched another 13-play drive, this time for 57 yards to Mirer's 7-yard touchdown pass to Kelvin Martin. That cut Seattle's deficit to 4 points with 1:17 to go, and the Seahawks appeared to have a chance to win when safety Eugene Robinson recovered the ensuing onside kickoff. But Robinson was ruled to have gone out of bounds before recovering the ball, and the Raiders covered the subsequent try. Hostetler completed 18 of 25 attempts before leaving early in the fourth quarter with a twisted knee.

| | | | | | | |
|---|---|---|---|---|---|---|
| **Seattle** | 0 | 9 | 0 | 14 | — | 23 |
| **L.A. Raiders** | 3 | 7 | 17 | 0 | — | 27 |

Raid — FG Jaeger 24
Sea — C. Warren 1 run (Kasay kick)
Sea — Safety, Stephens tackled Bell in end zone
Raid — Hostetler 4 run (Jaeger kick)
Raid — Brown 74 punt return (Jaeger kick)
Raid — FG Jaeger 48
Raid — Jett 56 pass from Hostetler (Jaeger kick)
Sea — Mirer 2 run (Kasay kick)
Sea — Martin 7 pass from Mirer (Kasay kick)

## SUNDAY NIGHT, DECEMBER 12

**GREEN BAY 20, SAN DIEGO 13**—at San Diego Jack Murphy Stadium, attendance 57,930. The Packers maintained a share of first place in the NFC Central Division while all but eliminating the defending AFC Western Division-champion Chargers from the playoff picture. Edgar Bennett's short touchdown run and a pair of field goals by Chris Jacke staked Green Bay to a 13-6 halftime lead. San Diego marched to the Packers' 34-yard line on its first possession of the second half, but linebacker Tony Bennett sacked quarterback Stan Humphries for an 11-yard loss on fourth-and-4, and Green Bay took over on its 45-yard line. Twelve plays later, Darrell Thompson ran 5 yards for the touchdown that proved to be the decisive score. The Packers converted three consecutive third-down situations on the 55-yard drive. The Chargers tried to rally behind the passing of Humphries, who completed 27 of a career-high 51 attempts for 257 yards. But Humphries also was intercepted 3 times, and suffered from the absence of a running attack. After his 10-yard touchdown pass to Nate Lewis in the final minute of the third quarter trimmed San Diego's deficit to 7 points, the Chargers best chance to tie the game was thwarted when Natrone Means was stopped for no gain on fourth-and-1 from the Packers' 37 with 4:42 to go. Interceptions by Terrell Buckley and Mike Prior ended San Diego's hopes after that.

| | | | | | | |
|---|---|---|---|---|---|---|
| **Green Bay** | 7 | 6 | 7 | 0 | — | 20 |
| **San Diego** | 3 | 3 | 7 | 0 | — | 13 |

GB — E. Bennett 3 run (Jacke kick)
SD — FG Carney 47
GB — FG Jacke 51
GB — FG Jacke 42
SD — FG Carney 43
GB — Thompson 5 run (Jacke kick)
SD — Lewis 10 pass from Humphries (Carney kick)

## MONDAY, DECEMBER 13

**PITTSBURGH 21, MIAMI 20**—at Joe Robbie Stadium, attendance 73,882. Running back Leroy Thompson had 142 yards from scrimmage and the Steelers held off a fourth-quarter rally to defeat the Dolphins. Thompson, playing in place of injured Barry Foster, ran for 81 yards on 28 carries and caught 4 passes for 61 yards. He had touchdown runs of 1 and 3 yards as Pittsburgh built a 21-6 advantage early in the fourth quarter. But Dolphins quarterback Steve DeBerg threw a 3-yard touchdown pass to tight end Keith Jackson 4:30 into the final period, and when rookie O.J. McDuffie returned a punt 72 yards for a touchdown with 6:37 remaining, Miami trailed by only a point. The Dolphins had two chances after that, but a sack by safety Carnell Lake and cornerback Rod Woodson's interception ended the threats. The 39-year-old DeBerg completed 27 of 44 passes for 344 yards, but was intercepted twice and pressured throughout the game. Linebacker Greg Lloyd had 2 of the Steelers' 5 sacks.

| | | | | | | |
|---|---|---|---|---|---|---|
| **Pittsburgh** | 0 | 7 | 7 | 7 | — | 21 |
| **Miami** | 3 | 3 | 0 | 14 | — | 20 |

Mia — FG Stoyanovich 31
Pitt — Thompson 1 run (Anderson kick)
Mia — FG Stoyanovich 22
Pitt — Thompson 3 run (Anderson kick)
Pitt — Hoge 2 pass from O'Donnell (Anderson kick)
Mia — K. Jackson 3 pass from DeBerg (Stoyanovich kick)
Mia — McDuffie 72 punt return (Stoyanovich kick)

## SIXTEENTH WEEK SUMMARIES

**AMERICAN FOOTBALL CONFERENCE**

| Eastern Division | W | L | T | Pct. | Pts. | OP |
|---|---|---|---|---|---|---|
| Buffalo | 10 | 4 | 0 | .714 | 283 | 218 |
| Miami | 9 | 5 | 0 | .643 | 302 | 273 |
| N.Y. Jets | 8 | 6 | 0 | .571 | 256 | 207 |
| Indianapolis | 4 | 10 | 0 | .286 | 179 | 310 |
| New England | 3 | 11 | 0 | .214 | 167 | 259 |
| **Central Division** | | | | | | |
| Houston | 10 | 4 | 0 | .714 | 334 | 231 |
| Pittsburgh | 8 | 6 | 0 | .571 | 286 | 256 |
| Cleveland | 6 | 8 | 0 | .429 | 253 | 277 |
| Cincinnati | 2 | 12 | 0 | .143 | 153 | 282 |
| **Western Division** | | | | | | |
| Kansas City | 10 | 4 | 0 | .714 | 284 | 237 |
| Denver | 9 | 5 | 0 | .643 | 333 | 234 |
| L.A. Raiders | 9 | 5 | 0 | .643 | 273 | 268 |
| San Diego | 6 | 8 | 0 | .429 | 245 | 253 |
| Seattle | 5 | 9 | 0 | .357 | 240 | 274 |

**NATIONAL FOOTBALL CONFERENCE**

| Eastern Division | W | L | T | Pct. | Pts. | OP |
|---|---|---|---|---|---|---|
| N.Y. Giants | 11 | 3 | 0 | .786 | 269 | 172 |
| Dallas | 10 | 4 | 0 | .714 | 322 | 213 |
| Philadelphia | 6 | 8 | 0 | .429 | 219 | 255 |
| Phoenix | 5 | 9 | 0 | .357 | 282 | 253 |
| Washington | 4 | 10 | 0 | .286 | 218 | 293 |
| **Central Division** | | | | | | |
| Detroit | 8 | 6 | 0 | .571 | 248 | 258 |
| Green Bay | 8 | 6 | 0 | .571 | 292 | 252 |
| Chicago | 7 | 7 | 0 | .500 | 214 | 190 |
| Minnesota | 7 | 7 | 0 | .500 | 233 | 271 |
| Tampa Bay | 4 | 10 | 0 | .286 | 203 | 334 |
| **Western Division** | | | | | | |
| San Francisco | 10 | 4 | 0 | .714 | 432 | 248 |
| New Orleans | 7 | 7 | 0 | .500 | 271 | 293 |
| Atlanta | 6 | 8 | 0 | .429 | 289 | 337 |
| L.A. Rams | 4 | 10 | 0 | .286 | 187 | 319 |

## SATURDAY, DECEMBER 18

**DENVER 13, CHICAGO 3**—at Soldier Field, attendance 53,056. Rod Bernstine rushed for 103 yards in the rain and the mud at Soldier Field as the Broncos moved a step closer to the playoffs by beating the Bears. Bernstine's 15-yard run late in the first half set up the only touchdown of the game, Robert Delpino's 1-yard run 1:24 before halftime. That broke a 3-3 tie and came after linebacker Mike Croel sacked Chicago quarterback Peter Tom Willis and recovered Willis's fumble at the Bears' 16-yard line. Chicago turned over the ball 5 times, including 3 on interceptions thrown by Willis, who was playing because Jim Harbaugh was nursing a bruised hand. Willis completed just 14 of 29 passes for 120 yards and was sacked 4 times as the Bears could muster only 185 total yards. Denver didn't fare much better, totaling only 234 yards, but the Broncos scored 10 points off the turnovers. They tied the score at 3-3 midway through the second quarter after linebacker David Wyman recovered Tim Worley's fumble at Chicago's 11. Though Denver was unable to move the ball, Jason Elam kicked a 29-yard field goal. Elam added a 24-yard field goal with 7:02 left in the third quarter.

| | | | | | | |
|---|---|---|---|---|---|---|
| **Denver** | 0 | 10 | 3 | 0 | — | 13 |
| **Chicago** | 3 | 0 | 0 | 0 | — | 3 |

Chi — FG Butler 31
Den — FG Elam 29
Den — Delpino 1 run (Elam kick)
Den — FG Elam 24

**DALLAS 28, N.Y. JETS 7**—at Giants Stadium, attendance 73,109. Troy Aikman threw for 252 yards and 2 touchdowns as the defending Super Bowl-champion Cowboys wrapped up a playoff berth by beating the Jets. Though he was intercepted 3 times, Aikman completed 21 of 27 passes, and broke a scoreless tie by throwing a 42-yard touchdown pass to Michael Irvin 36 seconds before intermission. The pair hooked up again at the end of a 95-yard drive late in the third quarter, this time on a 3-yard touchdown with 1:23 to go in the period. Fifty-one seconds later, cornerback Kevin Smith put the game out of reach by intercepting Boomer Esiason's pass and returning it 32 yards for a touchdown. Brad Baxter's 1-yard scoring run 3:32 into the fourth quarter was New York's first touchdown in four games.

| | | | | | | |
|---|---|---|---|---|---|---|
| **Dallas** | 0 | 7 | 14 | 7 | — | 28 |
| **N.Y. Jets** | 0 | 0 | 0 | 7 | — | 7 |

Dall — Irvin 42 pass from Aikman (Murray kick)
Dall — Irvin 3 pass from Aikman (Murray kick)
Dall — K. Smith 32 interception return (Murray kick)
Jets — B. Baxter 1 run (Blanchard kick)
Dall — Johnston 4 run (Murray kick)

## SUNDAY, DECEMBER 19

**WASHINGTON 30, ATLANTA 17**—at RFK Stadium, attendance 50,192. Cornerback AJ Johnson and linebacker Monte Coleman scored touchdowns as the Redskins dealt the Falcons' playoff hopes a severe blow. Atlanta entered the game with six wins in eight games since an 0-5 start, but left clinging to slim chances for a wild-card berth despite dominating Washington statistically. The Falcons doubled the Redskins in first downs (22-8), plays (85-42), total yards (378-167), and time of possession (40:40-19:20). But they also committed 6 turnovers (to Washington's 2), and were whistled for 10 penalties (Washington had none). Coleman, whose 29-yard touchdown return of quarterback Bobby Hebert's fumble sealed the victory with 2:11 remaining in the game, also recorded a safety, tackling Atlanta punter Harold Alexander after Harper Le Bel's snap from the 26-yard line sailed high. Quarterback Mark Rypien's 1-yard run and Johnson's 69-yard interception return with nine seconds left in the first half put the Redskins ahead 16-7. The Falcons rallied to go back in front on Steve Broussard's 2-yard touchdown run and Norm Johnson's 41-yard field goal with 4:39 to go in the game. But Desmond Howard returned the ensuing kickoff 33 yards, then caught a 17-yard pass from Rypien to set up Earnest Byner's 8-yard touchdown run at the 3:06 mark. Fifty-five seconds later, defensive end Sterling Palmer sacked Hebert, forcing the fumble that Coleman returned for a touchdown. Hebert completed 24 of 42 passes for 233 yards and a touchdown for Atlanta, but suffered 4 interceptions and 7 sacks. Broussard rushed for 162 yards on 26 carries, and Mike Pritchard caught 8 passes for 92 yards and a touchdown. Coleman, Palmer, and defensive end Al Noga each had 2 sacks for Washington.

| | | | | | | |
|---|---|---|---|---|---|---|
| **Atlanta** | 7 | 0 | 7 | 3 | — | 17 |
| **Washington** | 0 | 16 | 0 | 14 | — | 30 |

Atl — Pritchard 29 pass from Hebert (Johnson kick)
Wash — Safety, Coleman tackled Alexander in end zone
Wash — Rypien 1 run (Lohmiller kick)
Wash — Johnson 69 interception return (Lohmiller kick)
Atl — Broussard 2 run (Johnson kick)
Atl — FG Johnson 41
Wash — Byner 8 run (Lohmiller kick)
Wash — Coleman 29 fumble return (Lohmiller kick)

**BUFFALO 47, MIAMI 34**—at Joe Robbie Stadium, attendance 71,597. Kenneth Davis rushed for 3 touchdowns and the Bills converted 5 takeaways into 28 points while routing the Dolphins in a battle for first place in the AFC East. Miami led 17-16 until Steve Christie's 32-yard field goal with 1:27 remaining in the first half gave Buffalo the lead for good and started an avalanche of points. Eight seconds after Christie's field goal, cornerback Mickey Washington intercepted Scott Mitchell's pass and returned it 27 yards for a touchdown and a 26-17 advantage. The Dolphins' Pete Stoyanovich kicked an 18-yard field goal as time ran out in the first half to trim the margin to six points, but the Bills scored 3 touchdowns in the first 5:59 of the second half to to turn the game into a rout. On the first play of the third quarter, linebacker Darryl Talley stripped the ball from Miami tight end Keith Jackson. Cornerback Nate Odomes picked up the loose ball and returned it 25 yards for a touchdown. Two plays later, safety Matt Darby's interception and 32-yard return set up Davis's third touchdown of the game, a 1-yard run for a 40-20 lead. Four plays after that, running back Keith Byars fumbled and Buffalo nose tackle Mike Lodish recovered at the Dolphins' 37-yard line. Jim Kelly's 28-yard touchdown pass to Don Beebe made it 47-20. In all, the Bills scored 31 points in a span of 7:26, with each touchdown resulting from a turnover. Steve DeBerg tried to rally Miami with 2 touchdown passes, but after the Dolphins drove to Buffalo's 27-yard line midway through the fourth quarter, an interception by Odomes secured the victory for the Bills. Miami rolled up 424 total yards, but managed only 23 yards on the ground. Mitchell threw for 156 yards, and DeBerg completed 20 of 35 passes for 273 yards in less than two quarters of play. Running back Terry Kirby caught 9 passes for 148 yards. Kelly completed 20 of 30 passes for 245 yards for the Bills. Davis rushed for 64 yards on 13 carries.

| | | | | | | |
|---|---|---|---|---|---|---|
| **Buffalo** | 9 | 17 | 21 | 0 | — | 47 |
| **Miami** | 7 | 13 | 7 | 7 | — | 34 |

Buff — K. Davis 1 run (kick failed)
Mia — Ingram 14 pass from Mitchell (Stoyanovich kick)
Buff — FG Christie 38
Mia — FG Stoyanovich 41
Mia — Jackson 16 pass from Mitchell (Stoyanovich kick)
Buff — K. Davis 12 run (Christie kick)
Buff — FG Christie 32
Buff — M. Washington 27 interception return (Christie kick)
Mia — FG Stoyanovich 18
Buff — Odomes 25 fumble return (Christie kick)
Buff — K. Davis 1 run (Christie kick)
Buff — Beebe 28 pass from Kelly (Christie kick)
Mia — Kirby 30 pass from DeBerg (Stoyanovich kick)
Mia — Ingram 7 pass from DeBerg (Stoyanovich kick)

**HOUSTON 26, PITTSBURGH 17**—at Three Rivers Stadium, attendance 57,592. The Oilers completed a dramatic turnaround by beating the Steelers to clinch the AFC Central title. After starting the season 1-4, Houston won its ninth consecutive game, six of them against division rivals. The Oilers quieted the Three Rivers Stadium crowd early in this one, marching 80 yards in 8 plays, the last a 38-yard screen pass from Warren Moon to Gary Brown, to take a 7-0 lead just 3:53 into the game. Three plays later, Houston safety Bo Orlando intercepted Neil O'Donnell's pass and returned it 38 yards for a touchdown and a 14-0 advantage. The Oilers led 20-0 before 1992 division champ Pittsburgh scored. Brown rushed for 100 yards on 20 carries and caught 4 passes for 80 yards. Moon passed for 268 yards. O'Donnell and Mike Tomczak combined for 400 passing yards for the Steelers, but completed only 24 of 57 passes and were intercepted twice. Jeff Graham caught 7 passes for 192 yards. Houston's victory was tempered by the death of defensive tackle Jeff Alm earlier in the week.

| | | | | | | |
|---|---|---|---|---|---|---|
| **Houston** | 14 | 6 | 3 | 3 | — | 26 |
| **Pittsburgh** | 0 | 3 | 7 | 7 | — | 17 |

Hou — G. Brown 38 pass from Moon (Del Greco kick)
Hou — Orlando 38 interception return (Del Greco kick)
Hou — FG Del Greco 34
Hou — FG Del Greco 22
Pitt — FG Anderson 26
Hou — FG Del Greco 33
Pitt — Green 36 pass from O'Donnell (Anderson kick)
Hou — FG Del Greco 21
Pitt — Hoge 5 run (Anderson kick)

**CINCINNATI 15, L.A. RAMS 3**—at Riverfront Stadium, attendance 36,612. David Klingler passed for a career-high 223 yards and the Bengals compiled a season-high 393 total yards en route to beating the Rams. Cincinnati, which entered the game 1-12 and ranked last in the league in total offense, got a season-high 170 yards on the ground to complement Klingler's passing. Derrick Fenner rushed for 89 yards on 15 carries and Harold Green added 76 yards on 18 attempts. Fenner scored the game's only touchdown on a 1-yard run in the second quarter. Doug Pelfrey kicked 3 field goals, 2 in the second half to secure the victory. Los Angeles's Jerome Bettis had his fourth consecutive 100-yard game, gaining 124 yards on 24 attempts. The rookie took over the league lead with 1,227 yards.

| | | | | | | |
|---|---|---|---|---|---|---|
| **L.A. Rams** | 0 | 3 | 0 | 0 | — | 3 |
| **Cincinnati** | 3 | 6 | 3 | 3 | — | 15 |

Cin — FG Pelfrey 43
Cin — Fenner 1 run (kick failed)
Rams — FG Zendejas 32
Cin — FG Pelfrey 28
Cin — FG Pelfrey 25

**MINNESOTA 21, GREEN BAY 17**—at Milwaukee County Stadium, attendance 54,773. Jim McMahon threw 3 touchdown passes as the Vikings kept their playoff hopes alive by beating the Packers. McMahon, who completed 22 of 31 passes for 207 yards, erased Minnesota's 10-7 halftime deficit by teaming with Cris Carter on scoring plays of 6 and 25 yards. The veteran quarterback also tossed a 6-yard touchdown pass to Qadry Ismail early in the second quarter. Down 21-10 in the fourth quarter, Green Bay rallied, pulling within 4 points on Brett Favre's 11-yard touchdown pass to Mark Clayton with 5:51 left in the game. Minutes later, the Packers marched to a first-and-goal at the Vikings' 2-yard line. But Minnesota held, with safety Vencie Glenn knocking down Favre's fourth-down pass in the end zone with 1:14 remaining. Glenn also had an interception in the final minute to wrap up the victory. Vikings running back Scottie Graham, pressed into duty because of injuries, carried 30 times for 139 yards, just 6 short of his season total. Carter caught 6 passes for 106 yards. Green Bay wide receiver Sterling Sharpe also caught 6 passes for 106 yards. Favre completed 20 of 33 passes for 256 yards.

| | | | | | | |
|---|---|---|---|---|---|---|
| **Minnesota** | 0 | 7 | 7 | 7 | — | 21 |
| **Green Bay** | 3 | 7 | 0 | 7 | — | 17 |

GB — FG Jacke 20
Minn — Ismail 6 pass from McMahon (Reveiz kick)
GB — Sharpe 37 pass from Favre (Jacke kick)
Minn — C. Carter 6 pass from McMahon (Reveiz kick)
Minn — C. Carter 25 pass from McMahon (Reveiz kick)
GB — Clayton 11 pass from Favre (Jacke kick)

**NEW ENGLAND 20, CLEVELAND 17**—at Municipal Stadium, attendance 48,618. Leonard Russell's 4-yard touchdown run with 2:02 remaining lifted the Patriots to the victory and knocked the Browns out of the playoff picture. Cleveland led 17-13 and was driving to the apparent game-clinching touchdown when Vinny Testaverde's pass in the end zone was intercepted by New England safety Dion Lambert with 4:50 remaining. The Patriots then embarked on the winning 10-play, 80-yard drive, the key gain a 49-yard run by Kevin Turner. After Russell's touchdown run, any Browns' hopes were quashed when cornerback Maurice Hurst intercepted Testaverde's pass on the next play from scrimmage. Despite the 2 late thefts, Testaverde was productive, completing 21 of 31 passes for 297 yards and 2 touchdowns. Cleveland running back Eric Metcalf rushed for 48 yards and caught 8 passes for 81 yards. The Browns lost for the sixth time in the last seven games and missed the playoffs despite a 5-2 start.

| | | | | | | |
|---|---|---|---|---|---|---|
| **New England** | 0 | 10 | 3 | 7 | — | 20 |
| **Cleveland** | 7 | 7 | 0 | 3 | — | 17 |

Cle — McCardell 10 pass from Testaverde (Stover kick)
NE — FG Bahr 23
Cle — McCardell 10 pass from Testaverde (Stover kick)
NE — K. Turner 6 pass from Bledsoe (Bahr kick)
NE — FG Bahr 34
Cle — FG Stover 23
NE — Russell 4 run (Bahr kick)

**PHOENIX 30, SEATTLE 27**—at Kingdome, attendance 45,737. Greg Davis tied the game with a club-record 55-yard field goal as time ran out in regulation, then won it with a 41-yard kick 6:45 into overtime. Davis also kicked a 50-yard field goal to give the Cardinals a 24-20 lead with 5:09 to go in the fourth quarter. The Seahawks rallied, marching 93 yards in 15 plays to take a 27-24 advantage on quarterback Rick Mirer's 1-yard sneak for a touchdown. But 1:22 still remained, and Steve Beuerlein's 17-yard pass to Gary Clark positioned Davis for the tying kick. Phoenix took the kickoff in the extra session and drove 57 yards in 13 plays to the winning score. Beuerlein teamed with Clark and Anthony Edwards on key third-down completions. The Cardinals' quarterback completed 34 of 53 passes for 431 yards and 3 touchdowns. Clark caught 12 passes for 152 yards. Chris Warren carried 27 times for 168 yards, including a 45-yard touchdown 1:13 into the game, for Seattle. Mirer passed for 165 yards, giving him 2,576 yards for the season. He broke former Seahawks quarterback Jim Zorn's NFL record for passing yards by a rookie.

| | | | | | | | |
|---|---|---|---|---|---|---|---|
| **Phoenix** | 7 | 0 | 7 | 13 | 3 | — | 30 |
| **Seattle** | 10 | 10 | 0 | 7 | 0 | — | 27 |

Sea — Warren 45 run (Kasay kick)
Sea — FG Kasay 37
Phx — R. Hill 58 pass from Beuerlein (G. Davis kick)
Sea — FG Kasay 47
Sea — Edmunds 1 pass from Mirer (Kasay kick)
Phx — Clark 20 pass from Beuerlein (G. Davis kick)
Phx — Centers 16 pass from Beuerlein (G. Davis kick)
Phx — FG G. Davis 50
Sea — Mirer 1 run (Kasay kick)
Phx — FG G. Davis 55
Phx — FG G. Davis 41

**KANSAS CITY 28, SAN DIEGO 24**—at Arrowhead Stadium, attendance 74,778. The Chiefs rallied from a 17-point deficit to defeat the Chargers and maintain their hold on first place in the AFC West. San Diego jumped out to a 10-0 lead 3:47 into the game by converting an interception and a fumble recovery into Stan Humphries's 28-yard touchdown pass to Ronnie Harmon and John Carney's 38-yard field goal. Humphries was forced to leave the game with a concussion, but backup John Friesz threw a 3-yard touchdown pass to tight end Duane Young on the first play of the second quarter, increasing the Chargers' advantage to 17-0. Kansas City responded with touchdown drives of 77 and 66 yards to trim the margin to 17-14 by halftime, then took the lead for good on Joe Montana's 4-yard touchdown pass to J.J. Birden with 4:39 remaining in the third quarter. Montana also was forced from the game with a concussion, but Dave Krieg came on to throw a 28-yard touchdown pass to Willie Davis 2:06 into the fourth quarter for the decisive points.

| | | | | | | |
|---|---|---|---|---|---|---|
| **San Diego** | 10 | 7 | 0 | 7 | — | 24 |
| **Kansas City** | 0 | 14 | 7 | 7 | — | 28 |

SD — Harmon 28 pass from Humphries (Carney kick)
SD — FG Carney 38
SD — Young 3 pass from Friesz (Carney kick)
KC — Allen 1 run (Lowery kick)
KC — Davis 9 pass from Montana (Lowery kick)
KC — Birden 4 pass from Montana (Lowery kick)
KC — Davis 28 pass from Krieg (Lowery kick)
SD — Means 2 run (Carney kick)

**SAN FRANCISCO 55, DETROIT 17**—at Pontiac Silverdome, attendance 77,052. Steve Young threw 4 touchdown passes and the 49ers exploded for 565 total yards while wrapping up their tenth division championship in the last 12 years. San Francisco dominated from the start, scoring on a 68-yard pass from Young to Taylor on its third play from scrimmage. The 49ers did not punt, and scored on every possession except the two when time ran out in the first half and in the game. Young completed 17 of 23 passes for 354 yards in less than three quarters of play. Jerry Rice caught 4 passes for 132 yards and a touchdown, while Taylor had 4 receptions for 115 yards. Amp Lee rushed for 66 yards and caught 6 passes for 50 yards, including a 12-yard touchdown. Tom Rathman had 2 short scoring runs. Erik Kramer passed for 220 yards and 2 touchdowns for the Lions, who remained tied with the Packers atop the NFC Central.

| | | | | | | |
|---|---|---|---|---|---|---|
| **San Francisco** | 14 | 17 | 14 | 10 | — | 55 |
| **Detroit** | 0 | 10 | 0 | 7 | — | 17 |

SF — Taylor 68 pass from Young (Cofer kick)
SF — Beach 20 pass from Young (Cofer kick)
Det — FG Hanson 51
SF — Rice 80 pass from Young (Cofer kick)
SF — Rathman 2 run (Cofer kick)
SF — FG Cofer 43
Det — D. Moore 12 pass from Kramer (Hanson kick)
SF — Rathman 1 run (Cofer kick)
SF — Lee 12 pass from Young (Cofer kick)
SF — FG Cofer 21
Det — H. Moore 31 pass from Kramer (Hanson kick)
SF — Carter 50 run (Cofer kick)

**L.A. RAIDERS 27, TAMPA BAY 20**—at Los Angeles Memorial Coliseum, attendance 40,532. The Raiders converted a pair of fumble recoveries into the key touchdowns in their victory over the Buccaneers. Los Angeles led 7-0 in the first quarter when defensive end Greg Townsend sacked Tampa Bay quarterback Craig Erickson, forcing a fumble that was recovered by defensive tackle Chester McGlockton at the Buccaneers' 5-yard line. Napoleon McCallum ran for a touchdown on the next play to increase the Raiders' lead to 14-0. It was 20-10 in the fourth quarter when cornerback Torin Dorn forced Cobb to fumble, and end Aundray Bruce recovered at Tampa Bay's 16. Four plays later, Hostetler ran 1 yard for the decisive points. Los Angeles managed only 17 rushing yards, but Hostetler completed 19 of 30 passes for 260 yards. Alexander Wright caught 6 passes for 104 yards, including a 27-yard touchdown. Erickson completed 21 of 34 passes for 295 yards for the Buccaneers. Michael Husted's 57-yard field goal

10 seconds before halftime was the longest in franchise history.

| | | | | | | |
|---|---|---|---|---|---|---|
| **Tampa Bay** | 0 | 10 | 0 | 10 | — | 20 |
| **L.A. Raiders** | 14 | 3 | 0 | 10 | — | 27 |

Raid — Wright 27 pass from Hostetler (Jaeger kick)
Raid — McCallum 5 run (Jaeger kick)
TB — Cobb 5 run (Husted kick)
Raid — FG Jaeger 50
TB — FG Husted 57
Raid — FG Jaeger 33
Raid — Hostetler 1 run (Jaeger kick)
TB — Cobb 2 run (Husted kick)
TB — FG Husted 31

## SUNDAY NIGHT, DECEMBER 19

**PHILADELPHIA 20, INDIANAPOLIS 10**—at Hoosier Dome, attendance 44,952. The Eagles kept their slim playoff hopes alive by beating the Colts. Bubby Brister passed for 217 yards, including a 14-yard touchdown to Calvin Williams to break open the game. Philadelphia led 10-3 at halftime, but Eagles defensive tackle William Perry sacked Indianapolis quarterback Jeff George midway through the third quarter, forcing a fumble that linebacker William Thomas recovered. One play later, Brister and Williams teamed on the touchdown that made it 17-3. Philadelphia sacked George 4 times and forced 3 fumbles. The Eagles converted a first-quarter fumble by wide receiver Jessie Hester into a 21-yard field goal by Roger Ruzek. The Colts snapped a 20-quarter touchdown drought when George threw a 24-yard scoring pass to Reggie Langhorne with 4:18 to go in the game.

| | | | | | | |
|---|---|---|---|---|---|---|
| **Philadelphia** | 10 | 0 | 7 | 3 | — | 20 |
| **Indianapolis** | 3 | 0 | 0 | 7 | — | 10 |

Phil — FG Ruzek 21
Phil — Sherman 1 run (Ruzek kick)
Ind — FG Biasucci 39
Phil — Williams 14 pass from Brister (Ruzek kick)
Phil — FG Ruzek 25
Ind — Langhorne 24 pass from George (Biasucci kick)

## MONDAY, DECEMBER 20

**N.Y. GIANTS 24, NEW ORLEANS 14**—at Louisiana Superdome, attendance 69,036. Phil Simms threw 2 touchdown passes and David Meggett returned a punt 75 yards for a touchdown to lead the Giants past the slumping Saints. New York won its sixth in a row, while New Orleans lost its seventh in the last nine. After beginning the season 5-0, the Saints were in danger of falling out of the playoff chase. Simms, who completed 15 of 23 attempts for 166 yards, teamed with Mark Jackson on a 9-yard touchdown pass 10:15 into the game, then capped a 96-yard drive with a 17-yard touchdown pass to tight end Howard Cross to give the Giants a 14-0 advantage midway through the second quarter. It was 17-7 when Meggett effectively ended any doubts about the outcome with his punt return for a touchdown with 11:13 to go in the game.

| | | | | | | |
|---|---|---|---|---|---|---|
| **N.Y. Giants** | 7 | 7 | 3 | 7 | — | 24 |
| **New Orleans** | 0 | 7 | 0 | 7 | — | 14 |

Giants— M. Jackson 9 pass from Simms (Treadwell kick)
Giants— Cross 17 pass from Simms (Treadwell kick)
NO — Muster 1 run (Andersen kick)
Giants— FG Treadwell 22
Giants— Meggett 75 punt return (Treadwell kick)
NO — Hilliard 5 pass from Buck (Andersen kick)

## SEVENTEENTH WEEK SUMMARIES

**AMERICAN FOOTBALL CONFERENCE**

| Eastern Division | W | L | T | Pct. | Pts. | OP |
|---|---|---|---|---|---|---|
| Buffalo | 11 | 4 | 0 | .733 | 299 | 232 |
| Miami | 9 | 6 | 0 | .600 | 322 | 318 |
| N.Y. Jets | 8 | 7 | 0 | .533 | 270 | 223 |
| Indianapolis | 4 | 11 | 0 | .267 | 179 | 348 |
| New England | 4 | 11 | 0 | .267 | 205 | 259 |
| **Central Division** | | | | | | |
| Houston | 11 | 4 | 0 | .733 | 344 | 238 |
| Pittsburgh | 8 | 7 | 0 | .533 | 292 | 272 |
| Cleveland | 7 | 8 | 0 | .467 | 295 | 291 |
| Cincinnati | 3 | 12 | 0 | .200 | 174 | 299 |
| **Western Division** | | | | | | |
| Kansas City | 10 | 5 | 0 | .667 | 294 | 267 |
| Denver | 9 | 6 | 0 | .600 | 343 | 251 |
| L.A. Raiders | 9 | 6 | 0 | .600 | 273 | 296 |
| San Diego | 7 | 8 | 0 | .467 | 290 | 273 |
| Seattle | 6 | 9 | 0 | .400 | 256 | 280 |

**NATIONAL FOOTBALL CONFERENCE**

| Eastern Division | W | L | T | Pct. | Pts. | OP |
|---|---|---|---|---|---|---|
| Dallas | 11 | 4 | 0 | .733 | 360 | 216 |
| N.Y. Giants | 11 | 4 | 0 | .733 | 275 | 189 |
| Philadelphia | 7 | 8 | 0 | .467 | 256 | 281 |
| Phoenix | 6 | 9 | 0 | .400 | 299 | 259 |
| Washington | 4 | 11 | 0 | .267 | 221 | 331 |
| **Central Division** | | | | | | |
| Detroit | 9 | 6 | 0 | .600 | 268 | 272 |
| Green Bay | 9 | 6 | 0 | .600 | 320 | 252 |
| Minnesota | 8 | 7 | 0 | .533 | 263 | 281 |
| Chicago | 7 | 8 | 0 | .467 | 228 | 210 |
| Tampa Bay | 5 | 10 | 0 | .333 | 220 | 344 |
| **Western Division** | | | | | | |
| San Francisco | 10 | 5 | 0 | .667 | 439 | 258 |
| New Orleans | 7 | 8 | 0 | .467 | 297 | 330 |
| Atlanta | 6 | 9 | 0 | .400 | 306 | 358 |
| L.A. Rams | 4 | 11 | 0 | .267 | 201 | 361 |

## SATURDAY, DECEMBER 25

**HOUSTON 10, SAN FRANCISCO 7**—at Candlestick Park, attendance 61,744. The game matched the NFL's two highest scoring teams, but it was defense that carried the Oilers to the victory. Al Del Greco kicked a 24-yard field goal and Warren Moon threw a 7-yard touchdown pass to Ernest Givins to give Houston all the points it needed in the second quarter. From there, the Oilers' defense took over, using a steady stream of blitzes to knock the 49ers' number-one ranked offense off-balance. San Francisco didn't score until backup quarterback Steve Bono took over for Steve Young late in the third quarter. Bono's first drive was a 12-play, 73-yard march that resulted in Amp Lee's 8-yard touchdown run 2:49 into the fourth quarter. But the 49ers could not score again, and did not get the ball back after punting with 6:49 remaining in the game. Young completed 15 of 29 passes for 178 yards and was intercepted twice. Bono was 11 of 13 for 79 yards in his limited duty. Jerry Rice caught 10 passes for 83 yards. Moon completed only 11 of 26 attempts for 158 yards, with 3 interceptions. Gary Brown rushed for 114 yards on 19 carries. The Oilers won their tenth consecutive game and snapped the 49ers' club-record 13-game regular-season home winning streak.

| | | | | | | |
|---|---|---|---|---|---|---|
| **Houston** | 0 | 10 | 0 | 0 | — | 10 |
| **San Francisco** | 0 | 0 | 0 | 7 | — | 7 |

Hou — FG Del Greco 24
Hou — Givins 7 pass from Moon (Del Greco kick)
SF — Lee 8 run (Cofer kick)

## SUNDAY, DECEMBER 26

**CINCINNATI 21, ATLANTA 17**—at Riverfront Stadium, attendance 47,014. David Klingler threw a career-high 3 touchdown passes, including the game winner to Carl Pickens with one minute left, to lift the Bengals to the victory. Pickens' 6-yard touchdown catch was his second of the game. He also had a 24-yard scoring reception to give Cincinnati a 14-7 advantage late in the first half. The Falcons, fighting to stay alive in the playoff race, rallied behind a 49-yard field goal by Norm Johnson and Erric Pegram's 1-yard touchdown run to take a 17-14 lead with 6:58 to go in the game. But the Bengals countered with the game-winning drive, which covered 70 yards in 8 plays, the key gain Klingler's 26-yard scramble. Cincinnati cornerback Rod Jones ended Atlanta's last threat with an interception in the closing seconds. Klingler finished with 16 completions in 30 attempts for 174 yards. Pegram led all rushers with 180 yards on 37 carries. The Bengals won their third in a row at Riverfront Stadium. The Falcons, who won six of seven games after an 0-5 start to climb into playoff contention, were eliminated from the wild-card chase.

| | | | | | | |
|---|---|---|---|---|---|---|
| **Atlanta** | 7 | 0 | 3 | 7 | — | 17 |
| **Cincinnati** | 7 | 7 | 0 | 7 | — | 21 |

Atl — Rison 21 pass from Hebert (Johnson kick)
Cin — Thompson 3 pass from Klingler (Pelfrey kick)
Cin — Pickens 24 pass from Klingler (Pelfrey kick)
Atl — FG Johnson 49
Cin — Pickens 6 pass from Klingler (Pelfrey kick)
Atl — Pegram 1 run (Johnson kick)

**CLEVELAND 42, L.A. RAMS 14**—at Anaheim Stadium, attendance 34,155. Vinny Testaverde set an NFL record by completing 21 of 23 passes in the Browns' victory. Testaverde's completion percentage of .913 broke the old mark of .909 held by Cincinnati's Ken Anderson, who was 20 of 22 in a game against Pittsburgh in 1974. Testaverde passed for 216 yards, including touchdowns of 8 and 28 yards to Keenan McCardell, helping stake Cleveland to a 21-7 lead through three quarters. The Browns broke open the game with 3 touchdowns in a span of 4:13 early in the fourth period. Mark Carrier returned a punt 56 yards for a touchdown with 8:04 left in the game, Randy Hilliard's interception and 54-yard return set up Tommy Vardell's 1-yard touchdown run with 6:14 to go, and Selwyn Jones's fumble recovery on the ensuing kickoff positioned Kevin Mack for a 1-yard touchdown run with 3:51 remaining. The Rams outgained Cleveland 382-315, but much of that came after the issue was decided. Los Angeles quarterback T.J. Rubley completed 24 of 32 passes for 294 yards, including a 23-yard touchdown pass to Willie Anderson. Henry Ellard caught 8 passes for 114 yards. Jerome Bettis, who entered the game as the NFL's leading rusher, was limited to 56 yards on 16 carries.

| | | | | | | |
|---|---|---|---|---|---|---|
| **Cleveland** | 7 | 7 | 7 | 21 | — | 42 |
| **L.A. Rams** | 7 | 0 | 0 | 7 | — | 14 |

Rams — Bettis 1 run (Zendejas kick)
Cle — Vardell 1 run (Stover kick)
Cle — McCardell 8 pass from Testaverde (Stover kick)
Cle — McCardell 28 pass from Testaverde (Stover kick)
Cle — Carrier 56 punt return (Stover kick)
Cle — Vardell 1 run (Stover kick)
Cle — Mack 1 run (Stover kick)
Rams — Anderson 23 pass from Rubley (Zendejas kick)

**DETROIT 20, CHICAGO 14**—at Soldier Field, attendance 43,443. Erik Kramer's 1-yard touchdown pass to tight end Ty Hallock with 3:04 remaining clinched a playoff berth for the Lions, eliminated the Bears, and set up Detroit's showdown with the Packers for the NFC Central Division title one week later. Quarterback Jim Harbaugh's 1-yard dive 4:39 into the fourth quarter had given Chicago a 14-13 lead. But the Lions countered with a 12-play, 80-yard drive that took 7:17 off the clock, capping the march with Kramer's second touchdown pass of the game. The division rivals squared off in 13-degree temperatures with a wind-chill factor of minus-1. The Bears took the opening kickoff and maintained possession for 10:19, driving 65 yards in 16 plays to Tim Worley's 1-yard touchdown run. Detroit didn't get the ball until only 4:41 remained in the first quarter, but promptly reeled off a touchdown drive that lasted nearly seven minutes, finishing it off with Kramer's 20-yard scoring pass to Brett Perriman early in the second quarter. Despite the freezing conditions, Kramer completed 23 of 31 passes for 223 yards. Eric Lynch, playing only because of injuries to Barry Sanders and Derrick Moore, rushed for 85 yards and caught 7 passes for 46 yards. Chicago's offense faltered after its impressive opening drive, finishing with only 187 total yards.

| | | | | | | |
|---|---|---|---|---|---|---|
| **Detroit** | 0 | 10 | 3 | 7 | — | 20 |
| **Chicago** | 7 | 0 | 0 | 7 | — | 14 |

Chi — Worley 1 run (Butler kick)
Det — Perriman 20 pass from Kramer (Hanson kick)
Det — FG Hanson 40
Det — FG Hanson 37
Chi — Harbaugh 1 run (Butler kick)
Det — Hallock 1 pass from Kramer (Hanson kick)

**NEW ENGLAND 38, INDIANAPOLIS 0**—at Foxboro Stadium, attendance 26,571. Leonard Russell ran for 2 touchdowns and Drew Bledsoe passed for 2 as the Patriots posted their biggest rout in 14 years. Russell gained 97 yards in the first quarter and finished with 138 yards on 26 carries. Backfield mate Corey Croom rushed for 93 yards on 21 carries. Bolstered by 257 rushing yards, Bledsoe attempted only 11 passes. He completed 9 for 143 yards, including touchdowns of 1 yard to tight end Marv Cook and 30 yards to Michael Timpson. The statistics reflected the one-sidedness of the game: New England had 24 first downs to 7 for the Colts, limited Indianapolis to only 37 rushing yards and 99 passing yards, outgained the Colts 400-136, and maintained possession for 38:28. Wind gusts of up to 43 miles per hour produced a wind-chill factor of minus-21.

| | | | | | | |
|---|---|---|---|---|---|---|
| **Indianapolis** | 0 | 0 | 0 | 0 | — | 0 |
| **New England** | 7 | 10 | 14 | 7 | — | 38 |

NE — Russell 2 run (Bahr kick)
NE — FG Bahr 19
NE — Cook 1 pass from Bledsoe (Bahr kick)
NE — Timpson 30 pass from Bledsoe (Bahr kick)
NE — Russell 3 run (Bahr kick)
NE — Croom 5 run (Bahr kick)

**GREEN BAY 28, L.A. RAIDERS 0**—at Lambeau Field, attendance 54,482. The Packers sealed a playoff berth by breaking open a close game in the second half and beating the Raiders in zero-degree temperature. The game was scoreless until late in the first half, when Edgar Bennett capped a 48-yard drive with a 1-yard touchdown run just 1:01 before intermission. Green Bay then marched 74 yards with its first possession of the third quarter, increasing its lead to 14-0 on Brett Favre's 23-yard touchdown pass to Sterling Sharpe, who had 7 catches for 119 yards. Sharpe raised his season total to 106 receptions and became the first player in NFL history to record two seasons of more than 100. He also was on pace to break his season mark of 108 catches, which he set in 1992. Turnovers resulted in Green Bay's last 2 touchdowns, which came 1:50 apart early in the fourth quarter. Defensive end Reggie White scooped up a fumble forced by safety LeRoy Butler and ran 10 yards before lateraling to Butler, who scampered the remaining 25 yards for a score. Linebacker Wayne Simmons's interception preceded Darrell Thompson's 60-yard touchdown run. Thompson finished with 101 yards on 21 carries. Raiders quarterback Jeff Hostetler completed only 7 of 18 passes for 56 yards before leaving the game with a slight concussion early in the third quarter. Hostetler and backup Vince Evans were sacked 8 times. White, nose tackle John Jurkovic, and linebacker Tony Bennett each were credited with 2.5 sacks.

| | | | | | | |
|---|---|---|---|---|---|---|
| **L.A. Raiders** | 0 | 0 | 0 | 0 | — | 0 |
| **Green Bay** | 0 | 7 | 7 | 14 | — | 28 |

GB — E. Bennett 1 run (Jacke kick)
GB — Sharpe 23 pass from Favre (Jacke kick)
GB — Butler 25 fumble return (Jacke kick)
GB — Thompson 60 run (Jacke kick)

**PHILADELPHIA 37, NEW ORLEANS 26**—at Veterans Stadium, attendance 50,085. Eagles cornerback Eric Allen returned 2 interceptions for touchdowns and the Saints' slide continued. Allen returned thefts 33 yards and 25 yards for scores, giving him an NFL-record-tying 4 interception returns for touchdowns on the season. New Orleans, which began the season 5-0 but now was on the brink of elimination after falling to 7-8, sputtered all day offensively and managed only 158 total yards. Still, the Saints led 9-0 13 minutes into the game and trailed only 15-12 shortly before halftime because Morten Andersen kicked 4 field goals after short drives following poor punts, a bad punt snap, and a recovered fumble. But Roger Ruzek kicked a 46-yard field goal five seconds before intermission, and Allen returned his first interception for a touchdown 5:21 into the second half as Philadelphia increased its margin to 24-12. After New Orleans's Brad Muster closed the gap to 24-19 with a 2-yard touchdown run, the Eagles put the game away with a 17-play, 82-yard drive that resulted in Bubby Brister's 6-yard touchdown pass to tight end Mark Bavaro 1:28 into the fourth quarter. Less than a minute later, Allen scored his second touchdown to make it 37-19. Saints quarterback Mike Buck made his first NFL start in place of injured Wade Wilson but completed only 1 of 7 passes for 14 yards. He was relieved in the third quarter by Steve Walsh, who did not fare much better, completing only 5 of 11 attempts for 78 yards, with 2 interceptions.

| | | | | | | |
|---|---|---|---|---|---|---|
| **New Orleans** | 9 | 3 | 7 | 7 | — | 26 |
| **Philadelphia** | 0 | 18 | 6 | 13 | — | 37 |

NO — FG Andersen 41
NO — FG Andersen 56
NO — FG Andersen 35
Phil — Safety, Thomas sacked M. Buck in end zone
Phil — Young 49 pass from Brister (kick blocked)
Phil — Walker 11 pass from Brister (Ruzek kick)
NO — FG Andersen 37
Phil — FG Ruzek 46
Phil — Allen 33 interception return (kick failed)
NO — Muster 2 run (Andersen kick)
Phil — Bavaro 6 pass from Brister (kick failed)
Phil — Allen 25 interception return (Ruzek kick)
NO — Hughes 83 punt return (Andersen kick)

**PHOENIX 17, N.Y. GIANTS 6**—at Sun Devil Stadium, attendance 53,414. Ron Moore rushed for 2 second-half touchdowns to lead the Cardinals to an upset victory over the Giants. New York dominated the first half, holding a 224-85 edge in total offense and maintaining possession for more than 20 minutes. But the Giants managed only a pair of field goals by David Treadwell and led just 6-0 at intermission. Phoenix halved its deficit on a 20-yard field goal by Greg Davis 8:48 into the second half, then took the lead for good by marching 57 yards in 6 plays, the last of which was Moore's 19-yard touchdown run with 2:01 remaining in the third quarter. Moore's 1-yard run 2:51 into the fourth period put the game out of reach. The rookie running back finished with 135 yards on 23 carries. The Cardinals limited New York to 69 total yards in the second half and held the Giants' powerful rushing attack to only 78 yards for the game.

| | | | | | | |
|---|---|---|---|---|---|---|
| **N.Y. Giants** | 3 | 3 | 0 | 0 | — | 6 |
| **Phoenix** | 0 | 0 | 10 | 7 | — | 17 |

Giants— FG Treadwell 19
Giants— FG Treadwell 22
Phx — FG G. Davis 20
Phx — R. Moore 19 run (G. Davis kick)
Phx — R. Moore 1 run (G. Davis kick)

**BUFFALO 16, N.Y. JETS 14**—at Rich Stadium, attendance 70,817. The Bills clinched the AFC Eastern Division title when Steve Christie kicked a 40-yard field goal with 3:48 remaining and the Jets' Cary Blanchard missed a 42-yard try in the final minute. It's Buffalo's fifth division crown in the last six years; four times they clinched against New York. The Bills started quickly, taking the opening kickoff and driving 71 yards in 10 plays to Thurman Thomas's 2-yard touchdown run. But the Jets tied it later in the quarter on Boomer Esiason's 24-yard touchdown pass to running back Johnny Johnson. Esiason's second touchdown pass, a 6-yard toss to Chris Burkett, gave New York its only lead of the game, 14-13 midway through the third quarter. That held up until Christie's winning kick. Christie also converted 38- and 36-yard field goal tries despite swirling winds and a wind-chill factor of minus-23. Blanchard, however, was unsuccessful on attempts from 27 and 41 yards, in addition to his miss from 42. Jim Kelly passed for 256 yards for Buffalo. Johnson rushed for 94 yards and caught 8 passes for 81 yards for the Jets.

| | | | | | | |
|---|---|---|---|---|---|---|
| **N.Y. Jets** | 7 | 0 | 7 | 0 | — | 14 |
| **Buffalo** | 7 | 6 | 0 | 3 | — | 16 |

Buff — T. Thomas 2 run (Christie kick)
Jets — J. Johnson 24 pass from Esiason (Blanchard kick)
Buff — FG Christie 38
Buff — FG Christie 36
Jets — Burkett 6 pass from Esiason (Blanchard kick)
Buff — FG Christie 40

**SEATTLE 16, PITTSBURGH 6**—at Kingdome, attendance 51,814. Jon Vaughn ran for a career-high 131 yards as the Seahawks shredded the league's top-ranked rushing defense and put a dent in the Steelers' playoff hopes. Pittsburgh entered the game allowing only 74 yards per game on the ground. But in addition to Vaughn, playing because Chris Warren was out with a strained abdomen, John L. Williams rushed for 86 yards and quarterback Rick Mirer had 44 as Seattle ran for 267 yards on 45 attempts. Mirer had a 33-yard run on the Seahawks' first touchdown drive, which ended with his 2-yard touchdown pass to tight end Paul Green. After that, John Kasay kicked 3 field goals, and Seattle's defense limited the Steelers to 2 field goals by Gary Anderson. Quarterback Neil O'Donnell threw for 285 yards and Pittsburgh amassed 380 total yards, but could not crack the end zone. Tight end Eric Green caught 7 passes for 119 yards.

| | | | | | | |
|---|---|---|---|---|---|---|
| **Pittsburgh** | 0 | 3 | 0 | 3 | — | 6 |
| **Seattle** | 7 | 3 | 3 | 3 | — | 16 |

Sea — Green 2 pass from Mirer (Kasay kick)
Sea — FG Kasay 32
Pitt — FG Anderson 42
Sea — FG Kasay 48
Pitt — FG Anderson 43
Sea — FG Kasay 35

**TAMPA BAY 17, DENVER 10**—at Mile High Stadium, attendance 73,434. Craig Erickson threw 2 touchdown passes as the Buccaneers stunned the Broncos at Mile High Stadium. Despite the defeat, Denver qualified for the playoffs when Pittsburgh and the Jets also lost. The Broncos struck first, driving 84 yards to a touchdown the first time they had the ball, but Erickson's 19-yard touchdown pass to tight end Dave Moore and Michael Husted's 48-yard field goal 32 seconds before halftime put Tampa Bay ahead 10-7. The Buccaneers' first drive of the second half stalled, but Denver's Glyn Milburn fumbled the ensuing punt and Tampa Bay recovered at the Broncos' 15-yard line. Three plays later, Erickson teamed with Courtney Hawkins, who caught 8 passes for 105 yards, on a 14-yard touchdown pass for a 17-7 lead. Denver pulled within a touchdown, but could get no closer. The Broncos' last drive ended on downs with 1:23 remaining after reaching the Buccaneers' 29. Tampa Bay ended a 20-game losing streak to AFC teams on the road.

| | | | | | | |
|---|---|---|---|---|---|---|
| **Tampa Bay** | 0 | 10 | 7 | 0 | — | 17 |
| **Denver** | 7 | 0 | 3 | 0 | — | 10 |

Den — Rivers 5 run (Elam kick)
TB — Moore 19 pass from Erickson (Husted kick)
TB — FG Husted 48
TB — Hawkins 14 pass from Erickson (Husted kick)
Den — FG Elam 24

**DALLAS 38, WASHINGTON 3**—at Texas Stadium, attendance 64,497. Emmitt Smith rushed for 153 yards on 21 carries as the Cowboys blasted the Redskins to set up a showdown against the Giants for the NFC East title. Washington led 3-0 early on Chip Lohmiller's 32-yard field goal 4:30 into the game. But Dallas answered with an 80-yard touchdown march capped by Smith's 1-yard run, and the Cowboys never trailed after that. Troy Aikman threw a pair of touchdown passes in the second quarter to break open the game, and rookie Kevin Williams returned a punt 62 yards for a touchdown in the third period. Aikman passed for 193 yards as Dallas rolled up 380 total yards. The Redskins could muster only 198 yards. Mark Rypien completed just 12 of 30 passes for 91 yards and was intercepted twice. The 35-point margin of victory was the largest in the history of the 68-game series that began in 1960.

| | | | | | | |
|---|---|---|---|---|---|---|
| **Washington** | 3 | 0 | 0 | 0 | — | 3 |
| **Dallas** | 7 | 14 | 14 | 3 | — | 38 |

Wash — FG Lohmiller 32
Dall — E. Smith 1 run (Murray kick)
Dall — Irvin 8 pass from Aikman (Murray kick)
Dall — Harper 15 pass from Aikman (Murray kick)
Dall — Coleman 1 run (Murray kick)
Dall — K. Williams 62 punt return (Murray kick)
Dall — FG Murray 38

## SUNDAY NIGHT, DECEMBER 26

**MINNESOTA 30, KANSAS CITY 10**—at Metrodome, attendance 59,236. Scottie Graham ran for 166 yards and the Vikings turned 3 Chiefs turnovers into 13 points while taking a big step toward the playoffs. Though out of the race for the division title, Minnesota put itself in position to clinch the remaining wild-card playoff berth with a victory the following week at Washington. Because of losses by Denver and the Raiders earlier in the day, Kansas City had already clinched the AFC West title by the time it took the field, but the Chiefs fell behind Houston and Buffalo in the race for home-field advantage. Vikings cornerback Anthony Parker intercepted Joe Montana's pass on the second play from scrimmage and 11 plays later Minnesota took a lead it would never relinquish on Fuad Reveiz's 22-yard field goal. A pair of touchdown passes from Jim McMahon to Cris Carter helped turn the game into a rout, and Graham, who tied a club record with 33 carries, added a 6-yard touchdown run in the fourth quarter. McMahon completed 17 of 25 passes for 219 yards, and the Vikings outgained Kansas City 424-220.

| | | | | | | |
|---|---|---|---|---|---|---|
| **Kansas City** | 0 | 3 | 0 | 7 | — | 10 |
| **Minnesota** | 3 | 7 | 10 | 10 | — | 30 |

Minn — FG Reveiz 22
Minn — C. Carter 31 pass from McMahon (Reveiz kick)
KC — FG Lowery 42
Minn — C. Carter 29 pass from McMahon (Reveiz kick)
Minn — FG Reveiz 19
Minn — Graham 6 run (Reveiz kick)
Minn — FG Reveiz 34
KC — Cash 2 pass from Krieg (Lowery kick)

## MONDAY, DECEMBER 27

**SAN DIEGO 45, MIAMI 20**—at San Diego Jack Murphy Stadium, attendance 60,311. Stan Humphries broke open a close game with touchdown passes on 3 consecutive possessions, and the Chargers handed the Dolphins their fourth consecutive loss. Humphries and Anthony Miller teamed on a 41-yard touchdown pass as time ran out in the first half to give San Diego a 24-13 halftime lead. Humphries's desperation heave bounced off two Miami defenders and into the hands of Miller in the corner of the end zone. The Chargers' Nate Lewis then returned the second-half kickoff 40 yards and it took Humphries only three plays to toss a 21-yard touchdown pass to running back Ronnie Harmon, making it 31-13. It was 38-13 after Humphries and Miller teamed on a 14-yard touchdown 8:40 into the third quarter. Humphries finished with 19 completions in 29 attempts for 248 yards, while Miller caught 7 passes for 110 yards. Natrone Means had 118 of San Diego's 220 rushing yards. Dolphins quarterback Scott Mitchell completed 24 of 40 passes for 260 yards, but was intercepted 3 times. The 3 thefts—2 by safety Darren Carrington and 1 by cornerback Donald Frank—led to 17 points for the Chargers.

| | | | | | | |
|---|---|---|---|---|---|---|
| **Miami** | 3 | 10 | 7 | 0 | — | 20 |
| **San Diego** | 10 | 14 | 14 | 7 | — | 45 |

SD — FG Carney 32
Mia — FG Stoyanovich 31
SD — Means 1 run (Carney kick)
Mia — FG Stoyanovich 50
SD — Means 65 run (Carney kick)
Mia — Byars 1 run (Stoyanovich kick)
SD — A. Miller 41 pass from Humphries (Carney kick)
SD — Harmon 21 pass from Humphries (Carney kick)
SD — A. Miller 14 pass from Humphries (Carney kick)
Mia — Byars 13 pass from Mitchell (Stoyanovich kick)
SD — Means 2 run (Carney kick)

## EIGHTEENTH WEEK SUMMARIES

**AMERICAN FOOTBALL CONFERENCE**

| Eastern Division | W | L | T | Pct. | Pts. | OP |
|---|---|---|---|---|---|---|
| Buffalo | 12 | 4 | 0 | .750 | 329 | 242 |
| Miami | 9 | 7 | 0 | .563 | 349 | 351 |
| N.Y. Jets | 8 | 8 | 0 | .500 | 270 | 247 |
| New England | 5 | 11 | 0 | .313 | 238 | 286 |
| Indianapolis | 4 | 12 | 0 | .250 | 189 | 378 |
| **Central Division** | | | | | | |
| Houston | 12 | 4 | 0 | .750 | 368 | 238 |
| Pittsburgh | 9 | 7 | 0 | .563 | 308 | 281 |
| Cleveland | 7 | 9 | 0 | .438 | 304 | 307 |
| Cincinnati | 3 | 13 | 0 | .188 | 187 | 319 |
| **Western Division** | | | | | | |
| Kansas City | 11 | 5 | 0 | .688 | 328 | 291 |
| L.A. Raiders | 10 | 6 | 0 | .625 | 306 | 326 |
| Denver | 9 | 7 | 0 | .563 | 373 | 284 |
| San Diego | 8 | 8 | 0 | .500 | 322 | 290 |
| Seattle | 6 | 10 | 0 | .375 | 280 | 314 |

**NATIONAL FOOTBALL CONFERENCE**

| Eastern Division | W | L | T | Pct. | Pts. | OP |
|---|---|---|---|---|---|---|
| Dallas | 12 | 4 | 0 | .750 | 376 | 229 |
| N.Y. Giants | 11 | 5 | 0 | .688 | 288 | 205 |
| Philadelphia | 8 | 8 | 0 | .500 | 293 | 315 |
| Phoenix | 7 | 9 | 0 | .438 | 326 | 269 |
| Washington | 4 | 12 | 0 | .250 | 230 | 345 |
| **Central Division** | | | | | | |
| Detroit | 10 | 6 | 0 | .625 | 298 | 292 |
| Minnesota | 9 | 7 | 0 | .563 | 277 | 290 |
| Green Bay | 9 | 7 | 0 | .563 | 340 | 282 |
| Chicago | 7 | 9 | 0 | .438 | 234 | 230 |
| Tampa Bay | 5 | 11 | 0 | .313 | 237 | 376 |
| **Western Division** | | | | | | |
| San Francisco | 10 | 6 | 0 | .625 | 473 | 295 |
| New Orleans | 8 | 8 | 0 | .500 | 317 | 343 |
| Atlanta | 6 | 10 | 0 | .375 | 316 | 385 |
| L.A. Rams | 5 | 11 | 0 | .313 | 221 | 367 |

### FRIDAY, DECEMBER 31

**MINNESOTA 14, WASHINGTON 9**—at RFK Stadium, attendance 42,836. Jim McMahon passed for 225 yards and the decisive touchdown in the third quarter as the Vikings nailed down the final wild-card playoff berth in the NFC. Minnesota was clinging to a 7-6 advantage before marching 76 yards to McMahon's 11-yard touchdown pass to Anthony Carter in the final minute of the third quarter. The veteran quarterback converted four third-down situations with pass completions on the 14-play drive. The Redskins pulled within 5 points on Chip Lohmiller's third field goal of the game, from 34 yards 5:35 into the fourth quarter, but could get no closer. Their final possession reached the Vikings' 41-yard line inside of two minutes remaining before defensive end Roy Barker sacked quarterback Mark Rypien and recovered the Washington quarterback's fumble. McMahon, who was supported by only 45 rushing yards, completed 19 of 32 passes for 225 yards. Cris Carter caught 7 passes for 113 yards, including 24- and 30-yard receptions to set up each of Minnesota's touchdowns. Redskins rookie Reggie Brooks rushed for 68 yards to push his season total to 1,063. But Washington finished the season at 4-12, its worst record in 30 years.

| | | | | | | |
|---|---|---|---|---|---|---|
| **Minnesota** | 0 | 7 | 7 | 0 | — | 14 |
| **Washington** | 0 | 3 | 3 | 3 | — | 9 |

Minn — Graham 1 run (Reveiz kick)
Wash — FG Lohmiller 37
Wash — FG Lohmiller 35
Minn — A. Carter 11 pass from McMahon (Reveiz kick)
Wash — FG Lohmiller 34

### SUNDAY, JANUARY 2, 1994

**BUFFALO 30, INDIANAPOLIS 10**—at Hoosier Dome, attendance 43,028. Thurman Thomas rushed for 110 yards and the Bills clinched home-field advantage throughout the AFC playoffs by handing the Colts their eighth loss in nine games. Thomas's 3-yard touchdown run 45 seconds before halftime broke a 3-3 tie and gave Buffalo the lead for good. After Steve Christie kicked 2 field goals in the third quarter, the Bills put the game away with a pair of touchdowns in a span of 1:40 early in the fourth quarter. Jim Kelly threw a 1-yard touchdown pass to tight end Pete Metzelaars with 13:22 to play, and backup quarterback Frank Reich tossed a 30-yard scoring strike to Bill Brooks to make it 30-3 at the 11:42 mark. The final score came after Buffalo recovered 1 of Indianapolis's 4 lost fumbles. The Colts' lone touchdown came on Jeff George's 10-yard pass to Jessie Hester midway through the fourth quarter. It was just the second touchdown in the last seven games for Indianapolis. The Colts outgained the Bills 402-297, but were victimized by 4 sacks and 4 turnovers. George completed 30 of 48 passes for 338 yards.

| | | | | | | |
|---|---|---|---|---|---|---|
| **Buffalo** | 3 | 7 | 6 | 14 | — | 30 |
| **Indianapolis** | 0 | 3 | 0 | 7 | — | 10 |

Buff — FG Christie 39
Buff — Thomas 3 run (Christie kick)
Ind — FG Biasucci 22
Buff — FG Christie 49
Buff — FG Christie 40
Buff — Metzelaars 1 pass from Kelly (Christie kick)
Buff — Brooks 30 pass from Reich (Christie kick)
Ind — Hester 10 pass from George (Biasucci kick)

**L.A. RAMS 20, CHICAGO 6**—at Anaheim Stadium, attendance 39,147. Jerome Bettis carried a club-record 39 times for 146 yards to power the Rams past the Bears. Bettis finished the season with 1,429 rushing yards, second in the NFL and the sixth-highest total ever by a rookie. He did most of the damage on this game's decisive drive, which came after Chicago had pulled within 13-6 on Kevin Butler's 53-yard field goal with 8:20 left in the game. Bettis had a 13-yard run and a 25-yard reception on the ensuing 10-play, 78-yard drive, which he capped with a 4-yard scoring run with 1:56 to go. T.J. Rubley completed 18 of 28 passes for 213 yards for the Rams, who amassed 394 total yards to 163 for the Bears. Chicago converted just 1 of 9 third-down opportunities and maintained possession for only 19:20 of the game's 60 minutes.

| | | | | | | |
|---|---|---|---|---|---|---|
| **Chicago** | 0 | 3 | 0 | 3 | — | 6 |
| **L.A. Rams** | 3 | 3 | 0 | 14 | — | 20 |

Rams — FG Zendejas 29
Rams — FG Zendejas 29
Chi — FG Butler 27
Rams — Drayton 11 pass from Rubley (Zendejas kick)
Chi — FG Butler 53
Rams — Bettis 4 run (Zendejas kick)

**NEW ORLEANS 20, CINCINNATI 13**—at Louisiana Superdome, attendance 58,036. Steve Walsh, making his first start in more than two years, threw a 54-yard touchdown pass to Eric Martin 3:54 into the fourth quarter to provide the winning margin in the Saints' victory. The Bengals had rallied from a 13-3 deficit to tie the game on two scores just 14 seconds apart: a 31-yard field goal by Doug Pelfrey and safety Mike Brim's 23-yard interception return for a touchdown. But moments later, New Orleans's Tyrone Hughes returned a punt 34 yards to set up the winning score. Walsh finished with 15 completions in 27 attempts for 193 yards and 2 touchdowns. Martin caught 5 passes for 120 yards. The Saints finished the season at 8-8, becoming only the third team since the AFL-NFL merger in 1970 to miss the playoffs after starting the season 5-0.

| | | | | | | |
|---|---|---|---|---|---|---|
| **Cincinnati** | 0 | 3 | 0 | 10 | — | 13 |
| **New Orleans** | 0 | 6 | 7 | 7 | — | 20 |

NO — FG Andersen 43
NO — FG Andersen 49
Cin — FG Pelfrey 22
NO — Smith 9 pass from Walsh (Andersen kick)
Cin — FG Pelfrey 31
Cin — Brim 23 interception return (Pelfrey kick)
NO — E. Martin 54 pass from Walsh (Andersen kick)

**PITTSBURGH 16, CLEVELAND 9**—at Three Rivers Stadium, attendance 49,208. Neil O'Donnell's fourth-quarter touchdown pass to tight end Eric Green lifted the Steelers past the Browns and, coupled with losses by the Dolphins and Jets, into the playoffs. After 3 Matt Stover field goals enabled Cleveland to forge a 9-3 halftime lead, Pittsburgh pulled within 9-6 on Gary Anderson's 38-yard field goal 8:07 into the second half. The Steelers then marched 80 yards in 13 plays to O'Donnell's 14-yard touchdown pass to Green with 7:16 remaining in the game. It was Pittsburgh's first touchdown in eight quarters. Anderson's third field goal of the game, from 26 yards with 1:11 to go, increased the Steelers' advantage to 7 points. That held up despite the efforts of Browns quarterback Vinny Testaverde, who drove his team to Pittsburgh's 13-yard line, but had his fourth-down pass in the end zone broken up by cornerback D.J. Johnson with two seconds left. Testaverde passed for 249 yards and wide receiver Mark Carrier caught 4 passes for 118 yards for the Browns. O'Donnell threw for 226 yards but was sacked 7 times. Cleveland defensive end Anthony Pleasant had 3 of the sacks.

| | | | | | | |
|---|---|---|---|---|---|---|
| **Cleveland** | 0 | 9 | 0 | 0 | — | 9 |
| **Pittsburgh** | 0 | 3 | 3 | 10 | — | 16 |

Pitt — FG Anderson 36
Cle — FG Stover 36
Cle — FG Stover 47
Cle — FG Stover 44
Pitt — FG Anderson 38
Pitt — Green 14 pass from O'Donnell (Anderson kick)
Pitt — FG Anderson 26

**DALLAS 16, N.Y. GIANTS 13**—at Giants Stadium, attendance 77,356. Eddie Murray's 41-yard field goal 10:44 into overtime lifted the Cowboys to a dramatic victory in a showdown for the NFC Eastern Division title and home-field advantage throughout the playoffs. Dallas running back Emmitt Smith, who separated his shoulder when hit late in the first half, remained in the game and finished with 168 rushing yards on 32 carries and 61 yards on 10 receptions. He had an 11-yard run and an 11-yard catch on the winning field-goal drive, which covered 52 yards in 10 plays. The Giants had rallied from a 13-0 halftime deficit to tie the game on Jarrod Bunch's 1-yard touchdown run and a pair of field goals by David Treadwell, the second of which came from 32 yards with 10 seconds remaining in regulation. The Cowboys forged their first-half lead while outgaining New York 238-68 with a healthy Smith in the backfield. Dallas quarterback Troy Aikman completed 24 of 30 passes, but for only 180 yards. Most of his completions were dumpoffs to Smith, fullback Daryl Johnston (6 catches for 47 yards), or tight end Jay Novacek (4 for 19). Smith became only the fourth player to win three consecutive NFL rushing titles, finishing the season with 1,486 yards. Phil Simms passed for 207 yards and Rodney Hampton ran for 114 for the Giants. Hampton raised his season total to 1,077 yards and became the first player in franchise history to rush for more than 1,000 yards three straight years. Despite the loss, the Giants were assured of hosting a wild-card playoff game.

| | | | | | | | |
|---|---|---|---|---|---|---|---|
| **Dallas** | 3 | 10 | 0 | 0 | 3 | — | 16 |
| **N.Y. Giants** | 0 | 0 | 10 | 3 | 0 | — | 13 |

Dall — FG Murray 32
Dall — E. Smith 5 pass from Aikman (Murray kick)
Dall — FG Murray 38
Giants— Bunch 1 run (Treadwell kick)
Giants— FG Treadwell 29
Giants— FG Treadwell 32
Dall — FG Murray 41

**L.A. RAIDERS 33, DENVER 30**—at Los Angeles Memorial Coliseum, attendance 66,904. The Raiders battled back from the verge of playoff extinction to beat the Broncos on

Jeff Jaeger's 47-yard field goal 7:10 into overtime. Needing at least a tie to qualify for postseason play, Los Angeles fell behind by 17 points on two occasions, the last time at 30-13 after Denver drove 71 yards to a field goal following the second-half kickoff. The Broncos had scored on each of their six possessions to that point, but the Raiders' defense stiffened and shut out Denver the rest of the way. Meanwhile, Los Angeles quarterback Jeff Hostetler was rallying his team with a 24-yard touchdown pass to Tim Brown and a dramatic 4-yard touchdown pass to Alexander Wright sandwiched around another field goal by Jaeger. The latter touchdown capped a 14-play, 70-yard drive and came as time expired in regulation. Jaeger's extra point tied the score and forced the extra session. Denver, assured of a playoff berth but needing a victory to host a wild-card game, won the toss in overtime and marched to a 41-yard field-goal attempt by Jason Elam, but the rookie's kick hooked wide. The Raiders countered with their winning field-goal drive and earned the right to host the Broncos in the playoffs one week later. The wide-open game featured 671 passing yards between Denver's John Elway and Hostetler. Elway completed 25 of 36 passes for 361 yards and 3 touchdowns, 2 to tight end Shannon Sharpe, who caught 6 passes for 115 yards. Hostetler was 25 of 41 for 310 yards and 3 scores. Brown caught 11 passes for 173 yards and 2 touchdowns. Jaeger tied an NFL single-season record with 35 field goals.

| | | | | | | |
|---|---|---|---|---|---|---|
| **Denver** | 10 | 17 | 3 | 0 | 0 | — 30 |
| **L.A. Raiders** | 0 | 13 | 7 | 10 | 3 | — 33 |

Den — FG Elam 52
Den — Tillman 27 pass from Elway (Elam kick)
Den — FG Elam 25
Raid — Brown 4 pass from Hostetler (Jaeger kick)
Den — Sharpe 54 pass from Elway (Elam kick)
Raid — FG Jaeger 43
Den — Sharpe 1 pass from Elway (Elam kick)
Raid — FG Jaeger 50
Den — FG Elam 27
Raid — Brown 24 pass from Hostetler (Jaeger kick)
Raid — FG Jaeger 39
Raid — Wright 4 pass from Hostetler (Jaeger kick)
Raid — FG Jaeger 47

**DETROIT 30, GREEN BAY 20**—at Pontiac Silverdome, attendance 77,510. Free-agent running back Eric Lynch rushed for 115 yards and 2 touchdowns as the Lions beat the Packers to decide the NFC Central Division champion and set up a rematch in the same stadium one week later in the first round of the playoffs. Lynch, playing because Barry Sanders was nursing a knee injury and backup Derrick Moore had sore ribs, carried 30 times and scored on runs of 5 yards in the second quarter and 1 yard in the fourth. The latter came with 11:50 to go in the game and gave Detroit the lead for good at 23-20. Moments later, Lions linebacker Pat Swilling intercepted Brett Favre's pass, setting up Erik Kramer's 8-yard touchdown pass to tight end Rodney Holman with 9:19 left. Another interception thwarted Green Bay's last threat, which reached Detroit's 23-yard line. Favre completed 23 of 37 passes for 190 yards, including a 39-yard touchdown to Edgar Bennett in the first quarter, but was picked off 4 times. Packers wide receiver Sterling Sharpe caught 6 passes to raise his season total to an NFL-record 112, surpassing his own mark of 108 receptions that he set in 1992.

| | | | | | |
|---|---|---|---|---|---|
| **Green Bay** | 7 | 3 | 10 | 0 | — 20 |
| **Detroit** | 0 | 10 | 6 | 14 | — 30 |

GB — E. Bennett 39 pass from Favre (Jacke kick)
Det — Lynch 5 run (Hanson kick)
GB — FG Jacke 54
Det — FG Hanson 37
Det — FG Hanson 53
GB — E. Bennett 2 run (Jacke kick)
Det — FG Hanson 48
GB — FG Jacke 47
Det — Lynch 1 run (Hanson kick)
Det — Holman 8 pass from Kramer (Hanson kick)

**NEW ENGLAND 33, MIAMI 27**—at Foxboro Stadium, attendance 53,883. The Patriots' Drew Bledsoe threw a 36-yard touchdown pass to Michael Timpson 4:44 into overtime to stun the Dolphins. The loss was Miami's fifth in a row and, coupled with the Raiders' victory over Denver later in the day, knocked the Dolphins out of the playoffs. Before the losing skid started, Miami had the NFL's best record at 9-2. In this one, the lead see-sawed in a fourth quarter that began with the Patriots leading 17-10. It was 20-17 when the Dolphins' Terry Kirby ran 15 yards for a touchdown to give his team a 24-20 advantage with 4:40 remaining in the game. That lasted only 2:36, the time it took for New England to drive 75 yards and take back the lead on Bledsoe's 11-yard touchdown pass to tight end Ben Coates with 1:04 to go. Miami rallied again, as quarterback Scott Mitchell completed passes of 18 yards to running back O.J. McDuffie and 23 yards to Mark Ingram to march to a first-and-goal at the Patriots' 6-yard line. Three passes into the end zone fell incomplete, and Pete Stoyanovich kicked a 24-yard field goal to tie the game at 27-27 with six seconds left in regulation. In overtime, Bledsoe completed a short pass from his 32-yard line to Vincent Brisby. Brisby fumbled at the 42, but the ball was picked up by running back Leonard Russell, who scampered 22 yards to the Dolphins' 36. The winning touchdown pass came on the next play. Bledsoe completed 27 of 43 passes for 329 yards and 4 touchdowns. Mitchell completed 22 of 40 passes for 259 yards. New England closed the season with four consecutive victories.

| | | | | | | |
|---|---|---|---|---|---|---|
| **Miami** | 0 | 7 | 3 | 17 | 0 | — 27 |
| **New England** | 3 | 7 | 7 | 10 | 6 | — 33 |

NE — FG Bahr 31
NE — Coates 11 pass from Bledsoe (Bahr kick)
Mia — Higgs 5 run (Stoyanovich kick)
Mia — FG Stoyanovich 29
NE — Brisby 11 pass from Bledsoe (Bahr kick)
Mia — Ingram 9 pass from Mitchell (Stoyanovich kick)
NE — FG Bahr 37
Mia — Kirby 15 run (Stoyanovich kick)
NE — Coates 11 pass from Bledsoe (Bahr kick)
Mia — FG Stoyanovich 24
NE — Timpson 36 pass from Bledsoe

**PHOENIX 27, ATLANTA 10**—at Georgia Dome, attendance 44,360. Steve Beuerlein threw 3 touchdown passes as the Cardinals closed the season with their fourth victory in the last five games. Beuerlein, who set a club record by completing 14 passes in a row to start the game, finished 27 of 33 for 278 yards. Two of his scoring tosses went to Randal Hill in the first half and helped Phoenix build a 17-3 advantage at intermission. Gary Clark had 9 receptions for 121 yards, including a 20-yard score in the fourth quarter. Cardinals running back Ron Moore gained 96 yards to finish the season at 1,018. He didn't start until the sixth game of the year, when he took over for injured Garrison Hearst. The Falcons, who began the season with five consecutive losses before climbing into the playoff picture by winning six of their next eight, lost their third in a row.

| | | | | | |
|---|---|---|---|---|---|
| **Phoenix** | 7 | 10 | 3 | 7 | — 27 |
| **Atlanta** | 3 | 0 | 7 | 0 | — 10 |

Phx — Hill 7 pass from Beuerlein (Davis kick)
Atl — FG Johnson 24
Phx — Hill 9 pass from Beuerlein (Davis kick)
Phx — FG Davis 29
Atl — Pegram 19 run (Johnson kick)
Phx — FG Davis 20
Phx — Clark 20 pass from Beuerlein (Davis kick)

**SAN DIEGO 32, TAMPA BAY 17**—at Tampa Stadium, attendance 35,587. The defending AFC Western Division-champion Chargers closed a disappointing season at 8-8 by beating the Buccaneers. John Carney kicked 4 field goals, including a 45-yard kick with 6:17 remaining in the game that put San Diego ahead for good at 19-17. Subsequent interceptions by cornerbacks Darrien Gordon and Brian Davis set up touchdowns just 44 seconds apart to secure the victory. Tampa Bay had rallied from a 13-3 halftime deficit behind 2 touchdown passes from Craig Erickson, the second of which covered 42 yards to Courtney Hawkins 6:34 into the final quarter. But the Buccaneers' 17-16 advantage lasted only 2:09, the time it took the Chargers to drive 52 yards to Carney's go-ahead field goal. San Diego quarterback Stan Humphries completed 18 of 30 passes for 272 yards and 2 touchdowns. Anthony Miller caught 7 passes for 119 yards. Erickson was 21 of 41 for 272 yards, but was intercepted 3 times. Horace Copeland caught 7 passes for 101 yards.

| | | | | | |
|---|---|---|---|---|---|
| **San Diego** | 10 | 3 | 3 | 16 | — 32 |
| **Tampa Bay** | 0 | 3 | 7 | 7 | — 17 |

SD — FG Carney 48
SD — Miller 48 pass from Humphries (Carney kick)
TB — FG Husted 21
SD — FG Carney 38
TB — Thomas 20 pass from Erickson (Husted kick)
SD — FG Carney 43
TB — Hawkins 42 pass from Erickson (Husted kick)
SD — FG Carney 45
SD — Young 12 pass from Humphries (kick failed)
SD — Means 15 run (Carney kick)

**KANSAS CITY 34, SEATTLE 24**—at Arrowhead Stadium, attendance 72,136. Joe Montana threw for 210 yards and a touchdown as the Chiefs tuned up for the playoffs by beating the Seahawks. Montana's 14-yard touchdown pass to Willie Davis in the first quarter helped stake Kansas City to a 27-10 lead at halftime. Seattle rallied in the fourth quarter, pulling within 3 points on John L. Williams's 23-yard run and Rick Mirer's 4-yard touchdown pass to tight end Ferrell Edmunds with 6:27 remaining. But on the Seahawks' next possession, Chiefs linebacker Lonnie Marts sacked Mirer, forcing a fumble that defensive tackle Tim Newton recovered at the 11-yard line. Five plays later, Todd McNair ran 2 yards for the clinching touchdown with 46 seconds left.

| | | | | | |
|---|---|---|---|---|---|
| **Seattle** | 3 | 7 | 0 | 14 | — 24 |
| **Kansas City** | 10 | 17 | 0 | 7 | — 34 |

Sea — FG Kasay 55
KC — Davis 14 pass from Montana (Lowery kick)
KC — FG Lowery 23
KC — McNair 3 run (Lowery kick)
KC — Lewis recovered blocked punt in end zone (Lowery kick)
Sea — Johnson 2 pass from Mirer (Kasay kick)
KC — FG Lowery 47
Sea — Williams 23 run (Kasay kick)
Sea — Edmunds 4 pass from Mirer (Kasay kick)
KC — McNair 2 run (Lowery kick)

## SUNDAY NIGHT, JANUARY 2, 1994

**HOUSTON 24, N.Y. JETS 0**—at Astrodome, attendance 61,040. The Oilers routed the Jets to win their eleventh consecutive game and knock New York out of the playoffs. Reserve quarterback Cody Carlson, playing in place of injured Warren Moon, completed 23 of 38 passes for 247 yards, including touchdowns of 22 yards to Ernest Givins and 8 yards to Gary Brown to stake Houston to a 14-0 halftime advantage. Brown, subbing for the injured Lorenzo White the second half of the season, scored on a 16-yard touchdown run in the fourth quarter and rushed for 85 yards to finish the season at 1,002 despite starting only seven games. Wide receiver Gary Wellman, whose playing time increased after Webster Slaughter was lost for the season two weeks earlier, caught 8 passes for 106 yards. The Oilers' defense was dominant, limiting the Jets to 9 first downs and 164 total yards, and setting a club record with 6 sacks. Defensive end Ray Childress had 2.5 sacks and linebacker Lee Williams added 2. Miami's loss earlier in the day opened the door for the Jets to make the playoffs, but New York lost its third straight and finished at .500. Houston won 12 regular-season games for the first time.

| | | | | | |
|---|---|---|---|---|---|
| **N.Y. Jets** | 0 | 0 | 0 | 0 | — 0 |
| **Houston** | 7 | 7 | 3 | 7 | — 24 |

Hou — Givins 22 pass from Carlson (Del Greco kick)
Hou — Brown 8 pass from Carlson (Del Greco kick)
Hou — FG Del Greco 38
Hou — Brown 16 run (Del Greco kick)

## MONDAY, JANUARY 3, 1994

**PHILADELPHIA 37, SAN FRANCISCO 34**—at Candlestick Park, attendance 61,653. Roger Ruzek kicked a second-chance, 28-yard field goal after time had expired in overtime to lift the Eagles past the 49ers. Ruzek's winning kick came after he pushed a 38-yard attempt wide right as the final seconds ticked off the clock. But San Francisco's Merton Hanks was called for roughing the kicker on the play and Ruzek made good on his next try. Philadelphia, which won its last three games to finish the season at .500, jumped to a 24-3 lead in the first half and still led 34-24 late in the game. But the 49ers, playing with most of its starters on the bench, pulled within 3 points when quarterback Steve Bono scored on a 1-yard sneak with 4:41 remaining in regulation, then forced the overtime when Mike Cofer capped an 82-yard drive in the final two minutes by kicking a 29-yard field goal with 12 seconds left. San Francisco took the opening kickoff in the extra session and marched quickly to a 32-yard field-goal attempt to win the game, but Cofer's kick hooked wide left. The Eagles' winning score was set up by Bubby Brister's scramble and 32-yard completion to 37-year-old wide receiver James Lofton. It was Lofton's only catch of the game and enabled him to become the first player in league history to accumulate more than 14,000 career receiving yards. Brister finished with 26 completions in 43 attempts for 350 yards and 3 touchdowns. The 49ers' Steve Young completed 15 of 19 passes for 165 yards and gave way to Bono after throwing a 38-yard touchdown pass to John Taylor to tie the game at 24-24 midway through the third quarter. Young became the first player to win three consecutive NFL passing titles.

| | | | | | | | |
|---|---|---|---|---|---|---|---|
| **Philadelphia** | 10 | 14 | 10 | 0 | 3 | — | 37 |
| **San Francisco** | 3 | 7 | 14 | 10 | 0 | — | 34 |

Phil — FG Ruzek 34
Phil — Evans 30 fumble return (Ruzek kick)
SF — FG Cofer 30
Phil — C. Williams 13 pass from Brister (Ruzek kick)
Phil — M. Young 8 pass from Brister (Ruzek kick)
SF — Rice 3 pass from S. Young (Cofer kick)
SF — Watters 11 run (Cofer kick)
SF — Taylor 38 pass from S. Young (Cofer kick)
Phil — Walker 21 pass from Brister (Ruzek kick)
Phil — FG Ruzek 32
SF — Bono 1 run (Cofer kick)
SF — FG Cofer 29
Phil — FG Ruzek 28

## NINETEENTH WEEK SUMMARIES

### SATURDAY, JANUARY 8, 1994

**GREEN BAY 28, DETROIT 24**—at Pontiac Silverdome, attendance 68,479. Brett Favre's 40-yard touchdown pass to Sterling Sharpe with 55 seconds remaining lifted the Packers to victory in their first playoff game in 11 years. Favre, unable to find intended receiver Mark Clayton, scrambled left and threw across the field to Sharpe, who had gotten behind cornerback Kevin Scott down the right sideline. The quarterback's heroics offset brilliant individual performances by the Lions' Barry Sanders and Brett Perriman. Sanders, playing for first time since injuring his knee against the Bears on Thanksgiving Day, rushed for 169 yards on 27 carries. Perriman caught 10 passes for 150 yards, including a 1-yard touchdown from Erik Kramer late in the second quarter to give Detroit a 10-7 edge at halftime. The Lions increased that advantage to 17-7 when cornerback Melvin Jenkins intercepted Favre's pass and returned it 15 yards for a touchdown 6:40 into the third period. After Green Bay countered with a 28-yard touchdown pass from Favre to Sharpe, Detroit appeared poised to score again, driving to the Packers' 5-yard line. But Kramer's pass in the end zone was intercepted by rookie safety George Teague, who raced a playoff-record 101 yards to give Green Bay a 21-17 lead with 1:40 to go in the third quarter. The Lions then pieced together a 15-play, 89-yard drive that consumed more than 8 minutes, taking the lead for the last time on Derrick Moore's 5-yard touchdown run 6:33 into the fourth quarter. Kramer finished with 22 completions in 31 attempts for 248 yards for Detroit, which amassed 410 total yards but could not overcome the Packers' big plays. Sharpe, who set an NFL record with 112 receptions during the regular season, caught only 5 passes but made the most of them, gaining 101 yards and scoring 3 times.

| | | | | | | |
|---|---|---|---|---|---|---|
| **Green Bay** | 0 | 7 | 14 | 7 | — | 28 |
| **Detroit** | 3 | 7 | 7 | 7 | — | 24 |

Det — FG Hanson 47
GB — Sharpe 12 pass from Favre (Jacke kick)
Det — Perriman 1 pass from Kramer (Hanson kick)
Det — Jenkins 15 interception return (Hanson kick)
GB — Sharpe 28 pass from Favre (Jacke kick)
GB — Teague 101 interception return (Jacke kick)
Det — D. Moore 5 run (Hanson kick)
GB — Sharpe 40 pass from Favre (Jacke kick)

**KANSAS CITY 27, PITTSBURGH 24**—at Arrowhead Stadium, attendance 74,515. Nick Lowery kicked a 32-yard field goal 11:03 into overtime to give the Chiefs the come-from-behind victory. Kansas City rallied from a 10-point halftime deficit to tie the game at 17-17 in the fourth quarter, only to fall behind again before forcing the extra session when Joe Montana threw a 7-yard touchdown pass to Tim Barnett with 1:43 remaining in regulation. That came four plays after the Chiefs' Keith Cash blocked a punt and teammate Fred Jones returned it 31 yards to the Steelers' 9-yard line. Two running plays and an incomplete pass netted only 2 yards, but Montana teamed with Barnett on fourth down. Pittsburgh led 17-7 at intermission largely on the strength of 2 touchdown passes from Neil O'Donnell, the second of which was a 26-yard strike to Ernie Mills 18 seconds before halftime. That came six plays after the Steelers stopped Kansas City on downs near midfield. Lowery's 23-yard field goal and Marcus Allen's 2-yard run 6:02 into the fourth quarter tied the game, but Pittsburgh answered with a 74-yard drive capped by O'Donnell's 22-yard pass to tight end Eric Green to take back the lead. The Chiefs had a chance to win the game in regulation, forcing the Steelers to punt just 29 seconds after Barnett's touchdown catch. Montana quickly directed a 47-yard drive, setting up Lowery's 43-yard field-goal try in the closing seconds, but the kick was wide right. The teams exchanged punts in overtime, then Kansas City drove 66 yards in 11 plays to win it. Montana started slowly, completing only 1 of his first 8 passes, but wound up 28 of 43 for 276 yards. Backup Dave Krieg subbed briefly when Montana hurt his ribs in the first quarter, and completed his only pass attempt for a 23-yard touchdown to J.J. Birden. O'Donnell completed 23 of 42 attempts for 286 yards and 3 touchdowns. Pittsburgh nose tackle Gerald Williams had 3 sacks. There were no turnovers in the game.

| | | | | | | | |
|---|---|---|---|---|---|---|---|
| **Pittsburgh** | 7 | 10 | 0 | 7 | 0 | — | 24 |
| **Kansas City** | 7 | 0 | 3 | 14 | 3 | — | 27 |

Pitt — Cooper 10 pass from O'Donnell (Anderson kick)
KC — Birden 23 pass from Krieg (Lowery kick)
Pitt — FG Anderson 30
Pitt — Mills 26 pass from O'Donnell (Anderson kick)
KC — FG Lowery 23
KC — Allen 2 run (Lowery kick)
Pitt — Green 22 pass from O'Donnell (Anderson kick)
KC — Barnett 7 pass from Montana (Lowery kick)
KC — FG Lowery 32

### SUNDAY, JANUARY 9, 1994

**L.A. RAIDERS 42, DENVER 24**—at Los Angeles Memorial Coliseum, attendance 65,314. Napoleon McCallum rushed for 3 second-half touchdowns to decide what began as a shootout between quarterbacks Jeff Hostetler and John Elway. A wild first half ended in a 21-21 tie after the Raiders' Hostetler and the Broncos' Elway each traded 3 touchdown passes. But field position played a big role early in the third quarter: Los Angeles pinned Denver deep in its territory with a Jeff Gossett punt that was downed inside the 5, and moments later the Raiders took over at the Broncos' 35 after a short punt by Tom Rouen. Three plays later, McCallum turned a third-and-1 into a touchdown, scampering 26 yards—the team's longest run from scrimmage all year—for the score that put Los Angeles ahead for good with 8:08 left in the period. Another short punt set up McCallum's 2-yard touchdown run at the 4:27 mark, the key play on the 52-yard drive Hostetler's 33-yard completion to tight end Ethan Horton. After the Broncos closed within 35-24 early in the fourth quarter, the Raiders put the game out of reach with a time-consuming, 76-yard drive that culminated in McCallum's 1-yard run with 6:43 remaining in the game. McCallum finished with 81 yards on 13 carries and tied an NFL postseason record with his 3 touchdowns. Hostetler averaged better than 15 yards per attempt, throwing for 294 yards while completing 13 of 19 passes. James Jett had 111 yards on just 3 receptions, including a difficult over-the-shoulder grab to complete a 54-yard touchdown in the second quarter. Elway completed 29 of 47 passes for 302 yards. Tight end Shannon Sharpe tied a postseason record with 13 catches for 156 yards. The two teams combined for 814 total yards, including 427 by the Raiders.

| | | | | | | |
|---|---|---|---|---|---|---|
| **Denver** | 7 | 14 | 0 | 3 | — | 24 |
| **L.A. Raiders** | 14 | 7 | 14 | 7 | — | 42 |

Raid — Horton 9 pass from Hostetler (Jaeger kick)
Den — Sharpe 23 pass from Elway (Elam kick)
Raid — Brown 65 pass from Hostetler (Jaeger kick)
Den — R. Johnson 16 pass from Elway (Elam kick)
Raid — Jett 54 pass from Hostetler (Jaeger kick)
Den — Russell 6 pass from Elway (Elam kick)
Raid — McCallum 26 run (Jaeger kick)
Raid — McCallum 2 run (Jaeger kick)
Den — FG Elam 33
Raid — McCallum 1 run (Jaeger kick)

**N.Y. GIANTS 17, MINNESOTA 10**—at Giants Stadium, attendance 75,089. Rodney Hampton's 2 third-quarter touchdown runs erased a 7-point halftime deficit and lifted the Giants to the victory. Freezing temperatures and blustery winds limited the effectiveness of each team's offense, so much so that all the points in the game were scored by the team that had the wind at its back. New York, trailing 10-3, had such conditions in the third quarter when it rallied to win. The Giants tied the score on their first possession of the second half, as Hampton barreled over right end for 51 yards and a touchdown just 2:54 into the third period. Shortly after that, a 21-yard punt positioned New York at Minnesota's 26-yard line, and six plays later, Hampton ran 2 yards for the game's deciding score. Primarily on the strength of Hampton, the Giants controlled the game by rushing 41 times for 176 yards and maintaining possession for 35:23 of the game's 60 minutes. Vikings quarterbacks Jim McMahon and Sean Salisbury combined to complete only 15 of 34 passes for 192 yards.

| | | | | | | |
|---|---|---|---|---|---|---|
| **Minnesota** | 0 | 10 | 0 | 0 | — | 10 |
| **N.Y. Giants** | 3 | 0 | 14 | 0 | — | 17 |

Giants— FG Treadwell 26
Minn — C. Carter 40 pass from McMahon (Reveiz kick)
Minn — FG Reveiz 52
Giants— Hampton 51 run (Treadwell kick)
Giants— Hampton 2 run (Treadwell kick)

## TWENTIETH WEEK SUMMARIES

### SATURDAY, JANUARY 15, 1994

**BUFFALO 29, L.A. RAIDERS 23**—at Rich Stadium, attendance 61,923. Jim Kelly threw 2 second-half touchdown passes to Bill Brooks and the Bills overcame an 11-point deficit to advance to the AFC Championship Game for the fifth time in six years. Napoleon McCallum scored on a pair of 1-yard touchdown runs for the Raiders, the second of which gave Los Angeles a 17-6 advantage with 1:57 remaining in the first half. But Buffalo took only 67 seconds to march 76 yards and trim the deficit to 4 points at intermission. A 37-yard pass interference penalty preceded Thurman Thomas's 8-yard touchdown run with 50 seconds remaining in the second quarter. That set up a flurry of activity that saw the lead change three times in a span of 6:18 late in the third and early in the fourth quarters. Kelly gave the Bills a 19-17 edge with a 25-yard touchdown pass to Brooks with 3:23 left in the third period. Moments later, Buffalo safety Henry Jones recovered McCallum's fumble on the Raiders' 30-yard line, setting up Steve Christie's 29-yard field goal 59 seconds before the end of the quarter. Two plays after that, Raiders wide receiver Tim Brown took a short pass from a scrambling Jeff Hostetler and turned it into an 86-yard touchdown that put Los Angeles back on top 23-22. But the Bills responded by driving 71 yards to Kelly's 22-yard touchdown pass to Brooks 2:55 into the fourth quarter. That held up for the winning points as Buffalo's defense shut down the Raiders. After gaining 14 first downs in the first half, Los Angeles managed only 1 in the second half, that coming on the long touchdown pass. Kelly completed 27 of 37 passes for 287 yards for the Bills, while Brooks caught 6 passes for 96 yards. Hostetler was 14 of 20 for 230 yards for the Raiders. The game was played in frigid conditions. Temperature at kickoff was zero degrees, with the wind-chill at minus-32.

| | | | | | | |
|---|---|---|---|---|---|---|
| **L.A. Raiders** | 0 | 17 | 6 | 0 | — | 23 |
| **Buffalo** | 0 | 13 | 9 | 7 | — | 29 |

Raid — FG Jaeger 30
Buff — Davis 1 run (kick failed)
Raid — McCallum 1 run (Jaeger kick)
Raid — McCallum 1 run (Jaeger kick)
Buff — Thomas 8 run (Christie kick)
Buff — Brooks 25 pass from Kelly (kick failed)
Buff — FG Christie 29
Raid — Brown 86 pass from Hostetler (kick failed)
Buff — Brooks 22 pass from Kelly (Christie kick)

**SAN FRANCISCO 44, N.Y. GIANTS 3**—at Candlestick Park, attendance 67,143. Ricky Watters scored an NFL playoff-record 5 touchdowns to key the 49ers' victory. Watters ran for 118 yards on 24 carries, caught 5 passes for 46 yards, and scored all of his touchdowns on short runs. No player had scored more than 3 touchdowns in a postseason game. San Francisco started the rout early, with quarterback Steve Young completing all 4 of his passes for 63 yards on an 8-play, 80-yard touchdown drive following the opening kickoff, a march capped by Watters's 1-yard run 4:27 into the game. The Giants failed to make a first down on their initial possession, and the 49ers' Dexter Carter returned the ensuing punt 31 yards to set up Mike Cofer's 29-yard field goal. Safety Tim McDonald intercepted Phil Simms's pass on the next play, leading to another 1-yard touchdown run by Watters, and San Francisco led 16-0 two seconds into the second quarter. It was 23-3 at halftime and the 49ers never were threatened. Young completed 17 of 22 passes for 226 yards as San Francisco amassed 413 total yards to just 194 for the Giants. New York, which led the NFL by averaging 138 rushing yards per game during the regular season, managed only 41 yards on the ground. The 49ers' defense also recorded 4 sacks, including 2 by rookie end Dana Stubblefield.

| | | | | | | |
|---|---|---|---|---|---|---|
| **N.Y. Giants** | 0 | 3 | 0 | 0 | — | 3 |
| **San Francisco** | 9 | 14 | 14 | 7 | — | 44 |

SF — Watters 1 run (kick failed)
SF — FG Cofer 29
SF — Watters 1 run (Cofer kick)
SF — Watters 2 run (Cofer kick)
Giants— FG Treadwell 25
SF — Watters 6 run (Cofer kick)
SF — Watters 2 run (Cofer kick)
SF — Logan 2 run (Cofer kick)

## SUNDAY, JANUARY 16, 1994

**DALLAS 27, GREEN BAY 17**—at Texas Stadium, attendance 64,790. Troy Aikman passed for 302 yards and 3 touchdowns, and the Cowboys scored 10 points in a span of 18 seconds shortly before halftime to break open a close game. Aikman's 25-yard touchdown pass to Alvin Harper 5:53 into the second quarter put Dallas ahead 7-3, a lead the Cowboys would not relinquish. After Eddie Murray kicked a 41-yard field goal 23 seconds before halftime to stretch the advantage to 10-3, Kenneth Gant made the key play of the game on the ensuing kickoff. Gant knocked the ball loose from Packers kick returner Corey Harris, and Dallas's Joe Fishback recovered at Green Bay's 14-yard line. Aikman completed an 8-yard pass to Michael Irvin, then teamed with tight end Jay Novacek on a 6-yard touchdown pass with five seconds left in the first half to make it 17-3. Aikman's 19-yard touchdown pass to Michael Irvin 9:05 into the third quarter put the game out of reach. Aikman finished with 28 completions in 37 attempts, while Irvin caught 9 passes for 126 yards. Packers quarterback Brett Favre completed 28 of 45 passes for 331 yards, but most of it came after the issue was decided. Running back Edgar Bennett caught 9 passes. Wide receiver Sterling Sharpe had 6 receptions for 128 yards.

| | | | | | | |
|---|---|---|---|---|---|---|
| **Green Bay** | 3 | 0 | 7 | 7 | — | 17 |
| **Dallas** | 0 | 17 | 7 | 3 | — | 27 |

GB — FG Jacke 30
Dall — Harper 25 pass from Aikman (Murray kick)
Dall — FG Murray 41
Dall — Novacek 6 pass from Aikman (Murray kick)
Dall — Irvin 19 pass from Aikman (Murray kick)
GB — Brooks 13 pass from Favre (Jacke kick)
Dall — FG Murray 38
GB — Sharpe 29 pass from Favre (Jacke kick)

**KANSAS CITY 28, HOUSTON 20**—at Astrodome, attendance 64,011. Joe Montana threw 3 second-half touchdown passes, including 2 just 54 seconds apart in the fourth quarter, to rally the Chiefs past the Oilers. Houston, which entered the game with an 11-game winning streak, jumped out to a 10-0 lead in the opening quarter and still led 13-7 after Al Del Greco's 43-yard field goal with 9:37 remaining in the fourth quarter. But Kansas City marched 71 yards in only 59 seconds, the key play a 38-yard pass interference penalty against Oilers cornerback Cris Dishman, to take the lead for the first time on Montana's 11-yard touchdown pass to J.J. Birden. On the next play from scrimmage, Chiefs linebacker Derrick Thomas sacked Houston quarterback Warren Moon, forcing a fumble that defensive tackle Dan Saleaumua recovered at the Oilers' 12-yard line. On third down, Montana's 18-yard touchdown pass to Willie Davis put Kansas City ahead 21-13 with 7:44 left. Houston drove 80 yards to a touchdown to pull within 1 point with 3:45 to go, but Marcus Allen's 21-yard touchdown run at the 1:55 mark sealed the Oilers' fate. The key play on the Chiefs' 79-yard march came on third-and-1 from Kansas City's 30-yard line. Montana's arm was hit as he threw, but his wobbly pass was caught by tight end Keith Cash, who rumbled 41 yards to Houston's 29. Cash also had a 7-yard touchdown reception in the third quarter. Montana finished with 22 completions in 38 attempts for 299 yards. Allen rushed for 74 yards on only 14 carries. Moon completed 32 of 43 passes for 306 yards for the Oilers. But without the benefit of an effective rushing attack (Houston ran for only 39 yards), he was under pressure all afternoon and was sacked 9 times. Thomas, Joe Phillips, Albert Lewis, and Bennie Thompson each had 2 sacks for the Chiefs, who equaled the NFL record for sacks in a postseason game.

| | | | | | | |
|---|---|---|---|---|---|---|
| **Kansas City** | 0 | 0 | 7 | 21 | — | 28 |
| **Houston** | 10 | 0 | 0 | 10 | — | 20 |

Hou — FG Del Greco 49
Hou — Brown 2 run (Del Greco kick)
KC — Cash 7 pass from Montana (Lowery kick)
Hou — FG Del Greco 43
KC — Birden 11 pass from Montana (Lowery kick)
KC — Davis 18 pass from Montana (Lowery kick)
Hou — Givins 7 pass from Moon (Del Greco kick)
KC — Allen 21 run (Lowery kick)

## TWENTY-FIRST WEEK SUMMARIES
## SUNDAY, JANUARY 23, 1994

**BUFFALO 30, KANSAS CITY 13**—at Rich Stadium, attendance 76,642. Thurman Thomas rushed for 186 yards and 3 touchdowns as the Bills qualified for an unprecedented fourth consecutive Super Bowl. Thomas, who ran for 129 yards in the first two quarters, helped stake Buffalo to a 20-6 advantage at intermission by scoring on touchdown runs of 12 and 3 yards. The Chiefs had an opportunity to cut that deficit in half, marching 75 yards to the Bills' 5-yard line in the closing seconds of the first half. But Joe Montana's pass to a wide-open Kimble Anders near the goal line bounced off the running back's hands and was intercepted in the end zone by Buffalo safety Henry Jones. Montana, who completed only 9 of 23 passes for 125 yards, sat out most of the second half after suffering a concussion on the third play of the third quarter. Backup Dave Krieg, who completed 16 of 29 passes for 198 yards, came on and led a 90-yard touchdown drive that pulled Kansas City within 20-13 late in the third quarter. But Buffalo answered with a 14-play, 79-yard march capped by Steve Christie's 18-yard field goal 3:05 into the fourth quarter. Thomas's third touchdown, a 3-yard run with 5:30 remaining, put the game out of reach. Thomas averaged 5.6 yards on his 33 carries as the Bills overwhelmed the Chiefs on the ground, outrushing them 229 yards to 52.

| | | | | | | |
|---|---|---|---|---|---|---|
| **Kansas City** | 6 | 0 | 7 | 0 | — | 13 |
| **Buffalo** | 7 | 13 | 0 | 10 | — | 30 |

Buff — Thomas 12 run (Christie kick)
KC — FG Lowery 31
KC — FG Lowery 31
Buff — Thomas 3 run (Christie kick)
Buff — FG Christie 23
Buff — FG Christie 25
KC — Allen 1 run (Lowery kick)
Buff — FG Christie 18
Buff — Thomas 3 run (Christie kick)

**DALLAS 38, SAN FRANCISCO 21**—at Texas Stadium, attendance 64,902. Troy Aikman threw 2 touchdown passes and Emmitt Smith scored twice as the Cowboys scored on four of their first five possessions and easily handled the 49ers to win the NFC title. Dallas struck quickly, taking the opening kickoff and marching 75 yards in 11 plays to Smith's 5-yard touchdown run 6:19 into the game. San Francisco tied it when running back Tom Rathman caught a 7-yard touchdown pass from Steve Young on the first play of the second quarter, but the Cowboys broke open the game by scoring touchdowns the next three times they had the ball. They countered Rathman's score with an 11-play, 80-yard drive capped by Daryl Johnston's 4-yard touchdown run 5:12 into the second quarter. Three plays later, safety Thomas Everett intercepted a pass that was tipped by San Francisco's John Taylor, and returned it 14 yards to the 49ers' 24-yard line. It took Dallas only four plays to convert that into Aikman's 11-yard touchdown pass to Smith 6:04 before intermission. Aikman teamed with tight end Jay Novacek on a 19-yard touchdown pass in the final minute of the first half to give the Cowboys a 28-7 lead. San Francisco tried to make a game of it, pulling within 14 points on a 4-yard touchdown run by Ricky Watters, but Dallas put the game out of reach when Bernie Kosar teamed with Alvin Harper on a 42-yard touchdown pass with 2:24 remaining in the third quarter. Kosar, in the game because Aikman suffered a concussion early in the second half, kept the drive alive with a 12-yard completion to Michael Irvin on third-and-9 from the Cowboys' 19, and also had a 20-yard completion to Novacek on the 7-play, 82-yard drive. Aikman, who did not return, completed 14 of 18 passes for 177 yards. Kosar was 5 of 9 for 83 yards. Smith rushed for 88 yards on 23 carries and caught 7 passes for 85 yards. 49ers quarterback Steve Young completed 27 of 45 passes for 287 yards and led his team with 38 rushing yards. But he also suffered 4 sacks and was supported by only 46 yards from San Francisco's running backs. Dallas, which beat the 49ers 30-20 in the 1992 NFC Championship Game, qualified for its seventh Super Bowl, extending its NFL record. San Francisco lost in the NFC title game for the third time in four years.

| | | | | | | |
|---|---|---|---|---|---|---|
| **San Francisco** | 0 | 7 | 7 | 7 | — | 21 |
| **Dallas** | 7 | 21 | 7 | 3 | — | 38 |

Dall — E. Smith 5 run (Murray kick)
SF — Rathman 7 pass from Young (Cofer kick)
Dall — Johnston 4 run (Murray kick)
Dall — E. Smith 11 pass from Aikman (Murray kick)
Dall — Novacek 19 pass from Aikman (Murray kick)
SF — Watters 4 run (Cofer kick)
Dall — Harper 42 pass from Kosar (Murray kick)
Dall — FG Murray 50
SF — Young 1 run (Cofer kick)

## TWENTY-SECOND WEEK SUMMARY
## SUNDAY, JANUARY 30, 1994
## SUPER BOWL XXVIII
## ATLANTA, GEORGIA

**DALLAS 30, BUFFALO 13**—at Georgia Dome, attendance 72,817. Emmitt Smith rushed for 132 yards and 2 second-half touchdowns to power the Cowboys to their second consecutive NFL title. By winning, Dallas joined San Francisco and Pittsburgh as the only franchises with four Super Bowl victories. The Bills, meanwhile, extended a dubious string by losing in the Super Bowl for the fourth consecutive year. To win, the Cowboys had to rally from a 13-6 halftime deficit. Buffalo had forged its lead on Thurman Thomas's 4-yard touchdown run and a pair of field goals by Steve Christie, including a 54-yard kick, the longest in Super Bowl history. But just 55 seconds into the second half, Thomas was stripped of the ball by Dallas defensive tackle Leon Lett. Safety James Washington recovered and weaved his way 46 yards for a touchdown to tie the game at 13-13. After forcing the Bills to punt, the Cowboys began their next possession on their 36-yard line and Smith, the game's most valuable player, took over. He carried 7 times for 61 yards on the ensuing 8-play, 64-yard drive, capping the march with a 15-yard touchdown run to give Dallas the lead for good with 8:42 remaining in the third quarter. Early in the fourth quarter, Washington intercepted Jim Kelly's pass and returned it 12 yards to Buffalo's 34. A penalty moved the ball back to the 39, but Smith carried twice for 10 yards and caught a screen pass for 9, and quarterback Troy Aikman completed a 16-yard pass to Alvin Harper to give the Cowboys a first-and-goal at the 6. Smith took it from there, cracking the end zone on fourth-and-goal from the 1 to put Dallas ahead 27-13 with 9:50 remaining. Eddie Murray's third field goal, from 20 yards with 2:50 left, ended any doubt about the game's outcome. Smith had 30 carries in all, with 19 of his attempts and 92 yards coming after intermission. Washington, normally a reserve who played most of the game because the Cowboys used five defensive backs to combat the Bills' No-Huddle offense, had 11 tackles and forced another fumble by Thomas in the first quarter. Aikman completed 19 of 27 passes for 207 yards. Buffalo's Kelly completed a Super Bowl-record 31 passes in 50 attempts for 260 yards. Thomas and Bill Brooks each caught 7 passes, while Andre Reed and Don Beebe added 6 receptions each. Dallas, the first team in NFL history to begin the regular season 0-2 and go on to win the Super Bowl, also became the fifth to win back-to-back titles, following Green Bay, Miami, Pittsburgh (the Steelers did it twice), and San Francisco. Buffalo became the third team, along with Minnesota and Denver, to lose four

Super Bowls. The Cowboys' victory was the tenth in succession for NFC teams over AFC teams in the Super Bowl.

| | | | | | | |
|---|---|---|---|---|---|---|
| **Dallas** | 6 | 0 | 14 | 10 | — | 30 |
| **Buffalo** | 3 | 10 | 0 | 0 | — | 13 |

Dall — FG Murray 41
Buff — FG Christie 54
Dall — FG Murray 24
Buff — Thomas 4 run (Christie kick)
Buff — FG Christie 28
Dall — Washington 46 fumble return (Murray kick)
Dall — E. Smith 15 run (Murray kick)
Dall — E. Smith 1 run (Murray kick)
Dall — FG Murray 20

## TWENTY-THIRD WEEK SUMMARY
### SUNDAY, FEBRUARY 6, 1994
### PRO BOWL
### HONOLULU, HAWAII

**NFC 17, AFC 3**—at Aloha Stadium, attendance 50,026. The NFC converted a blocked punt and a fumble recovery into touchdowns just 2:20 apart in the second half of its victory over the AFC. With the score tied 3-3 late in the third quarter, Saints linebacker Renaldo Turnbull deflected a punt by the Oilers' Greg Montgomery, and the NFC took possession at the AFC's 48-yard line. A 32-yard pass from Bobby Hebert to Falcons teammate Andre Rison positioned Rams running back Jerome Bettis for a 4-yard touchdown run with 1:27 left in the third quarter. Moments later, Rams defensive tackle Sean Gilbert recovered a fumble by Oilers quarterback Warren Moon at the AFC's 19. Hebert then teamed with the Vikings' Cris Carter on a 15-yard touchdown pass 53 seconds into the fourth period. The NFC kept the AFC out of the end zone by maintaining possession for more than 38 minutes and forcing 6 turnovers. Rison earned the Dan McGuire Trophy as the player of the game by catching 6 passes for 86 yards. The victory was the fourth in the last six years for the NFC, which leads the series 14-10.

| | | | | | | |
|---|---|---|---|---|---|---|
| **NFC** | 3 | 0 | 7 | 7 | — | 17 |
| **AFC** | 0 | 3 | 0 | 0 | — | 3 |

NFC — FG N. Johnson 35
AFC — FG G. Anderson 25
NFC — Bettis 4 run (N. Johnson kick)
NFC — C. Carter 15 pass from Hebert (N. Johnson kick)

## 1993 PRO FOOTBALL AWARDS

| | NFL | AFC | NFC |
|---|---|---|---|
| **PRO FOOTBALL WRITERS OF AMERICA** | | | |
| Most Valuable Player | Emmitt Smith | | |
| Rookie of the Year | Jerome Bettis | | |
| Coach of the Year | Dan Reeves | | |
| **ASSOCIATED PRESS** | | | |
| Most Valuable Player | Emmitt Smith | | |
| Offensive Player of the Year | Jerry Rice | | |
| Defensive Player of the Year | Rod Woodson | | |
| Offensive Rookie of the Year | Jerome Bettis | | |
| Defensive Rookie of the Year | Dana Stubblefield | | |
| Coach of the Year | Dan Reeves | | |
| **UNITED PRESS INTERNATIONAL** | | | |
| Offensive Player of the Year | | John Elway | Emmitt Smith |
| Defensive Player of the Year | | Rod Woodson | Eric Allen |
| Coach of the Year | | Marv Levy | Dan Reeves |
| Rookie of the Year | | Rick Mirer | Jerome Bettis |
| **THE SPORTING NEWS** | | | |
| Player of the Year | Emmitt Smith | | |
| Rookie of the Year | Jerome Bettis | | |
| Coach of the Year | Dan Reeves | | |
| **FOOTBALL NEWS** | | | |
| Player of the Year | | John Elway | Emmitt Smith |
| Coach of the Year | | Don Shula | Dan Reeves |
| **PRO FOOTBALL WEEKLY** | | | |
| Most Valuable Player | Emmitt Smith | | |
| Offensive Player of the Year | Emmitt Smith | | |
| Defensive Player of the Year | Bruce Smith | | |
| Offensive Rookie of the Year | Jerome Bettis | | |
| Defensive Rookie of the Year | Dana Stubblefield | | |
| Coach of the Year | Dan Reeves | | |
| **FOOTBALL DIGEST** | | | |
| Player of the Year | Emmitt Smith | | |
| Defensive Player of the Year | Deion Sanders | | |
| Offensive Rookie of the Year | Rick Mirer | | |
| Defensive Rookie of the Year | Dana Stubblefield | | |
| Coach of the Year | Dan Reeves | | |
| **MAXWELL CLUB PLAYER OF THE YEAR** (Bert Bell Trophy) | Emmitt Smith | | |
| **MAXWELL CLUB COACH OF THE YEAR** (Earle "Greasy" Neale Trophy) | Dan Reeves | | |
| **SUPER BOWL MOST VALUABLE PLAYER** (Pete Rozelle Trophy) | Emmitt Smith | | |
| **AFC-NFC PRO BOWL PLAYER OF THE GAME** (Dan McGuire Award) | Andre Rison | | |

## 1993 AFC PLAYERS OF THE WEEK

| | Offense | | Defense | | Special Teams | |
|---|---|---|---|---|---|---|
| Week 1 | QB | Joe Montana, Kansas City | DE | Anthony Smith, L.A. Raiders | K | John Carney, San Diego |
| Week 2 | QB | Boomer Esiason, N.Y. Jets | S | Marcus Robertson, Houston | WR | Steve Tasker, Buffalo |
| Week 3 | RB | Chris Warren, Seattle | LB | Junior Seau, San Diego | K | John Carney, San Diego |
| Week 4 | QB | Dan Marino, Miami | LB | Duane Bickett, Indianapolis | KR | Rod Woodson, Pittsburgh |
| Week 5 | QB | Rick Mirer, Seattle | DE | Neil Smith, Kansas City | P | Rick Tuten, Seattle |
| Week 6 | QB | Scott Mitchell, Miami | LB | Greg Lloyd, Pittsburgh | P | Mike Saxon, New England |
| Week 7 | QB | Joe Montana, Kansas City | CB | Rod Woodson, Pittsburgh | P | Greg Montgomery, Houston |
| Week 8 | QB | Warren Moon, Houston | DE | Bruce Smith, Buffalo | PR | Eric Metcalf, Cleveland |
| Week 9 | QB | Scott Mitchell, Miami | CB | Donald Frank, San Diego | K | Dean Biasucci, Indianapolis |
| Week 10 | QB | John Elway, Denver | DT | Dan Saleaumua, Kansas City | LB | Kurt Barber, N.Y. Jets |
| Week 11 | RB | Gary Brown, Houston | S | Eugene Robinson, Seattle | P | Mark Royals, Pittsburgh |
| Week 12 | QB | John Elway, Denver | S | Marcus Robertson, Houston | P | Dale Hatcher, Miami |
| Week 13 | QB | Joe Montana, Kansas City | DE | William Fuller, Houston | K | Doug Pelfrey, Cincinnati |
| Week 14 | WR | Tim Brown, L.A. Raiders | CB | Steve Jackson, Houston | K | Dean Biasucci, Indianapolis |
| Week 15 | TE | Shannon Sharpe, Denver | LB | Greg Lloyd, Pittsburgh | RB | Reggie Rivers, Denver |
| Week 16 | RB | Gary Brown, Houston | CB | Nate Odomes, Buffalo | K | Jeff Jaeger, L.A. Raiders |
| Week 17 | QB | Vinny Testaverde, Cleveland | S | Blaine Bishop, Houston | K | Steve Christie, Buffalo |
| Week 18 | QB | Jeff Hostetler, L.A. Raiders | DT | Ray Childress, Houston | K | Jeff Jaeger, L.A. Raiders |

## 1993 AFC PLAYERS OF THE MONTH

| | Offense | | Defense | | Special Teams | |
|---|---|---|---|---|---|---|
| September | QB | Boomer Esiason, N.Y. Jets | DE | Anthony Smith, L.A. Raiders | K | John Carney, San Diego |
| October | QB | Scott Mitchell, Miami | DE | Bruce Smith, Buffalo | PR | Eric Metcalf, Cleveland |
| November | RB | Gary Brown, Houston | LB | Mo Lewis, N.Y. Jets | K | Al Del Greco, Houston |
| Dec.-Jan. | WR | Tim Brown, L.A. Raiders | CB | Cris Dishman, Houston | K | Jeff Jaeger, L.A. Raiders |

## 1993 NFC PLAYERS OF THE WEEK

| | Offense | | Defense | | Special Teams | |
|---|---|---|---|---|---|---|
| Week 1 | QB | Mark Rypien, Washington | LB | Lawrence Taylor, N.Y. Giants | K | Jason Hanson, Detroit |
| Week 2 | QB | Wade Wilson, New Orleans | DT | Sean Gilbert, L.A. Rams | KR | Johnny Bailey, Phoenix |
| Week 3 | WR | Calvin Williams, Philadelphia | LB | Renaldo Turnbull, New Orleans | P | Tommy Barnhardt, New Orleans |
| Week 4 | QB | Jim Everett, L.A. Rams | LB | Vaughan Johnson, New Orleans | K | Morten Andersen, New Orleans |
| Week 5 | QB | Troy Aikman, Dallas | CB | Eric Allen, Philadelphia | KR | Dexter Carter, San Francisco |
| Week 6 | TE | Jackie Harris, Green Bay | DE | Richard Dent, Chicago | K | Chris Jacke, Green Bay |
| Week 7 | WR | Michael Irvin, Dallas | DE | Eric Swann, Phoenix | LB | Darion Conner, Atlanta |
| Week 8 | WR | Sterling Sharpe, Green Bay | DT | John Randle, Minnesota | K | Norm Johnson, Atlanta |
| Week 9 | RB | Emmitt Smith, Dallas | LB | Hardy Nickerson, Tampa Bay | KR | Vernon Turner, Detroit |
| Week 10 | RB | Barry Sanders, Detroit | CB | Darrell Green, Washington | KR | Kevin Williams, Dallas |
| Week 11 | WR | Jerry Rice, San Francisco | DE | Reggie White, Green Bay | LB | Jessie Armstead, N.Y. Giants |
| Week 12 | QB | Bobby Hebert, Atlanta | CB | Merton Hanks, San Francisco | P | Sean Landeta, L.A. Rams |
| Week 13 | QB | Steve Young, San Francisco | DE | Trace Armstrong, Chicago | KR | Tyrone Hughes, New Orleans |
| Week 14 | RB | Ron Moore, Phoenix | LB | Dante Jones, Chicago | K | Brad Daluiso, N.Y. Giants |
| Week 15 | RB | Jerome Bettis, L.A. Rams | CB | Deion Sanders, Atlanta | K | Eddie Murray, Dallas |
| Week 16 | QB | Steve Young, San Francisco | CB | Kevin Smith, Dallas | RB | David Meggett, N.Y. Giants |
| Week 17 | RB | Ron Moore, Phoenix | CB | Eric Allen, Philadelphia | CB | Roger Jones, Tampa Bay |
| Week 18 | RB | Emmitt Smith, Dallas | CB | Ray Crockett, Detroit | P | Jim Arnold, Detroit |

## 1993 NFC PLAYERS OF THE MONTH

| | Offense | | Defense | | Special Teams | |
|---|---|---|---|---|---|---|
| September | QB | Randall Cunningham, Philadelphia | LB | Renaldo Turnbull, New Orleans | S | Pat Eilers, Washington |
| October | QB | Troy Aikman, Dallas | CB | Eric Davis, San Francisco | K | Jason Hanson, Detroit |
| November | QB | Steve Young, San Francisco | CB | Deion Sanders, Atlanta | LB | Jessie Armstead, N.Y. Giants |
| Dec.-Jan. | RB | Emmitt Smith, Dallas | DE | Chris Doleman, Minnesota | K | Jason Hanson, Detroit |

# 1993 ALL-PRO TEAMS

## 1993 PFWA ALL-PRO TEAM

*Selected by the Professional Football Writers of America*

**Offense**

| | |
|---|---|
| Jerry Rice, San Francisco | Wide Receiver |
| Sterling Sharpe, Green Bay | Wide Receiver |
| Shannon Sharpe, Denver | Tight End |
| Erik Williams, Dallas | Tackle |
| Harris Barton, San Francisco | Tackle |
| Randall McDaniel, Minnesota | Guard |
| Steve Wisniewski, Los Angeles Raiders | Guard |
| Bruce Matthews, Houston | Center |
| Steve Young, San Francisco | Quarterback |
| Jerome Bettis, Los Angeles Rams | Running Back |
| Emmitt Smith, Dallas | Running Back |

**Defense**

| | |
|---|---|
| Bruce Smith, Buffalo | End |
| Neil Smith, Kansas City | End |
| Cortez Kennedy, Seattle | Tackle |
| John Randle, Minnesota | Tackle |
| Greg Lloyd, Pittsburgh | Linebacker |
| Seth Joyner, Philadelphia | Linebacker |
| Junior Seau, San Diego | Linebacker |
| Hardy Nickerson, Tampa Bay | Linebacker |
| Rod Woodson, Pittsburgh | Cornerback |
| Deion Sanders, Atlanta | Cornerback |
| LeRoy Butler, Green Bay | Safety |
| Eugene Robinson, Seattle | Safety |

**Specialists**

| | |
|---|---|
| Norm Johnson, Atlanta | Kicker |
| Greg Montgomery, Houston | Punter |
| Tyrone Hughes, New Orleans | Kick Returner |
| Eric Metcalf, Cleveland | Punt Returner |
| Steve Tasker, Buffalo | Special Teams Player |

## 1993 ASSOCIATED PRESS ALL-PRO TEAM

**Offense**

| | |
|---|---|
| Jerry Rice, San Francisco | Wide Receiver |
| Sterling Sharpe, Green Bay | Wide Receiver |
| Shannon Sharpe, Denver | Tight End |
| Erik Williams, Dallas | Tackle |
| Harris Barton, San Francisco | Tackle |
| Randall McDaniel, Minnesota | Guard |
| Chris Hinton, Atlanta | Guard |
| Dermontti Dawson, Pittsburgh | Center |
| Steve Young, San Francisco | Quarterback |
| Jerome Bettis, L.A. Rams | Running Back |
| Emmitt Smith, Dallas | Running Back |

**Defense**

| | |
|---|---|
| Bruce Smith, Buffalo | End |
| Neil Smith, Kansas City | End |
| Cortez Kennedy, Seattle | Tackle |
| John Randle, Minnesota | Tackle |
| Greg Lloyd, Pittsburgh | Linebacker |
| Renaldo Turnbull, New Orleans | Linebacker |
| Junior Seau, San Diego | Linebacker |
| Hardy Nickerson, Tampa Bay | Linebacker |
| Rod Woodson, Pittsburgh | Cornerback |
| Deion Sanders, Atlanta | Cornerback |
| LeRoy Butler, Green Bay | Safety |
| Marcus Robertson, Houston | Safety |

**Specialists**

| | |
|---|---|
| Chris Jacke, Green Bay | Kicker |
| Greg Montgomery, Atlanta | Punter |
| Eric Metcalf, Cleveland | Kick Returner |

## 1993 ALL-NFL TEAM

*Selected by the Associated Press and the Professional Football Writers of America*

**Offense**

| | |
|---|---|
| Jerry Rice, San Francisco (AP, PFWA) | Wide Receiver |
| Sterling Sharpe, Green Bay (AP, PFWA) | Wide Receiver |
| Shannon Sharpe, Denver (AP, PFWA) | Tight End |
| Erik Williams, Dallas (AP, PFWA) | Tackle |
| Harris Barton, San Francisco (AP, PFWA) | Tackle |
| Randall McDaniel, Minnesota (AP, PFWA) | Guard |
| Chris Hinton, Atlanta (AP) | Guard |
| Steve Wisniewski, L.A. Raiders (PFWA) | Guard |
| Dermontti Dawson, Pittsburgh (AP) | Center |
| Bruce Matthews, Houston (PFWA) | Center |
| Steve Young, San Francisco (AP, PFWA) | Quarterback |
| Jerome Bettis, L.A. Rams (AP, PFWA) | Running Back |
| Emmitt Smith, Dallas (AP, PFWA) | Running Back |

**Defense**

| | |
|---|---|
| Bruce Smith, Buffalo (AP, PFWA) | End |
| Neil Smith, Kansas City (AP, PFWA) | End |
| Cortez Kennedy, Seattle (AP, PFWA) | Tackle |
| John Randle, Minnesota (AP, PFWA) | Tackle |
| Greg Lloyd, Pittsburgh (AP, PFWA) | Linebacker |
| Renaldo Turnbull (AP) | Linebacker |
| Seth Joyner, Philadelphia (PFWA) | Linebacker |
| Junior Seau, San Diego (AP, PFWA) | Linebacker |
| Hardy Nickerson, Tampa Bay (AP, PFWA) | Linebacker |
| Rod Woodson, Pittsburgh (AP, PFWA) | Cornerback |
| Deion Sanders, Atlanta (AP, PFWA) | Cornerback |
| LeRoy Butler, Green Bay (AP, PFWA) | Safety |
| Marcus Robertson, Houston (AP) | Safety |
| Eugene Robinson, Seattle (PFWA) | Safety |

**Specialists**

| | |
|---|---|
| Chris Jacke, Green Bay (AP) | Kicker |
| Norm Johnson, Atlanta (PFWA) | Kicker |
| Greg Montgomery, Houston (AP, PFWA) | Punter |
| Eric Metcalf, Cleveland (AP) | Kick Returner |
| Tyrone Hughes, New Orleans (PFWA) | Kick Returner |
| Eric Metcalf, Cleveland (PFWA) | Punt Returner |
| Steve Tasker, Buffalo (PFWA) | Special Teams Player |

## 1993 UPI ALL-AFC TEAM

*Selected by United Press International*

**Offense**

| | |
|---|---|
| Tim Brown, L.A. Raiders | Wide Receiver |
| Anthony Miller, San Diego | Wide Receiver |
| Shannon Sharpe, Denver | Tight End |
| Richmond Webb, Miami | Tackle |
| Howard Ballard, Buffalo | Tackle |
| Mike Munchak, Houston | Guard |
| Steve Wisniewski, L.A. Raiders | Guard |
| Bruce Matthews, Houston | Center |
| John Elway, Denver | Quarterback |
| Thurman Thomas, Buffalo | Running Back |
| Marcus Allen, Kansas City | Running Back |

**Defense**

| | |
|---|---|
| Bruce Smith, Buffalo | End |
| Neil Smith, Kansas City | End |
| Cortez Kennedy, Seattle | Tackle |
| Ray Childress, Houston | Tackle |
| Junior Seau, San Diego | Linebacker |
| Greg Lloyd, Pittsburgh | Linebacker |
| Derrick Thomas, Kansas City | Linebacker |
| Rod Woodson, Pittsburgh | Cornerback |
| Nate Odomes, Buffalo | Cornerback |
| Marcus Robertson, Houston | Safety |
| Steve Atwater, Denver | Safety |

**Specialists**

| | |
|---|---|
| Gary Anderson, Pittsburgh | Kicker |
| Greg Montgomery, Houston | Punter |
| Eric Metcalf, Cleveland | Kick Returner |

## 1993 UPI ALL-NFC TEAM

*Selected by United Press International*

**Offense**

| | |
|---|---|
| Sterling Sharpe, Green Bay | Wide Receiver |
| Jerry Rice, San Francisco | Wide Receiver |
| Brent Jones, San Francisco | Tight End |
| Erik Williams, Dallas | Tackle |
| Harris Barton, San Francisco | Tackle |
| Randall McDaniel, Minnesota | Guard |
| Chris Hinton, Atlanta | Guard |
| Mark Stepnoski, Dallas | Center |
| Steve Young, San Francisco | Quarterback |
| Jerome Bettis, Los Angeles Rams | Running Back |
| Emmitt Smith, Dallas | Running Back |

**Defense**

| | |
|---|---|
| Reggie White, Green Bay | End |
| Chris Doleman, Minnesota | End |
| John Randle, Minnesota | Tackle |
| Sean Gilbert, Los Angeles Rams | Tackle |
| Renaldo Turnbull, New Orleans | Linebacker |
| Rickey Jackson, New Orleans | Linebacker |
| Michael Brooks, New York Giants | Linebacker |
| Deion Sanders, Atlanta | Cornerback |
| Eric Allen, Philadelphia | Cornerback |
| LeRoy Butler, Green Bay | Safety |
| Tim McDonald, San Francisco | Safety |

**Specialists**

| | |
|---|---|
| Norm Johnson, Atlanta | Kicker |
| Rich Camarillo, Phoenix | Punter |
| Tyrone Hughes, New Orleans | Kick Returner |

## 1993 PFWA ALL-ROOKIE TEAM

*Selected by the Professional Football Writers of America*

**Offense**

| | |
|---|---|
| James Jett, Los Angeles Raiders | Wide Receiver |
| Vincent Brisby, New England | Wide Receiver |
| Tony McGee, Cincinnati | Tight End |
| William Roaf, New Orleans | Tackle |
| Brad Hopkins, Houston | Tackle |
| Lincoln Kennedy, Atlanta | Guard |
| Will Shields, Kansas City | Guard |
| Steve Everitt, Cleveland | Center |
| Rick Mirer, Seattle | Quarterback |
| Jerome Bettis, Los Angeles Rams | Running Back |
| Reggie Brooks, Washington | Running Back |

**Defense**

| | |
|---|---|
| John Copeland, Cincinnati | End |
| Eric Curry, Tampa Bay | End |
| Dana Stubblefield, San Francisco | Tackle |
| Leonard Renfro, Philadelphia | Tackle |
| Darrin Smith, Dallas | Linebacker |
| Wayne Simmons, Green Bay | Linebacker |
| Chad Brown, Pittsburgh | Linebacker |
| Steve Tovar, Cincinnati | Linebacker |
| Tom Carter, Washington | Cornerback |
| Darrien Gordon, San Diego | Cornerback |
| George Teague, Green Bay | Safety |
| Roger Harper, Atlanta | Safety |

**Specialists**

| | |
|---|---|
| Jason Elam, Denver | Kicker |
| Tyrone Hughes, New Orleans | Punt and Kick Returner |
| Jessie Armstead, New York Giants | Special Teams Player |

## 1993 BEST PERFORMANCES

### TEN BEST RUSHING PERFORMANCES, 1993

| | Att. | Yards | TD |
|---|---|---|---|
| 1. Emmitt Smith | | | |
| Dallas vs. Philadelphia, October 31 | 30 | 237 | 1 |
| 2. Jerome Bettis | | | |
| L.A. Rams vs. New Orleans, December 12 | 28 | 212 | 1 |
| 3. Gary Brown | | | |
| Houston vs. Cleveland, November 21 | 34 | 194 | 1 |
| 4. Erric Pegram | | | |
| Atlanta vs. San Francisco, September 19 | 27 | 192 | 0 |
| 5. Barry Sanders | | | |
| Detroit vs. Tampa Bay, November 7 | 29 | 187 | 0 |
| 6. Erric Pegram | | | |
| Atlanta vs. Cincinnati, December 26 | 37 | 180 | 1 |
| 7. Chris Warren | | | |
| Seattle vs. New England, September 19 | 36 | 174 | 1 |
| 8. Rodney Hampton | | | |
| N.Y. Giants vs. Indianapolis, December 12 | 33 | 173 | 1 |
| 9. Emmitt Smith | | | |
| Dallas vs. Philadelphia, December 6 | 23 | 172 | 0 |
| 10. Lewis Tillman | | | |
| N.Y. Giants vs. Philadelphia, October 17 | 20 | 169 | 2 |

### 100-YARD RUSHING PERFORMANCES, 1993

| | |
|---|---|
| **First Week** | |
| Brian Mitchell, Washington | 116 yards vs. Dallas |
| Thurman Thomas, Buffalo | 114 yards vs. New England |
| **Second Week** | |
| Barry Sanders, Detroit | 148 yards vs. New England |
| Rodney Hampton, N.Y. Giants | 134 yards vs. Tampa Bay |
| **Third Week** | |
| Erric Pegram, Atlanta | 192 yards vs. San Francisco |
| Chris Warren, Seattle | 174 yards vs. New England |
| Reggie Brooks, Washington | 154 yards vs. Philadelphia |
| Rodney Hampton, N.Y. Giants | 134 yards vs. L.A. Rams |
| Derek Brown, New Orleans | 125 yards vs. Detroit |
| Ricky Watters, San Francisco | 112 yards vs. Atlanta |
| Tommy Vardell, Cleveland | 104 yards vs. L.A. Raiders |
| Barry Foster, Pittsburgh | 103 yards vs. Cincinnati |
| **Fourth Week** | |
| Ricky Watters, San Francisco | 135 yards vs. New Orleans |
| Neal Anderson, Chicago | 104 yards vs. Tampa Bay |
| **Fifth Week** | |
| Barry Sanders, Detroit | 130 yards vs. Tampa Bay |
| Thurman Thomas, Buffalo | 122 yards vs. N.Y. Giants |
| Reggie Cobb, Tampa Bay | 113 yards vs. Detroit |
| Jerome Bettis, L.A. Rams | 102 yards vs. New Orleans |
| **Sixth Week** | |
| Leonard Russell, New England | 116 yards vs. Phoenix |
| Roosevelt Potts, Indianapolis | 113 yards vs. Dallas |
| Barry Foster, Pittsburgh | 110 yards vs. San Diego |
| Emmitt Smith, Dallas | 104 yards vs. Indianapolis |
| Lewis Tillman, N.Y. Giants | 104 yards vs. Washington |
| **Seventh Week** | |
| Lewis Tillman, N.Y. Giants | 169 yards vs. Philadelphia |
| Rod Bernstine, Denver | 101 yards vs. L.A. Raiders |
| Barry Sanders, Detroit | 101 yards vs. Seattle |
| Leroy Thompson, Pittsburgh | 101 yards vs. New Orleans |
| **Eighth Week** | |
| Erric Pegram, Atlanta | 132 yards vs. New Orleans |
| Thurman Thomas, Buffalo | 117 yards vs. N.Y. Jets |
| Mark Higgs, Miami | 114 yards vs. Indianapolis |
| Jerome Bettis, L.A. Rams | 113 yards vs. Detroit |
| Darrell Thompson, Green Bay | 105 yards vs. Tampa Bay |
| **Ninth Week** | |
| Emmitt Smith, Dallas | 237 yards vs. Philadelphia |
| Thurman Thomas, Buffalo | 129 yards vs. Washington |
| Reggie Brooks, Washington | 117 yards vs. Buffalo |
| Robert Smith, Minnesota | 115 yards vs. Detroit |
| **Tenth Week** | |
| Barry Sanders, Detroit | 187 yards vs. Tampa Bay |
| Ron Moore, Phoenix | 160 yards vs. Philadelphia |
| Barry Foster, Pittsburgh | 120 yards vs. Cincinnati |
| Emmitt Smith, Dallas | 117 yards vs. N.Y. Giants |
| Thurman Thomas, Buffalo | 111 yards vs. New England |
| Reggie Brooks, Washington | 105 yards vs. Indianapolis |
| Natrone Means, San Diego | 105 yards vs. Minnesota |
| **Eleventh Week** | |
| Gary Brown, Houston | 166 yards vs. Cincinnati |
| Johnny Johnson, N.Y. Jets | 141 yards vs. Indianapolis |
| Erric Pegram, Atlanta | 128 yards vs. L.A. Rams |
| Chris Warren, Seattle | 112 yards vs. Cleveland |
| Leroy Thompson, Pittsburgh | 108 yards vs. Buffalo |
| Derek Brown, New Orleans | 106 yards vs. Green Bay |
| **Twelfth Week** | |
| Gary Brown, Houston | 194 yards vs. Cleveland |
| Thurman Thomas, Buffalo | 116 yards vs. Indianapolis |
| Ricky Watters, San Francisco | 116 yards vs. New Orleans |
| Mark Higgs, Miami | 108 yards vs. New England |
| Rodney Hampton, N.Y. Giants | 101 yards vs. Philadelphia |
| **Thirteenth Week** | |
| Leonard Russell, New England | 147 yards vs. N.Y. Jets |
| Jerome Bettis, L.A. Rams | 133 yards vs. San Francisco |
| **Fourteenth Week** | |
| Emmitt Smith, Dallas | 172 yards vs. Philadelphia |
| Reggie Brooks, Washington | 128 yards vs. Tampa Bay |
| Ron Moore, Phoenix | 126 yards vs. L.A. Rams |
| Jerome Bettis, L.A. Rams | 115 yards vs. Phoenix |
| **Fifteenth Week** | |
| Jerome Bettis, L.A. Rams | 212 yards vs. New Orleans |
| Rodney Hampton, N.Y. Giants | 173 yards vs. Indianapolis |
| Johnny Johnson, N.Y. Jets | 155 yards vs. Washington |
| Gary Brown, Houston | 109 yards vs. Cleveland |
| Derrick Moore, Detroit | 107 yards vs. Phoenix |
| Emmitt Smith, Dallas | 104 yards vs. Minnesota |
| **Sixteenth Week** | |
| Chris Warren, Seattle | 168 yards vs. Phoenix |
| Steve Broussard, Atlanta | 162 yards vs. Washington |
| Scottie Graham, Minnesota | 139 yards vs. Green Bay |
| Jerome Bettis, L.A. Rams | 124 yards vs. Cincinnati |
| Gary Brown, Houston | 100 yards vs. Pittsburgh |
| **Seventeenth Week** | |
| Erric Pegram, Atlanta | 180 yards vs. Cincinnati |
| Scottie Graham, Minnesota | 166 yards vs. Kansas City |
| Emmitt Smith, Dallas | 153 yards vs. Washington |
| Leonard Russell, New England | 138 yards vs. Indianapolis |
| Ron Moore, Phoenix | 135 yards vs. N.Y. Giants |
| Jon Vaughn, Seattle | 131 yards vs. Pittsburgh |
| Natrone Means, San Diego | 118 yards vs. Miami |
| Darrell Thompson, Green Bay | 101 yards vs. L.A. Raiders |
| **Eighteenth Week** | |
| Emmitt Smith, Dallas | 168 yards vs. N.Y. Giants |
| Jerome Bettis, L.A. Rams | 146 yards vs. Chicago |
| Eric Lynch, Detroit | 115 yards vs. Green Bay |
| Rodney Hampton, N.Y. Giants | 114 yards vs. Dallas |
| Thurman Thomas, Buffalo | 110 yards vs. Indianapolis |
| John L. Williams, Seattle | 102 yards vs. Kansas City |
| Roosevelt Potts, Indianapolis | 100 yards vs. Buffalo |

**Times 100 or More (86)**
Bettis, E. Smith, T. Thomas, 7; Hampton, 5; Brooks, G. Brown, Pegram, Sanders, 4; Foster, R. Moore, Russell, C. Warren, Watters, 3; D. Brown, Graham, Higgs, J. Johnson, Means, Potts, D. Thompson, L. Thompson, Tillman, 2.

## TEN BEST PASSING PERFORMANCES, 1993

| | Att. | Comp. | Yards | TD |
|---|---|---|---|---|
| 1. Steve Young<br>San Francisco vs. L.A. Rams, November 28 | 32 | 26 | 462 | 4 |
| 2. Steve Beuerlein<br>Phoenix vs. Seattle, December 19 | 53 | 34 | 431 | 3 |
| 3. Jeff Hostetler<br>L.A. Raiders vs. San Diego, October 31 | 32 | 20 | 424 | 2 |
| 4. Brett Favre<br>Green Bay vs. Chicago, December 5 | 54 | 36 | 402 | 2 |
| 5. Jeff George<br>Indianapolis vs. Washington, November 7 | 59 | 37 | 376 | 3 |
| 6. Boomer Esiason<br>N.Y. Jets vs. Denver, September 5 | 40 | 29 | 371 | 2 |
| 7. Warren Moon<br>Houston vs. Seattle, November 7 | 55 | 36 | 369 | 2 |
| 8. John Elway<br>Denver vs. Green Bay, October 10 | 59 | 33 | 367 | 1 |
| 9. Sean Salisbury<br>Minnesota vs. Denver, November 14 | 37 | 19 | 366 | 2 |
| 10. Steve DeBerg<br>Miami vs. N.Y. Giants, December 5 | 41 | 26 | 365 | 1 |

## 300-YARD PASSING PERFORMANCES, 1993

**First Week**
Boomer Esiason, N.Y. Jets — 371 yards vs. Denver

**Second Week**
Wade Wilson, New Orleans — 341 yards vs. Atlanta
Boomer Esiason, N.Y. Jets — 323 yards vs. Miami

**Third Week**
Randall Cunningham, Philadelphia — 360 yards vs. Washington
John Elway, Denver — 300 yards vs. Kansas City

**Fourth Week**
Jim Everett, L.A. Rams — 316 yards vs. Houston
Warren Moon, Houston — 310 yards vs. L.A. Rams

**Fifth Week**
Troy Aikman, Dallas — 317 yards vs. Green Bay

**Sixth Week**
John Elway, Denver — 367 yards vs. Green Bay

**Seventh Week**
None

**Eighth Week**
Neil O'Donnell, Pittsburgh — 355 yards vs. Cleveland
Steve Beuerlein, Phoenix — 334 yards vs. San Francisco

**Ninth Week**
Jeff Hostetler, L.A. Raiders — 424 yards vs. San Diego
Scott Mitchell, Miami — 344 yards vs. Kansas City
Craig Erickson, Tampa Bay — 318 yards vs. Atlanta

**Tenth Week**
Jeff George, Indianapolis — 376 yards vs. Washington
Warren Moon, Houston — 369 yards vs. Seattle
Sean Salisbury, Minnesota — 347 yards vs. San Diego
Jim Kelly, Buffalo — 317 yards vs. New England

**Eleventh Week**
Sean Salisbury, Minnesota — 366 yards vs. Denver
Steve Young, San Francisco — 311 yards vs. Tampa Bay

**Twelfth Week**
Todd Philcox, Cleveland — 316 yards vs. Houston
Bobby Hebert, Atlanta — 315 yards vs. Dallas

**Thirteenth Week**
Steve Young, San Francisco — 462 yards vs. L.A. Rams
Phil Simms, N.Y. Giants — 337 yards vs. Phoenix

**Fourteenth Week**
Brett Favre, Green Bay — 402 yards vs. Chicago
Steve DeBerg, Miami — 365 yards vs. N.Y. Giants
Warren Moon, Houston — 342 yards vs. Atlanta
Bobby Hebert, Atlanta — 317 yards vs. Houston

**Fifteenth Week**
Steve DeBerg, Miami — 344 yards vs. Pittsburgh
Vinny Testaverde, Cleveland — 319 yards vs. Houston

**Sixteenth Week**
Steve Beuerlein, Phoenix — 431 yards vs. Seattle
Steve Young, San Francisco — 354 yards vs. Detroit

**Seventeenth Week**
None

**Eighteenth Week**
John Elway, Denver — 361 yards vs. L.A. Raiders
Bubby Brister, Philadelphia — 350 yards vs. San Francisco
Jeff George, Indianapolis — 330 yards vs. Buffalo
Drew Bledsoe, New England — 329 yards vs. Miami
Jeff Hostetler, L.A. Raiders — 310 yards vs. Denver

**Times 300 or More (37)**
Elway, Moon, Young, 3; Beuerlein, DeBerg, Esiason, George, Hebert, Hostetler, Salisbury, 2.

# 1993 BEST PERFORMANCES

## TEN BEST RECEIVING PERFORMANCES, 1993

| | Yards | No. | TD |
|---|---|---|---|
| 1. Reggie Langhorne<br>Indianapolis vs. Washington, November 7 | 203 | 12 | 1 |
| 2. Jeff Graham<br>Pittsburgh vs. Houston, December 19 | 192 | 7 | 0 |
| 3. Tim Brown<br>L.A. Raiders vs. Buffalo, December 5 | 183 | 10 | 1 |
| 4. Michael Haynes<br>Atlanta vs. New Orleans, September 12 | 182 | 7 | 2 |
| 5. Calvin Williams<br>Philadelphia vs. Washington, September 19 | 181 | 8 | 3 |
| 6. Tim Brown<br>L.A. Raiders vs. Denver, January 2 | 173 | 11 | 2 |
| 7. Jerry Rice<br>San Francisco vs. Tampa Bay, November 14 | 172 | 8 | 4 |
| 8. Michael Irvin<br>Dallas vs. San Francisco, October 17 | 168 | 12 | 1 |
| 9. Jerry Rice<br>San Francisco vs. L.A. Rams, November 28 | 166 | 8 | 2 |
| 10. Anthony Carter<br>Minnesota vs. San Diego, November 7 | 164 | 10 | 1 |

## 100-YARD RECEIVING PERFORMANCES, 1993

| | |
|---|---|
| **First Week** | |
| Alvin Harper, Dallas | 140 yards vs. Washington |
| Rob Moore, N.Y. Jets | 140 yards vs. Denver |
| Sterling Sharpe, Green Bay | 120 yards vs. L.A. Rams |
| Herman Moore, Detroit | 113 yards vs. Atlanta |
| Eric Martin, New Orleans | 111 yards vs. Houston |
| Andre Reed, Buffalo | 110 yards vs. New England |
| Andre Rison, Atlanta | 106 yards vs. Detroit |
| **Second Week** | |
| Michael Haynes, Atlanta | 182 yards vs. New Orleans |
| Henry Ellard, L.A. Rams | 127 yards vs. Pittsburgh |
| Rob Moore, N.Y. Jets | 124 yards vs. Miami |
| Nate Lewis, San Diego | 119 yards vs. Denver |
| Michael Irvin, Dallas | 115 yards vs. Buffalo |
| Jay Novacek, Dallas | 106 yards vs. Buffalo |
| Michael Jackson, Cleveland | 105 yards vs. San Francisco |
| **Third Week** | |
| Calvin Williams, Philadelphia | 181 yards vs. Washington |
| Willie Davis, Kansas City | 139 yards vs. Denver |
| Alvin Harper, Dallas | 136 yards vs. Phoenix |
| Derek Russell, Denver | 104 yards vs. Kansas City |
| **Fourth Week** | |
| Henry Ellard, L.A. Rams | 132 yards vs. Houston |
| Jessie Hester, Indianapolis | 110 yards vs. Cleveland |
| Ernest Givins, Houston | 107 yards vs. L.A. Rams |
| Irving Fryar, Miami | 103 yards vs. Buffalo |
| Willie Green, Detroit | 102 yards vs. Phoenix |
| Tony McGee, Cincinnati | 102 yards vs. Seattle |
| Lawrence Dawsey, Tampa Bay | 101 yards vs. Chicago |
| **Fifth Week** | |
| Michael Irvin, Dallas | 155 yards vs. Green Bay |
| Johnny Mitchell, N.Y. Jets | 146 yards vs. Philadelphia |
| Brian Blades, Seattle | 132 yards vs. San Diego |
| Anthony Miller, San Diego | 123 yards vs. Seattle |
| Tony Martin, Miami | 110 yards vs. Washington |
| Chris Burkett, N.Y. Jets | 103 yards vs. Philadelphia |
| **Sixth Week** | |
| Vance Johnson, Denver | 148 yards vs. Green Bay |
| Sean Dawkins, Indianapolis | 144 yards vs. Dallas |
| Jackie Harris, Green Bay | 128 yards vs. Denver |
| Mike Sherrard, N.Y. Giants | 124 yards vs. Washington |
| Michael Irvin, Dallas | 112 yards vs. Indianapolis |
| **Seventh Week** | |
| Michael Irvin, Dallas | 168 yards vs. San Francisco |
| Tim Brown, L.A. Raiders | 116 yards vs. Denver |
| Ricky Proehl, Phoenix | 115 yards vs. Washington |
| Derek Russell, Denver | 111 yards vs. L.A. Raiders |
| Anthony Miller, San Diego | 105 yards vs. Kansas City |
| **Eighth Week** | |
| Jerry Rice, San Francisco | 155 yards vs. Phoenix |
| Sterling Sharpe, Green Bay | 147 yards vs. Tampa Bay |
| Carl Pickens, Cincinnati | 127 yards vs. Houston |
| Herman Moore, Detroit | 120 yards vs. L.A. Rams |
| Anthony Edwards, Phoenix | 112 yards vs. San Francisco |
| Eric Green, Pittsburgh | 108 yards vs. Cleveland |
| Michael Jackson, Cleveland | 106 yards vs. Pittsburgh |
| **Ninth Week** | |
| Andre Reed, Buffalo | 159 yards vs. Washington |
| Tim Brown, L.A. Raiders | 156 yards vs. San Diego |
| Andre Rison, Atlanta | 147 yards vs. Tampa Bay |
| Herman Moore, Detroit | 113 yards vs. Minnesota |
| Ben Coates, New England | 108 yards vs. Indianapolis |
| Horace Copeland, Tampa Bay | 104 yards vs. Atlanta |
| Mark Ingram, Miami | 103 yards vs. Kansas City |
| **Tenth Week** | |
| Reggie Langhorne, Indianapolis | 203 yards vs. Washington |
| Anthony Carter, Minnesota | 164 yards vs. San Diego |
| Anthony Miller, San Diego | 142 yards vs. Minnesota |
| Webster Slaughter, Houston | 135 yards vs. Seattle |
| Irving Fryar, Miami | 111 yards vs. N.Y. Jets |
| **Eleventh Week** | |
| Jerry Rice, San Francisco | 172 yards vs. Tampa Bay |
| Cris Carter, Minnesota | 134 yards vs. Denver |
| Andre Rison, Atlanta | 120 yards vs. L.A. Rams |
| Willie Davis, Kansas City | 115 yards vs. L.A. Raiders |
| Reggie Langhorne, Indianapolis | 112 yards vs. N.Y. Jets |
| Anthony Carter, Minnesota | 111 yards vs. Denver |
| Shannon Sharpe, Denver | 104 yards vs. Minnesota |
| Emmitt Smith, Dallas | 102 yards vs. Phoenix |
| **Twelfth Week** | |
| James Jett, L.A. Raiders | 138 yards vs. San Diego |
| Mark Carrier, Cleveland | 123 yards vs. Houston |
| Anthony Carter, Minnesota | 104 yards vs. Tampa Bay |
| **Thirteenth Week** | |
| Jerry Rice, San Francisco | 166 yards vs. L.A. Rams |
| John Taylor, San Francisco | 150 yards vs. L.A. Rams |
| Haywood Jeffires, Houston | 139 yards vs. Pittsburgh |
| James Jett, L.A. Raiders | 117 yards vs. Cincinnati |
| Mark Jackson, N.Y. Giants | 113 yards vs. Phoenix |
| Herschel Walker, Philadelphia | 103 yards vs. Washington |
| Jeff Graham, Pittsburgh | 102 yards vs. Houston |
| **Fourteenth Week** | |
| Tim Brown, L.A. Raiders | 183 yards vs. Buffalo |
| Gary Clark, Phoenix | 159 yards vs. L.A. Rams |
| Brian Blades, Seattle | 134 yards vs. Kansas City |
| Don Beebe, Buffalo | 115 yards vs. L.A. Raiders |
| Sterling Sharpe, Green Bay | 114 yards vs. Chicago |
| Courtney Hawkins, Tampa Bay | 112 yards vs. Washington |
| Webster Slaughter, Houston | 108 yards vs. Atlanta |
| **Fifteenth Week** | |
| Michael Irvin, Dallas | 125 yards vs. Minnesota |
| Herschel Walker, Philadelphia | 109 yards vs. Buffalo |
| Terry Kirby, Miami | 107 yards vs. Pittsburgh |
| Andre Rison, Atlanta | 107 yards vs. San Francisco |
| Jerry Rice, San Francisco | 105 yards vs. Atlanta |
| Anthony Miller, San Diego | 103 yards vs. Green Bay |
| Eric Metcalf, Cleveland | 101 yards vs. Houston |

**Sixteenth Week**

| | |
|---|---|
| Jeff Graham, Pittsburgh | 192 yards vs. Houston |
| Gary Clark, Phoenix | 152 yards vs. Seattle |
| Terry Kirby, Miami | 148 yards vs. Buffalo |
| Jerry Rice, San Francisco | 132 yards vs. Detroit |
| John Taylor, San Francisco | 115 yards vs. Detroit |
| Cris Carter, Minnesota | 106 yards vs. Green Bay |
| Sterling Sharpe, Green Bay | 106 yards vs. Minnesota |
| Calvin Williams, Philadelphia | 105 yards vs. Indianapolis |
| Alexander Wright, L.A. Raiders | 104 yards vs. Tampa Bay |
| **Seventeenth Week** | |
| Eric Green, Pittsburgh | 119 yards vs. Seattle |
| Sterling Sharpe, Green Bay | 119 yards vs. L.A. Raiders |
| Henry Ellard, L.A. Rams | 114 yards vs. Cleveland |
| Anthony Miller, San Diego | 110 yards vs. Miami |
| Courtney Hawkins, Tampa Bay | 105 yards vs. Denver |
| Dwight Stone, Pittsburgh | 100 yards vs. Seattle |
| **Eighteenth Week** | |
| Tim Brown, L.A. Raiders | 173 yards vs. Denver |
| Gary Clark, Phoenix | 121 yards vs. Atlanta |
| Eric Martin, New Orleans | 120 yards vs. Cincinnati |
| Anthony Miller, San Diego | 119 yards vs. Tampa Bay |
| Mark Carrier, Cleveland | 118 yards vs. Pittsburgh |
| Shannon Sharpe, Denver | 115 yards vs. L.A. Raiders |
| James Joseph, Philadelphia | 109 yards vs. San Francisco |
| Gary Wellman, Houston | 106 yards vs. N.Y. Jets |
| Horace Copeland, Tampa Bay | 101 yards vs. San Diego |

**Times 100 or More (116)**
Miller, 6; Irvin, Rice, Sterling Sharpe, 5; Brown, Rison, 4; A. Carter, Clark, Ellard, H. Moore, 3; Blades, Carrier, C. Carter, Copeland, Davis, Fryar, Graham, Green, Harper, Hawkins, Michael Jackson, Jett, Kirby, Langhorne, E. Martin, R. Moore, Reed, Russell, Shannon Sharpe, Slaughter, J. Taylor, Walker, Williams, 2.

## TOP QUARTERBACK SACK PERFORMANCES, 1993

**(2.5 or More Sacks Per Game Needed to Qualify)**

| | |
|---|---|
| **First Week** | |
| Robert Young, L.A. Rams | 3.0 vs. Green Bay |
| **Second Week** | |
| Sean Gilbert, L.A. Rams | 4.0 vs. Pittsburgh |
| Anthony Smith, L.A. Raiders | 4.0 vs. Seattle |
| Keith Hamilton, N.Y. Giants | 3.0 vs. Tampa Bay |
| Ken Harvey, Phoenix | 3.0 vs. Washington |
| Chris Slade, New England | 3.0 vs. Detroit |
| **Third Week** | |
| Renaldo Turnbull, New Orleans | 3.0 vs. Detroit |
| **Fourth Week** | |
| Duane Bickett, Indianapolis | 3.0 vs. Cleveland |
| **Fifth Week** | |
| Neil Smith, Kansas City | 4.0 vs. L.A. Raiders |
| Michael Sinclair, Seattle | 3.0 vs. San Diego |
| Henry Thomas, Minnesota | 3.0 vs. San Francisco |
| Martin Harrison, San Francisco | 2.5 vs. Minnesota |
| **Sixth Week** | |
| Jeff Cross, Miami | 3.0 vs. Cleveland |
| Reggie White, Green Bay | 3.0 vs. Denver |
| Richard Dent, Chicago | 2.5 vs. Philadelphia |
| **Seventh Week** | |
| Andre Collins, Washington | 3.0 vs. Phoenix |
| Greg Townsend, L.A. Raiders | 3.0 vs. Denver |
| **Eighth Week** | |
| John Randle, Minnesota | 3.0 vs. Chicago |
| **Ninth Week** | |
| Renaldo Turnbull, New Orleans | 3.0 vs. Phoenix |
| Troy Wilson, San Francisco | 3.0 vs. L.A. Rams |
| **Tenth Week** | |
| Bryce Paup, Green Bay | 3.0 vs. Kansas City |
| **Eleventh Week** | |
| Jeff Cross, Miami | 3.0 vs. Philadelphia |
| Rickey Jackson, New Orleans | 3.0 vs. Green Bay |
| **Twelfth Week** | |
| Trace Armstrong, Chicago | 2.5 vs. Kansas City |
| **Thirteenth Week** | |
| William Fuller, Houston | 4.0 vs. Pittsburgh |
| Chester McGlockton, L.A. Raiders | 3.0 vs. Cincinnati |
| **Fourteenth Week** | |
| John Randle, Minnesota | 3.0 vs. Detroit |
| Andy Harmon, Philadelphia | 2.5 vs. Dallas |
| **Fifteenth Week** | |
| None | |
| **Sixteenth Week** | |
| None | |
| **Seventeenth Week** | |
| Kevin Greene, Pittsburgh | 3.0 vs. Seattle |
| Tony Bennett, Green Bay | 2.5 vs. L.A. Raiders |
| John Jurkovic, Green Bay | 2.5 vs. L.A. Raiders |
| Reggie White, Green Bay | 2.5 vs. L.A. Raiders |
| **Eighteenth Week** | |
| Ray Childress, Houston | 3.0 vs. N.Y. Jets |
| Andy Harmon, Philadelphia | 3.0 vs. San Francisco |
| Anthony Pleasant, Cleveland | 3.0 vs. Pittsburgh |
| Marvin Washington, N.Y. Jets | 2.5 vs. Houston |

## 1993 TEAM STATISTICS

### AMERICAN FOOTBALL CONFERENCE OFFENSE

| | Buff. | Cin. | Clev. | Den. | Hou. | Ind. | K.C. | Raid. | Mia. | N.E. | N.Y.J. | Pitt. | S.D. | Sea. |
|---|---|---|---|---|---|---|---|---|---|---|---|---|---|---|
| **First Downs** | 316 | 239 | 264 | 327 | 330 | 269 | 300 | 292 | 309 | 315 | 304 | 307 | 313 | 279 |
| Rushing | 117 | 89 | 91 | 105 | 101 | 71 | 94 | 95 | 85 | 116 | 106 | 116 | 120 | 114 |
| Passing | 176 | 133 | 152 | 187 | 208 | 180 | 180 | 168 | 207 | 169 | 173 | 180 | 171 | 144 |
| Penalty | 23 | 17 | 21 | 35 | 21 | 18 | 26 | 29 | 17 | 30 | 25 | 11 | 22 | 21 |
| **Rushes** | 550 | 423 | 425 | 468 | 409 | 365 | 445 | 433 | 419 | 502 | 521 | 491 | 455 | 473 |
| Net Yds. Gained | 1943 | 1511 | 1701 | 1693 | 1792 | 1288 | 1655 | 1425 | 1459 | 1780 | 1880 | 2003 | 1824 | 2015 |
| Avg. Gain | 3.5 | 3.6 | 4.0 | 3.6 | 4.4 | 3.5 | 3.7 | 3.3 | 3.5 | 3.5 | 3.6 | 4.1 | 4.0 | 4.3 |
| Avg. Yds. per Game | 121.4 | 94.4 | 106.3 | 105.8 | 112.0 | 80.5 | 103.4 | 89.1 | 91.2 | 111.3 | 117.5 | 125.2 | 114.0 | 125.9 |
| **Passes Attempted** | 497 | 510 | 478 | 553 | 614 | 594 | 490 | 495 | 581 | 566 | 489 | 540 | 563 | 498 |
| Completed | 304 | 272 | 262 | 350 | 357 | 332 | 287 | 281 | 342 | 289 | 294 | 299 | 301 | 280 |
| % Completed | 61.2 | 53.3 | 54.8 | 63.3 | 58.1 | 55.9 | 58.6 | 56.8 | 58.9 | 51.1 | 60.1 | 55.4 | 53.5 | 56.2 |
| Total Yds. Gained | 3535 | 2830 | 3328 | 4061 | 4145 | 3623 | 3384 | 3882 | 4564 | 3412 | 3492 | 3606 | 3383 | 2896 |
| Times Sacked | 31 | 53 | 45 | 39 | 43 | 29 | 35 | 50 | 30 | 23 | 21 | 48 | 32 | 48 |
| Yds. Lost | 218 | 289 | 289 | 293 | 279 | 206 | 204 | 293 | 211 | 127 | 160 | 374 | 240 | 242 |
| Net Yds. Gained | 3317 | 2541 | 3039 | 3768 | 3866 | 3417 | 3180 | 3589 | 4353 | 3285 | 3332 | 3232 | 3143 | 2654 |
| Avg. Yds. per Game | 207.3 | 158.8 | 189.9 | 235.5 | 241.6 | 213.6 | 198.8 | 224.3 | 272.1 | 205.3 | 208.3 | 202.0 | 196.4 | 165.9 |
| Net Yds. per Pass Play | 6.28 | 4.51 | 5.81 | 6.36 | 5.88 | 5.48 | 6.06 | 6.59 | 7.12 | 5.58 | 6.53 | 5.50 | 5.28 | 4.86 |
| Yds. Gained per Comp. | 11.63 | 10.40 | 12.70 | 11.60 | 11.61 | 10.91 | 11.79 | 13.81 | 13.35 | 11.81 | 11.88 | 12.06 | 11.24 | 10.34 |
| **Combined Net Yds. Gained** | 5260 | 4052 | 4740 | 5461 | 5658 | 4705 | 4835 | 5014 | 5812 | 5065 | 5212 | 5235 | 4967 | 4669 |
| % Total Yds. Rushing | 36.9 | 37.3 | 35.9 | 31.0 | 31.7 | 27.4 | 34.2 | 28.4 | 25.1 | 35.1 | 36.1 | 38.3 | 36.7 | 43.2 |
| % Total Yds. Passing | 63.1 | 62.7 | 64.1 | 69.0 | 68.3 | 72.6 | 65.8 | 71.6 | 74.9 | 64.9 | 63.9 | 61.7 | 63.3 | 56.8 |
| Avg. Yds. per Game | 328.8 | 253.3 | 296.3 | 341.3 | 353.6 | 294.1 | 302.2 | 313.4 | 363.3 | 316.6 | 325.8 | 327.2 | 310.4 | 291.8 |
| **Ball Control Plays** | 1078 | 986 | 948 | 1060 | 1066 | 988 | 970 | 978 | 1030 | 1091 | 1031 | 1079 | 1050 | 1019 |
| Avg. Yds. per Play | 4.9 | 4.1 | 5.0 | 5.2 | 5.3 | 4.8 | 5.0 | 5.1 | 5.6 | 4.6 | 5.1 | 4.9 | 4.7 | 4.6 |
| Avg. Time of Poss. | 27:30 | 28:58 | 29:32 | 31:35 | 31:48 | 27:55 | 29:28 | 30:21 | 28:59 | 29:43 | 32:16 | 32:15 | 29:52 | 29:03 |
| **Third Down Efficiency** | 43.6 | 34.5 | 32.8 | 43.6 | 44.5 | 29.2 | 40.4 | 36.6 | 45.9 | 38.8 | 41.8 | 39.1 | 39.7 | 35.7 |
| **Had Intercepted** | 18 | 11 | 19 | 10 | 25 | 15 | 10 | 14 | 18 | 24 | 12 | 12 | 14 | 18 |
| Yds. Opp Returned | 174 | 49 | 246 | 79 | 309 | 247 | 111 | 289 | 329 | 201 | 310 | 216 | 271 | 159 |
| Ret. by Opp. for TD | 0 | 0 | 0 | 0 | 0 | 1 | 0 | 2 | 2 | 1 | 3 | 2 | 2 | 0 |
| **Punts** | 74 | 90 | 84 | 68 | 56 | 83 | 77 | 71 | 58 | 76 | 73 | 89 | 74 | 91 |
| Yds. Punted | 2991 | 3954 | 3632 | 3017 | 2535 | 3595 | 3240 | 2971 | 2304 | 3096 | 2806 | 3781 | 3127 | 4007 |
| Avg. Yds. per Punt | 40.4 | 43.9 | 43.2 | 44.4 | 45.3 | 43.3 | 42.1 | 41.8 | 39.7 | 40.7 | 38.4 | 42.5 | 42.3 | 44.0 |
| **Punt Returns** | 33 | 48 | 42 | 41 | 41 | 30 | 37 | 40 | 28 | 51 | 31 | 47 | 34 | 33 |
| Yds. Returned | 277 | 321 | 563 | 425 | 275 | 173 | 348 | 465 | 326 | 462 | 256 | 353 | 412 | 280 |
| Avg. Yds. per Return | 8.4 | 6.7 | 13.4 | 10.4 | 6.7 | 5.8 | 9.4 | 11.6 | 11.6 | 9.1 | 8.3 | 7.5 | 12.1 | 8.5 |
| Returned for TD | 1 | 0 | 3 | 0 | 0 | 0 | 0 | 1 | 2 | 0 | 0 | 0 | 0 | 0 |
| **Kickoff Returns** | 45 | 61 | 58 | 39 | 31 | 57 | 45 | 52 | 49 | 47 | 46 | 52 | 47 | 50 |
| Yds. Returned | 746 | 1211 | 1119 | 717 | 589 | 1124 | 875 | 1061 | 1068 | 819 | 675 | 878 | 901 | 931 |
| Avg. Yds. per Return | 16.6 | 19.9 | 19.3 | 18.4 | 19.0 | 19.7 | 19.4 | 20.4 | 21.8 | 17.4 | 14.7 | 16.9 | 19.2 | 18.6 |
| Returned for TD | 0 | 0 | 0 | 0 | 0 | 0 | 0 | 0 | 0 | 0 | 0 | 0 | 0 | 0 |
| **Fumbles** | 26 | 24 | 27 | 29 | 37 | 34 | 28 | 23 | 32 | 30 | 38 | 28 | 13 | 25 |
| Lost | 17 | 9 | 17 | 18 | 20 | 20 | 18 | 11 | 16 | 10 | 16 | 15 | 5 | 13 |
| Out of Bounds | 0 | 2 | 2 | 1 | 5 | 3 | 3 | 1 | 1 | 1 | 2 | 4 | 1 | 2 |
| Own Rec. for TD | 0 | 0 | 0 | 1 | 0 | 0 | 0 | 0 | 0 | 0 | 0 | 0 | 0 | 0 |
| Opp. Rec. by | 24 | 14 | 9 | 13 | 17 | 11 | 17 | 9 | 14 | 9 | 18 | 14 | 12 | 15 |
| Opp. Rec. for TD | 1 | 0 | 1 | 0 | 3 | 2 | 2 | 0 | 0 | 0 | 0 | 2 | 0 | 2 |
| **Penalties** | 94 | 105 | 121 | 112 | 132 | 94 | 121 | 148 | 81 | 64 | 86 | 100 | 87 | 99 |
| Yds. Penalized | 630 | 773 | 842 | 822 | 1005 | 685 | 969 | 1181 | 663 | 468 | 555 | 861 | 699 | 745 |
| **Total Points Scored** | 329 | 187 | 304 | 373 | 368 | 189 | 328 | 306 | 349 | 238 | 270 | 308 | 322 | 280 |
| Total TDs | 37 | 16 | 36 | 42 | 40 | 16 | 37 | 29 | 40 | 26 | 31 | 32 | 33 | 29 |
| TDs Rushing | 12 | 3 | 8 | 13 | 11 | 4 | 14 | 10 | 10 | 9 | 14 | 13 | 14 | 13 |
| TDs Passing | 20 | 11 | 23 | 27 | 23 | 10 | 20 | 17 | 27 | 17 | 16 | 16 | 18 | 13 |
| TDs on Ret. and Rec. | 5 | 2 | 5 | 2 | 6 | 2 | 3 | 2 | 3 | 0 | 1 | 3 | 1 | 3 |
| Extra Points | 36 | 13 | 36 | 41 | 39 | 15 | 37 | 27 | 37 | 25 | 31 | 32 | 31 | 29 |
| Safeties | 1 | 3 | 2 | 1 | 1 | 0 | 0 | 0 | 0 | 0 | 1 | 0 | 0 | 4 |
| Field Goals Made | 23 | 24 | 16 | 26 | 29 | 26 | 23 | 35 | 24 | 19 | 17 | 28 | 31 | 23 |
| Field Goals Attempted | 32 | 31 | 22 | 35 | 34 | 31 | 29 | 44 | 32 | 31 | 26 | 30 | 40 | 28 |
| % Successful | 71.9 | 77.4 | 72.7 | 74.3 | 85.3 | 83.9 | 79.3 | 79.5 | 75.0 | 61.3 | 65.4 | 93.3 | 77.5 | 82.1 |

## AMERICAN FOOTBALL CONFERENCE DEFENSE

| | Buff. | Cin. | Clev. | Den. | Hou. | Ind. | K.C. | Raid. | Mia. | N.E. | N.Y.J. | Pitt. | S.D. | Sea. |
|---|---|---|---|---|---|---|---|---|---|---|---|---|---|---|
| **First Downs** | 331 | 306 | 290 | 280 | 289 | 334 | 300 | 302 | 332 | 269 | 266 | 267 | 299 | 322 |
| Rushing | 114 | 134 | 94 | 86 | 73 | 151 | 103 | 111 | 103 | 97 | 93 | 74 | 86 | 106 |
| Passing | 199 | 159 | 170 | 181 | 184 | 166 | 161 | 154 | 205 | 161 | 161 | 163 | 192 | 193 |
| Penalty | 18 | 13 | 26 | 13 | 32 | 17 | 36 | 37 | 24 | 11 | 12 | 30 | 21 | 23 |
| **Rushes** | 500 | 521 | 451 | 397 | 369 | 575 | 453 | 494 | 460 | 505 | 420 | 399 | 414 | 452 |
| Net Yds. Gained | 1921 | 2220 | 1654 | 1418 | 1273 | 2521 | 1620 | 1865 | 1665 | 1951 | 1473 | 1368 | 1314 | 1660 |
| Avg. Gain | 3.8 | 4.3 | 3.7 | 3.6 | 3.4 | 4.4 | 3.6 | 3.8 | 3.6 | 3.9 | 3.5 | 3.4 | 3.2 | 3.7 |
| Avg. Yds. per Game | 120.1 | 138.8 | 103.4 | 88.6 | 79.6 | 157.6 | 101.3 | 116.6 | 104.1 | 121.9 | 92.1 | 85.5 | 82.1 | 103.8 |
| **Passes Attempted** | 582 | 457 | 541 | 562 | 582 | 454 | 525 | 457 | 572 | 474 | 497 | 521 | 556 | 595 |
| Completed | 323 | 251 | 306 | 314 | 302 | 270 | 312 | 258 | 350 | 280 | 296 | 277 | 329 | 333 |
| % Completed | 55.5 | 54.9 | 56.6 | 55.9 | 51.9 | 59.5 | 59.4 | 56.5 | 61.2 | 59.1 | 59.6 | 53.2 | 59.2 | 56.0 |
| Total Yds. Gained | 3889 | 2952 | 3466 | 3969 | 3914 | 3238 | 3379 | 3141 | 3682 | 3087 | 3434 | 3440 | 3958 | 3897 |
| Times Sacked | 37 | 22 | 48 | 46 | 52 | 21 | 35 | 45 | 29 | 34 | 32 | 42 | 32 | 38 |
| Yds. Lost | 256 | 154 | 342 | 238 | 313 | 121 | 228 | 283 | 197 | 242 | 195 | 277 | 206 | 244 |
| Net Yds. Gained | 3633 | 2798 | 3124 | 3731 | 3601 | 3117 | 3151 | 2858 | 3485 | 2845 | 3239 | 3163 | 3752 | 3653 |
| Avg. Yds. per Game | 227.1 | 174.9 | 195.3 | 233.2 | 225.1 | 194.8 | 196.9 | 178.6 | 217.8 | 177.8 | 202.4 | 197.7 | 234.5 | 228.3 |
| Net Yds. per Pass Play | 5.87 | 5.84 | 5.30 | 6.14 | 5.68 | 6.56 | 5.63 | 5.69 | 5.80 | 5.60 | 6.12 | 5.62 | 6.38 | 5.77 |
| Yds. Gained per Comp. | 12.04 | 11.76 | 11.33 | 12.64 | 12.96 | 11.99 | 10.83 | 12.17 | 10.52 | 11.03 | 11.60 | 12.42 | 12.03 | 11.70 |
| **Combined Net Yds. Gained** | 5554 | 5018 | 4778 | 5149 | 4874 | 5638 | 4771 | 4723 | 5150 | 4796 | 4712 | 4531 | 5066 | 5313 |
| % Total Yds. Rushing | 34.6 | 44.2 | 34.6 | 27.5 | 26.1 | 44.7 | 34.0 | 39.5 | 32.3 | 40.7 | 31.3 | 30.2 | 25.9 | 31.2 |
| % Total Yds. Passing | 65.4 | 55.8 | 65.4 | 72.5 | 73.9 | 55.3 | 66.0 | 60.5 | 67.7 | 59.3 | 68.7 | 69.8 | 74.1 | 68.8 |
| Avg. Yds. per Game | 347.1 | 313.6 | 298.6 | 321.8 | 304.6 | 352.4 | 298.2 | 295.2 | 321.9 | 299.8 | 294.5 | 283.2 | 316.6 | 332.1 |
| **Ball Control Plays** | 1119 | 1000 | 1040 | 1005 | 1003 | 1050 | 1013 | 996 | 1061 | 1013 | 949 | 962 | 1002 | 1085 |
| Avg. Yds. per Play | 5.0 | 5.0 | 4.6 | 5.1 | 4.9 | 5.4 | 4.7 | 4.7 | 4.9 | 4.7 | 5.0 | 4.7 | 5.1 | 4.9 |
| Avg. Time of Poss. | 32:30 | 31:02 | 30:28 | 28:25 | 28:12 | 32:05 | 30:32 | 29:39 | 31:01 | 30:17 | 27:44 | 27:45 | 30:08 | 30:57 |
| **Third Down Efficiency** | 45.5 | 40.1 | 38.1 | 33.0 | 30.8 | 41.3 | 41.0 | 36.3 | 45.0 | 41.6 | 40.5 | 33.8 | 39.5 | 39.7 |
| **Intercepted By** | 23 | 12 | 13 | 18 | 26 | 10 | 21 | 14 | 13 | 13 | 19 | 24 | 22 | 22 |
| Yds. Returned By | 306 | 272 | 208 | 236 | 412 | 116 | 225 | 199 | 175 | 122 | 233 | 386 | 319 | 196 |
| Returned for TD | 3 | 2 | 1 | 1 | 3 | 0 | 0 | 1 | 1 | 0 | 1 | 1 | 1 | 1 |
| **Punts** | 65 | 74 | 85 | 81 | 79 | 71 | 68 | 80 | 76 | 90 | 66 | 82 | 72 | 73 |
| Yds. Punted | 2719 | 3123 | 3603 | 3541 | 3454 | 2855 | 3035 | 3369 | 3135 | 3709 | 2859 | 3600 | 3031 | 3097 |
| Avg. Yds. per Punt | 41.8 | 42.2 | 42.4 | 43.7 | 43.7 | 40.2 | 44.6 | 42.1 | 41.3 | 41.2 | 43.3 | 43.9 | 42.1 | 42.4 |
| **Punt Returns** | 29 | 47 | 49 | 33 | 28 | 41 | 43 | 35 | 32 | 34 | 26 | 50 | 36 | 47 |
| Yds. Returned | 247 | 416 | 438 | 337 | 249 | 352 | 352 | 301 | 359 | 313 | 156 | 678 | 292 | 475 |
| Avg. Yds. per Return | 8.5 | 8.9 | 8.9 | 10.2 | 8.9 | 8.6 | 8.2 | 8.6 | 11.2 | 9.2 | 6.0 | 13.6 | 8.1 | 10.1 |
| Returned for TD | 0 | 0 | 0 | 0 | 0 | 1 | 0 | 0 | 1 | 1 | 0 | 3 | 0 | 1 |
| **Kickoff Returns** | 43 | 38 | 46 | 63 | 60 | 37 | 49 | 45 | 62 | 44 | 47 | 54 | 64 | 52 |
| Yds. Returned | 850 | 831 | 814 | 1119 | 1062 | 551 | 1007 | 783 | 1239 | 921 | 911 | 1165 | 1063 | 967 |
| Avg. Yds. per Return | 19.8 | 21.9 | 17.7 | 17.8 | 17.7 | 14.9 | 20.6 | 17.4 | 20.0 | 20.9 | 19.4 | 21.6 | 16.6 | 18.6 |
| Returned for TD | 0 | 0 | 0 | 0 | 0 | 0 | 0 | 0 | 0 | 0 | 0 | 1 | 0 | 1 |
| **Fumbles** | 35 | 22 | 29 | 27 | 32 | 25 | 30 | 23 | 30 | 20 | 30 | 37 | 19 | 23 |
| Lost | 24 | 14 | 9 | 13 | 17 | 11 | 17 | 9 | 14 | 9 | 18 | 14 | 12 | 15 |
| Out of Bounds | 0 | 3 | 5 | 1 | 3 | 1 | 2 | 1 | 1 | 3 | 0 | 1 | 0 | 2 |
| Own Rec. for TD | 0 | 0 | 0 | 0 | 0 | 0 | 0 | 0 | 0 | 0 | 0 | 1 | 0 | 0 |
| Opp. Rec. by | 17 | 9 | 17 | 18 | 20 | 20 | 18 | 11 | 16 | 10 | 16 | 15 | 5 | 13 |
| Opp. Rec. for TD | 0 | 2 | 2 | 0 | 1 | 1 | 1 | 1 | 2 | 1 | 0 | 1 | 1 | 1 |
| **Penalties** | 99 | 73 | 105 | 128 | 103 | 87 | 127 | 105 | 92 | 111 | 86 | 77 | 94 | 109 |
| Yds. Penalized | 681 | 567 | 821 | 1019 | 791 | 610 | 1015 | 801 | 650 | 803 | 661 | 652 | 724 | 818 |
| **Total Points Scored** | 242 | 319 | 307 | 284 | 238 | 378 | 291 | 326 | 351 | 286 | 247 | 281 | 290 | 314 |
| Total TDs | 25 | 37 | 30 | 27 | 26 | 45 | 30 | 37 | 43 | 32 | 26 | 30 | 30 | 32 |
| TDs Rushing | 7 | 15 | 9 | 6 | 9 | 20 | 11 | 17 | 12 | 9 | 8 | 6 | 10 | 12 |
| TDs Passing | 18 | 20 | 19 | 21 | 16 | 22 | 18 | 17 | 26 | 20 | 15 | 16 | 17 | 16 |
| TDs on Ret. and Rec. | 0 | 2 | 2 | 0 | 1 | 3 | 1 | 3 | 5 | 3 | 3 | 8 | 3 | 4 |
| Extra Points | 23 | 37 | 30 | 27 | 25 | 43 | 27 | 37 | 40 | 32 | 26 | 29 | 30 | 31 |
| Safeties | 0 | 0 | 2 | 1 | 0 | 1 | 0 | 2 | 1 | 1 | 1 | 0 | 1 | 2 |
| Field Goals Made | 23 | 20 | 31 | 31 | 19 | 21 | 28 | 21 | 17 | 20 | 21 | 24 | 26 | 29 |
| Field Goals Attempted | 35 | 28 | 38 | 36 | 28 | 30 | 32 | 33 | 27 | 24 | 26 | 29 | 33 | 39 |
| % Successful | 65.7 | 71.4 | 81.6 | 86.1 | 67.9 | 70.0 | 87.5 | 63.6 | 63.0 | 83.3 | 80.8 | 82.8 | 78.8 | 74.4 |

# 1993 TEAM STATISTICS

## NATIONAL FOOTBALL CONFERENCE OFFENSE

| | Atl. | Chi. | Dall. | Det. | G.B. | Rams | Minn. | N.O. | N.Y.G. | Phil. | Phx. | S.F. | T.B. | Wash. |
|---|---|---|---|---|---|---|---|---|---|---|---|---|---|---|
| **First Downs** | 292 | 226 | 322 | 248 | 282 | 278 | 283 | 264 | 300 | 303 | 295 | 372 | 241 | 255 |
| Rushing | 91 | 98 | 120 | 101 | 98 | 117 | 85 | 94 | 127 | 104 | 107 | 134 | 80 | 92 |
| Passing | 185 | 113 | 172 | 139 | 166 | 147 | 182 | 158 | 153 | 184 | 173 | 212 | 141 | 143 |
| Penalty | 16 | 15 | 30 | 8 | 18 | 14 | 16 | 12 | 20 | 15 | 15 | 26 | 20 | 20 |
| **Rushes** | 395 | 477 | 490 | 456 | 448 | 449 | 447 | 414 | 560 | 456 | 452 | 463 | 402 | 396 |
| Net Yds. Gained | 1590 | 1677 | 2161 | 1944 | 1619 | 2014 | 1624 | 1766 | 2210 | 1761 | 1809 | 2133 | 1290 | 1728 |
| Avg. Gain | 4.0 | 3.5 | 4.4 | 4.3 | 3.6 | 4.5 | 3.6 | 4.3 | 3.9 | 3.9 | 4.0 | 4.6 | 3.2 | 4.4 |
| Avg. Yds. per Game | 99.4 | 104.8 | 135.1 | 121.5 | 101.2 | 125.9 | 101.5 | 110.4 | 138.1 | 110.1 | 113.1 | 133.3 | 80.6 | 108.0 |
| **Passes Attempted** | 573 | 388 | 475 | 435 | 528 | 473 | 526 | 481 | 424 | 556 | 522 | 524 | 508 | 533 |
| Completed | 334 | 230 | 317 | 264 | 322 | 247 | 315 | 274 | 257 | 328 | 310 | 354 | 262 | 287 |
| % Completed | 58.3 | 59.3 | 66.7 | 60.7 | 61.0 | 52.2 | 59.9 | 57.0 | 60.6 | 59.0 | 59.4 | 67.6 | 51.6 | 53.8 |
| Total Yds. Gained | 3787 | 2270 | 3617 | 2943 | 3330 | 3021 | 3381 | 3183 | 3180 | 3463 | 3635 | 4480 | 3295 | 2764 |
| Times Sacked | 40 | 48 | 29 | 46 | 30 | 31 | 35 | 40 | 40 | 42 | 33 | 35 | 39 | 40 |
| Yds. Lost | 267 | 230 | 163 | 229 | 199 | 231 | 181 | 242 | 245 | 302 | 231 | 178 | 274 | 219 |
| Net Yds. Gained | 3520 | 2040 | 3454 | 2714 | 3131 | 2790 | 3200 | 2941 | 2935 | 3161 | 3404 | 4302 | 3021 | 2545 |
| Avg. Yds. per Game | 220.0 | 127.5 | 215.9 | 169.6 | 195.7 | 174.4 | 200.0 | 183.8 | 183.4 | 197.6 | 212.8 | 268.9 | 188.8 | 159.1 |
| Net Yds. per Pass Play | 5.74 | 4.68 | 6.85 | 5.64 | 5.61 | 5.54 | 5.70 | 5.64 | 6.33 | 5.29 | 6.13 | 7.70 | 5.52 | 4.44 |
| Yds. Gained per Comp. | 11.34 | 9.87 | 11.41 | 11.15 | 10.34 | 12.23 | 10.73 | 11.62 | 12.37 | 10.56 | 11.73 | 12.66 | 12.58 | 9.63 |
| **Combined Net Yds. Gained** | 5110 | 3717 | 5615 | 4658 | 4750 | 4804 | 4824 | 4707 | 5145 | 4922 | 5213 | 6435 | 4311 | 4273 |
| % Total Yds. Rushing | 31.1 | 45.1 | 38.5 | 41.7 | 34.1 | 41.9 | 33.7 | 37.5 | 43.0 | 35.8 | 34.7 | 33.1 | 29.9 | 40.4 |
| % Total Yds. Passing | 68.9 | 54.9 | 61.5 | 58.3 | 65.9 | 58.1 | 66.3 | 62.5 | 57.0 | 64.2 | 65.3 | 66.9 | 70.1 | 59.6 |
| Avg. Yds. per Game | 319.4 | 232.3 | 350.9 | 291.1 | 296.9 | 300.3 | 301.5 | 294.2 | 321.6 | 307.6 | 325.8 | 402.2 | 269.4 | 267.1 |
| **Ball Control Plays** | 1008 | 913 | 994 | 937 | 1006 | 953 | 1008 | 935 | 1024 | 1054 | 1007 | 1022 | 949 | 969 |
| Avg. Yds. per Play | 5.1 | 4.1 | 5.6 | 5.0 | 4.7 | 5.0 | 4.8 | 5.0 | 5.0 | 4.7 | 5.2 | 6.3 | 4.5 | 4.4 |
| Avg. Time of Poss. | 31:23 | 28:36 | 30:56 | 29:27 | 30:53 | 28:18 | 30:28 | 28:32 | 32:18 | 31:00 | 31:54 | 30:24 | 28:38 | 27:58 |
| **Third Down Efficiency** | 38.3 | 34.6 | 41.9 | 34.6 | 37.2 | 39.1 | 34.0 | 35.5 | 40.7 | 41.1 | 46.2 | 47.8 | 34.7 | 34.7 |
| **Had Intercepted** | 25 | 16 | 6 | 19 | 24 | 19 | 14 | 21 | 9 | 13 | 20 | 17 | 25 | 21 |
| Yds. Opp Returned | 345 | 105 | 47 | 177 | 437 | 347 | 166 | 444 | 175 | 107 | 143 | 157 | 280 | 209 |
| Ret. by Opp. for TD | 2 | 1 | 0 | 1 | 3 | 2 | 3 | 6 | 1 | 0 | 0 | 0 | 1 | 2 |
| **Punts** | 72 | 80 | 56 | 72 | 74 | 80 | 90 | 77 | 78 | 83 | 73 | 42 | 94 | 83 |
| Yds. Punted | 3114 | 3080 | 2342 | 3207 | 3174 | 3271 | 3862 | 3356 | 3272 | 3323 | 3189 | 1718 | 3772 | 3644 |
| Avg. Yds. per Punt | 43.3 | 38.5 | 41.8 | 44.5 | 42.9 | 40.9 | 42.9 | 43.6 | 41.9 | 40.0 | 43.7 | 40.9 | 40.1 | 43.9 |
| **Punt Returns** | 35 | 35 | 37 | 40 | 45 | 19 | 39 | 38 | 32 | 33 | 47 | 35 | 38 | 35 |
| Yds. Returned | 276 | 289 | 381 | 349 | 404 | 102 | 280 | 517 | 331 | 284 | 384 | 411 | 311 | 245 |
| Avg. Yds. per Return | 7.9 | 8.3 | 10.3 | 8.7 | 9.0 | 5.4 | 7.2 | 13.6 | 10.3 | 8.6 | 8.2 | 11.7 | 8.2 | 7.0 |
| Returned for TD | 0 | 0 | 2 | 0 | 0 | 0 | 0 | 2 | 1 | 0 | 1 | 1 | 0 | 0 |
| **Kickoff Returns** | 55 | 45 | 36 | 52 | 60 | 49 | 55 | 62 | 32 | 54 | 45 | 40 | 58 | 59 |
| Yds. Returned | 1300 | 811 | 758 | 1204 | 1483 | 824 | 1086 | 1460 | 507 | 987 | 951 | 715 | 922 | 1166 |
| Avg. Yds. per Return | 23.6 | 18.0 | 21.1 | 23.2 | 24.7 | 16.8 | 19.7 | 23.5 | 15.8 | 18.3 | 21.1 | 17.9 | 15.9 | 19.8 |
| Returned for TD | 1 | 0 | 0 | 1 | 1 | 0 | 0 | 1 | 0 | 0 | 0 | 0 | 0 | 0 |
| **Fumbles** | 31 | 29 | 33 | 29 | 26 | 20 | 15 | 24 | 19 | 32 | 23 | 32 | 28 | 24 |
| Lost | 17 | 14 | 16 | 13 | 10 | 11 | 10 | 13 | 8 | 21 | 11 | 13 | 11 | 10 |
| Out of Bounds | 1 | 1 | 3 | 4 | 1 | 1 | 1 | 0 | 1 | 1 | 1 | 3 | 1 | 0 |
| Own Rec. for TD | 0 | 0 | 0 | 0 | 0 | 0 | 0 | 0 | 0 | 0 | 0 | 1 | 0 | 0 |
| Opp. Rec. by | 11 | 12 | 14 | 16 | 15 | 9 | 10 | 20 | 10 | 15 | 17 | 11 | 13 | 14 |
| Opp. Rec. for TD | 1 | 2 | 0 | 2 | 1 | 1 | 0 | 2 | 0 | 1 | 2 | 1 | 0 | 2 |
| **Penalties** | 111 | 68 | 94 | 93 | 85 | 71 | 109 | 81 | 90 | 101 | 77 | 95 | 89 | 90 |
| Yds. Penalized | 838 | 587 | 744 | 665 | 734 | 526 | 806 | 663 | 596 | 770 | 644 | 800 | 765 | 597 |
| **Total Points Scored** | 316 | 234 | 376 | 298 | 340 | 221 | 277 | 317 | 288 | 293 | 326 | 473 | 237 | 230 |
| Total TDs | 34 | 22 | 41 | 28 | 35 | 25 | 28 | 33 | 30 | 35 | 37 | 61 | 27 | 26 |
| TDs Rushing | 4 | 10 | 20 | 9 | 14 | 8 | 8 | 10 | 11 | 7 | 12 | 26 | 6 | 11 |
| TDs Passing | 28 | 7 | 18 | 15 | 19 | 16 | 18 | 18 | 17 | 23 | 21 | 29 | 19 | 11 |
| TDs on Ret. and Rec. | 2 | 5 | 3 | 4 | 2 | 1 | 2 | 5 | 2 | 5 | 4 | 6 | 2 | 4 |
| Extra Points | 34 | 21 | 40 | 28 | 35 | 23 | 27 | 33 | 28 | 31 | 37 | 59 | 27 | 24 |
| Safeties | 0 | 0 | 0 | 0 | 1 | 0 | 2 | 1 | 1 | 2 | 2 | 0 | 0 | 1 |
| Field Goals Made | 26 | 27 | 30 | 34 | 31 | 16 | 26 | 28 | 26 | 16 | 21 | 16 | 16 | 16 |
| Field Goals Attempted | 27 | 36 | 37 | 43 | 37 | 23 | 35 | 35 | 34 | 23 | 28 | 26 | 22 | 28 |
| % Successful | 96.3 | 75.0 | 81.1 | 79.1 | 83.8 | 69.6 | 74.3 | 80.0 | 76.5 | 69.6 | 75.0 | 61.5 | 72.7 | 57.1 |

## NATIONAL FOOTBALL CONFERENCE DEFENSE

| | Atl. | Chi. | Dall. | Det. | G.B. | Rams | Minn. | N.O. | N.Y.G. | Phil. | Phx. | S.F. | T.B. | Wash. |
|---|---|---|---|---|---|---|---|---|---|---|---|---|---|---|
| **First Downs** | 278 | 289 | 297 | 279 | 261 | 304 | 259 | 273 | 268 | 271 | 278 | 297 | 280 | 304 |
| Rushing | 79 | 112 | 94 | 108 | 88 | 117 | 98 | 116 | 89 | 91 | 106 | 109 | 109 | 127 |
| Passing | 180 | 163 | 176 | 154 | 157 | 179 | 139 | 145 | 161 | 155 | 158 | 171 | 152 | 157 |
| Penalty | 19 | 14 | 27 | 17 | 16 | 8 | 22 | 12 | 18 | 25 | 14 | 17 | 19 | 20 |
| **Rushes** | 419 | 476 | 423 | 433 | 424 | 480 | 415 | 513 | 395 | 467 | 433 | 404 | 479 | 513 |
| Net Yds. Gained | 1784 | 1835 | 1651 | 1649 | 1582 | 1851 | 1536 | 2090 | 1547 | 2080 | 1861 | 1800 | 1994 | 2112 |
| Avg. Gain | 4.3 | 3.9 | 3.9 | 3.8 | 3.7 | 3.9 | 3.7 | 4.1 | 3.9 | 4.5 | 4.3 | 4.5 | 4.2 | 4.1 |
| Avg. Yds. per Game | 111.5 | 114.7 | 103.2 | 103.1 | 98.9 | 115.7 | 96.0 | 130.6 | 96.7 | 130.0 | 116.3 | 112.5 | 124.6 | 132.0 |
| **Passes Attempted** | 505 | 504 | 555 | 514 | 529 | 488 | 478 | 444 | 514 | 463 | 495 | 564 | 503 | 483 |
| Completed | 308 | 306 | 334 | 309 | 290 | 299 | 310 | 259 | 298 | 251 | 281 | 314 | 300 | 291 |
| % Completed | 61.0 | 60.7 | 60.2 | 60.1 | 54.8 | 61.3 | 64.9 | 58.3 | 58.0 | 54.2 | 56.8 | 55.7 | 59.6 | 60.2 |
| Total Yds. Gained | 3786 | 3105 | 3347 | 3273 | 3201 | 3763 | 3146 | 2924 | 3354 | 3153 | 3511 | 3513 | 3384 | 3584 |
| Times Sacked | 27 | 46 | 34 | 43 | 46 | 35 | 45 | 51 | 41 | 36 | 34 | 44 | 29 | 31 |
| Yds. Lost | 149 | 287 | 231 | 253 | 301 | 203 | 276 | 318 | 238 | 214 | 205 | 316 | 132 | 197 |
| Net Yds. Gained | 3637 | 2818 | 3116 | 3020 | 2900 | 3560 | 2870 | 2606 | 3116 | 2939 | 3306 | 3197 | 3252 | 3387 |
| Avg. Yds. per Game | 227.3 | 176.1 | 194.8 | 188.8 | 181.3 | 222.5 | 179.4 | 162.9 | 194.8 | 183.7 | 206.6 | 199.8 | 203.3 | 211.7 |
| Net Yds. per Pass Play | 6.84 | 5.12 | 5.29 | 5.42 | 5.04 | 6.81 | 5.49 | 5.26 | 5.61 | 5.89 | 6.25 | 5.26 | 6.11 | 6.59 |
| Yds. Gained per Comp. | 12.29 | 10.15 | 10.02 | 10.59 | 11.04 | 12.59 | 10.15 | 11.29 | 11.26 | 12.56 | 12.49 | 11.19 | 11.28 | 12.32 |
| **Combined Net Yds. Gained** | 5421 | 4653 | 4767 | 4669 | 4482 | 5411 | 4406 | 4696 | 4663 | 5019 | 5167 | 4997 | 5246 | 5499 |
| % Total Yds. Rushing | 32.9 | 39.4 | 34.6 | 35.3 | 35.3 | 34.2 | 34.9 | 44.5 | 33.2 | 41.4 | 36.0 | 36.0 | 38.0 | 38.4 |
| % Total Yds. Passing | 67.1 | 60.6 | 65.4 | 64.7 | 64.7 | 65.8 | 65.1 | 55.5 | 66.8 | 58.6 | 64.0 | 64.0 | 62.0 | 61.6 |
| Avg. Yds. per Game | 338.8 | 290.8 | 297.9 | 291.8 | 280.1 | 338.2 | 275.4 | 293.5 | 291.4 | 313.7 | 322.9 | 312.3 | 327.9 | 343.7 |
| **Ball Control Plays** | 951 | 1026 | 1012 | 990 | 999 | 1003 | 938 | 1008 | 950 | 966 | 962 | 1012 | 1011 | 1027 |
| Avg. Yds. per Play | 5.7 | 4.5 | 4.7 | 4.7 | 4.5 | 5.4 | 4.7 | 4.7 | 4.9 | 5.2 | 5.4 | 4.9 | 5.2 | 5.4 |
| Avg. Time of Poss. | 28:37 | 31:24 | 29:04 | 30:33 | 29:07 | 31:42 | 29:33 | 31:28 | 27:42 | 29:00 | 28:06 | 29:36 | 31:22 | 32:02 |
| **Third Down Efficiency** | 36.5 | 37.4 | 39.7 | 40.9 | 32.3 | 46.8 | 39.1 | 40.5 | 34.2 | 32.2 | 36.9 | 40.7 | 37.9 | 42.8 |
| **Intercepted By** | 13 | 18 | 14 | 19 | 18 | 11 | 24 | 10 | 18 | 20 | 9 | 19 | 9 | 17 |
| Yds. Returned By | 160 | 300 | 171 | 156 | 255 | 127 | 211 | 133 | 184 | 324 | 124 | 267 | 71 | 241 |
| Returned for TD | 0 | 2 | 1 | 1 | 0 | 0 | 2 | 0 | 1 | 4 | 1 | 3 | 2 | 2 |
| **Punts** | 74 | 78 | 78 | 81 | 79 | 58 | 78 | 80 | 80 | 75 | 78 | 68 | 76 | 73 |
| Yds. Punted | 3029 | 3231 | 3219 | 3489 | 3176 | 2451 | 3307 | 3384 | 3224 | 3137 | 3333 | 2985 | 3290 | 2995 |
| Avg. Yds. per Punt | 40.9 | 41.4 | 41.3 | 43.1 | 40.2 | 42.3 | 42.4 | 42.3 | 40.3 | 41.8 | 42.7 | 43.9 | 43.3 | 41.0 |
| **Punt Returns** | 41 | 22 | 32 | 45 | 38 | 43 | 46 | 36 | 44 | 35 | 30 | 15 | 53 | 34 |
| Yds. Returned | 350 | 115 | 169 | 377 | 350 | 533 | 560 | 348 | 247 | 311 | 267 | 171 | 394 | 343 |
| Avg. Yds. per Return | 8.5 | 5.2 | 5.3 | 8.4 | 9.2 | 12.4 | 12.2 | 9.7 | 5.6 | 8.9 | 8.9 | 11.4 | 7.4 | 10.1 |
| Returned for TD | 0 | 0 | 0 | 0 | 0 | 2 | 1 | 1 | 0 | 1 | 0 | 0 | 0 | 2 |
| **Kickoff Returns** | 55 | 53 | 66 | 30 | 70 | 47 | 58 | 40 | 29 | 53 | 51 | 61 | 28 | 36 |
| Yds. Returned | 1064 | 918 | 1225 | 609 | 1407 | 984 | 1420 | 788 | 646 | 1133 | 994 | 1196 | 499 | 722 |
| Avg. Yds. per Return | 19.3 | 17.3 | 18.6 | 20.3 | 20.1 | 20.9 | 24.5 | 19.7 | 22.3 | 21.4 | 19.5 | 19.6 | 17.8 | 20.1 |
| Returned for TD | 0 | 0 | 1 | 0 | 0 | 0 | 1 | 0 | 0 | 0 | 0 | 0 | 0 | 0 |
| **Fumbles** | 25 | 24 | 22 | 34 | 33 | 26 | 24 | 30 | 27 | 33 | 27 | 20 | 27 | 25 |
| Lost | 11 | 12 | 14 | 16 | 15 | 9 | 10 | 20 | 10 | 15 | 17 | 11 | 13 | 14 |
| Out of Bounds | 5 | 0 | 1 | 2 | 2 | 0 | 1 | 1 | 4 | 0 | 2 | 1 | 4 | 1 |
| Own Rec. for TD | 0 | 0 | 0 | 0 | 0 | 0 | 0 | 0 | 0 | 0 | 0 | 0 | 1 | 0 |
| Opp. Rec. by | 17 | 14 | 16 | 13 | 10 | 11 | 10 | 13 | 8 | 21 | 11 | 13 | 11 | 10 |
| Opp. Rec. for TD | 3 | 0 | 1 | 0 | 2 | 1 | 1 | 3 | 0 | 1 | 0 | 1 | 1 | 0 |
| **Penalties** | 100 | 91 | 87 | 73 | 85 | 80 | 97 | 86 | 98 | 85 | 95 | 99 | 126 | 100 |
| Yds. Penalized | 874 | 783 | 653 | 500 | 712 | 542 | 768 | 590 | 820 | 610 | 730 | 743 | 913 | 782 |
| **Total Points Scored** | 385 | 230 | 229 | 292 | 282 | 367 | 290 | 343 | 205 | 315 | 269 | 295 | 376 | 345 |
| Total TDs | 46 | 22 | 23 | 32 | 27 | 40 | 31 | 39 | 22 | 35 | 27 | 30 | 40 | 42 |
| TDs Rushing | 14 | 9 | 7 | 12 | 6 | 18 | 14 | 7 | 7 | 11 | 13 | 6 | 15 | 14 |
| TDs Passing | 27 | 12 | 14 | 19 | 16 | 17 | 11 | 22 | 13 | 22 | 14 | 23 | 22 | 24 |
| TDs on Ret. and Rec. | 5 | 1 | 2 | 1 | 5 | 5 | 6 | 10 | 2 | 2 | 0 | 1 | 3 | 4 |
| Extra Points | 45 | 20 | 23 | 31 | 27 | 38 | 29 | 35 | 22 | 34 | 27 | 30 | 38 | 40 |
| Safeties | 2 | 0 | 1 | 0 | 0 | 1 | 0 | 1 | 0 | 1 | 1 | 2 | 1 | 1 |
| Field Goals Made | 20 | 26 | 22 | 23 | 31 | 29 | 25 | 24 | 17 | 23 | 26 | 27 | 32 | 17 |
| Field Goals Attempted | 31 | 34 | 27 | 30 | 40 | 37 | 33 | 30 | 23 | 34 | 35 | 30 | 35 | 22 |
| % Successful | 64.5 | 76.5 | 81.5 | 76.7 | 77.5 | 78.4 | 75.8 | 80.0 | 73.9 | 67.6 | 74.3 | 90.0 | 91.4 | 77.3 |

## 1993 TEAM STATISTICS

### AFC, NFC, AND NFL SUMMARY

| | AFC Offense Total | AFC Offense Average | AFC Defense Total | AFC Defense Average | NFC Offense Total | NFC Offense Average | NFC Defense Total | NFC Defense Average | NFL Total | NFL Average |
|---|---|---|---|---|---|---|---|---|---|---|
| **First Downs** | 4164 | 297.4 | 4187 | 299.1 | 3961 | 282.9 | 3938 | 281.3 | 8125 | 290.2 |
| Rushing | 1420 | 101.4 | 1425 | 101.8 | 1448 | 103.4 | 1443 | 103.1 | 2868 | 102.4 |
| Passing | 2428 | 173.4 | 2449 | 174.9 | 2268 | 162.0 | 2247 | 160.5 | 4696 | 167.7 |
| Penalty | 316 | 22.6 | 313 | 22.4 | 245 | 17.5 | 248 | 17.7 | 561 | 20.0 |
| **Rushes** | 6379 | 455.6 | 6410 | 457.9 | 6305 | 450.4 | 6274 | 448.1 | 12684 | 453.0 |
| Net Yds. Gained | 23969 | 1712.1 | 23923 | 1708.8 | 25326 | 1809.0 | 25372 | 1812.3 | 49295 | 1760.5 |
| Avg. Gain | — | 3.8 | — | 3.7 | — | 4.0 | — | 4.0 | — | 3.9 |
| Avg. Yds. per Game | — | 107.0 | — | 106.8 | — | 113.1 | — | 113.3 | — | 110.0 |
| **Passes Attempted** | 7468 | 533.4 | 7375 | 526.8 | 6946 | 496.1 | 7039 | 502.8 | 14414 | 514.8 |
| Completed | 4250 | 303.6 | 4201 | 300.1 | 4101 | 292.9 | 4150 | 296.4 | 8351 | 298.3 |
| % Completed | — | 56.9 | — | 57.0 | — | 59.0 | — | 59.0 | — | 57.9 |
| Total Yds. Gained | 50141 | 3581.5 | 49446 | 3531.9 | 46349 | 3310.6 | 47044 | 3360.3 | 96490 | 3446.1 |
| Times Sacked | 527 | 37.6 | 513 | 36.6 | 528 | 37.7 | 542 | 38.7 | 1055 | 37.7 |
| Yds. Lost | 3425 | 244.6 | 3296 | 235.4 | 3191 | 227.9 | 3320 | 237.1 | 6616 | 236.3 |
| Net Yds. Gained | 46716 | 3336.9 | 46150 | 3296.4 | 43158 | 3082.7 | 43724 | 3123.1 | 89874 | 3209.8 |
| Avg. Yds. per Game | — | 208.6 | — | 206.0 | — | 192.7 | — | 195.2 | — | 200.6 |
| Net Yds. per Pass Play | — | 5.84 | — | 5.85 | — | 5.77 | — | 5.77 | — | 5.81 |
| Yds. Gained per Comp. | — | 11.80 | — | 11.77 | — | 11.30 | — | 11.34 | — | 11.55 |
| **Combined Net Yds. Gained** | 70685 | 5048.9 | 70073 | 5005.2 | 68484 | 4891.7 | 69096 | 4935.4 | 139169 | 4970.3 |
| % Total Yds. Rushing | — | 33.9 | — | 34.1 | — | 37.0 | — | 36.7 | — | 35.4 |
| % Total Yds. Passing | — | 66.1 | — | 65.9 | — | 63.0 | — | 63.3 | — | 64.6 |
| Avg. Yds. per Game | — | 315.6 | — | 312.8 | — | 305.7 | — | 308.5 | — | 310.6 |
| **Ball Control Plays** | 14374 | 1026.7 | 14298 | 1021.3 | 13779 | 984.2 | 13855 | 989.6 | 28153 | 1005.5 |
| Avg. Yds. per Play | — | 4.9 | — | 4.9 | — | 5.0 | — | 5.0 | — | 4.9 |
| **Third Down Efficiency** | — | 39.1 | — | 39.1 | — | 38.5 | — | 38.5 | — | 38.8 |
| **Interceptions** | 220 | 15.7 | 250 | 17.9 | 249 | 17.8 | 219 | 15.6 | 469 | 16.8 |
| Yds. Returned | 2990 | 213.6 | 3405 | 243.2 | 3139 | 224.2 | 2724 | 194.6 | 6129 | 218.9 |
| Returned for TD | 13 | 0.9 | 16 | 1.1 | 22 | 1.6 | 19 | 1.4 | 35 | 1.3 |
| **Punts** | 1064 | 76.0 | 1062 | 75.9 | 1054 | 75.3 | 1056 | 75.4 | 2118 | 75.6 |
| Yds. Punted | 45056 | 3218.3 | 45130 | 3223.6 | 44324 | 3166.0 | 44250 | 3160.7 | 89380 | 3192.1 |
| Avg. Yds. per Punt | — | 42.3 | — | 42.5 | — | 42.1 | — | 41.9 | — | 42.2 |
| **Punt Returns** | 536 | 38.3 | 530 | 37.9 | 508 | 36.3 | 514 | 36.7 | 1044 | 37.3 |
| Yds. Returned | 4936 | 352.6 | 4965 | 354.6 | 4564 | 326.0 | 4535 | 323.9 | 9500 | 339.3 |
| Avg. Yds. per Return | — | 9.2 | — | 9.4 | — | 9.0 | — | 8.8 | — | 9.1 |
| Returned for TD | 7 | 0.5 | 7 | 0.5 | 7 | 0.5 | 7 | 0.5 | 14 | 0.5 |
| **Kickoff Returns** | 679 | 48.5 | 704 | 50.3 | 702 | 50.1 | 677 | 48.4 | 1381 | 49.3 |
| Yds. Returned | 12714 | 908.1 | 13283 | 948.8 | 14174 | 1012.4 | 13605 | 971.8 | 26888 | 960.3 |
| Avg. Yds. per Return | — | 18.7 | — | 18.9 | — | 20.2 | — | 20.1 | — | 19.5 |
| Returned for TD | 0 | 0.0 | 2 | 0.1 | 4 | 0.3 | 2 | 0.1 | 4 | 0.1 |
| **Fumbles** | 394 | 28.1 | 382 | 27.3 | 365 | 26.1 | 377 | 26.9 | 759 | 27.1 |
| Lost | 205 | 14.6 | 196 | 14.0 | 178 | 12.7 | 187 | 13.4 | 383 | 13.7 |
| Out of Bounds | 28 | 2.0 | 23 | 1.6 | 19 | 1.4 | 24 | 1.7 | 47 | 1.7 |
| Own Rec. for TD | 1 | 0.1 | 1 | 0.1 | 1 | 0.1 | 1 | 0.1 | 2 | 0.1 |
| Opp. Rec. | 196 | 14.0 | 205 | 14.6 | 187 | 13.4 | 178 | 12.7 | 383 | 13.7 |
| Opp. Rec. for TD | 13 | 0.9 | 14 | 1.0 | 15 | 1.1 | 14 | 1.0 | 28 | 1.0 |
| **Penalties** | 1444 | 103.1 | 1396 | 99.7 | 1254 | 89.6 | 1302 | 93.0 | 2698 | 96.4 |
| Yds. Penalized | 10898 | 778.4 | 10613 | 758.1 | 9735 | 695.4 | 10020 | 715.7 | 20633 | 736.9 |
| **Total Points Scored** | 4151 | 296.5 | 4154 | 296.7 | 4226 | 301.9 | 4223 | 301.6 | 8377 | 299.2 |
| Total TDs | 444 | 31.7 | 450 | 32.1 | 462 | 33.0 | 456 | 32.6 | 906 | 32.4 |
| TDs Rushing | 148 | 10.6 | 151 | 10.8 | 156 | 11.1 | 153 | 10.9 | 304 | 10.9 |
| TDs Passing | 258 | 18.4 | 261 | 18.6 | 259 | 18.5 | 256 | 18.3 | 517 | 18.5 |
| TDs on Ret. and Rec. | 38 | 2.7 | 38 | 2.7 | 47 | 3.4 | 47 | 3.4 | 85 | 3.0 |
| Extra Points | 429 | 30.6 | 437 | 31.2 | 447 | 31.9 | 439 | 31.4 | 876 | 31.3 |
| Safeties | 13 | 0.9 | 12 | 0.9 | 10 | 0.7 | 11 | 0.8 | 23 | 0.8 |
| Field Goals Made | 344 | 24.6 | 331 | 23.6 | 329 | 23.5 | 342 | 24.4 | 673 | 24.0 |
| Field Goals Attempted | 445 | 31.8 | 438 | 31.3 | 434 | 31.0 | 441 | 31.5 | 879 | 31.4 |
| % Successful | — | 77.3 | — | 75.6 | — | 75.8 | — | 77.6 | — | 76.6 |

## CLUB LEADERS

| | Offense | Defense |
|---|---|---|
| **First Downs** | S.F. 372 | Minn. 259 |
| Rushing | S.F. 134 | Hou. 73 |
| Passing | S.F. 212 | Minn. 139 |
| Penalty | Den. 35 | Rams 8 |
| **Rushes** | N.Y.G. 560 | Hou. 369 |
| Net Yds. Gained | N.Y.G. 2210 | Hou. 1273 |
| Avg. Gain | S.F. 4.6 | S.D. 3.2 |
| **Passes Attempted** | Hou. 614 | N.O. 444 |
| Completed | Hou. 357 | Cin. & Phil. 251 |
| % Completed | S.F. 67.6 | Hou. 51.9 |
| Total Yds. Gained | Mia. 4564 | N.O. 2924 |
| Times Sacked | N.Y.J. 21 | Hou. 52 |
| Yds. Lost | N.E. 127 | Clev. 342 |
| Net Yds. Gained | Mia. 4353 | N.O. 2606 |
| Net Yds. per Pass Play | S.F. 7.70 | G.B. 5.04 |
| Yds. Gained per Comp. | Raid. 1381 | Dall. 10.02 |
| **Combined Net Yds. Gained** | S.F. 6435 | Minn. 4406 |
| % Total Yds. Rushing | Chi. 45.1 | S.D. 25.9 |
| % Total Yds. Passing | Mia. 74.9 | Ind. 55.3 |
| **Ball Control Plays** | N.E. 1091 | Minn. 938 |
| Avg. Yds. per Play | S.F. 6.30 | G.B. 4.49 |
| Avg. Time of Poss. | N.Y.G. 32:18 | — |
| **Third Down Efficiency** | S.F. 47.8 | Hou. 30.8 |
| **Interceptions** | — | Hou. 26 |
| Yds. Returned | — | Hou. 412 |
| Returned for TD | — | Phil. 4 |
| **Punts** | T.B. 94 | — |
| Yds. Punted | Sea. 4007 | — |
| Avg. Yds. per Punt | Hou. 45.3 | — |
| **Punt Returns** | N.E. 51 | S.F. 15 |
| Yds. Returned | Clev. 563 | Chi. 115 |
| Avg. Yds. per Return | N.O. 13.6 | Chi. 5.2 |
| Returned for TD | Clev. 3 | — |
| **Kickoff Returns** | N.O. 62 | T.B. 28 |
| Yds. Returned | G.B. 1483 | T.B. 499 |
| Avg. Yds. per Return | G.B. 24.7 | Ind. 14.9 |
| Returned for TD | Four with 1 | — |
| **Total Points Scored** | S.F. 473 | N.Y.G. 205 |
| Total TDs | S.F. 61 | Chi. & N.Y.G. 22 |
| TDs Rushing | S.F. 26 | Four with 6 |
| TDs Passing | S.F. 29 | Minn. 11 |
| TDs on Ret. and Rec. | Hou. & S.F. 6 | Buff., Den., & Phx. 0 |
| Extra Points | S.F. 59 | Chi. 20 |
| Safeties | Sea. 4 | — |
| Field Goals Made | Raid. 35 | Mia., N.Y.G., & Wash. 17 |
| Field Goals Attempted | Raid. 44 | Wash. 22 |
| % Successful | Atl. 96.3 | Mia. 63.0 |

## NFL CLUB RANKINGS BY YARDS

| | Offense | | | Defense | | |
|---|---|---|---|---|---|---|
| | Total | Rush | Pass | Total | Rush | Pass |
| Atlanta | 11 | 23 | 6 | 25 | 15 | 25 |
| Buffalo | 6 | 8 | 11 | 27 | 21 | 24 |
| Chicago | 28 | 19 | 28 | 4 | 17 | 3 |
| Cincinnati | 27 | 24 | 27 | 16 | 27 | 2 |
| Cleveland | 20 | 17 | 19 | 12 | 12 | 13 |
| Dallas | 4 | 2 | 7 | 10 | 11 | 10T |
| Denver | 5 | 18 | 4 | 19 | 4 | 27 |
| Detroit | 24 | 7 | 24 | 6 | 10 | 9 |
| Green Bay | 19 | 22 | 18 | 2 | 8 | 7 |
| Houston | 3 | 12 | 3 | 14 | *1 | 23 |
| Indianapolis | 22 | 28 | 8 | 28 | 28 | 12 |
| Kansas City | 16 | 20 | 15 | 11 | 9 | 14 |
| L.A. Rams | 18 | 5 | 23 | 24 | 18 | 22 |
| L.A. Raiders | 13 | 26 | 5 | 9 | 20 | 5 |
| Miami | 2 | 25 | *1 | 20 | 14 | 21 |
| Minnesota | 17 | 21 | 14 | *1 | 6 | 6 |
| New England | 12 | 13 | 12 | 13 | 22 | 4 |
| New Orleans | 21 | 14 | 21 | 7 | 25 | *1 |
| N.Y. Giants | 10 | *1 | 22 | 5 | 7 | 10T |
| N.Y. Jets | 9 | 9 | 10 | 8 | 5 | 17 |
| Philadelphia | 15 | 15 | 16 | 17 | 24 | 8 |
| Phoenix | 8 | 11 | 9 | 21 | 19 | 19 |
| Pittsburgh | 7 | 6 | 13 | 3 | 3 | 15 |
| San Diego | 14 | 10 | 17 | 18 | 2 | 28 |
| San Francisco | *1 | 3 | 2 | 15 | 16 | 16 |
| Seattle | 23 | 4 | 25 | 23 | 13 | 26 |
| Tampa Bay | 25 | 27 | 20 | 22 | 23 | 18 |
| Washington | 26 | 16 | 26 | 26 | 26 | 20 |

*T = Tied for position*
** = League Leader*

## AFC TAKEAWAYS/GIVEAWAYS

| | Takeaways | | | Giveaways | | | Net |
|---|---|---|---|---|---|---|---|
| | Int | Fum | Total | Int | Fum | Total | Diff. |
| San Diego | 22 | 12 | 34 | 14 | 5 | 19 | +15 |
| Buffalo | 23 | 24 | 47 | 18 | 17 | 35 | +12 |
| Pittsburgh | 24 | 14 | 38 | 12 | 15 | 27 | +11 |
| Kansas City | 21 | 17 | 38 | 10 | 18 | 28 | +10 |
| N.Y. Jets | 19 | 18 | 37 | 12 | 16 | 28 | +9 |
| Seattle | 22 | 15 | 37 | 18 | 13 | 31 | +6 |
| Cincinnati | 12 | 14 | 26 | 11 | 9 | 20 | +6 |
| Denver | 18 | 13 | 31 | 10 | 18 | 28 | +3 |
| L.A. Raiders | 14 | 9 | 23 | 14 | 11 | 25 | -2 |
| Houston | 26 | 17 | 43 | 25 | 20 | 45 | -2 |
| Miami | 13 | 14 | 27 | 18 | 16 | 34 | -7 |
| New England | 13 | 9 | 22 | 24 | 10 | 34 | -12 |
| Indianapolis | 10 | 11 | 21 | 15 | 20 | 35 | -14 |
| Cleveland | 13 | 9 | 22 | 19 | 17 | 36 | -14 |

## NFC TAKEAWAYS/GIVEAWAYS

| | Takeaways | | | Giveaways | | | Net |
|---|---|---|---|---|---|---|---|
| | Int | Fum | Total | Int | Fum | Total | Diff. |
| N.Y. Giants | 18 | 10 | 28 | 9 | 8 | 17 | +11 |
| Minnesota | 24 | 10 | 34 | 14 | 10 | 24 | +10 |
| Dallas | 14 | 14 | 28 | 6 | 16 | 22 | +6 |
| Detroit | 19 | 16 | 35 | 19 | 13 | 32 | +3 |
| Philadelphia | 20 | 15 | 35 | 13 | 21 | 34 | +1 |
| San Francisco | 19 | 11 | 30 | 17 | 13 | 30 | 0 |
| Washington | 17 | 14 | 31 | 21 | 10 | 31 | 0 |
| Chicago | 18 | 12 | 30 | 16 | 14 | 30 | 0 |
| Green Bay | 18 | 15 | 33 | 24 | 10 | 34 | -1 |
| New Orleans | 10 | 20 | 30 | 21 | 13 | 34 | -4 |
| Phoenix | 9 | 17 | 26 | 20 | 11 | 31 | -5 |
| L.A. Rams | 11 | 9 | 20 | 19 | 11 | 30 | -10 |
| Tampa Bay | 9 | 13 | 22 | 25 | 11 | 36 | -14 |
| Atlanta | 13 | 11 | 24 | 25 | 17 | 42 | -18 |

# 1993 INDIVIDUAL STATISTICS

## SCORING

**Points**
- **AFC:** 132—Jeff Jaeger, Raiders
- **NFC:** 130—Jason Hanson Detroit

**Touchdowns**
- **NFC:** 16—Jerry Rice, San Francisco
- **AFC:** 15—Marcus Allen, Kansas City

**Extra Points**
- **NFC:** 59—Mike Cofer, San Francisco
- **AFC:** 41—Jason Elam, Denver

**Field Goals**
- **AFC:** 35—Jeff Jaeger, Raiders
- **NFC:** 34—Jason Hanson, Detroit

**Field Goal Attempts**
- **AFC:** 44—Jeff Jaeger, Raiders
- **NFC:** 43—Jason Hanson, Detroit

**Longest Field Goal**
- **AFC:** 59—Steve Christie, Buffalo vs. Miami, September 26
- **NFC:** 57—Michael Husted, Tampa Bay at Raiders, December 19

**Most Points, Game**
- **NFC:** 24—Sterling Sharpe, Green Bay at Tampa Bay, October 24, (4 TD)
  Jerry Rice, San Francisco at Tampa Bay, November 14, (4 TD)
  Ron Moore, Phoenix vs. Rams, December 5, (4 TD)
- **AFC:** 18—Andre Reed, Buffalo vs. New England, September 5, (3 TD)
  John Carney, San Diego vs. Seattle, September 5, (6 FG)
  John Carney, San Diego vs. Houston, September 19, (6 FG)
  Barry Foster, Pittsburgh at Atlanta, September 27, (3 TD)
  Johnny Mitchell, Jets vs. Philadelphia, October 3, (3 TD)
  Rodney Culver, Indianapolis at Miami, October 24, (3 TD)
  Haywood Jeffires, Houston at Cincinnati, November 14, (3 TD)
  Marcus Allen, Kansas City at Seattle, December 5, (3 TD)
  Shannon Sharpe, Denver vs. Kansas City, December 12, (3 TD)
  Kenneth Davis, Buffalo at Miami, December 19, (3 TD)
  Natrone Means, San Diego vs. Miami, December 27, (3 TD)

**Team Leaders, Points**
- **AFC:** BUFFALO: 105, Steve Christie; CINCINNATI: 85, Doug Pelfrey; CLEVELAND: 84, Matt Stover; DENVER: 119, Jason Elam; HOUSTON: 126, Al Del Greco; INDIANAPOLIS: 93, Dean Biasucci; KANSAS CITY: 106, Nick Lowery; L.A. RAIDERS: 132, Jeff Jaeger; MIAMI: 109, Pete Stoyanovich; NEW ENGLAND: 57, Scott Sisson; N.Y. JETS: 82, Cary Blanchard; PITTSBURGH: 116, Gary Anderson; SAN DIEGO: 124, John Carney; SEATTLE: 98, John Kasay
- **NFC:** ATLANTA: 112, Norm Johnson; CHICAGO: 102, Kevin Butler; DALLAS: 122, Ed Murray; DETROIT: 130, Jason Hanson ; GREEN BAY: 128, Chris Jacke ; L.A. RAMS: 71, Tony Zendejas; MINNESOTA: 105, Fuad Reveiz; NEW ORLEANS: 117, Morten Andersen; N.Y. GIANTS: 103, David Treadwell; PHILADELPHIA: 60, Calvin Williams; PHOENIX: 100, Greg Davis; SAN FRANCISCO: 107, Mike Cofer; TAMPA BAY: 75, Michael Husted; WASHINGTON: 72, Chip Lohmiller

**Team Champion**
- **NFC:** 473—San Francisco
- **AFC:** 373—Denver

### AFC SCORING—TEAM

| | TD | TDR | TDP | TDM | XP | XPA | FG | FGA | SAF | TP |
|---|---|---|---|---|---|---|---|---|---|---|
| Denver | 42 | 13 | 27 | 2 | 41 | 42 | 26 | 35 | 1 | 373 |
| Houston | 40 | 11 | 23 | 6 | 39 | 40 | 29 | 34 | 1 | 368 |
| Miami | 40 | 10 | 27 | 3 | 37 | 40 | 24 | 32 | 0 | 349 |
| Buffalo | 37 | 12 | 20 | 5 | 36 | 37 | 23 | 32 | 1 | 329 |
| Kansas City | 37 | 14 | 20 | 3 | 37 | 37 | 23 | 29 | 0 | 328 |
| San Diego | 33 | 14 | 18 | 1 | 31 | 33 | 31 | 40 | 0 | 322 |
| Pittsburgh | 32 | 13 | 16 | 3 | 32 | 32 | 28 | 30 | 0 | 308 |
| L.A. Raiders | 29 | 10 | 17 | 2 | 27 | 29 | 35 | 44 | 0 | 306 |
| Cleveland | 36 | 8 | 23 | 5 | 36 | 36 | 16 | 22 | 2 | 304 |
| Seattle | 29 | 13 | 13 | 3 | 29 | 29 | 23 | 28 | 4 | 280 |
| N.Y. Jets | 31 | 14 | 16 | 1 | 31 | 31 | 17 | 26 | 1 | 270 |
| New England | 26 | 9 | 17 | 0 | 25 | 25 | 19 | 31 | 0 | 238 |
| Indianapolis | 16 | 4 | 10 | 2 | 15 | 16 | 26 | 31 | 0 | 189 |
| Cincinnati | 16 | 3 | 11 | 2 | 13 | 16 | 24 | 31 | 3 | 187 |
| AFC Total | 444 | 148 | 258 | 38 | 429 | 443 | 344 | 445 | 13 | 4151 |
| AFC Average | 31.7 | 10.6 | 18.4 | 2.7 | 30.6 | 31.6 | 24.6 | 31.8 | 0.9 | 296.5 |

### NFC SCORING—TEAM

| | TD | TDR | TDP | TDM | XP | XPA | FG | FGA | SAF | TP |
|---|---|---|---|---|---|---|---|---|---|---|
| San Francisco | 61 | 26 | 29 | 6 | 59 | 61 | 16 | 26 | 0 | 473 |
| Dallas | 41 | 20 | 18 | 3 | 40 | 41 | 30 | 37 | 0 | 376 |
| Green Bay | 35 | 14 | 19 | 2 | 35 | 35 | 31 | 37 | 1 | 340 |
| Phoenix | 37 | 12 | 21 | 4 | 37 | 37 | 21 | 28 | 2 | 326 |
| New Orleans | 33 | 10 | 18 | 5 | 33 | 33 | 28 | 35 | 1 | 317 |
| Atlanta | 34 | 4 | 28 | 2 | 34 | 34 | 26 | 27 | 0 | 316 |
| Detroit | 28 | 9 | 15 | 4 | 28 | 28 | 34 | 43 | 0 | 298 |
| Philadelphia | 35 | 7 | 23 | 5 | 31 | 35 | 16 | 23 | 2 | 293 |
| N.Y. Giants | 30 | 11 | 17 | 2 | 28 | 30 | 26 | 34 | 1 | 288 |
| Minnesota | 28 | 8 | 18 | 2 | 27 | 28 | 26 | 35 | 2 | 277 |
| Tampa Bay | 27 | 6 | 19 | 2 | 27 | 27 | 16 | 22 | 0 | 237 |
| Chicago | 22 | 10 | 7 | 5 | 21 | 22 | 27 | 36 | 0 | 234 |
| Washington | 26 | 11 | 11 | 4 | 24 | 26 | 16 | 28 | 1 | 230 |
| L.A. Rams | 25 | 8 | 16 | 1 | 23 | 25 | 16 | 23 | 0 | 221 |
| NFC Total | 462 | 156 | 259 | 47 | 447 | 462 | 329 | 434 | 10 | 4226 |
| NFC Average | 33.0 | 11.1 | 18.5 | 3.4 | 31.9 | 33.0 | 23.5 | 31.0 | 0.7 | 301.9 |
| NFL Total | 906 | 304 | 517 | 85 | 876 | 905 | 673 | 879 | 23 | 8377 |
| NFL Average | 32.4 | 10.9 | 18.5 | 3.0 | 31.3 | 32.3 | 24.0 | 31.4 | 0.8 | 299.2 |

### NFL TOP TEN SCORERS—TOUCHDOWNS

| | TD | TDR | TDP | TDM | PTS |
|---|---|---|---|---|---|
| Rice, Jerry, S.F. | 16 | 1 | 15 | 0 | 96 |
| Allen, Marcus, K.C. | 15 | 12 | 3 | 0 | 90 |
| Rison, Andre, Atl. | 15 | 0 | 15 | 0 | 90 |
| Sharpe, Sterling, G.B. | 11 | 0 | 11 | 0 | 66 |
| Watters, Ricky, S.F. | 11 | 10 | 1 | 0 | 66 |
| Smith, Emmitt, Dall. | 10 | 9 | 1 | 0 | 60 |
| Bennett, Edgar, G.B. | 10 | 9 | 1 | 0 | 60 |
| Williams, Calvin, Phil. | 10 | 0 | 10 | 0 | 60 |
| Moore, Ron, Phx. | 9 | 9 | 0 | 0 | 54 |
| Carter, Cris, Minn. | 9 | 0 | 9 | 0 | 54 |
| Foster, Barry, Pitt. | 9 | 8 | 1 | 0 | 54 |
| Sharpe, Shannon, Den. | 9 | 0 | 9 | 0 | 54 |

### NFL TOP TEN SCORERS—KICKERS

| | XP | XPA | FG | FGA | PTS |
|---|---|---|---|---|---|
| Jaeger, Jeff, Raid. | 27 | 29 | 35 | 44 | 132 |
| Hanson, Jason, Det. | 28 | 28 | 34 | 43 | 130 |
| Jacke, Chris, G.B. | 35 | 35 | 31 | 37 | 128 |
| Del Greco, Al, Hou. | 39 | 40 | 29 | 34 | 126 |
| Carney, John, S.D. | 31 | 33 | 31 | 40 | 124 |
| Murray, Eddie, Dall. | 38 | 38 | 28 | 33 | 122 |
| Elam, Jason, Den. | 41 | 42 | 26 | 35 | 119 |
| Andersen, Morten, N.O. | 33 | 33 | 28 | 35 | 117 |
| Anderson, Gary, Pitt. | 32 | 32 | 28 | 30 | 116 |
| Johnson, Norm, Atl. | 34 | 34 | 26 | 27 | 112 |

### AFC SCORERS—INDIVIDUAL

**Kickers**

| | XP | XPA | FG | FGA | PTS |
|---|---|---|---|---|---|
| Jaeger, Jeff, Raid. | 27 | 29 | 35 | 44 | 132 |
| Del Greco, Al, Hou. | 39 | 40 | 29 | 34 | 126 |
| Carney, John, S.D. | 31 | 33 | 31 | 40 | 124 |
| Elam, Jason, Den. | 41 | 42 | 26 | 35 | 119 |
| Anderson, Gary, Pitt. | 32 | 32 | 28 | 30 | 116 |
| Stoyanovich, Pete, Mia. | 37 | 37 | 24 | 32 | 109 |
| Lowery, Nick, K.C. | 37 | 37 | 23 | 29 | 106 |
| Christie, Steve, Buff. | 36 | 37 | 23 | 32 | 105 |
| Kasay, John, Sea. | 29 | 29 | 23 | 28 | 98 |
| Biasucci, Dean, Ind. | 15 | 16 | 26 | 31 | 93 |
| Pelfrey, Doug, Cinn. | 13 | 16 | 24 | 31 | 85 |
| Stover, Matt, Clev. | 36 | 36 | 16 | 22 | 84 |
| Blanchard, Cary, N.Y.J. | 31 | 31 | 17 | 26 | 82 |
| Bahr, Matt, Phil.-N.E. | 28 | 29 | 13 | 18 | 67 |
| Sisson, Scott, N.E. | 15 | 15 | 14 | 26 | 57 |

**Non-kickers**

| | TD | TDR | TDP | TDM | PTS |
|---|---|---|---|---|---|
| Allen, Marcus, K.C. | 15 | 12 | 3 | 0 | 90 |
| Foster, Barry, Pitt. | 9 | 8 | 1 | 0 | 54 |
| Sharpe, Shannon, Den. | 9 | 0 | 9 | 0 | 54 |
| Brown, Gary, Hou. | 8 | 6 | 2 | 0 | 48 |
| Brown, Tim, Raid. | 8 | 0 | 7 | 1 | 48 |
| Coates, Ben, N.E. | 8 | 0 | 8 | 0 | 48 |
| Delpino, Robert, Den. | 8 | 8 | 0 | 0 | 48 |
| Jackson, Michael, Clev. | 8 | 0 | 8 | 0 | 48 |
| Means, Natrone, S.D. | 8 | 8 | 0 | 0 | 48 |
| Baxter, Brad, N.Y.J. | 7 | 7 | 0 | 0 | 42 |
| Davis, Willie, K.C. | 7 | 0 | 7 | 0 | 42 |

| | TD | TDR | TDP | TDM | PTS |
|---|---|---|---|---|---|
| Miller, Anthony, S.D. | 7 | 0 | 7 | 0 | 42 |
| Russell, Leonard, N.E. | 7 | 7 | 0 | 0 | 42 |
| Warren, Chris, Sea. | 7 | 7 | 0 | 0 | 42 |
| Byars, Keith, Mia. | 6 | 3 | 3 | 0 | 36 |
| Davis, Kenneth, Buff. | 6 | 6 | 0 | 0 | 36 |
| Ingram, Mark, Mia. | 6 | 0 | 6 | 0 | 36 |
| Jackson, Keith, Mia. | 6 | 0 | 6 | 0 | 36 |
| Jeffires, Haywood, Hou. | 6 | 0 | 6 | 0 | 36 |
| Kirby, Terry, Mia. | 6 | 3 | 3 | 0 | 36 |
| Mitchell, Johnny, N.Y.J. | 6 | 0 | 6 | 0 | 36 |
| Pickens, Carl, Cinn. | 6 | 0 | 6 | 0 | 36 |
| Reed, Andre, Buff. | 6 | 0 | 6 | 0 | 36 |
| Thomas, Thurman, Buff. | 6 | 6 | 0 | 0 | 36 |
| Brooks, Bill, Buff. | 5 | 0 | 5 | 0 | 30 |
| Carrier, Mark, Clev. | 5 | 1 | 3 | 1 | 30 |
| Culver, Rodney, Ind. | 5 | 3 | 1 | 1 | 30 |
| Fryar, Irving, Mia. | 5 | 0 | 5 | 0 | 30 |
| Green, Eric, Pitt. | 5 | 0 | 5 | 0 | 30 |
| Hoge, Merril, Pitt. | 5 | 1 | 4 | 0 | 30 |
| Hostetler, Jeff, Raid. | 5 | 5 | 0 | 0 | 30 |
| Johnson, Vance, Den. | 5 | 0 | 5 | 0 | 30 |
| Martin, Kelvin, Sea. | 5 | 0 | 5 | 0 | 30 |
| Metcalf, Eric, Clev. | 5 | 1 | 2 | 2 | 30 |
| Slaughter, Webster, Hou. | 5 | 0 | 5 | 0 | 30 |
| Bernstine, Rod, Den. | 4 | 4 | 0 | 0 | 24 |
| Burkett, Chris, N.Y.J.. | 4 | 0 | 4 | 0 | 24 |
| Butts, Marion, S.D. | 4 | 4 | 0 | 0 | 24 |
| Cash, Keith, K.C. | 4 | 0 | 4 | 0 | 24 |
| Givins, Ernest, Hou. | 4 | 0 | 4 | 0 | 24 |
| Johnson, Johnny, N.Y.J. | 4 | 3 | 1 | 0 | 24 |
| Lewis, Nate, S.D. | 4 | 0 | 4 | 0 | 24 |
| McCardell, Keenan, Clev. | 4 | 0 | 4 | 0 | 24 |
| Metzelaars, Pete, Buff. | 4 | 0 | 4 | 0 | 24 |
| Query, Jeff, Cinn. | 4 | 0 | 4 | 0 | 24 |
| Russell, Derek, Den. | 4 | 0 | 3 | 1 | 24 |
| Vardell, Tommy, Clev. | 4 | 3 | 1 | 0 | 24 |
| Williams, John L., Sea. | 4 | 3 | 1 | 0 | 24 |
| Wright, Alexander, Raid. | 4 | 0 | 4 | 0 | 24 |
| Beebe, Don, Buff. | 3 | 0 | 3 | 0 | 18 |
| Blades, Brian, Sea. | 3 | 0 | 3 | 0 | 18 |
| Cash, Kerry, Ind. | 3 | 0 | 3 | 0 | 18 |
| Duncan, Curtis, Hou. | 3 | 0 | 3 | 0 | 18 |
| Higgs, Mark, Mia. | 3 | 3 | 0 | 0 | 18 |
| Jett, James, Raid. | 3 | 0 | 3 | 0 | 18 |
| Langhorne, Reggie, Ind. | 3 | 0 | 3 | 0 | 18 |
| Martin, Tony, Mia. | 3 | 0 | 3 | 0 | 18 |
| McCallum, Napoleon, Raid. | 3 | 3 | 0 | 0 | 18 |
| Milburn, Glyn, Den. | 3 | 0 | 3 | 0 | 18 |
| Mirer, Rick, Sea. | 3 | 3 | 0 | 0 | 18 |
| Stone, Dwight, Pitt. | 3 | 1 | 2 | 0 | 18 |
| Thigpen, Yancey, Pitt. | 3 | 0 | 3 | 0 | 18 |
| Thompson, Leroy, Pitt. | 3 | 3 | 0 | 0 | 18 |
| Rivers, Reggie, Den. | 2 | 1 | 1 | 0 | *14 |
| Birden, J. J., K.C. | 2 | 0 | 2 | 0 | 12 |
| Brisby, Vincent, N.E. | 2 | 0 | 2 | 0 | 12 |
| Carlson, Cody, Hou. | 2 | 2 | 0 | 0 | 12 |
| Edmunds, Ferrell, Sea. | 2 | 0 | 2 | 0 | 12 |
| Harmon, Ronnie, S.D. | 2 | 0 | 2 | 0 | 12 |
| Jefferson, Shawn, S.D. | 2 | 0 | 2 | 0 | 12 |
| Kinchen, Brian, Clev. | 2 | 0 | 2 | 0 | 12 |
| Marshall, Arthur, Den. | 2 | 0 | 2 | 0 | 12 |
| McDuffie, O. J., Mia. | 2 | 0 | 0 | 2 | 12 |
| McNair, Todd, K.C. | 2 | 2 | 0 | 0 | 12 |
| Thornton, James, N.Y.J. | 2 | 0 | 2 | 0 | 12 |
| Tillman, Cedric, Den. | 2 | 0 | 2 | 0 | 12 |
| Timpson, Michael, N.E. | 2 | 0 | 2 | 0 | 12 |
| Turner, Kevin, N.E. | 2 | 0 | 2 | 0 | 12 |
| White, Lorenzo, Hou. | 2 | 2 | 0 | 0 | 12 |
| Young, Duane, S.D. | 2 | 0 | 2 | 0 | 12 |
| Stephens, Rod, Sea. | 1 | 0 | 0 | 1 | *10 |
| Jones, Henry, Buff. | 1 | 0 | 0 | 1 | *8 |
| Anders, Kimble, K.C. | 1 | 0 | 1 | 0 | 6 |
| Baldwin, Randy, Clev. | 1 | 0 | 1 | 0 | 6 |
| Ball, Eric, Cinn. | 1 | 1 | 0 | 0 | 6 |
| Barnett, Tim, K.C. | 1 | 0 | 1 | 0 | 6 |
| Baty, Greg, Mia. | 1 | 0 | 1 | 0 | 6 |
| Baxter, Fred, N.Y.J. | 1 | 0 | 1 | 0 | 6 |
| Bell, Nick, Raid. | 1 | 1 | 0 | 0 | 6 |
| Bieniemy, Eric, S.D. | 1 | 1 | 0 | 0 | 6 |
| Blackmon, Robert, Sea. | 1 | 0 | 0 | 1 | 6 |
| Brim, Michael, Cinn. | 1 | 0 | 0 | 1 | 6 |
| Chaffey, Pat, N.Y.J. | 1 | 0 | 1 | 0 | 6 |
| Childress, Ray, Hou. | 1 | 0 | 0 | 1 | 6 |
| Cook, Marv, N.E. | 1 | 0 | 1 | 0 | 6 |
| Copeland, Russell, Buff. | 1 | 0 | 0 | 1 | 6 |
| Crittenden, Ray, N.E. | 1 | 0 | 1 | 0 | 6 |
| Croel, Mike, Den. | 1 | 0 | 0 | 1 | 6 |
| Croom, Corey, N.E. | 1 | 1 | 0 | 0 | 6 |
| Davidson, Kenny, Pitt. | 1 | 0 | 0 | 1 | 6 |
| Dawkins, Sean, Ind. | 1 | 0 | 1 | 0 | 6 |
| Dishman, Cris, Hou. | 1 | 0 | 0 | 1 | 6 |
| Esiason, Boomer, N.Y.J. | 1 | 1 | 0 | 0 | 6 |
| Fenner, Derrick, Cinn. | 1 | 1 | 0 | 0 | 6 |
| Frank, Donald, S.D. | 1 | 0 | 0 | 1 | 6 |
| Gardner, Carwell, Buff. | 1 | 0 | 1 | 0 | 6 |
| Gash, Sam, N.E. | 1 | 1 | 0 | 0 | 6 |
| Glover, Andrew, Raid. | 1 | 0 | 1 | 0 | 6 |
| Green, Paul, Sea. | 1 | 0 | 1 | 0 | 6 |
| Harris, Leonard, Hou. | 1 | 0 | 1 | 0 | 6 |
| Hayes, Jonathan, K.C. | 1 | 0 | 1 | 0 | 6 |
| Herrod, Jeff, Ind. | 1 | 0 | 0 | 1 | 6 |
| Hester, Jessie, Ind. | 1 | 0 | 1 | 0 | 6 |
| Horton, Ethan, Raid. | 1 | 0 | 1 | 0 | 6 |
| Ismail, Raghib, Raid. | 1 | 0 | 1 | 0 | 6 |
| Jackson, Steve, Hou. | 1 | 0 | 0 | 1 | 6 |
| Johnson, Anthony, Ind. | 1 | 1 | 0 | 0 | 6 |
| Johnson, Reggie, Den. | 1 | 0 | 1 | 0 | 6 |
| Johnson, Tracy, Sea. | 1 | 0 | 1 | 0 | 6 |
| Jones, James, Clev. | 1 | 1 | 0 | 0 | 6 |
| Kidd, John, S.D. | 1 | 1 | 0 | 0 | 6 |
| Kirkland, Levon, Pitt. | 1 | 0 | 0 | 1 | 6 |
| Lewis, Albert, K.C. | 1 | 0 | 0 | 1 | 6 |
| Lewis, Darryll, Hou. | 1 | 0 | 0 | 1 | 6 |
| Mack, Kevin, Clev. | 1 | 1 | 0 | 0 | 6 |
| Marino, Dan, Mia. | 1 | 1 | 0 | 0 | 6 |
| Mathis, Terance, N.Y.J. | 1 | 1 | 0 | 0 | 6 |
| McDaniel, Terry, Raid. | 1 | 0 | 0 | 1 | 6 |
| McKeller, Keith, Buff. | 1 | 0 | 1 | 0 | 6 |
| McMurtry, Greg, N.E. | 1 | 0 | 1 | 0 | 6 |
| Miles, Ostell, Cinn. | 1 | 1 | 0 | 0 | 6 |
| Mills, Ernie, Pitt. | 1 | 0 | 1 | 0 | 6 |
| Moon, Warren, Hou. | 1 | 1 | 0 | 0 | 6 |
| Moore, Rob, N.Y.J. | 1 | 0 | 1 | 0 | 6 |
| Moore, Stevon, Clev. | 1 | 0 | 0 | 1 | 6 |
| Murrell, Adrian, N.Y.J. | 1 | 1 | 0 | 0 | 6 |
| Mustafaa, Najee, Clev. | 1 | 0 | 0 | 1 | 6 |
| Nash, Joe, Sea. | 1 | 0 | 0 | 1 | 6 |
| Odomes, Nate, Buff. | 1 | 0 | 0 | 1 | 6 |
| Oliver, Louis, Mia. | 1 | 0 | 0 | 1 | 6 |
| Orlando, Bo, Hou. | 1 | 0 | 0 | 1 | 6 |
| Philcox, Todd, Clev. | 1 | 1 | 0 | 0 | 6 |
| Robertson, Marcus, Hou. | 1 | 0 | 0 | 1 | 6 |
| Robinson, Greg, Raid. | 1 | 1 | 0 | 0 | 6 |
| Saleaumua, Dan, K.C. | 1 | 0 | 0 | 1 | 6 |
| Talley, Darryl, Buff. | 1 | 0 | 0 | 1 | 6 |
| Thomas, Blair, N.Y.J. | 1 | 1 | 0 | 0 | 6 |
| Thomas, Derrick, K.C. | 1 | 0 | 0 | 1 | 6 |
| Thompson, Craig, Cinn. | 1 | 0 | 1 | 0 | 6 |
| Tillman, Lawyer, Clev. | 1 | 0 | 1 | 0 | 6 |
| Tillman, Spencer, Hou. | 1 | 0 | 1 | 0 | 6 |
| Valerio, Joe, K.C. | 1 | 0 | 1 | 0 | 6 |
| Verdin, Clarence, Ind. | 1 | 0 | 1 | 0 | 6 |
| Walker, Derrick, S.D. | 1 | 0 | 1 | 0 | 6 |
| Washington, Brian, N.Y.J. | 1 | 0 | 0 | 1 | 6 |
| Washington, Mickey, Buff. | 1 | 0 | 0 | 1 | 6 |
| Wellman, Gary, Hou. | 1 | 0 | 1 | 0 | 6 |
| Williams, Darryl, Cinn. | 1 | 0 | 0 | 1 | 6 |
| Wolfley, Ron, Clev. | 1 | 0 | 1 | 0 | 6 |
| Woodson, Rod, Pitt. | 1 | 0 | 0 | 1 | 6 |
| Wyman, David, Den. | 1 | 0 | 1 | 0 | 6 |
| Edwards, Antonio, Sea. | 0 | 0 | 0 | 0 | *2 |
| Pleasant, Anthony, Clev. | 0 | 0 | 0 | 0 | *2 |
| Riddick, Louis, Clev. | 0 | 0 | 0 | 0 | *2 |
| Williams, Alfred, Cinn. | 0 | 0 | 0 | 0 | *2 |

** Safety*
*Team Safeties credited to Cincinnati (2), Houston, New York Jets and Seattle*

**NFC SCORERS—INDIVIDUAL**
**Kickers**

| | XP | XPA | FG | FGA | PTS |
|---|---|---|---|---|---|
| Hanson, Jason, Det. | 28 | 28 | 34 | 43 | 130 |
| Jacke, Chris, G.B. | 35 | 35 | 31 | 37 | 128 |
| Murray, Eddie, Dall. | 38 | 38 | 28 | 33 | 122 |

## 1993 INDIVIDUAL STATISTICS

| | XP | XPA | FG | FGA | PTS |
|---|---|---|---|---|---|
| Andersen, Morten, N.O. | 33 | 33 | 28 | 35 | 117 |
| Johnson, Norm, Atl. | 34 | 34 | 26 | 27 | 112 |
| Cofer, Mike, S.F. | 59 | 61 | 16 | 26 | 107 |
| Reveiz, Fuad, Minn. | 27 | 28 | 26 | 35 | 105 |
| Treadwell, David, N.Y.G. | 28 | 29 | 25 | 31 | 103 |
| Butler, Kevin, Chi. | 21 | 22 | 27 | 36 | 102 |
| Davis, Greg, Phx. | 37 | 37 | 21 | 28 | 100 |
| Husted, Michael, T.B. | 27 | 27 | 16 | 22 | 75 |
| Lohmiller, Chip, Wash. | 24 | 26 | 16 | 28 | 72 |
| Zendejas, Tony, Rams | 23 | 25 | 16 | 23 | 71 |
| Ruzek, Roger, Phil. | 13 | 16 | 8 | 10 | 37 |
| Elliott, Lin, Dall. | 2 | 3 | 2 | 4 | 8 |
| Daluiso, Brad, N.Y.G. | 0 | 0 | 1 | 3 | 3 |

**Non-kickers**

| | TD | TDR | TDP | TDM | PTS |
|---|---|---|---|---|---|
| Rice, Jerry, S.F. | 16 | 1 | 15 | 0 | 96 |
| Rison, Andre, Atl. | 15 | 0 | 15 | 0 | 90 |
| Sharpe, Sterling, G.B. | 11 | 0 | 11 | 0 | 66 |
| Watters, Ricky, S.F. | 11 | 10 | 1 | 0 | 66 |
| Bennett, Edgar, G.B. | 10 | 9 | 1 | 0 | 60 |
| Smith, Emmitt, Dall. | 10 | 9 | 1 | 0 | 60 |
| Williams, Calvin, Phil. | 10 | 0 | 10 | 0 | 60 |
| Carter, Cris, Minn. | 9 | 0 | 9 | 0 | 54 |
| Moore, Ron, Phx. | 9 | 9 | 0 | 0 | 54 |
| Bettis, Jerome, Rams | 7 | 7 | 0 | 0 | 42 |
| Irvin, Michael, Dall. | 7 | 0 | 7 | 0 | 42 |
| Logan, Marc, S.F. | 7 | 7 | 0 | 0 | 42 |
| Pritchard, Mike, Atl. | 7 | 0 | 7 | 0 | 42 |
| Proehl, Ricky, Phx. | 7 | 0 | 7 | 0 | 42 |
| Bavaro, Mark, Phil. | 6 | 0 | 6 | 0 | 36 |
| Early, Quinn, N.O. | 6 | 0 | 6 | 0 | 36 |
| Moore, Herman, Det. | 6 | 0 | 6 | 0 | 36 |
| Williams, Kevin, Dall. | 6 | 2 | 2 | 2 | 36 |
| Carter, Anthony, Minn. | 5 | 0 | 5 | 0 | 30 |
| Cross, Howard, N.Y.G. | 5 | 0 | 5 | 0 | 30 |
| Hampton, Rodney, N.Y.G. | 5 | 5 | 0 | 0 | 30 |
| Harper, Alvin, Dall. | 5 | 0 | 5 | 0 | 30 |
| Hawkins, Courtney, T.B. | 5 | 0 | 5 | 0 | 30 |
| Taylor, John, S.F. | 5 | 0 | 5 | 0 | 30 |
| Allen, Eric, Phil. | 4 | 0 | 0 | 4 | 24 |
| Anderson, Neal, Chi. | 4 | 4 | 0 | 0 | 24 |
| Anderson, Willie, Rams | 4 | 0 | 4 | 0 | 24 |
| Clark, Gary, Phx. | 4 | 0 | 4 | 0 | 24 |
| Cobb, Reggie, T.B. | 4 | 3 | 1 | 0 | 24 |
| Copeland, Horace, T.B. | 4 | 0 | 4 | 0 | 24 |
| Drayton, Troy, Rams | 4 | 0 | 4 | 0 | 24 |
| Harbaugh, Jim, Chi. | 4 | 4 | 0 | 0 | 24 |
| Harris, Jackie, G.B. | 4 | 0 | 4 | 0 | 24 |
| Haynes, Michael, Atl. | 4 | 0 | 4 | 0 | 24 |
| Hill, Randal, Phx. | 4 | 0 | 4 | 0 | 24 |
| Jackson, Mark, N.Y.G. | 4 | 0 | 4 | 0 | 24 |
| Johnston, Daryl, Dall. | 4 | 3 | 1 | 0 | 24 |
| Moore, Derrick, Det. | 4 | 3 | 1 | 0 | 24 |
| Sanders, Ricky, Wash. | 4 | 0 | 4 | 0 | 24 |
| Walker, Herschel, Phil. | 4 | 1 | 3 | 0 | 24 |
| Workman, Vince, T.B. | 4 | 2 | 2 | 0 | 24 |
| Brooks, Reggie, Wash. | 3 | 3 | 0 | 0 | 18 |
| Brown, Derek, N.O. | 3 | 2 | 1 | 0 | 18 |
| Bunch, Jarrod, N.Y.G. | 3 | 2 | 1 | 0 | 18 |
| Calloway, Chris, N.Y.G. | 3 | 0 | 3 | 0 | 18 |
| Centers, Larry, Phx. | 3 | 0 | 3 | 0 | 18 |
| Clayton, Mark, G.B. | 3 | 0 | 3 | 0 | 18 |
| Graham, Scottie, Minn. | 3 | 3 | 0 | 0 | 18 |
| Hebron, Vaughn, Phil. | 3 | 3 | 0 | 0 | 18 |
| Hilliard, Dalton, N.O. | 3 | 2 | 1 | 0 | 18 |
| Hughes, Tyrone, N.O. | 3 | 0 | 0 | 3 | 18 |
| Jones, Brent, S.F. | 3 | 0 | 3 | 0 | 18 |
| Lassic, Derrick, Dall. | 3 | 3 | 0 | 0 | 18 |
| Lee, Amp, S.F. | 3 | 1 | 2 | 0 | 18 |
| Martin, Eric, N.O. | 3 | 0 | 3 | 0 | 18 |
| McGee, Tim, Wash. | 3 | 0 | 3 | 0 | 18 |
| Mitchell, Brian, Wash. | 3 | 3 | 0 | 0 | 18 |
| Muster, Brad, N.O. | 3 | 3 | 0 | 0 | 18 |
| Obee, Terry, Chi. | 3 | 0 | 3 | 0 | 18 |
| Pegram, Erric, Atl. | 3 | 3 | 0 | 0 | 18 |
| Rathman, Tom, S.F. | 3 | 3 | 0 | 0 | 18 |
| Rypien, Mark, Wash. | 3 | 3 | 0 | 0 | 18 |
| Sanders, Barry, Det. | 3 | 3 | 0 | 0 | 18 |
| Thompson, Darrell, G.B. | 3 | 3 | 0 | 0 | 18 |
| Tillman, Lewis, N.Y.G. | 3 | 3 | 0 | 0 | 18 |
| Bailey, Johnny, Phx. | 2 | 1 | 0 | 1 | 12 |
| Baker, Myron, Chi. | 2 | 0 | 0 | 2 | 12 |
| Carter, Dexter, S.F. | 2 | 1 | 0 | 1 | 12 |
| Clay, Willie, Det. | 2 | 0 | 0 | 2 | 12 |
| Coleman, Lincoln, Dall. | 2 | 2 | 0 | 0 | 12 |
| Conway, Curtis, Chi. | 2 | 0 | 2 | 0 | 12 |
| Craig, Roger, Minn. | 2 | 1 | 1 | 0 | 12 |
| Davis, Eric, S.F. | 2 | 0 | 0 | 2 | 12 |
| Ellard, Henry, Rams | 2 | 0 | 2 | 0 | 12 |
| Gary, Cleveland, Rams | 2 | 1 | 1 | 0 | 12 |
| Green, Willie, Det. | 2 | 0 | 2 | 0 | 12 |
| Hallock, Ty, Det. | 2 | 0 | 2 | 0 | 12 |
| Holman, Rodney, Det. | 2 | 0 | 2 | 0 | 12 |
| Jones, Ernie, Rams | 2 | 0 | 2 | 0 | 12 |
| Lynch, Eric, Det. | 2 | 2 | 0 | 0 | 12 |
| McCaffrey, Ed, N.Y.G. | 2 | 0 | 2 | 0 | 12 |
| Middleton, Ron, Wash. | 2 | 0 | 2 | 0 | 12 |
| Monk, Art, Wash. | 2 | 0 | 2 | 0 | 12 |
| Novacek, Jay, Dall. | 2 | 1 | 1 | 0 | 12 |
| Perriman, Brett, Det. | 2 | 0 | 2 | 0 | 12 |
| Sherman, Heath, Phil. | 2 | 2 | 0 | 0 | 12 |
| Sherrard, Mike, N.Y.G. | 2 | 0 | 2 | 0 | 12 |
| Smith, Irv, N.O. | 2 | 0 | 2 | 0 | 12 |
| Smith, Robert, Minn. | 2 | 2 | 0 | 0 | 12 |
| Thomas, Lamar, T.B. | 2 | 0 | 2 | 0 | 12 |
| Williams, Aeneas, Phx. | 2 | 0 | 0 | 2 | 12 |
| Word, Barry, Minn. | 2 | 2 | 0 | 0 | 12 |
| Worley, Tim, Chi. | 2 | 2 | 0 | 0 | 12 |
| Young, Steve, S.F. | 2 | 2 | 0 | 0 | 12 |
| Young, Mike, Phil. | 2 | 0 | 2 | 0 | 12 |
| Anderson, Gary, T.B. | 1 | 0 | 1 | 0 | 6 |
| Armstrong, Tyji, T.B. | 1 | 0 | 1 | 0 | 6 |
| Bailey, Victor, Phil. | 1 | 0 | 1 | 0 | 6 |
| Beach, Sanjay, S.F. | 1 | 0 | 1 | 0 | 6 |
| Blount, Eric, Phx. | 1 | 1 | 0 | 0 | 6 |
| Bono, Steve, S.F. | 1 | 1 | 0 | 0 | 6 |
| Boykin, Deral, Rams | 1 | 0 | 0 | 1 | 6 |
| Brenner, Hoby, N.O. | 1 | 0 | 1 | 0 | 6 |
| Brooks, Robert, G.B. | 1 | 0 | 0 | 1 | 6 |
| Broussard, Steven, Atl. | 1 | 1 | 0 | 0 | 6 |
| Butler, LeRoy, G.B. | 1 | 0 | 0 | 1 | 6 |
| Byner, Earnest, Wash. | 1 | 1 | 0 | 0 | 6 |
| Carrier, Mark, Chi. | 1 | 0 | 0 | 1 | 6 |
| Carter, Pat, Rams | 1 | 0 | 1 | 0 | 6 |
| Clark, Vinnie, Atl. | 1 | 0 | 0 | 1 | 6 |
| Coleman, Monte, Wash. | 1 | 0 | 0 | 1 | 6 |
| Collins, Mark, N.Y.G. | 1 | 0 | 0 | 1 | 6 |
| Cunningham, Randall, Phil. | 1 | 1 | 0 | 0 | 6 |
| Dowdell, Marcus, N.O. | 1 | 0 | 1 | 0 | 6 |
| Edwards, Anthony, Phx. | 1 | 0 | 1 | 0 | 6 |
| Evans, Byron, Phil. | 1 | 0 | 0 | 1 | 6 |
| Favre, Brett, G.B. | 1 | 1 | 0 | 0 | 6 |
| Galbraith, Scott, Dall. | 1 | 0 | 1 | 0 | 6 |
| Gannon, Rich, Wash. | 1 | 1 | 0 | 0 | 6 |
| Gouveia, Kurt, Wash. | 1 | 0 | 0 | 1 | 6 |
| Gray, Mel, Det. | 1 | 0 | 0 | 1 | 6 |
| Green, Darrell, Wash. | 1 | 0 | 0 | 1 | 6 |
| Hall, Ron, T.B. | 1 | 0 | 1 | 0 | 6 |
| Hanks, Merton, S.F. | 1 | 0 | 0 | 1 | 6 |
| Hearst, Garrison, Phx. | 1 | 1 | 0 | 0 | 6 |
| Ismail, Qadry, Minn. | 1 | 0 | 1 | 0 | 6 |
| Jamison, George, Det. | 1 | 0 | 0 | 1 | 6 |
| Johnson, A. J., Wash. | 1 | 0 | 0 | 1 | 6 |
| Jones, Dante, Chi. | 1 | 0 | 0 | 1 | 6 |
| Jordan, Steve, Minn. | 1 | 0 | 1 | 0 | 6 |
| Joseph, James, Phil. | 1 | 0 | 1 | 0 | 6 |
| Kinchen, Todd, Rams | 1 | 0 | 1 | 0 | 6 |
| Lincoln, Jeremy, Chi. | 1 | 0 | 0 | 1 | 6 |
| Lynch, Lorenzo, Phx. | 1 | 0 | 0 | 1 | 6 |
| Mack, Milton, T.B. | 1 | 0 | 0 | 1 | 6 |
| McAfee, Fred, N.O. | 1 | 1 | 0 | 0 | 6 |
| McDowell, Anthony, T.B. | 1 | 0 | 1 | 0 | 6 |
| McGriggs, Lamar, Minn. | 1 | 0 | 0 | 1 | 6 |
| McGruder, Michael, S.F. | 1 | 0 | 0 | 1 | 6 |
| McMillian, Audray, Minn. | 1 | 0 | 0 | 1 | 6 |
| McNeal, Travis, Rams | 1 | 0 | 1 | 0 | 6 |
| Meggett, David, N.Y.G. | 1 | 0 | 0 | 1 | 6 |
| Mills, Sam, N.O. | 1 | 0 | 0 | 1 | 6 |
| Mims, David, Atl. | 1 | 0 | 1 | 0 | 6 |
| Moore, Dave, T.B. | 1 | 0 | 1 | 0 | 6 |
| Neal, Lorenzo, N.O. | 1 | 1 | 0 | 0 | 6 |
| Ned, Derrick, N.O. | 1 | 1 | 0 | 0 | 6 |
| Newman, Pat, N.O. | 1 | 0 | 1 | 0 | 6 |

| | TD | TDR | TDP | TDM | PTS |
|---|---|---|---|---|---|
| Peete, Rodney, Det. | 1 | 1 | 0 | 0 | 6 |
| Rasheed, Kenyon, N.Y.G. | 1 | 1 | 0 | 0 | 6 |
| Reeves, Walter, Phx. | 1 | 0 | 1 | 0 | 6 |
| Rolle, Butch, Phx. | 1 | 0 | 1 | 0 | 6 |
| Royster, Mazio, T.B. | 1 | 1 | 0 | 0 | 6 |
| Sanders, Deion, Atl. | 1 | 0 | 1 | 0 | 6 |
| Seals, Ray, T.B. | 1 | 0 | 0 | 1 | 6 |
| Singleton, Nate, S.F. | 1 | 0 | 1 | 0 | 6 |
| Small, Torrance, N.O. | 1 | 0 | 1 | 0 | 6 |
| Smith, Kevin, Dall. | 1 | 0 | 0 | 1 | 6 |
| Smith, Tony, Atl. | 1 | 0 | 0 | 1 | 6 |
| Stephens, John, G.B. | 1 | 1 | 0 | 0 | 6 |
| Tamm, Ralph, S.F. | 1 | 0 | 0 | 1 | 6 |
| Tice, Mike, Minn. | 1 | 0 | 1 | 0 | 6 |
| Turner, Floyd, N.O. | 1 | 0 | 1 | 0 | 6 |
| Waddle, Tom, Chi. | 1 | 0 | 1 | 0 | 6 |
| Warren, Frank, N.O. | 1 | 0 | 0 | 1 | 6 |
| Wetnight, Ryan, Chi. | 1 | 0 | 1 | 0 | 6 |
| Williams, Jamie, S.F. | 1 | 0 | 1 | 0 | 6 |
| Flores, Mike, Phil. | 0 | 0 | 0 | 0 | *2 |
| Hamilton, Keith, N.Y.G. | 0 | 0 | 0 | 0 | *2 |
| Stowers, Tommie, N.O. | 0 | 0 | 0 | 0 | *2 |
| Swann, Eric, Phx. | 0 | 0 | 0 | 0 | *2 |
| Thomas, Henry, Minn. | 0 | 0 | 0 | 0 | *2 |

** Indicates safety*
*Team Safeties credited to Green Bay, Minnesota, Philadelphia, Phoenix, and Washington.*

## FIELD GOALS

**Field Goal Percentage**
**NFC:** .963—Norm Johnson, Atlanta
**AFC:** .933—Gary Anderson, Pittsburgh

**Field Goals**
**AFC:** 35—Jeff Jaeger, Raiders
**NFC:** 34—Jason Hanson, Detroit

**Field Goal Attempts**
**AFC:** 44—Jeff Jaeger, Raiders
**NFC:** 43—Jason Hanson, Detroit

**Longest Field Goal**
**AFC:** 59—Steve Christie, Buffalo vs. Miami, September 26
**NFC:** 57—Michael Husted, Tampa Bay at Raiders, December 19

**Average Yards Made**
**NFC:** 37.1—Tony Zendejas, Rams
**AFC:** 36.6—Steve Christie, Buffalo

### AFC FIELD GOALS—TEAM

| | FG | FGA | Pct. | Long |
|---|---|---|---|---|
| Pittsburgh | 28 | 30 | .933 | 46 |
| Houston | 29 | 34 | .853 | 52 |
| Indianapolis | 26 | 31 | .839 | 53 |
| Seattle | 23 | 28 | .821 | 55 |
| L.A. Raiders | 35 | 44 | .795 | 53 |
| Kansas City | 23 | 29 | .793 | 52 |
| San Diego | 31 | 40 | .775 | 51 |
| Cincinnati | 24 | 31 | .774 | 53 |
| Miami | 24 | 32 | .750 | 52 |
| Denver | 26 | 35 | .743 | 54 |
| Cleveland | 16 | 22 | .727 | 53 |
| Buffalo | 23 | 32 | .719 | 59 |
| N.Y. Jets | 17 | 26 | .654 | 45 |
| New England | 19 | 31 | .613 | 40 |
| AFC Total | 344 | 445 | —— | 59 |
| AFC Average | 24.6 | 31.8 | .773 | — |

### NFC FIELD GOALS—TEAM

| | FG | FGA | Pct. | Long |
|---|---|---|---|---|
| Atlanta | 26 | 27 | .963 | 54 |
| Green Bay | 31 | 37 | .838 | 54 |
| Dallas | 30 | 37 | .811 | 52 |
| New Orleans | 28 | 35 | .800 | 56 |
| Detroit | 34 | 43 | .791 | 53 |
| N.Y. Giants | 26 | 34 | .765 | 54 |
| Phoenix | 21 | 28 | .750 | 55 |
| Chicago | 27 | 36 | .750 | 55 |
| Minnesota | 26 | 35 | .743 | 51 |
| Tampa Bay | 16 | 22 | .727 | 57 |
| Philadelphia | 16 | 23 | .696 | 48 |
| L.A. Rams | 16 | 23 | .696 | 54 |
| San Francisco | 16 | 26 | .615 | 46 |
| Washington | 16 | 28 | .571 | 51 |
| NFC Total | 329 | 434 | —— | 57 |
| NFC Average | 23.5 | 31.0 | .758 | — |
| League Total | 673 | 879 | —— | 59 |
| League Average | 24.0 | 31.4 | .766 | — |

# 1993 INDIVIDUAL STATISTICS

**AFC FIELD GOALS—INDIVIDUAL**

| | 1-19 Yards | 20-29 Yards | 30-39 Yards | 40-49 Yards | 50 or Longer | Totals | Avg. Yds. Att. | Avg. Yds. Made | Avg. Yds. Miss | Long |
|---|---|---|---|---|---|---|---|---|---|---|
| Anderson, Gary, Pitt. | 1-1 | 8-9 | 14-14 | 5-6 | 0-0 | 28-30 | 33.3 | 33.3 | 34.5 | 46 |
| | 1.000 | .889 | 1.000 | .833 | — | .933 | | | | |
| Del Greco, Al, Hou. | 0-0 | 13-13 | 8-9 | 4-5 | 4-7 | 29-34 | 35.9 | 34.0 | 46.6 | 52 |
| | — | 1.000 | .889 | .800 | .571 | .853 | | | | |
| Biasucci, Dean, Ind. | 1-1 | 14-14 | 7-8 | 3-6 | 1-2 | 26-31 | 33.3 | 30.8 | 46.2 | 53 |
| | 1.000 | 1.000 | .875 | .500 | .500 | .839 | | | | |
| Kasay, John, Sea. | 1-1 | 5-5 | 10-11 | 4-6 | 3-5 | 23-28 | 37.9 | 36.1 | 46.2 | 55 |
| | 1.000 | 1.000 | .909 | .667 | .600 | .821 | | | | |
| Jaeger, Jeff, Raid. | 0-0 | 12-12 | 13-15 | 6-10 | 4-7 | 35-44 | 36.5 | 34.5 | 44.2 | 53 |
| | — | 1.000 | .867 | .600 | .571 | .795 | | | | |
| Lowery, Nick, K.C. | 0-0 | 8-8 | 7-9 | 7-11 | 1-1 | 23-29 | 35.5 | 33.8 | 42.2 | 52 |
| | — | 1.000 | .778 | .636 | 1.000 | .793 | | | | |
| Carney, John, S.D. | 1-1 | 7-7 | 14-17 | 7-12 | 2-3 | 31-40 | 37.4 | 35.8 | 42.7 | 51 |
| | 1.000 | 1.000 | .824 | .583 | .667 | .775 | | | | |
| Pelfrey, Doug, Cinn. | 0-0 | 8-8 | 6-10 | 8-10 | 2-3 | 24-31 | 37.0 | 36.2 | 40.0 | 53 |
| | — | 1.000 | .600 | .800 | .667 | .774 | | | | |
| Stoyanovich, Pete, Mia. | 2-2 | 9-10 | 7-11 | 4-7 | 2-2 | 24-32 | 33.2 | 31.7 | 37.6 | 52 |
| | 1.000 | .900 | .636 | .571 | 1.000 | .750 | | | | |
| Elam, Jason, Den. | 0-0 | 11-12 | 7-7 | 4-10 | 4-6 | 26-35 | 36.7 | 34.8 | 42.4 | 54 |
| | — | .917 | 1.000 | .400 | .667 | .743 | | | | |
| Stover, Matt, Clev. | 0-0 | 4-4 | 5-6 | 6-8 | 1-4 | 16-22 | 39.9 | 36.4 | 49.2 | 53 |
| | — | 1.000 | .833 | .750 | .250 | .727 | | | | |
| Bahr, Matt, Phil.-N.E. | 1-1 | 5-7 | 5-5 | 2-5 | 0-0 | 13-18 | 32.6 | 31.0 | 36.8 | 48 |
| | 1.000 | .714 | 1.000 | .400 | — | .722 | | | | |
| Christie, Steve, Buff. | 0-0 | 4-5 | 12-12 | 6-9 | 1-6 | 23-32 | 39.4 | 36.6 | 46.7 | 59 |
| | — | .800 | 1.000 | .667 | .167 | .719 | | | | |
| Blanchard, Cary, N.Y.J. | 1-1 | 7-8 | 4-5 | 5-10 | 0-2 | 17-26 | 35.6 | 31.6 | 43.1 | 45 |
| | 1.000 | .875 | .800 | .500 | .000 | .654 | | | | |
| Sisson, Scott, N.E. | 1-1 | 8-13 | 3-4 | 2-6 | 0-2 | 14-26 | 33.1 | 28.8 | 38.2 | 40 |
| | 1.000 | .615 | .750 | .333 | .000 | .538 | | | | |
| AFC Totals | 9-9 | 119-129 | 120-141 | 71-116 | 25-50 | 344-445 | 36.0 | 34.0 | 42.8 | 59 |
| | 1.000 | .922 | .851 | .612 | .500 | .773 | | | | |
| League Totals | 28-28 | 229-246 | 219-263 | 136-222 | 61-120 | 673-879 | 36.2 | 34.1 | 43.3 | 59 |
| | 1.000 | .931 | .833 | .613 | .508 | .766 | | | | |

*Leader based on percentage, minimum 16 field goal attempts*

**NFC FIELD GOALS—INDIVIDUAL**

| | 1-19 Yards | 20-29 Yards | 30-39 Yards | 40-49 Yards | 50 or Longer | Totals | Avg. Yds. Att. | Avg. Yds. Made | Avg. Yds. Miss | Long |
|---|---|---|---|---|---|---|---|---|---|---|
| Johnson, Norm, Atl. | 1-1 | 7-7 | 9-10 | 7-7 | 2-2 | 26-27 | 35.4 | 35.3 | 38.0 | 54 |
| | 1.000 | 1.000 | .900 | 1.000 | 1.000 | .963 | | | | |
| Murray, Eddie, Dall. | 4-4 | 4-4 | 9-12 | 8-8 | 3-5 | 28-33 | 36.5 | 35.5 | 42.0 | 52 |
| | 1.000 | 1.000 | .750 | 1.000 | .600 | .848 | | | | |
| Jacke, Chris, G.B. | 1-1 | 12-12 | 6-10 | 6-7 | 6-7 | 31-37 | 35.4 | 34.8 | 38.5 | 54 |
| | 1.000 | 1.000 | .600 | .857 | .857 | .838 | | | | |
| Treadwell, David, NYG | 3-3 | 11-12 | 7-10 | 4-6 | 0-0 | 25-31 | 31.2 | 29.6 | 37.7 | 46 |
| | 1.000 | .917 | .700 | .667 | — | .806 | | | | |
| Andersen, Morten, N.O. | 2-2 | 7-7 | 7-7 | 11-14 | 1-5 | 28-35 | 38.7 | 36.5 | 47.7 | 56 |
| | 1.000 | 1.000 | 1.000 | .786 | .200 | .800 | | | | |
| Hanson, Jason, Det. | 1-1 | 8-8 | 15-15 | 7-12 | 3-7 | 34-43 | 38.3 | 35.6 | 48.8 | 53 |
| | 1.000 | 1.000 | 1.000 | .583 | .429 | .791 | | | | |
| Butler, Kevin, Chi. | 0-0 | 7-8 | 12-13 | 3-7 | 5-8 | 27-36 | 38.1 | 36.5 | 42.9 | 55 |
| | — | .875 | .923 | .429 | .625 | .750 | | | | |
| Davis, Greg, Phx. | 1-1 | 11-11 | 1-1 | 4-10 | 4-5 | 21-28 | 36.6 | 33.5 | 45.9 | 55 |
| | 1.000 | 1.000 | 1.000 | .400 | .800 | .750 | | | | |
| Reveiz, Fuad, Minn. | 4-4 | 12-12 | 6-6 | 3-7 | 1-6 | 26-35 | 34.7 | 29.4 | 50.0 | 51 |
| | 1.000 | 1.000 | 1.000 | .429 | .167 | .743 | | | | |
| Husted, Michael, T.B. | 0-0 | 5-5 | 5-6 | 3-6 | 3-5 | 16-22 | 39.1 | 36.0 | 47.3 | 57 |
| | — | 1.000 | .833 | .500 | .600 | .727 | | | | |
| Zendejas, Tony, Rams | 0-0 | 6-7 | 4-5 | 0-3 | 6-8 | 16-23 | 38.8 | 37.1 | 42.7 | 54 |
| | — | .857 | .800 | .000 | .750 | .696 | | | | |
| Cofer, Mike, S.F. | 0-0 | 7-9 | 5-7 | 4-7 | 0-3 | 16-26 | 35.9 | 32.5 | 41.4 | 46 |
| | — | .778 | .714 | .571 | .000 | .615 | | | | |
| Lohmiller, Chip, Wash. | 2-2 | 4-4 | 8-12 | 1-4 | 1-6 | 16-28 | 37.9 | 32.2 | 45.6 | 51 |
| | 1.000 | 1.000 | .667 | .250 | .167 | .571 | | | | |
| **Nonqualifiers:** | | | | | | | | | | |
| Ruzek, Roger, Phil. | 0-0 | 4-4 | 3-5 | 1-1 | 0-0 | 8-10 | 30.6 | 30.4 | 31.5 | 46 |
| | — | 1.000 | .600 | 1.000 | — | .800 | | | | |
| Elliott, Lin, Dall. | 0-0 | 1-1 | 0-1 | 1-2 | 0-0 | 2-4 | 36.0 | 32.5 | 39.5 | 43 |
| | — | 1.000 | .000 | .500 | — | .500 | | | | |
| Daluiso, Brad, NYG | 0-0 | 0-0 | 0-0 | 0-0 | 1-3 | 1-3 | 52.0 | 54.0 | 51.0 | 54 |
| | — | — | — | — | .333 | .333 | | | | |
| NFC Totals | 19-19 | 110-117 | 99-122 | 65-106 | 36-70 | 329-434 | 36.5 | 34.2 | 43.9 | 57 |
| | 1.000 | .940 | .811 | .613 | .514 | .758 | | | | |
| League Totals | 28-28 | 229-246 | 219-263 | 136-222 | 61-120 | 673-879 | 36.2 | 34.1 | 43.3 | 59 |
| | 1.000 | .931 | .833 | .613 | .508 | .766 | | | | |

*Leader based on percentage, minimum 16 field goal attempts*

## RUSHING

**Yards**
- **NFC:** 1486—Emmitt Smith, Dallas
- **AFC:** 1315—Thurman Thomas, Buffalo

**Yards, Game**
- **NFC:** 237—Emmitt Smith, Dallas at Philadelphia, October 31, (30 attempts, TD)
- **AFC:** 194—Gary Brown, Houston at Cleveland, November 21, (34 attempts, TD)

**Longest**
- **NFC:** 85—Reggie Brooks, Washington at Philadelphia, September 19 - TD
- **AFC:** 77—Keith Byars, Miami at Dallas, November 25 - TD

**Attempts**
- **AFC:** 355—Thurman Thomas, Buffalo
- **NFC:** 294—Jerome Bettis, Rams

**Attempts, Game**
- **NFC:** 41—Rodney Hampton, Giants vs. Rams, September 19, (134 yards)
- **AFC:** 36—Chris Warren, Seattle at New England, September 19, (174 yards)

**Yards Per Attempt**
- **NFC:** 5.3—Emmitt Smith, Dallas
- **AFC:** 5.1—Gary Brown, Houston

**Touchdowns**
- **AFC:** 12—Marcus Allen, Kansas City
- **NFC:** 10—Ricky Watters, San Francisco

**Team Leaders, Yards**
- **AFC:** BUFFALO: 1315, Thurman Thomas; CINCINNATI: 589, Harold Green; CLEVELAND: 644, Tommy Vardell; DENVER: 816, Rod Bernstine; HOUSTON: 1002, Gary Brown; INDIANAPOLIS: 711, Roosevelt Potts; KANSAS CITY: 764, Marcus Allen; L.A. RAIDERS: 591, Greg Robinson; MIAMI: 693, Mark Higgs; NEW ENGLAND: 1088, Leonard Russell; N.Y. JETS: 821, Johnny Johnson; PITTSBURGH: 763, Leroy Thompson; SAN DIEGO: 746, Marion Butts; SEATTLE: 1072, Chris Warren
- **NFC:** ATLANTA: 1185, Erric Pegram; CHICAGO: 646, Neal Anderson; DALLAS: 1486, Emmitt Smith; DETROIT: 1115, Barry Sanders; GREEN BAY: 654, Darrell Thompson; L.A. RAMS: 1429, Jerome Bettis; MINNESOTA: 487, Scottie Graham; NEW ORLEANS: 705, Derek Brown; N.Y. GIANTS: 1077, Rodney Hampton; PHILADELPHIA: 746, Herschel Walker; PHOENIX: 1018, Ron Moore; SAN FRANCISCO: 950, Ricky Watters; TAMPA BAY: 658, Reggie Cobb; WASHINGTON: 1063, Reggie Brooks

**Team Champion**
- **NFC:** 2210—Giants
- **AFC:** 2015—Seattle

**AFC RUSHING—TEAM**

| | Att | Yards | Avg | Long | TD |
|---|---|---|---|---|---|
| Seattle | 473 | 2015 | 4.3 | 45t | 13 |
| Pittsburgh | 491 | 2003 | 4.1 | 38t | 13 |
| Buffalo | 550 | 1943 | 3.5 | 27 | 12 |
| N.Y. Jets | 521 | 1880 | 3.6 | 57t | 14 |
| San Diego | 455 | 1824 | 4.0 | 65t | 14 |
| Houston | 409 | 1792 | 4.4 | 35 | 11 |
| New England | 502 | 1780 | 3.5 | 49 | 9 |
| Cleveland | 425 | 1701 | 4.0 | 55 | 8 |
| Denver | 468 | 1693 | 3.6 | 26 | 13 |
| Kansas City | 445 | 1655 | 3.7 | 47 | 14 |
| Cincinnati | 423 | 1511 | 3.6 | 29 | 3 |
| Miami | 419 | 1459 | 3.5 | 77t | 10 |
| L.A. Raiders | 433 | 1425 | 3.3 | 19 | 10 |
| Indianapolis | 365 | 1288 | 3.5 | 34 | 4 |
| AFC Total | 6379 | 23969 | 3.8 | 77t | 148 |
| AFC Average | 455.6 | 1712.1 | 3.8 | — | 10.6 |

## 1993 INDIVIDUAL STATISTICS

### NFC RUSHING—TEAM

| | Att. | Yards | Avg. | Long | TD |
|---|---|---|---|---|---|
| N.Y. Giants | 560 | 2210 | 3.9 | 58 | 11 |
| Dallas | 490 | 2161 | 4.4 | 62t | 20 |
| San Francisco | 463 | 2133 | 4.6 | 50t | 26 |
| L.A. Rams | 449 | 2014 | 4.5 | 71t | 8 |
| Detroit | 456 | 1944 | 4.3 | 48 | 9 |
| Phoenix | 452 | 1809 | 4.0 | 57 | 12 |
| New Orleans | 414 | 1766 | 4.3 | 74t | 10 |
| Philadelphia | 456 | 1761 | 3.9 | 35 | 7 |
| Washington | 396 | 1728 | 4.4 | 85t | 11 |
| Chicago | 477 | 1677 | 3.5 | 45 | 10 |
| Minnesota | 447 | 1624 | 3.6 | 31 | 8 |
| Green Bay | 448 | 1619 | 3.6 | 60t | 14 |
| Atlanta | 395 | 1590 | 4.0 | 29 | 4 |
| Tampa Bay | 402 | 1290 | 3.2 | 22 | 6 |
| NFC Total | 6305 | 25326 | 4.0 | 85t | 156 |
| NFC Average | 450.4 | 1809.0 | 4.0 | — | 11.1 |
| League Total | 12684 | 49295 | — | 85t | 304 |
| League Average | 453.0 | 1760.5 | 3.9 | — | 10.9 |

### NFL TOP TEN RUSHERS

| | Att. | Yards | Avg. | Long | TD |
|---|---|---|---|---|---|
| Smith, Emmitt, Dall. | 283 | 1486 | 5.3 | 62t | 9 |
| Bettis, Jerome, Rams | 294 | 1429 | 4.9 | 71t | 7 |
| Thomas, Thurman, Buff. | 355 | 1315 | 3.7 | 27 | 6 |
| Pegram, Erric, Atl. | 292 | 1185 | 4.1 | 29 | 3 |
| Sanders, Barry, Det. | 243 | 1115 | 4.6 | 42 | 3 |
| Russell, Leonard, N.E. | 300 | 1088 | 3.6 | 21 | 7 |
| Hampton, Rodney, N.Y.G. | 292 | 1077 | 3.7 | 20 | 5 |
| Warren, Chris, Sea. | 273 | 1072 | 3.9 | 45t | 7 |
| Brooks, Reggie, Wash. | 223 | 1063 | 4.8 | 85t | 3 |
| Moore, Ron, Phx. | 263 | 1018 | 3.9 | 20 | 9 |

### AFC RUSHERS—INDIVIDUAL

| | Att. | Yards | Avg. | Long | TD |
|---|---|---|---|---|---|
| Thomas, Thurman, Buff. | 355 | 1315 | 3.7 | 27 | 6 |
| Russell, Leonard, N.E. | 300 | 1088 | 3.6 | 21 | 7 |
| Warren, Chris, Sea. | 273 | 1072 | 3.9 | 45t | 7 |
| Brown, Gary, Hou. | 195 | 1002 | 5.1 | 26 | 6 |
| Johnson, Johnny, N.Y.J. | 198 | 821 | 4.1 | 57t | 3 |
| Bernstine, Rod, Den. | 223 | 816 | 3.7 | 24 | 4 |
| Allen, Marcus, K.C. | 206 | 764 | 3.7 | 39 | 12 |
| Thompson, Leroy, Pitt. | 205 | 763 | 3.7 | 36 | 3 |
| Butts, Marion, S.D. | 185 | 746 | 4.0 | 27 | 4 |
| Foster, Barry, Pitt. | 177 | 711 | 4.0 | 38 | 8 |
| Potts, Roosevelt, Ind. | 179 | 711 | 4.0 | 34 | 0 |
| Higgs, Mark, Mia. | 186 | 693 | 3.7 | 31 | 3 |
| Means, Natrone, S.D. | 160 | 645 | 4.0 | 65t | 8 |
| Vardell, Tommy, Clev. | 171 | 644 | 3.8 | 54 | 3 |
| Metcalf, Eric, Clev. | 129 | 611 | 4.7 | 55 | 1 |
| Robinson, Greg, Raid. | 156 | 591 | 3.8 | 16 | 1 |
| Green, Harold, Cinn. | 215 | 589 | 2.7 | 25 | 0 |
| Baxter, Brad, N.Y.J. | 174 | 559 | 3.2 | 16 | 7 |
| Fenner, Derrick, Cinn. | 121 | 482 | 4.0 | 26 | 1 |
| White, Lorenzo, Hou. | 131 | 465 | 3.5 | 14 | 2 |
| Delpino, Robert, Den. | 131 | 445 | 3.4 | 18 | 8 |
| Davis, Kenneth, Buff. | 109 | 391 | 3.6 | 19 | 6 |
| Kirby, Terry, Mia. | 119 | 390 | 3.3 | 20 | 3 |
| Williams, John L., Sea. | 82 | 371 | 4.5 | 38 | 3 |
| Mirer, Rick, Sea. | 68 | 343 | 5.0 | 33 | 3 |
| Johnson, Anthony, Ind. | 95 | 331 | 3.5 | 14 | 1 |
| Anders, Kimble, K.C. | 75 | 291 | 3.9 | 18 | 0 |
| Klingler, David, Cinn. | 41 | 282 | 6.9 | 29 | 0 |
| McNair, Todd, K.C. | 51 | 278 | 5.5 | 47 | 2 |
| Byars, Keith, Mia. | 64 | 269 | 4.2 | 77t | 3 |
| Hoge, Merril, Pitt. | 51 | 249 | 4.9 | 30 | 1 |
| Milburn, Glyn, Den. | 52 | 231 | 4.4 | 26 | 0 |
| Turner, Kevin, N.E. | 50 | 231 | 4.6 | 49 | 0 |
| Hoard, Leroy, Clev. | 56 | 227 | 4.1 | 30 | 0 |
| Thomas, Blair, N.Y.J. | 59 | 221 | 3.7 | 24 | 1 |
| Harmon, Ronnie, S.D. | 46 | 216 | 4.7 | 19 | 0 |
| Hostetler, Jeff, Raid. | 55 | 202 | 3.7 | 19 | 5 |
| Croom, Corey, N.E. | 60 | 198 | 3.3 | 22 | 1 |
| Stephens, John, G.B.-K.C. | 54 | 191 | 3.5 | 22 | 1 |
| Bell, Nick, Raid. | 67 | 180 | 2.7 | 12 | 1 |
| Murrell, Adrian, N.Y.J. | 34 | 157 | 4.6 | 37t | 1 |
| Smith, Steve, Raid. | 47 | 156 | 3.3 | 13 | 0 |
| Elway, John, Den. | 44 | 153 | 3.5 | 18 | 0 |

| | Att. | Yards | Avg. | Long | TD |
|---|---|---|---|---|---|
| Vaughn, Jon, Sea. | 36 | 153 | 4.3 | 37 | 0 |
| Culver, Rodney, Ind. | 65 | 150 | 2.3 | 9 | 3 |
| Gash, Sam, N.E. | 48 | 149 | 3.1 | 14 | 1 |
| Williams, Harvey, K.C. | 42 | 149 | 3.5 | 19 | 0 |
| Moon, Warren, Hou. | 48 | 145 | 3.0 | 35 | 1 |
| Bieniemy, Eric, S.D. | 33 | 135 | 4.1 | 12 | 1 |
| Stone, Dwight, Pitt. | 12 | 121 | 10.1 | 38t | 1 |
| Esiason, Boomer, N.Y.J. | 45 | 118 | 2.6 | 17 | 1 |
| McCallum, Napoleon, Raid. | 37 | 114 | 3.1 | 14 | 3 |
| O'Donnell, Neil, Pitt. | 26 | 111 | 4.3 | 27 | 0 |
| Montgomery, Tyrone, Raid. | 37 | 106 | 2.9 | 15 | 0 |
| Kelly, Jim, Buff. | 36 | 102 | 2.8 | 17 | 0 |
| Tillman, Spencer, Hou. | 9 | 94 | 10.4 | 34 | 0 |
| Mitchell, Scott, Mia. | 21 | 89 | 4.2 | 32 | 0 |
| Bledsoe, Drew, N.E. | 32 | 82 | 2.6 | 15 | 0 |
| Testaverde, Vinny, Clev. | 18 | 74 | 4.1 | 14 | 0 |
| Montana, Joe, K.C. | 25 | 64 | 2.6 | 17 | 0 |
| Baldwin, Randy, Clev. | 18 | 61 | 3.4 | 11 | 0 |
| Gardner, Carwell, Buff. | 20 | 56 | 2.8 | 8 | 0 |
| Miles, Ostell, Cinn. | 22 | 56 | 2.5 | 15 | 1 |
| Jefferson, Shawn, S.D. | 5 | 53 | 10.6 | 33 | 0 |
| Blades, Brian, Sea. | 5 | 52 | 10.4 | 26 | 0 |
| Evans, Vince, Raid. | 14 | 51 | 3.6 | 17 | 0 |
| Rivers, Reggie, Den. | 15 | 50 | 3.3 | 14 | 1 |
| Carlson, Cody, Hou. | 14 | 41 | 2.9 | 10t | 2 |
| Schroeder, Jay, Cinn. | 10 | 41 | 4.1 | 20 | 0 |
| George, Jeff, Ind. | 13 | 39 | 3.0 | 14 | 0 |
| Ball, Eric, Cinn. | 8 | 37 | 4.6 | 18 | 1 |
| Humphries, Stan, S.D. | 8 | 37 | 4.6 | 27 | 0 |
| Turner, Nate, Buff. | 11 | 36 | 3.3 | 10 | 0 |
| Jones, Fred, K.C. | 5 | 34 | 6.8 | 13 | 0 |
| Jordan, Randy, Raid. | 12 | 33 | 2.8 | 12 | 0 |
| Mack, Kevin, Clev. | 10 | 33 | 3.3 | 7 | 1 |
| Secules, Scott, N.E. | 8 | 33 | 4.1 | 13 | 0 |
| Verdin, Clarence, Ind. | 3 | 33 | 11.0 | 29 | 0 |
| Brooks, Bill, Buff. | 3 | 30 | 10.0 | 15 | 0 |
| Thompson, Ernie, K.C. | 11 | 28 | 2.5 | 14 | 0 |
| Carrier, Mark, Clev. | 4 | 26 | 6.5 | 15t | 1 |
| Krieg, Dave, K.C. | 21 | 24 | 1.1 | 20 | 0 |
| Reed, Andre, Buff. | 9 | 21 | 2.3 | 15 | 0 |
| Mathis, Terance, N.Y.J. | 2 | 20 | 10.0 | 17t | 1 |
| Givins, Ernest, Hou. | 6 | 19 | 3.2 | 16 | 0 |
| Chaffey, Pat, N.Y.J. | 5 | 17 | 3.4 | 7 | 0 |
| Parmalee, Bernie, Mia. | 4 | 16 | 4.0 | 12 | 0 |
| Query, Jeff, Cinn. | 2 | 13 | 6.5 | 8 | 0 |
| Saxon, James, Mia. | 5 | 13 | 2.6 | 9 | 0 |
| Bates, Michael, Sea. | 2 | 12 | 6.0 | 6 | 0 |
| Mills, Ernie, Pitt. | 3 | 12 | 4.0 | 19 | 0 |
| Stark, Rohn, Ind. | 1 | 11 | 11.0 | 11 | 0 |
| Maston, Le'Shai, Hou. | 1 | 10 | 10.0 | 10 | 0 |
| Richardson, Bucky, Hou. | 2 | 9 | 4.5 | 11 | 0 |
| Johnson, Tracy, Sea. | 2 | 8 | 4.0 | 5 | 0 |
| Brown, Tim, Raid. | 2 | 7 | 3.5 | 14 | 0 |
| Cuthbert, Randy, Pitt. | 1 | 7 | 7.0 | 7 | 0 |
| Martin, Tony, Mia. | 1 | 6 | 6.0 | 6 | 0 |
| Robinson, Patrick, Cinn. | 1 | 6 | 6.0 | 6 | 0 |
| Toner, Ed, Ind. | 2 | 6 | 3.0 | 6 | 0 |
| Wellman, Gary, Hou. | 2 | 6 | 3.0 | 4 | 0 |
| Benjamin, Ryan, Cinn. | 3 | 5 | 1.7 | 2 | 0 |
| Majkowski, Don, Ind. | 2 | 4 | 2.0 | 4 | 0 |
| Thomas, Doug, Sea. | 1 | 4 | 4.0 | 4 | 0 |
| Barnett, Tim, K.C. | 1 | 3 | 3.0 | 3 | 0 |
| Friesz, John, S.D. | 10 | 3 | 0.3 | 2 | 0 |
| Philcox, Todd, Clev. | 2 | 3 | 1.5 | 3t | 1 |
| Trudeau, Jack, Ind. | 5 | 3 | 0.6 | 2 | 0 |
| Carter, Dale, K.C. | 1 | 2 | 2.0 | 2 | 0 |
| Jones, James, Clev. | 2 | 2 | 1.0 | 1t | 1 |
| Lewis, Nate, S.D. | 3 | 2 | 0.7 | 7 | 0 |
| Mayes, Rueben, Sea. | 1 | 2 | 2.0 | 2 | 0 |
| Saxon, Mike, N.E. | 2 | 2 | 1.0 | 2 | 0 |
| Coleman, Pat, Hou. | 1 | 1 | 1.0 | 1 | 0 |
| Jackson, Michael, Clev. | 1 | 1 | 1.0 | 1 | 0 |
| Cash, Keith, K.C. | 1 | 0 | 0.0 | 0 | 0 |
| Hendrickson, Steve, S.D. | 1 | 0 | 0.0 | 0 | 0 |
| Jett, James, Raid. | 1 | 0 | 0.0 | 0 | 0 |
| Martin, Kelvin, Sea. | 1 | 0 | 0.0 | 0 | 0 |
| Miller, Anthony, S.D. | 1 | 0 | 0.0 | 0 | 0 |
| Rouen, Tom, Den. | 1 | 0 | 0.0 | 0 | 0 |
| Woodson, Rod, Pitt. | 1 | 0 | 0.0 | 0 | 0 |
| Zolak, Scott, N.E. | 1 | 0 | 0.0 | 0 | 0 |
| Gelbaugh, Stan, Sea. | 1 | -1 | -1.0 | -1 | 0 |
| McGwire, Dan, Sea. | 1 | -1 | -1.0 | -1 | 0 |

| | Att. | Yards | Avg. | Long | TD |
|---|---|---|---|---|---|
| Pederson, Doug, Mia. | 2 | -1 | -.5 | 0 | 0 |
| Fina, John, Buff. | 1 | -2 | -2.0 | -2 | 0 |
| Maddox, Tommy, Den. | 2 | -2 | -1.0 | -1 | 0 |
| Crittenden, Ray, N.E. | 1 | -3 | -3.0 | -3 | 0 |
| DeBerg, Steve, Mia. | 4 | -4 | -1.0 | -1 | 0 |
| Fryar, Irving, Mia. | 3 | -4 | -1.3 | 2 | 0 |
| Marino, Dan, Mia. | 9 | -4 | -.4 | 4t | 1 |
| McDuffie, O. J., Mia. | 1 | -4 | -4.0 | -4 | 0 |
| Tomczak, Mike, Pitt. | 5 | -4 | -.8 | 2 | 0 |
| Ismail, Raghib, Raid. | 4 | -5 | -1.2 | 10 | 0 |
| Moore, Rob, N.Y.J. | 1 | -6 | -6.0 | -6 | 0 |
| Reich, Frank, Buff. | 6 | -6 | -1.0 | -1 | 0 |
| Gossett, Jeff, Raid. | 1 | -10 | -10.0 | -10 | 0 |
| Kidd, John, S.D. | 3 | -13 | -4.3 | 2t | 1 |
| Aguiar, Louie, N.Y.J. | 3 | -27 | -9.0 | 5 | 0 |

*t = Touchdown*
*Leader based on most yards gained*

**NFC RUSHERS—INDIVIDUAL**

| | Att. | Yards | Avg. | Long | TD |
|---|---|---|---|---|---|
| Smith, Emmitt, Dall. | 283 | 1486 | 5.3 | 62t | 9 |
| Bettis, Jerome, Rams | 294 | 1429 | 4.9 | 71t | 7 |
| Pegram, Erric, Atl. | 292 | 1185 | 4.1 | 29 | 3 |
| Sanders, Barry, Det. | 243 | 1115 | 4.6 | 42 | 3 |
| Hampton, Rodney, N.Y.G. | 292 | 1077 | 3.7 | 20 | 5 |
| Brooks, Reggie, Wash. | 223 | 1063 | 4.8 | 85t | 3 |
| Moore, Ron, Phx. | 263 | 1018 | 3.9 | 20 | 9 |
| Watters, Ricky, S.F. | 208 | 950 | 4.6 | 39 | 10 |
| Walker, Herschel, Phil. | 174 | 746 | 4.3 | 35 | 1 |
| Brown, Derek, N.O. | 180 | 705 | 3.9 | 60 | 2 |
| Cobb, Reggie, T.B. | 221 | 658 | 3.0 | 16 | 3 |
| Thompson, Darrell, G.B. | 169 | 654 | 3.9 | 60t | 3 |
| Anderson, Neal, Chi. | 202 | 646 | 3.2 | 45 | 4 |
| Tillman, Lewis, N.Y.G. | 121 | 585 | 4.8 | 58 | 3 |
| Bennett, Edgar, G.B. | 159 | 550 | 3.5 | 19 | 9 |
| Graham, Scottie, Minn. | 118 | 488 | 4.1 | 31 | 3 |
| Worley, Tim, Pitt.-Chi. | 120 | 470 | 3.9 | 28 | 2 |
| Word, Barry, Minn. | 142 | 458 | 3.2 | 14 | 2 |
| Young, Steve, S.F. | 69 | 407 | 5.9 | 35 | 2 |
| Sherman, Heath, Phil. | 115 | 406 | 3.5 | 19 | 2 |
| Moore, Derrick, Det. | 88 | 405 | 4.6 | 48 | 3 |
| Smith, Robert, Minn. | 82 | 399 | 4.9 | 26t | 2 |
| Meggett, David, N.Y.G. | 69 | 329 | 4.8 | 23 | 0 |
| Hebron, Vaughn, Phil. | 84 | 297 | 3.5 | 33 | 3 |
| Gary, Cleveland, Rams | 79 | 293 | 3.7 | 15 | 1 |
| Workman, Vince, T.B. | 78 | 284 | 3.6 | 21 | 2 |
| Logan, Marc, S.F. | 58 | 280 | 4.8 | 45 | 7 |
| Harbaugh, Jim, Chi. | 60 | 277 | 4.6 | 25 | 4 |
| Lassic, Derrick, Dall. | 75 | 269 | 3.6 | 15 | 3 |
| Hearst, Garrison, Phx. | 76 | 264 | 3.5 | 57 | 1 |
| Bailey, Johnny, Phx. | 49 | 253 | 5.2 | 31 | 1 |
| Mitchell, Brian, Wash. | 63 | 246 | 3.9 | 29t | 3 |
| Lee, Amp, S.F. | 72 | 230 | 3.2 | 13 | 1 |
| Wilson, Wade, N.O. | 31 | 230 | 7.4 | 44 | 0 |
| Favre, Brett, G.B. | 58 | 216 | 3.7 | 27 | 1 |
| Muster, Brad, N.O. | 64 | 214 | 3.3 | 18 | 3 |
| Lynch, Eric, Det. | 53 | 207 | 3.9 | 15 | 2 |
| Broussard, Steven, Atl. | 39 | 206 | 5.3 | 26 | 1 |
| Heyward, Craig, Chi. | 68 | 206 | 3.0 | 11 | 0 |
| Ervins, Ricky, Wash. | 50 | 201 | 4.0 | 18 | 0 |
| Neal, Lorenzo, N.O. | 21 | 175 | 8.3 | 74t | 1 |
| Hilliard, Dalton, N.O. | 50 | 165 | 3.3 | 16 | 2 |
| Peete, Rodney, Det. | 45 | 165 | 3.7 | 28 | 1 |
| McAfee, Fred, N.O. | 51 | 160 | 3.1 | 27 | 1 |
| Centers, Larry, Phx. | 25 | 152 | 6.1 | 33 | 0 |
| Joseph, James, Phil. | 39 | 140 | 3.6 | 12 | 0 |
| Coleman, Lincoln, Dall. | 34 | 132 | 3.9 | 16 | 2 |
| Bunch, Jarrod, N.Y.G. | 33 | 128 | 3.9 | 13 | 2 |
| Aikman, Troy, Dall. | 32 | 125 | 3.9 | 20 | 0 |
| Craig, Roger, Minn. | 38 | 119 | 3.1 | 11 | 1 |
| Royster, Mazio, T.B. | 33 | 115 | 3.5 | 19 | 1 |
| Cunningham, Randall, Phil. | 18 | 110 | 6.1 | 26 | 1 |
| Byner, Earnest, Wash. | 23 | 105 | 4.6 | 16 | 1 |
| Rubley, T. J., Rams | 29 | 102 | 3.5 | 13 | 0 |
| Erickson, Craig, T.B. | 26 | 96 | 3.7 | 15 | 0 |
| McMahon, Jim, Minn. | 33 | 96 | 2.9 | 16 | 0 |
| Dickerson, Eric, Atl. | 26 | 91 | 3.5 | 10 | 0 |
| Gannon, Rich, Wash. | 21 | 88 | 4.2 | 12 | 1 |
| Rathman, Tom, S.F. | 19 | 80 | 4.2 | 19 | 3 |
| Johnston, Daryl, Dall. | 24 | 74 | 3.1 | 11 | 3 |
| Lester, Tim, Rams | 11 | 74 | 6.7 | 26 | 0 |
| Carter, Dexter, S.F. | 10 | 72 | 7.2 | 50t | 1 |
| Ned, Derrick, N.O. | 9 | 71 | 7.9 | 35t | 1 |
| Rice, Jerry, S.F. | 3 | 69 | 23.0 | 43t | 1 |
| Anderson, Gary, T.B. | 28 | 56 | 2.0 | 13 | 0 |
| Hebert, Bobby, Atl. | 24 | 49 | 2.0 | 14 | 0 |
| Tolliver, Billy Joe, Atl. | 7 | 48 | 6.9 | 24 | 0 |
| Proehl, Ricky, Phx. | 8 | 47 | 5.9 | 17 | 0 |
| Beuerlein, Steve, Phx. | 22 | 45 | 2.0 | 20 | 0 |
| Conway, Curtis, Chi. | 5 | 44 | 8.8 | 18 | 0 |
| Rasheed, Kenyon, N.Y.G. | 9 | 42 | 4.7 | 23t | 1 |
| Brister, Bubby, Phil. | 20 | 39 | 2.0 | 13 | 0 |
| Everett, Jim, Rams | 19 | 38 | 2.0 | 14 | 0 |
| Copeland, Horace, T.B. | 3 | 34 | 11.3 | 22 | 0 |
| Early, Quinn, N.O. | 2 | 32 | 16.0 | 26 | 0 |
| Evans, Chuck, Minn. | 14 | 32 | 2.3 | 5 | 0 |
| Simms, Phil, N.Y.G. | 28 | 31 | 1.1 | 9 | 0 |
| Gainer, Derrick, Dall. | 9 | 29 | 3.2 | 8 | 0 |
| Green, Robert, Chi. | 15 | 29 | 1.9 | 10 | 0 |
| Harris, Rudy, T.B. | 7 | 29 | 4.1 | 12 | 0 |
| Lang, David, Rams | 9 | 29 | 3.2 | 28 | 0 |
| Blount, Eric, Phx. | 5 | 28 | 5.6 | 7 | 1 |
| Kosar, Bernie, Clev.-Dall. | 23 | 26 | 1.1 | 10 | 0 |
| Williams, Kevin, Dall. | 7 | 26 | 3.7 | 12 | 2 |
| Jackson, Mark, N.Y.G. | 3 | 25 | 8.3 | 20 | 0 |
| Ware, Andre, Det. | 7 | 23 | 3.3 | 8 | 0 |
| Carter, Anthony, Minn. | 7 | 19 | 2.7 | 9 | 0 |
| Christian, Bob, Chi. | 8 | 19 | 2.4 | 12 | 0 |
| Barnhardt, Tommy, N.O. | 1 | 18 | 18.0 | 18 | 0 |
| Ellard, Henry, Rams | 2 | 18 | 9.0 | 15 | 0 |
| Brooks, Robert, G.B. | 3 | 17 | 5.7 | 21 | 0 |
| Howard, Desmond, Wash. | 2 | 17 | 8.5 | 9 | 0 |
| O'Brien, Ken, Phil. | 4 | 17 | 4.3 | 11 | 0 |
| Taylor, John, S.F. | 2 | 17 | 8.5 | 12 | 0 |
| Walker, Adam, S.F. | 5 | 17 | 3.4 | 11 | 0 |
| Perriman, Brett, Det. | 4 | 16 | 4.0 | 16 | 0 |
| Bono, Steve, S.F. | 12 | 14 | 1.2 | 10 | 1 |
| Ismail, Qadry, Minn. | 3 | 14 | 4.7 | 6 | 0 |
| Agee, Tommie, Dall. | 6 | 13 | 2.2 | 6 | 0 |
| Lewis, Darren, Chi. | 7 | 13 | 1.9 | 3 | 0 |
| Miller, Chris, Atl. | 2 | 11 | 5.5 | 6 | 0 |
| Kinchen, Todd, Rams | 2 | 10 | 5.0 | 8 | 0 |
| White, Russell, Rams | 2 | 10 | 5.0 | 5 | 0 |
| Sharpe, Sterling, G.B. | 4 | 8 | 2.0 | 5 | 0 |
| Drayton, Troy, Rams | 1 | 7 | 7.0 | 7 | 0 |
| Matthews, Aubrey, Det. | 2 | 7 | 3.5 | 9 | 0 |
| Sanders, Ricky, Wash. | 1 | 7 | 7.0 | 7 | 0 |
| Wilson, Charles, T.B. | 2 | 7 | 3.5 | 4 | 0 |
| Feagles, Jeff, Phil. | 2 | 6 | 3.0 | 6 | 0 |
| Irvin, Michael, Dall. | 2 | 6 | 3.0 | 9 | 0 |
| McDowell, Anthony, T.B. | 2 | 6 | 3.0 | 3 | 0 |
| Willis, Peter Tom, Chi. | 2 | 6 | 3.0 | 6 | 0 |
| Armstrong, Tyji, T.B. | 2 | 5 | 2.5 | 4 | 0 |
| Kramer, Erik, Det. | 10 | 5 | 0.5 | 4 | 0 |
| Jones, Ernie, Rams | 1 | 4 | 4.0 | 4 | 0 |
| Pritchard, Mike, Atl. | 2 | 4 | 2.0 | 4 | 0 |
| Rypien, Mark, Wash. | 9 | 4 | 0.4 | 5 | 3 |
| Mims, David, Atl. | 1 | 3 | 3.0 | 3 | 0 |
| Wilson, Marcus, G.B. | 6 | 3 | 0.5 | 5 | 0 |
| Chandler, Chris, Phx. | 3 | 2 | 0.7 | 1 | 0 |
| Novacek, Jay, Dall. | 1 | 2 | 2.0 | 2t | 1 |
| Richards, Curvin, Det. | 4 | 1 | 0.3 | 1 | 0 |
| Buck, Mike, N.O. | 1 | 0 | 0.0 | 0 | 0 |
| Camarillo, Rich, Phx. | 1 | 0 | 0.0 | 0 | 0 |
| Roby, Reggie, Wash. | 1 | 0 | 0.0 | 0 | 0 |
| Wilmsmeyer, Klaus, S.F. | 2 | 0 | 0.0 | 0 | 0 |
| Monk, Art, Wash. | 1 | -1 | -1.0 | -1 | 0 |
| Salisbury, Sean, Minn. | 10 | -1 | -0.1 | 6 | 0 |
| Conklin, Cary, Wash. | 2 | -2 | -1.0 | -1 | 0 |
| Detmer, Ty, G.B. | 1 | -2 | -2.0 | -2 | 0 |
| Graham, Kent, N.Y.G. | 2 | -3 | -1.5 | -1 | 0 |
| Musgrave, Bill, S.F. | 3 | -3 | -1.0 | -1 | 0 |
| Brown, Dave, N.Y.G. | 3 | -4 | -1.3 | -1 | 0 |
| Walsh, Steve, N.O. | 4 | -4 | -1.0 | -1 | 0 |
| Alexander, Harold, Atl. | 2 | -7 | -3.5 | 0 | 0 |
| Garrett, Jason, Dall. | 8 | -8 | -1.0 | 0 | 0 |

*t = Touchdown*
*Leader based on most yards gained*

## 1993 INDIVIDUAL STATISTICS

### PASSING

**Highest Rating**
- **NFC:** 101.5—Steve Young, San Francisco
- **AFC:** 92.8—John Elway, Denver

**Completion Percentage**
- **NFC:** 69.1—Troy Aikman, Dallas
- **AFC:** 63.2—John Elway, Denver

**Attempts**
- **AFC:** 551—John Elway, Denver
- **NFC:** 522—Brett Favre, Green Bay

**Completions**
- **AFC:** 348—John Elway, Denver
- **NFC:** 318—Brett Favre, Green Bay

**Yards**
- **AFC:** 4030—John Elway, Denver
- **NFC:** 4023—Steve Young, San Francisco

**Yards, Game**
- **NFC:** 462—Steve Young, San Francisco at Rams, November 28, (26-32, 4 TD)
- **AFC:** 424—Jeff Hostetler, Raiders vs. San Diego, October 31, (20-32, 2 TD)

**Longest**
- **NFC:** 98—Bobby Hebert (to Michael Haynes), Atlanta vs. New Orleans, September 12 - TD
- **AFC:** 82—Scott Secules (to Kevin Turner {13 yds} lateral to Leonard Russell {69 yds}), New England at Phoenix, October 10

**Yards Per Attempt**
- **NFC:** 8.71—Steve Young, San Francisco
- **AFC:** 7.81—Vinny Testaverde, Cleveland

**Touchdown Passes**
- **NFC:** 29—Steve Young, San Francisco
- **AFC:** 25—John Elway, Denver

**Touchdown Passes, Game**
- AFC: 4—Jim Kelly, Buffalo vs. New England, September 5, (13-22, 167 yards)
  - Boomer Esiason, Jets vs. Philadelphia, October 3, (19-33, 297 yards)
  - Warren Moon, Houston at Cincinnati, November 14, (23-31, 225 yards)
  - Drew Bledsoe, New England vs. Miami, January 2, (27-43, 329 yards) (OT)
- NFC: 4—Brett Favre, Green Bay at Tampa Bay, October 24, (20-35, 268 yards)
  - Craig Erickson, Tampa Bay at Atlanta, October 31, (18-28, 318 yards)
  - Steve Young, San Francisco at Tampa Bay. November 14, (23-29, 311 yards)
  - Steve Young, San Francisco at Rams, November 28, (26-32, 462 yards)
  - Steve Young, San Francisco at Detroit, December 19, (17-23, 354 yards)

**Lowest Interception Percentage**
- **AFC:** 1.4—Neil O'Donnell, Pittsburgh
- **NFC:** 1.5—Troy Aikman, Dallas

**Team Champion (Most Net Yards)**
- **AFC:** 4353—Miami
- **NFC:** 4302—San Francisco

### AFC PASSING—TEAM

| | Att. | Comp. | Pct. Comp. | Gross Yards | Sacked | Yds. Lost | Net Yards | Yds./ Att. | Yds./ Comp. | TD | Pct. TD | Long | Int. | Pct. Int. |
|---|---|---|---|---|---|---|---|---|---|---|---|---|---|---|
| Miami | 581 | 342 | 58.9 | 4564 | 30 | 211 | 4353 | 7.86 | 13.35 | 27 | 4.65 | 80t | 18 | 3.1 |
| Houston | 614 | 357 | 58.1 | 4145 | 43 | 279 | 3866 | 6.75 | 11.61 | 23 | 3.75 | 80t | 25 | 4.1 |
| Denver | 553 | 350 | 63.3 | 4061 | 39 | 293 | 3768 | 7.34 | 11.60 | 27 | 4.88 | 63 | 10 | 1.8 |
| L.A. Raiders | 495 | 281 | 56.8 | 3882 | 50 | 293 | 3589 | 7.84 | 13.81 | 17 | 3.43 | 74t | 14 | 2.8 |
| Indianapolis | 594 | 332 | 55.9 | 3623 | 29 | 206 | 3417 | 6.10 | 10.91 | 10 | 1.68 | 72t | 15 | 2.5 |
| Pittsburgh | 540 | 299 | 55.4 | 3606 | 48 | 374 | 3232 | 6.68 | 12.06 | 16 | 2.96 | 71t | 12 | 2.2 |
| Buffalo | 497 | 304 | 61.2 | 3535 | 31 | 218 | 3317 | 7.11 | 11.63 | 20 | 4.02 | 65t | 18 | 3.6 |
| N.Y. Jets | 489 | 294 | 60.1 | 3492 | 21 | 160 | 3332 | 7.14 | 11.88 | 16 | 3.27 | 77 | 12 | 2.5 |
| New England | 566 | 289 | 51.1 | 3412 | 23 | 127 | 3285 | 6.03 | 11.81 | 17 | 3.00 | 82 | 24 | 4.2 |
| Kansas City | 490 | 287 | 58.6 | 3384 | 35 | 204 | 3180 | 6.91 | 11.79 | 20 | 4.08 | 66t | 10 | 2.0 |
| San Diego | 563 | 301 | 53.5 | 3383 | 32 | 240 | 3143 | 6.01 | 11.24 | 18 | 3.20 | 66t | 14 | 2.5 |
| Cleveland | 478 | 262 | 54.8 | 3328 | 45 | 289 | 3039 | 6.96 | 12.70 | 23 | 4.81 | 62t | 19 | 4.0 |
| Seattle | 498 | 280 | 56.2 | 2896 | 48 | 242 | 2654 | 5.82 | 10.34 | 13 | 2.61 | 53t | 18 | 3.6 |
| Cincinnati | 510 | 272 | 53.3 | 2830 | 53 | 289 | 2541 | 5.55 | 10.40 | 11 | 2.16 | 51 | 11 | 2.2 |
| AFC Total | 7468 | 4250 | — | 50141 | 527 | 3425 | 46716 | — | — | 258 | — | 82 | 220 | — |
| AFC Average | 533.4 | 303.6 | 56.9 | 3581.5 | 37.6 | 244.6 | 3336.9 | 6.71 | 11.80 | 18.4 | 3.5 | — | 15.7 | 2.9 |

### NFC PASSING—TEAM

| | Att. | Comp. | Pct. Comp. | Gross Yards | Sacked | Yds. Lost | Net Yards | Yds./ Att. | Yds./ Comp. | TD | Pct. TD | Long | Int. | Pct. Int. |
|---|---|---|---|---|---|---|---|---|---|---|---|---|---|---|
| San Francisco | 524 | 354 | 67.6 | 4480 | 35 | 178 | 4302 | 8.55 | 12.66 | 29 | 5.53 | 80t | 17 | 3.2 |
| Atlanta | 573 | 334 | 58.3 | 3787 | 40 | 267 | 3520 | 6.61 | 11.34 | 28 | 4.89 | 98t | 25 | 4.4 |
| Phoenix | 522 | 310 | 59.4 | 3635 | 33 | 231 | 3404 | 6.96 | 11.73 | 21 | 4.02 | 65t | 20 | 3.8 |
| Dallas | 475 | 317 | 66.7 | 3617 | 29 | 163 | 3454 | 7.61 | 11.41 | 18 | 3.79 | 86 | 6 | 1.3 |
| Philadelphia | 556 | 328 | 59.0 | 3463 | 42 | 302 | 3161 | 6.23 | 10.56 | 23 | 4.14 | 80t | 13 | 2.3 |
| Minnesota | 526 | 315 | 59.9 | 3381 | 35 | 181 | 3200 | 6.43 | 10.73 | 18 | 3.42 | 58 | 14 | 2.7 |
| Green Bay | 528 | 322 | 61.0 | 3330 | 30 | 199 | 3131 | 6.31 | 10.34 | 19 | 3.60 | 66t | 24 | 4.5 |
| Tampa Bay | 508 | 262 | 51.6 | 3295 | 39 | 274 | 3021 | 6.49 | 12.58 | 19 | 3.74 | 67t | 25 | 4.9 |
| New Orleans | 481 | 274 | 57.0 | 3183 | 40 | 242 | 2941 | 6.62 | 11.62 | 18 | 3.74 | 63t | 21 | 4.4 |
| N.Y. Giants | 424 | 257 | 60.6 | 3180 | 40 | 245 | 2935 | 7.50 | 12.37 | 17 | 4.01 | 62 | 9 | 2.1 |
| L.A. Rams | 473 | 247 | 52.2 | 3021 | 31 | 231 | 2790 | 6.39 | 12.23 | 16 | 3.38 | 60t | 19 | 4.0 |
| Detroit | 435 | 264 | 60.7 | 2943 | 46 | 229 | 2714 | 6.77 | 11.15 | 15 | 3.45 | 93t | 19 | 4.4 |
| Washington | 533 | 287 | 53.8 | 2764 | 40 | 219 | 2545 | 5.19 | 9.63 | 11 | 2.06 | 54 | 21 | 3.9 |
| Chicago | 388 | 230 | 59.3 | 2270 | 48 | 230 | 2040 | 5.85 | 9.87 | 7 | 1.80 | 48 | 16 | 4.1 |
| NFC Total | 6946 | 4101 | — | 46349 | 528 | 3191 | 43158 | — | — | 259 | — | 98t | 249 | — |
| NFC Average | 496.1 | 292.9 | 59.0 | 3310.6 | 37.7 | 227.9 | 3082.7 | 6.67 | 11.30 | 18.5 | 3.7 | — | 17.8 | 3.6 |
| League Total | 14414 | 8351 | — | 96490 | 1055 | 6616 | 89874 | — | — | 517 | — | 98t | 469 | — |
| League Average | 514.8 | 298.3 | 57.9 | 3446.1 | 37.7 | 236.3 | 3209.8 | 6.69 | 11.55 | 18.5 | 3.6 | — | 16.8 | 3.3 |

*Leader based on net yards*

**NFL TOP TEN PASSERS**

| | Att. | Comp. | Pct. Comp. | Yds. | Avg. Gain | TD | Pct. TD | Long | Int. | Pct. Int. | Sack | Yds. Lost | Rating Points |
|---|---|---|---|---|---|---|---|---|---|---|---|---|---|
| Young, Steve, S.F. | 462 | 314 | 68.0 | 4023 | 8.71 | 29 | 6.3 | 80t | 16 | 3.5 | 31 | 160 | 101.5 |
| Aikman, Troy, Dall. | 392 | 271 | 69.1 | 3100 | 7.91 | 15 | 3.8 | 80t | 6 | 1.5 | 26 | 153 | 99.0 |
| Elway, John, Den. | 551 | 348 | 63.2 | 4030 | 7.31 | 25 | 4.5 | 63 | 10 | 1.8 | 39 | 293 | 92.8 |
| Simms, Phil, N.Y.G. | 400 | 247 | 61.8 | 3038 | 7.60 | 15 | 3.8 | 62 | 9 | 2.3 | 37 | 217 | 88.3 |
| Montana, Joe, K.C. | 298 | 181 | 60.7 | 2144 | 7.19 | 13 | 4.4 | 50t | 7 | 2.3 | 12 | 61 | 87.4 |
| Testaverde, Vinny, Clev. | 230 | 130 | 56.5 | 1797 | 7.81 | 14 | 6.1 | 62t | 9 | 3.9 | 17 | 101 | 85.7 |
| Brister, Bubby, Phil. | 309 | 181 | 58.6 | 1905 | 6.17 | 14 | 4.5 | 58 | 5 | 1.6 | 19 | 148 | 84.9 |
| Esiason, Boomer, N.Y.J. | 473 | 288 | 60.9 | 3421 | 7.23 | 16 | 3.4 | 77 | 11 | 2.3 | 18 | 139 | 84.5 |
| Mitchell, Scott, Mia. | 233 | 133 | 57.1 | 1773 | 7.61 | 12 | 5.2 | 77t | 8 | 3.4 | 7 | 49 | 84.2 |
| Hebert, Bobby, Atl. | 430 | 263 | 61.2 | 2978 | 6.93 | 24 | 5.6 | 98t | 17 | 4.0 | 29 | 190 | 84.0 |

**AFC PASSING—INDIVIDUAL**

| | Att. | Comp. | Pct. Comp. | Yds. | Avg. Gain | TD | Pct. TD | Long | Int. | Pct. Int. | Sack | Yds. Lost | Rating Points |
|---|---|---|---|---|---|---|---|---|---|---|---|---|---|
| Elway, John, Den. | 551 | 348 | 63.2 | 4030 | 7.31 | 25 | 4.5 | 63 | 10 | 1.8 | 39 | 293 | 92.8 |
| Montana, Joe, K.C. | 298 | 181 | 60.7 | 2144 | 7.19 | 13 | 4.4 | 50t | 7 | 2.3 | 12 | 61 | 87.4 |
| Testaverde, Vinny, Clev. | 230 | 130 | 56.5 | 1797 | 7.81 | 14 | 6.1 | 62t | 9 | 3.9 | 17 | 101 | 85.7 |
| Esiason, Boomer, N.Y.J. | 473 | 288 | 60.9 | 3421 | 7.23 | 16 | 3.4 | 77 | 11 | 2.3 | 18 | 139 | 84.5 |
| Mitchell, Scott, Mia. | 233 | 133 | 57.1 | 1773 | 7.61 | 12 | 5.2 | 77t | 8 | 3.4 | 7 | 49 | 84.2 |
| Hostetler, Jeff, Raid. | 419 | 236 | 56.3 | 3242 | 7.74 | 14 | 3.3 | 74t | 10 | 2.4 | 38 | 206 | 82.5 |
| Kelly, Jim, Buff. | 470 | 288 | 61.3 | 3382 | 7.20 | 18 | 3.8 | 65t | 18 | 3.8 | 25 | 171 | 79.9 |
| O'Donnell, Neil, Pitt. | 486 | 270 | 55.6 | 3208 | 6.60 | 14 | 2.9 | 71t | 7 | 1.4 | 41 | 331 | 79.5 |
| George, Jeff, Ind. | 407 | 234 | 57.5 | 2526 | 6.21 | 8 | 2.0 | 72t | 6 | 1.5 | 26 | 190 | 76.3 |
| DeBerg, Steve, T.B.-Mia. | 227 | 136 | 59.9 | 1707 | 7.52 | 7 | 3.1 | 47 | 10 | 4.4 | 18 | 143 | 75.3 |
| Moon, Warren, Hou. | 520 | 303 | 58.3 | 3485 | 6.70 | 21 | 4.0 | 80t | 21 | 4.0 | 34 | 218 | 75.2 |
| Friesz, John, S.D. | 238 | 128 | 53.8 | 1402 | 5.89 | 6 | 2.5 | 66t | 4 | 1.7 | 14 | 98 | 72.8 |
| Humphries, Stan, S.D. | 324 | 173 | 53.4 | 1981 | 6.11 | 12 | 3.7 | 48t | 10 | 3.1 | 18 | 142 | 71.5 |
| Mirer, Rick, Sea. | 486 | 274 | 56.4 | 2833 | 5.83 | 12 | 2.5 | 53t | 17 | 3.5 | 47 | 235 | 67.0 |
| Klingler, David, Cinn. | 343 | 190 | 55.4 | 1935 | 5.64 | 6 | 1.7 | 51 | 9 | 2.6 | 40 | 202 | 66.6 |
| Bledsoe, Drew, N.E. | 429 | 214 | 49.9 | 2494 | 5.81 | 15 | 3.5 | 54t | 15 | 3.5 | 16 | 99 | 65.0 |
| **Nonqualifiers** | | | | | | | | | | | | | |
| Reich, Frank, Buff. | 26 | 16 | 61.5 | 153 | 5.88 | 2 | 7.7 | 30t | 0 | 0.0 | 6 | 47 | 103.5 |
| Marino, Dan, Mia. | 150 | 91 | 60.7 | 1218 | 8.12 | 8 | 5.3 | 80t | 3 | 2.0 | 7 | 42 | 95.9 |
| Krieg, Dave, K.C. | 189 | 105 | 55.6 | 1238 | 6.55 | 7 | 3.7 | 66t | 3 | 1.6 | 22 | 138 | 81.4 |
| Evans, Vince, Raid. | 76 | 45 | 59.2 | 640 | 8.42 | 3 | 3.9 | 68t | 4 | 5.3 | 12 | 87 | 77.7 |
| Schroeder, Jay, Cinn. | 159 | 78 | 49.1 | 832 | 5.23 | 5 | 3.1 | 37 | 2 | 1.3 | 13 | 87 | 70.0 |
| Carlson, Cody, Hou. | 90 | 51 | 56.7 | 605 | 6.72 | 2 | 2.2 | 47 | 4 | 4.4 | 8 | 53 | 66.2 |
| Nagle, Browning, N.Y.J. | 14 | 6 | 42.9 | 71 | 5.07 | 0 | 0.0 | 18 | 0 | 0.0 | 3 | 21 | 58.9 |
| Trudeau, Jack, Ind. | 162 | 85 | 52.5 | 992 | 6.12 | 2 | 1.2 | 68 | 7 | 4.3 | 2 | 11 | 57.4 |
| Philcox, Todd, Clev. | 108 | 52 | 48.1 | 699 | 6.47 | 4 | 3.7 | 56 | 7 | 6.5 | 7 | 60 | 54.5 |
| Secules, Scott, N.E. | 134 | 75 | 56.0 | 918 | 6.85 | 2 | 1.5 | 82 | 9 | 6.7 | 7 | 28 | 54.3 |
| Tomczak, Mike, Pitt. | 54 | 29 | 53.7 | 398 | 7.37 | 2 | 3.7 | 39t | 5 | 9.3 | 7 | 43 | 51.3 |
| Majkowski, Don, Ind. | 24 | 13 | 54.2 | 105 | 4.38 | 0 | 0.0 | 17 | 1 | 4.2 | 1 | 5 | 48.1 |
| **Fewer than 10 attempts** | | | | | | | | | | | | | |
| Aguiar, Louie, N.Y.J. | 2 | 0 | 0.0 | 0 | 0.00 | 0 | 0.0 | 0 | 1 | 50.0 | 0 | 0 | 0.0 |
| Anders, Kimble, K.C. | 0 | 0 | — | 0 | — | 0 | — | — | 0 | — | 1 | 5 | — |
| Blundin, Matt, K.C. | 3 | 1 | 33.3 | 2 | 0.67 | 0 | 0.0 | 2 | 0 | 0.0 | 0 | 0 | 42.4 |
| Byars, Keith, Mia. | 2 | 1 | 50.0 | 11 | 5.50 | 1 | 50.0 | 11t | 0 | 0.0 | 0 | 0 | 106.3 |
| Gelbaugh, Stan, Sea. | 5 | 3 | 60.0 | 39 | 7.80 | 0 | 0.0 | 22 | 1 | 20.0 | 1 | 7 | 45.0 |
| Hoard, Leroy, Clev. | 1 | 0 | 0.0 | 0 | 0.00 | 0 | 0.0 | 0 | 0 | 0.0 | 0 | 0 | 39.6 |
| Jackson, Michael, Clev. | 1 | 1 | 100.0 | 25 | 25.00 | 0 | 0.0 | 25 | 0 | 0.0 | 0 | 0 | 118.8 |
| Johnson, Anthony, Ind. | 1 | 0 | 0.0 | 0 | 0.00 | 0 | 0.0 | 0 | 1 | 100.0 | 0 | 0 | 0.0 |
| Johnson, Lee, Cinn. | 1 | 0 | 0.0 | 0 | 0.00 | 0 | 0.0 | 0 | 0 | 0.0 | 0 | 0 | 39.6 |
| Maddox, Tommy, Den. | 1 | 1 | 100.0 | 1 | 1.00 | 1 | 100.0 | 1t | 0 | 0.0 | 0 | 0 | 118.8 |
| Marshall, Arthur, Den. | 1 | 1 | 100.0 | 30 | 30.00 | 1 | 100.0 | 30t | 0 | 0.0 | 0 | 0 | 158.3 |
| McGwire, Dan, Sea. | 5 | 3 | 60.0 | 24 | 4.80 | 1 | 20.0 | 17t | 0 | 0.0 | 0 | 0 | 111.7 |
| Means, Natrone, S.D. | 1 | 0 | 0.0 | 0 | 0.00 | 0 | 0.0 | 0 | 0 | 0.0 | 0 | 0 | 39.6 |
| Pederson, Doug, Mia. | 8 | 4 | 50.0 | 41 | 5.13 | 0 | 0.0 | 12 | 0 | 0.0 | 1 | 4 | 65.1 |
| Pickens, Carl, Cinn. | 1 | 0 | 0.0 | 0 | 0.00 | 0 | 0.0 | 0 | 0 | 0.0 | 0 | 0 | 39.6 |
| Richardson, Bucky, Hou. | 4 | 3 | 75.0 | 55 | 13.75 | 0 | 0.0 | 34 | 0 | 0.0 | 1 | 8 | 116.7 |
| Thomas, Thurman, Buff. | 1 | 0 | 0.0 | 0 | 0.00 | 0 | 0.0 | 0 | 0 | 0.0 | 0 | 0 | 39.6 |
| Turner, Kevin, N.E. | 1 | 0 | 0.0 | 0 | 0.00 | 0 | 0.0 | 0 | 0 | 0.0 | 0 | 0 | 39.6 |
| Tuten, Rick, Sea. | 1 | 0 | 0.0 | 0 | 0.00 | 0 | 0.0 | 0 | 0 | 0.0 | 0 | 0 | 39.6 |
| Wilhelm, Erik, Cinn. | 6 | 4 | 66.7 | 63 | 10.50 | 0 | 0.0 | 27 | 0 | 0.0 | 0 | 0 | 101.4 |
| Williams, John L., Sea. | 1 | 0 | 0.0 | 0 | 0.00 | 0 | 0.0 | 0 | 0 | 0.0 | 0 | 0 | 39.6 |
| Zolak, Scott, N.E. | 2 | 0 | 0.0 | 0 | 0.00 | 0 | 0.0 | 0 | 0 | 0.0 | 0 | 0 | 39.6 |

*t = Touchdown*
*Leader based on rating points, minimum 224 attempts*

# 1993 INDIVIDUAL STATISTICS

**NFC PASSING—INDIVIDUAL**

| | Att. | Comp. | Pct. Comp. | Yds. | Avg. Gain | TD | Pct. TD | Long | Int. | Pct. Int. | Sack | Yds. Lost | Rating Points |
|---|---|---|---|---|---|---|---|---|---|---|---|---|---|
| Young, Steve, S.F. | 462 | 314 | 68.0 | 4023 | 8.71 | 29 | 6.3 | 80t | 16 | 3.5 | 31 | 160 | 101.5 |
| Aikman, Troy, Dall. | 392 | 271 | 69.1 | 3100 | 7.91 | 15 | 3.8 | 80t | 6 | 1.5 | 26 | 153 | 99.0 |
| Simms, Phil, N.Y.G. | 400 | 247 | 61.8 | 3038 | 7.60 | 15 | 3.8 | 62 | 9 | 2.3 | 37 | 217 | 88.3 |
| Brister, Bubby, Phil. | 309 | 181 | 58.6 | 1905 | 6.17 | 14 | 4.5 | 58 | 5 | 1.6 | 19 | 148 | 84.9 |
| Hebert, Bobby, Atl. | 430 | 263 | 61.2 | 2978 | 6.93 | 24 | 5.6 | 98t | 17 | 4.0 | 29 | 190 | 84.0 |
| Beuerlein, Steve, Phx. | 418 | 258 | 61.7 | 3164 | 7.57 | 18 | 4.3 | 65t | 17 | 4.1 | 29 | 206 | 82.5 |
| McMahon, Jim, Minn. | 331 | 200 | 60.4 | 1968 | 5.95 | 9 | 2.7 | 58 | 8 | 2.4 | 23 | 104 | 76.2 |
| Favre, Brett, G.B. | 522 | 318 | 60.9 | 3303 | 6.33 | 19 | 3.6 | 66t | 24 | 4.6 | 30 | 199 | 72.2 |
| Harbaugh, Jim, Chi. | 325 | 200 | 61.5 | 2002 | 6.16 | 7 | 2.2 | 48 | 11 | 3.4 | 43 | 210 | 72.1 |
| Wilson, Wade, N.O. | 388 | 221 | 57.0 | 2457 | 6.33 | 12 | 3.1 | 42t | 15 | 3.9 | 37 | 225 | 70.1 |
| Erickson, Craig, T.B. | 457 | 233 | 51.0 | 3054 | 6.68 | 18 | 3.9 | 67t | 21 | 4.6 | 35 | 236 | 66.4 |
| Peete, Rodney, Det. | 252 | 157 | 62.3 | 1670 | 6.63 | 6 | 2.4 | 93t | 14 | 5.6 | 34 | 174 | 66.4 |
| Everett, Jim, Rams | 274 | 135 | 49.3 | 1652 | 6.03 | 8 | 2.9 | 60t | 12 | 4.4 | 18 | 125 | 59.7 |
| Rypien, Mark, Wash. | 319 | 166 | 52.0 | 1514 | 4.75 | 4 | 1.3 | 43 | 10 | 3.1 | 16 | 87 | 56.3 |
| **Nonqualifiers** | | | | | | | | | | | | | |
| Kramer, Erik, Det. | 138 | 87 | 63.0 | 1002 | 7.26 | 8 | 5.8 | 48 | 3 | 2.2 | 5 | 35 | 95.1 |
| Cunningham, Randall, Phil. | 110 | 76 | 69.1 | 850 | 7.73 | 5 | 4.5 | 80t | 5 | 4.5 | 7 | 33 | 88.1 |
| Buck, Mike, N.O. | 54 | 32 | 59.3 | 448 | 8.30 | 4 | 7.4 | 63t | 3 | 5.6 | 3 | 17 | 87.6 |
| Salisbury, Sean, Minn. | 195 | 115 | 59.0 | 1413 | 7.25 | 9 | 4.6 | 55 | 6 | 3.1 | 12 | 77 | 84.0 |
| Kosar, Bernie, Clev.-Dall. | 201 | 115 | 57.2 | 1217 | 6.05 | 8 | 4.0 | 86 | 3 | 1.5 | 23 | 132 | 82.0 |
| Rubley, T. J., Rams | 189 | 108 | 57.1 | 1338 | 7.08 | 8 | 4.2 | 54 | 6 | 3.2 | 13 | 106 | 80.1 |
| Bono, Steve, S.F. | 61 | 39 | 63.9 | 416 | 6.82 | 0 | 0.0 | 33 | 1 | 1.6 | 4 | 18 | 76.9 |
| Conklin, Cary, Wash. | 87 | 46 | 52.9 | 496 | 5.70 | 4 | 4.6 | 34t | 3 | 3.4 | 8 | 45 | 70.9 |
| O'Brien, Ken, Phil. | 137 | 71 | 51.8 | 708 | 5.17 | 4 | 2.9 | 41 | 3 | 2.2 | 15 | 116 | 67.4 |
| Chandler, Chris, Phx. | 103 | 52 | 50.5 | 471 | 4.57 | 3 | 2.9 | 27t | 2 | 1.9 | 4 | 25 | 64.8 |
| Walsh, Steve, N.O. | 38 | 20 | 52.6 | 271 | 7.13 | 2 | 5.3 | 54t | 3 | 7.9 | 0 | 0 | 60.3 |
| Gannon, Rich, Wash. | 125 | 74 | 59.2 | 704 | 5.63 | 3 | 2.4 | 54 | 7 | 5.6 | 16 | 87 | 59.6 |
| Tolliver, Billy Joe, Atl. | 76 | 39 | 51.3 | 464 | 6.11 | 3 | 3.9 | 42t | 5 | 6.6 | 3 | 15 | 56.0 |
| Garrett, Jason, Dall. | 19 | 9 | 47.4 | 61 | 3.21 | 0 | 0.0 | 16 | 0 | 0.0 | 1 | 6 | 54.9 |
| Ware, Andre, Det. | 45 | 20 | 44.4 | 271 | 6.02 | 1 | 2.2 | 47 | 2 | 4.4 | 7 | 20 | 53.1 |
| Miller, Chris, Atl. | 66 | 32 | 48.5 | 345 | 5.23 | 1 | 1.5 | 32t | 3 | 4.5 | 8 | 62 | 50.4 |
| Graham, Kent, N.Y.G. | 22 | 8 | 36.4 | 79 | 3.59 | 0 | 0.0 | 18 | 0 | 0.0 | 3 | 28 | 47.3 |
| Weldon, Casey, T.B. | 11 | 6 | 54.5 | 55 | 5.00 | 0 | 0.0 | 20 | 1 | 9.1 | 1 | 11 | 30.5 |
| Willis, Peter Tom, Chi. | 60 | 30 | 50.0 | 268 | 4.47 | 0 | 0.0 | 29 | 5 | 8.3 | 5 | 20 | 27.6 |
| **Fewer than 10 attempts** | | | | | | | | | | | | | |
| Anderson, Neal, Chi. | 1 | 0 | 0.0 | 0 | 0.00 | 0 | 0.0 | 0 | 0 | 0.0 | 0 | 0 | 39.6 |
| Barnhardt, Tommy, N.O. | 1 | 1 | 100.0 | 7 | 7.00 | 0 | 0.0 | 7 | 0 | 0.0 | 0 | 0 | 95.8 |
| Detmer, Ty, G.B. | 5 | 3 | 60.0 | 26 | 5.20 | 0 | 0.0 | 25 | 0 | 0.0 | 0 | 0 | 73.8 |
| Gardocki, Chris, Chi. | 2 | 0 | 0.0 | 0 | 0.00 | 0 | 0.0 | 0 | 0 | 0.0 | 0 | 0 | 39.6 |
| Gary, Cleveland, Rams | 1 | 1 | 100.0 | 8 | 8.00 | 0 | 0.0 | 8 | 0 | 0.0 | 0 | 0 | 100.0 |
| Harper, Alvin, Dall. | 1 | 1 | 100.0 | 46 | 46.00 | 0 | 0.0 | 46 | 0 | 0.0 | 0 | 0 | 118.8 |
| Hearst, Garrison, Phx. | 1 | 0 | 0.0 | 0 | 0.00 | 0 | 0.0 | 0 | 1 | 100.0 | 0 | 0 | 0.0 |
| Meggett, David, N.Y.G. | 2 | 2 | 100.0 | 63 | 31.50 | 2 | 100.0 | 42t | 0 | 0.0 | 0 | 0 | 158.3 |
| Mitchell, Brian, Wash. | 2 | 1 | 50.0 | 50 | 25.00 | 0 | 0.0 | 50 | 1 | 50.0 | 0 | 0 | 56.3 |
| Moore, Dave, T.B. | 1 | 0 | 0.0 | 0 | 0.00 | 0 | 0.0 | 0 | 0 | 0.0 | 0 | 0 | 39.6 |
| Pagel, Mike, Rams | 9 | 3 | 33.3 | 23 | 2.56 | 0 | 0.0 | 10 | 1 | 11.1 | 0 | 0 | 2.8 |
| Sanders, Deion, Atl. | 1 | 0 | 0.0 | 0 | 0.00 | 0 | 0.0 | 0 | 0 | 0.0 | 0 | 0 | 39.6 |
| Sharpe, Sterling, G.B. | 1 | 1 | 100.0 | 1 | 1.00 | 0 | 0.0 | 1 | 0 | 0.0 | 0 | 0 | 79.2 |
| Taylor, John, S.F. | 1 | 1 | 100.0 | 41 | 41.00 | 0 | 0.0 | 41 | 0 | 0.0 | 0 | 0 | 118.8 |
| Walker, Herschel, Phil. | 0 | 0 | — | 0 | — | 0 | — | — | 0 | — | 1 | 5 | — |

*t = Touchdown*
*Leader based on rating points, minimum 224 attempts*

## PASS RECEIVING

**Receptions**
- **NFC:** 112—Sterling Sharpe, Green Bay
- **AFC:** 85—Reggie Langhorne, Indianapolis

**Receptions, Game**
- **AFC:** 12—Reggie Langhorne, Indianapolis at Washington, November 7, (203 yards - TD)
- **NFC:** 12—Michael Irvin, Dallas vs. San Francisco, October 17, (168 yards - TD)
  Gary Clark, Phoenix at Seattle, December 19, (152 yards - TD) (OT)

**Yards**
- **NFC:** 1503—Jerry Rice, San Francisco
- **AFC:** 1180—Tim Brown, Raiders

**Yards, Game**
- **AFC:** 203—Reggie Langhorne, Indianapolis at Washington, November 7, (12 receptions - TD)
- **NFC:** 182—Michael Haynes, Atlanta vs. New Orleans, September 12, (7 receptions - 2 TD)

**Longest**
- **NFC:** 98—Michael Haynes (from Bobby Hebert), Atlanta vs. New Orleans, September 12 - TD
- **AFC:** 82—Kevin Turner {13 yds} lateral to Leonard Russell {69 yds} (from Scott Secules), New England at Phoenix, October 10

**Yards Per Reception**
- **AFC:** 23.4—James Jett, Raiders
- **NFC:** 21.6—Alvin Harper, Dallas

**Touchdowns**
- **NFC:** 15—Jerry Rice, San Francisco
  Andre Rison, Atlanta
- **AFC:** 9—Shannon Sharpe, Denver

**Team Leaders, Receptions**
- **AFC:** BUFFALO: 68, Pete Metzelaars; CINCINNATI: 56, Jeff Query; CLEVELAND: 63, Eric Metcalf; DENVER: 81, Shannon Sharpe; HOUSTON: 77, Webster Slaughter; INDIANAPOLIS: 85, Reggie Langhorne; KANSAS CITY: 52, Willie Davis; L.A. RAIDERS: 80, Tim Brown; MIAMI: 75, Terry Kirby; NEW ENGLAND: 53, Ben Coates; N.Y. JETS: 67, Johnny Johnson; PITTSBURGH: 63, Eric Green; SAN DIEGO: 84, Anthony Miller; SEATTLE: 80, Brian Blades
- **NFC:** ATLANTA: 86, Andre Rison; CHICAGO: 44, Tom Waddle; DALLAS: 88, Michael Irvin; DETROIT: 61, Herman Moore; GREEN BAY: 112, Sterling Sharpe; L.A. RAMS: 61, Henry Ellard; MINNESOTA: 86, Cris Carter; NEW ORLEANS: 66, Eric Martin; N.Y. GIANTS: 58, Mark Jackson; PHILADELPHIA: 75, Herschel Walker; PHOENIX: 66, Larry Centers; SAN FRANCISCO: 98, Jerry Rice; TAMPA BAY: 62, Courtney Hawkins; WASHINGTON: 58, Ricky Sanders

### NFL TOP TEN PASS RECEIVERS

| | No. | Yards | Avg. | Long | TD |
|---|---|---|---|---|---|
| Sharpe, Sterling, G.B. | 112 | 1274 | 11.4 | 54 | 11 |
| Rice, Jerry, S.F. | 98 | 1503 | 15.3 | 80t | 15 |
| Irvin, Michael, Dall. | 88 | 1330 | 15.1 | 61t | 7 |
| Carter, Cris, Minn. | 86 | 1071 | 12.5 | 58 | 9 |
| Rison, Andre, Atl. | 86 | 1242 | 14.4 | 53t | 15 |
| Langhorne, Reggie, Ind. | 85 | 1038 | 12.2 | 72t | 3 |
| Miller, Anthony, S.D. | 84 | 1162 | 13.8 | 66t | 7 |
| Sharpe, Shannon, Den. | 81 | 995 | 12.3 | 63 | 9 |
| Blades, Brian, Sea. | 80 | 945 | 11.8 | 41 | 3 |
| Brown, Tim, Raid. | 80 | 1180 | 14.8 | 71t | 7 |

### NFL TOP TEN RECEIVERS BY YARDS

| | Yards | No. | Avg. | Long | TD |
|---|---|---|---|---|---|
| Rice, Jerry, S.F. | 1503 | 98 | 15.3 | 80t | 15 |
| Irvin, Michael, Dall. | 1330 | 88 | 15.1 | 61t | 7 |
| Sharpe, Sterling, G.B. | 1274 | 112 | 11.4 | 54 | 11 |
| Rison, Andre, Atl. | 1242 | 86 | 14.4 | 53t | 15 |
| Brown, Tim, Raid. | 1180 | 80 | 14.8 | 71t | 7 |
| Miller, Anthony, S.D. | 1162 | 84 | 13.8 | 66t | 7 |
| Carter, Cris, Minn. | 1071 | 86 | 12.5 | 58 | 9 |
| Langhorne, Reggie, Ind. | 1038 | 85 | 12.2 | 72t | 3 |
| Fryar, Irving, Mia. | 1010 | 64 | 15.8 | 65t | 5 |
| Sharpe, Shannon, Den. | 995 | 81 | 12.3 | 63 | 9 |

### AFC RECEIVERS—INDIVIDUAL

| | No. | Yards | Avg. | Long | TD |
|---|---|---|---|---|---|
| Langhorne, Reggie, Ind. | 85 | 1038 | 12.2 | 72t | 3 |
| Miller, Anthony, S.D. | 84 | 1162 | 13.8 | 66t | 7 |
| Sharpe, Shannon, Den. | 81 | 995 | 12.3 | 63 | 9 |
| Brown, Tim, Raid. | 80 | 1180 | 14.8 | 71t | 7 |
| Blades, Brian, Sea. | 80 | 945 | 11.8 | 41 | 3 |
| Slaughter, Webster, Hou. | 77 | 904 | 11.7 | 41 | 5 |
| Kirby, Terry, Mia. | 75 | 874 | 11.7 | 47 | 3 |
| Harmon, Ronnie, S.D. | 73 | 671 | 9.2 | 37 | 2 |
| Givins, Ernest, Hou. | 68 | 887 | 13.0 | 80t | 4 |
| Metzelaars, Pete, Buff. | 68 | 609 | 9.0 | 51 | 4 |
| Johnson, Johnny, N.Y.J. | 67 | 641 | 9.6 | 48 | 1 |
| Jeffires, Haywood, Hou. | 66 | 753 | 11.4 | 66t | 6 |
| Fryar, Irving, Mia. | 64 | 1010 | 15.8 | 65t | 5 |
| Moore, Rob, N.Y.J. | 64 | 843 | 13.2 | 51 | 1 |
| Hester, Jessie, Ind. | 64 | 835 | 13.0 | 58 | 1 |
| Green, Eric, Pitt. | 63 | 942 | 15.0 | 71t | 5 |
| Metcalf, Eric, Clev. | 63 | 539 | 8.6 | 49t | 2 |
| Byars, Keith, Mia. | 61 | 613 | 10.0 | 27 | 3 |
| Brooks, Bill, Buff. | 60 | 714 | 11.9 | 32 | 5 |
| Williams, John L., Sea. | 58 | 450 | 7.8 | 25 | 1 |
| Martin, Kelvin, Sea. | 57 | 798 | 14.0 | 53t | 5 |
| Query, Jeff, Cinn. | 56 | 654 | 11.7 | 51 | 4 |
| Johnson, Anthony, Ind. | 55 | 443 | 8.1 | 36 | 0 |
| Coates, Ben, N.E. | 53 | 659 | 12.4 | 54t | 8 |
| Davis, Willie, K.C. | 52 | 909 | 17.5 | 66t | 7 |
| Reed, Andre, Buff. | 52 | 854 | 16.4 | 65t | 6 |
| Birden, J. J., K.C. | 51 | 721 | 14.1 | 50t | 2 |
| Fenner, Derrick, Cinn. | 48 | 427 | 8.9 | 40 | 0 |
| Thomas, Thurman, Buff. | 48 | 387 | 8.1 | 37 | 0 |
| Brisby, Vincent, N.E. | 45 | 626 | 13.9 | 39 | 2 |
| Russell, Derek, Den. | 44 | 719 | 16.3 | 43 | 3 |
| Ingram, Mark, Mia. | 44 | 707 | 16.1 | 77t | 6 |
| McGee, Tony, Cinn. | 44 | 525 | 11.9 | 37 | 0 |
| Bernstine, Rod, Den. | 44 | 372 | 8.5 | 41 | 0 |
| Carrier, Mark, Clev. | 43 | 746 | 17.3 | 55 | 3 |
| Pickens, Carl, Cinn. | 43 | 565 | 13.1 | 36 | 6 |
| Horton, Ethan, Raid. | 43 | 467 | 10.9 | 32 | 1 |
| Cash, Kerry, Ind. | 43 | 402 | 9.3 | 37 | 3 |
| Timpson, Michael, N.E. | 42 | 654 | 15.6 | 48 | 2 |
| Jackson, Michael, Clev. | 41 | 756 | 18.4 | 62t | 8 |
| Stone, Dwight, Pitt. | 41 | 587 | 14.3 | 44 | 2 |
| Duncan, Curtis, Hou. | 41 | 456 | 11.1 | 47 | 3 |
| Burkett, Chris, N.Y.J. | 40 | 531 | 13.3 | 77 | 4 |
| Anders, Kimble, K.C. | 40 | 326 | 8.2 | 27 | 1 |
| Mitchell, Johnny, N.Y.J. | 39 | 630 | 16.2 | 65t | 6 |
| Jackson, Keith, Mia. | 39 | 613 | 15.7 | 57t | 6 |
| Turner, Kevin, N.E. | 39 | 333 | 8.5 | 26 | 2 |
| Graham, Jeffrey, Pitt. | 38 | 579 | 15.2 | 51 | 0 |
| Lewis, Nate, S.D. | 38 | 463 | 12.2 | 47 | 4 |
| Milburn, Glyn, Den. | 38 | 300 | 7.9 | 50 | 3 |
| Thompson, Leroy, Pitt. | 38 | 259 | 6.8 | 28 | 0 |
| Johnson, Vance, Den. | 36 | 517 | 14.4 | 56 | 5 |
| Hoard, Leroy, Clev. | 35 | 351 | 10.0 | 41 | 0 |
| Allen, Marcus, K.C. | 34 | 238 | 7.0 | 18t | 3 |
| White, Lorenzo, Hou. | 34 | 229 | 6.7 | 20 | 0 |
| Jett, James, Raid. | 33 | 771 | 23.4 | 74t | 3 |
| Hoge, Merril, Pitt. | 33 | 247 | 7.5 | 18 | 4 |
| Beebe, Don, Buff. | 31 | 504 | 16.3 | 65t | 3 |
| Wellman, Gary, Hou. | 31 | 430 | 13.9 | 44 | 1 |
| Jefferson, Shawn, S.D. | 30 | 391 | 13.0 | 39t | 2 |
| Mills, Ernie, Pitt. | 29 | 386 | 13.3 | 30 | 1 |
| Kinchen, Brian, Clev. | 29 | 347 | 12.0 | 40 | 2 |
| Marshall, Arthur, Den. | 28 | 360 | 12.9 | 40 | 2 |
| Wright, Alexander, Raid. | 27 | 462 | 17.1 | 68t | 4 |
| Foster, Barry, Pitt. | 27 | 217 | 8.0 | 21 | 1 |
| Dawkins, Sean, Ind. | 26 | 430 | 16.5 | 68 | 1 |
| Ismail, Raghib, Raid. | 26 | 353 | 13.6 | 43t | 1 |
| Russell, Leonard, N.E. | 26 | 245 | 9.4 | 69 | 0 |
| Delpino, Robert, Den. | 26 | 195 | 7.5 | 25 | 0 |
| Potts, Roosevelt, Ind. | 26 | 189 | 7.3 | 24 | 0 |
| Mathis, Terance, N.Y.J. | 24 | 352 | 14.7 | 46 | 0 |
| Hayes, Jonathan, K.C. | 24 | 331 | 13.8 | 49 | 1 |
| Cash, Keith, K.C. | 24 | 242 | 10.1 | 24 | 4 |
| Edmunds, Ferrell, Sea. | 24 | 239 | 10.0 | 32 | 2 |
| Green, Paul, Sea. | 23 | 178 | 7.7 | 20 | 1 |
| McMurtry, Greg, N.E. | 22 | 241 | 11.0 | 20 | 1 |
| Cook, Marv, N.E. | 22 | 154 | 7.0 | 17 | 1 |
| Green, Harold, Cinn. | 22 | 115 | 5.2 | 16 | 0 |
| Brown, Gary, Hou. | 21 | 240 | 11.4 | 38t | 2 |
| Walker, Derrick, S.D. | 21 | 212 | 10.1 | 25t | 1 |
| Davis, Kenneth, Buff. | 21 | 95 | 4.5 | 28 | 0 |
| Martin, Tony, Mia. | 20 | 347 | 17.4 | 80t | 3 |
| Johnson, Reggie, Den. | 20 | 243 | 12.2 | 38 | 1 |
| Baxter, Brad, N.Y.J. | 20 | 158 | 7.9 | 24 | 0 |
| McDuffie, O. J., Mia. | 19 | 197 | 10.4 | 18 | 0 |
| Vardell, Tommy, Clev. | 19 | 151 | 7.9 | 28t | 1 |
| Smith, Steve, Raid. | 18 | 187 | 10.4 | 22 | 0 |
| Tillman, Cedric, Den. | 17 | 193 | 11.4 | 30 | 2 |
| Barnett, Tim, K.C. | 17 | 182 | 10.7 | 25 | 1 |
| Thompson, Craig, Cinn. | 17 | 87 | 5.1 | 10 | 1 |

# 1993 INDIVIDUAL STATISTICS

| | No. | Yards | Avg. | Long | TD |
|---|---|---|---|---|---|
| Crittenden, Ray, N.E. | 16 | 293 | 18.3 | 44 | 1 |
| Robinson, Greg, Raid. | 15 | 142 | 9.5 | 58 | 0 |
| Butts, Marion, S.D. | 15 | 105 | 7.0 | 23 | 0 |
| Warren, Chris, Sea. | 15 | 99 | 6.6 | 21 | 0 |
| Arbuckle, Charles, Ind. | 15 | 90 | 6.0 | 23 | 0 |
| Gash, Sam, N.E. | 14 | 93 | 6.6 | 15 | 0 |
| Copeland, Russell, Buff. | 13 | 242 | 18.6 | 60 | 0 |
| McCardell, Keenan, Clev. | 13 | 234 | 18.0 | 43 | 4 |
| Pupunu, Alfred, S.D. | 13 | 142 | 10.9 | 28 | 0 |
| Thornton, James, N.Y.J. | 12 | 108 | 9.0 | 22 | 2 |
| Culver, Rodney, Ind. | 11 | 112 | 10.2 | 26 | 1 |
| Bell, Nick, Raid. | 11 | 111 | 10.1 | 18 | 0 |
| Thomas, Doug, Sea. | 11 | 95 | 8.6 | 20 | 0 |
| Barnes, Johnnie, S.D. | 10 | 137 | 13.7 | 21 | 0 |
| McNair, Todd, K.C. | 10 | 74 | 7.4 | 24 | 0 |
| Higgs, Mark, Mia. | 10 | 72 | 7.2 | 15 | 0 |
| Means, Natrone, S.D. | 10 | 59 | 5.9 | 11 | 0 |
| Montgomery, Tyrone, Raid. | 10 | 43 | 4.3 | 9 | 0 |
| Thigpen, Yancey, Pitt. | 9 | 154 | 17.1 | 39t | 3 |
| Coleman, Pat, Hou. | 9 | 129 | 14.3 | 25 | 0 |
| Cooper, Adrian, Pitt. | 9 | 112 | 12.4 | 38 | 0 |
| Jones, Fred, K.C. | 9 | 111 | 12.3 | 19 | 0 |
| Rembert, Reggie, Cinn. | 8 | 101 | 12.6 | 21 | 0 |
| Croom, Corey, N.E. | 8 | 92 | 11.5 | 21 | 0 |
| Kimbrough, Tony, Den. | 8 | 79 | 9.9 | 16 | 0 |
| Robinson, Patrick, Cinn. | 8 | 72 | 9.0 | 14 | 0 |
| Gault, Willie, Raid. | 8 | 64 | 8.0 | 12 | 0 |
| Jones, Hassan, K.C. | 7 | 91 | 13.0 | 22 | 0 |
| Dyal, Mike, K.C. | 7 | 83 | 11.9 | 31 | 0 |
| Thomas, Robb, Sea. | 7 | 67 | 9.6 | 16 | 0 |
| Williams, Harvey, K.C. | 7 | 42 | 6.0 | 14 | 0 |
| Thomas, Blair, N.Y.J. | 7 | 25 | 3.6 | 7 | 0 |
| Miles, Ostell, Cinn. | 6 | 89 | 14.8 | 27 | 0 |
| Carpenter, Rob, N.Y.J. | 6 | 83 | 13.8 | 18 | 0 |
| Carroll, Wesley, Cinn. | 6 | 81 | 13.5 | 28 | 0 |
| Rivers, Reggie, Den. | 6 | 59 | 9.8 | 17 | 1 |
| Frisch, David, Cinn. | 6 | 43 | 7.2 | 12 | 0 |
| Young, Duane, S.D. | 6 | 41 | 6.8 | 12t | 2 |
| Baty, Greg, Mia. | 5 | 78 | 15.6 | 32 | 1 |
| Tillman, Lawyer, Clev. | 5 | 68 | 13.6 | 18 | 1 |
| Wolfley, Ron, Clev. | 5 | 25 | 5.0 | 9 | 1 |
| Murrell, Adrian, N.Y.J. | 5 | 12 | 2.4 | 8 | 0 |
| Cox, Aaron, Ind. | 4 | 59 | 14.8 | 24 | 0 |
| Chaffey, Pat, N.Y.J. | 4 | 55 | 13.8 | 20t | 1 |
| Glover, Andrew, Raid. | 4 | 55 | 13.8 | 26 | 1 |
| Smith, Rico, Clev. | 4 | 55 | 13.8 | 17 | 0 |
| Harris, Leonard, Hou. | 4 | 53 | 13.3 | 17t | 1 |
| Davenport, Charles, Pitt. | 4 | 51 | 12.8 | 19 | 0 |
| Gardner, Carwell, Buff. | 4 | 50 | 12.5 | 22 | 1 |
| Jordan, Randy, Raid. | 4 | 42 | 10.5 | 33 | 0 |
| Ball, Eric, Cinn. | 4 | 39 | 9.8 | 24 | 0 |
| Thompson, Ernie, K.C. | 4 | 33 | 8.3 | 13 | 0 |
| Baxter, Fred, N.Y.J. | 3 | 48 | 16.0 | 25 | 1 |
| Hastings, Andre, Pitt. | 3 | 44 | 14.7 | 18 | 0 |
| Rowe, Patrick, Clev. | 3 | 37 | 12.3 | 16 | 0 |
| McKeller, Keith, Buff. | 3 | 35 | 11.7 | 13t | 1 |
| Johnson, Tracy, Sea. | 3 | 15 | 5.0 | 8 | 1 |
| Brown, Reggie, Hou. | 2 | 30 | 15.0 | 26 | 0 |
| Tasker, Steve, Buff. | 2 | 26 | 13.0 | 22 | 0 |
| Brown, Troy, N.E. | 2 | 22 | 11.0 | 14 | 0 |
| Verdin, Clarence, Ind. | 2 | 20 | 10.0 | 19 | 1 |
| Awalt, Robert, Buff. | 2 | 19 | 9.5 | 10 | 0 |
| Miller, Scott, Mia. | 2 | 15 | 7.5 | 8 | 0 |
| Sadowski, Troy, N.Y.J. | 2 | 14 | 7.0 | 11 | 0 |
| Thomason, Jeff, Cinn. | 2 | 8 | 4.0 | 5 | 0 |
| McCallum, Napoleon, Raid. | 2 | 5 | 2.5 | 3 | 0 |
| Taylor, Kitrick, Den. | 1 | 28 | 28.0 | 28 | 0 |
| Benjamin, Ryan, Cinn. | 1 | 16 | 16.0 | 16 | 0 |
| Maston, Le'Shai, Hou. | 1 | 14 | 14.0 | 14 | 0 |
| Williams, Clarence, Clev. | 1 | 14 | 14.0 | 14 | 0 |
| Norgard, Erik, Hou. | 1 | 13 | 13.0 | 13 | 0 |
| Jorden, Tim, Pitt. | 1 | 12 | 12.0 | 12 | 0 |
| Williams, Mike, Mia. | 1 | 11 | 11.0 | 11 | 0 |
| Stegall, Milt, Cinn. | 1 | 8 | 8.0 | 8 | 0 |
| Bates, Michael, Sea. | 1 | 6 | 6.0 | 6 | 0 |
| Baldwin, Randy, Clev. | 1 | 5 | 5.0 | 5t | 1 |
| Toner, Ed, Ind. | 1 | 5 | 5.0 | 5 | 0 |
| Roberts, Ray, Sea. | 1 | 4 | 4.0 | 4 | 0 |
| Tillman, Spencer, Hou. | 1 | 4 | 4.0 | 4t | 1 |
| Cuthbert, Randy, Pitt. | 1 | 3 | 3.0 | 3 | 0 |
| Drewrey, Willie, Hou. | 1 | 3 | 3.0 | 3 | 0 |
| Parmalee, Bernie, Mia. | 1 | 1 | 1.0 | 1 | 0 |
| Valerio, Joe, K.C. | 1 | 1 | 1.0 | 1t | 1 |
| Wyman, David, Den. | 1 | 1 | 1.0 | 1t | 1 |
| Bieniemy, Eric, S.D. | 1 | 0 | 0.0 | 0 | 0 |
| Esiason, Boomer, N.Y.J. | 1 | -8 | -8.0 | -8 | 0 |

*t = Touchdown*
*Leader based on receptions*

**NFC RECEIVERS—INDIVIDUAL**

| | No. | Yards | Avg. | Long | TD |
|---|---|---|---|---|---|
| Sharpe, Sterling, G.B. | 112 | 1274 | 11.4 | 54 | 11 |
| Rice, Jerry, S.F. | 98 | 1503 | 15.3 | 80t | 15 |
| Irvin, Michael, Dall. | 88 | 1330 | 15.1 | 61t | 7 |
| Rison, Andre, Atl. | 86 | 1242 | 14.4 | 53t | 15 |
| Carter, Cris, Minn. | 86 | 1071 | 12.5 | 58 | 9 |
| Walker, Herschel, Phil. | 75 | 610 | 8.1 | 55 | 3 |
| Pritchard, Mike, Atl. | 74 | 736 | 9.9 | 34 | 7 |
| Haynes, Michael, Atl. | 72 | 778 | 10.8 | 98t | 4 |
| Jones, Brent, S.F. | 68 | 735 | 10.8 | 29 | 3 |
| Martin, Eric, N.O. | 66 | 950 | 14.4 | 54t | 3 |
| Centers, Larry, Phx. | 66 | 603 | 9.1 | 29 | 3 |
| Proehl, Ricky, Phx. | 65 | 877 | 13.5 | 51t | 7 |
| Clark, Gary, Phx. | 63 | 818 | 13.0 | 55 | 4 |
| Hawkins, Courtney, T.B. | 62 | 933 | 15.0 | 67 | 5 |
| Ellard, Henry, Rams | 61 | 945 | 15.5 | 54 | 2 |
| Moore, Herman, Det. | 61 | 935 | 15.3 | 93t | 6 |
| Carter, Anthony, Minn. | 60 | 775 | 12.9 | 39 | 5 |
| Williams, Calvin, Phil. | 60 | 725 | 12.1 | 80t | 10 |
| Bennett, Edgar, G.B. | 59 | 457 | 7.7 | 39t | 1 |
| Jackson, Mark, N.Y.G. | 58 | 708 | 12.2 | 40t | 4 |
| Sanders, Ricky, Wash. | 58 | 638 | 11.0 | 50 | 4 |
| Smith, Emmitt, Dall. | 57 | 414 | 7.3 | 86 | 1 |
| Taylor, John, S.F. | 56 | 940 | 16.8 | 76t | 5 |
| Jordan, Steve, Minn. | 56 | 542 | 9.7 | 53 | 1 |
| Workman, Vince, T.B. | 54 | 411 | 7.6 | 42t | 2 |
| Johnston, Daryl, Dall. | 50 | 372 | 7.4 | 20 | 1 |
| Perriman, Brett, Det. | 49 | 496 | 10.1 | 34 | 2 |
| Early, Quinn, N.O. | 45 | 670 | 14.9 | 63t | 6 |
| Waddle, Tom, Chi. | 44 | 552 | 12.5 | 38 | 1 |
| Novacek, Jay, Dall. | 44 | 445 | 10.1 | 30 | 1 |
| Bavaro, Mark, Phil. | 43 | 481 | 11.2 | 27 | 6 |
| Harris, Jackie, G.B. | 42 | 604 | 14.4 | 66t | 4 |
| Bailey, Victor, Phil. | 41 | 545 | 13.3 | 58 | 1 |
| Monk, Art, Wash. | 41 | 398 | 9.7 | 29 | 2 |
| Hilliard, Dalton, N.O. | 40 | 296 | 7.4 | 34 | 1 |
| McGee, Tim, Wash. | 39 | 500 | 12.8 | 54 | 3 |
| Meggett, David, N.Y.G. | 38 | 319 | 8.4 | 50 | 0 |
| Anderson, Willie, Rams | 37 | 552 | 14.9 | 56t | 4 |
| Logan, Marc, S.F. | 37 | 348 | 9.4 | 24 | 0 |
| Harper, Alvin, Dall. | 36 | 777 | 21.6 | 80t | 5 |
| Gary, Cleveland, Rams | 36 | 289 | 8.0 | 60t | 1 |
| Sanders, Barry, Det. | 36 | 205 | 5.7 | 17 | 0 |
| Hill, Randal, Phx. | 35 | 519 | 14.8 | 58t | 4 |
| Calloway, Chris, N.Y.G. | 35 | 513 | 14.7 | 47 | 3 |
| Hill, Drew, Atl. | 34 | 384 | 11.3 | 30 | 0 |
| Pegram, Erric, Atl. | 33 | 302 | 9.2 | 30 | 0 |
| Clayton, Mark, G.B. | 32 | 331 | 10.3 | 32 | 3 |
| Bailey, Johnny, Phx. | 32 | 243 | 7.6 | 30 | 0 |
| Watters, Ricky, S.F. | 31 | 326 | 10.5 | 48t | 1 |
| Anderson, Neal, Chi. | 31 | 160 | 5.2 | 35 | 0 |
| Copeland, Horace, T.B. | 30 | 633 | 21.1 | 67t | 4 |
| Joseph, James, Phil. | 29 | 291 | 10.0 | 48 | 1 |
| Green, Willie, Det. | 28 | 462 | 16.5 | 47 | 2 |
| McCaffrey, Ed, N.Y.G. | 27 | 335 | 12.4 | 31 | 2 |
| Drayton, Troy, Rams | 27 | 319 | 11.8 | 27 | 4 |
| Byner, Earnest, Wash. | 27 | 194 | 7.2 | 20 | 0 |
| Obee, Terry, Chi. | 26 | 351 | 13.5 | 48 | 3 |
| Bettis, Jerome, Rams | 26 | 244 | 9.4 | 28 | 0 |
| West, Ed, G.B. | 25 | 253 | 10.1 | 24 | 0 |
| Holman, Rodney, Det. | 25 | 244 | 9.8 | 28t | 2 |
| Sherrard, Mike, N.Y.G. | 24 | 433 | 18.0 | 55t | 2 |
| Middleton, Ron, Wash. | 24 | 154 | 6.4 | 18 | 2 |
| Smith, Robert, Minn. | 24 | 111 | 4.6 | 12 | 0 |
| Howard, Desmond, Wash. | 23 | 286 | 12.4 | 27 | 0 |
| Hall, Ron, T.B. | 23 | 268 | 11.7 | 37t | 1 |
| Muster, Brad, N.O. | 23 | 195 | 8.5 | 31 | 0 |
| Cross, Howard, N.Y.G. | 21 | 272 | 13.0 | 32 | 5 |
| Brooks, Reggie, Wash. | 21 | 186 | 8.9 | 43 | 0 |
| Brown, Derek, N.O. | 21 | 170 | 8.1 | 19 | 1 |
| Moore, Derrick, Det. | 21 | 169 | 8.0 | 20 | 1 |
| Brooks, Robert, G.B. | 20 | 180 | 9.0 | 25 | 0 |
| Mitchell, Brian, Wash. | 20 | 157 | 7.9 | 18 | 0 |

| | No. | Yards | Avg. | Long | TD |
|---|---|---|---|---|---|
| Williams, Kevin, Dall. | 20 | 151 | 7.6 | 33 | 2 |
| Conway, Curtis, Chi. | 19 | 231 | 12.2 | 38t | 2 |
| Ismail, Qadry, Minn. | 19 | 212 | 11.2 | 37 | 1 |
| Craig, Roger, Minn. | 19 | 169 | 8.9 | 31 | 1 |
| Hampton, Rodney, N.Y.G. | 18 | 210 | 11.7 | 62 | 0 |
| Lester, Tim, Rams | 18 | 154 | 8.6 | 21 | 0 |
| Thompson, Darrell, G.B. | 18 | 129 | 7.2 | 34 | 0 |
| Barnett, Fred, Phil. | 17 | 170 | 10.0 | 21 | 0 |
| Smith, Irv, N.O. | 16 | 180 | 11.3 | 23 | 2 |
| Small, Torrance, N.O. | 16 | 164 | 10.3 | 17 | 1 |
| Christian, Bob, Chi. | 16 | 160 | 10.0 | 36 | 0 |
| Heyward, Craig, Chi. | 16 | 132 | 8.3 | 20 | 0 |
| Williams, Jamie, S.F. | 16 | 132 | 8.3 | 15 | 1 |
| Ervins, Ricky, Wash. | 16 | 123 | 7.7 | 20 | 0 |
| Lee, Amp, S.F. | 16 | 115 | 7.2 | 22 | 2 |
| Wycheck, Frank, Wash. | 16 | 113 | 7.1 | 20 | 0 |
| Wilson, Charles, T.B. | 15 | 225 | 15.0 | 24 | 0 |
| Dawsey, Lawrence, T.B. | 15 | 203 | 13.5 | 24 | 0 |
| Tennell, Derek, Minn. | 15 | 122 | 8.1 | 17 | 0 |
| Young, Mike, Phil. | 14 | 186 | 13.3 | 49t | 2 |
| Lofton, James, Rams-Phil. | 14 | 183 | 13.1 | 32 | 0 |
| Carter, Pat, Rams | 14 | 166 | 11.9 | 38 | 1 |
| Jennings, Keith, Chi. | 14 | 150 | 10.7 | 29 | 0 |
| Edwards, Anthony, Phx. | 13 | 326 | 25.1 | 65t | 1 |
| Bunch, Jarrod, N.Y.G. | 13 | 98 | 7.5 | 15 | 1 |
| Lynch, Eric, Det. | 13 | 82 | 6.3 | 11 | 0 |
| Green, Robert, Chi. | 13 | 63 | 4.8 | 9 | 0 |
| Pierce, Aaron, N.Y.G. | 12 | 212 | 17.7 | 54 | 0 |
| Turner, Floyd, N.O. | 12 | 163 | 13.6 | 52 | 1 |
| Davis, Wendell, Chi. | 12 | 132 | 11.0 | 17 | 0 |
| Mims, David, Atl. | 12 | 107 | 8.9 | 19 | 1 |
| Sherman, Heath, Phil. | 12 | 78 | 6.5 | 21 | 0 |
| Brenner, Hoby, N.O. | 11 | 171 | 15.5 | 27 | 1 |
| Matthews, Aubrey, Det. | 11 | 171 | 15.5 | 40 | 0 |
| Anderson, Gary, T.B. | 11 | 89 | 8.1 | 28 | 1 |
| Hebron, Vaughn, Phil. | 11 | 82 | 7.5 | 12 | 0 |
| Worley, Tim, Pitt.-Chi. | 11 | 62 | 5.6 | 15 | 0 |
| Gedney, Chris, Chi. | 10 | 98 | 9.8 | 24 | 0 |
| Rathman, Tom, S.F. | 10 | 86 | 8.6 | 17 | 0 |
| Johnson, Maurice, Phil. | 10 | 81 | 8.1 | 17 | 0 |
| Rolle, Butch, Phx. | 10 | 67 | 6.7 | 22 | 1 |
| Word, Barry, Minn. | 9 | 105 | 11.7 | 27 | 0 |
| Wetnight, Ryan, Chi. | 9 | 93 | 10.3 | 25t | 1 |
| Armstrong, Tyji, T.B. | 9 | 86 | 9.6 | 29 | 1 |
| Reeves, Walter, Phx. | 9 | 67 | 7.4 | 18 | 1 |
| Cobb, Reggie, T.B. | 9 | 61 | 6.8 | 19 | 1 |
| Ned, Derrick, N.O. | 9 | 54 | 6.0 | 14 | 0 |
| Lassic, Derrick, Dall. | 9 | 37 | 4.1 | 9 | 0 |
| Thomas, Lamar, T.B. | 8 | 186 | 23.3 | 62t | 2 |
| Kinchen, Todd, Rams | 8 | 137 | 17.1 | 35t | 1 |
| Singleton, Nate, S.F. | 8 | 126 | 15.8 | 33 | 1 |
| Newman, Pat, N.O. | 8 | 121 | 15.1 | 32 | 1 |
| Hallock, Ty, Det. | 8 | 88 | 11.0 | 24 | 2 |
| McNeal, Travis, Rams | 8 | 75 | 9.4 | 22t | 1 |
| Lyons, Mitch, Atl. | 8 | 63 | 7.9 | 14 | 0 |
| McDowell, Anthony, T.B. | 8 | 26 | 3.3 | 9 | 1 |
| Brown, Derek, N.Y.G. | 7 | 56 | 8.0 | 14 | 0 |
| Campbell, Jeff, Det. | 7 | 55 | 7.9 | 12 | 0 |
| Graham, Scottie, Minn. | 7 | 46 | 6.6 | 11 | 0 |
| Sanders, Deion, Atl. | 6 | 106 | 17.7 | 70t | 1 |
| Dickerson, Eric, Atl. | 6 | 58 | 9.7 | 30 | 0 |
| Whitaker, Danta, Chi. | 6 | 53 | 8.8 | 18 | 0 |
| Dowdell, Marcus, N.O. | 6 | 46 | 7.7 | 11t | 1 |
| Tice, Mike, Minn. | 6 | 39 | 6.5 | 21 | 1 |
| Gainer, Derrick, Dall. | 6 | 37 | 6.2 | 8 | 0 |
| Hearst, Garrison, Phx. | 6 | 18 | 3.0 | 9 | 0 |
| Reed, Jake, Minn. | 5 | 65 | 13.0 | 18 | 0 |
| Claiborne, Robert, T.B. | 5 | 61 | 12.2 | 16 | 0 |
| Beach, Sanjay, S.F. | 5 | 59 | 11.8 | 20t | 1 |
| Jones, Ernie, Rams | 5 | 56 | 11.2 | 21t | 2 |
| Blount, Eric, Phx. | 5 | 36 | 7.2 | 9 | 0 |
| Stephens, John, G.B. | 5 | 31 | 6.2 | 10 | 0 |
| Royster, Mazio, T.B. | 5 | 18 | 3.6 | 10 | 0 |
| Harris, Rudy, T.B. | 4 | 48 | 12.0 | 25 | 0 |
| Moore, Dave, T.B. | 4 | 47 | 11.8 | 19t | 1 |
| Lang, David, Rams | 4 | 45 | 11.3 | 21 | 0 |
| Truitt, Olanda, Minn. | 4 | 40 | 10.0 | 13 | 0 |
| Evans, Chuck, Minn. | 4 | 39 | 9.8 | 21 | 0 |
| Lewis, Darren, Chi. | 4 | 26 | 6.5 | 18 | 0 |
| Coleman, Lincoln, Dall. | 4 | 24 | 6.0 | 10 | 0 |
| Turner, Odessa, S.F. | 3 | 64 | 21.3 | 32 | 0 |
| Ware, Derek, Phx. | 3 | 45 | 15.0 | 27 | 0 |

| | No. | Yards | Avg. | Long | TD |
|---|---|---|---|---|---|
| Carter, Dexter, S.F. | 3 | 40 | 13.3 | 14 | 0 |
| Moore, Ron, Phx. | 3 | 16 | 5.3 | 6 | 0 |
| Banks, Fred, Mia.-Chi. | 2 | 45 | 22.5 | 26 | 0 |
| Sydner, Jeff, Phil. | 2 | 42 | 21.0 | 31 | 0 |
| LaChapelle, Sean, Rams | 2 | 23 | 11.5 | 14 | 0 |
| Lewis, Ron, G.B. | 2 | 21 | 10.5 | 17 | 0 |
| Johnson, Jimmy, Det. | 2 | 18 | 9.0 | 9 | 0 |
| Wilson, Marcus, G.B. | 2 | 18 | 9.0 | 11 | 0 |
| Clifton, Gregory, Wash. | 2 | 15 | 7.5 | 10 | 0 |
| Chmura, Mark, G.B. | 2 | 13 | 6.5 | 7 | 0 |
| Harris, Corey, G.B. | 2 | 11 | 5.5 | 6 | 0 |
| Young, Steve, S.F. | 2 | 2 | 1.0 | 6 | 0 |
| Guliford, Eric, Minn. | 1 | 45 | 45.0 | 45 | 0 |
| Williams, Tyrone, Dall. | 1 | 25 | 25.0 | 25 | 0 |
| Tillman, Lewis, N.Y.G. | 1 | 21 | 21.0 | 21 | 0 |
| Phillips, Jason, Atl. | 1 | 15 | 15.0 | 15 | 0 |
| Thompson, Marty, Det. | 1 | 15 | 15.0 | 15 | 0 |
| Morgan, Anthony, G.B. | 1 | 8 | 8.0 | 8 | 0 |
| Turner, Vernon, Det. | 1 | 7 | 7.0 | 7 | 0 |
| Crawford, Keith, N.Y.G. | 1 | 6 | 6.0 | 6 | 0 |
| Lawrence, Reggie, Phil. | 1 | 5 | 5.0 | 5 | 0 |
| Broussard, Steven, Atl. | 1 | 4 | 4.0 | 4 | 0 |
| Price, Jim, Dall. | 1 | 4 | 4.0 | 4 | 0 |
| Walker, Adam, S.F. | 1 | 4 | 4.0 | 4 | 0 |
| McAfee, Fred, N.O. | 1 | 3 | 3.0 | 3 | 0 |
| Rasheed, Kenyon, N.Y.G. | 1 | 3 | 3.0 | 3 | 0 |
| Galbraith, Scott, Dall. | 1 | 1 | 1.0 | 1t | 1 |
| Harbaugh, Jim, Chi. | 1 | 1 | 1.0 | 1 | 0 |
| Fralic, Bill, Det. | 1 | -4 | -4.0 | -4 | 0 |
| Simms, Phil, N.Y.G. | 1 | -6 | -6.0 | -6 | 0 |
| Hinton, Chris, Atl. | 1 | -8 | -8.0 | -8 | 0 |

*t = Touchdown*
*Leader based on receptions*

## INTERCEPTIONS

**Interceptions**
**AFC:** 9—Nate Odomes, Buffalo
Eugene Robinson, Seattle
**NFC:** 7—Deion Sanders, Atlanta

**Interceptions, Game**
**AFC:** 3—Marcus Robertson, Houston at Cleveland, November 21
**NFC:** 3—Jack Del Rio, Minnesota at Detroit, December 5

**Yards**
**NFC:** 201—Eric Allen, Philadelphia
**AFC:** 138—Rod Woodson, Pittsburgh

**Longest**
**AFC:** 102—Donald Frank, San Diego at Raiders, October 31 - TD
**NFC:** 94—Eric Allen, Philadelphia at Jets, October 3 - TD

**Touchdowns**
**NFC:** 4—Eric Allen, Philadelphia
**AFC:** 1—Mike Brim, Cincinnati
Mike Croel, Denver
Donald Frank, San Diego
Steve Jackson, Houston
Henry Jones, Buffalo
Darryll Lewis, Houston
Terry McDaniel, Raiders
Najee Mustafaa, Cleveland
Joe Nash, Seattle
Louis Oliver, Miami
Bo Orlando, Houston
Darryl Talley, Buffalo
Brian Washington, Jets
Mickey Washington, Buffalo
Darryl Williams, Cincinnati
Rod Woodson, Pittsburgh

**Team Leaders, Interceptions**
**AFC:** BUFFALO: 9, Nate Odomes; CINCINNATI: 3, Mike Brim; CLEVELAND: 5, Eric Turner; DENVER: 3, Tyrone Braxton, Dennis Smith; HOUSTON: 7, Marcus Robertson; INDIANAPOLIS: 4, Ray Buchanan; KANSAS CITY: 6, Albert Lewis; L.A. RAIDERS: 5, Terry McDaniel; MIAMI: 5, J.B. Brown; NEW ENGLAND: 4, Maurice Hurst; N.Y. JETS: 6, Brian Washington; PITTSBURGH: 8, Rod Woodson; SAN DIEGO: 7, Darren Carrington; SEATTLE: 9, Eugene Robinson
**NFC:** ATLANTA: 7, Deion Sanders; CHICAGO: 4, Mark Carrier, Dante Jones; DALLAS: 6, Kevin Smith; DETROIT: 3, Pat Swilling; GREEN BAY: 6, LeRoy Butler; L.A. RAMS: 2, Robert Bailey, Todd Lyght, Henry Rolling, Pat Terrell; MINNESOTA: 5, Vencie Glenn; NEW ORLEANS: 3, Gene Atkins; N.Y. GIANTS: 4, Mark Collins, Greg Jackson; PHILADELPHIA: 6, Eric Allen ; PHOENIX: 3, Lorenzo Lynch; SAN FRANCISCO : 5, Michael McGruder; TAMPA BAY: 3, Joe King; WASHINGTON: 6, Tom Carter

## 1993 INDIVIDUAL STATISTICS

**Team Champions**
**AFC:** 26—Houston
**NFC:** 24—Minnesota

### AFC INTERCEPTIONS—TEAM

| | No. | Yards | Avg. | Long | TD |
|---|---|---|---|---|---|
| Houston | 26 | 412 | 15.8 | 69 | 3 |
| Pittsburgh | 24 | 386 | 16.1 | 78 | 1 |
| Buffalo | 23 | 306 | 13.3 | 85t | 3 |
| San Diego | 22 | 319 | 14.5 | 102t | 1 |
| Seattle | 22 | 196 | 8.9 | 34 | 1 |
| Kansas City | 21 | 225 | 10.7 | 48 | 0 |
| N.Y. Jets | 19 | 233 | 12.3 | 62t | 1 |
| Denver | 18 | 236 | 13.1 | 68 | 1 |
| L.A. Raiders | 14 | 199 | 14.2 | 36t | 1 |
| New England | 13 | 122 | 9.4 | 40 | 0 |
| Miami | 13 | 175 | 13.5 | 56t | 1 |
| Cleveland | 13 | 208 | 16.0 | 97t | 1 |
| Cincinnati | 12 | 272 | 22.7 | 97t | 2 |
| Indianapolis | 10 | 116 | 11.6 | 29 | 0 |
| AFC Total | 250 | 3405 | 13.6 | 102t | 16 |
| AFC Average | 17.9 | 243.2 | 13.6 | — | 1.1 |

### NFC INTERCEPTIONS—TEAM

| | No. | Yards | Avg. | Long | TD |
|---|---|---|---|---|---|
| Minnesota | 24 | 211 | 8.8 | 63t | 2 |
| Philadelphia | 20 | 324 | 16.2 | 94t | 4 |
| San Francisco | 19 | 267 | 14.1 | 67t | 3 |
| Detroit | 19 | 156 | 8.2 | 35t | 1 |
| Chicago | 18 | 300 | 16.7 | 86t | 2 |
| N.Y. Giants | 18 | 184 | 10.2 | 50t | 1 |
| Green Bay | 18 | 255 | 14.2 | 39 | 0 |
| Washington | 17 | 241 | 14.2 | 69t | 2 |
| Dallas | 14 | 171 | 12.2 | 32t | 1 |
| Atlanta | 13 | 160 | 12.3 | 44 | 0 |
| L.A. Rams | 11 | 127 | 11.5 | 41 | 0 |
| New Orleans | 10 | 133 | 13.3 | 37 | 0 |
| Tampa Bay | 9 | 71 | 7.9 | 28 | 2 |
| Phoenix | 9 | 124 | 13.8 | 46t | 1 |
| NFC Total | 219 | 2724 | 12.4 | 94t | 19 |
| NFC Average | 15.6 | 194.6 | 12.4 | — | 1.4 |
| League Total | 469 | 6129 | — | 102t | 35 |
| League Average | 16.8 | 218.9 | 13.1 | — | 1.3 |

### NFL TOP TEN INTERCEPTORS

| | No. | Yards | Avg. | Long | TD |
|---|---|---|---|---|---|
| Odomes, Nate, Buff. | 9 | 65 | 7.2 | 25 | 0 |
| Robinson, Eugene, Sea. | 9 | 80 | 8.9 | 28 | 0 |
| Woodson, Rod, Pitt. | 8 | 138 | 17.3 | 63t | 1 |
| Carrington, Darren, S.D. | 7 | 104 | 14.9 | 28 | 0 |
| Robertson, Marcus, Hou. | 7 | 137 | 19.6 | 69 | 0 |
| Sanders, Deion, Atl. | 7 | 91 | 13.0 | 41 | 0 |
| Allen, Eric, Phil. | 6 | 201 | 33.5 | 94t | 4 |
| Butler, LeRoy, G.B. | 6 | 131 | 21.8 | 39 | 0 |
| Carter, Tom, Wash. | 6 | 54 | 9.0 | 29 | 0 |
| Dishman, Cris, Hou. | 6 | 74 | 12.3 | 30 | 0 |
| Lewis, Albert, K.C. | 6 | 61 | 10.2 | 24 | 0 |
| Smith, Kevin, Dall. | 6 | 56 | 9.3 | 32t | 1 |
| Washington, Brian, N.Y.J. | 6 | 128 | 21.3 | 62t | 1 |

### AFC INTERCEPTIONS—INDIVIDUAL

| | No. | Yards | Avg. | Long | TD |
|---|---|---|---|---|---|
| Robinson, Eugene, Sea. | 9 | 80 | 8.9 | 28 | 0 |
| Odomes, Nate, Buff. | 9 | 65 | 7.2 | 25 | 0 |
| Woodson, Rod, Pitt. | 8 | 138 | 17.3 | 63t | 1 |
| Robertson, Marcus, Hou. | 7 | 137 | 19.6 | 69 | 0 |
| Carrington, Darren, S.D. | 7 | 104 | 14.9 | 28 | 0 |
| Washington, Brian, N.Y.J. | 6 | 128 | 21.3 | 62t | 1 |
| Dishman, Cris, Hou. | 6 | 74 | 12.3 | 30 | 0 |
| Lewis, Albert, K.C. | 6 | 61 | 10.2 | 24 | 0 |
| McDaniel, Terry, Raid. | 5 | 87 | 17.4 | 36t | 1 |
| Jackson, Steve, Hou. | 5 | 54 | 10.8 | 22t | 1 |
| Mincy, Charles, K.C. | 5 | 44 | 8.8 | 20 | 0 |
| Brown, J. B., Mia. | 5 | 43 | 8.6 | 29 | 0 |
| Turner, Eric, Clev. | 5 | 25 | 5.0 | 19 | 0 |
| Perry, Darren, Pitt. | 4 | 61 | 15.3 | 30 | 0 |
| Hunter, Patrick, Sea. | 4 | 54 | 13.5 | 34 | 0 |
| Hurst, Maurice, N.E. | 4 | 53 | 13.3 | 24 | 0 |
| Buchanan, Ray, Ind. | 4 | 45 | 11.3 | 28 | 0 |
| Lake, Carnell, Pitt. | 4 | 31 | 7.8 | 26 | 0 |
| Frank, Donald, S.D. | 3 | 119 | 39.7 | 102t | 1 |
| Brim, Michael, Cinn. | 3 | 74 | 24.7 | 30 | 1 |
| Talley, Darryl, Buff. | 3 | 74 | 24.7 | 61t | 1 |
| Orlando, Bo, Hou. | 3 | 68 | 22.7 | 38t | 1 |
| Smith, Dennis, Den. | 3 | 57 | 19.0 | 36 | 0 |
| Johnson, David, Pitt. | 3 | 51 | 17.0 | 26 | 0 |
| Braxton, Tyrone, Den. | 3 | 37 | 12.3 | 25 | 0 |
| Lott, Ronnie, N.Y.J. | 3 | 35 | 11.7 | 29 | 0 |
| Gray, Carlton, Sea. | 3 | 33 | 11.0 | 16 | 0 |
| McDowell, Bubba, Hou. | 3 | 31 | 10.3 | 13 | 0 |
| Baylor, John, Ind. | 3 | 11 | 3.7 | 7 | 0 |
| Jones, Selwyn, Clev. | 3 | 0 | 0.0 | 0 | 0 |
| Wren, Darryl, N.E. | 3 | -7 | -2.3 | 2 | 0 |
| Williams, Darryl, Cinn. | 2 | 126 | 63.0 | 97t | 1 |
| Jones, Henry, Buff. | 2 | 92 | 46.0 | 85t | 1 |
| Atwater, Steve, Den. | 2 | 81 | 40.5 | 68 | 0 |
| Oliver, Louis, Mia. | 2 | 60 | 30.0 | 56t | 1 |
| Seau, Junior, S.D. | 2 | 58 | 29.0 | 42 | 0 |
| Anderson, Eddie, Raid. | 2 | 52 | 26.0 | 27 | 0 |
| Ross, Kevin, K.C. | 2 | 49 | 24.5 | 48 | 0 |
| Hoskins, Derrick, Raid. | 2 | 34 | 17.0 | 20 | 0 |
| Darby, Matt, Buff. | 2 | 32 | 16.0 | 32 | 0 |
| Vincent, Troy, Mia. | 2 | 29 | 14.5 | 23 | 0 |
| Hasty, James, N.Y.J. | 2 | 22 | 11.0 | 22 | 0 |
| Thomas, Eric, N.Y.J. | 2 | 20 | 10.0 | 20 | 0 |
| White, Sheldon, Cinn. | 2 | 19 | 9.5 | 14 | 0 |
| Bayless, Martin, K.C. | 2 | 14 | 7.0 | 16 | 0 |
| Pope, Marquez, S.D. | 2 | 14 | 7.0 | 12 | 0 |
| Dronett, Shane, Den. | 2 | 13 | 6.5 | 7 | 0 |
| Francis, James, Cinn. | 2 | 12 | 6.0 | 12 | 0 |
| Jones, Gary, Pitt. | 2 | 11 | 5.5 | 11 | 0 |
| Williams, James, Buff. | 2 | 11 | 5.5 | 6 | 0 |
| Plummer, Gary, S.D. | 2 | 7 | 3.5 | 6 | 0 |
| Lang, Le-Lo, Den. | 2 | 4 | 2.0 | 4 | 0 |
| Lewis, Mo, N.Y.J. | 2 | 4 | 2.0 | 3 | 0 |
| Blackmon, Robert, Sea. | 2 | 0 | 0.0 | 0 | 0 |
| Green, Chris, Mia. | 2 | 0 | 0.0 | 0 | 0 |
| Patton, Marvcus, Buff. | 2 | 0 | 0.0 | 0 | 0 |
| Vanhorse, Sean, S.D. | 2 | 0 | 0.0 | 0 | 0 |
| Washington, Lionel, Raid. | 2 | 0 | 0.0 | 0 | 0 |
| Mustafaa, Najee, Clev. | 1 | 97 | 97.0 | 97t | 1 |
| Figures, Deon, Pitt. | 1 | 78 | 78.0 | 78 | 0 |
| Hilliard, Randy, Clev. | 1 | 54 | 54.0 | 54 | 0 |
| Lewis, Darryll, Hou. | 1 | 47 | 47.0 | 47t | 1 |
| Barnett, Harlon, N.E. | 1 | 40 | 40.0 | 40 | 0 |
| Herrod, Jeff, Ind. | 1 | 29 | 29.0 | 29 | 0 |
| Washington, Mickey, Buff. | 1 | 27 | 27.0 | 27t | 1 |
| Cox, Bryan, Mia. | 1 | 26 | 26.0 | 26 | 0 |
| Brown, Vincent, N.E. | 1 | 24 | 24.0 | 24 | 0 |
| Croel, Mike, Den. | 1 | 22 | 22.0 | 22t | 1 |
| Speer, Del, Clev. | 1 | 22 | 22.0 | 22 | 0 |
| Terry, Doug, K.C. | 1 | 21 | 21.0 | 21 | 0 |
| Marts, Lonnie, K.C. | 1 | 20 | 20.0 | 20 | 0 |
| McGlockton, Chester, Raid. | 1 | 19 | 19.0 | 19 | 0 |
| Daniel, Eugene, Ind. | 1 | 17 | 17.0 | 17 | 0 |
| Grant, Alan, Cinn. | 1 | 17 | 17.0 | 17 | 0 |
| Hobley, Liffort, Mia. | 1 | 17 | 17.0 | 17 | 0 |
| Hendrickson, Steve, S.D. | 1 | 16 | 16.0 | 16 | 0 |
| Lageman, Jeff, N.Y.J. | 1 | 15 | 15.0 | 15 | 0 |
| Belser, Jason, Ind. | 1 | 14 | 14.0 | 11 | 0 |
| Nash, Joe, Sea. | 1 | 13 | 13.0 | 13t | 1 |
| Robinson, Frank, Den. | 1 | 13 | 13.0 | 13 | 0 |
| Saleaumua, Dan, K.C. | 1 | 13 | 13.0 | 13 | 0 |
| Jefferson, James, Sea. | 1 | 12 | 12.0 | 12 | 0 |
| Henry, Kevin, Pitt. | 1 | 10 | 10.0 | 10 | 0 |
| Matthews, Clay Jr., Clev. | 1 | 10 | 10.0 | 10 | 0 |
| Wyman, David, Den. | 1 | 9 | 9.0 | 9 | 0 |
| Collins, Todd, N.E. | 1 | 8 | 8.0 | 8 | 0 |
| Trapp, James, Raid. | 1 | 7 | 7.0 | 7 | 0 |
| Davidson, Kenny, Pitt. | 1 | 6 | 6.0 | 6 | 0 |
| Young, Lonnie, N.Y.J. | 1 | 6 | 6.0 | 6 | 0 |
| Bennett, Cornelius, Buff. | 1 | 5 | 5.0 | 5 | 0 |
| Porter, Rufus, Sea. | 1 | 4 | 4.0 | 4 | 0 |
| Thompson, Reyna, N.E. | 1 | 4 | 4.0 | 4 | 0 |
| Clifton, Kyle, N.Y.J. | 1 | 3 | 3.0 | 3 | 0 |
| Gordon, Darrien, S.D. | 1 | 3 | 3.0 | 3 | 0 |
| Smith, Neil, K.C. | 1 | 3 | 3.0 | 3 | 0 |
| Bishop, Blaine, Hou. | 1 | 1 | 1.0 | 1 | 0 |
| Bates, Patrick, Raid. | 1 | 0 | 0.0 | 0 | 0 |

| | No. | Yards | Avg. | Long | TD |
|---|---|---|---|---|---|
| Bradford, Ronnie, Den. | 1 | 0 | 0.0 | 0 | 0 |
| Carter, Dale, K.C. | 1 | 0 | 0.0 | 0 | 0 |
| Davis, Brian, S.D. | 1 | 0 | 0.0 | 0 | 0 |
| Dimry, Charles, Den. | 1 | 0 | 0.0 | 0 | 0 |
| Hall, Darryl, Den. | 1 | 0 | 0.0 | 0 | 0 |
| Harper, Dwayne, Sea. | 1 | 0 | 0.0 | 0 | 0 |
| Houston, Bobby, N.Y.J. | 1 | 0 | 0.0 | 0 | 0 |
| Johnson, Mike, Clev. | 1 | 0 | 0.0 | 0 | 0 |
| Jones, Rod, Cinn. | 1 | 0 | 0.0 | 0 | 0 |
| Lambert, Dion, N.E. | 1 | 0 | 0.0 | 0 | 0 |
| Ray, Terry, N.E. | 1 | 0 | 0.0 | 0 | 0 |
| Smith, Bruce, Buff. | 1 | 0 | 0.0 | 0 | 0 |
| Taylor, Jay, K.C. | 1 | 0 | 0.0 | 0 | 0 |
| Tovar, Steve, Cinn. | 1 | 0 | 0.0 | 0 | 0 |
| Richard, Stanley, S.D. | 1 | -2 | -2.0 | -2 | 0 |
| Wheeler, Leonard, Cinn. | 0 | 24 | — | 24 | 0 |

*t = Touchdown*
*Leader based on interceptions*

**NFC INTERCEPTIONS—INDIVIDUAL**

| | No. | Yards | Avg. | Long | TD |
|---|---|---|---|---|---|
| Sanders, Deion, Atl. | 7 | 91 | 13.0 | 41 | 0 |
| Allen, Eric, Phil. | 6 | 201 | 33.5 | 94t | 4 |
| Butler, LeRoy, G.B. | 6 | 131 | 21.8 | 39 | 0 |
| Smith, Kevin, Dall. | 6 | 56 | 9.3 | 32t | 1 |
| Carter, Tom, Wash. | 6 | 54 | 9.0 | 29 | 0 |
| McGruder, Michael, S.F. | 5 | 89 | 17.8 | 37 | 1 |
| Glenn, Vencie, Minn. | 5 | 49 | 9.8 | 23 | 0 |
| Carrier, Mark, Chi. | 4 | 94 | 23.5 | 34t | 1 |
| Collins, Mark, N.Y.G. | 4 | 77 | 19.3 | 50t | 1 |
| Jones, Dante, Chi. | 4 | 52 | 13.0 | 22 | 0 |
| Davis, Eric, S.F. | 4 | 45 | 11.3 | 41t | 1 |
| McMillian, Audray, Minn. | 4 | 45 | 11.3 | 22t | 1 |
| Jackson, Greg, N.Y.G. | 4 | 32 | 8.0 | 29 | 0 |
| Miano, Rich, Phil. | 4 | 26 | 6.5 | 16 | 0 |
| Green, Darrell, Wash. | 4 | 10 | 2.5 | 6 | 0 |
| Del Rio, Jack, Minn. | 4 | 3 | 0.8 | 3 | 0 |
| Lincoln, Jeremy, Chi. | 3 | 109 | 36.3 | 80t | 1 |
| Hanks, Merton, S.F. | 3 | 104 | 34.7 | 67t | 1 |
| Atkins, Gene, N.O. | 3 | 59 | 19.7 | 37 | 0 |
| King, Joe, T.B. | 3 | 29 | 9.7 | 28 | 0 |
| McDonald, Tim, S.F. | 3 | 23 | 7.7 | 21 | 0 |
| Lee, Carl, Minn. | 3 | 20 | 6.7 | 19 | 0 |
| Swilling, Pat, Det. | 3 | 16 | 5.3 | 14 | 0 |
| Lynch, Lorenzo, Phx. | 3 | 13 | 4.3 | 13 | 0 |
| Walker, Darnell, Atl. | 3 | 7 | 2.3 | 7 | 0 |
| Griffin, Don, S.F. | 3 | 6 | 2.0 | 3 | 0 |
| Williams, Aeneas, Phx. | 2 | 87 | 43.5 | 46t | 1 |
| Clark, Vinnie, Atl. | 2 | 59 | 29.5 | 38 | 0 |
| Jamison, George, Det. | 2 | 48 | 24.0 | 35t | 1 |
| Bailey, Robert, Rams | 2 | 41 | 20.5 | 41 | 0 |
| Holland, Johnny, G.B. | 2 | 41 | 20.5 | 30 | 0 |
| Thomas, William, Phil. | 2 | 39 | 19.5 | 21 | 0 |
| Guyton, Myron, N.Y.G. | 2 | 34 | 17.0 | 19 | 0 |
| Taylor, Keith, N.O. | 2 | 32 | 16.0 | 30 | 0 |
| Buckley, Terrell, G.B. | 2 | 31 | 15.5 | 31 | 0 |
| Crockett, Ray, Det. | 2 | 31 | 15.5 | 31 | 0 |
| Buck, Vince, N.O. | 2 | 28 | 14.0 | 28 | 0 |
| Colon, Harry, Det. | 2 | 28 | 14.0 | 27 | 0 |
| Coleman, Monte, Wash. | 2 | 27 | 13.5 | 14 | 0 |
| Scott, Todd, Minn. | 2 | 26 | 13.0 | 26 | 0 |
| Bates, Bill, Dall. | 2 | 25 | 12.5 | 22 | 0 |
| Everett, Thomas, Dall. | 2 | 25 | 12.5 | 17 | 0 |
| McMillian, Mark, Phil. | 2 | 25 | 12.5 | 17 | 0 |
| Booty, John, Phx. | 2 | 24 | 12.0 | 19 | 0 |
| Rolling, Henry, Rams | 2 | 21 | 10.5 | 12 | 0 |
| Simmons, Wayne, G.B. | 2 | 21 | 10.5 | 19 | 0 |
| McNeil, Ryan, Det. | 2 | 19 | 9.5 | 16 | 0 |
| Miller, Corey, N.Y.G. | 2 | 18 | 9.0 | 11 | 0 |
| Woolford, Donnell, Chi. | 2 | 18 | 9.0 | 18 | 0 |
| Raymond, Corey, N.Y.G. | 2 | 11 | 5.5 | 11 | 0 |
| McKyer, Tim, Det. | 2 | 10 | 5.0 | 10 | 0 |
| Jenkins, Carlos, Minn. | 2 | 7 | 3.5 | 4 | 0 |
| Blaylock, Anthony, Chi. | 2 | 3 | 1.5 | 3 | 0 |
| Terrell, Pat, Rams | 2 | 1 | 0.5 | 1 | 0 |
| Lyght, Todd, Rams | 2 | 0 | 0.0 | 0 | 0 |
| Spielman, Chris, Det. | 2 | -2 | -1.0 | 0 | 0 |
| Johnson, A. J., Wash. | 1 | 69 | 69.0 | 69t | 1 |
| McGriggs, Lamar, Minn. | 1 | 63 | 63.0 | 63t | 1 |
| Gouveia, Kurt, Wash. | 1 | 59 | 59.0 | 59t | 1 |
| Washington, James, Dall. | 1 | 38 | 38.0 | 24 | 0 |
| Stewart, Michael, Rams | 1 | 30 | 30.0 | 30 | 0 |
| Conlan, Shane, Rams | 1 | 28 | 28.0 | 28 | 0 |
| Mack, Milton, T.B. | 1 | 27 | 27.0 | 27t | 1 |
| Norton, Ken, Dall. | 1 | 25 | 25.0 | 25 | 0 |
| Dent, Richard, Chi. | 1 | 24 | 24.0 | 24 | 0 |
| Teague, George, G.B. | 1 | 22 | 22.0 | 22 | 0 |
| Hager, Britt, Phil. | 1 | 19 | 19.0 | 19 | 0 |
| Edwards, Brad, Wash. | 1 | 17 | 17.0 | 17 | 0 |
| Jones, Reggie, N.O. | 1 | 12 | 12.0 | 12 | 0 |
| Tate, David, N.Y.G. | 1 | 12 | 12.0 | 12 | 0 |
| Evans, Byron, Phil. | 1 | 8 | 8.0 | 7 | 0 |
| Paup, Bryce, G.B. | 1 | 8 | 8.0 | 8 | 0 |
| Anderson, Darren, T.B. | 1 | 6 | 6.0 | 6 | 0 |
| Homco, Thomas, Rams | 1 | 6 | 6.0 | 6 | 0 |
| Joyner, Seth, Phil. | 1 | 6 | 6.0 | 6 | 0 |
| Nickerson, Hardy, T.B. | 1 | 6 | 6.0 | 6 | 0 |
| Collins, Andre, Wash. | 1 | 5 | 5.0 | 5 | 0 |
| White, William, Det. | 1 | 5 | 5.0 | 5 | 0 |
| Reynolds, Ricky, T.B. | 1 | 3 | 3.0 | 3 | 0 |
| Marion, Brock, Dall. | 1 | 2 | 2.0 | 2 | 0 |
| Turnbull, Renaldo, N.O. | 1 | 2 | 2.0 | 2 | 0 |
| Owens, Dan, Det. | 1 | 1 | 1.0 | 1 | 0 |
| Parker, Anthony, Minn. | 1 | 1 | 1.0 | 1 | 0 |
| Prior, Mike, G.B. | 1 | 1 | 1.0 | 1 | 0 |
| Armstead, Jessie, N.Y.G. | 1 | 0 | 0.0 | 0 | 0 |
| Beamon, Willie, N.Y.G. | 1 | 0 | 0.0 | 0 | 0 |
| Brock, Matt, G.B. | 1 | 0 | 0.0 | 0 | 0 |
| Campbell, Jesse, N.Y.G. | 1 | 0 | 0.0 | 0 | 0 |
| Carter, Marty, T.B. | 1 | 0 | 0.0 | 0 | 0 |
| Cook, Toi, N.O. | 1 | 0 | 0.0 | 0 | 0 |
| Copeland, Danny, Wash. | 1 | 0 | 0.0 | 0 | 0 |
| Eaton, Tracey, Atl. | 1 | 0 | 0.0 | 0 | 0 |
| Evans, Doug, G.B. | 1 | 0 | 0.0 | 0 | 0 |
| Gant, Kenneth, Dall. | 1 | 0 | 0.0 | 0 | 0 |
| Gibson, Dennis, Det. | 1 | 0 | 0.0 | 0 | 0 |
| Hopkins, Wes, Phil. | 1 | 0 | 0.0 | 0 | 0 |
| Johnson, John, S.F. | 1 | 0 | 0.0 | 0 | 0 |
| Mangum, John, Chi. | 1 | 0 | 0.0 | 0 | 0 |
| McMichael, Steve, Chi. | 1 | 0 | 0.0 | 0 | 0 |
| Mitchell, Roland, G.B. | 1 | 0 | 0.0 | 0 | 0 |
| Oldham, Chris, Phx. | 1 | 0 | 0.0 | 0 | 0 |
| Pearson, J. C., Minn. | 1 | 0 | 0.0 | 0 | 0 |
| Scroggins, Tracy, Det. | 1 | 0 | 0.0 | 0 | 0 |
| Seals, Ray, T.B. | 1 | 0 | 0.0 | 0t | 1 |
| Simmons, Clyde, Phil. | 1 | 0 | 0.0 | 0 | 0 |
| Smith, Otis, Phil. | 1 | 0 | 0.0 | 0 | 0 |
| Zordich, Mike, Phx. | 1 | 0 | 0.0 | 0 | 0 |
| Doleman, Chris, Minn. | 1 | -3 | -3.0 | -3 | 0 |
| Case, Scott, Atl. | 0 | 3 | — | 3 | 0 |

*t = Touchdown*
*Leader based on interceptions*

## PUNTING

**Average Yards Per Punt**
- **AFC:** 45.6—Greg Montgomery, Houston
- **NFC:** 44.5—Jim Arnold, Detroit

**Net Average Yards Per Punt**
- **NFC:** 39.9—Mike Horan, Giants
- **AFC:** 39.1—Greg Montgomery, Houston

**Longest**
- **AFC:** 77—Greg Montgomery, Houston at San Diego, September 19
- **NFC:** 75—Harold Alexander, Atlanta at Chicago, October 3

**Punts**
- **NFC:** 93—Dan Stryzinski, Tampa Bay
- **AFC:** 90—Rick Tuten, Seattle
  Lee Johnson, Cincinnati

**Punts, Game**
- **AFC:** 12—Rick Tuten, Seattle vs. Denver, November 28, (559 yards)
- **NFC:** 10—Tommy Barnhardt, New Orleans at Cleveland, December 5, (428 yards)
  Dan Stryzinski, Tampa Bay at Green Bay, November 28, (336 yards)

**Team Champion**
- **AFC:** 45.3—Houston
- **NFC:** 44.5—Detroit

### AFC PUNTING—TEAM

| | Total Punts | Yards | Long | Avg. | TB | Blk. | Opp. Ret. | Return Yards | Inside the 20 | Net. Avg. |
|---|---|---|---|---|---|---|---|---|---|---|
| Houston | 56 | 2535 | 77 | 45.3 | 6 | 0 | 28 | 249 | 14 | 38.7 |
| Denver | 68 | 3017 | 62 | 44.4 | 8 | 1 | 33 | 337 | 17 | 37.1 |
| Seattle | 91 | 4007 | 64 | 44.0 | 7 | 1 | 47 | 475 | 21 | 37.3 |
| Cincinnati | 90 | 3954 | 60 | 43.9 | 12 | 0 | 47 | 416 | 24 | 36.6 |
| Indianapolis | 83 | 3595 | 65 | 43.3 | 13 | 0 | 41 | 352 | 18 | 35.9 |
| Cleveland | 84 | 3632 | 72 | 43.2 | 10 | 2 | 49 | 438 | 15 | 35.6 |
| Pittsburgh | 89 | 3781 | 61 | 42.5 | 3 | 0 | 50 | 678 | 28 | 34.2 |
| San Diego | 74 | 3127 | 67 | 42.3 | 7 | 0 | 36 | 292 | 20 | 36.4 |
| Kansas City | 77 | 3240 | 59 | 42.1 | 8 | 1 | 43 | 352 | 19 | 35.4 |
| L.A. Raiders | 71 | 2971 | 61 | 41.8 | 9 | 0 | 35 | 301 | 19 | 35.1 |
| New England | 76 | 3096 | 59 | 40.7 | 7 | 3 | 34 | 313 | 25 | 34.8 |
| Buffalo | 74 | 2991 | 58 | 40.4 | 4 | 0 | 29 | 247 | 19 | 36.0 |
| Miami | 58 | 2304 | 56 | 39.7 | 4 | 0 | 32 | 359 | 13 | 32.2 |
| N.Y. Jets | 73 | 2806 | 71 | 38.4 | 7 | 0 | 26 | 156 | 21 | 34.4 |
| AFC Total | 1064 | 45056 | 77 | —— | 105 | 8 | 530 | 4965 | 273 | —— |
| AFC Average | 76.0 | 3218.3 | — | 42.3 | 7.5 | 0.6 | 37.9 | 354.6 | 19.5 | 35.7 |

### NFC PUNTING—TEAM

| | Total Punts | Yards | Long | Avg. | TB | Blk. | Opp. Ret. | Return Yards | Inside the 20 | Net. Avg. |
|---|---|---|---|---|---|---|---|---|---|---|
| Detroit | 72 | 3207 | 68 | 44.5 | 9 | 0 | 45 | 377 | 15 | 36.8 |
| Washington | 83 | 3644 | 60 | 43.9 | 10 | 0 | 34 | 343 | 28 | 37.4 |
| Phoenix | 73 | 3189 | 61 | 43.7 | 8 | 0 | 30 | 267 | 23 | 37.8 |
| New Orleans | 77 | 3356 | 58 | 43.6 | 6 | 0 | 36 | 348 | 26 | 37.5 |
| Atlanta | 72 | 3114 | 75 | 43.3 | 3 | 0 | 41 | 350 | 21 | 37.6 |
| Minnesota | 90 | 3862 | 64 | 42.9 | 6 | 0 | 46 | 560 | 25 | 35.4 |
| Green Bay | 74 | 3174 | 60 | 42.9 | 7 | 0 | 38 | 350 | 19 | 36.3 |
| N.Y. Giants | 78 | 3272 | 60 | 41.9 | 4 | 1 | 44 | 247 | 24 | 37.8 |
| Dallas | 56 | 2342 | 59 | 41.8 | 3 | 0 | 32 | 169 | 22 | 37.7 |
| San Francisco | 42 | 1718 | 61 | 40.9 | 5 | 0 | 15 | 171 | 11 | 34.5 |
| L.A. Rams | 80 | 3271 | 66 | 40.9 | 10 | 0 | 43 | 533 | 15 | 31.7 |
| Tampa Bay | 94 | 3772 | 57 | 40.1 | 3 | 1 | 53 | 394 | 24 | 35.3 |
| Philadelphia | 83 | 3323 | 60 | 40.0 | 4 | 0 | 35 | 311 | 31 | 35.3 |
| Chicago | 80 | 3080 | 58 | 38.5 | 2 | 0 | 22 | 115 | 28 | 36.6 |
| NFC Total | 1054 | 44324 | 75 | —— | 80 | 2 | 514 | 4535 | 312 | —— |
| NFC Average | 75.3 | 3166.0 | — | 42.1 | 5.7 | 0.1 | 36.7 | 323.9 | 22.3 | 36.2 |
| League Total | 2118 | 89380 | 77 | —— | 185 | 10 | 1044 | 9500 | 585 | —— |
| League Average | 75.6 | 3192.1 | — | 42.2 | 6.6 | 0.4 | 37.3 | 339.3 | 20.9 | 36.0 |

### NFL TOP TEN PUNTERS

| | No. | Yards | Long | Avg. | Total Punts | TB | Blk. | Opp. Ret. | Ret. Yds. | In 20 | Net. Avg. |
|---|---|---|---|---|---|---|---|---|---|---|---|
| Montgomery, Greg, Hou. | 54 | 2462 | 77 | 45.6 | 54 | 5 | 0 | 28 | 249 | 13 | 39.1 |
| Rouen, Tom, Den. | 67 | 3017 | 62 | 45.0 | 68 | 8 | 1 | 33 | 337 | 17 | 37.1 |
| Arnold, Jim, Det. | 72 | 3207 | 68 | 44.5 | 72 | 9 | 0 | 45 | 377 | 15 | 36.8 |
| Tuten, Rick, Sea. | 90 | 4007 | 64 | 44.5 | 91 | 7 | 1 | 47 | 475 | 21 | 37.3 |
| Hansen, Brian, Clev. | 82 | 3632 | 72 | 44.3 | 84 | 10 | 2 | 49 | 438 | 15 | 35.6 |
| Roby, Reggie, Wash. | 78 | 3447 | 60 | 44.2 | 78 | 10 | 0 | 31 | 343 | 25 | 37.2 |
| Johnson, Lee, Cinn. | 90 | 3954 | 60 | 43.9 | 90 | 12 | 0 | 47 | 416 | 24 | 36.6 |
| Camarillo, Rich, Phx. | 73 | 3189 | 61 | 43.7 | 73 | 8 | 0 | 30 | 267 | 23 | 37.8 |
| Barnhardt, Tommy, N.O. | 77 | 3356 | 58 | 43.6 | 77 | 6 | 0 | 36 | 348 | 26 | 37.5 |
| Stark, Rohn, Ind. | 83 | 3595 | 65 | 43.3 | 83 | 13 | 0 | 41 | 352 | 18 | 35.9 |

### AFC PUNTERS—INDIVIDUAL

| | No. | Yards | Long | Avg. | Total Punts | TB | Blk. | Opp. Ret. | Ret. Yds. | In 20 | Net. Avg. |
|---|---|---|---|---|---|---|---|---|---|---|---|
| Montgomery, Greg, Hou. | 54 | 2462 | 77 | 45.6 | 54 | 5 | 0 | 28 | 249 | 13 | 39.1 |
| Rouen, Tom, Den. | 67 | 3017 | 62 | 45.0 | 68 | 8 | 1 | 33 | 337 | 17 | 37.1 |
| Tuten, Rick, Sea. | 90 | 4007 | 64 | 44.5 | 91 | 7 | 1 | 47 | 475 | 21 | 37.3 |
| Hansen, Brian, Clev. | 82 | 3632 | 72 | 44.3 | 84 | 10 | 2 | 49 | 438 | 15 | 35.6 |
| Johnson, Lee, Cinn. | 90 | 3954 | 60 | 43.9 | 90 | 12 | 0 | 47 | 416 | 24 | 36.6 |
| Stark, Rohn, Ind. | 83 | 3595 | 65 | 43.3 | 83 | 13 | 0 | 41 | 352 | 18 | 35.9 |
| Kidd, John, S.D. | 57 | 2431 | 67 | 42.6 | 57 | 7 | 0 | 28 | 243 | 16 | 35.9 |
| Barker, Bryan, K.C. | 76 | 3240 | 59 | 42.6 | 77 | 8 | 1 | 43 | 352 | 19 | 35.4 |
| Royals, Mark, Pitt. | 89 | 3781 | 61 | 42.5 | 89 | 3 | 0 | 50 | 678 | 28 | 34.2 |
| Saxon, Mike, N.E. | 73 | 3096 | 59 | 42.4 | 76 | 7 | 3 | 34 | 313 | 25 | 34.8 |
| Gossett, Jeff, Raid. | 71 | 2971 | 61 | 41.8 | 71 | 9 | 0 | 35 | 301 | 19 | 35.1 |
| Mohr, Chris, Buff. | 74 | 2991 | 58 | 40.4 | 74 | 4 | 0 | 29 | 247 | 19 | 36.0 |
| Hatcher, Dale, Mia. | 58 | 2304 | 56 | 39.7 | 58 | 4 | 0 | 32 | 359 | 13 | 32.2 |
| Aguiar, Louie, N.Y.J. | 73 | 2806 | 71 | 38.4 | 73 | 7 | 0 | 26 | 156 | 21 | 34.4 |
| **Nonqualifiers** | | | | | | | | | | | |
| Sullivan, Kent, S.D.-Hou.-S.D. | 15 | 614 | 50 | 40.9 | 15 | 1 | 0 | 6 | 33 | 4 | 37.4 |
| Carney, John, S.D. | 4 | 155 | 46 | 38.8 | 4 | 0 | 0 | 2 | 16 | 1 | 34.8 |

*Leader based on average, minimum 40 punts*

### NFC PUNTERS—INDIVIDUAL

| | No. | Yards | Long | Avg. | Total Punts | TB | Blk. | Opp. Ret. | Ret. Yds. | In 20 | Net. Avg. |
|---|---|---|---|---|---|---|---|---|---|---|---|
| Arnold, Jim, Det. | 72 | 3207 | 68 | 44.5 | 72 | 9 | 0 | 45 | 377 | 15 | 36.8 |
| Roby, Reggie, Wash. | 78 | 3447 | 60 | 44.2 | 78 | 10 | 0 | 31 | 343 | 25 | 37.2 |
| Camarillo, Rich, Phx. | 73 | 3189 | 61 | 43.7 | 73 | 8 | 0 | 30 | 267 | 23 | 37.8 |
| Barnhardt, Tommy, N.O. | 77 | 3356 | 58 | 43.6 | 77 | 6 | 0 | 36 | 348 | 26 | 37.5 |
| Alexander, Harold, Atl. | 72 | 3114 | 75 | 43.3 | 72 | 3 | 0 | 41 | 350 | 21 | 37.6 |
| Newsome, Harry, Minn. | 90 | 3862 | 64 | 42.9 | 90 | 6 | 0 | 46 | 560 | 25 | 35.4 |

| | No. | Yards | Long | Avg. | Total Punts | TB | Blk | Opp. Ret. | Ret. Yds. | In 20 | Net. Avg. |
|---|---|---|---|---|---|---|---|---|---|---|---|
| Wagner, Bryan, G.B. | 74 | 3174 | 60 | 42.9 | 74 | 7 | 0 | 38 | 350 | 19 | 36.3 |
| Landeta, Sean, N.Y.G.-Rams | 75 | 3215 | 66 | 42.9 | 76 | 10 | 1 | 44 | 444 | 18 | 33.8 |
| Horan, Mike, N.Y.G. | 44 | 1882 | 60 | 42.8 | 44 | 1 | 0 | 25 | 107 | 13 | 39.9 |
| Jett, John, Dall. | 56 | 2342 | 59 | 41.8 | 56 | 3 | 0 | 32 | 169 | 22 | 37.7 |
| Wilmsmeyer, Klaus, S.F. | 42 | 1718 | 61 | 40.9 | 42 | 5 | 0 | 15 | 171 | 11 | 34.5 |
| Stryzinski, Dan, T.B. | 93 | 3772 | 57 | 40.6 | 94 | 3 | 1 | 53 | 394 | 24 | 35.3 |
| Feagles, Jeff, Phil. | 83 | 3323 | 60 | 40.0 | 83 | 4 | 0 | 35 | 311 | 31 | 35.3 |
| Gardocki, Chris, Chi. | 80 | 3080 | 58 | 38.5 | 80 | 2 | 0 | 22 | 115 | 28 | 36.6 |
| **Nonqualifiers** | | | | | | | | | | | |
| McJulien, Paul, Rams | 21 | 795 | 56 | 37.9 | 21 | 3 | 0 | 10 | 143 | 5 | 28.2 |
| Bracken, Don, Rams | 17 | 651 | 51 | 38.3 | 17 | 0 | 0 | 8 | 86 | 3 | 33.2 |
| Goodburn, Kelly, Wash. | 5 | 197 | 49 | 39.4 | 5 | 0 | 0 | 3 | 0 | 3 | 39.4 |

*Leader based on average, minimum 40 punts*

## PUNT RETURNS

**Yards Per Return**
- **NFC:** 13.6—Tyrone Hughes, New Orleans
- **AFC:** 12.9—Eric Metcalf, Cleveland

**Yards**
- **NFC:** 503—Tyrone Hughes, New Orleans
- **AFC:** 465—Tim Brown, Raiders

**Yards, Game**
- **AFC:** 166—Eric Metcalf, Cleveland vs. Pittsburgh, October 24, (2 returns - 2 TD)
- **NFC:** 131—Dexter Carter, San Francisco vs. Minnesota, October 3, (5 returns - TD)

**Longest**
- **AFC:** 91—Eric Metcalf, Cleveland vs. Pittsburgh, October 24 - TD
- **NFC:** 83—Tyrone Hughes, New Orleans at Philadelphia December 26 - TD

**Returns**
- **AFC:** 43—Patrick Robinson, Cincinnati
- **NFC:** 37—Tyrone Hughes, New Orleans

**Returns, Game**
- **AFC:** 10—Ron Harris, New England at Pittsburgh, December 5, (74 yards)
- **NFC:** 6—Mel Gray, Detroit vs. Atlanta, September 5, (52 yards)
  Vernon Turner, Detroit vs. Tampa Bay, November 7, (17 yards)
  Brian Mitchell, Washington at Rams, November 21, (30 yards)
  Vai Sikahema, Philadelphia vs. Giants, November 21, (29 yards)
  Robert Brooks, Green Bay vs. Tampa Bay, November 28, (39 yards)

**Fair Catches**
- **AFC:** 22—O.J. McDuffie, Miami
- **NFC:** 21—Tyrone Hughes, New Orleans

**Touchdowns**
- **AFC:** 2—O.J. McDuffie, Miami
  Eric Metcalf, Cleveland
- **NFC:** 2—Tyrone Hughes, New Orleans
  Kevin Williams, Dallas

**Team Champion**
- **NFC:** 13.6—New Orleans
- **AFC:** 13.4—Cleveland

### AFC PUNT RETURNS—TEAM

| | No. | FC | Yards | Avg. | Long | TD |
|---|---|---|---|---|---|---|
| Cleveland | 42 | 12 | 563 | 13.4 | 91t | 3 |
| San Diego | 34 | 17 | 412 | 12.1 | 54 | 0 |
| Miami | 28 | 22 | 326 | 11.6 | 72t | 2 |
| L.A. Raiders | 40 | 20 | 465 | 11.6 | 74t | 1 |
| Denver | 41 | 11 | 425 | 10.4 | 54 | 0 |
| Kansas City | 37 | 7 | 348 | 9.4 | 30 | 0 |
| New England | 51 | 14 | 462 | 9.1 | 30 | 0 |
| Seattle | 33 | 15 | 280 | 8.5 | 33 | 0 |
| Buffalo | 33 | 7 | 277 | 8.4 | 47t | 1 |
| N.Y. Jets | 31 | 12 | 256 | 8.3 | 20 | 0 |
| Pittsburgh | 47 | 12 | 353 | 7.5 | 39 | 0 |
| Houston | 41 | 19 | 275 | 6.7 | 18 | 0 |
| Cincinnati | 48 | 8 | 321 | 6.7 | 36 | 0 |
| Indianapolis | 30 | 17 | 173 | 5.8 | 24 | 0 |
| AFC Total | 536 | 193 | 4936 | 9.2 | 91t | 7 |
| AFC Average | 38.3 | 13.8 | 352.6 | 9.2 | — | 0.5 |

### NFC PUNT RETURNS—TEAM

| | No. | FC | Yards | Avg. | Long | TD |
|---|---|---|---|---|---|---|
| New Orleans | 38 | 21 | 517 | 13.6 | 83t | 2 |
| San Francisco | 35 | 20 | 411 | 11.7 | 72t | 1 |
| N.Y. Giants | 32 | 20 | 331 | 10.3 | 75t | 1 |
| Dallas | 37 | 14 | 381 | 10.3 | 64t | 2 |
| Green Bay | 45 | 12 | 404 | 9.0 | 39 | 0 |
| Detroit | 40 | 18 | 349 | 8.7 | 53 | 0 |
| Philadelphia | 33 | 20 | 284 | 8.6 | 25 | 0 |
| Chicago | 35 | 20 | 289 | 8.3 | 28 | 0 |
| Tampa Bay | 38 | 15 | 311 | 8.2 | 35 | 0 |
| Phoenix | 47 | 11 | 384 | 8.2 | 58t | 1 |
| Atlanta | 35 | 18 | 276 | 7.9 | 51 | 0 |
| Minnesota | 39 | 23 | 280 | 7.2 | 50 | 0 |
| Washington | 35 | 8 | 245 | 7.0 | 48 | 0 |
| L.A. Rams | 19 | 15 | 102 | 5.4 | 13 | 0 |
| NFC Total | 508 | 235 | 4564 | 9.0 | 83t | 7 |
| NFC Average | 36.3 | 16.8 | 326.0 | 9.0 | — | 0.5 |
| League Total | 1044 | 428 | 9500 | — | 91t | 14 |
| League Average | 37.3 | 15.3 | 339.3 | 9.1 | — | 0.5 |

### NFL TOP TEN PUNT RETURNERS

| | No. | FC | Yards | Avg. | Long | TD |
|---|---|---|---|---|---|---|
| Hughes, Tyrone, N.O. | 37 | 21 | 503 | 13.6 | 83t | 2 |
| Metcalf, Eric, Clev. | 36 | 11 | 464 | 12.9 | 91t | 2 |
| Gordon, Darrien, S.D. | 31 | 15 | 395 | 12.7 | 54 | 0 |
| Carter, Dexter, S.F. | 34 | 20 | 411 | 12.1 | 72t | 1 |
| Brown, Tim, Raid. | 40 | 20 | 465 | 11.6 | 74t | 1 |
| McDuffie, O. J., Mia. | 28 | 22 | 317 | 11.3 | 72t | 2 |
| Milburn, Glyn, Den. | 40 | 11 | 425 | 10.6 | 54 | 0 |
| Williams, Kevin, Dall. | 36 | 14 | 381 | 10.6 | 64t | 2 |
| Meggett, David, N.Y.G. | 32 | 20 | 331 | 10.3 | 75t | 1 |
| Carter, Dale, K.C. | 27 | 4 | 247 | 9.1 | 30 | 0 |

### AFC - INDIVIDUAL PUNT RETURNERS

| | No. | FC | Yards | Avg. | Long | TD |
|---|---|---|---|---|---|---|
| Metcalf, Eric, Clev. | 36 | 11 | 464 | 12.9 | 91t | 2 |
| Gordon, Darrien, S.D. | 31 | 15 | 395 | 12.7 | 54 | 0 |
| Brown, Tim, Raid. | 40 | 20 | 465 | 11.6 | 74t | 1 |
| McDuffie, O. J., Mia. | 28 | 22 | 317 | 11.3 | 72t | 2 |
| Milburn, Glyn, Den. | 40 | 11 | 425 | 10.6 | 54 | 0 |
| Carter, Dale, K.C. | 27 | 4 | 247 | 9.1 | 30 | 0 |
| Brown, Troy, N.E. | 25 | 9 | 224 | 9.0 | 19 | 0 |
| Copeland, Russell, Buff. | 31 | 7 | 274 | 8.8 | 47t | 1 |
| Harris, Ronnie, N.E. | 23 | 4 | 201 | 8.7 | 21 | 0 |
| Martin, Kelvin, Sea. | 32 | 15 | 270 | 8.4 | 33 | 0 |
| Woodson, Rod, Pitt. | 42 | 10 | 338 | 8.0 | 39 | 0 |
| Robinson, Patrick, Cinn. | 43 | 6 | 305 | 7.1 | 36 | 0 |
| Drewrey, Willie, Hou. | 41 | 19 | 275 | 6.7 | 18 | 0 |
| Verdin, Clarence, Ind. | 30 | 17 | 173 | 5.8 | 24 | 0 |
| **Nonqualifiers** | | | | | | |
| Hicks, Cliff, N.Y.J. | 17 | 4 | 157 | 9.2 | 20 | 0 |
| Mathis, Terance, N.Y.J. | 14 | 8 | 99 | 7.1 | 16 | 0 |
| Carrier, Mark, Clev. | 6 | 1 | 92 | 15.3 | 56t | 1 |
| Birden, J. J., K.C. | 5 | 3 | 43 | 8.6 | 12 | 0 |
| Figures, Deon, Pitt. | 5 | 2 | 15 | 3.0 | 6 | 0 |
| Pickens, Carl, Cinn. | 4 | 2 | 16 | 4.0 | 9 | 0 |
| Hughes, Danan, K.C. | 3 | 0 | 49 | 16.3 | 29 | 0 |
| Lewis, Nate, S.D. | 3 | 2 | 17 | 5.7 | 7 | 0 |
| Crittenden, Ray, N.E. | 2 | 1 | 37 | 18.5 | 30 | 0 |

| | No. | FC | Yards | Avg. | Long | TD |
|---|---|---|---|---|---|---|
| Mincy, Charles, K.C. | 2 | 0 | 9 | 4.5 | 9 | 0 |
| McCloughan, Dave, Sea. | 1 | 0 | 10 | 10.0 | 10 | 0 |
| Brooks, Bill, Buff. | 1 | 0 | 3 | 3.0 | 3 | 0 |
| Bradford, Ronnie, Den. | 1 | 0 | 0 | 0.0 | 0 | 0 |
| Simmons, Marcello, Cinn. | 1 | 0 | 0 | 0.0 | 0 | 0 |
| Smith, Rod, N.E. | 1 | 0 | 0 | 0.0 | 0 | 0 |
| Tasker, Steve, Buff. | 1 | 0 | 0 | 0.0 | 0 | 0 |
| Vincent, Troy, Mia. | 0 | 0 | 9 | — | 9 | 0 |
| Turner, Eric, Clev. | 0 | 0 | 7 | — | 7 | 0 |

*t = Touchdown*
*Leader based on average return, minimum 20 returns*

**NFC - INDIVIDUAL PUNT RETURNERS**

| | No. | FC | Yards | Avg. | Long | TD |
|---|---|---|---|---|---|---|
| Hughes, Tyrone, N.O. | 37 | 21 | 503 | 13.6 | 83t | 2 |
| Carter, Dexter, S.F. | 34 | 20 | 411 | 12.1 | 72t | 1 |
| Williams, Kevin, Dall. | 36 | 14 | 381 | 10.6 | 64t | 2 |
| Meggett, David, N.Y.G. | 32 | 20 | 331 | 10.3 | 75t | 1 |
| Gray, Mel, Det. | 23 | 14 | 197 | 8.6 | 35 | 0 |
| Sikahema, Vai, Phil. | 33 | 20 | 275 | 8.3 | 25 | 0 |
| Obee, Terry, Chi. | 35 | 20 | 289 | 8.3 | 28 | 0 |
| Bailey, Johnny, Phx. | 35 | 5 | 282 | 8.1 | 58t | 1 |
| Smith, Tony, Atl. | 32 | 17 | 255 | 8.0 | 51 | 0 |
| Guliford, Eric, Minn. | 29 | 15 | 212 | 7.3 | 50 | 0 |
| Mitchell, Brian, Wash. | 29 | 7 | 193 | 6.7 | 48 | 0 |
| **Nonqualifiers** | | | | | | |
| Prior, Mike, G.B. | 17 | 3 | 194 | 11.4 | 24 | 0 |
| Turner, Vernon, Det. | 17 | 4 | 152 | 8.9 | 53 | 0 |
| Anderson, Gary, T.B. | 17 | 1 | 113 | 6.6 | 15 | 0 |
| Brooks, Robert, G.B. | 16 | 4 | 135 | 8.4 | 35 | 0 |
| Hawkins, Courtney, T.B. | 15 | 8 | 166 | 11.1 | 35 | 0 |
| Buckley, Terrell, G.B. | 11 | 5 | 76 | 6.9 | 39 | 0 |
| Blount, Eric, Phx. | 9 | 3 | 90 | 10.0 | 25 | 0 |
| Parker, Anthony, Minn. | 9 | 6 | 64 | 7.1 | 20 | 0 |
| Buchanan, Richard, Rams | 8 | 1 | 41 | 5.1 | 12 | 0 |
| Kinchen, Todd, Rams | 7 | 4 | 32 | 4.6 | 8 | 0 |
| Claiborne, Robert, T.B. | 6 | 6 | 32 | 5.3 | 13 | 0 |
| Howard, Desmond, Wash. | 4 | 0 | 25 | 6.3 | 13 | 0 |
| Edwards, Anthony, Phx. | 3 | 3 | 12 | 4.0 | 11 | 0 |
| Sanders, Deion, Atl. | 2 | 1 | 21 | 10.5 | 16 | 0 |
| Ellard, Henry, Rams | 2 | 8 | 18 | 9.0 | 13 | 0 |
| Green, Darrell, Wash. | 1 | 1 | 27 | 27.0 | 24 | 0 |
| Newman, Pat, N.O. | 1 | 0 | 14 | 14.0 | 14 | 0 |
| Henley, Darryl, Rams | 1 | 0 | 8 | 8.0 | 8 | 0 |
| Smith, Robert, Minn. | 1 | 2 | 4 | 4.0 | 4 | 0 |
| Price, Mitchell, Rams | 1 | 2 | 3 | 3.0 | 3 | 0 |
| Clark, Vinnie, Atl. | 1 | 0 | 0 | 0.0 | 0 | 0 |
| Kelm, Larry, S.F. | 1 | 0 | 0 | 0.0 | 0 | 0 |
| Mays, Alvoid, Wash. | 1 | 0 | 0 | 0.0 | 0 | 0 |
| Washington, James, Dall. | 1 | 0 | 0 | 0.0 | 0 | 0 |
| Teague, George, G.B. | 1 | 0 | -1 | -1.0 | -1 | 0 |
| Smith, Otis, Phil. | 0 | 0 | 9 | — | 9 | 0 |

*t = Touchdown*
*Leader based on average return, minimum 20 returns*

## KICKOFF RETURNS

**Yards Per Return**
- **NFC:** 26.6—Robert Brooks, Green Bay
- **AFC:** 24.2—Raghib Ismail, Raiders

**Yards**
- **AFC:** 1050—Clarence Verdin, Indianapolis
- **NFC:** 948—Tony Smith, Atlanta

**Yards, Game**
- **NFC:** 249—Tony Smith, Atlanta vs. Pittsburgh, September 27, (6 returns - TD)
- **AFC:** 117—Nate Lewis, San Diego at Kansas City, December 19, (4 returns)

**Longest**
- **NFC:** 99—Tyrone Hughes, New Orleans at Minnesota, November 28 - TD
- **AFC:** 66—Raghib Ismail, Raiders at Cincinnati, November 28

**Returns**
- **AFC:** 50—Clarence Verdin, Indianapolis
- **NFC:** 42—Qadry Ismail, Minnesota

**Returns, Game**
- **NFC:** 7—Johnny Bailey, Phoenix at Seattle, December 19, (137 yards)
- **AFC:** 6—Adrian Murrell, Jets vs. Denver, September 5, (83 yards)
  Clarence Verdin, Indianapolis at Miami, October 24, (151 yards)
  Eric Ball, Cincinnati vs. Houston, November 14, (121 yards)
  Michael Bates, Seattle vs. Kansas City, December 5, (164 yards)
  O.J. McDuffie, Miami at New England, January 2, (150 yards)

**Touchdowns**
- **NFC:** 1—Robert Brooks, Green Bay
  Mel Gray, Detroit
  Tyrone Hughes, New Orleans
  Tony Smith, Atlanta
- **AFC:** None

**Team Champion**
- **NFC:** 24.7—Green Bay
- **AFC:** 21.8—Miami

**AFC KICKOFF RETURNS—TEAM**

| | No. | Yards | Avg. | Long | TD |
|---|---|---|---|---|---|
| Miami | 49 | 1068 | 21.8 | 48 | 0 |
| L.A. Raiders | 52 | 1061 | 20.4 | 66 | 0 |
| Cincinnati | 61 | 1211 | 19.9 | 45 | 0 |
| Indianapolis | 57 | 1124 | 19.7 | 38 | 0 |
| Kansas City | 45 | 875 | 19.4 | 47 | 0 |
| Cleveland | 58 | 1119 | 19.3 | 47 | 0 |
| San Diego | 47 | 901 | 19.2 | 60 | 0 |
| Houston | 31 | 589 | 19.0 | 37 | 0 |
| Seattle | 50 | 931 | 18.6 | 46 | 0 |
| Denver | 39 | 717 | 18.4 | 49 | 0 |
| New England | 47 | 819 | 17.4 | 44 | 0 |
| Pittsburgh | 52 | 878 | 16.9 | 44 | 0 |
| Buffalo | 45 | 746 | 16.6 | 28 | 0 |
| N.Y. Jets | 46 | 675 | 14.7 | 28 | 0 |
| AFC Total | 679 | 12714 | 18.7 | 66 | 0 |
| AFC Average | 48.5 | 908.1 | 18.7 | — | 0.0 |

**NFC KICKOFF RETURNS—TEAM**

| | No. | Yards | Avg. | Long | TD |
|---|---|---|---|---|---|
| Green Bay | 60 | 1483 | 24.7 | 95t | 1 |
| Atlanta | 55 | 1300 | 23.6 | 97t | 1 |
| New Orleans | 62 | 1460 | 23.5 | 99t | 1 |
| Detroit | 52 | 1204 | 23.2 | 95t | 1 |
| Phoenix | 45 | 951 | 21.1 | 48 | 0 |
| Dallas | 36 | 758 | 21.1 | 49 | 0 |
| Washington | 59 | 1166 | 19.8 | 68 | 0 |
| Minnesota | 55 | 1086 | 19.7 | 47 | 0 |
| Philadelphia | 54 | 987 | 18.3 | 36 | 0 |
| Chicago | 45 | 811 | 18.0 | 55 | 0 |
| San Francisco | 40 | 715 | 17.9 | 60 | 0 |
| L.A. Rams | 49 | 824 | 16.8 | 35 | 0 |
| Tampa Bay | 58 | 922 | 15.9 | 42 | 0 |
| N.Y. Giants | 32 | 507 | 15.8 | 35 | 0 |
| NFC Total | 702 | 14174 | 20.2 | 99t | 4 |
| NFC Average | 50.1 | 1012.4 | 20.2 | — | 0.3 |
| League Total | 1381 | 26888 | — | 99t | 4 |
| League Average | 49.3 | 960.3 | 19.5 | — | 0.1 |

**TOP TEN KICKOFF RETURNERS**

| | No. | Yards | Avg. | Long | TD |
|---|---|---|---|---|---|
| Brooks, Robert, G.B. | 23 | 611 | 26.6 | 95t | 1 |
| Hughes, Tyrone, N.O. | 30 | 753 | 25.1 | 99t | 1 |
| Smith, Tony, Atl. | 38 | 948 | 24.9 | 97t | 1 |
| Gray, Mel, Det. | 28 | 688 | 24.6 | 95t | 1 |
| Ismail, Raghib, Raid. | 25 | 605 | 24.2 | 66 | 0 |
| McDuffie, O. J., Mia. | 32 | 755 | 23.6 | 48 | 0 |
| Bailey, Johnny, Phx. | 31 | 699 | 22.5 | 48 | 0 |
| Williams, Kevin, Dall. | 31 | 689 | 22.2 | 49 | 0 |
| Ball, Eric, Cinn. | 23 | 501 | 21.8 | 45 | 0 |
| Ismail, Qadry, Minn. | 42 | 902 | 21.5 | 47 | 0 |

### AFC KICKOFF RETURNERS—INDIVIDUAL

| | No. | Yards | Avg. | Long | TD |
|---|---|---|---|---|---|
| Ismail, Raghib, Raid. | 25 | 605 | 24.2 | 66 | 0 |
| McDuffie, O. J., Mia. | 32 | 755 | 23.6 | 48 | 0 |
| Ball, Eric, Cinn. | 23 | 501 | 21.8 | 45 | 0 |
| Verdin, Clarence, Ind. | 50 | 1050 | 21.0 | 38 | 0 |
| Crittenden, Ray, N.E. | 23 | 478 | 20.8 | 44 | 0 |
| Lewis, Nate, S.D. | 33 | 684 | 20.7 | 60 | 0 |
| Bates, Michael, Sea. | 30 | 603 | 20.1 | 46 | 0 |
| Robinson, Patrick, Cinn. | f30 | 567 | 18.9 | 42 | 0 |
| Baldwin, Randy, Clev. | 24 | 444 | 18.5 | 31 | 0 |
| Copeland, Russell, Buff. | 24 | 436 | 18.2 | 28 | 0 |
| Murrell, Adrian, N.Y.J. | 23 | 342 | 14.9 | 23 | 0 |
| **Nonqualifiers** | | | | | |
| Russell, Derek, Den. | 18 | 374 | 20.8 | 49 | 0 |
| Vaughn, Jon, Sea. | 16 | 280 | 17.5 | 31 | 0 |
| Metcalf, Eric, Clev. | 15 | 318 | 21.2 | 47 | 0 |
| Woodson, Rod, Pitt. | 15 | 294 | 19.6 | 44 | 0 |
| Drewrey, Willie, Hou. | 15 | 293 | 19.5 | 34 | 0 |
| Brown, Troy, N.E. | 15 | 243 | 16.2 | 29 | 0 |
| Hughes, Danan, K.C. | 14 | 266 | 19.0 | 30 | 0 |
| Hoard, Leroy, Clev. | 13 | 286 | 22.0 | 39 | 0 |
| Milburn, Glyn, Den. | 12 | 188 | 15.7 | 26 | 0 |
| Hastings, Andre, Pitt. | 12 | 177 | 14.8 | 22 | 0 |
| Dickerson, Ron, K.C. | 11 | 237 | 21.5 | 44 | 0 |
| Mills, John Henry, Hou. | 11 | 230 | 20.9 | 37 | 0 |
| Stone, Dwight, Pitt. | 11 | 168 | 15.3 | 30 | 0 |
| Wright, Alexander, Raid. | 10 | 167 | 16.7 | 28 | 0 |
| Beebe, Don, Buff. | 10 | 160 | 16.0 | 22 | 0 |
| Jones, Fred, K.C. | 9 | 156 | 17.3 | 29 | 0 |
| Prior, Anthony, N.Y.J. | 9 | 126 | 14.0 | 27 | 0 |
| Williams, Mike, Mia. | 8 | 180 | 22.5 | 39 | 0 |
| Davis, Kenneth, Buff. | 8 | 100 | 12.5 | 18 | 0 |
| Gault, Willie, Raid. | 7 | 187 | 26.7 | 60 | 0 |
| Delpino, Robert, Den. | 7 | 146 | 20.9 | 49 | 0 |
| Bieniemy, Eric, S.D. | 7 | 110 | 15.7 | 18 | 0 |
| Mathis, Terance, N.Y.J. | 7 | 102 | 14.6 | 28 | 0 |
| Harris, Ronnie, N.E. | 6 | 90 | 15.0 | 19 | 0 |
| Stephens, John, K.C. | 5 | 88 | 17.6 | 25 | 0 |
| Kirby, Terry, Mia. | 4 | 85 | 21.3 | 26 | 0 |
| Benjamin, Ryan, Cinn. | 4 | 78 | 19.5 | 24 | 0 |
| Thompson, Leroy, Pitt. | 4 | 77 | 19.3 | 27 | 0 |
| Anderson, Richie, N.Y.J. | 4 | 66 | 16.5 | 22 | 0 |
| Miles, Ostell, Cinn. | 4 | 65 | 16.3 | 24 | 0 |
| Vardell, Tommy, Clev. | 4 | 58 | 14.5 | 16 | 0 |
| Robinson, Greg, Raid. | 4 | 57 | 14.3 | 33 | 0 |
| Williams, Harvey, K.C. | 3 | 53 | 17.7 | 26 | 0 |
| Culver, Rodney, Ind. | 3 | 51 | 17.0 | 20 | 0 |
| Martin, Kelvin, Sea. | 3 | 38 | 12.7 | 15 | 0 |
| Coleman, Pat, Hou. | 3 | 37 | 12.3 | 16 | 0 |
| Hoge, Merril, Pitt. | 3 | 33 | 11.0 | 15 | 0 |
| Miller, Anthony, S.D. | 2 | 42 | 21.0 | 29 | 0 |
| Lamb, Brad, Buff. | 2 | 40 | 20.0 | 23 | 0 |
| Thomas, Blair, N.Y.J. | 2 | 39 | 19.5 | 28 | 0 |
| Brown, Gary, Hou. | 2 | 29 | 14.5 | 16 | 0 |
| Hendrickson, Steve, S.D. | 2 | 25 | 12.5 | 13 | 0 |
| Means, Natrone, S.D. | 2 | 22 | 11.0 | 14 | 0 |
| Miller, Scott, Mia. | 2 | 22 | 11.0 | 16 | 0 |
| Peat, Todd, Raid. | 2 | 18 | 9.0 | 10 | 0 |
| Smith, Kevin, Raid. | 2 | 15 | 7.5 | 8 | 0 |
| Butcher, Paul, Ind. | 2 | 2 | 1.0 | 2 | 0 |
| Sabb, Dwayne, N.E. | 2 | 0 | 0.0 | 0 | 0 |
| Anders, Kimble, K.C. | 1 | 47 | 47.0 | 47 | 0 |
| McNair, Todd, K.C. | 1 | 28 | 28.0 | 28 | 0 |
| Thigpen, Yancey, Pitt. | 1 | 23 | 23.0 | 23 | 0 |
| Williams, Willie, Pitt. | 1 | 19 | 19.0 | 19 | 0 |
| Harmon, Ronnie, S.D. | 1 | 18 | 18.0 | 18 | 0 |
| Smith, Rico, Clev. | 1 | 13 | 13.0 | 13 | 0 |
| McCallum, Napoleon, Raid. | 1 | 12 | 12.0 | 12 | 0 |
| Cash, Kerry, Ind. | 1 | 11 | 11.0 | 11 | 0 |
| Fryar, Irving, Mia. | 1 | 10 | 10.0 | 10 | 0 |
| Radecic, Scott, Ind. | 1 | 10 | 10.0 | 10 | 0 |
| Tuatagaloa, Natu, Sea. | 1 | 10 | 10.0 | 10 | 0 |
| Turner, Nate, Buff. | 1 | 10 | 10.0 | 10 | 0 |
| Meeks, Bob, Den. | 1 | 9 | 9.0 | 9 | 0 |
| Cook, Marv, N.E. | 1 | 8 | 8.0 | 8 | 0 |
| Baty, Greg, Mia. | 1 | 7 | 7.0 | 7 | 0 |
| Saxon, James, Mia. | 1 | 7 | 7.0 | 7 | 0 |
| Cooper, Adrian, Pitt. | 1 | 2 | 2.0 | 2 | 0 |
| Kinchen, Brian, Clev. | 1 | 0 | 0.0 | 0 | 0 |
| Marts, Lonnie, K.C. | 1 | 0 | 0.0 | 0 | 0 |
| Sadowski, Troy, N.Y.J. | 1 | 0 | 0.0 | 0 | 0 |
| Sharpe, Shannon, Den. | 1 | 0 | 0.0 | 0 | 0 |
| Turk, Daniel, Raid. | 1 | 0 | 0.0 | 0 | 0 |
| Vincent, Troy, Mia. | 0 | 2 | — | 2 | 0 |
| Birden, J. J., K.C. | f0 | 0 | — | — | 0 |
| Coates, Ben, N.E. | f0 | 0 | — | — | 0 |
| Shaw, Eric, Cinn. | f0 | 0 | — | — | 0 |

*t = Touchdown*
*f = Fair Catch (Shaw, Eric, Cinn.: 2 fair catches)*
*Leader based on average return, minimum 20 returns*

### NFC KICKOFF RETURNERS—INDIVIDUAL

| | No. | Yards | Avg. | Long | TD |
|---|---|---|---|---|---|
| Brooks, Robert, G.B. | 23 | 611 | 26.6 | 95t | 1 |
| Hughes, Tyrone, N.O. | 30 | 753 | 25.1 | 99t | 1 |
| Smith, Tony, Atl. | 38 | 948 | 24.9 | 97t | 1 |
| Gray, Mel, Det. | 28 | 688 | 24.6 | 95t | 1 |
| Bailey, Johnny, Phx. | 31 | 699 | 22.5 | 48 | 0 |
| Williams, Kevin, Dall. | 31 | 689 | 22.2 | 49 | 0 |
| Ismail, Qadry, Minn. | 42 | 902 | 21.5 | 47 | 0 |
| Conway, Curtis, Chi. | 21 | 450 | 21.4 | 55 | 0 |
| McAfee, Fred, N.O. | 28 | 580 | 20.7 | 55 | 0 |
| Mitchell, Brian, Wash. | 33 | 678 | 20.5 | 68 | 0 |
| Carter, Dexter, S.F. | f25 | 494 | 19.8 | 60 | 0 |
| Wilson, Charles, T.B. | f23 | 454 | 19.7 | 42 | 0 |
| Sikahema, Vai, Phil. | 30 | 579 | 19.3 | 35 | 0 |
| Howard, Desmond, Wash. | 21 | 405 | 19.3 | 33 | 0 |
| Turner, Vernon, Det.-T.B. | 21 | 391 | 18.6 | 46 | 0 |
| Meggett, David, N.Y.G. | f24 | 403 | 16.8 | 35 | 0 |
| **Nonqualifiers** | | | | | |
| Harris, Corey, G.B. | 16 | 482 | 30.1 | 65 | 0 |
| Anderson, Gary, T.B.-Det. | 15 | 232 | 15.5 | 24 | 0 |
| Boykin, Deral, Rams | 13 | 216 | 16.6 | 29 | 0 |
| Walker, Herschel, Phil. | 11 | 184 | 16.7 | 30 | 0 |
| Lee, Amp, S.F. | 10 | 160 | 16.0 | 28 | 0 |
| Wilson, Marcus, G.B. | 9 | 197 | 21.9 | 37 | 0 |
| Thompson, Darrell, G.B. | 9 | 171 | 19.0 | 42 | 0 |
| Obee, Terry, Chi. | 9 | 159 | 17.7 | 34 | 0 |
| Sydner, Jeff, Phil. | 9 | 158 | 17.6 | 36 | 0 |
| Green, Robert, Chi. | 9 | 141 | 15.7 | 30 | 0 |
| Griffith, Howard, Rams | 8 | 169 | 21.1 | 29 | 0 |
| Blount, Eric, Phx. | 8 | 163 | 20.4 | 27 | 0 |
| Price, Mitchell, Rams | 8 | 144 | 18.0 | 23 | 0 |
| White, Russell, Rams | 8 | 122 | 15.3 | 35 | 0 |
| Royster, Mazio, T.B. | 8 | 102 | 12.8 | 26 | 0 |
| Sanders, Deion, Atl. | 7 | 169 | 24.1 | 31 | 0 |
| Worley, Tim, Pitt.-Chi. | 6 | 121 | 20.2 | 26 | 0 |
| Kinchen, Todd, Rams | 6 | 96 | 16.0 | 22 | 0 |
| Calloway, Chris, N.Y.G. | 6 | 89 | 14.8 | 21 | 0 |
| Guliford, Eric, Minn. | 5 | 101 | 20.2 | 29 | 0 |
| Israel, Steve, Rams | 5 | 92 | 18.4 | 23 | 0 |
| Workman, Vince, T.B. | 5 | 67 | 13.4 | 19 | 0 |
| Pegram, Erric, Atl. | 4 | 63 | 15.8 | 28 | 0 |
| Claiborne, Robert, T.B. | 4 | 57 | 14.3 | 33 | 0 |
| Brown, Derek, N.O. | 3 | 58 | 19.3 | 23 | 0 |
| Edwards, Anthony, Phx. | 3 | 51 | 17.0 | 20 | 0 |
| Walker, Adam, S.F. | 3 | 51 | 17.0 | 30 | 0 |
| Smith, Robert, Minn. | 3 | 41 | 13.7 | 16 | 0 |
| Hebron, Vaughn, Phil. | 3 | 35 | 11.7 | 18 | 0 |
| Montgomery, Alton, Atl. | 2 | 53 | 26.5 | 33 | 0 |
| Phillips, Jason, Atl. | 2 | 38 | 19.0 | 29 | 0 |
| Clay, Willie, Det. | 2 | 34 | 17.0 | 20 | 0 |
| Ervins, Ricky, Wash. | 2 | 29 | 14.5 | 18 | 0 |
| Jurkovic, John, G.B. | 2 | 22 | 11.0 | 13 | 0 |
| Cross, Howard, N.Y.G. | 2 | 15 | 7.5 | 13 | 0 |
| Moore, Derrick, Det. | 1 | 68 | 68.0 | 68 | 0 |
| Smith, Kevin, Dall. | 1 | 33 | 33.0 | 33 | 0 |
| Bowles, Todd, Wash. | 1 | 27 | 27.0 | 27 | 0 |
| Lynch, Eric, Det. | 1 | 22 | 22.0 | 22 | 0 |
| Mims, David, Atl. | 1 | 22 | 22.0 | 22 | 0 |
| Gant, Kenneth, Dall. | 1 | 18 | 18.0 | 18 | 0 |
| Lofton, Steve, Phx. | 1 | 18 | 18.0 | 18 | 0 |
| Hilliard, Dalton, N.O. | 1 | 17 | 17.0 | 17 | 0 |
| Graham, Scottie, Minn. | 1 | 16 | 16.0 | 16 | 0 |
| Buck, Jason, Wash. | 1 | 15 | 15.0 | 15 | 0 |
| Brooks, Reggie, Wash. | 1 | 12 | 12.0 | 12 | 0 |
| Heyward, Craig, Chi. | 1 | 12 | 12.0 | 12 | 0 |
| Jones, Robert, Dall. | 1 | 12 | 12.0 | 12 | 0 |
| Craig, Roger, Minn. | 1 | 11 | 11.0 | 11 | 0 |
| Evans, Chuck, Minn. | 1 | 11 | 11.0 | 11 | 0 |
| Hallock, Ty, Det. | 1 | 11 | 11.0 | 11 | 0 |
| Smith, Lance, Phx. | 1 | 11 | 11.0 | 11 | 0 |
| Brandes, John, S.F. | 1 | 10 | 10.0 | 10 | 0 |

| | No. | Yards | Avg. | Long | TD |
|---|---|---|---|---|---|
| Moore, Ron, Phx. | 1 | 9 | 9.0 | 9 | 0 |
| Fontenot, Albert, Chi. | 1 | 8 | 8.0 | 8 | 0 |
| Hennings, Chad, Dall. | 1 | 7 | 7.0 | 7 | 0 |
| Johnson, Maurice, Phil. | 1 | 7 | 7.0 | 7 | 0 |
| Ruether, Mike, Atl. | 1 | 7 | 7.0 | 7 | 0 |
| Ryan, Tim, Chi. | 1 | 5 | 5.0 | 5 | 0 |
| Del Rio, Jack, Minn. | 1 | 4 | 4.0 | 4 | 0 |
| Chmura, Mark, G.B. | 1 | 0 | 0.0 | 0 | 0 |
| Jamison, George, Det. | 1 | 0 | 0.0 | 0 | 0 |
| Kelm, Larry, S.F. | 1 | 0 | 0.0 | 0 | 0 |
| Mangum, John, Chi. | 1 | 0 | 0.0 | 0 | 0 |
| McMillian, Audray, Minn. | 1 | 0 | 0.0 | 0 | 0 |
| Novacek, Jay, Dall. | 1 | -1 | -1.0 | -1 | 0 |
| Drayton, Troy, Rams | 1 | -15 | -15.0 | -15 | 0 |
| Dowdell, Marcus, N.O. | 0 | 52 | — | 52 | 0 |
| Smith, Otis, Phil. | 0 | 24 | — | 24 | 0 |
| Jones, Victor, Det. | f0 | 0 | — | — | 0 |
| Vanderbeek, Matt, Dall. | f0 | 0 | — | — | 0 |
| Walls, Wesley, S.F. | f0 | 0 | — | — | 0 |
| Williams, Jamie, S.F. | f0 | 0 | — | — | 0 |

*t = Touchdown*
*f = Fair Catch (Vanderbeek, Matt, Dall.: 2 fair catches)*
*Leader based on average return, minimum 20 returns*

## FUMBLES

**Most Fumbles**
**NFC:** 15—Jim Harbaugh, Chicago
**AFC:** 13—Boomer Esiason, Jets
Rick Mirer, Seattle
Warren Moon, Houston

**Most Fumbles, Game**
**AFC:** 3—David Klingler, Cincinnati at Cleveland, September 5
Vince Evans, Raiders at Kansas City, October 3
Rick Mirer, Seattle at Detroit, October 17
Scott Secules, New England at Indianapolis, October 31
Leroy Thompson, Pittsburgh at Denver, November 21
Drew Bledsoe, New England at Pittsburgh, December 5
Glyn Milburn, Denver vs. Tampa Bay, December 26
Boomer Esiason, Jets at Houston, January 2
Leroy Hoard, Cleveland at Pittsburgh, January 2
**NFC:** 3—Jim Harbaugh, Chicago vs. Giants, September 5
Randall Cunningham, Philadelphia at Green Bay, September 12
Rodney Peete, Detroit at New Orleans, September 19
Bobby Hebert, Atlanta vs. Pittsburgh, September 27
Brett Favre, Green Bay at Kansas City, November 8
Craig Erickson, Tampa Bay at Denver, December 26
Mark Rypien, Washington vs. Minnesota, December 31

**Own Fumbles Recovered**
**NFC:** 6—Craig Erickson, Tampa Bay
**AFC:** 5—Drew Bledsoe, New England
John Elway, Denver
Boomer Esiason, Jets
Rick Mirer, Seattle
Warren Moon, Houston

**Most Own Fumbles Recovered, Game**
**NFC:** 3—Craig Erickson, Tampa Bay at Denver, December 26
**AFC:** 2—Drew Bledsoe, New England at Buffalo, September 5
Dan Marino, Miami at Indianapolis, September 5
Terry Kirby, Miami vs. Jets, September 12
Nate Lewis, San Diego at Pittsburgh, October 10
Jim Kelly, Buffalo vs. Houston, October 11
Rick Mirer, Seattle vs. New England, October 24
Scott Secules, New England at Indianapolis, October 31
Boomer Esiason, Jets vs. Miami, November 7
John Elway, Denver at Seattle, November 28
Warren Moon, Houston vs. Pittsburgh, November 28
Drew Bledsoe, New England at Pittsburgh, December 5

**Opponents' Fumbles Recovered**
**NFC:** 5—Michael Bankston, Phoenix
**AFC:** 4—Bryan Cox, Miami
Andre Tippett, New England

**Most Opponents' Fumples Recovered, Game**
**AFC:** 2—Bill Pickel, Jets at Raiders, October 10
Bryan Cox, Miami vs. Kansas City, October 31
Andre Tippett, New England vs. Buffalo, November 7 (OT)
Patrick Hunter, Seattle vs. Cleveland, November 14
Tim Newton, Kansas City vs. Seattle, January 2
**NFC:** 2—Lorenzo Lynch, Phoenix at Philadelphia, September 5
Jimmy Spencer, New Orleans vs. Houston, September 5
Pat Eilers, Washington vs. Dallas, September 6
Rickey Jackson, New Orleans vs. Detroit, September 19
Myron Baker, Chicago vs. Tampa Bay, September 26
Michael Bankston, Phoenix vs. Washington, October 17
Trace Armstrong, Chicago at Detroit, November 25

**Yards**
**AFC:** 107—Marcus Robertson, Houston
**NFC:** 86—Darrell Green, Washington

**Longest**
**AFC:** 86—Derrick Thomas, Kansas City at Seattle, December 5 - TD
**NFC:** 78—Darrell Green, Washington vs. Indianapolis, November 7 - TD

### AFC FUMBLES—TEAM

| | Fum. | Own. Rec. | Fum. OB | TD | Opp. Rec. | TD | Fum. Yards | Tot. Rec. |
|---|---|---|---|---|---|---|---|---|
| San Diego | 13 | 7 | 1 | 0 | 12 | 0 | 29 | 19 |
| L.A. Raiders | 23 | 11 | 1 | 0 | 9 | 0 | 4 | 20 |
| Cincinnati | 24 | 13 | 2 | 0 | 14 | 0 | -24 | 27 |
| Seattle | 25 | 10 | 2 | 0 | 15 | 2 | -6 | 25 |
| Buffalo | 26 | 9 | 0 | 0 | 24 | 1 | 87 | 33 |
| Cleveland | 27 | 8 | 2 | 0 | 9 | 1 | 12 | 17 |
| Pittsburgh | 28 | 9 | 4 | 0 | 14 | 2 | 57 | 23 |
| Kansas City | 28 | 7 | 3 | 0 | 17 | 2 | 122 | 24 |
| Denver | 29 | 10 | 1 | 1 | 13 | 0 | -24 | 23 |
| New England | 30 | 19 | 1 | 0 | 9 | 0 | -29 | 28 |
| Miami | 32 | 15 | 1 | 0 | 14 | 0 | -23 | 29 |
| Indianapolis | 34 | 11 | 3 | 0 | 11 | 2 | 45 | 22 |
| Houston | 37 | 12 | 5 | 0 | 17 | 3 | 178 | 29 |
| N.Y. Jets | 38 | 20 | 2 | 0 | 18 | 0 | 22 | 38 |
| AFC Total | 394 | 161 | 28 | 1 | 196 | 13 | 450 | 357 |
| AFC Average | 28.1 | 11.5 | 2.0 | 0.1 | 14.0 | 0.9 | 32.1 | 25.5 |

### NFC FUMBLES—TEAM

| | Fum. | Own. Rec. | Fum. OB | TD | Opp. Rec. | TD | Fum. Yards | Tot. Rec. |
|---|---|---|---|---|---|---|---|---|
| Minnesota | 15 | 4 | 1 | 0 | 10 | 0 | -12 | 14 |
| N.Y. Giants | 19 | 10 | 1 | 0 | 10 | 0 | -17 | 20 |
| L.A. Rams | 20 | 8 | 1 | 0 | 9 | 1 | 61 | 17 |
| Phoenix | 23 | 11 | 1 | 0 | 17 | 2 | 56 | 28 |
| New Orleans | 24 | 11 | 0 | 0 | 20 | 2 | 118 | 31 |
| Washington | 24 | 14 | 0 | 0 | 14 | 2 | 114 | 28 |
| Green Bay | 26 | 15 | 1 | 0 | 15 | 1 | 34 | 30 |
| Tampa Bay | 28 | 16 | 1 | 0 | 13 | 0 | 7 | 29 |
| Chicago | 29 | 14 | 1 | 0 | 12 | 2 | 42 | 26 |
| Detroit | 29 | 12 | 4 | 0 | 16 | 2 | 110 | 28 |
| Atlanta | 31 | 13 | 1 | 0 | 11 | 1 | 11 | 24 |
| San Francisco | 32 | 16 | 3 | 1 | 11 | 1 | 56 | 27 |
| Philadelphia | 32 | 10 | 1 | 0 | 15 | 1 | 29 | 25 |
| Dallas | 33 | 14 | 3 | 0 | 14 | 0 | 14 | 28 |
| NFC Total | 365 | 168 | 19 | 1 | 187 | 15 | 623 | 355 |
| NFC Average | 26.1 | 12.0 | 1.4 | 0.1 | 13.4 | 1.1 | 44.5 | 25.4 |
| League Total | 759 | 329 | 47 | 2 | 383 | 28 | 1073 | 712 |
| League Average | 27.1 | 11.8 | 1.7 | 0.1 | 13.7 | 1.0 | 38.3 | 25.4 |

*Fum OB= Fumbled out of bounds, includes fumbled through the end zone.*
*Yards includes aborted plays, own recoveries, and oppponents' recoveries.*

### AFC FUMBLES - INDIVIDUAL

| | Fum. | Own Rec. | Opp. Rec. | Yards | Tot. Rec. |
|---|---|---|---|---|---|
| Aguiar, Louie, N.Y.J. | 2 | 1 | 0 | -10 | 1 |
| Alexander, Bruce, Mia. | 0 | 0 | 1 | 0 | 1 |
| Allen, Marcus, K.C. | 4 | 1 | 0 | 0 | 1 |
| Anders, Kimble, K.C. | 1 | 0 | 0 | 0 | 0 |
| Anderson, Eddie, Raid. | 0 | 0 | 1 | 0 | 1 |
| Anderson, Richie, N.Y.J. | 1 | 1 | 0 | 0 | 1 |
| Arbuckle, Charles, Ind. | 1 | 0 | 0 | 0 | 0 |
| Armstrong, Bruce, N.E. | 0 | 1 | 0 | 0 | 1 |

| | Fum. | Own Rec. | Opp. Rec. | Yards | Tot. Rec. |
|---|---|---|---|---|---|
| Arthur, Mike, N.E. | 0 | 1 | 0 | 0 | 1 |
| Baldwin, Randy, Clev. | 2 | 1 | 0 | 0 | 1 |
| Bates, Michael, Sea. | 1 | 0 | 2 | 3 | 2 |
| Bavaro, David, N.E. | 0 | 1 | 1 | 0 | 2 |
| Baxter, Brad, N.Y.J. | 3 | 2 | 0 | 0 | 2 |
| Beebe, Don, Buff. | 1 | 1 | 0 | 0 | 1 |
| Bell, Nick, Raid. | 2 | 0 | 0 | 0 | 0 |
| Belser, Jason, Ind. | 0 | 0 | 3 | 0 | 3 |
| Bennett, Cornelius, Buff. | 1 | 1 | 1 | 40 | 2 |
| Bernstine, Rod, Den. | 3 | 1 | 0 | 0 | 1 |
| Bickett, Duane, Ind. | 0 | 0 | 1 | 0 | 1 |
| Bieniemy, Eric, S.D. | 1 | 0 | 0 | 0 | 0 |
| Birden, J. J., K.C. | 1 | 0 | 0 | 0 | 0 |
| Bishop, Blaine, Hou. | 1 | 0 | 1 | 0 | 1 |
| Blackmon, Robert, Sea. | 0 | 0 | 1 | 5 | 1 |
| Blades, Brian, Sea. | 1 | 0 | 0 | 0 | 0 |
| Bledsoe, Drew, N.E. | 8 | 5 | 0 | -23 | 5 |
| Bowden, Joe, Hou. | 0 | 0 | 1 | 0 | 1 |
| Bradford, Ronnie, Den. | 1 | 0 | 0 | 0 | 0 |
| Brady, Jeff, S.D. | 0 | 0 | 1 | 0 | 1 |
| Braxton, Tyrone, Den. | 0 | 0 | 2 | 6 | 2 |
| Brim, Michael, Cinn. | 0 | 1 | 1 | 0 | 2 |
| Brisby, Vincent, N.E. | 1 | 1 | 0 | 0 | 1 |
| Brown, Corwin, N.E. | 0 | 0 | 1 | 0 | 1 |
| Brown, Gary, Hou. | 4 | 2 | 0 | 4 | 2 |
| Brown, J. B., Mia. | 1 | 0 | 0 | 0 | 0 |
| Brown, Tim, Raid. | 1 | 0 | 0 | 0 | 0 |
| Brown, Troy, N.E. | 2 | 1 | 0 | 0 | 1 |
| Bruce, Aundray, Raid. | 0 | 0 | 1 | 0 | 1 |
| Burkett, Chris, N.Y.J. | 1 | 0 | 0 | 0 | 0 |
| Burnett, Rob, Clev. | 0 | 0 | 2 | 0 | 2 |
| Byars, Keith, Mia. | 3 | 0 | 0 | 0 | 0 |
| Caldwell, Mike, Clev. | 0 | 0 | 1 | 0 | 1 |
| Carlson, Cody, Hou. | 3 | 2 | 0 | -2 | 2 |
| Carrington, Darren, S.D. | 1 | 0 | 1 | 0 | 1 |
| Carter, Dale, K.C. | 4 | 2 | 0 | 0 | 2 |
| Cash, Keith, K.C. | 1 | 1 | 1 | 0 | 2 |
| Cash, Kerry, Ind. | 2 | 1 | 0 | 0 | 1 |
| Childress, Ray, Hou. | 0 | 0 | 3 | 0 | 3 |
| Clancy, Sam, Ind. | 0 | 0 | 1 | 0 | 1 |
| Clifton, Kyle, N.Y.J. | 0 | 0 | 2 | 0 | 2 |
| Collins, Todd, N.E. | 0 | 0 | 1 | 2 | 1 |
| Cook, Marv, N.E. | 1 | 0 | 0 | -2 | 0 |
| Cooper, Adrian, Pitt. | 1 | 0 | 0 | 0 | 0 |
| Copeland, Russell, Buff. | 1 | 0 | 0 | 0 | 0 |
| Cox, Bryan, Mia. | 0 | 0 | 4 | 1 | 4 |
| Croel, Mike, Den. | 0 | 0 | 2 | 0 | 2 |
| Croom, Corey, N.E. | 1 | 0 | 0 | 0 | 0 |
| Cross, Jeff, Mia. | 0 | 0 | 2 | 0 | 2 |
| Culver, Rodney, Ind. | 3 | 1 | 1 | 56 | 2 |
| Dahl, Bob, Clev. | 0 | 1 | 0 | 0 | 1 |
| Darby, Matt, Buff. | 0 | 0 | 1 | 0 | 1 |
| Davidson, Kenny, Pitt. | 0 | 0 | 1 | 18 | 1 |
| Davis, Kenneth, Buff. | 3 | 1 | 0 | 0 | 1 |
| Dawson, Dermontti, Pitt. | 1 | 0 | 0 | 0 | 0 |
| DeBerg, Steve, T.B.-Mia. | 2 | 0 | 0 | 0 | 0 |
| Dellenbach, Jeff, Mia. | 1 | 0 | 1 | -6 | 1 |
| Delpino, Robert, Den. | 1 | 0 | 0 | 0 | 0 |
| Dennis, Mark, Mia. | 0 | 1 | 0 | 0 | 1 |
| Dishman, Cris, Hou. | 0 | 0 | 2 | 69 | 2 |
| Donaldson, Ray, Sea. | 1 | 0 | 0 | -7 | 0 |
| Drewrey, Willie, Hou. | 2 | 1 | 0 | 0 | 1 |
| Duffy, Roger, N.Y.J. | 0 | 1 | 0 | 0 | 1 |
| Dyal, Mike, K.C. | 1 | 0 | 0 | 0 | 0 |
| Edmunds, Ferrell, Sea. | 1 | 0 | 0 | 0 | 0 |
| Elway, John, Den. | 8 | 5 | 0 | -5 | 5 |
| Esiason, Boomer, N.Y.J. | 13 | 5 | 0 | -10 | 5 |
| Evans, Vince, Raid. | 4 | 0 | 0 | 0 | 0 |
| Everitt, Steve, Clev. | 0 | 2 | 0 | 0 | 2 |
| Fenner, Derrick, Cinn. | 1 | 2 | 0 | 0 | 2 |
| Figures, Deon, Pitt. | 2 | 0 | 2 | 6 | 2 |
| Fletcher, Simon, Den. | 0 | 0 | 1 | 0 | 1 |
| Foster, Barry, Pitt. | 3 | 0 | 0 | 0 | 0 |
| Francis, James, Cinn. | 0 | 0 | 1 | 0 | 1 |
| Frase, Paul, N.Y.J. | 0 | 0 | 2 | 0 | 2 |
| Friesz, John, S.D. | 2 | 1 | 0 | -3 | 1 |
| Gardner, Carwell, Buff. | 1 | 0 | 0 | 0 | 0 |
| Gash, Sam, N.E. | 1 | 0 | 0 | 0 | 0 |
| Gelbaugh, Stan, Sea. | 1 | 0 | 0 | 0 | 0 |
| George, Jeff, Ind. | 4 | 0 | 0 | -1 | 0 |
| Givins, Ernest, Hou. | 2 | 0 | 0 | 0 | 0 |
| Goad, Tim, N.E. | 0 | 0 | 1 | 0 | 1 |
| Goganious, Keith, Buff. | 0 | 0 | 1 | 0 | 1 |
| Gordon, Darrien, S.D. | 4 | 1 | 1 | -2 | 2 |
| Gray, Derwin, Ind. | 0 | 0 | 1 | 0 | 1 |
| Green, Eric, Pitt. | 3 | 0 | 0 | 0 | 0 |
| Green, Harold, Cinn. | 3 | 0 | 0 | 0 | 0 |
| Greene, Kevin, Pitt. | 0 | 0 | 3 | 5 | 3 |
| Grossman, Burt, S.D. | 0 | 0 | 1 | 0 | 1 |
| Grunhard, Tim, K.C. | 1 | 0 | 0 | -1 | 0 |
| Gunn, Lance, Cinn. | 0 | 0 | 1 | 0 | 1 |
| Harper, Dwayne, Sea. | 0 | 0 | 1 | 0 | 1 |
| Harris, Ronnie, N.E. | 2 | 1 | 0 | 0 | 1 |
| Harrison, Nolan, Raid. | 0 | 0 | 1 | 5 | 1 |
| Hasty, James, N.Y.J. | 0 | 0 | 2 | 28 | 2 |
| Hayes, Jonathan, K.C. | 1 | 0 | 0 | 0 | 0 |
| Heck, Andy, Sea. | 0 | 2 | 0 | 0 | 2 |
| Heller, Ron, Mia. | 0 | 1 | 0 | 0 | 1 |
| Henderson, Jerome, Buff. | 0 | 0 | 1 | 0 | 1 |
| Hendrickson, Steve, S.D. | 0 | 0 | 1 | 0 | 1 |
| Herrod, Jeff, Ind. | 0 | 0 | 1 | 0 | 1 |
| Hester, Jessie, Ind. | 1 | 0 | 0 | 0 | 0 |
| Hicks, Cliff, N.Y.J. | 2 | 1 | 0 | 0 | 1 |
| Higgs, Mark, Mia. | 1 | 0 | 0 | 0 | 0 |
| Hoard, Leroy, Clev. | 4 | 0 | 0 | 0 | 0 |
| Hoge, Merril, Pitt. | 0 | 1 | 0 | 4 | 1 |
| Hollier, Dwight, Mia. | 0 | 0 | 1 | 0 | 1 |
| Hoover, Houston, Clev. | 0 | 1 | 0 | 0 | 1 |
| Horton, Ethan, Raid. | 0 | 1 | 0 | 0 | 1 |
| Hoskins, Derrick, Raid. | 0 | 0 | 1 | 0 | 1 |
| Hostetler, Jeff, Raid. | 6 | 2 | 0 | -1 | 2 |
| Houston, Bobby, N.Y.J. | 0 | 0 | 1 | 0 | 1 |
| Humphries, Stan, S.D. | 2 | 1 | 0 | 0 | 1 |
| Hunter, Patrick, Sea. | 0 | 0 | 3 | 0 | 3 |
| Ingram, Mark, Mia. | 3 | 1 | 0 | 0 | 1 |
| Ismail, Raghib, Raid. | 0 | 1 | 0 | 0 | 1 |
| Jackson, John, Pitt. | 0 | 1 | 0 | 0 | 1 |
| Jackson, Keith, Mia. | 2 | 0 | 0 | 0 | 0 |
| Jackson, Michael, Clev. | 1 | 0 | 1 | 0 | 1 |
| Jeffires, Haywood, Hou. | 5 | 0 | 0 | 0 | 0 |
| Jett, James, Raid. | 1 | 0 | 0 | 0 | 0 |
| Johnson, Anthony, Ind. | 5 | 2 | 0 | 0 | 2 |
| Johnson, Johnny, N.Y.J. | 5 | 2 | 0 | 0 | 2 |
| Johnson, Reggie, Den. | 1 | 0 | 0 | 0 | 0 |
| Jones, Fred, K.C. | 1 | 0 | 0 | 0 | 0 |
| Jones, Gary, Pitt. | 0 | 1 | 0 | 0 | 1 |
| Jones, Henry, Buff. | 0 | 1 | 1 | 0 | 2 |
| Jones, Marvin, N.Y.J. | 0 | 0 | 1 | 0 | 1 |
| Jones, Rod, Cinn. | 0 | 0 | 1 | 0 | 1 |
| Jones, Sean, Hou. | 0 | 0 | 2 | 0 | 2 |
| Jones, Selwyn, Clev. | 0 | 0 | 1 | 0 | 1 |
| Jordan, Randy, Raid. | 2 | 0 | 0 | 0 | 0 |
| Jorden, Tim, Pitt. | 0 | 1 | 0 | 2 | 1 |
| Junior, E. J., Sea. | 0 | 1 | 0 | 0 | 1 |
| Kartz, Keith, Den. | 2 | 0 | 0 | -17 | 0 |
| Kasay, John, Sea. | 0 | 0 | 1 | 0 | 1 |
| Kelly, Jim, Buff. | 7 | 3 | 0 | -17 | 3 |
| Kelly, Joe, Raid. | 0 | 0 | 1 | 0 | 1 |
| Kelso, Mark, Buff. | 0 | 0 | 1 | 0 | 1 |
| Kennedy, Cortez, Sea. | 0 | 0 | 1 | 0 | 1 |
| Kinchen, Brian, Clev. | 1 | 0 | 0 | 0 | 0 |
| Kirby, Terry, Mia. | 5 | 4 | 0 | 0 | 4 |
| Kirkland, Levon, Pitt. | 0 | 0 | 2 | 24 | 2 |
| Klingler, David, Cinn. | 7 | 2 | 0 | -10 | 2 |
| Kozerski, Bruce, Cinn. | 3 | 1 | 0 | -14 | 1 |
| Kragen, Greg, Den. | 0 | 0 | 1 | 0 | 1 |
| Krieg, Dave, K.C. | 6 | 1 | 0 | 0 | 1 |
| Lake, Carnell, Pitt. | 0 | 0 | 2 | 0 | 2 |
| Langhorne, Reggie, Ind. | 4 | 1 | 1 | 0 | 2 |
| Lathon, Lamar, Hou. | 0 | 0 | 1 | 0 | 1 |
| Lee, Shawn, S.D. | 0 | 0 | 1 | 0 | 1 |
| Lewis, Albert, K.C. | 0 | 0 | 2 | 0 | 2 |
| Lewis, Bill, N.E. | 2 | 0 | 0 | -43 | 0 |
| Lewis, Nate, S.D. | 2 | 2 | 0 | 0 | 2 |
| Lloyd, Greg, Pitt. | 0 | 0 | 1 | 0 | 1 |
| Lodish, Mike, Buff. | 0 | 0 | 1 | 0 | 1 |
| Lott, Ronnie, N.Y.J. | 0 | 0 | 2 | 0 | 2 |
| Lowdermilk, Kirk, Ind. | 0 | 1 | 0 | 0 | 1 |
| Maddox, Mark, Buff. | 0 | 0 | 2 | 0 | 2 |
| Majkowski, Don, Ind. | 1 | 1 | 0 | -7 | 1 |
| Malamala, Siupeli, N.Y.J. | 0 | 1 | 0 | 0 | 1 |
| Marino, Dan, Mia. | 4 | 2 | 0 | -13 | 2 |

## 1993 INDIVIDUAL STATISTICS

| | Fum. | Own Rec. | Opp. Rec. | Yards | Tot. Rec. |
|---|---|---|---|---|---|
| Marshall, Leonard, N.Y.J. | 0 | 0 | 1 | 0 | 1 |
| Marshall, Wilber, Hou. | 0 | 0 | 1 | 0 | 1 |
| Martin, Kelvin, Sea. | 1 | 1 | 0 | 0 | 1 |
| Martin, Tony, Mia. | 1 | 0 | 0 | 0 | 0 |
| Marts, Lonnie, K.C. | 0 | 0 | 1 | 0 | 1 |
| Maston, Le'Shai, Hou. | 1 | 0 | 0 | 0 | 0 |
| Mathis, Terance, N.Y.J. | 5 | 1 | 0 | 0 | 1 |
| McCallum, Napoleon, Raid. | 1 | 0 | 0 | 0 | 0 |
| McClendon, Skip, Ind. | 0 | 0 | 2 | 0 | 2 |
| McDuffie, O. J., Mia. | 4 | 1 | 0 | 0 | 1 |
| McGee, Tony, Cinn. | 1 | 0 | 0 | 0 | 0 |
| McGlockton, Chester, Raid. | 0 | 0 | 1 | 0 | 1 |
| McMurtry, Greg, N.E. | 1 | 1 | 0 | 0 | 1 |
| McNair, Todd, K.C. | 2 | 0 | 0 | 0 | 0 |
| Means, Natrone, S.D. | 1 | 1 | 0 | 0 | 1 |
| Mecklenburg, Karl, Den. | 0 | 0 | 2 | 0 | 2 |
| Metcalf, Eric, Clev. | 4 | 0 | 0 | 0 | 0 |
| Metzelaars, Pete, Buff. | 1 | 0 | 0 | 0 | 0 |
| Mickell, Darren, K.C. | 0 | 0 | 1 | 0 | 1 |
| Milburn, Glyn, Den. | 9 | 1 | 0 | 0 | 1 |
| Mims, Chris, S.D. | 0 | 0 | 2 | 0 | 2 |
| Mincy, Charles, K.C. | 0 | 0 | 2 | 0 | 2 |
| Mirer, Rick, Sea. | 13 | 5 | 0 | -14 | 5 |
| Mitchell, Scott, Mia. | 3 | 1 | 0 | -4 | 1 |
| Mohr, Chris, Buff. | 1 | 1 | 0 | 0 | 1 |
| Montana, Joe, K.C. | 1 | 0 | 0 | -1 | 0 |
| Montgomery, Glenn, Hou. | 0 | 0 | 3 | 0 | 3 |
| Montgomery, Tyrone, Raid. | 2 | 1 | 0 | 0 | 1 |
| Moon, Warren, Hou. | 13 | 5 | 0 | -7 | 5 |
| Moore, Rob, N.Y.J. | 2 | 0 | 0 | 0 | 0 |
| Moore, Stevon, Clev. | 0 | 0 | 1 | 22 | 1 |
| Murrell, Adrian, N.Y.J. | 4 | 2 | 0 | 0 | 2 |
| Newton, Tim, K.C. | 0 | 0 | 3 | 0 | 3 |
| Norgard, Erik, Hou. | 0 | 1 | 0 | 0 | 1 |
| Odomes, Nate, Buff. | 0 | 0 | 1 | 25 | 1 |
| O'Donnell, Neil, Pitt. | 5 | 0 | 0 | -2 | 0 |
| Oliver, Louis, Mia. | 0 | 0 | 1 | 0 | 1 |
| O'Neal, Leslie, S.D. | 0 | 0 | 1 | 13 | 1 |
| Patton, Marvcus, Buff. | 0 | 0 | 3 | 5 | 3 |
| Pederson, Doug, Mia. | 2 | 1 | 0 | -1 | 1 |
| Perry, Gerald, Raid. | 0 | 1 | 0 | 0 | 1 |
| Perry, Michael Dean, Clev. | 0 | 0 | 2 | 4 | 2 |
| Philcox, Todd, Clev. | 2 | 0 | 0 | -1 | 0 |
| Pickel, Bill, N.Y.J. | 0 | 0 | 3 | 7 | 3 |
| Pickens, Carl, Cinn. | 1 | 0 | 0 | 0 | 0 |
| Pool, David, Buff. | 0 | 0 | 1 | 12 | 1 |
| Potts, Roosevelt, Ind. | 8 | 2 | 0 | 0 | 2 |
| Prior, Anthony, N.Y.J. | 0 | 1 | 0 | 0 | 1 |
| Pupunu, Alfred, S.D. | 0 | 1 | 0 | 0 | 1 |
| Query, Jeff, Cinn. | 1 | 0 | 0 | 0 | 0 |
| Rayam, Thomas, Cinn. | 0 | 2 | 0 | 0 | 2 |
| Reed, Andre, Buff. | 3 | 0 | 0 | 0 | 0 |
| Richard, Stanley, S.D. | 0 | 0 | 1 | 0 | 1 |
| Rivers, Reggie, Den. | 0 | 0 | 1 | 0 | 1 |
| Robertson, Marcus, Hou. | 0 | 0 | 3 | 107 | 3 |
| Robinson, Eugene, Sea. | 0 | 0 | 2 | 7 | 2 |
| Robinson, Greg, Raid. | 3 | 1 | 0 | 0 | 1 |
| Robinson, Jeff, Den. | 1 | 0 | 1 | -10 | 1 |
| Robinson, Patrick, Cinn. | 2 | 1 | 0 | 0 | 1 |
| Robinson, Rafael, Sea. | 0 | 0 | 1 | 0 | 1 |
| Rogers, Tracy, K.C. | 0 | 0 | 1 | 0 | 1 |
| Ross, Kevin, K.C. | 0 | 0 | 1 | 22 | 1 |
| Rowe, Patrick, Clev. | 1 | 0 | 0 | 0 | 0 |
| Russell, Derek, Den. | 1 | 1 | 0 | 0 | 1 |
| Russell, Leonard, N.E. | 4 | 2 | 0 | 22 | 2 |
| Saleaumua, Dan, K.C. | 0 | 0 | 1 | 16 | 1 |
| Saxon, Mike, N.E. | 1 | 1 | 0 | 0 | 1 |
| Schroeder, Jay, Cinn. | 5 | 1 | 0 | 0 | 1 |
| Scott, Tom, Cinn. | 0 | 2 | 0 | 0 | 2 |
| Searcy, Leon, Pitt. | 0 | 1 | 0 | 0 | 1 |
| Seau, Junior, S.D. | 0 | 0 | 1 | 21 | 1 |
| Secules, Scott, N.E. | 4 | 2 | 0 | -5 | 2 |
| Sharpe, Shannon, Den. | 1 | 0 | 0 | 0 | 0 |
| Shaw, Eric, Cinn. | 0 | 0 | 1 | 0 | 1 |
| Shields, Will, K.C. | 0 | 2 | 0 | 0 | 2 |
| Sims, Keith, Mia. | 0 | 1 | 0 | 0 | 1 |
| Slade, Chris, N.E. | 0 | 0 | 1 | 0 | 1 |
| Slaughter, Webster, Hou. | 4 | 0 | 0 | 0 | 0 |
| Smith, Bruce, Buff. | 0 | 0 | 1 | 0 | 1 |
| Smith, Neil, K.C. | 0 | 0 | 3 | 0 | 3 |
| Smith, Steve, Raid. | 1 | 3 | 0 | 0 | 3 |

| | Fum. | Own Rec. | Opp. Rec. | Yards | Tot. Rec. |
|---|---|---|---|---|---|
| Smith, Thomas, Buff. | 0 | 0 | 1 | 0 | 1 |
| Speer, Del, Clev. | 1 | 0 | 1 | 0 | 1 |
| Steed, Joel, Pitt. | 0 | 0 | 1 | 0 | 1 |
| Stephens, John, G.B.-K.C. | 1 | 1 | 0 | 0 | 1 |
| Stephens, Rod, Sea. | 0 | 0 | 1 | 0 | 1 |
| Stone, Dwight, Pitt. | 2 | 1 | 0 | 0 | 1 |
| Strzelczyk, Justin, Pitt. | 0 | 0 | 1 | 0 | 1 |
| Stubbs, Danny, Cinn. | 0 | 0 | 1 | 0 | 1 |
| Talley, Darryl, Buff. | 0 | 0 | 2 | 4 | 2 |
| Tasker, Steve, Buff. | 1 | 0 | 1 | 0 | 1 |
| Testaverde, Vinny, Clev. | 4 | 0 | 0 | 0 | 0 |
| Thomas, Blair, N.Y.J. | 0 | 1 | 0 | 0 | 1 |
| Thomas, Derrick, K.C. | 0 | 0 | 1 | 86 | 1 |
| Thomas, Eric, N.Y.J. | 0 | 1 | 0 | 0 | 1 |
| Thomas, Thurman, Buff. | 6 | 1 | 0 | 0 | 1 |
| Thompson, Craig, Cinn. | 0 | 1 | 0 | 0 | 1 |
| Thompson, Leroy, Pitt. | 7 | 1 | 0 | 0 | 1 |
| Tillman, Cedric, Den. | 1 | 1 | 0 | 0 | 1 |
| Timpson, Michael, N.E. | 1 | 0 | 0 | 0 | 0 |
| Tippett, Andre, N.E. | 0 | 0 | 4 | 14 | 4 |
| Tomczak, Mike, Pitt. | 2 | 1 | 0 | 0 | 1 |
| Tovar, Steve, Cinn. | 0 | 0 | 1 | 0 | 1 |
| Trudeau, Jack, Ind. | 2 | 1 | 0 | -3 | 1 |
| Tuatagaloa, Natu, Sea. | 0 | 0 | 1 | 0 | 1 |
| Turk, Daniel, Raid. | 0 | 0 | 1 | 0 | 1 |
| Turner, Kevin, N.E. | 1 | 2 | 0 | 6 | 2 |
| Turner, Marcus, N.Y.J. | 0 | 0 | 1 | 7 | 1 |
| Vardell, Tommy, Clev. | 3 | 0 | 0 | 0 | 0 |
| Vaughn, Jon, Sea. | 1 | 0 | 0 | 0 | 0 |
| Verdin, Clarence, Ind. | 3 | 1 | 0 | 0 | 1 |
| Vincent, Troy, Mia. | 0 | 0 | 1 | 0 | 1 |
| Vinson, Fernandus, Cinn. | 0 | 0 | 3 | 0 | 3 |
| Wallace, Aaron, Raid. | 0 | 0 | 2 | 0 | 2 |
| Warren, Chris, Sea. | 3 | 0 | 0 | 0 | 0 |
| Washington, Brian, N.Y.J. | 0 | 0 | 1 | 0 | 1 |
| Washington, Mickey, Buff. | 0 | 0 | 2 | 6 | 2 |
| Webster, Larry, Mia. | 0 | 0 | 1 | 0 | 1 |
| Weidner, Bert, Mia. | 0 | 1 | 0 | 0 | 1 |
| Wellman, Gary, Hou. | 1 | 0 | 0 | 0 | 0 |
| Wheeler, Leonard, Cinn. | 0 | 0 | 1 | 0 | 1 |
| White, Lorenzo, Hou. | 1 | 0 | 0 | 0 | 0 |
| White, Sheldon, Cinn. | 0 | 0 | 1 | 0 | 1 |
| Wilkerson, Bruce, Raid. | 0 | 1 | 0 | 0 | 1 |
| Williams, Dan, Den. | 0 | 0 | 1 | 0 | 1 |
| Williams, Darryl, Cinn. | 0 | 0 | 2 | 0 | 2 |
| Williams, David, Hou. | 0 | 1 | 0 | 7 | 1 |
| Williams, Harvey, K.C. | 3 | 0 | 0 | 0 | 0 |
| Williams, James, Buff. | 0 | 0 | 2 | 12 | 2 |
| Williams, Jarvis, Mia. | 0 | 0 | 2 | 0 | 2 |
| Williams, John L., Sea. | 2 | 1 | 0 | 0 | 1 |
| Williams, Mike, Mia. | 1 | 0 | 0 | 0 | 0 |
| Williams, Ronnie, Mia. | 0 | 1 | 0 | 0 | 1 |
| Wilson, Karl, N.Y.J. | 0 | 0 | 1 | 0 | 1 |
| Winter, Blaise, S.D. | 0 | 0 | 1 | 0 | 1 |
| Wooden, Terry, Sea. | 0 | 0 | 1 | 0 | 1 |
| Woodson, Rod, Pitt. | 2 | 1 | 0 | 0 | 1 |
| Wright, Jeff, Buff. | 0 | 0 | 1 | 0 | 1 |
| Wyman, David, Den. | 0 | 0 | 2 | 2 | 2 |
| Young, Lonnie, N.Y.J. | 0 | 0 | 1 | 0 | 1 |
| Zgonina, Jeff, Pitt. | 0 | 0 | 1 | 0 | 1 |
| Zimmerman, Gary, Den. | 0 | 1 | 0 | 0 | 1 |

*Yards includes aborted plays, own recoveries, and opponents' recoveries.*

### NFC FUMBLES - INDIVIDUAL

| | Fum. | Own Rec. | Opp. Rec. | Yards | Tot. Rec. |
|---|---|---|---|---|---|
| Aikman, Troy, Dall. | 7 | 3 | 0 | -3 | 3 |
| Alexander, Harold, Atl. | 0 | 1 | 0 | 0 | 1 |
| Anderson, Neal, Chi. | 2 | 1 | 0 | 0 | 1 |
| Anderson, Gary, T.B.-Det. | 4 | 0 | 0 | 0 | 0 |
| Anderson, Willie, Rams | 0 | 1 | 0 | 0 | 1 |
| Armstrong, Trace, Chi. | 0 | 0 | 3 | 3 | 3 |
| Atkins, Gene, N.O. | 0 | 0 | 2 | 4 | 2 |
| Bailey, Carlton, N.Y.G. | 1 | 1 | 0 | 0 | 1 |
| Bailey, Johnny, Phx. | 4 | 0 | 0 | 0 | 0 |
| Baker, Myron, Chi. | 0 | 0 | 2 | 8 | 2 |
| Bankston, Michael, Phx. | 0 | 0 | 5 | 16 | 5 |
| Barker, Roy, Minn. | 0 | 0 | 1 | 0 | 1 |
| Barlow, Corey, Phil. | 0 | 1 | 0 | 0 | 1 |
| Barnett, Fred, Phil. | 1 | 0 | 0 | 0 | 0 |

| | Fum. | Own Rec. | Opp. Rec. | Yards | Tot. Rec. |
|---|---|---|---|---|---|
| Bates, Bill, Dall. | 0 | 0 | 1 | 0 | 1 |
| Beach, Sanjay, S.F. | 0 | 0 | 1 | 0 | 1 |
| Beckles, Ian, T.B. | 0 | 1 | 0 | 0 | 1 |
| Bennett, Edgar, G.B. | 0 | 1 | 0 | 0 | 1 |
| Bettis, Jerome, Rams | 4 | 0 | 0 | 0 | 0 |
| Beuerlein, Steve, Phx. | 8 | 2 | 0 | 0 | 2 |
| Bingham, Guy, Wash. | 1 | 0 | 0 | -9 | 0 |
| Bortz, Mark, Chi. | 0 | 1 | 0 | 0 | 1 |
| Boutte, Marc, Rams | 0 | 0 | 1 | 0 | 1 |
| Bowles, Todd, Wash. | 0 | 0 | 1 | 0 | 1 |
| Boykin, Deral, Rams | 1 | 1 | 1 | 6 | 2 |
| Brandes, John, S.F. | 1 | 0 | 1 | 0 | 1 |
| Brister, Bubby, Phil. | 3 | 0 | 0 | 0 | 0 |
| Brock, Matt, G.B. | 0 | 0 | 1 | 0 | 1 |
| Brooks, Michael, N.Y.G. | 0 | 0 | 1 | 0 | 1 |
| Brooks, Reggie, Wash. | 4 | 1 | 0 | 0 | 1 |
| Brooks, Robert, G.B. | 1 | 1 | 0 | 0 | 1 |
| Brostek, Bern, Rams | 1 | 0 | 0 | 0 | 0 |
| Brown, Derek, N.O. | 1 | 0 | 0 | 0 | 0 |
| Buck, Mike, N.O. | 2 | 0 | 0 | -8 | 0 |
| Buck, Vince, N.O. | 0 | 0 | 2 | 6 | 2 |
| Buckley, Marcus, N.Y.G. | 0 | 0 | 1 | 0 | 1 |
| Buckley, Terrell, G.B. | 1 | 0 | 0 | 0 | 0 |
| Bunch, Jarrod, N.Y.G. | 2 | 0 | 0 | 0 | 0 |
| Bussey, Barney, T.B. | 0 | 0 | 1 | 0 | 1 |
| Butler, LeRoy, G.B. | 0 | 0 | 1 | 25 | 1 |
| Byner, Earnest, Wash. | 0 | 1 | 0 | 0 | 1 |
| Calloway, Chris, N.Y.G. | 0 | 1 | 0 | 0 | 1 |
| Camarillo, Rich, Phx. | 0 | 1 | 0 | 0 | 1 |
| Campen, James, G.B. | 0 | 1 | 0 | 0 | 1 |
| Carter, Anthony, Minn. | 1 | 0 | 0 | 0 | 0 |
| Carter, Cris, Minn. | 0 | 1 | 0 | 0 | 1 |
| Carter, Dexter, S.F. | 5 | 1 | 0 | 0 | 1 |
| Carter, Marty, T.B. | 0 | 0 | 2 | 0 | 2 |
| Casillas, Tony, Dall. | 0 | 0 | 1 | 0 | 1 |
| Centers, Larry, Phx. | 1 | 2 | 0 | 0 | 2 |
| Chandler, Chris, Phx. | 2 | 0 | 0 | 0 | 0 |
| Chmura, Mark, G.B. | 1 | 1 | 0 | 0 | 1 |
| Claiborne, Robert, T.B. | 2 | 0 | 0 | 0 | 0 |
| Clark, Gary, Phx. | 1 | 0 | 0 | 0 | 0 |
| Clark, Vinnie, Atl. | 1 | 0 | 1 | 46 | 1 |
| Clay, Willie, Det. | 0 | 0 | 2 | 54 | 2 |
| Cobb, Reggie, T.B. | 5 | 1 | 0 | 0 | 1 |
| Coleman, Keo, G.B. | 0 | 0 | 1 | 0 | 1 |
| Coleman, Lincoln, Dall. | 1 | 0 | 0 | 0 | 0 |
| Coleman, Monte, Wash. | 0 | 0 | 2 | 29 | 2 |
| Collins, Shane, Wash. | 0 | 0 | 1 | 0 | 1 |
| Conklin, Cary, Wash. | 1 | 0 | 0 | 0 | 0 |
| Conway, Curtis, Chi. | 1 | 0 | 0 | 0 | 0 |
| Cook, Toi, N.O. | 0 | 0 | 3 | 0 | 3 |
| Cooper, Richard, N.O. | 0 | 1 | 0 | 0 | 1 |
| Cox, Ron, Chi. | 0 | 0 | 1 | 0 | 1 |
| Craig, Roger, Minn. | 1 | 0 | 0 | 0 | 0 |
| Crockett, Ray, Det. | 0 | 0 | 1 | 0 | 1 |
| Cross, Howard, N.Y.G. | 0 | 0 | 1 | 0 | 1 |
| Cunningham, Randall, Phil. | 3 | 0 | 0 | 0 | 0 |
| Cunningham, Rick, Phx. | 0 | 1 | 0 | 0 | 1 |
| Curry, Eric, T.B. | 0 | 0 | 1 | 0 | 1 |
| Dalman, Chris, S.F. | 0 | 1 | 0 | 0 | 1 |
| Davis, Eric, S.F. | 0 | 0 | 1 | 47 | 1 |
| Davis, Reuben, Phx. | 0 | 0 | 1 | 0 | 1 |
| DeLong, Keith, S.F. | 0 | 0 | 1 | 0 | 1 |
| Dickerson, Eric, Atl. | 0 | 1 | 0 | 0 | 1 |
| Dill, Scott, T.B. | 0 | 1 | 0 | 0 | 1 |
| Doleman, Chris, Minn. | 0 | 0 | 1 | 0 | 1 |
| Dowdell, Marcus, N.O. | 1 | 0 | 0 | 0 | 0 |
| Drayton, Troy, Rams | 1 | 0 | 0 | 0 | 0 |
| Dukes, Jamie, Atl. | 0 | 0 | 1 | 0 | 1 |
| Early, Quinn, N.O. | 1 | 0 | 0 | 0 | 0 |
| Eatman, Irv, Rams | 0 | 1 | 0 | 0 | 1 |
| Edwards, Brad, Wash. | 0 | 0 | 1 | 0 | 1 |
| Edwards, Dixon, Dall. | 0 | 0 | 1 | 0 | 1 |
| Eilers, Pat, Wash. | 0 | 0 | 3 | 0 | 3 |
| Elewonibi, Mohammed, Wash. | 0 | 2 | 0 | 10 | 2 |
| Erickson, Craig, T.B. | 9 | 6 | 0 | -2 | 6 |
| Ervins, Ricky, Wash. | 2 | 0 | 0 | 0 | 0 |
| Evans, Byron, Phil. | 0 | 0 | 3 | 30 | 3 |
| Evans, Doug, G.B. | 0 | 0 | 2 | 0 | 2 |
| Everett, Jim, Rams | 7 | 1 | 0 | -1 | 1 |
| Favre, Brett, G.B. | 14 | 2 | 0 | -1 | 2 |
| Feagles, Jeff, Phil. | 0 | 1 | 0 | 0 | 1 |
| Flores, Mike, Phil. | 0 | 0 | 1 | 0 | 1 |
| Floyd, Eric, Phil. | 0 | 1 | 0 | 5 | 1 |
| Fontenot, Jerry, Chi. | 0 | 1 | 0 | 0 | 1 |
| Fox, Mike, N.Y.G. | 0 | 0 | 1 | 2 | 1 |
| Gannon, Rich, Wash. | 3 | 1 | 0 | 0 | 1 |
| Gardocki, Chris, Chi. | 1 | 1 | 0 | 0 | 1 |
| Garrett, Jason, Dall. | 1 | 0 | 0 | -2 | 0 |
| Gary, Cleveland, Rams | 1 | 0 | 0 | 0 | 0 |
| Gedney, Chris, Chi. | 1 | 0 | 0 | 0 | 0 |
| Gibson, Dennis, Det. | 0 | 0 | 1 | 2 | 1 |
| Gordon, Dwayne, Atl. | 1 | 0 | 0 | 0 | 0 |
| Gray, Jerry, T.B. | 0 | 1 | 0 | 3 | 1 |
| Gray, Mel, Det. | 3 | 0 | 0 | 0 | 0 |
| Green, Darrell, Wash. | 0 | 0 | 2 | 86 | 2 |
| Guliford, Eric, Minn. | 1 | 0 | 0 | 0 | 0 |
| Guyton, Myron, N.Y.G. | 0 | 1 | 0 | 0 | 1 |
| Haley, Charles, Dall. | 0 | 0 | 1 | 0 | 1 |
| Hamilton, Keith, N.Y.G. | 0 | 0 | 1 | 10 | 1 |
| Hamilton, Rick, Wash. | 0 | 0 | 1 | 0 | 1 |
| Hampton, Rodney, N.Y.G. | 2 | 1 | 0 | 0 | 1 |
| Hanks, Merton, S.F. | 0 | 1 | 0 | 0 | 1 |
| Harbaugh, Jim, Chi. | 15 | 4 | 0 | -1 | 4 |
| Harmon, Andy, Phil. | 0 | 0 | 2 | 0 | 2 |
| Harper, Alvin, Dall. | 1 | 0 | 0 | 0 | 0 |
| Harper, Roger, Atl. | 1 | 0 | 1 | 0 | 1 |
| Hauck, Tim, G.B. | 0 | 0 | 1 | 0 | 1 |
| Hawkins, Courtney, T.B. | 2 | 0 | 0 | 0 | 0 |
| Haynes, Michael, Atl. | 1 | 0 | 0 | 0 | 0 |
| Hearst, Garrison, Phx. | 2 | 0 | 0 | 0 | 0 |
| Hebert, Bobby, Atl. | 11 | 3 | 0 | -9 | 3 |
| Hebron, Vaughn, Phil. | 5 | 1 | 0 | 0 | 1 |
| Henley, Darryl, Rams | 0 | 0 | 1 | 0 | 1 |
| Heyward, Craig, Chi. | 1 | 0 | 0 | 0 | 0 |
| Hilgenberg, Jay, N.O. | 1 | 0 | 0 | -2 | 0 |
| Hilgenberg, Joel, N.O. | 1 | 0 | 0 | -19 | 0 |
| Hill, Eric, Phx. | 0 | 0 | 1 | 0 | 1 |
| Hilliard, Dalton, N.O. | 2 | 3 | 0 | 0 | 3 |
| Holland, Johnny, G.B. | 2 | 0 | 2 | 0 | 2 |
| Holman, Rodney, Det. | 1 | 0 | 0 | 0 | 0 |
| Holmes, Lester, Phil. | 0 | 1 | 0 | 0 | 1 |
| Hopkins, Wes, Phil. | 0 | 0 | 2 | 8 | 2 |
| Hudson, John, Phil. | 1 | 0 | 0 | -14 | 0 |
| Irwin, Tim, Minn. | 0 | 1 | 0 | 0 | 1 |
| Ismail, Qadry, Minn. | 1 | 0 | 0 | 0 | 0 |
| Jackson, Greg, N.Y.G. | 0 | 1 | 2 | 3 | 3 |
| Jackson, Mark, N.Y.G. | 1 | 0 | 0 | 0 | 0 |
| Jackson, Rickey, N.O. | 0 | 0 | 3 | 3 | 3 |
| Jeffries, Greg, Det. | 0 | 1 | 0 | 0 | 1 |
| Jenkins, Carlos, Minn. | 0 | 0 | 1 | 0 | 1 |
| Jenkins, Mel, Atl. | 0 | 0 | 1 | 0 | 1 |
| Jennings, Keith, Chi. | 1 | 1 | 0 | 0 | 1 |
| Johnson, A. J., Wash. | 0 | 1 | 0 | 0 | 1 |
| Johnson, John, S.F. | 0 | 0 | 1 | 7 | 1 |
| Johnson, Maurice, Phil. | 1 | 1 | 0 | 0 | 1 |
| Johnson, Tim, Wash. | 0 | 0 | 1 | 0 | 1 |
| Johnston, Daryl, Dall. | 1 | 1 | 0 | 0 | 1 |
| Jones, Brent, S.F. | 2 | 2 | 0 | 0 | 2 |
| Jones, Dante, Chi. | 1 | 1 | 2 | 32 | 3 |
| Jones, Roger, T.B. | 0 | 1 | 2 | 12 | 3 |
| Kauahi, Kani, Phx. | 1 | 0 | 0 | -35 | 0 |
| Kelm, Larry, S.F. | 1 | 1 | 0 | 0 | 1 |
| Kennedy, Lincoln, Atl. | 0 | 1 | 0 | 0 | 1 |
| Kinchen, Todd, Rams | 1 | 0 | 0 | 0 | 0 |
| King, Joe, T.B. | 0 | 0 | 2 | 0 | 2 |
| Koonce, George, G.B. | 0 | 0 | 1 | 0 | 1 |
| Kosar, Bernie, Clev.-Dall. | 6 | 3 | 0 | -13 | 3 |
| Kramer, Erik, Det. | 1 | 0 | 0 | 0 | 0 |
| Lassic, Derrick, Dall. | 2 | 1 | 0 | 0 | 1 |
| LeBel, Harper, Atl. | 1 | 0 | 0 | -26 | 0 |
| Lee, Amp, S.F. | 1 | 0 | 0 | 0 | 0 |
| Lee, Carl, Minn. | 0 | 0 | 1 | 0 | 1 |
| Lett, Leon, Dall. | 1 | 0 | 0 | 0 | 0 |
| Logan, Marc, S.F. | 2 | 1 | 0 | 0 | 1 |
| Lyght, Todd, Rams | 0 | 0 | 1 | 13 | 1 |
| Lynch, Eric, Det. | 1 | 0 | 0 | 0 | 0 |
| Lynch, Lorenzo, Phx. | 0 | 0 | 3 | 55 | 3 |
| Marion, Brock, Dall. | 0 | 0 | 1 | 0 | 1 |
| Martin, Chris, Rams | 0 | 0 | 1 | 0 | 1 |
| Martin, Wayne, N.O. | 0 | 0 | 2 | 7 | 2 |
| Maryland, Russell, Dall. | 0 | 0 | 2 | 0 | 2 |
| Massey, Robert, Phx. | 0 | 0 | 2 | 0 | 2 |

# 1993 INDIVIDUAL STATISTICS

| | Fum. | Own Rec. | Opp. Rec. | Yards | Tot. Rec. |
|---|---|---|---|---|---|
| May, Mark, Phx. | 0 | 1 | 0 | 0 | 1 |
| Mayberry, Tony, T.B. | 1 | 1 | 0 | -6 | 1 |
| Mays, Alvoid, Wash. | 1 | 0 | 0 | 0 | 0 |
| McAfee, Fred, N.O. | 3 | 0 | 0 | 0 | 0 |
| McDonald, Tim, S.F. | 0 | 0 | 1 | 15 | 1 |
| McDowell, Anthony, T.B. | 2 | 1 | 0 | 0 | 1 |
| McIntyre, Guy, S.F. | 0 | 2 | 0 | 0 | 2 |
| McKyer, Tim, Det. | 0 | 0 | 1 | 23 | 1 |
| McMahon, Jim, Minn. | 4 | 1 | 0 | -7 | 1 |
| McMichael, Steve, Chi. | 0 | 0 | 2 | 0 | 2 |
| McMillian, Audray, Minn. | 0 | 0 | 1 | 0 | 1 |
| McMillian, Mark, Phil. | 1 | 0 | 1 | 0 | 1 |
| McNeal, Travis, Rams | 0 | 1 | 0 | 0 | 1 |
| Meggett, David, N.Y.G. | 1 | 1 | 0 | 0 | 1 |
| Miano, Rich, Phil. | 0 | 0 | 1 | 0 | 1 |
| Middleton, Ron, Wash. | 0 | 1 | 0 | 0 | 1 |
| Millard, Keith, Phil. | 0 | 0 | 1 | 0 | 1 |
| Miller, Chris, Atl. | 2 | 0 | 0 | 0 | 0 |
| Miller, Corey, N.Y.G. | 1 | 0 | 2 | 0 | 2 |
| Mills, Sam, N.O. | 0 | 0 | 1 | 30 | 1 |
| Mitchell, Brian, Wash. | 3 | 1 | 0 | 0 | 1 |
| Moore, Dave, T.B. | 0 | 0 | 1 | 0 | 1 |
| Moore, Derrick, Det. | 4 | 3 | 0 | 0 | 3 |
| Moore, Herman, Det. | 2 | 0 | 0 | 0 | 0 |
| Moore, Ron, Phx. | 3 | 1 | 0 | 0 | 1 |
| Morrissey, Jim, G.B. | 0 | 0 | 1 | 0 | 1 |
| Muster, Brad, N.O. | 0 | 0 | 1 | 0 | 1 |
| Neal, Lorenzo, N.O. | 1 | 0 | 0 | 0 | 0 |
| Ned, Derrick, N.O. | 1 | 0 | 0 | 0 | 0 |
| Newberry, Tom, Rams | 0 | 1 | 0 | 0 | 1 |
| Nickerson, Hardy, T.B. | 0 | 0 | 1 | 0 | 1 |
| Noble, Brian, G.B. | 0 | 0 | 1 | 0 | 1 |
| Noga, Al, Wash. | 0 | 0 | 1 | 0 | 1 |
| Norton, Ken, Dall. | 0 | 0 | 1 | 3 | 1 |
| Novacek, Jay, Dall. | 3 | 1 | 0 | 0 | 1 |
| Nunn, Freddie Joe, Phx. | 0 | 0 | 1 | 0 | 1 |
| Obee, Terry, Chi. | 1 | 1 | 0 | 0 | 1 |
| O'Brien, Ken, Phil. | 4 | 0 | 0 | 0 | 0 |
| Owens, Dan, Det. | 0 | 0 | 2 | 17 | 2 |
| Peete, Rodney, Det. | 11 | 4 | 0 | -8 | 4 |
| Pegram, Erric, Atl. | 6 | 4 | 0 | 0 | 4 |
| Perriman, Brett, Det. | 1 | 0 | 0 | 0 | 0 |
| Pete, Lawrence, Det. | 0 | 0 | 2 | 0 | 2 |
| Phifer, Roman, Rams | 0 | 0 | 2 | 10 | 2 |
| Pierce, Aaron, N.Y.G. | 2 | 0 | 0 | 0 | 0 |
| Port, Chris, N.O. | 0 | 1 | 0 | 0 | 1 |
| Prior, Mike, G.B. | 3 | 2 | 0 | 0 | 2 |
| Pritchard, Mike, Atl. | 1 | 0 | 0 | 0 | 0 |
| Proehl, Ricky, Phx. | 1 | 0 | 0 | 0 | 0 |
| Reeves, Walter, Phx. | 0 | 1 | 0 | 0 | 1 |
| Rice, Jerry, S.F. | 3 | 1 | 0 | 0 | 1 |
| Richards, David, Det. | 0 | 1 | 0 | 0 | 1 |
| Rison, Andre, Atl. | 2 | 0 | 0 | 0 | 0 |
| Roberts, William, N.Y.G. | 0 | 1 | 0 | 0 | 1 |
| Roby, Reggie, Wash. | 0 | 1 | 0 | 0 | 1 |
| Romanowski, Bill, S.F. | 0 | 0 | 1 | 0 | 1 |
| Roper, John, Phil. | 0 | 0 | 1 | 0 | 1 |
| Rose, Ken, Phil. | 0 | 1 | 0 | 0 | 1 |
| Rubley, T. J., Rams | 4 | 2 | 0 | -18 | 2 |
| Rucker, Keith, Phx. | 0 | 0 | 1 | 0 | 1 |
| Ruettgers, Ken, G.B. | 0 | 2 | 0 | 0 | 2 |
| Russell, Damien, S.F. | 0 | 0 | 1 | 0 | 1 |
| Rypien, Mark, Wash. | 7 | 0 | 0 | -2 | 0 |
| Salisbury, Sean, Minn. | 3 | 1 | 0 | -9 | 1 |
| Sanders, Barry, Det. | 3 | 3 | 0 | 0 | 3 |
| Sanders, Ricky, Wash. | 1 | 1 | 0 | 0 | 1 |
| Schad, Mike, Phil. | 0 | 1 | 0 | 0 | 1 |
| Schlereth, Mark, Wash. | 0 | 1 | 0 | 0 | 1 |
| Scott, Kevin, Det. | 0 | 0 | 1 | 22 | 1 |
| Scott, Todd, Minn. | 0 | 0 | 1 | 0 | 1 |
| Scroggins, Tracy, Det. | 0 | 0 | 1 | 0 | 1 |
| Seals, Ray, T.B. | 0 | 0 | 1 | 0 | 1 |
| Sharpe, Sterling, G.B. | 1 | 0 | 0 | 0 | 0 |
| Sherman, Heath, Phil. | 3 | 0 | 0 | 0 | 0 |
| Sikahema, Vai, Phil. | 4 | 0 | 0 | 0 | 0 |
| Simmons, Ed, Wash. | 0 | 1 | 0 | 0 | 1 |
| Simmons, Wayne, G.B. | 0 | 1 | 0 | 0 | 1 |
| Simms, Phil, N.Y.G. | 7 | 3 | 0 | -13 | 3 |
| Smith, Chuck, Atl. | 0 | 0 | 2 | 0 | 2 |
| Smith, Darrin, Dall. | 0 | 0 | 1 | 0 | 1 |
| Smith, Emmitt, Dall. | 4 | 3 | 0 | 0 | 3 |
| Smith, Irv, N.O. | 1 | 1 | 0 | 0 | 1 |
| Smith, Kevin, Dall. | 0 | 0 | 1 | 14 | 1 |
| Smith, Lance, Phx. | 0 | 2 | 0 | 0 | 2 |
| Smith, Tony, Atl. | 4 | 1 | 0 | 0 | 1 |
| Solomon, Jesse, Atl. | 0 | 0 | 1 | 0 | 1 |
| Spencer, Jimmy, N.O. | 0 | 0 | 3 | 53 | 3 |
| Spielman, Chris, Det. | 0 | 0 | 2 | 0 | 2 |
| Spindler, Marc, Det. | 0 | 0 | 2 | 0 | 2 |
| Stepnoski, Mark, Dall. | 1 | 0 | 0 | -1 | 0 |
| Stokes, Fred, Rams | 0 | 0 | 2 | 51 | 2 |
| Strickland, Fred, Minn. | 0 | 0 | 4 | 4 | 4 |
| Swann, Eric, Phx. | 0 | 0 | 1 | 0 | 1 |
| Swilling, Pat, Det. | 0 | 0 | 1 | 0 | 1 |
| Sydner, Jeff, Phil. | 3 | 0 | 0 | 0 | 0 |
| Tamm, Ralph, S.F. | 0 | 1 | 0 | 1 | 1 |
| Tate, David, N.Y.G. | 1 | 0 | 0 | 0 | 0 |
| Taylor, John, S.F. | 1 | 0 | 0 | 0 | 0 |
| Taylor, Keith, N.O. | 0 | 1 | 0 | 0 | 1 |
| Taylor, Lawrence, N.Y.G. | 0 | 0 | 1 | 0 | 1 |
| Teague, George, G.B. | 0 | 0 | 2 | 0 | 2 |
| Thomas, Broderick, T.B. | 0 | 0 | 1 | 0 | 1 |
| Thomas, Johnny, Wash. | 0 | 1 | 1 | 0 | 2 |
| Thomas, Mark, S.F. | 0 | 0 | 1 | 0 | 1 |
| Thomas, William, Phil. | 0 | 0 | 3 | 0 | 3 |
| Thompson, Darrell, G.B. | 2 | 1 | 0 | 0 | 1 |
| Tice, Mike, Minn. | 1 | 0 | 0 | 0 | 0 |
| Tillman, Lewis, N.Y.G. | 1 | 0 | 0 | -19 | 0 |
| Tippins, Kenny, Atl. | 0 | 0 | 1 | 0 | 1 |
| Tuggle, Jessie, Atl. | 0 | 0 | 1 | 0 | 1 |
| Tuinei, Mark, Dall. | 0 | 1 | 0 | 0 | 1 |
| Turnbull, Renaldo, N.O. | 0 | 0 | 2 | 0 | 2 |
| Turner, Odessa, S.F. | 1 | 0 | 0 | 0 | 0 |
| Turner, Vernon, Det. | 1 | 0 | 0 | 0 | 0 |
| Walker, Herschel, Phil. | 3 | 2 | 0 | 0 | 2 |
| Wallace, Steve, S.F. | 0 | 0 | 1 | 0 | 1 |
| Walls, Wesley, S.F. | 0 | 1 | 0 | 0 | 1 |
| Warren, Frank, N.O. | 0 | 0 | 1 | 47 | 1 |
| Washington, Charles, Atl. | 0 | 0 | 2 | 0 | 2 |
| Washington, James, Dall. | 1 | 0 | 1 | 0 | 1 |
| Washington, Ted, S.F. | 0 | 0 | 1 | 0 | 1 |
| Watters, Ricky, S.F. | 5 | 1 | 0 | 0 | 1 |
| White, Reggie, G.B. | 0 | 1 | 1 | 10 | 2 |
| Whitfield, Bob, Atl. | 0 | 2 | 0 | 0 | 2 |
| Williams, Aeneas, Phx. | 0 | 0 | 2 | 20 | 2 |
| Williams, Jimmy, T.B. | 0 | 0 | 1 | 0 | 1 |
| Williams, Kevin, Dall. | 8 | 4 | 0 | 0 | 4 |
| Willis, James, G.B. | 0 | 1 | 0 | 0 | 1 |
| Willis, Peter Tom, Chi. | 2 | 1 | 0 | 0 | 1 |
| Wilmsmeyer, Klaus, S.F. | 2 | 1 | 0 | -10 | 1 |
| Wilson, Charles, T.B. | 1 | 2 | 0 | 0 | 2 |
| Wilson, Marcus, G.B. | 1 | 0 | 1 | 0 | 1 |
| Wilson, Wade, N.O. | 9 | 4 | 0 | -3 | 4 |
| Wojciechowski, John, Chi. | 0 | 2 | 0 | 0 | 2 |
| Woodson, Darren, Dall. | 0 | 0 | 3 | 3 | 3 |
| Word, Barry, Minn. | 3 | 0 | 0 | 0 | 0 |
| Workman, Vince, T.B. | 2 | 1 | 0 | 0 | 1 |
| Worley, Tim, Chi. | 3 | 0 | 0 | 0 | 0 |
| Wycheck, Frank, Wash. | 1 | 1 | 0 | 0 | 1 |
| Young, Steve, S.F. | 8 | 2 | 0 | -4 | 2 |
| Zorich, Chris, Chi. | 0 | 0 | 2 | 0 | 2 |

*Yards includes aborted plays, own recoveries, and opponents' recoveries.*

## SACKS

**Most Sacks**

**AFC:** 15.0—Neil Smith, Kansas City
**NFC:** 13.0—Renaldo Turnbull, New Orleans
Reggie White, Green Bay

**Most Sacks, Game**

**AFC:** 4.0—Anthony Smith, Raiders at Seattle, September 12
Neil Smith, Kansas City vs. Raiders, October 3
William Fuller, Houston vs. Pittsburgh, November 28
**NFC:** 4.0—Sean Gilbert, Rams vs. Pittsburgh, September 12

**Team Champion**

**AFC:** 52—Houston
**NFC:** 51—New Orleans

### AFC SACKS—TEAM

| | Sacks | Yards |
|---|---|---|
| Houston | 52 | 313 |
| Cleveland | 48 | 342 |
| Denver | 46 | 238 |
| L.A. Raiders | 45 | 283 |
| Pittsburgh | 42 | 277 |
| Seattle | 38 | 244 |
| Buffalo | 37 | 256 |
| Kansas City | 35 | 228 |
| New England | 34 | 242 |
| San Diego | 32 | 206 |
| N.Y. Jets | 32 | 195 |
| Miami | 29 | 197 |
| Cincinnati | 22 | 154 |
| Indianapolis | 21 | 121 |
| AFC Total | 513 | 3296 |
| AFC Average | 36.6 | 235.4 |

### NFC SACKS—TEAM

| | Sacks | Yards |
|---|---|---|
| New Orleans | 51 | 318 |
| Green Bay | 46 | 301 |
| Chicago | 46 | 287 |
| Minnesota | 45 | 276 |
| San Francisco | 44 | 316 |
| Detroit | 43 | 253 |
| N.Y. Giants | 41 | 238 |
| Philadelphia | 36 | 214 |
| L.A. Rams | 35 | 203 |
| Phoenix | 34 | 205 |
| Dallas | 34 | 231 |
| Washington | 31 | 197 |
| Tampa Bay | 29 | 132 |
| Atlanta | 27 | 149 |
| NFC Total | 542 | 3320 |
| NFC Average | 38.7 | 237.1 |
| League Total | 1055 | 6616 |
| League Average | 37.7 | 236.3 |

### NFL TOP TEN LEADERS - SACKS

| | Total |
|---|---|
| Smith, Neil, K.C. | 15.0 |
| Smith, Bruce, Buff. | 14.0 |
| Fletcher, Simon, Den. | 13.5 |
| Jones, Sean, Hou. | 13.0 |
| Turnbull, Renaldo, N.O. | 13.0 |
| White, Reggie, G.B. | 13.0 |
| Dent, Richard, Chi. | 12.5 |
| Doleman, Chris, Minn. | 12.5 |
| Greene, Kevin, Pitt. | 12.5 |
| Randle, John, Minn. | 12.5 |
| Smith, Anthony, Raid. | 12.5 |

### AFC SACKS—INDIVIDUAL

| | |
|---|---|
| Smith, Neil, K.C. | 15.0 |
| Smith, Bruce, Buff. | 14.0 |
| Fletcher, Simon, Den. | 13.5 |
| Jones, Sean, Hou. | 13.0 |
| Greene, Kevin, Pitt. | 12.5 |
| Smith, Anthony, Raid. | 12.5 |
| O'Neal, Leslie, S.D. | 12.0 |
| Pleasant, Anthony, Clev. | 11.0 |
| Cross, Jeff, Mia. | 10.5 |
| Fuller, William, Hou. | 10.0 |
| Burnett, Rob, Clev. | 9.0 |
| Childress, Ray, Hou. | 9.0 |
| Mecklenburg, Karl, Den. | 9.0 |
| Slade, Chris, N.E. | 9.0 |
| Lageman, Jeff, N.Y.J. | 8.5 |
| Tippett, Andre, N.E. | 8.5 |
| Sinclair, Mike, Sea. | 8.0 |
| Thomas, Derrick, K.C. | 8.0 |
| Townsend, Greg, Raid. | 7.5 |
| Dronett, Shane, Den. | 7.0 |
| McGlockton, Chester, Raid. | 7.0 |
| Mims, Chris, S.D. | 7.0 |
| Evans, Donald, Pitt. | 6.5 |
| Kennedy, Cortez, Sea. | 6.5 |
| Lloyd, Greg, Pitt. | 6.0 |
| Long, Howie, Raid. | 6.0 |
| Montgomery, Glenn, Hou. | 6.0 |
| Perry, Michael Dean, Clev. | 6.0 |
| Coleman, Marco, Mia. | 5.5 |
| Hand, Jon, Ind. | 5.5 |
| Jones, James, Clev. | 5.5 |
| Matthews, Clay, Clev. | 5.5 |
| Washington, Marvin, N.Y.J. | 5.5 |
| Bennett, Cornelius, Buff. | 5.0 |
| Cox, Bryan, Mia. | 5.0 |
| Croel, Mike, Den. | 5.0 |
| Lake, Carnell, Pitt. | 5.0 |
| Stubbs, Danny, Cinn. | 5.0 |
| Grossman, Burt, S.D. | 4.5 |
| Wright, Jeff, Buff. | 4.5 |
| Johnson, Mike, Clev. | 4.0 |
| Lewis, Mo, N.Y.J. | 4.0 |
| McCrary, Michael, Sea. | 4.0 |
| Williams, Alfred, Cinn. | 4.0 |
| Bickett, Duane, Ind. | 3.5 |
| Hansen, Phil, Buff. | 3.5 |
| Jones, Aaron, N.E. | 3.5 |
| Robinson, Jeff, Den. | 3.5 |
| Saleaumua, Dan, K.C. | 3.5 |
| Tuatagaloa, Natu, Sea. | 3.5 |
| Ball, Jerry, Clev. | 3.0 |
| Brown, Chad, Pitt. | 3.0 |
| Copeland, John, Cinn. | 3.0 |
| Edwards, Antonio, Sea. | 3.0 |
| Harrison, Nolan, Raid. | 3.0 |
| Houston, Bobby, N.Y.J. | 3.0 |
| Hunter, Jeff, Mia. | 3.0 |
| Kragen, Greg, Den. | 3.0 |
| Krumrie, Tim, Cinn. | 3.0 |
| Lee, Shawn, S.D. | 3.0 |
| Pitts, Mike, N.E. | 3.0 |
| Williams, Lee, Hou. | 3.0 |
| Davidson, Kenny, Pitt. | 2.5 |
| Stephens, Rod, Sea. | 2.5 |
| Wooden, Terry, Sea. | 2.5 |
| Barnett, Oliver, Buff. | 2.0 |
| Bruce, Aundray, Raid. | 2.0 |
| Francis, James, Cinn. | 2.0 |
| Herrod, Jeff, Ind. | 2.0 |
| Jones, Henry, Buff. | 2.0 |
| Lathon, Lamar, Hou. | 2.0 |
| Marshall, Leonard, N.Y.J. | 2.0 |
| Marshall, Wilber, Hou. | 2.0 |
| Marts, Lonnie, K.C. | 2.0 |
| Peguese, Willis, Ind. | 2.0 |
| Richard, Stanley, S.D. | 2.0 |
| Robinson, Eugene, Sea. | 2.0 |
| Sabb, Dwayne, N.E. | 2.0 |
| Talley, Darryl, Buff. | 2.0 |
| Veasey, Craig, Mia. | 2.0 |
| Wallace, Aaron, Raid. | 2.0 |
| Williams, Brent, N.E. | 2.0 |
| Williams, Darryl, Cinn. | 2.0 |
| Winter, Blaise, S.D. | 2.0 |
| Woodson, Rod, Pitt. | 2.0 |
| Wyman, David, Den. | 2.0 |
| Agnew, Ray, N.E. | 1.5 |
| Klingbeil, Chuck, Mia. | 1.5 |
| McClendon, Skip, Ind. | 1.5 |
| Phillips, Joe, K.C. | 1.5 |
| Robinson, Rafael, Sea. | 1.5 |
| Siragusa, Tony, Ind. | 1.5 |
| Steed, Joel, Pitt. | 1.5 |
| Alexander, Bruce, Mia. | 1.0 |
| Anderson, Eddie, Raid. | 1.0 |
| Atwater, Steve, Den. | 1.0 |
| Barrow, Micheal, Hou. | 1.0 |
| Bayless, Martin, K.C. | 1.0 |
| Bishop, Blaine, Hou. | 1.0 |
| Bowden, Joe, Hou. | 1.0 |
| Broughton, Willie, Raid. | 1.0 |
| Brown, Vincent, N.E. | 1.0 |
| Bryant, Jeff, Sea. | 1.0 |
| Carrington, Darren, S.D. | 1.0 |
| Clancy, Sam, Ind. | 1.0 |
| Clifton, Kyle, N.Y.J. | 1.0 |
| Collins, Todd, N.E. | 1.0 |
| Coryatt, Quentin, Ind. | 1.0 |
| Emtman, Steve, Ind. | 1.0 |
| Footman, Dan, Clev. | 1.0 |
| Frase, Paul, N.Y.J. | 1.0 |
| Frier, Mike, Cinn. | 1.0 |
| Goganious, Keith, Buff. | 1.0 |
| Gray, Carlton, Sea. | 1.0 |
| Henry, Kevin, Pitt. | 1.0 |
| Hinkle, George, Cinn. | 1.0 |
| Hurst, Maurice, N.E. | 1.0 |
| Johnson, Pepper, Clev. | 1.0 |
| Johnson, William, Clev. | 1.0 |
| Jones, Don, N.Y.J. | 1.0 |
| Kelly, Joe, Raid. | 1.0 |
| Kirkland, Levon, Pitt. | 1.0 |
| Lott, Ronnie, N.Y.J. | 1.0 |
| McDonald, Ricardo, Cinn. | 1.0 |
| McDowell, Bubba, Hou. | 1.0 |
| Mersereau, Scott, N.Y.J. | 1.0 |
| Mickell, Darren, K.C. | 1.0 |
| Newton, Tim, K.C. | 1.0 |
| Oshodin, Willie, Den. | 1.0 |
| Parrella, John, Buff. | 1.0 |
| Patton, Marvcus, Buff. | 1.0 |
| Porter, Rufus, Sea. | 1.0 |
| Robinson, Eddie, Hou. | 1.0 |
| Rodgers, Tyrone, Sea. | 1.0 |
| Sims, Tom, Ind. | 1.0 |
| Stargell, Tony, Ind. | 1.0 |
| Teeter, Mike, Hou. | 1.0 |
| Terry, Doug, K.C. | 1.0 |
| Thompson, Reyna, N.E. | 1.0 |
| Turner, Marcus, N.Y.J. | 1.0 |
| Walls, Everson, Clev. | 1.0 |
| Washington, Lionel, Raid. | 1.0 |
| Williams, Dan, Den. | 1.0 |
| Williams, Gerald, Pitt. | 1.0 |
| Young, Lonnie, N.Y.J. | 1.0 |
| Goad, Tim, N.E. | 0.5 |
| Griggs, David, Mia. | 0.5 |
| Lodish, Mike, Buff. | 0.5 |
| Nash, Joe, Sea. | 0.5 |
| Pope, Marquez, S.D. | 0.5 |
| Ross, Kevin, K.C. | 0.5 |
| Thompson, Bennie, K.C. | 0.5 |
| Washington, Mickey, Buff. | 0.5 |

### NFC SACKS—INDIVIDUAL

| | |
|---|---|
| Turnbull, Renaldo, N.O. | 13.0 |
| White, Reggie, G.B. | 13.0 |
| Dent, Richard, Chi. | 12.5 |
| Doleman, Chris, Minn. | 12.5 |
| Randle, John, Minn. | 12.5 |
| Armstrong, Trace, Chi. | 11.5 |
| Hamilton, Keith, N.Y.G. | 11.5 |
| Harmon, Andy, Phil. | 11.5 |
| Jackson, Rickey, N.O. | 11.5 |
| Paup, Bryce, G.B. | 11.0 |

## 1993 INDIVIDUAL STATISTICS

| | |
|---|---|
| Gilbert, Sean, Rams | 10.5 |
| Stubblefield, Dana, S.F. | 10.5 |
| Harvey, Ken, Phx. | 9.5 |
| Stokes, Fred, Rams | 9.5 |
| Thomas, Henry, Minn. | 9.0 |
| Porcher, Robert, Det. | 8.5 |
| Seals, Ray, T.B. | 8.5 |
| Scroggins, Tracy, Det. | 8.0 |
| Tolbert, Tony, Dall. | 7.5 |
| Young, Robert, Rams | 7.0 |
| Zorich, Chris, Chi. | 7.0 |
| Bennett, Tony, G.B. | 6.5 |
| Holt, Pierce, Atl. | 6.5 |
| Miller, Corey, N.Y.G. | 6.5 |
| Nunn, Freddie Joe, Phx. | 6.5 |
| Swilling, Pat, Det. | 6.5 |
| Thomas, William, Phil. | 6.5 |
| Barker, Roy, Minn. | 6.0 |
| Coleman, Monte, Wash. | 6.0 |
| Collins, Andre, Wash. | 6.0 |
| Harrison, Martin, S.F. | 6.0 |
| Jeffcoat, Jim, Dall. | 6.0 |
| McMichael, Steve, Chi. | 6.0 |
| Taylor, Lawrence, N.Y.G. | 6.0 |
| Brown, Dennis, S.F. | 5.5 |
| Jones, Jimmie, Dall. | 5.5 |
| Jurkovic, John, G.B. | 5.5 |
| Wilson, Troy, S.F. | 5.5 |
| Curry, Eric, T.B. | 5.0 |
| Dotson, Santana, T.B. | 5.0 |
| Johnson, Vaughan, N.O. | 5.0 |
| Martin, Wayne, N.O. | 5.0 |
| Simmons, Clyde, Phil. | 5.0 |
| Fox, Mike, N.Y.G. | 4.5 |
| Palmer, Sterling, Wash. | 4.5 |
| Haley, Charles, Dall. | 4.0 |
| Johnson, Tim, Wash. | 4.0 |
| Millard, Keith, Phil. | 4.0 |
| Noga, Al, Wash. | 4.0 |
| Pritchett, Kelvin, Det. | 4.0 |
| Geathers, James, Atl. | 3.5 |
| Howard, Erik, N.Y.G. | 3.5 |
| Smith, Chuck, Atl. | 3.5 |
| Swann, Eric, Phx. | 3.5 |
| Bankston, Michael, Phx. | 3.0 |
| Booty, John, Phx. | 3.0 |
| Buck, Vince, N.O. | 3.0 |
| Dillard, Stacey, N.Y.G. | 3.0 |
| Flores, Mike, Phil. | 3.0 |
| Jones, Mike, Phx. | 3.0 |
| Koonce, George, G.B. | 3.0 |
| Owens, Dan, Det. | 3.0 |
| Price, Shawn, T.B. | 3.0 |
| Robinson, Gerald, Rams | 3.0 |
| Romanowski, Bill, S.F. | 3.0 |
| Washington, Ted, S.F. | 3.0 |
| Wilson, Karl, S.F. | 3.0 |
| Agee, Mel, Atl. | 2.5 |
| Jenkins, Carlos, Minn. | 2.5 |
| Maryland, Russell, Dall. | 2.5 |
| Miller, Les, N.O. | 2.5 |
| Spellman, Alonzo, Chi. | 2.5 |
| Allen, Eric, Phil. | 2.0 |
| Brock, Matt, G.B. | 2.0 |
| Casillas, Tony, Dall. | 2.0 |
| Cox, Ron, Chi. | 2.0 |
| Gardner, Moe, Atl. | 2.0 |
| Goff, Robert, N.O. | 2.0 |
| Hayworth, Tracy, Det. | 2.0 |
| Holland, Johnny, G.B. | 2.0 |
| Jamison, George, Det. | 2.0 |
| Johnson, John, S.F. | 2.0 |
| Joyner, Seth, Phil. | 2.0 |
| Mills, Sam, N.O. | 2.0 |
| Norton, Ken, Dall. | 2.0 |
| Roper, John, Dall. | 2.0 |
| Spindler, Marc, Det. | 2.0 |
| Tuggle, Jessie, Atl. | 2.0 |
| Wheeler, Mark, T.B. | 2.0 |
| Williams, James, N.O. | 2.0 |
| Wilson, Bobby, Wash. | 2.0 |
| Ahanotu, Chidi, T.B. | 1.5 |
| Bailey, Carlton, N.Y.G. | 1.5 |
| Case, Scott, Atl. | 1.5 |
| Conner, Darion, Atl. | 1.5 |
| Edwards, Dixon, Dall. | 1.5 |
| Gouveia, Kurt, Wash. | 1.5 |
| McGhee, Kanavis, N.Y.G. | 1.5 |
| Roberts, Larry, S.F. | 1.5 |
| Smith, Artie, S.F. | 1.5 |
| Stowe, Tyronne, Phx. | 1.5 |
| White, William, Det. | 1.5 |
| Atkins, Gene, N.O. | 1.0 |
| Banks, Carl, Wash. | 1.0 |
| Boutte, Marc, Rams | 1.0 |
| Brooks, Michael, N.Y.G. | 1.0 |
| Butler, LeRoy, G.B. | 1.0 |
| Clay, Willie, Det. | 1.0 |
| Collins, Mark, N.Y.G. | 1.0 |
| Colon, Harry, Det. | 1.0 |
| Cook, Toi, N.O. | 1.0 |
| Crockett, Ray, Det. | 1.0 |
| Davis, Reuben, Phx. | 1.0 |
| Fagan, Kevin, S.F. | 1.0 |
| Faulkner, Jeff, Wash. | 1.0 |
| Fontenot, Albert, Chi. | 1.0 |
| Gann, Mike, Atl. | 1.0 |
| Gayle, Shaun, Chi. | 1.0 |
| George, Ron, Atl. | 1.0 |
| Gibson, Dennis, Det. | 1.0 |
| Hager, Britt, Phil. | 1.0 |
| Harris, Robert, Minn. | 1.0 |
| Henderson, Wymon, Rams | 1.0 |
| Hill, Eric, Phx. | 1.0 |
| Jones, Dante, Chi. | 1.0 |
| Jones, Reggie, N.O. | 1.0 |
| Jones, Roger, T.B. | 1.0 |
| Kelly, Todd, S.F. | 1.0 |
| Logan, Ernie, Atl. | 1.0 |
| London, Antonio, Det. | 1.0 |
| Lynch, Lorenzo, Phx. | 1.0 |
| Mann, Charles, Wash. | 1.0 |
| Nickerson, Hardy, T.B. | 1.0 |
| Oldham, Chris, Phx. | 1.0 |
| Patterson, Shawn, G.B. | 1.0 |
| Perry, William, Phil. | 1.0 |
| Reynolds, Ricky, T.B. | 1.0 |
| Rocker, David, Rams | 1.0 |
| Sheppard, Ashley, Minn. | 1.0 |
| Simmons, Wayne, G.B. | 1.0 |
| Smeenge, Joel, N.O. | 1.0 |
| Smith, Darrin, Dall. | 1.0 |
| Stewart, Michael, Rams | 1.0 |
| Strahan, Michael, N.Y.G. | 1.0 |
| Thomas, Broderick, T.B. | 1.0 |
| Warren, Frank, N.O. | 1.0 |
| Woods, Tony, Rams | 1.0 |
| Del Rio, Jack, Minn. | 0.5 |
| Simpson, Carl, Chi. | 0.5 |
| Spielman, Chris, Det. | 0.5 |
| Thomas, Mark, S.F. | 0.5 |

## 1993 NFL PAID ATTENDANCE BREAKDOWN

| | Games | Attendance | Average |
|---|---|---|---|
| AFC Preseason | 10 | 517,195 | 51,720 |
| NFC Preseason | 14 | 755,187 | 53,942 |
| AFC-NFC Preseason, Interconference | 37 | 1,897,999 | 51,297 |
| **NFL Preseason Total** | **61** | **3,170,381** | **51,973** |
| AFC Regular Season | 86 | 5,474,280 | 63,654 |
| NFC Regular Season | 86 | 5,264,255 | 61,212 |
| AFC-NFC Regular Season, Interconference | 52 | 3,228,308 | 62,083 |
| **NFL Regular Season Total** | **224** | ***13,966,843** | ***62,352** |
| AFC Wild Card Playoffs | 2 | | |
| Denver at Los Angeles Raiders | | 63,236 | |
| Pittsburgh at Kansas City | | 77,588 | |
| AFC Divisional Playoffs | 2 | | |
| Los Angeles Raiders at Buffalo | | 71,123 | |
| Kansas City at Houston | | 63,712 | |
| AFC Championship Game | 1 | | |
| Kansas City at Buffalo | | 77,824 | |
| NFC Wild Card Playoffs | 2 | | |
| Minnesota at New York Giants | | 76,828 | |
| Green Bay at Detroit | | 69,789 | |
| NFC Divisional Playoffs | 2 | | |
| Green Bay at Dallas | | 64,142 | |
| New York Giants at San Francisco | | 67,130 | |
| NFC Championship Game | 1 | | |
| San Francisco at Dallas | | 64,552 | |
| Super Bowl XXVIII at Atlanta, Georgia | 1 | | |
| Buffalo vs. Dallas | | 70,783 | |
| AFC-NFC Pro Bowl at Honolulu, Hawaii | 1 | 47,900 | |
| **NFL Postseason Total** | **12** | **814,607** | **67,884** |
| **NFL All Games** | **297** | ***17,951,831** | **60,444** |

**All-time record*

## ONE MILLION PLUS CLUB

During the 1993 season, 13 clubs drew a combined home and away paid attendance of more than 1 million. The Kansas City Chiefs drew an NFL-leading 1,144,109 fans in 1993.

| Team | Total Paid Home Attendance | Total Paid Visiting Attendance | Total Paid Attendance |
|---|---|---|---|
| Kansas City | 617,795 | 526,314 | 1,144,109 |
| Buffalo | 624,349 | 518,636 | 1,142,985 |
| New York Giants | 611,057 | 525,806 | 1,136,863 |
| Denver | 585,986 | 544,542 | 1,130,528 |
| Miami | 561,627 | 531,982 | 1,093,609 |
| New York Jets | 606,377 | 486,045 | 1,092,422 |
| San Francisco | 537,718 | 527,824 | 1,065,542 |
| Dallas | 505,422 | 536,434 | 1,041,856 |
| Chicago | 527,515 | 508,313 | 1,035,828 |
| Cleveland | 572,281 | 451,307 | 1,023,588 |
| New Orleans | 533,407 | 475,918 | 1,009,325 |
| Philadelphia | 521,804 | 483,083 | 1,004,887 |
| Pittsburgh | 473,910 | 529,669 | 1,003,579 |

***Note:*** *For complete year-by-year paid attendance and attendance records,* *see page 337.*

# Inside the Numbers

# INSIDE THE NUMBERS

## 75 NOTES FOR THE NFL'S 75TH SEASON

1 Phil Simms of the New York Giants needs 1 touchdown pass to become the sixteenth player to throw 200 touchdown passes in his NFL career.
2 In the first change in scoring rules in NFL history, teams may opt for a 2-point conversion following touchdowns this season.
3 With 3 more touchdowns, San Francisco's Jerry Rice would break Jim Brown's all-time NFL record of 126 touchdowns.
4 If he recovers 4 more opponents' fumbles, the Saints' Rickey Jackson would break the all-time record of 29 held by Jim Marshall.
5 Five NFL teams have new head coaches: Arizona, Buddy Ryan; Atlanta, June Jones; Dallas, Barry Switzer; New York Jets, Pete Carroll; Washington, Norv Turner.
6 The Pro Football Hall of Fame enshrines six former players and coaches this year: Tony Dorsett, Bud Grant, JImmy Johnson, Leroy Kelly, Jackie Smith, and Randy White.
7 The Houston Oilers are the only NFL team that has reached the playoffs in each of the past 7 seasons.
8 Eight Super Bowl champions have failed to reach the playoffs the following season, most recently the New York Giants in 1991.
9 With 9 more rushing touchdowns, Kansas City's Marcus Allen would become just the fourth player in NFL history to score 100 touchdowns on the ground.
10 The New York Giants have allowed the fewest points in the league in 10 different seasons, an all-time NFL record.
11 Minnesota's Roger Craig needs 11 more carries to become the eleventh player in NFL history with 2,000 career carries.
12 With 12 more kickoff returns, Detroit's Mel Gray would break the all-time NFL record of 275 kickoff returns held by Ron Smith.
13 The San Francisco 49ers have won 13 division titles since the 1970 AFL-NFL merger, the most by any team.
14 The most successful 2-point conversions in any one season in the 10-year history of the American Football League was 14 in 1961.
15 Buffalo's Thurman Thomas has scored 15 touchdowns in postseason play, 2 shy of the NFL record held by Franco Harris.
16 The AFC-NFC Pro Bowl will be played in Honolulu for the sixteenth consecutive year on February 5, 1995.
17 The 1994 regular season will be played over 17 weeks, with each team having only one bye week, instead of two as in 1993.
18 The Cleveland Browns have finished the regular season in first place in their division or conference 18 times, an all-time NFL record.
19 This is the nineteenth season for the Seattle Seahawks and Tampa Bay Buccaneers, the most recent expansion teams prior to the Carolina Panthers and Jacksonville Jaguars, who were selected in 1993.
20 The San Diego Chargers are the only NFL team that did not allow a 20-yard rushing play last season.
21 The youngest player to appear in the NFL in 1993 was Tom Carter of the Washington Redskins; he turned 21 last September 5.
22 Morten Andersen of the New Orleans Saints has made 22 field goals of 50-or-more yards, the highest career total by any player in NFL history.
23 The New York Giants have reached postseason play 23 times, the most such appearances by any team in NFL history.
24 There have been 24 games played in the AFC-NFC Pro Bowl series, with the NFC holding a 14-10 series advantage.
25 This is the twenty-fifth season of ABC's NFL Monday Night Football, the longest-running prime-time series in the history of the ABC network.
26 The Dallas Cowboys have won 26 postseason games since the 1970 AFL-NFL merger, the most by any team.
27 The Miami Dolphins won an NFL-record 27 consecutive home games, 1971-74. In the 20 years since, the longest streak is 18 by Dallas, 1979-1981.
28 The Saints' Morten Andersen has scored in 158 consecutive games; that's 28 games shy of the NFL record, held by Jim Breech.
29 The Green Bay Packers allowed only 29 points in the first quarter last season, the fewest by any NFL team.
30 The Raiders have won 30 games on ABC's NFL Monday Night Football, the most by any team in the history of the series.
31 Philadelphia's Jeff Feagles's 31 punts inside-the-20 were the most by any player in the NFL in 1993.
32 Miami's Don Shula is in his thirty-second season as an NFL head coach, 8 years shy of George Halas's record.
33 Paul Hornung's NFL single-season scoring record of 176 points, established in a 12-game schedule in 1960, has survived for 33 years.
34 There have been 34 players in NFL history who have passed for 25,000-or-more yards; Jim Everett (23,758) of the Saints could be the next to reach that mark.
35 Steve DeBerg needs 35 more passes to become the sixth player in NFL history with 5,000 career passes.
36 The Bills' Thurman Thomas has 36 career 100-yard rushing games, the most by any active NFL player.
37 The San Francisco 49ers have retired uniform number 37 in honor of former defensive back Jimmy Johnson, a 1994 Hall of Fame inductee.
38 Phil Simms of the Giants, who turned 38 during the 1993 season, was the oldest NFL player to start every game last season.
39 At age 39, Steve DeBerg was the oldest player in the NFL in 1993; he turned 40 on January 19, 1994.
40 1994 Pro Football Hall of Fame inductee Jackie Smith had 40 touchdown receptions in his NFL career.
41 Dick (Night Train) Lane's NFL single-season record of 14 interceptions, set in a 12-game schedule in 1952, has survived for 41 years.
42 The Buffalo Bills allowed only 42 points in the fourth quarter last season, the fewest by any team in the NFL.
43 Kansas City's Joe Montana has thrown 43 touchdown passes in postseason play; no other player in NFL history has thrown more than 30.
44 Miami's Dan Marino starts the season with 298 touchdown passes; that's 44 behind the total of all-time NFL record-holder Fran Tarkenton.
45 Kansas City's Nick Lowery needs 45 more field goals to break the NFL record of 373, established by Hall of Famer Jan Stenerud.
46 Once again in 1994, NFL teams will be permitted to dress 46 players (including an emergency quarterback) for each NFL game.
47 The Buffalo Bills led the NFL with 47 takeaways last season.
48 Dan Marino threw an NFL-record 48 touchdown passes in 1984. The only other over-40 total in NFL history: Marino's 44 in 1986.
49 In 1949, two NFL players rushed for 1,000-or-more yards in a season for the first time: Philadelphia's Steve Van Buren and Green Bay's Tony Canadeo.
50 Winning teams (335.6 yards per game) averaged 50 more yards per game than did losing teams (285.7) in the NFL in 1993.
51 It has been 51 years since the NFL's last scoreless tie was played between the Giants and the Lions on November 7, 1943.
52 Of 201 regular-season overtime games over the past 20 years, 52 have ended on touchdowns, 135 on field goals, 1 on a safety, and 13 have ended tied.
53 Elmer Layden was named the first Commissioner of the NFL 53 years ago.
54 1994 Pro Football Hall of Fame inductee Randy White wore uniform number 54 during his career with the Dallas Cowboys.
55 The San Francisco 49ers scored 55 points at Detroit last December 19, the highest single-game total by any NFL team in 1993.
56 All 56 teams that have played in a Super Bowl played their home games (that season) in an outdoor stadium.
57 Michael Husted's 57-yard field goal in 1993 was the longest in the history of the Tampa Bay Buccaneers.
58 Of the NFL's 224 regular-season games in 1994, 58 have been designated for national television.
59 Jerry Rice of the 49ers needs 59 more yards on receptions to surpass Don Maynard's career total of 11,834 and move into fifth place in NFL history.
60 The first Thanksgiving Day game hosted by the Detroit Lions was played 60 years ago. The visiting Chicago Bears won 19-16 on November 29, 1934.
61 The San Francisco 49ers scored 61 touchdowns in 1993, leading the NFL in that category for the second year in a row.
62 The San Francisco 49ers have won an NFL-high 62 games over the past 5 seasons, 4 more than the runner-up Buffalo Bills.
63 In 13 seasons in the NFL, Ronnie Lott of the New York Jets has made 63 interceptions, the highest total by any active NFL player.
64 Only 64 penalties were enforced against the New England Patriots last season, the fewest against any NFL team.
65 An NFL team has scored 65-or-more points in a regular-season NFL game 4 times; the Los Angeles Rams did it in consecutive weeks in 1950.
66 The NFL record for most takeaways in one season is 66 by the San Diego Chargers in a 14-game season in 1961.
67 In 1967, the NFL adopted as standard the single-stem style of goalpost and a 6-foot border around the playing field.
68 Six feet, eight inches is the height of Seattle Seahawks quarterback Dan McGwire; he's the tallest active quarterback in the NFL.
69 Troy Aikman completed 69 percent of his passes in 1993, the highest rating by any quarterback in the NFL.
70 The New York Giants are in their seventieth season in the NFL. They made their debut on October 11, 1925.
71 Bob Hayes holds the Dallas Cowboys record with 71 touchdown receptions; Michael Irvin, with 34, is less than halfway to that mark.
72 An NFL team played a turnover-free game 72 times last season, or slightly less than one-sixth of the time.
73 The Chicago Bear's 73-0 win over the Washington Redskins in the 1940 NFL Championship Game represents the NFL record for points in a postseason game.
74 1994 Pro Football Hall of Fame inductee Leroy Kelly scored 74 rushing touchdowns in his career, tied for eleventh place on the all-time list.
75 Chicago is the only city that has been represented in each of the NFL's 75 seasons.

## COMPARISON OF JOE MONTANA'S CAREER STATISTICS WITH HALL OF FAME QUARTERBACKS WHOSE CAREERS ENDED SINCE 1945

| PASSING | Att. | Comp. | Pct. | Yds. | Avg. | Lng. | TD | Pct. | Int. | Pct. | Rating |
|---|---|---|---|---|---|---|---|---|---|---|---|
| Joe Montana | 4898 | 3110 | 63.5 | 37,268 | 7.61 | 96t | 257 | 5.2 | 130 | 2.7 | 93.1 |
| Sammy Baugh | 2995 | 1693 | 56.5 | 21,886 | 7.31 | 86t | 187 | 6.2 | 203 | 6.8 | 72.0 |
| George Blanda | 4007 | 1911 | 47.7 | 26,920 | 6.72 | 95t | 236 | 5.9 | 277 | 6.9 | 60.8 |
| Terry Bradshaw | 3901 | 2025 | 51.9 | 27,989 | 7.17 | 90t | 212 | 5.4 | 210 | 5.4 | 70.9 |
| Len Dawson | 3741 | 2136 | 57.1 | 28,711 | 7.67 | 92t | 239 | 6.4 | 183 | 4.9 | 82.6 |
| Dan Fouts | 5604 | 3297 | 58.8 | 43,040 | 7.68 | 81t | 254 | 4.5 | 242 | 4.3 | 80.2 |
| Otto Graham | 1565 | 872 | 55.7 | 13,499 | 8.63 | 81t | 88 | 5.6 | 94 | 6.0 | 78.1 |
| Bob Griese | 3429 | 1926 | 56.2 | 25,092 | 7.32 | 86t | 192 | 5.6 | 172 | 5.0 | 77.1 |
| Arnie Herber* | 1175 | 481 | 40.9 | 8,041 | 6.84 | 92t | 78 | 6.6 | 106 | 9.0 | 49.3 |
| Sonny Jurgensen | 4262 | 2433 | 57.1 | 32,224 | 7.56 | 99t | 255 | 6.0 | 189 | 4.4 | 82.8 |
| Bobby Layne | 3700 | 1814 | 49.0 | 26,768 | 7.23 | 97t | 196 | 5.3 | 243 | 6.6 | 63.4 |
| Sid Luckman | 1744 | 904 | 51.8 | 14,686 | 8.42 | 86t | 137 | 7.9 | 132 | 7.6 | 75.0 |
| Joe Namath | 3762 | 1886 | 50.1 | 27,663 | 7.35 | 91 | 173 | 4.6 | 220 | 5.8 | 65.6 |
| Bart Starr | 3149 | 1808 | 57.4 | 24,718 | 7.85 | 91t | 152 | 4.8 | 138 | 4.4 | 80.5 |
| Roger Staubach | 2958 | 1685 | 57.0 | 22,700 | 7.67 | 91t | 153 | 5.2 | 109 | 3.7 | 83.4 |
| Fran Tarkenton | 6467 | 3686 | 57.0 | 47,003 | 7.27 | 89t | 342 | 5.3 | 266 | 4.1 | 80.4 |
| Y.A. Tittle | 3817 | 2118 | 55.5 | 28,339 | 7.42 | 78t | 212 | 5.6 | 221 | 5.8 | 73.8 |
| Johnny Unitas | 5186 | 2830 | 54.6 | 40,239 | 7.76 | 89t | 290 | 5.6 | 253 | 4.9 | 78.2 |
| Norm Van Brocklin | 2895 | 1553 | 53.6 | 23,611 | 8.16 | 91t | 173 | 6.0 | 178 | 6.1 | 75.3 |
| Bob Waterfield | 1617 | 814 | 50.3 | 11,849 | 7.33 | 91t | 97 | 6.0 | 128 | 7.9 | 61.6 |

| RUSHING | Years | Last Year | Games | Att. | Yds. | Avg. | Lng. | TD |
|---|---|---|---|---|---|---|---|---|
| Joe Montana | 14 | 1993 | 178 | 439 | 1659 | 3.8 | 21 | 20 |
| Sammy Baugh | 16 | 1952 | 165 | 324 | 325 | 1.0 | 41t | 9 |
| George Blanda | 26 | 1975 | 340 | 135 | 344 | 2.5 | 19 | 9 |
| Terry Bradshaw | 14 | 1983 | 168 | 444 | 2257 | 5.1 | 39 | 32 |
| Len Dawson | 19 | 1975 | 211 | 294 | 1293 | 4.4 | 43 | 9 |
| Dan Fouts | 15 | 1987 | 142 | 224 | 476 | 2.1 | 32 | 13 |
| Otto Graham | 6 | 1955 | 72 | 306 | 682 | 2.2 | 36 | 33 |
| Bob Griese | 14 | 1980 | 161 | 261 | 994 | 3.8 | 35 | 7 |
| Arnie Herber* | 13 | 1945 | x | 250 | 116 | 0.5 | x | 2 |
| Sonny Jurgensen | 18 | 1974 | 218 | 181 | 492 | 2.7 | 33 | 15 |
| Bobby Layne | 15 | 1962 | 175 | 611 | 2451 | 4.0 | 36 | 25 |
| Sid Luckman | 12 | 1950 | 128 | 204 | –239 | –1.2 | 40t | 4 |
| Joe Namath | 13 | 1977 | 140 | 71 | 140 | 2.0 | 39 | 7 |
| Bart Starr | 16 | 1971 | 196 | 247 | 1308 | 5.3 | 39 | 15 |
| Roger Staubach | 11 | 1979 | 131 | 410 | 2264 | 5.5 | 33 | 20 |
| Fran Tarkenton | 18 | 1978 | 246 | 675 | 3674 | 5.4 | 52t | 32 |
| Y.A. Tittle | 15 | 1964 | 178 | 291 | 999 | 3.4 | 45 | 33 |
| Johnny Unitas | 18 | 1973 | 211 | 450 | 1777 | 3.9 | 34 | 13 |
| Norm Van Brocklin | 12 | 1960 | 140 | 102 | 40 | 0.4 | 16 | 11 |
| Bob Waterfield | 8 | 1952 | 91 | 75 | 21 | 0.3 | 25 | 13 |

**statistics do not include 1930-31 seasons. xUnavailable.*

## JOE MONTANA'S GAME-BY-GAME POSTSEASON CAREER

| Date | Game | Opponent | Att. | Comp. | Pct. | Yds. | Avg. | TD | Int. | Rating |
|---|---|---|---|---|---|---|---|---|---|---|
| Jan. 3, 1982 | NFC Divisional Playoff | N.Y. Giants | 31 | 20 | 64.5 | 304 | 9.81 | 2 | 1 | 104.8 |
| Jan. 10, 1982 | NFC Championship Game | Dallas | 35 | 22 | 62.9 | 286 | 8.17 | 3 | 3 | 81.4 |
| Jan. 24, 1982 | Super Bowl XVI | Cincinnati | 22 | 14 | 63.6 | 157 | 7.14 | 1 | 0 | 100.0 |
| Dec. 31, 1983 | NFC Divisional Playoff | Detroit | 31 | 18 | 58.1 | 201 | 6.48 | 1 | 1 | 74.8 |
| Jan. 8, 1984 | NFC Championship Game | Washington | 48 | 27 | 56.3 | 347 | 7.23 | 3 | 1 | 91.2 |
| Dec. 29, 1984 | NFC Divisional Playoff | N.Y. Giants | 39 | 25 | 64.1 | 309 | 7.92 | 3 | 3 | 82.1 |
| Jan. 6, 1985 | NFC Championship Game | Chicago | 34 | 18 | 52.9 | 233 | 6.85 | 1 | 2 | 60.0 |
| Jan. 20, 1985 | Super Bowl XIX | Miami | 35 | 24 | 68.6 | 331 | 9.46 | 3 | 0 | 127.2 |
| Dec. 29, 1985 | NFC First-Round Game | N.Y. Giants | 47 | 26 | 55.3 | 296 | 6.30 | 0 | 1 | 65.6 |
| Jan. 4, 1987 | NFC Divisional Playoff | N.Y. Giants | 15 | 8 | 53.3 | 98 | 6.53 | 0 | 2 | 34.2 |
| Jan. 9, 1988 | NFC Divisional Playoff | Minnesota | 26 | 12 | 46.2 | 109 | 4.19 | 0 | 1 | 42.0 |
| Jan. 1, 1989 | NFC Divisional Playoff | Minnesota | 27 | 16 | 59.3 | 178 | 6.59 | 3 | 1 | 100.5 |
| Jan. 8, 1989 | NFC Championship Game | Chicago | 27 | 17 | 63.0 | 288 | 10.67 | 3 | 0 | 136.0 |
| Jan. 22, 1989 | Super Bowl XXIII | Cincinnati | 36 | 23 | 63.9 | 357 | 9.92 | 2 | 0 | 115.2 |
| Jan. 6, 1990 | NFC Divisional Playoff | Minnesota | 24 | 17 | 70.8 | 241 | 10.04 | 4 | 0 | 142.5 |
| Jan. 14, 1990 | NFC Championship Game | L.A. Rams | 30 | 26 | 86.7 | 262 | 8.73 | 2 | 0 | 125.3 |
| Jan. 28, 1990 | Super Bowl XXIV | Denver | 29 | 22 | 75.9 | 297 | 10.24 | 5 | 0 | 147.6 |
| Jan. 12, 1991 | NFC Divisional Playoff | Washington | 31 | 22 | 71.0 | 274 | 8.84 | 2 | 1 | 106.1 |
| Jan. 20, 1991 | NFC Championship Game | N.Y. Giants | 26 | 18 | 69.2 | 190 | 7.31 | 1 | 0 | 103.0 |
| Jan. 8, 1994 | AFC First-Round Game | Pittsburgh | 43 | 28 | 65.1 | 276 | 6.42 | 1 | 0 | 90.8 |
| Jan. 16, 1994 | AFC Divisional Playoff | Houston | 38 | 22 | 57.9 | 299 | 7.87 | 3 | 2 | 87.5 |
| Jan. 23, 1994 | AFC Championship Game | Buffalo | 23 | 9 | 39.1 | 125 | 5.43 | 0 | 1 | 39.2 |
| Totals (22 games) | | | 697 | 434 | 62.3 | 5458 | 7.83 | 43 | 20 | 95.2 |

## HIGHEST NFL POSTSEASON PASSER RATINGS (MINIMUM: 150 ATTEMPTS)

| | Games | Att. | Comp. | Pct. | Yds. | Avg. Gain | TD | Int. | Rating |
|---|---|---|---|---|---|---|---|---|---|
| Troy Aikman | 7 | 187 | 133 | 71.1 | 1595 | 8.53 | 13 | 4 | 111.2 |
| Bart Starr | 10 | 213 | 130 | 61.0 | 1753 | 8.23 | 15 | 3 | 104.8 |
| Joe Montana | 22 | 697 | 434 | 62.3 | 5458 | 7.83 | 43 | 20 | 95.2 |
| Ken Anderson | 6 | 166 | 110 | 66.3 | 1321 | 7.96 | 9 | 6 | 93.5 |
| Joe Theismann | 10 | 211 | 128 | 60.7 | 1782 | 8.45 | 11 | 7 | 91.4 |
| Steve Young | 12 | 156 | 106 | 67.9 | 1261 | 8.08 | 5 | 5 | 89.7 |
| Warren Moon | 9 | 351 | 230 | 65.5 | 2578 | 7.34 | 15 | 12 | 87.3 |
| Ken Stabler | 13 | 351 | 203 | 57.8 | 2641 | 7.52 | 19 | 13 | 84.2 |

| | | | | | | | | | |
|---|---|---|---|---|---|---|---|---|---|
| Bernie Kosar | 9 | 269 | 151 | 56.1 | 1943 | 7.22 | 16 | 10 | 83.3 |
| Terry Bradshaw | 19 | 456 | 261 | 57.2 | 3833 | 8.41 | 30 | 26 | 83.0 |

## HIGHEST NFL POSTSEASON PASSER RATINGS, ACTIVE PLAYERS (MINIMUM: 150 ATTEMPTS)

| | Games | Att. | Comp. | Pct. | Yds. | Avg. | TD | Int. | Rating |
|---|---|---|---|---|---|---|---|---|---|
| Troy Aikman | 7 | 187 | 133 | 71.1 | 1595 | 8.53 | 13 | 4 | 111.2 |
| Joe Montana | 22 | 697 | 434 | 62.3 | 5458 | 7.83 | 43 | 20 | 95.2 |
| Steve Young | 12 | 156 | 106 | 67.9 | 1261 | 8.08 | 5 | 5 | 89.7 |
| Warren Moon | 9 | 351 | 230 | 65.5 | 2578 | 7.34 | 15 | 12 | 87.3 |
| Bernie Kosar | 9 | 269 | 151 | 56.1 | 1943 | 7.22 | 16 | 10 | 83.3 |
| Dan Marino | 10 | 387 | 212 | 54.8 | 2659 | 6.87 | 22 | 14 | 80.2 |
| Phil Simms | 10 | 279 | 157 | 56.3 | 1679 | 6.02 | 10 | 6 | 77.0 |
| Jim McMahon | 8 | 155 | 82 | 52.9 | 1112 | 7.17 | 5 | 4 | 76.1 |
| John Elway | 14 | 431 | 229 | 53.1 | 3321 | 7.71 | 19 | 18 | 75.8 |
| Wade Wilson | 6 | 185 | 99 | 53.5 | 1322 | 7.15 | 7 | 6 | 75.6 |

## ALL-TIME RANKINGS OF PLAYERS IN FOUR CATEGORIES THAT DETERMINE NFL PASSER RATING

*Minimum: 1500 Attempts*

| COMPLETION PERCENTAGE | Pct. | Att. | Comp. |
|---|---|---|---|
| Joe Montana | 63.50 | 4898 | 3110 |
| Steve Young | 62.09 | 1968 | 1222 |
| Troy Aikman | 62.03 | 1920 | 1191 |
| Jim Kelly | 60.45 | 3494 | 2112 |
| Ken Stabler | 59.85 | 3793 | 2270 |
| Danny White | 59.69 | 2950 | 1761 |
| Ken Anderson | 59.31 | 4475 | 2654 |
| Dan Marino | 59.24 | 5434 | 3219 |
| Bobby Hebert | 58.95 | 2485 | 1465 |
| Dan Fouts | 58.83 | 5604 | 3297 |

| TOUCHDOWN PERCENTAGE | Pct. | Att. | TD |
|---|---|---|---|
| Sid Luckman | 7.86 | 1744 | 137 |
| Frank Ryan | 6.99 | 2133 | 149 |
| Len Dawson | 6.39 | 3741 | 239 |
| Daryle Lamonica | 6.31 | 2601 | 164 |
| Sammy Baugh | 6.24 | 2995 | 187 |
| Charley Conerly | 6.11 | 2833 | 173 |
| Bob Waterfield | 6.00 | 1617 | 97 |
| Earl Morrall | 5.99 | 2689 | 161 |
| Sonny Jurgensen | 5.98 | 4262 | 255 |
| Norm Van Brocklin | 5.98 | 2895 | 173 |

| AVERAGE YARDS PER PASS | Avg. | Att. | Yards |
|---|---|---|---|
| Otto Graham | 8.63 | 1565 | 13,499 |
| Sid Luckman | 8.42 | 1744 | 14,686 |
| Norm Van Brocklin | 8.16 | 2895 | 23,611 |
| Steve Young | 8.08 | 1968 | 15,900 |
| Ed Brown | 7.85 | 1987 | 15,600 |
| Bart Starr | 7.85 | 3149 | 24,718 |
| Johnny Unitas | 7.76 | 5186 | 40,239 |
| Earl Morrall | 7.74 | 2689 | 20,809 |
| Dan Fouts | 7.68 | 5604 | 43,040 |
| Len Dawson | 7.67 | 3741 | 28,711 |

| INTERCEPTION PERCENTAGE | Pct. | Att. | Int. |
|---|---|---|---|
| Bernie Kosar | 2.52 | 3213 | 81 |
| Joe Montana | 2.65 | 4898 | 130 |
| Ken O'Brien | 2.72 | 3602 | 98 |
| Neil Lomax | 2.85 | 3153 | 90 |
| Steve Young | 2.95 | 1968 | 58 |
| Jeff George | 3.00 | 1532 | 46 |
| Dan Marino | 3.09 | 5434 | 168 |
| Randall Cunningham | 3.16 | 2751 | 87 |
| Jim Harbaugh | 3.18 | 1759 | 56 |
| Tony Eason | 3.26 | 1564 | 51 |

## TEAMS THAT FINISHED IN FIRST PLACE IN THEIR DIVISION THE SEASON AFTER FINISHING IN LAST PLACE

| Season | Team | Record | Previous Season |
|---|---|---|---|
| 1967 | Houston | 9 - 4 - 1 | *3 - 11 |
| 1968 | Minnesota | 8 - 6 | 3 - 8 - 3 |
| 1970 | Cincinnati | 8 - 6 | 4 - 9 - 1 |
| 1970 | San Francisco | 10 - 3 - 1 | 4 - 8 - 2 |
| 1972 | Green Bay | 10 - 4 | 4 - 8 - 2 |
| 1975 | Baltimore | 10 - 4 | 2 - 12 |
| 1979 | Tampa Bay | 10 - 6 | 5 - 11 |
| 1981 | Cincinnati | 12 - 4 | 6 - 10 |
| 1987 | Indianapolis | 9 - 6 | 3 - 13 |
| 1988 | Cincinnati | 12 - 4 | 4 - 11 |
| 1990 | Cincinnati | 9 - 7 | 8 - 8 |
| 1991 | Denver | 12 - 4 | 5 - 11 |
| 1992 | San Diego | 11 - 5 | 4 - 12 |
| 1993 | Detroit | 10 - 6 | 5 - 11 |

**tied for last place*

## RECORDS OF NFL TEAMS, 1984-93

| AFC | W - L - T | Pct. | Division Titles | Playoff Berths | Postseason Record | Super Bowl Record |
|---|---|---|---|---|---|---|
| Denver | 98 - 60 - 1 | .619 | 5 | 6 | 7-6 | 0-3 |
| Miami | 96 - 63 - 0 | .604 | 3 | 4 | 5-4 | 0-1 |
| L.A. Raiders | 89 - 70 - 0 | .560 | 2 | 5 | 2-5 | 0-0 |
| Buffalo | 85 - 74 - 0 | .535 | 5 | 6 | 10-6 | 0-4 |
| Houston | 83 - 76 - 0 | .522 | 2 | 7 | 3-7 | 0-0 |
| Kansas City | 82 - 75 - 2 | .522 | 1 | 5 | 3-5 | 0-0 |
| Pittsburgh | 80 - 79 - 0 | .503 | 2 | 4 | 2-4 | 0-0 |
| Seattle | 79 - 80 - 0 | .497 | 1 | 3 | 1-3 | 0-0 |
| Cleveland | 77 - 81 - 1 | .487 | 4 | 5 | 3-5 | 0-0 |
| N.Y. Jets | 72 - 86 - 1 | .456 | 0 | 3 | 1-3 | 0-0 |
| Cincinnati | 69 - 90 - 0 | .434 | 2 | 2 | 3-2 | 0-1 |
| San Diego | 68 - 91 - 0 | .428 | 1 | 1 | 1-1 | 0-0 |
| New England | 67 - 92 - 0 | .421 | 1 | 2 | 3-2 | 0-1 |
| Indianapolis | 59 - 100 - 0 | .371 | 1 | 1 | 0-1 | 0-0 |

| NFC | W - L - T | Pct. | Division Titles | Playoff Berths | Postseason Record | Super Bowl Record |
|---|---|---|---|---|---|---|
| San Francisco | 120 - 38 - 1 | .758 | 8 | 9 | 12-6 | 3-0 |
| Chicago | 102 - 57 - 0 | .642 | 6 | 7 | 6-6 | 1-0 |
| N.Y. Giants | 99 - 60 - 0 | .623 | 3 | 6 | 9-4 | 2-0 |
| Washington | 98 - 61 - 0 | .616 | 3 | 6 | 10-4 | 2-0 |
| New Orleans | 89 - 70 - 0 | .560 | 1 | 4 | 0-4 | 0-0 |
| Philadelphia | 85 - 72 - 2 | .541 | 1 | 4 | 1-4 | 0-0 |
| Minnesota | 82 - 77 - 0 | .516 | 2 | 5 | 3-5 | 0-0 |
| Dallas | 80 - 79 - 0 | .503 | 3 | 4 | 7-2 | 2-0 |
| L.A. Rams | 77 - 82 - 0 | .484 | 1 | 5 | 3-5 | 0-0 |
| Green Bay | 67 - 91 - 1 | .425 | 0 | 1 | 1-1 | 0-0 |
| Detroit | 64 - 94 - 1 | .406 | 2 | 2 | 1-2 | 0-0 |
| Arizona | 57 - 101 - 1 | .362 | 0 | 0 | 0-0 | 0-0 |
| Atlanta | 53 - 105 - 1 | .336 | 0 | 1 | 1-1 | 0-0 |
| Tampa Bay | 43 - 116 - 0 | .270 | 0 | 0 | 0-0 | 0-0 |

*Arizona totals include St. Louis, 1984-87, and Phoenix, 1988-93*

## HOME RECORDS, 1984-93

| AFC | W-L-T | Pct. | NFC | W-L-T | Pct. |
|---|---|---|---|---|---|
| Denver | 62-18-0 | .775 | San Francisco | 60-19-0 | .759 |
| Kansas City | 54-25-0 | .684 | N.Y. Giants | 59-21-0 | .738 |
| Houston | 53-26-0 | .671 | Chicago | 58-22-0 | .725 |
| Miami | 53-26-0 | .671 | Washington | 56-23-0 | .709 |
| Buffalo | 52-28-0 | .650 | Minnesota | 48-32-0 | .600 |
| Pittsburgh | 51-28-0 | .646 | New Orleans | 47-32-0 | .595 |
| L.A. Raiders | 50-30-0 | .625 | Philadelphia | 47-32-1 | .594 |
| Seattle | 48-32-0 | .600 | Dallas | 43-36-0 | .544 |
| Cincinnati | 44-36-0 | .550 | L.A. Rams | 41-38-0 | .519 |
| Cleveland | 42-36-1 | .538 | Green Bay | 38-41-1 | .481 |
| San Diego | 39-40-0 | .494 | Detroit | 35-43-1 | .449 |
| New England | 39-41-0 | .488 | Atlanta | 34-45-1 | .431 |
| N.Y. Jets | 38-41-1 | .481 | Arizona | 34-45-0 | .430 |
| Indianapolis | 32-48-0 | .400 | Tampa Bay | 29-50-0 | .367 |

## ROAD RECORDS, 1984-93

| AFC | W-L-T | Pct. | NFC | W-L-T | Pct. |
|---|---|---|---|---|---|
| Miami | 43-37-0 | .538 | San Francisco | 60-19-1 | .756 |
| L.A. Raiders | 39-40-0 | .494 | Chicago | 44-35-0 | .557 |
| Denver | 36-42-1 | .462 | New Orleans | 42-38-0 | .525 |
| Cleveland | 35-45-0 | .438 | Washington | 42-38-0 | .525 |
| N.Y. Jets | 34-45-0 | .430 | N.Y. Giants | 40-39-0 | .506 |
| Buffalo | 33-46-0 | .418 | Philadelphia | 38-40-1 | .487 |

| AFC | | | NFC | | |
|---|---|---|---|---|---|
| Seattle | 31-48-0 | .392 | Dallas | 37-43-0 | .463 |
| Houston | 30-50-0 | .375 | L.A. Rams | 36-44-0 | .450 |
| Kansas City | 28-50-2 | .363 | Minnesota | 34-45-0 | .430 |
| Pittsburgh | 29-51-0 | .363 | Green Bay | 29-50-0 | .367 |
| San Diego | 29-51-0 | .363 | Detroit | 29-51-0 | .363 |
| New England | 28-51-0 | .354 | Arizona | 23-56-1 | .294 |
| Indianapolis | 27-52-0 | .342 | Atlanta | 19-60-0 | .241 |
| Cincinnati | 25-54-0 | .316 | Tampa Bay | 14-66-0 | .175 |

## RECORDS BY MONTHS, 1984-93

| | Sept. | Oct. | Nov. | Dec. | Total | |
|---|---|---|---|---|---|---|
| AFC | W-L-T | W-L-T | W-L-T | W-L-T | W-L-T | Pct. |
| Denver | 26-11-1 | 26-14 | 26-16 | 20-19 | 98-60-1 | .619 |
| Miami | 22-15 | 27-13 | 26-17 | 21-18 | 96-63-0 | .604 |
| L.A. Raiders | 21-17 | 26-15 | 20-21 | 22-17 | 89-70-0 | .560 |
| Buffalo | 22-16 | 21-17 | 25-19 | 17-22 | 85-74-0 | .535 |
| Houston | 16-22 | 21-19 | 24-18 | 22-17 | 83-76-0 | .522 |
| Kansas City | 23-15 | 14-26-1 | 19-21-1 | 26-13 | 82-75-2 | .522 |
| Pittsburgh | 16-21 | 20-21 | 22-21 | 22-16 | 80-79-0 | .503 |
| Seattle | 18-20 | 24-18 | 18-22 | 19-20 | 79-80-0 | .497 |
| Cleveland | 17-21 | 23-17 | 19-22-1 | 18-21 | 77-81-1 | .487 |
| N.Y. Jets | 21-17 | 18-21-1 | 22-22 | 11-26 | 72-86-1 | .456 |
| Cincinnati | 15-21 | 17-25 | 17-25 | 20-19 | 69-90-0 | .434 |
| San Diego | 13-25 | 14-27 | 23-19 | 18-20 | 68-91-0 | .428 |
| New England | 13-25 | 18-22 | 19-23 | 17-22 | 67-92-0 | .421 |
| Indianapolis | 9-28 | 17-23 | 14-29 | 19-20 | 59-100-0 | .371 |
| | Sept. | Oct. | Nov. | Dec. | Total | |
| NFC | W-L-T | W-L-T | W-L-T | W-L-T | W-L-T | Pct. |
| San Francisco | 27-11 | 30-9-1 | 30-11 | 33-7 | 120-38-1 | .758 |
| Chicago | 29-9 | 28-11 | 29-15 | 16-22 | 102-57-0 | .642 |
| N.Y. Giants | 24-13 | 25-15 | 27-15 | 23-17 | 99-60-0 | .623 |
| Washington | 23-14 | 24-15 | 26-19 | 25-13 | 98-61-0 | .616 |
| New Orleans | 23-15 | 21-19 | 25-17 | 20-19 | 89-70-0 | .560 |
| Philadelphia | 17-20 | 21-19 | 24-18-1 | 23-15-1 | 85-72-2 | .541 |
| Minnesota | 22-16 | 16-24 | 25-19 | 19-18 | 82-77-0 | .516 |
| Dallas | 21-16 | 21-20 | 20-25 | 18-18 | 80-79-0 | .503 |
| L.A. Rams | 24-14 | 17-23 | 18-24 | 18-21 | 77-82-0 | .484 |
| Green Bay | 9-28-1 | 17-22 | 22-21 | 19-20 | 67-91-1 | .425 |
| Detroit | 15-24 | 17-22 | 15-28-1 | 17-20 | 64-94-1 | .406 |
| Arizona | 15-23 | 15-26 | 14-29 | 13-23-1 | 57-101-1 | .362 |
| Atlanta | 13-25 | 13-26-1 | 15-27 | 12-27 | 53-105-1 | .336 |
| Tampa Bay | 13-25 | 9-31 | 11-32 | 10-28 | 43-116-0 | .270 |

*Arizona totals include St. Louis, 1984-87, and Phoenix, 1988-93*
*December totals include January*

## TAKEAWAYS/GIVEAWAYS IN 1984-93

| | Takeaways | | | Giveaways | | | |
|---|---|---|---|---|---|---|---|
| AFC | Int. | Fum. | Total | Int. | Fum. | Total | Net.Diff. |
| Kansas City | 212 | 166 | 378 | 165 | 146 | 311 | 67 |
| Pittsburgh | 228 | 152 | 380 | 187 | 148 | 335 | 45 |
| Denver | 204 | 161 | 365 | 186 | 138 | 324 | 41 |
| N.Y. Jets | 190 | 157 | 347 | 159 | 159 | 318 | 29 |
| Seattle | 204 | 176 | 380 | 214 | 151 | 365 | 15 |
| Cincinnati | 178 | 148 | 326 | 175 | 143 | 318 | 8 |
| Cleveland | 180 | 134 | 314 | 159 | 158 | 317 | -3 |
| Indianapolis | 160 | 163 | 323 | 199 | 142 | 341 | -18 |
| Houston | 197 | 154 | 351 | 209 | 163 | 372 | -21 |
| San Diego | 199 | 135 | 334 | 216 | 143 | 359 | -25 |
| New England | 171 | 160 | 331 | 207 | 153 | 360 | -29 |
| Buffalo | 188 | 155 | 343 | 205 | 176 | 381 | -38 |
| Miami | 169 | 127 | 296 | 191 | 151 | 342 | -46 |
| L.A. Raiders | 168 | 127 | 295 | 202 | 149 | 351 | -56 |
| | Takeaways | | | Giveaways | | | |
| NFC | Int. | Fum. | Total | Int. | Fum. | Total | Net.Diff. |
| San Francisco | 215 | 137 | 352 | 137 | 138 | 275 | 77 |
| Philadelphia | 233 | 164 | 397 | 177 | 149 | 326 | 71 |
| N.Y. Giants | 191 | 137 | 328 | 144 | 129 | 273 | 55 |
| Minnesota | 228 | 149 | 377 | 198 | 133 | 331 | 46 |
| New Orleans | 193 | 172 | 365 | 198 | 144 | 342 | 23 |
| Chicago | 231 | 136 | 367 | 189 | 163 | 352 | 15 |
| Washington | 215 | 125 | 340 | 187 | 139 | 326 | 14 |
| L.A. Rams | 185 | 145 | 330 | 176 | 164 | 340 | -10 |
| Detroit | 180 | 160 | 340 | 208 | 156 | 364 | -24 |
| Green Bay | 189 | 174 | 363 | 224 | 170 | 394 | -31 |
| Dallas | 172 | 146 | 318 | 206 | 144 | 350 | -32 |
| Atlanta | 175 | 141 | 316 | 200 | 159 | 359 | -43 |
| Arizona | 148 | 142 | 290 | 204 | 144 | 348 | -58 |
| Tampa Bay | 172 | 163 | 335 | 253 | 154 | 407 | -72 |

*Arizona totals include St. Louis, 1984-87, and Phoenix, 1988-93*

## HIGH AND LOW SINGLE-GAME YARDAGE TOTALS, 1984-93

**Most Total Yards, Game**
676 Washington vs. Detroit, Nov. 4, 1990 (OT)
621 Cincinnati vs. N.Y. Jets, Dec. 21, 1986
598 San Francisco vs. Buffalo, Sept. 13, 1992
597 N.Y. Jets vs. Miami, Nov. 27, 1988
593 San Diego vs. L.A. Raiders, Nov. 10, 1985 (OT)

**Fewest Total Yards, Game**
53 Pittsburgh vs. Cleveland, Sept. 10, 1989
60 Detroit vs. Minnesota, Nov. 24, 1988
62 Seattle vs. Dallas, Oct. 11, 1992
65 Tampa Bay vs. Green Bay, Dec. 1, 1985
65 Seattle vs. New England, Dec. 4, 1988

**Most Yards Rushing, Game**
356 L.A. Raiders vs. Seattle, Nov. 30, 1987
315 Buffalo vs. Atlanta, Nov. 22, 1992
310 Kansas City vs. Detroit, Oct. 14, 1990
307 Washington vs. Atlanta, Nov. 3, 1985
305 Pittsburgh vs. Miami, Dec. 18, 1988

**Fewest Yards Rushing, Game**
0 Buffalo vs. Chicago, Oct. 2, 1988
1 Tampa Bay vs. Washington, Oct. 22, 1989
2 New England vs. New Orleans, Nov. 30, 1986
4 Indianapolis vs. Detroit, Sept. 22, 1991
6 N.Y. Giants vs. L.A. Rams, Nov. 12, 1989

**Most Yards Passing, Game**
521 Miami vs. N.Y. Jets, Oct. 23, 1988
505 Houston vs. Kansas City, Dec. 16, 1990
494 San Diego vs. Seattle, Sept. 15, 1985
483 Cincinnati vs. L.A. Rams, Oct. 7, 1990
482 Washington vs. Detroit, Nov. 4, 1990 (OT)

**Fewest Yards Passing, Game**
–22 Atlanta vs. Chicago, Nov. 24, 1985
–13 Cincinnati vs. San Diego, Oct. 4, 1987
4 St. Louis vs. New Orleans, Oct. 11, 1987
11 Tampa Bay vs. Green Bay, Dec. 1, 1985
15 New England vs. Atlanta, Nov. 29, 1992

## NFL INDIVIDUAL LEADERS, 1984-93

| Points | Touchdowns | Field Goals |
|---|---|---|
| 1,099, Morten Andersen | 124, Jerry Rice | 254, Morten Andersen |
| 1,068, Gary Anderson | 87, Marcus Allen | 248, Gary Anderson |
| 1,064, Nick Lowery | 83, Mark Clayton | 240, Nick Lowery |
| 964, Norm Johnson | 76, Eric Dickerson | 199, Kevin Butler |
| 915, Kevin Butler | 72, Herschel Walker | 194, Norm Johnson |

| Rushes | Rushing Yards | Rushing TDs |
|---|---|---|
| 2,606, Eric Dickerson | 11,451, Eric Dickerson | 72, Eric Dickerson |
| 1,870, Marcus Allen | 7,631, Thurman Thomas | 71, Marcus Allen |
| 1,815, Roger Craig | 7,468, Herschel Walker | 56, Gerald Riggs |
| 1,811, Gerald Riggs | 7,464, Roger Craig | 55, Barry Sanders |
| 1,794, Herschel Walker | 7,452, Gerald Riggs | 55, Herschel Walker |

| Passes | Completions | Passing Yards |
|---|---|---|
| 5,138, Dan Marino | 3,046, Dan Marino | 38,510, Dan Marino |
| 4,631, John Elway | 2,632, Warren Moon | 33,685, Warren Moon |
| 4,546, Warren Moon | 2,600, John Elway | 32,583, John Elway |
| 3,851, Boomer Esiason | 2,185, Boomer Esiason | 29,092, Boomer Esiason |
| 3,743, Dave Krieg | 2,171, Dave Krieg | 27,237, Phil Simms |

| TD Passes | Receptions | Reception Yards |
|---|---|---|
| 278, Dan Marino | 708, Jerry Rice | 11,776, Jerry Rice |
| 196, Warren Moon | 692, Art Monk | 9,560, Gary Clark |
| 190, Boomer Esiason | 612, Gary Clark | 9,493, Henry Ellard |
| 190, Dave Krieg | 588, Drew Hill | 9,142, Art Monk |
| 179, Jim Kelly | 586, Andre Reed | 8,874, Drew Hill |
| 179, Joe Montana | | |

| Receiving TDs | Interceptions | Sacks |
|---|---|---|
| 118, Jerry Rice | 50, Ronnie Lott | 137.0, Reggie White |
| 83, Mark Clayton | 44, Dave Waymer | 121.5, Richard Dent |
| 62, Gary Clark | 42, Deron Cherry | 116.0, Lawrence Taylor |
| 58, Andre Reed | 41, Gil Byrd | 106.0, Bruce Smith |
| 54, Drew Hill | 38, Eugene Robinson | 98.5, Rickey Jackson |

## INSIDE THE NUMBERS

### RECORDS FOR EACH CURRENT NFL TEAM FOR MOST POINTS IN A GAME (REGULAR SEASON ONLY)

***Note:*** *When the record has been achieved more than once, only the most recent game is shown; summaries are listed in alphabetical order by conference. Bold face indicates team holding record.*

**BUFFALO BILLS**
**September 18, 1966, at Buffalo**
Miami ............................ 3 7 0 14 — 24
**Buffalo** .......................... 21 27 3 7 — 58
TDs: Buff—Bobby Burnett 2, Butch Byrd 2, Jack Spikes 2, Bobby Crockett, Jack Kemp; Mia—Dave Kocourek, Bo Roberson, John Roderick. TD Passes: Buff—Jack Kemp, Daryle Lamonica; Mia—George Wilson 3. FGs: Buff—Booth Lusteg; Mia—Gene Mingo.

**CINCINNATI BENGALS**
**December 17, 1989, at Cincinnati**
Houston ......................... 0 0 0 7 — 7
**Cincinnati** ..................... 21 10 21 9 — 61
TDs: Cin—Eddie Brown 2, Eric Ball, James Brooks, Ira Hillary, Rodney Holman, Tim McGee, Craig Taylor; Hou—Lorenzo White. TD Passes: Cin—Boomer Esiason 4, Erik Wilhelm. FGs: Cin—Jim Breech 2.

**CLEVELAND BROWNS**
**November 7, 1954, at Cleveland**
Washington ................... 0 3 0 0 — 3
**Cleveland** ..................... 13 14 21 14 — 62
TDs: Clev—Darrell Brewster 2, Mo Bassett, Ken Gorgal, Otto Graham, Dub Jones, Dante Lavelli, Curley Morrison. TD Passes: Clev—George Ratterman 3, Otto Graham. FGs: Clev—Lou Groza 2; Wash—Vic Janowicz.

**DENVER BRONCOS**
**October 6, 1963, at Denver**
San Diego ..................... 13 7 0 14 — 34
**Denver** .......................... 3 14 9 24 — 50
TDs: Den—Lionel Taylor 2, Goose Gonsoulin, Gene Prebola, Donnie Stone; SD—Keith Lincoln 2, Lance Alworth, Paul Lowe, Jacque MacKinnon. TD Passes: Den—John McCormick 3; SD—Tobin Rote 3, John Hadl 2. FGs: Den—Gene Mingo 5.

**HOUSTON OILERS**
**December 9, 1990, at Houston**
Cleveland ...................... 0 7 7 0 — 14
**Houston** ........................ 14 31 7 6 — 58
TDs: Hou—Lorenzo White 4, Ernest Givins, Leonard Harris, Tony Jones, Terry Kinard; Clev—Eric Metcalf 2. TD Passes: Hou—Warren Moon 2, Cody Carlson; Clev—Bernie Kosar. FG: Hou—Teddy Garcia.

**INDIANAPOLIS COLTS**
**December 12, 1976, at Baltimore**
Buffalo ........................... 3 3 7 7 — 20
**Baltimore Colts** ........... 7 13 28 10 — 58
TDs: Balt—Roger Carr, Raymond Chester, Glenn Doughty, Roosevelt Leaks, Derrel Luce, Lydell Mitchell, Howard Stevens; Buff—Bob Chandler, O.J. Simpson. TD Passes: Balt—Bert Jones 3; Buff—Gary Marangi. FGs: Balt—Toni Linhart 3; Buff—George Jakowenko 2.

**KANSAS CITY CHIEFS**
**September 7, 1963, at Denver**
**Kansas City** .................. 14 14 21 10 — 59
Denver ........................... 0 7 0 0 — 7
TDs: KC—Chris Burford 2, Frank Jackson 2, Dave Grayson, Abner Haynes, Sherrill Headrick, Curtis McClinton; Den—Lionel Taylor. TD Passes: KC—Len Dawson 4, Curtis McClinton; Den—Mickey Slaughter. FG: KC—Tommy Brooker.

**LOS ANGELES RAIDERS**
**December 22, 1963, at Oakland**
Houston ......................... 14 21 14 0 — 49
**Oakland Raiders** .......... 7 28 7 10 — 52
TDs: Oak—Art Powell 4, Clem Daniels, Claude Gibson, Ken Herock; Hou—Willard Dewveall 2, Dave Smith 2, Charley Hennigan, Bob McLeod, Charley Tolar. TD Passes: Oak—Tom Flores 6; Hou—George Blanda 5. FG: Oak—Mike Mercer.

**MIAMI DOLPHINS**
**November 24, 1977, at St. Louis**
**Miami** ............................ 14 14 20 7 — 55
St. Louis ........................ 7 0 0 7 — 14
TDs: Mia—Nat Moore 3, Gary Davis, Duriel Harris, Leroy Harris, Benny Malone, Andre Tillman; StL—Ike Harris, Terry Metcalf. TD Passes: Mia—Bob Griese 6; StL—Jim Hart.

**NEW ENGLAND PATRIOTS**
**September 9, 1979, at New England**
New York Jets ............... 3 0 0 0 — 3
**New England** ............... 14 21 7 14 — 56
TDs: NE—Harold Jackson 3, Stanley Morgan 2, Allan Clark, Andy Johnson, Don Westbrook. TD Passes: NE—Steve Grogan 5, Tom Owen. FG: NYJ—Pat Leahy.

**NEW YORK JETS**
**November 17, 1985, at New York**
Tampa Bay .................... 14 7 7 0 — 28
**New York Jets** .............. 17 24 14 7 — 62
TDs: NYJ—Mickey Shuler 3, Johnny Hector 2, Tony Paige, Al Toon, Wesley Walker; TB—James Wilder 2, Kevin House, Calvin Magee. TD Passes: NYJ—Ken O'Brien 5; TB—Steve DeBerg 2. FGs: NYJ—Pat Leahy 2.

**PITTSBURGH STEELERS**
**November 30, 1952, at Pittsburgh**
New York Giants ........... 0 0 7 0 — 7
**Pittsburgh** .................... 14 14 7 28 — 63
TDs: Pitt—Lynn Chandnois 2, Dick Hensley 2, Jack Butler, George Hays, Ray Mathews, Ed Modzelewski, Elbie Nickel; NYG—Bill Stribling. TD Passes: Pitt—Jim Finks 4, Gary Kerkorian; NYG—Tom Landry.

**SAN DIEGO CHARGERS**
**December 22, 1963, at San Diego**
Denver .......................... 7 10 3 0 — 20
**San Diego** ..................... 10 16 10 22 — 58
TDs: SD—Paul Lowe 2, Chuck Allen, Bobby Jackson, Dave Kocourek, Keith Lincoln, Jacque MacKinnon; Den—Billy Joe, Donnie Stone. TD Passes: SD—John Hadl, Tobin Rote; Den—Don Breaux. FGs: SD—George Blair 3; Den—Gene Mingo 2.

**SEATTLE SEAHAWKS**
**October 30, 1977, at Seattle**
Buffalo .......................... 3 0 7 7 — 17
**Seattle** ........................... 14 28 7 7 — 56
TDs: Sea—Steve Largent 2, Duke Fergerson, Al Hunter, David Sims, Sherman Smith, Don Testerman, Jim Zorn; Buff—Joe Ferguson, John Kimbrough. TD Passes: Sea—Jim Zorn 4; Buff—Joe Ferguson. FG: Buff—Carson Long.

**ARIZONA CARDINALS**
**November 13, 1949, at New York**
**Chicago Cardinals** ....... 7 31 14 13 — 65
New York Bulldogs ........ 7 0 6 7 — 20
TDs: Chi—Red Cochran 2, Pat Harder 2, Bill Dewell, Mel Kutner, Bob Ravensburg, Vic Schwall, Charlie Trippi; NY—Joe Golding, Frank Muehlheuser, Johnny Rauch. TD Passes: Chi—Paul Christman 3, Jim Hardy 3; NY—Bobby Layne. FG: Chi—Pat Harder.

**ATLANTA FALCONS**
**September 16, 1973, at New Orleans**
**Atlanta** .......................... 0 24 21 17 — 62
New Orleans ................. 0 0 7 0 — 7
TDs: Atl—Ken Burrow 2, Eddie Ray 2, Wes Chesson, Tom Hayes, Art Malone, Joe Profit; NO—Bill Butler. TD Passes: Atl—Dick Shiner 3, Bob Lee; NO—Archie Manning. FGs: Atl—Nick Mike-Mayer 2.

**CHICAGO BEARS**
**December 7, 1980, at Chicago**
Green Bay ..................... 0 7 0 0 — 7
**Chicago** ......................... 0 28 13 20 — 61
TDs: Chi—Walter Payton 3, Brian Baschnagel, Robin Earl, Roland Harper, Willie McClendon, Len Walterscheid, Rickey Watts; GB—James Lofton. TD Passes: Chi—Vince Evans 3; GB—Lynn Dickey.

**DALLAS COWBOYS**
**October 12, 1980, at Dallas**
San Francisco ............... 0 7 0 7 — 14
**Dallas** ............................ 14 24 14 7 — 59
TDs: Dall—Drew Pearson 3, Ron Springs 2, Tony Dorsett, Billy Joe DuPree, Robert Newhouse; SF—Dwight Clark 2. TD Passes: Dall—Danny White 4; SF—Steve DeBerg 2. FG: Dall—Rafael Septien.

**DETROIT LIONS**
**October 26, 1952, at Green Bay**
**Detroit** ........................... 14 14 14 10 — 52
Green Bay ..................... 7 3 7 0 — 17
TDs: Det—Jug Girard 2, Bob Hoernschemeyer 2, Jack Christiansen, Jim Smith, Bill Swiacki; GB—Billy Howton, Jim Keane. TD Passes: Det—Bobby Layne 3; GB—Babe Parilli, Tobin Rote. FGs: Det—Pat Harder; GB—Bill Reichardt.

**GREEN BAY PACKERS**
**October 7, 1945, at Milwaukee**
Detroit ............................ 0 7 7 7 — 21
**Green Bay** ..................... 0 41 9 7 — 57
TDs: GB—Don Hutson 4, Charley Brock, Irv Comp, Ted Fritsch, Clyde Goodnight; Det—Chuck Fenenbock, John Greene, Bob Westfall. TD Passes: GB—Tex McKay 4, Lou Brock, Irv Comp; Det—Dave Ryan.

**LOS ANGELES RAMS**
**October 22, 1950, at Los Angeles**
Baltimore ....................... 13 0 7 7 — 27
**Los Angeles** .................. 21 14 14 21 — 70
TDs: LA—Bob Boyd 2, Vitamin T. Smith 2, Tom Fears, Elroy (Crazylegs) Hirsch, Dick Hoerner, Ralph Pasquariello, Dan Towler, Bob Waterfield; Balt—Chet Mutryn 2, Adrian Burk, Billy Stone. TD Passes: LA—Norm Van Brocklin 2, Bob Waterfield 2, Glenn Davis; Balt—Adrian Burk 3.

**MINNESOTA VIKINGS**
**October 18, 1970, at Minnesota**
Dallas ............................. 3 3 0 7 — 13
**Minnesota** ...................... 14 20 17 3 — 54
TDs: Minn—Clint Jones 2, Ed Sharockman 2, John Beasley, Dave Osborn; Dall—Calvin Hill. TD Pass: Minn—Gary Cuozzo. FGs: Minn—Fred Cox 4; Dall—Mike Clark 2.

**NEW ORLEANS SAINTS**
**November 21, 1976, at Seattle**
**New Orleans** ................. 3 17 28 3 — 51
Seattle ............................ 6 0 7 14 — 27
TDs: NO—Bobby Douglass 2, Tony Galbreath, Chuck Muncie, Tom Myers, Elex Price; Sea—Sherman Smith 2, Steve Largent, Jim Zorn. TD Pass: Sea—Bill Munson. FGs: NO—Rich Szaro 3.

**NEW YORK GIANTS**
**November 26, 1972, at New York**
Philadelphia .................. 3 7 0 0 — 10
**New York Giants** ........... 14 24 10 14 — 62
TDs: NYG—Don Herrmann 2, Ron Johnson 2, Bob Tucker 2, Randy Johnson; Phil—Harold Jackson. TD Passes: NYG—Norm Snead 3, Randy Johnson 2; Phil—John Reaves. FGs: NYG—Pete Gogolak 2; Phil—Tom Dempsey.

**PHILADELPHIA EAGLES**
**November 6, 1934, at Philadelphia**
Cincinnati Reds ............. 0 0 0 0 — 0
**Philadelphia** .................. 26 6 12 20 — 64
TDs: Phil—Joe Carter 3, Swede Hanson 3, Marvin Ellstrom, Roger Kirkman, Ed Matesic, Ed Storm. TD Passes: Phil—Ed Matesic 2, Albert Weiner 2, Marvin Elstrom.

**SAN FRANCISCO 49ERS**
**October 18, 1992, at San Francisco**
Atlanta ........................... 7 3 0 7 — 17
**San Francisco** ............... 21 21 14 0 — 56
TDs: SF—Jerry Rice 3, Ricky Watters 3, Brent Jones, Tom Rathman; Atl—Michael Haynes, Jason Phillips. TD Passes: SF—Steve Young 3; Atl—Chris Miller, Wade Wilson. FG: Atl—Norm Johnson.

**TAMPA BAY BUCCANEERS**
**September 13, 1987, at Tampa Bay**
Atlanta ........................... 0 3 0 7 — 10
**Tampa Bay** .................... 14 13 7 14 — 48
TDs: TB—Gerald Carter 2, Cliff Austin, Steve Bartalo, Mark Carrier, Phil Freeman, Calvin Magee; Atl—Stacey Bailey. TD Passes: TB—Steve DeBerg 5; Atl—Scott Campbell. FG: Atl—Mick Luckhurst.

**WASHINGTON REDSKINS**
**November 27, 1966, at Washington**
New York Giants ........... 0 14 14 13 — 41
**Washington** .................. 13 21 14 24 — 72
TDs: Wash—A.D. Whitfield 3, Brig Owens 2, Charley Taylor 2, Rickie Harris, Joe Don Looney, Bobby Mitchell; NYG—Allen Jacobs, Homer Jones, Dan Lewis, Joe Morrison, Aaron Thomas, Gary Wood. TD Passes: Wash—Sonny Jurgensen 3; NYG—Gary Wood 2, Tom Kennedy. FG: Wash—Charlie Gogolak.

## NFL GAMES IN WHICH A TEAM HAS SCORED 60 OR MORE POINTS

*(Home team in capitals)*

**Regular Season**

WASHINGTON 72, New York Giants 41 .......... November 27, 1966
LOS ANGELES RAMS 70, Baltimore 27 .......... October 22, 1950
Chicago Cardinals 65, NEW YORK BULLDOGS 20 .......... November 13, 1949
LOS ANGELES RAMS 65, Detroit 24 .......... October 29, 1950
PHILADELPHIA 64, Cincinnati 0 .......... November 6, 1934
CHICAGO CARDINALS 63, New York Giants 35 .......... October 17, 1948
AKRON 62, Oorang 0 .......... October 29,1922
PITTSBURGH 62, New York Giants 7 .......... November 30, 1952
CLEVELAND 62, New York Giants 14 .......... December 6, 1953
CLEVELAND 62, Washington 3 .......... November 7, 1954
NEW YORK GIANTS 62, Philadelphia 10 .......... November 26, 1972
Atlanta 62, NEW ORLEANS 7 .......... September 16, 1973
NEW YORK JETS 62, Tampa Bay 28 .......... November 17, 1985
CHICAGO 61, San Francisco 20 .......... December 12, 1965
Cincinnati 61, HOUSTON 17 .......... December 17, 1972
CHICAGO 61, Green Bay 7 .......... December 7, 1980
CINCINNATI 61, Houston 7 .......... December 17, 1989
ROCK ISLAND 60, Evansville 0 .......... October 15, 1922
CHICAGO CARDINALS 60, Rochester 0 .......... October 7, 1923

**Postseason**

Chicago Bears 73, WASHINGTON 0 .......... December 8, 1940

## YOUNGEST AND OLDEST PLAYERS IN NFL IN 1993

| Ten Youngest Players | Birthdate | Games | Starts | Position |
|---|---|---|---|---|
| Tom Carter, Washington | 9/5/72 | 14 | 11 | CB |
| James Willis, Green Bay | 9/2/72 | 13 | 0 | LB |
| Othello Henderson, New Orleans | 8/23/72 | 5 | 1 | DB |
| Marvin Jones, N.Y. Jets | 6/28/72 | 9 | 0 | LB |
| Natrone Means, San Diego | 4/26/72 | 16 | 0 | RB |
| Robert Smith, Minnesota | 3/4/72 | 10 | 2 | RB |
| Jerome Bettis, L.A. Rams | 2/16/72 | 16 | 12 | RB |
| Drew Bledsoe, New England | 2/14/72 | 13 | 12 | QB |
| Michael Strahan, N.Y. Giants | 11/21/71 | 9 | 0 | DE |
| Russell Copeland, Buffalo | 11/4/71 | 16 | 2 | WR |

| Ten Oldest Players | Birthdate | Games | Starts | Position |
|---|---|---|---|---|
| Steve DeBerg, Tampa Bay-Miami | 1/19/54 | 8 | 5 | QB |
| Jackie Slater, L.A. Rams | 5/27/54 | 8 | 8 | T |
| Vince Evans, L.A. Raiders | 6/14/55 | 8 | 1 | QB |
| Phil Simms, N.Y. Giants | 11/3/55 | 16 | 16 | QB |
| Mike Kenn, Atlanta | 2/9/56 | 16 | 16 | T |
| Clay Matthews, Cleveland | 3/15/56 | 16 | 15 | LB |
| Max Montoya, L.A. Raiders | 5/12/56 | 16 | 16 | G |
| Nick Lowery, Kansas City | 5/27/56 | 16 | 0 | K |
| Joe Montana, Kansas City | 6/11/56 | 11 | 11 | QB |
| James Lofton, L.A. Rams-Phil. | 7/5/56 | 10 | 2 | WR |

## YOUNGEST AND OLDEST REGULAR STARTERS BY POSITION IN 1993

*Minimum: 8 Games Started*

| | Youngest | Oldest |
|---|---|---|
| QB | 2/14/72 Drew Bledsoe, N.E. | 11/3/55 Phil Simms, N.Y. Giants |
| RB | 2/16/72 Jerome Bettis, L.A. Rams | 3/26/60 Marcus Allen, K.C. |
| WR | 1/25/71 Vincent Brisby, N.E. | 9/17/60 Anthony Carter, Minn. |
| TE | 10/13/71 Irv Smith, N.O. | 2/2/59 Mike Tice, Minn. |
| C | 8/21/70 Steve Everitt, Clev. | 5/18/58 Ray Donaldson, Sea. |
| G | 9/15/71 Will Shields, K.C. | 5/12/56 Max Montoya, L.A. Raiders |
| T | 10/18/71 Bob Whitfield, Atl. | 5/27/54 Jackie Slater, L.A. Rams |
| DE | 5/25/71 Keith Hamilton, N.Y. Giants | 1/6/60 Howie Long, L.A. Raiders |
| DT | 11/14/70 Dana Stubblefield, S.F. | 10/17/57 Steve McMichael, Chi. |
| LB | 9/17/71 Eric Shaw, Cin. | 3/15/56 Clay Matthews, Clev. |
| CB | 9/2/72 Tom Carter, Wash. | 2/15/60 Darrell Green, Wash. |
| S | 2/18/71 George Teague, G.B. | 2/3/59 Dennis Smith, Den. |

## MARCUS ALLEN'S CAREER RUSHING VS. EACH OPPONENT

| Opponent | Games | Rushes | Yards | Yards Per Rush | Yards Per Game | TD |
|---|---|---|---|---|---|---|
| Arizona | 2 | 22 | 96 | 4.4 | 48.0 | 1 |
| Atlanta | 3 | 47 | 230 | 4.9 | 76.7 | 1 |
| Buffalo | 7 | 120 | 412 | 3.4 | 58.9 | 4 |
| Chicago | 4 | 61 | 252 | 4.1 | 63.0 | 4 |
| Cincinnati | 8 | 101 | 363 | 3.6 | 45.4 | 5 |
| Cleveland | 4 | 55 | 224 | 4.1 | 56.0 | 0 |
| Dallas | 3 | 25 | 93 | 3.7 | 31.0 | 1 |
| Denver | 20 | 281 | 1,189 | 4.2 | 59.5 | 7 |
| Detroit | 3 | 46 | 153 | 3.3 | 51.0 | 2 |
| Green Bay | 4 | 75 | 269 | 3.6 | 67.3 | 5 |
| Houston | 5 | 74 | 281 | 3.8 | 56.2 | 3 |
| Indianapolis | 2 | 28 | 141 | 5.0 | 70.5 | 0 |
| Kansas City | 17 | 264 | 961 | 3.6 | 56.5 | 8 |
| L.A. Raiders | 2 | 34 | 109 | 3.2 | 54.5 | 2 |
| L.A. Rams | 3 | 63 | 269 | 4.3 | 89.7 | 3 |
| Miami | 6 | 87 | 451 | 5.2 | 75.2 | 6 |
| Minnesota | 4 | 44 | 150 | 3.4 | 37.5 | 1 |
| New England | 2 | 37 | 139 | 3.8 | 69.5 | 1 |
| New Orleans | 3 | 53 | 234 | 4.4 | 78.0 | 2 |
| N.Y. Giants | 4 | 30 | 117 | 3.9 | 29.3 | 1 |
| N.Y. Jets | 2 | 30 | 119 | 4.0 | 59.5 | 2 |
| Philadelphia | 2 | 30 | 82 | 2.7 | 41.0 | 0 |
| Pittsburgh | 2 | 24 | 82 | 3.4 | 41.0 | 1 |
| San Diego | 20 | 315 | 1,297 | 4.1 | 64.9 | 20 |
| San Francisco | 3 | 49 | 233 | 4.8 | 77.7 | 1 |
| Seattle | 22 | 260 | 1,140 | 4.4 | 51.8 | 10 |
| Tampa Bay | 1 | 13 | 79 | 6.1 | 79.0 | 0 |
| Washington | 3 | 28 | 144 | 5.1 | 48.0 | 0 |
| Totals | 161 | 2,296 | 9,309 | 4.1 | 57.8 | 91 |

*Arizona totals include one game vs. St. Louis, one game vs. Phoenix*

## EMMITT SMITH'S CAREER RUSHING VS. EACH OPPONENT

| Opponent | Games | Rushes | Yards | Yards Per Rush | Yards Per Game | TD |
|---|---|---|---|---|---|---|
| Arizona | 8 | 162 | 716 | 4.4 | 89.5 | 11 |
| Atlanta | 4 | 73 | 369 | 5.1 | 92.3 | 4 |
| Chicago | 1 | 20 | 131 | 6.6 | 131.0 | 1 |
| Cincinnati | 1 | 19 | 62 | 3.3 | 62.0 | 1 |
| Cleveland | 1 | 32 | 112 | 3.5 | 112.0 | 0 |
| Denver | 1 | 26 | 62 | 2.4 | 62.0 | 1 |
| Detroit | 2 | 35 | 133 | 3.8 | 66.5 | 3 |
| Green Bay | 2 | 45 | 193 | 4.3 | 96.5 | 1 |
| Houston | 1 | 12 | 49 | 4.1 | 49.0 | 0 |
| Indianapolis | 1 | 25 | 104 | 4.2 | 104.0 | 1 |
| Kansas City | 1 | 24 | 95 | 4.0 | 95.0 | 1 |
| L.A. Raiders | 1 | 29 | 152 | 5.2 | 152.0 | 3 |
| L.A. Rams | 2 | 40 | 134 | 3.4 | 67.0 | 1 |
| Miami | 1 | 16 | 51 | 3.2 | 51.0 | 0 |
| Minnesota | 1 | 19 | 104 | 5.5 | 104.0 | 1 |
| New Orleans | 2 | 47 | 197 | 4.2 | 98.5 | 1 |
| N.Y. Giants | 8 | 149 | 697 | 4.7 | 87.1 | 6 |
| N.Y. Jets | 2 | 35 | 146 | 4.2 | 73.0 | 0 |
| Philadelphia | 8 | 168 | 871 | 5.2 | 108.9 | 2 |
| Pittsburgh | 1 | 32 | 109 | 3.4 | 109.0 | 1 |
| San Diego | 1 | 2 | 2 | 1.0 | 2.0 | 0 |
| San Francisco | 2 | 33 | 132 | 4.0 | 66.0 | 1 |
| Seattle | 1 | 22 | 78 | 3.5 | 78.0 | 2 |
| Tampa Bay | 2 | 39 | 169 | 4.3 | 84.5 | 1 |
| Washington | 7 | 158 | 831 | 5.3 | 118.7 | 7 |
| Totals | 62 | 1,262 | 5,699 | 4.5 | 91.9 | 50 |

*Arizona totals include eight games vs. Phoenix*

## BARRY SANDERS'S CAREER RUSHING VS. EACH OPPONENT

| Opponent | Games | Rushes | Yards | Yards Per Rush | Yards Per Game | TD |
|---|---|---|---|---|---|---|
| Arizona | 2 | 32 | 161 | 5.0 | 80.5 | 1 |
| Atlanta | 3 | 64 | 303 | 4.7 | 101.0 | 5 |
| Buffalo | 1 | 26 | 108 | 4.2 | 108.0 | 1 |
| Chicago | 9 | 171 | 784 | 4.6 | 87.1 | 6 |
| Cincinnati | 2 | 47 | 265 | 5.6 | 132.5 | 2 |
| Cleveland | 2 | 58 | 232 | 4.0 | 116.0 | 1 |
| Dallas | 2 | 39 | 163 | 4.2 | 81.5 | 0 |
| Denver | 1 | 23 | 147 | 6.4 | 147.0 | 1 |
| Green Bay | 9 | 175 | 834 | 4.8 | 92.7 | 4 |
| Houston | 2 | 41 | 145 | 3.5 | 72.5 | 3 |
| Indianapolis | 1 | 30 | 179 | 6.0 | 179.0 | 2 |
| Kansas City | 1 | 16 | 90 | 5.6 | 90.0 | 1 |
| L.A. Raiders | 1 | 25 | 176 | 7.0 | 176.0 | 2 |
| L.A. Rams | 2 | 52 | 148 | 2.8 | 74.0 | 1 |
| Miami | 1 | 32 | 143 | 4.5 | 143.0 | 0 |
| Minnesota | 9 | 169 | 820 | 4.9 | 91.1 | 7 |
| New England | 1 | 32 | 148 | 4.6 | 148.0 | 0 |
| New Orleans | 4 | 57 | 194 | 3.4 | 48.5 | 2 |
| N.Y. Giants | 2 | 23 | 126 | 5.5 | 63.0 | 1 |
| N.Y. Jets | 1 | 20 | 114 | 5.7 | 114.0 | 2 |
| Pittsburgh | 2 | 26 | 95 | 3.7 | 47.5 | 1 |
| San Francisco | 2 | 26 | 130 | 5.0 | 65.0 | 0 |
| Seattle | 2 | 31 | 124 | 4.0 | 62.0 | 1 |
| Tampa Bay | 9 | 192 | 1022 | 5.3 | 113.6 | 10 |
| Washington | 2 | 25 | 138 | 5.5 | 69.0 | 1 |
| Totals | 73 | 1,432 | 6,789 | 4.7 | 93.0 | 55 |

*Arizona totals include two games vs. Phoenix*

## INSIDE THE NUMBERS

### THURMAN THOMAS'S CAREER RUSHING VS. EACH OPPONENT

| Opponent | Games | Rushes | Yards | Yards Per Rush | Yards Per Game | TD |
|---|---|---|---|---|---|---|
| Arizona | 1 | 26 | 112 | 4.3 | 112.0 | 0 |
| Atlanta | 2 | 34 | 198 | 5.8 | 99.0 | 1 |
| Chicago | 2 | 30 | 129 | 4.3 | 64.5 | 1 |
| Cincinnati | 3 | 50 | 234 | 4.7 | 78.0 | 0 |
| Cleveland | 1 | 17 | 58 | 3.4 | 58.0 | 2 |
| Dallas | 1 | 25 | 75 | 3.0 | 75.0 | 0 |
| Denver | 3 | 50 | 194 | 3.9 | 64.7 | 1 |
| Green Bay | 2 | 47 | 222 | 4.7 | 111.0 | 1 |
| Houston | 4 | 69 | 301 | 4.4 | 75.3 | 2 |
| Indianapolis | 12 | 213 | 936 | 4.4 | 78.0 | 6 |
| Kansas City | 2 | 28 | 76 | 2.7 | 38.0 | 0 |
| L.A. Raiders | 5 | 79 | 356 | 4.5 | 71.2 | 3 |
| L.A. Rams | 2 | 46 | 208 | 4.5 | 104.0 | 3 |
| Miami | 11 | 218 | 997 | 4.6 | 90.6 | 4 |
| Minnesota | 1 | 18 | 86 | 4.8 | 86.0 | 1 |
| New England | 12 | 265 | 1,207 | 4.6 | 100.6 | 7 |
| New Orleans | 2 | 40 | 155 | 3.9 | 77.5 | 2 |
| N.Y. Giants | 2 | 47 | 182 | 3.9 | 91.0 | 1 |
| N.Y. Jets | 12 | 208 | 1,094 | 5.3 | 91.2 | 3 |
| Philadelphia | 2 | 31 | 84 | 2.7 | 42.0 | 0 |
| Pittsburgh | 4 | 81 | 351 | 4.3 | 87.8 | 1 |
| San Francisco | 2 | 25 | 92 | 3.7 | 46.0 | 1 |
| Seattle | 2 | 27 | 100 | 3.7 | 50.0 | 0 |
| Tampa Bay | 2 | 24 | 55 | 2.3 | 27.5 | 0 |
| Washington | 2 | 33 | 129 | 3.9 | 64.5 | 1 |
| Totals | 94 | 1,731 | 7,631 | 4.4 | 81.2 | 41 |

*Arizona totals include one game vs. Phoenix*

### JOE MONTANA'S CAREER PASSING VS. EACH OPPONENT

| Opponent | Games | Att. | Cmp. | Pct. | Yards | Avg. Gain | TD | Int. | Sacked |
|---|---|---|---|---|---|---|---|---|---|
| Arizona | 6 | 141 | 95 | 67.4 | 1,389 | 9.85 | 13 | 5 | 7/53 |
| Atlanta | 21 | 567 | 370 | 65.3 | 4,436 | 7.82 | 36 | 17 | 33/235 |
| Buffalo | 3 | 96 | 61 | 63.5 | 589 | 6.14 | 4 | 1 | 6/46 |
| Chicago | 7 | 162 | 90 | 55.6 | 1,023 | 6.31 | 5 | 4 | 20/144 |
| Cincinnati | 4 | 141 | 90 | 63.8 | 923 | 6.55 | 7 | 6 | 9/75 |
| Cleveland | 4 | 140 | 88 | 62.9 | 1,003 | 7.16 | 7 | 6 | 6/48 |
| Dallas | 5 | 126 | 84 | 66.7 | 1,114 | 8.84 | 9 | 3 | 7/48 |
| Denver | 6 | 172 | 96 | 55.8 | 1,289 | 7.49 | 6 | 4 | 10/72 |
| Detroit | 6 | 141 | 89 | 63.1 | 839 | 5.95 | 4 | 2 | 10/63 |
| Green Bay | 5 | 149 | 104 | 69.8 | 1,264 | 8.48 | 7 | 2 | 8/50 |
| Houston | 4 | 135 | 95 | 70.4 | 1,164 | 8.62 | 10 | 4 | 5/31 |
| Indianapolis | 1 | 26 | 15 | 57.7 | 233 | 8.96 | 1 | 0 | 3/29 |
| Kansas City | 2 | 69 | 43 | 62.3 | 488 | 7.07 | 2 | 2 | 3/16 |
| L.A. Raiders | 5 | 105 | 58 | 55.2 | 727 | 6.92 | 6 | 1 | 11/92 |
| L.A. Rams | 23 | 693 | 446 | 64.4 | 5,632 | 8.13 | 37 | 15 | 47/297 |
| Miami | 3 | 47 | 29 | 61.7 | 357 | 7.60 | 1 | 0 | 3/22 |
| Minnesota | 6 | 128 | 83 | 64.8 | 950 | 7.42 | 9 | 5 | 8/34 |
| New England | 4 | 108 | 69 | 63.9 | 791 | 7.32 | 6 | 2 | 6/39 |
| New Orleans | 20 | 508 | 314 | 61.8 | 3,704 | 7.29 | 31 | 14 | 38/225 |
| N.Y. Giants | 8 | 210 | 132 | 62.9 | 1,435 | 6.83 | 10 | 3 | 7/38 |
| N.Y. Jets | 3 | 79 | 48 | 60.8 | 538 | 6.81 | 3 | 3 | 3/17 |
| Philadelphia | 3 | 54 | 35 | 64.8 | 546 | 10.11 | 5 | 2 | 9/52 |
| Pittsburgh | 4 | 150 | 100 | 66.7 | 919 | 6.13 | 4 | 8 | 3/20 |
| San Diego | 5 | 139 | 84 | 60.4 | 1,079 | 7.76 | 9 | 4 | 7/32 |
| Seattle | 5 | 120 | 75 | 62.5 | 988 | 8.23 | 7 | 5 | 4/25 |
| Tampa Bay | 9 | 275 | 190 | 69.1 | 2,106 | 7.66 | 11 | 6 | 12/76 |
| Washington | 6 | 217 | 127 | 58.5 | 1,742 | 8.03 | 7 | 6 | 9/84 |
| Totals | 178 | 4,898 | 3,110 | 63.5 | 37,268 | 7.61 | 257 | 130 | 294/1,963 |

*Arizona totals include six games vs. St. Louis*
*L.A. Raiders totals include one game vs. Oakland*

### PHIL SIMMS'S CAREER PASSING VS. EACH OPPONENT

| Opponent | Games | Att. | Cmp. | Pct. | Yards | Avg. Gain | TD | Int. | Sacked |
|---|---|---|---|---|---|---|---|---|---|
| Arizona | 18 | 509 | 263 | 51.7 | 3,404 | 6.69 | 29 | 10 | 47/294 |
| Atlanta | 4 | 116 | 66 | 56.9 | 910 | 7.84 | 4 | 3 | 12/81 |
| Buffalo | 2 | 38 | 18 | 47.4 | 219 | 5.76 | 2 | 3 | 3/7 |
| Chicago | 3 | 91 | 58 | 63.7 | 678 | 7.45 | 5 | 0 | 13/82 |
| Cincinnati | 2 | 106 | 66 | 62.3 | 809 | 7.63 | 4 | 2 | 10/88 |
| Cleveland | 1 | 37 | 23 | 62.2 | 289 | 7.81 | 1 | 2 | 4/22 |
| Dallas | 23 | 604 | 322 | 53.3 | 4,804 | 7.95 | 34 | 29 | 59/427 |
| Denver | 3 | 78 | 43 | 55.1 | 519 | 6.65 | 1 | 1 | 8/64 |
| Detroit | 4 | 112 | 78 | 69.6 | 935 | 8.35 | 6 | 0 | 11/73 |
| Green Bay | 5 | 156 | 97 | 62.2 | 1,302 | 8.35 | 11 | 4 | 16/111 |
| Houston | 2 | 41 | 28 | 68.3 | 434 | 10.59 | 3 | 1 | 1/8 |
| Indianapolis | 3 | 50 | 33 | 66.0 | 324 | 6.48 | 2 | 5 | 5/33 |
| Kansas City | 3 | 82 | 42 | 51.2 | 587 | 7.16 | 5 | 5 | 7/52 |
| L.A. Raiders | 3 | 84 | 50 | 59.5 | 604 | 7.19 | 2 | 3 | 8/62 |
| L.A. Rams | 8 | 262 | 152 | 58.0 | 1,782 | 6.80 | 7 | 6 | 32/257 |
| Miami | 2 | 49 | 30 | 61.2 | 439 | 8.96 | 1 | 0 | 4/19 |
| Minnesota | 3 | 58 | 33 | 56.9 | 428 | 7.38 | 1 | 2 | 4/27 |
| New Orleans | 6 | 178 | 105 | 59.0 | 1,177 | 6.61 | 7 | 7 | 17/110 |
| N.Y. Jets | 5 | 165 | 98 | 59.4 | 1,070 | 6.48 | 5 | 3 | 22/168 |
| Philadelphia | 21 | 595 | 296 | 49.7 | 4,111 | 6.91 | 24 | 23 | 58/414 |
| Pittsburgh | 1 | 16 | 10 | 62.5 | 106 | 6.63 | 1 | 1 | 3/24 |
| San Diego | 3 | 99 | 54 | 54.5 | 667 | 6.74 | 1 | 4 | 8/72 |
| San Francisco | 8 | 295 | 163 | 55.3 | 2,025 | 6.86 | 8 | 9 | 35/212 |
| Seattle | 3 | 78 | 43 | 55.1 | 487 | 6.24 | 3 | 5 | 9/59 |
| Tampa Bay | 8 | 217 | 123 | 56.7 | 1,264 | 5.82 | 7 | 6 | 20/201 |
| Washington | 20 | 531 | 282 | 53.1 | 4,088 | 7.70 | 25 | 23 | 61/451 |
| Totals | 164 | 4,647 | 2,576 | 55.4 | 33,462 | 7.20 | 199 | 157 | 477/3,418 |

*Arizona totals include 12 games vs. St. Louis, six games vs. Phoenix*
*Indianapolis totals include one game vs. Baltimore*

### DAN MARINO'S CAREER PASSING VS. EACH OPPONENT

| Opponent | Games | Att. | Cmp. | Pct. | Yards | Avg. Gain | TD | Int. | Sacked |
|---|---|---|---|---|---|---|---|---|---|
| Arizona | 2 | 61 | 42 | 68.9 | 634 | 10.39 | 5 | 0 | 1/9 |
| Atlanta | 2 | 80 | 40 | 50.0 | 553 | 6.91 | 2 | 4 | 1/2 |
| Buffalo | 20 | 681 | 432 | 63.4 | 5,375 | 7.89 | 39 | 27 | 25/210 |
| Chicago | 3 | 79 | 39 | 49.4 | 566 | 7.16 | 5 | 3 | 6/36 |
| Cincinnati | 4 | 136 | 84 | 61.8 | 1,026 | 7.54 | 7 | 1 | 5/39 |
| Cleveland | 6 | 205 | 126 | 61.5 | 1,661 | 8.10 | 11 | 5 | 4/33 |
| Dallas | 3 | 115 | 66 | 57.4 | 860 | 7.48 | 6 | 3 | 4/36 |
| Denver | 1 | 43 | 25 | 58.1 | 390 | 9.07 | 3 | 0 | 3/25 |
| Detroit | 2 | 78 | 39 | 50.0 | 421 | 5.40 | 2 | 2 | 3/28 |
| Green Bay | 4 | 146 | 95 | 65.1 | 1,151 | 7.88 | 9 | 6 | 4/22 |
| Houston | 7 | 220 | 116 | 52.7 | 1,464 | 6.65 | 10 | 11 | 7/36 |
| Indianapolis | 21 | 687 | 412 | 60.0 | 5,108 | 7.44 | 37 | 11 | 16/115 |
| Kansas City | 4 | 148 | 84 | 56.8 | 1,031 | 6.97 | 8 | 3 | 2/20 |
| L.A. Raiders | 6 | 204 | 116 | 56.9 | 1,469 | 7.20 | 12 | 6 | 8/70 |
| L.A. Rams | 3 | 121 | 75 | 62.0 | 905 | 7.48 | 9 | 3 | 1/4 |
| Minnesota | 1 | 37 | 20 | 54.1 | 264 | 7.14 | 2 | 3 | 0/0 |
| New England | 19 | 649 | 376 | 57.9 | 4,544 | 7.00 | 30 | 29 | 13/101 |
| New Orleans | 3 | 105 | 65 | 61.9 | 650 | 6.19 | 5 | 2 | 6/42 |
| N.Y. Giants | 1 | 30 | 14 | 46.7 | 115 | 3.83 | 0 | 2 | 1/7 |
| N.Y. Jets | 19 | 712 | 417 | 58.6 | 5,724 | 8.04 | 49 | 22 | 28/153 |
| Philadelphia | 3 | 127 | 72 | 56.7 | 987 | 7.77 | 6 | 2 | 5/45 |
| Pittsburgh | 6 | 175 | 110 | 62.9 | 1,333 | 7.62 | 9 | 9 | 1/4 |
| San Diego | 4 | 163 | 103 | 63.2 | 1,243 | 7.63 | 9 | 2 | 6/42 |
| San Francisco | 3 | 106 | 61 | 57.5 | 687 | 6.48 | 3 | 4 | 4/36 |
| Seattle | 2 | 68 | 40 | 58.8 | 504 | 7.41 | 3 | 4 | 3/21 |
| Tampa Bay | 3 | 117 | 74 | 63.2 | 875 | 7.48 | 7 | 1 | 1/10 |
| Washington | 4 | 141 | 76 | 53.9 | 1,180 | 8.37 | 10 | 3 | 2/7 |
| Totals | 156 | 5,434 | 3,219 | 59.2 | 40,720 | 7.49 | 298 | 168 | 160/1,157 |

*Arizona totals include one game vs. St. Louis, one game vs. Phoenix*
*Indianapolis totals include two games vs. Baltimore*

### JOHN ELWAY'S CAREER PASSING VS. EACH OPPONENT

| Opponent | Games | Att. | Cmp. | Pct. | Yards | Avg. Gain | TD | Int. | Sacked |
|---|---|---|---|---|---|---|---|---|---|
| Arizona | 2 | 62 | 39 | 62.9 | 492 | 7.94 | 3 | 5 | 3/16 |
| Atlanta | 2 | 64 | 35 | 54.7 | 526 | 8.22 | 4 | 2 | 4/26 |
| Buffalo | 4 | 109 | 55 | 50.5 | 739 | 6.78 | 5 | 4 | 8/70 |
| Chicago | 5 | 118 | 65 | 55.1 | 763 | 6.47 | 3 | 4 | 12/73 |
| Cincinnati | 3 | 75 | 48 | 64.0 | 617 | 8.23 | 6 | 1 | 2/13 |
| Cleveland | 8 | 210 | 117 | 55.7 | 1,656 | 7.89 | 12 | 7 | 15/120 |
| Dallas | 1 | 24 | 12 | 50.0 | 200 | 8.33 | 3 | 0 | 1/2 |
| Detroit | 3 | 88 | 56 | 63.6 | 699 | 7.94 | 2 | 2 | 7/72 |
| Green Bay | 4 | 153 | 88 | 57.5 | 913 | 5.97 | 2 | 5 | 5/38 |
| Houston | 3 | 98 | 54 | 55.1 | 749 | 7.64 | 6 | 4 | 11/109 |
| Indianapolis | 7 | 213 | 118 | 55.4 | 1,545 | 7.25 | 8 | 2 | 17/129 |
| Kansas City | 20 | 626 | 341 | 54.5 | 4,311 | 6.89 | 17 | 29 | 52/388 |
| L.A. Raiders | 19 | 560 | 306 | 54.6 | 3,811 | 6.81 | 22 | 23 | 51/417 |
| L.A. Rams | 2 | 74 | 39 | 52.7 | 501 | 6.77 | 5 | 2 | 3/24 |
| Miami | 1 | 37 | 18 | 48.6 | 250 | 6.76 | 0 | 1 | 3/24 |
| Minnesota | 5 | 130 | 84 | 64.6 | 923 | 7.10 | 10 | 2 | 13/100 |
| New England | 6 | 192 | 108 | 56.3 | 1,286 | 6.70 | 7 | 4 | 8/54 |
| New Orleans | 2 | 79 | 46 | 58.2 | 519 | 6.57 | 4 | 2 | 4/35 |
| N.Y. Giants | 3 | 103 | 58 | 56.3 | 724 | 7.03 | 2 | 3 | 3/19 |
| N.Y. Jets | 3 | 90 | 51 | 56.7 | 675 | 7.50 | 3 | 3 | 7/42 |
| Philadelphia | 4 | 102 | 52 | 51.0 | 626 | 6.14 | 4 | 6 | 16/119 |
| Pittsburgh | 7 | 192 | 105 | 54.7 | 1,366 | 7.11 | 6 | 5 | 14/109 |
| San Diego | 21 | 646 | 357 | 55.3 | 4,327 | 6.70 | 17 | 26 | 50/340 |
| San Francisco | 2 | 81 | 41 | 50.6 | 425 | 5.25 | 3 | 3 | 5/43 |
| Seattle | 20 | 656 | 369 | 56.3 | 4,968 | 7.57 | 28 | 20 | 47/329 |
| Tampa Bay | 1 | 41 | 26 | 63.4 | 225 | 5.49 | 0 | 0 | 1/0 |
| Washington | 2 | 67 | 35 | 52.2 | 410 | 6.12 | 1 | 2 | 8/59 |
| Totals | 160 | 4,890 | 2,723 | 55.7 | 34,246 | 7.00 | 183 | 167 | 370/2,770 |

*Arizona totals include two games vs. Phoenix*

## BOOMER ESIASON'S CAREER PASSING VS. EACH OPPONENT

| Opponent | Games | Att. | Cmp. | Pct. | Yards | Avg. Gain | TD | Int. | Sacked |
|---|---|---|---|---|---|---|---|---|---|
| Arizona | 2 | 38 | 24 | 63.2 | 356 | 9.37 | 4 | 1 | 3/22 |
| Atlanta | 3 | 67 | 34 | 50.7 | 367 | 5.48 | 1 | 2 | 3/3 |
| Buffalo | 8 | 183 | 109 | 59.6 | 1,410 | 7.70 | 8 | 6 | 8/72 |
| Chicago | 3 | 95 | 48 | 50.5 | 568 | 5.98 | 5 | 5 | 9/88 |
| Cincinnati | 1 | 26 | 17 | 65.4 | 192 | 7.38 | 0 | 0 | 2/15 |
| Cleveland | 16 | 369 | 198 | 53.7 | 2,561 | 6.94 | 18 | 13 | 19/134 |
| Dallas | 4 | 122 | 69 | 56.6 | 855 | 7.01 | 6 | 3 | 5/35 |
| Denver | 3 | 90 | 61 | 67.8 | 883 | 9.81 | 6 | 5 | 5/37 |
| Detroit | 3 | 91 | 55 | 60.4 | 630 | 6.92 | 3 | 4 | 5/24 |
| Green Bay | 2 | 47 | 26 | 55.3 | 335 | 7.13 | 4 | 2 | 3/24 |
| Houston | 17 | 461 | 266 | 57.7 | 3,740 | 8.11 | 25 | 21 | 36/255 |
| Indianapolis | 6 | 153 | 84 | 54.9 | 1,059 | 6.92 | 6 | 6 | 9/72 |
| Kansas City | 4 | 121 | 67 | 55.4 | 940 | 7.77 | 5 | 3 | 7/71 |
| L.A. Raiders | 6 | 147 | 81 | 55.1 | 1,029 | 7.00 | 5 | 2 | 8/70 |
| L.A. Rams | 1 | 45 | 31 | 68.9 | 490 | 10.89 | 3 | 0 | 1/7 |
| Miami | 5 | 151 | 92 | 60.9 | 1,196 | 7.92 | 7 | 2 | 6/69 |
| Minnesota | 3 | 100 | 59 | 59.0 | 747 | 7.47 | 4 | 8 | 9/78 |
| New England | 8 | 241 | 133 | 55.2 | 1,968 | 8.17 | 13 | 7 | 11/79 |
| New Orleans | 3 | 75 | 33 | 44.0 | 309 | 4.12 | 3 | 2 | 9/71 |
| N.Y. Giants | 3 | 71 | 44 | 62.0 | 526 | 7.41 | 4 | 0 | 4/36 |
| N.Y. Jets | 7 | 180 | 93 | 51.7 | 1,410 | 7.83 | 12 | 8 | 16/123 |
| Philadelphia | 3 | 83 | 49 | 59.0 | 770 | 9.28 | 9 | 5 | 5/45 |
| Pittsburgh | 16 | 437 | 261 | 59.7 | 3,589 | 8.21 | 18 | 17 | 28/230 |
| San Diego | 3 | 97 | 56 | 57.7 | 748 | 7.71 | 8 | 5 | 10/84 |
| San Francisco | 2 | 49 | 26 | 53.1 | 294 | 6.00 | 2 | 2 | 5/28 |
| Seattle | 6 | 167 | 90 | 53.9 | 1,093 | 6.54 | 2 | 6 | 14/109 |
| Tampa Bay | 1 | 28 | 17 | 60.7 | 197 | 7.04 | 5 | 0 | 1/1 |
| Washington | 4 | 117 | 62 | 53.0 | 861 | 7.36 | 4 | 3 | 9/72 |
| Totals | 143 | 3,851 | 2,185 | 56.7 | 29,092 | 7.55 | 190 | 140 | 248/1,954 |

*Arizona totals include one game vs. St. Louis, one game vs. Phoenix*

## WARREN MOON'S CAREER PASSING VS. EACH OPPONENT

| Opponent | Games | Att. | Cmp. | Pct. | Yards | Avg. Gain | TD | Int. | Sacked |
|---|---|---|---|---|---|---|---|---|---|
| Arizona | 2 | 61 | 31 | 50.8 | 453 | 7.43 | 4 | 2 | 3/21 |
| Atlanta | 4 | 156 | 87 | 55.8 | 1,189 | 7.62 | 9 | 5 | 9/43 |
| Buffalo | 7 | 172 | 96 | 55.8 | 1,267 | 7.37 | 7 | 9 | 12/94 |
| Chicago | 2 | 55 | 28 | 50.9 | 521 | 9.47 | 3 | 3 | 5/49 |
| Cincinnati | 19 | 606 | 357 | 58.9 | 4,608 | 7.60 | 35 | 22 | 36/301 |
| Cleveland | 18 | 561 | 316 | 56.3 | 4,048 | 7.22 | 23 | 21 | 41/308 |
| Dallas | 3 | 111 | 67 | 60.4 | 873 | 7.86 | 2 | 4 | 16/105 |
| Denver | 3 | 87 | 50 | 57.5 | 777 | 8.93 | 5 | 2 | 9/66 |
| Detroit | 2 | 76 | 51 | 67.1 | 743 | 9.78 | 3 | 4 | 0/0 |
| Green Bay | 1 | 21 | 14 | 66.7 | 218 | 10.38 | 2 | 1 | 0/0 |
| Indianapolis | 7 | 255 | 160 | 62.7 | 2,156 | 8.45 | 13 | 7 | 14/97 |
| Kansas City | 8 | 267 | 166 | 62.2 | 2,006 | 7.51 | 10 | 7 | 26/180 |
| L.A. Raiders | 4 | 138 | 68 | 49.3 | 1,004 | 7.28 | 6 | 5 | 13/115 |
| L.A. Rams | 4 | 157 | 85 | 54.1 | 1,163 | 7.41 | 4 | 7 | 10/71 |
| Miami | 5 | 111 | 76 | 68.5 | 910 | 8.20 | 5 | 6 | 9/97 |
| Minnesota | 3 | 95 | 58 | 61.1 | 592 | 6.23 | 2 | 2 | 14/106 |
| New England | 3 | 94 | 50 | 53.2 | 597 | 6.35 | 5 | 4 | 4/31 |
| New Orleans | 4 | 113 | 63 | 55.8 | 737 | 6.52 | 3 | 3 | 8/65 |
| N.Y. Giants | 2 | 83 | 48 | 57.8 | 566 | 6.82 | 3 | 2 | 5/46 |
| N.Y. Jets | 3 | 121 | 85 | 70.2 | 1,011 | 8.36 | 6 | 2 | 7/60 |
| Philadelphia | 1 | 46 | 24 | 52.2 | 262 | 5.70 | 0 | 0 | 4/36 |
| Pittsburgh | 19 | 591 | 333 | 56.3 | 4,208 | 7.12 | 22 | 27 | 41/315 |
| San Diego | 6 | 201 | 108 | 53.7 | 1,362 | 6.78 | 7 | 6 | 10/71 |
| San Francisco | 4 | 128 | 71 | 55.5 | 903 | 7.05 | 7 | 8 | 8/46 |
| Seattle | 3 | 115 | 73 | 63.5 | 783 | 6.81 | 4 | 4 | 5/34 |
| Tampa Bay | 1 | 23 | 14 | 60.9 | 149 | 6.48 | 2 | 0 | 0/0 |
| Washington | 3 | 102 | 53 | 52.0 | 579 | 5.68 | 4 | 3 | 6/46 |
| Totals | 141 | 4,546 | 2,632 | 57.9 | 33,685 | 7.41 | 196 | 166 | 315/2,403 |

*Arizona totals include one game vs. St. Louis, one game vs. Phoenix*

## JIM KELLY'S CAREER PASSING VS. EACH OPPONENT

| Opponent | Games | Att. | Cmp. | Pct. | Yards | Avg. Gain | TD | Int. | Sacked |
|---|---|---|---|---|---|---|---|---|---|
| Arizona | 2 | 26 | 17 | 65.4 | 270 | 10.38 | 4 | 1 | 5/34 |
| Atlanta | 2 | 37 | 24 | 64.9 | 324 | 8.76 | 4 | 2 | 3/18 |
| Chicago | 2 | 66 | 39 | 59.1 | 576 | 8.73 | 3 | 1 | 9/79 |
| Cincinnati | 4 | 99 | 65 | 65.7 | 1,008 | 10.18 | 10 | 7 | 5/49 |
| Cleveland | 3 | 93 | 56 | 60.2 | 737 | 7.93 | 5 | 0 | 6/31 |
| Dallas | 1 | 27 | 16 | 59.3 | 155 | 5.74 | 1 | 1 | 4/26 |
| Denver | 4 | 124 | 71 | 57.3 | 813 | 6.56 | 3 | 7 | 8/58 |
| Green Bay | 2 | 49 | 27 | 55.1 | 312 | 6.37 | 3 | 2 | 5/23 |
| Houston | 6 | 179 | 110 | 61.5 | 1,435 | 8.02 | 14 | 6 | 19/141 |
| Indianapolis | 15 | 407 | 241 | 59.2 | 3,015 | 7.41 | 26 | 10 | 14/112 |
| Kansas City | 4 | 131 | 81 | 61.8 | 884 | 6.75 | 3 | 7 | 12/101 |
| L.A. Raiders | 6 | 208 | 125 | 60.1 | 1,550 | 7.45 | 8 | 5 | 12/89 |
| L.A. Rams | 1 | 19 | 13 | 68.4 | 106 | 5.58 | 2 | 1 | 1/0 |
| Miami | 14 | 450 | 286 | 63.6 | 3,358 | 7.46 | 17 | 12 | 22/173 |
| Minnesota | 1 | 31 | 17 | 54.8 | 204 | 6.58 | 0 | 1 | 1/8 |
| New England | 15 | 426 | 252 | 59.2 | 3,235 | 7.59 | 20 | 19 | 41/329 |
| New Orleans | 2 | 63 | 30 | 47.6 | 346 | 5.49 | 2 | 4 | 3/16 |
| N.Y. Giants | 2 | 36 | 21 | 58.3 | 257 | 7.14 | 2 | 1 | 5/30 |
| N.Y. Jets | 15 | 472 | 281 | 59.5 | 3,566 | 7.56 | 26 | 18 | 24/170 |
| Philadelphia | 3 | 98 | 56 | 57.1 | 698 | 7.12 | 4 | 5 | 3/26 |
| Pittsburgh | 5 | 149 | 95 | 63.8 | 1,129 | 7.58 | 11 | 3 | 9/62 |
| San Francisco | 2 | 75 | 48 | 64.0 | 668 | 8.91 | 3 | 4 | 5/32 |
| Seattle | 2 | 48 | 26 | 54.2 | 324 | 6.75 | 1 | 2 | 2/21 |
| Tampa Bay | 3 | 114 | 72 | 63.2 | 913 | 8.01 | 4 | 3 | 5/54 |
| Washington | 2 | 67 | 43 | 64.2 | 530 | 7.91 | 3 | 4 | 3/33 |
| Totals | 118 | 3,494 | 2,112 | 60.4 | 26,413 | 7.56 | 179 | 126 | 226/1,715 |

*Arizona totals include one game vs. St. Louis, one game vs. Phoenix*

## TROY AIKMAN'S CAREER PASSING VS. EACH OPPONENT

| Opponent | Games | Att. | Cmp. | Pct. | Yards | Avg. Gain | TD | Int. | Sacked |
|---|---|---|---|---|---|---|---|---|---|
| Arizona | 8 | 210 | 131 | 62.4 | 1,726 | 8.22 | 8 | 8 | 12/85 |
| Atlanta | 2 | 44 | 31 | 70.5 | 480 | 10.91 | 4 | 2 | 0/0 |
| Buffalo | 1 | 45 | 28 | 62.2 | 297 | 6.60 | 0 | 2 | 1/7 |
| Chicago | 1 | 20 | 10 | 50.0 | 78 | 3.90 | 0 | 0 | 1/2 |
| Cincinnati | 1 | 22 | 14 | 63.6 | 276 | 12.55 | 1 | 2 | 1/12 |
| Cleveland | 1 | 37 | 24 | 64.9 | 274 | 7.41 | 2 | 0 | 2/9 |
| Denver | 1 | 35 | 25 | 71.4 | 231 | 6.60 | 3 | 0 | 2/9 |
| Detroit | 2 | 67 | 44 | 65.7 | 545 | 8.13 | 2 | 3 | 2/16 |
| Green Bay | 3 | 92 | 67 | 72.8 | 729 | 7.92 | 2 | 4 | 4/29 |
| Houston | 1 | 39 | 24 | 61.5 | 260 | 6.67 | 1 | 0 | 3/19 |
| Indianapolis | 1 | 28 | 21 | 75.0 | 245 | 8.75 | 1 | 0 | 2/14 |
| Kansas City | 1 | 29 | 21 | 72.4 | 192 | 6.62 | 1 | 2 | 1/9 |
| L.A. Raiders | 1 | 25 | 16 | 64.0 | 234 | 9.36 | 0 | 0 | 5/27 |
| L.A. Rams | 3 | 103 | 58 | 56.3 | 754 | 7.32 | 7 | 2 | 4/25 |
| Miami | 2 | 76 | 53 | 69.7 | 442 | 5.82 | 2 | 2 | 0/0 |
| Minnesota | 1 | 29 | 19 | 65.5 | 208 | 7.17 | 1 | 0 | 0/0 |
| New Orleans | 2 | 56 | 32 | 57.1 | 357 | 6.38 | 1 | 2 | 4/46 |
| N.Y. Giants | 10 | 231 | 155 | 67.1 | 1,587 | 6.87 | 9 | 5 | 15/91 |
| N.Y. Jets | 2 | 67 | 46 | 68.7 | 501 | 7.48 | 2 | 5 | 6/40 |
| Philadelphia | 9 | 232 | 121 | 52.2 | 1,295 | 5.58 | 6 | 11 | 31/191 |
| San Diego | 1 | 29 | 13 | 44.8 | 193 | 6.66 | 1 | 1 | 5/32 |
| San Francisco | 2 | 56 | 30 | 53.6 | 339 | 6.05 | 1 | 1 | 4/29 |
| Seattle | 1 | 23 | 15 | 65.2 | 173 | 7.52 | 0 | 2 | 1/3 |
| Tampa Bay | 2 | 53 | 30 | 56.6 | 332 | 6.26 | 2 | 2 | 5/38 |
| Washington | 9 | 272 | 163 | 59.9 | 1,879 | 6.91 | 12 | 10 | 28/199 |
| Totals | 68 | 1,920 | 1,191 | 62.0 | 13,627 | 7.10 | 69 | 66 | 139/932 |

*Arizona totals include eight games vs. Phoenix*

## JERRY RICE'S CAREER RECEIVING VS. EACH OPPONENT

| Opponent | Games | Rec. | Yards | Yards Per Rec. | Yards Per Game | TD |
|---|---|---|---|---|---|---|
| Arizona | 5 | 25 | 465 | 18.6 | 93.0 | 5 |
| Atlanta | 17 | 89 | 1,523 | 17.1 | 89.6 | 17 |
| Buffalo | 2 | 6 | 72 | 12.0 | 36.0 | 1 |
| Chicago | 5 | 24 | 424 | 17.7 | 84.8 | 7 |
| Cincinnati | 3 | 16 | 269 | 16.8 | 89.7 | 2 |
| Cleveland | 3 | 19 | 275 | 14.5 | 91.7 | 4 |
| Dallas | 4 | 28 | 368 | 13.1 | 92.0 | 2 |
| Denver | 2 | 7 | 145 | 20.7 | 72.5 | 0 |
| Detroit | 5 | 17 | 267 | 15.7 | 53.4 | 2 |
| Green Bay | 4 | 23 | 432 | 18.8 | 108.0 | 4 |
| Houston | 3 | 23 | 238 | 10.3 | 79.3 | 2 |
| Indianapolis | 2 | 12 | 335 | 27.9 | 167.5 | 4 |
| Kansas City | 2 | 8 | 100 | 12.5 | 50.0 | 2 |
| L.A. Raiders | 3 | 11 | 193 | 17.5 | 64.3 | 0 |
| L.A. Rams | 18 | 84 | 1,527 | 18.2 | 84.8 | 11 |
| Miami | 2 | 10 | 155 | 15.5 | 77.5 | 3 |
| Minnesota | 7 | 32 | 552 | 17.3 | 78.9 | 6 |
| New England | 3 | 13 | 207 | 15.9 | 69.0 | 3 |
| New Orleans | 18 | 86 | 1,280 | 14.9 | 75.3 | 9 |
| N.Y. Giants | 6 | 27 | 454 | 16.8 | 75.7 | 4 |
| N.Y. Jets | 3 | 15 | 265 | 17.7 | 88.3 | 2 |
| Philadelphia | 5 | 25 | 424 | 17.0 | 84.8 | 5 |
| Pittsburgh | 3 | 19 | 215 | 11.3 | 71.7 | 3 |
| San Diego | 2 | 15 | 321 | 21.4 | 160.5 | 4 |
| Seattle | 3 | 14 | 272 | 19.4 | 90.7 | 4 |
| Tampa Bay | 6 | 39 | 615 | 15.8 | 102.5 | 10 |
| Washington | 4 | 21 | 383 | 18.2 | 95.8 | 2 |
| Totals | 140 | 708 | 11,776 | 16.6 | 84.1 | 118 |

*Arizona totals include one game vs. St. Louis, four games vs. Phoenix*

## ART MONK'S CAREER RECEIVING VS. EACH OPPONENT

| Opponent | Games | Rec. | Yards | Yards Per Rec. | Yards Per Game | TD |
|---|---|---|---|---|---|---|
| Arizona | 27 | 112 | 1,555 | 13.9 | 59.6 | 14 |
| Atlanta | 9 | 42 | 600 | 14.3 | 66.7 | 7 |
| Buffalo | 5 | 31 | 305 | 9.8 | 61.0 | 2 |
| Chicago | 7 | 36 | 496 | 13.8 | 70.9 | 4 |
| Cincinnati | 3 | 21 | 366 | 17.4 | 122.0 | 1 |
| Cleveland | 3 | 11 | 146 | 13.3 | 48.7 | 1 |
| Dallas | 24 | 94 | 1,334 | 14.2 | 55.6 | 3 |
| Denver | 4 | 21 | 261 | 12.4 | 65.3 | 2 |
| Detroit | 8 | 39 | 426 | 10.9 | 53.3 | 2 |
| Green Bay | 3 | 10 | 148 | 14.8 | 49.3 | 1 |
| Houston | 3 | 16 | 147 | 9.2 | 49.0 | 0 |
| Indianapolis | 4 | 22 | 351 | 16.0 | 87.8 | 5 |
| Kansas City | 1 | 2 | 19 | 9.5 | 19.0 | 0 |
| L.A. Raiders | 5 | 14 | 258 | 18.4 | 51.6 | 1 |
| L.A. Rams | 5 | 16 | 310 | 19.4 | 62.0 | 2 |
| Miami | 4 | 20 | 219 | 11.0 | 54.8 | 2 |
| Minnesota | 5 | 21 | 243 | 11.6 | 48.6 | 1 |
| New England | 3 | 9 | 100 | 11.1 | 33.3 | 0 |
| New Orleans | 7 | 32 | 440 | 13.8 | 62.9 | 2 |
| N.Y. Giants | 26 | 101 | 1,313 | 13.0 | 50.5 | 3 |
| N.Y. Jets | 2 | 6 | 94 | 15.7 | 47.0 | 0 |
| Philadelphia | 27 | 101 | 1,299 | 12.9 | 48.1 | 9 |
| Pittsburgh | 3 | 23 | 281 | 12.2 | 93.7 | 1 |
| San Diego | 4 | 23 | 361 | 15.7 | 90.3 | 0 |
| San Francisco | 6 | 40 | 583 | 14.6 | 97.2 | 2 |
| Seattle | 4 | 12 | 226 | 18.8 | 56.5 | 0 |
| Tampa Bay | 3 | 13 | 145 | 11.2 | 48.3 | 0 |
| Totals | 205 | 888 | 12,026 | 13.5 | 58.7 | 65 |

*Arizona totals include 15 games vs. St. Louis, 12 games vs. Phoenix*
*Indianapolis totals include one game vs. Baltimore*
*L.A. Raiders totals include one game vs. Oakland*

## ANDRE REED'S CAREER RECEIVING VS. EACH OPPONENT

| Opponent | Games | Rec. | Yards | Yards Per Rec. | Yards Per Game | TD |
|---|---|---|---|---|---|---|
| Arizona | 2 | 0 | 0 | — | 0.0 | 0 |
| Atlanta | 2 | 9 | 170 | 18.9 | 85.0 | 1 |
| Chicago | 2 | 11 | 131 | 11.9 | 65.5 | 0 |
| Cincinnati | 5 | 11 | 171 | 15.5 | 42.8 | 2 |
| Cleveland | 4 | 16 | 250 | 15.6 | 62.5 | 1 |
| Dallas | 1 | 1 | 10 | 10.0 | 10.0 | 0 |
| Denver | 4 | 21 | 258 | 12.3 | 64.5 | 1 |
| Detroit | 1 | 2 | 31 | 15.5 | 31.0 | 1 |
| Green Bay | 2 | 6 | 58 | 9.7 | 29.0 | 1 |
| Houston | 7 | 35 | 536 | 15.3 | 76.6 | 5 |
| Indianapolis | 17 | 78 | 1,065 | 13.7 | 62.6 | 13 |
| Kansas City | 4 | 21 | 262 | 12.5 | 65.5 | 2 |
| L.A. Raiders | 5 | 28 | 406 | 14.5 | 81.2 | 1 |
| L.A. Rams | 2 | 10 | 135 | 13.5 | 67.5 | 1 |
| Miami | 18 | 80 | 1,103 | 13.8 | 68.9 | 7 |
| Minnesota | 2 | 9 | 86 | 9.6 | 43.0 | 0 |
| New England | 16 | 67 | 1,041 | 15.5 | 65.1 | 5 |
| New Orleans | 2 | 6 | 54 | 9.0 | 27.0 | 0 |
| N.Y. Giants | 2 | 7 | 95 | 13.6 | 47.5 | 1 |
| N.Y. Jets | 18 | 74 | 1,016 | 13.7 | 56.4 | 8 |
| Philadelphia | 3 | 15 | 161 | 10.7 | 53.7 | 3 |
| Pittsburgh | 6 | 22 | 295 | 13.4 | 49.2 | 2 |
| San Diego | 2 | 9 | 138 | 15.3 | 69.0 | 0 |
| San Francisco | 2 | 20 | 259 | 13.0 | 129.5 | 0 |
| Seattle | 2 | 5 | 116 | 23.2 | 58.0 | 1 |
| Tampa Bay | 3 | 8 | 119 | 14.9 | 39.7 | 0 |
| Washington | 3 | 15 | 267 | 17.8 | 89.0 | 2 |
| Totals | 137 | 586 | 8,233 | 14.0 | 60.1 | 58 |

*Arizona totals include one game vs. St. Louis, one game vs. Phoenix*

## MICHAEL IRVIN'S CAREER RECEIVING VS. EACH OPPONENT

| Opponent | Games | Rec. | Yards | Yards Per Rec. | Yards Per Game | TD |
|---|---|---|---|---|---|---|
| Arizona | 10 | 30 | 623 | 20.8 | 77.9 | 4 |
| Atlanta | 6 | 24 | 406 | 16.9 | 67.7 | 2 |
| Buffalo | 1 | 8 | 115 | 14.4 | 115.0 | 0 |
| Chicago | 1 | 5 | 46 | 9.2 | 46.0 | 0 |
| Cincinnati | 2 | 10 | 242 | 24.2 | 121.0 | 0 |
| Cleveland | 2 | 11 | 160 | 14.5 | 80.0 | 1 |
| Denver | 1 | 6 | 62 | 10.3 | 62.0 | 2 |
| Detroit | 2 | 13 | 257 | 19.8 | 128.5 | 1 |
| Green Bay | 3 | 18 | 296 | 16.4 | 98.7 | 2 |
| Houston | 2 | 8 | 106 | 13.3 | 53.0 | 1 |
| Indianapolis | 1 | 7 | 112 | 16.0 | 112.0 | 0 |
| Kansas City | 1 | 6 | 84 | 14.0 | 84.0 | 0 |
| L.A. Raiders | 1 | 3 | 54 | 18.0 | 54.0 | 0 |
| L.A. Rams | 2 | 10 | 239 | 23.9 | 119.5 | 2 |
| Miami | 1 | 3 | 31 | 10.3 | 31.0 | 0 |
| Minnesota | 2 | 10 | 167 | 16.7 | 83.5 | 1 |
| New Orleans | 4 | 11 | 197 | 17.9 | 49.3 | 0 |
| N.Y. Giants | 9 | 32 | 497 | 15.5 | 62.1 | 3 |
| N.Y. Jets | 2 | 10 | 184 | 18.4 | 92.0 | 2 |
| Philadelphia | 10 | 25 | 427 | 17.1 | 53.4 | 2 |
| Pittsburgh | 2 | 11 | 230 | 20.9 | 115.0 | 2 |
| San Francisco | 3 | 19 | 238 | 12.5 | 79.3 | 1 |
| Seattle | 1 | 6 | 113 | 18.8 | 113.0 | 0 |
| Tampa Bay | 2 | 2 | 42 | 21.0 | 21.0 | 1 |
| Washington | 9 | 49 | 766 | 15.6 | 85.1 | 7 |
| Totals | 80 | 337 | 5,694 | 16.9 | 71.2 | 34 |

*Arizona totals include 10 games vs. Phoenix*

## STARTING RECORDS OF ACTIVE NFL QUARTERBACKS

*Minimum: 10 starts*

| | W- | L- | T | Pct. |
|---|---|---|---|---|
| Joe Montana | 108- | 42 | | .720 |
| Cody Carlson | 10- | 4 | | .714 |
| Jim McMahon | 67- | 29 | | .698 |
| Stan Humphries | 20- | 10 | | .667 |
| Jeff Hostetler | 26- | 14 | | .650 |
| Erik Kramer | 11- | 6 | | .647 |
| Jim Kelly | 76- | 42 | | .644 |
| Dan Marino | 97- | 57 | | .630 |
| Jay Schroeder | 57- | 34 | | .626 |
| Mark Rypien | 45- | 27 | | .625 |
| Randall Cunningham | 55- | 33 | -1 | .624 |
| John Elway | 98- | 59 | -1 | .623 |
| Bobby Hebert | 53- | 34 | | .609 |
| Phil Simms | 95- | 64 | | .597 |
| Dave Krieg | 83- | 57 | | .593 |
| Brett Favre | 17- | 12 | | .586 |
| Mike Tomczak | 27- | 20 | | .574 |
| Neil O'Donnell | 20- | 15 | | .571 |
| Troy Aikman | 38- | 30 | | .559 |
| Steve Young | 39- | 32 | | .549 |
| Steve Beuerlein | 18- | 15 | | .545 |
| Bob Gagliano | 7- | 6 | | .538 |
| Jim Harbaugh | 35- | 30 | | .538 |
| Wade Wilson | 35- | 30 | | .538 |
| Rich Gannon | 20- | 19 | | .513 |
| Bernie Kosar | 53- | 52 | -1 | .505 |
| Warren Moon | 70- | 69 | | .504 |
| Boomer Esiason | 66- | 68 | | .493 |
| Bubby Brister | 32- | 33 | | .492 |
| Billy Joe Tolliver | 13- | 15 | | .464 |
| Ken O'Brien | 50- | 59 | -1 | .459 |
| Don Majkowski | 22- | 26 | -1 | .459 |
| Steve Walsh | 11- | 13 | | .458 |
| Rodney Peete | 21- | 26 | | .447 |
| Jim Everett | 46- | 59 | | .438 |
| Drew Bledsoe | 5- | 7 | | .417 |
| Steve DeBerg | 53- | 85 | -1 | .385 |
| Chris Chandler | 15- | 24 | | .385 |
| Jack Trudeau | 18- | 29 | | .383 |
| Rick Mirer | 6- | 10 | | .375 |
| Vince Evans | 13- | 23 | | .361 |
| Chris Miller | 23- | 43 | | .348 |
| Vinny Testaverde | 27- | 51 | | .346 |
| Craig Erickson | 5- | 10 | | .333 |
| Hugh Millen | 7- | 16 | | .304 |
| Jeff George | 14- | 35 | | .286 |
| John Friesz | 6- | 17 | | .261 |
| David Klingler | 4- | 13 | | .235 |
| Browning Nagle | 3- | 10 | | .231 |
| Chuck Long | 4- | 17 | | .190 |
| Stan Gelbaugh | 0- | 11 | | .000 |

## NFL INDIVIDUAL LEADERS OVER RECENT SEASONS

| Last 2 Seasons | Last 3 Seasons | Last 4 Seasons |
|---|---|---|
| **Points** | | |
| 237, Morten Andersen | 354, Pete Stoyanovich | 472, Chip Lohmiller |
| 237, John Carney | 350, Morten Andersen | 460, Nick Lowery |
| 233, Pete Stoyanovich | 341, Chip Lohmiller | 454, Pete Stoyanovich |
| 230, Al Del Greco | 329, Gary Anderson | 442, Morten Andersen |
| 229, Gary Anderson | 325, John Carney | 421, Gary Anderson |

**Touchdowns**

| Last 2 Seasons | Last 3 Seasons | Last 4 Seasons |
|---|---|---|
| 29, Emmitt Smith | 42, Emmitt Smith | 54, Jerry Rice |
| 27, Jerry Rice | 41, Jerry Rice | 53, Emmitt Smith |
| 26, Andre Rison | 38, Andre Rison | 48, Andre Rison |
| 24, Sterling Sharpe | 30, Barry Sanders | 46, Barry Sanders |
| 22, Ricky Watters | 30, Thurman Thomas | 43, Thurman Thomas |

**Field Goals**

| Last 2 Seasons | Last 3 Seasons | Last 4 Seasons |
|---|---|---|
| 57, Morten Andersen | 85, Pete Stoyanovich | 107, Chip Lohmiller |
| 57, John Carney | 82, Morten Andersen | 106, Pete Stoyanovich |
| 56, Gary Anderson | 79, Gary Anderson | 104, Nick Lowery |
| 55, Jason Hanson | 79, Jeff Jaeger | 103, Morten Andersen |
| 54, Pete Stoyanovich | 77, Chip Lohmiller | 99, Gary Anderson |

**Rushes**

| Last 2 Seasons | Last 3 Seasons | Last 4 Seasons |
|---|---|---|
| 667, Thurman Thomas | 1021, Emmitt Smith | 1262, Emmitt Smith |
| 656, Emmitt Smith | 955, Thurman Thomas | 1226, Thurman Thomas |
| 567, Barry Foster | 897, Barry Sanders | 1152, Barry Sanders |
| 555, Barry Sanders | 805, Rodney Hampton | 914, Rodney Hampton |
| 549, Rodney Hampton | 727, Reggie Cobb | 878, Reggie Cobb |

**Rushing Yards**

| Last 2 Seasons | Last 3 Seasons | Last 4 Seasons |
|---|---|---|
| 3199, Emmitt Smith | 4762, Emmitt Smith | 5699, Emmitt Smith |
| 2802, Thurman Thomas | 4209, Thurman Thomas | 5506, Thurman Thomas |
| 2467, Barry Sanders | 4015, Barry Sanders | 5319, Barry Sanders |
| 2401, Barry Foster | 3277, Rodney Hampton | 3732, Rodney Hampton |
| 2218, Rodney Hampton | 2889, Barry Foster | 3614, Marion Butts |

**Rushing TDs**

| Last 2 Seasons | Last 3 Seasons | Last 4 Seasons |
|---|---|---|
| 27, Emmitt Smith | 39, Emmitt Smith | 50, Emmitt Smith |
| 19, Barry Foster | 29, Rodney Hampton | 41, Barry Sanders |
| 19, Rodney Hampton | 28, Barry Sanders | 33, Thurman Thomas |
| 19, Ricky Watters | 24, Brad Baxter | 31, Rodney Hampton |
| 15, Thurman Thomas | 22, Thurman Thomas | 30, Brad Baxter |

**Passes**

| Last 2 Seasons | Last 3 Seasons | Last 4 Seasons |
|---|---|---|
| 993, Brett Favre | 1521, Warren Moon | 2105, Warren Moon |
| 932, Jim Kelly | 1406, Jim Kelly | 1820, John Elway |
| 867, John Elway | 1318, John Elway | 1793, Jim Everett |
| 866, Warren Moon | 1253, Dan Marino | 1784, Dan Marino |
| 865, Troy Aikman | 1239, Jim Everett | 1752, Jim Kelly |

**Completions**

| Last 2 Seasons | Last 3 Seasons | Last 4 Seasons |
|---|---|---|
| 620, Brett Favre | 931, Warren Moon | 1293, Warren Moon |
| 582, Steve Young | 861, Jim Kelly | 1080, Jim Kelly |
| 573, Troy Aikman | 810, Troy Aikman | 1058, John Elway |
| 557, Jim Kelly | 764, John Elway | 1045, Dan Marino |
| 527, Warren Moon | 762, Steve Young | 1036, Troy Aikman |

**Passing Yards**

| Last 2 Seasons | Last 3 Seasons | Last 4 Seasons |
|---|---|---|
| 7488, Steve Young | 10696, Warren Moon | 15385, Warren Moon |
| 6839, Jim Kelly | 10683, Jim Kelly | 13512, Jim Kelly |
| 6545, Troy Aikman | 10005, Steve Young | 13051, John Elway |
| 6530, Brett Favre | 9525, John Elway | 12867, Dan Marino |
| 6272, John Elway | 9304, Dan Marino | 12402, Jim Everett |

**Touchdown Passes**

| Last 2 Seasons | Last 3 Seasons | Last 4 Seasons |
|---|---|---|
| 54, Steve Young | 74, Jim Kelly | 98, Jim Kelly |
| 43, Bobby Hebert | 71, Steve Young | 95, Warren Moon |
| 41, Jim Kelly | 62, Warren Moon | 78, Dan Marino |
| 39, Warren Moon | 57, Dan Marino | 73, Steve Young |
| 38, Troy Aikman | 52, Bobby Hebert | 64, Boomer Esiason |
| | | 64, Jim Everett |

**Receptions**

| Last 2 Seasons | Last 3 Seasons | Last 4 Seasons |
|---|---|---|
| 220, Sterling Sharpe | 289, Sterling Sharpe | 362, Jerry Rice |
| 182, Jerry Rice | 262, Jerry Rice | 356, Sterling Sharpe |
| 179, Andre Rison | 260, Andre Rison | 342, Andre Rison |
| 166, Michael Irvin | 259, Michael Irvin | 330, Haywood Jeffires |
| 156, Haywood Jeffires | 256, Haywood Jeffires | 279, Michael Irvin |
| 156, Anthony Miller | | |

**Reception Yards**

| Last 2 Seasons | Last 3 Seasons | Last 4 Seasons |
|---|---|---|
| 2735, Sterling Sharpe | 4249, Michael Irvin | 5412, Jerry Rice |
| 2726, Michael Irvin | 3910, Jerry Rice | 4801, Sterling Sharpe |
| 2704, Jerry Rice | 3696, Sterling Sharpe | 4662, Michael Irvin |
| 2361, Andre Rison | 3337, Andre Rison | 4545, Andre Rison |
| 2222, Anthony Miller | 3070, Gary Clark | 4182, Gary Clark |

**Receiving Touchdowns**

| Last 2 Seasons | Last 3 Seasons | Last 4 Seasons |
|---|---|---|
| 26, Andre Rison | 39, Jerry Rice | 52, Jerry Rice |
| 25, Jerry Rice | 38, Andre Rison | 48, Andre Rison |
| 24, Sterling Sharpe | 28, Sterling Sharpe | 34, Sterling Sharpe |
| 17, Calvin Williams | 25, Michael Haynes | 30, Haywood Jeffires |
| 15, three players | 22, Michael Irvin | 29, Calvin Williams |
| | 22, Haywood Jeffires | |

**Interceptions**

| Last 2 Seasons | Last 3 Seasons | Last 4 Seasons |
|---|---|---|
| 16, Eugene Robinson | 21, Eugene Robinson | 24, Eugene Robinson |
| 14, Nate Odomes | 19, Nate Odomes | 20, Nate Odomes |
| 13, Darren Carrington | 16, Darren Carrington | 20, Rod Woodson |
| 12, Audray McMillian | 16, Audray McMillian | 19, Cris Dishman |
| 12, Brian Washington | 16, Deion Sanders | 19, Audray McMillian |
| 12, Rod Woodson | | 19, Deion Sanders |

**Sacks**

| Last 2 Seasons | Last 3 Seasons | Last 4 Seasons |
|---|---|---|
| 29.5, Simon Fletcher | 43.0, Simon Fletcher | 56.0, Derrick Thomas |
| 29.5, Neil Smith | 42.0, Reggie White | 56.0, Reggie White |
| 29.0, Leslie O'Neal | 38.0, Leslie O'Neal | 54.0, Simon Fletcher |
| 28.0, Bruce Smith | 37.5, Neil Smith | 51.5, Leslie O'Neal |
| 27.0, Chris Doleman | 37.0, Clyde Simmons | 48.5, Bruce Smith |
| 27.0, Reggie White | | |

## NFL TEAM LEADERS OVER RECENT SEASONS

**Highest Won-Lost Percentage**

| Last 2 Seasons | Last 3 Seasons | Last 4 Seasons |
|---|---|---|
| .781, Dallas | .750, Buffalo | .766, Buffalo |
| .750, San Francisco | .750, Dallas | .750, San Francisco |
| .719, Buffalo | .708, San Francisco | .672, Dallas |
| .688, Houston | .688, Houston | .656, Houston |
| .656, Kansas City | .646, Kansas City | .656, Kansas City |
| | .646, New Orleans | |

**Most Points**

| Last 2 Seasons | Last 3 Seasons | Last 4 Seasons |
|---|---|---|
| 904, San Francisco | 1297, San Francisco | 1650, San Francisco |
| 785, Dallas | 1168, Buffalo | 1596, Buffalo |
| 720, Houston | 1127, Dallas | 1511, Houston |
| 710, Buffalo | 1106, Houston | 1396, Washington |
| 689, Miami | 1032, Miami | 1371, Dallas |

**Most Total Yards**

| Last 2 Seasons | Last 3 Seasons | Last 4 Seasons |
|---|---|---|
| 12630, San Francisco | 18488, San Francisco | 24383, San Francisco |
| 11313, Houston | 17405, Buffalo | 23522, Houston |
| 11312, Miami | 17300, Houston | 22681, Buffalo |
| 11221, Dallas | 16553, Miami | 21600, Miami |
| 11153, Buffalo | 16322, Dallas | 20466, Washington |

**Most Rushing Yards**

| Last 2 Seasons | Last 3 Seasons | Last 4 Seasons |
|---|---|---|
| 4448, San Francisco | 6760, Buffalo | 8840, Buffalo |
| 4379, Buffalo | 6351, N.Y. Giants | 8400, N.Y. Giants |
| 4287, N.Y. Giants | 6309, San Francisco | 8204, San Diego |
| 4282, Dallas | 5993, Dallas | 8101, Philadelphia |
| 4159, Pittsburgh | 5947, San Diego | 8027, San Francisco |

**Most Passing Yards**

| Last 2 Seasons | Last 3 Seasons | Last 4 Seasons |
|---|---|---|
| 8328, Miami | 12516, Houston | 17321, Houston |
| 8182, San Francisco | 12217, Miami | 16356, San Francisco |
| 7895, Houston | 12179, San Francisco | 15729, Miami |
| 7153, Atlanta | 10645, Buffalo | 14063, Atlanta |
| 6939, Dallas | 10602, Atlanta | 13841, Buffalo |

**Fewest Turnovers**

| Last 2 Seasons | Last 3 Seasons | Last 4 Seasons |
|---|---|---|
| 40, N.Y. Giants | 63, N.Y. Giants | 77, N.Y. Giants |
| 46, Dallas | 70, Dallas | 90, Kansas City |
| 47, Cincinnati | 71, Kansas City | 103, Dallas |
| 49, Kansas City | 78, Washington | 106, Washington |
| 52, San Diego | 80, San Diego | 112, San Diego |
| 52, San Francisco | | |

**Fewest Points Allowed**

| Last 2 Seasons | Last 3 Seasons | Last 4 Seasons |
|---|---|---|
| 472, Dallas | 747, Houston | 1009, San Francisco |
| 496, Houston | 756, New Orleans | 1031, New Orleans |
| 506, Pittsburgh | 770, San Francisco | 1054, Houston |
| 525, Buffalo | 782, Dallas | 1080, N.Y. Giants |
| 531, San Diego | 804, Philadelphia | 1082, Kansas City |
| 531, San Francisco | | |

**Fewest Total Yards Allowed**

| Last 2 Seasons | Last 3 Seasons | Last 4 Seasons |
|---|---|---|
| 8698, Dallas | 12704, New Orleans | 17582, New Orleans |
| 8771, New Orleans | 12979, Philadelphia | 17639, Philadelphia |
| 8921, Minnesota | 13764, Dallas | 18379, Dallas |
| 9085, Houston | 13842, Houston | 18472, Pittsburgh |
| 9095, Kansas City | 13937, Minnesota | 18477, Houston |

**Fewest Rushing Yards Allowed**

| | | |
|---|---|---|
| 2709, San Diego | 4375, San Diego | 5866, Philadelphia |
| 2895, Dallas | 4447, Houston | 5890, San Diego |
| 2907, Houston | 4466, Dallas | 5988, San Francisco |
| 3209, Pittsburgh | 4697, Philadelphia | 6022, Houston |
| 3218, San Francisco | 4730, San Francisco | 6406, Pittsburgh |

**Fewest Passing Yards Allowed**

| | | |
|---|---|---|
| 5076, New Orleans | 7796, New Orleans | 11115, New Orleans |
| 5652, Minnesota | 8282, Philadelphia | 11474, Minnesota |
| 5688, Kansas City | 8749, Chicago | 11664, L.A. Raiders |
| 5691, L.A. Raiders | 8817, Indianapolis | 11669, Chicago |
| 5803, Dallas | 8831, Minnesota | 11768, N.Y. Giants |

**Most Opponents' Turnovers**

| | | |
|---|---|---|
| 82, Buffalo | 120, Philadelphia | 155, Kansas City |
| 81, Pittsburgh | 119, Buffalo | 154, Buffalo |
| 77, Kansas City | 116, New Orleans | 153, Pittsburgh |
| 76, Minnesota | 113, N.Y. Jets | 150, Philadelphia |
| 76, N.Y. Jets | 112, Houston | 145, Houston |

## RECORDS OF TEAMS ON OPENING DAY, 1933-93

| AFC | W | L | T | Pct. | Longest W Strk. | Longest L Strk. | Current Streak |
|---|---|---|---|---|---|---|---|
| Denver | 21 | 12 | 1 | .636 | 3 | 4 | W-3 |
| L.A. Raiders | 20 | 14 | 0 | .588 | 5 | 5 | W-1 |
| Cleveland | 25 | 19 | 0 | .568 | 5 | 5 | W-1 |
| Kansas City | 19 | 15 | 0 | .559 | 5 | 4 | W-4 |
| San Diego | 19 | 15 | 0 | .559 | 6 | 6 | W-1 |
| Pittsburgh | 29 | 26 | 4 | .527 | 4 | 3 | L-1 |
| Indianapolis | 21 | 20 | 0 | .512 | 8 | 8 | L-1 |
| Cincinnati | 13 | 13 | 0 | .500 | 4 | 4 | L-1 |
| Houston | 17 | 17 | 0 | .500 | 4 | 3 | L-2 |
| Miami | 13 | 14 | 1 | .481 | 4 | 5 | W-2 |
| New England | 16 | 18 | 0 | .471 | 6 | 3 | L-2 |
| Buffalo | 15 | 19 | 0 | .441 | 6 | 5 | W-6 |
| N.Y. Jets | 14 | 20 | 0 | .412 | 3 | 5 | L-2 |
| Seattle | 4 | 14 | 0 | .222 | 3 | 8 | L-5 |

| NFC | W | L | T | Pct. | Longest W Strk. | Longest L Strk. | Current Streak |
|---|---|---|---|---|---|---|---|
| Dallas | 25 | 8 | 1 | .758 | 17 | 3 | L-1 |
| N.Y. Giants | 34 | 23 | 4 | .596 | 4 | 3 | W-1 |
| Chicago | 35 | 25 | 1 | .583 | 9 | 6 | L-1 |
| Minnesota | 18 | 14 | 1 | .563 | 4 | 2 | L-1 |
| Atlanta | 15 | 13 | 0 | .536 | 5 | 3 | L-1 |
| Washington | 30 | 27 | 4 | .526 | 6 | 5 | W-1 |
| Detroit | 31 | 28 | 2 | .525 | 7 | 4 | W-1 |
| L.A. Rams | 29 | 27 | 0 | .518 | 5 | 6 | L-4 |
| Green Bay | 30 | 28 | 3 | .517 | 5 | 6 | W-1 |
| San Francisco | 21 | 22 | 1 | .488 | 4 | 3 | W-2 |
| Arizona | 26 | 33 | 1 | .441 | 6 | 6 | L-2 |
| Philadelphia | 25 | 34 | 1 | .424 | 5 | 9 | W-3 |
| Tampa Bay | 7 | 11 | 0 | .389 | 3 | 5 | L-1 |
| New Orleans | 7 | 20 | 0 | .259 | 1 | 6 | W-1 |

*NOTE: All tied games occurred prior to 1972, when calculation of ties in percentages as half-win, half-loss was begun.*

## OLDEST INDIVIDUAL SINGLE-SEASON OR SINGLE-GAME RECORDS IN NFL RECORD & FACT BOOK

**Regular-Season Records That Have Not Been Surpassed or Tied**

Most Points, Game—40, Ernie Nevers, Chi. Cardinals vs. Chi. Bears, Nov. 28, 1929 (6-td, 4-pat)
Most Touchdowns Rushing, Game—6, Ernie Nevers, Chi. Cardinals vs. Chi. Bears, Nov. 28, 1929
Highest Punting Average, Season (Qualifiers)—51.40, Sammy Baugh, Washington, 1940 (35-1,799)
Highest Punting Average, Game (minimum: 4 punts)—61.75, Bob Cifers, Detroit vs. Chi. Bears, Nov. 24, 1946 (4-247)
Highest Average Gain, Pass Receptions, Season (minimum: 24 receptions)—32.58, Don Currivan, Boston, 1947 (24-782)
Highest Average Gain, Passing, Game (minimum: 20 passes)—18.58, Sammy Baugh, Washington vs. Boston, Oct. 31, 1948 (24-446)
Most Touchdowns, Fumble Recoveries, Game—2, Fred (Dippy) Evans, Chi. Bears vs. Washington, Nov. 28, 1948
Most Yards Gained, Intercepted Passes, Rookie, Season—301, Don Doll, Detroit, 1949
Most Passes Had Intercepted, Game—8, Jim Hardy, Chi. Cardinals vs. Philadelphia, Sept. 24, 1950
Highest Average Gain, Rushing, Game (minimum: 10 attempts)—17.09, Marion Motley, Cleveland vs. Pittsburgh, Oct. 29, 1950 (11-188)
Most Yards Gained, Kickoff Returns, Game—294, Wally Triplett, Detroit vs. Los Angeles, Oct. 29, 1950
Highest Kickoff Return Average, Game (minimum: 3 returns)—73.50, Wally Triplett, Detroit vs. Los Angeles, Oct. 29, 1950 (4-294)
Most Pass Receptions, Game—18, Tom Fears, Los Angeles vs. Green Bay, Dec. 3, 1950
Highest Punt Return Average, Season (Qualifiers)—23.00, Herb Rich, Baltimore, 1950 (12-276)
Highest Punt Return Average, Rookie, Season (Qualifiers)—23.00, Herb Rich, Baltimore, 1950 (12-276)
Most Yards Passing, Game—554, Norm Van Brocklin, Los Angeles vs. N.Y. Yanks, Sept. 28, 1951
Most Touchdowns, Punt Returns, Rookie, Season—4, Jack Christiansen, Detroit, 1951
Most Interceptions By, Season—14, Dick (Night Train) Lane, Los Angeles, 1952
Most Interceptions By, Rookie, Season—14, Dick (Night Train) Lane, Los Angeles, 1952
Highest Average Gain, Passing, Season (Qualifiers)—11.17, Tommy O'Connell, Cleveland, 1957 (110-1,229)
Most Points, Season—176, Paul Hornung, Green Bay, 1960 (15-td, 41-pat,15-fg)
Most Yards Gained, Pass Receptions, Rookie, Season—1,473, Bill Groman, Houston, 1960

## LARGEST TRADES IN NFL HISTORY

**(Based on number of players or draft choices involved)**

**18—October 13, 1989**—RB Herschel Walker from the Dallas Cowboys to Minnesota. Dallas also traded its third-round choice in 1990, its tenth-round choice in 1990, and its third-round choice in 1991 to Minnesota. Minnesota traded LB Jesse Solomon, LB David Howard, CB Issiac Holt, and DE Alex Stewart along with its first-round choice in 1990, its second-round choice in 1990, its sixth-round choice in 1990, its first-round choice in 1991, its second-round choice in 1991, its first-round choice in 1992, its second-round choice in 1992, and its third-round choice in 1992 to Dallas. Minnesota traded RB Darrin Nelson to Dallas, which traded Nelson to San Diego for the Chargers' fifth-round choice in 1990, which Dallas then sent to Minnesota.

**15—March 26, 1953**—T Mike McCormack, DT Don Colo, LB Tom Catlin, DB John Petitbon, and G Herschell Forester from Baltimore to Cleveland for DB Don Shula, DB Bert Rechichar, DB Carl Taseff, LB Ed Sharkey, E Gern Nagler, QB Harry Agganis, T Dick Batten, T Stu Sheets, G Art Spinney, and G Elmer Willhoite.

**15—January 28, 1971**—LB Marlin McKeever, first- and third-round choices in 1971, and third-, fourth-, fifth-, sixth-, and seventh-round choices in 1972 from Washington to the Los Angeles Rams for LB Maxie Baughan, LB Jack Pardee, LB Myron Pottios, RB Jeff Jordan, G John Wilbur, DT Diron Talbert, and a fifth-round choice in 1971.

**12—June 13, 1952**—Selection rights to Les Richter from the Dallas Texans to the Los Angeles Rams for RB Dick Hoerner, DB Tom Keane, DB George Sims, C Joe Reid, HB Billy Baggett, T Jack Halliday, FB Dick McKissack, LB Vic Vasicek, E Richard Wilkins, C Aubrey Phillips, and RB Dave Anderson.

**10—March 23, 1959**—HB Ollie Matson from the Chicago Cardinals to the Los Angeles Rams for T Frank Fuller, DE Glenn Holtzman, T Ken Panfil, DT Art Hauser, E John Tracey, FB Larry Hickman, HB Don Brown, the Rams second-round choice in 1960, and a player to be delivered during the 1959 training camp.

**10—October 31, 1987**—RB Eric Dickerson from the Los Angeles Rams to Indianapolis. The rights to LB Cornelius Bennett from Indianapolis to Buffalo. Indianapolis running back Owen Gill and the Colts' first- and second-round choices in 1988 and second-round choice in 1989, plus Bills running back Greg Bell and Buffalo's first-round choice in 1988 and first- and second-round choices in 1989 to the Rams.

## RETIRED UNIFORM NUMBERS IN NFL

**AFC**

| | | |
|---|---|---|
| Buffalo: | None | |
| Cincinnati: | Bob Johnson | 54 |
| Cleveland: | Otto Graham | 14 |
| | Jim Brown | 32 |
| | Ernie Davis | 45 |
| | Don Fleming | 46 |
| | Lou Groza | 76 |
| Denver: | Frank Tripucka | 18 |
| | Floyd Little | 44 |
| Houston: | Earl Campbell | 34 |
| | Jim Norton | 43 |
| | Elvin Bethea | 65 |
| Indianapolis: | Johnny Unitas | 19 |
| | Buddy Young | 22 |
| | Lenny Moore | 24 |
| | Art Donovan | 70 |
| | Jim Parker | 77 |
| | Raymond Berry | 82 |
| | Gino Marchetti | 89 |

| Team | Player | No. |
|---|---|---|
| Kansas City: | Jan Stenerud | 3 |
| | Len Dawson | 16 |
| | Abner Haynes | 28 |
| | Stone Johnson | 33 |
| | Mack Lee Hill | 36 |
| | Willie Lanier | 63 |
| | Bobby Bell | 78 |
| | Buck Buchanan | 86 |
| Los Angeles Raiders: | None | |
| Miami: | Bob Griese | 12 |
| New England: | Gino Cappelletti | 20 |
| | Steve Nelson | 57 |
| | John Hannah | 73 |
| | Jim Hunt | 79 |
| | Bob Dee | 89 |
| New York Jets: | Joe Namath | 12 |
| | Don Maynard | 13 |
| Pittsburgh: | None | |
| San Diego: | Dan Fouts | 14 |
| Seattle: | "Fans/the twelfth man" | 12 |
| **NFC** | | |
| Arizona: | Larry Wilson | 8 |
| | Stan Mauldin | 77 |
| | J.V. Cain | 88 |
| | Marshall Goldberg | 99 |
| Atlanta: | Steve Bartowski | 10 |
| | William Andrews | 31 |
| | Jeff Van Note | 57 |
| | Tommy Nobis | 60 |
| Chicago: | Bronko Nagurski | 3 |
| | George McAfee | 5 |
| | George Halas | 7 |
| | Willie Galimore | 28 |
| | Walter Payton | 34 |
| | Brian Piccolo | 41 |
| | Sid Luckman | 42 |
| | Bill Hewitt | 56 |
| | Bill George | 61 |
| | Bulldog Turner | 66 |
| | Red Grange | 77 |
| Dallas: | None | |
| Detroit: | Dutch Clark | 7 |
| | Bobby Layne | 22 |
| | Doak Walker | 37 |
| | Joe Schmidt | 56 |
| | Chuck Hughes | 85 |
| | Charlie Sanders | 88 |
| Green Bay: | Tony Canadeo | 3 |
| | Don Hutson | 14 |
| | Bart Starr | 15 |
| | Ray Nitschke | 66 |
| Los Angeles Rams: | Bob Waterfield | 7 |
| | Merlin Olsen | 74 |
| Minnesota: | Fran Tarkenton | 10 |
| | Alan Page | 88 |
| New Orleans: | Jim Taylor | 31 |
| | Doug Atkins | 81 |
| New York Giants: | Ray Flaherty | 1 |
| | Mel Hein | 7 |
| | Y.A. Tittle | 14 |
| | Al Blozis | 32 |
| | Joe Morrison | 40 |
| | Charlie Conerly | 42 |
| | Ken Strong | 50 |
| Philadelphia: | Steve Van Buren | 15 |
| | Tom Brookshier | 40 |
| | Pete Retzlaff | 44 |
| | Chuck Bednarik | 60 |
| | Al Wistert | 70 |
| | Jerome Brown | 99 |
| San Francisco: | John Brodie | 12 |
| | Joe Perry | 34 |
| | Jimmy Johnson | 37 |
| | Hugh McElhenny | 39 |
| | Charlie Krueger | 70 |
| | Leo Nomellini | 73 |
| | Dwight Clark | 87 |
| Tampa Bay: | Lee Roy Selmon | 63 |
| Washington | Sammy Baugh | 33 |

## 1993 NFL SCORE BY QUARTERS

| AFC Offense | 1 | 2 | 3 | 4 | OT | PTS |
|---|---|---|---|---|---|---|
| Denver | 66 | 147 | 91 | 69 | 0 | 373 |
| Houston | 68 | 131 | 75 | 94 | 0 | 368 |
| Miami | 100 | 76 | 85 | 88 | 0 | 349 |
| Buffalo | 64 | 113 | 51 | 98 | 3 | 329 |
| Kansas City | 71 | 108 | 82 | 67 | 0 | 328 |
| San Diego | 66 | 76 | 67 | 113 | 0 | 322 |
| Pittsburgh | 38 | 110 | 79 | 81 | 0 | 308 |
| L.A. Raiders | 77 | 93 | 50 | 83 | 3 | 306 |
| Cleveland | 56 | 99 | 58 | 91 | 0 | 304 |
| Seattle | 72 | 64 | 45 | 99 | 0 | 280 |
| N.Y. Jets | 65 | 105 | 37 | 63 | 0 | 270 |
| New England | 33 | 60 | 54 | 85 | 6 | 238 |
| Indianapolis | 19 | 60 | 29 | 81 | 0 | 189 |
| Cincinnati | 41 | 74 | 18 | 54 | 0 | 187 |

| NFC Offense | 1 | 2 | 3 | 4 | OT | PTS |
|---|---|---|---|---|---|---|
| San Francisco | 97 | 158 | 108 | 110 | 0 | 473 |
| Dallas | 76 | 124 | 86 | 87 | 3 | 376 |
| Green Bay | 97 | 95 | 77 | 71 | 0 | 340 |
| Phoenix | 54 | 98 | 79 | 92 | 3 | 326 |
| New Orleans | 66 | 80 | 60 | 111 | 0 | 317 |
| Atlanta | 60 | 77 | 68 | 111 | 0 | 316 |
| Detroit | 44 | 102 | 62 | 87 | 3 | 298 |
| Philadelphia | 36 | 101 | 56 | 97 | 3 | 293 |
| N.Y. Giants | 61 | 112 | 43 | 72 | 0 | 288 |
| Minnesota | 49 | 81 | 83 | 64 | 0 | 277 |
| Tampa Bay | 19 | 74 | 89 | 55 | 0 | 237 |
| Chicago | 37 | 85 | 56 | 56 | 0 | 234 |
| Washington | 23 | 77 | 59 | 71 | 0 | 230 |
| L.A. Rams | 52 | 40 | 40 | 89 | 0 | 221 |

| AFC Defense | 1 | 2 | 3 | 4 | OT | PTS |
|---|---|---|---|---|---|---|
| Houston | 40 | 73 | 50 | 75 | 0 | 238 |
| Buffalo | 71 | 62 | 67 | 42 | 0 | 242 |
| N.Y. Jets | 36 | 77 | 68 | 66 | 0 | 247 |
| Pittsburgh | 75 | 102 | 40 | 64 | 0 | 281 |
| Denver | 53 | 82 | 62 | 84 | 3 | 284 |
| New England | 41 | 103 | 26 | 110 | 6 | 286 |
| San Diego | 50 | 102 | 83 | 55 | 0 | 290 |
| Kansas City | 51 | 86 | 50 | 104 | 0 | 291 |
| Cleveland | 64 | 110 | 52 | 81 | 0 | 307 |
| Seattle | 65 | 104 | 66 | 76 | 3 | 314 |
| Cincinnati | 42 | 119 | 63 | 95 | 0 | 319 |
| L.A. Raiders | 34 | 108 | 57 | 127 | 0 | 326 |
| Miami | 56 | 126 | 71 | 92 | 6 | 351 |
| Indianapolis | 96 | 96 | 98 | 88 | 0 | 378 |

| NFC Defense | 1 | 2 | 3 | 4 | OT | PTS |
|---|---|---|---|---|---|---|
| N.Y. Giants | 40 | 60 | 40 | 62 | 3 | 205 |
| Dallas | 43 | 46 | 79 | 61 | 0 | 229 |
| Chicago | 45 | 83 | 38 | 64 | 0 | 230 |
| Phoenix | 58 | 84 | 53 | 74 | 0 | 269 |
| Green Bay | 29 | 76 | 90 | 87 | 0 | 282 |
| Minnesota | 67 | 93 | 36 | 94 | 0 | 290 |
| Detroit | 61 | 86 | 78 | 67 | 0 | 292 |
| San Francisco | 44 | 106 | 57 | 85 | 3 | 295 |
| Philadelphia | 65 | 94 | 55 | 101 | 0 | 315 |
| New Orleans | 78 | 106 | 72 | 87 | 0 | 343 |
| Washington | 81 | 92 | 69 | 103 | 0 | 345 |
| L.A. Rams | 72 | 95 | 92 | 108 | 0 | 367 |
| Tampa Bay | 72 | 133 | 75 | 96 | 0 | 376 |
| Atlanta | 78 | 116 | 100 | 91 | 0 | 385 |

| NFL Totals | 1 | 2 | 3 | 4 | OT | PTS |
|---|---|---|---|---|---|---|
| | 1,607 | 2,620 | 1,787 | 2,339 | 24 | 8,377 |

## TEAM LEADERS

| Offense | Most Scored | Fewest Scored |
|---|---|---|
| 1st Quarter | 100, Miami | 19, Ind. & T.B. |
| 2nd Quarter | 158, San Francisco | 40, L.A. Rams |
| 3rd Quarter | 108, San Francisco | 18, Cincinnati |
| 4th Quarter | 113, San Diego | 54, Cincinnati |

| Defense | Most Allowed | Fewest Allowed |
|---|---|---|
| 1st Quarter | 96, Indianapolis | 29, Green Bay |
| 2nd Quarter | 133, Tampa Bay | 46, Dallas |
| 3rd Quarter | 100, Atlanta | 26, New England |
| 4th Quarter | 127, L.A. Raiders | 42, Buffalo |

## INSIDE THE NUMBERS

### GREATEST COMEBACKS IN NFL HISTORY

**(Most Points Overcome To Win Game)**

### REGULAR SEASON GAMES

**FROM 28 POINTS BEHIND TO WIN:**
**December 7, 1980, at San Francisco**

| | | | | | | |
|---|---|---|---|---|---|---|
| New Orleans | 14 | 21 | 0 | 0 | 0 | — 35 |
| San Francisco | 0 | 7 | 14 | 14 | 3 | — 38 |

NO — Harris 33 pass from Manning (Ricardo kick)
NO — Childs 21 pass from Manning (Ricardo kick)
NO — Holmes 1 run (Ricardo kick)
SF — Solomon 57 punt return (Wersching kick)
NO — Holmes 1 run (Ricardo kick)
NO — Harris 41 pass from Manning (Ricardo kick)
SF — Montana 1 run (Wersching kick)
SF — Clark 71 pass from Montana (Wersching kick)
SF — Solomon 14 pass from Montana (Wersching kick)
SF — Elliott 7 run (Wersching kick)
SF — FG Wersching 36

| | N.O. | S.F. |
|---|---|---|
| First Downs | 27 | 24 |
| Total Yards | 519 | 430 |
| Yards Rushing | 143 | 176 |
| Yards Passing | 376 | 254 |
| Turnovers | 3 | 0 |

**FROM 25 POINTS BEHIND TO WIN:**
**November 8, 1987, at St. Louis**

| | | | | | |
|---|---|---|---|---|---|
| Tampa Bay | 7 | 7 | 14 | 0 | — 28 |
| St. Louis | 0 | 3 | 0 | 28 | — 31 |

TB — Carrier 5 pass from DeBerg (Igwebuike kick)
TB — Carter 3 pass from DeBerg (Igwebuike kick)
StL — FG Gallery 31
TB — Smith 34 pass from DeBerg (Igwebuike kick)
TB — Smith 3 run (Igwebuike kick)
StL — Awalt 4 pass from Lomax (Gallery kick)
StL — Noga 23 fumble recovery (Gallery kick)
StL — J. Smith 11 pass from Lomax (Gallery kick)
StL — J. Smith 17 pass from Lomax (Gallery kick)

| | T.B. | St.L. |
|---|---|---|
| First Downs | 26 | 26 |
| Total Yards | 377 | 415 |
| Yards Rushing | 83 | 137 |
| Yards Passing | 294 | 278 |
| Turnovers | 1 | 2 |

**FROM 24 POINTS BEHIND TO WIN:**
**October 27, 1946, at Washington**

| | | | | | |
|---|---|---|---|---|---|
| Philadelphia | 0 | 0 | 14 | 14 | — 28 |
| Washington | 10 | 14 | 0 | 0 | — 24 |

Wash — Rosato 2 run (Poillon kick)
Wash — FG Poillon 28
Wash — Rosato 4 run (Poillon kick)
Wash — Lapka recovered fumble in end zone (Poillon kick)
Phil — Steele 1 run (Lio kick)
Phil — Pritchard 45 pass from Thompson (Lio kick)
Phil — Steinke 7 pass from Thompson (Lio kick)
Phil — Ferrante 30 pass from Thompson (Lio kick)

| | Phil. | Wash. |
|---|---|---|
| First Downs | 14 | 8 |
| Total Yards | 262 | 127 |
| Yards Rushing | 34 | 66 |
| Yards Passing | 228 | 61 |
| Turnovers | 6 | 3 |

**FROM 24 POINTS BEHIND TO WIN:**
**October 20, 1957, at Detroit**

| | | | | | |
|---|---|---|---|---|---|
| Baltimore | 7 | 14 | 6 | 0 | — 27 |
| Detroit | 0 | 3 | 7 | 21 | — 31 |

Balt — Mutscheller 15 pass from Unitas (Rechichar kick)
Det — FG Martin 47
Balt — Moore 72 pass from Unitas (Rechichar kick)
Balt — Mutscheller 52 pass from Unitas (Rechichar kick)
Balt — Moore 4 pass from Unitas (kick failed)
Det — Junker 14 pass from Rote (Layne kick)
Det — Cassady 26 pass from Layne (Layne kick)
Det — Johnson 1 run (Layne kick)
Det — Cassady 29 pass from Layne (Layne kick)

| | Balt. | Det. |
|---|---|---|
| First Downs | 15 | 20 |
| Total Yards | 322 | 369 |
| Yards Rushing | 117 | 178 |
| Yards Passing | 205 | 191 |
| Turnovers | 6 | 4 |

**FROM 24 POINTS BEHIND TO WIN:**
**October 25, 1959, at Chicago**

| | | | | | |
|---|---|---|---|---|---|
| Philadelphia | 0 | 0 | 21 | 7 | — 28 |
| Chicago Cardinals | 7 | 10 | 7 | 0 | — 24 |

Cardinals — Crow 10 pass from Roach (Conrad kick)
Cardinals — J. Hill 77 blocked field goal return (Conrad kick)
Cardinals — FG Conrad 15
Cardinals — Lane 37 interception return (Conrad kick)
Phil — Barnes 1 run (Walston kick)
Phil — McDonald 29 pass from Van Brocklin (Walston kick)
Phil — Barnes 2 run (Walston kick)
Phil — McDonald 22 pass from Van Brocklin (Walston kick)

| | Phil. | Cardinals |
|---|---|---|
| First Downs | 22 | 14 |
| Total Yards | 399 | 313 |
| Yards Rushing | 168 | 163 |
| Yards Passing | 231 | 150 |
| Turnovers | 2 | 6 |

**FROM 24 POINTS BEHIND TO WIN:**
**October 23, 1960, at Denver**

| | | | | | |
|---|---|---|---|---|---|
| Boston | 10 | 7 | 7 | 0 | — 24 |
| Denver | 0 | 0 | 14 | 17 | — 31 |

Bos — FG Cappelletti 12
Bos — Colclough 10 pass from Songin (Cappelletti kick)
Bos — Wells 6 pass from Songin (Cappelletti kick)
Bos — Miller 47 pass from Songin (Cappelletti kick)
Den — Carmichael 21 pass from Tripucka (Mingo kick)
Den — Jessup 19 pass from Tripucka (Mingo kick)
Den — Carmichael 35 lateral from Taylor, pass from Tripucka (Mingo kick)
Den — Taylor 8 pass from Tripucka (Mingo kick)
Den — FG Mingo 9

| | Bos. | Den. |
|---|---|---|
| First Downs | 19 | 16 |
| Total Yards | 434 | 326 |
| Yards Rushing | 211 | 65 |
| Yards Passing | 223 | 261 |
| Turnovers | 7 | 4 |

**FROM 24 POINTS BEHIND TO WIN:**
**December 15, 1974, at Miami**

| | | | | | |
|---|---|---|---|---|---|
| New England | 21 | 3 | 0 | 3 | — 27 |
| Miami | 0 | 17 | 7 | 10 | — 34 |

NE — Hannah recovered fumble in end zone (J. Smith kick)
NE — Sanders 23 interception return (J. Smith kick)
NE — Herron 4 pass from Plunkett (J. Smith kick)
NE — FG J. Smith 46
Mia — Nottingham 1 run (Yepremian kick)
Mia — Baker 37 pass from Morrall (Yepremian kick)
Mia — FG Yepremian 28
Mia — Baker 46 pass from Morrall (Yepremian kick)
NE — FG J. Smith 34
Mia — Nottingham 2 run (Yepremian kick)
Mia — FG Yepremian 40

| | N.E. | Mia. |
|---|---|---|
| First Downs | 18 | 18 |
| Total Yards | 333 | 333 |
| Yards Rushing | 114 | 61 |
| Yards Passing | 219 | 272 |
| Turnovers | 3 | 4 |

**FROM 24 POINTS BEHIND TO WIN:**
**December 4, 1977, at Minnesota**

| | | | | | |
|---|---|---|---|---|---|
| San Francisco | 0 | 10 | 14 | 3 | — 27 |
| Minnesota | 0 | 0 | 7 | 21 | — 28 |

SF — Delvin Williams 2 run (Wersching kick)
SF — FG Wersching 31
SF — Dave Williams 80 kickoff return (Wersching kick)
SF — Delvin Williams 5 run (Wersching kick)
Minn — McClanahan 15 pass from Lee (Cox kick)
Minn — Rashad 8 pass from Kramer (Cox kick)
Minn — Tucker 9 pass from Kramer (Cox kick)
SF — FG Wersching 31
Minn — S. White 69 pass from Kramer (Cox kick)

| | S.F. | Minn. |
|---|---|---|
| First Downs | 19 | 18 |
| Total Yards | 243 | 309 |
| Yards Rushing | 196 | 52 |
| Yards Passing | 47 | 257 |
| Turnovers | 2 | 5 |

**FROM 24 POINTS BEHIND TO WIN:**
**September 23, 1979, at Denver**

| | | | | | |
|---|---|---|---|---|---|
| Seattle | 10 | 10 | 14 | 0 | — 34 |
| Denver | 0 | 10 | 21 | 6 | — 37 |

Sea — FG Herrera 28
Sea — Doornink 5 run (Herrera kick)
Den — FG Turner 27
Sea — Doornink 5 run (Herrera kick)
Den — Armstrong 2 run (Turner kick)
Sea — FG Herrera 22
Sea — McCullum 13 pass from Zorn (Herrera kick)
Sea — Smith 1 run (Herrera kick)
Den — Studdard 2 pass from Morton (Turner kick)
Den — Moses 11 pass from Morton (Turner kick)
Den — Upchurch 35 pass from Morton (Turner kick)
Den — Lytle 1 run (kick failed)

| | Sea. | Den. |
|---|---|---|
| First Downs | 22 | 23 |
| Total Yards | 350 | 344 |
| Yards Rushing | 153 | 90 |
| Yards Passing | 197 | 254 |
| Turnovers | 4 | 3 |

**FROM 24 POINTS BEHIND TO WIN:**
**September 23, 1979, at Cincinnati**

| | | | | | | |
|---|---|---|---|---|---|---|
| Houston | 0 | 10 | 17 | 0 | 3 | —30 |
| Cincinnati | 14 | 10 | 0 | 3 | 0 | —27 |

Cin — Johnson 1 run (Bahr kick)
Cin — Alexander 2 run (Bahr kick)
Cin — Johnson 1 run (Bahr kick)
Cin — FG Bahr 52
Hou — Burrough 35 pass from Pastorini (Fritsch kick)
Hou — FG Fritsch 33
Hou — Campbell 8 run (Fritsch kick)
Hou — Caster 22 pass from Pastorini (Fritsch kick)
Hou — FG Fritsch 47
Cin — FG Bahr 55
Hou — FG Fritsch 29

| | Hou. | Cin. |
|---|---|---|
| First Downs | 19 | 21 |
| Total Yards | 361 | 265 |
| Yards Rushing | 177 | 165 |
| Yards Passing | 184 | 100 |
| Turnovers | 3 | 2 |

**FROM 24 POINTS BEHIND TO WIN:**
**November 22, 1982, at Los Angeles**

| | | | | | |
|---|---|---|---|---|---|
| San Diego | 10 | 14 | 0 | 0 | — 24 |
| L.A. Raiders | 0 | 7 | 14 | 7 | — 28 |

SD — FG Benirschke 19
SD — Scales 29 pass from Fouts (Benirschke kick)
SD — Muncie 2 run (Benirschke kick)
SD — Muncie 1 run (Benirschke kick)
Raiders — Christensen 1 pass from Plunkett (Bahr kick)

Raiders — Allen 3 run (Bahr kick)
Raiders — Allen 6 run (Bahr kick)
Raiders — Hawkins 1 run (Bahr kick)

| | S.D. | Raiders |
|---|---|---|
| First Downs | 26 | 23 |
| Total Yards | 411 | 326 |
| Yards Rushing | 72 | 181 |
| Yards Passing | 339 | 145 |
| Turnovers | 4 | 2 |

**FROM 24 POINTS BEHIND TO WIN:**
**September 26, 1988, at Denver**

| | | | | | |
|---|---|---|---|---|---|
| L.A. Raiders | 0 | 0 | 14 | 13 | 3 — 30 |
| Denver | 7 | 17 | 0 | 3 | 0 — 27 |

Den — Dorsett 1 run (Karlis kick)
Den — Dorsett 1 run (Karlis kick)
Den — Sewell 7 pass from Elway (Karlis kick)
Den — FG Karlis 39
Raiders — Smith 40 pass from Schroeder (Bahr kick)
Raiders — Smith 42 pass from Schroeder (Bahr kick)
Raiders — FG Bahr 28
Raiders — Allen 4 run (Bahr kick)
Den — FG Karlis 25
Raiders — FG Bahr 44
Raiders — FG Bahr 35

| | Raiders | Den. |
|---|---|---|
| First Downs | 20 | 23 |
| Total Yards | 363 | 398 |
| Yards Rushing | 128 | 189 |
| Yards Passing | 235 | 209 |
| Turnovers | 1 | 5 |

**FROM 24 POINTS BEHIND TO WIN:**
**December 6, 1992, at Tampa**

| | | | | | |
|---|---|---|---|---|---|
| L.A. Rams | 0 | 3 | 21 | 7 | — 31 |
| Tampa Bay | 6 | 21 | 0 | 0 | — 27 |

TB — FG Murray 34
TB — FG Murray 47
TB — Armstrong 81 pass from Testaverde (Murray kick)
TB — Jones 26 fumble recovery (Murray kick)
Rams — FG Zendejas 18
TB — Carrier 10 pass from Testaverde (Murray kick)
Rams — Anderson 40 pass from Everett (Zendejas kick)
Rams — Chadwick 27 pass from Everett (Zendejas kick)
Rams — Lang 1 run (Zendejas kick)
Rams — Carter 8 pass from Everett (Zendejas kick)

| | Rams | T.B. |
|---|---|---|
| First Downs | 21 | 16 |
| Total Yards | 405 | 313 |
| Yards Rushing | 63 | 150 |
| Yards Passing | 342 | 163 |
| Turnovers | 3 | 3 |

## POSTSEASON GAMES

**FROM 32 POINTS BEHIND TO WIN:**
**AFC First-Round Playoff Game**
**January 3, 1993, at Buffalo**

| | | | | | | |
|---|---|---|---|---|---|---|
| Houston | 7 | 21 | 7 | 3 | 0 — 38 |
| Buffalo | 3 | 0 | 28 | 7 | 3 — 41 |

Hou — Jeffires 3 pass from Moon (Del Greco kick)
Buff — FG Christie 36
Hou — Slaughter 7 pass from Moon (Del Greco kick)
Hou — Duncan 26 pass from Moon (Del Greco kick)
Hou — Jeffires 27 pass from Moon (Del Greco kick)
Hou — McDowell 58 interception return (Del Greco kick)
Buff — Davis 1 run (Christie kick)
Buff — Beebe 38 pass from Reich (Christie kick)
Buff — Reed 26 pass from Reich (Christie kick)
Buff — Reed 18 pass from Reich (Christie kick)
Buff — Reed 17 pass from Reich (Christie kick)
Hou — FG Del Greco 26
Buff — FG Christie 32

| | Hou. | Buff. |
|---|---|---|
| First Downs | 27 | 19 |
| Total Yards | 429 | 366 |
| Yards Rushing | 82 | 98 |
| Yards Passing | 347 | 268 |
| Turnovers | 2 | 1 |

**FROM 20 POINTS BEHIND TO WIN:**
**Western Conference Playoff Game**
**December 22, 1957, at San Francisco**

| | | | | | |
|---|---|---|---|---|---|
| Detroit | 0 | 7 | 14 | 10 | — 31 |
| San Francisco | 14 | 10 | 3 | 0 | — 27 |

SF — Owens 34 pass from Tittle (Soltau kick)
SF — McElhenny 47 pass from Tittle (Soltau kick)
Det — Junker 4 pass from Rote (Martin kick)
SF — Wilson 12 pass from Tittle (Soltau kick)
SF — FG Soltau 25
SF — FG Soltau 10
Det — Tracy 2 run (Martin kick)
Det — Tracy 58 run (Martin kick)
Det — Gedman 3 run (Martin kick)
Det — FG Martin 14

| | Det. | S.F. |
|---|---|---|
| First Downs | 22 | 20 |
| Total Yards | 324 | 351 |
| Yards Rushing | 129 | 127 |
| Yards Passing | 195 | 224 |
| Turnovers | 5 | 4 |

**FROM 18 POINTS BEHIND TO WIN:**
**NFC Divisional Playoff Game**
**December 23, 1972, at San Francisco**

| | | | | | |
|---|---|---|---|---|---|
| Dallas | 3 | 10 | 0 | 17 | — 30 |
| San Francisco | 7 | 14 | 7 | 0 | — 28 |

SF — Washington 97 kickoff return (Gossett kick)
Dall — FG Fritsch 37
SF — Schreiber 1 run (Gossett kick)
SF — Schreiber 1 run (Gossett kick)
Dall — FG Fritsch 45
Dall — Alworth 28 pass from Morton (Fritsch kick)
SF — Schreiber 1 run (Gossett kick)
Dall — FG Fritsch 27
Dall — Parks 20 pass from Staubach (Fritsch kick)
Dall — Sellers 10 pass from Staubach (Fritsch kick)

| | Dall. | S.F. |
|---|---|---|
| First Downs | 22 | 13 |
| Total Yards | 402 | 255 |
| Yards Rushing | 165 | 105 |
| Yards Passing | 237 | 150 |
| Turnovers | 5 | 3 |

**FROM 18 POINTS BEHIND TO WIN:**
**AFC Divisional Playoff Game**
**January 4, 1986, at Miami**

| | | | | | |
|---|---|---|---|---|---|
| Cleveland | 7 | 7 | 7 | 0 | — 21 |
| Miami | 3 | 0 | 14 | 7 | — 24 |

Mia — FG Reveiz 51
Clev — Newsome 16 pass from Kosar (Bahr kick)
Clev — Byner 21 run (Bahr kick)
Clev — Byner 66 run (Bahr kick)
Mia — Moore 6 pass from Marino (Reveiz kick)
Mia — Davenport 31 run (Reveiz kick)
Mia — Davenport 1 run (Reveiz kick)

| | Clev. | Mia. |
|---|---|---|
| First Downs | 17 | 20 |
| Total Yards | 313 | 330 |
| Yards Rushing | 251 | 92 |
| Yards Passing | 62 | 238 |
| Turnovers | 1 | 1 |

## RECORDS OF NFL TEAMS SINCE 1970 AFL-NFL MERGER

| AFC | W - L - T | Pct. | Division Titles | Playoff Berths | Post-season Record | Super Bowl Record |
|---|---|---|---|---|---|---|
| Miami | 238-120-2 | .664 | 10 | 14 | 16-12 | 2-3 |
| L.A. Raiders | 227-127-6 | .640 | 9 | 15 | 18-12 | 3-0 |
| Pittsburgh | 212-147-1 | .590 | 10 | 14 | 16-10 | 4-0 |
| Denver | 202-152-6 | .570 | 7 | 10 | 9-10 | 0-4 |
| Cleveland | 178-179-3 | .499 | 6 | 9 | 3-9 | 0-0 |
| Cincinnati | 175-185-0 | .486 | 5 | 7 | 5-7 | 0-2 |
| Kansas City | 168-185-7 | .476 | 2 | 6 | 3-6 | 0-0 |
| Buffalo | 169-189-2 | .472 | 6 | 9 | 11-9 | 0-4 |
| Seattle* | 127-149-0 | .460 | 1 | 4 | 3-4 | 0-0 |
| Houston | 164-194-2 | .458 | 2 | 10 | 7-10 | 0-0 |
| San Diego | 159-196-5 | .448 | 4 | 5 | 4-5 | 0-0 |
| New England | 158-202-0 | .439 | 2 | 5 | 3-5 | 0-1 |
| N.Y. Jets | 152-206-2 | .425 | 0 | 5 | 3-5 | 0-0 |
| Indianapolis | 148-210-2 | .414 | 5 | 6 | 4-5 | 1-0 |

| NFC | W - L - T | Pct. | Division Titles | Playoff Berths | Post-season Record | Super Bowl Record |
|---|---|---|---|---|---|---|
| Dallas | 227-133-0 | .631 | 11 | 17 | 26-13 | 4-3 |
| Washington | 225-134-1 | .627 | 5 | 13 | 18-10 | 3-2 |
| San Francisco | 212-145-3 | .593 | 13 | 14 | 18-10 | 4-0 |
| Minnesota | 210-148-2 | .589 | 11 | 15 | 11-15 | 0-3 |
| L.A. Rams | 203-153-4 | .570 | 8 | 14 | 10-14 | 0-1 |
| Chicago | 186-173-1 | .519 | 6 | 9 | 6-8 | 1-0 |
| Philadelphia | 171-183-6 | .483 | 2 | 8 | 4-8 | 0-1 |
| N.Y. Giants | 169-189-2 | .472 | 3 | 7 | 10-5 | 2-0 |
| Detroit | 160-196-4 | .450 | 3 | 5 | 1-5 | 0-0 |
| Arizona | 151-203-6 | .427 | 2 | 3 | 0-3 | 0-0 |
| Green Bay | 150-202-8 | .427 | 1 | 3 | 2-3 | 0-0 |
| New Orleans | 148-208-4 | .416 | 1 | 4 | 0-4 | 0-0 |
| Atlanta | 144-212-4 | .405 | 1 | 4 | 2-4 | 0-0 |
| Tampa Bay* | 81-194-1 | .295 | 2 | 3 | 1-3 | 0-0 |

*entered NFL in 1976.
Indianapolis totals include Baltimore, 1970-83.
L.A. Raiders totals include Oakland, 1970-81.
Arizona totals include St. Louis, 1970-87, and Phoenix, 1988-93.

Tie games before 1972 are not calculated in won-lost percentage.
In 1982, due to players' strike, the divisional format was abandoned.
(L.A. Raiders and Washington won regular-season conference titles, not included in "Division Titles" totals listed above. Sixteen teams were awarded playoff berths, included in totals listed above.)

## LONGEST WINNING STREAKS SINCE 1970

**Regular-season games**

| | | |
|---|---|---|
| 16 | Miami, 1971-73 | (1 in 1971, 14 in 1972, 1 in 1973) |
| 16 | Miami, 1983-84 | (5 in 1983, 11 in 1984) |
| 15 | San Francisco, 1989-90 | (5 in 1989, 10 in 1990) |
| 14 | Oakland, 1976-77 | (10 in 1976, 4 in 1977) |
| 13 | Minnesota, 1974-75 | (3 in 1974, 10 in 1975) |
| 13 | Chicago, 1984-85 | (1 in 1984, 12 in 1985) |
| 13 | N.Y. Giants, 1989-90 | (3 in 1989, 10 in 1990) |
| 12 | Washington, 1990-91 | (1 in 1990, 11 in 1991) |
| 11 | Pittsburgh, 1975 | |
| 11 | Baltimore, 1975-76 | (9 in 1975, 2 in 1976) |
| 11 | Chicago, 1986-87 | (7 in 1986, 4 in 1987) |
| 10 | Miami, 1973 | |
| 10 | Pittsburgh, 1976-77 | (9 in 1976, 1 in 1977) |
| 10 | Denver, 1984 | |
| 10 | Houston, 1993 | |

## NFL PLAYOFF APPEARANCES BY SEASONS

| Team | Number of Seasons in Playoffs |
|---|---|
| N.Y. Giants | 23 |
| Cleveland | 22 |
| L.A. Rams | 22 |
| Dallas | 21 |
| Chicago | 20 |
| Washington | 19 |
| L.A. Raiders | 18 |
| Minnesota | 17 |
| Houston | 15 |
| Pittsburgh | 15 |
| San Francisco | 15 |
| Green Bay | 14 |
| Miami | 14 |
| Buffalo | 13 |
| Philadelphia | 12 |
| Indianapolis | 11 |
| Denver | 10 |
| Detroit | 10 |
| Kansas City | 10 |
| San Diego | 10 |
| Cincinnati | 7 |
| N.Y. Jets | 7 |
| New England | 6 |
| Arizona | 5 |
| Atlanta | 4 |
| New Orleans | 4 |
| Seattle | 4 |
| Tampa Bay | 3 |

## TEAMS IN SUPER BOWL CONTENTION, 1978-93

| | With 3 Weeks to Play | With 2 Weeks to Play | With 1 Week to Play |
|---|---|---|---|
| 1993 | 20 | 18 | 16 |
| 1992 | 20 | 16 | 14 |
| 1991 | 20 | 18 | 13 |
| 1990 | 23 | 20 | 15 |
| 1989 | 21 | 18 | 17 |
| 1988 | 21 | 18 | 15 |
| 1987 | 19 | 19 | 15 |
| 1986 | 19 | 17 | 14 |
| 1985 | 21 | 18 | 13 |
| 1984 | 18 | 14 | 13 |
| 1983 | 24 | 19 | 15 |
| 1982 | 20 | 17 | 16 |
| 1981 | 21 | 20 | 16 |
| 1980 | 20 | 14 | 12 |
| 1979 | 19 | 15 | 13 |
| 1978 | 20 | 17 | 12 |

## GAMES DECIDED BY 7 POINTS OR LESS AND 3 POINTS OR LESS (1970-93)

| | Games Decided by 7 Points or Less | Games Decided by 3 Points or Less |
|---|---|---|
| 1970 | 59 of 182 (32.4%) | 34 of 182 (18.7%) |
| 1971 | 76 of 182 (41.8%) | 35 of 182 (19.2%) |
| 1972 | 71 of 182 (39.0%) | 38 of 182 (20.9%) |
| 1973 | 60 of 182 (32.9%) | 28 of 182 (15.4%) |
| 1974 | 91 of 182 (50.0%) | 37 of 182 (20.3%) |
| 1975 | 62 of 182 (34.1%) | 35 of 182 (19.2%) |
| 1976 | 73 of 196 (37.2%) | 38 of 196 (19.4%) |
| 1977 | 85 of 196 (43.4%) | 36 of 196 (18.4%) |
| 1978 | 108 of 224 (48.2%) | 49 of 224 (21.9%) |
| 1979 | 104 of 224 (46.4%) | 51 of 224 (22.8%) |
| 1980 | 108 of 224 (48.2%) | 58 of 224 (25.9%) |
| 1981 | 91 of 224 (40.6%) | 60 of 224 (26.8%) |
| 1982 | 61 of 126 (48.4%) | 33 of 126 (26.2%) |
| 1983 | 106 of 224 (47.3%) | 54 of 224 (24.1%) |
| 1984 | 95 of 224 (42.4%) | 58 of 224 (25.9%) |
| 1985 | 87 of 224 (38.8%) | 38 of 224 (17.0%) |
| 1986 | 106 of 224 (47.3%) | 48 of 224 (21.4%) |
| 1987 | 99 of 210 (47.1%) | 40 of 210 (19.0%) |
| 1988 | 113 of 224 (50.4%) | 62 of 224 (27.7%) |
| 1989 | 107 of 224 (47.8%) | 55 of 224 (24.6%) |
| 1990 | 97 of 224 (43.3%) | 54 of 224 (24.1%) |
| 1991 | 112 of 224 (50.0%) | 57 of 224 (25.4%) |
| 1992 | 88 of 224 (39.3%) | 48 of 224 (21.4%) |
| 1993 | 105 of 224 (46.9%) | 53 of 224 (23.7%) |

## 1993 RECORDS OF TEAMS IN CLOSE GAMES

| AFC | Overall Record | Decided by 7 Pts. or Less | Decided By 3 Pts. or Less |
|---|---|---|---|
| Buffalo | 12-4 | 5-1 | 5-1 |
| Cincinnati | 3-13 | 2-5 | 0-2 |
| Cleveland | 7-9 | 3-5 | 1-3 |
| Denver | 9-7 | 2-6 | 0-5 |
| Houston | 12-4 | 3-1 | 2-1 |
| Indianapolis | 4-12 | 3-2 | 3-0 |
| Kansas City | 11-5 | 4-2 | 2-1 |
| L.A. Raiders | 10-6 | 9-3 | 4-1 |
| Miami | 9-7 | 5-3 | 1-1 |
| New England | 5-11 | 4-8 | 2-6 |
| N.Y. Jets | 8-8 | 4-5 | 1-2 |
| Pittsburgh | 9-7 | 3-1 | 2-0 |
| San Diego | 8-8 | 4-5 | 2-2 |
| Seattle | 6-10 | 2-4 | 2-1 |

| NFC | Overall Record | Decided by 7 Pts. or Less | Decided By 3 Pts. or Less |
|---|---|---|---|
| Atlanta | 6-10 | 3-5 | 2-1 |
| Chicago | 7-9 | 4-6 | 2-3 |
| Dallas | 12-4 | 4-2 | 1-2 |
| Detroit | 10-6 | 6-1 | 3-0 |
| Green Bay | 9-7 | 4-4 | 3-2 |
| L.A. Rams | 5-11 | 2-2 | 1-1 |
| Minnesota | 9-7 | 6-2 | 2-2 |
| New Orleans | 8-8 | 5-3 | 4-2 |
| N.Y. Giants | 11-5 | 4-3 | 1-2 |
| Philadelphia | 8-8 | 6-4 | 4-1 |
| Phoenix | 7-9 | 2-8 | 1-3 |
| San Francisco | 10-6 | 1-4 | 0-4 |
| Tampa Bay | 5-11 | 3-3 | 2-1 |
| Washington | 4-12 | 2-7 | 0-3 |

## SUPER BOWL CHAMPIONS WHO DID NOT MAKE PLAYOFFS THE FOLLOWING YEAR

**N.Y. Giants**—Super Bowl XXV champions did not make playoffs in the 1991 season.

**Washington**—Super Bowl XXII champions did not make playoffs in the 1988 season.

**N.Y. Giants**—Super Bowl XXI champions did not make playoffs in the 1987 season.

**San Francisco**—Super Bowl XVI champions did not make playoffs in the 1982 season.

**Oakland**—Super Bowl XV champions did not make playoffs in the 1981 season.

**Pittsburgh**—Super Bowl XIV champions did not make playoffs in the 1980 season.

**Kansas City**—Super Bowl IV champions did not make playoffs in the 1970 season.

**Green Bay**—Super Bowl II champions did not make playoffs in the 1968 season.

## ALL-TIME RECORDS OF CURRENT NFL TEAMS

### AFC

BUFFALO BILLS

| | All Games | | | Home Games | | | Road Games | | |
|---|---|---|---|---|---|---|---|---|---|
| Season | W | L | T | W | L | T | W | L | T |
| 1960 | 5 | 8 | 1 | 3 | 4 | | 2 | 4 | 1 |
| 1961 | 6 | 8 | | 2 | 5 | | 4 | 3 | |
| 1962 | 7 | 6 | 1 | 3 | 3 | 1 | 4 | 3 | |
| 1963 | 7 | 6 | 1 | 4 | 2 | 1 | 3 | 4 | |
| 1964 | 12 | 2 | | 6 | 1 | | 6 | 1 | |
| 1965 | 10 | 3 | 1 | 5 | 2 | | 5 | 1 | 1 |
| 1966 | 9 | 4 | 1 | 4 | 2 | 1 | 5 | 2 | |
| 1967 | 4 | 10 | | 2 | 5 | | 2 | 5 | |
| 1968 | 1 | 12 | 1 | 1 | 6 | | 0 | 6 | 1 |
| 1969 | 4 | 10 | | 4 | 3 | | 0 | 7 | |
| 1970 | 3 | 10 | 1 | 1 | 6 | | 2 | 4 | 1 |
| 1971 | 1 | 13 | | 1 | 6 | | 0 | 7 | |
| 1972 | 4 | 9 | 1 | 2 | 4 | 1 | 2 | 5 | |
| 1973 | 9 | 5 | | 5 | 2 | | 4 | 3 | |
| 1974 | 9 | 5 | | 5 | 2 | | 4 | 3 | |
| 1975 | 8 | 6 | | 3 | 4 | | 5 | 2 | |
| 1976 | 2 | 12 | | 1 | 6 | | 1 | 6 | |
| 1977 | 3 | 11 | | 1 | 6 | | 2 | 5 | |
| 1978 | 5 | 11 | | 4 | 4 | | 1 | 7 | |
| 1979 | 7 | 9 | | 3 | 5 | | 4 | 4 | |
| 1980 | 11 | 5 | | 6 | 2 | | 5 | 3 | |
| 1981 | 10 | 6 | | 7 | 1 | | 3 | 5 | |
| 1982 | 4 | 5 | | 4 | 1 | | 0 | 4 | |
| 1983 | 8 | 8 | | 3 | 5 | | 5 | 3 | |
| 1984 | 2 | 14 | | 2 | 6 | | 0 | 8 | |
| 1985 | 2 | 14 | | 2 | 6 | | 0 | 8 | |
| 1986 | 4 | 12 | | 3 | 5 | | 1 | 7 | |
| 1987 | 7 | 8 | | 4 | 4 | | 3 | 4 | |
| 1988 | 12 | 4 | | 8 | 0 | | 4 | 4 | |
| 1989 | 9 | 7 | | 6 | 2 | | 3 | 5 | |
| 1990 | 13 | 3 | | 8 | 0 | | 5 | 3 | |
| 1991 | 13 | 3 | | 7 | 1 | | 6 | 2 | |
| 1992 | 11 | 5 | | 6 | 2 | | 5 | 3 | |
| 1993 | 12 | 4 | | 6 | 2 | | 6 | 2 | |
| Total | 234 | 258 | 8 | 132 | 115 | 4 | 102 | 143 | 4 |

CINCINNATI BENGALS

| | All Games | | | Home Games | | | Road Games | | |
|---|---|---|---|---|---|---|---|---|---|
| Season | W | L | T | W | L | T | W | L | T |
| 1968 | 3 | 11 | | 2 | 5 | | 1 | 6 | |
| 1969 | 4 | 9 | 1 | 4 | 3 | | 0 | 6 | 1 |
| 1970 | 8 | 6 | | 5 | 2 | | 3 | 4 | |
| 1971 | 4 | 10 | | 3 | 4 | | 1 | 6 | |
| 1972 | 8 | 6 | | 4 | 3 | | 4 | 3 | |
| 1973 | 10 | 4 | | 7 | 0 | | 3 | 4 | |
| 1974 | 7 | 7 | | 4 | 3 | | 3 | 4 | |
| 1975 | 11 | 3 | | 6 | 1 | | 5 | 2 | |
| 1976 | 10 | 4 | | 6 | 1 | | 4 | 3 | |
| 1977 | 8 | 6 | | 5 | 2 | | 3 | 4 | |
| 1978 | 4 | 12 | | 3 | 5 | | 1 | 7 | |
| 1979 | 4 | 12 | | 4 | 4 | | 0 | 8 | |
| 1980 | 6 | 10 | | 3 | 5 | | 3 | 5 | |
| 1981 | 12 | 4 | | 6 | 2 | | 6 | 2 | |
| 1982 | 7 | 2 | | 4 | 0 | | 3 | 2 | |
| 1983 | 7 | 9 | | 4 | 4 | | 3 | 5 | |
| 1984 | 8 | 8 | | 5 | 3 | | 3 | 5 | |
| 1985 | 7 | 9 | | 5 | 3 | | 2 | 6 | |
| 1986 | 10 | 6 | | 6 | 2 | | 4 | 4 | |
| 1987 | 4 | 11 | | 1 | 7 | | 3 | 4 | |
| 1988 | 12 | 4 | | 8 | 0 | | 4 | 4 | |
| 1989 | 8 | 8 | | 5 | 3 | | 3 | 5 | |
| 1990 | 9 | 7 | | 5 | 3 | | 4 | 4 | |
| 1991 | 3 | 13 | | 3 | 5 | | 0 | 8 | |
| 1992 | 5 | 11 | | 3 | 5 | | 2 | 6 | |
| 1993 | 3 | 13 | | 3 | 5 | | 0 | 8 | |
| Total | 182 | 205 | 1 | 114 | 80 | | 68 | 125 | 1 |

CLEVELAND BROWNS

| | All Games | | | Home Games | | | Road Games | | |
|---|---|---|---|---|---|---|---|---|---|
| Season | W | L | T | W | L | T | W | L | T |
| 1950 | 10 | 2 | | 5 | 1 | | 5 | 1 | |
| 1951 | 11 | 1 | | 6 | 0 | | 5 | 1 | |
| 1952 | 8 | 4 | | 4 | 2 | | 4 | 2 | |
| 1953 | 11 | 1 | | 6 | 0 | | 5 | 1 | |
| 1954 | 9 | 3 | | 5 | 1 | | 4 | 2 | |
| 1955 | 9 | 2 | 1 | 5 | 1 | | 4 | 1 | 1 |
| 1956 | 5 | 7 | | 1 | 5 | | 4 | 2 | |

| | All Games | | | Home Games | | | Road Games | | |
|---|---|---|---|---|---|---|---|---|---|
| Season | W | L | T | W | L | T | W | L | T |
| 1957 | 9 | 2 | 1 | 6 | 0 | | 3 | 2 | 1 |
| 1958 | 9 | 3 | | 4 | 2 | | 5 | 1 | |
| 1959 | 7 | 5 | | 3 | 3 | | 4 | 2 | |
| 1960 | 8 | 3 | 1 | 4 | 2 | | 4 | 1 | 1 |
| 1961 | 8 | 5 | 1 | 4 | 3 | | 4 | 2 | 1 |
| 1962 | 7 | 6 | 1 | 4 | 2 | 1 | 3 | 4 | |
| 1963 | 10 | 4 | | 5 | 2 | | 5 | 2 | |
| 1964 | 10 | 3 | 1 | 5 | 1 | 1 | 5 | 2 | |
| 1965 | 11 | 3 | | 5 | 2 | | 6 | 1 | |
| 1966 | 9 | 5 | | 5 | 2 | | 4 | 3 | |
| 1967 | 9 | 5 | | 6 | 1 | | 3 | 4 | |
| 1968 | 10 | 4 | | 5 | 2 | | 5 | 2 | |
| 1969 | 10 | 3 | 1 | 5 | 1 | 1 | 5 | 2 | |
| 1970 | 7 | 7 | | 4 | 3 | | 3 | 4 | |
| 1971 | 9 | 5 | | 4 | 3 | | 5 | 2 | |
| 1972 | 10 | 4 | | 4 | 3 | | 6 | 1 | |
| 1973 | 7 | 5 | 2 | 5 | 1 | 1 | 2 | 4 | 1 |
| 1974 | 4 | 10 | | 3 | 4 | | 1 | 6 | |
| 1975 | 3 | 11 | | 3 | 4 | | 0 | 7 | |
| 1976 | 9 | 5 | | 6 | 1 | | 3 | 4 | |
| 1977 | 6 | 8 | | 2 | 5 | | 4 | 3 | |
| 1978 | 8 | 8 | | 5 | 3 | | 3 | 5 | |
| 1979 | 9 | 7 | | 5 | 3 | | 4 | 4 | |
| 1980 | 11 | 5 | | 6 | 2 | | 5 | 3 | |
| 1981 | 5 | 11 | | 3 | 5 | | 2 | 6 | |
| 1982 | 4 | 5 | | 2 | 2 | | 2 | 3 | |
| 1983 | 9 | 7 | | 6 | 2 | | 3 | 5 | |
| 1984 | 5 | 11 | | 2 | 6 | | 3 | 5 | |
| 1985 | 8 | 8 | | 5 | 3 | | 3 | 5 | |
| 1986 | 12 | 4 | | 6 | 2 | | 6 | 2 | |
| 1987 | 10 | 5 | | 5 | 2 | | 5 | 3 | |
| 1988 | 10 | 6 | | 6 | 2 | | 4 | 4 | |
| 1989 | 9 | 6 | 1 | 5 | 2 | 1 | 4 | 4 | |
| 1990 | 3 | 13 | | 2 | 6 | | 1 | 7 | |
| 1991 | 6 | 10 | | 3 | 5 | | 3 | 5 | |
| 1992 | 7 | 9 | | 4 | 4 | | 3 | 5 | |
| 1993 | 7 | 9 | | 4 | 4 | | 3 | 5 | |
| Total | 358 | 250 | 10 | 193 | 110 | 5 | 165 | 140 | 5 |

**DENVER BRONCOS**

| | All Games | | | Home Games | | | Road Games | | |
|---|---|---|---|---|---|---|---|---|---|
| Season | W | L | T | W | L | T | W | L | T |
| 1960 | 4 | 9 | 1 | 2 | 4 | 1 | 2 | 5 | |
| 1961 | 3 | 11 | | 2 | 5 | | 1 | 6 | |
| 1962 | 7 | 7 | | 3 | 4 | | 4 | 3 | |
| 1963 | 2 | 11 | 1 | 2 | 5 | | 0 | 6 | 1 |
| 1964 | 2 | 11 | 1 | 2 | 4 | 1 | 0 | 7 | |
| 1965 | 4 | 10 | | 2 | 5 | | 2 | 5 | |
| 1966 | 4 | 10 | | 3 | 4 | | 1 | 6 | |
| 1967 | 3 | 11 | | 1 | 6 | | 2 | 5 | |
| 1968 | 5 | 9 | | 3 | 4 | | 2 | 5 | |
| 1969 | 5 | 8 | 1 | 4 | 2 | 1 | 1 | 6 | |
| 1970 | 5 | 8 | 1 | 3 | 3 | 1 | 2 | 5 | |
| 1971 | 4 | 9 | 1 | 2 | 4 | 1 | 2 | 5 | |
| 1972 | 5 | 9 | | 3 | 4 | | 2 | 5 | |
| 1973 | 7 | 5 | 2 | 3 | 3 | 1 | 4 | 2 | 1 |
| 1974 | 7 | 6 | 1 | 3 | 3 | 1 | 4 | 3 | |
| 1975 | 6 | 8 | | 5 | 2 | | 1 | 6 | |
| 1976 | 9 | 5 | | 6 | 1 | | 3 | 4 | |
| 1977 | 12 | 2 | | 6 | 1 | | 6 | 1 | |
| 1978 | 10 | 6 | | 6 | 2 | | 4 | 4 | |
| 1979 | 10 | 6 | | 6 | 2 | | 4 | 4 | |
| 1980 | 8 | 8 | | 4 | 4 | | 4 | 4 | |
| 1981 | 10 | 6 | | 8 | 0 | | 2 | 6 | |
| 1982 | 2 | 7 | | 1 | 4 | | 1 | 3 | |
| 1983 | 9 | 7 | | 6 | 2 | | 3 | 5 | |
| 1984 | 13 | 3 | | 7 | 1 | | 6 | 2 | |
| 1985 | 11 | 5 | | 6 | 2 | | 5 | 3 | |
| 1986 | 11 | 5 | | 7 | 1 | | 4 | 4 | |
| 1987 | 10 | 4 | 1 | 7 | 1 | | 3 | 3 | 1 |
| 1988 | 8 | 8 | | 6 | 2 | | 2 | 6 | |
| 1989 | 11 | 5 | | 6 | 2 | | 5 | 3 | |
| 1990 | 5 | 11 | | 4 | 4 | | 1 | 7 | |
| 1991 | 12 | 4 | | 7 | 1 | | 5 | 3 | |
| 1992 | 8 | 8 | | 7 | 1 | | 1 | 7 | |
| 1993 | 9 | 7 | | 5 | 3 | | 4 | 4 | |
| Total | 241 | 249 | 10 | 148 | 96 | 7 | 93 | 153 | 3 |

**HOUSTON OILERS**

| | All Games | | | Home Games | | | Road Games | | |
|---|---|---|---|---|---|---|---|---|---|
| Season | W | L | T | W | L | T | W | L | T |
| 1960 | 10 | 4 | | 6 | 1 | | 4 | 3 | |
| 1961 | 10 | 3 | 1 | 6 | 1 | | 4 | 2 | 1 |
| 1962 | 11 | 3 | | 6 | 1 | | 5 | 2 | |
| 1963 | 6 | 8 | | 4 | 3 | | 2 | 5 | |
| 1964 | 4 | 10 | | 3 | 4 | | 1 | 6 | |
| 1965 | 4 | 10 | | 3 | 4 | | 1 | 6 | |
| 1966 | 3 | 11 | | 3 | 4 | | 0 | 7 | |
| 1967 | 9 | 4 | 1 | 5 | 2 | | 4 | 2 | 1 |
| 1968 | 7 | 7 | | 3 | 4 | | 4 | 3 | |
| 1969 | 6 | 6 | 2 | 4 | 2 | 1 | 2 | 4 | 1 |
| 1970 | 3 | 10 | 1 | 1 | 6 | | 2 | 4 | 1 |
| 1971 | 4 | 9 | 1 | 3 | 3 | 1 | 1 | 6 | |
| 1972 | 1 | 13 | | 1 | 6 | | 0 | 7 | |
| 1973 | 1 | 13 | | 0 | 7 | | 1 | 6 | |
| 1974 | 7 | 7 | | 3 | 4 | | 4 | 3 | |
| 1975 | 10 | 4 | | 5 | 2 | | 5 | 2 | |
| 1976 | 5 | 9 | | 3 | 4 | | 2 | 5 | |
| 1977 | 8 | 6 | | 5 | 2 | | 3 | 4 | |
| 1978 | 10 | 6 | | 5 | 3 | | 5 | 3 | |
| 1979 | 11 | 5 | | 6 | 2 | | 5 | 3 | |
| 1980 | 11 | 5 | | 6 | 2 | | 5 | 3 | |
| 1981 | 7 | 9 | | 5 | 3 | | 2 | 6 | |
| 1982 | 1 | 8 | | 1 | 4 | | 0 | 4 | |
| 1983 | 2 | 14 | | 2 | 6 | | 0 | 8 | |
| 1984 | 3 | 13 | | 2 | 6 | | 1 | 7 | |
| 1985 | 5 | 11 | | 4 | 4 | | 1 | 7 | |
| 1986 | 5 | 11 | | 4 | 4 | | 1 | 7 | |
| 1987 | 9 | 6 | | 5 | 2 | | 4 | 4 | |
| 1988 | 10 | 6 | | 7 | 1 | | 3 | 5 | |
| 1989 | 9 | 7 | | 6 | 2 | | 3 | 5 | |
| 1990 | 9 | 7 | | 6 | 2 | | 3 | 5 | |
| 1991 | 11 | 5 | | 7 | 1 | | 4 | 4 | |
| 1992 | 10 | 6 | | 5 | 3 | | 5 | 3 | |
| 1993 | 12 | 4 | | 7 | 1 | | 5 | 3 | |
| Total | 234 | 260 | 6 | 142 | 106 | 2 | 92 | 154 | 4 |

**INDIANAPOLIS COLTS***

| | All Games | | | Home Games | | | Road Games | | |
|---|---|---|---|---|---|---|---|---|---|
| Season | W | L | T | W | L | T | W | L | T |
| 1953 | 3 | 9 | | 2 | 4 | | 1 | 5 | |
| 1954 | 3 | 9 | | 2 | 4 | | 1 | 5 | |
| 1955 | 5 | 6 | 1 | 4 | 1 | 1 | 1 | 5 | |
| 1956 | 5 | 7 | | 4 | 2 | | 1 | 5 | |
| 1957 | 7 | 5 | | 4 | 2 | | 3 | 3 | |
| 1958 | 9 | 3 | | 6 | 0 | | 3 | 3 | |
| 1959 | 9 | 3 | | 4 | 2 | | 5 | 1 | |
| 1960 | 6 | 6 | | 4 | 2 | | 2 | 4 | |
| 1961 | 8 | 6 | | 5 | 2 | | 3 | 4 | |
| 1962 | 7 | 7 | | 3 | 4 | | 4 | 3 | |
| 1963 | 8 | 6 | | 4 | 3 | | 4 | 3 | |
| 1964 | 12 | 2 | | 7 | 1 | | 5 | 1 | |
| 1965 | 10 | 3 | 1 | 5 | 2 | | 5 | 1 | 1 |
| 1966 | 9 | 5 | | 5 | 2 | | 4 | 3 | |
| 1967 | 11 | 1 | 2 | 6 | 0 | 1 | 5 | 1 | 1 |
| 1968 | 13 | 1 | | 6 | 1 | | 7 | 0 | |
| 1969 | 8 | 5 | 1 | 4 | 2 | 1 | 4 | 3 | |
| 1970 | 11 | 2 | 1 | 5 | 1 | 1 | 6 | 1 | |
| 1971 | 10 | 4 | | 5 | 2 | | 5 | 2 | |
| 1972 | 5 | 9 | | 2 | 5 | | 3 | 4 | |
| 1973 | 4 | 10 | | 3 | 4 | | 1 | 6 | |
| 1974 | 2 | 12 | | 0 | 7 | | 2 | 5 | |
| 1975 | 10 | 4 | | 5 | 2 | | 5 | 2 | |
| 1976 | 11 | 3 | | 6 | 1 | | 5 | 2 | |
| 1977 | 10 | 4 | | 6 | 1 | | 4 | 3 | |
| 1978 | 5 | 11 | | 2 | 6 | | 3 | 5 | |
| 1979 | 5 | 11 | | 3 | 5 | | 2 | 6 | |
| 1980 | 7 | 9 | | 2 | 6 | | 5 | 3 | |
| 1981 | 2 | 14 | | 1 | 7 | | 1 | 7 | |
| 1982 | 0 | 8 | 1 | 0 | 3 | 1 | 0 | 5 | |
| 1983 | 7 | 9 | | 3 | 5 | | 4 | 4 | |
| 1984 | 4 | 12 | | 2 | 6 | | 2 | 6 | |
| 1985 | 5 | 11 | | 4 | 4 | | 1 | 7 | |
| 1986 | 3 | 13 | | 1 | 7 | | 2 | 6 | |
| 1987 | 9 | 6 | | 4 | 4 | | 5 | 2 | |
| 1988 | 9 | 7 | | 6 | 2 | | 3 | 5 | |
| 1989 | 8 | 8 | | 6 | 2 | | 2 | 6 | |
| 1990 | 7 | 9 | | 3 | 5 | | 4 | 4 | |
| 1991 | 1 | 15 | | 0 | 8 | | 1 | 7 | |
| 1992 | 9 | 7 | | 4 | 4 | | 5 | 3 | |
| 1993 | 4 | 12 | | 2 | 6 | | 2 | 6 | |
| Total | 281 | 294 | 7 | 150 | 137 | 5 | 131 | 157 | 2 |

*includes Baltimore Colts (1953-83).*

**KANSAS CITY CHIEFS***

| | All Games | | | Home Games | | | Road Games | | |
|---|---|---|---|---|---|---|---|---|---|
| Season | W | L | T | W | L | T | W | L | T |
| 1960 | 8 | 6 | | 5 | 2 | | 3 | 4 | |
| 1961 | 6 | 8 | | 4 | 3 | | 2 | 5 | |
| 1962 | 11 | 3 | | 6 | 1 | | 5 | 2 | |
| 1963 | 5 | 7 | 2 | 4 | 3 | | 1 | 4 | 2 |
| 1964 | 7 | 7 | | 4 | 3 | | 3 | 4 | |
| 1965 | 7 | 5 | 2 | 5 | 2 | | 2 | 3 | 2 |
| 1966 | 11 | 2 | 1 | 4 | 2 | 1 | 7 | 0 | |
| 1967 | 9 | 5 | | 4 | 3 | | 5 | 2 | |
| 1968 | 12 | 2 | | 6 | 1 | | 6 | 1 | |
| 1969 | 11 | 3 | | 6 | 1 | | 5 | 2 | |
| 1970 | 7 | 5 | 2 | 4 | 1 | 2 | 3 | 4 | |
| 1971 | 10 | 3 | 1 | 7 | 0 | | 3 | 3 | 1 |
| 1972 | 8 | 6 | | 3 | 4 | | 5 | 2 | |
| 1973 | 7 | 5 | 2 | 5 | 1 | 1 | 2 | 4 | 1 |
| 1974 | 5 | 9 | | 1 | 6 | | 4 | 3 | |
| 1975 | 5 | 9 | | 3 | 4 | | 2 | 5 | |
| 1976 | 5 | 9 | | 1 | 6 | | 4 | 3 | |
| 1977 | 2 | 12 | | 1 | 6 | | 1 | 6 | |
| 1978 | 4 | 12 | | 3 | 5 | | 1 | 7 | |
| 1979 | 7 | 9 | | 3 | 5 | | 4 | 4 | |
| 1980 | 8 | 8 | | 3 | 5 | | 5 | 3 | |
| 1981 | 9 | 7 | | 5 | 3 | | 4 | 4 | |
| 1982 | 3 | 6 | | 2 | 2 | | 1 | 4 | |
| 1983 | 6 | 10 | | 5 | 3 | | 1 | 7 | |
| 1984 | 8 | 8 | | 5 | 3 | | 3 | 5 | |
| 1985 | 6 | 10 | | 5 | 3 | | 1 | 7 | |
| 1986 | 10 | 6 | | 6 | 2 | | 4 | 4 | |
| 1987 | 4 | 11 | | 3 | 4 | | 1 | 7 | |
| 1988 | 4 | 11 | 1 | 4 | 4 | | 0 | 7 | 1 |
| 1989 | 8 | 7 | 1 | 5 | 3 | | 3 | 4 | 1 |
| 1990 | 11 | 5 | | 6 | 2 | | 5 | 3 | |
| 1991 | 10 | 6 | | 6 | 2 | | 4 | 4 | |
| 1992 | 10 | 6 | | 7 | 1 | | 3 | 5 | |
| 1993 | 11 | 5 | | 7 | 1 | | 4 | 4 | |
| Total | 255 | 233 | 12 | 148 | 97 | 4 | 107 | 136 | 8 |

*includes Dallas Texans (1960-62).*

**LOS ANGELES RAIDERS***

| | All Games | | | Home Games | | | Road Games | | |
|---|---|---|---|---|---|---|---|---|---|
| Season | W | L | T | W | L | T | W | L | T |
| 1960 | 6 | 8 | | 3 | 4 | | 3 | 4 | |
| 1961 | 2 | 12 | | 1 | 6 | | 1 | 6 | |
| 1962 | 1 | 13 | | 1 | 6 | | 0 | 7 | |
| 1963 | 10 | 4 | | 6 | 1 | | 4 | 3 | |
| 1964 | 5 | 7 | 2 | 5 | 2 | | 0 | 5 | 2 |
| 1965 | 8 | 5 | 1 | 5 | 2 | | 3 | 3 | 1 |
| 1966 | 8 | 5 | 1 | 3 | 3 | 1 | 5 | 2 | |
| 1967 | 13 | 1 | | 7 | 0 | | 6 | 1 | |
| 1968 | 12 | 2 | | 6 | 1 | | 6 | 1 | |
| 1969 | 12 | 1 | 1 | 7 | 0 | | 5 | 1 | 1 |
| 1970 | 8 | 4 | 2 | 6 | 1 | | 2 | 3 | 2 |
| 1971 | 8 | 4 | 2 | 5 | 1 | 1 | 3 | 3 | 1 |
| 1972 | 10 | 3 | 1 | 5 | 1 | 1 | 5 | 2 | |
| 1973 | 9 | 4 | 1 | 5 | 2 | | 4 | 2 | 1 |
| 1974 | 12 | 2 | | 6 | 1 | | 6 | 1 | |
| 1975 | 11 | 3 | | 6 | 1 | | 5 | 2 | |
| 1976 | 13 | 1 | | 7 | 0 | | 6 | 1 | |
| 1977 | 11 | 3 | | 6 | 1 | | 5 | 2 | |
| 1978 | 9 | 7 | | 4 | 4 | | 5 | 3 | |
| 1979 | 9 | 7 | | 6 | 2 | | 3 | 5 | |
| 1980 | 11 | 5 | | 6 | 2 | | 5 | 3 | |
| 1981 | 7 | 9 | | 4 | 4 | | 3 | 5 | |
| 1982 | 8 | 1 | | 4 | 0 | | 4 | 1 | |
| 1983 | 12 | 4 | | 6 | 2 | | 6 | 2 | |
| 1984 | 11 | 5 | | 6 | 2 | | 5 | 3 | |
| 1985 | 12 | 4 | | 7 | 1 | | 5 | 3 | |
| 1986 | 8 | 8 | | 3 | 5 | | 5 | 3 | |
| 1987 | 5 | 10 | | 3 | 5 | | 2 | 5 | |
| 1988 | 7 | 9 | | 3 | 5 | | 4 | 4 | |
| 1989 | 8 | 8 | | 7 | 1 | | 1 | 7 | |
| 1990 | 12 | 4 | | 6 | 2 | | 6 | 2 | |
| 1991 | 9 | 7 | | 5 | 3 | | 4 | 4 | |

| | All Games | | | Home Games | | | Road Games | | |
|---|---|---|---|---|---|---|---|---|---|
| Season | W | L | T | W | L | T | W | L | T |
| 1992 | 7 | 9 | | 5 | 3 | | 2 | 6 | |
| 1993 | 10 | 6 | | 5 | 3 | | 5 | 3 | |
| Total | 304 | 185 | 11 | 170 | 77 | 3 | 134 | 108 | 8 |

*includes Oakland Raiders (1960-81).*

**MIAMI DOLPHINS**

| | All Games | | | Home Games | | | Road Games | | |
|---|---|---|---|---|---|---|---|---|---|
| Season | W | L | T | W | L | T | W | L | T |
| 1966 | 3 | 11 | | 2 | 5 | | 1 | 6 | |
| 1967 | 4 | 10 | | 4 | 3 | | 0 | 7 | |
| 1968 | 5 | 8 | 1 | 1 | 5 | 1 | 4 | 3 | |
| 1969 | 3 | 10 | 1 | 2 | 4 | 1 | 1 | 6 | |
| 1970 | 10 | 4 | | 6 | 1 | | 4 | 3 | |
| 1971 | 10 | 3 | 1 | 6 | 1 | | 4 | 2 | 1 |
| 1972 | 14 | 0 | | 7 | 0 | | 7 | 0 | |
| 1973 | 12 | 2 | | 7 | 0 | | 5 | 2 | |
| 1974 | 11 | 3 | | 7 | 0 | | 4 | 3 | |
| 1975 | 10 | 4 | | 5 | 2 | | 5 | 2 | |
| 1976 | 6 | 8 | | 3 | 4 | | 3 | 4 | |
| 1977 | 10 | 4 | | 6 | 1 | | 4 | 3 | |
| 1978 | 11 | 5 | | 7 | 1 | | 4 | 4 | |
| 1979 | 10 | 6 | | 6 | 2 | | 4 | 4 | |
| 1980 | 8 | 8 | | 5 | 3 | | 3 | 5 | |
| 1981 | 11 | 4 | 1 | 6 | 1 | 1 | 5 | 3 | |
| 1982 | 7 | 2 | | 4 | 0 | | 3 | 2 | |
| 1983 | 12 | 4 | | 7 | 1 | | 5 | 3 | |
| 1984 | 14 | 2 | | 7 | 1 | | 7 | 1 | |
| 1985 | 12 | 4 | | 8 | 0 | | 4 | 4 | |
| 1986 | 8 | 8 | | 4 | 4 | | 4 | 4 | |
| 1987 | 8 | 7 | | 4 | 3 | | 4 | 4 | |
| 1988 | 6 | 10 | | 4 | 4 | | 2 | 6 | |
| 1989 | 8 | 8 | | 4 | 4 | | 4 | 4 | |
| 1990 | 12 | 4 | | 7 | 1 | | 5 | 3 | |
| 1991 | 8 | 8 | | 5 | 3 | | 3 | 5 | |
| 1992 | 11 | 5 | | 6 | 2 | | 5 | 3 | |
| 1993 | 9 | 7 | | 4 | 4 | | 5 | 3 | |
| Total | 253 | 159 | 4 | 144 | 60 | 3 | 109 | 99 | 1 |

**NEW ENGLAND PATRIOTS***

| | All Games | | | Home Games | | | Road Games | | |
|---|---|---|---|---|---|---|---|---|---|
| Season | W | L | T | W | L | T | W | L | T |
| 1960 | 5 | 9 | | 3 | 4 | | 2 | 5 | |
| 1961 | 9 | 4 | 1 | 4 | 2 | 1 | 5 | 2 | |
| 1962 | 9 | 4 | 1 | 6 | 1 | | 3 | 3 | 1 |
| 1963 | 7 | 6 | 1 | 5 | 1 | 1 | 2 | 5 | |
| 1964 | 10 | 3 | 1 | 4 | 2 | 1 | 6 | 1 | |
| 1965 | 4 | 8 | 2 | 1 | 4 | 2 | 3 | 4 | |
| 1966 | 8 | 4 | 2 | 4 | 2 | 1 | 4 | 2 | 1 |
| 1967 | 3 | 10 | 1 | 2 | 4 | | 1 | 6 | 1 |
| 1968 | 4 | 10 | | 2 | 5 | | 2 | 5 | |
| 1969 | 4 | 10 | | 2 | 5 | | 2 | 5 | |
| 1970 | 2 | 12 | | 1 | 6 | | 1 | 6 | |
| 1971 | 6 | 8 | | 5 | 2 | | 1 | 6 | |
| 1972 | 3 | 11 | | 2 | 5 | | 1 | 6 | |
| 1973 | 5 | 9 | | 3 | 4 | | 2 | 5 | |
| 1974 | 7 | 7 | | 3 | 4 | | 4 | 3 | |
| 1975 | 3 | 11 | | 2 | 5 | | 1 | 6 | |
| 1976 | 11 | 3 | | 6 | 1 | | 5 | 2 | |
| 1977 | 9 | 5 | | 6 | 1 | | 3 | 4 | |
| 1978 | 11 | 5 | | 5 | 3 | | 6 | 2 | |
| 1979 | 9 | 7 | | 6 | 2 | | 3 | 5 | |
| 1980 | 10 | 6 | | 6 | 2 | | 4 | 4 | |
| 1981 | 2 | 14 | | 2 | 6 | | 0 | 8 | |
| 1982 | 5 | 4 | | 3 | 1 | | 2 | 3 | |
| 1983 | 8 | 8 | | 5 | 3 | | 3 | 5 | |
| 1984 | 9 | 7 | | 5 | 3 | | 4 | 4 | |
| 1985 | 11 | 5 | | 7 | 1 | | 4 | 4 | |
| 1986 | 11 | 5 | | 4 | 4 | | 7 | 1 | |
| 1987 | 8 | 7 | | 5 | 3 | | 3 | 4 | |
| 1988 | 9 | 7 | | 7 | 1 | | 2 | 6 | |
| 1989 | 5 | 11 | | 3 | 5 | | 2 | 6 | |
| 1990 | 1 | 15 | | 0 | 8 | | 1 | 7 | |
| 1991 | 6 | 10 | | 4 | 4 | | 2 | 6 | |
| 1992 | 2 | 14 | | 1 | 7 | | 1 | 7 | |
| 1993 | 5 | 11 | | 3 | 5 | | 2 | 6 | |
| Total | 221 | 270 | 9 | 127 | 116 | 6 | 94 | 154 | 3 |

*includes Boston Patriots (1960-70).*

**NEW YORK JETS***

| | All Games | | | Home Games | | | Road Games | | |
|---|---|---|---|---|---|---|---|---|---|
| Season | W | L | T | W | L | T | W | L | T |
| 1960 | 7 | 7 | | 3 | 4 | | 4 | 3 | |
| 1961 | 7 | 7 | | 5 | 2 | | 2 | 5 | |
| 1962 | 5 | 9 | | 2 | 5 | | 3 | 4 | |
| 1963 | 5 | 8 | 1 | 4 | 2 | 1 | 1 | 6 | |
| 1964 | 5 | 8 | 1 | 5 | 1 | 1 | 0 | 7 | |
| 1965 | 5 | 8 | 1 | 3 | 3 | 1 | 2 | 5 | |
| 1966 | 6 | 6 | 2 | 4 | 3 | | 2 | 3 | 2 |
| 1967 | 8 | 5 | 1 | 4 | 2 | 1 | 4 | 3 | |
| 1968 | 11 | 3 | | 6 | 1 | | 5 | 2 | |
| 1969 | 10 | 4 | | 5 | 2 | | 5 | 2 | |
| 1970 | 4 | 10 | | 2 | 5 | | 2 | 5 | |
| 1971 | 6 | 8 | | 4 | 3 | | 2 | 5 | |
| 1972 | 7 | 7 | | 4 | 3 | | 3 | 4 | |
| 1973 | 4 | 10 | | 2 | 4 | | 2 | 6 | |
| 1974 | 7 | 7 | | 3 | 4 | | 4 | 3 | |
| 1975 | 3 | 11 | | 1 | 6 | | 2 | 5 | |
| 1976 | 3 | 11 | | 2 | 5 | | 1 | 6 | |
| 1977 | 3 | 11 | | 1 | 6 | | 2 | 5 | |
| 1978 | 8 | 8 | | 4 | 4 | | 4 | 4 | |
| 1979 | 8 | 8 | | 6 | 2 | | 2 | 6 | |
| 1980 | 4 | 12 | | 2 | 6 | | 2 | 6 | |
| 1981 | 10 | 5 | 1 | 6 | 2 | | 4 | 3 | 1 |
| 1982 | 6 | 3 | | 3 | 1 | | 3 | 2 | |
| 1983 | 7 | 9 | | 2 | 6 | | 5 | 3 | |
| 1984 | 7 | 9 | | 3 | 5 | | 4 | 4 | |
| 1985 | 11 | 5 | | 7 | 1 | | 4 | 4 | |
| 1986 | 10 | 6 | | 5 | 3 | | 5 | 3 | |
| 1987 | 6 | 9 | | 4 | 4 | | 2 | 5 | |
| 1988 | 8 | 7 | 1 | 5 | 2 | 1 | 3 | 5 | |
| 1989 | 4 | 12 | | 1 | 7 | | 3 | 5 | |
| 1990 | 6 | 10 | | 3 | 5 | | 3 | 5 | |
| 1991 | 8 | 8 | | 4 | 4 | | 4 | 4 | |
| 1992 | 4 | 12 | | 3 | 5 | | 1 | 7 | |
| 1993 | 8 | 8 | | 3 | 5 | | 5 | 3 | |
| Total | 221 | 271 | 8 | 121 | 123 | 5 | 100 | 148 | 3 |

*includes New York Titans (1960-62).*

**PITTSBURGH STEELERS***

| | All Games | | | Home Games | | | Road Games | | |
|---|---|---|---|---|---|---|---|---|---|
| Season | W | L | T | W | L | T | W | L | T |
| 1933 | 3 | 6 | 2 | 2 | 3 | | 1 | 3 | 2 |
| 1934 | 2 | 10 | | 1 | 5 | | 1 | 5 | |
| 1935 | 4 | 8 | | 2 | 5 | | 2 | 3 | |
| 1936 | 6 | 6 | | 4 | 1 | | 2 | 5 | |
| 1937 | 4 | 7 | | 2 | 4 | | 2 | 3 | |
| 1938 | 2 | 9 | | 0 | 5 | | 2 | 4 | |
| 1939 | 1 | 9 | 1 | 1 | 4 | | 0 | 5 | 1 |
| 1940 | 2 | 7 | 2 | 1 | 2 | 2 | 1 | 5 | |
| 1941 | 1 | 9 | 1 | 1 | 4 | | 0 | 5 | 1 |
| 1942 | 7 | 4 | | 3 | 2 | | 4 | 2 | |
| 1945 | 2 | 8 | | 1 | 4 | | 1 | 4 | |
| 1946 | 5 | 5 | 1 | 4 | 1 | | 1 | 4 | 1 |
| 1947 | 8 | 4 | | 5 | 1 | | 3 | 3 | |
| 1948 | 4 | 8 | | 4 | 2 | | 0 | 6 | |
| 1949 | 6 | 5 | 1 | 3 | 2 | 1 | 3 | 3 | |
| 1950 | 6 | 6 | | 2 | 4 | | 4 | 2 | |
| 1951 | 4 | 7 | 1 | 1 | 4 | 1 | 3 | 3 | |
| 1952 | 5 | 7 | | 2 | 4 | | 3 | 3 | |
| 1953 | 6 | 6 | | 3 | 3 | | 3 | 3 | |
| 1954 | 5 | 7 | | 4 | 2 | | 1 | 5 | |
| 1955 | 4 | 8 | | 3 | 2 | | 1 | 6 | |
| 1956 | 5 | 7 | | 3 | 3 | | 2 | 4 | |
| 1957 | 6 | 6 | | 4 | 2 | | 2 | 4 | |
| 1958 | 7 | 4 | 1 | 5 | 1 | | 2 | 3 | 1 |
| 1959 | 6 | 5 | 1 | 3 | 2 | 1 | 3 | 3 | |
| 1960 | 5 | 6 | 1 | 4 | 2 | | 1 | 4 | 1 |
| 1961 | 6 | 8 | | 4 | 3 | | 2 | 5 | |
| 1962 | 9 | 5 | | 4 | 3 | | 5 | 2 | |
| 1963 | 7 | 4 | 3 | 5 | 0 | 2 | 2 | 4 | 1 |
| 1964 | 5 | 9 | | 2 | 5 | | 3 | 4 | |
| 1965 | 2 | 12 | | 1 | 6 | | 1 | 6 | |
| 1966 | 5 | 8 | 1 | 3 | 3 | 1 | 2 | 5 | |
| 1967 | 4 | 9 | 1 | 1 | 6 | | 3 | 3 | 1 |
| 1968 | 2 | 11 | 1 | 1 | 6 | | 1 | 5 | 1 |
| 1969 | 1 | 13 | | 1 | 6 | | 0 | 7 | |
| 1970 | 5 | 9 | | 4 | 3 | | 1 | 6 | |
| 1971 | 6 | 8 | | 5 | 2 | | 1 | 6 | |
| 1972 | 11 | 3 | | 7 | 0 | | 4 | 3 | |
| 1973 | 10 | 4 | | 7 | 1 | | 3 | 3 | |
| 1974 | 10 | 3 | 1 | 5 | 2 | | 5 | 1 | 1 |
| 1975 | 12 | 2 | | 6 | 1 | | 6 | 1 | |
| 1976 | 10 | 4 | | 6 | 1 | | 4 | 3 | |
| 1977 | 9 | 5 | | 6 | 1 | | 3 | 4 | |
| 1978 | 14 | 2 | | 7 | 1 | | 7 | 1 | |
| 1979 | 12 | 4 | | 8 | 0 | | 4 | 4 | |
| 1980 | 9 | 7 | | 6 | 2 | | 3 | 5 | |
| 1981 | 8 | 8 | | 5 | 3 | | 3 | 5 | |
| 1982 | 6 | 3 | | 4 | 0 | | 2 | 3 | |
| 1983 | 10 | 6 | | 4 | 4 | | 6 | 2 | |
| 1984 | 9 | 7 | | 6 | 2 | | 3 | 5 | |
| 1985 | 7 | 9 | | 5 | 3 | | 2 | 6 | |
| 1986 | 6 | 10 | | 4 | 4 | | 2 | 6 | |
| 1987 | 8 | 7 | | 4 | 3 | | 4 | 4 | |
| 1988 | 5 | 11 | | 4 | 4 | | 1 | 7 | |
| 1989 | 9 | 7 | | 4 | 4 | | 5 | 3 | |
| 1990 | 9 | 7 | | 6 | 2 | | 3 | 5 | |
| 1991 | 7 | 9 | | 5 | 3 | | 2 | 6 | |
| 1992 | 11 | 5 | | 7 | 1 | | 4 | 4 | |
| 1993 | 9 | 7 | | 6 | 2 | | 3 | 5 | |
| Total | 369 | 400 | 19 | 221 | 161 | 8 | 148 | 239 | 11 |

*includes Pittsburgh Pirates (1933-40).*

**SAN DIEGO CHARGERS***

| | All Games | | | Home Games | | | Road Games | | |
|---|---|---|---|---|---|---|---|---|---|
| Season | W | L | T | W | L | T | W | L | T |
| 1960 | 10 | 4 | | 5 | 2 | | 5 | 2 | |
| 1961 | 12 | 2 | | 6 | 1 | | 6 | 1 | |
| 1962 | 4 | 10 | | 3 | 4 | | 1 | 6 | |
| 1963 | 11 | 3 | | 6 | 1 | | 5 | 2 | |
| 1964 | 8 | 5 | 1 | 4 | 3 | | 4 | 2 | 1 |
| 1965 | 9 | 2 | 3 | 4 | 1 | 2 | 5 | 1 | 1 |
| 1966 | 7 | 6 | 1 | 5 | 2 | | 2 | 4 | 1 |
| 1967 | 8 | 5 | 1 | 5 | 2 | 1 | 3 | 3 | |
| 1968 | 9 | 5 | | 4 | 3 | | 5 | 2 | |
| 1969 | 8 | 6 | | 5 | 2 | | 3 | 4 | |
| 1970 | 5 | 6 | 3 | 2 | 3 | 2 | 3 | 3 | 1 |
| 1971 | 6 | 8 | | 6 | 1 | | 0 | 7 | |
| 1972 | 4 | 9 | 1 | 2 | 5 | | 2 | 4 | 1 |
| 1973 | 2 | 11 | 1 | 2 | 5 | | 0 | 6 | 1 |
| 1974 | 5 | 9 | | 3 | 4 | | 2 | 5 | |
| 1975 | 2 | 12 | | 1 | 6 | | 1 | 6 | |
| 1976 | 6 | 8 | | 3 | 4 | | 3 | 4 | |
| 1977 | 7 | 7 | | 3 | 4 | | 4 | 3 | |
| 1978 | 9 | 7 | | 5 | 3 | | 4 | 4 | |
| 1979 | 12 | 4 | | 7 | 1 | | 5 | 3 | |
| 1980 | 11 | 5 | | 6 | 2 | | 5 | 3 | |
| 1981 | 10 | 6 | | 5 | 3 | | 5 | 3 | |
| 1982 | 6 | 3 | | 3 | 1 | | 3 | 2 | |
| 1983 | 6 | 10 | | 4 | 4 | | 2 | 6 | |
| 1984 | 7 | 9 | | 4 | 4 | | 3 | 5 | |
| 1985 | 8 | 8 | | 6 | 2 | | 2 | 6 | |
| 1986 | 4 | 12 | | 2 | 6 | | 2 | 6 | |
| 1987 | 8 | 7 | | 4 | 3 | | 4 | 4 | |
| 1988 | 6 | 10 | | 3 | 5 | | 3 | 5 | |
| 1989 | 6 | 10 | | 4 | 4 | | 2 | 6 | |
| 1990 | 6 | 10 | | 3 | 5 | | 3 | 5 | |
| 1991 | 4 | 12 | | 3 | 5 | | 1 | 7 | |
| 1992 | 11 | 5 | | 6 | 2 | | 5 | 3 | |
| 1993 | 8 | 8 | | 4 | 4 | | 4 | 4 | |
| Total | 245 | 244 | 11 | 138 | 107 | 5 | 107 | 137 | 6 |

*includes Los Angeles Chargers (1960).*

**SEATTLE SEAHAWKS**

| | All Games | | | Home Games | | | Road Games | | |
|---|---|---|---|---|---|---|---|---|---|
| Season | W | L | T | W | L | T | W | L | T |
| 1976 | 2 | 12 | | 1 | 6 | | 1 | 6 | |
| 1977 | 5 | 9 | | 3 | 4 | | 2 | 5 | |
| 1978 | 9 | 7 | | 5 | 3 | | 4 | 4 | |
| 1979 | 9 | 7 | | 5 | 3 | | 4 | 4 | |
| 1980 | 4 | 12 | | 0 | 8 | | 4 | 4 | |
| 1981 | 6 | 10 | | 5 | 3 | | 1 | 7 | |
| 1982 | 4 | 5 | | 3 | 2 | | 1 | 3 | |
| 1983 | 9 | 7 | | 5 | 3 | | 4 | 4 | |
| 1984 | 12 | 4 | | 7 | 1 | | 5 | 3 | |
| 1985 | 8 | 8 | | 5 | 3 | | 3 | 5 | |
| 1986 | 10 | 6 | | 7 | 1 | | 3 | 5 | |
| 1987 | 9 | 6 | | 6 | 2 | | 3 | 4 | |
| 1988 | 9 | 7 | | 5 | 3 | | 4 | 4 | |
| 1989 | 7 | 9 | | 3 | 5 | | 4 | 4 | |
| 1990 | 9 | 7 | | 5 | 3 | | 4 | 4 | |
| 1991 | 7 | 9 | | 5 | 3 | | 2 | 6 | |

| | All Games | | | Home Games | | | Road Games | | |
|---|---|---|---|---|---|---|---|---|---|
| Season | W | L | T | W | L | T | W | L | T |
| 1992 | 2 | 14 | | 1 | 7 | | 1 | 7 | |
| 1993 | 6 | 10 | | 4 | 4 | | 2 | 6 | |
| Total | 127 | 149 | | 75 | 64 | | 52 | 85 | |

## NFC

### ARIZONA CARDINALS*

| | All Games | | | Home Games | | | Road Games | | |
|---|---|---|---|---|---|---|---|---|---|
| Season | W | L | T | W | L | T | W | L | T |
| 1920 | 6 | 2 | 2 | 5 | 1 | 1 | 1 | 1 | 1 |
| 1921 | 3 | 3 | 2 | 3 | 3 | 1 | 0 | 0 | 1 |
| 1922 | 8 | 3 | | 8 | 3 | | 0 | 0 | |
| 1923 | 8 | 4 | | 8 | 3 | | 0 | 1 | |
| 1924 | 5 | 4 | 1 | 5 | 3 | 1 | 0 | 1 | |
| 1925 | 11 | 2 | 1 | 11 | 2 | | 0 | 0 | 1 |
| 1926 | 5 | 6 | 1 | 3 | 3 | | 2 | 3 | 1 |
| 1927 | 3 | 7 | 1 | 2 | 3 | 1 | 1 | 4 | |
| 1928 | 1 | 5 | | 1 | 1 | | 0 | 4 | |
| 1929 | 6 | 6 | 1 | 3 | 2 | | 3 | 4 | 1 |
| 1930 | 5 | 6 | 2 | 3 | 2 | | 2 | 4 | 2 |
| 1931 | 5 | 4 | | 3 | 0 | | 2 | 4 | |
| 1932 | 2 | 6 | 2 | 1 | 2 | 1 | 1 | 4 | 1 |
| 1933 | 1 | 9 | 1 | 0 | 4 | 1 | 1 | 5 | |
| 1934 | 5 | 6 | | 2 | 2 | | 3 | 4 | |
| 1935 | 6 | 4 | 2 | 2 | 2 | | 4 | 2 | 2 |
| 1936 | 3 | 8 | 1 | 3 | 1 | 1 | 0 | 7 | |
| 1937 | 5 | 5 | 1 | 1 | 3 | | 4 | 2 | 1 |
| 1938 | 2 | 9 | | 1 | 4 | | 1 | 5 | |
| 1939 | 1 | 10 | | 0 | 4 | | 1 | 6 | |
| 1940 | 2 | 7 | 2 | 2 | 1 | 1 | 0 | 6 | 1 |
| 1941 | 3 | 7 | 1 | 0 | 3 | 1 | 3 | 4 | |
| 1942 | 3 | 8 | | 2 | 2 | | 1 | 6 | |
| 1943 | 0 | 10 | | 0 | 3 | | 0 | 7 | |
| 1945 | 1 | 9 | | 0 | 3 | | 1 | 6 | |
| 1946 | 6 | 5 | | 2 | 2 | | 4 | 3 | |
| 1947 | 9 | 3 | | 5 | 0 | | 4 | 3 | |
| 1948 | 11 | 1 | | 5 | 1 | | 6 | 0 | |
| 1949 | 6 | 5 | 1 | 2 | 3 | 1 | 4 | 2 | |
| 1950 | 5 | 7 | | 3 | 3 | | 2 | 4 | |
| 1951 | 3 | 9 | | 1 | 5 | | 2 | 4 | |
| 1952 | 4 | 8 | | 2 | 4 | | 2 | 4 | |
| 1953 | 1 | 10 | 1 | 0 | 5 | 1 | 1 | 5 | |
| 1954 | 2 | 10 | | 2 | 4 | | 0 | 6 | |
| 1955 | 4 | 7 | 1 | 3 | 2 | 1 | 1 | 5 | |
| 1956 | 7 | 5 | | 4 | 2 | | 3 | 3 | |
| 1957 | 3 | 9 | | 0 | 6 | | 3 | 3 | |
| 1958 | 2 | 9 | 1 | 1 | 4 | 1 | 1 | 5 | |
| 1959 | 2 | 10 | | 2 | 4 | | 0 | 6 | |
| 1960 | 6 | 5 | 1 | 3 | 2 | 1 | 3 | 3 | |
| 1961 | 7 | 7 | | 3 | 4 | | 4 | 3 | |
| 1962 | 4 | 9 | 1 | 2 | 4 | 1 | 2 | 5 | |
| 1963 | 9 | 5 | | 3 | 4 | | 6 | 1 | |
| 1964 | 9 | 3 | 2 | 4 | 1 | 1 | 5 | 2 | 1 |
| 1965 | 5 | 9 | | 2 | 5 | | 3 | 4 | |
| 1966 | 8 | 5 | 1 | 5 | 1 | 1 | 3 | 4 | |
| 1967 | 6 | 7 | 1 | 3 | 3 | 1 | 3 | 4 | |
| 1968 | 9 | 4 | 1 | 4 | 2 | 1 | 5 | 2 | |
| 1969 | 4 | 9 | 1 | 3 | 4 | | 1 | 5 | 1 |
| 1970 | 8 | 5 | 1 | 6 | 1 | | 2 | 4 | 1 |
| 1971 | 4 | 9 | 1 | 1 | 5 | 1 | 3 | 4 | |
| 1972 | 4 | 9 | 1 | 2 | 5 | | 2 | 4 | 1 |
| 1973 | 4 | 9 | 1 | 2 | 4 | 1 | 2 | 5 | |
| 1974 | 10 | 4 | | 5 | 2 | | 5 | 2 | |
| 1975 | 11 | 3 | | 6 | 1 | | 5 | 2 | |
| 1976 | 10 | 4 | | 6 | 1 | | 4 | 3 | |
| 1977 | 7 | 7 | | 4 | 3 | | 3 | 4 | |
| 1978 | 6 | 10 | | 3 | 5 | | 3 | 5 | |
| 1979 | 5 | 11 | | 3 | 5 | | 2 | 6 | |
| 1980 | 5 | 11 | | 2 | 6 | | 3 | 5 | |
| 1981 | 7 | 9 | | 5 | 3 | | 2 | 6 | |
| 1982 | 5 | 4 | | 1 | 3 | | 4 | 1 | |
| 1983 | 8 | 7 | 1 | 4 | 3 | 1 | 4 | 4 | |
| 1984 | 9 | 7 | | 5 | 3 | | 4 | 4 | |
| 1985 | 5 | 11 | | 4 | 4 | | 1 | 7 | |
| 1986 | 4 | 11 | 1 | 3 | 5 | | 1 | 6 | 1 |
| 1987 | 7 | 8 | | 4 | 3 | | 3 | 5 | |
| 1988 | 7 | 9 | | 4 | 4 | | 3 | 5 | |
| 1989 | 5 | 11 | | 2 | 6 | | 3 | 5 | |
| 1990 | 5 | 11 | | 3 | 5 | | 2 | 6 | |
| 1991 | 4 | 12 | | 2 | 6 | | 2 | 6 | |
| 1992 | 4 | 12 | | 3 | 5 | | 1 | 7 | |
| 1993 | 7 | 9 | | 4 | 4 | | 3 | 5 | |
| Total | 383 | 514 | 39 | 217 | 227 | 22 | 166 | 287 | 17 |

*includes Chicago Cardinals (1920-59), St. Louis Cardinals (1960-87), and Phoenix Cardinals (1988-1993).*

### ATLANTA FALCONS

| | All Games | | | Home Games | | | Road Games | | |
|---|---|---|---|---|---|---|---|---|---|
| Season | W | L | T | W | L | T | W | L | T |
| 1966 | 3 | 11 | | 1 | 6 | | 2 | 5 | |
| 1967 | 1 | 12 | 1 | 1 | 5 | 1 | 0 | 7 | |
| 1968 | 2 | 12 | | 1 | 6 | | 1 | 6 | |
| 1969 | 6 | 8 | | 4 | 3 | | 2 | 5 | |
| 1970 | 4 | 8 | 2 | 3 | 4 | | 1 | 4 | 2 |
| 1971 | 7 | 6 | 1 | 4 | 3 | | 3 | 3 | 1 |
| 1972 | 7 | 7 | | 4 | 3 | | 3 | 4 | |
| 1973 | 9 | 5 | | 4 | 3 | | 5 | 2 | |
| 1974 | 3 | 11 | | 2 | 5 | | 1 | 6 | |
| 1975 | 4 | 10 | | 3 | 4 | | 1 | 6 | |
| 1976 | 4 | 10 | | 3 | 4 | | 1 | 6 | |
| 1977 | 7 | 7 | | 4 | 3 | | 3 | 4 | |
| 1978 | 9 | 7 | | 7 | 1 | | 2 | 6 | |
| 1979 | 6 | 10 | | 3 | 5 | | 3 | 5 | |
| 1980 | 12 | 4 | | 6 | 2 | | 6 | 2 | |
| 1981 | 7 | 9 | | 4 | 4 | | 3 | 5 | |
| 1982 | 5 | 4 | | 2 | 3 | | 3 | 1 | |
| 1983 | 7 | 9 | | 4 | 4 | | 3 | 5 | |
| 1984 | 4 | 12 | | 2 | 6 | | 2 | 6 | |
| 1985 | 4 | 12 | | 3 | 5 | | 1 | 7 | |
| 1986 | 7 | 8 | 1 | 2 | 5 | 1 | 5 | 3 | |
| 1987 | 3 | 12 | | 2 | 6 | | 1 | 6 | |
| 1988 | 5 | 11 | | 2 | 6 | | 3 | 5 | |
| 1989 | 3 | 13 | | 3 | 5 | | 0 | 8 | |
| 1990 | 5 | 11 | | 5 | 3 | | 0 | 8 | |
| 1991 | 10 | 6 | | 6 | 2 | | 4 | 4 | |
| 1992 | 6 | 10 | | 5 | 3 | | 1 | 7 | |
| 1993 | 6 | 10 | | 4 | 4 | | 2 | 6 | |
| Total | 156 | 255 | 5 | 94 | 113 | 2 | 62 | 142 | 3 |

### CHICAGO BEARS*

| | All Games | | | Home Games | | | Road Games | | |
|---|---|---|---|---|---|---|---|---|---|
| Season | W | L | T | W | L | T | W | L | T |
| 1920 | 10 | 1 | 2 | 6 | 0 | 1 | 4 | 1 | 1 |
| 1921 | 9 | 1 | 1 | 9 | 1 | 1 | 0 | 0 | |
| 1922 | 9 | 3 | | 7 | 1 | | 2 | 2 | |
| 1923 | 9 | 2 | 1 | 7 | 1 | 1 | 2 | 1 | |
| 1924 | 6 | 1 | 4 | 5 | 0 | 3 | 1 | 1 | 1 |
| 1925 | 9 | 5 | 3 | 7 | 1 | 1 | 2 | 4 | 2 |
| 1926 | 12 | 1 | 3 | 10 | 0 | 2 | 2 | 1 | 1 |
| 1927 | 9 | 3 | 2 | 7 | 1 | 1 | 2 | 2 | 1 |
| 1928 | 7 | 5 | 1 | 6 | 3 | | 1 | 2 | 1 |
| 1929 | 4 | 9 | 2 | 1 | 5 | 2 | 3 | 4 | |
| 1930 | 9 | 4 | 1 | 5 | 2 | 1 | 4 | 2 | |
| 1931 | 8 | 5 | | 6 | 3 | | 2 | 2 | |
| 1932 | 7 | 1 | 6 | 6 | 1 | 1 | 1 | 0 | 5 |
| 1933 | 10 | 2 | 1 | 6 | 0 | | 4 | 2 | 1 |
| 1934 | 13 | 0 | | 5 | 0 | | 8 | 0 | |
| 1935 | 6 | 4 | 2 | 1 | 2 | 2 | 5 | 2 | |
| 1936 | 9 | 3 | | 3 | 1 | | 6 | 2 | |
| 1937 | 9 | 1 | 1 | 4 | 1 | | 5 | 0 | 1 |
| 1938 | 6 | 5 | | 2 | 3 | | 4 | 2 | |
| 1939 | 8 | 3 | | 4 | 1 | | 4 | 2 | |
| 1940 | 8 | 3 | | 5 | 0 | | 3 | 3 | |
| 1941 | 10 | 1 | | 5 | 1 | | 5 | 0 | |
| 1942 | 11 | 0 | | 6 | 0 | | 5 | 0 | |
| 1943 | 8 | 1 | 1 | 5 | 0 | | 3 | 1 | 1 |
| 1944 | 6 | 3 | 1 | 4 | 0 | 1 | 2 | 3 | |
| 1945 | 3 | 7 | | 2 | 3 | | 1 | 4 | |
| 1946 | 8 | 2 | 1 | 4 | 1 | 1 | 4 | 1 | |
| 1947 | 8 | 4 | | 4 | 2 | | 4 | 2 | |
| 1948 | 10 | 2 | | 5 | 1 | | 5 | 1 | |
| 1949 | 9 | 3 | | 5 | 1 | | 4 | 2 | |
| 1950 | 9 | 3 | | 6 | 0 | | 3 | 3 | |
| 1951 | 7 | 5 | | 3 | 3 | | 4 | 2 | |
| 1952 | 5 | 7 | | 3 | 3 | | 2 | 4 | |
| 1953 | 3 | 8 | 1 | 1 | 4 | 1 | 2 | 4 | |
| 1954 | 8 | 4 | | 4 | 2 | | 4 | 2 | |
| 1955 | 8 | 4 | | 5 | 1 | | 3 | 3 | |
| 1956 | 9 | 2 | 1 | 6 | 0 | | 3 | 2 | 1 |
| 1957 | 5 | 7 | | 2 | 4 | | 3 | 3 | |
| 1958 | 8 | 4 | | 5 | 1 | | 3 | 3 | |
| 1959 | 8 | 4 | | 4 | 2 | | 4 | 2 | |
| 1960 | 5 | 6 | 1 | 4 | 2 | | 1 | 4 | 1 |
| 1961 | 8 | 6 | | 5 | 2 | | 3 | 4 | |
| 1962 | 9 | 5 | | 4 | 3 | | 5 | 2 | |
| 1963 | 11 | 1 | 2 | 6 | 0 | 1 | 5 | 1 | 1 |
| 1964 | 5 | 9 | | 2 | 5 | | 3 | 4 | |
| 1965 | 9 | 5 | | 5 | 2 | | 4 | 3 | |
| 1966 | 5 | 7 | 2 | 4 | 1 | 2 | 1 | 6 | |
| 1967 | 7 | 6 | 1 | 3 | 3 | 1 | 4 | 3 | |
| 1968 | 7 | 7 | | 2 | 5 | | 5 | 2 | |
| 1969 | 1 | 13 | | 1 | 6 | | 0 | 7 | |
| 1970 | 6 | 8 | | 3 | 4 | | 3 | 4 | |
| 1971 | 6 | 8 | | 4 | 3 | | 2 | 5 | |
| 1972 | 4 | 9 | 1 | 1 | 5 | 1 | 3 | 4 | |
| 1973 | 3 | 11 | | 1 | 6 | | 2 | 5 | |
| 1974 | 4 | 10 | | 4 | 3 | | 0 | 7 | |
| 1975 | 4 | 10 | | 3 | 4 | | 1 | 6 | |
| 1976 | 7 | 7 | | 4 | 3 | | 3 | 4 | |
| 1977 | 9 | 5 | | 5 | 2 | | 4 | 3 | |
| 1978 | 7 | 9 | | 4 | 4 | | 3 | 5 | |
| 1979 | 10 | 6 | | 6 | 2 | | 4 | 4 | |
| 1980 | 7 | 9 | | 5 | 3 | | 2 | 6 | |
| 1981 | 6 | 10 | | 4 | 4 | | 2 | 6 | |
| 1982 | 3 | 6 | | 2 | 2 | | 1 | 4 | |
| 1983 | 8 | 8 | | 5 | 3 | | 3 | 5 | |
| 1984 | 10 | 6 | | 6 | 2 | | 4 | 4 | |
| 1985 | 15 | 1 | | 8 | 0 | | 7 | 1 | |
| 1986 | 14 | 2 | | 7 | 1 | | 7 | 1 | |
| 1987 | 11 | 4 | | 6 | 2 | | 5 | 2 | |
| 1988 | 12 | 4 | | 7 | 1 | | 5 | 3 | |
| 1989 | 6 | 10 | | 4 | 4 | | 2 | 6 | |
| 1990 | 11 | 5 | | 7 | 1 | | 4 | 4 | |
| 1991 | 11 | 5 | | 6 | 2 | | 5 | 3 | |
| 1992 | 5 | 11 | | 4 | 4 | | 1 | 7 | |
| 1993 | 7 | 9 | | 3 | 5 | | 4 | 4 | |
| Total | 573 | 371 | 42 | 336 | 155 | 24 | 237 | 216 | 18 |

*includes Decatur Staleys (1920) and Chicago Staleys (1921).*

### DALLAS COWBOYS

| | All Games | | | Home Games | | | Road Games | | |
|---|---|---|---|---|---|---|---|---|---|
| Season | W | L | T | W | L | T | W | L | T |
| 1960 | 0 | 11 | 1 | 0 | 6 | | 0 | 5 | 1 |
| 1961 | 4 | 9 | 1 | 2 | 4 | 1 | 2 | 5 | |
| 1962 | 5 | 8 | 1 | 2 | 4 | 1 | 3 | 4 | |
| 1963 | 4 | 10 | | 3 | 4 | | 1 | 6 | |
| 1964 | 5 | 8 | 1 | 2 | 4 | 1 | 3 | 4 | |
| 1965 | 7 | 7 | | 5 | 2 | | 2 | 5 | |
| 1966 | 10 | 3 | 1 | 6 | 1 | | 4 | 2 | 1 |
| 1967 | 9 | 5 | | 5 | 2 | | 4 | 3 | |
| 1968 | 12 | 2 | | 5 | 2 | | 7 | 0 | |
| 1969 | 11 | 2 | 1 | 6 | 0 | 1 | 5 | 2 | |
| 1970 | 10 | 4 | | 6 | 1 | | 4 | 3 | |
| 1971 | 11 | 3 | | 6 | 1 | | 5 | 2 | |
| 1972 | 10 | 4 | | 5 | 2 | | 5 | 2 | |
| 1973 | 10 | 4 | | 6 | 1 | | 4 | 3 | |
| 1974 | 8 | 6 | | 5 | 2 | | 3 | 4 | |
| 1975 | 10 | 4 | | 5 | 2 | | 5 | 2 | |
| 1976 | 11 | 3 | | 6 | 1 | | 5 | 2 | |
| 1977 | 12 | 2 | | 6 | 1 | | 6 | 1 | |
| 1978 | 12 | 4 | | 7 | 1 | | 5 | 3 | |
| 1979 | 11 | 5 | | 6 | 2 | | 5 | 3 | |
| 1980 | 12 | 4 | | 8 | 0 | | 4 | 4 | |
| 1981 | 12 | 4 | | 8 | 0 | | 4 | 4 | |
| 1982 | 6 | 3 | | 3 | 2 | | 3 | 1 | |
| 1983 | 12 | 4 | | 6 | 2 | | 6 | 2 | |
| 1984 | 9 | 7 | | 5 | 3 | | 4 | 4 | |
| 1985 | 10 | 6 | | 7 | 1 | | 3 | 5 | |
| 1986 | 7 | 9 | | 3 | 5 | | 4 | 4 | |
| 1987 | 7 | 8 | | 3 | 4 | | 4 | 4 | |
| 1988 | 3 | 13 | | 1 | 7 | | 2 | 6 | |
| 1989 | 1 | 15 | | 0 | 8 | | 1 | 7 | |
| 1990 | 7 | 9 | | 5 | 3 | | 2 | 6 | |
| 1991 | 11 | 5 | | 6 | 2 | | 5 | 3 | |
| 1992 | 13 | 3 | | 7 | 1 | | 6 | 2 | |
| 1993 | 12 | 4 | | 6 | 2 | | 6 | 2 | |
| Total | 294 | 198 | 6 | 162 | 83 | 4 | 132 | 115 | 2 |

### DETROIT LIONS*

| | All Games | | | Home Games | | | Road Games | | |
|---|---|---|---|---|---|---|---|---|---|
| Season | W | L | T | W | L | T | W | L | T |
| 1930 | 5 | 6 | 3 | 5 | 1 | 2 | 0 | 5 | 1 |

| | All Games | | | Home Games | | | Road Games | | |
|---|---|---|---|---|---|---|---|---|---|
| Season | W | L | T | W | L | T | W | L | T |
| 1931 | 11 | 3 | | 8 | 0 | | 3 | 3 | |
| 1932 | 6 | 2 | 4 | 3 | 0 | 2 | 3 | 2 | 2 |
| 1933 | 6 | 5 | | 4 | 1 | | 2 | 4 | |
| 1934 | 10 | 3 | | 6 | 2 | | 4 | 1 | |
| 1935 | 7 | 3 | 2 | 5 | 0 | 1 | 2 | 3 | 1 |
| 1936 | 8 | 4 | | 5 | 1 | | 3 | 3 | |
| 1937 | 7 | 4 | | 4 | 2 | | 3 | 2 | |
| 1938 | 7 | 4 | | 4 | 3 | | 3 | 1 | |
| 1939 | 6 | 5 | | 4 | 2 | | 2 | 3 | |
| 1940 | 5 | 5 | 1 | 3 | 3 | | 2 | 2 | 1 |
| 1941 | 4 | 6 | 1 | 3 | 2 | | 1 | 4 | 1 |
| 1942 | 0 | 11 | | 0 | 7 | | 0 | 4 | |
| 1943 | 3 | 6 | 1 | 2 | 2 | 1 | 1 | 4 | |
| 1944 | 6 | 3 | 1 | 4 | 2 | | 2 | 1 | 1 |
| 1945 | 7 | 3 | | 4 | 1 | | 3 | 2 | |
| 1946 | 1 | 10 | | 1 | 5 | | 0 | 5 | |
| 1947 | 3 | 9 | | 2 | 4 | | 1 | 5 | |
| 1948 | 2 | 10 | | 2 | 4 | | 0 | 6 | |
| 1949 | 4 | 8 | | 2 | 4 | | 2 | 4 | |
| 1950 | 6 | 6 | | 4 | 2 | | 2 | 4 | |
| 1951 | 7 | 4 | 1 | 3 | 3 | 1 | 4 | 1 | |
| 1952 | 9 | 3 | | 6 | 1 | | 3 | 2 | |
| 1953 | 10 | 2 | | 5 | 1 | | 5 | 1 | |
| 1954 | 9 | 2 | 1 | 5 | 0 | 1 | 4 | 2 | |
| 1955 | 3 | 9 | | 3 | 4 | | 0 | 5 | |
| 1956 | 9 | 3 | | 5 | 1 | | 4 | 2 | |
| 1957 | 8 | 4 | | 5 | 1 | | 3 | 3 | |
| 1958 | 4 | 7 | 1 | 2 | 4 | | 2 | 3 | 1 |
| 1959 | 3 | 8 | 1 | 2 | 4 | | 1 | 4 | 1 |
| 1960 | 7 | 5 | | 5 | 1 | | 2 | 4 | |
| 1961 | 8 | 5 | 1 | 2 | 5 | | 6 | 0 | 1 |
| 1962 | 11 | 3 | | 7 | 0 | | 4 | 3 | |
| 1963 | 5 | 8 | 1 | 3 | 3 | 1 | 2 | 5 | |
| 1964 | 7 | 5 | 2 | 3 | 3 | 1 | 4 | 2 | 1 |
| 1965 | 6 | 7 | 1 | 2 | 4 | 1 | 4 | 3 | |
| 1966 | 4 | 9 | 1 | 3 | 4 | | 1 | 5 | 1 |
| 1967 | 5 | 7 | 2 | 3 | 4 | | 2 | 3 | 2 |
| 1968 | 4 | 8 | 2 | 1 | 4 | 2 | 3 | 4 | |
| 1969 | 9 | 4 | 1 | 5 | 2 | | 4 | 2 | 1 |
| 1970 | 10 | 4 | | 6 | 1 | | 4 | 3 | |
| 1971 | 7 | 6 | 1 | 3 | 4 | | 4 | 2 | 1 |
| 1972 | 8 | 5 | 1 | 5 | 2 | | 3 | 3 | 1 |
| 1973 | 6 | 7 | 1 | 4 | 3 | | 2 | 4 | 1 |
| 1974 | 7 | 7 | | 5 | 2 | | 2 | 5 | |
| 1975 | 7 | 7 | | 4 | 3 | | 3 | 4 | |
| 1976 | 6 | 8 | | 5 | 2 | | 1 | 6 | |
| 1977 | 6 | 8 | | 5 | 2 | | 1 | 6 | |
| 1978 | 7 | 9 | | 5 | 3 | | 2 | 6 | |
| 1979 | 2 | 14 | | 2 | 6 | | 0 | 8 | |
| 1980 | 9 | 7 | | 6 | 2 | | 3 | 5 | |
| 1981 | 8 | 8 | | 7 | 1 | | 1 | 7 | |
| 1982 | 4 | 5 | | 2 | 3 | | 2 | 2 | |
| 1983 | 9 | 7 | | 6 | 2 | | 3 | 5 | |
| 1984 | 4 | 11 | 1 | 2 | 5 | 1 | 2 | 6 | |
| 1985 | 7 | 9 | | 6 | 2 | | 1 | 7 | |
| 1986 | 5 | 11 | | 1 | 7 | | 4 | 4 | |
| 1987 | 4 | 11 | | 1 | 6 | | 3 | 5 | |
| 1988 | 4 | 12 | | 2 | 6 | | 2 | 6 | |
| 1989 | 7 | 9 | | 4 | 4 | | 3 | 5 | |
| 1990 | 6 | 10 | | 3 | 5 | | 3 | 5 | |
| 1991 | 12 | 4 | | 8 | 0 | | 4 | 4 | |
| 1992 | 5 | 11 | | 3 | 5 | | 2 | 6 | |
| 1993 | 10 | 6 | | 5 | 3 | | 5 | 3 | |
| Total | 402 | 415 | 32 | 245 | 176 | 14 | 157 | 239 | 18 |

*includes Portsmouth Spartans (1930-33)

### GREEN BAY PACKERS

| | All Games | | | Home Games | | | Road Games | | |
|---|---|---|---|---|---|---|---|---|---|
| Season | W | L | T | W | L | T | W | L | T |
| 1921 | 3 | 2 | 1 | 2 | 1 | | 1 | 1 | 1 |
| 1922 | 4 | 3 | 3 | 4 | 1 | 1 | 0 | 2 | 2 |
| 1923 | 7 | 2 | 1 | 4 | 2 | 1 | 3 | 0 | |
| 1924 | 7 | 4 | | 5 | 0 | | 2 | 4 | |
| 1925 | 8 | 5 | | 6 | 0 | | 2 | 5 | |
| 1926 | 7 | 3 | 3 | 4 | 1 | 2 | 3 | 2 | 1 |
| 1927 | 7 | 2 | 1 | 6 | 1 | | 1 | 1 | 1 |
| 1928 | 6 | 4 | 3 | 2 | 2 | 2 | 4 | 2 | 1 |
| 1929 | 12 | 0 | 1 | 5 | 0 | | 7 | 0 | 1 |
| 1930 | 10 | 3 | 1 | 6 | 0 | | 4 | 3 | 1 |
| 1931 | 12 | 2 | | 8 | 0 | | 4 | 2 | |
| 1932 | 10 | 3 | 1 | 5 | 0 | 1 | 5 | 3 | |
| 1933 | 5 | 7 | 1 | 3 | 2 | 1 | 2 | 5 | |
| 1934 | 7 | 6 | | 4 | 2 | | 3 | 4 | |
| 1935 | 8 | 4 | | 5 | 2 | | 3 | 2 | |
| 1936 | 10 | 1 | 1 | 5 | 1 | | 5 | 0 | 1 |
| 1937 | 7 | 4 | | 3 | 2 | | 4 | 2 | |
| 1938 | 8 | 3 | | 4 | 2 | | 4 | 1 | |
| 1939 | 9 | 2 | | 4 | 1 | | 5 | 1 | |
| 1940 | 6 | 4 | 1 | 4 | 2 | | 2 | 2 | 1 |
| 1941 | 10 | 1 | | 4 | 1 | | 6 | 0 | |
| 1942 | 8 | 2 | 1 | 4 | 1 | | 4 | 1 | 1 |
| 1943 | 7 | 2 | 1 | 2 | 1 | 1 | 5 | 1 | |
| 1944 | 8 | 2 | | 5 | 0 | | 3 | 2 | |
| 1945 | 6 | 4 | | 4 | 1 | | 2 | 3 | |
| 1946 | 6 | 5 | | 2 | 3 | | 4 | 2 | |
| 1947 | 6 | 5 | 1 | 4 | 2 | | 2 | 3 | 1 |
| 1948 | 3 | 9 | | 2 | 4 | | 1 | 5 | |
| 1949 | 2 | 10 | | 1 | 5 | | 1 | 5 | |
| 1950 | 3 | 9 | | 3 | 3 | | 0 | 6 | |
| 1951 | 3 | 9 | | 2 | 4 | | 1 | 5 | |
| 1952 | 6 | 6 | | 3 | 3 | | 3 | 3 | |
| 1953 | 2 | 9 | 1 | 1 | 5 | | 1 | 4 | 1 |
| 1954 | 4 | 8 | | 2 | 4 | | 2 | 4 | |
| 1955 | 6 | 6 | | 5 | 1 | | 1 | 5 | |
| 1956 | 4 | 8 | | 2 | 4 | | 2 | 4 | |
| 1957 | 3 | 9 | | 1 | 5 | | 2 | 4 | |
| 1958 | 1 | 10 | 1 | 1 | 4 | 1 | 0 | 6 | |
| 1959 | 7 | 5 | | 4 | 2 | | 3 | 3 | |
| 1960 | 8 | 4 | | 4 | 2 | | 4 | 2 | |
| 1961 | 11 | 3 | | 6 | 1 | | 5 | 2 | |
| 1962 | 13 | 1 | | 7 | 0 | | 6 | 1 | |
| 1963 | 11 | 2 | 1 | 6 | 1 | | 5 | 1 | 1 |
| 1964 | 8 | 5 | 1 | 4 | 3 | | 4 | 2 | 1 |
| 1965 | 10 | 3 | 1 | 6 | 1 | | 4 | 2 | 1 |
| 1966 | 12 | 2 | | 6 | 1 | | 6 | 1 | |
| 1967 | 9 | 4 | 1 | 4 | 2 | 1 | 5 | 2 | |
| 1968 | 6 | 7 | 1 | 2 | 5 | | 4 | 2 | 1 |
| 1969 | 8 | 6 | | 5 | 2 | | 3 | 4 | |
| 1970 | 6 | 8 | | 4 | 3 | | 2 | 5 | |
| 1971 | 4 | 8 | 2 | 3 | 3 | 1 | 1 | 5 | 1 |
| 1972 | 10 | 4 | | 4 | 3 | | 6 | 1 | |
| 1973 | 5 | 7 | 2 | 3 | 2 | 2 | 2 | 5 | |
| 1974 | 6 | 8 | | 4 | 3 | | 2 | 5 | |
| 1975 | 4 | 10 | | 3 | 4 | | 1 | 6 | |
| 1976 | 5 | 9 | | 4 | 3 | | 1 | 6 | |
| 1977 | 4 | 10 | | 2 | 5 | | 2 | 5 | |
| 1978 | 8 | 7 | 1 | 5 | 2 | 1 | 3 | 5 | |
| 1979 | 5 | 11 | | 4 | 4 | | 1 | 7 | |
| 1980 | 5 | 10 | 1 | 4 | 4 | | 1 | 6 | 1 |
| 1981 | 8 | 8 | | 4 | 4 | | 4 | 4 | |
| 1982 | 5 | 3 | 1 | 3 | 1 | | 2 | 2 | 1 |
| 1983 | 8 | 8 | | 5 | 3 | | 3 | 5 | |
| 1984 | 8 | 8 | | 5 | 3 | | 3 | 5 | |
| 1985 | 8 | 8 | | 5 | 3 | | 3 | 5 | |
| 1986 | 4 | 12 | | 1 | 7 | | 3 | 5 | |
| 1987 | 5 | 9 | 1 | 2 | 5 | 1 | 3 | 4 | |
| 1988 | 4 | 12 | | 2 | 6 | | 2 | 6 | |
| 1989 | 10 | 6 | | 6 | 2 | | 4 | 4 | |
| 1990 | 6 | 10 | | 3 | 5 | | 3 | 5 | |
| 1991 | 4 | 12 | | 2 | 6 | | 2 | 6 | |
| 1992 | 9 | 7 | | 6 | 2 | | 3 | 5 | |
| 1993 | 9 | 7 | | 6 | 2 | | 3 | 5 | |
| Total | 494 | 422 | 36 | 281 | 178 | 16 | 213 | 244 | 20 |

### LOS ANGELES RAMS*

| | All Games | | | Home Games | | | Road Games | | |
|---|---|---|---|---|---|---|---|---|---|
| Season | W | L | T | W | L | T | W | L | T |
| 1937 | 1 | 10 | | 0 | 5 | | 1 | 5 | |
| 1938 | 4 | 7 | | 2 | 2 | | 2 | 5 | |
| 1939 | 5 | 5 | 1 | 3 | 2 | 1 | 2 | 3 | |
| 1940 | 4 | 6 | 1 | 3 | 1 | 1 | 1 | 5 | |
| 1941 | 2 | 9 | | 1 | 4 | | 1 | 5 | |
| 1942 | 5 | 6 | | 3 | 2 | | 2 | 4 | |
| 1944 | 4 | 6 | | 1 | 2 | | 3 | 4 | |
| 1945 | 9 | 1 | | 4 | 0 | | 5 | 1 | |
| 1946 | 6 | 4 | 1 | 3 | 2 | | 3 | 2 | 1 |
| 1947 | 6 | 6 | | 3 | 3 | | 3 | 3 | |
| 1948 | 6 | 5 | 1 | 3 | 2 | 1 | 3 | 3 | |
| 1949 | 8 | 2 | 2 | 5 | 1 | | 3 | 1 | 2 |
| 1950 | 9 | 3 | | 5 | 1 | | 4 | 2 | |
| 1951 | 8 | 4 | | 5 | 2 | | 3 | 2 | |
| 1952 | 9 | 3 | | 5 | 1 | | 4 | 2 | |
| 1953 | 8 | 3 | 1 | 5 | 1 | | 3 | 2 | 1 |
| 1954 | 6 | 5 | 1 | 3 | 2 | 1 | 3 | 3 | |
| 1955 | 8 | 3 | 1 | 5 | 1 | | 3 | 2 | 1 |
| 1956 | 4 | 8 | | 4 | 2 | | 0 | 6 | |
| 1957 | 6 | 6 | | 5 | 1 | | 1 | 5 | |
| 1958 | 8 | 4 | | 4 | 2 | | 4 | 2 | |
| 1959 | 2 | 10 | | 0 | 6 | | 2 | 4 | |
| 1960 | 4 | 7 | 1 | 2 | 3 | 1 | 2 | 4 | |
| 1961 | 4 | 10 | | 4 | 3 | | 0 | 7 | |
| 1962 | 1 | 12 | 1 | 0 | 7 | | 1 | 5 | 1 |
| 1963 | 5 | 9 | | 3 | 4 | | 2 | 5 | |
| 1964 | 5 | 7 | 2 | 3 | 2 | 2 | 2 | 5 | |
| 1965 | 4 | 10 | | 3 | 4 | | 1 | 6 | |
| 1966 | 8 | 6 | | 5 | 2 | | 3 | 4 | |
| 1967 | 11 | 1 | 2 | 5 | 1 | 1 | 6 | 0 | 1 |
| 1968 | 10 | 3 | 1 | 5 | 2 | | 5 | 1 | 1 |
| 1969 | 11 | 3 | | 5 | 2 | | 6 | 1 | |
| 1970 | 9 | 4 | 1 | 3 | 3 | 1 | 6 | 1 | |
| 1971 | 8 | 5 | 1 | 4 | 2 | 1 | 4 | 3 | |
| 1972 | 6 | 7 | 1 | 4 | 3 | | 2 | 4 | 1 |
| 1973 | 12 | 2 | | 7 | 0 | | 5 | 2 | |
| 1974 | 10 | 4 | | 6 | 1 | | 4 | 3 | |
| 1975 | 12 | 2 | | 6 | 1 | | 6 | 1 | |
| 1976 | 10 | 3 | 1 | 5 | 2 | | 5 | 1 | 1 |
| 1977 | 10 | 4 | | 7 | 0 | | 3 | 4 | |
| 1978 | 12 | 4 | | 6 | 2 | | 6 | 2 | |
| 1979 | 9 | 7 | | 4 | 4 | | 5 | 3 | |
| 1980 | 11 | 5 | | 6 | 2 | | 5 | 3 | |
| 1981 | 6 | 10 | | 4 | 4 | | 2 | 6 | |
| 1982 | 2 | 7 | | 1 | 4 | | 1 | 3 | |
| 1983 | 9 | 7 | | 5 | 3 | | 4 | 4 | |
| 1984 | 10 | 6 | | 5 | 3 | | 5 | 3 | |
| 1985 | 11 | 5 | | 6 | 2 | | 5 | 3 | |
| 1986 | 10 | 6 | | 6 | 2 | | 4 | 4 | |
| 1987 | 6 | 9 | | 3 | 4 | | 3 | 5 | |
| 1988 | 10 | 6 | | 4 | 4 | | 6 | 2 | |
| 1989 | 11 | 5 | | 6 | 2 | | 5 | 3 | |
| 1990 | 5 | 11 | | 2 | 6 | | 3 | 5 | |
| 1991 | 3 | 13 | | 2 | 6 | | 1 | 7 | |
| 1992 | 6 | 10 | | 4 | 4 | | 2 | 6 | |
| 1993 | 5 | 11 | | 3 | 5 | | 2 | 6 | |
| Total | 394 | 337 | 20 | 216 | 144 | 10 | 178 | 193 | 10 |

*includes Cleveland Rams (1937-42, 1944-45).

### MINNESOTA VIKINGS

| | All Games | | | Home Games | | | Road Games | | |
|---|---|---|---|---|---|---|---|---|---|
| Season | W | L | T | W | L | T | W | L | T |
| 1961 | 3 | 11 | | 3 | 4 | | 0 | 7 | |
| 1962 | 2 | 11 | 1 | 1 | 5 | 1 | 1 | 6 | |
| 1963 | 5 | 8 | 1 | 3 | 4 | | 2 | 4 | 1 |
| 1964 | 8 | 5 | 1 | 4 | 3 | | 4 | 2 | 1 |
| 1965 | 7 | 7 | | 2 | 5 | | 5 | 2 | |
| 1966 | 4 | 9 | 1 | 2 | 5 | | 2 | 4 | 1 |
| 1967 | 3 | 8 | 3 | 1 | 4 | 2 | 2 | 4 | 1 |
| 1968 | 8 | 6 | | 4 | 3 | | 4 | 3 | |
| 1969 | 12 | 2 | | 7 | 0 | | 5 | 2 | |
| 1970 | 12 | 2 | | 7 | 0 | | 5 | 2 | |
| 1971 | 11 | 3 | | 5 | 2 | | 6 | 1 | |
| 1972 | 7 | 7 | | 3 | 4 | | 4 | 3 | |
| 1973 | 12 | 2 | | 7 | 0 | | 5 | 2 | |
| 1974 | 10 | 4 | | 4 | 3 | | 6 | 1 | |
| 1975 | 12 | 2 | | 7 | 0 | | 5 | 2 | |
| 1976 | 11 | 2 | 1 | 6 | 0 | 1 | 5 | 2 | |
| 1977 | 9 | 5 | | 5 | 2 | | 4 | 3 | |
| 1978 | 8 | 7 | 1 | 5 | 3 | | 3 | 4 | 1 |
| 1979 | 7 | 9 | | 5 | 3 | | 2 | 6 | |
| 1980 | 9 | 7 | | 5 | 3 | | 4 | 4 | |
| 1981 | 7 | 9 | | 5 | 3 | | 2 | 6 | |
| 1982 | 5 | 4 | | 4 | 1 | | 1 | 3 | |
| 1983 | 8 | 8 | | 3 | 5 | | 5 | 3 | |
| 1984 | 3 | 13 | | 2 | 6 | | 1 | 7 | |
| 1985 | 7 | 9 | | 4 | 4 | | 3 | 5 | |
| 1986 | 9 | 7 | | 5 | 3 | | 4 | 4 | |
| 1987 | 8 | 7 | | 5 | 3 | | 3 | 4 | |
| 1988 | 11 | 5 | | 7 | 1 | | 4 | 4 | |
| 1989 | 10 | 6 | | 8 | 0 | | 2 | 6 | |
| 1990 | 6 | 10 | | 4 | 4 | | 2 | 6 | |
| 1991 | 8 | 8 | | 4 | 4 | | 4 | 4 | |
| 1992 | 11 | 5 | | 5 | 3 | | 6 | 2 | |
| 1993 | 9 | 7 | | 4 | 4 | | 5 | 3 | |
| Total | 262 | 215 | 9 | 146 | 94 | 4 | 116 | 121 | 5 |

## NEW ORLEANS SAINTS

| Season | All Games W | L | T | Home Games W | L | T | Road Games W | L | T |
|---|---|---|---|---|---|---|---|---|---|
| 1967 | 3 | 11 | | 2 | 5 | | 1 | 6 | |
| 1968 | 4 | 9 | 1 | 3 | 4 | | 1 | 5 | 1 |
| 1969 | 5 | 9 | | 3 | 4 | | 2 | 5 | |
| 1970 | 2 | 11 | 1 | 2 | 5 | | 0 | 6 | 1 |
| 1971 | 4 | 8 | 2 | 2 | 4 | 1 | 2 | 4 | 1 |
| 1972 | 2 | 11 | 1 | 2 | 5 | | 0 | 6 | 1 |
| 1973 | 5 | 9 | | 5 | 2 | | 0 | 7 | |
| 1974 | 5 | 9 | | 4 | 3 | | 1 | 6 | |
| 1975 | 2 | 12 | | 2 | 5 | | 0 | 7 | |
| 1976 | 4 | 10 | | 2 | 5 | | 2 | 5 | |
| 1977 | 3 | 11 | | 2 | 5 | | 1 | 6 | |
| 1978 | 7 | 9 | | 3 | 5 | | 4 | 4 | |
| 1979 | 8 | 8 | | 3 | 5 | | 5 | 3 | |
| 1980 | 1 | 15 | | 0 | 8 | | 1 | 7 | |
| 1981 | 4 | 12 | | 2 | 6 | | 2 | 6 | |
| 1982 | 4 | 5 | | 2 | 3 | | 2 | 2 | |
| 1983 | 8 | 8 | | 5 | 3 | | 3 | 5 | |
| 1984 | 7 | 9 | | 3 | 5 | | 4 | 4 | |
| 1985 | 5 | 11 | | 3 | 5 | | 2 | 6 | |
| 1986 | 7 | 9 | | 4 | 4 | | 3 | 5 | |
| 1987 | 12 | 3 | | 6 | 1 | | 6 | 2 | |
| 1988 | 10 | 6 | | 5 | 3 | | 5 | 3 | |
| 1989 | 9 | 7 | | 5 | 3 | | 4 | 4 | |
| 1990 | 8 | 8 | | 5 | 3 | | 3 | 5 | |
| 1991 | 11 | 5 | | 6 | 2 | | 5 | 3 | |
| 1992 | 12 | 4 | | 6 | 2 | | 6 | 2 | |
| 1993 | 8 | 8 | | 4 | 4 | | 4 | 4 | |
| Total | 160 | 237 | 5 | 91 | 109 | 1 | 69 | 128 | 4 |

## NEW YORK GIANTS

| Season | All Games W | L | T | Home Games W | L | T | Road Games W | L | T |
|---|---|---|---|---|---|---|---|---|---|
| 1925 | 8 | 4 | | 7 | 2 | | 1 | 2 | |
| 1926 | 8 | 4 | 1 | 5 | 2 | 1 | 3 | 2 | |
| 1927 | 11 | 1 | 1 | 7 | 1 | | 4 | 0 | 1 |
| 1928 | 4 | 7 | 2 | 1 | 2 | 2 | 3 | 5 | |
| 1929 | 13 | 1 | 1 | 7 | 1 | | 6 | 0 | 1 |
| 1930 | 13 | 4 | | 6 | 2 | | 7 | 2 | |
| 1931 | 7 | 6 | 1 | 4 | 2 | 1 | 3 | 4 | |
| 1932 | 4 | 6 | 2 | 3 | 2 | 1 | 1 | 4 | 1 |
| 1933 | 11 | 3 | | 7 | 0 | | 4 | 3 | |
| 1934 | 8 | 5 | | 5 | 1 | | 3 | 4 | |
| 1935 | 9 | 3 | | 4 | 2 | | 5 | 1 | |
| 1936 | 5 | 6 | 1 | 3 | 3 | 1 | 2 | 3 | |
| 1937 | 6 | 3 | 2 | 4 | 2 | 1 | 2 | 1 | 1 |
| 1938 | 8 | 2 | 1 | 6 | 1 | | 2 | 1 | 1 |
| 1939 | 9 | 1 | 1 | 6 | 0 | | 3 | 1 | 1 |
| 1940 | 6 | 4 | 1 | 4 | 3 | | 2 | 1 | 1 |
| 1941 | 8 | 3 | | 5 | 2 | | 3 | 1 | |
| 1942 | 5 | 5 | 1 | 3 | 2 | 1 | 2 | 3 | |
| 1943 | 6 | 3 | 1 | 4 | 2 | | 2 | 1 | 1 |
| 1944 | 8 | 1 | 1 | 5 | 1 | | 3 | 0 | 1 |
| 1945 | 3 | 6 | 1 | 2 | 4 | | 1 | 2 | 1 |
| 1946 | 7 | 3 | 1 | 5 | 1 | 1 | 2 | 2 | |
| 1947 | 2 | 8 | 2 | 2 | 3 | 1 | 0 | 5 | 1 |
| 1948 | 4 | 8 | | 2 | 4 | | 2 | 4 | |
| 1949 | 6 | 6 | | 2 | 4 | | 4 | 2 | |
| 1950 | 10 | 2 | | 5 | 1 | | 5 | 1 | |
| 1951 | 9 | 2 | 1 | 5 | 1 | | 4 | 1 | 1 |
| 1952 | 7 | 5 | | 2 | 4 | | 5 | 1 | |
| 1953 | 3 | 9 | | 2 | 4 | | 1 | 5 | |
| 1954 | 7 | 5 | | 4 | 2 | | 3 | 3 | |
| 1955 | 6 | 5 | 1 | 4 | 1 | 1 | 2 | 4 | |
| 1956 | 8 | 3 | 1 | 4 | 1 | 1 | 4 | 2 | |
| 1957 | 7 | 5 | | 3 | 3 | | 4 | 2 | |
| 1958 | 9 | 3 | | 5 | 1 | | 4 | 2 | |
| 1959 | 10 | 2 | | 5 | 1 | | 5 | 1 | |
| 1960 | 6 | 4 | 2 | 1 | 3 | 2 | 5 | 1 | |
| 1961 | 10 | 3 | 1 | 4 | 2 | 1 | 6 | 1 | |
| 1962 | 12 | 2 | | 6 | 1 | | 6 | 1 | |
| 1963 | 11 | 3 | | 5 | 2 | | 6 | 1 | |
| 1964 | 2 | 10 | 2 | 2 | 5 | | 0 | 5 | 2 |
| 1965 | 7 | 7 | | 3 | 4 | | 4 | 3 | |
| 1966 | 1 | 12 | 1 | 1 | 6 | | 0 | 6 | 1 |
| 1967 | 7 | 7 | | 5 | 2 | | 2 | 5 | |
| 1968 | 7 | 7 | | 3 | 4 | | 4 | 3 | |
| 1969 | 6 | 8 | | 5 | 2 | | 1 | 6 | |
| 1970 | 9 | 5 | | 5 | 2 | | 4 | 3 | |
| 1971 | 4 | 10 | | 1 | 6 | | 3 | 4 | |
| 1972 | 8 | 6 | | 4 | 3 | | 4 | 3 | |
| 1973 | 2 | 11 | 1 | 2 | 4 | 1 | 0 | 7 | |
| 1974 | 2 | 12 | | 0 | 7 | | 2 | 5 | |
| 1975 | 5 | 9 | | 2 | 5 | | 3 | 4 | |
| 1976 | 3 | 11 | | 3 | 4 | | 0 | 7 | |
| 1977 | 5 | 9 | | 3 | 4 | | 2 | 5 | |
| 1978 | 6 | 10 | | 5 | 3 | | 1 | 7 | |
| 1979 | 6 | 10 | | 4 | 4 | | 2 | 6 | |
| 1980 | 4 | 12 | | 2 | 6 | | 2 | 6 | |
| 1981 | 9 | 7 | | 4 | 4 | | 5 | 3 | |
| 1982 | 4 | 5 | | 2 | 3 | | 2 | 2 | |
| 1983 | 3 | 12 | 1 | 1 | 7 | | 2 | 5 | 1 |
| 1984 | 9 | 7 | | 6 | 2 | | 3 | 5 | |
| 1985 | 10 | 6 | | 6 | 2 | | 4 | 4 | |
| 1986 | 14 | 2 | | 8 | 0 | | 6 | 2 | |
| 1987 | 6 | 9 | | 5 | 3 | | 1 | 6 | |
| 1988 | 10 | 6 | | 5 | 3 | | 5 | 3 | |
| 1989 | 12 | 4 | | 7 | 1 | | 5 | 3 | |
| 1990 | 13 | 3 | | 7 | 1 | | 6 | 2 | |
| 1991 | 8 | 8 | | 5 | 3 | | 3 | 5 | |
| 1992 | 6 | 10 | | 4 | 4 | | 2 | 6 | |
| 1993 | 11 | 5 | | 6 | 2 | | 5 | 3 | |
| Total | 493 | 396 | 32 | 280 | 182 | 16 | 213 | 214 | 16 |

## PHILADELPHIA EAGLES

| Season | All Games W | L | T | Home Games W | L | T | Road Games W | L | T |
|---|---|---|---|---|---|---|---|---|---|
| 1933 | 3 | 5 | 1 | 2 | 3 | 1 | 1 | 2 | |
| 1934 | 4 | 7 | | 2 | 4 | | 2 | 3 | |
| 1935 | 2 | 9 | | 0 | 5 | | 2 | 4 | |
| 1936 | 1 | 11 | | 1 | 6 | | 0 | 5 | |
| 1937 | 2 | 8 | 1 | 0 | 5 | 1 | 2 | 3 | |
| 1938 | 5 | 6 | | 2 | 3 | | 3 | 3 | |
| 1939 | 1 | 9 | 1 | 1 | 3 | 1 | 0 | 6 | |
| 1940 | 1 | 10 | | 1 | 4 | | 0 | 6 | |
| 1941 | 2 | 8 | 1 | 1 | 4 | 1 | 1 | 4 | |
| 1942 | 2 | 9 | | 0 | 5 | | 2 | 4 | |
| 1944 | 7 | 1 | 2 | 3 | 1 | 2 | 4 | 0 | |
| 1945 | 7 | 3 | | 6 | 0 | | 1 | 3 | |
| 1946 | 6 | 5 | | 3 | 2 | | 3 | 3 | |
| 1947 | 8 | 4 | | 6 | 1 | | 2 | 3 | |
| 1948 | 9 | 2 | 1 | 6 | 0 | | 3 | 2 | 1 |
| 1949 | 11 | 1 | | 6 | 0 | | 5 | 1 | |
| 1950 | 6 | 6 | | 2 | 4 | | 4 | 2 | |
| 1951 | 4 | 8 | | 1 | 5 | | 3 | 3 | |
| 1952 | 7 | 5 | | 4 | 2 | | 3 | 3 | |
| 1953 | 7 | 4 | 1 | 5 | 0 | 1 | 2 | 4 | |
| 1954 | 7 | 4 | 1 | 5 | 1 | | 2 | 3 | 1 |
| 1955 | 4 | 7 | 1 | 4 | 2 | | 0 | 5 | 1 |
| 1956 | 3 | 8 | 1 | 2 | 3 | 1 | 1 | 5 | |
| 1957 | 4 | 8 | | 3 | 3 | | 1 | 5 | |
| 1958 | 2 | 9 | 1 | 2 | 4 | | 0 | 5 | 1 |
| 1959 | 6 | 5 | | 4 | 1 | | 2 | 4 | |
| 1960 | 10 | 2 | | 5 | 1 | | 5 | 1 | |
| 1961 | 10 | 4 | | 5 | 2 | | 5 | 2 | |
| 1962 | 3 | 10 | 1 | 2 | 5 | | 1 | 5 | 1 |
| 1963 | 2 | 10 | 2 | 1 | 5 | 1 | 1 | 5 | 1 |
| 1964 | 6 | 8 | | 3 | 4 | | 3 | 4 | |
| 1965 | 5 | 9 | | 2 | 5 | | 3 | 4 | |
| 1966 | 9 | 5 | | 5 | 2 | | 4 | 3 | |
| 1967 | 6 | 7 | 1 | 5 | 2 | | 1 | 5 | 1 |
| 1968 | 2 | 12 | | 1 | 6 | | 1 | 6 | |
| 1969 | 4 | 9 | 1 | 2 | 5 | | 2 | 4 | 1 |
| 1970 | 3 | 10 | 1 | 3 | 3 | 1 | 0 | 7 | |
| 1971 | 6 | 7 | 1 | 3 | 4 | | 3 | 3 | 1 |
| 1972 | 2 | 11 | 1 | 0 | 6 | 1 | 2 | 5 | |
| 1973 | 5 | 8 | 1 | 4 | 3 | | 1 | 5 | 1 |
| 1974 | 7 | 7 | | 5 | 2 | | 2 | 5 | |
| 1975 | 4 | 10 | | 2 | 5 | | 2 | 5 | |
| 1976 | 4 | 10 | | 2 | 5 | | 2 | 5 | |
| 1977 | 5 | 9 | | 4 | 3 | | 1 | 6 | |
| 1978 | 9 | 7 | | 5 | 3 | | 4 | 4 | |
| 1979 | 11 | 5 | | 5 | 3 | | 6 | 2 | |
| 1980 | 12 | 4 | | 7 | 1 | | 5 | 3 | |
| 1981 | 10 | 6 | | 6 | 2 | | 4 | 4 | |
| 1982 | 3 | 6 | | 1 | 4 | | 2 | 2 | |
| 1983 | 5 | 11 | | 1 | 7 | | 4 | 4 | |
| 1984 | 6 | 9 | 1 | 5 | 3 | | 1 | 6 | 1 |
| 1985 | 7 | 9 | | 4 | 4 | | 3 | 5 | |
| 1986 | 5 | 10 | 1 | 2 | 5 | 1 | 3 | 5 | |
| 1987 | 7 | 8 | | 4 | 4 | | 3 | 4 | |
| 1988 | 10 | 6 | | 5 | 3 | | 5 | 3 | |
| 1989 | 11 | 5 | | 6 | 2 | | 5 | 3 | |
| 1990 | 10 | 6 | | 6 | 2 | | 4 | 4 | |
| 1991 | 10 | 6 | | 4 | 4 | | 6 | 2 | |
| 1992 | 11 | 5 | | 8 | 0 | | 3 | 5 | |
| 1993 | 8 | 8 | | 3 | 5 | | 5 | 3 | |
| Total | 349 | 421 | 23 | 198 | 191 | 12 | 151 | 230 | 11 |

## SAN FRANCISCO 49ERS

| Season | All Games W | L | T | Home Games W | L | T | Road Games W | L | T |
|---|---|---|---|---|---|---|---|---|---|
| 1950 | 3 | 9 | | 3 | 3 | | 0 | 6 | |
| 1951 | 7 | 4 | 1 | 5 | 1 | | 2 | 3 | 1 |
| 1952 | 7 | 5 | | 3 | 3 | | 4 | 2 | |
| 1953 | 9 | 3 | | 5 | 1 | | 4 | 2 | |
| 1954 | 7 | 4 | 1 | 4 | 2 | | 3 | 2 | 1 |
| 1955 | 4 | 8 | | 2 | 4 | | 2 | 4 | |
| 1956 | 5 | 6 | 1 | 3 | 3 | | 2 | 3 | 1 |
| 1957 | 8 | 4 | | 5 | 1 | | 3 | 3 | |
| 1958 | 6 | 6 | | 4 | 2 | | 2 | 4 | |
| 1959 | 7 | 5 | | 4 | 2 | | 3 | 3 | |
| 1960 | 7 | 5 | | 3 | 3 | | 4 | 2 | |
| 1961 | 7 | 6 | 1 | 5 | 1 | 1 | 2 | 5 | |
| 1962 | 6 | 8 | | 1 | 6 | | 5 | 2 | |
| 1963 | 2 | 12 | | 2 | 5 | | 0 | 7 | |
| 1964 | 4 | 10 | | 3 | 4 | | 1 | 6 | |
| 1965 | 7 | 6 | 1 | 4 | 2 | 1 | 3 | 4 | |
| 1966 | 6 | 6 | 2 | 4 | 2 | 1 | 2 | 4 | 1 |
| 1967 | 7 | 7 | | 3 | 4 | | 4 | 3 | |
| 1968 | 7 | 6 | 1 | 3 | 3 | 1 | 4 | 3 | |
| 1969 | 4 | 8 | 2 | 3 | 3 | 1 | 1 | 5 | 1 |
| 1970 | 10 | 3 | 1 | 5 | 1 | 1 | 5 | 2 | |
| 1971 | 9 | 5 | | 4 | 3 | | 5 | 2 | |
| 1972 | 8 | 5 | 1 | 4 | 2 | 1 | 4 | 3 | |
| 1973 | 5 | 9 | | 3 | 4 | | 2 | 5 | |
| 1974 | 6 | 8 | | 3 | 4 | | 3 | 4 | |
| 1975 | 5 | 9 | | 2 | 5 | | 3 | 4 | |
| 1976 | 8 | 6 | | 4 | 3 | | 4 | 3 | |
| 1977 | 5 | 9 | | 3 | 4 | | 2 | 5 | |
| 1978 | 2 | 14 | | 2 | 6 | | 0 | 8 | |
| 1979 | 2 | 14 | | 2 | 6 | | 0 | 8 | |
| 1980 | 6 | 10 | | 4 | 4 | | 2 | 6 | |
| 1981 | 13 | 3 | | 7 | 1 | | 6 | 2 | |
| 1982 | 3 | 6 | | 0 | 5 | | 3 | 1 | |
| 1983 | 10 | 6 | | 4 | 4 | | 6 | 2 | |
| 1984 | 15 | 1 | | 7 | 1 | | 8 | 0 | |
| 1985 | 10 | 6 | | 5 | 3 | | 5 | 3 | |
| 1986 | 10 | 5 | 1 | 6 | 2 | | 4 | 3 | 1 |
| 1987 | 13 | 2 | | 6 | 1 | | 7 | 1 | |
| 1988 | 10 | 6 | | 4 | 4 | | 6 | 2 | |
| 1989 | 14 | 2 | | 6 | 2 | | 8 | 0 | |
| 1990 | 14 | 2 | | 6 | 2 | | 8 | 0 | |
| 1991 | 10 | 6 | | 7 | 1 | | 3 | 5 | |
| 1992 | 14 | 2 | | 7 | 1 | | 7 | 1 | |
| 1993 | 10 | 6 | | 6 | 2 | | 4 | 4 | |
| Total | 332 | 273 | 13 | 176 | 126 | 7 | 156 | 147 | 6 |

## TAMPA BAY BUCCANEERS

| Season | All Games W | L | T | Home Games W | L | T | Road Games W | L | T |
|---|---|---|---|---|---|---|---|---|---|
| 1976 | 0 | 14 | | 0 | 7 | | 0 | 7 | |
| 1977 | 2 | 12 | | 1 | 6 | | 1 | 6 | |
| 1978 | 5 | 11 | | 3 | 5 | | 2 | 6 | |
| 1979 | 10 | 6 | | 5 | 3 | | 5 | 3 | |
| 1980 | 5 | 10 | 1 | 2 | 5 | 1 | 3 | 5 | |
| 1981 | 9 | 7 | | 6 | 2 | | 3 | 5 | |
| 1982 | 5 | 4 | | 4 | 1 | | 1 | 3 | |
| 1983 | 2 | 14 | | 1 | 7 | | 1 | 7 | |
| 1984 | 6 | 10 | | 6 | 2 | | 0 | 8 | |
| 1985 | 2 | 14 | | 2 | 6 | | 0 | 8 | |
| 1986 | 2 | 14 | | 1 | 7 | | 1 | 7 | |
| 1987 | 4 | 11 | | 2 | 5 | | 2 | 6 | |
| 1988 | 5 | 11 | | 3 | 5 | | 2 | 6 | |
| 1989 | 5 | 11 | | 2 | 6 | | 3 | 5 | |
| 1990 | 6 | 10 | | 4 | 4 | | 2 | 6 | |
| 1991 | 3 | 13 | | 3 | 5 | | 0 | 8 | |
| 1992 | 5 | 11 | | 3 | 5 | | 2 | 6 | |
| 1993 | 5 | 11 | | 3 | 5 | | 2 | 6 | |
| Total | 81 | 194 | 1 | 51 | 86 | 1 | 30 | 108 | |

**WASHINGTON REDSKINS***

| | All Games | | | Home Games | | | Road Games | | |
|---|---|---|---|---|---|---|---|---|---|
| **Season** | **W** | **L** | **T** | **W** | **L** | **T** | **W** | **L** | **T** |
| 1932 | 4 | 4 | 2 | 2 | 3 | 1 | 2 | 1 | 1 |
| 1933 | 5 | 5 | 2 | 4 | 2 | | 1 | 3 | 2 |
| 1934 | 6 | 6 | | 4 | 3 | | 2 | 3 | |
| 1935 | 2 | 8 | 1 | 2 | 5 | | 0 | 3 | 1 |
| 1936 | 7 | 5 | | 4 | 3 | | 3 | 2 | |
| 1937 | 8 | 3 | | 4 | 2 | | 4 | 1 | |
| 1938 | 6 | 3 | 2 | 3 | 1 | 1 | 3 | 2 | 1 |
| 1939 | 8 | 2 | 1 | 5 | 0 | 1 | 3 | 2 | |
| 1940 | 9 | 2 | | 6 | 0 | | 3 | 2 | |
| 1941 | 6 | 5 | | 4 | 2 | | 2 | 3 | |
| 1942 | 10 | 1 | | 5 | 1 | | 5 | 0 | |
| 1943 | 6 | 3 | 1 | 4 | 2 | | 2 | 1 | 1 |
| 1944 | 6 | 3 | 1 | 4 | 2 | | 2 | 1 | 1 |
| 1945 | 8 | 2 | | 6 | 0 | | 2 | 2 | |
| 1946 | 5 | 5 | 1 | 3 | 2 | 1 | 2 | 3 | |
| 1947 | 4 | 8 | | 4 | 2 | | 0 | 6 | |
| 1948 | 7 | 5 | | 4 | 2 | | 3 | 3 | |
| 1949 | 4 | 7 | 1 | 3 | 3 | | 1 | 4 | 1 |
| 1950 | 3 | 9 | | 1 | 5 | | 2 | 4 | |
| 1951 | 5 | 7 | | 2 | 4 | | 3 | 3 | |
| 1952 | 4 | 8 | | 1 | 5 | | 3 | 3 | |
| 1953 | 6 | 5 | 1 | 3 | 3 | | 3 | 2 | 1 |
| 1954 | 3 | 9 | | 3 | 3 | | 0 | 6 | |
| 1955 | 8 | 4 | | 3 | 3 | | 5 | 1 | |
| 1956 | 6 | 6 | | 4 | 2 | | 2 | 4 | |
| 1957 | 5 | 6 | 1 | 2 | 3 | 1 | 3 | 3 | |
| 1958 | 4 | 7 | 1 | 3 | 2 | 1 | 1 | 5 | |
| 1959 | 4 | 8 | | 2 | 4 | | 2 | 4 | |
| 1960 | 1 | 9 | 2 | 1 | 4 | 1 | 0 | 5 | 1 |
| 1961 | 1 | 12 | 1 | 1 | 6 | | 0 | 6 | 1 |
| 1962 | 5 | 7 | 2 | 3 | 4 | | 2 | 3 | 2 |
| 1963 | 3 | 11 | | 1 | 6 | | 2 | 5 | |
| 1964 | 6 | 8 | | 4 | 3 | | 2 | 5 | |
| 1965 | 6 | 8 | | 3 | 4 | | 3 | 4 | |
| 1966 | 7 | 7 | | 4 | 3 | | 3 | 4 | |
| 1967 | 5 | 6 | 3 | 2 | 4 | 1 | 3 | 2 | 2 |
| 1968 | 5 | 9 | | 3 | 4 | | 2 | 5 | |
| 1969 | 7 | 5 | 2 | 4 | 2 | 1 | 3 | 3 | 1 |
| 1970 | 6 | 8 | | 4 | 3 | | 2 | 5 | |
| 1971 | 9 | 4 | 1 | 4 | 2 | 1 | 5 | 2 | |
| 1972 | 11 | 3 | | 6 | 1 | | 5 | 2 | |
| 1973 | 10 | 4 | | 7 | 0 | | 3 | 4 | |
| 1974 | 10 | 4 | | 6 | 1 | | 4 | 3 | |
| 1975 | 8 | 6 | | 5 | 2 | | 3 | 4 | |
| 1976 | 10 | 4 | | 5 | 2 | | 5 | 2 | |
| 1977 | 9 | 5 | | 5 | 2 | | 4 | 3 | |
| 1978 | 8 | 8 | | 5 | 3 | | 3 | 5 | |
| 1979 | 10 | 6 | | 6 | 2 | | 4 | 4 | |
| 1980 | 6 | 10 | | 4 | 4 | | 2 | 6 | |
| 1981 | 8 | 8 | | 5 | 3 | | 3 | 5 | |
| 1982 | 8 | 1 | | 3 | 1 | | 5 | 0 | |
| 1983 | 14 | 2 | | 7 | 1 | | 7 | 1 | |
| 1984 | 11 | 5 | | 7 | 1 | | 4 | 4 | |
| 1985 | 10 | 6 | | 5 | 3 | | 5 | 3 | |
| 1986 | 12 | 4 | | 7 | 1 | | 5 | 3 | |
| 1987 | 11 | 4 | | 6 | 1 | | 5 | 3 | |
| 1988 | 7 | 9 | | 4 | 4 | | 3 | 5 | |
| 1989 | 10 | 6 | | 4 | 4 | | 6 | 2 | |
| 1990 | 10 | 6 | | 7 | 1 | | 3 | 5 | |
| 1991 | 14 | 2 | | 7 | 1 | | 7 | 1 | |
| 1992 | 9 | 7 | | 6 | 2 | | 3 | 5 | |
| 1993 | 4 | 12 | | 3 | 5 | | 1 | 7 | |
| Total | 430 | 362 | 26 | 249 | 159 | 10 | 181 | 203 | 16 |

*includes Boston Braves (1932) and Boston Redskins (1933-36).*

# History

# PRO FOOTBALL HALL OF FAME

The Professional Football Hall of Fame is located in Canton, Ohio, site of the organizational meeting on September 17, 1920, from which the National Football League evolved. The NFL recognized Canton as the Hall of Fame site on April 27, 1961. Canton area individuals, foundations, and companies donated almost $400,000 in cash and services to provide funds for the construction of the original two-building complex, which was dedicated on September 7, 1963. The original Hall of Fame complex was almost doubled in size with the completion of a $620,000 expansion project that was dedicated on May 10, 1971. A second expansion project was completed on November 20, 1978. It now features four exhibition areas and a theater twice the size of the original one.

The Hall represents the sport of pro football in many ways—through four large and colorful exhibition galleries, in the twin enshrinement halls, with numerous fan-participation electronic devices, a research library, and a museum store.

In recent years, the Pro Football Hall of Fame has become an extremely popular tourist attraction. At the end of 1993, a total of 5,466,279 fans had visited the Hall of Fame.

New members of the Pro Football Hall of Fame are elected annually by a 34-member National Board of Selectors, made up of media representatives from every league city, 5 at-large representatives, and a representative of the Pro Football Writers of America. Between four and seven new members are elected each year. An affirmative vote of approximately 80 percent is needed for election.

Any fan may nominate any eligible player or contributor simply by writing to the Pro Football Hall of Fame. Players must be retired five years to be eligible, while a coach need only to be retired with no time limit specified. Contributors (administrators, owners, *et al.*) may be elected while they are still active.

The charter class of 17 enshrinees was elected in 1963 and the honor roll now stands at 175 with the election of a six-man class in 1994. That class consists of Tony Dorsett, Bud Grant, Jimmy Johnson, Leroy Kelly, Jackie Smith, and Randy White.

## ROSTER OF MEMBERS

**HERB ADDERLEY**
Defensive back. 6-1, 200. Born in Philadelphia, Pennsylvania, June 8, 1939. Michigan State. Inducted in 1980. 1961-69 Green Bay Packers, 1970-72 Dallas Cowboys.

**LANCE ALWORTH**
Wide receiver. 6-0, 184. Born in Houston, Texas, August 3, 1940. Arkansas. Inducted in 1978. 1962-70 San Diego Chargers, 1971-72 Dallas Cowboys.

**DOUG ATKINS**
Defensive end. 6-8, 275. Born in Humboldt, Tennessee, May 8, 1930. Tennessee. Inducted in 1982. 1953-54 Cleveland Browns, 1955-66 Chicago Bears, 1967-69 New Orleans Saints.

**MORRIS (RED) BADGRO**
End. 6-0, 190. Born in Orilla, Washington, December 1, 1902. Southern California. Inducted in 1981. 1927 New York Yankees, 1930-35 New York Giants, 1936 Brooklyn Dodgers.

**LEM BARNEY**
Cornerback. 6-0, 190. Born in Gulfport, Mississippi, September 9, 1945. Jackson State. Inducted in 1992. 1967-77 Detroit Lions.

**CLIFF BATTLES**
Halfback. 6-1, 201. Born in Akron, Ohio, May 1, 1910. Died April 28, 1981. West Virginia Wesleyan. Inducted in 1968. 1932 Boston Braves, 1933-36 Boston Redskins, 1937 Washington Redskins.

**SAMMY BAUGH**
Quarterback. 6-2, 180. Born in Temple, Texas, March 17, 1914. Texas Christian. Inducted in 1963. 1937-52 Washington Redskins.

**CHUCK BEDNARIK**
Center-linebacker. 6-3, 230. Born in Bethlehem, Pennsylvania, May 1, 1925. Pennsylvania. Inducted in 1967. 1949-62 Philadelphia Eagles.

**BERT BELL**
Team owner. Commissioner. Born in Philadelphia, Pennsylvania, February 25, 1895. Died October 11, 1959. Pennsylvania. Inducted in 1963. 1933-40 Philadelphia Eagles, 1941-42 Pittsburgh Steelers, 1943 Phil-Pitt, 1944-46 Pittsburgh Steelers. Commissioner, 1946-59.

**BOBBY BELL**
Linebacker. 6-4, 225. Born in Shelby, North Carolina, June 17, 1940. Minnesota. Inducted in 1983. 1963-74 Kansas City Chiefs.

**RAYMOND BERRY**
End. 6-2, 187. Born in Corpus Christi, Texas, February 27, 1933. Southern Methodist. Inducted in 1973. 1955-67 Baltimore Colts.

**CHARLES W. BIDWILL, SR.**
Team owner. Born in Chicago, Illinois, September 16, 1895. Died April 19, 1947. Loyola of Chicago. Inducted in 1967. 1933-43 Chicago Cardinals, 1944 Card-Pitt, 1945-47 Chicago Cardinals.

**FRED BILETNIKOFF**
Wide receiver. 6-1, 190. Born in Erie, Pennsylvania, February 23, 1943. Florida State. Inducted in 1988. 1965-78 Oakland Raiders.

**GEORGE BLANDA**
Quarterback-kicker. 6-2, 215. Born in Youngwood, Pennsylvania, September 17, 1927. Kentucky. Inducted in 1981. 1949-58 Chicago Bears, 1950 Baltimore Colts, 1960-66 Houston Oilers, 1967-75 Oakland Raiders.

**MEL BLOUNT**
Cornerback. 6-3, 205. Born in Vidalia, Georgia, April 10, 1948. Southern University. Inducted in 1989. 1970-83 Pittsburgh Steelers.

**TERRY BRADSHAW**
Quarterback. 6-3, 210. Born in Shreveport, Louisiana, September 2, 1948. Louisiana Tech. Inducted in 1989. 1970-83 Pittsburgh Steelers.

**JIM BROWN**
Fullback. 6-2, 232. Born in St. Simons, Georgia, February 17, 1936. Syracuse. Inducted in 1971. 1957-65 Cleveland Browns.

**PAUL BROWN**
Coach. Born in Norwalk, Ohio, September 7, 1908. Died August 5, 1991. Miami, Ohio. Inducted in 1967. 1946-49 Cleveland Browns (AAFC), 1950-62 Cleveland Browns, 1968-75 Cincinnati Bengals.

**ROOSEVELT BROWN**
Tackle. 6-3, 255. Born in Charlottesville, Virginia, October 20, 1932. Morgan State. Inducted in 1975. 1953-65 New York Giants.

**WILLIE BROWN**
Defensive back. 6-1, 210. Born in Yazoo City, Mississippi, December 2, 1940. Grambling. Inducted in 1984. 1963-66 Denver Broncos, 1967-78 Oakland Raiders.

**BUCK BUCHANAN**
Defensive tackle. 6-7, 274. Born in Gainesville, Alabama, September 10, 1940. Grambling. Inducted in 1990. 1963-75 Kansas City Chiefs.

**DICK BUTKUS**
Linebacker. 6-3, 245. Born in Chicago, Illinois, December 9, 1942. Illinois. Inducted in 1979. 1965-73 Chicago Bears.

**EARL CAMPBELL**
Running back. 5-11, 233. Born in Tyler, Texas, March 29, 1955. Texas. Inducted in 1991. 1978-84 Houston Oilers, 1984-85 New Orleans Saints.

**TONY CANADEO**
Halfback. 5-11, 195. Born in Chicago, Illinois, May 5, 1919. Gonzaga. Inducted in 1974. 1941-44, 1946-52 Green Bay Packers.

**JOE CARR**
NFL president. Born in Columbus, Ohio, October 22, 1880. Died May 20, 1939. Did not attend college. Inducted in 1963. President, 1921-39 National Football League.

**GUY CHAMBERLIN**
End. Coach. 6-2, 210. Born in Blue Springs, Nebraska, January 16, 1894. Died April 4, 1967. Nebraska. Inducted in 1965. 1920 Decatur Staleys, 1921 Chicago Staleys, player-coach 1922-23 Canton Bulldogs, 1924 Cleveland Bulldogs, 1925-26 Frankford Yellow Jackets, 1927 Chicago Cardinals.

**JACK CHRISTIANSEN**
Defensive back. 6-1, 185. Born in Sublette, Kansas, December 20, 1928. Died June 29, 1986. Colorado State. Inducted in 1970. 1951-58 Detroit Lions.

**EARL (DUTCH) CLARK**
Quarterback. 6-0, 185. Born in Fowler, Colorado, October 11, 1906. Died August 5, 1978. Colorado College. Inducted in 1963. 1931-32 Portsmouth Spartans, 1934-38 Detroit Lions.

**GEORGE CONNOR**
Tackle-linebacker. 6-3, 240. Born in Chicago, Illinois, January 21, 1925. Holy Cross, Notre Dame. Inducted in 1975. 1948-55 Chicago Bears.

**JIMMY CONZELMAN**
Quarterback. Coach. Team owner. 6-0, 180. Born in St. Louis, Missouri,March 6, 1898. Died July 31, 1970. Washington, Missouri. Inducted in 1964. 1920 Decatur Staleys, 1921-22 Rock Island, Ill., Independents, 1923-24 Milwaukee Badgers; owner-coach, 1925-26 Detroit Panthers; player-coach 1927-29, coach 1930 Providence Steam Roller; coach, 1940-42 Chicago Cardinals, 1946-48 Chicago Cardinals.

**LARRY CSONKA**
Running back. 6-3, 235. Born in Stow, Ohio, December 25, 1946. Syracuse. Inducted in 1987. Miami Dolphins 1968-74, 1979, New York Giants 1976-78.

**AL DAVIS**
Team, League Administrator. Born in Brockton, Massachusetts, July 4, 1929. Wittenberg, Syracuse. Inducted in 1992. 1963-81 Oakland Raiders, 1982-92 Los Angeles Raiders, 1966 American Football League.

**WILLIE DAVIS**
Defensive end. 6-3, 245. Born in Lisbon, Louisiana, July 24, 1934. Grambling. Inducted in 1981. 1958-59 Cleveland Browns, 1960-69 Green Bay Packers.

**LEN DAWSON**
Quarterback. 6-0, 190. Born in Alliance, Ohio, June 20, 1935. Purdue. Inducted in 1987. 1957-59 Pittsburgh Steelers, 1960-61 Cleveland Browns, 1962 Dallas Texans, 1963-75 Kansas City Chiefs.

**MIKE DITKA**
Tight end. 6-3, 225. Born in Carnegie, Pennsylvania, October 18, 1939. Pittsburgh. Inducted in 1988. 1961-66 Chicago Bears, 1967-68 Philadelphia Eagles, 1969-72 Dallas Cowboys.

**ART DONOVAN**
Defensive tackle. 6-3, 265. Born in Bronx, New York, June 5, 1925. Boston College. Inducted in 1968. 1950 Baltimore Colts, 1951 New York Yanks, 1952 Dallas Texans, 1953-61 Baltimore Colts.

**TONY DORSETT**
Running back. 5-11, 184. Born in Rochester, Pennsylvania, April 7, 1954. Pittsburgh. Inducted in 1994. 1977-87 Dallas Cowboys, 1988 Denver Broncos.

**JOHN (PADDY) DRISCOLL**
Quarterback. 5-11, 160. Born in Evanston, Illinois, January 11, 1896. Died June 29, 1968. Northwestern. Inducted in 1965. 1920 Decatur Sta-

leys, 1920-25 Chicago Cardinals, 1926-29 Chicago Bears. Coach, 1956-57 Chicago Bears.

**BILL DUDLEY**
Halfback. 5-10, 176. Born in Bluefield, Virginia, December 24, 1921. Virginia. Inducted in 1966. 1942, 1945-46 Pittsburgh Steelers, 1947-49 Detroit Lions, 1950-51, 1953 Washington Redskins.

**GLEN (TURK) EDWARDS**
Tackle. 6-2, 260. Born in Mold, Washington, September 28, 1907. Died January 12, 1973. Washington State. Inducted in 1969. 1932 Boston Braves, 1933-36 Boston Redskins, 1937-40 Washington Redskins.

**WEEB EWBANK**
Coach. Born in Richmond, Indiana, May 6, 1907. Miami, Ohio. Inducted in 1978. 1954-62 Baltimore Colts, 1963-73 New York Jets.

**TOM FEARS**
End. 6-2, 215. Born in Los Angeles, California, December 3, 1923. Santa Clara, UCLA. Inducted in 1970. 1948-56 Los Angeles Rams.

**RAY FLAHERTY**
End. Coach. Born in Spokane, Washington, September 1, 1904. Gonzaga. Inducted in 1976. 1926 Los Angeles Wildcats (AFL), 1927-28 New York Yankees, 1928-29, 1931-35 New York Giants. Coach, 1936 Boston Redskins, 1937-42 Washington Redskins, 1946-48 New York Yankees (AAFC), 1949 Chicago Hornets (AAFC).

**LEN FORD**
End. 6-5, 260. Born in Washington, D.C., February 18, 1926. Died March 14, 1972. Michigan. Inducted in 1976. 1948-49 Los Angeles Dons (AAFC), 1950-57 Cleveland Browns, 1958 Green Bay Packers.

**DAN FORTMANN**
Guard. 6-0, 207. Born in Pearl River, New York, April 11, 1916. Colgate. Inducted in 1965. 1936-43 Chicago Bears.

**DAN FOUTS**
Quarterback. 6-3, 210. Born in San Francisco, California, June 10, 1951. Oregon. Inducted in 1993. 1973-1987 San Diego Chargers.

**FRANK GATSKI**
Center. 6-3, 240. Born in Farmington, West Virginia, March 18, 1922. Marshall, Auburn. Inducted in 1985. 1946-49 Cleveland Browns (AAFC), 1950-56 Cleveland Browns, 1957 Detroit Lions.

**BILL GEORGE**
Linebacker. 6-2, 230. Born in Waynesburg, Pennsylvania, October 27, 1930. Died September 30, 1982. Wake Forest. Inducted in 1974. 1952-65 Chicago Bears, 1966 Los Angeles Rams.

**FRANK GIFFORD**
Halfback. 6-1, 195. Born in Santa Monica, California, August 16, 1930. Southern California. Inducted in 1977. 1952-60, 1962-64 New York Giants.

**SID GILLMAN**
Coach. Born in Minneapolis, Minnesota, October 26, 1911. Ohio State. Inducted in 1983. 1955-59 Los Angeles Rams, 1960 Los Angeles Chargers, 1961-69 San Diego Chargers, 1973-74 Houston Oilers.

**OTTO GRAHAM**
Quarterback. 6-1, 195. Born in Waukegan, Illinois, December 6, 1921. Northwestern. Inducted in 1965. 1946-49 Cleveland Browns (AAFC), 1950-55 Cleveland Browns.

**HAROLD (RED) GRANGE**
Halfback. 6-0, 185. Born in Forksville, Pennsylvania, June 13, 1903. Died January 28, 1991. Illinois. Inducted in 1963. 1925 Chicago Bears, 1926 New York Yankees (AFL), 1927 New York Yankees, 1929-34 Chicago Bears.

**BUD GRANT**
Coach. Born in Superior, Wisconsin, May 20, 1927. Minnesota. Inducted in 1994. 1967-83, 1985 Minnesota Vikings.

**JOE GREENE**
Defensive tackle. 6-4, 260. Born in Temple, Texas, September 24, 1946. North Texas State. Inducted in 1987. 1969-81 Pittsburgh Steelers.

**FORREST GREGG**
Tackle. 6-4, 250. Born in Birthright, Texas, October 18, 1933. Southern Methodist. Inducted in 1977. 1956, 1958-70 Green Bay Packers, 1971 Dallas Cowboys.

**BOB GRIESE**
Quarterback. 6-1, 190. Born in Evansville, Indiana, February 3, 1945. Purdue. Inducted in 1990. 1967-80 Miami Dolphins.

**LOU GROZA**
Tackle-kicker. 6-3, 250. Born in Martin's Ferry, Ohio, January 25, 1924. Ohio State. Inducted in 1974. 1946-49 Cleveland Browns (AAFC), 1950-59, 1961-67 Cleveland Browns.

**JOE GUYON**
Halfback. 6-1, 180. Born in Mahnomen, Minnesota, November 26, 1892. Died November 27, 1971. Carlisle, Georgia Tech. Inducted in 1966. 1920 Canton Bulldogs, 1921 Cleveland Indians, 1922-23 Oorang Indians, 1924 Rock Island, Ill., Independents, 1924-25 Kansas City Cowboys, 1927 New York Giants.

**GEORGE HALAS**
End. Coach. Team owner. Born in Chicago, Illinois, February 2, 1895. Died October 31, 1983. Illinois. Inducted in 1963. 1920 Decatur Staleys, 1921 Chicago Staleys, 1922-29 Chicago Bears; coach, 1933-42, 1946-55, 1958-67 Chicago Bears.

**JACK HAM**
Linebacker. 6-1, 225. Born in Johnstown, Pennsylvania, December 23, 1948. Penn State. Inducted in 1988. 1971-82 Pittsburgh Steelers.

**JOHN HANNAH**
Guard. 6-3, 265. Born in Canton, Georgia, April 4, 1951. Alabama. Inducted in 1991. 1973-85 New England Patriots.

**FRANCO HARRIS**
Running back. 6-2, 225. Born in Fort Dix, New Jersey, March 7, 1950. Penn State. Inducted in 1990. 1972-83 Pittsburgh Steelers, 1984 Seattle Seahawks.

**ED HEALEY**
Tackle. 6-3, 220. Born in Indian Orchard, Massachusetts, December 28, 1894. Died December 9, 1978. Dartmouth. Inducted in 1964. 1920-22 Rock Island, Ill., Independents, 1922-27 Chicago Bears.

**MEL HEIN**
Center. 6-2, 225. Born in Redding, California, August 22, 1909. Died January 31, 1992. Washington State. Inducted in 1963. 1931-45 New York Giants.

**TED HENDRICKS**
Linebacker. 6-7, 235. Born in Guatemala City, Guatemala, November 1, 1947. Miami. Inducted in 1990. 1969-73 Baltimore Colts, 1974 Green Bay Packers, 1975-81 Oakland Raiders, 1982-83 Los Angeles Raiders.

**WILBUR (PETE) HENRY**
Tackle. 6-0, 250. Born in Mansfield, Ohio, October 31, 1897. Died February 7, 1952. Washington & Jefferson. Inducted in 1963. 1920-23, 1925-26 Canton Bulldogs, 1927 New York Giants, 1927-28 Pottsville Maroons.

**ARNIE HERBER**
Quarterback. 6-1, 200. Born in Green Bay, Wisconsin, April 2, 1910. Died October 14, 1969. Wisconsin, Regis College. Inducted in 1966. 1930-40 Green Bay Packers, 1944-45 New York Giants.

**BILL HEWITT**
End. 5-11, 191. Born in Bay City, Michigan, October 8, 1909. Died January 14, 1947. Michigan. Inducted in 1971. 1932-36 Chicago Bears, 1937-39 Philadelphia Eagles, 1943 Phil-Pitt.

**CLARKE HINKLE**
Fullback. 5-11, 201. Born in Toronto, Ohio, April 10, 1909. Died November 9, 1988. Bucknell. Inducted in 1964. 1932-41 Green Bay Packers.

**ELROY (CRAZYLEGS) HIRSCH**
Halfback-end. 6-2, 190. Born in Wausau, Wisconsin, June 17, 1923. Wisconsin, Michigan. Inducted in1968. 1946-48 Chicago Rockets (AAFC), 1949-57 Los Angeles Rams.

**PAUL HORNUNG**
Halfback. 6-2, 220. Born in Louisville, Kentucky, December 23, 1935. Notre Dame. Inducted in 1986. 1957-62, 1964-66 Green Bay Packers.

**KEN HOUSTON**
Safety. 6-3, 198. Born in Lufkin, Texas, November 12, 1944. Prairie View A&M. Inducted in 1986. 1967-72 Houston Oilers, 1973-80 Washington Redskins.

**CAL HUBBARD**
Tackle. 6-5, 250. Born in Keytesville, Missouri, October 31, 1900. Died October 17, 1977. Centenary, Geneva. Inducted in 1963. 1927-28 New York Giants, 1929-33, 1935 Green Bay Packers, 1936 New York Giants, 1936 Pittsburgh Pirates.

**SAM HUFF**
Linebacker. 6-1, 230. Born in Morgantown, West Virginia, October 4, 1934. West Virginia. Inducted in 1982. 1956-63 New York Giants, 1964-67, 1969 Washington Redskins.

**LAMAR HUNT**
Team owner. Born in El Dorado, Arkansas, August 2, 1932. Southern Methodist. Inducted in 1972. 1960-62 Dallas Texans, 1963-90 Kansas City Chiefs.

**DON HUTSON**
End. 6-1, 180. Born in Pine Bluff, Arkansas, January 31, 1913. Alabama. Inducted in 1963. 1935-45 Green Bay Packers.

**JIMMY JOHNSON**
Cornerback. 6-2, 187. Born in Dallas, Texas, March 31, 1938. UCLA. Inducted in 1994. 1961-76 San Francisco 49ers.

**JOHN HENRY JOHNSON**
Fullback. 6-2, 225. Born in Waterproof, Louisiana, November 24, 1929. St. Mary's, Arizona State. Inducted in 1987. 1954-56 San Francisco 49ers, 1957-59 Detroit Lions, 1960-65 Pittsburgh Steelers, 1966 Houston Oilers.

**DAVID (DEACON) JONES**
Defensive end. 6-5, 250. Born in Eatonville, Florida, December 9, 1938. Mississippi Vocational. Inducted in 1980. 1961-71 Los Angeles Rams, 1972-73 San Diego Chargers, 1974 Washington Redskins.

**STAN JONES**
Guard-defensive tackle. 6-1, 250. Born in Altoona, Pennsylvania, November 24, 1931. Maryland. Inducted in 1991. 1954-65 Chicago Bears, 1966 Washington Redskins.

**SONNY JURGENSEN**
Quarterback. 6-0, 203. Born in Wilmington, North Carolina, August 23, 1934. Duke. Inducted in 1983. 1957-63 Philadelphia Eagles, 1964-74 Washington Redskins.

**LEROY KELLY**
Running back. 6-0, 205. Born in Philadelphia, Pennsylvania, May 20, 1942. Morgan State. Inducted in 1994. 1964-73 Cleveland Browns.

**WALT KIESLING**
Guard. Coach. 6-2, 245. Born in St. Paul, Minnesota, March 27, 1903. Died March 2, 1962. St. Thomas (Minnesota). Inducted in 1966. 1926-27 Duluth Eskimos, 1928 Pottsville Maroons, 1929-33 Chicago Cardinals, 1934 Chicago Bears, 1935-36 Green Bay Packers, 1937-38 Pittsburgh Pirates; coach, 1939-42 Pittsburgh Steelers;

co-coach, 1943 Phil-Pitt, 1944 Card-Pitt; coach, 1954-56 Pittsburgh Steelers.

**FRANK (BRUISER) KINARD**
Tackle. 6-1, 210. Born in Pelahatchie, Mississippi, October 23, 1914. Died September 7, 1985. Mississippi. Inducted in 1971. 1938-44 Brooklyn Dodgers-Tigers, 1946-47 New York Yankees (AAFC).

**EARL (CURLY) LAMBEAU**
Coach. Born in Green Bay, Wisconsin, April 9, 1898. Died June 1, 1965. Notre Dame. Inducted in 1963. 1919-49 Green Bay Packers, 1950-51 Chicago Cardinals, 1952-53 Washington Redskins.

**JACK LAMBERT**
Linebacker. 6-4, 220. Born in Mantua, Ohio, July 8, 1952. Kent State. Inducted in 1990. 1974-84 Pittsburgh Steelers.

**TOM LANDRY**
Coach. Born in Mission, Texas, September 11, 1924. Texas. Inducted in 1990. 1960-88 Dallas Cowboys.

**DICK (NIGHT TRAIN) LANE**
Defensive back. 6-2, 210. Born in Austin, Texas, April 16, 1928. Scottsbluff Junior College. Inducted in 1974. 1952-53 Los Angeles Rams, 1954-59 Chicago Cardinals, 1960-65 Detroit Lions.

**JIM LANGER**
Center. 6-2, 255. Born in Little Falls, Minnesota, May 16, 1948. South Dakota State. Inducted in 1987. 1970-79 Miami Dolphins, 1980-81 Minnesota Vikings.

**WILLIE LANIER**
Linebacker. 6-1, 245. Born in Clover, Virginia, August 21, 1945. Morgan State. Inducted in 1986. 1967-77 Kansas City Chiefs.

**YALE LARY**
Defensive back-punter. 5-11, 189. Born in Fort Worth, Texas, November 24, 1930. Texas A&M. Inducted in 1979. 1952-53, 1956-64 Detroit Lions.

**DANTE LAVELLI**
End. 6-0, 199. Born in Hudson, Ohio, February 23, 1923. Ohio State. Inducted in 1975. 1946-49 Cleveland Browns (AAFC), 1950-56 Cleveland Browns.

**BOBBY LAYNE**
Quarterback. 6-2, 190. Born in Santa Anna, Texas, December 19, 1926. Died December 1, 1986. Texas. Inducted in 1967. 1948 Chicago Bears, 1949 New York Bulldogs, 1950-58 Detroit Lions, 1958-62 Pittsburgh Steelers.

**ALPHONSE (TUFFY) LEEMANS**
Fullback. 6-0, 200. Born in Superior, Wisconsin, November 12, 1912. Died January 19, 1979. George Washington. Inducted in 1978. 1936-43 New York Giants.

**BOB LILLY**
Defensive tackle. 6-5, 260. Born in Olney, Texas, July 26, 1939. Texas Christian. Inducted in 1980. 1961-74 Dallas Cowboys.

**LARRY LITTLE**
Guard. 6-1, 255. Born in Groveland, Georgia, November 2, 1945. Bethune-Cookman. Inducted in 1993. 1967-68 San Diego Chargers, 1969-80 Miami Dolphins.

**VINCE LOMBARDI**
Coach. Born in Brooklyn, New York, June 11, 1913. Died September 3, 1970. Fordham. Inducted in 1971. 1959-67 Green Bay Packers, 1969 Washington Redskins.

**SID LUCKMAN**
Quarterback. 6-0, 195. Born in Brooklyn, New York, November 21, 1916. Columbia. Inducted in 1965. 1939-50 Chicago Bears.

**ROY (LINK) LYMAN**
Tackle. 6-2, 252. Born in Table Rock, Nebraska, November 30, 1898. Died December 16, 1972. Nebraska. Inducted in 1964. 1922-23, 1925 Canton Bulldogs, 1924 Cleveland Bulldogs, 1925 Frankford Yellow Jackets, 1926-28, 1930-31, 1933-34 Chicago Bears.

**JOHN MACKEY**
Tight end. 6-2, 224. Born in New York, New York, September 24, 1941. Syracuse. Inducted in 1992. 1963-71 Baltimore Colts, 1972 San Diego Chargers.

**TIM MARA**
Team owner. Born in New York, New York, July 29, 1887. Died February 17, 1959. Did not attend college. Inducted in 1963. 1925-59 New York Giants.

**GINO MARCHETTI**
Defensive end. 6-4, 245. Born in Smithers, West Virginia, January 2, 1927. San Francisco. Inducted in 1972. 1952 Dallas Texans, 1953-64, 1966 Baltimore Colts.

**GEORGE PRESTON MARSHALL**
Team owner. Born in Grafton, West Virginia, October 11, 1897. Died August 9, 1969. Randolph-Macon. Inducted in 1963. 1932 Boston Braves, 1933-36 Boston Redskins, 1937-69 Washington Redskins.

**OLLIE MATSON**
Halfback. 6-2, 220. Born in Trinity, Texas, May 1, 1930. San Francisco. Inducted in 1972. 1952, 1954-58 Chicago Cardinals, 1959-62 Los Angeles Rams, 1963 Detroit Lions, 1964-66 Philadelphia Eagles.

**DON MAYNARD**
Wide receiver. 6-1, 175. Born in Crosbyton, Texas, January 25, 1935. Texas Western. Inducted in 1987. 1958 New York Giants, 1960-62 New York Titans, 1963-72 New York Jets, 1973 St. Louis Cardinals.

**GEORGE McAFEE**
Halfback. 6-0, 177. Born in Ironton, Ohio, March 13, 1918. Duke. Inducted in 1966. 1940-41, 1945-50 Chicago Bears.

**MIKE McCORMACK**
Tackle. 6-4, 248. Born in Chicago, Illinois, June 21, 1930. Kansas. Inducted in 1984. 1951 New York Yanks, 1954-62 Cleveland Browns.

**HUGH McELHENNY**
Halfback. 6-1, 198. Born in Los Angeles, California, December 31, 1928. Washington. Inducted in 1970. 1952-60 San Francisco 49ers, 1961-62 Minnesota Vikings, 1963 New York Giants, 1964 Detroit Lions.

**JOHNNY BLOOD (McNALLY)**
Halfback. 6-0, 185. Born in New Richmond, Wisconsin, November 27, 1903. Died November 28, 1985. St. John's (Minnesota). Inducted in 1963. 1925-26 Milwaukee Badgers, 1926-27 Duluth Eskimos, 1928 Pottsville Maroons, 1929-33, 1935-36 Green Bay Packers, 1934 Pittsburgh Pirates; player-coach, 1937-39 Pittsburgh Pirates.

**MIKE MICHALSKE**
Guard. 6-0, 209. Born in Cleveland, Ohio, April 24, 1903. Died October 26, 1983. Penn State. Inducted in 1964. 1926 New York Yankees (AFL), 1927-28 New York Yankees, 1929-35, 1937 Green Bay Packers.

**WAYNE MILLNER**
End. 6-0, 191. Born in Roxbury, Massachusetts, January 31, 1913. Died November 19, 1976. Notre Dame. Inducted in 1968. 1936 Boston Redskins, 1937-41, 1945 Washington Redskins.

**BOBBY MITCHELL**
Running back-wide receiver. 6-0, 195. Born in Hot Springs, Arkansas, June 6, 1935. Illinois. Inducted in 1983. 1958-61 Cleveland Browns, 1962-68 Washington Redskins.

**RON MIX**
Tackle. 6-4, 250. Born in Los Angeles, California, March 10, 1938. Southern California. Inducted in 1979. 1960 Los Angeles Chargers, 1961-69 San Diego Chargers, 1971 Oakland Raiders.

**LENNY MOORE**
Back. 6-1, 198. Born in Reading, Pennsylvania, November 25, 1933. Penn State. Inducted in 1975. 1956-67 Baltimore Colts.

**MARION MOTLEY**
Fullback. 6-1, 238. Born in Leesburg, Georgia, June 5, 1920. South Carolina State, Nevada. Inducted in 1968. 1946-49 Cleveland Browns (AAFC), 1950-53 Cleveland Browns, 1955 Pittsburgh Steelers.

**GEORGE MUSSO**
Guard-tackle. 6-2, 270. Born in Collinsville, Illinois. April 8, 1910. Millikin. Inducted in 1982. 1933-44 Chicago Bears.

**BRONKO NAGURSKI**
Fullback. 6-2, 225. Born in Rainy River, Ontario, Canada, November 3, 1908. Died January 7, 1990. Minnesota. Inducted in 1963. 1930-37, 1943 Chicago Bears.

**JOE NAMATH**
Quarterback. 6-2, 200. Born in Beaver Falls, Pennsylvania, May 31, 1943. Alabama. Inducted in 1985. 1965-76 New York Jets, 1977 Los Angeles Rams.

**EARLE (GREASY) NEALE**
Coach. Born in Parkersburg, West Virginia, November 5, 1891. Died November 2, 1973. West Virginia Wesleyan. Inducted in 1969. 1941-42, 1944-50 Philadelphia Eagles; co-coach, Phil-Pitt 1943.

**ERNIE NEVERS**
Fullback. 6-1, 205. Born in Willow River, Minnesota, June 11, 1903. Died May 3, 1976. Stanford. Inducted in 1963. 1926-27 Duluth Eskimos, 1929-31 Chicago Cardinals.

**RAY NITSCHKE**
Linebacker. 6-3, 235. Born in Elmwood Park, Illinois, December 29, 1936. Illinois. Inducted in 1978. 1958-72 Green Bay Packers.

**CHUCK NOLL**
Coach. Born in Cleveland, Ohio, January 5, 1932. Dayton. Inductedin 1993. 1969-91 Pittsburgh Steelers.

**LEO NOMELLINI**
Defensive tackle. 6-3, 250. Born in Lucca, Italy, June 19, 1924. Minnesota. Inducted in 1969. 1950-63 San Francisco 49ers.

**MERLIN OLSEN**
Defensive tackle. 6-5, 270. Born in Logan, Utah, September 15, 1940. Utah State. Inducted in 1982. 1962-76 Los Angeles Rams.

**JIM OTTO**
Center. 6-2, 255. Born in Wausau, Wisconsin, January 5, 1938. Miami. Inducted in 1980. 1960-74 Oakland Raiders.

**STEVE OWEN**
Tackle. Coach. 6-0, 235. Born in Cleo Springs, Oklahoma, April 21, 1898. Died May 17, 1964. Phillips. Inducted in 1966. 1924-25 Kansas City Cowboys, 1926-30 New York Giants; coach, 1931-53 New York Giants.

**ALAN PAGE**
Defensive tackle. 6-4, 225. Born in Canton, Ohio, August 7, 1945. Notre Dame. Inducted in 1988. 1967-78 Minnesota Vikings, 1978-81 Chicago Bears.

**CLARENCE (ACE) PARKER**
Quarterback. 5-11, 168. Born in Portsmouth, Virginia, May 17, 1912. Duke. Inducted in 1972. 1937-41 Brooklyn Dodgers, 1945 Boston Yanks, 1946 New York Yankees (AAFC).

**JIM PARKER**
Guard-tackle. 6-3, 273. Born in Macon, Georgia, April 3, 1934. Ohio State. Inducted in 1973. 1957-67 Baltimore Colts.

**WALTER PAYTON**
Running back. 5-10, 202. Born in Columbia, Mississippi, July 25, 1954.

Jackson State. Inducted in 1993. 1975-87 Chicago Bears.

**JOE PERRY**
Fullback. 6-0, 200. Born in Stevens, Arkansas, January 22, 1927. Compton Junior College. Inducted in 1969. 1948-49 San Francisco 49ers (AAFC), 1950-60, 1963 San Francisco 49ers, 1961-62 Baltimore Colts.

**PETE PIHOS**
End. 6-1, 210. Born in Orlando, Florida, October 22, 1923. Indiana. Inducted in 1970. 1947-55 Philadelphia Eagles.

**HUGH (SHORTY) RAY**
Supervisor of officials 1938-56. Born in Highland Park, Illinois, September 21, 1884. Died September 16, 1956. Illinois. Inducted in 1966.

**DAN REEVES**
Team owner. Born in New York, New York, June 30, 1912. Died April 15, 1971. Georgetown. Inducted in 1967. 1941-45 Cleveland Rams, 1946-71 Los Angeles Rams.

**JOHN RIGGINS**
Running back. 6-2, 240. Born in Seneca, Kansas, August 4, 1949. Kansas. Inducted in 1992. 1971-75 New York Jets, 1976-79, 1981-85 Washington Redskins.

**JIM RINGO**
Center. 6-1, 235. Born in Orange, New Jersey, November 21, 1931. Syracuse. Inducted in 1981. 1953-63 Green Bay Packers, 1964-67 Philadelphia Eagles.

**ANDY ROBUSTELLI**
Defensive end. 6-0, 230. Born in Stamford, Connecticut, December 6, 1925. Arnold College. Inducted in 1971. 1951-55 Los Angeles Rams, 1956-64 New York Giants.

**ART ROONEY**
Team owner. Born in Coulterville, Pennsylvania, January 27, 1901. Died August 25, 1988. Georgetown, Duquesne. Inducted in 1964. 1933-40 Pittsburgh Pirates, 1941-42, 1945-88 Pittsburgh Steelers, 1943 Phil-Pitt, 1944 Card-Pitt.

**PETE ROZELLE**
Commissioner. Born in South Gate, California, March 1, 1926. San Francisco. Inducted in 1985. Commissioner, 1960-89.

**BOB ST. CLAIR**
Tackle. 6-9, 265. Born in San Francisco, California, February 18, 1931. San Francisco, Tulsa. Inducted in 1990. 1953-63 San Francisco 49ers.

**GALE SAYERS**
Running back. 6-0, 200. Born in Wichita, Kansas, May 30, 1943. Kansas. Inducted in 1977. 1965-71 Chicago Bears.

**JOE SCHMIDT**
Linebacker. 6-0, 222. Born in Pittsburgh, Pennsylvania, January 19,1932. Pittsburgh. Inducted in 1973. 1953-65 Detroit Lions.

**TEX SCHRAMM**
Team president-general manager. Born in San Gabriel, California, June 2, 1920. Texas. Inducted in 1991. 1947-57 Los Angeles Rams. 1960-88 Dallas Cowboys.

**ART SHELL**
Tackle. 6-5, 285. Born in Charleston, South Carolina, November 25, 1946. Maryland State-Eastern Shore. Inducted in 1989. 1968-81 Oakland Raiders, 1982 Los Angeles Raiders.

**O.J. SIMPSON**
Running back. 6-1, 212. Born in San Francisco, California, July 9, 1947. Southern California. Inducted in 1985. 1969-77 Buffalo Bills, 1978-79 San Francisco 49ers.

**JACKIE SMITH**
Tight end. 6-4, 232. Born in Columbia, Mississippi, February 23, 1940. Northwestern Louisiana. Inducted in 1994. 1963-77 St. Louis Cardinals, 1978 Dallas Cowboys.

**BART STARR**
Quarterback. 6-1, 200. Born in Montgomery, Alabama, January 9, 1934. Alabama. Inducted in 1977. 1956-71 Green Bay Packers.

**ROGER STAUBACH**
Quarterback. 6-3, 202. Born in Cincinnati, Ohio, February 5, 1942. Navy. Inducted in 1985. 1969-79 Dallas Cowboys.

**ERNIE STAUTNER**
Defensive tackle. 6-2, 235. Born in Prinzing-by-Cham, Bavaria, Germany, April 20, 1925. Boston College. Inducted in 1969. 1950-63 Pittsburgh Steelers.

**JAN STENERUD**
Kicker. 6-2, 190. Born in Fetsund, Norway, November 26, 1942. Montana State. Inducted in 1991. 1967-79 Kansas City Chiefs, 1980-83 Green Bay Packers, 1984-85 Minnesota Vikings.

**KEN STRONG**
Halfback. 5-11, 210. Born in New Haven, Connecticut, August 6, 1906. Died October 5, 1979. New York University. Inducted in 1967. 1929-32 Staten Island Stapletons, 1933-35, 1939, 1944-47 New York Giants, 1936-37 New York Yanks (AFL).

**JOE STYDAHAR**
Tackle. 6-4, 230. Born in Kaylor,Pennsylvania, March 3, 1912. Died March 23, 1977. West Virginia. Inducted in 1967. 1936-42, 1945-46 Chicago Bears.

**FRAN TARKENTON**
Quarterback. 6-0, 185. Born in Richmond, Virginia, February 3, 1940. Georgia. Inducted in 1986. 1961-66, 1972-78 Minnesota Vikings, 1967-71 New York Giants.

**CHARLEY TAYLOR**
Running back-wide receiver. 6-3, 210. Born in Grand Prairie, Texas, September 28, 1941. Arizona State. Inducted in 1984. 1964-75, 1977 Washington Redskins.

**JIM TAYLOR**
Fullback. 6-0, 216. Born in Baton Rouge, Louisiana, September 20, 1935. Louisiana State. Inducted in 1976. 1958-66 Green Bay Packers, 1967 New Orleans Saints.

**JIM THORPE**
Halfback. 6-1, 190. Born in Prague, Oklahoma, May 28, 1888. Died March 28, 1953. Carlisle. Inducted in 1963. 1915-17, 1919-20, 1926 Canton Bulldogs, 1921 Cleveland Indians, 1922-23 Oorang Indians, 1924 Rock Island, Ill., Independents, 1925 New York Giants, 1928 Chicago Cardinals.

**Y.A. TITTLE**
Quarterback. 6-0, 200. Born in Marshall, Texas, October 24, 1926. Louisiana State. Inducted in 1971. 1948-49 Baltimore Colts (AAFC), 1950 Baltimore Colts, 1951-60 San Francisco 49ers, 1961-64 New York Giants.

**GEORGE TRAFTON**
Center. 6-2, 235. Born in Chicago, Illinois, December 6, 1896. Died September 5, 1971. Notre Dame. Inducted in 1964. 1920 Decatur Staleys, 1921 Chicago Staleys, 1922-32 Chicago Bears.

**CHARLEY TRIPPI**
Halfback. 6-0, 185. Born in Pittston, Pennsylvania, December 14, 1922. Georgia. Inducted in 1968. 1947-55 Chicago Cardinals.

**EMLEN TUNNELL**
Safety. 6-1, 200. Born in Bryn Mawr, Pennsylvania, March 29, 1925. Died July 23, 1975. Toledo, Iowa. Inducted in 1967. 1948-58 New York Giants, 1959-61 Green Bay Packers.

**CLYDE (BULLDOG) TURNER**
Center. 6-2, 235. Born in Sweetwater, Texas, November 10, 1919. Hardin-Simmons. Inducted in 1966. 1940-52 Chicago Bears.

**JOHNNY UNITAS**
Quarterback. 6-1, 195. Born in Pittsburgh, Pennsylvania, May 7, 1933. Louisville. Inducted in 1979. 1956-72 Baltimore Colts, 1973 San Diego Chargers.

**GENE UPSHAW**
Guard. 6-5, 255. Born in Robstown, Texas, August 15, 1945. Texas A & I. Inducted in 1987. 1967-81 Oakland Raiders.

**NORM VAN BROCKLIN**
Quarterback. 6-1, 190. Born in Eagle Butte, South Dakota, March 15, 1926. Died May 2, 1983. Oregon. Inducted in 1971. 1949-57 Los Angeles Rams, 1958-60 Philadelphia Eagles.

**STEVE VAN BUREN**
Halfback. 6-1, 200. Born in La Ceiba, Honduras, December 28, 1920. Louisiana State. Inducted in 1965. 1944-51 Philadelphia Eagles.

**DOAK WALKER**
Halfback. 5-10, 172. Born in Dallas, Texas, January 1, 1927. Southern Methodist. Inducted in 1986. 1950-55 Detroit Lions.

**BILL WALSH**
Coach. Born in Los Angeles, California, November 30, 1931. San Jose State. Inducted in 1993. 1979-88 San Francisco 49ers.

**PAUL WARFIELD**
Wide receiver. 6-0, 188. Born in Warren, Ohio, November 28, 1942. Ohio State. Inducted in 1983. 1964-69, 1976-77 Cleveland Browns, 1970-74 Miami Dolphins.

**BOB WATERFIELD**
Quarterback. 6-2, 200. Born in Elmira, New York, July 26, 1920. Died March 25, 1983. UCLA. Inducted in 1965. 1945 Cleveland Rams, 1946-52 Los Angeles Rams.

**ARNIE WEINMEISTER**
Defensive tackle. 6-4, 235. Born in Rhein, Saskatchewan, Canada, March 23, 1923. Washington. Inducted in 1984. 1948-49 New York Yankees (AAFC), 1950-53 New York Giants.

**RANDY WHITE**
Defensive tackle. 6-4, 265. Born in Wilmington, Delaware, January 15, 1953. Maryland. Inducted in 1994. 1975-88 Dallas Cowboys.

**BILL WILLIS**
Guard. 6-2, 215. Born in Columbus, Ohio, October 5, 1921. Ohio State. Inducted in 1977. 1946-49 Cleveland Browns (AAFC), 1950-53 Cleveland Browns.

**LARRY WILSON**
Safety. 6-0, 190. Born in Rigby, Idaho, March 24, 1938. Utah. Inducted in 1978. 1960-72 St. Louis Cardinals.

**ALEX WOJCIECHOWICZ**
Center. 6-0, 235. Born in South River, New Jersey, August 12, 1915. Fordham. Inducted in 1968. 1938-46 Detroit Lions, 1946-50 Philadelphia Eagles.

**WILLIE WOOD**
Safety. 5-10, 190. Born in Washington, D.C., December 23, 1936. Southern California. Inducted in 1989. 1960-71 Green Bay Packers.

# CHRONOLOGY OF PROFESSIONAL FOOTBALL

**1869**
Rutgers and Princeton played a college soccer football game, the first ever, November 6. The game used modified London Football Association rules. During the next seven years, rugby gained favor with the major eastern schools over soccer, and modern football began to develop from rugby.

**1876**
At the Massasoit convention, the first rules for American football were written. Walter Camp, who would become known as the father of American football, first became involved with the game.

**1892**
In an era in which football was a major attraction of local athletic clubs, an intense competition between two Pittsburgh-area clubs, the Allegheny Athletic Association (AAA) and the Pittsburgh Athletic Club (PAC), led to the making of the first professional football player. Former Yale All-America guard William (Pudge) Heffelfinger was paid $500 by the AAA to play in a game against the PAC, becoming the first person to be paid to play football, November 12. The AAA won the game 4-0 when Heffelfinger picked up a PAC fumble and ran 25 yards for a touchdown.

**1893**
The Pittsburgh Athletic Club signed one of its players, probably halfback Grant Dibert, to the first known pro football contract, which covered all of the PAC's games for the year.

**1895**
John Brallier became the first football player to openly turn pro, accepting $10 and expenses to play for the Latrobe YMCA against the Jeannette Athletic Club.

**1896**
The Allegheny Athletic Association team fielded the first completely professional team for its abbreviated two-game season.

**1897**
The Latrobe Athletic Association football team went entirely professional, becoming the first team to play a full season with only professionals.

**1898**
A touchdown was changed from four points to five.

**1899**
Chris O'Brien formed a neighborhood team, which played under the name the Morgan Athletic Club, on the south side of Chicago. The team later became known as the Normals, then the Racine (for a street in Chicago) Cardinals, the Chicago Cardinals, the St. Louis Cardinals, the Phoenix Cardinals, and, in 1994, the Arizona Cardinals. The team remains the oldest continuing operation in pro football.

**1900**
William C. Temple took over the team payments for the Duquesne Country and Athletic Club, becoming the first known individual club owner.

**1902**
Baseball's Philadelphia Athletics, managed by Connie Mack, and the Philadelphia Phillies formed professional football teams, joining the Pittsburgh Stars in the first attempt at a pro football league, named the National Football League. The Athletics won the first night football game ever played, 39-0 over Kanaweola AC at Elmira, New York, November 21.

All three teams claimed the pro championship for the year, but the league president, Dave Berry, named the Stars the champions. Pitcher Rube Waddell was with the Athletics, and pitcher Christy Mathewson a fullback for Pittsburgh.

The first World Series of pro football, actually a five-team tournament, was played among a team made up of players from both the Athletics and the Phillies, but simply named New York; the New York Knickerbockers; the Syracuse AC; the Warlow AC; and the Orange (New Jersey) AC at New York's original Madison Square Garden. New York and Syracuse played the first indoor football game before 3,000, December 28. Syracuse, with Glen (Pop) Warner at guard, won 6-0 and went on to win the tournament.

**1903**
The Franklin (Pa.) Athletic Club won the second and last World Series of pro football over the Oreos AC of Asbury Park, New Jersey; the Watertown Red and Blacks; and the Orange AC.

Pro football was popularized in Ohio when the Massillon Tigers, a strong amateur team, hired four Pittsburgh pros to play in the season-ending game against Akron. At the same time, pro football declined in the Pittsburgh area, and the emphasis on the pro game moved west from Pennsylvania to Ohio.

**1904**
A field goal was changed from five points to four.

Ohio had at least seven pro teams, with Massillon winning the Ohio Independent Championship, that is, the pro title. Talk surfaced about forming a state-wide league to end spiraling salaries brought about by constant bidding for players and to write universal rules for the game. The feeble attempt to start the league failed.

Halfback Charles Follis signed a contract with the Shelby AC, making him the first known black pro football player.

**1905**
The Canton AC, later to become known as the Bulldogs, became a professional team. Massillon again won the Ohio League championship.

**1906**
The forward pass was legalized. The first authenticated pass completion in a pro game came on October 27, when George (Peggy) Parratt of Massillon threw a completion to Dan (Bullet) Riley in a victory over a combined Benwood-Moundsville team.

Arch-rivals Canton and Massillon, the two best pro teams in America, played twice, with Canton winning the first game but Massillon winning the second and the Ohio League championship. A betting scandal and the financial disaster wrought upon the two clubs by paying huge salaries caused a temporary decline in interest in pro football in the two cities and, somewhat, throughout Ohio.

**1909**
A field goal dropped from four points to three.

**1912**
A touchdown was increased from five points to six.

Jack Cusack revived a strong pro team in Canton.

**1913**
Jim Thorpe, a former football and track star at the Carlisle Indian School (Pa.) and a double gold medal winner at the 1912 Olympics in Stockholm, played for the Pine Village Pros in Indiana.

**1915**
Massillon again fielded a major team, reviving the old rivalry with Canton. Cusack signed Thorpe to play for Canton for $250 a game.

**1916**
With Thorpe and former Carlisle teammate Pete Calac starring, Canton went 9-0-1, won the Ohio League championship, and was acclaimed the pro football champion.

**1917**
Despite an upset by Massillon, Canton again won the Ohio League championship.

**1919**
Canton again won the Ohio League championship, despite the team having been turned over from Cusack to Ralph Hay. Thorpe and Calac were joined in the backfield by Joe Guyon.

Earl (Curly) Lambeau and George Calhoun organized the Green Bay Packers. Lambeau's employer at the Indian Packing Company provided $500 for equipment and allowed the team to use the company field for practices. The Packers went 10-1.

**1920**
Pro football was in a state of confusion due to three major problems: dramatically rising salaries; players continually jumping from one team to another following the highest offer; and the use of college players still enrolled in school. A league in which all the members would follow the same rules seemed the answer. An organizational meeting, at which the Akron Pros, Canton Bulldogs, Cleveland Indians, and Dayton Triangles were represented, was held in Canton, Ohio, August 20. This meeting resulted in the formation of the American Professional Football Conference.

A second organizational meeting was held in Canton, September 17. The teams were from four states—Akron, Canton, Cleveland, and Dayton from Ohio; the Hammond Pros and Muncie Flyers from Indiana; the Rochester Jeffersons from New York; and the Rock Island Independents, Decatur Staleys, and Racine Cardinals from Illinois. The name of the league was changed to the American Professional Football Association. Hoping to capitalize on his fame, the members elected Thorpe president; Stanley Cofall of Cleveland was elected vice president. A membership fee of $100 per team was charged to give an appearance of respectability, but no team ever paid it. Scheduling was left up to the teams, and there were wide variations, both in the overall number of games played and in the number played against APFA member teams.

Four other teams—the Buffalo All-Americans, Chicago Tigers, Columbus Panhandles, and Detroit Heralds—joined the league sometime during the year. On September 26, the first game featuring an APFA team was played at Rock Island's Douglas Park. A crowd of 800 watched the Independents defeat the St. Paul Ideals 48-0. A week later, October 3, the first game matching two APFA teams was held. At Triangle Park, Dayton defeated Columbus 14-0, with Lou Partlow of Dayton scoring the first touchdown in a game between Association teams. The same day, Rock Island defeated Muncie 45-0.

By the beginning of December, most of the teams in the APFA had abandoned their hopes for a championship, and some of them, including the Chicago Tigers and the Detroit Heralds, had finished their seasons, disbanded, and had their franchises canceled by the Association. Four teams—Akron, Buffalo, Canton, and Decatur—still had championship aspirations, but a series of late-season games among them left Akron as the only undefeated team in the Association. At one of these games, Akron sold tackle Bob Nash to Buffalo for $300 and five percent of the gate receipts—the first APFA player deal.

**1921**
At the league meeting in Akron, April 30, the championship of the 1920 season was awarded to the Akron Pros. The APFA was reorganized, with Joe Carr of the Columbus Panhandles named president and Carl Storck of Dayton secretary-treasurer. Carr moved the Association's headquarters to Columbus, drafted a league constitution and by-laws, gave teams territorial rights, restricted player movements, developed membership criteria for the franchises, and issued standings for the first time, so that the APFA would have a clear champion.

The Association's membership increased to 22 teams, including the Green Bay Packers, who were awarded to John Clair of the Acme Packing Company.

Thorpe moved from Canton to the Cleveland Indians, but he was hurt early in the season and played very little.

A.E. Staley turned the Decatur Staleys over to player-coach George Halas, who moved the team to Cubs Park in Chicago. Staley paid Halas

$5,000 to keep the name Staleys for one more year. Halas made halfback Ed (Dutch) Sternaman his partner.

The Staleys claimed the APFA championship with a 9-1-1 record, as did Buffalo at 9-1-2. Carr ruled in favor of the Staleys, giving Halas his first championship.

**1922**

After admitting the use of players who had college eligibility remaining during the 1921 season, Clair and the Green Bay management withdrew from the APFA, January 28. Curly Lambeau promised to obey league rules and then used $50 of his own money to buy back the franchise. Bad weather and low attendance plagued the Packers, and Lambeau went broke, but local merchants arranged a $2,500 loan for the club. A public nonprofit corporation was set up to operate the team, with Lambeau as head coach and manager.

The American Professional Football Association changed its name to the National Football League, June 24. The Chicago Staleys became the Chicago Bears.

The NFL fielded 18 teams, including the new Oorang Indians of Marion, Ohio, an all-Indian team featuring Thorpe, Joe Guyon, and Pete Calac, and sponsored by the Oorang dog kennels.

Canton, led by player-coach Guy Chamberlin and tackles Link Lyman and Wilbur (Pete) Henry, emerged as the league's first true powerhouse, going 10-0-2.

**1923**

For the first time, all of the franchises considered to be part of the NFL fielded teams. Thorpe played first for Oorang, then for the Toledo Maroons. Against the Bears, Thorpe fumbled, and Halas picked up the ball and returned it 98 yards for a touchdown, a record that would last until 1972.

Canton had its second consecutive undefeated season, going 11-0-1 for the NFL title.

**1924**

The league had 18 franchises, including new ones in Kansas City, Kenosha, and Frankford, a section of Philadelphia. League champion Canton, successful on the field but not at the box office, was purchased by the owner of the Cleveland franchise, who kept the Canton franchise inactive, while using the best players for his Cleveland team, which he renamed the Bulldogs. Cleveland won the title with a 7-1-1 record.

**1925**

Five new franchises were admitted to the NFL—the New York Giants, who were awarded to Tim Mara and Billy Gibson for $500; the Detroit Panthers, featuring Jimmy Conzelman as owner, coach, and tailback; the Providence Steam Roller; a new Canton Bulldogs team; and the Pottsville Maroons, who had been perhaps the most successful independent pro team. The NFL established its first player limit, at 16 players.

Late in the season, the NFL made its greatest coup in gaining national recognition. Shortly after the University of Illinois season ended in November, All-America halfback Harold (Red) Grange signed a contract to play with the Chicago Bears. On Thanksgiving Day, a crowd of 36,000—the largest in pro football history—watched Grange and the Bears play the Chicago Cardinals to a scoreless tie at Wrigley Field. At the beginning of December, the Bears left on a barnstorming tour that saw them play eight games in 12 days, in St. Louis, Philadelphia, New York City, Washington, Boston, Pittsburgh, Detroit, and Chicago. A crowd of 73,000 watched the game against the Giants at the Polo Grounds, helping assure the future of the troubled NFL franchise in New York. The Bears then played nine more games in the South and West, including a game in Los Angeles, in which 75,000 fans watched them defeat the Los Angeles Tigers in the Los Angeles Memorial Coliseum.

Pottsville and the Chicago Cardinals were the top contenders for the league title, with Pottsville winning a late-season meeting 21-7. Pottsville scheduled a game against a team of former Notre Dame players for Shibe Park in Philadelphia. Frankford lodged a protest not only because the game was in Frankford's protected territory, but because it was being played the same day as a Yellow Jackets home game. Carr gave three different notices forbidding Pottsville to play the game, but Pottsville played anyway, December 12. That day, Carr fined the club, suspended it from all rights and privileges (including the right to play for the NFL championship), and returned its franchise to the league. The Cardinals, who ended the season with the best record in the league, were named the 1925 champions.

**1926**

Grange's manager, C.C. Pyle, told the Bears that Grange wouldn't play for them unless he was paid a five-figure salary and given one-third ownership of the team. The Bears refused. Pyle leased Yankee Stadium in New York City, then petitioned for an NFL franchise. After he was refused, he started the first American Football League. It lasted one season and included Grange's New York Yankees and eight other teams. The AFL champion Philadelphia Quakers played a December game against the New York Giants, seventh in the NFL, and the Giants won 31-0. At the end of the season, the AFL folded.

Halas pushed through a rule that prohibited any team from signing a player whose college class had not graduated.

The NFL grew to 22 teams, including the Duluth Eskimos, who signed All-America fullback Ernie Nevers of Stanford, giving the league a gate attraction to rival Grange. The 15-member Eskimos, dubbed the Iron Men of the North, played 29 exhibition and league games, 28 on the road, and Nevers played in all but 29 minutes of them.

Frankford edged the Bears for the championship, despite Halas having obtained John (Paddy) Driscoll from the Cardinals. On December 4, the Yellow Jackets scored in the final two minutes to defeat the Bears 7-6 and move ahead of them in the standings.

**1927**

At a special meeting in Cleveland, April 23, Carr decided to secure the NFL's future by eliminating the financially weaker teams and consolidating the quality players onto a limited number of more successful teams. The new-look NFL dropped to 12 teams, and the center of gravity of the league left the Midwest, where the NFL had started, and began to emerge in the large cities of the East. One of the new teams was Grange's New York Yankees, but Grange suffered a knee injury and the Yankees finished in the middle of the pack. The NFL championship was won by the cross-town rival New York Giants, who posted 10 shutouts in 13 games.

**1928**

Grange and Nevers both retired from pro football, and Duluth disbanded, as the NFL was reduced to only 10 teams. The Providence Steam Roller of Jimmy Conzelman and Pearce Johnson won the championship, playing in the Cycledrome, a 10,000-seat oval that had been built for bicycle races.

**1929**

Chris O'Brien sold the Chicago Cardinals to David Jones, July 27.

The NFL added a fourth official, the field judge, July 28.

Grange and Nevers returned to the NFL. Nevers scored six rushing touchdowns and four extra points as the Cardinals beat Grange's Bears 40-6, November 28. The 40 points set a record that remains the NFL's oldest.

Providence became the first NFL team to host a game at night under floodlights, against the Cardinals, November 3.

The Packers added back Johnny Blood (McNally), tackle Cal Hubbard, and guard Mike Michalske, and won their first NFL championship, edging the Giants, who featured quarterback Benny Friedman.

**1930**

Dayton, the last of the NFL's original franchises, was purchased by John Dwyer, moved to Brooklyn, and renamed the Dodgers. The Portsmouth, Ohio, Spartans entered the league.

The Packers edged the Giants for the title, but the most improved team was the Bears. Halas retired as a player and replaced himself as coach of the Bears with Ralph Jones, who refined the T-formation by introducing wide ends and a halfback in motion. Jones also introduced rookie All-America fullback-tackle Bronko Nagurski.

The Giants defeated a team of former Notre Dame players coached by Knute Rockne 22-0 before 55,000 at the Polo Grounds, December 14. The proceeds went to the New York Unemployment Fund to help those suffering because of the Great Depression, and the easy victory helped give the NFL credibility with the press and the public.

**1931**

The NFL decreased to 10 teams, and halfway through the season the Frankford franchise folded. Carr fined the Bears, Packers, and Portsmouth $1,000 each for using players whose college classes had not graduated.

The Packers won an unprecedented third consecutive title, beating out the Spartans, who were led by rookie backs Earl (Dutch) Clark and Glenn Presnell.

**1932**

George Preston Marshall, Vincent Bendix, Jay O'Brien, and M. Dorland Doyle were awarded a franchise for Boston, July 9. Despite the presence of two rookies—halfback Cliff Battles and tackle Glen (Turk) Edwards—the new team, named the Braves, lost money and Marshall was left as the sole owner at the end of the year.

NFL membership dropped to eight teams, the lowest in history. Official statistics were kept for the first time. The Bears and the Spartans finished the season in the first-ever tie for first place. After the season finale, the league office arranged for the first playoff game in NFL history. The game was moved indoors to Chicago Stadium because of bitter cold and heavy snow. The arena allowed only an 80-yard field that came right to the walls. The goal posts were moved from the end lines to the goal lines and, for safety, inbounds lines or hashmarks where the ball would be put in play were drawn 10 yards from the walls that butted against the sidelines. The Bears won 9-0, December 18, scoring the winning touchdown on a two-yard pass from Nagurski to Grange. The Spartans claimed Nagurski's pass was thrown from less than five yards behind the line of scrimmage, violating the existing passing rule, but the play stood.

**1933**

The NFL, which long had followed the rules of college football, made a number of significant changes from the college game for the first time and began to develop rules serving its needs and the style of play it preferred. The innovations from the 1932 championship game—inbounds line or hashmarks and goal posts on the goal lines—were adopted. Also the forward pass was legalized from anywhere behind the line of scrimmage, February 25.

Marshall and Halas pushed through a proposal that divided the NFL into two divisions, with the winners to meet in an annual championship game, July 8.

Three new franchises joined the league—the Pittsburgh Pirates of Art Rooney, the Philadelphia Eagles of Bert Bell and Lud Wray, and the Cincinnati Reds. The Staten Island Stapletons suspended operations for a year, but never returned to the league.

Halas bought out Sternaman, became sole owner of the Bears, and reinstated himself as head coach. Marshall changed the name of the Boston Braves to the Redskins. David Jones sold the Chicago Cardinals to Charles W. Bidwill.

# CHRONOLOGY OF PROFESSIONAL FOOTBALL

In the first NFL Championship Game scheduled before the season, the Western Division champion Bears defeated the Eastern Division champion Giants 23-21 at Wrigley Field, December 17.

**1934**
G.A. (Dick) Richards purchased the Portsmouth Spartans, moved them to Detroit, and renamed them the Lions.

Professional football gained new prestige when the Bears were matched against the best college football players in the first Chicago College All-Star Game, August 31. The game ended in a scoreless tie before 79,432 at Soldier Field.

The Cincinnati Reds lost their first eight games, then were suspended from the league for defaulting on payments. The St. Louis Gunners, an independent team, joined the NFL by buying the Cincinnati franchise and went 1-2 the last three weeks.

Rookie Beattie Feathers of the Bears became the NFL's first 1,000-yard rusher, gaining 1,004 on 101 carries. The Thanksgiving Day game between the Bears and the Lions became the first NFL game broadcast nationally, with Graham McNamee the announcer for CBS radio.

In the championship game, on an extremely cold and icy day at the Polo Grounds, the Giants trailed the Bears 13-3 in the third quarter before changing to basketball shoes for better footing. The Giants won 30-13 in what has come to be known as the Sneakers Game, December 9.

The player waiver rule was adopted, December 10.

**1935**
The NFL adopted Bert Bell's proposal to hold an annual draft of college players, to begin in 1936, with teams selecting in an inverse order of finish, May 19. The inbounds line or hashmarks were moved nearer the center of the field, 15 yards from the sidelines.

All-America end Don Hutson of Alabama joined Green Bay. The Lions defeated the Giants 26-7 in the NFL Championship Game, December 15.

**1936**
There were no franchise transactions for the first year since the formation of the NFL. It also was the first year in which all member teams played the same number of games.

The Eagles made University of Chicago halfback and Heisman Trophy winner Jay Berwanger the first player ever selected in the NFL draft, February 8. The Eagles traded his rights to the Bears, but Berwanger never played pro football. The first player selected to actually sign was the number-two pick, Riley Smith of Alabama, who was selected by Boston.

A rival league was formed, and it became the second to call itself the American Football League. The Boston Shamrocks were its champions.

Because of poor attendance, Marshall, the owner of the host team, moved the Championship Game from Boston to the Polo Grounds in New York. Green Bay defeated the Redskins 21-6, December 13.

**1937**
Homer Marshman was granted a Cleveland franchise, named the Rams, February 12. Marshall moved the Redskins to Washington, D.C., February 13. The Redskins signed TCU All-America tailback Sammy Baugh, who led them to a 28-21 victory over the Bears in the NFL Championship Game, December 12.

The Los Angeles Bulldogs had an 8-0 record to win the AFL title, but then the 2-year-old league folded.

**1938**
At the suggestion of Halas, Hugh (Shorty) Ray became a technical advisor on rules and officiating to the NFL. A new rule called for a 15-yard penalty for roughing the passer.

Rookie Byron (Whizzer) White of the Pittsburgh Pirates led the NFL in rushing. The Giants defeated the Packers 23-17 for the NFL title, December 11.

Marshall, *Los Angeles Times* sports editor Bill Henry, and promoter Tom Gallery established the Pro Bowl game between the NFL champion and a team of pro all-stars.

**1939**
The New York Giants defeated the Pro All-Stars 13-10 in the first Pro Bowl, at Wrigley Field, Los Angeles, January 15.

Carr, NFL president since 1921, died in Columbus, May 20. Carl Storck was named acting president, May 25.

An NFL game was televised for the first time when NBC broadcast the Brooklyn Dodgers-Philadelphia Eagles game from Ebbets Field to the approximately 1,000 sets then in New York.

Green Bay defeated New York 27-0 in the NFL Championship Game, December 10 at Milwaukee. NFL attendance exceeded 1 million in a season for the first time, reaching 1,071,200.

**1940**
A six-team rival league, the third to call itself the American Football League, was formed, and the Columbus Bullies won its championship.

Halas's Bears, with additional coaching by Clark Shaughnessy of Stanford, defeated the Redskins 73-0 in the NFL Championship Game, December 8. The game, which was the most decisive victory in NFL history, popularized the Bears' T-formation with a man-in-motion. It was the first championship carried on network radio, broadcast by Red Barber to 120 stations of the Mutual Broadcasting System, which paid $2,500 for the rights.

Art Rooney sold the Pittsburgh franchise to Alexis Thompson, December 9, then bought part interest in the Philadelphia Eagles.

**1941**
Elmer Layden was named the first Commissioner of the NFL, March 1; Storck, the acting president, resigned, April 5. NFL headquarters were moved to Chicago.

Bell and Rooney traded the Eagles to Thompson for the Pirates, then re-named their new team the Steelers. Homer Marshman sold the Rams to Daniel F. Reeves and Fred Levy, Jr.

The league by-laws were revised to provide for playoffs in case there were ties in division races, and sudden-death overtimes in case a playoff game was tied after four quarters. An official *NFL Record Manual* was published for the first time.

Columbus again won the championship of the AFL, but the two-year-old league then folded.

The Bears and the Packers finished in a tie for the Western Division championship, setting up the first divisional playoff game in league history. The Bears won 33-14, then defeated the Giants 37-9 for the NFL championship, December 21.

**1942**
Players departing for service in World War II depleted the rosters of NFL teams. Halas left the Bears in midseason to join the Navy, and Luke Johnsos and Heartley (Hunk) Anderson served as co-coaches as the Bears went 11-0 in the regular season. The Redskins defeated the Bears 14-6 in the NFL Championship Game, December 13.

**1943**
The Cleveland Rams, with co-owners Reeves and Levy in the service, were granted permission to suspend operations for one season, April 6. Levy transferred his stock in the team to Reeves, April 16.

The NFL adopted free substitution, April 7. The league also made the wearing of helmets mandatory and approved a 10-game schedule for all teams.

Philadelphia and Pittsburgh were granted permission to merge for one season, June 19. The team, known as Phil-Pitt (and called the Steagles by fans), divided home games between the two cities, and Earle (Greasy) Neale of Philadelphia and Walt Kiesling of Pittsburgh served as co-coaches. The merger automatically dissolved the last day of the season, December 5.

Ted Collins was granted a franchise for Boston, to become active in 1944.

Sammy Baugh led the league in passing, punting, and interceptions. He led the Redskins to a tie with the Giants for the Eastern Division title, and then to a 28-0 victory in a divisional playoff game. The Bears beat the Redskins 41-21 in the NFL Championship Game, December 26.

**1944**
Collins, who had wanted a franchise in Yankee Stadium in New York, named his new team in Boston the Yanks. Cleveland resumed operations. The Brooklyn Dodgers changed their name to the Tigers.

Coaching from the bench was legalized, April 20.

The Cardinals and the Steelers were granted permission to merge for one year under the name Card-Pitt, April 21. Phil Handler of the Cardinals and Walt Kiesling of the Steelers served as co-coaches. The merger automatically dissolved the last day of the season, December 3.

In the NFL Championship Game, Green Bay defeated the New York Giants 14-7, December 17.

**1945**
The inbounds lines or hashmarks were moved from 15 yards away from the sidelines to nearer the center of the field—20 yards from the sidelines.

Brooklyn and Boston merged into a team that played home games in both cities and was known simply as The Yanks. The team was coached by former Boston head coach Herb Kopf. In December, the Brooklyn franchise withdrew from the NFL to join the new All-America Football Conference; all the players on its active and reserve lists were assigned to The Yanks, who once again became the Boston Yanks.

Halas rejoined the Bears late in the season after service with the U.S. Navy. Although Halas took over much of the coaching duties, Anderson and Johnsos remained the coaches of record throughout the season.

Steve Van Buren of Philadelphia led the NFL in rushing, kickoff returns, and scoring.

After the Japanese surrendered ending World War II, a count showed that the NFL service roster, limited to men who had played in league games, totaled 638, 21 of whom had died in action.

Rookie quarterback Bob Waterfield led Cleveland to a 15-14 victory over Washington in the NFL Championship Game, December 16.

**1946**
The contract of Commissioner Layden was not renewed, and Bert Bell, the co-owner of the Steelers, replaced him, January 11. Bell moved the league headquarters from Chicago to the Philadelphia suburb of Bala-Cynwyd.

Free substitution was withdrawn and substitutions were limited to no more than three men at a time. Forward passes were made automatically incomplete upon striking the goal posts, January 11.

The NFL took on a truly national appearance for the first time when Reeves was granted permission by the league to move his NFL champion Rams to Los Angeles.

The rival All-America Football Conference began play with eight teams. The Cleveland Browns, coached by Paul Brown, won the AAFC's first championship, defeating the New York Yankees 14-9.

Bill Dudley of the Steelers led the NFL in rushing, interceptions, and punt returns, and won the league's most valuable player award.

Backs Frank Filchock and Merle Hapes of the Giants were questioned about an attempt by a New York man to fix the championship game with the Bears. Bell suspended Hapes but allowed Filchock to play; he played well, but Chicago won 24-14, December 15.

**1947**
The NFL added a fifth official, the back judge.

A bonus choice was made for the first time in the NFL draft. One team each year would select the special choice before the first round began. The Chicago Bears won a lottery and the rights to the first choice and drafted back Bob Fenimore of Oklahoma A&M.

The Cleveland Browns again won the AAFC title, defeating the New York Yankees 14-3.

Charles Bidwill, Sr., owner of the Cardinals, died April 19, but his wife and sons retained ownership of the team. On December 28, the Cardinals won the NFL Championship Game 28-21 over the Philadelphia Eagles, who had beaten Pittsburgh 21-0 in a playoff.

**1948**

Plastic helmets were prohibited. A flexible artificial tee was permitted at the kickoff. Officials other than the referee were equipped with whistles, not horns, January 14.

Fred Mandel sold the Detroit Lions to a syndicate headed by D. Lyle Fife, January 15.

Halfback Fred Gehrke of the Los Angeles Rams painted horns on the Rams' helmets, the first modern helmet emblems in pro football.

The Cleveland Browns won their third straight championship in the AAFC, going 14-0 and then defeating the Buffalo Bills 49-7.

In a blizzard, the Eagles defeated the Cardinals 7-0 in the NFL Championship Game, December 19.

**1949**

Alexis Thompson sold the champion Eagles to a syndicate headed by James P. Clark, January 15. The Boston Yanks became the New York Bulldogs, sharing the Polo Grounds with the Giants.

Free substitution was adopted for one year, January 20.

The NFL had two 1,000-yard rushers in the same season for the first time—Steve Van Buren of Philadelphia and Tony Canadeo of Green Bay.

The AAFC played its season with a one-division, seven-team format. On December 9, Bell announced a merger agreement in which three AAFC franchises—Cleveland, San Francisco, and Baltimore—would join the NFL in 1950. The Browns won their fourth consecutive AAFC title, defeating the 49ers 21-7, December 11.

In a heavy rain, the Eagles defeated the Rams 14-0 in the NFL Championship Game, December 18.

**1950**

Unlimited free substitution was restored, opening the way for the era of two platoons and specialization in pro football, January 20.

Curly Lambeau, founder of the franchise and Green Bay's head coach since 1921, resigned under fire, February 1.

The name National Football League was restored after about three months as the National-American Football League. The American and National conferences were created to replace the Eastern and Western divisions, March 3.

The New York Bulldogs became the Yanks and divided the players of the former AAFC Yankees with the Giants. A special allocation draft was held in which the 13 teams drafted the remaining AAFC players, with special consideration for Baltimore, which received 15 choices compared to 10 for other teams.

The Los Angeles Rams became the first NFL team to have all of its games—both home and away—televised. The Washington Redskins followed the Rams in arranging to televise their games; other teams made deals to put selected games on television.

In the first game of the season, former AAFC champion Cleveland defeated NFL champion Philadelphia 35-10. For the first time, deadlocks occurred in both conferences and playoffs were necessary. The Browns defeated the Giants in the American and the Rams defeated the Bears in the National. Cleveland defeated Los Angeles 30-28 in the NFL Championship Game, December 24.

**1951**

The Pro Bowl game, dormant since 1942, was revived under a new format matching the all-stars of each conference at the Los Angeles Memorial Coliseum. The American Conference defeated the National Conference 28-27, January 14.

Abraham Watner returned the Baltimore franchise and its player contracts back to the NFL for $50,000. Baltimore's former players were made available for drafting at the same time as college players, January 18.

A rule was passed that no tackle, guard, or center would be eligible to catch a forward pass, January 18.

The Rams reversed their television policy and televised only road games.

The NFL Championship Game was televised coast-to-coast for the first time, December 23. The DuMont Network paid $75,000 for the rights to the game, in which the Rams defeated the Browns 24-17.

**1952**

Ted Collins sold the New York Yanks' franchise back to the NFL, January 19. A new franchise was awarded to a group in Dallas after it purchased the assets of the Yanks, January 24. The new Texans went 1-11, with the owners turning the franchise back to the league in midseason. For the last five games of the season, the commissioner's office operated the Texans as a road team, using Hershey, Pennsylvania, as a home base. At the end of the season the franchise was canceled, the last time an NFL team failed.

The Pittsburgh Steelers abandoned the Single-Wing for the T-formation, the last pro team to do so.

The Detroit Lions won their first NFL championship in 17 years, defeating the Browns 17-7 in the title game, December 28.

**1953**

A Baltimore group headed by Carroll Rosenbloom was granted a franchise and was awarded the holdings of the defunct Dallas organization, January 23. The team, named the Colts, put together the largest trade in league history, acquiring 10 players from Cleveland in exchange for five.

The names of the American and National conferences were changed to the Eastern and Western conferences, January 24.

Jim Thorpe died, March 28.

Mickey McBride, founder of the Cleveland Browns, sold the franchise to a syndicate headed by Dave R. Jones, June 10.

The NFL policy of blacking out home games was upheld by Judge Allan K. Grim of the U.S. District Court in Philadelphia, November 12.

The Lions again defeated the Browns in the NFL Championship Game, winning 17-16, December 27.

**1954**

The Canadian Football League began a series of raids on NFL teams, signing quarterback Eddie LeBaron and defensive end Gene Brito of Washington and defensive tackle Arnie Weinmeister of the Giants, among others.

Fullback Joe Perry of the 49ers became the first player in league history to gain 1,000 yards rushing in consecutive seasons.

Cleveland defeated Detroit 56-10 in the NFL Championship Game, December 26.

**1955**

The sudden-death overtime rule was used for the first time in a preseason game between the Rams and Giants at Portland, Oregon, August 28. The Rams won 23-17 three minutes into overtime.

A rule change declared the ball dead immediately if the ball carrier touched the ground with any part of his body except his hands or feet while in the grasp of an opponent.

The Baltimore Colts made an 80-cent phone call to Johnny Unitas and signed him as a free agent. Another quarterback, Otto Graham, played his last game as the Browns defeated the Rams 38-14 in the NFL Championship Game, December 26. Graham had quarterbacked the Browns to 10 championship-game appearances in 10 years.

NBC replaced DuMont as the network for the title game, paying a rights fee of $100,000.

**1956**

The NFL Players Association was founded.

Grabbing an opponent's facemask (other than the ball carrier) was made illegal. Using radio receivers to communicate with players on the field was prohibited. A natural leather ball with white end stripes replaced the white ball with black stripes for night games.

The Giants moved from the Polo Grounds to Yankee Stadium.

Halas retired as coach of the Bears, and was replaced by Paddy Driscoll.

CBS became the first network to broadcast some NFL regular-season games to selected television markets across the nation.

The Giants routed the Bears 47-7 in the NFL Championship Game, December 30.

**1957**

Pete Rozelle was named general manager of the Rams. Anthony J. Morabito, founder and co-owner of the 49ers, died of a heart attack during a game against the Bears at Kezar Stadium, October 28. An NFL-record crowd of 102,368 saw the 49ers-Rams game at the Los Angeles Memorial Coliseum, November 10.

The Lions came from 20 points down to post a 31-27 playoff victory over the 49ers, December 22. Detroit defeated Cleveland 59-14 in the NFL Championship Game, December 29.

**1958**

The bonus selection in the draft was eliminated, January 29. The last selection was quarterback King Hill of Rice by the Chicago Cardinals.

Halas reinstated himself as coach of the Bears.

Jim Brown of Cleveland gained an NFL-record 1,527 yards rushing. In a divisional playoff game, the Giants held Brown to eight yards and defeated Cleveland 10-0.

Baltimore, coached by Weeb Ewbank, defeated the Giants 23-17 in the first sudden-death overtime in an NFL Championship Game, December 28. The game ended when Colts fullback Alan Ameche scored on a one-yard touchdown run after 8:15 of overtime.

**1959**

Vince Lombardi was named head coach of the Green Bay Packers, January 28. Tim Mara, the co-founder of the Giants, died, February 17.

Lamar Hunt of Dallas announced his intentions to form a second pro football league. The first meeting was held in Chicago, August 14, and consisted of Hunt representing Dallas; Bob Howsam, Denver; K.S. (Bud) Adams, Houston; Barron Hilton, Los Angeles; Max Winter and Bill Boyer, Minneapolis; and Harry Wismer, New York City. They made plans to begin play in 1960.

The new league was named the American Football League, August 22. Buffalo, owned by Ralph Wilson, became the seventh franchise, October 28. Boston, owned by William H. Sullivan, became the eighth team, November 22. The first AFL draft, lasting 33 rounds, was held, November 22. Joe Foss was named AFL Commissioner, November 30. An additional draft of 20 rounds was held by the AFL, December 2.

NFL Commissioner Bert Bell died of a heart attack suffered at Franklin Field, Philadelphia, during the last two minutes of a game between the Eagles and the Steelers, October 11. Treasurer Austin Gunsel was named president in the office of the commissioner, October 14.

The Colts again defeated the Giants in the NFL Championship Game, 31-16, December 27.

**1960**

Pete Rozelle was elected NFL Commissioner as a compromise choice on the twenty-third ballot, January 26. Rozelle moved the league offices to New York City.

Hunt was elected AFL president for

1960, January 26. Minneapolis withdrew from the AFL, January 27, and the same ownership was given an NFL franchise for Minnesota (to start in 1961), January 28. Dallas received an NFL franchise for 1960, January 28. Oakland received an AFL franchise, January 30.

The AFL adopted the two-point option on points after touchdown, January 28. A no-tampering verbal pact, relative to players' contracts, was agreed to between the NFL and AFL, February 9.

The NFL owners voted to allow the transfer of the Chicago Cardinals to St. Louis, March 13.

The AFL signed a five-year television contract with ABC, June 9.

The Boston Patriots defeated the Buffalo Bills 28-7 before 16,000 at Buffalo in the first AFL preseason game, July 30. The Denver Broncos defeated the Patriots 13-10 before 21,597 at Boston in the first AFL regular-season game, September 9.

Philadelphia defeated Green Bay 17-13 in the NFL Championship Game, December 26.

**1961**

The Houston Oilers defeated the Los Angeles Chargers 24-16 before 32,183 in the first AFL Championship Game, January 1.

Detroit defeated Cleveland 17-16 in the first Playoff Bowl, or Bert Bell Benefit Bowl, between second-place teams in each conference in Miami, January 7.

End Willard Dewveall of the Bears played out his option and joined the Oilers, becoming the first player to move deliberately from one league to the other, January 14.

Ed McGah, Wayne Valley, and Robert Osborne bought out their partners in the ownership of the Raiders, January 17. The Chargers were transferred to San Diego, February 10. Dave R. Jones sold the Browns to a group headed by Arthur B. Modell, March 22. The Howsam brothers sold the Broncos to a group headed by Calvin Kunz and Gerry Phipps, May 26.

NBC was awarded a two-year contract for radio and television rights to the NFL Championship Game for $615,000 annually, $300,000 of which was to go directly into the NFL Player Benefit Plan, April 5.

Canton, Ohio, where the league that became the NFL was formed in 1920, was chosen as the site of the Pro Football Hall of Fame, April 27. Dick McCann, a former Redskins executive, was named executive director.

A bill legalizing single-network television contracts by professional sports leagues was introduced in Congress by Representative Emanuel Celler. It passed the House and Senate and was signed into law by President John F. Kennedy, September 30.

Houston defeated San Diego 10-3 for the AFL championship, December 24. Green Bay won its first NFL championship since 1944, defeating the New York Giants 37-0, December 31.

**1962**

The Western Division defeated the Eastern Division 47-27 in the first AFL All-Star Game, played before 20,973 in San Diego, January 7.

Both leagues prohibited grabbing any player's facemask. The AFL voted to make the scoreboard clock the official timer of the game.

The NFL entered into a single-network agreement with CBS for telecasting all regular-season games for $4.65 million annually, January 10.

Judge Roszel Thompson of the U.S. District Court in Baltimore ruled against the AFL in its antitrust suit against the NFL, May 21. The AFL had charged the NFL with monopoly and conspiracy in areas of expansion, television, and player signings. The case lasted two and a half years, the trial two months.

McGah and Valley acquired controlling interest in the Raiders, May 24. The AFL assumed financial responsibility for the New York Titans, November 8. With Commissioner Rozelle as referee, Daniel F. Reeves regained the ownership of the Rams, outbidding his partners in sealed-envelope bidding for the team, November 27.

The Dallas Texans defeated the Oilers 20-17 for the AFL championship at Houston after 17 minutes, 54 seconds of overtime on a 25-yard field goal by Tommy Brooker, December 23. The game lasted a record 77 minutes, 54 seconds.

Judge Edward Weinfeld of the U.S. District Court in New York City upheld the legality of the NFL's television blackout within a 75-mile radius of home games and denied an injunction that would have forced the championship game between the Giants and the Packers to be televised in the New York City area, December 28. The Packers beat the Giants 16-7 for the NFL title, December 30.

**1963**

The Dallas Texans transferred to Kansas City, becoming the Chiefs, February 8. The New York Titans were sold to a five-man syndicate headed by David (Sonny) Werblin, March 28. Weeb Ewbank became the Titans' new head coach and the team's name was changed to the Jets, April 15. They began play in Shea Stadium.

NFL Properties, Inc., was founded to serve as the licensing arm of the NFL.

Rozelle indefinitely suspended Green Bay halfback Paul Hornung and Detroit defensive tackle Alex Karras for placing bets on their own teams and on other NFL games; he also fined five other Detroit players $2,000 each for betting on one game in which they did not participate, and the Detroit Lions Football Company $2,000 on each of two counts for failure to report information promptly and for lack of sideline supervision.

Paul Brown, head coach of the Browns since their inception, was fired and replaced by Blanton Collier. Don Shula replaced Weeb Ewbank as head coach of the Colts.

The AFL allowed the Jets and Raiders to select players from other franchises in hopes of giving the league more competitive balance, May 11.

NBC was awarded exclusive network broadcasting rights for the 1963 AFL Championship Game for $926,000, May 23.

The Pro Football Hall of Fame was dedicated at Canton, Ohio, September 7.

The U.S. Fourth Circuit Court of Appeals reaffirmed the lower court's finding for the NFL in the $10-million suit brought by the AFL, ending three and a half years of litigation, November 21.

Jim Brown of Cleveland rushed for an NFL single-season record 1,863 yards.

Boston defeated Buffalo 26-8 in the first divisional playoff game in AFL history, December 28.

The Bears defeated the Giants 14-10 in the NFL Championship Game, a record sixth and last title for Halas in his thirty-sixth season as the Bears' coach, December 29.

**1964**

The Chargers defeated the Patriots 51-10 in the AFL Championship Game, January 5.

William Clay Ford, the Lions' president since 1961, purchased the team, January 10. A group representing the late James P. Clark sold the Eagles to a group headed by Jerry Wolman, January 21. Carroll Rosenbloom, the majority owner of the Colts since 1953, acquired complete ownership of the team, January 23.

The AFL signed a five-year, $36-million television contract with NBC to begin with the 1965 season, January 29.

Commissioner Rozelle negotiated an agreement on behalf of the NFL clubs to purchase Ed Sabol's Blair Motion Pictures, which was renamed NFL Films, March 5.

Hornung and Karras were reinstated by Rozelle, March 16.

CBS submitted the winning bid of $14.1 million per year for the NFL regular-season television rights for 1964 and 1965, January 24. CBS acquired the rights to the championship games for 1964 and 1965 for $1.8 million per game, April 17.

Pete Gogolak of Cornell signed a contract with Buffalo, becoming the first soccer-style kicker in pro football.

Buffalo defeated San Diego 20-7 in the AFL Championship Game, December 26. Cleveland defeated Baltimore 27-0 in the NFL Championship Game, December 27.

**1965**

The NFL teams pledged not to sign college seniors until completion of all their games, including bowl games, and empowered the Commissioner to discipline the clubs up to as much as the loss of an entire draft list for a violation of the pledge, February 15.

The NFL added a sixth official, the line judge, February 19. The color of the officials' penalty flags was changed from white to bright gold, April 5.

Atlanta was awarded an NFL franchise for 1966, with Rankin Smith, Sr., as owner, June 30. Miami was awarded an AFL franchise for 1966, with Joe Robbie and Danny Thomas as owners, August 16.

Green Bay defeated Baltimore 13-10 in sudden-death overtime in a Western Conference playoff game. Don Chandler kicked a 25-yard field goal for the Packers after 13 minutes, 39 seconds of overtime, December 26. The Packers then defeated the Browns 23-12 in the NFL Championship Game, January 2.

In the AFL Championship Game, the Bills again defeated the Chargers, 23-0, December 26.

CBS acquired the rights to the NFL regular-season games in 1966 and 1967, with an option for 1968, for $18.8 million per year, December 29.

**1966**

The AFL-NFL war reached its peak, as the leagues spent a combined $7 million to sign their 1966 draft choices. The NFL signed 75 percent of its 232 draftees, the AFL 46 percent of its 181. Of the 111 common draft choices, 79 signed with the NFL, 28 with the AFL, and 4 went unsigned.

The rights to the 1966 and 1967 NFL Championship Games were sold to CBS for $2 million per game, February 14.

Foss resigned as AFL Commissioner, April 7. Al Davis, the head coach and general manager of the Raiders, was named to replace him, April 8.

Goal posts offset from the goal line, painted bright yellow, and with uprights 20 feet above the cross-bar were made standard in the NFL, May 16.

A series of secret meetings regarding a possible AFL-NFL merger were held in the spring between Hunt of Kansas City and Tex Schramm of Dallas. Rozelle announced the merger, June 8. Under the agreement, the two leagues would combine to form an expanded league with 24 teams, to be increased to 26 in 1968 and to 28 by 1970 or soon thereafter. All existing franchises would be retained, and no franchises would be transferred outside their metropolitan areas. While maintaining separate schedules through 1969, the leagues agreed to play an annual AFL-NFL World Championship Game beginning in January, 1967, and to hold a combined draft, also beginning in 1967. Preseason games would be held between teams of each league starting in 1967. Official regular-season play would start in 1970 when the two leagues would officially merge to form one league with two conferences. Rozelle was named Commissioner of the expanded league setup.

Davis rejoined the Raiders, and Milt Woodard was named president of the AFL, July 25.

The St. Louis Cardinals moved into newly constructed Busch Memorial Stadium.

Barron Hilton sold the Chargers to a group headed by Eugene Klein and Sam Schulman, August 25.

Congress approved the AFL-NFL merger, passing legislation exempting the agreement itself from antitrust action, October 21.

New Orleans was awarded an NFL franchise to begin play in 1967, November 1. John Mecom, Jr., of Houston was designated majority stockholder and president of the franchise, December 15.

The NFL was realigned for the 1967-69 seasons into the Capitol and Century Divisions in the Eastern Conference and the Central and Coastal Divisions in the Western Conference, December 2. New Orleans and the New York Giants agreed to switch divisions in 1968 and return to the 1967 alignment in 1969.

The rights to the Super Bowl for four years were sold to CBS and NBC for $9.5 million, December 13.

**1967**

Green Bay earned the right to represent the NFL in the first AFL-NFL World Championship Game by defeating Dallas 34-27, January 1. The same day, Kansas City defeated Buffalo 31-7 to represent the AFL. The Packers defeated the Chiefs 35-10 before 61,946 fans at the Los Angeles Memorial Coliseum in the first game between AFL and NFL teams, January 15. The winning players' share for the Packers was $15,000 each, and the losing players' share for the Chiefs was $7,500 each. The game was televised by both CBS and NBC.

The "sling-shot" goal post and a six-foot-wide border around the field were made standard in the NFL, February 22.

Baltimore made Bubba Smith, a Michigan State defensive lineman, the first choice in the first combined AFL-NFL draft, March 14.

The AFL awarded a franchise to begin play in 1968 to Cincinnati, May 24. A group with Paul Brown as part owner, general manager, and head coach, was awarded the Cincinnati franchise, September 27.

Arthur B. Modell, the president of the Cleveland Browns, was elected president of the NFL, May 28.

An AFL team defeated an NFL team for the first time, when Denver beat Detroit 13-7 in a preseason game, August 5.

Green Bay defeated Dallas 21-17 for the NFL championship on a last-minute 1-yard quarterback sneak by Bart Starr in 13-below-zero temperature at Green Bay, December 31. The same day, Oakland defeated Houston 40-7 for the AFL championship.

**1968**

Green Bay defeated Oakland 33-14 in Super Bowl II at Miami, January 14. The game had the first $3-million gate in pro football history.

Vince Lombardi resigned as head coach of the Packers, but remained as general manager, January 28.

Werblin sold his shares in the Jets to his partners Don Lillis, Leon Hess, Townsend Martin, and Phil Iselin, May 21. Lillis assumed the presidency of the club, but then died July 23. Iselin was appointed president, August 6.

Halas retired for the fourth and last time as head coach of the Bears, May 27.

The Oilers left Rice Stadium for the Astrodome and became the first NFL team to play its home games in a domed stadium.

The movie "Heidi" became a footnote in sports history when NBC didn't show the last 1:05 of the Jets-Raiders game in order to permit the children's special to begin on time. The Raiders scored two touchdowns in the last 42 seconds to win 43-32, November 17.

Ewbank became the first coach to win titles in both the NFL and AFL when his Jets defeated the Raiders 27-23 for the AFL championship, December 29. The same day, Baltimore defeated Cleveland 34-0.

**1969**

The AFL established a playoff format for the 1969 season, with the winner in one division playing the runner-up in the other, January 11.

An AFL team won the Super Bowl for the first time, as the Jets defeated the Colts 16-7 at Miami, January 12 in Super Bowl III. The title Super Bowl was recognized by the NFL for the first time.

Vince Lombardi became part owner, executive vice-president, and head coach of the Washington Redskins, February 7.

Wolman sold the Eagles to Leonard Tose, May 1.

Baltimore, Cleveland, and Pittsburgh agreed to join the AFL teams to form the 13-team American Football Conference of the NFL in 1970, May 17. The NFL also agreed on a playoff format that would include one "wild-card" team per conference—the second-place team with the best record.

Monday Night Football was signed for 1970. ABC acquired the rights to televise 13 NFL regular-season Monday night games in 1970, 1971, and 1972.

George Preston Marshall, president emeritus of the Redskins, died at 72, August 9.

The NFL marked its fiftieth year by the wearing of a special patch by each of the 16 teams.

**1970**

Kansas City defeated Minnesota 23-7 in Super Bowl IV at New Orleans, January 11. The gross receipts of approximately $3.8 million were the largest ever for a one-day sports event.

Four-year television contracts, under which CBS would televise all NFC games and NBC all AFC games (except Monday night games) and the two would divide televising the Super Bowl and AFC-NFC Pro Bowl games, were announced, January 26.

Art Modell resigned as president of the NFL, March 12. Milt Woodard resigned as president of the AFL, March 13. Lamar Hunt was elected president of the AFC and George Halas was elected president of the NFC, March 19.

The merged 26-team league adopted rules changes putting names on the backs of players' jerseys, making a point after touchdown worth only one point, and making the scoreboard clock the official timing device of the game, March 18.

The Players Negotiating Committee and the NFL Players Association announced a four-year agreement guaranteeing approximately $4,535,000 annually to player pension and insurance benefits, August 3. The owners also agreed to contribute $250,000 annually to improve or implement items such as disability payments, widows' benefits, maternity benefits, and dental benefits. The agreement also provided for increased preseason game and per diem payments, averaging approximately $2.6 million annually.

The Pittsburgh Steelers moved into Three Rivers Stadium. The Cincinnati Bengals moved to Riverfront Stadium.

Lombardi died of cancer at 57, September 3.

Tom Dempsey of New Orleans kicked a game-winning NFL-record 63-yard field goal against Detroit, November 8.

**1971**

Baltimore defeated Dallas 16-13 on Jim O'Brien's 32-yard field goal with five seconds to go in Super Bowl V at Miami, January 17. The NBC telecast was viewed in an estimated 23,980,000 homes, the largest audience ever for a one-day sports event.

The NFC defeated the AFC 27-6 in the first AFC-NFC Pro Bowl at Los Angeles, January 24.

The Boston Patriots changed their name to the New England Patriots, March 25. Their new stadium, Schaefer Stadium, was dedicated in a 20-14 preseason victory over the Giants.

The Philadelphia Eagles left Franklin Field and played their games at the new Veterans Stadium.

The San Francisco 49ers left Kezar Stadium and moved their games to Candlestick Park.

Daniel F. Reeves, the president and general manager of the Rams, died at 58, April 15.

The Dallas Cowboys moved from the Cotton Bowl into their new home, Texas Stadium, October 24.

Miami defeated Kansas City 27-24 in sudden-death overtime in an AFC Divisional Playoff Game, December 25. Garo Yepremian kicked a 37-yard field goal for the Dolphins after 22 minutes, 40 seconds of overtime, as the game lasted 82 minutes, 40 seconds overall, making it the longest game in history.

**1972**

Dallas defeated Miami 24-3 in Super Bowl VI at New Orleans, January 16. The CBS telecast was viewed in an estimated 27,450,000 homes, the top-rated one-day telecast ever.

The inbounds lines or hashmarks were moved nearer the center of the field, 23 yards, 1 foot, 9 inches from the sidelines, March 23. The method of determining won-lost percentage in standings changed. Tie games, previously not counted in the standings, were made equal to a half-game won and a half-game lost, May 24.

Robert Irsay purchased the Los Angeles Rams and transferred ownership of the club to Carroll Rosenbloom in exchange for the Baltimore Colts, July 13.

William V. Bidwill purchased the stock of his brother Charles (Stormy) Bidwill to become the sole owner of the St. Louis Cardinals, September 2.

The National District Attorneys Association endorsed the position of professional leagues in opposing proposed legalization of gambling on professional team sports, September 28.

Franco Harris's "Immaculate Reception" gave the Steelers their first postseason win ever, 13-7 over the Raiders, December 23.

**1973**

Rozelle announced that all Super Bowl VII tickets were sold and that the game would be telecast in Los Angeles, the site of the game, on an experimental basis, January 3.

Miami defeated Washington 14-7 in Super Bowl VII at Los Angeles, completing a 17-0 season, the first perfect-record regular-season and post-season mark in NFL history, January 14. The NBC telecast was viewed by approximately 75 million people.

The AFC defeated the NFC 33-28 in the Pro Bowl in Dallas, the first time since 1942 that the game was played outside Los Angeles, January 21.

A jersey numbering system was adopted, April 5: 1-19 for quarterbacks and specialists, 20-49 for running backs and defensive backs, 50-59 for centers and linebackers, 60-79 for defensive linemen and interior offensive linemen other than centers, and 80-89 for wide receivers and tight ends. Players who had been in the NFL in 1972 could continue to use old numbers.

NFL Charities, a nonprofit organization, was created to derive an income from monies generated from NFL Properties' licensing of NFL trademarks and team names, June 26. NFL Charities was set up to support education and charitable activities and to supply economic support to persons formerly associated with professional football who were no longer able to support themselves.

Congress adopted experimental legislation (for three years) requiring any NFL game that had been declared a sellout 72 hours prior to kickoff to be made available for local televising, September 14. The legislation provided for an annual review to be made by the Federal Communications Commission.

The Buffalo Bills moved their home games from War Memorial Stadium to Rich Stadium in nearby Orchard Park.

The Giants tied the Eagles 23-23 in the final game in Yankee Stadium, September 23. The Giants played the rest of their home games at the Yale Bowl in New Haven, Connecticut.

A rival league, the World Football League, was formed and was reported in operation, October 2. It had plans to start play in 1974.

O.J. Simpson of Buffalo became the first player to rush for more than 2,000 yards in a season, gaining 2,003.

**1974**

Miami defeated Minnesota 24-7 in Super Bowl VIII at Houston, the second consecutive Super Bowl championship for the Dolphins, January 13. The CBS telecast was viewed by approximately 75 million people.

Rozelle was given a 10-year contract effective January 1, 1973, February 27.

Tampa Bay was awarded a franchise to begin operation in 1976, April 24.

Sweeping rules changes were adopted to add action and tempo to games: one sudden-death overtime period was added for preseason and regular-season games; the goal posts were moved from the goal line to the end lines; kickoffs were moved from the 40- to the 35-yard line; after missed field goals from beyond the 20, the ball was to be returned to the line of scrimmage; restrictions were placed on members of the punting team to open up return possibilities; roll-blocking and cutting of wide receivers was eliminated; the extent of downfield contact a defender could have with an eligible receiver was restricted; the penalties for offensive holding, illegal use of the hands, and tripping were reduced from 15 to 10 yards; wide receivers blocking back toward the ball within three yards of the line of scrimmage were prevented from blocking below the waist, April 25.

The Toronto Northmen of the WFL signed Larry Csonka, Jim Kiick, and Paul Warfield of Miami, March 31.

Seattle was awarded an NFL franchise to begin play in 1976, June 4. Lloyd W. Nordstrom, president of the Seattle Seahawks, and Hugh Culverhouse, president of the Tampa Bay Buccaneers, signed franchise agreements, December 5.

The Birmingham Americans defeated the Florida Blazers 22-21 in the WFL World Bowl, winning the league championship, December 5.

**1975**
Pittsburgh defeated Minnesota 16-6 in Super Bowl IX at New Orleans, the Steelers' first championship since entering the NFL in 1933. The NBC telecast was viewed by approximately 78 million people.

The divisional winners with the highest won-loss percentage were made the home team for the divisional playoffs, and the surviving winners with the highest percentage made home teams for the championship games, June 26.

Referees were equipped with wireless microphones for all preseason, regular-season, and playoff games.

The Lions moved to the new Pontiac Silverdome. The Giants played their home games in Shea Stadium. The Saints moved into the Louisiana Superdome.

The World Football League folded, October 22.

**1976**
Pittsburgh defeated Dallas 21-17 in Super Bowl X in Miami. The Steelers joined Green Bay and Miami as the only teams to win two Super Bowls; the Cowboys became the first wild-card team to play in the Super Bowl. The CBS telecast was viewed by an estimated 80 million people, the largest television audience in history.

Lloyd Nordstrom, the president of the Seahawks, died at 66, January 20. His brother Elmer succeeded him as majority representative of the team.

The owners awarded Super Bowl XII, to be played on January 15, 1978, to New Orleans. They also adopted the use of two 30-second clocks for all games, visible to both players and fans to note the official time between the ready-for-play signal and snap of the ball, March 16.

A veteran player allocation was held to stock the Seattle and Tampa Bay franchises with 39 players each, March 30-31. In the college draft, Seattle and Tampa Bay each received eight extra choices, April 8-9.

The Giants moved into new Giants Stadium in East Rutherford, New Jersey.

The Steelers defeated the College All-Stars in a storm-shortened Chicago College All-Star Game, the last of the series, July 23. St. Louis defeated San Diego 20-10 in a preseason game before 38,000 in Korakuen Stadium, Tokyo, in the first NFL game outside of North America, August 16.

**1977**
Oakland defeated Minnesota 32-14 before a record crowd of 100,421 in Super Bowl XI at Pasadena, January 9. The paid attendance was a pro record 103,438. The NBC telecast was viewed by 81.9 million people, the largest ever to view a sports event. The victory was the fifth consecutive for the AFC in the Super Bowl.

The NFL Players Association and the NFL Management Council ratified a collective bargaining agreement extending until 1982, covering five football seasons while continuing the pension plan—including years 1974, 1975, and 1976—with contributions totaling more than $55 million. The total cost of the agreement was estimated at $107 million. The agreement called for a college draft at least through 1986; contained a no-strike, no-suit clause; established a 43-man active player limit; reduced pension vesting to four years; provided for increases in minimum salaries and preseason and postseason pay; improved insurance, medical, and dental benefits; modified previous practices in player movement and control; and reaffirmed the NFL Commissioner's disciplinary authority. Additionally, the agreement called for the NFL member clubs to make payments totaling $16 million the next 10 years to settle various legal disputes, February 25.

The San Francisco 49ers were sold to Edward J. DeBartolo, Jr., March 28.

A 16-game regular season, 4-game preseason was adopted to begin in 1978, March 29. A second wild-card team was adopted for the playoffs beginning in 1978, with the wild-card teams to play each other and the winners advancing to a round of eight postseason series.

The Seahawks were permanently aligned in the AFC Western Division and the Buccaneers in the NFC Central Division, March 31.

The owners awarded Super Bowl XIII, to be played on January 21, 1979, to Miami, to be played in the Orange Bowl; Super Bowl XIV, to be played January 20, 1980, was awarded to Pasadena, to be played in the Rose Bowl, June 14.

Rules changes were adopted to open up the passing game and to cut down on injuries. Defenders were permitted to make contact with eligible receivers only once; the head slap was outlawed; offensive linemen were prohibited from thrusting their hands to an opponent's neck, face, or head; and wide receivers were prohibited from clipping, even in the legal clipping zone.

Rozelle negotiated contracts with the three television networks to televise all NFL regular-season and postseason games, plus selected preseason games, for four years beginning with the 1978 season. ABC was awarded yearly rights to 16 Monday night games, four prime-time games, the AFC-NFC Pro Bowl, and the Hall of Fame games. CBS received the rights to all NFC regular-season and postseason games (except those in the ABC package) and to Super Bowls XIV and XVI. NBC received the rights to all AFC regular-season and postseason games (except those in the ABC package) and to Super Bowls XIII and XV. Industry sources considered it the largest single television package ever negotiated, October 12.

Chicago's Walter Payton set a single-game rushing record with 275 yards (40 carries) against Minnesota, November 20.

**1978**
Dallas defeated Denver 27-10 in Super Bowl XII, held indoors for the first time, at the Louisiana Superdome in New Orleans, January 15. The CBS telecast was viewed by more than 102 million people, meaning the game was watched by more viewers than any other show of any kind in the history of television. Dallas's victory was the first for the NFC in six years.

According to a Louis Harris Sports Survey, 70 percent of the nation's sports fans said they followed football, compared to 54 percent who followed baseball. Football increased its lead as the country's favorite, 26 percent to 16 percent for baseball, January 19.

A seventh official, the side judge, was added to the officiating crew, March 14.

The NFL continued a trend toward opening up the game. Rules changes permitted a defender to maintain contact with a receiver within five yards of the line of scrimmage, but restricted contact beyond that point. The pass-blocking rule was interpreted to permit the extending of arms and open hands, March 17.

A study on the use of instant replay as an officiating aid was made during seven nationally televised preseason games.

The NFL played for the first time in Mexico City, with the Saints defeating the Eagles 14-7 in a preseason game, August 5.

Bolstered by the expansion of the regular-season schedule from 14 to 16 weeks, NFL paid attendance exceeded 12 million (12,771,800) for the first time. The per-game average of 57,017 was the third-highest in league history and the most since 1973.

**1979**
Pittsburgh defeated Dallas 35-31 in Super Bowl XIII at Miami to become the first team ever to win three Super Bowls, January 21. The NBC telecast was viewed in 35,090,000 homes, by an estimated 96.6 million fans.

The owners awarded three future Super Bowl sites: Super Bowl XV to the Louisiana Superdome in New Orleans, to be played on January 25, 1981; Super Bowl XVI to the Pontiac Silverdome in Pontiac, Michigan, to be played on January 24, 1982; and Super Bowl XVII to Pasadena's Rose Bowl, to be played on January 30, 1983, March 13.

NFL rules changes emphasized additional player safety. The changes prohibited players on the receiving team from blocking below the waist during kickoffs, punts, and field-goal attempts; prohibited the wearing of torn or altered equipment and exposed pads that could be hazardous; extended the zone in which there could be no crackback blocks; and instructed officials to quickly whistle a play dead when a quarterback was clearly in the grasp of a tackler, March 16.

Rosenbloom, the president of the Rams, drowned at 72, April 2. His widow, Georgia, assumed control of the club.

**1980**
Pittsburgh defeated the Los Angeles Rams 31-19 in Super Bowl XIV at Pasadena to become the first team to win four Super Bowls, January 20. The game was viewed in a record 35,330,000 homes.

The AFC-NFC Pro Bowl, won 37-27 by the NFC, was played before 48,060 fans at Aloha Stadium in Honolulu, Hawaii. It was the first time in the 30-year history of the Pro Bowl that the game was played in a non-NFL city.

Rules changes placed greater restrictions on contact in the area of the head, neck, and face. Under the heading of "personal foul," players were prohibited from directly striking, swinging, or clubbing on the head, neck, or face. Starting in 1980, a penalty could be called for such contact whether or not the initial contact was made below the neck area.

CBS, with a record bid of $12 million, won the national radio rights to 26 NFL regular-season games and all 10 postseason games for the 1980-83 seasons.

The Los Angeles Rams moved their home games to Anaheim Stadium in nearby Orange County, California.

The Oakland Raiders joined the Los Angeles Coliseum Commission's antitrust suit against the NFL. The suit contended the league violated antitrust laws in declining to approve a proposed move by the Raiders from Oakland to Los Angeles.

NFL regular-season attendance of nearly 13.4 million set a record for the third year in a row. The average paid attendance for the 224-game 1980 regular season was 59,787, the highest in the league's 61-year history. NFL games in 1980 were played before 92.4 percent of total stadium capacity.

Television ratings in 1980 were the second-best in NFL history, trailing only the combined ratings of the 1976 season. All three networks posted gains, and NBC's 15.0 rating was its best ever. CBS and ABC had their best ratings since 1977, with 15.3 and 20.8 ratings, respectively. CBS Radio reported a record audience of 7 million for Monday night and special games.

**1981**

Oakland defeated Philadelphia 27-10 in Super Bowl XV at the Louisiana Superdome in New Orleans, to become the first wild-card team to win a Super Bowl, January 25.

Edgar F. Kaiser, Jr., purchased the Denver Broncos from Gerald and Allan Phipps, February 26.

The owners adopted a disaster plan for re-stocking a team should the club be involved in a fatal accident, March 20.

The owners awarded Super Bowl XVIII to Tampa, to be played in Tampa Stadium on January 22, 1984, June 3.

A CBS-New York Times poll showed that 48 percent of sports fans preferred football to 31 percent for baseball.

The NFL teams hosted 167 representatives from 44 predominantly black colleges during training camps for a total of 289 days. The program was adopted for renewal during each training camp period.

NFL regular-season attendance—13.6 million for an average of 60,745—set a record for the fourth year in a row. It also was the first time the per-game average exceeded 60,000. NFL games in 1981 were played before 93.8 percent of total stadium capacity.

ABC and CBS set all-time rating highs. ABC finished with a 21.7 rating and CBS with a 17.5 rating. NBC was down slightly to 13.9.

**1982**

San Francisco defeated Cincinnati 26-21 in Super Bowl XVI at the Pontiac Silverdome, in the first Super Bowl held in the North, January 24. The CBS telecast achieved the highest rating of any televised sports event ever, 49.1 with a 73.0 share. The game was viewed by a record 110.2 million fans. CBS Radio reported a record 14 million listeners for the game.

The NFL signed a five-year contract with the three television networks (ABC, CBS, and NBC) to televise all NFL regular-season and postseason games starting with the 1982 season.

The owners awarded the 1983, 1984, and 1985 AFC-NFC Pro Bowls to Honolulu's Aloha Stadium.

A jury ruled against the NFL in the antitrust trial brought by the Los Angeles Coliseum Commission and the Oakland Raiders, May 7. The verdict cleared the way for the Raiders to move to Los Angeles, where they defeated Green Bay 24-3 in their first preseason game, August 29.

The 1982 season was reduced from a 16-game schedule to nine as the result of a 57-day players' strike. The strike was called by the NFLPA at midnight on Monday, September 20, following the Green Bay at New York Giants game. Play resumed November 21-22 following ratification of the Collective Bargaining Agreement by NFL owners, November 17 in New York.

Under the Collective Bargaining Agreement, which was to run through the 1986 season, the NFL draft was extended through 1992 and the veteran free-agent system was left basically unchanged. A minimum salary schedule for years of experience was established; training camp and postseason pay were increased; players' medical, insurance, and retirement benefits were increased; and a severance-pay system was introduced to aid in career transition, a first in professional sports.

Despite the players' strike, the average paid attendance in 1982 was 58,472, the fifth-highest in league history.

The owners awarded the sites of two Super Bowls, December 14: Super Bowl XIX, to be played on January 20, 1985, to Stanford University Stadium in Stanford, California, with San Francisco as host team; and Super Bowl XX, to be played on January 26, 1986, to the Louisiana Superdome in New Orleans.

**1983**

Because of the shortened season, the NFL adopted a format of 16 teams competing in a Super Bowl Tournament for the 1982 playoffs. The NFC's number-one seed, Washington, defeated the AFC's number-two seed, Miami, 27-17 in Super Bowl XVII at the Rose Bowl in Pasadena, January 30.

Super Bowl XVII was the second-highest rated live television program of all time, giving the NFL a sweep of the top 10 live programs in television history. The game was viewed in more than 40 million homes, the largest ever for a live telecast.

Halas, the owner of the Bears and the last surviving member of the NFL's second organizational meeting, died at 88, October 31.

**1984**

The Los Angeles Raiders defeated Washington 38-9 in Super Bowl XVIII at Tampa Stadium, January 22. The game achieved a 46.4 rating and 71.0 share.

An 11-man group headed by H.R. (Bum) Bright purchased the Dallas Cowboys from Clint Murchison, Jr., March 20. Club president Tex Schramm was designated as managing general partner.

Patrick Bowlen purchased a majority interest in the Denver Broncos from Edgar Kaiser, Jr., March 21.

The Colts relocated to Indianapolis, March 28. Their new home became the Hoosier Dome.

The owners awarded two Super Bowl sites at their May 23-25 meetings: Super Bowl XXI, to be played on January 25, 1987, to the Rose Bowl in Pasadena; and Super Bowl XXII, to be played on January 31, 1988, to San Diego Jack Murphy Stadium.

The New York Jets moved their home games to Giants Stadium in East Rutherford, New Jersey.

Alex G. Spanos purchased a majority interest in the San Diego Chargers from Eugene V. Klein, August 28.

Houston defeated Pittsburgh 23-20 to mark the one-hundredth overtime game in regular-season play since overtime was adopted in 1974, December 2.

On the field, many all-time records were set: Dan Marino of Miami passed for 5,084 yards and 48 touchdowns; Eric Dickerson of the Los Angeles Rams rushed for 2,105 yards; Art Monk of Washington caught 106 passes; and Walter Payton of Chicago broke Jim Brown's career rushing mark, finishing the season with 13,309 yards.

According to a CBS Sports/*New York Times* survey, 53 percent of the nation's sports fans said they most enjoyed watching football, compared to 18 percent for baseball, December 2-4.

NFL paid attendance exceeded 13 million for the fifth consecutive complete regular season when 13,398,112, an average of 59,813, attended games. The figure was the second-highest in league history. Teams averaged 42.4 points per game, the second-highest total since the 1970 merger.

**1985**

San Francisco defeated Miami 38-16 in Super Bowl XIX at Stanford Stadium in Stanford, California, January 20. The game was viewed on television by more people than any other live event in history. President Ronald Reagan, who took his second oath of office before tossing the coin for the game, was one of 115,936,000 viewers. The game drew a 46.4 rating and a 63.0 share. In addition, 6 million people watched the Super Bowl in the United Kingdom and a similar number in Italy. Super Bowl XIX had a direct economic impact of $113.5 million on the San Francisco Bay area.

NBC Radio and the NFL entered into a two-year agreement granting NBC the radio rights to a 37-game package in each of the 1985-86 seasons, March 6. The package included 27 regular-season games and 10 postseason games.

The owners awarded two Super Bowl sites at their annual meeting, March 10-15: Super Bowl XXIII, to be played on January 22, 1989, to the proposed Dolphins Stadium in Miami; and Super Bowl XXIV, to be played on January 28, 1990, to the Louisiana Superdome in New Orleans.

Norman Braman, in partnership with Edward Leibowitz, bought the Philadelphia Eagles from Leonard Tose, April 29.

Bruce Smith, a Virginia Tech defensive lineman selected by Buffalo, was the first player chosen in the fiftieth NFL draft, April 30.

A group headed by Tom Benson, Jr., was approved to purchase the New Orleans Saints from John W. Mecom, Jr., June 3.

The NFL owners adopted a resolution calling for a series of overseas preseason games, beginning in 1986, with one game to be played in England/Europe and/or one game in Japan each year. The game would be a fifth preseason game for the clubs involved and all arrangements and selection of the clubs would be under the control of the Commissioner, May 23.

The league-wide conversion to videotape from movie film for coaching study was approved.

Commissioner Rozelle was authorized to extend the commitment to Honolulu's Aloha Stadium for the AFC-NFC Pro Bowl for 1988, 1989, and 1990, October 15.

The NFL set a single-weekend paid attendance record when 902,657 tickets were sold for the weekend of October 27-28.

A Louis Harris poll in December revealed that pro football remained the sport most followed by Americans. Fifty-nine percent of those surveyed followed pro football, compared with 54 percent who followed baseball.

The Chicago-Miami Monday game had the highest rating, 29.6, and share, 46.0, of any prime-time game in NFL history, December 2. The game was viewed in more than 25 million homes.

The NFL showed a ratings increase on all three networks for the season, gaining 4 percent on NBC, 10 on CBS, and 16 on ABC.

**1986**

Chicago defeated New England 46-10 in Super Bowl XX at the Louisiana Superdome, January 26. The Patriots had earned the right to play the Bears by becoming the first wild-card team to win three consecutive games on the road. The NBC telecast replaced the final episode of M*A*S*H as the most-viewed television program in history, with an audience of 127 million viewers, according to A.C. Nielsen figures. In addition to drawing a 48.3 rating and a 70 percent share in the United States, Super Bowl XX was televised to 59 foreign countries and beamed via satellite to the QE II. An estimated 300 million Chinese viewed a tape delay of the game in March. NBC Radio figures indicated an audience of 10 million for the game.

Super Bowl XX injected more than $100 million into the New Orleans-area economy, and fans spent $250 per day and a record $17.69 per person on game day.

The owners adopted limited use of instant replay as an officiating aid, prohibited players from wearing or otherwise displaying equipment, apparel, or other items that carry commercial names, names of organizations, or personal messages of any type, March 11.

After an 11-week trial, a jury in U.S. District Court in New York awarded the United States Football League one dollar in its $1.7 billion antitrust suit against the NFL. The jury rejected all of the USFL's television-related claims, which were the self-proclaimed heart of the USFL's case, July 29.

Chicago defeated Dallas 17-6 at Wembley Stadium in London in the first American Bowl. The game drew a sellout crowd of 82,699 and the NBC national telecast in this country produced a 12.4 rating and 36 percent share, making it the second-highest-rated daytime preseason game and highest daytime preseason television audience ever with 10.65-million viewers, August 3.

Monday Night Football became the longest-running prime-time series in the history of the ABC network.

Instant replay was used to reverse two plays in 31 preseason games. During the regular season, 374 plays were closely reviewed by replay officials, leading to 38 reversals in 224 games. Eighteen plays were closely reviewed by instant replay in 10 postseason games with three reversals.

**1987**

The New York Giants defeated Denver 39-20 in Super Bowl XXI and captured their first NFL title since 1956. The game, played in Pasadena's Rose Bowl, drew a sellout crowd of 101,063. According to A.C. Nielsen figures, the CBS broadcast of the game was viewed in the U.S. on television by 122.64-million people, making the telecast the second most-watched television show of all-time behind Super Bowl XX. The game was watched live or on tape in 55 foreign countries and NBC Radio's broadcast of the game was heard by a record 10.1 million people.

The NFL set an all-time paid attendance mark of 17,304,463 for all games, including preseason, regular-season, and postseason. Average regular-season game attendance (60,663) exceeded the 60,000 figure for only the second time in league history.

New three-year TV contracts with ABC, CBS, and NBC were announced for 1987-89 at the NFL annual meeting in Maui, Hawaii, March 15. Commissioner Rozelle and Broadcast Committee Chairman Art Modell also announced a three-year contract with ESPN to televise 13 prime-time games each season. The ESPN contract was the first with a cable network. However, NFL games on ESPN also were scheduled for regular television in the city of the visiting team and in the home city if the game was sold out 72 hours in advance.

Owners also voted to continue in effect for one year the instant replay system used during the 1986 season.

A special payment program was adopted to benefit nearly 1,000 former NFL players who participated in the League before the current Bert Bell NFL Pension Plan was created and made retroactive to the 1959 season. Players covered by the new program spent at least five years in the League and played all or part of their career prior to 1959. Each vested player would receive $60 per month for each year of service in the League for life.

Possible sites for Super Bowl XXV were reduced to five locations by the NFL Super Bowl XXV Site Selection Committee: Anaheim Stadium, Los Angeles Memorial Coliseum, Joe Robbie Stadium, San Diego Jack Murphy Stadium, and Tampa Stadium.

NFL and CBS Radio jointly announced agreement granting CBS the radio rights to a 40-game package in each of the next three NFL seasons, 1987-89, April 7.

NFL owners awarded Super Bowl XXV, to be played on January 27, 1991, to Tampa Stadium, May 20.

Over 400 former NFL players from the pre-1959 era received first payments from NFL owners, July 1.

The NFL's debut on ESPN produced the two highest-rated and most-watched sports programs in basic cable history. The Chicago at Miami game on August 16 drew an 8.9 rating in 3.81 million homes. Those records fell two weeks later when the Los Angeles Raiders at Dallas game achieved a 10.2 cable rating in 4.36 million homes.

Fifty-eight preseason games drew a record paid attendance of 3,116,870.

The 1987 season was reduced from a 16-game season to 15 as the result of a 24-day players' strike. The strike was called by the NFLPA on Tuesday, September 22, following the New England at New York Jets game. Games scheduled for the third weekend were canceled but the games of weeks four, five, and six were played with replacement teams. Striking players returned for the seventh week of the season, October 25.

In a three-team deal involving 10 players and/or draft choices, the Los Angeles Rams traded running back Eric Dickerson to the Indianapolis Colts for six draft choices and two players. Buffalo obtained the rights to linebacker Cornelius Bennett from Indianapolis, sending Greg Bell and three draft choices to the Rams. The Colts added Owen Gill and three draft choices of their own to complete the deal with the Rams, October 31.

The Chicago at Minnesota game became the highest-rated and most-watched sports program in basic cable history when it drew a 14.4 cable rating in 6.5 million homes, December 6.

Instant replay was used to reverse eight plays in 52 preseason games. During the strike-shortened 210-game regular season, 490 plays were closely reviewed by replay officials, leading to 57 reversals. Eighteen plays were closely reviewed by instant replay in 10 postseason games, with three reversals.

**1988**

Washington defeated Denver 42-10 in Super Bowl XXII to earn its second victory this decade in the NFL Championship Game. The game, played for the first time in San Diego Jack Murphy Stadium, drew a sellout crowd of 73,302. According to A.C. Nielsen figures, the ABC broadcast of the game was viewed in the U.S. on television by 115,000,000 people. The game was seen live or on tape in 60 foreign countries, including the People's Republic of China, and CBS's radio broadcast of the game was heard by 13.7 million people.

A total of 811 players shared in the postseason pool of $16.9 million, the most ever distributed in a single season.

In a unanimous 3-0 decision, the 2nd Circuit Court of Appeals in New York upheld the verdict of the jury that in July, 1986, had awarded the United States Football League one dollar in its $1.7 billion antitrust suit against the NFL. In a 91-page opinion, Judge Ralph K. Winter said the USFL sought through court decree the success it failed to gain among football fans, March 10.

By a 23-5 margin, owners voted to continue the instant replay system for the third consecutive season with the Instant Replay Official to be assigned to a regular seven-man, on-the-field crew. At the NFL annual meeting in Phoenix, Arizona, a 45-second clock was also approved to replace the 30-second clock. For a normal sequence of plays, the interval between plays was changed to 45 seconds from the time the ball is signaled dead until it is snapped on the succeeding play.

NFL owners approved the transfer of the Cardinals' franchise from St. Louis to Phoenix; approved two supplemental drafts each year—one prior to training camp and one prior to the regular season; and voted to initiate an annual series of games in Japan/Asia as early as the 1989 preseason, March 14-18.

The NFL Annual Selection Meeting returned to a separate two-day format and for the first time originated on a Sunday. ESPN drew a 3.6 rating during their seven-hour coverage of the draft, which was viewed in 1.6 million homes, April 24-25.

Art Rooney, founder and owner of the Steelers, died at 87, August 25.

Paid and average attendance of 934,271 and 66,734 at 14 games on October 16-17 set single weekend records.

Commissioner Rozelle announced that two teams would play a preseason game as part of the American Bowl series on August 6, 1989, in the Korakuen Tokyo Dome in Japan, December 16.

NFL regular-season paid attendance of 13,535,335 and the average of 60,427 was the third highest all-time. Buffalo set an NFL team single-season, in-house attendance mark of 622,793.

**1989**

San Francisco defeated Cincinnati 20-16 in Super Bowl XXIII. The game, played for the first time at Joe Robbie Stadium in Miami, was attended by a sellout crowd of 75,129. NBC's telecast of the game was watched by an estimated 110,780,000 viewers, according to A.C. Nielsen, making it the sixth most-watched program in television history. The game was seen live or on tape in 60 foreign countries, including an estimated 300 million in China. The CBS Radio broadcast of the game was heard by 11.2 million people.

Commissioner Rozelle announced his retirement, pending the naming of a successor, March 22 at the NFL annual meeting in Palm Desert, California.

Following the announcement, AFC president Lamar Hunt and NFC president Wellington Mara announced the formation of a six-man search committee composed of Art Modell, Robert Parins, Dan Rooney, and Ralph Wilson. Hunt and Mara served as co-chairmen.

By a 24-4 margin, owners voted to continue the instant replay system for the fourth straight season. A strengthened policy regarding anabolic steroids and masking agents was announced by Commissioner Rozelle. NFL clubs called for strong disciplinary measures in cases of feigned injuries and adopted a joint proposal by the Long-Range Planning and Finance committees regarding player personnel rules, March 19-23.

Two hundred twenty-nine unconditional free agents signed with new teams under management's Plan B system, April 1.

Jerry Jones purchased a majority interest in the Dallas Cowboys from H.R. (Bum) Bright, April 18.

Tex Schramm was named president of the new World League of American Football to work with a six-man committee of Dan Rooney, chairman; Norman Braman, Lamar Hunt, Victor Kiam, Mike Lynn, and Bill Walsh, April 18.

NFL and CBS Radio jointly announced agreement extending CBS's radio rights to an annual 40-game package through the 1994 season, April 18.

NFL owners awarded Super Bowl XXVI, to be played on January 26, 1992, to Minneapolis, May 24.

As of opening day, September 10, of the 229 Plan B free agents, 111 were active and 23 others were on teams' reserve lists. Ninety-two others were waived and three retired.

Art Shell was named head coach of the Los Angeles Raiders making him the NFL's first black head coach since Fritz Pollard coached the Akron Pros in 1921, October 3.

The site of the New England Patriots at San Francisco 49ers game scheduled for Candlestick Park on October 22 was switched to Stanford Stadium in the aftermath of the Bay Area Earthquake of October 17. The change was announced on October 19.

Paul Tagliabue became the seventh chief executive of the NFL on October 26 when he was chosen to succeed Commissioner Pete Rozelle on the sixth ballot of a three-day meeting in Cleveland, Ohio.

In all, 12 ballots were required to select Tagliabue. Two were conducted at a meeting in Chicago on July 6, and four at a meeting in Dallas on October 10-11. On the twelfth ballot, with Seattle absent, Tagliabue received more than the 19 affirmative votes required for election from among the 27 clubs present.

The transfer from Commissioner Rozelle to Commissioner Tagliabue took place at 12:01 A.M. on Sunday, November 5.

NFL Charities donated $1 million through United Way to benefit Bay Area earthquake victims, November 6.

NFL paid attendance of 17,399,538 was the highest total in league history. This included a total of 13,625,662 for an average of 60,829—both NFL records—for the 224-game regular season.

**1990**

San Francisco defeated Denver 55-10 in Super Bowl XXIV at the Louisiana Superdome, January 28. San Francisco joined Pittsburgh as the NFL's only teams to win four Super Bowls.

The NFL announced revisions in its

1990 draft eligibility rules. College juniors became eligible but must renounce their collegiate football eligibility before applying for the NFL Draft, February 16.

Commissioner Tagliabue announced NFL teams will play their 16-game schedule over 17 weeks in 1990 and 1991 and 16 games over 18 weeks in 1992 and 1993, February 27.

The NFL revised its playoff format to include two additional wild-card teams (one per conference).

Commissioner Tagliabue and Broadcast Committee Chairman Art Modell announced a four-year contract with Turner Broadcasting to televise nine Sunday-night games.

New four-year TV agreements were ratified for 1990-93 for ABC, CBS, NBC, ESPN, and TNT at the NFL annual meeting in Orlando, Florida, March 12. The contracts totaled $3.6 billion, the largest in TV history.

The NFL announced plans to expand its American Bowl series of preseason games. In addition to games in London and Tokyo, American Bowl games were scheduled for Berlin, Germany, and Montreal, Canada, in 1990.

For the fifth straight year, NFL owners voted to continue a limited system of Instant Replay. Beginning in 1990, the replay official will have a two-minute time limit to make a decision. The vote was 21-7, March 12.

Commissioner Tagliabue announced the formation of a Committee on Expansion and Realignment, March 13. He also named a Player Advisory Council, comprised of 12 former NFL players, March 14.

One-hundred eighty-four Plan B unconditional free agents signed with new teams, April 2.

Commissioner Tagliabue appointed Dr. John Lombardo as the League's Drug Advisor for Anabolic Steroids, April 25 and named Dr. Lawrence Brown as the League's Advisor for Drugs of Abuse, May 17.

NFL owners awarded Super Bowl XXVIII, to be played in 1994, to the proposed Georgia Dome, May 23.

Commissioner Tagliabue named NFL referee Jerry Seeman as NFL Director of Officiating, replacing Art McNally, who announced his retirement, July 12.

NFL International Week was celebrated with four preseason games in seven days in Tokyo, London, Berlin, and Montreal. More than 200,000 fans on three continents attended the four games, August 4-11.

Commissioner Tagliabue announced the NFL Teacher of the Month program in which the League furnishes grants and scholarships in recognition of teachers who provided a positive influence upon NFL players in elementary and secondary schools, September 20.

For the first time since 1957, every NFL club won at least one of its first four games, October 1.

NFL total paid attendance of 17,665,671 was the highest total in League history. The regular-season total paid attendance of 13,959,896 and average of 62,321 for 224 games were the highest ever, surpassing the previous records set in the 1989 season.

**1991**

The New York Giants defeated Buffalo 20-19 in Super Bowl XXV to capture their second title in five years. The game was played before a sellout crowd of 73,813 at Tampa Stadium and became the first Super Bowl decided by one point, January 26. The ABC broadcast of the game was seen by more than 112-million people in the United States and was seen live or taped in 60 other countries.

NFL playoff games earned the top television rating spot of the week for each week of the month-long playoffs, January 29.

A total of 693 players shared in the postseason pool of $14.9 million.

New York businessman Robert Tisch purchased a 50 percent interest in the New York Giants from Mrs. Helen Mara Nugent and her children, Tim Mara and Maura Mara Concannon, February 2.

Commissioner Tagliabue named Neil Austrian to the newly created position of President of the NFL to be chief operating officer for League-wide business and financial operations, February 27.

NFL clubs voted to continue a limited system of Instant Replay for the sixth consecutive year. The vote was 21-7, March 19.

The NFL launched the World League of American Football, the first sports league to operate on a weekly basis on two separate continents, March 23.

NFL Charities presented a $250,000 donation to the United Service Organization. The donation was the second largest single grant ever by NFL Charities, April 5.

Commissioner Tagliabue named Harold Henderson as Executive Vice President for Labor Relations and Chairman of the NFL Management Council Executive Committee, April 8.

Russell Maryland, a University of Miami defensive lineman, was selected by Dallas, becoming the first player chosen in the 1991 NFL draft, April 21.

NFL clubs approved a recommendation by the Expansion and Realignment Committee to add two teams for the 1994 season, resulting in six divisions of five teams each, May 22.

NFL clubs awarded Super Bowl XXIX, to be played on January 29, 1995, to Miami, May 23.

"NFL International Week" featured six 1990 playoff teams playing nationally televised games in London, Berlin, and Tokyo on July 28 and August 3-4. The games drew more than 150,000 fans.

Paul Brown, founder of the Cleveland Browns and Cincinnati Bengals, died at age 82, August 5.

NFL clubs approved a resolution establishing an international division, reporting to the President of the NFL. A three-year financial plan for the World League was approved by NFL clubs at a meeting in Dallas, October 23.

**1992**

The NFL agreed to provide a minimum of $2.5 million in financial support to the NFL Alumni Association and assistance to NFL Alumni-related programs. The agreement included contributions from NFL Charities to the Pre-59ers and Dire Need Programs for former players, January 25.

The Washington Redskins defeated the Buffalo Bills 37-24 in Super Bowl XXVI to capture their third world championship in 10 years, January 26. The game was played before a sellout crowd of 63,130 at the Hubert H. Humphrey Metrodome in Minneapolis and attracted the second largest television audience in Super Bowl history. The CBS broadcast was seen by more than 123 million people nationally, second only to the 127 million who viewed Super Bowl XX.

For the third consecutive season, NFL total paid attendance reached a record level. Total paid attendance was 17,752,139 for the 296 preseason, regular-season, and postseason games, February 3.

The use in officiating of a limited system of Instant Replay for a seventh consecutive year was not approved. The vote was 17-11 in favor of approval (21 votes were required), March 18.

Steve Emtman, a University of Washington defensive lineman, was selected by Indianapolis, becoming the first player chosen in the 1992 NFL draft, April 26.

St. Louis businessman James Orthwein purchased controlling interest in the New England Patriots from Victor Kiam, May 11.

In a Harris Poll taken during the NFL offseason, professional football again was declared the nation's most popular sport. Professional football finished atop similar surveys conducted by Harris in 1985 and 1989, May 23.

NFL clubs accepted the report of the Expansion Committee at a league meeting in Pasadena. The report names five cities as finalists for the two expansion teams—Baltimore, Charlotte, Jacksonville, Memphis, and St. Louis, May 19.

At a league meeting in Dallas, NFL clubs approved a proposal by the World League Board of Directors to restructure the World League and place future emphasis on its international success, September 17.

**1993**

The NFL and lawyers for the players announced a settlement of various lawsuits and an agreement on the terms of a seven-year deal that included a new player system to be in place through the 1999 season, January 6.

Commissioner Tagliabue announced the establishment of the "NFL World Partnership Program" to develop amateur football internationally through a series of clinics conducted by former NFL players and coaches, January 14.

As part of Super Bowl XXVII, the NFL announced the creation of the first NFL Youth Education Town, a facility located in south central Los Angeles for inner city youth, January 25.

The Dallas Cowboys defeated the Buffalo Bills 52-17 in Super Bowl XXVII to capture their first NFL title since 1978. The game was played before a crowd of 98,374 at the Rose Bowl in Pasadena, California. The NBC broadcast of the game was the most watched program in television history and was seen by 133,400,000 people in the United States. The game also was seen live or taped in 101 other countries. The rating for the game was 45.1, the tenth highest for any televised sports event, January 31.

A total of 695 players shared in the postseason pool of $14.9 million, February 15.

For the fourth consecutive season, the NFL total paid attendance reached a record level. Total paid attendance was 17,784,354 for the 296 preseason, regular-season, and postseason games, March 4.

NFL clubs awarded Super Bowl XXX to the city of Phoenix, to be played on January 28, 1996, at Sun Devil Stadium, March 23.

Drew Bledsoe, a quarterback from Washington State, was selected by New England, becoming the first player chosen in the 1993 NFL draft, April 25.

The NFL and the NFL Players Association officially signed a 7-year Collective Bargaining Agreement in Washington, D.C., which guarantees more than $1 billion in pension, health, and post-career benefits for current and retired players—the most extensive benefits plan in pro sports. It was the NFL's first CBA since the 1982 agreement expired in 1987, June 29.

Ron Bernard was named president of NFL Enterprises, a newly formed division of the NFL responsible for NFL Films, home video, and special domestic and international television programming, August 19.

NFL announced plans to allow fans, for the first time ever, to join players and coaches in selecting the annual AFC and NFC Pro Bowl teams, October 12.

NFL clubs unanimously awarded the league's twenty-ninth franchise to the Carolina Panthers at a meeting in Chicago. NFL clubs also awarded Super Bowl XXXI to New Orleans and Super Bowl XXXII to San Diego, October 26.

At the same meeting in Chicago, NFL clubs approved a plan to form a European league with joint venture partners, October 27.

Don Shula became the winningest coach in NFL history when Miami beat Philadelphia to give Shula his 325th victory, one more than George Halas, November 14.

NFL clubs awarded the league's thirtieth franchise to the Jacksonville Jaguars at a meeting in Chicago, November 30.

The NFL announced new 4-year television agreements with ABC, ESPN, TNT, and NFL newcomer FOX, which took over the NFC package from CBS, December 18.

The NFL completed its new TV agreements by announcing that NBC would retain the rights to the AFC package, December 20.

**1994**

The NFL announced that a regular-season paid attendance record was set in 1993. Attendance averaged 62,354, topping the previous record of 62,321 set in 1990, January 6.

The Dallas Cowboys defeated the Buffalo Bills 30-13 in Super Bowl

XXVIII to become the fifth team to win back-to-back Super Bowl titles. The game was viewed by the largest U.S. audience in television history—134.8 million people. The game's 45.5 rating was the highest for a Super Bowl since 1987 and the tenth highest-rated Super Bowl ever, January 30.

NFL clubs unanimously approved the transfer of the New England Patriots from James Orthwein to Robert Kraft at a meeting in Orlando, February 22.

In an effort to increase offensive production, NFL clubs at the league's annual meeting in Orlando adopted a package of changes, including modifications in line play, chucking rules, and the roughing-the-passer rule, plus the adoption of the two-point conversion and moving the spot of the kickoff back to the 30-yard line, March 22.

NFL clubs approved the transfer of the majority interest in the Miami Dolphins from the Robbie family to H. Wayne Huizenga, March 23.

The NFL and FOX announced the formation of a joint venture to create a six-team World League to begin play in Europe in April, 1995, March 23.

The NFL announced a total paid attendance record for the fifth consecutive year, with 17,951,831 in paid attendance for all 1993 games, March 23.

Dan Wilkinson, a defensive tackle from Ohio State, was selected by Cincinnati as the first overall selection in the draft, April 24.

The Carolina Panthers earned the right to select first in the 1995 NFL draft by winning a coin toss with the Jacksonville Jaguars. The Jaguars received the second selection in the 1995 draft, April 24.

NFL clubs approved the transfer of the Philadelphia Eagles from Norman Braman to Jeffrey Lurie, May 6.

The NFL launched "NFL Sunday Ticket," a new season subscription service for satellite television dish owners, June 1.

**NFL COMMISSIONERS AND PRESIDENTS***

1920.................Jim Thorpe, President
1921-39.................Joe Carr, President
1939-41 ...........Carl Storck, President
1941-46........................Elmer Layden, Commissioner
1946-59 ........Bert Bell, Commissioner
1960-89 ..........................Pete Rozelle, Commissioner
1989-present...............Paul Tagliabue, Commissioner

**NFL treasurer Austin Gunsel served as president in the office of the commissioner following the death of Bert Bell (Oct. 11, 1959) until the election of Pete Rozelle (Jan. 26, 1960).*

## PAST STANDINGS

### 1993

**AMERICAN CONFERENCE**

**Eastern Division**

| | W | L | T | Pct. | Pts. | OP |
|---|---|---|---|---|---|---|
| Buffalo | 12 | 4 | 0 | .750 | 329 | 242 |
| Miami | 9 | 7 | 0 | .563 | 349 | 351 |
| N.Y. Jets | 8 | 8 | 0 | .500 | 270 | 247 |
| New England | 5 | 11 | 0 | .313 | 238 | 286 |
| Indianapolis | 4 | 12 | 0 | .250 | 189 | 378 |

**Central Division**

| | W | L | T | Pct. | Pts. | OP |
|---|---|---|---|---|---|---|
| Houston | 12 | 4 | 0 | .750 | 368 | 238 |
| Pittsburgh* | 9 | 7 | 0 | .563 | 308 | 281 |
| Cleveland | 7 | 9 | 0 | .438 | 304 | 307 |
| Cincinnati | 3 | 13 | 0 | .188 | 187 | 319 |

**Western Division**

| | W | L | T | Pct. | Pts. | OP |
|---|---|---|---|---|---|---|
| Kansas City | 11 | 5 | 0 | .688 | 328 | 291 |
| L.A. Raiders* | 10 | 6 | 0 | .625 | 306 | 326 |
| Denver* | 9 | 7 | 0 | .563 | 373 | 284 |
| San Diego | 8 | 8 | 0 | .500 | 322 | 290 |
| Seattle | 6 | 10 | 0 | .375 | 280 | 314 |

**NATIONAL CONFERENCE**

**Eastern Division**

| | W | L | T | Pct. | Pts. | OP |
|---|---|---|---|---|---|---|
| Dallas | 12 | 4 | 0 | .750 | 376 | 229 |
| N.Y. Giants* | 11 | 5 | 0 | .688 | 288 | 205 |
| Philadelphia | 8 | 8 | 0 | .500 | 293 | 315 |
| Phoenix | 7 | 9 | 0 | .438 | 326 | 269 |
| Washington | 4 | 12 | 0 | .250 | 230 | 345 |

**Central Division**

| | W | L | T | Pct. | Pts. | OP |
|---|---|---|---|---|---|---|
| Detroit | 10 | 6 | 0 | .625 | 298 | 292 |
| Minnesota* | 9 | 7 | 0 | .563 | 277 | 290 |
| Green Bay* | 9 | 7 | 0 | .563 | 340 | 282 |
| Chicago | 7 | 9 | 0 | .438 | 234 | 230 |
| Tampa Bay | 5 | 11 | 0 | .313 | 237 | 376 |

**Western Division**

| | W | L | T | Pct. | Pts. | OP |
|---|---|---|---|---|---|---|
| San Francisco | 10 | 6 | 0 | .625 | 473 | 295 |
| New Orleans | 8 | 8 | 0 | .500 | 317 | 343 |
| Atlanta | 6 | 10 | 0 | .375 | 316 | 385 |
| L.A. Rams | 5 | 11 | 0 | .313 | 221 | 367 |

**Wild-Card qualifier for playoffs*

*Minnesota finished ahead of Green Bay based on a head-to-head sweep (2-0).*

Wild Card playoffs: KANSAS CITY 27, Pittsburgh 24 (OT); L.A. RAIDERS 42, Denver 24

Divisional playoffs: BUFFALO 29, L.A. Raiders 23; Kansas City 28, HOUSTON 20

AFC championship: BUFFALO 30, Kansas City 13

Wild Card playoffs: Green Bay 28, DETROIT 24; N.Y. GIANTS 17, Minnesota 10

Divisional playoffs: SAN FRANCISCO 44, N.Y. Giants 3; DALLAS 27, Green Bay 17

NFC championship: DALLAS 38, San Francisco 21

Super Bowl XXVIII: Dallas (NFC) 30, Buffalo (AFC) 13, at Georgia Dome, Atlanta, Georgia

*In Past Standings section, home teams in playoff games are indicated by capital letters.*

### 1992

**AMERICAN CONFERENCE**

**Eastern Division**

| | W | L | T | Pct. | Pts. | OP |
|---|---|---|---|---|---|---|
| Miami | 11 | 5 | 0 | .688 | 340 | 281 |
| Buffalo* | 11 | 5 | 0 | .688 | 381 | 283 |
| Indianapolis | 9 | 7 | 0 | .563 | 216 | 302 |
| N.Y. Jets | 4 | 12 | 0 | .250 | 220 | 315 |
| New England | 2 | 14 | 0 | .125 | 205 | 363 |

**Central Division**

| | W | L | T | Pct. | Pts. | OP |
|---|---|---|---|---|---|---|
| Pittsburgh | 11 | 5 | 0 | .688 | 299 | 225 |
| Houston* | 10 | 6 | 0 | .625 | 352 | 258 |
| Cleveland | 7 | 9 | 0 | .438 | 272 | 275 |
| Cincinnati | 5 | 11 | 0 | .313 | 274 | 364 |

**Western Division**

| | W | L | T | Pct. | Pts. | OP |
|---|---|---|---|---|---|---|
| San Diego | 11 | 5 | 0 | .688 | 335 | 241 |
| Kansas City* | 10 | 6 | 0 | .625 | 348 | 282 |
| Denver | 8 | 8 | 0 | .500 | 262 | 329 |
| L.A. Raiders | 7 | 9 | 0 | .438 | 249 | 281 |
| Seattle | 2 | 14 | 0 | .125 | 140 | 312 |

**NATIONAL CONFERENCE**

**Eastern Division**

| | W | L | T | Pct. | Pts. | OP |
|---|---|---|---|---|---|---|
| Dallas | 13 | 3 | 0 | .813 | 409 | 243 |
| Philadelphia* | 11 | 5 | 0 | .688 | 354 | 245 |
| Washington* | 9 | 7 | 0 | .563 | 300 | 255 |
| N.Y. Giants | 6 | 10 | 0 | .375 | 306 | 367 |
| Phoenix | 4 | 12 | 0 | .250 | 243 | 332 |

**Central Division**

| | W | L | T | Pct. | Pts. | OP |
|---|---|---|---|---|---|---|
| Minnesota | 11 | 5 | 0 | .688 | 374 | 249 |
| Green Bay | 9 | 7 | 0 | .563 | 276 | 296 |
| Tampa Bay | 5 | 11 | 0 | .313 | 267 | 365 |
| Chicago | 5 | 11 | 0 | .313 | 295 | 361 |
| Detroit | 5 | 11 | 0 | .313 | 273 | 332 |

**Western Division**

| | W | L | T | Pct. | Pts. | OP |
|---|---|---|---|---|---|---|
| San Francisco | 14 | 2 | 0 | .875 | 431 | 236 |
| New Orleans* | 12 | 4 | 0 | .750 | 330 | 202 |
| Atlanta | 6 | 10 | 0 | .375 | 327 | 414 |
| L.A. Rams | 6 | 10 | 0 | .375 | 313 | 383 |

**Wild-Card qualifier for playoffs*

*Miami finished ahead of Buffalo based on better conference record (9-3 to 7-5). Tampa Bay finished ahead of Chicago and Detroit based on better conference record (5-9 to Bears' 4-8 and Lions' 3-9). Atlanta finished ahead of L.A. Rams based on better record versus common opponents (5-7 to 4-8).*

Wild Card playoffs: SAN DIEGO 17, Kansas City 0; BUFFALO 41, Houston 38 (OT)

Divisional playoffs: Buffalo 24, PITTSBURGH 3; MIAMI 31, San Diego 0

AFC championship: Buffalo 29, MIAMI 10

Wild Card playoffs: Washington 24, MINNESOTA 7; Philadelphia 36, NEW ORLEANS 20

Divisional playoffs: SAN FRANCISCO 20, Washington 13; DALLAS 34, Philadelphia 10

NFC championship: Dallas 30, SAN FRANCISCO 20

Super Bowl XXVII: Dallas (NFC) 52, Buffalo (AFC) 17, at Rose Bowl, Pasadena, California.

### 1991

**AMERICAN CONFERENCE**

**Eastern Division**

| | W | L | T | Pct. | Pts. | OP |
|---|---|---|---|---|---|---|
| Buffalo | 13 | 3 | 0 | .813 | 458 | 318 |
| N.Y. Jets* | 8 | 8 | 0 | .500 | 314 | 293 |
| Miami | 8 | 8 | 0 | .500 | 343 | 349 |
| New England | 6 | 10 | 0 | .375 | 211 | 305 |
| Indianapolis | 1 | 15 | 0 | .063 | 143 | 381 |

**Central Division**

| | W | L | T | Pct. | Pts. | OP |
|---|---|---|---|---|---|---|
| Houston | 11 | 5 | 0 | .688 | 386 | 251 |
| Pittsburgh | 7 | 9 | 0 | .438 | 292 | 344 |
| Cleveland | 6 | 10 | 0 | .375 | 293 | 298 |
| Cincinnati | 3 | 13 | 0 | .188 | 263 | 435 |

**Western Division**

| | W | L | T | Pct. | Pts. | OP |
|---|---|---|---|---|---|---|
| Denver | 12 | 4 | 0 | .750 | 304 | 235 |
| Kansas City* | 10 | 6 | 0 | .625 | 322 | 252 |
| L.A. Raiders* | 9 | 7 | 0 | .563 | 298 | 297 |
| Seattle | 7 | 9 | 0 | .438 | 276 | 261 |
| San Diego | 4 | 12 | 0 | .250 | 274 | 342 |

**NATIONAL CONFERENCE**

**Eastern Division**

| | W | L | T | Pct. | Pts. | OP |
|---|---|---|---|---|---|---|
| Washington | 14 | 2 | 0 | .875 | 485 | 224 |
| Dallas* | 11 | 5 | 0 | .688 | 342 | 310 |
| Philadelphia | 10 | 6 | 0 | .625 | 285 | 244 |
| N.Y. Giants | 8 | 8 | 0 | .500 | 281 | 297 |
| Phoenix | 4 | 12 | 0 | .250 | 196 | 344 |

**Central Division**

| | W | L | T | Pct. | Pts. | OP |
|---|---|---|---|---|---|---|
| Detroit | 12 | 4 | 0 | .750 | 339 | 295 |
| Chicago* | 11 | 5 | 0 | .688 | 299 | 269 |
| Minnesota | 8 | 8 | 0 | .500 | 301 | 306 |
| Green Bay | 4 | 12 | 0 | .250 | 273 | 313 |
| Tampa Bay | 3 | 13 | 0 | .188 | 199 | 365 |

**Western Division**

| | W | L | T | Pct. | Pts. | OP |
|---|---|---|---|---|---|---|
| New Orleans | 11 | 5 | 0 | .688 | 341 | 211 |
| Atlanta* | 10 | 6 | 0 | .625 | 361 | 338 |
| San Francisco | 10 | 6 | 0 | .625 | 393 | 239 |
| L.A. Rams | 3 | 13 | 0 | .188 | 234 | 390 |

**Wild-Card qualifiers for playoffs*

*New York Jets finished ahead of Miami based on head-to-head sweep (2-0). Atlanta finished ahead of San Francisco based on head-to-head sweep (2-0).*

Wild Card playoffs: KANSAS CITY 10, L.A. Raiders 6; HOUSTON 17, N.Y. Jets 10

Divisional playoffs: DENVER 26, Houston 24; BUFFALO 37, Kansas City 14

AFC championship: BUFFALO 10, Denver 7

Wild Card playoffs: Atlanta 27, NEW ORLEANS 20; Dallas 17, CHICAGO 13

Divisional playoffs: WASHINGTON 24, Atlanta 7; DETROIT 38, Dallas 6

NFC championship: WASHINGTON 41, Detroit 10

Super Bowl XXVI: Washington (NFC) 37, Buffalo (AFC) 24, at Hubert H. Humphrey Metrodome, Minneapolis, Minnesota.

### 1990

**AMERICAN CONFERENCE**

**Eastern Division**

| | W | L | T | Pct. | Pts. | OP |
|---|---|---|---|---|---|---|
| Buffalo | 13 | 3 | 0 | .813 | 428 | 263 |
| Miami* | 12 | 4 | 0 | .750 | 336 | 242 |
| Indianapolis | 7 | 9 | 0 | .438 | 281 | 353 |
| N.Y. Jets | 6 | 10 | 0 | .375 | 295 | 345 |
| New England | 1 | 15 | 0 | .063 | 181 | 446 |

**Central Division**

| | W | L | T | Pct. | Pts. | OP |
|---|---|---|---|---|---|---|
| Cincinnati | 9 | 7 | 0 | .563 | 360 | 352 |
| Houston* | 9 | 7 | 0 | .563 | 405 | 307 |
| Pittsburgh | 9 | 7 | 0 | .563 | 292 | 240 |
| Cleveland | 3 | 13 | 0 | .188 | 228 | 462 |

**Western Division**

| | W | L | T | Pct. | Pts. | OP |
|---|---|---|---|---|---|---|
| L.A. Raiders | 12 | 4 | 0 | .750 | 337 | 268 |
| Kansas City* | 11 | 5 | 0 | .688 | 369 | 257 |
| Seattle | 9 | 7 | 0 | .563 | 306 | 286 |
| San Diego | 6 | 10 | 0 | .375 | 315 | 281 |
| Denver | 5 | 11 | 0 | .313 | 331 | 374 |

**NATIONAL CONFERENCE**

**Eastern Division**

| | W | L | T | Pct. | Pts. | OP |
|---|---|---|---|---|---|---|
| N.Y. Giants | 13 | 3 | 0 | .813 | 335 | 211 |
| Philadelphia* | 10 | 6 | 0 | .625 | 396 | 299 |
| Washington* | 10 | 6 | 0 | .625 | 381 | 301 |
| Dallas | 7 | 9 | 0 | .438 | 244 | 308 |
| Phoenix | 5 | 11 | 0 | .313 | 268 | 396 |

**Central Division**

| | W | L | T | Pct. | Pts. | OP |
|---|---|---|---|---|---|---|
| Chicago | 11 | 5 | 0 | .688 | 348 | 280 |
| Tampa Bay | 6 | 10 | 0 | .375 | 264 | 367 |
| Detroit | 6 | 10 | 0 | .375 | 373 | 413 |
| Green Bay | 6 | 10 | 0 | .375 | 271 | 347 |
| Minnesota | 6 | 10 | 0 | .375 | 351 | 326 |

**Western Division**

| | W | L | T | Pct. | Pts. | OP |
|---|---|---|---|---|---|---|
| San Francisco | 14 | 2 | 0 | .875 | 353 | 239 |
| New Orleans* | 8 | 8 | 0 | .500 | 274 | 275 |
| L.A. Rams | 5 | 11 | 0 | .313 | 345 | 412 |
| Atlanta | 5 | 11 | 0 | .313 | 348 | 365 |

**Wild-Card qualifiers for playoffs*

*Cincinnati won AFC Central title based on best head-to-head record (3-1) vs. Houston (2-2) and Pittsburgh (1-3). Houston was Wild Card based on better conference record (8-4) than Seattle (7-5) and Pittsburgh (6-6). Philadelphia finished second in the NFC East based on better division record (5-3) than Washington (4-4). Tampa Bay was second in NFC Central based on 5-1 record vs. Detroit, Green Bay, and Minnesota. Detroit finished third based on best net division points (minus 8) vs. Green Bay (minus 40) in fourth. Minnesota was fifth based on 4-8 conference record. The Los Angeles Rams finished third in NFC West based on net points in division (plus 1) vs. Atlanta (minus 31).*

Wild Card playoffs: MIAMI 17, Kansas City 16; CINCINNATI 41, Houston 14

Divisional playoffs: BUFFALO 44, Miami 34; L.A. RAIDERS 20, Cincinnati 10

AFC championship: BUFFALO 51, L.A. Raiders 3

Wild Card playoffs: Washington 20, PHILADELPHIA 6; CHICAGO 16, New Orleans 6

Divisional playoffs: SAN FRANCISCO 28, Washington 10; N.Y. GIANTS 31, Chicago 3

NFC championship: N.Y. Giants 15, SAN FRANCISCO 13

Super Bowl XXV: N.Y. Giants (NFC) 20, Buffalo (AFC) 19, at Tampa Stadium, Tampa, Florida.

# PAST STANDINGS

## 1989

### AMERICAN CONFERENCE

**Eastern Division**

| | W | L | T | Pct. | Pts. | OP |
|---|---|---|---|---|---|---|
| Buffalo | 9 | 7 | 0 | .563 | 409 | 317 |
| Indianapolis | 8 | 8 | 0 | .500 | 298 | 301 |
| Miami | 8 | 8 | 0 | .500 | 331 | 379 |
| New England | 5 | 11 | 0 | .313 | 297 | 391 |
| N.Y. Jets | 4 | 12 | 0 | .250 | 253 | 411 |

**Central Division**

| | W | L | T | Pct. | Pts. | OP |
|---|---|---|---|---|---|---|
| Cleveland | 9 | 6 | 1 | .594 | 334 | 254 |
| Houston* | 9 | 7 | 0 | .563 | 365 | 412 |
| Pittsburgh* | 9 | 7 | 0 | .563 | 265 | 326 |
| Cincinnati | 8 | 8 | 0 | .500 | 404 | 285 |

**Western Division**

| | W | L | T | Pct. | Pts. | OP |
|---|---|---|---|---|---|---|
| Denver | 11 | 5 | 0 | .688 | 362 | 226 |
| Kansas City | 8 | 7 | 1 | .531 | 318 | 286 |
| L.A. Raiders | 8 | 8 | 0 | .500 | 315 | 297 |
| Seattle | 7 | 9 | 0 | .438 | 241 | 327 |
| San Diego | 6 | 10 | 0 | .375 | 266 | 290 |

### NATIONAL CONFERENCE

**Eastern Division**

| | W | L | T | Pct. | Pts. | OP |
|---|---|---|---|---|---|---|
| N.Y. Giants | 12 | 4 | 0 | .750 | 348 | 252 |
| Philadelphia* | 11 | 5 | 0 | .688 | 342 | 274 |
| Washington | 10 | 6 | 0 | .625 | 386 | 308 |
| Phoenix | 5 | 11 | 0 | .313 | 258 | 377 |
| Dallas | 1 | 15 | 0 | .063 | 204 | 393 |

**Central Division**

| | W | L | T | Pct. | Pts. | OP |
|---|---|---|---|---|---|---|
| Minnesota | 10 | 6 | 0 | .625 | 351 | 275 |
| Green Bay | 10 | 6 | 0 | .625 | 362 | 356 |
| Detroit | 7 | 9 | 0 | .438 | 312 | 364 |
| Chicago | 6 | 10 | 0 | .375 | 358 | 377 |
| Tampa Bay | 5 | 11 | 0 | .313 | 320 | 419 |

**Western Division**

| | W | L | T | Pct. | Pts. | OP |
|---|---|---|---|---|---|---|
| San Francisco | 14 | 2 | 0 | .875 | 442 | 253 |
| L.A. Rams* | 11 | 5 | 0 | .688 | 426 | 344 |
| New Orleans | 9 | 7 | 0 | .563 | 386 | 301 |
| Atlanta | 3 | 13 | 0 | .188 | 279 | 437 |

**Wild-Card qualifiers for playoffs*

*Indianapolis finished ahead of Miami in AFC East because of better conference record (7-5 vs. 6-8). Houston finished ahead of Pittsburgh in AFC Central because of head-to-head sweep (2-0). Minnesota finished ahead of Green Bay in NFC Central because of better division record (6-2 vs. 5-3).*

Wild Card playoff: Pittsburgh 26, HOUSTON 23 (OT)
Divisional playoffs: CLEVELAND 34, Buffalo 30; DENVER 24, Pittsburgh 23
AFC championship: DENVER 37, Cleveland 21
Wild Card playoff: L.A. Rams 21, PHILADELPHIA 7
Divisional playoffs: L.A. Rams 19, N.Y. GIANTS 13 (OT); SAN FRANCISCO 41, Minnesota 13
NFC championship: SAN FRANCISCO 30, L.A. Rams 3
Super Bowl XXIV: San Francisco (NFC) 55, Denver (AFC) 10, at Louisiana Superdome, New Orleans, Louisiana.

## 1988

### AMERICAN CONFERENCE

**Eastern Division**

| | W | L | T | Pct. | Pts. | OP |
|---|---|---|---|---|---|---|
| Buffalo | 12 | 4 | 0 | .750 | 329 | 237 |
| Indianapolis | 9 | 7 | 0 | .563 | 354 | 315 |
| New England | 9 | 7 | 0 | .563 | 250 | 284 |
| N.Y. Jets | 8 | 7 | 1 | .531 | 372 | 354 |
| Miami | 6 | 10 | 0 | .375 | 319 | 380 |

**Central Division**

| | W | L | T | Pct. | Pts. | OP |
|---|---|---|---|---|---|---|
| Cincinnati | 12 | 4 | 0 | .750 | 448 | 329 |
| Cleveland* | 10 | 6 | 0 | .625 | 304 | 288 |
| Houston* | 10 | 6 | 0 | .625 | 424 | 365 |
| Pittsburgh | 5 | 11 | 0 | .313 | 336 | 421 |

**Western Division**

| | W | L | T | Pct. | Pts. | OP |
|---|---|---|---|---|---|---|
| Seattle | 9 | 7 | 0 | .563 | 339 | 329 |
| Denver | 8 | 8 | 0 | .500 | 327 | 352 |
| L.A. Raiders | 7 | 9 | 0 | .438 | 325 | 369 |
| San Diego | 6 | 10 | 0 | .375 | 231 | 332 |
| Kansas City | 4 | 11 | 1 | .281 | 254 | 320 |

### NATIONAL CONFERENCE

**Eastern Division**

| | W | L | T | Pct. | Pts. | OP |
|---|---|---|---|---|---|---|
| Philadelphia | 10 | 6 | 0 | .625 | 379 | 319 |
| N.Y. Giants | 10 | 6 | 0 | .625 | 359 | 304 |
| Washington | 7 | 9 | 0 | .438 | 345 | 387 |
| Phoenix | 7 | 9 | 0 | .438 | 344 | 398 |
| Dallas | 3 | 13 | 0 | .188 | 265 | 381 |

**Central Division**

| | W | L | T | Pct. | Pts. | OP |
|---|---|---|---|---|---|---|
| Chicago | 12 | 4 | 0 | .750 | 312 | 215 |
| Minnesota* | 11 | 5 | 0 | .688 | 406 | 233 |
| Tampa Bay | 5 | 11 | 0 | .313 | 261 | 350 |
| Detroit | 4 | 12 | 0 | .250 | 220 | 313 |
| Green Bay | 4 | 12 | 0 | .250 | 240 | 315 |

**Western Division**

| | W | L | T | Pct. | Pts. | OP |
|---|---|---|---|---|---|---|
| San Francisco | 10 | 6 | 0 | .625 | 369 | 294 |
| L.A. Rams* | 10 | 6 | 0 | .625 | 407 | 293 |
| New Orleans | 10 | 6 | 0 | .625 | 312 | 283 |
| Atlanta | 5 | 11 | 0 | .313 | 244 | 315 |

**Wild-Card qualifiers for playoffs*

*Indianapolis finished second in AFC East on basis of better record versus common opponents (7-5) over New England (6-6). Cleveland gained first AFC Wild-Card position based on better division record (4-2) over Houston (3-3). Philadelphia finished first in NFC East on basis of head-to-head sweep over New York Giants. Washington finished third in NFC East on basis of better division record (4-4) over Phoenix (3-5). Detroit finished fourth in NFC Central on basis of head-to-head sweep over Green Bay. San Francisco finished first in NFC West based on better head-to-head record (3-1) over Los Angeles Rams (2-2) and New Orleans (1-3). Los Angeles Rams finished second in NFC West on basis of better division record (4-2) over New Orleans (3-3) and earned Wild-Card position based on better conference record (8-4) over New York Giants (9-5) and New Orleans (6-6).*

Wild Card playoff: Houston 24, CLEVELAND 23
Divisional playoffs: CINCINNATI 21, Seattle 13; BUFFALO 17, Houston 10
AFC championship: CINCINNATI 21, Buffalo 10
Wild Card playoff: MINNESOTA 28, Los Angeles Rams 17
Divisional playoffs: CHICAGO 20, Philadelphia 12
SAN FRANCISCO 34, Minnesota 9
NFC championship: San Francisco 28, CHICAGO 3
Super Bowl XXIII: San Francisco (NFC) 20, Cincinnati (AFC) 16, at Joe Robbie Stadium, Miami, Florida.

## 1987

### AMERICAN CONFERENCE

**Eastern Division**

| | W | L | T | Pct. | Pts. | OP |
|---|---|---|---|---|---|---|
| Indianapolis | 9 | 6 | 0 | .600 | 300 | 238 |
| New England | 8 | 7 | 0 | .533 | 320 | 293 |
| Miami | 8 | 7 | 0 | .533 | 362 | 335 |
| Buffalo | 7 | 8 | 0 | .467 | 270 | 305 |
| N.Y. Jets | 6 | 9 | 0 | .400 | 334 | 360 |

**Central Division**

| | W | L | T | Pct. | Pts. | OP |
|---|---|---|---|---|---|---|
| Cleveland | 10 | 5 | 0 | .667 | 390 | 239 |
| Houston* | 9 | 6 | 0 | .600 | 345 | 349 |
| Pittsburgh | 8 | 7 | 0 | .533 | 285 | 299 |
| Cincinnati | 4 | 11 | 0 | .267 | 285 | 370 |

**Western Division**

| | W | L | T | Pct. | Pts. | OP |
|---|---|---|---|---|---|---|
| Denver | 10 | 4 | 1 | .700 | 379 | 288 |
| Seattle* | 9 | 6 | 0 | .600 | 371 | 314 |
| San Diego | 8 | 7 | 0 | .533 | 253 | 317 |
| L.A. Raiders | 5 | 10 | 0 | .333 | 301 | 289 |
| Kansas City | 4 | 11 | 0 | .267 | 273 | 388 |

### NATIONAL CONFERENCE

**Eastern Division**

| | W | L | T | Pct. | Pts. | OP |
|---|---|---|---|---|---|---|
| Washington | 11 | 4 | 0 | .733 | 379 | 285 |
| Dallas | 7 | 8 | 0 | .467 | 340 | 348 |
| St. Louis | 7 | 8 | 0 | .467 | 362 | 368 |
| Philadelphia | 7 | 8 | 0 | .467 | 337 | 380 |
| N.Y. Giants | 6 | 9 | 0 | .400 | 280 | 312 |

**Central Division**

| | W | L | T | Pct. | Pts. | OP |
|---|---|---|---|---|---|---|
| Chicago | 11 | 4 | 0 | .733 | 356 | 282 |
| Minnesota* | 8 | 7 | 0 | .533 | 336 | 335 |
| Green Bay | 5 | 9 | 1 | .367 | 255 | 300 |
| Tampa Bay | 4 | 11 | 0 | .267 | 286 | 360 |
| Detroit | 4 | 11 | 0 | .267 | 269 | 384 |

**Western Division**

| | W | L | T | Pct. | Pts. | OP |
|---|---|---|---|---|---|---|
| San Francisco | 13 | 2 | 0 | .867 | 459 | 253 |
| New Orleans* | 12 | 3 | 0 | .800 | 422 | 283 |
| L.A. Rams | 6 | 9 | 0 | .400 | 317 | 361 |
| Atlanta | 3 | 12 | 0 | .200 | 205 | 436 |

**Wild-Card qualifiers for playoffs*

*Houston gained first AFC Wild-Card position on better conference record (7-4) over Seattle (5-6).*

Wild Card playoff: HOUSTON 23, Seattle 20 (OT)
Divisional playoffs: CLEVELAND 38, Indianapolis 21; DENVER 34, Houston 10
AFC championship: DENVER 38, Cleveland 33
Wild Card playoff: Minnesota 44, NEW ORLEANS 10
Divisional playoffs: Minnesota 36, SAN FRANCISCO 24; Washington 21, CHICAGO 17
NFC championship: WASHINGTON 17, Minnesota 10
Super Bowl XXII: Washington (NFC) 42, Denver (AFC) 10, at San Diego Jack Murphy Stadium, San Diego, California.
*Note: 1987 regular season was reduced from 16 to 15 games for each team due to players' strike.*

## 1986

### AMERICAN CONFERENCE

**Eastern Division**

| | W | L | T | Pct. | Pts. | OP |
|---|---|---|---|---|---|---|
| New England | 11 | 5 | 0 | .688 | 412 | 307 |
| N.Y. Jets* | 10 | 6 | 0 | .625 | 364 | 386 |
| Miami | 8 | 8 | 0 | .500 | 430 | 405 |
| Buffalo | 4 | 12 | 0 | .250 | 287 | 348 |
| Indianapolis | 3 | 13 | 0 | .188 | 229 | 400 |

**Central Division**

| | W | L | T | Pct. | Pts. | OP |
|---|---|---|---|---|---|---|
| Cleveland | 12 | 4 | 0 | .750 | 391 | 310 |
| Cincinnati | 10 | 6 | 0 | .625 | 409 | 394 |
| Pittsburgh | 6 | 10 | 0 | .375 | 307 | 336 |
| Houston | 5 | 11 | 0 | .313 | 274 | 329 |

**Western Division**

| | W | L | T | Pct. | Pts. | OP |
|---|---|---|---|---|---|---|
| Denver | 11 | 5 | 0 | .688 | 378 | 327 |
| Kansas City* | 10 | 6 | 0 | .625 | 358 | 326 |
| Seattle | 10 | 6 | 0 | .625 | 366 | 293 |
| L.A. Raiders | 8 | 8 | 0 | .500 | 323 | 346 |
| San Diego | 4 | 12 | 0 | .250 | 335 | 396 |

### NATIONAL CONFERENCE

**Eastern Division**

| | W | L | T | Pct. | Pts. | OP |
|---|---|---|---|---|---|---|
| N.Y. Giants | 14 | 2 | 0 | .875 | 371 | 236 |
| Washington* | 12 | 4 | 0 | .750 | 368 | 296 |
| Dallas | 7 | 9 | 0 | .438 | 346 | 337 |
| Philadelphia | 5 | 10 | 1 | .344 | 256 | 312 |
| St. Louis | 4 | 11 | 1 | .281 | 218 | 351 |

**Central Division**

| | W | L | T | Pct. | Pts. | OP |
|---|---|---|---|---|---|---|
| Chicago | 14 | 2 | 0 | .875 | 352 | 187 |
| Minnesota | 9 | 7 | 0 | .563 | 398 | 273 |
| Detroit | 5 | 11 | 0 | .313 | 277 | 326 |
| Green Bay | 4 | 12 | 0 | .250 | 254 | 418 |
| Tampa Bay | 2 | 14 | 0 | .125 | 239 | 473 |

**Western Division**

| | W | L | T | Pct. | Pts. | OP |
|---|---|---|---|---|---|---|
| San Francisco | 10 | 5 | 1 | .656 | 374 | 247 |
| L.A. Rams* | 10 | 6 | 0 | .625 | 309 | 267 |
| Atlanta | 7 | 8 | 1 | .469 | 280 | 280 |
| New Orleans | 7 | 9 | 0 | .438 | 288 | 287 |

**Wild-Card qualifiers for playoffs*

*New York Jets gained first AFC Wild-Card position on better conference record (8-4) over Kansas City (9-5), Seattle (7-5), and Cincinnati (7-5). Kansas City gained second Wild Card based on better conference record (9-5) over Seattle (7-5) and Cincinnati (7-5).*

Wild Card playoff: NEW YORK JETS 35, Kansas City 15
Divisional playoffs: CLEVELAND 23, New York Jets 20 (OT)
DENVER 22, New England 17
AFC championship: Denver 23, CLEVELAND 20 (OT)
Wild Card playoff: WASHINGTON 19, Los Angeles Rams 7
Divisional playoffs: Washington 27, CHICAGO 13
NEW YORK GIANTS 49, San Francisco 3
NFC championship: NEW YORK GIANTS 17, Washington 0
Super Bowl XXI: New York Giants (NFC) 39, Denver (AFC) 20, at Rose Bowl, Pasadena, California.

## 1985

### AMERICAN CONFERENCE

**Eastern Division**

| | W | L | T | Pct. | Pts. | OP |
|---|---|---|---|---|---|---|
| Miami | 12 | 4 | 0 | .750 | 428 | 320 |
| N.Y. Jets* | 11 | 5 | 0 | .688 | 393 | 264 |
| New England* | 11 | 5 | 0 | .688 | 362 | 290 |
| Indianapolis | 5 | 11 | 0 | .313 | 320 | 386 |
| Buffalo | 2 | 14 | 0 | .125 | 200 | 381 |

**Central Division**

| | W | L | T | Pct. | Pts. | OP |
|---|---|---|---|---|---|---|
| Cleveland | 8 | 8 | 0 | .500 | 287 | 294 |
| Cincinnati | 7 | 9 | 0 | .438 | 441 | 437 |
| Pittsburgh | 7 | 9 | 0 | .438 | 379 | 355 |
| Houston | 5 | 11 | 0 | .313 | 284 | 412 |

**Western Division**

| | W | L | T | Pct. | Pts. | OP |
|---|---|---|---|---|---|---|
| L.A. Raiders | 12 | 4 | 0 | .750 | 354 | 308 |
| Denver | 11 | 5 | 0 | .688 | 380 | 329 |
| Seattle | 8 | 8 | 0 | .500 | 349 | 303 |
| San Diego | 8 | 8 | 0 | .500 | 467 | 435 |
| Kansas City | 6 | 10 | 0 | .375 | 317 | 360 |

### NATIONAL CONFERENCE

**Eastern Division**

| | W | L | T | Pct. | Pts. | OP |
|---|---|---|---|---|---|---|
| Dallas | 10 | 6 | 0 | .625 | 357 | 333 |
| N.Y. Giants* | 10 | 6 | 0 | .625 | 399 | 283 |
| Washington | 10 | 6 | 0 | .625 | 297 | 312 |
| Philadelphia | 7 | 9 | 0 | .438 | 286 | 310 |
| St. Louis | 5 | 11 | 0 | .313 | 278 | 414 |

**Central Division**

| | W | L | T | Pct. | Pts. | OP |
|---|---|---|---|---|---|---|
| Chicago | 15 | 1 | 0 | .938 | 456 | 198 |
| Green Bay | 8 | 8 | 0 | .500 | 337 | 355 |
| Minnesota | 7 | 9 | 0 | .438 | 346 | 359 |
| Detroit | 7 | 9 | 0 | .438 | 307 | 366 |
| Tampa Bay | 2 | 14 | 0 | .125 | 294 | 448 |

**Western Division**

| | W | L | T | Pct. | Pts. | OP |
|---|---|---|---|---|---|---|
| L.A. Rams | 11 | 5 | 0 | .688 | 340 | 277 |
| San Francisco* | 10 | 6 | 0 | .625 | 411 | 263 |
| New Orleans | 5 | 11 | 0 | .313 | 294 | 401 |
| Atlanta | 4 | 12 | 0 | .250 | 282 | 452 |

**Wild-Card qualifiers for playoffs*

*New York Jets gained first AFC Wild-Card position on better conference record (9-3) over New England (8-4) and Denver (8-4). New England gained second AFC Wild-Card position based on better record vs. common opponents (4-2) than Denver (3-3). Dallas won NFC Eastern Division title based on better record (4-0) vs. New York Giants (1-3) and Washington (1-3). New York Giants gained first NFC Wild Card position based on better conference record (8-4) over San Francisco (7-5) and Washington (6-6). San Francisco gained second NFC Wild-Card position based on head-to-head victory over Washington.*

Wild Card playoff: New England 26, NEW YORK JETS 14
Divisional playoffs: MIAMI 24, Cleveland 21;
New England 27, LOS ANGELES RAIDERS 20
AFC championship: New England 31, MIAMI 14
Wild Card playoff: NEW YORK GIANTS 17, San Francisco 3
Divisional playoffs: LOS ANGELES RAMS 20, Dallas 0;
CHICAGO 21, New York Giants 0
NFC championship: CHICAGO 24, Los Angeles Rams 0
Super Bowl XX: Chicago (NFC) 46, New England (AFC) 10, at Louisiana Superdome, New Orleans, Louisiana.

## 1984

### AMERICAN CONFERENCE

**Eastern Division**

| | W | L | T | Pct. | Pts. | OP |
|---|---|---|---|---|---|---|
| Miami | 14 | 2 | 0 | .875 | 513 | 298 |
| New England | 9 | 7 | 0 | .563 | 362 | 352 |
| N.Y. Jets | 7 | 9 | 0 | .438 | 332 | 364 |
| Indianapolis | 4 | 12 | 0 | .250 | 239 | 414 |
| Buffalo | 2 | 14 | 0 | .125 | 250 | 454 |

**Central Division**

| | W | L | T | Pct. | Pts. | OP |
|---|---|---|---|---|---|---|
| Pittsburgh | 9 | 7 | 0 | .563 | 387 | 310 |
| Cincinnati | 8 | 8 | 0 | .500 | 339 | 339 |
| Cleveland | 5 | 11 | 0 | .313 | 250 | 297 |
| Houston | 3 | 13 | 0 | .188 | 240 | 437 |

**Western Division**

| | W | L | T | Pct. | Pts. | OP |
|---|---|---|---|---|---|---|
| Denver | 13 | 3 | 0 | .813 | 353 | 241 |
| Seattle* | 12 | 4 | 0 | .750 | 418 | 282 |
| L.A. Raiders* | 11 | 5 | 0 | .688 | 368 | 278 |
| Kansas City | 8 | 8 | 0 | .500 | 314 | 324 |
| San Diego | 7 | 9 | 0 | .438 | 394 | 413 |

### NATIONAL CONFERENCE

**Eastern Division**

| | W | L | T | Pct. | Pts. | OP |
|---|---|---|---|---|---|---|
| Washington | 11 | 5 | 0 | .688 | 426 | 310 |
| N.Y. Giants* | 9 | 7 | 0 | .563 | 299 | 301 |
| St. Louis | 9 | 7 | 0 | .563 | 423 | 345 |
| Dallas | 9 | 7 | 0 | .563 | 308 | 308 |
| Philadelphia | 6 | 9 | 1 | .406 | 278 | 320 |

**Central Division**

| | W | L | T | Pct. | Pts. | OP |
|---|---|---|---|---|---|---|
| Chicago | 10 | 6 | 0 | .625 | 325 | 248 |
| Green Bay | 8 | 8 | 0 | .500 | 390 | 309 |
| Tampa Bay | 6 | 10 | 0 | .375 | 335 | 380 |
| Detroit | 4 | 11 | 1 | .281 | 283 | 408 |
| Minnesota | 3 | 13 | 0 | .188 | 276 | 484 |

**Western Division**

| | W | L | T | Pct. | Pts. | OP |
|---|---|---|---|---|---|---|
| San Francisco | 15 | 1 | 0 | .938 | 475 | 227 |
| L.A. Rams* | 10 | 6 | 0 | .625 | 346 | 316 |
| New Orleans | 7 | 9 | 0 | .438 | 298 | 361 |
| Atlanta | 4 | 12 | 0 | .250 | 281 | 382 |

**Wild-Card qualifiers for playoffs*

*New York Giants clinched Wild-Card berth based on 3-1 record vs. St. Louis's 2-2 and Dallas's 1-3. St. Louis finished ahead of Dallas based on better division record (5-3 to 3-5).*

Wild Card playoff: SEATTLE 13, Los Angeles Raiders 7
Divisional playoffs: MIAMI 31, Seattle 10; Pittsburgh 24, DENVER 17
AFC championship: MIAMI 45, Pittsburgh 28
Wild Card playoff: New York Giants 16, LOS ANGELES RAMS 13
Divisional playoffs: SAN FRANCISCO 21, New York Giants 10;
Chicago 23, WASHINGTON 19
NFC championship: SAN FRANCISCO 23, Chicago 0
Super Bowl XIX: San Francisco (NFC) 38, Miami (AFC) 16, at Stanford Stadium, Stanford, California.

## 1983

### AMERICAN CONFERENCE

**Eastern Division**

| | W | L | T | Pct. | Pts. | OP |
|---|---|---|---|---|---|---|
| Miami | 12 | 4 | 0 | .750 | 389 | 250 |
| New England | 8 | 8 | 0 | .500 | 274 | 289 |
| Buffalo | 8 | 8 | 0 | .500 | 283 | 351 |
| Baltimore | 7 | 9 | 0 | .438 | 264 | 354 |
| N.Y. Jets | 7 | 9 | 0 | .438 | 313 | 331 |

**Central Division**

| | W | L | T | Pct. | Pts. | OP |
|---|---|---|---|---|---|---|
| Pittsburgh | 10 | 6 | 0 | .625 | 355 | 303 |
| Cleveland | 9 | 7 | 0 | .563 | 356 | 342 |
| Cincinnati | 7 | 9 | 0 | .438 | 346 | 302 |
| Houston | 2 | 14 | 0 | .125 | 288 | 460 |

**Western Division**

| | W | L | T | Pct. | Pts. | OP |
|---|---|---|---|---|---|---|
| L.A. Raiders | 12 | 4 | 0 | .750 | 442 | 338 |
| Seattle* | 9 | 7 | 0 | .563 | 403 | 397 |
| Denver* | 9 | 7 | 0 | .563 | 302 | 327 |
| San Diego | 6 | 10 | 0 | .375 | 358 | 462 |
| Kansas City | 6 | 10 | 0 | .375 | 386 | 367 |

### NATIONAL CONFERENCE

**Eastern Division**

| | W | L | T | Pct. | Pts. | OP |
|---|---|---|---|---|---|---|
| Washington | 14 | 2 | 0 | .875 | 541 | 332 |
| Dallas* | 12 | 4 | 0 | .750 | 479 | 360 |
| St. Louis | 8 | 7 | 1 | .531 | 374 | 428 |
| Philadelphia | 5 | 11 | 0 | .313 | 233 | 322 |
| N.Y. Giants | 3 | 12 | 1 | .219 | 267 | 347 |

**Central Division**

| | W | L | T | Pct. | Pts. | OP |
|---|---|---|---|---|---|---|
| Detroit | 9 | 7 | 0 | .563 | 347 | 286 |
| Green Bay | 8 | 8 | 0 | .500 | 429 | 439 |
| Chicago | 8 | 8 | 0 | .500 | 311 | 301 |
| Minnesota | 8 | 8 | 0 | .500 | 316 | 348 |
| Tampa Bay | 2 | 14 | 0 | .125 | 241 | 380 |

**Western Division**

| | W | L | T | Pct. | Pts. | OP |
|---|---|---|---|---|---|---|
| San Francisco | 10 | 6 | 0 | .625 | 432 | 293 |
| L.A. Rams* | 9 | 7 | 0 | .563 | 361 | 344 |
| New Orleans | 8 | 8 | 0 | .500 | 319 | 337 |
| Atlanta | 7 | 9 | 0 | .438 | 370 | 389 |

**Wild-Card qualifiers for playoffs*

*Seattle and Denver gained Wild-Card berths over Cleveland because of their victories over the Browns.*

Wild Card playoff: SEATTLE 31, Denver 7
Divisional playoffs: Seattle 27, MIAMI 20; LOS ANGELES RAIDERS 38, Pittsburgh 10
AFC championship: LOS ANGELES RAIDERS 30, Seattle 14
Wild Card playoff: Los Angeles Rams 24, DALLAS 17
Divisional playoffs: SAN FRANCISCO 24, Detroit 23; WASHINGTON 51, L.A. Rams 7
NFC championship: WASHINGTON 24, San Francisco 21
Super Bowl XVIII: Los Angeles Raiders (AFC) 38, Washington (NFC) 9, at Tampa Stadium, Tampa, Florida.

## 1982

### AMERICAN CONFERENCE

| | W | L | T | Pct. | Pts. | OP |
|---|---|---|---|---|---|---|
| L.A. Raiders | 8 | 1 | 0 | .889 | 260 | 200 |
| Miami | 7 | 2 | 0 | .778 | 198 | 131 |
| Cincinnati | 7 | 2 | 0 | .778 | 232 | 177 |
| Pittsburgh | 6 | 3 | 0 | .667 | 204 | 146 |
| San Diego | 6 | 3 | 0 | .667 | 288 | 221 |
| N.Y. Jets | 6 | 3 | 0 | .667 | 245 | 166 |
| New England | 5 | 4 | 0 | .556 | 143 | 157 |
| Cleveland | 4 | 5 | 0 | .444 | 140 | 182 |
| Buffalo | 4 | 5 | 0 | .444 | 150 | 154 |
| Seattle | 4 | 5 | 0 | .444 | 127 | 147 |
| Kansas City | 3 | 6 | 0 | .333 | 176 | 184 |
| Denver | 2 | 7 | 0 | .222 | 148 | 226 |
| Houston | 1 | 8 | 0 | .111 | 136 | 245 |
| Baltimore | 0 | 8 | 1 | .056 | 113 | 236 |

### NATIONAL CONFERENCE

| | W | L | T | Pct. | Pts. | OP |
|---|---|---|---|---|---|---|
| Washington | 8 | 1 | 0 | .889 | 190 | 128 |
| Dallas | 6 | 3 | 0 | .667 | 226 | 145 |
| Green Bay | 5 | 3 | 1 | .611 | 226 | 169 |
| Minnesota | 5 | 4 | 0 | .556 | 187 | 198 |
| Atlanta | 5 | 4 | 0 | .556 | 183 | 199 |
| St. Louis | 5 | 4 | 0 | .556 | 135 | 170 |
| Tampa Bay | 5 | 4 | 0 | .556 | 158 | 178 |
| Detroit | 4 | 5 | 0 | .444 | 181 | 176 |
| New Orleans | 4 | 5 | 0 | .444 | 129 | 160 |
| N.Y. Giants | 4 | 5 | 0 | .444 | 164 | 160 |
| San Francisco | 3 | 6 | 0 | .333 | 209 | 206 |
| Chicago | 3 | 6 | 0 | .333 | 141 | 174 |
| Philadelphia | 3 | 6 | 0 | .333 | 191 | 195 |
| L.A. Rams | 2 | 7 | 0 | .222 | 200 | 250 |

*As the result of a 57-day players' strike, the 1982 NFL regular season schedule was reduced from 16 weeks to 9. At the conclusion of the regular season, the NFL conducted a 16-team postseason Super Bowl Tournament. Eight teams from each conference were seeded 1-8 based on their records during the season.*

*Miami finished ahead of Cincinnati based on better conference record (6-1 to 6-2). Pittsburgh won common games tie-breaker with San Diego (3-1 to 2-1) after New York Jets were eliminated from three-way tie based on conference record (Pittsburgh and San Diego 5-3 vs. Jets 2-3). Cleveland finished ahead of Buffalo and Seattle based on better conference record (4-3 to 3-3 to 3-5). Minnesota (4-1), Atlanta (4-3), St. Louis (5-4), Tampa Bay (3-3) seeds were determined by best won-lost record in conference games. Detroit finished ahead of New Orleans and the New York Giants based on better conference record (4-4 to 3-5 to 3-5).*

First round playoff: MIAMI 28, New England 13
LOS ANGELES RAIDERS 27, Cleveland 10
New York Jets 44, CINCINNATI 17
San Diego 31, PITTSBURGH 28
Second round playoff: New York Jets 17, LOS ANGELES RAIDERS 14
MIAMI 34, San Diego 13
AFC championship: MIAMI 14, New York Jets 0
First round playoff: WASHINGTON 31, Detroit 7
GREEN BAY 41, St. Louis 16
MINNESOTA 30, Atlanta 24
DALLAS 30, Tampa Bay 17
Second round playoff: WASHINGTON 21, Minnesota 7
DALLAS 37, Green Bay 26
NFC championship: WASHINGTON 31, Dallas 17
Super Bowl XVII: Washington (NFC) 27, Miami (AFC) 17, at Rose Bowl, Pasadena, California.

# PAST STANDINGS

## 1981

### AMERICAN CONFERENCE

**Eastern Division**

| | W | L | T | Pct. | Pts. | OP |
|---|---|---|---|---|---|---|
| Miami | 11 | 4 | 1 | .719 | 345 | 275 |
| N.Y. Jets* | 10 | 5 | 1 | .656 | 355 | 287 |
| Buffalo* | 10 | 6 | 0 | .625 | 311 | 276 |
| Baltimore | 2 | 14 | 0 | .125 | 259 | 533 |
| New England | 2 | 14 | 0 | .125 | 322 | 370 |

**Central Division**

| | W | L | T | Pct. | Pts. | OP |
|---|---|---|---|---|---|---|
| Cincinnati | 12 | 4 | 0 | .750 | 421 | 304 |
| Pittsburgh | 8 | 8 | 0 | .500 | 356 | 297 |
| Houston | 7 | 9 | 0 | .438 | 281 | 355 |
| Cleveland | 5 | 11 | 0 | .313 | 276 | 375 |

**Western Division**

| | W | L | T | Pct. | Pts. | OP |
|---|---|---|---|---|---|---|
| San Diego | 10 | 6 | 0 | .625 | 478 | 390 |
| Denver | 10 | 6 | 0 | .625 | 321 | 289 |
| Kansas City | 9 | 7 | 0 | .563 | 343 | 290 |
| Oakland | 7 | 9 | 0 | .438 | 273 | 343 |
| Seattle | 6 | 10 | 0 | .375 | 322 | 388 |

### NATIONAL CONFERENCE

**Eastern Division**

| | W | L | T | Pct. | Pts. | OP |
|---|---|---|---|---|---|---|
| Dallas | 12 | 4 | 0 | .750 | 367 | 277 |
| Philadelphia* | 10 | 6 | 0 | .625 | 368 | 221 |
| N.Y. Giants* | 9 | 7 | 0 | .563 | 295 | 257 |
| Washington | 8 | 8 | 0 | .500 | 347 | 349 |
| St. Louis | 7 | 9 | 0 | .438 | 315 | 408 |

**Central Division**

| | W | L | T | Pct. | Pts. | OP |
|---|---|---|---|---|---|---|
| Tampa Bay | 9 | 7 | 0 | .563 | 315 | 268 |
| Detroit | 8 | 8 | 0 | .500 | 397 | 322 |
| Green Bay | 8 | 8 | 0 | .500 | 324 | 361 |
| Minnesota | 7 | 9 | 0 | .438 | 325 | 369 |
| Chicago | 6 | 10 | 0 | .375 | 253 | 324 |

**Western Division**

| | W | L | T | Pct. | Pts. | OP |
|---|---|---|---|---|---|---|
| San Francisco | 13 | 3 | 0 | .813 | 357 | 250 |
| Atlanta | 7 | 9 | 0 | .438 | 426 | 355 |
| Los Angeles | 6 | 10 | 0 | .375 | 303 | 351 |
| New Orleans | 4 | 12 | 0 | .250 | 207 | 378 |

**Wild-Card qualifiers for playoffs*

*San Diego won AFC Western title over Denver on the basis of a better division record (6-2 to 5-3). Buffalo won a Wild-Card playoff berth over Denver as the result of a 9-7 victory in head-to-head competition.*

Wild Card playoff: Buffalo 31, NEW YORK JETS 27
Divisional playoffs: San Diego 41, MIAMI 38 (OT); CINCINNATI 28, Buffalo 21
AFC championship: CINCINNATI 27, San Diego 7
Wild Card playoff: New York Giants 27, PHILADELPHIA 21
Divisional playoffs: DALLAS 38, Tampa Bay 0; SAN FRANCISCO 38, New York Giants 24
NFC championship: SAN FRANCISCO 28, Dallas 27
Super Bowl XVI: San Francisco (NFC) 26, Cincinnati (AFC) 21, at Silverdome, Pontiac, Michigan.

## 1980

### AMERICAN CONFERENCE

**Eastern Division**

| | W | L | T | Pct. | Pts. | OP |
|---|---|---|---|---|---|---|
| Buffalo | 11 | 5 | 0 | .688 | 320 | 260 |
| New England | 10 | 6 | 0 | .625 | 441 | 325 |
| Miami | 8 | 8 | 0 | .500 | 266 | 305 |
| Baltimore | 7 | 9 | 0 | .438 | 355 | 387 |
| N.Y. Jets | 4 | 12 | 0 | .250 | 302 | 395 |

**Central Division**

| | W | L | T | Pct. | Pts. | OP |
|---|---|---|---|---|---|---|
| Cleveland | 11 | 5 | 0 | .688 | 357 | 310 |
| Houston* | 11 | 5 | 0 | .688 | 295 | 251 |
| Pittsburgh | 9 | 7 | 0 | .563 | 352 | 313 |
| Cincinnati | 6 | 10 | 0 | .375 | 244 | 312 |

**Western Division**

| | W | L | T | Pct. | Pts. | OP |
|---|---|---|---|---|---|---|
| San Diego | 11 | 5 | 0 | .688 | 418 | 327 |
| Oakland* | 11 | 5 | 0 | .688 | 364 | 306 |
| Kansas City | 8 | 8 | 0 | .500 | 319 | 336 |
| Denver | 8 | 8 | 0 | .500 | 310 | 323 |
| Seattle | 4 | 12 | 0 | .250 | 291 | 408 |

### NATIONAL CONFERENCE

**Eastern Division**

| | W | L | T | Pct. | Pts. | OP |
|---|---|---|---|---|---|---|
| Philadelphia | 12 | 4 | 0 | .750 | 384 | 222 |
| Dallas* | 12 | 4 | 0 | .750 | 454 | 311 |
| Washington | 6 | 10 | 0 | .375 | 261 | 293 |
| St. Louis | 5 | 11 | 0 | .313 | 299 | 350 |
| N.Y. Giants | 4 | 12 | 0 | .250 | 249 | 425 |

**Central Division**

| | W | L | T | Pct. | Pts. | OP |
|---|---|---|---|---|---|---|
| Minnesota | 9 | 7 | 0 | .563 | 317 | 308 |
| Detroit | 9 | 7 | 0 | .563 | 334 | 272 |
| Chicago | 7 | 9 | 0 | .438 | 304 | 264 |
| Tampa Bay | 5 | 10 | 1 | .344 | 271 | 341 |
| Green Bay | 5 | 10 | 1 | .344 | 231 | 371 |

**Western Division**

| | W | L | T | Pct. | Pts. | OP |
|---|---|---|---|---|---|---|
| Atlanta | 12 | 4 | 0 | .750 | 405 | 272 |
| Los Angeles* | 11 | 5 | 0 | .688 | 424 | 289 |
| San Francisco | 6 | 10 | 0 | .375 | 320 | 415 |
| New Orleans | 1 | 15 | 0 | .063 | 291 | 487 |

**Wild-Card qualifiers for playoffs*

*Philadelphia won division title over Dallas on the basis of best net points in division games (plus 84 net points to plus 50). Minnesota won division title because of a better conference record than Detroit (8-4 to 9-5). Cleveland won division title because of a better conference record than Houston (8-4 to 7-5). San Diego won division title over Oakland on the basis of best net points in division games (plus 60 net points to plus 37).*

Wild Card playoff: OAKLAND 27, Houston 7
Divisional playoffs: SAN DIEGO 20, Buffalo 14; Oakland 14, CLEVELAND 12
AFC championship: Oakland 34, SAN DIEGO 27
Wild Card playoff: DALLAS 34, Los Angeles 13
Divisional playoffs: PHILADELPHIA 31, Minnesota 16; Dallas 30, ATLANTA 27
NFC championship: PHILADELPHIA 20, Dallas 7
Super Bowl XV: Oakland (AFC) 27, Philadelphia (NFC) 10, at Louisiana Superdome, New Orleans, Louisiana.

## 1979

### AMERICAN CONFERENCE

**Eastern Division**

| | W | L | T | Pct. | Pts. | OP |
|---|---|---|---|---|---|---|
| Miami | 10 | 6 | 0 | .625 | 341 | 257 |
| New England | 9 | 7 | 0 | .563 | 411 | 326 |
| N.Y. Jets | 8 | 8 | 0 | .500 | 337 | 383 |
| Buffalo | 7 | 9 | 0 | .438 | 268 | 279 |
| Baltimore | 5 | 11 | 0 | .313 | 271 | 351 |

**Central Division**

| | W | L | T | Pct. | Pts. | OP |
|---|---|---|---|---|---|---|
| Pittsburgh | 12 | 4 | 0 | .750 | 416 | 262 |
| Houston* | 11 | 5 | 0 | .688 | 362 | 331 |
| Cleveland | 9 | 7 | 0 | .563 | 359 | 352 |
| Cincinnati | 4 | 12 | 0 | .250 | 337 | 421 |

**Western Division**

| | W | L | T | Pct. | Pts. | OP |
|---|---|---|---|---|---|---|
| San Diego | 12 | 4 | 0 | .750 | 411 | 246 |
| Denver* | 10 | 6 | 0 | .625 | 289 | 262 |
| Seattle | 9 | 7 | 0 | .563 | 378 | 372 |
| Oakland | 9 | 7 | 0 | .563 | 365 | 337 |
| Kansas City | 7 | 9 | 0 | .438 | 238 | 262 |

### NATIONAL CONFERENCE

**Eastern Division**

| | W | L | T | Pct. | Pts. | OP |
|---|---|---|---|---|---|---|
| Dallas | 11 | 5 | 0 | .688 | 371 | 313 |
| Philadelphia* | 11 | 5 | 0 | .688 | 339 | 282 |
| Washington | 10 | 6 | 0 | .625 | 348 | 295 |
| N.Y. Giants | 6 | 10 | 0 | .375 | 237 | 323 |
| St. Louis | 5 | 11 | 0 | .313 | 307 | 358 |

**Central Division**

| | W | L | T | Pct. | Pts. | OP |
|---|---|---|---|---|---|---|
| Tampa Bay | 10 | 6 | 0 | .625 | 273 | 237 |
| Chicago* | 10 | 6 | 0 | .625 | 306 | 249 |
| Minnesota | 7 | 9 | 0 | .438 | 259 | 337 |
| Green Bay | 5 | 11 | 0 | .313 | 246 | 316 |
| Detroit | 2 | 14 | 0 | .125 | 219 | 365 |

**Western Division**

| | W | L | T | Pct. | Pts. | OP |
|---|---|---|---|---|---|---|
| Los Angeles | 9 | 7 | 0 | .563 | 323 | 309 |
| New Orleans | 8 | 8 | 0 | .500 | 370 | 360 |
| Atlanta | 6 | 10 | 0 | .375 | 300 | 388 |
| San Francisco | 2 | 14 | 0 | .125 | 308 | 416 |

**Wild-Card qualifiers for playoffs*

*Dallas won division title because of a better conference record than Philadelphia (10-2 to 9-3). Tampa Bay won division title because of a better division record than Chicago (6-2 to 5-3). Chicago won a Wild-Card berth over Washington on the basis of best net points in all games (plus 57 net points to plus 53).*

Wild Card playoff: HOUSTON 13, Denver 7
Divisional playoffs: Houston 17, SAN DIEGO 14; PITTSBURGH 34, Miami 14
AFC championship: PITTSBURGH 27, Houston 13
Wild Card playoff: PHILADELPHIA 27, Chicago 17
Divisional playoffs: TAMPA BAY 24, Philadelphia 17; Los Angeles 21, DALLAS 19
NFC championship: Los Angeles 9, TAMPA BAY 0
Super Bowl XIV: Pittsburgh (AFC) 31, Los Angeles (NFC) 19, at Rose Bowl, Pasadena, California.

## 1978

### AMERICAN CONFERENCE

**Eastern Division**

| | W | L | T | Pct. | Pts. | OP |
|---|---|---|---|---|---|---|
| New England | 11 | 5 | 0 | .688 | 358 | 286 |
| Miami* | 11 | 5 | 0 | .688 | 372 | 254 |
| N.Y. Jets | 8 | 8 | 0 | .500 | 359 | 364 |
| Buffalo | 5 | 11 | 0 | .313 | 302 | 354 |
| Baltimore | 5 | 11 | 0 | .313 | 239 | 421 |

**Central Division**

| | W | L | T | Pct. | Pts. | OP |
|---|---|---|---|---|---|---|
| Pittsburgh | 14 | 2 | 0 | .875 | 356 | 195 |
| Houston* | 10 | 6 | 0 | .625 | 283 | 298 |
| Cleveland | 8 | 8 | 0 | .500 | 334 | 356 |
| Cincinnati | 4 | 12 | 0 | .250 | 252 | 284 |

**Western Division**

| | W | L | T | Pct. | Pts. | OP |
|---|---|---|---|---|---|---|
| Denver | 10 | 6 | 0 | .625 | 282 | 198 |
| Oakland | 9 | 7 | 0 | .563 | 311 | 283 |
| Seattle | 9 | 7 | 0 | .563 | 345 | 358 |
| San Diego | 9 | 7 | 0 | .563 | 355 | 309 |
| Kansas City | 4 | 12 | 0 | .250 | 243 | 327 |

### NATIONAL CONFERENCE

**Eastern Division**

| | W | L | T | Pct. | Pts. | OP |
|---|---|---|---|---|---|---|
| Dallas | 12 | 4 | 0 | .750 | 384 | 208 |
| Philadelphia* | 9 | 7 | 0 | .563 | 270 | 250 |
| Washington | 8 | 8 | 0 | .500 | 273 | 283 |
| St. Louis | 6 | 10 | 0 | .375 | 248 | 296 |
| N.Y. Giants | 6 | 10 | 0 | .375 | 264 | 298 |

**Central Division**

| | W | L | T | Pct. | Pts. | OP |
|---|---|---|---|---|---|---|
| Minnesota | 8 | 7 | 1 | .531 | 294 | 306 |
| Green Bay | 8 | 7 | 1 | .531 | 249 | 269 |
| Detroit | 7 | 9 | 0 | .438 | 290 | 300 |
| Chicago | 7 | 9 | 0 | .438 | 253 | 274 |
| Tampa Bay | 5 | 11 | 0 | .313 | 241 | 259 |

**Western Division**

| | W | L | T | Pct. | Pts. | OP |
|---|---|---|---|---|---|---|
| Los Angeles | 12 | 4 | 0 | .750 | 316 | 245 |
| Atlanta* | 9 | 7 | 0 | .563 | 240 | 290 |
| New Orleans | 7 | 9 | 0 | .438 | 281 | 298 |
| San Francisco | 2 | 14 | 0 | .125 | 219 | 350 |

**Wild-Card qualifiers for playoffs*

*New England won division title on the basis of a better division record than Miami (6-2 to 5-3). Minnesota won division title because of a better head-to-head record against Green Bay (1-0-1).*

Wild Card playoff: Houston 17, MIAMI 9
Divisional playoffs: Houston 31, NEW ENGLAND 14; PITTSBURGH 33, Denver 10
AFC championship: PITTSBURGH 34, Houston 5
Wild Card playoff: ATLANTA 14, Philadelphia 13
Divisional playoffs: DALLAS 27, Atlanta 20; LOS ANGELES 34, Minnesota 10
NFC championship: Dallas 28, LOS ANGELES 0
Super Bowl XIII: Pittsburgh (AFC) 35, Dallas (NFC) 31, at Orange Bowl, Miami, Florida.

## 1977

### AMERICAN CONFERENCE

**Eastern Division**

| | W | L | T | Pct. | Pts. | OP |
|---|---|---|---|---|---|---|
| Baltimore | 10 | 4 | 0 | .714 | 295 | 221 |
| Miami | 10 | 4 | 0 | .714 | 313 | 197 |
| New England | 9 | 5 | 0 | .643 | 278 | 217 |
| N.Y. Jets | 3 | 11 | 0 | .214 | 191 | 300 |
| Buffalo | 3 | 11 | 0 | .214 | 160 | 313 |

**Central Division**

| | W | L | T | Pct. | Pts. | OP |
|---|---|---|---|---|---|---|
| Pittsburgh | 9 | 5 | 0 | .643 | 283 | 243 |
| Houston | 8 | 6 | 0 | .571 | 299 | 230 |
| Cincinnati | 8 | 6 | 0 | .571 | 238 | 235 |
| Cleveland | 6 | 8 | 0 | .429 | 269 | 267 |

**Western Division**

| | W | L | T | Pct. | Pts. | OP |
|---|---|---|---|---|---|---|
| Denver | 12 | 2 | 0 | .857 | 274 | 148 |
| Oakland* | 11 | 3 | 0 | .786 | 351 | 230 |
| San Diego | 7 | 7 | 0 | .500 | 222 | 205 |
| Seattle | 5 | 9 | 0 | .357 | 282 | 373 |
| Kansas City | 2 | 12 | 0 | .143 | 225 | 349 |

### NATIONAL CONFERENCE

**Eastern Division**

| | W | L | T | Pct. | Pts. | OP |
|---|---|---|---|---|---|---|
| Dallas | 12 | 2 | 0 | .857 | 345 | 212 |
| Washington | 9 | 5 | 0 | .643 | 196 | 189 |
| St. Louis | 7 | 7 | 0 | .500 | 272 | 287 |
| Philadelphia | 5 | 9 | 0 | .357 | 220 | 207 |
| N.Y. Giants | 5 | 9 | 0 | .357 | 181 | 265 |

**Central Division**

| | W | L | T | Pct. | Pts. | OP |
|---|---|---|---|---|---|---|
| Minnesota | 9 | 5 | 0 | .643 | 231 | 227 |
| Chicago* | 9 | 5 | 0 | .643 | 255 | 253 |
| Detroit | 6 | 8 | 0 | .429 | 183 | 252 |
| Green Bay | 4 | 10 | 0 | .286 | 134 | 219 |
| Tampa Bay | 2 | 12 | 0 | .143 | 103 | 223 |

**Western Division**

| | W | L | T | Pct. | Pts. | OP |
|---|---|---|---|---|---|---|
| Los Angeles | 10 | 4 | 0 | .714 | 302 | 146 |
| Atlanta | 7 | 7 | 0 | .500 | 179 | 129 |
| San Francisco | 5 | 9 | 0 | .357 | 220 | 260 |
| New Orleans | 3 | 11 | 0 | .214 | 232 | 336 |

**Wild-Card qualifier for playoffs*

*Baltimore won division title on the basis of a better conference record than Miami (9-3 to 8-4). Chicago won a Wild-Card berth over Washington on the basis of best net points in conference games (plus 48 net points to plus 4).*

Divisional playoffs: DENVER 34, Pittsburgh 21; Oakland 37, BALTIMORE 31 (OT)

AFC championship: DENVER 20, Oakland 17

Divisional playoffs: DALLAS 37, Chicago 7; Minnesota 14, LOS ANGELES 7

NFC championship: DALLAS 23, Minnesota 6

Super Bowl XII: Dallas (NFC) 27, Denver (AFC) 10, at Louisiana Superdome, New Orleans, Louisiana.

## 1976

### AMERICAN CONFERENCE

**Eastern Division**

| | W | L | T | Pct. | Pts. | OP |
|---|---|---|---|---|---|---|
| Baltimore | 11 | 3 | 0 | .786 | 417 | 246 |
| New England* | 11 | 3 | 0 | .786 | 376 | 236 |
| Miami | 6 | 8 | 0 | .429 | 263 | 264 |
| N.Y. Jets | 3 | 11 | 0 | .214 | 169 | 383 |
| Buffalo | 2 | 12 | 0 | .143 | 245 | 363 |

**Central Division**

| | W | L | T | Pct. | Pts. | OP |
|---|---|---|---|---|---|---|
| Pittsburgh | 10 | 4 | 0 | .714 | 342 | 138 |
| Cincinnati | 10 | 4 | 0 | .714 | 335 | 210 |
| Cleveland | 9 | 5 | 0 | .643 | 267 | 287 |
| Houston | 5 | 9 | 0 | .357 | 222 | 273 |

**Western Division**

| | W | L | T | Pct. | Pts. | OP |
|---|---|---|---|---|---|---|
| Oakland | 13 | 1 | 0 | .929 | 350 | 237 |
| Denver | 9 | 5 | 0 | .643 | 315 | 206 |
| San Diego | 6 | 8 | 0 | .429 | 248 | 285 |
| Kansas City | 5 | 9 | 0 | .357 | 290 | 376 |
| Tampa Bay | 0 | 14 | 0 | .000 | 125 | 412 |

### NATIONAL CONFERENCE

**Eastern Division**

| | W | L | T | Pct. | Pts. | OP |
|---|---|---|---|---|---|---|
| Dallas | 11 | 3 | 0 | .786 | 296 | 194 |
| Washington* | 10 | 4 | 0 | .714 | 291 | 217 |
| St. Louis | 10 | 4 | 0 | .714 | 309 | 267 |
| Philadelphia | 4 | 10 | 0 | .286 | 165 | 286 |
| N.Y. Giants | 3 | 11 | 0 | .214 | 170 | 250 |

**Central Division**

| | W | L | T | Pct. | Pts. | OP |
|---|---|---|---|---|---|---|
| Minnesota | 11 | 2 | 1 | .821 | 305 | 176 |
| Chicago | 7 | 7 | 0 | .500 | 253 | 216 |
| Detroit | 6 | 8 | 0 | .429 | 262 | 220 |
| Green Bay | 5 | 9 | 0 | .357 | 218 | 299 |

**Western Division**

| | W | L | T | Pct. | Pts. | OP |
|---|---|---|---|---|---|---|
| Los Angeles | 10 | 3 | 1 | .750 | 351 | 190 |
| San Francisco | 8 | 6 | 0 | .571 | 270 | 190 |
| Atlanta | 4 | 10 | 0 | .286 | 172 | 312 |
| New Orleans | 4 | 10 | 0 | .286 | 253 | 346 |
| Seattle | 2 | 12 | 0 | .143 | 229 | 429 |

**Wild-Card qualifier for playoffs*

*Baltimore won division title on the basis of a better division record than New England (7-1 to 6-2). Pittsburgh won division title because of a two-game sweep over Cincinnati. Washington won Wild-Card berth over St. Louis because of a two-game sweep over Cardinals.*

Divisional playoffs: OAKLAND 24, New England 21; Pittsburgh 40, BALTIMORE 14

AFC championship: OAKLAND 24, Pittsburgh 7

Divisional playoffs: MINNESOTA 35, Washington 20; Los Angeles 14, DALLAS 12

NFC championship: MINNESOTA 24, Los Angeles 13

Super Bowl XI: Oakland (AFC) 32, Minnesota (NFC) 14, at Rose Bowl, Pasadena, California.

## 1975

### AMERICAN CONFERENCE

**Eastern Division**

| | W | L | T | Pct. | Pts. | OP |
|---|---|---|---|---|---|---|
| Baltimore | 10 | 4 | 0 | .714 | 395 | 269 |
| Miami | 10 | 4 | 0 | .714 | 357 | 222 |
| Buffalo | 8 | 6 | 0 | .571 | 420 | 355 |
| New England | 3 | 11 | 0 | .214 | 258 | 358 |
| N.Y. Jets | 3 | 11 | 0 | .214 | 258 | 433 |

**Central Division**

| | W | L | T | Pct. | Pts. | OP |
|---|---|---|---|---|---|---|
| Pittsburgh | 12 | 2 | 0 | .857 | 373 | 162 |
| Cincinnati* | 11 | 3 | 0 | .786 | 340 | 246 |
| Houston | 10 | 4 | 0 | .714 | 293 | 226 |
| Cleveland | 3 | 11 | 0 | .214 | 218 | 372 |

**Western Division**

| | W | L | T | Pct. | Pts. | OP |
|---|---|---|---|---|---|---|
| Oakland | 11 | 3 | 0 | .786 | 375 | 255 |
| Denver | 6 | 8 | 0 | .429 | 254 | 307 |
| Kansas City | 5 | 9 | 0 | .357 | 282 | 341 |
| San Diego | 2 | 12 | 0 | .143 | 189 | 345 |

### NATIONAL CONFERENCE

**Eastern Division**

| | W | L | T | Pct. | Pts. | OP |
|---|---|---|---|---|---|---|
| St. Louis | 11 | 3 | 0 | .786 | 356 | 276 |
| Dallas* | 10 | 4 | 0 | .714 | 350 | 268 |
| Washington | 8 | 6 | 0 | .571 | 325 | 276 |
| N.Y. Giants | 5 | 9 | 0 | .357 | 216 | 306 |
| Philadelphia | 4 | 10 | 0 | .286 | 225 | 302 |

**Central Division**

| | W | L | T | Pct. | Pts. | OP |
|---|---|---|---|---|---|---|
| Minnesota | 12 | 2 | 0 | .857 | 377 | 180 |
| Detroit | 7 | 7 | 0 | .500 | 245 | 262 |
| Chicago | 4 | 10 | 0 | .286 | 191 | 379 |
| Green Bay | 4 | 10 | 0 | .286 | 226 | 285 |

**Western Division**

| | W | L | T | Pct. | Pts. | OP |
|---|---|---|---|---|---|---|
| Los Angeles | 12 | 2 | 0 | .857 | 312 | 135 |
| San Francisco | 5 | 9 | 0 | .357 | 255 | 286 |
| Atlanta | 4 | 10 | 0 | .286 | 240 | 289 |
| New Orleans | 2 | 12 | 0 | .143 | 165 | 360 |

**Wild-Card qualifier for playoffs*

*Baltimore won division title on the basis of a two-game sweep over Miami.*

Divisional playoffs: PITTSBURGH 28, Baltimore 10; OAKLAND 31, Cincinnati 28

AFC championship: PITTSBURGH 16, Oakland 10

Divisional playoffs: LOS ANGELES 35, St. Louis 23; Dallas 17, MINNESOTA 14

NFC championship: Dallas 37, LOS ANGELES 7

Super Bowl X: Pittsburgh (AFC) 21, Dallas (NFC) 17, at Orange Bowl, Miami, Florida.

## 1974

### AMERICAN CONFERENCE

**Eastern Division**

| | W | L | T | Pct. | Pts. | OP |
|---|---|---|---|---|---|---|
| Miami | 11 | 3 | 0 | .786 | 327 | 216 |
| Buffalo* | 9 | 5 | 0 | .643 | 264 | 244 |
| New England | 7 | 7 | 0 | .500 | 348 | 289 |
| N.Y. Jets | 7 | 7 | 0 | .500 | 279 | 300 |
| Baltimore | 2 | 12 | 0 | .143 | 190 | 329 |

**Central Division**

| | W | L | T | Pct. | Pts. | OP |
|---|---|---|---|---|---|---|
| Pittsburgh | 10 | 3 | 1 | .750 | 305 | 189 |
| Cincinnati | 7 | 7 | 0 | .500 | 283 | 259 |
| Houston | 7 | 7 | 0 | .500 | 236 | 282 |
| Cleveland | 4 | 10 | 0 | .286 | 251 | 344 |

**Western Division**

| | W | L | T | Pct. | Pts. | OP |
|---|---|---|---|---|---|---|
| Oakland | 12 | 2 | 0 | .857 | 355 | 228 |
| Denver | 7 | 6 | 1 | .536 | 302 | 294 |
| Kansas City | 5 | 9 | 0 | .357 | 233 | 293 |
| San Diego | 5 | 9 | 0 | .357 | 212 | 285 |

### NATIONAL CONFERENCE

**Eastern Division**

| | W | L | T | Pct. | Pts. | OP |
|---|---|---|---|---|---|---|
| St. Louis | 10 | 4 | 0 | .714 | 285 | 218 |
| Washington* | 10 | 4 | 0 | .714 | 320 | 196 |
| Dallas | 8 | 6 | 0 | .571 | 297 | 235 |
| Philadelphia | 7 | 7 | 0 | .500 | 242 | 217 |
| N.Y. Giants | 2 | 12 | 0 | .143 | 195 | 299 |

**Central Division**

| | W | L | T | Pct. | Pts. | OP |
|---|---|---|---|---|---|---|
| Minnesota | 10 | 4 | 0 | .714 | 310 | 195 |
| Detroit | 7 | 7 | 0 | .500 | 256 | 270 |
| Green Bay | 6 | 8 | 0 | .429 | 210 | 206 |
| Chicago | 4 | 10 | 0 | .286 | 152 | 279 |

**Western Division**

| | W | L | T | Pct. | Pts. | OP |
|---|---|---|---|---|---|---|
| Los Angeles | 10 | 4 | 0 | .714 | 263 | 181 |
| San Francisco | 6 | 8 | 0 | .429 | 226 | 236 |
| New Orleans | 5 | 9 | 0 | .357 | 166 | 263 |
| Atlanta | 3 | 11 | 0 | .214 | 111 | 271 |

**Wild-Card qualifier for playoffs*

*St. Louis won division title because of a two-game sweep over Washington.*

Divisional playoffs: OAKLAND 28, Miami 26; PITTSBURGH 32, Buffalo 14

AFC championship: Pittsburgh 24, OAKLAND 13

Divisional playoffs: MINNESOTA 30, St. Louis 14; LOS ANGELES 19, Washington 10

NFC championship: MINNESOTA 14, Los Angeles 10

Super Bowl IX: Pittsburgh (AFC) 16, Minnesota (NFC) 6, at Tulane Stadium, New Orleans, Louisiana.

## 1973

### AMERICAN CONFERENCE

**Eastern Division**

| | W | L | T | Pct. | Pts. | OP |
|---|---|---|---|---|---|---|
| Miami | 12 | 2 | 0 | .857 | 343 | 150 |
| Buffalo | 9 | 5 | 0 | .643 | 259 | 230 |
| New England | 5 | 9 | 0 | .357 | 258 | 300 |
| Baltimore | 4 | 10 | 0 | .286 | 226 | 341 |
| N.Y. Jets | 4 | 10 | 0 | .286 | 240 | 306 |

**Central Division**

| | W | L | T | Pct. | Pts. | OP |
|---|---|---|---|---|---|---|
| Cincinnati | 10 | 4 | 0 | .714 | 286 | 231 |
| Pittsburgh* | 10 | 4 | 0 | .714 | 347 | 210 |
| Cleveland | 7 | 5 | 2 | .571 | 234 | 255 |
| Houston | 1 | 13 | 0 | .071 | 199 | 447 |

**Western Division**

| | W | L | T | Pct. | Pts. | OP |
|---|---|---|---|---|---|---|
| Oakland | 9 | 4 | 1 | .679 | 292 | 175 |
| Denver | 7 | 5 | 2 | .571 | 354 | 296 |
| Kansas City | 7 | 5 | 2 | .571 | 231 | 192 |
| San Diego | 2 | 11 | 1 | .179 | 188 | 386 |

### NATIONAL CONFERENCE

**Eastern Division**

| | W | L | T | Pct. | Pts. | OP |
|---|---|---|---|---|---|---|
| Dallas | 10 | 4 | 0 | .714 | 382 | 203 |
| Washington* | 10 | 4 | 0 | .714 | 325 | 198 |
| Philadelphia | 5 | 8 | 1 | .393 | 310 | 393 |
| St. Louis | 4 | 9 | 1 | .321 | 286 | 365 |
| N.Y. Giants | 2 | 11 | 1 | .179 | 226 | 362 |

**Central Division**

| | W | L | T | Pct. | Pts. | OP |
|---|---|---|---|---|---|---|
| Minnesota | 12 | 2 | 0 | .857 | 296 | 168 |
| Detroit | 6 | 7 | 1 | .464 | 271 | 247 |
| Green Bay | 5 | 7 | 2 | .429 | 202 | 259 |
| Chicago | 3 | 11 | 0 | .214 | 195 | 334 |

**Western Division**

| | W | L | T | Pct. | Pts. | OP |
|---|---|---|---|---|---|---|
| Los Angeles | 12 | 2 | 0 | .857 | 388 | 178 |
| Atlanta | 9 | 5 | 0 | .643 | 318 | 224 |
| New Orleans | 5 | 9 | 0 | .357 | 163 | 312 |
| San Francisco | 5 | 9 | 0 | .357 | 262 | 319 |

**Wild-Card qualifier for playoffs*

*Cincinnati won division title on the basis of a better conference record than Pittsburgh (8-3 to 7-4). Dallas won division title on the basis of a better point differential vs. Washington (net 13 points).*

Divisional playoffs: OAKLAND 33, Pittsburgh 14; MIAMI 34, Cincinnati 16
AFC championship: MIAMI 27, Oakland 10
Divisional playoffs: MINNESOTA 27, Washington 20; DALLAS 27, Los Angeles 16
NFC championship: Minnesota 27, DALLAS 10
Super Bowl VIII: Miami (AFC) 24, Minnesota (NFC) 7, at Rice Stadium, Houston, Texas.

## 1972

### AMERICAN CONFERENCE

**Eastern Division**

| | W | L | T | Pct. | Pts. | OP |
|---|---|---|---|---|---|---|
| Miami | 14 | 0 | 0 | 1.000 | 385 | 171 |
| N.Y. Jets | 7 | 7 | 0 | .500 | 367 | 324 |
| Baltimore | 5 | 9 | 0 | .357 | 235 | 252 |
| Buffalo | 4 | 9 | 1 | .321 | 257 | 377 |
| New England | 3 | 11 | 0 | .214 | 192 | 446 |

**Central Division**

| | W | L | T | Pct. | Pts. | OP |
|---|---|---|---|---|---|---|
| Pittsburgh | 11 | 3 | 0 | .786 | 343 | 175 |
| Cleveland* | 10 | 4 | 0 | .714 | 268 | 249 |
| Cincinnati | 8 | 6 | 0 | .571 | 299 | 229 |
| Houston | 1 | 13 | 0 | .071 | 164 | 380 |

**Western Division**

| | W | L | T | Pct. | Pts. | OP |
|---|---|---|---|---|---|---|
| Oakland | 10 | 3 | 1 | .750 | 365 | 248 |
| Kansas City | 8 | 6 | 0 | .571 | 287 | 254 |
| Denver | 5 | 9 | 0 | .357 | 325 | 350 |
| San Diego | 4 | 9 | 1 | .321 | 264 | 344 |

### NATIONAL CONFERENCE

**Eastern Division**

| | W | L | T | Pct. | Pts. | OP |
|---|---|---|---|---|---|---|
| Washington | 11 | 3 | 0 | .786 | 336 | 218 |
| Dallas* | 10 | 4 | 0 | .714 | 319 | 240 |
| N.Y. Giants | 8 | 6 | 0 | .571 | 331 | 247 |
| St. Louis | 4 | 9 | 1 | .321 | 193 | 303 |
| Philadelphia | 2 | 11 | 1 | .179 | 145 | 352 |

**Central Division**

| | W | L | T | Pct. | Pts. | OP |
|---|---|---|---|---|---|---|
| Green Bay | 10 | 4 | 0 | .714 | 304 | 226 |
| Detroit | 8 | 5 | 1 | .607 | 339 | 290 |
| Minnesota | 7 | 7 | 0 | .500 | 301 | 252 |
| Chicago | 4 | 9 | 1 | .321 | 225 | 275 |

**Western Division**

| | W | L | T | Pct. | Pts. | OP |
|---|---|---|---|---|---|---|
| San Francisco | 8 | 5 | 1 | .607 | 353 | 249 |
| Atlanta | 7 | 7 | 0 | .500 | 269 | 274 |
| Los Angeles | 6 | 7 | 1 | .464 | 291 | 286 |
| New Orleans | 2 | 11 | 1 | .179 | 215 | 361 |

**Wild-Card qualifier for playoffs*

Divisional playoffs: PITTSBURGH 13, Oakland 7; MIAMI 20, Cleveland 14
AFC championship: Miami 21, PITTSBURGH 17
Divisional playoffs: Dallas 30, SAN FRANCISCO 28; WASHINGTON 16, Green Bay 3
NFC championship: WASHINGTON 26, Dallas 3
Super Bowl VII: Miami (AFC) 14, Washington (NFC) 7, at Memorial Coliseum, Los Angeles, California.

## 1971

### AMERICAN CONFERENCE

**Eastern Division**

| | W | L | T | Pct. | Pts. | OP |
|---|---|---|---|---|---|---|
| Miami | 10 | 3 | 1 | .769 | 315 | 174 |
| Baltimore* | 10 | 4 | 0 | .714 | 313 | 140 |
| New England | 6 | 8 | 0 | .429 | 238 | 325 |
| N.Y. Jets | 6 | 8 | 0 | .429 | 212 | 299 |
| Buffalo | 1 | 13 | 0 | .071 | 184 | 394 |

**Central Division**

| | W | L | T | Pct. | Pts. | OP |
|---|---|---|---|---|---|---|
| Cleveland | 9 | 5 | 0 | .643 | 285 | 273 |
| Pittsburgh | 6 | 8 | 0 | .429 | 246 | 292 |
| Houston | 4 | 9 | 1 | .308 | 251 | 330 |
| Cincinnati | 4 | 10 | 0 | .286 | 284 | 265 |

**Western Division**

| | W | L | T | Pct. | Pts. | OP |
|---|---|---|---|---|---|---|
| Kansas City | 10 | 3 | 1 | .769 | 302 | 208 |
| Oakland | 8 | 4 | 2 | .667 | 344 | 278 |
| San Diego | 6 | 8 | 0 | .429 | 311 | 341 |
| Denver | 4 | 9 | 1 | .308 | 203 | 275 |

### NATIONAL CONFERENCE

**Eastern Division**

| | W | L | T | Pct. | Pts. | OP |
|---|---|---|---|---|---|---|
| Dallas | 11 | 3 | 0 | .786 | 406 | 222 |
| Washington* | 9 | 4 | 1 | .692 | 276 | 190 |
| Philadelphia | 6 | 7 | 1 | .462 | 221 | 302 |
| St. Louis | 4 | 9 | 1 | .308 | 231 | 279 |
| N.Y. Giants | 4 | 10 | 0 | .286 | 228 | 362 |

**Central Division**

| | W | L | T | Pct. | Pts. | OP |
|---|---|---|---|---|---|---|
| Minnesota | 11 | 3 | 0 | .786 | 245 | 139 |
| Detroit | 7 | 6 | 1 | .538 | 341 | 286 |
| Chicago | 6 | 8 | 0 | .429 | 185 | 276 |
| Green Bay | 4 | 8 | 2 | .333 | 274 | 298 |

**Western Division**

| | W | L | T | Pct. | Pts. | OP |
|---|---|---|---|---|---|---|
| San Francisco | 9 | 5 | 0 | .643 | 300 | 216 |
| Los Angeles | 8 | 5 | 1 | .615 | 313 | 260 |
| Atlanta | 7 | 6 | 1 | .538 | 274 | 277 |
| New Orleans | 4 | 8 | 2 | .333 | 266 | 347 |

**Wild-Card qualifier for playoffs*

Divisional playoffs: Miami 27, KANSAS CITY 24 (OT); Baltimore 20, CLEVELAND 3
AFC championship: MIAMI 21, Baltimore 0
Divisional playoffs: Dallas 20, MINNESOTA 12; SAN FRANCISCO 24, Washington 20
NFC championship: DALLAS 14, San Francisco 3
Super Bowl VI: Dallas (NFC) 24, Miami (AFC) 3, at Tulane Stadium, New Orleans, Louisiana.

## 1970

### AMERICAN CONFERENCE

**Eastern Division**

| | W | L | T | Pct. | Pts. | OP |
|---|---|---|---|---|---|---|
| Baltimore | 11 | 2 | 1 | .846 | 321 | 234 |
| Miami* | 10 | 4 | 0 | .714 | 297 | 228 |
| N.Y. Jets | 4 | 10 | 0 | .286 | 255 | 286 |
| Buffalo | 3 | 10 | 1 | .231 | 204 | 337 |
| Boston Patriots | 2 | 12 | 0 | .143 | 149 | 361 |

**Central Division**

| | W | L | T | Pct. | Pts. | OP |
|---|---|---|---|---|---|---|
| Cincinnati | 8 | 6 | 0 | .571 | 312 | 255 |
| Cleveland | 7 | 7 | 0 | .500 | 286 | 265 |
| Pittsburgh | 5 | 9 | 0 | .357 | 210 | 272 |
| Houston | 3 | 10 | 1 | .231 | 217 | 352 |

**Western Division**

| | W | L | T | Pct. | Pts. | OP |
|---|---|---|---|---|---|---|
| Oakland | 8 | 4 | 2 | .667 | 300 | 293 |
| Kansas City | 7 | 5 | 2 | .583 | 272 | 244 |
| San Diego | 5 | 6 | 3 | .455 | 282 | 278 |
| Denver | 5 | 8 | 1 | .385 | 253 | 264 |

### NATIONAL CONFERENCE

**Eastern Division**

| | W | L | T | Pct. | Pts. | OP |
|---|---|---|---|---|---|---|
| Dallas | 10 | 4 | 0 | .714 | 299 | 221 |
| N.Y. Giants | 9 | 5 | 0 | .643 | 301 | 270 |
| St. Louis | 8 | 5 | 1 | .615 | 325 | 228 |
| Washington | 6 | 8 | 0 | .429 | 297 | 314 |
| Philadelphia | 3 | 10 | 1 | .231 | 241 | 332 |

**Central Division**

| | W | L | T | Pct. | Pts. | OP |
|---|---|---|---|---|---|---|
| Minnesota | 12 | 2 | 0 | .857 | 335 | 143 |
| Detroit* | 10 | 4 | 0 | .714 | 347 | 202 |
| Chicago | 6 | 8 | 0 | .429 | 256 | 261 |
| Green Bay | 6 | 8 | 0 | .429 | 196 | 293 |

**Western Division**

| | W | L | T | Pct. | Pts. | OP |
|---|---|---|---|---|---|---|
| San Francisco | 10 | 3 | 1 | .769 | 352 | 267 |
| Los Angeles | 9 | 4 | 1 | .692 | 325 | 202 |
| Atlanta | 4 | 8 | 2 | .333 | 206 | 261 |
| New Orleans | 2 | 11 | 1 | .154 | 172 | 347 |

**Wild-Card qualifier for playoffs*

Divisional playoffs: BALTIMORE 17, Cincinnati 0; OAKLAND 21, Miami 14
AFC championship: BALTIMORE 27, Oakland 17
Divisional playoffs: DALLAS 5, Detroit 0; San Francisco 17, MINNESOTA 14
NFC championship: Dallas 17, SAN FRANCISCO 10
Super Bowl V: Baltimore (AFC) 16, Dallas (NFC) 13, at Orange Bowl, Miami, Florida.

## 1969 NFL

### EASTERN CONFERENCE

**Capitol Division**

| | W | L | T | Pct. | Pts. | OP |
|---|---|---|---|---|---|---|
| Dallas | 11 | 2 | 1 | .846 | 369 | 223 |
| Washington | 7 | 5 | 2 | .583 | 307 | 319 |
| New Orleans | 5 | 9 | 0 | .357 | 311 | 393 |
| Philadelphia | 4 | 9 | 1 | .308 | 279 | 377 |

**Century Division**

| | W | L | T | Pct. | Pts. | OP |
|---|---|---|---|---|---|---|
| Cleveland | 10 | 3 | 1 | .769 | 351 | 300 |
| N.Y. Giants | 6 | 8 | 0 | .429 | 264 | 298 |
| St. Louis | 4 | 9 | 1 | .308 | 314 | 389 |
| Pittsburgh | 1 | 13 | 0 | .071 | 218 | 404 |

### WESTERN CONFERENCE

**Coastal Division**

| | W | L | T | Pct. | Pts. | OP |
|---|---|---|---|---|---|---|
| Los Angeles | 11 | 3 | 0 | .786 | 320 | 243 |
| Baltimore | 8 | 5 | 1 | .615 | 279 | 268 |
| Atlanta | 6 | 8 | 0 | .429 | 276 | 268 |
| San Francisco | 4 | 8 | 2 | .333 | 277 | 319 |

**Central Division**

| | W | L | T | Pct. | Pts. | OP |
|---|---|---|---|---|---|---|
| Minnesota | 12 | 2 | 0 | .857 | 379 | 133 |
| Detroit | 9 | 4 | 1 | .692 | 259 | 188 |
| Green Bay | 8 | 6 | 0 | .571 | 269 | 221 |
| Chicago | 1 | 13 | 0 | .071 | 210 | 339 |

Conference championships: Cleveland 38, DALLAS 14; MINNESOTA 23, Los Angeles 20
NFL championship: MINNESOTA 27, Cleveland 7
Super Bowl IV: Kansas City (AFL) 23, Minnesota (NFL) 7, at Tulane Stadium, New Orleans, Louisiana

## 1969 AFL

**EASTERN DIVISION**

| | W | L | T | Pct. | Pts. | OP |
|---|---|---|---|---|---|---|
| N.Y. Jets | 10 | 4 | 0 | .714 | 353 | 269 |
| Houston | 6 | 6 | 2 | .500 | 278 | 279 |
| Boston Patriots | 4 | 10 | 0 | .286 | 266 | 316 |
| Buffalo | 4 | 10 | 0 | .286 | 230 | 359 |
| Miami | 3 | 10 | 1 | .231 | 233 | 332 |

**WESTERN DIVISION**

| | W | L | T | Pct. | Pts. | OP |
|---|---|---|---|---|---|---|
| Oakland | 12 | 1 | 1 | .923 | 377 | 242 |
| Kansas City | 11 | 3 | 0 | .786 | 359 | 177 |
| San Diego | 8 | 6 | 0 | .571 | 288 | 276 |
| Denver | 5 | 8 | 1 | .385 | 297 | 344 |
| Cincinnati | 4 | 9 | 1 | .308 | 280 | 367 |

Divisional playoffs: Kansas City 13, N.Y. JETS 6; OAKLAND 56, Houston 7
AFL championship: Kansas City 17, OAKLAND 7

## 1968 NFL

**EASTERN CONFERENCE**

**Capitol Division**

| | W | L | T | Pct. | Pts. | OP |
|---|---|---|---|---|---|---|
| Dallas | 12 | 2 | 0 | .857 | 431 | 186 |
| N.Y. Giants | 7 | 7 | 0 | .500 | 294 | 325 |
| Washington | 5 | 9 | 0 | .357 | 249 | 358 |
| Philadelphia | 2 | 12 | 0 | .143 | 202 | 351 |

**Century Division**

| | W | L | T | Pct. | Pts. | OP |
|---|---|---|---|---|---|---|
| Cleveland | 10 | 4 | 0 | .714 | 394 | 273 |
| St. Louis | 9 | 4 | 1 | .692 | 325 | 289 |
| New Orleans | 4 | 9 | 1 | .308 | 246 | 327 |
| Pittsburgh | 2 | 11 | 1 | .154 | 244 | 397 |

**WESTERN CONFERENCE**

**Coastal Division**

| | W | L | T | Pct. | Pts. | OP |
|---|---|---|---|---|---|---|
| Baltimore | 13 | 1 | 0 | .929 | 402 | 144 |
| Los Angeles | 10 | 3 | 1 | .769 | 312 | 200 |
| San Francisco | 7 | 6 | 1 | .538 | 303 | 310 |
| Atlanta | 2 | 12 | 0 | .143 | 170 | 389 |

**Central Division**

| | W | L | T | Pct. | Pts. | OP |
|---|---|---|---|---|---|---|
| Minnesota | 8 | 6 | 0 | .571 | 282 | 242 |
| Chicago | 7 | 7 | 0 | .500 | 250 | 333 |
| Green Bay | 6 | 7 | 1 | .462 | 281 | 227 |
| Detroit | 4 | 8 | 2 | .333 | 207 | 241 |

Conference championships: CLEVELAND 31, Dallas 20; BALTIMORE 24, Minnesota 14
NFL championship: Baltimore 34, CLEVELAND 0
Super Bowl III: N.Y. Jets (AFL) 16, Baltimore (NFL) 7, at Orange Bowl, Miami, Florida.

## 1968 AFL

**EASTERN DIVISION**

| | W | L | T | Pct. | Pts. | OP |
|---|---|---|---|---|---|---|
| N.Y. Jets | 11 | 3 | 0 | .786 | 419 | 280 |
| Houston | 7 | 7 | 0 | .500 | 303 | 248 |
| Miami | 5 | 8 | 1 | .385 | 276 | 355 |
| Boston Patriots | 4 | 10 | 0 | .286 | 229 | 406 |
| Buffalo | 1 | 12 | 1 | .077 | 199 | 367 |

**WESTERN DIVISION**

| | W | L | T | Pct. | Pts. | OP |
|---|---|---|---|---|---|---|
| Oakland | 12 | 2 | 0 | .857 | 453 | 233 |
| Kansas City | 12 | 2 | 0 | .857 | 371 | 170 |
| San Diego | 9 | 5 | 0 | .643 | 382 | 310 |
| Denver | 5 | 9 | 0 | .357 | 255 | 404 |
| Cincinnati | 3 | 11 | 0 | .214 | 215 | 329 |

Western Division playoff: OAKLAND 41, Kansas City 6
AFL championship: N.Y. JETS 27, Oakland 23

## 1967 NFL

**EASTERN CONFERENCE**

**Capitol Division**

| | W | L | T | Pct. | Pts. | OP |
|---|---|---|---|---|---|---|
| Dallas | 9 | 5 | 0 | .643 | 342 | 268 |
| Philadelphia | 6 | 7 | 1 | .462 | 351 | 409 |
| Washington | 5 | 6 | 3 | .455 | 347 | 353 |
| New Orleans | 3 | 11 | 0 | .214 | 233 | 379 |

**Century Division**

| | W | L | T | Pct. | Pts. | OP |
|---|---|---|---|---|---|---|
| Cleveland | 9 | 5 | 0 | .643 | 334 | 297 |
| N.Y. Giants | 7 | 7 | 0 | .500 | 369 | 379 |
| St. Louis | 6 | 7 | 1 | .462 | 333 | 356 |
| Pittsburgh | 4 | 9 | 1 | .308 | 281 | 320 |

**WESTERN CONFERENCE**

**Coastal Division**

| | W | L | T | Pct. | Pts. | OP |
|---|---|---|---|---|---|---|
| Los Angeles | 11 | 1 | 2 | .917 | 398 | 196 |
| Baltimore | 11 | 1 | 2 | .917 | 394 | 198 |
| San Francisco | 7 | 7 | 0 | .500 | 273 | 337 |
| Atlanta | 1 | 12 | 1 | .077 | 175 | 422 |

**Central Division**

| | W | L | T | Pct. | Pts. | OP |
|---|---|---|---|---|---|---|
| Green Bay | 9 | 4 | 1 | .692 | 332 | 209 |
| Chicago | 7 | 6 | 1 | .538 | 239 | 218 |
| Detroit | 5 | 7 | 2 | .417 | 260 | 259 |
| Minnesota | 3 | 8 | 3 | .273 | 233 | 294 |

*Los Angeles won division title on the basis of advantage in points (58-34) in two games vs. Baltimore.*
Conference championships: DALLAS 52, Cleveland 14; GREEN BAY 28, Los Angeles 7
NFL championship: GREEN BAY 21, Dallas 17
Super Bowl II: Green Bay (NFL) 33, Oakland (AFL) 14, at Orange Bowl, Miami, Florida.

## 1967 AFL

**EASTERN DIVISION**

| | W | L | T | Pct. | Pts. | OP |
|---|---|---|---|---|---|---|
| Houston | 9 | 4 | 1 | .692 | 258 | 199 |
| N.Y. Jets | 8 | 5 | 1 | .615 | 371 | 329 |
| Buffalo | 4 | 10 | 0 | .286 | 237 | 285 |
| Miami | 4 | 10 | 0 | .286 | 219 | 407 |
| Boston Patriots | 3 | 10 | 1 | .231 | 280 | 389 |

**WESTERN DIVISION**

| | W | L | T | Pct. | Pts. | OP |
|---|---|---|---|---|---|---|
| Oakland | 13 | 1 | 0 | .929 | 468 | 233 |
| Kansas City | 9 | 5 | 0 | .643 | 408 | 254 |
| San Diego | 8 | 5 | 1 | .615 | 360 | 352 |
| Denver | 3 | 11 | 0 | .214 | 256 | 409 |

AFL championship: OAKLAND 40, Houston 7

## 1966 NFL

**EASTERN CONFERENCE**

| | W | L | T | Pct. | Pts. | OP |
|---|---|---|---|---|---|---|
| Dallas | 10 | 3 | 1 | .769 | 445 | 239 |
| Cleveland | 9 | 5 | 0 | .643 | 403 | 259 |
| Philadelphia | 9 | 5 | 0 | .643 | 326 | 340 |
| St. Louis | 8 | 5 | 1 | .615 | 264 | 265 |
| Washington | 7 | 7 | 0 | .500 | 351 | 355 |
| Pittsburgh | 5 | 8 | 1 | .385 | 316 | 347 |
| Atlanta | 3 | 11 | 0 | .214 | 204 | 437 |
| N.Y. Giants | 1 | 12 | 1 | .077 | 263 | 501 |

**WESTERN CONFERENCE**

| | W | L | T | Pct. | Pts. | OP |
|---|---|---|---|---|---|---|
| Green Bay | 12 | 2 | 0 | .857 | 335 | 163 |
| Baltimore | 9 | 5 | 0 | .643 | 314 | 226 |
| Los Angeles | 8 | 6 | 0 | .571 | 289 | 212 |
| San Francisco | 6 | 6 | 2 | .500 | 320 | 325 |
| Chicago | 5 | 7 | 2 | .417 | 234 | 272 |
| Detroit | 4 | 9 | 1 | .308 | 206 | 317 |
| Minnesota | 4 | 9 | 1 | .308 | 292 | 304 |

NFL championship: Green Bay 34, DALLAS 27
Super Bowl I: Green Bay (NFL) 35, Kansas City (AFL) 10, at Memorial Coliseum, Los Angeles, California.

## 1966 AFL

**EASTERN DIVISION**

| | W | L | T | Pct. | Pts. | OP |
|---|---|---|---|---|---|---|
| Buffalo | 9 | 4 | 1 | .692 | 358 | 255 |
| Boston Patriots | 8 | 4 | 2 | .677 | 315 | 283 |
| N.Y. Jets | 6 | 6 | 2 | .500 | 322 | 312 |
| Houston | 3 | 11 | 0 | .214 | 335 | 396 |
| Miami | 3 | 11 | 0 | .214 | 213 | 362 |

**WESTERN DIVISION**

| | W | L | T | Pct. | Pts. | OP |
|---|---|---|---|---|---|---|
| Kansas City | 11 | 2 | 1 | .846 | 448 | 276 |
| Oakland | 8 | 5 | 1 | .615 | 315 | 288 |
| San Diego | 7 | 6 | 1 | .538 | 335 | 284 |
| Denver | 4 | 10 | 0 | .286 | 196 | 381 |

AFL championship: Kansas City 31, BUFFALO 7

## 1965 NFL

**EASTERN CONFERENCE**

| | W | L | T | Pct. | Pts. | OP |
|---|---|---|---|---|---|---|
| Cleveland | 11 | 3 | 0 | .786 | 363 | 325 |
| Dallas | 7 | 7 | 0 | .500 | 325 | 280 |
| N.Y. Giants | 7 | 7 | 0 | .500 | 270 | 338 |
| Washington | 6 | 8 | 0 | .429 | 257 | 301 |
| Philadelphia | 5 | 9 | 0 | .357 | 363 | 359 |
| St. Louis | 5 | 9 | 0 | .357 | 296 | 309 |
| Pittsburgh | 2 | 12 | 0 | .143 | 202 | 397 |

**WESTERN CONFERENCE**

| | W | L | T | Pct. | Pts. | OP |
|---|---|---|---|---|---|---|
| Green Bay | 10 | 3 | 1 | .769 | 316 | 224 |
| Baltimore | 10 | 3 | 1 | .769 | 389 | 284 |
| Chicago | 9 | 5 | 0 | .643 | 409 | 275 |
| San Francisco | 7 | 6 | 1 | .538 | 421 | 402 |
| Minnesota | 7 | 7 | 0 | .500 | 383 | 403 |
| Detroit | 6 | 7 | 1 | .462 | 257 | 295 |
| Los Angeles | 4 | 10 | 0 | .286 | 269 | 328 |

Western Conference playoff: GREEN BAY 13, Baltimore 10 (OT)
NFL championship: GREEN BAY 23, Cleveland 12

## 1965 AFL

**EASTERN DIVISION**

| | W | L | T | Pct. | Pts. | OP |
|---|---|---|---|---|---|---|
| Buffalo | 10 | 3 | 1 | .769 | 313 | 226 |
| N.Y. Jets | 5 | 8 | 1 | .385 | 285 | 303 |
| Boston Patriots | 4 | 8 | 2 | .333 | 244 | 302 |
| Houston | 4 | 10 | 0 | .286 | 298 | 429 |

**WESTERN DIVISION**

| | W | L | T | Pct. | Pts. | OP |
|---|---|---|---|---|---|---|
| San Diego | 9 | 2 | 3 | .818 | 340 | 227 |
| Oakland | 8 | 5 | 1 | .615 | 298 | 239 |
| Kansas City | 7 | 5 | 2 | .583 | 322 | 285 |
| Denver | 4 | 10 | 0 | .286 | 303 | 392 |

AFL championship: Buffalo 23, SAN DIEGO 0

## 1964 NFL

**EASTERN CONFERENCE**

| | W | L | T | Pct. | Pts. | OP |
|---|---|---|---|---|---|---|
| Cleveland | 10 | 3 | 1 | .769 | 415 | 293 |
| St. Louis | 9 | 3 | 2 | .750 | 357 | 331 |
| Philadelphia | 6 | 8 | 0 | .429 | 312 | 313 |
| Washington | 6 | 8 | 0 | .429 | 307 | 305 |
| Dallas | 5 | 8 | 1 | .385 | 250 | 289 |
| Pittsburgh | 5 | 9 | 0 | .357 | 253 | 315 |
| N.Y. Giants | 2 | 10 | 2 | .167 | 241 | 399 |

**WESTERN CONFERENCE**

| | W | L | T | Pct. | Pts. | OP |
|---|---|---|---|---|---|---|
| Baltimore | 12 | 2 | 0 | .857 | 428 | 225 |
| Green Bay | 8 | 5 | 1 | .615 | 342 | 245 |
| Minnesota | 8 | 5 | 1 | .615 | 355 | 296 |
| Detroit | 7 | 5 | 2 | .583 | 280 | 260 |
| Los Angeles | 5 | 7 | 2 | .417 | 283 | 339 |
| Chicago | 5 | 9 | 0 | .357 | 260 | 379 |
| San Francisco | 4 | 10 | 0 | .286 | 236 | 330 |

NFL championship: CLEVELAND 27, Baltimore 0

## 1964 AFL

**EASTERN DIVISION**

| | W | L | T | Pct. | Pts. | OP |
|---|---|---|---|---|---|---|
| Buffalo | 12 | 2 | 0 | .857 | 400 | 242 |
| Boston Patriots | 10 | 3 | 1 | .769 | 365 | 297 |
| N.Y. Jets | 5 | 8 | 1 | .385 | 278 | 315 |
| Houston | 4 | 10 | 0 | .286 | 310 | 355 |

**WESTERN DIVISION**

| | W | L | T | Pct. | Pts. | OP |
|---|---|---|---|---|---|---|
| San Diego | 8 | 5 | 1 | .615 | 341 | 300 |
| Kansas City | 7 | 7 | 0 | .500 | 366 | 306 |
| Oakland | 5 | 7 | 2 | .417 | 303 | 350 |
| Denver | 2 | 11 | 1 | .154 | 240 | 438 |

AFL championship: BUFFALO 20, San Diego 7

## 1963 NFL

**EASTERN CONFERENCE**

| | W | L | T | Pct. | Pts. | OP |
|---|---|---|---|---|---|---|
| N.Y. Giants | 11 | 3 | 0 | .786 | 448 | 280 |
| Cleveland | 10 | 4 | 0 | .714 | 343 | 262 |
| St. Louis | 9 | 5 | 0 | .643 | 341 | 283 |
| Pittsburgh | 7 | 4 | 3 | .636 | 321 | 295 |
| Dallas | 4 | 10 | 0 | .286 | 305 | 378 |
| Washington | 3 | 11 | 0 | .214 | 279 | 398 |
| Philadelphia | 2 | 10 | 2 | .167 | 242 | 381 |

**WESTERN CONFERENCE**

| | W | L | T | Pct. | Pts. | OP |
|---|---|---|---|---|---|---|
| Chicago | 11 | 1 | 2 | .917 | 301 | 144 |
| Green Bay | 11 | 2 | 1 | .846 | 369 | 206 |
| Baltimore | 8 | 6 | 0 | .571 | 316 | 285 |
| Detroit | 5 | 8 | 1 | .385 | 326 | 265 |
| Minnesota | 5 | 8 | 1 | .385 | 309 | 390 |
| Los Angeles | 5 | 9 | 0 | .357 | 210 | 350 |
| San Francisco | 2 | 12 | 0 | .143 | 198 | 391 |

NFL championship: CHICAGO 14, N.Y. Giants 10

# PAST STANDINGS

## 1963 AFL

**EASTERN DIVISION**

| | W | L | T | Pct. | Pts. | OP |
|---|---|---|---|---|---|---|
| Boston Patriots | 7 | 6 | 1 | .538 | 327 | 257 |
| Buffalo | 7 | 6 | 1 | .538 | 304 | 291 |
| Houston | 6 | 8 | 0 | .429 | 302 | 372 |
| N.Y. Jets | 5 | 8 | 1 | .385 | 249 | 399 |

**WESTERN DIVISION**

| | W | L | T | Pct. | Pts. | OP |
|---|---|---|---|---|---|---|
| San Diego | 11 | 3 | 0 | .786 | 399 | 256 |
| Oakland | 10 | 4 | 0 | .714 | 363 | 288 |
| Kansas City | 5 | 7 | 2 | .417 | 347 | 263 |
| Denver | 2 | 11 | 1 | .154 | 301 | 473 |

Eastern Division playoff: Boston 26, BUFFALO 8
AFL championship: SAN DIEGO 51, Boston 10

## 1962 NFL

**EASTERN CONFERENCE**

| | W | L | T | Pct. | Pts. | OP |
|---|---|---|---|---|---|---|
| N.Y. Giants | 12 | 2 | 0 | .857 | 398 | 283 |
| Pittsburgh | 9 | 5 | 0 | .643 | 312 | 363 |
| Cleveland | 7 | 6 | 1 | .538 | 291 | 257 |
| Washington | 5 | 7 | 2 | .417 | 305 | 376 |
| Dallas Cowboys | 5 | 8 | 1 | .385 | 398 | 402 |
| St. Louis | 4 | 9 | 1 | .308 | 287 | 361 |
| Philadelphia | 3 | 10 | 1 | .231 | 282 | 356 |

**WESTERN CONFERENCE**

| | W | L | T | Pct. | Pts. | OP |
|---|---|---|---|---|---|---|
| Green Bay | 13 | 1 | 0 | .929 | 415 | 148 |
| Detroit | 11 | 3 | 0 | .786 | 315 | 177 |
| Chicago | 9 | 5 | 0 | .643 | 321 | 287 |
| Baltimore | 7 | 7 | 0 | .500 | 293 | 288 |
| San Francisco | 6 | 8 | 0 | .429 | 282 | 331 |
| Minnesota | 2 | 11 | 1 | .154 | 254 | 410 |
| Los Angeles | 1 | 12 | 1 | .077 | 220 | 334 |

NFL championship: Green Bay 16, N.Y. GIANTS 7

## 1962 AFL

**EASTERN DIVISION**

| | W | L | T | Pct. | Pts. | OP |
|---|---|---|---|---|---|---|
| Houston | 11 | 3 | 0 | .786 | 387 | 270 |
| Boston Patriots | 9 | 4 | 1 | .692 | 346 | 295 |
| Buffalo | 7 | 6 | 1 | .538 | 309 | 272 |
| N.Y. Titans | 5 | 9 | 0 | .357 | 278 | 423 |

**WESTERN DIVISION**

| | W | L | T | Pct. | Pts. | OP |
|---|---|---|---|---|---|---|
| Dallas Texans | 11 | 3 | 0 | .786 | 389 | 233 |
| Denver | 7 | 7 | 0 | .500 | 353 | 334 |
| San Diego | 4 | 10 | 0 | .286 | 314 | 392 |
| Oakland | 1 | 13 | 0 | .071 | 213 | 370 |

AFL championship: Dallas Texans 20, HOUSTON 17 (OT)

## 1961 NFL

**EASTERN CONFERENCE**

| | W | L | T | Pct. | Pts. | OP |
|---|---|---|---|---|---|---|
| N.Y. Giants | 10 | 3 | 1 | .769 | 368 | 220 |
| Philadelphia | 10 | 4 | 0 | .714 | 361 | 297 |
| Cleveland | 8 | 5 | 1 | .615 | 319 | 270 |
| St. Louis | 7 | 7 | 0 | .500 | 279 | 267 |
| Pittsburgh | 6 | 8 | 0 | .429 | 295 | 287 |
| Dallas Cowboys | 4 | 9 | 1 | .308 | 236 | 380 |
| Washington | 1 | 12 | 1 | .077 | 174 | 392 |

**WESTERN CONFERENCE**

| | W | L | T | Pct. | Pts. | OP |
|---|---|---|---|---|---|---|
| Green Bay | 11 | 3 | 0 | .786 | 391 | 223 |
| Detroit | 8 | 5 | 1 | .615 | 270 | 258 |
| Baltimore | 8 | 6 | 0 | .571 | 302 | 307 |
| Chicago | 8 | 6 | 0 | .571 | 326 | 302 |
| San Francisco | 7 | 6 | 1 | .538 | 346 | 272 |
| Los Angeles | 4 | 10 | 0 | .286 | 263 | 333 |
| Minnesota | 3 | 11 | 0 | .214 | 285 | 407 |

NFL championship: GREEN BAY 37, N.Y. Giants 0

## 1961 AFL

**EASTERN DIVISION**

| | W | L | T | Pct. | Pts. | OP |
|---|---|---|---|---|---|---|
| Houston | 10 | 3 | 1 | .769 | 513 | 242 |
| Boston Patriots | 9 | 4 | 1 | .692 | 413 | 313 |
| N.Y. Titans | 7 | 7 | 0 | .500 | 301 | 390 |
| Buffalo | 6 | 8 | 0 | .429 | 294 | 342 |

**WESTERN DIVISION**

| | W | L | T | Pct. | Pts. | OP |
|---|---|---|---|---|---|---|
| San Diego | 12 | 2 | 0 | .857 | 396 | 219 |
| Dallas Texans | 6 | 8 | 0 | .429 | 334 | 343 |
| Denver | 3 | 11 | 0 | .214 | 251 | 432 |
| Oakland | 2 | 12 | 0 | .143 | 237 | 458 |

AFL championship: Houston 10, SAN DIEGO 3

## 1960 NFL

**EASTERN CONFERENCE**

| | W | L | T | Pct. | Pts. | OP |
|---|---|---|---|---|---|---|
| Philadelphia | 10 | 2 | 0 | .833 | 321 | 246 |
| Cleveland | 8 | 3 | 1 | .727 | 362 | 217 |
| N.Y. Giants | 6 | 4 | 2 | .600 | 271 | 261 |
| St. Louis | 6 | 5 | 1 | .545 | 288 | 230 |
| Pittsburgh | 5 | 6 | 1 | .455 | 240 | 275 |
| Washington | 1 | 9 | 2 | .100 | 178 | 309 |

**WESTERN CONFERENCE**

| | W | L | T | Pct. | Pts. | OP |
|---|---|---|---|---|---|---|
| Green Bay | 8 | 4 | 0 | .667 | 332 | 209 |
| Detroit | 7 | 5 | 0 | .583 | 239 | 212 |
| San Francisco | 7 | 5 | 0 | .583 | 208 | 205 |
| Baltimore | 6 | 6 | 0 | .500 | 288 | 234 |
| Chicago | 5 | 6 | 1 | .455 | 194 | 299 |
| L.A. Rams | 4 | 7 | 1 | .364 | 265 | 297 |
| Dallas Cowboys | 0 | 11 | 1 | .000 | 177 | 369 |

NFL championship: PHILADELPHIA 17, Green Bay 13

## 1960 AFL

**EASTERN CONFERENCE**

| | W | L | T | Pct. | Pts. | OP |
|---|---|---|---|---|---|---|
| Houston | 10 | 4 | 0 | .714 | 379 | 285 |
| N.Y. Titans | 7 | 7 | 0 | .500 | 382 | 399 |
| Buffalo | 5 | 8 | 1 | .385 | 296 | 303 |
| Boston | 5 | 9 | 0 | .357 | 286 | 349 |

**WESTERN CONFERENCE**

| | W | L | T | Pct. | Pts. | OP |
|---|---|---|---|---|---|---|
| L.A. Chargers | 10 | 4 | 0 | .714 | 373 | 336 |
| Dallas Texans | 8 | 6 | 0 | .571 | 362 | 253 |
| Oakland | 6 | 8 | 0 | .429 | 319 | 388 |
| Denver | 4 | 9 | 1 | .308 | 309 | 393 |

AFL championship: HOUSTON 24, L.A. Chargers 16

## 1959

**EASTERN CONFERENCE**

| | W | L | T | Pct. | Pts. | OP |
|---|---|---|---|---|---|---|
| N.Y. Giants | 10 | 2 | 0 | .833 | 284 | 170 |
| Cleveland | 7 | 5 | 0 | .583 | 270 | 214 |
| Philadelphia | 7 | 5 | 0 | .583 | 268 | 278 |
| Pittsburgh | 6 | 5 | 1 | .545 | 257 | 216 |
| Washington | 3 | 9 | 0 | .250 | 185 | 350 |
| Chi. Cardinals | 2 | 10 | 0 | .167 | 234 | 324 |

**WESTERN CONFERENCE**

| | W | L | T | Pct. | Pts. | OP |
|---|---|---|---|---|---|---|
| Baltimore | 9 | 3 | 0 | .750 | 374 | 251 |
| Chi. Bears | 8 | 4 | 0 | .667 | 252 | 196 |
| Green Bay | 7 | 5 | 0 | .583 | 248 | 246 |
| San Francisco | 7 | 5 | 0 | .583 | 255 | 237 |
| Detroit | 3 | 8 | 1 | .273 | 203 | 275 |
| Los Angeles | 2 | 10 | 0 | .167 | 242 | 315 |

NFL championship: BALTIMORE 31, N.Y. Giants 16

## 1958

**EASTERN CONFERENCE**

| | W | L | T | Pct. | Pts. | OP |
|---|---|---|---|---|---|---|
| N.Y. Giants | 9 | 3 | 0 | .750 | 246 | 183 |
| Cleveland | 9 | 3 | 0 | .750 | 302 | 217 |
| Pittsburgh | 7 | 4 | 1 | .636 | 261 | 230 |
| Washington | 4 | 7 | 1 | .364 | 214 | 268 |
| Chi. Cardinals | 2 | 9 | 1 | .182 | 261 | 356 |
| Philadelphia | 2 | 9 | 1 | .182 | 235 | 306 |

**WESTERN CONFERENCE**

| | W | L | T | Pct. | Pts. | OP |
|---|---|---|---|---|---|---|
| Baltimore | 9 | 3 | 0 | .750 | 381 | 203 |
| Chi. Bears | 8 | 4 | 0 | .667 | 298 | 230 |
| Los Angeles | 8 | 4 | 0 | .667 | 344 | 278 |
| San Francisco | 6 | 6 | 0 | .500 | 257 | 324 |
| Detroit | 4 | 7 | 1 | .364 | 261 | 276 |
| Green Bay | 1 | 10 | 1 | .091 | 193 | 382 |

Eastern Conference playoff: N.Y. GIANTS 10, Cleveland 0
NFL championship: Baltimore 23, N.Y. GIANTS 17 (OT)

## 1957

**EASTERN CONFERENCE**

| | W | L | T | Pct. | Pts. | OP |
|---|---|---|---|---|---|---|
| Cleveland | 9 | 2 | 1 | .818 | 269 | 172 |
| N.Y. Giants | 7 | 5 | 0 | .583 | 254 | 211 |
| Pittsburgh | 6 | 6 | 0 | .500 | 161 | 178 |
| Washington | 5 | 6 | 1 | .455 | 251 | 230 |
| Philadelphia | 4 | 8 | 0 | .333 | 173 | 230 |
| Chi. Cardinals | 3 | 9 | 0 | .250 | 200 | 299 |

**WESTERN CONFERENCE**

| | W | L | T | Pct. | Pts. | OP |
|---|---|---|---|---|---|---|
| Detroit | 8 | 4 | 0 | .667 | 251 | 231 |
| San Francisco | 8 | 4 | 0 | .667 | 260 | 264 |
| Baltimore | 7 | 5 | 0 | .583 | 303 | 235 |
| Los Angeles | 6 | 6 | 0 | .500 | 307 | 278 |
| Chi. Bears | 5 | 7 | 0 | .417 | 203 | 211 |
| Green Bay | 3 | 9 | 0 | .250 | 218 | 311 |

Western Conference playoff: Detroit 31, SAN FRANCISCO 27
NFL championship: DETROIT 59, Cleveland 14

## 1956

**EASTERN CONFERENCE**

| | W | L | T | Pct. | Pts. | OP |
|---|---|---|---|---|---|---|
| N.Y. Giants | 8 | 3 | 1 | .727 | 264 | 197 |
| Chi. Cardinals | 7 | 5 | 0 | .583 | 240 | 182 |
| Washington | 6 | 6 | 0 | .500 | 183 | 225 |
| Cleveland | 5 | 7 | 0 | .417 | 167 | 177 |
| Pittsburgh | 5 | 7 | 0 | .417 | 217 | 250 |
| Philadelphia | 3 | 8 | 1 | .273 | 143 | 215 |

**WESTERN CONFERENCE**

| | W | L | T | Pct. | Pts. | OP |
|---|---|---|---|---|---|---|
| Chi. Bears | 9 | 2 | 1 | .818 | 363 | 246 |
| Detroit | 9 | 3 | 0 | .750 | 300 | 188 |
| San Francisco | 5 | 6 | 1 | .455 | 233 | 284 |
| Baltimore | 5 | 7 | 0 | .417 | 270 | 322 |
| Green Bay | 4 | 8 | 0 | .333 | 264 | 342 |
| Los Angeles | 4 | 8 | 0 | .333 | 291 | 307 |

NFL championship: N.Y. GIANTS 47, Chi. Bears 7

## 1955

**EASTERN CONFERENCE**

| | W | L | T | Pct. | Pts. | OP |
|---|---|---|---|---|---|---|
| Cleveland | 9 | 2 | 1 | .818 | 349 | 218 |
| Washington | 8 | 4 | 0 | .667 | 246 | 222 |
| N.Y. Giants | 6 | 5 | 1 | .545 | 267 | 223 |
| Chi. Cardinals | 4 | 7 | 1 | .364 | 224 | 252 |
| Philadelphia | 4 | 7 | 1 | .364 | 248 | 231 |
| Pittsburgh | 4 | 8 | 0 | .333 | 195 | 285 |

**WESTERN CONFERENCE**

| | W | L | T | Pct. | Pts. | OP |
|---|---|---|---|---|---|---|
| Los Angeles | 8 | 3 | 1 | .727 | 260 | 231 |
| Chi. Bears | 8 | 4 | 0 | .667 | 294 | 251 |
| Green Bay | 6 | 6 | 0 | .500 | 258 | 276 |
| Baltimore | 5 | 6 | 1 | .455 | 214 | 239 |
| San Francisco | 4 | 8 | 0 | .333 | 216 | 298 |
| Detroit | 3 | 9 | 0 | .250 | 230 | 275 |

NFL championship: Cleveland 38, LOS ANGELES 14

## 1954

**EASTERN CONFERENCE**

| | W | L | T | Pct. | Pts. | OP |
|---|---|---|---|---|---|---|
| Cleveland | 9 | 3 | 0 | .750 | 336 | 162 |
| Philadelphia | 7 | 4 | 1 | .636 | 284 | 230 |
| N.Y. Giants | 7 | 5 | 0 | .583 | 293 | 184 |
| Pittsburgh | 5 | 7 | 0 | .417 | 219 | 263 |
| Washington | 3 | 9 | 0 | .250 | 207 | 432 |
| Chi. Cardinals | 2 | 10 | 0 | .167 | 183 | 347 |

**WESTERN CONFERENCE**

| | W | L | T | Pct. | Pts. | OP |
|---|---|---|---|---|---|---|
| Detroit | 9 | 2 | 1 | .818 | 337 | 189 |
| Chi. Bears | 8 | 4 | 0 | .667 | 301 | 279 |
| San Francisco | 7 | 4 | 1 | .636 | 313 | 251 |
| Los Angeles | 6 | 5 | 1 | .545 | 314 | 285 |
| Green Bay | 4 | 8 | 0 | .333 | 234 | 251 |
| Baltimore | 3 | 9 | 0 | .250 | 131 | 279 |

NFL championship: CLEVELAND 56, Detroit 10

## 1953

**EASTERN CONFERENCE**

| | W | L | T | Pct. | Pts. | OP |
|---|---|---|---|---|---|---|
| Cleveland | 11 | 1 | 0 | .917 | 348 | 162 |
| Philadelphia | 7 | 4 | 1 | .636 | 352 | 215 |
| Washington | 6 | 5 | 1 | .545 | 208 | 215 |
| Pittsburgh | 6 | 6 | 0 | .500 | 211 | 263 |
| N.Y. Giants | 3 | 9 | 0 | .250 | 179 | 277 |
| Chi. Cardinals | 1 | 10 | 1 | .091 | 190 | 337 |

**WESTERN CONFERENCE**

| | W | L | T | Pct. | Pts. | OP |
|---|---|---|---|---|---|---|
| Detroit | 10 | 2 | 0 | .833 | 271 | 205 |
| San Francisco | 9 | 3 | 0 | .750 | 372 | 237 |
| Los Angeles | 8 | 3 | 1 | .727 | 366 | 236 |
| Chi. Bears | 3 | 8 | 1 | .273 | 218 | 262 |
| Baltimore | 3 | 9 | 0 | .250 | 182 | 350 |
| Green Bay | 2 | 9 | 1 | .182 | 200 | 338 |

NFL championship: DETROIT 17, Cleveland 16

## 1952

**AMERICAN CONFERENCE**

| | W | L | T | Pct. | Pts. | OP |
|---|---|---|---|---|---|---|
| Cleveland | 8 | 4 | 0 | .667 | 310 | 213 |
| N.Y. Giants | 7 | 5 | 0 | .583 | 234 | 231 |
| Philadelphia | 7 | 5 | 0 | .583 | 252 | 271 |
| Pittsburgh | 5 | 7 | 0 | .417 | 300 | 273 |
| Chi. Cardinals | 4 | 8 | 0 | .333 | 172 | 221 |
| Washington | 4 | 8 | 0 | .333 | 240 | 287 |

**NATIONAL CONFERENCE**

| | W | L | T | Pct. | Pts. | OP |
|---|---|---|---|---|---|---|
| Detroit | 9 | 3 | 0 | .750 | 344 | 192 |
| Los Angeles | 9 | 3 | 0 | .750 | 349 | 234 |
| San Francisco | 7 | 5 | 0 | .583 | 285 | 221 |
| Green Bay | 6 | 6 | 0 | .500 | 295 | 312 |
| Chi. Bears | 5 | 7 | 0 | .417 | 245 | 326 |
| Dallas Texans | 1 | 11 | 0 | .083 | 182 | 427 |

National Conference playoff: DETROIT 31, Los Angeles 21
NFL championship: Detroit 17, CLEVELAND 7

## 1951

**AMERICAN CONFERENCE**

| | W | L | T | Pct. | Pts. | OP |
|---|---|---|---|---|---|---|
| Cleveland | 11 | 1 | 0 | .917 | 331 | 152 |
| N.Y. Giants | 9 | 2 | 1 | .818 | 254 | 161 |
| Washington | 5 | 7 | 0 | .417 | 183 | 296 |
| Pittsburgh | 4 | 7 | 1 | .364 | 183 | 235 |
| Philadelphia | 4 | 8 | 0 | .333 | 234 | 264 |
| Chi. Cardinals | 3 | 9 | 0 | .250 | 210 | 287 |

**NATIONAL CONFERENCE**

| | W | L | T | Pct. | Pts. | OP |
|---|---|---|---|---|---|---|
| Los Angeles | 8 | 4 | 0 | .667 | 392 | 261 |
| Detroit | 7 | 4 | 1 | .636 | 336 | 259 |
| San Francisco | 7 | 4 | 1 | .636 | 255 | 205 |
| Chi. Bears | 7 | 5 | 0 | .583 | 286 | 282 |
| Green Bay | 3 | 9 | 0 | .250 | 254 | 375 |
| N.Y. Yanks | 1 | 9 | 2 | .100 | 241 | 382 |

NFL championship: LOS ANGELES 24, Cleveland 17

## 1950

**AMERICAN CONFERENCE**

| | W | L | T | Pct. | Pts. | OP |
|---|---|---|---|---|---|---|
| Cleveland | 10 | 2 | 0 | .833 | 310 | 144 |
| N.Y. Giants | 10 | 2 | 0 | .833 | 268 | 150 |
| Philadelphia | 6 | 6 | 0 | .500 | 254 | 141 |
| Pittsburgh | 6 | 6 | 0 | .500 | 180 | 195 |
| Chi. Cardinals | 5 | 7 | 0 | .417 | 233 | 287 |
| Washington | 3 | 9 | 0 | .250 | 232 | 326 |

**NATIONAL CONFERENCE**

| | W | L | T | Pct. | Pts. | OP |
|---|---|---|---|---|---|---|
| Los Angeles | 9 | 3 | 0 | .750 | 466 | 309 |
| Chi. Bears | 9 | 3 | 0 | .750 | 279 | 207 |
| N.Y. Yanks | 7 | 5 | 0 | .583 | 366 | 367 |
| Detroit | 6 | 6 | 0 | .500 | 321 | 285 |
| Green Bay | 3 | 9 | 0 | .250 | 244 | 406 |
| San Francisco | 3 | 9 | 0 | .250 | 213 | 300 |
| Baltimore | 1 | 11 | 0 | .083 | 213 | 462 |

American Conference playoff: CLEVELAND 8, N.Y. Giants 3
National Conference playoff: LOS ANGELES 24, Chi. Bears 14
NFL championship: CLEVELAND 30, Los Angeles 28

## 1949

**EASTERN DIVISION**

| | W | L | T | Pct. | Pts. | OP |
|---|---|---|---|---|---|---|
| Philadelphia | 11 | 1 | 0 | .917 | 364 | 134 |
| Pittsburgh | 6 | 5 | 1 | .545 | 224 | 214 |
| N.Y. Giants | 6 | 6 | 0 | .500 | 287 | 298 |
| Washington | 4 | 7 | 1 | .364 | 268 | 339 |
| N.Y. Bulldogs | 1 | 10 | 1 | .091 | 153 | 365 |

**WESTERN DIVISION**

| | W | L | T | Pct. | Pts. | OP |
|---|---|---|---|---|---|---|
| Los Angeles | 8 | 2 | 2 | .800 | 360 | 239 |
| Chi. Bears | 9 | 3 | 0 | .750 | 332 | 218 |
| Chi. Cardinals | 6 | 5 | 1 | .545 | 360 | 301 |
| Detroit | 4 | 8 | 0 | .333 | 237 | 259 |
| Green Bay | 2 | 10 | 0 | .167 | 114 | 329 |

NFL championship: Philadelphia 14, LOS ANGELES 0

## 1948

**EASTERN DIVISION**

| | W | L | T | Pct. | Pts. | OP |
|---|---|---|---|---|---|---|
| Philadelphia | 9 | 2 | 1 | .818 | 376 | 156 |
| Washington | 7 | 5 | 0 | .583 | 291 | 287 |
| N.Y. Giants | 4 | 8 | 0 | .333 | 297 | 388 |
| Pittsburgh | 4 | 8 | 0 | .333 | 200 | 243 |
| Boston | 3 | 9 | 0 | .250 | 174 | 372 |

**WESTERN DIVISION**

| | W | L | T | Pct. | Pts. | OP |
|---|---|---|---|---|---|---|
| Chi. Cardinals | 11 | 1 | 0 | .917 | 395 | 226 |
| Chi. Bears | 10 | 2 | 0 | .833 | 375 | 151 |
| Los Angeles | 6 | 5 | 1 | .545 | 327 | 269 |
| Green Bay | 3 | 9 | 0 | .250 | 154 | 290 |
| Detroit | 2 | 10 | 0 | .167 | 200 | 407 |

NFL championship: PHILADELPHIA 7, Chi. Cardinals 0

## 1947

**EASTERN DIVISION**

| | W | L | T | Pct. | Pts. | OP |
|---|---|---|---|---|---|---|
| Philadelphia | 8 | 4 | 0 | .667 | 308 | 242 |
| Pittsburgh | 8 | 4 | 0 | .667 | 240 | 259 |
| Boston | 4 | 7 | 1 | .364 | 168 | 256 |
| Washington | 4 | 8 | 0 | .333 | 295 | 367 |
| N.Y. Giants | 2 | 8 | 2 | .200 | 190 | 309 |

**WESTERN DIVISION**

| | W | L | T | Pct. | Pts. | OP |
|---|---|---|---|---|---|---|
| Chi. Cardinals | 9 | 3 | 0 | .750 | 306 | 231 |
| Chi. Bears | 8 | 4 | 0 | .667 | 363 | 241 |
| Green Bay | 6 | 5 | 1 | .545 | 274 | 210 |
| Los Angeles | 6 | 6 | 0 | .500 | 259 | 214 |
| Detroit | 3 | 9 | 0 | .250 | 231 | 305 |

Eastern Division playoff: Philadelphia 21, PITTSBURGH 0
NFL championship: CHI. CARDINALS 28, Philadelphia 21

## 1946

**EASTERN DIVISION**

| | W | L | T | Pct. | Pts. | OP |
|---|---|---|---|---|---|---|
| N.Y. Giants | 7 | 3 | 1 | .700 | 236 | 162 |
| Philadelphia | 6 | 5 | 0 | .545 | 231 | 220 |
| Washington | 5 | 5 | 1 | .500 | 171 | 191 |
| Pittsburgh | 5 | 5 | 1 | .500 | 136 | 117 |
| Boston | 2 | 8 | 1 | .200 | 189 | 273 |

**WESTERN DIVISION**

| | W | L | T | Pct. | Pts. | OP |
|---|---|---|---|---|---|---|
| Chi. Bears | 8 | 2 | 1 | .800 | 289 | 193 |
| Los Angeles | 6 | 4 | 1 | .600 | 277 | 257 |
| Green Bay | 6 | 5 | 0 | .545 | 148 | 158 |
| Chi. Cardinals | 6 | 5 | 0 | .545 | 260 | 198 |
| Detroit | 1 | 10 | 0 | .091 | 142 | 310 |

NFL championship: Chi. Bears 24, N.Y. GIANTS 14

## 1945

**EASTERN DIVISION**

| | W | L | T | Pct. | Pts. | OP |
|---|---|---|---|---|---|---|
| Washington | 8 | 2 | 0 | .800 | 209 | 121 |
| Philadelphia | 7 | 3 | 0 | .700 | 272 | 133 |
| N.Y. Giants | 3 | 6 | 1 | .333 | 179 | 198 |
| Boston | 3 | 6 | 1 | .333 | 123 | 211 |
| Pittsburgh | 2 | 8 | 0 | .200 | 79 | 220 |

**WESTERN DIVISION**

| | W | L | T | Pct. | Pts. | OP |
|---|---|---|---|---|---|---|
| Cleveland | 9 | 1 | 0 | .900 | 244 | 136 |
| Detroit | 7 | 3 | 0 | .700 | 195 | 194 |
| Green Bay | 6 | 4 | 0 | .600 | 258 | 173 |
| Chi. Bears | 3 | 7 | 0 | .300 | 192 | 235 |
| Chi. Cardinals | 1 | 9 | 0 | .100 | 98 | 228 |

NFL championship: CLEVELAND 15, Washington 14

## 1944

**EASTERN DIVISION**

| | W | L | T | Pct. | Pts. | OP |
|---|---|---|---|---|---|---|
| N.Y. Giants | 8 | 1 | 1 | .889 | 206 | 75 |
| Philadelphia | 7 | 1 | 2 | .875 | 267 | 131 |
| Washington | 6 | 3 | 1 | .667 | 169 | 180 |
| Boston | 2 | 8 | 0 | .200 | 82 | 233 |
| Brooklyn | 0 | 10 | 0 | .000 | 69 | 166 |

**WESTERN DIVISION**

| | W | L | T | Pct. | Pts. | OP |
|---|---|---|---|---|---|---|
| Green Bay | 8 | 2 | 0 | .800 | 238 | 141 |
| Chi. Bears | 6 | 3 | 1 | .667 | 258 | 172 |
| Detroit | 6 | 3 | 1 | .667 | 216 | 151 |
| Cleveland | 4 | 6 | 0 | .400 | 188 | 224 |
| Card-Pitt | 0 | 10 | 0 | .000 | 108 | 328 |

NFL championship: Green Bay 14, N.Y. GIANTS 7

## 1943

**EASTERN DIVISION**

| | W | L | T | Pct. | Pts. | OP |
|---|---|---|---|---|---|---|
| Washington | 6 | 3 | 1 | .667 | 229 | 137 |
| N.Y. Giants | 6 | 3 | 1 | .667 | 197 | 170 |
| Phil-Pitt | 5 | 4 | 1 | .556 | 225 | 230 |
| Brooklyn | 2 | 8 | 0 | .200 | 65 | 234 |

**WESTERN DIVISION**

| | W | L | T | Pct. | Pts. | OP |
|---|---|---|---|---|---|---|
| Chi. Bears | 8 | 1 | 1 | .889 | 303 | 157 |
| Green Bay | 7 | 2 | 1 | .778 | 264 | 172 |
| Detroit | 3 | 6 | 1 | .333 | 178 | 218 |
| Chi. Cardinals | 0 | 10 | 0 | .000 | 95 | 238 |

Eastern Division playoff: Washington 28, N.Y. GIANTS 0
NFL championship: CHI. BEARS 41, Washington 21

## 1942

**EASTERN DIVISION**

| | W | L | T | Pct. | Pts. | OP |
|---|---|---|---|---|---|---|
| Washington | 10 | 1 | 0 | .909 | 227 | 102 |
| Pittsburgh | 7 | 4 | 0 | .636 | 167 | 119 |
| N.Y. Giants | 5 | 5 | 1 | .500 | 155 | 139 |
| Brooklyn | 3 | 8 | 0 | .273 | 100 | 168 |
| Philadelphia | 2 | 9 | 0 | .182 | 134 | 239 |

**WESTERN DIVISION**

| | W | L | T | Pct. | Pts. | OP |
|---|---|---|---|---|---|---|
| Chi. Bears | 11 | 0 | 0 | 1.000 | 376 | 84 |
| Green Bay | 8 | 2 | 1 | .800 | 300 | 215 |
| Cleveland | 5 | 6 | 0 | .455 | 150 | 207 |
| Chi. Cardinals | 3 | 8 | 0 | .273 | 98 | 209 |
| Detroit | 0 | 11 | 0 | .000 | 38 | 263 |

NFL championship: WASHINGTON 14, Chi. Bears 6

## 1941

**EASTERN DIVISION**

| | W | L | T | Pct. | Pts. | OP |
|---|---|---|---|---|---|---|
| N.Y. Giants | 8 | 3 | 0 | .727 | 238 | 114 |
| Brooklyn | 7 | 4 | 0 | .636 | 158 | 127 |
| Washington | 6 | 5 | 0 | .545 | 176 | 174 |
| Philadelphia | 2 | 8 | 1 | .200 | 119 | 218 |
| Pittsburgh | 1 | 9 | 1 | .100 | 103 | 276 |

**WESTERN DIVISION**

| | W | L | T | Pct. | Pts. | OP |
|---|---|---|---|---|---|---|
| Chi. Bears | 10 | 1 | 0 | .909 | 396 | 147 |
| Green Bay | 10 | 1 | 0 | .909 | 258 | 120 |
| Detroit | 4 | 6 | 1 | .400 | 121 | 195 |
| Chi. Cardinals | 3 | 7 | 1 | .300 | 127 | 197 |
| Cleveland | 2 | 9 | 0 | .182 | 116 | 244 |

Western Division playoff: CHI. BEARS 33, Green Bay 14
NFL championship: CHI. BEARS 37, N.Y. Giants 9

## 1940

**EASTERN DIVISION**

| | W | L | T | Pct. | Pts. | OP |
|---|---|---|---|---|---|---|
| Washington | 9 | 2 | 0 | .818 | 245 | 142 |
| Brooklyn | 8 | 3 | 0 | .727 | 186 | 120 |
| N.Y. Giants | 6 | 4 | 1 | .600 | 131 | 133 |
| Pittsburgh | 2 | 7 | 2 | .222 | 60 | 178 |
| Philadelphia | 1 | 10 | 0 | .091 | 111 | 211 |

**WESTERN DIVISION**

| | W | L | T | Pct. | Pts. | OP |
|---|---|---|---|---|---|---|
| Chi. Bears | 8 | 3 | 0 | .727 | 238 | 152 |
| Green Bay | 6 | 4 | 1 | .600 | 238 | 155 |
| Detroit | 5 | 5 | 1 | .500 | 138 | 153 |
| Cleveland | 4 | 6 | 1 | .400 | 171 | 191 |
| Chi. Cardinals | 2 | 7 | 2 | .222 | 139 | 222 |

NFL championship: Chi. Bears 73, WASHINGTON 0

## 1939

**EASTERN DIVISION**

| | W | L | T | Pct. | Pts. | OP |
|---|---|---|---|---|---|---|
| N.Y. Giants | 9 | 1 | 1 | .900 | 168 | 85 |
| Washington | 8 | 2 | 1 | .800 | 242 | 94 |
| Brooklyn | 4 | 6 | 1 | .400 | 108 | 219 |
| Philadelphia | 1 | 9 | 1 | .100 | 105 | 200 |
| Pittsburgh | 1 | 9 | 1 | .100 | 114 | 216 |

**WESTERN DIVISION**

| | W | L | T | Pct. | Pts. | OP |
|---|---|---|---|---|---|---|
| Green Bay | 9 | 2 | 0 | .818 | 233 | 153 |
| Chi. Bears | 8 | 3 | 0 | .727 | 298 | 157 |
| Detroit | 6 | 5 | 0 | .545 | 145 | 150 |
| Cleveland | 5 | 5 | 1 | .500 | 195 | 164 |
| Chi. Cardinals | 1 | 10 | 0 | .091 | 84 | 254 |

NFL championship: GREEN BAY 27, N.Y. Giants 0

## 1938

**EASTERN DIVISION**

| | W | L | T | Pct. | Pts. | OP |
|---|---|---|---|---|---|---|
| N.Y. Giants | 8 | 2 | 1 | .800 | 194 | 79 |
| Washington | 6 | 3 | 2 | .667 | 148 | 154 |
| Brooklyn | 4 | 4 | 3 | .500 | 131 | 161 |
| Philadelphia | 5 | 6 | 0 | .455 | 154 | 164 |
| Pittsburgh | 2 | 9 | 0 | .182 | 79 | 169 |

**WESTERN DIVISION**

| | W | L | T | Pct. | Pts. | OP |
|---|---|---|---|---|---|---|
| Green Bay | 8 | 3 | 0 | .727 | 223 | 118 |
| Detroit | 7 | 4 | 0 | .636 | 119 | 108 |
| Chi. Bears | 6 | 5 | 0 | .545 | 194 | 148 |
| Cleveland | 4 | 7 | 0 | .364 | 131 | 215 |
| Chi. Cardinals | 2 | 9 | 0 | .182 | 111 | 168 |

NFL championship: N.Y. GIANTS 23, Green Bay 17

## 1937

**EASTERN DIVISION**

| | W | L | T | Pct. | Pts. | OP |
|---|---|---|---|---|---|---|
| Washington | 8 | 3 | 0 | .727 | 195 | 120 |
| N.Y. Giants | 6 | 3 | 2 | .667 | 128 | 109 |
| Pittsburgh | 4 | 7 | 0 | .364 | 122 | 145 |
| Brooklyn | 3 | 7 | 1 | .300 | 82 | 174 |
| Philadelphia | 2 | 8 | 1 | .200 | 86 | 177 |

**WESTERN DIVISION**

| | W | L | T | Pct. | Pts. | OP |
|---|---|---|---|---|---|---|
| Chi. Bears | 9 | 1 | 1 | .900 | 201 | 100 |
| Green Bay | 7 | 4 | 0 | .636 | 220 | 122 |
| Detroit | 7 | 4 | 0 | .636 | 180 | 105 |
| Chi. Cardinals | 5 | 5 | 1 | .500 | 135 | 165 |
| Cleveland | 1 | 10 | 0 | .091 | 75 | 207 |

NFL championship: Washington 28, CHI. BEARS 21

# PAST STANDINGS

## 1936

**EASTERN DIVISION**

| | W | L | T | Pct. | Pts. | OP |
|---|---|---|---|---|---|---|
| Boston | 7 | 5 | 0 | .583 | 149 | 110 |
| Pittsburgh | 6 | 6 | 0 | .500 | 98 | 187 |
| N.Y. Giants | 5 | 6 | 1 | .455 | 115 | 163 |
| Brooklyn | 3 | 8 | 1 | .273 | 92 | 161 |
| Philadelphia | 1 | 11 | 0 | .083 | 51 | 206 |

**WESTERN DIVISION**

| | W | L | T | Pct. | Pts. | OP |
|---|---|---|---|---|---|---|
| Green Bay | 10 | 1 | 1 | .909 | 248 | 118 |
| Chi. Bears | 9 | 3 | 0 | .750 | 222 | 94 |
| Detroit | 8 | 4 | 0 | .667 | 235 | 102 |
| Chi. Cardinals | 3 | 8 | 1 | .273 | 74 | 143 |

NFL championship: Green Bay 21, Boston 6, at Polo Grounds, N.Y.

## 1935

**EASTERN DIVISION**

| | W | L | T | Pct. | Pts. | OP |
|---|---|---|---|---|---|---|
| N. Y. Giants | 9 | 3 | 0 | .750 | 180 | 96 |
| Brooklyn | 5 | 6 | 1 | .455 | 90 | 141 |
| Pittsburgh | 4 | 8 | 0 | .333 | 100 | 209 |
| Boston | 2 | 8 | 1 | .200 | 65 | 123 |
| Philadelphia | 2 | 9 | 0 | .182 | 60 | 179 |

**WESTERN DIVISION**

| | W | L | T | Pct. | Pts. | OP |
|---|---|---|---|---|---|---|
| Detroit | 7 | 3 | 2 | .700 | 191 | 111 |
| Green Bay | 8 | 4 | 0 | .667 | 181 | 96 |
| Chi. Bears | 6 | 4 | 2 | .600 | 192 | 106 |
| Chi. Cardinals | 6 | 4 | 2 | .600 | 99 | 97 |

NFL championship: DETROIT 26, N.Y. Giants 7
One game between Boston and Philadelphia was canceled.

## 1934

**EASTERN DIVISION**

| | W | L | T | Pct. | Pts. | OP |
|---|---|---|---|---|---|---|
| N.Y. Giants | 8 | 5 | 0 | .615 | 147 | 107 |
| Boston | 6 | 6 | 0 | .500 | 107 | 94 |
| Brooklyn | 4 | 7 | 0 | .364 | 61 | 153 |
| Philadelphia | 4 | 7 | 0 | .364 | 127 | 85 |
| Pittsburgh | 2 | 10 | 0 | .167 | 51 | 206 |

**WESTERN DIVISION**

| | W | L | T | Pct. | Pts. | OP |
|---|---|---|---|---|---|---|
| Chi. Bears | 13 | 0 | 0 | 1.000 | 286 | 86 |
| Detroit | 10 | 3 | 0 | .769 | 238 | 59 |
| Green Bay | 7 | 6 | 0 | .538 | 156 | 112 |
| Chi. Cardinals | 5 | 6 | 0 | .455 | 80 | 84 |
| St. Louis | 1 | 2 | 0 | .333 | 27 | 61 |
| Cincinnati | 0 | 8 | 0 | .000 | 10 | 243 |

NFL championship: N.Y. GIANTS 30, Chi. Bears 13

## 1933

**EASTERN DIVISION**

| | W | L | T | Pct. | Pts. | OP |
|---|---|---|---|---|---|---|
| N.Y. Giants | 11 | 3 | 0 | .786 | 244 | 101 |
| Brooklyn | 5 | 4 | 1 | .556 | 93 | 54 |
| Boston | 5 | 5 | 2 | .500 | 103 | 97 |
| Philadelphia | 3 | 5 | 1 | .375 | 77 | 158 |
| Pittsburgh | 3 | 6 | 2 | .333 | 67 | 208 |

**WESTERN DIVISION**

| | W | L | T | Pct. | Pts. | OP |
|---|---|---|---|---|---|---|
| Chi. Bears | 10 | 2 | 1 | .833 | 133 | 82 |
| Portsmouth | 6 | 5 | 0 | .545 | 128 | 87 |
| Green Bay | 5 | 7 | 1 | .417 | 170 | 107 |
| Cincinnati | 3 | 6 | 1 | .333 | 38 | 110 |
| Chi. Cardinals | 1 | 9 | 1 | .100 | 52 | 101 |

NFL championship: CHI. BEARS 23, N.Y. Giants 21

## 1932

| | W | L | T | Pct. |
|---|---|---|---|---|
| Chicago Bears | 7 | 1 | 6 | .875 |
| Green Bay Packers | 10 | 3 | 1 | .769 |
| Portsmouth Spartans | 6 | 2 | 4 | .750 |
| Boston Braves | 4 | 4 | 2 | .500 |
| New York Giants | 4 | 6 | 2 | .400 |
| Brooklyn Dodgers | 3 | 9 | 0 | .250 |
| Chicago Cardinals | 2 | 6 | 2 | .250 |
| Staten Island Stapletons | 2 | 7 | 3 | .222 |

*Chicago Bears and Portsmouth finished regularly scheduled games tied for first place. Bears won playoff game, which counted in standings, 9-0.*

## 1931

| | W | L | T | Pct. |
|---|---|---|---|---|
| Green Bay Packers | 12 | 2 | 0 | .857 |
| Portsmouth Spartans | 11 | 3 | 0 | .786 |
| Chicago Bears | 8 | 5 | 0 | .615 |
| Chicago Cardinals | 5 | 4 | 0 | .556 |
| New York Giants | 7 | 6 | 1 | .538 |
| Providence Steam Roller | 4 | 4 | 3 | .500 |
| Staten Island Stapletons | 4 | 6 | 1 | .400 |
| Cleveland Indians | 2 | 8 | 0 | .200 |
| Brooklyn Dodgers | 2 | 12 | 0 | .143 |
| Frankford Yellow Jackets | 1 | 6 | 1 | .143 |

## 1930

| | W | L | T | Pct. |
|---|---|---|---|---|
| Green Bay Packers | 10 | 3 | 1 | .769 |
| New York Giants | 13 | 4 | 0 | .765 |
| Chicago Bears | 9 | 4 | 1 | .692 |
| Brooklyn Dodgers | 7 | 4 | 1 | .636 |
| Providence Steam Roller | 6 | 4 | 1 | .600 |
| Staten Island Stapletons | 5 | 5 | 2 | .500 |
| Chicago Cardinals | 5 | 6 | 2 | .455 |
| Portsmouth Spartans | 5 | 6 | 3 | .455 |
| Frankford Yellow Jackets | 4 | 13 | 1 | .222 |
| Minneapolis Red Jackets | 1 | 7 | 1 | .125 |
| Newark Tornadoes | 1 | 10 | 1 | .091 |

## 1929

| | W | L | T | Pct. |
|---|---|---|---|---|
| Green Bay Packers | 12 | 0 | 1 | 1.000 |
| New York Giants | 13 | 1 | 1 | .929 |
| Frankford Yellow Jackets | 9 | 4 | 5 | .692 |
| Chicago Cardinals | 6 | 6 | 1 | .500 |
| Boston Bulldogs | 4 | 4 | 0 | .500 |
| Orange Tornadoes | 3 | 4 | 4 | .429 |
| Staten Island Stapletons | 3 | 4 | 3 | .429 |
| Providence Steam Roller | 4 | 6 | 2 | .400 |
| Chicago Bears | 4 | 9 | 2 | .308 |
| Buffalo Bisons | 1 | 7 | 1 | .125 |
| Minneapolis Red Jackets | 1 | 9 | 0 | .100 |
| Dayton Triangles | 0 | 6 | 0 | .000 |

## 1928

| | W | L | T | Pct. |
|---|---|---|---|---|
| Providence Steam Roller | 8 | 1 | 2 | .889 |
| Frankford Yellow Jackets | 11 | 3 | 2 | .786 |
| Detroit Wolverines | 7 | 2 | 1 | .778 |
| Green Bay Packers | 6 | 4 | 3 | .600 |
| Chicago Bears | 7 | 5 | 1 | .583 |
| New York Giants | 4 | 7 | 2 | .364 |
| New York Yankees | 4 | 8 | 1 | .333 |
| Pottsville Maroons | 2 | 8 | 0 | .200 |
| Chicago Cardinals | 1 | 5 | 0 | .167 |
| Dayton Triangles | 0 | 7 | 0 | .000 |

## 1927

| | W | L | T | Pct. |
|---|---|---|---|---|
| New York Giants | 11 | 1 | 1 | .917 |
| Green Bay Packers | 7 | 2 | 1 | .778 |
| Chicago Bears | 9 | 3 | 2 | .750 |
| Cleveland Bulldogs | 8 | 4 | 1 | .667 |
| Providence Steam Roller | 8 | 5 | 1 | .615 |
| New York Yankees | 7 | 8 | 1 | .467 |
| Frankford Yellow Jackets | 6 | 9 | 3 | .400 |
| Pottsville Maroons | 5 | 8 | 0 | .385 |
| Chicago Cardinals | 3 | 7 | 1 | .300 |
| Dayton Triangles | 1 | 6 | 1 | .143 |
| Duluth Eskimos | 1 | 8 | 0 | .111 |
| Buffalo Bisons | 0 | 5 | 0 | .000 |

## 1926

| | W | L | T | Pct. |
|---|---|---|---|---|
| Frankford Yellow Jackets | 14 | 1 | 1 | .933 |
| Chicago Bears | 12 | 1 | 3 | .923 |
| Pottsville Maroons | 10 | 2 | 1 | .833 |
| Kansas City Cowboys | 8 | 3 | 0 | .727 |
| Green Bay Packers | 7 | 3 | 3 | .700 |
| Los Angeles Buccaneers | 6 | 3 | 1 | .667 |
| New York Giants | 8 | 4 | 1 | .667 |
| Duluth Eskimos | 6 | 5 | 3 | .545 |
| Buffalo Rangers | 4 | 4 | 2 | .500 |
| Chicago Cardinals | 5 | 6 | 1 | .455 |
| Providence Steam Roller | 5 | 7 | 1 | .417 |
| Detroit Panthers | 4 | 6 | 2 | .400 |
| Hartford Blues | 3 | 7 | 0 | .300 |
| Brooklyn Lions | 3 | 8 | 0 | .273 |
| Milwaukee Badgers | 2 | 7 | 0 | .222 |
| Akron Pros | 1 | 4 | 3 | .200 |
| Dayton Triangles | 1 | 4 | 1 | .200 |
| Racine Tornadoes | 1 | 4 | 0 | .200 |
| Columbus Tigers | 1 | 6 | 0 | .143 |
| Canton Bulldogs | 1 | 9 | 3 | .100 |
| Hammond Pros | 0 | 4 | 0 | .000 |
| Louisville Colonels | 0 | 4 | 0 | .000 |

## 1925

| | W | L | T | Pct. |
|---|---|---|---|---|
| Chicago Cardinals | 11 | 2 | 1 | .846 |
| Pottsville Maroons | 10 | 2 | 0 | .833 |
| Detroit Panthers | 8 | 2 | 2 | .800 |
| New York Giants | 8 | 4 | 0 | .667 |
| Akron Indians | 4 | 2 | 2 | .667 |
| Frankford Yellow Jackets | 13 | 7 | 0 | .650 |
| Chicago Bears | 9 | 5 | 3 | .643 |
| Rock Island Independents | 5 | 3 | 3 | .625 |
| Green Bay Packers | 8 | 5 | 0 | .615 |
| Providence Steam Roller | 6 | 5 | 1 | .545 |
| Canton Bulldogs | 4 | 4 | 0 | .500 |
| Cleveland Bulldogs | 5 | 8 | 1 | .385 |
| Kansas City Cowboys | 2 | 5 | 1 | .286 |
| Hammond Pros | 1 | 4 | 0 | .200 |
| Buffalo Bisons | 1 | 6 | 2 | .143 |
| Duluth Kelleys | 0 | 3 | 0 | .000 |
| Rochester Jeffersons | 0 | 6 | 1 | .000 |
| Milwaukee Badgers | 0 | 6 | 0 | .000 |
| Dayton Triangles | 0 | 7 | 1 | .000 |
| Columbus Tigers | 0 | 9 | 0 | .000 |

## 1924

| | W | L | T | Pct. |
|---|---|---|---|---|
| Cleveland Bulldogs | 7 | 1 | 1 | .875 |
| Chicago Bears | 6 | 1 | 4 | .857 |
| Frankford Yellow Jackets | 11 | 2 | 1 | .846 |
| Duluth Kelleys | 5 | 1 | 0 | .833 |
| Rock Island Independents | 6 | 2 | 2 | .750 |
| Green Bay Packers | 7 | 4 | 0 | .636 |
| Racine Legion | 4 | 3 | 3 | .571 |
| Chicago Cardinals | 5 | 4 | 1 | .556 |
| Buffalo Bisons | 6 | 5 | 0 | .545 |
| Columbus Tigers | 4 | 4 | 0 | .500 |
| Hammond Pros | 2 | 2 | 1 | .500 |
| Milwaukee Badgers | 5 | 8 | 0 | .385 |
| Akron Indians | 2 | 6 | 0 | .250 |
| Dayton Triangles | 2 | 6 | 0 | .250 |
| Kansas City Blues | 2 | 7 | 0 | .222 |
| Kenosha Maroons | 0 | 5 | 1 | .000 |
| Minneapolis Marines | 0 | 6 | 0 | .000 |
| Rochester Jeffersons | 0 | 7 | 0 | .000 |

## 1923

| | W | L | T | Pct. |
|---|---|---|---|---|
| Canton Bulldogs | 11 | 0 | 1 | 1.000 |
| Chicago Bears | 9 | 2 | 1 | .818 |
| Green Bay Packers | 7 | 2 | 1 | .778 |
| Milwaukee Badgers | 7 | 2 | 3 | .778 |
| Cleveland Indians | 3 | 1 | 3 | .750 |
| Chicago Cardinals | 8 | 4 | 0 | .667 |
| Duluth Kelleys | 4 | 3 | 0 | .571 |
| Columbus Tigers | 5 | 4 | 1 | .556 |
| Buffalo All-Americans | 4 | 4 | 3 | .500 |
| Racine Legion | 4 | 4 | 2 | .500 |
| Toledo Maroons | 2 | 3 | 2 | .400 |
| Rock Island Independents | 2 | 3 | 3 | .400 |
| Minneapolis Marines | 2 | 5 | 2 | .286 |
| St. Louis All-Stars | 1 | 4 | 2 | .200 |
| Hammond Pros | 1 | 5 | 1 | .167 |
| Dayton Triangles | 1 | 6 | 1 | .143 |
| Akron Indians | 1 | 6 | 0 | .143 |
| Oorang Indians | 1 | 10 | 0 | .091 |
| Rochester Jeffersons | 0 | 2 | 0 | .000 |
| Louisville Brecks | 0 | 3 | 0 | .000 |

## 1922

| | W | L | T | Pct. |
|---|---|---|---|---|
| Canton Bulldogs | 10 | 0 | 2 | 1.000 |
| Chicago Bears | 9 | 3 | 0 | .750 |
| Chicago Cardinals | 8 | 3 | 0 | .727 |
| Toledo Maroons | 5 | 2 | 2 | .714 |
| Rock Island Independents | 4 | 2 | 1 | .667 |
| Racine Legion | 6 | 4 | 1 | .600 |
| Dayton Triangles | 4 | 3 | 1 | .571 |
| Green Bay Packers | 4 | 3 | 3 | .571 |
| Buffalo All-Americans | 5 | 4 | 1 | .556 |
| Akron Pros | 3 | 5 | 2 | .375 |
| Milwaukee Badgers | 2 | 4 | 3 | .333 |
| Oorang Indians | 2 | 6 | 0 | .250 |
| Minneapolis Marines | 1 | 3 | 0 | .250 |
| Louisville Brecks | 1 | 3 | 0 | .250 |
| Evansville Crimson Giants | 0 | 3 | 0 | .000 |
| Rochester Jeffersons | 0 | 4 | 1 | .000 |
| Hammond Pros | 0 | 5 | 1 | .000 |
| Columbus Panhandles | 0 | 7 | 0 | .000 |

## 1921

| | W | L | T | Pct. |
|---|---|---|---|---|
| Chicago Staleys | 9 | 1 | 1 | .900 |
| Buffalo All-Americans | 9 | 1 | 2 | .900 |
| Akron Pros | 8 | 3 | 1 | .727 |
| Canton Bulldogs | 5 | 2 | 3 | .714 |
| Rock Island Independents | 4 | 2 | 1 | .667 |
| Evansville Crimson Giants | 3 | 2 | 0 | .600 |
| Green Bay Packers | 3 | 2 | 1 | .600 |
| Dayton Triangles | 4 | 4 | 1 | .500 |
| Chicago Cardinals | 3 | 3 | 2 | .500 |
| Rochester Jeffersons | 2 | 3 | 0 | .400 |
| Cleveland Indians | 3 | 5 | 0 | .375 |
| Washington Senators | 1 | 2 | 0 | .333 |
| Cincinnati Celts | 1 | 3 | 0 | .250 |
| Hammond Pros | 1 | 3 | 1 | .250 |
| Minneapolis Marines | 1 | 3 | 1 | .250 |
| Detroit Heralds | 1 | 5 | 1 | .167 |
| Columbus Panhandles | 1 | 8 | 0 | .111 |
| Tonawanda Kardex | 0 | 1 | 0 | .000 |
| Muncie Flyers | 0 | 2 | 0 | .000 |
| Louisville Brecks | 0 | 2 | 0 | .000 |
| New York Giants | 0 | 2 | 0 | .000 |

## 1920*

| | W | L | T | Pct. |
|---|---|---|---|---|
| Akron Pros | 8 | 0 | 3 | 1.000 |
| Decatur Staleys | 10 | 1 | 2 | .909 |
| Buffalo All-Americans | 9 | 1 | 1 | .900 |
| Chicago Cardinals | 6 | 2 | 2 | .750 |
| Rock Island Independents | 6 | 2 | 2 | .750 |
| Dayton Triangles | 5 | 2 | 2 | .714 |
| Rochester Jeffersons | 6 | 3 | 2 | .667 |
| Canton Bulldogs | 7 | 4 | 2 | .636 |
| Detroit Heralds | 2 | 3 | 3 | .400 |
| Cleveland Tigers | 2 | 4 | 2 | .333 |
| Chicago Tigers | 2 | 5 | 1 | .286 |
| Hammond Pros | 2 | 5 | 0 | .286 |
| Columbus Panhandles | 2 | 6 | 2 | .250 |
| Muncie Flyers | 0 | 1 | 0 | .000 |

**No official standing was maintained for the 1920 season, and the championship was awarded to the Akron Pros in a League meeting on April 30, 1921. Clubs played schedules which included games against non-league opponents. Records of clubs against all opponents are listed above.*

**RS=REGULAR SEASON**
**PS=POSTSEASON**
***ARIZONA vs. ATLANTA**
RS: Cardinals lead series, 11-5
1966—Falcons, 16-10 (A)
1968—Cardinals, 17-12 (StL)
1971—Cardinals, 26-9 (A)
1973—Cardinals, 32-10 (A)
1975—Cardinals, 23-20 (StL)
1978—Cardinals, 42-21 (StL)
1980—Falcons, 33-27 (StL) OT
1981—Falcons, 41-20 (A)
1982—Cardinals, 23-20 (A)
1986—Falcons, 33-13 (A)
1987—Cardinals, 34-21 (A)
1989—Cardinals, 34-20 (P)
1990—Cardinals, 24-13 (A)
1991—Cardinals, 16-10 (P)
1992—Falcons, 20-17 (A)
1993—Cardinals, 27-10 (A)
(RS Pts.—Cardinals 385, Falcons 309)
**Franchise known as Phoenix prior to 1994 and in St. Louis prior to 1988*
***ARIZONA vs. BUFFALO**
RS: Series tied, 3-3
1971—Cardinals, 28-23 (B)
1975—Bills, 32-14 (StL)
1981—Cardinals, 24-0 (StL)
1984—Cardinals, 37-7 (StL)
1986—Bills, 17-10 (B)
1990—Bills, 45-14 (B)
(RS Pts.—Cardinals 127, Bills 124)
**Franchise known as Phoenix prior to 1994 and in St. Louis prior to 1988*
***ARIZONA vs. **CHICAGO**
RS: Bears lead series, 51-25-6
(NP denotes Normal Park;
Wr denotes Wrigley Field;
Co denotes Comiskey Park;
So denotes Soldier Field;
all Chicago)
1920—Cardinals, 7-6 (NP)
Staleys, 10-0 (Wr)
1921—Tie, 0-0 (Wr)
1922—Cardinals, 6-0 (Co)
Cardinals, 9-0 (Co)
1923—Bears, 3-0 (Wr)
1924—Bears, 6-0 (Wr)
Bears, 21-0 (Co)
1925—Cardinals, 9-0 (Co)
Tie, 0-0 (Wr)
1926—Bears, 16-0 (Wr)
Bears, 10-0 (So)
Tie, 0-0 (Wr)
1927—Bears, 9-0 (NP)
Cardinals, 3 0 (Wr)
1928—Bears, 15-0 (NP)
Bears, 34-0 (Wr)
1929—Tie, 0-0 (Wr)
Cardinals, 40-6 (Co)
1930—Bears, 32-6 (Co)
Bears, 6-0 (Wr)
1931—Bears, 26-13 (Wr)
Bears, 18-7 (Wr)
1932—Tie, 0-0 (Wr)
Bears, 34-0 (Wr)
1933—Bears, 12-9 (Wr)
Bears, 22-6 (Wr)
1934—Bears, 20-0 (Wr)
Bears, 17-6 (Wr)
1935—Tie, 7-7 (Wr)
Bears, 13-0 (Wr)
1936—Bears, 7-3 (Wr)
Cardinals, 14-7 (Wr)
1937—Bears, 16-7 (Wr)
Bears, 42-28 (Wr)
1938—Bears, 16-13 (So)
Bears, 34-28 (Wr)
1939—Bears, 44-7 (Wr)
Bears, 48-7 (Co)
1940—Cardinals, 21-7 (Co)
Bears, 31-23 (Wr)
1941—Bears, 53-7 (Wr)
Bears, 34-24 (Co)
1942—Bears, 41-14 (Wr)
Bears, 21-7 (Co)
1943—Bears, 20-0 (Wr)
Bears, 35-24 (Co)
1945—Cardinals, 16-7 (Wr)
Bears, 28-20 (Co)
1946—Bears, 34-17 (Co)
Cardinals, 35-28 (Wr)
1947—Cardinals, 31-7 (Co)
Cardinals, 30-21 (Wr)
1948—Bears, 28-17 (Co)
Cardinals, 24-21 (Wr)
1949—Bears, 17-7 (Co)
Bears, 52-21 (Wr)
1950—Bears, 27-6 (Wr)
Cardinals, 20-10 (Co)
1951—Cardinals, 28-14 (Co)
Cardinals, 24-14 (Wr)
1952—Cardinals, 21-10 (Co)
Bears, 10-7 (Wr)
1953—Cardinals, 24-17 (Wr)
1954—Bears, 29-7 (Co)
1955—Cardinals, 53-14 (Co)
1956—Bears, 10-3 (Wr)
1957—Bears, 14-6 (Co)
1958—Bears, 30-14 (Wr)
1959—Bears, 31-7 (So)
1965—Bears, 34-13 (Wr)
1966—Cardinals, 24-17 (StL)
1967—Bears, 30-3 (Wr)
1969—Cardinals, 20-17 (StL)
1972—Bears, 27-10 (StL)
1975—Cardinals, 34-20 (So)
1977—Cardinals, 16-13 (StL)
1978—Bears, 17-10 (So)
1979—Bears, 42-6 (So)
1982—Cardinals, 10-7 (So)
1984—Cardinals, 38-21 (StL)
1990—Bears, 31-21 (P)
(RS Pts.—Bears 1,548, Cardinals 998)
**Franchise known as Phoenix prior to 1994, in St. Louis prior to 1988, and in Chicago prior to 1960*
***Franchise in Decatur prior to 1921 and known as Staleys prior to 1922*
***ARIZONA vs. CINCINNATI**
RS: Bengals lead series, 3-1
1973—Bengals, 42-24 (C)
1979—Bengals, 34-28 (C)
1985—Cardinals, 41-27 (StL)
1988—Bengals, 21-14 (C)
(RS Pts.—Bengals 124, Cardinals 107)
**Franchise known as Phoenix prior to 1994 and in St. Louis prior to 1988*
***ARIZONA vs. CLEVELAND**
RS: Browns lead series, 31-10-3
1950—Browns, 34-24 (Cle)
Browns, 10-7 (Chi)
1951—Browns, 34-17 (Chi)
Browns, 49-28 (Cle)
1952—Browns, 28-13 (Cle)
Browns, 10-0 (Chi)
1953—Browns, 27-7 (Chi)
Browns, 27-16 (Cle)
1954—Browns, 31-7 (Cle)
Browns, 35-3 (Chi)
1955—Browns, 26-20 (Chi)
Browns, 35-24 (Cle)
1956—Cardinals, 9-7 (Chi)
Cardinals, 24-7 (Cle)
1957—Browns, 17-7 (Chi)
Browns, 31-0 (Cle)
1958—Browns, 35-28 (Cle)
Browns, 38-24 (Chi)
1959—Browns, 34-7 (Chi)
Browns, 17-7 (Cle)
1960—Browns, 28-27 (Cle)
Tie, 17-17 (StL)
1961—Browns, 20-17 (Cle)
Browns, 21-10 (StL)
1962—Browns, 34-7 (StL)
Browns, 38-14 (Cle)
1963—Cardinals, 20-14 (Cle)
Browns, 24-10 (StL)
1964—Tie, 33-33 (Cle)
Cardinals, 28-19 (StL)
1965—Cardinals, 49-13 (Cle)
Browns, 27-24 (StL)
1966—Cardinals, 34-28 (Cle)
Browns, 38-10 (StL)
1967—Browns, 20-16 (Cle)
Browns, 20-16 (StL)
1968—Cardinals, 27-21 (Cle)
Cardinals, 27-16 (StL)
1969—Tie, 21-21 (Cle)
Browns, 27-21 (StL)
1974—Cardinals, 29-7 (StL)
1979—Browns, 38-20 (StL)
1985—Cardinals, 27-24 (Cle) OT
1988—Browns, 29-21 (P)
(RS Pts.—Browns 1,109, Cardinals 797)
**Franchise known as Phoenix prior to 1994, in St. Louis prior to 1988, and in Chicago prior to 1960*
***ARIZONA vs. DALLAS**
RS: Cowboys lead series, 40-22-1
1960—Cardinals, 12-10 (StL)
1961—Cardinals, 31-17 (D)
Cardinals, 31-13 (StL)
1962—Cardinals, 28-24 (D)
Cardinals, 52-20 (StL)
1963—Cardinals, 34-7 (D)
Cowboys, 28-24 (StL)
1964—Cardinals, 16-6 (D)
Cowboys, 31-13 (StL)
1965—Cardinals, 20-13 (StL)
Cowboys, 27-13 (D)
1966—Tie, 10-10 (StL)
Cowboys, 31-17 (D)
1967—Cowboys, 46-21 (D)
1968—Cowboys, 27-10 (StL)
1969—Cowboys, 24-3 (D)
1970—Cardinals, 20-7 (StL)
Cardinals, 38-0 (D)
1971—Cowboys, 16-13 (StL)
Cowboys, 31-12 (D)
1972—Cowboys, 33-24 (D)
Cowboys, 27-6 (StL)
1973—Cowboys, 45-10 (D)
Cowboys, 30-3 (StL)
1974—Cardinals, 31-28 (StL)
Cowboys, 17-14 (D)
1975—Cowboys, 37-31 (D) OT
Cardinals, 31-17 (StL)
1976—Cardinals, 21-17 (StL)
Cowboys, 19-14 (D)
1977—Cowboys, 30-24 (StL)
Cardinals, 24-17 (D)
1978—Cowboys, 21-12 (D)
Cowboys, 24-21 (StL) OT
1979—Cowboys, 22-21 (StL)
Cowboys, 22-13 (D)
1980—Cowboys, 27-24 (StL)
Cowboys, 31-21 (D)
1981—Cowboys, 30-17 (D)
Cardinals, 20-17 (StL)
1982—Cowboys, 24-7 (StL)
1983—Cowboys, 34-17 (StL)
Cowboys, 35-17 (D)
1984—Cardinals, 31-20 (D)
Cowboys, 24-17 (StL)
1985—Cardinals, 21-10 (StL)
Cowboys, 35-17 (D)
1986—Cowboys, 31-7 (StL)
Cowboys, 37-6 (D)
1987—Cardinals, 24-13 (StL)
Cowboys, 21-16 (D)
1988—Cowboys, 17-14 (P)
Cardinals, 16-10 (D)
1989—Cardinals, 19-10 (D)
Cardinals, 24-20 (P)
1990—Cardinals, 20-3 (P)
Cowboys, 41-10 (D)
1991—Cowboys, 17-9 (P)
Cowboys, 27-7 (D)
1992—Cowboys, 31-20 (D)
Cowboys, 16-10 (P)
1993—Cowboys, 17-10 (P)
Cowboys, 20-15 (D)
(RS Pts.—Cowboys 1,412, Cardinals 1,154)
**Franchise known as Phoenix prior to 1994 and in St. Louis prior to 1988*
***ARIZONA vs. DENVER**
RS: Broncos lead series, 3-0-1
1973—Tie, 17-17 (StL)
1977—Broncos, 7-0 (D)
1989—Broncos, 37-0 (P)
1991—Broncos, 24-19 (D)
(RS Pts.—Broncos 85, Cardinals 36)
**Franchise known as Phoenix prior to 1994 and in St. Louis prior to 1988*
***ARIZONA vs. **DETROIT**
RS: Lions lead series, 27-16-5
1930—Tie, 0-0 (Port)
Cardinals, 23-0 (C)
1931—Cardinals, 20-19 (C)
1932—Tie, 7-7 (Port)
1933—Spartans, 7-6 (Port)
1934—Lions, 6-0 (D)
Lions, 17-13 (C)
1935—Tie, 10-10 (D)
Lions, 7-6 (C)
1936—Lions, 39-0 (D)
Lions, 14-7 (C)
1937—Lions, 16-7 (C)
Lions, 16-7 (D)
1938—Lions, 10-0 (D)
Lions, 7-3 (C)
1939—Lions, 21-3 (D)
Lions, 17-3 (C)
1940—Tie, 0-0 (Buffalo)
Lions, 43-14 (C)
1941—Tie, 14-14 (C)
Lions, 21-3 (D)
1942—Cardinals, 13-0 (C)
Cardinals, 7-0 (D)
1943—Lions, 35-17 (D)
Lions, 7-0 (C)
1945—Lions, 10-0 (C)
Lions, 26-0 (D)
1946—Cardinals, 34-14 (C)
Cardinals, 36-14 (D)
1947—Cardinals, 45-21 (C)
Cardinals, 17-7 (D)
1948—Cardinals, 56-20 (C)
Cardinals, 28-14 (D)
1949—Lions, 24-7 (C)
Cardinals, 42-19 (D)
1959—Lions, 45-21 (D)
1961—Lions, 45-14 (StL)
1967—Cardinals, 38-28 (StL)
1969—Lions, 20-0 (D)
1970—Lions, 16-3 (D)
1973—Lions, 20-16 (StL)
1975—Cardinals, 24-13 (D)
1978—Cardinals, 21-14 (StL)
1980—Lions, 20-7 (D)
Cardinals, 24-23 (StL)
1989—Cardinals, 16-13 (D)
1993—Lions, 26-20 (D)
Lions, 21-14 (Phx)
(RS Pts.—Lions 806, Cardinals 676)
**Franchise known as Phoenix prior to 1994, in St. Louis prior to 1988, and in Chicago prior to 1960*
***Franchise in Portsmouth prior to 1934 and known as the Spartans*
***ARIZONA vs. GREEN BAY**
RS: Packers lead series, 39-21-4
PS: Packers lead series, 1-0
1921—Tie, 3-3 (C)
1922—Cardinals, 16-3 (C)
1924—Cardinals, 3-0 (C)
1925—Cardinals, 9-6 (C)
1926—Cardinals, 13-7 (GB)
Packers, 3-0 (C)
1927—Packers, 13-0 (GB)
Tie, 6-6 (C)

1928—Packers, 20-0 (GB)
1929—Packers, 9-2 (GB)
Packers, 7-6 (C)
Packers, 12-0 (C)
1930—Packers, 14-0 (GB)
Cardinals, 13-6 (C)
1931—Packers, 26-7 (GB)
Cardinals, 21-13 (C)
1932—Packers, 15-7 (GB)
Packers, 19-9 (C)
1933—Packers, 14-6 (C)
1934—Packers, 15-0 (GB)
Cardinals, 9-0 (Mil)
Cardinals, 6-0 (C)
1935—Cardinals, 7-6 (GB)
Cardinals, 3-0 (Mil)
Cardinals, 9-7 (C)
1936—Packers, 10-7 (GB)
Packers, 24-0 (Mil)
Tie, 0-0 (C)
1937—Cardinals, 14-7 (GB)
Packers, 34-13 (Mil)
1938—Packers, 28-7 (Mil)
Packers, 24-22 (Buffalo)
1939—Packers, 14-10 (GB)
Packers, 27-20 (Mil)
1940—Packers, 31-6 (Mil)
Packers, 28-7 (C)
1941—Packers, 14-13 (Mil)
Packers, 17-9 (GB)
1942—Packers, 17-13 (C)
Packers, 55-24 (GB)
1943—Packers, 28-7 (C)
Packers, 35-14 (Mil)
1945—Packers, 33-14 (GB)
1946—Packers, 19-7 (C)
Cardinals, 24-6 (GB)
1947—Cardinals, 14-10 (GB)
Cardinals, 21-20 (C)
1948—Cardinals, 17-7 (Mil)
Cardinals, 42-7 (C)
1949—Cardinals, 39-17 (Mil)
Cardinals, 41-21 (C)
1955—Packers, 31-14 (GB)
1956—Packers, 24-21 (C)
1962—Packers, 17-0 (Mil)
1963—Packers, 30-7 (StL)
1967—Packers, 31-23 (StL)
1969—Packers, 45-28 (GB)
1971—Tie, 16-16 (StL)
1973—Packers, 25-21 (GB)
1976—Cardinals, 29-0 (StL)
1982—**Packers, 41-16 (GB)
1984—Packers, 24-23 (GB)
1985—Cardinals, 43-28 (StL)
1988—Packers, 26-17 (P)
1990—Packers, 24-21 (P)
(RS Pts.—Packers 1,078, Cardinals 823)
(PS Pts.—Packers 41, Cardinals 16)
*Franchise known as Phoenix prior to 1994, in St. Louis prior to 1988, and in Chicago prior to 1960*
***NFC First-Round Playoff*

***ARIZONA vs. HOUSTON**
RS: Cardinals lead series, 3-2
1970—Cardinals, 44-0 (StL)
1974—Cardinals, 31-27 (H)
1979—Cardinals, 24-17 (H)
1985—Oilers, 20-10 (StL)
1988—Oilers, 38-20 (H)
(RS Pts.—Cardinals 129, Oilers 102)
*Franchise known as Phoenix prior to 1994 and in St. Louis prior to 1988*

***ARIZONA vs. **INDIANAPOLIS**
RS: Cardinals lead series, 6-5
1961—Colts, 16-0 (B)
1964—Colts, 47-27 (B)
1968—Colts, 27-0 (B)
1972—Cardinals, 10-3 (B)
1976—Cardinals, 24-17 (StL)
1978—Colts, 30-17 (StL)
1980—Cardinals, 17-10 (B)
1981—Cardinals, 35-24 (B)
1984—Cardinals, 34-33 (I)
1990—Cardinals, 20-17 (P)
1992—Colts, 16-13 (I)
(RS Pts.—Colts 240, Cardinals 197)
*Franchise known as Phoenix prior to 1994 and in St. Louis prior to 1988*
***Franchise in Baltimore prior to 1984*

***ARIZONA vs. KANSAS CITY**
RS: Chiefs lead series, 3-1-1
1970—Tie, 6-6 (KC)
1974—Chiefs, 17-13 (StL)
1980—Chiefs, 21-13 (StL)
1983—Chiefs, 38-14 (KC)
1986—Cardinals, 23-14 (StL)
(RS Pts.—Chiefs 96, Cardinals 69)
*Franchise known as Phoenix prior to 1994 and in St. Louis prior to 1988*

***ARIZONA vs. **L. A. RAIDERS**
RS: Raiders lead series, 2-1
1973—Raiders, 17-10 (StL)
1983—Cardinals, 34-24 (LA)
1989—Raiders, 16-14 (LA)
(RS Pts.—Cardinals 58, Raiders 57)
*Franchise known as Phoenix prior to 1994 and in St. Louis prior to 1988*
***Franchise in Oakland prior to 1982*

***ARIZONA vs. **L.A. RAMS**
RS: Rams lead series, 22-19-2
PS: Rams lead series, 1-0
1937—Cardinals, 6-0 (Clev)
Cardinals, 13-7 (Chi)
1938—Cardinals, 7-6 (Clev)
Cardinals, 31-17 (Chi)
1939—Rams, 24-0 (Chi)
Rams, 14-0 (Clev)
1940—Rams, 26-14 (Clev)
Cardinals, 17-7 (Chi)
1941—Rams, 10-6 (Clev)
Cardinals, 7-0 (Chi)
1942—Cardinals, 7-0 (Chi)
Rams, 7-3 (Clev)
1945—Rams, 21-0 (Clev)
Rams, 35-21 (Chi)
1946—Cardinals, 34-10 (Chi)
Rams, 17-14 (LA)
1947—Rams, 27-7 (LA)
Cardinals, 17-10 (Chi)
1948—Cardinals, 27-22 (LA)
Cardinals, 27-24 (Chi)
1949—Tie, 28-28 (Chi)
Cardinals, 31-27 (LA)
1951—Rams, 45-21 (LA)
1953—Tie, 24-24 (Chi)
1954—Rams, 28-17 (LA)
1958—Rams, 20-14 (Chi)
1960—Cardinals, 43-21 (LA)
1965—Rams, 27-3 (StL)
1968—Rams, 24-13 (StL)
1970—Rams, 34-13 (LA)
1972—Cardinals, 24-14 (StL)
1975—***Rams, 35-23 (LA)
1976—Cardinals, 30-28 (LA)
1979—Rams, 21-0 (LA)
1980—Rams, 21-13 (StL)
1984—Rams, 16-13 (StL)
1985—Rams, 46-14 (LA)
1986—Rams, 16-10 (StL)
1987—Rams, 27-24 (StL)
1988—Cardinals, 41-27 (LA)
1989—Rams, 37-14 (LA)
1991—Cardinals, 24-14 (LA)
1992—Cardinals, 20-14 (LA)
1993—Cardinals, 38-10 (P)
(RS Pts.—Rams 853, Cardinals 730)
(PS Pts.—Rams 35, Cardinals 23)
*Franchise known as Phoenix prior to 1994, in St. Louis prior to 1988, and in Chicago prior to 1960*
***Franchise in Cleveland prior to 1946*
****NFC Divisional Playoff*

***ARIZONA vs. MIAMI**
RS: Dolphins lead series, 6-0
1972—Dolphins, 31-10 (M)
1977—Dolphins, 55-14 (StL)
1978—Dolphins, 24-10 (M)
1981—Dolphins, 20-7 (StL)
1984—Dolphins, 36-28 (StL)
1990—Dolphins, 23-3 (M)
(RS Pts.—Dolphins 189, Cardinals 72)
*Franchise known as Phoenix prior to 1994 and in St. Louis prior to 1988*

***ARIZONA vs. MINNESOTA**
RS: Cardinals lead series, 7-4
PS: Vikings lead series, 1-0
1963—Cardinals, 56-14 (M)
1967—Cardinals, 34-24 (M)
1969—Vikings, 27-10 (StL)
1972—Cardinals, 19-17 (M)
1974—Vikings, 28-24 (StL)
**Vikings, 30-14 (M)
1977—Cardinals, 27-7 (M)
1979—Cardinals, 37-7 (StL)
1981—Cardinals, 30-17 (StL)
1983—Cardinals, 41-31 (StL)
1991—Vikings, 34-7 (M)
Vikings, 28-0 (P)
(RS Pts.—Cardinals 285, Vikings 234)
(PS Pts.—Vikings 30, Cardinals 14)
*Franchise known as Phoenix prior to 1994 and in St. Louis prior to 1988*
***NFC Divisional Playoff*

***ARIZONA vs. **NEW ENGLAND**
RS: Cardinals lead series, 6-2
1970—Cardinals, 31-0 (StL)
1975—Cardinals, 24-17 (StL)
1978—Patriots, 16-6 (StL)
1981—Cardinals, 27-20 (NE)
1984—Cardinals, 33-10 (NE)
1990—Cardinals, 34-14 (P)
1991—Cardinals, 24-10 (P)
1993—Patriots, 23-21 (P)
(RS Pts.—Cardinals 200, Patriots 110)
*Franchise known as Phoenix prior to 1994 and in St. Louis prior to 1988*
***Franchise in Boston prior to 1971*

***ARIZONA vs. NEW ORLEANS**
RS: Cardinals lead series, 10-9
1967—Cardinals, 31-20 (StL)
1968—Cardinals, 21-20 (NO)
Cardinals, 31-17 (StL)
1969—Saints, 51-42 (StL)
1970—Cardinals, 24-17 (StL)
1974—Saints, 14-0 (NO)
1977—Cardinals, 49-31 (StL)
1980—Cardinals, 40-7 (NO)
1981—Cardinals, 30-3 (StL)
1982—Cardinals, 21-7 (NO)
1983—Saints, 28-17 (NO)
1984—Saints, 34-24 (NO)
1985—Cardinals, 28-16 (StL)
1986—Saints, 16-7 (StL)
1987—Cardinals, 24-19 (StL)
1990—Saints, 28-7 (NO)
1991—Saints, 27-3 (P)
1992—Saints, 30-21 (P)
1993—Saints, 20-17 (P)
(RS Pts.—Cardinals 437, Saints 405)
*Franchise known as Phoenix prior to 1994 and in St. Louis prior to 1988*

***ARIZONA vs. N.Y. GIANTS**
RS: Giants lead series, 65-35-2
1926—Giants, 20-0 (NY)
1927—Giants, 28-7 (NY)
1929—Giants, 24-21 (NY)
1930—Giants, 25-12 (NY)
Giants, 13-7 (C)
1935—Cardinals, 14-13 (NY)
1936—Giants, 14-6 (NY)
1938—Giants, 6-0 (NY)
1939—Giants, 17-7 (NY)
1941—Cardinals, 10-7 (NY)
1942—Giants, 21-7 (NY)
1943—Giants, 24-13 (NY)
1946—Giants, 28-24 (NY)
1947—Giants, 35-31 (NY)
1948—Cardinals, 63-35 (NY)
1949—Giants, 41-38 (C)
1950—Cardinals, 17-3 (C)
Giants, 51-21 (NY)
1951—Giants, 28-17 (NY)
Giants, 10-0 (C)
1952—Cardinals, 24-23 (NY)
Giants, 28-6 (C)
1953—Giants, 21-7 (NY)
Giants, 23-20 (C)
1954—Giants, 41-10 (C)
Giants, 31-17 (NY)
1955—Cardinals, 28-17 (C)
Giants, 10-0 (NY)
1956—Cardinals, 35-27 (C)
Giants, 23-10 (NY)
1957—Giants, 27-14 (NY)
Giants, 28-21 (C)
1958—Giants, 37-7 (Buffalo)
Cardinals, 23-6 (NY)
1959—Giants, 9-3 (NY)
Giants, 30-20 (Minn)
1960—Giants, 35-14 (StL)
Cardinals, 20-13 (NY)
1961—Cardinals, 21-10 (NY)
Giants, 24-9 (StL)
1962—Giants, 31-14 (StL)
Giants, 31-28 (NY)
1963—Giants, 38-21 (StL)
Cardinals, 24-17 (NY)
1964—Giants, 34-17 (NY)
Tie, 10-10 (StL)
1965—Giants, 14-10 (NY)
Giants, 28-15 (StL)
1966—Cardinals, 24-19 (StL)
Cardinals, 20-17 (NY)
1967—Giants, 37-20 (StL)
Giants, 37-14 (NY)
1968—Cardinals, 28-21 (NY)
1969—Cardinals, 42-17 (StL)
Giants, 49-6 (NY)
1970—Giants, 35-17 (NY)
Giants, 34-17 (StL)
1971—Giants, 21-20 (StL)
Cardinals, 24-7 (NY)
1972—Giants, 27-21 (NY)
Giants, 13-7 (StL)
1973—Cardinals, 35-27 (StL)
Giants, 24-13 (New Haven)
1974—Cardinals, 23-21 (New Haven)
Cardinals, 26-14 (StL)
1975—Cardinals, 26-14 (StL)
Cardinals, 20-13 (NY)
1976—Cardinals, 27-21 (StL)
Cardinals, 17-14 (NY)
1977—Cardinals, 28-0 (StL)
Giants, 27-7 (NY)
1978—Cardinals, 20-10 (StL)
Giants, 17-0 (NY)
1979—Cardinals, 27-14 (NY)
Cardinals, 29-20 (StL)
1980—Giants, 41-35 (StL)
Cardinals, 23-7 (NY)
1981—Giants, 34-14 (NY)
Giants, 20-10 (StL)
1982—Cardinals, 24-21 (StL)
1983—Tie, 20-20 (StL) OT
Cardinals, 10-6 (NY)
1984—Giants, 16-10 (NY)
Cardinals, 31-21 (StL)
1985—Giants, 27-17 (NY)
Giants, 34-3 (StL)
1986—Giants, 13-6 (StL)
Giants, 27-7 (NY)
1987—Giants, 30-7 (NY)
Cardinals, 27-24 (StL)
1988—Cardinals, 24-17 (P)
Giants, 44-7 (NY)
1989—Giants, 35-7 (NY)
Giants, 20-13 (P)
1990—Giants, 20-19 (NY)
Giants, 24-21 (P)
1991—Giants, 20-9 (NY)
Giants, 21-14 (P)

1992—Giants, 31-21 (NY)
Cardinals, 19-0 (P)
1993—Giants, 19-17 (NY)
Cardinals, 17-6 (P)
(RS Pts.—Giants 2,277, Cardinals 1,753)
*Franchise known as Phoenix prior to 1994, in St. Louis prior to 1988, and in Chicago prior to 1960*

***ARIZONA vs. N.Y. JETS**
RS: Cardinals lead series, 2-1
1971—Cardinals, 17-10 (StL)
1975—Cardinals, 37-6 (NY)
1978—Jets, 23-10 (NY)
(RS Pts.—Cardinals 64, Jets 39)
*Franchise known as Phoenix prior to 1994 and in St. Louis prior to 1988*

***ARIZONA vs. PHILADELPHIA**
RS: Cardinals lead series, 44-43-5
PS: Series tied, 1-1
1935—Cardinals, 12-3 (C)
1936—Cardinals, 13-0 (C)
1937—Tie, 6-6 (P)
1938—Eagles, 7-0 (Erie, Pa.)
1941—Eagles, 21-14 (P)
1945—Eagles, 21-6 (P)
1947—Cardinals, 45-21 (P)
**Cardinals, 28-21 (C)
1948—Cardinals, 21-14 (C)
**Eagles, 7-0 (P)
1949—Eagles, 28-3 (P)
1950—Eagles, 45-7 (C)
Cardinals, 14-10 (P)
1951—Eagles, 17-14 (C)
1952—Eagles, 10-7 (P)
Cardinals, 28-22 (C)
1953—Eagles, 56-17 (C)
Eagles, 38-0 (P)
1954—Eagles, 35-16 (C)
Eagles, 30-14 (P)
1955—Tie, 24-24 (C)
Eagles, 27-3 (P)
1956—Cardinals, 20-6 (P)
Cardinals, 28-17 (C)
1957—Eagles, 38-21 (C)
Cardinals, 31-27 (P)
1958—Tie, 21-21 (C)
Eagles, 49-21 (P)
1959—Eagles, 28-24 (Minn)
Eagles, 27-17 (P)
1960—Eagles, 31-27 (P)
Eagles, 20-6 (StL)
1961—Cardinals, 30-27 (P)
Eagles, 20-7 (StL)
1962—Cardinals, 27-21 (P)
Cardinals, 45-35 (StL)
1963—Cardinals, 28-24 (P)
Cardinals, 38-14 (StL)
1964—Cardinals, 38-13 (P)
Cardinals, 36-34 (StL)
1965—Eagles, 34-27 (P)
Eagles, 28-24 (StL)
1966—Cardinals, 16-13 (StL)
Cardinals, 41-10 (P)
1967—Cardinals, 48-14 (StL)
1968—Cardinals, 45-17 (P)
1969—Eagles, 34-30 (StL)
1970—Cardinals, 35-20 (P)
Cardinals, 23-14 (StL)
1971—Eagles, 37-20 (StL)
Eagles, 19-7 (P)
1972—Tie, 6-6 (P)
Cardinals, 24-23 (StL)
1973—Cardinals, 34-23 (P)
Eagles, 27-24 (StL)
1974—Cardinals, 7-3 (StL)
Cardinals, 13-3 (P)
1975—Cardinals, 31-20 (StL)
Cardinals, 24-23 (P)
1976—Cardinals, 33-14 (StL)
Cardinals, 17-14 (P)
1977—Cardinals, 21-17 (P)
Cardinals, 21-16 (StL)
1978—Cardinals, 16-10 (P)
Eagles, 14-10 (StL)
1979—Eagles, 24-20 (StL)
Eagles, 16-13 (P)
1980—Cardinals, 24-14 (StL)
Eagles, 17-3 (P)
1981—Eagles, 52-10 (StL)
Eagles, 38-0 (P)
1982—Cardinals, 23-20 (P)
1983—Cardinals, 14-11 (P)
Cardinals, 31-7 (StL)
1984—Cardinals, 34-14 (P)
Cardinals, 17-16 (StL)
1985—Eagles, 30-7 (P)
Eagles, 24-14 (StL)
1986—Cardinals, 13-10 (StL)
Tie, 10-10 (P) OT
1987—Eagles, 28-23 (StL)
Cardinals, 31-19 (P)
1988—Eagles, 31-21 (P)
Eagles, 23-17 (Phx)
1989—Eagles, 17-5 (Phx)
Eagles, 31-14 (P)
1990—Cardinals, 23-21 (P)
Eagles, 23-21 (Phx)
1991—Cardinals, 26-10 (P)
Eagles, 34-14 (Phx)
1992—Eagles, 31-14 (Phx)
Eagles, 7-3 (P)
1993—Eagles, 23-17 (P)
Cardinals, 16-3 (Phx)
(RS Pts.—Eagles 1,972, Cardinals 1,832)
(PS Pts.—Tie 28, 28)
*Franchise known as Phoenix prior to 1994, in St. Louis prior to 1988, and in Chicago prior to 1960*
***NFL Championship*

***ARIZONA vs. **PITTSBURGH**
RS: Steelers lead series, 29-21-3
1933—Pirates, 14-13 (C)
1935—Pirates, 17-13 (P)
1936—Cardinals, 14-6 (C)
1937—Cardinals, 13-7 (P)
1939—Cardinals, 10-0 (P)
1940—Tie, 7-7 (P)
1942—Steelers, 19-3 (P)
1945—Steelers, 23-0 (P)
1946—Steelers, 14-7 (P)
1948—Cardinals, 24-7 (P)
1950—Steelers, 28-17 (C)
Steelers, 28-7 (P)
1951—Steelers, 28-14 (C)
1952—Steelers, 34-28 (C)
Steelers, 17-14 (P)
1953—Steelers, 31-28 (P)
Steelers, 21-17 (C)
1954—Cardinals, 17-14 (C)
Steelers, 20-17 (P)
1955—Steelers, 14-7 (P)
Cardinals, 27-13 (C)
1956—Steelers, 14-7 (P)
Cardinals, 38-27 (C)
1957—Steelers, 29-20 (P)
Steelers, 27-2 (C)
1958—Steelers, 27-20 (C)
Steelers, 38-21 (P)
1959—Cardinals, 45-24 (C)
Steelers, 35-20 (P)
1960—Steelers, 27-14 (P)
Cardinals, 38-7 (StL)
1961—Steelers, 30-27 (P)
Cardinals, 20-0 (StL)
1962—Steelers, 26-17 (StL)
Steelers, 19-7 (P)
1963—Steelers, 23-10 (P)
Cardinals, 24-23 (StL)
1964—Cardinals, 34-30 (StL)
Cardinals, 21-20 (P)
1965—Cardinals, 20-7 (P)
Cardinals, 21-17 (StL)
1966—Steelers, 30-9 (P)
Cardinals, 6-3 (StL)
1967—Cardinals, 28-14 (P)
Tie, 14-14 (StL)
1968—Tie, 28-28 (StL)
Cardinals, 20-10 (P)
1969—Cardinals, 27-14 (P)
Cardinals, 47-10 (StL)
1972—Steelers, 25-19 (StL)
1979—Steelers, 24-21 (StL)
1985—Steelers, 23-10 (P)
1988—Cardinals, 31-14 (Phx)
(RS Pts.—Steelers 1,021, Cardinals 983)
*Franchise known as Phoenix prior to 1994, in St. Louis prior to 1988, and in Chicago prior to 1960*
***Steelers known as Pirates prior to 1941*

***ARIZONA vs. SAN DIEGO**
RS: Chargers lead series, 5-1
1971—Chargers, 20-17 (SD)
1976—Chargers, 43-24 (SD)
1983—Cardinals, 44-14 (StL)
1987—Chargers, 28-24 (SD)
1989—Chargers, 24-13 (P)
1992—Chargers, 27-21 (P)
(RS Pts.—Chargers 156, Cardinals 143)
*Franchise known as Phoenix prior to 1994, in St. Louis prior to 1988,*

***ARIZONA vs. SAN FRANCISCO**
RS: 49ers lead series, 10-9
1951—Cardinals, 27-21 (SF)
1957—Cardinals, 20-10 (SF)
1962—49ers, 24-17 (StL)
1964—Cardinals, 23-13 (SF)
1968—49ers, 35-17 (SF)
1971—49ers, 26-14 (StL)
1974—Cardinals, 34-9 (SF)
1976—Cardinals, 23-20 (StL) OT
1978—Cardinals, 16-10 (SF)
1979—Cardinals, 13-10 (StL)
1980—49ers, 24-21 (SF) OT
1982—49ers, 31-20 (StL)
1983—49ers, 42-27 (StL)
1986—49ers, 43-17 (SF)
1987—49ers, 34-28 (SF)
1988—Cardinals, 24-23 (P)
1991—49ers, 14-10 (SF)
1992—Cardinals, 24-14 (P)
1993—49ers, 28-14 (SF)
(RS Pts.—49ers 431, Cardinals 389)
*Franchise known as Phoenix prior to 1994, in St. Louis prior to 1988, and in Chicago prior to 1960*

***ARIZONA vs. SEATTLE**
RS: Cardinals lead series, 4-0
1976—Cardinals, 30-24 (S)
1983—Cardinals, 33-28 (StL)
1989—Cardinals, 34-24 (S)
1993—Cardinals, 30-27 (S) OT
(RS Pts.—Cardinals 127, Seahawks 103)
*Franchise known as Phoenix prior to 1994 and in St. Louis prior to 1988*

***ARIZONA vs. TAMPA BAY**
RS: Series tied, 6-6
1977—Buccaneers, 17-7 (TB)
1981—Buccaneers, 20-10 (TB)
1983—Cardinals, 34-27 (TB)
1985—Buccaneers, 16-0 (TB)
1986—Cardinals, 30-19 (TB)
Cardinals, 21-17 (StL)
1987—Cardinals, 31-28 (StL)
Cardinals, 31-14 (TB)
1988—Cardinals, 30-24 (TB)
1989—Buccaneers, 14-13 (P)
1992—Buccaneers, 23-7 (TB)
Buccaneers, 7-3 (P)
(RS Pts.—Buccaneers 226, Cardinals 217)
*Franchise known as Phoenix prior to 1994 and in St. Louis prior to 1988*

***ARIZONA vs. **WASHINGTON**
RS: Redskins lead series, 61-36-2
1932—Cardinals, 9-0 (B)
Braves, 8-6 (C)
1933—Redskins, 10-0 (C)
Tie, 0-0 (B)
1934—Redskins, 9-0 (B)
1935—Cardinals, 6-0 (B)
1936—Redskins, 13-10 (B)
1937—Cardinals, 21-14 (W)
1939—Redskins, 28-7 (W)
1940—Redskins, 28-21 (W)
1942—Redskins, 28-0 (W)
1943—Redskins, 13-7 (W)
1945—Redskins, 24-21 (W)
1947—Redskins, 45-21 (W)
1949—Cardinals, 38-7 (C)
1950—Cardinals, 38-28 (W)
1951—Redskins, 7-3 (C)
Redskins, 20-17 (W)
1952—Redskins, 23-7 (C)
Cardinals, 17-6 (W)
1953—Redskins, 24-13 (C)
Redskins, 28-17 (W)
1954—Cardinals, 38-16 (C)
Redskins, 37-20 (W)
1955—Cardinals, 24-10 (W)
Redskins, 31-0 (C)
1956—Cardinals, 31-3 (W)
Redskins, 17-14 (C)
1957—Redskins, 37-14 (C)
Cardinals, 44-14 (W)
1958—Cardinals, 37-10 (C)
Redskins, 45-31 (W)
1959—Cardinals, 49-21 (C)
Redskins, 23-14 (W)
1960—Cardinals, 44-7 (StL)
Cardinals, 26-14 (W)
1961—Cardinals, 24-0 (W)
Cardinals, 38-24 (StL)
1962—Redskins, 24-14 (W)
Tie, 17-17 (StL)
1963—Cardinals, 21-7 (W)
Cardinals, 24-20 (StL)
1964—Cardinals, 23-17 (W)
Cardinals, 38-24 (StL)
1965—Cardinals, 37-16 (W)
Redskins, 24-20 (StL)
1966—Cardinals, 23-7 (StL)
Redskins, 26-20 (W)
1967—Cardinals, 27-21 (W)
1968—Cardinals, 41-14 (StL)
1969—Redskins, 33-17 (W)
1970—Cardinals, 27-17 (StL)
Redskins, 28-27 (W)
1971—Redskins, 24-17 (StL)
Redskins, 20-0 (W)
1972—Redskins, 24-10 (W)
Redskins, 33-3 (StL)
1973—Cardinals, 34-27 (StL)
Redskins, 31-13 (W)
1974—Cardinals, 17-10 (W)
Cardinals, 23-20 (StL)
1975—Redskins, 27-17 (W)
Cardinals, 20-17 (StL) OT
1976—Redskins, 20-10 (W)
Redskins, 16-10 (StL)
1977—Redskins, 24-14 (W)
Redskins, 26-20 (StL)
1978—Redskins, 28-10 (StL)
Cardinals, 27-17 (W)
1979—Redskins, 17-7 (StL)
Redskins, 30-28 (W)
1980—Redskins, 23-0 (W)
Redskins, 31-7 (StL)
1981—Cardinals, 40-30 (StL)
Redskins, 42-21 (W)
1982—Redskins, 12-7 (StL)
Redskins, 28-0 (W)
1983—Redskins, 38-14 (StL)
Redskins, 45-7 (W)
1984—Cardinals, 26-24 (StL)
Redskins, 29-27 (W)
1985—Redskins, 27-10 (W)
Redskins, 27-16 (StL)
1986—Redskins, 28-21 (W)
Redskins, 20-17 (StL)
1987—Redskins, 28-21 (W)
Redskins, 34-17 (StL)
1988—Cardinals, 30-21 (P)

Redskins, 33-17 (W)
1989—Redskins, 30-28 (W)
Redskins, 29-10 (P)
1990—Redskins, 31-0 (W)
Redskins, 38-10 (P)
1991—Redskins, 34-0 (W)
Redskins, 20-14 (P)
1992—Cardinals, 27-24 (P)
Redskins, 41-3 (W)
1993—Cardinals, 17-10 (W)
Cardinals, 36-6 (P)
(RS Pts.—Redskins 2,161, Cardinals 1,826)
*Franchise known as Phoenix prior to 1994, in St. Louis prior to 1988, and in Chicago prior to 1960*
**Franchise in Boston prior to 1937 and known as Braves prior to 1933*

**ATLANTA vs. ARIZONA**
RS: Cardinals lead series, 11-5;
See Arizona vs. Atlanta

**ATLANTA vs. BUFFALO**
RS: Series tied, 3-3
1973—Bills, 17-6 (A)
1977—Bills, 3-0 (B)
1980—Falcons, 30-14 (B)
1983—Falcons, 31-14 (A)
1989—Falcons, 30-28 (A)
1992—Bills, 41-14 (B)
(RS Pts.—Bills 117, Falcons 111)

**ATLANTA vs. CHICAGO**
RS: Series tied, 9-9
1966—Bears, 23-6 (C)
1967—Bears, 23-14 (A)
1968—Falcons, 16-13 (C)
1969—Falcons, 48-31 (A)
1970—Bears, 23-14 (A)
1972—Falcons, 37-21 (C)
1973—Falcons, 46-6 (A)
1974—Falcons, 13-10 (A)
1976—Falcons, 10-0 (C)
1977—Falcons, 16-10 (C)
1978—Bears, 13-7 (C)
1980—Falcons, 28-17 (A)
1983—Falcons, 20-17 (C)
1985—Bears, 36-0 (C)
1986—Bears, 13-10 (A)
1990—Bears, 30-24 (C)
1992—Bears, 41-31 (C)
1993—Bears, 6-0 (C)
(RS Pts.—Falcons 340, Bears 333)

**ATLANTA vs. CINCINNATI**
RS: Bengals lead series, 6-2
1971—Falcons, 9-6 (C)
1975—Bengals, 21-14 (A)
1978—Bengals, 37-7 (C)
1981—Bengals, 30-28 (A)
1984—Bengals, 35-14 (C)
1987—Bengals, 16-10 (A)
1990—Falcons, 38-17 (A)
1993—Bengals, 21-17 (C)
(RS Pts.—Bengals 183, Falcons 137)

**ATLANTA vs. CLEVELAND**
RS: Browns lead series, 8-2
1966—Browns, 49-17 (A)
1968—Browns, 30-7 (C)
1971—Falcons, 31-14 (C)
1976—Browns, 20-17 (A)
1978—Browns, 24-16 (A)
1981—Browns, 28-17 (C)
1984—Browns, 23-7 (A)
1987—Browns, 38-3 (C)
1990—Browns, 13-10 (C)
1993—Falcons, 17-14 (A)
(RS Pts.—Browns 253, Falcons 142)

**ATLANTA vs. DALLAS**
RS: Cowboys lead series, 9-6
PS: Cowboys lead series, 2-0
1966—Cowboys, 47-14 (A)
1967—Cowboys, 37-7 (D)
1969—Cowboys, 24-17 (A)
1970—Cowboys, 13-0 (D)
1974—Cowboys, 24-0 (A)
1976—Falcons, 17-10 (A)
1978—*Cowboys, 27-20 (D)
1980—*Cowboys, 30-27 (A)
1985—Cowboys, 24-10 (D)
1986—Falcons, 37-35 (D)
1987—Falcons, 21-10 (D)
1988—Cowboys, 26-20 (D)
1989—Falcons 27-21 (A)
1990—Falcons, 26-7 (A)
1991—Cowboys, 31-27 (D)
1992—Cowboys, 41-17 (A)
1993—Falcons, 27-14 (A)
(RS Pts.—Cowboys 364, Falcons 267)
(PS Pts.—Cowboys 57, Falcons 47)
*NFC Divisional Playoff*

**ATLANTA vs. DENVER**
RS: Broncos lead series, 4-3
1970—Broncos, 24-10 (D)
1972—Falcons, 23-20 (A)
1975—Falcons, 35-21 (A)
1979—Broncos, 20-17 (A) OT
1982—Falcons, 34-27 (D)
1985—Broncos, 44-28 (A)
1988—Broncos, 30-14 (D)
(RS Pts.—Broncos 186, Falcons 161)

**ATLANTA vs. DETROIT**
RS: Lions lead series, 17-5
1966—Lions, 28-10 (D)
1967—Lions, 24-3 (D)
1968—Lions, 24-7 (A)
1969—Lions, 27-21 (D)
1971—Lions, 41-38 (D)
1972—Lions, 26-23 (A)
1973—Lions, 31-6 (D)
1975—Lions, 17-14 (A)
1976—Lions, 24-10 (D)
1977—Falcons, 17-6 (A)
1978—Falcons, 14-0 (A)
1979—Lions, 24-23 (D)
1980—Falcons, 43-28 (A)
1983—Falcons, 30-14 (D)
1984—Lions, 27-24 (A) OT
1985—Lions, 28-27 (A)
1986—Falcons, 20-6 (D)
1987—Lions, 30-13 (A)
1988—Lions, 31-17 (D)
1989—Lions, 31-24 (A)
1990—Lions, 21-14 (D)
1993—Lions, 30-13 (D)
(RS Pts.—Lions 518, Falcons 411)

**ATLANTA vs. GREEN BAY**
RS: Series tied, 9-9
1966—Packers, 56-3 (Mil)
1967—Packers, 23-0 (Mil)
1968—Packers, 38-7 (A)
1969—Packers, 28-10 (GB)
1970—Packers, 27-24 (GB)
1971—Falcons, 28-21 (A)
1972—Falcons, 10-9 (Mil)
1974—Falcons, 10-3 (A)
1975—Packers, 22-13 (GB)
1976—Packers, 24-20 (A)
1979—Falcons, 25-7 (A)
1981—Falcons, 31-17 (GB)
1982—Packers, 38-7 (A)
1983—Falcons, 47-41 (A) OT
1988—Falcons, 20-0 (A)
1989—Packers, 23-21 (Mil)
1991—Falcons, 35-31 (A)
1992—Falcons, 24-10 (A)
(RS Pts.—Packers 418, Falcons 335)

**ATLANTA vs. HOUSTON**
RS: Falcons lead series, 5-3
1972—Falcons, 20-10 (A)
1976—Oilers, 20-14 (H)
1978—Falcons, 20-14 (A)
1981—Falcons, 31-27 (H)
1984—Falcons, 42-10 (A)
1987—Oilers, 37-33 (H)
1990—Falcons, 47-27 (A)
1993—Oilers, 33-17 (H)
(RS Pts.—Falcons 224, Oilers 178)

**ATLANTA vs. *INDIANAPOLIS**
RS: Colts lead series, 10-0
1966—Colts, 19-7 (A)
1967—Colts, 38-31 (B)
Colts, 49-7 (A)
1968—Colts, 28-20 (A)
Colts, 44-0 (B)
1969—Colts, 21-14 (A)
Colts, 13-6 (B)
1974—Colts, 17-7 (A)
1986—Colts, 28-23 (A)
1989—Colts, 13-9 (I)
(RS Pts.—Colts 270, Falcons 124)
*Franchise in Baltimore prior to 1984*

**ATLANTA vs. KANSAS CITY**
RS: Chiefs lead series, 3-0
1972—Chiefs, 17-14 (A)
1985—Chiefs, 38-10 (KC)
1991—Chiefs, 14-3 (KC)
(RS Pts.—Chiefs 69, Falcons 27)

**ATLANTA vs. *L.A. RAIDERS**
RS: Raiders lead series, 4-3
1971—Falcons, 24-13 (A)
1975—Raiders, 37-34 (O) OT
1979—Raiders, 50-19 (O)
1982—Raiders, 38-14 (A)
1985—Raiders, 34-24 (A)
1988—Falcons, 12-6 (LA)
1991—Falcons, 21-17 (A)
(RS Pts.—Raiders 195, Falcons 148)
*Franchise in Oakland prior to 1982*

**ATLANTA vs. L.A. RAMS**
RS: Rams lead series, 36-16-2
1966—Rams, 19-14 (A)
1967—Rams, 31-3 (A)
Rams, 20-3 (LA)
1968—Rams, 27-14 (LA)
Rams, 17-10 (A)
1969—Rams, 17-7 (LA)
Rams, 38-6 (A)
1970—Tie, 10-10 (LA)
Rams, 17-7 (A)
1971—Tie, 20-20 (LA)
Rams, 24-16 (A)
1972—Falcons, 31-3 (A)
Rams, 20-7 (LA)
1973—Rams, 31-0 (LA)
Falcons, 15-13 (A)
1974—Rams, 21-0 (LA)
Rams, 30-7 (A)
1975—Rams, 22-7 (LA)
Rams, 16-7 (A)
1976—Rams, 30-14 (A)
Rams, 59-0 (LA)
1977—Falcons, 17-6 (A)
Rams, 23-7 (LA)
1978—Rams, 10-0 (LA)
Falcons, 15-7 (A)
1979—Rams, 20-14 (LA)
Rams, 34-13 (A)
1980—Falcons, 13-10 (A)
Rams, 20-17 (LA) OT
1981—Rams, 37-35 (A)
Rams, 21-16 (LA)
1982—Falcons, 34-17 (A)
1983—Rams, 27-21 (LA)
Rams, 36-13 (A)
1984—Falcons, 30-28 (LA)
Rams, 24-10 (A)
1985—Rams, 17-6 (LA)
Falcons, 30-14 (A)
1986—Falcons, 26-14 (A)
Rams, 14-7 (LA)
1987—Falcons, 24-20 (A)
Rams, 33-0 (LA)
1988—Rams, 33-0 (A)
Rams, 22-7 (LA)
1989—Rams, 31-21 (A)
Rams, 26-14 (LA)
1990—Rams, 44-24 (LA)
Falcons, 20-13 (A)
1991—Falcons, 31-14 (A)
Falcons, 31-14 (LA)
1992—Falcons, 30-28 (A)
Rams, 38-27 (LA)
1993—Falcons, 30-24 (A)
Falcons, 13-0 (LA)
(RS Pts.—Rams 1,204, Falcons 794)

**ATLANTA vs. MIAMI**
RS: Dolphins lead series, 5-1
1970—Dolphins, 20-7 (A)
1974—Dolphins, 42-7 (M)
1980—Dolphins, 20-17 (A)
1983—Dolphins, 31-24 (M)
1986—Falcons, 20-14 (M)
1992—Dolphins, 21-17 (M)
(RS Pts.—Dolphins 148, Falcons 92)

**ATLANTA vs. MINNESOTA**
RS: Vikings lead series, 11-6
PS: Vikings lead series, 1-0
1966—Falcons, 20-13 (M)
1967—Falcons, 21-20 (A)
1968—Vikings, 47-7 (M)
1969—Falcons, 10-3 (A)
1970—Vikings, 37-7 (A)
1971—Vikings, 24-7 (M)
1973—Falcons, 20-14 (A)
1974—Vikings, 23-10 (M)
1975—Vikings, 38-0 (M)
1977—Vikings, 14-7 (A)
1980—Vikings, 24-23 (M)
1981—Falcons, 31-30 (A)
1982—*Vikings, 30-24 (M)
1984—Vikings, 27-20 (M)
1985—Falcons, 14-13 (A)
1987—Vikings, 24-13 (M)
1989—Vikings, 43-17 (M)
1991—Vikings, 20-19 (A)
(RS Pts.—Vikings 414, Falcons 246)
(PS Pts.—Vikings 30, Falcons 24)
*NFC First-Round Playoff*

**ATLANTA vs. NEW ENGLAND**
RS: Falcons lead series, 4-3
1972—Patriots, 21-20 (NE)
1977—Patriots, 16-10 (A)
1980—Falcons, 37-21 (NE)
1983—Falcons, 24-13 (A)
1986—Patriots, 25-17 (NE)
1989—Falcons, 16-15 (A)
1992—Falcons, 34-0 (A)
(RS Pts.—Falcons 158, Patriots 111)

**ATLANTA vs. NEW ORLEANS**
RS: Falcons lead series, 27-22
PS: Falcons lead series, 1-0
1967—Saints, 27-24 (NO)
1969—Falcons, 45-17 (A)
1970—Falcons, 14-3 (NO)
Falcons, 32-14 (A)
1971—Falcons, 28-6 (A)
Falcons, 24-20 (NO)
1972—Falcons, 21-14 (NO)
Falcons, 36-20 (A)
1973—Falcons, 62-7 (NO)
Falcons, 14-10 (A)
1974—Saints, 14-13 (NO)
Saints, 13-3 (A)
1975—Falcons, 14-7 (A)
Saints, 23-7 (NO)
1976—Saints, 30-0 (NO)
Falcons, 23-20 (A)
1977—Saints, 21-20 (NO)
Falcons, 35-7 (A)
1978—Falcons, 20-17 (NO)
Falcons, 20-17 (A)
1979—Falcons, 40-34 (NO) OT
Saints, 37-6 (A)
1980—Falcons, 41-14 (NO)
Falcons, 31-13 (A)
1981—Falcons, 27-0 (A)
Falcons, 41-10 (NO)
1982—Falcons, 35-0 (A)
Saints, 35-6 (NO)
1983—Saints, 19-17 (A)
Saints, 27-10 (NO)
1984—Falcons, 36-28 (NO)
Saints, 17-13 (A)
1985—Falcons, 31-24 (A)

Falcons, 16-10 (NO)
1986—Falcons, 31-10 (NO)
Saints, 14-9 (A)
1987—Saints, 38-0 (A)
1988—Saints, 29-21 (A)
Saints, 10-9 (NO)
1989—Saints, 20-13 (NO)
Saints, 26-17 (A)
1990—Falcons, 28-27 (A)
Saints, 10-7 (NO)
1991—Saints, 27-6 (A)
Falcons, 23-20 (NO) OT
*Falcons, 27-20 (NO)
1992—Saints, 10-7 (A)
Saints, 22-14 (NO)
1993—Saints, 34-31 (A)
Falcons, 26-15 (NO)
(RS Pts.—Falcons 1,047, Saints 887)
(PS Pts.—Falcons 27, Saints 20)
*NFC First-Round Playoff*

**ATLANTA vs. N.Y. GIANTS**
RS: Series tied, 6-6
1966—Falcons, 27-16 (NY)
1968—Falcons, 24-21 (A)
1971—Giants, 21-17 (A)
1974—Falcons, 14-7 (New Haven)
1977—Falcons, 17-3 (A)
1978—Falcons, 23-20 (A)
1979—Giants, 24-3 (NY)
1981—Giants, 27-24 (A) OT
1982—Falcons, 16-14 (NY)
1983—Giants, 16-13 (A) OT
1984—Giants, 19-7 (A)
1988—Giants, 23-16 (A)
(RS Pts.—Giants 211, Falcons 201)

**ATLANTA vs. N.Y. JETS**
RS: Series tied, 3-3
1973—Falcons, 28-20 (NY)
1980—Jets, 14-7 (A)
1983—Falcons, 27-21 (NY)
1986—Jets, 28-14 (A)
1989—Jets, 27-7 (NY)
1992—Falcons, 20-17 (A)
(RS Pts.—Jets 127, Falcons 103)

**ATLANTA vs. PHILADELPHIA**
RS: Eagles lead series, 8-6-1
PS: Falcons lead series, 1-0
1966—Eagles, 23-10 (P)
1967—Eagles, 38-7 (A)
1969—Falcons, 27-3 (P)
1970—Tie, 13-13 (P)
1973—Falcons, 44-27 (P)
1976—Eagles, 14-13 (A)
1978—*Falcons, 14-13 (A)
1979—Falcons, 14-10 (P)
1980—Falcons, 20-17 (P)
1981—Eagles, 16-13 (P)
1983—Eagles, 28-24 (A)
1984—Falcons, 26-10 (A)
1985—Eagles, 23-17 (P) OT
1986—Eagles, 16-0 (A)
1988—Falcons, 27-24 (P)
1990—Eagles, 24-23 (A)
(RS Pts.—Eagles 286, Falcons 278)
(PS Pts.—Falcons 14, Eagles 13)
*NFC First-Round Playoff*

**ATLANTA vs. PITTSBURGH**
RS: Steelers lead series, 9-1
1966—Steelers, 57-33 (A)
1968—Steelers, 41-21 (A)
1970—Falcons, 27-16 (A)
1974—Steelers, 24-17 (P)
1978—Steelers, 31-7 (P)
1981—Steelers, 34-20 (A)
1984—Steelers, 35-10 (P)
1987—Steelers, 28-12 (A)
1990—Steelers, 21-9 (P)
1993—Steelers, 45-17 (A)
(RS Pts.—Steelers 332, Falcons 173)

**ATLANTA vs. SAN DIEGO**
RS: Falcons lead series, 3-1
1973—Falcons, 41-0 (SD)
1979—Falcons, 28-26 (SD)
1988—Chargers, 10-7 (A)
1991—Falcons, 13-10 (SD)
(RS Pts.—Falcons 89, Chargers 46)

**ATLANTA vs. SAN FRANCISCO**
RS: 49ers lead series, 32-21-1
1966—49ers, 44-7 (A)
1967—49ers, 38-7 (SF)
49ers, 34-28 (A)
1968—49ers, 28-13 (SF)
49ers, 14-12 (A)
1969—Falcons, 24-12 (A)
Falcons, 21-7 (SF)
1970—Falcons, 21-20 (A)
49ers, 24-20 (SF)
1971—Falcons, 20-17 (A)
49ers, 24-3 (SF)
1972—49ers, 49-14 (A)
49ers, 20-0 (SF)
1973—49ers, 13-9 (A)
Falcons, 17-3 (SF)
1974—49ers, 16-10 (A)
49ers, 27-0 (SF)
1975—Falcons, 17-3 (SF)
Falcons, 31-9 (A)
1976—49ers, 15-0 (SF)
Falcons, 21-16 (A)
1977—Falcons, 7-0 (SF)
49ers, 10-3 (A)
1978—Falcons, 20-17 (SF)
Falcons, 21-10 (A)
1979—49ers, 20-15 (SF)
Falcons, 31-21 (A)
1980—Falcons, 20-17 (SF)
Falcons, 35-10 (A)
1981—Falcons, 34-17 (A)
49ers, 17-14 (SF)
1982—Falcons, 17-7 (SF)
1983—49ers, 24-20 (SF)
Falcons, 28-24 (A)
1984—49ers, 14-5 (SF)
49ers, 35-17 (A)
1985—49ers, 35-16 (SF)
49ers, 38-17 (A)
1986—Tie, 10-10 (A) OT
49ers, 20-0 (SF)
1987—49ers, 25-17 (A)
49ers, 35-7 (SF)
1988—Falcons, 34-17 (SF)
49ers, 13-3 (A)
1989—49ers, 45-3 (SF)
49ers, 23-10 (A)
1990—49ers, 19-13 (SF)
49ers, 45-35 (A)
1991—Falcons, 39-34 (SF)
Falcons, 17-14 (A)
1992—49ers, 56-17 (SF)
49ers, 41-3 (A)
1993—49ers, 37-30 (SF)
Falcons, 27-24 (A)
(RS Pts.—49ers 1,207, Falcons 880)

**ATLANTA vs. SEATTLE**
RS: Seahawks lead series, 4-1
1976—Seahawks, 30-13 (S)
1979—Seahawks, 31-28 (A)
1985—Seahawks, 30-26 (S)
1988—Seahawks, 31-20 (A)
1991—Falcons, 26-13 (A)
(RS Pts.—Seahawks 135, Falcons 113)

**ATLANTA vs. TAMPA BAY**
RS: Series tied, 6-6
1977—Falcons, 17-0 (TB)
1978—Buccaneers, 14-9 (TB)
1979—Falcons, 17-14 (A)
1981—Buccaneers, 24-23 (TB)
1984—Buccaneers, 23-6 (TB)
1986—Falcons, 23-20 (TB) OT
1987—Buccaneers, 48-10 (TB)
1988—Falcons, 17-10 (A)
1990—Buccaneers, 23-17 (TB)
1991—Falcons, 43-7 (A)
1992—Falcons, 35-7 (TB)
1993—Buccaneers, 31-24 (A)
(RS Pts.—Falcons 241, Buccaneers 221)

**ATLANTA vs. WASHINGTON**
RS: Redskins lead series, 13-3-1
PS: Redskins lead series, 1-0
1966—Redskins, 33-20 (W)
1967—Tie, 20-20 (A)
1969—Redskins, 27-20 (W)
1972—Redskins, 24-13 (W)
1975—Redskins, 30-27 (A)
1977—Redskins, 10-6 (W)
1978—Falcons, 20-17 (A)
1979—Redskins, 16-7 (A)
1980—Falcons, 10-6 (A)
1983—Redskins, 37-21 (W)
1984—Redskins, 27-14 (W)
1985—Redskins, 44-10 (A)
1987—Falcons, 21-20 (A)
1989—Redskins, 31-30 (A)
1991—Redskins, 56-17 (W)
*Redskins, 24-7 (W)
1992—Redskins, 24-17 (W)
1993—Redskins, 30-17 (W)
(RS Pts.—Redskins 452, Falcons 290)
(PS Pts.—Redskins 24, Falcons 7)
*NFC Divisional Playoff*

---

**BUFFALO vs. ARIZONA**
RS: Series tied, 3-3;
See Arizona vs. Buffalo

**BUFFALO vs. ATLANTA**
RS: Series tied 3-3;
See Atlanta vs. Buffalo

**BUFFALO vs. CHICAGO**
RS: Bears lead series, 3-2
1970—Bears, 31-13 (C)
1974—Bills, 16-6 (B)
1979—Bears, 7-0 (B)
1988—Bears, 24-3 (C)
1991—Bills, 35-20 (B)
(RS Pts.—Bears 88, Bills 67)

**BUFFALO vs. CINCINNATI**
RS: Bengals lead series, 9-7
PS: Bengals lead series, 2-0
1968—Bengals, 34-23 (C)
1969—Bills, 16-13 (B)
1970—Bengals, 43-14 (B)
1973—Bengals, 16-13 (B)
1975—Bengals, 33-24 (C)
1978—Bills, 5-0 (B)
1979—Bills, 51-24 (B)
1980—Bills, 14-0 (C)
1981—Bengals, 27-24 (C) OT
*Bengals, 28-21 (C)
1983—Bills, 10-6 (C)
1984—Bengals, 52-21 (C)
1985—Bengals, 23-17 (B)
1986—Bengals, 36-33 (C) OT
1988—Bengals, 35-21 (C)
**Bengals, 21-10 (C)
1989—Bills, 24-7 (B)
1991—Bills, 35-16 (B)
(RS Pts.—Bengals 365, Bills 345)
(PS Pts.—Bengals 49, Bills 31)
*AFC Divisional Playoff*
***AFC Championship*

**BUFFALO vs. CLEVELAND**
RS: Browns lead series, 7-3
PS: Browns lead series, 1-0
1972—Browns, 27-10 (C)
1974—Bills, 15-10 (C)
1977—Browns, 27-16 (B)
1978—Browns, 41-20 (C)
1981—Bills, 22-13 (B)
1984—Browns, 13-10 (B)
1985—Browns, 17-7 (C)
1986—Browns, 21-17 (B)
1987—Browns, 27-21 (C)
1989—*Browns, 34-30 (C)
1990—Bills, 42-0 (C)
(RS Pts.—Browns 196, Bills 180)
(PS Pts.—Browns 34, Bills 30)
*AFC Divisional Playoff*

**BUFFALO vs. DALLAS**
RS: Cowboys lead series, 3-2
PS: Cowboys lead series, 2-0
1971—Cowboys, 49-37 (B)
1976—Cowboys, 17-10 (D)
1981—Cowboys, 27-14 (D)
1984—Bills, 14-3 (B)
1992—*Cowboys, 52-17 (Pasadena)
1993—Bills, 13-10 (D)
**Cowboys, 30-13 (Atlanta)
(RS Pts.—Cowboys 106, Bills 88)
(PS Pts.—Cowboys 82, Bills 30)
*Super Bowl XXVII*
***Super Bowl XXVIII*

**BUFFALO vs. DENVER**
RS: Bills lead series, 16-10-1
PS: Bills lead series, 1-0
1960—Broncos, 27-21 (B)
Tie, 38-38 (D)
1961—Broncos, 22-10 (B)
Bills, 23-10 (D)
1962—Broncos, 23-20 (B)
Bills, 45-38 (D)
1963—Bills, 30-28 (D)
Bills, 27-17 (B)
1964—Bills, 30-13 (B)
Bills, 30-19 (D)
1965—Bills, 30-15 (D)
Bills, 31-13 (B)
1966—Bills, 38-21 (B)
1967—Bills, 17-16 (D)
Broncos, 21-20 (B)
1968—Broncos, 34-32 (D)
1969—Bills, 41-28 (B)
1970—Broncos, 25-10 (B)
1975—Bills, 38-14 (B)
1977—Broncos, 26-6 (D)
1979—Broncos, 19-16 (B)
1981—Bills, 9-7 (B)
1984—Broncos, 37-7 (B)
1987—Bills, 21-14 (B)
1989—Broncos, 28-14 (B)
1990—Bills, 29-28 (B)
1991—*Bills, 10-7 (B)
1992—Bills, 27-17 (B)
(RS Pts.—Bills 660, Broncos 598)
(PS Pts.—Bills 10, Broncos 7)
*AFC Championship

**BUFFALO vs. DETROIT**
RS: Lions lead series, 2-1-1
1972—Tie, 21-21 (B)
1976—Lions, 27-14 (D)
1979—Bills, 20-17 (D)
1991—Lions, 17-14 (B) OT
(RS Pts.—Lions 82, Bills 69)

**BUFFALO vs. GREEN BAY**
RS: Bills lead series, 4-1
1974—Bills, 27-7 (GB)
1979—Bills, 19-12 (B)
1982—Packers, 33-21 (Mil)
1988—Bills, 28-0 (B)
1991—Bills, 34-24 (Mil)
(RS Pts.—Bills 129, Packers 76)

**BUFFALO vs. HOUSTON**
RS: Oilers lead series, 20-12
PS: Bills lead series, 2-0
1960—Bills, 25-24 (B)
Oilers, 31-23 (H)
1961—Bills, 22-12 (H)
Oilers, 28-16 (B)
1962—Oilers, 28-23 (B)
Oilers, 17-14 (H)
1963—Oilers, 31-20 (B)
Oilers, 28-14 (H)
1964—Bills, 48-17 (H)
Bills, 24-10 (B)
1965—Oilers, 19-17 (B)
Bills, 29-18 (H)
1966—Bills, 27-20 (B)
Bills, 42-20 (H)
1967—Oilers, 20-3 (B)
Oilers, 10-3 (H)
1968—Oilers, 30-7 (B)
Oilers, 35-6 (H)
1969—Oilers, 17-3 (B)

# ALL-TIME TEAM VS. TEAM RESULTS

Oilers, 28-14 (H)
1971—Oilers, 20-14 (B)
1974—Oilers, 21-9 (B)
1976—Oilers, 13-3 (B)
1978—Oilers, 17-10 (H)
1983—Bills, 30-13 (B)
1985—Bills, 20-0 (B)
1986—Oilers, 16-7 (H)
1987—Bills, 34-30 (B)
1988—*Bills, 17-10 (B)
1989—Bills, 47-41 (H) OT
1990—Oilers, 27-24 (H)
1992—Oilers, 27-3 (H)
**Bills, 41-38 (B) OT
1993—Bills, 35-7 (B)
(RS Pts.—Oilers 675, Bills 616)
(PS Pts.—Bills 58, Oilers 48)
*AFC Divisional Playoff*
***AFC First-Round Game*

**BUFFALO vs. *INDIANAPOLIS**
RS: Bills lead series, 26-20-1
1970—Tie, 17-17 (Balt)
Colts, 20-14 (Buff)
1971—Colts, 43-0 (Buff)
Colts, 24-0 (Balt)
1972—Colts, 17-0 (Buff)
Colts, 35-7 (Balt)
1973—Bills, 31-13 (Buff)
Bills, 24-17 (Balt)
1974—Bills, 27-14 (Balt)
Bills, 6-0 (Buff)
1975—Bills, 38-31 (Balt)
Colts, 42-35 (Buff)
1976—Colts, 31-13 (Buff)
Colts, 58-20 (Balt)
1977—Colts, 17-14 (Balt)
Colts, 31-13 (Buff)
1978—Bills, 24-17 (Buff)
Bills, 21-14 (Balt)
1979—Bills, 31-13 (Balt)
Colts, 14-13 (Buff)
1980—Colts, 17-12 (Buff)
Colts, 28-24 (Balt)
1981—Bills, 35-3 (Balt)
Bills, 23-17 (Buff)
1982—Bills, 20-0 (Buff)
1983—Bills, 28-23 (Buff)
Bills, 30-7 (Balt)
1984—Colts, 31-17 (I)
Bills, 21-15 (Buff)
1985—Colts, 49-17 (I)
Bills, 21-9 (Buff)
1986—Bills, 24-13 (Buff)
Colts, 24-14 (I)
1987—Colts, 47-6 (Buff)
Bills, 27-3 (I)
1988—Bills, 34-23 (Buff)
Colts, 17-14 (I)
1989—Colts, 37-14 (I)
Bills, 30-7 (Buff)
1990—Bills, 26-10 (Buff)
Bills, 31-7 (I)
1991—Bills, 42-6 (Buff)
Bills, 35-7 (I)
1992—Bills, 38-0 (Buff)
Colts, 16-13 (I) OT
1993—Bills, 23-9 (Buff)
Bills, 30-10 (I)
(RS Pts.—Bills 997, Colts 903)
*Franchise in Baltimore prior to 1984*

**BUFFALO vs. *KANSAS CITY**
RS: Bills lead series, 15-13-1
PS: Bills lead series, 2-1
1960—Texans, 45-28 (B)
Texans, 24-7 (D)
1961—Bills, 27-24 (B)
Bills, 30-20 (D)
1962—Texans, 41-21 (D)
Bills, 23-14 (B)
1963—Tie, 27-27 (B)
Bills, 35-26 (KC)
1964—Bills, 34-17 (B)
Bills, 35-22 (KC)
1965—Bills, 23-7 (KC)
Bills, 34-25 (B)
1966—Chiefs, 42-20 (B)
Bills, 29-14 (KC)
**Chiefs, 31-7 (B)
1967—Chiefs, 23-13 (KC)
1968—Chiefs, 18-7 (B)
1969—Chiefs, 29-7 (B)
Chiefs, 22-19 (KC)
1971—Chiefs, 22-9 (KC)
1973—Bills, 23-14 (B)
1976—Bills, 50-17 (B)
1978—Bills, 28-13 (B)
Chiefs, 14-10 (KC)
1982—Bills, 14-9 (B)
1983—Bills, 14-9 (KC)
1986—Chiefs, 20-17 (B)
Bills, 17-14 (KC)
1991—Chiefs, 33-6 (KC)
***Bills, 37-14 (B)
1993—Chiefs, 23-7 (KC)
****Bills, 30-13 (B)
(RS Pts.—Chiefs 633, Bills 609)
(PS Pts.—Bills 74, Chiefs 58)
*Franchise in Dallas prior to 1963 and known as Texans*
***AFL Championship*
****AFC Divisional Playoff*
*****AFC Championship*

**BUFFALO vs. *L.A. RAIDERS**
RS: Raiders lead series, 15-14
PS: Bills lead series, 2-0
1960—Bills, 38-9 (B)
Raiders, 20-7 (O)
1961—Raiders, 31-22 (B)
Bills, 26-21 (O)
1962—Bills, 14-6 (B)
Bills, 10-6 (O)
1963—Raiders, 35-17 (O)
Bills, 12-0 (B)
1964—Bills, 23-20 (B)
Raiders, 16-13 (O)
1965—Bills, 17-12 (B)
Bills, 17-14 (O)
1966—Bills, 31-10 (O)
1967—Raiders, 24-20 (B)
Raiders, 28-21 (O)
1968—Raiders, 48-6 (B)
Raiders, 13-10 (O)
1969—Raiders, 50-21 (O)
1972—Raiders, 28-16 (O)
1974—Bills, 21-20 (B)
1977—Raiders, 34-13 (O)
1980—Bills, 24-7 (B)
1983—Raiders, 27-24 (B)
1987—Raiders, 34-21 (LA)
1988—Bills, 37-21 (B)
1990—Bills, 38-24 (B)
**Bills, 51-3 (B)
1991—Bills, 30-27 (LA) OT
1992—Raiders, 20-3 (LA)
1993—Raiders, 25-24 (B)
***Bills, 29-23 (B)
(RS Pts.—Raiders 630, Bills 576)
(PS Pts.—Bills 80, Raiders 26)
*Franchise in Oakland prior to 1982*
***AFC Championship*
****AFC Divisional Playoff*

**BUFFALO vs. L.A. RAMS**
RS: Series tied, 3-3
1970—Rams, 19-0 (B)
1974—Rams, 19-14 (LA)
1980—Bills, 10-7 (B) OT
1983—Rams, 41-17 (LA)
1989—Bills, 23-20 (B)
1992—Bills, 40-7 (B)
(RS Pts.—Rams 113, Bills 104)

**BUFFALO vs. MIAMI**
RS: Dolphins lead series, 37-18-1
PS: Bills lead series, 2-0
1966—Bills, 58-24 (B)
Bills, 29-0 (M)
1967—Bills, 35-13 (B)
Dolphins, 17-14 (M)
1968—Tie, 14-14 (M)
Dolphins, 21-17 (B)
1969—Dolphins, 24-6 (M)
Bills, 28-3 (B)
1970—Dolphins, 33-14 (B)
Dolphins, 45-7 (M)
1971—Dolphins, 29-14 (B)
Dolphins, 34-0 (M)
1972—Dolphins, 24-23 (M)
Dolphins, 30-16 (B)
1973—Dolphins, 27-6 (M)
Dolphins, 17-0 (B)
1974—Dolphins, 24-16 (B)
Dolphins, 35-28 (M)
1975—Dolphins, 35-30 (B)
Dolphins, 31-21 (M)
1976—Dolphins, 30-21 (B)
Dolphins, 45-27 (M)
1977—Dolphins, 13-0 (B)
Dolphins, 31-14 (M)
1978—Dolphins, 31-24 (M)
Dolphins, 25-24 (B)
1979—Dolphins, 9-7 (B)
Dolphins, 17-7 (M)
1980—Bills, 17-7 (B)
Dolphins, 17-14 (M)
1981—Bills, 31-21 (B)
Dolphins, 16-6 (M)
1982—Dolphins, 9-7 (B)
Dolphins, 27-10 (M)
1983—Dolphins, 12-0 (B)
Bills, 38-35 (M) OT
1984—Dolphins, 21-17 (B)
Dolphins, 38-7 (M)
1985—Dolphins, 23-14 (B)
Dolphins, 28-0 (M)
1986—Dolphins, 27-14 (M)
Dolphins, 34-24 (B)
1987—Bills, 34-31 (M) OT
Bills, 27-0 (B)
1988—Bills, 9-6 (B)
Bills, 31-6 (M)
1989—Bills, 27-24 (M)
Bills, 31-17 (B)
1990—Dolphins, 30-7 (M)
Bills, 24-14 (B)
*Bills, 44-34 (B)
1991—Bills, 35-31 (B)
Bills, 41-27 (M)
1992—Dolphins, 37-10 (B)
Bills, 26-20 (M)
**Bills, 29-10 (M)
1993—Dolphins, 22-13 (B)
Bills, 47-34 (M)
(RS Pts.—Dolphins 1,295, Bills 1,061)
(PS Pts.—Bills 73, Dolphins 44)
*AFC Divisional Playoff*
***AFC Championship*

**BUFFALO vs. MINNESOTA**
RS: Vikings lead series, 4-2
1971—Vikings, 19-0 (M)
1975—Vikings, 35-13 (B)
1979—Vikings, 10-3 (M)
1982—Bills, 23-22 (B)
1985—Vikings, 27-20 (B)
1988—Bills, 13-10 (B)
(RS Pts.—Vikings 123, Bills 72)

**BUFFALO vs. *NEW ENGLAND**
RS: Series tied, 33-33-1
PS: Patriots lead series, 1-0
1960—Bills, 13-0 (Bos)
Bills, 38-14 (Buff)
1961—Patriots, 23-21 (Buff)
Patriots, 52-21 (Bos)
1962—Tie, 28-28 (Buff)
Patriots, 21-10 (Bos)
1963—Bills, 28-21 (Buff)
Patriots, 17-7 (Bos)
**Patriots, 26-8 (Buff)
1964—Patriots, 36-28 (Buff)
Bills, 24-14 (Bos)
1965—Bills, 24-7 (Buff)
Bills, 23-7 (Bos)
1966—Patriots, 20-10 (Buff)
Patriots, 14-3 (Bos)
1967—Patriots, 23-0 (Buff)
Bills, 44-16 (Bos)
1968—Patriots, 16-7 (Buff)
Patriots, 23-6 (Bos)
1969—Bills, 23-16 (Buff)
Patriots, 35-21 (Bos)
1970—Bills, 45-10 (Bos)
Patriots, 14-10 (Buff)
1971—Patriots, 38-33 (NE)
Bills, 27-20 (Buff)
1972—Bills, 38-14 (Buff)
Bills, 27-24 (NE)
1973—Bills, 31-13 (NE)
Bills, 37-13 (Buff)
1974—Bills, 30-28 (Buff)
Bills, 29-28 (NE)
1975—Bills, 45-31 (Buff)
Bills, 34-14 (NE)
1976—Patriots, 26-22 (Buff)
Patriots, 20-10 (NE)
1977—Bills, 24-14 (NE)
Patriots, 20-7 (Buff)
1978—Patriots, 14-10 (Buff)
Patriots, 26-24 (NE)
1979—Patriots, 26-6 (Buff)
Bills, 16-13 (NE) OT
1980—Bills, 31-13 (Buff)
Patriots, 24-2 (NE)
1981—Bills, 20-17 (Buff)
Bills, 19-10 (NE)
1982—Patriots, 30-19 (NE)
1983—Patriots, 31-0 (Buff)
Patriots, 21-7 (NE)
1984—Patriots, 21-17 (Buff)
Patriots, 38-10 (NE)
1985—Patriots, 17-14 (Buff)
Patriots, 14-3 (NE)
1986—Patriots, 23-3 (Buff)
Patriots, 22-19 (NE)
1987—Patriots, 14-7 (NE)
Patriots, 13-7 (Buff)
1988—Bills, 16-14 (NE)
Bills, 23-20 (Buff)
1989—Bills, 31-10 (Buff)
Patriots, 33-24 (NE)
1990—Bills, 27-10 (NE)
Bills, 14-0 (Buff)
1991—Bills, 22-17 (Buff)
Patriots, 16-13 (NE)
1992—Bills, 41-7 (NE)
Bills, 16-7 (Buff)
1993—Bills, 38-14 (Buff)
Bills, 13-10 (NE) OT
(RS Pts.—Bills 1,340, Patriots 1,275)
(PS Pts.—Patriots 26, Bills 8)
*Franchise in Boston prior to 1971*
***Division Playoff*

**BUFFALO vs. NEW ORLEANS**
RS: Bills lead series, 3-2
1973—Saints, 13-0 (NO)
1980—Bills, 35-26 (NO)
1983—Bills, 27-21 (B)
1989—Saints, 22-19 (B)
1992—Bills, 20-16 (NO)
(RS Pts.—Bills 101, Saints 98)

**BUFFALO vs. N.Y. GIANTS**
RS: Bills lead series, 4-2
PS: Giants lead series, 1-0
1970—Giants, 20-6 (NY)
1975—Giants, 17-14 (B)
1978—Bills, 41-17 (B)
1987—Bills, 6-3 (B) OT
1990—Bills, 17-13 (NY)
*Giants, 20-19 (Tampa)
1993—Bills, 17-14 (B)
(RS Pts.—Bills 101, Giants 84)
(PS Pts.—Giants 20, Bills 19)
*Super Bowl XXV*

**BUFFALO vs. *N.Y. JETS**
RS: Bills lead series, 37-29

PS: Bills lead series, 1-0
1960—Titans, 27-3 (NY)
Titans, 17-13 (B)
1961—Bills, 41-31 (B)
Titans, 21-14 (NY)
1962—Titans, 17-6 (B)
Bills, 20-3 (NY)
1963—Bills, 45-14 (B)
Bills, 19-10 (NY)
1964—Bills, 34-24 (B)
Bills, 20-7 (NY)
1965—Bills, 33-21 (B)
Jets, 14-12 (NY)
1966—Bills, 33-23 (NY)
Bills, 14-3 (B)
1967—Bills, 20-17 (B)
Jets, 20-10 (NY)
1968—Bills, 37-35 (B)
Jets, 25-21 (NY)
1969—Jets, 33-19 (B)
Jets, 16-6 (NY)
1970—Bills, 34-31 (B)
Bills, 10-6 (NY)
1971—Jets, 28-17 (NY)
Jets, 20-7 (B)
1972—Jets, 41-24 (B)
Jets, 41-3 (NY)
1973—Bills, 9-7 (B)
Bills, 34-14 (NY)
1974—Bills, 16-12 (B)
Jets, 20-10 (NY)
1975—Bills, 42-14 (B)
Bills, 24-23 (NY)
1976—Jets, 17-14 (NY)
Jets, 19-14 (B)
1977—Jets, 24-19 (B)
Bills, 14-10 (NY)
1978—Jets, 21-20 (B)
Jets, 45-14 (NY)
1979—Bills, 46-31 (B)
Bills, 14-12 (NY)
1980—Bills, 20-10 (B)
Bills, 31-24 (NY)
1981—Bills, 31-0 (B)
Jets, 33-14 (NY)
**Bills, 31-27 (NY)
1983—Jets, 34-10 (B)
Bills, 24-17 (NY)
1984—Jets, 28-26 (B)
Jets, 21-17 (NY)
1985—Jets, 42-3 (NY)
Jets, 27-7 (B)
1986—Jets, 28-24 (B)
Jets, 14-13 (NY)
1987—Jets, 31-28 (B)
Bills, 17-14 (NY)
1988—Bills, 37-14 (NY)
Bills, 9-6 (B) OT
1989—Bills, 34-3 (B)
Bills, 37-0 (NY)
1990—Bills, 30-7 (NY)
Bills, 30-27 (B)
1991—Bills, 23-20 (NY)
Bills, 24-13 (B)
1992—Bills, 24-20 (NY)
Jets, 24-17 (B)
1993—Bills, 19-10 (NY)
Bills, 16-14 (B)
(RS Pts.—Bills, 1,370, Jets 1,295)
(PS Pts.—Bills 31, Jets 27)
*Jets known as Titans prior to 1963*
***AFC First-Round Playoff*

**BUFFALO vs. PHILADELPHIA**
RS: Eagles lead series, 4-3
1973—Bills, 27-26 (B)
1981—Eagles, 20-14 (B)
1984—Eagles, 27-17 (B)
1985—Eagles, 21-17 (P)
1987—Eagles, 17-7 (P)
1990—Bills, 30-23 (B)
1993—Bills, 10-7 (P)
(RS Pts.—Eagles 141, Bills 122)

**BUFFALO vs. PITTSBURGH**
RS: Bills lead series, 7-6
PS: Series tied, 1-1
1970—Steelers, 23-10 (P)
1972—Steelers, 38-21 (B)
1974—*Steelers, 32-14 (P)
1975—Bills, 30-21 (P)
1978—Steelers, 28-17 (B)
1979—Steelers, 28-0 (P)
1980—Bills, 28-13 (B)
1982—Bills, 13-0 (B)
1985—Steelers, 30-24 (P)
1986—Bills, 16-12 (B)
1988—Bills, 36-28 (B)
1991—Bills, 52-34 (B)
1992—Bills, 28-20 (B)
*Bills, 24-3 (P)
1993—Steelers, 23-0 (P)
(RS Pts.—Steelers 298, Bills 275)
(PS Pts.—Bills 38, Steelers 35)
**AFC Divisional Playoff*

**BUFFALO vs. *SAN DIEGO**
RS: Chargers lead series, 16-7-2
PS: Bills lead series, 2-1
1960—Chargers, 24-10 (B)
Bills, 32-3 (LA)
1961—Chargers, 19-11 (B)
Chargers, 28-10 (SD)
1962—Bills, 35-10 (B)
Bills, 40-20 (SD)
1963—Chargers, 14-10 (SD)
Chargers, 23-13 (B)
1964—Bills, 30-3 (B)
Bills, 27-24 (SD)
**Bills, 20-7 (B)
1965—Chargers, 34-3 (B)
Tie, 20-20 (SD)
**Bills, 23-0 (SD)
1966—Chargers, 27-7 (SD)
Tie, 17-17 (B)
1967—Chargers, 37-17 (B)
1968—Chargers, 21-6 (B)
1969—Chargers, 45-6 (SD)
1971—Chargers, 20-3 (SD)
1973—Chargers, 34-7 (SD)
1976—Chargers, 34-13 (B)
1979—Chargers, 27-19 (SD)
1980—Bills, 26-24 (SD)
***Chargers, 20-14 (SD)
1981—Bills, 28-27 (SD)
1985—Chargers, 14-9 (B)
Chargers, 40-7 (SD)
(RS Pts.—Chargers 589, Bills 406)
(PS Pts.—Bills 57, Chargers 27)
**Franchise in Los Angeles prior to 1961*
***AFL Championship*
****AFC Divisional Playoff*

**BUFFALO vs. SAN FRANCISCO**
RS: Bills lead series 3-2
1972—Bills, 27-20 (B)
1980—Bills, 18-13 (SF)
1983—49ers, 23-10 (B)
1989—49ers, 21-10 (SF)
1992—Bills, 34-31 (SF)
(RS Pts.—49ers 108, Bills 99)

**BUFFALO vs. SEATTLE**
RS: Seahawks lead series, 3-1
1977—Seahawks, 56-17 (S)
1984—Seahawks, 31-28 (S)
1988—Bills, 13-3 (S)
1989—Seahawks, 17-16 (S)
(RS Pts.—Seahawks 107, Bills 74)

**BUFFALO vs. TAMPA BAY**
RS: Buccaneers lead series, 4-2
1976—Bills, 14-9 (TB)
1978—Buccaneers, 31-10 (TB)
1982—Buccaneers, 24-23 (TB)
1986—Buccaneers, 34-28 (TB)
1988—Buccaneers, 10-5 (TB)
1991—Bills, 17-10 (TB)
(RS Pts.—Buccaneers 118, Bills 97)

**BUFFALO vs. WASHINGTON**
RS: Redskins lead series, 4-3
PS: Redskins lead series, 1-0
1972—Bills, 24-17 (W)
1977—Redskins, 10-0 (B)
1981—Bills, 21-14 (B)
1984—Redskins, 41-14 (W)
1987—Redskins, 27-7 (B)
1990—Redskins, 29-14 (W)
1991—*Redskins, 37-24 (Minneapolis)
1993—Bills, 24-10 (B)
(RS Pts.—Redskins 148, Bills 104)
(PS Pts.—Redskins 37, Bills 24)
**Super Bowl XXVI*

---

**CHICAGO vs. ARIZONA**
RS: Bears lead series, 51-25-6;
See Arizona vs. Chicago

**CHICAGO vs. ATLANTA**
RS: Series tied, 9-9;
See Atlanta vs. Chicago

**CHICAGO vs. BUFFALO**
RS: Bears lead series, 3-2;
See Buffalo vs. Chicago

**CHICAGO vs. CINCINNATI**
RS: Bengals lead series, 3-2
1972—Bengals, 13-3 (Chi)
1980—Bengals, 17-14 (Chi) OT
1986—Bears, 44-7 (Cin)
1989—Bears, 17-14 (Chi)
1992—Bengals, 31-28 (Chi) OT
(RS Pts.—Bears 106, Bengals 82)

**CHICAGO vs. CLEVELAND**
RS: Browns lead series, 8-3
1951—Browns, 42-21 (Cle)
1954—Browns, 39-10 (Chi)
1960—Browns, 42-0 (Cle)
1961—Bears, 17-14 (Chi)
1967—Browns, 24-0 (Cle)
1969—Browns, 28-24 (Chi)
1972—Bears, 17-0 (Cle)
1980—Browns, 27-21 (Cle)
1986—Bears, 41-31 (Chi)
1989—Browns, 27-7 (Cle)
1992—Browns, 27-14 (Cle)
(RS Pts.—Browns 301, Bears 172)

**CHICAGO vs. DALLAS**
RS: Cowboys lead series, 8-6
PS: Cowboys lead series, 2-0
1960—Bears, 17-7 (C)
1962—Bears, 34-33 (D)
1964—Cowboys, 24-10 (C)
1968—Cowboys, 34-3 (C)
1971—Bears, 23-19 (C)
1973—Cowboys, 20-17 (C)
1976—Cowboys, 31-21 (D)
1977—*Cowboys, 37-7 (D)
1979—Cowboys, 24-20 (D)
1981—Cowboys, 10-9 (D)
1984—Cowboys, 23-14 (C)
1985—Bears, 44-0 (D)
1986—Bears, 24-10 (D)
1988—Bears, 17-7 (C)
1991—**Cowboys, 17-13 (C)
1992—Cowboys, 27-14 (D)
(RS Pts.—Cowboys 269, Bears 267)
(PS Pts.—Cowboys 54, Bears 20)
**NFC Divisional Playoff*
***NFC First-Round Playoff*

**CHICAGO vs. DENVER**
RS: Series tied, 5-5
1971—Broncos, 6-3 (D)
1973—Bears, 33-14 (D)
1976—Broncos, 28-14 (C)
1978—Broncos, 16-7 (D)
1981—Bears, 35-24 (C)
1983—Bears, 31-14 (C)
1984—Bears, 27-0 (C)
1987—Broncos, 31-29 (D)
1990—Bears, 16-13 (D) OT
1993—Broncos, 13-3 (C)
(RS Pts.—Bears 198, Broncos 159)

**CHICAGO vs. *DETROIT**
RS: Bears lead series, 74-49-5
1930—Spartans, 7-6 (P)
Bears, 14-6 (C)
1931—Bears, 9-6 (C)
Spartans, 3-0 (P)
1932—Tie, 13-13 (C)
Tie, 7-7 (P)
Bears, 9-0 (C)
1933—Bears, 17-14 (C)
Bears, 17-7 (P)
1934—Bears, 19-16 (D)
Bears, 10-7 (C)
1935—Tie, 20-20 (C)
Lions, 14-2 (D)
1936—Bears, 12-10 (C)
Lions, 13-7 (D)
1937—Bears, 28-20 (C)
Bears, 13-0 (D)
1938—Lions, 13-7 (C)
Lions, 14-7 (D)
1939—Lions, 10-0 (C)
Bears, 23-13 (D)
1940—Bears, 7-0 (C)
Lions, 17-14 (D)
1941—Bears, 49-0 (C)
Bears, 24-7 (D)
1942—Bears, 16-0 (C)
Bears, 42-0 (D)
1943—Bears, 27-21 (D)
Bears, 35-14 (C)
1944—Tie, 21-21 (C)
Lions, 41-21 (D)
1945—Lions, 16-10 (D)
Lions, 35-28 (C)
1946—Bears, 42-6 (C)
Bears, 45-24 (D)
1947—Bears, 33-24 (C)
Bears, 34-14 (D)
1948—Bears, 28-0 (C)
Bears, 42-14 (D)
1949—Bears, 27-24 (C)
Bears, 28-7 (D)
1950—Bears, 35-21 (D)
Bears, 6-3 (C)
1951—Bears, 28-23 (D)
Lions, 41-28 (C)
1952—Bears, 24-23 (C)
Lions, 45-21 (D)
1953—Lions, 20-16 (C)
Lions, 13-7 (D)
1954—Lions, 48-23 (D)
Bears, 28-24 (C)
1955—Bears, 24-14 (D)
Bears, 21-20 (C)
1956—Lions, 42-10 (D)
Bears, 38-21 (C)
1957—Bears, 27-7 (D)
Lions, 21-13 (C)
1958—Bears, 20-7 (D)
Bears, 21-16 (C)
1959—Bears, 24-14 (D)
Bears, 25-14 (C)
1960—Bears, 28-7 (C)
Lions, 36-0 (D)
1961—Bears, 31-17 (D)
Lions, 16-15 (C)
1962—Lions, 11-3 (D)
Bears, 3-0 (C)
1963—Bears, 37-21 (D)
Bears, 24-14 (C)
1964—Lions, 10-0 (C)
Bears, 27-24 (D)
1965—Bears, 38-10 (C)
Bears, 17-10 (D)
1966—Lions, 14-3 (D)
Tie, 10-10 (C)
1967—Bears, 14-3 (C)
Bears, 27-13 (D)
1968—Lions, 42-0 (D)
Lions, 28-10 (C)
1969—Lions, 13-7 (D)
Lions, 20-3 (C)
1970—Lions, 28-14 (D)
Lions, 16-10 (C)
1971—Bears, 28-23 (D)
Lions, 28-3 (C)

1972—Lions, 38-24 (C)
Lions, 14-0 (D)
1973—Lions, 30-7 (C)
Lions, 40-7 (D)
1974—Bears, 17-9 (C)
Lions, 34-17 (D)
1975—Lions, 27-7 (D)
Bears, 25-21 (C)
1976—Bears, 10-3 (C)
Lions, 14-10 (D)
1977—Bears, 30-20 (C)
Bears, 31-14 (D)
1978—Bears, 19-0 (D)
Lions, 21-17 (C)
1979—Bears, 35-7 (C)
Lions, 20-0 (D)
1980—Bears, 24-7 (C)
Bears, 23-17 (D) OT
1981—Lions, 48-17 (D)
Lions, 23-7 (C)
1982—Lions, 17-10 (D)
Bears, 20-17 (C)
1983—Lions, 31-17 (D)
Lions, 38-17 (C)
1984—Bears, 16-14 (C)
Bears, 30-13 (D)
1985—Bears, 24-3 (C)
Bears, 37-17 (D)
1986—Bears, 13-7 (C)
Bears, 16-13 (D)
1987—Bears, 30-10 (C)
1988—Bears, 24-7 (D)
Bears, 13-12 (C)
1989—Bears, 47-27 (D)
Lions, 27-17 (C)
1990—Bears, 23-17 (C) OT
Lions, 38-21 (D)
1991—Bears, 20-10 (C)
Lions, 16-6 (D)
1992—Bears, 27-24 (C)
Lions, 16-3 (D)
1993—Bears, 10-6 (D)
Lions, 20-14 (C)
(RS Pts.—Bears 2,386, Lions 2,156)
*Franchise in Portsmouth prior to 1934 and known as the Spartans*

***CHICAGO vs. GREEN BAY**
RS: Bears lead series, 81-59-6
PS: Bears lead series, 1-0
1921—Staleys, 20-0 (C)
1923—Bears, 3-0 (GB)
1924—Bears, 3-0 (C)
1925—Packers, 14-10 (GB)
Bears, 21-0 (C)
1926—Tie, 6-6 (GB)
Bears, 19-13 (C)
Tie, 3-3 (C)
1927—Bears, 7-6 (GB)
Bears, 14-6 (C)
1928—Tie, 12-12 (GB)
Packers, 16-6 (C)
Packers, 6-0 (C)
1929—Packers, 23-0 (GB)
Packers, 14-0 (C)
Packers, 25-0 (C)
1930—Packers, 7-0 (GB)
Packers, 13-12 (C)
Bears, 21-0 (C)
1931—Packers, 7-0 (GB)
Packers, 6-2 (C)
Bears, 7-6 (C)
1932—Tie, 0-0 (GB)
Packers, 2-0 (C)
Bears, 9-0 (C)
1933—Bears, 14-7 (GB)
Bears, 10-7 (C)
Bears, 7-6 (C)
1934—Bears, 24-10 (GB)
Bears, 27-14 (C)
1935—Packers, 7-0 (GB)
Packers, 17-14 (C)
1936—Bears, 30-3 (GB)
Packers, 21-10 (C)
1937—Bears, 14-2 (GB)
Packers, 24-14 (C)
1938—Bears, 2-0 (GB)
Packers, 24-17 (C)
1939—Packers, 21-16 (GB)
Bears, 30-27 (C)
1940—Bears, 41-10 (GB)
Bears, 14-7 (C)
1941—Bears, 25-17 (GB)
Packers, 16-14 (C)
**Bears, 33-14 (C)
1942—Bears, 44-28 (GB)
Bears, 38-7 (C)
1943—Tie, 21-21 (GB)
Bears, 21-7 (C)
1944—Packers, 42-28 (GB)
Bears, 21-0 (C)
1945—Packers, 31-21 (GB)
Bears, 28-24 (C)
1946—Bears, 30-7 (GB)
Bears, 10-7 (C)
1947—Packers, 29-20 (GB)
Bears, 20-17 (C)
1948—Bears, 45-7 (GB)
Bears, 7-6 (C)
1949—Bears, 17-0 (GB)
Bears, 24-3 (C)
1950—Packers, 31-21 (GB)
Bears, 28-14 (C)
1951—Bears, 31-20 (GB)
Bears, 24-13 (C)
1952—Bears, 24-14 (GB)
Packers, 41-28 (C)
1953—Bears, 17-13 (GB)
Tie, 21-21 (C)
1954—Bears, 10-3 (GB)
Bears, 28-23 (C)
1955—Packers, 24-3 (GB)
Bears, 52-31 (C)
1956—Bears, 37-21 (GB)
Bears, 38-14 (C)
1957—Packers, 21-17 (GB)
Bears, 21-14 (C)
1958—Bears, 34-20 (GB)
Bears, 24-10 (C)
1959—Packers, 9-6 (GB)
Bears, 28-17 (C)
1960—Bears, 17-14 (GB)
Packers, 41-13 (C)
1961—Packers, 24-0 (GB)
Packers, 31-28 (C)
1962—Packers, 49-0 (GB)
Packers, 38-7 (C)
1963—Bears, 10-3 (GB)
Bears, 26-7 (C)
1964—Packers, 23-12 (GB)
Packers, 17-3 (C)
1965—Packers, 23-14 (GB)
Bears, 31-10 (C)
1966—Packers, 17-0 (C)
Packers, 13-6 (GB)
1967—Packers, 13-10 (GB)
Packers, 17-13 (C)
1968—Bears, 13-10 (GB)
Packers, 28-27 (C)
1969—Packers, 17-0 (GB)
Packers, 21-3 (C)
1970—Packers, 20-19 (GB)
Bears, 35-17 (C)
1971—Packers, 17-14 (C)
Packers, 31-10 (GB)
1972—Packers, 20-17 (GB)
Packers, 23-17 (C)
1973—Bears, 31-17 (GB)
Packers, 21-0 (C)
1974—Bears, 10-9 (C)
Packers, 20-3 (Mil)
1975—Bears, 27-14 (C)
Packers, 28-7 (GB)
1976—Bears, 24-13 (C)
Bears, 16-10 (GB)
1977—Bears, 26-0 (GB)
Bears, 21-10 (C)
1978—Packers, 24-14 (GB)
Bears, 14-0 (C)
1979—Bears, 6-3 (C)
Bears, 15-14 (GB)
1980—Packers, 12-6 (GB) OT
Bears, 61-7 (C)
1981—Packers, 16-9 (C)
Packers, 21-17 (GB)
1983—Packers, 31-28 (GB)
Bears, 23-21 (C)
1984—Bears, 9-7 (GB)
Packers, 20-14 (C)
1985—Bears, 23-7 (C)
Bears, 16-10 (GB)
1986—Bears, 25-12 (GB)
Bears, 12-10 (C)
1987—Bears, 26-24 (GB)
Bears, 23-10 (C)
1988—Bears, 24-6 (GB)
Bears, 16-0 (C)
1989—Packers, 14-13 (GB)
Packers, 40-28 (C)
1990—Bears, 31-13 (GB)
Bears, 27-13 (C)
1991—Bears, 10-0 (GB)
Bears, 27-13 (C)
1992—Bears, 30-10 (GB)
Packers, 17-3 (C)
1993—Packers, 17-3 (GB)
Bears, 30-17 (C)
(RS Pts.—Bears 2,478, Packers 2,130)
(PS Pts.—Bears 33, Packers 14)
**Bears known as Staleys prior to 1922*
***Division Playoff*

**CHICAGO vs. HOUSTON**
RS: Oilers lead series, 4-2
1973—Bears, 35-14 (C)
1977—Oilers, 47-0 (H)
1980—Oilers, 10-6 (C)
1986—Bears, 20-7 (H)
1989—Oilers, 33-28 (C)
1992—Oilers, 24-7 (H)
(RS Pts.—Oilers 135, Bears 96)

**CHICAGO vs. *INDIANAPOLIS**
RS: Colts lead series, 21-16
1953—Colts, 13-9 (B)
Colts, 16-14 (C)
1954—Bears, 28-9 (C)
Bears, 28-13 (B)
1955—Colts, 23-17 (B)
Bears, 38-10 (C)
1956—Colts, 28-21 (B)
Bears, 58-27 (C)
1957—Colts, 21-10 (B)
Colts, 29-14 (C)
1958—Colts, 51-38 (B)
Colts, 17-0 (C)
1959—Bears, 26-21 (B)
Colts, 21-7 (C)
1960—Colts, 42-7 (B)
Colts, 24-20 (C)
1961—Bears, 24-10 (C)
Bears, 21-20 (B)
1962—Bears, 35-15 (C)
Bears, 57-0 (B)
1963—Bears, 10-3 (C)
Bears, 17-7 (B)
1964—Colts, 52-0 (B)
Colts, 40-24 (C)
1965—Colts, 26-21 (C)
Bears, 13-0 (B)
1966—Bears, 27-17 (C)
Colts, 21-16 (B)
1967—Colts, 24-3 (C)
1968—Colts, 28-7 (B)
1969—Colts, 24-21 (C)
1970—Colts, 21-20 (B)
1975—Colts, 35-7 (C)
1983—Colts, 22-19 (B) OT
1985—Bears, 17-10 (C)
1988—Bears, 17-13 (I)
1991—Bears, 31-17 (I)
(RS Pts.—Colts 770, Bears 742)
**Franchise in Baltimore prior to 1984*

**CHICAGO vs. KANSAS CITY**
RS: Bears lead series, 4-2
1973—Chiefs, 19-7 (KC)
1977—Bears, 28-27 (C)
1981—Bears, 16-13 (KC) OT
1987—Bears, 31-28 (C)
1990—Chiefs, 21-10 (C)
1993—Bears, 19-17 (KC)
(RS Pts.—Chiefs 125, Bears 111)

**CHICAGO vs. *L.A. RAIDERS**
RS: Raiders lead series, 5-3
1972—Raiders, 28-21 (O)
1976—Raiders, 28-27 (C)
1978—Raiders, 25-19 (C) OT
1981—Bears, 23-6 (O)
1984—Bears, 17-6 (C)
1987—Bears, 6-3 (LA)
1990—Raiders, 24-10 (LA)
1993—Raiders, 16-14 (C)
(RS Pts.—Bears 137, Raiders 136)
**Franchise in Oakland prior to 1982*

**CHICAGO vs. *L.A. RAMS**
RS: Bears lead series, 44-29-3
PS: Series tied, 1-1
1937—Bears, 20-2 (Clev)
Bears, 15-7 (C)
1938—Rams, 14-7 (C)
Rams, 23-21 (Clev)
1939—Bears, 30-21 (Clev)
Bears, 35-21 (C)
1940—Bears, 21-14 (Clev)
Bears, 47-25 (C)
1941—Bears, 48-21 (Clev)
Bears, 31-13 (C)
1942—Bears, 21-7 (Clev)
Bears, 47-0 (C)
1944—Rams, 19-7 (Clev)
Bears, 28-21 (C)
1945—Rams, 17-0 (Clev)
Rams, 41-21 (C)
1946—Tie, 28-28 (C)
Bears, 27-21 (LA)
1947—Bears, 41-21 (LA)
Rams, 17-14 (C)
1948—Bears, 42-21 (C)
Bears, 21-6 (LA)
1949—Rams, 31-16 (C)
Rams, 27-24 (LA)
1950—Bears, 24-20 (LA)
Bears, 24-14 (C)
**Rams, 24-14 (LA)
1951—Rams, 42-17 (C)
1952—Rams, 31-7 (LA)
Rams, 40-24 (C)
1953—Rams, 38-24 (LA)
Bears, 24-21 (C)
1954—Rams, 42-38 (LA)
Bears, 24-13 (C)
1955—Bears, 31-20 (LA)
Bears, 24-3 (C)
1956—Bears, 35-24 (LA)
Bears, 30-21 (C)
1957—Bears, 34-26 (C)
Bears, 16-10 (LA)
1958—Bears, 31-10 (C)
Rams, 41-35 (LA)
1959—Rams, 28-21 (C)
Bears, 26-21 (LA)
1960—Bears, 34-27 (C)
Tie, 24-24 (LA)
1961—Bears, 21-17 (LA)
Bears, 28-24 (C)
1962—Bears, 27-23 (LA)
Bears, 30-14 (C)
1963—Bears, 52-14 (LA)
Bears, 6-0 (C)
1964—Bears, 38-17 (C)
Bears, 34-24 (LA)
1965—Rams, 30-28 (LA)
Bears, 31-6 (C)
1966—Rams, 31-17 (LA)
Bears, 17-10 (C)

1967—Rams, 28-17 (C)
1968—Bears, 17-16 (LA)
1969—Rams, 9-7 (C)
1971—Rams, 17-3 (LA)
1972—Tie, 13-13 (C)
1973—Rams, 26-0 (C)
1975—Rams, 38-10 (LA)
1976—Rams, 20-12 (LA)
1977—Bears, 24-23 (C)
1979—Bears, 27-23 (C)
1981—Rams, 24-7 (C)
1982—Bears, 34-26 (LA)
1983—Rams, 21-14 (LA)
1984—Rams, 29-13 (LA)
1985—***Bears, 24-0 (C)
1986—Rams, 20-17 (C)
1988—Rams, 23-3 (LA)
1989—Bears, 20-10 (C)
1990—Bears, 38-9 (C)
1993—Rams, 20-6 (LA)
(RS Pts.—Bears 1,770, Rams 1,559)
(PS Pts.—Bears 38, Rams 24)
*Franchise in Cleveland prior to 1946*
***Conference Playoff*
****NFC Championship*

**CHICAGO vs. MIAMI**
RS: Dolphins lead series, 5-1
1971—Dolphins, 34-3 (M)
1975—Dolphins, 46-13 (C)
1979—Dolphins, 31-16 (M)
1985—Dolphins, 38-24 (M)
1988—Bears, 34-7 (C)
1991—Dolphins, 16-13 (C) OT
(RS Pts.—Dolphins 172, Bears 103)

**CHICAGO vs. MINNESOTA**
RS: Vikings lead series, 34-29-2
1961—Vikings, 37-13 (M)
Bears, 52-35 (C)
1962—Bears, 13-0 (M)
Bears, 31-30 (C)
1963—Bears, 28-7 (M)
Tie, 17-17 (C)
1964—Bears, 34-28 (M)
Vikings, 41-14 (C)
1965—Bears, 45-37 (M)
Vikings, 24-17 (C)
1966—Bears, 13-10 (M)
Bears, 41-28 (C)
1967—Bears, 17-7 (M)
Tie, 10-10 (C)
1968—Bears, 27-17 (M)
Bears, 26-24 (C)
1969—Vikings, 31-0 (C)
Vikings, 31-14 (M)
1970—Vikings, 24-0 (C)
Vikings, 16-13 (M)
1971—Bears, 20-17 (M)
Vikings, 27-10 (C)
1972—Bears, 13-10 (C)
Vikings, 23-10 (M)
1973—Vikings, 22-13 (C)
Vikings, 31-13 (M)
1974—Vikings, 11-7 (M)
Vikings, 17-0 (C)
1975—Vikings, 28-3 (M)
Vikings, 13-9 (C)
1976—Vikings, 20-19 (M)
Bears, 14-13 (C)
1977—Vikings, 22-16 (M) OT
Bears, 10-7 (C)
1978—Vikings, 24-20 (C)
Vikings, 17-14 (M)
1979—Bears, 26-7 (C)
Vikings, 30-27 (M)
1980—Vikings, 34-14 (C)
Vikings, 13-7 (M)
1981—Vikings, 24-21 (M)
Bears, 10-9 (C)
1982—Vikings, 35-7 (M)
1983—Vikings, 23-14 (C)
Bears, 19-13 (M)
1984—Bears, 16-7 (C)
Bears, 34-3 (M)
1985—Bears, 33-24 (M)
Bears, 27-9 (C)
1986—Bears, 23-0 (C)
Vikings, 23-7 (M)
1987—Bears, 27-7 (C)
Bears, 30-24 (M)
1988—Vikings, 31-7 (C)
Vikings, 28-27 (M)
1989—Bears, 38-7 (C)
Vikings, 27-16 (M)
1990—Bears, 19-16 (C)
Vikings, 41-13 (M)
1991—Bears, 10-6 (C)
Bears, 34-17 (M)
1992—Vikings, 21-20 (M)
Vikings, 38-10 (C)
1993—Vikings, 10-7 (M)
Vikings, 19-12 (C)
(RS Pts.—Vikings 1,302, Bears 1,171)

**CHICAGO vs. NEW ENGLAND**
RS: Patriots lead series, 3-2
PS: Bears lead series, 1-0
1973—Patriots, 13-10 (C)
1979—Patriots, 27-7 (C)
1982—Bears, 26-13 (C)
1985—Bears, 20-7 (C)
*Bears, 46-10 (New Orleans)
1988—Patriots, 30-7 (NE)
(RS Pts.—Patriots 100, Bears 70)
(PS Pts.—Bears 46, Patriots 10)
**Super Bowl XX*

**CHICAGO vs. NEW ORLEANS**
RS: Bears lead series, 8-6
PS: Bears lead series, 1-0
1968—Bears, 23-17 (NO)
1970—Bears, 24-3 (NO)
1971—Bears, 35-14 (C)
1973—Saints, 21-16 (NO)
1974—Bears, 24-10 (C)
1975—Bears, 42-17 (NO)
1977—Saints, 42-24 (C)
1980—Bears, 22-3 (C)
1982—Saints, 10-0 (C)
1983—Saints, 34-31 (NO) OT
1984—Bears, 20-7 (C)
1987—Saints, 19-17 (C)
1990—*Bears, 16-6 (C)
1991—Bears, 20-17 (NO)
1992—Saints, 28-6 (NO)
(RS Pts.—Bears 304, Saints 242)
(PS Pts.—Bears 16, Saints 6)
**NFC First-Round Playoff*

**CHICAGO vs. N.Y. GIANTS**
RS: Bears lead series, 24-16-2
PS: Bears lead series, 5-3
1925—Bears, 19-7 (NY)
Giants, 9-0 (C)
1926—Bears, 7-0 (C)
1927—Giants, 13-7 (NY)
1928—Bears, 13-0 (C)
1929—Giants, 26-14 (C)
Giants, 34-0 (NY)
Giants, 14-9 (C)
1930—Giants, 12-0 (C)
Bears, 12-0 (NY)
1931—Bears, 6-0 (C)
Bears, 12-6 (NY)
Giants, 25-6 (C)
1932—Bears, 28-8 (NY)
Bears, 6-0 (C)
1933—Bears, 14-10 (C)
Giants, 3-0 (NY)
*Bears, 23-21 (C)
1934—Bears, 27-7 (C)
Bears, 10-9 (NY)
*Giants, 30-13 (NY)
1935—Bears, 20-3 (NY)
Giants, 3-0 (C)
1936—Bears, 25-7 (NY)
1937—Tie, 3-3 (NY)
1939—Giants, 16-13 (NY)
1940—Bears, 37-21 (NY)
1941—*Bears, 37-9 (C)
1942—Bears, 26-7 (NY)
1943—Bears, 56-7 (NY)
1946—Giants, 14-0 (NY)
*Bears, 24-14 (NY)
1948—Bears, 35-14 (C)
1949—Giants, 35-28 (NY)
1956—Tie, 17-17 (NY)
*Giants, 47-7 (NY)
1962—Giants, 26-24 (C)
1963—*Bears, 14-10 (C)
1965—Bears, 35-14 (NY)
1967—Bears, 34-7 (C)
1969—Giants, 28-24 (NY)
1970—Bears, 24-16 (NY)
1974—Bears, 16-13 (C)
1977—Bears, 12-9 (NY) OT
1985—**Bears, 21-0 (C)
1987—Bears, 34-19 (C)
1990—**Giants, 31-3 (NY)
1991—Bears, 20-17 (C)
1992—Giants, 27-14 (C)
1993—Giants, 26-20 (C)
(RS Pts.—Bears 707, Giants 532)
(PS Pts.—Giants 162, Bears 142)
**NFL Championship*
***NFC Divisional Playoff*

**CHICAGO vs. N.Y. JETS**
RS: Bears lead series, 3-1
1974—Jets, 23-21 (C)
1979—Bears, 23-13 (C)
1985—Bears, 19-6 (NY)
1991—Bears, 19-13 (C) OT
(RS Pts.—Bears 82, Jets 55)

**CHICAGO vs. PHILADELPHIA**
RS: Bears lead series, 23-3-1
PS: Series tied, 1-1
1933—Tie, 3-3 (P)
1935—Bears, 39-0 (P)
1936—Bears, 17-0 (P)
Bears, 28-7 (P)
1938—Bears, 28-6 (P)
1939—Bears, 27-14 (C)
1941—Bears, 49-14 (P)
1942—Bears, 45-14 (C)
1944—Bears, 28-7 (P)
1946—Bears, 21-14 (C)
1947—Bears, 40-7 (C)
1948—Eagles, 12-7 (P)
1949—Bears, 38-21 (C)
1955—Bears, 17-10 (C)
1961—Eagles, 16-14 (P)
1963—Bears, 16-7 (C)
1968—Bears, 29-16 (P)
1970—Bears, 20-16 (C)
1972—Bears, 21-12 (P)
1975—Bears, 15-13 (C)
1979—*Eagles, 27-17 (P)
1980—Eagles, 17-14 (P)
1983—Bears, 7-6 (P)
Bears, 17-14 (C)
1986—Bears, 13-10 (C) OT
1987—Bears, 35-3 (P)
1988—**Bears, 20-12 (C)
1989—Bears, 27-13 (C)
1993—Bears, 17-6 (P)
(RS Pts.—Bears 632, Eagles 278)
(PS Pts.—Eagles 39, Bears 37)
**NFC First-Round Playoff*
***NFC Divisional Playoff*

**CHICAGO vs. *PITTSBURGH**
RS: Bears lead series, 16-4-1
1934—Bears, 28-0 (P)
1935—Bears, 23-7 (P)
1936—Bears, 27-9 (P)
Bears, 26-6 (C)
1937—Bears, 7-0 (P)
1939—Bears, 32-0 (P)
1941—Bears, 34-7 (C)
1945—Bears, 28-7 (P)
1947—Bears, 49-7 (C)
1949—Bears, 30-21 (C)
1958—Steelers, 24-10 (P)
1959—Bears, 27-21 (C)
1963—Tie, 17-17 (P)
1967—Steelers, 41-13 (P)
1969—Bears, 38-7 (C)
1971—Bears, 17-15 (C)
1975—Steelers, 34-3 (P)
1980—Steelers, 38-3 (P)
1986—Bears, 13-10 (C) OT
1989—Bears, 20-0 (P)
1992—Bears, 30-6 (C)
(RS Pts.—Bears 475, Steelers 277)
**Steelers known as Pirates prior to 1941*

**CHICAGO vs. SAN DIEGO**
RS: Chargers lead series, 4-2
1970—Chargers, 20-7 (C)
1974—Chargers, 28-21 (SD)
1978—Chargers, 40-7 (SD)
1981—Bears, 20-17 (C) OT
1984—Chargers, 20-7 (SD)
1993—Bears, 16-13 (SD)
(RS Pts.—Chargers 138, Bears 78)

**CHICAGO vs. SAN FRANCISCO**
RS: Series tied, 25-25-1
PS: 49ers lead series, 2-0
1950—Bears, 32-20 (SF)
Bears, 17-0 (C)
1951—Bears, 13-7 (C)
1952—49ers, 40-16 (C)
Bears, 20-17 (SF)
1953—49ers, 35-28 (C)
49ers, 24-14 (SF)
1954—49ers, 31-24 (C)
Bears, 31-27 (SF)
1955—49ers, 20-19 (C)
Bears, 34-23 (SF)
1956—Bears, 31-7 (C)
Bears, 38-21 (SF)
1957—49ers, 21-17 (C)
49ers, 21-17 (SF)
1958—Bears, 28-6 (C)
Bears, 27-14 (SF)
1959—49ers, 20-17 (SF)
Bears, 14-3 (C)
1960—Bears, 27-10 (C)
49ers, 25-7 (SF)
1961—Bears, 31-0 (C)
49ers, 41-31 (SF)
1962—Bears, 30-14 (SF)
49ers, 34-27 (C)
1963—49ers, 20-14 (SF)
Bears, 27-7 (C)
1964—49ers, 31-21 (SF)
Bears, 23-21 (C)
1965—49ers, 52-24 (SF)
Bears, 61-20 (C)
1966—Tie, 30-30 (C)
49ers, 41-14 (SF)
1967—Bears, 28-14 (SF)
1968—Bears, 27-19 (C)
1969—49ers, 42-21 (SF)
1970—49ers, 37-16 (C)
1971—49ers, 13-0 (SF)
1972—49ers, 34-21 (C)
1974—49ers, 34-0 (C)
1975—49ers, 31-3 (SF)
1976—Bears, 19-12 (SF)
1978—Bears, 16-13 (SF)
1979—Bears, 28-27 (SF)
1981—49ers, 28-17 (SF)
1983—Bears, 13-3 (C)
1984—*49ers, 23-0 (SF)
1985—Bears, 26-10 (SF)
1987—49ers, 41-0 (SF)
1988—Bears, 10-9 (C)
*49ers, 28-3 (C)
1989—49ers, 26-0 (SF)
1991—49ers, 52-14 (SF)
(RS Pts.—49ers 1,148, Bears 1,063)
(PS Pts.—49ers 51, Bears 3)
**NFC Championship*

**CHICAGO vs. SEATTLE**
RS: Seahawks lead series, 4-2
1976—Bears, 34-7 (S)
1978—Seahawks, 31-29 (C)

1982—Seahawks, 20-14 (S)
1984—Seahawks, 38-9 (S)
1987—Seahawks, 34-21 (C)
1990—Bears, 17-0 (C)
(RS Pts.—Seahawks 130, Bears 124)

**CHICAGO vs. TAMPA BAY**
RS: Bears lead series, 24-8
1977—Bears, 10-0 (TB)
1978—Buccaneers, 33-19 (TB)
Bears, 14-3 (C)
1979—Buccaneers, 17-13 (C)
Bears, 14-0 (TB)
1980—Bears, 23-0 (C)
Bears, 14-13 (TB)
1981—Bears, 28-17 (C)
Buccaneers, 20-10 (TB)
1982—Buccaneers, 26-23 (TB) OT
1983—Bears, 17-10 (C)
Bears, 27-0 (TB)
1984—Bears, 34-14 (C)
Bears, 44-9 (TB)
1985—Bears, 38-28 (C)
Bears, 27-19 (TB)
1986—Bears, 23-3 (TB)
Bears, 48-14 (C)
1987—Bears, 20-3 (C)
Bears, 27-26 (TB)
1988—Bears, 28-10 (C)
Bears, 27-15 (TB)
1989—Buccaneers, 42-35 (TB)
Buccaneers, 32-31 (C)
1990—Bears, 26-6 (TB)
Bears, 27-14 (C)
1991—Bears, 21-20 (TB)
Bears, 27-0 (C)
1992—Bears, 31-14 (C)
Buccaneers, 20-17 (TB)
1993—Bears, 47-17 (C)
Buccaneers, 13-10 (TB)
(RS Pts.—Bears 800, Buccaneers 458)

**CHICAGO vs. *WASHINGTON**
RS: Bears lead series, 18-12-1
PS: Redskins lead series, 4-3
1932—Tie, 7-7 (B)
1933—Bears, 7-0 (C)
Redskins, 10-0 (B)
1934—Bears, 21-0 (B)
1935—Bears, 30-14 (B)
1936—Bears, 26-0 (B)
1937—**Redskins, 28-21 (C)
1938—Bears, 31-7 (C)
1940—Redskins, 7-3 (W)
**Bears, 73-0 (W)
1941—Bears, 35-21 (C)
1942—**Redskins, 14-6 (W)
1943—Redskins, 21-7 (W)
**Bears, 41-21 (C)
1945—Redskins, 28-21 (W)
1946—Bears, 24-20 (C)
1947—Bears, 56-20 (W)
1948—Bears, 48-13 (C)
1949—Bears, 31-21 (W)
1951—Bears, 27-0 (W)
1953—Bears, 27-24 (W)
1957—Redskins, 14-3 (C)
1964—Redskins, 27-20 (W)
1968—Redskins, 38-28 (C)
1971—Bears, 16-15 (C)
1974—Redskins, 42-0 (W)
1976—Bears, 33-7 (C)
1978—Bears, 14-10 (W)
1980—Bears, 35-21 (C)
1981—Redskins, 24-7 (C)
1984—***Bears, 23-19 (W)
1985—Bears, 45-10 (C)
1986—***Redskins, 27-13 (C)
1987—***Redskins, 21-17 (C)
1988—Bears, 34-14 (W)
1989—Redskins, 38-14 (W)
1990—Redskins, 10-9 (W)
1991—Redskins, 20-7 (C)
(RS Pts.—Bears 666, Redskins 503)
(PS Pts.—Bears 194, Redskins 130)
*Franchise in Boston prior to 1937 and known as Braves prior to 1933
**NFL Championship
***NFC Divisional Playoff

---

**CINCINNATI vs. ARIZONA**
RS: Bengals lead series, 3-1;
See Arizona vs. Cincinnati

**CINCINNATI vs. ATLANTA**
RS: Bengals lead series, 6-2;
See Atlanta vs. Cincinnati

**CINCINNATI vs. BUFFALO**
RS: Bengals lead series, 9-7
PS: Bengals lead series, 2-0;
See Buffalo vs. Cincinnati

**CINCINNATI vs. CHICAGO**
RS: Bengals lead series, 3-2;
See Chicago vs. Cincinnati

**CINCINNATI vs. CLEVELAND**
RS: Bengals lead series, 24-23
1970—Browns, 30-27 (Cle)
Bengals, 14-10 (Cin)
1971—Browns, 27-24 (Cin)
Browns, 31-27 (Cle)
1972—Browns, 27-6 (Cle)
Browns, 27-24 (Cin)
1973—Browns, 17-10 (Cle)
Bengals, 34-17 (Cin)
1974—Bengals, 33-7 (Cin)
Bengals, 34-24 (Cle)
1975—Bengals, 24-17 (Cin)
Browns, 35-23 (Cle)
1976—Bengals, 45-24 (Cle)
Bengals, 21-6 (Cin)
1977—Browns, 13-3 (Cin)
Bengals, 10-7 (Cle)
1978—Browns, 13-10 (Cle) OT
Bengals, 48-16 (Cin)
1979—Browns, 28-27 (Cle)
Bengals, 16-12 (Cin)
1980—Browns, 31-7 (Cle)
Browns, 27-24 (Cin)
1981—Browns, 20-17 (Cin)
Bengals, 41-21 (Cle)
1982—Bengals, 23-10 (Cin)
1983—Browns, 17-7 (Cle)
Bengals, 28-21 (Cin)
1984—Bengals, 12-9 (Cin)
Bengals, 20-17 (Cle) OT
1985—Bengals, 27-10 (Cin)
Browns, 24-6 (Cle)
1986—Bengals, 30-13 (Cle)
Browns, 34-3 (Cin)
1987—Browns, 34-0 (Cin)
Browns, 38-24 (Cle)
1988—Bengals, 24-17 (Cin)
Browns, 23-16 (Cle)
1989—Bengals, 21-14 (Cin)
Bengals, 21-0 (Cle)
1990—Bengals, 34-13 (Cle)
Bengals, 21-14 (Cin)
1991—Browns, 14-13 (Cle)
Bengals, 23-21 (Cin)
1992—Bengals, 30-10 (Cin)
Browns, 37-21 (Cle)
1993—Browns, 27-14 (Cle)
Browns, 28-17 (Cin)
(RS Pts.—Bengals 984, Browns 932)

**CINCINNATI vs. DALLAS**
RS: Cowboys lead series, 3-2
1973—Cowboys, 38-10 (D)
1979—Cowboys, 38-13 (D)
1985—Bengals, 50-24 (C)
1988—Bengals, 38-24 (D)
1991—Cowboys, 35-23 (D)
(RS Pts.—Cowboys 159, Bengals 134)

**CINCINNATI vs. DENVER**
RS: Broncos lead series, 10-6
1968—Bengals, 24-10 (C)
Broncos, 10-7 (D)
1969—Broncos, 30-23 (C)
Broncos, 27-16 (D)
1971—Bengals, 24-10 (D)
1972—Bengals, 21-10 (C)
1973—Broncos, 28-10 (D)
1975—Bengals, 17-16 (D)
1976—Bengals, 17-7 (C)
1977—Broncos, 24-13 (C)
1979—Broncos, 10-0 (D)
1981—Bengals, 38-21 (C)
1983—Broncos, 24-17 (D)
1984—Broncos, 20-17 (D)
1986—Broncos, 34-28 (D)
1991—Broncos, 45-14 (D)
(RS Pts.—Broncos 326, Bengals 286)

**CINCINNATI vs. DETROIT**
RS: Series tied, 3-3
1970—Lions, 38-3 (D)
1974—Lions, 23-19 (C)
1983—Bengals, 17-9 (C)
1986—Bengals, 24-17 (D)
1989—Bengals, 42-7 (C)
1992—Lions, 19-13 (C)
(RS Pts.—Bengals 118, Lions 113)

**CINCINNATI vs. GREEN BAY**
RS: Bengals lead series, 4-3
1971—Packers, 20-17 (GB)
1976—Bengals, 28-7 (C)
1977—Bengals, 17-7 (Mil)
1980—Packers, 14-9 (GB)
1983—Bengals, 34-14 (C)
1986—Bengals, 34-28 (Mil)
1992—Packers, 24-23 (GB)
(RS Pts.—Bengals 162, Packers 114)

**CINCINNATI vs. HOUSTON**
RS: Oilers lead series, 25-24-1
PS: Bengals lead series, 1-0
1968—Oilers, 27-17 (C)
1969—Tie, 31-31 (H)
1970—Oilers, 20-13 (C)
Bengals, 30-20 (H)
1971—Oilers, 10-6 (H)
Bengals, 28-13 (C)
1972—Bengals, 30-7 (C)
Bengals, 61-17 (H)
1973—Bengals, 24-10 (C)
Bengals, 27-24 (H)
1974—Oilers, 34-21 (C)
Oilers, 20-3 (H)
1975—Bengals, 21-19 (H)
Bengals, 23-19 (C)
1976—Bengals, 27-7 (H)
Bengals, 31-27 (C)
1977—Bengals, 13-10 (C) OT
Oilers, 21-16 (H)
1978—Bengals, 28-13 (C)
Oilers, 17-10 (H)
1979—Oilers, 30-27 (C) OT
Oilers, 42-21 (H)
1980—Oilers, 13-10 (C)
Oilers, 23-3 (H)
1981—Oilers, 17-10 (H)
Bengals, 34-21 (C)
1982—Bengals, 27-6 (C)
Bengals, 35-27 (H)
1983—Bengals, 55-14 (H)
Bengals, 38-10 (C)
1984—Bengals, 13-3 (C)
Bengals, 31-13 (H)
1985—Oilers, 44-27 (H)
Bengals, 45-27 (C)
1986—Bengals, 31-28 (C)
Oilers, 32-28 (H)
1987—Oilers, 31-29 (C)
Oilers, 21-17 (H)
1988—Bengals, 44-21 (C)
Oilers, 41-6 (H)
1989—Oilers, 26-24 (H)
Bengals, 61-7 (C)
1990—Oilers, 48-17 (H)
Bengals, 40-20 (C)
*Bengals, 41-14 (C)
1991—Oilers, 30-7 (C)
Oilers, 35-3 (H)
1992—Oilers, 38-24 (C)
Oilers, 26-10 (H)
1993—Oilers, 28-12 (H)
Oilers, 38-3 (C)
(RS Pts.—Bengals 1,192, Oilers 1,126)
(PS Pts.—Bengals 41, Oilers 14)
*AFC First Round Playoff

**CINCINNATI vs.*INDIANAPOLIS**
RS: Colts lead series, 8-5
PS: Colts lead series, 1-0
1970—**Colts, 17-0 (B)
1972—Colts, 20-19 (C)
1974—Bengals, 24-14 (B)
1976—Colts, 28-27 (B)
1979—Colts, 38-28 (B)
1980—Bengals, 34-33 (C)
1981—Bengals, 41-19 (B)
1982—Bengals, 20-17 (B)
1983—Colts, 34-31 (C)
1987—Bengals, 23-21 (I)
1989—Colts, 23-12 (C)
1990—Colts, 34-20 (C)
1992—Colts, 21-17 (C)
1993—Colts, 9-6 (C)
(RS Pts.—Colts 311, Bengals 302)
(PS Pts.—Colts 17, Bengals 0)
*Franchise in Baltimore prior to 1984
**AFC Divisional Playoff

**CINCINNATI vs. KANSAS CITY**
RS: Chiefs lead series, 11-9
1968—Chiefs, 13-3 (KC)
Chiefs, 16-9 (C)
1969—Bengals, 24-19 (C)
Chiefs, 42-22 (KC)
1970—Chiefs, 27-19 (C)
1972—Bengals, 23-16 (KC)
1973—Bengals, 14-6 (C)
1974—Bengals, 33-6 (C)
1976—Bengals, 27-24 (KC)
1977—Bengals, 27-7 (KC)
1978—Chiefs, 24-23 (C)
1979—Chiefs, 10-7 (C)
1980—Bengals, 20-6 (KC)
1983—Chiefs, 20-15 (KC)
1984—Chiefs, 27-22 (C)
1986—Chiefs, 24-14 (KC)
1987—Bengals, 30-27 (C) OT
1988—Chiefs, 31-28 (KC)
1989—Bengals, 21-17 (KC)
1993—Chiefs, 17-15 (KC)
(RS Pts.—Bengals 396, Chiefs 379)

**CINCINNATI vs. *L.A. RAIDERS**
RS: Raiders lead series, 14-7
PS: Raiders lead series, 2-0
1968—Raiders, 31-10 (O)
Raiders, 34-0 (C)
1969—Bengals, 31-17 (C)
Raiders, 37-17 (O)
1970—Bengals, 31-21 (C)
1971—Raiders, 31-27 (O)
1972—Raiders, 20-14 (C)
1974—Raiders, 30-27 (O)
1975—Bengals, 14-10 (C)
**Raiders, 31-28 (O)
1976—Raiders, 35-20 (O)
1978—Raiders, 34-21 (C)
1980—Raiders, 28-17 (O)
1982—Bengals, 31-17 (C)
1983—Raiders, 20-10 (C)
1985—Raiders, 13-6 (LA)
1988—Bengals, 45-21 (LA)
1989—Raiders, 28-7 (LA)
1990—Raiders, 24-7 (LA)
**Raiders, 20-10 (LA)
1991—Raiders, 38-14 (C)
1992—Bengals, 24-21 (C) OT
1993—Bengals, 16-10 (C)
(RS Pts.—Raiders 520, Bengals 389)
(PS Pts.—Raiders 51, Bengals 38)
*Franchise in Oakland prior to 1982
**AFC Divisional Playoff

**CINCINNATI vs. L.A. RAMS**
RS: Bengals lead series, 5-2
1972—Rams, 15-12 (LA)
1976—Bengals, 20-12 (C)

1978—Bengals, 20-19 (LA)
1981—Bengals, 24-10 (C)
1984—Rams, 24-14 (C)
1990—Bengals, 34-31 (LA) OT
1993—Bengals, 15-3 (C)
(RS Pts.—Bengals 139, Rams 114)

**CINCINNATI vs. MIAMI**
RS: Dolphins lead series, 9-3
PS: Dolphins lead series, 1-0
1968—Dolphins, 24-22 (C)
Bengals, 38-21 (M)
1969—Bengals, 27-21 (C)
1971—Dolphins, 23-13 (C)
1973—*Dolphins, 34-16 (M)
1974—Dolphins, 24-3 (M)
1977—Bengals, 23-17 (C)
1978—Dolphins, 21-0 (M)
1980—Dolphins, 17-16 (M)
1983—Dolphins, 38-14 (M)
1987—Dolphins, 20-14 (C)
1989—Dolphins, 20-13 (C)
1991—Dolphins, 37-13 (M)
(RS Pts.—Dolphins 317, Bengals 212)
(PS Pts.—Dolphins 34, Bengals 16)
*AFC Divisional Playoff*

**CINCINNATI vs. MINNESOTA**
RS: Vikings lead series, 4-3
1973—Bengals, 27-0 (C)
1977—Vikings, 42-10 (M)
1980—Bengals, 14-0 (C)
1983—Vikings, 20-14 (M)
1986—Bengals, 24-20 (C)
1989—Vikings, 29-21 (M)
1992—Vikings, 42-7 (C)
(RS Pts.—Vikings 153, Bengals 117)

**CINCINNATI vs. *NEW ENGLAND**
RS: Patriots lead series, 8-7
1968—Patriots, 33-14 (B)
1969—Patriots, 25-14 (C)
1970—Bengals, 45-7 (C)
1972—Bengals, 31-7 (NE)
1975—Bengals, 27-10 (C)
1978—Patriots, 10-3 (C)
1979—Patriots, 20-14 (C)
1984—Patriots, 20-14 (NE)
1985—Patriots, 34-23 (NE)
1986—Bengals, 31-7 (NE)
1988—Patriots, 27-21 (NE)
1990—Bengals, 41-7 (C)
1991—Bengals, 29-7 (C)
1992—Bengals, 20-10 (C)
1993—Patriots, 7-2 (NE)
(RS Pts.—Bengals 329, Patriots 231)
*Franchise in Boston prior to 1971*

**CINCINNATI vs. NEW ORLEANS**
RS: Saints lead series, 5-3
1970—Bengals, 26-6 (C)
1975—Bengals, 21-0 (NO)
1978—Saints, 20-18 (C)
1981—Saints, 17-7 (NO)
1984—Bengals, 24-21 (NO)
1987—Saints, 41-24 (C)
1990—Saints, 21-7 (C)
1993—Saints, 20-13 (NO)
(RS Pts.—Saints 146, Bengals 140)

**CINCINNATI vs. N.Y. GIANTS**
RS: Bengals lead series, 4-0
1972—Bengals, 13-10 (C)
1977—Bengals, 30-13 (C)
1985—Bengals, 35-30 (C)
1991—Bengals, 27-24 (C)
(RS Pts.—Bengals 105, Giants 77)

**CINCINNATI vs. N.Y. JETS**
RS: Jets lead series, 9-6
PS: Jets lead series, 1-0
1968—Jets, 27-14 (NY)
1969—Jets, 21-7 (C)
Jets, 40-7 (NY)
1971—Jets, 35-21 (NY)
1973—Bengals, 20-14 (C)
1976—Bengals, 42-3 (NY)
1981—Bengals, 31-30 (NY)
1982—*Jets, 44-17 (C)
1984—Jets, 43-23 (NY)
1985—Jets, 29-20 (C)
1986—Bengals, 52-21 (C)
1987—Jets, 27-20 (NY)
1988—Bengals, 36-19 (C)
1990—Bengals, 25-20 (C)
1992—Jets, 17-14 (NY)
1993—Jets, 17-12 (NY)
(RS Pts.—Jets 363, Bengals 344)
(PS Pts.—Jets 44, Bengals 17)
*AFC First-Round Playoff*

**CINCINNATI vs. PHILADELPHIA**
RS: Bengals lead series, 5-1
1971—Bengals, 37-14 (C)
1975—Bengals, 31-0 (P)
1979—Bengals, 37-13 (C)
1982—Bengals, 18-14 (P)
1988—Bengals, 28-24 (P)
1991—Eagles, 17-10 (P)
(RS Pts.—Bengals 161, Eagles 82)

**CINCINNATI vs. PITTSBURGH**
RS: Steelers lead series, 26-21
1970—Steelers, 21-10 (P)
Bengals, 34-7 (C)
1971—Steelers, 21-10 (P)
Steelers, 21-13 (C)
1972—Bengals, 15-10 (C)
Steelers, 40-17 (P)
1973—Bengals, 19-7 (C)
Steelers, 20-13 (P)
1974—Bengals, 17-10 (C)
Steelers, 27-3 (P)
1975—Steelers, 30-24 (C)
Steelers, 35-14 (P)
1976—Steelers, 23-6 (P)
Steelers, 7-3 (C)
1977—Steelers, 20-14 (P)
Bengals, 17-10 (C)
1978—Steelers, 28-3 (C)
Steelers, 7-6 (P)
1979—Bengals, 34-10 (C)
Steelers, 37-17 (P)
1980—Bengals, 30-28 (C)
Bengals, 17-16 (P)
1981—Bengals, 34-7 (C)
Bengals, 17-10 (P)
1982—Steelers, 26-20 (P) OT
1983—Steelers, 24-14 (C)
Bengals, 23-10 (P)
1984—Steelers, 38-17 (P)
Bengals, 22-20 (C)
1985—Bengals, 37-24 (P)
Bengals, 26-21 (C)
1986—Bengals, 24-22 (C)
Steelers, 30-9 (P)
1987—Steelers, 23-20 (P)
Steelers, 30-16 (C)
1988—Bengals, 17-12 (P)
Bengals, 42-7 (C)
1989—Bengals, 41-10 (C)
Bengals, 26-16 (P)
1990—Bengals, 27-3 (C)
Bengals, 16-12 (P)
1991—Steelers, 33-27 (C) OT
Steelers, 17-10 (P)
1992—Steelers, 20-0 (P)
Steelers, 21-9 (C)
1993—Steelers, 34-7 (P)
Steelers, 24-16 (C)
(RS Pts.—Steelers 929, Bengals 853)

**CINCINNATI vs. SAN DIEGO**
RS: Chargers lead series, 12-8
PS: Bengals lead series, 1-0
1968—Chargers, 29-13 (SD)
Chargers, 31-10 (C)
1969—Bengals, 34-20 (C)
Chargers, 21-14 (SD)
1970—Bengals, 17-14 (SD)
1971—Bengals, 31-0 (C)
1973—Bengals, 20-13 (SD)
1974—Chargers, 20-17 (C)
1975—Bengals, 47-17 (C)
1977—Chargers, 24-3 (SD)
1978—Chargers, 22-13 (SD)
1979—Chargers, 26-24 (C)
1980—Chargers, 31-14 (C)
1981—Bengals, 40-17 (SD)
*Bengals, 27-7 (C)
1982—Chargers, 50-34 (SD)
1985—Chargers, 44-41 (C)
1987—Chargers, 10-9 (C)
1988—Bengals, 27-10 (C)
1990—Bengals, 21-16 (SD)
1992—Chargers, 27-10 (SD)
(RS Pts.—Chargers 442, Bengals 439)
(PS Pts.—Bengals 27, Chargers 7)
*AFC Championship*

**CINCINNATI vs. SAN FRANCISCO**
RS: 49ers lead series, 6-1
PS: 49ers lead series, 2-0
1974—Bengals, 21-3 (SF)
1978—49ers, 28-12 (SF)
1981—49ers, 21-3 (C)
*49ers, 26-21 (Detroit)
1984—49ers, 23-17 (SF)
1987—49ers, 27-26 (C)
1988—**49ers, 20-16 (Miami)
1990—49ers, 20-17 (C)
1993—49ers, 21-8 (SF)
(RS Pts.—49ers 143, Bengals 104)
(PS Pts.—49ers 46, Bengals 37)
*Super Bowl XVI*
***Super Bowl XXIII*

**CINCINNATI vs. SEATTLE**
RS: Series tied, 6-6
PS: Bengals lead series, 1-0
1977—Bengals, 42-20 (C)
1981—Bengals, 27-21 (C)
1982—Bengals, 24-10 (C)
1984—Seahawks, 26-6 (C)
1985—Seahawks, 28-24 (C)
1986—Bengals, 34-7 (C)
1987—Bengals, 17-10 (S)
1988—*Bengals, 21-13 (C)
1989—Seahawks, 24-17 (C)
1990—Seahawks, 31-16 (S)
1991—Seahawks, 13-7 (C)
1992—Bengals, 21-3 (S)
1993—Seahawks, 19-10 (C)
(RS Pts.—Bengals 245, Seahawks 212)
(PS Pts.—Bengals 21, Seahawks 13)
*AFC Divisional Playoff*

**CINCINNATI vs. TAMPA BAY**
RS: Bengals lead series, 3-1
1976—Bengals, 21-0 (C)
1980—Buccaneers, 17-12 (C)
1983—Bengals, 23-17 (TB)
1989—Bengals, 56-23 (C)
(RS Pts.—Bengals 112, Buccaneers 57)

**CINCINNATI vs. WASHINGTON**
RS: Redskins lead series, 4-2
1970—Redskins, 20-0 (W)
1974—Bengals, 28-17 (C)
1979—Redskins, 28-14 (W)
1985—Redskins, 27-24 (W)
1988—Bengals, 20-17 (C) OT
1991—Redskins, 34-27 (C)
(RS Pts.—Redskins 143, Bengals 113)

---

**CLEVELAND vs. ARIZONA**
RS: Browns lead series, 31-10-3;
See Arizona vs. Cleveland

**CLEVELAND vs. ATLANTA**
RS: Browns lead series, 8-2;
See Atlanta vs. Cleveland

**CLEVELAND vs. BUFFALO**
RS: Browns lead series, 7-3
PS: Browns lead series, 1-0;
See Buffalo vs. Cleveland

**CLEVELAND vs. CHICAGO**
RS: Browns lead series, 8-3;
See Chicago vs. Cleveland

**CLEVELAND vs. CINCINNATI**
RS: Bengals lead series, 24-23;
See Cincinnati vs. Cleveland

**CLEVELAND vs. DALLAS**
RS: Browns lead series, 14-9
PS: Browns lead series, 2-1
1960—Browns, 48-7 (D)
1961—Browns, 25-7 (C)
Browns, 38-17 (D)
1962—Browns, 19-10 (C)
Cowboys, 45-21 (D)
1963—Browns, 41-24 (D)
Browns, 27-17 (C)
1964—Browns, 27-6 (C)
Browns, 20-16 (D)
1965—Browns, 23-17 (C)
Browns, 24-17 (D)
1966—Browns, 30-21 (C)
Cowboys, 26-14 (D)
1967—Cowboys, 21-14 (C)
*Cowboys, 52-14 (D)
1968—Cowboys, 28-7 (C)
*Browns, 31-20 (C)
1969—Browns, 42-10 (C)
*Browns, 38-14 (D)
1970—Cowboys, 6-2 (C)
1974—Cowboys, 41-17 (D)
1979—Browns, 26-7 (C)
1982—Cowboys, 31-14 (D)
1985—Cowboys, 20-7 (D)
1988—Browns, 24-21 (C)
1991—Cowboys, 26-14 (C)
(RS Pts.—Browns 524, Cowboys 441)
(PS Pts.—Cowboys 86, Browns 83)
*Conference Championship*

**CLEVELAND vs. DENVER**
RS: Broncos lead series, 12-5
PS: Broncos lead series, 3-0
1970—Browns, 27-13 (D)
1971—Broncos, 27-0 (C)
1972—Browns, 27-20 (D)
1974—Browns, 23-21 (C)
1975—Broncos, 16-15 (D)
1976—Broncos, 44-13 (D)
1978—Broncos, 19-7 (C)
1980—Broncos, 19-16 (C)
1981—Broncos, 23-20 (D) OT
1983—Broncos, 27-6 (D)
1984—Broncos, 24-14 (C)
1986—*Broncos, 23-20 (C) OT
1987—*Broncos, 38-33 (D)
1988—Broncos, 30-7 (D)
1989—Browns, 16-13 (C)
*Broncos, 37-21 (D)
1990—Browns, 30-29 (D)
1991—Broncos, 17-7 (C)
1992—Broncos, 12-0 (C)
1993—Broncos, 29-14 (C)
(RS Pts.—Broncos 383, Browns 242)
(PS Pts.—Broncos 98, Browns 74)
*AFC Championship*

**CLEVELAND vs. DETROIT**
RS: Lions lead series, 11-3
PS: Lions lead series, 3-1
1952—Lions, 17-6 (D)
*Lions, 17-7 (C)
1953—*Lions, 17-16 (D)
1954—Lions, 14-10 (C)
*Browns, 56-10 (C)
1957—Lions, 20-7 (D)
*Lions, 59-14 (D)
1958—Lions, 30-10 (C)
1963—Lions, 38-10 (D)
1964—Browns, 37-21 (C)
1967—Lions, 31-14 (D)
1969—Lions, 28-21 (C)
1970—Lions, 41-24 (C)
1975—Lions, 21-10 (D)
1983—Browns, 31-26 (D)
1986—Browns, 24-21 (C)
1989—Lions, 13-10 (D)
1992—Lions, 24-14 (D)
(RS Pts.—Lions 345, Browns 228)
(PS Pts.—Lions 103, Browns 93)
*NFL Championship*

**CLEVELAND vs. GREEN BAY**
RS: Packers lead series, 7-6

## ALL-TIME TEAM VS. TEAM RESULTS

PS: Packers lead series, 1-0
1953—Browns, 27-0 (Mil)
1955—Browns, 41-10 (C)
1956—Browns, 24-7 (Mil)
1961—Packers, 49-17 (C)
1964—Packers, 28-21 (Mil)
1965—*Packers, 23-12 (GB)
1966—Packers, 21-20 (C)
1967—Packers, 55-7 (Mil)
1969—Browns, 20-7 (C)
1972—Packers, 26-10 (C)
1980—Browns, 26-21 (C)
1983—Packers, 35-21 (Mil)
1986—Packers, 17-14 (C)
1992—Browns, 17-6 (C)
(RS Pts.—Packers 282, Browns 265)
(PS Pts.—Packers 23, Browns 12)
*NFL Championship*

**CLEVELAND vs. HOUSTON**
RS: Browns lead series, 27-20
PS: Oilers lead series, 1-0
1970—Browns, 28-14 (C)
Browns, 21-10 (H)
1971—Browns, 31-0 (C)
Browns, 37-24 (H)
1972—Browns, 23-17 (H)
Browns, 20-0 (C)
1973—Browns, 42-13 (C)
Browns, 23-13 (H)
1974—Browns, 20-7 (C)
Oilers, 28-24 (H)
1975—Oilers, 40-10 (C)
Oilers, 21-10 (H)
1976—Browns, 21-7 (H)
Browns, 13-10 (C)
1977—Browns, 24-23 (H)
Oilers, 19-15 (C)
1978—Oilers, 16-13 (C)
Oilers, 14-10 (H)
1979—Oilers, 31-10 (H)
Browns, 14-7 (C)
1980—Oilers, 16-7 (C)
Browns, 17-14 (H)
1981—Oilers, 9-3 (C)
Oilers, 17-13 (H)
1982—Browns, 20-14 (H)
1983—Browns, 25-19 (C) OT
Oilers, 34-27 (H)
1984—Browns, 27-10 (C)
Browns, 27-20 (H)
1985—Browns, 21-6 (H)
Browns, 28-21 (C)
1986—Browns, 23-20 (H)
Browns, 13-10 (C) OT
1987—Oilers, 15-10 (C)
Browns, 40-7 (H)
1988—Oilers, 24-17 (H)
Browns, 28-23 (C)
*Oilers, 24-23 (C)
1989—Browns, 28-17 (C)
Browns, 24-20 (H)
1990—Oilers, 35-23 (C)
Oilers, 58-14 (H)
1991—Oilers, 28-24 (H)
Oilers, 17-14 (C)
1992—Browns, 24-14 (H)
Oilers, 17-14 (C)
1993—Oilers, 27-20 (C)
Oilers, 19-17 (H)
(RS Pts.—Browns 957, Oilers 845)
(PS Pts.—Oilers 24, Browns 23)
*AFC First-Round Playoff*

**CLEVELAND vs. *INDIANAPOLIS**
RS: Browns lead series, 12-7
PS: Series tied, 2-2
1956—Colts, 21-7 (C)
1959—Browns, 38-31 (B)
1962—Colts, 36-14 (C)
1964—**Browns, 27-0 (C)
1968—Browns, 30-20 (B)
**Colts, 34-0 (C)
1971—Browns, 14-13 (B)
***Colts, 20-3 (C)
1973—Browns, 24-14 (C)
1975—Colts, 21-7 (B)
1978—Browns, 45-24 (B)
1979—Browns, 13-10 (C)
1980—Browns, 28-27 (B)
1981—Browns, 42-28 (C)
1983—Browns, 41-23 (C)
1986—Browns, 24-9 (I)
1987—Colts, 9-7 (C)
***Browns, 38-21 (C)
1988—Browns, 23-17 (C)
1989—Colts, 23-17 (I) OT
1991—Browns, 31-0 (I)
1992—Colts, 14-3 (I)
1993—Colts, 23-10 (I)
(RS Pts.—Browns 418, Colts 363)
(PS Pts.—Colts 75, Browns 68)
*Franchise in Baltimore prior to 1984*
**NFL Championship*
***AFC Divisional Playoff*

**CLEVELAND vs. KANSAS CITY**
RS: Browns lead series, 7-6-2
1971—Chiefs, 13-7 (KC)
1972—Chiefs, 31-7 (C)
1973—Tie, 20-20 (KC)
1975—Browns, 40-14 (C)
1976—Chiefs, 39-14 (KC)
1977—Browns, 44-7 (C)
1978—Chiefs, 17-3 (KC)
1979—Browns, 27-24 (KC)
1980—Browns, 20-13 (C)
1984—Chiefs, 10-6 (KC)
1986—Browns, 20-7 (C)
1988—Browns, 6-3 (KC)
1989—Tie, 10-10 (C) OT
1990—Chiefs, 34-0 (KC)
1991—Browns, 20-15 (C)
(RS Pts.—Chiefs 257, Browns 244)

**CLEVELAND vs. *L.A.RAIDERS**
RS: Raiders lead series, 8-4
PS: Raiders lead series, 2-0
1970—Raiders, 23-20 (O)
1971—Raiders, 34-20 (C)
1973—Browns, 7-3 (O)
1974—Raiders, 40-24 (C)
1975—Raiders, 38-17 (O)
1977—Raiders, 26-10 (C)
1979—Raiders, 19-14 (O)
1980—**Raiders, 14-12 (C)
1982—***Raiders, 27-10 (LA)
1985—Raiders, 21-20 (C)
1986—Raiders, 27-14 (LA)
1987—Browns, 24-17 (LA)
1992—Browns, 28-16 (LA)
1993—Browns, 19-16 (LA)
(RS Pts.—Raiders 280, Browns 217)
(PS Pts.—Raiders 41, Browns 22)
*Franchise in Oakland prior to 1982*
**AFC Divisional Playoff*
***AFC First-Round Playoff*

**CLEVELAND vs. L.A. RAMS**
RS: Browns lead series, 8-7
PS: Browns lead series, 2-1
1950—*Browns, 30-28 (C)
1951—Browns, 38-23 (LA)
*Rams, 24-17 (LA)
1952—Browns, 37-7 (C)
1955—*Browns, 38-14 (LA)
1957—Browns, 45-31 (C)
1958—Browns, 30-27 (LA)
1963—Browns, 20-6 (C)
1965—Rams, 42-7 (LA)
1968—Rams, 24-6 (C)
1973—Rams, 30-17 (LA)
1977—Rams, 9-0 (C)
1978—Browns, 30-19 (C)
1981—Rams, 27-16 (LA)
1984—Rams, 20-17 (LA)
1987—Browns, 30-17 (C)
1990—Rams, 38-23 (C)
1993—Browns, 42-14 (LA)
(RS Pts.—Browns 358, Rams 334)
(PS Pts.—Browns 85, Rams 66)
*NFL Championship*

**CLEVELAND vs. MIAMI**
RS: Dolphins lead series, 6-4
PS: Dolphins lead series, 2-0
1970—Browns, 28-0 (M)
1972—*Dolphins, 20-14 (M)
1973—Dolphins, 17-9 (C)
1976—Browns, 17-13 (C)
1979—Browns, 30-24 (C) OT
1985—*Dolphins, 24-21 (M)
1986—Browns, 26-16 (C)
1988—Dolphins, 38-31 (M)
1989—Dolphins, 13-10 (M) OT
1990—Dolphins, 30-13 (C)
1992—Dolphins, 27-23 (C)
1993—Dolphins, 24-14 (C)
(RS Pts.—Dolphins 202, Browns 201)
(PS Pts.—Dolphins 44, Browns 35)
*AFC Divisional Playoff*

**CLEVELAND vs. MINNESOTA**
RS: Vikings lead series, 7-3
PS: Vikings lead series, 1-0
1965—Vikings, 27-17 (C)
1967—Browns, 14-10 (C)
1969—Vikings, 51-3 (M)
*Vikings, 27-7 (M)
1973—Vikings, 26-3 (M)
1975—Vikings, 42-10 (C)
1980—Vikings, 28-23 (M)
1983—Vikings, 27-21 (C)
1986—Browns, 23-20 (M)
1989—Browns, 23-17 (C) OT
1992—Vikings, 17-13 (M)
(RS Pts.—Vikings 265, Browns 150)
(PS Pts.—Vikings 27, Browns 7)
*NFL Championship*

**CLEVELAND vs. NEW ENGLAND**
RS: Browns lead series, 9-3
1971—Browns, 27-7 (C)
1974—Browns, 21-14 (NE)
1977—Browns, 30-27 (C) OT
1980—Patriots, 34-17 (NE)
1982—Browns, 10-7 (C)
1983—Browns, 30-0 (NE)
1984—Patriots, 17-16 (C)
1985—Browns, 24-20 (C)
1987—Browns, 20-10 (NE)
1991—Browns, 20-0 (NE)
1992—Browns, 19-17 (NE)
1993—Patriots, 20-17 (C)
(RS Pts.—Browns 251, Patriots 173)

**CLEVELAND vs. NEW ORLEANS**
RS: Browns lead series, 9-3
1967—Browns, 42-7 (NO)
1968—Browns, 24-10 (NO)
Browns, 35-17 (C)
1969—Browns, 27-17 (NO)
1971—Browns, 21-17 (NO)
1975—Browns, 17-16 (C)
1978—Browns, 24-16 (NO)
1981—Browns, 20-17 (C)
1984—Saints, 16-14 (C)
1987—Saints, 28-21 (NO)
1990—Saints, 25-20 (NO)
1993—Browns, 17-13 (C)
(RS Pts.—Browns 282, Saints 199)

**CLEVELAND vs. N.Y. GIANTS**
RS: Browns lead series, 25-16-2
PS: Series tied, 1-1
1950—Giants, 6-0 (C)
Giants, 17-13 (NY)
*Browns, 8-3 (C)
1951—Browns, 14-13 (C)
Browns, 10-0 (NY)
1952—Giants, 17-9 (C)
Giants, 37-34 (NY)
1953—Browns, 7-0 (NY)
Browns, 62-14 (C)
1954—Browns, 24-14 (C)
Browns, 16-7 (NY)
1955—Browns, 24-14 (C)
Tie, 35-35 (NY)
1956—Giants, 21-9 (C)
Browns, 24-7 (NY)
1957—Browns, 6-3 (C)
Browns, 34-28 (NY)
1958—Giants, 21-17 (C)
Giants, 13-10 (NY)
*Giants, 10-0 (NY)
1959—Giants, 10-6 (C)
Giants, 48-7 (NY)
1960—Giants, 17-13 (C)
Browns, 48-34 (NY)
1961—Giants, 37-21 (C)
Tie, 7-7 (NY)
1962—Browns, 17-7 (C)
Giants, 17-13 (NY)
1963—Browns, 35-24 (NY)
Giants, 33-6 (C)
1964—Browns, 42-20 (C)
Browns, 52-20 (NY)
1965—Browns, 38-14 (NY)
Browns, 34-21 (C)
1966—Browns, 28-7 (NY)
Browns, 49-40 (C)
1967—Giants, 38-34 (NY)
Browns, 24-14 (C)
1968—Browns, 45-10 (C)
1969—Browns, 28-17 (C)
Giants, 27-14 (NY)
1973—Browns, 12-10 (C)
1977—Browns, 21-7 (NY)
1985—Browns, 35-33 (NY)
1991—Giants, 13-10 (NY)
(RS Pts.—Browns 987, Giants 792)
(PS Pts.—Giants 13, Browns 8)
*Conference Playoff*

**CLEVELAND vs. N.Y. JETS**
RS: Browns lead series, 8-6
PS: Browns lead series, 1-0
1970—Browns, 31-21 (C)
1972—Browns, 26-10 (NY)
1976—Browns, 38-17 (C)
1978—Browns, 37-34 (C) OT
1979—Browns, 25-22 (NY) OT
1980—Browns, 17-14 (C)
1981—Jets, 14-13 (C)
1983—Browns, 10-7 (C)
1984—Jets, 24-20 (C)
1985—Jets, 37-10 (NY)
1986—*Browns, 23-20 (C) OT
1988—Jets, 23-3 (C)
1989—Browns, 38-24 (C)
1990—Jets, 24-21 (NY)
1991—Jets, 17-14 (C)
(RS Pts.—Browns 303, Jets 288)
(PS Pts.—Browns 23, Jets 20)
*AFC Divisional Playoff*

**CLEVELAND vs. PHILADELPHIA**
RS: Browns lead series, 30-12-1
1950—Browns, 35-10 (P)
Browns, 13-7 (C)
1951—Browns, 20-17 (C)
Browns, 24-9 (P)
1952—Browns, 49-7 (P)
Eagles, 28-20 (C)
1953—Browns, 37-13 (C)
Eagles, 42-27 (P)
1954—Eagles, 28-10 (P)
Browns, 6-0 (C)
1955—Browns, 21-17 (C)
Eagles, 33-17 (P)
1956—Browns, 16-0 (P)
Browns, 17-14 (C)
1957—Browns, 24-7 (C)
Eagles, 17-7 (P)
1958—Browns, 28-14 (C)
Browns, 21-14 (P)
1959—Browns, 28-7 (C)
Browns, 28-21 (P)
1960—Browns, 41-24 (P)
Eagles, 31-29 (C)
1961—Eagles, 27-20 (P)
Browns, 45-24 (C)
1962—Eagles, 35-7 (P)
Tie, 14-14 (C)

1963—Browns, 37-7 (C)
Browns, 23-17 (P)
1964—Browns, 28-20 (P)
Browns, 38-24 (C)
1965—Browns, 35-17 (P)
Browns, 38-34 (C)
1966—Browns, 27-7 (C)
Eagles, 33-21 (P)
1967—Eagles, 28-24 (P)
1968—Browns, 47-13 (C)
1969—Browns, 27-20 (P)
1972—Browns, 27-17 (P)
1976—Browns, 24-3 (C)
1979—Browns, 24-19 (P)
1982—Eagles, 24-21 (C)
1988—Browns, 19-3 (C)
1991—Eagles, 32-30 (C)
(RS Pts.—Browns 1,094, Eagles 778)

**CLEVELAND vs. PITTSBURGH**
RS: Browns lead series, 52-36
1950—Browns, 30-17 (P)
Browns, 45-7 (C)
1951—Browns, 17-0 (C)
Browns, 28-0 (P)
1952—Browns, 21-20 (P)
Browns, 29-28 (C)
1953—Browns, 34-16 (C)
Browns, 20-16 (P)
1954—Steelers, 55-27 (P)
Browns, 42-7 (C)
1955—Browns, 41-14 (C)
Browns, 30-7 (P)
1956—Browns, 14-10 (P)
Steelers, 24-16 (C)
1957—Browns, 23-12 (P)
Browns, 24-0 (C)
1958—Browns, 45-12 (P)
Browns, 27-10 (C)
1959—Steelers, 17-7 (P)
Steelers, 21-20 (C)
1960—Browns, 28-20 (C)
Steelers, 14-10 (P)
1961—Browns, 30-28 (P)
Steelers, 17-13 (C)
1962—Browns, 41-14 (P)
Browns, 35-14 (C)
1963—Browns, 35-23 (C)
Steelers, 9-7 (P)
1964—Steelers, 23-7 (C)
Browns, 30-17 (P)
1965—Browns, 24-19 (C)
Browns, 42-21 (P)
1966—Browns, 41-10 (C)
Steelers, 16-6 (P)
1967—Browns, 21-10 (C)
Browns, 34-14 (P)
1968—Browns, 31-24 (C)
Browns, 45-24 (P)
1969—Browns, 42-31 (C)
Browns, 24-3 (P)
1970—Browns, 15-7 (C)
Steelers, 28-9 (P)
1971—Browns, 27-17 (C)
Steelers, 26-9 (P)
1972—Browns, 26-24 (C)
Steelers, 30-0 (P)
1973—Steelers, 33-6 (P)
Browns, 21-16 (C)
1974—Steelers, 20-16 (P)
Steelers, 26-16 (C)
1975—Steelers, 42-6 (C)
Steelers, 31-17 (P)
1976—Steelers, 31-14 (P)
Browns, 18-16 (C)
1977—Steelers, 28-14 (C)
Steelers, 35-31 (P)
1978—Steelers, 15-9 (P) OT
Steelers, 34-14 (C)
1979—Steelers, 51-35 (C)
Steelers, 33-30 (P) OT
1980—Browns, 27-26 (C)
Steelers, 16-13 (P)
1981—Steelers, 13-7 (P)
Steelers, 32-10 (C)
1982—Browns, 10-9 (C)
Steelers, 37-21 (P)
1983—Steelers, 44-17 (P)
Browns, 30-17 (C)
1984—Browns, 20-10 (C)
Steelers, 23-20 (P)
1985—Browns, 17-7 (C)
Steelers, 10-9 (P)
1986—Browns, 27-24 (P)
Browns, 37-31 (C) OT
1987—Browns, 34-10 (C)
Browns, 19-13 (P)
1988—Browns, 23-9 (P)
Browns, 27-7 (C)
1989—Browns, 51-0 (P)
Steelers, 17-7 (C)
1990—Browns, 13-3 (C)
Steelers, 35-0 (P)
1991—Browns, 17-14 (C)
Steelers, 17-10 (P)
1992—Browns, 17-9 (C)
Steelers, 23-13 (P)
1993—Browns, 28-23 (C)
Steelers, 16-9 (P)
(RS Pts.—Browns 1,952, Steelers 1,682)

**CLEVELAND vs. SAN DIEGO**
RS: Chargers lead series, 8-6-1
1970—Chargers, 27-10 (C)
1972—Browns, 21-17 (SD)
1973—Tie, 16-16 (C)
1974—Chargers, 36-35 (SD)
1976—Browns, 21-17 (C)
1977—Chargers, 37-14 (SD)
1981—Chargers, 44-14 (C)
1982—Chargers, 30-13 (C)
1983—Browns, 30-24 (SD) OT
1985—Browns, 21-7 (SD)
1986—Browns, 47-17 (C)
1987—Chargers, 27-24 (SD) OT
1990—Chargers, 24-14 (C)
1991—Browns, 30-24 (SD) OT
1992—Chargers, 14-13 (C)
(RS Pts.—Chargers 361, Browns 323)

**CLEVELAND vs. SAN FRANCISCO**
RS: Browns lead series, 9-6
1950—Browns, 34-14 (C)
1951—49ers, 24-10 (SF)
1953—Browns, 23-21 (C)
1955—Browns, 38-3 (SF)
1959—49ers, 21-20 (C)
1962—Browns, 13-10 (SF)
1968—Browns, 33-21 (SF)
1970—49ers, 34-31 (SF)
1974—Browns, 7-0 (C)
1978—Browns, 24-7 (C)
1981—Browns, 15-12 (SF)
1984—49ers, 41-7 (C)
1987—49ers, 38-24 (SF)
1990—49ers, 20-17 (SF)
1993—Browns, 23-13 (C)
(RS Pts.—Browns 319, 49ers 279)

**CLEVELAND vs. SEATTLE**
RS: Seahawks lead series, 9-3
1977—Seahawks, 20-19 (S)
1978—Seahawks, 47-24 (S)
1979—Seahawks, 29-24 (C)
1980—Browns, 27-3 (S)
1981—Seahawks, 42-21 (S)
1982—Browns, 21-7 (S)
1983—Seahawks, 24-9 (C)
1984—Seahawks, 33-0 (S)
1985—Seahawks, 31-13 (S)
1988—Seahawks, 16-10 (C)
1989—Browns, 17-7 (S)
1993—Seahawks, 22-5 (S)
(RS Pts.—Seahawks 281, Browns 190)

**CLEVELAND vs. TAMPA BAY**
RS: Browns lead series, 4-0
1976—Browns, 24-7 (TB)
1980—Browns, 34-27 (TB)
1983—Browns, 20-0 (C)
1989—Browns, 42-31 (TB)
(RS Pts.—Browns 120, Buccaneers 65)

**CLEVELAND vs. WASHINGTON**
RS: Browns lead series, 32-9-1
1950—Browns, 20-14 (C)
Browns, 45-21 (W)
1951—Browns, 45-0 (C)
1952—Browns, 19-15 (C)
Browns, 48-24 (W)
1953—Browns, 30-14 (W)
Browns, 27-3 (C)
1954—Browns, 62-3 (C)
Browns, 34-14 (W)
1955—Redskins, 27-17 (C)
Browns, 24-14 (W)
1956—Redskins, 20-9 (W)
Redskins, 20-17 (C)
1957—Browns, 21-17 (C)
Tie, 30-30 (W)
1958—Browns, 20-10 (W)
Browns, 21-14 (C)
1959—Browns, 34-7 (C)
Browns, 31-17 (W)
1960—Browns, 31-10 (W)
Browns, 27-16 (C)
1961—Browns, 31-7 (C)
Browns, 17-6 (W)
1962—Redskins, 17-16 (C)
Redskins, 17-9 (W)
1963—Browns, 37-14 (C)
Browns, 27-20 (W)
1964—Browns, 27-13 (W)
Browns, 34-24 (C)
1965—Browns, 17-7 (W)
Browns, 24-16 (C)
1966—Browns, 38-14 (W)
Browns, 14-3 (C)
1967—Browns, 42-37 (C)
1968—Browns, 24-21 (W)
1969—Browns, 27-23 (C)
1971—Browns, 20-13 (W)
1975—Redskins, 23-7 (C)
1979—Redskins, 13-9 (C)
1985—Redskins, 14-7 (C)
1988—Browns, 17-13 (W)
1991—Redskins, 42-17 (W)
(RS Pts.—Browns 1,073, Redskins 667)

---

**DALLAS vs. ARIZONA**
RS: Cowboys lead series, 40-22-1;
See Arizona vs. Dallas

**DALLAS vs. ATLANTA**
RS: Cowboys lead series, 9-6
PS: Cowboys lead series, 2-0;
See Atlanta vs. Dallas

**DALLAS vs. BUFFALO**
RS: Cowboys lead series, 3-2
PS: Cowboys lead series, 2-0;
See Buffalo vs. Dallas

**DALLAS vs. CHICAGO**
RS: Cowboys lead series, 8-6
PS: Cowboys lead series, 2-0;
See Chicago vs. Dallas

**DALLAS vs. CINCINNATI**
RS: Cowboys lead series, 3-2;
See Cincinnati vs. Dallas

**DALLAS vs. CLEVELAND**
RS: Browns lead series, 14-9
PS: Browns lead series, 2-1;
See Cleveland vs. Dallas

**DALLAS vs. DENVER**
RS: Cowboys lead series, 3-2
PS: Cowboys lead series, 1-0
1973—Cowboys, 22-10 (Den)
1977—Cowboys, 14-6 (Dal)
*Cowboys, 27-10 (New Orleans)
1980—Broncos, 41-20 (Den)
1986—Broncos, 29-14 (Den)
1992—Cowboys, 31-27 (Den)
(RS Pts.—Broncos 113, Cowboys 101)
(PS Pts.—Cowboys 27, Broncos 10)
**Super Bowl XII*

**DALLAS vs. DETROIT**
RS: Cowboys lead series, 7-5
PS: Series tied, 1-1
1960—Lions, 23-14 (Det)
1963—Cowboys, 17-14 (Dal)
1968—Cowboys, 59-13 (Dal)
1970—*Cowboys, 5-0 (Dal)
1972—Cowboys, 28-24 (Dal)
1975—Cowboys, 36-10 (Det)
1977—Cowboys, 37-0 (Dal)
1981—Lions, 27-24 (Det)
1985—Lions, 26-21 (Det)
1986—Cowboys, 31-7 (Det)
1987—Lions, 27-17 (Det)
1991—Lions, 34-10 (Det)
*Lions, 38-6 (Det)
1992—Cowboys, 37-3 (Det)
(RS Pts.—Cowboys 331, Lions 208)
(PS Pts.—Lions 38, Cowboys 11)
**NFC Divisional Playoff*

**DALLAS vs. GREEN BAY**
RS: Packers lead series, 8-6
PS: Series tied, 2-2
1960—Packers, 41-7 (GB)
1964—Packers, 45-21 (D)
1965—Packers, 13-3 (Mil)
1966—*Packers, 34-27 (D)
1967—*Packers, 21-17 (GB)
1968—Packers, 28-17 (D)
1970—Cowboys, 16-3 (D)
1972—Packers, 16-13 (Mil)
1975—Packers, 19-17 (D)
1978—Cowboys, 42-14 (Mil)
1980—Cowboys, 28-7 (Mil)
1982—**Cowboys, 37-26 (D)
1984—Cowboys, 20-6 (D)
1989—Packers, 31-13 (GB)
Packers, 20-10 (D)
1991—Cowboys, 20-17 (Mil)
1993—Cowboys, 36-14 (D)
***Cowboys, 27-17 (D)
(RS Pts.—Packers 274, Cowboys 263)
(PS Pts.—Cowboys 108, Packers 98)
**NFL Championship*
***NFC Second-Round Playoff*
****NFC Divisional Playoff*

**DALLAS vs. HOUSTON**
RS: Cowboys lead series, 4-3
1970—Cowboys, 52-10 (D)
1974—Cowboys, 10-0 (H)
1979—Oilers, 30-24 (D)
1982—Cowboys, 37-7 (H)
1985—Cowboys, 17-10 (H)
1988—Oilers, 25-17 (D)
1991—Oilers, 26-23 (H) OT
(RS Pts.—Cowboys 180, Oilers 108)

**DALLAS vs. *INDIANAPOLIS**
RS: Cowboys lead series, 7-2
PS: Colts lead series, 1-0
1960—Colts, 45-7 (D)
1967—Colts, 23-17 (B)
1969—Cowboys, 27-10 (D)
1970—**Colts, 16-13 (Miami)
1972—Cowboys, 21-0 (B)
1976—Cowboys, 30-27 (D)
1978—Cowboys, 38-0 (D)
1981—Cowboys, 37-13 (B)
1984—Cowboys, 22-3 (D)
1993—Cowboys, 27-3 (I)
(RS Pts.—Cowboys 226, Colts 124)
(PS Pts.—Colts 16, Cowboys 13)
**Franchise in Baltimore prior to 1984*
***Super Bowl V*

**DALLAS vs. KANSAS CITY**
RS: Cowboys lead series, 3-2
1970—Cowboys, 27-16 (KC)
1975—Chiefs, 34-31 (D)
1983—Cowboys, 41-21 (D)
1989—Chiefs, 36-28 (KC)
1992—Cowboys, 17-10 (D)
(RS Pts.—Cowboys 144, Chiefs 117)

**DALLAS vs. *L.A. RAIDERS**
RS: Raiders lead series, 3-2
1974—Raiders, 27-23 (O)
1980—Cowboys, 19-13 (O)

1983—Raiders, 40-38 (D)
1986—Raiders, 17-13 (D)
1992—Cowboys, 28-13 (LA)
(RS Pts.—Cowboys 121, Raiders 110)
*Franchise in Oakland prior to 1982*

**DALLAS vs. L.A. RAMS**
RS: Rams lead series, 9-8
PS: Series tied, 4-4
1960—Rams, 38-13 (D)
1962—Cowboys, 27-17 (LA)
1967—Rams, 35-13 (D)
1969—Rams, 24-23 (LA)
1971—Cowboys, 28-21 (D)
1973—Rams, 37-31 (LA)
*Cowboys, 27-16 (D)
1975—Cowboys, 18-7 (D)
**Cowboys, 37-7 (LA)
1976—*Rams, 14-12 (D)
1978—Rams, 27-14 (LA)
**Cowboys, 28-0 (LA)
1979—Cowboys, 30-6 (D)
*Rams, 21-19 (D)
1980—Rams, 38-14 (LA)
***Cowboys, 34-13 (D)
1981—Cowboys, 29-17 (D)
1983—***Rams, 24-17 (D)
1984—Cowboys, 20-13 (LA)
1985—*Rams, 20-0 (LA)
1986—Rams, 29-10 (LA)
1987—Cowboys, 29-21 (LA)
1989—Rams, 35-31 (D)
1990—Cowboys, 24-21 (LA)
1992—Rams, 27-23 (D)
(RS Pts.—Rams 413, Cowboys 377)
(PS Pts.—Cowboys 174, Rams 115)
**NFC Divisional Playoff*
***NFC Championship*
***NFC First-Round Playoff

**DALLAS vs. MIAMI**
RS: Dolphins lead series, 6-1
PS: Cowboys lead series, 1-0
1971—*Cowboys, 24-3 (New Orleans)
1973—Dolphins, 14-7 (D)
1978—Dolphins, 23-16 (M)
1981—Cowboys, 28-27 (D)
1984—Dolphins, 28-21 (M)
1987—Dolphins, 20-14 (D)
1989—Dolphins, 17-14 (D)
1993—Dolphins, 16-14 (D)
(RS Pts.—Dolphins 145, Cowboys 114)
(PS Pts.—Cowboys 24, Dolphins 3)
**Super Bowl VI*

**DALLAS vs. MINNESOTA**
RS: Cowboys lead series, 8-6
PS: Cowboys lead series, 3-1
1961—Cowboys, 21-7 (D)
Cowboys, 28-0 (M)
1966—Cowboys, 28-17 (D)
1968—Cowboys, 20-7 (M)
1970—Vikings, 54-13 (M)
1971—*Cowboys, 20-12 (M)
1973—**Vikings, 27-10 (D)
1974—Vikings, 23-21 (D)
1975—*Cowboys, 17-14 (M)
1977—Cowboys, 16-10 (M) OT
**Cowboys, 23-6 (D)
1978—Vikings, 21-10 (D)
1979—Cowboys, 36-20 (M)
1982—Vikings, 31-27 (M)
1983—Cowboys, 37-24 (M)
1987—Vikings, 44-38 (D) OT
1988—Vikings, 43-3 (D)
1993—Cowboys, 37-20 (M)
(RS Pts.—Cowboys 335, Vikings 321)
(PS Pts.—Cowboys 70, Vikings 59)
**NFC Divisional Playoff*
***NFC Championship*

**DALLAS vs. NEW ENGLAND**
RS: Cowboys lead series, 6-0
1971—Cowboys, 44-21 (D)
1975—Cowboys, 34-31 (NE)
1978—Cowboys, 17-10 (D)
1981—Cowboys, 35-21 (NE)
1984—Cowboys, 20-17 (D)
1987—Cowboys, 23-17 (NE) OT
(RS Pts.—Cowboys 173, Patriots 117)

**DALLAS vs. NEW ORLEANS**
RS: Cowboys lead series, 13-3
1967—Cowboys, 14-10 (D)
Cowboys, 27-10 (NO)
1968—Cowboys, 17-3 (NO)
1969—Cowboys, 21-17 (NO)
Cowboys, 33-17 (D)
1971—Saints, 24-14 (NO)
1973—Cowboys, 40-3 (D)
1976—Cowboys, 24-6 (NO)
1978—Cowboys, 27-7 (D)
1982—Cowboys, 21-7 (D)
1983—Cowboys, 21-20 (D)
1984—Cowboys, 30-27 (D) OT
1988—Saints, 20-17 (NO)
1989—Saints, 28-0 (NO)
1990—Cowboys, 17-13 (D)
1991—Cowboys, 23-14 (D)
(RS Pts.—Cowboys 346, Saints 226)

**DALLAS vs. N.Y. GIANTS**
RS: Cowboys lead series, 40-21-2
1960—Tie, 31-31 (NY)
1961—Giants, 31-10 (D)
Cowboys, 17-16 (NY)
1962—Giants, 41-10 (D)
Giants, 41-31 (NY)
1963—Giants, 37-21 (NY)
Giants, 34-27 (D)
1964—Tie, 13-13 (D)
Cowboys, 31-21 (NY)
1965—Cowboys, 31-2 (D)
Cowboys, 38-20 (NY)
1966—Cowboys, 52-7 (D)
Cowboys, 17-7 (NY)
1967—Cowboys, 38-24 (D)
1968—Giants, 27-21 (D)
Cowboys, 28-10 (NY)
1969—Cowboys, 25-3 (D)
1970—Cowboys, 28-10 (D)
Giants, 23-20 (NY)
1971—Cowboys, 20-13 (D)
Cowboys, 42-14 (NY)
1972—Cowboys, 23-14 (NY)
Giants, 23-3 (D)
1973—Cowboys, 45-28 (D)
Cowboys, 23-10 (New Haven)
1974—Giants, 14-6 (D)
Cowboys, 21-7 (New Haven)
1975—Cowboys, 13-7 (NY)
Cowboys, 14-3 (D)
1976—Cowboys, 24-14 (NY)
Cowboys, 9-3 (D)
1977—Cowboys, 41-21 (D)
Cowboys, 24-10 (NY)
1978—Cowboys, 34-24 (NY)
Cowboys, 24-3 (D)
1979—Cowboys, 16-14 (NY)
Cowboys, 28-7 (D)
1980—Cowboys, 24-3 (D)
Giants, 38-35 (NY)
1981—Cowboys, 18-10 (D)
Giants, 13-10 (NY) OT
1983—Cowboys, 28-13 (D)
Cowboys, 38-20 (NY)
1984—Giants, 28-7 (NY)
Giants, 19-7 (D)
1985—Cowboys, 30-29 (NY)
Cowboys, 28-21 (D)
1986—Cowboys, 31-28 (D)
Giants, 17-14 (NY)
1987—Cowboys, 16-14 (NY)
Cowboys, 33-24 (D)
1988—Giants, 12-10 (D)
Giants, 29-21 (NY)
1989—Giants, 30-13 (D)
Giants, 15-0 (NY)
1990—Giants, 28-7 (D)
Giants, 31-17 (NY)
1991—Cowboys, 21-16 (D)
Giants, 22-9 (NY)
1992—Cowboys, 34-28 (NY)
Cowboys, 30-3 (D)
1993—Cowboys, 31-9 (D)
Cowboys, 16-13 (NY) OT
(RS Pts.—Cowboys 1,427, Giants 1,140)

**DALLAS vs. N.Y. JETS**
RS: Cowboys lead series, 5-1
1971—Cowboys, 52-10 (D)
1975—Cowboys, 31-21 (NY)
1978—Cowboys, 30-7 (NY)
1987—Cowboys, 38-24 (NY)
1990—Jets, 24-9 (NY)
1993—Cowboys, 28-7 (NY)
(RS Pts.—Cowboys 188, Jets 93)

**DALLAS vs. PHILADELPHIA**
RS: Cowboys lead series, 40-26
PS: Series tied, 1-1
1960—Eagles, 27-25 (D)
1961—Eagles, 43-7 (D)
Eagles, 35-13 (P)
1962—Cowboys, 41-19 (D)
Eagles, 28-14 (P)
1963—Eagles, 24-21 (P)
Cowboys, 27-20 (D)
1964—Eagles, 17-14 (D)
Eagles, 24-14 (P)
1965—Eagles, 35-24 (D)
Cowboys, 21-19 (P)
1966—Cowboys, 56-7 (D)
Eagles, 24-23 (P)
1967—Eagles, 21-14 (P)
Cowboys, 38-17 (D)
1968—Cowboys, 45-13 (P)
Cowboys, 34-14 (D)
1969—Cowboys, 38-7 (P)
Cowboys, 49-14 (D)
1970—Cowboys, 17-7 (P)
Cowboys, 21-17 (D)
1971—Cowboys, 42-7 (P)
Cowboys, 20-7 (D)
1972—Cowboys, 28-6 (D)
Cowboys, 28-7 (P)
1973—Eagles, 30-16 (P)
Cowboys, 31-10 (D)
1974—Eagles, 13-10 (P)
Cowboys, 31-24 (D)
1975—Cowboys, 20-17 (P)
Cowboys, 27-17 (D)
1976—Cowboys, 27-7 (D)
Cowboys, 26-7 (P)
1977—Cowboys, 16-10 (P)
Cowboys, 24-14 (D)
1978—Cowboys, 14-7 (D)
Cowboys, 31-13 (P)
1979—Eagles, 31-21 (D)
Cowboys, 24-17 (P)
1980—Eagles, 17-10 (P)
Cowboys, 35-27 (D)
*Eagles, 20-7 (P)
1981—Cowboys, 17-14 (P)
Cowboys, 21-10 (D)
1982—Eagles, 24-20 (D)
1983—Cowboys, 37-7 (D)
Cowboys, 27-20 (P)
1984—Cowboys, 23-17 (D)
Cowboys, 26-10 (P)
1985—Eagles, 16-14 (P)
Cowboys, 34-17 (D)
1986—Cowboys, 17-14 (P)
Eagles, 23-21 (D)
1987—Cowboys, 41-22 (D)
Eagles, 37-20 (P)
1988—Eagles, 24-23 (P)
Eagles, 23-7 (D)
1989—Eagles, 27-0 (D)
Eagles, 20-10 (P)
1990—Eagles, 21-20 (D)
Eagles, 17-3 (P)
1991—Eagles, 24-0 (D)
Cowboys, 25-13 (P)
1992—Eagles, 31-7 (P)
Cowboys, 20-10 (D)
**Cowboys, 34-10 (D)
1993—Cowboys, 23-10 (P)
Cowboys, 23-17 (D)
(RS Pts.—Cowboys 1,516, Eagles 1,188)
(PS Pts.—Cowboys 41, Eagles 30)
**NFC Championship*
***NFC Divisional Playoff*

**DALLAS vs. PITTSBURGH**
RS: Cowboys lead series, 12-11
PS: Steelers lead series, 2-0
1960—Steelers, 35-28 (D)
1961—Cowboys, 27-24 (D)
Steelers, 37-7 (P)
1962—Steelers, 30-28 (D)
Cowboys, 42-27 (P)
1963—Steelers, 27-21 (P)
Steelers, 24-19 (D)
1964—Steelers, 23-17 (P)
Cowboys, 17-14 (D)
1965—Steelers, 22-13 (P)
Cowboys, 24-17 (D)
1966—Cowboys, 52-21 (D)
Cowboys, 20-7 (P)
1967—Cowboys, 24-21 (P)
1968—Cowboys, 28-7 (D)
1969—Cowboys, 10-7 (P)
1972—Cowboys, 17-13 (D)
1975—*Steelers, 21-17 (Miami)
1977—Steelers, 28-13 (P)
1978—**Steelers, 35-31 (Miami)
1979—Steelers, 14-3 (P)
1982—Steelers, 36-28 (D)
1985—Cowboys, 27-13 (D)
1988—Steelers, 24-21 (P)
1991—Cowboys, 20-10 (D)
(RS Pts.—Cowboys 506, Steelers 481)
(PS Pts.—Steelers 56, Cowboys 48)
**Super Bowl X*
***Super Bowl XIII*

**DALLAS vs. SAN DIEGO**
RS: Cowboys lead series, 4-1
1972—Cowboys, 34-28 (SD)
1980—Cowboys, 42-31 (D)
1983—Chargers, 24-23 (SD)
1986—Cowboys, 24-21 (SD)
1990—Cowboys, 17-14 (D)
(RS Pts.—Cowboys 140, Chargers 118)

**DALLAS vs. SAN FRANCISCO**
RS: 49ers lead series, 9-6-1
PS: Cowboys lead series, 5-1
1960—49ers, 26-14 (D)
1963—49ers, 31-24 (SF)
1965—Cowboys, 39-31 (D)
1967—49ers, 24-16 (SF)
1969—Tie, 24-24 (D)
1970—*Cowboys, 17-10 (SF)
1971—*Cowboys, 14-3 (D)
1972—49ers, 31-10 (D)
**Cowboys, 30-28 (SF)
1974—Cowboys, 20-14 (D)
1977—Cowboys, 42-35 (SF)
1979—Cowboys, 21-13 (SF)
1980—Cowboys, 59-14 (D)
1981—49ers, 45-14 (SF)
*49ers, 28-27 (SF)
1983—49ers, 42-17 (SF)
1985—49ers, 31-16 (SF)
1989—49ers, 31-14 (D)
1990—49ers, 24-6 (D)
1992—**Cowboys, 30-20 (SF)
1993—Cowboys, 26-17 (D)
*Cowboys, 38-21 (D)
(RS Pts.—49ers 433, Cowboys 362)
(PS Pts.—Cowboys 156, 49ers 110)
**NFC Championship*
***NFC Divisional Playoff*

**DALLAS vs. SEATTLE**
RS: Cowboys lead series, 4-1
1976—Cowboys, 28-13 (S)
1980—Cowboys, 51-7 (D)
1983—Cowboys, 35-10 (S)
1986—Seahawks, 31-14 (D)
1992—Cowboys, 27-0 (D)
(RS Pts.—Cowboys 155, Seahawks 61)

**DALLAS vs. TAMPA BAY**
RS: Cowboys lead series, 6-0
PS: Cowboys lead series, 2-0
1977—Cowboys, 23-7 (D)
1980—Cowboys, 28-17 (D)
1981—*Cowboys, 38-0 (D)
1982—Cowboys, 14-9 (D)
**Cowboys, 30-17 (D)
1983—Cowboys, 27-24 (D) OT
1990—Cowboys, 14-10 (D)
Cowboys, 17-13 (TB)
(RS Pts.—Cowboys 123, Buccaneers 80)
(PS Pts.—Cowboys 68, Buccaneers 17)
*NFC Divisional Playoff*
***NFC First-Round Playoff*

**DALLAS vs. WASHINGTON**
RS: Cowboys lead series, 37-27-2
PS: Redskins lead series, 2-0
1960—Redskins, 26-14 (W)
1961—Tie, 28-28 (D)
Redskins, 34-24 (W)
1962—Tie, 35-35 (D)
Cowboys, 38-10 (W)
1963—Redskins, 21-17 (W)
Cowboys, 35-20 (D)
1964—Cowboys, 24-18 (D)
Redskins, 28-16 (W)
1965—Cowboys, 27-7 (D)
Redskins, 34-31 (W)
1966—Cowboys, 31-30 (W)
Redskins, 34-31 (D)
1967—Cowboys, 17-14 (W)
Redskins, 27-20 (D)
1968—Cowboys, 44-24 (W)
Cowboys, 29-20 (D)
1969—Cowboys, 41-28 (W)
Cowboys, 20-10 (D)
1970—Cowboys, 45-21 (W)
Cowboys, 34-0 (D)
1971—Redskins, 20-16 (D)
Cowboys, 13-0 (W)
1972—Redskins, 24-20 (W)
Cowboys, 34-24 (D)
*Redskins, 26-3 (W)
1973—Redskins, 14-7 (W)
Cowboys, 27-7 (D)
1974—Redskins, 28-21 (W)
Cowboys, 24-23 (D)
1975—Redskins, 30-24 (W) OT
Cowboys, 31-10 (D)
1976—Cowboys, 20-7 (W)
Redskins, 27-14 (D)
1977—Cowboys, 34-16 (D)
Cowboys, 14-7 (W)
1978—Redskins, 9-5 (W)
Cowboys, 37-10 (D)
1979—Redskins, 34-20 (W)
Cowboys, 35-34 (D)
1980—Cowboys, 17-3 (W)
Cowboys, 14-10 (D)
1981—Cowboys, 26-10 (W)
Cowboys, 24-10 (D)
1982—Cowboys, 24-10 (W)
*Redskins, 31-17 (W)
1983—Cowboys, 31-30 (W)
Redskins, 31-10 (D)
1984—Redskins, 34-14 (W)
Redskins, 30-28 (D)
1985—Cowboys, 44-14 (D)
Cowboys, 13-7 (W)
1986—Cowboys, 30-6 (D)
Redskins, 41-14 (W)
1987—Redskins, 13-7 (D)
Redskins, 24-20 (W)
1988—Redskins, 35-17 (D)
Cowboys, 24-17 (W)
1989—Redskins, 30-7 (D)
Cowboys, 13-3 (W)
1990—Redskins, 19-15 (W)
Cowboys, 27-17 (D)
1991—Redskins, 33-31 (D)
Cowboys, 24-21 (W)
1992—Cowboys, 23-10 (D)
Redskins, 20-17 (W)
1993—Redskins, 35-16 (W)
Cowboys, 38-3 (D)
(RS Pts.—Cowboys, 1,565, Redskins 1,309)
(PS Pts.—Redskins 57, Cowboys 20)
*NFC Championship*

---

**DENVER vs. ARIZONA**
RS: Broncos lead series, 3-0-1;
See Arizona vs. Denver

**DENVER vs. ATLANTA**
RS: Broncos lead series, 4-3;
See Atlanta vs. Denver

**DENVER vs. BUFFALO**
RS: Bills lead series, 16-10-1
PS: Bills lead series, 1-0;
See Buffalo vs. Denver

**DENVER vs. CHICAGO**
RS: Series tied, 5-5;
See Chicago vs. Denver

**DENVER vs. CINCINNATI**
RS: Broncos lead series, 10-6;
See Cincinnati vs. Denver

**DENVER vs. CLEVELAND**
RS: Broncos lead series, 12-5
PS: Broncos lead series, 3-0;
See Cleveland vs. Denver

**DENVER vs. DALLAS**
RS: Cowboys lead series, 3-2
PS: Cowboys lead series, 1-0;
See Dallas vs. Denver

**DENVER vs. DETROIT**
RS: Broncos lead series, 4-3
1971—Lions, 24-20 (Den)
1974—Broncos, 31-27 (Det)
1978—Lions, 17-14 (Det)
1981—Broncos, 27-21 (Den)
1984—Broncos, 28-7 (Det)
1987—Broncos, 34-0 (Den)
1990—Lions, 40-27 (Det)
(RS Pts.—Broncos 181, Lions 136)

**DENVER vs. GREEN BAY**
RS: Broncos lead series, 4-2-1
1971—Packers, 34-13 (Mil)
1975—Broncos, 23-13 (D)
1978—Broncos, 16-3 (D)
1984—Broncos, 17-14 (D)
1987—Tie, 17-17 (Mil) OT
1990—Broncos, 22-13 (D)
1993—Packers, 30-27 (GB)
(RS Pts.—Broncos 135, Packers 124)

**DENVER vs. HOUSTON**
RS: Oilers lead series, 19-11-1
PS: Broncos lead series, 2-1
1960—Oilers, 45-25 (D)
Oilers, 20 10 (H)
1961—Oilers, 55-14 (D)
Oilers, 45-14 (H)
1962—Broncos, 20-10 (D)
Oilers, 34-17 (H)
1963—Oilers, 20-14 (H)
Oilers, 33-24 (D)
1964—Oilers, 38-17 (D)
Oilers, 34-15 (H)
1965—Broncos, 28-17 (D)
Broncos, 31-21 (H)
1966—Oilers, 45-7 (H)
Broncos, 40-38 (D)
1967—Oilers, 10-6 (H)
Oilers, 20-18 (D)
1968—Oilers, 38-17 (H)
1969—Oilers, 24-21 (H)
Tie, 20-20 (D)
1970—Oilers, 31-21 (H)
1972—Broncos, 30-17 (D)
1973—Broncos, 48-20 (H)
1974—Broncos, 37-14 (D)
1976—Oilers, 17-3 (H)
1977—Broncos, 24-14 (H)
1979—*Oilers, 13-7 (H)
1980—Oilers, 20-16 (D)
1983—Broncos, 26-14 (H)
1985—Broncos, 31-20 (D)
1987—Oilers, 40-10 (D)
**Broncos, 34-10 (D)
1991—Oilers, 42-14 (H)
**Broncos, 26-24 (D)
1992—Broncos, 27-21 (D)
(RS Pts.—Oilers 837, Broncos 645)
(PS Pts.—Broncos 67, Oilers 47)
*AFC First-Round Playoff*
***AFC Divisional Playoff*

**DENVER vs. *INDIANAPOLIS**
RS: Broncos lead series, 9-2
1974—Broncos, 17-6 (B)
1977—Broncos, 27-13 (D)
1978—Colts, 7-6 (B)
1981—Broncos, 28-10 (D)
1983—Broncos, 17-10 (B)
Broncos, 21-19 (D)
1985—Broncos, 15-10 (I)
1988—Colts, 55-23 (I)
1989—Broncos, 14-3 (D)
1990—Broncos, 27-17 (I)
1993—Broncos, 35-13 (D)
(RS Pts.—Broncos 230, Colts 163)
*Franchise in Baltimore prior to 1984*

**DENVER vs. *KANSAS CITY**
RS: Chiefs lead series, 38-29
1960—Texans, 17-14 (D)
Texans, 34-7 (Dal)
1961—Texans, 19-12 (D)
Texans, 49-21 (Dal)
1962—Texans, 24-3 (D)
Texans, 17-10 (Dal)
1963—Chiefs, 59-7 (D)
Chiefs, 52-21 (KC)
1964—Broncos, 33-27 (D)
Chiefs, 49-39 (KC)
1965—Chiefs, 31-23 (D)
Chiefs, 45-35 (KC)
1966—Chiefs, 37-10 (KC)
Chiefs, 56-10 (D)
1967—Chiefs, 52-9 (KC)
Chiefs, 38-24 (D)
1968—Chiefs, 34-2 (KC)
Chiefs, 30-7 (D)
1969—Chiefs, 26-13 (D)
Chiefs, 31-17 (KC)
1970—Broncos, 26-13 (D)
Chiefs, 16-0 (KC)
1971—Chiefs, 16-3 (D)
Chiefs, 28-10 (KC)
1972—Chiefs, 45-24 (D)
Chiefs, 24-21 (KC)
1973—Chiefs, 16-14 (KC)
Broncos, 14-10 (D)
1974—Broncos, 17-14 (KC)
Chiefs, 42-34 (D)
1975—Broncos, 37-33 (D)
Chiefs, 26-13 (KC)
1976—Broncos, 35-26 (KC)
Broncos, 17-16 (D)
1977—Broncos, 23-7 (D)
Broncos, 14-7 (KC)
1978—Broncos, 23-17 (KC) OT
Broncos, 24-3 (D)
1979—Broncos, 24-10 (KC)
Broncos, 20-3 (D)
1980—Chiefs, 23-17 (D)
Chiefs, 31-14 (KC)
1981—Chiefs, 28-14 (KC)
Broncos, 16-13 (D)
1982—Chiefs, 37-16 (D)
1983—Broncos, 27-24 (D)
Chiefs, 48-17 (KC)
1984—Broncos, 21-0 (D)
Chiefs, 16-13 (KC)
1985—Broncos, 30-10 (KC)
Broncos, 14-13 (D)
1986—Broncos, 38-17 (D)
Chiefs, 37-10 (KC)
1987—Broncos, 26-17 (KC)
Broncos, 20-17 (D)
1988—Chiefs, 20-13 (KC)
Broncos, 17-11 (D)
1989—Broncos, 34-20 (D)
Broncos, 16-13 (KC)
1990—Broncos, 24-23 (D)
Chiefs, 31-20 (KC)
1991—Broncos, 19-16 (D)
Broncos, 24-20 (KC)
1992—Broncos, 20-19 (D)
Chiefs, 42-20 (KC)
1993—Chiefs, 15-7 (KC)
Broncos, 27-21 (D)
(RS Pts.—Chiefs 1,681, Broncos 1,244)
*Franchise in Dallas prior to 1963 and known as Texans*

**DENVER vs. *L.A. RAIDERS**
RS: Raiders lead series, 46-19-2
PS: Series tied, 1-1
1960—Broncos, 31-14 (D)
Raiders, 48-10 (O)
1961—Raiders, 33-19 (O)
Broncos, 27-24 (D)
1962—Broncos, 44-7 (D)
Broncos, 23-6 (O)
1963—Raiders, 26-10 (D)
Raiders, 35-31 (O)
1964—Raiders, 40-7 (O)
Tie, 20-20 (D)
1965—Raiders, 28-20 (D)
Raiders, 24-13 (O)
1966—Raiders, 17-3 (D)
Raiders, 28-10 (O)
1967—Raiders, 51-0 (O)
Raiders, 21-17 (D)
1968—Raiders, 43-7 (D)
Raiders, 33-27 (O)
1969—Raiders, 24-14 (D)
Raiders, 41-10 (O)
1970—Raiders, 35-23 (O)
Raiders, 24-19 (D)
1971—Raiders, 27-16 (D)
Raiders, 21-13 (O)
1972—Broncos, 30-23 (O)
Raiders, 37-20 (D)
1973—Tie, 23-23 (D)
Raiders, 21-17 (O)
1974—Raiders, 28-17 (D)
Broncos, 20-17 (O)
1975—Raiders, 42-17 (D)
Raiders, 17-10 (O)
1976—Raiders, 17-10 (D)
Raiders, 19-6 (O)
1977—Broncos, 30-7 (O)
Raiders, 24-14 (D)
**Broncos, 20-17 (D)
1978—Broncos, 14-6 (D)
Broncos, 21-6 (O)
1979—Raiders, 27-3 (O)
Raiders, 14-10 (D)
1980—Raiders, 9-3 (O)
Raiders, 24-21 (D)
1981—Broncos, 9-7 (D)
Broncos, 17-0 (O)
1982—Raiders, 27-10 (LA)
1983—Raiders, 22-7 (D)
Raiders, 22-20 (LA)
1984—Broncos, 16-13 (D)
Broncos, 22-19 (LA) OT
1985—Raiders, 31-28 (LA) OT
Raiders, 17-14 (D) OT
1986—Broncos, 38-36 (D)
Broncos, 21-10 (LA)
1987—Broncos, 30-14 (D)
Broncos, 23-17 (LA)
1988—Raiders, 30-27 (D) OT
Raiders, 21-20 (LA)
1989—Broncos, 31-21 (D)
Raiders, 16-13 (LA) OT
1990—Raiders, 14-9 (LA)
Raiders, 23-20 (D)
1991—Raiders, 16-13 (LA)
Raiders, 17-16 (D)
1992—Broncos, 17-13 (D)
Raiders, 24-0 (LA)
1993—Raiders, 23-20 (D)

Raiders, 33-30 (LA) OT
***Raiders, 42-24 (LA)
(RS Pts.—Raiders 1,517, Broncos 1,171)
(PS Pts.—Raiders 59, Broncos 44)
*Franchise in Oakland prior to 1982*
***AFC Championship*
****AFC First-Round Playoff*

**DENVER vs. L.A. RAMS**
RS: Series tied, 3-3
1972—Broncos, 16-10 (LA)
1974—Rams, 17-10 (D)
1979—Rams, 13-9 (D)
1982—Broncos, 27-24 (LA)
1985—Rams, 20-16 (LA)
1988—Broncos, 35-24 (D)
(RS Pts.—Broncos 113, Rams 108)

**DENVER vs. MIAMI**
RS: Dolphins lead series, 5-2-1
1966—Dolphins, 24-7 (M)
Broncos, 17-7 (D)
1967—Dolphins, 35-21 (M)
1968—Broncos, 21-14 (D)
1969—Dolphins, 27-24 (M)
1971—Tie, 10-10 (D)
1975—Dolphins, 14-13 (M)
1985—Dolphins, 30-26 (D)
(RS Pts.—Dolphins 161, Broncos 139)

**DENVER vs. MINNESOTA**
RS: Vikings lead series, 5-3
1972—Vikings, 23-20 (D)
1978—Vikings, 12-9 (M) OT
1981—Broncos, 19-17 (D)
1984—Broncos, 42-21 (D)
1987—Vikings, 34-27 (M)
1990—Vikings, 27-22 (M)
1991—Broncos, 13-6 (M)
1993—Vikings, 26-23 (D)
(RS Pts.—Broncos 175, Vikings 166)

**DENVER vs. *NEW ENGLAND**
RS: Broncos lead series, 16-12
PS: Broncos lead series, 1-0
1960—Broncos, 13-10 (B)
Broncos, 31-24 (D)
1961—Patriots, 45-17 (B)
Patriots, 28-24 (D)
1962—Patriots, 41-16 (B)
Patriots, 33-29 (D)
1963—Broncos, 14-10 (D)
Patriots, 40-21 (B)
1964—Patriots, 39-10 (D)
Patriots, 12-7 (B)
1965—Broncos, 27-10 (B)
Patriots, 28-20 (D)
1966—Patriots, 24-10 (D)
Broncos, 17-10 (B)
1967—Broncos, 26-21 (D)
1968—Patriots, 20-17 (D)
Broncos, 35-14 (B)
1969—Broncos, 35-7 (D)
1972—Broncos, 45-21 (D)
1976—Patriots, 38-14 (NE)
1979—Broncos, 45-10 (D)
1980—Patriots, 23-14 (NE)
1984—Broncos, 26-19 (D)
1986—Broncos, 27-20 (D)
**Broncos, 22-17 (D)
1987—Broncos, 31-20 (D)
1988—Broncos, 21-10 (D)
1991—Broncos, 9-6 (NE)
Broncos, 20-3 (D)
(RS Pts.—Broncos 621, Patriots 586)
(PS Pts.—Broncos 22, Patriots 17)
*Franchise in Boston prior to 1971*
***AFC Divisional Playoff*

**DENVER vs. NEW ORLEANS**
RS: Broncos lead series, 4-1
1970—Broncos, 31-6 (NO)
1974—Broncos, 33-17 (D)
1979—Broncos, 10-3 (D)
1985—Broncos, 34-23 (D)
1988—Saints, 42-0 (NO)
(RS Pts.—Broncos 108, Saints 91)

**DENVER vs. N.Y. GIANTS**
RS: Series tied, 3-3
PS: Giants lead series, 1-0
1972—Giants, 29-17 (NY)
1976—Broncos, 14-13 (D)
1980—Broncos, 14-9 (NY)
1986—Giants, 19-16 (NY)
*Giants, 39-20 (Pasadena)
1989—Giants, 14-7 (D)
1992—Broncos, 27-13 (D)
(RS Pts.—Giants 97, Broncos 95)
(PS Pts.—Giants 39, Broncos 20)
*Super Bowl XXI*

**DENVER vs. *N.Y. JETS**
RS: Broncos lead series, 12-11-1
1960—Titans, 28-24 (NY)
Titans, 30-27 (D)
1961—Titans, 35-28 (NY)
Broncos, 27-10 (D)
1962—Broncos, 32-10 (NY)
Titans, 46-45 (D)
1963—Tie, 35-35 (NY)
Jets, 14-9 (D)
1964—Jets, 30-6 (NY)
Broncos, 20-16 (D)
1965—Broncos, 16-13 (D)
Jets, 45-10 (NY)
1966—Jets, 16-7 (D)
1967—Jets, 38-24 (D)
Broncos, 33-24 (NY)
1968—Broncos, 21-13 (NY)
1969—Broncos, 21-19 (D)
1973—Broncos, 40-28 (NY)
1976—Broncos, 46-3 (D)
1978—Jets, 31-28 (D)
1980—Broncos, 31-24 (D)
1986—Jets, 22-10 (NY)
1992—Broncos, 27-16 (D)
1993—Broncos, 26-20 (NY)
(RS Pts.—Broncos 593, Jets 566)
*Jets known as Titans prior to 1963*

**DENVER vs. PHILADELPHIA**
RS: Eagles lead series, 5-2
1971—Eagles, 17-16 (P)
1975—Broncos, 25-10 (D)
1980—Eagles, 27-6 (P)
1983—Eagles, 13-10 (D)
1986—Broncos, 33-7 (P)
1989—Eagles, 28-24 (D)
1992—Eagles, 30-0 (P)
(RS Pts.—Eagles 132, Broncos 114)

**DENVER vs. PITTSBURGH**
RS: Broncos lead series, 10-5-1
PS: Series tied, 2-2
1970—Broncos, 16-13 (D)
1971—Broncos, 22-10 (P)
1973—Broncos, 23-13 (P)
1974—Tie, 35-35 (D) OT
1975—Steelers, 20-9 (P)
1977—Broncos, 21-7 (D)
*Broncos, 34-21 (D)
1978—Steelers, 21-17 (D)
*Steelers, 33-10 (P)
1979—Steelers, 42-7 (P)
1983—Broncos, 14-10 (P)
1984—*Steelers, 24-17 (D)
1985—Broncos, 31-23 (P)
1986—Broncos, 21-10 (P)
1988—Steelers, 39-21 (P)
1989—Broncos, 34-7 (D)
*Broncos, 24-23 (D)
1990—Steelers, 34-17 (D)
1991—Broncos, 20-13 (D)
1993—Broncos, 37-13 (D)
(RS Pts.—Broncos 345, Steelers 310)
(PS Pts.—Steelers 101, Broncos 85)
*AFC Divisional Playoff*

**DENVER vs. *SAN DIEGO**
RS: Broncos lead series, 35-32-1
1960—Chargers, 23-19 (D)
Chargers, 41-33 (LA)
1961—Chargers, 37-0 (SD)
Chargers, 19-16 (D)
1962—Broncos, 30-21 (D)
Broncos, 23-20 (SD)
1963—Broncos, 50-34 (D)
Chargers, 58-20 (SD)
1964—Chargers, 42-14 (SD)
Chargers, 31-20 (D)
1965—Chargers, 34-31 (SD)
Chargers, 33-21 (D)
1966—Chargers, 24-17 (SD)
Broncos, 20-17 (D)
1967—Chargers, 38-21 (D)
Chargers, 24-20 (SD)
1968—Chargers, 55-24 (SD)
Chargers, 47-23 (D)
1969—Broncos, 13-0 (D)
Chargers, 45-24 (SD)
1970—Chargers, 24-21 (SD)
Tie, 17-17 (D)
1971—Broncos, 20-16 (D)
Chargers, 45-17 (SD)
1972—Chargers, 37-14 (SD)
Broncos, 38-13 (D)
1973—Broncos, 30-19 (D)
Broncos, 42-28 (SD)
1974—Broncos, 27-7 (D)
Chargers, 17-0 (SD)
1975—Broncos, 27-17 (SD)
Broncos, 13-10 (D) OT
1976—Broncos, 26-0 (D)
Broncos, 17-0 (SD)
1977—Broncos, 17-14 (SD)
Broncos, 17-9 (D)
1978—Broncos, 27-14 (D)
Chargers, 23-0 (SD)
1979—Broncos, 7-0 (D)
Chargers, 17-7 (SD)
1980—Chargers, 30-13 (D)
Broncos, 20-13 (SD)
1981—Broncos, 42-24 (D)
Chargers, 34-17 (SD)
1982—Chargers, 23-3 (D)
Chargers, 30-20 (SD)
1983—Broncos, 14-6 (D)
Chargers, 31-7 (SD)
1984—Broncos, 16-13 (SD)
Broncos, 16-13 (D)
1985—Chargers, 30-10 (SD)
Broncos, 30-24 (D) OT
1986—Broncos, 31-14 (SD)
Chargers, 9-3 (D)
1987—Broncos, 31-17 (SD)
Broncos, 24-0 (D)
1988—Broncos, 34-3 (D)
Broncos, 12-0 (SD)
1989—Broncos, 16-10 (D)
Chargers, 19-16 (SD)
1990—Chargers, 19-7 (SD)
Broncos, 20-10 (D)
1991—Broncos, 27-19 (D)
Broncos, 17-14 (SD)
1992—Broncos, 21-13 (D)
Chargers, 24-21 (SD)
1993—Broncos, 34-17 (D)
Chargers, 13-10 (SD)
(RS Pts.—Chargers 1,442, Broncos 1,355)
*Franchise in Los Angeles prior to 1961*

**DENVER vs. SAN FRANCISCO**
RS: Broncos lead series, 4-2
PS: 49ers lead series, 1-0
1970—49ers, 19-14 (SF)
1973—49ers, 36-34 (D)
1979—Broncos, 38-28 (SF)
1982—Broncos, 24-21 (D)
1985—Broncos, 17-16 (D)
1988—Broncos, 16-13 (SF) OT
1989—*49ers, 55-10 (New Orleans)
(RS Pts.—Broncos 143, 49ers 133)
(PS Pts.—49ers 55, Broncos 10)
*Super Bowl XXIV*

**DENVER vs. SEATTLE**
RS: Broncos lead series, 20-13
PS: Seahawks lead series, 1-0
1977—Broncos, 24-13 (S)
1978—Broncos, 28-7 (D)
Broncos, 20-17 (S) OT
1979—Broncos, 37-34 (D)
Seahawks, 28-23 (S)
1980—Broncos, 36-20 (D)
Broncos, 25-17 (S)
1981—Seahawks, 13-10 (S)
Broncos, 23-13 (D)
1982—Seahawks, 17-10 (D)
Seahawks, 13-11 (S)
1983—Seahawks, 27-19 (S)
Broncos, 38-27 (D)
*Seahawks, 31-7 (S)
1984—Seahawks, 27-24 (D)
Broncos, 31-14 (S)
1985—Broncos, 13-10 (D) OT
Broncos, 27-24 (S)
1986—Broncos, 20-13 (D)
Seahawks, 41-16 (S)
1987—Broncos, 40-17 (D)
Seahawks, 28-21 (S)
1988—Seahawks, 21-14 (D)
Seahawks, 42-14 (S)
1989—Broncos, 24-21 (S) OT
Broncos, 41-14 (D)
1990—Broncos, 34-31 (D) OT
Seahawks, 17-12 (S)
1991—Broncos, 16-10 (D)
Seahawks, 13-10 (S)
1992—Seahawks, 16-13 (S) OT
Broncos, 10-6 (D)
1993—Broncos, 28-17 (D)
Broncos, 17-9 (S)
(RS Pts.—Broncos 729, Seahawks 637)
(PS Pts.—Seahawks 31, Broncos 7)
*AFC First-Round Playoff*

**DENVER vs. TAMPA BAY**
RS: Broncos lead series, 2-1
1976—Broncos, 48-13 (D)
1981—Broncos, 24-7 (TB)
1993—Buccaneers, 17-10 (D)
(RS Pts.—Broncos 82, Buccaneers 37)

**DENVER vs. WASHINGTON**
RS: Series tied, 3-3
PS: Redskins lead series, 1-0
1970—Redskins, 19-3 (D)
1974—Redskins, 30-3 (W)
1980—Broncos, 20-17 (D)
1986—Broncos, 31-30 (D)
1987—*Redskins, 42-10 (San Diego)
1989—Broncos, 14-10 (W)
1992—Redskins, 34-3 (W)
(RS Pts.—Redskins 140, Broncos 74)
(PS Pts.—Redskins 42, Broncos 10)
*Super Bowl XXII*

---

**DETROIT vs. ARIZONA**
RS: Lions lead series, 27-16-5;
See Arizona vs. Detroit

**DETROIT vs. ATLANTA**
RS: Lions lead series, 17-5;
See Atlanta vs. Detroit

**DETROIT vs. BUFFALO**
RS: Lions lead series, 2-1-1;
See Buffalo vs. Detroit

**DETROIT vs. CHICAGO**
RS: Bears lead series, 74-49-5;
See Chicago vs. Detroit

**DETROIT vs. CINCINNATI**
RS: Series tied, 3-3;
See Cincinnati vs. Detroit

**DETROIT vs. CLEVELAND**
RS: Lions lead series, 11-3
PS: Lions lead series, 3-1;
See Cleveland vs. Detroit

**DETROIT vs. DALLAS**
RS: Cowboys lead series, 7-5
PS: Series tied, 1-1;
See Dallas vs. Detroit

**DETROIT vs. DENVER**
RS: Broncos lead series, 4-3;
See Denver vs. Detroit

***DETROIT vs. GREEN BAY**
RS: Packers lead series, 64-56-7

PS: Packers lead series, 1-0
1930—Packers, 47-13 (GB)
Tie, 6-6 (P)
1932—Packers, 15-10 (GB)
Spartans, 19-0 (P)
1933—Packers, 17-0 (GB)
Spartans, 7-0 (P)
1934—Lions, 3-0 (GB)
Packers, 3-0 (D)
1935—Packers, 13-9 (Mil)
Packers, 31-7 (GB)
Lions, 20-10 (D)
1936—Packers, 20-18 (GB)
Packers, 26-17 (D)
1937—Packers, 26-6 (GB)
Packers, 14-13 (D)
1938—Lions, 17-7 (GB)
Packers, 28-7 (D)
1939—Packers, 26-7 (GB)
Packers, 12-7 (D)
1940—Lions, 23-14 (GB)
Packers, 50-7 (D)
1941—Packers, 23-0 (GB)
Packers, 24-7 (D)
1942—Packers, 38-7 (Mil)
Packers, 28-7 (D)
1943—Packers, 35-14 (GB)
Packers, 27-6 (D)
1944—Packers, 27-6 (Mil)
Packers, 14-0 (D)
1945—Packers, 57-21 (Mil)
Lions, 14-3 (D)
1946—Packers, 10-7 (Mil)
Packers, 9-0 (D)
1947—Packers, 34-17 (GB)
Packers, 35-14 (D)
1948—Packers, 33-21 (GB)
Lions, 24-20 (D)
1949—Packers, 16-14 (Mil)
Lions, 21-7 (D)
1950—Lions, 45-7 (GB)
Lions, 24-21 (D)
1951—Lions, 24-17 (GB)
Lions, 52-35 (D)
1952—Lions, 52-17 (GB)
Lions, 48-24 (D)
1953—Lions, 14-7 (GB)
Lions, 34-15 (D)
1954—Lions, 21-17 (GB)
Lions, 28-24 (D)
1955—Packers, 20-17 (GB)
Lions, 24-10 (D)
1956—Lions, 20-16 (GB)
Packers, 24-20 (D)
1957—Lions, 24-14 (GB)
Lions, 18-6 (D)
1958—Tie, 13-13 (GB)
Lions, 24-14 (D)
1959—Packers, 28-10 (GB)
Packers, 24-17 (D)
1960—Packers, 28-9 (GB)
Lions, 23-10 (D)
1961—Lions, 17-13 (Mil)
Packers, 17-9 (D)
1962—Packers, 9-7 (GB)
Lions, 26-14 (D)
1963—Packers, 31-10 (Mil)
Tie, 13-13 (D)
1964—Packers, 14-10 (D)
Packers, 30-7 (GB)
1965—Packers, 31-21 (D)
Lions, 12-7 (GB)
1966—Packers, 23-14 (GB)
Packers, 31-7 (D)
1967—Tie, 17-17 (GB)
Packers, 27-17 (D)
1968—Lions, 23-17 (GB)
Tie, 14-14 (D)
1969—Packers, 28-17 (D)
Lions, 16-10 (GB)
1970—Lions, 40-0 (GB)
Lions, 20-0 (D)
1971—Lions, 31-28 (D)
Tie, 14-14 (Mil)
1972—Packers, 24-23 (D)
Packers, 33-7 (GB)
1973—Tie, 13-13 (GB)
Lions, 34-0 (D)
1974—Packers, 21-19 (Mil)
Lions, 19-17 (D)
1975—Lions, 30-16 (Mil)
Lions, 13-10 (D)
1976—Packers, 24-14 (GB)
Lions, 27-6 (D)
1977—Lions, 10-6 (D)
Packers, 10-9 (GB)
1978—Packers, 13-7 (D)
Packers, 35-14 (Mil)
1979—Packers, 24-16 (Mil)
Packers, 18-13 (D)
1980—Lions, 29-7 (Mil)
Lions, 24-3 (D)
1981—Lions, 31-27 (D)
Packers, 31-17 (GB)
1982—Lions, 30-10 (GB)
Lions, 27-24 (D)
1983—Lions, 38-14 (D)
Lions, 23-20 (Mil) OT
1984—Packers, 41-9 (GB)
Lions, 31-28 (D)
1985—Packers, 43-10 (GB)
Packers, 26-23 (D)
1986—Lions, 21-14 (GB)
Packers, 44-40 (D)
1987—Lions, 19-16 (GB) OT
Packers, 34-33 (D)
1988—Lions, 19-9 (Mil)
Lions, 30-14 (D)
1989—Packers, 23-20 (Mil) OT
Lions, 31-22 (D)
1990—Packers, 24-21 (D)
Lions, 24-17 (GB)
1991—Lions, 23-14 (D)
Lions, 21-17 (GB)
1992—Packers, 27-13 (D)
Packers, 38-10 (Mil)
1993—Packers, 26-17 (Mil)
Lions, 30-20 (D)
**Packers, 28-24 (D)
(RS Pts.—Packers 2,487, Lions 2,271)
(PS Pts.—Packers 28, Lions 24)
*Franchise in Portsmouth prior to 1934 and known as the Spartans*
***NFC First-Round Playoff*

**DETROIT vs. HOUSTON**
RS: Oilers lead series, 4-2
1971—Lions, 31-7 (H)
1975—Oilers, 24-8 (H)
1983—Oilers, 27-17 (H)
1986—Lions, 24-13 (D)
1989—Oilers, 35-31 (H)
1992—Oilers, 24-21 (D)
(RS Pts.—Lions 132, Oilers 130)

**DETROIT vs. *INDIANAPOLIS**
RS: Series tied, 17-17-2
1953—Lions, 27-17 (B)
Lions, 17-7 (D)
1954—Lions, 35-0 (D)
Lions, 27-3 (B)
1955—Colts, 28-13 (B)
Lions, 24-14 (D)
1956—Lions, 31-14 (B)
Lions, 27-3 (D)
1957—Colts, 34-14 (B)
Lions, 31-27 (D)
1958—Colts, 28-15 (B)
Colts, 40-14 (D)
1959—Colts, 21-9 (B)
Colts, 31-24 (D)
1960—Lions, 30-17 (D)
Lions, 20-15 (B)
1961—Lions, 16-15 (B)
Colts, 17-14 (D)
1962—Lions, 29-20 (B)
Lions, 21-14 (D)
1963—Colts, 25-21 (D)
Colts, 24-21 (B)
1964—Colts, 34-0 (D)
Lions, 31-14 (B)
1965—Colts, 31-7 (B)
Tie, 24-24 (D)
1966—Colts, 45-14 (B)
Lions, 20-14 (D)
1967—Colts, 41-7 (B)
1968—Colts, 27-10 (D)
1969—Tie, 17-17 (B)
1973—Colts, 29-27 (D)
1977—Lions, 13-10 (B)
1980—Colts, 10-9 (D)
1985—Colts, 14-6 (I)
1991—Lions, 33-24 (I)
(RS Pts.—Colts 748, Lions 698)
*Franchise in Baltimore prior to 1984*

**DETROIT vs. KANSAS CITY**
RS: Chiefs lead series, 4-3
1971—Lions, 32-21 (D)
1975—Chiefs, 24-21 (KC) OT
1980—Chiefs, 20-17 (KC)
1981—Lions, 27-10 (D)
1987—Chiefs, 27-20 (D)
1988—Lions, 7-6 (KC)
1990—Chiefs, 43-24 (KC)
(RS Pts.—Chiefs 151, Lions 148)

**DETROIT vs. *L.A. RAIDERS**
RS: Raiders lead series, 5-2
1970—Lions, 28-14 (D)
1974—Raiders, 35-13 (O)
1978—Raiders, 29-17 (O)
1981—Lions, 16-0 (D)
1984—Raiders, 24-3 (D)
1987—Raiders, 27-7 (LA)
1990—Raiders, 38-31 (D)
(RS Pts.—Raiders 167, Lions 115)
*Franchise in Oakland prior to 1982*

**DETROIT vs. *L.A. RAMS**
RS: Rams lead series, 39-35-1
PS: Lions lead series, 1-0
1937—Lions, 28-0 (C)
Lions, 27-7 (D)
1938—Rams, 21-17 (C)
Lions, 6-0 (D)
1939—Lions, 15-7 (D)
Rams, 14-3 (C)
1940—Lions, 6-0 (D)
Rams, 24-0 (C)
1941—Lions, 17-7 (D)
Lions, 14-0 (C)
1942—Rams, 14-0 (D)
Rams, 27-7 (C)
1944—Rams, 20-17 (D)
Lions, 26-14 (C)
1945—Rams, 28-21 (D)
1946—Rams, 35-14 (LA)
Rams, 41-20 (D)
1947—Rams, 27-13 (D)
Rams, 28-17 (LA)
1948—Rams, 44-7 (LA)
Rams, 34-27 (D)
1949—Rams, 27-24 (LA)
Rams, 21-10 (D)
1950—Rams, 30-28 (D)
Rams, 65-24 (LA)
1951—Rams, 27-21 (D)
Lions, 24-22 (LA)
1952—Lions, 17-14 (LA)
Lions, 24-16 (D)
**Lions, 31-21 (D)
1953—Rams, 31-19 (D)
Rams, 37-24 (LA)
1954—Lions, 21-3 (D)
Lions, 27-24 (LA)
1955—Rams, 17-10 (D)
Rams, 24-13 (LA)
1956—Lions, 24-21 (D)
Lions, 16-7 (LA)
1957—Lions, 10-7 (D)
Rams, 35-17 (LA)
1958—Rams, 42-28 (D)
Lions, 41-24 (LA)
1959—Lions, 17-7 (LA)
Lions, 23-17 (D)
1960—Rams, 48-35 (LA)
Lions, 12-10 (D)
1961—Lions, 14-13 (D)
Lions, 28-10 (LA)
1962—Lions, 13-10 (D)
Lions, 12-3 (LA)
1963—Lions, 23-2 (LA)
Rams, 28-21 (D)
1964—Tie, 17-17 (LA)
Lions, 37-17 (D)
1965—Lions, 20-0 (D)
Lions, 31-7 (LA)
1966—Rams, 14-7 (D)
Rams, 23-3 (LA)
1967—Rams, 31-7 (D)
1968—Rams, 10-7 (LA)
1969—Lions, 28-0 (D)
1970—Lions, 28-23 (LA)
1971—Rams, 21-13 (D)
1972—Lions, 34-17 (LA)
1974—Rams, 16-13 (LA)
1975—Rams, 20-0 (D)
1976—Rams, 20-17 (D)
1980—Lions, 41-20 (LA)
1981—Rams, 20-13 (LA)
1982—Lions, 19-14 (LA)
1983—Rams, 21-10 (LA)
1986—Rams, 14-10 (LA)
1987—Rams, 37-16 (D)
1988—Rams, 17-10 (LA)
1991—Lions, 21-10 (D)
1993—Lions, 16-13 (LA)
(RS Pts.—Rams 1,436, Lions 1,340)
(PS Pts.—Lions 31, Rams 21)
*Franchise in Cleveland prior to 1946*
***Conference Playoff*

**DETROIT vs. MIAMI**
RS: Series tied, 2-2
1973—Dolphins, 34-7 (M)
1979—Dolphins, 28-10 (D)
1985—Lions, 31-21 (D)
1991—Lions, 17-13 (D)
(RS Pts.—Dolphins 96, Lions 65)

**DETROIT vs. MINNESOTA**
RS: Vikings lead series, 40-23-2
1961—Lions, 37-10 (M)
Lions, 13-7 (D)
1962—Lions, 17-6 (M)
Lions, 37-23 (D)
1963—Lions, 28-10 (D)
Vikings, 34-31 (M)
1964—Lions, 24-20 (M)
Tie, 23-23 (D)
1965—Lions, 31-29 (M)
Vikings, 29-7 (D)
1966—Lions, 32-31 (M)
Vikings, 28-16 (D)
1967—Tie, 10-10 (M)
Lions, 14-3 (D)
1968—Vikings, 24-10 (M)
Vikings, 13-6 (D)
1969—Vikings, 24-10 (M)
Vikings, 27-0 (D)
1970—Vikings, 30-17 (D)
Vikings, 24-20 (M)
1971—Vikings, 16-13 (D)
Vikings, 29-10 (M)
1972—Vikings, 34-10 (D)
Vikings, 16-14 (M)
1973—Vikings, 23-9 (D)
Vikings, 28-7 (M)
1974—Vikings, 7-6 (D)
Lions, 20-16 (M)
1975—Vikings, 25-19 (M)
Lions, 17-10 (D)
1976—Vikings, 10-9 (D)
Vikings, 31-23 (M)
1977—Vikings, 14-7 (M)
Vikings, 30-21 (D)
1978—Vikings, 17-7 (M)
Lions, 45-14 (D)

1979—Vikings, 13-10 (D)
Vikings, 14-7 (M)
1980—Lions, 27-7 (D)
Vikings, 34-0 (M)
1981—Vikings, 26-24 (M)
Lions, 45-7 (D)
1982—Vikings, 34-31 (D)
1983—Vikings, 20-17 (M)
Lions, 13-2 (D)
1984—Vikings, 29-28 (D)
Lions, 16-14 (M)
1985—Vikings, 16-13 (M)
Lions, 41-21 (D)
1986—Lions, 13-10 (M)
Vikings, 24-10 (D)
1987—Vikings, 34-19 (M)
Vikings, 17-14 (D)
1988—Vikings, 44-17 (M)
Vikings, 23-0 (D)
1989—Vikings, 24-17 (M)
Vikings, 20-7 (D)
1990—Lions, 34-27 (M)
Vikings, 17-7 (D)
1991—Lions, 24-20 (D)
Lions, 34-14 (M)
1992—Lions, 31-17 (D)
Vikings, 31-14 (M)
1993—Lions, 30-27 (M)
Vikings, 13-0 (D)
(RS Pts.—Vikings 1,327, Lions 1,163)

**DETROIT vs. NEW ENGLAND**
RS: Lions lead series, 3-2
1971—Lions, 34-7 (NE)
1976—Lions, 30-10 (D)
1979—Patriots, 24-17 (NE)
1985—Patriots, 23-6 (NE)
1993—Lions, 19-16 (NE) OT
(RS Pts.—Lions 106, Patriots 80)

**DETROIT vs. NEW ORLEANS**
RS: Saints lead series, 7-6-1
1968—Tie, 20-20 (D)
1970—Saints, 19-17 (NO)
1972—Lions, 27-14 (D)
1973—Saints, 20-13 (NO)
1974—Lions, 19-14 (D)
1976—Saints, 17-16 (NO)
1977—Lions, 23-19 (D)
1979—Saints, 17-7 (NO)
1980—Lions, 24-13 (D)
1988—Saints, 22-14 (D)
1989—Lions, 21-14 (D)
1990—Lions, 27-10 (NO)
1992—Saints, 13-7 (D)
1993—Saints, 14-3 (NO)
(RS Pts.—Lions 238, Saints 226)

***DETROIT vs. N.Y. GIANTS**
RS: Lions lead series, 17-15-1
PS: Lions lead series, 1-0
1930—Giants, 19-6 (P)
1931—Spartans, 14-6 (P)
Giants, 14-0 (NY)
1932—Spartans, 7-0 (P)
Spartans, 6-0 (NY)
1933—Spartans, 17-7 (P)
Giants, 13-10 (NY)
1934—Lions, 9-0 (D)
1935—**Lions, 26-7 (D)
1936—Giants, 14-7 (NY)
Lions, 38-0 (D)
1937—Lions, 17-0 (NY)
1939—Lions, 18-14 (D)
1941—Giants, 20-13 (NY)
1943—Tie, 0-0 (D)
1945—Giants, 35-14 (NY)
1947—Lions, 35-7 (D)
1949—Lions, 45-21 (NY)
1953—Lions, 27-16 (NY)
1955—Giants, 24-19 (D)
1958—Giants, 19-17 (D)
1962—Giants, 17-14 (NY)
1964—Lions, 26-3 (D)
1967—Lions, 30-7 (NY)
1969—Lions, 24-0 (D)
1972—Lions, 30-16 (D)
1974—Lions, 20-19 (D)
1976—Giants, 24-10 (NY)
1982—Giants, 13-6 (D)
1983—Lions, 15-9 (D)
1988—Giants, 30-10 (NY)
Giants, 13-10 (D) OT
1989—Giants, 24-14 (NY)
1990—Giants, 20-0 (NY)
(RS Pts.—Lions, 528, Giants 424)
(PS Pts.—Lions 26, Giants 7)
**Franchise in Portsmouth prior to 1934 and known as the Spartans*
***NFL Championship*

**DETROIT vs. N.Y. JETS**
RS: Series tied, 3-3
1972—Lions, 37-20 (D)
1979—Jets, 31-10 (NY)
1982—Jets, 28-13 (D)
1985—Lions, 31-20 (D)
1988—Jets, 17-10 (D)
1991—Lions, 34-20 (D)
(RS Pts.—Jets 136, Lions 135)

***DETROIT vs. PHILADELPHIA**
RS: Lions lead series, 12-9-2
1933—Spartans, 25-0 (P)
1934—Lions, 10-0 (P)
1935—Lions, 35-0 (D)
1936—Lions, 23-0 (P)
1938—Eagles, 21-7 (D)
1940—Lions, 21-0 (P)
1941—Lions, 21-17 (D)
1945—Lions, 28-24 (D)
1948—Eagles, 45-21 (P)
1949—Eagles, 22-14 (D)
1951—Lions, 28-10 (P)
1954—Tie, 13-13 (D)
1957—Lions, 27-16 (P)
1960—Eagles, 28-10 (P)
1961—Eagles, 27-24 (D)
1965—Lions, 35-28 (P)
1968—Eagles, 12-0 (D)
1971—Eagles, 23-20 (D)
1974—Eagles, 28-17 (P)
1977—Lions, 17-13 (D)
1979—Eagles, 44-7 (P)
1984—Tie, 23-23 (D) OT
1986—Lions, 13-11 (P)
(RS Pts.—Lions 439, Eagles 405)
**Franchise in Portsmouth prior to 1934 and known as the Spartans*

**DETROIT vs. *PITTSBURGH**
RS: Lions lead series, 13-11-1
1934—Lions, 40-7 (D)
1936—Lions, 28-3 (D)
1937—Lions, 7-3 (D)
1938—Lions, 16-7 (D)
1940—Pirates, 10-7 (D)
1942—Steelers, 35-7 (D)
1946—Lions, 17-7 (D)
1947—Steelers, 17-10 (P)
1948—Lions, 17-14 (D)
1949—Steelers, 14-7 (P)
1950—Lions, 10-7 (D)
1952—Lions, 31-6 (P)
1953—Lions, 38-21 (D)
1955—Lions, 31-28 (P)
1956—Lions, 45-7 (D)
1959—Tie, 10-10 (P)
1962—Lions, 45-7 (D)
1966—Steelers, 17-3 (P)
1967—Steelers, 24-14 (D)
1969—Steelers, 16-13 (P)
1973—Steelers, 24-10 (P)
1983—Lions, 45-3 (D)
1986—Steelers, 27-17 (P)
1989—Steelers, 23-3 (D)
1992—Steelers, 17-14 (P)
(RS Pts.—Lions 485, Steelers 354)
**Steelers known as Pirates prior to 1941*

**DETROIT vs. SAN DIEGO**
RS: Lions lead series, 3-2
1972—Lions, 34-20 (D)
1977—Lions, 20-0 (D)
1978—Lions, 31-14 (D)
1981—Chargers, 28-23 (SD)
1984—Chargers, 27-24 (SD)
(RS Pts.—Lions 132, Chargers 89)

**DETROIT vs. SAN FRANCISCO**
RS: 49ers lead series, 26-25-1
PS: Series tied, 1-1
1950—Lions, 24-7 (D)
49ers, 28-27 (SF)
1951—49ers, 20-10 (D)
49ers, 21-17 (SF)
1952—49ers, 17-3 (SF)
49ers, 28-0 (D)
1953—Lions, 24-21 (D)
Lions, 14-10 (SF)
1954—49ers, 37-31 (SF)
Lions, 48-7 (D)
1955—49ers, 27-24 (D)
49ers, 38-21 (SF)
1956—Lions, 20-17 (D)
Lions, 17-13 (SF)
1957—49ers, 35-31 (SF)
Lions, 31-10 (D)
*Lions, 31-27 (SF)
1958—49ers, 24-21 (SF)
Lions, 35-21 (D)
1959—49ers, 34-13 (D)
49ers, 33-7 (SF)
1960—49ers, 14-10 (D)
Lions, 24-0 (SF)
1961—49ers, 49-0 (D)
Tie, 20-20 (SF)
1962—Lions, 45-24 (D)
Lions, 38-24 (SF)
1963—Lions, 26-3 (D)
Lions, 45-7 (SF)
1964—Lions, 26-17 (SF)
Lions, 24-7 (D)
1965—49ers, 27-21 (D)
49ers, 17-14 (SF)
1966—49ers, 27-24 (SF)
49ers, 41-14 (D)
1967—Lions, 45-3 (SF)
1968—49ers, 14-7 (D)
1969—Lions, 26-14 (SF)
1970—Lions, 28-7 (D)
1971—49ers, 31-27 (SF)
1973—Lions, 30-20 (D)
1974—Lions, 17-13 (D)
1975—Lions, 28-17 (SF)
1977—49ers, 28-7 (SF)
1978—Lions, 33-14 (D)
1980—Lions, 17-13 (D)
1981—Lions, 24-17 (D)
1983—**49ers, 24-23 (SF)
1984—49ers, 30-27 (D)
1985—Lions, 23-21 (D)
1988—49ers, 20-13 (SF)
1991—49ers, 35-3 (SF)
1992—49ers, 24-6 (SF)
1993—49ers, 55-17 (D)
(RS Pts.—Lions 1,127, 49ers 1,101)
(PS Pts.—Lions 54, 49ers 51)
**Conference Playoff*
***NFC Divisional Playoff*

**DETROIT vs. SEATTLE**
RS: Seahawks lead series, 4-2
1976—Lions, 41-14 (S)
1978—Seahawks, 28-16 (S)
1984—Seahawks, 38-17 (S)
1987—Seahawks, 37-14 (D)
1990—Seahawks, 30-10 (S)
1993—Lions, 30-10 (D)
(RS Pts.—Seahawks 157, Lions 128)

**DETROIT vs. TAMPA BAY**
RS: Series tied, 16-16
1977—Lions, 16-7 (D)
1978—Lions, 15-7 (TB)
Lions, 34-23 (D)
1979—Buccaneers, 31-16 (TB)
Buccaneers, 16-14 (D)
1980—Lions, 24-10 (TB)
Lions, 27-14 (D)
1981—Buccaneers, 28-10 (TB)
Buccaneers, 20-17 (D)
1982—Buccaneers, 23-21 (TB)
1983—Lions, 11-0 (TB)
Lions, 23-20 (D)
1984—Buccaneers, 21-17 (TB)
Lions, 13-7 (D) OT
1985—Lions, 30-9 (D)
Buccaneers, 19-16 (TB) OT
1986—Buccaneers, 24-20 (D)
Lions, 38-17 (TB)
1987—Buccaneers, 31-27 (D)
Lions, 20-10 (TB)
1988—Buccaneers, 23-20 (D)
Buccaneers, 21-10 (TB)
1989—Lions, 17-16 (TB)
Lions, 33-7 (D)
1990—Buccaneers, 38-21 (D)
Buccaneers, 23-20 (TB)
1991—Lions, 31-3 (D)
Buccaneers, 30-21 (TB)
1992—Buccaneers, 27-23 (D)
Lions, 38-7 (TB)
1993—Buccaneers, 27-10 (TB)
Lions, 23-0 (D)
(RS Pts.—Lions 676, Buccaneers 559)

***DETROIT vs. **WASHINGTON**
RS: Redskins lead series, 22-8
PS: Redskins lead series, 2-0
1932—Spartans, 10-0 (P)
1933—Spartans, 13-0 (B)
1934—Lions, 24-0 (D)
1935—Lions, 17-7 (B)
Lions, 14-0 (D)
1938—Redskins, 7-5 (D)
1939—Redskins, 31-7 (W)
1940—Redskins, 20-14 (D)
1942—Redskins, 15-3 (D)
1943—Redskins, 42-20 (W)
1946—Redskins, 17-16 (W)
1947—Lions, 38-21 (D)
1948—Redskins, 46-21 (W)
1951—Lions, 35-17 (D)
1956—Redskins, 18-17 (W)
1965—Lions, 14-10 (D)
1968—Redskins, 14-3 (W)
1970—Redskins, 31-10 (W)
1973—Redskins, 20-0 (D)
1976—Redskins, 20-7 (W)
1978—Redskins, 21-19 (D)
1979—Redskins, 27-24 (D)
1981—Redskins, 33-31 (W)
1982—***Redskins, 31-7 (W)
1983—Redskins, 38-17 (W)
1984—Redskins, 28-14 (W)
1985—Redskins, 24-3 (W)
1987—Redskins, 20-13 (W)
1990—Redskins, 41-38 (D)
1991—Redskins, 45-0 (W)
****Redskins, 41-10 (W)
1992—Redskins, 13-10 (W)
(RS Pts.—Redskins 626, Lions 457)
(PS Pts.—Redskins 72, Lions 17)
**Franchise in Portsmouth prior to 1934 and known as the Spartans.*
***Franchise in Boston prior to 1937*
****NFC First-Round Playoff*
*****NFC Championship*

---

**GREEN BAY vs. ARIZONA**
RS: Packers lead series, 39-21-4
PS: Packers lead series, 1-0;
See Arizona vs. Green Bay

**GREEN BAY vs. ATLANTA**
RS: Series tied, 9-9;
See Atlanta vs. Green Bay

**GREEN BAY vs. BUFFALO**
RS: Bills lead series, 4-1;
See Buffalo vs. Green Bay

**GREEN BAY vs. CHICAGO**
RS: Bears lead series, 81-59-6
PS: Bears lead series, 1-0;

See Chicago vs. Green Bay
**GREEN BAY vs. CINCINNATI**
RS: Bengals lead series, 4-3;
See Cincinnati vs. Green Bay
**GREEN BAY vs. CLEVELAND**
RS: Packers lead series, 7-6
PS: Packers lead series, 1-0;
See Cleveland vs. Green Bay
**GREEN BAY vs. DALLAS**
RS: Packers lead series, 8-6
PS: Series tied, 2-2;
See Dallas vs. Green Bay
**GREEN BAY vs. DENVER**
RS: Broncos lead series, 4-2-1;
See Denver vs. Green Bay
**GREEN BAY vs. DETROIT**
RS: Packers lead series, 64-56-7
PS: Packers lead series, 1-0;
See Detroit vs. Green Bay
**GREEN BAY vs. HOUSTON**
RS: Series tied, 3-3
1972—Packers, 23-10 (H)
1977—Oilers, 16-10 (GB)
1980—Oilers, 22-3 (GB)
1983—Packers, 41-38 (H) OT
1986—Oilers, 31-3 (GB)
1992—Packers, 16-14 (H)
(RS Pts.—Oilers 131, Packers 96)
**GREEN BAY vs. *INDIANAPOLIS**
RS: Series tied, 18-18-1
PS: Packers lead series, 1-0
1953—Packers, 37-14 (GB)
Packers, 35-24 (B)
1954—Packers, 7-6 (B)
Packers, 24-13 (Mil)
1955—Colts, 24-20 (Mil)
Colts, 14-10 (B)
1956—Packers, 38-33 (Mil)
Colts, 28-21 (B)
1957—Colts, 45-17 (Mil)
Packers, 24-21 (B)
1958—Colts, 24-17 (Mil)
Colts, 56-0 (B)
1959—Colts, 38-21 (B)
Colts, 28-24 (Mil)
1960—Packers, 35-21 (GB)
Colts, 38-24 (B)
1961—Packers, 45-7 (GB)
Colts, 45-21 (B)
1962—Packers, 17-6 (B)
Packers, 17-13 (GB)
1963—Packers, 31-20 (GB)
Packers, 34-20 (B)
1964—Colts, 21-20 (GB)
Colts, 24-21 (B)
1965—Packers, 20-17 (Mil)
Packers, 42-27 (B)
**Packers, 13-10 (GB) OT
1966—Packers, 24-3 (Mil)
Packers, 14-10 (B)
1967—Colts, 13-10 (B)
1968—Colts, 16-3 (GB)
1969—Colts, 14-6 (B)
1970—Colts, 13-10 (Mil)
1974—Packers, 20-13 (B)
1982—Tie, 20-20 (B) OT
1985—Colts, 37-10 (I)
1988—Colts, 20-13 (GB)
1991—Packers, 14-10 (Mil)
(RS Pts.—Colts 796, Packers 766)
(PS Pts.—Packers 13, Colts 10)
*Franchise in Baltimore prior to 1984*
***Conference Playoff*
**GREEN BAY vs. KANSAS CITY**
RS: Chiefs lead series, 4-1-1
PS: Packers lead series, 1-0
1966—*Packers, 35-10 (Los Angeles)
1973—Tie, 10-10 (Mil)
1977—Chiefs, 20-10 (KC)
1987—Packers, 23-3 (KC)
1989—Chiefs, 21-3 (GB)
1990—Chiefs, 17-3 (GB)
1993—Chiefs, 23-16 (KC)
(RS Pts.—Chiefs 94, Packers 65)
(PS Pts.—Packers 35, Chiefs 10)
**Super Bowl I*
**GREEN BAY vs. *L.A. RAIDERS**
RS: Raiders lead series, 5-2
PS: Packers lead series, 1-0
1967—**Packers, 33-14 (Miami)
1972—Raiders, 20-14 (GB)
1976—Raiders, 18-14 (O)
1978—Raiders, 28-3 (GB)
1984—Raiders, 28-7 (LA)
1987—Raiders, 20-0 (GB)
1990—Packers, 29-16 (LA)
1993—Packers, 28-0 (GB)
(RS Pts.—Raiders 130, Packers 95)
(PS Pts.—Packers 33, Raiders 14)
*Franchise in Oakland prior to 1982*
***Super Bowl II*
**GREEN BAY vs. *L.A. RAMS**
RS: Rams lead series, 42-36-2
PS: Packers lead series, 1-0
1937—Packers, 35-10 (C)
Packers, 35-7 (GB)
1938—Packers, 26-17 (GB)
Packers, 28-7 (C)
1939—Rams, 27-24 (GB)
Packers, 7-6 (C)
1940—Packers, 31-14 (GB)
Tie, 13-13 (C)
1941—Packers, 24-7 (Mil)
Packers, 17-14 (C)
1942—Packers, 45-28 (GB)
Packers, 30-12 (C)
1944—Packers, 30-21 (GB)
Packers, 42-7 (C)
1945—Rams, 27-14 (GB)
Rams, 20-7 (C)
1946—Rams, 21-17 (Mil)
Rams, 38-17 (LA)
1947—Packers, 17-14 (Mil)
Packers, 30-10 (LA)
1948—Packers, 16-0 (GB)
Rams, 24-10 (LA)
1949—Rams, 48-7 (GB)
Rams, 35-7 (LA)
1950—Rams, 45-14 (Mil)
Rams, 51-14 (LA)
1951—Rams, 28-0 (Mil)
Rams, 42-14 (LA)
1952—Rams, 30-28 (Mil)
Rams, 45-27 (LA)
1953—Rams, 38-20 (Mil)
Rams, 33-17 (LA)
1954—Packers, 35-17 (Mil)
Rams, 35-27 (LA)
1955—Packers, 30-28 (Mil)
Rams, 31-17 (LA)
1956—Packers, 42-17 (Mil)
Rams, 49-21 (LA)
1957—Rams, 31-27 (Mil)
Rams, 42-17 (LA)
1958—Rams, 20-7 (GB)
Rams, 34-20 (LA)
1959—Rams, 45-6 (Mil)
Packers, 38-20 (LA)
1960—Rams, 33-31 (Mil)
Packers, 35-21 (LA)
1961—Packers, 35-17 (GB)
Packers, 24-17 (LA)
1962—Packers, 41-10 (Mil)
Packers, 20-17 (LA)
1963—Packers, 42-10 (GB)
Packers, 31-14 (LA)
1964—Rams, 27-17 (Mil)
Tie, 24-24 (LA)
1965—Packers, 6-3 (Mil)
Rams, 21-10 (LA)
1966—Packers, 24-13 (GB)
Packers, 27-23 (LA)
1967—Rams, 27-24 (LA)
**Packers, 28-7 (Mil)
1968—Rams, 16-14 (Mil)
1969—Rams, 34-21 (LA)
1970—Rams, 31-21 (GB)
1971—Rams, 30-13 (LA)
1973—Rams, 24-7 (LA)
1974—Packers, 17-6 (Mil)
1975—Rams, 22-5 (LA)
1977—Rams, 24-6 (Mil)
1978—Rams, 31-14 (LA)
1980—Rams, 51-21 (LA)
1981—Rams, 35-23 (LA)
1982—Packers, 35-23 (Mil)
1983—Packers, 27-24 (Mil)
1984—Packers, 31-6 (Mil)
1985—Rams, 34-17 (LA)
1988—Rams, 34-7 (GB)
1989—Rams, 41-38 (LA)
1990—Packers, 36-24 (GB)
1991—Rams, 23-21 (LA)
1992—Packers, 28-13 (GB)
1993—Packers, 36-6 (Mil)
(RS Pts.—Rams 1,917, Packers 1,779)
(PS Pts.—Packers 28, Rams 7)
*Franchise in Cleveland prior to 1946*
***Conference Championship*
**GREEN BAY vs. MIAMI**
RS: Dolphins lead series, 7-0
1971—Dolphins, 27-6 (Mia)
1975—Dolphins, 31-7 (GB)
1979—Dolphins, 27-7 (Mia)
1985—Dolphins, 34-24 (GB)
1988—Dolphins, 24-17 (Mia)
1989—Dolphins, 23-20 (Mia)
1991—Dolphins, 16-13 (Mia)
(RS Pts.—Dolphins 182, Packers 94)
**GREEN BAY vs. MINNESOTA**
RS: Vikings lead series, 33-31-1
1961—Packers, 33-7 (Minn)
Packers, 28-10 (Mil)
1962—Packers, 34-7 (GB)
Packers, 48-21 (Minn)
1963—Packers, 37-28 (Minn)
Packers, 28-7 (GB)
1964—Vikings, 24-23 (GB)
Packers, 42-13 (Minn)
1965—Packers, 38-13 (Minn)
Packers, 24-19 (GB)
1966—Vikings, 20-17 (GB)
Packers, 28-16 (Minn)
1967—Vikings, 10-7 (Mil)
Packers, 30-27 (Minn)
1968—Vikings, 26-13 (Mil)
Vikings, 14-10 (Minn)
1969—Vikings, 19-7 (Minn)
Vikings, 9-7 (Mil)
1970—Packers, 13-10 (Mil)
Vikings, 10-3 (Minn)
1971—Vikings, 24-13 (GB)
Vikings, 3-0 (Minn)
1972—Vikings, 27-13 (GB)
Packers, 23-7 (Minn)
1973—Vikings, 11-3 (Minn)
Vikings, 31-7 (GB)
1974—Vikings, 32-17 (GB)
Packers, 19-7 (Minn)
1975—Vikings, 28-17 (GB)
Vikings, 24-3 (Minn)
1976—Vikings, 17-10 (Mil)
Vikings, 20-9 (Minn)
1977—Vikings, 19-7 (Minn)
Vikings, 13-6 (GB)
1978—Vikings, 21-7 (Minn)
Tie, 10-10 (GB) OT
1979—Vikings, 27-21 (Minn) OT
Packers, 19-7 (Mil)
1980—Packers, 16-3 (GB)
Packers, 25-13 (Minn)
1981—Vikings, 30-13 (Mil)
Packers, 35-23 (Minn)
1982—Packers, 26-7 (Mil)
1983—Vikings, 20-17 (GB) OT
Packers, 29-21 (Minn)
1984—Packers, 45-17 (Mil)
Packers, 38-14 (Minn)
1985—Packers, 20-17 (Mil)
Packers, 27-17 (Minn)
1986—Vikings, 42-7 (Minn)
Vikings, 32-6 (GB)
1987—Packers, 23-16 (Minn)
Packers, 16-10 (Mil)
1988—Packers, 34-14 (Minn)
Packers, 18-6 (GB)
1989—Vikings, 26-14 (Minn)
Packers, 20-19 (Mil)
1990—Packers, 24-10 (Mil)
Vikings, 23-7 (Minn)
1991—Vikings, 35-21 (GB)
Packers, 27-7 (Minn)
1992—Vikings, 23-20 (GB) OT
Vikings, 27-7 (Minn)
1993—Vikings, 15-13 (Minn)
Vikings, 21-17 (Mil)
(RS Pts.—Packers 1,239, Vikings 1,146)
**GREEN BAY vs. NEW ENGLAND**
RS: Series tied, 2-2
1973—Patriots, 33-24 (NE)
1979—Packers, 27-14 (GB)
1985—Patriots, 26-20 (NE)
1988—Packers, 45-3 (Mil)
(RS Pts.—Packers 116, Patriots 76)
**GREEN BAY vs. NEW ORLEANS**
RS: Packers lead series, 12-4
1968—Packers, 29-7 (Mil)
1971—Saints, 29-21 (Mil)
1972—Packers, 30-20 (NO)
1973—Packers, 30-10 (Mil)
1975—Saints, 20-19 (NO)
1976—Packers, 32-27 (Mil)
1977—Packers, 24-20 (NO)
1978—Packers, 28-17 (Mil)
1979—Packers, 28-19 (Mil)
1981—Packers, 35-7 (NO)
1984—Packers, 23-13 (NO)
1985—Packers, 38-14 (Mil)
1986—Saints, 24-10 (NO)
1987—Saints, 33-24 (NO)
1989—Packers, 35-34 (GB)
1993—Packers, 19-17 (NO)
(RS Pts.—Packers 425, Saints 311)
**GREEN BAY vs. N.Y. GIANTS**
RS: Packers lead series, 21-20-2
PS: Packers lead series, 4-1
1928—Giants, 6-0 (GB)
Packers, 7-0 (NY)
1929—Packers, 20-6 (NY)
1930—Packers, 14-7 (GB)
Giants, 13-6 (NY)
1931—Packers, 27-7 (GB)
Packers, 14-10 (NY)
1932—Packers, 13-0 (GB)
Giants, 6-0 (NY)
1933—Giants, 10-7 (Mil)
Giants, 17-6 (NY)
1934—Packers, 20-6 (Mil)
Giants, 17-3 (NY)
1935—Packers, 16-7 (GB)
1936—Packers, 26-14 (NY)
1937—Giants, 10-0 (NY)
1938—Giants, 15-3 (NY)
*Giants, 23-17 (NY)
1939—*Packers, 27-0 (Mil)
1940—Giants, 7-3 (NY)
1942—Tie, 21-21 (NY)
1943—Packers, 35-21 (NY)
1944—Giants, 24-0 (NY)
*Packers, 14-7 (NY)
1945—Packers, 23-14 (NY)
1947—Tie, 24-24 (NY)
1948—Giants, 49-3 (Mil)
1949—Giants, 30-10 (GB)
1952—Packers, 17-3 (NY)
1957—Giants, 31-17 (GB)
1959—Giants, 20-3 (NY)
1961—Packers, 20-17 (Mil)
*Packers, 37-0 (GB)
1962—*Packers, 16-7 (NY)
1967—Packers, 48-21 (NY)
1969—Packers, 20-10 (Mil)

1971—Giants, 42-40 (GB)
1973—Packers, 16-14 (New Haven)
1975—Packers, 40-14 (Mil)
1980—Giants, 27-21 (NY)
1981—Packers, 27-14 (NY)
Packers, 26-24 (Mil)
1982—Packers, 27-19 (NY)
1983—Giants, 27-3 (NY)
1985—Packers, 23-20 (GB)
1986—Giants, 55-24 (NY)
1987—Giants, 20-10 (NY)
1992—Giants, 27-7 (NY)
(RS Pts.—Giants 746, Packers 690)
(PS Pts.—Packers 111, Giants 37)
*NFL Championship*

**GREEN BAY vs. N.Y. JETS**
RS: Jets lead series, 5-1
1973—Packers, 23-7 (Mil)
1979—Jets, 27-22 (GB)
1981—Jets, 28-3 (NY)
1982—Jets, 15-13 (NY)
1985—Jets, 24-3 (Mil)
1991—Jets, 19-16 (NY) OT
(RS Pts.—Jets 120, Packers 80)

**GREEN BAY vs. PHILADELPHIA**
RS: Packers lead series, 19-7
PS: Eagles lead series, 1-0
1933—Packers, 35-9 (GB)
Packers, 10-0 (P)
1934—Packers, 19-6 (GB)
1935—Packers, 13-6 (P)
1937—Packers, 37-7 (Mil)
1939—Packers, 23-16 (P)
1940—Packers, 27-20 (GB)
1942—Packers, 7-0 (P)
1946—Packers, 19-7 (P)
1947—Eagles, 28-14 (P)
1951—Packers, 37-24 (GB)
1952—Packers, 12-10 (Mil)
1954—Packers, 37-14 (P)
1958—Packers, 38-35 (GB)
1960—*Eagles, 17-13 (P)
1962—Packers, 49-0 (P)
1968—Packers, 30-13 (GB)
1970—Packers, 30-17 (Mil)
1974—Eagles, 36-14 (P)
1976—Packers, 28-13 (GB)
1978—Eagles, 10-3 (P)
1979—Eagles, 21-10 (GB)
1987—Packers, 16-10 (GB) OT
1990—Eagles, 31-0 (P)
1991—Eagles, 20-3 (GB)
1992—Packers, 27-24 (Mil)
1993—Eagles, 20-17 (GB)
(RS Pts.—Packers 555, Eagles 397)
(PS Pts.—Eagles 17, Packers 13)
*NFL Championship*

**GREEN BAY vs. *PITTSBURGH**
RS: Packers lead series, 17-11
1933—Packers, 47-0 (GB)
1935—Packers, 27-0 (GB)
Packers, 34-14 (P)
1936—Packers, 42-10 (Mil)
1938—Packers, 20-0 (GB)
1940—Packers, 24-3 (Mil)
1941—Packers, 54-7 (P)
1942—Packers, 24-21 (Mil)
1946—Packers, 17-7 (GB)
1947—Steelers, 18-17 (Mil)
1948—Steelers, 38-7 (P)
1949—Steelers, 30-7 (Mil)
1951—Packers, 35-33 (Mil)
Steelers, 28-7 (P)
1953—Steelers, 31-14 (P)
1954—Steelers, 21-20 (GB)
1957—Packers, 27-10 (P)
1960—Packers, 19-13 (P)
1963—Packers, 33-14 (Mil)
1965—Packers, 41-9 (P)
1967—Steelers, 24-17 (GB)
1969—Packers, 38-34 (P)
1970—Packers, 20-12 (P)
1975—Steelers, 16-13 (Mil)
1980—Steelers, 22-20 (P)
1983—Steelers, 25-21 (GB)
1986—Steelers, 27-3 (P)
1992—Packers, 17-3 (GB)
(RS Pts.—Packers 665, Steelers 470)
*Steelers known as Pirates prior to 1941*

**GREEN BAY vs. SAN DIEGO**
RS: Packers lead series, 4-1
1970—Packers, 22-20 (SD)
1974—Packers, 34-0 (GB)
1978—Packers, 24-3 (SD)
1984—Chargers, 34-28 (GB)
1993—Packers, 20-13 (SD)
(RS Pts.—Packers 128, Chargers 70)

**GREEN BAY vs. SAN FRANCISCO**
RS: 49ers lead series, 25-21-1
1950—Packers, 25-21 (GB)
49ers, 30-14 (SF)
1951—49ers, 31-19 (SF)
1952—49ers, 24-14 (SF)
1953—49ers, 37-7 (Mil)
49ers, 48-14 (SF)
1954—49ers, 23-17 (Mil)
49ers, 35-0 (SF)
1955—Packers, 27-21 (Mil)
Packers, 28-7 (SF)
1956—49ers, 17-16 (GB)
49ers, 38-20 (SF)
1957—49ers, 24-14 (Mil)
49ers, 27-20 (SF)
1958—49ers, 33-12 (Mil)
49ers, 48-21 (SF)
1959—Packers, 21-20 (GB)
Packers, 36-14 (SF)
1960—Packers, 41-14 (Mil)
Packers, 13-0 (SF)
1961—Packers, 30-10 (GB)
49ers, 22-21 (SF)
1962—Packers, 31-13 (Mil)
Packers, 31-21 (SF)
1963—Packers, 28-10 (Mil)
Packers, 21-17 (SF)
1964—Packers, 24-14 (Mil)
49ers, 24-14 (SF)
1965—Packers, 27-10 (GB)
Tie, 24-24 (SF)
1966—49ers, 21-20 (SF)
Packers, 20-7 (Mil)
1967—Packers, 13-0 (GB)
1968—49ers, 27-20 (SF)
1969—Packers, 14-7 (Mil)
1970—49ers, 26-10 (SF)
1972—Packers, 34-24 (Mil)
1973—49ers, 20-6 (SF)
1974—49ers, 7-6 (SF)
1976—49ers, 26-14 (GB)
1977—Packers, 16-14 (Mil)
1980—Packers, 23-16 (Mil)
1981—49ers, 13-3 (Mil)
1986—49ers, 31-17 (Mil)
1987—49ers, 23-12 (GB)
1989—Packers, 21-17 (SF)
1990—49ers, 24-20 (GB)
(RS Pts.—49ers 980, Packers 899)

**GREEN BAY vs. SEATTLE**
RS: Series tied, 3-3
1976—Packers, 27-20 (Mil)
1978—Packers, 45-28 (Mil)
1981—Packers, 34-24 (GB)
1984—Seahawks, 30-24 (Mil)
1987—Seahawks, 24-13 (S)
1990—Seahawks, 20-14 (Mil)
(RS Pts.—Packers 157, Seahawks 146)

**GREEN BAY vs. TAMPA BAY**
RS: Packers lead series, 17-12-1
1977—Packers, 13-0 (TB)
1978—Packers, 9-7 (GB)
Packers, 17-7 (TB)
1979—Buccaneers, 21-10 (GB)
Buccaneers, 21-3 (TB)
1980—Tie, 14-14 (TB) OT
Buccaneers, 20-17 (Mil)
1981—Buccaneers, 21-10 (GB)
Buccaneers, 37-3 (TB)
1983—Packers, 55-14 (GB)
Packers, 12-9 (TB) OT
1984—Buccaneers, 30-27 (TB) OT
Packers, 27-14 (GB)
1985—Packers, 21-0 (GB)
Packers, 20-17 (TB)
1986—Packers, 31-7 (Mil)
Packers, 21-7 (TB)
1987—Buccaneers, 23-17 (Mil)
1988—Buccaneers, 13-10 (GB)
Buccaneers, 27-24 (TB)
1989—Buccaneers, 23-21 (GB)
Packers, 17-16 (TB)
1990—Buccaneers, 26-14 (TB)
Packers, 20-10 (Mil)
1991—Packers, 15-13 (GB)
Packers, 27-0 (TB)
1992—Buccaneers, 31-3 (TB)
Packers, 19-14 (Mil)
1993—Packers, 37-14 (TB)
Packers, 13-10 (GB)
(RS Pts.—Packers 547, Buccaneers 466)

**GREEN BAY vs. *WASHINGTON**
RS: Packers lead series, 13-12-1
PS: Series tied, 1-1
1932—Packers, 21-0 (B)
1933—Tie, 7-7 (GB)
Redskins, 20-7 (B)
1934—Packers, 10-0 (B)
1936—Packers, 31-2 (GB)
Packers, 7-3 (B)
**Packers, 21-6 (New York)
1937—Redskins, 14-6 (W)
1939—Packers, 24-14 (Mil)
1941—Packers, 22-17 (W)
1943—Redskins, 33-7 (Mil)
1946—Packers, 20-7 (W)
1947—Packers, 27-10 (Mil)
1948—Redskins, 23-7 (Mil)
1949—Redskins, 30-0 (W)
1950—Packers, 35-21 (Mil)
1952—Packers, 35-20 (Mil)
1958—Redskins, 37-21 (W)
1959—Packers, 21-0 (GB)
1968—Packers, 27-7 (W)
1972—Redskins, 21-16 (W)
***Redskins, 16-3 (W)
1974—Redskins, 17-6 (GB)
1977—Redskins, 10-9 (W)
1979—Redskins, 38-21 (W)
1983—Packers, 48-47 (GB)
1986—Redskins, 16-7 (GB)
1988—Redskins, 20-17 (Mil)
(RS Pts.—Packers 459, Redskins 434)
(PS Pts.—Packers 24, Redskins 22)
*Franchise in Boston prior to 1937 and known as Braves prior to 1933*
***NFL Championship*
****NFC Divisional Playoff*

---

**HOUSTON vs. ARIZONA**
RS: Cardinals lead series, 3-2;
See Arizona vs. Houston

**HOUSTON vs. ATLANTA**
RS: Falcons lead series, 5-3;
See Atlanta vs. Houston

**HOUSTON vs. BUFFALO**
RS: Oilers lead series, 20-12
PS: Bills lead series, 2-0;
See Buffalo vs. Houston

**HOUSTON vs. CHICAGO**
RS: Oilers lead series, 4-2;
See Chicago vs. Houston

**HOUSTON vs. CINCINNATI**
RS: Oilers lead series, 25-24-1
PS: Bengals lead series, 1-0;
See Cincinnati vs. Houston

**HOUSTON vs. CLEVELAND**
RS: Browns lead series, 27-20
PS: Oilers lead series, 1-0;
See Cleveland vs. Houston

**HOUSTON vs. DALLAS**
RS: Cowboys lead series, 4-3;
See Dallas vs. Houston

**HOUSTON vs. DENVER**
RS: Oilers lead series, 19-11-1
PS: Broncos lead series, 2-1;
See Denver vs. Houston

**HOUSTON vs. DETROIT**
RS: Oilers lead series, 4-2;
See Detroit vs. Houston

**HOUSTON vs. GREEN BAY**
RS: Series tied, 3-3;
See Green Bay vs. Houston

**HOUSTON vs. *INDIANAPOLIS**
RS: Oilers lead series, 7-6
1970—Colts, 24-20 (H)
1973—Oilers, 31-27 (B)
1976—Colts, 38-14 (B)
1979—Oilers, 28-16 (B)
1980—Oilers, 21-16 (H)
1983—Colts, 20-10 (B)
1984—Colts, 35-21 (H)
1985—Colts, 34-16 (I)
1986—Oilers, 31-17 (H)
1987—Colts, 51-27 (I)
1988—Oilers, 17-14 (I) OT
1990—Oilers, 24-10 (H)
1992—Oilers, 20-10 (I)
(RS Pts.—Colts 312, Oilers 280)
*Franchise in Baltimore prior to 1984*

**HOUSTON vs. *KANSAS CITY**
RS: Chiefs lead series, 21-17
PS: Chiefs lead series, 2-0
1960—Oilers, 20-10 (H)
Texans, 24-0 (D)
1961—Texans, 26-21 (D)
Oilers, 38-7 (H)
1962—Texans, 31-7 (H)
Oilers, 14-6 (D)
**Texans, 20-17 (H) OT
1963—Chiefs, 28-7 (KC)
Oilers, 28-7 (H)
1964—Chiefs, 28-7 (KC)
Chiefs, 28-19 (H)
1965—Chiefs, 52-21 (KC)
Oilers, 38-36 (H)
1966—Chiefs, 48-23 (KC)
1967—Chiefs, 25-20 (H)
Oilers, 24-19 (KC)
1968—Chiefs, 26-21 (H)
Chiefs, 24-10 (KC)
1969—Chiefs, 24-0 (KC)
1970—Chiefs, 24-9 (KC)
1971—Chiefs, 20-16 (H)
1973—Chiefs, 38-14 (KC)
1974—Chiefs, 17-7 (H)
1975—Oilers, 17-13 (KC)
1977—Oilers, 34-20 (H)
1978—Oilers, 20-17 (KC)
1979—Oilers, 20-6 (H)
1980—Chiefs, 21-20 (KC)
1981—Chiefs, 23-10 (KC)
1983—Chiefs, 13-10 (H) OT
1984—Oilers, 17-16 (KC)
1985—Oilers, 23-20 (H)
1986—Chiefs, 27-13 (KC)
1988—Oilers, 7-6 (H)
1989—Chiefs, 34-0 (KC)
1990—Oilers, 27-10 (KC)
1991—Oilers, 17-7 (H)
1992—Oilers, 23-20 (H) OT
1993—Oilers, 30-0 (H)
***Chiefs, 28-20 (H)
(RS Pts.—Chiefs 801, Oilers 652)
(PS Pts.—Chiefs 48, Oilers 37)
*Franchise in Dallas prior to 1963 and known as Texans*
***AFL Championship*
****AFC Divisional Playoff*

**HOUSTON vs. *L.A. RAIDERS**
RS: Raiders lead series, 19-13
PS: Raiders lead series, 3-0
1960—Oilers, 37-22 (O)
Raiders, 14-13 (H)

1961—Oilers, 55-0 (H)
Oilers, 47-16 (O)
1962—Oilers, 28-20 (O)
Oilers, 32-17 (H)
1963—Raiders, 24-13 (H)
Raiders, 52-49 (O)
1964—Oilers, 42-28 (H)
Raiders, 20-10 (O)
1965—Raiders, 21-17 (O)
Raiders, 33-21 (H)
1966—Oilers, 31-0 (H)
Raiders, 38-23 (O)
1967—Raiders, 19-7 (H)
**Raiders, 40-7 (O)
1968—Raiders, 24-15 (H)
1969—Raiders, 21-17 (O)
***Raiders, 56-7 (O)
1971—Raiders, 41-21 (O)
1972—Raiders, 34-0 (H)
1973—Raiders, 17-6 (H)
1975—Oilers, 27-26 (O)
1976—Raiders, 14-13 (H)
1977—Raiders, 34-29 (O)
1978—Raiders, 21-17 (O)
1979—Oilers, 31-17 (H)
1980—****Raiders, 27-7 (O)
1981—Oilers, 17-16 (H)
1983—Raiders, 20-6 (LA)
1984—Raiders, 24-14 (H)
1986—Raiders, 28-17 (H)
1988—Oilers, 38-35 (H)
1989—Oilers, 23-7 (H)
1991—Oilers, 47-17 (H)
(RS Pts.—Oilers 763, Raiders 720)
(PS Pts.—Raiders 123, Oilers 21)
*Franchise in Oakland prior to 1982*
***AFL Championship*
****Inter-Divisional Playoff*
*****AFC First-Round Playoff*

**HOUSTON vs. L.A. RAMS**
RS: Rams lead series, 5-2
1973—Rams, 31-26 (H)
1978—Rams, 10-6 (H)
1981—Oilers, 27-20 (LA)
1984—Rams, 27-16 (LA)
1987—Oilers, 20-16 (H)
1990—Rams, 17-13 (LA)
1993—Rams, 28-13 (H)
(RS Pts.—Rams 149, Oilers 121)

**HOUSTON vs. MIAMI**
RS: Series tied, 11-11
PS: Oilers lead series, 1-0
1966—Dolphins, 20-13 (H)
Dolphins, 29-28 (M)
1967—Oilers, 17-14 (H)
Oilers, 41-10 (M)
1968—Oilers, 24-10 (M)
Dolphins, 24-7 (H)
1969—Oilers, 22-10 (H)
Oilers, 32-7 (M)
1970—Dolphins, 20-10 (H)
1972—Dolphins, 34-13 (M)
1975—Oilers, 20-19 (H)
1977—Dolphins, 27-7 (M)
1978—Oilers, 35-30 (H)
*Oilers, 17-9 (M)
1979—Oilers, 9-6 (M)
1981—Dolphins, 16-10 (H)
1983—Dolphins, 24-17 (H)
1984—Dolphins, 28-10 (M)
1985—Oilers, 26-23 (H)
1986—Dolphins, 28-7 (M)
1989—Oilers, 39-7 (H)
1991—Oilers, 17-13 (M)
1992—Dolphins, 19-16 (M)
(RS Pts.—Oilers 420, Dolphins 418)
(PS Pts.—Oilers 17, Dolphins 9)
**AFC First Round Playoff*

**HOUSTON vs. MINNESOTA**
RS: Series tied, 3-3
1974—Vikings, 51-10 (M)
1980—Oilers, 20-16 (H)
1983—Vikings, 34-14 (M)
1986—Oilers, 23-10 (H)
1989—Vikings, 38-7 (M)
1992—Oilers, 17-13 (M)
(RS Pts.—Vikings 162, Oilers 91)

**HOUSTON vs. *NEW ENGLAND**
RS: Patriots lead series, 17-14-1
PS: Oilers lead series, 1-0
1960—Oilers, 24-10 (B)
Oilers, 37-21 (H)
1961—Tie, 31-31 (B)
Oilers, 27-15 (H)
1962—Patriots, 34-21 (B)
Oilers, 21-17 (H)
1963—Patriots, 45-3 (B)
Patriots, 46-28 (H)
1964—Patriots, 25-24 (B)
Patriots, 34-17 (H)
1965—Oilers, 31-10 (H)
Patriots, 42-14 (B)
1966—Patriots, 27-21 (B)
Patriots, 38-14 (H)
1967—Patriots, 18-7 (B)
Oilers, 27-6 (H)
1968—Oilers, 16-0 (B)
Oilers, 45-17 (H)
1969—Patriots, 24-0 (B)
Oilers, 27-23 (H)
1971—Patriots, 28-20 (NE)
1973—Patriots, 32-0 (H)
1975—Oilers, 7-0 (NE)
1978—Oilers, 26-23 (NE)
**Oilers, 31-14 (NE)
1980—Oilers, 38-34 (H)
1981—Patriots, 38-10 (NE)
1982—Patriots, 29-21 (NE)
1987—Patriots, 21-7 (H)
1988—Oilers, 31-6 (H)
1989—Patriots, 23-13 (NE)
1991—Patriots, 24-20 (NE)
1993—Oilers, 28-14 (NE)
(RS Pts.—Patriots 755, Oilers 656)
(PS Pts.—Oilers 31, Patriots 14)
*Franchise in Boston prior to 1971*
***AFC Divisional Playoff*

**HOUSTON vs. NEW ORLEANS**
RS: Saints lead series, 4-3-1
1971—Tie, 13-13 (H)
1976—Oilers, 31-26 (NO)
1978—Oilers, 17-12 (NO)
1981—Saints, 27-24 (H)
1984—Saints, 27-10 (H)
1987—Saints, 24-10 (NO)
1990—Oilers, 23-10 (H)
1993—Saints, 33-21 (NO)
(RS Pts.—Saints 172, Oilers 149)

**HOUSTON vs. N.Y. GIANTS**
RS: Giants lead series, 4-0
1973—Giants, 34-14 (NY)
1982—Giants, 17-14 (NY)
1985—Giants, 35-14 (H)
1991—Giants, 24-20 (NY)
(RS Pts.—Giants 110, Oilers 62)

**HOUSTON vs. *N.Y. JETS**
RS: Oilers lead series, 17-12-1
PS: Oilers lead series, 1-0
1960—Oilers, 27-21 (H)
Oilers, 42-28 (NY)
1961—Oilers, 49-13 (H)
Oilers, 48-21 (NY)
1962—Oilers, 56-17 (H)
Oilers, 44-10 (NY)
1963—Jets, 24-17 (NY)
Oilers, 31-27 (H)
1964—Jets, 24-21 (NY)
Oilers, 33-17 (H)
1965—Oilers, 27-21 (H)
Jets, 41-14 (NY)
1966—Jets, 52-13 (NY)
Oilers, 24-0 (H)
1967—Tie, 28-28 (NY)
1968—Jets, 20-14 (H)
Jets, 26-7 (NY)
1969—Jets, 26-17 (NY)
Jets, 34-26 (H)
1972—Oilers, 26-20 (H)
1974—Oilers, 27-22 (NY)
1977—Oilers, 20-0 (H)
1979—Oilers, 27-24 (H) OT
1980—Jets, 31-28 (NY) OT
1981—Jets, 33-17 (NY)
1984—Oilers, 31-20 (H)
1988—Jets, 45-3 (NY)
1990—Jets, 17-12 (H)
1991—Oilers, 23-20 (NY)
**Oilers, 17-10 (H)
1993—Oilers, 24-0 (H)
(RS Pts.—Oilers 776, Jets 682)
(PS Pts.—Oilers 17, Jets 10)
*Jets known as Titans prior to 1963*
***AFC First-Round Playoff*

**HOUSTON vs. PHILADELPHIA**
RS: Eagles lead series, 5-0
1972—Eagles, 18-17 (H)
1979—Eagles, 26-20 (H)
1982—Eagles, 35-14 (P)
1988—Eagles, 32-23 (P)
1991—Eagles, 13-6 (H)
(RS Pts.—Eagles 124, Oilers 80)

**HOUSTON vs. PITTSBURGH**
RS: Steelers lead series, 29-18
PS: Steelers lead series, 3-0
1970—Oilers, 19-7 (P)
Steelers, 7-3 (H)
1971—Steelers, 23-16 (P)
Oilers, 29-3 (H)
1972—Steelers, 24-7 (P)
Steelers, 9-3 (H)
1973—Steelers, 36-7 (H)
Steelers, 33-7 (P)
1974—Steelers, 13-7 (H)
Oilers, 13-10 (P)
1975—Steelers, 24-17 (P)
Steelers, 32-9 (H)
1976—Steelers, 32-16 (P)
Steelers, 21-0 (H)
1977—Oilers, 27-10 (H)
Steelers, 27-10 (P)
1978—Oilers, 24-17 (P)
Steelers, 13-3 (H)
*Steelers, 34-5 (P)
1979—Steelers, 38-7 (P)
Oilers, 20-17 (H)
*Steelers, 27-13 (P)
1980—Steelers, 31-17 (P)
Oilers, 6-0 (H)
1981—Steelers, 26-13 (P)
Oilers, 21-20 (H)
1982—Steelers, 24-10 (H)
1983—Steelers, 40-28 (H)
Steelers, 17-10 (P)
1984—Steelers, 35-7 (P)
Oilers, 23-20 (H) OT
1985—Steelers, 20-0 (P)
Steelers, 30-7 (H)
1986—Steelers, 22-16 (H) OT
Steelers, 21-10 (P)
1987—Oilers, 23-3 (P)
Oilers, 24-16 (H)
1988—Oilers, 34-14 (P)
Steelers, 37-34 (H)
1989—Oilers, 27-0 (H)
Oilers, 23-16 (P)
**Steelers, 26-23 (H)
1990—Steelers, 20-9 (P)
Oilers, 34-14 (H)
1991—Steelers, 26-14 (P)
Oilers, 31-6 (H)
1992—Steelers, 29-24 (H)
Steelers, 21-20 (P)
1993—Oilers, 23-3 (H)
Oilers, 26-17 (P)
(RS Pts.—Steelers 924, Oilers 758)
(PS Pts.—Steelers 87, Oilers 41)
**AFC Championship*
***AFC First-Round Playoff*

**HOUSTON vs. *SAN DIEGO**
RS: Chargers lead series, 18-13-1
PS: Oilers lead series, 3-0
1960—Oilers, 38-28 (H)
Chargers, 24-21 (LA)
**Oilers, 24-16 (H)
1961—Chargers, 34-24 (SD)
Oilers, 33-13 (H)
**Oilers, 10-3 (SD)
1962—Oilers, 42-17 (SD)
Oilers, 33-27 (H)
1963—Chargers, 27-0 (SD)
Chargers 20-14 (H)
1964—Chargers, 27-21 (SD)
Chargers, 20-17 (H)
1965—Chargers, 31-14 (SD)
Chargers, 37-26 (H)
1966—Chargers, 28-22 (H)
1967—Chargers, 13-3 (SD)
Oilers, 24-17 (H)
1968—Chargers, 30-14 (SD)
1969—Chargers, 21-17 (H)
1970—Tie, 31-31 (SD)
1971—Oilers, 49-33 (H)
1972—Chargers, 34-20 (SD)
1974—Oilers, 21-14 (H)
1975—Oilers, 33-17 (H)
1976—Chargers, 30-27 (SD)
1978—Chargers, 45-24 (H)
1979—***Oilers, 17-14 (SD)
1984—Chargers, 31-14 (SD)
1985—Oilers, 37-35 (H)
1986—Chargers, 27-0 (SD)
1987—Oilers, 33-18 (H)
1989—Oilers, 34-27 (SD)
1990—Oilers, 17-7 (SD)
1992—Oilers, 27-0 (H)
1993—Chargers, 18-17 (SD)
(RS Pts.—Chargers 781, Oilers 747)
(PS Pts.—Oilers 51, Chargers 33)
*Franchise in Los Angeles prior to 1961*
***AFL Championship*
****AFC Divisional Playoff*

**HOUSTON vs. SAN FRANCISCO**
RS: 49ers lead series, 5-3
1970—49ers, 30-20 (H)
1975—Oilers, 27-13 (SF)
1978—Oilers, 20-19 (H)
1981—49ers, 28-6 (SF)
1984—49ers, 34-21 (H)
1987—49ers, 27-20 (SF)
1990—49ers, 24-21 (H)
1993—Oilers, 10-7 (SF)
(RS Pts.—49ers 182, Oilers 145)

**HOUSTON vs. SEATTLE**
RS: Series tied, 4-4
PS: Oilers lead series, 1-0
1977—Oilers, 22-10 (S)
1979—Seahawks, 34-14 (S)
1980—Seahawks, 26-7 (H)
1981—Oilers, 35-17 (H)
1982—Oilers, 23-21 (H)
1987—*Oilers, 23-20 (H) OT
1988—Seahawks, 27-24 (S)
1990—Seahawks, 13-10 (S) OT
1993—Oilers, 24-14 (H)
(RS Pts.—Seahawks 162, Oilers 159)
(PS Pts.—Oilers 23, Seahawks 20)
**AFC First-Round Playoff*

**HOUSTON vs. TAMPA BAY**
RS: Oilers lead series, 3-1
1976—Oilers, 20-0 (H)
1980—Oilers, 20-14 (H)
1983—Buccaneers, 33-24 (TB)
1989—Oilers, 20-17 (H)
(RS Pts.—Oilers 84, Buccaneers 64)

**HOUSTON vs. WASHINGTON**
RS: Series tied, 3-3
1971—Redskins, 22-13 (W)
1975—Oilers, 13-10 (H)
1979—Oilers, 29-27 (W)
1985—Redskins, 16-13 (W)
1988—Oilers, 41-17 (H)
1991—Redskins, 16-13 (W) OT

# ALL-TIME TEAM VS. TEAM RESULTS

(RS Pts.—Oilers 122, Redskins 108)

**INDIANAPOLIS vs. ARIZONA**
RS: Cardinals lead series, 6-5;
See Arizona vs. Indianapolis
**INDIANAPOLIS vs. ATLANTA**
RS: Colts lead series, 10-0;
See Atlanta vs. Indianapolis
**INDIANAPOLIS vs. BUFFALO**
RS: Bills lead series, 26-20-1;
See Buffalo vs. Indianapolis
**INDIANAPOLIS vs. CHICAGO**
RS: Colts lead series, 21-16;
See Chicago vs. Indianapolis
**INDIANAPOLIS vs. CINCINNATI**
RS: Colts lead series, 8-5
PS: Colts lead series, 1-0;
See Cincinnati vs. Indianapolis
**INDIANAPOLIS vs. CLEVELAND**
RS: Browns lead series, 12-7
PS: Series tied, 2-2;
See Cleveland vs. Indianapolis
**INDIANAPOLIS vs. DALLAS**
RS: Cowboys lead series, 7-2
PS: Colts lead series, 1-0;
See Dallas vs. Indianapolis
**INDIANAPOLIS vs. DENVER**
RS: Broncos lead series, 9-2;
See Denver vs. Indianapolis
**INDIANAPOLIS vs. DETROIT**
RS: Series tied, 17-17-2;
See Detroit vs. Indianapolis
**INDIANAPOLIS vs. GREEN BAY**
RS: Series tied, 18-18-1
PS: Packers lead series, 1-0;
See Green Bay vs. Indianapolis
**INDIANAPOLIS vs. HOUSTON**
RS: Oilers lead series, 7-6;
See Houston vs. Indianapolis
***INDIANAPOLIS vs. KANSAS CITY**
RS: Chiefs lead series, 6-4
1970—Chiefs, 44-24 (B)
1972—Chiefs, 24-10 (KC)
1975—Colts, 28-14 (B)
1977—Colts, 17-6 (KC)
1979—Chiefs, 14-0 (KC)
Chiefs, 10-7 (B)
1980—Colts, 31-24 (KC)
Chiefs, 38-28 (B)
1985—Chiefs, 20-7 (KC)
1990—Colts, 23-19 (I)
(RS Pts.—Chiefs 213, Colts 175)
**Franchise in Baltimore prior to 1984*
***INDIANAPOLIS vs **L.A. RAIDERS**
RS: Raiders lead series, 4-2
PS: Series tied, 1-1
1970—***Colts, 27-17 (B)
1971—Colts, 37-14 (O)
1973—Raiders, 34-21 (B)
1975—Raiders, 31-20 (B)
1977—****Raiders, 37-31 (B) OT
1984—Raiders, 21-7 (LA)
1986—Colts, 30-24 (LA)
1991—Raiders, 16-0 (LA)
(RS Pts.—Raiders 140, Colts 115)
(PS Pts.—Colts 58, Raiders 54)
**Franchise in Baltimore prior to 1984*
***Franchise in Oakland prior to 1982*
****AFC Championship*
*****AFC Divisional Playoff*
***INDIANAPOLIS vs. L.A. RAMS**
RS: Colts lead series, 20-16-2
1953—Rams, 21-13 (B)
Rams, 45-2 (LA)
1954—Rams, 48-0 (B)
Colts, 22-21 (LA)
1955—Tie, 17-17 (B)
Rams, 20-14 (LA)
1956—Colts, 56-21 (B)
Rams, 31-7 (LA)
1957—Colts, 31-14 (B)
Rams, 37-21 (LA)
1958—Colts, 34-7 (B)
Rams, 30-28 (LA)
1959—Colts, 35-21 (B)
Colts, 45-26 (LA)
1960—Colts, 31-17 (B)
Rams, 10-3 (LA)
1961—Colts, 27-24 (B)
Rams, 34-17 (LA)
1962—Colts, 30-27 (B)
Colts, 14-2 (LA)
1963—Rams, 17-16 (LA)
Colts, 19-16 (B)
1964—Colts, 35-20 (B)
Colts, 24-7 (LA)
1965—Colts, 35-20 (B)
Colts, 20-17 (LA)
1966—Colts, 17-3 (LA)
Rams, 23-7 (B)
1967—Tie, 24-24 (B)
Rams, 34-10 (LA)
1968—Colts, 27-10 (B)
Colts, 28-24 (LA)
1969—Rams, 27-20 (B)
Colts, 13-7 (LA)
1971—Colts, 24-17 (B)
1975—Rams, 24-13 (LA)
1986—Rams, 24-7 (I)
1989—Rams, 31-17 (LA)
(RS Pts.—Rams 818, Colts 803)
**Franchise in Baltimore prior to 1984*
***INDIANAPOLIS vs. MIAMI**
RS: Dolphins lead series, 34-14
PS: Dolphins lead series, 1-0
1970—Colts, 35-0 (B)
Dolphins, 34-17 (M)
1971—Dolphins, 17-14 (M)
Colts, 14-3 (B)
**Dolphins, 21-0 (M)
1972—Dolphins, 23-0 (B)
Dolphins, 16-0 (M)
1973—Dolphins, 44-0 (M)
Colts, 16-3 (B)
1974—Dolphins, 17-7 (M)
Dolphins, 17-16 (B)
1975—Colts, 33-17 (M)
Colts, 10-7 (B) OT
1976—Colts, 28-14 (B)
Colts, 17-16 (M)
1977—Colts, 45-28 (B)
Dolphins, 17-6 (M)
1978—Dolphins, 42-0 (B)
Dolphins, 26-8 (M)
1979—Dolphins, 19-0 (M)
Dolphins, 28-24 (B)
1980—Colts, 30-17 (M)
Dolphins, 24-14 (B)
1981—Dolphins, 31-28 (B)
Dolphins, 27-10 (M)
1982—Dolphins, 24-20 (M)
Dolphins, 34-7 (B)
1983—Dolphins, 21-7 (B)
Dolphins, 37-0 (M)
1984—Dolphins, 44-7 (M)
Dolphins, 35-17 (I)
1985—Dolphins, 30-13 (M)
Dolphins, 34-20 (I)
1986—Dolphins, 30-10 (M)
Dolphins, 17-13 (I)
1987—Dolphins, 23-10 (I)
Colts, 40-21 (M)
1988—Colts, 15-13 (I)
Colts, 31-28 (M)
1989—Dolphins, 19-13 (M)
Colts, 42-13 (I)
1990—Dolphins, 27-7 (I)
Dolphins, 23-17 (M)
1991—Dolphins, 17-6 (M)
Dolphins, 10-6 (I)
1992—Colts, 31-20 (M)
Dolphins, 28-0 (I)
1993—Dolphins, 24-20 (I)
Dolphins, 41-27 (M)
(RS Pts.—Dolphins 1,100, Colts 751)
(PS Pts.—Dolphins 21, Colts 0)
**Franchise in Baltimore prior to 1984*
***AFC Championship*
***INDIANAPOLIS vs. MINNESOTA**
RS: Colts lead series, 11-6-1
PS: Colts lead series, 1-0
1961—Colts, 34-33 (B)
Vikings, 28-20 (M)
1962—Colts, 34-7 (M)
Colts, 42-17 (B)
1963—Colts, 37-34 (M)
Colts, 41-10 (B)
1964—Vikings, 34-24 (M)
Colts, 17-14 (B)
1965—Colts, 35-16 (B)
Colts, 41-21 (M)
1966—Colts, 38-23 (M)
Colts, 20-17 (B)
1967—Tie, 20-20 (M)
1968—Colts, 21-9 (B)
**Colts, 24-14 (B)
1969—Vikings, 52-14 (M)
1971—Vikings, 10-3 (M)
1982—Vikings, 13-10 (M)
1988—Vikings, 12-3 (M)
(RS Pts.—Colts 454, Vikings 370)
(PS Pts.—Colts 24, Vikings 14)
**Franchise in Baltimore prior to 1984*
***Conference Championship*
***INDIANAPOLIS vs. **NEW ENGLAND**
RS: Patriots lead series, 27-20
1970—Colts, 14-6 (Bos)
Colts, 27-3 (Balt)
1971—Colts, 23-3 (NE)
Patriots, 21-17 (Balt)
1972—Colts, 24-17 (NE)
Colts, 31-0 (Balt)
1973—Patriots, 24-16 (NE)
Colts, 18-13 (Balt)
1974—Patriots, 42-3 (NE)
Patriots, 27-17 (Balt)
1975—Patriots, 21-10 (NE)
Colts, 34-21 (Balt)
1976—Colts, 27-13 (NE)
Patriots, 21-14 (Balt)
1977—Patriots, 17-3 (NE)
Colts, 30-24 (Balt)
1978—Colts, 34-27 (NE)
Patriots, 35-14 (Balt)
1979—Colts, 31-26 (Balt)
Patriots, 50-21 (NE)
1980—Patriots, 37-21 (Balt)
Patriots, 47-21 (NE)
1981—Colts, 29-28 (NE)
Colts, 23-21 (Balt)
1982—Patriots, 24-13 (Balt)
1983—Colts, 29-23 (NE) OT
Colts, 12-7 (Balt)
1984—Patriots, 50-17 (I)
Patriots, 16-10 (NE)
1985—Patriots, 34-15 (NE)
Patriots, 38-31 (I)
1986—Patriots, 33-3 (NE)
Patriots, 30-21 (I)
1987—Colts, 30-16 (I)
Patriots, 24-0 (NE)
1988—Patriots, 21-17 (NE)
Colts, 24-21 (I)
1989—Patriots, 23-20 (I) OT
Patriots, 22-16 (NE)
1990—Patriots, 16-14 (I)
Colts, 13-10 (NE)
1991—Patriots, 16-7 (I)
Patriots, 23-17 (NE) OT
1992—Patriots, 37-34 (I) OT
Colts, 6-0 (NE)
1993—Colts, 9-6 (I)
Patriots, 38-0 (NE)
(RS Pts.—Patriots 1,072, Colts 860)
**Franchise in Baltimore prior to 1984*
***Franchise in Boston prior to 1971*
***INDIANAPOLIS vs. NEW ORLEANS**
RS: Colts lead series, 3-2
1967—Colts, 30-10 (B)
1969—Colts, 30-10 (NO)
1973—Colts, 14-10 (B)
1986—Saints, 17-14 (I)
1989—Saints, 41-6 (NO)
(RS Pts.—Colts 94, Saints 88)
**Franchise in Baltimore prior to 1984*
***INDIANAPOLIS vs. N.Y. GIANTS**
RS: Series tied, 5-5
PS: Colts lead series, 2-0
1954—Colts, 20-14 (B)
1955—Giants, 17-7 (NY)
1958—Giants, 24-21 (NY)
**Colts, 23-17 (NY) OT
1959—**Colts, 31-16 (B)
1963—Giants, 37-28 (B)
1968—Colts, 26-0 (NY)
1971—Colts, 31-7 (NY)
1975—Colts, 21-0 (NY)
1979—Colts, 31-7 (NY)
1990—Giants, 24-7 (I)
1993—Giants, 20-6 (NY)
(RS Pts.—Colts 198, Giants 150)
(PS Pts.—Colts 54, Giants 33)
**Franchise in Baltimore prior to 1984*
***NFL Championship*
***INDIANAPOLIS vs. N.Y. JETS**
RS: Colts lead series, 27-20
PS: Jets lead series, 1-0
1968—**Jets 16-7 (Miami)
1970—Colts, 29-22 (NY)
Colts, 35-20 (B)
1971—Colts, 22-0 (B)
Colts, 14-13 (NY)
1972—Jets, 44-34 (B)
Jets, 24-20 (NY)
1973—Jets, 34-10 (B)
Jets, 20-17 (NY)
1974—Colts, 35-20 (NY)
Jets, 45-38 (B)
1975—Colts, 45-28 (NY)
Colts, 52-19 (B)
1976—Colts, 20-0 (NY)
Colts, 33-16 (B)
1977—Colts, 20-12 (NY)
Colts, 33-12 (B)
1978—Jets, 33-10 (B)
Jets, 24-16 (NY)
1979—Colts, 10-8 (B)
Jets, 30-17 (NY)
1980—Colts, 17-14 (NY)
Colts, 35-21 (B)
1981—Jets, 41-14 (B)
Jets, 25-0 (NY)
1982—Jets, 37-0 (NY)
1983—Colts, 17-14 (NY)
Jets, 10-6 (B)
1984—Jets, 23-14 (I)
Colts, 9-5 (NY)
1985—Jets, 25-20 (NY)
Jets, 35-17 (I)
1986—Jets, 26-7 (I)
Jets, 31-16 (NY)
1987—Colts, 6-0 (I)
Colts, 19-14 (NY)
1988—Colts, 38-14 (I)
Jets, 34-16 (NY)
1989—Colts, 17-10 (NY)
Colts, 27-10 (I)
1990—Colts, 17-14 (I)
Colts, 29-21 (NY)
1991—Jets, 17-6 (I)
Colts, 28-27 (NY)
1992—Colts, 6-3 (I) OT
Colts, 10-6 (NY)
1993—Jets, 31-17 (I)
Colts, 9-6 (NY)
(RS Pts.—Jets 938,Colts 927)
(PS Pts.—Jets 16, Colts 7)
**Franchise in Baltimore prior to 1984*
***Super Bowl III*
***INDIANAPOLIS vs. PHILADELPHIA**
RS: Series tied, 6-6
1953—Eagles, 45-14 (P)

1965—Colts, 34-24 (B)
1967—Colts, 38-6 (P)
1969—Colts, 24-20 (B)
1970—Colts, 29-10 (B)
1974—Eagles, 30-10 (P)
1978—Eagles, 17-14 (B)
1981—Eagles, 38-13 (P)
1983—Colts, 22-21 (P)
1984—Eagles, 16-7 (P)
1990—Colts, 24-23 (P)
1993—Eagles, 20-10 (I)
(RS Pts.—Eagles 270, Colts 239)
*Franchise in Baltimore prior to 1984*

***INDIANAPOLIS vs. PITTSBURGH**
RS: Steelers lead series, 10-4
PS: Steelers lead series, 2-0
1957—Steelers, 19-13 (B)
1968—Colts, 41-7 (P)
1971—Colts, 34-21 (B)
1974—Steelers, 30-0 (B)
1975—**Steelers, 28-10 (P)
1976—**Steelers, 40-14 (B)
1977—Colts, 31-21 (B)
1978—Steelers, 35-13 (P)
1979—Steelers, 17-13 (P)
1980—Steelers, 20-17 (B)
1983—Steelers, 24-13 (B)
1984—Colts, 17-16 (I)
1985—Steelers, 45-3 (P)
1987—Steelers, 21-7 (P)
1991—Steelers, 21-3 (I)
1992—Steelers, 30-14 (P)
(RS Pts.—Steelers 327, Colts 219)
(PS Pts.—Steelers 68, Colts 24)
*Franchise in Baltimore prior to 1984*
***AFC Divisional Playoff*

***INDIANAPOLIS vs. SAN DIEGO**
RS: Chargers lead series, 9-5
1970—Colts, 16-14 (SD)
1972—Chargers, 23-20 (B)
1976—Colts, 37-21 (SD)
1981—Chargers, 43-14 (B)
1982—Chargers, 44-26 (SD)
1984—Chargers, 38-10 (I)
1986—Chargers, 17-3 (I)
1987—Chargers, 16-13 (I)
Colts, 20-7 (SD)
1988—Colts, 16-0 (SD)
1989—Colts, 10-6 (I)
1992—Chargers, 34-14 (I)
Chargers, 26-0 (SD)
1993—Chargers, 31-0 (I)
(RS Pts.—Chargers 320, Colts 199)
*Franchise in Baltimore prior to 1984*

***INDIANAPOLIS vs. SAN FRANCISCO**
RS: Colts lead series, 21-16
1953—49ers, 38-21 (B)
49ers, 45-14 (SF)
1954—Colts, 17-13 (B)
49ers, 10-7 (SF)
1955—Colts, 26-14 (B)
49ers, 35-24 (SF)
1956—49ers, 20-17 (B)
49ers, 30-17 (SF)
1957—Colts, 27-21 (B)
49ers, 17-13 (SF)
1958—Colts, 35-27 (B)
49ers, 21-12 (SF)
1959—Colts, 45-14 (B)
Colts, 34-14 (SF)
1960—49ers, 30-22 (B)
49ers, 34-10 (SF)
1961—Colts, 20-17 (B)
Colts, 27-24 (SF)
1962—49ers, 21-13 (B)
Colts, 22-3 (SF)
1963—Colts, 20-14 (SF)
Colts, 20-3 (B)
1964—Colts, 37-7 (B)
Colts, 14-3 (SF)
1965—Colts, 27-24 (B)
Colts, 34-28 (SF)
1966—Colts, 36-14 (B)
Colts, 30-14 (SF)
1967—Colts, 41-7 (B)
Colts, 26-9 (SF)
1968—Colts, 27-10 (B)
Colts, 42-14 (SF)
1969—49ers, 24-21 (B)
49ers, 20-17 (SF)
1972—49ers, 24-21 (SF)
1986—49ers, 35-14 (SF)
1989—49ers, 30-24 (I)
(RS Pts.—Colts 874, 49ers 728)
*Franchise in Baltimore prior to 1984*

***INDIANAPOLIS vs. SEATTLE**
RS: Colts lead series, 2-1
1977—Colts, 29-14 (S)
1978—Colts, 17-14 (S)
1991—Seahawks, 31-3 (S)
(RS Pts.—Seahawks 59, Colts 49)
*Franchise in Baltimore prior to 1984*

***INDIANAPOLIS vs. TAMPA BAY**
RS: Colts lead series, 5-2
1976—Colts, 42-17 (B)
1979—Buccaneers, 29-26 (B) OT
1985—Colts, 31-23 (TB)
1987—Colts, 24-6 (I)
1988—Colts, 35-31 (I)
1991—Buccaneers, 17-3 (TB)
1992—Colts, 24-14 (TB)
(RS Pts.—Colts 185, Buccaneers 137)
*Franchise in Baltimore prior to 1984*

***INDIANAPOLIS vs. WASHINGTON**
RS: Colts lead series, 16-7
1953—Colts, 27-17 (B)
1954—Redskins, 24-21 (W)
1955—Redskins, 14-13 (B)
1956—Colts, 19-17 (B)
1957—Colts, 21-17 (W)
1958—Colts, 35-10 (B)
1959—Redskins, 27-24 (W)
1960—Colts, 20-0 (B)
1961—Colts, 27-6 (W)
1962—Colts, 34-21 (B)
1963—Colts, 36-20 (W)
1964—Colts, 45-17 (B)
1965—Colts, 38-7 (W)
1966—Colts, 37-10 (B)
1967—Colts, 17-13 (W)
1969—Colts, 41-17 (B)
1973—Redskins, 22-14 (W)
1977—Colts, 10-3 (B)
1978—Colts, 21-17 (B)
1981—Redskins, 38-14 (W)
1984—Redskins, 35-7 (I)
1990—Colts, 35-28 (I)
1993—Redskins, 30-24 (W)
(RS Pts.—Colts 580, Redskins 410)
*Franchise in Baltimore prior to 1984*

**KANSAS CITY vs. ARIZONA**
RS: Chiefs lead series, 3-1-1;
See Arizona vs. Kansas City

**KANSAS CITY vs. ATLANTA**
RS: Chiefs lead series, 3-0;
See Atlanta vs. Kansas City

**KANSAS CITY vs. BUFFALO**
RS: Bills lead series, 15-13-1
PS: Bills lead series, 2-1;
See Buffalo vs. Kansas City

**KANSAS CITY vs. CHICAGO**
RS: Bears lead series, 4-2;
See Chicago vs. Kansas City

**KANSAS CITY vs. CINCINNATI**
RS: Chiefs lead series, 11-9;
See Cincinnati vs. Kansas City

**KANSAS CITY vs. CLEVELAND**
RS: Browns lead series, 7-6-2;
See Cleveland vs. Kansas City

**KANSAS CITY vs. DALLAS**
RS: Cowboys lead series, 3-2;
See Dallas vs. Kansas City

**KANSAS CITY vs. DENVER**
RS: Chiefs lead series, 38-29;
See Denver vs. Kansas City

**KANSAS CITY vs. DETROIT**
RS: Chiefs lead series, 4-3;
See Detroit vs. Kansas City

**KANSAS CITY vs. GREEN BAY**
RS: Chiefs lead series, 4-1-1
PS: Packers lead series, 1-0;
See Green Bay vs. Kansas City

**KANSAS CITY vs. HOUSTON**
RS: Chiefs lead series, 21-17
PS: Chiefs lead series, 2-0;
See Houston vs. Kansas City

**KANSAS CITY vs. INDIANAPOLIS**
RS: Chiefs lead series, 6-4;
See Indianapolis vs. Kansas City

***KANSAS CITY vs. **L.A. RAIDERS**
RS: Raiders lead series, 35-30-2
PS: Chiefs lead series, 2-1
1960—Texans, 34-16 (O)
Raiders, 20-19 (D)
1961—Texans, 42-35 (O)
Texans, 43-11 (D)
1962—Texans, 26-16 (O)
Texans, 35-7 (D)
1963—Raiders, 10-7 (O)
Raiders, 22-7 (KC)
1964—Chiefs, 21-9 (O)
Chiefs, 42-7 (KC)
1965—Raiders, 37-10 (O)
Chiefs, 14-7 (KC)
1966—Chiefs, 32-10 (O)
Raiders, 34-13 (KC)
1967—Raiders, 23-21 (O)
Raiders, 44-22 (KC)
1968—Chiefs, 24-10 (KC)
Raiders, 38-21 (O)
***Raiders, 41-6 (O)
1969—Raiders, 27-24 (KC)
Raiders, 10-6 (O)
****Chiefs, 17-7 (O)
1970—Tie, 17-17 (KC)
Raiders, 20-6 (O)
1971—Tie, 20-20 (O)
Chiefs, 16-14 (KC)
1972—Chiefs, 27-14 (KC)
Raiders, 26-3 (O)
1973—Chiefs, 16-3 (KC)
Raiders, 37-7 (O)
1974—Raiders, 27-7 (O)
Raiders, 7-6 (KC)
1975—Chiefs, 42-10 (KC)
Raiders, 28-20 (O)
1976—Raiders, 24-21 (KC)
Raiders, 21-10 (O)
1977—Raiders, 37-28 (KC)
Raiders, 21-20 (O)
1978—Raiders, 28-6 (O)
Raiders, 20-10 (KC)
1979—Chiefs, 35-7 (KC)
Chiefs, 24-21 (O)
1980—Raiders, 27-14 (KC)
Chiefs, 31-17 (O)
1981—Chiefs, 27-0 (KC)
Chiefs, 28-17 (O)
1982—Raiders, 21-16 (KC)
1983—Raiders, 21-20 (LA)
Raiders, 28-20 (KC)
1984—Raiders, 22-20 (KC)
Raiders, 17-7 (LA)
1985—Chiefs, 36-20 (KC)
Raiders, 19-10 (LA)
1986—Raiders, 24-17 (KC)
Chiefs, 20-17 (LA)
1987—Raiders, 35-17 (LA)
Chiefs, 16-10 (KC)
1988—Raiders, 27-17 (KC)
Raiders, 17-10 (LA)
1989—Chiefs, 24-19 (KC)
Raiders, 20-14 (LA)
1990—Chiefs, 9-7 (KC)
Chiefs, 27-24 (LA)
1991—Chiefs, 24-21 (KC)
Chiefs, 27-21 (LA)
†Chiefs, 10-6 (KC)
1992—Chiefs, 27-7 (KC)
Raiders, 28-7 (LA)
1993—Chiefs, 24-9 (KC)
Chiefs, 31-20 (LA)
(RS Pts.—Chiefs 1,344, Raiders 1,310)
(PS Pts.—Raiders 54, Chiefs 33)
**Franchise in Dallas prior to 1963 and known as Texans*
***Franchise in Oakland prior to 1982*
****Division Playoff*
*****AFL Championship*
*†AFC First-Round Playoff*

**KANSAS CITY vs. L.A. RAMS**
RS: Rams lead series, 3-1
1973—Rams, 23-13 (KC)
1982—Rams, 20-14 (LA)
1985—Rams, 16-0 (KC)
1991—Chiefs, 27-20 (LA)
(RS Pts.—Rams 79, Chiefs 54)

**KANSAS CITY vs. MIAMI**
RS: Chiefs lead series, 10-7
PS: Dolphins lead series, 2-0
1966—Chiefs, 34-16 (KC)
Chiefs, 19-18 (M)
1967—Chiefs, 24-0 (M)
Chiefs, 41-0 (KC)
1968—Chiefs, 48-3 (M)
1969—Chiefs, 17-10 (KC)
1971—*Dolphins, 27-24 (KC) OT
1972—Dolphins, 20-10 (KC)
1974—Dolphins, 9-3 (M)
1976—Chiefs, 20-17 (M) OT
1981—Dolphins, 17-7 (KC)
1983—Dolphins, 14-6 (M)
1985—Dolphins, 31-0 (M)
1987—Dolphins, 42-0 (M)
1989—Chiefs, 26-21 (KC)
Chiefs, 27-24 (M)
1990—**Dolphins, 17-16 (M)
1991—Chiefs, 42-7 (KC)
1993—Dolphins, 30-10 (M)
(RS Pts.—Chiefs 334, Dolphins 279)
(PS Pts.—Dolphins 44, Chiefs 40)
**AFC Divisional Playoff*
***AFC First-Round Playoff*

**KANSAS CITY vs. MINNESOTA**
RS: Vikings lead series, 3-2
PS: Chiefs lead series, 1-0
1969—*Chiefs, 23-7 (New Orleans)
1970—Vikings, 27-10 (M)
1974—Vikings, 35-15 (KC)
1981—Chiefs, 10-6 (M)
1990—Chiefs, 24-21 (KC)
1993—Vikings, 30-10 (M)
(RS Pts.—Vikings 119, Chiefs 69)
(PS Pts.—Chiefs 23, Vikings 7)
**Super Bowl IV*

***KANSAS CITY vs. **NEW ENGLAND**
RS: Chiefs lead series, 13-7-3
1960—Patriots, 42-14 (B)
Texans, 34-0 (D)
1961—Patriots, 18-17 (D)
Patriots, 28-21 (B)
1962—Texans, 42-28 (D)
Texans, 27-7 (B)
1963—Tie, 24-24 (B)
Chiefs, 35-3 (KC)
1964—Patriots, 24-7 (B)
Patriots, 31-24 (KC)
1965—Chiefs, 27-17 (KC)
Tie, 10-10 (B)
1966—Chiefs, 43-24 (B)
Tie, 27-27 (KC)
1967—Chiefs, 33-10 (B)
1968—Chiefs, 31-17 (KC)
1969—Chiefs, 31-0 (B)
1970—Chiefs, 23-10 (KC)
1973—Chiefs, 10-7 (NE)
1977—Patriots, 21-17 (NE)
1981—Patriots, 33-17 (NE)
1990—Chiefs, 37-7 (NE)
1992—Chiefs, 27-20 (KC)
(RS Pts.—Chiefs 578, Patriots 408)

## ALL-TIME TEAM VS. TEAM RESULTS

**Franchise located in Dallas prior to 1963 and known as Texans*
***Franchise in Boston prior to 1971*

**KANSAS CITY vs. NEW ORLEANS**
RS: Saints lead series, 3-2
1972—Chiefs, 20-17 (NO)
1976—Saints, 27-17 (KC)
1982—Saints, 27-17 (NO)
1985—Chiefs, 47-27 (NO)
1991—Saints, 17-10 (KC)
(RS Pts.—Saints 115, Chiefs 111)

**KANSAS CITY vs. N.Y. GIANTS**
RS: Giants lead series, 6-1
1974—Giants, 33-27 (KC)
1978—Giants, 26-10 (NY)
1979—Giants, 21-17 (KC)
1983—Chiefs, 38-17 (KC)
1984—Giants, 28-27 (NY)
1988—Giants, 28-12 (NY)
1992—Giants, 35-21 (NY)
(RS Pts.—Giants 188, Chiefs 152)

***KANSAS CITY vs. **N.Y. JETS**
RS: Chiefs lead series, 14-12-1
PS: Series tied, 1-1
1960—Titans, 37-35 (D)
Titans, 41-35 (NY)
1961—Titans, 28-7 (NY)
Texans, 35-24 (D)
1962—Texans, 20-17 (D)
Texans, 52-31 (NY)
1963—Jets, 17-0 (NY)
Chiefs, 48-0 (KC)
1964—Jets, 27-14 (NY)
Chiefs, 24-7 (KC)
1965—Chiefs, 14-10 (NY)
Jets, 13-10 (KC)
1966—Chiefs, 32-24 (NY)
1967—Chiefs, 42-18 (KC)
Chiefs, 21-7 (NY)
1968—Jets, 20-19 (KC)
1969—Chiefs, 34-16 (NY)
***Chiefs, 13-6 (NY)
1971—Jets, 13-10 (NY)
1974—Chiefs, 24-16 (KC)
1975—Jets, 30-24 (KC)
1982—Chiefs, 37-13 (KC)
1984—Jets, 17-16 (KC)
Jets, 28-7 (NY)
1986—****Jets, 35-15 (NY)
1987—Jets, 16-9 (KC)
1988—Tie, 17-17 (NY)
Chiefs, 38-34 (KC)
1992—Chiefs, 23-7 (NY)
(RS Pts.—Chiefs 647, Jets 528)
(PS Pts.—Jets 41, Chiefs 28)
**Franchise in Dallas prior to 1963 and known as Texans*
***Jets known as Titans prior to 1963*
****Inter-Divisional Playoff*
*****AFC First-Round Playoff*

**KANSAS CITY vs. PHILADELPHIA**
RS: Series tied, 1-1
1972—Eagles, 21-20 (KC)
1992—Chiefs, 24-17 (KC)
(RS Pts.—Chiefs 44, Eagles 38)

**KANSAS CITY vs. PITTSBURGH**
RS: Steelers lead series, 13-5
PS: Chiefs lead series, 1-0
1970—Chiefs, 31-14 (P)
1971—Chiefs, 38-16 (KC)
1972—Steelers, 16-7 (P)
1974—Steelers, 34-24 (KC)
1975—Steelers, 28-3 (P)
1976—Steelers, 45-0 (KC)
1978—Steelers, 27-24 (P)
1979—Steelers, 30-3 (KC)
1980—Steelers, 21-16 (P)
1981—Chiefs, 37-33 (P)
1982—Steelers, 35-14 (P)
1984—Chiefs, 37-27 (P)
1985—Steelers, 36-28 (KC)
1986—Chiefs, 24-19 (P)
1987—Steelers, 17-16 (KC)
1988—Steelers, 16-10 (P)
1989—Steelers, 23-17 (P)
1992—Steelers, 27-3 (KC)
1993—*Chiefs, 27-24 (KC) OT
(RS Pts.—Steelers 464, Chiefs 332)
(PS Pts.—Chiefs 27, Steelers 24)
**AFC First-Round Playoff*

***KANSAS CITY vs. **SAN DIEGO**
RS: Chiefs lead series, 35-31-1
PS: Chargers lead series, 1-0
1960—Chargers, 21-20 (LA)
Texans, 17-0 (D)
1961—Chargers, 26-10 (D)
Chargers, 24-14 (SD)
1962—Chargers, 32-28 (SD)
Texans, 26-17 (D)
1963—Chargers, 24-10 (SD)
Chargers, 38-17 (KC)
1964—Chargers, 28-14 (KC)
Chiefs, 49-6 (SD)
1965—Tie, 10-10 (SD)
Chiefs, 31-7 (KC)
1966—Chiefs, 24-14 (KC)
Chiefs, 27-17 (SD)
1967—Chargers, 45-31 (SD)
Chargers, 17-16 (KC)
1968—Chiefs, 27-20 (KC)
Chiefs, 40-3 (SD)
1969—Chiefs, 27-9 (SD)
Chiefs, 27-3 (KC)
1970—Chiefs, 26-14 (KC)
Chargers, 31-13 (SD)
1971—Chargers, 21-14 (SD)
Chiefs, 31-10 (KC)
1972—Chiefs, 26-14 (SD)
Chargers, 27-17 (KC)
1973—Chiefs, 19-0 (SD)
Chiefs, 33-6 (KC)
1974—Chiefs, 24-14 (SD)
Chargers, 14-7 (KC)
1975—Chiefs, 12-10 (SD)
Chargers, 28-20 (KC)
1976—Chargers, 30-16 (KC)
Chiefs, 23-20 (SD)
1977—Chargers, 23-7 (KC)
Chiefs, 21-16 (SD)
1978—Chargers, 29-23 (SD) OT
Chiefs, 23-0 (KC)
1979—Chargers, 20-14 (KC)
Chargers, 28-7 (SD)
1980—Chargers, 24-7 (KC)
Chargers, 20-7 (SD)
1981—Chargers, 42-31 (KC)
Chargers, 22-20 (SD)
1982—Chiefs, 19-12 (KC)
1983—Chargers, 17-14 (KC)
Chargers, 41-38 (SD)
1984—Chiefs, 31-13 (KC)
Chiefs, 42-21 (SD)
1985—Chargers, 31-20 (SD)
Chiefs, 38-34 (KC)
1986—Chiefs, 42-41 (KC)
Chiefs, 24-23 (SD)
1987—Chiefs, 20-13 (KC)
Chargers, 42-21 (SD)
1988—Chargers, 24-23 (KC)
Chargers, 24-13 (SD)
1989—Chargers, 21-6 (SD)
Chargers, 20-13 (KC)
1990—Chiefs, 27-10 (KC)
Chiefs, 24-21 (SD)
1991—Chiefs, 14-13 (SD)
Chiefs, 20-17 (KC) OT
1992—Chiefs, 24-10 (SD)
Chiefs, 16-14 (KC)
***Chargers, 17-0 (SD)
1993—Chiefs, 17-14 (SD)
Chiefs, 28-24 (KC)
(RS Pts.—Chiefs 1,440, Chargers 1,324)
(PS Pts.—Chargers 17, Chiefs 0)
**Franchise in Dallas prior to 1963 and known as Texans*
***Franchise in Los Angeles prior to 1961*
****AFC First-Round Playoff*

**KANSAS CITY vs. SAN FRANCISCO**
RS: 49ers lead series, 4-1
1971—Chiefs, 26-17 (SF)
1975—49ers, 20-3 (KC)
1982—49ers, 26-13 (KC)
1985—49ers, 31-3 (SF)
1991—49ers, 28-14 (SF)
(RS Pts.—49ers 122, Chiefs 59)

**KANSAS CITY vs. SEATTLE**
RS: Chiefs lead series, 19-12
1977—Seahawks, 34-31 (KC)
1978—Seahawks, 13-10 (KC)
Seahawks, 23-19 (S)
1979—Chiefs, 24-6 (S)
Chiefs, 37-21 (KC)
1980—Seahawks, 17-16 (KC)
Chiefs, 31-30 (S)
1981—Chiefs, 20-14 (S)
Chiefs, 40-13 (KC)
1983—Chiefs, 17-13 (KC)
Seahawks, 51-48 (S) OT
1984—Seahawks, 45-0 (S)
Chiefs, 34-7 (KC)
1985—Chiefs, 28-7 (KC)
Seahawks, 24-6 (S)
1986—Seahawks, 23-17 (S)
Chiefs, 27-7 (KC)
1987—Seahawks, 43-14 (S)
Chiefs, 41-20 (KC)
1988—Seahawks, 31-10 (S)
Chiefs, 27-24 (KC)
1989—Chiefs, 20-16 (S)
Chiefs, 20-10 (KC)
1990—Seahawks, 19-7 (S)
Seahawks, 17-16 (KC)
1991—Chiefs, 20-13 (KC)
Chiefs, 19-6 (S)
1992—Chiefs, 26-7 (KC)
Chiefs, 24-14 (S)
1993—Chiefs, 31-16 (S)
Chiefs, 34-24 (KC)
(RS Pts.—Chiefs 714, Seahawks 608)

**KANSAS CITY vs. TAMPA BAY**
RS: Chiefs lead series, 5-2
1976—Chiefs, 28-19 (TB)
1978—Buccaneers, 30-13 (KC)
1979—Buccaneers, 3-0 (TB)
1981—Chiefs, 19-10 (KC)
1984—Chiefs, 24-20 (KC)
1986—Chiefs, 27-20 (KC)
1993—Chiefs, 27-3 (TB)
(RS Pts.—Chiefs 138, Buccaneers 105)

**KANSAS CITY vs. WASHINGTON**
RS: Chiefs lead series, 3-1
1971—Chiefs, 27-20 (KC)
1976—Chiefs, 33-30 (W)
1983—Redskins, 27-12 (W)
1992—Chiefs, 35-16 (KC)
(RS Pts.—Chiefs 107, Redskins 93)

---

**L.A. RAIDERS vs. ARIZONA**
RS: Raiders lead series, 2-1;
See Arizona vs. L.A. Raiders

**L.A. RAIDERS vs. ATLANTA**
RS: Raiders lead series, 4-3;
See Atlanta vs. L.A. Raiders

**L.A. RAIDERS vs. BUFFALO**
RS: Raiders lead series, 15-14
PS: Bills lead series, 2-0;
See Buffalo vs. L.A. Raiders

**L.A. RAIDERS vs. CHICAGO**
RS: Raiders lead series, 5-3;
See Chicago vs. L.A. Raiders

**L.A. RAIDERS vs. CINCINNATI**
RS: Raiders lead series, 14-7
PS: Raiders lead series, 2-0;
See Cincinnati vs. L.A. Raiders

**L.A. RAIDERS vs. CLEVELAND**
RS: Raiders lead series, 8-4
PS: Raiders lead series, 2-0;
See Cleveland vs. L.A. Raiders

**L.A. RAIDERS vs. DALLAS**
RS: Raiders lead series, 3-2;
See Dallas vs. L.A. Raiders

**L.A. RAIDERS vs. DENVER**
RS: Raiders lead series, 46-19-2
PS: Series tied, 1-1;
See Denver vs. L.A. Raiders

**L.A. RAIDERS vs. DETROIT**
RS: Raiders lead series, 5-2;
See Detroit vs. L.A. Raiders

**L.A. RAIDERS vs. GREEN BAY**
RS: Raiders lead series, 5-2
PS: Packers lead series, 1-0;
See Green Bay vs. L.A. Raiders

**L.A. RAIDERS vs. HOUSTON**
RS: Raiders lead series, 19-13
PS: Raiders lead series, 3-0;
See Houston vs. L.A. Raiders

**L.A. RAIDERS vs. INDIANAPOLIS**
RS: Raiders lead series, 4-2
PS: Series tied, 1-1;
See Indianapolis vs. L.A. Raiders

**L.A. RAIDERS vs. KANSAS CITY**
RS: Raiders lead series, 35-30-2
PS: Chiefs lead series, 2-1;
See Kansas City vs. L.A. Raiders

***L.A. RAIDERS vs. L.A. RAMS**
RS: Raiders lead series, 5-2
1972—Raiders, 45-17 (O)
1977—Rams, 20-14 (LA)
1979—Raiders, 24-17 (LA)
1982—Raiders, 37-31 (LA Raiders)
1985—Raiders, 16-6 (LA Rams)
1988—Rams, 22-17 (LA Raiders)
1991—Raiders, 20-17 (LA Raiders)
(RS Pts.—Raiders 173, Rams 130)
**Franchise in Oakland prior to 1982*

***L.A. RAIDERS vs. MIAMI**
RS: Raiders lead series, 14-4-1
PS: Raiders lead series, 2-1
1966—Raiders, 23-14 (M)
Raiders, 21-10 (O)
1967—Raiders, 31-17 (O)
1968—Raiders, 47-21 (M)
1969—Raiders, 20-17 (O)
Tie, 20-20 (M)
1970—Dolphins, 20-13 (M)
**Raiders, 21-14 (O)
1973—Raiders, 12-7 (O)
***Dolphins, 27-10 (M)
1974—**Raiders, 28-26 (O)
1975—Raiders, 31-21 (M)
1978—Dolphins, 23-6 (M)
1979—Raiders, 13-3 (O)
1980—Raiders, 16-10 (O)
1981—Raiders, 33-17 (M)
1983—Raiders, 27-14 (LA)
1984—Raiders, 45-34 (M)
1986—Raiders, 30-28 (M)
1988—Dolphins, 24-14 (LA)
1990—Raiders, 13-10 (M)
1992—Dolphins, 20-7 (M)
(RS Pts.—Raiders 422, Dolphins 330)
(PS Pts.—Dolphins 67, Raiders 59)
**Franchise in Oakland prior to 1982*
***AFC Divisional Playoff*
****AFC Championship*

***L.A. RAIDERS vs. MINNESOTA**
RS: Raiders lead series, 6-2
PS: Raiders lead series, 1-0
1973—Vikings, 24-16 (M)
1976—**Raiders, 32-14 (Pasadena)
1977—Raiders, 35-13 (O)
1978—Raiders, 27-20 (O)
1981—Raiders, 36-10 (M)
1984—Raiders, 23-20 (LA)
1987—Vikings, 31-20 (M)
1990—Raiders, 28-24 (M)
1993—Raiders, 24-7 (LA)
(RS Pts.—Raiders 209, Vikings 149)
(PS Pts.—Raiders 32, Vikings 14)
**Franchise in Oakland prior to 1982*
***Super Bowl XI*

***L.A. RAIDERS vs. **NEW ENGLAND**

RS: Series tied, 12-12-1
PS: Series tied, 1-1
1960—Raiders, 27-14 (O)
Patriots, 34-28 (B)
1961—Patriots, 20-17 (B)
Patriots, 35-21 (O)
1962—Patriots, 26-16 (B)
Raiders, 20-0 (O)
1963—Patriots, 20-14 (O)
Patriots, 20-14 (B)
1964—Patriots, 17-14 (O)
Tie, 43-43 (B)
1965—Raiders, 24-10 (B)
Raiders, 30-21 (O)
1966—Patriots, 24-21 (B)
1967—Raiders, 35-7 (O)
Raiders, 48-14 (B)
1968—Raiders, 41-10 (O)
1969—Raiders, 38-23 (B)
1971—Patriots, 20-6 (NE)
1974—Raiders, 41-26 (O)
1976—Patriots, 48-17 (NE)
***Raiders, 24-21 (O)
1978—Patriots, 21-14 (O)
1981—Raiders, 27-17 (O)
1985—Raiders, 35-20 (NE)
***Patriots, 27-20 (LA)
1987—Patriots, 26-23 (NE)
1989—Raiders, 24-21 (LA)
(RS Pts.—Raiders 638, Patriots 537)
(PS Pts.—Patriots 48, Raiders 44)
*Franchise in Oakland prior to 1982*
***Franchise in Boston prior to 1971*
****AFC Divisional Playoff*

***L.A. RAIDERS vs. NEW ORLEANS**
RS: Raiders lead series, 3-2-1
1971—Tie, 21-21 (NO)
1975—Raiders, 48-10 (O)
1979—Raiders, 42-35 (NO)
1985—Raiders, 23-13 (LA)
1988—Saints, 20-6 (NO)
1991—Saints, 27-0 (NO)
(RS Pts.—Raiders 140, Saints 126)
*Franchise in Oakland prior to 1982*

***L.A. RAIDERS vs. N.Y. GIANTS**
RS: Raiders lead series, 4-2
1973—Raiders, 42-0 (O)
1980—Raiders, 33-17 (NY)
1983—Raiders, 27-12 (LA)
1986—Giants, 14-9 (LA)
1989—Giants, 34-17 (NY)
1992—Raiders, 13-10 (LA)
(RS Pts.—Raiders 141, Giants 87)
*Franchise in Oakland prior to 1982*

***L.A. RAIDERS vs. **N.Y. JETS**
RS: Raiders lead series, 14-9-2
PS: Jets lead series, 2-0
1960—Raiders, 28-27 (NY)
Titans, 31-28 (O)
1961—Titans, 14-6 (O)
Titans, 23-12 (NY)
1962—Titans, 28-17 (O)
Titans, 31-21 (NY)
1963—Jets, 10-7 (NY)
Raiders, 49-26 (O)
1964—Jets, 35-13 (NY)
Raiders, 35-26 (O)
1965—Tie, 24-24 (NY)
Raiders, 24-14 (O)
1966—Raiders, 24-21 (NY)
Tie, 28-28 (O)
1967—Jets, 27-14 (NY)
Raiders, 38-29 (O)
1968—Raiders, 43-32 (O)
***Jets, 27-23 (NY)
1969—Raiders, 27-14 (NY)
1970—Raiders, 14-13 (NY)
1972—Raiders, 24-16 (O)
1977—Raiders, 28-27 (NY)
1979—Jets, 28-19 (NY)
1982—****Jets, 17-14 (LA)
1985—Raiders, 31-0 (LA)
1989—Raiders, 14-7 (NY)
1993—Raiders, 24-20 (LA)
(RS Pts.—Raiders 592, Jets 551)
(PS Pts.—Jets 44, Raiders 37)
*Franchise in Oakland prior to 1982*
***Jets known as Titans prior to 1963*
****AFL Championship*
*****AFC Second-Round Playoff*

***L.A. RAIDERS vs. PHILADELPHIA**
RS: Eagles lead series, 4-2
PS: Raiders lead series, 1-0
1971—Raiders, 34-10 (O)
1976—Raiders, 26-7 (P)
1980—Eagles, 10-7 (P)
**Raiders, 27-10 (New Orleans)
1986—Eagles, 33-27 (LA) OT
1989—Eagles, 10-7 (P)
1992—Eagles, 31-10 (P)
(RS Pts.—Raiders 111, Eagles 101)
(PS Pts.—Raiders 27, Eagles 10)
*Franchise in Oakland prior to 1982*
***Super Bowl XV*

***L.A. RAIDERS vs. PITTSBURGH**
RS: Raiders lead series, 7-3
PS: Series tied, 3-3
1970—Raiders, 31-14 (O)
1972—Steelers, 34-28 (P)
**Steelers, 13-7 (P)
1973—Steelers, 17-9 (O)
**Raiders, 33-14 (O)
1974—Raiders, 17-0 (P)
***Steelers, 24-13 (O)
1975—***Steelers, 16-10 (P)
1976—Raiders, 31-28 (O)
***Raiders, 24-7 (O)
1977—Raiders, 16-7 (P)
1980—Raiders, 45-34 (P)
1981—Raiders, 30-27 (O)
1983—**Raiders, 38-10 (LA)
1984—Steelers, 13-7 (LA)
1990—Raiders, 20-3 (LA)
(RS Pts.—Raiders 234, Steelers 177)
(PS Pts.—Raiders 125, Steelers 84)
*Franchise in Oakland prior to 1982*
***AFC Divisional Playoff*
****AFC Championship*

***L.A. RAIDERS vs. **SAN DIEGO**
RS: Raiders lead series, 41-25-2
PS: Raiders lead series, 1-0
1960—Chargers, 52-28 (LA)
Chargers, 41-17 (O)
1961—Chargers, 44-0 (SD)
Chargers, 41-10 (O)
1962—Chargers, 42-33 (O)
Chargers, 31-21 (SD)
1963—Raiders, 34-33 (SD)
Raiders, 41-27 (O)
1964—Chargers, 31-17 (O)
Raiders, 21-20 (SD)
1965—Chargers, 17-6 (O)
Chargers, 24-14 (SD)
1966—Chargers, 29-20 (O)
Raiders, 41-19 (SD)
1967—Raiders, 51-10 (O)
Raiders, 41-21 (SD)
1968—Chargers, 23-14 (O)
Raiders, 34-27 (SD)
1969—Raiders, 24-12 (SD)
Raiders, 21-16 (O)
1970—Tie, 27-27 (SD)
Raiders, 20-17 (O)
1971—Raiders, 34-0 (SD)
Raiders, 34-33 (O)
1972—Tie, 17-17 (O)
Raiders, 21-19 (SD)
1973—Raiders, 27-17 (SD)
Raiders, 31-3 (O)
1974—Raiders, 14-10 (SD)
Raiders, 17-10 (O)
1975—Raiders, 6-0 (SD)
Raiders, 25-0 (O)
1976—Raiders, 27-17 (SD)
Raiders, 24-0 (O)
1977—Raiders, 24-0 (O)
Chargers, 12-7 (SD)
1978—Raiders, 21-20 (SD)
Chargers, 27-23 (O)
1979—Chargers, 30-10 (SD)
Raiders, 45-22 (O)
1980—Chargers, 30-24 (SD) OT
Raiders, 38-24 (O)
***Raiders, 34-27 (SD)
1981—Chargers, 55-21 (O)
Chargers, 23-10 (SD)
1982—Raiders, 28-24 (LA)
Raiders, 41-34 (SD)
1983—Raiders, 42-10 (SD)
Raiders, 30-14 (LA)
1984—Raiders, 33-30 (LA)
Raiders, 44-37 (SD)
1985—Raiders, 34-21 (LA)
Chargers, 40-34 (SD) OT
1986—Raiders, 17-13 (LA)
Raiders, 37-31 (SD) OT
1987—Chargers, 23-17 (LA)
Chargers, 16-14 (SD)
1988—Raiders, 24-13 (LA)
Raiders, 13-3 (SD)
1989—Raiders, 40-14 (LA)
Chargers, 14-12 (SD)
1990—Raiders, 24-9 (SD)
Raiders, 17-12 (LA)
1991—Chargers, 21-13 (LA)
Raiders, 9-7 (SD)
1992—Chargers, 27-3 (SD)
Chargers, 36-14 (LA)
1993—Chargers, 30-23 (LA)
Raiders, 12-7 (SD)
(RS Pts.—Raiders 1,610, Chargers, 1,459)
(PS Pts.—Raiders 34, Chargers 27)
*Franchise in Oakland prior to 1982*
***Franchise in Los Angeles prior to 1961*
****AFC Championship*

***L.A. RAIDERS vs. SAN FRANCISCO**
RS: Raiders lead series, 5-2
1970—49ers, 38-7 (O)
1974—Raiders, 35-24 (SF)
1979—Raiders, 23-10 (O)
1982—Raiders, 23-17 (SF)
1985—49ers, 34-10 (LA)
1988—Raiders, 9-3 (SF)
1991—Raiders, 12-6 (LA)
(RS Pts.—49ers 132, Raiders 119)
*Franchise in Oakland prior to 1982*

***L.A. RAIDERS vs. SEATTLE**
RS: Raiders lead series, 18-14
PS: Series tied, 1-1
1977—Raiders, 44-7 (O)
1978—Seahawks, 27-7 (S)
Seahawks, 17-16 (O)
1979—Seahawks, 27-10 (S)
Seahawks, 29-24 (O)
1980—Raiders, 33-14 (O)
Raiders, 19-17 (S)
1981—Raiders, 20-10 (O)
Raiders, 32-31 (S)
1982—Raiders, 28-23 (LA)
1983—Seahawks, 38-36 (S)
Seahawks, 34-21 (LA)
**Raiders, 30-14 (LA)
1984—Raiders, 28-14 (LA)
Seahawks, 17-14 (S)
***Seahawks, 13-7 (S)
1985—Seahawks, 33-3 (S)
Raiders, 13-3 (LA)
1986—Raiders, 14-10 (LA)
Seahawks, 37-0 (S)
1987—Seahawks, 35-13 (LA)
Raiders, 37-14 (S)
1988—Seahawks, 35-27 (S)
Seahawks, 43-37 (LA)
1989—Seahawks, 24-20 (LA)
Seahawks, 23-17 (S)
1990—Raiders, 17-13 (S)
Raiders, 24-17 (LA)
1991—Raiders, 23-20 (S) OT
Raiders, 31-7 (LA)
1992—Raiders, 19-0 (S)
Raiders, 20-3 (LA)
1993—Raiders, 17-13 (S)
Raiders, 27-23 (LA)
(RS Pts.—Raiders 691, Seahawks 658)
(PS Pts.—Raiders 37, Seahawks 27)
*Franchise in Oakland prior to 1982*
***AFC Championship*
****AFC First-Round Playoff*

***L.A. RAIDERS vs. TAMPA BAY**
RS: Raiders lead series, 3-0
1976—Raiders, 49-16 (O)
1981—Raiders, 18-16 (O)
1993—Raiders, 27-20 (LA)
(RS Pts.—Raiders 94, Buccaneers 52)
*Franchise in Oakland prior to 1982*

***L.A. RAIDERS vs. WASHINGTON**
RS: Raiders lead series, 5-2
PS: Raiders lead series, 1-0
1970—Raiders, 34-20 (O)
1975—Raiders, 26-23 (W) OT
1980—Raiders, 24-21 (O)
1983—Redskins, 37-35 (W)
**Raiders, 38-9 (Tampa)
1986—Redskins, 10-6 (W)
1989—Raiders, 37-24 (LA)
1992—Raiders, 21-20 (W)
(RS Pts.—Raiders 183, Redskins 155)
(PS Pts.—Raiders 38, Redskins 9)
*Franchise in Oakland prior to 1982*
***Super Bowl XVIII*

---

**L.A. RAMS vs. ARIZONA**
RS: Rams lead series, 22-19-2
PS: Rams lead series, 1-0;
See Arizona vs. L.A. Rams

**L.A. RAMS vs. ATLANTA**
RS: Rams lead series, 36-16-2;
See Atlanta vs. L.A. Rams

**L.A. RAMS vs. BUFFALO**
RS: Series tied, 3-3;
See Buffalo vs. L.A. Rams

**L.A. RAMS vs. CHICAGO**
RS: Bears lead series, 44-29-3
PS: Series tied, 1-1;
See Chicago vs. L.A. Rams

**L.A. RAMS vs. CINCINNATI**
RS: Bengals lead series, 5-2;
See Cincinnati vs. L.A. Rams

**L.A. RAMS vs. CLEVELAND**
RS: Browns lead series, 8-7
PS: Browns lead series, 2-1;
See Cleveland vs. L.A. Rams

**L.A. RAMS vs. DALLAS**
RS: Rams lead series, 9-8
PS: Series tied, 4-4;
See Dallas vs. L.A. Rams

**L.A. RAMS vs. DENVER**
RS: Series tied, 3-3;
See Denver vs. L.A. Rams

**L.A. RAMS vs. DETROIT**
RS: Rams lead series, 39-35-1
PS: Lions lead series, 1-0;
See Detroit vs. L.A. Rams

**L.A. RAMS vs. GREEN BAY**
RS: Rams lead series, 42-36-2
PS: Packers lead series, 1-0;
See Green Bay vs. L.A. Rams

**L.A. RAMS vs. HOUSTON**
RS: Rams lead series, 5-2;
See Houston vs. L.A. Rams

**L.A. RAMS vs. INDIANAPOLIS**
RS: Colts lead series, 20-16-2;
See Indianapolis vs. L.A. Rams

**L.A. RAMS vs. KANSAS CITY**
RS: Rams lead series, 3-1;
See Kansas City vs. L.A. Rams

**L.A. RAMS VS. L.A. RAIDERS**
RS: Raiders lead series, 5-2;
See L.A. Raiders vs. L.A. Rams

**L.A. RAMS vs. MIAMI**
RS: Dolphins lead series, 5-1

1971—Dolphins, 20-14 (LA)
1976—Rams, 31-28 (M)
1980—Dolphins, 35-14 (LA)
1983—Dolphins, 30-14 (M)
1986—Dolphins, 37-31 (LA) OT
1992—Dolphins, 26-10 (M)
(RS Pts.—Dolphins 176, Rams 114)

**L.A. RAMS vs. MINNESOTA**
RS: Vikings lead series, 15-11-2
PS: Vikings lead series, 5-1
1961—Rams, 31-17 (LA)
Vikings, 42-21 (M)
1962—Vikings, 38-14 (LA)
Tie, 24-24 (M)
1963—Rams, 27-24 (LA)
Vikings, 21-13 (M)
1964—Rams, 22-13 (LA)
Vikings, 34-13 (M)
1965—Vikings, 38-35 (LA)
Vikings, 24-13 (M)
1966—Vikings, 35-7 (M)
Rams, 21-6 (LA)
1967—Rams, 39-3 (LA)
1968—Rams, 31-3 (M)
1969—Vikings, 20-13 (LA)
*Vikings, 23-20 (M)
1970—Vikings, 13-3 (M)
1972—Vikings, 45-41 (LA)
1973—Vikings, 10-9 (M)
1974—Rams, 20-17 (LA)
**Vikings, 14-10 (M)
1976—Tie, 10-10 (M) OT
**Vikings, 24-13 (M)
1977—Rams, 35-3 (LA)
***Vikings, 14-7 (LA)
1978—Rams, 34-17 (M)
***Rams, 34-10 (LA)
1979—Rams, 27-21 (LA) OT
1985—Rams, 13-10 (LA)
1987—Vikings, 21-16 (LA)
1988—****Vikings, 28-17 (M)
1989—Vikings, 23-21 (M) OT
1991—Vikings, 20-14 (M)
1992—Vikings, 31-17 (LA)
(RS Pts.—Rams 584, Vikings 583)
(PS Pts.—Vikings 113, Rams 101)
*Conference Championship*
***NFC Championship*
****NFC Divisional Playoff*
*****NFC First-Round Playoff*

**L.A. RAMS vs. NEW ENGLAND**
RS: Series tied, 3-3
1974—Patriots, 20-14 (NE)
1980—Rams, 17-14 (NE)
1983—Patriots, 21-7 (LA)
1986—Patriots, 30-28 (LA)
1989—Rams, 24-20 (NE)
1992—Rams, 14-0 (LA)
(RS Pts.—Patriots 105, Rams 104)

**L.A. RAMS vs. NEW ORLEANS**
RS: Rams lead series, 27-21
1967—Rams, 27-13 (NO)
1969—Rams, 36-17 (LA)
1970—Rams, 30-17 (NO)
Rams, 34-16 (LA)
1971—Saints, 24-20 (NO)
Rams, 45-28 (LA)
1972—Rams, 34-14 (LA)
Saints, 19-16 (NO)
1973—Rams, 29-7 (LA)
Rams, 24-13 (NO)
1974—Rams, 24-0 (LA)
Saints, 20-7 (NO)
1975—Rams, 38-14 (LA)
Rams, 14-7 (NO)
1976—Rams, 16-10 (NO)
Rams, 33-14 (LA)
1977—Rams, 14-7 (LA)
Saints, 27-26 (NO)
1978—Rams, 26-20 (NO)
Saints, 10-3 (LA)
1979—Rams, 35-17 (NO)
Saints, 29-14 (LA)
1980—Rams, 45-31 (LA)
Rams, 27-7 (NO)
1981—Saints, 23-17 (NO)
Saints, 21-13 (LA)
1983—Rams, 30-27 (LA)
Rams, 26-24 (NO)
1984—Rams, 28-10 (NO)
Rams, 34-21 (LA)
1985—Rams, 28-10 (LA)
Saints, 29-3 (NO)
1986—Saints, 6-0 (NO)
Rams, 26-13 (LA)
1987—Saints, 37-10 (NO)
Saints, 31-14 (LA)
1988—Rams, 12-10 (NO)
Saints, 14-10 (LA)
1989—Saints, 40-21 (LA)
Rams, 20-17 (NO) OT
1990—Saints, 24-20 (LA)
Saints, 20-17 (NO)
1991—Saints, 24-7 (NO)
Saints, 24-17 (LA)
1992—Saints, 13-10 (NO)
Saints, 37-14 (LA)
1993—Saints, 37-6 (LA)
Rams, 23-20 (NO)
(RS Pts.—Rams 1,023, Saints 913)

***L.A. RAMS vs. N.Y. GIANTS**
RS: Rams lead series, 20-9
PS: Series tied, 1-1
1938—Giants, 28-0 (NY)
1940—Rams, 13-0 (NY)
1941—Giants, 49-14 (NY)
1945—Rams, 21-17 (NY)
1946—Rams, 31-21 (NY)
1947—Rams, 34-10 (LA)
1948—Rams, 52-37 (NY)
1953—Rams, 21-7 (LA)
1954—Rams, 17-16 (NY)
1959—Giants, 23-21 (LA)
1961—Giants, 24-14 (NY)
1966—Rams, 55-14 (LA)
1968—Rams, 24-21 (LA)
1970—Rams, 31-3 (NY)
1973—Rams, 40-6 (LA)
1976—Rams, 24-10 (LA)
1978—Rams, 20-17 (NY)
1979—Giants, 20-14 (LA)
1980—Rams, 28-7 (NY)
1981—Giants, 10-7 (NY)
1983—Rams, 16-6 (NY)
1984—Rams, 33-12 (LA)
**Giants, 16-13 (LA)
1985—Giants, 24-19 (NY)
1988—Rams, 45-31 (NY)
1989—Rams, 31-10 (LA)
***Rams, 19-13 (NY) OT
1990—Giants, 31-7 (LA)
1991—Rams, 19-13 (NY)
1992—Rams, 38-17 (LA)
1993—Giants, 20-10 (NY)
(RS Pts.—Rams 699, Giants 504)
(PS Pts.—Rams 32, Giants 29)
**Franchise in Cleveland prior to 1946*
***NFC First-Round Playoff*
****NFC Divisional Playoff*

**L.A. RAMS vs. N.Y. JETS**
RS: Rams lead series, 5-2
1970—Jets, 31-20 (LA)
1974—Rams, 20-13 (NY)
1980—Rams, 38-13 (LA)
1983—Jets, 27-24 (NY) OT
1986—Rams, 17-3 (NY)
1989—Rams, 38-14 (LA)
1992—Rams, 18-10 (LA)
(RS Pts.—Rams 175, Jets 111)

***L.A. RAMS vs. PHILADELPHIA**
RS: Rams lead series, 15-11-1
PS: Series tied, 1-1
1937—Rams, 21-3 (P)
1939—Rams, 35-13 (Colorado Springs)
1940—Rams, 21-13 (C)
1942—Rams, 24-14 (Akron)
1944—Eagles, 26-13 (P)
1945—Eagles, 28-14 (P)
1946—Eagles, 25-14 (LA)
1947—Eagles, 14-7 (P)
1948—Tie, 28-28 (LA)
1949—Eagles, 38-14 (P)
**Eagles, 14-0 (LA)
1950—Eagles, 56-20 (P)
1955—Rams, 23-21 (P)
1956—Rams, 27-7 (LA)
1957—Rams, 17-13 (LA)
1959—Eagles, 23-20 (P)
1964—Rams, 20-10 (LA)
1967—Rams, 33-17 (LA)
1969—Rams, 23-17 (P)
1972—Rams, 34-3 (P)
1975—Rams, 42-3 (P)
1977—Rams, 20-0 (LA)
1978—Rams, 16-14 (P)
1983—Eagles, 13-9 (P)
1985—Rams, 17-6 (P)
1986—Eagles, 34-20 (P)
1988—Eagles, 30-24 (P)
1989—***Rams, 21-7 (P)
1990—Eagles, 27-21 (LA)
(RS Pts.—Rams 577, Eagles 496)
(PS Pts.—Rams 21, Eagles 21)
**Franchise in Cleveland prior to 1946*
***NFL Championship*
****NFC First-Round Playoff*

***L.A. RAMS vs. **PITTSBURGH**
RS: Rams lead series, 14-4-2
PS: Steelers lead series, 1-0
1938—Rams, 13-7 (New Orleans)
1939—Tie, 14-14 (C)
1941—Rams, 17-14 (Akron)
1947—Rams, 48-7 (P)
1948—Rams, 31-14 (LA)
1949—Tie, 7-7 (P)
1952—Rams, 28-14 (LA)
1955—Rams, 27-26 (LA)
1956—Steelers, 30-13 (P)
1961—Rams, 24-14 (LA)
1964—Rams, 26-14 (P)
1968—Rams, 45-10 (LA)
1971—Rams, 23-14 (P)
1975—Rams, 10-3 (LA)
1978—Rams, 10-7 (LA)
1979—***Steelers, 31-19 (Pasadena)
1981—Steelers, 24-0 (P)
1984—Steelers, 24-14 (P)
1987—Rams, 31-21 (LA)
1990—Steelers, 41-10 (P)
1993—Rams, 27-0 (LA)
(RS Pts.—Rams 418, Steelers 305)
(PS Pts.—Steelers 31, Rams 19)
**Franchise in Cleveland prior to 1946*
***Steelers known as Pirates prior to 1941*
****Super Bowl XIV*

**L.A. RAMS vs. SAN DIEGO**
RS: Rams lead series, 3-2
1970—Rams, 37-10 (LA)
1975—Rams, 13-10 (SD) OT
1979—Chargers, 40-16 (LA)
1988—Chargers, 38-24 (LA)
1991—Rams, 30-24 (LA)
(RS Pts.—Chargers 122, Rams 120)

**L.A. RAMS vs. SAN FRANCISCO**
RS: Rams lead series, 48-38-2
PS: 49ers lead series, 1-0
1950—Rams, 35-14 (SF)
Rams, 28-21 (LA)
1951—49ers, 44-17 (SF)
Rams, 23-16 (LA)
1952—Rams, 35-9 (LA)
Rams, 34-21 (SF)
1953—49ers, 31-30 (SF)
49ers, 31-27 (LA)
1954—Tie, 24-24 (LA)
Rams, 42-34 (SF)
1955—Rams, 23-14 (SF)
Rams, 27-14 (LA)
1956—49ers, 33-30 (SF)
Rams, 30-6 (LA)
1957—49ers, 23-20 (SF)
Rams, 37-24 (LA)
1958—Rams, 33-3 (SF)
Rams, 56-7 (LA)
1959—49ers, 34-0 (SF)
49ers, 24-16 (LA)
1960—49ers, 13-9 (SF)
49ers, 23-7 (LA)
1961—49ers, 35-0 (SF)
Rams, 17-7 (LA)
1962—Rams, 28-14 (SF)
49ers, 24-17 (LA)
1963—Rams, 28-21 (LA)
Rams, 21-17 (SF)
1964—Rams, 42-14 (LA)
49ers, 28-7 (SF)
1965—49ers, 45-21 (LA)
49ers, 30-27 (SF)
1966—Rams, 34-3 (LA)
49ers, 21-13 (SF)
1967—49ers, 27-24 (LA)
Rams, 17-7 (SF)
1968—Rams, 24-10 (LA)
Tie, 20-20 (SF)
1969—Rams, 27-21 (SF)
Rams, 41-30 (LA)
1970—49ers, 20-6 (LA)
Rams, 30-13 (SF)
1971—Rams, 20-13 (SF)
Rams, 17-6 (LA)
1972—Rams, 31-7 (LA)
Rams, 26-16 (SF)
1973—Rams, 40-20 (SF)
Rams, 31-13 (LA)
1974—Rams, 37-14 (LA)
Rams, 15-13 (SF)
1975—Rams, 23-14 (SF)
49ers, 24-23 (LA)
1976—49ers, 16-0 (LA)
Rams, 23-3 (SF)
1977—Rams, 34-14 (LA)
Rams, 23-10 (SF)
1978—Rams, 27-10 (LA)
Rams, 31-28 (SF)
1979—Rams, 27-24 (LA)
Rams, 26-20 (SF)
1980—Rams, 48-26 (LA)
Rams, 31-17 (SF)
1981—49ers, 20-17 (SF)
49ers, 33-31 (LA)
1982—49ers, 30-24 (LA)
Rams, 21-20 (SF)
1983—Rams, 10-7 (SF)
49ers, 45-35 (LA)
1984—49ers, 33-0 (LA)
49ers, 19-16 (SF)
1985—49ers, 28-14 (LA)
Rams, 27-20 (SF)
1986—Rams, 16-13 (LA)
49ers, 24-14 (SF)
1987—49ers, 31-10 (LA)
49ers, 48-0 (SF)
1988—49ers, 24-21 (LA)
Rams, 38-16 (SF)
1989—Rams, 13-12 (SF)
49ers, 30-27 (LA)
*49ers, 30-3 (SF)
1990—Rams, 28-17 (SF)
49ers, 26-10 (LA)
1991—49ers, 27-10 (SF)
49ers, 33-10 (LA)
1992—49ers, 27-24 (SF)
49ers, 27-10 (LA)
1993—49ers, 40-17 (SF)
49ers, 35-10 (LA)
(RS Pts.—Rams 2,013, 49ers 1,863)
(PS Pts.—49ers 30, Rams 3)
**NFC Championship*

**L.A. RAMS vs. SEATTLE**
RS: Rams lead series, 4-1
1976—Rams, 45-6 (LA)
1979—Rams, 24-0 (S)

1985—Rams, 35-24 (S)
1988—Rams, 31-10 (LA)
1991—Seahawks, 23-9 (S)
(RS Pts.—Rams 144, Seahawks 63)

**L.A. RAMS vs. TAMPA BAY**
RS: Rams lead series, 8-2
PS: Rams lead series, 1-0
1977—Rams, 31-0 (LA)
1978—Rams, 26-23 (LA)
1979—Buccaneers, 21-6 (TB)
*Rams, 9-0 (TB)
1980—Buccaneers, 10-9 (TB)
1984—Rams, 34-33 (TB)
1985—Rams, 31-27 (TB)
1986—Rams, 26-20 (LA) OT
1987—Rams, 35-3 (LA)
1990—Rams, 35-14 (TB)
1992—Rams, 31-27 (TB)
(RS Pts.—Rams 264, Buccaneers 178)
(PS Pts.—Rams 9, Buccaneers 0)
*NFC Championship*

***L.A. RAMS vs. WASHINGTON**
RS: Redskins lead series, 14-5-1
PS: Series tied, 2-2
1937—Redskins, 16-7 (C)
1938—Redskins, 37-13 (W)
1941—Redskins, 17-13 (W)
1942—Redskins, 33-14 (W)
1944—Redskins, 14-10 (W)
1945—**Rams, 15-14 (C)
1948—Rams, 41-13 (W)
1949—Rams, 53-27 (LA)
1951—Redskins, 31-21 (W)
1962—Redskins, 20-14 (W)
1963—Redskins, 37-14 (LA)
1967—Tie, 28-28 (LA)
1969—Rams, 24-13 (W)
1971—Redskins, 38-24 (LA)
1974—Redskins, 23-17 (LA)
***Rams, 19-10 (LA)
1977—Redskins, 17-14 (W)
1981—Redskins, 30-7 (LA)
1983—Redskins, 42-20 (LA)
***Redskins, 51-7 (W)
1986—****Redskins, 19-7 (W)
1987—Rams, 30-26 (W)
1991—Redskins, 27-6 (LA)
1993—Rams, 10-6 (LA)
(RS Pts.—Redskins 495, Rams 380)
(PS Pts.—Redskins 94, Rams 48)
*Franchise in Cleveland prior to 1946*
***NFL Championship*
****NFC Divisional Playoff*
*****NFC First-Round Playoff*

---

**MIAMI vs. ARIZONA**
RS: Dolphins lead series, 6-0;
See Arizona vs. Miami

**MIAMI vs. ATLANTA**
RS: Dolphins lead series, 5-1;
See Atlanta vs. Miami

**MIAMI vs. BUFFALO**
RS: Dolphins lead series, 37-18-1
PS: Bills lead series, 2-0;
See Buffalo vs. Miami

**MIAMI vs. CHICAGO**
RS: Dolphins lead series, 5-1;
See Chicago vs. Miami

**MIAMI vs. CINCINNATI**
RS: Dolphins lead series, 9-3
PS: Dolphins lead series, 1-0;
See Cincinnati vs. Miami

**MIAMI vs. CLEVELAND**
RS: Dolphins lead series, 6-4
PS: Dolphins lead series, 2-0;
See Cleveland vs. Miami

**MIAMI vs. DALLAS**
RS: Dolphins lead series, 6-1
PS: Cowboys lead series, 1-0;
See Dallas vs. Miami

**MIAMI vs. DENVER**
RS: Dolphins lead series, 5-2-1;
See Denver vs. Miami

**MIAMI vs. DETROIT**
RS: Series tied, 2-2;
See Detroit vs. Miami

**MIAMI vs. GREEN BAY**
RS: Dolphins lead series, 7-0;
See Green Bay vs. Miami

**MIAMI vs. HOUSTON**
RS: Series tied, 11-11
PS: Oilers lead series, 1-0;
See Houston vs. Miami

**MIAMI vs. INDIANAPOLIS**
RS: Dolphins lead series, 34-14
PS: Dolphins lead series, 1-0;
See Indianapolis vs. Miami

**MIAMI vs. KANSAS CITY**
RS: Chiefs lead series, 10-7
PS: Dolphins lead series, 2-0;
See Kansas City vs. Miami

**MIAMI vs. L.A. RAIDERS**
RS: Raiders lead series, 14-4-1
PS: Raiders lead series, 2-1;
See L.A. Raiders vs. Miami

**MIAMI vs. L.A. RAMS**
RS: Dolphins lead series, 5-1;
See L.A. Rams vs. Miami

**MIAMI vs. MINNESOTA**
RS: Dolphins lead series, 4-1
PS: Dolphins lead series, 1-0
1972—Dolphins, 16-14 (Minn)
1973—*Dolphins, 24-7 (Houston)
1976—Vikings, 29-7 (Mia)
1979—Dolphins, 27-12 (Minn)
1982—Dolphins, 22-14 (Mia)
1988—Dolphins, 24-7 (Mia)
(RS Pts.—Dolphins 96, Vikings 76)
(PS Pts.—Dolphins 24, Vikings 7)
*Super Bowl VIII*

**MIAMI vs. *NEW ENGLAND**
RS: Dolphins lead series, 33-21
PS: Series tied, 1-1
1966—Patriots, 20-14 (M)
1967—Patriots, 41-10 (B)
Dolphins, 41-32 (M)
1968—Dolphins, 34-10 (B)
Dolphins, 38-7 (M)
1969—Dolphins, 17-16 (B)
Patriots, 38-23 (Tampa)
1970—Patriots, 27-14 (B)
Dolphins, 37-20 (M)
1971—Dolphins, 41-3 (M)
Patriots, 34-13 (NE)
1972—Dolphins, 52-0 (M)
Dolphins, 37-21 (NE)
1973—Dolphins, 44-23 (M)
Dolphins, 30-14 (NE)
1974—Patriots, 34-24 (NE)
Dolphins, 34-27 (M)
1975—Dolphins, 22-14 (NE)
Dolphins, 20-7 (M)
1976—Patriots, 30-14 (NE)
Dolphins, 10-3 (M)
1977—Dolphins, 17-5 (M)
Patriots, 14-10 (NE)
1978—Patriots, 33-24 (NE)
Dolphins, 23-3 (M)
1979—Patriots, 28-13 (NE)
Dolphins, 39-24 (M)
1980—Patriots, 34-0 (NE)
Dolphins, 16-13 (M) OT
1981—Dolphins, 30-27 (NE) OT
Dolphins, 24-14 (M)
1982—Patriots, 3-0 (NE)
**Dolphins, 28-13 (M)
1983—Dolphins, 34-24 (M)
Patriots, 17-6 (NE)
1984—Dolphins, 28-7 (M)
Dolphins, 44-24 (NE)
1985—Patriots, 17-13 (NE)
Dolphins, 30-27 (M)
***Patriots, 31-14 (M)
1986—Patriots, 34-7 (NE)
Patriots, 34-27 (M)
1987—Patriots, 28-21 (NE)
Patriots, 24-10 (M)
1988—Patriots, 21-10 (NE)
Patriots, 6-3 (M)
1989—Dolphins, 24-10 (NE)
Dolphins, 31-10 (M)
1990—Dolphins, 27-24 (NE)
Dolphins, 17-10 (M)
1991—Dolphins, 20-10 (NE)
Dolphins, 30-20 (M)
1992—Dolphins, 38-17 (M)
Dolphins, 16-13 (NE) OT
1993—Dolphins, 17-13 (M)
Patriots, 33-27 (NE) OT
(RS Pts.—Dolphins 1,245, Patriots 1,042)
(PS Pts.—Patriots 44, Dolphins 42)
*Franchise in Boston prior to 1971*
***AFC First-Round Playoff*
****AFC Championship*

**MIAMI vs. NEW ORLEANS**
RS: Dolphins lead series, 4-2
1970—Dolphins, 21-10 (M)
1974—Dolphins, 21-0 (NO)
1980—Dolphins, 21-16 (M)
1983—Saints, 17-7 (NO)
1986—Dolphins, 31-27 (NO)
1992—Saints, 24-13 (NO)
(RS Pts.—Dolphins 114, Saints 94)

**MIAMI vs. N.Y. GIANTS**
RS: Giants lead series, 2-1
1972—Dolphins, 23-13 (NY)
1990—Giants, 20-3 (NY)
1993—Giants, 19-14 (M)
(RS Pts.—Giants 52, Dolphins 40)

**MIAMI vs. N.Y. JETS**
RS: Jets lead series, 28-27-1
PS: Dolphins lead series, 1-0
1966—Jets, 19-14 (M)
Jets, 30-13 (NY)
1967—Jets, 29-7 (NY)
Jets, 33-14 (M)
1968—Jets, 35-17 (NY)
Jets, 31-7 (M)
1969—Jets, 34-31 (NY)
Jets, 27-9 (M)
1970—Dolphins, 20-6 (NY)
Dolphins, 16-10 (M)
1971—Jets, 14-10 (M)
Dolphins, 30-14 (NY)
1972—Dolphins, 27-17 (NY)
Dolphins, 28-24 (M)
1973—Dolphins, 31-3 (M)
Dolphins, 24-14 (NY)
1974—Dolphins, 21-17 (M)
Jets, 17-14 (NY)
1975—Dolphins, 43-0 (NY)
Dolphins, 27 7 (M)
1976—Dolphins, 16-0 (M)
Dolphins, 27-7 (NY)
1977—Dolphins, 21-17 (M)
Dolphins, 14-10 (NY)
1978—Jets, 33-20 (NY)
Jets, 24-13 (M)
1979—Jets, 33-27 (NY)
Jets, 27-24 (M)
1980—Jets, 17-14 (NY)
Jets, 24-17 (M)
1981—Tie, 28-28 (M) OT
Jets, 16-15 (NY)
1982—Dolphins, 45-28 (NY)
Dolphins, 20-19 (M)
*Dolphins, 14-0 (M)
1983—Dolphins, 32-14 (NY)
Dolphins, 34-14 (M)
1984—Dolphins, 31-17 (NY)
Dolphins, 28-17 (M)
1985—Jets, 23-7 (NY)
Dolphins, 21-17 (M)
1986—Jets, 51-45 (NY) OT
Dolphins, 45-3 (M)
1987—Jets, 37-31 (NY) OT
Dolphins, 37-28 (M)
1988—Jets, 44-30 (M)
Jets, 38-34 (NY)
1989—Jets, 40-33 (M)
Dolphins, 31-23 (NY)
1990—Dolphins, 20-16 (M)
Dolphins, 17-3 (NY)
1991—Jets, 41-23 (NY)
Jets, 23-20 (M) OT
1992—Jets, 26-14 (NY)
Dolphins, 19-17 (M)
1993—Jets, 24-14 (M)
Jets, 27-10 (NY)
(RS Pts.—Dolphins 1,280, Jets 1,207)
(PS Pts.—Dolphins 14, Jets 0)
*AFC Championship*

**MIAMI vs. PHILADELPHIA**
RS: Dolphins lead series, 6-2
1970—Eagles, 24-17 (P)
1975—Dolphins, 24-16 (M)
1978—Eagles, 17-3 (P)
1981—Dolphins, 13-10 (M)
1984—Dolphins, 24-23 (M)
1987—Dolphins, 28-10 (P)
1990—Dolphins, 23-20 (M) OT
1993—Dolphins, 19-14 (P)
(RS Pts.—Dolphins 151, Eagles 134)

**MIAMI vs. PITTSBURGH**
RS: Dolphins lead series, 7-5
PS: Dolphins lead series, 2-1
1971—Dolphins, 24-21 (M)
1972—*Dolphins, 21-17 (P)
1973—Dolphins, 30-26 (M)
1976—Steelers, 14-3 (P)
1979—**Steelers, 34-14 (P)
1980—Steelers, 23-10 (P)
1981—Dolphins, 30-10 (M)
1984—Dolphins, 31-7 (P)
*Dolphins, 45-28 (M)
1985—Dolphins, 24-20 (M)
1987—Dolphins, 35-24 (M)
1988—Steelers, 40-24 (P)
1989—Steelers, 34-14 (M)
1990—Dolphins, 28-6 (P)
1993—Steelers, 21-20 (M)
(RS Pts.—Dolphins 273, Steelers 246)
(PS Pts.—Dolphins 80, Steelers 79)
*AFC Championship*
***AFC Divisional Playoff*

**MIAMI vs. SAN DIEGO**
RS: Chargers lead series, 10-5
PS: Dolphins lead series, 2-1
1966—Chargers, 44-10 (SD)
1967—Chargers, 24-0 (SD)
Dolphins, 41-24 (M)
1968—Chargers, 34-28 (SD)
1969—Chargers, 21-14 (M)
1972—Dolphins, 24-10 (M)
1974 Dolphins, 28-21 (SD)
1977—Chargers, 14-13 (M)
1978—Dolphins, 28-21 (SD)
1980—Chargers, 27-24 (M) OT
1981—*Chargers, 41-38 (M) OT
1982—**Dolphins, 34-13 (M)
1984—Chargers, 34-28 (SD) OT
1986—Chargers, 50-28 (SD)
1988—Dolphins, 31-28 (M)
1991—Chargers, 38-30 (SD)
1992—*Dolphins, 31-0 (M)
1993—Chargers, 45-20 (SD)
(RS Pts.—Chargers 435, Dolphins 347)
(PS Pts.—Dolphins 103, Chargers 54)
*AFC Divisional Playoff*
***AFC Second-Round Playoff*

**MIAMI vs. SAN FRANCISCO**
RS: Dolphins lead series, 4-2
PS: 49ers lead series, 1-0
1973—Dolphins, 21-13 (M)
1977—Dolphins, 19-15 (SF)
1980—Dolphins, 17-13 (M)
1983—Dolphins, 20-17 (SF)
1984—*49ers, 38-16 (Stanford)
1986—49ers, 31-16 (M)
1992—49ers, 27-3 (SF)
(RS Pts.—49ers 116, Dolphins 96)
(PS Pts.—49ers 38, Dolphins 16)

*Super Bowl XIX*
**MIAMI vs. SEATTLE**
RS: Dolphins lead series, 4-1
PS: Series tied, 1-1
1977—Dolphins, 31-13 (M)
1979—Dolphins, 19-10 (M)
1983—*Seahawks, 27-20 (M)
1984—*Dolphins, 31-10 (M)
1987—Seahawks, 24-20 (S)
1990—Dolphins, 24-17 (M)
1992—Dolphins, 19-17 (S)
(RS Pts.—Dolphins 113, Seahawks 81)
(PS Pts.—Dolphins 51, Seahawks 37)
*AFC Divisional Playoff*
**MIAMI vs. TAMPA BAY**
RS: Dolphins lead series, 4-1
1976—Dolphins, 23-20 (TB)
1982—Buccaneers, 23-17 (TB)
1985—Dolphins, 41-38 (M)
1988—Dolphins, 17-14 (TB)
1991—Dolphins, 33-14 (M)
(RS Pts.—Dolphins 131, Buccaneers 109)
**MIAMI vs. WASHINGTON**
RS: Dolphins lead series, 5-2
PS: Series tied, 1-1
1972—*Dolphins, 14-7 (Los Angeles)
1974—Redskins, 20-17 (W)
1978—Dolphins, 16-0 (W)
1981—Dolphins, 13-10 (M)
1982—**Redskins, 27-17 (Pasadena)
1984—Dolphins, 35-17 (W)
1987—Dolphins, 23-21 (M)
1990—Redskins, 42-20 (W)
1993—Dolphins, 17-10 (M)
(RS Pts.—Dolphins 141, Redskins 120)
(PS Pts.—Redskins 34, Dolphins 31)
*Super Bowl VII*
**Super Bowl XVII*

---

**MINNESOTA vs. ARIZONA**
RS: Cardinals lead series, 7-4
PS: Vikings lead series, 1-0;
See Arizona vs. Minnesota
**MINNESOTA vs. ATLANTA**
RS: Vikings lead series, 11-6
PS: Vikings lead series, 1-0;
See Atlanta vs. Minnesota
**MINNESOTA vs. BUFFALO**
RS: Vikings lead series, 4-2;
See Buffalo vs. Minnesota
**MINNESOTA vs. CHICAGO**
RS: Vikings lead series, 34-29-2;
See Chicago vs. Minnesota
**MINNESOTA vs. CINCINNATI**
RS: Vikings lead series, 4-3;
See Cincinnati vs. Minnesota
**MINNESOTA vs. CLEVELAND**
RS: Vikings lead series, 7-3
PS: Vikings lead series, 1-0;
See Cleveland vs. Minnesota
**MINNESOTA vs. DALLAS**
RS: Cowboys lead series, 8-6
PS: Cowboys lead series, 3-1;
See Dallas vs. Minnesota
**MINNESOTA vs. DENVER**
RS: Vikings lead series, 5-3;
See Denver vs. Minnesota
**MINNESOTA vs. DETROIT**
RS: Vikings lead series, 40-23-2;
See Detroit vs. Minnesota
**MINNESOTA vs. GREEN BAY**
RS: Vikings lead series, 33-31-1;
See Green Bay vs. Minnesota
**MINNESOTA vs. HOUSTON**
RS: Series tied, 3-3;
See Houston vs. Minnesota
**MINNESOTA vs. INDIANAPOLIS**
RS: Colts lead series, 11-6-1
PS: Colts lead series, 1-0;
See Indianapolis vs. Minnesota
**MINNESOTA vs. KANSAS CITY**
RS: Vikings lead series, 3-2
PS: Chiefs lead series, 1-0;
See Kansas City vs. Minnesota
**MINNESOTA vs. L.A. RAIDERS**
RS: Raiders lead series, 6-2
PS: Raiders lead series, 1-0;
See L.A. Raiders vs. Minnesota
**MINNESOTA vs. L.A. RAMS**
RS: Vikings lead series, 15-11-2
PS: Vikings lead series, 5-1;
See L.A. Rams vs. Minnesota
**MINNESOTA vs. MIAMI**
RS: Dolphins lead series, 4-1
PS: Dolphins lead series, 1-0;
See Miami vs. Minnesota
**MINNESOTA vs. *NEW ENGLAND**
RS: Patriots lead series, 3-2
1970—Vikings, 35-14 (B)
1974—Patriots, 17-14 (M)
1979—Patriots, 27-23 (NE)
1988—Vikings, 36-6 (M)
1991—Patriots, 26-23 (NE) OT
(RS Pts.—Vikings 131, Patriots 90)
*Franchise in Boston prior to 1971*
**MINNESOTA vs. NEW ORLEANS**
RS: Vikings lead series, 11-6
PS: Vikings lead series, 1-0
1968—Saints, 20-17 (NO)
1970—Vikings, 26-0 (M)
1971—Vikings, 23-10 (NO)
1972—Vikings, 37-6 (M)
1974—Vikings, 29-9 (M)
1975—Vikings, 20-7 (NO)
1976—Vikings, 40-9 (NO)
1978—Saints, 31-24 (NO)
1980—Vikings, 23-20 (NO)
1981—Vikings, 20-10 (M)
1983—Saints, 17-16 (NO)
1985—Saints, 30-23 (M)
1986—Vikings, 33-17 (M)
1987—*Vikings, 44-10 (NO)
1988—Vikings, 45-3 (M)
1990—Vikings, 32-3 (M)
1991—Saints, 26-0 (NO)
1993—Saints, 17-14 (M)
(RS Pts.—Vikings 422, Saints 235)
(PS Pts.—Vikings 44, Saints 10)
*NFC First-Round Playoff*
**MINNESOTA vs. N.Y. GIANTS**
RS: Vikings lead series, 6-4
PS: Giants lead series, 1-0
1964—Vikings, 30-21 (NY)
1965—Vikings, 40-14 (M)
1967—Vikings, 27-24 (M)
1969—Giants, 24-23 (NY)
1971—Vikings, 17-10 (NY)
1973—Vikings, 31-7 (New Haven)
1976—Vikings, 24-7 (M)
1986—Giants, 22-20 (M)
1989—Giants, 24-14 (NY)
1990—Giants, 23-15 (NY)
1993—*Giants, 17-10 (NY)
(RS Pts.—Vikings 241, Giants 176)
(PS Pts.—Giants 17, Vikings 10)
*NFC First-Round Playoff*
**MINNESOTA vs. N.Y. JETS**
RS: Jets lead series, 3-1
1970—Jets, 20-10 (NY)
1975—Vikings, 29-21 (M)
1979—Jets, 14-7 (NY)
1982—Jets, 42-14 (M)
(RS Pts.—Jets 97, Vikings 60)
**MINNESOTA vs. PHILADELPHIA**
RS: Vikings lead series, 10-6
PS: Eagles lead series, 1-0
1962—Vikings, 31-21 (M)
1963—Vikings, 34-13 (P)
1968—Vikings, 24-17 (P)
1971—Vikings, 13-0 (P)
1973—Vikings, 28-21 (M)
1976—Vikings, 31-12 (P)
1978—Vikings, 28-27 (M)
1980—Eagles, 42-7 (M)
*Eagles, 31-16 (P)
1981—Vikings, 35-23 (M)
1984—Eagles, 19-17 (P)
1985—Vikings, 28-23 (P)
Eagles, 37-35 (M)
1988—Vikings, 23-21 (M)
1989—Eagles, 10-9 (P)
1990—Eagles, 32-24 (P)
1992—Eagles, 28-17 (P)
(RS Pts.—Vikings 384, Eagles 346)
(PS Pts.—Eagles 31, Vikings 16)
*NFC Divisional Playoff*
**MINNESOTA vs. PITTSBURGH**
RS: Vikings lead series, 7-4
PS: Steelers lead series, 1-0
1962—Steelers, 39-31 (P)
1964—Vikings, 30-10 (M)
1967—Vikings, 41-27 (P)
1969—Vikings, 52-14 (M)
1972—Steelers, 23-10 (P)
1974—*Steelers, 16-6 (New Orleans)
1976—Vikings, 17-6 (M)
1980—Steelers, 23-17 (M)
1983—Vikings, 17-14 (P)
1986—Vikings, 31-7 (M)
1989—Steelers, 27-14 (P)
1992—Vikings, 6-3 (P)
(RS Pts.—Vikings 266, Steelers 193)
(PS Pts.—Steelers 16, Vikings 6)
*Super Bowl IX*
**MINNESOTA vs. SAN DIEGO**
RS: Chargers lead series, 4-3
1971—Chargers, 30-14 (SD)
1975—Vikings, 28-13 (M)
1978—Chargers, 13-7 (M)
1981—Vikings, 33-31 (SD)
1984—Chargers, 42-13 (M)
1985—Vikings, 21-17 (M)
1993—Chargers, 30-17 (M)
(RS Pts.—Chargers 176, Vikings 133)
**MINNESOTA vs. SAN FRANCISCO**
RS: Series tied, 15-15-1
PS: 49ers lead series, 3-1
1961—49ers, 38-24 (M)
49ers, 38-28 (SF)
1962—49ers, 21-7 (SF)
49ers, 35-12 (M)
1963—Vikings, 24-20 (SF)
Vikings, 45-14 (M)
1964—Vikings, 27-22 (SF)
Vikings, 24-7 (M)
1965—Vikings, 42-41 (SF)
49ers, 45-24 (M)
1966—Tie, 20-20 (SF)
Vikings, 28-3 (SF)
1967—49ers, 27-21 (M)
1968—Vikings, 30-20 (SF)
1969—Vikings, 10-7 (M)
1970—*49ers, 17-14 (M)
1971—49ers, 13-9 (M)
1972—49ers, 20-17 (SF)
1973—Vikings, 17-13 (SF)
1975—Vikings, 27-17 (M)
1976—49ers, 20-16 (SF)
1977—Vikings, 28-27 (M)
1979—Vikings, 28-22 (M)
1983—49ers, 48-17 (M)
1984—49ers, 51-7 (SF)
1985—Vikings, 28-21 (M)
1986—Vikings, 27-24 (SF) OT
1987—*Vikings, 36-24 (SF)
1988—49ers, 24-21 (SF)
*49ers, 34-9 (SF)
1989—*49ers, 41-13 (SF)
1990—49ers, 20-17 (M)
1991—Vikings, 17-14 (M)
1992—49ers, 20-17 (M)
1993—49ers, 38-19 (SF)
(RS Pts.—49ers 750, Vikings 678)
(PS Pts.—49ers 116, Vikings 72)
*NFC Divisional Playoff*
**MINNESOTA vs. SEATTLE**
RS: Seahawks lead series, 3-2
1976—Vikings, 27-21 (M)
1978—Seahawks, 29-28 (S)
1984—Seahawks, 20-12 (M)
1987—Seahawks, 28-17 (S)
1990—Vikings, 24-21 (S)
(RS Pts.—Seahawks 119, Vikings 108)
**MINNESOTA vs. TAMPA BAY**
RS: Vikings lead series, 23-9
1977—Vikings, 9-3 (TB)
1978—Buccaneers, 16-10 (M)
Vikings, 24-7 (TB)
1979—Buccaneers, 12-10 (M)
Vikings, 23-22 (TB)
1980—Vikings, 38-30 (M)
Vikings, 21-10 (TB)
1981—Buccaneers, 21-13 (TB)
Vikings, 25-10 (M)
1982—Vikings, 17-10 (M)
1983—Vikings, 19-16 (TB) OT
Buccaneers, 17-12 (M)
1984—Buccaneers, 35-31 (TB)
Vikings, 27-24 (M)
1985—Vikings, 31-16 (TB)
Vikings, 26-7 (M)
1986—Vikings, 23-10 (TB)
Vikings, 45-13 (M)
1987—Buccaneers, 20-10 (TB)
Vikings, 23-17 (M)
1988—Vikings, 14-13 (M)
Vikings, 49-20 (TB)
1989—Vikings, 17-3 (M)
Vikings, 24-10 (TB)
1990—Buccaneers, 23-20 (M) OT
Buccaneers, 26-13 (TB)
1991—Vikings, 28-13 (M)
Vikings, 26-24 (TB)
1992—Vikings, 26-20 (M)
Vikings, 35-7 (TB)
1993—Vikings, 15-0 (M)
Buccaneers, 23-10 (TB)
(RS Pts.—Vikings 714, Buccaneers 498)
**MINNESOTA vs. WASHINGTON**
RS: Redskins lead series, 6-4
PS: Redskins lead series, 3-2
1968—Vikings, 27-14 (M)
1970—Vikings, 19-10 (W)
1972—Redskins, 24-21 (M)
1973—*Vikings, 27-20 (M)
1975—Redskins, 31-30 (W)
1976—*Vikings, 35-20 (M)
1980—Vikings, 39-14 (W)
1982—**Redskins, 21-7 (W)
1984—Redskins, 31-17 (M)
1986—Redskins, 44-38 (W) OT
1987—Redskins, 27-24 (M) OT
***Redskins, 17-10 (W)
1992—Redskins, 15-13 (M)
****Redskins, 24-7 (M)
1993—Vikings, 14-9 (W)
(RS Pts.—Vikings 242, Redskins 219)
(PS Pts.—Redskins 102, Vikings 86)
*NFC Divisional Playoff*
**NFC Second-Round Playoff*
***NFC Championship*
****NFC First-Round Playoff*

---

**NEW ENGLAND vs. ARIZONA**
RS: Cardinals lead series, 6-2;
See Arizona vs. New England
**NEW ENGLAND vs. ATLANTA**
RS: Falcons lead series, 4-3;
See Atlanta vs. New England
**NEW ENGLAND vs. BUFFALO**
RS: Series tied, 33-33-1
PS: Patriots lead series, 1-0;
See Buffalo vs. New England
**NEW ENGLAND vs. CHICAGO**
RS: Patriots lead series, 3-2
PS: Bears lead series, 1-0;
See Chicago vs. New England
**NEW ENGLAND vs. CINCINNATI**
RS: Patriots lead series, 8-7;
See Cincinnati vs. New England
**NEW ENGLAND vs. CLEVELAND**

RS: Browns lead series, 9-3;
See Cleveland vs. New England
**NEW ENGLAND vs. DALLAS**
RS: Cowboys lead series, 6-0;
See Dallas vs. New England
**NEW ENGLAND vs. DENVER**
RS: Broncos lead series, 16-12
PS: Broncos lead series, 1-0;
See Denver vs. New England
**NEW ENGLAND vs. DETROIT**
RS: Lions lead series, 3-2;
See Detroit vs. New England
**NEW ENGLAND vs. GREEN BAY**
RS: Series tied, 2-2;
See Green Bay vs. New England
**NEW ENGLAND vs. HOUSTON**
RS: Patriots lead series, 17-14-1
PS: Oilers lead series, 1-0;
See Houston vs. New England
**NEW ENGLAND vs. INDIANAPOLIS**
RS: Patriots lead series, 27-20;
See Indianapolis vs. New England
**NEW ENGLAND vs. KANSAS CITY**
RS: Chiefs lead series, 13-7-3;
See Kansas City vs. New England
**NEW ENGLAND vs. L.A. RAIDERS**
RS: Series tied, 12-12-1
PS: Series tied, 1-1;
See L.A. Raiders vs. New England
**NEW ENGLAND vs. L.A. RAMS**
RS: Series tied, 3-3;
See L.A. Rams vs. New England
**NEW ENGLAND vs. MIAMI**
RS: Dolphins lead series, 33-21
PS: Series tied, 1-1;
See Miami vs. New England
**NEW ENGLAND vs. MINNESOTA**
RS: Patriots lead series, 3-2;
See Minnesota vs. New England
**NEW ENGLAND vs. NEW ORLEANS**
RS: Patriots lead series, 5-2
1972—Patriots, 17-10 (NO)
1976—Patriots, 27-6 (NE)
1980—Patriots, 38-27 (NO)
1983—Patriots, 7-0 (NE)
1986—Patriots, 21-20 (NO)
1989—Saints, 28-24 (NE)
1992—Saints, 31-14 (NE)
(RS Pts.—Patriots 148, Saints 122)
***NEW ENGLAND vs. N.Y. GIANTS**
RS: Giants lead series, 3-1
1970—Giants, 16-0 (B)
1974—Patriots, 28-20 (New Haven)
1987—Giants, 17-10 (NY)
1990—Giants, 13-10 (NE)
(RS Pts.—Giants 66, Patriots 48)
**Franchise in Boston prior to 1971*
***NEW ENGLAND vs. **N.Y. JETS**
RS: Jets lead series, 38-28-1
PS: Patriots lead series, 1-0
1960—Patriots, 28-24 (NY)
Patriots, 38-21 (B)
1961—Titans, 21-20 (B)
Titans, 37-30 (NY)
1962—Patriots, 43-14 (NY)
Patriots, 24-17 (B)
1963—Patriots, 38-14 (B)
Jets, 31-24 (NY)
1964—Patriots, 26-10 (B)
Jets, 35-14 (NY)
1965—Jets, 30-20 (B)
Patriots, 27-23 (NY)
1966—Tie, 24-24 (B)
Jets, 38-28 (NY)
1967—Jets, 30-23 (NY)
Jets, 29-24 (B)
1968—Jets, 47-31 (Birmingham)
Jets, 48-14 (NY)
1969—Jets, 23-14 (B)
Jets, 23-17 (NY)
1970—Jets, 31-21 (B)
Jets, 17-3 (NY)
1971—Patriots, 20-0 (NE)
Jets, 13-6 (NY)
1972—Jets, 41-13 (NE)
Jets, 34-10 (NY)
1973—Jets, 9-7 (NE)
Jets, 33-13 (NY)
1974—Patriots, 24-0 (NY)
Jets, 21-16 (NE)
1975—Jets, 36-7 (NY)
Jets, 30-28 (NE)
1976—Patriots, 41-7 (NE)
Patriots, 38-24 (NY)
1977—Jets, 30-27 (NY)
Patriots, 24-13 (NE)
1978—Patriots, 55-21 (NE)
Patriots, 19-17 (NY)
1979—Patriots, 56-3 (NE)
Jets, 27-26 (NY)
1980—Patriots, 21-11 (NY)
Patriots, 34-21 (NE)
1981—Jets, 28-24 (NY)
Jets, 17-6 (NE)
1982—Jets, 31-7 (NE)
1983—Patriots, 23-13 (NE)
Jets, 26-3 (NY)
1984—Patriots, 28-21 (NY)
Patriots, 30-20 (NE)
1985—Patriots, 20-13 (NE)
Jets, 16-13 (NY) OT
***Patriots, 26-14 (NY)
1986—Patriots, 20-6 (NY)
Jets, 31-24 (NE)
1987—Jets, 43-24 (NY)
Patriots, 42-20 (NE)
1988—Patriots, 28-3 (NE)
Patriots, 14-13 (NY)
1989—Patriots, 27-24 (NY)
Jets, 27-26 (NE)
1990—Jets, 37-13 (NE)
Jets, 42-7 (NY)
1991—Jets, 28-21 (NE)
Patriots, 6-3 (NY)
1992—Jets, 30-21 (NY)
Patriots, 24-3 (NE)
1993—Jets, 45-7 (NY)
Jets, 6-0 (NE)
(RS Pts.—Jets 1,524, Patriots 1,474)
(PS Pts.—Patriots 26, Jets 14)
**Franchise in Boston prior to 1971*
***Jets known as Titans prior to 1963*
****AFC First-Round Playoff*
**NEW ENGLAND vs. PHILADELPHIA**
RS: Eagles lead series, 5-2
1973—Eagles, 24-23 (P)
1977—Patriots, 14-6 (NE)
1978—Patriots, 24-14 (NE)
1981—Eagles, 13-3 (P)
1984—Eagles, 27-17 (P)
1987—Eagles, 34-31 (NE) OT
1990—Eagles, 48-20 (P)
(RS Pts.—Eagles 166, Patriots 132)
**NEW ENGLAND vs. PITTSBURGH**
RS: Steelers lead series, 9-3
1972—Steelers, 33-3 (P)
1974—Steelers, 21-17 (NE)
1976—Patriots, 30-27 (P)
1979—Steelers, 16-13 (NE) OT
1981—Steelers, 27-21 (P) OT
1982—Steelers, 37-14 (P)
1983—Patriots, 28-23 (P)
1986—Patriots, 34-0 (P)
1989—Steelers, 28-10 (P)
1990—Steelers, 24-3 (P)
1991—Steelers, 20-6 (P)
1993—Steelers, 17-14 (P)
(RS Pts.—Steelers 273, Patriots 193)
***NEW ENGLAND vs. **SAN DIEGO**
RS: Patriots lead series, 13-11-2
PS: Chargers lead series, 1-0
1960—Patriots, 35-0 (LA)
Chargers, 45-16 (B)
1961—Chargers, 38-27 (B)
Patriots, 41-0 (SD)
1962—Patriots, 24-20 (B)
Patriots, 20-14 (SD)
1963—Chargers, 17-13 (SD)
Chargers, 7-6 (B)
***Chargers, 51-10 (SD)
1964—Patriots, 33-28 (SD)
Chargers, 26-17 (B)
1965—Tie, 10-10 (B)
Patriots, 22-6 (SD)
1966—Chargers, 24-0 (SD)
Patriots, 35-17 (B)
1967—Chargers, 28-14 (SD)
Tie, 31-31 (SD)
1968—Chargers, 27-17 (B)
1969—Chargers, 13-10 (B)
Chargers, 28-18 (SD)
1970—Chargers, 16-14 (B)
1973—Patriots, 30-14 (NE)
1975—Patriots, 33-19 (SD)
1977—Patriots, 24-20 (SD)
1978—Patriots, 28-23 (NE)
1979—Patriots, 27-21 (NE)
1983—Patriots, 37-21 (NE)
(RS Pts.—Patriots 582, Chargers 513)
(PS Pts.—Chargers 51, Patriots 10)
**Franchise in Boston prior to 1971*
***Franchise in Los Angeles prior to 1961*
****AFL Championship*
**NEW ENGLAND vs. SAN FRANCISCO**
RS: 49ers lead series, 6-1
1971—49ers, 27-10 (SF)
1975—Patriots, 24-16 (NE)
1980—49ers, 21-17 (SF)
1983—49ers, 33-13 (NE)
1986—49ers, 29-24 (NE)
1989—49ers, 37-20 (SF)
1992—49ers, 24-12 (NE)
(RS Pts.—49ers 187, Patriots 120)
**NEW ENGLAND vs. SEATTLE**
RS: Seahawks lead series, 7-6
1977—Patriots, 31-0 (NE)
1980—Patriots, 37-31 (S)
1982—Patriots, 16-0 (S)
1983—Seahawks, 24-6 (S)
1984—Patriots, 38-23 (NE)
1985—Patriots, 20-13 (S)
1986—Seahawks, 38-31 (NE)
1988—Patriots, 13-7 (NE)
1989—Seahawks, 24-3 (NE)
1990—Seahawks, 33-20 (NE)
1992—Seahawks, 10-6 (NE)
1993—Seahawks, 17-14 (NE)
Seahawks, 10-9 (S)
(RS Pts.—Patriots 244, Seahawks 230)
**NEW ENGLAND vs. TAMPA BAY**
RS: Patriots lead series, 3-0
1976—Patriots, 31-14 (TB)
1985—Patriots, 32-14 (TB)
1988—Patriots, 10-7 (NE) OT
(RS Pts.—Patriots 73, Buccaneers 35)
**NEW ENGLAND vs. WASHINGTON**
RS: Redskins lead series, 4-1
1972—Patriots, 24-23 (NE)
1978—Redskins, 16-14 (NE)
1981—Redskins, 24-22 (W)
1984—Redskins, 26-10 (NE)
1990—Redskins, 25-10 (NE)
(RS Pts.—Redskins 114, Patriots 80)

---

**NEW ORLEANS vs. ARIZONA**
RS: Cardinals lead series, 10-9;
See Arizona vs. New Orleans
**NEW ORLEANS vs. ATLANTA**
RS: Falcons lead series, 27-22
PS: Falcons lead series, 1-0;
See Atlanta vs. New Orleans
**NEW ORLEANS vs. BUFFALO**
RS: Bills lead series, 3-2;
See Buffalo vs. New Orleans
**NEW ORLEANS vs. CHICAGO**
RS: Bears lead series, 8-6
PS: Bears lead series, 1-0;
See Chicago vs. New Orleans
**NEW ORLEANS vs. CINCINNATI**
RS: Saints lead series, 5-3;
See Cincinnati vs. New Orleans
**NEW ORLEANS vs. CLEVELAND**
RS: Browns lead series, 9-3;
See Cleveland vs. New Orleans
**NEW ORLEANS vs. DALLAS**
RS: Cowboys lead series, 13-3;
See Dallas vs. New Orleans
**NEW ORLEANS vs. DENVER**
RS: Broncos lead series, 4-1;
See Denver vs. New Orleans
**NEW ORLEANS vs. DETROIT**
RS: Saints lead series, 7-6-1;
See Detroit vs. New Orleans
**NEW ORLEANS vs. GREEN BAY**
RS: Packers lead series, 12-4;
See Green Bay vs. New Orleans
**NEW ORLEANS vs. HOUSTON**
RS: Saints lead series, 4-3-1;
See Houston vs. New Orleans
**NEW ORLEANS vs. INDIANAPOLIS**
RS: Colts lead series, 3-2;
See Indianapolis vs. New Orleans
**NEW ORLEANS vs. KANSAS CITY**
RS: Saints lead series, 3-2;
See Kansas City vs. New Orleans
**NEW ORLEANS vs. L.A. RAIDERS**
RS: Raiders lead series, 3-2-1;
See L.A. Raiders vs. New Orleans
**NEW ORLEANS vs. L.A. RAMS**
RS: Rams lead series, 27-21;
See L.A. Rams vs. New Orleans
**NEW ORLEANS vs. MIAMI**
RS: Dolphins lead series, 4-2;
See Miami vs. New Orleans
**NEW ORLEANS vs. MINNESOTA**
RS: Vikings lead series, 11-6
PS: Vikings lead series, 1-0;
See Minnesota vs. New Orleans
**NEW ORLEANS vs. NEW ENGLAND**
RS: Patriots lead series, 5-2;
See New England vs. New Orleans
**NEW ORLEANS vs. N.Y. GIANTS**
RS: Giants lead series, 9-6
1967—Giants, 27-21 (NY)
1968—Giants, 38-21 (NY)
1969—Saints, 25-24 (NY)
1970—Saints, 14-10 (NO)
1972—Giants, 45-21 (NY)
1975—Giants, 28-14 (NY)
1978—Saints, 28-17 (NO)
1979—Saints, 24-14 (NO)
1981—Giants, 20-7 (NY)
1984—Saints, 10-3 (NY)
1985—Giants, 21-13 (NO)
1986—Giants, 20-17 (NY)
1987—Saints, 23-14 (NO)
1988—Giants, 13-12 (NO)
1993—Giants, 24-14 (NO)
(RS Pts.—Giants 318, Saints 264)
**NEW ORLEANS vs. N.Y. JETS**
RS: Jets lead series, 4-3
1972—Jets, 18-17 (NY)
1977—Jets, 16-13 (NO)
1980—Saints, 21-20 (NY)
1983—Jets, 31-28 (NO)
1986—Jets, 28-23 (NY)
1989—Saints, 29-14 (NO)
1992—Saints, 20-0 (NY)
(RS Pts.—Saints 151, Jets 127)
**NEW ORLEANS vs. PHILADELPHIA**
RS: Eagles lead series, 11-8
PS: Eagles lead series, 1-0
1967—Saints, 31-24 (NO)
Eagles, 48-21 (P)
1968—Eagles, 29-17 (P)
1969—Eagles, 13-10 (P)
Saints, 26-17 (NO)
1972—Saints, 21-3 (NO)
1974—Saints, 14-10 (NO)
1977—Eagles, 28-7 (P)
1978—Eagles, 24-17 (NO)
1979—Eagles, 26-14 (NO)

# ALL-TIME TEAM VS. TEAM RESULTS

1980—Eagles, 34-21 (NO)
1981—Eagles, 31-14 (NO)
1983—Saints, 20-17 (P) OT
1985—Saints, 23-21 (NO)
1987—Eagles, 27-17 (P)
1989—Saints, 30-20 (NO)
1991—Saints, 13-6 (P)
1992—Eagles, 15-13 (P)
*Eagles, 36-20 (NO)
1993—Eagles, 37-26 (P)
(RS Pts.—Eagles 430, Saints 355)
(PS Pts.—Eagles 36, Saints 20)
*NFC First-Round Playoff

**NEW ORLEANS vs. PITTSBURGH**
RS: Steelers lead series, 6-5
1967—Steelers, 14-10 (NO)
1968—Saints, 16-12 (P)
Saints, 24-14 (NO)
1969—Saints, 27-24 (NO)
1974—Steelers, 28-7 (NO)
1978—Steelers, 20-14 (P)
1981—Steelers, 20-6 (NO)
1984—Saints, 27-24 (NO)
1987—Saints, 20-16 (P)
1990—Steelers, 9-6 (NO)
1993—Steelers, 37-14 (P)
(RS Pts.—Steelers 218, Saints 171)

**NEW ORLEANS vs. SAN DIEGO**
RS: Chargers lead series, 4-1
1973—Chargers, 17-14 (SD)
1977—Chargers, 14-0 (NO)
1979—Chargers, 35-0 (NO)
1988—Saints, 23-17 (SD)
1991—Chargers, 24-21 (SD)
(RS Pts.—Chargers 107, Saints 58)

**NEW ORLEANS vs. SAN FRANCISCO**
RS: 49ers lead series, 33-14-2
1967—49ers, 27-13 (SF)
1969—Saints, 43-38 (NO)
1970—Tie, 20-20 (SF)
49ers, 38-27 (NO)
1971—49ers, 38-20 (NO)
Saints, 26-20 (SF)
1972—49ers, 37-2 (NO)
Tie, 20-20 (SF)
1973—49ers, 40-0 (SF)
Saints, 16-10 (NO)
1974—49ers, 17-13 (NO)
49ers, 35-21 (SF)
1975—49ers, 35-21 (SF)
49ers, 16-6 (NO)
1976—49ers, 33-3 (SF)
49ers, 27-7 (NO)
1977—49ers, 10-7 (NO) OT
49ers, 20-17 (SF)
1978—Saints, 14-7 (SF)
Saints, 24-13 (NO)
1979—Saints, 30-21 (SF)
Saints, 31-20 (NO)
1980—49ers, 26-23 (NO)
49ers, 38-35 (SF) OT
1981—49ers, 21-14 (SF)
49ers, 21-17 (NO)
1982—Saints, 23-20 (SF)
1983—49ers, 32-13 (NO)
49ers, 27-0 (SF)
1984—49ers, 30-20 (SF)
49ers, 35-3 (NO)
1985—Saints, 20-17 (SF)
49ers, 31-19 (NO)
1986—49ers, 26-17 (SF)
Saints, 23-10 (NO)
1987—49ers, 24-22 (NO)
Saints, 26-24 (SF)
1988—49ers, 34-33 (NO)
49ers, 30-17 (SF)
1989—49ers, 24-20 (NO)
49ers, 31-13 (SF)
1990—49ers, 13-12 (NO)
Saints, 13-10 (SF)
1991—Saints, 10-3 (NO)
49ers, 38-24 (SF)
1992—49ers, 16-10 (NO)
49ers, 21-20 (SF)
1993—Saints, 16-13 (NO)
49ers, 42-7 (SF)
(RS Pts.—49ers, 1,199, Saints 851)

**NEW ORLEANS vs. SEATTLE**
RS: Saints lead series, 3-2
1976—Saints, 51-27 (S)
1979—Seahawks, 38-24 (S)
1985—Seahawks, 27-3 (NO)
1988—Saints, 20-19 (S)
1991—Saints, 27-24 (NO)
(RS Pts.—Seahawks 135, Saints 125)

**NEW ORLEANS vs. TAMPA BAY**
RS: Saints lead series, 11-4
1977—Buccaneers, 33-14 (NO)
1978—Saints, 17-10 (TB)
1979—Saints, 42-14 (TB)
1981—Buccaneers, 31-14 (NO)
1982—Buccaneers, 13-10 (NO)
1983—Saints, 24-21 (TB)
1984—Saints, 17-13 (NO)
1985—Saints, 20-13 (NO)
1986—Saints, 38-7 (NO)
1987—Saints, 44-34 (NO)
1988—Saints, 13-9 (NO)
1989—Buccaneers, 20-10 (TB)
1990—Saints, 35-7 (NO)
1991—Saints, 23-7 (NO)
1992—Saints, 23-21 (NO)
(RS Pts.—Saints 344, Buccaneers 253)

**NEW ORLEANS vs. WASHINGTON**
RS: Redskins lead series, 11-5
1967—Redskins, 30-10 (NO)
Saints, 30-14 (W)
1968—Saints, 37-17 (NO)
1969—Redskins, 26-20 (NO)
Redskins, 17-14 (W)
1971—Redskins, 24-14 (W)
1973—Saints, 19-3 (NO)
1975—Redskins, 41-3 (W)
1979—Saints, 14-10 (W)
1980—Redskins, 22-14 (W)
1982—Redskins, 27-10 (NO)
1986—Redskins, 14-6 (NO)
1988—Redskins, 27-24 (W)
1989—Redskins, 16-14 (NO)
1990—Redskins, 31-17 (W)
1992—Saints, 20-3 (NO)
(RS Pts.—Redskins 322, Saints 266)

---

**N.Y. GIANTS vs. ARIZONA**
RS: Giants lead series, 65-35-2;
See Arizona vs. N.Y. Giants

**N.Y. GIANTS vs. ATLANTA**
RS: Series tied, 6-6;
See Atlanta vs. N.Y. Giants

**N.Y. GIANTS vs. BUFFALO**
RS: Bills lead series, 4-2
PS: Giants lead series, 1-0;
See Buffalo vs. N.Y. Giants

**N.Y. GIANTS vs. CHICAGO**
RS: Bears lead series, 24-16-2
PS: Bears lead series, 5-3;
See Chicago vs. N.Y. Giants

**N.Y. GIANTS vs. CINCINNATI**
RS: Bengals lead series, 4-0;
See Cincinnati vs. N.Y. Giants

**N.Y. GIANTS vs. CLEVELAND**
RS: Browns lead series, 25-16-2
PS: Series tied, 1-1;
See Cleveland vs. N.Y. Giants

**N.Y. GIANTS vs. DALLAS**
RS: Cowboys lead series, 40-21-2;
See Dallas vs. N.Y. Giants

**N.Y. GIANTS vs. DENVER**
RS: Series tied, 3-3
PS: Giants lead series, 1-0;
See Denver vs. N.Y. Giants

**N.Y. GIANTS vs. DETROIT**
RS: Lions lead series, 17-15-1
PS: Lions lead series, 1-0;
See Detroit vs. N.Y. Giants

**N.Y. GIANTS vs. GREEN BAY**
RS: Packers lead series, 21-20-2
PS: Packers lead series, 4-1;
See Green Bay vs. N.Y. Giants

**N.Y. GIANTS vs. HOUSTON**
RS: Giants lead series, 4-0;
See Houston vs. N.Y. Giants

**N.Y. GIANTS vs. INDIANAPOLIS**
RS: Series tied, 5-5
PS: Colts lead series, 2-0;
See Indianapolis vs. N.Y. Giants

**N.Y. GIANTS vs. KANSAS CITY**
RS: Giants lead series, 6-1;
See Kansas City vs. N.Y. Giants

**N.Y. GIANTS vs. L.A. RAIDERS**
RS: Raiders lead series, 4-2;
See L.A. Raiders vs. N.Y. Giants

**N.Y. GIANTS vs. L.A. RAMS**
RS: Rams lead series, 20-9
PS: Series tied, 1-1;
See L.A. Rams vs. N.Y. Giants

**N.Y. GIANTS vs. MIAMI**
RS: Giants lead series, 2-1;
See Miami vs. N.Y. Giants

**N.Y. GIANTS vs. MINNESOTA**
RS: Vikings lead series, 6-4
PS: Giants lead series, 1-0;
See Minnesota vs. N.Y. Giants

**N.Y. GIANTS vs. NEW ENGLAND**
RS: Giants lead series, 3-1;
See New England vs. N.Y. Giants

**N.Y. GIANTS vs. NEW ORLEANS**
RS: Giants lead series, 9-6;
See New Orleans vs. N.Y. Giants

**N.Y. GIANTS vs. N.Y. JETS**
RS: Jets lead series, 4-3
1970—Giants, 22-10 (NYJ)
1974—Jets, 26-20 (New Haven) OT
1981—Jets, 26-7 (NYG)
1984—Giants, 20-10 (NYJ)
1987—Giants, 20-7 (NYG)
1988—Jets, 27-21 (NYJ)
1993—Jets, 10-6 (NYG)
(RS Pts.—Giants 116, Jets 116)

**N.Y. GIANTS vs. PHILADELPHIA**
RS: Giants lead series, 62-54-2
PS: Giants lead series, 1-0
1933—Giants, 56-0 (NY)
Giants, 20-14 (P)
1934—Giants, 17-0 (NY)
Eagles, 6-0 (P)
1935—Giants, 10-0 (NY)
Giants, 21-14 (P)
1936—Eagles, 10-7 (P)
Giants, 21-17 (NY)
1937—Giants, 16-7 (P)
Giants, 21-0 (NY)
1938—Eagles, 14-10 (P)
Giants, 17-7 (NY)
1939—Giants, 13-3 (P)
Giants, 27-10 (NY)
1940—Giants, 20-14 (P)
Giants, 17-7 (NY)
1941—Giants, 24-0 (P)
Giants, 16-0 (NY)
1942—Giants, 35-17 (NY)
Giants, 14-0 (P)
1944—Eagles, 24-17 (NY)
Tie, 21-21 (P)
1945—Eagles, 38-17 (P)
Giants, 28-21 (NY)
1946—Eagles, 24-14 (P)
Giants, 45-17 (NY)
1947—Eagles, 23-0 (P)
Eagles, 41-24 (NY)
1948—Eagles, 45-0 (P)
Eagles, 35-14 (NY)
1949—Eagles, 24-3 (NY)
Eagles, 17-3 (P)
1950—Giants, 7-3 (NY)
Giants, 9-7 (P)
1951—Giants, 26-24 (NY)
Giants, 23-7 (P)
1952—Giants, 31-7 (P)
Eagles, 14-10 (NY)
1953—Eagles, 30-7 (P)
Giants, 37-28 (NY)
1954—Giants, 27-14 (NY)
Eagles, 29-14 (P)
1955—Eagles, 27-17 (P)
Giants, 31-7 (NY)
1956—Giants, 20-3 (NY)
Giants, 21-7 (P)
1957—Giants, 24-20 (P)
Giants, 13-0 (NY)
1958—Eagles, 27-24 (P)
Giants, 24-10 (NY)
1959—Eagles, 49-21 (P)
Giants, 24-7 (NY)
1960—Eagles, 17-10 (NY)
Eagles, 31-23 (P)
1961—Giants, 38-21 (NY)
Giants, 28-24 (P)
1962—Giants, 29-13 (P)
Giants, 19-14 (NY)
1963—Giants, 37-14 (P)
Giants, 42-14 (NY)
1964—Eagles, 38-7 (P)
Eagles, 23-17 (NY)
1965—Giants, 16-14 (P)
Giants, 35-27 (NY)
1966—Eagles, 35-17 (P)
Eagles, 31-3 (NY)
1967—Giants, 44-7 (NY)
1968—Giants, 34-25 (P)
Giants, 7-6 (NY)
1969—Eagles, 23-20 (NY)
1970—Giants, 30-23 (NY)
Eagles, 23-20 (P)
1971—Eagles, 23-7 (P)
Eagles, 41-28 (NY)
1972—Giants, 27-12 (P)
Giants, 62-10 (NY)
1973—Tie, 23-23 (NY)
Eagles, 20-16 (P)
1974—Eagles, 35-7 (P)
Eagles, 20-7 (New Haven)
1975—Giants, 23-14 (P)
Eagles, 13-10 (NY)
1976—Eagles, 20-7 (P)
Eagles, 10-0 (NY)
1977—Eagles, 28-10 (NY)
Eagles, 17-14 (P)
1978—Eagles, 19-17 (NY)
Eagles, 20-3 (P)
1979—Eagles, 23-17 (P)
Eagles, 17-13 (NY)
1980—Eagles, 35-3 (P)
Eagles, 31-16 (NY)
1981—Eagles, 24-10 (NY)
Giants, 20-10 (P)
*Giants, 27-21 (P)
1982—Giants, 23-7 (NY)
Giants, 26-24 (P)
1983—Eagles, 17-13 (NY)
Giants, 23-0 (P)
1984—Giants, 28-27 (NY)
Eagles, 24-10 (P)
1985—Giants, 21-0 (NY)
Giants, 16-10 (P) OT
1986—Giants, 35-3 (NY)
Giants, 17-14 (P)
1987—Giants, 20-17 (P)
Giants, 23-20 (NY) OT
1988—Eagles, 24-13 (P)
Eagles, 23-17 (NY) OT
1989—Eagles, 21-19 (P)
Eagles, 24-17 (NY)
1990—Giants, 27-20 (NY)
Eagles, 31-13 (P)
1991—Eagles, 30-7 (P)
Eagles, 19-14 (NY)
1992—Eagles, 47-34 (NY)
Eagles, 20-10 (P)
1993—Giants, 21-10 (NY)
Giants, 7-3 (P)
(RS Pts.—Giants 2,248, Eagles 2,113)

(PS Pts.—Giants 27, Eagles 21)
*NFC First-Round Playoff*

**N.Y. GIANTS vs. *PITTSBURGH**
RS: Giants lead series, 42-26-3
1933—Giants, 23-2 (P)
Giants, 27-3 (NY)
1934—Giants, 14-12 (P)
Giants, 17-7 (NY)
1935—Giants, 42-7 (P)
Giants, 13-0 (NY)
1936—Pirates, 10-7 (P)
1937—Giants, 10-7 (P)
Giants, 17-0 (NY)
1938—Giants, 27-14 (P)
Pirates, 13-10 (NY)
1939—Giants, 14-7 (P)
Giants, 23-7 (NY)
1940—Tie, 10-10 (P)
Giants, 12-0 (NY)
1941—Giants, 37-10 (P)
Giants, 28-7 (NY)
1942—Steelers, 13-10 (P)
Steelers, 17-9 (NY)
1945—Giants, 34-6 (P)
Steelers, 21-7 (NY)
1946—Giants, 17-14 (P)
Giants, 7-0 (NY)
1947—Steelers, 38-21 (NY)
Steelers, 24-7 (P)
1948—Giants, 34-27 (NY)
Steelers, 38-28 (P)
1949—Steelers, 28-7 (P)
Steelers, 21-17 (NY)
1950—Giants, 18-7 (P)
Steelers, 17-6 (NY)
1951—Tie, 13-13 (P)
Giants, 14-0 (NY)
1952—Steelers, 63-7 (P)
1953—Steelers, 24-14 (P)
Steelers, 14-10 (NY)
1954—Giants, 30-6 (P)
Giants, 24-3 (NY)
1955—Steelers, 30-23 (P)
Steelers, 19-17 (NY)
1956—Giants, 38-10 (NY)
Giants, 17-14 (P)
1957—Giants, 35-0 (NY)
Steelers, 21-10 (P)
1958—Giants, 17-6 (NY)
Steelers, 31-10 (P)
1959—Giants, 21-16 (P)
Steelers, 14-9 (NY)
1960—Giants, 19-17 (P)
Giants, 27-24 (NY)
1961—Giants, 17-14 (P)
Giants, 42-21 (NY)
1962—Giants, 31-27 (P)
Steelers, 20-17 (NY)
1963—Steelers, 31-0 (P)
Giants, 33-17 (NY)
1964—Steelers, 27-24 (P)
Steelers, 44-17 (NY)
1965—Giants, 23-13 (P)
Giants, 35-10 (NY)
1966—Tie, 34-34 (P)
Steelers, 47-28 (NY)
1967—Giants, 27-24 (P)
Giants, 28-20 (NY)
1968—Giants, 34-20 (P)
1969—Giants, 10-7 (NY)
Giants, 21-17 (P)
1971—Steelers, 17-13 (P)
1976—Steelers, 27-0 (NY)
1985—Giants, 28-10 (NY)
1991—Giants, 23-20 (P)
(RS Pts.—Giants 1,393, Steelers 1,179)
*Steelers known as Pirates prior to 1941*

**N.Y. GIANTS vs. SAN DIEGO**
RS: Giants lead series, 4-2
1971—Giants, 35-17 (NY)
1975—Giants, 35-24 (NY)
1980—Chargers, 44-7 (SD)
1983—Chargers, 41-34 (NY)
1986—Giants, 20-7 (NY)
1989—Giants, 20-13 (SD)
(RS Pts.—Giants 151, Chargers 146)

**N.Y. GIANTS vs. SAN FRANCISCO**
RS: Giants lead series, 11-10
PS: Series tied, 3-3
1952—Giants, 23-14 (NY)
1956—Giants, 38-21 (SF)
1957—49ers, 27-17 (NY)
1960—Giants, 21-19 (SF)
1963—Giants, 48-14 (NY)
1968—49ers, 26-10 (NY)
1972—Giants, 23-17 (SF)
1975—Giants, 26-23 (SF)
1977—Giants, 20-17 (NY)
1978—Giants, 27-10 (NY)
1979—Giants, 32-16 (NY)
1980—49ers, 12-0 (SF)
1981—49ers, 17-10 (SF)
*49ers, 38-24 (SF)
1984—49ers, 31-10 (NY)
*49ers, 21-10 (SF)
1985—**Giants, 17-3 (NY)
1986—Giants, 21-17 (SF)
*Giants, 49-3 (NY)
1987—49ers, 41-21 (NY)
1988—49ers, 20-17 (NY)
1989—49ers, 34-24 (SF)
1990—49ers, 7-3 (SF)
***Giants, 15-13 (SF)
1991—Giants, 16-14 (NY)
1992—49ers, 31-14 (NY)
1993—*49ers, 44-3 (SF)
(RS Pts.—49ers 431, Giants 421)
(PS Pts.—49ers 119, Giants 118)
*NFC Divisional Playoff
**NFC First-Round Playoff
***NFC Championship*

**N.Y. GIANTS vs. SEATTLE**
RS: Giants lead series, 5-2
1976—Giants, 28-16 (NY)
1980—Giants, 27-21 (S)
1981—Giants, 32-0 (S)
1983—Seahawks, 17-12 (NY)
1986—Seahawks, 17-12 (S)
1989—Giants, 15-3 (NY)
1992—Giants, 23-10 (NY)
(RS Pts.—Giants 149, Seahawks 84)

**N.Y. GIANTS vs. TAMPA BAY**
RS: Giants lead series, 8-3
1977—Giants, 10-0 (TB)
1978—Giants, 19-13 (TB)
Giants, 17-14 (NY)
1979—Giants, 17-14 (NY)
Buccaneers, 31-3 (TB)
1980—Buccaneers, 30-13 (TB)
1984—Giants, 17-14 (NY)
Buccaneers, 20-17 (TB)
1985—Giants, 22-20 (NY)
1991—Giants, 21-14 (TB)
1993—Giants, 23-7 (NY)
(RS Pts.—Giants 179, Buccaneers 177)

**N.Y. GIANTS vs. *WASHINGTON**
RS: Giants lead series, 69-50-3
PS: Series tied, 1-1
1932—Braves, 14-6 (B)
Tie, 0-0 (NY)
1933—Redskins, 21-20 (B)
Giants, 7-0 (NY)
1934—Giants, 16-13 (B)
Giants, 3-0 (NY)
1935—Giants, 20-12 (B)
Giants, 17-6 (NY)
1936—Giants, 7-0 (B)
Redskins, 14-0 (NY)
1937—Redskins, 13-3 (W)
Redskins, 49-14 (NY)
1938—Giants, 10-7 (W)
Giants, 36-0 (NY)
1939—Tie, 0-0 (W)
Giants, 9-7 (NY)
1940—Redskins, 21-7 (W)
Giants, 21-7 (NY)
1941—Giants, 17-10 (W)
Giants, 20-13 (NY)
1942—Giants, 14-7 (W)
Redskins, 14-7 (NY)
1943—Giants, 14-10 (NY)
Giants, 31-7 (W)
**Redskins, 28-0 (NY)
1944—Giants, 16-13 (NY)
Giants, 31-0 (W)
1945—Redskins, 24-14 (NY)
Redskins, 17-0 (W)
1946—Redskins, 24-14 (W)
Giants, 31-0 (NY)
1947—Redskins, 28-20 (W)
Giants, 35-10 (NY)
1948—Redskins, 41-10 (W)
Redskins, 28-21 (NY)
1949—Giants, 45-35 (W)
Giants, 23-7 (NY)
1950—Giants, 21-17 (W)
Giants, 24-21 (NY)
1951—Giants, 35-14 (W)
Giants, 28-14 (NY)
1952—Giants, 14-10 (W)
Redskins, 27-17 (NY)
1953—Redskins, 13-9 (W)
Redskins, 24-21 (NY)
1954—Giants, 51-21 (W)
Giants, 24-7 (NY)
1955—Giants, 35-7 (NY)
Giants, 27-20 (W)
1956—Redskins, 33-7 (W)
Giants, 28-14 (NY)
1957—Giants, 24-20 (W)
Redskins, 31-14 (NY)
1958—Giants, 21-14 (W)
Giants, 30-0 (NY)
1959—Giants, 45-14 (NY)
Giants, 24-10 (W)
1960—Tie, 24-24 (NY)
Giants, 17-3 (W)
1961—Giants, 24-21 (W)
Giants, 53-0 (NY)
1962—Giants, 49-34 (NY)
Giants, 42-24 (W)
1963—Giants, 24-14 (W)
Giants, 44-14 (NY)
1964—Giants, 13-10 (NY)
Redskins, 36-21 (W)
1965—Redskins, 23-7 (NY)
Giants, 27-10 (W)
1966—Giants, 13-10 (NY)
Redskins, 72-41 (W)
1967—Redskins, 38-34 (W)
1968—Giants, 48-21 (NY)
Giants, 13-10 (W)
1969—Redskins, 20-14 (W)
1970—Giants, 35-33 (NY)
Giants, 27-24 (W)
1971—Redskins, 30-3 (NY)
Redskins, 23-7 (W)
1972—Redskins, 23-16 (NY)
Redskins, 27-13 (W)
1973—Redskins, 21-3 (New Haven)
Redskins, 27-24 (W)
1974—Redskins, 13-10 (New Haven)
Redskins, 24-3 (W)
1975—Redskins, 49-13 (W)
Redskins, 21-13 (NY)
1976—Redskins, 19-17 (W)
Giants, 12-9 (NY)
1977—Giants, 20-17 (NY)
Giants, 17-6 (W)
1978—Giants, 17-6 (NY)
Redskins, 16-13 (W) OT
1979—Redskins, 27-0 (W)
Giants, 14-6 (NY)
1980—Redskins, 23-21 (NY)
Redskins, 16-13 (W)
1981—Giants, 17-7 (W)
Redskins, 30-27 (NY) OT
1982—Redskins, 27-17 (NY)
Redskins, 15-14 (W)
1983—Redskins, 33-17 (NY)
Redskins, 31-22 (W)
1984—Redskins, 30-14 (W)
Giants, 37-13 (NY)
1985—Giants, 17-3 (NY)
Redskins, 23-21 (W)
1986—Giants, 27-20 (NY)
Giants, 24-14 (W)
***Giants, 17-0 (NY)
1987—Redskins, 38-12 (NY)
Redskins, 23-19 (W)
1988—Giants, 27-20 (NY)
Giants, 24-23 (W)
1989—Giants, 27-24 (W)
Giants, 20-17 (NY)
1990—Giants, 24-20 (W)
Giants, 21-10 (NY)
1991—Redskins, 17-13 (NY)
Redskins, 34-17 (W)
1992—Giants, 24-7 (W)
Redskins, 28-10 (NY)
1993—Giants, 41-7 (W)
Giants, 20-6 (NY)
(RS Pts.—Giants 2,430, Redskins 2,167)
(PS Pts.—Redskins 28, Giants 17)
*Franchise in Boston prior to 1937 and known as Braves prior to 1933
**Division Playoff
***NFC Championship*

---

**N.Y. JETS vs. ARIZONA**
RS: Cardinals lead series, 2-1;
See Arizona vs. N.Y. Jets

**N.Y. JETS vs. ATLANTA**
RS: Series tied, 3-3;
See Atlanta vs. N.Y. Jets

**N.Y. JETS vs. BUFFALO**
RS: Bills lead series, 37-29
PS: Bills lead series, 1-0;
See Buffalo vs. N.Y. Jets

**N.Y. JETS vs. CHICAGO**
RS: Bears lead series, 3-1;
See Chicago vs. N.Y. Jets

**N.Y. JETS vs. CINCINNATI**
RS: Jets lead series, 9-6
PS: Jets lead series, 1-0;
See Cincinnati vs. N.Y. Jets

**N.Y. JETS vs. CLEVELAND**
RS: Browns lead series, 8-6
PS: Browns lead series, 1-0;
See Cleveland vs. N.Y. Jets

**N.Y. JETS vs. DALLAS**
RS: Cowboys lead series, 5-1;
See Dallas vs. N.Y. Jets

**N.Y. JETS vs. DENVER**
RS: Broncos lead series, 12-11-1;
See Denver vs. N.Y. Jets

**N.Y. JETS vs. DETROIT**
RS: Series tied, 3-3;
See Detroit vs. N.Y. Jets

**N.Y. JETS vs. GREEN BAY**
RS: Jets lead series, 5-1;
See Green Bay vs. N.Y. Jets

**N.Y. JETS vs. HOUSTON**
RS: Oilers lead series, 17-12-1
PS: Oilers lead series, 1-0;
See Houston vs. N.Y. Jets

**N.Y. JETS vs. INDIANAPOLIS**
RS: Colts lead series, 27-20
PS: Jets lead series, 1-0;
See Indianapolis vs. N.Y. Jets

**N.Y. JETS vs. KANSAS CITY**
RS: Chiefs lead series, 14-12-1
PS: Series tied, 1-1;
See Kansas City vs. N.Y. Jets

**N.Y. JETS vs. L.A. RAIDERS**
RS: Raiders lead series, 14-9-2
PS: Jets lead series, 2-0;
See L.A. Raiders vs. N.Y. Jets

**N.Y. JETS vs. L.A. RAMS**
RS: Rams lead series, 5-2;
See L.A. Rams vs. N.Y. Jets

**N.Y. JETS vs. MIAMI**

# ALL-TIME TEAM VS. TEAM RESULTS

RS: Jets lead series, 28-27-1
PS: Dolphins lead series, 1-0;
See Miami vs. N.Y. Jets
**N.Y. JETS vs. MINNESOTA**
RS: Jets lead series, 3-1;
See Minnesota vs. N.Y. Jets
**N.Y. JETS vs. NEW ENGLAND**
RS: Jets lead series, 38-28-1
PS: Patriots lead series, 1-0;
See New England vs. N.Y. Jets
**N.Y. JETS vs. NEW ORLEANS**
RS: Jets lead series, 4-3;
See New Orleans vs. N.Y. Jets
**N.Y. JETS vs. N.Y. GIANTS**
RS: Jets lead series, 4-3;
See N.Y. Giants vs. N.Y. Jets
**N.Y. JETS vs. PHILADELPHIA**
RS: Eagles lead series, 5-0
1973—Eagles, 24-23 (P)
1977—Eagles, 27-0 (P)
1978—Eagles, 17-9 (P)
1987—Eagles, 38-27 (NY)
1993—Eagles, 35-30 (NY)
(RS Pts.—Eagles 141, Jets 89)
**N.Y. JETS vs. PITTSBURGH**
RS: Steelers lead series, 12-1
1970—Steelers, 21-17 (P)
1973—Steelers, 26-14 (P)
1975—Steelers, 20-7 (NY)
1977—Steelers, 23-20 (NY)
1978—Steelers, 28-17 (NY)
1981—Steelers, 38-10 (P)
1983—Steelers, 34-7 (NY)
1984—Steelers, 23-17 (NY)
1986—Steelers, 45-24 (NY)
1988—Jets, 24-20 (NY)
1989—Steelers, 13-0 (NY)
1990—Steelers, 24-7 (NY)
1992—Steelers, 27-10 (P)
(RS Pts.—Steelers 342, Jets 174)
***N.Y. JETS vs. **SAN DIEGO**
RS: Chargers lead series, 16-9-1
1960—Chargers, 21-7 (NY)
Chargers, 50-43 (LA)
1961—Chargers, 25-10 (NY)
Chargers, 48-13 (SD)
1962—Chargers, 40-14 (SD)
Titans, 23-3 (NY)
1963—Chargers, 24-20 (SD)
Chargers, 53-7 (NY)
1964—Tie, 17-17 (NY)
Chargers, 38-3 (SD)
1965—Chargers, 34-9 (NY)
Chargers, 38-7 (SD)
1966—Jets, 17-16 (NY)
Chargers, 42-27 (SD)
1967—Jets, 42-31 (SD)
1968—Jets, 23-20 (NY)
Jets, 37-15 (SD)
1969—Chargers, 34-27 (SD)
1971—Chargers, 49-21 (SD)
1974—Jets, 27-14 (NY)
1975—Chargers, 24-16 (SD)
1983—Jets, 41-29 (SD)
1989—Jets, 20-17 (SD)
1990—Chargers, 39-3 (NY)
Chargers, 38-17 (SD)
1991—Jets, 24-3 (NY)
(RS Pts.—Chargers 762, Jets 515)
**Jets known as Titans prior to 1963*
***Franchise in Los Angeles prior to 1961*
**N.Y. JETS vs. SAN FRANCISCO**
RS: 49ers lead series, 6-1
1971—49ers, 24-21 (NY)
1976—49ers, 17-6 (SF)
1980—49ers, 37-27 (NY)
1983—Jets, 27-13 (SF)
1986—49ers, 24-10 (SF)
1989—49ers, 23-10 (NY)
1992—49ers, 31-14 (NY)
(RS Pts.—49ers 169, Jets 115)
**N.Y. JETS vs. SEATTLE**
RS: Seahawks lead series, 8-3
1977—Seahawks, 17-0 (NY)
1978—Seahawks, 24-17 (NY)
1979—Seahawks, 30-7 (S)
1980—Seahawks, 27-17 (NY)
1981—Seahawks, 19-3 (NY)
Seahawks, 27-23 (S)
1983—Seahawks, 17-10 (NY)
1985—Jets, 17-14 (NY)
1986—Jets, 38-7 (S)
1987—Jets, 30-14 (NY)
1991—Seahawks, 20-13 (S)
(RS Pts.—Seahawks 216, Jets 175)
**N.Y. JETS vs. TAMPA BAY**
RS: Jets lead series, 5-1
1976—Jets, 34-0 (NY)
1982—Jets, 32-17 (NY)
1984—Buccaneers, 41-21 (TB)
1985—Jets, 62-28 (NY)
1990—Jets, 16-14 (TB)
1991—Jets, 16-13 (NY)
(RS Pts.—Jets 181, Buccaneers 113)
**N.Y. JETS vs. WASHINGTON**
RS: Redskins lead series, 4-1
1972—Redskins, 35-17 (NY)
1976—Redskins, 37-16 (NY)
1978—Redskins, 23-3 (W)
1987—Redskins, 17-16 (W)
1993—Jets, 3-0 (W)
(RS Pts.—Redskins 112, Jets 55)

---

**PHILADELPHIA vs. ARIZONA**
RS: Cardinals lead series, 44-43-5
PS: Series tied, 1-1;
See Arizona vs. Philadelphia
**PHILADELPHIA vs. ATLANTA**
RS: Eagles lead series, 8-6-1
PS: Falcons lead series, 1-0;
See Atlanta vs. Philadelphia
**PHILADELPHIA vs. BUFFALO**
RS: Eagles lead series, 4-3;
See Buffalo vs. Philadelphia
**PHILADELPHIA vs. CHICAGO**
RS: Bears lead series, 23-3-1
PS: Series tied, 1-1;
See Chicago vs. Philadelphia
**PHILADELPHIA vs. CINCINNATI**
RS: Bengals lead series, 5-1;
See Cincinnati vs. Philadelphia
**PHILADELPHIA vs. CLEVELAND**
RS: Browns lead series, 30-12-1;
See Cleveland vs. Philadelphia
**PHILADELPHIA vs. DALLAS**
RS: Cowboys lead series, 40-26
PS: Series tied, 1-1;
See Dallas vs. Philadelphia
**PHILADELPHIA vs. DENVER**
RS: Eagles lead series, 5-2;
See Denver vs. Philadelphia
**PHILADELPHIA vs. DETROIT**
RS: Lions lead series, 12-9-2;
See Detroit vs. Philadelphia
**PHILADELPHIA vs. GREEN BAY**
RS: Packers lead series, 19-7
PS: Eagles lead series, 1-0;
See Green Bay vs. Philadelphia
**PHILADELPHIA vs. HOUSTON**
RS: Eagles lead series, 5-0;
See Houston vs. Philadelphia
**PHILADELPHIA vs. INDIANAPOLIS**
RS: Series tied, 6-6;
See Indianapolis vs. Philadelphia
**PHILADELPHIA vs. KANSAS CITY**
RS: Series tied, 1-1;
See Kansas City vs. Philadelphia
**PHILADELPHIA vs. L.A. RAIDERS**
RS: Eagles lead series, 4-2
PS: Raiders lead series, 1-0;
See L.A. Raiders vs. Philadelphia
**PHILADELPHIA vs. L.A. RAMS**
RS: Rams lead series, 15-11-1
PS: Series tied, 1-1;
See L.A. Rams vs. Philadelphia
**PHILADELPHIA vs. MIAMI**
RS: Dolphins lead series, 6-2;
See Miami vs. Philadelphia
**PHILADELPHIA vs. MINNESOTA**
RS: Vikings lead series, 10-6
PS: Eagles lead series, 1-0;
See Minnesota vs. Philadelphia
**PHILADELPHIA vs. NEW ENGLAND**
RS: Eagles lead series, 5-2;
See New England vs. Philadelphia
**PHILADELPHIA vs. NEW ORLEANS**
RS: Eagles lead series, 11-8
PS; Eagles lead series, 1-0;
See New Orleans vs. Philadelphia
**PHILADELPHIA vs. N.Y. GIANTS**
RS: Giants lead series, 62-54-2
PS: Giants lead series, 1-0;
See N.Y. Giants vs. Philadelphia
**PHILADELPHIA vs. N.Y. JETS**
RS: Eagles lead series, 5-0;
See N.Y. Jets vs. Philadelphia
**PHILADELPHIA vs. *PITTSBURGH**
RS: Eagles lead series, 43-25-3
PS: Eagles lead series, 1-0
1933—Eagles, 25-6 (Phila)
1934—Eagles, 17-0 (Pitt)
Pirates, 9-7 (Phila)
1935—Pirates, 17-7 (Phila)
Eagles, 17-6 (Pitt)
1936—Pirates, 17-0 (Pitt)
Pirates, 6-0 (Johnstown, Pa.)
1937—Pirates, 27-14 (Pitt)
Pirates, 16-7 (Pitt)
1938—Eagles, 27-7 (Buffalo)
Eagles, 14-7 (Charleston, W. Va.)
1939—Eagles, 17-14 (Phila)
Pirates, 24-12 (Pitt)
1940—Pirates, 7-3 (Pitt)
Eagles, 7-0 (Phila)
1941—Eagles, 10-7 (Pitt)
Tie, 7-7 (Phila)
1942—Eagles, 24-14 (Pitt)
Steelers, 14-0 (Phila)
1945—Eagles, 45-3 (Pitt)
Eagles, 30-6 (Phila)
1946—Steelers, 10-7 (Pitt)
Eagles, 10-7 (Phila)
1947—Steelers, 35-24 (Pitt)
Eagles, 21-0 (Phila)
**Eagles, 21-0 (Pitt)
1948—Eagles, 34-7 (Pitt)
Eagles, 17-0 (Phila)
1949—Eagles, 38-7 (Pitt)
Eagles, 34-17 (Phila)
1950—Eagles, 17-10 (Pitt)
Steelers, 9-7 (Phila)
1951—Eagles, 34-13 (Pitt)
Steelers, 17-13 (Phila)
1952—Eagles, 31-25 (Pitt)
Eagles, 26-21 (Phila)
1953—Eagles, 23-17 (Phila)
Eagles, 35-7 (Pitt)
1954—Eagles, 24-22 (Phila)
Steelers, 17-7 (Pitt)
1955—Steelers, 13-7 (Pitt)
Eagles, 24-0 (Phila)
1956—Eagles, 35-21 (Pitt)
Eagles, 14-7 (Phila)
1957—Steelers, 6-0 (Pitt)
Eagles, 7-6 (Phila)
1958—Steelers, 24-3 (Pitt)
Steelers, 31-24 (Phila)
1959—Eagles, 28-24 (Phila)
Steelers, 31-0 (Pitt)
1960—Eagles, 34-7 (Phila)
Steelers, 27-21 (Pitt)
1961—Eagles, 21-16 (Phila)
Eagles, 35-24 (Pitt)
1962—Steelers, 13-7 (Pitt)
Steelers, 26-17 (Phila)
1963—Tie, 21-21 (Phila)
Tie, 20-20 (Pitt)
1964—Eagles, 21-7 (Phila)
Eagles, 34-10 (Pitt)
1965—Steelers, 20-14 (Phila)
Eagles, 47-13 (Pitt)
1966—Eagles, 31-14 (Pitt)
Eagles, 27-23 (Phila)
1967—Eagles, 34-24 (Phila)
1968—Steelers, 6-3 (Pitt)
1969—Eagles, 41-27 (Phila)
1970—Eagles, 30-20 (Phila)
1974—Steelers, 27-0 (Pitt)
1979—Eagles, 17-14 (Phila)
1988—Eagles, 27-26 (Pitt)
1991—Eagles, 23-14 (Phila)
(RS Pts.—Eagles 1,359, Steelers 1,007)
(PS Pts.—Eagles 21, Steelers 0)
**Steelers known as Pirates prior to 1941*
***Division Playoff*
**PHILADELPHIA vs. SAN DIEGO**
RS: Chargers lead series, 3-2
1974—Eagles, 13-7 (SD)
1980—Chargers, 22-21 (SD)
1985—Chargers, 20-14 (SD)
1986—Eagles, 23-7 (P)
1989—Chargers, 20-17 (SD)
(RS Pts.—Eagles 88, Chargers 76)
**PHILADELPHIA vs. SAN FRANCISCO**
RS: 49ers lead series, 13-5-1
1951—Eagles, 21-14 (P)
1953—49ers, 31-21 (SF)
1956—Tie, 10-10 (P)
1958—49ers, 30-24 (P)
1959—49ers, 24-14 (SF)
1964—49ers, 28-24 (P)
1966—Eagles, 35-34 (SF)
1967—49ers, 28-27 (P)
1969—49ers, 14-13 (SF)
1971—49ers, 31-3 (P)
1973—49ers, 38-28 (SF)
1975—Eagles, 27-17 (P)
1983—Eagles, 22-17 (SF)
1984—49ers, 21-9 (P)
1985—49ers, 24-13 (SF)
1989—49ers, 38-28 (P)
1991—49ers, 23-7 (P)
1992—49ers, 20-14 (SF)
1993—Eagles, 37-34 (SF) OT
(RS Pts.—49ers 476, Eagles 377)
**PHILADELPHIA vs. SEATTLE**
RS: Eagles lead series, 4-1
1976—Eagles, 27-10 (P)
1980—Eagles, 27-20 (S)
1986—Seahawks, 24-20 (S)
1989—Eagles, 31-7 (P)
1992—Eagles, 20-17 (S) OT
(RS Pts.—Eagles 125, Seahawks 78)
**PHILADELPHIA vs. TAMPA BAY**
RS: Eagles lead series, 3-1
PS: Buccaneers lead series, 1-0
1977—Eagles, 13-3 (P)
1979—*Buccaneers, 24-17 (TB)
1981—Eagles, 20-10 (P)
1988—Eagles, 41-14 (TB)
1991—Buccaneers, 14-13 (TB)
(RS Pts.—Eagles 87, Buccaneers 41)
(PS Pts.—Buccaneers 24, Eagles 17)
**NFC Divisional Playoff*
**PHILADELPHIA vs. *WASHINGTON**
RS: Redskins lead series, 66-46-5
PS: Redskins lead series, 1-0
1934—Redskins, 6-0 (B)
Redskins, 14-7 (P)
1935—Eagles, 7-6 (B)
1936—Redskins, 26-3 (P)
Redskins, 17-7 (B)
1937—Eagles, 14-0 (W)
Redskins, 10-7 (P)
1938—Redskins, 26-23 (P)
Redskins, 20-14 (W)
1939—Redskins, 7-0 (P)
Redskins, 7-6 (W)
1940—Redskins, 34-17 (P)
Redskins, 13-6 (W)
1941—Redskins, 21-17 (P)
Redskins, 20-14 (W)

1942—Redskins, 14-10 (P)
Redskins, 30-27 (W)
1944—Tie, 31-31 (P)
Eagles, 37-7 (W)
1945—Redskins, 24-14 (W)
Eagles, 16-0 (P)
1946—Eagles, 28-24 (W)
Redskins, 27-10 (P)
1947—Eagles, 45-42 (P)
Eagles, 38-14 (W)
1948—Eagles, 45-0 (W)
Eagles, 42-21 (P)
1949—Eagles, 49-14 (P)
Eagles, 44-21 (W)
1950—Eagles, 35-3 (P)
Eagles, 33-0 (W)
1951—Redskins, 27-23 (P)
Eagles, 35-21 (W)
1952—Eagles, 38-20 (P)
Redskins, 27-21 (W)
1953—Tie, 21-21 (P)
Redskins, 10-0 (W)
1954—Eagles, 49-21 (W)
Eagles, 41-33 (P)
1955—Redskins, 31-30 (P)
Redskins, 34-21 (W)
1956—Eagles, 13-9 (P)
Redskins, 19-17 (W)
1957—Eagles, 21-12 (P)
Redskins, 42-7 (W)
1958—Redskins, 24-14 (P)
Redskins, 20-0 (W)
1959—Eagles, 30-23 (P)
Eagles, 34-14 (W)
1960—Eagles, 19-13 (P)
Eagles, 38-28 (W)
1961—Eagles, 14-7 (P)
Eagles, 27-24 (W)
1962—Redskins, 27-21 (P)
Eagles, 37-14 (W)
1963—Eagles, 37-24 (W)
Redskins, 13-10 (P)
1964—Redskins, 35-20 (W)
Redskins, 21-10 (P)
1965—Redskins, 23-21 (W)
Eagles, 21-14 (P)
1966—Redskins, 27-13 (P)
Eagles, 37-28 (W)
1967—Eagles, 35-24 (P)
Tie, 35-35 (W)
1968—Redskins, 17-14 (W)
Redskins, 16-10 (P)
1969—Tie, 28-28 (W)
Redskins, 34-29 (P)
1970—Redskins, 33-21 (P)
Redskins, 24-6 (W)
1971—Tie, 7-7 (W)
Redskins, 20-13 (P)
1972—Redskins, 14-0 (W)
Redskins, 23-7 (P)
1973—Redskins, 28-7 (P)
Redskins, 38-20 (W)
1974—Redskins, 27-20 (P)
Redskins, 26-7 (W)
1975—Eagles, 26-10 (P)
Eagles, 26-3 (W)
1976—Redskins, 20-17 (P) OT
Redskins, 24-0 (W)
1977—Redskins, 23-17 (W)
Redskins, 17-14 (P)
1978—Redskins, 35-30 (W)
Eagles, 17-10 (P)
1979—Eagles, 28-17 (P)
Redskins, 17-7 (W)
1980—Eagles, 24-14 (P)
Eagles, 24-0 (W)
1981—Eagles, 36-13 (P)
Redskins, 15-13 (W)
1982—Redskins, 37-34 (P) OT
Redskins, 13-9 (W)
1983—Redskins, 23-13 (P)
Redskins, 28-24 (W)
1984—Redskins, 20-0 (W)
Eagles, 16-10 (P)
1985—Eagles, 19-6 (W)
Redskins, 17-12 (P)
1986—Redskins, 41-14 (W)
Redskins, 21-14 (P)
1987—Redskins, 34-24 (W)
Eagles, 31-27 (P)
1988—Redskins, 17-10 (W)
Redskins, 20-19 (P)
1989—Eagles, 42-37 (W)
Redskins, 10-3 (P)
1990—Redskins, 13-7 (W)
Eagles, 28-14 (P)
**Redskins, 20-6 (P)
1991—Redskins, 23-0 (W)
Eagles, 24-22 (P)
1992—Redskins, 16-12 (W)
Eagles, 17-13 (P)
1993—Eagles, 34-31 (P)
Eagles, 17-14 (W)
(RS Pts.—Eagles 2,347, Redskins 2,324)
(PS Pts.—Redskins 20, Eagles 6)
*Franchise in Boston prior to 1937*
***NFC First-Round Playoff*

**PITTSBURGH vs. ARIZONA**
RS: Steelers lead series, 29-21-3;
See Arizona vs. Pittsburgh
**PITTSBURGH vs. ATLANTA**
RS: Steelers lead series, 9-1;
See Atlanta vs. Pittsburgh
**PITTSBURGH vs. BUFFALO**
RS: Bills lead series, 7-6
PS: Series tied, 1-1;
See Buffalo vs. Pittsburgh
**PITTSBURGH vs. CHICAGO**
RS: Bears lead series, 16-4-1;
See Chicago vs. Pittsburgh
**PITTSBURGH vs. CINCINNATI**
RS: Steelers lead series, 26-21;
See Cincinnati vs. Pittsburgh
**PITTSBURGH vs. CLEVELAND**
RS: Browns lead series, 52-36;
See Cleveland vs. Pittsburgh
**PITTSBURGH vs. DALLAS**
RS: Cowboys lead series, 12-11
PS: Steelers lead series, 2-0;
See Dallas vs. Pittsburgh
**PITTSBURGH vs. DENVER**
RS: Broncos lead series, 10-5-1
PS: Series tied, 2-2;
See Denver vs. Pittsburgh
**PITTSBURGH vs. DETROIT**
RS: Lions lead series, 13-11-1;
See Detroit vs. Pittsburgh
**PITTSBURGH vs. GREEN BAY**
RS: Packers lead series, 17-11;
See Green Bay vs. Pittsburgh
**PITTSBURGH vs. HOUSTON**
RS: Steelers lead series, 29-18
PS: Steelers lead series, 3-0;
See Houston vs. Pittsburgh
**PITTSBURGH vs. INDIANAPOLIS**
RS: Steelers lead series, 10-4
PS: Steelers lead series, 2-0;
See Indianapolis vs. Pittsburgh
**PITTSBURGH vs. KANSAS CITY**
RS: Steelers lead series, 13-5
PS: Chiefs lead series, 1-0;
See Kansas City vs. Pittsburgh
**PITTSBURGH vs. L.A. RAIDERS**
RS: Raiders lead series, 7-3
PS: Series tied, 3-3;
See L.A. Raiders vs. Pittsburgh
**PITTSBURGH vs. L.A. RAMS**
RS: Rams lead series, 14-4-2
PS: Steelers lead series, 1-0;
See L.A. Rams vs. Pittsburgh
**PITTSBURGH vs. MIAMI**
RS: Dolphins lead series, 7-5
PS: Dolphins lead series, 2-1;
See Miami vs. Pittsburgh
**PITTSBURGH vs. MINNESOTA**
RS: Vikings lead series, 7-4
PS: Steelers lead series, 1-0;
See Minnesota vs. Pittsburgh
**PITTSBURGH vs. NEW ENGLAND**
RS: Steelers lead series, 9-3;
See New England vs. Pittsburgh
**PITTSBURGH vs. NEW ORLEANS**
RS: Steelers lead series, 6-5;
See New Orleans vs. Pittsburgh
**PITTSBURGH vs. N.Y. GIANTS**
RS: Giants lead series, 42-26-3;
See N.Y. Giants vs. Pittsburgh
**PITTSBURGH vs. N.Y. JETS**
RS: Steelers lead series, 12-1;
See N.Y. Jets vs. Pittsburgh
**PITTSBURGH vs. PHILADELPHIA**
RS: Eagles lead series, 43-25-3
PS: Eagles lead series, 1-0;
See Philadelphia vs. Pittsburgh
**PITTSBURGH vs. SAN DIEGO**
RS: Steelers lead series, 14-4
PS: Chargers lead series, 1-0
1971—Steelers, 21-17 (P)
1972—Steelers, 24-2 (SD)
1973—Steelers, 38-21 (P)
1975—Steelers, 37-0 (SD)
1976—Steelers, 23-0 (P)
1977—Steelers, 10-9 (SD)
1979—Chargers, 35-7 (SD)
1980—Chargers, 26-17 (SD)
1982—*Chargers, 31-28 (P)
1983—Steelers, 26-3 (P)
1984—Steelers, 52-24 (P)
1985—Chargers, 54-44 (SD)
1987—Steelers, 20-16 (SD)
1988—Chargers, 20-14 (SD)
1989—Steelers, 20-17 (P)
1990—Steelers, 36-14 (P)
1991—Steelers, 26-20 (P)
1992—Steelers, 23-6 (SD)
1993—Steelers,.16-3 (P)
(RS Pts.—Steelers 454, Chargers 287)
(PS Pts.—Chargers 31, Steelers 28)
**AFC First-Round Playoff*
**PITTSBURGH vs. SAN FRANCISCO**
RS: 49ers lead series, 8-7
1951—49ers, 28-24 (P)
1952—Steelers, 24-7 (SF)
1954—49ers, 31-3 (SF)
1958—49ers, 23-20 (SF)
1961—Steelers, 20-10 (P)
1965—49ers, 27-17 (SF)
1968—49ers, 45-28 (P)
1973—Steelers, 37-14 (SF)
1977—Steelers, 27-0 (P)
1978—Steelers, 24-7 (SF)
1981—49ers, 17-14 (P)
1984—Steelers, 20-17 (SF)
1987—Steelers, 30-17 (P)
1990—49ers, 27-7 (SF)
1993—49ers, 24-13 (P)
(RS Pts.—Steelers 308, 49ers 294)
**PITTSBURGH vs. SEATTLE**
RS: Series tied, 5-5
1977—Steelers, 30-20 (P)
1978—Steelers, 21-10 (P)
1981—Seahawks, 24-21 (S)
1982—Seahawks, 16-0 (S)
1983—Steelers, 27-21 (S)
1986—Seahawks, 30-0 (S)
1987—Steelers, 13-9 (P)
1991—Seahawks, 27-7 (P)
1992—Steelers, 20-14 (P)
1993—Seahawks, 16-6 (S)
(RS Pts.—Seahawks 187, Steelers 145)
**PITTSBURGH vs. TAMPA BAY**
RS: Steelers lead series, 4-0
1976—Steelers, 42-0 (P)
1980—Steelers, 24-21 (TB)
1983—Steelers, 17-12 (P)
1989—Steelers, 31-22 (TB)
(RS Pts.—Steelers 114, Buccaneers 55)
***PITTSBURGH vs. **WASHINGTON**
RS: Redskins lead series, 42-27-3
1933—Redskins, 21-6 (P)
Pirates, 16-14 (B)
1934—Redskins, 7-0 (P)
Redskins, 39-0 (B)
1935—Pirates, 6-0 (P)
Redskins, 13-3 (B)
1936—Pirates, 10-0 (P)
Redskins, 30-0 (B)
1937—Redskins, 34-20 (W)
Pirates, 21-13 (P)
1938—Redskins, 7-0 (P)
Redskins, 15-0 (W)
1939—Redskins, 44-14 (W)
Redskins, 21-14 (P)
1940—Redskins, 40-10 (P)
Redskins, 37-10 (W)
1941—Redskins, 24-20 (P)
Redskins, 23-3 (W)
1942—Redskins, 28-14 (W)
Redskins, 14-0 (P)
1945—Redskins, 14-0 (P)
Redskins, 24-0 (W)
1946—Tie, 14-14 (W)
Steelers, 14-7 (P)
1947—Redskins, 27-26 (W)
Steelers, 21-14 (P)
1948—Redskins, 17-14 (W)
Steelers, 10-7 (P)
1949—Redskins, 27-14 (P)
Redskins, 27-14 (W)
1950—Steelers, 26-7 (W)
Redskins, 24-7 (P)
1951—Redskins, 22-7 (P)
Steelers, 20-10 (W)
1952—Redskins, 28-24 (P)
Steelers, 24-23 (W)
1953—Redskins, 17-9 (P)
Steelers, 14-13 (W)
1954—Steelers, 37-7 (P)
Redskins, 17-14 (W)
1955—Redskins, 23-14 (P)
Redskins, 28-17 (W)
1956—Steelers, 30-13 (P)
Steelers, 23-0 (W)
1957—Steelers, 28-7 (P)
Redskins, 10-3 (W)
1958—Steelers, 24-16 (P)
Tie, 14-14 (W)
1959—Redskins, 23-17 (P)
Steelers, 27-6 (W)
1960—Tie, 27-27 (W)
Steelers, 22-10 (P)
1961—Steelers, 20-0 (P)
Steelers, 30-14 (W)
1962—Steelers, 23-21 (P)
Steelers, 27-24 (W)
1963—Steelers, 38-27 (P)
Steelers, 34-28 (W)
1964—Redskins, 30-0 (P)
Steelers, 14-7 (W)
1965—Redskins, 31-3 (P)
Redskins, 35-14 (W)
1966—Redskins, 33-27 (P)
Redskins, 24-10 (W)
1967—Redskins, 15-10 (P)
1968—Redskins, 16-13 (W)
1969—Redskins, 14-7 (P)
1973—Steelers, 21-16 (P)
1979—Steelers, 38-7 (P)
1985—Redskins, 30-23 (P)
1988—Redskins, 30-29 (W)
1991—Redskins, 41-14 (P)
(RS Pts.—Redskins 1,390, Steelers 1,117)
**Steelers known as Pirates prior to 1941*
***Franchise in Boston prior to 1937*

**SAN DIEGO vs. ARIZONA**
RS: Chargers lead series, 5-1;
See Arizona vs. San Diego
**SAN DIEGO vs. ATLANTA**
RS: Falcons lead series, 3-1;

See Atlanta vs. San Diego
**SAN DIEGO vs. BUFFALO**
RS: Chargers lead series, 16-7-2
PS: Bills lead series, 2-1;
See Buffalo vs. San Diego
**SAN DIEGO vs. CHICAGO**
RS: Chargers lead series, 4-2;
See Chicago vs. San Diego
**SAN DIEGO vs. CINCINNATI**
RS: Chargers lead series, 12-8
PS: Bengals lead series, 1-0;
See Cincinnati vs. San Diego
**SAN DIEGO vs. CLEVELAND**
RS: Chargers lead series, 8-6-1;
See Cleveland vs. San Diego
**SAN DIEGO vs. DALLAS**
RS: Cowboys lead series, 4-1;
See Dallas vs. San Diego
**SAN DIEGO vs. DENVER**
RS: Broncos lead series, 35-32-1;
See Denver vs. San Diego
**SAN DIEGO vs. DETROIT**
RS: Lions lead series, 3-2;
See Detroit vs. San Diego
**SAN DIEGO vs. GREEN BAY**
RS: Packers lead series, 4-1;
See Green Bay vs. San Diego
**SAN DIEGO vs. HOUSTON**
RS: Chargers lead series, 18-13-1
PS: Oilers lead series, 3-0;
See Houston vs. San Diego
**SAN DIEGO vs. INDIANAPOLIS**
RS: Chargers lead series, 9-5;
See Indianapolis vs. San Diego
**SAN DIEGO vs. KANSAS CITY**
RS: Chiefs lead series, 35-31-1
PS: Chargers lead series, 1-0;
See Kansas City vs. San Diego
**SAN DIEGO vs. L.A. RAIDERS**
RS: Raiders lead series, 41-25-2
PS: Raiders lead series, 1-0;
See L.A. Raiders vs. San Diego
**SAN DIEGO vs. L.A. RAMS**
RS: Rams lead series, 3-2;
See L.A. Rams vs. San Diego
**SAN DIEGO vs. MIAMI**
RS: Chargers lead series, 10-5
PS: Dolphins lead series, 2-1;
See Miami vs. San Diego
**SAN DIEGO vs. MINNESOTA**
RS: Chargers lead series, 4-3;
See Minnesota vs. San Diego
**SAN DIEGO vs. NEW ENGLAND**
RS: Patriots lead series, 13-11-2
PS: Chargers lead series, 1-0;
See New England vs. San Diego
**SAN DIEGO vs. NEW ORLEANS**
RS: Chargers lead series, 4-1;
See New Orleans vs. San Diego
**SAN DIEGO vs. N.Y. GIANTS**
RS: Giants lead series, 4-2;
See N.Y. Giants vs. San Diego
**SAN DIEGO vs. N.Y. JETS**
RS: Chargers lead series, 16-9-1;
See N.Y. Jets vs. San Diego
**SAN DIEGO vs. PHILADELPHIA**
RS: Chargers lead series, 3-2;
See Philadelphia vs. San Diego
**SAN DIEGO vs. PITTSBURGH**
RS: Steelers lead series, 14-4
PS: Chargers lead series, 1-0;
See Pittsburgh vs. San Diego
**SAN DIEGO vs. SAN FRANCISCO**
RS: Series tied, 3-3
1972—49ers, 34-3 (SF)
1976—Chargers, 13-7 (SD) OT
1979—Chargers, 31-9 (SD)
1982—Chargers, 41-37 (SF)
1988—49ers, 48-10 (SD)
1991—49ers, 34-14 (SF)
(RS Pts.—49ers 169, Chargers 112)
**SAN DIEGO vs. SEATTLE**
RS: Series tied, 15-15
1977—Chargers, 30-28 (S)
1978—Chargers, 24-20 (S)
Chargers, 37-10 (SD)
1979—Chargers, 33-16 (S)
Chargers, 20-10 (SD)
1980—Chargers, 34-13 (S)
Chargers, 21-14 (SD)
1981—Chargers, 24-10 (SD)
Seahawks, 44-23 (S)
1983—Seahawks, 34-31 (S)
Chargers, 28-21 (SD)
1984—Seahawks, 31-17 (S)
Seahawks, 24-0 (SD)
1985—Seahawks, 49-35 (SD)
Seahawks, 26-21 (S)
1986—Seahawks, 33-7 (S)
Seahawks, 34-24 (SD)
1987—Seahawks, 34-3 (S)
1988—Chargers, 17-6 (SD)
Seahawks, 17-14 (S)
1989—Seahawks, 17-16 (SD)
Seahawks, 10-7 (S)
1990—Chargers, 31-14 (S)
Seahawks, 13-10 (SD) OT
1991—Seahawks, 20-9 (S)
Chargers, 17-14 (SD)
1992—Chargers, 17-6 (SD)
Chargers, 31-14 (S)
1993—Chargers, 18-12 (SD)
Seahawks, 31-14 (S)
(RS Pts.—Seahawks 625, Chargers 613)
**SAN DIEGO vs. TAMPA BAY**
RS: Chargers lead series, 6-0
1976—Chargers, 23-0 (TB)
1981—Chargers, 24-23 (TB)
1987—Chargers, 17-13 (TB)
1990—Chargers, 41-10 (SD)
1992—Chargers, 29-14 (SD)
1993—Chargers, 32-17 (TB)
(RS Pts.—Chargers 166, Buccaneers 77)
**SAN DIEGO vs. WASHINGTON**
RS: Redskins lead series, 5-0
1973—Redskins, 38-0 (W)
1980—Redskins, 40-17 (W)
1983—Redskins, 27-24 (SD)
1986—Redskins, 30-27 (SD)
1989—Redskins, 26-21 (W)
(RS Pts.—Redskins 161, Chargers 89)

---

**SAN FRANCISCO vs. ARIZONA**
RS: 49ers lead series, 10-9;
See Arizona vs. San Francisco
**SAN FRANCISCO vs. ATLANTA**
RS: 49ers lead series, 32-21-1;
See Atlanta vs. San Francisco
**SAN FRANCISCO vs. BUFFALO**
RS: Bills lead series, 3-2;
See Buffalo vs. San Francisco
**SAN FRANCISCO vs. CHICAGO**
RS: Series tied, 25-25-1
PS: 49ers lead series, 2-0;
See Chicago vs. San Francisco
**SAN FRANCISCO vs. CINCINNATI**
RS: 49ers lead series, 6-1
PS: 49ers lead series, 2-0;
See Cincinnati vs. San Francisco
**SAN FRANCISCO vs. CLEVELAND**
RS: Browns lead series, 9-6;
See Cleveland vs. San Francisco
**SAN FRANCISCO vs. DALLAS**
RS: 49ers lead series, 9-6-1
PS: Cowboys lead series, 5-1;
See Dallas vs. San Francisco
**SAN FRANCISCO vs. DENVER**
RS: Broncos lead series, 4-2
PS: 49ers lead series, 1-0;
See Denver vs. San Francisco
**SAN FRANCISCO vs. DETROIT**
RS: 49ers lead series, 26-25-1
PS: Series tied, 1-1;
See Detroit vs. San Francisco
**SAN FRANCISCO vs. GREEN BAY**
RS: 49ers lead series, 25-21-1;
See Green Bay vs. San Francisco
**SAN FRANCISCO vs. HOUSTON**
RS: 49ers lead series, 5-3;
See Houston vs. San Francisco
**SAN FRANCISCO vs. INDIANAPOLIS**
RS: Colts lead series, 21-16;
See Indianapolis vs. San Francisco
**SAN FRANCISCO vs. KANSAS CITY**
RS: 49ers lead series, 4-1;
See Kansas City vs. San Francisco
**SAN FRANCISCO vs. L.A RAIDERS**
RS: Raiders lead series, 5-2;
See L.A. Raiders vs. San Francisco
**SAN FRANCISCO vs. L.A. RAMS**
RS: Rams lead series, 48-38-2
PS: 49ers lead series, 1-0;
See L.A. Rams vs. San Francisco
**SAN FRANCISCO vs. MIAMI**
RS: Dolphins lead series, 4-2
PS: 49ers lead series, 1-0;
See Miami vs. San Francisco
**SAN FRANCISCO vs. MINNESOTA**
RS: Series tied, 15-15-1
PS: 49ers lead series, 3-1;
See Minnesota vs. San Francisco
**SAN FRANCISCO vs. NEW ENGLAND**
RS: 49ers lead series, 6-1;
See New England vs. San Francisco
**SAN FRANCISCO vs. NEW ORLEANS**
RS: 49ers lead series, 33-14-2;
See New Orleans vs. San Francisco
**SAN FRANCISCO vs. N.Y. GIANTS**
RS: Giants lead series, 11-10
PS: Series tied, 3-3;
See N.Y. Giants vs. San Francisco
**SAN FRANCISCO vs. N.Y. JETS**
RS: 49ers lead series, 6-1;
See N.Y. Jets vs. San Francisco
**SAN FRANCISCO vs. PHILADELPHIA**
RS: 49ers lead series, 13-5-1;
See Philadelphia vs. San Francisco
**SAN FRANCISCO vs. PITTSBURGH**
RS: 49ers lead series, 8-7;
See Pittsburgh vs. San Francisco
**SAN FRANCISCO vs. SAN DIEGO**
RS: Series tied, 3-3;
See San Diego vs. San Francisco
**SAN FRANCISCO vs. SEATTLE**
RS: 49ers lead series, 4-1
1976—49ers, 37-21 (S)
1979—Seahawks, 35-24 (SF)
1985—49ers, 19-6 (SF)
1988—49ers, 38-7 (S)
1991—49ers, 24-22 (S)
(RS Pts.—49ers 142, Seahawks 91)
**SAN FRANCISCO vs. TAMPA BAY**
RS: 49ers lead series, 11-1
1977—49ers, 20-10 (SF)
1978—49ers, 6-3 (SF)
1979—49ers, 23-7 (SF)
1980—Buccaneers, 24-23 (SF)
1983—49ers, 35-21 (SF)
1984—49ers, 24-17 (SF)
1986—49ers, 31-7 (TB)
1987—49ers, 24-10 (TB)
1989—49ers, 20-16 (TB)
1990—49ers, 31-7 (SF)
1992—49ers, 21-14 (SF)
1993—49ers, 45-21 (TB)
(RS. Pts.—49ers 303, Buccaneers 157)
**SAN FRANCISCO vs. WASHINGTON**
RS: 49ers lead series, 9-6-1
PS: 49ers lead series, 3-1
1952—49ers, 23-17 (W)
1954—49ers, 41-7 (SF)
1955—Redskins, 7-0 (W)
1961—49ers, 35-3 (SF)
1967—Redskins, 31-28 (W)
1969—Tie, 17-17 (SF)
1970—49ers, 26-17 (SF)
1971—*49ers, 24-20 (SF)
1973—Redskins, 33-9 (W)
1976—Redskins, 24-21 (SF)
1978—Redskins, 38-20 (W)
1981—49ers, 30-17 (W)
1983—**Redskins, 24-21 (W)
1984—49ers, 37-31 (SF)
1985—49ers, 35-8 (W)
1986—Redskins, 14-6 (W)
1988—49ers, 37-21 (SF)
1990—49ers, 26-13 (SF)
*49ers, 28-10 (SF)
1992—*49ers, 20-13 (SF)
(RS Pts.—49ers 391, Redskins 298)
(PS Pts.—49ers 93, Redskins 67)
**NFC Divisional Playoff*
***NFC Championship*

---

**SEATTLE vs. ARIZONA**
RS: Cardinals lead series, 4-0;
See Arizona vs. Seattle
**SEATTLE vs. ATLANTA**
RS: Seahawks lead series, 4-1;
See Atlanta vs. Seattle
**SEATTLE vs. BUFFALO**
RS: Seahawks lead series, 3-1;
See Buffalo vs. Seattle
**SEATTLE vs. CHICAGO**
RS: Seahawks lead series, 4-2;
See Chicago vs. Seattle
**SEATTLE vs. CINCINNATI**
RS: Series tied, 6-6
PS: Bengals lead series, 1-0;
See Cincinnati vs. Seattle
**SEATTLE vs. CLEVELAND**
RS: Seahawks lead series, 9-3;
See Cleveland vs. Seattle
**SEATTLE vs. DALLAS**
RS: Cowboys lead series, 4-1;
See Dallas vs. Seattle
**SEATTLE vs. DENVER**
RS: Broncos lead series, 20-13
PS: Seahawks lead series, 1-0;
See Denver vs. Seattle
**SEATTLE vs. DETROIT**
RS: Seahawks lead series, 4-2;
See Detroit vs. Seattle
**SEATTLE vs. GREEN BAY**
RS: Series tied, 3-3;
See Green Bay vs. Seattle
**SEATTLE vs. HOUSTON**
RS: Series tied, 4-4
PS: Oilers lead series, 1-0;
See Houston vs. Seattle
**SEATTLE vs. INDIANAPOLIS**
RS: Colts lead series, 2-1;
See Indianapolis vs. Seattle
**SEATTLE vs. KANSAS CITY**
RS: Chiefs lead series, 19-12;
See Kansas City vs. Seattle
**SEATTLE vs. L.A. RAIDERS**
RS: Raiders lead series, 18-14
PS: Series tied, 1-1;
See L.A. Raiders vs. Seattle
**SEATTLE vs. L.A. RAMS**
RS: Rams lead series, 4-1;
See L.A. Rams vs. Seattle
**SEATTLE vs. MIAMI**
RS: Dolphins lead series, 4-1
PS: Series tied, 1-1;
See Miami vs. Seattle
**SEATTLE vs. MINNESOTA**
RS: Seahawks lead series, 3-2;
See Minnesota vs. Seattle
**SEATTLE vs. NEW ENGLAND**
RS: Seahawks lead series, 7-6;
See New England vs. Seattle
**SEATTLE vs. NEW ORLEANS**
RS: Saints lead series, 3-2;
See New Orleans vs. Seattle
**SEATTLE vs. N.Y. GIANTS**
RS: Giants lead series, 5-2;
See N.Y. Giants vs. Seattle
**SEATTLE vs. N.Y. JETS**
RS: Seahawks lead series, 8-3;
See N.Y. Jets vs. Seattle

**SEATTLE vs. PHILADELPHIA**
RS: Eagles lead series, 4-1;
See Philadelphia vs. Seattle
**SEATTLE vs. PITTSBURGH**
RS: Series tied, 5-5;
See Pittsburgh vs. Seattle
**SEATTLE vs. SAN DIEGO**
RS: Series tied, 15-15;
See San Diego vs. Seattle
**SEATTLE vs. SAN FRANCISCO**
RS: 49ers lead series, 4-1;
See San Francisco vs. Seattle
**SEATTLE vs. TAMPA BAY**
RS: Seahawks lead series, 2-0
1976—Seahawks, 13-10 (TB)
1977—Seahawks, 30-23 (S)
(RS Pts.—Seahawks 43, Buccaneers 33)
**SEATTLE vs. WASHINGTON**
RS: Redskins lead series, 5-1
1976—Redskins, 31-7 (W)
1980—Seahawks, 14-0 (W)
1983—Redskins, 27-17 (S)
1986—Redskins, 19-14 (W)
1989—Redskins, 29-0 (S)
1992—Redskins, 16-3 (S)
(RS Pts.—Redskins 122, Seahawks 55)

**TAMPA BAY vs. ARIZONA**
RS: Series tied, 6-6;
See Arizona vs. Tampa Bay
**TAMPA BAY vs. ATLANTA**
RS: Series tied,6-6;
See Atlanta vs. Tampa Bay
**TAMPA BAY vs. BUFFALO**
RS: Buccaneers lead series, 4-2;
See Buffalo vs. Tampa Bay
**TAMPA BAY vs. CHICAGO**
RS: Bears lead series, 24-8;
See Chicago vs. Tampa Bay
**TAMPA BAY vs. CINCINNATI**
RS: Bengals lead series, 3-1;
See Cincinnati vs. Tampa Bay
**TAMPA BAY vs. CLEVELAND**
RS: Browns lead series, 4-0;
See Cleveland vs. Tampa Bay
**TAMPA BAY vs. DALLAS**
RS: Cowboys lead series, 6-0
PS: Cowboys lead series, 2-0;
See Dallas vs. Tampa Bay
**TAMPA BAY vs. DENVER**
RS: Broncos lead series, 2-1;
See Denver vs. Tampa Bay
**TAMPA BAY vs. DETROIT**
RS: Series tied, 16-16;
See Detroit vs. Tampa Bay
**TAMPA BAY vs. GREEN BAY**
RS: Packers lead series, 17-12-1;
See Green Bay vs. Tampa Bay
**TAMPA BAY vs. HOUSTON**
RS: Oilers lead series, 3-1;
See Houston vs. Tampa Bay
**TAMPA BAY vs. INDIANAPOLIS**
RS: Colts lead series, 5-2;
See Indianapolis vs. Tampa Bay
**TAMPA BAY vs. KANSAS CITY**
RS: Chiefs lead series, 5-2;
See Kansas City vs. Tampa Bay
**TAMPA BAY vs. L.A. RAIDERS**
RS: Raiders lead series, 3-0;
See L.A. Raiders vs. Tampa Bay
**TAMPA BAY vs. L.A. RAMS**
RS: Rams lead series, 8-2
PS: Rams lead series, 1-0;
See L.A. Rams vs. Tampa Bay
**TAMPA BAY vs. MIAMI**
RS: Dolphins lead series, 4-1;
See Miami vs. Tampa Bay
**TAMPA BAY vs. MINNESOTA**
RS: Vikings lead series, 23-9;
See Minnesota vs. Tampa Bay
**TAMPA BAY vs. NEW ENGLAND**
RS: Patriots lead series, 3-0;
See New England vs. Tampa Bay
**TAMPA BAY vs. NEW ORLEANS**
RS: Saints lead series, 11-4;
See New Orleans vs. Tampa Bay
**TAMPA BAY vs. N.Y. GIANTS**
RS: Giants lead series, 8-3;
See N.Y. Giants vs. Tampa Bay
**TAMPA BAY vs. N.Y. JETS**
RS: Jets lead series, 5-1;
See N.Y. Jets vs. Tampa Bay
**TAMPA BAY vs. PHILADELPHIA**
RS: Eagles lead series, 3-1
PS: Buccaneers lead series, 1-0;
See Philadelphia vs. Tampa Bay
**TAMPA BAY vs. PITTSBURGH**
RS: Steelers lead series, 4-0;
See Pittsburgh vs. Tampa Bay
**TAMPA BAY vs. SAN DIEGO**
RS: Chargers lead series, 6-0;
See San Diego vs. Tampa Bay
**TAMPA BAY vs. SAN FRANCISCO**
RS: 49ers lead series, 11-1;
See San Francisco vs. Tampa Bay
**TAMPA BAY vs. SEATTLE**
RS: Seahawks lead series, 2-0;
See Seattle vs. Tampa Bay
**TAMPA BAY vs. WASHINGTON**
RS: Redskins lead series, 4-0
1977—Redskins, 10-0 (TB)
1982—Redskins, 21-13 (TB)
1989—Redskins, 32-28 (W)
1993—Redskins, 23-17 (TB)
(RS Pts.—Redskins 86, Buccaneers 58)

**WASHINGTON vs. ARIZONA**
RS: Redskins lead series, 61-36-2;
See Arizona vs. Washington
**WASHINGTON vs. ATLANTA**
RS: Redskins lead series, 13-3-1
PS: Redskins lead series, 1-0;
See Atlanta vs. Washington
**WASHINGTON vs. BUFFALO**
RS: Redskins lead series, 4-3
PS: Redskins lead series, 1-0;
See Buffalo vs. Washington
**WASHINGTON vs. CHICAGO**
RS: Bears lead series, 18-12-1
PS: Redskins lead series, 4-3;
See Chicago vs. Washington
**WASHINGTON vs. CINCINNATI**
RS: Redskins lead series, 4-2;
See Cincinnati vs. Washington
**WASHINGTON vs. CLEVELAND**
RS: Browns lead series, 32-9-1;
See Cleveland vs. Washington
**WASHINGTON vs. DALLAS**
RS: Cowboys lead series, 37-27-2
PS: Redskins lead series, 2-0;
See Dallas vs. Washington
**WASHINGTON vs. DENVER**
RS: Series tied 3-3
PS: Redskins lead series, 1-0;
See Denver vs. Washington
**WASHINGTON vs. DETROIT**
RS: Redskins lead series, 22-8
PS: Redskins lead series, 2-0;
See Detroit vs. Washington
**WASHINGTON vs. GREEN BAY**
RS: Packers lead series, 13-12-1
PS: Series tied 1-1;
See Green Bay vs. Washington
**WASHINGTON vs. HOUSTON**
RS: Series tied 3-3;
See Houston vs. Washington
**WASHINGTON vs. INDIANAPOLIS**
RS: Colts lead series, 16-7;
See Indianapolis vs. Washington
**WASHINGTON vs. KANSAS CITY**
RS: Chiefs lead series, 3-1;
See Kansas City vs. Washington
**WASHINGTON vs. L.A. RAIDERS**
RS: Raiders lead series, 5-2
PS: Raiders lead series, 1-0;
See L.A. Raiders vs. Washington
**WASHINGTON vs. L.A. RAMS**
RS: Redskins lead series, 14-5-1
PS: Series tied 2-2;
See L.A. Rams vs. Washington
**WASHINGTON vs. MIAMI**
RS: Dolphins lead series, 5-2
PS: Series tied 1-1;
See Miami vs. Washington
**WASHINGTON vs. MINNESOTA**
RS: Redskins lead series, 6-4
PS: Redskins lead series, 3-2;
See Minnesota vs. Washington
**WASHINGTON vs. NEW ENGLAND**
RS: Redskins lead series, 4-1;
See New England vs. Washington
**WASHINGTON vs. NEW ORLEANS**
RS: Redskins lead series, 11-5;
See New Orleans vs. Washington
**WASHINGTON vs. N.Y. GIANTS**
RS: Giants lead series, 69-50-3
PS: Series tied 1-1;
See N.Y. Giants vs. Washington
**WASHINGTON vs. N.Y. JETS**
RS: Redskins lead series, 4-1;
See N.Y. Jets vs. Washington
**WASHINGTON vs. PHILADELPHIA**
RS: Redskins lead series, 66-46-5
PS: Redskins lead series, 1-0;
See Philadelphia vs. Washington
**WASHINGTON vs. PITTSBURGH**
RS: Redskins lead series, 42-27-3;
See Pittsburgh vs. Washington
**WASHINGTON vs. SAN DIEGO**
RS: Redskins lead series, 5-0;
See San Diego vs. Washington
**WASHINGTON vs. SAN FRANCISCO**
RS: 49ers lead series, 9-6-1
PS: 49ers lead series, 3-1;
See San Francisco vs. Washington
**WASHINGTON vs. SEATTLE**
RS: Redskins lead series, 5-1;
See Seattle vs. Washington
**WASHINGTON vs. TAMPA BAY**
RS: Redskins lead series, 4-0;
See Tampa Bay vs. Washington

## SUPER BOWL SUMMARIES

### RESULTS

| Season | Date | Winner (Share) | Loser (Share) | Score | Site | Attendance |
|---|---|---|---|---|---|---|
| XXVIII | 1-30-94 | Dallas ($38,000) | Buffalo ($23,500) | 30-13 | Atlanta | 72,817 |
| XXVII | 1-31-93 | Dallas ($36,000) | Buffalo ($18,000) | 52-17 | Pasadena | 98,374 |
| XXVI | 1-26-92 | Washington ($36,000) | Buffalo ($18,000) | 37-24 | Minneapolis | 63,130 |
| XXV | 1-27-91 | N.Y. Giants ($36,000) | Buffalo ($18,000) | 20-19 | Tampa | 73,813 |
| XXIV | 1-28-90 | San Francisco ($36,000) | Denver ($18,000) | 55-10 | New Orleans | 72,919 |
| XXIII | 1-22-89 | San Francisco ($36,000) | Cincinnati ($18,000) | 20-16 | Miami | 75,129 |
| XXII | 1-31-88 | Washington ($36,000) | Denver ($18,000) | 42-10 | San Diego | 73,302 |
| XXI | 1-25-87 | N.Y. Giants ($36,000) | Denver ($18,000) | 39-20 | Pasadena | 101,063 |
| XX | 1-26-86 | Chicago ($36,000) | New England ($18,000) | 46-10 | New Orleans | 73,818 |
| XIX | 1-20-85 | San Francisco ($36,000) | Miami ($18,000) | 38-16 | Stanford | 84,059 |
| XVIII | 1-22-84 | L.A. Raiders ($36,000) | Washington ($18,000) | 38-9 | Tampa | 72,920 |
| XVII | 1-30-83 | Washington ($36,000) | Miami ($18,000) | 27-17 | Pasadena | 103,667 |
| XVI | 1-24-82 | San Francisco ($18,000) | Cincinnati ($9,000) | 26-21 | Pontiac | 81,270 |
| XV | 1-25-81 | Oakland ($18,000) | Philadelphia ($9,000) | 27-10 | New Orleans | 76,135 |
| XIV | 1-20-80 | Pittsburgh ($18,000) | Los Angeles ($9,000) | 31-19 | Pasadena | 103,985 |
| XIII | 1-21-79 | Pittsburgh ($18,000) | Dallas ($9,000) | 35-31 | Miami | 79,484 |
| XII | 1-15-78 | Dallas ($18,000) | Denver ($9,000) | 27-10 | New Orleans | 75,583 |
| XI | 1-9-77 | Oakland ($15,000) | Minnesota ($7,500) | 32-14 | Pasadena | 103,438 |
| X | 1-18-76 | Pittsburgh ($15,000) | Dallas ($7,500) | 21-17 | Miami | 80,187 |
| IX | 1-12-75 | Pittsburgh ($15,000) | Minnesota ($7,500) | 16-6 | New Orleans | 80,997 |
| VIII | 1-13-74 | Miami ($15,000) | Minnesota ($7,500) | 24-7 | Houston | 71,882 |
| VII | 1-14-73 | Miami ($15,000) | Washington ($7,500) | 14-7 | Los Angeles | 90,182 |
| VI | 1-16-72 | Dallas ($15,000) | Miami ($7,500) | 24-3 | New Orleans | 81,023 |
| V | 1-17-71 | Baltimore ($15,000) | Dallas ($7,500) | 16-13 | Miami | 79,204 |
| IV | 1-11-70 | Kansas City ($15,000) | Minnesota ($7,500) | 23-7 | New Orleans | 80,562 |
| III | 1-12-69 | N.Y. Jets ($15,000) | Baltimore ($7,500) | 16-7 | Miami | 75,389 |
| II | 1-14-68 | Green Bay ($15,000) | Oakland ($7,500) | 33-14 | Miami | 75,546 |
| I | 1-15-67 | Green Bay ($15,000) | Kansas City ($7,500) | 35-10 | Los Angeles | 61,946 |

### SUPER BOWL COMPOSITE STANDINGS

| | W | L | Pct. | Pts. | OP |
|---|---|---|---|---|---|
| Pittsburgh Steelers | 4 | 0 | 1.000 | 103 | 73 |
| San Francisco 49ers | 4 | 0 | 1.000 | 139 | 63 |
| Green Bay Packers | 2 | 0 | 1.000 | 68 | 24 |
| New York Giants | 2 | 0 | 1.000 | 59 | 39 |
| Chicago Bears | 1 | 0 | 1.000 | 46 | 10 |
| New York Jets | 1 | 0 | 1.000 | 16 | 7 |
| Oakland/L.A. Raiders | 3 | 1 | .750 | 111 | 66 |
| Washington Redskins | 3 | 2 | .600 | 122 | 103 |
| Dallas Cowboys | 4 | 3 | .571 | 194 | 115 |
| Baltimore Colts | 1 | 1 | .500 | 23 | 29 |
| Kansas City Chiefs | 1 | 1 | .500 | 33 | 42 |
| Miami Dolphins | 2 | 3 | .400 | 74 | 103 |
| Los Angeles Rams | 0 | 1 | .000 | 19 | 31 |
| New England Patriots | 0 | 1 | .000 | 10 | 46 |
| Philadelphia Eagles | 0 | 1 | .000 | 10 | 27 |
| Cincinnati Bengals | 0 | 2 | .000 | 37 | 46 |
| Buffalo Bills | 0 | 4 | .000 | 73 | 139 |
| Denver Broncos | 0 | 4 | .000 | 50 | 163 |
| Minnesota Vikings | 0 | 4 | .000 | 34 | 95 |

### SUPER BOWL MOST VALUABLE PLAYERS*

Super Bowl I — QB Bart Starr, Green Bay
Super Bowl II — QB Bart Starr, Green Bay
Super Bowl III — QB Joe Namath, N.Y. Jets
Super Bowl IV — QB Len Dawson, Kansas City
Super Bowl V — LB Chuck Howley, Dallas
Super Bowl VI — QB Roger Staubach, Dallas
Super Bowl VII — S Jake Scott, Miami
Super Bowl VIII — RB Larry Csonka, Miami
Super Bowl IX — RB Franco Harris, Pittsburgh
Super Bowl X — WR Lynn Swann, Pittsburgh
Super Bowl XI — WR Fred Biletnikoff, Oakland
Super Bowl XII — DT Randy White and DE Harvey Martin, Dallas
Super Bowl XIII — QB Terry Bradshaw, Pittsburgh
Super Bowl XIV — QB Terry Bradshaw, Pittsburgh
Super Bowl XV — QB Jim Plunkett, Oakland
Super Bowl XVI — QB Joe Montana, San Francisco
Super Bowl XVII — RB John Riggins, Washington
Super Bowl XVIII — RB Marcus Allen, L.A. Raiders
Super Bowl XIX — QB Joe Montana, San Francisco
Super Bowl XX — DE Richard Dent, Chicago
Super Bowl XXI — QB Phil Simms, N.Y. Giants
Super Bowl XXII — QB Doug Williams, Washington
Super Bowl XXIII — WR Jerry Rice, San Francisco
Super Bowl XXIV — QB Joe Montana, San Francisco
Super Bowl XXV — RB Ottis Anderson, N.Y. Giants
Super Bowl XXVI — QB Mark Rypien, Washington
Super Bowl XXVII — QB Troy Aikman, Dallas
Super Bowl XXVIII — RB Emmitt Smith, Dallas

** Award named Pete Rozelle Trophy since Super Bowl XXV.*

### SUPER BOWL XXVIII

Georgia Dome, Atlanta, Georgia
January 30, 1994, Attendance: 72,817

**DALLAS 30, BUFFALO 13**—Emmitt Smith rushed for 132 yards and 2 second-half touchdowns to power the Cowboys to their second consecutive NFL title. By winning, Dallas joined San Francisco and Pittsburgh as the only franchises with four Super Bowl victories. The Bills, meanwhile, extended a dubious string by losing in the Super Bowl for the fourth consecutive year. To win, the Cowboys had to rally from a 13-6 halftime deficit. Buffalo had forged its lead on Thurman Thomas's 4-yard touchdown run and a pair of field goals by Steve Christie, including a 54-yard kick, the longest in Super Bowl history. But just 55 seconds into the second half, Thomas was stripped of the ball by Dallas defensive tackle Leon Lett. Safety James Washington recovered and weaved his way 46 yards for a touchdown to tie the game at 13-13. After forcing the Bills to punt, the Cowboys began their next possession on their 36-yard line and Smith, the game's most valuable player, took over. He carried 7 times for 61 yards on the ensuing 8-play, 64-yard drive, capping the march with a 15-yard touchdown run to give Dallas the lead for good with 8:42 remaining in the third quarter. Early in the fourth quarter, Washington intercepted Jim Kelly's pass and returned it 12 yards to Buffalo's 34. A penalty moved the ball back to the 39, but Smith carried twice for 10 yards and caught a screen pass for 9, and quarterback Troy Aikman completed a 16-yard pass to Alvin Harper to give the Cowboys a first-and-goal at the 6. Smith took it from there, cracking the end zone on fourth-and-goal from the 1 to put Dallas ahead 27-13 with 9:50 remaining. Eddie Murray's third field goal, from 20 yards with 2:50 left, ended any doubt about the game's outcome. Smith had 30 carries in all, with 19 of his attempts and 92 yards coming after intermission. Washington, normally a reserve who played most of the game because the Cowboys used five defensive backs to combat the Bills' No-Huddle offense, had 11 tackles and forced another fumble by Thomas in the first quarter. Aikman completed 19 of 27 passes for 207 yards. Buffalo's Kelly completed a Super Bowl-record 31 passes in 50 attempts for 260 yards. Dallas, the first team in NFL history to begin the regular season 0-2 and go on to win the Super Bowl, also became the fifth to win back-to-back titles, following Green Bay, Miami, Pittsburgh (the Steelers did it twice), and San Francisco. Buffalo became the third team, along with Minnesota and Denver, to lose four Super Bowls. The Cowboys' victory was the tenth in succession for the NFC over the AFC.

| Dallas (30) | Offense | Buffalo (13) |
|---|---|---|
| Alvin Harper | WR | Don Beebe |
| Mark Tuinei | LT | John Fina |
| Nate Newton | LG | Glenn Parker |
| John Gesek | C | Kent Hull |
| Kevin Gogan | RG | John Davis |
| Erik Williams | RT | Howard Ballard |
| Jay Novacek | TE | Pete Metzelaars |
| Michael Irvin | WR | Bill Brooks |
| Troy Aikman | QB | Jim Kelly |
| Emmitt Smith | RB | Thurman Thomas |
| Daryl Johnston | RB-WR | Andre Reed |
| | **Defense** | |
| Tony Tolbert | LE | Phil Hansen |
| Tony Casillas | LT-NT | Jeff Wright |
| Leon Lett | RT-RE | Bruce Smith |
| Charles Haley | RE-RILB | Cornelius Bennett |
| Darrin Smith | LLB-RILB | Mark Maddox |
| Darren Woodson | DB-LOLB | Marvcus Patton |
| Ken Norton | RLB-LOLB | Darryl Talley |
| Kevin Smith | LCB | Mickey Washington |
| Larry Brown | RCB | Nate Odomes |
| Thomas Everett | SS | Henry Jones |
| James Washington | FS | Mark Kelso |

#### SUBSTITUTIONS

**Dallas**—Offense: K—Eddie Murray. P—John Jett. QB—Bernie Kosar. RB—Lincoln Coleman, Derrick Gainer. WR—Kevin Williams. TE—Scott Galbraith. G-C—Frank Cornish, Dale Hellestrae. Defense: E—Jim Jeffcoat. T—Chad Hennings, Russell Maryland. DL—Jimmie Jones. DB—Bill Bates, Joe Fishback, Elvis Patterson. LB—Dixon Edwards, Robert Jones, Godfrey Myles, Matt Vanderbeek. CB—Dave Thomas. S—Kenneth Gant. DNP: RB—Derrick Lassic.

**Buffalo**—Offense: K—Steve Christie. P—Chris

Mohr. QB—Frank Reich. RB—Kenneth Davis, Carwell Gardner. WR—Russell Copeland, Steve Tasker. TE—Keith McKeller. T—Jerry Crafts. G—Jim Ritcher. C—Mike Devlin, Adam Lingner. Defense: E—Oliver Barnett, Mark Pike. NT—Mike Lodish. LB—Monty Brown, Keith Goganious, Richard Harvey. CB—Jerome Henderson, Thomas Smith. S—Matt Darby, Kurt Schulz. DNP: RB—Nate Turner.

**OFFICIALS**

Referee—Bob McElwee. Umpire—Art Demmas. Head Linesman—Sid Semon. Line Judge—Tom Barnes. Back Judge—Al Jury. Field Judge—Don Orr. Side Judge—Nate Jones.

**SCORING**

| | | | | | | |
|---|---|---|---|---|---|---|
| **Dallas (NFC)** | 6 | 0 | 14 | 10 | — | 30 |
| **Buffalo (AFC)** | 3 | 10 | 0 | 0 | — | 13 |

Dall — FG Murray 41
Buff — FG Christie 54
Dall — FG Murray 24
Buff — Thomas 4 run (Christie kick)
Buff — FG Christie 28
Dall — Washington 46 fumble return (Murray kick)
Dall — E. Smith 15 run (Murray kick)
Dall — E. Smith 1 run (Murray kick)
Dall — FG Murray 20

| **TEAM STATISTICS** | **Dallas** | **Buffalo** |
|---|---|---|
| Total First Downs | 20 | 22 |
| Rushing | 6 | 6 |
| Passing | 14 | 15 |
| Penalty | 0 | 1 |
| Total Net Yardage | 341 | 314 |
| Total Offensive Plays | 64 | 80 |
| Average Gain per Offensive Play | 5.3 | 3.9 |
| Rushes | 35 | 27 |
| Yards Gained Rushing (Net) | 137 | 87 |
| Average Yards per Rush | 3.9 | 3.2 |
| Passes Attempted | 27 | 50 |
| Passes Completed | 19 | 31 |
| Had Intercepted | 1 | 1 |
| Tackled Attempting to Pass | 2 | 3 |
| Yards Lost Attempting to Pass | 3 | 33 |
| Yards Gained Passing (Net) | 204 | 227 |
| Punts | 4 | 5 |
| Average Distance | 43.8 | 37.6 |
| Punt Returns | 1 | 1 |
| Punt Return Yardage | 5 | 5 |
| Kickoff Returns | 2 | 6 |
| Kickoff Return Yardage | 72 | 144 |
| Interception Return Yardage | 12 | 41 |
| Total Return Yardage | 89 | 190 |
| Fumbles | 0 | 3 |
| Own Fumbles Recovered | 0 | 1 |
| Opponent Fumbles Recovered | 2 | 0 |
| Penalties | 6 | 1 |
| Yards Penalized | 50 | 10 |
| Total Points Scored | 30 | 13 |
| Touchdowns | 3 | 1 |
| Rushing | 2 | 1 |
| Passing | 0 | 0 |
| Returns | 1 | 0 |
| Extra Points | 3 | 1 |
| Field Goals | 3 | 2 |
| Field Goals Attempted | 3 | 2 |
| Safeties | 0 | 0 |
| Third-Down Efficiency | 5/13 | 5/17 |
| Fourth-Down Efficiency | 1/1 | 2/3 |
| Time of Possession | 34:29 | 25:31 |

**INDIVIDUAL STATISTICS**

**Rushing**

| **Dallas** | **No.** | **Yds.** | **LG** | **TD** |
|---|---|---|---|---|
| E. Smith | 30 | 132 | 15t | 2 |
| K. Williams | 1 | 6 | 6 | 0 |
| Aikman | 1 | 3 | 3 | 0 |
| Johnston | 1 | 0 | 0 | 0 |
| Kosar | 1 | -1 | -1 | 0 |
| Coleman | 1 | -3 | -3 | 0 |
| **Buffalo** | **No.** | **Yds.** | **LG** | **TD** |
| Thomas | 16 | 37 | 6 | 1 |
| K. Davis | 9 | 38 | 11 | 0 |
| Kelly | 2 | 12 | 8 | 0 |

**Passing**

| **Dallas** | **Att.** | **Comp.** | **Yds.** | **TD** | **Int.** |
|---|---|---|---|---|---|
| Aikman | 27 | 19 | 207 | 0 | 1 |
| **Buffalo** | **Att.** | **Comp.** | **Yds.** | **TD** | **Int.** |
| Kelly | 50 | 31 | 260 | 0 | 1 |

**Receiving**

| **Dallas** | **No.** | **Yds.** | **LG** | **TD** |
|---|---|---|---|---|
| Irvin | 5 | 66 | 20 | 0 |
| Novacek | 5 | 26 | 9 | 0 |
| E. Smith | 4 | 26 | 10 | 0 |
| Harper | 3 | 75 | 35 | 0 |
| Johnston | 2 | 14 | 11 | 0 |
| **Buffalo** | **No.** | **Yds.** | **LG** | **TD** |
| Brooks | 7 | 63 | 15 | 0 |
| Thomas | 7 | 52 | 24 | 0 |
| Reed | 6 | 75 | 22 | 0 |
| Beebe | 6 | 60 | 18 | 0 |
| K. Davis | 3 | -5 | 7 | 0 |
| Metzelaars | 1 | 8 | 8 | 0 |
| McKeller | 1 | 7 | 7 | 0 |

**Interceptions**

| **Dallas** | **No.** | **Yds.** | **LG** | **TD** |
|---|---|---|---|---|
| Washington | 1 | 12 | 12 | 0 |
| **Buffalo** | **No.** | **Yds.** | **LG** | **TD** |
| Odomes | 1 | 41 | 41 | 0 |

**Punting**

| **Dallas** | **No.** | **Avg.** | **LG** | **Blk.** |
|---|---|---|---|---|
| Jett | 4 | 43.8 | 47 | 0 |
| **Buffalo** | **No.** | **Avg.** | **LG** | **Blk.** |
| Mohr | 5 | 37.6 | 52 | 0 |

**Punt Returns**

| **Dallas** | **No.** | **FC** | **Yds.** | **LG** | **TD** |
|---|---|---|---|---|---|
| K. Williams | 1 | 1 | 5 | 5 | 0 |
| **Buffalo** | **No.** | **FC** | **Yds.** | **LG** | **TD** |
| Copeland | 1 | 1 | 5 | 5 | 0 |

**Kickoff Returns**

| **Dallas** | **No.** | **Yds.** | **LG** | **TD** |
|---|---|---|---|---|
| K. Williams | 1 | 50 | 50 | 0 |
| Gant | 1 | 22 | 22 | 0 |
| **Buffalo** | **No.** | **Yds.** | **LG** | **TD** |
| Copeland | 4 | 82 | 22 | 0 |
| Beebe | 2 | 62 | 34 | 0 |

## SUPER BOWL XXVII

Rose Bowl, Pasadena, California
January 31, 1993, Attendance: 98,374

**DALLAS 52, BUFFALO 17**—Troy Aikman threw 4 touchdown passes, Emmitt Smith rushed for 108 yards, and the Cowboys converted 9 turnovers into 35 points while coasting to the victory. Dallas's win was its third in its record sixth Super Bowl appearance; the Bills became the first team to drop three in succession. Buffalo led 7-0 until the first 2 of its record number of turnovers helped the Cowboys take the lead for good late in the opening quarter. First, Dallas safety James Washington intercepted a Jim Kelly pass and returned it 13 yards to the Bills' 47, setting up Aikman's 23-yard touchdown pass to tight end Jay Novacek with 1:36 remaining in the period. On the next play from scrimmage, Kelly was sacked by Charles Haley and fumbled at the Bills' 2-yard line where the Cowboys' Jimmie Jones picked up the loose ball and ran 2 yards for a touchdown. Dallas, which recovered 5 fumbles and intercepted 4 passes, struck just as quickly late in the first half, when Aikman tossed 19- and 18-yard touchdown passes to Michael Irvin 15 seconds apart to give the Cowboys a 28-10 lead at intermission. The second score was set up when Bills running back Thurman Thomas lost a fumble at his 19-yard line. Buffalo scored for the last time when backup quarterback Frank Reich, playing because Kelly was injured while attempting to pass midway through the second quarter, threw a 40-yard touchdown pass to Don Beebe on the final play of the third period to trim the deficit to 31-17. But Dallas put the game out of reach by scoring three times in a span of 2:33 of the fourth quarter. Aikman, the game's most valuable player, completed 22 of 30 passes for 273 yards and was not intercepted. The victory was the ninth in succession for the NFC over the AFC.

| | | | | | | |
|---|---|---|---|---|---|---|
| **Buffalo (AFC)** | 7 | 3 | 7 | 0 | — | 17 |
| **Dallas (NFC)** | 14 | 14 | 3 | 21 | — | 52 |

Buff — Thomas 2 run (Christie kick)
Dall — Novacek 23 pass from Aikman (Elliott kick)
Dall — J. Jones 2 fumble recovery return (Elliott kick)
Buff — FG Christie 21
Dall — Irvin 19 pass from Aikman (Elliott kick)
Dall — Irvin 18 pass from Aikman (Elliott kick)
Dall — FG Elliott 20
Buff — Beebe 40 pass from Reich (Christie kick)
Dall — Harper 45 pass from Aikman (Elliott kick)
Dall — E. Smith 10 run (Elliott kick)
Dall — Norton 9 fumble recovery return (Elliott kick)

## SUPER BOWL XXVI

Metrodome, Minneapolis, Minnesota
January 26, 1992, Attendance: 63,130

**WASHINGTON 37, BUFFALO 24**—Mark Rypien passed for 292 yards and 2 touchdowns as the Redskins overwhelmed the Bills to win their third Super Bowl in the past 10 years. Rypien, the game's most valuable player, completed 18 of 33 passes, including a 10-yard scoring strike to Earnest Byner and a 30-yard touchdown to Gary Clark. The latter came late in the third quarter after Buffalo had trimmed a 24-0 deficit to 24-10, and effectively put the game out of reach. Washington went on to lead by as much as 37-10 before the Bills made it close wih a pair of touchdowns in the final six minutes. Though the Redskins struggled early, converting their first three drives inside the Bills' 20-yard line into only 3 points, they built a 17-0 halftime lead. And they made it 24-0 just 16 seconds into the second half, after Kurt Gouveia intercepted Buffalo quarterback Jim Kelly's pass on the first play of the third quarter and returned it 23 yards to the Bills' 2. One play later, Gerald Riggs scored his second touchdown of the game to make it 24-0. Kelly, forced to bring Buffalo from behind, completed 28 of a Super Bowl-record 58 passes for 275 yards and 2 touchdowns, but was intercepted 4 times. Bills running back Thurman Thomas, who had an AFC-high 1,407 yards rushing and an NFL-best 2,038 total yards from scrimmage during the regular season, ran for only 13 yards on 10 carries and was limited to 27 yards on 4 receptions. Clark had 7 catches for 114 yards and Art Monk added 7 for 113 for the Redskins, who amassed 417 yards of total offense while limiting the explosive Bills to 283. Washington's Joe Gibbs became only the third head coach to win three Super Bowls.

| | | | | | | |
|---|---|---|---|---|---|---|
| **Washington (NFC)** | 0 | 17 | 14 | 6 | — | 37 |
| **Buffalo (AFC)** | 0 | 0 | 10 | 14 | — | 24 |

Wash — FG Lohmiller 34
Wash — Byner 10 pass from Rypien (Lohmiller kick)
Wash — Riggs 1 run (Lohmiller kick)
Wash — Riggs 2 run (Lohmiller kick)
Buff — FG Norwood 21
Buff — Thomas 1 run (Norwood kick)
Wash — Clark 30 pass from Rypien(Lohmiller kick)
Wash — FG Lohmiller 25
Wash — FG Lohmiller 39
Buff — Metzelaars 2 pass from Kelly (Norwood kick)
Buff — Beebe 4 pass from Kelly (Norwood kick)

## SUPER BOWL XXV

Tampa Stadium, Tampa, Florida
January 27, 1991, Attendance: 73,813

**NEW YORK GIANTS 20, BUFFALO 19**—The NFC champion New York Giants won their second Super Bowl in five years with a 20-19 victory over AFC titlist Buffalo. New York, employing its ball-control offense, had possession for 40 minutes, 33 seconds, a Super Bowl record. The Bills, who scored 95 points in their previous two playoff games leading to Super Bowl XXV, had the ball for less than eight minutes in the second half and just 19:27 for the game. Fourteen of New York's 73 plays came on its initial drive of the third quarter, which covered 75 yards and consumed a Super Bowl-record 9:29 before running back Ottis Anderson ran 1 yard for a touchdown. Giants quarterback Jeff Hostetler kept the long drive going by converting three third-down plays—an 11-yard pass to running back David Meggett on third-and-eight, a 14-yard toss to wide receiver Mark Ingram on third-and-13, and a 9-yard pass to Howard Cross on third-and-four—to give New York a 17-12 lead in the third quarter. Buffalo jumped to a 12-3 lead midway through the second quarter before Hostetler completed a 14-yard scoring strike to wide receiver Stephen Baker to close the score to 12-10 at halftime. Buffalo's Thurman Thomas ran 31 yards for a touchdown on the opening play of the fourth quarter to help Buffalo recapture the lead 19-17. Matt Bahr's 21-yard field goal gave the Giants a 20-19 lead, but Buffalo's Scott Norwood had a chance to win the game with seconds remaining before his 47-yard field-goal attempt sailed wide right. Hostetler completed 20 of 32 passes for 222 yards and 1 touchdown. Anderson rushed 21 times for 102 yards and 1 touchdown to capture the most-valuable-player honors. Thomas totaled 190 scrimmage yards, rushing 15 times for 135 yards and catching 5 passes for 55 yards.

| | | | | | | |
|---|---|---|---|---|---|---|
| **Buffalo (AFC)** | 3 | 9 | 0 | 7 | — | 19 |
| **N.Y. Giants (NFC)** | 3 | 7 | 7 | 3 | — | 20 |

NYG — FG Bahr 28
Buff — FG Norwood 23
Buff — D. Smith 1 run (Norwood kick)
Buff — Safety, B. Smith tackled Hostetler in end zone
NYG — Baker 14 pass from Hostetler (Bahr kick)
NYG — Anderson 1 run (Bahr kick)
Buff — Thomas 31 run (Norwood kick)
NYG — FG Bahr 21

## SUPER BOWL XXIV

Louisiana Superdome, New Orleans, Louisiana
January 28, 1990, Attendance: 72,919

**SAN FRANCISCO 55, DENVER 10**—NFC titlist San Francisco won its fourth Super Bowl championship with a 55-10 victory over AFC champion Denver. The 49ers, who also won Super Bowls XVI, XIX, and XXIII, tied the Pittsburgh Steelers for most Super Bowl victories. The Steelers captured Super Bowls IX, X, XIII, and XIV. San Francisco's 55 points broke the previous Super Bowl scoring mark of 46 points by Chicago in Super Bowl XX. San Francisco scored touchdowns on four of its six first-half possessions to hold a 27-3 lead at halftime. Interceptions by Michael Walter and Chet Brooks ended the Broncos' first two possessions of the second half. San Francisco quarterback Joe Montana was named the Super Bowl most valuable player for a record third time. Montana completed 22 of 29 passes for 297 yards and a Super Bowl-record 5 touchdowns. Jerry Rice, Super Bowl XXIII most valuable player, caught 7 passes for 148 yards and three touchdowns. The 49ers' domination included first downs (28 to 12), net yards (461 to 167), and time of possession (39:31 to 20:29).

| | | | | | | |
|---|---|---|---|---|---|---|
| **San Francisco (NFC)** | 13 | 14 | 14 | 14 | — | 55 |
| **Denver (AFC)** | 3 | 0 | 7 | 0 | — | 10 |

SF — Rice 20 pass from Montana (Cofer kick)
Den — FG Treadwell 42
SF — Jones 7 pass from Montana (kick failed)
SF — Rathman 1 run (Cofer kick)
SF — Rice 38 pass from Montana (Cofer kick)
SF — Rice 28 pass from Montana (Cofer kick)
SF — Taylor 35 pass from Montana (Cofer kick)
Den — Elway 3 run (Treadwell kick)
SF — Rathman 3 run (Cofer kick)
SF — Craig 1 run (Cofer kick)

## SUPER BOWL XXIII

Joe Robbie Stadium, Miami, Florida
January 22, 1989, Attendance: 75,129

**SAN FRANCISCO 20, CINCINNATI 16**—NFC champion San Francisco captured its third Super Bowl of the 1980s by defeating AFC champion Cincinnati 20-16. The 49ers, who also won Super Bowls XVI and XIX, are the first NFC team to win three Super Bowls. Pittsburgh, with four Super Bowl titles (IX, X, XIII, and XIV), and the Oakland/Los Angeles Raiders, with three (XI, XV, and XVIII), lead AFC franchises. Even though San Francisco held an advantage in total net yards (453 to 229), the 49ers found themselves trailing the Bengals late in the game. With the score 13-13, Cincinnati took a 16-13 lead on Jim Breech's 40-yard field goal with 3:20 remaining. It was Breech's third field goal of the day, following earlier successes from 34 and 43 yards. The 49ers started their winning drive at their 8-yard line. Over the next 11 plays, San Francisco covered 92 yards with the decisive score coming on a 10-yard pass from quarterback Joe Montana to wide receiver John Taylor with 34 seconds remaining. At halftime, the score was 3-3, the first time in Super Bowl history the game was tied at intermission. After the teams traded third-period field goals, the Bengals jumped ahead 13-6 on Stanford Jennings's 93-yard kickoff return for a touchdown with 34 seconds remaining in the quarter. The 49ers didn't waste any time coming back as they covered 85 yards in four plays, concluding with Montana's 14-yard scoring pass to Jerry Rice 57 seconds into the final stanza. Rice was named the game's most valuable player after compiling 11 catches for a Super Bowl-record 215 yards. Montana completed 23 of 36 passes for a Super Bowl-record 357 yards and 2 touchdowns.

| | | | | | | |
|---|---|---|---|---|---|---|
| **Cincinnati (AFC)** | 0 | 3 | 10 | 3 | — | 16 |
| **San Francisco (NFC)** | 3 | 0 | 3 | 14 | — | 20 |

SF — FG Cofer 41
Cin — FG Breech 34
Cin — FG Breech 43
SF — FG Cofer 32
Cin — Jennings 93 kickoff return (Breech kick)
SF — Rice 14 pass from Montana (Cofer kick)
Cin — FG Breech 40
SF — Taylor 10 pass from Montana (Cofer kick)

## SUPER BOWL XXII

San Diego Jack Murphy Stadium, San Diego,California
January 31, 1988, Attendance: 73,302

**WASHINGTON 42, DENVER 10**—NFC champion Washington won Super Bowl XXII and its second NFL championship of the 1980s with a 42-10 decision over AFC champion Denver. The Redskins, who also won Super Bowl XVII, enjoyed a record-setting second quarter en route to the victory. The Broncos broke in front 10-0 when quarterback John Elway threw a 56-yard touchdown pass to wide receiver Ricky Nattiel on the Broncos' first play from scrimmage. Following a Washington punt, Denver's Rich Karlis kicked a 24-yard field goal to cap a seven-play, 61-yard scoring drive. The Redskins then erupted for 35 points on five straight possessions in the second period and coasted thereafter. The 35 points established an NFL postseason mark for most points in a period, bettering the previous total of 21 by San Francisco in Super Bowl XIX and Chicago in Super Bowl XX. Redskins quarterback Doug Williams led the second-period explosion by throwing a Super Bowl record-tying 4 touchdown passes, including 80- and 50-yard passes to wide receiver Ricky Sanders, a 27-yard toss to wide receiver Gary Clark, and an 8-yard pass to tight end Clint Didier. Washington scored 5 touchdowns in 18 plays with total time of possession of only 5:47. Overall, Williams completed 18 of 29 passes for 340 yards and was named the game's most valuable player. His passyardage total eclipsed the Super Bowl record of 331 yards by Joe Montana of San Francisco in Super Bowl XIX. Sanders ended with 193 yards on 8 catches, breaking the previous Super Bowl yardage record of 161 yards by Lynn Swann of Pittsburgh in Game X. Rookie running back Timmy Smith was the game's leading rusher with 22 carries for a Super Bowl-record 204 yards, breaking the previous mark of 191 yards by Marcus Allen of the Raiders in Game XVIII. Smith also scored twice on runs of 58 and 4 yards. Washington's 6 touchdowns and 602 total yards gained also set Super Bowl records. Redskins cornerback Barry Wilburn had 2 of the team's 3 interceptions, and strong safety Alvin Walton had 2 of Washington's 5 sacks.

| | | | | | | |
|---|---|---|---|---|---|---|
| **Washington (NFC)** | 0 | 35 | 0 | 7 | — | 42 |
| **Denver (AFC)** | 10 | 0 | 0 | 0 | — | 10 |

Den — Nattiel 56 pass from Elway (Karlis kick)
Den — FG Karlis 24
Wash — Sanders 80 pass from Williams (Haji-Sheikh kick)
Wash — Clark 27 pass from Williams (Haji-Sheikh kick)
Wash — Smith 58 run (Haji-Sheikh kick)
Wash — Sanders 50 pass from Williams (Haji-Sheikh kick)
Wash — Didier 8 pass from Williams (Haji-Sheikh kick)
Wash — Smith 4 run (Haji-Sheikh kick)

## SUPER BOWL XXI

Rose Bowl, Pasadena, California
January 25, 1987, Attendance: 101,063

**NEW YORK GIANTS 39, DENVER 20**—The NFC champion New York Giants captured their first NFL title since 1956 when they downed the AFC champion Denver Broncos 39-20 in Super Bowl XXI. The victory marked the NFC's fifth NFL title in the past six seasons. The Broncos, behind the passing of quarterback John Elway, who was 13 of 20 for 187 yards in the first half, held a 10-9 lead at intermission, the narrowest halftime margin in Super Bowl history. Denver's Rich Karlis opened the scoring with a Super Bowl record-tying 48-yard field goal. New York drove 78 yards in nine plays on the next series to take a 7-3 lead on quarterback Phil Simms's 6-yard touchdown pass to tight end Zeke Mowatt. The Broncos came right back with a 58-yard scoring drive on six plays capped by Elway's 4-yard touchdown run. The only scoring in the second period was the sack of Elway in the end zone by defensive end George Martin for a New York safety. The Giants produced a key defensive stand early in the second quarter when the Broncos had a first down at the New York 1-yard line, but failed to score on three running plays and Karlis's 23-yard missed field-goal attempt. The Giants took command of the game in the third period en route to a 30-point second half, the most ever scored in one half of Super Bowl play. New York took the lead for good on tight end Mark Bavaro's 13-yard touchdown catch 4:52 into the third period. The nine-play, 63-yard scoring drive included the successful conversion of a fourth-and-1 play on the New York 46-yard line. Denver was limited to only 2 net yards on 10 offensive plays in the third period. Simms set Super Bowl records for most consecutive completions (10) and highest completion percentage (88 percent on 22 completions in 25 attempts). He also passed for 268 yards and 3 touchdowns and was named the game's most valuable player. New York running back Joe Morris was the game's leading rusher with 20 carries for 67 yards. Denver wide receiver Vance Johnson led all receivers with 5 catches for 121 yards. The Giants defeated their three playoff opponents by a cumulative total of 82 points (New York 105, opponents 23), the largest such margin by a Super Bowl winner.

| | | | | | | |
|---|---|---|---|---|---|---|
| **Denver (AFC)** | 10 | 0 | 0 | 10 | — | 20 |
| **N.Y. Giants (NFC)** | 7 | 2 | 17 | 13 | — | 39 |

Den — FG Karlis 48
NYG — Mowatt 6 pass from Simms (Allegre kick)
Den — Elway 4 run (Karlis kick)
NYG — Safety, Martin tackled Elway in end zone
NYG — Bavaro 13 pass from Simms (Allegre kick)
NYG — FG Allegre 21
NYG — Morris 1 run (Allegre kick)
NYG — McConkey 6 pass from Simms (Allegre kick)
Den — FG Karlis 28
NYG — Anderson 2 run (kick failed)
Den — V. Johnson 47 pass from Elway (Karlis kick)

## SUPER BOWL XX

Louisiana Superdome, New Orleans, Louisiana
January 26, 1986, Attendance: 73,818

**CHICAGO 46, NEW ENGLAND 10**—The NFC champion Chicago Bears, seeking their first NFL title since 1963, scored a Super Bowl-record 46 points in downing AFC champion New England 46-10 in Super Bowl XX. The previous record for most points in a Super Bowl was 38, shared by San Francisco in XIX and the Los Angeles Raiders in XVIII. The Bears' league-leading defense tied the Super Bowl record for sacks (7) and limited the Patriots to a record-low 7 rushing yards. New England took the quickest lead in Super Bowl history when Tony Franklin kicked a 36-yard field goal with 1:19 elapsed in the first period. The score came about because of Larry McGrew's fumble recovery at the Chicago 19-yard line. However, the Bears rebounded for a 23-3 first-half lead, while building a yardage advantage of 236 total yards to New England's minus 19. Running back Matt Suhey rushed 8 times for 37 yards, including an 11-yard touchdown run, and caught 1 pass for 24 yards in the first half. After the Patriots first drive of the second half ended with a punt to the Bears' 4-yard line, Chicago marched 96 yards in nine plays with quarterback Jim McMahon's 1-yard scoring run capping the drive. McMahon became the first quarterback in Super Bowl history to rush for a pair of touchdowns. The Bears completed their scoring via a 28-yard interception return by reserve cornerback Reggie Phillips, a 1-yard run by defensive tackle/fullback William Perry, and a safety when defensive end Henry Waechter tackled Patriots quarterback Steve Grogan in the end zone. Bears defensive end Richard Dent became the fourth defender to be named the game's most valuable player after contributing 1½ sacks. The Bears' victory margin of 36 points was the largest in Super Bowl history, bettering the previous mark of 29 by the Los Angeles Raiders when they topped Washington 38-9 in Game XVIII. McMahon completed 12 of 20 passes for 256 yards before leaving the game in the fourth period with a wrist injury. The NFL's all-time leading rusher, Bears running back Walter Payton, carried 22 times for 61 yards. Wide receiver Willie Gault caught 4 passes for 129 yards, the fourth-most receiving yards in a Super Bowl. Chicago coach Mike Ditka became the second man (Tom Flores of Raiders was the other) who played in a Super Bowl and coached a team to a victory in the game.

| | | | | | |
|---|---|---|---|---|---|
| **Chicago (NFC)** | 13 | 10 | 21 | 2 | — 46 |
| **New England (AFC)** | 3 | 0 | 0 | 7 | — 10 |

NE — FG Franklin 36
Chi — FG Butler 28
Chi — FG Butler 24
Chi — Suhey 11 run (Butler kick)
Chi — McMahon 2 run (Butler kick)
Chi — FG Butler 24
Chi — McMahon 1 run (Butler kick)
Chi — Phillips 28 interception return (Butler kick)
Chi — Perry 1 run (Butler kick)
NE — Fryar 8 pass from Grogan (Franklin kick)
Chi — Safety, Waechter tackled Grogan in end zone

## SUPER BOWL XIX

Stanford Stadium, Stanford, California
January 20, 1985, Attendance: 84,059

**SAN FRANCISCO 38, MIAMI 16**—The San Francisco 49ers captured their second Super Bowl title with a dominating offense and a defense that tamed Miami's explosive passing attack. The Dolphins held a 10-7 lead at the end of the first period, which represented the most points scored by two teams in an opening quarter of a Super Bowl. However, the 49ers used excellent field position in the second period to build a 28-16 halftime lead. Running back Roger Craig set a Super Bowl record by scoring 3 touchdowns on pass receptions of 8 and 16 yards and a run of 2 yards. San Francisco's Joe Montana was voted the game's most valuable player. He joined Green Bay's Bart Starr and Pittsburgh's Terry Bradshaw as the only two-time Super Bowl most valuable players. Montana completed 24 of 35 passes for a Super Bowl-record 331 yards and 3 touchdowns, and rushed 5 times for 59 yards, including a 6-yard touchdown. Craig had 58 yards on 15 carries and caught 7 passes for 77 yards. Wendell Tyler rushed 13 times for 65 yards and had 4 catches for 70 yards. Dwight Clark had 6 receptions for 77 yards, while Russ Francis had 5 for 60. San Francisco's 537 total net yards bettered the previous Super Bowl record of 429 yards by Oakland in Super Bowl XI. The 49ers also held a time of possession advantage over the Dolphins of 37:11 to 22:49.

| | | | | | |
|---|---|---|---|---|---|
| **Miami (AFC)** | 10 | 6 | 0 | 0 | — 16 |
| **San Francisco (NFC)** | 7 | 21 | 10 | 0 | — 38 |

Mia — FG von Schamann 37
SF — Monroe 33 pass from Montana (Wersching kick)
Mia — D. Johnson 2 pass from Marino (von Schamann kick)
SF — Craig 8 pass from Montana (Wersching kick)
SF — Montana 6 run (Wersching kick)
SF — Craig 2 run (Wersching kick)
Mia — FG von Schamann 31
Mia — FG von Schamann 30
SF — FG Wersching 27
SF — Craig 16 pass from Montana (Wersching kick)

## SUPER BOWL XVIII

Tampa Stadium, Tampa, Florida
January 22, 1984, Attendance: 72,920

**LOS ANGELES RAIDERS 38, WASHINGTON 9**—The Los Angeles Raiders dominated the Washington Redskins from the beginning in Super Bowl XVIII and achieved the most lopsided victory in Super Bowl history, surpassing Green Bay's 35-10 win over Kansas City in Super Bowl I. The Raiders took a 7-0 lead 4:52 into the game when Derrick Jensen blocked a Jeff Hayes punt and recovered it in the end zone for a touchdown. With 9:14 remaining in the first half, Raiders quarterback Jim Plunkett threw a 12-yard touchdown pass to wide receiver Cliff Branch to complete a three-play, 65-yard drive. Washington cut the Raiders' lead to 14-3 on a 24-yard field goal by Mark Moseley. With seven seconds left in the first half, Raiders linebacker Jack Squirek intercepted a Joe Theismann pass at the Redskins' 5-yard line and ran it in for a touchdown to give Los Angeles a 21-3 halftime lead. In the third period, running back Marcus Allen, who rushed for a Super Bowl-record 191 yards on 20 carries, increased the Raiders' lead to 35-9 on touchdown runs of 5 and 74 yards, the latter erasing the Super Bowl record of 58 yards set by Baltimore's Tom Matte in Game III. Allen was named the game's most valuable player. The victory over Washington raised Raiders coach Tom Flores' playoff record to 8-1, including a 27-10 win against Philadelphia in Super Bowl XV. The 38 points scored by the Raiders were the highest total by a Super Bowl team. The previous high was 35 points by Green Bay in Game I.

| | | | | | |
|---|---|---|---|---|---|
| **Washington (NFC)** | 0 | 3 | 6 | 0 | — 9 |
| **L.A. Raiders (AFC)** | 7 | 14 | 14 | 3 | — 38 |

Raiders — Jensen recovered blocked punt in end zone (Bahr kick)
Raiders — Branch 12 pass from Plunkett (Bahr kick)
Wash — FG Moseley 24
Raiders — Squirek 5 interception return (Bahr kick)
Wash — Riggins 1 run (kick blocked)
Raiders — Allen 5 run (Bahr kick)
Raiders — Allen 74 run (Bahr kick)
Raiders — FG Bahr 21

## SUPER BOWL XVII

Rose Bowl, Pasadena, California
January 30, 1983, Attendance: 103,667

**WASHINGTON 27, MIAMI 17**—Fullback John Riggins ran for a Super Bowl-record 166 yards on 38 carries to spark Washington to a 27-17 victory over AFC champion Miami. It was Riggins's fourth straight 100-yard rushing game during the playoffs, also a record. The win marked Washington's first NFL title since 1942, and was only the second time in Super Bowl history NFL/NFC teams scored consecutive victories (Green Bay did it in Super Bowls I and II and San Francisco won Super Bowl XVI). The Redskins, under second-year head coach Joe Gibbs, used a balanced offense that accounted for 400 total yards (a Super Bowl-record 276 yards rushing and 124 passing), second in Super Bowl history to 429 yards by Oakland in Super Bowl XI. The Dolphins built a 17-10 halftime lead on a 76-yard touchdown pass from quarterback David Woodley to wide receiver Jimmy Cefalo 6:49 into the first period, a 20-yard field goal by Uwe von Schamann with 6:00 left in the half, and a Super Bowl-record 98-yard kickoff return by Fulton Walker with 1:38 remaining. Washington had tied the score at 10-10 with 1:51 left on a four-yard touchdown pass from Joe Theismann to wide receiver Alvin Garrett. Mark Moseley started the Redskins' scoring with a 31-yard field goal late in the first period, and added a 20-yarder midway through the third period to cut the Dolphins' lead to 17-13. Riggins, who was voted the game's most valuable player, gave Washington its first lead of the game with 10:01 left when he ran 43 yards off left tackle for a touchdown in a fourth-and-1 situation. Wide receiver Charlie Brown caught a six-yard scoring pass from Theismann with 1:55 left to complete the scoring. The Dolphins managed only 176 yards (142 in first half). Theismann completed 15 of 23 passes for 143 yards, with 2 touchdowns and 2 interceptions. For Miami, Woodley was 4 of 14 for 97 yards, with 1 touchdown, and 1 interception. Don Strock was 0 for 3 in relief.

| | | | | | |
|---|---|---|---|---|---|
| **Miami (AFC)** | 7 | 10 | 0 | 0 | — 17 |
| **Washington (NFC)** | 0 | 10 | 3 | 14 | — 27 |

Mia — Cefalo 76 pass from Woodley (von Schamann kick)
Wash — FG Moseley 31
Mia — FG von Schamann 20
Wash — Garrett 4 pass from Theismann (Moseley kick)
Mia — Walker 98 kickoff return (von Schamann kick)
Wash — FG Moseley 20
Wash — Riggins 43 run (Moseley kick)
Wash — Brown 6 pass from Theismann (Moseley kick)

## SUPER BOWL XVI

Pontiac Silverdome, Pontiac, Michigan
January 24, 1982, Attendance: 81,270

**SAN FRANCISCO 26, CINCINNATI 21**—Ray Wersching's Super Bowl record-tying 4 field goals and Joe Montana's controlled passing helped lift the San Francisco 49ers to their first NFL championship with a 26-21 victory over Cincinnati. The 49ers built a game-record 20-0 halftime lead via Montana's 1-yard touchdown run, which capped an 11-play, 68-yard drive; fullback Earl Cooper's 11-yard scoring-pass from Montana, which climaxed a Super Bowl record 92-yard drive on 12 plays; and Wersching's 22- and 26-yard field goals. The Bengals rebounded in the second half, closing the gap to 20-14 on quarterback Ken Anderson's 5-yard run and Dan Ross's 4-yard reception from Anderson, who established Super Bowl passing records for completions (25) and completion percentage (73.5 percent on 25 of 34). Wersching added early fourth-period field goals of 40 and 23 yards to increase the 49ers' lead to 26-14. The Bengals managed to score on an Anderson-to-Ross 3-yard pass with only 16 seconds remaining. Ross set a Super Bowl record with 11 receptions for 104 yards. Montana, the game's most valuable player, completed 14 of 22 passes for 157 yards. Cincinnati compiled 356 yards to San Francisco's 275, which marked the first time in Super Bowl history that the team that gained the most yards from scrimmage lost the game.

| | | | | | |
|---|---|---|---|---|---|
| **San Francisco (NFC)** | 7 | 13 | 0 | 6 | — 26 |
| **Cincinnati (AFC)** | 0 | 0 | 7 | 14 | — 21 |

SF — Montana 1 run (Wersching kick)
SF — Cooper 11 pass from Montana (Wersching kick)

SF — FG Wersching 22
SF — FG Wersching 26
Cin — Anderson 5 run (Breech kick)
Cin — Ross 4 pass from Anderson (Breech kick)
SF — FG Wersching 40
SF — FG Wersching 23
Cin — Ross 3 pass from Anderson (Breech kick)

## SUPER BOWL XV

Louisiana Superdome, New Orleans, Louisiana
January 25, 1981, Attendance: 76,135

**OAKLAND 27, PHILADELPHIA 10**—Jim Plunkett threw 3 touchdown passes, including an 80-yard strike to Kenny King, as the Raiders became the first wild-card team to win the Super Bowl. Plunkett's touchdown bomb to King—the longest play in Super Bowl history—gave Oakland a decisive 14-0 lead with nine seconds left in the first period. Linebacker Rod Martin had set up Oakland's first touchdown, a 2-yard reception by Cliff Branch, with a 17-yard interception return to the Eagles' 30-yard line. The Eagles never recovered from that early deficit, managing only a Tony Franklin field goal (30 yards) and an 8-yard touchdown pass from Ron Jaworski to Keith Krepfle. Plunkett, who became a starter in the sixth game of the season, completed 13 of 21 for 261 yards and was named the game's most valuable player. Oakland won 9 of 11 games with Plunkett starting, but that was good enough only for second place in the AFC West, although they tied division winner San Diego with an 11-5 record. The Raiders, who had previously won Super Bowl XI over Minnesota, had to win three playoff games to get to the championship game. Oakland defeated Houston 27-7 at home followed by road victories over Cleveland (14-12) and San Diego (34-27). Oakland's Mark van Eeghen was the game's leading rusher with 75 yards on 18 carries. Philadelphia's Wilbert Montgomery led all receivers with 6 receptions for 91 yards. Branch had 5 for 67 and Harold Carmichael of Philadelphia 5 for 83. Martin finished the game with 3 interceptions, a Super Bowl record.

| | | | | | | |
|---|---|---|---|---|---|---|
| **Oakland (AFC)** | 14 | 0 | 10 | 3 | — | 27 |
| **Philadelphia (NFC)** | 0 | 3 | 0 | 7 | — | 10 |

Oak — Branch 2 pass from Plunkett (Bahr kick)
Oak — King 80 pass from Plunkett (Bahr kick)
Phil — FG Franklin 30
Oak — Branch 29 pass from Plunkett (Bahr kick)
Oak — FG Bahr 46
Phil — Krepfle 8 pass from Jaworski (Franklin kick)
Oak — FG Bahr 35

## SUPER BOWL XIV

Rose Bowl, Pasadena, California
January 20, 1980, Attendance: 103,985

**PITTSBURGH 31, LOS ANGELES 19**—Terry Bradshaw completed 14 of 21 passes for 309 yards and set two passing records as the Steelers became the first team to win four Super Bowls. Despite 3 interceptions by the Rams, Bradshaw kept his poise and brought the Steelers from behind twice in the second half. Trailing 13-10 at halftime, Pittsburgh went ahead 17-13 when Bradshaw hit Lynn Swann with a 47-yard touchdown pass after 2:48 of the third quarter. On the Rams' next possession Vince Ferragamo, who completed 15 of 25 passes for 212 yards, responded with a 50-yard pass to Billy Waddy that moved Los Angeles from its 26 to the Steelers' 24. On the following play, Lawrence McCutcheon connected with Ron Smith on a halfback option pass that gave the Rams a 19-17 lead. On Pittsburgh's initial possession of the final period, Bradshaw lofted a 73-yard scoring pass to John Stallworth to put the Steelers in front to stay 24-19. Franco Harris scored on a 1-yard run later in the quarter to seal the verdict. A 45-yard pass from Bradshaw to Stallworth was the key play in the drive to Harris's score. Bradshaw, the game's most valuable player for the second straight year, set career Super Bowl records for most touchdown passes (9) and most passing yards (932). Larry Anderson gave the Steelers excellent field position throughout the game with 5 kickoff returns for a record 162 yards.

| | | | | | | |
|---|---|---|---|---|---|---|
| **Los Angeles (NFC)** | 7 | 6 | 6 | 0 | — | 19 |
| **Pittsburgh (AFC)** | 3 | 7 | 7 | 14 | — | 31 |

Pitt — FG Bahr 41
LA — Bryant 1 run (Corral kick)
Pitt — Harris 1 run (Bahr kick)
LA — FG Corral 31
LA — FG Corral 45
Pitt — Swann 47 pass from Bradshaw (Bahr kick)
LA — Smith 24 pass from McCutcheon (kick failed)
Pitt — Stallworth 73 pass from Bradshaw (Bahr kick)
Pitt — Harris 1 run (Bahr kick)

## SUPER BOWL XIII

Orange Bowl, Miami, Florida
January 21, 1979, Attendance: 79,484

**PITTSBURGH 35, DALLAS 31**—Terry Bradshaw threw a record 4 touchdown passes to lead the Steelers to victory. The Steelers became the first team to win three Super Bowls, mostly because of Bradshaw's accurate arm. Bradshaw, voted the game's most valuable player, completed 17 of 30 passes for 318 yards, a personal high. Four of those passes went for touchdowns—2 to John Stallworth and the third, with 26 seconds remaining in the second period, to Rocky Bleier for a 21-14 halftime lead. The Cowboys scored twice before intermission on Roger Staubach's 39-yard pass to Tony Hill and a 37-yard fumble return by linebacker Mike Hegman, who stole the ball from Bradshaw. The Steelers broke open the contest with 2 touchdowns in a span of 19 seconds midway through the final period. Franco Harris rambled 22 yards up the middle to give the Steelers a 28-17 lead with 7:10 left. Pittsburgh got the ball right back when Randy White fumbled the kickoff and Dennis Winston recovered for the Steelers. On first down, Bradshaw fired his fourth touchdown pass, an 18-yard pass to Lynn Swann to boost the Steelers' lead to 35-17 with 6:51 to play. The Cowboys refused to let the Steelers run away with the contest. Staubach connected with Billy Joe DuPree on a 7-yard scoring pass with 2:23 left. Then the Cowboys recovered an onside kick and Staubach took them in for another score, passing 4 yards to Butch Johnson with 22 seconds remaining. Bleier recovered another onside kick with 17 seconds left to seal the victory for the Steelers.

| | | | | | | |
|---|---|---|---|---|---|---|
| **Pittsburgh (AFC)** | 7 | 14 | 0 | 14 | — | 35 |
| **Dallas (NFC)** | 7 | 7 | 3 | 14 | — | 31 |

Pitt — Stallworth 28 pass from Bradshaw (Gerela kick)
Dall — Hill 39 pass from Staubach (Septien kick)
Dall — Hegman 37 fumble recovery return (Septien kick)
Pitt — Stallworth 75 pass from Bradshaw (Gerela kick)
Pitt — Bleier 7 pass from Bradshaw (Gerela kick)
Dall — FG Septien 27
Pitt — Harris 22 run (Gerela kick)
Pitt — Swann 18 pass from Bradshaw (Gerela kick)
Dall — DuPree 7 pass from Staubach (Septien kick)
Dall — B. Johnson 4 pass from Staubach (Septien kick)

## SUPER BOWL XII

Louisiana Superdome, New Orleans, Louisiana
January 15, 1978, Attendance: 75,583

**DALLAS 27, DENVER 10**—The Cowboys evened their Super Bowl record at 2-2 by defeating Denver before a sellout crowd of 75,583, plus 102,010,000 television viewers, the largest audience ever to watch a sporting event. Dallas converted 2 interceptions into 10 points and Efren Herrera added a 35-yard field goal for a 13-0 halftime advantage. In the third period Craig Morton engineered a drive to the Cowboys' 30 and Jim Turner's 47-yard field goal made the score 13-3. After an exchange of punts, Butch Johnson made a spectacular diving catch in the end zone to complete a 45-yard pass from Roger Staubach and put the Cowboys ahead 20-3. Following Rick Upchurch's 67-yard kickoff return, Norris Weese guided the Broncos to a touchdown to cut the Dallas lead to 20-10. Dallas clinched the victory when running back Robert Newhouse threw a 29-yard touchdown pass to Golden Richards with 7:04 remaining in the game. It was the first pass thrown by Newhouse since 1975. Harvey Martin and Randy White, who were named co-most valuable players, led the Cowboys' defense, which recovered 4 fumbles and intercepted 4 passes.

| | | | | | | |
|---|---|---|---|---|---|---|
| **Dallas (NFC)** | 10 | 3 | 7 | 7 | — | 27 |
| **Denver (AFC)** | 0 | 0 | 10 | 0 | — | 10 |

Dall — Dorsett 3 run (Herrera kick)
Dall — FG Herrera 35
Dall — FG Herrera 43
Den — FG Turner 47
Dall — Johnson 45 pass from Staubach (Herrera kick)
Den — Lytle 1 run (Turner kick)
Dall — Richards 29 pass from Newhouse (Herrera kick)

## SUPER BOWL XI

Rose Bowl, Pasadena, California
January 9, 1977, Attendance: 103,438

**OAKLAND 32, MINNESOTA 14**—The Raiders won their first NFL championship before a record Super Bowl crowd plus 81 million television viewers, the largest audience ever to watch a sporting event. The Raiders gained a record-breaking 429 yards, including running back Clarence Davis's 137 rushing yards. Wide receiver Fred Biletnikoff made 4 key receptions, which earned him the game's most valuable player trophy. Oakland scored on three successive possessions in the second quarter to build a 16-0 halftime lead. Errol Mann's 24-yard field goal opened the scoring, then the AFC champions put together drives of 64 and 35 yards, scoring on a 1-yard pass from Ken Stabler to Dave Casper and a 1-yard run by Pete Banaszak. The Raiders increased their lead to 19-0 on a 40-yard field goal in the third quarter, but Minnesota responded with a 12-play, 58-yard drive late in the period, with Fran Tarkenton passing 8 yards to wide receiver Sammy White to cut the deficit to 19-7. Two fourth-quarter interceptions clinched the title for the Raiders. One set up Banaszak's second touchdown run, the other resulted in cornerback Willie Brown's Super Bowl-record 75-yard interception return.

| | | | | | | |
|---|---|---|---|---|---|---|
| **Oakland (AFC)** | 0 | 16 | 3 | 13 | — | 32 |
| **Minnesota (NFC)** | 0 | 0 | 7 | 7 | — | 14 |

Oak — FG Mann 24
Oak — Casper 1 pass from Stabler (Mann kick)
Oak — Banaszak 1 run (kick failed)
Oak — FG Mann 40
Minn — S. White 8 pass from Tarkenton (Cox kick)
Oak — Banaszak 2 run (Mann kick)
Oak — Brown 75 interception return (kick failed)
Minn — Voigt 13 pass from Lee (Cox kick)

## SUPER BOWL X

Orange Bowl, Miami, Florida
January 18, 1976, Attendance: 80,187

**PITTSBURGH 21, DALLAS 17**—The Steelers won the Super Bowl for the second year in a row on Terry Bradshaw's 64-yard touchdown pass to Lynn Swann and an aggressive defense that snuffed out a late rally by the Cowboys with an end-zone interception on the final play of the game. In the fourth quarter, Pittsburgh ran on fourth down and gave up the ball on the Cowboys' 39 with 1:22 to play. Roger Staubach ran and passed for 2 first downs but his last desperation pass was picked off by Glen Edwards. Dallas's scoring was the result of 2 touchdown passes by Staubach, one to Drew Pearson for 29 yards and the other to Percy Howard for 34 yards. Toni Fritsch had a 36-yard field goal. The Steelers scored on 2 touchdown passes by Bradshaw, 1 to Randy Grossman for 7 yards and the long bomb to Swann. Roy Gerela had 36- and 18-yard field goals. Reggie Harrison blocked a punt through the end zone for a safety. Swann set a Super Bowl record by gaining 161 yards on his 4 receptions.

| | | | | | |
|---|---|---|---|---|---|
| **Dallas (NFC)** | 7 | 3 | 0 | 7 — | 17 |
| **Pittsburgh (AFC)** | 7 | 0 | 0 | 14 — | 21 |

Dall — D. Pearson 29 pass from Staubach (Fritsch kick)
Pitt — Grossman 7 pass from Bradshaw (Gerela kick)
Dall — FG Fritsch 36
Pitt — Safety, Harrison blocked Hoopes's punt through end zone
Pitt — FG Gerela 36
Pitt — FG Gerela 18
Pitt — Swann 64 pass from Bradshaw (kick failed)
Dall — P. Howard 34 pass from Staubach (Fritsch kick)

## SUPER BOWL IX

Tulane Stadium, New Orleans, Louisiana
January 12, 1975, Attendance: 80,997

**PITTSBURGH 16, MINNESOTA 6**—AFC champion Pittsburgh, in its initial Super Bowl appearance, and NFC champion Minnesota, making a third bid for its first Super Bowl title, struggled through a first half in which the only score was produced by the Steelers' defense when Dwight White downed Vikings' quarterback Fran Tarkenton in the end zone for a safety 7:49 into the second period. The Steelers forced another break and took advantage on the second-half kickoff when Minnesota's Bill Brown fumbled and Marv Kellum recovered for Pittsburgh on the Vikings' 30. After Rocky Bleier failed to gain on first down, Franco Harris carried 3 consecutive times for 24 yards, a loss of 3, and a 9-yard touchdown and a 9-0 lead. Though its offense was completely stymied by Pittsburgh's defense, Minnesota managed to move into a threatening position after 4:27 of the final period when Matt Blair blocked Bobby Walden's punt and Terry Brown recovered the ball in the end zone for a touchdown. Fred Cox's kick failed and the Steelers led 9-6. Pittsburgh wasted no time putting the victory away. The Steelers took the ensuing kickoff and marched 66 yards in 11 plays, climaxed by Terry Bradshaw's 4-yard scoring pass to Larry Brown with 3:31 left. Pittsburgh's defense permitted Minnesota only 119 yards total offense, including a Super Bowl low of 17 rushing yards. The Steelers, meanwhile, gained 333 yards, including Harris's record 158 yards on 34 carries.

| | | | | | |
|---|---|---|---|---|---|
| **Pittsburgh (AFC)** | 0 | 2 | 7 | 7 — | 16 |
| **Minnesota (NFC)** | 0 | 0 | 0 | 6 — | 6 |

Pitt — Safety, White downed Tarkenton in end zone
Pitt — Harris 9 run (Gerela kick)
Minn — T. Brown recovered blocked punt in end zone (kick failed)
Pitt — L. Brown 4 pass from Bradshaw (Gerela kick)

## SUPER BOWL VIII

Rice Stadium, Houston, Texas
January 13, 1974, Attendance: 71,882

**MIAMI 24, MINNESOTA 7**—The defending NFL champion Dolphins, representing the AFC for the third straight year, scored the first two times they had possession on marches of 62 and 56 yards while the Miami defense limited the Vikings to only seven plays in the first period. Larry Csonka climaxed the initial 10-play drive with a 5-yard touchdown bolt through right guard after 5:27 had elapsed. Four plays later, Miami began another 10-play scoring drive, which ended with Jim Kiick bursting 1 yard through the middle for another touchdown after 13:38 of the period. Garo Yepremian added a 28-yard field goal midway in the second period for a 17-0 Miami lead. Minnesota then drove from its 20 to a second-and-2 situation on the Miami 7 yard line with 1:18 left in the half. But on two plays, Miami limited Oscar Reed to 1 yard. On fourth-and-1 from the 6, Reed went over right tackle, but Dolphins middle linebacker Nick Buoniconti jarred the ball loose and Jake Scott recovered for Miami to halt the Minnesota threat. The Vikings were unable to muster enough offense in the second half to threaten the Dolphins. Csonka rushed 33 times for a Super Bowl-record 145 yards. Bob Griese of Miami completed 6 of 7 passes for 73 yards.

| | | | | | |
|---|---|---|---|---|---|
| **Minnesota (NFC)** | 0 | 0 | 0 | 7 — | 7 |
| **Miami (AFC)** | 14 | 3 | 7 | 0 — | 24 |

Mia — Csonka 5 run (Yepremian kick)
Mia — Kiick 1 run (Yepremian kick)
Mia — FG Yepremian 28
Mia — Csonka 2 run (Yepremian kick)
Minn — Tarkenton 4 run (Cox kick)

## SUPER BOWL VII

Memorial Coliseum, Los Angeles, California
January 14, 1973, Attendance: 90,182

**MIAMI 14, WASHINGTON 7**—The Dolphins played virtually perfect football in the first half as their defense permitted the Redskins to cross midfield only once and their offense turned good field position into 2 touchdowns. On its third possession, Miami opened its first scoring drive from the Dolphins' 37 yard line. An 18-yard pass from Bob Griese to Paul Warfield preceded by three plays Griese's 28-yard touchdown pass to Howard Twilley. After Washington moved from its 17 to the Miami 48 with two minutes remaining in the first half, Dolphins linebacker Nick Buoniconti intercepted a Billy Kilmer pass at the Miami 41 and returned it to the Washington 27. Jim Kiick ran for 3 yards, Larry Csonka for 3, Griese passed to Jim Mandich for 19, and Kiick gained 1 to the 1-yard line. With 18 seconds left until intermission, Kiick scored from the 1. Washington's only touchdown came with 2:07 left in the game and resulted from a misplayed field-goal attempt and fumble by Garo Yepremian, with the Redskins' Mike Bass picking the ball out of the air and running 49 yards for the score. Dolphins safety Jake Scott, who had 2 interceptions, including 1 in the end zone to kill a Redskins' drive, was voted the game's most valuable player.

| | | | | | |
|---|---|---|---|---|---|
| **Miami (AFC)** | 7 | 7 | 0 | 0 — | 14 |
| **Washington (NFC)** | 0 | 0 | 0 | 7 — | 7 |

Mia — Twilley 28 pass from Griese (Yepremian kick)
Mia — Kiick 1 run (Yepremian kick)
Wash — Bass 49 fumble recovery return (Knight kick)

## SUPER BOWL VI

Tulane Stadium, New Orleans, Louisiana
January 16, 1972, Attendance: 81,023

**DALLAS 24, MIAMI 3**—The Cowboys rushed for a record 252 yards and their defense limited the Dolphins to a low of 185 yards while not permitting a touchdown for the first time in Super Bowl history. Dallas converted Chuck Howley's recovery of Larry Csonka's first fumble of the season into a 3-0 advantage and led at halftime 10-3. After Dallas received the second-half kickoff, Duane Thomas led a 71-yard march in eight plays for a 17-3 margin. Howley intercepted Bob Griese's pass at the 50 and returned it to the Miami 9 early in the fourth period, and three plays later Roger Staubach passed 7 yards to Mike Ditka for the final touchdown. Thomas rushed for 95 yards and Walt Garrison gained 74. Staubach, voted the game's most valuable player, completed 12 of 19 passes for 119 yards and 2 touchdowns.

| | | | | | |
|---|---|---|---|---|---|
| **Dallas (NFC)** | 3 | 7 | 7 | 7 — | 24 |
| **Miami (AFC)** | 0 | 3 | 0 | 0 — | 3 |

Dall — FG Clark 9
Dall — Alworth 7 pass from Staubach (Clark kick)
Mia — FG Yepremian 31
Dall — D. Thomas 3 run (Clark kick)
Dall — Ditka 7 pass from Staubach (Clark kick)

## SUPER BOWL V

Orange Bowl, Miami, Florida
January 17, 1971, Attendance: 79,204

**BALTIMORE 16, DALLAS 13**—A 32-yard field goal by rookie kicker Jim O'Brien brought the Baltimore Colts a victory over the Dallas Cowboys in the final five seconds of Super Bowl V. The game between the champions of the AFC and NFC was played on artificial turf for the first time. Dallas led13-6 at the half but interceptions by Rick Volk and Mike Curtis set up a Baltimore touchdown and O'Brien's decisive kick in the fourth period. Earl Morrell relieved an injured Johnny Unitas late in the firsthalf, although Unitas completed the Colts' only scoring pass. It caromed off receiver Eddie Hinton's fingertips, off Dallas defensive back Mel Renfro, and finally settled into the grasp of John Mackey, who went 45 yards to score on a 75-yard play.

| | | | | | |
|---|---|---|---|---|---|
| **Baltimore (AFC)** | 0 | 6 | 0 | 10 — | 16 |
| **Dallas (NFC)** | 3 | 10 | 0 | 0 — | 13 |

Dall — FG Clark 14
Dall — FG Clark 30
Balt — Mackey 75 pass from Unitas (kick blocked)
Dall — Thomas 7 pass from Morton (Clark kick)
Balt — Nowatzke 2 run (O'Brien kick)
Balt — FG O'Brien 32

## SUPER BOWL IV

Tulane Stadium, New Orleans, Louisiana
January 11, 1970, Attendance: 80,562

**KANSAS CITY 23, MINNESOTA 7**—The AFL squared the Super Bowl at two games apiece with the NFL, building a 16-0 halftime lead behind Len Dawson's superb quarterbacking and a powerful defense. Dawson, the fourth consecutive quarterback to be chosen the Super Bowl's top player, called an almost flawless game, completing 12 of 17 passes and hitting Otis Taylor on a 46-yard play for the final Chiefs touchdown. The Kansas City defense limited Minnesota's strong rushing game to 67 yards and had 3 interceptions and 2 fumble recoveries. The crowd of 80,562 set a Super Bowl record, as did the gross receipts of $3,817,872.69.

| | | | | | |
|---|---|---|---|---|---|
| **Minnesota (NFL)** | 0 | 0 | 7 | 0 — | 7 |
| **Kansas City (AFL)** | 3 | 13 | 7 | 0 — | 23 |

KC — FG Stenerud 48
KC — FG Stenerud 32
KC — FG Stenerud 25
KC — Garrett 5 run (Stenerud kick)
Minn — Osborn 4 run (Cox kick)
KC — Taylor 46 pass from Dawson (Stenerud kick)

## SUPER BOWL III

Orange Bowl, Miami, Florida
January 12, 1969, Attendance: 75,389

**NEW YORK JETS 16, BALTIMORE 7**—Jets quarterback Joe Namath "guaranteed" victory on the Thursday before the game, then went out and led the AFL to its first Super Bowl victory over a Baltimore team that had lost only once in 16 games all season. Namath, chosen the outstanding player, completed 17 of 28 passes for 206 yards and directed a steady attack that dominated the NFL champions after the Jets' defense had intercepted Colts quarterback Earl Morrall 3 times in the first half. The Jets had 337 total yards, including 121 rushing yards by Matt Snell. Johnny Unitas, who had missed most of the season with a sore elbow, came off the bench and led Baltimore to its only touchdown late in the fourth quarter after New York led 16-0.

| | | | | | |
|---|---|---|---|---|---|
| **New York Jets (AFL)** | 0 | 7 | 6 | 3 — | 16 |
| **Baltimore (NFL)** | 0 | 0 | 0 | 7 — | 7 |

NYJ — Snell 4 run (Turner kick)
NYJ — FG Turner 32
NYJ — FG Turner 30
NYJ — FG Turner 9
Balt — Hill 1 run (Michaels kick)

## SUPER BOWL II

Orange Bowl, Miami, Florida
January 14, 1968, Attendance: 75,546

**GREEN BAY 33, OAKLAND 14**—Green Bay, after winning its third consecutive NFL championship, won the Super Bowl title for the second straight year, defeating the AFL champion Raiders in a game that drew the first $3-million gate in football history. Bart Starr again was chosen the game's most valuable player as he completed 13 of 24 passes for 202 yards and 1 touchdown and directed a Packers attack that was in control all the way after building a 16-7 halftime lead. Don Chandler kicked 4 field goals and all-pro cornerback Herb Adderley capped the Green Bay scoring with a 60-yard interception return. The game marked the last for Vince Lombardi as Packers coach, ending nine years at Green Bay in which he won six Western Conference championships, five NFL championships, and two Super Bowls.

| | | | | | |
|---|---|---|---|---|---|
| **Green Bay (NFL)** | 3 | 13 | 10 | 7 | — 33 |
| **Oakland (AFL)** | 0 | 7 | 0 | 7 | — 14 |

GB — FG Chandler 39
GB — FG Chandler 20
GB — Dowler 62 pass from Starr (Chandler kick)
Oak — Miller 23 pass from Lamonica (Blanda kick)
GB — FG Chandler 43
GB — Anderson 2 run (Chandler kick)
GB — FG Chandler 31
GB — Adderley 60 interception return (Chandler kick)
Oak — Miller 23 pass from Lamonica (Blanda kick)

## SUPER BOWL I

Memorial Coliseum, Los Angeles, California
January 15, 1967, Attendance: 61,946

**GREEN BAY 35, KANSAS CITY 10**—The Green Bay Packers opened the Super Bowl series by defeating the AFL champion Chiefs behind the passing of Bart Starr, the receiving of Max McGee, and a key interception by all-pro safety Willie Wood. Green Bay broke open the game with 3 second-half touchdowns, the first of which was set up by Wood's 50-yard return of an interception to the Chiefs' 5 yard line. McGee, filling in for ailing Boyd Dowler after having caught only 4 passes all season, caught 7 from Starr for 138 yards and 2 touchdowns. Elijah Pitts ran for two other scores. The Chiefs' 10 points came in the second quarter, the only touchdown on a 7-yard pass from Len Dawson to Curtis McClinton. Starr completed 16 of 23 passes for 250 yards and 2 touchdowns and was chosen the most valuable player. The Packers collected $15,000 per man and the Chiefs $7,500—the largest single-game shares in the history of team sports.

| | | | | | |
|---|---|---|---|---|---|
| **Kansas City (AFL)** | 0 | 10 | 0 | 0 | — 10 |
| **Green Bay (NFL)** | 7 | 7 | 14 | 7 | — 35 |

GB — McGee 37 pass from Starr (Chandler kick)
KC — McClinton 7 pass from Dawson (Mercer kick)
GB — Taylor 14 run (Chandler kick)
KC — FG Mercer 31
GB — Pitts 5 run (Chandler kick)
GB — McGee 13 pass from Starr (Chandler kick)
GB — Pitts 1 run (Chandler kick)

## AFC CHAMPIONSHIP GAME RESULTS

*Includes AFL Championship Games (1960-69)*

| Season | Date | Winner (Share) | Loser (Share) | Score | Site | Attendance |
|---|---|---|---|---|---|---|
| 1993 | Jan. 23 | Buffalo ($23,500) | Kansas City ($23,500) | 30-13 | Buffalo | 76,642 |
| 1992 | Jan. 17 | Buffalo ($18,000) | Miami ($18,000) | 29-10 | Miami | 72,703 |
| 1991 | Jan. 12 | Buffalo ($18,000) | Denver ($18,000) | 10-7 | Buffalo | 80,272 |
| 1990 | Jan. 20 | Buffalo ($18,000) | L.A. Raiders ($18,000) | 51-3 | Buffalo | 80,325 |
| 1989 | Jan. 14 | Denver ($18,000) | Cleveland ($18,000) | 37-21 | Denver | 76,046 |
| 1988 | Jan. 8 | Cincinnati ($18,000) | Buffalo ($18,000) | 21-10 | Cincinnati | 59,747 |
| 1987 | Jan. 17 | Denver ($18,000) | Cleveland ($18,000) | 38-33 | Denver | 76,197 |
| 1986 | Jan. 11 | Denver ($18,000) | Cleveland ($18,000) | 23-20* | Cleveland | 79,973 |
| 1985 | Jan. 12 | New England ($18,000) | Miami ($18,000) | 31-14 | Miami | 75,662 |
| 1984 | Jan. 6 | Miami ($18,000) | Pittsburgh ($18,000) | 45-28 | Miami | 76,029 |
| 1983 | Jan. 8 | L.A. Raiders ($18,000) | Seattle ($18,000) | 30-14 | Los Angeles | 91,445 |
| 1982 | Jan. 23 | Miami ($18,000) | N.Y. Jets ($18,000) | 14-0 | Miami | 67,396 |
| 1981 | Jan. 10 | Cincinnati ($9,000) | San Diego ($9,000) | 27-7 | Cincinnati | 46,302 |
| 1980 | Jan. 11 | Oakland ($9,000) | San Diego ($9,000) | 34-27 | San Diego | 52,675 |
| 1979 | Jan. 6 | Pittsburgh ($9,000) | Houston ($9,000) | 27-13 | Pittsburgh | 50,475 |
| 1978 | Jan. 7 | Pittsburgh ($9,000) | Houston ($9,000) | 34-5 | Pittsburgh | 50,725 |
| 1977 | Jan. 1 | Denver ($9,000) | Oakland ($9,000) | 20-17 | Denver | 75,044 |
| 1976 | Dec. 26 | Oakland ($8,500) | Pittsburgh ($5,500) | 24-7 | Oakland | 53,821 |
| 1975 | Jan. 4 | Pittsburgh ($8,500) | Oakland ($5,500) | 16-10 | Pittsburgh | 50,609 |
| 1974 | Dec. 29 | Pittsburgh ($8,500) | Oakland ($5,500) | 24-13 | Oakland | 53,800 |
| 1973 | Dec. 30 | Miami ($8,500) | Oakland ($5,500) | 27-10 | Miami | 79,325 |
| 1972 | Dec. 31 | Miami ($8,500) | Pittsburgh ($5,500) | 21-17 | Pittsburgh | 50,845 |
| 1971 | Jan. 2 | Miami ($8,500) | Baltimore ($5,500) | 21-0 | Miami | 76,622 |
| 1970 | Jan. 3 | Baltimore ($8,500) | Oakland ($5,500) | 27-17 | Baltimore | 54,799 |
| 1969 | Jan. 4 | Kansas City ($7,755) | Oakland ($6,252) | 17-7 | Oakland | 53,564 |
| 1968 | Dec. 29 | N.Y. Jets ($7,007) | Oakland ($5,349) | 27-23 | New York | 62,627 |
| 1967 | Dec. 31 | Oakland ($6,321) | Houston ($4,996) | 40-7 | Oakland | 53,330 |
| 1966 | Jan. 1 | Kansas City ($5,309) | Buffalo ($3,799) | 31-7 | Buffalo | 42,080 |
| 1965 | Dec. 26 | Buffalo ($5,189) | San Diego ($3,447) | 23-0 | San Diego | 30,361 |
| 1964 | Dec. 26 | Buffalo ($2,668) | San Diego ($1,738) | 20-7 | Buffalo | 40,242 |
| 1963 | Jan. 5 | San Diego ($2,498) | Boston ($1,596) | 51-10 | San Diego | 30,127 |
| 1962 | Dec. 23 | Dallas ($2,206) | Houston ($1,471) | 20-17* | Houston | 37,981 |
| 1961 | Dec. 24 | Houston ($1,792) | San Diego ($1,111) | 10-3 | San Diego | 29,556 |
| 1960 | Jan. 1 | Houston ($1,025) | L.A. Chargers ($718) | 24-16 | Houston | 32,183 |

**Sudden death overtime.*

## AFC CHAMPIONSHIP GAME COMPOSITE STANDINGS

| | W | L | Pct. | Pts. | OP |
|---|---|---|---|---|---|
| Cincinnati Bengals | 2 | 0 | 1.000 | 48 | 17 |
| Denver Broncos | 4 | 1 | .800 | 125 | 101 |
| Buffalo Bills | 6 | 2 | .750 | 180 | 92 |
| Kansas City Chiefs* | 3 | 1 | .750 | 81 | 61 |
| Miami Dolphins | 5 | 2 | .714 | 152 | 115 |
| Pittsburgh Steelers | 4 | 3 | .571 | 153 | 131 |
| Baltimore Colts | 1 | 1 | .500 | 27 | 38 |
| New England Patriots** | 1 | 1 | .500 | 41 | 65 |
| New York Jets | 1 | 1 | .500 | 27 | 37 |
| Houston Oilers | 2 | 4 | .333 | 76 | 140 |
| Oakland/L.A. Raiders | 4 | 8 | .333 | 228 | 264 |
| San Diego Chargers*** | 1 | 6 | .143 | 111 | 148 |
| Seattle Seahawks | 0 | 1 | .000 | 14 | 30 |
| Cleveland Browns | 0 | 3 | .000 | 74 | 98 |

**One game played when franchise was in Dallas (Texans). (Won 20-17)*
***One game played when franchise was in Boston. (Lost 51-10)*
****One game played when franchise was in Los Angeles. (Lost 24-16)*

## 1993 AFC CHAMPIONSHIP GAME

Rich Stadium, Buffalo, New York
January 23, 1994, Attendance: 76,642

**BUFFALO 30, KANSAS CITY 13**—Thurman Thomas rushed for 186 yards and 3 touchdowns as the Bills qualified for an unprecedented fourth consecutive Super Bowl. Thomas, who ran for 129 yards in the first two quarters, helped stake Buffalo to a 20-6 advantage at intermission by scoring on touchdown runs of 12 and 3 yards. The Chiefs had an opportunity to cut that deficit in half, marching 75 yards to the Bills' 5-yard line in the closing seconds of the first half. But Joe Montana's pass to a wide-open Kimble Anders near the goal line bounced off the running back's hands and was intercepted in the end zone by Buffalo safety Henry Jones. Montana, who completed only 9 of 23 passes for 125 yards, sat out most of the second half after suffering a concussion on the third play of the third quarter. Backup Dave Krieg, who completed 16 of 29 passes for 198 yards, came on and led a 90-yard touchdown drive that pulled Kansas City within 20-13 late in the third quarter. But Buffalo answered with a 14-play, 79-yard march capped by Steve Christie's 18-yard field goal 3:05 into the fourth quarter. Thomas's third touchdown, a 3-yard run with 5:30 remaining, put the game out of reach. Thomas averaged 5.6 yards on his 33 carries as the Bills overwhelmed the Chiefs on the ground, outrushing them 229 yards to 52.

| Kansas City (13) | Offense | Buffalo (30) |
|---|---|---|
| J.J. Birden | WR | Don Beebe |
| John Alt | LT | John Fina |
| David Szott | LG | Glenn Parker |
| Tim Grunhard | C | Kent Hull |
| Will Shields | RG | John Davis |
| Rickey Siglar | RT | Howard Ballard |
| Jonathan Hayes | TE | Pete Metzelaars |
| Keith Cash | TE-WR | Andre Reed |
| Joe Montana | QB | Jim Kelly |
| Marcus Allen | RB | Thurman Thomas |
| Willie Davis | WR | Bill Brooks |
| | **Defense** | |
| Neil Smith | LE | Phil Hansen |
| Joe Phillips | NT | Jeff Wright |
| Dan Saleaumua | RE | Bruce Smith |
| Derrick Thomas | LOLB | Cornelius Bennett |
| Martin Bayless | MLB-LILB | Marvcus Patton |
| Lonnie Marts | ROLB-RILB | Mark Maddox |
| Charles Mincy | DB-ROLB | Darryl Talley |
| Albert Lewis | LCB | Mickey Washington |
| Jay Taylor | RCB | Nate Odomes |
| Bruce Pickens | SS | Henry Jones |
| Kevin Ross | FS | Mark Kelso |

### SUBSTITUTIONS

**Kansas City**—Offense: K—Nick Lowery. P—Bryan Barker. QB—Dave Krieg. RB—Kimble Anders, Todd McNair, John Stephens, Ernie Thompson. WR—Tim Barnett, Danan Hughes, Fred Jones. T—Derrick Graham, Joe Valerio. G—Danny Villa. Defense: E—Pellom McDaniels. DT—Darren Mickell, Tim Newton. LB—Erick Anderson, Tracy Rogers, Tracy Simien, Santo Stephens. S—Bennie Thompson, Tim Watson, Felix Wright. DNP: None.

**Buffalo**—Offense: K—Steve Christie. P—Chris Mohr. QB—Frank Reich. RB—Kenneth Davis, Carwell Gardner. WR—Russell Copeland, Steve Tasker. TE—Keith McKeller. T—Jerry Crafts. G—Jim Ritcher. C—Mike Devlin, Adam Lingner. Defense: E—Oliver Barnett, Mark Pike. NT—Mike Lodish. LB—Monty Brown, Keith Goganious, Richard Harvey. CB—Thomas Smith, James Williams. S—Matt Darby, Kurt Schulz. DNP: RB—Nate Turner.

### OFFICIALS

Referee—Johnny Grier. Umpire—Ron Botchan. Head Linesman—Ron Phares. Line Judge—Jim Quirk. Back Judge—Dick Creed. Field Judge—Phil Luckett. Side Judge—Tom Fincken.

### SCORING

| | | | | | | |
|---|---|---|---|---|---|---|
| **Kansas City** | 6 | 0 | 7 | 0 | – | 13 |
| **Buffalo** | 7 | 13 | 0 | 10 | – | 30 |

| | | |
|---|---|---|
| Buff | — | Thomas 12 run (Christie kick) |
| KC | — | FG Lowery 31 |
| KC | — | FG Lowery 31 |
| Buff | — | Thomas 3 run (Christie kick) |
| Buff | — | FG Christie 23 |
| Buff | — | FG Christie 25 |
| KC | — | Allen 1 run (Lowery kick) |
| Buff | — | FG Christie 18 |
| Buff | — | Thomas 3 run (Christie kick) |

### TEAM STATISTICS

| | Kansas City | Buffalo |
|---|---|---|
| Total First Downs | 22 | 30 |
| Rushing | 3 | 17 |
| Passing | 18 | 9 |
| Penalty | 1 | 4 |
| Total Net Yardage | 338 | 389 |
| Total Offensive Plays | 77 | 73 |
| Average Gain per Offensive Play | 4.4 | 5.3 |
| Rushes | 21 | 46 |

## PLAYOFF GAMES SUMMARIES

| | | |
|---|---|---|
| Yards Gained Rushing (Net) | 52 | 229 |
| Average Yards per Rush | 2.5 | 5.0 |
| Passes Attempted | 52 | 27 |
| Passes Completed | 25 | 17 |
| Had Intercepted | 2 | 0 |
| Tackled Attempting to Pass | 4 | 0 |
| Yards Lost Attempting to Pass | 37 | 0 |
| Yards Gained Passing (Net) | 286 | 160 |
| Punts | 6 | 4 |
| Average Distance | 40.8 | 33.3 |
| Punt Returns | 1 | 5 |
| Punt Return Yardage | 11 | 70 |
| Kickoff Returns | 5 | 4 |
| Kickoff Return Yardage | 89 | 68 |
| Interception Return Yardage | 0 | 15 |
| Total Return Yardage | 100 | 153 |
| Fumbles | 1 | 1 |
| Own Fumbles Recovered | 1 | 0 |
| Opponents Fumbles Recovered | 1 | 0 |
| Penalties | 6 | 2 |
| Yards Penalized | 29 | 10 |
| Total Points Scored | 13 | 30 |
| Touchdowns | 1 | 3 |
| Rushing | 1 | 3 |
| Passing | 0 | 0 |
| Returns | 0 | 0 |
| Extra Points | 1 | 3 |
| Field Goals | 2 | 3 |
| Field Goals Attempted | 2 | 3 |
| Safeties | 0 | 0 |
| Third-Down Efficiency | 7/17 | 5/12 |
| Fourth-Down Efficiency | 1/1 | 0/0 |
| Time of Possession | 29:20 | 30:40 |

**INDIVIDUAL STATISTICS**

**Rushing**

| **Kansas City** | **No.** | **Yds.** | **LG** | **TD** |
|---|---|---|---|---|
| Allen | 18 | 50 | 24 | 1 |
| Anders | 2 | 1 | 3 | 0 |
| Montana | 1 | 1 | 1 | 0 |
| **Buffalo** | **No.** | **Yds.** | **LG** | **TD** |
| Thomas | 33 | 186 | 33 | 3 |
| K. Davis | 10 | 32 | 15 | 0 |
| Reed | 1 | 8 | 8 | 0 |
| Kelly | 2 | 3 | 4 | 0 |

**Passing**

| **Kansas City** | **Att.** | **Comp.** | **Yds.** | **TD** | **Int.** |
|---|---|---|---|---|---|
| Krieg | 29 | 16 | 198 | 0 | 1 |
| Montana | 23 | 9 | 125 | 0 | 1 |
| **Buffalo** | **Att.** | **Comp.** | **Yds.** | **TD** | **Int.** |
| Kelly | 27 | 17 | 160 | 0 | 0 |

**Receiving**

| **Kansas City** | **No.** | **Yds.** | **LG** | **TD** |
|---|---|---|---|---|
| Cash | 6 | 87 | 19 | 0 |
| W. Davis | 5 | 57 | 17 | 0 |
| Birden | 4 | 60 | 26 | 0 |
| Allen | 2 | 36 | 27 | 0 |
| McNair | 2 | 33 | 31 | 0 |
| Hayes | 2 | 14 | 10 | 0 |
| E. Thompson | 1 | 12 | 12 | 0 |
| Hughes | 1 | 11 | 11 | 0 |
| Anders | 1 | 7 | 7 | 0 |
| Szott | 1 | 6 | 6 | 0 |
| **Buffalo** | **No.** | **Yds.** | **LG** | **TD** |
| Reed | 4 | 49 | 28 | 0 |
| Brooks | 4 | 34 | 11 | 0 |
| Metzelaars | 4 | 29 | 12 | 0 |
| Thomas | 2 | 22 | 15 | 0 |
| Beebe | 2 | 19 | 11 | 0 |
| McKeller | 1 | 7 | 7 | 0 |

**Interceptions**

| **Kansas City** | **No.** | **Yds.** | **LG** | **TD** |
|---|---|---|---|---|
| None | | | | |
| **Buffalo** | **No.** | **Yds.** | **LG** | **TD** |
| Jones | 1 | 15 | 15 | 0 |
| Williams | 1 | 0 | 0 | 0 |

**Punting**

| **Kansas City** | **No.** | **Avg.** | **LG** | **Blk.** |
|---|---|---|---|---|
| Barker | 6 | 40.8 | 51 | 0 |
| **Buffalo** | **No.** | **Avg.** | **LG** | **Blk.** |
| Mohr | 4 | 33.3 | 41 | 0 |

**Punt Returns**

| **Kansas City** | **No.** | **FC** | **Yds.** | **LG** | **TD** |
|---|---|---|---|---|---|
| Hughes | 1 | 1 | 11 | 11 | 0 |
| **Buffalo** | **No.** | **FC** | **Yds.** | **LG** | **TD** |
| Copeland | 5 | 0 | 70 | 26 | 0 |

**Kickoff Returns**

| **Kansas City** | **No.** | **Yds.** | **LG** | **TD** |
|---|---|---|---|---|
| J. Stephens | 5 | 89 | 31 | 0 |
| **Buffalo** | **No.** | **Yds.** | **LG** | **TD** |
| Copeland | 4 | 68 | 22 | 0 |

### NFC CHAMPIONSHIP GAME RESULTS

*Includes NFL Championship Games (1933-69)*

| Season | Date | Winner (Share) | Loser (Share) | Score | Site | Attendance |
|---|---|---|---|---|---|---|
| 1993 | Jan. 23 | Dallas ($23,500) | San Francisco ($23,500) | 38-21 | Dallas | 64,902 |
| 1992 | Jan. 17 | Dallas ($18,000) | San Francisco ($18,000) | 30-20 | San Francisco | 64,920 |
| 1991 | Jan. 12 | Washington ($18,000) | Detroit ($18,000) | 41-10 | Washington | 55,585 |
| 1990 | Jan. 20 | N.Y. Giants ($18,000) | San Francisco ($18,000) | 15-13 | San Francisco | 65,750 |
| 1989 | Jan. 14 | San Francisco ($18,000) | L.A. Rams ($18,000) | 30-3 | San Francisco | 65,634 |
| 1988 | Jan. 8 | San Francisco ($18,000) | Chicago ($18,000) | 28-3 | Chicago | 66,946 |
| 1987 | Jan. 17 | Washington ($18,000) | Minnesota ($18,000) | 17-10 | Washington | 55,212 |
| 1986 | Jan. 11 | New York Giants ($18,000) | Washington ($18,000) | 17-0 | East Rutherford | 76,891 |
| 1985 | Jan. 12 | Chicago ($18,000) | L.A. Rams ($18,000) | 24-0 | Chicago | 66,030 |
| 1984 | Jan. 6 | San Francisco ($18,000) | Chicago ($18,000) | 23-0 | San Francisco | 61,336 |
| 1983 | Jan. 8 | Washington ($18,000) | San Francisco ($18,000) | 24-21 | Washington | 55,363 |
| 1982 | Jan. 22 | Washington ($18,000) | Dallas ($18,000) | 31-17 | Washington | 55,045 |
| 1981 | Jan. 10 | San Francisco ($9,000) | Dallas ($9,000) | 28-27 | San Francisco | 60,525 |
| 1980 | Jan. 11 | Philadelphia ($9,000) | Dallas ($9,000) | 20-7 | Philadelphia | 71,522 |
| 1979 | Jan. 6 | Los Angeles ($9,000) | Tampa Bay ($9,000) | 9-0 | Tampa Bay | 72,033 |
| 1978 | Jan. 7 | Dallas ($9,000) | Los Angeles ($9,000) | 28-0 | Los Angeles | 71,086 |
| 1977 | Jan. 1 | Dallas ($9,000) | Minnesota ($9,000) | 23-6 | Dallas | 64,293 |
| 1976 | Dec. 26 | Minnesota ($8,500) | Los Angeles ($5,500) | 24-13 | Minnesota | 48,379 |
| 1975 | Jan. 4 | Dallas ($8,500) | Los Angeles ($5,500) | 37-7 | Los Angeles | 88,919 |
| 1974 | Dec. 29 | Minnesota ($8,500) | Los Angeles ($5,500) | 14-10 | Minnesota | 48,444 |
| 1973 | Dec. 30 | Minnesota ($8,500) | Dallas ($5,500) | 27-10 | Dallas | 64,422 |
| 1972 | Dec. 31 | Washington ($8,500) | Dallas ($5,500) | 26-3 | Washington | 53,129 |
| 1971 | Jan. 2 | Dallas ($8,500) | San Francisco ($5,500) | 14-3 | Dallas | 63,409 |
| 1970 | Jan. 3 | Dallas ($8,500) | San Francisco ($5,500) | 17-10 | San Francisco | 59,364 |
| 1969 | Jan. 4 | Minnesota ($7,930) | Cleveland ($5,118) | 27-7 | Minnesota | 46,503 |
| 1968 | Dec. 29 | Baltimore ($9,306) | Cleveland ($5,963) | 34-0 | Cleveland | 78,410 |
| 1967 | Dec. 31 | Green Bay ($7,950) | Dallas ($5,299) | 21-17 | Green Bay | 50,861 |
| 1966 | Jan. 1 | Green Bay ($9,813) | Dallas ($6,527) | 34-27 | Dallas | 74,152 |
| 1965 | Jan. 2 | Green Bay ($7,819) | Cleveland ($5,288) | 23-12 | Green Bay | 50,777 |
| 1964 | Dec. 27 | Cleveland ($8,052) | Baltimore ($5,571) | 27-0 | Cleveland | 79,544 |
| 1963 | Dec. 29 | Chicago ($5,899) | New York ($4,218) | 14-10 | Chicago | 45,801 |
| 1962 | Dec. 30 | Green Bay ($5,888) | New York ($4,166) | 16-7 | New York | 64,892 |
| 1961 | Dec. 31 | Green Bay ($5,195) | New York ($3,339) | 37-0 | Green Bay | 39,029 |
| 1960 | Dec. 26 | Philadelphia ($5,116) | Green Bay ($3,105) | 17-13 | Philadelphia | 67,325 |
| 1959 | Dec. 27 | Baltimore ($4,674) | New York ($3,083) | 31-16 | Baltimore | 57,545 |
| 1958 | Dec. 28 | Baltimore ($4,718) | New York ($3,111) | 23-17* | New York | 64,185 |
| 1957 | Dec. 29 | Detroit ($4,295) | Cleveland ($2,750) | 59-14 | Detroit | 55,263 |
| 1956 | Dec. 30 | New York ($3,779) | Chi. Bears ($2,485) | 47-7 | New York | 56,836 |
| 1955 | Dec. 26 | Cleveland ($3,508) | Los Angeles ($2,316) | 38-14 | Los Angeles | 85,693 |
| 1954 | Dec. 26 | Cleveland ($2,478) | Detroit ($1,585) | 56-10 | Cleveland | 43,827 |
| 1953 | Dec. 27 | Detroit ($2,424) | Cleveland ($1,654) | 17-16 | Detroit | 54,577 |
| 1952 | Dec. 28 | Detroit ($2,274) | Cleveland ($1,712) | 17-7 | Cleveland | 50,934 |

| Season | Date | Winner (Share) | Loser (Share) | Score | Site | Attendance |
|---|---|---|---|---|---|---|
| 1951 | Dec. 23 | Los Angeles ($2,108) | Cleveland ($1,483) | 24-17 | Los Angeles | 57,522 |
| 1950 | Dec. 24 | Cleveland ($1,113) | Los Angeles ($686) | 30-28 | Cleveland | 29,751 |
| 1949 | Dec. 18 | Philadelphia ($1,094) | Los Angeles ($739) | 14-0 | Los Angeles | 27,980 |
| 1948 | Dec. 19 | Philadelphia ($1,540) | Chi. Cardinals ($874) | 7-0 | Philadelphia | 36,309 |
| 1947 | Dec. 28 | Chi. Cardinals ($1,132) | Philadelphia ($754) | 28-21 | Chicago | 30,759 |
| 1946 | Dec. 15 | Chi. Bears ($1,975) | New York ($1,295) | 24-14 | New York | 58,346 |
| 1945 | Dec. 16 | Cleveland ($1,469) | Washington ($902) | 15-14 | Cleveland | 32,178 |
| 1944 | Dec. 17 | Green Bay ($1,449) | New York ($814) | 14-7 | New York | 46,016 |
| 1943 | Dec. 26 | Chi. Bears ($1,146) | Washington ($765) | 41-21 | Chicago | 34,320 |
| 1942 | Dec. 13 | Washington ($965) | Chi. Bears ($637) | 14-6 | Washington | 36,006 |
| 1941 | Dec. 21 | Chi. Bears ($430) | New York ($288) | 37-9 | Chicago | 13,341 |
| 1940 | Dec. 8 | Chi. Bears ($873) | Washington ($606) | 73-0 | Washington | 36,034 |
| 1939 | Dec. 10 | Green Bay ($703.97) | New York ($455.57) | 27-0 | Milwaukee | 32,279 |
| 1938 | Dec. 11 | New York ($504.45) | Green Bay ($368.81) | 23-17 | New York | 48,120 |
| 1937 | Dec. 12 | Washington ($225.90) | Chi. Bears ($127.78) | 28-21 | Chicago | 15,870 |
| 1936 | Dec. 13 | Green Bay ($250) | Boston ($180) | 21-6 | New York | 29,545 |
| 1935 | Dec. 15 | Detroit ($313.35) | New York ($200.20) | 26-7 | Detroit | 15,000 |
| 1934 | Dec. 9 | New York ($621) | Chi. Bears ($414.02) | 30-13 | New York | 35,059 |
| 1933 | Dec. 17 | Chi. Bears ($210.34) | New York ($140.22) | 23-21 | Chicago | 26,000 |

*Sudden death overtime.*

## NFC CHAMPIONSHIP GAME COMPOSITE STANDINGS

| | W | L | Pct. | Pts. | OP |
|---|---|---|---|---|---|
| Green Bay Packers | 8 | 2 | .800 | 223 | 116 |
| Philadelphia Eagles | 4 | 1 | .800 | 79 | 48 |
| Baltimore Colts | 3 | 1 | .750 | 88 | 60 |
| Detroit Lions | 4 | 2 | .667 | 139 | 141 |
| Minnesota Vikings | 4 | 2 | .667 | 108 | 80 |
| Washington Redskins* | 7 | 5 | .583 | 222 | 255 |
| Chicago Bears | 7 | 6 | .538 | 286 | 245 |
| Dallas Cowboys | 7 | 7 | .500 | 295 | 254 |
| Phoenix Cardinals** | 1 | 1 | .500 | 28 | 28 |
| San Francisco 49ers | 4 | 6 | .400 | 197 | 171 |
| Cleveland Browns | 4 | 7 | .364 | 224 | 253 |
| New York Giants | 5 | 11 | .313 | 240 | 322 |
| Los Angeles Rams*** | 3 | 9 | .250 | 123 | 270 |
| Tampa Bay Buccaneers | 0 | 1 | .000 | 0 | 9 |

*One game played when franchise was in Boston. (Lost 21-6)
**Both games played when franchise was in Chicago. (Won 28-21, lost 7-0)
***One game played when franchise was in Cleveland. (Won 15-14)

## 1993 NFC CHAMPIONSHIP GAME

Texas Stadium, Irving, Texas
January 23, 1994, Attendance: 64,902

**DALLAS 38, SAN FRANCISCO 21**—Troy Aikman threw 2 touchdown passes and Emmitt Smith scored twice as the Cowboys scored on four of their first five possessions and easily handled the 49ers 38-21 to win the NFC title. Dallas struck quickly, taking the opening kickoff and marching 75 yards in 11 plays to Smith's 5-yard touchdown run 6:19 into the game. San Francisco tied it when running back Tom Rathman caught a 7-yard touchdown pass from Steve Young on the first play of the second quarter, but the Cowboys broke open the game by scoring touchdowns the next three times they had the ball. They countered Rathman's score with an 11-play, 80-yard drive capped by Daryl Johnston's 4-yard touchdown run 5:12 into the second quarter. Three plays later, safety Thomas Everett intercepted a pass that was tipped by San Francisco's John Taylor, and returned it 14 yards to the 49ers' 24-yard line. It took Dallas only four plays to convert that into Aikman's 11-yard touchdown pass to Smith 6:04 before intermission. Aikman teamed with tight end Jay Novacek on a 19-yard touchdown pass in the final minute of the first half to give the Cowboys a 28-7 lead. San Francisco pulled within 14 points on a 4-yard touchdown run by Ricky Watters, but Dallas put the game out of reach when Bernie Kosar teamed with Alvin Harper on a 42-yard touchdown pass with 2:24 remaining in the third quarter. Kosar, in the game because Aikman suffered a concussion early in the second half, kept the drive alive with a 12-yard completion to Michael Irvin on third-and-9 from the Cowboys' 19, and also had a 20-yard completion to Novacek on the 7-play, 82-yard drive. Aikman, who did not return, completed 14 of 18 passes for 177 yards. Kosar was 5 of 9 for 83 yards. Smith rushed for 88 yards on 23 carries and caught 7 passes for 85 yards. 49ers quarterback Steve Young completed 27 of 45 passes for 287 yards and led his team with 38 rushing yards. But he also suffered 4 sacks and was supported by only 46 yards from San Francisco's running backs. Dallas, which beat the 49ers 30-20 in the 1992 NFC Championship Game, qualified for its seventh Super Bowl, extending its NFL record. San Francisco lost in the NFC title game for the third time in four years.

| San Francisco (21) | Offense | Dallas (38) |
|---|---|---|
| John Taylor | WR | Alvin Harper |
| Steve Wallace | LT | Mark Tuinei |
| Guy McIntyre | LG | Nate Newton |
| Jesse Sapolu | C | John Gesek |
| Ralph Tamm | RG | Kevin Gogan |
| Harris Barton | RT | Erik Williams |
| Brent Jones | TE | Jay Novacek |
| Jerry Rice | WR | Michael Irvin |
| Steve Young | QB | Troy Aikman |
| Ricky Watters | RB | Emmitt Smith |
| Tom Rathman | FB | Daryl Johnston |
| | Defense | |
| Dennis Brown | LE | Tony Tolbert |
| Dana Stubblefield | LT | Tony Casillas |
| Ted Washington | RT | Leon Lett |
| Karl Wilson | RE | Charles Haley |
| John Johnson | LLB | Dixon Edwards |
| Michael Walter | MLB | Ken Norton |
| Bill Romanowski | RLB | Darrin Smith |
| Eric Davis | LCB | Kevin Smith |
| Don Griffin | RCB | Larry Brown |
| Tim McDonald | SS | Darren Woodson |
| Merton Hanks | FS | Thomas Everett |

**SUBSTITUTIONS**

**San Francisco**—Offense: K—Mike Cofer. P—Klaus Wilmsmeyer. QB—Steve Bono. RB—Dexter Carter, Amp Lee, Marc Logan. WR—Sanjay Beach, Odessa Turner. TE—John Brandes, Jamie Williams. T—Harry Boatswain. G—Brian Bollinger, Chris Dalman. Defense: E—Larry Roberts, Artie Smith, Troy Wilson. LB—Ravin Caldwell, Antonio Goss,Todd Kelly, Larry Kelm. CB—Michael McGruder. S—Dana Hall, Damien Russell. DNP: None.

**Dallas**—Offense: K—Eddie Murray. P—John Jett. QB—Bernie Kosar. RB—Derrick Gainer, Derrick Lassic. WR—Kevin Williams. TE—Scott Galbraith. C—Frank Cornish. T—Dale Hellestrae. Defense: E—Jim Jeffcoat. T—Jimmie Jones, Russell Maryland. DB—Bill Bates, Joe Fishback, Brock Marion, Elvis Patterson. LB—Robert Jones, Godfrey Myles, Matt Vanderbeek. CB—Dave Thomas. S—Kenneth Gant, James Washington. DNP: RB—Lincoln Coleman.

**OFFICIALS**

Referee—Jerry Markbreit. Umpire—Bob Boylston. Head Linesman—John Schleyer. Line Judge—Dale Orem. Back Judge—Jim Poole. Field Judge—Donnie Hampton. Side Judge—Mike Carey.

**SCORING**

| | | | | | | |
|---|---|---|---|---|---|---|
| **San Francisco** | 0 | 7 | 7 | 7 | — | 21 |
| **Dallas** | 7 | 21 | 7 | 3 | — | 38 |

Dall — E. Smith 5 run (Murray kick)
SF — Rathman 7 pass from Young (Cofer kick)
Dall — Johnston 4 run (Murray kick)
Dall — E. Smith 11 pass from Aikman (Murray kick)
Dall — Novacek 19 pass from Aikman (Murray kick)
SF — Watters 4 run (Cofer kick)
Dall — Harper 42 pass from Kosar (Murray kick)
Dall — FG Murray 50
SF — Young 1 run (Cofer kick)

**TEAM STATISTICS**

| | San Francisco | Dallas |
|---|---|---|
| Total First Downs | 23 | 24 |
| Rushing | 5 | 9 |
| Passing | 15 | 15 |
| Penalty | 3 | 0 |
| Total Net Yardage | 359 | 377 |
| Total Offensive Plays | 70 | 63 |
| Average Gain per Offensive Play | 5.1 | 6.0 |
| Rushes | 21 | 33 |
| Yards Gained Rushing (Net) | 84 | 124 |
| Average Yards per Rush | 4.0 | 3.8 |
| Passes Attempted | 45 | 28 |
| Passes Completed | 27 | 19 |
| Had Intercepted | 1 | 0 |
| Tackled Attempting to Pass | 4 | 2 |
| Yards Lost Attempting to Pass | 12 | 7 |
| Yards Gained Passing (Net) | 275 | 253 |
| Punts | 4 | 4 |
| Average Distance | 45.5 | 41.0 |
| Punt Returns | 1 | 1 |
| Punt Return Yardage | 9 | 6 |
| Kickoff Returns | 6 | 2 |
| Kickoff Return Yardage | 82 | 29 |
| Interception Return Yardage | 0 | 14 |
| Total Return Yardage | 91 | 49 |
| Fumbles | 2 | 0 |
| Own Fumbles Recovered | 2 | 0 |
| Opponents Fumbles Recovered | 0 | 0 |
| Penalties | 6 | 4 |
| Yards Penalized | 40 | 29 |
| Total Points Scored | 21 | 38 |
| Touchdowns | 3 | 5 |
| Rushing | 2 | 2 |
| Passing | 1 | 3 |
| Returns | 0 | 0 |
| Extra Points | 3 | 5 |
| Field Goals | 0 | 1 |
| Field Goals Attempted | 0 | 1 |
| Safeties | 0 | 0 |

## PLAYOFF GAMES SUMMARIES

| | | |
|---|---|---|
| Third-Down Efficiency | 5/15 | 8/13 |
| Fourth-Down Efficiency | 1/2 | 0/0 |
| Time of Possession | 26:27 | 33:33 |

**INDIVIDUAL STATISTICS**

**Rushing**

| San Francisco | No. | Yds. | LG | TD |
|---|---|---|---|---|
| Watters | 12 | 37 | 8 | 1 |
| Young | 7 | 38 | 18 | 1 |
| Rathman | 2 | 9 | 6 | 0 |
| **Dallas** | **No.** | **Yds.** | **LG** | **TD** |
| E. Smith | 23 | 88 | 9 | 1 |
| Aikman | 3 | 25 | 12 | 0 |
| Johnston | 4 | 13 | 4t | 1 |
| Lassic | 1 | 1 | 1 | 0 |
| Kosar | 2 | -3 | -1 | 0 |

**Passing**

| San Francisco | Att. | Comp. | Yds. | TD | Int. |
|---|---|---|---|---|---|
| Young | 45 | 27 | 287 | 1 | 1 |
| **Dallas** | **Att.** | **Comp.** | **Yds.** | **TD** | **Int.** |
| Aikman | 18 | 14 | 177 | 2 | 0 |
| Kosar | 9 | 5 | 83 | 1 | 0 |
| Harper | 1 | 0 | 0 | 0 | 0 |

**Receiving**

| San Francisco | No. | Yds. | LG | TD |
|---|---|---|---|---|
| Watters | 7 | 33 | 9 | 0 |
| Rice | 6 | 83 | 23 | 0 |
| J. Taylor | 3 | 61 | 22 | 0 |
| J. Williams | 3 | 44 | 25 | 0 |
| Jones | 3 | 26 | 13 | 0 |
| Logan | 3 | 21 | 8 | 0 |
| Turner | 1 | 12 | 12 | 0 |
| Rathman | 1 | 7 | 7t | 1 |
| **Dallas** | **No.** | **Yds.** | **LG** | **TD** |
| E. Smith | 7 | 85 | 28 | 1 |
| Harper | 4 | 78 | 42t | 1 |
| Novacek | 4 | 57 | 20 | 1 |
| Irvin | 2 | 23 | 12 | 0 |
| Johnston | 2 | 17 | 9 | 0 |

**Interceptions**

| San Francisco | No. | Yds. | LG | TD |
|---|---|---|---|---|
| None | — | — | — | — |
| **Dallas** | **No.** | **Yds.** | **LG** | **TD** |
| Everett | 1 | 14 | 14 | 0 |

**Punting**

| San Francisco | No. | Avg. | LG | Blk. |
|---|---|---|---|---|
| Wilmsmeyer | 4 | 45.5 | 52 | 0 |
| **Dallas** | **No.** | **Avg.** | **LG** | **Blk.** |
| Jett | 4 | 41.0 | 46 | 0 |

**Punt Returns**

| San Francisco | No. | FC | Yds. | LG | TD |
|---|---|---|---|---|---|
| Carter | 1 | 1 | 9 | 9 | 0 |
| **Dallas** | **No.** | **FC** | **Yds.** | **LG** | **TD** |
| K. Williams | 1 | 2 | 6 | 6 | 0 |

**Kickoff Returns**

| San Francisco | No. | Yds. | LG | TD |
|---|---|---|---|---|
| Carter | 4 | 62 | 20 | 0 |
| Logan | 2 | 20 | 14 | 0 |
| **Dallas** | **No.** | **Yds.** | **LG** | **TD** |
| Marion | 1 | 15 | 15 | 0 |
| K. Williams | 1 | 14 | 14 | 0 |

### AFC DIVISIONAL PLAYOFFS RESULTS

*Includes Second-Round Playoff Games (1982), AFC Inter-Divisional Games (1969), and special playoff games to break ties for AFL Division Championships (1963, 1968)*

| Season | Date | Winner (Share) | Loser (Share) | Score | Site | Attendance |
|---|---|---|---|---|---|---|
| 1993 | Jan. 16 | Kansas City ($12,000) | Houston ($12,000) | 28-20 | Houston | 64,011 |
| | Jan. 15 | Buffalo ($12,000) | L.A. Raiders ($12,000) | 29-23 | Buffalo | 61,923 |
| 1992 | Jan. 10 | Miami ($10,000) | San Diego ($10,000) | 31-0 | Miami | 71,224 |
| | Jan. 9 | Buffalo ($10,000) | Pittsburgh ($10,000) | 24-3 | Pittsburgh | 60,407 |
| 1991 | Jan. 5 | Buffalo ($10,000) | Kansas City ($10,000) | 37-14 | Buffalo | 80,182 |
| | Jan. 4 | Denver ($10,000) | Houston ($10,000) | 26-24 | Denver | 75,301 |
| 1990 | Jan. 13 | L.A. Raiders ($10,000) | Cincinnati ($10,000) | 20-10 | Los Angeles | 92,045 |
| | Jan. 12 | Buffalo ($10,000) | Miami ($10,000) | 44-34 | Buffalo | 77,087 |
| 1989 | Jan. 7 | Denver ($10,000) | Pittsburgh ($10,000) | 24-23 | Denver | 75,477 |
| | Jan. 6 | Cleveland ($10,000) | Buffalo ($10,000) | 34-30 | Cleveland | 78,921 |
| 1988 | Jan. 1 | Buffalo ($10,000) | Houston ($10,000) | 17-10 | Buffalo | 79,532 |
| | Dec. 31 | Cincinnati ($10,000) | Seattle ($10,000) | 21-13 | Cincinnati | 58,560 |
| 1987 | Jan. 10 | Denver ($10,000) | Houston ($10,000) | 34-10 | Denver | 75,440 |
| | Jan. 9 | Cleveland ($10,000) | Indianapolis ($10,000) | 38-21 | Cleveland | 79,372 |
| 1986 | Jan. 4 | Denver ($10,000) | New England ($10,000) | 22-17 | Denver | 75,262 |
| | Jan. 3 | Cleveland ($10,000) | N.Y. Jets ($10,000) | 23-20* | Cleveland | 79,720 |
| 1985 | Jan. 5 | New England ($10,000) | L.A. Raiders ($10,000) | 27-20 | Los Angeles | 87,163 |
| | Jan. 4 | Miami ($10,000) | Cleveland ($10,000) | 24-21 | Miami | 74,667 |
| 1984 | Dec. 30 | Pittsburgh ($10,000) | Denver ($10,000) | 24-17 | Denver | 74,981 |
| | Dec. 29 | Miami ($10,000) | Seattle ($10,000) | 31-10 | Miami | 73,469 |
| 1983 | Jan. 1 | L.A. Raiders ($10,000) | Pittsburgh ($10,000) | 38-10 | Los Angeles | 90,380 |
| | Dec. 31 | Seattle ($10,000) | Miami ($10,000) | 27-20 | Miami | 74,136 |
| 1982 | Jan. 16 | Miami ($10,000) | San Diego ($10,000) | 34-13 | Miami | 71,383 |
| | Jan. 15 | N.Y. Jets ($10,000) | L.A. Raiders ($10,000) | 17-14 | Los Angeles | 90,038 |
| 1981 | Jan. 3 | Cincinnati ($5,000) | Buffalo ($5,000) | 28-21 | Cincinnati | 55,420 |
| | Jan. 2 | San Diego ($5,000) | Miami ($5,000) | 41-38* | Miami | 73,735 |
| 1980 | Jan. 4 | Oakland ($5,000) | Cleveland ($5,000) | 14-12 | Cleveland | 78,245 |
| | Jan. 3 | San Diego ($5,000) | Buffalo ($5,000) | 20-14 | San Diego | 52,253 |
| 1979 | Dec. 30 | Pittsburgh ($5,000) | Miami ($5,000) | 34-14 | Pittsburgh | 50,214 |
| | Dec. 29 | Houston ($5,000) | San Diego ($5,000) | 17-14 | San Diego | 51,192 |
| 1978 | Dec. 31 | Houston ($5,000) | New England ($5,000) | 31-14 | New England | 60,735 |
| | Dec. 30 | Pittsburgh ($5,000) | Denver ($5,000) | 33-10 | Pittsburgh | 50,230 |
| 1977 | Dec. 24 | Oakland ($5,000) | Baltimore ($5,000) | 37-31* | Baltimore | 59,925 |
| | Dec. 24 | Denver ($5,000) | Pittsburgh ($5,000) | 34-21 | Denver | 75,059 |
| 1976 | Dec. 19 | Pittsburgh ($) | Baltimore ($) | 40-14 | Baltimore | 59,296 |
| | Dec. 18 | Oakland ($) | New England ($) | 24-21 | Oakland | 53,050 |
| 1975 | Dec. 28 | Oakland ($) | Cincinnati ($) | 31-28 | Oakland | 53,030 |
| | Dec. 27 | Pittsburgh ($) | Baltimore ($) | 28-10 | Pittsburgh | 49,557 |
| 1974 | Dec. 22 | Pittsburgh ($) | Buffalo ($) | 32-14 | Pittsburgh | 49,841 |
| | Dec. 21 | Oakland ($) | Miami ($) | 28-26 | Oakland | 53,023 |
| 1973 | Dec. 23 | Miami ($) | Cincinnati ($) | 34-16 | Miami | 78,928 |
| | Dec. 22 | Oakland ($) | Pittsburgh ($) | 33-14 | Oakland | 52,646 |
| 1972 | Dec. 24 | Miami ($) | Cleveland ($) | 20-14 | Miami | 78,916 |
| | Dec. 23 | Pittsburgh ($) | Oakland ($) | 13-7 | Pittsburgh | 50,327 |
| 1971 | Dec. 26 | Baltimore ($) | Cleveland ($) | 20-3 | Cleveland | 70,734 |
| | Dec. 25 | Miami ($) | Kansas City ($) | 27-24* | Kansas City | 45,822 |
| 1970 | Dec. 27 | Oakland ($) | Miami ($) | 21-14 | Oakland | 52,594 |
| | Dec. 26 | Baltimore ($) | Cincinnati ($) | 17-0 | Baltimore | 49,694 |
| 1969 | Dec. 21 | Oakland ($) | Houston ($) | 56-7 | Oakland | 53,539 |
| | Dec. 20 | Kansas City ($) | N.Y. Jets ($) | 13-6 | New York | 62,977 |
| 1968 | Dec. 22 | Oakland ($) | Kansas City ($) | 41-6 | Oakland | 53,605 |
| 1963 | Dec. 28 | Boston ($) | Buffalo ($) | 26-8 | Buffalo | 33,044 |

**Sudden Death Overtime.*

*$ Players received 1/14 of annual salary for playoff appearances.*

## 1993 AFC DIVISIONAL PLAYOFF GAMES

Rich Stadium, Buffalo, New York
January 15, 1994, Attendance: 61,923

**BUFFALO 29, L.A. RAIDERS 23**—Jim Kelly threw 2 second-half touchdown passes to Bill Brooks and the Bills overcame an 11-point deficit to advance to the AFC Championship Game for the fifth time in six years. Napoleon McCallum scored on a pair of 1-yard touchdown runs for the Raiders, the second of which gave Los Angeles a 17-6 advantage with 1:57 remaining in the first half. But Buffalo took only 67 seconds to march 76 yards and trim the deficit to 4 points at intermission. A 37-yard pass interference penalty preceded Thurman Thomas's 8-yard touchdown run with 50 seconds remaining in the second quarter. That set up a flurry of activity that saw the lead change three times in a span of 6:18 late in the third and early in the fourth quarters. Kelly gave the Bills a 19-17 edge with a 25-yard touchdown pass to Brooks with 3:23 left in the third period. Moments later, Buffalo safety Henry Jones recovered McCallum's fumble on the Raiders' 30-yard line, setting up Steve Christie's 29-yard field goal 59 seconds before the end of the quarter. Two plays after that, Raiders wide receiver Tim Brown took a short pass from a scrambling Jeff Hostetler and turned it into an 86-yard touchdown that put Los Angeles back on top 23-22. But the Bills responded by driving 71 yards to Kelly's 22-yard touchdown pass to Brooks 2:55 into the fourth quarter. That held up for the winning points as Buffalo's defense shut down the Raiders. After gaining 14 first downs in the first half, Los Angeles managed only 1 in the second half, that coming on the long touchdown pass. Kelly completed 27 of 37 passes for 287 yards for the Bills, while Brooks caught 6 passes for 96 yards. Hostetler was 14 of 20 for 230 yards for the Raiders. The game was played in frigid conditions. Temperature at kickoff was zero degrees, with the wind-chill at minus-32.

| | | | | | | |
|---|---|---|---|---|---|---|
| **L.A. Raiders** | 0 | 17 | 6 | 0 | — | 23 |
| **Buffalo** | 0 | 13 | 9 | 7 | — | 29 |

Raid — FG Jaeger 30
Buff — Davis 1 run (kick failed)
Raid — McCallum 1 run (Jaeger kick)
Raid — McCallum 1 run (Jaeger kick)
Buff — Thomas 8 run (Christie kick)
Buff — Brooks 25 pass from Kelly (kick failed)
Buff — FG Christie 29
Raid — Brown 86 pass from Hostetler (kick failed)
Buff — Brooks 22 pass from Kelly (Christie kick)

Astrodome, Houston, Texas
January 16, 1994, Attendance: 64,011

**KANSAS CITY 28, HOUSTON 20**—Joe Montana threw 3 second-half touchdown passes, including 2 just 54 seconds apart in the fourth quarter, to rally the Chiefs past the Oilers. Houston, which entered the game with an 11-game winning streak, jumped out to a 10-0 lead in the opening quarter and still led 13-7 after Al Del Greco's 43-yard field goal with 9:37 remaining in the fourth quarter. But Kansas City marched 71 yards in only 59 seconds, the key play a 38-yard pass interference penalty against Oilers cornerback Cris Dishman, to take the lead for the first time on Montana's 11-yard touchdown pass to J.J. Birden. On the next play from scrimmage, Chiefs linebacker Derrick Thomas sacked Houston quarterback Warren Moon, forcing a fumble that defensive tackle Dan Saleaumua recovered at the Oilers' 12-yard line. On third down, Montana's 18-yard touchdown pass to Willie Davis put Kansas City ahead 21-13 with 7:44 left. Houston drove 80 yards to a touchdown to pull within 1 point with 3:45 to go, but Marcus Allen's 21-yard touchdown run at the 1:55 mark sealed the Oilers' fate. The key play on the Chiefs' 79-yard march came on third-and-1 from Kansas City's 30-yard line. Montana's arm was hit as he threw, but his wobbly pass was caught by tight end Keith Cash, who rumbled 41 yards to Houston's 29. Cash also had a 7-yard touchdown reception in the third quarter. Montana finished with 22 completions in 38 attempts for 299 yards. Allen rushed for 74 yards on only 14 carries. Moon completed 32 of 43 passes for 306 yards for the Oilers. But without the benefit of an effective rushing attack (Houston ran for only 39 yards), he was under pressure all afternoon and was sacked 9 times. Thomas, Joe Phillips, Albert Lewis, and Bennie Thompson each had 2 sacks for the Chiefs, who equaled the NFL record for sacks in a postseason game.

| | | | | | | |
|---|---|---|---|---|---|---|
| **Kansas City** | 0 | 0 | 7 | 21 | — | 28 |
| **Houston** | 10 | 0 | 0 | 10 | — | 20 |

Hou — FG Del Greco 49
Hou — Brown 2 run (Del Greco kick)
KC — Cash 7 pass from Montana (Lowery kick)
Hou — FG Del Greco 43
KC — Birden 11 pass from Montana (Lowery kick)
KC — Davis 18 pass from Montana (Lowery kick)
Hou — Givins 7 pass from Moon (Del Greco kick)
KC — Allen 21 run (Lowery kick)

## NFC DIVISIONAL PLAYOFFS RESULTS

*Includes Second-Round Playoff Games (1982), NFL Conference Championship Games (1967-69), and special playoff games to break ties for NFL Division or Conference Championships (1941, 1943, 1947, 1950, 1952, 1957, 1958, 1965)*

| Season | Date | Winner (Share) | Loser (Share) | Score | Site | Attendance |
|---|---|---|---|---|---|---|
| 1993 | Jan. 16 | Dallas ($12,000) | Green Bay ($12,000) | 27-17 | Dallas | 64,790 |
| | Jan. 15 | San Francisco ($12,000) | N.Y. Giants ($12,000) | 44-3 | San Francisco | 67,143 |
| 1992 | Jan. 10 | Dallas ($10,000) | Philadelphia ($10,000) | 34-10 | Dallas | 63,721 |
| | Jan. 9 | San Francisco ($10,000) | Washington ($10,000) | 20-13 | San Francisco | 64,991 |
| 1991 | Jan. 5 | Detroit ($10,000) | Dallas ($10,000) | 38-6 | Detroit | 78,290 |
| | Jan. 4 | Washington ($10,000) | Atlanta ($10,000) | 24-7 | Washington | 55,181 |
| 1990 | Jan. 13 | N.Y. Giants ($10,000) | Chicago ($10,000) | 31-3 | East Rutherford | 77,025 |
| | Jan. 12 | San Francisco ($10,000) | Washington ($10,000) | 28-10 | San Francisco | 65,292 |
| 1989 | Jan. 7 | L.A. Rams ($10,000) | N.Y. Giants ($10,000) | 19-13* | East Rutherford | 76,526 |
| | Jan. 6 | San Francisco ($10,000) | Minnesota ($10,000) | 41-13 | San Francisco | 64,918 |
| 1988 | Jan. 1 | San Francisco ($10,000) | Minnesota ($10,000) | 34-9 | San Francisco | 61,848 |
| | Dec. 31 | Chicago ($10,000) | Philadelphia ($10,000) | 20-12 | Chicago | 65,534 |
| 1987 | Jan. 10 | Washington ($10,000) | Chicago ($10,000) | 21-17 | Chicago | 65,268 |
| | Jan. 9 | Minnesota ($10,000) | San Francisco ($10,000) | 36-24 | San Francisco | 63,008 |
| 1986 | Jan. 4 | N.Y. Giants ($10,000) | San Francisco ($10,000) | 49-3 | East Rutherford | 75,691 |
| | Jan. 3 | Washington ($10,000) | Chicago ($10,000) | 27-13 | Chicago | 65,524 |
| 1985 | Jan. 5 | Chicago ($10,000) | N.Y. Giants ($10,000) | 21-0 | Chicago | 65,670 |
| | Jan. 4 | L.A. Rams ($10,000) | Dallas ($10,000) | 20-0 | Anaheim | 66,581 |
| 1984 | Dec. 30 | Chicago ($10,000) | Washington ($10,000) | 23-19 | Washington | 55,431 |
| | Dec. 29 | San Francisco ($10,000) | N.Y. Giants ($10,000) | 21-10 | San Francisco | 60,303 |
| 1983 | Jan. 1 | Washington ($10,000) | L.A. Rams ($10,000) | 51-7 | Washington | 54,440 |
| | Dec. 31 | San Francisco ($10,000) | Detroit ($10,000) | 24-23 | San Francisco | 59,979 |
| 1982 | Jan. 16 | Dallas ($10,000) | Green Bay ($10,000) | 37-26 | Dallas | 63,972 |
| | Jan. 15 | Washington ($10,000) | Minnesota ($10,000) | 21-7 | Washington | 54,593 |
| 1981 | Jan. 3 | San Francisco ($5,000) | N.Y. Giants ($5,000) | 38-24 | San Francisco | 58,360 |
| | Jan. 2 | Dallas ($5,000) | Tampa Bay ($5,000) | 38-0 | Dallas | 64,848 |
| 1980 | Jan. 4 | Dallas ($5,000) | Atlanta ($5,000) | 30-27 | Atlanta | 59,793 |
| | Jan. 3 | Philadelphia ($5,000) | Minnesota ($5,000) | 31-16 | Philadelphia | 70,178 |
| 1979 | Dec. 30 | Los Angeles ($5,000) | Dallas ($5,000) | 21-19 | Dallas | 64,792 |
| | Dec. 29 | Tampa Bay ($5,000) | Philadelphia ($5,000) | 24-17 | Tampa Bay | 71,402 |
| 1978 | Dec. 31 | Los Angeles ($5,000) | Minnesota ($5,000) | 34-10 | Los Angeles | 70,436 |
| | Dec. 30 | Dallas ($5,000) | Atlanta ($5,000) | 27-20 | Dallas | 63,406 |
| 1977 | Dec. 26 | Dallas ($5,000) | Chicago ($5,000) | 37-7 | Dallas | 63,260 |
| | Dec. 26 | Minnesota ($5,000) | Los Angeles ($5,000) | 14-7 | Los Angeles | 70,203 |
| 1976 | Dec. 19 | Los Angeles ($) | Dallas ($) | 14-12 | Dallas | 63,283 |
| | Dec. 18 | Minnesota ($) | Washington ($) | 35-20 | Minnesota | 47,466 |
| 1975 | Dec. 28 | Dallas ($) | Minnesota ($) | 17-14 | Minnesota | 48,050 |
| | Dec. 27 | Los Angeles ($) | St. Louis ($) | 35-23 | Los Angeles | 73,459 |
| 1974 | Dec. 22 | Los Angeles ($) | Washington ($) | 19-10 | Los Angeles | 77,925 |
| | Dec. 21 | Minnesota ($) | St. Louis ($) | 30-14 | Minnesota | 48,150 |
| 1973 | Dec. 23 | Dallas ($) | Los Angeles ($) | 27-16 | Dallas | 63,272 |

| | | | | | | |
|---|---|---|---|---|---|---|
| | Dec. 22 | Minnesota ($) | Washington ($) | 27-20 | Minnesota | 48,040 |
| 1972 | Dec. 24 | Washington ($) | Green Bay ($) | 16-3 | Washington | 52,321 |
| | Dec. 23 | Dallas ($) | San Francisco ($) | 30-28 | San Francisco | 59,746 |
| 1971 | Dec. 26 | San Francisco ($) | Washington ($) | 24-20 | San Francisco | 45,327 |
| | Dec. 25 | Dallas ($) | Minnesota ($) | 20-12 | Minnesota | 47,307 |
| 1970 | Dec. 27 | San Francisco ($) | Minnesota ($) | 17-14 | Minnesota | 45,103 |
| | Dec. 26 | Dallas ($) | Detroit ($) | 5-0 | Dallas | 69,613 |
| 1969 | Dec. 28 | Cleveland ($) | Dallas ($) | 38-14 | Dallas | 69,321 |
| | Dec. 27 | Minnesota ($) | Los Angeles ($) | 23-20 | Minnesota | 47,900 |
| 1968 | Dec. 22 | Baltimore ($) | Minnesota ($) | 24-14 | Baltimore | 60,238 |
| | Dec. 21 | Cleveland ($) | Dallas ($) | 31-20 | Cleveland | 81,497 |
| 1967 | Dec. 24 | Dallas ($) | Cleveland ($) | 52-14 | Dallas | 70,786 |
| | Dec. 23 | Green Bay ($) | Los Angeles ($) | 28-7 | Milwaukee | 49,861 |
| 1965 | Dec. 26 | Green Bay ($) | Baltimore ($) | 13-10* | Green Bay | 50,484 |
| 1958 | Dec. 21 | N.Y. Giants (#) | Cleveland (#) | 10-0 | New York | 61,274 |
| 1957 | Dec. 22 | Detroit (#) | San Francisco (#) | 31-27 | San Francisco | 60,118 |
| 1952 | Dec. 21 | Detroit (#) | Los Angeles (#) | 31-21 | Detroit | 47,645 |
| 1950 | Dec. 17 | Los Angeles (#) | Chicago Bears (#) | 24-14 | Los Angeles | 83,501 |
| | Dec. 17 | Cleveland (#) | N.Y. Giants (#) | 8-3 | Cleveland | 33,054 |
| 1947 | Dec. 21 | Philadelphia (#) | Pittsburgh (#) | 21-0 | Pittsburgh | 35,729 |
| 1943 | Dec. 19 | Washington (¢) | N.Y. Giants (¢) | 28-0 | New York | 42,800 |
| 1941 | Dec. 14 | Chicago Bears (¢) | Green Bay (¢) | 33-14 | Chicago | 43,425 |

** Sudden Death Overtime.*
*$ Players received 1/14 of annual salary for playoff appearances.*
*# Players received 1/12 of annual salary for playoff appearances.*
*¢ Players received 1/10 of annual salary for playoff appearances.*

## 1993 NFC DIVISIONAL PLAYOFF GAMES

Candlestick Park, San Francisco, California
January 15, 1994, Attendance: 67,143

**SAN FRANCISCO 44, N.Y. GIANTS 3**—Ricky Watters scored an NFL playoff-record 5 touchdowns to key the 49ers' victory. Watters ran for 118 yards on 24 carries, caught 5 passes for 46 yards, and scored all of his touchdowns on short runs. No player had scored more than 3 touchdowns in a postseason game. San Francisco started the rout early, with quarterback Steve Young completing all 4 of his passes for 63 yards on an 8-play, 80-yard touchdown drive following the opening kickoff, a march capped by Watters's 1-yard run 4:27 into the game. The Giants failed to make a first down on their initial possession, and the 49ers' Dexter Carter returned the ensuing punt 31 yards to set up Mike Cofer's 29-yard field goal. Safety Tim McDonald intercepted Phil Simms's pass on the next play, leading to another 1-yard touchdown run by Watters, and San Francisco led 16-0 two seconds into the second quarter. It was 23-3 at halftime and the 49ers never were threatened. Young completed 17 of 22 passes for 226 yards as San Francisco amassed 413 total yards to just 194 for the Giants. New York, which led the NFL by averaging 138 rushing yards per game during the regular season, managed only 41 yards on the ground. The 49ers' defense also recorded 4 sacks, including 2 by rookie end Dana Stubblefield.

| | | | | | | |
|---|---|---|---|---|---|---|
| **N.Y. Giants** | 0 | 3 | 0 | 0 | — | 3 |
| **San Francisco** | 9 | 14 | 14 | 7 | — | 44 |

SF — Watters 1 run (kick failed)
SF — FG Cofer 29
SF — Watters 1 run (Cofer kick)
SF — Watters 2 run (Cofer kick)
NYG — FG Treadwell 25
SF — Watters 6 run (Cofer kick)
SF — Watters 2 run (Cofer kick)
SF — Logan 2 run (Cofer kick)

Texas Stadium, Irving, Texas
January 16, 1994, Attendance: 64,790

**DALLAS 27, GREEN BAY 17**—Troy Aikman passed for 302 yards and 3 touchdowns, and the Cowboys scored 10 points in a span of 18 seconds shortly before halftime to break open a close game. Aikman's 25-yard touchdown pass to Alvin Harper 5:53 into the second quarter put Dallas ahead 7-3, a lead the Cowboys would not relinquish. After Eddie Murray kicked a 41-yard field goal 23 seconds before halftime to stretch the advantage to 10-3, Kenneth Gant made the key play of the game on the ensuing kickoff. Gant knocked the ball loose from Packers kick returner Corey Harris, and Dallas's Joe Fishback recovered at Green Bay's 14-yard line. Aikman completed an 8-yard pass to Michael Irvin, then teamed with tight end Jay Novacek on a 6-yard touchdown pass with five seconds left in the first half to make it 17-3. Aikman's 19-yard touchdown pass to Michael Irvin 9:05 into the third quarter put the game out of reach. Aikman finished with 28 completions in 37 attempts, while Irvin caught 9 passes for 126 yards. Packers quarterback Brett Favre completed 28 of 45 passes for 331 yards, but most of it came after the issue was decided. Running back Edgar Bennett caught 9 passes. Wide receiver Sterling Sharpe had 6 receptions for 128 yards.

| | | | | | | |
|---|---|---|---|---|---|---|
| **Green Bay** | 3 | 0 | 7 | 7 | — | 17 |
| **Dallas** | 0 | 17 | 7 | 3 | — | 27 |

GB — FG Jacke 30
Dall — Harper 25 pass from Aikman (Murray kick)
Dall — FG Murray 41
Dall — Novacek 6 pass from Aikman (Murray kick)
Dall — Irvin 19 pass from Aikman (Murray kick)
GB — Brooks 13 pass from Favre (Jacke kick)
Dall — FG Murray 38
GB — Sharpe 29 pass from Favre (Jacke kick)

## AFC WILD CARD PLAYOFF GAMES RESULTS

| Season | Date | Winner (Share) | Loser (Share) | Score | Site | Attendance |
|---|---|---|---|---|---|---|
| 1993 | Jan. 9 | L.A. Raiders ($7,500) | Denver ($7,500) | 42-24 | Los Angeles | 65,314 |
| | Jan. 8 | Kansas City ($12,000) | Pittsburgh ($7,500) | 27-24* | Kansas City | 74,515 |
| 1992 | Jan. 3 | Buffalo ($6,000) | Houston ($6,000) | 41-38* | Buffalo | 75,141 |
| | Jan. 2 | San Diego ($10,000) | Kansas City ($6,000) | 17-0 | San Diego | 58,278 |
| 1991 | Dec. 29 | Houston ($10,000) | N.Y. Jets ($6,000) | 17-10 | Houston | 61,485 |
| | Dec. 28 | Kansas City ($6,000) | L.A. Raiders ($6,000) | 10-6 | Kansas City | 75,827 |
| 1990 | Jan. 6 | Cincinnati ($10,000) | Houston ($6,000) | 41-14 | Cincinnati | 60,012 |
| | Jan. 5 | Miami ($6,000) | Kansas City ($6,000) | 17-16 | Miami | 67,276 |
| 1989 | Dec. 31 | Pittsburgh ($6,000) | Houston ($6,000) | 26-23* | Houston | 59,406 |
| 1988 | Dec. 26 | Houston ($6,000) | Cleveland ($6,000) | 24-23 | Cleveland | 75,896 |
| 1987 | Jan. 3 | Houston ($6,000) | Seattle ($6,000) | 23-20* | Houston | 50,519 |
| 1986 | Dec. 28 | N.Y. Jets ($6,000) | Kansas City ($6,000) | 35-15 | East Rutherford | 75,210 |
| 1985 | Dec. 28 | New England ($6,000) | N.Y. Jets ($6,000) | 26-14 | East Rutherford | 75,945 |
| 1984 | Dec. 22 | Seattle ($6,000) | L.A. Raiders ($6,000) | 13-7 | Seattle | 62,049 |
| 1983 | Dec. 24 | Seattle ($6,000) | Denver ($6,000) | 31-7 | Seattle | 64,275 |
| 1982 | Jan. 9 | N.Y. Jets ($6,000) | Cincinnati ($6,000) | 44-17 | Cincinnati | 57,560 |
| | Jan. 9 | San Diego ($6,000) | Pittsburgh ($6,000) | 31-28 | Pittsburgh | 53,546 |
| | Jan. 8 | L.A. Raiders ($6,000) | Cleveland ($6,000) | 27-10 | Los Angeles | 56,555 |
| | Jan. 8 | Miami ($6,000) | New England ($6,000) | 28-13 | Miami | 68,842 |
| 1981 | Dec. 27 | Buffalo ($3,000) | N.Y. Jets ($3,000) | 31-27 | New York | 57,050 |
| 1980 | Dec. 28 | Oakland ($3,000) | Houston ($3,000) | 27-7 | Oakland | 53,333 |
| 1979 | Dec. 23 | Houston ($3,000) | Denver ($3,000) | 13-7 | Houston | 48,776 |
| 1978 | Dec. 24 | Houston ($3,000) | Miami ($3,000) | 17-9 | Miami | 72,445 |

**Sudden death overtime.*

## 1993 AFC WILD CARD PLAYOFF GAMES

Arrowhead Stadium, Kansas City, Missouri
January 8, 1994, Attendance: 74,515

**KANSAS CITY 27, PITTSBURGH 24**—Nick Lowery kicked a 32-yard field goal 11:03 into overtime to give the Chiefs the come-from-behind victory. Kansas City rallied from a 10-point halftime deficit to tie the game at 17-17 in the fourth quarter, only to fall behind again before forcing the extra session when Joe Montana threw a 7-yard touchdown pass to Tim Barnett with 1:43 remaining in regulation. That came four plays after the Chiefs' Keith Cash blocked a punt and teammate Fred Jones returned it 31 yards to the Steelers' 9-yard line. Two running plays and an incomplete pass netted only 2 yards, but Montana teamed with Barnett on fourth down. Pittsburgh led 17-7 at intermission largely on the strength of 2 touchdown passes from Neil O'Donnell, the second of which was a 26-yard strike to Ernie Mills 18 seconds before halftime. That came six plays after the Steelers stopped Kansas City on downs near midfield. Lowery's 23-yard field goal and Marcus Allen's 2-yard run 6:02 into the fourth quarter tied the game, but Pittsburgh answered with a 74-yard drive capped by O'Donnell's 22-yard pass to tight end Eric Green to take back the lead. The Chiefs had a chance to win the game in regulation, forcing the Steelers to punt just 29 seconds after Barnett's touchdown catch. Montana quickly directed a 47-yard drive, setting up Lowery's 43-yard field-goal try in the closing seconds, but the kick was wide right. The teams exchanged punts in overtime, then Kansas City drove 66 yards in 11 plays to win it. Montana started slowly, completing only 1 of his first 8 passes, but wound up 28 of 43 for 276 yards. Backup Dave Krieg subbed briefly when Montana hurt his ribs in the first quarter, and completed his only pass attempt for a 23-yard touchdown to J.J. Birden. O'Donnell completed 23 of 42 attempts for 286 yards and 3 touchdowns. Pittsburgh nose tackle Gerald Williams had 3 sacks. There were no turnovers in the game.

| | | | | | | |
|---|---|---|---|---|---|---|
| **Pittsburgh** | 7 | 10 | 0 | 7 | 0 | — 24 |
| **Kansas City** | 7 | 0 | 3 | 14 | 3 | — 27 |

Pitt — Cooper 10 pass from O'Donnell (Anderson kick)
KC — Birden 23 pass from Krieg (Lowery kick)
Pitt — FG Anderson 30
Pitt — Mills 26 pass from O'Donnell (Anderson kick)
KC — FG Lowery 23
KC — Allen 2 run (Lowery kick)
Pitt — Green 22 pass from O'Donnell (Anderson kick)
KC — Barnett 7 pass from Montana (Lowery kick)
KC — FG Lowery 32

Memorial Coliseum, Los Angeles, California
January 9, 1994, Attendance: 65,314

**L.A. RAIDERS 42, DENVER 24**—Napoleon McCallum rushed for 3 second-half touchdowns to decide what began as a shootout between quarterbacks Jeff Hostetler and John Elway. A wild first half ended in a 21-21 tie after the Raiders' Hostetler and the Broncos' Elway each traded 3 touchdown passes. But field position played a big role early in the third quarter: Los Angeles pinned Denver deep in its territory with a Jeff Gossett punt that was downed inside the 5, and moments later the Raiders took over at the Broncos' 35 after a short punt by Tom Rouen. Three plays later, McCallum turned a third-and-1 into a touchdown, scampering 26 yards—the team's longest run from scrimmage all year—for the score that put Los Angeles ahead for good with 8:08 left in the period. Another short punt set up McCallum's 2-yard touchdown run at the 4:27 mark, the key play on the 52-yard drive Hostetler's 33-yard completion to tight end Ethan Horton. After the Broncos closed within 35-24 early in the fourth quarter, the Raiders put the game out of reach with a time-consuming, 76-yard drive that culminated in McCallum's 1-yard run with 6:43 remaining in the game. McCallum finished with 81 yards on 13 carries and tied an NFL postseason record with his 3 touchdowns. Hostetler averaged better than 15 yards per attempt, throwing for 294 yards while completing 13 of 19 passes. James Jett had 111 yards on just 3 receptions, including a difficult over-the-shoulder grab to complete a 54-yard touchdown in the second quarter. Elway completed 29 of 47 passes for 302 yards. Tight end Shannon Sharpe tied a postseason record with 13 catches for 156 yards. The two teams combined for 814 total yards, including 427 by the Raiders.

| | | | | | |
|---|---|---|---|---|---|
| **Denver** | 7 | 14 | 0 | 3 | — 24 |
| **L.A. Raiders** | 14 | 7 | 14 | 7 | — 42 |

Raid — Horton 9 pass from Hostetler (Jaeger kick)
Den — Sharpe 23 pass from Elway (Elam kick)
Raid — Brown 65 pass from Hostetler (Jaeger kick)
Den — R. Johnson 16 pass from Elway (Elam kick)
Raid — Jett 54 pass from Hostetler (Jaeger kick)
Den — Russell 6 pass from Elway (Elam kick)
Raid — McCallum 26 run (Jaeger kick)
Raid — McCallum 2 run (Jaeger kick)
Den — FG Elam 33
Raid — McCallum 1 run (Jaeger kick)

## NFC WILD CARD PLAYOFF GAMES RESULTS

| Season | Date | Winner (Share) | Loser (Share) | Score | Site | Attendance |
|---|---|---|---|---|---|---|
| 1993 | Jan. 9 | N.Y. Giants ($7,500) | Minnesota ($7,500) | 17-10 | East Rutherford | 75,089 |
| | Jan. 8 | Green Bay ($7,500) | Detroit ($12,000) | 28-24 | Detroit | 68,479 |
| 1992 | Jan. 3 | Philadelphia ($6,000) | New Orleans ($6,000) | 36-20 | New Orleans | 68,893 |
| | Jan. 2 | Washington ($6,000) | Minnesota ($10,000) | 24-7 | Minneapolis | 57,353 |
| 1991 | Dec. 29 | Dallas ($6,000) | Chicago ($6,000) | 17-13 | Chicago | 62,594 |
| | Dec. 28 | Atlanta ($6,000) | New Orleans ($10,000) | 27-20 | New Orleans | 68,794 |
| 1990 | Jan. 6 | Chicago ($10,000) | New Orleans ($6,000) | 16-6 | Chicago | 60,767 |
| | Jan. 5 | Washington ($6,000) | Philadelphia ($6,000) | 20-6 | Philadelphia | 65,287 |
| 1989 | Dec. 31 | L.A. Rams ($6,000) | Philadelphia ($6,000) | 21-7 | Philadelphia | 65,479 |
| 1988 | Dec. 26 | Minnesota ($6,000) | L.A. Rams ($6,000) | 28-17 | Minnesota | 61,204 |
| 1987 | Jan. 3 | Minnesota ($6,000) | New Orleans ($6,000) | 44-10 | New Orleans | 68,546 |
| 1986 | Dec. 28 | Washington ($6,000) | L.A. Rams ($6,000) | 19-7 | Washington | 54,567 |
| 1985 | Dec. 29 | N.Y. Giants ($6,000) | San Francisco ($6,000) | 17-3 | East Rutherford | 75,131 |
| 1984 | Dec. 23 | N.Y. Giants ($6,000) | L.A. Rams ($6,000) | 16-3 | Anaheim | 67,037 |
| 1983 | Dec. 26 | L.A. Rams ($6,000) | Dallas ($6,000) | 24-17 | Dallas | 62,118 |
| 1982 | Jan. 9 | Dallas ($6,000) | Tampa Bay ($6,000) | 30-17 | Dallas | 65,042 |
| | Jan. 9 | Minnesota ($6,000) | Atlanta ($6,000) | 30-24 | Minnesota | 60,560 |
| | Jan. 8 | Green Bay ($6,000) | St. Louis ($6,000) | 41-16 | Green Bay | 54,282 |
| | Jan. 8 | Washington ($6,000) | Detroit ($6,000) | 31-7 | Washington | 55,045 |
| 1981 | Dec. 27 | N.Y. Giants ($3,000) | Philadelphia ($3,000) | 27-21 | Philadelphia | 71,611 |
| 1980 | Dec. 28 | Dallas ($3,000) | Los Angeles ($3,000) | 34-13 | Dallas | 63,052 |
| 1979 | Dec. 23 | Philadelphia ($3,000) | Chicago ($3,000) | 27-17 | Philadelphia | 69,397 |
| 1978 | Dec. 24 | Atlanta ($3,000) | Philadelphia ($3,000) | 14-13 | Atlanta | 59,403 |

## 1993 NFC WILD CARD PLAYOFF GAMES

Silverdome, Pontiac, Michigan
January 8, 1994, Attendance: 68,479

**GREEN BAY 28, DETROIT 24**—Brett Favre's 40-yard touchdown pass to Sterling Sharpe with 55 seconds remaining lifted the Packers to victory in their first playoff game in 11 years. Favre, unable to find intended receiver Mark Clayton, scrambled left and threw across the field to Sharpe, who had gotten behind cornerback Kevin Scott down the right sideline. The quarterback's heroics offset brilliant individual performances by the Lions' Barry Sanders and Brett Perriman. Sanders, playing for first time since injuring his knee against the Bears on Thanksgiving Day, rushed for 169 yards on 27 carries. Perriman caught 10 passes for 150 yards, including a 1-yard touchdown from Erik Kramer late in the second quarter to give Detroit a 10-7 edge at halftime. The Lions increased that advantage to 17-7 when cornerback Melvin Jenkins intercepted Favre's pass and returned it 15 yards for a touchdown 6:40 into the third period. After Green Bay countered with a 28-yard touchdown pass from Favre to Sharpe, Detroit appeared poised to score again, driving to the Packers' 5-yard line. But Kramer's pass in the end zone was intercepted by rookie safety George Teague, who raced a playoff-record 101 yards to give Green Bay a 21-17 lead with 1:40 to go in the third quarter. The Lions then pieced together a 15-play, 89-yard drive that consumed more than 8 minutes, taking the lead for the last time on Derrick Moore's 5-yard touchdown run 6:33 into the fourth quarter. Kramer finished with 22 completions in 31 attempts for 248 yards for Detroit, which amassed 410 total yards but could not overcome the Packers' big plays. Sharpe, who set an NFL record with 112 receptions during the regular season, caught only 5 passes but made the most of them, gaining 101 yards and scoring 3 times.

| | | | | | |
|---|---|---|---|---|---|
| **Green Bay** | 0 | 7 | 14 | 7 | — 28 |
| **Detroit** | 3 | 7 | 7 | 7 | — 24 |

Det — FG Hanson 47
GB — Sharpe 12 pass from Favre (Jacke kick)
Det — Perriman 1 pass from Kramer (Hanson kick)
Det — Jenkins 15 interception return (Hanson kick)
GB — Sharpe 28 pass from Favre (Jacke kick)
GB — Teague 101 interception return (Jacke kick)
Det — D. Moore 5 run (Hanson kick)
GB — Sharpe 40 pass from Favre (Jacke kick)

# PLAYOFF GAMES SUMMARIES

Giants Stadium, East Rutherford, New Jersey
January 9, 1994, Attendance: 75,089

**N.Y. GIANTS 17, MINNESOTA 10**—Rodney Hampton's 2 third-quarter touchdown runs erased a 7-point halftime deficit and lifted the Giants to the victory. Freezing temperatures and blustery winds limited the effectiveness of each team's offense, so much so that all the points in the game were scored by the team that had the wind at its back. New York, trailing 10-3, had such conditions in the third quarter when it rallied to win. The Giants tied the score on their first possession of the second half, as Hampton barreled over right end for 51 yards and a touchdown just 2:54 into the third period. Shortly after that, a 21-yard punt positioned New York at Minnesota's 26-yard line, and six plays later, Hampton ran 2 yards for the game's deciding score. Primarily on the strength of Hampton, the Giants controlled the game by rushing 41 times for 176 yards and maintaining possession for 35:23 of the game's 60 minutes. Vikings quarterbacks Jim McMahon and Sean Salisbury combined to complete only 15 of 34 passes for 192 yards.

| | | | | | |
|---|---|---|---|---|---|
| **Minnesota** | 0 | 10 | 0 | 0 | — 10 |
| **N.Y. Giants** | 3 | 0 | 14 | 0 | — 17 |

NYG — FG Treadwell 26
Minn — C. Carter 40 pass from McMahon (Reveiz kick)
Minn — FG Reveiz 52
NYG — Hampton 51 run (Treadwell kick)
NYG — Hampton 2 run (Treadwell kick)

## AFC-NFC PRO BOWL AT A GLANCE RESULTS (1971-1994)

*NFC leads series, 14-10*

| Year | Date | Winner (Share) | Loser (Share) | Score | Site | Attendance |
|---|---|---|---|---|---|---|
| 1994 | Feb. 6 | NFC ($20,000) | AFC ($10,000) | 17-3 | Honolulu | 50,026 |
| 1993 | Feb. 7 | AFC ($10,000) | NFC ($5,000) | 23-20 (OT) | Honolulu | 50,007 |
| 1992 | Feb. 2 | NFC ($10,000) | AFC ($5,000) | 21-15 | Honolulu | 50,209 |
| 1991 | Feb. 3 | AFC ($10,000) | NFC ($5,000) | 23-21 | Honolulu | 50,345 |
| 1990 | Feb. 4 | NFC ($10,000) | AFC ($5,000) | 27-21 | Honolulu | 50,445 |
| 1989 | Jan. 29 | NFC ($10,000) | AFC ($5,000) | 34-3 | Honolulu | 50,113 |
| 1988 | Feb. 7 | AFC ($10,000) | NFC ($5,000) | 15-6 | Honolulu | 50,113 |
| 1987 | Feb. 1 | AFC ($10,000) | NFC ($5,000) | 10-6 | Honolulu | 50,101 |
| 1986 | Feb. 2 | NFC ($10,000) | AFC ($5,000) | 28-24 | Honolulu | 50,101 |
| 1985 | Jan. 27 | AFC ($10,000) | NFC ($5,000) | 22-14 | Honolulu | 50,385 |
| 1984 | Jan. 29 | NFC ($10,000) | AFC ($5,000) | 45-3 | Honolulu | 50,445 |
| 1983 | Feb. 6 | NFC ($10,000) | AFC ($5,000) | 20-19 | Honolulu | 49,883 |
| 1982 | Jan. 31 | AFC ($5,000) | NFC ($2,500) | 16-13 | Honolulu | 50,402 |
| 1981 | Feb. 1 | NFC ($5,000) | AFC ($2,500) | 21-7 | Honolulu | 50,360 |
| 1980 | Jan. 27 | NFC ($5,000) | AFC ($2,500) | 37-27 | Honolulu | 49,800 |
| 1979 | Jan. 29 | NFC ($5,000) | AFC ($2,500) | 13-7 | Los Angeles | 46,281 |
| 1978 | Jan. 23 | NFC ($5,000) | AFC ($2,500) | 14-13 | Tampa | 51,337 |
| 1977 | Jan. 17 | AFC ($2,000) | NFC ($1,500) | 24-14 | Seattle | 64,752 |
| 1976 | Jan. 26 | NFC ($2,000) | AFC ($1,500) | 23-20 | New Orleans | 30,546 |
| 1975 | Jan. 20 | NFC ($2,000) | AFC ($1,500) | 17-10 | Miami | 26,484 |
| 1974 | Jan. 20 | AFC ($2,000) | NFC ($1,500) | 15-13 | Kansas City | 66,918 |
| 1973 | Jan. 21 | AFC ($2,000) | NFC ($1,500) | 33-28 | Dallas | 37,091 |
| 1972 | Jan. 23 | AFC ($2,000) | NFC ($1,500) | 26-13 | Los Angeles | 53,647 |
| 1971 | Jan. 24 | NFC ($2,000) | AFC ($1,500) | 27-6 | Los Angeles | 48,222 |

## 1994 AFC-NFC PRO BOWL

Aloha Stadium, Honolulu, Hawaii
February 6, 1994, Attendance: 50,026

**NFC 17, AFC 3—**The NFC converted a blocked punt and a fumble recovery into touchdowns just 2:20 apart in the second half of its victory over the AFC. With the score tied 3-3 late in the third quarter, Saints linebacker Renaldo Turnbull deflected a punt by the Oilers' Greg Montgomery, and the NFC took possession at the AFC's 48-yard line. A 32-yard pass from Bobby Hebert to Falcons teammate Andre Rison positioned Rams running back Jerome Bettis for a 4-yard touchdown run with 1:27 left in the third quarter. Moments later, Rams defensive tackle Sean Gilbert recovered a fumble by Oilers quarterback Warren Moon at the AFC's 19. Hebert then teamed with the Vikings' Cris Carter on a 15-yard touchdown pass 53 seconds into the fourth period. The NFC kept the AFC out of the end zone by maintaining possession for more than 38 minutes and forcing 6 turnovers. Rison earned the Dan McGuire Trophy as the player of the game by catching 6 passes for 86 yards. The victory was the fourth in the last six years for the NFC, which leads the series 14-10.

| NFC (17) | Offense | AFC (3) |
|---|---|---|
| Jerry Rice (San Francisco) | WR | Tim Brown (L.A. Raiders) |
| Erik Williams (Dallas) | LT | Richmond Webb (Miami) |
| Nate Newton (Dallas) | LG | Keith Sims (Miami) |
| Jesse Sapolu (San Francisco) | C | Bruce Matthews (Houston) |
| Randall McDaniel (Minnesota) | RG | Steve Wisniewski (L.A. Raiders) |
| Harris Barton (San Francisco) | RT | Howard Ballard (Buffalo) |
| Jay Novacek (Dallas) | TE | Shannon Sharpe (Denver) |
| Michael Irvin (Dallas) | WR | Anthony Miller (San Diego) |
| Steve Young (San Francisco) | QB | John Elway (Denver) |
| Jerome Bettis (L.A. Rams) | RB | Thurman Thomas (Buffalo) |
| Daryl Johnston (Dallas) | RB | Marcus Allen (Kansas City) |
| | **Defense** | |
| Reggie White (Green Bay) | LE | Neil Smith (Kansas City) |
| Sean Gilbert (L.A. Rams) | LT | Cortez Kennedy (Seattle) |
| John Randle (Minnesota) | RT | Ray Childress (Houston) |
| Richard Dent (Chicago) | RE | Howie Long (L.A. Raiders) |
| Rickey Jackson (New Orleans) | LOLB | Derrick Thomas (Kansas City) |
| Hardy Nickerson (Tampa Bay) | LILB | Junior Seau (San Diego) |
| Renaldo Turnbull (New Orleans) | ROLB | Greg Lloyd (Pittsburgh) |
| Deion Sanders (Atlanta) | LCB | Rod Woodson (Pittsburgh) |
| Eric Allen (Philadelphia) | RCB | Nate Odomes (Buffalo) |
| Tim McDonald (San Francisco) | SS | Dennis Smith (Denver) |
| Mark Carrier (Chicago) | FS | Steve Atwater (Denver) |

**SUBSTITUTIONS**

**NFC—**Offense: K—Norm Johnson (Atlanta). P—Rich Camarillo (Phoenix). QB—Brett Favre (Green Bay), Bobby Hebert (Atlanta). RB—Rodney Hampton (N.Y. Giants), Ricky Watters (San Francisco). WR—Cris Carter (Minnesota), Andre Rison (Atlanta). TE—Brent Jones (San Francisco). ST—Elbert Shelley (Atlanta). KR—Tyrone Hughes (New Orleans). T—Lomas Brown (Detroit). G—Guy McIntyre (San Francisco). C—Bart Oates (N.Y. Giants). Defense: E—Chris Doleman (Minnesota). T—Russell Maryland (Dallas). LB—Seth Joyner (Philadelphia), Ken Norton (Dallas), Pat Swilling (Detroit), CB—Donnell Woolford (Chicago). S—LeRoy Butler (Green Bay). DNP—None.

**AFC—**Offense: K—Gary Anderson (Pittsburgh). P—Greg Montgomery (Houston). QB—Boomer Esiason (N.Y. Jets), Warren Moon (Houston). RB—Keith Byars (Miami), Chris Warren (Seattle). WR—Irving Fryar (Miami), Haywood Jeffires (Houston). TE—Eric Green (Pittsburgh). ST—Steve Tasker (Buffalo). KR—Eric Metcalf (Cleveland). T—John Alt (Kansas City). G—Max Montoya (L.A. Raiders). C—Dermontti Dawson (Pittsburgh). Defense: E—Sean Jones (Houston), Leslie O'Neal (San Diego). T—Michael Dean Perry (Cleveland). LB—Cornelius Bennett (Buffalo), Karl Mecklenburg (Denver). CB—Terry McDaniel (L.A. Raiders). S—Eugene Robinson (Seattle). DNP—None.

**HEAD COACHES**

**NFC—**George Seifert (San Francisco)
**AFC—**Marty Schottenheimer (Kansas City)

**OFFICIALS**

Referee—Gordon McCarter. Umpire—Dave Hamilton. Head Linesman—Tom Johnson. Line Judge—Bama Glass. Back Judge—Jim Daopoulos. Field Judge—Pat Mallette. Side Judge—Howard Slavin.

**SCORING**

| | | | | | |
|---|---|---|---|---|---|
| **NFC** | 3 | 0 | 7 | 7 | — 17 |
| **AFC** | 0 | 3 | 0 | 0 | — 3 |

NFC — FG Johnson 35
AFC — FG Anderson 25
NFC — Bettis 4 run (Johnson kick)
NFC — Carter 15 pass from Hebert (Johnson kick)

| TEAM STATISTICS | NFC | AFC |
|---|---|---|
| Total First Downs | 27 | 16 |
| Rushing | 10 | 3 |
| Passing | 13 | 11 |
| Penalty | 4 | 2 |
| Total Net Yardage | 350 | 271 |
| Total Offensive Plays | 82 | 60 |
| Average Gain per Offensive Play | 4.3 | 4.7 |
| Rushes | 37 | 14 |
| Yards Gained Rushing (Net) | 110 | 81 |
| Average Yards per Rush | 3.0 | 5.8 |
| Passes Attempted | 44 | 43 |
| Passes Completed | 22 | 21 |
| Had Intercepted | 2 | 4 |
| Tackled Attempting to Pass | 1 | 3 |
| Yards Lost Attempting to Pass | 11 | 10 |
| Yards Gained Passing (Net) | 240 | 190 |
| Punts | 5 | 5 |
| Average Distance | 43.0 | 42.4 |
| Punt Returns | 3 | 3 |
| Punt Return Yardage | 3 | 36 |
| Kickoff Returns | 1 | 4 |
| Kickoff Return Yardage | 24 | 80 |
| Interception Return Yardage | 13 | 103 |
| Total Return Yardage | 40 | 219 |
| Fumbles | 1 | 2 |
| Own Fumbles Recovered | 1 | 0 |
| Opponent Fumbles Recovered | 2 | 0 |
| Penalties | 9 | 9 |
| Yards Penalized | 42 | 48 |
| Total Points Scored | 17 | 3 |
| Touchdowns | 2 | 0 |
| Rushing | 1 | 0 |
| Passing | 1 | 0 |
| Returns | 0 | 0 |
| Extra Points | 2 | 0 |
| Field Goals | 1 | 1 |
| Field Goals Attempted | 3 | 1 |
| Safeties | 0 | 0 |
| Third-Down Efficiency | 6/17 | 2/13 |
| Fourth-Down Efficiency | 2/2 | 1/1 |
| Time of Possession | 38:22 | 21:38 |

INDIVIDUAL STATISTICS

**Rushing**

| NFC | No. | Yds. | LG | TD |
|---|---|---|---|---|
| Bettis | 14 | 49 | 10 | 1 |
| Watters | 11 | 25 | 8 | 0 |
| Rice | 1 | 12 | 12 | 0 |
| Hampton | 5 | 11 | 5 | 0 |
| Young | 1 | 7 | 7 | 0 |
| Johnston | 3 | 5 | 3 | 0 |
| Favre | 1 | 2 | 2 | 0 |
| Hebert | 1 | -1 | -1 | 0 |
| **AFC** | **No.** | **Yds.** | **LG** | **TD** |
| Warren | 4 | 64 | 39 | 0 |
| Thomas | 4 | 11 | 5 | 0 |
| Byars | 3 | 8 | 4 | 0 |
| Moon | 1 | 3 | 3 | 0 |
| Esiason | 1 | 2 | 2 | 0 |
| Allen | 1 | -7 | -7 | 0 |

**Passing**

| NFC | Att. | Comp. | Yds. | TD | Int. |
|---|---|---|---|---|---|
| Favre | 24 | 14 | 135 | 0 | 2 |
| Young | 14 | 4 | 48 | 0 | 0 |
| Hebert | 6 | 4 | 68 | 1 | 0 |
| **AFC** | **Att.** | **Comp.** | **Yds.** | **TD** | **Int.** |
| Esiason | 22 | 13 | 129 | 0 | 2 |
| Elway | 13 | 5 | 45 | 0 | 2 |
| Moon | 8 | 3 | 26 | 0 | 0 |

**Receiving**

| NFC | No. | Yds. | LG | TD |
|---|---|---|---|---|
| Rison | 6 | 86 | 32 | 0 |
| Carter | 3 | 52 | 22 | 1 |
| Novacek | 3 | 21 | 9 | 0 |
| Hampton | 3 | 13 | 6 | 0 |
| Rice | 2 | 30 | 19 | 0 |
| Jones | 1 | 13 | 13 | 0 |
| Irvin | 1 | 12 | 12 | 0 |
| Bettis | 1 | 10 | 10 | 0 |
| Watters | 1 | 9 | 5 | 0 |
| Johnston | 1 | 5 | 5 | 0 |
| **AFC** | **No.** | **Yds.** | **LG** | **TD** |
| Byars | 6 | 53 | 19 | 0 |
| Sharpe | 3 | 28 | 11 | 0 |
| Green | 2 | 35 | 26 | 0 |
| Fryar | 2 | 20 | 11 | 0 |
| Brown | 2 | 19 | 12 | 0 |
| Miller | 2 | 19 | 11 | 0 |
| Allen | 2 | 14 | 12 | 0 |
| Metcalf | 1 | 9 | 9 | 0 |
| Jeffires | 1 | 3 | 3 | 0 |

**Interceptions**

| NFC | No. | Yds. | LG | TD |
|---|---|---|---|---|
| Jackson | 1 | 7 | 7 | 0 |
| Sanders | 1 | 6 | 6 | 0 |
| Allen | 1 | 0 | 0 | 0 |
| Woolford | 1 | 0 | 0 | 0 |
| **AFC** | **No.** | **Yds.** | **LG** | **TD** |
| McDaniel | 1 | 20 | 20 | 0 |
| Robinson | 1 | 10 | 10 | 0 |
| Woodson | 0 | 73 | 73 | 0 |

**Punting**

| NFC | No. | Avg. | LG | Blk. |
|---|---|---|---|---|
| Camarillo | 5 | 43.0 | 51 | 0 |
| **AFC** | **No.** | **Avg.** | **LG** | **Blk.** |
| Montgomery | 5 | 42.4 | 53 | 0 |

**Punt Returns**

| NFC | No. | FC | Yds. | LG | TD |
|---|---|---|---|---|---|
| Hughes | 2 | 0 | 6 | 5 | 0 |
| Sanders | 1 | 0 | -3 | -3 | 0 |
| **AFC** | **No.** | **FC** | **Yds.** | **LG** | **TD** |
| Metcalf | 3 | 0 | 36 | 13 | 0 |

**Kickoff Returns**

| NFC | No. | Yds. | LG | TD |
|---|---|---|---|---|
| Sanders | 1 | 24 | 24 | 0 |
| **AFC** | **No.** | **Yds.** | **LG** | **TD** |
| Metcalf | 4 | 80 | 31 | 0 |

## 1993 AFC-NFC PRO BOWL

Aloha Stadium, Honolulu, Hawaii
February 7, 1993, Attendance: 50,007

**AFC 23, NFC 20—**Nick Lowery's 33-yard field goal 4:09 into overtime gave the American Conference all-stars an unlikely 23-20 victory over the National Conference. Despite being overwhelmed by the NFC in first downs (30-9), total yards (471-114), and time of possession (10:19-23:50), the AFC won because it forced 6 turnovers, bocked a pair of field goals (1 of which was returned for a touchdown), and returned an interception for a score. Special-teams star Steve Tasker of the Bills earned the Dan McGuire Trophy as the player of the game for making 4 tackles, forcing a fumble, and blocking a field goal. The block came with eight minutes left in regulation and the game tied at 13-13. The Raiders' Terry McDaniel picked up the loose ball and ran 28 yards for a touchdown and a 20-13 AFC lead. The NFC rallied behind 49ers quarterback Steve Young, whose fourth-down, 23-yard touchdown pass to Giants running back Rodney Hampton tied the game at 20-20 with 10 seconds left in regulation. Young completed 18 of 32 passes for 196 yards but was intercepted 3 times and lost a fumble when sacked in overtime. Raiders defensive end Howie Long fell on that fumble at the NFC 28-yard line, and five plays later, Lowery converted the winning field goal.

| | | | | | | |
|---|---|---|---|---|---|---|
| **AFC** | 0 | 10 | 3 | 7 | 3 | — 23 |
| **NFC** | 3 | 10 | 0 | 7 | 0 | — 20 |

NFC — FG Andersen 27
AFC — Seau 31 interception return (Lowery kick)
NFC — FG Andersen 37
NFC — Irvin 9 pass from Aikman (Andersen kick)
AFC — FG Lowery 42
AFC — FG Lowery 29
AFC — McDaniel 28 blocked field goal return (Lowery kick)
NFC — Hampton 23 pass from Young (Andersen kick)
AFC — FG Lowery 33

## 1992 AFC-NFC PRO BOWL

Aloha Stadium, Honolulu, Hawaii
February 2, 1992, Attendance: 50,209

**NFC 21, AFC 15—**Atlanta's Chris Miller threw an 11-yard touchdown pass to San Francisco's Jerry Rice with 4:04 remaining in the game to lift the NFC over the AFC. It was the NFC's thirteenth win in the 22-game series. The AFC had taken a 15-14 lead when the Raiders' Jeff Jaeger kicked a 27-yard field goal 1:49 into the fourth quarter. But the NFC, aided by a key roughing-the-passer penalty on a third-down incompletion from the AFC 24-yard line, drove 85 yards to the winning score. The Cowboys' Michael Irvin, playing in his first Pro Bowl, caught 8 passes for 125 yards, including a 13-yard touchdown in the first quarter, and was named the player of the game. Rice had 7 catches for 77 yards. Mark Rypien of Washington, the Super Bowl most valuable player one week earlier, completed 11 of 18 passes for 165 yards and 2 touchdowns for the NFC, including a 35-yard pass to Redskins teammate Gary Clark just 26 seconds before halftime. Miller completed 7 of his 10 attempts for 85 yards.

| | | | | | | |
|---|---|---|---|---|---|---|
| **NFC** | 7 | 7 | 0 | 7 | — | 21 |
| **AFC** | 7 | 5 | 0 | 3 | — | 15 |

AFC — Clayton 4 pass from Kelly (Jaeger kick)
NFC — Irvin 13 pass from Rypien (Lohmiller kick)
AFC — Safety, Townsend tackled Byner in end zone
AFC — FG Jaeger 48
NFC — Clark 35 pass from Rypien (Lohmiller kick)
AFC — FG Jaeger 27
NFC — Rice 11 pass from Miller (Lohmiller kick)

## 1991 AFC-NFC PRO BOWL

Aloha Stadium, Honolulu, Hawaii
February 3, 1991, Attendance: 50,345

**AFC 23, NFC 21—**Buffalo's Jim Kelly and Houston's Ernest Givins combined for a 13-yard scoring pass late in the fourth quarter to rally the AFC over the NFC. Phoenix rookie Johnny Johnson scored on runs of 1 and 9 yards to put the NFC ahead 14-3 in the third quarter. Buffalo's Andre Reed, who led all receivers with 4 catches for 80 yards, caught a 20-yard scoring reception from Kelly early in the fourth quarter to move the AFC to within 1 point. Barry Sanders ran 22 yards for a touchdown to increase the NFC's lead to 21-13. Miami's Jeff Cross blocked a 46-yard field-goal attempt by New Orleans's Morten Andersen with seven seconds remaining to preserve the win. Buffalo's Bruce Smith recorded 3 sacks and also had a blocked field goal. Kelly, who completed 13 of 19 passes for 210 yards and 2 touchdowns, was presented the Dan McGuire Award as player of the game. The AFC's victory narrowed the NFC's Pro Bowl series lead to 12-9.

| | | | | | | |
|---|---|---|---|---|---|---|
| **AFC** | 3 | 0 | 3 | 17 | — | 23 |
| **NFC** | 0 | 7 | 7 | 7 | — | 21 |

AFC — FG Lowery 26
NFC — J. Johnson 1 run (Andersen kick)
AFC — FG Lowery 43
NFC — J. Johnson 9 run (Andersen kick)
AFC — Reed 20 pass from Kelly (Lowery kick)
NFC — Sanders 22 run (Andersen kick)
AFC — FG Lowery 34
AFC — Givins 13 pass from Kelly (Lowery kick)

## 1990 AFC-NFC PRO BOWL

Aloha Stadium, Honolulu, Hawaii
February 4, 1990, Attendance: 50,445

**NFC 27, AFC 21—**The NFC captured its second straight Pro Bowl as the defense accounted for a pair of touchdowns and forced 5 turnovers before the eleventh consecutive sellout crowd at Aloha Stadium. The AFC held a 7-6 halftime edge on a 1-yard scoring run by Christian Okoye of the Chiefs. The NFC then rallied with 21 unanswered points in the third quarter. David Meggett of the Giants began the comeback with an 11-yard touchdown reception from Philadelphia's Randall Cunningham. The Rams' Jerry Gray followed with a 51-yard interception return for a score and the Vikings' Keith Millard added an 8-yard fumble return for a touchdown four minutes later to give the NFC a commanding 27-7 lead. Seattle's Dave Krieg rallied the AFC with a 5-yard touchdown pass to Miami's Ferrell Edmunds. Cleveland's Mike Johnson then returned an interception 22 yards for a score to pull the AFC to within 27-21. Gray, who was credited with 7 tackles, was given the Dan McGuire Award as player of the game. Krieg led all quarterbacks by completing 15 of 23 for 148 yards and 1 touchdown. Buffalo's Thurman Thomas topped all receivers with 5 catches for 47 yards, while Indianapolis's Eric Dickerson led all rushers with 46 yards on 15 carries. The win gave the NFC a 12-8 advantage in Pro Bowl games since 1971.

| | | | | | | |
|---|---|---|---|---|---|---|
| **NFC** | 3 | 3 | 21 | 0 | — | 27 |
| **AFC** | 0 | 7 | 0 | 14 | — | 21 |

NFC — FG Murray 23
NFC — FG Murray 41
AFC — Okoye 1 run (Treadwell kick)
NFC — Meggett 11 pass from Cunningham (Murray kick)
NFC — Gray 51 interception return (Murray kick)
NFC — Millard 8 fumble recovery return (Murray kick)
AFC — Edmunds 5 pass from Krieg (Treadwell kick)
AFC — M. Johnson 22 interception return (Treadwell kick)

## 1989 AFC-NFC PRO BOWL

Aloha Stadium, Honolulu, Hawaii
January 29, 1989, Attendance: 50,113

**NFC 34, AFC 3—**The NFC scored 34 unanswered points to snap a two-game losing streak to the AFC before the tenth straight sellout crowd in Honolulu's Aloha Stadium. Bills kicker Scott Norwood provided the AFC's only points on a 38-yard field goal 6:23 into the game. Touchdown runs by Dallas's Herschel Walker (4 yards) and Atlanta's John Settle (1) brought the NFC a 14-3 halftime lead. Walker added a 7-yard scoring run, the Saints' Morten Andersen kicked field goals of 27 and 51 yards, and Los Angeles Rams' wide receiver Henry Ellard caught an 8-yard scoring pass from Minnesota quarterback Wade Wilson in the second half to complete the scoring. Chicago running back Neal Anderson and Philadelphia quarterback Randall Cunningham, who were both appearing in their first Pro Bowl, also played major roles in the NFC's victory. Anderson rushed 13 times for 85 yards and had 2 receptions for 17. Cunningham, who was voted the game's outstanding player, completed 10 of 14 passes for 63 yards and rushed for 49 yards. The NFC, which had 5 takeaways, outgained the AFC 355 yards to 167 and held a time-of-possession advantage of 35:18 to 24:42. Houston quarterback Warren Moon completed 13 of 20 passes for 134 yards for the AFC. The win gave the NFC an 11-8 advantage in Pro Bowl games.

| | | | | | | |
|---|---|---|---|---|---|---|
| **AFC** | 3 | 0 | 0 | 0 | — | 3 |
| **NFC** | 7 | 7 | 10 | 10 | — | 34 |

AFC — FG Norwood 38
NFC — Walker 4 run (Andersen kick)
NFC — Settle 1 run (Andersen kick)
NFC — FG Andersen 27
NFC — Walker 7 run (Andersen kick)
NFC — FG Andersen 51
NFC — Ellard 8 pass from Wilson (Andersen kick)

## 1988 AFC-NFC PRO BOWL

Aloha Stadium, Honolulu, Hawaii
February 7, 1988, Attendance: 50,113

**AFC 15, NFC 6**—Led by a tenacious pass rush, the AFC defeated the NFC for the second consecutive year before the ninth straight sellout crowd in Honolulu's Aloha Stadium. Buffalo quarterback Jim Kelly scored the game's lone touchdown on a 1-yard run for a 7-6 halftime lead. Colts kicker Dean Biasucci added field goals from 37 and 30 yards to complete the AFC's scoring. Saints kicker Morten Andersen had 25- and 36-yard field goals to account for the NFC's points. AFC defenders held the NFC to 213 yards and recorded 8 sacks. Bills defensive end Bruce Smith, who had 2 sacks among his 5 tackles, was voted the game's outstanding player. Oilers running back Mike Rozier led all rushers with 49 yards on 9 carries. Jets wide receiver Al Toon had 5 receptions for 75 yards. The AFC generated 341 yards total offense and held a time-of-possession advantage of 34:14 to 25:46. By winning, the AFC cut the NFC's lead in the Pro Bowl series to 10-8.

| | | | | | | |
|---|---|---|---|---|---|---|
| **NFC** | 0 | 6 | 0 | 0 | — | 6 |
| **AFC** | 0 | 7 | 6 | 2 | — | 15 |

NFC — FG Andersen 25
AFC — Kelly 1 run (Biasucci kick)
NFC — FG Andersen 36
AFC — FG Biasucci 37
AFC — FG Biasucci 30
AFC — Safety, Montana forced out of end zone

## 1987 AFC-NFC PRO BOWL

Aloha Stadium, Honolulu, Hawaii
February 1, 1987, Attendance: 50,101

**AFC 10, NFC 6**—The AFC defeated the NFC in the lowest-scoring game in AFC-NFC Pro Bowl history. The AFC took a 10-0 halftime lead on Broncos quarterback John Elway's 10-yard touchdown pass to Raiders tight end Todd Christensen and Patriots kicker Tony Franklin's 26-yard field goal. The AFC defense made the lead stand by forcing the NFC to settle for a pair of field goals from 38 and 19 yards by Saints kicker Morten Andersen after the NFC had first downs at the AFC 31-, 7-, 16-, 15-, 5-, and 7-yard lines. Both AFC scores were set up by fumble recoveries by Seahawks linebacker Fredd Young and Dolphins linebacker John Offerdahl, respectively. Eagles defensive end Reggie White, who tied a Pro Bowl record with 4 sacks among his 7 solo tackles, was voted the game's outstanding player. The AFC victory cut the NFC's lead in the Pro Bowl series to 10-7.

| | | | | | | |
|---|---|---|---|---|---|---|
| **AFC** | 7 | 3 | 0 | 0 | — | 10 |
| **NFC** | 0 | 0 | 3 | 3 | — | 6 |

AFC — Christensen 10 pass from Elway (Franklin kick)
AFC — FG Franklin 26
NFC — FG Andersen 38
NFC — FG Andersen 19

## 1986 AFC-NFC PRO BOWL

Aloha Stadium, Honolulu, Hawaii
February 2, 1986, Attendance: 50,101

**NFC 28, AFC 24**—New York Giants quarterback Phil Simms brought the NFC back from a 24-7 halftime deficit to defeat the AFC. Simms, who completed 15 of 27 passes for 212 yards and 3 touchdowns, was named the most valuable player of the game. The AFC had taken its first-half lead behind a 2-yard run by Los Angeles Raiders running back Marcus Allen, who also threw a 51-yard scoring pass to San Diego wide receiver Wes Chandler, an 11-yard touchdown catch by Pittsburgh wide receiver Louis Lipps, and a 34-yard field goal by Steelers kicker Gary Anderson. Minnesota's Joey Browner accounted for the NFC's only score before halftime with a 48-yard interception return. After intermission, the NFC blanked the AFC while scoring 3 touchdowns via a 15-yard catch by Washington wide receiver Art Monk, a 2-yard reception by Dallas tight end Doug Cosbie, and a 15-yard catch by Tampa Bay tight end Jimmie Giles with 2:47 remaining in the game. The victory gave the NFC a 10-6 Pro Bowl record against the AFC.

| | | | | | | |
|---|---|---|---|---|---|---|
| **NFC** | 0 | 7 | 7 | 14 | — | 28 |
| **AFC** | 7 | 17 | 0 | 0 | — | 24 |

AFC — Allen 2 run (Anderson kick)
NFC — Browner 48 interception return (Andersen kick)
AFC — Chandler 51 pass from Allen (Anderson kick)
AFC — FG Anderson 34
AFC — Lipps 11 pass from O'Brien (Anderson kick)
NFC — Monk 15 pass from Simms (Andersen kick)
NFC — Cosbie 2 pass from Simms (Andersen kick)
NFC — Giles 15 pass from Simms (Andersen kick)

## 1985 AFC-NFC PRO BOWL

Aloha Stadium, Honolulu, Hawaii
January 27, 1985, Attendance: 50,385

**AFC 22, NFC 14**—Defensive end Art Still of the Kansas City Chiefs recovered a fumble and returned it 83 yards for a touchdown to clinch the AFC's victory over the NFC. Still's touchdown came in the fourth period with the AFC trailing 14-12 and was one of several outstanding defensive plays in a Pro Bowl dominated by two record-breaking defenses. The teams combined for a Pro Bowl-record 17 sacks, including 4 by New York Jets defensive end Mark Gastineau, who was named the game's outstanding player. The AFC's first score came on a safety when Gastineau tackled running back Eric Dickerson of the Los Angeles Rams in the end zone. The AFC's second score, a 6-yard pass from Miami's Dan Marino to Los Angeles Raiders running back Marcus Allen, was set up by a partial block of a punt by Seahawks linebacker Fredd Young. The NFC leads the series 9-6.

| | | | | | | |
|---|---|---|---|---|---|---|
| **AFC** | 0 | 9 | 0 | 13 | — | 22 |
| **NFC** | 0 | 0 | 7 | 7 | — | 14 |

AFC — Safety, Gastineau tackled Dickerson in end zone
AFC — Allen 6 pass from Marino (Johnson kick)
NFC — Lofton 13 pass from Montana (Stenerud kick)
NFC — Payton 1 run (Stenerud kick)
AFC — FG Johnson 33
AFC — Still 83 fumble recovery return (Johnson kick)
AFC — FG Johnson 22

## 1984 AFC-NFC PRO BOWL

Aloha Stadium, Honolulu, Hawaii
January 29, 1984, Attendance: 50,445

**NFC 45, AFC 3**—The NFC won its sixth Pro Bowl in the last seven seasons by routing the AFC. The NFC was led by the passing of most valuable player Joe Theismann of Washington, who completed 21 of 27 passes for 242 yards and 3 touchdowns. Theismann set Pro Bowl records for completions and touchdown passes. The NFC established Pro Bowl marks for most points scored and fewest points allowed. Running back William Andrews of Atlanta had 6 carries for 43 yards and caught 4 passes for 49 yards, including scoring receptions of 16 and 2 yards. Los Angeles Rams rookie Eric Dickerson gained 46 yards on 11 carries, including a 14-yard touchdown run, and had 45 yards on 5 catches. Rams safety Nolan Cromwell had a 44-yard interception return for a touchdown early in the third period to give the NFC a commanding 24-3 lead. Green Bay wide receiver James Lofton caught an 8-yard touchdown pass, while tight end teammate Paul Coffman had a 6-yard scoring catch.

| | | | | | | |
|---|---|---|---|---|---|---|
| **NFC** | 3 | 14 | 14 | 14 | — | 45 |
| **AFC** | 0 | 3 | 0 | 0 | — | 3 |

NFC — FG Haji-Sheikh 23
NFC — Andrews 16 pass from Theismann (Haji-Sheikh kick)
NFC — Andrews 2 pass from Montana (Haji-Sheikh kick)
AFC — FG Anderson 43
NFC — Cromwell 44 interception return (Haji-Sheikh kick)
NFC — Lofton 8 pass from Theismann (Haji-Sheikh kick)
NFC — Coffman 6 pass from Theismann (Haji-Sheikh kick)
NFC — Dickerson 14 run (Haji-Sheikh kick)

## 1983 AFC-NFC PRO BOWL

Aloha Stadium, Honolulu, Hawaii
February 6, 1983, Attendance: 49,883

**NFC 20, AFC 19**—Dallas's Danny White threw an 11-yard touchdown pass to the Packers' John Jefferson with 35 seconds remaining to rally the NFC over the AFC. White, who completed 14 of 26 passes for 162 yards, kept the winning 65-yard drive alive with a 14-yard completion to Jefferson on a fourth-and-7 play at the AFC 25. The AFC was ahead 12-10 at halftime and increased the lead to 19-10 in the third period, when Marcus Allen scored on a 1-yard run. San Diego's Dan Fouts, who attempted 30 passes, set Pro Bowl records for most completions (17) and yards (274). Pittsburgh's John Stallworth was the AFC's leading receiver with 7 catches for 67 yards. William Andrews topped the NFC with 5 receptions for 48 yards. Fouts and Jefferson were co-winners of the player of the game award.

| | | | | | | |
|---|---|---|---|---|---|---|
| **AFC** | 9 | 3 | 7 | 0 | — | 19 |
| **NFC** | 0 | 10 | 0 | 10 | — | 20 |

AFC — Walker 34 pass from Fouts (Benirschke kick)
AFC — Safety, Still tackled Theismann in end zone
NFC — Andrews 3 run (Moseley kick)
NFC — FG Moseley 35
AFC — FG Benirschke 29
AFC — Allen 1 run (Benirschke kick)
NFC — FG Moseley 41
NFC — Jefferson 11 pass from D. White (Moseley kick)

## 1982 AFC-NFC PRO BOWL

Aloha Stadium, Honolulu, Hawaii
January 31, 1982, Attendance: 50,402

**AFC 16, NFC 13**—Nick Lowery of Kansas City kicked a 23-yard field goal with three seconds remaining to give the AFC a last-second victory over the NFC. Lowery's kick climaxed a 69-yard drive directed by quarterback Dan Fouts. The NFC gained a 13-13 tie with 2:43 to go when Dallas's Tony Dorsett ran 4 yards for a touchdown. In the drive to the winning field goal, Fouts completed 3 passes, including a 23-yard toss to San Diego teammate Kellen Winslow that put the ball on the NFC's 5-yard line. Two plays later, Lowery kicked the field goal. Winslow, who caught 6 passes for 86 yards, was named co-player of the game along with Tampa Bay defensive end Lee Roy Selmon.

| | | | | | | |
|---|---|---|---|---|---|---|
| **NFC** | 0 | 6 | 0 | 7 | — | 13 |
| **AFC** | 0 | 0 | 13 | 3 | — | 16 |

NFC — Giles 4 pass from Montana (kick blocked)
AFC — Muncie 2 run (kick failed)
AFC — Campbell 1 run (Lowery kick)

NFC — Dorsett 4 run (Septien kick)
AFC — FG Lowery 23

### 1981 AFC-NFC PRO BOWL

Aloha Stadium, Honolulu, Hawaii
February 1, 1981, Attendance: 50,360

**NFC 21, AFC 7**—Eddie Murray kicked 4 field goals and Steve Bartkowski fired a 55-yard scoring pass to Alfred Jenkins to lead the NFC to its fourth straight victory over the AFC and a 7-4 edge in the series. Murray was named the game's most valuable player and missed tying Garo Yepremian's Pro Bowl record of 5 field goals when a 37-yard attempt hit the crossbar with 22 seconds remaining. The AFC's only score came on a 9-yard pass from Brian Sipe to Stanley Morgan in the second period. Bartkowski completed 9 of 21 passes for 173 yards, while Sipe connected on 10 of 15 for 142 yards. Ottis Anderson led all rushers with 70 yards on 10 carries. Earl Campbell, the NFL's leading rusher in 1980, was limited to 24 yards on 8 attempts.

| | | | | | | |
|---|---|---|---|---|---|---|
| **AFC** | 0 | 7 | 0 | 0 | — | 7 |
| **NFC** | 3 | 6 | 0 | 12 | — | 21 |

NFC — FG Murray 31
AFC — Morgan 9 pass from Sipe (J. Smith kick)
NFC — FG Murray 31
NFC — FG Murray 34
NFC — Jenkins 55 pass from Bartkowski (Murray kick)
NFC — FG Murray 36
NFC — Safety, Shell called for holding in end zone

### 1980 AFC-NFC PRO BOWL

Aloha Stadium, Honolulu, Hawaii
January 27, 1980, Attendance: 49,800

**NFC 37, AFC 27**—Running back Chuck Muncie of New Orleans ran for 2 touchdowns and threw a 25-yard option pass for another score to give the NFC its third consecutive victory over the AFC. Muncie, who was selected the game's most valuable player, snapped a 3-3 tie on a 1-yard touchdown run at 1:41 of the second quarter, then scored on an 11-yard run in the fourth quarter for the NFC's final touchdown. Two scoring records were set in the game— 37 points by the NFC, eclipsing the 33 by the AFC in 1973, and the 64 points by both teams, surpassing the 61 scored in 1973.

| | | | | | | |
|---|---|---|---|---|---|---|
| **NFC** | 3 | 20 | 7 | 7 | — | 37 |
| **AFC** | 3 | 7 | 10 | 7 | — | 27 |

NFC — FG Moseley 37
AFC — FG Fritsch 19
NFC — Muncie 1 run (Moseley kick)
AFC — Pruitt 1 pass from Bradshaw (Fritsch kick)
NFC — D. Hill 13 pass from Manning (kick failed)
NFC — T. Hill 25 pass from Muncie (Moseley kick)
NFC — Henry 86 punt return (Moseley kick)
AFC — Campbell 2 run (Fritsch kick)
AFC — FG Fritsch 29
NFC — Muncie 11 run (Moseley kick)
AFC — Campbell 1 run (Fritsch kick)

### 1979 AFC-NFC PRO BOWL

Memorial Coliseum, Los Angeles, California
January 29, 1979, Attendance: 46,281

**NFC 13, AFC 7**—Roger Staubach completed 9 of 15 passes for 125 yards, including the winning touchdown on a 19-yard strike to Dallas Cowboys teammate Tony Hill in the third period. The winning drive began at the AFC's 45-yard line after a shanked punt. Staubach hit Ahmad Rashad with passes of 15 and 17 yards to set up Hill's decisive catch. The victory gave the NFC a 5-4 advantage in Pro Bowl games. Rashad, who accounted for 89 yards on 5 receptions, was named the player of the game. The AFC led 7-6 at halftime on Bob Griese's 8-yard scoring toss to Steve Largent late in the second quarter. Largent finished the game with 5 receptions for 75 yards. The NFC scored first as Archie Manning marched his team 70 yards in 11 plays, capped by Wilbert Montgomery's 2-yard touchdown run. The AFC's Earl Campbell was the game's leading rusher with 66 yards on 12 carries.

| | | | | | | |
|---|---|---|---|---|---|---|
| **AFC** | 0 | 7 | 0 | 0 | — | 7 |
| **NFC** | 0 | 6 | 7 | 0 | — | 13 |

NFC — Montgomery 2 run (kick failed)
AFC — Largent 8 pass from Griese (Yepremian kick)
NFC — T. Hill 19 pass from Staubach (Corral kick)

### 1978 AFC-NFC PRO BOWL

Tampa Stadium, Tampa, Florida
January 23, 1978, Attendance: 51,337

**NFC 14, AFC 13**—Walter Payton, the NFL's leading rusher in 1977, sparked a second-half comeback to give the NFC the win and tie the series between the two conferences at four victories each. Payton, who was the game's most valuable player, gained 77 yards on 13 carries and scored the tying touchdown on a 1-yard burst with 7:37 left in the game. Efren Herrera kicked the winning extra point. The AFC dominated the first half of the game, taking a 13-0 lead on field goals of 21 and 39 yards by Toni Linhart and a 10-yard touchdown pass from Ken Stabler to Oakland teammate Cliff Branch. On the NFC's first possession of the second half, Pat Haden put together the first touchdown drive after Eddie Brown returned Ray Guy's punt to the AFC 46-yard line. Haden connected on all 4 of his passes on that drive, finally hitting Terry Metcalf with a 4-yard scoring toss. The NFC continued to rally and, with Jim Hart at quarterback, moved 63 yards in 12 plays for the go-ahead score. During the winning drive, Hart completed 5 of 6 passes for 38 yards and Payton picked up 20 more on the ground.

| | | | | | | |
|---|---|---|---|---|---|---|
| **AFC** | 3 | 10 | 0 | 0 | — | 13 |
| **NFC** | 0 | 0 | 7 | 7 | — | 14 |

AFC — FG Linhart 21
AFC — Branch 10 pass from Stabler (Linhart kick)
AFC — FG Linhart 39
NFC — Metcalf 4 pass from Haden (Herrera kick)
NFC — Payton 1 run (Herrera kick)

### 1977 AFC-NFC PRO BOWL

Kingdome, Seattle, Washington
January 17, 1977, Attendance: 64,752

**AFC 24, NFC 14**—O.J. Simpson's 3-yard touchdown burst at 7:03 of the first quarter gave the AFC a lead it would not surrender, the victory breaking a two-game NFC win streak and giving the American Conference stars a 4-3 series lead. The AFC took a 17-7 lead midway through the second period on the first of 2 Ken Anderson touchdown passes, a 12-yard toss to Charlie Joiner. But the NFC mounted a 73-yard drive capped by Lawrence McCutcheon's 1-yard touchdown plunge to pull within 17-14 at the half. Following a scoreless third quarter, player of the game Mel Blount thwarted a possible NFC score when he intercepted Jim Hart's pass in the end zone. Less than three minutes later, Blount again picked off a Hart pass, returning it 16 yards to the NFC 27. That set up Anderson's 27-yard touchdown strike to the Raiders' Cliff Branch for the final score.

| | | | | | | |
|---|---|---|---|---|---|---|
| **NFC** | 0 | 14 | 0 | 0 | — | 14 |
| **AFC** | 10 | 7 | 0 | 7 | — | 24 |

AFC — Simpson 3 run (Linhart kick)
AFC — FG Linhart 31
NFC — Thomas 15 run (Bakken kick)
AFC — Joiner 12 pass from Anderson (Linhart kick)
NFC — McCutcheon 1 run (Bakken kick)
AFC — Branch 27 pass from Anderson (Linhart kick)

### 1976 AFC-NFC PRO BOWL

Superdome, New Orleans, Louisiana
January 26, 1976, Attendance: 30,546

**NFC 23, AFC 20**—Mike Boryla, a late substitute who did not enter the game until 5:39 remained, lifted the National Football Conference to the victory over the American Football Conference with 2 touchdown passes in the final minutes. It was the second straight NFC win, squaring the series at 3-3. Until Boryla started firing the ball the AFC was in control, leading 13-0 at the half. Boryla entered the game after Billy Johnson had raced 90 yards with a punt to make the score 20-9 in favor of the AFC. He floated a 14-yard touchdown pass to Terry Metcalf and later fired an 8-yard scoring pass to Mel Gray for the winner.

| | | | | | | |
|---|---|---|---|---|---|---|
| **AFC** | 0 | 13 | 0 | 7 | — | 20 |
| **NFC** | 0 | 0 | 9 | 14 | — | 23 |

AFC — FG Stenerud 20
AFC — FG Stenerud 35
AFC — Burrough 64 pass from Pastorini (Stenerud kick)
NFC — FG Bakken 42
NFC — Foreman 4 pass from Hart (kick blocked)
AFC — Johnson 90 punt return (Stenerud kick)
NFC — Metcalf 14 pass from Boryla (Bakken kick)
NFC — Gray 8 pass from Boryla (Bakken kick)

### 1975 AFC-NFC PRO BOWL

Orange Bowl, Miami, Florida
January 20, 1975, Attendance: 26,484

**NFC 17, AFC 10**—Los Angeles quarterback James Harris, who took over the NFC offense after Jim Hart of St. Louis suffered a laceration above his right eye in the second period, threw 2 touchdown passes early in the fourth period to pace the NFC to its second victory in the five-game Pro Bowl series. The NFC win snapped a three-game AFC victory string. Harris, who was named the player of the game, connected with St. Louis's Mel Gray for an 8-yard touchdown 2:03 into the final period. One minute and 24 seconds later, following a fumble recovery by Washington's Ken Houston, Harris tossed another 8-yard scoring pass to Washington's Charley Taylor for the decisive points.

| | | | | | | |
|---|---|---|---|---|---|---|
| **NFC** | 0 | 3 | 0 | 14 | — | 17 |
| **AFC** | 0 | 0 | 10 | 0 | — | 10 |

NFC — FG Marcol 33
AFC — Warfield 32 pass from Griese (Gerela kick)
AFC — FG Gerela 33
NFC — Gray 8 pass from J. Harris (Marcol kick)
NFC — Taylor 8 pass from J. Harris (Marcol kick)

### 1974 AFC-NFC PRO BOWL

Arrowhead Stadium, Kansas City, Missouri
January 20, 1974, Attendance: 66,918

**AFC 15, NFC 13**—Miami's Garo Yepremian's fifth field goal—a 42-yard kick with 21 seconds remaining—gave the AFC its third straight victory since the NFC won the inaugural game following the 1970 season. The field goal by Yepremian, who was voted the game's outstanding player, offset a 21-yard field goal by Atlanta's Nick Mike-Mayer that had given the NFC a 13-12 advantage with 1:41 remaining. The only touchdown in the game was scored by the NFC on a 14-yard pass from Philadelphia's Roman Gabriel to Lawrence McCutcheon of the Los Angeles Rams.

| | | | | | | |
|---|---|---|---|---|---|---|
| **NFC** | 0 | 10 | 0 | 3 | — | 13 |
| **AFC** | 3 | 3 | 3 | 6 | — | 15 |

AFC — FG Yepremian 16
NFC — FG Mike-Mayer 27
NFC — McCutcheon 14 pass from Gabriel (Mike-Mayer kick)
AFC — FG Yepremian 37
AFC — FG Yepremian 27
AFC — FG Yepremian 41
NFC — FG Mike-Mayer 21
AFC — FG Yepremian 42

### 1973 AFC-NFC PRO BOWL

Texas Stadium, Irving, Texas
January 21, 1973, Attendance: 37,091

**AFC 33, NFC 28**—Paced by the rushing and receiving of player of the game O.J. Simpson, the AFC erased a 14-0 first period deficit and built a commanding 33-14 lead midway through the fourth period before the NFC managed 2 touchdowns in the final minute of play. Simpson rushed for 112 yards and caught 3 passes for 58 more to gain unanimous recognition in the balloting for player of the game. John Brockington scored 3 touchdowns for the NFC.

| | | | | | | |
|---|---|---|---|---|---|---|
| **AFC** | 0 | 10 | 10 | 13 | — | 33 |
| **NFC** | 14 | 0 | 0 | 14 | — | 28 |

NFC — Brockington 1 run (Marcol kick)
NFC — Brockington 3 pass from Kilmer (Marcol kick)
AFC — Simpson 7 run (Gerela kick)
AFC — FG Gerela 18
AFC — FG Gerela 22

AFC — Hubbard 11 run (Gerela kick)
AFC — O. Taylor 5 pass from Lamonica (kick failed)
AFC — Bell 12 interception return (Gerela kick)
NFC — Brockington 1 run (Marcol kick)
NFC — Kwalick 12 pass from Snead (Marcol kick)

### 1972 AFC-NFC PRO BOWL

Memorial Coliseum, Los Angeles, California
January 23, 1972, Attendance: 53,647
**AFC 26, NFC 13**—Kansas City's Jan Stenerud kicked 4 field goals to lead the AFC from a 6-0 deficit to victory. The AFC defense picked off 3 passes. Stenerud was selected as the outstanding offensive player and his Kansas City teammate, linebacker Willie Lanier, was the game's outstanding defensive player.

| | | | | | | |
|---|---|---|---|---|---|---|
| **AFC** | 0 | 3 | 13 | 10 | — | 26 |
| **NFC** | 0 | 6 | 0 | 7 | — | 13 |

NFC — Grim 50 pass from Landry (kick failed)
AFC — FG Stenerud 25
AFC — FG Stenerud 23
AFC — FG Stenerud 48
AFC — Morin 5 pass from Dawson (Stenerud kick)
AFC — FG Stenerud 42
NFC — V. Washington 2 run (Knight kick)
AFC — F. Little 6 run (Stenerud kick)

### 1971 AFC-NFC PRO BOWL

Memorial Coliseum, Los Angeles, California
January 24, 1971, Attendance: 48,222
**NFC 27, AFC 6**—Mel Renfro of Dallas broke open the first meeting between the American Football Conference and National Football Conference all-star teams as he returned a pair of punts 82 and 56 yards for touchdowns in the final period to clinch the NFC victory over the AFC. Renfro was voted the game's outstanding back and linebacker Fred Carr of Green Bay the outstanding lineman.

| | | | | | | |
|---|---|---|---|---|---|---|
| **AFC** | 0 | 3 | 3 | 0 | — | 6 |
| **NFC** | 0 | 3 | 10 | 14 | — | 27 |

AFC — FG Stenerud 37
NFC — FG Cox 13
NFC — Osborn 23 pass from Brodie (Cox kick)
NFC — FG Cox 35
AFC — FG Stenerud 16
NFC — Renfro 82 punt return (Cox kick)
NFC — Renfro 56 punt return (Cox kick)

## PRO BOWL ALL-TIME RESULTS

| Date | Result | Site (attendance) | Honored players |
|---|---|---|---|
| Jan. 15, 1939 | New York Giants 13, Pro All-Stars 10 | Wrigley Field, Los Angeles (20,000) | |
| Jan. 14, 1940 | Green Bay 16, NFL All-Stars 7 | Gilmore Stadium, Los Angeles (18,000) | |
| Dec. 29, 1940 | Chicago Bears 28, NFL All-Stars 14 | Gilmore Stadium, Los Angeles (21,624) | |
| Jan. 4, 1942 | Chicago Bears 35, NFL All-Stars 24 | Polo Grounds, New York (17,725) | |
| Dec. 27, 1942 | NFL All-Stars 17, Washington 14 | Shibe Park, Philadelphia (18,671) | |
| Jan. 14, 1951 | American Conf. 28, National Conf. 27 | Los Angeles Memorial Coliseum (53,676) | Otto Graham, Cleveland, player of the game |
| Jan. 12, 1952 | National Conf. 30, American Conf. 13 | Los Angeles Memorial Coliseum (19,400) | Dan Towler, Los Angeles, player of the game |
| Jan. 10, 1953 | National Conf. 27, American Conf. 7 | Los Angeles Memorial Coliseum (34,208) | Don Doll, Detroit, player of the game |
| Jan. 17, 1954 | East 20, West 9 | Los Angeles Memorial Coliseum (44,214) | Chuck Bednarik, Philadelphia, player of the game |
| Jan. 16, 1955 | West 26, East 19 | Los Angeles Memorial Coliseum (43,972) | Billy Wilson, San Francisco, player of the game |
| Jan. 15, 1956 | East 31, West 30 | Los Angeles Memorial Coliseum (37,867) | Ollie Matson, Chi. Cardinals, player of the game |
| Jan. 13, 1957 | West 19, East 10 | Los Angeles Memorial Coliseum (44,177) | Bert Rechichar, Baltimore, outstanding back<br>Ernie Stautner, Pittsburgh, outstanding lineman |
| Jan. 12, 1958 | West 26, East 7 | Los Angeles Memorial Coliseum (66,634) | Hugh McElhenny, San Francisco, outstanding back<br>Gene Brito, Washington, outstanding lineman |
| Jan. 11, 1959 | East 28, West 21 | Los Angeles Memorial Coliseum (72,250) | Frank Gifford, N.Y. Giants, outstanding back<br>Doug Atkins, Chi. Bears, outstanding lineman |
| Jan. 17, 1960 | West 38, East 21 | Los Angeles Memorial Coliseum (56,876) | Johnny Unitas, Baltimore, outstanding back<br>Gene (Big Daddy) Lipscomb, Baltimore, outstanding lineman |
| Jan. 15, 1961 | West 35, East 31 | Los Angeles Memorial Coliseum (62,971) | Johnny Unitas, Baltimore, outstanding back<br>Sam Huff, N.Y. Giants, outstanding lineman |
| Jan. 7, 1962 | AFL West 47, East 27 | Balboa Stadium, San Diego (20,973) | Cotton Davidson, Dallas Texans, player of the game |
| Jan. 14, 1962 | NFL West 31, East 30 | Los Angeles Memorial Coliseum (57,409) | Jim Brown, Cleveland, outstanding back<br>Henry Jordan, Green Bay, outstanding lineman |
| Jan. 13, 1963 | AFL West 21, East 14 | Balboa Stadium, San Diego (27,641) | Curtis McClinton, Dallas Texans, outstanding offensive player<br>Earl Faison, San Diego, outstanding defensive player |
| Jan. 13, 1963 | NFL East 30, West 20 | Los Angeles Memorial Coliseum (61,374) | Jim Brown, Cleveland, outstanding back<br>Gene (Big Daddy) Lipscomb, Pittsburgh, outstanding lineman |
| Jan. 12, 1964 | NFL West 31, East 17 | Los Angeles Memorial Coliseum (67,242) | Johnny Unitas, Baltimore, player of the game<br>Gino Marchetti, Baltimore, outstanding lineman |
| Jan. 19, 1964 | AFL West 27, East 24 | Balboa Stadium, San Diego (20,016) | Keith Lincoln, San Diego, outstanding offensive player<br>Archie Matsos, Oakland, outstanding defensive player |
| Jan. 10, 1965 | NFL West 34, East 14 | Los Angeles Memorial Coliseum (60,598) | Fran Tarkenton, Minnesota, outstanding back<br>Terry Barr, Detroit, outstanding lineman |
| Jan. 16, 1965 | AFL West 38, East 14 | Jeppesen Stadium, Houston (15,446) | Keith Lincoln, San Diego, outstanding offensive player<br>Willie Brown, Denver, outstanding defensive player |
| Jan. 15, 1966 | AFL All-Stars 30, Buffalo 19 | Rice Stadium, Houston (35,572) | Joe Namath, N.Y. Jets, most valuable player, offense<br>Frank Buncom, San Diego, most valuable player, defense |
| Jan. 15, 1966 | NFL East 36, West 7 | Los Angeles Memorial Coliseum (60,124) | Jim Brown, Cleveland, outstanding back<br>Dale Meinert, St. Louis, outstanding lineman |
| Jan. 21, 1967 | AFL East 30, West 23 | Oakland-Alameda County Coliseum (18,876) | Babe Parilli, Boston, outstanding offensive player<br>Verlon Biggs, N.Y. Jets, outstanding defensive player |
| Jan. 22, 1967 | NFL East 20, West 10 | Los Angeles Memorial Coliseum (15,062) | Gale Sayers, Chicago, outstanding back<br>Floyd Peters, Philadelphia, outstanding lineman |
| Jan. 21, 1968 | AFL East 25, West 24 | Gator Bowl, Jacksonville, Fla. (40,103) | Joe Namath and Don Maynard, N.Y. Jets, out. off. players<br>Leslie (Speedy) Duncan, San Diego, out. def. player |
| Jan. 21, 1968 | NFL West 38, East 20 | Los Angeles Memorial Coliseum (53,289) | Gale Sayers, Chicago, outstanding back<br>Dave Robinson, Green Bay, outstanding lineman |
| Jan. 19, 1969 | AFL West 38, East 25 | Gator Bowl, Jacksonville, Fla. (41,058) | Len Dawson, Kansas City, outstanding offensive player<br>George Webster, Houston, outstanding defensive player |
| Jan. 19, 1969 | NFL West 10, East 7 | Los Angeles Memorial Coliseum (32,050) | Roman Gabriel, Los Angeles, outstanding back<br>Merlin Olsen, Los Angeles, outstanding lineman |
| Jan. 17, 1970 | AFL West 26, East 3 | Astrodome, Houston (30,170) | John Hadl, San Diego, player of the game |
| Jan. 18, 1970 | NFL West 16, East 13 | Los Angeles Memorial Coliseum (57,786) | Gale Sayers, Chicago, outstanding back<br>George Andrie, Dallas, outstanding lineman |
| Jan. 24, 1971 | NFC 27, AFC 6 | Los Angeles Memorial Coliseum (48,222) | Mel Renfro, Dallas, outstanding back<br>Fred Carr, Green Bay, outstanding lineman |
| Jan. 23, 1972 | AFC 26, NFC 13 | Los Angeles Memorial Coliseum (53,647) | Jan Stenerud, Kansas City, outstanding offensive player<br>Willie Lanier, Kansas City, outstanding defensive player |
| Jan. 21, 1973 | AFC 33, NFC 28 | Texas Stadium, Irving (37,091) | O.J. Simpson, Buffalo, player of the game |
| Jan. 20, 1974 | AFC 15, NFC 13 | Arrowhead Stadium, Kansas City (66,918) | Garo Yepremian, Miami, player of the game |
| Jan. 20, 1975 | NFC 17, AFC 10 | Orange Bowl, Miami (26,484) | James Harris, Los Angeles, player of the game |
| Jan. 26, 1976 | NFC 23, AFC 20 | Louisiana Superdome, New Orleans (30,546) | Billy Johnson, Houston, player of the game |
| Jan. 17, 1977 | AFC 24, NFC 14 | Kingdome, Seattle (64,752) | Mel Blount, Pittsburgh, player of the game |
| Jan. 23, 1978 | NFC 14, AFC 13 | Tampa Stadium (51,337) | Walter Payton, Chicago, player of the game |
| Jan. 29, 1979 | NFC 13, AFC 7 | Los Angeles Memorial Coliseum (46,281) | Ahmad Rashad, Minnesota, player of the game |
| Jan. 27, 1980 | NFC 37, AFC 27 | Aloha Stadium, Honolulu (49,800) | Chuck Muncie, New Orleans, player of the game |
| Feb. 1, 1981 | NFC 21, AFC 7 | Aloha Stadium, Honolulu (50,360) | Eddie Murray, Detroit, player of the game |
| Jan. 31, 1982 | AFC 16, NFC 13 | Aloha Stadium, Honolulu (50,402) | Kellen Winslow, San Diego, and Lee Roy Selmon, Tampa Bay, players of the game |
| Feb. 6, 1983 | NFC 20, AFC 19 | Aloha Stadium, Honolulu (49,883) | Dan Fouts, San Diego, and John Jefferson, Green Bay, players of the game |
| Jan. 29, 1984 | NFC 45, AFC 3 | Aloha Stadium, Honolulu (50,445) | Joe Theismann, Washington, player of the game |
| Jan. 27, 1985 | AFC 22, NFC 14 | Aloha Stadium, Honolulu (50,385) | Mark Gastineau, N.Y. Jets, player of the game |
| Feb. 2, 1986 | NFC 28, AFC 24 | Aloha Stadium, Honolulu (50,101) | Phil Simms, N.Y. Giants, player of the game |
| Feb. 1, 1987 | AFC 10, NFC 6 | Aloha Stadium, Honolulu (50,101) | Reggie White, Philadelphia, player of the game |
| Feb. 7, 1988 | AFC 15, NFC 6 | Aloha Stadium, Honolulu (50,113) | Bruce Smith, Buffalo, player of the game |
| Jan. 29, 1989 | NFC 34, AFC 3 | Aloha Stadium, Honolulu (50,113) | Randall Cunningham, Philadelphia, player of the game |
| Feb. 4, 1990 | NFC 27, AFC 21 | Aloha Stadium, Honolulu (50,445) | Jerry Gray, L.A. Rams, player of the game |
| Feb. 3, 1991 | AFC 23, NFC 21 | Aloha Stadium, Honolulu (50,345) | Jim Kelly, Buffalo, player of the game |
| Feb. 2, 1992 | NFC 21, AFC 15 | Aloha Stadium, Honolulu (50,209) | Michael Irvin, Dallas, player of the game |
| Feb. 7, 1993 | AFC 23, NFC 20 (OT) | Aloha Stadium, Honolulu (50,007) | Steve Tasker, Buffalo, player of the game |
| Feb. 6, 1994 | NFC 17, AFC 3 | Aloha Stadium, Honolulu (50,026) | Andre Rison, Atlanta, player of the game |

## PRO FOOTBALL HALL OF FAME GAME

| | |
|---|---|
| 1962 | New York Giants 21, St. Louis Cardinals 21 |
| 1963 | Pittsburgh Steelers 16, Cleveland Browns 7 |
| 1964 | Baltimore Colts 48, Pittsburgh Steelers 17 |
| 1965 | Washington Redskins 20, Detroit Lions 3 |
| 1966 | No game |
| 1967 | Philadelphia Eagles 28, Cleveland Browns 13 |
| 1968 | Chicago Bears 30, Dallas Cowboys 24 |
| 1969 | Green Bay Packers 38, Atlanta Falcons 24 |
| 1970 | New Orleans Saints 14, Minnesota Vikings 13 |
| 1971 | Los Angeles Rams (NFC) 17, Houston Oilers (AFC) 6 |
| 1972 | Kansas City Chiefs (AFC) 23, New York Giants (NFC) 17 |
| 1973 | San Francisco 49ers (NFC) 20, New England Patriots (AFC) 7 |
| 1974 | St. Louis Cardinals (NFC) 21, Buffalo Bills (AFC) 13 |
| 1975 | Washington Redskins (NFC) 17, Cincinnati Bengals (AFC) 9 |
| 1976 | Denver Broncos (AFC) 10, Detroit Lions (NFC) 7 |
| 1977 | Chicago Bears (NFC) 20, New York Jets (AFC) 6 |
| 1978 | Philadelphia Eagles (NFC) 17, Miami Dolphins (AFC) 3 |
| 1979 | Oakland Raiders (AFC) 20, Dallas Cowboys (NFC) 13 |
| 1980* | San Diego Chargers (AFC) 0, Green Bay Packers (NFC) 0 |
| 1981 | Cleveland Browns (AFC) 24, Atlanta Falcons (NFC) 10 |
| 1982 | Minnesota Vikings (NFC) 30, Baltimore Colts (AFC) 14 |
| 1983 | Pittsburgh Steelers (AFC) 27, New Orleans Saints (NFC) 14 |
| 1984 | Seattle Seahawks (AFC) 38, Tampa Bay Buccaneers (NFC) 0 |
| 1985 | New York Giants (NFC) 21, Houston Oilers (AFC) 20 |
| 1986 | New England Patriots (AFC) 21, St. Louis Cardinals (NFC) 16 |
| 1987 | San Francisco 49ers (NFC) 20, Kansas City Chiefs (AFC) 7 |
| 1988 | Cincinnati Bengals (AFC) 14, Los Angeles Rams (NFC) 7 |
| 1989 | Washington Redskins (NFC) 31, Buffalo Bills (AFC) 6 |
| 1990 | Chicago Bears (NFC) 13, Cleveland Browns (AFC) 0 |
| 1991 | Detroit Lions (NFC) 14, Denver Broncos (AFC) 3 |
| 1992 | New York Jets (AFC) 41, Philadelphia Eagles (NFC) 14 |
| 1993 | Los Angeles Raiders (AFC) 19, Green Bay Packers (NFC) 3 |

*Game called with 5:29 remaining due to severe thunder and lightning.*

## NFL INTERNATIONAL GAMES

| Date | Site | Teams |
|---|---|---|
| Aug. 12, 1950 | Ottawa, Canada | N.Y. Giants 27, Ottawa Roughriders 6 |
| Aug. 11, 1951 | Ottawa, Canada | N.Y. Giants 41, Ottawa Roughriders 18 |
| Aug. 5, 1959 | Toronto, Canada | Chi. Cardinals 55, Tor. Argonauts 26 |
| Aug. 3, 1960 | Toronto, Canada | Pittsburgh 43, Toronto Argonauts 16 |
| Aug. 15, 1960 | Toronto, Canada | Chicago 16, N.Y. Giants 7 |
| Aug. 2, 1961 | Toronto, Canada | St. Louis 36, Toronto Argonauts 7 |
| Aug. 5, 1961 | Montreal, Canada | Chicago 34, Montreal Allouettes 16 |
| Aug. 8, 1961 | Hamilton, Canada | Hamilton Tiger-Cats 38, Buffalo 21 |
| Sept. 11, 1969 | Montreal, Canada | Pittsburgh 17, N.Y. Giants 13 |
| Aug. 25, 1969 | Montreal, Canada | Detroit 22, Boston 9 |
| Aug. 16, 1976 | Tokyo, Japan | St. Louis 20, San Diego 10 |
| Aug. 5, 1978 | Mexico City, Mexico | New Orleans 14, Philadelphia 7 |
| Aug. 6, 1983 | London, England | Minnesota 28, St. Louis 10 |
| *Aug. 3, 1986 | London, England | Chicago 17, Dallas 6 |
| *Aug. 9, 1987 | London, England | L.A. Rams 28, Denver 27 |
| *July 31, 1988 | London, England | Miami 27, San Francisco 21 |
| Aug. 14, 1988 | Goteborg, Sweden | Minnesota 28, Chicago 21 |
| Aug. 18, 1988 | Montreal, Canada | N.Y. Jets 11, Cleveland 7 |
| *Aug. 5, 1989 | Tokyo, Japan | L.A. Rams 16, San Francisco 13 (OT) |
| *Aug. 6, 1989 | London, England | Philadelphia 17, Cleveland 13 |
| *Aug. 4, 1990 | Tokyo, Japan | Denver 10, Seattle 7 |
| *Aug. 5, 1990 | London, England | New Orleans 17, L.A. Raiders 10 |
| *Aug. 9, 1990 | Montreal, Canada | Pittsburgh 30, New England 14 |
| *Aug. 11, 1990 | Berlin, Germany | L.A. Rams 19, Kansas City 3 |
| *July 28, 1991 | London, England | Buffalo 17, Philadelphia 13 |
| *Aug. 3, 1991 | Berlin, Germany | San Francisco 21, Chicago 7 |
| *Aug. 3, 1991 | Tokyo, Japan | Miami 19, L.A. Raiders 17 |
| *Aug. 1, 1992 | Tokyo, Japan | Houston 34, Dallas 23 |
| *Aug. 15, 1992 | Berlin, Germany | Miami 31, Denver 27 |
| *Aug. 16, 1992 | London, England | San Francisco 17, Washington 15 |
| *July 31, 1993 | Tokyo, Japan | New Orleans 28, Philadelphia 16 |
| *Aug. 1, 1993 | Barcelona, Spain | San Francisco 21, Pittsburgh 14 |
| *Aug. 7, 1993 | Berlin, Germany | Minnesota 20, Buffalo 6 |
| *Aug. 8, 1993 | London, England | Dallas 13, Detroit 13 (OT) |
| Aug. 14, 1993 | Toronto, Canada | Cleveland 12, New England 9 |

**American Bowl Game*

## CHICAGO ALL-STAR GAME

*Pro teams won 31, lost 9, and tied 2. The game was discontinued after 1976.*

| Year | Date | Winner | Loser | Attendance |
|---|---|---|---|---|
| 1976* | July 23 | Pittsburgh 24 | All-Stars 0 | 52,895 |
| 1975 | Aug. 1 | Pittsburgh 21 | All-Stars 14 | 54,103 |
| 1974 | | No game was played | | |
| 1973 | July 27 | Miami 14 | All-Stars 3 | 54,103 |
| 1972 | July 28 | Dallas 20 | All-Stars 7 | 54,162 |
| 1971 | July 30 | Baltimore 24 | All-Stars 17 | 52,289 |
| 1970 | July 31 | Kansas City 24 | All-Stars 3 | 69,940 |
| 1969 | Aug. 1 | N.Y. Jets 26 | All-Stars 24 | 74,208 |
| 1968 | Aug. 2 | Green Bay 34 | All-Stars 17 | 69,917 |
| 1967 | Aug. 4 | Green Bay 27 | All-Stars 0 | 70,934 |
| 1966 | Aug. 5 | Green Bay 38 | All-Stars 0 | 72,000 |
| 1965 | Aug. 6 | Cleveland 24 | All-Stars 16 | 68,000 |
| 1964 | Aug. 7 | Chicago 28 | All-Stars 17 | 65,000 |
| 1963 | Aug. 2 | All-Stars 20 | Green Bay 17 | 65,000 |
| 1962 | Aug. 3 | Green Bay 42 | All-Stars 20 | 65,000 |
| 1961 | Aug. 4 | Philadelphia 28 | All-Stars 14 | 66,000 |
| 1960 | Aug. 12 | Baltimore 32 | All-Stars 7 | 70,000 |
| 1959 | Aug. 14 | Baltimore 29 | All-Stars 0 | 70,000 |
| 1958 | Aug. 15 | All-Stars 35 | Detroit 19 | 70,000 |
| 1957 | Aug. 9 | N.Y. Giants 22 | All-Stars 12 | 75,000 |
| 1956 | Aug. 10 | Cleveland 26 | All-Stars 0 | 75,000 |
| 1955 | Aug. 12 | All-Stars 30 | Cleveland 27 | 75,000 |
| 1954 | Aug. 13 | Detroit 31 | All-Stars 6 | 93,470 |
| 1953 | Aug. 14 | Detroit 24 | All-Stars 10 | 93,818 |
| 1952 | Aug. 15 | Los Angeles 10 | All-Stars 7 | 88,316 |
| 1951 | Aug. 17 | Cleveland 33 | All-Stars 0 | 92,180 |
| 1950 | Aug. 11 | All-Stars 17 | Philadelphia 7 | 88,885 |
| 1949 | Aug. 12 | Philadelphia 38 | All-Stars 0 | 93,780 |
| 1948 | Aug. 20 | Chi. Cardinals 28 | All-Stars 0 | 101,220 |
| 1947 | Aug. 22 | All-Stars 16 | Chi. Bears 0 | 105,840 |
| 1946 | Aug. 23 | All-Stars 16 | Los Angeles 0 | 97,380 |
| 1945 | Aug. 30 | Green Bay 19 | All-Stars 7 | 92,753 |
| 1944 | Aug. 30 | Chi. Bears 24 | All-Stars 21 | 48,769 |
| 1943 | Aug. 25 | All-Stars 27 | Washington 7 | 48,471 |
| 1942 | Aug. 28 | Chi. Bears 21 | All-Stars 0 | 101,100 |
| 1941 | Aug. 28 | Chi. Bears 37 | All-Stars 13 | 98,203 |
| 1940 | Aug. 29 | Green Bay 45 | All-Stars 28 | 84,567 |
| 1939 | Aug. 30 | N.Y. Giants 9 | All-Stars 0 | 81,456 |
| 1938 | Aug. 31 | All-Stars 28 | Washington 16 | 74,250 |
| 1937 | Sept. 1 | All-Stars 6 | Green Bay 0 | 84,560 |
| 1936 | Sept. 3 | All-Stars 7 | Detroit 7 (tie) | 76,000 |
| 1935 | Aug. 29 | Chi. Bears 5 | All-Stars 0 | 77,450 |
| 1934 | Aug. 31 | Chi. Bears 0 | All-Stars 0 (tie) | 79,432 |

**Game shortened due to thunderstorms.*

## NFL PLAYOFF BOWL

*Western Conference won 8, Eastern Conference won 2.*
*All games played at Miami's Orange Bowl.*

| | |
|---|---|
| 1970 | Los Angeles Rams 31, Dallas Cowboys 0 |
| 1969 | Dallas Cowboys 17, Minnesota Vikings 13 |
| 1968 | Los Angeles Rams 30, Cleveland Browns 6 |
| 1967 | Baltimore Colts 20, Philadelphia Eagles 14 |
| 1966 | Baltimore Colts 35, Dallas Cowboys 3 |
| 1965 | St. Louis Cardinals 24, Green Bay Packers 17 |
| 1964 | Green Bay Packers 40, Cleveland Browns 23 |
| 1963 | Detroit Lions 17, Pittsburgh Steelers 10 |
| 1962 | Detroit Lions 28, Philadelphia Eagles 10 |
| 1961 | Detroit Lions 17, Cleveland Browns 16 |

# INTERCONFERENCE GAMES

## AFC VS. NFC (REGULAR SEASON), 1970-1993

| | 1970 | 1971 | 1972 | 1973 | 1974 | 1975 | 1976 | 1977 | 1978 | 1979 | 1980 | 1981 | 1982 | 1983 | 1984 | 1985 | 1986 | 1987 | 1988 | 1989 | 1990 | 1991 | 1992 | 1993 | Totals |
|---|---|---|---|---|---|---|---|---|---|---|---|---|---|---|---|---|---|---|---|---|---|---|---|---|---|
| Miami | 2-1 | 3-0 | 3-0 | 3-0 | 2-1 | 3-0 | 0-2 | 2-0 | 3-1 | 4-0 | 4-0 | 3-1 | 1-1 | 3-1 | 4-0 | 3-1 | 2-2 | 3-0 | 3-1 | 2-0 | 2-2 | 3-1 | 2-2 | 3-1 | 63-18 |
| L.A. Raiders | 1-2 | 1-1-1 | 3-0 | 2-1 | 3-0 | 3-0 | 3-0 | 1-1 | 4-0 | 4-0 | 2-2 | 2-2 | 3-0 | 2-2 | 3-1 | 3-1 | 1-3 | 2-2 | 1-3 | 2-2 | 3-1 | 2-2 | 2-2 | 3-1 | 56-29-1 |
| Pittsburgh | 0-3 | 1-2 | 2-1 | 3-0 | 3-0 | 2-1 | 1-1 | 2-0 | 3-1 | 3-1 | 4-0 | 3-1 | 1-0 | 2-2 | 3-1 | 1-3 | 2-2 | 2-2 | 1-3 | 3-1 | 3-1 | 0-4 | 1-3 | 2-2 | 48-35 |
| Cincinnati | 1-2 | 1-2 | 2-1 | 2-1 | 2-1 | 3-0 | 2-0 | 2-1 | 2-2 | 2-2 | 2-2 | 2-2 | 1-0 | 3-1 | 2-2 | 2-2 | 3-1 | 1-2 | 4-0 | 2-2 | 1-3 | 1-3 | 1-3 | 2-2 | 46-37 |
| Denver | 2-2 | 1-3 | 1-3 | 0-3-1 | 2-2 | 2-1 | 2-0 | 1-1 | 2-2 | 3-1 | 3-1 | 3-1 | 2-1 | 0-2 | 3-1 | 3-1 | 3-1 | 2-1-1 | 3-1 | 2-2 | 1-3 | 2-0 | 1-3 | 1-3 | 45-39-2 |
| Cleveland | 0-3 | 2-1 | 1-2 | 1-2 | 1-2 | 1-3 | 2-0 | 1-1 | 4-0 | 3-1 | 3-1 | 3-1 | 0-2 | 2-2 | 1-3 | 1-3 | 2-2 | 2-2 | 4-0 | 3-1 | 1-3 | 0-4 | 2-2 | 3-1 | 43-42 |
| San Diego | 1-2 | 2-1 | 0-3 | 1-2 | 1-2 | 0-3 | 2-0 | 1-1 | 2-2 | 3-1 | 2-2 | 2-2 | 1-0 | 2-2 | 4-0 | 1-1 | 0-4 | 2-0 | 2-2 | 2-2 | 1-1 | 1-3 | 2-0 | 2-2 | 37-38 |
| Kansas City | 0-2-1 | 2-1 | 2-1 | 1-1-1 | 1-2 | 2-1 | 1-1 | 1-1 | 0-2 | 0-2 | 2-0 | 2-2 | 0-3 | 2-2 | 1-1 | 2-2 | 1-1 | 1-2 | 0-2 | 2-0 | 4-0 | 2-2 | 2-2 | 2-2 | 33-35-2 |
| Buffalo | 0-3 | 0-3 | 2-0-1 | 2-1 | 2-1 | 1-2 | 0-2 | 1-1 | 1-1 | 2-2 | 3-1 | 1-3 | 1-2 | 1-3 | 1-3 | 0-2 | 1-1 | 1-2 | 2-2 | 1-3 | 3-1 | 3-1 | 4-0 | 4-0 | 37-40-1 |
| Seattle | | | | | | | | 1-0 | 3-1 | 3-1 | 1-3 | 0-2 | 1-0 | 1-3 | 4-0 | 2-2 | 3-1 | 4-0 | 1-3 | 0-4 | 2-2 | 1-3 | 0-4 | 0-2 | 27-31 |
| N.Y. Jets | 2-1 | 0-3 | 1-2 | 0-3 | 2-1 | 0-3 | 0-2 | 1-1 | 1-3 | 3-1 | 1-3 | 2-0 | 4-0 | 3-1 | 0-2 | 2-2 | 2-2 | 0-4 | 2-0 | 1-3 | 2-0 | 2-2 | 0-4 | 2-2 | 33-45 |
| Houston | 0-3 | 0-2-1 | 0-3 | 0-3 | 0-3 | 3-0 | 2-0 | 2-0 | 2-2 | 2-2 | 4-0 | 1-3 | 0-3 | 1-3 | 0-4 | 1-3 | 2-2 | 2-2 | 3-1 | 3-1 | 1-3 | 1-3 | 3-1 | 2-2 | 35-49-1 |
| Indianapolis | 3-0 | 2-1 | 0-3 | 2-1 | 1-2 | 2-1 | 0-2 | 1-1 | 2-2 | 1-1 | 1-1 | 0-4 | 0-1-1 | 2-0 | 0-4 | 3-1 | 1-3 | 1-0 | 2-2 | 1-3 | 2-2 | 0-4 | 2-0 | 0-4 | 29-43-1 |
| New England | 0-3 | 0-3 | 3-0 | 2-1 | 3-0 | 1-2 | 1-1 | 2-0 | 2-2 | 3-1 | 1-3 | 0-4 | 0-1 | 2-2 | 0-4 | 3-1 | 3-1 | 0-3 | 2-2 | 0-4 | 0-4 | 1-1 | 0-4 | 1-1 | 30-48 |
| Tampa Bay | | | | | | | 0-1 | | | | | | | | | | | | | | | | | | 0-1 |
| TOTALS | 12-27-1 | 15-23-2 | 20-19-1 | 19-19-2 | 23-17 | 23-17 | 16-12 | 19-9 | 31-21 | 36-16 | 33-19 | 24-28 | 15-14-1 | 26-26 | 26-26 | 27-25 | 26-26 | 23-22-1 | 30-22 | 24-28 | 26-26 | 19-33 | 22-30 | 27-25 | 562-530-8 |

## NFC VS. AFC (REGULAR SEASON), 1970-1993

| | 1970 | 1971 | 1972 | 1973 | 1974 | 1975 | 1976 | 1977 | 1978 | 1979 | 1980 | 1981 | 1982 | 1983 | 1984 | 1985 | 1986 | 1987 | 1988 | 1989 | 1990 | 1991 | 1992 | 1993 | Totals |
|---|---|---|---|---|---|---|---|---|---|---|---|---|---|---|---|---|---|---|---|---|---|---|---|---|---|
| Dallas | 3-0 | 3-0 | 3-0 | 2-1 | 2-1 | 2-1 | 2-0 | 1-1 | 3-1 | 1-3 | 3-1 | 4-0 | 2-1 | 2-2 | 2-2 | 3-1 | 1-3 | 2-1 | 0-4 | 0-2 | 1-1 | 3-1 | 4-0 | 2-2 | 51-29 |
| Philadelphia | 2-1 | 1-2 | 2-1 | 2-1 | 2-1 | 0-3 | 0-2 | 1-1 | 3-1 | 2-2 | 3-1 | 3-1 | 2-1 | 1-1 | 3-1 | 1-1 | 2-2 | 3-1 | 2-2 | 3-1 | 1-3 | 4-0 | 3-1 | 2-2 | 48-33 |
| San Francisco | 4-0 | 2-1 | 2-1 | 1-2 | 0-3 | 1-2 | 1-1 | 0-2 | 1-3 | 0-4 | 2-2 | 3-1 | 1-3 | 2-2 | 3-1 | 3-1 | 4-0 | 3-1 | 2-2 | 4-0 | 4-0 | 3-1 | 3-1 | 2-2 | 51-36 |
| Washington | 2-1 | 1-2 | 1-2 | 2-1 | 2-1 | 1-2 | 1-1 | 1-1 | 2-2 | 2-2 | 1-3 | 2-2 | | 4-0 | 3-1 | 4-0 | 3-1 | 2-1 | 1-3 | 2-2 | 3-1 | 4-0 | 2-2 | 1-3 | 47-34 |
| L.A. Rams | 2-1 | 1-2 | 1-2 | 3-0 | 3-1 | 3-0 | 1-1 | 2-0 | 2-2 | 2-2 | 2-2 | 1-3 | 1-2 | 1-3 | 3-1 | 3-1 | 2-2 | 1-2 | 2-2 | 3-1 | 2-2 | 1-3 | 2-2 | 2-2 | 46-39 |
| N.Y. Giants | 3-0 | 1-2 | 1-2 | 1-2 | 1-2 | 2-1 | 0-2 | 0-2 | 1-1 | 1-1 | 1-3 | 1-1 | 1-0 | 0-4 | 2-0 | 2-2 | 3-1 | 2-1 | 1-1 | 4-0 | 3-1 | 3-1 | 2-2 | 2-2 | 38-34 |
| Minnesota | 2-1 | 2-1 | 1-2 | 2-1 | 2-1 | 4-0 | 2-0 | 1-1 | 1-3 | 1-3 | 1-3 | 1-3 | 1-3 | 4-0 | 0-4 | 2-0 | 1-3 | 2-1 | 2-2 | 2-2 | 2-2 | 0-2 | 3-1 | 2-2 | 41-41 |
| Arizona | 2-0-1 | 2-1 | 1-2 | 0-2-1 | 2-1 | 2-1 | 1-1 | 0-2 | 0-4 | 1-3 | 1-1 | 3-1 | | 3-1 | 3-1 | 2-2 | 1-1 | 0-1 | 1-3 | 1-3 | 2-2 | 1-1 | 0-2 | 1-1 | 30-37-2 |
| Chicago | 1-2 | 1-2 | 1-2 | 2-2 | 0-3 | 0-3 | 0-2 | 1-1 | 0-4 | 2-2 | 0-4 | 4-0 | 1-1 | 1-1 | 2-2 | 3-1 | 4-0 | 2-2 | 3-1 | 2-2 | 2-2 | 2-2 | 1-3 | 2-2 | 37-46 |
| Detroit | 3-0 | 4-0 | 2-0-1 | 0-3 | 1-2 | 1-2 | 2-0 | 2-0 | 2-2 | 0-4 | 0-2 | 2-2 | 0-1 | 1-3 | 0-4 | 2-2 | 1-3 | 0-4 | 1-1 | 1-3 | 1-3 | 4-0 | 2-2 | 2-0 | 34-43-1 |
| New Orleans | 0-3 | 0-1-2 | 0-3 | 1-2 | 0-3 | 0-3 | 1-2 | 0-2 | 1-3 | 0-4 | 1-3 | 2-2 | 1-0 | 1-3 | 3-1 | 0-4 | 1-3 | 4-0 | 4-0 | 4-0 | 2-2 | 3-1 | 3-1 | 2-2 | 34-48-2 |
| Atlanta | 1-2 | 3-0 | 2-2 | 2-1 | 0-3 | 1-2 | 0-2 | 0-2 | 1-3 | 1-3 | 2-2 | 1-3 | 1-1 | 3-1 | 1-3 | 0-4 | 1-3 | 0-4 | 1-3 | 2-2 | 2-2 | 3-1 | 2-2 | 1-3 | 31-54 |
| Green Bay | 2-1 | 2-1 | 2-1 | 1-1-1 | 2-1 | 0-3 | 0-2 | 0-3 | 2-2 | 1-3 | 1-3 | 1-1 | 1-1-1 | 2-2 | 0-4 | 0-4 | 1-3 | 1-2-1 | 1-3 | 0-2 | 1-3 | 1-3 | 3-1 | 3-1 | 28-51-3 |
| Tampa Bay | | | | | | | | 0-1 | 2-0 | 2-0 | 1-3 | 0-4 | 2-1 | 1-3 | 1-1 | 0-4 | 1-1 | 0-2 | 1-3 | 0-4 | 0-2 | 1-3 | 0-2 | 1-3 | 13-37 |
| Seattle | | | | | | | 1-0 | | | | | | | | | | | | | | | | | | 1-0 |
| TOTALS | 27-12-1 | 23-15-2 | 19-20-1 | 19-19-2 | 17-23 | 17-23 | 12-16 | 9-19 | 21-31 | 16-36 | 19-33 | 28-24 | 14-15-1 | 26-26 | 26-26 | 25-27 | 26-26 | 22-23-1 | 22-30 | 28-24 | 26-26 | 33-19 | 30-22 | 25-27 | 530-562-8 |

## 1993 INTERCONFERENCE GAMES

*(Home Team in capital letters)*

**AFC 27, NFC 25**

**AFC Victories**

Kansas City 27, TAMPA BAY 3
LOS ANGELES RAIDERS 24, Minnesota 7
Buffalo 13, DALLAS 10
CLEVELAND 23, San Francisco 13
Pittsburgh 45, ATLANTA 17
BUFFALO 17, New York Giants 14
MIAMI 17, Washington 10
New England 23, PHOENIX 21
PITTSBURGH 37, New Orleans 14
New York Jets 10, NEW YORK GIANTS 6
BUFFALO 24, Washington 10
Los Angeles Raiders 16, CHICAGO 14
San Diego 30, MINNESOTA 17
KANSAS CITY 23, Green Bay 16
Miami 19, PHILADELPHIA 14
Miami 16, DALLAS 14
HOUSTON 33, Atlanta 17
CLEVELAND 17, New Orleans 13
New York Jets 3, WASHINGTON 0
Buffalo 10, PHILADELPHIA 7
Denver 13, CHICAGO 3
CINCINNATI 15, Los Angeles Rams 3
LOS ANGELES RAIDERS 27, Tampa Bay 20
Houston 10, SAN FRANCISCO 7
CINCINNATI 21, Atlanta 17
Cleveland 42, LOS ANGELES RAMS 14
San Diego 32, TAMPA BAY 17

**NFC Victories**

NEW ORLEANS 33, Houston 21
San Francisco 24, PITTSBURGH 13
Detroit 19, NEW ENGLAND 16 (OT)
LOS ANGELES RAMS 27, Pittsburgh 0
Los Angeles Rams 28, HOUSTON 13
Philadelphia 35, NEW YORK JETS 30
Dallas 27, INDIANAPOLIS 3
GREEN BAY 30, Denver 27
DETROIT 30, Seattle 10
WASHINGTON 30, Indianapolis 24
Chicago 16, SAN DIEGO 13
Minnesota 26, DENVER 23
Chicago 19, KANSAS CITY 17
ATLANTA 17, Cleveland 14
SAN FRANCISCO 21, Cincinnati 8
New York Giants 19, MIAMI 14
Green Bay 20, SAN DIEGO 13
NEW YORK GIANTS 20, Indianapolis 6
Dallas 28, NEW YORK JETS 7
Philadelphia 20, INDIANAPOLIS 10
Phoenix 30, SEATTLE 27 (OT)
MINNESOTA 30, Kansas City 10
GREEN BAY 28, Los Angeles Raiders 0
Tampa Bay 17, DENVER 10
NEW ORLEANS 20, Cincinnati 13

## REGULAR SEASON INTERCONFERENCE RECORDS, 1970-1993

### AMERICAN FOOTBALL CONFERENCE

| Eastern Division | W | L | T | Pct. |
|---|---|---|---|---|
| Miami | 63 | 18 | 0 | .778 |
| Buffalo | 37 | 40 | 1 | .481 |
| New York Jets | 33 | 45 | 0 | .423 |
| Indianapolis | 29 | 43 | 1 | .404 |
| New England | 30 | 48 | 0 | .385 |
| **Central Division** | | | | |
| Pittsburgh | 48 | 35 | 0 | .578 |
| Cincinnati | 46 | 37 | 0 | .554 |
| Cleveland | 43 | 42 | 0 | .506 |
| Houston | 35 | 49 | 1 | .418 |
| **Western Division** | | | | |
| Los Angeles Raiders | 56 | 29 | 1 | .657 |
| Denver | 45 | 39 | 2 | .535 |
| San Diego | 37 | 38 | 0 | .493 |
| Kansas City | 33 | 35 | 2 | .486 |
| Seattle | 27 | 31 | 0 | .466 |

### NATIONAL FOOTBALL CONFERENCE

| Eastern Division | W | L | T | Pct. |
|---|---|---|---|---|
| Dallas | 51 | 29 | 0 | .638 |
| Philadelphia | 48 | 33 | 0 | .593 |
| Washington | 47 | 34 | 0 | .580 |
| New York Giants | 38 | 34 | 0 | .528 |
| Arizona | 30 | 37 | 2 | .449 |
| **Central Division** | | | | |
| Minnesota | 41 | 41 | 0 | .500 |
| Chicago | 37 | 46 | 0 | .446 |
| Detroit | 34 | 43 | 1 | .442 |
| Green Bay | 28 | 51 | 3 | .360 |
| Tampa Bay | 13 | 37 | 0 | .260 |
| **Western Division** | | | | |
| San Francisco | 51 | 36 | 0 | .586 |
| Los Angeles Rams | 46 | 39 | 0 | .541 |
| New Orleans | 34 | 48 | 2 | .417 |
| Atlanta | 31 | 54 | 0 | .365 |

## INTERCONFERENCE VICTORIES, 1970-1993

### REGULAR SEASON

| | AFC | NFC | Tie |
|---|---|---|---|
| 1970 | 12 | 27 | 1 |
| 1971 | 15 | 23 | 2 |
| 1972 | 20 | 19 | 1 |
| 1973 | 19 | 19 | 2 |
| 1974 | 23 | 17 | 0 |
| 1975 | 23 | 17 | 0 |
| 1976 | 16 | 12 | 0 |
| 1977 | 19 | 9 | 0 |
| 1978 | 31 | 21 | 0 |
| 1979 | 36 | 16 | 0 |
| 1980 | 33 | 19 | 0 |
| 1981 | 24 | 28 | 0 |
| 1982 | 15 | 14 | 1 |
| 1983 | 26 | 26 | 0 |
| 1984 | 26 | 26 | 0 |
| 1985 | 27 | 25 | 0 |
| 1986 | 26 | 26 | 0 |
| 1987 | 23 | 22 | 1 |
| 1988 | 30 | 22 | 0 |
| 1989 | 24 | 28 | 0 |
| 1990 | 26 | 26 | 0 |
| 1991 | 19 | 33 | 0 |
| 1992 | 22 | 30 | 0 |
| 1993 | 27 | 25 | 0 |
| Total | 562 | 530 | 8 |

### PRESEASON

| | AFC | NFC | Tie |
|---|---|---|---|
| 1970 | 21 | 28 | 1 |
| 1971 | 28 | 28 | 3 |
| 1972 | 27 | 25 | 4 |
| 1973 | 23 | 35 | 2 |
| 1974 | 35 | 25 | 0 |
| 1975 | 30 | 26 | 1 |
| 1976 | 30 | 31 | 0 |
| 1977 | 38 | 25 | 0 |
| 1978 | 20 | 19 | 0 |
| 1979 | 25 | 18 | 0 |
| 1980 | 22 | 20 | 1 |
| 1981 | 18 | 19 | 0 |
| 1982 | 25 | 16 | 0 |
| 1983 | 15 | 24 | 0 |
| 1984 | 16 | 19 | 0 |
| 1985 | 10 | 22 | 1 |
| 1986 | 22 | 17 | 0 |
| 1987 | 22 | 22 | 0 |
| 1988 | 23 | 16 | 1 |
| 1989 | 16 | 27 | 0 |
| 1990 | 15 | 29 | 0 |
| 1991 | 19 | 27 | 0 |
| 1992 | 30 | 22 | 0 |
| 1993 | 17 | 22 | 0 |
| Total | 547 | 562 | 14 |

## MONDAY NIGHT FOOTBALL, 1970-1993

*(Home Team in capitals, games listed in chronological order.)*

**1993**
WASHINGTON 35, Dallas 16
CLEVELAND 23, San Francisco 13
KANSAS CITY 15, Denver 7
Pittsburgh 45, ATLANTA 17
MIAMI 17, Washington 10
BUFFALO 35, Houston 7
Los Angeles Raiders 23, DENVER 20
Minnesota 19, CHICAGO 12
BUFFALO 24, Washington 10
KANSAS CITY 23, Green Bay 16
PITTSBURGH 23, Buffalo 0
SAN FRANCISCO 42, New Orleans 7
San Diego 31, INDIANAPOLIS 0
DALLAS 23, Philadelphia 17
Pittsburgh 21, MIAMI 20
New York Giants 24, NEW ORLEANS 14
SAN DIEGO 45, Miami 20
Philadelphia 37, SAN FRANCISCO 34 (OT)

**1992**
DALLAS 23, Washington 10
Miami 27, CLEVELAND 23
New York Giants 27, CHICAGO 14
KANSAS CITY 27, Los Angeles Raiders 7
PHILADELPHIA 31, Dallas 7
WASHINGTON 34, Denver 3
PITTSBURGH 20, Cincinnati 0
Buffalo 24, NEW YORK JETS 20
Minnesota 38, CHICAGO 10
San Francisco 41, ATLANTA 3
Buffalo 26, MIAMI 20
NEW ORLEANS 20, Washington 3
SEATTLE 16, Denver 13 (OT)
HOUSTON 24, Chicago 7
MIAMI 20, Los Angeles Raiders 7
Dallas 41, ATLANTA 17
SAN FRANCISCO 24, Detroit 6

**1991**
NEW YORK GIANTS 16, San Francisco 14
Washington 33, DALLAS 31
HOUSTON 17, Kansas City 7
CHICAGO 19, New York Jets 13 (OT)
WASHINGTON 23, Philadelphia 0
KANSAS CITY 33, Buffalo 6
New York Giants 23, PITTSBURGH 20
BUFFALO 35, Cincinnati 16
KANSAS CITY 24, Los Angeles Raiders 21
PHILADELPHIA 30, New York Giants 7
Chicago 34, MINNESOTA 17
Buffalo 41, MIAMI 27
San Francisco 33, LOS ANGELES RAMS 10
Philadelphia 13, HOUSTON 6
MIAMI 37, Cincinnati 13
NEW ORLEANS 27, Los Angeles Raiders 0
SAN FRANCISCO 52, Chicago 14

**1990**
San Francisco 13, NEW ORLEANS 12
DENVER 24, Kansas City 23
Buffalo 30, NEW YORK JETS 7
SEATTLE 31, Cincinnati 16
Cleveland 30, DENVER 29
PHILADELPHIA 32, Minnesota 24
Cincinnati 34, CLEVELAND 13
PITTSBURGH 41, Los Angeles Rams 10
New York Giants 24, INDIANAPOLIS 7
PHILADELPHIA 28, Washington 14
Los Angeles Raiders 13, MIAMI 10
HOUSTON 27, Buffalo 24
SAN FRANCISCO 7, New York Giants 3
Los Angeles Raiders 38, DETROIT 31
San Francisco 26, LOS ANGELES RAMS 10
NEW ORLEANS 20, Los Angeles Rams 17

**1989**
New York Giants 27, WASHINGTON 24
Denver 28, BUFFALO 14
CINCINNATI 21, Cleveland 14
CHICAGO 27, Philadelphia 13
Los Angeles Raiders 14, NEW YORK JETS 7
BUFFALO 23, Los Angeles Rams 20
CLEVELAND 27, Chicago 7
NEW YORK GIANTS 24, Minnesota 14
SAN FRANCISCO 31, New Orleans 13
HOUSTON 26, Cincinnati 24
Denver 14, WASHINGTON 10
SAN FRANCISCO 34, New York Giants 24
SEATTLE 17, Buffalo 16
San Francisco 30, LOS ANGELES RAMS 27
NEW ORLEANS 30, Philadelphia 20
MINNESOTA 29, Cincinnati 21

**1988**
NEW YORK GIANTS 27, Washington 20
Dallas 17, PHOENIX 14
CLEVELAND 23, Indianapolis 17
Los Angeles Raiders 30, DENVER 27 (OT)
NEW ORLEANS 20, Dallas 17
PHILADELPHIA 24, New York Giants 13
Buffalo 37, NEW YORK JETS 14
CHICAGO 10, San Francisco 9
INDIANAPOLIS 55, Denver 23
HOUSTON 24, Cleveland 17
Buffalo 31, MIAMI 6
SAN FRANCISCO 37, Washington 21
SEATTLE 35, Los Angeles Raiders 27
LOS ANGELES RAMS 23, Chicago 3
MIAMI 38, Cleveland 31
MINNESOTA 28, Chicago 27

**1987**
CHICAGO 34, New York Giants 19
NEW YORK JETS 43, New England 24
San Francisco 41, NEW YORK GIANTS 21
DENVER 30, Los Angeles Raiders 14
Washington 13, DALLAS 7
CLEVELAND 30, Los Angeles Rams 17
MINNESOTA 34, Denver 27
DALLAS 33, New York Giants 24
NEW YORK JETS 30, Seattle 14
DENVER 31, Chicago 29
Los Angeles Rams 30, WASHINGTON 26
Los Angeles Raiders 37, SEATTLE 14
MIAMI 37, New York Jets 28
SAN FRANCISCO 41, Chicago 0
Dallas 29, LOS ANGELES RAMS 21
New England 24, MIAMI 10

**1986**
DALLAS 31, New York Giants 28
Denver 21, PITTSBURGH 10
Chicago 25, GREEN BAY 12
Dallas 31, ST. LOUIS 7
SEATTLE 33, San Diego 7
CINCINNATI 24, Pittsburgh 22
NEW YORK JETS 22, Denver 10
NEW YORK GIANTS 27, Washington 20
Los Angeles Rams 20, CHICAGO 17
CLEVELAND 26, Miami 16
WASHINGTON 14, San Francisco 6
MIAMI 45, New York Jets 3
New York Giants 21, SAN FRANCISCO 17
SEATTLE 37, Los Angeles Raiders 0
Chicago 16, DETROIT 13
New England 34, MIAMI 27

**1985**
DALLAS 44, Washington 14
CLEVELAND 17, Pittsburgh 7
Los Angeles Rams 35, SEATTLE 24
Cincinnati 37, PITTSBURGH 24
WASHINGTON 27, St. Louis 10
NEW YORK JETS 23, Miami 7
CHICAGO 23, Green Bay 7
LOS ANGELES RAIDERS 34, San Diego 21
ST. LOUIS 21, Dallas 10
DENVER 17, San Francisco 16
WASHINGTON 23, New York Giants 21
SAN FRANCISCO 19, Seattle 6
MIAMI 38, Chicago 24
Los Angeles Rams 27, SAN FRANCISCO 20
MIAMI 30, New England 27
L.A. Raiders 16, L.A. RAMS 6

**1984**
Dallas 20, LOS ANGELES RAMS 13
SAN FRANCISCO 37, Washington 31
Miami 21, BUFFALO 17
LOS ANGELES RAIDERS 33, San Diego 30
PITTSBURGH 38, Cincinnati 17
San Francisco 31, NEW YORK GIANTS 10
DENVER 17, Green Bay 14
Los Angeles Rams 24, ATLANTA 10
Seattle 24, SAN DIEGO 0
WASHINGTON 27, Atlanta 14
SEATTLE 17, Los Angeles Raiders 14
NEW ORLEANS 27, Pittsburgh 24
MIAMI 28, New York Jets 17
SAN DIEGO 20, Chicago 7
Los Angeles Raiders 24, DETROIT 3
MIAMI 28, Dallas 21

**1983**
Dallas 31, WASHINGTON 30
San Diego 17, KANSAS CITY 14
LOS ANGELES RAIDERS 27, Miami 14
NEW YORK GIANTS 27, Green Bay 3
New York Jets 34, BUFFALO 10
Pittsburgh 24, CINCINNATI 14
GREEN BAY 48, Washington 47
ST. LOUIS 20, New York Giants 20 (OT)
Washington 27, SAN DIEGO 24
DETROIT 15, New York Giants 9
Los Angeles Rams 36, ATLANTA 13
New York Jets 31, NEW ORLEANS 28
MIAMI 38, Cincinnati 14
DETROIT 13, Minnesota 2
Green Bay 12, TAMPA BAY 9 (OT)
SAN FRANCISCO 42, Dallas 17

**1982**
Pittsburgh 36, DALLAS 28
Green Bay 27, NEW YORK GIANTS 19
LOS ANGELES RAIDERS 28, San Diego 24
TAMPA BAY 23, Miami 17
New York Jets 28, DETROIT 13
Dallas 37, HOUSTON 7
SAN DIEGO 50, Cincinnati 34
MIAMI 27, Buffalo 10
MINNESOTA 31, Dallas 27

**1981**
San Diego 44, CLEVELAND 14
Oakland 36, MINNESOTA 10
Dallas 35, NEW ENGLAND 21
Los Angeles 24, CHICAGO 7
PHILADELPHIA 16, Atlanta 13
BUFFALO 31, Miami 21
DETROIT 48, Chicago 17
PITTSBURGH 26, Houston 13
DENVER 19, Minnesota 17
DALLAS 27, Buffalo 14
SEATTLE 44, San Diego 23
ATLANTA 31, Minnesota 30
MIAMI 13, Philadelphia 10
OAKLAND 30, Pittsburgh 27
LOS ANGELES 21, Atlanta 16
SAN DIEGO 23, Oakland 10

**1980**
Dallas 17, WASHINGTON 3
Houston 16, CLEVELAND 7
PHILADELPHIA 35, New York Giants 3
NEW ENGLAND 23, Denver 14
CHICAGO 23, Tampa Bay 0
DENVER 20, Washington 17
Oakland 45, PITTSBURGH 34
NEW YORK JETS 17, Miami 14
CLEVELAND 27, Chicago 21
HOUSTON 38, New England 34
Oakland 19, SEATTLE 17
Los Angeles 27, NEW ORLEANS 7
OAKLAND 9, Denver 3

MIAMI 16, New England 13 (OT)
LOS ANGELES 38, Dallas 14
SAN DIEGO 26, Pittsburgh 17

**1979**
Pittsburgh 16, NEW ENGLAND 13 (OT)
Atlanta 14, PHILADELPHIA 10
WASHINGTON 27, New York Giants 0
CLEVELAND 26, Dallas 7
GREEN BAY 27, New England 14
OAKLAND 13, Miami 3
NEW YORK JETS 14, Minnesota 7
PITTSBURGH 42, Denver 7
Seattle 31, ATLANTA 28
Houston 9, MIAMI 6
Philadelphia 31, DALLAS 21
LOS ANGELES 20, Atlanta 14
SEATTLE 30, New York Jets 7
Oakland 42, NEW ORLEANS 35
HOUSTON 20, Pittsburgh 17
SAN DIEGO 17, Denver 7

**1978**
DALLAS 38, Baltimore 0
MINNESOTA 12, Denver 9 (OT)
Baltimore 34, NEW ENGLAND 27
Minnesota 24, CHICAGO 20
WASHINGTON 9, Dallas 5
MIAMI 21, Cincinnati 0
DENVER 16, Chicago 7
Houston 24, PITTSBURGH 17
ATLANTA 15, Los Angeles 7
BALTIMORE 21, Washington 17
Oakland 34, CINCINNATI 21
HOUSTON 35, Miami 30
Pittsburgh 24, SAN FRANCISCO 7
SAN DIEGO 40, Chicago 7
Cincinnati 20, LOS ANGELES 19
MIAMI 23, New England 3

**1977**
PITTSBURGH 27, San Francisco 0
CLEVELAND 30, New England 27 (OT)
Oakland 37, KANSAS CITY 28
CHICAGO 24, Los Angeles 23
PITTSBURGH 20, Cincinnati 14
LOS ANGELES 35, Minnesota 3
ST. LOUIS 28, New York Giants 0
BALTIMORE 10, Washington 3
St. Louis 24, DALLAS 17
WASHINGTON 10, Green Bay 9
OAKLAND 34, Buffalo 13
MIAMI 17, Baltimore 6
Dallas 42, SAN FRANCISCO 35

**1976**
Miami 30, BUFFALO 21
Oakland 24, KANSAS CITY 21
Washington 20, PHILADELPHIA 17 (OT)
MINNESOTA 17, Pittsburgh 6
San Francisco 16, LOS ANGELES 0
NEW ENGLAND 41, New York Jets 7
WASHINGTON 20, St. Louis 10
BALTIMORE 38, Houston 14
CINCINNATI 20, Los Angeles 12
DALLAS 17, Buffalo 10
Baltimore 17, MIAMI 16
SAN FRANCISCO 20, Minnesota 16
OAKLAND 35, Cincinnati 20

**1975**
Oakland 31, MIAMI 21
DENVER 23, Green Bay 13
Dallas 36, DETROIT 10
WASHINGTON 27, St. Louis 17
New York Giants 17, BUFFALO 14
Minnesota 13, CHICAGO 9
Los Angeles 42, PHILADELPHIA 3
Kansas City 34, DALLAS 31
CINCINNATI 33, Buffalo 24
Pittsburgh 32, HOUSTON 9
MIAMI 20, New England 7
OAKLAND 17, Denver 10
SAN DIEGO 24, New York Jets 16

**1974**
BUFFALO 21, Oakland 20
PHILADELPHIA 13, Dallas 10
WASHINGTON 30, Denver 3
MIAMI 21, New York Jets 17
DETROIT 17, San Francisco 13
CHICAGO 10, Green Bay 9
PITTSBURGH 24, Atlanta 17
Los Angeles 15, SAN FRANCISCO 13
Minnesota 28, ST. LOUIS 24
Kansas City 42, DENVER 34
Pittsburgh 28, NEW ORLEANS 7
MIAMI 24, Cincinnati 3
Washington 23, LOS ANGELES 17

**1973**
GREEN BAY 23, New York Jets 7
DALLAS 40, New Orleans 3
DETROIT 31, Atlanta 6
WASHINGTON 14, Dallas 7
Miami 17, CLEVELAND 9
DENVER 23, Oakland 23
BUFFALO 23, Kansas City 14
PITTSBURGH 21, Washington 16
KANSAS CITY 19, Chicago 7
ATLANTA 20, Minnesota 14
SAN FRANCISCO 20, Green Bay 6
MIAMI 30, Pittsburgh 26
LOS ANGELES 40, New York Giants 6

**1972**
Washington 24, MINNESOTA 21
Kansas City 20, NEW ORLEANS 17
New York Giants 27, PHILADELPHIA 12
Oakland 34, HOUSTON 0
Green Bay 24, DETROIT 23
CHICAGO 13, Minnesota 10
DALLAS 28, Detroit 24
Baltimore 24, NEW ENGLAND 17
Cleveland 21, SAN DIEGO 17
WASHINGTON 24, Atlanta 13
MIAMI 31, St. Louis 10
Los Angeles 26, SAN FRANCISCO 16
OAKLAND 24, New York Jets 16

**1971**
Minnesota 16, DETROIT 13
ST. LOUIS 17, New York Jets 10
Oakland 34, CLEVELAND 20
DALLAS 20, New York Giants 13
KANSAS CITY 38, Pittsburgh 16
MINNESOTA 10, Baltimore 3
GREEN BAY 14, Detroit 14
BALTIMORE 24, Los Angeles 17
SAN DIEGO 20, St. Louis 17
ATLANTA 28, Green Bay 21
MIAMI 34, Chicago 3
Kansas City 26, SAN FRANCISCO 17
Washington 38, LOS ANGELES 24

**1970**
CLEVELAND 31, New York Jets 21
Kansas City 44, BALTIMORE 24
DETROIT 28, Chicago 14
Green Bay 22, SAN DIEGO 20
OAKLAND 34, Washington 20
MINNESOTA 13, Los Angeles 3
PITTSBURGH 21, Cincinnati 10
Baltimore 13, GREEN BAY 10
St. Louis 38, DALLAS 0
PHILADELPHIA 23, New York Giants 20
Miami 20, ATLANTA 7
Cleveland 21, HOUSTON 10
Detroit 28, LOS ANGELES 23

## MONDAY NIGHT SYNDROME

**1993**

Of the 17 winning teams:
- 8 won the next week
- 5 lost the next week
- 0 tied the next week
- 4 had an Open Date the next week

Of the 17 losing teams:
- 7 won the next week
- 8 lost the next week
- 0 tied the next week
- 2 had an Open Date the next week

Of the 34 NFL teams:
- 15 won the next week
- 13 lost the next week
- 0 tied the next week
- 6 had an Open Date the next week

**1970-1993**

Of the 338 winning teams:
- 195 won the next week
- 132 lost the next week
- 3 tied the next week
- 8 had Open Dates the next week

Of the 338 losing teams:
- 182 won the next week
- 151 lost the next week
- 1 tied the next week
- 4 had Open Dates the next week

Of the 6 tying teams:
- 5 won the next week
- 1 lost the next week
- 0 tied the next week

Of the 682 NFL teams:
- 382 won the next week
- 284 lost the next week
- 4 tied the next week
- 12 had Open Dates the next week

## MONDAY NIGHT WON-LOST RECORDS, 1970-1992

### AMERICAN FOOTBALL CONFERENCE

| | Buff. | Cin. | Clev. | Den. | Hou. | Ind. | K.C. | Raid. | Mia. | N.E. | N.Y.J. | Pitt. | S.D. | Sea. |
|---|---|---|---|---|---|---|---|---|---|---|---|---|---|---|
| Total | 13-14 | 7-16 | 13-9 | 12-17-1 | 11-8 | 9-7 | 12-6 | 30-10-1 | 28-19 | 4-12 | 9-16 | 19-14 | 12-9 | 11-5 |
| 1993 | 2-1 | | 1-0 | 0-2 | 0-1 | 0-1 | 2-0 | 1-0 | 1-2 | | | 3-0 | 2-0 | |
| 1992 | 2-0 | 0-1 | 0-1 | 0-2 | 1-0 | | 1-0 | 0-2 | 2-1 | | 0-1 | 1-0 | | 1-0 |
| 1991 | 2-1 | 0-2 | | | 1-1 | | 2-1 | 0-2 | 1-1 | | 0-1 | 0-1 | | |
| 1990 | 1-1 | 1-1 | 1-1 | 1-1 | 1-0 | 0-1 | 0-1 | 2-0 | 0-1 | | 0-1 | 1-0 | | 1-0 |
| 1989 | 1-2 | 1-2 | 1-1 | 2-0 | 1-0 | | | 1-0 | | | 0-1 | | | 1-0 |
| 1988 | 2-0 | | 1-2 | 0-2 | 1-0 | 1-1 | | 1-1 | 1-1 | | 0-1 | | | 1-0 |
| 1987 | | | 1-0 | 2-1 | | | | 1-1 | 1-1 | 1-1 | 2-1 | | | 0-2 |
| 1986 | | 1-0 | 1-0 | 1-1 | | | | 0-1 | 1-2 | 1-0 | 1-1 | 0-2 | 0-1 | 2-0 |
| 1985 | | 1-0 | 1-0 | 1-0 | | | | 2-0 | 2-1 | 0-1 | 1-0 | 0-2 | 0-1 | 0-2 |
| 1984 | 0-1 | 0-1 | | 1-0 | | | | 2-1 | 3-0 | | 0-1 | 1-1 | 1-2 | 2-0 |
| 1983 | 0-1 | 0-2 | | | | | 0-1 | 1-0 | 1-1 | | 2-0 | 1-0 | 1-1 | |
| 1982 | 0-1 | 0-1 | | | 0-1 | | | 1-0 | 1-1 | | 1-0 | 1-0 | 1-1 | |
| 1981 | 1-1 | | 0-1 | 1-0 | 0-1 | | | 2-1 | 1-1 | 0-1 | | 1-1 | 2-1 | 1-0 |
| 1980 | | | 1-1 | 1-2 | 2-0 | | | 3-0 | 1-1 | 1-2 | 1-0 | 0-2 | 1-0 | 0-1 |
| 1979 | | | 1-0 | 0-2 | 2-0 | | | 2-0 | 0-2 | 0-2 | 1-1 | 2-1 | 1-0 | 2-0 |
| 1978 | | 1-2 | | 1-1 | 2-0 | 2-1 | | 1-0 | 2-1 | 0-2 | | 1-1 | 1-0 | |
| 1977 | 0-1 | 0-1 | 1-0 | | | 1-1 | 0-1 | 2-0 | 1-0 | 0-1 | | 2-0 | | |
| 1976 | 0-2 | 1-1 | | | 0-1 | 2-0 | 0-1 | 2-0 | 1-1 | 1-0 | 0-1 | 0-1 | | |
| 1975 | 0-2 | 1-0 | | 1-1 | 0-1 | | 1-0 | 2-0 | 1-1 | 0-1 | 0-1 | 1-0 | 1-0 | |
| 1974 | 1-0 | 0-1 | | 0-2 | | | 1-0 | 0-1 | 2-0 | | 0-1 | 2-0 | | |
| 1973 | 1-0 | | 0-1 | 0-0-1 | | | 1-1 | 0-0-1 | 2-0 | | 0-1 | 1-1 | | |
| 1972 | | | 1-0 | | 0-1 | 1-0 | 1-0 | 2-0 | 1-0 | 0-1 | 0-1 | | 0-1 | |
| 1971 | | | 0-1 | | | 1-1 | 2-0 | 1-0 | 1-0 | | 0-1 | 0-1 | 1-0 | |
| 1970 | | 0-1 | 2-0 | | 0-1 | 1-1 | 1-0 | 1-0 | 1-0 | | 0-1 | 1-0 | 0-1 | |

### NATIONAL FOOTBALL CONFERENCE

| | Atl. | Chi. | Dall. | Det. | G.B. | Rams | Minn. | N.O. | N.Y.G. | Phil. | Phx. | S.F. | T.B. | Wash. |
|---|---|---|---|---|---|---|---|---|---|---|---|---|---|---|
| Total | 5-14 | 12-23 | 22-19 | 7-9-1 | 7-11-1 | 17-20 | 14-13 | 6-10 | 13-18-1 | 12-9 | 5-8-1 | 21-14 | 1-2 | 22-21 |
| 1993 | 0-1 | 0-1 | 1-1 | | 0-1 | | 1-0 | 0-2 | 1-0 | 1-1 | | 1-2 | | 1-2 |
| 1992 | 0-2 | 0-3 | 2-1 | 0-1 | | | 1-0 | 1-0 | 1-0 | 1-0 | | 2-0 | | 1-2 |
| 1991 | | 2-1 | 0-1 | | | 0-1 | 0-1 | 1-0 | 2-1 | 2-1 | | 2-1 | | 2-0 |
| 1990 | | | | 0-1 | | 0-3 | 0-1 | 1-1 | 1-1 | 2-0 | | 3-0 | | 0-1 |
| 1989 | | 1-1 | | | | 0-2 | 1-1 | 1-1 | 2-1 | 0-2 | | 3-0 | | 0-2 |
| 1988 | | 1-2 | 1-1 | | | 1-0 | 1-0 | 1-0 | 1-1 | 1-0 | 0-1 | 1-1 | | 0-2 |
| 1987 | | 1-2 | 2-1 | | | 1-2 | 1-0 | | 0-3 | | | 2-0 | | 1-1 |
| 1986 | | 2-1 | 2-0 | 0-1 | 0-1 | 1-0 | | | 2-1 | | 0-1 | 0-2 | | 1-1 |
| 1985 | | 1-1 | 1-1 | | 0-1 | 2-1 | | | 0-1 | | 1-1 | 1-2 | | 2-1 |
| 1984 | 0-2 | 0-1 | 1-1 | 0-1 | 0-1 | 1-1 | | 1-0 | 0-1 | | | 2-0 | | 1-1 |
| 1983 | 0-1 | | 1-1 | 2-0 | 2-1 | 1-0 | 0-1 | 0-1 | 1-1-1 | | 0-0-1 | 1-0 | 0-1 | 1-2 |
| 1982 | | | 1-2 | 0-1 | 1-0 | | 1-0 | | 0-1 | | | | 1-0 | |
| 1981 | 1-2 | 0-2 | 2-0 | 1-0 | | 2-0 | 0-3 | | | 1-1 | | | | |
| 1980 | | 1-1 | 1-1 | | | 2-0 | | 0-1 | 0-1 | 1-0 | | | 0-1 | 0-2 |
| 1979 | 1-2 | | 0-2 | | 1-0 | 1-0 | 0-1 | 0-1 | 0-1 | 1-1 | | | | 1-0 |
| 1978 | 1-0 | 0-3 | 1-1 | | | 0-2 | 2-0 | | | | 2-0 | 0-1 | | 1-1 |
| 1977 | | 1-0 | 1-1 | | 0-1 | 1-1 | 0-1 | | 0-1 | | 0-1 | 0-2 | | 1-1 |
| 1976 | | | 1-0 | | | 0-2 | 1-1 | | | 0-1 | 0-1 | 2-0 | | 2-0 |
| 1975 | | 0-1 | 1-1 | 0-1 | 0-1 | 1-0 | 1-0 | | 1-0 | 0-1 | 0-1 | | | 1-0 |
| 1974 | 0-1 | 1-0 | 0-1 | 1-0 | 0-1 | 1-1 | 1-0 | 0-1 | | 1-0 | | 0-2 | | 2-0 |
| 1973 | 1-1 | 0-1 | 1-1 | 1-0 | 1-1 | 1-0 | 0-1 | 0-1 | 0-1 | | 0-1 | 1-0 | | 1-1 |
| 1972 | 0-1 | 1-0 | 1-0 | 0-2 | 1-0 | 1-0 | 0-2 | 0-1 | 1-0 | 0-1 | 1-1 | 0-1 | | 2-0 |
| 1971 | 1-0 | 0-1 | 1-0 | 0-1-1 | 0-1-1 | 0-2 | 2-0 | | 0-1 | | 1-0 | 0-1 | | 1-0 |
| 1970 | 0-1 | 0-1 | 0-1 | 2-0 | 1-1 | 0-2 | 1-0 | | 0-1 | 1-0 | | | | 0-1 |

## THURSDAY-SUNDAY NIGHT FOOTBALL, 1974-1993

*(Home Team in capitals, games listed in chronological order.)*

**1993**
NEW ORLEANS 33, Houston 21 (Sun.)
Los Angeles Raiders 17, SEATTLE 13 (Sun.)
Dallas 17, PHOENIX 10 (Sun.)
NEW YORK JETS 45, New England 7 (Sun.)
BUFFALO 17, New York Giants 14 (Sun.)
GREEN BAY 30, Denver 27 (Sun.)
ATLANTA 30, Los Angeles Rams 24 (Thurs.)
MIAMI 41, Indianapolis 27 (Sun.)
Detroit 30, MINNESOTA 27 (Sun.)
WASHINGTON 30, Indianapolis 24 (Sun.)
Chicago 16, SAN DIEGO 13 (Sun.)
TAMPA BAY 23, Minnesota 10 (Sun.)
HOUSTON 23, Pittsburgh 3 (Sun.)
SAN FRANCISCO 21, Cincinnati 8 (Sun.)
Green Bay 20, SAN DIEGO 13 (Sun.)
Philadelphia 20, INDIANAPOLIS 10 (Sun.)
MINNESOTA 30, Kansas City 10 (Sun.)
HOUSTON 24, New York Jets 0 (Sun.)

**1992**
DENVER 17, Los Angeles Raiders 13 (Sun.)
Philadelphia 31, PHOENIX 14 (Sun.)
BUFFALO 38, Indianapolis 0 (Sun.)
San Francisco 16, NEW ORLEANS 10 (Sun.)
NEW YORK JETS 30, New England 21 (Sun.)
NEW ORLEANS 13, Los Angeles Rams 10 (Sun.)
MINNESOTA 31, Detroit 14 (Thurs.)
Pittsburgh 27, KANSAS CITY 3 (Sun.)
New York Giants 24, WASHINGTON 7 (Sun.)
Cincinnati 31, CHICAGO 28 (OT) (Sun.)
DENVER 27, New York Giants 13 (Sun.)
Kansas City 24, SEATTLE 14 (Sun.)
Houston 24, DETROIT 21 (Thurs.)
DALLAS 30, New York Giants 3 (Thurs.)
SAN DIEGO 27, Los Angeles Raiders 3 (Sun.)
NEW ORLEANS 22, Atlanta 14 (Thurs.)
Los Angeles Rams 31, TAMPA BAY 27 (Sun.)
Green Bay 16, HOUSTON 14 (Sun.)
MIAMI 19, New York Jets 17 (Sun.)
Los Angeles Raiders 21, WASHINGTON 20 (Sat.)
HOUSTON 27, Buffalo 3 (Sun.)

**1991**
WASHINGTON 45, Detroit 0 (Sun.)
Houston 30, CINCINNATI 7 (Sun.)
NEW ORLEANS 24, Los Angeles Rams 7 (Sun.)
Dallas 17, PHOENIX 9 (Sun.)
Denver 13, MINNESOTA 6 (Sun.)
Pittsburgh 21, INDIANAPOLIS 3 (Sun.)
Los Angeles Raiders 23, SEATTLE 20 (Sun.)
Chicago 10, GREEN BAY 0 (Thurs.)
Washington 17, NEW YORK GIANTS 13 (Sun.)
DENVER 20, Pittsburgh 13 (Sun.)
MIAMI 30, New England 20 (Sun.)
HOUSTON 28, Cleveland 24 (Sun.)
Atlanta 23, NEW ORLEANS 20 (OT) (Sun.)
Los Angeles Raiders 9, SAN DIEGO 7 (Sun.)
Minnesota 26, TAMPA BAY 24 (Sun.)
Buffalo 35, INDIANAPOLIS 7 (Sun.)
SEATTLE 23, Los Angeles Rams 9 (Sun.)

**1990**
NEW YORK GIANTS 27, Philadelphia 20 (Sun.)
PITTSBURGH 20, Houston 9 (Sun.)
TAMPA BAY 23, Detroit 20 (Sun.)
Washington 38, PHOENIX 10 (Sun.)
BUFFALO 38, Los Angeles Raiders 24 (Sun.)
CHICAGO 38, Los Angeles Rams 9 (Sun.)
MIAMI 17, New England 10 (Thurs.)
ATLANTA 38, Cincinnati 17 (Sun.)
MINNESOTA 27, Denver 22 (Sun.)
San Francisco 24, DALLAS 6 (Sun.)
CINCINNATI 27, Pittsburgh 3 (Sun.)
Seattle 13, SAN DIEGO 10 (Sun.)
MINNESOTA 23, Green Bay 7 (Sun.)
MIAMI 23, Philadelphia 20 (Sun.)
DETROIT 38, Chicago 21 (Sun.)
INDIANAPOLIS 35, Washington 28 (Sat.)
SEATTLE 17, Denver 12 (Sun.)
HOUSTON 34, Pittsburgh 14 (Sun.)

**1989**
Dallas 13, WASHINGTON 3 (Sun.)
SAN DIEGO 14, Los Angeles Raiders 12 (Sun.)
INDIANAPOLIS 27, New York Jets 10 (Sun.)
Los Angeles Rams 20, NEW ORLEANS 17 (Sun.)
MINNESOTA 27, Chicago 16 (Sun.)
MIAMI 31, New England 10 (Sun.)
SEATTLE 23, Los Angeles Raiders 17 (Sun.)
Cleveland 24, HOUSTON 20 (Sat.)

**1988**
HOUSTON 41, Washington 17 (Sun.)
Los Angeles Raiders 13, SAN DIEGO 3 (Sun.)
Minnesota 34, DALLAS 3 (Sun.)
New England 6, MIAMI 3 (Sun.)
New York Giants 13, NEW ORLEANS 12 (Sun.)
Pittsburgh 37, HOUSTON 34 (Sun.)
SEATTLE 42, Denver 14 (Sun.)
Los Angeles Rams 38, SAN FRANCISCO 16 (Sun.)

**1987**
NEW YORK GIANTS 17, New England 10 (Sun.)
SAN DIEGO 16, Los Angeles Raiders 14 (Sun.)
Miami 20, DALLAS 14 (Sun.)
SAN FRANCISCO 38, Cleveland 24 (Sun.)
Chicago 30, MINNESOTA 24 (Sun.)
SEATTLE 28, Denver 21 (Sun.)
MIAMI 23, Washington 21 (Sun.)
SAN FRANCISCO 48, Los Angeles Rams 0 (Sun.)

**1986**
New England 20, NEW YORK JETS 6 (Thurs.)
Cincinnati 30, CLEVELAND 13 (Thurs.)
Los Angeles Raiders 37, SAN DIEGO 31 (OT) (Thurs.)
LOS ANGELES RAMS 29, Dallas 10 (Sun.)
SAN FRANCISCO 24, Los Angeles Rams 14 (Fri.)

**1985**
KANSAS CITY 36, Los Angeles Raiders 20 (Thurs.)
Chicago 33, MINNESOTA 24 (Thurs.)
Dallas 30, NEW YORK GIANTS 29 (Sun.)
SAN DIEGO 54, Pittsburgh 44 (Sun.)
Denver 27, SEATTLE 24 (Fri.)

**1984**
Pittsburgh 23, NEW YORK JETS 17 (Thurs.)
Denver 24, CLEVELAND 14 (Sun.)
DALLAS 30, New Orleans 27 (Sun.)
Washington 31, MINNESOTA 17 (Thurs.)
SAN FRANCISCO 19, Los Angeles Rams 16 (Fri.)

**1983**
San Francisco 48, MINNESOTA 17 (Thurs.)
CLEVELAND 17, Cincinnati 7 (Thurs.)
Los Angeles Raiders 40, DALLAS 38 (Sun.)
Los Angeles Raiders 42, SAN DIEGO 10 (Thurs.)
MIAMI 34, New York Jets 14 (Fri.)

**1982**
BUFFALO 23, Minnesota 22 (Thurs.)
SAN FRANCISCO 30, Los Angeles Rams 24 (Thurs.)
ATLANTA 17, San Francisco 7 (Sun.)

**1981**
MIAMI 30, Pittsburgh 10 (Thurs.)
Philadelphia 20, BUFFALO 14 (Thurs.)
DALLAS 29, Los Angeles 17 (Sun.)
HOUSTON 17, Cleveland 13 (Thurs.)

**1980**
TAMPA BAY 10, Los Angeles 9 (Thurs.)
DALLAS 42, San Diego 31 (Sun.)
San Diego 27, MIAMI 24 (OT) (Thurs.)
HOUSTON 6, Pittsburgh 0 (Thurs.)

**1979**
Los Angeles 13, DENVER 9 (Thurs.)
DALLAS 30, Los Angeles 6 (Sun.)
OAKLAND 45, San Diego 22 (Thurs.)
MIAMI 39, New England 24 (Thurs.)

**1978**
New England 21, OAKLAND 14 (Sun.)
Minnesota 21, DALLAS 10 (Thurs.)
LOS ANGELES 10, Pittsburgh 7 (Sun.)
Denver 21, OAKLAND 6 (Sun.)

**1977**
Minnesota 30, DETROIT 21 (Sat.)

**1976**
Los Angeles 20, DETROIT 17 (Sat.)

**1975**
LOS ANGELES 10, Pittsburgh 3 (Sat.)

**1974**
OAKLAND 27, Dallas 23 (Sat.)

# OVERTIME GAMES

## HISTORY OF OVERTIME GAMES

### PRESEASON

| | |
|---|---|
| Aug. 28, 1955 | Los Angeles 23, New York Giants 17, at Portland, Oregon |
| Aug. 24, 1962 | Denver 27, Dallas Texans 24, at Fort Worth, Texas |
| Aug. 10, 1974 | San Diego 20, New York Jets 14, at San Diego |
| Aug. 17, 1974 | Pittsburgh 33, Philadelphia 30, at Philadelphia |
| Aug. 17, 1974 | Dallas 19, Houston 13, at Dallas |
| Aug. 17, 1974 | Cincinnati 13, Atlanta 7, at Atlanta |
| Sept. 6, 1974 | Buffalo 23, New York Giants 17, at Buffalo |
| Aug. 9, 1975 | Baltimore 23, Denver 20, at Denver |
| Aug. 30, 1975 | New England 20, Green Bay 17, at Milwaukee |
| Sept. 13, 1975 | Minnesota 14, San Diego 14, at San Diego |
| Aug. 1, 1976 | New England 13, New York Giants 7, at New England |
| Aug. 2, 1976 | Kansas City 9, Houston 3, at Kansas City |
| Aug. 20, 1976 | New Orleans 26, Baltimore 20, at Baltimore |
| Sept. 4, 1976 | Dallas 26, Houston 20, at Dallas |
| Aug. 13, 1977 | Seattle 23, Dallas 17, at Seattle |
| Aug. 28, 1977 | New England 13, Pittsburgh 10, at New England |
| Aug. 28, 1977 | New York Giants 24, Buffalo 21, at East Rutherford, N.J. |
| Aug. 2, 1979 | Seattle 12, Minnesota 9, at Minnesota |
| Aug. 4, 1979 | Los Angeles 20, Oakland 14, at Los Angeles |
| Aug. 24, 1979 | Denver 20, New England 17, at Denver |
| Aug. 23, 1980 | Tampa Bay 20, Cincinnati 14, at Tampa Bay |
| Aug. 5, 1981 | San Francisco 27, Seattle 24, at Seattle |
| Aug. 29, 1981 | New Orleans 20, Detroit 17, at New Orleans |
| Aug. 28, 1982 | Miami 17, Kansas City 17, at Kansas City |
| Sept. 3, 1982 | Miami 16, New York Giants 13, at Miami |
| Aug. 6, 1983 | L.A. Raiders 26, San Francisco 23, at Los Angeles |
| Aug. 6, 1983 | Atlanta 13, Washington 10, at Atlanta |
| Aug. 13, 1983 | St. Louis 27, Chicago 24, at St. Louis |
| Aug. 18, 1983 | New York Jets 20, Cincinnati 17, at Cincinnati |
| Aug. 27, 1983 | Chicago 20, Kansas City 17, at Chicago |
| Aug. 11, 1984 | Pittsburgh 20, Philadelphia 17, at Pittsburgh |
| Aug. 9, 1985 | Buffalo 10, Detroit 10, at Pontiac, Mich. |
| Aug. 10, 1985 | Minnesota 16, Miami 13, at Miami |
| Aug. 17, 1985 | Dallas 27, San Diego 24, at San Diego |
| Aug. 24, 1985 | N.Y. Giants 34, N.Y. Jets 31, at East Rutherford, N.J. |
| Aug. 15, 1986 | Washington 27, Pittsburgh 24, at Washington |
| Aug. 15, 1986 | Detroit 30, Seattle 27, at Detroit |
| Aug. 23, 1986 | Los Angeles Rams 20, San Diego 17, at Anaheim |
| Aug. 30, 1986 | Minnesota 23, Indianapolis 20, at Indianapolis |
| Aug. 23, 1987 | Philadelphia 19, New England 13, at New England |
| Sept. 5, 1987 | Cleveland 30, Green Bay 24, at Milwaukee |
| Sept. 6, 1987 | Kansas City 13, St. Louis 10, at Memphis, Tenn. |
| Aug. 11, 1988 | Seattle 16, Detroit 13, at Detroit |
| Aug. 19, 1988 | Miami 16, Denver 13, at Miami |
| Aug. 19, 1988 | Green Bay 21, Kansas City 21, at Milwaukee |
| Aug. 20, 1988 | Houston 20, Los Angeles Rams 17, at Anaheim |
| Aug. 21, 1988 | Minnesota 19, Phoenix 16, at Phoenix |
| Aug. 5, 1989 | Los Angeles Rams 16, San Francisco 13, at Tokyo, Japan |
| Aug. 26, 1989 | Denver 24, Dallas 21, at Denver |
| Sept. 1, 1989 | N.Y. Jets 15, Kansas City 13, at Kansas City |
| Aug. 24, 1990 | Cincinnati 13, New England 10, at New England |
| Aug. 16, 1991 | Cleveland 24, Washington 21, at Washington |
| Aug. 17, 1991 | Cincinnati 27, Minnesota 24, at Cincinnati |
| Aug. 23, 1991 | Dallas 20, Atlanta 17, at Dallas |
| Aug. 24, 1991 | Cincinnati 19, Green Bay 16, at Green Bay |
| Aug. 22, 1992 | Los Angeles Rams 16, Green Bay 13, at Anaheim |
| Aug. 8, 1993 | Dallas 13, Detroit 13, at London, England |

### REGULAR SEASON

**Sept. 22, 1974—Pittsburgh 35, Denver 35,** at Denver; Steelers win toss. Gilliam's pass intercepted and returned by Rowser to Denver's 42. Turner misses 41-yard field goal. Walden punts and Greer returns to Broncos' 39. Van Heusen punts and Edwards returns to Steelers' 16. Game ends with Steelers on own 26.

**Nov. 10, 1974—New York Jets 26, New York Giants 20,** at New Haven, Conn.; Giants win toss. Gogolak misses 42-yard field goal. Namath passes to Boozer for five yards and touchdown at 6:53.

**Sept. 28, 1975—Dallas 37, St. Louis 31,** at Dallas; Cardinals win toss. Hart's pass intercepted and returned by Jordan to Cardinals' 37. Staubach passes to DuPree for three yards and touchdown at 7:53.

**Oct. 12, 1975—Los Angeles 13, San Diego 10,** at San Diego; Chargers win toss. Partee punts to Rams' 14. Dempsey kicks 22-yard field goal at 9:27.

**Nov. 2, 1975—Washington 30, Dallas 24,** at Washington; Cowboys win toss. Staubach's pass intercepted and returned by Houston to Cowboys' 35. Kilmer runs one yard for touchdown at 6:34.

**Nov. 16, 1975—St. Louis 20, Washington 17,** at St. Louis; Cardinals win toss. Bakken kicks 37-yard field goal at 7:00.

**Nov. 23, 1975—Kansas City 24, Detroit 21,** at Kansas City; Lions win toss. Chiefs take over on downs at own 38. Stenerud kicks 26-yard field goal at 6:44.

**Nov. 23, 1975—Oakland 26, Washington 23,** at Washington; Redskins win toss. Bragg punts to Raiders' 42. Blanda kicks 27-yard field goal at 7:13.

**Nov. 30, 1975—Denver 13, San Diego 10,** at Denver; Broncos win toss. Turner kicks 25-yard field goal at 4:13.

**Nov. 30, 1975—Oakland 37, Atlanta 34,** at Oakland; Falcons win toss. James punts to Raiders' 16. Guy punts and Herron returns to Falcons' 41. Nick Mike-Mayer misses 45-yard field goal. Guy punts into Falcons' end zone. James punts to Raiders' 39. Blanda kicks 36-yard field goal at 15:00.

**Dec. 14, 1975—Baltimore 10, Miami 7,** at Baltimore; Dolphins win toss. Seiple punts to Colts' 4. Linhart kicks 31-yard field goal at 12:44.

**Sept. 19, 1976—Minnesota 10, Los Angeles 10,** at Minnesota; Vikings win toss. Tarkenton's pass intercepted by Monte Jackson and returned to Minnesota 16. Allen blocks Dempsey's 30-yard field goal attempt, ball rolls into end zone for touchback. Clabo punts and Scribner returns to Rams' 20. Rusty Jackson punts to Vikings' 35. Tarkenton's pass intercepted by Kay at Rams' 1, no return. Game ends with Rams on own 3.

***Sept. 27, 1976—Washington 20, Philadelphia 17,** at Philadelphia; Eagles win toss. Jones punts and E. Brown loses one yard on return to Redskins' 40. Bragg punts 51 yards into end zone for touchback. Jones punts and E. Brown returns to Redskins' 42. Bragg punts and Marshall returns to Eagles' 41. Boryla's pass intercepted by Dusek at Redskins' 37, no return. Bragg punts and Bradley returns. Philadelphia holding penalty moves ball back to Eagles' 8. Boryla pass intercepted by E. Brown and returned to Eagles' 22. Moseley kicks 29-yard field goal at 12:49.

**Oct. 17, 1976—Kansas City 20, Miami 17,** at Miami; Chiefs win toss. Wilson punts into end zone for touchback. Bulaich fumbles into Kansas City end zone, Collier recovers for touchback. Stenerud kicks 34-yard field goal at 14:48.

**Oct. 31, 1976—St. Louis 23, San Francisco 20,** at St. Louis; Cardinals win toss. Joyce punts and Leonard fumbles on return, Jones recovers at 49ers' 43. Bakken kicks 21-yard field goal at 6:42.

**Dec. 5, 1976—San Diego 13, San Francisco 7,** at San Diego; Chargers win toss. Morris runs 13 yards for touchdown at 5:12.

**Sept. 18, 1977—Dallas 16, Minnesota 10,** at Minnesota; Vikings win toss. Dallas starts on Vikings' 47 after a punt early in the overtime period. Staubach scores seven plays later on a four-yard run at 6:14.

***Sept. 26, 1977—Cleveland 30, New England 27,** at Cleveland; Browns win toss. Sipe throws a 22-yard pass to Logan at Patriots' 19. Cockroft kicks 35-yard field goal at 4:45.

**Oct. 16, 1977—Minnesota 22, Chicago 16,** at Minnesota; Bears win toss. Parsons punts 53 yards to Vikings' 18. Minnesota drives to Bears' 11. On a first-and-10, Vikings fake a field goal and holder Krause hits Voigt with a touchdown pass at 6:45.

**Oct. 30, 1977—Cincinnati 13, Houston 10,** at Cincinnati; Bengals win toss. Bahr kicks a 22-yard field goal at 5:51.

**Nov. 13, 1977—San Francisco 10, New Orleans 7,** at New Orleans; Saints win toss. Saints fail to move ball and Blanchard punts to 49ers' 41. Wersching kicks a 33-yard field goal at 6:33.

**Dec. 18, 1977—Chicago 12, New York Giants 9,** at East Rutherford, N.J.; Giants win toss. The ball changes hands eight times before Thomas kicks a 28-yard field goal at 14:51.

**Sept. 10, 1978—Cleveland 13, Cincinnati 10,** at Cleveland; Browns win toss. Collins returns kickoff 41 yards to Browns' 47. Cockroft kicks 27-yard field goal at 4:30.

***Sept. 11, 1978—Minnesota 12, Denver 9,** at Minnesota; Vikings win toss. Danmeier kicks 44-yard field goal at 2:56.

**Sept. 24, 1978—Pittsburgh 15, Cleveland 9,** at Pittsburgh; Steelers win toss. Cunningham scores on a 37-yard "gadget" pass from Bradshaw at 3:43. Steelers start winning drive on their 21.

**Sept. 24, 1978—Denver 23, Kansas City 17,** at Kansas City; Broncos win toss. Dilts punts to Kansas City. Chiefs advance to Broncos' 40 where Reed fails to make first down on fourth-and-one situation. Broncos march downfield. Preston scores two-yard touchdown at 10:28.

**Oct. 1, 1978—Oakland 25, Chicago 19,** at Chicago; Bears win toss. Both teams punt on first possession. On Chicago's second offensive series, Colzie intercepts Avellini's pass and returns it to Bears' 3. Three plays later, Whittington runs two yards for a touchdown at 5:19.

**Oct. 15, 1978—Dallas 24, St. Louis 21,** at St. Louis; Cowboys win toss. Dallas drives from its 23 into field goal range. Septien kicks 27-yard field goal at 3:28.

**Oct. 29, 1978—Denver 20, Seattle 17,** at Seattle; Broncos win toss. Ball changes hands four times before Turner kicks 18-yard field goal at 12:59.

**Nov. 12, 1978—San Diego 29, Kansas City 23,** at San Diego; Chiefs win toss. Fouts hits Jefferson for decisive 14-yard touchdown pass on the last play (15:00) of overtime period.

**Nov. 12, 1978—Washington 16, New York Giants 13,** at Washington; Redskins win toss. Moseley kicks winning 45-yard field goal at 8:32 after missing first down field goal attempt of 35 yards at 4:50.

**Nov. 26, 1978—Green Bay 10, Minnesota 10,** at Green Bay; Packers win toss. Both teams have possession of the ball four times.

**Dec. 9, 1978—Cleveland 37, New York Jets 34,** at Cleveland; Browns win toss. Cockroft kicks 22-yard field goal at 3:07.

**Sept. 2, 1979—Atlanta 40, New Orleans 34,** at New Orleans; Falcons win toss. Bartkowski's pass intercepted by Myers and returned to Falcons' 46. Erxleben punts to Falcons' 4. James punts to Chandler on Saints' 43. Erxleben punts and Ryckman returns to Falcons' 28. James punts and Chandler returns to Saints' 36. Erxleben retrieves punt snap on Saints' 1 and attempts pass. Mayberry

intercepts and returns six yards for touchdown at 8:22.
**Sept. 2, 1979—Cleveland 25, New York Jets 22,** at New York; Jets win toss. Leahy's 43-yard field goal attempt goes wide right at 4:41. Evans's punt blocked by Dykes is recovered by Newton. Ramsey punts into end zone for touchback. Evans punts and Harper returns to Jets' 24. Robinson's pass intercepted by Davis and returned 33 yards to Jets' 31. Cockroft kicks 27-yard field goal at 14:45.
***Sept. 3, 1979—Pittsburgh 16, New England 13,** at Foxboro; Patriots win toss. Hare punts to Swann at Steelers' 31. Bahr kicks 41-yard field goal at 5:10.
**Sept. 9, 1979—Tampa Bay 29, Baltimore 26,** at Baltimore; Colts win toss. Landry fumbles, recovered by Kollar at Colts' 14. O'Donoghue kicks 31-yard, first-down field goal at 1:41.
**Sept. 16, 1979—Denver 20, Atlanta 17,** at Atlanta; Broncos win toss. Broncos march 65 yards to Falcons' 7. Turner kicks 24-yard field goal at 6:15.
**Sept. 23, 1979—Houston 30, Cincinnati 27,** at Cincinnati; Oilers win toss. Parsley punts and Lusby returns to Bengals' 33. Bahr's 32-yard field goal attempt is wide right at 8:05. Parsley's punt downed on Bengals' 5. McInally punts and Ellender returns to Bengals' 42. Fritsch's third down, 29-yard field goal attempt hits left upright and bounces through at 14:28.
**Sept. 23, 1979—Minnesota 27, Green Bay 21,** at Minnesota; Vikings win toss. Kramer throws 50-yard touchdown pass to Rashad at 3:18.
**Oct. 28, 1979—Houston 27, New York Jets 24,** at Houston; Oilers win toss. Oilers march 58 yards to Jets' 18. Fritsch kicks 35-yard field goal at 5:10.
**Nov. 18, 1979—Cleveland 30, Miami 24,** at Cleveland; Browns win toss. Sipe passes 39 yards to Rucker for touchdown at 1:59.
**Nov. 25, 1979—Pittsburgh 33, Cleveland 30,** at Pittsburgh; Browns win toss. Sipe's pass intercepted by Blount on Steelers' 4. Bradshaw pass intercepted by Bolton on Browns' 12. Evans punts and Bell returns to Steelers' 17. Bahr kicks 37-yard field goal at 14:51.
**Nov. 25, 1979—Buffalo 16, New England 13,** at Foxboro; Patriots win toss. Hare's punt downed on Bills' 38. Jackson punts and Morgan returns to Patriots' 20. Grogan's pass intercepted by Haslett and returned to Bills' 42. Ferguson's 51-yard pass to Butler sets up N. Mike-Mayer's 29-yard field goal at 9:15.
**Dec. 2, 1979—Los Angeles 27, Minnesota 21,** at Los Angeles; Rams win toss. Clark punts and Miller returns to Vikings' 25. Kramer's pass intercepted by Brown and returned to Rams' 40. Cromwell, holding for 22-yard field goal attempt, runs around left end untouched for winning score at 6:53.
**Sept. 7, 1980—Green Bay 12, Chicago 6,** at Green Bay; Bears win toss. Parsons punts and Nixon returns 16 yards. Five plays later, Marcol returns own blocked field goal attempt 24 yards for touchdown at 6:00.
**Sept. 14, 1980—San Diego 30, Oakland 24,** at San Diego; Raiders win toss. Pastorini's first-down pass intercepted by Edwards. Millen intercepts Fouts' first-down pass and returns to San Diego 46. Bahr's 50-yard field goal attempt partially blocked by Williams and recovered on Chargers' 32. Eight plays later, Fouts throws 24-yard touchdown pass to Jefferson at 8:09.
**Sept. 14, 1980—San Francisco 24, St. Louis 21,** at San Francisco; Cardinals win toss. Swider punts and Robinson returns to 49ers' 32. San Francisco drives 52 yards to St. Louis 16, where Wersching kicks 33-yard field goal at 4:12.
**Oct. 12, 1980—Green Bay 14, Tampa Bay 14,** at Tampa Bay; Packers win toss. Teams trade punts twice. Lee returns second Tampa Bay punt to Green Bay 42. Dickey completes three passes to Buccaneers' 18, where Birney's 36-yard field goal attempt is wide right as time expires.
**Nov. 9, 1980—Atlanta 33, St. Louis 27,** at St. Louis; Falcons win toss. Strong runs 21 yards for touchdown at 4:20.
**#Nov. 20, 1980—San Diego 27, Miami 24,** at Miami; Chargers win toss. Partridge punts into end zone, Dolphins take over on their own 20. Woodley's pass for Nathan intercepted by Lowe and returned 28 yards to Dolphins' 12. Benirschke kicks 28-yard field goal at 7:14.
**Nov. 23, 1980—New York Jets 31, Houston 28,** at New York; Jets win toss. Leahy kicks 38-yard field goal at 3:58.
**Nov. 27, 1980—Chicago 23, Detroit 17,** at Detroit; Bears win toss. Williams returns kickoff 95 yards for touchdown at 0:21.
**Dec. 7, 1980—Buffalo 10, Los Angeles 7,** at Buffalo; Rams win toss. Corral punts and Hooks returns to Bills' 34. Ferguson's 30-yard pass to Lewis sets up N. Mike-Mayer's 30-yard field goal at 5:14.
**Dec. 7, 1980—San Francisco 38, New Orleans 35,** at San Francisco; Saints win toss. Erxleben's punt downed by Hardy on 49ers' 27. Wersching kicks 36-yard field goal at 7:40.
***Dec. 8, 1980—Miami 16, New England 13,** at Miami; Dolphins win toss. Von Schamann kicks 23-yard field goal at 3:20.
**Dec. 14, 1980—Cincinnati 17, Chicago 14,** at Chicago; Bengals win toss. Breech kicks 28-yard field goal at 4:23.
**Dec. 21, 1980—Los Angeles 20, Atlanta 17,** at Los Angeles; Rams win toss. Corral's punt downed at Rams' 37. James punts into end zone for touchback. Corral's punt downed on Falcons' 17. Bartkowski fumbles when hit by Harris, recovered by Delaney. Corral kicks 23-yard field goal on first play of possession at 7:00.
**Sept. 27, 1981—Cincinnati 27, Buffalo 24,** at Cincinnati; Bills win toss. Cater punts into end zone for touchback. Bengals drive to the Bills' 10 where Breech kicks 28-yard field goal at 9:33.
**Sept. 27, 1981—Pittsburgh 27, New England 21,** at Pittsburgh; Patriots win toss. Hubach punts and Smith returns five yards to midfield. Four plays later Bradshaw throws 24-yard touchdown pass to Swann at 3:19.
**Oct. 4, 1981—Miami 28, New York Jets 28,** at Miami; Jets win toss. Teams trade punts twice. Leahy's 48-yard field goal attempt is wide right as time expires.
**Oct. 25, 1981—New York Giants 27, Atlanta 24,** at Atlanta; Giants win toss. Jennings' punt goes out of bounds at New York 47. Bright returns Atlanta punt to Giants' 14. Woerner fair catches punt at own 28. Andrews fumbles on first play, recovered by Van Pelt. Danelo kicks 40-yard field goal four plays later at 9:20.
**Oct. 25, 1981—Chicago 20, San Diego 17,** at Chicago; Bears win toss. Teams trade punts. Bears' second punt returned by Brooks to Chargers' 33. Fouts pass intercepted by Fencik and returned 32 yards to San Diego 27. Roveto kicks 27-yard field goal seven plays later at 9:30.
**Nov. 8, 1981—Chicago 16, Kansas City 13,** at Kansas City; Bears win toss. Teams trade punts. Kansas City takes over on downs on its own 38. Fuller's fumble recovered by Harris on Chicago 36. Roveto's 37-yard field goal wide, but Chiefs penalized for leverage. Roveto's 22-yard field goal attempt three plays later is good at 13:07.
**Nov. 8, 1981—Denver 23, Cleveland 20,** at Denver; Browns win toss. D. Smith recovers Hill's fumble at Denver 48. Morton's 33-yard pass to Upchurch and 6-yard run by Preston set up Steinfort's 30-yard field goal at 4:10.
**Nov. 8, 1981—Miami 30, New England 27,** at New England; Dolphins win toss. Orosz punts and Morgan returns six yards to New England 26. Grogan's pass intercepted by Brudzinski who returns 19 yards to Patriots' 26. Von Schamann kicks 30-yard field goal on first down at 7:09.
**Nov. 15, 1981—Washington 30, New York Giants 27,** at New York; Giants win toss. Nelms returns Giants' punt 26 yards to New York 47. Five plays later Moseley kicks 48-yard field goal at 3:44.
**Dec. 20, 1981—New York Giants 13, Dallas 10,** at New York; Cowboys win toss and kick off. Jennings punts to Dallas 40. Taylor recovers Dorsett's fumble on second down. Danelo's 33-yard field goal attempt hits right upright and bounces back. White's pass for Pearson intercepted by Hunt and returned seven yards to Dallas 24. Four plays later Danelo kicks 35-yard field goal at 6:19.
**Sept. 12, 1982—Washington 37, Philadelphia 34,** at Philadelphia; Redskins win toss. Theismann completes five passes for 63 yards to set up Moseley's 26-yard field goal at 4:47.
**Sept. 19, 1982—Pittsburgh 26, Cincinnati 20,** at Pittsburgh; Bengals win toss. Anderson's pass intended for Kreider intercepted by Woodruff and returned 30 yards to Cincinnati 2. Bradshaw completes two-yard touchdown pass to Stallworth on first down at 1:08.
**Dec. 19, 1982—Baltimore 20, Green Bay 20,** at Baltimore; Packers win toss. K. Anderson intercepts Dickey's first-down pass and returns to Packers' 42. Miller's 44-yard field goal attempt blocked by G. Lewis. Teams trade punts before Stenerud's 47-yard field goal attempt is wide right. Teams trade punts again before time expires in Colts possession.
**Jan. 2, 1983—Tampa Bay 26, Chicago 23,** at Tampa; Bears win toss. Parsons punts to T. Bell at Buccaneers' 40. Capece kicks 33-yard field goal at 3:14.
**Sept. 4, 1983—Baltimore 29, New England 23,** at New England; Patriots win toss. Cooks runs 52 yards with fumble recovery three plays into overtime at 0:30.
**Sept. 4, 1983—Green Bay 41, Houston 38,** at Houston; Packers win toss. Stenerud kicks 42-yard field goal at 5:55.
**Sept. 11, 1983—New York Giants 16, Atlanta 13,** at Atlanta; Giants win toss. Dennis returns kickoff 54 yards to Atlanta 41. Haji-Sheikh kicks 30-yard field goal at 3:38.
**Sept. 18, 1983—New Orleans 34, Chicago 31,** at New Orleans; Bears win toss. Parsons punts and Groth returns five yards to New Orleans 34. Stabler pass intercepted by Schmidt at Chicago 47. Parsons punt downed by Gentry at New Orleans 2. Stabler gains 36 yards in four passes; Wilson 38 on six carries. Andersen kicks 41-yard field goal at 10:57.
**Sept. 18, 1983—Minnesota 19, Tampa Bay 16,** at Tampa; Vikings win toss. Coleman punts and Bell returns eight yards to Tampa Bay 47. Capece's 33-yard field goal attempt sails wide at 7:26. Dils and Young combine for 48-yard gain to Tampa Bay 27. Ricardo kicks 42-yard field goal at 9:27.
**Sept. 25, 1983—Baltimore 22, Chicago 19,** at Baltimore; Colts win toss. Allegre kicks 33-yard field goal nine plays later at 4:51.
**Sept. 25, 1983—Cleveland 30, San Diego 24,** at San Diego; Browns win toss. Walker returns kickoff 33 yards to Cleveland 37. Sipe completes 48-yard touchdown pass to Holt four plays later at 1:53.
**Sept. 25, 1983—New York Jets 27, Los Angeles Rams 24,** at New York; Jets win toss. Ramsey punts to Irvin who returns to 25 but penalty puts Rams on own 13. Holmes 30-yard interception return sets up Leahy's 26-yard field goal at 3:22.
**Oct. 9, 1983—Buffalo 38, Miami 35,** at Miami; Dolphins win toss. Von Schamann's 52-yard field goal attempt goes wide at 12:36. Cater punts to Clayton who loses 11 to own 13. Von Schamann's 43-yard field goal attempt sails wide at 5:15. Danelo kicks 36-yard field goal nine plays later at 13:58.
**Oct. 9, 1983—Dallas 27, Tampa Bay 24,** at Dallas; Cowboys win toss. Septien's 51-yard field goal attempt goes wide but Buccaneers penalized for roughing kicker. Septien kicks 42-yard field goal at 4:38.
**Oct. 23, 1983—Kansas City 13, Houston 10,** at Houston; Chiefs win toss. Lowery kicks 41-yard field goal 13 plays later at 7:41.
**Oct. 23, 1983—Minnesota 20, Green Bay 17,** at Green Bay; Packers win toss. Scribner's punt downed on Vikings' 42. Ricardo kicks 32-yard field goal eight plays later at 5:05.
***Oct. 24, 1983—New York Giants 20, St. Louis 20,** at St. Louis; Cardinals win toss. Teams trade punts before O'Donoghue's 44-yard field goal attempt is wide

left. Jennings' punt returned by Bird to St. Louis 21. Lomax pass intercepted by Haynes who loses six yards to New York 33. Jennings' punt downed on St. Louis 17. O'Donoghue's 19-yard field goal attempt is wide right. Rutledge's pass intercepted by L. Washington who returns 25 yards to New York 25. O'Donoghue's 42-yard field goal attempt is wide right. Rutledge's pass intercepted by W. Smith at St. Louis 33 to end game.

**Oct. 30, 1983—Cleveland 25, Houston 19,** at Cleveland; Oilers win toss. Teams trade punts. Nielsen's pass intercepted by Whitwell who returns to Houston 20. Green runs 20 yards for touchdown on first down at 6:34.

**Nov. 20, 1983—Detroit 23, Green Bay 20,** at Milwaukee; Packers win toss. Scribner punts and Jenkins returns 14 yards to Green Bay 45. Murray's 33-yard field goal attempt is wide left at 9:32. Whitehurst's pass intercepted by Watkins and returned to Green Bay 27. Murray kicks 37-yard field goal four plays later at 8:30.

**Nov. 27, 1983—Atlanta 47, Green Bay 41,** at Atlanta; Packers win toss. K. Johnson returns interception 31 yards for touchdown at 2:13.

**Nov. 27, 1983—Seattle 51, Kansas City 48,** at Seattle; Seahawks win toss. Dixon's 47-yard kickoff return sets up N. Johnson's 42-yard field goal at 1:36.

**Dec. 11, 1983—New Orleans 20, Philadelphia 17,** at Philadelphia; Eagles win toss. Runager punts to Groth who fair catches on New Orleans 32. Stabler completes two passes for 36 yards to Goodlow to set up Andersen's 50-yard field goal at 5:30.

***Dec. 12, 1983—Green Bay 12, Tampa Bay 9,** at Tampa; Packers win toss. Stenerud kicks 23-yard field goal 11 plays later at 4:07.

**Sept. 9, 1984—Detroit 27, Atlanta 24,** at Atlanta; Lions win toss. Murray kicks 48-yard field goal nine plays later at 5:06.

**Sept. 30, 1984—Tampa Bay 30, Green Bay 27,** at Tampa; Packers win toss. Scribner punts 44 yards to Tampa Bay 2. Epps returns Garcia's punt three yards to Green Bay 27. Scribner's punt downed on Buccaneers' 33. Ariri kicks 46-yard field goal 11 plays later at 10:32.

**Oct. 14, 1984—Detroit 13, Tampa Bay 7,** at Detroit; Buccaneers win toss. Tampa Bay drives to Lions' 39 before Wilder fumbles. Five plays later Danielson hits Thompson with 37-yard touchdown pass at 4:34.

**Oct. 21, 1984—Dallas 30, New Orleans 27,** at Dallas; Cowboys win toss. Septien kicks 41-yard field goal eight plays later at 3:42.

**Oct. 28, 1984—Denver 22, Los Angeles Raiders 19,** at Los Angeles; Raiders win toss. Hawkins fumble recovered by Foley at Denver 7. Teams trade punts. Karlis's 42-yard field goal attempt is wide left. Teams trade punts. Wilson pass intercepted by R. Jackson at Los Angeles 45, returned 23 yards to Los Angeles 22. Karlis kicks 35-yard field goal two plays later at 15:00.

**Nov. 4, 1984—Philadelphia 23, Detroit 23,** at Detroit; Lions win toss. Lions drive to Eagles' 3 in eight plays. Murray's 21-yard field goal attempt hits right upright and bounces back. Jaworski's pass intercepted by Watkins at Detroit 5. Teams trade punts. Cooper returns Black's punt five yards to Eagles' 14. Time expires four plays later with Eagles on own 21.

**Nov. 18, 1984—San Diego 34, Miami 28,** at San Diego; Chargers win toss. McGee scores eight plays later on a 25-yard run at 3:17.

**Dec. 2, 1984—Cincinnati 20, Cleveland 17,** at Cleveland; Browns win toss. Simmons returns Cox's punt 30 yards to Cleveland 35. Breech kicks 35-yard field goal seven plays later at 4:34.

**Dec. 2, 1984—Houston 23, Pittsburgh 20,** at Houston; Oilers win toss. Cooper kicks 30-yard field goal 16 plays later at 5:53.

**Sept. 8, 1985—St. Louis 27, Cleveland 24,** at Cleveland; Cardinals win toss. O'Donoghue kicks 35-yard field goal nine plays later at 5:27.

**Sept. 29, 1985—New York Giants 16, Philadelphia 10,** at Philadelphia; Eagles win toss. Jaworski's pass tipped by Quick and intercepted by Patterson who returns 29 yards for touchdown at 0:55.

**Oct. 20, 1985—Denver 13, Seattle 10,** at Denver; Seahawks win toss. Teams trade punts twice. Krieg's pass intercepted by Hunter and returned to Seahawks' 15. Karlis kicks 24-yard field goal four plays later at 9:19.

**Nov. 10, 1985—Philadelphia 23, Atlanta 17,** at Philadelphia; Falcons win toss. Donnelly's 62-yard punt goes out of bounds at Eagles' 1. Jaworski completes 99-yard touchdown pass to Quick two plays later at 1:49.

**Nov. 10, 1985—San Diego 40, Los Angeles Raiders 34,** at San Diego; Chargers win toss. James scores on 17-yard run seven plays later at 3:44.

**Nov. 17, 1985—Denver 30, San Diego 24,** at Denver; Chargers win toss. Thomas' 40-yard field goal attempt blocked by Smith and returned 60 yards by Wright for touchdown at 4:45.

**Nov. 24, 1985—New York Jets 16, New England 13,** at New York; Jets win toss. Teams trade punts twice. Patriots' second punt returned 46 yards by Sohn to Patriots' 15. Leahy kicks 32-yard field goal one play later at 10:05.

**Nov. 24, 1985—Tampa Bay 19, Detroit 16,** at Tampa; Lions win toss. Teams trade punts. Lions' punt downed on Buccaneers' 38. Igwebuike kicks 24-yard field goal 11 plays later at 12:31.

**Nov. 24, 1985—Los Angeles Raiders 31, Denver 28,** at Los Angeles; Raiders win toss. Bahr kicks 32-yard field goal six plays later at 2:42.

**Dec. 8, 1985—Los Angeles Raiders 17, Denver 14,** at Denver; Broncos win toss. Teams trade punts twice. Elway's fumble recovered by Townsend at Broncos' 8. Bahr kicks 26-yard field goal one play later at 4:55.

**Sept. 14, 1986—Chicago 13, Philadelphia 10,** at Chicago; Eagles win toss. Crawford's fumble of kickoff recovered by Jackson at Eagles' 35. Butler kicks 23-yard field goal 10 plays later at 5:56.

**Sept. 14, 1986—Cincinnati 36, Buffalo 33,** at Cincinnati; Bills win toss. Zander intercepts Kelly's first-down pass and returns it to Bills' 17. Breech kicks 20-yard field goal two plays later at 0:56.

**Sept. 21, 1986—New York Jets 51, Miami 45,** at New York; Jets win toss. O'Brien completes 43-yard touchdown pass to Walker five plays later at 2:35.

**Sept. 28, 1986—Pittsburgh 22, Houston 16,** at Houston; Oilers win toss. Johnson's punt returned 41 yards by Woods to Oilers' 15. Abercrombie scores on three-yard run three plays later at 2:35.

**Sept. 28, 1986—Atlanta 23, Tampa Bay 20,** at Tampa; Falcons win toss. Teams trade punts. Luckhurst kicks 34-yard field goal 10 plays later at 12:35.

**Oct. 5, 1986—Los Angeles Rams 26, Tampa Bay 20,** at Anaheim; Rams win toss. Dickerson scores four plays later on 42-yard run at 2:16.

**Oct. 12, 1986—Minnesota 27, San Francisco 24,** at San Francisco; Vikings win toss. C. Nelson kicks 28-yard field goal nine plays later at 4:27.

**Oct. 19, 1986—San Francisco 10, Atlanta 10,** at Atlanta; Falcons win toss. Teams trade punts twice. Donnelly punts to 49ers' 27. The following play Wilson recovers Rice's fumble at 49ers' 46 as time expires.

**Nov. 2, 1986—Washington 44, Minnesota 38,** at Washington; Redskins win toss. Schroeder completes 38-yard touchdown pass to Clark four plays later at 1:46.

**Nov. 20, 1986—Los Angeles Raiders 37, San Diego 31,** at San Diego; Raiders win toss. Teams trade punts. Allen scores five plays later on 28-yard run at 8:33.

**Nov. 23, 1986—Cleveland 37, Pittsburgh 31,** at Cleveland; Browns win toss. Teams trade punts. Six plays later Kosar hits Slaughter with 36-yard touchdown pass at 6:37.

**Nov. 30, 1986—Chicago 13, Pittsburgh 10,** at Chicago; Bears win toss and kick off. Newsome's punt returned by Barnes to Chicago 49. Butler kicks 42-yard field goal five plays later at 3:55.

**Nov. 30, 1986—Philadelphia 33, Los Angeles Raiders 27,** at Los Angeles; Eagles win toss. Teams trade punts. Long recovers Cunningham's fumble at Philadelphia 42. Waters returns Allen's fumble 81 yards to Los Angeles 4. Cunningham scores on one-yard run two plays later at 6:53.

**Nov. 30, 1986—Cleveland 13, Houston 10,** at Cleveland; Oilers win toss and kick off. Gossett punts to Houston 39. Luck's pass intercepted by Minnifield at Cleveland 21. Gossett punts to Houston 34. Luck's pass intercepted by Minnifield at Cleveland 43 who returns 20 yards to Houston 37. Moseley kicks 29-yard field goal nine plays later at 14:44.

**Dec. 7, 1986—St. Louis 10, Philadelphia 10,** at Philadelphia; Cardinals win toss. White blocks Schubert's 40-yard field goal attempt. Teams trade punts. McFadden's 43-yard field goal attempt is wide left. Schubert's 37-yard field goal attempt is wide right. Cavanaugh's pass intercepted by Carter and returned to Eagles' 48 to end game.

**Dec. 14, 1986—Miami 37, Los Angeles Rams 31,** at Anaheim; Dolphins win toss. Marino completes 20-yard touchdown pass to Duper six plays later at 3:04.

**Sept. 20, 1987—Denver 17, Green Bay 17,** at Milwaukee; Packers win toss. Del Greco's 47-yard field goal attempt is short. Teams trade punts. Elway intercepted by Noble who returns 10 yards to Green Bay 34. Davis fumbles on next play and Smith recovers. Two plays later, Karlis's 40-yard field goal attempt is wide left. Time expires two plays later with Packers on own 23.

**Oct. 11, 1987—Detroit 19, Green Bay 16,** at Green Bay; Lions win toss. Prindle's 42-yard field goal attempt is wide left. Packers punt downed on Detroit 17. Prindle kicks 31-yard field goal 16 plays later at 12:26.

**Oct. 18, 1987—New York Jets 37, Miami 31,** at New York; Jets win toss. Teams trade punts. Ryan intercepted by Hooper at Jets' 47 who returns 11 yards. Mackey intercepted by Haslett at Jets' 37 who returns 9 yards. Jets punt. Mackey intercepted by Radachowsky who returns 45 yards to Miami 24. Ryan completes eight-yard touchdown pass to Hunter five plays later at 14:26.

**Oct. 18, 1987—Green Bay 16, Philadelphia 10,** at Green Bay; Packers win toss. Hargrove scores on seven-yard run 10 plays later at 5:04.

**Oct. 18, 1987—Buffalo 6, New York Giants 3,** at Buffalo; Bills win toss. Schlopy's 28-yard field goal attempt is wide left. Teams trade punts. Rutledge intercepted by Clark who returns 23 yards to Buffalo 40. Schlopy kicks 27-yard field goal nine plays later at 14:41.

**Oct. 25, 1987—Buffalo 34, Miami 31,** at Miami; Bills win toss. Norwood kicks 27-yard field goal seven plays later at 4:12.

**Nov. 1, 1987—San Diego 27, Cleveland 24,** at San Diego; Browns win toss. Kosar intercepted by Glenn who returns 20 yards to Browns' 25. Abbott kicks 33-yard field goal three plays later at 2:16.

**Nov. 15, 1987—Dallas 23, New England 17,** at New England; Cowboys win toss. Walker scores on 60-yard run four plays later at 1:50.

**Nov. 26, 1987—Minnesota 44, Dallas 38,** at Dallas; Vikings win toss. Coleman's punt downed by Hilton at Cowboys' 37. White intercepted by Studwell who returns 12 yards to Vikings' 37. D. Nelson scores on 24-yard run seven plays later at 7:51.

**Nov. 29, 1987—Philadelphia 34, New England 31,** at New England; Patriots win toss. Ramsey intercepted by Joyner who returns 29 yards to Eagles' 32. Fryar fair catches Teltschik's punt at Patriots' 13. Franklin's 46-yard field goal attempt is short. McFadden's 39-yard field goal attempt is wide left. Tatupu fumbles on next play and Cobb recovers. McFadden kicks 38-yard field goal four plays later at 12:16.

**Dec. 6, 1987—New York Giants 23, Philadelphia 20,** at New York; Giants win toss and kick off. Teams trade punts twice. Teltschik's punt is returned 16 yards by McConkey to Eagles' 33. Three plays later, Allegre's 50-yard field goal attempt is blocked by Joyner and returned 25 yards by Hoage to Eagles' 30. McConkey returns Teltschik's punt four yards to Giants' 44. Allegre kicks 28-yard field goal four plays later at 10:42.

**Dec. 6, 1987—Cincinnati 30, Kansas City 27,** at Cincinnati; Bengals win toss. Teams trade punts. Breech kicks 32-yard field goal 16 plays later at 9:44.

**Dec. 26, 1987—Washington 27, Minnesota 24,** at Minnesota; Redskins win toss. Haji-Sheikh kicks 26-yard field goal six plays later at 2:09.

**Sept. 4, 1988—Houston 17, Indianapolis 14,** at Indianapolis; Colts win toss. Dickerson fumble recovered by Lyles who returns six yards to Colts' 42. Zendejas kicks 35-yard field goal six plays later at 3:51.

***Sept. 26, 1988—Los Angeles Raiders 30, Denver 27,** at Denver; Broncos win toss. Teams trade punts twice. Elway intercepted by Lee who returns 20 yards to Broncos' 31. Bahr kicks 35-yard field goal four plays later at 12:35.

**Oct. 2, 1988—New York Jets 17, Kansas City 17,** at New York; Chiefs win toss. Chiefs punt goes into end zone for touchback. Leahy's 44-yard field goal attempt is wide right. Chiefs punt is returned by Townsell to Jets' 26. Burruss recovers McNeil's fumble at Chiefs' 11. DeBerg intercepted by Humphery at Jets' 49. Three plays later, time expires.

**Oct. 9, 1988—Denver 16, San Francisco 13,** at San Francisco; Broncos win toss and kick off. Young intercepted by Haynes at Broncos' 32. Denver punt downed at 49ers' 5. Young intercepted by Wilson who returns seven yards to 49ers' 5. Karlis kicks 22-yard field goal two plays later at 8:11.

**Oct. 30, 1988—New York Giants 13, Detroit 10,** at Detroit; Lions win toss. James's fumble recovered by Taylor at Lions' 22. Three plays later, McFadden kicks 33-yard field goal at 1:13.

**Nov. 20, 1988—Buffalo 9, New York Jets 6,** at Buffalo; Jets win toss. Vick's fumble recovered by Bennett at Bills' 32. Norwood kicks 30-yard field goal five plays later at 3:47.

**Nov. 20, 1988—Philadelphia 23, New York Giants 17,** at New York; Eagles win toss. Philadelphia's punt goes into end zone for touchback. Hostetler intercepted by Hoage who returns 11 yards to Giants' 41. Six plays later, Zendejas's 30-yard field-goal attempt is blocked and ball is recovered behind line of scrimmage by Eagles' Simmons, who runs 15 yards for touchdown at 3:09.

**Dec. 11, 1988—New England 10, Tampa Bay 7,** at New England; Buccaneers win toss and kick off. Staurovsky kicks 27-yard field goal six plays later at 3:08.

**Dec. 17, 1988—Cincinnati 20, Washington 17,** at Cincinnati; Bengals win toss. Cincinnati's punt returned by Oliphant to Redskins' 16. Grant recovers Williams's fumble at Redskins' 17. Breech kicks 20-yard field goal three plays later at 7:01.

**Sept. 24, 1989—Buffalo 47, Houston 41,** at Houston; Oilers win toss. Johnson returns Brady's kickoff 17 yards to Oilers' 19. Oilers drive to Buffalo 25, Zendejas's 37-yard field goal blocked, but Bills offsides and Zendejas's second attempt is wide left. Bills' ball and Kelly completes series of passes, including 28-yard game-winner to Andre Reed, at 8:42.

**Oct. 8, 1989—Miami 13, Cleveland 10,** at Miami; Browns win toss. Metcalf returns Stoyanovich's kickoff 20 yards to Browns' 28. Browns drive ball 46 yards in eight plays; Bahr wide left on 44-yard field goal attempt. Dolphins ball. Browns called for pass interference on Marino pass to Banks at Cleveland 47. Two plays later, Banks's 20-yard reception at Browns' 23 sets up winning 35-yard field goal by Stoyanovich at 6:23.

**Oct. 22, 1989—Denver 24, Seattle 21,** at Seattle; Seahawks win toss. Treadwell's 56-yard kickoff returned 18 yards by Jefferson to Seahawks' 27. Seahawks drive to Broncos' 22 in 10 plays, but Johnson's 40-yard field goal attempt wide left. Smith intercepts a Krieg pass and returns it 28 yards to Seahawks' 10. Treadwell kicks winning 27-yard field goal at 7:46.

**Oct. 29, 1989—New England 23, Indianapolis 20,** at Indianapolis; Patriots win toss. Biasucci kickoff returned 13 yards to Patriots' 23 by Martin. Holding penalty brings ball back to Patriots' 13. After six plays, Feagles punt returned 11 yards by Verdin to Colts' 28. Six plays later, Colts punt to Martin at Patriots' 12. Grogan completes three straight passes to Patriots' 44. Five consecutive runs put New England on Colts' 33. Davis kicks a 51-yard winning field goal for Patriots at 9:46.

**Oct. 29, 1989—Green Bay 23, Detroit 20,** at Milwaukee; Lions win toss. Sanders touchback on Jacke kickoff. On first play, Murphy intercepts Lions' Peete and returns it three yards to Lions' 26. Fullwood gains five yards on three plays to set up Jacke's 38-yard field goal at 2:14.

**Nov. 5, 1989—Minnesota 23, Los Angeles Rams 21,** at Minneapolis; Rams win toss. Karlis's kick returned 18 yards by Delpino to Rams' 19. Drive stops at Rams' 28. Merriweather blocks Hatcher's punt at 12. Ball rolls out of end zone for safety.

**Nov. 19, 1989—Cleveland 10, Kansas City 10,** at Cleveland; Browns win toss. Browns punt three times; Chiefs twice; before Kansas City's Lowery misses 47-yard field goal with 17 seconds remaining in overtime. Kosar's pass intercepted as time expired.

**Nov. 26, 1989—Los Angeles Rams 20, New Orleans 17,** at New Orleans; Saints win toss. Lansford's kickoff returned 27 yards to Saints' 30. After four plays, Barnhardt punts to Rams' 15. Saints penalized 35 yards for interference to Rams' 43. Three plays later, Everett hits Anderson with 14-yard pass to Saints' 40, then 26-yarder to put Rams in field goal position. Lansford kicks 31-yard field goal at 6:38.

**Dec. 3, 1989—Los Angeles Raiders 16, Denver 13,** at Los Angeles; Broncos win toss. Bell returns Jaeger kickoff 14 yards to Broncos' 18. Broncos' penalized for illegal block to Broncos' 9. Elway completes three passes for two first downs. On third and eight Elway sacked for 10-yard loss. Horan punts, Adams calls for fair catch at Raiders' 29. Dyal's 26-yard reception moves Raiders to Denver 43. Raiders move ball 34 yards in three plays to set up Jaeger's 26-yard field goal at 7:02.

**Dec. 10, 1989—Indianapolis 23, Cleveland 17,** at Indianapolis; Browns win toss. Teams trade punts. McNeil returns Colts' punt 42 yards to 42. Seven plays later, Bahr misses 35-yard field goal attempt. Three plays later, Stark punts and McNeil returns ball to 50-yard line. Two plays later, Prior intercepts Kosar's pass at Colts' 42 and returns it 58 yards for touchdown at 10:54.

**Dec. 17, 1989—Cleveland 23, Minnesota 17,** at Cleveland; Browns win toss. Browns punt to Vikings' 18. Six plays later, Vikings punt to Browns' 22. Nine plays later, Bahr lines up to attempt 31-yard field goal. Holder Pagel takes snap and passes 14 yards to Waiters for touchdown at 9:30.

**Sept. 23, 1990—Denver 34, Seattle 31,** at Denver; Seahawks win toss. Loville returns kickoff 19 yards to Seahawks' 27. Seahawks drive to Broncos' 26, where Johnson misses 44-yard field goal wide right. Broncos take over and Elway completes series of passes to set up Treadwell's 25-yard field goal at 9:14.

**Sept. 30, 1990—Tampa Bay 23, Minnesota 20,** at Minnesota; Vikings win toss. Vikings drive to Buccaneers' 31; Igwebuike's 48-yard field goal attempt wide left. Buccaneers drive to Vikings' 43 and punt. Gannon's pass is intercepted at Vikings' 26 by Wayne Haddix. Buccaneers drive to Vikings' 19 to set up Christie's 36-yard field goal at 9:11.

**Oct. 7, 1990—Cincinnati 34, Los Angeles Rams 31,** at Anaheim; Rams win toss. Berry returns kickoff to Rams' 21. After 3 plays, English punts and Green downs ball at Bengals' 25. After 3 plays, Johnson punts and Sutton downs ball at Rams' 29-yard line. After 3 plays, English punts and Price signals fair catch at Bengals' 47. Esiason completes series of passes to 26-yard line to set up Breech's 44-yard field goal at 11:56.

**Nov. 4, 1990—Washington 41, Detroit 38,** at Detroit; Redskins win toss. Howard downs kickoff on Redskins' 15. After 3 plays, Mojsiejenko punts to Redskins' 45. After 3 plays, Arnold punts to Redskins' 10. Rutledge completes series of passes to set up Lohmiller's 34-yard field goal at 9:10.

**Nov. 18, 1990—Chicago 16, Denver 13,** at Denver; Broncos win toss. Ezor returns kickoff to Broncos' 12. Both teams have ball twice and have to punt after each possession. Broncos punt after third possession of overtime and Bailey returns 20 yards to Broncos' 34. Harbaugh completes 10-yard pass to Thornton to set up Butler's 44-yard field goal at 13:14.

**Nov. 25, 1990—Seattle 13, San Diego 10,** at San Diego; Chargers win toss. Lewis returns kickoff to Chargers' 22. After 2 plays, Cox fumbles and ball is recovered by Porter at Chargers' 23. After two plays, Johnson kicks 40-yard field goal at 3:01.

**Dec. 2, 1990—Chicago 23, Detroit 17,** at Chicago; Lions win toss. Gray returns kickoff to Lions' 35. After 10 plays, Murray misses 35-yard field goal. Bears take possession at Chicago 20. Harbaugh completes 50-yard game-winning pass to Anderson at 10:57.

**Dec. 2, 1990—Seattle 13, Houston 10,** at Seattle; Seahawks win toss. Warren returns kickoff to Seahawks' 13. After 5 plays, Donnelly punts to Oilers' 23-yard line. Ford's fumble recovered by Wyman. Seahawks take possession at Oilers' 27. After 2 plays, Johnson kicks 42-yard field goal at 4:25.

**Dec. 9, 1990—Miami 23, Philadelphia 20,** at Miami; Eagles win toss. After 11 plays, Feagles punts to Dolphins' 26. After 6 plays, Roby punts to Eagles' 14 and Harris returns to 25. After 3 plays, Feagles punts to Dolphins' 43. Marino completes series of passes to Eagles' 22. Stoyanovich kicks 39-yard field goal at 12:32.

**Dec. 9, 1990—San Francisco 20, Cincinnati 17,** at Cincinnati; 49ers win toss. Carter returns kickoff to 49ers' 19. After 10 plays, Cofer kicks 23-yard field goal at 6:12.

**Sept. 24, 1991—Chicago 19, New York Jets 13,** at Chicago; Jets win toss. Mathis returns kickoff seven yards to New York's 12. Jets drive to New York 26; Bailey returns punt to Chicago 39. Bears drive to Jets' 44-yard line and punt into the end zone. Jets drive to Bears' 11 where Leahy's 28-yard field goal attempt is wide left. Bears drive from 20 to Jets' 1 where Harbaugh runs for touchdown at 14:42.

**Oct. 13, 1991—Los Angeles Raiders 23, Seattle 20,** at Seattle. Seahawks win toss. Seahawks begin on 20. After 5 plays, Tuten punts and Brown signals fair catch at Raiders' 24. After 3 plays, Gossett punts and Land downs ball at Seattle 9. After 1 play, Lott intercepts at Seahawks' 19 to set up Jaeger's game-winning 37-yard field goal at 6:37.

**Oct. 20, 1991—Cleveland 30, San Diego 24,** at San Diego; Chargers win toss. After kickoff, Chargers drive to Browns' 45 and punt to Browns' 6 where Hendrickson downs ball. Browns drive to 38 and punt; Taylor fair catches on Chargers' 14. After 3 plays, Brandon intercepts at Chargers' 30 and scores at 5:58.

**Oct. 20, 1991—New England 26, Minnesota 23,** at New England; Patriots win toss. Martin returns kickoff 18 yards to New England 22. Patriots drive to Minnesota 19. Staurovsky's 36-yard field goal attempt is wide left. Minnesota drives to the 50 where Newsome punts into end zone. On first play, McMillian intercepts at the 40 for Minnesota. After 2 plays, Marion causes Jordan fumble and Pool recovers at New England 20. New England drives to Minnesota 24 where Staurovsky kicks 42-yard field goal as time expires.

**Nov. 3, 1991—New York Jets 19, Green Bay 16,** at New York; Packers win toss. Thompson returns kickoff 30 yards to Packers' 39. Green Bay drives to New York 24 where Jacke's 42-yard field goal attempt is wide right. Jets drive to 50. Aguiar's punt is fumbled by Sikahema and recovered by New York at Packers' 23. After 2 plays, Leahy kicks 37-yard field goal at 9:40.

**Nov. 3, 1991—Washington 16, Houston 13,** at Washington; Redskins win toss. Mitchell returns kickoff 9 yards to Washington 14. After 4 plays, Goodburn punts

and Givins returns to Houston 31. After 1 play, Moon's pass is intercepted by Green at Oilers' 35. After 3 plays, Lohmiller kicks 41-yard field goal at 4:01.
**Nov. 10, 1991—Houston 26, Dallas 23,** at Houston; Oilers win toss. Pinkett returns kickoff 20 yards to Houston 24. After 6 plays, Montgomery punts and Martin returns to Dallas 24. Cowboys drive to Oilers' 24 where Smith fumbles and McDowell recovers at Oilers' 15. Houston drives to Dallas 5 where Del Greco kicks 23-yard field goal at 14:31.
**Nov. 10, 1991—Pittsburgh 33, Cincinnati 27,** at Cincinnati; Pittsburgh wins toss. Woodson downs kickoff for touchback. After 3 plays, Stryzinski punts and Barber returns 7 yards to Cincinnati 38. Bengals drive to Pittsburgh 37 where Woods fumbles and Lloyd returns recovery to Cincinnati 44. After 2 plays, O'Donnell passes to Green for 26-yard touchdown at 6:32.
**Nov. 24, 1991—Atlanta 23, New Orleans 20,** at New Orleans; Atlanta wins toss. Falcons begin at 20. After 3 plays, Fulhage punts and Fenerty signals fair catch at New Orleans 43. After 3 plays, Barnhardt punts and Thompson downs ball at Atlanta 23. After 3 plays, Fulhage punts and Fenerty fair catches at New Orleans 25. Saints drive to Atlanta 38 where Andersen misses 55-yard field-goal attempt. After 1 play, Rozier fumbles and Martin recovers on 50. Saints drive to Atlanta 38 where Barnhardt punts to Falcons' 2. Atlanta drives to New Orleans 33 where Johnson kicks 50-yard field goal at 13:03.
**Nov. 24, 1991—Miami 16, Chicago 13,** at Chicago; Miami wins toss. Butler kicks to Miami 20 where Paige returns kickoff 15 yards to 35. Miami drives to Chicago 9 where Stoyanovich kicks 27-yard field goal at 4:11.
**Dec. 8, 1991—Buffalo 30, Los Angeles Raiders 27,** at Los Angeles; Raiders win toss. Daluiso kicks into end zone for touchback. On third play, Kelso intercepts for Buffalo and returns ball to Bills' 36. Bills drive to Los Angeles 24 where Norwood kicks 42-yard field goal at 2:34.
**Dec. 8, 1991—Kansas City 20, San Diego 17,** at Kansas City; Chiefs win toss. Carney kicks to Kansas City 10 where Stradford returns 23 yards to 33. After 3 plays, Barker punts to San Diego 4. Chargers drive to 40 where Kidd punts 60 yards into end zone for touchback. Kansas City drives to San Diego 39 where Barker punts 38 yards to 1. After 3 plays, Kidd punts 41 yards to San Diego 42 where Stradford returns 12 yards to 30. Chiefs drive to San Diego 1 where Lowery kicks 18-yard field goal at 11:26.
**Dec. 8, 1991—New England 23, Indianapolis 17,** at New England; Indianapolis wins toss. Baumann kicks off to Indianapolis 2 where Martin returns 23 yards to 25. After 3 downs, Stark punts to New England 17 where Henderson returns 8 yards to 25. New England drives to 50 where McCarthy punts and Prior signals fair catch at Indianapolis 15. After 3 plays, Stark punts to New England 40 where Henderson returns 7 yards to 47. After 2 plays, Millen passes to Timpson for 45-yard touchdown at 8:55.
**Dec. 22, 1991—Detroit 17, Buffalo 14,** at Buffalo; Detroit wins toss. Daluiso kicks off to Detroit 20 where Dozier returns 15 yards to Lions 35. Lions drive to Bills' 3 where Murray kicks 21-yard field goal at 4:23.
**Dec. 22, 1991—New York Jets 23, Miami 20,** at Miami; Jets win toss. Aguiar kicks to Miami's 30 where Logan returns 3 yards to the 33. After 4 downs, Stoyanovich punts to Jets' 15 where Baty returns 8 yards to 23. Jets drive to Miami 12 where Allegre kicks 30-yard field goal at 6:33.
**Sept. 6, 1992—Minnesota 23, Green Bay 20,** at Green Bay. Vikings win toss. Nelson returns kickoff 14 yards to the Minnesota 23. After 5 plays, Newsome punts 49 yards to Green Bay 21 where Brooks returns 12 yards to the 33. After 2 plays, Glenn intercepts pass at the Vikings' 48. On first play, Allen fumbles and Billups recovers at Green Bay 35. After 3 plays, McJulien punts 33 yards to Vikings' 35. Vikings drive to Minnesota 48; Newsome punts 52 yards for touchback. After 3 plays, McJulien punts and Parker returns 10 yards to Green Bay 48. Vikings drive to Packers' 9 where Reveiz kicks 26-yard field goal at 10:20.
**Sept. 13, 1992—Cincinnati 24, Los Angeles Raiders 21,** at Cincinnati. Raiders win toss. Land returns kickoff 13 yards but fumbles at Los Angeles's 20; ball recovered by Bengals' Bennett at Raiders' 21. After 1 play, Breech kicks 34-yard field goal at 1:01.
**Sept. 20, 1992—Houston 23, Kansas City 20,** at Houston. Chiefs win toss. Carter returns kickoff 25 yards to Kansas City 28. On third play of drive, Birden fumbles at Kansas City 34; ball recovered by Houston's D. Smith at Chiefs' 23. After one play, Del Greco kicks 39-yard field goal at 1:55.
**Oct. 11, 1992—Indianapolis 6, New York Jets 3,** at Indianapolis. Colts win toss. Verdin returns kickoff 33 yards to Colts' 36. Colts drive to Jets' 30 where Biasucci kicks 47-yard field goal at 3:01.
**Nov. 8, 1992—Cincinnati 31, Chicago 28,** at Chicago. Bears win toss. Lewis returns kickoff 22 yards to Chicago's 29. Bears drive to Chicago's 46 where Gardocki punts; fair catch by Wright at the Cincinnati 17. Bengals drive to Bears' 18 where Breech kicks 36-yard field goal at 8:39.
**Nov. 15, 1992—New England 37, Indianapolis 34,** at Indianapolis. Colts win toss. Verdin returns kickoff 10 yards to Colts' 20; holding penalty brings ball back to Colts' 10. After two plays, Henderson intercepts pass at Colts' 38 and returns it 9 yards to the 29. In three plays, Patriots drive to 1 where Baumann kicks 18-yard field goal at 3:25.
**Nov. 29, 1992—Indianapolis 16, Buffalo 13,** at Indianapolis. Colts win toss. Verdin returns kickoff 24 yards to Colts' 22. Colts drive to Buffalo 22 where Biasucci kicks 40-yard field goal at 3:51.
***Nov. 30, 1992—Seattle 16, Denver 13,** at Seattle. Seahawks win toss. Daluiso kicks through end zone for touchback. After three plays, Tuten punts 53 yards to Denver 18 where Marshall returns for no gain. After three plays, Rodriguez punts 29 yards to Seattle 45 where Warren signals fair catch.Seahawks drive to Denver 15 where Kasay's 33-yard field goal attempt misses. Broncos take over at Denver 20. After three plays, Rodriguez punts 43 yards to Seattle 38 where Warren signals for fair catch. After four plays, Tuten punts 39 yards to Denver 4 where Daniels downs punt. After three plays, Rodriguez punts 46 yards to Denver 48 where Warren returns 10 yards to the 38. Seahawks drive to Denver 14 where Kasay kicks 32-yard field goal at 11:10.
**Dec. 13, 1992—Philadelphia 20, Seattle 17,** at Seattle. Eagles win toss. Sydner returns kick 12 yards to Eagles' 16; illegal block penalty brings ball back to 8. Eagles drive to Philadelphia 45 where Feagles punts for a touchback. After 6 plays, Tuten punts 45 yards to Philadelphia 22 where Sydner returns 7 yards to 29. After 6 plays, Feagles punts 44 yards to Seattle 26 where Warren returns 5 yards to 31. After 5 plays, Tuten punts 32 yards to Philadelphia 20 where Sydner signals for fair catch. Eagles drive to Seattle 27 where Ruzek kicks 44-yard field goal with no time remaining.
**Dec. 27, 1992—Miami 16, New England 13,** at New England. Patriots win toss. Lockwood returns kickoff 15 yards to Patriots' 21. After three plays, McCarthy punts 39 yards to Miami 33 where Miller returns 2 yards to the 35. Miami drives to New England 18 where Stoyanovich kicks 35-yard field goal at 8:17.
**Sept. 12, 1993—Detroit 19, New England 16,** at New England. Patriots win toss. Patriots begin at 20. After 3 plays, Saxon punts 42 yards to Detroit 29 where Gray returns 12 yards to the 41. After 3 plays, Arnold punts 41 yards to New England 12 where Brown returns 16 yards to the 28. Patriots drive to Detroit 44 where Saxon punts into the end zone for a touchback. Detroit drives to New England 20 where Hanson kicks 38-yard field goal at 11:04.
**Nov. 7, 1993—Buffalo 13, New England 10,** at New England. Patriots win toss. T. Brown returns kickoff 27 yards to Patriots 30. Patriots drive to Buffalo 48 where Bills take over on downs. Bills drive to New England 25 where Metzelaars fumbles, and C. Brown recovers. After 3 plays, Saxon punts 46 yards to Buffalo 24 where Copeland returns 11 yards to the 35. Bills drive to New England 14 where Christie kicks 32-yard field goal at 9:22.
**Dec. 19, 1993—Phoenix 30, Seattle 27,** at Seattle. Cardinals win toss. Bailey returns kickoff 14 yards to Cardinals 20. Cardinals drive to Seattle 23 where Davis kicks 41-yard field goal at 6:45.
**Jan. 2, 1994—Dallas 16, New York Giants 13,** at New York. Giants win toss. Meggett returns kickoff 19 yards to Giants 19. After 6 plays, Horan punts 45 yards to Cowboys 25 where Widmer downs punt. Cowboys drive to Giants' 23 where Murray kicks 41-yard field goal at 10:44.
**Jan. 2, 1994—New England 33, Miami 27,** at New England. Dolphins win toss. McDuffie returns kickoff 21 yards to Miami 27. After 3 plays, Hatcher punts 43 yards to New England 29 where Harris returns 6 yards to the 35. After 2 plays, Brown intercepts pass from Bledsoe and returns 3 yards to Miami 49. After 3 plays, Hatcher punts 37 yards to New England 14 where Harris returns 18 yards to the 32. After 2 plays, Bledsoe passes 36 yards to Timpson for touchdown at 4:44.
**Jan. 2, 1994—Los Angeles Raiders 33, Denver 30,** at Los Angeles. Broncos win toss. Delpino returns kickoff 12 yards to Denver 25. Broncos drive to Los Angeles 22 where Elam's 40-yard field goal attempt is wide left. Raiders drive to Denver 29 where Jaeger kicks 47-yard field goal at 7:10.
***Jan. 3, 1994—Philadelphia 37, San Francisco 34,** at San Francisco. 49ers win toss. Walker returns kickoff, 19 yards to San Francisco 27. 49ers drive to Philadelphia 14 where Cofer misses 32-yard field goal. Eagles start at their 20-yard line, and, after 3 plays, Feagles punts 48 yards to San Francisco 36 where Carter fumbles and 49ers recover. After 7 plays, Wilmsmeyer punts 57 yards to Philadelphia 6 where Sikahema returns 16 yards to the 22. Eagles drive to San Francisco 10 where Ruzek kicks 28-yard field goal with no time remaining.

**indicates Monday night game*
*#indicates Thursday night game*

**POSTSEASON**
**Dec. 28, 1958—Baltimore 23, New York Giants 17,** at New York in NFL Championship Game. Giants win toss. Maynard returns kickoff to Giants' 20. Chandler punts and Taseff returns one yard to Colts' 20. Colts win at 8:15 on a 1-yard run by Ameche.
**Dec. 23, 1962—Dallas Texans 20, Houston Oilers 17,** at Houston in AFL Championship Game. Texans win toss and kick off. Jancik returns kickoff to Oilers' 33. Norton punts and Jackson makes fair catch on Texans' 22. Wilson punts and Jancik makes fair catch on Oilers' 45. Robinson intercepts Blanda's pass and returns 13 yards to Oilers' 47. Wilson's punt rolls dead at Oilers' 12. Hull intercepts Blanda's pass and returns 23 yards to midfield. Texans win at 17:54 on a 25-yard field goal by Brooker.
**Dec. 26, 1965—Green Bay 13, Baltimore 10,** at Green Bay in NFL Divisional Playoff Game. Packers win toss. Moore returns kickoff to Packers' 22. Chandler punts and Haymond returns nine yards to Colts' 41. Gilburg punts and Wood makes fair catch at Packers' 21. Chandler punts and Haymond returns one yard to Colts' 41. Michaels misses 47-yard field goal. Packers win at 13:39 on 25-yard field goal by Chandler.
**Dec. 25, 1971—Miami 27, Kansas City 24,** at Kansas City in AFC Divisional Playoff Game. Chiefs win toss. Podolak, after a lateral from Buchanan, returns kickoff to Chiefs' 46. Stenerud's 42-yard field goal is blocked. Seiple punts and Podolak makes fair catch at Chiefs' 17. Wilson punts and Scott returns 18 yards to Dolphins' 39. Yepremian misses 62-yard field goal. Scott intercepts Dawson's pass and returns 13 yards to Dolphins' 46. Seiple punts and Podolak loses one

yard to Chiefs' 15. Wilson punts and Scott makes fair catch on Dolphins' 30. Dolphins win at 22:40 on a 37-yard field goal by Yepremian.

**Dec. 24, 1977—Oakland 37, Baltimore 31,** at Baltimore in AFC Divisional Playoff Game. Colts win toss. Raiders start on own 42 following a punt late in the first overtime. Oakland works way into field-goal range on Stabler's 19-yard pass to Branch at Colts' 26. Four plays later, on the second play of the second overtime, Stabler hits Casper with a 10-yard touchdown pass at 15:43.

**Jan. 2, 1982—San Diego 41, Miami 38,** at Miami in AFC Divisional Playoff Game. Chargers win toss. San Diego drives from its 13 to Miami 8. On second-and-goal, Benirschke misses 27-yard field goal attempt wide left at 9:15. Miami has the ball twice and San Diego twice more before the Dolphins get their third possession. Miami drives from the San Diego 46 to Chargers' 17 and on fourth-and-two, von Schamann's 34-yard field goal attempt is blocked by San Diego's Winslow after 11:27. Fouts then completes four of five passes, including a 39-yarder to Joiner that puts the ball on Dolphins' 10. On first down, Benirschke kicks a 29-yard field goal at 13:52. San Diego's winning drive covered 74 yards in six plays.

**Jan. 3, 1987—Cleveland 23, New York Jets 20,** at Cleveland in AFC Divisional Playoff Game. Jets win toss. Jets' punt downed at Browns' 26. Moseley's 23-yard field goal attempt is wide right. Teams trade punts. Jets' second punt downed at Browns' 31. First overtime period expires eight plays later with Browns in possession at Jets' 42. Moseley kicks 27-yard field goal four plays into second overtime at 17:02.

**Jan. 11, 1987—Denver 23, Cleveland 20,** at Cleveland in AFC Championship Game. Browns win toss. Broncos hold Browns on four downs. Browns' punt returned four yards to Denver's 25. Elway completes 22- and 28-yard passes to set up Karlis's 33-yard field goal nine plays into drive at 5:38.

**Jan. 3, 1988—Houston 23, Seattle 20,** at Houston in AFC Wild Card Game. Seahawks win toss. Rodriguez punts to K. Johnson who returns one yard to Houston 15. Zendejas kicks 32-yard field goal 12 plays later at 8:05.

**Dec. 31, 1989—Pittsburgh 26, Houston 23,** at Houston in AFC Wild Card Playoff Game. Steelers win toss. Steelers punt to Oilers. Oilers' fumble recovered by Woodson and returned three yards. Four plays and 13 yards later, Anderson kicks a 50-yard field goal at 3:26.

**Jan. 7, 1990—Los Angeles Rams 19, New York Giants 13,** at New York in NFC Wild Card Game. Rams win toss. Everett completes two passes to move ball to Giants' 48. White called for pass interference; ball spotted on Giants' 25. Everett hits Anderson with a 30-yard touchdown pass at 1:06.

**Jan. 3, 1993—Buffalo 41, Houston 38,** at Buffalo in AFC Wild Card Game. Houston wins toss. Oilers begin at 20. After 2 plays, Moon's pass is intercepted by Odomes who returns ball 2 yards to Houston 35. After 2 plays, Christie kicks 32-yard field goal at 3:06.

**Jan. 8, 1994—Kansas City 27, Pittsburgh 24,** at Kansas City. Kansas City wins toss. Hughes returns kickoff 20 yards to Kansas City 25. After 3 plays, Barker punts 48 yards to Pittsburgh 18 where Woodson returns 8 yards to the 26. After 6 plays, Royals punts 30 yards to Kansas City 20. Kansas City drives to Pittsburgh 14 where Lowery kicks 32-yard field goal at 11:03.

## NFL POSTSEASON OVERTIME GAMES
**(BY LENGTH OF GAME)**

| | | |
|---|---|---|
| Dec. 25, 1971 | Miami 27, KANSAS CITY 24 | 82:40 |
| Dec. 23, 1962 | Dallas Texans 20, HOUSTON 17 | 77:54 |
| Jan. 3, 1987 | CLEVELAND 23, New York Jets 20 | 77:02 |
| Dec. 24, 1977 | Oakland 37, BALTIMORE 31 | 75:43 |
| Jan. 2, 1982 | San Diego 41, MIAMI 38 | 73:52 |
| Dec. 26, 1965 | GREEN BAY 13, Baltimore 10 | 73:39 |
| Jan. 8, 1994 | KANSAS CITY 27, Pittsburgh 24 | 71:03 |
| Dec. 28, 1958 | Baltimore 23, N.Y. GIANTS 17 | 68:15 |
| Jan. 3, 1988 | HOUSTON 23, Seattle 20 | 68:05 |
| Jan. 11, 1987 | Denver 23, CLEVELAND 20 | 65:38 |
| Dec. 31, 1989 | Pittsburgh 26, HOUSTON 23 | 63:26 |
| Jan. 7, 1990 | Los Angeles Rams 19, N.Y. GIANTS 13 | 61:06 |

*Home team in CAPS*

## OVERTIME WON-LOST RECORDS, 1974-1993
**(REGULAR SEASON)**

| AFC | W | L | T |
|---|---|---|---|
| Buffalo | 9 | 4 | 0 |
| Cincinnati | 10 | 5 | 0 |
| Cleveland | 11 | 8 | 1 |
| Denver | 11 | 8 | 2 |
| Houston | 6 | 10 | 0 |
| Indianapolis | 6 | 5 | 1 |
| Kansas City | 4 | 6 | 2 |
| Los Angeles Raiders | 10 | 6 | 0 |
| Miami | 7 | 11 | 1 |
| New England | 6 | 13 | 0 |
| New York Jets | 8 | 6 | 2 |
| Pittsburgh | 7 | 3 | 1 |
| San Diego | 7 | 9 | 0 |
| Seattle | 4 | 7 | 0 |

| NFC | W | L | T |
|---|---|---|---|
| Atlanta | 5 | 7 | 1 |
| Chicago | 9 | 9 | 0 |
| Dallas | 7 | 4 | 0 |
| Detroit | 6 | 7 | 1 |
| Green Bay | 5 | 8 | 4 |
| Los Angeles Rams | 5 | 5 | 1 |
| Minnesota | 9 | 7 | 2 |
| New Orleans | 2 | 6 | 0 |
| New York Giants | 6 | 7 | 1 |
| Philadelphia | 6 | 8 | 2 |
| Phoenix | 4 | 4 | 2 |
| San Francisco | 4 | 5 | 1 |
| Tampa Bay | 5 | 7 | 1 |
| Washington | 9 | 3 | 0 |

## OVERTIME GAMES BY YEAR
**(REGULAR SEASON)**

| | | | |
|---|---|---|---|
| 1993-7 | 1988- 9 | 1983-19 | 1978-11 |
| 1992-10 | 1987-13 | 1982- 4 | 1977- 6 |
| 1991-15 | 1986-16 | 1981-10 | 1976- 5 |
| 1990-10 | 1985-10 | 1980-13 | 1975- 9 |
| 1989-11 | 1984- 9 | 1979-12 | 1974- 2 |

## OVERTIME GAME SUMMARY—1974-1993
There have been 201 overtime games in regular-season play since the rule was adopted in 1974 (7 in 1993 season). Breakdown follows:

150 (6) times both teams had at least one possession (75%)
51 (1) times the team which won the toss drove for winning score (36 FG, 15 TD) (25%)
94 (1) times the team which won the toss won the game (47%)
94 (6) times the team which lost the toss won the game (47%)
135 (6) games were decided by a field goal (67%)
52 (1) games were decided by a touchdown (26%)
1 (0) game was decided by a safety (.5%)
13 (0) games ended tied (6.5%). Last time: Nov. 19, 1989, Cleveland 10, Kansas City 10, at Cleveland

*Note: The number in parentheses represents the 1993 season total in each category.*

## MOST OVERTIME GAMES, SEASON
5 Green Bay Packers, 1983
4 Denver Broncos, 1985
4 Cleveland Browns, 1989
3 By many teams, last time: New England Patriots, 1993

## LONGEST CONSECUTIVE GAME STREAKS WITHOUT OVERTIME (Current)
60 Tampa Bay Buccaneers (last OT game, 9/30/90 vs. Minnesota)
60 Los Angeles Rams (last OT game, 10/7/90 vs. Cincinnati)
41 Cleveland Browns (last OT game, 10/20/91 vs. San Diego)
(Record: 110, Phoenix Cardinals, 12/7/86-12/19/93)

## SHORTEST OVERTIME GAMES
0:21 (Chicago 23, Detroit 17; 11/27/80)—only kickoff return for TD
0:30 (Baltimore 29, New England 23; 9/4/83)
0:55 (New York Giants 16, Philadelphia 10; 9/29/85)

There have been 13 overtime postseason games dating back to 1958. In 12 cases, both teams had at least one possession. Last time: 1/8/94, Kansas City 27, Pittsburgh 24.

## OVERTIME GAMES

### LONGEST OVERTIME GAMES
**(All Postseason Games)**

22:40 Miami 27, Kansas City 24; 12/25/71
17:54 Dallas Texans 20, Houston 17; 12/23/62
17:02 Cleveland 23, New York Jets 20; 1/3/87

### OVERTIME SCORING SUMMARY

135 were decided by a field goal
22 were decided by a touchdown pass
17 were decided by a touchdown run
5 were decided by interceptions (Atlanta 40, New Orleans 34, 9/2/79; Atlanta 47, Green Bay 41, 11/27/83; New York Giants 16, Philadelphia 10, 9/29/85; Indianapolis 23, Cleveland 17, 12/10/89; Cleveland 30, San Diego 24, 10/20/91)
2 were decided on a fake field goal/touchdown pass (Minnesota 22, Chicago 16, 10/16/77; Cleveland 23, Minnesota 17, 12/17/89)
1 was decided by a kickoff return (Chicago 23, Detroit 17, 11/27/80)
1 was decided by a fumble recovery (Baltimore 29, New England 23, 9/4/83)
1 was decided on a fake field goal/touchdown run (Los Angeles Rams 27, Minnesota 21, 12/2/79)
1 was decided on a blocked field goal (Denver 30, San Diego 24, 11/17/85)
1 was decided on a blocked field goal/recovery by kicker (Green Bay 12, Chicago 6, 9/7/80)
1 was decided on a blocked field goal/recovery by kicking team (Philadelphia 23, New York Giants 17, 11/20/88)
1 was decided by a safety (Minnesota 23, Los Angeles Rams 21, 11/5/89)
13 ended tied

### OVERTIME RECORDS

**Longest Touchdown Pass**
99 Yards — Ron Jaworski to Mike Quick, Philadelphia 23, Atlanta 17 (11/10/85)
50 Yards — Tommy Kramer to Ahmad Rashad, Minnesota 27, Green Bay 21 (9/23/79)
50 Yards — Jim Harbaugh to Neal Anderson, Chicago 23, Detroit 17 (12/2/90)

**Longest Touchdown Run**
60 Yards — Herschel Walker, Dallas 23, New England 17 (11/15/87)
42 Yards — Eric Dickerson, Los Angeles Rams 26, Tampa Bay 20 (10/5/86)
28 Yards — Marcus Allen, Los Angeles Raiders 37, San Diego 31 (11/20/86)

**Longest Field Goal**
51 Yards — Greg Davis, New England 23, Indianapolis 20 (10/29/89)
50 Yards — Morten Andersen, New Orleans 20, Philadelphia 17 (12/11/83); Norm Johnson, Atlanta 23, New Orleans 20 (11/24/91)
48 Yards — Eddie Murray, Detroit 27, Atlanta 24 (9/9/84); Mark Moseley, Washington 30, New York Giants 27 (11/15/81)

**Longest Touchdown Plays**
99 Yards — (Pass) Ron Jaworski to Mike Quick, Philadelphia 23, Atlanta 17 (11/10/85)
60 Yards — (Blocked field goal return) Louis Wright, Denver 30, San Diego 24 (11/17/85)
(Run) Herschel Walker, Dallas 23, New England 17 (11/15/87)
58 Yards — (Interception return) Mike Prior, Indianapolis 23, Cleveland 17 (12/10/89)

## NFL PAID ATTENDANCE

*For detailed 1993 attendance, see page 217.*

| Year | Regular Season | | Average | Postseason | Total |
|---|---|---|---|---|---|
| 1993 | #13,966,843 | (224 games) | #62,352 | 814,607 (12) | 14,781,450 |
| 1992 | 13,828,887 | (224 games) | 61,736 | 815,910 (12) | 14,644,797 |
| 1991 | 13,841,459 | (224 games) | 61,792 | 813,247 (12) | 14,654,706 |
| 1990 | 13,959,896 | (224 games) | 62,321 | 847,543 (12) | 14,807,439 |
| 1989 | 13,625,662 | (224 games) | 60,829 | 685,771 (10) | 14,311,433 |
| 1988 | 13,539,848 | (224 games) | 60,446 | 658,317 (10) | 14,198,165 |
| 1987 | *11,406,166 | (210 games) | 54,315 | 656,977 (10) | 12,063,143 |
| 1986 | 13,588,551 | (224 games) | 60,663 | 734,002 (10) | 14,322,553 |
| 1985 | 13,345,047 | (224 games) | 59,567 | 710,768 (10) | 14,055,815 |
| 1984 | 13,398,112 | (224 games) | 59,813 | 665,194 (10) | 14,063,306 |
| 1983 | 13,277,222 | (224 games) | 59,273 | 675,513 (10) | 13,952,735 |
| 1982 | **7,367,438 | (126 games) | 58,472 | 1,033,153 (16) | 8,400,591 |
| 1981 | 13,606,990 | (224 games) | 60,745 | 637,763 (10) | 14,244,753 |
| 1980 | 13,392,230 | (224 games) | 59,787 | 624,430 (10) | 14,016,660 |
| 1979 | 13,182,039 | (224 games) | 58,848 | 630,326 (10) | 13,812,365 |
| 1978 | 12,771,800 | (224 games) | 57,017 | 624,388 (10) | 13,396,188 |
| 1977 | 11,018,632 | (196 games) | 56,218 | 534,925 (8) | 11,553,557 |
| 1976 | 11,070,543 | (196 games) | 56,482 | 492,884 (8) | 11,563,427 |
| 1975 | 10,213,193 | (182 games) | 56,116 | 475,919 (8) | 10,689,112 |
| 1974 | 10,236,322 | (182 games) | 56,244 | 438,664 (8) | 10,674,986 |
| 1973 | 10,730,933 | (182 games) | 58,961 | 525,433 (8) | 11,256,366 |
| 1972 | 10,445,827 | (182 games) | 57,395 | 483,345 (8) | 10,929,172 |
| 1971 | 10,076,035 | (182 games) | 55,363 | 483,891 (8) | 10,559,926 |
| 1970 | 9,533,333 | (182 games) | 52,381 | 458,493 (8) | 9,991,826 |
| 1969 | 6,096,127 | (112 games) NFL | 54,430 | 162,279 (3) | 6,258,406 |
| | 2,843,373 | (70 games) AFL | 40,620 | 167,088 (3) | 3,010,461 |
| 1968 | 5,882,313 | (112 games) NFL | 52,521 | 215,902 (3) | 6,098,215 |
| | 2,635,004 | (70 games) AFL | 37,643 | 114,438 (2) | 2,749,442 |
| 1967 | 5,938,924 | (112 games) NFL | 53,026 | 166,208 (3) | 6,105,132 |
| | 2,295,697 | (63 games) AFL | 36,439 | 53,330 (1) | 2,349,027 |
| 1966 | 5,337,044 | (105 games) NFL | 50,829 | 74,152 (1) | 5,411,196 |
| | 2,160,369 | (63 games) AFL | 34,291 | 42,080 (1) | 2,202,449 |
| 1965 | 4,634,021 | (98 games) NFL | 47,286 | 100,304 (2) | 4,734,325 |
| | 1,782,384 | (56 games) AFL | 31,828 | 30,361 (1) | 1,812,745 |
| 1964 | 4,563,049 | (98 games) NFL | 46,562 | 79,544 (1) | 4,642,593 |
| | 1,447,875 | (56 games) AFL | 25,855 | 40,242 (1) | 1,488,117 |
| 1963 | 4,163,643 | (98 games) NFL | 42,486 | 45,801 (1) | 4,209,444 |
| | 1,208,697 | (56 games) AFL | 21,584 | 63,171 (2) | 1,271,868 |
| 1962 | 4,003,421 | (98 games) NFL | 40,851 | 64,892 (1) | 4,068,313 |
| | 1,147,302 | (56 games) AFL | 20,487 | 37,981 (1) | 1,185,283 |
| 1961 | 3,986,159 | (98 games) NFL | 40,675 | 39,029 (1) | 4,025,188 |
| | 1,002,657 | (56 games) AFL | 17,904 | 29,556 (1) | 1,032,213 |
| 1960 | 3,128,296 | (78 games) NFL | 40,106 | 67,325 (1) | 3,195,621 |
| | 926,156 | (56 games) AFL | 16,538 | 32,183 (1) | 958,339 |
| 1959 | 3,140,000 | (72 games) | 43,617 | 57,545 (1) | 3,197,545 |
| 1958 | 3,006,124 | (72 games) | 41,752 | 123,659 (2) | 3,129,783 |
| 1957 | 2,836,318 | (72 games) | 39,393 | 119,579 (2) | 2,955,897 |
| 1956 | 2,551,263 | (72 games) | 35,434 | 56,836 (1) | 2,608,099 |
| 1955 | 2,521,836 | (72 games) | 35,026 | 85,693 (1) | 2,607,529 |
| 1954 | 2,190,571 | (72 games) | 30,425 | 43,827 (1) | 2,234,398 |
| 1953 | 2,164,585 | (72 games) | 30,064 | 54,577 (1) | 2,219,162 |
| 1952 | 2,052,126 | (72 games) | 28,502 | 97,507 (2) | 2,149,633 |
| 1951 | 1,913,019 | (72 games) | 26,570 | 57,522 (1) | 1,970,541 |
| 1950 | 1,977,753 | (78 games) | 25,356 | 136,647 (3) | 2,114,400 |
| 1949 | 1,391,735 | (60 games) | 23,196 | 27,980 (1) | 1,419,715 |
| 1948 | 1,525,243 | (60 games) | 25,421 | 36,309 (1) | 1,561,552 |
| 1947 | 1,837,437 | (60 games) | 30,624 | 66,268 (2) | 1,903,705 |
| 1946 | 1,732,135 | (55 games) | 31,493 | 58,346 (1) | 1,790,481 |
| 1945 | 1,270,401 | (50 games) | 25,408 | 32,178 (1) | 1,302,579 |
| 1944 | 1,019,649 | (50 games) | 20,393 | 46,016 (1) | 1,065,665 |
| 1943 | 969,128 | (40 games) | 24,228 | 71,315 (2) | 1,040,443 |
| 1942 | 887,920 | (55 games) | 16,144 | 36,006 (1) | 923,926 |
| 1941 | 1,108,615 | (55 games) | 20,157 | 55,870 (2) | 1,164,485 |
| 1940 | 1,063,025 | (55 games) | 19,328 | 36,034 (1) | 1,099,059 |
| 1939 | 1,071,200 | (55 games) | 19,476 | 32,279 (1) | 1,103,479 |
| 1938 | 937,197 | (55 games) | 17,040 | 48,120 (1) | 985,317 |
| 1937 | 963,039 | (55 games) | 17,510 | 15,878 (1) | 978,917 |
| 1936 | 816,007 | (54 games) | 15,111 | 29,545 (1) | 845,552 |
| 1935 | 638,178 | (53 games) | 12,041 | 15,000 (1) | 653,178 |
| 1934 | 492,684 | (60 games) | 8,211 | 35,059 (1) | 527,743 |

*# Record*
**Players' 24-day strike reduced 224-game schedule to 210 games.*
***Players' 57-day strike reduced 224-game schedule to 126 games.*

## NFL'S 10 BIGGEST ATTENDANCE WEEKENDS

**(Paid Count)**

| Weekend | Games | Attedance |
|---|---|---|
| October 16-17, 1988 | 14 | 934,211 |
| September 1-2, 1991 | 14 | 922,076 |
| November 8-9, 1992 | 14 | 917,384 |
| November 4-5, 1990 | 14 | 916,127 |
| October 29-30, 1989 | 14 | 915,401 |
| November 17-18, 1990 | 14 | 905,486 |
| October 27-28, 1985 | 14 | 902,128 |
| October 12-13, 1980 | 14 | 898,223 |
| September 12-13, 1993 | 14 | 898,703 |
| September 23-24, 1984 | 14 | 894,402 |

## NFL'S 10 HIGHEST SCORING WEEKENDS

| Point Total | Date | Weekend |
|---|---|---|
| 761 | October 16-17, 1983 | 7th |
| 736 | October 25-26, 1987 | 7th |
| 732 | November 9-10, 1980 | 10th |
| 725 | November 24, 27-28, 1983 | 13th |
| 714 | September 17-18, 1989 | 2nd |
| 711 | November 26, 29-30, 1987 | 12th |
| 710 | November 28, December 1-2, 1985 | 13th |
| 696 | October 2-3, 1983 | 5th |
| 693 | September 24-25, 1989 | 3rd |
| 676 | September 21-22, 1980 | 3rd |

## TOP 10 TELEVISED SPORTS EVENTS OF ALL-TIME

*(Based on A.C. Nielsen Figures)*

| Program | Date | Network | Share | Rating |
|---|---|---|---|---|
| Super Bowl XVI | 1/24/82 | CBS | 73.0 | 49.1 |
| Super Bowl XVII | 1/30/83 | NBC | 69.0 | 48.6 |
| Winter Olympics | 2/23/94 | CBS | 64.0 | 48.5 |
| Super Bowl XX | 1/26/86 | NBC | 70.0 | 48.3 |
| Super Bowl XII | 1/15/78 | CBS | 67.0 | 47.2 |
| Super Bowl XIII | 1/21/79 | NBC | 74.0 | 47.1 |
| Super Bowl XVIII | 1/22/84 | CBS | 71.0 | 46.4 |
| Super Bowl XIX | 1/20/85 | ABC | 63.0 | 46.4 |
| Super Bowl XIV | 1/20/80 | CBS | 67.0 | 46.3 |
| Super Bowl XXI | 1/25/87 | CBS | 66.0 | 45.8 |

## TEN MOST WATCHED TV PROGRAMS & ESTIMATED TOTAL NUMBER OF VIEWERS

*(Based on A.C. Nielsen Figures)*

| Program | Date | Network | *Total Viewers |
|---|---|---|---|
| Super Bowl XXVIII | Jan. 30, 1994 | NBC | 134,800,000 |
| Super Bowl XXVII | Jan. 31, 1993 | NBC | 133,400,000 |
| Super Bowl XX | Jan. 26, 1986 | NBC | 127,000,000 |
| Winter Olympics | Feb. 23, 1994 | CBS | 126,686,000 |
| Super Bowl XXI | Jan. 25, 1987 | CBS | 122,640,000 |
| M*A*S*H (Special) | Feb. 28, 1983 | CBS | 121,624,000 |
| Winter Olympics | Feb. 25, 1994 | CBS | 119,900,000 |
| Super Bowl XXVI | Jan. 26, 1992 | CBS | 119,680,000 |
| Super Bowl XIX | Jan. 20, 1985 | ABC | 115,936,000 |
| Super Bowl XXII | Jan. 31, 1988 | ABC | 115,000,000 |

**Watched some portion of the broadcast*

## NFL'S 10 BIGGEST TEAM SINGLE-SEASON HOME ATTENDANCE TOTALS

**(Paid Count)**

| Year | Club | Games | Attendance |
|---|---|---|---|
| 1980 | Detroit Lions | 8 | 634,204 |
| 1988 | Buffalo Bills | 8 | 631,818 |
| 1991 | Buffalo Bills | 8 | 631,786 |
| 1992 | Buffalo Bills | 8 | 630,978 |
| 1989 | Buffalo Bills | 8 | 626,399 |
| 1989 | Cleveland Browns | 8 | 625,240 |
| 1993 | Buffalo Bills | 8 | 624,349 |
| 1988 | Cleveland Browns | 8 | 624,154 |
| 1980 | Cleveland Browns | 8 | 623,351 |
| 1990 | Buffalo Bills | 8 | 621,528 |

## NUMBER-ONE DRAFT CHOICES

| Season | Team | Player | Position | College |
|---|---|---|---|---|
| 1994 | Cincinnati | Dan Wilkinson | DT | Ohio State |
| 1993 | New England | Drew Bledsoe | QB | Washington State |
| 1992 | Indianapolis | Steve Emtman | DT | Washington |
| 1991 | Dallas | Russell Maryland | DT | Miami |
| 1990 | Indianapolis | Jeff George | QB | Illinois |
| 1989 | Dallas | Troy Aikman | QB | UCLA |
| 1988 | Atlanta | Aundray Bruce | LB | Auburn |
| 1987 | Tampa Bay | Vinny Testaverde | QB | Miami |
| 1986 | Tampa Bay | Bo Jackson | RB | Auburn |
| 1985 | Buffalo | Bruce Smith | DE | Virginia Tech |
| 1984 | New England | Irving Fryar | WR | Nebraska |
| 1983 | Baltimore | John Elway | QB | Stanford |
| 1982 | New England | Kenneth Sims | DT | Texas |
| 1981 | New Orleans | George Rogers | RB | South Carolina |
| 1980 | Detroit | Billy Sims | RB | Oklahoma |
| 1979 | Buffalo | Tom Cousineau | LB | Ohio State |
| 1978 | Houston | Earl Campbell | RB | Texas |
| 1977 | Tampa Bay | Ricky Bell | RB | Southern California |
| 1976 | Tampa Bay | Lee Roy Selmon | DE | Oklahoma |
| 1975 | Atlanta | Steve Bartkowski | QB | California |
| 1974 | Dallas | Ed Jones | DE | Tennessee State |
| 1973 | Houston | John Matuszak | DE | Tampa |
| 1972 | Buffalo | Walt Patulski | DE | Notre Dame |
| 1971 | New England | Jim Plunkett | QB | Stanford |
| 1970 | Pittsburgh | Terry Bradshaw | QB | Louisiana Tech |
| 1969 | Buffalo (AFL) | O.J. Simpson | RB | Southern California |
| 1968 | Minnesota | Ron Yary | T | Southern California |
| 1967 | Baltimore | Bubba Smith | DT | Michigan State |
| 1966 | Atlanta | Tommy Nobis | LB | Texas |
| | Miami (AFL) | Jim Grabowski | RB | Illinois |
| 1965 | New York Giants | Tucker Frederickson | RB | Auburn |
| | Houston (AFL) | Lawrence Elkins | E | Baylor |
| 1964 | San Francisco | Dave Parks | E | Texas Tech |
| | Boston (AFL) | Jack Concannon | QB | Boston College |
| 1963 | Los Angeles | Terry Baker | QB | Oregon State |
| | Kansas City (AFL) | Buck Buchanan | DT | Grambling |
| 1962 | Washington | Ernie Davis | RB | Syracuse |
| | Oakland (AFL) | Roman Gabriel | QB | North Carolina State |
| 1961 | Minnesota | Tommy Mason | RB | Tulane |
| | Buffalo (AFL) | Ken Rice | G | Auburn |
| 1960 | Los Angeles | Billy Cannon | RB | Louisiana State |
| | (AFL had no formal first pick) | | | |
| 1959 | Green Bay | Randy Duncan | QB | Iowa |
| 1958 | Chicago Cardinals | King Hill | QB | Rice |
| 1957 | Green Bay | Paul Hornung | HB | Notre Dame |
| 1956 | Pittsburgh | Gary Glick | DB | Colorado A&M |
| 1955 | Baltimore | George Shaw | QB | Oregon |
| 1954 | Cleveland | Bobby Garrett | QB | Stanford |
| 1953 | San Francisco | Harry Babcock | E | Georgia |
| 1952 | Los Angeles | Bill Wade | QB | Vanderbilt |
| 1951 | New York Giants | Kyle Rote | HB | Southern Methodist |
| 1950 | Detroit | Leon Hart | E | Notre Dame |
| 1949 | Philadelphia | Chuck Bednarik | C | Pennsylvania |
| 1948 | Washington | Harry Gilmer | QB | Alabama |
| 1947 | Chicago Bears | Bob Fenimore | HB | Oklahoma A&M |
| 1946 | Boston | Frank Dancewicz | QB | Notre Dame |
| 1945 | Chicago Cardinals | Charley Trippi | HB | Georgia |
| 1944 | Boston | Angelo Bertelli | QB | Notre Dame |
| 1943 | Detroit | Frank Sinkwich | HB | Georgia |
| 1942 | Pittsburgh | Bill Dudley | HB | Virginia |
| 1941 | Chicago Bears | Tom Harmon | HB | Michigan |
| 1940 | Chicago Cardinals | George Cafego | HB | Tennessee |
| 1939 | Chicago Cardinals | Ki Aldrich | C | Texas Christian |
| 1938 | Cleveland | Corbett Davis | FB | Indiana |
| 1937 | Philadelphia | Sam Francis | FB | Nebraska |
| 1936 | Philadelphia | Jay Berwanger | HB | Chicago |

*Note: From 1947 through 1958, the first selection in the draft was a Bonus pick, awarded to the winner of a random draw. That club, in turn, forfeited its last-round draft choice. The winner of the Bonus choice was eliminated from future draws. The system was abolished after 1958, by which time all clubs had received a Bonus choice.*

## FIRST-ROUND SELECTIONS

*If club had no first-round selection, first player drafted is listed with round in parentheses.*

### ARIZONA CARDINALS

| Year | Player, College, Position |
|---|---|
| 1936 | Jim Lawrence, Texas Christian, B |
| 1937 | Ray Buivid, Marquette, B |
| 1938 | Jack Robbins, Arkansas, B |
| 1939 | Charles (Ki) Aldrich, Texas Christian, C |
| 1940 | George Cafego, Tennessee, B |
| 1941 | John Kimbrough, Texas A&M, B |
| 1942 | Steve Lach, Duke, B |
| 1943 | Glenn Dobbs, Tulsa, B |
| 1944 | Pat Harder, Wisconsin, B |
| 1945 | Charley Trippi, Georgia, B |
| 1946 | Dub Jones, Louisiana State, B |
| 1947 | DeWitt (Tex) Coulter, Army, T |
| 1948 | Jim Spavital, Oklahoma A&M, B |
| 1949 | Bill Fischer, Notre Dame, G |
| 1950 | Jack Jennings, Ohio State, T (2) |
| 1951 | Jerry Groom, Notre Dame, C |
| 1952 | Ollie Matson, San Francisco, B |
| 1953 | Johnny Olszewski, California, B |
| 1954 | Lamar McHan, Arkansas, B |
| 1955 | Max Boydston, Oklahoma, E |
| 1956 | Joe Childress, Auburn, B |
| 1957 | Jerry Tubbs, Oklahoma, C |
| 1958 | King Hill, Rice, B |
| | John David Crow, Texas A&M, B |
| 1959 | Bill Stacy, Mississippi State, B |
| 1960 | George Izo, Notre Dame, QB |
| 1961 | Ken Rice, Auburn, T |
| 1962 | Fate Echols, Northwestern, DT |
| | Irv Goode, Kentucky, C |
| 1963 | Jerry Stovall, Louisiana State, S |
| | Don Brumm, Purdue, DE |
| 1964 | Ken Kortas, Louisville, DT |
| 1965 | Joe Namath, Alabama, QB |
| 1966 | Carl McAdams, Oklahoma, LB |
| 1967 | Dave Williams, Washington, WR |
| 1968 | MacArthur Lane, Utah State, RB |
| 1969 | Roger Wehrli, Missouri, DB |
| 1970 | Larry Stegent, Texas A&M, RB |
| 1971 | Norm Thompson, Utah, CB |
| 1972 | Bobby Moore, Oregon, RB-WR |
| 1973 | Dave Butz, Purdue, DT |
| 1974 | J.V. Cain, Colorado, TE |
| 1975 | Tim Gray, Texas A&M, DB |
| 1976 | Mike Dawson, Arizona, DT |
| 1977 | Steve Pisarkiewicz, Missouri, QB |
| 1978 | Steve Little, Arkansas, K |
| | Ken Greene, Washington State, DB |
| 1979 | Ottis Anderson, Miami, RB |
| 1980 | Curtis Greer, Michigan, DE |
| 1981 | E.J. Junior, Alabama, LB |
| 1982 | Luis Sharpe, UCLA, T |
| 1983 | Leonard Smith, McNeese State, DB |
| 1984 | Clyde Duncan, Tennessee, WR |
| 1985 | Freddie Joe Nunn, Mississippi, LB |
| 1986 | Anthony Bell, Michigan State, LB |
| 1987 | Kelly Stouffer, Colorado State, QB |
| 1988 | Ken Harvey, California, LB |
| 1989 | Eric Hill, Louisiana State, LB |
| | Joe Wolf, Boston College, G |
| 1990 | Anthony Thompson, Indiana, RB (2) |
| 1991 | Eric Swann, No College, DE |
| 1992 | Tony Sacca, Penn State, QB (2) |
| 1993 | Garrison Hearst, Georgia, RB |
| | Ernest Dye, South Carolina, T |
| 1994 | Jamir Miller, UCLA, LB |

### ATLANTA FALCONS

| Year | Player, College, Position |
|---|---|
| 1966 | Tommy Nobis, Texas, LB |
| | Randy Johnson, Texas A&I, QB |
| 1967 | Leo Carroll, San Diego State, DE (2) |
| 1968 | Claude Humphrey, Tennessee State, DE |
| 1969 | George Kunz, Notre Dame, T |
| 1970 | John Small, Citadel, LB |
| 1971 | Joe Profit, Northeast Louisiana, RB |
| 1972 | Clarence Ellis, Notre Dame, DB |
| 1973 | Greg Marx, Notre Dame, DT (2) |
| 1974 | Gerald Tinker, Kent State, WR (2) |
| 1975 | Steve Bartkowski, California, QB |
| 1976 | Bubba Bean, Texas A&M, RB |
| 1977 | Warren Bryant, Kentucky, T |
| | Wilson Faumuina, San Jose State, DT |
| 1978 | Mike Kenn, Michigan, T |
| 1979 | Don Smith, Miami, DE |
| 1980 | Junior Miller, Nebraska, TE |
| 1981 | Bobby Butler, Florida State, DB |
| 1982 | Gerald Riggs, Arizona State, RB |
| 1983 | Mike Pitts, Alabama, DE |
| 1984 | Rick Bryan, Oklahoma, DT |
| 1985 | Bill Fralic, Pittsburgh, T |
| 1986 | Tony Casillas, Oklahoma, NT |
| | Tim Green, Syracuse, LB |
| 1987 | Chris Miller, Oregon, QB |
| 1988 | Aundray Bruce, Auburn, LB |
| 1989 | Deion Sanders, Florida State, DB |
| | Shawn Collins, Northern Arizona, WR |
| 1990 | Steve Broussard, Washington State, RB |
| 1991 | Bruce Pickens, Nebraska, DB |
| | Mike Pritchard, Colorado, WR |
| 1992 | Bob Whitfield, Stanford, T |
| | Tony Smith, Southern Mississippi, RB |
| 1993 | Lincoln Kennedy, Washington, T |
| 1994 | Bert Emanuel, Rice, WR (2) |

### BUFFALO BILLS

| Year | Player, College, Position |
|---|---|
| 1960 | Richie Lucas, Penn State, QB |
| 1961 | Ken Rice, Auburn, T |
| 1962 | Ernie Davis, Syracuse, RB |
| 1963 | Dave Behrman, Michigan State, C |
| 1964 | Carl Eller, Minnesota, DE |
| 1965 | Jim Davidson, Ohio State, T |
| 1966 | Mike Dennis, Mississippi, RB |
| 1967 | John Pitts, Arizona State, S |
| 1968 | Haven Moses, San Diego State, WR |
| 1969 | O.J. Simpson, Southern California, RB |
| 1970 | Al Cowlings, Southern California, DE |
| 1971 | J.D. Hill, Arizona State, WR |
| 1972 | Walt Patulski, Notre Dame, DE |
| 1973 | Paul Seymour, Michigan, TE |
| | Joe DeLamielleure, Michigan State, G |
| 1974 | Reuben Gant, Oklahoma State, TE |
| 1975 | Tom Ruud, Nebraska, LB |
| 1976 | Mario Clark, Oregon, DB |
| 1977 | Phil Dokes, Oklahoma State, DT |
| 1978 | Terry Miller, Oklahoma State, RB |
| 1979 | Tom Cousineau, Ohio State, LB |
| | Jerry Butler, Clemson, WR |
| 1980 | Jim Ritcher, North Carolina State, C |
| 1981 | Booker Moore, Penn State, RB |
| 1982 | Perry Tuttle, Clemson, WR |
| 1983 | Tony Hunter, Notre Dame, TE |
| | Jim Kelly, Miami, QB |
| 1984 | Greg Bell, Notre Dame, RB |
| 1985 | Bruce Smith, Virginia Tech, DE |
| | Derrick Burroughs, Memphis State, DB |
| 1986 | Ronnie Harmon, Iowa, RB |
| | Will Wolford, Vanderbilt, T |
| 1987 | Shane Conlan, Penn State, LB |
| 1988 | Thurman Thomas, Oklahoma State, RB (2) |
| 1989 | Don Beebe, Chadron, Neb., WR (3) |
| 1990 | James Williams, Fresno State, DB |
| 1991 | Henry Jones, Illinois, DB |
| 1992 | John Fina, Arizona, T |
| 1993 | Thomas Smith, North Carolina, DB |
| 1994 | Jeff Burris, Notre Dame, DB |

### CHICAGO BEARS

| Year | Player, College, Position |
|---|---|
| 1936 | Joe Stydahar, West Virginia, T |
| 1937 | Les McDonald, Nebraska, E |
| 1938 | Joe Gray, Oregon State, B |
| 1939 | Sid Luckman, Columbia, QB |
| | Bill Osmanski, Holy Cross, B |
| 1940 | Clyde (Bulldog) Turner, Hardin-Simmons, C |
| 1941 | Tom Harmon, Michigan, B |
| | Norm Standlee, Stanford, B |
| | Don Scott, Ohio State, B |
| 1942 | Frankie Albert, Stanford, B |
| 1943 | Bob Steber, Missouri, B |
| 1944 | Ray Evans, Kansas, B |
| 1945 | Don Lund, Michigan, B |
| 1946 | Johnny Lujack, Notre Dame, QB |
| 1947 | Bob Fenimore, Oklahoma State, B |
| | Don Kindt, Wisconsin, B |
| 1948 | Bobby Layne, Texas, QB |
| | Max Bumgardner, Texas, E |
| 1949 | Dick Harris, Texas, C |
| 1950 | Chuck Hunsinger, Florida, B |
| | Fred Morrison, Ohio State, B |
| 1951 | Bob Williams, Notre Dame, B |
| | Billy Stone, Bradley, B |
| | Gene Schroeder, Virginia, E |
| 1952 | Jim Dooley, Miami, B |
| 1953 | Billy Anderson, Compton (Calif.) J.C., B |
| 1954 | Stan Wallace, Illinois, B |
| 1955 | Ron Drzewiecki, Marquette, B |
| 1956 | Menan (Tex) Schriewer, Texas, E |
| 1957 | Earl Leggett, Louisiana State, T |
| 1958 | Chuck Howley, West Virginia, G |
| 1959 | Don Clark, Ohio State, B |
| 1960 | Roger Davis, Syracuse, G |
| 1961 | Mike Ditka, Pittsburgh, E |
| 1962 | Ronnie Bull, Baylor, RB |
| 1963 | Dave Behrman, Michigan State, C |
| 1964 | Dick Evey, Tennessee, DT |
| 1965 | Dick Butkus, Illinois, LB |
| | Gale Sayers, Kansas, RB |
| | Steve DeLong, Tennessee, T |
| 1966 | George Rice, Louisiana State, DT |
| 1967 | Loyd Phillips, Arkansas, DE |
| 1968 | Mike Hull, Southern California, RB |
| 1969 | Rufus Mayes, Ohio State, T |
| 1970 | George Farmer, UCLA, WR (3) |
| 1971 | Joe Moore, Missouri, RB |
| 1972 | Lionel Antoine, Southern Illinois, T |
| | Craig Clemons, Iowa, DB |
| 1973 | Wally Chambers, Eastern Kentucky, DE |
| 1974 | Waymond Bryant, Tennessee State, LB |
| | Dave Gallagher, Michigan, DT |
| 1975 | Walter Payton, Jackson State, RB |
| 1976 | Dennis Lick, Wisconsin, T |
| 1977 | Ted Albrecht, California, T |
| 1978 | Brad Shearer, Texas, DT (3) |
| 1979 | Dan Hampton, Arkansas, DT |
| | Al Harris, Arizona State, DE |
| 1980 | Otis Wilson, Louisville, LB |
| 1981 | Keith Van Horne, Southern California, T |
| 1982 | Jim McMahon, Brigham Young, QB |
| 1983 | Jim Covert, Pittsburgh, T |
| | Willie Gault, Tennessee, WR |
| 1984 | Wilber Marshall, Florida, LB |
| 1985 | William Perry, Clemson, DT |
| 1986 | Neal Anderson, Florida, RB |
| 1987 | Jim Harbaugh, Michigan, QB |
| 1988 | Brad Muster, Stanford, RB |
| | Wendell Davis, Louisiana State, WR |
| 1989 | Donnell Woolford, Clemson, DB |
| | Trace Armstrong, Florida, DE |
| 1990 | Mark Carrier, Southern California, DB |
| 1991 | Stan Thomas, Texas, T |
| 1992 | Alonzo Spellman, Ohio State, DE |
| 1993 | Curtis Conway, Southern California, WR |
| 1994 | John Thierry, Alcorn State, DE |

### CINCINNATI BENGALS

| Year | Player, College, Position |
|---|---|
| 1968 | Bob Johnson, Tennessee, C |
| 1969 | Greg Cook, Cincinnati, QB |
| 1970 | Mike Reid, Penn State, DT |
| 1971 | Vernon Holland, Tennessee State, T |
| 1972 | Sherman White, California, DE |
| 1973 | Isaac Curtis, San Diego State, WR |
| 1974 | Bill Kollar, Montana State, DT |
| 1975 | Glenn Cameron, Florida, LB |
| 1976 | Billy Brooks, Oklahoma, WR |
| | Archie Griffin, Ohio State, RB |
| 1977 | Eddie Edwards, Miami, DT |
| | Wilson Whitley, Houston, DT |
| | Mike Cobb, Michigan State, TE |
| 1978 | Ross Browner, Notre Dame, DT |
| | Blair Bush, Washington, C |
| 1979 | Jack Thompson, Washington State, QB |

Charles Alexander, Louisiana State, RB
1980 Anthony Muñoz, Southern California, T
1981 David Verser, Kansas, WR
1982 Glen Collins, Mississippi State, DE
1983 Dave Rimington, Nebraska, C
1984 Ricky Hunley, Arizona, LB
Pete Koch, Maryland, DE
Brian Blados, North Carolina, T
1985 Eddie Brown, Miami, WR
Emanuel King, Alabama, LB
1986 Joe Kelly, Washington, LB
Tim McGee, Tennessee, WR
1987 Jason Buck, Brigham Young, DE
1988 Rickey Dixon, Oklahoma, DB
1989 Eric Ball, UCLA, RB (2)
1990 James Francis, Baylor, LB
1991 Alfred Williams, Colorado, LB
1992 David Klingler, Houston, QB
Darryl Williams, Miami, DB
1993 John Copeland, Alabama, DE
1994 Dan Wilkinson, Ohio State, DT

**CLEVELAND BROWNS**

**Year Player, College, Position**
1950 Ken Carpenter, Oregon State, B
1951 Ken Konz, Louisiana State, B
1952 Bert Rechichar, Tennessee, DB
Harry Agganis, Boston U., QB
1953 Doug Atkins, Tennessee, DE
1954 Bobby Garrett, Stanford, QB
John Bauer, Illinois, G
1955 Kurt Burris, Oklahoma, C
1956 Preston Carpenter, Arkansas, B
1957 Jim Brown, Syracuse, RB
1958 Jim Shofner, Texas Christian, DB
1959 Rich Kreitling, Illinois, DE
1960 Jim Houston, Ohio State, DE
1961 Bobby Crespino, Mississippi, TE
1962 Gary Collins, Maryland, WR
Leroy Jackson, Western Illinois, RB
1963 Tom Hutchinson, Kentucky, WR
1964 Paul Warfield, Ohio State, WR
1965 James Garcia, Purdue, T (2)
1966 Milt Morin, Massachusetts, TE
1967 Bob Matheson, Duke, LB
1968 Marvin Upshaw, Trinity, Tex., DT-DE
1969 Ron Johnson, Michigan, RB
1970 Mike Phipps, Purdue, QB
Bob McKay, Texas, T
1971 Clarence Scott, Kansas State, CB
1972 Thom Darden, Michigan, DB
1973 Steve Holden, Arizona State, WR
Pete Adams, Southern California, T
1974 Billy Corbett, Johnson C. Smith, T (2)
1975 Mack Mitchell, Houston, DE
1976 Mike Pruitt, Purdue, RB
1977 Robert Jackson, Texas A&M, LB
1978 Clay Matthews, Southern California, LB
Ozzie Newsome, Alabama, TE
1979 Willis Adams, Houston, WR
1980 Charles White, Southern California, RB
1981 Hanford Dixon, Southern Mississippi, DB
1982 Chip Banks, Southern California, LB
1983 Ron Brown, Arizona State, WR (2)
1984 Don Rogers, UCLA, DB
1985 Greg Allen, Florida State, RB (2)
1986 Webster Slaughter, San Diego State, WR (2)
1987 Mike Junkin, Duke, LB
1988 Clifford Charlton, Florida, LB
1989 Eric Metcalf, Texas, RB
1990 Leroy Hoard, Michigan, RB (2)
1991 Eric Turner, UCLA, DB
1992 Tommy Vardell, Stanford, RB
1993 Steve Everitt, Michigan, C
1994 Antonio Langham, Alabama, DB
Derrick Alexander, Michigan, WR

**DALLAS COWBOYS**

**Year Player, College, Position**
1960 None
1961 Bob Lilly, Texas Christian, DT
1962 Sonny Gibbs, Texas Christian, QB (2)
1963 Lee Roy Jordan, Alabama, LB
1964 Scott Appleton, Texas, DT
1965 Craig Morton, California, QB
1966 John Niland, Iowa, G
1967 Phil Clark, Northwestern, DB (3)
1968 Dennis Homan, Alabama, WR
1969 Calvin Hill, Yale, RB
1970 Duane Thomas, West Texas State, RB
1971 Tody Smith, Southern California, DE
1972 Bill Thomas, Boston College, RB
1973 Billy Joe DuPree, Michigan State, TE
1974 Ed (Too Tall) Jones, Tennessee State, DE
Charley Young, North Carolina State, RB
1975 Randy White, Maryland, LB
Thomas Henderson, Langston, LB
1976 Aaron Kyle, Wyoming, DB
1977 Tony Dorsett, Pittsburgh, RB
1978 Larry Bethea, Michigan State, DE
1979 Robert Shaw, Tennessee, C
1980 Bill Roe, Colorado, LB (3)
1981 Howard Richards, Missouri, T
1982 Rod Hill, Kentucky State, DB
1983 Jim Jeffcoat, Arizona State, DE
1984 Billy Cannon, Jr., Texas A&M, LB
1985 Kevin Brooks, Michigan, DE
1986 Mike Sherrard, UCLA, WR
1987 Danny Noonan, Nebraska, DT
1988 Michael Irvin, Miami, WR
1989 Troy Aikman, UCLA, QB
1990 Emmitt Smith, Florida, RB
1991 Russell Maryland, Miami, DT
Alvin Harper, Tennessee, WR
Kelvin Pritchett, Mississippi, DT
1992 Kevin Smith, Texas A&M, DB
Robert Jones, East Carolina, LB
1993 Kevin Williams, Miami, WR (2)
1994 Shante Carver, Arizona State, DE

**DENVER BRONCOS**

**Year Player, College, Position**
1960 Roger LeClerc, Trinity, Conn., C
1961 Bob Gaiters, New Mexico State, RB
1962 Merlin Olsen, Utah State, DT
1963 Kermit Alexander, UCLA, CB
1964 Bob Brown, Nebraska, T
1965 Dick Butkus, Illinois, LB (2)
1966 Jerry Shay, Purdue, DT
1967 Floyd Little, Syracuse, RB
1968 Curley Culp, Arizona State, DE (2)
1969 Grady Cavness, Texas-El Paso, DB (2)
1970 Bob Anderson, Colorado, RB
1971 Marv Montgomery, Southern California, T
1972 Riley Odoms, Houston, TE
1973 Otis Armstrong, Purdue, RB
1974 Randy Gradishar, Ohio State, LB
1975 Louis Wright, San Jose State, DB
1976 Tom Glassic, Virginia, G
1977 Steve Schindler, Boston College, G
1978 Don Latimer, Miami, DT
1979 Kelvin Clark, Nebraska, T
1980 Rulon Jones, Utah State, DE (2)
1981 Dennis Smith, Southern California, DB
1982 Gerald Willhite, San Jose State, RB
1983 Chris Hinton, Northwestern, G
1984 Andre Townsend, Mississippi, DE (2)
1985 Steve Sewell, Oklahoma, RB
1986 Jim Juriga, Illinois, T (4)
1987 Ricky Nattiel, Florida, WR
1988 Ted Gregory, Syracuse, NT
1989 Steve Atwater, Arkansas, DB
1990 Alton Montgomery, Houston, DB (2)
1991 Mike Croel, Nebraska, LB
1992 Tommy Maddox, UCLA, QB
1993 Dan Williams, Toledo, DE
1994 Allen Aldridge, Houston, LB (2)

**DETROIT LIONS**

**Year Player, College, Position**
1936 Sid Wagner, Michigan State, G
1937 Lloyd Cardwell, Nebraska, B
1938 Alex Wojciechowicz, Fordham, C
1939 John Pingel, Michigan State, B
1940 Doyle Nave, Southern California, B
1941 Jim Thomason, Texas A&M, B
1942 Bob Westfall, Michigan, B
1943 Frank Sinkwich, Georgia, B
1944 Otto Graham, Northwestern, B
1945 Frank Szymanski, Notre Dame, C
1946 Bill Dellastatious, Missouri, B
1947 Glenn Davis, Army, B
1948 Y.A. Tittle, Louisiana State, B
1949 John Rauch, Georgia, B
1950 Leon Hart, Notre Dame, E
Joe Watson, Rice, C
1951 Dick Stanfel, San Francisco, G (2)
1952 Yale Lary, Texas A&M, B (3)
1953 Harley Sewell, Texas, G
1954 Dick Chapman, Rice, T
1955 Dave Middleton, Auburn, B
1956 Hopalong Cassady, Ohio State, B
1957 Bill Glass, Baylor, G
1958 Alex Karras, Iowa, T
1959 Nick Pietrosante, Notre Dame, B
1960 John Robinson, Louisiana State, S
1961 Danny LaRose, Missouri, T (2)
1962 John Hadl, Kansas, QB
1963 Daryl Sanders, Ohio State, T
1964 Pete Beathard, Southern California, QB
1965 Tom Nowatzke, Indiana, RB
1966 Nick Eddy, Notre Dame, RB (2)
1967 Mel Farr, UCLA, RB
1968 Greg Landry, Massachusetts, QB
Earl McCullouch, Southern California, WR
1969 Altie Taylor, Utah State, RB (2)
1970 Steve Owens, Oklahoma, RB
1971 Bob Bell, Cincinnati, DT
1972 Herb Orvis, Colorado, DE
1973 Ernie Price, Texas A&I, DE
1974 Ed O'Neil, Penn State, LB
1975 Lynn Boden, South Dakota State, G
1976 James Hunter, Grambling, DB
Lawrence Gaines, Wyoming, RB
1977 Walt Williams, New Mexico State, DB (2)
1978 Luther Bradley, Notre Dame, DB
1979 Keith Dorney, Penn State, T
1980 Billy Sims, Oklahoma, RB
1981 Mark Nichols, San Jose State, WR
1982 Jimmy Williams, Nebraska, LB
1983 James Jones, Florida, RB
1984 David Lewis, California, TE
1985 Lomas Brown, Florida, T
1986 Chuck Long, Iowa, QB
1987 Reggie Rogers, Washington, DE
1988 Bennie Blades, Miami, DB
1989 Barry Sanders, Oklahoma State, RB
1990 Andre Ware, Houston, QB
1991 Herman Moore, Virginia, WR
1992 Robert Porcher, South Carolina State, DE
1993 Ryan McNeil, Miami, DB (2)
1994 Johnnie Morton, Southern California, WR

**GREEN BAY PACKERS**

**Year Player, College, Position**
1936 Russ Letlow, San Francisco, G
1937 Eddie Jankowski, Wisconsin, B
1938 Cecil Isbell, Purdue, B
1939 Larry Buhler, Minnesota, B
1940 Harold Van Every, Minnesota, B
1941 George Paskvan, Wisconsin, B
1942 Urban Odson, Minnesota, T
1943 Dick Wildung, Minnesota, T
1944 Merv Pregulman, Michigan, G
1945 Walt Schlinkman, Texas Tech, B
1946 Johnny (Strike) Strzykalski, Marquette, B
1947 Ernie Case, UCLA, B
1948 Earl (Jug) Girard, Wisconsin, B
1949 Stan Heath, Nevada, B
1950 Clayton Tonnemaker, Minnesota, C
1951 Bob Gain, Kentucky, T
1952 Babe Parilli, Kentucky, QB
1953 Al Carmichael, Southern California, B
1954 Art Hunter, Notre Dame, T
Veryl Switzer, Kansas State, B
1955 Tom Bettis, Purdue, G
1956 Jack Losch, Miami, B
1957 Paul Hornung, Notre Dame, B
Ron Kramer, Michigan, E

1958 Dan Currie, Michigan State, C
1959 Randy Duncan, Iowa, B
1960 Tom Moore, Vanderbilt, RB
1961 Herb Adderley, Michigan State, CB
1962 Earl Gros, Louisiana State, RB
1963 Dave Robinson, Penn State, LB
1964 Lloyd Voss, Nebraska, DT
1965 Donny Anderson, Texas Tech, RB
Lawrence Elkins, Baylor, E
1966 Jim Grabowski, Illinois, RB
Gale Gillingham, Minnesota, T
1967 Bob Hyland, Boston College, C
Don Horn, San Diego State, QB
1968 Fred Carr, Texas-El Paso, LB
Bill Lueck, Arizona, G
1969 Rich Moore, Villanova, DT
1970 Mike McCoy, Notre Dame, DT
Rich McGeorge, Elon, TE
1971 John Brockington, Ohio State, RB
1972 Willie Buchanon, San Diego State, DB
Jerry Tagge, Nebraska, QB
1973 Barry Smith, Florida State, WR
1974 Barty Smith, Richmond, RB
1975 Bill Bain, Southern California, G (2)
1976 Mark Koncar, Colorado, T
1977 Mike Butler, Kansas, DE
Ezra Johnson, Morris Brown, DE
1978 James Lofton, Stanford, WR
John Anderson, Michigan, LB
1979 Eddie Lee Ivery, Georgia Tech, RB
1980 Bruce Clark, Penn State, DE
George Cumby, Oklahoma, LB
1981 Rich Campbell, California, QB
1982 Ron Hallstrom, Iowa, G
1983 Tim Lewis, Pittsburgh, DB
1984 Alphonso Carreker, Florida State, DE
1985 Ken Ruettgers, Southern California, T
1986 Kenneth Davis, Texas Christian, RB (2)
1987 Brent Fullwood, Auburn, RB
1988 Sterling Sharpe, South Carolina, WR
1989 Tony Mandarich, Michigan State, T
1990 Tony Bennett, Mississippi, LB
Darrell Thompson, Minnesota, RB
1991 Vinnie Clark, Ohio State, DB
1992 Terrell Buckley, Florida State, DB
1993 Wayne Simmons, Clemson, LB
George Teague, Alabama, DB
1994 Aaron Taylor, Notre Dame, T

**HOUSTON OILERS**

**Year Player, College, Position**

1960 Billy Cannon, Louisiana State, RB
1961 Mike Ditka, Pittsburgh, E
1962 Ray Jacobs, Howard Payne, DT
1963 Danny Brabham, Arkansas, LB
1964 Scott Appleton, Texas, DT
1965 Lawrence Elkins, Baylor, WR
1966 Tommy Nobis, Texas, LB
1967 George Webster, Michigan State, LB
Tom Regner, Notre Dame, G
1968 Mac Haik, Mississippi, WR (2)
1969 Ron Pritchard, Arizona State, LB
1970 Doug Wilkerson, N. Carolina Central, G
1971 Dan Pastorini, Santa Clara, QB
1972 Greg Sampson, Stanford, DE
1973 John Matuszak, Tampa, DE
George Amundson, Iowa State, RB
1974 Steve Manstedt, Nebraska, LB (4)
1975 Robert Brazile, Jackson State, LB
Don Hardeman, Texas A&I, RB
1976 Mike Barber, Louisiana Tech, TE (2)
1977 Morris Towns, Missouri, T
1978 Earl Campbell, Texas, RB
1979 Mike Stensrud, Iowa State, DE (2)
1980 Angelo Fields, Michigan State, T (2)
1981 Michael Holston, Morgan State, WR (3)
1982 Mike Munchak, Penn State, G
1983 Bruce Matthews, Southern California, T
1984 Dean Steinkuhler, Nebraska, T
1985 Ray Childress, Texas A&M, DE
Richard Johnson, Wisconsin, DB
1986 Jim Everett, Purdue, QB
1987 Alonzo Highsmith, Miami, RB
Haywood Jeffires, North Carolina St., WR
1988 Lorenzo White, Michigan State, RB
1989 David Williams, Florida, T
1990 Lamar Lathon, Houston, LB
1991 Mike Dumas, Indiana, DB (2)
1992 Eddie Robinson, Alabama State, LB (2)
1993 Brad Hopkins, Illinois, T
1994 Henry Ford, Arkansas, DE

**INDIANAPOLIS COLTS**

**Year Player, College, Position**

1953 Billy Vessels, Oklahoma, B
1954 Cotton Davidson, Baylor, B
1955 George Shaw, Oregon, B
Alan Ameche, Wisconsin, FB
1956 Lenny Moore, Penn State, B
1957 Jim Parker, Ohio State, G
1958 Lenny Lyles, Louisville, B
1959 Jackie Burkett, Auburn, C
1960 Ron Mix, Southern California, T
1961 Tom Matte, Ohio State, RB
1962 Wendell Harris, Louisiana State, S
1963 Bob Vogel, Ohio State, T
1964 Marv Woodson, Indiana, CB
1965 Mike Curtis, Duke, LB
1966 Sam Ball, Kentucky, T
1967 Bubba Smith, Michigan State, DT
Jim Detwiler, Michigan, RB
1968 John Williams, Minnesota, G
1969 Eddie Hinton, Oklahoma, WR
1970 Norman Bulaich, Texas Christian, RB
1971 Don McCauley, North Carolina, RB
Leonard Dunlap, North Texas State, DB
1972 Tom Drougas, Oregon, T
1973 Bert Jones, Louisiana State, QB
Joe Ehrmann, Syracuse, DT
1974 John Dutton, Nebraska, DE
Roger Carr, Louisiana Tech, WR
1975 Ken Huff, North Carolina, G
1976 Ken Novak, Purdue, DT
1977 Randy Burke, Kentucky, WR
1978 Reese McCall, Auburn, TE
1979 Barry Krauss, Alabama, LB
1980 Curtis Dickey, Texas A&M, RB
Derrick Hatchett, Texas, DB
1981 Randy McMillan, Pittsburgh, RB
Donnell Thompson, North Carolina, DT
1982 Johnie Cooks, Mississippi State, LB
Art Schlichter, Ohio State, QB
1983 John Elway, Stanford, QB
1984 Leonard Coleman, Vanderbilt, DB
Ron Solt, Maryland, G
1985 Duane Bickett, Southern California, LB
1986 Jon Hand, Alabama, DE
1987 Cornelius Bennett, Alabama, LB
1988 Chris Chandler, Washington, QB (3)
1989 Andre Rison, Michigan State, WR
1990 Jeff George, Illinois, QB
1991 Shane Curry, Miami, DE (2)
1992 Steve Emtman, Washington, DT
Quentin Coryatt, Texas A&M, LB
1993 Sean Dawkins, California, WR
1994 Marshall Faulk, San Diego State, RB
Trev Alberts, Nebraska, LB

**KANSAS CITY CHIEFS**

**Year Player, College, Position**

1960 Don Meredith, Southern Methodist, QB
1961 E.J. Holub, Texas Tech, C
1962 Ronnie Bull, Baylor, RB
1963 Buck Buchanan, Grambling, DT
Ed Budde, Michigan State, G
1964 Pete Beathard, Southern California, QB
1965 Gale Sayers, Kansas, RB
1966 Aaron Brown, Minnesota, DE
1967 Gene Trosch, Miami, DE-DT
1968 Mo Moorman, Texas A&M, G
George Daney, Texas-El Paso, G
1969 Jim Marsalis, Tennessee State, CB
1970 Sid Smith, Southern California, T
1971 Elmo Wright, Houston, WR
1972 Jeff Kinney, Nebraska, RB
1973 Gary Butler, Rice, TE (2)
1974 Woody Green, Arizona State, RB
1975 Elmore Stephens, Kentucky, TE (2)
1976 Rod Walters, Iowa, G
1977 Gary Green, Baylor, DB
1978 Art Still, Kentucky, DE
1979 Mike Bell, Colorado State, DE
Steve Fuller, Clemson, QB
1980 Brad Budde, Southern California, G
1981 Willie Scott, South Carolina, TE
1982 Anthony Hancock, Tennessee, WR
1983 Todd Blackledge, Penn State, QB
1984 Bill Maas, Pittsburgh, DT
John Alt, Iowa, T
1985 Ethan Horton, North Carolina, RB
1986 Brian Jozwiak, West Virginia, T
1987 Paul Palmer, Temple, RB
1988 Neil Smith, Nebraska, DE
1989 Derrick Thomas, Alabama, LB
1990 Percy Snow, Michigan State, LB
1991 Harvey Williams, Louisiana State, RB
1992 Dale Carter, Tennessee, DB
1993 Will Shields, Nebraska, G (3)
1994 Greg Hill, Texas A&M, RB

**LOS ANGELES RAIDERS**

**Year Player, College, Position**

1960 Dale Hackbart, Wisconsin, CB
1961 Joe Rutgens, Illinois, DT
1962 Roman Gabriel, North Carolina State, QB
1963 George Wilson, Alabama, RB (6)
1964 Tony Lorick, Arizona State, RB
1965 Harry Schuh, Memphis State, T
1966 Rodger Bird, Kentucky, S
1967 Gene Upshaw, Texas A&I, G
1968 Eldridge Dickey, Tennessee State, QB
1969 Art Thoms, Syracuse, DT
1970 Raymond Chester, Morgan State, TE
1971 Jack Tatum, Ohio State, S
1972 Mike Siani, Villanova, WR
1973 Ray Guy, Southern Mississippi, P
1974 Henry Lawrence, Florida A&M, T
1975 Neal Colzie, Ohio State, DB
1976 Charles Philyaw, Texas Southern, DT (2)
1977 Mike Davis, Colorado, DB (2)
1978 Dave Browning, Washington, DE (2)
1979 Willie Jones, Florida State, DE (2)
1980 Marc Wilson, Brigham Young, QB
1981 Ted Watts, Texas Tech, DB
Curt Marsh, Washington, T
1982 Marcus Allen, Southern California, RB
1983 Don Mosebar, Southern California, T
1984 Sean Jones, Northeastern, DE (2)
1985 Jessie Hester, Florida State, WR
1986 Bob Buczkowski, Pittsburgh, DE
1987 John Clay, Missouri, T
1988 Tim Brown, Notre Dame, WR
Terry McDaniel, Tennessee, DB
Scott Davis, Illinois, DE
1989 Jeff Francis, Tennessee, QB (6)
1990 Anthony Smith, Arizona, DE
1991 Todd Marinovich, Southern California, QB
1992 Chester McGlockton, Clemson, DE
1993 Patrick Bates, Texas A&M, DB
1994 Rob Fredrickson, Michigan State, LB

**LOS ANGELES RAMS**

**Year Player, College, Position**

1937 Johnny Drake, Purdue, B
1938 Corbett Davis, Indiana, B
1939 Parker Hall, Mississippi, B
1940 Ollie Cordill, Rice, B
1941 Rudy Mucha, Washington, C
1942 Jack Wilson, Baylor, B
1943 Mike Holovak, Boston College, B
1944 Tony Butkovich, Illinois, B
1945 Elroy (Crazylegs) Hirsch, Wisconsin, B
1946 Emil Sitko, Notre Dame, B
1947 Herman Wedemeyer, St. Mary's, Calif., B
1948 Tom Keane, West Virginia, B (2)
1949 Bobby Thomason, Virginia Military, B
1950 Ralph Pasquariello, Villanova, B
Stan West, Oklahoma, G
1951 Bud McFadin, Texas, G

## FIRST-ROUND SELECTIONS

| | |
|---|---|
| 1952 | Bill Wade, Vanderbilt, QB |
| | Bob Carey, Michigan State, E |
| 1953 | Donn Moomaw, UCLA, C |
| | Ed Barker, Washington State, E |
| 1954 | Ed Beatty, Cincinnati, C |
| 1955 | Larry Morris, Georgia Tech, C |
| 1956 | Joe Marconi, West Virginia, B |
| | Charles Horton, Vanderbilt, B |
| 1957 | Jon Arnett, Southern California, B |
| | Del Shofner, Baylor, E |
| 1958 | Lou Michaels, Kentucky, T |
| | Jim Phillips, Auburn, E |
| 1959 | Dick Bass, Pacific, B |
| | Paul Dickson, Baylor, T |
| 1960 | Billy Cannon, Louisiana State, RB |
| 1961 | Marlin McKeever, So. California, E-LB |
| 1962 | Roman Gabriel, North Carolina State, QB |
| | Merlin Olsen, Utah State, DT |
| 1963 | Terry Baker, Oregon State, QB |
| | Rufus Guthrie, Georgia Tech, G |
| 1964 | Bill Munson, Utah State, QB |
| 1965 | Clancy Williams, Washington State, CB |
| 1966 | Tom Mack, Michigan, G |
| 1967 | Willie Ellison, Texas Southern, RB (2) |
| 1968 | Gary Beban, UCLA, QB (2) |
| 1969 | Larry Smith, Florida, RB |
| | Jim Seymour, Notre Dame, WR |
| | Bob Klein, Southern California, TE |
| 1970 | Jack Reynolds, Tennessee, LB |
| 1971 | Isiah Robertson, Southern, LB |
| | Jack Youngblood, Florida, DE |
| 1972 | Jim Bertelsen, Texas, RB (2) |
| 1973 | Cullen Bryant, Colorado, DB (2) |
| 1974 | John Cappelletti, Penn State, RB |
| 1975 | Mike Fanning, Notre Dame, DT |
| | Dennis Harrah, Miami, T |
| | Doug France, Ohio State, T |
| 1976 | Kevin McLain, Colorado State, LB |
| 1977 | Bob Brudzinski, Ohio State, LB |
| 1978 | Elvis Peacock, Oklahoma, RB |
| 1979 | George Andrews, Nebraska, LB |
| | Kent Hill, Georgia Tech, T |
| 1980 | Johnnie Johnson, Texas, DB |
| 1981 | Mel Owens, Michigan, LB |
| 1982 | Barry Redden, Richmond, RB |
| 1983 | Eric Dickerson, Southern Methodist, RB |
| 1984 | Hal Stephens, East Carolina, DE (5) |
| 1985 | Jerry Gray, Texas, DB |
| 1986 | Mike Schad, Queen's University, Canada, T |
| 1987 | Donald Evans, Winston-Salem, DE (2) |
| 1988 | Gaston Green, UCLA, RB |
| | Aaron Cox, Arizona State, WR |
| 1989 | Bill Hawkins, Miami, DE |
| | Cleveland Gary, Miami, RB |
| 1990 | Bern Brostek, Washington, C |
| 1991 | Todd Lyght, Notre Dame, DB |
| 1992 | Sean Gilbert, Pittsburgh, DE |
| 1993 | Jerome Bettis, Notre Dame, RB |
| 1994 | Wayne Gandy, Auburn, T |

**MIAMI DOLPHINS**

| Year | Player, College, Position |
|---|---|
| 1966 | Jim Grabowski, Illinois, RB |
| | Rick Norton, Kentucky, QB |
| 1967 | Bob Griese, Purdue, QB |
| 1968 | Larry Csonka, Syracuse, RB |
| | Doug Crusan, Indiana, T |
| 1969 | Bill Stanfill, Georgia, DE |
| 1970 | Jim Mandich, Michigan, TE (2) |
| 1971 | Otto Stowe, Iowa State, WR (2) |
| 1972 | Mike Kadish, Notre Dame, DT |
| 1973 | Chuck Bradley, Oregon, C (2) |
| 1974 | Donald Reese, Jackson State, DE |
| 1975 | Darryl Carlton, Tampa, T |
| 1976 | Larry Gordon, Arizona State, LB |
| | Kim Bokamper, San Jose State, LB |
| 1977 | A.J. Duhe, Louisiana State, DT |
| 1978 | Guy Benjamin, Stanford, QB (2) |
| 1979 | Jon Giesler, Michigan, T |
| 1980 | Don McNeal, Alabama, DB |
| 1981 | David Overstreet, Oklahoma, RB |
| 1982 | Roy Foster, Southern California, G |
| 1983 | Dan Marino, Pittsburgh, QB |
| 1984 | Jackie Shipp, Oklahoma, LB |
| 1985 | Lorenzo Hampton, Florida, RB |
| 1986 | John Offerdahl, Western Michigan, LB (2) |
| 1987 | John Bosa, Boston College, DE |
| 1988 | Eric Kumerow, Ohio State, DE |
| 1989 | Sammie Smith, Florida State, RB |
| | Louis Oliver, Florida, DB |
| 1990 | Richmond Webb, Texas A&M, T |
| 1991 | Randal Hill, Miami, WR |
| 1992 | Troy Vincent, Wisconsin, DB |
| | Marco Coleman, Georgia Tech, LB |
| 1993 | O.J. McDuffie, Penn State, WR |
| 1994 | Tim Bowens, Mississippi, DT |

**MINNESOTA VIKINGS**

| Year | Player, College, Position |
|---|---|
| 1961 | Tommy Mason, Tulane, RB |
| 1962 | Bill Miller, Miami, WR (3) |
| 1963 | Jim Dunaway, Mississippi, T |
| 1964 | Carl Eller, Minnesota, DE |
| 1965 | Jack Snow, Notre Dame, WR |
| 1966 | Jerry Shay, Purdue, DT |
| 1967 | Clint Jones, Michigan State, RB |
| | Gene Washington, Michigan State, WR |
| | Alan Page, Notre Dame, DT |
| 1968 | Ron Yary, Southern California, T |
| 1969 | Ed White, California, G (2) |
| 1970 | John Ward, Oklahoma State, DT |
| 1971 | Leo Hayden, Ohio State, RB |
| 1972 | Jeff Siemon, Stanford, LB |
| 1973 | Chuck Foreman, Miami, RB |
| 1974 | Fred McNeill, UCLA, LB |
| | Steve Riley, Southern California, T |
| 1975 | Mark Mullaney, Colorado State, DE |
| 1976 | James White, Oklahoma State, DT |
| 1977 | Tommy Kramer, Rice, QB |
| 1978 | Randy Holloway, Pittsburgh, DE |
| 1979 | Ted Brown, North Carolina State, RB |
| 1980 | Doug Martin, Washington, DT |
| 1981 | Mardye McDole, Mississippi State, WR (2) |
| 1982 | Darrin Nelson, Stanford, RB |
| 1983 | Joey Browner, Southern California, DB |
| 1984 | Keith Millard, Washington State, DE |
| 1985 | Chris Doleman, Pittsburgh, LB |
| 1986 | Gerald Robinson, Auburn, DE |
| 1987 | D.J. Dozier, Penn State, RB |
| 1988 | Randall McDaniel, Arizona State, G |
| 1989 | David Braxton, Wake Forest, LB (2) |
| 1990 | Mike Jones, Texas A&M, TE (3) |
| 1991 | Carlos Jenkins, Michigan State, LB (3) |
| 1992 | Robert Harris, Southern University, DE (2) |
| 1993 | Robert Smith, Ohio State, RB |
| 1994 | DeWayne Washington, N. Carolina St., DB |
| | Todd Steussie, California, T |

**NEW ENGLAND PATRIOTS**

| Year | Player, College, Position |
|---|---|
| 1960 | Ron Burton, Northwestern, RB |
| 1961 | Tommy Mason, Tulane, RB |
| 1962 | Gary Collins, Maryland, WR |
| 1963 | Art Graham, Boston College, WR |
| 1964 | Jack Concannon, Boston College, QB |
| 1965 | Jerry Rush, Michigan State, DE |
| 1966 | Karl Singer, Purdue, T |
| 1967 | John Charles, Purdue, S |
| 1968 | Dennis Byrd, North Carolina State, DE |
| 1969 | Ron Sellers, Florida State, WR |
| 1970 | Phil Olsen, Utah State, DE |
| 1971 | Jim Plunkett, Stanford, QB |
| 1972 | Tom Reynolds, San Diego State, WR (2) |
| 1973 | John Hannah, Alabama, G |
| | Sam Cunningham, So. California, RB |
| | Darryl Stingley, Purdue, WR |
| 1974 | Steve Corbett, Boston College, G (2) |
| 1975 | Russ Francis, Oregon, TE |
| 1976 | Mike Haynes, Arizona State, DB |
| | Pete Brock, Colorado, C |
| | Tim Fox, Ohio State, DB |
| 1977 | Raymond Clayborn, Texas, DB |
| | Stanley Morgan, Tennessee, WR |
| 1978 | Bob Cryder, Alabama, G |
| 1979 | Rick Sanford, South Carolina, DB |
| 1980 | Roland James, Tennessee, DB |
| | Vagas Ferguson, Notre Dame, RB |
| 1981 | Brian Holloway, Stanford, T |
| 1982 | Kenneth Sims, Texas, DT |
| | Lester Williams, Miami, DT |
| 1983 | Tony Eason, Illinois, QB |
| 1984 | Irving Fryar, Nebraska, WR |
| 1985 | Trevor Matich, Brigham Young, C |
| 1986 | Reggie Dupard, Southern Methodist, RB |
| 1987 | Bruce Armstrong, Louisville, T |
| 1988 | John Stephens, Northwestern St., La., RB |
| 1989 | Hart Lee Dykes, Oklahoma State, WR |
| 1990 | Chris Singleton, Arizona, LB |
| | Ray Agnew, North Carolina State, DE |
| 1991 | Pat Harlow, Southern California, T |
| | Leonard Russell, Arizona State, RB |
| 1992 | Eugene Chung, Virginia Tech, T |
| 1993 | Drew Bledsoe, Washington State, QB |
| 1994 | Willie McGinest, Southern California, DE |

**NEW ORLEANS SAINTS**

| Year | Player, College, Position |
|---|---|
| 1967 | Les Kelley, Alabama, RB |
| 1968 | Kevin Hardy, Notre Dame, DE |
| 1969 | John Shinners, Xavier, G |
| 1970 | Ken Burrough, Texas Southern, WR |
| 1971 | Archie Manning, Mississippi, QB |
| 1972 | Royce Smith, Georgia, G |
| 1973 | Derland Moore, Oklahoma, DE (2) |
| 1974 | Rick Middleton, Ohio State, LB |
| 1975 | Larry Burton, Purdue, WR |
| | Kurt Schumacher, Ohio State, T |
| 1976 | Chuck Muncie, California, RB |
| 1977 | Joe Campbell, Maryland, DE |
| 1978 | Wes Chandler, Florida, WR |
| 1979 | Russell Erxleben, Texas, P-K |
| 1980 | Stan Brock, Colorado, T |
| 1981 | George Rogers, South Carolina, RB |
| 1982 | Lindsay Scott, Georgia, WR |
| 1983 | Steve Korte, Arkansas, G (2) |
| 1984 | James Geathers, Wichita State, DE |
| 1985 | Alvin Toles, Tennessee, LB |
| 1986 | Jim Dombrowski, Virginia, T |
| 1987 | Shawn Knight, Brigham Young, DT |
| 1988 | Craig Heyward, Pittsburgh, RB |
| 1989 | Wayne Martin, Arkansas, DE |
| 1990 | Renaldo Turnbull, West Virginia, DE |
| 1991 | Wesley Carroll, Miami, WR (2) |
| 1992 | Vaughn Dunbar, Indiana, RB |
| 1993 | Willie Roaf, Louisiana Tech, T |
| | Irv Smith, Notre Dame, TE |
| 1994 | Joe Johnson, Louisville, DE |

**NEW YORK GIANTS**

| Year | Player, College, Position |
|---|---|
| 1936 | Art Lewis, Ohio U., T |
| 1937 | Ed Widseth, Minnesota, T |
| 1938 | George Karamatic, Gonzaga, B |
| 1939 | Walt Neilson, Arizona, B |
| 1940 | Grenville Lansdell, Southern California, B |
| 1941 | George Franck, Minnesota, B |
| 1942 | Merle Hapes, Mississippi, B |
| 1943 | Steve Filipowicz, Fordham, B |
| 1944 | Billy Hillenbrand, Indiana, B |
| 1945 | Elmer Barbour, Wake Forest, B |
| 1946 | George Connor, Notre Dame, T |
| 1947 | Vic Schwall, Northwestern, B |
| 1948 | Tony Minisi, Pennsylvania, B |
| 1949 | Paul Page, Southern Methodist, B |
| 1950 | Travis Tidwell, Auburn, B |
| 1951 | Kyle Rote, Southern Methodist, B |
| | Jim Spavital, Oklahoma A&M, B |
| 1952 | Frank Gifford, Southern California, B |
| 1953 | Bobby Marlow, Alabama, B |
| 1954 | Ken Buck, Pacific, C (2) |
| 1955 | Joe Heap, Notre Dame, B |
| 1956 | Henry Moore, Arkansas, B (2) |
| 1957 | Sam DeLuca, South Carolina, T (2) |
| 1958 | Phil King, Vanderbilt, B |
| 1959 | Lee Grosscup, Utah, B |
| 1960 | Lou Cordileone, Clemson, G |
| 1961 | Bruce Tarbox, Syracuse, G (2) |
| 1962 | Jerry Hillebrand, Colorado, LB |
| 1963 | Frank Lasky, Florida, T (2) |

1964 Joe Don Looney, Oklahoma, RB
1965 Tucker Frederickson, Auburn, RB
1966 Francis Peay, Missouri, T
1967 Louis Thompson, Alabama, DT (4)
1968 Dick Buzin, Penn State, T (2)
1969 Fred Dryer, San Diego State, DE
1970 Jim Files, Oklahoma, LB
1971 Rocky Thompson, West Texas State, WR
1972 Eldridge Small, Texas A&I, DB
Larry Jacobson, Nebraska, DE
1973 Brad Van Pelt, Michigan State, LB (2)
1974 John Hicks, Ohio State, G
1975 Al Simpson, Colorado State, T (2)
1976 Troy Archer, Colorado, DE
1977 Gary Jeter, Southern California, DT
1978 Gordon King, Stanford, T
1979 Phil Simms, Morehead State, QB
1980 Mark Haynes, Colorado, DB
1981 Lawrence Taylor, North Carolina, LB
1982 Butch Woolfolk, Michigan, RB
1983 Terry Kinard, Clemson, DB
1984 Carl Banks, Michigan State, LB
William Roberts, Ohio State, T
1985 George Adams, Kentucky, RB
1986 Eric Dorsey, Notre Dame, DE
1987 Mark Ingram, Michigan State, WR
1988 Eric Moore, Indiana, T
1989 Brian Williams, Minnesota, C-G
1990 Rodney Hampton, Georgia, RB
1991 Jarrod Bunch, Michigan, RB
1992 Derek Brown, Notre Dame, TE
1993 Michael Strahan, Texas Southern, DE (2)
1994 Thomas Lewis, Indiana, WR

**NEW YORK JETS**

**Year Player, College, Position**
1960 George Izo, Notre Dame, QB
1961 Tom Brown, Minnesota, G
1962 Sandy Stephens, Minnesota, QB
1963 Jerry Stovall, Louisiana State, S
1964 Matt Snell, Ohio State, RB
1965 Joe Namath, Alabama, QB
Tom Nowatzke, Indiana, RB
1966 Bill Yearby, Michigan, DT
1967 Paul Seiler, Notre Dame, T
1968 Lee White, Weber State, RB
1969 Dave Foley, Ohio State, T
1970 Steve Tannen, Florida, CB
1971 John Riggins, Kansas, RB
1972 Jerome Barkum, Jackson State, WR
Mike Taylor, Michigan, LB
1973 Burgess Owens, Miami, DB
1974 Carl Barzilauskas, Indiana, DT
1975 Anthony Davis, Southern California, RB (2)
1976 Richard Todd, Alabama, QB
1977 Marvin Powell, Southern California, T
1978 Chris Ward, Ohio State, T
1979 Marty Lyons, Alabama, DE
1980 Johnny (Lam) Jones, Texas, WR
1981 Freeman McNeil, UCLA, RB
1982 Bob Crable, Notre Dame, LB
1983 Ken O'Brien, Cal-Davis, QB
1984 Russell Carter, Southern Methodist, DB
Ron Faurot, Arkansas, DE
1985 Al Toon, Wisconsin, WR
1986 Mike Haight, Iowa, T
1987 Roger Vick, Texas A&M, RB
1988 Dave Cadigan, Southern California, T
1989 Jeff Lageman, Virginia, LB
1990 Blair Thomas, Penn State, RB
1991 Browning Nagle, Louisville, QB (2)
1992 Johnny Mitchell, Nebraska, TE
1993 Marvin Jones, Florida State, LB
1994 Aaron Glenn, Texas A&M, DB

**PHILADELPHIA EAGLES**

**Year Player, College, Position**
1936 Jay Berwanger, Chicago, B
1937 Sam Francis, Nebraska, B
1938 Jim McDonald, Ohio State, B
1939 Davey O'Brien, Texas Christian, B
1940 George McAfee, Duke, B
1941 Art Jones, Richmond, B (2)
1942 Pete Kmetovic, Stanford, B
1943 Joe Muha, Virginia Military, B
1944 Steve Van Buren, Louisiana State, B
1945 John Yonaker, Notre Dame, E
1946 Leo Riggs, Southern California, B
1947 Neill Armstrong, Oklahoma A&M, E
1948 Clyde (Smackover) Scott, Arkansas, B
1949 Chuck Bednarik, Pennsylvania, C
Frank Tripucka, Notre Dame, B
1950 Harry (Bud) Grant, Minnesota, E
1951 Ebert Van Buren, Louisiana State, B
Chet Mutryn, Xavier, B
1952 Johnny Bright, Drake, B
1953 Al Conway, Army, B (2)
1954 Neil Worden, Notre Dame, B
1955 Dick Bielski, Maryland, B
1956 Bob Pellegrini, Maryland, C
1957 Clarence Peaks, Michigan State, B
1958 Walt Kowalczyk, Michigan State, B
1959 J.D. Smith, Rice, T (2)
1960 Ron Burton, Northwestern, RB
1961 Art Baker, Syracuse, RB
1962 Pete Case, Georgia, G (2)
1963 Ed Budde, Michigan State, G
1964 Bob Brown, Nebraska, T
1965 Ray Rissmiller, Georgia, T (2)
1966 Randy Beisler, Indiana, DE
1967 Harry Jones, Arkansas, RB
1968 Tim Rossovich, Southern California, DE
1969 Leroy Keyes, Purdue, RB
1970 Steve Zabel, Oklahoma, TE
1971 Richard Harris, Grambling, DE
1972 John Reaves, Florida, QB
1973 Jerry Sisemore, Texas, T
Charle Young, Southern California, TE
1974 Mitch Sutton, Kansas, DT (3)
1975 Bill Capraun, Miami, T (7)
1976 Mike Smith, Florida, DE (4)
1977 Skip Sharp, Kansas, DB (5)
1978 Reggie Wilkes, Georgia Tech, LB (3)
1979 Jerry Robinson, UCLA, LB
1980 Roynell Young, Alcorn State, DB
1981 Leonard Mitchell, Houston, DE
1982 Mike Quick, North Carolina State, WR
1983 Michael Haddix, Mississippi State, RB
1984 Kenny Jackson, Penn State, WR
1985 Kevin Allen, Indiana, T
1986 Keith Byars, Ohio State, RB
1987 Jerome Brown, Miami, DT
1988 Keith Jackson, Oklahoma, TE
1989 Jessie Small, Eastern Kentucky, LB (2)
1990 Ben Smith, Georgia, DB
1991 Antone Davis, Tennessee, T
1992 Siran Stacy, Alabama, RB (2)
1993 Lester Holmes, Jackson State, T
Leonard Renfro, Colorado, DT
1994 Bernard Williams, Georgia, T

**PITTSBURGH STEELERS**

**Year Player, College, Position**
1936 Bill Shakespeare, Notre Dame, B
1937 Mike Basrak, Duquesne, C
1938 Byron (Whizzer) White, Colorado, B
1939 Bill Patterson, Baylor, B (3)
1940 Kay Eakin, Arkansas, B
1941 Chet Gladchuk, Boston College, C (2)
1942 Bill Dudley, Virginia, B
1943 Bill Daley, Minnesota, B
1944 Johnny Podesto, St. Mary's, Calif., B
1945 Paul Duhart, Florida, B
1946 Felix (Doc) Blanchard, Army, B
1947 Hub Bechtol, Texas, E
1948 Dan Edwards, Georgia, E
1949 Bobby Gage, Clemson, B
1950 Lynn Chandnois, Michigan State, B
1951 Butch Avinger, Alabama, B
1952 Ed Modzelewski, Maryland, B
1953 Ted Marchibroda, St. Bonaventure, B
1954 Johnny Lattner, Notre Dame, B
1955 Frank Varrichione, Notre Dame, T
1956 Gary Glick, Colorado A&M, B
Art Davis, Mississippi State, B
1957 Len Dawson, Purdue, B
1958 Larry Krutko, West Virginia, B (2)
1959 Tom Barnett, Purdue, B (8)
1960 Jack Spikes, Texas Christian, RB
1961 Myron Pottios, Notre Dame, LB (2)
1962 Bob Ferguson, Ohio State, RB
1963 Frank Atkinson, Stanford, T (8)
1964 Paul Martha, Pittsburgh, S
1965 Roy Jefferson, Utah, WR (2)
1966 Dick Leftridge, West Virginia, RB
1967 Don Shy, San Diego State, RB (2)
1968 Mike Taylor, Southern California, T
1969 Joe Greene, North Texas State, DT
1970 Terry Bradshaw, Louisiana Tech, QB
1971 Frank Lewis, Grambling, WR
1972 Franco Harris, Penn State, RB
1973 J.T. Thomas, Florida State, DB
1974 Lynn Swann, Southern California, WR
1975 Dave Brown, Michigan, DB
1976 Bennie Cunningham, Clemson, TE
1977 Robin Cole, New Mexico, LB
1978 Ron Johnson, Eastern Michigan, DB
1979 Greg Hawthorne, Baylor, RB
1980 Mark Malone, Arizona State, QB
1981 Keith Gary, Oklahoma, DE
1982 Walter Abercrombie, Baylor, RB
1983 Gabriel Rivera, Texas Tech, DT
1984 Louis Lipps, Southern Mississippi, WR
1985 Darryl Sims, Wisconsin, DE
1986 John Rienstra, Temple, G
1987 Rod Woodson, Purdue, DB
1988 Aaron Jones, Eastern Kentucky, DE
1989 Tim Worley, Georgia, RB
Tom Ricketts, Pittsburgh, T
1990 Eric Green, Liberty, TE
1991 Huey Richardson, Florida, DE
1992 Leon Searcy, Miami, T
1993 Deon Figures, Colorado, DB
1994 Charles Johnson, Colorado, WR

**SAN DIEGO CHARGERS**

**Year Player, College, Position**
1960 Monty Stickles, Notre Dame, E
1961 Earl Faison, Indiana, DE
1962 Bob Ferguson, Ohio State, RB
1963 Walt Sweeney, Syracuse, G
1964 Ted Davis, Georgia Tech, LB
1965 Steve DeLong, Tennessee, DE
1966 Don Davis, Cal State-Los Angeles, DT
1967 Ron Billingsley, Wyoming, DE
1968 Russ Washington, Missouri, DT
Jimmy Hill, Texas A&I, DB
1969 Marty Domres, Columbia, QB
Bob Babich, Miami, Ohio, LB
1970 Walker Gillette, Richmond, WR
1971 Leon Burns, Long Beach State, RB
1972 Pete Lazetich, Stanford, DE (2)
1973 Johnny Rodgers, Nebraska, WR
1974 Bo Matthews, Colorado, RB
Don Goode, Kansas, LB
1975 Gary Johnson, Grambling, DT
Mike Williams, Louisiana State, DB
1976 Joe Washington, Oklahoma, RB
1977 Bob Rush, Memphis State, C
1978 John Jefferson, Arizona State, WR
1979 Kellen Winslow, Missouri, TE
1980 Ed Luther, San Jose State, QB (4)
1981 James Brooks, Auburn, RB
1982 Hollis Hall, Clemson, DB (7)
1983 Billy Ray Smith, Arkansas, LB
Gary Anderson, Arkansas, WR
Gill Byrd, San Jose State, DB
1984 Mossy Cade, Texas, DB
1985 Jim Lachey, Ohio State, G
1986 Leslie O'Neal, Oklahoma State, DE
James FitzPatrick, Southern California, T
1987 Rod Bernstine, Texas A&M, TE
1988 Anthony Miller, Tennessee, WR
1989 Burt Grossman, Pittsburgh, DE
1990 Junior Seau, Southern California, LB
1991 Stanley Richard, Texas, DB
1992 Chris Mims, Tennessee, DE
1993 Darrien Gordon, Stanford, DB
1994 Isaac Davis, Arkansas, G (2)

## FIRST-ROUND SELECTIONS

**SAN FRANCISCO 49ERS**

| Year | Player, College, Position |
|---|---|
| 1950 | Leo Nomellini, Minnesota, T |
| 1951 | Y.A. Tittle, Louisiana State, B |
| 1952 | Hugh McElhenny, Washington, B |
| 1953 | Harry Babcock, Georgia, E |
| | Tom Stolhandske, Texas, E |
| 1954 | Bernie Faloney, Maryland, B |
| 1955 | Dickie Moegle, Rice, B |
| 1956 | Earl Morrall, Michigan State, B |
| 1957 | John Brodie, Stanford, B |
| 1958 | Jim Pace, Michigan, B |
| | Charlie Krueger, Texas A&M, T |
| 1959 | Dave Baker, Oklahoma, B |
| | Dan James, Ohio State, C |
| 1960 | Monty Stickles, Notre Dame, E |
| 1961 | Jimmy Johnson, UCLA, CB |
| | Bernie Casey, Bowling Green, WR |
| | Bill Kilmer, UCLA, QB |
| 1962 | Lance Alworth, Arkansas, WR |
| 1963 | Kermit Alexander, UCLA, CB |
| 1964 | Dave Parks, Texas Tech, WR |
| 1965 | Ken Willard, North Carolina, RB |
| | George Donnelly, Illinois, DB |
| 1966 | Stan Hindman, Mississippi, DE |
| 1967 | Steve Spurrier, Florida, QB |
| | Cas Banaszek, Northwestern, T |
| 1968 | Forrest Blue, Auburn, C |
| 1969 | Ted Kwalick, Penn State, TE |
| | Gene Washington, Stanford, WR |
| 1970 | Cedrick Hardman, North Texas State, DE |
| | Bruce Taylor, Boston U., DB |
| 1971 | Tim Anderson, Ohio State, DB |
| 1972 | Terry Beasley, Auburn, WR |
| 1973 | Mike Holmes, Texas Southern, DB |
| 1974 | Wilbur Jackson, Alabama, RB |
| | Bill Sandifer, UCLA, DT |
| 1975 | Jimmy Webb, Mississippi State, DT |
| 1976 | Randy Cross, UCLA, C (2) |
| 1977 | Elmo Boyd, Eastern Kentucky, WR (3) |
| 1978 | Ken MacAfee, Notre Dame, TE |
| | Dan Bunz, Cal State-Long Beach, LB |
| 1979 | James Owens, UCLA, WR (2) |
| 1980 | Earl Cooper, Rice, RB |
| | Jim Stuckey, Clemson, DT |
| 1981 | Ronnie Lott, Southern California, DB |
| 1982 | Bubba Paris, Michigan, T (2) |
| 1983 | Roger Craig, Nebraska, RB (2) |
| 1984 | Todd Shell, Brigham Young, LB |
| 1985 | Jerry Rice, Mississippi Valley State, WR |
| 1986 | Larry Roberts, Alabama, DE (2) |
| 1987 | Harris Barton, North Carolina, T |
| | Terrence Flagler, Clemson, RB |
| 1988 | Danny Stubbs, Miami, DE (2) |
| 1989 | Keith DeLong, Tennessee, LB |
| 1990 | Dexter Carter, Florida State, RB |
| 1991 | Ted Washington, Louisville, DT |
| 1992 | Dana Hall, Washington, DB |
| 1993 | Dana Stubblefield, Kansas, DT |
| | Todd Kelly, Tennessee, DE |
| 1994 | Bryant Young, Notre Dame, DT |
| | William Floyd, Florida State, RB |

**SEATTLE SEAHAWKS**

| Year | Player, College, Position |
|---|---|
| 1976 | Steve Niehaus, Notre Dame, DT |
| 1977 | Steve August, Tulsa, G |
| 1978 | Keith Simpson, Memphis State, DB |
| 1979 | Manu Tuiasosopo, UCLA, DT |
| 1980 | Jacob Green, Texas A&M, DE |
| 1981 | Ken Easley, UCLA, DB |
| 1982 | Jeff Bryant, Clemson, DE |
| 1983 | Curt Warner, Penn State, RB |
| 1984 | Terry Taylor, Southern Illinois, DB |
| 1985 | Owen Gill, Iowa, RB (2) |
| 1986 | John L. Williams, Florida, RB |
| 1987 | Tony Woods, Pittsburgh, LB |
| 1988 | Brian Blades, Miami, WR (2) |
| 1989 | Andy Heck, Notre Dame, T |
| 1990 | Cortez Kennedy, Miami, DT |
| 1991 | Dan McGwire, San Diego State, QB |
| 1992 | Ray Roberts, Virginia, T |
| 1993 | Rick Mirer, Notre Dame, QB |
| 1994 | Sam Adams, Texas A&M, DT |

**TAMPA BAY BUCCANEERS**

| Year | Player, College, Position |
|---|---|
| 1976 | Lee Roy Selmon, Oklahoma, DT |
| 1977 | Ricky Bell, Southern California, RB |
| 1978 | Doug Williams, Grambling, QB |
| 1979 | Greg Roberts, Oklahoma, G (2) |
| 1980 | Ray Snell, Wisconsin, G |
| 1981 | Hugh Green, Pittsburgh, LB |
| 1982 | Sean Farrell, Penn State, G |
| 1983 | Randy Grimes, Baylor, C (2) |
| 1984 | Keith Browner, Southern California, LB (2) |
| 1985 | Ron Holmes, Washington, DE |
| 1986 | Bo Jackson, Auburn, RB |
| | Roderick Jones, Southern Methodist, DB |
| 1987 | Vinny Testaverde, Miami, QB |
| 1988 | Paul Gruber, Wisconsin, T |
| 1989 | Broderick Thomas, Nebraska, LB |
| 1990 | Keith McCants, Alabama, LB |
| 1991 | Charles McRae, Tennessee, T |
| 1992 | Courtney Hawkins, Michigan State, WR (2) |
| 1993 | Eric Curry, Alabama, DE |
| 1994 | Trent Dilfer, Fresno State, QB |

**WASHINGTON REDSKINS**

| Year | Player, College, Position |
|---|---|
| 1936 | Riley Smith, Alabama, B |
| 1937 | Sammy Baugh, Texas Christian, B |
| 1938 | Andy Farkas, Detroit, B |
| 1939 | I.B. Hale, Texas Christian, T |
| 1940 | Ed Boell, New York U., B |
| 1941 | Forest Evashevski, Michigan, B |
| 1942 | Orban (Spec) Sanders, Texas, B |
| 1943 | Jack Jenkins, Missouri, B |
| 1944 | Mike Micka, Colgate, B |
| 1945 | Jim Hardy, Southern California, B |
| 1946 | Casl Rossi, UCLA, B* |
| 1947 | Casl Rossi, UCLA, B |
| 1948 | Harry Gilmer, Alabama, B |
| | Lowell Tew, Alabama, B |
| 1949 | Rob Goode, Texas A&M, B |
| 1950 | George Thomas, Oklahoma, B |
| 1951 | Leon Heath, Oklahoma, B |
| 1952 | Larry Isbell, Baylor, B |
| 1953 | Jack Scarbath, Maryland, B |
| 1954 | Steve Meilinger, Kentucky, E |
| 1955 | Ralph Guglielmi, Notre Dame, B |
| 1956 | Ed Vereb, Maryland, B |
| 1957 | Don Bosseler, Miami, B |
| 1958 | Mike Sommer, George Washington, B (2) |
| 1959 | Don Allard, Boston College, B |
| 1960 | Richie Lucas, Penn State, QB |
| 1961 | Norman Snead, Wake Forest, QB |
| | Joe Rutgens, Illinois, DT |
| 1962 | Ernie Davis, Syracuse, RB |
| 1963 | Pat Richter, Wisconsin, TE |
| 1964 | Charley Taylor, Arizona State, RB-WR |
| 1965 | Bob Breitenstein, Tulsa, T (2) |
| 1966 | Charlie Gogolak, Princeton, K |
| 1967 | Ray McDonald, Idaho, RB |
| 1968 | Jim Smith, Oregon, DB |
| 1969 | Eugene Epps, Texas-El Paso, DB (2) |
| 1970 | Bill Bundige, Colorado, DT (2) |
| 1971 | Cotton Speyrer, Texas, WR (2) |
| 1972 | Moses Denson, Maryland State, RB (8) |
| 1973 | Charles Cantrell, Lamar, G (5) |
| 1974 | Jon Keyworth, Colorado, TE (6) |
| 1975 | Mike Thomas, Nevada-Las Vegas, RB (6) |
| 1976 | Mike Hughes, Baylor, G (5) |
| 1977 | Duncan McColl, Stanford, DE (4) |
| 1978 | Tony Green, Florida, RB (6) |
| 1979 | Don Warren, San Diego State, TE (4) |
| 1980 | Art Monk, Syracuse, WR |
| 1981 | Mark May, Pittsburgh, T |
| 1982 | Vernon Dean, San Diego State, DB (2) |
| 1983 | Darrell Green, Texas A&I, DB |
| 1984 | Bob Slater, Oklahoma, DT (2) |
| 1985 | Tory Nixon, San Diego State, DB (2) |
| 1986 | Markus Koch, Boise State, DE (2) |
| 1987 | Brian Davis, Nebraska, DB (2) |
| 1988 | Chip Lohmiller, Minnesota, K (2) |
| 1989 | Tracy Rocker, Auburn, DT (3) |
| 1990 | Andre Collins, Penn State, LB (2) |
| 1991 | Bobby Wilson, Michigan State, DT |
| 1992 | Desmond Howard, Michigan, WR |
| 1993 | Tom Carter, Notre Dame, DB |
| 1994 | Heath Shuler, Tennessee, QB |

**Choice lost due to ineligibility*

# Records

# ALL-TIME RECORDS

*Compiled by Elias Sports Bureau*
*The following records reflect all available official information on the National Football League from its formation in 1920 to date. Also included are all applicable records from the American Football League, 1960-69.*

## INDIVIDUAL RECORDS

### SERVICE

**Most Seasons**
26 George Blanda, Chi. Bears, 1949, 1950-58; Baltimore, 1950; Houston, 1960-66; Oakland, 1967-75
21 Earl Morrall, San Francisco, 1956; Pittsburgh, 1957-58; Detroit, 1958-64; N.Y. Giants, 1965-67; Baltimore, 1968-71; Miami, 1972-76
20 Jim Marshall, Cleveland, 1960; Minnesota, 1961-79

**Most Seasons, One Club**
19 Jim Marshall, Minnesota, 1961-79
18 Jim Hart, St. Louis, 1966-83
Jeff Van Note, Atlanta, 1969-86
Pat Leahy, N.Y. Jets, 1974-91
Jackie Slater, L.A. Rams, 1976-93
17 Lou Groza, Cleveland, 1950-59, 1961-67
Johnny Unitas, Baltimore, 1956-72
John Brodie, San Francisco, 1957-73
Jim Bakken, St. Louis, 1962-78
Mick Tingelhoff, Minnesota, 1962-78

**Most Games Played, Career**
340 George Blanda, Chi. Bears, 1949, 1950-58; Baltimore, 1950; Houston, 1960-66; Oakland, 1967-75
282 Jim Marshall, Cleveland, 1960; Minnesota, 1961-79
263 Jan Stenerud, Kansas City, 1967-79; Green Bay, 1980-83; Minnesota, 1984-85

**Most Consecutive Games Played, Career**
282 Jim Marshall, Cleveland, 1960; Minnesota, 1961-79
240 Mick Tingelhoff, Minnesota, 1962-78
234 Jim Bakken, St. Louis, 1962-78

### SCORING

**Most Seasons Leading League**
5 Don Hutson, Green Bay, 1940-44
Gino Cappelletti, Boston, 1961, 1963-66
3 Earl (Dutch) Clark, Portsmouth, 1932; Detroit, 1935-36
Pat Harder, Chi. Cardinals, 1947-49
Paul Hornung, Green Bay, 1959-61
2 Jack Manders, Chi. Bears, 1934, 1937
Gordy Soltau, San Francisco, 1952-53
Doak Walker, Detroit, 1950, 1955
Gene Mingo, Denver, 1960, 1962
Jim Turner, N.Y. Jets, 1968-69
Fred Cox, Minnesota, 1969-70
Chester Marcol, Green Bay, 1972, 1974
John Smith, New England, 1979-80

**Most Consecutive Seasons Leading League**
5 Don Hutson, Green Bay, 1940-44
4 Gino Cappelletti, Boston, 1963-66
3 Pat Harder, Chi. Cardinals, 1947-49
Paul Hornung, Green Bay, 1959-61

### POINTS

**Most Points, Career**
2,002 George Blanda, Chi. Bears, 1949, 1950-58; Baltimore, 1950; Houston, 1960-66; Oakland, 1967-75 (9-td, 943-pat, 335-fg)
1,699 Jan Stenerud, Kansas City, 1967-79; Green Bay, 1980-83; Minnesota, 1984-85 (580-pat, 373-fg)
1,473 Nick Lowery, New England, 1978; Kansas City, 1980-93

**Most Points, Season**
176 Paul Hornung, Green Bay, 1960 (15-td, 41-pat, 15-fg)
161 Mark Moseley, Washington, 1983 (62-pat, 33-fg)
155 Gino Cappelletti, Boston, 1964 (7-td, 38-pat, 25-fg)

**Most Points, No Touchdowns, Season**
161 Mark Moseley, Washington, 1983 (62-pat, 33-fg)
149 Chip Lohmiller, Washington, 1991 (56-pat, 31-fg)
145 Jim Turner, N.Y. Jets, 1968 (43-pat, 34-fg)

**Most Seasons, 100 or More Points**
11 Nick Lowery, Kansas City, 1981, 1983-86, 1988-93
8 Morten Andersen, New Orleans, 1985-89, 1991-93
7 Jan Stenerud, Kansas City, 1967-71; Green Bay, 1981, 1983
Gary Anderson, Pittsburgh, 1983-85, 1988, 1991-93

**Most Points, Rookie, Season**
144 Kevin Butler, Chicago, 1985 (51-pat, 31-fg)
132 Gale Sayers, Chicago, 1965 (22-td)
128 Doak Walker, Detroit, 1950 (11-td, 38-pat, 8-fg)
Chester Marcol, Green Bay, 1972 (29-pat, 33-fg)

**Most Points, Game**
40 Ernie Nevers, Chi. Cardinals vs. Chi. Bears, Nov. 28, 1929 (6-td, 4-pat)
36 Dub Jones, Cleveland vs. Chi. Bears, Nov. 25, 1951 (6-td)
Gale Sayers, Chicago vs. San Francisco, Dec. 12, 1965 (6-td)
33 Paul Hornung, Green Bay vs. Baltimore, Oct. 8, 1961 (4-td, 6-pat, 1-fg)

**Most Consecutive Games Scoring**
186 Jim Breech, Oakland, 1979; Cincinnati, 1980-92
158 Morten Andersen, New Orleans, 1982-93 (current)
151 Fred Cox, Minnesota, 1963-73

### TOUCHDOWNS

**Most Seasons Leading League**
8 Don Hutson, Green Bay, 1935-38, 1941-44
3 Jim Brown, Cleveland, 1958-59, 1963
Lance Alworth, San Diego, 1964-66
2 By many players

**Most Consecutive Seasons Leading League**
4 Don Hutson, Green Bay, 1935-38, 1941-44
3 Lance Alworth, San Diego, 1964-66
2 By many players

**Most Touchdowns, Career**
126 Jim Brown, Cleveland, 1957-65 (106-r, 20-p)
125 Walter Payton, Chicago, 1975-87 (110-r, 15-p)
124 Jerry Rice, San Francisco, 1985-93 (6-r, 118-p)

**Most Touchdowns, Season**
24 John Riggins, Washington, 1983 (24-r)
23 O.J. Simpson, Buffalo, 1975 (16-r, 7-p)
Jerry Rice, San Francisco, 1987 (1-r, 22-p)
22 Gale Sayers, Chicago, 1965 (14-r, 6-p, 2-ret)
Chuck Foreman, Minnesota, 1975 (13-r, 9-p)

**Most Touchdowns, Rookie, Season**
22 Gale Sayers, Chicago, 1965 (14-r, 6-p, 2-ret)
20 Eric Dickerson, L.A. Rams, 1983 (18-r, 2-p)
16 Billy Sims, Detroit, 1980 (13-r, 3-p)

**Most Touchdowns, Game**
6 Ernie Nevers, Chi. Cardinals vs. Chi. Bears, Nov. 28, 1929 (6-r)
Dub Jones, Cleveland vs. Chi. Bears, Nov. 25, 1951 (4-r, 2-p)
Gale Sayers, Chicago vs. San Francisco, Dec. 12, 1965 (4-r, 1-p, 1-ret)
5 Bob Shaw, Chi. Cardinals vs. Baltimore, Oct. 2, 1950 (5-p)
Jim Brown, Cleveland vs. Baltimore, Nov. 1, 1959 (5-r)
Abner Haynes, Dall. Texans vs. Oakland, Nov. 26, 1961 (4-r, 1-p)
Billy Cannon, Houston vs. N.Y. Titans, Dec. 10, 1961 (3-r, 2-p)
Cookie Gilchrist, Buffalo vs. N.Y. Jets, Dec. 8, 1963 (5-r)
Paul Hornung, Green Bay vs. Baltimore, Dec. 12, 1965 (3-r, 2-p)
Kellen Winslow, San Diego vs. Oakland, Nov. 22, 1981 (5-p)
Jerry Rice, San Francisco vs. Atlanta, Oct. 14, 1990 (5-p)
4 By many players. Last time: Ron Moore, Phoenix vs. L.A. Rams, Dec. 5, 1993 (4-r)

**Most Consecutive Games Scoring Touchdowns**
18 Lenny Moore, Baltimore, 1963-65
14 O.J. Simpson, Buffalo, 1975
13 John Riggins, Washington, 1982-83
George Rogers, Washington, 1985-86
Jerry Rice, San Francisco, 1986-87

### POINTS AFTER TOUCHDOWN

**Most Seasons Leading League**
8 George Blanda, Chi. Bears, 1956; Houston, 1961-62; Oakland, 1967-69, 1972, 1974
4 Bob Waterfield, Cleveland, 1945; Los Angeles, 1946, 1950, 1952
3 Earl (Dutch) Clark, Portsmouth, 1932; Detroit, 1935-36
Jack Manders, Chi. Bears, 1933-35
Don Hutson, Green Bay, 1941-42, 1945

**Most Points After Touchdown Attempted, Career**
959 George Blanda, Chi. Bears, 1949, 1950-58; Baltimore, 1950; Houston, 1960-66; Oakland, 1967-75
657 Lou Groza, Cleveland, 1950-59, 1961-67
601 Jan Stenerud, Kansas City, 1967-79; Green Bay, 1980-83; Minnesota, 1984-85

**Most Points After Touchdown Attempted, Season**
70 Uwe von Schamann, Miami, 1984
65 George Blanda, Houston, 1961
63 Mark Moseley, Washington, 1983

**Most Points After Touchdown Attempted, Game**
10 Charlie Gogolak, Washington vs. N.Y. Giants, Nov. 27, 1966
9 Pat Harder, Chi. Cardinals vs. N.Y. Giants, Oct. 17, 1948; vs. N.Y. Bulldogs, Nov. 13, 1949
Bob Waterfield, Los Angeles vs. Baltimore, Oct. 22, 1950
Bob Thomas, Chicago vs. Green Bay, Dec. 7, 1980
8 By many players

**Most Points After Touchdown, Career**
943 George Blanda, Chi. Bears, 1949, 1950-58; Baltimore, 1950; Houston, 1960-66; Oakland, 1967-75

641 Lou Groza, Cleveland, 1950-59, 1961-67
580 Jan Stenerud, Kansas City, 1967-79; Green Bay, 1980-83; Minnesota, 1984-85

**Most Points After Touchdown, Season**
66 Uwe von Schamann, Miami, 1984
64 George Blanda, Houston, 1961
62 Mark Moseley, Washington, 1983

**Most Points After Touchdown, Game**
9 Pat Harder, Chi. Cardinals vs. N.Y. Giants, Oct. 17, 1948
Bob Waterfield, Los Angeles vs. Baltimore, Oct. 22, 1950
Charlie Gogolak, Washington vs. N.Y. Giants, Nov. 27, 1966
8 By many players

**Most Consecutive Points After Touchdown**
234 Tommy Davis, San Francisco, 1959-65
221 Jim Turner, N.Y. Jets, 1967-70; Denver, 1971-74
213 Chip Lohmiller, Washington, 1988-93

**Highest Points After Touchdown Percentage, Career (200 points after touchdown)**
99.43 Tommy Davis, San Francisco, 1959-69 (350-348)
99.18 Nick Lowery, New England, 1978; Kansas City, 1980-93 (490-486)
98.97 Gary Anderson, Pittsburgh, 1982-93 (388-384)

**Most Points After Touchdown, No Misses, Season**
56 Danny Villanueva, Dallas, 1966
Ray Wersching, San Francisco, 1984
Chip Lohmiller, Washington, 1991
54 Mike Clark, Dallas, 1968
George Blanda, Oakland, 1968
53 Pat Harder, Chi. Cardinals, 1948

**Most Points After Touchdown, No Misses, Game**
9 Pat Harder, Chi. Cardinals vs. N.Y. Giants, Oct. 17, 1948
Bob Waterfield, Los Angeles vs. Baltimore, Oct. 22, 1950
8 By many players

## FIELD GOALS

**Most Seasons Leading League**
5 Lou Groza, Cleveland, 1950, 1952-54, 1957
4 Jack Manders, Chi. Bears, 1933-34, 1936-37
Ward Cuff, N.Y. Giants, 1938-39, 1943; Green Bay, 1947
Mark Moseley, Washington, 1976-77, 1979, 1982
3 Bob Waterfield, Los Angeles, 1947, 1949, 1951
Gino Cappelletti, Boston, 1961, 1963-64
Fred Cox, Minnesota, 1965, 1969-70
Jan Stenerud, Kansas City, 1967, 1970, 1975

**Most Consecutive Seasons Leading League**
3 Lou Groza, Cleveland, 1952-54
2 Jack Manders, Chi. Bears, 1933-34
Armand Niccolai, Pittsburgh, 1935-36
Jack Manders, Chi. Bears, 1936-37
Ward Cuff, N.Y. Giants, 1938-39
Clark Hinkle, Green Bay, 1940-41
Cliff Patton, Philadelphia, 1948-49
Gino Cappelletti, Boston, 1963-64
Jim Turner, N.Y. Jets, 1968-69
Fred Cox, Minnesota, 1969-70
Mark Moseley, Washington, 1976-77
Chip Lohmiller, Washington, 1991-92
Pete Stoyanovich, Miami, 1991-92

**Most Field Goals Attempted, Career**
637 George Blanda, Chi. Bears, 1949, 1950-58; Baltimore, 1950; Houston, 1960-66; Oakland, 1967-75
558 Jan Stenerud, Kansas City, 1967-79; Green Bay, 1980-83; Minnesota, 1984-85
488 Jim Turner, N.Y. Jets, 1964-70; Denver, 1971-79

**Most Field Goals Attempted, Season**
49 Bruce Gossett, Los Angeles, 1966
Curt Knight, Washington, 1971
48 Chester Marcol, Green Bay, 1972
47 Jim Turner, N.Y. Jets, 1969
David Ray, Los Angeles, 1973
Mark Moseley, Washington, 1983

**Most Field Goals Attempted, Game**
9 Jim Bakken, St. Louis vs. Pittsburgh, Sept. 24, 1967
8 Lou Michaels, Pittsburgh vs. St. Louis, Dec. 2, 1962
Garo Yepremian, Detroit vs. Minnesota, Nov. 13, 1966
Jim Turner, N.Y. Jets vs. Buffalo, Nov. 3, 1968
7 By many players

**Most Field Goals, Career**
373 Jan Stenerud, Kansas City, 1967-79; Green Bay, 1980-83; Minnesota, 1984-85
335 George Blanda, Chi. Bears, 1949, 1950-58; Baltimore, 1950; Houston, 1960-66; Oakland, 1967-75
329 Nick Lowery, New England, 1978; Kansas City, 1980-93

**Most Field Goals, Season**
35 Ali Haji-Sheikh, N.Y. Giants, 1983
Jeff Jaeger, L.A. Raiders, 1993
34 Jim Turner, N.Y. Jets, 1968
Nick Lowery, Kansas City, 1990
Jason Hanson, Detroit, 1993
33 Chester Marcol, Green Bay, 1972
Mark Moseley, Washington, 1983
Gary Anderson, Pittsburgh, 1985

**Most Field Goals, Rookie, Season**
35 Ali Haji-Sheikh, N.Y. Giants, 1983
33 Chester Marcol, Green Bay, 1972
31 Kevin Butler, Chicago, 1985

**Most Field Goals, Game**
7 Jim Bakken, St. Louis vs. Pittsburgh, Sept. 24, 1967
Rich Karlis, Minnesota vs. L.A. Rams, Nov. 5, 1989 (OT)
6 Gino Cappelletti, Boston vs. Denver, Oct. 4, 1964
Garo Yepremian, Detroit vs. Minnesota, Nov. 13, 1966
Jim Turner, N.Y. Jets vs. Buffalo, Nov. 3, 1968
Tom Dempsey, Philadelphia vs. Houston, Nov. 12, 1972
Bobby Howfield, N.Y. Jets vs. New Orleans, Dec. 3, 1972
Jim Bakken, St. Louis vs. Atlanta, Dec. 9, 1973
Joe Danelo, N.Y. Giants vs. Seattle, Oct. 18, 1981
Ray Wersching, San Francisco vs. New Orleans, Oct. 16, 1983
Gary Anderson, Pittsburgh vs. Denver, Oct. 23, 1988
John Carney, San Diego vs. Seattle, Sept. 5, 1993
John Carney, San Diego vs. Houston, Sept. 19, 1993
5 By many players

**Most Field Goals, One Quarter**
4 Garo Yepremian, Detroit vs. Minnesota, Nov. 13, 1966 (second quarter)
Curt Knight, Washington vs. N.Y. Giants, Nov. 15, 1970 (second quarter)
Roger Ruzek, Dallas vs. N.Y. Giants, Nov. 2, 1987 (fourth quarter)
3 By many players

**Most Consecutive Games Scoring Field Goals**
31 Fred Cox, Minnesota, 1968-70
28 Jim Turner, N.Y. Jets, 1970; Denver, 1971-72
Chip Lohmiller, Washington, 1988-90
23 Morten Andersen, New Orleans, 1986-88

**Most Consecutive Field Goals**
29 John Carney, San Diego, 1992-93
26 Norm Johnson, Atlanta, 1992-93
25 Morten Andersen, New Orleans, 1992-93

**Longest Field Goal**
63 Tom Dempsey, New Orleans vs. Detroit, Nov. 8, 1970
60 Steve Cox, Cleveland vs. Cincinnati, Oct. 21, 1984
Morten Andersen, New Orleans vs. Chicago, Oct. 27, 1991
59 Tony Franklin, Philadelphia vs. Dallas, Nov. 12, 1979
Pete Stoyanovich, Miami vs. N.Y. Jets, Nov. 12, 1989
Steve Christie, Buffalo vs. Miami, Sept. 26, 1993

**Highest Field Goal Percentage, Career (100 field goals)**
80.05 Nick Lowery, New England, 1978; Kansas City, 1980-93 (411-329)
79.62 Pete Stoyanovich, Miami, 1989-93 (157-125)
78.48 David Treadwell, Denver, 1989-92; N.Y. Giants, 1993 (158-124)

**Highest Field Goal Percentage, Season (Qualifiers)**
100.00 Tony Zendejas, L.A. Rams, 1991 (17-17)
96.30 Norm Johnson, Atlanta, 1993 (27-26)
95.24 Mark Moseley, Washington, 1982 (21-20)
Eddie Murray, Detroit, 1988 (21-20)
Eddie Murray, Detroit, 1989 (21-20)

**Most Field Goals, No Misses, Game**
7 Rich Karlis, Minnesota vs. L.A. Rams, Nov. 5, 1989 (OT)
6 Gino Cappelletti, Boston vs. Denver, Oct. 4, 1964
Joe Danelo, N.Y. Giants vs. Seattle, Oct. 18, 1981
Ray Wersching, San Francisco vs. New Orleans, Oct. 16, 1983
Gary Anderson, Pittsburgh vs. Denver, Oct. 23, 1988
John Carney, San Diego vs. Seattle, Sept. 5, 1993
John Carney, San Diego vs. Houston, Sept. 19, 1993
5 By many players

**Most Field Goals, 50 or More Yards, Career**
22 Morten Andersen, New Orleans, 1982-93
20 Nick Lowery, New England, 1978; Kansas City, 1980-93
Eddie Murray, Detroit, 1980-91; Kansas City, 1992; Tampa Bay, 1992; Dallas, 1993
17 Jan Stenerud, Kansas City, 1967-79; Green Bay, 1980-83; Minnesota, 1984-85
Norm Johnson, Seattle, 1982-90; Atlanta, 1991-93
Tony Zendejas, Houston, 1985-90; L.A. Rams, 1991-93

**Most Field Goals, 50 or More Yards, Season**
6 Dean Biasucci, Indianapolis, 1988
Chris Jacke, Green Bay, 1993
Tony Zendejas, L.A. Rams, 1993
5 Fred Steinfort, Denver, 1980
Norm Johnson, Seattle, 1986

Kevin Butler, Chicago, 1993
4 By many players

**Most Field Goals, 50 or More Yards, Game**

2 Jim Martin, Detroit vs. Baltimore, Oct. 23, 1960
Tom Dempsey, New Orleans vs. Los Angeles, Dec. 6, 1970
Chris Bahr, Cincinnati vs. Houston, Sept. 23, 1979
Nick Lowery, Kansas City vs. Seattle, Sept. 14, 1980
Mark Moseley, Washington vs. New Orleans, Oct. 26, 1980
Fred Steinfort, Denver vs. Seattle, Dec. 21, 1980
Mick Luckhurst, Atlanta vs. Denver, Dec. 5, 1982
Morten Andersen, New Orleans vs. Philadelphia, Dec. 11, 1983
Mick Luckhurst, Atlanta vs. L.A. Rams, Oct. 7, 1984
Paul McFadden, Philadelphia vs. Detroit, Nov. 4, 1984
Nick Lowery, Kansas City vs. New Orleans, Sept. 8, 1985
Pat Leahy, N.Y. Jets vs. New England, Oct. 20, 1985
Tony Zendejas, Houston vs. San Diego, Nov. 24, 1985
Norm Johnson, Seattle vs. L.A. Raiders, Dec. 8, 1986
Raul Allegre, N.Y. Giants vs. Philadelphia, Nov. 15, 1987
Nick Lowery, Kansas City vs. Detroit, Nov. 26, 1987
Dean Biasucci, Indianapolis vs. Miami, Sept. 25, 1988
Paul McFadden, Atlanta vs. Buffalo, Nov. 5, 1989
Kevin Butler, Chicago vs. Minnesota, Sept. 23, 1990
Kevin Butler, Chicago vs. Green Bay, Oct. 7, 1990
Chip Lohmiller, Washington vs. Indianapolis, Dec. 22, 1990
Chip Lohmiller, Washington vs. Dallas, Sept. 9, 1991
John Kasay, Seattle vs. San Diego, October 27, 1991
Fuad Reveiz, Minnesota vs. Tampa Bay, Dec. 8, 1991
John Carney, San Diego vs. Seattle, Sept. 5, 1993
Tony Zendejas, L.A. Rams vs. Pittsburgh, Sept. 12, 1993
Doug Pelfrey, Cincinnati vs. Houston, Oct. 24, 1993
Eddie Murray, Dallas vs. Minnesota, Dec. 12, 1993
Greg Davis, Phoenix vs. Seattle, Dec. 19, 1993 (OT)

### SAFETIES

**Most Safeties, Career**

4 Ted Hendricks, Baltimore, 1969-73; Green Bay, 1974; Oakland, 1975-81; L.A. Raiders, 1982-83
Doug English, Detroit, 1975-79, 1981-85
3 Bill McPeak, Pittsburgh, 1949-57
Charlie Krueger, San Francisco, 1959-73
Ernie Stautner, Pittsburgh, 1950-63
Jim Katcavage, N.Y. Giants, 1956-68
Roger Brown, Detroit, 1960-66; Los Angeles, 1967-69
Bruce Maher, Detroit, 1960-67; N.Y. Giants, 1968-69
Ron McDole, St. Louis, 1961; Houston, 1962; Buffalo, 1963-70; Washington, 1971-78
Alan Page, Minnesota, 1967-78; Chicago, 1979-81
Lyle Alzado, Denver, 1971-78; Cleveland, 1979-81; L.A. Raiders, 1982-85
Rulon Jones, Denver, 1980-88
Steve McMichael, New England, 1980; Chicago, 1981-93
Kevin Greene, L.A. Rams, 1985-92; Pittsburgh, 1993
Burt Grossman, San Diego, 1989-93
2 By many players

**Most Safeties, Season**

2 Tom Nash, Green Bay, 1932
Roger Brown, Detroit, 1962
Ron McDole, Buffalo, 1964
Alan Page, Minnesota, 1971
Fred Dryer, Los Angeles, 1973
Benny Barnes, Dallas, 1973
James Young, Houston, 1977
Tom Hannon, Minnesota, 1981
Doug English, Detroit, 1983
Don Blackmon, New England, 1985
Tim Harris, Green Bay, 1988
Brian Jordan, Atlanta, 1991
Burt Grossman, San Diego, 1992
Rod Stephens, Seattle, 1993

**Most Safeties, Game**

2 Fred Dryer, Los Angeles vs. Green Bay, Oct. 21, 1973

## RUSHING

**Most Seasons Leading League**

8 Jim Brown, Cleveland, 1957-61, 1963-65
4 Steve Van Buren, Philadelphia, 1945, 1947-49
O.J. Simpson, Buffalo, 1972-73, 1975-76
Eric Dickerson, L.A. Rams, 1983-84, 1986; Indianapolis, 1988
3 Earl Campbell, Houston, 1978-80
Emmitt Smith, Dallas, 1991-93

**Most Consecutive Seasons Leading League**

5 Jim Brown, Cleveland, 1957-61
3 Steve Van Buren, Philadelphia, 1947-49
Jim Brown, Cleveland, 1963-65
Earl Campbell, Houston, 1978-80
Emmitt Smith, Dallas, 1991-93
2 Bill Paschal, N.Y. Giants, 1943-44
Joe Perry, San Francisco, 1953-54
Jim Nance, Boston, 1966-67
Leroy Kelly, Cleveland, 1967-68
O.J. Simpson, Buffalo, 1972-73; 1975-76
Eric Dickerson, L.A. Rams, 1983-84

### ATTEMPTS

**Most Seasons Leading League**

6 Jim Brown, Cleveland, 1958-59, 1961, 1963-65
4 Steve Van Buren, Philadelphia, 1947-50
Walter Payton, Chicago, 1976-79
3 Cookie Gilchrist, Buffalo, 1963-64; Denver, 1965
Jim Nance, Boston, 1966-67, 1969
O.J. Simpson, Buffalo, 1973-75
Eric Dickerson, L.A. Rams, 1983, 1986; Indianapolis, 1988

**Most Consecutive Seasons Leading League**

4 Steve Van Buren, Philadelphia, 1947-50
Walter Payton, Chicago, 1976-79
3 Jim Brown, Cleveland, 1963-65
Cookie Gilchrist, Buffalo, 1963-64; Denver, 1965
O.J. Simpson, Buffalo, 1973-75
2 By many players

**Most Attempts, Career**

3,838 Walter Payton, Chicago, 1975-87
2,996 Eric Dickerson, L.A. Rams, 1983-87; Indianapolis, 1987-91; L.A. Raiders, 1992; Atlanta, 1993
2,949 Franco Harris, Pittsburgh, 1972-83; Seattle, 1984

**Most Attempts, Season**

407 James Wilder, Tampa Bay, 1984
404 Eric Dickerson, L.A. Rams, 1986
397 Gerald Riggs, Atlanta, 1985

**Most Attempts, Rookie, Season**

390 Eric Dickerson, L.A. Rams, 1983
378 George Rogers, New Orleans, 1981
335 Curt Warner, Seattle, 1983

**Most Attempts, Game**

45 Jamie Morris, Washington vs. Cincinnati, Dec. 17, 1988 (OT)
43 Butch Woolfolk, N.Y. Giants vs. Philadelphia, Nov. 20, 1983
James Wilder, Tampa Bay vs. Green Bay, Sept. 30, 1984 (OT)
42 James Wilder, Tampa Bay vs. Pittsburgh, Oct. 30, 1983

### YARDS GAINED

**Most Yards Gained, Career**

16,726 Walter Payton, Chicago, 1975-87
13,259 Eric Dickerson, L.A. Rams, 1983-87; Indianapolis, 1987-91; L.A. Raiders, 1992; Atlanta, 1993
12,739 Tony Dorsett, Dallas, 1977-87; Denver, 1988

**Most Seasons, 1,000 or More Yards Rushing**

10 Walter Payton, Chicago, 1976-81, 1983-86
8 Franco Harris, Pittsburgh, 1972, 1974-79, 1983
Tony Dorsett, Dallas, 1977-81, 1983-85
7 Jim Brown, Cleveland, 1958-61, 1963-65
Eric Dickerson, L.A. Rams, 1983-86; L.A. Rams-Indianapolis, 1987; Indianapolis, 1988-89

**Most Consecutive Seasons, 1,000 or More Yards Rushing**

7 Eric Dickerson, L.A. Rams, 1983-86; L.A. Rams-Indianapolis, 1987; Indianapolis, 1988-89
6 Franco Harris, Pittsburgh, 1974-79
Walter Payton, Chicago, 1976-81
5 Jim Taylor, Green Bay, 1960-64
O.J. Simpson, Buffalo, 1972-76
Tony Dorsett, Dallas, 1977-81
Barry Sanders, Detroit, 1989-93
Thurman Thomas, Buffalo, 1989-93

**Most Yards Gained, Season**

2,105 Eric Dickerson, L.A. Rams, 1984
2,003 O.J. Simpson, Buffalo, 1973
1,934 Earl Campbell, Houston, 1980

**Most Yards Gained, Rookie, Season**

1,808 Eric Dickerson, L.A. Rams, 1983
1,674 George Rogers, New Orleans, 1981
1,605 Ottis Anderson, St. Louis, 1979

**Most Yards Gained, Game**

275 Walter Payton, Chicago vs. Minnesota, Nov. 20, 1977
273 O.J. Simpson, Buffalo vs. Detroit, Nov. 25, 1976
250 O.J. Simpson, Buffalo vs. New England, Sept. 16, 1973

**Most Games, 200 or More Yards Rushing, Career**

6 O.J. Simpson, Buffalo, 1969-77; San Francisco, 1978-79
4 Jim Brown, Cleveland, 1957-65

Earl Campbell, Houston, 1978-84; New Orleans, 1984-85
3 Eric Dickerson, L.A. Rams, 1983-87; Indianapolis, 1987-91; L.A. Raiders, 1992; Atlanta, 1993
Greg Bell, Buffalo, 1984-87; L.A. Rams, 1987-89; L.A. Raiders, 1990

**Most Games, 200 or More Yards Rushing, Season**
4 Earl Campbell, Houston, 1980
3 O.J. Simpson, Buffalo, 1973
2 Jim Brown, Cleveland, 1963
O.J. Simpson, Buffalo, 1976
Walter Payton, Chicago, 1977
Eric Dickerson, L.A. Rams, 1984
Greg Bell, L.A. Rams, 1989

**Most Consecutive Games, 200 or More Yards Rushing**
2 O.J. Simpson, Buffalo, 1973, 1976
Earl Campbell, Houston, 1980

**Most Games, 100 or More Yards Rushing, Career**
77 Walter Payton, Chicago, 1975-87
64 Eric Dickerson, L.A. Rams, 1983-87; Indianapolis, 1987-91; L.A. Raiders, 1992; Atlanta, 1993
58 Jim Brown, Cleveland, 1957-65

**Most Games, 100 or More Yards Rushing, Season**
12 Eric Dickerson, L.A. Rams, 1984
Barry Foster, Pittsburgh, 1992
11 O.J. Simpson, Buffalo, 1973
Earl Campbell, Houston, 1979
Marcus Allen, L.A. Raiders, 1985
Eric Dickerson, L.A. Rams, 1986
10 Walter Payton, Chicago, 1977, 1985
Earl Campbell, Houston, 1980

**Most Consecutive Games, 100 or More Yards Rushing**
11 Marcus Allen, L.A. Raiders, 1985-86
9 Walter Payton, Chicago, 1985
7 O.J. Simpson, Buffalo, 1972-73
Earl Campbell, Houston, 1979

**Longest Run From Scrimmage**
99 Tony Dorsett, Dallas vs. Minnesota, Jan. 3, 1983 (TD)
97 Andy Uram, Green Bay vs. Chi. Cardinals, Oct. 8, 1939 (TD)
Bob Gage, Pittsburgh vs. Chi. Bears, Dec. 4, 1949 (TD)
96 Jim Spavital, Baltimore vs. Green Bay, Nov. 5, 1950 (TD)
Bob Hoernschemeyer, Detroit vs. N.Y. Yanks, Nov. 23, 1950 (TD)

## AVERAGE GAIN

**Highest Average Gain, Career (750 attempts)**
5.22 Jim Brown, Cleveland, 1957-65 (2,359-12,312)
5.14 Eugene (Mercury) Morris, Miami, 1969-75; San Diego, 1976 (804-4,133)
5.00 Gale Sayers, Chicago, 1965-71 (991-4,956)

**Highest Average Gain, Season (Qualifiers)**
8.44 Beattie Feathers, Chi. Bears, 1934 (119-1,004)
7.98 Randall Cunningham, Philadelphia 1990 (118-942)
6.87 Bobby Douglass, Chicago, 1972 (141-968)

**Highest Average Gain, Game (10 attempts)**
17.09 Marion Motley, Cleveland vs. Pittsburgh, Oct. 29, 1950 (11-188)
16.70 Bill Grimes, Green Bay vs. N.Y. Yanks, Oct. 8, 1950 (10-167)
16.57 Bobby Mitchell, Cleveland vs. Washington, Nov. 15, 1959 (14-232)

## TOUCHDOWNS

**Most Seasons Leading League**
5 Jim Brown, Cleveland, 1957-59, 1963, 1965
4 Steve Van Buren, Philadelphia, 1945, 1947-49
3 Abner Haynes, Dall. Texans, 1960-62
Cookie Gilchrist, Buffalo, 1962-64
Paul Lowe, L.A. Chargers, 1960; San Diego, 1961, 1965
Leroy Kelly, Cleveland, 1966-68

**Most Consecutive Seasons Leading League**
3 Steve Van Buren, Philadelphia, 1947-49
Jim Brown, Cleveland, 1957-59
Abner Haynes, Dall. Texans, 1960-62
Cookie Gilchrist, Buffalo, 1962-64
Leroy Kelly, Cleveland, 1966-68

**Most Touchdowns, Career**
110 Walter Payton, Chicago, 1975-87
106 Jim Brown, Cleveland, 1957-65
104 John Riggins, N.Y. Jets, 1971-75; Washington, 1976-79, 1981-85

**Most Touchdowns, Season**
24 John Riggins, Washington, 1983
21 Joe Morris, N.Y. Giants, 1985
19 Jim Taylor, Green Bay, 1962
Earl Campbell, Houston, 1979
Chuck Muncie, San Diego, 1981

**Most Touchdowns, Rookie, Season**
18 Eric Dickerson, L.A. Rams, 1983
15 Ickey Woods, Cincinnati, 1988
14 Gale Sayers, Chicago, 1965
Barry Sanders, Detroit, 1989

**Most Touchdowns, Game**
6 Ernie Nevers, Chi. Cardinals vs. Chi. Bears, Nov. 28, 1929
5 Jim Brown, Cleveland vs. Baltimore, Nov. 1, 1959
Cookie Gilchrist, Buffalo vs. N.Y. Jets, Dec. 8, 1963
4 By many players

**Most Consecutive Games Rushing for Touchdowns**
13 John Riggins, Washington, 1982-83
George Rogers, Washington, 1985-86
11 Lenny Moore, Baltimore, 1963-64
10 Greg Bell, L.A. Rams, 1988-89

## PASSING

**Most Seasons Leading League**
6 Sammy Baugh, Washington, 1937, 1940, 1943, 1945, 1947, 1949
4 Len Dawson, Dall. Texans; 1962; Kansas City, 1964, 1966, 1968
Roger Staubach, Dallas, 1971, 1973, 1978-79
Ken Anderson, Cincinnati, 1974-75, 1981-82
3 Arnie Herber, Green Bay, 1932, 1934, 1936
Norm Van Brocklin, Los Angeles, 1950, 1952, 1954
Bart Starr, Green Bay, 1962, 1964, 1966
Steve Young, San Francisco, 1991-93

**Most Consecutive Seasons Leading League**
3 Steve Young, San Francisco, 1991-93
2 Cecil Isbell, Green Bay, 1941-42
Milt Plum, Cleveland, 1960-61
Ken Anderson, Cincinnati, 1974-75, 1981-82
Roger Staubach, Dallas, 1978-79

## PASS RATING

**Highest Pass Rating, Career (1,500 attempts)**
93.1 Joe Montana, San Francisco, 1979-90, 1992; Kansas City, 1993
93.0 Steve Young, Tampa Bay, 1985-86; San Francisco, 1987-93
88.1 Dan Marino, Miami, 1983-93

**Highest Pass Rating, Season (Qualifiers)**
112.4 Joe Montana, San Francisco, 1989
110.4 Milt Plum, Cleveland, 1960
109.9 Sammy Baugh, Washington, 1945

**Highest Pass Rating, Rookie, Season (Qualifiers)**
96.0 Dan Marino, Miami, 1983
88.2 Greg Cook, Cincinnati, 1969
84.0 Charlie Conerly, N.Y. Giants, 1948

## ATTEMPTS

**Most Seasons Leading League**
4 Sammy Baugh, Washington, 1937, 1943, 1947-48
Johnny Unitas, Baltimore, 1957, 1959-61
George Blanda, Chi. Bears, 1953; Houston, 1963-65
Dan Marino, Miami, 1984, 1986, 1988, 1992
3 Arnie Herber, Green Bay, 1932, 1934, 1936
Sonny Jurgensen, Washington, 1966-67, 1969
2 By many players

**Most Consecutive Seasons Leading League**
3 Johnny Unitas, Baltimore, 1959-61
George Blanda, Houston, 1963-65
2 By many players

**Most Passes Attempted, Career**
6,467 Fran Tarkenton, Minnesota, 1961-66, 1972-78; N.Y. Giants, 1967-71
5,604 Dan Fouts, San Diego, 1973-87
5,434 Dan Marino, Miami, 1983-93

**Most Passes Attempted, Season**
655 Warren Moon, Houston, 1991
623 Dan Marino, Miami, 1986
609 Dan Fouts, San Diego, 1981

**Most Passes Attempted, Rookie, Season**
486 Rick Mirer, Seattle, 1993
439 Jim Zorn, Seattle, 1976
429 Drew Bledsoe, New England, 1993

**Most Passes Attempted, Game**
68 George Blanda, Houston vs. Buffalo, Nov. 1, 1964
66 Chris Miller, Atlanta vs. Detroit, Dec. 24, 1989
63 Rich Gannon, Minnesota vs. New England, Oct. 20, 1991 (OT)

## COMPLETIONS

**Most Seasons Leading League**
5 Sammy Baugh, Washington, 1937, 1943, 1945, 1947-48
Dan Marino, Miami, 1984-86, 1988, 1992
4 George Blanda, Chi. Bears, 1953; Houston, 1963-65
Sonny Jurgensen, Philadelphia, 1961; Washington, 1966-67, 1969
3 Arnie Herber, Green Bay, 1932, 1934, 1936
Johnny Unitas, Baltimore, 1959-60, 1963
John Brodie, San Francisco, 1965, 1968, 1970

Fran Tarkenton, Minnesota, 1975-76, 1978

**Most Consecutive Seasons Leading League**

3 George Blanda, Houston, 1963-65
Dan Marino, Miami, 1984-86
2 By many players

**Most Passes Completed, Career**

3,686 Fran Tarkenton, Minnesota, 1961-66, 1972-78; N.Y. Giants, 1967-71
3,297 Dan Fouts, San Diego, 1973-87
3,219 Dan Marino, Miami, 1983-93

**Most Passes Completed, Season**

404 Warren Moon, Hosuton, 1991
378 Dan Marino, Miami, 1986
362 Dan Marino, Miami, 1984
Warren Moon, Houston, 1990

**Most Passes Completed, Rookie, Season**

274 Rick Mirer, Seattle, 1993
214 Drew Bledsoe, New England, 1993
208 Jim Zorn, Seattle, 1976

**Most Passes Completed, Game**

42 Richard Todd, N.Y. Jets vs. San Francisco, Sept. 21, 1980
41 Warren Moon, Houston vs. Dallas, Nov. 10, 1991 (OT)
40 Ken Anderson, Cincinnati vs. San Diego, Dec. 20, 1982
Phil Simms, N.Y. Giants vs. Cincinnati, Oct. 13, 1985

**Most Consecutive Passes Completed**

22 Joe Montana, San Francisco vs. Cleveland (5), Nov. 29, 1987; vs. Green Bay (17), Dec. 6, 1987
20 Ken Anderson, Cincinnati vs. Houston, Jan. 2, 1983
18 Steve DeBerg, Denver vs. L.A. Rams (17), Dec. 12, 1982; vs. Kansas City (1), Dec. 19, 1982
Lynn Dickey, Green Bay vs. Houston, Sept. 4, 1983
Joe Montana, San Francisco vs. L.A. Rams (13), Oct. 28, 1984; vs. Cincinnati (5), Nov. 4, 1984
Don Majkowski, Green Bay vs. New Orleans, Sept. 18, 1989
Boomer Esiason, N.Y. Jets vs. Miami (5), Sept. 12, 1993; vs. New England (13), Sept. 26, 1993

## COMPLETION PERCENTAGE

**Most Seasons Leading League**

8 Len Dawson, Dall. Texans, 1962; Kansas City, 1964-69, 1975
7 Sammy Baugh, Washington, 1940, 1942-43, 1945, 1947-49
5 Joe Montana, San Francisco, 1980-81, 1985, 1987, 1989

**Most Consecutive Seasons Leading League**

6 Len Dawson, Kansas City, 1964-69
3 Sammy Baugh, Washington, 1947-49
Otto Graham, Cleveland, 1953-55
Milt Plum, Cleveland, 1959-61
2 By many players

**Highest Completion Percentage, Career (1,500 attempts)**

63.50 Joe Montana, San Francisco, 1979-90, 1992; Kansas City, 1993 (4,898-3,110)
62.09 Steve Young, Tampa Bay, 1985-86; San Francisco, 1987-93 (1,968-1,222)
62.03 Troy Aikman, Dallas, 1989-93 (1,920-1,191)

**Highest Completion Percentage, Season (Qualifiers)**

70.55 Ken Anderson, Cincinnati, 1982 (309-218)
70.33 Sammy Baugh, Washington, 1945 (182-128)
70.21 Joe Montana, San Francisco, 1989 (386-271)

**Highest Completion Percentage, Rookie, Season (Qualifiers)**

58.45 Dan Marino, Miami, 1983 (296-173)
57.14 Jim McMahon, Chicago, 1982 (210-120)
56.38 Rick Mirer, Seattle, 1993 (486-274)

**Highest Completion Percentage, Game (20 attempts)**

91.30 Vinny Testaverde, Cleveland vs. L.A. Rams, Dec. 26, 1993 (23-21)
90.91 Ken Anderson, Cincinnati vs. Pittsburgh, Nov. 10, 1974 (22-20)
90.48 Lynn Dickey, Green Bay vs. New Orleans, Dec. 13, 1981 (21-19)

## YARDS GAINED

**Most Seasons Leading League**

5 Sonny Jurgensen, Philadelphia, 1961-62; Washington, 1966-67, 1969
Dan Marino, Miami, 1984-86, 1988, 1992
4 Sammy Baugh, Washington, 1937, 1940, 1947-48
Johnny Unitas, Baltimore, 1957, 1959-60, 1963
Dan Fouts, San Diego, 1979-82
3 Arnie Herber, Green Bay, 1932, 1934, 1936
Sid Luckman, Chi. Bears, 1943, 1945-46
John Brodie, San Francisco, 1965, 1968, 1970
John Hadl, San Diego, 1965, 1968, 1971
Joe Namath, N.Y. Jets, 1966-67, 1972

**Most Consecutive Seasons Leading League**

4 Dan Fouts, San Diego, 1979-82
3 Dan Marino, Miami, 1984-86
2 By many players

**Most Yards Gained, Career**

47,003 Fran Tarkenton, Minnesota, 1961-66, 1972-78; N.Y. Giants, 1967-71
43,040 Dan Fouts, San Diego, 1973-87
40,720 Dan Marino, Miami, 1983-93

**Most Seasons, 3,000 or More Yards Passing**

9 Dan Marino, Miami, 1984-92
8 John Elway, Denver, 1985-91, 1993
7 Joe Montana, San Francisco, 1981, 1983-85, 1987, 1989-90
Boomer Esiason, Cincinnati, 1985-90; N.Y. Jets, 1993

**Most Yards Gained, Season**

5,084 Dan Marino, Miami, 1984
4,802 Dan Fouts, San Diego, 1981
4,746 Dan Marino, Miami, 1986

**Most Yards Gained, Rookie, Season**

2,833 Rick Mirer, Seattle, 1993
2,571 Jim Zorn, Seattle, 1976
2,507 Dennis Shaw, Buffalo, 1970

**Most Yards Gained, Game**

554 Norm Van Brocklin, Los Angeles vs. N.Y. Yanks, Sept. 28, 1951
527 Warren Moon, Houston vs. Kansas City, Dec. 16, 1990
521 Dan Marino, Miami vs. N.Y. Jets, Oct. 23, 1988

**Most Games, 400 or More Yards Passing, Career**

10 Dan Marino, Miami, 1983-93
7 Joe Montana, San Francisco, 1979-90, 1992; Kansas City, 1993
6 Dan Fouts, San Diego, 1973-87

**Most Games, 400 or More Yards Passing, Season**

4 Dan Marino, Miami, 1984
3 Dan Marino, Miami, 1986
2 George Blanda, Houston, 1961
Sonny Jurgensen, Philadelphia, 1961
Joe Namath, N.Y. Jets, 1972
Dan Fouts, San Diego, 1982
Dan Fouts, San Diego, 1985
Phil Simms, N.Y. Giants, 1985
Ken O'Brien, N.Y. Jets, 1986
Bernie Kosar, Cleveland, 1986
Dan Marino, Miami, 1988
Randall Cunningham, Philadelphia, 1989
Joe Montana, San Francisco, 1989
Joe Montana, San Francisco, 1990
Warren Moon, Houston, 1991

**Most Consecutive Games, 400 or More Yards Passing**

2 Dan Fouts, San Diego, 1982
Dan Marino, Miami, 1984
Phil Simms, N.Y. Giants, 1985

**Most Games, 300 or More Yards Passing, Career**

51 Dan Fouts, San Diego, 1973-87
44 Dan Marino, Miami, 1983-93
38 Warren Moon, Houston, 1984-93

**Most Games, 300 or More Yards Passing, Season**

9 Dan Marino, Miami, 1984
Warren Moon, Houston, 1990
8 Dan Fouts, San Diego, 1980
7 Dan Fouts, San Diego, 1981
Bill Kenney, Kansas City, 1983
Neil Lomax, St. Louis, 1984
Dan Fouts, San Diego, 1985

**Most Consecutive Games, 300 or More Yards Passing, Season**

5 Joe Montana, San Francisco, 1982
4 Dan Fouts, San Diego, 1979
Bill Kenney, Kansas City, 1983
Joe Montana, San Francisco, 1990
Warren Moon, Houston, 1990
3 By many players

**Longest Pass Completion (All TDs except as noted)**

99 Frank Filchock (to Farkas), Washington vs. Pittsburgh, Oct. 15, 1939
George Izo (to Mitchell), Washington vs. Cleveland, Sept. 15, 1963
Karl Sweetan (to Studstill), Detroit vs. Baltimore, Oct. 16, 1966
Sonny Jurgensen (to Allen), Washington vs. Chicago, Sept. 15, 1968
Jim Plunkett (to Branch), L.A. Raiders vs. Washington, Oct. 2, 1983
Ron Jaworski (to Quick), Philadelphia vs. Atlanta, Nov. 10, 1985
98 Doug Russell (to Tinsley), Chi. Cardinals vs. Cleveland, Nov. 27, 1938
Ogden Compton (to Lane), Chi. Cardinals vs. Green Bay, Nov. 13, 1955
Bill Wade (to Farrington), Chicago Bears vs. Detroit, Oct. 8, 1961
Jacky Lee (to Dewveall), Houston vs. San Diego, Nov. 25, 1962
Earl Morrall (to Jones), N.Y. Giants vs. Pittsburgh, Sept. 11, 1966
Jim Hart (to Moore), St. Louis vs. Los Angeles, Dec. 10, 1972 (no TD)
Bobby Hebert (to Haynes), Atlanta vs. New Orleans, Sept. 12, 1993
97 Pat Coffee (to Tinsley), Chi. Cardinals vs. Chi. Bears, Dec. 5, 1937
Bobby Layne (to Box), Detroit vs. Green Bay, Nov. 26, 1953
George Shaw (to Tarr), Denver vs. Boston, Sept. 21, 1962
Bernie Kosar (to Slaughter), Cleveland vs. Chicago, Oct. 23, 1989
Steve Young (to Taylor), San Francisco vs. Atlanta, Nov. 3, 1991

**AVERAGE GAIN**

**Most Seasons Leading League**

7 Sid Luckman, Chi. Bears, 1939-43, 1946-47
3 Arnie Herber, Green Bay, 1932, 1934, 1936
Norm Van Brocklin, Los Angeles, 1950, 1952, 1954
Len Dawson, Dall. Texans, 1962; Kansas City, 1966, 1968
Bart Starr, Green Bay, 1966-68
Steve Young, San Francisco, 1991-93

**Most Consecutive Seasons Leading League**

5 Sid Luckman, Chi. Bears, 1939-43
3 Bart Starr, Green Bay, 1966-68
Steve Young, San Francisco, 1991-93
2 Bernie Masterson, Chi. Bears, 1937-38
Sid Luckman, Chi. Bears, 1946-47
Johnny Unitas, Baltimore, 1964-65
Terry Bradshaw, Pittsburgh, 1977-78
Steve Grogan, New England, 1980-81

**Highest Average Gain, Career (1,500 attempts)**

8.63 Otto Graham, Cleveland, 1950-55 (1,565-13,499)
8.42 Sid Luckman, Chi. Bears, 1939-50 (1,744-14,686)
8.16 Norm Van Brocklin, Los Angeles, 1949-57; Philadelphia, 1958-60 (2,895-23,611)

**Highest Average Gain, Season (Qualifiers)**

11.17 Tommy O'Connell, Cleveland, 1957 (110-1,229)
10.86 Sid Luckman, Chi. Bears, 1943 (202-2,194)
10.55 Otto Graham, Cleveland, 1953 (258-2,722)

**Highest Average Gain, Rookie, Season (Qualifiers)**

9.411 Greg Cook, Cincinnati, 1969 (197-1,854)
9.409 Bob Waterfield, Cleveland, 1945 (171-1,609)
8.36 Zeke Bratkowski, Chi. Bears, 1954 (130-1,087)

**Highest Average Gain, Game (20 attempts)**

18.58 Sammy Baugh, Washington vs. Boston, Oct. 31, 1948 (24-446)
18.50 Johnny Unitas, Baltimore vs. Atlanta, Nov. 12, 1967 (20-370)
17.71 Joe Namath, N.Y. Jets vs. Baltimore, Sept. 24, 1972 (28-496)

**TOUCHDOWNS**

**Most Seasons Leading League**

4 Johnny Unitas, Baltimore, 1957-60
Len Dawson, Dall. Texans, 1962; Kansas City, 1963, 1965-66
3 Arnie Herber, Green Bay, 1932, 1934, 1936
Sid Luckman, Chi. Bears, 1943, 1945-46
Y.A. Tittle, San Francisco, 1955; N.Y. Giants, 1962-63
Dan Marino, Miami, 1984-86
2 By many players

**Most Consecutive Seasons Leading League**

4 Johnny Unitas, Baltimore, 1957-60
3 Dan Marino, Miami, 1984-86
2 By many players

**Most Touchdown Passes, Career**

342 Fran Tarkenton, Minnesota, 1961-66, 1972-78; N.Y. Giants, 1967-71
298 Dan Marino, Miami, 1983-93
290 Johnny Unitas, Baltimore, 1956-72: San Diego, 1973

**Most Touchdown Passes, Season**

48 Dan Marino, Miami, 1984
44 Dan Marino, Miami, 1986
36 George Blanda, Houston, 1961
Y.A. Tittle, N.Y. Giants, 1963

**Most Touchdown Passes, Rookie, Season**

22 Charlie Conerly, N.Y. Giants, 1948
20 Dan Marino, Miami, 1983
19 Jim Plunkett, New England, 1971

**Most Touchdown Passes, Game**

7 Sid Luckman, Chi. Bears vs. N.Y. Giants, Nov. 14, 1943
Adrian Burk, Philadelphia vs. Washington, Oct. 17, 1954
George Blanda, Houston vs. N.Y. Titans, Nov. 19, 1961
Y.A. Tittle, N.Y. Giants vs. Washington, Oct. 28, 1962
Joe Kapp, Minnesota vs. Baltimore, Sept. 28, 1969
6 By many players. Last time: Mark Rypien, Washington vs. Atlanta, Nov. 10, 1991

**Most Games, Four or More Touchdown Passes, Career**

17 Johnny Unitas, Baltimore, 1956-72; San Diego, 1973
Dan Marino, Miami, 1983-93
13 George Blanda, Chi. Bears, 1949, 1950-58; Baltimore, 1950; Houston, 1960-66; Oakland, 1967-75
12 Sonny Jurgensen, Philadelphia, 1957-63; Washington, 1964-74
Fran Tarkenton, Minnesota, 1961-66, 1972-78; N.Y. Giants, 1967-71
Dan Fouts, San Diego, 1973-87

**Most Games, Four or More Touchdown Passes, Season**

6 Dan Marino, Miami, 1984
5 Dan Marino, Miami, 1986
4 George Blanda, Houston, 1961
Vince Ferragamo, Los Angeles, 1980

**Most Consecutive Games, Four or More Touchdown Passes**

4 Dan Marino, Miami, 1984
2 By many players

**Most Consecutive Games, Touchdown Passes**

47 Johnny Unitas, Baltimore, 1956-60
30 Dan Marino, Miami, 1985-87
28 Dave Krieg, Seattle, 1983-85

**HAD INTERCEPTED**

**Most Consecutive Passes Attempted, None Intercepted**

308 Bernie Kosar, Cleveland, 1990-91
294 Bart Starr, Green Bay, 1964-65
233 Steve DeBerg, Kansas City, 1990

**Most Passes Had Intercepted, Career**

277 George Blanda, Chi. Bears, 1949, 1950-58; Baltimore, 1950; Houston, 1960-66; Oakland, 1967-75
268 John Hadl, San Diego, 1962-72; Los Angeles, 1973-74; Green Bay, 1974-75; Houston, 1976-77
266 Fran Tarkenton, Minnesota, 1961-66, 1972-78; N.Y. Giants, 1967-71

**Most Passes Had Intercepted, Season**

42 George Blanda, Houston, 1962
35 Vinny Testaverde, Tampa Bay, 1988
34 Frank Tripucka, Denver, 1960

**Most Passes Had Intercepted, Game**

8 Jim Hardy, Chi. Cardinals vs. Philadelphia, Sept. 24, 1950
7 Parker Hall, Cleveland vs. Green Bay, Nov. 8, 1942
Frank Sinkwich, Detroit vs. Green Bay, Oct. 24, 1943
Bob Waterfield, Los Angeles vs. Green Bay, Oct. 17, 1948
Zeke Bratkowski, Chicago vs. Baltimore, Oct. 2, 1960
Tommy Wade, Pittsburgh vs. Philadelphia, Dec. 12, 1965
Ken Stabler, Oakland vs. Denver, Oct. 16, 1977
Steve DeBerg, Tampa Bay vs. San Francisco, Sept. 7, 1986
6 By many players

**Most Attempts, No Interceptions, Game**

63 Rich Gannon, Minnesota vs. New England, Oct. 20, 1991 (OT)
60 Davey O'Brien, Philadelphia vs. Washington, Dec. 1, 1940
57 Joe Montana, San Francisco vs. Atlanta, Oct. 6, 1985

**LOWEST PERCENTAGE, PASSES HAD INTERCEPTED**

**Most Seasons Leading League, Lowest Percentage, Passes Had Intercepted**

5 Sammy Baugh, Washington, 1940, 1942, 1944-45, 1947
3 Charlie Conerly, N.Y. Giants, 1950, 1956, 1959
Bart Starr, Green Bay, 1962, 1964, 1966
Roger Staubach, Dallas, 1971, 1977, 1979
Ken Anderson, Cincinnati, 1972, 1981-82
Ken O'Brien, N.Y. Jets, 1985, 1987-88
2 By many players

**Lowest Percentage, Passes Had Intercepted, Career (1,500 attempts)**

2.52 Bernie Kosar, Cleveland, 1985-93; Dallas, 1993 (3,213-81)
2.65 Joe Montana, San Francisco, 1979-90, 1992; Kansas City, 1993 (4,898-130)
2.72 Ken O'Brien, N.Y. Jets, 1984-92; Philadelphia, 1993 (3,602-98)

**Lowest Percentage, Passes Had Intercepted, Season (Qualifiers)**

0.66 Joe Ferguson, Buffalo, 1976 (151-1)
0.90 Steve DeBerg, Kansas City, 1990 (444-4)
1.16 Steve Bartkowski, Atlanta, 1983 (432-5)

**Lowest Percentage, Passes Had Intercepted, Rookie, Season (Qualifiers)**

2.03 Dan Marino, Miami, 1983 (296-6)
2.10 Gary Wood, N.Y. Giants, 1964 (143-3)
2.82 Bernie Kosar, Cleveland, 1985 (248-7)

**TIMES SACKED**

Times Sacked has been compiled since 1963.

**Most Times Sacked, Career**

483 Fran Tarkenton, Minnesota, 1961-66, 1972-78; N.Y. Giants, 1967-71
477 Phil Simms, N.Y. Giants, 1979-81, 1983-93
411 Dave Krieg, Seattle, 1980-91; Kansas City, 1992-93

**Most Times Sacked, Season**

72 Randall Cunningham, Philadelphia, 1986
62 Ken O'Brien, N.Y. Jets, 1985
61 Neil Lomax, St. Louis, 1985

**Most Times Sacked, Game**

12 Bert Jones, Baltimore vs. St. Louis, Oct. 26, 1980
Warren Moon, Houston vs. Dallas, Sept. 29, 1985
11 Charley Johnson, St. Louis vs. N.Y. Giants, Nov. 1, 1964
Bart Starr, Green Bay vs. Detroit, Nov. 7, 1965
Jack Kemp, Buffalo vs. Oakland, Oct. 15, 1967
Bob Berry, Atlanta vs. St. Louis, Nov. 24, 1968
Greg Landry, Detroit vs. Dallas, Oct. 6, 1975
Ron Jaworski, Philadelphia vs. St. Louis, Dec. 18, 1983
Paul McDonald, Cleveland vs. Kansas City, Sept. 30, 1984
Archie Manning, Minnesota vs. Chicago, Oct. 28, 1984
Steve Pelluer, Dallas vs. San Diego, Nov. 16, 1986
Randall Cunningham, Philadelphia vs. L.A. Raiders, Nov. 30, 1986 (OT)

David Norrie, N.Y. Jets vs. Dallas, Oct. 4, 1987
Troy Aikman, Dallas vs. Philadelphia, Sept. 15, 1991
Bernie Kosar, Cleveland vs. Indianapolis, Sept. 6, 1992
10 By many players

## PASS RECEIVING

**Most Seasons Leading League**
8 Don Hutson, Green Bay, 1936-37, 1939, 1941-45
5 Lionel Taylor, Denver, 1960-63, 1965
3 Tom Fears, Los Angeles, 1948-50
Pete Pihos, Philadelphia, 1953-55
Billy Wilson, San Francisco, 1954, 1956-57
Raymond Berry, Baltimore, 1958-60
Lance Alworth, San Diego, 1966, 1968-69
Sterling Sharpe, Green Bay, 1989, 1992-93

**Most Consecutive Seasons Leading League**
5 Don Hutson, Green Bay, 1941-45
4 Lionel Taylor, Denver, 1960-63
3 Tom Fears, Los Angeles, 1948-50
Pete Pihos, Philadelphia, 1953-55
Raymond Berry, Baltimore, 1958-60

**Most Pass Receptions, Career**
888 Art Monk, Washington, 1980-93
819 Steve Largent, Seattle, 1976-89
764 James Lofton, Green Bay, 1978-86; L.A. Raiders, 1987-88; Buffalo, 1989-92; L.A. Rams, 1993; Philadelphia, 1993

**Most Seasons, 50 or More Pass Receptions**
10 Steve Largent, Seattle, 1976, 1978-81, 1983-87
9 Art Monk, Washington, 1980-81, 1984-86, 1988-91
James Lofton, Green Bay, 1979-81, 1983-86; Buffalo, 1991-92
Gary Clark, Washington, 1985-92; Phoenix, 1993
8 Andre Reed, Buffalo, 1986-93
Jerry Rice, San Francisco, 1986-93

**Most Pass Receptions, Season**
112 Sterling Sharpe, Green Bay, 1993
108 Sterling Sharpe, Green Bay, 1992
106 Art Monk, Washington, 1984

**Most Pass Receptions, Rookie, Season**
83 Earl Cooper, San Francisco, 1980
81 Keith Jackson, Philadelphia, 1988
75 Terry Kirby, Miami, 1993

**Most Pass Receptions, Game**
18 Tom Fears, Los Angeles vs. Green Bay, Dec. 3, 1950
17 Clark Gaines, N.Y. Jets vs. San Francisco, Sept. 21, 1980
16 Sonny Randle, St. Louis vs. N.Y. Giants, Nov. 4, 1962

**Most Consecutive Games, Pass Receptions**
177 Steve Largent, Seattle, 1977-89
164 Art Monk, Washington, 1980-93 (current)
150 Ozzie Newsome, Cleveland, 1979-89

## YARDS GAINED

**Most Seasons Leading League**
7 Don Hutson, Green Bay, 1936, 1938-39, 1941-44
4 Jerry Rice, San Francisco, 1986, 1989-90, 1993
3 Raymond Berry, Baltimore, 1957, 1959-60
Lance Alworth, San Diego, 1965-66, 1968

**Most Consecutive Seasons Leading League**
4 Don Hutson, Green Bay, 1941-44
2 By many players

**Most Yards Gained, Career**
14,004 James Lofton, Green Bay, 1978-86; L.A. Raiders, 1987-88; Buffalo, 1989-92; L.A. Rams, 1993; Philadelphia, 1993
13,089 Steve Largent, Seattle, 1976-89
12,146 Charlie Joiner, Houston, 1969-72; Cincinnati, 1972-75; San Diego, 1976-86

**Most Seasons, 1,000 or More Yards, Pass Receiving**
8 Steve Largent, Seattle, 1978-81, 1983-86
Jerry Rice, San Francisco, 1986-93
7 Lance Alworth, San Diego, 1963-69
6 James Lofton, Green Bay, 1980-81, 1983-85; Buffalo, 1991

**Most Yards Gained, Season**
1,746 Charley Hennigan, Houston, 1961
1,602 Lance Alworth, San Diego, 1965
1,570 Jerry Rice, San Francisco, 1986

**Most Yards Gained, Rookie, Season**
1,473 Bill Groman, Houston, 1960
1,231 Bill Howton, Green Bay, 1952
1,131 Bill Brooks, Indianapolis, 1986

**Most Yards Gained, Game**
336 Willie Anderson, L.A. Rams vs. New Orleans, Nov. 26, 1989 (OT)
309 Stephone Paige, Kansas City vs. San Diego, Dec. 22, 1985
303 Jim Benton, Cleveland vs. Detroit, Nov. 22, 1945

**Most Games, 200 or More Yards Pass Receiving, Career**
5 Lance Alworth, San Diego, 1962-70; Dallas, 1971-72
4 Don Hutson, Green Bay, 1935-45
Charley Hennigan, Houston, 1960-66
3 Don Maynard, N.Y. Giants, 1958; N.Y. Jets, 1960-72; St. Louis, 1973
Wes Chandler, New Orleans, 1978-81; San Diego, 1981-87; San Francisco, 1988
Jerry Rice, San Francisco, 1985-93

**Most Games, 200 or More Yards Pass Receiving, Season**
3 Charley Hennigan, Houston, 1961
2 Don Hutson, Green Bay, 1942
Gene Roberts, N.Y. Giants, 1949
Lance Alworth, San Diego, 1963
Don Maynard, N.Y. Jets, 1968

**Most Games, 100 or More Yards Pass Receiving, Career**
50 Don Maynard, N.Y. Giants, 1958; N.Y. Jets, 1960-72; St. Louis, 1973
44 Jerry Rice, San Francisco, 1985-93
43 James Lofton, Green Bay, 1978-86; L.A. Raiders, 1987-88; Buffalo, 1989-92; L.A. Rams, 1993; Philadelphia, 1993

**Most Games, 100 or More Yards Pass Receiving, Season**
10 Charley Hennigan, Houston, 1961
9 Elroy (Crazylegs) Hirsch, Los Angeles, 1951
Bill Groman, Houston, 1960
Lance Alworth, San Diego, 1965
Don Maynard, N.Y. Jets, 1967
Stanley Morgan, New England, 1986
Mark Carrier, Tampa Bay, 1989
8 Charley Hennigan, Houston, 1964
Lance Alworth, San Diego, 1967
Mark Duper, Miami, 1986
Jerry Rice, San Francisco, 1989

**Most Consecutive Games, 100 or More Yards Pass Receiving**
7 Charley Hennigan, Houston, 1961
Bill Groman, Houston, 1961
6 Raymond Berry, Baltimore, 1960
Pat Studstill, Detroit, 1966
5 Elroy (Crazylegs) Hirsch, Los Angeles, 1951
Bob Boyd, Los Angeles, 1954
Terry Barr, Detroit, 1963
Lance Alworth, San Diego, 1966

**Longest Pass Reception (All TDs except as noted)**
99 Andy Farkas (from Filchock), Washington vs. Pittsburgh, Oct. 15, 1939
Bobby Mitchell (from Izo), Washington vs. Cleveland, Sept. 15, 1963
Pat Studstill (from Sweetan), Detroit vs. Baltimore, Oct. 16, 1966
Gerry Allen (from Jurgensen), Washington vs. Chicago, Sept. 15, 1968
Cliff Branch (from Plunkett), L.A. Raiders vs. Washington, Oct. 2, 1983
Mike Quick (from Jaworski), Philadelphia vs. Atlanta, Nov. 10, 1985
98 Gaynell Tinsley (from Russell), Chi. Cardinals vs. Cleveland, Nov. 17, 1938
Dick (Night Train) Lane (from Compton), Chi. Cardinals vs. Green Bay, Nov. 13, 1955
John Farrington (from Wade), Chicago vs. Detroit, Oct. 8, 1961
Willard Dewveall (from Lee), Houston vs. San Diego, Nov. 25, 1962
Homer Jones (from Morrall), N.Y. Giants vs. Pittsburgh, Sept. 11, 1966
Bobby Moore (from Hart), St. Louis vs. Los Angeles, Dec. 10, 1972 (no TD)
Michael Haynes (from Hebert), Atlanta vs. New Orleans, Sept. 12, 1993
97 Gaynell Tinsley (from Coffee), Chi. Cardinals vs. Chi. Bears, Dec. 5, 1937
Cloyce Box (from Layne), Detroit vs. Green Bay, Nov. 26, 1953
Jerry Tarr (from Shaw), Denver vs. Boston, Sept. 21, 1962
Webster Slaughter (from Kosar), Cleveland vs. Chicago, Oct. 23, 1989
John Taylor (from Young), San Francisco vs. Atlanta, Nov. 3, 1991

## AVERAGE GAIN

**Highest Average Gain, Career (200 receptions)**
22.26 Homer Jones, N.Y. Giants, 1964-69; Cleveland, 1970 (224-4,986)
20.83 Buddy Dial, Pittsburgh, 1959-63; Dallas, 1964-66 (261-5,436)
20.24 Harlon Hill, Chicago, 1954-61; Pittsburgh, 1962; Detroit, 1962 (233-4,717)

**Highest Average Gain, Season (24 receptions)**
32.58 Don Currivan, Boston, 1947 (24-782)
31.44 Bucky Pope, Los Angeles, 1964 (25-786)
28.60 Bobby Duckworth, San Diego, 1984 (25-715)

**Highest Average Gain, Game (3 receptions)**
60.67 Bill Groman, Houston vs. Denver, Nov. 20, 1960 (3-182)
Homer Jones, N.Y. Giants vs. Washington, Dec. 12, 1965 (3-182)
60.33 Don Currivan, Boston vs. Washington, Nov. 30, 1947 (3-181)
59.67 Bobby Duckworth, San Diego vs. Chicago, Dec. 3, 1984 (3-179)

## TOUCHDOWNS

**Most Seasons Leading League**
9 Don Hutson, Green Bay, 1935-38, 1940-44

6 Jerry Rice, San Francisco, 1986-87, 1989-91, 1993
3 Lance Alworth, San Diego, 1964-66

**Most Consecutive Seasons Leading League**

5 Don Hutson, Green Bay, 1940-44
4 Don Hutson, Green Bay, 1935-38
3 Lance Alworth, San Diego, 1964-66
Jerry Rice, San Francisco, 1989-91

**Most Touchdowns, Career**

118 Jerry Rice, San Francisco, 1985-93
100 Steve Largent, Seattle, 1976-89
99 Don Hutson, Green Bay, 1935-45

**Most Touchdowns, Season**

22 Jerry Rice, San Francisco, 1987
18 Mark Clayton, Miami, 1984
17 Don Hutson, Green Bay, 1942
Elroy (Crazylegs) Hirsch, Los Angeles, 1951
Bill Groman, Houston, 1961
Jerry Rice, San Francisco, 1989

**Most Touchdowns, Rookie, Season**

13 Bill Howton, Green Bay, 1952
John Jefferson, San Diego, 1979
12 Harlon Hill, Chi. Bears, 1954
Bill Groman, Houston, 1960
Mike Ditka, Chicago, 1961
Bob Hayes, Dallas, 1965
10 Bill Swiacki, N.Y. Giants, 1948
Bucky Pope, Los Angeles, 1964
Sammy White, Minnesota, 1976
Daryl Turner, Seattle, 1984

**Most Touchdowns, Game**

5 Bob Shaw, Chi. Cardinals vs. Baltimore, Oct. 2, 1950
Kellen Winslow, San Diego vs. Oakland, Nov. 22, 1981
Jerry Rice, San Francisco vs. Atlanta, Oct. 14, 1990
4 By many players. Last time: Jerry Rice, San Francisco vs. Tampa Bay, Nov. 14, 1993

**Most Consecutive Games, Touchdowns**

13 Jerry Rice, San Francisco, 1986-87
11 Elroy (Crazylegs) Hirsch, Los Angeles, 1950-51
Buddy Dial, Pittsburgh, 1959-60
9 Lance Alworth, San Diego, 1963

## INTERCEPTIONS BY

**Most Seasons Leading League**

3 Everson Walls, Dallas, 1981-82, 1985
2 Dick (Night Train) Lane, Los Angeles, 1952; Chi. Cardinals, 1954
Jack Christiansen, Detroit, 1953, 1957
Milt Davis, Baltimore, 1957, 1959
Dick Lynch, N.Y. Giants, 1961, 1963
Johnny Robinson, Kansas City, 1966, 1970
Bill Bradley, Philadelphia, 1971-72
Emmitt Thomas, Kansas City, 1969, 1974
Ronnie Lott, San Francisco, 1986; L.A. Raiders, 1991

**Most Interceptions By, Career**

81 Paul Krause, Washington, 1964-67; Minnesota, 1968-79
79 Emlen Tunnell, N.Y. Giants, 1948-58; Green Bay, 1959-61
68 Dick (Night Train) Lane, Los Angeles, 1952-53; Chi. Cardinals, 1954-59; Detroit, 1960-65

**Most Interceptions By, Season**

14 Dick (Night Train) Lane, Los Angeles, 1952
13 Dan Sandifer, Washington, 1948
Orban (Spec) Sanders, N.Y. Yanks, 1950
Lester Hayes, Oakland, 1980
12 By nine players

**Most Interceptions By, Rookie, Season**

14 Dick (Night Train) Lane, Los Angeles, 1952
13 Dan Sandifer, Washington, 1948
12 Woodley Lewis, Los Angeles, 1950
Paul Krause, Washington, 1964

**Most Interceptions By, Game**

4 Sammy Baugh, Washington vs. Detroit, Nov. 14, 1943
Dan Sandifer, Washington vs. Boston, Oct. 31, 1948
Don Doll, Detroit vs. Chi. Cardinals, Oct. 23, 1949
Bob Nussbaumer, Chi. Cardinals vs. N.Y. Bulldogs, Nov. 13, 1949
Russ Craft, Philadelphia vs. Chi. Cardinals, Sept. 24, 1950
Bobby Dillon, Green Bay vs. Detroit, Nov. 26, 1953
Jack Butler, Pittsburgh vs. Washington, Dec. 13, 1953
Austin (Goose) Gonsoulin, Denver vs. Buffalo, Sept. 18, 1960
Jerry Norton, St. Louis vs. Washington, Nov. 20, 1960; vs. Pittsburgh, Nov. 26, 1961
Dave Baker, San Francisco vs. L.A. Rams, Dec. 4, 1960
Bobby Ply, Dall. Texans vs. San Diego, Dec. 16, 1962
Bobby Hunt, Kansas City vs. Houston, Oct. 4, 1964
Willie Brown, Denver vs. N.Y. Jets, Nov. 15, 1964
Dick Anderson, Miami vs. Pittsburgh, Dec. 3, 1973
Willie Buchanon, Green Bay vs. San Diego, Sept. 24, 1978
Deron Cherry, Kansas City vs. Seattle, Sept. 29, 1985

**Most Consecutive Games, Passes Intercepted By**

8 Tom Morrow, Oakland, 1962-63
7 Paul Krause, Washington, 1964
Larry Wilson, St. Louis, 1966
Ben Davis, Cleveland, 1968
6 Dick (Night Train) Lane, Chi. Cardinals, 1954-55
Will Sherman, Los Angeles, 1954-55
Jim Shofner, Cleveland, 1960
Paul Krause, Minnesota, 1968
Willie Williams, N.Y. Giants, 1968
Kermit Alexander, San Francisco, 1968-69
Mel Blount, Pittsburgh, 1975
Eric Harris, Kansas City, 1980
Lester Hayes, Oakland, 1980
Barry Wilburn, Washington, 1987

### YARDS GAINED

**Most Seasons Leading League**

2 Dick (Night Train) Lane, Los Angeles, 1952; Chi. Cardinals, 1954
Herb Adderley, Green Bay, 1965, 1969
Dick Anderson, Miami, 1968, 1970

**Most Yards Gained, Career**

1,282 Emlen Tunnell, N.Y. Giants, 1948-58; Green Bay, 1959-61
1,207 Dick (Night Train) Lane, Los Angeles, 1952-53; Chi. Cardinals, 1954-59; Detroit, 1960-65
1,185 Paul Krause, Washington, 1964-67; Minnesota, 1968-79

**Most Yards Gained, Season**

349 Charlie McNeil, San Diego, 1961
301 Don Doll, Detroit, 1949
298 Dick (Night Train) Lane, Los Angeles, 1952

**Most Yards Gained, Rookie, Season**

301 Don Doll, Detroit, 1949
298 Dick (Night Train) Lane, Los Angeles, 1952
275 Woodley Lewis, Los Angeles, 1950

**Most Yards Gained, Game**

177 Charlie McNeil, San Diego vs. Houston, Sept. 24, 1961
170 Louis Oliver, Miami vs. Buffalo, Oct. 4, 1992
167 Dick Jauron, Detroit vs. Chicago, Nov. 18, 1973

**Longest Return (All TDs)**

103 Vencie Glenn, San Diego vs. Denver, Nov. 29, 1987
Louis Oliver, Miami vs. Buffalo, Oct. 4, 1992
102 Bob Smith, Detroit vs. Chi. Bears, Nov. 24, 1949
Erich Barnes, N.Y. Giants vs. Dall. Cowboys, Oct. 15, 1961
Gary Barbaro, Kansas City vs. Seattle, Dec. 11, 1977
Louis Breeden, Cincinnati vs. San Diego, Nov. 8, 1981
Eddie Anderson, L.A. Raiders vs. Miami, Dec. 14, 1992
Donald Frank, San Diego vs. L.A. Raiders, Oct. 31, 1993
101 Richie Petitbon, Chicago vs Los Angeles, Dec. 9, 1962
Henry Carr, N.Y. Giants vs. Los Angeles, Nov. 13, 1966
Tony Greene, Buffalo vs. Kansas City, Oct. 3, 1976
Tom Pridemore, Atlanta vs. San Francisco, Sept. 20, 1981

### TOUCHDOWNS

**Most Touchdowns, Career**

9 Ken Houston, Houston, 1967-72; Washington, 1973-80
7 Herb Adderley, Green Bay, 1961-69; Dallas, 1970-72
Erich Barnes, Chi. Bears, 1958-60; N.Y. Giants, 1961-64; Cleveland, 1965-70
Lem Barney, Detroit, 1967-77
6 Tom Janik, Denver, 1963-64; Buffalo, 1965-68; Boston, 1969-70; New England, 1971
Miller Farr, Denver, 1965; San Diego, 1965-66; Houston, 1967-69; St. Louis, 1970-72; Detroit, 1973
Bobby Bell, Kansas City, 1963-74

**Most Touchdowns, Season**

4 Ken Houston, Houston, 1971
Jim Kearney, Kansas City, 1972
Eric Allen, Philadelphia, 1993
3 Dick Harris, San Diego, 1961
Dick Lynch, N.Y. Giants, 1963
Herb Adderley, Green Bay, 1965
Lem Barney, Detroit, 1967
Miller Farr, Houston, 1967
Monte Jackson, Los Angeles, 1976
Rod Perry, Los Angeles, 1978
Ronnie Lott, San Francisco, 1981
Lloyd Burruss, Kansas City, 1986
Wayne Haddix, Tampa Bay, 1990
Robert Massey, Phoenix, 1992
2 By many players

**Most Touchdowns, Rookie, Season**

3 Lem Barney, Detroit, 1967
Ronnie Lott, San Francisco, 1981
2 By many players

**Most Touchdowns, Game**

2 Bill Blackburn, Chi. Cardinals vs. Boston, Oct. 24, 1948
Dan Sandifer, Washington vs. Boston, Oct. 31, 1948
Bob Franklin, Cleveland vs. Chicago, Dec. 11, 1960
Bill Stacy, St. Louis vs. Dall. Cowboys, Nov. 5, 1961
Jerry Norton, St. Louis vs. Pittsburgh, Nov. 26, 1961
Miller Farr, Houston vs. Buffalo, Dec. 7, 1968
Ken Houston, Houston vs. San Diego, Dec. 19, 1971
Jim Kearney, Kansas City vs. Denver, Oct. 1, 1972
Lemar Parrish, Cincinnati vs. Houston, Dec. 17, 1972
Dick Anderson, Miami vs. Pittsburgh, Dec. 3, 1973
Prentice McCray, New England vs. N.Y. Jets, Nov. 21, 1976
Kenny Johnson, Atlanta vs. Green Bay, Nov. 27, 1983 (OT)
Mike Kozlowski, Miami vs. N.Y. Jets, Dec. 16, 1983
Dave Brown, Seattle vs. Kansas City, Nov. 4, 1984
Lloyd Burruss, Kansas City vs. San Diego, Oct. 19, 1986
Henry Jones, Buffalo vs. Indianapolis, Sept. 20, 1992
Robert Massey, Phoenix vs. Washington, Oct. 4, 1992
Eric Allen, Philadelphia vs. New Orleans, Dec. 26, 1993

## PUNTING

**Most Seasons Leading League**

4 Sammy Baugh, Washington, 1940-43
Jerrel Wilson, Kansas City, 1965, 1968, 1972-73
3 Yale Lary, Detroit, 1959, 1961, 1963
Jim Fraser, Denver, 1962-64
Ray Guy, Oakland, 1974-75, 1977
Rohn Stark, Baltimore, 1983; Indianapolis, 1985-86
2 By many players

**Most Consecutive Seasons Leading League**

4 Sammy Baugh, Washington, 1940-43
3 Jim Fraser, Denver, 1962-64
2 By many players

### PUNTS

**Most Punts, Career**

1,154 Dave Jennings, N.Y. Giants, 1974-84; N.Y. Jets, 1985-87
1,083 John James, Atlanta, 1972-81; Detroit, 1982, Houston, 1982-84
1,072 Jerrel Wilson, Kansas City, 1963-77; New England, 1978

**Most Punts, Season**

114 Bob Parsons, Chicago, 1981
109 John James, Atlanta, 1978
108 John Teltschik, Philadelphia, 1986
Rick Tuten, Seattle, 1992

**Most Punts, Rookie, Season**

108 John Teltschik, Philadelphia, 1986
99 Lewis Colbert, Kansas City, 1986
96 Mike Connell, San Francisco, 1978
Chris Norman, Denver, 1984

**Most Punts, Game**

15 John Teltschik, Philadelphia vs. N.Y. Giants, Dec. 6, 1987 (OT)
14 Dick Nesbitt, Chi. Cardinals vs. Chi. Bears, Nov. 30, 1933
Keith Molesworth, Chi. Bears vs. Green Bay, Dec. 10, 1933
Sammy Baugh, Washington vs. Philadelphia, Nov. 5, 1939
Carl Kinscherf, N.Y. Giants vs. Detroit, Nov. 7, 1943
George Taliaferro, N.Y. Yanks vs. Los Angeles, Sept. 28, 1951
12 By many players. Last time: Rick Tuten, Seattle vs. Denver, Nov. 28, 1993

**Longest Punt**

98 Steve O'Neal, N.Y. Jets vs. Denver, Sept. 21, 1969
94 Joe Lintzenich, Chi. Bears vs. N.Y. Giants, Nov. 16, 1931
93 Shawn McCarthy, New England vs. Buffalo, Nov. 3, 1991

### AVERAGE YARDAGE

**Highest Average, Punting, Career (250 punts)**

45.10 Sammy Baugh, Washington, 1937-52 (338-15,245)
44.68 Tommy Davis, San Francisco, 1959-69 (511-22,833)
44.29 Yale Lary, Detroit, 1952-53, 1956-64 (503-22,279)

**Highest Average, Punting, Season (Qualifiers)**

51.40 Sammy Baugh, Washington, 1940 (35-1,799)
48.94 Yale Lary, Detroit, 1963 (35-1,713)
48.73 Sammy Baugh, Washington, 1941 (30-1,462)

**Highest Average, Punting, Rookie, Season (Qualifiers)**

45.92 Frank Sinkwich, Detroit, 1943 (12-551)
45.66 Tommy Davis, San Francisco, 1959 (59-2,694)
45.57 David Lee, Baltimore, 1966 (49-2,233)

**Highest Average, Punting, Game (4 punts)**

61.75 Bob Cifers, Detroit vs. Chi. Bears, Nov. 24, 1946 (4-247)
61.60 Roy McKay, Green Bay vs. Chi. Cardinals, Oct. 28, 1945 (5-308)
59.40 Sammy Baugh, Washington vs. Detroit, Oct. 27, 1940 (5-297)

### PUNTS HAD BLOCKED

**Most Consecutive Punts, None Blocked**

623 Dave Jennings, N.Y. Giants, 1976-83
619 Ray Guy, Oakland, 1979-81; L.A. Raiders, 1982-86
578 Bobby Walden, Minnesota, 1964-67; Pittsburgh, 1968-72

**Most Punts Had Blocked, Career**

14 Herman Weaver, Detroit, 1970-76; Seattle, 1977-80
Harry Newsome, Pittsburgh, 1985-89; Minnesota, 1990-93
12 Jerrel Wilson, Kansas City, 1963-77; New England, 1978
Tom Blanchard, N.Y. Giants, 1971-73; New Orleans, 1974-78; Tampa Bay, 1979-81
11 David Lee, Baltimore, 1966-78

**Most Punts Had Blocked, Season**

6 Harry Newsome, Pittsburgh, 1988
4 Bryan Wagner, Cleveland, 1990
3 By many players

## PUNT RETURNS

**Most Seasons Leading League**

3 Les (Speedy) Duncan, San Diego, 1965-66; Washington, 1971
Rick Upchurch, Denver, 1976, 1978, 1982
2 Dick Christy, N.Y. Titans, 1961-62
Claude Gibson, Oakland, 1963-64
Billy Johnson, Houston, 1975, 1977
Mel Gray, New Orleans, 1987; Detroit, 1991

### PUNT RETURNS

**Most Punt Returns, Career**

292 Vai Sikahema, St. Louis, 1986-87; Phoenix, 1988-90; Green Bay, 1991; Philadelphia, 1992-93
282 Billy Johnson, Houston, 1974-80; Atlanta, 1982-87; Washington, 1988
267 J.T. Smith, Washington, 1978; Kansas City, 1978-84; St. Louis, 1985-87; Phoenix, 1988-90

**Most Punt Returns, Season**

70 Danny Reece, Tampa Bay, 1979
62 Fulton Walker, Miami-L.A. Raiders, 1985
58 J.T. Smith, Kansas City, 1979
Greg Pruitt, L.A. Raiders, 1983
Leo Lewis, Minnesota, 1988

**Most Punt Returns, Rookie, Season**

57 Lew Barnes, Chicago, 1986
54 James Jones, Dallas, 1980
53 Louis Lipps, Pittsburgh, 1984

**Most Punt Returns, Game**

11 Eddie Brown, Washington vs. Tampa Bay, Oct. 9, 1977
10 Theo Bell, Pittsburgh vs. Buffalo, Dec. 16, 1979
Mike Nelms, Washington vs. New Orleans, Dec. 26, 1982
Ronnie Harris, New England vs. Pittsburgh, Dec. 5, 1993
9 Rodger Bird, Oakland vs. Denver, Sept. 10, 1967
Ralph McGill, San Francisco vs. Atlanta, Oct. 29, 1972
Ed Podolak, Kansas City vs. San Diego, Nov. 10, 1974
Anthony Leonard, San Francisco vs. New Orleans, Oct. 17, 1976
Butch Johnson, Dallas vs. Buffalo, Nov. 15, 1976
Larry Marshall, Philadelphia vs. Tampa Bay, Sept. 18, 1977
Nesby Glasgow, Baltimore vs. Kansas City, Sept. 2, 1979
Mike Nelms, Washington vs. St. Louis, Dec. 21, 1980
Leon Bright, N.Y. Giants vs. Philadelphia, Dec. 11, 1982
Pete Shaw, N.Y. Giants vs. Philadelphia, Nov. 20, 1983
Cleotha Montgomery, L.A. Raiders vs. Detroit, Dec. 10, 1984
Phil McConkey, N.Y. Giants vs. Philadelphia, Dec. 6, 1987 (OT)

### FAIR CATCHES

**Most Fair Catches, Career**

102 Willie Wood, Green Bay, 1960-71
99 Phil McConkey, N.Y. Giants, 1984-88; Green Bay, 1986; San Diego, 1989
98 Leo Lewis, Minnesota, 1981-90, 1991; Cleveland, 1990

**Most Fair Catches, Season**

27 Leo Lewis, Minnesota, 1989
25 Mark Konecny, Philadelphia, 1988
Phil McConkey, N.Y. Giants, 1988
Chris Warren, Seattle, 1992
24 Ken Graham, San Diego, 1969

**Most Fair Catches, Game**

7 Lem Barney, Detroit vs. Chicago, Nov. 21, 1976
Bobby Morse, Philadelphia vs. Buffalo, Dec. 27, 1987
6 Jake Scott, Miami vs. Buffalo, Dec. 20, 1970
Greg Pruitt, L.A. Raiders vs. Seattle, Oct. 7, 1984
Phil McConkey, San Diego vs. Kansas City, Dec. 17, 1989
Gerald McNeil, Houston vs. Pittsburgh, Sept. 16, 1990
5 By many players

**YARDS GAINED**

**Most Seasons Leading League**

3 Alvin Haymond, Baltimore, 1965-66; Los Angeles, 1969
2 Bill Dudley, Pittsburgh, 1942, 1946
Emlen Tunnell, N.Y. Giants, 1951-52
Dick Christy, N.Y. Titans, 1961-62
Claude Gibson, Oakland, 1963-64
Rodger Bird, Oakland, 1966-67
J.T. Smith, Kansas City, 1979-80
Vai Sikahema, St. Louis, 1986-87
David Meggett, N.Y. Giants, 1989-90

**Most Yards Gained, Career**

3,317 Billy Johnson, Houston, 1974-80; Atlanta, 1982-87; Washington, 1988
3,169 Vai Sikahema, St. Louis, 1986-87; Phoenix, 1988-90; Green Bay, 1991; Philadelphia, 1992-93
3,008 Rick Upchurch, Denver, 1975-83

**Most Yards Gained, Season**

692 Fulton Walker, Miami-L.A. Raiders, 1985
666 Greg Pruitt, L.A. Raiders, 1983
656 Louis Lipps, Pittsburgh, 1984

**Most Yards Gained, Rookie, Season**

656 Louis Lipps, Pittsburgh, 1984
655 Neal Colzie, Oakland, 1975
608 Mike Haynes, New England, 1976

**Most Yards Gained, Game**

207 LeRoy Irvin, Los Angeles vs. Atlanta, Oct. 11, 1981
205 George Atkinson, Oakland vs. Buffalo, Sept. 15, 1968
184 Tom Watkins, Detroit vs. San Francisco, Oct. 6, 1963

**Longest Punt Return (All TDs)**

98 Gil LeFebvre, Cincinnati vs. Brooklyn, Dec. 3, 1933
Charlie West, Minnesota vs. Washington, Nov. 3, 1968
Dennis Morgan, Dallas vs. St. Louis, Oct. 13, 1974
Terance Mathis, N.Y. Jets vs. Dallas, Nov. 4, 1990
97 Greg Pruitt, L.A. Raiders vs. Washington, Oct. 2, 1983
96 Bill Dudley, Washington vs. Pittsburgh, Dec. 3, 1950

**AVERAGE YARDAGE**

**Highest Average, Career (75 returns)**

12.78 George McAfee, Chi. Bears, 1940-41, 1945-50 (112-1,431)
12.75 Jack Christiansen, Detroit, 1951-58 (85-1,084)
12.55 Claude Gibson, San Diego, 1961-62; Oakland, 1963-65 (110-1,381)

**Highest Average, Season (Qualifiers)**

23.00 Herb Rich, Baltimore, 1950 (12-276)
21.47 Jack Christiansen, Detroit, 1952 (15-322)
21.28 Dick Christy, N.Y. Titans, 1961 (18-383)

**Highest Average, Rookie, Season (Qualifiers)**

23.00 Herb Rich, Baltimore, 1950 (12-276)
20.88 Jerry Davis, Chi. Cardinals, 1948 (16-334)
20.73 Frank Sinkwich, Detroit, 1943 (11-228)

**Highest Average, Game (3 returns)**

47.67 Chuck Latourette, St. Louis vs. New Orleans, Sept. 29, 1968 (3-143)
47.33 Johnny Roland, St. Louis vs. Philadelphia, Oct. 2, 1966 (3-142)
45.67 Dick Christy, N.Y. Titans vs. Denver, Sept. 24, 1961 (3-137)

**TOUCHDOWNS**

**Most Touchdowns, Career**

8 Jack Christiansen, Detroit, 1951-58
Rick Upchurch, Denver, 1975-83
6 Billy Johnson, Houston, 1974-80; Atlanta, 1982-87; Washington, 1988
5 Emlen Tunnell, N.Y. Giants, 1948-58; Green Bay, 1959-61

**Most Touchdowns, Season**

4 Jack Christiansen, Detroit, 1951
Rick Upchurch, Denver, 1976
3 Emlen Tunnell, N.Y. Giants, 1951
Billy Johnson, Houston, 1975
LeRoy Irvin, Los Angeles, 1981
2 By many players

**Most Touchdowns, Rookie, Season**

4 Jack Christiansen, Detroit, 1951
2 By 10 players

**Most Touchdowns, Game**

2 Jack Christiansen, Detroit vs. Los Angeles, Oct. 14, 1951; vs. Green Bay, Nov. 22, 1951
Dick Christy, N.Y. Titans vs. Denver, Sept. 24, 1961
Rick Upchurch, Denver vs. Cleveland, Sept. 26, 1976
LeRoy Irvin, Los Angeles vs. Atlanta, Oct. 11, 1981
Vai Sikahema, St. Louis vs. Tampa Bay, Dec. 21, 1986
Todd Kinchen, L.A. Rams vs. Atlanta, Dec. 27, 1992
Eric Metcalf, Cleveland vs. Pittsburgh, Oct. 24, 1993

## KICKOFF RETURNS

**Most Seasons Leading League**

3 Abe Woodson, San Francisco, 1959, 1962-63
2 Lynn Chandnois, Pittsburgh, 1951-52
Bobby Jancik, Houston, 1962-63
Travis Williams, Green Bay, 1967; Los Angeles, 1971

**KICKOFF RETURNS**

**Most Kickoff Returns, Career**

275 Ron Smith, Chicago, 1965, 1970-72; Atlanta, 1966-67; Los Angeles, 1968-69; San Diego, 1973; Oakland, 1974
264 Mel Gray, New Orleans, 1986-88; Detroit, 1989-93
243 Bruce Harper, N.Y. Jets, 1977-84

**Most Kickoff Returns, Season**

60 Drew Hill, Los Angeles, 1981
55 Bruce Harper, N.Y. Jets, 1978, 1979
David Turner, Cincinnati, 1979
Stump Mitchell, St. Louis, 1981
53 Eddie Payton, Minnesota, 1980
Buster Rhymes, Minnesota, 1985

**Most Kickoff Returns, Rookie, Season**

55 Stump Mitchell, St. Louis, 1981
53 Buster Rhymes, Minnesota, 1985
50 Nesby Glasgow, Baltimore, 1979
Dino Hall, Cleveland, 1979

**Most Kickoff Returns, Game**

9 Noland Smith, Kansas City vs. Oakland, Nov. 23, 1967
Dino Hall, Cleveland vs. Pittsburgh, Oct. 7, 1979
Paul Palmer, Kansas City vs. Seattle, Sept. 20, 1987
8 George Taliaferro, N.Y. Yanks vs. N.Y. Giants, Dec. 3, 1950
Bobby Jancik, Houston vs. Boston, Dec. 8, 1963
Bobby Jancik, Houston vs. Oakland, Dec. 22, 1963
Mel Renfro, Dallas vs. Green Bay, Nov. 29, 1964
Willie Porter, Boston vs. N.Y. Jets, Sept. 22, 1968
Keith Moody, Buffalo vs. Seattle, Oct. 30, 1977
Brian Baschnagel, Chicago vs. Houston, Nov. 6, 1977
Bruce Harper, N.Y. Jets vs. New England, Oct. 29, 1978
Bruce Harper, N.Y. Jets vs. New England, Sept. 9, 1979
Dino Hall, Cleveland vs. Pittsburgh, Nov. 25, 1979
Terry Metcalf, Washington vs. St. Louis, Sept. 20, 1981
Harlan Huckleby, Green Bay vs. Washington, Oct. 17, 1983
Gary Ellerson, Green Bay vs. St. Louis, Sept. 29, 1985
Bobby Humphery, N.Y. Jets vs. Cincinnati, Dec. 21, 1986
Bobby Joe Edmonds, Seattle vs. L.A. Raiders, Nov. 30, 1987
Joe Cribbs, Miami vs. Pittsburgh, Dec. 18, 1988
Erric Pegram, Atlanta vs. Washington, Nov. 10, 1991
Mel Gray, Detroit vs. Dallas, Nov. 8, 1992
7 By many players

**YARDS GAINED**

**Most Seasons Leading League**

3 Bruce Harper, N.Y. Jets, 1977-79
2 Marshall Goldberg, Chi. Cardinals, 1941-42
Woodley Lewis, Los Angeles, 1953-54
Al Carmichael, Green Bay, 1956-57
Timmy Brown, Philadelphia, 1961, 1963
Bobby Jancik, Houston, 1963, 1966
Ron Smith, Atlanta, 1966-67

**Most Yards Gained, Career**

6,922 Ron Smith, Chicago, 1965, 1970-72; Atlanta, 1966-67; Los Angeles, 1968-69; San Diego, 1973; Oakland, 1974
6,374 Mel Gray, New Orleans, 1986-88; Detroit, 1989-93
5,538 Abe Woodson, San Francisco, 1958-64; St. Louis, 1965-66

**Most Yards Gained, Season**

1,345 Buster Rhymes, Minnesota, 1985
1,317 Bobby Jancik, Houston, 1963
1,314 Dave Hampton, Green Bay, 1971

**Most Yards Gained, Rookie, Season**

1,345 Buster Rhymes, Minnesota, 1985
1,292 Stump Mitchell, St. Louis, 1981
1,245 Odell Barry, Denver, 1964

**Most Yards Gained, Game**

294 Wally Triplett, Detroit vs. Los Angeles, Oct. 29, 1950
249 Tony Smith, Atlanta vs. Pittsburgh, Sept. 27, 1993
247 Timmy Brown, Philadelphia vs. Dallas, Nov. 6, 1966

**Longest Kickoff Return (All TDs)**

106 Al Carmichael, Green Bay vs. Chi. Bears, Oct. 7, 1956
Noland Smith, Kansas City vs. Denver, Dec. 17, 1967
Roy Green, St. Louis vs. Dallas, Oct. 21, 1979
105 Frank Seno, Chi. Cardinals vs. N.Y. Giants, Oct. 20, 1946
Ollie Matson, Chi. Cardinals vs. Washington, Oct. 14, 1956
Abe Woodson, San Francisco vs. Los Angeles, Nov. 8, 1959
Timmy Brown, Philadelphia vs. Cleveland, Sept. 17, 1961
Jon Arnett, Los Angeles vs. Detroit, Oct. 29, 1961
Eugene (Mercury) Morris, Miami vs. Cincinnati, Sept. 14, 1969

Travis Williams, Los Angeles vs. New Orleans, Dec. 5, 1971
104 By many players

### AVERAGE YARDAGE

**Highest Average, Career (75 returns)**
30.56 Gale Sayers, Chicago, 1965-71 (91-2,781)
29.57 Lynn Chandnois, Pittsburgh, 1950-56 (92-2,720)
28.69 Abe Woodson, San Francisco, 1958-64; St. Louis, 1965-66 (193-5,538)

**Highest Average, Season (Qualifiers)**
41.06 Travis Williams, Green Bay, 1967 (18-739)
37.69 Gale Sayers, Chicago, 1967 (16-603)
35.50 Ollie Matson, Chi. Cardinals, 1958 (14-497)

**Highest Average, Rookie, Season (Qualifiers)**
41.06 Travis Williams, Green Bay, 1967 (18-739)
33.08 Tom Moore, Green Bay, 1960 (12-397)
32.88 Duriel Harris, Miami, 1976 (17-559)

**Highest Average, Game (3 returns)**
73.50 Wally Triplett, Detroit vs. Los Angeles, Oct. 29, 1950 (4-294)
67.33 Lenny Lyles, San Francisco vs. Baltimore, Dec. 18, 1960 (3-202)
65.33 Ken Hall, Houston vs. N.Y. Titans, Oct. 23, 1960 (3-196)

### TOUCHDOWNS

**Most Touchdowns, Career**
6 Ollie Matson, Chi. Cardinals, 1952, 1954-58; L.A. Rams, 1959-62; Detroit, 1963; Philadelphia, 1964
Gale Sayers, Chicago, 1965-71
Travis Williams, Green Bay, 1967-70; Los Angeles, 1971
5 Bobby Mitchell, Cleveland, 1958-61; Washington, 1962-68
Abe Woodson, San Francisco, 1958-64; St. Louis, 1965-66
Timmy Brown, Green Bay, 1959; Philadelphia, 1960-67; Baltimore, 1968
4 Cecil Turner, Chicago, 1968-73
Ron Brown, L.A. Rams, 1984-89, 1991; L.A. Raiders, 1990

**Most Touchdowns, Season**
4 Travis Williams, Green Bay, 1967
Cecil Turner, Chicago, 1970
3 Verda (Vitamin T) Smith, Los Angeles, 1950
Abe Woodson, San Francisco, 1963
Gale Sayers, Chicago, 1967
Raymond Clayborn, New England, 1977
Ron Brown, L.A. Rams, 1985
2 By many players

**Most Touchdowns, Rookie, Season**
4 Travis Williams, Green Bay, 1967
3 Raymond Clayborn, New England, 1977
2 By seven players

**Most Touchdowns, Game**
2 Timmy Brown, Philadelphia vs. Dallas, Nov. 6, 1966
Travis Williams, Green Bay vs. Cleveland, Nov. 12, 1967
Ron Brown, L.A. Rams vs. Green Bay, Nov. 24, 1985

## COMBINED KICK RETURNS

**Most Combined Kick Returns, Career**
527 Vai Sikahema, St. Louis, 1986-87; Phoenix, 1988-90; Green Bay, 1991; Philadelphia, 1992-93 (p-292, k-235)
510 Ron Smith, Chicago, 1965, 1970-72; Atlanta, 1966-67; Los Angeles, 1968-69; San Diego, 1973; Oakland, 1974 (p-235, k-275)
426 Bruce Harper, N.Y. Jets, 1977-84 (p-183, k-243)

**Most Combined Kick Returns, Season**
100 Larry Jones, Washington, 1975 (p-53, k-47)
97 Stump Mitchell, St. Louis, 1981 (p-42, k-55)
94 Nesby Glasgow, Baltimore, 1979 (p-44, k-50)

**Most Combined Kick Returns, Game**
13 Stump Mitchell, St. Louis vs. Atlanta, Oct. 18, 1981 (p-6, k-7)
Ronnie Harris, New England vs. Pittsburgh, Dec. 5, 1993 (p-10, k-3)
12 Mel Renfro, Dallas vs. Green Bay, Nov. 29, 1964 (p-4, k-8)
Larry Jones, Washington vs. Dallas, Dec. 13, 1975 (p-6, k-6)
Eddie Brown, Washington vs. Tampa Bay, Oct. 9, 1977 (p-11, k-1)
Nesby Glasgow, Baltimore vs. Denver, Sept. 2, 1979 (p-9, k-3)
11 By many players

### YARDS GAINED

**Most Yards Returned, Career**
8,710 Ron Smith, Chicago, 1965, 1970-72; Atlanta, 1966-67; Los Angeles, 1968-69; San Diego, 1973; Oakland, 1974 (p-1,788, k-6,922)
8,225 Mel Gray, New Orleans, 1986-88; Detroit, 1989-93 (p-1,851, k-6,374)
8,102 Vai Sikahema, St. Louis, 1986-87; Phoenix, 1988-90; Green Bay, 1991; Philadelphia, 1992-93 (p-3,169, k-4,933)

**Most Yards Returned, Season**
1,737 Stump Mitchell, St. Louis, 1981 (p-445, k-1,292)
1,658 Bruce Harper, N.Y. Jets, 1978 (p-378, k-1,280)
1,591 Mike Nelms, Washington, 1981 (p-492, k-1,099)

**Most Yards Returned, Game**
294 Wally Triplett, Detroit vs. Los Angeles, Oct. 29, 1950 (k-294)
Woodley Lewis, Los Angeles vs. Detroit, Oct. 18, 1953 (p-120, k-174)
289 Eddie Payton, Detroit vs. Minnesota, Dec. 17, 1977 (p-105, k-184)
282 Les (Speedy) Duncan, San Diego vs. N.Y. Jets, Nov. 24, 1968 (p-102, k-180)

### TOUCHDOWNS

**Most Touchdowns, Career**
9 Ollie Matson, Chi. Cardinals, 1952, 1954-58; Los Angeles, 1959-62; Detroit, 1963; Philadelphia, 1964-66 (p-3, k-6)
8 Jack Christiansen, Detroit, 1951-58 (p-8)
Bobby Mitchell, Cleveland, 1958-61; Washington, 1962-68 (p-3, k-5)
Gale Sayers, Chicago, 1965-71 (p-2, k-6)
Rick Upchurch, Denver, 1975-83 (p-8)
Billy Johnson, Houston, 1974-80; Atlanta, 1982-87; Washington, 1988 (p-6, k-2)
7 Abe Woodson, San Francisco, 1958-64; St. Louis, 1965-66 (p-2, k-5)
Travis Williams, Green Bay, 1967-70; Los Angeles, 1971 (p-1, k-6)

**Most Touchdowns, Season**
4 Jack Christiansen, Detroit, 1951 (p-4)
Emlen Tunnell, N.Y. Giants, 1951 (p-3, k-1)
Gale Sayers, Chicago, 1967 (p-1, k-3)
Travis Williams, Green Bay, 1967 (k-4)
Cecil Turner, Chicago, 1970 (k-4)
Billy Johnson, Houston, 1975 (p-3, k-1)
Rick Upchurch, Denver, 1976 (p-4)
3 Verda (Vitamin T) Smith, Los Angeles, 1950 (k-3)
Abe Woodson, San Francisco, 1963 (k-3)
Raymond Clayborn, New England, 1977 (k-3)
Billy Johnson, Houston, 1977 (p-2, k-1)
LeRoy Irvin, Los Angeles, 1981 (p-3)
Ron Brown, L.A. Rams, 1985 (k-3)
Tyrone Hughes, New Orleans, 1993 (p-2, k-1)
2 By many players

**Most Touchdowns, Game**
2 Jack Christiansen, Detroit vs. Los Angeles, Oct. 14, 1951 (p-2); vs. Green Bay, Nov. 22, 1951 (p-2)
Jim Patton, N.Y. Giants vs. Washington, Oct. 30, 1955 (p-1, k-1)
Bobby Mitchell, Cleveland vs. Philadelphia, Nov. 23, 1958 (p-1, k-1)
Dick Christy, N.Y. Titans vs. Denver, Sept. 24, 1961 (p-2)
Al Frazier, Denver vs. Boston, Dec. 3, 1961 (p-1, k-1)
Timmy Brown, Philadelphia vs. Dallas, Nov. 6, 1966 (k-2)
Travis Williams, Green Bay vs. Cleveland, Nov. 12, 1967 (k-2); vs. Pittsburgh, Nov. 2, 1969 (p-1, k-1)
Gale Sayers, Chicago vs. San Francisco, Dec. 3, 1967 (p-1, k-1)
Rick Upchurch, Denver vs. Cleveland, Sept. 26, 1976 (p-2)
Eddie Payton, Detroit vs. Minnesota, Dec. 17, 1977 (p-1, k-1)
LeRoy Irvin, Los Angeles vs. Atlanta, Oct. 11, 1981 (p-2)
Ron Brown, L.A. Rams vs. Green Bay, Nov. 24, 1985 (k-2)
Vai Sikahema, St. Louis vs. Tampa Bay, Dec. 21, 1986 (p-2)
Eric Metcalf, Cleveland vs. Pittsburgh, Oct. 24, 1993 (p-2)

## FUMBLES

**Most Fumbles, Career**
124 Dave Krieg, Seattle, 1980-91; Kansas City, 1992-93
116 Warren Moon, Houston, 1984-93
106 Dan Fouts, San Diego, 1973-87

**Most Fumbles, Season**
18 Dave Krieg, Seattle, 1989
Warren Moon, Houston, 1990
17 Dan Pastorini, Houston, 1973
Warren Moon, Houston, 1984
Randall Cunningham, Philadelphia, 1989
16 Don Meredith, Dallas, 1964
Joe Cribbs, Buffalo, 1980
Steve Fuller, Kansas City, 1980
Paul McDonald, Cleveland, 1984
Phil Simms, N.Y. Giants, 1985

**Most Fumbles, Game**
7 Len Dawson, Kansas City vs. San Diego, Nov. 15, 1964
6 Sam Etcheverry, St. Louis vs. N.Y. Giants, Sept, 17, 1961
Dave Krieg, Seattle vs. Kansas City, Nov. 5, 1989
5 Paul Christman, Chi. Cardinals vs. Green Bay, Nov. 10, 1946
Charlie Conerly, N.Y. Giants vs. San Francisco, Dec. 1, 1957
Jack Kemp, Buffalo vs. Houston, Oct. 29, 1967
Roman Gabriel, Philadelphia vs. Oakland, Nov. 21, 1976
Randall Cunningham, Philadelphia vs. L.A. Raiders, Nov. 30, 1986 (OT)
Willie Totten, Buffalo vs. Indianapolis, Oct. 4, 1987
Dave Walter, Cincinnati vs. Seattle, Oct. 11, 1987
Dave Krieg, Seattle vs. San Diego, Nov. 25, 1990 (OT)
Andre Ware, Detroit vs. Green Bay, Dec. 6, 1992

## FUMBLES RECOVERED

**Most Fumbles Recovered, Career, Own and Opponents'**

44 Warren Moon, Houston, 1984-93 (44 own)
43 Fran Tarkenton, Minnesota, 1961-66, 1972-78; N.Y. Giants, 1967-71 (43 own)
38 Jack Kemp, Pittsburgh, 1957; L.A. Chargers, 1960; San Diego, 1961-62; Buffalo, 1962-67, 1969 (38 own)
Dan Fouts, San Diego, 1973-87 (37 own, 1 opp)

**Most Fumbles Recovered, Season, Own and Opponents'**

9 Don Hultz, Minnesota, 1963 (9 opp)
Dave Krieg, Seattle, 1989 (9 own)
8 Paul Christman, Chi. Cardinals, 1945 (8 own)
Joe Schmidt, Detroit, 1955 (8 opp)
Bill Butler, Minnesota, 1963 (8 own)
Kermit Alexander, San Francisco, 1965 (4 own, 4 opp)
Jack Lambert, Pittsburgh, 1976 (1 own, 7 opp)
Danny White, Dallas, 1981 (8 own)
Dan Marino, Miami, 1988 (7 own, 1 opp)
7 By many players

**Most Fumbles Recovered, Game, Own and Opponents'**

4 Otto Graham, Cleveland vs. N.Y. Giants, Oct. 25, 1953 (4 own)
Sam Etcheverry, St. Louis vs. N.Y. Giants, Sept. 17, 1961 (4 own)
Roman Gabriel, Los Angeles vs. San Francisco, Oct. 12, 1969 (4 own)
Joe Ferguson, Buffalo vs. Miami, Sept. 18, 1977 (4 own)
Randall Cunningham, Philadelphia vs. L.A. Raiders, Nov. 30, 1986 (OT) (4 own)
3 By many players

## OWN FUMBLES RECOVERED

**Most Own Fumbles Recovered, Career**

44 Warren Moon, Houston, 1984-93
43 Fran Tarkenton, Minnesota, 1961-66, 1972-78; N.Y. Giants, 1967-71
38 Jack Kemp, Pittsburgh, 1957; L.A. Chargers, 1960; San Diego, 1961-62; Buffalo, 1962-67, 1969

**Most Own Fumbles Recovered, Season**

9 Dave Krieg, Seattle, 1989
8 Paul Christman, Chi. Cardinals, 1945
Bill Butler, Minnesota, 1963
Danny White, Dallas, 1981
7 By many players

**Most Own Fumbles Recovered, Game**

4 Otto Graham, Cleveland vs. N.Y. Giants, Oct. 25, 1953
Sam Etcheverry, St. Louis vs. N.Y. Giants, Sept. 17, 1961
Roman Gabriel, Los Angeles vs. San Francisco, Oct. 12, 1969
Joe Ferguson, Buffalo vs. Miami, Sept. 18, 1977
Randall Cunningham, Philadelphia vs. L.A. Raiders, Nov. 30, 1986 (OT)
3 By many players

## OPPONENTS' FUMBLES RECOVERED

**Most Opponents' Fumbles Recovered, Career**

29 Jim Marshall, Cleveland, 1960; Minnesota, 1961-79
26 Rickey Jackson, New Orleans, 1981-93
25 Dick Butkus, Chicago, 1965-73

**Most Opponents' Fumbles Recovered, Season**

9 Don Hultz, Minnesota, 1963
8 Joe Schmidt, Detroit, 1955
7 Alan Page, Minnesota, 1970
Jack Lambert, Pittsburgh, 1976
Ray Childress, Houston, 1988
Rickey Jackson, New Orleans, 1990

**Most Opponents' Fumbles Recovered, Game**

3 Corwin Clatt, Chi. Cardinals vs. Detroit, Nov. 6, 1949
Vic Sears, Philadelphia vs. Green Bay, Nov. 2, 1952
Ed Beatty, San Francisco vs. Los Angeles, Oct. 7, 1956
Ron Carroll, Houston vs. Cincinnati, Oct. 27, 1974
Maurice Spencer, New Orleans vs. Atlanta, Oct. 10, 1976
Steve Nelson, New England vs. Philadelphia, Oct. 8, 1978
Charles Jackson, Kansas City vs. Pittsburgh, Sept. 6, 1981
Willie Buchanon, San Diego vs. Denver, Sept. 27, 1981
Joey Browner, Minnesota vs. San Francisco, Sept. 8, 1985
Ray Childress, Houston vs. Washington, Oct. 30, 1988
2 By many players

## YARDS RETURNING FUMBLES

**Longest Fumble Run (All TDs)**

104 Jack Tatum, Oakland vs. Green Bay, Sept. 24, 1972
100 Chris Martin, Kansas City vs. Miami, Oct. 13, 1991
99 Don Griffin, San Francisco vs. Chicago, Dec. 23, 1991

## TOUCHDOWNS

**Most Touchdowns, Career (Total)**

4 Bill Thompson, Denver, 1969-81
Jessie Tuggle, Atlanta, 1987-93
3 Ralph Heywood, Detroit, 1947-48; Boston, 1948; N.Y. Bulldogs, 1949
Leo Sugar, Chi. Cardinals, 1954-59; St. Louis, 1960; Philadelphia, 1961; Detroit, 1962
Bud McFadin, Los Angeles, 1952-56; Denver, 1960-63; Houston, 1964-65
Doug Cline, Houston, 1960-66; San Diego, 1966
Bob Lilly, Dall. Cowboys, 1961-74
Chris Hanburger, Washington, 1965-78
Lemar Parrish, Cincinnati, 1970-77; Washington, 1978-81; Buffalo, 1982
Paul Krause, Washington, 1964-67; Minnesota, 1968-79
Brad Dusek, Washington, 1974-81
David Logan, Tampa Bay, 1979-86; Green Bay, 1987
Thomas Howard, Kansas City, 1977-83; St. Louis, 1984-85
Greg Townsend, L.A. Raiders, 1983-93
Les Miller, San Diego, 1987-90; New Orleans, 1991-93
Chris Martin, New Orleans, 1983; Minnesota, 1984-88; Kansas City, 1989-92; L.A. Rams, 1993
Seth Joyner, Philadelphia, 1986-93
Derrick Thomas, Kansas City, 1989-93
2 By many players

**Most Touchdowns, Season (Total)**

2 Harold McPhail, Boston, 1934
Harry Ebding, Detroit, 1937
John Morelli, Boston, 1944
Frank Maznicki, Boston, 1947
Fred (Dippy) Evans, Chi. Bears, 1948
Ralph Heywood, Boston, 1948
Art Tait, N.Y. Yanks, 1951
John Dwyer, Los Angeles, 1952
Leo Sugar, Chi. Cardinals, 1957
Doug Cline, Houston, 1961
Jim Bradshaw, Pittsburgh, 1964
Royce Berry, Cincinnati, 1970
Ahmad Rashad, Buffalo, 1974
Tim Gray, Kansas City, 1977
Charles Phillips, Oakland, 1978
Kenny Johnson, Atlanta, 1981
George Martin, N.Y. Giants, 1981
Del Rodgers, Green Bay, 1982
Mike Douglass, Green Bay, 1983
Shelton Robinson, Seattle, 1983
Erik McMillan, N.Y. Jets, 1989
Les Miller, San Diego, 1990
Seth Joyner, Philadelphia, 1991
Robert Goff, New Orleans, 1992
Willie Clay, Detroit, 1993

**Most Touchdowns, Career (Own recovered)**

2 Ken Kavanaugh, Chi. Bears, 1940-41, 1945-50
Mike Ditka, Chicago, 1961-66; Philadelphia, 1967-68; Dallas, 1969-72
Gail Cogdill, Detroit, 1960-68; Baltimore, 1968; Atlanta, 1969-70
Ahmad Rashad, St. Louis, 1972-73; Buffalo, 1974; Minnesota, 1976-82
Jim Mitchell, Atlanta, 1969-79
Drew Pearson, Dallas, 1973-83
Del Rodgers, Green Bay, 1982, 1984; San Francisco, 1987-88

**Most Touchdowns, Season (Own recovered)**

2 Ahmad Rashad, Buffalo, 1974
Del Rodgers, Green Bay, 1982
1 By many players

**Most Touchdowns, Career (Opponents' recovered)**

4 Jessie Tuggle, Atlanta, 1987-93
3 Leo Sugar, Chi. Cardinals, 1954-59; St. Louis, 1960; Philadelphia, 1961; Detroit, 1962
Doug Cline, Houston, 1960-66; San Diego, 1966
Bud McFadin, Los Angeles, 1952-56; Denver, 1960-63; Houston, 1964-65
Bob Lilly, Dall. Cowboys, 1961-74
Chris Hanburger, Washington, 1965-78
Paul Krause, Washington, 1964-67; Minnesota, 1968-79
Lemar Parrish, Cincinnati, 1970-77; Washington, 1978-81; Buffalo, 1982
Bill Thompson, Denver, 1969-81
Brad Dusek, Washington, 1974-81
David Logan, Tampa Bay, 1979-86; Green Bay, 1987
Thomas Howard, Kansas City, 1977-83; St. Louis, 1984-85
Greg Townsend, L.A. Raiders, 1983-93
Les Miller, San Diego, 1987-90; New Orleans, 1991-93
Chris Martin, New Orleans, 1983; Minnesota, 1984-88; Kansas City, 1989-92; L.A. Rams, 1993
Seth Joyner, Philadelphia, 1986-93
Derrick Thomas, Kansas City, 1989-93
2 By many players

**Most Touchdowns, Season (Opponents' recovered)**

2 Harold McPhail, Boston, 1934

Harry Ebding, Detroit, 1937
John Morelli, Boston, 1944
Frank Maznicki, Boston, 1947
Fred (Dippy) Evans, Chi. Bears, 1948
Ralph Heywood, Boston, 1948
Art Tait, N.Y. Yanks, 1951
John Dwyer, Los Angeles, 1952
Leo Sugar, Chi. Cardinals, 1957
Doug Cline, Houston, 1961
Jim Bradshaw, Pittsburgh, 1964
Royce Berry, Cincinnati, 1970
Tim Gray, Kansas City, 1977
Charles Phillips, Oakland, 1978
Kenny Johnson, Atlanta, 1981
George Martin, N.Y. Giants, 1981
Mike Douglass, Green Bay, 1983
Shelton Robinson, Seattle, 1983
Erik McMillan, N.Y. Jets, 1989
Les Miller, San Diego, 1990
Seth Joyner, Philadelphia, 1991
Robert Goff, New Orleans, 1992
Willie Clay, Detroit, 1993

**Most Touchdowns, Game (Opponents' recovered)**
2 Fred (Dippy) Evans, Chi. Bears vs. Washington, Nov. 28, 1948

## COMBINED NET YARDS GAINED

Rushing, receiving, interception returns, punt returns, kickoff returns, and fumble returns

**Most Seasons Leading League**
5 Jim Brown, Cleveland, 1958-61, 1964
3 Cliff Battles, Boston, 1932-33; Washington, 1937
Gale Sayers, Chicago, 1965-67
Eric Dickerson, L.A. Rams, 1983-84, 1986
Thurman Thomas, Buffalo, 1989, 1991-92
2 By many players

**Most Consecutive Seasons Leading League**
4 Jim Brown, Cleveland, 1958-61
3 Gale Sayers, Chicago, 1965-67
2 Cliff Battles, Boston, 1932-33
Charley Trippi, Chi. Cardinals, 1948-49
Timmy Brown, Philadelphia, 1962-63
Floyd Little, Denver, 1967-68
James Brooks, San Diego, 1981-82
Eric Dickerson, L.A. Rams, 1983-84
Thurman Thomas, Buffalo, 1991-92

### ATTEMPTS

**Most Attempts, Career**
4,368 Walter Payton, Chicago, 1975-87
3,351 Tony Dorsett, Dallas, 1977-87; Denver, 1988
3,293 Eric Dickerson, L.A. Rams, 1983-87; Indianapolis, 1987-91; L.A. Raiders, 1992; Atlanta, 1993

**Most Attempts, Season**
496 James Wilder, Tampa Bay, 1984
449 Marcus Allen, L.A. Raiders, 1985
442 Eric Dickerson, L.A. Rams, 1983

**Most Attempts, Rookie, Season**
442 Eric Dickerson, L.A. Rams, 1983
395 George Rogers, New Orleans, 1981
390 Joe Cribbs, Buffalo, 1980

**Most Attempts, Game**
48 James Wilder, Tampa Bay vs. Pittsburgh, Oct. 30, 1983
47 James Wilder, Tampa Bay vs. Green Bay, Sept. 30, 1984 (OT)
46 Gerald Riggs, Atlanta vs. L.A. Rams, Nov. 17, 1985

### YARDS GAINED

**Most Yards Gained, Career**
21,803 Walter Payton, Chicago, 1975-87
16,326 Tony Dorsett, Dallas, 1977-87; Denver, 1988
15,459 Jim Brown, Cleveland, 1957-65

**Most Yards Gained, Season**
2,535 Lionel James, San Diego, 1985
2,462 Terry Metcalf, St. Louis, 1975
2,444 Mack Herron, New England, 1974

**Most Yards Gained, Rookie, Season**
2,317 Tim Brown, L.A. Raiders, 1988
2,272 Gale Sayers, Chicago, 1965
2,212 Eric Dickerson, L.A. Rams, 1983

**Most Yards Gained, Game**
373 Billy Cannon, Houston vs. N.Y. Titans, Dec. 10, 1961
345 Lionel James, San Diego vs. L.A. Raiders, Nov. 10, 1985 (OT)
341 Timmy Brown, Philadelphia vs. St. Louis, Dec. 16, 1962

## SACKS

Sacks have been compiled since 1982.

**Most Sacks, Career**
137 Reggie White, Philadelphia, 1985-92; Green Bay, 1993
132.5 Lawrence Taylor, N.Y. Giants, 1982-93
124.5 Richard Dent, Chicago, 1983-93

**Most Sacks, Season**
22 Mark Gastineau, N.Y. Jets, 1984
21 Reggie White, Philadelphia, 1987
Chris Doleman, Minnesota, 1989
20.5 Lawrence Taylor, N.Y. Giants, 1986

**Most Sacks, Rookie, Season**
12.5 Leslie O'Neal, San Diego, 1986
12 Charles Haley, San Francisco, 1986
11 Vernon Maxwell, Baltimore, 1983

**Most Sacks, Game**
7 Derrick Thomas, Kansas City vs. Seattle, Nov. 11, 1990
6 Fred Dean, San Francisco vs. New Orleans, Nov. 13, 1983
5.5 William Gay, Detroit vs. Tampa Bay, Sept. 4, 1983

## MISCELLANEOUS

**Longest Return of Missed Field Goal (All TDs)**
101 Al Nelson, Philadelphia vs. Dallas, Sept. 26, 1971
100 Al Nelson, Philadelphia vs. Cleveland, Dec. 11, 1966
Ken Ellis, Green Bay vs. N.Y. Giants, Sept. 19, 1971
99 Jerry Williams, Los Angeles vs. Green Bay, Dec. 16, 1951
Carl Taseff, Baltimore vs. Los Angeles, Dec. 12, 1959
Timmy Brown, Philadelphia vs. St. Louis, Sept. 16, 1962

## TEAM RECORDS

## CHAMPIONSHIPS

**Most Seasons League Champion**
11 Green Bay, 1929-31, 1936, 1939, 1944, 1961-62, 1965-67
9 Chi. Bears, 1921, 1932-33, 1940-41, 1943, 1946, 1963, 1985
6 N.Y. Giants, 1927, 1934, 1938, 1956, 1986, 1990

**Most Consecutive Seasons League Champion**
3 Green Bay, 1929-31
Green Bay, 1965-67
2 Canton, 1922-23
Chi. Bears, 1932-33
Chi. Bears, 1940-41
Philadelphia, 1948-49
Detroit, 1952-53
Cleveland, 1954-55
Baltimore, 1958-59
Houston, 1960-61
Green Bay, 1961-62
Buffalo, 1964-65
Miami, 1972-73
Pittsburgh, 1974-75
Pittsburgh, 1978-79
San Francisco, 1988-89
Dallas, 1992-93

**Most Times Finishing First, Regular Season (Since 1933)**
18 Clev. Browns, 1950-55, 1957, 1964-65, 1967-69, 1971, 1980, 1985-87, 1989
17 N.Y. Giants, 1933-35, 1938-39, 1941, 1944, 1946, 1956, 1958-59, 1961-63, 1986, 1989-90
16 Chi. Bears, 1933-34, 1937, 1940-43, 1946, 1956, 1963, 1984-88, 1990

**Most Consecutive Times Finishing First, Regular Season (Since 1933)**
7 Los Angeles, 1973-79
6 Cleveland, 1950-55
Dallas, 1966-71
Minnesota, 1973-78
Pittsburgh, 1974-79
5 Oakland, 1972-76
Chicago, 1984-88
San Francisco, 1986-90

## GAMES WON

**Most Consecutive Games Won**
17 Chi. Bears, 1933-34
16 Chi. Bears, 1941-42
Miami, 1971-73
Miami, 1983-84
15 L.A. Chargers/San Diego, 1960-61
San Francisco, 1989-90

**Most Consecutive Games Without Defeat**
25 Can ton, 1921-23 (won 22, tied 3)
24 Chi. Bears, 1941-43 (won 23, tied 1)
23 Green Bay, 1928-30 (won 21, tied 2)

**Most Games Won, Season**
15 San Francisco, 1984
Chicago, 1985
14 Miami, 1972
Pittsburgh, 1978
Washington, 1983
Miami, 1984
Chicago, 1986
N.Y. Giants, 1986
San Francisco, 1989
San Francisco, 1990
Washington, 1991
San Francisco, 1992
13 By many teams

**Most Consecutive Games Won, Season**
14 Miami, 1972
13 Chi. Bears, 1934
12 Minnesota, 1969
Chicago, 1985

**Most Consecutive Games Won, Start of Season**
14 Miami, 1972, entire season
13 Chi. Bears, 1934, entire season
12 Chicago, 1985

**Most Consecutive Games Won, End of Season**
14 Miami, 1972, entire season
13 Chi. Bears, 1934, entire season
11 Chi. Bears, 1942, entire season
Cleveland, 1951
Houston, 1993

**Most Consecutive Games Without Defeat, Season**
14 Miami, 1972 (won 14)
13 Chi. Bears, 1926 (won 11, tied 2)
Green Bay, 1929 (won 12, tied 1)
Chi. Bears, 1934 (won 13)
Baltimore, 1967 (won 11, tied 2)
12 Canton, 1922 (won 10, tied 2)
Canton, 1923 (won 11, tied 1)
Minnesota, 1969 (won 12)
Chicago, 1985 (won 12)

**Most Consecutive Games Without Defeat, Start of Season**
14 Miami, 1972 (won 14), entire season
13 Chi. Bears, 1926 (won 11, tied 2)
Green Bay, 1929 (won 12, tied 1), entire season
Chi. Bears, 1934 (won 13), entire season
Baltimore, 1967 (won 11, tied 2)
12 Canton, 1922 (won 10, tied 2), entire season
Canton, 1923 (won 11, tied 1), entire season
Chicago, 1985 (won 12)

**Most Consecutive Games Without Defeat, End of Season**
14 Miami, 1972 (won 14), entire season
13 Green Bay, 1929 (won 12, tied 1), entire season
Chi. Bears, 1934 (won 13), entire season
12 Canton, 1922 (won 10, tied 2), entire season
Canton, 1923 (won 11, tied 1), entire season

**Most Consecutive Home Games Won**
27 Miami, 1971-74
20 Green Bay, 1929-32
18 Oakland, 1968-70
Dallas, 1979-81

**Most Consecutive Home Games Without Defeat**
30 Green Bay, 1928-33 (won 27, tied 3)
27 Miami, 1971-74 (won 27)
25 Chi. Bears, 1923-25 (won 19, tied 6)

**Most Consecutive Road Games Won**
18 San Francisco, 1988-90
11 L.A. Chargers/San Diego, 1960-61
San Francisco, 1987-88
10 Chi. Bears, 1941-42
Dallas, 1968-69
New Orleans, 1987-88

**Most Consecutive Road Games Without Defeat**
18 San Francisco, 1988-90 (won 18)
13 Chi. Bears, 1941-43 (won 12, tied 1)
12 Green Bay, 1928-30 (won 10, tied 2)

**Most Shutout Games Won or Tied, Season**
10 Pottsville, 1926 (won 9, tied 1)
N.Y. Giants, 1927 (won 9, tied 1)
9 Akron, 1921 (won 8, tied 1)
Canton, 1922 (won 7, tied 2)
Frankford, 1926 (won 9)
Frankford, 1929 (won 6, tied 3)
8 By many teams

**Most Consecutive Shutout Games Won or Tied**
13 Akron, 1920-21 (won 10, tied 3)
7 Pottsville, 1926 (won 6, tied 1)
Detroit, 1934 (won 7)
6 Buffalo, 1920-21 (won 5, tied 1)
Frankford, 1926 (won 6)
Detroit, 1926 (won 4, tied 2)
N.Y. Giants, 1926-27 (won 5, tied 1)

## GAMES LOST

**Most Consecutive Games Lost**
26 Tampa Bay, 1976-77
19 Chi. Cardinals, 1942-43, 1945
Oakland, 1961-62
18 Houston, 1972-73

**Most Consecutive Games Without Victory**
26 Tampa Bay, 1976-77 (lost 26)
23 Rochester, 1922-25 (lost 21, tied 2)
Washington, 1960-61 (lost 20, tied 3)
19 Dayton, 1927-29 (lost 18, tied 1)
Chi. Cardinals, 1942-43, 1945 (lost 19)
Oakland, 1961-62 (lost 19)

**Most Games Lost, Season**
15 New Orleans, 1980
Dallas, 1989
New England, 1990
Indianapolis, 1991
14 By many teams

**Most Consecutive Games Lost, Season**
14 Tampa Bay, 1976
New Orleans, 1980
Baltimore, 1981
New England, 1990
13 Oakland, 1962
Pittsburgh, 1969
Indianapolis, 1986
12 Tampa Bay, 1977

**Most Consecutive Games Lost, Start of Season**
14 Tampa Bay, 1976, entire season
New Orleans, 1980
13 Oakland, 1962
Indianapolis, 1986
12 Tampa Bay, 1977

**Most Consecutive Games Lost, End of Season**
14 Tampa Bay, 1976, entire season
New England, 1990
13 Pittsburgh, 1969
11 Philadelphia, 1936
Detroit, 1942, entire season
Houston, 1972

**Most Consecutive Games Without Victory, Season**
14 Tampa Bay, 1976 (lost 14), entire season
New Orleans, 1980 (lost 14)
Baltimore, 1981 (lost 14)
New England, 1990 (lost 14)
13 Washington, 1961 (lost 12, tied 1)
Oakland, 1962 (lost 13)
Pittsburgh, 1969 (lost 13)
Indianapolis, 1986 (lost 13)
12 Dall. Cowboys, 1960 (lost 11, tied 1), entire season
Tampa Bay, 1977 (lost 12)

**Most Consecutive Games Without Victory, Start of Season**
14 Tampa Bay, 1976 (lost 14), entire season
New Orleans, 1980 (lost 14)
13 Washington, 1961 (lost 12, tied 1)
Oakland, 1962 (lost 13)
Indianapolis, 1986 (lost 13)
12 Dall. Cowboys, 1960 (lost 11, tied 1), entire season
Tampa Bay, 1977 (lost 12)

**Most Consecutive Games Without Victory, End of Season**
14 Tampa Bay, 1976, (lost 14), entire season
New England, 1990 (lost 14)
13 Pittsburgh, 1969 (lost 13)
12 Dall. Cowboys, 1960 (lost 11, tied 1), entire season

**Most Consecutive Home Games Lost**
14 Dallas, 1988-89
13 Houston, 1972-73
Tampa Bay, 1976-77
11 Oakland, 1961-62
Los Angeles, 1961-63

**Most Consecutive Home Games Without Victory**
14 Dallas, 1988-89 (lost 14)
13 Houston, 1972-73 (lost 13)

Tampa Bay, 1976-77 (lost 13)
12 Philadelphia, 1936-38 (lost 11, tied 1)

**Most Consecutive Road Games Lost**
23 Houston, 1981-84
22 Buffalo, 1983-86
19 Tampa Bay, 1983-85
Atlanta, 1988-91

**Most Consecutive Road Games Without Victory**
23 Houston, 1981-84 (lost 23)
22 Buffalo, 1983-86 (lost 22)
19 Tampa Bay, 1983-85 (lost 19)
Atlanta, 1988-91 (lost 19)

**Most Shutout Games Lost or Tied, Season**
8 Frankford, 1927 (lost 6, tied 2)
Brooklyn, 1931 (lost 8)
7 Dayton, 1925 (lost 6, tied 1)
Orange, 1929 (lost 4, tied 3)
Frankford, 1931 (lost 6, tied 1)
6 By many teams

**Most Consecutive Shutout Games Lost or Tied**
8 Rochester, 1922-24 (lost 8)
7 Hammond, 1922-23 (lost 6, tied 1)
6 Providence, 1926-27 (lost 5, tied 1)
Brooklyn, 1942-43 (lost 6)

## TIE GAMES

**Most Tie Games, Season**
6 Chi. Bears, 1932
5 Frankford, 1929
4 Chi. Bears, 1924
Orange, 1929
Portsmouth, 1932

**Most Consecutive Tie Games**
3 Chi. Bears, 1932
2 By many teams

## SCORING

**Most Seasons Leading League**
10 Chi. Bears, 1932, 1934-35, 1939, 1941-43, 1946-47, 1956
7 San Francisco, 1953, 1965, 1970, 1987, 1989, 1992-93
6 Green Bay, 1931, 1936-38, 1961-62
L.A. Rams, 1950-52, 1957, 1967, 1973

**Most Consecutive Seasons Leading League**
3 Green Bay, 1936-38
Chi. Bears, 1941-43
Los Angeles, 1950-52
Oakland, 1967-69

### POINTS

**Most Points, Season**
541 Washington, 1983
513 Houston, 1961
Miami, 1984
485 Washington, 1991

**Fewest Points, Season (Since 1932)**
37 Cincinnati/St. Louis, 1934
38 Cincinnati, 1933
Detroit, 1942
51 Pittsburgh, 1934
Philadelphia, 1936

**Most Points, Game**
72 Washington vs. N.Y. Giants, Nov. 27, 1966
70 Los Angeles vs. Baltimore, Oct. 22, 1950
65 Chi. Cardinals vs. N.Y. Bulldogs, Nov. 13, 1949
Los Angeles vs. Detroit, Oct. 29, 1950

**Most Points, Both Teams, Game**
113 Washington (72) vs. N.Y. Giants (41), Nov. 27, 1966
101 Oakland (52) vs. Houston (49), Dec. 22, 1963
99 Seattle (51) vs. Kansas City (48), Nov. 27, 1983 (OT)

**Fewest Points, Both Teams, Game**
0 In many games. Last time: N.Y. Giants vs. Detroit, Nov. 7, 1943

**Most Points, Shutout Victory, Game**
64 Philadelphia vs. Cincinnati, Nov. 6, 1934
62 Akron vs. Oorang, Oct. 29, 1922
60 Rock Island vs. Evansville, Oct. 15, 1922
Chi. Cardinals vs. Rochester, Oct. 7, 1923

**Fewest Points, Shutout Victory, Game**
2 Green Bay vs. Chi. Bears, Oct. 16, 1932
Chi. Bears vs. Green Bay, Sept. 18, 1938

**Most Points Overcome to Win Game**
28 San Francisco vs. New Orleans, Dec. 7, 1980 (OT) (trailed 7-35, won 38-35)
25 St. Louis vs. Tampa Bay, Nov. 8, 1987 (trailed 3-28, won 31-28)
24 Philadelphia vs. Washington, Oct. 27, 1946 (trailed 0-24, won 28-24)
Detroit vs. Baltimore, Oct. 20, 1957 (trailed 3-27, won 31-27)
Philadelphia vs. Chi. Cardinals, Oct. 25, 1959 (trailed 0-24, won 28-24)
Denver vs. Boston, Oct. 23, 1960 (trailed 0-24, won 31-24)
Miami vs. New England, Dec. 15, 1974 (trailed 0-24, won 34-27)
Minnesota vs. San Francisco, Dec. 4, 1977 (trailed 0-24, won 28-27)
Denver vs. Seattle, Sept. 23, 1979 (trailed 10-34, won 37-34)
Houston vs. Cincinnati, Sept. 23, 1979 (OT) (trailed 0-24, won 30-27)
L.A. Raiders vs. San Diego, Nov. 22, 1982 (trailed 0-24, won 28-24)
L.A. Raiders vs. Denver, Sept. 26, 1988 (OT) (trailed 0-24, won 30-27)
L.A. Rams vs. Tampa Bay, Dec. 6, 1992 (trailed 3-27, won 31-27)

**Most Points Overcome to Tie Game**
31 Denver vs. Buffalo, Nov. 27, 1960 (trailed 7-38, tied 38-38)
28 Los Angeles vs. Philadelphia, Oct. 3, 1948 (trailed 0-28, tied 28-28)

**Most Points, Each Half**
1st: 49 Green Bay vs. Tampa Bay, Oct. 2, 1983
48 Buffalo vs. Miami, Sept. 18, 1966
45 Green Bay vs. Cleveland, Nov. 12, 1967
Indianapolis vs. Denver, Oct. 31, 1988
Houston vs. Cleveland, Dec. 9, 1990
2nd: 49 Chi. Bears vs. Philadelphia, Nov. 30, 1941
48 Chi. Cardinals vs. Baltimore, Oct. 2, 1950
N.Y. Giants vs. Baltimore, Nov. 19, 1950
45 Cincinnati vs. Houston, Dec. 17, 1972

**Most Points, Both Teams, Each Half**
1st: 70 Houston (35) vs. Oakland (35), Dec. 22, 1963
62 N.Y. Jets (41) vs. Tampa Bay (21), Nov. 17, 1985
59 St. Louis (31) vs. Philadelphia (28), Dec. 16, 1962
2nd: 65 Washington (38) vs. N.Y. Giants (27), Nov. 27, 1966
62 L.A. Raiders (31) vs. San Diego (31), Jan. 2, 1983
58 New England (37) vs. Baltimore (21), Nov. 23, 1980
N.Y. Jets (37) vs. New England (21), Sept. 21, 1987

**Most Points, One Quarter**
41 Green Bay vs. Detroit, Oct. 7, 1945 (second quarter)
Los Angeles vs. Detroit, Oct. 29, 1950 (third quarter)
37 Los Angeles vs. Green Bay, Sept. 21, 1980 (second quarter)
35 Chi. Cardinals vs. Boston, Oct. 24, 1948 (third quarter)
Green Bay vs. Cleveland, Nov. 12, 1967 (first quarter)
Green Bay vs. Tampa Bay, Oct. 2, 1983 (second quarter)

**Most Points, Both Teams, One Quarter**
49 Oakland (28) vs. Houston (21), Dec. 22, 1963 (second quarter)
48 Green Bay (41) vs. Detroit (7), Oct. 7, 1945 (second quarter)
Los Angeles (41) vs. Detroit (7), Oct. 29, 1950 (third quarter)
47 St. Louis (27) vs. Philadelphia (20), Dec. 13, 1964 (second quarter)

**Most Points, Each Quarter**
1st: 35 Green Bay vs. Cleveland, Nov. 12, 1967
31 Buffalo vs. Kansas City, Sept. 13, 1964
28 By seven teams
2nd: 41 Green Bay vs. Detroit, Oct. 7, 1945
37 Los Angeles vs. Green Bay, Sept. 21, 1980
35 Green Bay vs. Tampa Bay, Oct. 2, 1983
3rd: 41 Los Angeles vs. Detroit, Oct. 29, 1950
35 Chi. Cardinals vs. Boston, Oct. 24, 1948
28 By nine teams
4th: 31 Oakland vs. Denver, Dec. 17, 1960
Oakland vs. San Diego, Dec. 8, 1963
Atlanta vs. Green Bay, Sept. 13, 1981
28 By many teams

**Most Points, Both Teams, Each Quarter**
1st: 42 Green Bay (35) vs. Cleveland (7), Nov. 12, 1967
35 Dall. Texans (21) vs. N.Y. Titans (14), Nov. 11, 1962
Dallas (28) vs. Philadelphia (7), Oct. 19, 1969
Kansas City (21) vs. Seattle (14), Dec. 11, 1977
Detroit (21) vs. L.A. Raiders (14), Dec. 10, 1990
Dallas (21) vs. Atlanta (14), Dec. 22, 1991
34 Los Angeles (21) vs. Baltimore (13), Oct. 22, 1950
Oakland (21) vs. Atlanta (13), Nov. 30, 1975
2nd: 49 Oakland (28) vs. Houston (21), Dec. 22, 1963
48 Green Bay (41) vs. Detroit (7), Oct. 7, 1945
47 St. Louis (27) vs. Philadelphia (20), Dec. 13, 1964
3rd: 48 Los Angeles (41) vs. Detroit (7), Oct. 29, 1950
42 Washington (28) vs. Philadelphia (14), Oct. 1, 1955
41 Green Bay (21) vs. N.Y. Yanks (20), Oct. 8, 1950
4th: 42 Chi. Cardinals (28) vs. Philadelphia (14), Dec. 7, 1947
Green Bay (28) vs. Chi. Bears (14), Nov. 6, 1955
N.Y. Jets (28) vs. Boston (14), Oct. 27, 1968
Pittsburgh (21) vs. Cleveland (21), Oct. 18, 1969
41 Baltimore (27) vs. New England (14), Sept. 18, 1978
New England (27) vs. Baltimore (14), Nov. 23, 1980
40 Chicago (21) vs. Tampa Bay (19), Nov. 19, 1989

**Most Consecutive Games Scoring**
274 Cleveland, 1950-71
258 San Francisco, 1977-93 (current)

218 Dallas, 1970-85

### TOUCHDOWNS

**Most Seasons Leading League, Touchdowns**
13 Chi. Bears, 1932, 1934-35, 1939, 1941-44, 1946-48, 1956, 1965
7 Dallas, 1966, 1968, 1971, 1973, 1977-78, 1980
6 Oakland, 1967-69, 1972, 1974, 1977
San Diego, 1963, 1965, 1979, 1981-82, 1985

**Most Consecutive Seasons Leading League, Touchdowns**
4 Chi. Bears, 1941-44
Los Angeles, 1949-52
3 Chi. Bears, 1946-48
Baltimore, 1957-59
Oakland, 1967-69
2 By many teams

**Most Touchdowns, Season**
70 Miami, 1984
66 Houston, 1961
64 Los Angeles, 1950

**Fewest Touchdowns, Season (Since 1932)**
3 Cincinnati, 1933
4 Cincinnati/St. Louis, 1934
5 Detroit, 1942

**Most Touchdowns, Game**
10 Philadelphia vs. Cincinnati, Nov. 6, 1934
Los Angeles vs. Baltimore, Oct. 22, 1950
Washington vs. N.Y. Giants, Nov. 27, 1966
9 Chi. Cardinals vs. Rochester, Oct. 7, 1923
Chi. Cardinals vs. N.Y. Giants, Oct. 17, 1948
Chi. Cardinals vs. N.Y. Bulldogs, Nov. 13, 1949
Los Angeles vs. Detroit, Oct. 29, 1950
Pittsburgh vs. N.Y. Giants, Nov. 30, 1952
Chicago vs. San Francisco, Dec. 12, 1965
Chicago vs. Green Bay, Dec. 7, 1980
8 By many teams.

**Most Touchdowns, Both Teams, Game**
16 Washington (10) vs. N.Y. Giants (6), Nov. 27, 1966
14 Chi. Cardinals (9) vs. N.Y. Giants (5), Oct. 17, 1948
Los Angeles (10) vs. Baltimore (4), Oct. 22, 1950
Houston (7) vs. Oakland (7), Dec. 22, 1963
13 New Orleans (7) vs. St. Louis (6), Nov. 2, 1969
Kansas City (7) vs. Seattle (6), Nov. 27, 1983 (OT)
San Diego (8) vs. Pittsburgh (5), Dec. 8, 1985
N.Y. Jets (7) vs. Miami (6), Sept. 21, 1986 (OT)

**Most Consecutive Games Scoring Touchdowns**
166 Cleveland, 1957-69
97 Oakland, 1966-73
96 Kansas City, 1963-70

### POINTS AFTER TOUCHDOWN

**Most Points After Touchdown, Season**
66 Miami, 1984
65 Houston, 1961
62 Washington, 1983

**Fewest Points After Touchdown, Season**
2 Chi. Cardinals, 1933
3 Cincinnati, 1933
Pittsburgh, 1934
4 Cincinnati/St. Louis, 1934

**Most Points After Touchdown, Game**
10 Los Angeles vs. Baltimore, Oct. 22, 1950
9 Chi. Cardinals vs. N.Y. Giants, Oct. 17, 1948
Pittsburgh vs. N.Y. Giants, Nov. 30, 1952
Washington vs. N.Y. Giants, Nov. 27, 1966
8 By many teams

**Most Points After Touchdown, Both Teams, Game**
14 Chi. Cardinals (9) vs. N.Y. Giants (5), Oct. 17, 1948
Houston (7) vs. Oakland (7), Dec. 22, 1963
Washington (9) vs. N.Y. Giants (5), Nov. 27, 1966
13 Los Angeles (10) vs. Baltimore (3), Oct. 22, 1950
12 In many games

### FIELD GOALS

**Most Seasons Leading League, Field Goals**
11 Green Bay, 1935-36, 1940-43, 1946-47, 1955, 1972, 1974
8 Washington, 1945, 1956, 1971, 1976-77, 1979, 1982, 1992
7 N.Y. Giants, 1933, 1937, 1939, 1941, 1944, 1959, 1983

**Most Consecutive Seasons Leading League, Field Goals**
4 Green Bay, 1940-43
3 Cleveland, 1952-54
2 By many teams

**Most Field Goals Attempted, Season**
49 Los Angeles, 1966
Washington, 1971
48 Green Bay, 1972
47 N.Y. Jets, 1969
Los Angeles, 1973
Washington, 1983

**Fewest Field Goals Attempted, Season (Since 1938)**
0 Chi. Bears, 1944
2 Cleveland, 1939
Card-Pitt, 1944
Boston, 1946
Chi. Bears, 1947
3 Chi. Bears, 1945
Cleveland, 1945

**Most Field Goals Attempted, Game**
9 St. Louis vs. Pittsburgh, Sept. 24, 1967
8 Pittsburgh vs. St. Louis, Dec. 2, 1962
Detroit vs. Minnesota, Nov. 13, 1966
N.Y. Jets vs. Buffalo, Nov. 3, 1968
7 By many teams

**Most Field Goals Attempted, Both Teams, Game**
11 St. Louis (6) vs. Pittsburgh (5), Nov. 13, 1966
Washington (6) vs. Chicago (5), Nov. 14, 1971
Green Bay (6) vs. Detroit (5), Sept. 29, 1974
Washington (6) vs. N.Y. Giants (5), Nov. 14, 1976
10 Denver (5) vs. Boston (5), Nov. 11, 1962
Boston (7) vs. San Diego (3), Sept. 20, 1964
Buffalo (7) vs. Houston (3), Dec. 5, 1965
St. Louis (7) vs. Atlanta (3), Dec. 11, 1966
Boston (7) vs. Buffalo (3), Sept. 24, 1967
Detroit (7) vs. Minnesota (3), Sept. 20, 1971
Washington (7) vs. Houston (3), Oct. 10, 1971
Green Bay (5) vs. St. Louis (5), Dec. 5, 1971
Kansas City (7) vs. Buffalo (3), Dec. 19, 1971
Kansas City (5) vs. San Diego (5), Oct. 29, 1972
Minnesota (6) vs. Chicago (4), Sept. 23, 1973
Cleveland (7) vs. Denver (3), Oct. 19, 1975
Cleveland (5) vs. Denver (5), Oct. 5, 1980
9 In many games

**Most Field Goals, Season**
35 N.Y. Giants, 1983
L.A. Raiders, 1993
34 N.Y. Jets, 1968
Kansas City, 1990
Detroit, 1993
33 Green Bay, 1972
Washington, 1983
Pittsburgh, 1985
New Orleans, 1987
Miami, 1991

**Fewest Field Goals, Season (Since 1932)**
0 Boston, 1932, 1935
Chi. Cardinals, 1932, 1945
Green Bay, 1932, 1944
N.Y. Giants, 1932
Brooklyn, 1944
Card-Pitt, 1944
Chi. Bears, 1944, 1947
Boston, 1946
Baltimore, 1950
Dallas, 1952

**Most Field Goals, Game**
7 St. Louis vs. Pittsburgh, Sept. 24, 1967
Minnesota vs. L.A. Rams, Nov. 5, 1989 (OT)
6 Boston vs. Denver, Oct. 4, 1964
Detroit vs. Minnesota, Nov. 13, 1966
N.Y. Jets vs. Buffalo, Nov. 3, 1968
Philadelphia vs. Houston, Nov. 12, 1972
N.Y. Jets vs. New Orleans, Dec. 3, 1972
St. Louis vs. Atlanta, Dec. 9, 1973
N.Y. Giants vs. Seattle, Oct. 18, 1981
San Francisco vs. New Orleans, Oct. 16, 1983
Pittsburgh vs. Denver, Oct. 23, 1988
San Diego vs. Seattle, Sept. 5, 1993
San Diego vs. Houston, Sept. 19, 1993
5 By many teams

**Most Field Goals, Both Teams, Game**
8 Cleveland (4) vs. St. Louis (4), Sept. 20, 1964
Chicago (5) vs. Philadelphia (3), Oct. 20, 1968
Washington (5) vs. Chicago (3), Nov. 14, 1971
Kansas City (5) vs. Buffalo (3), Dec. 19, 1971
Detroit (4) vs. Green Bay (4), Sept. 29, 1974
Cleveland (5) vs. Denver (3), Oct. 19, 1975
New England (4) vs. San Diego (4), Nov. 9, 1975

San Francisco (6) vs. New Orleans (2), Oct. 16, 1983
Seattle (5) vs. L.A. Raiders (3), Dec. 18, 1988
7 In many games

**Most Consecutive Games Scoring Field Goals**
31 Minnesota, 1968-70
28 Washington, 1988-90
22 San Francisco, 1988-89

## SAFETIES

**Most Safeties, Season**
4 Cleveland, 1927
Detroit, 1962
3 By many teams

**Most Safeties, Game**
3 L.A. Rams vs. N.Y. Giants, Sept. 30, 1984
2 N.Y. Giants vs. Pottsville, Oct. 30, 1927
Chi. Bears vs. Pottsville, Nov. 13, 1927
Detroit vs. Brooklyn, Dec. 1, 1935
N.Y. Giants vs. Pittsburgh, Sept. 17, 1950
N.Y. Giants vs. Washington, Nov. 5, 1961
Chicago vs. Pittsburgh, Nov. 9, 1969
Dallas vs. Philadelphia, Nov. 19, 1972
Los Angeles vs. Green Bay, Oct. 21, 1973
Oakland vs. San Diego, Oct. 26, 1975
Denver vs. Seattle, Jan. 2, 1983
New Orleans vs. Cleveland, Sept. 13, 1987
Buffalo vs. Denver, Nov. 8, 1987

**Most Safeties, Both Teams, Game**
3 L.A. Rams (3) vs. N.Y. Giants (0), Sept. 30, 1984
2 Chi. Cardinals (1) vs. Frankford (1), Nov. 19, 1927
Chi. Cardinals (1) vs. Cincinnati (1), Nov. 12, 1933
Chi. Bears (1) vs. San Francisco (1), Oct. 19, 1952
Cincinnati (1) vs. Los Angeles (1), Oct. 22, 1972
Chi. Bears (1) vs. San Francisco (1), Sept. 19, 1976
Baltimore (1) vs. Miami (1), Oct. 29, 1978
Atlanta (1) vs. Detroit (1), Oct. 5, 1980
Houston (1) vs. Philadelphia (1), Oct. 2, 1988
Cleveland (1) vs. Seattle (1), Nov. 14, 1993
(Also see previous record)

## FIRST DOWNS

**Most Seasons Leading League**
9 Chi. Bears, 1935, 1939, 1941, 1943, 1945, 1947-49, 1955
7 San Diego, 1965, 1969, 1980-83, 1985
6 L.A. Rams, 1946, 1950-51, 1954, 1957, 1973

**Most Consecutive Seasons Leading League**
4 San Diego, 1980-83
3 Chi. Bears, 1947-49
2 By many teams

**Most First Downs, Season**
387 Miami, 1984
380 San Diego, 1985
379 San Diego, 1981

**Fewest First Downs, Season**
51 Cincinnati, 1933
64 Pittsburgh, 1935
67 Philadelphia, 1937

**Most First Downs, Game**
39 N.Y. Jets vs. Miami, Nov. 27, 1988
Washington vs. Detroit, Nov. 4, 1990 (OT)
38 Los Angeles vs. N.Y. Giants, Nov. 13, 1966
37 Green Bay vs. Philadelphia, Nov. 11, 1962

**Fewest First Downs, Game**
0 N.Y. Giants vs. Green Bay, Oct. 1, 1933
Pittsburgh vs. Boston, Oct. 29, 1933
Philadelphia vs. Detroit, Sept. 20, 1935
N.Y. Giants vs. Washington, Sept. 27, 1942
Denver vs. Houston, Sept. 3, 1966

**Most First Downs, Both Teams, Game**
62 San Diego (32) vs. Seattle (30), Sept. 15, 1985
59 Miami (31) vs. Buffalo (28), Oct. 9, 1983 (OT)
Seattle (33) vs. Kansas City (26), Nov. 27, 1983 (OT)
N.Y. Jets (32) vs. Miami (27), Sept. 21, 1986 (OT)
N.Y. Jets (39) vs. Miami (20), Nov. 27, 1988
58 Los Angeles (30) vs. Chi. Bears (28), Oct. 24, 1954
Denver (34) vs. Kansas City (24), Nov. 18, 1974
Atlanta (35) vs. New Orleans (23), Sept. 2, 1979 (OT)
Pittsburgh (36) vs. Cleveland (22), Nov. 25, 1979 (OT)
San Diego (34) vs. Miami (24), Nov. 18, 1984 (OT)
Cincinnati (32) vs. San Diego (26), Sept. 22, 1985

**Fewest First Downs, Both Teams, Game**
7 Chi. Cardinals (2) vs. Detroit (5), Sept. 15, 1940
9 Pittsburgh (1) vs. Boston (8), Oct. 27, 1935
Boston (4) vs. Brooklyn (5), Nov. 24, 1935
N.Y. Giants (3) vs. Detroit (6), Nov. 7, 1943
Pittsburgh (4) vs. Chi. Cardinals (5), Nov. 11, 1945
N.Y. Bulldogs (1) vs. Philadelphia (8), Sept. 22, 1949
10 N.Y. Giants (4) vs. Washington (6), Dec. 11, 1960

**Most First Downs, Rushing, Season**
181 New England, 1978
177 Los Angeles, 1973
176 Chicago, 1985

**Fewest First Downs, Rushing, Season**
36 Cleveland, 1942
Boston, 1944
39 Brooklyn, 1943
40 Philadelphia, 1940
Detroit, 1945

**Most First Downs, Rushing, Game**
25 Philadelphia vs. Washington, Dec. 2, 1951
23 St. Louis vs. New Orleans, Oct. 5, 1980
21 Cleveland vs. Philadelphia, Dec. 13, 1959
Green Bay vs. Philadelphia, Nov. 11, 1962
Los Angeles vs. New Orleans, Nov. 25, 1973
Pittsburgh vs. Kansas City, Nov. 7, 1976
New England vs. Denver, Nov. 28, 1976
Oakland vs. Green Bay, Sept. 17, 1978

**Fewest First Downs, Rushing, Game**
0 By many teams. Last time: Tampa Bay vs. Phoenix, Dec. 27, 1992

**Most First Downs, Rushing, Both Teams, Game**
36 Philadelphia (25) vs. Washington (11), Dec. 2, 1951
31 Detroit (18) vs. Washington (13), Sept. 30, 1951
30 Los Angeles (17) vs. Minnesota (13), Nov. 5, 1961
New Orleans (17) vs. Green Bay (13), Sept. 9, 1979
New Orleans (16) vs. San Francisco (14), Nov. 11, 1979
New England (16) vs. Kansas City (14), Oct. 4, 1981

**Fewest First Downs, Rushing, Both Teams, Game**
2 Houston (0) vs. Denver (2), Dec. 2, 1962
3 Philadelphia (1) vs. Pittsburgh (2), Oct. 27, 1957
Boston (1) vs. Buffalo (2), Nov. 15, 1964
Los Angeles (0) vs. San Francisco (3), Dec. 6, 1964
Pittsburgh (1) vs. St. Louis (2), Nov. 13, 1966
Seattle (1) vs. New Orleans (2), Sept. 1, 1991
4 In many games

**Most First Downs, Passing, Season**
259 San Diego, 1985
251 Houston, 1990
250 Miami, 1986

**Fewest First Downs, Passing, Season**
18 Pittsburgh, 1941
23 Brooklyn, 1942
N.Y. Giants, 1944
24 N.Y. Giants, 1943

**Most First Downs, Passing, Game**
29 N.Y. Giants vs. Cincinnati, Oct. 13, 1985
27 San Diego vs. Seattle, Sept. 15, 1985
26 Miami vs. Cleveland, Dec. 12, 1988

**Fewest First Downs, Passing, Game**
0 By many teams. Last time: Houston vs. Kansas City, Oct. 9, 1988

**Most First Downs, Passing, Both Teams, Game**
43 San Diego (23) vs. Cincinnati (20), Dec. 20, 1982
Miami (24) vs. N.Y. Jets (19), Sept. 21, 1986 (OT)
42 San Francisco (22) vs. San Diego (20), Dec. 11, 1982
41 San Diego (27) vs. Seattle (14), Sept. 15, 1985
Miami (26) vs. Cleveland (15), Dec. 12, 1988

**Fewest First Downs, Passing, Both Teams, Game**
0 Brooklyn vs. Pittsburgh, Nov. 29, 1942
1 Green Bay (0) vs. Cleveland (1), Sept. 21, 1941
Pittsburgh (0) vs. Brooklyn (1), Oct. 11, 1942
N.Y. Giants (0) vs. Detroit (1), Nov. 7, 1943
Pittsburgh (0) vs. Chi. Cardinals (1), Nov. 11, 1945
N.Y. Bulldogs (0) vs. Philadelphia (1), Sept. 22, 1949
Chicago (0) vs. Buffalo (1), Oct. 7, 1979
2 In many games

**Most First Downs, Penalty, Season**
42 Chicago, 1987
41 Denver, 1986
39 Seattle, 1978

**Fewest First Downs, Penalty, Season**
2 Brooklyn, 1940
4 Chi. Cardinals, 1940
N.Y. Giants, 1942, 1944
Washington, 1944
Cleveland, 1952
Kansas City, 1969
5 Brooklyn, 1939

Chi. Bears, 1939
Detroit, 1953
Los Angeles, 1953
Houston, 1982

**Most First Downs, Penalty, Game**
11 Denver vs. Houston, Oct. 6, 1985
9 Chi. Bears vs. Cleveland, Nov. 25, 1951
Baltimore vs. Pittsburgh, Oct. 30, 1977
N.Y. Jets vs. Houston, Sept. 18, 1988
8 Philadelphia vs. Detroit, Dec. 2, 1979
Cincinnati vs. N.Y. Jets, Oct. 6, 1985
Buffalo vs. Houston, Sept. 20, 1987
Houston vs. Atlanta, Sept. 9, 1990
Kansas City vs. L.A. Raiders, Oct. 3, 1993

**Fewest First Downs, Penalty, Game**
0 By many teams

**Most First Downs, Penalty, Both Teams, Game**
11 Chi. Bears (9) vs. Cleveland (2), Nov. 25, 1951
Cincinnati (8) vs. N.Y. Jets (3), Oct. 6, 1985
Denver (11) vs. Houston (0), Oct. 6, 1985
Detroit (6) vs. Dallas (5), Nov. 8, 1987
N.Y. Jets (9) vs. Houston (2), Sept. 18, 1988
Kansas City (8) vs. L.A. Raiders (3), Oct. 3, 1993
10 In many games

## NET YARDS GAINED RUSHING AND PASSING

**Most Seasons Leading League**
12 Chi. Bears, 1932, 1934-35, 1939, 1941-44, 1947, 1949, 1955-56
7 San Diego, 1963, 1965, 1980-83, 1985
6 L.A. Rams, 1946, 1950-51, 1954, 1957, 1973
Baltimore, 1958-60, 1964, 1967, 1976
Dall. Cowboys, 1966, 1968-69, 1971, 1974, 1977

**Most Consecutive Seasons Leading League**
4 Chi. Bears, 1941-44
San Diego, 1980-83
3 Baltimore, 1958-60
Houston, 1960-62
Oakland, 1968-70
2 By many teams

**Most Yards Gained, Season**
6,936 Miami, 1984
6,744 San Diego, 1981
6,535 San Diego, 1985

**Fewest Yards Gained, Season**
1,150 Cincinnati, 1933
1,443 Chi. Cardinals, 1934
1,486 Chi. Cardinals, 1933

**Most Yards Gained, Game**
735 Los Angeles vs. N.Y. Yanks, Sept. 28, 1951
683 Pittsburgh vs. Chi. Cardinals, Dec. 13, 1958
682 Chi. Bears vs. N.Y. Giants, Nov. 14, 1943

**Fewest Yards Gained, Game**
–7 Seattle vs. Los Angeles, Nov. 4, 1979
–5 Denver vs. Oakland, Sept. 10, 1967
14 Chi. Cardinals vs. Detroit, Sept. 15, 1940

**Most Yards Gained, Both Teams, Game**
1,133 Los Angeles (636) vs. N.Y. Yanks (497), Nov. 19, 1950
1,102 San Diego (661) vs. Cincinnati (441), Dec. 20, 1982
1,087 St. Louis (589) vs. Philadelphia (498), Dec. 16, 1962

**Fewest Yards Gained, Both Teams, Game**
30 Chi. Cardinals (14) vs. Detroit (16), Sept. 15, 1940
136 Chi. Cardinals (50) vs. Green Bay (86), Nov. 18, 1934
154 N.Y. Giants (51) vs. Washington (103), Dec. 11, 1960

**Most Consecutive Games, 400 or More Yards Gained**
11 San Diego, 1982-83
6 Houston, 1961-62
San Diego, 1981
San Francisco, 1987
5 Chi. Bears, 1947
Philadelphia, 1953
Chi. Bears, 1955
Oakland, 1968
New England, 1981
Cincinnati, 1986

**Most Consecutive Games, 300 or More Yards Gained**
29 Los Angeles, 1949-51
26 Miami, 1983-85
19 Cleveland, 1978-79
San Diego, 1980-82
San Francisco, 1988-89

## RUSHING

**Most Seasons Leading League**
16 Chi. Bears, 1932, 1934-35, 1939-42, 1951, 1955-56, 1968, 1977, 1983-86
7 Buffalo, 1962, 1964, 1973, 1975, 1982, 1991-92
6 Cleveland, 1958-59, 1963, 1965-67

**Most Consecutive Seasons Leading League**
4 Chi. Bears, 1939-42
Chi. Bears, 1983-86
3 Detroit, 1936-38
San Francisco, 1952-54
Cleveland, 1965-67
2 By many teams

### ATTEMPTS

**Most Rushing Attempts, Season**
681 Oakland, 1977
674 Chicago, 1984
671 New England, 1978

**Fewest Rushing Attempts, Season**
211 Philadelphia, 1982
219 San Francisco, 1982
225 Houston, 1982

**Most Rushing Attempts, Game**
72 Chi. Bears vs. Brooklyn, Oct. 20, 1935
70 Chi. Cardinals vs. Green Bay, Dec. 5, 1948
69 Chi. Cardinals vs. Green Bay, Dec. 6, 1936
Kansas City vs. Cincinnati, Sept. 3, 1978

**Fewest Rushing Attempts, Game**
6 Chi. Cardinals vs. Boston, Oct. 29, 1933
7 Oakland vs. Buffalo, Oct. 15, 1963
Houston vs. N.Y. Giants, Dec. 8, 1985
Seattle vs. L.A. Raiders, Nov. 17, 1991
8 Denver vs. Oakland, Dec. 17, 1960
Buffalo vs. St. Louis, Sept. 9, 1984
Detroit vs. San Francisco, Oct. 20, 1991
Atlanta vs. Detroit, Sept. 5, 1993

**Most Rushing Attempts, Both Teams, Game**
108 Chi. Cardinals (70) vs. Green Bay (38), Dec. 5, 1948
105 Oakland (62) vs. Atlanta (43), Nov. 30, 1975 (OT)
104 Chi. Bears (64) vs. Pittsburgh (40), Oct. 18, 1936

**Fewest Rushing Attempts, Both Teams, Game**
34 Atlanta (12) vs. Houston (22), Dec. 5, 1993
35 Seattle (15) vs. New Orleans (20), Sept. 1, 1991
36 Houston (15) vs. N.Y. Jets (21), Oct. 13, 1991

### YARDS GAINED

**Most Yards Gained Rushing, Season**
3,165 New England, 1978
3,088 Buffalo, 1973
2,986 Kansas City, 1978

**Fewest Yards Gained Rushing, Season**
298 Philadelphia, 1940
467 Detroit, 1946
471 Boston, 1944

**Most Yards Gained Rushing, Game**
426 Detroit vs. Pittsburgh, Nov. 4, 1934
423 N.Y. Giants vs. Baltimore, Nov. 19, 1950
420 Boston vs. N.Y. Giants, Oct. 8, 1933

**Fewest Yards Gained Rushing, Game**
–53 Detroit vs. Chi. Cardinals, Oct. 17, 1943
–36 Philadelphia vs. Chi. Bears, Nov. 19, 1939
–33 Phil-Pitt vs. Brooklyn, Oct. 2, 1943

**Most Yards Gained Rushing, Both Teams, Game**
595 Los Angeles (371) vs. N.Y. Yanks (224), Nov. 18, 1951
574 Chi. Bears (396) vs. Pittsburgh (178), Oct. 10, 1934
558 Boston (420) vs. N.Y. Giants (138), Oct. 8, 1933

**Fewest Yards Gained Rushing, Both Teams, Game**
–15 Detroit (–53) vs. Chi. Cardinals (38), Oct. 17, 1943
4 Detroit (–10) vs. Chi. Cardinals (14), Sept. 15, 1940
62 L.A. Rams (15) vs. San Francisco (47), Dec. 6, 1964

### AVERAGE GAIN

**Highest Average Gain, Rushing, Season**
5.74 Cleveland, 1963
5.65 San Francisco, 1954
5.56 San Diego, 1963

**Lowest Average Gain, Rushing, Season**
0.94 Philadelphia, 1940
1.45 Boston, 1944
1.55 Pittsburgh, 1935

# ALL-TIME RECORDS

**TOUCHDOWNS**

**Most Touchdowns, Rushing, Season**

36Green Bay, 1962
33 Pittsburgh, 1976
30 Chi. Bears, 1941
New England, 1978
Washington, 1983

**Fewest Touchdowns, Rushing, Season**

1 Brooklyn, 1934
2 Chi. Cardinals, 1933
Cincinnati, 1933
Pittsburgh, 1934
Philadelphia, 1935
Philadelphia, 1936
Philadelphia, 1937
Philadelphia, 1938
Pittsburgh, 1940
Philadelphia, 1972
3 By many teams

**Most Touchdowns, Rushing, Game**

7 Los Angeles vs. Atlanta, Dec. 4, 1976
6 By many teams

**Most Touchdowns, Rushing, Both Teams, Game**

8 Los Angeles (6) vs. N.Y. Yanks (2), Nov. 18, 1951
Chi. Bears (5) vs. Green Bay (3), Nov. 6, 1955
Cleveland (6) vs. Los Angeles (2), Nov. 24, 1957
7 In many games

## PASSING

**ATTEMPTS**

**Most Passes Attempted, Season**

709 Minnesota, 1981
667 Houston, 1991
662 San Diego, 1984

**Fewest Passes Attempted, Season**

102 Cincinnati, 1933
106 Boston, 1933
120 Detroit, 1937

**Most Passes Attempted, Game**

68 Houston vs. Buffalo, Nov 1, 1964
66 Atlanta vs. Detroit, Dec. 24, 1989
65 San Diego vs. Kansas City, Oct. 19, 1986

**Fewest Passes Attempted, Game**

0 Green Bay vs. Portsmouth, Oct. 8, 1933
Detroit vs. Cleveland, Sept. 10, 1937
Pittsburgh vs. Brooklyn, Nov. 16, 1941
Pittsburgh vs. Los Angeles, Nov. 13, 1949
Cleveland vs. Philadelphia, Dec. 3, 1950

**Most Passes Attempted, Both Teams, Game**

104 Miami (55) vs. N.Y. Jets (49), Oct. 18, 1987 (OT)
102 San Francisco (57) vs. Atlanta (45), Oct. 6, 1985
100 Tampa Bay (54) vs. Kansas City (46), Oct. 28, 1984
San Francisco (60) vs. Washington (40), Nov. 17, 1986
Philadelphia (62) vs. Chicago (38), Oct. 2, 1989

**Fewest Passes Attempted, Both Teams, Game**

4 Chi. Cardinals (1) vs. Detroit (3), Nov. 3, 1935
Detroit (0) vs. Cleveland (4), Sept. 10, 1937
6 Chi. Cardinals (2) vs. Detroit (4), Sept. 15, 1940
8 Brooklyn (2) vs. Philadelphia (6), Oct. 1, 1939

**COMPLETIONS**

**Most Passes Completed, Season**

411 Houston, 1991
401 San Diego, 1984
399 Houston, 1990

**Fewest Passes Completed, Season**

25 Cincinnati, 1933
33 Boston, 1933
34 Chi. Cardinals, 1934
Detroit, 1934

**Most Passes Completed, Game**

42 N.Y. Jets vs. San Francisco, Sept. 21, 1980
41 Houston vs. Dallas, Nov. 10, 1991 (OT)
40 Cincinnati vs. San Diego, Dec. 20, 1982
Dallas vs. Detroit, Sept. 15, 1985
N.Y. Giants vs. Cincinnati, Oct. 13, 1985

**Fewest Passes Completed, Game**

0 By many teams. Last time: Buffalo vs. N.Y. Jets, Sept. 29, 1974

**Most Passes Completed, Both Teams, Game**

68 San Francisco (37) vs. Atlanta (31), Oct. 6, 1985
66 Cincinnati (40) vs. San Diego (26), Dec. 20, 1982
65 San Diego (33) vs. San Francisco (32), Dec. 11, 1982
San Diego (37) vs. Miami (28), Nov. 18, 1984 (OT)
Houston (41) vs. Dallas (24), Nov. 10, 1991 (OT)

**Fewest Passes Completed, Both Teams, Game**

1 Chi. Cardinals (0) vs. Philadelphia (1), Nov. 8, 1936
Detroit (0) vs. Cleveland (1), Sept. 10, 1937
Chi. Cardinals (0) vs. Detroit (1), Sept. 15, 1940
Brooklyn (0) vs. Pittsburgh (1), Nov. 29, 1942
2 Chi. Cardinals (0) vs. Detroit (2), Nov. 3, 1935
Buffalo (0) vs. N.Y. Jets (2), Sept. 29, 1974
Chi. Cardinals (0) vs. Green Bay (2), Nov. 18, 1934
3 In seven games

**YARDS GAINED**

**Most Seasons Leading League, Passing Yardage**

10 San Diego, 1965, 1968, 1971, 1978-83, 1985
8 Chi. Bears, 1932, 1939, 1941, 1943, 1945, 1949, 1954, 1964
Washington, 1938, 1940, 1944, 1947-48, 1967, 1974, 1989
7 Houston, 1960-61, 1963-64, 1990-92

**Most Consecutive Seasons Leading League, Passing Yardage**

6 San Diego, 1978-83
4 Green Bay, 1934-37
3 Miami, 1986-88
Houston, 1990-92

**Most Yards Gained, Passing, Season**

5,018 Miami, 1984
4,870 San Diego, 1985
4,805 Houston, 1990

**Fewest Yards Gained, Passing, Season**

302 Chi. Cardinals, 1934
357 Cincinnati, 1933
459 Boston, 1934

**Most Yards Gained, Passing, Game**

554 Los Angeles vs. N.Y. Yanks, Sept. 28, 1951
530 Minnesota vs. Baltimore, Sept. 28, 1969
521 Miami vs. N.Y. Jets, Oct. 23, 1988

**Fewest Yards Gained, Passing, Game**

–53 Denver vs. Oakland, Sept. 10, 1967
–52 Cincinnati vs. Houston, Oct. 31, 1971
–39 Atlanta vs. San Francisco, Oct. 23, 1976

**Most Yards Gained, Passing, Both Teams, Game**

884 N.Y. Jets (449) vs. Miami (435), Sept. 21, 1986 (OT)
883 San Diego (486) vs. Cincinnati (397), Dec. 20, 1982
849 Minnesota (471) vs. Washington (378), Nov. 2, 1986 (OT)

**Fewest Yards Gained, Passing, Both Teams, Game**

–11 Green Bay (–10) vs. Dallas (–1), Oct. 24, 1965
1 Chi. Cardinals (0) vs. Philadelphia (1), Nov. 8, 1936
7 Brooklyn (0) vs. Pittsburgh (7), Nov. 29, 1942

**TIMES SACKED**

**Most Seasons Leading League, Fewest Times Sacked**

10 Miami, 1973, 1982-90
4 San Diego, 1963-64, 1967-68
San Francisco, 1964-65, 1970-71
N.Y. Jets, 1965-66, 1968, 1993
3 Houston, 1961-62, 1978
St. Louis, 1974-76
Washington, 1966-67, 1991

**Most Consecutive Seasons Leading League, Fewest Times Sacked**

9 Miami, 1982-90
3 St. Louis, 1974-76
2 By many teams

**Most Times Sacked, Season**

104 Philadelphia, 1986
72 Philadelphia, 1987
70 Atlanta, 1968

**Fewest Times Sacked, Season**

7 Miami, 1988
8 San Francisco, 1970
St. Louis, 1975
9 N.Y. Jets, 1966
Washington, 1991

**Most Times Sacked, Game**

12 Pittsburgh vs. Dallas, Nov. 20, 1966
Baltimore vs. St. Louis, Oct. 26, 1980
Detroit vs. Chicago, Dec. 16, 1984
Houston vs. Dallas, Sept. 29, 1985
11 St. Louis vs. N.Y. Giants, Nov. 1, 1964
Los Angeles vs. Baltimore, Nov. 22, 1964
Denver vs. Buffalo, Dec. 13, 1964
Green Bay vs. Detroit, Nov. 7, 1965
Buffalo vs. Oakland, Oct. 15, 1967
Denver vs. Oakland, Nov. 5, 1967
Atlanta vs. St. Louis, Nov. 24, 1968
Detroit vs. Dallas, Oct. 6, 1975

Philadelphia vs. St. Louis, Dec. 18, 1983
Cleveland vs. Kansas City, Sept. 30, 1984
Minnesota vs. Chicago, Oct. 28, 1984
Atlanta vs. Cleveland, Nov. 18, 1984
Dallas vs. San Diego, Nov. 16, 1986
Philadelphia vs. Detroit, Nov. 16, 1986
Philadelphia vs. L.A. Raiders, Nov. 30, 1986 (OT)
L.A. Raiders vs. Seattle, Dec. 8, 1986
N.Y. Jets vs. Dallas, Oct. 4, 1987
Philadelphia vs. Chicago, Oct. 4, 1987
Dallas vs. Philadelphia, Sept. 15, 1991
Cleveland vs. Indianapolis, Sept. 6, 1992
10 By many teams

**Most Times Sacked, Both Teams, Game**
18 Green Bay (10) vs. San Diego (8), Sept. 24, 1978
17 Buffalo (10) vs. N.Y. Titans (7), Nov. 23, 1961
Pittsburgh (12) vs. Dallas (5), Nov. 20, 1966
Atlanta (9) vs. Philadelphia (8), Dec. 16, 1984
Philadelphia (11) vs. L.A. Raiders (6), Nov. 30, 1986 (OT)
16 Los Angeles (11) vs. Baltimore (5), Nov. 22, 1964
Buffalo (11) vs. Oakland (5), Oct. 15, 1967

## COMPLETION PERCENTAGE

**Most Seasons Leading League, Completion Percentage**
11 Washington, 1937, 1939-40, 1942-45, 1947-48, 1969-70
10 San Francisco, 1952, 1957-58, 1965, 1981, 1983, 1987, 1989, 1992-93
7 Green Bay, 1936, 1941, 1961-62, 1964, 1966, 1968

**Most Consecutive Seasons Leading League, Completion Percentage**
4 Washington, 1942-45
Kansas City, 1966-69
3 Cleveland, 1953-55
2 By many teams

**Highest Completion Percentage, Season**
70.65 Cincinnati, 1982 (310-219)
70.19 San Francisco, 1989 (483-339)
67.56 San Francisco, 1993 (524-354)

**Lowest Completion Percentage, Season**
22.9 Philadelphia, 1936 (170-39)
24.5 Cincinnati, 1933 (102-25)
25.0 Pittsburgh, 1941 (168-42)

## TOUCHDOWNS

**Most Touchdowns, Passing, Season**
49 Miami, 1984
48 Houston, 1961
46 Miami, 1986

**Fewest Touchdowns, Passing, Season**
0 Cincinnati, 1933
Pittsburgh, 1945
1 Boston, 1932
Boston, 1933
Chi. Cardinals, 1934
Cincinnati/St. Louis, 1934
Detroit, 1942
2 Chi. Cardinals, 1932
Stapleton, 1932
Chi. Cardinals, 1935
Brooklyn, 1936
Pittsburgh, 1942

**Most Touchdowns, Passing, Game**
7 Chi. Bears vs. N.Y. Giants, Nov. 14, 1943
Philadelphia vs. Washington, Oct. 17, 1954
Houston vs. N.Y. Titans, Nov. 19, 1961
Houston vs. N.Y. Titans, Oct. 14, 1962
N.Y. Giants vs. Washington, Oct. 28, 1962
Minnesota vs. Baltimore, Sept. 28, 1969
San Diego vs. Oakland, Nov. 22, 1981
6 By many teams.

**Most Touchdowns, Passing, Both Teams, Game**
12 New Orleans (6) vs. St. Louis (6), Nov. 2, 1969
11 N.Y. Giants (7) vs. Washington (4), Oct. 28, 1962
Oakland (6) vs. Houston (5), Dec. 22, 1963
10 San Diego (5) vs. Seattle (5), Sept. 15, 1985
Miami (6) vs. N.Y. Jets (4), Sept. 21, 1986 (OT)

## PASSES HAD INTERCEPTED

**Most Passes Had Intercepted, Season**
48 Houston, 1962
45* Denver, 1961
41 Card-Pitt, 1944

**Fewest Passes Had Intercepted, Season**
5 Cleveland, 1960
Green Bay, 1966
Kansas City, 1990
N.Y. Giants, 1990
6 Green Bay, 1964
St. Louis, 1982
Dallas, 1993
7 Los Angeles, 1969

**Most Passes Had Intercepted, Game**
9 Detroit vs. Green Bay, Oct. 24, 1943
Pittsburgh vs. Philadelphia, Dec. 12, 1965
8 Green Bay vs. N.Y. Giants, Nov. 21, 1948
Chi. Cardinals vs. Philadelphia, Sept. 24, 1950
N.Y. Yanks vs. N.Y. Giants, Dec. 16, 1951
Denver vs. Houston, Dec. 2, 1962
Chi. Bears vs. Detroit, Sept. 22, 1968
Baltimore vs. N.Y. Jets, Sept. 23, 1973
7 By many teams. Last time: Green Bay vs. New Orleans, Sept. 14, 1986

**Most Passes Had Intercepted, Both Teams, Game**
13 Denver (8) vs. Houston (5), Dec. 2, 1962
11 Philadelphia (7) vs. Boston (4), Nov. 3, 1935
Boston (6) vs. Pittsburgh (5), Dec. 1, 1935
Cleveland (7) vs. Green Bay (4), Oct. 30, 1938
Green Bay (7) vs. Detroit (4), Oct. 20, 1940
Detroit (7) vs. Chi. Bears (4), Nov. 22, 1942
Detroit (7) vs. Cleveland (4), Nov. 26, 1944
Chi. Cardinals (8) vs. Philadelphia (3), Sept. 24, 1950
Washington (7) vs. N.Y. Giants (4), Dec. 8, 1963
Pittsburgh (9) vs. Philadelphia (2), Dec 12, 1965
10 In many games

## PUNTING

**Most Seasons Leading League (Average Distance)**
7 Denver, 1962-64, 1966-67, 1982, 1988
6 Washington, 1940-43, 1945, 1958
Kansas City, 1968, 1971-73, 1979, 1984
4 L.A. Rams, 1946, 1949, 1955-56
Baltimore/Indianapolis, 1966, 1969, 1983, 1985

**Most Consecutive Seasons Leading League (Average Distance)**
4 Washington, 1940-43
3 Cleveland, 1950-52
Denver, 1962-64
Kansas City, 1971-73

**Most Punts, Season**
114 Chicago, 1981
113 Boston, 1934
Brooklyn, 1934
112 Boston, 1935

**Fewest Punts, Season**
23 San Diego, 1982
31 Cincinnati, 1982
32 Chi. Bears, 1941

**Most Punts, Game**
17 Chi. Bears vs. Green Bay, Oct. 22, 1933
Cincinnati vs. Pittsburgh, Oct. 22, 1933
16 Cincinnati vs. Portsmouth, Sept. 17, 1933
Chi. Cardinals vs. Chi. Bears, Nov. 30, 1933
Chi. Cardinals vs. Detroit, Sept. 15, 1940
15 N.Y. Giants vs. Chi. Bears, Nov. 17, 1935
Philadelphia vs. N.Y. Giants, Dec. 6, 1987 (OT)

**Fewest Punts, Game**
0 By many teams. Last time: San Francisco vs. Detroit, Dec. 19, 1993

**Most Punts, Both Teams, Game**
31 Chi. Bears (17) vs. Green Bay (14), Oct. 22, 1933
Cincinnati (17), vs. Pittsburgh (14), Oct. 22, 1933
29 Chi. Cardinals (15) vs. Cincinnati (14), Nov. 12, 1933
Chi. Cardinals (16) vs. Chi. Bears (13), Nov. 30, 1933
Chi. Cardinals (16) vs. Detroit (13), Sept. 15, 1940
28 Philadelphia (14) vs. Washington (14), Nov. 5, 1939

**Fewest Punts, Both Teams, Game**
0 Buffalo vs. San Francisco, Sept. 13, 1992
1 Baltimore (0) vs. Cleveland (1), Nov. 1, 1959
Dall. Cowboys (0) vs. Cleveland (1), Dec. 3, 1961
Chicago (0) vs. Detroit (1), Oct. 1, 1972
San Francisco (0) vs. N.Y. Giants (1), Oct. 15, 1972
Green Bay (0) vs. Buffalo (1), Dec. 5, 1982
Miami (0) vs. Buffalo (1), Oct. 12, 1986
Green Bay (0) vs. Chicago (1), Dec. 17, 1989
2 In many games

## AVERAGE YARDAGE

**Highest Average Distance, Punting, Season**
47.6 Detroit, 1961 (56-2,664)

47.0 Pittsburgh, 1961 (73-3,431)
46.9 Pittsburgh, 1953 (80-3,752)

**Lowest Average Distance, Punting, Season**
32.7 Card-Pitt, 1944 (60-1,964)
33.8 Cincinnati, 1986 (59-1,996)
33.9 Detroit, 1969 (74-2,510)

## PUNT RETURNS

**Most Seasons Leading League (Average Return)**
9 Detroit, 1943-45, 1951-52, 1962, 1966, 1969, 1991
7 Chi. Cardinals/St. Louis, 1948-49, 1955-56, 1959, 1986-87
5 Cleveland, 1958, 1960, 1964-65, 1967
Green Bay, 1950, 1953-54, 1961, 1972
Dall. Texans/Kansas City, 1960, 1968, 1970, 1979-80

**Most Consecutive Seasons Leading League (Average Return)**
3 Detroit, 1943-45
2 By many teams

**Most Punt Returns, Season**
71 Pittsburgh, 1976
Tampa Bay, 1979
L.A. Raiders, 1985
67 Pittsburgh, 1974
Los Angeles, 1978
L.A. Raiders, 1984
65 San Francisco, 1976

**Fewest Punt Returns, Season**
12 Baltimore, 1981
San Diego, 1982
14 Los Angeles, 1961
Philadelphia, 1962
Baltimore, 1982
15 Houston, 1960
Washington, 1960
Oakland, 1961
N.Y. Giants, 1969
Philadelphia, 1973
Kansas City, 1982

**Most Punt Returns, Game**
12 Philadelphia vs. Cleveland, Dec. 3, 1950
11 Chi. Bears vs. Chi. Cardinals, Oct. 8, 1950
Washington vs. Tampa Bay, Oct. 9, 1977
10 Philadelphia vs. N.Y. Giants, Nov. 26, 1950
Philadelphia vs. Tampa Bay, Sept. 18, 1977
Pittsburgh vs. Buffalo, Dec. 16, 1979
Washington vs. New Orleans, Dec. 26, 1982
Philadelphia vs. Seattle, Dec. 13, 1992 (OT)
New England vs. Pittsburgh, Dec. 5, 1993

**Most Punt Returns, Both Teams, Game**
17 Philadelphia (12) vs. Cleveland (5), Dec. 3, 1950
16 N.Y. Giants (9) vs. Philadelphia (7), Dec. 12, 1954
Washington (11) vs. Tampa Bay (5), Oct. 9, 1977
15 Detroit (8) vs. Cleveland (7), Sept. 27, 1942
Los Angeles (8) vs. Baltimore (7), Nov. 27, 1966
Pittsburgh (8) vs. Houston (7), Dec. 1, 1974
Philadelphia (10) vs. Tampa Bay (5), Sept. 18, 1977
Baltimore (9) vs. Kansas City (6), Sept. 2, 1979
Washington (10) vs. New Orleans (5), Dec. 26, 1982
L.A. Raiders (8) vs. Cleveland (7), Nov. 16, 1986

### FAIR CATCHES

**Most Fair Catches, Season**
34 Baltimore, 1971
32 San Diego, 1969
30 St. Louis, 1967
Minnesota, 1971

**Fewest Fair Catches, Season**
0 San Diego, 1975
New England, 1976
Tampa Bay, 1976
Pittsburgh, 1977
Dallas, 1982
1 Cleveland, 1974
San Francisco, 1975
Kansas City, 1976
St. Louis, 1976
San Diego, 1976
L.A. Rams, 1982
St. Louis, 1982
Tampa Bay, 1982
2 By many teams

**Most Fair Catches, Game**
7 Minnesota vs. Dallas, Sept. 25, 1966
Detroit vs. Chicago, Nov. 21, 1976
Philadelphia vs. Buffalo, Dec. 27, 1987
6 By many teams

### YARDS GAINED

**Most Yards, Punt Returns, Season**
785 L.A. Raiders, 1985
781 Chi. Bears, 1948
774 Pittsburgh, 1974

**Fewest Yards, Punt Returns, Season**
27 St. Louis, 1965
35 N.Y. Giants, 1965
37 New England, 1972

**Most Yards, Punt Returns, Game**
231 Detroit vs. San Francisco, Oct. 6, 1963
225 Oakland vs. Buffalo, Sept. 15, 1968
219 Los Angeles vs. Atlanta, Oct. 11, 1981

**Fewest Yards, Punt Returns, Game**
-28 Washington vs. Dallas, Dec. 11, 1966
-23 N.Y. Giants vs. Buffalo, Oct. 20, 1975
Pittsburgh vs. Houston, Sept. 20, 1970
-20 New Orleans vs. Pittsburgh, Oct. 20, 1968

**Most Yards, Punt Returns, Both Teams, Game**
282 Los Angeles (219) vs. Atlanta (63), Oct. 11, 1981
245 Detroit (231) vs. San Francisco (14), Oct. 6, 1963
244 Oakland (225) vs. Buffalo (19), Sept. 15, 1968

**Fewest Yards, Punt Returns, Both Teams, Game**
-18 Buffalo (-18) vs. Pittsburgh (0), Oct. 29, 1972
-14 Miami (-14) vs. Boston (0), Nov. 30, 1969
-13 N.Y. Giants (-13) vs. Cleveland (0), Nov. 14, 1965

### AVERAGE YARDS RETURNING PUNTS

**Highest Average, Punt Returns, Season**
20.2 Chi. Bears, 1941 (27-546)
19.1 Chi. Cardinals, 1948 (35-669)
18.2 Chi. Cardinals, 1949 (30-546)

**Lowest Average, Punt Returns, Season**
1.2 St. Louis, 1965 (23-27)
1.5 N.Y. Giants, 1965 (24-35)
1.7 Washington, 1970 (27-45)

### TOUCHDOWNS RETURNING PUNTS

**Most Touchdowns, Punt Returns, Season**
5 Chi. Cardinals, 1959
4 Chi. Cardinals, 1948
Detroit, 1951
N.Y. Giants, 1951
Denver, 1976
3 Washington, 1941
Detroit, 1952
Pittsburgh, 1952
Houston, 1975
Los Angeles, 1981
Cleveland, 1993

**Most Touchdowns, Punt Returns, Game**
2 Detroit vs. Los Angeles, Oct. 14, 1951
Detroit vs. Green Bay, Nov. 22, 1951
Chi. Cardinals vs. Pittsburgh, Nov. 1, 1959
Chi. Cardinals vs. N.Y. Giants, Nov. 22, 1959
N.Y. Titans vs. Denver, Sept. 24, 1961
Denver vs. Cleveland, Sept. 26, 1976
Los Angeles vs. Atlanta, Oct. 11, 1981
St. Louis vs. Tampa Bay, Dec. 21, 1986
L.A. Rams vs. Atlanta, Dec. 27, 1992
Cleveland vs. Pittsburgh, Oct. 24, 1993

**Most Touchdowns, Punt Returns, Both Teams, Game**
2 Philadelphia (1) vs. Washington (1), Nov. 9, 1952
Kansas City (1) vs. Buffalo (1), Sept. 11, 1966
Baltimore (1) vs. New England (1), Nov. 18, 1979
L.A. Raiders (1) vs. Philadelphia (1), Nov. 30, 1986 (OT)
Cincinnati (1) vs. Green Bay (1), Sept. 20, 1992
(Also see previous record)

## KICKOFF RETURNS

**Most Seasons Leading League (Average Return)**
7 Washington, 1942, 1947, 1962-63, 1973-74, 1981
6 Chicago Bears, 1943, 1948, 1958, 1966, 1972, 1985
5 N.Y. Giants, 1944, 1946, 1949, 1951, 1953

**Most Consecutive Seasons Leading League (Average Return)**
3 Denver, 1965-67
2 By many teams

**Most Kickoff Returns, Season**
88 New Orleans, 1980

86 Minnesota, 1984
84 Baltimore, 1981

**Fewest Kickoff Returns, Season**
17 N.Y. Giants, 1944
20 N.Y. Giants, 1941, 1943
Chi. Bears, 1942
23 Washington, 1942

**Most Kickoff Returns, Game**
12 N.Y. Giants vs. Washington, Nov. 27, 1966
10 By many teams

**Most Kickoff Returns, Both Teams, Game**
19 N.Y. Giants (12) vs. Washington (7), Nov. 27, 1966
18 Houston (10) vs. Oakland (8), Dec. 22, 1963
17 Washington (9) vs. Green Bay (8), Oct. 17, 1983
San Diego (9) vs. Pittsburgh (8), Dec. 8, 1985
Detroit (9) vs. Green Bay (8), Nov. 27, 1986
L.A. Raiders (9) vs. Seattle (8), Dec. 18, 1988

### YARDS GAINED

**Most Yards, Kickoff Returns, Season**
1,973 New Orleans, 1980
1,824 Houston, 1963
1,801 Denver, 1963

**Fewest Yards, Kickoff Returns, Season**
282 N.Y. Giants, 1940
381 Green Bay, 1940
424 Chicago, 1963

**Most Yards, Kickoff Returns, Game**
362 Detroit vs. Los Angeles, Oct. 29, 1950
304 Chi. Bears vs. Green Bay, Nov. 9, 1952
295 Denver vs. Boston, Oct. 4, 1964

**Most Yards, Kickoff Returns, Both Teams, Game**
560 Detroit (362) vs. Los Angeles (198), Oct. 29, 1950
453 Washington (236) vs. Philadelphia (217), Sept. 28, 1947
447 N.Y. Giants (236) vs. Cleveland (211), Dec. 4, 1966

### AVERAGE YARDAGE

**Highest Average, Kickoff Returns, Season**
29.4 Chicago, 1972 (52-1,528)
28.9 Pittsburgh, 1952 (39-1,128)
28.2 Washington, 1962 (61-1,720)

**Lowest Average, Kickoff Returns, Season**
14.7 N.Y. Jets, 1993 (46-675)
15.8 N.Y. Giants, 1993 (32-507)
15.9 Tampa Bay, 1993 (58-922)

### TOUCHDOWNS

**Most Touchdowns, Kickoff Returns, Season**
4 Green Bay, 1967
Chicago, 1970
3 Los Angeles, 1950
Chi. Cardinals, 1954
San Francisco, 1963
Denver, 1966
Chicago, 1967
New England, 1977
L.A. Rams, 1985
2 By many teams

**Most Touchdowns, Kickoff Returns, Game**
2 Chi. Bears vs. Green Bay, Sept. 22, 1940
Chi. Bears vs. Green Bay, Nov. 9, 1952
Philadelphia vs. Dallas, Nov. 6, 1966
Green Bay vs. Cleveland, Nov. 12, 1967
L.A. Rams vs. Green Bay, Nov. 24, 1985

**Most Touchdowns, Kickoff Returns, Both Teams, Game**
2 Washington (1) vs. Philadelphia (1), Nov. 1, 1942
Washington (1) vs. Philadelphia (1), Sept. 28, 1947
Los Angeles (1) vs. Detroit (1), Oct. 29, 1950
N.Y. Yanks (1) vs. N.Y. Giants (1), Nov. 4, 1951 (consecutive)
Baltimore (1) vs. Chi. Bears (1), Oct. 4, 1958
Buffalo (1) vs. Boston (1), Nov. 3, 1962
Pittsburgh (1) vs. Dallas (1), Oct. 30, 1966
St. Louis (1) vs. Washington (1), Sept. 23, 1973 (consecutive)
Atlanta (1) vs. San Francisco (1), Dec. 20, 1987 (consecutive)
Houston (1) vs. Pittsburgh (1), Dec. 4, 1988
(Also see previous record)

## FUMBLES

**Most Fumbles, Season**
56 Chi. Bears, 1938
San Francisco, 1978
54 Philadelphia, 1946
51 New England, 1973

**Fewest Fumbles, Season**
8 Cleveland, 1959
11 Green Bay, 1944
12 Brooklyn, 1934
Detroit, 1943
Cincinnati, 1982
Minnesota, 1982

**Most Fumbles, Game**
10 Phil-Pitt vs. N.Y. Giants, Oct. 9, 1943
Detroit vs. Minnesota, Nov. 12, 1967
Kansas City vs. Houston, Oct. 12, 1969
San Francisco vs. Detroit, Dec. 17, 1978
9 Philadelphia vs. Green Bay, Oct. 13, 1946
Kansas City vs. San Diego, Nov. 15, 1964
N.Y. Giants vs. Buffalo, Oct. 20, 1975
St. Louis vs. Washington, Oct. 25, 1976
San Diego vs. Green Bay, Sept. 24, 1978
Pittsburgh vs. Cincinnati, Oct. 14, 1979
Cleveland vs. Seattle, Dec. 20, 1981
Cleveland vs. Pittsburgh, Dec. 23, 1990
8 By many teams

**Most Fumbles, Both Teams, Game**
14 Washington (8) vs. Pittsburgh (6), Nov. 14, 1937
Chi. Bears (7) vs. Cleveland (7), Nov. 24, 1940
St. Louis (8) vs. N.Y. Giants (6), Sept. 17, 1961
Kansas City (10) vs. Houston (4), Oct. 12, 1969
13 Washington (8) vs. Pittsburgh (5), Nov. 14, 1937
Philadelphia (7) vs. Boston (6), Dec. 8, 1946
N.Y. Giants (7) vs. Washington (6), Nov. 5, 1950
Kansas City (9) vs. San Diego (4), Nov. 15, 1964
Buffalo (7) vs. Denver (6), Dec. 13, 1964
N.Y. Jets (7) vs. Houston (6), Sept. 12, 1965
Houston (8) vs. Pittsburgh (5), Dec. 9, 1973
St. Louis (9) vs. Washington (4), Oct. 25, 1976
Cleveland (9) vs. Seattle (4), Dec. 20, 1981
Green Bay (7) vs. Detroit (6), Oct. 6, 1985
12 In many games

### FUMBLES LOST

**Most Fumbles Lost, Season**
36 Chi. Cardinals, 1959
31 Green Bay, 1952
29 Chi. Cardinals, 1946
Pittsburgh, 1950

**Fewest Fumbles Lost, Season**
3 Philadelphia, 1938
Minnesota, 1980
4 San Francisco, 1960
Kansas City, 1982
5 Chi. Cardinals, 1943
Detroit, 1943
N.Y. Giants, 1943
Cleveland, 1959
Minnesota, 1982
San Diego, 1993

**Most Fumbles Lost, Game**
8 St. Louis vs. Washington, Oct. 25, 1976
Cleveland vs. Pittsburgh, Dec. 23, 1990
7 Cincinnati vs. Buffalo, Nov. 30, 1969
Pittsburgh vs. Cincinnati, Oct. 14, 1979
Cleveland vs. Seattle, Dec. 20, 1981
6 By many teams

### FUMBLES RECOVERED

**Most Fumbles Recovered, Season, Own and Opponents'**
58 Minnesota, 1963 (27 own, 31 opp)
51 Chi. Bears, 1938 (37 own, 14 opp)
San Francisco, 1978 (24 own, 27 opp)
50 Philadelphia, 1987 (23 own, 27 opp)

**Fewest Fumbles Recovered, Season, Own and Opponents'**
9 San Francisco, 1982 (5 own, 4 opp)
11 Cincinnati, 1982 (5 own, 6 opp)
13 Baltimore, 1967 (5 own, 8 opp)
N.Y. Jets, 1967 (7 own, 6 opp)
Philadelphia, 1968 (6 own, 7 opp)
Miami, 1973 (5 own, 8 opp)
Chicago, 1982 (6 own, 7 opp)
Denver, 1982 (6 own, 7 opp)
Miami, 1982 (5 own, 8 opp)
N.Y. Giants, 1982 (7 own, 6 opp)

**Most Fumbles Recovered, Game, Own and Opponents'**
10 Denver vs. Buffalo, Dec. 13, 1964 (5 own, 5 opp)
Pittsburgh vs. Houston, Dec. 9, 1973 (5 own, 5 opp)
Washington vs. St. Louis, Oct. 25, 1976 (2 own, 8 opp)
9 St. Louis vs. N.Y. Giants, Sept. 17, 1961 (6 own, 3 opp)
Houston vs. Cincinnati, Oct. 27, 1974 (4 own, 5 opp)
Kansas City vs. Dallas, Nov. 10, 1975 (4 own, 5 opp)
Green Bay vs. Detroit, Oct. 6, 1985 (5 own, 4 opp)
8 By many teams

**Most Own Fumbles Recovered, Season**
37 Chi. Bears, 1938
28 Pittsburgh, 1987
27 Philadelphia, 1946
Minnesota, 1963

**Fewest Own Fumbles Recovered, Season**
2 Washington, 1958
3 Detroit, 1956
Cleveland, 1959
Houston, 1982
4 By many teams

**Most Opponents' Fumbles Recovered, Season**
31 Minnesota, 1963
29 Cleveland, 1951
28 Green Bay, 1946
Houston, 1977
Seattle, 1983

**Fewest Opponents' Fumbles Recovered, Season**
3 Los Angeles, 1974
4 Philadelphia, 1944
San Francisco, 1982
5 Baltimore, 1982

**Most Opponents' Fumbles Recovered, Game**
8 Washington vs. St. Louis, Oct. 25, 1976
Pittsburgh vs. Cleveland, Dec. 23, 1990
7 Buffalo vs. Cincinnati, Nov. 30, 1969
Cincinnati vs. Pittsburgh, Oct. 14, 1979
Seattle vs. Cleveland, Dec. 20, 1981
6 By many teams

### TOUCHDOWNS

**Most Touchdowns, Fumbles Recovered, Season, Own and Opponents'**
5 Chi. Bears, 1942 (1 own, 4 opp)
Los Angeles, 1952 (1 own, 4 opp)
San Francisco, 1965 (1 own, 4 opp)
Oakland, 1978 (2 own, 3 opp)
4 Chi. Bears, 1948 (1 own, 3 opp)
Boston, 1948 (4 opp)
Denver, 1979 (1 own, 3 opp)
Atlanta, 1981 (1 own, 3 opp)
Denver, 1984 (4 opp)
St. Louis, 1987 (4 opp)
Minnesota, 1989 (4 opp)
Atlanta, 1991 (4 opp)
3 By many teams

**Most Touchdowns, Own Fumbles Recovered, Season**
2 Chi. Bears, 1953
New England, 1973
Buffalo, 1974
Denver, 1975
Oakland, 1978
Green Bay, 1982
New Orleans, 1983
Cleveland, 1986
Green Bay, 1989

**Most Touchdowns, Opponents' Fumbles Recovered, Season**
4 Detroit, 1937
Chi. Bears, 1942
Boston, 1948
Los Angeles, 1952
San Francisco, 1965
Denver, 1984
St. Louis, 1987
Minnesota, 1989
Atlanta, 1991
3 By many teams

**Most Touchdowns, Fumbles Recovered, Game, Own and Opponents'**
2 By many teams

**Most Touchdowns, Fumbled Recovered, Game, Both Teams, Own and Opponents'**
3 Detroit (2) vs. Minnesota (1), Dec. 9, 1962 (2 own, 1 opp)
Green Bay (2) vs. Dallas (1), Nov. 29, 1964 (3 opp)
Oakland (2) vs. Buffalo (1), Dec. 24, 1967 (3 opp)

**Most Touchdowns, Own Fumbles Recovered, Game**
1 By many teams

**Most Touchdowns, Opponents' Fumbles Recovered, Game**
2 Detroit vs. Cleveland, Nov. 7, 1937
Philadelphia vs. N.Y. Giants, Sept. 25, 1938
Chi. Bears vs. Washington, Nov. 28, 1948
N.Y. Giants vs. Pittsburgh, Sept. 17, 1950
Cleveland vs. Dall. Cowboys, Dec. 3, 1961
Cleveland vs. N.Y. Giants, Oct. 25, 1964
Green Bay vs. Dallas, Nov. 29, 1964
San Francisco vs. Detroit, Nov. 14, 1965
Oakland vs. Buffalo, Dec. 24, 1967
N.Y. Giants vs. Green Bay, Sept. 19, 1971
Washington vs. San Diego, Sept. 16, 1973
New Orleans vs. San Francisco, Oct. 19, 1975
Cincinnati vs. Pittsburgh, Oct. 14, 1979
Atlanta vs. Detroit, Oct. 5, 1980
Kansas City vs. Oakland, Oct. 5, 1980
New England vs. Baltimore, Nov. 23, 1980
Denver vs. Green Bay, Oct. 15, 1984
Miami vs. Kansas City, Oct. 11, 1987
St. Louis vs. New Orleans, Oct. 11, 1987
Minnesota vs. Atlanta, Dec. 10, 1989
Philadelphia vs. Phoenix, Nov. 24, 1991
Cincinnati vs. Seattle, Sept. 6, 1992

**Most Touchdowns, Opponents' Fumbled Recovered, Game, Both Teams**
3 Green Bay (2) vs. Dallas (1), Nov. 29, 1964
Oakland (2) vs. Buffalo (1), Dec. 24, 1967

### TURNOVERS

(Number of times losing the ball on interceptions and fumbles.)

**Most Turnovers, Season**
63 San Francisco, 1978
58 Chi. Bears, 1947
Pittsburgh, 1950
N.Y. Giants, 1983
57 Green Bay, 1950
Houston, 1962, 1963
Pittsburgh, 1965

**Fewest Turnovers, Season**
12 Kansas City, 1982
14 N.Y. Giants, 1943
Cleveland, 1959
N.Y. Giants, 1990
16 San Francisco, 1960
Cincinnati, 1982
St. Louis, 1982
Washington, 1982

**Most Turnovers, Game**
12 Detroit vs. Chi. Bears, Nov. 22, 1942
Chi. Cardinals vs. Philadelphia, Sept. 24, 1950
Pittsburgh vs. Philadelphia, Dec. 12, 1965
11 San Diego vs. Green Bay, Sept. 24, 1978
10 Washington vs. N.Y. Giants, Dec. 4, 1938
Pittsburgh vs. Green Bay, Nov. 23, 1941
Detroit vs. Green Bay, Oct. 24, 1943
Chi. Cardinals vs. Green Bay, Nov. 10, 1946
Chi. Cardinals vs. N.Y. Giants, Nov. 2, 1952
Minnesota vs. Detroit, Dec. 9, 1962
Houston vs. Oakland, Sept. 7, 1963
Washington vs. N.Y. Giants, Dec. 8, 1963
Chicago vs. Detroit, Sept. 22, 1968
St. Louis vs. Washington, Oct. 25, 1976
N.Y. Jets vs. New England, Nov. 21, 1976
San Francisco vs. Dallas, Oct. 12, 1980
Cleveland vs. Seattle, Dec. 20, 1981
Detroit vs. Denver, Oct. 7, 1984

**Most Turnovers, Both Teams, Game**
17 Detroit (12) vs. Chi. Bears (5), Nov. 22, 1942
Boston (9) vs. Philadelphia (8), Dec. 8, 1946
16 Chi. Cardinals (12) vs. Philadelphia (4), Sept. 24, 1950
Chi. Cardinals (8) vs. Chi. Bears (8), Dec. 7, 1958
Minnesota (10) vs. Detroit (6), Dec. 9, 1962
Houston (9) vs. Kansas City (7), Oct. 12, 1969
15 Philadelphia (8) vs. Chi. Cardinals (7), Oct. 3, 1954
Denver (9) vs. Houston (6), Dec. 2, 1962
Washington (10) vs. N.Y. Giants (5), Dec. 8, 1963
St. Louis (9) vs. Kansas City (6), Oct. 2, 1983

### PENALTIES

**Most Seasons Leading League, Fewest Penalties**
13 Miami, 1968, 1976-84, 1986, 1990-91
9 Pittsburgh, 1946-47, 1950-52, 1954, 1963, 1965, 1968

7 Boston/New England, 1962, 1964-65, 1973, 1987, 1989, 1993

**Most Consecutive Seasons Leading League, Fewest Penalties**

9 Miami, 1976-84
3 Pittsburgh, 1950-52
2 By many teams

**Most Seasons Leading League, Most Penalties**

16 Chi. Bears, 1941-44, 1946-49, 1951, 1959-61, 1963, 1965, 1968, 1976
9 Oakland/L.A. Raiders, 1963, 1966, 1968-69, 1975, 1982, 1984, 1991, 1993
6 L.A. Rams, 1950, 1952, 1962, 1969, 1978, 1980

**Most Consecutive Seasons Leading League, Most Penalties**

4 Chi. Bears, 1941-44, 1946-49
3 Chi. Cardinals, 1954-56
Chi. Bears, 1959-61
Houston, 1988-90

**Fewest Penalties, Season**

19 Detroit, 1937
21 Boston, 1935
24 Philadelphia, 1936

**Most Penalties, Season**

149 Houston, 1989
148 L.A. Raiders, 1993
144 Buffalo, 1983

**Fewest Penalties, Game**

0 By many teams. Last time: Washington vs. Atlanta, Dec. 19, 1993

**Most Penalties, Game**

22 Brooklyn vs. Green Bay, Sept. 17, 1944
Chi. Bears vs. Philadelphia, Nov. 26, 1944
21 Cleveland vs. Chi. Bears, Nov. 25, 1951
20 Tampa Bay vs. Seattle, Oct. 17, 1976

**Fewest Penalties, Both Teams, Game**

0 Brooklyn vs. Pittsburgh, Oct. 28, 1934
Brooklyn vs. Boston, Sept. 28, 1936
Cleveland vs. Chi. Bears, Oct. 9, 1938
Pittsburgh vs. Philadelphia, Nov. 10, 1940

**Most Penalties, Both Teams, Game**

37 Cleveland (21) vs. Chi. Bears (16), Nov. 25, 1951
35 Tampa Bay (20) vs. Seattle (15), Oct. 17, 1976
33 Brooklyn (22) vs. Green Bay (11), Sept. 17, 1944

### YARDS PENALIZED

**Most Seasons Leading League, Fewest Yards Penalized**

13 Miami, 1967-68, 1973, 1977-84, 1990-91
8 Boston/Washington, 1935, 1953-54, 1956-58, 1970, 1985
7 Pittsburgh, 1946-47, 1950, 1952, 1962, 1965, 1968
Boston/New England, 1962, 1964-66, 1987, 1989, 1993

**Most Consecutive Seasons Leading League, Fewest Yards Penalized**

8 Miami, 1977-84
3 Washington, 1956-58
Boston, 1964-66
2 By many teams

**Most Seasons Leading League, Most Yards Penalized**

15 Chi. Bears, 1935, 1937, 1939-44, 1946-47, 1949, 1951, 1961-62, 1968
9 Oakland/L.A. Raiders, 1963-64, 1968-69, 1975, 1982, 1984, 1991, 1993
6 Buffalo, 1962, 1967, 1970, 1972, 1981, 1983
Houston, 1961, 1985-86, 1988-90

**Most Consecutive Seasons Leading League, Most Yards Penalized**

6 Chi. Bears, 1939-44
3 Cleveland, 1976-78
Houston, 1988-90
2 By many teams

**Fewest Yards Penalized, Season**

139 Detroit, 1937
146 Philadelphia, 1937
159 Philadelphia, 1936

**Most Yards Penalized, Season**

1,274 Oakland, 1969
1,239 Baltimore, 1979
1,209 L.A. Raiders, 1984

**Fewest Yards Penalized, Game**

0 By many teams. Last time: Washington vs. Atlanta, Dec. 19, 1993

**Most Yards Penalized, Game**

209 Cleveland vs. Chi. Bears, Nov. 25, 1951
191 Philadelphia vs. Seattle, Dec. 13, 1992 (OT)
190 Tampa Bay vs. Seattle, Oct. 17, 1976

**Fewest Yards Penalized, Both Teams, Game**

0 Brooklyn vs. Pittsburgh, Oct. 28, 1934
Brooklyn vs. Boston, Sept. 28, 1936
Cleveland vs. Chi. Bears, Oct. 9, 1938
Pittsburgh vs. Philadelphia, Nov. 10, 1940

**Most Yards Penalized, Both Teams, Game**

374 Cleveland (209) vs. Chi. Bears (165), Nov. 25, 1951
310 Tampa Bay (190) vs. Seattle (120), Oct. 17, 1976
309 Green Bay (184) vs. Boston (125), Oct. 21, 1945

## DEFENSE

### SCORING

**Most Seasons Leading League, Fewest Points Allowed**

10 N.Y. Giants, 1935, 1938-39, 1941, 1944, 1958-59, 1961, 1990, 1993
9 Chi. Bears, 1932, 1936-37, 1942, 1948, 1963, 1985-86, 1988
6 Cleveland, 1951, 1953-57

**Most Consecutive Seasons Leading League, Fewest Points Allowed**

5 Cleveland, 1953-57
3 Buffalo, 1964-66
Minnesota, 1969-71
2 By many teams

**Fewest Points Allowed, Season (Since 1932)**

44 Chi. Bears, 1932
54 Brooklyn, 1933
59 Detroit, 1934

**Most Points Allowed, Season**

533 Baltimore, 1981
501 N.Y. Giants, 1966
487 New Orleans, 1980

**Fewest Touchdowns Allowed, Season (Since 1932)**

6 Chi. Bears, 1932
Brooklyn, 1933
7 Detroit, 1934
8 Green Bay, 1932

**Most Touchdowns Allowed, Season**

68 Baltimore, 1981
66 N.Y. Giants, 1966
63 Baltimore, 1950

### FIRST DOWNS

**Fewest First Downs Allowed Season**

77 Detroit, 1935
79 Boston, 1935
82 Washington, 1937

**Most First Downs Allowed, Season**

406 Baltimore, 1981
371 Seattle, 1981
366 Green Bay, 1983

**Fewest First Downs Allowed, Rushing, Season**

35 Chi. Bears, 1942
40 Green Bay, 1939
41 Brooklyn, 1944

**Most First Downs Allowed, Rushing, Season**

179 Detroit, 1985
178 New Orleans, 1980
175 Seattle, 1981

**Fewest First Downs Allowed, Passing, Season**

33 Chi. Bears, 1943
34 Pittsburgh, 1941
Washington, 1943
35 Detroit, 1940
Philadelphia, 1940, 1944

**Most First Downs Allowed, Passing, Season**

218 San Diego, 1985
216 San Diego, 1981
N.Y. Jets, 1986
214 Baltimore, 1981

**Fewest First Downs Allowed, Penalty, Season**

1 Boston, 1944
3 Philadelphia, 1940
Pittsburgh, 1945
Washington, 1957
4 Cleveland, 1940
Green Bay, 1943
N.Y. Giants, 1943

**Most First Downs Allowed, Penalty, Season**

48 Houston, 1985
46 Houston, 1986
43 L.A. Raiders, 1984

### NET YARDS ALLOWED RUSHING AND PASSING

**Most Seasons Leading League, Fewest Yards Allowed**

8 Chi. Bears, 1942-43, 1948, 1958, 1963, 1984-86
6 N.Y. Giants, 1938, 1940-41, 1951, 1956, 1959
Philadelphia, 1944-45, 1949, 1953, 1981, 1991
Minnesota, 1969-70, 1975, 1988-89, 1993
5 Boston/Washington, 1935-37, 1939, 1946

**Most Consecutive Seasons Leading League, Fewest Yards Allowed**

3 Boston/Washington, 1935-37

Chicago, 1984-86
2 By many teams

**Fewest Yards Allowed, Season**
1,539 Chi. Cardinals, 1934
1,703 Chi. Bears, 1942
1,789 Brooklyn, 1933

**Most Yards Allowed, Season**
6,793 Baltimore, 1981
6,403 Green Bay, 1983
6,352 Minnesota, 1984

## RUSHING

**Most Seasons Leading League, Fewest Yards Allowed**
10 Chi. Bears, 1937, 1939, 1942, 1946, 1949, 1963, 1984-85, 1987-88
7 Detroit, 1938, 1950, 1952, 1962, 1970, 1980-81
Philadelphia, 1944-45, 1947-48, 1953, 1990-91
Dallas, 1966-69, 1972, 1978, 1992
5 N.Y. Giants, 1940, 1951, 1956, 1959, 1986

**Most Consecutive Seasons Leading League, Fewest Yards Allowed**
4 Dallas, 1966-69
2 By many teams

**Fewest Yards Allowed, Rushing, Season**
519 Chi. Bears, 1942
558 Philadelphia, 1944
762 Pittsburgh, 1982

**Most Yards Allowed, Rushing, Season**
3,228 Buffalo, 1978
3,106 New Orleans, 1980
3,010 Baltimore, 1978

**Fewest Touchdowns Allowed, Rushing, Season**
2 Detroit, 1934
Dallas, 1968
Minnesota, 1971
3 By many teams

**Most Touchdowns Allowed, Rushing, Season**
36 Oakland, 1961
31 N.Y. Giants, 1980
Tampa Bay, 1986
30 Baltimore, 1981

## PASSING

**Most Seasons Leading League, Fewest Yards Allowed**
8 Green Bay, 1947-48, 1962, 1964-68
7 Washington, 1939, 1942, 1945, 1952-53, 1980, 1985
6 Chi. Bears, 1938, 1943-44, 1958, 1960, 1963
Minnesota, 1969-70, 1972, 1975-76, 1989
Pittsburgh, 1941, 1946, 1951, 1955, 1974, 1990
Philadelphia, 1934, 1936, 1940, 1949, 1981, 1991

**Most Consecutive Seasons Leading League, Fewest Yards Allowed**
5 Green Bay, 1964-68
2 By many teams

**Fewest Yards Allowed, Passing, Season**
545 Philadelphia, 1934
558 Portsmouth, 1933
585 Chi. Cardinals, 1934

**Most Yards Allowed, Passing, Season**
4,389 N.Y. Jets, 1986
4,311 San Diego, 1981
4,293 San Diego, 1985

**Fewest Touchdowns Allowed, Passing, Season**
1 Portsmouth, 1932
Philadelphia, 1934
2 Brooklyn, 1933
Chi. Bears, 1934
3 Chi. Bears, 1932
Green Bay, 1932
Green Bay, 1934
Chi. Bears, 1936
New York, 1939
New York, 1944

**Most Touchdowns Allowed, Passing, Season**
40 Denver, 1963
38 St. Louis, 1969
37 Washington, 1961
Baltimore, 1981

## SACKS

**Most Seasons Leading League**
5 Oakland/L.A. Raiders, 1966-68, 1982, 1986
4 Boston/New England, 1961, 1963, 1977, 1979
Dallas, 1966, 1968-69, 1978
Dallas/Kansas City, 1960, 1965, 1969, 1990
3 San Francisco, 1967, 1972, 1976
L.A. Rams, 1968, 1970, 1988

**Most Consecutive Seasons Leading League**
3 Oakland, 1966-68
2 Dallas, 1968-69

**Most Sacks, Season**
72 Chicago, 1984
71 Minnesota, 1989
70 Chicago, 1987

**Fewest Sacks, Season**
11 Baltimore, 1982
12 Buffalo, 1982
13 Baltimore, 1981

**Most Sacks, Game**
12 Dallas vs. Pittsburgh, Nov. 20, 1966
St. Louis vs. Baltimore, Oct. 26, 1980
Chicago vs. Detroit, Dec. 16, 1984
Dallas vs. Houston, Sept. 29, 1985
11 N.Y. Giants vs. St. Louis, Nov. 1, 1964
Baltimore vs. Los Angeles, Nov. 22, 1964
Buffalo vs. Denver, Dec. 13, 1964
Detroit vs. Green Bay, Nov. 7, 1965
Oakland vs. Buffalo, Oct. 15, 1967
Oakland vs. Denver, Nov. 5, 1967
St. Louis vs. Atlanta, Nov. 24, 1968
Dallas vs. Detroit, Oct. 6, 1975
St. Louis vs. Philadelphia, Dec. 18, 1983
Kansas City vs. Cleveland, Sept. 30, 1984
Chicago vs. Minnesota, Oct. 28, 1984
Cleveland vs. Atlanta, Nov. 18, 1984
Detroit vs. Philadelphia, Nov. 16, 1986
San Diego vs. Dallas, Nov. 16, 1986
L.A. Raiders vs. Philadelphia, Nov. 30, 1986 (OT)
Seattle vs. L.A. Raiders, Dec. 8, 1986
Chicago vs. Philadelphia, Oct. 4, 1987
Dallas vs. N.Y. Jets, Oct. 4, 1987
Indianapolis vs. Cleveland, Sept. 6, 1992
10 By many teams

**Most Opponents Yards Lost Attempting to Pass, Season**
666 Oakland, 1967
583 Chicago, 1984
573 San Francisco, 1976

**Fewest Opponents Yards Lost Attempting to Pass, Season**
75 Green Bay, 1956
77 N.Y. Bulldogs, 1949
78 Green Bay, 1958

## INTERCEPTIONS BY

**Most Seasons Leading League**
9 N.Y. Giants, 1933, 1937-39, 1944, 1948, 1951, 1954, 1961
8 Green Bay, 1940, 1942-43, 1947, 1955, 1957, 1962, 1965
Chi. Bears, 1935-36, 1941-42, 1946, 1963, 1985, 1990
6 Kansas City, 1966-70, 1974

**Most Consecutive Seasons Leading League**
5 Kansas City, 1966-70
3 N.Y. Giants, 1937-39
2 By many teams

**Most Passes Intercepted By, Season**
49 San Diego, 1961
42 Green Bay, 1943
41 N.Y. Giants, 1951

**Fewest Passes Intercepted By, Season**
3 Houston, 1982
5 Baltimore, 1982
6 Houston, 1972
St. Louis, 1982

**Most Passes Intercepted By, Game**
9 Green Bay vs. Detroit, Oct. 24, 1943
Philadelphia vs. Pittsburgh, Dec. 12, 1965
8 N.Y. Giants vs. Green Bay, Nov. 21, 1948
Philadelphia vs. Chi. Cardinals, Sept. 24, 1950
N.Y. Giants vs. N.Y. Yanks, Dec. 16, 1951
Houston vs. Denver, Dec. 2, 1962
Detroit vs. Chicago, Sept. 22, 1968
N.Y. Jets vs. Baltimore, Sept. 23, 1973
7 By many teams. Last time: New Orleans vs. Green Bay, Sept. 14, 1986

**Most Consecutive Games, One or More Interceptions By**
46 L.A. Chargers/San Diego, 1960-63
37 Detroit, 1960-63
36 Boston, 1944-47

**Most Yards Returning Interceptions, Season**
929 San Diego, 1961
712 Los Angeles, 1952

697 Seattle, 1984

**Fewest Yards Returning Interceptions, Season**

5 Los Angeles, 1959
37 Dallas, 1989
42 Philadelphia, 1982

**Most Yards Returning Interceptions, Game**

325 Seattle vs. Kansas City, Nov. 4, 1984
314 Los Angeles vs. San Francisco, Oct. 18, 1964
245 Houston vs. N.Y. Jets, Oct. 15, 1967

**Most Yards Returning Interceptions, Both Teams, Game**

356 Seattle (325) vs. Kansas City (31), Nov. 4, 1984
338 Los Angeles (314) vs. San Francisco (24), Oct. 18, 1964
308 Dallas (182) vs. Los Angeles (126), Nov. 2, 1952

**Most Touchdowns, Returning Interceptions, Season**

9 San Diego, 1961
7 Seattle, 1984
6 Cleveland, 1960
Green Bay, 1966
Detroit, 1967
Houston, 1967

**Most Touchdowns Returning Interceptions, Game**

4 Seattle vs. Kansas City, Nov. 4, 1984
3 Baltimore vs. Green Bay, Nov. 5, 1950
Cleveland vs. Chicago, Dec. 11, 1960
Philadelphia vs. Pittsburgh, Dec. 12, 1965
Baltimore vs. Pittsburgh, Sept. 29, 1968
Buffalo vs. N.Y. Jets, Sept. 29, 1968
Houston vs. San Diego, Dec. 19, 1971
Cincinnati vs. Houston, Dec. 17, 1972
Tampa Bay vs. New Orleans, Dec. 11, 1977
2 By many teams

**Most Touchdown Returning Interceptions, Both Teams, Game**

4 Philadelphia (3) vs. Pittsburgh (1), Dec. 12, 1965
Seattle (4) vs. Kansas City (0), Nov. 4, 1984
3 Los Angeles (2) vs. Detroit (1), Nov. 1, 1953
Cleveland (2) vs. N.Y. Giants (1), Dec. 18, 1960
Pittsburgh (2) vs. Cincinnati (1), Oct. 10, 1983
Kansas City (2) vs. San Diego (1), Oct. 19, 1986
(Also see previous record)

## PUNT RETURNS

**Fewest Opponents Punt Returns, Season**

7 Washington, 1962
San Diego, 1982
10 Buffalo, 1982
11 Boston, 1962

**Most Opponents Punt Returns, Season**

71 Tampa Bay, 1976, 1977
69 N.Y. Giants, 1953
68 Cleveland, 1974

**Fewest Yards Allowed, Punt Returns, Season**

22 Green Bay, 1967
34 Washington, 1962
39 Cleveland, 1959
Washington, 1972

**Most Yards Allowed, Punt Returns, Season**

932 Green Bay, 1949
913 Boston, 1947
906 New Orleans, 1974

**Lowest Average Allowed, Punt Returns, Season**

1.20 Chi. Cardinals, 1954 (46-55)
1.22 Cleveland, 1959 (32-39)
1.55 Chi. Cardinals, 1953 (44-68)

**Highest Average Allowed, Punt Returns, Season**

18.6 Green Bay, 1949 (50-932)
18.0 Cleveland, 1977 (31-558)
17.9 Boston, 1960 (20-357)

**Most Touchdowns Allowed, Punt Returns, Season**

4 New York, 1959
Atlanta, 1992
3 Green Bay, 1949
Chi. Cardinals, 1951
Los Angeles, 1951
Washington, 1952
Dallas, 1952
Pittsburgh, 1959, 1993
N.Y. Jets, 1968
Cleveland, 1977
Atlanta, 1986
Tampa Bay, 1986
2 By many teams

## KICKOFF RETURNS

**Fewest Opponents Kickoff Returns, Season**

10 Brooklyn, 1943
13 Denver, 1992
15 Detroit, 1942
Brooklyn, 1944

**Most Opponents Kickoff Returns, Season**

91 Washington, 1983
89 New England, 1980
88 San Diego, 1981

**Fewest Yards Allowed, Kickoff Returns, Season**

225 Brooklyn, 1943
254 Denver, 1992
293 Brooklyn, 1944

**Most Yards Allowed, Kickoff Returns, Season**

2,045 Kansas City, 1966
1,827 Chicago, 1985
1,816 N.Y. Giants, 1963

**Lowest Average Allowed, Kickoff Returns, Season**

14.3 Cleveland, 1980 (71-1,018)
14.9 Indianapolis, 1993 (37-551)
15.0 Seattle, 1982 (24-361)

**Highest Average Allowed, Kickoff Returns, Season**

29.5 N.Y. Jets, 1972 (47-1,386)
29.4 Los Angeles, 1950 (48-1,411)
29.1 New England, 1971 (49-1,427)

**Most Touchdowns Allowed, Kickoff Returns, Season**

3 Minnesota, 1963, 1970
Dallas, 1966
Detroit, 1980
Pittsburgh, 1986
2 By many teams

## FUMBLES

**Fewest Opponents Fumbles, Season**

11 Cleveland, 1956
Baltimore, 1982
13 Los Angeles, 1956
Chicago, 1960
Cleveland, 1963
Cleveland, 1965
Detroit, 1967
San Diego, 1969
14 Baltimore, 1970
Oakland, 1975
Buffalo, 1982
St. Louis, 1982
San Francisco, 1982

**Most Opponents Fumbles, Season**

50 Minnesota, 1963
San Francisco, 1978
48 N.Y. Giants, 1980
N.Y. Jets, 1986
47 N.Y. Giants, 1977
Seattle, 1984

## TURNOVERS

(Number of times losing the ball on interceptions and fumbles.)

**Fewest Opponents Turnovers, Season**

11 Baltimore, 1982
13 San Francisco, 1982
15 St. Louis, 1982

**Most Opponents Turnovers, Season**

66 San Diego, 1961
63 Seattle, 1984
61 Washington, 1983

**Most Opponents Turnovers, Game**

12 Chi. Bears vs. Detroit, Nov. 22, 1942
Philadelphia vs. Chi. Cardinals, Sept. 24, 1950
Philadelphia vs. Pittsburgh, Dec. 12, 1965
11 Green Bay vs. San Diego, Sept. 24, 1978
10 N.Y. Giants vs. Washington, Dec.4, 1938
Green Bay vs. Pittsburgh, Nov. 23, 1941
Green Bay vs. Detroit, Oct. 24, 1943
Green Bay vs. Chi. Cardinals, Nov. 10, 1946
N.Y. Giants vs. Chi. Cardinals, Nov. 2, 1952
Detroit vs. Minnesota, Dec. 9, 1962
Oakland vs. Houston, Sept. 7, 1963
N.Y. Giants vs. Washington, Dec. 8, 1963
Detroit vs. Chicago, Sept. 22, 1968
Washington vs. St. Louis, Oct. 25, 1976
New England vs. N.Y. Jets, Nov. 21, 1976
Dallas vs. San Francisco, Oct. 12, 1980
Seattle vs. Cleveland, Dec. 20, 1981
Denver vs. Detroit, Oct. 7, 1984

# OUTSTANDING PERFORMERS

## 1,000 YARDS RUSHING IN A SEASON

| Year | Player, Team | Att. | Yards | Avg. | Long | TD |
|---|---|---|---|---|---|---|
| 1993 | Emmitt Smith, Dallas[3] | 283 | 1,486 | 5.3 | 62 | 9 |
| | *Jerome Bettis, L.A. Rams | 294 | 1,429 | 4.9 | 71 | 7 |
| | Thurman Thomas, Buffalo[5] | 355 | 1,315 | 3.7 | 27 | 6 |
| | Erric Pegram, Atlanta | 292 | 1,185 | 4.1 | 29 | 3 |
| | Barry Sanders, Detroit[5] | 243 | 1,115 | 4.6 | 42 | 3 |
| | Leonard Russell, New England | 300 | 1,088 | 3.6 | 21 | 7 |
| | Rodney Hampton, N.Y. Giants[3] | 292 | 1,077 | 3.7 | 20 | 5 |
| | Chris Warren, Seattle[2] | 273 | 1,072 | 3.9 | 45 | 7 |
| | *Reggie Brooks, Washington | 223 | 1,063 | 4.8 | 85 | 3 |
| | *Ron Moore, Phoenix | 263 | 1,018 | 3.9 | 20 | 9 |
| | Gary Brown, Houston | 195 | 1,002 | 5.1 | 26 | 6 |
| 1992 | Emmitt Smith, Dallas[2] | 373 | 1,713 | 4.6 | 68 | 18 |
| | Barry Foster, Pittsburgh | 390 | 1,690 | 4.3 | 69 | 11 |
| | Thurman Thomas, Buffalo[4] | 312 | 1,487 | 4.8 | 44 | 9 |
| | Barry Sanders, Detroit[4] | 312 | 1,352 | 4.3 | 55 | 9 |
| | Lorenzo White, Houston | 265 | 1,226 | 4.6 | 44 | 7 |
| | Terry Allen, Minnesota | 266 | 1,201 | 4.5 | 51 | 13 |
| | Reggie Cobb, Tampa Bay | 310 | 1,171 | 3.8 | 25 | 9 |
| | Harold Green, Cincinnati | 265 | 1,170 | 4.4 | 53 | 2 |
| | Rodney Hampton, N.Y. Giants[2] | 257 | 1,141 | 4.4 | 63 | 14 |
| | Cleveland Gary, L.A. Rams | 279 | 1,125 | 4.0 | 63 | 7 |
| | Herschel Walker, Philadelphia[2] | 267 | 1,070 | 4.0 | 38 | 8 |
| | Chris Warren, Seattle | 223 | 1,017 | 4.6 | 52 | 3 |
| | *Ricky Watters, San Francisco | 206 | 1,013 | 4.9 | 43 | 9 |
| 1991 | Emmitt Smith, Dallas | 365 | 1,563 | 4.3 | 75 | 12 |
| | Barry Sanders, Detroit[3] | 342 | 1,548 | 4.5 | 69 | 16 |
| | Thurman Thomas, Buffalo[3] | 288 | 1,407 | 4.9 | 33 | 7 |
| | Rodney Hampton, N.Y. Giants | 256 | 1,059 | 4.1 | 44 | 10 |
| | Earnest Byner, Washington[3] | 274 | 1,048 | 3.8 | 32 | 5 |
| | Gaston Green, Denver | 261 | 1,037 | 4.0 | 63 | 4 |
| | Christian Okoye, Kansas City[2] | 225 | 1,031 | 4.6 | 48 | 9 |
| 1990 | Barry Sanders, Detroit[2] | 255 | 1,304 | 5.1 | 45 | 13 |
| | Thurman Thomas, Buffalo[2] | 271 | 1,297 | 4.8 | 80 | 11 |
| | Marion Butts, San Diego | 265 | 1,225 | 4.6 | 52 | 8 |
| | Earnest Byner, Washington[2] | 297 | 1,219 | 4.1 | 22 | 6 |
| | Bobby Humphrey, Denver[2] | 288 | 1,202 | 4.2 | 37 | 7 |
| | Neal Anderson, Chicago[3] | 260 | 1,078 | 4.1 | 52 | 10 |
| | Barry Word, Kansas City | 204 | 1,015 | 5.0 | 53 | 4 |
| | James Brooks, Cincinnati[3] | 195 | 1,004 | 5.1 | 56 | 5 |
| 1989 | Christian Okoye, Kansas City | 370 | 1,480 | 4.0 | 59 | 12 |
| | *Barry Sanders, Detroit | 280 | 1,470 | 5.3 | 34 | 14 |
| | Eric Dickerson, Indianapolis[7] | 314 | 1,311 | 4.2 | 21 | 7 |
| | Neal Anderson, Chicago[2] | 274 | 1,275 | 4.7 | 73 | 11 |
| | Dalton Hilliard, New Orleans | 344 | 1,262 | 3.7 | 40 | 13 |
| | Thurman Thomas, Buffalo | 298 | 1,244 | 4.2 | 38 | 6 |
| | James Brooks, Cincinnati[2] | 221 | 1,239 | 5.6 | 65 | 7 |
| | *Bobby Humphrey, Denver | 294 | 1,151 | 3.9 | 40 | 7 |
| | Greg Bell, L.A. Rams[3] | 272 | 1,137 | 4.2 | 47 | 15 |
| | Roger Craig, San Francisco[3] | 271 | 1,054 | 3.9 | 27 | 6 |
| | Ottis Anderson, N.Y. Giants[6] | 325 | 1,023 | 3.1 | 36 | 14 |
| 1988 | Eric Dickerson, Indianapolis[6] | 388 | 1,659 | 4.3 | 41 | 14 |
| | Herschel Walker, Dallas | 361 | 1,514 | 4.2 | 38 | 5 |
| | Roger Craig, San Francisco[2] | 310 | 1,502 | 4.8 | 46 | 9 |
| | Greg Bell, L.A. Rams[2] | 288 | 1,212 | 4.2 | 44 | 16 |
| | *John Stephens, New England | 297 | 1,168 | 3.9 | 52 | 4 |
| | Gary Anderson, San Diego | 225 | 1,119 | 5.0 | 36 | 3 |
| | Neal Anderson, Chicago | 249 | 1,106 | 4.4 | 80 | 12 |
| | Joe Morris, N.Y. Giants[3] | 307 | 1,083 | 3.5 | 27 | 5 |
| | *Ickey Woods, Cincinnati | 203 | 1,066 | 5.3 | 56 | 15 |
| | Curt Warner, Seattle[4] | 266 | 1,025 | 3.9 | 29 | 10 |
| | John Settle, Atlanta | 232 | 1,024 | 4.4 | 62 | 7 |
| | Mike Rozier, Houston | 251 | 1,002 | 4.0 | 28 | 10 |
| 1987 | Charles White, L.A. Rams | 324 | 1,374 | 4.2 | 58 | 11 |
| | Eric Dickerson, L.A. Rams-Indianapolis[5] | 283 | 1,288 | 4.6 | 57 | 6 |
| 1986 | Eric Dickerson, L.A. Rams[4] | 404 | 1,821 | 4.5 | 42 | 11 |
| | Joe Morris, N.Y. Giants[2] | 341 | 1,516 | 4.4 | 54 | 14 |
| | Curt Warner, Seattle[3] | 319 | 1,481 | 4.6 | 60 | 13 |
| | *Rueben Mayes, New Orleans | 286 | 1,353 | 4.7 | 50 | 8 |
| | Walter Payton, Chicago[10] | 321 | 1,333 | 4.2 | 41 | 8 |
| | Gerald Riggs, Atlanta[3] | 343 | 1,327 | 3.9 | 31 | 9 |
| | George Rogers, Washington[4] | 303 | 1,203 | 4.0 | 42 | 18 |
| | James Brooks, Cincinnati | 205 | 1,087 | 5.3 | 56 | 5 |
| 1985 | Marcus Allen, L.A. Raiders[3] | 390 | 1,759 | 4.6 | 61 | 11 |
| | Gerald Riggs, Atlanta[2] | 397 | 1,719 | 4.3 | 50 | 10 |
| | Walter Payton, Chicago[9] | 324 | 1,551 | 4.8 | 40 | 9 |
| | Joe Morris, N.Y. Giants | 294 | 1,336 | 4.5 | 65 | 21 |
| | Freeman McNeil, N.Y. Jets[2] | 294 | 1,331 | 4.5 | 69 | 3 |
| | Tony Dorsett, Dallas[8] | 305 | 1,307 | 4.3 | 60 | 7 |
| | James Wilder, Tampa Bay[2] | 365 | 1,300 | 3.6 | 28 | 10 |
| | Eric Dickerson, L.A. Rams[3] | 292 | 1,234 | 4.2 | 43 | 12 |
| | Craig James, New England | 263 | 1,227 | 4.7 | 65 | 5 |
| | Kevin Mack, Cleveland | 222 | 1,104 | 5.0 | 61 | 7 |
| | Curt Warner, Seattle[2] | 291 | 1,094 | 3.8 | 38 | 8 |
| | George Rogers, Washington[3] | 231 | 1,093 | 4.7 | 35 | 7 |
| | Roger Craig, San Francisco | 214 | 1,050 | 4.9 | 62 | 9 |
| | Earnest Jackson, Philadelphia[2] | 282 | 1,028 | 3.6 | 59 | 5 |
| | Stump Mitchell, St. Louis | 183 | 1,006 | 5.5 | 64 | 7 |
| | Earnest Byner, Cleveland | 244 | 1,002 | 4.1 | 36 | 8 |
| 1984 | Eric Dickerson, L.A. Rams[2] | 379 | 2,105 | 5.6 | 66 | 14 |
| | Walter Payton, Chicago[8] | 381 | 1,684 | 4.4 | 72 | 11 |
| | James Wilder, Tampa Bay | 407 | 1,544 | 3.8 | 37 | 13 |
| | Gerald Riggs, Atlanta | 353 | 1,486 | 4.2 | 57 | 13 |
| | Wendell Tyler, San Francisco[3] | 246 | 1,262 | 5.1 | 40 | 7 |
| | John Riggins, Washington[5] | 327 | 1,239 | 3.8 | 24 | 14 |
| | Tony Dorsett, Dallas[7] | 302 | 1,189 | 3.9 | 31 | 6 |
| | Earnest Jackson, San Diego | 296 | 1,179 | 4.0 | 32 | 8 |
| | Ottis Anderson, St. Louis[5] | 289 | 1,174 | 4.1 | 24 | 6 |
| | Marcus Allen, L.A. Raiders[2] | 275 | 1,168 | 4.2 | 52 | 13 |
| | Sammy Winder, Denver | 296 | 1,153 | 3.9 | 24 | 4 |
| | *Greg Bell, Buffalo | 262 | 1,100 | 4.2 | 85 | 7 |
| | Freeman McNeil, N.Y. Jets | 229 | 1,070 | 4.7 | 53 | 5 |
| 1983 | *Eric Dickerson, L.A. Rams | 390 | 1,808 | 4.6 | 85 | 18 |
| | William Andrews, Atlanta[4] | 331 | 1,567 | 4.7 | 27 | 7 |
| | *Curt Warner, Seattle | 335 | 1,449 | 4.3 | 60 | 13 |
| | Walter Payton, Chicago[7] | 314 | 1,421 | 4.5 | 49 | 6 |
| | John Riggins, Washington[4] | 375 | 1,347 | 3.6 | 44 | 24 |
| | Tony Dorsett, Dallas[6] | 289 | 1,321 | 4.6 | 77 | 8 |
| | Earl Campbell, Houston[5] | 322 | 1,301 | 4.0 | 42 | 12 |
| | Ottis Anderson, St. Louis[4] | 296 | 1,270 | 4.3 | 43 | 5 |
| | Mike Pruitt, Cleveland[4] | 293 | 1,184 | 4.0 | 27 | 10 |
| | George Rogers, New Orleans[2] | 256 | 1,144 | 4.5 | 76 | 5 |
| | Joe Cribbs, Buffalo[3] | 263 | 1,131 | 4.3 | 45 | 3 |
| | Curtis Dickey, Baltimore | 254 | 1,122 | 4.4 | 56 | 4 |
| | Tony Collins, New England | 219 | 1,049 | 4.8 | 50 | 10 |
| | Billy Sims, Detroit[3] | 220 | 1,040 | 4.7 | 41 | 7 |
| | Marcus Allen, L.A. Raiders | 266 | 1,014 | 3.8 | 19 | 9 |
| | Franco Harris, Pittsburgh[8] | 279 | 1,007 | 3.6 | 19 | 5 |
| 1981 | *George Rogers, New Orleans | 378 | 1,674 | 4.4 | 79 | 13 |
| | Tony Dorsett, Dallas[5] | 342 | 1,646 | 4.8 | 75 | 4 |
| | Billy Sims, Detroit[2] | 296 | 1,437 | 4.9 | 51 | 13 |
| | Wilbert Montgomery, Philadelphia[3] | 286 | 1,402 | 4.9 | 41 | 8 |
| | Ottis Anderson, St. Louis[3] | 328 | 1,376 | 4.2 | 28 | 9 |
| | Earl Campbell, Houston[4] | 361 | 1,376 | 3.8 | 43 | 10 |
| | William Andrews, Atlanta[3] | 289 | 1,301 | 4.5 | 29 | 10 |
| | Walter Payton, Chicago[6] | 339 | 1,222 | 3.6 | 39 | 6 |
| | Chuck Muncie, San Diego[2] | 251 | 1,144 | 4.6 | 73 | 19 |
| | *Joe Delaney, Kansas City | 234 | 1,121 | 4.8 | 82 | 3 |
| | Mike Pruitt, Cleveland[3] | 247 | 1,103 | 4.5 | 21 | 7 |
| | Joe Cribbs, Buffalo[2] | 257 | 1,097 | 4.3 | 35 | 3 |
| | Pete Johnson, Cincinnati | 274 | 1,077 | 3.9 | 39 | 12 |
| | Wendell Tyler, Los Angeles[2] | 260 | 1,074 | 4.1 | 69 | 12 |
| | Ted Brown, Minnesota | 274 | 1,063 | 3.9 | 34 | 6 |
| 1980 | Earl Campbell, Houston[3] | 373 | 1,934 | 5.2 | 55 | 13 |
| | Walter Payton, Chicago[5] | 317 | 1,460 | 4.6 | 69 | 6 |
| | Ottis Anderson, St. Louis[2] | 301 | 1,352 | 4.5 | 52 | 9 |
| | William Andrews, Atlanta[2] | 265 | 1,308 | 4.9 | 33 | 4 |
| | *Billy Sims, Detroit | 313 | 1,303 | 4.2 | 52 | 13 |
| | Tony Dorsett, Dallas[4] | 278 | 1,185 | 4.3 | 56 | 11 |
| | *Joe Cribbs, Buffalo | 306 | 1,185 | 3.9 | 48 | 11 |
| | Mike Pruitt, Cleveland[2] | 249 | 1,034 | 4.2 | 56 | 6 |
| 1979 | Earl Campbell, Houston[2] | 368 | 1,697 | 4.6 | 61 | 19 |
| | Walter Payton, Chicago[4] | 369 | 1,610 | 4.4 | 43 | 14 |
| | *Ottis Anderson, St. Louis | 331 | 1,605 | 4.8 | 76 | 8 |
| | Wilbert Montgomery, Philadelphia[2] | 338 | 1,512 | 4.5 | 62 | 9 |
| | Mike Pruitt, Cleveland | 264 | 1,294 | 4.9 | 77 | 9 |
| | Ricky Bell, Tampa Bay | 283 | 1,263 | 4.5 | 49 | 7 |
| | Chuck Muncie, New Orleans | 238 | 1,198 | 5.0 | 69 | 11 |
| | Franco Harris, Pittsburgh[7] | 267 | 1,186 | 4.4 | 71 | 11 |
| | John Riggins, Washington[3] | 260 | 1,153 | 4.4 | 66 | 9 |
| | Wendell Tyler, Los Angeles | 218 | 1,109 | 5.1 | 63 | 9 |
| | Tony Dorsett, Dallas[3] | 250 | 1,107 | 4.4 | 41 | 6 |
| | *William Andrews, Atlanta | 239 | 1,023 | 4.3 | 23 | 3 |
| 1978 | *Earl Campbell, Houston | 302 | 1,450 | 4.8 | 81 | 13 |
| | Walter Payton, Chicago[3] | 333 | 1,395 | 4.2 | 76 | 11 |
| | Tony Dorsett, Dallas[2] | 290 | 1,325 | 4.6 | 63 | 7 |
| | Delvin Williams, Miami[2] | 272 | 1,258 | 4.6 | 58 | 8 |
| | Wilbert Montgomery, Philadelphia | 259 | 1,220 | 4.7 | 47 | 9 |
| | Terdell Middleton, Green Bay | 284 | 1,116 | 3.9 | 76 | 11 |
| | Franco Harris, Pittsburgh[6] | 310 | 1,082 | 3.5 | 37 | 8 |
| | Mark van Eeghen, Oakland[3] | 270 | 1,080 | 4.0 | 34 | 9 |
| | *Terry Miller, Buffalo | 238 | 1,060 | 4.5 | 60 | 7 |
| | Tony Reed, Kansas City | 206 | 1,053 | 5.1 | 62 | 5 |
| | John Riggins, Washington[2] | 248 | 1,014 | 4.1 | 31 | 5 |
| 1977 | Walter Payton, Chicago[2] | 339 | 1,852 | 5.5 | 73 | 14 |

| | | | | | | |
|---|---|---|---|---|---|---|
| | Mark van Eeghen, Oakland[2] | 324 | 1,273 | 3.9 | 27 | 7 |
| | Lawrence McCutcheon, Los Angeles[4] | 294 | 1,238 | 4.2 | 48 | 7 |
| | Franco Harris, Pittsburgh[5] | 300 | 1,162 | 3.9 | 61 | 11 |
| | Lydell Mitchell, Baltimore[3] | 301 | 1,159 | 3.9 | 64 | 3 |
| | Chuck Foreman, Minnesota[3] | 270 | 1,112 | 4.1 | 51 | 6 |
| | Greg Pruitt, Cleveland[3] | 236 | 1,086 | 4.6 | 78 | 3 |
| | Sam Cunningham, New England | 270 | 1,015 | 3.8 | 31 | 4 |
| | *Tony Dorsett, Dallas | 208 | 1,007 | 4.8 | 84 | 12 |
| 1976 | O.J. Simpson, Buffalo[5] | 290 | 1,503 | 5.2 | 75 | 8 |
| | Walter Payton, Chicago | 311 | 1,390 | 4.5 | 60 | 13 |
| | Delvin Williams, San Francisco | 248 | 1,203 | 4.9 | 80 | 7 |
| | Lydell Mitchell, Baltimore[2] | 289 | 1,200 | 4.2 | 43 | 5 |
| | Lawrence McCutcheon, Los Angeles[3] | 291 | 1,168 | 4.0 | 40 | 9 |
| | Chuck Foreman, Minnesota[2] | 278 | 1,155 | 4.2 | 46 | 13 |
| | Franco Harris, Pittsburgh[4] | 289 | 1,128 | 3.9 | 30 | 14 |
| | Mike Thomas, Washington | 254 | 1,101 | 4.3 | 28 | 5 |
| | Rocky Bleier, Pittsburgh | 220 | 1,036 | 4.7 | 28 | 5 |
| | Mark van Eeghen, Oakland | 233 | 1,012 | 4.3 | 21 | 3 |
| | Otis Armstrong, Denver[2] | 247 | 1,008 | 4.1 | 31 | 5 |
| | Greg Pruitt, Cleveland[2] | 209 | 1,000 | 4.8 | 64 | 4 |
| 1975 | O.J. Simpson, Buffalo[4] | 329 | 1,817 | 5.5 | 88 | 16 |
| | Franco Harris, Pittsburgh[3] | 262 | 1,246 | 4.8 | 36 | 10 |
| | Lydell Mitchell, Baltimore | 289 | 1,193 | 4.1 | 70 | 11 |
| | Jim Otis, St. Louis | 269 | 1,076 | 4.0 | 30 | 5 |
| | Chuck Foreman, Minnesota | 280 | 1,070 | 3.8 | 31 | 13 |
| | Greg Pruitt, Cleveland | 217 | 1,067 | 4.9 | 50 | 8 |
| | John Riggins, N.Y. Jets | 238 | 1,005 | 4.2 | 42 | 8 |
| | Dave Hampton, Atlanta | 250 | 1,002 | 4.0 | 22 | 5 |
| 1974 | Otis Armstrong, Denver | 263 | 1,407 | 5.3 | 43 | 9 |
| | *Don Woods, San Diego | 227 | 1,162 | 5.1 | 56 | 7 |
| | O.J. Simpson, Buffalo[3] | 270 | 1,125 | 4.2 | 41 | 3 |
| | Lawrence McCutcheon, Los Angeles[2] | 236 | 1,109 | 4.7 | 23 | 3 |
| | Franco Harris, Pittsburgh[2] | 208 | 1,006 | 4.8 | 54 | 5 |
| 1973 | O.J. Simpson, Buffalo[2] | 332 | 2,003 | 6.0 | 80 | 12 |
| | John Brockington, Green Bay[3] | 265 | 1,144 | 4.3 | 53 | 3 |
| | Calvin Hill, Dallas[2] | 273 | 1,142 | 4.2 | 21 | 6 |
| | Lawrence McCutcheon, Los Angeles | 210 | 1,097 | 5.2 | 37 | 2 |
| | Larry Csonka, Miami[3] | 219 | 1,003 | 4.6 | 25 | 5 |
| 1972 | O.J. Simpson, Buffalo | 292 | 1,251 | 4.3 | 94 | 6 |
| | Larry Brown, Washington[2] | 285 | 1,216 | 4.3 | 38 | 8 |
| | Ron Johnson, N.Y. Giants[2] | 298 | 1,182 | 4.0 | 35 | 9 |
| | Larry Csonka, Miami[2] | 213 | 1,117 | 5.2 | 45 | 6 |
| | Marv Hubbard, Oakland | 219 | 1,100 | 5.0 | 39 | 4 |
| | *Franco Harris, Pittsburgh | 188 | 1,055 | 5.6 | 75 | 10 |
| | Calvin Hill, Dallas | 245 | 1,036 | 4.2 | 26 | 6 |
| | Mike Garrett, San Diego[2] | 272 | 1,031 | 3.8 | 41 | 6 |
| | John Brockington, Green Bay[2] | 274 | 1,027 | 3.7 | 30 | 8 |
| | Eugene (Mercury) Morris, Miami | 190 | 1,000 | 5.3 | 33 | 12 |
| 1971 | Floyd Little, Denver | 284 | 1,133 | 4.0 | 40 | 6 |
| | *John Brockington, Green Bay | 216 | 1,105 | 5.1 | 52 | 4 |
| | Larry Csonka, Miami | 195 | 1,051 | 5.4 | 28 | 7 |
| | Steve Owens, Detroit | 246 | 1,035 | 4.2 | 23 | 8 |
| | Willie Ellison, Los Angeles | 211 | 1,000 | 4.7 | 80 | 4 |
| 1970 | Larry Brown, Washington | 237 | 1,125 | 4.7 | 75 | 5 |
| | Ron Johnson, N.Y. Giants | 263 | 1,027 | 3.9 | 68 | 8 |
| 1969 | Gale Sayers, Chicago[2] | 236 | 1,032 | 4.4 | 28 | 8 |
| 1968 | Leroy Kelly, Cleveland[3] | 248 | 1,239 | 5.0 | 65 | 16 |
| | *Paul Robinson, Cincinnati | 238 | 1,023 | 4.3 | 87 | 8 |
| 1967 | Jim Nance, Boston[2] | 269 | 1,216 | 4.5 | 53 | 7 |
| | Leroy Kelly, Cleveland[2] | 235 | 1,205 | 5.1 | 42 | 11 |
| | Hoyle Granger, Houston | 236 | 1,194 | 5.1 | 67 | 6 |
| | Mike Garrett, Kansas City | 236 | 1,087 | 4.6 | 58 | 9 |
| 1966 | Jim Nance, Boston | 299 | 1,458 | 4.9 | 65 | 11 |
| | Gale Sayers, Chicago | 229 | 1,231 | 5.4 | 58 | 8 |
| | Leroy Kelly, Cleveland | 209 | 1,141 | 5.5 | 70 | 15 |
| | Dick Bass, Los Angeles[2] | 248 | 1,090 | 4.4 | 50 | 8 |
| 1965 | Jim Brown, Cleveland[7] | 289 | 1,544 | 5.3 | 67 | 17 |
| | Paul Lowe, San Diego[2] | 222 | 1,121 | 5.0 | 59 | 7 |
| 1964 | Jim Brown, Cleveland[6] | 280 | 1,446 | 5.2 | 71 | 7 |
| | Jim Taylor, Green Bay[5] | 235 | 1,169 | 5.0 | 84 | 12 |
| | John Henry Johnson, Pittsburgh[2] | 235 | 1,048 | 4.5 | 45 | 7 |
| 1963 | Jim Brown, Cleveland[5] | 291 | 1,863 | 6.4 | 80 | 12 |
| | Clem Daniels, Oakland | 215 | 1,099 | 5.1 | 74 | 3 |
| | Jim Taylor, Green Bay[4] | 248 | 1,018 | 4.1 | 40 | 9 |
| | Paul Lowe, San Diego | 177 | 1,010 | 5.7 | 66 | 8 |
| 1962 | Jim Taylor, Green Bay[3] | 272 | 1,474 | 5.4 | 51 | 19 |
| | John Henry Johnson, Pittsburgh | 251 | 1,141 | 4.5 | 40 | 7 |
| | Cookie Gilchrist, Buffalo | 214 | 1,096 | 5.1 | 44 | 13 |
| | Abner Haynes, Dall. Texans | 221 | 1,049 | 4.7 | 71 | 13 |
| | Dick Bass, Los Angeles | 196 | 1,033 | 5.3 | 57 | 6 |
| | Charlie Tolar, Houston | 244 | 1,012 | 4.1 | 25 | 7 |
| 1961 | Jim Brown, Cleveland[4] | 305 | 1,408 | 4.6 | 38 | 8 |
| | Jim Taylor, Green Bay[2] | 243 | 1,307 | 5.4 | 53 | 15 |
| 1960 | Jim Brown, Cleveland[3] | 215 | 1,257 | 5.8 | 71 | 9 |
| | Jim Taylor, Green Bay | 230 | 1,101 | 4.8 | 32 | 11 |
| | John David Crow, St. Louis | 183 | 1,071 | 5.9 | 57 | 6 |
| 1959 | Jim Brown, Cleveland[2] | 290 | 1,329 | 4.6 | 70 | 14 |
| | J.D. Smith, San Francisco | 207 | 1,036 | 5.0 | 73 | 10 |
| 1958 | Jim Brown, Cleveland | 257 | 1,527 | 5.9 | 65 | 17 |
| 1956 | Rick Casares, Chi. Bears | 234 | 1,126 | 4.8 | 68 | 12 |
| 1954 | Joe Perry, San Francisco[2] | 173 | 1,049 | 6.1 | 58 | 8 |
| 1953 | Joe Perry, San Francisco | 192 | 1,018 | 5.3 | 51 | 10 |
| 1949 | Steve Van Buren, Philadelphia[2] | 263 | 1,146 | 4.4 | 41 | 11 |
| | Tony Canadeo, Green Bay | 208 | 1,052 | 5.1 | 54 | 4 |
| 1947 | Steve Van Buren, Philadelphia | 217 | 1,008 | 4.6 | 45 | 13 |
| 1934 | *Beattie Feathers, Chi. Bears | 119 | 1,004 | 8.4 | 82 | 8 |

**First season of professional football.*

## 200 YARDS RUSHING IN A GAME

| Date | Player, Team, Opponent | Att. | Yards | TD |
|---|---|---|---|---|
| Dec. 12, 1993 | *Jerome Bettis, L.A. Rams vs. New Orleans | 28 | 212 | 1 |
| Oct. 31, 1993 | Emmitt Smith, Dallas vs. Philadelphia | 30 | 237 | 1 |
| Nov. 24, 1991 | Barry Sanders, Detroit vs. Minnesota | 23 | 220 | 4 |
| Dec. 23, 1990 | James Brooks, Cincinnati vs. Houston | 20 | 201 | 1 |
| Oct. 14, 1990 | Barry Word, Kansas City vs. Detroit | 18 | 200 | 2 |
| Sept. 24, 1990 | Thurman Thomas, Buffalo vs. N.Y. Jets | 18 | 214 | 0 |
| Dec. 24, 1989 | Greg Bell, L.A. Rams vs. New England | 26 | 210 | 1 |
| Sept. 24, 1989 | Greg Bell, L.A. Rams vs. Green Bay | 28 | 221 | 2 |
| Sept. 17, 1989 | Gerald Riggs, Washington vs. Philadelphia | 29 | 221 | 1 |
| Dec. 18, 1988 | Gary Anderson, San Diego vs. Kansas City | 34 | 217 | 1 |
| Nov. 30, 1987 | *Bo Jackson, L.A. Raiders vs. Seattle | 18 | 221 | 2 |
| Nov. 15, 1987 | Charles White, L.A. Rams vs. St. Louis | 34 | 213 | 1 |
| Dec. 7, 1986 | Rueben Mayes, New Orleans vs. Miami | 28 | 203 | 2 |
| Oct. 5, 1986 | Eric Dickerson, L.A. Rams vs. Tampa Bay (OT) | 30 | 207 | 2 |
| Dec. 21, 1985 | George Rogers, Washington vs. St. Louis | 34 | 206 | 1 |
| Dec. 21, 1985 | Joe Morris, N.Y. Giants vs. Pittsburgh | 36 | 202 | 3 |
| Dec. 9, 1984 | Eric Dickerson, L.A. Rams vs. Houston | 27 | 215 | 2 |
| Nov. 18, 1984 | *Greg Bell, Buffalo vs. Dallas | 27 | 206 | 1 |
| Nov. 4, 1984 | Eric Dickerson, L.A. Rams vs. St. Louis | 21 | 208 | 0 |
| Sept. 2, 1984 | Gerald Riggs, Atlanta vs. New Orleans | 35 | 202 | 2 |
| Nov. 27, 1983 | *Curt Warner, Seattle vs. Kansas City (OT) | 32 | 207 | 3 |
| Nov. 6, 1983 | James Wilder, Tampa Bay vs. Minnesota | 31 | 219 | 1 |
| Sept. 18, 1983 | Tony Collins, New England vs. N.Y. Jets | 23 | 212 | 3 |
| Sept. 4, 1983 | George Rogers, New Orleans vs. St. Louis | 24 | 206 | 2 |
| Dec. 21, 1980 | Earl Campbell, Houston vs. Minnesota | 29 | 203 | 1 |
| Nov. 16, 1980 | Earl Campbell, Houston vs. Chicago | 31 | 206 | 0 |
| Oct. 26, 1980 | Earl Campbell, Houston vs. Cincinnati | 27 | 202 | 2 |
| Oct. 19, 1980 | Earl Campbell, Houston vs. Tampa Bay | 33 | 203 | 0 |
| Nov. 26, 1978 | *Terry Miller, Buffalo vs. N.Y. Giants | 21 | 208 | 2 |
| Dec. 4, 1977 | *Tony Dorsett, Dallas vs. Philadelphia | 23 | 206 | 2 |
| Nov. 20, 1977 | Walter Payton, Chicago vs. Minnesota | 40 | 275 | 1 |
| Oct. 30, 1977 | Walter Payton, Chicago vs. Green Bay | 23 | 205 | 2 |
| Dec. 5, 1976 | O.J. Simpson, Buffalo vs. Miami | 24 | 203 | 1 |
| Nov. 25, 1976 | O.J. Simpson, Buffalo vs. Detroit | 29 | 273 | 2 |
| Oct. 24, 1976 | Chuck Foreman, Minnesota vs. Philadelphia | 28 | 200 | 2 |
| Dec. 14, 1975 | Greg Pruitt, Cleveland vs. Kansas City | 26 | 214 | 3 |
| Sept. 28, 1975 | O.J. Simpson, Buffalo vs. Pittsburgh | 28 | 227 | 1 |
| Dec. 16, 1973 | O.J. Simpson, Buffalo vs. N.Y. Jets | 34 | 200 | 1 |
| Dec. 9, 1973 | O.J. Simpson, Buffalo vs. New England | 22 | 219 | 1 |
| Sept. 16, 1973 | O.J. Simpson, Buffalo vs. New England | 29 | 250 | 2 |
| Dec. 5, 1971 | Willie Ellison, Los Angeles vs. New Orleans | 26 | 247 | 1 |
| Dec. 20, 1970 | John (Frenchy) Fuqua, Pittsburgh vs. Philadelphia | 20 | 218 | 2 |
| Nov. 3, 1968 | Gale Sayers, Chicago vs. Green Bay | 24 | 205 | 0 |
| Oct. 30, 1966 | Jim Nance, Boston vs. Oakland | 38 | 208 | 2 |
| Oct. 10, 1964 | John Henry Johnson, Pittsburgh vs. Cleveland | 30 | 200 | 3 |
| Dec. 8, 1963 | Cookie Gilchrist, Buffalo vs. N.Y. Jets | 36 | 243 | 5 |
| Nov. 3, 1963 | Jim Brown, Cleveland vs. Philadelphia | 28 | 223 | 1 |
| Oct. 20, 1963 | Clem Daniels, Oakland vs. N.Y. Jets | 27 | 200 | 2 |
| Sept. 22, 1963 | Jim Brown, Cleveland vs. Dallas | 20 | 232 | 2 |
| Dec. 10, 1961 | Billy Cannon, Houston vs. N.Y. Titans | 25 | 216 | 3 |
| Nov. 19, 1961 | Jim Brown, Cleveland vs. Philadelphia | 34 | 237 | 4 |
| Dec. 18, 1960 | John David Crow, St. Louis vs. Pittsburgh | 24 | 203 | 0 |
| Nov. 15, 1959 | Bobby Mitchell, Cleveland vs. Washington | 14 | 232 | 3 |
| Nov. 24, 1957 | *Jim Brown, Cleveland vs. Los Angeles | 31 | 237 | 4 |
| Dec. 16, 1956 | *Tom Wilson, Los Angeles vs. Green Bay | 23 | 223 | 0 |
| Nov. 22, 1953 | Dan Towler, Los Angeles vs. Baltimore | 14 | 205 | 1 |
| Nov. 12, 1950 | Gene Roberts, N.Y. Giants vs. Chi. Cardinals | 26 | 218 | 2 |
| Nov. 27, 1949 | Steve Van Buren, Philadelphia vs. Pittsburgh | 27 | 205 | 0 |
| Oct. 8, 1933 | Cliff Battles, Boston vs. N.Y. Giants | 16 | 215 | 1 |

**First season of professional football.*

**TIMES 200 OR MORE**

59 times by 41 players...Simpson 6; Brown, Campbell 4; Bell, Dickerson 3; Payton, Riggs, Rogers 2.

# OUTSTANDING PERFORMERS

## 4,000 YARDS PASSING IN A SEASON

| Year | Player, Team | Att. | Comp. | Pct. | Yards | TD | Int. |
|---|---|---|---|---|---|---|---|
| 1993 | John Elway, Denver | 551 | 348 | 63.2 | 4,030 | 25 | 10 |
| | Steve Young, San Francisco | 462 | 314 | 68.0 | 4,023 | 29 | 16 |
| 1992 | Dan Marino, Miami[5] | 554 | 330 | 59.6 | 4,116 | 24 | 16 |
| 1991 | Warren Moon, Houston[2] | 655 | 404 | 61.7 | 4,690 | 23 | 21 |
| 1990 | Warren Moon, Houston | 584 | 362 | 62.0 | 4,689 | 33 | 13 |
| 1989 | Don Majkowski, Green Bay | 599 | 353 | 58.9 | 4,318 | 27 | 20 |
| | Jim Everett, L.A. Rams | 518 | 304 | 58.7 | 4,310 | 29 | 17 |
| 1988 | Dan Marino, Miami[4] | 606 | 354 | 58.4 | 4,434 | 28 | 23 |
| 1986 | Dan Marino, Miami[3] | 623 | 378 | 60.7 | 4,746 | 44 | 23 |
| | Jay Schroeder, Washington | 541 | 276 | 51.0 | 4,109 | 22 | 22 |
| 1985 | Dan Marino, Miami[2] | 567 | 336 | 59.3 | 4,137 | 30 | 21 |
| 1984 | Dan Marino, Miami | 564 | 362 | 64.2 | 5,084 | 48 | 17 |
| | Neil Lomax, St. Louis | 560 | 345 | 61.6 | 4,614 | 28 | 16 |
| | Phil Simms, N.Y. Giants | 533 | 286 | 53.7 | 4,044 | 22 | 18 |
| 1983 | Lynn Dickey, Green Bay | 484 | 289 | 59.7 | 4,458 | 32 | 29 |
| | Bill Kenney, Kansas City | 603 | 346 | 57.4 | 4,348 | 24 | 18 |
| 1981 | Dan Fouts, San Diego[3] | 609 | 360 | 59.1 | 4,802 | 33 | 17 |
| 1980 | Dan Fouts, San Diego[2] | 589 | 348 | 59.1 | 4,715 | 30 | 24 |
| | Brian Sipe, Cleveland | 554 | 337 | 60.8 | 4,132 | 30 | 14 |
| 1979 | Dan Fouts, San Diego | 530 | 332 | 62.6 | 4,082 | 24 | 24 |
| 1967 | Joe Namath, N.Y. Jets | 491 | 258 | 52.5 | 4,007 | 26 | 28 |

## 400 YARDS PASSING IN A GAME

| Date | Player, Team, Opponent | Att. | Comp. | Yards | TD |
|---|---|---|---|---|---|
| Dec. 19, 1993 | Steve Beuerlein, Phoenix vs. Seattle | 53 | 34 | 431 | 3 |
| Dec. 5, 1993 | Brett Favre, Green Bay vs. Chicago | 54 | 36 | 402 | 2 |
| Nov. 28, 1993 | Steve Young, San Francisco vs. L.A. Rams | 32 | 26 | 462 | 4 |
| Oct. 31, 1993 | Jeff Hostetler, L.A. Raiders vs. San Diego | 32 | 20 | 424 | 2 |
| Sept. 13, 1992 | Steve Young, San Francisco vs. Buffalo | 37 | 26 | 449 | 3 |
| Sept. 13, 1992 | Jim Kelly, Buffalo vs. San Francisco | 33 | 22 | 403 | 3 |
| Nov. 10, 1991 | Warren Moon, Houston vs. Dallas (OT) | 56 | 41 | 432 | 0 |
| Nov. 10, 1991 | Mark Rypien, Washington vs. Atlanta | 31 | 16 | 442 | 6 |
| Oct. 13, 1991 | Warren Moon, Houston vs. N.Y. Jets | 50 | 35 | 423 | 2 |
| Dec. 16, 1990 | Warren Moon, Houston vs. Kansas City | 45 | 27 | 527 | 3 |
| Nov. 4, 1990 | Joe Montana, San Francisco vs. Green Bay | 40 | 25 | 411 | 3 |
| Oct. 14, 1990 | Joe Montana, San Francisco vs. Atlanta | 49 | 32 | 476 | 6 |
| Oct. 7, 1990 | Boomer Esiason, Cincinnati vs. L.A. Rams (OT) | 45 | 31 | 490 | 3 |
| Dec. 23, 1989 | Warren Moon, Houston vs. Cleveland | 51 | 32 | 414 | 2 |
| Dec. 11, 1989 | Joe Montana, San Francisco vs. L.A. Rams | 42 | 30 | 458 | 3 |
| Nov. 26, 1989 | Jim Everett, L.A. Rams vs. New Orleans (OT) | 51 | 29 | 454 | 1 |
| Nov. 26, 1989 | Mark Rypien, Washington vs. Chicago | 47 | 30 | 401 | 4 |
| Oct. 2, 1989 | Randall Cunningham, Philadelphia vs. Chicago | 62 | 32 | 401 | 1 |
| Sept. 24, 1989 | Joe Montana, San Francisco vs. Philadelphia | 34 | 25 | 428 | 5 |
| Sept. 24, 1989 | Dan Marino, Miami vs. N.Y. Jets | 55 | 33 | 427 | 3 |
| Sept. 17, 1989 | Randall Cunningham, Phil. vs. Washington | 46 | 34 | 447 | 5 |
| Dec. 18, 1988 | Dave Krieg, Seattle vs. L.A. Raiders | 32 | 19 | 410 | 4 |
| Dec. 12, 1988 | Dan Marino, Miami vs. Cleveland | 50 | 30 | 404 | 4 |
| Oct. 23, 1988 | Dan Marino, Miami vs. N.Y. Jets | 60 | 35 | 521 | 3 |
| Oct. 16, 1988 | Vinny Testaverde, Tampa Bay vs. Indianapolis | 42 | 25 | 469 | 2 |
| Sept. 11, 1988 | Doug Williams, Washington vs. Pittsburgh | 52 | 30 | 430 | 2 |
| Nov. 29, 1987 | Tom Ramsey, New England vs. Philadelphia | 53 | 34 | 402 | 3 |
| Nov. 22, 1987 | Boomer Esiason, Cincinnati vs. Pittsburgh | 53 | 30 | 409 | 0 |
| Sept. 20, 1987 | Neil Lomax, St. Louis vs. San Diego | 61 | 32 | 457 | 3 |
| Dec. 21, 1986 | Boomer Esiason, Cincinnati vs. N.Y. Jets | 30 | 23 | 425 | 5 |
| Dec. 14, 1986 | Dan Marino, Miami vs. L.A. Rams (OT) | 46 | 29 | 403 | 5 |
| Nov. 23, 1986 | Bernie Kosar, Cleveland vs. Pittsburgh (OT) | 46 | 28 | 414 | 2 |
| Nov. 17, 1986 | Joe Montana, San Francisco vs. Washington | 60 | 33 | 441 | 0 |
| Nov. 16, 1986 | Dan Marino, Miami vs. Buffalo | 54 | 39 | 404 | 4 |
| Nov. 10, 1986 | Bernie Kosar, Cleveland vs. Miami | 50 | 32 | 401 | 0 |
| Nov. 2, 1986 | Tommy Kramer, Minnesota vs. Washington (OT) | 35 | 20 | 490 | 4 |
| Nov. 2, 1986 | Ken O'Brien, N.Y. Jets vs. Seattle | 32 | 26 | 431 | 4 |
| Oct. 27, 1986 | Jay Schroeder, Washington vs. N.Y. Giants | 40 | 22 | 420 | 1 |
| Oct. 12, 1986 | Steve Grogan, New England vs. N.Y. Jets | 42 | 23 | 401 | 3 |
| Sept. 21, 1986 | Ken O'Brien, N.Y. Jets vs. Miami (OT) | 43 | 29 | 479 | 4 |
| Sept. 21, 1986 | Dan Marino, Miami vs. N.Y. Jets (OT) | 50 | 30 | 448 | 6 |
| Sept. 21, 1986 | Tony Eason, New England vs. Seattle | 45 | 26 | 414 | 3 |
| Dec. 20, 1985 | John Elway, Denver vs. Seattle | 42 | 24 | 432 | 1 |
| Nov. 10, 1985 | Dan Fouts, San Diego vs. L.A. Raiders (OT) | 41 | 26 | 436 | 4 |
| Oct. 13, 1985 | Phil Simms, N.Y. Giants vs. Cincinnati | 62 | 40 | 513 | 1 |
| Oct. 13, 1985 | Dave Krieg, Seattle vs. Atlanta | 51 | 33 | 405 | 4 |
| Oct. 6, 1985 | Phil Simms, N.Y. Giants vs. Dallas | 36 | 18 | 432 | 3 |
| Oct. 6, 1985 | Joe Montana, San Francisco vs. Atlanta | 57 | 37 | 429 | 5 |
| Sept. 19, 1985 | Tommy Kramer, Minnesota vs. Chicago | 55 | 28 | 436 | 3 |
| Sept. 15, 1985 | Dan Fouts, San Diego vs. Seattle | 43 | 29 | 440 | 4 |
| Dec. 16, 1984 | Neil Lomax, St. Louis vs. Washington | 46 | 37 | 468 | 2 |
| Dec. 9, 1984 | Dan Marino, Miami vs. Indianapolis | 41 | 29 | 404 | 4 |
| Dec. 2, 1984 | Dan Marino, Miami vs. L.A. Raiders | 57 | 35 | 470 | 4 |
| Nov. 25, 1984 | Dave Krieg, Seattle vs. Denver | 44 | 30 | 406 | 3 |
| Nov. 4, 1984 | Dan Marino, Miami vs. N.Y. Jets | 42 | 23 | 422 | 2 |
| Oct. 21, 1984 | Dan Fouts, San Diego vs. L.A. Raiders | 45 | 24 | 410 | 3 |
| Sept. 30, 1984 | Dan Marino, Miami vs. St. Louis | 36 | 24 | 429 | 3 |
| Sept. 2, 1984 | Phil Simms, N.Y. Giants vs. Philadelphia | 30 | 23 | 409 | 4 |
| Dec. 11, 1983 | Bill Kenney, Kansas City vs. San Diego | 41 | 31 | 411 | 4 |
| Nov. 20, 1983 | Dave Krieg, Seattle vs. Denver | 42 | 31 | 418 | 3 |
| Oct. 9, 1983 | Joe Ferguson, Buffalo vs. Miami (OT) | 55 | 38 | 419 | 5 |
| Oct. 2, 1983 | Joe Theismann, Washington vs. L.A. Raiders | 39 | 23 | 417 | 3 |
| Sept. 25, 1983 | Richard Todd, N.Y. Jets vs. L.A. Rams (OT) | 50 | 37 | 446 | 2 |
| Dec. 26, 1982 | Vince Ferragamo, L.A. Rams vs. Chicago | 46 | 30 | 509 | 3 |
| Dec. 20, 1982 | Dan Fouts, San Diego vs. Cincinnati | 40 | 25 | 435 | 1 |
| Dec. 20, 1982 | Ken Anderson, Cincinnati vs. San Diego | 56 | 40 | 416 | 2 |
| Dec. 11, 1982 | Dan Fouts, San Diego vs. San Francisco | 48 | 33 | 444 | 5 |
| Nov. 21, 1982 | Joe Montana, San Francisco vs. St. Louis | 39 | 26 | 408 | 3 |
| Nov. 15, 1981 | Steve Bartkowski, Atlanta vs. Pittsburgh | 50 | 33 | 416 | 2 |
| Oct. 25, 1981 | Brian Sipe, Cleveland vs. Baltimore | 41 | 30 | 444 | 4 |
| Oct. 25, 1981 | David Woodley, Miami vs. Dallas | 37 | 21 | 408 | 3 |
| Oct. 11, 1981 | Tommy Kramer, Minnesota vs. San Diego | 43 | 27 | 444 | 4 |
| Dec. 14, 1980 | Tommy Kramer, Minnesota vs. Cleveland | 49 | 38 | 456 | 4 |
| Nov. 16, 1980 | Doug Williams, Tampa Bay vs. Minnesota | 55 | 30 | 486 | 4 |
| Oct. 19, 1980 | Dan Fouts, San Diego vs. N.Y. Giants | 41 | 26 | 444 | 3 |
| Oct. 12, 1980 | Lynn Dickey, Green Bay vs. Tampa Bay (OT) | 51 | 35 | 418 | 1 |
| Sept. 21, 1980 | Richard Todd, N.Y. Jets vs. San Francisco | 60 | 42 | 447 | 3 |
| Oct. 3, 1976 | James Harris, Los Angeles vs. Miami | 29 | 17 | 436 | 2 |
| Nov. 17, 1975 | Ken Anderson, Cincinnati vs. Buffalo | 46 | 30 | 447 | 2 |
| Nov. 18, 1974 | Charley Johnson, Denver vs. Kansas City | 42 | 28 | 445 | 2 |
| Dec. 11, 1972 | Joe Namath, N.Y. Jets vs. Oakland | 46 | 25 | 403 | 1 |
| Sept. 24, 1972 | Joe Namath, N.Y. Jets vs. Baltimore | 28 | 15 | 496 | 6 |
| Dec. 21, 1969 | Don Horn, Green Bay vs. St. Louis | 31 | 22 | 410 | 5 |
| Sept. 28, 1969 | Joe Kapp, Minnesota vs. Baltimore | 43 | 28 | 449 | 7 |
| Sept. 9, 1968 | Pete Beathard, Houston vs. Kansas City | 48 | 23 | 413 | 2 |
| Nov. 26, 1967 | Sonny Jurgensen, Washington vs. Cleveland | 50 | 32 | 418 | 3 |
| Oct. 1, 1967 | Joe Namath, N.Y. Jets vs. Miami | 39 | 23 | 415 | 3 |
| Sept. 17, 1967 | Johnny Unitas, Baltimore vs. Atlanta | 32 | 22 | 401 | 2 |
| Nov. 13, 1966 | Don Meredith, Dallas vs. Washington | 29 | 21 | 406 | 2 |
| Nov. 28, 1965 | Sonny Jurgensen, Washington vs. Dallas | 43 | 26 | 411 | 3 |
| Oct. 24, 1965 | Fran Tarkenton, Minnesota vs. San Francisco | 35 | 21 | 407 | 3 |
| Nov. 1, 1964 | Len Dawson, Kansas City vs. Denver | 38 | 23 | 435 | 6 |
| Oct. 25, 1964 | Cotton Davidson, Oakland vs. Denver | 36 | 23 | 427 | 5 |
| Oct. 16, 1964 | Babe Parilli, Boston vs. Oakland | 47 | 25 | 422 | 4 |
| Dec. 22, 1963 | Tom Flores, Oakland vs. Houston | 29 | 17 | 407 | 6 |
| Nov. 17, 1963 | Norm Snead, Washington vs. Pittsburgh | 40 | 23 | 424 | 2 |
| Nov. 10, 1963 | Don Meredith, Dallas vs. San Francisco | 48 | 30 | 460 | 3 |
| Oct. 13, 1963 | Charley Johnson, St. Louis vs. Pittsburgh | 41 | 20 | 428 | 2 |
| Dec. 16, 1962 | Sonny Jurgensen, Philadelphia vs. St. Louis | 34 | 15 | 419 | 5 |
| Nov. 18, 1962 | Bill Wade, Chicago vs. Dall. Cowboys | 46 | 28 | 466 | 2 |
| Oct. 28, 1962 | Y.A. Tittle, N.Y. Giants vs. Washington | 39 | 27 | 505 | 7 |
| Sept. 15, 1962 | Frank Tripucka, Denver vs. Buffalo | 56 | 29 | 447 | 2 |
| Dec. 17, 1961 | Sonny Jurgensen, Philadelphia vs. Detroit | 42 | 27 | 403 | 3 |
| Nov. 19, 1961 | George Blanda, Houston vs. N.Y. Titans | 32 | 20 | 418 | 7 |
| Oct. 29, 1961 | George Blanda, Houston vs. Buffalo | 32 | 18 | 464 | 4 |
| Oct. 29, 1961 | Sonny Jurgensen, Philadelphia vs. Washington | 41 | 27 | 436 | 3 |
| Oct. 13, 1961 | Jacky Lee, Houston vs. Boston | 41 | 27 | 457 | 2 |
| Dec. 13, 1958 | Bobby Layne, Pittsburgh vs. Chi. Cardinals | 49 | 23 | 409 | 2 |
| Nov. 8, 1953 | Bobby Thomason, Philadelphia vs. N.Y. Giants | 44 | 22 | 437 | 4 |
| Oct. 4, 1952 | Otto Graham, Cleveland vs. Pittsburgh | 49 | 21 | 401 | 3 |
| Sept. 28, 1951 | Norm Van Brocklin, Los Angeles vs. N.Y. Yanks | 41 | 27 | 554 | 5 |
| Dec. 11, 1949 | Johnny Lujack, Chi. Bears vs. Chi. Cardinals | 39 | 24 | 468 | 6 |
| Oct. 31, 1948 | Sammy Baugh, Washington vs. Boston | 24 | 17 | 446 | 4 |
| Oct. 31, 1948 | Jim Hardy, Los Angeles vs. Chi. Cardinals | 53 | 28 | 406 | 3 |
| Nov. 14, 1943 | Sid Luckman, Chi. Bears vs. N.Y. Giants | 32 | 21 | 433 | 7 |

### TIMES 400 OR MORE

113 times by 62 players...Marino 10; Montana 7; Fouts 6; Jurgensen 5; Kramer, Krieg, Moon 4; Esiason, Namath, Simms 3; Anderson, Blanda, Cunningham, Johnson, Kosar, Lomax, Meredith, O'Brien, Rypien, Todd, Williams, Young 2.

## 1,000 YARDS PASS RECEIVING IN A SEASON

| Year | Player, Team | No. | Yards | Avg. | Long | TD |
|---|---|---|---|---|---|---|
| 1993 | Jerry Rice, San Francisco[8] | 98 | 1,503 | 15.3 | 80 | 15 |
| | Michael Irvin, Dallas[3] | 88 | 1,330 | 15.1 | 61 | 7 |
| | Sterling Sharpe, Green Bay[4] | 112 | 1,274 | 11.4 | 54 | 11 |
| | Andre Rison, Atlanta[3] | 86 | 1,242 | 14.4 | 53 | 15 |
| | Tim Brown, L.A. Raiders | 80 | 1,180 | 14.8 | 71 | 7 |
| | Anthony Miller, San Diego[3] | 84 | 1,162 | 13.8 | 66 | 7 |
| | Cris Carter, Minnesota | 86 | 1,071 | 12.5 | 58 | 9 |
| | Reggie Langhorne, Indianapolis | 85 | 1,038 | 12.2 | 72 | 3 |
| | Irving Fryar, Miami[2] | 64 | 1,010 | 15.8 | 65 | 5 |
| 1992 | Sterling Sharpe, Green Bay[3] | 108 | 1,461 | 13.5 | 76 | 13 |
| | Michael Irvin, Dallas[2] | 78 | 1,396 | 17.9 | 87 | 7 |
| | Jerry Rice, San Francisco[7] | 84 | 1,201 | 14.3 | 80 | 10 |
| | Andre Rison, Atlanta[2] | 93 | 1,119 | 12.0 | 71 | 11 |
| | Fred Barnett, Philadelphia | 67 | 1,083 | 16.2 | 71 | 6 |

| | | | | | | |
|---|---|---|---|---|---|---|
| | Anthony Miller, San Diego[2] | 72 | 1,060 | 14.7 | 67 | 7 |
| | Eric Martin, New Orleans[3] | 68 | 1,041 | 15.3 | 52 | 5 |
| 1991 | Michael Irvin, Dallas | 93 | 1,523 | 16.4 | 66 | 8 |
| | Gary Clark, Washington[5] | 70 | 1,340 | 19.1 | 82 | 10 |
| | Jerry Rice, San Francisco[6] | 80 | 1,206 | 15.1 | 73 | 14 |
| | Haywood Jeffires, Houston[2] | 100 | 1,181 | 11.8 | 44 | 7 |
| | Michael Haynes, Atlanta | 50 | 1,122 | 22.4 | 80 | 11 |
| | Andre Reed, Buffalo[2] | 81 | 1,113 | 13.7 | 55 | 10 |
| | Drew Hill, Houston[5] | 90 | 1,109 | 12.3 | 61 | 4 |
| | Mark Duper, Miami[4] | 70 | 1,085 | 15.5 | 43 | 5 |
| | James Lofton, Buffalo[6] | 57 | 1,072 | 18.8 | 77 | 8 |
| | Mark Clayton, Miami[5] | 70 | 1,053 | 15.0 | 43 | 12 |
| | Henry Ellard, L.A. Rams[4] | 64 | 1,052 | 16.4 | 38 | 3 |
| | Art Monk, Washington[5] | 71 | 1,049 | 14.8 | 64 | 8 |
| | Irving Fryar, New England | 68 | 1,014 | 14.9 | 56 | 3 |
| | John Taylor, San Francisco[2] | 64 | 1,011 | 15.8 | 97 | 9 |
| | Brian Blades, Seattle[2] | 70 | 1,003 | 14.3 | 52 | 2 |
| 1990 | Jerry Rice, San Francisco[5] | 100 | 1,502 | 15.0 | 64 | 13 |
| | Henry Ellard, L.A. Rams[3] | 76 | 1,294 | 17.0 | 50 | 4 |
| | Andre Rison, Atlanta | 82 | 1,208 | 14.7 | 75 | 10 |
| | Gary Clark, Washington[4] | 75 | 1,112 | 14.8 | 53 | 8 |
| | Sterling Sharpe, Green Bay[2] | 67 | 1,105 | 16.5 | 76 | 6 |
| | Willie Anderson, L.A. Rams[2] | 51 | 1,097 | 21.5 | 55 | 4 |
| | Haywood Jeffires, Houston | 74 | 1,048 | 14.2 | 87 | 8 |
| | Stephone Paige, Kansas City | 65 | 1,021 | 15.7 | 86 | 5 |
| | Drew Hill, Houston[4] | 74 | 1,019 | 13.8 | 57 | 5 |
| | Anthony Carter, Minnesota[3] | 70 | 1,008 | 14.4 | 56 | 8 |
| 1989 | Jerry Rice, San Francisco[4] | 82 | 1,483 | 18.1 | 68 | 17 |
| | Sterling Sharpe, Green Bay | 90 | 1,423 | 15.8 | 79 | 12 |
| | Mark Carrier, Tampa Bay | 86 | 1,422 | 16.5 | 78 | 9 |
| | Henry Ellard, L.A. Rams[2] | 70 | 1,382 | 19.7 | 53 | 8 |
| | Andre Reed, Buffalo | 88 | 1,312 | 14.9 | 78 | 9 |
| | Anthony Miller, San Diego | 75 | 1,252 | 16.7 | 69 | 10 |
| | Webster Slaughter, Cleveland | 65 | 1,236 | 19.0 | 97 | 6 |
| | Gary Clark, Washington[3] | 79 | 1,229 | 15.6 | 80 | 9 |
| | Tim McGee, Cincinnati | 65 | 1,211 | 18.6 | 74 | 8 |
| | Art Monk, Washington[4] | 86 | 1,186 | 13.8 | 60 | 8 |
| | Willie Anderson, L.A. Rams | 44 | 1,146 | 26.0 | 78 | 5 |
| | Ricky Sanders, Washington[2] | 80 | 1,138 | 14.2 | 68 | 4 |
| | Vance Johnson, Denver | 76 | 1,095 | 14.4 | 69 | 7 |
| | Richard Johnson, Detroit | 70 | 1,091 | 15.6 | 75 | 8 |
| | Eric Martin, New Orleans[2] | 68 | 1,090 | 16.0 | 53 | 8 |
| | John Taylor, San Francisco | 60 | 1,077 | 18.0 | 95 | 10 |
| | Mervyn Fernandez, L.A. Raiders | 57 | 1,069 | 18.8 | 75 | 9 |
| | Anthony Carter, Minnesota[2] | 65 | 1,066 | 16.4 | 50 | 4 |
| | Brian Blades, Seattle | 77 | 1,063 | 13.8 | 60 | 5 |
| | Mark Clayton, Miami[4] | 64 | 1,011 | 15.8 | 78 | 9 |
| 1988 | Henry Ellard, L.A. Rams | 86 | 1,414 | 16.4 | 68 | 10 |
| | Jerry Rice, San Francisco[3] | 64 | 1,306 | 20.4 | 96 | 9 |
| | Eddie Brown, Cincinnati | 53 | 1,273 | 24.0 | 86 | 9 |
| | Anthony Carter, Minnesota | 72 | 1,225 | 17.0 | 67 | 6 |
| | Ricky Sanders, Washington | 73 | 1,148 | 15.7 | 55 | 12 |
| | Drew Hill, Houston[3] | 72 | 1,141 | 15.8 | 57 | 10 |
| | Mark Clayton, Miami[3] | 86 | 1,129 | 13.1 | 45 | 14 |
| | Roy Green, Phoenix[3] | 68 | 1,097 | 16.1 | 52 | 7 |
| | Eric Martin, New Orleans | 85 | 1,083 | 12.7 | 40 | 7 |
| | Al Toon, N.Y. Jets[2] | 93 | 1,067 | 11.5 | 42 | 5 |
| | Bruce Hill, Tampa Bay | 58 | 1,040 | 17.9 | 42 | 9 |
| | Lionel Manuel, N.Y. Giants | 65 | 1,029 | 15.8 | 46 | 4 |
| 1987 | J.T. Smith, St. Louis[2] | 91 | 1,117 | 12.3 | 38 | 8 |
| | Jerry Rice, San Francisco[2] | 65 | 1,078 | 16.6 | 57 | 22 |
| | Gary Clark, Washington[2] | 56 | 1,066 | 19.0 | 84 | 7 |
| | Carlos Carson, Kansas City[3] | 55 | 1,044 | 19.0 | 81 | 7 |
| 1986 | Jerry Rice, San Francisco | 86 | 1,570 | 18.3 | 66 | 15 |
| | Stanley Morgan, New England[3] | 84 | 1,491 | 17.8 | 44 | 10 |
| | Mark Duper, Miami[3] | 67 | 1,313 | 19.6 | 85 | 11 |
| | Gary Clark, Washington | 74 | 1,265 | 17.1 | 55 | 7 |
| | Al Toon, N.Y. Jets | 85 | 1,176 | 13.8 | 62 | 8 |
| | Todd Christensen, L.A. Raiders[3] | 95 | 1,153 | 12.1 | 35 | 8 |
| | Mark Clayton, Miami[2] | 60 | 1,150 | 19.2 | 68 | 10 |
| | *Bill Brooks, Indianapolis | 65 | 1,131 | 17.4 | 84 | 8 |
| | Drew Hill, Houston[2] | 65 | 1,112 | 17.1 | 81 | 5 |
| | Steve Largent, Seattle[8] | 70 | 1,070 | 15.3 | 38 | 9 |
| | Art Monk, Washington[3] | 73 | 1,068 | 14.6 | 69 | 4 |
| | *Ernest Givins, Houston | 61 | 1,062 | 17.4 | 60 | 3 |
| | Cris Collinsworth, Cincinnati[4] | 62 | 1,024 | 16.5 | 46 | 10 |
| | Wesley Walker, N.Y. Jets[2] | 49 | 1,016 | 20.7 | 83 | 12 |
| | J.T. Smith, St. Louis | 80 | 1,014 | 12.7 | 45 | 6 |
| | Mark Bavaro, N.Y. Giants | 66 | 1,001 | 15.2 | 41 | 4 |
| 1985 | Steve Largent, Seattle[7] | 79 | 1,287 | 16.3 | 43 | 6 |
| | Mike Quick, Philadelphia[3] | 73 | 1,247 | 17.1 | 99 | 11 |
| | Art Monk, Washington[2] | 91 | 1,226 | 13.5 | 53 | 2 |
| | Wes Chandler, San Diego[4] | 67 | 1,199 | 17.9 | 75 | 10 |
| | Drew Hill, Houston | 64 | 1,169 | 18.3 | 57 | 9 |
| | James Lofton, Green Bay[5] | 69 | 1,153 | 16.7 | 56 | 4 |
| | Louis Lipps, Pittsburgh | 59 | 1,134 | 19.2 | 51 | 12 |
| | Cris Collinsworth, Cincinnati[3] | 65 | 1,125 | 17.3 | 71 | 5 |
| | Tony Hill, Dallas[3] | 74 | 1,113 | 15.0 | 53 | 7 |
| | Lionel James, San Diego | 86 | 1,027 | 11.9 | 67 | 6 |
| | Roger Craig, San Francisco | 92 | 1,016 | 11.0 | 73 | 6 |
| 1984 | Roy Green, St. Louis[2] | 78 | 1,555 | 19.9 | 83 | 12 |
| | John Stallworth, Pittsburgh[3] | 80 | 1,395 | 17.4 | 51 | 11 |
| | Mark Clayton, Miami | 73 | 1,389 | 19.0 | 65 | 18 |
| | Art Monk, Washington | 106 | 1,372 | 12.9 | 72 | 7 |
| | James Lofton, Green Bay[4] | 62 | 1,361 | 22.0 | 79 | 7 |
| | Mark Duper, Miami[2] | 71 | 1,306 | 18.4 | 80 | 8 |
| | Steve Watson, Denver[3] | 69 | 1,170 | 17.0 | 73 | 7 |
| | Steve Largent, Seattle[6] | 74 | 1,164 | 15.7 | 65 | 12 |
| | Tim Smith, Houston[2] | 69 | 1,141 | 16.5 | 75 | 4 |
| | Stacey Bailey, Atlanta | 67 | 1,138 | 17.0 | 61 | 6 |
| | Carlos Carson, Kansas City[2] | 57 | 1,078 | 18.9 | 57 | 4 |
| | Mike Quick, Philadelphia[2] | 61 | 1,052 | 17.2 | 90 | 9 |
| | Todd Christensen, L.A. Raiders[2] | 80 | 1,007 | 12.6 | 38 | 7 |
| | Kevin House, Tampa Bay[2] | 76 | 1,005 | 13.2 | 55 | 5 |
| | Ozzie Newsome, Cleveland[2] | 89 | 1,001 | 11.2 | 52 | 5 |
| 1983 | Mike Quick, Philadelphia | 69 | 1,409 | 20.4 | 83 | 13 |
| | Carlos Carson, Kansas City | 80 | 1,351 | 16.9 | 50 | 7 |
| | James Lofton, Green Bay[3] | 58 | 1,300 | 22.4 | 74 | 8 |
| | Todd Christensen, L.A. Raiders | 92 | 1,247 | 13.6 | 45 | 12 |
| | Roy Green, St. Louis | 78 | 1,227 | 15.7 | 71 | 14 |
| | Charlie Brown, Washington | 78 | 1,225 | 15.7 | 75 | 8 |
| | Tim Smith, Houston | 83 | 1,176 | 14.2 | 47 | 6 |
| | Kellen Winslow, San Diego[3] | 88 | 1,172 | 13.3 | 46 | 8 |
| | Earnest Gray, N.Y. Giants | 78 | 1,139 | 14.6 | 62 | 5 |
| | Steve Watson, Denver[2] | 59 | 1,133 | 19.2 | 78 | 5 |
| | Cris Collinsworth, Cincinnati[2] | 66 | 1,130 | 17.1 | 63 | 5 |
| | Steve Largent, Seattle[5] | 72 | 1,074 | 14.9 | 46 | 11 |
| | Mark Duper, Miami | 51 | 1,003 | 19.7 | 85 | 10 |
| 1982 | Wes Chandler, San Diego[3] | 49 | 1,032 | 21.1 | 66 | 9 |
| 1981 | Alfred Jenkins, Atlanta[2] | 70 | 1,358 | 19.4 | 67 | 13 |
| | James Lofton, Green Bay[2] | 71 | 1,294 | 18.2 | 75 | 8 |
| | Steve Watson, Denver | 60 | 1,244 | 20.7 | 95 | 13 |
| | Frank Lewis, Buffalo[2] | 70 | 1,244 | 17.8 | 33 | 4 |
| | Steve Largent, Seattle[4] | 75 | 1,224 | 16.3 | 57 | 9 |
| | Charlie Joiner, San Diego[4] | 70 | 1,188 | 17.0 | 57 | 7 |
| | Kevin House, Tampa Bay | 56 | 1,176 | 21.0 | 84 | 9 |
| | Wes Chandler, N.O.-San Diego[2] | 69 | 1,142 | 16.6 | 51 | 6 |
| | Dwight Clark, San Francisco | 85 | 1,105 | 13.0 | 78 | 4 |
| | John Stallworth, Pittsburgh[2] | 63 | 1,098 | 17.4 | 55 | 5 |
| | Kellen Winslow, San Diego[2] | 88 | 1,075 | 12.2 | 67 | 10 |
| | Pat Tilley, St. Louis | 66 | 1,040 | 15.8 | 75 | 3 |
| | Stanley Morgan, New England[2] | 44 | 1,029 | 23.4 | 76 | 6 |
| | Harold Carmichael, Philadelphia[3] | 61 | 1,028 | 16.9 | 85 | 6 |
| | Freddie Scott, Detroit | 53 | 1,022 | 19.3 | 48 | 5 |
| | *Cris Collinsworth, Cincinnati | 67 | 1,009 | 15.1 | 74 | 8 |
| | Joe Senser, Minnesota | 79 | 1,004 | 12.7 | 53 | 8 |
| | Ozzie Newsome, Cleveland | 69 | 1,002 | 14.5 | 62 | 6 |
| | Sammy White, Minnesota | 66 | 1,001 | 15.2 | 53 | 3 |
| 1980 | John Jefferson, San Diego[3] | 82 | 1,340 | 16.3 | 58 | 13 |
| | Kellen Winslow, San Diego | 89 | 1,290 | 14.5 | 65 | 9 |
| | James Lofton, Green Bay | 71 | 1,226 | 17.3 | 47 | 4 |
| | Charlie Joiner, San Diego[3] | 71 | 1,132 | 15.9 | 51 | 4 |
| | Ahmad Rashad, Minnesota[2] | 69 | 1,095 | 15.9 | 76 | 5 |
| | Steve Largent, Seattle[3] | 66 | 1,064 | 16.1 | 67 | 6 |
| | Tony Hill, Dallas[2] | 60 | 1,055 | 17.6 | 58 | 8 |
| | Alfred Jenkins, Atlanta | 57 | 1,026 | 18.0 | 57 | 6 |
| 1979 | Steve Largent, Seattle[2] | 66 | 1,237 | 18.7 | 55 | 9 |
| | John Stallworth, Pittsburgh | 70 | 1,183 | 16.9 | 65 | 8 |
| | Ahmad Rashad, Minnesota | 80 | 1,156 | 14.5 | 52 | 9 |
| | John Jefferson, San Diego[2] | 61 | 1,090 | 17.9 | 65 | 10 |
| | Frank Lewis, Buffalo | 54 | 1,082 | 20.0 | 55 | 2 |
| | Wes Chandler, New Orleans | 65 | 1,069 | 16.4 | 85 | 6 |
| | Tony Hill, Dallas | 60 | 1,062 | 17.7 | 75 | 10 |
| | Drew Pearson, Dallas[2] | 55 | 1,026 | 18.7 | 56 | 8 |
| | Wallace Francis, Atlanta | 74 | 1,013 | 13.7 | 42 | 8 |
| | Harold Jackson, New England[3] | 45 | 1,013 | 22.5 | 59 | 7 |
| | Charlie Joiner, San Diego[2] | 72 | 1,008 | 14.0 | 39 | 4 |
| | Stanley Morgan, New England | 44 | 1,002 | 22.8 | 63 | 12 |
| 1978 | Wesley Walker, N.Y. Jets | 48 | 1,169 | 24.4 | 77 | 8 |
| | Steve Largent, Seattle | 71 | 1,168 | 16.5 | 57 | 8 |
| | Harold Carmichael, Philadelphia[2] | 55 | 1,072 | 19.5 | 56 | 8 |
| | *John Jefferson, San Diego | 56 | 1,001 | 17.9 | 46 | 13 |
| 1976 | Roger Carr, Baltimore | 43 | 1,112 | 25.9 | 79 | 11 |
| | Cliff Branch, Oakland[2] | 46 | 1,111 | 24.2 | 88 | 12 |
| | Charlie Joiner, San Diego | 50 | 1,056 | 21.1 | 81 | 7 |
| 1975 | Ken Burrough, Houston | 53 | 1,063 | 20.1 | 77 | 8 |

| | | | | | | |
|---|---|---|---|---|---|---|
| 1974 | Cliff Branch, Oakland | 60 | 1,092 | 18.2 | 67 | 13 |
| | Drew Pearson, Dallas | 62 | 1,087 | 17.5 | 50 | 2 |
| 1973 | Harold Carmichael, Philadelphia | 67 | 1,116 | 16.7 | 73 | 9 |
| 1972 | Harold Jackson, Philadelphia[2] | 62 | 1,048 | 16.9 | 77 | 4 |
| | John Gilliam, Minnesota | 47 | 1,035 | 22.0 | 66 | 7 |
| 1971 | Otis Taylor, Kansas City[2] | 57 | 1,110 | 19.5 | 82 | 7 |
| 1970 | Gene Washington, San Francisco | 53 | 1,100 | 20.8 | 79 | 12 |
| | Marlin Briscoe, Buffalo | 57 | 1,036 | 18.2 | 48 | 8 |
| | Dick Gordon, Chicago | 71 | 1,026 | 14.5 | 69 | 13 |
| | Gary Garrison, San Diego[2] | 44 | 1,006 | 22.9 | 67 | 12 |
| 1969 | Warren Wells, Oakland[2] | 47 | 1,260 | 26.8 | 80 | 14 |
| | Harold Jackson, Philadelphia | 65 | 1,116 | 17.2 | 65 | 9 |
| | Roy Jefferson, Pittsburgh[2] | 67 | 1,079 | 16.1 | 63 | 9 |
| | Dan Abramowicz, New Orleans | 73 | 1,015 | 13.9 | 49 | 7 |
| | Lance Alworth, San Diego[7] | 64 | 1,003 | 15.7 | 76 | 4 |
| 1968 | Lance Alworth, San Diego[6] | 68 | 1,312 | 19.3 | 80 | 10 |
| | Don Maynard, N.Y. Jets[5] | 57 | 1,297 | 22.8 | 87 | 10 |
| | George Sauer, N.Y. Jets[3] | 66 | 1,141 | 17.3 | 43 | 3 |
| | Warren Wells, Oakland | 53 | 1,137 | 21.5 | 94 | 11 |
| | Gary Garrison, San Diego | 52 | 1,103 | 21.2 | 84 | 10 |
| | Roy Jefferson, Pittsburgh | 58 | 1,074 | 18.5 | 62 | 11 |
| | Paul Warfield, Cleveland | 50 | 1,067 | 21.3 | 65 | 12 |
| | Homer Jones, N.Y. Giants[3] | 45 | 1,057 | 23.5 | 84 | 7 |
| | Fred Biletnikoff, Oakland | 61 | 1,037 | 17.0 | 82 | 6 |
| | Lance Rentzel, Dallas | 54 | 1,009 | 18.7 | 65 | 6 |
| 1967 | Don Maynard, N.Y. Jets[4] | 71 | 1,434 | 20.2 | 75 | 10 |
| | Ben Hawkins, Philadelphia | 59 | 1,265 | 21.4 | 87 | 10 |
| | Homer Jones, N.Y. Giants[2] | 49 | 1,209 | 24.7 | 70 | 13 |
| | Jackie Smith, St. Louis | 56 | 1,205 | 21.5 | 76 | 9 |
| | George Sauer, N.Y. Jets[2] | 75 | 1,189 | 15.9 | 61 | 6 |
| | Lance Alworth, San Diego[5] | 52 | 1,010 | 19.4 | 71 | 9 |
| 1966 | Lance Alworth, San Diego[4] | 73 | 1,383 | 18.9 | 78 | 13 |
| | Otis Taylor, Kansas City | 58 | 1,297 | 22.4 | 89 | 8 |
| | Pat Studstill, Detroit | 67 | 1,266 | 18.9 | 99 | 5 |
| | Bob Hayes, Dallas[2] | 64 | 1,232 | 19.3 | 95 | 13 |
| | Charlie Frazier, Houston | 57 | 1,129 | 19.8 | 79 | 12 |
| | Charley Taylor, Washington | 72 | 1,119 | 15.5 | 86 | 12 |
| | George Sauer, N.Y. Jets | 63 | 1,081 | 17.2 | 77 | 5 |
| | Homer Jones, N.Y. Giants | 48 | 1,044 | 21.8 | 98 | 8 |
| | Art Powell, Oakland[5] | 53 | 1,026 | 19.4 | 46 | 11 |
| 1965 | Lance Alworth, San Diego[3] | 69 | 1,602 | 23.2 | 85 | 14 |
| | Dave Parks, San Francisco | 80 | 1,344 | 16.8 | 53 | 12 |
| | Don Maynard, N.Y. Jets[3] | 68 | 1,218 | 17.9 | 56 | 14 |
| | Pete Retzlaff, Philadelphia | 66 | 1,190 | 18.0 | 78 | 10 |
| | Lionel Taylor, Denver[4] | 85 | 1,131 | 13.3 | 63 | 6 |
| | Tommy McDonald, Los Angeles[3] | 67 | 1,036 | 15.5 | 51 | 9 |
| | *Bob Hayes, Dallas | 46 | 1,003 | 21.8 | 82 | 12 |
| 1964 | Charley Hennigan, Houston[3] | 101 | 1,546 | 15.3 | 53 | 8 |
| | Art Powell, Oakland[4] | 76 | 1,361 | 17.9 | 77 | 11 |
| | Lance Alworth, San Diego[2] | 61 | 1,235 | 20.2 | 82 | 13 |
| | Johnny Morris, Chicago | 93 | 1,200 | 12.9 | 63 | 10 |
| | Elbert Dubenion, Buffalo | 42 | 1,139 | 27.1 | 72 | 10 |
| | Terry Barr, Detroit[2] | 57 | 1,030 | 18.1 | 58 | 9 |
| 1963 | Bobby Mitchell, Washington[2] | 69 | 1,436 | 20.8 | 99 | 7 |
| | Art Powell, Oakland[3] | 73 | 1,304 | 17.9 | 85 | 16 |
| | Buddy Dial, Pittsburgh[2] | 60 | 1,295 | 21.6 | 83 | 9 |
| | Lance Alworth, San Diego | 61 | 1,205 | 19.8 | 85 | 11 |
| | Del Shofner, N.Y. Giants[4] | 64 | 1,181 | 18.5 | 70 | 9 |
| | Lionel Taylor, Denver[3] | 78 | 1,101 | 14.1 | 72 | 10 |
| | Terry Barr, Detroit | 66 | 1,086 | 16.5 | 75 | 13 |
| | Charley Hennigan, Houston[2] | 61 | 1,051 | 17.2 | 83 | 10 |
| | Sonny Randle, St. Louis[2] | 51 | 1,014 | 19.9 | 68 | 12 |
| | Bake Turner, N.Y. Jets | 71 | 1,009 | 14.2 | 53 | 6 |
| 1962 | Bobby Mitchell, Washington | 72 | 1,384 | 19.2 | 81 | 11 |
| | Sonny Randle, St. Louis | 63 | 1,158 | 18.4 | 86 | 7 |
| | Tommy McDonald, Philadelphia[2] | 58 | 1,146 | 19.8 | 60 | 10 |
| | Del Shofner, N.Y. Giants[3] | 53 | 1,133 | 21.4 | 69 | 12 |
| | Art Powell, N.Y. Titans[2] | 64 | 1,130 | 17.7 | 80 | 8 |
| | Frank Clarke, Dall. Cowboys | 47 | 1,043 | 22.2 | 66 | 14 |
| | Don Maynard, N.Y. Titans[2] | 56 | 1,041 | 18.6 | 86 | 8 |
| 1961 | Charley Hennigan, Houston | 82 | 1,746 | 21.3 | 80 | 12 |
| | Lionel Taylor, Denver[2] | 100 | 1,176 | 11.8 | 52 | 4 |
| | Bill Groman, Houston[2] | 50 | 1,175 | 23.5 | 80 | 17 |
| | Tommy McDonald, Philadelphia | 64 | 1,144 | 17.9 | 66 | 13 |
| | Del Shofner, N.Y. Giants[2] | 68 | 1,125 | 16.5 | 46 | 11 |
| | Jim Phillips, Los Angeles | 78 | 1,092 | 14.0 | 69 | 5 |
| | *Mike Ditka, Chicago | 56 | 1,076 | 19.2 | 76 | 12 |
| | Dave Kocourek, San Diego | 55 | 1,055 | 19.2 | 76 | 4 |
| | Buddy Dial, Pittsburgh | 53 | 1,047 | 19.8 | 88 | 12 |
| | R.C. Owens, San Francisco | 55 | 1,032 | 18.8 | 54 | 5 |
| 1960 | *Bill Groman, Houston | 72 | 1,473 | 20.5 | 92 | 12 |
| | Raymond Berry, Baltimore | 74 | 1,298 | 17.5 | 70 | 10 |
| | Don Maynard, N.Y. Titans | 72 | 1,265 | 17.6 | 65 | 6 |
| | Lionel Taylor, Denver | 92 | 1,235 | 13.4 | 80 | 12 |
| | Art Powell, N.Y. Titans | 69 | 1,167 | 16.9 | 76 | 14 |
| 1958 | Del Shofner, Los Angeles | 51 | 1,097 | 21.5 | 92 | 8 |
| 1956 | Bill Howton, Green Bay[2] | 55 | 1,188 | 21.6 | 66 | 12 |
| | Harlon Hill, Chi. Bears[2] | 47 | 1,128 | 24.0 | 79 | 11 |
| 1954 | Bob Boyd, Los Angeles | 53 | 1,212 | 22.9 | 80 | 6 |
| | *Harlon Hill, Chi. Bears | 45 | 1,124 | 25.0 | 76 | 12 |
| 1953 | Pete Pihos, Philadelphia | 63 | 1,049 | 16.7 | 59 | 10 |
| 1952 | *Bill Howton, Green Bay | 53 | 1,231 | 23.2 | 90 | 13 |
| 1951 | Elroy (Crazylegs) Hirsch, Los Angeles | 66 | 1,495 | 22.7 | 91 | 17 |
| 1950 | Tom Fears, Los Angeles[2] | 84 | 1,116 | 13.3 | 53 | 7 |
| | Cloyce Box, Detroit | 50 | 1,009 | 20.2 | 82 | 11 |
| 1949 | Bob Mann, Detroit | 66 | 1,014 | 15.4 | 64 | 4 |
| | Tom Fears, Los Angeles | 77 | 1,013 | 13.2 | 51 | 9 |
| 1945 | Jim Benton, Cleveland | 45 | 1,067 | 23.7 | 84 | 8 |
| 1942 | Don Hutson, Green Bay | 74 | 1,211 | 16.4 | 73 | 17 |

**First season of professional football.*

## 250 YARDS PASS RECEIVING IN A GAME

| Date | Player, Team, Opponent | No. | Yards | TD |
|---|---|---|---|---|
| Dec. 11, 1989 | John Taylor, San Francisco vs. L.A. Rams | 11 | 286 | 2 |
| Nov. 26, 1989 | Willie Anderson, L.A. Rams vs. New Orleans (OT) | 15 | 336 | 1 |
| Oct. 18, 1987 | Steve Largent, Seattle vs. Detroit | 15 | 261 | 3 |
| Oct. 4, 1987 | Anthony Allen, Washington vs. St. Louis | 7 | 255 | 3 |
| Dec. 22, 1985 | Stephone Paige, Kansas City vs. San Diego | 8 | 309 | 2 |
| Dec. 20, 1982 | Wes Chandler, San Diego vs. Cincinnati | 10 | 260 | 2 |
| Sept. 23, 1979 | *Jerry Butler, Buffalo vs. N.Y. Jets | 10 | 255 | 4 |
| Nov. 4, 1962 | Sonny Randle, St. Louis vs. N.Y. Giants | 16 | 256 | 1 |
| Oct. 28, 1962 | Del Shofner, N.Y. Giants vs. Washington | 11 | 269 | 1 |
| Oct. 13, 1961 | Charley Hennigan, Houston vs. Boston | 13 | 272 | 1 |
| Oct. 21, 1956 | Billy Howton, Green Bay vs. Los Angeles | 7 | 257 | 2 |
| Dec. 3, 1950 | Cloyce Box, Detroit vs. Baltimore | 12 | 302 | 4 |
| Nov. 22, 1945 | Jim Benton, Cleveland vs. Detroit | 10 | 303 | 1 |

**First season of professional football.*

## 2,000 COMBINED NET YARDS GAINED IN A SEASON

| Year | Player, Team | Rushing Att.-Yds. | Pass Rec. | Punt Ret. | Kickoff Ret. | Fum. Runs | Total Yds. |
|---|---|---|---|---|---|---|---|
| 1992 | Thurman Thomas, Buffalo | 312-1,487 | 58-626 | 0-0 | 0-0 | 1-0 | 371-2,113 |
| | Emmitt Smith, Dallas | 373-1,713 | 59-335 | 0-0 | 0-0 | 1-0 | 433-2,048 |
| | Barry Foster, Pittsburgh | 390-1,690 | 36-344 | 0-0 | 0-0 | 2-(–20) | 428-2,014 |
| 1991 | Thurman Thomas, Buffalo | 288-1,407 | 62-631 | 0-0 | 0-0 | 0-0 | 350-2,038 |
| 1990 | Herschel Walker, Minnesota | 184-770 | 35-315 | 0-0 | 44-966 | 4-0 | 267-2,051 |
| 1988 | *Tim Brown, L.A. Raiders | 14-50 | 43-725 | 49-444 | 41-1,098 | 7-0 | 154-2,317 |
| | Roger Craig, San Fran. | 310-1,502 | 76-534 | 0-0 | 2-32 | 2-0 | 390-2,068 |
| | Eric Dickerson, Indianapolis | 388-1,659 | 36-377 | 0-0 | 0-0 | 1-0 | 425-2,036 |
| | Herschel Walker, Dallas | 361-1,514 | 53-505 | 0-0 | 0-0 | 3-0 | 417-2,019 |
| 1986 | Eric Dickerson, L.A. Rams | 404-1,821 | 26-205 | 0-0 | 0-0 | 2-0 | 432-2,026 |
| | Gary Anderson, San Diego | 127-442 | 80-871 | 25-227 | 24-482 | 2-0 | 258-2,022 |
| 1985 | Lionel James, San Diego | 105-516 | 86-1,027 | 25-213 | 36-779 | 1-0 | 253-2,535 |
| | Marcus Allen, L.A. Raiders | 380-1,759 | 67-555 | 0-0 | 0-0 | 2-(–6) | 449-2,308 |
| | Roger Craig, San Fran. | 214-1,050 | 92-1,016 | 0-0 | 0-0 | 0-0 | 306-2,066 |
| | Walter Payton, Chicago | 324-1,551 | 49-483 | 0-0 | 0-0 | 1-0 | 374-2,034 |
| 1984 | Eric Dickerson, L.A. Rams | 379-2,105 | 21-139 | 0-0 | 0-0 | 4-15 | 404-2,259 |
| | James Wilder, Tampa Bay | 407-1,544 | 85-685 | 0-0 | 0-0 | 4-0 | 496-2,229 |
| | Walter Payton, Chicago | 381-1,684 | 45-368 | 0-0 | 0-0 | 1-0 | 427-2,052 |
| 1983 | *Eric Dickerson, L.A. Rams | 390-1,808 | 51-404 | 0-0 | 0-0 | 1-0 | 442-2,212 |
| | William Andrews, Atlanta | 331-1,567 | 59-609 | 0-0 | 0-0 | 2-0 | 392-2,176 |
| | Walter Payton, Chicago | 314-1,421 | 53-607 | 0-0 | 0-0 | 2-0 | 369-2,028 |
| 1981 | *James Brooks, San Diego | 109-525 | 46-329 | 22-290 | 40-949 | 2-0 | 219-2,093 |
| | William Andrews, Atlanta | 289-1,301 | 81-735 | 0-0 | 0-0 | 0-0 | 370-2,036 |
| 1980 | Bruce Harper, N.Y. Jets | 45-126 | 50-634 | 28-242 | 49-1,070 | 3-0 | 175-2,072 |
| 1979 | Wilbert Montgomery, Phil. | 338-1,512 | 41-494 | 0-0 | 1-6 | 2-0 | 382-2,012 |
| 1978 | Bruce Harper, N.Y. Jets | 58-303 | 13-196 | 30-378 | 55-1,280 | 1-0 | 157-2,157 |
| 1977 | Walter Payton, Chicago | 339-1,852 | 27-269 | 0-0 | 2-95 | 5-0 | 373-2,216 |
| | Terry Metcalf, St. Louis | 149-739 | 34-403 | 14-108 | 32-772 | 1-0 | 230-2,022 |
| 1975 | Terry Metcalf, St. Louis | 165-816 | 43-378 | 23-285 | 35-960 | 2-23 | 268-2,462 |
| | O.J. Simpson, Buffalo | 329-1,817 | 28-426 | 0-0 | 0-0 | 1-0 | 358-2,243 |
| 1974 | Mack Herron, New England | 231-824 | 38-474 | 35-517 | 28-629 | 3-0 | 335-2,444 |
| | Otis Armstrong, Denver | 263-1,407 | 38-405 | 0-0 | 16-386 | 1-0 | 318-2,198 |
| | Terry Metcalf, St. Louis | 152-718 | 50-377 | 26-340 | 20-623 | 7-0 | 255-2,058 |
| 1973 | O.J. Simpson, Buffalo | 332-2,003 | 6-70 | 0-0 | 0-0 | 0-0 | 338-2,073 |
| 1966 | Gale Sayers, Chicago | 229-1,231 | 34-447 | 6-44 | 23-718 | 3-0 | 295-2,440 |
| | Leroy Kelly, Cleveland | 209-1,141 | 32-366 | 13-104 | 19-403 | 0-0 | 273-2,014 |
| 1965 | *Gale Sayers, Chicago | 166-867 | 29-507 | 16-238 | 21-660 | 4-0 | 236-2,272 |
| 1963 | Timmy Brown, Philadelphia | 192-841 | 36-487 | 16-152 | 33-945 | 2-3 | 279-2,428 |
| | Jim Brown, Cleveland | 291-1,863 | 24-268 | 0-0 | 0-0 | 0-0 | 315-2,131 |
| 1962 | Timmy Brown, Philadelphia | 137-545 | 52-849 | 6-81 | 30-831 | 4-0 | 229-2,306 |
| | Dick Christy, N.Y. Titans | 114-535 | 62-538 | 15-250 | 38-824 | 2-0 | 231-2,147 |
| 1961 | Billy Cannon, Houston | 200-948 | 43-586 | 9-70 | 18-439 | 2-0 | 272-2,043 |
| 1960 | *Abner Haynes, Dall. Texans | 156-875 | 55-576 | 14-215 | 19-434 | 4-0 | 248-2,100 |

**First season of professional football.*

## 300 COMBINED NET YARDS GAINED IN A GAME

| Date | Player, Team, Opponent | No. | Yards | TD |
|---|---|---|---|---|
| Dec. 11, 1989 | John Taylor, San Francisco vs. L.A. Rams | 14 | 321 | 2 |
| Nov. 26, 1989 | Willie Anderson, L.A. Rams vs. New Orleans (OT) | 15 | 336 | 1 |
| Nov. 28, 1988 | *Tim Brown, L.A. Raiders vs. San Diego | 12 | 306 | 1 |
| Dec. 22, 1985 | Stephone Paige, Kansas City vs. San Diego | 8 | 309 | 2 |
| Nov. 10, 1985 | Lionel James, San Diego vs. L.A. Raiders (OT) | 23 | 345 | 0 |
| Sept. 22, 1985 | Lionel James, San Diego vs. Cincinnati | 20 | 316 | 2 |
| Dec. 21, 1975 | *Walter Payton, Chicago vs. New Orleans | 32 | 300 | 1 |
| Nov. 23, 1975 | Greg Pruitt, Cleveland vs. Cincinnati | 28 | 304 | 2 |
| Nov. 1, 1970 | Eugene (Mercury) Morris, Miami vs. Baltimore | 17 | 302 | 0 |
| Oct. 4, 1970 | O.J. Simpson, Buffalo vs. N.Y. Jets | 26 | 303 | 2 |
| Dec. 6, 1969 | Jerry LeVias, Houston vs. N.Y. Jets | 18 | 329 | 1 |
| Nov. 2, 1969 | Travis Williams, Green Bay vs. Pittsburgh | 11 | 314 | 3 |
| Dec. 18, 1966 | Gale Sayers, Chicago vs. Minnesota | 20 | 339 | 2 |
| Dec. 12, 1965 | *Gale Sayers, Chicago vs. San Francisco | 17 | 336 | 6 |
| Nov. 17, 1963 | Gary Ballman, Pittsburgh vs. Washington | 12 | 320 | 2 |
| Dec. 16, 1962 | Timmy Brown, Philadelphia vs. St. Louis | 19 | 341 | 2 |
| Dec. 10, 1961 | Billy Cannon, Houston vs. N.Y. Titans | 32 | 373 | 5 |
| Nov. 19, 1961 | Jim Brown, Cleveland vs. Philadelphia | 38 | 313 | 4 |
| Dec. 3, 1950 | Cloyce Box, Detroit vs. Baltimore | 13 | 302 | 4 |
| Oct. 29, 1950 | Wally Triplett, Detroit vs. Los Angeles | 11 | 331 | 1 |
| Nov. 22, 1945 | Jim Benton, Cleveland vs. Detroit | 10 | 303 | 1 |

**First season of professional football.*

## TOP 20 SCORERS

| Player | Years | TD | FG | PAT | TP |
|---|---|---|---|---|---|
| George Blanda | 26 | 9 | 335 | 943 | 2,002 |
| Jan Stenerud | 19 | 0 | 373 | 580 | 1,699 |
| Nick Lowery | 15 | 0 | 329 | 486 | 1,473 |
| Pat Leahy | 18 | 0 | 304 | 558 | 1,470 |
| Jim Turner | 16 | 1 | 304 | 521 | 1,439 |
| Mark Moseley | 16 | 0 | 300 | 482 | 1,382 |
| Jim Bakken | 17 | 0 | 282 | 534 | 1,380 |
| Fred Cox | 15 | 0 | 282 | 519 | 1,365 |
| Lou Groza | 17 | 1 | 234 | 641 | 1,349 |
| Eddie Murray | 16 | 0 | 277 | 432 | 1,263 |
| Jim Breech | 14 | 0 | 243 | 517 | 1,246 |
| Gary Anderson | 12 | 0 | 285 | 384 | 1,239 |
| Chris Bahr | 14 | 0 | 241 | 490 | 1,213 |
| Matt Bahr | 15 | 0 | 250 | 459 | 1,209 |
| Morten Andersen | 12 | 0 | 274 | 380 | 1,202 |
| Gino Cappelletti | 11 | 42 | 176 | 350 | 1,130 |
| Ray Wersching | 15 | 0 | 222 | 456 | 1,122 |
| Norm Johnson | 12 | 0 | 222 | 444 | 1,110 |
| Don Cockroft | 13 | 0 | 216 | 432 | 1,080 |
| Garo Yepremian | 14 | 0 | 210 | 444 | 1,074 |

*Cappelletti's total includes four two-point conversions.*

## TOP 20 TOUCHDOWN SCORERS

| Player | Years | Rush | Rec. | Returns | Total TD |
|---|---|---|---|---|---|
| Jim Brown | 9 | 106 | 20 | 0 | 126 |
| Walter Payton | 13 | 110 | 15 | 0 | 125 |
| Jerry Rice | 9 | 6 | 118 | 0 | 124 |
| John Riggins | 14 | 104 | 12 | 0 | 116 |
| Marcus Allen | 12 | 91 | 21 | 1 | 113 |
| Lenny Moore | 12 | 63 | 48 | 2 | 113 |
| Don Hutson | 11 | 3 | 99 | 3 | 105 |
| Steve Largent | 14 | 1 | 100 | 0 | 101 |
| Franco Harris | 13 | 91 | 9 | 0 | 100 |
| Eric Dickerson | 11 | 90 | 6 | 0 | 96 |
| Jim Taylor | 10 | 83 | 10 | 0 | 93 |
| Tony Dorsett | 12 | 77 | 13 | 1 | 91 |
| Bobby Mitchell | 11 | 18 | 65 | 8 | 91 |
| Leroy Kelly | 10 | 74 | 13 | 3 | 90 |
| Charley Taylor | 13 | 11 | 79 | 0 | 90 |
| Don Maynard | 15 | 0 | 88 | 0 | 88 |
| Lance Alworth | 11 | 2 | 85 | 0 | 87 |
| Ottis Anderson | 14 | 81 | 5 | 0 | 86 |
| Paul Warfield | 13 | 1 | 85 | 0 | 86 |
| Mark Clayton | 11 | 0 | 84 | 1 | 85 |
| Tommy McDonald | 12 | 0 | 84 | 1 | 85 |

## TOP 20 RUSHERS

| Player | Years | Att. | Yards | Avg. | Long | TD |
|---|---|---|---|---|---|---|
| Walter Payton | 13 | 3,838 | 16,726 | 4.4 | 76 | 110 |
| Eric Dickerson | 11 | 2,996 | 13,259 | 4.4 | 85 | 90 |
| Tony Dorsett | 12 | 2,936 | 12,739 | 4.3 | 99 | 77 |
| Jim Brown | 9 | 2,359 | 12,312 | 5.2 | 80 | 106 |
| Franco Harris | 13 | 2,949 | 12,120 | 4.1 | 75 | 91 |
| John Riggins | 14 | 2,916 | 11,352 | 3.9 | 66 | 104 |
| O.J. Simpson | 11 | 2,404 | 11,236 | 4.7 | 94 | 61 |
| Ottis Anderson | 14 | 2,562 | 10,273 | 4.0 | 76 | 81 |
| Earl Campbell | 8 | 2,187 | 9,407 | 4.3 | 81 | 74 |
| Marcus Allen | 12 | 2,296 | 9,309 | 4.1 | 61 | 91 |
| Jim Taylor | 10 | 1,941 | 8,597 | 4.4 | 84 | 83 |
| Joe Perry | 14 | 1,737 | 8,378 | 4.8 | 78 | 53 |
| Roger Craig | 11 | 1,991 | 8,189 | 4.1 | 71 | 56 |
| Gerald Riggs | 10 | 1,989 | 8,188 | 4.1 | 58 | 69 |
| Larry Csonka | 11 | 1,891 | 8,081 | 4.3 | 54 | 64 |
| Freeman McNeil | 12 | 1,798 | 8,074 | 4.5 | 69 | 38 |
| James Brooks | 12 | 1,685 | 7,962 | 4.7 | 65 | 49 |
| Thurman Thomas | 6 | 1,731 | 7,631 | 4.4 | 80 | 41 |
| Herschel Walker | 8 | 1,794 | 7,468 | 4.2 | 84 | 55 |
| Mike Pruitt | 11 | 1,844 | 7,378 | 4.0 | 77 | 51 |

## TOP 20 COMBINED YARDS GAINED

| | Years | Tot. | Rush. | Rec. | Int. Ret. | Punt Ret. | Kickoff Ret. | Fumble Ret. |
|---|---|---|---|---|---|---|---|---|
| Walter Payton | 13 | 21,803 | 16,726 | 4,538 | 0 | 0 | 539 | 0 |
| Tony Dorsett | 12 | 16,326 | 12,739 | 3,554 | 0 | 0 | 0 | 33 |
| Jim Brown | 9 | 15,459 | 12,312 | 2,499 | 0 | 0 | 648 | 0 |
| Eric Dickerson | 11 | 15,411 | 13,259 | 2,137 | 0 | 0 | 0 | 15 |
| James Brooks | 12 | 14,910 | 7,962 | 3,621 | 0 | 565 | 2,762 | 0 |
| Franco Harris | 13 | 14,622 | 12,120 | 2,287 | 0 | 0 | 233 | –18 |
| O.J. Simpson | 11 | 14,368 | 11,236 | 2,142 | 0 | 0 | 990 | 0 |
| James Lofton | 16 | 14,277 | 246 | 14,004 | 0 | 0 | 0 | 27 |
| Bobby Mitchell | 11 | 14,078 | 2,735 | 7,954 | 0 | 699 | 2,690 | 0 |
| Marcus Allen | 12 | 13,799 | 9,309 | 4,496 | 0 | 0 | 0 | –6 |
| John Riggins | 14 | 13,435 | 11,352 | 2,090 | 0 | 0 | 0 | –7 |
| Steve Largent | 14 | 13,396 | 83 | 13,089 | 0 | 68 | 156 | 0 |
| Ottis Anderson | 14 | 13,364 | 10,273 | 3,062 | 0 | 0 | 0 | 29 |
| Drew Hill | 14 | 13,337 | 19 | 9,831 | 0 | 22 | 3,460 | 5 |
| Greg Pruitt | 12 | 13,262 | 5,672 | 3,069 | 0 | 2,007 | 2,514 | 0 |
| Roger Craig | 11 | 13,143 | 8,189 | 4,911 | 0 | 0 | 43 | 0 |
| Herschel Walker | 8 | 13,031 | 7,468 | 3,887 | 0 | 0 | 1,676 | 0 |
| Ollie Matson | 14 | 12,884 | 5,173 | 3,285 | 51 | 595 | 3,746 | 34 |
| Tim Brown | 10 | 12,684 | 3,862 | 3,399 | 0 | 639 | 4,781 | 3 |
| Lenny Moore | 12 | 12,451 | 5,174 | 6,039 | 0 | 56 | 1,180 | 2 |

## TOP 20 PASSERS

| Player | Years | Att. | Comp. | Pct. Comp. | Yards | TD | Pct. TD | Int. | Pct. Int. | Avg. Gain | Rating |
|---|---|---|---|---|---|---|---|---|---|---|---|
| Joe Montana | 14 | 4,898 | 3,110 | 63.5 | 37,268 | 257 | 5.2 | 58 | 2.7 | 7.61 | 93.1 |
| Steve Young | 9 | 1,968 | 1,222 | 62.1 | 15,900 | 105 | 5.3 | 58 | 2.9 | 8.08 | 93.0 |
| Dan Marino | 11 | 5,434 | 3,219 | 59.2 | 40,720 | 298 | 5.5 | 168 | 3.1 | 7.49 | 88.1 |
| Jim Kelly | 8 | 3,494 | 2,112 | 60.4 | 26,413 | 179 | 5.1 | 126 | 3.6 | 7.56 | 86.0 |
| R. Staubach | 11 | 2,958 | 1,685 | 57.0 | 22,700 | 153 | 5.2 | 109 | 3.7 | 7.67 | 83.4 |
| Neil Lomax | 8 | 3,153 | 1,817 | 57.6 | 22,771 | 136 | 4.3 | 90 | 2.9 | 7.22 | 82.7 |
| S. Jurgensen | 18 | 4,262 | 2,433 | 57.1 | 32,224 | 255 | 6.0 | 189 | 4.4 | 7.56 | 82.6 |
| Len Dawson | 19 | 3,741 | 2,136 | 57.1 | 28,711 | 239 | 6.4 | 183 | 4.9 | 7.67 | 82.6 |
| B. Esiason | 10 | 3,851 | 2,185 | 56.7 | 29,092 | 190 | 4.9 | 140 | 3.6 | 7.55 | 82.1 |
| Dave Krieg | 14 | 4,178 | 2,431 | 58.2 | 30,485 | 217 | 5.2 | 163 | 3.9 | 7.30 | 82.0 |
| Ken Anderson | 16 | 4,475 | 2,654 | 59.3 | 32,838 | 197 | 4.4 | 160 | 3.6 | 7.34 | 81.9 |
| Bernie Kosar | 9 | 3,213 | 1,889 | 58.8 | 22,314 | 119 | 3.7 | 81 | 2.5 | 6.94 | 81.9 |
| Danny White | 13 | 2,950 | 1,761 | 59.7 | 21,959 | 155 | 5.3 | 132 | 4.5 | 7.44 | 81.7 |
| Troy Aikman | 5 | 1,920 | 1,191 | 62.0 | 13,627 | 69 | 3.6 | 66 | 3.4 | 7.10 | 81.0 |
| Bart Starr | 16 | 3,149 | 1,808 | 57.4 | 24,718 | 152 | 4.8 | 138 | 4.4 | 7.85 | 80.5 |
| Ken O'Brien | 10 | 3,602 | 2,110 | 58.6 | 25,094 | 128 | 3.6 | 98 | 2.7 | 6.97 | 80.4 |
| Warren Moon | 10 | 4,546 | 2,632 | 57.9 | 33,685 | 196 | 4.3 | 166 | 3.7 | 7.41 | 80.4 |
| F. Tarkenton | 18 | 6,467 | 3,686 | 57.0 | 47,003 | 342 | 5.3 | 266 | 4.1 | 7.27 | 80.4 |
| R. Cunningham | 9 | 2,751 | 1,540 | 56.0 | 19,043 | 131 | 4.8 | 87 | 3.2 | 6.92 | 80.3 |
| Dan Fouts | 15 | 5,604 | 3,297 | 58.8 | 43,040 | 254 | 4.5 | 242 | 4.3 | 7.68 | 80.2 |

*1,500 or more attempts. The passing ratings are based on performance standards established for completion percentage, interception percentage, touchdown percentage, and average gain. Passers are allocated points according to how their marks compare with those standards.*

## TOP 20 PASS RECEIVERS

| Player | Years | No. | Yards | Avg. | Long | TD |
|---|---|---|---|---|---|---|
| Art Monk | 14 | 888 | 12,026 | 13.5 | 79 | 65 |
| Steve Largent | 14 | 819 | 13,089 | 16.0 | 74 | 100 |
| James Lofton | 16 | 764 | 14,004 | 18.3 | 80 | 75 |
| Charlie Joiner | 18 | 750 | 12,146 | 16.2 | 87 | 65 |
| Jerry Rice | 9 | 708 | 11,776 | 16.6 | 96 | 118 |
| Ozzie Newsome | 13 | 662 | 7,980 | 12.1 | 74 | 47 |
| Charley Taylor | 13 | 649 | 9,110 | 14.0 | 88 | 79 |
| Drew Hill | 14 | 634 | 9,831 | 15.5 | 81 | 60 |
| Don Maynard | 15 | 633 | 11,834 | 18.7 | 87 | 88 |
| Raymond Berry | 13 | 631 | 9,275 | 14.7 | 70 | 68 |
| Gary Clark | 9 | 612 | 9,560 | 15.6 | 84 | 62 |
| Henry Ellard | 11 | 593 | 9,761 | 16.5 | 81 | 48 |
| Harold Carmichael | 14 | 590 | 8,985 | 15.2 | 85 | 79 |
| Fred Biletnikoff | 14 | 589 | 8,974 | 15.2 | 82 | 76 |
| Andre Reed | 9 | 586 | 8,233 | 14.0 | 78 | 58 |

| | | | | | | |
|---|---|---|---|---|---|---|
| Mark Clayton | 11 | 582 | 8,974 | 15.4 | 78 | 84 |
| Harold Jackson | 16 | 579 | 10,372 | 17.9 | 79 | 76 |
| Lionel Taylor | 10 | 567 | 7,195 | 12.7 | 80 | 45 |
| Roger Craig | 11 | 566 | 4,911 | 8.7 | 73 | 17 |
| Wes Chandler | 11 | 559 | 8,966 | 16.0 | 85 | 56 |
| Roy Green | 14 | 559 | 8,965 | 16.0 | 83 | 66 |

### TOP 20 INTERCEPTORS

| Player | Years | No. | Yards | Avg. | Long | TD |
|---|---|---|---|---|---|---|
| Paul Krause | 16 | 81 | 1,185 | 14.6 | 81 | 3 |
| Emlen Tunnell | 14 | 79 | 1,282 | 16.2 | 55 | 4 |
| Dick (Night Train) Lane | 14 | 68 | 1,207 | 17.8 | 80 | 5 |
| Ken Riley | 15 | 65 | 596 | 9.2 | 66 | 5 |
| Ronnie Lott | 13 | 63 | 730 | 11.6 | 83 | 5 |
| Dick LeBeau | 13 | 62 | 762 | 12.3 | 70 | 3 |
| Dave Brown | 15 | 62 | 698 | 11.3 | 90 | 5 |
| Emmitt Thomas | 13 | 58 | 937 | 16.2 | 73 | 5 |
| Bobby Boyd | 9 | 57 | 994 | 17.4 | 74 | 4 |
| Johnny Robinson | 12 | 57 | 741 | 13.0 | 57 | 1 |
| Mel Blount | 14 | 57 | 736 | 12.9 | 52 | 2 |
| Everson Walls | 13 | 57 | 504 | 8.8 | 40 | 1 |
| Lem Barney | 11 | 56 | 1,077 | 19.2 | 71 | 7 |
| Pat Fischer | 17 | 56 | 941 | 16.8 | 69 | 4 |
| Willie Brown | 16 | 54 | 472 | 8.7 | 45 | 2 |
| Bobby Dillon | 8 | 52 | 976 | 18.8 | 61 | 5 |
| Jack Butler | 9 | 52 | 826 | 15.9 | 52 | 4 |
| Larry Wilson | 13 | 52 | 800 | 15.4 | 96 | 5 |
| Jim Patton | 12 | 52 | 712 | 13.7 | 51 | 2 |
| Mel Renfro | 14 | 52 | 626 | 12.0 | 90 | 3 |

### TOP 20 PUNTERS

| Player | Years | No. | Yards | Avg. | Long | Blk. |
|---|---|---|---|---|---|---|
| Sammy Baugh | 16 | 338 | 15,245 | 45.1 | 85 | 9 |
| Tommy Davis | 11 | 511 | 22,833 | 44.7 | 82 | 2 |
| Yale Lary | 11 | 503 | 22,279 | 44.3 | 74 | 4 |
| Rohn Stark | 12 | 912 | 40,070 | 43.9 | 72 | 6 |
| Bob Scarpitto | 8 | 283 | 12,408 | 43.8 | 87 | 4 |
| Horace Gillom | 7 | 385 | 16,872 | 43.8 | 80 | 5 |
| Jerry Norton | 11 | 358 | 15,671 | 43.8 | 78 | 2 |
| David Lewis | 4 | 285 | 12,447 | 43.7 | 63 | 0 |
| Greg Montgomery | 6 | 310 | 13,529 | 43.6 | 77 | 6 |
| Don Chandler | 12 | 660 | 28,678 | 43.5 | 90 | 4 |
| Reggie Roby | 11 | 633 | 27,483 | 43.4 | 77 | 3 |
| Sean Landeta | 9 | 568 | 24,631 | 43.4 | 71 | 4 |
| Rick Tuten | 5 | 307 | 13,236 | 43.1 | 65 | 1 |
| Jerrel Wilson | 16 | 1,072 | 46,139 | 43.0 | 72 | 12 |
| Rich Camarillo | 13 | 854 | 36,615 | 42.9 | 76 | 5 |
| Norm Van Brocklin | 12 | 523 | 22,413 | 42.9 | 72 | 3 |
| Tommy Barnhardt | 7 | 387 | 16,562 | 42.8 | 65 | 2 |
| Danny Villanueva | 8 | 488 | 20,862 | 42.8 | 68 | 2 |
| Bobby Joe Green | 14 | 970 | 41,317 | 42.6 | 75 | 3 |
| Sam Baker | 15 | 703 | 29,938 | 42.6 | 72 | 2 |

*250 or more punts*

### TOP 20 PUNT RETURNERS

| Player | Years | No. | Yards | Avg. | Long | TD |
|---|---|---|---|---|---|---|
| George McAfee | 8 | 112 | 1,431 | 12.8 | 74 | 2 |
| Jack Christiansen | 8 | 85 | 1,084 | 12.8 | 89 | 8 |
| Claude Gibson | 5 | 110 | 1,381 | 12.6 | 85 | 3 |
| Bill Dudley | 9 | 124 | 1,515 | 12.2 | 96 | 3 |
| Rick Upchurch | 9 | 248 | 3,008 | 12.1 | 92 | 8 |
| Billy Johnson | 14 | 282 | 3,317 | 11.8 | 87 | 6 |
| Mack Herron | 3 | 84 | 982 | 11.7 | 66 | 0 |
| Mel Gray | 8 | 160 | 1,851 | 11.6 | 80 | 3 |
| Billy Thompson | 13 | 157 | 1,814 | 11.6 | 60 | 0 |
| Henry Ellard | 10 | 135 | 1,527 | 11.3 | 83 | 4 |
| Rodger Bird | 3 | 94 | 1,063 | 11.3 | 78 | 0 |
| Bosh Pritchard | 6 | 95 | 1,072 | 11.3 | 81 | 2 |
| Bobby Joe Edmonds | 4 | 105 | 1,178 | 11.2 | 75 | 1 |
| Terry Metcalf | 6 | 84 | 936 | 11.1 | 69 | 1 |
| Bob Hayes | 11 | 104 | 1,158 | 11.1 | 90 | 3 |
| Floyd Little | 9 | 81 | 893 | 11.0 | 72 | 2 |
| Louis Lipps | 9 | 112 | 1,234 | 11.0 | 76 | 3 |
| Les (Speedy) Duncan | 11 | 202 | 2,201 | 10.9 | 95 | 4 |
| Verda (Vitamin T) Smith | 5 | 75 | 814 | 10.9 | 85 | 1 |
| Vai Sikahema | 8 | 292 | 3,169 | 10.9 | 87 | 4 |

*75 or more returns*

### TOP 20 KICKOFF RETURNERS

| Player | Years | No. | Yards | Avg. | Long | TD |
|---|---|---|---|---|---|---|
| Gale Sayers | 7 | 91 | 2,781 | 30.6 | 103 | 6 |
| Lynn Chandnois | 7 | 92 | 2,720 | 29.6 | 93 | 3 |
| Abe Woodson | 9 | 193 | 5,538 | 28.7 | 105 | 5 |
| Claude (Buddy) Young | 6 | 90 | 2,514 | 27.9 | 104 | 2 |
| Travis Williams | 5 | 102 | 2,801 | 27.5 | 105 | 6 |
| Joe Arenas | 7 | 139 | 3,798 | 27.3 | 96 | 1 |
| Clarence Davis | 8 | 79 | 2,140 | 27.1 | 76 | 0 |
| Steve Van Buren | 8 | 76 | 2,030 | 26.7 | 98 | 3 |
| Lenny Lyles | 12 | 81 | 2,161 | 26.7 | 103 | 3 |
| Eugene (Mercury) Morris | 8 | 111 | 2,947 | 26.5 | 105 | 3 |
| Bobby Jancik | 6 | 158 | 4,185 | 26.5 | 61 | 0 |
| Mel Renfro | 14 | 85 | 2,246 | 26.4 | 100 | 2 |
| Bobby Mitchell | 11 | 102 | 2,690 | 26.4 | 98 | 5 |
| Ollie Matson | 14 | 143 | 3,746 | 26.2 | 105 | 6 |
| Alvin Haymond | 10 | 170 | 4,438 | 26.1 | 98 | 2 |
| Noland Smith | 3 | 82 | 2,137 | 26.1 | 106 | 1 |
| Al Nelson | 9 | 101 | 2,625 | 26.0 | 78 | 0 |
| Tim Brown | 10 | 184 | 4,781 | 26.0 | 105 | 5 |
| Vic Washington | 6 | 129 | 3,341 | 25.9 | 98 | 1 |
| Dave Hampton | 8 | 113 | 2,923 | 25.9 | 101 | 3 |

*75 or more returns*

## ANNUAL SCORING LEADERS

| Year | Player, Team | TD | FG | PAT | TP |
|---|---|---|---|---|---|
| 1993 | Jeff Jaeger, L.A. Raiders, AFC | 0 | 35 | 27 | 132 |
| | Jason Hanson, Detroit, NFC | 0 | 34 | 28 | 130 |
| 1992 | Pete Stoyanovich, Miami, AFC | 0 | 30 | 34 | 124 |
| | Morten Andersen, New Orleans, NFC | 0 | 29 | 33 | 120 |
| | Chip Lohmiller, Washington, NFC | 0 | 30 | 30 | 120 |
| 1991 | Chip Lohmiller, Washington, NFC | 0 | 31 | 56 | 149 |
| | Pete Stoyanovich, Miami, AFC | 0 | 31 | 28 | 121 |
| 1990 | Nick Lowery, Kansas City, AFC | 0 | 34 | 37 | 139 |
| | Chip Lohmiller, Washington, NFC | 0 | 30 | 41 | 131 |
| 1989 | Mike Cofer, San Francisco, NFC | 0 | 29 | 49 | 136 |
| | *David Treadwell, Denver, AFC | 0 | 27 | 39 | 120 |
| 1988 | Scott Norwood, Buffalo, AFC | 0 | 32 | 33 | 129 |
| | Mike Cofer, San Francisco, NFC | 0 | 27 | 40 | 121 |
| 1987 | Jerry Rice, San Francisco, NFC | 23 | 0 | 0 | 138 |
| | Jim Breech, Cincinnati, AFC | 0 | 24 | 25 | 97 |
| 1986 | Tony Franklin, New England, AFC | 0 | 32 | 44 | 140 |
| | Kevin Butler, Chicago, NFC | 0 | 28 | 36 | 120 |
| 1985 | *Kevin Butler, Chicago, NFC | 0 | 31 | 51 | 144 |
| | Gary Anderson, Pittsburgh, AFC | 0 | 33 | 40 | 139 |
| 1984 | Ray Wersching, San Francisco, NFC | 0 | 25 | 56 | 131 |
| | Gary Anderson, Pittsburgh, AFC | 0 | 24 | 45 | 117 |
| 1983 | Mark Moseley, Washington, NFC | 0 | 33 | 62 | 161 |
| | Gary Anderson, Pittsburgh, AFC | 0 | 27 | 38 | 119 |
| 1982 | *Marcus Allen, L.A. Raiders, AFC | 14 | 0 | 0 | 84 |
| | Wendell Tyler, L.A. Rams, NFC | 13 | 0 | 0 | 78 |
| 1981 | Ed Murray, Detroit, NFC | 0 | 25 | 46 | 121 |
| | Rafael Septien, Dallas, NFC | 0 | 27 | 40 | 121 |
| | Jim Breech, Cincinnati, AFC | 0 | 22 | 49 | 115 |
| | Nick Lowery, Kansas City, AFC | 0 | 26 | 37 | 115 |
| 1980 | John Smith, New England, AFC | 0 | 26 | 51 | 129 |
| | *Ed Murray, Detroit, NFC | 0 | 27 | 35 | 116 |
| 1979 | John Smith, New England, AFC | 0 | 23 | 46 | 115 |
| | Mark Moseley, Washington, NFC | 0 | 25 | 39 | 114 |
| 1978 | *Frank Corral, Los Angeles, NFC | 0 | 29 | 31 | 118 |
| | Pat Leahy, N.Y. Jets, AFC | 0 | 22 | 41 | 107 |
| 1977 | Errol Mann, Oakland, AFC | 0 | 20 | 39 | 99 |
| | Walter Payton, Chicago, NFC | 16 | 0 | 0 | 96 |
| 1976 | Toni Linhart, Baltimore, AFC | 0 | 20 | 49 | 109 |
| | Mark Moseley, Washington, NFC | 0 | 22 | 31 | 97 |
| 1975 | O.J. Simpson, Buffalo, AFC | 23 | 0 | 0 | 138 |
| | Chuck Foreman, Minnesota, NFC | 22 | 0 | 0 | 132 |
| 1974 | Chester Marcol, Green Bay, NFC | 0 | 25 | 19 | 94 |
| | Roy Gerela, Pittsburgh, AFC | 0 | 20 | 33 | 93 |
| 1973 | David Ray, Los Angeles, NFC | 0 | 30 | 40 | 130 |
| | Roy Gerela, Pittsburgh, AFC | 0 | 29 | 36 | 123 |
| 1972 | *Chester Marcol, Green Bay, NFC | 0 | 33 | 29 | 128 |
| | Bobby Howfield, N.Y. Jets, AFC | 0 | 27 | 40 | 121 |
| 1971 | Garo Yepremian, Miami, AFC | 0 | 28 | 33 | 117 |
| | Curt Knight, Washington, NFC | 0 | 29 | 27 | 114 |
| 1970 | Fred Cox, Minnesota, NFC | 0 | 30 | 35 | 125 |
| | Jan Stenerud, Kansas City, AFC | 0 | 30 | 26 | 116 |
| 1969 | Jim Turner, N.Y. Jets, AFL | 0 | 32 | 33 | 129 |
| | Fred Cox, Minnesota, NFL | 0 | 26 | 43 | 121 |
| 1968 | Jim Turner, N.Y. Jets, AFL | 0 | 34 | 43 | 145 |
| | Leroy Kelly, Cleveland, NFL | 20 | 0 | 0 | 120 |
| 1967 | Jim Bakken, St. Louis, NFL | 0 | 27 | 36 | 117 |
| | George Blanda, Oakland, AFL | 0 | 20 | 56 | 116 |
| 1966 | Gino Cappelletti, Boston, AFL | 6 | 16 | 35 | 119 |
| | Bruce Gossett, Los Angeles, NFL | 0 | 28 | 29 | 113 |
| 1965 | *Gale Sayers, Chicago, NFL | 22 | 0 | 0 | 132 |
| | Gino Cappelletti, Boston, AFL | 9 | 17 | 27 | 132 |
| 1964 | Gino Cappelletti, Boston, AFL | 7 | 25 | 36 | #155 |
| | Lenny Moore, Baltimore, NFL | 20 | 0 | 0 | 120 |
| 1963 | Gino Cappelletti, Boston, AFL | 2 | 22 | 35 | 113 |
| | Don Chandler, N.Y. Giants, NFL | 0 | 18 | 52 | 106 |
| 1962 | Gene Mingo, Denver, AFL | 4 | 27 | 32 | 137 |
| | Jim Taylor, Green Bay, NFL | 19 | 0 | 0 | 114 |
| 1961 | Gino Cappelletti, Boston, AFL | 8 | 17 | 48 | 147 |
| | Paul Hornung, Green Bay, NFL | 10 | 15 | 41 | 146 |
| 1960 | Paul Hornung, Green Bay, NFL | 15 | 15 | 41 | 176 |
| | *Gene Mingo, Denver, AFL | 6 | 18 | 33 | 123 |
| 1959 | Paul Hornung, Green Bay | 7 | 7 | 31 | 94 |
| 1958 | Jim Brown, Cleveland | 18 | 0 | 0 | 108 |
| 1957 | Sam Baker, Washington | 1 | 14 | 29 | 77 |
| | Lou Groza, Cleveland | 0 | 15 | 32 | 77 |
| 1956 | Bobby Layne, Detroit | 5 | 12 | 33 | 99 |
| 1955 | Doak Walker, Detroit | 7 | 9 | 27 | 96 |
| 1954 | Bobby Walston, Philadelphia | 11 | 4 | 36 | 114 |
| 1953 | Gordy Soltau, San Francisco | 6 | 10 | 48 | 114 |
| 1952 | Gordy Soltau, San Francisco | 7 | 6 | 34 | 94 |
| 1951 | Elroy (Crazylegs) Hirsch, Los Angeles | 17 | 0 | 0 | 102 |
| 1950 | *Doak Walker, Detroit | 11 | 8 | 38 | 128 |
| 1949 | Pat Harder, Chi. Cardinals | 8 | 3 | 45 | 102 |
| | Gene Roberts, N.Y. Giants | 17 | 0 | 0 | 102 |
| 1948 | Pat Harder, Chi. Cardinals | 6 | 7 | 53 | 110 |
| 1947 | Pat Harder, Chi. Cardinals | 7 | 7 | 39 | 102 |
| 1946 | Ted Fritsch, Green Bay | 10 | 9 | 13 | 100 |
| 1945 | Steve Van Buren, Philadelphia | 18 | 0 | 2 | 110 |
| 1944 | Don Hutson, Green Bay | 9 | 0 | 31 | 85 |
| 1943 | Don Hutson, Green Bay | 12 | 3 | 36 | 117 |
| 1942 | Don Hutson, Green Bay | 17 | 1 | 33 | 138 |
| 1941 | Don Hutson, Green Bay | 12 | 1 | 20 | 95 |
| 1940 | Don Hutson, Green Bay | 7 | 0 | 15 | 57 |
| 1939 | Andy Farkas, Washington | 11 | 0 | 2 | 68 |
| 1938 | Clarke Hinkle, Green Bay | 7 | 3 | 7 | 58 |
| 1937 | Jack Manders, Chi. Bears | 5 | 8 | 15 | 69 |
| 1936 | Earl (Dutch) Clark, Detroit | 7 | 4 | 19 | 73 |
| 1935 | Earl (Dutch) Clark, Detroit | 6 | 1 | 16 | 55 |
| 1934 | Jack Manders, Chi. Bears | 3 | 10 | 31 | 79 |
| 1933 | Ken Strong, N.Y. Giants | 6 | 5 | 13 | 64 |
| | Glenn Presnell, Portsmouth | 6 | 6 | 10 | 64 |
| 1932 | Earl (Dutch) Clark, Portsmouth | 6 | 3 | 10 | 55 |

**First season of professional football.*

*#Cappelletti's total includes a two-point conversion.*

## ANNUAL TOUCHDOWN LEADERS

| Year | Player, Team | TD | Rush | Pass | Ret. |
|---|---|---|---|---|---|
| 1993 | Jerry Rice, San Francisco, NFC | 16 | 1 | 15 | 0 |
| | Marcus Allen, Kansas City, AFC | 15 | 12 | 3 | 0 |
| 1992 | Emmitt Smith, Dallas, NFC | 19 | 18 | 1 | 0 |
| | Thurman Thomas, Buffalo, AFC | 12 | 9 | 3 | 0 |
| 1991 | Barry Sanders, Detroit, NFC | 17 | 16 | 1 | 0 |
| | Mark Clayton, Miami, AFC | 12 | 0 | 12 | 0 |
| | Thurman Thomas, Buffalo, AFC | 12 | 7 | 5 | 0 |
| 1990 | Barry Sanders, Detroit, NFC | 16 | 13 | 3 | 0 |
| | Derrick Fenner, Seattle, AFC | 15 | 14 | 1 | 0 |
| 1989 | Dalton Hilliard, New Orleans, NFC | 18 | 13 | 5 | 0 |
| | Christian Okoye, Kansas City, AFC | 12 | 12 | 0 | 0 |
| | Thurman Thomas, Buffalo, AFC | 12 | 6 | 6 | 0 |
| 1988 | Greg Bell, L.A. Rams, NFC | 18 | 16 | 2 | 0 |
| | Eric Dickerson, Indianapolis, AFC | 15 | 14 | 1 | 0 |
| | *Ickey Woods, Cincinnati, AFC | 15 | 15 | 0 | 0 |
| 1987 | Jerry Rice, San Francisco, NFC | 23 | 1 | 22 | 0 |
| | Johnny Hector, N.Y. Jets, AFC | 11 | 11 | 0 | 0 |
| 1986 | George Rogers, Washington, NFC | 18 | 18 | 0 | 0 |
| | Sammy Winder, Denver, AFC | 14 | 9 | 5 | 0 |
| 1985 | Joe Morris, N.Y. Giants, NFC | 21 | 21 | 0 | 0 |
| | Louis Lipps, Pittsburgh, AFC | 15 | 1 | 12 | 2 |
| 1984 | Marcus Allen, L.A. Raiders, AFC | 18 | 13 | 5 | 0 |
| | Mark Clayton, Miami, AFC | 18 | 0 | 18 | 0 |
| | Eric Dickerson, L.A. Rams, NFC | 14 | 14 | 0 | 0 |
| | John Riggins, Washington, NFC | 14 | 14 | 0 | 0 |
| 1983 | John Riggins, Washington, NFC | 24 | 24 | 0 | 0 |
| | Pete Johnson, Cincinnati, AFC | 14 | 14 | 0 | 0 |
| | *Curt Warner, Seattle, AFC | 14 | 13 | 1 | 0 |
| 1982 | *Marcus Allen, L.A. Raiders, AFC | 14 | 11 | 3 | 0 |
| | Wendell Tyler, L.A. Rams, NFC | 13 | 9 | 4 | 0 |
| 1981 | Chuck Muncie, San Diego, AFC | 19 | 19 | 0 | 0 |
| | Wendell Tyler, Los Angeles, NFC | 17 | 12 | 5 | 0 |
| 1980 | *Billy Sims, Detroit, NFC | 16 | 13 | 3 | 0 |
| | Earl Campbell, Houston, AFC | 13 | 13 | 0 | 0 |
| | *Curtis Dickey, Baltimore, AFC | 13 | 11 | 2 | 0 |
| | John Jefferson, San Diego, AFC | 13 | 0 | 13 | 0 |
| 1979 | Earl Campbell, Houston, AFC | 19 | 19 | 0 | 0 |
| | Walter Payton, Chicago, NFC | 16 | 14 | 2 | 0 |
| 1978 | David Sims, Seattle, AFC | 15 | 14 | 1 | 0 |
| | Terdell Middleton, Green Bay, NFC | 12 | 11 | 1 | 0 |
| 1977 | Walter Payton, Chicago, NFC | 16 | 14 | 2 | 0 |
| | Nat Moore, Miami, AFC | 13 | 1 | 12 | 0 |
| 1976 | Chuck Foreman, Minnesota, NFC | 14 | 13 | 1 | 0 |
| | Franco Harris, Pittsburgh, AFC | 14 | 14 | 0 | 0 |
| 1975 | O.J. Simpson, Buffalo, AFC | 23 | 16 | 7 | 0 |
| | Chuck Foreman, Minnesota, NFC | 22 | 13 | 9 | 0 |
| 1974 | Chuck Foreman, Minnesota, NFC | 15 | 9 | 6 | 0 |
| | Cliff Branch, Oakland, AFC | 13 | 0 | 13 | 0 |
| 1973 | Larry Brown, Washington, NFC | 14 | 8 | 6 | 0 |
| | Floyd Little, Denver, AFC | 13 | 12 | 1 | 0 |
| 1972 | Emerson Boozer, N.Y. Jets, AFC | 14 | 11 | 3 | 0 |
| | Ron Johnson, N.Y. Giants, NFC | 14 | 9 | 5 | 0 |
| 1971 | Duane Thomas, Dallas, NFC | 13 | 11 | 2 | 0 |
| | Leroy Kelly, Cleveland, AFC | 12 | 10 | 2 | 0 |
| 1970 | Dick Gordon, Chicago, NFC | 13 | 0 | 13 | 0 |
| | MacArthur Lane, St. Louis, NFC | 13 | 11 | 2 | 0 |
| | Gary Garrison, San Diego, AFC | 12 | 0 | 12 | 0 |

| | | | | | |
|---|---|---|---|---|---|
| 1969 | Warren Wells, Oakland, AFL | 14 | 0 | 14 | 0 |
| | Tom Matte, Baltimore, NFL | 13 | 11 | 2 | 0 |
| | Lance Rentzel, Dallas, NFL | 13 | 0 | 12 | 1 |
| 1968 | Leroy Kelly, Cleveland, NFL | 20 | 16 | 4 | 0 |
| | Warren Wells, Oakland, AFL | 12 | 1 | 11 | 0 |
| 1967 | Homer Jones, N.Y. Giants, NFL | 14 | 1 | 13 | 0 |
| | Emerson Boozer, N.Y. Jets, AFL | 13 | 10 | 3 | 0 |
| 1966 | Leroy Kelly, Cleveland, NFL | 16 | 15 | 1 | 0 |
| | Dan Reeves, Dallas, NFL | 16 | 8 | 8 | 0 |
| | Lance Alworth, San Diego, AFL | 13 | 0 | 13 | 0 |
| 1965 | *Gale Sayers, Chicago, NFL | 22 | 14 | 6 | 2 |
| | Lance Alworth, San Diego, AFL | 14 | 0 | 14 | 0 |
| | Don Maynard, N.Y. Jets, AFL | 14 | 0 | 14 | 0 |
| 1964 | Lenny Moore, Baltimore, NFL | 20 | 16 | 3 | 1 |
| | Lance Alworth, San Diego, AFL | 15 | 2 | 13 | 0 |
| 1963 | Art Powell, Oakland, AFL | 16 | 0 | 16 | 0 |
| | Jim Brown, Cleveland, NFL | 15 | 12 | 3 | 0 |
| 1962 | Abner Haynes, Dallas, AFL | 19 | 13 | 6 | 0 |
| | Jim Taylor, Green Bay, NFL | 19 | 19 | 0 | 0 |
| 1961 | Bill Groman, Houston, AFL | 18 | 1 | 17 | 0 |
| | Jim Taylor, Green Bay, NFL | 16 | 15 | 1 | 0 |
| 1960 | Paul Hornung, Green Bay, NFL | 15 | 13 | 2 | 0 |
| | Sonny Randle, St. Louis, NFL | 15 | 0 | 15 | 0 |
| | Art Powell, N.Y. Titans, AFL | 14 | 0 | 14 | 0 |
| 1959 | Raymond Berry, Baltimore | 14 | 0 | 14 | 0 |
| | Jim Brown, Cleveland | 14 | 14 | 0 | 0 |
| 1958 | Jim Brown, Cleveland | 18 | 17 | 1 | 0 |
| 1957 | Lenny Moore, Baltimore | 11 | 3 | 7 | 1 |
| 1956 | Rick Casares, Chi. Bears | 14 | 12 | 2 | 0 |
| 1955 | *Alan Ameche, Baltimore | 9 | 9 | 0 | 0 |
| | Harlon Hill, Chi. Bears | 9 | 0 | 9 | 0 |
| 1954 | *Harlon Hill, Chi. Bears | 12 | 0 | 12 | 0 |
| 1953 | Joseph Perry, San Francisco | 13 | 10 | 3 | 0 |
| 1952 | Cloyce Box, Detroit | 15 | 0 | 15 | 0 |
| 1951 | Elroy (Crazylegs) Hirsch, Los Angeles | 17 | 0 | 17 | 0 |
| 1950 | Bob Shaw, Chi. Cardinals | 12 | 0 | 12 | 0 |
| 1949 | Gene Roberts, N.Y. Giants | 17 | 9 | 8 | 0 |
| 1948 | Mal Kutner, Chi. Cardinals | 15 | 1 | 14 | 0 |
| 1947 | Steve Van Buren, Philadelphia | 14 | 13 | 0 | 1 |
| 1946 | Ted Fritsch, Green Bay | 10 | 9 | 1 | 0 |
| 1945 | Steve Van Buren, Philadelphia | 18 | 15 | 2 | 1 |
| 1944 | Don Hutson, Green Bay | 9 | 0 | 9 | 0 |
| | Bill Paschal, N.Y. Giants | 9 | 9 | 0 | 0 |
| 1943 | Don Hutson, Green Bay | 12 | 0 | 11 | 1 |
| | *Bill Paschal, N.Y. Giants | 12 | 10 | 2 | 0 |
| 1942 | Don Hutson, Green Bay | 17 | 0 | 17 | 0 |
| 1941 | Don Hutson, Green Bay | 12 | 2 | 10 | 0 |
| | George McAfee, Chi. Bears | 12 | 6 | 3 | 3 |
| 1940 | John Drake, Cleveland | 9 | 9 | 0 | 0 |
| | Richard Todd, Washington | 9 | 4 | 4 | 1 |
| 1939 | Andrew Farkas, Washington | 11 | 5 | 5 | 1 |
| 1938 | Don Hutson, Green Bay | 9 | 0 | 9 | 0 |
| 1937 | Cliff Battles, Washington | 7 | 5 | 1 | 1 |
| | Clarke Hinkle, Green Bay | 7 | 5 | 2 | 0 |
| | Don Hutson, Green Bay | 7 | 0 | 7 | 0 |
| 1936 | Don Hutson, Green Bay | 9 | 0 | 8 | 1 |
| 1935 | *Don Hutson, Green Bay | 7 | 0 | 6 | 1 |
| 1934 | *Beattie Feathers, Chi. Bears | 9 | 8 | 1 | 0 |
| 1933 | *Charlie (Buckets) Goldenberg, Green Bay | 7 | 4 | 1 | 2 |
| | John (Shipwreck) Kelly, Brooklyn | 7 | 2 | 3 | 2 |
| | *Elvin (Kink) Richards, N.Y. Giants | 7 | 4 | 3 | 0 |
| 1932 | Earl (Dutch) Clark, Portsmouth | 6 | 3 | 3 | 0 |
| | Red Grange, Chi. Bears | 6 | 3 | 3 | 0 |

**First season of professional football.*

## ANNUAL LEADERS—MOST FIELD GOALS MADE

| Year | Player, Team | Att. | Made. | Pct. |
|---|---|---|---|---|
| 1993 | Jeff Jaeger, L.A. Raiders, AFC | 44 | 35 | 79.5 |
| | Jason Hanson, Detroit, NFC | 43 | 34 | 79.1 |
| 1992 | Pete Stoyanovich, Miami, AFC | 37 | 30 | 81.1 |
| | Chip Lohmiller, Washington, NFC | 40 | 30 | 75.0 |
| 1991 | Pete Stoyanovich, Miami, AFC | 37 | 31 | 83.8 |
| | Chip Lohmiller, Washington, NFC | 43 | 31 | 72.1 |
| 1990 | Nick Lowery, Kansas City, AFC | 37 | 34 | 91.9 |
| | Chip Lohmiller, Washington, NFC | 40 | 30 | 75.0 |
| 1989 | Rich Karlis, Minnesota, NFC | 39 | 31 | 79.5 |
| | *David Treadwell, Denver, AFC | 33 | 27 | 81.8 |
| 1988 | Scott Norwood, Buffalo, AFC | 37 | 32 | 86.5 |
| | Mike Cofer, San Francisco, NFC | 38 | 27 | 71.1 |
| 1987 | Morten Andersen, New Orleans, NFC | 36 | 28 | 77.8 |
| | Dean Biasucci, Indianapolis, AFC | 27 | 24 | 88.9 |
| | Jim Breech, Cincinnati, AFC | 30 | 24 | 80.0 |
| 1986 | Tony Franklin, New England, AFC | 41 | 32 | 78.0 |
| | Kevin Butler, Chicago, NFC | 41 | 28 | 68.3 |
| 1985 | Gary Anderson, Pittsburgh, AFC | 42 | 33 | 78.6 |
| | Morten Andersen, New Orleans, NFC | 35 | 31 | 88.6 |
| | *Kevin Butler, Chicago, NFC | 37 | 31 | 83.8 |
| 1984 | *Paul McFadden, Philadelphia, NFC | 37 | 30 | 81.1 |
| | Gary Anderson, Pittsburgh, AFC | 32 | 24 | 75.0 |
| | Matt Bahr, Cleveland, AFC | 32 | 24 | 75.0 |
| 1983 | *Ali-Haji-Sheikh, N.Y. Giants, NFC | 42 | 35 | 83.3 |
| | *Raul Allegre, Baltimore, AFC | 35 | 30 | 85.7 |
| 1982 | Mark Moseley, Washington, NFC | 21 | 20 | 95.2 |
| | Nick Lowery, Kansas City, AFC | 24 | 19 | 79.2 |
| 1981 | Rafael Septien, Dallas, NFC | 35 | 27 | 77.1 |
| | Nick Lowery, Kansas City, AFC | 36 | 26 | 72.2 |
| 1980 | *Ed Murray, Detroit, NFC | 42 | 27 | 64.3 |
| | John Smith, New England, AFC | 34 | 26 | 76.5 |
| | Fred Steinfort, Denver, AFC | 34 | 26 | 76.5 |
| 1979 | Mark Moseley, Washington, NFC | 33 | 25 | 75.8 |
| | John Smith, New England, AFC | 33 | 23 | 69.7 |
| 1978 | *Frank Corral, Los Angeles, NFC | 43 | 29 | 67.4 |
| | Pat Leahy, N.Y. Jets, AFC | 30 | 22 | 73.3 |
| 1977 | Mark Moseley, Washington, NFC | 37 | 21 | 56.8 |
| | Errol Mann, Oakland, AFC | 28 | 20 | 71.4 |
| 1976 | Mark Moseley, Washington, NFC | 34 | 22 | 64.7 |
| | Jan Stenerud, Kansas City, AFC | 38 | 21 | 55.3 |
| 1975 | Jan Stenerud, Kansas City, AFC | 32 | 22 | 68.8 |
| | Toni Fritsch, Dallas, NFC | 35 | 22 | 62.9 |
| 1974 | Chester Marcol, Green Bay, NFC | 39 | 25 | 64.1 |
| | Roy Gerela, Pittsburgh, AFC | 29 | 20 | 69.0 |
| 1973 | David Ray, Los Angeles, NFC | 47 | 30 | 63.8 |
| | Roy Gerela, Pittsburgh, AFC | 43 | 29 | 67.4 |
| 1972 | *Chester Marcol, Green Bay, NFC | 48 | 33 | 68.8 |
| | Roy Gerela, Pittsburgh, AFC | 41 | 28 | 68.3 |
| 1971 | Curt Knight, Washington, NFC | 49 | 29 | 59.2 |
| | Garo Yepremian, Miami, AFC | 40 | 28 | 70.0 |
| 1970 | Jan Stenerud, Kansas City, AFC | 42 | 30 | 71.4 |
| | Fred Cox, Minnesota, NFC | 46 | 30 | 65.2 |
| 1969 | Jim Turner, N.Y. Jets, AFL | 47 | 32 | 68.1 |
| | Fred Cox, Minnesota, NFL | 37 | 26 | 70.3 |
| 1968 | Jim Turner, N.Y. Jets, AFL | 46 | 34 | 73.9 |
| | Mac Percival, Chicago, NFL | 36 | 25 | 69.4 |
| 1967 | Jim Bakken, St. Louis, NFL | 39 | 27 | 69.2 |
| | Jan Stenerud, Kansas City, AFL | 36 | 21 | 58.3 |
| 1966 | Bruce Gossett, Los Angeles, NFL | 49 | 28 | 57.1 |
| | Mike Mercer, Oakland-Kansas City, AFL | 30 | 21 | 70.0 |
| 1965 | Pete Gogolak, Buffalo, AFL | 46 | 28 | 60.9 |
| | Fred Cox, Minnesota, NFL | 35 | 23 | 65.7 |
| 1964 | Jim Bakken, St. Louis, NFL | 38 | 25 | 65.8 |
| | Gino Cappelletti, Boston, AFL | 39 | 25 | 64.1 |
| 1963 | Jim Martin, Baltimore, NFL | 39 | 24 | 61.5 |
| | Gino Cappelletti, Boston, AFL | 38 | 22 | 57.9 |
| 1962 | Gene Mingo, Denver, AFL | 39 | 27 | 69.2 |
| | Lou Michaels, Pittsburgh, NFL | 42 | 26 | 61.9 |
| 1961 | Steve Myhra, Baltimore, NFL | 39 | 21 | 53.8 |
| | Gino Cappelletti, Boston, AFL | 32 | 17 | 53.1 |
| 1960 | Tommy Davis, San Francisco, NFL | 32 | 19 | 59.4 |
| | *Gene Mingo, Denver, AFL | 28 | 18 | 64.3 |
| 1959 | Pat Summerall, N.Y. Giants | 29 | 20 | 69.0 |
| 1958 | Paige Cothren, Los Angeles | 25 | 14 | 56.0 |
| | *Tom Miner, Pittsburgh | 28 | 14 | 50.0 |
| 1957 | Lou Groza, Cleveland | 22 | 15 | 68.2 |
| 1956 | Sam Baker, Washington | 25 | 17 | 68.0 |
| 1955 | Fred Cone, Green Bay | 24 | 16 | 66.7 |
| 1954 | Lou Groza, Cleveland | 24 | 16 | 66.7 |
| 1953 | Lou Groza, Cleveland | 26 | 23 | 88.5 |
| 1952 | Lou Groza, Cleveland | 33 | 19 | 57.6 |
| 1951 | Bob Waterfield, Los Angeles | 23 | 13 | 56.5 |
| 1950 | Lou Groza, Cleveland | 19 | 13 | 68.4 |
| 1949 | Cliff Patton, Philadelphia | 18 | 9 | 50.0 |
| | Bob Waterfield, Los Angeles | 16 | 9 | 56.3 |
| 1948 | Cliff Patton, Philadelphia | 12 | 8 | 66.7 |
| 1947 | Ward Cuff, Green Bay | 16 | 7 | 43.8 |
| | Pat Harder, Chi. Cardinals | 10 | 7 | 70.0 |
| | Bob Waterfield, Los Angeles | 16 | 7 | 43.8 |
| 1946 | Ted Fritsch, Green Bay | 17 | 9 | 52.9 |
| 1945 | Joe Aguirre, Washington | 13 | 7 | 53.8 |
| 1944 | Ken Strong, N.Y. Giants | 12 | 6 | 50.0 |
| 1943 | Ward Cuff, N.Y. Giants | 9 | 3 | 33.3 |
| | Don Hutson, Green Bay | 5 | 3 | 60.0 |
| 1942 | Bill Daddio, Chi. Cardinals | 10 | 5 | 50.0 |
| 1941 | Clarke Hinkle, Green Bay | 14 | 6 | 42.9 |
| 1940 | Clarke Hinkle, Green Bay | 14 | 9 | 64.3 |
| 1939 | Ward Cuff, N.Y. Giants | 16 | 7 | 43.8 |
| 1938 | Ward Cuff, N.Y. Giants | 9 | 5 | 55.6 |

| | | | | |
|---|---|---|---|---|
| | Ralph Kercheval, Brooklyn | 13 | 5 | 38.5 |
| 1937 | Jack Manders, Chi. Bears | | 8 | |
| 1936 | Jack Manders, Chi. Bears | | 7 | |
| | Armand Niccolai, Pittsburgh | | 7 | |
| 1935 | Armand Niccolai, Pittsburgh | | 6 | |
| | Bill Smith, Chi. Cardinals | | 6 | |
| 1934 | Jack Manders, Chi. Bears | | 10 | |
| 1933 | *Jack Manders, Chi. Bears | | 6 | |
| | Glenn Presnell, Portsmouth | | 6 | |
| 1932 | Earl (Dutch) Clark, Portsmouth | | 3 | |

*First season of professional football.*

## ANNUAL RUSHING LEADERS

| Year | Player, Team | Att. | Yards | Avg. | TD |
|---|---|---|---|---|---|
| 1993 | Emmitt Smith, Dallas, NFC | 283 | 1,486 | 5.3 | 9 |
| | Thurman Thomas, Buffalo, AFC | 355 | 1,315 | 3.7 | 6 |
| 1992 | Emmitt Smith, Dallas, NFC | 373 | 1,713 | 4.6 | 18 |
| | Barry Foster, Pittsburgh, AFC | 390 | 1,690 | 4.3 | 11 |
| 1991 | Emmitt Smith, Dallas, NFC | 365 | 1,563 | 4.3 | 12 |
| | Thurman Thomas, Buffalo, AFC | 288 | 1,407 | 4.9 | 7 |
| 1980 | Barry Sanders, Detroit, NFC | 255 | 1,304 | 5.1 | 13 |
| | Thurman Thomas, Buffalo, AFC | 271 | 1,297 | 4.8 | 11 |
| 1989 | Christian Okoye, Kansas City, AFC | 370 | 1,480 | 4.0 | 12 |
| | *Barry Sanders, Detroit, NFC | 280 | 1,470 | 5.3 | 14 |
| 1988 | Eric Dickerson, Indianapolis, AFC | 388 | 1,659 | 4.3 | 14 |
| | Herschel Walker, Dallas, NFC | 361 | 1,514 | 4.2 | 5 |
| 1987 | Charles White, L.A. Rams, NFC | 324 | 1,374 | 4.2 | 11 |
| | Eric Dickerson, Indianapolis, AFC | 223 | 1,011 | 4.5 | 5 |
| 1986 | Eric Dickerson, L.A. Rams, NFC | 404 | 1,821 | 4.5 | 11 |
| | Curt Warner, Seattle, AFC | 319 | 1,481 | 4.6 | 13 |
| 1985 | Marcus Allen, L.A. Raiders, AFC | 380 | 1,759 | 4.6 | 11 |
| | Gerald Riggs, Atlanta, NFC | 397 | 1,719 | 4.3 | 10 |
| 1984 | Eric Dickerson, L.A. Rams, NFC | 379 | 2,105 | 5.6 | 14 |
| | Earnest Jackson, San Diego, AFC | 296 | 1,179 | 4.0 | 8 |
| 1983 | *Eric Dickerson, L.A. Rams, NFC | 390 | 1,808 | 4.6 | 18 |
| | *Curt Warner, Seattle, AFC | 335 | 1,449 | 4.3 | 13 |
| 1982 | Freeman McNeil, N.Y. Jets, AFC | 151 | 786 | 5.2 | 6 |
| | Tony Dorsett, Dallas, NFC | 177 | 745 | 4.2 | 5 |
| 1981 | *George Rogers, New Orleans, NFC | 378 | 1,674 | 4.4 | 13 |
| | Earl Campbell, Houston, AFC | 361 | 1,376 | 3.8 | 10 |
| 1980 | Earl Campbell, Houston, AFC | 373 | 1,934 | 5.2 | 13 |
| | Walter Payton, Chicago, NFC | 317 | 1,460 | 4.6 | 6 |
| 1979 | Earl Campbell, Houston, AFC | 368 | 1,697 | 4.6 | 19 |
| | Walter Payton, Chicago, NFC | 369 | 1,610 | 4.4 | 14 |
| 1978 | *Earl Campbell, Houston, AFC | 302 | 1,450 | 4.8 | 13 |
| | Walter Payton, Chicago, NFC | 333 | 1,395 | 4.2 | 11 |
| 1977 | Walter Payton, Chicago, NFC | 339 | 1,852 | 5.5 | 14 |
| | Mark van Eeghen, Oakland, AFC | 324 | 1,273 | 3.9 | 7 |
| 1976 | O.J. Simpson, Buffalo, AFC | 290 | 1,503 | 5.2 | 8 |
| | Walter Payton, Chicago, NFC | 311 | 1,390 | 4.5 | 13 |
| 1975 | O.J. Simpson, Buffalo, AFC | 329 | 1,817 | 5.5 | 16 |
| | Jim Otis, St. Louis, NFC | 269 | 1,076 | 4.0 | 5 |
| 1974 | Otis Armstrong, Denver, AFC | 263 | 1,407 | 5.3 | 9 |
| | Lawrence McCutcheon, Los Angeles, NFC | 236 | 1,109 | 4.7 | 3 |
| 1973 | O.J. Simpson, Buffalo, AFC | 332 | 2,003 | 6.0 | 12 |
| | John Brockington, Green Bay, NFC | 265 | 1,144 | 4.3 | 3 |
| 1972 | O.J. Simpson, Buffalo, AFC | 292 | 1,251 | 4.3 | 6 |
| | Larry Brown, Washington, NFC | 285 | 1,216 | 4.3 | 8 |
| 1971 | Floyd Little, Denver, AFC | 284 | 1,133 | 4.0 | 6 |
| | *John Brockington, Green Bay, NFC | 216 | 1,105 | 5.1 | 4 |
| 1970 | Larry Brown, Washington, NFC | 237 | 1,125 | 4.7 | 5 |
| | Floyd Little, Denver, AFC | 209 | 901 | 4.3 | 3 |
| 1969 | Gale Sayers, Chicago, NFL | 236 | 1,032 | 4.4 | 8 |
| | Dickie Post, San Diego, AFL | 182 | 873 | 4.8 | 6 |
| 1968 | Leroy Kelly, Cleveland, NFL | 248 | 1,239 | 5.0 | 16 |
| | *Paul Robinson, Cincinnati, AFL | 238 | 1,023 | 4.3 | 8 |
| 1967 | Jim Nance, Boston, AFL | 269 | 1,216 | 4.5 | 7 |
| | Leroy Kelly, Cleveland, NFL | 235 | 1,205 | 5.1 | 11 |
| 1966 | Jim Nance, Boston, AFL | 299 | 1,458 | 4.9 | 11 |
| | Gale Sayers, Chicago, NFL | 229 | 1,231 | 5.4 | 8 |
| 1965 | Jim Brown, Cleveland, NFL | 289 | 1,544 | 5.3 | 17 |
| | Paul Lowe, San Diego, AFL | 222 | 1,121 | 5.0 | 7 |
| 1964 | Jim Brown, Cleveland, NFL | 280 | 1,446 | 5.2 | 7 |
| | Cookie Gilchrist, Buffalo, AFL | 230 | 981 | 4.3 | 6 |
| 1963 | Jim Brown, Cleveland, NFL | 291 | 1,863 | 6.4 | 12 |
| | Clem Daniels, Oakland, AFL | 215 | 1,099 | 5.1 | 3 |
| 1962 | Jim Taylor, Green Bay, NFL | 272 | 1,474 | 5.4 | 19 |
| | Cookie Gilchrist, Buffalo, AFL | 214 | 1,096 | 5.1 | 13 |
| 1961 | Jim Brown, Cleveland, NFL | 305 | 1,408 | 4.6 | 8 |
| | Billy Cannon, Houston, AFL | 200 | 948 | 4.7 | 6 |
| 1960 | Jim Brown, Cleveland, NFL | 215 | 1,257 | 5.8 | 9 |
| | *Abner Haynes, Dall. Texans, AFL | 156 | 875 | 5.6 | 9 |
| 1959 | Jim Brown, Cleveland | 290 | 1,329 | 4.6 | 14 |
| 1958 | Jim Brown, Cleveland | 257 | 1,527 | 5.9 | 17 |
| 1957 | *Jim Brown, Cleveland | 202 | 942 | 4.7 | 9 |
| 1956 | Rick Casares, Chi. Bears | 234 | 1,126 | 4.8 | 12 |
| 1955 | *Alan Ameche, Baltimore | 213 | 961 | 4.5 | 9 |
| 1954 | Joe Perry, San Francisco | 173 | 1,049 | 6.1 | 8 |
| 1953 | Joe Perry, San Francisco | 192 | 1,018 | 5.3 | 10 |
| 1952 | Dan Towler, Los Angeles | 156 | 894 | 5.7 | 10 |
| 1951 | Eddie Price, N.Y. Giants | 271 | 971 | 3.6 | 7 |
| 1950 | Marion Motley, Cleveland | 140 | 810 | 5.8 | 3 |
| 1949 | Steve Van Buren, Philadelphia | 263 | 1,146 | 4.4 | 11 |
| 1948 | Steve Van Buren, Philadelphia | 201 | 945 | 4.7 | 10 |
| 1947 | Steve Van Buren, Philadelphia | 217 | 1,008 | 4.6 | 13 |
| 1946 | Bill Dudley, Pittsburgh | 146 | 604 | 4.1 | 3 |
| 1945 | Steve Van Buren, Philadelphia | 143 | 832 | 5.8 | 15 |
| 1944 | Bill Paschal, N.Y. Giants | 196 | 737 | 3.8 | 9 |
| 1943 | *Bill Paschal, N.Y. Giants | 147 | 572 | 3.9 | 10 |
| 1942 | *Bill Dudley, Pittsburgh | 162 | 696 | 4.3 | 5 |
| 1941 | Clarence (Pug) Manders, Brooklyn | 111 | 486 | 4.4 | 5 |
| 1940 | Byron (Whizzer) White, Detroit | 146 | 514 | 3.5 | 5 |
| 1939 | *Bill Osmanski, Chicago | 121 | 699 | 5.8 | 7 |
| 1938 | *Byron (Whizzer) White, Pittsburgh | 152 | 567 | 3.7 | 4 |
| 1937 | Cliff Battles, Washington | 216 | 874 | 4.0 | 5 |
| 1936 | *Alphonse (Tuffy) Leemans, N.Y. Giants | 206 | 830 | 4.0 | 2 |
| 1935 | Doug Russell, Chi. Cardinals | 140 | 499 | 3.6 | 0 |
| 1934 | *Beattie Feathers, Chi. Bears | 119 | 1,004 | 8.4 | 8 |
| 1933 | Jim Musick, Boston | 173 | 809 | 4.7 | 5 |
| 1932 | *Cliff Battles, Boston | 148 | 576 | 3.9 | 3 |

*First season of professional football.*

## ANNUAL PASSING LEADERS

**(Current rating system implemented in 1973)**

| Year | Player, Team | Att. | Comp. | Yards | TD | Int. | Rating |
|---|---|---|---|---|---|---|---|
| 1993 | Steve Young, San Francisco, NFC | 462 | 314 | 4,023 | 29 | 16 | 101.5 |
| | John Elway, Denver, AFC | 551 | 348 | 4,030 | 25 | 10 | 92.8 |
| 1992 | Steve Young, San Francisco, NFC | 402 | 268 | 3,465 | 25 | 7 | 107.0 |
| | Warren Moon, Houston, AFC | 346 | 224 | 2,521 | 18 | 12 | 89.3 |
| 1991 | Steve Young, San Francisco, NFC | 279 | 180 | 2,517 | 17 | 8 | 101.8 |
| | Jim Kelly, Buffalo, AFC | 474 | 304 | 3,844 | 33 | 17 | 97.6 |
| 1990 | Jim Kelly, Buffalo, AFC | 346 | 219 | 2,829 | 24 | 9 | 101.2 |
| | Phil Simms, N.Y. Giants, NFC | 311 | 184 | 2,284 | 15 | 4 | 92.7 |
| 1989 | Joe Montana, San Francisco, NFC | 386 | 271 | 3,521 | 26 | 8 | 112.4 |
| | Boomer Esiason, Cincinnati, AFC | 455 | 258 | 3,525 | 28 | 11 | 92.1 |
| 1988 | Boomer Esiason, Cincinnati, AFC | 388 | 223 | 3,572 | 28 | 14 | 97.4 |
| | Wade Wilson, Minnesota, NFC | 332 | 204 | 2,746 | 15 | 9 | 91.5 |
| 1987 | Joe Montana, San Francisco, NFC | 398 | 266 | 3,054 | 31 | 13 | 102.1 |
| | Bernie Kosar, Cleveland, AFC | 389 | 241 | 3,033 | 22 | 9 | 95.4 |
| 1986 | Tommy Kramer, Minnesota, NFC | 372 | 208 | 3,000 | 24 | 10 | 92.6 |
| | Dan Marino, Miami, AFC | 623 | 378 | 4,746 | 44 | 23 | 92.5 |
| 1985 | Ken O'Brien, N.Y. Jets, AFC | 488 | 297 | 3,888 | 25 | 8 | 96.2 |
| | Joe Montana, San Francisco, NFC | 494 | 303 | 3,653 | 27 | 13 | 91.3 |
| 1984 | Dan Marino, Miami, AFC | 564 | 362 | 5,084 | 48 | 17 | 108.9 |
| | Joe Montana, San Francisco, NFC | 432 | 279 | 3,630 | 28 | 10 | 102.9 |
| 1983 | Steve Bartkowski, Atlanta, NFC | 432 | 274 | 3,167 | 22 | 5 | 97.6 |
| | *Dan Marino, Miami, AFC | 296 | 173 | 2,210 | 20 | 6 | 96.0 |
| 1982 | Ken Anderson, Cincinnati, AFC | 309 | 218 | 2,495 | 12 | 9 | 95.5 |
| | Joe Theismann, Washington, NFC | 252 | 161 | 2,033 | 13 | 9 | 91.3 |
| 1981 | Ken Anderson, Cincinnati, AFC | 479 | 300 | 3,754 | 29 | 10 | 98.5 |
| | Joe Montana, San Francisco, NFC | 488 | 311 | 3,565 | 19 | 12 | 88.2 |
| 1980 | Brian Sipe, Cleveland, AFC | 554 | 337 | 4,132 | 30 | 14 | 91.4 |
| | Ron Jaworski, Philadelphia, NFC | 451 | 257 | 3,529 | 27 | 12 | 90.9 |
| 1979 | Roger Staubach, Dallas, NFC | 461 | 267 | 3,586 | 27 | 11 | 92.4 |
| | Dan Fouts, San Diego, AFC | 530 | 332 | 4,082 | 24 | 24 | 82.6 |
| 1978 | Roger Staubach, Dallas, NFC | 413 | 231 | 3,190 | 25 | 16 | 84.9 |
| | Terry Bradshaw, Pittsburgh, AFC | 368 | 207 | 2,915 | 28 | 20 | 84.8 |
| 1977 | Bob Griese, Miami, AFC | 307 | 180 | 2,252 | 22 | 13 | 88.0 |
| | Roger Staubach, Dallas, NFC | 361 | 210 | 2,620 | 18 | 9 | 87.1 |
| 1976 | Ken Stabler, Oakland, AFC | 291 | 194 | 2,737 | 27 | 17 | 103.4 |
| | James Harris, Los Angeles, NFC | 158 | 91 | 1,460 | 8 | 6 | 89.8 |
| 1975 | Ken Anderson, Cincinnati, AFC | 377 | 228 | 3,169 | 21 | 11 | 94.1 |
| | Fran Tarkenton, Minnesota, NFC | 425 | 273 | 2,994 | 25 | 13 | 91.7 |
| 1974 | Ken Anderson, Cincinnati, AFC | 328 | 213 | 2,667 | 18 | 10 | 95.9 |
| | Sonny Jurgensen, Washington, NFC | 167 | 107 | 1,185 | 11 | 5 | 94.6 |
| 1973 | Roger Staubach, Dallas, NFC | 286 | 179 | 2,428 | 23 | 15 | 94.6 |
| | Ken Stabler, Oakland, AFC | 260 | 163 | 1,997 | 14 | 10 | 88.5 |
| 1972 | Norm Snead, N.Y. Giants, NFC | 325 | 196 | 2,307 | 17 | 12 | |
| | Earl Morrall, Miami, AFC | 150 | 83 | 1,360 | 11 | 7 | |
| 1971 | Roger Staubach, Dallas, NFC | 211 | 126 | 1,882 | 15 | 4 | |
| | Bob Griese, Miami, AFC | 263 | 145 | 2,089 | 19 | 9 | |
| 1970 | John Brodie, San Francisco, NFC | 378 | 223 | 2,941 | 24 | 10 | |
| | Daryle Lamonica, Oakland, AFC | 356 | 179 | 2,516 | 22 | 15 | |
| 1969 | Sonny Jurgensen, Washington, NFL | 442 | 274 | 3,102 | 22 | 15 | |
| | *Greg Cook, Cincinnati, AFL | 197 | 106 | 1,854 | 15 | 11 | |
| 1968 | Len Dawson, Kansas City, AFL | 224 | 131 | 2,109 | 17 | 9 | |

| | | | | | | |
|---|---|---|---|---|---|---|
| | Earl Morrall, Baltimore, NFL | 317 | 182 | 2,909 | 26 | 17 |
| 1967 | Sonny Jurgensen, Washington, NFL | 508 | 288 | 3,747 | 31 | 16 |
| | Daryle Lamonica, Oakland, AFL | 425 | 220 | 3,228 | 30 | 20 |
| 1966 | Bart Starr, Green Bay, NFL | 251 | 156 | 2,257 | 14 | 3 |
| | Len Dawson, Kansas City, AFL | 284 | 159 | 2,527 | 26 | 10 |
| 1965 | Rudy Bukich, Chicago, NFL | 312 | 176 | 2,641 | 20 | 9 |
| | John Hadl, San Diego, AFL | 348 | 174 | 2,798 | 20 | 21 |
| 1964 | Len Dawson, Kansas City, AFL | 354 | 199 | 2,879 | 30 | 18 |
| | Bart Starr, Green Bay, NFL | 272 | 163 | 2,144 | 15 | 4 |
| 1963 | Y.A. Tittle, N.Y. Giants, NFL | 367 | 221 | 3,145 | 36 | 14 |
| | Tobin Rote, San Diego, AFL | 286 | 170 | 2,510 | 20 | 17 |
| 1962 | Len Dawson, Dall. Texans, AFL | 310 | 189 | 2,759 | 29 | 17 |
| | Bart Starr, Green Bay, NFL | 285 | 178 | 2,438 | 12 | 9 |
| 1961 | George Blanda, Houston, AFL | 362 | 187 | 3,330 | 36 | 22 |
| | Milt Plum, Cleveland, NFL | 302 | 177 | 2,416 | 18 | 10 |
| 1960 | Milt Plum, Cleveland, NFL | 250 | 151 | 2,297 | 21 | 5 |
| | Jack Kemp, L.A. Chargers, AFL | 406 | 211 | 3,018 | 20 | 25 |
| 1959 | Charlie Conerly, N.Y. Giants | 194 | 113 | 1,706 | 14 | 4 |
| 1958 | Eddie LeBaron, Washington | 145 | 79 | 1,365 | 11 | 10 |
| 1957 | Tommy O'Connell, Cleveland | 110 | 63 | 1,229 | 9 | 8 |
| 1956 | Ed Brown, Chi. Bears | 168 | 96 | 1,667 | 11 | 12 |
| 1955 | Otto Graham, Cleveland | 185 | 98 | 1,721 | 15 | 8 |
| 1954 | Norm Van Brocklin, Los Angeles | 260 | 139 | 2,637 | 13 | 21 |
| 1953 | Otto Graham, Cleveland | 258 | 167 | 2,722 | 11 | 9 |
| 1952 | Norm Van Brocklin, Los Angeles | 205 | 113 | 1,736 | 14 | 17 |
| 1951 | Bob Waterfield, Los Angeles | 176 | 88 | 1,566 | 13 | 10 |
| 1950 | Norm Van Brocklin, Los Angeles | 233 | 127 | 2,061 | 18 | 14 |
| 1949 | Sammy Baugh, Washington | 255 | 145 | 1,903 | 18 | 14 |
| 1948 | Tommy Thompson, Philadelphia | 246 | 141 | 1,965 | 25 | 11 |
| 1947 | Sammy Baugh, Washington | 354 | 210 | 2,938 | 25 | 15 |
| 1946 | Bob Waterfield, Los Angeles | 251 | 127 | 1,747 | 18 | 17 |
| 1945 | Sammy Baugh, Washington | 182 | 128 | 1,669 | 11 | 4 |
| | Sid Luckman, Chi. Bears | 217 | 117 | 1,725 | 14 | 10 |
| 1944 | Frank Filchock, Washington | 147 | 84 | 1,139 | 13 | 9 |
| 1943 | Sammy Baugh, Washington | 239 | 133 | 1,754 | 23 | 19 |
| 1942 | Cecil Isbell, Green Bay | 268 | 146 | 2,021 | 24 | 14 |
| 1941 | Cecil Isbell, Green Bay | 206 | 117 | 1,479 | 15 | 11 |
| 1940 | Sammy Baugh, Washington | 177 | 111 | 1,367 | 12 | 10 |
| 1939 | *Parker Hall, Cleveland | 208 | 106 | 1,227 | 9 | 13 |
| 1938 | Ed Danowski, N.Y. Giants | 129 | 70 | 848 | 7 | 8 |
| 1937 | *Sammy Baugh, Washington | 171 | 81 | 1,127 | 8 | 14 |
| 1936 | Arnie Herber, Green Bay | 173 | 77 | 1,239 | 11 | 13 |
| 1935 | Ed Danowski, N.Y. Giants | 113 | 57 | 794 | 10 | 9 |
| 1934 | Arnie Herber, Green Bay | 115 | 42 | 799 | 8 | 12 |
| 1933 | *Harry Newman, N.Y. Giants | 136 | 53 | 973 | 11 | 17 |
| 1932 | Arnie Herber, Green Bay | 101 | 37 | 639 | 9 | 9 |

*First season of professional football.*

## ANNUAL PASSING TOUCHDOWN LEADERS

| Year | Player, Team | TD |
|---|---|---|
| 1993 | Steve Young, San Francisco, NFC | 29 |
| | John Elway, Denver, AFC | 25 |
| 1992 | Steve Young, San Francisco, NFC | 25 |
| | Dan Marino, Miami, AFC | 24 |
| 1991 | Jim Kelly, Buffalo, AFC | 33 |
| | Mark Rypien, Washington, NFC | 28 |
| 1990 | Warren Moon, Houston, AFC | 33 |
| | Randall Cunningham, Philadelphia, NFC | 30 |
| 1989 | Jim Everett, L.A. Rams, NFC | 29 |
| | Boomer Esiason, Cincinnati, AFC | 28 |
| 1988 | Jim Everett, L.A. Rams, NFC | 31 |
| | Boomer Esiason, Cincinnati, AFC | 28 |
| | Dan Marino, Miami, AFC | 28 |
| 1987 | Joe Montana, San Francisco, NFC | 31 |
| | Dan Marino, Miami, AFC | 26 |
| 1986 | Dan Marino, Miami, AFC | 44 |
| | Tommy Kramer, Minnesota, NFC | 24 |
| 1985 | Dan Marino, Miami, AFC | 30 |
| | Joe Montana, San Francisco, NFC | 27 |
| 1984 | Dan Marino, Miami, AFC | 48 |
| | Neil Lomax, St. Louis, NFC | 28 |
| | Joe Montana, San Francisco, NFC | 28 |
| 1983 | Lynn Dickey, Green Bay, NFC | 32 |
| | Joe Ferguson, Buffalo, AFC | 26 |
| | Brian Sipe, Cleveland, AFC | 26 |
| 1982 | Terry Bradshaw, Pittsburgh, AFC | 17 |
| | Dan Fouts, San Diego, AFC | 17 |
| | Joe Montana, San Francisco, NFC | 17 |
| 1981 | Dan Fouts, San Diego, AFC | 33 |
| | Steve Bartkowski, Atlanta, NFC | 30 |
| 1980 | Steve Bartkowski, Atlanta, NFC | 31 |
| | Dan Fouts, San Diego, AFC | 30 |
| | Brian Sipe, Cleveland, AFC | 30 |
| 1979 | Steve Grogan, New England, AFC | 28 |
| | Brian Sipe, Cleveland, AFC | 28 |
| | Roger Staubach, Dallas, NFC | 27 |
| 1978 | Terry Bradshaw, Pittsburgh, AFC | 28 |
| | Roger Staubach, Dallas, NFC | 25 |
| | Fran Tarkenton, Minnesota, NFC | 25 |
| 1977 | Bob Griese, Miami, AFC | 22 |
| | Ron Jaworski, Philadelphia, NFC | 18 |
| | Roger Staubach, Dallas, NFC | 18 |
| 1976 | Ken Stabler, Oakland, AFC | 27 |
| | Jim Hart, St. Louis, NFC | 18 |
| 1975 | Joe Ferguson, Buffalo, AFC | 25 |
| | Fran Tarkenton, Minnesota, NFC | 25 |
| 1974 | Ken Stabler, Oakland, AFC | 26 |
| | Jim Hart, St. Louis, NFC | 20 |
| 1973 | Roman Gabriel, Philadelphia, NFC | 23 |
| | Roger Staubach, Dallas, NFC | 23 |
| | Charley Johnson, Denver, AFC | 20 |
| 1972 | Billy Kilmer, Washington, NFC | 19 |
| | Joe Namath, N.Y. Jets, AFC | 19 |
| 1971 | John Hadl, San Diego, AFC | 21 |
| | John Brodie, San Francisco, NFC | 18 |
| 1970 | John Brodie, San Francisco, NFC | 24 |
| | John Hadl, San Diego, AFC | 22 |
| | Daryle Lamonica, Oakland, AFC | 22 |
| 1969 | Daryle Lamonica, Oakland, AFL | 34 |
| | Roman Gabriel, Los Angeles, NFL | 24 |
| 1968 | John Hadl, San Diego, AFL | 27 |
| | Earl Morrall, Baltimore, NFL | 26 |
| 1967 | Sonny Jurgensen, Washington, NFL | 31 |
| | Daryle Lamonica, Oakland, AFL | 30 |
| 1966 | Frank Ryan, Cleveland, NFL | 29 |
| | Len Dawson, Kansas City, AFL | 26 |
| 1965 | John Brodie, San Francisco, NFL | 30 |
| | Len Dawson, Kansas City, AFL | 21 |
| 1964 | Babe Parilli, Boston, AFL | 31 |
| | Frank Ryan, Cleveland, NFL | 25 |
| 1963 | Y.A. Tittle, N.Y. Giants, NFL | 36 |
| | Len Dawson, Kansas City, AFL | 26 |
| 1962 | Y.A. Tittle, N.Y. Giants, NFL | 33 |
| | Len Dawson, Dallas, AFL | 29 |
| 1961 | George Blanda, Houston, AFL | 36 |
| | Sonny Jurgensen, Philadelphia, NFL | 32 |
| 1960 | Al Dorow, N.Y. Titans, AFL | 26 |
| | Johnny Unitas, Baltimore, NFL | 25 |
| 1959 | Johnny Unitas, Baltimore | 32 |
| 1958 | Johnny Unitas, Baltimore | 19 |
| 1957 | Johnny Unitas, Baltimore | 24 |
| 1956 | Tobin Rote, Green Bay | 18 |
| 1955 | Tobin Rote, Green Bay | 17 |
| | Y.A. Tittle, San Francisco | 17 |
| 1954 | Adrian Burk, Philadelphia | 23 |
| 1953 | Robert Thomason, Philadelphia | 21 |
| 1952 | Jim Finks, Pittsburgh | 20 |
| | Otto Graham, Cleveland | 20 |
| 1951 | Bobby Layne, Detroit | 26 |
| 1950 | George Ratterman, N.Y. Yanks | 22 |
| 1949 | Johnny Lujack, Chi. Bears | 23 |
| 1948 | Tommy Thompson, Philadelphia | 25 |
| 1947 | Sammy Baugh, Washington | 25 |
| 1946 | Sid Luckman, Chi. Bears | 17 |
| | Bob Waterfield, Los Angeles | 17 |
| 1945 | Sid Luckman, Chi. Bears | 14 |
| | *Bob Waterfield, Cleveland | 14 |
| 1944 | Frank Filchock, Washington | 13 |
| 1943 | Sid Luckman, Chi. Bears | 28 |
| 1942 | Cecil Isbell, Green Bay | 24 |
| 1941 | Cecil Isbell, Green Bay | 15 |
| 1940 | Sammy Baugh, Washington | 12 |
| 1939 | Frank Filchock, Washington | 11 |
| 1938 | Bob Monnett, Green Bay | 9 |
| 1937 | Bernie Masterson, Chi. Bears | 9 |
| 1936 | Arnie Herber, Green Bay | 11 |
| 1935 | Ed Danowski, N.Y. Giants | 10 |
| 1934 | Arnie Herber, Green Bay | 8 |
| 1933 | *Harry Newman, N.Y. Giants | 11 |
| 1932 | Arnie Herber, Green Bay | 9 |

*First season of professional football.*

## ANNUAL PASS RECEIVING LEADERS

| Year | Player, Team | No. | Yards | Avg. | TD |
|---|---|---|---|---|---|
| 1993 | Sterling Sharpe, Green Bay, NFC | 112 | 1,274 | 11.4 | 11 |
| | Reggie Langhorne, Indianapolis, AFC | 85 | 1,038 | 12.2 | 3 |

| | | | | | |
|---|---|---|---|---|---|
| 1992 | Sterling Sharpe, Green Bay, NFC | 108 | 1,461 | 13.5 | 13 |
| | Haywood Jeffires, Houston, AFC | 90 | 913 | 10.1 | 9 |
| 1991 | Haywood Jeffires, Houston, AFC | 100 | 1,181 | 11.8 | 7 |
| | Michael Irvin, Dallas, NFC | 93 | 1,523 | 16.4 | 8 |
| 1990 | Jerry Rice, San Francisco, NFC | 100 | 1,502 | 15.0 | 13 |
| | Haywood Jeffires, Houston, AFC | 74 | 1,048 | 14.2 | 8 |
| | Drew Hill, Houston, AFC | 74 | 1,019 | 13.8 | 5 |
| 1989 | Sterling Sharpe, Green Bay, NFC | 90 | 1,423 | 15.8 | 12 |
| | Andre Reed, Buffalo, AFC | 88 | 1,312 | 14.9 | 9 |
| 1988 | Al Toon, N.Y. Jets, AFC | 93 | 1,067 | 11.5 | 5 |
| | Henry Ellard, L.A. Rams, NFC | 86 | 1,414 | 16.4 | 10 |
| 1987 | J.T. Smith, St. Louis, NFC | 91 | 1,117 | 12.3 | 8 |
| | Al Toon, N.Y. Jets, AFC | 68 | 976 | 14.4 | 5 |
| 1986 | Todd Christensen, L.A. Raiders, AFC | 95 | 1,153 | 12.1 | 8 |
| | Jerry Rice, San Francisco, NFC | 86 | 1,570 | 18.3 | 15 |
| 1985 | Roger Craig, San Francisco, NFC | 92 | 1,016 | 11.0 | 6 |
| | Lionel James, San Diego, AFC | 86 | 1,027 | 11.9 | 6 |
| 1984 | Art Monk, Washington, NFC | 106 | 1,372 | 12.9 | 7 |
| | Ozzie Newsome, Cleveland, AFC | 89 | 1,001 | 11.2 | 5 |
| 1983 | Todd Christensen, L.A. Raiders, AFC | 92 | 1,247 | 13.6 | 12 |
| | Roy Green, St. Louis, NFC | 78 | 1,227 | 15.7 | 14 |
| | Charlie Brown, Washington, NFC | 78 | 1,225 | 15.7 | 8 |
| | Earnest Gray, N.Y. Giants, NFC | 78 | 1,139 | 14.6 | 5 |
| 1982 | Dwight Clark, San Francisco, NFC | 60 | 913 | 15.2 | 5 |
| | Kellen Winslow, San Diego, AFC | 54 | 721 | 13.4 | 6 |
| 1981 | Kellen Winslow, San Diego, AFC | 88 | 1,075 | 12.2 | 10 |
| | Dwight Clark, San Francisco, NFC | 85 | 1,105 | 13.0 | 4 |
| 1980 | Kellen Winslow, San Diego, AFC | 89 | 1,290 | 14.5 | 9 |
| | *Earl Cooper, San Francisco, NFC | 83 | 567 | 6.8 | 4 |
| 1979 | Joe Washington, Baltimore, AFC | 82 | 750 | 9.1 | 3 |
| | Ahmad Rashad, Minnesota, NFC | 80 | 1,156 | 14.5 | 9 |
| 1978 | Rickey Young, Minnesota, NFC | 88 | 704 | 8.0 | 5 |
| | Steve Largent, Seattle, AFC | 71 | 1,168 | 16.5 | 8 |
| 1977 | Lydell Mitchell, Baltimore, AFC | 71 | 620 | 8.7 | 4 |
| | Ahmad Rashad, Minnesota, NFC | 51 | 681 | 13.4 | 2 |
| 1976 | MacArthur Lane, Kansas City, AFC | 66 | 686 | 10.4 | 1 |
| | Drew Pearson, Dallas, NFC | 58 | 806 | 13.9 | 6 |
| 1975 | Chuck Foreman, Minnesota, NFC | 73 | 691 | 9.5 | 9 |
| | Reggie Rucker, Cleveland, AFC | 60 | 770 | 12.8 | 3 |
| | Lydell Mitchell, Baltimore, AFC | 60 | 544 | 9.1 | 4 |
| 1974 | Lydell Mitchell, Baltimore, AFC | 72 | 544 | 7.6 | 2 |
| | Charles Young, Philadelphia, NFC | 63 | 696 | 11.0 | 3 |
| 1973 | Harold Carmichael, Philadelphia, NFC | 67 | 1,116 | 16.7 | 9 |
| | Fred Willis, Houston, AFC | 57 | 371 | 6.5 | 1 |
| 1972 | Harold Jackson, Philadelphia, NFC | 62 | 1,048 | 16.9 | 4 |
| | Fred Biletnikoff, Oakland, AFC | 58 | 802 | 13.8 | 7 |
| 1971 | Fred Biletnikoff, Oakland, AFC | 61 | 929 | 15.2 | 9 |
| | Bob Tucker, N.Y. Giants, NFC | 59 | 791 | 13.4 | 4 |
| 1970 | Dick Gordon, Chicago, NFC | 71 | 1,026 | 14.5 | 13 |
| | Marlin Briscoe, Buffalo, AFC | 57 | 1,036 | 18.2 | 8 |
| 1969 | Dan Abramowicz, New Orleans, NFL | 73 | 1,015 | 13.9 | 7 |
| | Lance Alworth, San Diego, AFL | 64 | 1,003 | 15.7 | 4 |
| 1968 | Clifton McNeil, San Francisco, NFL | 71 | 994 | 14.0 | 7 |
| | Lance Alworth, San Diego, AFL | 68 | 1,312 | 19.3 | 10 |
| 1967 | George Sauer, N.Y. Jets, AFL | 75 | 1,189 | 15.9 | 6 |
| | Charley Taylor, Washington, NFL | 70 | 990 | 14.1 | 9 |
| 1966 | Lance Alworth, San Diego, AFL | 73 | 1,383 | 18.9 | 13 |
| | Charley Taylor, Washington, NFL | 72 | 1,119 | 15.5 | 12 |
| 1965 | Lionel Taylor, Denver, AFL | 85 | 1,131 | 13.3 | 6 |
| | Dave Parks, San Francisco, NFL | 80 | 1,344 | 16.8 | 12 |
| 1964 | Charley Hennigan, Houston, AFL | 101 | 1,546 | 15.3 | 8 |
| | Johnny Morris, Chicago, NFL | 93 | 1,200 | 12.9 | 10 |
| 1963 | Lionel Taylor, Denver, AFL | 78 | 1,101 | 14.1 | 10 |
| | Bobby Joe Conrad, St. Louis, NFL | 73 | 967 | 13.2 | 10 |
| 1962 | Lionel Taylor, Denver, AFL | 77 | 908 | 11.8 | 4 |
| | Bobby Mitchell, Washington, NFL | 72 | 1,384 | 19.2 | 11 |
| 1961 | Lionel Taylor, Denver, AFL | 100 | 1,176 | 11.8 | 4 |
| | Jim (Red) Phillips, Los Angeles, NFL | 78 | 1,092 | 14.0 | 5 |
| 1960 | Lionel Taylor, Denver, AFL | 92 | 1,235 | 13.4 | 12 |
| | Raymond Berry, Baltimore, NFL | 74 | 1,298 | 17.5 | 10 |
| 1959 | Raymond Berry, Baltimore | 66 | 959 | 14.5 | 14 |
| 1958 | Raymond Berry, Baltimore | 56 | 794 | 14.2 | 9 |
| | Pete Retzlaff, Philadelphia | 56 | 766 | 13.7 | 2 |
| 1957 | Billy Wilson, San Francisco | 52 | 757 | 14.6 | 6 |
| 1956 | Billy Wilson, San Francisco | 60 | 889 | 14.8 | 5 |
| 1955 | Pete Pihos, Philadelphia | 62 | 864 | 13.9 | 7 |
| 1954 | Pete Pihos, Philadelphia | 60 | 872 | 14.5 | 10 |
| | Billy Wilson, San Francisco | 60 | 830 | 13.8 | 5 |
| 1953 | Pete Pihos, Philadelphia | 63 | 1,049 | 16.7 | 10 |
| 1952 | Mac Speedie, Cleveland | 62 | 911 | 14.7 | 5 |
| 1951 | Elroy (Crazylegs) Hirsch, Los Angeles | 66 | 1,495 | 22.7 | 17 |
| 1950 | Tom Fears, Los Angeles | 84 | 1,116 | 13.3 | 7 |
| 1949 | Tom Fears, Los Angeles | 77 | 1,013 | 13.2 | 9 |
| 1948 | *Tom Fears, Los Angeles | 51 | 698 | 13.7 | 4 |
| 1947 | Jim Keane, Chi. Bears | 64 | 910 | 14.2 | 10 |
| 1946 | Jim Benton, Los Angeles | 63 | 981 | 15.6 | 6 |
| 1945 | Don Hutson, Green Bay | 47 | 834 | 17.7 | 9 |
| 1944 | Don Hutson, Green Bay | 58 | 866 | 14.9 | 9 |
| 1943 | Don Hutson, Green Bay | 47 | 776 | 16.5 | 11 |
| 1942 | Don Hutson, Green Bay | 74 | 1,211 | 16.4 | 17 |
| 1941 | Don Hutson, Green Bay | 58 | 738 | 12.7 | 10 |
| 1940 | *Don Looney, Philadelphia | 58 | 707 | 12.2 | 4 |
| 1939 | Don Hutson, Green Bay | 34 | 846 | 24.9 | 6 |
| 1938 | Gaynell Tinsley, Chi. Cardinals | 41 | 516 | 12.6 | 1 |
| 1937 | Don Hutson, Green Bay | 41 | 552 | 13.5 | 7 |
| 1936 | Don Hutson, Green Bay | 34 | 536 | 15.8 | 8 |
| 1935 | *Tod Goodwin, N.Y. Giants | 26 | 432 | 16.6 | 4 |
| 1934 | Joe Carter, Philadelphia | 16 | 238 | 14.9 | 4 |
| | Morris (Red) Badgro, N.Y. Giants | 16 | 206 | 12.9 | 1 |
| 1933 | John (Shipwreck) Kelly, Brooklyn | 22 | 246 | 11.2 | 3 |
| 1932 | Ray Flaherty, N.Y. Giants | 21 | 350 | 16.7 | 3 |

*First season of professional football.*

## ANNUAL PASS RECEIVING LEADERS (YARDS)

| Year | Player, Team | No. | Yards | Avg. | TD |
|---|---|---|---|---|---|
| 1993 | Jerry Rice, San Francisco, NFC | 98 | 1,503 | 15.3 | 15 |
| | Tim Brown, L.A. Raiders, AFC | 80 | 1,180 | 14.8 | 7 |
| 1992 | Sterling Sharpe, Green Bay, NFC | 108 | 1,461 | 13.5 | 13 |
| | Anthony Miller, San Diego, AFC | 72 | 1,060 | 14.7 | 7 |
| 1991 | Michael Irvin, Dallas, NFC | 93 | 1,523 | 16.4 | 8 |
| | Haywood Jeffires, Houston, AFC | 100 | 1,181 | 11.8 | 7 |
| 1990 | Jerry Rice, San Francisco, NFC | 100 | 1,502 | 15.0 | 13 |
| | Haywood Jeffires, Houston, AFC | 74 | 1,048 | 14.2 | 8 |
| 1989 | Jerry Rice, San Francisco, NFC | 82 | 1,483 | 18.1 | 17 |
| | Andre Reed, Buffalo, AFC | 88 | 1,312 | 14.9 | 9 |
| 1988 | Henry Ellard, L.A. Rams, NFC | 86 | 1,414 | 16.4 | 10 |
| | Eddie Brown, Cincinnati, AFC | 53 | 1,273 | 24.0 | 9 |
| 1987 | J.T. Smith, St. Louis, NFC | 91 | 1,117 | 12.3 | 8 |
| | Carlos Carson, Kansas City, AFC | 55 | 1,044 | 19.0 | 7 |
| 1986 | Jerry Rice, San Francisco, NFC | 86 | 1,570 | 18.3 | 15 |
| | Stanley Morgan, New England, AFC | 84 | 1,491 | 17.8 | 10 |
| 1985 | Steve Largent, Seattle, AFC | 79 | 1,287 | 16.3 | 6 |
| | Mike Quick, Philadelphia, NFC | 73 | 1,247 | 17.1 | 11 |
| 1984 | Roy Green, St. Louis, NFC | 78 | 1,555 | 19.9 | 12 |
| | John Stallworth, Pittsburgh, AFC | 80 | 1,395 | 17.4 | 11 |
| 1983 | Mike Quick, Philadelphia, NFC | 69 | 1,409 | 20.4 | 13 |
| | Carlos Carson, Kansas City, AFC | 80 | 1,351 | 16.9 | 7 |
| 1982 | Wes Chandler, San Diego, AFC | 49 | 1,032 | 21.1 | 9 |
| | Dwight Clark, San Francisco, NFC | 60 | 913 | 15.2 | 5 |
| 1981 | Alfred Jenkins, Atlanta, NFC | 70 | 1,358 | 19.4 | 13 |
| | Frank Lewis, Buffalo, AFC | 70 | 1,244 | 17.8 | 4 |
| | Steve Watson, Denver, AFC | 60 | 1,244 | 20.7 | 13 |
| 1980 | John Jefferson, San Diego, AFC | 82 | 1,340 | 16.3 | 13 |
| | James Lofton, Green Bay, NFC | 71 | 1,226 | 17.3 | 4 |
| 1979 | Steve Largent, Seattle, AFC | 66 | 1,237 | 18.7 | 9 |
| | Ahmad Rashad, Minnesota, NFC | 80 | 1,156 | 14.5 | 9 |
| 1978 | Wesley Walker, N.Y. Jets, AFC | 48 | 1,169 | 24.4 | 8 |
| | Harold Carmichael, Philadelphia, NFC | 55 | 1,072 | 19.5 | 8 |
| 1977 | Drew Pearson, Dallas, NFC | 48 | 870 | 18.1 | 2 |
| | Ken Burrough, Houston, AFC | 43 | 816 | 19.0 | 8 |
| 1976 | Roger Carr, Baltimore, AFC | 43 | 1,112 | 25.9 | 11 |
| | *Sammy White, Minnesota, NFC | 51 | 906 | 17.8 | 10 |
| 1975 | Ken Burrough, Houston, AFC | 53 | 1,063 | 20.1 | 8 |
| | Mel Gray, St. Louis, NFC | 48 | 926 | 19.3 | 11 |
| 1974 | Cliff Branch, Oakland, AFC | 60 | 1,092 | 18.2 | 13 |
| | Drew Pearson, Dallas, NFC | 62 | 1,087 | 17.5 | 2 |
| 1973 | Harold Carmichael, Philadelphia, NFC | 67 | 1,116 | 16.7 | 9 |
| | *Isaac Curtis, Cincinnati, AFC | 45 | 843 | 18.7 | 9 |
| 1972 | Harold Jackson, Philadelphia, NFC | 62 | 1,048 | 16.9 | 4 |
| | Rich Caster, N.Y. Jets, AFC | 39 | 833 | 21.4 | 10 |
| 1971 | Otis Taylor, Kansas City, AFC | 57 | 1,110 | 19.5 | 7 |
| | Gene Washington, San Francisco, NFC | 46 | 884 | 19.2 | 4 |
| 1970 | Gene Washington, San Francisco, NFC | 53 | 1,100 | 20.8 | 12 |
| | Marlin Briscoe, Buffalo, AFC | 57 | 1,036 | 18.2 | 8 |
| 1969 | Warren Wells, Oakland, AFL | 47 | 1,260 | 26.8 | 14 |
| | Harold Jackson, Philadelphia, NFL | 65 | 1,116 | 17.2 | 9 |
| 1968 | Lance Alworth, San Diego, AFL | 68 | 1,312 | 19.3 | 10 |
| | Roy Jefferson, Pittsburgh, NFL | 58 | 1,074 | 18.5 | 11 |
| 1967 | Don Maynard, N.Y. Jets, AFL | 71 | 1,434 | 20.3 | 10 |
| | Ben Hawkins, Philadelphia, NFL | 59 | 1,265 | 21.4 | 10 |
| 1966 | Lance Alworth, San Diego, AFL | 73 | 1,383 | 18.9 | 13 |
| | Pat Studstill, Detroit, NFL | 67 | 1,266 | 18.9 | 5 |
| 1965 | Lance Alworth, San Diego, AFL | 69 | 1,602 | 23.2 | 14 |
| | Dave Parks, San Francisco, NFL | 80 | 1,344 | 16.8 | 12 |
| 1964 | Charley Hennigan, Houston, AFL | 101 | 1,546 | 15.3 | 8 |
| | Johnny Morris, Chicago, NFL | 93 | 1,200 | 12.9 | 10 |

## YEARLY STATISTICAL LEADERS

| | | | | | |
|---|---|---|---|---|---|
| 1963 | Bobby Mitchell, Washington, NFL | 69 | 1,436 | 20.8 | 7 |
| | Art Powell, Oakland, AFL | 73 | 1,304 | 17.8 | 16 |
| 1962 | Bobby Mitchel, Washington, NFL | 72 | 1,384 | 19.2 | 11 |
| | Art Powell, N.Y. Titans, AFL | 64 | 1,130 | 17.6 | 8 |
| 1961 | Charley Hennigan, Houston, AFL | 82 | 1,746 | 21.3 | 12 |
| | Tommy McDonald, Philadelphia, NFL | 64 | 1,144 | 17.9 | 13 |
| 1960 | *Bill Groman, Houston, AFL | 72 | 1,473 | 20.5 | 12 |
| | Raymond Berry, Baltimore, NFL | 74 | 1,298 | 17.5 | 10 |
| 1959 | Raymond Berry, Baltimore | 66 | 959 | 14.5 | 14 |
| 1958 | Del Shofner, Los Angeles | 51 | 1,097 | 21.5 | 8 |
| 1957 | Raymond Berry, Baltimore | 47 | 800 | 17.0 | 6 |
| 1956 | Billy Howton, Green Bay | 55 | 1,188 | 21.6 | 12 |
| 1955 | Pete Pihos, Philadelphia | 62 | 864 | 13.9 | 7 |
| 1954 | Bob Boyd, Los Angeles | 53 | 1,212 | 22.9 | 6 |
| 1953 | Pete Pihos, Philadelphia | 63 | 1,049 | 16.7 | 10 |
| 1952 | *Bill Howton, Green Bay | 53 | 1,231 | 23.2 | 13 |
| 1951 | Elroy (Crazylegs) Hirsch, Los Angeles | 66 | 1,495 | 22.7 | 17 |
| 1950 | Tom Fears, Los Angeles | 84 | 1,116 | 13.3 | 7 |
| 1949 | Bob Mann, Detroit | 66 | 1,014 | 15.4 | 4 |
| 1948 | Mal Kutner, Chi. Cardinals | 41 | 943 | 23.0 | 14 |
| 1947 | Mal Kutner, Chi. Cardinals | 43 | 944 | 21.9 | 7 |
| 1946 | Jim Benton, Los Angeles | 63 | 981 | 15.5 | 6 |
| 1945 | Jim Benton, Cleveland | 45 | 1,067 | 23.7 | 8 |
| 1944 | Don Hutson, Green Bay | 58 | 866 | 14.6 | 9 |
| 1943 | Don Hutson, Green Bay | 47 | 776 | 16.5 | 11 |
| 1942 | Don Hutson, Green Bay | 74 | 1,211 | 16.4 | 17 |
| 1941 | Don Hutson, Green Bay | 58 | 738 | 12.7 | 10 |
| 1940 | *Don Looney, Philadelphia | 58 | 707 | 12.2 | 4 |
| 1939 | Don Hutson, Green Bay | 34 | 846 | 24.9 | 6 |
| 1938 | Don Hutson, Green Bay | 32 | 548 | 17.1 | 9 |
| 1937 | *Gaynell Tinsley, Chi. Cardinals | 36 | 675 | 18.8 | 5 |
| 1936 | Don Hutson, Green Bay | 34 | 526 | 15.5 | 8 |
| 1935 | Charley Malone, Boston | 22 | 433 | 19.7 | 2 |
| 1934 | Harry Ebding, Detroit | 9 | 257 | 28.6 | 2 |
| 1933 | *Paul Moss, Pittsburgh | 18 | 383 | 21.3 | 2 |
| 1932 | Johnny Blood (McNally), Green Bay | 19 | 326 | 17.2 | 3 |

**First season of professional football.*

### ANNUAL INTERCEPTION LEADERS

| Year | Player, Team | No. | Yards | TD |
|---|---|---|---|---|
| 1993 | Eugene Robinson, Seattle, AFC | 9 | 80 | 0 |
| | Nate Odomes, Buffalo, AFC | 9 | 65 | 0 |
| | Deion Sanders, Atlanta, NFC | 7 | 91 | 0 |
| 1992 | Henry Jones, Buffalo, AFC | 8 | 263 | 2 |
| | Audray McMillan, Minnesota, NFC | 8 | 157 | 2 |
| 1991 | Ronnie Lott, L.A. Raiders, AFC | 8 | 52 | 0 |
| | Ray Crockett, Detroit, NFC | 6 | 141 | 1 |
| | Deion Sanders, Atlanta, AFC | 6 | 119 | 1 |
| | *Aeneas Williams, Phoenix, NFC | 6 | 60 | 0 |
| | Tim McKyer, Atlanta, NFC | 6 | 24 | 0 |
| 1990 | *Mark Carrier, Chicago, NFC | 10 | 39 | 0 |
| | Richard Johnson, Houston, AFC | 8 | 100 | 1 |
| 1989 | Felix Wright, Cleveland, AFC | 9 | 91 | 1 |
| | Eric Allen, Philadelphia, NFC | 8 | 38 | 0 |
| 1988 | Scott Case, Atlanta, NFC | 10 | 47 | 0 |
| | Erik McMillan, N.Y. Jets, AFC | 8 | 168 | 2 |
| 1987 | Barry Wilburn, Washington, NFC | 9 | 135 | 1 |
| | Mike Prior, Indianapolis, AFC | 6 | 57 | 0 |
| | Mark Kelso, Buffalo, AFC | 6 | 25 | 0 |
| | Keith Bostic, Houston, AFC | 6 | -14 | 0 |
| 1986 | Ronnie Lott, San Francisco, NFC | 10 | 134 | 1 |
| | Deron Cherry, Kansas City, AFC | 9 | 150 | 0 |
| 1985 | Everson Walls, Dallas, NFC | 9 | 31 | 0 |
| | Albert Lewis, Kansas City, AFC | 8 | 59 | 0 |
| | Eugene Daniel, Indianapolis, AFC | 8 | 53 | 0 |
| 1984 | Ken Easley, Seattle, AFC | 10 | 126 | 2 |
| | *Tom Flynn, Green Bay, NFC | 9 | 106 | 0 |
| 1983 | Mark Murphy, Washington, NFC | 9 | 127 | 0 |
| | Ken Riley, Cincinnati, AFC | 8 | 89 | 2 |
| | Vann McElroy, L.A. Raiders, AFC | 8 | 68 | 0 |
| 1982 | Everson Walls, Dallas, NFC | 7 | 61 | 0 |
| | Ken Riley, Cincinnati, AFC | 5 | 88 | 1 |
| | Bobby Jackson, N.Y Jets, AFC | 5 | 84 | 1 |
| | Dwayne Woodruff, Pittsburgh, AFC | 5 | 53 | 0 |
| | Donnie Shell, Pittsburgh, AFC | 5 | 27 | 0 |
| 1981 | *Everson Walls, Dallas, NFC | 11 | 133 | 0 |
| | John Harris, Seattle, AFC | 10 | 155 | 2 |
| 1980 | Lester Hayes, Oakland, AFC | 13 | 273 | 1 |
| | Nolan Cromwell, Los Angeles, NFC | 8 | 140 | 1 |
| 1979 | Mike Reinfeldt, Houston, AFC | 12 | 205 | 0 |
| | Lemar Parrish, Washington, NFC | 9 | 65 | 0 |
| 1978 | Thom Darden, Cleveland, AFC | 10 | 200 | 0 |
| | Ken Stone, St. Louis, NFC | 9 | 139 | 0 |
| | Willie Buchanon, Green Bay, NFC | 9 | 93 | 1 |
| 1977 | Lyle Blackwood, Baltimore, AFC | 10 | 163 | 0 |
| | Rolland Lawrence, Atlanta, NFC | 7 | 138 | 0 |
| 1976 | Monte Jackson, Los Angeles, NFC | 10 | 173 | 3 |
| | Ken Riley, Cincinnati, AFC | 9 | 141 | 1 |
| 1975 | Mel Blount, Pittsburgh, AFC | 11 | 121 | 0 |
| | Paul Krause, Minnesota, NFC | 10 | 201 | 0 |
| 1974 | Emmitt Thomas, Kansas City, AFC | 12 | 214 | 2 |
| | Ray Brown, Atlanta, NFC | 8 | 164 | 1 |
| 1973 | Dick Anderson, Miami, AFC | 8 | 163 | 2 |
| | Mike Wagner, Pittsburgh, AFC | 8 | 134 | 0 |
| | Bobby Bryant, Minnesota, NFC | 7 | 105 | 1 |
| 1972 | Bill Bradley, Philadelphia, NFC | 9 | 73 | 0 |
| | Mike Sensibaugh, Kansas City, AFC | 8 | 65 | 0 |
| 1971 | Bill Bradley, Philadelphia, NFC | 11 | 248 | 0 |
| | Ken Houston, Houston, AFC | 9 | 220 | 4 |
| 1970 | Johnny Robinson, Kansas City, AFC | 10 | 155 | 0 |
| | Dick LeBeau, Detroit, NFC | 9 | 96 | 0 |
| 1969 | Mel Renfro, Dallas, NFL | 10 | 118 | 0 |
| | Emmitt Thomas, Kansas City, AFL | 9 | 146 | 1 |
| 1968 | Dave Grayson, Oakland, AFL | 10 | 195 | 1 |
| | Willie Williams, N.Y. Giants, NFL | 10 | 103 | 0 |
| 1967 | Miller Farr, Houston, AFL | 10 | 264 | 3 |
| | *Lem Barney, Detroit, NFL | 10 | 232 | 3 |
| | Tom Janik, Buffalo, AFL | 10 | 222 | 2 |
| | Dave Whitsell, New Orleans, NFL | 10 | 178 | 2 |
| | Dick Westmoreland, Miami, AFL | 10 | 127 | 1 |
| 1966 | Larry Wilson, St. Louis, NFL | 10 | 180 | 2 |
| | Johnny Robinson, Kansas City, AFL | 10 | 136 | 1 |
| | Bobby Hunt, Kansas City, AFL | 10 | 113 | 0 |
| 1965 | W.K. Hicks, Houston, AFL | 9 | 156 | 0 |
| | Bobby Boyd, Baltimore, NFL | 9 | 78 | 1 |
| 1964 | Dainard Paulson, N.Y. Jets, AFL | 12 | 157 | 1 |
| | *Paul Krause, Washington, NFL | 12 | 140 | 1 |
| 1963 | Fred Glick, Houston, AFL | 12 | 180 | 1 |
| | Dick Lynch, N.Y. Giants, NFL | 9 | 251 | 3 |
| | Roosevelt Taylor, Chicago, NFL | 9 | 172 | 1 |
| 1962 | Lee Riley, N.Y. Titans, AFL | 11 | 122 | 0 |
| | Willie Wood, Green Bay, NFL | 9 | 132 | 0 |
| 1961 | Billy Atkins, Buffalo, AFL | 10 | 158 | 0 |
| | Dick Lynch, N.Y. Giants, NFL | 9 | 60 | 0 |
| 1960 | *Austin (Goose) Gonsoulin, Denver, AFL | 11 | 98 | 0 |
| | Dave Baker, San Francisco, NFL | 10 | 96 | 0 |
| | Jerry Norton, St. Louis, NFL | 10 | 96 | 0 |
| 1959 | Dean Derby, Pittsburgh | 7 | 127 | 0 |
| | Milt Davis, Baltimore | 7 | 119 | 1 |
| | Don Shinnick, Baltimore | 7 | 70 | 0 |
| 1958 | Jim Patton, N.Y. Giants | 11 | 183 | 0 |
| 1957 | Milt Davis, Baltimore | 10 | 219 | 2 |
| | Jack Christiansen, Detroit | 10 | 137 | 1 |
| | Jack Butler, Pittsburgh | 10 | 85 | 0 |
| 1956 | Linden Crow, Chi. Cardinals | 11 | 170 | 0 |
| 1955 | Will Sherman, Los Angeles | 11 | 101 | 0 |
| 1954 | Dick (Night Train) Lane, Chi. Cardinals | 10 | 181 | 0 |
| 1953 | Jack Christiansen, Detroit | 12 | 238 | 1 |
| 1952 | *Dick (Night Train) Lane, Los Angeles | 14 | 298 | 2 |
| 1951 | Otto Schnellbacher, N.Y. Giants | 11 | 194 | 2 |
| 1950 | Orban (Spec) Sanders, N.Y. Yanks | 13 | 199 | 0 |
| 1949 | Bob Nussbaumer, Chi. Cardinals | 12 | 157 | 0 |
| 1948 | *Dan Sandifer, Washington | 13 | 258 | 2 |
| 1947 | Frank Reagan, N.Y. Giants | 10 | 203 | 0 |
| | Frank Seno, Boston | 10 | 100 | 0 |
| 1946 | Bill Dudley, Pittsburgh | 10 | 242 | 1 |
| 1945 | Roy Zimmerman, Philadelphia | 7 | 90 | 0 |
| 1944 | *Howard Livingston, N.Y. Giants | 9 | 172 | 1 |
| 1943 | Sammy Baugh, Washington | 11 | 112 | 0 |
| 1942 | Clyde (Bulldog) Turner, Chi. Bears | 8 | 96 | 1 |
| 1941 | Marshall Goldberg, Chi. Cardinals | 7 | 54 | 0 |
| | *Art Jones, Pittsburgh | 7 | 35 | 0 |
| 1940 | Clarence (Ace) Parker, Brooklyn | 6 | 146 | 1 |
| | Kent Ryan, Detroit | 6 | 65 | 0 |
| | Don Hutson, Green Bay | 6 | 24 | 0 |

**First season of professional football.*

### ANNUAL PUNTING LEADERS

| Year | Player, Team | No. | Avg. | Long |
|---|---|---|---|---|
| 1993 | Greg Montgomery, Houston, AFC | 54 | 45.6 | 77 |
| | Jim Arnold, Detroit, NFC | 72 | 44.5 | 68 |
| 1992 | Greg Montgomery, Houston, AFC | 53 | 46.9 | 66 |
| | Harry Newsome, Minnesota, NFC | 72 | 45.0 | 84 |
| 1991 | Reggie Roby, Miami, AFC | 54 | 45.7 | 64 |
| | Harry Newsome, Minnesota, AFC | 68 | 45.5 | 65 |
| 1990 | Mike Horan, Denver, AFC | 58 | 44.4 | 67 |

| | | | | |
|---|---|---|---|---|
| | Sean Landeta, N.Y. Giants, NFC | 75 | 44.1 | 67 |
| 1989 | Rich Camarillo, Phoenix, NFC | 76 | 43.4 | 58 |
| | Greg Montgomery, Hounton, AFC | 56 | 43.3 | 63 |
| 1988 | Harry Newsome, Pittsburgh, AFC | 65 | 45.4 | 62 |
| | Jim Arnold, Detroit, NFC | 97 | 42.4 | 69 |
| 1987 | Rick Donnelly, Atlanta, NFC | 61 | 44.0 | 62 |
| | Ralf Mojsiejenko, San Diego, AFC | 67 | 42.9 | 57 |
| 1986 | Rohn Stark, Indianapolis, AFC | 76 | 45.2 | 63 |
| | Sean Landeta, N.Y. Giants, NFC | 79 | 44.8 | 61 |
| 1985 | Rohn Stark, Indianapolis, AFC | 78 | 45.9 | 68 |
| | *Rick Donnelly, Atlanta, NFC | 59 | 43.6 | 68 |
| 1984 | Jim Arnold, Kansas City, AFC | 98 | 44.9 | 63 |
| | *Brian Hansen, New Orleans, NFC | 69 | 43.8 | 66 |
| 1983 | Rohn Stark, Baltimore, AFC | 91 | 45.3 | 68 |
| | Frank Garcia, Tampa Bay, NFC | 95 | 42.2 | 64 |
| 1982 | Luke Prestridge, Denver, AFC | 45 | 45.0 | 65 |
| | Carl Birdsong, St. Louis, NFC | 54 | 43.8 | 65 |
| 1981 | Pat McInally, Cincinnati, AFC | 72 | 45.4 | 62 |
| | Tom Skladany, Detroit, NFC | 64 | 43.5 | 74 |
| 1980 | Dave Jennings, N.Y. Giants, NFC | 94 | 44.8 | 63 |
| | Luke Prestridge, Denver, AFC | 70 | 43.9 | 57 |
| 1979 | *Bob Grupp, Kansas City, AFC | 89 | 43.6 | 74 |
| | Dave Jennings, N.Y. Giants, NFC | 104 | 42.7 | 72 |
| 1978 | Pat McInally, Cincinnati, AFC | 91 | 43.1 | 65 |
| | *Tom Skladany, Detroit, NFC | 86 | 42.5 | 63 |
| 1977 | Ray Guy, Oakland, AFC | 59 | 43.3 | 74 |
| | Tom Blanchard, New Orleans, NFC | 82 | 42.4 | 66 |
| 1976 | Marv Bateman, Buffalo, AFC | 86 | 42.8 | 78 |
| | John James, Atlanta, NFC | 101 | 42.1 | 67 |
| 1975 | Ray Guy, Oakland, AFC | 68 | 43.8 | 64 |
| | Herman Weaver, Detroit, NFC | 80 | 42.0 | 61 |
| 1974 | Ray Guy, Oakland, AFC | 74 | 42.2 | 66 |
| | Tom Blanchard, New Orleans, NFC | 88 | 42.1 | 71 |
| 1973 | Jerrel Wilson, Kansas City, AFC | 80 | 45.5 | 68 |
| | *Tom Wittum, San Francisco, NFC | 79 | 43.7 | 62 |
| 1972 | Jerrel Wilson, Kansas City, AFC | 66 | 44.8 | 69 |
| | Dave Chapple, Los Angeles, NFC | 53 | 44.2 | 70 |
| 1971 | Dave Lewis, Cincinnati, AFC | 72 | 44.8 | 56 |
| | Tom McNeill, Philadelphia, NFC | 73 | 42.0 | 64 |
| 1970 | Dave Lewis, Cincinnati, AFC | 79 | 46.2 | 63 |
| | *Julian Fagan, New Orleans, NFC | 77 | 42.5 | 64 |
| 1969 | David Lee, Baltimore, NFL | 57 | 45.3 | 66 |
| | Dennis Partee, San Diego, AFL | 71 | 44.6 | 62 |
| 1968 | Jerrel Wilson, Kansas City, AFL | 63 | 45.1 | 70 |
| | Billy Lothridge, Atlanta, NFL | 75 | 44.3 | 70 |
| 1967 | Bob Scarpitto, Denver, AFL | 105 | 44.9 | 73 |
| | Billy Lothridge, Atlanta, NFL | 87 | 43.7 | 62 |
| 1966 | Bob Scarpitto, Denver, AFL | 76 | 45.8 | 70 |
| | *David Lee, Baltimore, NFL | 49 | 45.6 | 64 |
| 1965 | Gary Collins, Cleveland, NFL | 65 | 46.7 | 71 |
| | Jerrel Wilson, Kansas City, AFL | 69 | 45.4 | 64 |
| 1964 | *Bobby Walden, Minnesota, NFL | 72 | 46.4 | 73 |
| | Jim Fraser, Denver, AFL | 73 | 44.2 | 67 |
| 1963 | Yale Lary, Detroit, NFL | 35 | 48.9 | 73 |
| | Jim Fraser, Denver, AFL | 81 | 44.4 | 66 |
| 1962 | Tommy Davis, San Francisco, NFL | 48 | 45.6 | 82 |
| | Jim Fraser, Denver, AFL | 55 | 43.6 | 75 |
| 1961 | Yale Lary, Detroit, NFL | 52 | 48.4 | 71 |
| | Billy Atkins, Buffalo, AFL | 85 | 44.5 | 70 |
| 1960 | Jerry Norton, St. Louis, NFL | 39 | 45.6 | 62 |
| | *Paul Maguire, L.A. Chargers, AFL | 43 | 40.5 | 61 |
| 1959 | Yale Lary, Detroit | 45 | 47.1 | 67 |
| 1958 | Sam Baker, Washington | 48 | 45.4 | 64 |
| 1957 | Don Chandler, N.Y. Giants | 60 | 44.6 | 61 |
| 1956 | Norm Van Brocklin, Los Angeles | 48 | 43.1 | 72 |
| 1955 | Norm Van Brocklin, Los Angeles | 60 | 44.6 | 61 |
| 1954 | Pat Brady, Pittsburgh | 66 | 43.2 | 72 |
| 1953 | Pat Brady, Pittsburgh | 80 | 46.9 | 64 |
| 1952 | Horace Gillom, Cleveland | 61 | 45.7 | 73 |
| 1951 | Horace Gillom, Cleveland | 73 | 45.5 | 66 |
| 1950 | *Fred (Curly) Morrison, Chi. Bears | 57 | 43.3 | 65 |
| 1949 | *Mike Boyda, N.Y. Bulldogs | 56 | 44.2 | 61 |
| 1948 | Joe Muha, Philadelphia | 57 | 47.3 | 82 |
| 1947 | Jack Jacobs, Green Bay | 57 | 43.5 | 74 |
| 1946 | Roy McKay, Green Bay | 64 | 42.7 | 64 |
| 1945 | Roy McKay, Green Bay | 44 | 41.2 | 73 |
| 1944 | Frank Sinkwich, Detroit | 45 | 41.0 | 73 |
| 1943 | Sammy Baugh, Washington | 50 | 45.9 | 81 |
| 1942 | Sammy Baugh, Washington | 37 | 48.2 | 74 |
| 1941 | Sammy Baugh, Washington | 30 | 48.7 | 75 |
| 1940 | Sammy Baugh, Washington | 35 | 51.4 | 85 |
| 1939 | *Parker Hall, Cleveland | 58 | 40.8 | 80 |

**First season of professional football.*

## ANNUAL PUNT RETURN LEADERS

| Year | Player, Team | No. | Yards | Avg. | Long | TD |
|---|---|---|---|---|---|---|
| 1993 | *Tyrone Hughes, New Orleans, NFC | 37 | 503 | 13.6 | 83 | 2 |
| | Eric Metcalf, Cleveland, AFC | 36 | 464 | 12.9 | 91 | 2 |
| 1992 | Johnny Bailey, Phoenix, NFC | 20 | 263 | 13.2 | 65 | 0 |
| | Rod Woodson, Pittsburgh, AFC | 32 | 364 | 11.4 | 80 | 1 |
| 1991 | Mel Gray, Detroit, NFC | 25 | 385 | 15.4 | 78 | 1 |
| | Rod Woodson, Pittsburgh, AFC | 28 | 320 | 11.4 | 40 | 0 |
| 1990 | Clarence Verdin, Indianapolis, AFC | 31 | 396 | 12.8 | 36 | 0 |
| | *Johnny Bailey, Chicago, NFC | 36 | 399 | 11.1 | 95 | 1 |
| 1989 | Walter Stanley, Detroit, NFC | 36 | 496 | 13.8 | 74 | 0 |
| | Clarence Verdin, Indianapolis, AFC | 23 | 296 | 12.9 | 49 | 1 |
| 1988 | John Taylor, San Francisco, NFC | 44 | 556 | 12.6 | 95 | 2 |
| | JoJo Townsell, N.Y. Jets, AFC | 35 | 409 | 11.7 | 59 | 1 |
| 1987 | Mel Gray, New Orleans, NFC | 24 | 352 | 14.7 | 80 | 0 |
| | Bobby Joe Edmonds, Seattle, AFC | 20 | 251 | 12.6 | 40 | 0 |
| 1986 | *Bobby Joe Edmonds, Seattle, AFC | 34 | 419 | 12.3 | 75 | 1 |
| | *Vai Sikahema, St. Louis, NFC | 43 | 522 | 12.1 | 71 | 2 |
| 1985 | Irving Fryar, New England, AFC | 37 | 520 | 14.1 | 85 | 2 |
| | Henry Ellard, L.A. Rams, NFC | 37 | 501 | 13.5 | 80 | 1 |
| 1984 | Mike Martin, Cincinnati, AFC | 24 | 376 | 15.7 | 55 | 0 |
| | Henry Ellard, L.A. Rams, NFC | 30 | 403 | 13.4 | 83 | 2 |
| 1983 | *Henry Ellard, L.A. Rams, NFC | 16 | 217 | 13.6 | 72 | 1 |
| | Kirk Springs, N.Y. Jets, AFC | 23 | 287 | 12.5 | 76 | 1 |
| 1982 | Rick Upchurch, Denver, AFC | 15 | 242 | 16.1 | 78 | 2 |
| | Billy Johnson, Atlanta, NFC | 24 | 273 | 11.4 | 71 | 0 |
| 1981 | LeRoy Irvin, Los Angeles, NFC | 46 | 615 | 13.4 | 84 | 3 |
| | *James Brooks, San Diego, AFC | 22 | 290 | 13.2 | 42 | 0 |
| 1980 | J.T. Smith, Kansas City, AFC | 40 | 581 | 14.5 | 75 | 2 |
| | *Kenny Johnson, Atlanta, NFC | 23 | 281 | 12.2 | 56 | 0 |
| 1979 | John Sciarra, Philadelphia, NFC | 16 | 182 | 11.4 | 38 | 0 |
| | *Tony Nathan, Miami, AFC | 28 | 306 | 10.9 | 86 | 1 |
| 1978 | Rick Upchurch, Denver, AFC | 36 | 493 | 13.7 | 75 | 1 |
| | Jackie Wallace, Los Angeles, NFC | 52 | 618 | 11.9 | 58 | 0 |
| 1977 | Billy Johnson, Houston, AFC | 35 | 539 | 15.4 | 87 | 2 |
| | Larry Marshall, Philadelphia, NFC | 46 | 489 | 10.6 | 48 | 0 |
| 1976 | Rick Upchurch, Denver, AFC | 39 | 536 | 13.7 | 92 | 4 |
| | Eddie Brown, Washington, NFC | 48 | 646 | 13.5 | 71 | 1 |
| 1975 | Billy Johnson, Houston, AFC | 40 | 612 | 15.3 | 83 | 3 |
| | Terry Metcalf, St. Louis, NFC | 23 | 285 | 12.4 | 69 | 1 |
| 1974 | Lemar Parrish, Cincinnati, AFC | 18 | 338 | 18.8 | 90 | 2 |
| | Dick Jauron, Detroit, NFC | 17 | 286 | 16.8 | 58 | 0 |
| 1973 | Bruce Taylor, San Francisco, NFC | 15 | 207 | 13.8 | 61 | 0 |
| | Ron Smith, San Diego, AFC | 27 | 352 | 13.0 | 84 | 2 |
| 1972 | Ken Ellis, Green Bay, NFC | 14 | 215 | 15.4 | 80 | 1 |
| | Chris Farasopoulos, N.Y. Jets, AFC | 17 | 179 | 10.5 | 65 | 1 |
| 1971 | Les (Speedy) Duncan, Washington, NFC | 22 | 233 | 10.6 | 33 | 0 |
| | Leroy Kelly, Cleveland, AFC | 30 | 292 | 9.7 | 74 | 0 |
| 1970 | Ed Podolak, Kansas City, AFC | 23 | 311 | 13.5 | 60 | 0 |
| | *Bruce Taylor, San Francisco, NFC | 43 | 516 | 12.0 | 76 | 0 |
| 1969 | Alvin Haymond, Los Angeles, NFL | 33 | 435 | 13.2 | 52 | 0 |
| | *Bill Thompson, Denver, AFL | 25 | 288 | 11.5 | 40 | 0 |
| 1968 | Bob Hayes, Dallas, NFL | 15 | 312 | 20.8 | 90 | 2 |
| | Noland Smith, Kansas City, AFL | 18 | 270 | 15.0 | 80 | 1 |
| 1967 | Floyd Little, Denver, AFL | 16 | 270 | 16.9 | 72 | 1 |
| | Ben Davis, Cleveland, NFL | 18 | 229 | 12.7 | 52 | 1 |
| 1966 | Les (Speedy) Duncan, San Diego, AFL | 18 | 238 | 13.2 | 81 | 1 |
| | Johnny Roland, St. Louis, NFL | 20 | 221 | 11.1 | 86 | 1 |
| 1965 | Leroy Kelly, Cleveland, NFL | 17 | 265 | 15.6 | 67 | 2 |
| | Les (Speedy) Duncan, San Diego, AFL | 30 | 464 | 15.5 | 66 | 2 |
| 1964 | Bobby Jancik, Houston, AFL | 12 | 220 | 18.3 | 82 | 1 |
| | Tommy Watkins, Detroit, NFL | 16 | 238 | 14.9 | 68 | 2 |
| 1963 | Dick James, Washington, NFL | 16 | 214 | 13.4 | 39 | 0 |
| | Claude (Hoot) Gibson, Oakland, AFL | 26 | 307 | 11.8 | 85 | 2 |
| 1962 | Dick Christy, N.Y. Titans, AFL | 15 | 250 | 16.7 | 73 | 2 |
| | Pat Studstill, Detroit, NFL | 29 | 457 | 15.8 | 44 | 0 |
| 1961 | Dick Christy, N.Y. Titans, AFL | 18 | 383 | 21.3 | 70 | 2 |
| | Willie Wood, Green Bay, NFL | 14 | 225 | 16.1 | 72 | 2 |
| 1960 | *Abner Haynes, Dall. Texans, AFL | 14 | 215 | 15.4 | 46 | 0 |
| | Abe Woodson, San Francisco, NFL | 13 | 174 | 13.4 | 48 | 0 |
| 1959 | Johnny Morris, Chi. Bears | 14 | 171 | 12.2 | 78 | 1 |
| 1958 | Jon Arnett, Los Angeles | 18 | 223 | 12.4 | 58 | 0 |
| 1957 | Bert Zagers, Washington | 14 | 217 | 15.5 | 76 | 2 |
| 1956 | Ken Konz, Cleveland | 13 | 187 | 14.4 | 65 | 1 |
| 1955 | Ollie Matson, Chi. Cardinals | 13 | 245 | 18.8 | 78 | 2 |
| 1954 | *Veryl Switzer, Green Bay | 24 | 306 | 12.8 | 93 | 1 |
| 1953 | Charley Trippi, Chi. Cardinals | 21 | 239 | 11.4 | 38 | 0 |
| 1952 | Jack Christiansen, Detroit | 15 | 322 | 21.5 | 79 | 2 |
| 1951 | Claude (Buddy) Young, N.Y. Yanks | 12 | 231 | 19.3 | 79 | 1 |
| 1950 | *Herb Rich, Baltimore | 12 | 276 | 23.0 | 86 | 1 |
| 1949 | Verda (Vitamin T) Smith, Los Angeles | 27 | 427 | 15.8 | 85 | 1 |
| 1948 | George McAfee, Chi. Bears | 30 | 417 | 13.9 | 60 | 1 |
| 1947 | *Walt Slater, Pittsburgh | 28 | 435 | 15.5 | 33 | 0 |

| | | | | | | |
|---|---|---|---|---|---|---|
| 1946 | Bill Dudley, Pittsburgh | 27 | 385 | 14.3 | 52 | 0 |
| 1945 | *Dave Ryan, Detroit | 15 | 220 | 14.7 | 56 | 0 |
| 1944 | *Steve Van Buren, Philadelphia | 15 | 230 | 15.3 | 55 | 1 |
| 1943 | Andy Farkas, Washington | 15 | 168 | 11.2 | 33 | 0 |
| 1942 | Merlyn Condit, Brooklyn | 21 | 210 | 10.0 | 23 | 0 |
| 1941 | Byron (Whizzer) White, Detroit | 19 | 262 | 13.8 | 64 | 0 |

**First season of professional football.*

## ANNUAL KICKOFF RETURN LEADERS

| Year | Player, Team | No. | Yards | Avg. | Long | TD |
|---|---|---|---|---|---|---|
| 1993 | Robert Brooks, Green Bay, NFC | 23 | 611 | 26.6 | 95 | 1 |
| | *Raghib Ismail, L.A. Raiders, AFC | 25 | 605 | 24.2 | 66 | 0 |
| 1992 | Jon Vaughn, New England, AFC | 20 | 564 | 28.2 | 100 | 1 |
| | Deion Sanders, Atlanta, NFC | 40 | 1,067 | 26.7 | 99 | 2 |
| 1991 | Mel Gray, Detroit, NFC | 36 | 929 | 25.8 | 71 | 0 |
| | Nate Lewis, San Diego, AFC | 23 | 578 | 25.1 | 95 | 1 |
| 1990 | Kevin Clark, Denver, AFC | 20 | 505 | 25.3 | 75 | 0 |
| | David Meggett, N.Y. Giants, NFC | 21 | 492 | 23.4 | 58 | 0 |
| 1989 | Rod Woodson, Pittsburgh, AFC | 36 | 982 | 27.3 | 84 | 1 |
| | Mel Gray, Detroit, NFC | 24 | 640 | 26.7 | 57 | 0 |
| 1988 | *Tim Brown, L.A. Raiders, AFC | 41 | 1,098 | 26.8 | 97 | 1 |
| | Donnie Elder, Tampa Bay, NFC | 34 | 772 | 22.7 | 51 | 0 |
| 1987 | Sylvester Stamps, Atlanta, NFC | 24 | 660 | 27.5 | 97 | 1 |
| | Paul Palmer, Kansas City, AFC | 38 | 923 | 24.3 | 95 | 2 |
| 1986 | Dennis Gentry, Chicago, NFC | 20 | 576 | 28.8 | 91 | 1 |
| | Lupe Sanchez, Pittsburgh, AFC | 25 | 591 | 23.6 | 64 | 0 |
| 1985 | Ron Brown, L.A. Rams, NFC | 28 | 918 | 32.8 | 98 | 3 |
| | Glen Young, Cleveland, AFC | 35 | 898 | 25.7 | 63 | 0 |
| 1984 | *Bobby Humphery, N.Y. Jets, AFC | 22 | 675 | 30.7 | 97 | 1 |
| | Barry Redden, L.A. Rams, NFC | 23 | 530 | 23.0 | 40 | 0 |
| 1983 | Fulton Walker, Miami, AFC | 36 | 962 | 26.7 | 78 | 0 |
| | Darrin Nelson, Minnesota, NFC | 18 | 445 | 24.7 | 50 | 0 |
| 1982 | *Mike Mosley, Buffalo, AFC | 18 | 487 | 27.1 | 66 | 0 |
| | Alvin Hall, Detroit, NFC | 16 | 426 | 26.6 | 96 | 1 |
| 1981 | Mike Nelms, Washington, NFC | 37 | 1,099 | 29.7 | 84 | 0 |
| | Carl Roaches, Houston, AFC | 28 | 769 | 27.5 | 96 | 1 |
| 1980 | Horace Ivory, New England, AFC | 36 | 992 | 27.6 | 98 | 1 |
| | Rich Mauti, New Orleans, NFC | 31 | 798 | 25.7 | 52 | 0 |
| 1979 | Larry Brunson, Oakland, AFC | 17 | 441 | 25.9 | 89 | 0 |
| | Jimmy Edwards, Minnesota, NFC | 44 | 1,103 | 25.1 | 83 | 0 |
| 1978 | Steve Odom, Green Bay, NFC | 25 | 677 | 27.1 | 95 | 1 |
| | *Keith Wright, Cleveland, AFC | 30 | 789 | 26.3 | 86 | 0 |
| 1977 | *Raymond Clayborn, New England, AFC | 28 | 869 | 31.0 | 101 | 3 |
| | *Wilbert Montgomery, Philadelphia, NFC | 23 | 619 | 26.9 | 99 | 1 |
| 1976 | *Duriel Harris, Miami, AFC | 17 | 559 | 32.9 | 69 | 0 |
| | Cullen Bryant, Los Angeles, NFC | 16 | 459 | 28.7 | 90 | 1 |
| 1975 | *Walter Payton, Chicago, NFC | 14 | 444 | 31.7 | 70 | 0 |
| | Harold Hart, Oakland, AFC | 17 | 518 | 30.5 | 102 | 1 |
| 1974 | Terry Metcalf, St. Louis, NFC | 20 | 623 | 31.2 | 94 | 1 |
| | Greg Pruitt, Cleveland, AFC | 22 | 606 | 27.5 | 88 | 1 |
| 1973 | Carl Garrett, Chicago, NFC | 16 | 486 | 30.4 | 67 | 0 |
| | *Wallace Francis, Buffalo, AFC | 23 | 687 | 29.9 | 101 | 2 |
| 1972 | Ron Smith, Chicago, NFC | 30 | 924 | 30.8 | 94 | 1 |
| | *Bruce Laird, Baltimore, AFC | 29 | 843 | 29.1 | 73 | 0 |
| 1971 | Travis Williams, Los Angeles, NFC | 25 | 743 | 29.7 | 105 | 1 |
| | Eugene (Mercury) Morris, Miami, AFC | 15 | 423 | 28.2 | 94 | 1 |
| 1970 | Jim Duncan, Baltimore, AFC | 20 | 707 | 35.4 | 99 | 1 |
| | Cecil Turner, Chicago, NFC | 23 | 752 | 32.7 | 96 | 4 |
| 1969 | Bobby Williams, Detroit, NFL | 17 | 563 | 33.1 | 96 | 1 |
| | *Bill Thompson, Denver, AFL | 18 | 513 | 28.5 | 63 | 0 |
| 1968 | Preston Pearson, Baltimore, NFL | 15 | 527 | 35.1 | 102 | 2 |
| | *George Atkinson, Oakland, AFL | 32 | 802 | 25.1 | 60 | 0 |
| 1967 | *Travis Williams, Green Bay, NFL | 18 | 739 | 41.1 | 104 | 4 |
| | *Zeke Moore, Houston, AFL | 14 | 405 | 28.9 | 92 | 1 |
| 1966 | Gale Sayers, Chicago, NFL | 23 | 718 | 31.2 | 93 | 2 |
| | *Goldie Sellers, Denver, AFL | 19 | 541 | 28.5 | 100 | 2 |
| 1965 | Tommy Watkins, Detroit, NFL | 17 | 584 | 34.4 | 94 | 0 |
| | Abner Haynes, Denver, AFL | 34 | 901 | 26.5 | 60 | 0 |
| 1964 | *Clarence Childs, N.Y. Giants, NFL | 34 | 987 | 29.0 | 100 | 1 |
| | Bo Roberson, Oakland, AFL | 36 | 975 | 27.1 | 59 | 0 |
| 1963 | Abe Woodson, San Francisco, NFL | 29 | 935 | 32.2 | 103 | 3 |
| | Bobby Jancik, Houston, AFL | 45 | 1,317 | 29.3 | 53 | 0 |
| 1962 | Abe Woodson, San Francisco, NFL | 37 | 1,157 | 31.3 | 79 | 0 |
| | *Bobby Jancik, Houston, AFL | 24 | 826 | 30.3 | 61 | 0 |
| 1961 | Dick Bass, Los Angeles, NFL | 23 | 698 | 30.3 | 64 | 0 |
| | *Dave Grayson, Dall. Texans, AFL | 16 | 453 | 28.3 | 73 | 0 |
| 1960 | *Tom Moore, Green Bay, NFL | 12 | 397 | 33.1 | 84 | 0 |
| | Ken Hall, Houston, AFL | 19 | 594 | 31.3 | 104 | 1 |
| 1959 | Abe Woodson, San Francisco | 13 | 382 | 29.4 | 105 | 1 |
| 1958 | Ollie Matson, Chi. Cardinals | 14 | 497 | 35.5 | 101 | 2 |
| 1957 | *Jon Arnett, Los Angeles | 18 | 504 | 28.0 | 98 | 1 |
| 1956 | *Tom Wilson, Los Angeles | 15 | 477 | 31.8 | 103 | 1 |
| 1955 | Al Carmichael, Green Bay | 14 | 418 | 29.9 | 100 | 1 |
| 1954 | Billy Reynolds, Cleveland | 14 | 413 | 29.5 | 51 | 0 |
| 1953 | Joe Arenas, San Francisco | 16 | 551 | 34.4 | 82 | 0 |
| 1952 | Lynn Chandnois, Pittsburgh | 17 | 599 | 35.2 | 93 | 2 |
| 1951 | Lynn Chandnois, Pittsburgh | 12 | 390 | 32.5 | 55 | 0 |
| 1950 | Verda (Vitamin T) Smith, Los Angeles | 22 | 742 | 33.7 | 97 | 3 |
| 1949 | *Don Doll, Detroit | 21 | 536 | 25.5 | 56 | 0 |
| 1948 | *Joe Scott, N.Y. Giants | 20 | 569 | 28.5 | 99 | 1 |
| 1947 | Eddie Saenz, Washington | 29 | 797 | 27.5 | 94 | 2 |
| 1946 | Abe Karnofsky, Boston | 21 | 599 | 28.5 | 97 | 1 |
| 1945 | Steve Van Buren, Philadelphia | 13 | 373 | 28.7 | 98 | 1 |
| 1944 | Bob Thurbon, Card.-Pitt. | 12 | 291 | 24.3 | 55 | 0 |
| 1943 | Ken Heineman, Brooklyn | 16 | 444 | 27.8 | 69 | 0 |
| 1942 | Marshall Goldberg, Chi. Cardinals | 15 | 393 | 26.2 | 95 | 1 |
| 1941 | Marshall Goldberg, Chi. Cardinals | 12 | 290 | 24.2 | 41 | 0 |

**First season of professional football.*

## ANNUAL LEADERS IN SACKS (SINCE 1982)

| Year | Player, Team | Sacks |
|---|---|---|
| 1993 | Neil Smith, K.C., AFC | 15 |
| | Renaldo Turnbull, N.O., NFC | 13 |
| | Reggie White, G.B., NFC | 13 |
| 1992 | Clyde Simmons, Phil., NFC | 19 |
| | Leslie O'Neal, S.D., AFC | 17 |
| 1991 | Pat Swilling, N.O., NFC | 17 |
| | William Fuller, Hou., AFC | 15 |
| 1990 | Derrick Thomas, K.C., AFC | 20 |
| | Charles Haley, S.F., NFC | 16 |
| 1989 | Chris Doleman, Minn., NFC | 21 |
| | Lee Williams, S.D., AFC | 14 |
| 1988 | Reggie White, Phil., NFC | 18 |
| | G. Townsend, Raiders, AFC | 11.5 |
| 1987 | Reggie White, Phil., NFC | 21 |
| | Andre Tippett, N.E., AFC | 12.5 |
| 1986 | Lawrence Taylor, N.Y.G., NFC | 20.5 |
| | Sean Jones, Raiders, AFC | 15.5 |
| 1985 | Richard Dent, Chi., NFC | 17 |
| | Andre Tippett, N.E., AFC | 16.5 |
| 1984 | Mark Gastineau, N.Y.J., AFC | 22 |
| | Richard Dent, Chi., NFC | 17.5 |
| 1983 | Mark Gastineau, N.Y.J., AFC | 19 |
| | Fred Dean, San Fran., NFC | 17.5 |
| 1982 | Doug Martin, Minn., NFC | 11.5 |
| | Jesse Baker, Hou., AFC | 7.5 |

## POINTS SCORED

| Year | Team | Points |
|---|---|---|
| 1993 | San Francisco, NFC | 473 |
| | Denver, AFC | 373 |
| 1992 | San Francisco, NFC | 431 |
| | Buffalo, AFC | 381 |
| 1991 | Washington, NFC | 485 |
| | Buffalo, AFC | 458 |
| 1990 | Buffalo, AFC | 428 |
| | Philadelphia, NFC | 396 |
| 1989 | San Francisco, NFC | 442 |
| | Buffalo, AFC | 409 |
| 1988 | Cincinnati, AFC | 448 |
| | L.A. Rams, NFC | 407 |
| 1987 | San Francisco, NFC | 459 |
| | Cleveland, AFC | 390 |
| 1986 | Miami, AFC | 430 |
| | Minnesota, NFC | 398 |
| 1985 | San Diego, AFC | 467 |
| | Chicago, NFC | 456 |
| 1984 | Miami, AFC | 513 |
| | San Francisco, NFC | 475 |
| 1983 | Washington, NFC | 541 |
| | L.A. Raiders, AFC | 442 |
| 1982 | San Diego, AFC | 288 |
| | Dallas, NFC | 226 |
| | Green Bay, NFC | 226 |
| 1981 | San Diego, AFC | 478 |
| | Atlanta, NFC | 426 |
| 1980 | Dallas, NFC | 454 |
| | New England, AFC | 441 |
| 1979 | Pittsburgh, AFC | 416 |
| | Dallas, NFC | 371 |
| 1978 | Dallas, NFC | 384 |
| | Miami, AFC | 372 |
| 1977 | Oakland, AFC | 351 |
| | Dallas, NFC | 345 |
| 1976 | Baltimore, AFC | 417 |
| | Los Angeles, NFC | 351 |
| 1975 | Buffalo, AFC | 420 |
| | Minnesota, NFC | 377 |
| 1974 | Oakland, AFC | 355 |
| | Washington, NFC | 320 |
| 1973 | Los Angeles, NFC | 388 |
| | Denver, AFC | 354 |
| 1972 | Miami, AFC | 385 |
| | San Francisco, NFC | 353 |
| 1971 | Dallas, NFC | 406 |
| | Oakland, AFC | 344 |
| 1970 | San Francisco, NFC | 352 |
| | Baltimore, AFC | 321 |
| 1969 | Minnesota, NFL | 379 |
| | Oakland, AFL | 377 |
| 1968 | Oakland, AFL | 453 |
| | Dallas, NFL | 431 |
| 1967 | Oakland, AFL | 468 |
| | Los Angeles, NFL | 398 |
| 1966 | Kansas City, AFL | 448 |
| | Dallas, NFL | 445 |
| 1965 | San Francisco, NFL | 421 |
| | San Diego, AFL | 340 |
| 1964 | Baltimore, NFL | 428 |
| | Buffalo, AFL | 400 |
| 1963 | N.Y. Giants, NFL | 448 |
| | San Diego, AFL | 399 |
| 1962 | Green Bay, NFL | 415 |
| | Dall. Texans, AFL | 389 |
| 1961 | Houston, AFL | 513 |
| | Green Bay, NFL | 391 |
| 1960 | N.Y. Titans, AFL | 382 |
| | Cleveland, NFL | 362 |
| 1959 | Baltimore | 374 |
| 1958 | Baltimore | 381 |
| 1957 | Los Angeles | 307 |
| 1956 | Chi. Bears | 363 |
| 1955 | Cleveland | 349 |
| 1954 | Detroit | 337 |
| 1953 | San Francisco | 372 |
| 1952 | Los Angeles | 349 |
| 1951 | Los Angeles | 392 |
| 1950 | Los Angeles | 466 |
| 1949 | Philadelphia | 364 |
| 1948 | Chi. Cardinals | 395 |
| 1947 | Chi. Bears | 363 |
| 1946 | Chi. Bears | 289 |
| 1945 | Philadelphia | 272 |
| 1944 | Philadelphia | 267 |
| 1943 | Chi. Bears | 303 |
| 1942 | Chi. Bears | 376 |
| 1941 | Chi. Bears | 396 |
| 1940 | Washington | 245 |
| 1939 | Chi. Bears | 298 |
| 1938 | Green Bay | 223 |
| 1937 | Green Bay | 220 |
| 1936 | Green Bay | 248 |
| 1935 | Chi. Bears | 192 |
| 1934 | Chi. Bears | 286 |
| 1933 | N.Y. Giants | 244 |
| 1932 | Chicago Bears | 160 |

## TOTAL YARDS GAINED

| Year | Team | Yards |
|---|---|---|
| 1993 | San Francisco, NFC | 6,435 |
| | Miami, AFC | 5,812 |
| 1992 | San Francisco, NFC | 6,195 |
| | Buffalo, AFC | 5,893 |
| 1991 | Buffalo, AFC | 6,252 |
| | San Francisco, NFC | 5,858 |
| 1990 | Houston, AFC | 6,222 |
| | San Francisco, NFC | 5,895 |
| 1989 | San Francisco, NFC | 6,268 |
| | Cincinnati, AFC | 6,101 |
| 1988 | Cincinnati, AFC | 6,057 |
| | San Francisco, NFC | 5,900 |
| 1987 | San Francisco, NFC | 5,987 |
| | Denver, AFC | 5,624 |
| 1986 | Cincinnati, AFC | 6,490 |
| | San Francisco, NFC | 6,082 |
| 1985 | San Diego, AFC | 6,535 |
| | San Francisco, NFC | 5,920 |
| 1984 | Miami, AFC | 6,936 |
| | San Francisco, NFC | 6,366 |
| 1983 | San Diego, AFC | 6,197 |
| | Green Bay, NFC | 6,172 |
| 1982 | San Diego, AFC | 4,048 |
| | San Francisco, NFC | 3,242 |
| 1981 | San Diego, AFC | 6,744 |
| | Detroit, NFC | 5,933 |
| 1980 | San Diego, AFC | 6,410 |
| | Los Angeles, NFC | 6,006 |
| 1979 | Pittsburgh, AFC | 6,258 |
| | Dallas, NFC | 5,968 |
| 1978 | New England, AFC | 5,965 |
| | Dallas, NFC | 5,959 |
| 1977 | Dallas, NFC | 4,812 |
| | Oakland, AFC | 4,736 |
| 1976 | Baltimore, AFC | 5,236 |
| | St. Louis, NFC | 5,136 |
| 1975 | Buffalo, AFC | 5,467 |
| | Dallas, NFC | 5,025 |
| 1974 | Dallas, NFC | 4,983 |
| | Oakland, AFC | 4,718 |
| 1973 | Los Angeles, NFC | 4,906 |
| | Oakland, AFC | 4,773 |
| 1972 | Miami, AFC | 5,036 |
| | N.Y. Giants, NFC | 4,483 |
| 1971 | Dallas, NFC | 5,035 |
| | San Diego, AFC | 4,738 |
| 1970 | Oakland, AFC | 4,829 |
| | San Francisco, NFC | 4,503 |
| 1969 | Dallas, NFL | 5,122 |
| | Oakland, AFL | 5,036 |
| 1968 | Oakland, AFL | 5,696 |
| | Dallas, NFL | 5,117 |
| 1967 | N.Y. Jets, AFL | 5,152 |
| | Baltimore, NFL | 5,008 |
| 1966 | Dallas, NFL | 5,145 |
| | Kansas City, AFL | 5,114 |
| 1965 | San Francisco, NFL | 5,270 |
| | San Diego, AFL | 5,188 |
| 1964 | Buffalo, AFL | 5,206 |
| | Baltimore, NFL | 4,779 |
| 1963 | San Diego, AFL | 5,153 |
| | N.Y. Giants, NFL | 5,024 |
| 1962 | N.Y. Giants, NFL | 5,005 |
| | Houston, AFL | 4,971 |
| 1961 | Houston, AFL | 6,288 |
| | Philadelphia, NFL | 5,112 |
| 1960 | Houston, AFL | 4,936 |
| | Baltimore, NFL | 4,245 |
| 1959 | Baltimore | 4,458 |
| 1958 | Baltimore | 4,539 |
| 1957 | Los Angeles | 4,143 |
| 1956 | Chi. Bears | 4,537 |
| 1955 | Chi. Bears | 4,316 |
| 1954 | Los Angeles | 5,187 |
| 1953 | Philadelphia | 4,811 |
| 1952 | Cleveland | 4,352 |
| 1951 | Los Angeles | 5,506 |
| 1950 | Los Angeles | 5,420 |
| 1949 | Chi. Bears | 4,873 |
| 1948 | Chi. Cardinals | 4,705 |
| 1947 | Chi. Bears | 5,053 |
| 1946 | Los Angeles | 3,793 |
| 1945 | Washington | 3,549 |
| 1944 | Chi. Bears | 3,239 |
| 1943 | Chi. Bears | 4,045 |
| 1942 | Chi. Bears | 3,900 |
| 1941 | Chi. Bears | 4,265 |
| 1940 | Green Bay | 3,400 |
| 1939 | Chi. Bears | 3,988 |
| 1938 | Green Bay | 3,037 |
| 1937 | Green Bay | 3,201 |
| 1936 | Detroit | 3,703 |
| 1935 | Chi. Bears | 3,454 |
| 1934 | Chi. Bears | 3,900 |
| 1933 | N.Y. Giants | 2,973 |
| 1932 | Chi. Bears | 2,755 |

## YARDS RUSHING

| Year | Team | Yards |
|---|---|---|
| 1993 | N.Y. Giants, NFC | 2,210 |
| | Seattle, AFC | 2,015 |
| 1992 | Buffalo, AFC | 2,436 |
| | Philadelphia, NFC | 2,388 |
| 1991 | Buffalo, AFC | 2,381 |
| | Minnesota, NFC | 2,201 |
| 1990 | Philadelphia, NFC | 2,556 |
| | San Diego, AFC | 2,257 |
| 1989 | Cincinnati, AFC | 2,483 |
| | Chicago, NFC | 2,287 |
| 1988 | Cincinnati, AFC | 2,710 |
| | San Francisco, NFC | 2,523 |
| 1987 | San Francisco, NFC | 2,237 |
| | L.A. Raiders, AFC | 2,197 |
| 1986 | Chicago, NFC | 2,700 |
| | Cincinnati, AFC | 2,533 |
| 1985 | Chicago, NFC | 2,761 |
| | Indianapolis, AFC | 2,439 |
| 1984 | Chicago, NFC | 2,974 |
| | N.Y. Jets, AFC | 2,189 |
| 1983 | Chicago, NFC | 2,727 |
| | Baltimore, AFC | 2,695 |
| 1982 | Buffalo, AFC | 1,371 |
| | Dallas, NFC | 1,313 |
| 1981 | Detroit, NFC | 2,795 |
| | Kansas City, AFC | 2,633 |
| 1980 | Los Angeles, NFC | 2,799 |
| | Houston, AFC | 2,635 |
| 1979 | N.Y. Jets, AFC | 2,646 |
| | St. Louis, NFC | 2,582 |
| 1978 | New England, AFC | 3,165 |
| | Dallas, NFC | 2,783 |
| 1977 | Chicago, NFC | 2,811 |
| | Oakland, AFC | 2,627 |
| 1976 | Pittsburgh, AFC | 2,971 |
| | Los Angeles, NFC | 2,528 |
| 1975 | Buffalo, AFC | 2,974 |
| | Dallas, NFC | 2,432 |
| 1974 | Dallas, NFC | 2,454 |
| | Pittsburgh, AFC | 2,417 |
| 1973 | Buffalo, AFC | 3,088 |
| | Los Angeles, NFC | 2,925 |
| 1972 | Miami, AFC | 2,960 |
| | Chicago, NFC | 2,360 |
| 1971 | Miami, AFC | 2,429 |
| | Detroit, NFC | 2,376 |
| 1970 | Dallas, NFC | 2,300 |
| | Miami, AFC | 2,082 |
| 1969 | Dallas, NFL | 2,276 |
| | Kansas City, AFL | 2,220 |
| 1968 | Chicago, NFL | 2,377 |
| | Kansas City, AFL | 2,227 |
| 1967 | Cleveland, NFL | 2,139 |
| | Houston, AFL | 2,122 |
| 1966 | Kansas City, AFL | 2,274 |
| | Cleveland, NFL | 2,166 |
| 1965 | Cleveland, NFL | 2,331 |
| | San Diego, AFL | 2,085 |
| 1964 | Green Bay, NFL | 2,276 |
| | Buffalo, AFL | 2,040 |
| 1963 | Cleveland, NFL | 2,639 |
| | San Diego, AFL | 2,203 |
| 1962 | Buffalo, AFL | 2,480 |
| | Green Bay, NFL | 2,460 |
| 1961 | Green Bay, NFL | 2,350 |
| | Dall. Texans, AFL | 2,189 |
| 1960 | St. Louis, NFL | 2,356 |
| | Oakland, AFL | 2,056 |
| 1959 | Cleveland | 2,149 |
| 1958 | Cleveland | 2,526 |
| 1957 | Los Angeles | 2,142 |
| 1956 | Chi. Bears | 2,468 |
| 1955 | Chi. Bears | 2,388 |
| 1954 | San Francisco | 2,498 |
| 1953 | San Francisco | 2,230 |
| 1952 | San Francisco | 1,905 |
| 1951 | Chi. Bears | 2,408 |
| 1950 | N.Y. Giants | 2,336 |
| 1949 | Philadelphia | 2,607 |
| 1948 | Chi. Cardinals | 2,560 |
| 1947 | Los Angeles | 2,171 |
| 1946 | Green Bay | 1,765 |
| 1945 | Cleveland | 1,714 |
| 1944 | Philadelphia | 1,661 |
| 1943 | Phil-Pitt | 1,730 |
| 1942 | Chi. Bears | 1,881 |
| 1941 | Chi. Bears | 2,263 |
| 1940 | Chi. Bears | 1,818 |
| 1939 | Chi. Bears | 2,043 |
| 1938 | Detroit | 1,893 |
| 1937 | Detroit | 2,074 |
| 1936 | Detroit | 2,885 |
| 1935 | Chi. Bears | 2,096 |
| 1934 | Chi. Bears | 2,847 |
| 1933 | Boston | 2,260 |
| 1932 | Chi. Bears | 1,770 |

## YARDS PASSING

Leadership in this category has been based on net yards since 1952.

| Year | Team | Yards |
|---|---|---|
| 1993 | Miami, AFC | 4,353 |

| | | |
|---|---|---|
| | San Francisco, NFC | 4,302 |
| 1992 | Houston, AFC | 4,029 |
| | San Francisco, NFC | 3,880 |
| 1991 | Houston, AFC | 4,621 |
| | San Francisco, NFC | 3,997 |
| 1990 | Houston, AFC | 4,805 |
| | San Francisco, NFC | 4,177 |
| 1989 | Washington, NFC | 4,349 |
| | Miami, AFC | 4,216 |
| 1988 | Miami, AFC | 4,516 |
| | Washington, NFC | 4,136 |
| 1987 | Miami, AFC | 3,876 |
| | San Francisco, NFC | 3,750 |
| 1986 | Miami, AFC | 4,779 |
| | San Francisco, NFC | 4,096 |
| 1985 | San Diego, AFC | 4,870 |
| | Dallas, NFC | 3,861 |
| 1984 | Miami, AFC | 5,018 |
| | St. Louis, NFC | 4,257 |
| 1983 | San Diego, AFC | 4,661 |
| | Green Bay, NFC | 4,365 |
| 1982 | San Diego, AFC | 2,927 |
| | San Francisco, NFC | 2,502 |
| 1981 | San Diego, AFC | 4,739 |
| | Minnesota, NFC | 4,333 |
| 1980 | San Diego, AFC | 4,531 |
| | Minnesota, NFC | 3,688 |
| 1979 | San Diego, AFC | 3,915 |
| | San Francisco, NFC | 3,641 |
| 1978 | San Diego, AFC | 3,375 |
| | Minnesota, NFC | 3,243 |
| 1977 | Buffalo, AFC | 2,530 |
| | St. Louis, NFC | 2,499 |
| 1976 | Baltimore, AFC | 2,933 |
| | Minnesota, NFC | 2,855 |
| 1975 | Cincinnati, AFC | 3,241 |
| | Washington, NFC | 2,917 |
| 1974 | Washington, NFC | 2,978 |
| | Cincinnati, AFC | 2,804 |
| 1973 | Philadelphia, NFC | 2,998 |
| | Denver, AFC | 2,519 |
| 1972 | N.Y. Jets, AFC | 2,777 |
| | San Francisco, NFC | 2,735 |
| 1971 | San Diego, AFC | 3,134 |
| | Dallas, NFC | 2,786 |
| 1970 | San Francisco, NFC | 2,923 |
| | Oakland, AFC | 2,865 |
| 1969 | Oakland, AFL | 3,271 |
| | San Francisco, NFL | 3,158 |
| 1968 | San Diego, AFL | 3,623 |
| | Dallas, NFL | 3,026 |
| 1967 | N.Y. Jets, AFL | 3,845 |
| | Washington, NFL | 3,730 |
| 1966 | N.Y. Jets, AFL | 3,464 |
| | Dallas, NFL | 3,023 |
| 1965 | San Francisco, NFL | 3,487 |
| | San Diego, AFL | 3,103 |
| 1964 | Houston, AFL | 3,527 |
| | Chicago, NFL | 2,841 |
| 1963 | Baltimore, NFL | 3,296 |
| | Houston, AFL | 3,222 |
| 1962 | Denver, AFL | 3,404 |
| | Philadelphia, NFL | 3,385 |
| 1961 | Houston, AFL | 4,392 |
| | Philadelphia, NFL | 3,605 |
| 1960 | Houston, AFL | 3,203 |
| | Baltimore, NFL | 2,956 |
| 1959 | Baltimore | 2,753 |
| 1958 | Pittsburgh | 2,752 |
| 1957 | Baltimore | 2,388 |
| 1956 | Los Angeles | 2,419 |
| 1955 | Philadelphia | 2,472 |
| 1954 | Chi. Bears | 3,104 |
| 1953 | Philadelphia | 3,089 |
| 1952 | Cleveland | 2,566 |
| 1951 | Los Angeles | 3,296 |
| 1950 | Los Angeles | 3,709 |
| 1949 | Chi. Bears | 3,055 |
| 1948 | Washington | 2,861 |
| 1947 | Washington | 3,336 |
| 1946 | Los Angeles | 2,080 |
| 1945 | Chi. Bears | 1,857 |
| 1944 | Washington | 2,021 |
| 1943 | Chi. Bears | 2,310 |
| 1942 | Green Bay | 2,407 |
| 1941 | Chi. Bears | 2,002 |
| 1940 | Washington | 1,887 |
| 1939 | Chi. Bears | 1,965 |
| 1938 | Washington | 1,536 |
| 1937 | Green Bay | 1,398 |
| 1936 | Green Bay | 1,629 |
| 1935 | Green Bay | 1,449 |
| 1934 | Green Bay | 1,165 |
| 1933 | N.Y. Giants | 1,348 |
| 1932 | Chi. Bears | 1,013 |

## FEWEST POINTS ALLOWED

| Year | Team | Points |
|---|---|---|
| 1993 | N.Y. Giants, NFC | 205 |
| | Houston, AFC | 238 |
| 1992 | New Orleans, NFC | 202 |
| | Pittsburgh, AFC | 225 |
| 1991 | New Orleans, NFC | 211 |
| | Denver, AFC | 235 |
| 1990 | N.Y. Giants, NFC | 211 |
| | Pittsburgh, AFC | 240 |
| 1989 | Denver, AFC | 226 |
| | N.Y. Giants, NFC | 252 |
| 1988 | Chicago, NFC | 215 |
| | Buffalo, AFC | 237 |
| 1987 | Indianapolis, AFC | 238 |
| | San Francisco, NFC | 253 |
| 1986 | Chicago, NFC | 187 |
| | Seattle, AFC | 293 |
| 1985 | Chicago, NFC | 198 |
| | N.Y. Jets, AFC | 264 |
| 1984 | San Francisco, NFC | 227 |
| | Denver, AFC | 241 |
| 1983 | Miami, AFC | 250 |
| | Detroit, NFC | 286 |
| 1982 | Washington, NFC | 128 |
| | Miami, AFC | 131 |
| 1981 | Philadelphia, NFC | 221 |
| | Miami, AFC | 275 |
| 1980 | Philadelphia, NFC | 222 |
| | Houston, AFC | 251 |
| 1979 | Tampa Bay, NFC | 237 |
| | San Diego, AFC | 246 |
| 1978 | Pittsburgh, AFC | 195 |
| | Dallas, NFC | 208 |
| 1977 | Atlanta, NFC | 129 |
| | Denver, AFC | 148 |
| 1976 | Pittsburgh, AFC | 138 |
| | Minnesota, NFC | 176 |
| 1975 | Los Angeles, NFC | 135 |
| | Pittsburgh, AFC | 162 |
| 1974 | Los Angeles, NFC | 181 |
| | Pittsburgh, AFC | 189 |
| 1973 | Miami, AFC | 150 |
| | Minnesota, NFC | 168 |
| 1972 | Miami, AFC | 171 |
| | Washington, NFC | 218 |
| 1971 | Minnesota, NFC | 139 |
| | Baltimore, AFC | 140 |
| 1970 | Minnesota, NFC | 143 |
| | Miami, AFC | 228 |
| 1969 | Minnesota, NFL | 133 |
| | Kansas City, AFL | 177 |
| 1968 | Baltimore, NFL | 144 |
| | Kansas City, AFL | 170 |
| 1967 | Los Angeles, NFL | 196 |
| | Houston, AFL | 199 |
| 1966 | Green Bay, NFL | 163 |
| | Buffalo, AFL | 255 |
| 1965 | Green Bay, NFL | 224 |
| | Buffalo, AFL | 226 |
| 1964 | Baltimore, NFL | 225 |
| | Buffalo, AFL | 242 |
| 1963 | Chicago, NFL | 144 |
| | San Diego, AFL | 255 |
| 1962 | Green Bay, NFL | 148 |
| | Dall. Texans, AFL | 233 |
| 1961 | San Diego, AFL | 219 |
| | N.Y. Giants, NFL | 220 |
| 1960 | San Francisco, NFL | 205 |
| | Dall. Texans, AFL | 253 |
| 1959 | N.Y. Giants | 170 |
| 1958 | N.Y. Giants | 183 |
| 1957 | Cleveland | 172 |
| 1956 | Cleveland | 177 |
| 1955 | Cleveland | 218 |
| 1954 | Cleveland | 162 |
| 1953 | Cleveland | 162 |
| 1952 | Detroit | 192 |
| 1951 | Cleveland | 152 |
| 1950 | Philadelphia | 141 |
| 1949 | Philadelphia | 134 |
| 1948 | Chi. Bears | 151 |
| 1947 | Green Bay | 210 |
| 1946 | Pittsburgh | 117 |
| 1945 | Washington | 121 |
| 1944 | N.Y. Giants | 75 |
| 1943 | Washington | 137 |
| 1942 | Chi. Bears | 84 |
| 1941 | N.Y. Giants | 114 |
| 1940 | Brooklyn | 120 |
| 1939 | N.Y. Giants | 85 |
| 1938 | N.Y. Giants | 79 |
| 1937 | Chi. Bears | 100 |
| 1936 | Chi. Bears | 94 |
| 1935 | Green Bay | 96 |
| | N.Y. Giants | 96 |
| 1934 | Detroit | 59 |
| 1933 | Brooklyn | 54 |
| 1932 | Chi. Bears | 44 |

## FEWEST TOTAL YARDS ALLOWED

| Year | Team | Yards |
|---|---|---|
| 1993 | Minnesota, NFC | 4,406 |
| | Pittsburgh, AFC | 4,531 |
| 1992 | Dallas, NFC | 3,931 |
| | Houston, AFC | 4,211 |
| 1991 | Philadelphia, NFC | 3,549 |
| | Denver, AFC | 4,549 |
| 1990 | Pittsburgh, AFC | 4,115 |
| | N.Y. Giants, NFC | 4,206 |
| 1989 | Minnesota, NFC | 4,184 |
| | Kansas City, AFC | 4,293 |
| 1988 | Minnesota, NFC | 4,091 |
| | Buffalo, AFC | 4,578 |
| 1987 | San Francisco, NFC | 4,095 |
| | Cleveland, AFC | 4,264 |
| 1986 | Chicago, NFC | 4,130 |
| | L.A. Raiders, AFC | 4,804 |
| 1985 | Chicago, NFC | 4,135 |
| | L.A. Raiders, AFC | 4,603 |
| 1984 | Chicago, NFC | 3,863 |
| | Cleveland, AFC | 4,641 |
| 1983 | Cincinnati, AFC | 4,327 |
| | New Orleans, NFC | 4,691 |
| 1982 | Miami, AFC | 2,312 |
| | Tampa Bay, NFC | 2,442 |
| 1981 | Philadelphia, NFC | 4,447 |
| | N.Y. Jets, AFC | 4,871 |
| 1980 | Buffalo, AFC | 4,101 |
| | Philadelphia, NFC | 4,443 |
| 1979 | Tampa Bay, NFC | 3,949 |
| | Pittsburgh, AFC | 4,270 |
| 1978 | Los Angeles, NFC | 3,893 |
| | Pittsburgh, AFC | 4,168 |
| 1977 | Dallas, NFC | 3,213 |
| | New England, AFC | 3,638 |
| 1976 | Pittsburgh, AFC | 3,323 |
| | San Francisco, NFC | 3,562 |
| 1975 | Minnesota, NFC | 3,153 |
| | Oakland, AFC | 3,629 |
| 1974 | Pittsburgh, AFC | 3,074 |
| | Washington, NFC | 3,285 |
| 1973 | Los Angeles, NFC | 2,951 |
| | Oakland, AFC | 3,160 |
| 1972 | Miami, AFC | 3,297 |
| | Green Bay, NFC | 3,474 |
| 1971 | Baltimore, AFC | 2,852 |
| | Minnesota, NFC | 3,406 |
| 1970 | Minnesota, NFC | 2,803 |
| | N.Y. Jets, AFC | 3,655 |
| 1969 | Minnesota, NFL | 2,720 |
| | Kansas City, AFL | 3,163 |
| 1968 | Los Angeles, NFL | 3,118 |
| | N.Y. Jets, AFL | 3,363 |
| 1967 | Oakland, AFL | 3,294 |
| | Green Bay, NFL | 3,300 |
| 1966 | St. Louis, NFL | 3,492 |
| | Oakland, AFL | 3,910 |
| 1965 | San Diego, AFL | 3,262 |
| | Detroit, NFL | 3,557 |
| 1964 | Green Bay, NFL | 3,179 |
| | Buffalo, AFL | 3,878 |
| 1963 | Chicago, NFL | 3,176 |
| | Boston, AFL | 3,834 |
| 1962 | Detroit, NFL | 3,217 |
| | Dall. Texans, AFL | 3,951 |
| 1961 | San Diego, AFL | 3,726 |
| | Baltimore, NFL | 3,782 |
| 1960 | St. Louis, NFL | 3,029 |
| | Buffalo, AFL | 3,866 |
| 1959 | N.Y. Giants | 2,843 |
| 1958 | Chi. Bears | 3,066 |
| 1957 | Pittsburgh | 2,791 |
| 1956 | N.Y. Giants | 3,081 |
| 1955 | Cleveland | 2,841 |
| 1954 | Cleveland | 2,658 |
| 1953 | Philadelphia | 2,998 |
| 1952 | Cleveland | 3,075 |
| 1951 | N.Y. Giants | 3,250 |
| 1950 | Cleveland | 3,154 |
| 1949 | Philadelphia | 2,831 |
| 1948 | Chi. Bears | 2,931 |
| 1947 | Green Bay | 3,396 |
| 1946 | Washington | 2,451 |
| 1945 | Philadelphia | 2,073 |
| 1944 | Philadelphia | 1,943 |
| 1943 | Chi. Bears | 2,262 |
| 1942 | Chi. Bears | 1,703 |
| 1941 | N.Y. Giants | 2,368 |
| 1940 | N.Y. Giants | 2,219 |
| 1939 | Washington | 2,116 |
| 1938 | N.Y. Giants | 2,029 |
| 1937 | Washington | 2,123 |
| 1936 | Boston | 2,181 |
| 1935 | Boston | 1,996 |
| 1934 | Chi. Cardinals | 1,539 |
| 1933 | Brooklyn | 1,789 |

## FEWEST RUSHING YARDS ALLOWED

| Year | Team | Yards |
|---|---|---|
| 1993 | Houston, AFC | 1,273 |
| | Minnesota, NFC | 1,536 |
| 1992 | Dallas, NFC | 1,244 |
| | Buffalo, AFC | 1,395 |
| | San Diego, AFC | 1,395 |
| 1991 | Philadelphia, NFC | 1,136 |
| | N.Y. Jets, AFC | 1,442 |
| 1990 | Philadelphia, NFC | 1,169 |
| | San Diego, AFC | 1,515 |
| 1989 | New Orleans, NFC | 1,326 |
| | Denver, AFC | 1,580 |
| 1988 | Chicago, NFC | 1,326 |
| | Houston, AFC | 1,592 |
| 1987 | Chicago, NFC | 1,413 |
| | Cleveland, AFC | 1,433 |
| 1986 | N.Y. Giants, NFC | 1,284 |
| | Denver, AFC | 1,651 |
| 1985 | Chicago, NFC | 1,319 |
| | N.Y. Jets, AFC | 1,516 |
| 1984 | Chicago, NFC | 1,377 |
| | Pittsburgh, AFC | 1,617 |
| 1983 | Washington, NFC | 1,289 |
| | Cincinnati, AFC | 1,499 |
| 1982 | Pittsburgh, AFC | 762 |
| | Detroit, NFC | 854 |
| 1981 | Detroit, NFC | 1,623 |
| | Kansas City, AFC | 1,747 |
| 1980 | Detroit, NFC | 1,599 |
| | Cincinnati, AFC | 1,680 |
| 1979 | Denver, AFC | 1,693 |
| | Tampa Bay, NFC | 1,873 |
| 1978 | Dallas, NFC | 1,721 |
| | Pittsburgh, AFC | 1,774 |

| | | |
|---|---|---|
| 1977 | Denver, AFC | 1,531 |
| | Dallas, NFC | 1,651 |
| 1976 | Pittsburgh, AFC | 1,457 |
| | Los Angeles, NFC | 1,564 |
| 1975 | Minnesota, NFC | 1,532 |
| | Houston, AFC | 1,680 |
| 1974 | Los Angeles, NFC | 1,302 |
| | New England, AFC | 1,587 |
| 1973 | Los Angeles, NFC | 1,270 |
| | Oakland, AFC | 1,470 |
| 1972 | Dallas, NFC | 1,515 |
| | Miami, AFC | 1,548 |
| 1971 | Baltimore, AFC | 1,113 |
| | Dallas, NFC | 1,144 |
| 1970 | Detroit, NFC | 1,152 |
| | N.Y. Jets, AFC | 1,283 |
| 1969 | Dallas, NFL | 1,050 |
| | Kansas City, AFL | 1,091 |
| 1968 | Dallas, NFL | 1,195 |
| | N.Y. Jets, AFL | 1,195 |
| 1967 | Dallas, NFL | 1,081 |
| | Oakland, AFL | 1,129 |
| 1966 | Buffalo, AFL | 1,051 |
| | Dallas, NFL | 1,176 |
| 1965 | San Diego, AFL | 1,094 |
| | Los Angeles, NFL | 1,409 |
| 1964 | Buffalo, AFL | 913 |
| | Los Angeles, NFL | 1,501 |
| 1963 | Boston, AFL | 1,107 |
| | Chicago, NFL | 1,442 |
| 1962 | Detroit, NFL | 1,231 |
| | Dall. Texans, AFL | 1,250 |
| 1961 | Boston, AFL | 1,041 |
| | Pittsburgh, NFL | 1,463 |
| 1960 | St. Louis, NFL | 1,212 |
| | Dall. Texans, AFL | 1,338 |
| 1959 | N.Y. Giants | 1,261 |
| 1958 | Baltimore | 1,291 |
| 1957 | Baltimore | 1,174 |
| 1956 | N.Y. Giants | 1,443 |
| 1955 | Cleveland | 1,189 |
| 1954 | Cleveland | 1,050 |
| 1953 | Philadelphia | 1,117 |
| 1952 | Detroit | 1,145 |
| 1951 | N.Y. Giants | 913 |
| 1950 | Detroit | 1,367 |
| 1949 | Chi. Bears | 1,196 |
| 1948 | Philadelphia | 1,209 |
| 1947 | Philadelphia | 1,329 |
| 1946 | Chi. Bears | 1,060 |
| 1945 | Philadelphia | 817 |
| 1944 | Philadelphia | 558 |
| 1943 | Phil-Pitt | 793 |
| 1942 | Chi. Bears | 519 |
| 1941 | Washington | 1,042 |
| 1940 | N.Y. Giants | 977 |
| 1939 | Chi. Bears | 812 |
| 1938 | Detroit | 1,081 |
| 1937 | Chi. Bears | 933 |
| 1936 | Boston | 1,148 |
| 1935 | Boston | 998 |
| 1934 | Chi. Cardinals | 954 |
| 1933 | Brooklyn | 964 |

## FEWEST PASSING YARDS ALLOWED

Leadership in this category has been based on net yards since 1952.

| Year | Team | Yards |
|---|---|---|
| 1993 | New Orleans, NFC | 2,606 |
| | Cincinnati, AFC | 2,798 |
| 1992 | New Orleans, NFC | 2,470 |
| | Kansas City, AFC | 2,537 |
| 1991 | Philadelphia, NFC | 2,413 |
| | Denver, AFC | 2,755 |
| 1990 | Pittsburgh, AFC | 2,500 |
| | Dallas, NFC | 2,639 |
| 1989 | Minnesota, NFC | 2,501 |
| | Kansas City, AFC | 2,527 |
| 1988 | Kansas City, AFC | 2,434 |
| | Minnesota, NFC | 2,489 |
| 1987 | San Francisco, NFC | 2,484 |
| | L.A. Raiders, AFC | 2,727 |
| 1986 | St. Louis, NFC | 2,637 |
| | New England, AFC | 2,978 |
| 1985 | Washington, NFC | 2,746 |
| | Pittsburgh, AFC | 2,783 |
| 1984 | New Orleans, NFC | 2,453 |
| | Cleveland, AFC | 2,696 |
| 1983 | New Orleans, NFC | 2,691 |
| | Cincinnati, AFC | 2,828 |
| 1982 | Miami, AFC | 1,027 |
| | Tampa Bay, NFC | 1,384 |
| 1981 | Philadelphia, NFC | 2,696 |
| | Buffalo, AFC | 2,870 |
| 1980 | Washington, NFC | 2,171 |
| | Buffalo, AFC | 2,282 |
| 1979 | Tampa Bay, NFC | 2,076 |
| | Buffalo, AFC | 2,530 |
| 1978 | Buffalo, AFC | 1,960 |
| | Los Angeles, NFC | 2,048 |
| 1977 | Atlanta, NFC | 1,384 |
| | San Diego, AFC | 1,725 |
| 1976 | Minnesota, NFC | 1,575 |
| | Cincinnati, AFC | 1,758 |
| 1975 | Minnesota, NFC | 1,621 |
| | Cincinnati, AFC | 1,729 |
| 1974 | Pittsburgh, AFC | 1,466 |
| | Atlanta, NFC | 1,572 |
| 1973 | Miami, AFC | 1,290 |
| | Atlanta, NFC | 1,430 |
| 1972 | Minnesota, NFC | 1,699 |
| | Cleveland, AFC | 1,736 |
| 1971 | Atlanta, NFC | 1,638 |
| | Baltimore, AFC | 1,739 |
| 1970 | Minnesota, NFC | 1,438 |
| | Kansas City, AFC | 2,010 |
| 1969 | Minnesota, NFL | 1,631 |
| | Kansas City, AFL | 2,072 |
| 1968 | Houston, AFL | 1,671 |
| | Green Bay, NFL | 1,796 |
| 1967 | Green Bay, NFL | 1,377 |
| | Buffalo, AFL | 1,825 |
| 1966 | Green Bay, NFL | 1,959 |
| | Oakland, AFL | 2,118 |
| 1965 | Green Bay, NFL | 1,981 |
| | San Diego, AFL | 2,168 |
| 1964 | Green Bay, NFL | 1,647 |
| | San Diego, AFL | 2,518 |
| 1963 | Chicago, NFL | 1,734 |
| | Oakland, AFL | 2,589 |
| 1962 | Green Bay, NFL | 1,746 |
| | Oakland, AFL | 2,306 |
| 1961 | Baltimore, NFL | 1,913 |
| | San Diego, AFL | 2,363 |
| 1960 | Chicago, NFL | 1,388 |
| | Buffalo, AFL | 2,124 |
| 1959 | N.Y. Giants | 1,582 |
| 1958 | Chi. Bears | 1,769 |
| 1957 | Cleveland | 1,300 |
| 1956 | Cleveland | 1,103 |
| 1955 | Pittsburgh | 1,295 |
| 1954 | Cleveland | 1,608 |
| 1953 | Washington | 1,751 |
| 1952 | Washington | 1,580 |
| 1951 | Pittsburgh | 1,687 |
| 1950 | Cleveland | 1,581 |
| 1949 | Philadelphia | 1,607 |
| 1948 | Green Bay | 1,626 |
| 1947 | Green Bay | 1,790 |
| 1946 | Pittsburgh | 939 |
| 1945 | Washington | 1,121 |
| 1944 | Chi. Bears | 1,052 |
| 1943 | Chi. Bears | 980 |
| 1942 | Washington | 1,093 |
| 1941 | Pittsburgh | 1,168 |
| 1940 | Philadelphia | 1,012 |
| 1939 | Washington | 1,116 |
| 1938 | Chi. Bears | 897 |
| 1937 | Detroit | 804 |
| 1936 | Philadelphia | 853 |
| 1935 | Chi. Cardinals | 793 |
| 1934 | Philadelphia | 545 |
| 1933 | Portsmouth | 558 |

# SUPER BOWL RECORDS

Compiled by Elias Sports Bureau

| | | |
|---|---|---|
| 1967: Super Bowl I | 1977: Super Bowl XI | 1987: Super Bowl XXI |
| 1968: Super Bowl II | 1978: Super Bowl XII | 1988: Super Bowl XXII |
| 1969: Super Bowl III | 1979: Super Bowl XIII | 1989: Super Bowl XXIII |
| 1970: Super Bowl IV | 1980: Super Bowl XIV | 1990: Super Bowl XXIV |
| 1971: Super Bowl V | 1981: Super Bowl XV | 1991: Super Bowl XXV |
| 1972: Super Bowl VI | 1982: Super Bowl XVI | 1992: Super Bowl XXVI |
| 1973: Super Bowl VII | 1983: Super Bowl XVII | 1993: Super Bowl XXVII |
| 1974: Super Bowl VIII | 1984: Super Bowl XVIII | 1994: Super Bowl XXVIII |
| 1975: Super Bowl IX | 1985: Super Bowl XIX | |
| 1976: Super Bowl X | 1986: Super Bowl XX | |

## INDIVIDUAL RECORDS

### SERVICE

**Most Games**

5 Marv Fleming, Green Bay, 1967-68; Miami, 1972-74
Larry Cole, Dallas, 1971-72, 1976, 1978-79
Cliff Harris, Dallas, 1971-72, 1976, 1978-79
D.D. Lewis, Dallas, 1971-72, 1976, 1978-79
Preston Pearson, Baltimore, 1969; Pittsburgh, 1975; Dallas, 1976, 1978-79
Charlie Waters, Dallas, 1971-72, 1976, 1978-79
Rayfield Wright, Dallas, 1971-72, 1976, 1978-79
4 By many players

**Most Games, Winning Team**

4 By many players

**Most Games, Coach**

6 Don Shula, Baltimore, 1969; Miami, 1972-74, 1983, 1985
5 Tom Landry, Dallas, 1971-72, 1976, 1978-79
4 Bud Grant, Minnesota, 1970, 1974-75, 1977
Chuck Noll, Pittsburgh, 1975-76, 1979-80
Joe Gibbs, Washington, 1983-84, 1988, 1992
Marv Levy, Buffalo, 1991-94

**Most Games, Winning Team, Coach**

4 Chuck Noll, Pittsburgh, 1975-76, 1979-80
3 Bill Walsh, San Francisco, 1982, 1985, 1989
Joe Gibbs, Washington, 1983, 1988, 1992
2 Vince Lombardi, Green Bay, 1967-68
Tom Landry, Dallas, 1972, 1978
Don Shula, Miami, 1973-74
Tom Flores, Oakland, 1981; L.A. Raiders, 1984
Bill Parcells, N.Y. Giants, 1987, 1991
Jimmy Johnson, Dallas, 1993-94

**Most Games, Losing Team, Coach**

4 Bud Grant, Minnesota, 1970, 1974-75, 1977
Don Shula, Baltimore, 1969; Miami, 1972, 1983, 1985
Marv Levy, Buffalo, 1991-94
3 Tom Landry, Dallas, 1971, 1976, 1979
Dan Reeves, Denver, 1987-88, 1990

### SCORING

#### POINTS

**Most Points, Career**

24 Franco Harris, Pittsburgh, 4 games (4-td)
Roger Craig, San Francisco, 3 games (4-td)
Jerry Rice, San Francisco, 2 games (4-td)
Thurman Thomas, Buffalo, 4 games (4-td)
22 Ray Wersching, San Francisco, 2 games (7-pat, 5-fg)
20 Don Chandler, Green Bay, 2 games (8-pat, 4-fg)

**Most Points, Game**

18 Roger Craig, San Francisco vs. Miami, 1985 (3-td)
Jerry Rice, San Francisco vs. Denver, 1990 (3-td)
15 Don Chandler, Green Bay vs. Oakland, 1968 (3-pat, 4-fg)
14 Ray Wersching, San Francisco vs. Cincinnati, 1982 (2-pat, 4-fg)
Kevin Butler, Chicago vs. New England, 1986 (5-pat, 3-fg)

#### TOUCHDOWNS

**Most Touchdowns, Career**

4 Franco Harris, Pittsburgh, 4 games (4-r)
Roger Craig, San Francisco, 3 games (2-r, 2-p)
Jerry Rice, San Francisco, 2 games (4-p)
Thurman Thomas, Buffalo, 4 games (4-r)
3 John Stallworth, Pittsburgh, 4 games (3-p)
Lynn Swann, Pittsburgh, 4 games (3-p)
Cliff Branch, Oakland-L.A. Raiders, 3 games (3-p)
Emmitt Smith, Dallas, 3 games (3-r)

**Most Touchdowns, Game**

3 Roger Craig, San Francisco vs. Miami, 1985 (1-r, 2-p)
Jerry Rice, San Francisco vs. Denver, 1990 (3-p)
2 Max McGee, Green Bay vs. Kansas City, 1967 (2-p)
Elijah Pitts, Green Bay vs. Kansas City, 1967 (2-r)
Bill Miller, Oakland vs. Green Bay, 1968 (2-p)
Larry Csonka, Miami vs. Minnesota, 1974 (2-r)
Pete Banaszak, Oakland vs. Minnesota, 1977 (2-r)
John Stallworth, Pittsburgh vs. Dallas, 1979 (2-p)
Franco Harris, Pittsburgh vs. Los Angeles, 1980 (2-r)
Cliff Branch, Oakland vs. Philadelphia, 1981 (2-p)
Dan Ross, Cincinnati vs. San Francisco, 1982 (2-p)
Marcus Allen, L.A. Raiders vs. Washington, 1984 (2-r)
Jim McMahon, Chicago vs. New England, 1986 (2-r)
Ricky Sanders, Washington vs. Denver, 1988 (2-p)
Timmy Smith, Washington vs. Denver, 1988 (2-r)
Tom Rathman, San Francisco vs. Denver, 1990 (2-r)
Gerald Riggs, Washington vs. Buffalo, 1992 (2-r)
Michael Irvin, Dallas vs. Buffalo, 1993 (2-p)
Emmitt Smith, Dallas vs. Buffalo, 1994 (2-r)

#### POINTS AFTER TOUCHDOWN

**Most Points After Touchdown, Career**

9 Mike Cofer, San Francisco, 2 games (10 att)
8 Don Chandler, Green Bay, 2 games (8 att)
Roy Gerela, Pittsburgh, 3 games (9 att)
Chris Bahr, Oakland-L.A. Raiders, 2 games (8 att)
7 Ray Wersching, San Francisco, 2 games (7 att)
Lin Elliott, Dallas, 1 game (7 att)

**Most Points After Touchdown, Game**

7 Mike Cofer, San Francisco vs. Denver, 1990 (8 att)
Lin Elliott, Dallas vs. Buffalo, 1993 (7 att)
6 Ali Haji-Sheikh, Washington vs. Denver, 1988 (6 att)
5 Don Chandler, Green Bay vs. Kansas City, 1967 (5 att)
Roy Gerela, Pittsburgh vs. Dallas, 1979 (5 att)
Chris Bahr, L.A. Raiders vs. Washington, 1984 (5 att)
Ray Wersching, San Francisco vs. Miami, 1985 (5 att)
Kevin Butler, Chicago vs. New England, 1986 (5 att)

#### FIELD GOALS

**Field Goals Attempted, Career**

6 Jim Turner, N.Y. Jets-Denver, 2 games
Roy Gerela, Pittsburgh, 3 games
Rich Karlis, Denver, 2 games
5 Efren Herrera, Dallas, 1 game
Ray Wersching, San Francisco, 2 games

**Most Field Goals Attempted, Game**

5 Jim Turner, N.Y. Jets vs. Baltimore, 1969
Efren Herrera, Dallas vs. Denver, 1978
4 Don Chandler, Green Bay vs. Oakland, 1968
Roy Gerela, Pittsburgh vs. Dallas, 1976
Ray Wersching, San Francisco vs. Cincinnati, 1982
Rich Karlis, Denver vs. N.Y. Giants, 1987
Mike Cofer, San Francisco vs. Cincinnati, 1989

**Most Field Goals, Career**

5 Ray Wersching, San Francisco, 2 games (5 att)
4 Don Chandler, Green Bay, 2 games (4 att)
Jim Turner, N.Y. Jets-Denver, 2 games (6 att)
Uwe von Schamann, Miami, 2 games (4 att)
3 Mike Clark, Dallas, 2 games (3 att)
Jan Stenerud, Kansas City, 1 game (3 att)
Chris Bahr, Oakland-L.A. Raiders, 2 games (4 att)
Mark Moseley, Washington, 2 games (4 att)
Kevin Butler, Chicago, 1 game (3 att)
Rich Karlis, Denver, 2 games (6 att)
Jim Breech, Cincinnati, 2 games (3 att)
Matt Bahr, Pittsburgh-N.Y. Giants, 2 games (3 att)
Chip Lohmiller, Washington, 1 game (3 att)
Steve Christie, Buffalo, 2 games (3 att)
Eddie Murray, Dallas, 1 game (3 att)

**Most Field Goals, Game**

4 Don Chandler, Green Bay vs. Oakland, 1968
Ray Wersching, San Francisco vs. Cincinnati, 1982
3 Jim Turner, N.Y. Jets vs. Baltimore, 1969
Jan Stenerud, Kansas City vs. Minnesota, 1970
Uwe von Schamann, Miami vs. San Francisco, 1985
Kevin Butler, Chicago vs. New England, 1986
Jim Breech, Cincinnati vs. San Francisco, 1989
Chip Lohmiller, Washington vs. Buffalo, 1992
Eddie Murray, Dallas vs. Buffalo, 1994

**Longest Field Goal**

54 Steve Christie, Buffalo vs. Dallas, 1994
48 Jan Stenerud, Kansas City vs. Minnesota, 1970
Rich Karlis, Denver vs. N.Y. Giants, 1987
47 Jim Turner, Denver vs. Dallas, 1978

#### SAFETIES

**Most Safeties, Game**

1 Dwight White, Pittsburgh vs. Minnesota, 1975

Reggie Harrison, Pittsburgh vs. Dallas, 1976
Henry Waechter, Chicago vs. New England, 1986
George Martin, N.Y. Giants vs. Denver, 1987
Bruce Smith, Buffalo vs. N.Y. Giants, 1991

## RUSHING

### ATTEMPTS

**Most Attempts, Career**

101 Franco Harris, Pittsburgh, 4 games
64 John Riggins, Washington, 2 games
57 Larry Csonka, Miami, 3 games

**Most Attempts, Game**

38 John Riggins, Washington vs. Miami, 1983
34 Franco Harris, Pittsburgh vs. Minnesota, 1975
33 Larry Csonka, Miami vs. Minnesota, 1974

### YARDS GAINED

**Most Yards Gained, Career**

354 Franco Harris, Pittsburgh, 4 games
297 Larry Csonka, Miami, 3 games
240 Emmitt Smith, Dallas, 2 games

**Most Yards Gained, Game**

204 Timmy Smith, Washington vs. Denver, 1988
191 Marcus Allen, L.A. Raiders vs. Washington, 1984
166 John Riggins, Washington vs. Miami, 1983

**Longest Run From Scrimmage**

74 Marcus Allen, L.A. Raiders vs. Washington, 1984 (TD)
58 Tom Matte, Baltimore vs. N.Y. Jets, 1969
Timmy Smith, Washington vs. Denver, 1988 (TD)
49 Larry Csonka, Miami vs. Washington, 1973

### AVERAGE GAIN

**Highest Average Gain, Career (20 attempts)**

9.6 Marcus Allen, L.A. Raiders, 1 game (20-191)
9.3 Timmy Smith, Washington, 1 game (22-204)
5.3 Walt Garrison, Dallas, 2 games (26-139)

**Highest Average Gain, Game (10 attempts)**

10.5 Tom Matte, Baltimore vs. N.Y. Jets, 1969 (11-116)
9.6 Marcus Allen, L.A. Raiders vs. Washington, 1984 (20-191)
9.3 Timmy Smith, Washington vs. Denver, 1988 (22-204)

### TOUCHDOWNS

**Most Touchdowns, Career**

4 Franco Harris, Pittsburgh, 4 games
Thurman Thomas, Buffalo, 4 games
3 Emmitt Smith, Dallas, 2 games
2 Elijah Pitts, Green Bay, 1 game
Jim Kiick, Miami, 3 games
Larry Csonka, Miami, 3 games
Pete Banaszak, Oakland, 2 games
Marcus Allen, L.A. Raiders, 1 game
John Riggins, Washington, 2 games
Jim McMahon, Chicago, 1 game
Timmy Smith, Washington, 1 game
Roger Craig, San Francisco, 3 games
Tom Rathman, San Francisco, 2 games
John Elway, Denver, 3 games
Ottis Anderson, N.Y. Giants, 2 games
Gerald Riggs, Washington, 1 game
Joe Montana, San Francisco, 4 games

**Most Touchdowns, Game**

2 Elijah Pitts, Green Bay vs. Kansas City, 1967
Larry Csonka, Miami vs. Minnesota, 1974
Pete Banaszak, Oakland vs. Minnesota, 1977
Franco Harris, Pittsburgh vs. Los Angeles, 1980
Marcus Allen, L.A. Raiders vs. Washington, 1984
Jim McMahon, Chicago vs. New England, 1986
Timmy Smith, Washington vs. Denver, 1988
Tom Rathman, San Francisco vs. Denver, 1990
Gerald Riggs, Washington vs. Buffalo, 1992
Emmitt Smith, Dallas vs. Buffalo, 1994

## PASSING

### PASSER RATING

**Highest Passer Rating, Career (40 attempts)**

127.8 Joe Montana, San Francisco, 4 games
122.8 Jim Plunkett, Oakland-L.A. Raiders, 2 games
113.2 Troy Aikman, Dallas, 2 games

### ATTEMPTS

**Most Passes Attempted, Career**

145 Jim Kelly, Buffalo, 4 games
122 Joe Montana, San Francisco, 4 games
101 John Elway, Denver, 3 games

**Most Passes Attempted, Game**

58 Jim Kelly, Buffalo vs. Washington, 1992
50 Dan Marino, Miami vs. San Francisco, 1985
Jim Kelly, Buffalo vs. Dallas, 1994
38 Ron Jaworski, Philadelphia vs. Oakland, 1981
John Elway, Denver vs. Washington, 1988

### COMPLETIONS

**Most Passes Completed, Career**

83 Joe Montana, San Francisco, 4 games
81 Jim Kelly, Buffalo, 4 games
61 Roger Staubach, Dallas, 4 games

**Most Passes Completed, Game**

31 Jim Kelly, Buffalo vs. Dallas, 1994
29 Dan Marino, Miami vs. San Francisco, 1985
28 Jim Kelly, Buffalo vs. Washington, 1992

**Most Consecutive Completions, Game**

13 Joe Montana, San Francisco vs. Denver, 1990
10 Phil Simms, N.Y. Giants vs. Denver, 1987
9 Jim Kelly, Buffalo vs. Dallas, 1994

### COMPLETION PERCENTAGE

**Highest Completion Percentage, Career (40 attempts)**

71.9 Troy Aikman, Dallas, 2 games (57-41)
68.0 Joe Montana, San Francisco, 4 games (122-83)
63.6 Len Dawson, Kansas City, 2 games (44-28)

**Highest Completion Percentage, Game (20 attempts)**

88.0 Phil Simms, N.Y. Giants vs. Denver, 1987 (25-22)
75.9 Joe Montana, San Francisco vs. Denver, 1990 (29-22)
73.5 Ken Anderson, Cincinnati vs. San Francisco, 1982 (34-25)

### YARDS GAINED

**Most Yards Gained, Career**

1,142 Joe Montana, San Francisco, 4 games
932 Terry Bradshaw, Pittsburgh, 4 games
829 Jim Kelly, Buffalo, 4 games

**Most Yards Gained, Game**

357 Joe Montana, San Francisco vs. Cincinnati, 1989
340 Doug Williams, Washington vs. Denver, 1988
331 Joe Montana, San Francisco vs. Miami, 1985

**Longest Pass Completion**

80 Jim Plunkett (to King), Oakland vs. Philadelphia, 1981 (TD)
Doug Williams (to Sanders), Washington vs. Denver, 1988 (TD)
76 David Woodley (to Cefalo), Miami vs. Washington, 1983 (TD)
75 Johnny Unitas (to Mackey), Baltimore vs. Dallas, 1971 (TD)
Terry Bradshaw (to Stallworth), Pittsburgh vs. Dallas, 1979 (TD)

### AVERAGE GAIN

**Highest Average Gain, Career (40 attempts)**

11.10 Terry Bradshaw, Pittsburgh, 4 games (84-932)
9.62 Bart Starr, Green Bay, 2 games (47-452)
9.41 Jim Plunkett, Oakland-L.A. Raiders, 2 games (46-433)

**Highest Average Gain, Game (20 attempts)**

14.71 Terry Bradshaw, Pittsburgh vs. Los Angeles, 1980 (21-309)
12.80 Jim McMahon, Chicago vs. New England, 1986 (20-256)
12.43 Jim Plunkett, Oakland vs. Philadelphia, 1981 (21-261)

### TOUCHDOWNS

**Most Touchdown Passes, Career**

11 Joe Montana, San Francisco, 4 games
9 Terry Bradshaw, Pittsburgh, 4 games
8 Roger Staubach, Dallas, 4 games

**Most Touchdown Passes, Game**

5 Joe Montana, San Francisco vs. Denver, 1990
4 Terry Bradshaw, Pittsburgh vs. Dallas, 1979
Doug Williams, Washington vs. Denver, 1988
Troy Aikman, Dallas vs. Buffalo, 1993
3 Roger Staubach, Dallas vs. Pittsburgh, 1979
Jim Plunkett, Oakland vs. Philadelphia, 1981
Joe Montana, San Francisco vs. Miami, 1985
Phil Simms, N.Y. Giants vs. Denver, 1987

### HAD INTERCEPTED

**Lowest Percentage, Passes Had Intercepted, Career (40 attempts)**

0.00 Jim Plunkett, Oakland-L.A. Raiders, 2 games (46-0)
Joe Montana, San Francisco, 4 games (122-0)
1.75 Troy Aikman, Dallas, 2 games (57-1)
2.13 Bart Starr, Green Bay, 2 games (47-1)

**Most Attempts, Without Interception, Game**

36 Joe Montana, San Francisco vs. Cincinnati, 1989
35 Joe Montana, San Francisco vs. Miami, 1985
32 Jeff Hostetler, N.Y. Giants vs. Buffalo, 1991

**Most Passes Had Intercepted, Career**

7 Craig Morton, Dallas-Denver, 2 games

Jim Kelly, Buffalo, 4 games
6 Fran Tarkenton, Minnesota, 3 games
John Elway, Denver, 3 games
4 Earl Morrall, Baltimore-Miami, 4 games
Roger Staubach, Dallas, 4 games
Terry Bradshaw, Pittsburgh, 4 games
Joe Theismann, Washington, 2 games

**Most Passes Had Intercepted, Game**
4 Craig Morton, Denver vs. Dallas, 1978
Jim Kelly, Buffalo vs. Washington, 1992
3 By eight players

## PASS RECEIVING

### RECEPTIONS

**Most Receptions, Career**
27 Andre Reed, Buffalo, 4 games
20 Roger Craig, San Francisco, 3 games
Thurman Thomas, Buffalo, 4 games
18 Jerry Rice, San Francisco, 2 games

**Most Receptions, Game**
11 Dan Ross, Cincinnati vs. San Francisco, 1982
Jerry Rice, San Francisco vs. Cincinnati, 1989
10 Tony Nathan, Miami vs. San Francisco, 1985
9 Ricky Sanders, Washington vs. Denver, 1988

### YARDS GAINED

**Most Yards Gained, Career**
364 Lynn Swann, Pittsburgh, 4 games
363 Jerry Rice, San Francisco, 2 games
323 Andre Reed, Buffalo, 4 games

**Most Yards Gained, Game**
215 Jerry Rice, San Francisco vs. Cincinnati, 1989
193 Ricky Sanders, Washington vs. Denver, 1988
161 Lynn Swann, Pittsburgh vs. Dallas, 1976

**Longest Reception**
80 Kenny King (from Plunkett), Oakland vs. Philadelphia, 1981 (TD)
Ricky Sanders (from Williams), Washington vs. Denver, 1988 (TD)
76 Jimmy Cefalo (from Woodley), Miami vs. Washington, 1983 (TD)
75 John Mackey (from Unitas), Baltimore vs. Dallas, 1971 (TD)
John Stallworth (from Bradshaw), Pittsburgh vs. Dallas, 1979 (TD)

### AVERAGE GAIN

**Highest Average Gain, Career (8 receptions)**
24.4 John Stallworth, Pittsburgh, 4 games (11-268)
23.4 Ricky Sanders, Washington, 2 games (10-234)
22.8 Lynn Swann, Pittsburgh, 4 games (16-364)

**Highest Average Gain, Game (3 receptions)**
40.33 John Stallworth, Pittsburgh vs. Los Angeles, 1980 (3-121)
40.25 Lynn Swann, Pittsburgh vs. Dallas, 1979 (4-161)
38.33 John Stallworth, Pittsburgh vs. Dallas, 1979 (3-115)

### TOUCHDOWNS

**Most Touchdowns, Career**
4 Jerry Rice, San Francisco, 2 games
3 John Stallworth, Pittsburgh, 4 games
Lynn Swann, Pittsburgh, 4 games
Cliff Branch, Oakland-L.A. Raiders, 3 games
2 Max McGee, Green Bay, 2 games
Bill Miller, Oakland, 1 game
Butch Johnson, Dallas, 2 games
Dan Ross, Cincinnati, 1 game
Roger Craig, San Francisco, 3 games
Ricky Sanders, Washington, 2 games
John Taylor, San Francisco, 2 games
Gary Clark, Washington, 2 games
Don Beebe, Buffalo, 3 games
Michael Irvin, Dallas, 2 games

**Most Touchdowns, Game**
3 Jerry Rice, San Francisco vs. Denver, 1990
2 Max McGee, Green Bay vs. Kansas City, 1967
Bill Miller, Oakland vs. Green Bay, 1968
John Stallworth, Pittsburgh vs. Dallas, 1979
Cliff Branch, Oakland vs. Philadelphia, 1981
Dan Ross, Cincinnati vs. San Francisco, 1982
Roger Craig, San Francisco vs. Miami, 1985
Ricky Sanders, Washington vs. Denver, 1988
Michael Irvin, Dallas vs. Buffalo, 1993

## INTERCEPTIONS BY

**Most Interceptions By, Career**
3 Chuck Howley, Dallas, 2 games
Rod Martin, Oakland-L.A. Raiders, 2 games
2 Randy Beverly, N.Y. Jets, 1 game
Jake Scott, Miami, 3 games
Mike Wagner, Pittsburgh, 3 games
Mel Blount, Pittsburgh, 4 games
Eric Wright, San Francisco, 4 games
Barry Wilburn, Washington, 1 game
Brad Edwards, Washington, 1 game
Thomas Everett, Dallas, 2 games
James Washington, Dallas, 2 games

**Most Interceptions By, Game**
3 Rod Martin, Oakland vs. Philadelphia, 1981
2 Randy Beverly, N.Y. Jets vs. Baltimore, 1969
Chuck Howley, Dallas vs. Baltimore, 1971
Jake Scott, Miami vs. Washington, 1973
Barry Wilburn, Washington vs. Denver, 1988
Brad Edwards, Washington vs. Buffalo, 1992
Thomas Everett, Dallas vs. Buffalo, 1993

### YARDS GAINED

**Most Yards Gained, Career**
75 Willie Brown, Oakland, 2 games
63 Chuck Howley, Dallas, 2 games
Jake Scott, Miami, 3 games
60 Herb Adderley, Green Bay-Dallas, 4 games

**Most Yards Gained, Game**
75 Willie Brown, Oakland vs. Minnesota, 1977
63 Jake Scott, Miami vs. Washington, 1973
60 Herb Adderley, Green Bay vs. Oakland, 1968

**Longest Return**
75 Willie Brown, Oakland vs. Minnesota, 1977 (TD)
60 Herb Adderley, Green Bay vs. Oakland, 1968 (TD)
55 Jake Scott, Miami vs. Washington, 1973

### TOUCHDOWNS

**Most Touchdowns, Game**
1 Herb Adderley, Green Bay vs. Oakland, 1968
Willie Brown, Oakland vs. Minnesota, 1977
Jack Squirek, L.A. Raiders vs. Washington, 1984
Reggie Phillips, Chicago vs. New England, 1986

## PUNTING

**Most Punts, Career**
17 Mike Eischeid, Oakland-Minnesota, 3 games
15 Larry Seiple, Miami, 3 games
Mike Horan, Denver, 3 games
14 Ron Widby, Dallas, 2 games
Ray Guy, Oakland-L.A. Raiders, 3 games
Chris Mohr, Buffalo, 3 games

**Most Punts, Game**
9 Ron Widby, Dallas vs. Baltimore, 1971
7 By eight players

**Longest Punt**
63 Lee Johnson, Cincinnati vs. San Francisco, 1989
62 Rich Camarillo, New England vs. Chicago, 1986
61 Jerrel Wilson, Kansas City vs. Green Bay, 1967

### AVERAGE YARDAGE

**Highest Average, Punting, Career (10 punts)**
46.5 Jerrel Wilson, Kansas City, 2 games (11-511)
41.9 Ray Guy, Oakland-L.A. Raiders, 3 games (14-587)
41.3 Larry Seiple, Miami, 3 games (15-620)

**Highest Average, Punting, Game (4 punts)**
48.5 Jerrel Wilson, Kansas City vs. Minnesota, 1970 (4-194)
46.3 Jim Miller, San Francisco vs. Cincinnati, 1982 (4-185)
45.3 Jerrel Wilson, Kansas City vs. Green Bay, 1967 (7-317)

## PUNT RETURNS

**Most Punt Returns, Career**
6 Willie Wood, Green Bay, 2 games
Jake Scott, Miami, 3 games
Theo Bell, Pittsburgh, 2 games
Mike Nelms, Washington, 1 game
John Taylor, San Francisco, 2 games
5 Dana McLemore, San Francisco, 1 game
4 By eight players

**Most Punt Returns, Game**
6 Mike Nelms, Washington vs. Miami, 1983
5 Willie Wood, Green Bay vs. Oakland, 1968
Dana McLemore, San Francisco vs. Miami, 1985
4 By six players

**Most Fair Catches, Game**
3 Ron Gardin, Baltimore vs. Dallas, 1971
Golden Richards, Dallas vs. Pittsburgh, 1976
Greg Pruitt, L.A. Raiders vs. Washington, 1984

Al Edwards, Buffalo vs. N.Y. Giants, 1991
David Meggett, N.Y. Giants vs. Buffalo, 1991

**YARDS GAINED**

**Most Yards Gained, Career**
94 John Taylor, San Francisco, 2 games
52 Mike Nelms, Washington, 1 game
51 Dana McLemore, San Francisco, 1 game

**Most Yards Gained, Game**
56 John Taylor, San Francisco vs. Cincinnati, 1989
52 Mike Nelms, Washington vs. Miami, 1983
51 Dana McLemore, San Francisco vs. Miami, 1985

**Longest Return**
45 John Taylor, San Francisco vs. Cincinnati, 1989
34 Darrell Green, Washington vs. L.A. Raiders, 1984
31 Willie Wood, Green Bay vs. Oakland, 1968

**AVERAGE YARDAGE**

**Highest Average, Career (4 returns)**
15.7 John Taylor, San Francisco, 2 games (6-94)
10.8 Neal Colzie, Oakland, 1 game (4-43)
10.2 Dana McLemore, San Francisco, 1 game (5-51)

**Highest Average, Game (3 returns)**
18.7 John Taylor, San Francisco vs. Cincinnati, 1989 (3-56)
12.7 John Taylor, San Francisco vs. Denver, 1990 (3-38)
11.7 Kelvin Martin, Dallas vs. Buffalo, 1993 (3-35)

**TOUCHDOWNS**

**Most Touchdowns, Game**
None

## KICKOFF RETURNS

**Most Kickoff Returns, Career**
10 Ken Bell, Denver, 3 games
8 Larry Anderson, Pittsburgh, 2 games
Fulton Walker, Miami, 2 games
7 Preston Pearson, Baltimore-Pittsburgh-Dallas, 5 games
Stephen Starring, New England, 1 game

**Most Kickoff Returns, Game**
7 Stephen Starring, New England vs. Chicago, 1986
6 Darren Carrington, Denver vs. San Francisco, 1990
5 Larry Anderson, Pittsburgh vs. Los Angeles, 1980
Billy Campfield, Philadelphia vs. Oakland, 1981
David Verser, Cincinnati vs. San Francisco, 1982
Alvin Garrett, Washington vs. L.A. Raiders, 1984
Ken Bell, Denver vs. Washington, 1988

**YARDS GAINED**

**Most Yards Gained, Career**
283 Fulton Walker, Miami, 2 games
207 Larry Anderson, Pittsburgh, 2 games
177 Ken Bell, Denver, 3 games

**Most Yards Gained, Game**
190 Fulton Walker, Miami vs. Washington, 1983
162 Larry Anderson, Pittsburgh vs. Los Angeles, 1980
153 Stephen Starring, New England vs. Chicago, 1986

**Longest Return**
98 Fulton Walker, Miami vs. Washington, 1983 (TD)
93 Stanford Jennings, Cincinnati vs. San Francisco, 1989 (TD)
67 Rick Upchurch, Denver vs. Dallas, 1978

**AVERAGE YARDAGE**

**Highest Average, Career (4 returns)**
35.4 Fulton Walker, Miami, 2 games (8-283)
25.9 Larry Anderson, Pittsburgh, 2 games (8-207)
24.3 Darren Carrington, Denver, 1 game (6-146)

**Highest Average, Game (3 returns)**
47.5 Fulton Walker, Miami vs. Washington, 1983 (4-190)
32.4 Larry Anderson, Pittsburgh vs. Los Angeles, 1980 (5-162)
31.3 Rick Upchurch, Denver vs. Dallas, 1978 (3-94)

**TOUCHDOWNS**

**Most Touchdowns, Game**
1 Fulton Walker, Miami vs. Washington, 1983
Stanford Jennings, Cincinnati vs. San Francisco, 1989

## FUMBLES

**Most Fumbles, Career**
5 Roger Staubach, Dallas, 4 games
4 Jim Kelly, Buffalo, 4 games
3 Franco Harris, Pittsburgh, 4 games
Terry Bradshaw, Pittsburgh, 4 games
John Elway, Denver, 3 games
Frank Reich, Buffalo, 4 games
Thurman Thomas, Buffalo, 4 games

**Most Fumbles, Game**
3 Roger Staubach, Dallas vs. Pittsburgh, 1976
Jim Kelly, Buffalo vs. Washington, 1992
Frank Reich, Buffalo vs. Dallas, 1993
2 Franco Harris, Pittsburgh vs. Minnesota, 1975
Butch Johnson, Dallas vs. Denver, 1978
Terry Bradshaw, Pittsburgh vs. Dallas, 1979
Joe Montana, San Francisco vs. Cincinnati, 1989
John Elway, Denver vs. San Francisco, 1990
Thurman Thomas, Buffalo vs. Dallas, 1994

**RECOVERIES**

**Most Fumbles Recovered, Career**
2 Jake Scott, Miami, 3 games (1 own, 1 opp)
Fran Tarkenton, Minnesota, 3 games (2 own)
Franco Harris, Pittsburgh, 4 games (2 own)
Roger Staubach, Dallas, 4 games (2 own)
Bobby Walden, Pittsburgh, 2 games (2 own)
John Fitzgerald, Dallas, 4 games (2 own)
Randy Hughes, Dallas, 3 games (2 opp)
Butch Johnson, Dallas, 2 games (2 own)
Mike Singletary, Chicago, 1 game (2 opp)
John Elway, Denver, 3 games (2 own)
Jimmie Jones, Dallas, 2 games (2 opp)
Kenneth Davis, Buffalo, 4 games (2 own)

**Most Fumbles Recovered, Game**
2 Jake Scott, Miami vs. Minnesota, 1974 (1 own, 1 opp)
Roger Staubach, Dallas vs. Pittsburgh, 1976 (2 own)
Randy Hughes, Dallas vs. Denver, 1978 (2 opp)
Butch Johnson, Dallas vs. Denver, 1978 (2 own)
Mike Singletary, Chicago vs. New England, 1986 (2 opp)
Jimmie Jones, Dallas vs. Buffalo, 1993 (2 opp)

**YARDS GAINED**

**Most Yards Gained, Game**
64 Leon Lett, Dallas vs. Buffalo, 1993 (opp)
49 Mike Bass, Washington vs. Miami, 1973 (opp)
46 James Washington, Dallas vs. Buffalo, 1994 (opp)

**Longest Return**
64 Leon Lett, Dallas vs. Buffalo, 1993
49 Mike Bass, Washington vs. Miami, 1973 (TD)
46 James Washington, Dallas vs. Buffalo, 1994 (TD)

**TOUCHDOWNS**

**Most Touchdowns, Game**
1 Mike Bass, Washington vs. Miami, 1973 (opp 49 yds)
Mike Hegman, Dallas vs. Pittsburgh, 1979 (opp 37 yds)
Jimmie Jones, Dallas vs. Buffalo, 1993 (opp 2 yds)
Ken Norton, Dallas vs. Buffalo, 1993 (opp 9 yds)
James Washington, Dallas vs. Buffalo, 1994 (opp 46 yds)

## COMBINED NET YARDS GAINED

(Rushing, receiving, interception returns, punt returns, kickoff returns, and fumble returns)

**ATTEMPTS**

**Most Attempts, Career**
108 Franco Harris, Pittsburgh, 4 games
72 Roger Craig, San Francisco, 3 games
Thurman Thomas, Buffalo, 4 games
66 John Riggins, Washington, 2 games

**Most Attempts, Game**
39 John Riggins, Washington vs. Miami, 1983
35 Franco Harris, Pittsburgh vs. Minnesota, 1975
34 Matt Snell, N.Y. Jets vs. Baltimore, 1969
Emmitt Smith, Dallas vs. Buffalo, 1994

**YARDS GAINED**

**Most Yards Gained, Career**
468 Franco Harris, Pittsburgh, 4 games
410 Roger Craig, San Francisco, 3 games
391 Lynn Swann, Pittsburgh, 4 games

**Most Yards Gained, Game**
235 Ricky Sanders, Washington vs. Denver, 1988
220 Jerry Rice, San Francisco vs. Cincinnati, 1989
213 Timmy Smith, Washington vs. Denver, 1988

## SACKS

Sacks have been compiled since 1983.

**Most Sacks, Career**
3.5 Charles Haley, San Francisco-Dallas, 4 games
3 Danny Stubbs, San Francisco, 2 games

Leonard Marshall, N.Y. Giants, 2 games
Jeff Wright, Buffalo, 4 games
2.5 Dexter Manley, Washington, 3 games

**Most Sacks, Game**
2 Dwaine Board, San Francisco vs. Miami, 1985
Dennis Owens, New England vs. Chicago, 1986
Otis Wilson, Chicago vs. New England, 1986
Leonard Marshall, N.Y. Giants vs. Denver, 1987
Alvin Walton, Washington vs. Denver, 1988
Charles Haley, San Francisco vs. Cincinnati, 1989
Danny Stubbs, San Francisco vs. Denver, 1990
Jeff Wright, Buffalo vs. Dallas, 1994

## TEAM RECORDS

### GAMES, VICTORIES, DEFEATS

**Most Games**
7 Dallas, 1971-72, 1976, 1978-79, 1993-94
5 Miami, 1972-74, 1983, 1985
Washington, 1973, 1983-84, 1988, 1992
4 Minnesota, 1970, 1974-75, 1977
Pittsburgh, 1975-76, 1979-80
Oakland/L.A. Raiders, 1968, 1977, 1981, 1984
Denver, 1978, 1987-88, 1990
San Francisco, 1982, 1985, 1989-90
Buffalo, 1991-94

**Most Consecutive Games**
4 Buffalo, 1991-94
3 Miami, 1972-74
2 Green Bay, 1967-68
Dallas, 1971-72; 1978-79; 1993-94
Minnesota, 1974-75
Pittsburgh, 1975-76, 1979-80
Washington, 1983-84
Denver, 1987-88
San Francisco 1989-90

**Most Games Won**
4 Pittsburgh, 1975-76, 1979-80
San Francisco, 1982, 1985, 1989-90
Dallas, 1972, 1978, 1993-94
3 Oakland/L.A. Raiders, 1977, 1981, 1984
Washington, 1983, 1988, 1992
2 Green Bay, 1967-68
Miami, 1973-74
N.Y. Giants, 1987, 1991

**Most Consecutive Games Won**
2 Green Bay, 1967-68
Miami, 1973-74
Pittsburgh, 1975-76, 1979-80
San Francisco, 1989-90
Dallas, 1993-94

**Most Games Lost**
4 Minnesota, 1970, 1974-75, 1977
Denver, 1978, 1987-88, 1990
Buffalo, 1991-94
3 Dallas, 1971, 1976, 1979
Miami, 1972, 1983, 1985
2 Washington, 1973, 1984
Cincinnati, 1982, 1989

**Most Consecutive Games Lost**
4 Buffalo, 1991-94
2 Minnesota, 1974-75
Denver, 1987-88

### SCORING

**Most Points, Game**
55 San Francisco vs. Denver, 1990
52 Dallas vs. Buffalo, 1993
46 Chicago vs. New England, 1986

**Fewest Points, Game**
3 Miami vs. Dallas, 1972
6 Minnesota vs. Pittsburgh, 1975
7 By four teams

**Most Points, Both Teams, Game**
69 Dallas (52) vs. Buffalo (17), 1993
66 Pittsburgh (35) vs. Dallas (31), 1979
65 San Francisco (55) vs. Denver (10), 1990

**Fewest Points, Both Teams, Game**
21 Washington (7) vs. Miami (14), 1973
22 Minnesota (6) vs. Pittsburgh (16), 1975
23 Baltimore (7) vs. N.Y. Jets (16), 1969

**Largest Margin of Victory, Game**
45 San Francisco vs. Denver, 1990 (55-10)
36 Chicago vs. New England, 1986 (46-10)
35 Dallas vs. Buffalo, 1993 (52-17)

**Most Points, Each Half**
1st: 35 Washington vs. Denver, 1988
2nd: 30 N.Y. Giants vs. Denver, 1987

**Most Points, Each Quarter**
1st: 14 Miami vs. Minnesota, 1974
Oakland vs. Philadelphia, 1981
Dallas vs. Buffalo, 1993
2nd: 35 Washington vs. Denver, 1988
3rd: 21 Chicago vs. New England, 1986
4th: 21 Dallas vs. Buffalo, 1993

**Most Points, Both Teams, Each Half**
1st: 45 Washington (35) vs. Denver (10), 1988
2nd: 44 Buffalo (24) vs. Washington (20), 1992

**Fewest Points, Both Teams, Each Half**
1st: 2 Minnesota (0) vs. Pittsburgh (2), 1975
2nd: 7 Miami (0) vs. Washington (7), 1973
Denver (0) vs. Washington (7), 1988

**Most Points, Both Teams, Each Quarter**
1st: 21 Dallas (14) vs. Buffalo (7), 1993
2nd: 35 Washington (35) vs. Denver (0), 1988
3rd: 24 Washington (14) vs. Buffalo (10), 1992
4th: 28 Dallas (14) vs. Pittsburgh (14), 1979

### TOUCHDOWNS

**Most Touchdowns, Game**
8 San Francisco vs. Denver, 1990
7 Dallas vs. Buffalo, 1993
6 Washington vs. Denver, 1988

**Fewest Touchdowns, Game**
0 Miami vs. Dallas, 1972
1 By 17 teams

**Most Touchdowns, Both Teams, Game**
9 Pittsburgh (5) vs. Dallas (4), 1979
San Francisco (8) vs. Denver (1), 1990
Dallas (7) vs. Buffalo (2), 1993
7 N.Y. Giants (5) vs. Denver (2), 1987
Washington (6) vs. Denver (1), 1988
Washington (4) vs. Buffalo (3), 1992
6 Green Bay (5) vs. Kansas City (1), 1967
Oakland (4) vs. Minnesota (2), 1977
Pittsburgh (4) vs. Los Angeles (2), 1980
L.A. Raiders (5) vs. Washington (1), 1984
San Francisco (5) vs. Miami (1), 1985
Chicago (5) vs. New England (1), 1986

**Fewest Touchdowns, Both Teams, Game**
2 Baltimore (1) vs. N.Y. Jets (1), 1969
3 In six games

### POINTS AFTER TOUCHDOWN

**Most Points After Touchdown, Game**
7 San Francisco vs. Denver, 1990
Dallas vs. Buffalo, 1993
6 Washington vs. Denver, 1988
5 Green Bay vs. Kansas City, 1967
Pittsburgh vs. Dallas, 1979
L.A. Raiders vs. Washington, 1984
San Francisco vs. Miami, 1985
Chicago vs. New England, 1986

**Most Points After Touchdown, Both Teams, Game**
9 Pittsburgh (5) vs. Dallas (4), 1979
Dallas (7) vs. Buffalo (2), 1993
8 San Francisco (7) vs. Denver (1), 1990
7 Washington (6) vs. Denver (1), 1988
Washington (4) vs. Buffalo (3), 1992

**Fewest Points After Touchdown, Both Teams, Game**
2 Baltimore (1) vs. N.Y. Jets (1), 1969
Baltimore (1) vs. Dallas (1), 1971
Minnesota (0) vs. Pittsburgh (2), 1975

### FIELD GOALS

**Most Field Goals Attempted, Game**
5 N.Y. Jets vs. Baltimore, 1969
Dallas vs. Denver, 1978
4 Green Bay vs. Oakland, 1968
Pittsburgh vs. Dallas, 1976
San Francisco vs. Cincinnati, 1982; 1989
Denver vs. N.Y. Giants, 1987

**Most Field Goals Attempted, Both Teams, Game**
7 N.Y. Jets (5) vs. Baltimore (2), 1969
San Francisco (4) vs. Cincinnati (3), 1989
6 Dallas (5) vs. Denver (1), 1978

5 Green Bay (4) vs. Oakland (1), 1968
Pittsburgh (4) vs. Dallas (1), 1976
Oakland (3) vs. Philadelphia (2), 1981
Denver (4) vs. N.Y. Giants (1), 1987
Dallas (3) vs. Buffalo (2), 1994

**Fewest Field Goals Attempted, Both Teams, Game**
1 Minnesota (0) vs. Miami (1), 1974
San Francisco (0) vs. Denver (1), 1990
2 Green Bay (0) vs. Kansas City (2), 1967
Miami (1) vs. Washington (1), 1973
Dallas (1) vs. Pittsburgh (1), 1979
Dallas (1) vs. Buffalo (1), 1993

**Most Field Goals, Game**
4 Green Bay vs. Oakland, 1968
San Francisco vs. Cincinnati, 1982
3 N.Y. Jets vs. Baltimore, 1969
Kansas City vs. Minnesota, 1970
Miami vs. San Francisco, 1985
Chicago vs. New England, 1986
Cincinnati vs. San Francisco, 1989
Washington vs. Buffalo, 1992
Dallas vs. Buffalo, 1994

**Most Field Goals, Both Teams, Game**
5 Cincinnati (3) vs. San Francisco (2), 1989
Dallas (3) vs. Buffalo (2), 1994
4 Green Bay (4) vs. Oakland (0), 1968
San Francisco (4) vs. Cincinnati (0), 1982
Miami (3) vs. San Francisco (1), 1985
Chicago (3) vs. New England (1), 1986
Buffalo (2) vs. N.Y. Giants (2), 1991
Washington (3) vs. Buffalo (1), 1992
3 In eight games

**Fewest Field Goals, Both Teams, Game**
0 Miami vs. Washington, 1973
Pittsburgh vs. Minnesota, 1975
1 Green Bay (0) vs. Kansas City (1), 1967
Minnesota (0) vs. Miami (1), 1974
Pittsburgh (0) vs. Dallas (1), 1979
Washington (0) vs. Denver (1), 1988
San Francisco (0) vs. Denver (1), 1990

### SAFETIES

**Most Safeties, Game**
1 Pittsburgh vs. Minnesota, 1975; vs. Dallas, 1976
Chicago vs. New England, 1986
N.Y. Giants vs. Denver, 1987
Buffalo vs. N.Y. Giants, 1991

## FIRST DOWNS

**Most First Downs, Game**
31 San Francisco vs. Miami, 1985
28 San Francisco vs. Denver, 1990
25 Washington vs. Denver, 1988
Buffalo vs. Washington, 1992

**Fewest First Downs, Game**
9 Minnesota vs. Pittsburgh, 1975
Miami vs. Washington, 1983
10 Dallas vs. Baltimore, 1971
Miami vs. Dallas, 1972
11 Denver vs. Dallas, 1978

**Most First Downs, Both Teams, Game**
50 San Francisco (31) vs. Miami (19), 1985
49 Buffalo (25) vs. Washington (24), 1992
47 N.Y. Giants (24) vs. Denver (23), 1987

**Fewest First Downs, Both Teams, Game**
24 Dallas (10) vs. Baltimore (14), 1971
26 Minnesota (9) vs. Pittsburgh (17), 1975
27 Pittsburgh (13) vs. Dallas (14), 1976

### RUSHING

**Most First Downs, Rushing, Game**
16 San Francisco vs. Miami, 1985
15 Dallas vs. Miami, 1972
14 Washington vs. Miami, 1983
San Francisco vs. Denver, 1990

**Fewest First Downs, Rushing, Game**
1 New England vs. Chicago, 1986
2 Minnesota vs. Kansas City, 1970; vs. Pittsburgh, 1975; vs. Oakland, 1977
Pittsburgh vs. Dallas, 1979
Miami vs. San Francisco, 1985
3 Miami vs. Dallas, 1972
Philadelphia vs. Oakland, 1981

**Most First Downs, Rushing, Both Teams, Game**
21 Washington (14) vs. Miami (7), 1983
19 Washington (13) vs. Denver (6), 1988
San Francisco (14) vs. Denver (5), 1990
18 Dallas (15) vs. Miami (3), 1972
Miami (13) vs. Minnesota (5), 1974
San Francisco (16) vs. Miami (2), 1985
N.Y. Giants (10) vs. Buffalo (8), 1991

**Fewest First Downs, Rushing, Both Teams, Game**
8 Baltimore (4) vs. Dallas (4), 1971
Pittsburgh (2) vs. Dallas (6), 1979
9 Philadelphia (3) vs. Oakland (6), 1981
10 Minnesota (2) vs. Kansas City (8), 1970

### PASSING

**Most First Downs, Passing, Game**
18 Buffalo vs. Washington, 1992
17 Miami vs. San Francisco, 1985
16 Denver vs. N.Y. Giants, 1987
San Francisco vs. Cincinnati, 1989

**Fewest First Downs, Passing, Game**
1 Denver vs. Dallas, 1978
2 Miami vs. Washington, 1983
4 Miami vs. Minnesota, 1974

**Most First Downs, Passing, Both Teams, Game**
32 Miami (17) vs. San Francisco (15), 1985
30 Buffalo (18) vs. Washington (12), 1992
29 Denver (16) vs. N.Y. Giants (13), 1987
Buffalo (15) vs. Dallas (14), 1994

**Fewest First Downs, Passing, Both Teams, Game**
9 Denver (1) vs. Dallas (8), 1978
10 Minnesota (5) vs. Pittsburgh (5), 1975
11 Dallas (5) vs. Baltimore (6), 1971
Miami (2) vs. Washington (9), 1983

### PENALTY

**Most First Downs, Penalty, Game**
4 Baltimore vs. Dallas, 1971
Miami vs. Minnesota, 1974
Cincinnati vs. San Francisco, 1982
Buffalo vs. Dallas, 1993
3 Kansas City vs. Minnesota, 1970
Minnesota vs. Oakland, 1977
Buffalo vs. Washington, 1992

**Most First Downs, Penalty, Both Teams, Game**
6 Cincinnati (4) vs. San Francisco (2), 1982
5 Baltimore (4) vs. Dallas (1), 1971
Miami (4) vs. Minnesota (1), 1974
Buffalo (3) vs. Washington (2), 1992
4 Kansas City (3) vs. Minnesota (1), 1970
Buffalo (4) vs. Dallas (0), 1993

**Fewest First Downs, Penalty, Both Teams, Game**
0 Dallas vs. Miami, 1972
Miami vs. Washington, 1973
Dallas vs. Pittsburgh, 1976
Miami vs. San Francisco, 1985
1 Green Bay (0) vs. Kansas City (1), 1967
Miami (0) vs. Washington (1), 1983
Cincinnati (0) vs. San Francisco (1), 1989
San Francisco (0) vs. Denver (1), 1990
Dallas (0) vs. Buffalo (1), 1994

## NET YARDS GAINED RUSHING AND PASSING

**Most Yards Gained, Game**
602 Washington vs. Denver, 1988
537 San Francisco vs. Miami, 1985
461 San Francisco vs. Denver, 1990

**Fewest Yards Gained, Game**
119 Minnesota vs. Pittsburgh, 1975
123 New England vs. Chicago, 1986
156 Denver vs. Dallas, 1978

**Most Yards Gained, Both Teams, Game**
929 Washington (602) vs. Denver (327), 1988
851 San Francisco (537) vs. Miami (314), 1985
782 Oakland (429) vs. Minnesota (353), 1977

**Fewest Yards Gained, Both Teams, Game**
452 Minnesota (119) vs. Pittsburgh (333), 1975
481 Washington (228) vs. Miami (253), 1973
Denver (156) vs. Dallas (325), 1978
497 Minnesota (238) vs. Miami (259), 1974

## SUPER BOWL RECORDS

### RUSHING

**ATTEMPTS**

**Most Attempts, Game**

57 Pittsburgh vs. Minnesota, 1975
53 Miami vs. Minnesota, 1974
52 Oakland vs. Minnesota, 1977
Washington vs. Miami, 1983

**Fewest Attempts, Game**

9 Miami vs. San Francisco, 1985
11 New England vs. Chicago, 1986
17 Denver vs. Washington, 1988; vs. San Francisco, 1990

**Most Attempts, Both Teams, Game**

81 Washington (52) vs. Miami (29), 1983
78 Pittsburgh (57) vs. Minnesota (21), 1975
Oakland (52) vs. Minnesota (26), 1977
77 Miami (53) vs. Minnesota (24), 1974
Pittsburgh (46) vs. Dallas (31), 1976

**Fewest Attempts, Both Teams, Game**

49 Miami (9) vs. San Francisco (40), 1985
53 Kansas City (19) vs. Green Bay (34), 1967
55 San Francisco (27) vs. Cincinnati (28), 1989

**YARDS GAINED**

**Most Yards Gained, Game**

280 Washington vs. Denver, 1988
276 Washington vs. Miami, 1983
266 Oakland vs. Minnesota, 1977

**Fewest Yards Gained, Game**

7 New England vs. Chicago, 1986
17 Minnesota vs. Pittsburgh, 1975
25 Miami vs. San Francisco, 1985

**Most Yards Gained, Both Teams, Game**

377 Washington (280) vs. Denver (97), 1988
372 Washington (276) vs. Miami (96), 1983
338 N.Y. Giants (172) vs. Buffalo (166), 1991

**Fewest Yards Gained, Both Teams, Game**

168 Buffalo (43) vs. Washington (125), 1992
171 Baltimore (69) vs. Dallas (102), 1971
174 New England (7) vs. Chicago (167), 1986

**AVERAGE GAIN**

**Highest Average Gain, Game**

7.00 L.A. Raiders vs. Washington, 1984 (33-231)
Washington vs. Denver, 1988 (40-280)
6.64 Buffalo vs. N.Y. Giants, 1991 (25-166)
6.22 Baltimore vs. N.Y. Jets, 1969 (23-143)

**Lowest Average Gain, Game**

0.64 New England vs. Chicago, 1986 (11-7)
0.81 Minnesota vs. Pittsburgh, 1975 (21-17)
2.23 Baltimore vs. Dallas, 1971 (31-69)

**TOUCHDOWNS**

**Most Touchdowns, Game**

4 Chicago vs. New England, 1986
3 Green Bay vs. Kansas City, 1967
Miami vs. Minnesota, 1974
San Francisco vs. Denver, 1990
2 Oakland vs. Minnesota, 1977
Pittsburgh vs. Los Angeles, 1980
L.A. Raiders vs. Washington, 1984
San Francisco vs. Miami, 1985
N.Y. Giants vs. Denver, 1987
Washington vs. Denver, 1988; vs. Buffalo, 1992
Buffalo vs. N.Y. Giants, 1991

**Fewest Touchdowns, Game**

0 By 17 teams

**Most Touchdowns, Both Teams, Game**

4 Miami (3) vs. Minnesota (1), 1974
Chicago (4) vs. New England (0), 1986
San Francisco (3) vs. Denver (1), 1990
3 Green Bay (3) vs. Kansas City (0), 1967
Pittsburgh (2) vs. Los Angeles (1), 1980
L.A. Raiders (2) vs. Washington (1), 1984
N.Y. Giants (2) vs. Denver (1), 1987
Buffalo (2) vs. N.Y. Giants (1), 1991
Washington (2) vs. Buffalo (1), 1992
Dallas (2) vs. Buffalo (1), 1994

**Fewest Touchdowns, Both Teams, Game**

0 Pittsburgh vs. Dallas, 1976
Oakland vs. Philadelphia, 1981
Cincinnati vs. San Francisco, 1989
1 In seven games

### PASSING

**ATTEMPTS**

**Most Passes Attempted, Game**

59 Buffalo vs. Washington, 1992
50 Miami vs. San Francisco, 1985
Buffalo vs. Dallas, 1994
44 Minnesota vs. Oakland, 1977

**Fewest Passes Attempted, Game**

7 Miami vs. Minnesota, 1974
11 Miami vs. Washington, 1973
14 Pittsburgh vs. Minnesota, 1975

**Most Passes Attempted, Both Teams, Game**

92 Buffalo (59) vs. Washington (33), 1992
85 Miami (50) vs. San Francisco (35), 1985
77 Buffalo (50) vs. Dallas (27), 1994

**Fewest Passes Attempted, Both Teams, Game**

35 Miami (7) vs. Minnesota (28), 1974
39 Miami (11) vs. Washington (28), 1973
40 Pittsburgh (14) vs. Minnesota (26), 1975
Miami (17) vs. Washington (23), 1983

**COMPLETIONS**

**Most Passes Completed, Game**

31 Buffalo vs. Dallas, 1994
29 Miami vs. San Francisco, 1985
Buffalo vs. Washington, 1992
26 Denver vs. N.Y. Giants, 1987

**Fewest Passes Completed, Game**

4 Miami vs. Washington, 1983
6 Miami vs. Minnesota, 1974
8 Miami vs. Washington, 1973
Denver vs. Dallas, 1978

**Most Passes Completed, Both Teams, Game**

53 Miami (29) vs. San Francisco (24), 1985
50 Buffalo (31) vs. Dallas (19), 1994
48 Denver (26) vs. N.Y. Giants (22), 1987

**Fewest Passes Completed, Both Teams, Game**

19 Miami (4) vs. Washington (15), 1983
20 Pittsburgh (9) vs. Minnesota (11), 1975
22 Miami (8) vs. Washington (14), 1973

**COMPLETION PERCENTAGE**

**Highest Completion Percentage, Game (20 attempts)**

88.0 N.Y. Giants vs. Denver, 1987 (25-22)
75.0 San Francisco vs. Denver, 1990 (32-24)
73.5 Cincinnati vs. San Francisco, 1982 (34-25)

**Lowest Completion Percentage, Game (20 attempts)**

32.0 Denver vs. Dallas, 1978 (25-8)
37.9 Denver vs. San Francisco, 1990 (29-11)
38.5 Denver vs. Washington, 1988 (39-15)

**YARDS GAINED**

**Most Yards Gained, Game**

341 San Francisco vs. Cincinnati, 1989
326 San Francisco vs. Miami, 1985
322 Washington vs. Denver, 1988

**Fewest Yards Gained, Game**

35 Denver vs. Dallas, 1978
63 Miami vs. Minnesota, 1974
69 Miami vs. Washington, 1973

**Most Yards Gained, Both Teams, Game**

615 San Francisco (326) vs. Miami (289), 1985
583 Denver (320) vs. N.Y. Giants (263), 1987
552 Washington (322) vs. Denver (230), 1988

**Fewest Yards Gained, Both Teams, Game**

156 Miami (69) vs. Washington (87), 1973
186 Pittsburgh (84) vs. Minnesota (102), 1975
205 Dallas (100) vs. Miami (105), 1972

**TIMES SACKED**

**Most Times Sacked, Game**

7 Dallas vs. Pittsburgh, 1976
New England vs. Chicago, 1986
6 Kansas City vs. Green Bay, 1967
Washington vs. L.A. Raiders, 1984
Denver vs. San Francisco, 1990
5 Dallas vs. Denver, 1978; vs. Pittsburgh, 1979
Cincinnati vs. San Francisco, 1982; 1989
Denver vs. Washington, 1988
Buffalo vs. Washington, 1992

**Fewest Times Sacked, Game**

0 Baltimore vs. N.Y. Jets, 1969; vs. Dallas, 1971
Minnesota vs. Pittsburgh, 1975

Pittsburgh vs. Los Angeles, 1980
Philadelphia vs. Oakland, 1981
Washington vs. Buffalo, 1992
1 By 11 teams

**Most Times Sacked, Both Teams, Game**
10 New England (7) vs. Chicago (3), 1986
9 Kansas City (6) vs. Green Bay (3), 1967
Dallas (7) vs. Pittsburgh (2), 1976
Dallas (5) vs. Denver (4), 1978
Dallas (5) vs. Pittsburgh (4), 1979
Cincinnati (5) vs. San Francisco (4), 1989
8 Washington (6) vs. L.A. Raiders (2), 1984

**Fewest Times Sacked, Both Teams, Game**
1 Philadelphia (0) vs. Oakland (1), 1981
2 Baltimore (0) vs. N.Y. Jets (2), 1969
Baltimore (0) vs. Dallas (2), 1971
Minnesota (0) vs. Pittsburgh (2), 1975
3 In four games

### TOUCHDOWNS

**Most Touchdowns, Game**
5 San Francisco vs. Denver, 1990
4 Pittsburgh vs. Dallas, 1979
Washington vs. Denver, 1988
Dallas vs. Buffalo, 1993
3 Dallas vs. Pittsburgh, 1979
Oakland vs. Philadelphia, 1981
San Francisco vs. Miami, 1985
N.Y. Giants vs. Denver, 1987

**Fewest Touchdowns, Game**
0 By 16 teams

**Most Touchdowns, Both Teams, Game**
7 Pittsburgh (4) vs. Dallas (3), 1979
5 Washington (4) vs. Denver (1), 1988
San Francisco (5) vs. Denver (0), 1990
Dallas (4) vs. Buffalo (1), 1993
4 Dallas (2) vs. Pittsburgh (2), 1976
Oakland (3) vs. Philadelphia (1), 1981
San Francisco (3) vs. Miami (1), 1985
N.Y. Giants (3) vs. Denver (1), 1987
Washington (2) vs. Buffalo (2), 1992

**Fewest Touchdowns, Both Teams, Game**
0 N.Y. Jets vs. Baltimore, 1969
Miami vs. Minnesota, 1974
Buffalo vs. Dallas, 1994
1 In six games

## INTERCEPTIONS BY

**Most Interceptions By, Game**
4 N.Y. Jets vs. Baltimore, 1969
Dallas vs. Denver, 1978
Washington vs. Buffalo, 1992
Dallas vs. Buffalo, 1993
3 By nine teams

**Most Interceptions By, Both Teams, Game**
6 Baltimore (3) vs. Dallas (3), 1971
5 Washington (4) vs. Buffalo (1), 1992
4 In seven games

**Fewest Interceptions By, Both Teams, Game**
0 Buffalo vs. N.Y. Giants, 1991
1 Oakland (0) vs. Green Bay (1), 1968
Miami (0) vs. Dallas (1), 1972
Minnesota (0) vs. Miami (1), 1974
N.Y. Giants (0) vs. Denver (1), 1987
San Francisco (1) vs. Cincinnati (0), 1989

### YARDS GAINED

**Most Yards Gained, Game**
95 Miami vs. Washington, 1973
91 Oakland vs. Minnesota, 1977
89 Pittsburgh vs. Dallas, 1976

**Most Yards Gained, Both Teams, Game**
95 Miami (95) vs. Washington (0), 1973
91 Oakland (91) vs. Minnesota (0), 1977
89 Pittsburgh (89) vs. Dallas (0), 1976

### TOUCHDOWNS

**Most Touchdowns, Game**
1 Green Bay vs. Oakland, 1968
Oakland vs. Minnesota, 1977
L.A. Raiders vs. Washington, 1984
Chicago vs. New England, 1986

## PUNTING

**Most Punts, Game**
9 Dallas vs. Baltimore, 1971
8 Washington vs. L.A. Raiders, 1984
7 By seven teams

**Fewest Punts, Game**
2 Pittsburgh vs. Los Angeles, 1980
Denver vs. N.Y. Giants, 1987
3 By 10 teams

**Most Punts, Both Teams, Game**
15 Washington (8) vs. L.A. Raiders (7), 1984
13 Dallas (9) vs. Baltimore (4), 1971
Pittsburgh (7) vs. Minnesota (6), 1975
12 In three games

**Fewest Punts, Both Teams, Game**
5 Denver (2) vs. N.Y. Giants (3), 1987
6 Oakland (3) vs. Philadelphia (3), 1981
7 In five games

### AVERAGE YARDAGE

**Highest Average, Game (4 punts)**
48.50 Kansas City vs. Minnesota, 1970 (4-194)
46.25 San Francisco vs. Cincinnati, 1982 (4-185)
45.29 Kansas City vs. Green Bay, 1967 (7-317)

**Lowest Average, Game (4 punts)**
31.20 Washington vs. Miami, 1973 (5-156)
32.38 Washington vs. L.A. Raiders, 1984 (8-259)
32.40 Oakland vs. Minnesota, 1977 (5-162)

## PUNT RETURNS

**Most Punt Returns, Game**
6 Washington vs. Miami, 1983
5 By five teams

**Fewest Punt Returns, Game**
0 Minnesota vs. Miami, 1974
Buffalo vs. N.Y. Giants, 1991
Washington vs. Buffalo, 1992
1 By 12 teams

**Most Punt Returns, Both Teams, Game**
9 Pittsburgh (5) vs. Minnesota (4), 1975
8 Green Bay (5) vs. Oakland (3), 1968
Baltimore (5) vs. Dallas (3), 1971
Washington (6) vs. Miami (2), 1983
7 Green Bay (4) vs. Kansas City (3), 1967
Oakland (4) vs. Minnesota (3), 1977
San Francisco (5) vs. Miami (2), 1985

**Fewest Punt Returns, Both Teams, Game**
2 Dallas (1) vs. Miami (1), 1972
Denver (1) vs. N.Y. Giants (1), 1987
Buffalo (0) vs. N.Y. Giants (2), 1991
Buffalo (1) vs. Dallas (1), 1994
3 Kansas City (1) vs. Minnesota (2), 1970
Minnesota (0) vs. Miami (3), 1974
Washington (1) vs. Denver (2), 1988
Washington (0) vs. Buffalo (3), 1992
4 L.A. Raiders (2) vs. Washington (2), 1984
Chicago (2) vs. New England (2), 1986
Buffalo (1) vs. Dallas (3), 1993

### YARDS GAINED

**Most Yards Gained, Game**
56 San Francisco vs. Cincinnati, 1989
52 Washington vs. Miami, 1983
51 San Francisco vs. Miami, 1985

**Fewest Yards Gained, Game**
–1 Dallas vs. Miami, 1972
0 By eight teams

**Most Yards Gained, Both Teams, Game**
74 Washington (52) vs. Miami (22), 1983
66 San Francisco (51) vs. Miami (15), 1985
61 San Francisco (56) vs. Cincinnati (5), 1989

**Fewest Yards Gained, Both Teams, Game**
9 Washington (0) vs. Bufffalo (9), 1992
10 Buffalo (5) vs. Dallas (5), 1994
13 Miami (4) vs. Washington (9), 1973

### AVERAGE RETURN

**Highest Average, Game (3 returns)**
18.7 San Francisco vs. Cincinnati, 1989 (3-56)
12.7 San Francisco vs. Denver, 1990 (3-38)
11.7 Dallas vs. Buffalo, 1993 (3-35)

# SUPER BOWL RECORDS

**TOUCHDOWNS**
**Most Touchdowns, Game**
None

## KICKOFF RETURNS
**Most Kickoff Returns, Game**
9 Denver vs. San Francisco, 1990
7 Oakland vs. Green Bay, 1968
Minnesota vs. Oakland, 1977
Cincinnati vs. San Francisco, 1982
Washington vs. L.A. Raiders, 1984
Miami vs. San Francisco, 1985
New England vs. Chicago, 1986
6 By eight teams
**Fewest Kickoff Returns, Game**
1 N.Y. Jets vs. Baltimore, 1969
L.A. Raiders vs. Washington, 1984
Washington vs. Buffalo, 1992
2 By seven teams
**Most Kickoff Returns, Both Teams, Game**
12 Denver (9) vs. San Francisco (3), 1990
11 Los Angeles (6) vs. Pittsburgh (5), 1980
Miami (7) vs. San Francisco (4), 1985
New England (7) vs. Chicago (4), 1986
10 Oakland (7) vs. Green Bay (3), 1968
**Fewest Kickoff Returns, Both Teams, Game**
5 N.Y. Jets (1) vs. Baltimore (4), 1969
Miami (2) vs. Washington (3), 1973
Washington (1) vs. Buffalo (4), 1992
6 In three games

**YARDS GAINED**
**Most Yards Gained, Game**
222 Miami vs. Washington, 1983
196 Denver vs. San Francisco, 1990
173 Denver vs. Dallas, 1978
**Fewest Yards Gained, Game**
16 Washington vs. Buffalo, 1992
17 L.A. Raiders vs. Washington, 1984
25 N.Y. Jets vs. Baltimore, 1969
**Most Yards Gained, Both Teams, Game**
279 Miami (222) vs. Washington (57), 1983
245 Denver (196) vs. San Francisco (49), 1990
231 Pittsburgh (162) vs. Los Angeles (79), 1980
**Fewest Yards Gained, Both Teams, Game**
78 Miami (33) vs. Washington (45), 1973
82 Pittsburgh (32) vs. Minnesota (50), 1975
92 San Francisco (40) vs. Cincinnati (52), 1982

**AVERAGE GAIN**
**Highest Average, Game (3 returns)**
44.0 Cincinnati vs. San Francisco, 1989 (3-132)
37.0 Miami vs. Washington, 1983 (6-222)
32.4 Pittsburgh vs. Los Angeles, 1980 (5-162)

**TOUCHDOWNS**
**Most Touchdowns, Game**
1 Miami vs. Washington, 1983
Cincinnati vs. San Francisco, 1989

## PENALTIES
**Most Penalties, Game**
12 Dallas vs. Denver, 1978
10 Dallas vs. Baltimore, 1971
9 Dallas vs. Pittsburgh, 1979
**Fewest Penalties, Game**
0 Miami vs. Dallas, 1972
Pittsburgh vs. Dallas, 1976
Denver vs. San Francisco, 1990
1 Green Bay vs. Oakland, 1968
Miami vs. Minnesota, 1974; vs. San Francisco, 1985
Buffalo vs. Dallas, 1994
2 By four teams
**Most Penalties, Both Teams, Game**
20 Dallas (12) vs. Denver (8), 1978
16 Cincinnati (8) vs. San Francisco (8), 1982
14 Dallas (10) vs. Baltimore (4), 1971
Dallas (9) vs. Pittsburgh (5), 1979
**Fewest Penalties, Both Teams, Game**
2 Pittsburgh (0) vs. Dallas (2), 1976
3 Miami (0) vs. Dallas (3), 1972
Miami (1) vs. San Francisco (2), 1985
4 Denver (0) vs. San Francisco (4), 1990

**YARDS PENALIZED**
**Most Yards Penalized, Game**
133 Dallas vs. Baltimore, 1971
122 Pittsburgh vs. Minnesota, 1975
94 Dallas vs. Denver, 1978
**Fewest Yards Penalized, Game**
0 Miami vs. Dallas, 1972
Pittsburgh vs. Dallas, 1976
Denver vs. San Francisco, 1990
4 Miami vs. Minnesota, 1974
10 Miami vs. San Francisco, 1985
San Francisco vs. Miami, 1985
Buffalo vs. Dallas, 1994
**Most Yards Penalized, Both Teams, Game**
164 Dallas (133) vs. Baltimore (31), 1971
154 Dallas (94) vs. Denver (60), 1978
140 Pittsburgh (122) vs. Minnesota (18), 1975
**Fewest Yards Penalized, Both Teams, Game**
15 Miami (0) vs. Dallas (15), 1972
20 Pittsburgh (0) vs. Dallas (20), 1976
Miami (10) vs. San Francisco (10), 1985
38 Denver (0) vs. San Francisco (38), 1990

## FUMBLES
**Most Fumbles, Game**
8 Buffalo vs. Dallas, 1993
6 Dallas vs. Denver, 1978
Buffalo vs. Washington, 1992
5 Baltimore vs. Dallas, 1971
**Fewest Fumbles, Game**
0 By 11 teams
**Most Fumbles, Both Teams, Game**
12 Buffalo (8) vs. Dallas (4), 1993
10 Dallas (6) vs. Denver (4), 1978
8 Dallas (4) vs. Pittsburgh (4), 1976
**Fewest Fumbles, Both Teams, Game**
0 Los Angeles vs. Pittsburgh, 1980
1 Oakland (0) vs. Minnesota (1), 1977
Oakland (0) vs. Philadelphia (1), 1981
Denver (0) vs. Washington (1), 1988
N.Y. Giants (0) vs. Buffalo (1), 1991
2 In four games
**Most Fumbles Lost, Game**
5 Buffalo vs. Dallas, 1993
4 Baltimore vs. Dallas, 1971
Denver vs. Dallas, 1978
New England vs. Chicago, 1986
2 In many games
**Most Fumbles Lost, Both Teams, Game**
7 Buffalo (5) vs. Dallas (2), 1993
6 Denver (4) vs. Dallas (2), 1978
New England (4) vs. Chicago (2), 1986
5 Baltimore (4) vs. Dallas (1), 1971
**Fewest Fumbles Lost, Both Teams, Game**
0 Green Bay vs. Kansas City, 1967
Dallas vs. Pittsburgh, 1976
Los Angeles vs. Pittsburgh, 1980
Denver vs. N.Y. Giants, 1987
Denver vs. Washington, 1988
Buffalo vs. N.Y. Giants, 1991
**Most Fumbles Recovered, Game**
8 Dallas vs. Denver, 1978 (4 own, 4 opp.)
6 Dallas vs. Buffalo, 1993 (1 own, 5 opp.)
5 Chicago vs. New England, 1986 (1 own, 4 opp.)

## TURNOVERS
(Number of times losing the ball on interceptions and fumbles.)
**Most Turnovers, Game**
9 Buffalo vs. Dallas, 1993
8 Denver vs. Dallas, 1978
7 Baltimore vs. Dallas, 1971
**Fewest Turnovers, Game**
0 Green Bay vs. Oakland, 1968
Miami vs. Minnesota, 1974
Pittsburgh vs. Dallas, 1976
Oakland vs. Minnesota, 1977; vs. Philadelphia, 1981
N.Y. Giants vs. Denver, 1987; vs. Buffalo, 1991
San Francisco vs. Denver, 1990
Buffalo vs. N.Y. Giants, 1991
1 By many teams
**Most Turnovers, Both Teams, Game**
11 Baltimore (7) vs. Dallas (4), 1971
Buffalo (9) vs. Dallas (2), 1993

10 Denver (8) vs. Dallas (2), 1978
8 New England (6) vs. Chicago (2), 1986

**Fewest Turnovers, Both Teams, Game**

0 Buffalo vs. N.Y. Giants, 1991
1 N.Y. Giants (0) vs. Denver (1), 1987
2 Green Bay (1) vs. Kansas City (1), 1967
Miami (0) vs. Minnesota (2), 1974
Cincinnati (1) vs. San Francisco (1), 1989

# POSTSEASON GAME RECORDS

Compiled by Elias Sports Bureau

Throughout this all-time postseason record section, the following abbreviations are used to indicate various levels of postseason games:

SB Super Bowl (1966 to date)

AFC AFC Championship Game (1970 to date) or AFL Championship Game (1960-69)

NFC NFC Championship Game (1970 to date) or NFL Championship Game (1933-69)

AFC-D AFC Divisional Playoff Game (1970 to date), AFC Second-Round Playoff Game (1982), AFL Inter-Divisional Playoff Game (1969), or special playoff game to break tie for AFL Division Championship (1963, 1968)

NFC-D NFC Divisional Playoff Game (1970 to date), NFC Second-Round Playoff Game (1982), NFL Conference Championship Game (1967-69), or special playoff game to break tie for NFL Division or Conference Championship (1941, 1943, 1947, 1950, 1952, 1957, 1958, 1965)

AFC FR AFC First-Round Playoff Game (1978 to date)

NFC-FR NFC First-Round Playoff Game (1978 to date)

## POSTSEASON GAME COMPOSITE STANDINGS

| | W | L | PCT. | PTS. | OP |
|---|---|---|---|---|---|
| Green Bay Packers | 14 | 6 | .700 | 461 | 310 |
| San Francisco 49ers | 18 | 11 | .621 | 712 | 536 |
| Dallas Cowboys | 27 | 17 | .614 | 1039 | 789 |
| Washington Redskins* | 21 | 14 | .600 | 738 | 625 |
| Pittsburgh Steelers | 16 | 11 | .593 | 609 | 545 |
| Los Angeles Raiders** | 21 | 15 | .583 | 855 | 659 |
| Miami Dolphins | 16 | 12 | .571 | 627 | 557 |
| Buffalo Bills | 13 | 11 | .542 | 563 | 520 |
| Detroit Lions | 7 | 6 | .538 | 293 | 283 |
| Chicago Bears | 13 | 13 | .500 | 529 | 490 |
| Indianapolis Colts*** | 8 | 8 | .500 | 285 | 300 |
| Kansas City Chiefs**** | 8 | 8 | .500 | 267 | 333 |
| Denver Broncos | 9 | 10 | .474 | 380 | 502 |
| Philadelphia Eagles | 8 | 9 | .471 | 290 | 288 |
| New York Jets | 5 | 6 | .455 | 216 | 200 |
| New York Giants | 14 | 18 | .438 | 529 | 593 |
| Minnesota Vikings | 13 | 17 | .433 | 535 | 611 |
| Seattle Seahawks | 3 | 4 | .429 | 128 | 139 |
| Cincinnati Bengals | 5 | 7 | .417 | 246 | 257 |
| Houston Oilers | 9 | 13 | .409 | 371 | 533 |
| New England Patriots† | 4 | 6 | .400 | 195 | 258 |
| Los Angeles Rams†† | 13 | 20 | .394 | 501 | 697 |
| Cleveland Browns | 10 | 18 | .357 | 567 | 650 |
| San Diego Chargers††† | 5 | 9 | .357 | 247 | 310 |
| Atlanta Falcons | 2 | 4 | .333 | 119 | 144 |
| Tampa Bay Buccaneers | 1 | 3 | .250 | 41 | 94 |
| Phoenix Cardinals†††† | 1 | 4 | .200 | 81 | 134 |
| New Orleans Saints | 0 | 4 | .000 | 56 | 123 |

**One game played when franchise was in Boston (lost 21-6).*

***24 games played when franchise was in Oakland (won 15, lost 9, 587 points scored, 435 points allowed).*

****15 games played when franchise was in Baltimore (won 8, lost 7, 264 points scored, 262 points allowed).*

*****One game played when franchise was Dallas Texans (won 20-17).*

*†Two games played when franchise was in Boston (won 26-8, lost 51-10).*

*††One game played when franchise was in Cleveland (won 15-14).*

*†††One game played when franchise was in Los Angeles (lost 24-16).*

*††††Two games played when franchise was in Chicago (won 28-21, lost 7-0), three games played when franchise was in St. Louis (lost 30-14, lost 35-23, lost 41-16).*

## INDIVIDUAL RECORDS

### SERVICE

**Most Games, Career**

27 D.D. Lewis, Dallas (SB 5, NFC 9, NFC-D 12, NFC-FR 1)
26 Larry Cole, Dallas (SB 5, NFC 8, NFC-D 12, NFC-FR 1)
25 Charlie Waters, Dallas (SB 5, NFC 9, NFC-D 10, NFC-FR 1)

**Most Games, Head Coach**

36 Tom Landry, Dallas
33 Don Shula, Baltimore-Miami
24 Chuck Noll, Pittsburgh

**Most Games Won, Head Coach**

20 Tom Landry, Dallas
18 Don Shula, Baltimore-Miami
16 Chuck Noll, Pittsburgh
Joe Gibbs, Washington

**Most Games Lost, Head Coach**

16 Tom Landry, Dallas
15 Don Shula, Baltimore-Miami
12 Bud Grant, Minnesota

### SCORING

#### POINTS

**Most Points, Career**

115 George Blanda, Chi. Bears-Houston-Oakland, 19 games (49-pat, 22-fg)
102 Franco Harris, Pittsburgh, 19 games (17-td)
96 Matt Bahr, Pittsburgh-Cleveland-N.Y. Giants, 13 games (39-pat, 19-fg)

**Most Points, Game**

30 Ricky Watters, NFC-D:San Francisco vs. N.Y. Giants, 1993 (5-td)
19 Pat Harder, NFC-D: Detroit vs. Los Angeles, 1952 (2-td, 4-pat, 1-fg)
Paul Hornung, NFC: Green Bay vs. N.Y. Giants, 1961 (1-td, 4-pat, 3-fg)
18 By 22 players

#### TOUCHDOWNS

**Most Touchdowns, Career**

17 Franco Harris, Pittsburgh, 19 games (16-r, 1-p)
15 Thurman Thomas, Buffalo, 16 games (12-r, 3-p)
13 Jerry Rice, San Francisco, 15 games (13-p)
Marcus Allen, L.A. Raiders-Kansas City, 13 games (11-r, 2-p)

**Most Touchdowns, Game**

5 Ricky Watters, NFC-D:San Francisco vs. N.Y. Giants, 1993 (5-r)
3 Andy Farkas, NFC-D: Washington vs. N.Y. Giants, 1943 (3-r)
Tom Fears, NFC-D: Los Angeles vs. Chi. Bears, 1950 (3-p)
Otto Graham, NFC: Cleveland vs. Detroit, 1954 (3-r)
Gary Collins, NFC: Cleveland vs. Baltimore, 1964 (3-p)
Craig Baynham, NFC-D: Dallas vs. Cleveland, 1967 (2-r, 1-p)
Fred Biletnikoff, AFC-D: Oakland vs. Kansas City, 1968 (3-p)
Tom Matte, NFC: Baltimore vs. Cleveland, 1968 (3-r)
Larry Schreiber, NFC-D: San Francisco vs. Dallas, 1972 (3-r)
Larry Csonka, AFC: Miami vs. Oakland, 1973 (3-r)
Franco Harris, AFC-D: Pittsburgh vs. Buffalo, 1974 (3-r)
Preston Pearson, NFC: Dallas vs. Los Angeles, 1975 (3-p)
Dave Casper, AFC-D: Oakland vs. Baltimore, 1977 (OT) (3-p)
Alvin Garrett, NFC-FR: Washington vs. Detroit, 1982 (3-p)
John Riggins, NFC-D: Washington vs. L.A. Rams, 1983 (3-r)
Roger Craig, SB: San Francisco vs. Miami, 1984 (1-r, 2-p)
Jerry Rice, NFC-D: San Francisco vs. Minnesota, 1988 (3-p)
Jerry Rice, SB: San Francisco vs. Denver, 1989 (3-p)
Kenneth Davis, AFC: Buffalo vs. L.A. Raiders, 1990 (3-r)
Andre Reed, AFC-FR: Buffalo vs. Houston, 1992 (OT) (3-p)
Sterling Sharpe, NFC-FR: Green Bay vs. Detroit, 1993 (3-p)
Napoleon McCallum, AFC-FR: L.A. Raiders vs. Denver, 1993 (3-r)
Thurman Thomas, AFC: Buffalo vs. Kansas City, 1993 (3-r)

**Most Consecutive Games Scoring Touchdowns**

8 John Stallworth, Pittsburgh, 1978-83
7 John Riggins, Washington, 1982-84
Marcus Allen, L.A. Raiders, 1982-85
5 Duane Thomas, Dallas, 1970-71
Franco Harris, Pittsburgh, 1974-75
Franco Harris, Pittsburgh, 1977-79
James Lofton, Green Bay-Buffalo, 1982-90
Thurman Thomas, Buffalo, 1992-93 (current)

#### POINTS AFTER TOUCHDOWN

**Most Points After Touchdown, Career**

49 George Blanda, Chi. Bears-Houston-Oakland, 19 games (49 att)
42 Mike Cofer, San Francisco, 12 games (46 att)
41 Rafael Septien, L.A. Rams-Dallas, 15 games (41 att)

**Most Points After Touchdown, Game**

8 Lou Groza, NFC: Cleveland vs. Detroit, 1954 (8 att)
Jim Martin, NFC: Detroit vs. Cleveland, 1957 (8 att)
George Blanda, AFC-D: Oakland vs. Houston, 1969 (8 att)
7 Danny Villanueva, NFC-D: Dallas vs. Cleveland, 1967 (7 att)
Raul Allegre, NFC-D: N.Y. Giants vs. San Francisco, 1986 (7 att)
Mike Cofer, SB: San Francisco vs. Denver, 1989 (8 att)
Lin Elliott, SB: Dallas vs. Buffalo, 1992 (7 att)
6 George Blair, AFC: San Diego vs. Boston, 1963 (6 att)
Mark Moseley, NFC-D: Washington vs. L.A. Rams, 1983 (6 att)
Uwe von Schamann, AFC: Miami vs. Pittsburgh, 1984 (6 att)
Ali Haji-Sheikh, SB: Washington vs. Denver, 1987 (6 att)
Scott Norwood, AFC: Buffalo vs. L.A. Raiders, 1990 (7 att)
Jeff Jaeger, AFC-FR: L.A. Raiders vs. Denver, 1993 (6 att)

**Most Points After Touchdown, No Misses, Career**

49 George Blanda, Chi. Bears-Houston-Oakland, 19 games
41 Rafael Septien, L.A. Rams-Dallas, 14 games
39 Matt Bahr, Pittsburgh-Cleveland-N.Y. Giants, 13 games

#### FIELD GOALS

**Most Field Goals Attempted, Career**

39 George Blanda, Chi. Bears-Houston-Oakland, 19 games
31 Mark Moseley, Washington-Cleveland, 11 games
26 Roy Gerela, Houston-Pittsburgh, 15 games

**Most Field Goals Attempted, Game**

6 George Blanda, AFC: Oakland vs. Houston, 1967
David Ray, NFC-D: Los Angeles vs. Dallas, 1973
Mark Moseley, AFC-D: Cleveland vs. N.Y. Jets, 1986 (OT)
Matt Bahr, NFC: N.Y. Giants vs. San Francisco, 1990
Steve Christie, AFC: Buffalo vs. Miami, 1992
5 Jerry Kramer, NFC: Green Bay vs. N.Y. Giants, 1962
Gino Cappelletti, AFC-D: Boston vs. Buffalo, 1963
Pete Gogolak, AFC: Buffalo vs. San Diego, 1965
Jim Turner, SB: N.Y. Jets vs. Baltimore, 1968
Jan Stenerud, AFC-D: Kansas City vs. N.Y. Jets, 1969
George Blanda, AFC-D: Oakland vs. Pittsburgh, 1973
Ed Murray, NFC-D: Detroit vs. San Francisco, 1983
Mark Moseley, NFC: Washington vs. San Francisco, 1983
Tony Franklin, AFC-FR: New England vs. N.Y. Jets, 1985
Tony Zendejas, AFC-FR: Houston vs. Seattle, 1987 (OT)
Chuck Nelson, NFC-D: Minnesota vs. San Francisco, 1987
Luis Zendejas, NFC-D: Philadelphia vs. Chicago, 1988
4 By many players

**Most Field Goals, Career**

22 George Blanda, Chi. Bears-Houston-Oakland, 19 games
20 Toni Fritsch, Dallas-Houston, 14 games
19 Matt Bahr, Pittsburgh-Cleveland-N.Y. Giants, 13 games

**Most Field Goals, Game**

5 Chuck Nelson, NFC-D: Minnesota vs. San Francisco, 1987
Matt Bahr, NFC: N.Y. Giants vs. San Francisco, 1990
Steve Christie, AFC: Buffalo vs. Miami, 1992
4 Gino Cappelletti, AFC-D: Boston vs. Buffalo, 1963
George Blanda, AFC: Oakland vs. Houston, 1967
Don Chandler, SB: Green Bay vs. Oakland, 1967
Curt Knight, NFC: Washington vs. Dallas, 1972
George Blanda, AFC-D: Oakland vs. Pittsburgh, 1973
Ray Wersching, SB: San Francisco vs. Cincinnati, 1981
Tony Franklin, AFC-FR: New England vs. N.Y. Jets, 1985
Jess Atkinson, NFC-FR: Washington vs. L.A. Rams, 1986
Luis Zendejas, NFC-D: Philadelphia vs. Chicago, 1988
Gary Anderson, AFC-FR: Pittsburgh vs. Houston, 1989 (OT)
3 By many players

**Most Consecutive Field Goals**

15 Rafael Septien, Dallas, 1978-82
9 Chuck Nelson, Minnesota, 1987
Gary Anderson, Pittsburgh, 1989-93 (current)
8 Tony Fritsch, Houston, 1978-79

**Longest Field Goal**

58 Pete Stoyanovich, AFC-FR: Miami vs. Kansas City, 1990
54 Ed Murray, NFC-D: Detroit vs. San Francisco, 1983
Steve Christie, SB: Buffalo vs. Dallas, 1993
53 Al Del Greco, AFC-FR: Houston vs. N.Y. Jets, 1991

**Highest Field Goal Percentage, Career (10 field goals)**

90.9 Chuck Nelson, L.A. Rams-Minnesota, 6 games (10-11)
88.2 Steve Christie, Buffalo, 7 games (15-17)
85.7 Rafael Septien, L.A. Rams-Dallas, 15 games (18-21)

### SAFETIES

**Most Safeties, Game**

1 Bill Willis, NFC-D: Cleveland vs. N.Y. Giants, 1950
Carl Eller, NFC-D: Minnesota vs. Los Angeles, 1969
George Andrie, NFC-D: Dallas vs. Detroit, 1970
Alan Page, NFC-D: Minnesota vs. Dallas, 1971
Dwight White, SB: Pittsburgh vs. Minnesota, 1974
Reggie Harrison, SB: Pittsburgh vs. Dallas, 1975
Jim Jensen, NFC-D: Dallas vs. Los Angeles, 1976
Ted Washington, AFC: Houston vs. Pittsburgh, 1978
Randy White, NFC-D: Dallas vs. Los Angeles, 1979
Henry Waechter, SB: Chicago vs. New England, 1985
Rulon Jones, AFC-FR: Denver vs. New England, 1986
George Martin, SB: N.Y. Giants vs. Denver, 1986
D.D. Hoggard, AFC: Cleveland vs. Denver, 1987
Bruce Smith, SB: Buffalo vs. N.Y. Giants, 1990
Reggie White, NFC-FR: Philadelphia vs. New Orleans, 1992

## RUSHING

### ATTEMPTS

**Most Attempts, Career**

400 Franco Harris, Pittsburgh, 19 games
302 Tony Dorsett, Dallas, 17 games
275 Thurman Thomas, Buffalo, 16 games

**Most Attempts, Game**

38 Ricky Bell, NFC-D: Tampa Bay vs. Philadelphia, 1979
John Riggins, SB: Washington vs. Miami, 1982
37 Lawrence McCutcheon, NFC-D: Los Angeles vs. St. Louis, 1975
John Riggins, NFC-D: Washington vs. Minnesota, 1982
36 John Riggins, NFC: Washington vs. Dallas, 1982
John Riggins, NFC: Washington vs. San Francisco, 1983

### YARDS GAINED

**Most Yards Gained, Career**

1,556 Franco Harris, Pittsburgh, 19 games
1,383 Tony Dorsett, Dallas, 17 games
1,152 Marcus Allen, L.A. Raiders-Kansas City, 13 games

**Most Yards Gained, Game**

248 Eric Dickerson, NFC-D: L.A. Rams vs. Dallas, 1985
206 Keith Lincoln, AFC: San Diego vs. Boston, 1963
204 Timmy Smith, SB: Washington vs. Denver, 1987

**Most Games, 100 or More Yards Rushing, Career**

6 John Riggins, Washington, 9 games
5 Franco Harris, Pittsburgh, 19 games
Marcus Allen, L.A. Raiders-Kansas City, 13 games
Thurman Thomas, Buffalo, 16 games
Emmitt Smith, Dallas, 8 games
4 Larry Csonka, Miami, 12 games
Chuck Foreman, Minnesota, 13 games

**Most Consecutive Games, 100 or More Yards Rushing**

6 John Riggins, Washington, 1982-83
4 Thurman Thomas, Buffalo, 1990-91
3 Larry Csonka, Miami, 1973-74
Franco Harris, Pittsburgh, 1974-75
Marcus Allen, L.A. Raiders, 1983
Emmitt Smith, Dallas, 1992

**Longest Run From Scrimmage**

80 Roger Craig, NFC-D: San Francisco vs. Minnesota, 1988 (TD)
74 Marcus Allen, SB: L.A. Raiders vs. Washington, 1983 (TD)
71 Hugh McElhenny, NFC-D: San Francisco vs. Detroit, 1957
James Lofton, NFC-D: Green Bay vs. Dallas, 1982 (TD)

### AVERAGE GAIN

**Highest Average Gain, Career (75 attempts)**

5.68 Roger Staubach, Dallas, 20 games (76-432)
5.24 Marcus Allen, L.A. Raiders-Kansas City, 13 games (220-1,152)
4.89 Eric Dickerson, L.A. Rams-Indianapolis, 7 games (148-724)

**Highest Average Gain, Game (10 attempts)**

15.90 Elmer Angsman, NFC: Chi. Cardinals vs. Philadelphia, 1947 (10-159)
15.85 Keith Lincoln, AFC: San Diego vs. Boston, 1963 (13-206)
10.90 Bill Osmanski, NFC: Chi. Bears vs. Washington, 1940 (10-109)

### TOUCHDOWNS

**Most Touchdowns, Career**

16 Franco Harris, Pittsburgh, 19 games
12 John Riggins, Washington, 9 games
Thurman Thomas, Buffalo, 16 games
11 Marcus Allen, L.A. Raiders-Kansas City, 13 games

**Most Touchdowns, Game**

5 Ricky Watters, NFC-D: San Francisco vs. N.Y. Giants, 1993
3 Andy Farkas, NFC-D: Washington vs. N.Y. Giants, 1943
Otto Graham, NFC: Cleveland vs. Detroit, 1954
Tom Matte, NFC: Baltimore vs. Cleveland, 1968
Larry Schreiber, NFC-D: San Francisco vs. Dallas, 1972
Larry Csonka, AFC: Miami vs. Oakland, 1973
Franco Harris, AFC-D: Pittsburgh vs. Buffalo, 1974
John Riggins, NFC-D: Washington vs. L.A. Rams, 1983
Kenneth Davis, AFC: Buffalo vs. L.A. Raiders, 1990
Napoleon McCallum, AFC-FR: L.A. Raiders vs. Denver, 1993
Thuman Thomas, AFC: Buffalo vs. Kansas City, 1993

**Most Consecutive Games Rushing for Touchdowns**

7 John Riggins, Washington, 1982-84
5 Franco Harris, Pittsburgh, 1974-75
Franco Harris, Pittsburgh, 1977-79
4 Thurman Thomas, Buffalo, 1992-93 (current)

## PASSING

### PASSER RATING

**Highest Passer Rating, Career (150 attempts)**

111.2 Troy Aikman, Dallas, 7 games
104.8 Bart Starr, Green Bay, 10 games
95.2 Joe Montana, San Francisco-Kansas City, 22 games

### ATTEMPTS

**Most Passes Attempted, Career**

697 Joe Montana, San Francisco-Kansas City, 22 games
462 Jim Kelly, Buffalo, 14 games
456 Terry Bradshaw, Pittsburgh, 19 games

**Most Passes Attempted, Game**

64 Bernie Kosar, AFC-D: Cleveland vs. N.Y. Jets, 1986 (OT)
58 Jim Kelly, SB: Buffalo vs. Washington, 1991
54 Randall Cunningham, NFC-D: Philadelphia vs. Chicago, 1988
Jim Kelly, AFC-D: Buffalo vs. Cleveland, 1989

## POSTSEASON GAME RECORDS

**COMPLETIONS**

**Most Passes Completed, Career**

434 Joe Montana, San Francisco-Kansas City, 22 games
275 Jim Kelly, Buffalo, 14 games
261 Terry Bradshaw, Pittsburgh, 19 games

**Most Passes Completed, Game**

36 Warren Moon, AFC-FR: Houston vs. Buffalo, 1992 (OT)
33 Dan Fouts, AFC-D: San Diego vs. Miami, 1981 (OT)
Bernie Kosar, AFC-D: Cleveland vs. N.Y. Jets, 1986 (OT)
32 Neil Lomax, NFC-FR: St. Louis vs. Green Bay, 1982
Danny White, NFC-FR: Dallas vs. L.A. Rams, 1983
Warren Moon, AFC-D: Houston vs. Kansas City, 1993

**COMPLETION PERCENTAGE**

**Highest Completion Percentage, Career (150 attempts)**

71.1 Troy Aikman, Dallas, 7 games (187-133)
67.9 Steve Young, San Francisco, 12 games (156-106)
66.3 Ken Anderson, Cincinnati, 6 games (166-110)

**Highest Completion Percentage, Game (15 completions)**

88.0 Phil Simms, SB: N.Y. Giants vs. Denver, 1986 (25-22)
86.7 Joe Montana, NFC: San Francisco vs. L.A. Rams, 1989 (30-26)
84.2 David Woodley, AFC-FR: Miami vs. New England, 1982 (19-16)

**YARDS GAINED**

**Most Yards Gained, Career**

5,458 Joe Montana, San Francisco-Kansas City, 22 games
3,833 Terry Bradshaw, Pittsburgh, 19 games
3,321 John Elway, Denver, 14 games

**Most Yards Gained, Game**

489 Bernie Kosar, AFC-D: Cleveland vs. N.Y. Jets, 1986 (OT)
433 Dan Fouts, AFC-D: San Diego vs. Miami, 1981 (OT)
421 Dan Marino, AFC: Miami vs. Pittsburgh, 1984

**Most Games, 300 or More Yards Passing, Career**

5 Dan Fouts, San Diego, 7 games
Joe Montana, San Francisco-Kansas City, 22 games
4 Warren Moon, Houston, 9 games
3 Terry Bradshaw, Pittsburgh, 19 games
Danny White, Dallas, 17 games
Dan Marino, Miami, 10 games
Jim Kelly, Buffalo, 14 games
John Elway, Denver, 14 games

**Most Consecutive Games, 300 or More Yards Passing**

4 Dan Fouts, San Diego, 1979-81
3 Jim Kelly, Buffalo, 1989-90
Warren Moon, Houston, 1991-93 (current)
2 Daryle Lamonica, Oakland, 1968
Ken Anderson, Cincinnati, 1981-82
Terry Bradshaw, Pittsburgh, 1979-82
Joe Montana, San Francisco, 1983-84
Dan Marino, Miami, 1984

**Longest Pass Completion**

93 Daryle Lamonica (to Dubenion), AFC-D: Buffalo vs. Boston, 1963 (TD)
88 George Blanda (to Cannon), AFC: Houston vs. L.A. Chargers, 1960 (TD)
86 Don Meredith (to Hayes), NFC-D: Dallas vs. Cleveland, 1967 (TD)
Jeff Hostetler (to Brown), AFC-D: L.A. Raiders vs. Buffalo, 1993 (TD)

**AVERAGE GAIN**

**Highest Average Gain, Career (150 attempts)**

8.53 Troy Aikman, Dallas, 7 games (187-1,595)
8.45 Joe Theismann, Washington, 10 games (211-1,782)
8.43 Jim Plunkett, Oakland-L.A. Raiders, 10 games (272-2,293)

**Highest Average Gain, Game (20 attempts)**

14.71 Terry Bradshaw, SB: Pittsburgh vs. Los Angeles, 1979 (21-309)
13.33 Bob Waterfield, NFC-D: Los Angeles vs. Chi. Bears, 1950 (21-280)
13.16 Dan Marino, AFC: Miami vs. Pittsburgh, 1984 (32-421)

**TOUCHDOWNS**

**Most Touchdown Passes, Career**

43 Joe Montana, San Francisco-Kansas City, 22 games
30 Terry Bradshaw, Pittsburgh, 19 games
24 Roger Staubach, Dallas, 20 games

**Most Touchdown Passes, Game**

6 Daryle Lamonica, AFC-D: Oakland vs. Houston, 1969
5 Sid Luckman, NFC: Chi. Bears vs. Washington, 1943
Daryle Lamonica, AFC-D: Oakland vs. Kansas City, 1968
Joe Montana, SB: San Francisco vs. Denver, 1989
4 Otto Graham, NFC: Cleveland vs. Los Angeles, 1950
Tobin Rote, NFC: Detroit vs. Cleveland, 1957
Bart Starr, NFC: Green Bay vs. Dallas, 1966
Ken Stabler, AFC-D: Oakland vs. Miami, 1974
Roger Staubach, NFC: Dallas vs. Los Angeles, 1975
Terry Bradshaw, SB: Pittsburgh vs. Dallas, 1978
Don Strock, AFC-D: Miami vs. San Diego, 1981 (OT)
Lynn Dickey, NFC-FR: Green Bay vs. St. Louis, 1982
Dan Marino, AFC: Miami vs. Pittsburgh, 1984
Phil Simms, NFC-D: N.Y. Giants vs. San Francisco, 1986
Doug Williams, SB: Washington vs. Denver, 1987
Jim Kelly, AFC-D: Buffalo vs. Cleveland, 1989
Joe Montana, NFC-D: San Francisco vs. Minnesota, 1989
Warren Moon, AFC-FR: Houston vs. Buffalo, 1992 (OT)
Frank Reich, AFC-FR: Buffalo vs. Houston, 1992 (OT)
Troy Aikman, SB: Dallas vs. Buffalo, 1992

**Most Consecutive Games, Touchdown Passes**

10 Ken Stabler, Oakland, 1973-77
Dan Marino, Miami, 1983-92 (current)
Joe Montana, San Francisco-Kansas City, 1988-93
9 John Elway, Denver, 1984-89
8 Terry Bradshaw, Pittsburgh, 1977-82
Joe Montana, San Francisco, 1981-84
Bernie Kosar, Cleveland-Dallas, 1985-93

**HAD INTERCEPTED**

**Lowest Percentage, Passes Had Intercepted, Career (150 attempts)**

1.41 Bart Starr, Green Bay, 10 games (213-3)
2.14 Troy Aikman, Dallas, 7 games (187-4)
2.15 Phil Simms, N.Y. Giants, 10 games (279-6)

**Most Attempts Without Interception, Game**

48 Warren Moon, AFC-FR: Houston vs. Pittsburgh, 1989 (OT)
47 Daryle Lamonica, AFC: Oakland vs. N.Y. Jets, 1968
43 Joe Montana, AFC-FR: Kansas City vs. Pittsburgh, 1993 (OT)

**Most Passes Had Intercepted, Career**

26 Terry Bradshaw, Pittsburgh, 19 games
22 Jim Kelly, Buffalo, 14 games
20 Joe Montana, San Francisco-Kansas City, 22 games

**Most Passes Had Intercepted, Game**

6 Frank Filchock, NFC: N.Y. Giants vs. Chi. Bears, 1946
Bobby Layne, NFC: Detroit vs. Cleveland, 1954
Norm Van Brocklin, NFC: Los Angeles vs. Cleveland, 1955
5 Frank Filchock, NFC: Washington vs. Chi. Bears, 1940
George Blanda, AFC: Houston vs. San Diego, 1961
George Blanda, AFC: Houston vs. Dall. Texans, 1962 (OT)
Y.A. Tittle, NFC: N.Y. Giants vs. Chicago, 1963
Mike Phipps, AFC-D: Cleveland vs. Miami, 1972
Dan Pastorini, AFC: Houston vs. Pittsburgh, 1978
Dan Fouts, AFC-D: San Diego vs. Houston, 1979
Tommy Kramer, NFC-D: Minnesota vs. Philadelphia, 1980
Dan Fouts, AFC-D: San Diego vs. Miami, 1982
Richard Todd, AFC: N.Y. Jets vs Miami, 1982
Gary Danielson, NFC-D: Detroit vs. San Francisco, 1983
Jay Schroeder, AFC: L.A. Raiders vs. Buffalo, 1990
4 By many players

## PASS RECEIVING

**RECEPTIONS**

**Most Receptions, Career**

84 Jerry Rice, San Francisco, 15 games
75 Andre Reed, Buffalo, 16 games
73 Cliff Branch, Oakland-L.A. Raiders, 22 games

**Most Receptions, Game**

13 Kellen Winslow, AFC-D: San Diego vs. Miami, 1981 (OT)
Thurman Thomas, AFC-D: Buffalo vs. Cleveland, 1989
Shannon Sharpe, AFC-FR: Denver vs. L.A. Raiders, 1993
12 Raymond Berry, NFC: Baltimore vs. N.Y. Giants, 1958
11 Dante Lavelli, NFC: Cleveland vs. Los Angeles, 1950
Dan Ross, SB: Cincinnati vs. San Francisco, 1981
Franco Harris, AFC-FR: Pittsburgh vs. San Diego, 1982
Steve Watson, AFC-D: Denver vs. Pittsburgh, 1984
John L. Williams, AFC-D: Seattle vs. Cincinnati, 1988
Jerry Rice, SB: San Francisco vs. Cincinnati, 1988
Ernest Givins, AFC-FR: Houston vs. Pittsburgh, 1989 (OT)

**Most Consecutive Games, Pass Receptions**

22 Drew Pearson, Dallas, 1973-83
18 Paul Warfield, Cleveland-Miami, 1964-74
Cliff Branch, Oakland-L.A. Raiders, 1974-83
17 John Stallworth, Pittsburgh, 1974-84

**YARDS GAINED**

**Most Yards Gained, Career**

1,306 Jerry Rice, San Francisco, 15 games
1,289 Cliff Branch, Oakland-L.A. Raiders, 22 games
1,167 Fred Biletnikoff, Oakland, 19 games

**Most Yards Gained, Game**

227 Anthony Carter, NFC-D: Minnesota vs. San Francisco, 1987
215 Jerry Rice, SB: San Francisco vs. Cincinnati, 1988
198 Tom Fears, NFC-D: Los Angeles vs. Chi. Bears, 1950

**Most Games, 100 or More Yards Receiving, Career**
5 John Stallworth, Pittsburgh, 18 games
Jerry Rice, San Francisco, 15 games
Andre Reed, Buffalo, 16 games
4 Fred Biletnikoff, Oakland, 19 games
Dwight Clark, San Francisco, 7 games
Art Monk, Washington, 15 games
3 Tom Fears, L.A. Rams, 6 games
Cliff Branch, Oakland-L.A. Raiders, 22 games
Tony Nathan, Miami, 10 games
Mark Duper, Miami, 10 games
James Lofton, Green Bay-Buffalo, 13 games
Vance Johnson, Denver, 11 games
Ernest Givins, Houston, 10 games

**Most Consecutive Games, 100 or More Yards Receiving, Career**
3 Tom Fears, Los Angeles, 1950-51
Jerry Rice, San Francisco, 1988-89
2 Lenny Moore, Baltimore, 1958-59
Fred Biletnikoff, Oakland, 1968
Paul Warfield, Miami, 1971
Charlie Joiner, San Diego, 1980-81
Dwight Clark, San Francisco, 1981
Cris Collinsworth, Cincinnati, 1981-82
John Stallworth, Pittsburgh, 1979-82
Wesley Walker, N.Y. Jets, 1982
Charlie Brown, Washington, 1983
Steve Largent, Seattle, 1984-87
Vance Johnson, Denver, 1986-87
Andre Reed, Buffalo, 1989-90
James Lofton, Buffalo, 1990
Ernest Givins, Houston, 1991-92
Michael Irvin, Dallas, 1992-93
Sterling Sharpe, Green Bay, 1993 (current)

**Longest Reception**
93 Elbert Dubenion (from Lamonica), AFC-D: Buffalo vs. Boston, 1963 (TD)
88 Billy Cannon (from Blanda), AFC: Houston vs. L.A. Chargers, 1960 (TD)
86 Bob Hayes (from Meredith), NFC: Dallas vs. Cleveland, 1967 (TD)
Tim Brown (from Hostetler), AFC-D: L.A. Raiders vs. Buffalo, 1993 (TD)

### AVERAGE GAIN

**Highest Average Gain, Career (20 receptions)**
25.4 Alvin Harper, Dallas, 8 games (21-533)
23.7 Willie Gault, Chicago-L.A. Raiders, 10 games (21-497)
22.8 Harold Jackson, L.A. Rams-New England-Minnesota-Seattle, 14 games (24-548)

**Highest Average Gain, Game (3 receptions)**
46.3 Harold Jackson, NFC: Los Angeles vs. Minnesota, 1974 (3-139)
42.7 Billy Cannon, AFC: Houston vs. L.A. Chargers, 1960 (3-128)
42.0 Lenny Moore, NFC: Baltimore vs. N.Y. Giants, 1959 (3-126)

### TOUCHDOWNS

**Most Touchdowns, Career**
13 Jerry Rice, San Francisco, 15 games
12 John Stallworth, Pittsburgh, 18 games
10 Fred Biletnikoff, Oakland, 19 games

**Most Touchdowns, Game**
3 Tom Fears, NFC-D: Los Angeles vs. Chi. Bears, 1950
Gary Collins, NFC: Cleveland vs. Baltimore, 1964
Fred Biletnikoff, AFC-D: Oakland vs. Kansas City, 1968
Preston Pearson, NFC: Dallas vs. Los Angeles, 1975
Dave Casper, AFC-D: Oakland vs. Baltimore, 1977 (OT)
Alvin Garrett, NFC-FR: Washington vs. Detroit, 1982
Jerry Rice, NFC-D: San Francisco vs. Minnesota, 1988
Jerry Rice, SB: San Francisco vs. Denver, 1989
Andre Reed, AFC-FR: Buffalo vs. Houston, 1992 (OT)
Sterling Sharpe, NFC-FR: Green Bay vs. Detroit, 1993

**Most Consecutive Games, Touchdown Passes Caught**
8 John Stallworth, Pittsburgh, 1978-83
5 James Lofton, Green Bay-Buffalo, 1982-90
4 Lynn Swann, Pittsburgh, 1978-79
Harold Carmichael, Philadelphia, 1978-80
Fred Solomon, San Francisco, 1983-84
Jerry Rice, San Francisco, 1988-89
John Taylor, San Francisco, 1988-89

## INTERCEPTIONS BY

**Most Interceptions, Career**
9 Charlie Waters, Dallas, 25 games
Bill Simpson, Los Angeles-Buffalo, 11 games
Ronnie Lott, San Francisco-L.A. Raiders, 20 games
8 Lester Hayes, Oakland-L.A. Raiders, 13 games
7 Willie Brown, Oakland, 17 games
Dennis Thurman, Dallas, 14 games

**Most Interceptions, Game**
4 Vernon Perry, AFC-D: Houston vs. San Diego, 1979
3 Joe Laws, NFC: Green Bay vs. N.Y. Giants, 1944
Charlie Waters, NFC-D: Dallas vs. Chicago, 1977
Rod Martin, SB: Oakland vs. Philadelphia, 1980
Dennis Thurman, NFC-D: Dallas vs. Green Bay, 1982
A.J. Duhe, AFC: Miami vs. N.Y. Jets, 1982
2 By many players

**Most Consecutive Games, Interceptions**
3 Warren Lahr, Cleveland, 1950-51
Ken Gorgal, Cleveland, 1950-53
Joe Schmidt, Detroit, 1954-57
Emmitt Thomas, Kansas City, 1969
Mel Renfro, Dallas, 1970
Rick Volk, Baltimore, 1970-71
Mike Wagner, Pittsburgh, 1975-76
Randy Hughes, Dallas, 1977-78
Vernon Perry, Houston, 1979-80
Lester Hayes, Oakland, 1980
Gerald Small, Miami, 1982
Lester Hayes, L.A. Raiders, 1982-83
Fred Marion, New England, 1985
John Harris, Seattle-Minnesota, 1984-87
Felix Wright, Cleveland, 1987-88
Kurt Gouveia, Washington, 1991

### YARDS GAINED

**Most Yards Gained, Career**
196 Willie Brown, Oakland, 17 games
187 Ronnie Lott, San Francisco-L.A. Raiders, 20 games
151 Glen Edwards, Pittsburgh-San Diego, 17 games

**Most Yards Gained, Game**
101 George Teague, NFC-FR: Green Bay vs. Detroit, 1993
98 Darrol Ray, AFC-FR: N.Y. Jets vs. Cincinnati, 1982
94 LeRoy Irvin, NFC-FR: L.A. Rams vs. Dallas, 1983

**Longest Return**
101 George Teague, NFC-FR: Green Bay vs. Detroit, 1993 (TD)
98 Darrol Ray, AFC-FR: N.Y. Jets vs. Cincinnati, 1982 (TD)
94 LeRoy Irvin, NFC-FR: L.A. Rams vs. Dallas, 1983

### TOUCHDOWNS

**Most Touchdowns, Career**
3 Willie Brown, Oakland, 17 games
2 Lester Hayes, Oakland-L.A. Raiders, 13 games
Ronnie Lott, San Francisco-L.A. Raiders, 20 games
Darrell Green, Washington, 16 games
Melvin Jenkins, Seattle-Detroit, 5 games

**Most Touchdowns, Game**
1 By many players.

## PUNTING

**Most Punts, Career**
111 Ray Guy, Oakland-L.A. Raiders, 22 games
84 Danny White, Dallas, 18 games
73 Mike Eischeid, Oakland-Minnesota, 14 games

**Most Punts, Game**
14 Dave Jennings, AFC-D: N.Y. Jets vs. Cleveland, 1986 (OT)
12 David Lee, AFC-D: Baltimore vs. Oakland, 1977 (OT)
11 Ken Strong, NFC: N.Y. Giants vs. Chi. Bears, 1933
Jim Norton, AFC: Houston vs. Oakland, 1967
Ode Burrell, AFC-D: Houston vs. Oakland, 1969
Dale Hatcher, NFC: L.A. Rams vs. Chicago, 1985

**Longest Punt**
76 Ed Danowski, NFC: N.Y. Giants vs. Detroit, 1935
Mike Horan, AFC: Denver vs. Buffalo, 1991
72 Charlie Conerly, NFC-D: N.Y. Giants vs. Cleveland, 1950
Yale Lary, NFC: Detroit vs. Cleveland, 1953
71 Ray Guy, AFC: Oakland vs. San Diego, 1980

### AVERAGE YARDAGE

**Highest Average, Career (25 punts)**
44.5 Rich Camarillo, New England, 6 games (35-1,559)
44.4 Lee Johnson, Cleveland-Cincinnati, 7 games (28-1,244)
43.8 John Kidd, Buffalo-San Diego, 5 games (26-1,139)

**Highest Average, Game (4 punts)**
56.0 Ray Guy, AFC: Oakland vs. San Diego, 1980 (4-224)
52.5 Sammy Baugh, NFC: Washington vs. Chi. Bears, 1942 (6-315)
51.6 Lee Johnson, AFC-D: Cincinnati vs. L.A. Raiders, 1990 (5-258)

## PUNT RETURNS

**Most Punt Returns, Career**
25 Theo Bell, Pittsburgh-Tampa Bay, 10 games
21 Gerald McNeil, Cleveland-Houston, 8 games

19 Willie Wood, Green Bay, 10 games
Butch Johnson, Dallas-Denver, 18 games
Phil McConkey, N.Y. Giants, 5 games

**Most Punt Returns, Game**
7 Ron Gardin, AFC-D: Baltimore vs. Cincinnati, 1970
Carl Roaches, AFC-FR: Houston vs. Oakland, 1980
Gerald McNeil, AFC-D: Cleveland vs. N.Y. Jets, 1986 (OT)
Phil McConkey, NFC-D: N.Y. Giants vs. San Francisco, 1986
6 George McAfee, NFC-D: Chi. Bears vs. Los Angeles, 1950
Eddie Brown, NFC-D: Washington vs. Minnesota, 1976
Theo Bell, AFC: Pittsburgh vs. Houston, 1978
Eddie Brown, NFC: Los Angeles vs. Tampa Bay, 1979
John Sciarra, NFC: Philadelphia vs. Dallas, 1980
Kurt Sohn, AFC: N.Y. Jets vs. Miami, 1982
Mike Nelms, SB: Washington vs. Miami, 1982
Anthony Carter, NFC-FR: Minnesota vs. New Orleans, 1987
5 By many players

### YARDS GAINED
**Most Yards Gained, Career**
259 Anthony Carter, Minnesota, 8 games
221 Neal Colzie, Oakland-Miami-Tampa Bay, 10 games
211 Gerald McNeil, Cleveland-Houston, 8 games

**Most Yards Gained, Game**
143 Anthony Carter, NFC-FR: Minnesota vs. New Orleans, 1987
141 Bob Hayes, NFC-D: Dallas vs. Cleveland, 1967
102 Charley Trippi, NFC: Chi. Cardinals vs. Philadelphia, 1947

**Longest Return**
84 Anthony Carter, NFC-FR: Minnesota vs. New Orleans, 1987 (TD)
81 Hugh Gallarneau, NFC-D: Chi. Bears vs. Green Bay, 1941 (TD)
79 Bosh Pritchard, NFC-D: Philadelphia vs. Pittsburgh, 1947 (TD)

### AVERAGE YARDAGE
**Highest Average, Career (10 returns)**
15.2 Anthony Carter, Minnesota, 8 games (17-259)
12.9 Brian Mitchell, Washington, 7 games (11-142)
12.6 Bob Hayes, Dallas, 15 games (12-151)

**Highest Average Gain, Game (3 returns)**
47.0 Bob Hayes, NFC-D: Dallas vs. Cleveland, 1967 (3-141)
29.0 George (Butch) Byrd, AFC: Buffalo vs. San Diego, 1965 (3-87)
25.3 Bosh Pritchard, NFC-D: Philadelphia vs. Pittsburgh, 1947 (4-101)

### TOUCHDOWNS
**Most Touchdowns**
1 Hugh Gallarneau, NFC-D: Chicago Bears vs. Green Bay, 1941
Bosh Pritchard, NFC-D: Philadelphia vs. Pittsburgh, 1947
Charley Trippi, NFC: Chicago Cardinals vs. Philadelphia, 1947
Verda (Vitamin T) Smith, NFC-D: Los Angeles vs. Detroit, 1952
George (Butch) Byrd, AFC: Buffalo vs. San Diego, 1965
Golden Richards, NFC: Dallas vs. Minnesota, 1973
Wes Chandler, AFC-D: San Diego vs. Miami, 1981 (OT)
Shaun Gayle, NFC-D: Chicago vs. N.Y. Giants, 1985
Anthony Carter, NFC-FR: Minnesota vs. New Orleans, 1987
Darrell Green, NFC-D: Washington vs. Chicago, 1987

## KICKOFF RETURNS
**Most Kickoff Returns, Career**
29 Fulton Walker, Miami-L.A. Raiders, 10 games
21 Ken Bell, Denver, 9 games
19 Preston Pearson, Baltimore-Pittsburgh-Dallas, 22 games
James Brooks, San Diego-Cincinnati, 9 games

**Most Kickoff Returns, Game**
8 Marc Logan, AFC-D: Miami vs. Buffalo, 1990
7 Don Bingham, NFC: Chi. Bears vs. N.Y. Giants, 1956
Reggie Brown, NFC-FR: Atlanta vs. Minnesota, 1982
David Verser, AFC-FR: Cincinnati vs. N.Y. Jets, 1982
Del Rodgers, NFC-D: Green Bay vs. Dallas, 1982
Henry Ellard, NFC-D: L.A. Rams vs. Washington, 1983
Stephen Starring, SB: New England vs. Chicago, 1985
6 By many players

### YARDS GAINED
**Most Yards Gained, Career**
677 Fulton Walker, Miami-L.A. Raiders, 10 games
481 Carl Garrett, Oakland, 5 games
435 Dennis Gentry, Chicago, 12 games

**Most Yards Gained, Game**
190 Fulton Walker, SB: Miami vs. Washington, 1982
170 Les (Speedy) Duncan, NFC-D: Washington vs. San Francisco, 1971
169 Carl Garrett, AFC-D: Oakland vs. Baltimore, 1977 (OT)

**Longest Return**
98 Fulton Walker, SB: Miami vs. Washington, 1982 (TD)
97 Vic Washington, NFC-D: San Francisco vs. Dallas, 1972 (TD)
93 Stanford Jennings, SB: Cincinnati vs. San Francisco, 1988 (TD)

### AVERAGE YARDAGE
**Highest Average, Career (10 returns)**
30.1 Carl Garrett, Oakland, 5 games (16-481)
27.9 George Atkinson, Oakland, 16 games (12-335)
27.7 Eric Metcalf, Cleveland, 2 games (10-277)

**Highest Average, Game (3 returns)**
56.7 Les (Speedy) Duncan, NFC-D: Washington vs. San Francisco, 1971 (3-170)
51.3 Ed Podolak, AFC-D: Kansas City vs. Miami, 1971 (OT) (3-154)
49.0 Les (Speedy) Duncan, AFC: San Diego vs. Buffalo, 1964 (3-147)

### TOUCHDOWNS
**Most Touchdowns**
1 Vic Washington, NFC-D: San Francisco vs. Dallas, 1972
Nat Moore, AFC-D: Miami vs. Oakland, 1974
Marshall Johnson, AFC-D: Baltimore vs. Oakland, 1977 (OT)
Fulton Walker, SB: Miami vs. Washington, 1982
Stanford Jennings, SB: Cincinnati vs. San Francisco, 1988
Eric Metcalf, AFC-D: Cleveland vs. Buffalo, 1989

## FUMBLES
**Most Fumbles, Career**
15 Warren Moon, Houston, 9 games
13 Tony Dorsett, Dallas, 17 games
10 Franco Harris, Pittsburgh, 19 games
Terry Bradshaw, Pittsburgh, 19 games
Roger Staubach, Dallas, 20 games

**Most Fumbles, Game**
5 Warren Moon, AFC-D: Houston vs. Kansas City, 1993
4 Brian Sipe, AFC-D: Cleveland vs. Oakland, 1980
3 By many players

### RECOVERIES
**Most Own Fumbles Recovered, Career**
7 Warren Moon, Houston, 9 games
6 John Elway, Denver, 14 games
5 Roger Staubach, Dallas, 20 games

**Most Opponents' Fumbles Recovered, Career**
4 Cliff Harris, Dallas, 21 games
Harvey Martin, Dallas, 22 games
Ted Hendricks, Baltimore-Oakland-L.A. Raiders, 21 games
Alvin Walton, Washington, 9 games
Monte Coleman, Washington, 21 games
3 Paul Krause, Minnesota, 19 games
Jack Lambert, Pittsburgh, 18 games
Fred Dryer, Los Angeles, 14 games
Charlie Waters, Dallas, 25 games
Jack Ham, Pittsburgh, 16 games
Mike Hegman, Dallas, 16 games
Tom Jackson, Denver, 10 games
Rich Milot, Washington, 13 games
Mike Singletary, Chicago, 12 games
Darryl Grant, Washington, 16 games
Wes Hopkins, Philadelphia, 3 games
Wilber Marshall, Chicago-Washington, 14 games
2 By many players

**Most Fumbles Recovered, Game, Own and Opponents'**
3 Jack Lambert, AFC: Pittsburgh vs. Oakland, 1975 (3 opp)
Ron Jaworski, NFC-FR: Philadelphia vs. N.Y. Giants, 1981 (3 own)
2 By many players

### YARDS GAINED
**Longest Return**
93 Andy Russell, AFC-D: Pittsburgh vs. Baltimore, 1975 (opp, TD)
64 Leon Lett, SB: Dallas vs. Buffalo, 1992 (opp)
60 Mike Curtis, NFC-D: Baltimore vs. Minnesota, 1968 (opp, TD)
Hugh Green, NFC-FR: Tampa Bay vs. Dallas, 1982 (opp, TD)

### TOUCHDOWNS
**Most Touchdowns**
1 By many players

## COMBINED NET YARDS GAINED
Rushing, receiving, interception returns, punt returns, kickoff returns, and fumble returns.

### ATTEMPTS
**Most Attempts, Career**
454 Franco Harris, Pittsburgh, 19 games
350 Tony Dorsett, Dallas, 17 games
342 Thurman Thomas, Buffalo, 16 games

**Most Attempts, Game**
40 Lawrence McCutcheon, NFC-D: Los Angeles vs. St. Louis, 1975
39 John Riggins, SB: Washington vs. Miami, 1982
Rodney Hampton, NFC-FR: N.Y. Giants vs. Minnesota, 1993
38 Ricky Bell, NFC-D: Tampa Bay vs. Philadelphia, 1979
Rob Carpenter, NFC-FR: N.Y. Giants vs. Philadelphia, 1981

### YARDS GAINED
**Most Yards Gained, Career**
2,060 Franco Harris, Pittsburgh, 19 games
1,786 Tony Dorsett, Dallas, 17 games
1,736 Thurman Thomas, Buffalo, 16 games
**Most Yards Gained, Game**
350 Ed Podolak, AFC-D: Kansas City vs. Miami, 1971 (OT)
329 Keith Lincoln, AFC: San Diego vs. Boston, 1963
285 Bob Hayes, NFC-D: Dallas vs. Cleveland, 1967

## SACKS
Sacks have been compiled since 1982
**Most Sacks, Career**
12 Bruce Smith, Buffalo, 16 games
10.5 Richard Dent, Chicago, 10 games
10 Charles Mann, Washington, 17 games
Charles Haley, San Francisco-Dallas, 16 games
**Most Sacks, Game**
3.5 Rich Milot, NFC-D: Washington vs. Chicago, 1984
Richard Dent, NFC-D: Chicago vs. N.Y. Giants, 1985
3 Richard Dent, NFC-D: Chicago vs. Washington, 1984
Garin Veris, AFC-FR: New England vs. N.Y. Jets, 1985
Gary Jeter, NFC-D: L.A. Rams vs. Dallas, 1985
Carl Hairston, AFC-D: Cleveland vs. N.Y. Jets, 1986 (OT)
Charles Mann, NFC-D: Washington vs. Chicago, 1987
Kevin Greene, NFC-FR: L.A. Rams vs. Minnesota, 1988
Greg Townsend, AFC-D: L.A. Raiders vs. Cincinnati, 1990
Wilber Marshall, NFC: Washington vs. Detroit, 1991
Fred Stokes, NFC-FR: Washington vs. Minnesota, 1992
Pierce Holt, NFC-D: San Francisco vs. Washington, 1992
Tony Casillas, NFC: Dallas vs. San Francisco, 1992
Gerald Williams, AFC-FR: Pittsburgh vs. Kansas City, 1993
2.5 Lyle Alzado, AFC-D: L.A. Raiders vs. Pittsburgh, 1983
Jacob Green, AFC-FR: Seattle vs. L.A. Raiders, 1984
Larry Roberts, NFC-D: San Francisco vs. Minnesota, 1988
Leslie O'Neal, AFC-FR: San Diego vs. Kansas City, 1992

## TEAM RECORDS

## GAMES, VICTORIES, DEFEATS
**Most Seasons Participating in Postseason Games**
23 N.Y. Giants, 1933-35, 1938-39, 1941, 1943-44, 1946, 1950, 1956, 1958-59,1961-63, 1981, 1984-86, 1989-90, 1993
22 Cleveland/L.A. Rams, 1945, 1949-52, 1955, 1967, 1969, 1973-80, 1983-86, 1988-89
Cleveland, 1950-55, 1957-58, 1964-65, 1967-69, 1971-72, 1980, 1982, 1985-89
21 Dallas, 1966-73, 1975-83, 1985, 1991-93
**Most Consecutive Seasons Participating in Postseason Games**
9 Dallas, 1975-83
8 Dallas, 1966-73
Pittsburgh, 1972-79
Los Angeles, 1973-80
San Francisco, 1983-90
7 Houston, 1987-93
**Most Games**
44 Dallas, 1966-73, 1975-83, 1985, 1991-93
36 Oakland/L.A. Raiders, 1967-70, 1973-77, 1980, 1982-85, 1990-91, 1993
35 Boston/Washington, 1936-37, 1940, 1942-43, 1945, 1971-74, 1976-77, 1982-84, 1986-87, 1990-92
**Most Games Won**
27 Dallas, 1967, 1970-73, 1975, 1977-78, 1980-82, 1991-93
21 Washington, 1937, 1942-43, 1972, 1982-83, 1986-87, 1990-92
Oakland/L.A. Raiders, 1967-70, 1973-77, 1980, 1982-83, 1990, 1993
18 San Francisco, 1970-71, 1981, 1983-84, 1988-90, 1992-93
**Most Consecutive Games Won**
9 Green Bay, 1961-62, 1965-67
7 Pittsburgh, 1974-76
San Francisco, 1988-90
6 Miami, 1972-73
Pittsburgh, 1978-79
Washington, 1982-83
Dallas, 1992-93

**Most Games Lost**
20 L.A. Rams, 1949-50, 1952, 1955, 1967, 1969, 1973-80, 1983-86, 1988-89
18 Cleveland, 1951-53, 1957-58, 1965, 1967-69, 1971-72, 1980, 1982, 1985-89
N.Y. Giants, 1933, 1935, 1939, 1941, 1943-44, 1946, 1950, 1958-59, 1961-63, 1981, 1984-85, 1989, 1993
17 Dallas, 1966-70, 1972-73, 1975-76, 1978-83, 1985, 1991
Minnesota, 1968-71, 1973-78, 1980, 1982, 1987-89, 1992-93
**Most Consecutive Games Lost**
6 N.Y. Giants, 1939, 1941, 1943-44, 1946, 1950
Cleveland, 1969, 1971-72, 1980, 1982, 1985
5 N.Y. Giants, 1958-59, 1961-63
Los Angeles, 1952, 1955, 1967, 1969, 1973
Denver, 1977-79, 1983-84
Baltimore/Indianapolis, 1971, 1975-77, 1987 (current)
Philadelphia, 1980-81, 1988-90
4 Washington, 1972-74, 1976
Miami, 1974, 1978-79, 1981
Chi. Cardinals/St. Louis, 1948, 1974-75, 1982 (current)
Boston/New England, 1963, 1976, 1978, 1982
New Orleans, 1987, 1990-92 (current)
Minnesota, 1988-89, 1992-93

## SCORING
**Most Points, Game**
73 NFC: Chi. Bears vs. Washington, 1940
59 NFC: Detroit vs. Cleveland, 1957
56 NFC: Cleveland vs. Detroit, 1954
AFC-D: Oakland vs. Houston, 1969
**Most Points, Both Teams, Game**
79 AFC-D: San Diego (41) vs. Miami (38), 1981 (OT)
AFC-FR: Buffalo (41) vs. Houston (38), 1992 (OT)
78 AFC-D: Buffalo (44) vs. Miami (34), 1990
73 NFC: Chi. Bears (73) vs. Washington (0), 1940
NFC: Detroit (59) vs. Cleveland (14), 1957
AFC: Miami (45) vs. Pittsburgh (28), 1984
**Fewest Points, Both Teams, Game**
5 NFC-D: Detroit (0) vs. Dallas (5), 1970
7 NFC: Chi. Cardinals (0) vs. Philadelphia (7), 1948
9 NFC: Tampa Bay (0) vs. Los Angeles (9), 1979
**Largest Margin of Victory, Game**
73 NFC: Chi. Bears vs. Washington, 1940 (73-0)
49 AFC-D: Oakland vs. Houston, 1969 (56-7)
48 AFC: Buffalo vs. L.A. Raiders, 1990 (51-3)
**Most Points, Shutout Victory, Game**
73 NFC: Chi. Bears vs. Washington, 1940
38 NFC-D: Dallas vs. Tampa Bay, 1981
37 NFC: Green Bay vs. N.Y. Giants, 1961
**Most Points Overcome to Win Game**
32 AFC-FR: Buffalo vs. Houston, 1992 (trailed 3-35, won 41-38) (OT)
20 NFC-D: Detroit vs. San Francisco, 1957 (trailed 7-27, won 31-27)
18 NFC-D: Dallas vs. San Francisco, 1972 (trailed 3-21, won 30-28)
AFC-D: Miami vs. Cleveland, 1985 (trailed 3-21, won 24-21)
**Most Points, Each Half**
1st: 41 AFC: Buffalo vs. L.A. Raiders, 1990
38 NFC-D: Washington vs. L.A. Rams, 1983
35 NFC: Cleveland vs. Detroit, 1954
AFC-D: Oakland vs. Houston, 1969
SB: Washington vs. Denver, 1987
2nd: 45 NFC: Chi. Bears vs. Washington, 1940
35 AFC-FR: Buffalo vs. Houston, 1992
30 SB: N.Y. Giants vs. Denver, 1986
AFC: Cleveland vs. Denver, 1987
**Most Points, Each Quarter**
1st: 28 AFC-D: Oakland vs. Houston, 1969
24 AFC-D: San Diego vs. Miami, 1981
21 NFC: Chi. Bears vs. Washington, 1940
AFC: San Diego vs. Boston, 1963
AFC-D: Oakland vs. Kansas City, 1968
AFC: Oakland vs. San Diego, 1980
AFC: Buffalo vs. L.A. Raiders, 1990
2nd: 35 SB: Washington vs. Denver, 1987
26 AFC-D: Pittsburgh vs. Buffalo, 1974
24 NFC-D: Chi. Bears vs. Green Bay, 1941
NFC: Green Bay vs. N.Y. Giants, 1961
3rd: 28 AFC-FR: Buffalo vs. Houston, 1992
26 NFC: Chi. Bears vs. Washington, 1940
21 NFC-D: Dallas vs. Cleveland, 1967
NFC-D: Dallas vs. Tampa Bay, 1981
AFC-D: L.A. Raiders vs. Pittsburgh, 1983
SB: Chicago vs. New England, 1985
NFC-D: N.Y. Giants vs. San Francisco, 1986

AFC: Cleveland vs. Denver, 1987
AFC: Cleveland vs. Denver, 1989
4th: 27 NFC: N.Y. Giants vs. Chi. Bears, 1934
26 NFC-FR: Philadelphia vs. New Orleans, 1992
24 NFC: Baltimore vs. N.Y. Giants, 1959
OT: 6 NFC: Baltimore vs. N.Y. Giants, 1958
AFC-D: Oakland vs. Baltimore, 1977
NFC-D: L.A. Rams vs. N.Y. Giants, 1989

## TOUCHDOWNS

**Most Touchdowns, Game**

11 NFC: Chi. Bears vs. Washington, 1940
8 NFC: Cleveland vs. Detroit, 1954
NFC: Detroit vs. Cleveland, 1957
AFC-D: Oakland vs. Houston, 1969
SB: San Francisco vs. Denver, 1989
7 AFC: San Diego vs. Boston, 1963
NFC-D: Dallas vs. Cleveland, 1967
NFC-D: N.Y. Giants vs. San Francisco, 1986
AFC: Buffalo vs. L.A. Raiders, 1990
SB: Dallas vs. Buffalo, 1992

**Most Touchdowns, Both Teams, Game**

11 NFC: Chi. Bears (11) vs. Washington (0), 1940
10 NFC: Detroit (8) vs. Cleveland (2), 1957
AFC-D: Miami (5) vs. San Diego (5), 1981 (OT)
AFC: Miami (6) vs. Pittsburgh (4), 1984
AFC-FR: Buffalo (5) vs. Houston (5), 1992 (OT)
9 NFC: Chi. Bears (6) vs. Washington (3), 1943
NFC: Cleveland (8) vs. Detroit (1), 1954
NFC-D: Dallas (7) vs. Cleveland (2), 1967
AFC-D: Oakland (8) vs. Houston (1), 1969
AFC-D: Oakland (5) vs. Baltimore (4), 1977 (OT)
SB: Pittsburgh (5) vs. Dallas (4), 1978
AFC: Denver (5) vs. Cleveland (4), 1987
SB: San Francisco (8) vs. Denver (1), 1989
AFC-D: Buffalo (5) vs. Miami (4), 1990
SB: Dallas (7) vs. Buffalo (2), 1992
AFC-FR: L.A. Raiders (6) vs. Denver (3), 1993

**Fewest Touchdowns, Both Teams, Game**

0 NFC-D: N.Y. Giants vs. Cleveland, 1950
NFC-D: Dallas vs. Detroit, 1970
NFC: Los Angeles vs. Tampa Bay, 1979
1 NFC: Chi. Cardinals (0) vs. Philadelphia (1), 1948
NFC-D: Cleveland (0) vs. N.Y. Giants (1), 1958
AFC: San Diego (0) vs. Houston (1), 1961
AFC-D: N.Y. Jets (0) vs. Kansas City (1), 1969
NFC-D: Green Bay (0) vs. Washington (1), 1972
NFC-FR: New Orleans (0) vs. Chicago (1), 1990
NFC: N.Y. Giants (0) vs. San Francisco (1), 1990
AFC-FR: L.A. Raiders (0) vs. Kansas City (1), 1991
2 In many games

## POINTS AFTER TOUCHDOWN

**Most Points After Touchdown, Game**

8 NFC: Cleveland vs. Detroit, 1954
NFC: Detroit vs. Cleveland, 1957
AFC-D: Oakland vs. Houston, 1969
7 NFC: Chi. Bears vs. Washington, 1940
NFC-D: Dallas vs. Cleveland, 1967
NFC-D: N.Y. Giants vs. San Francisco, 1986
SB: San Francisco vs. Denver, 1989
SB: Dallas vs. Buffalo, 1992
6 AFC: San Diego vs. Boston, 1963
NFC-D: Washington vs. L.A. Rams, 1983
AFC: Miami vs. Pittsburgh, 1984
SB: Washington vs. Denver, 1987
AFC: Buffalo vs. L.A. Raiders, 1990
AFC-FR: L.A. Raiders vs. Denver, 1993

**Most Points After Touchdown, Both Teams, Game**

10 NFC: Detroit (8) vs. Cleveland (2), 1957
AFC-D: Miami (5) vs. San Diego (5), 1981 (OT)
AFC: Miami (6) vs. Pittsburgh (4), 1984
AFC-FR: Buffalo (5) vs. Houston (5), 1992 (OT)
9 In many games

**Fewest Points After Touchdown, Both Teams, Game**

0 NFC-D: N.Y. Giants vs. Cleveland, 1950
NFC-D: Dallas vs. Detroit, 1970
NFC: Los Angeles vs. Tampa Bay, 1979

## FIELD GOALS

**Most Field Goals, Game**

5 NFC-D: Minnesota vs. San Francisco, 1987
NFC: N.Y. Giants vs. San Francisco, 1990
AFC: Buffalo vs. Miami, 1992
4 AFC-D: Boston vs. Buffalo, 1963
AFC: Oakland vs. Houston, 1967
SB: Green Bay vs. Oakland, 1967
NFC: Washington vs. Dallas, 1972
AFC-D: Oakland vs. Pittsburgh, 1973
SB: San Francisco vs. Cincinnati, 1981
AFC-FR: New England vs. N.Y. Jets, 1985
NFC-FR: Washington vs. L.A. Rams, 1986
NFC-D: Philadelphia vs. Chicago, 1988
AFC-FR: Pittsburgh vs. Houston, 1989 (OT)
3 By many teams

**Most Field Goals, Both Teams, Game**

7 AFC-FR: Pittsburgh (4) vs. Houston (3), 1989 (OT)
NFC: N.Y. Giants (5) vs. San Francisco (2), 1990
6 NFC-D: Minnesota (5) vs. San Francisco (1), 1987
NFC-D: Philadelphia (4) vs. Chicago (2), 1988
AFC: Buffalo (5) vs. Miami (1), 1992
5 In many games

**Most Field Goals Attempted, Game**

6 AFC: Oakland vs. Houston, 1967
NFC-D: Los Angeles vs. Dallas, 1973
AFC-D: Cleveland vs. N.Y. Jets, 1986 (OT)
NFC: N.Y. Giants vs. San Francisco, 1990
5 By many teams

**Most Field Goals Attempted, Both Teams, Game**

9 NFC-D: Philadelphia (5) vs. Chicago (4), 1988
8 NFC-D: Los Angeles (6) vs. Dallas (2), 1973
NFC-D: Detroit (5) vs. San Francisco (3), 1983
AFC-D: Cleveland (6) vs. N.Y. Jets (2), 1986 (OT)
NFC-D: Minnesota (5) vs. San Francisco (3), 1987
AFC-FR: Houston (4) vs. Pittsburgh (4), 1989 (OT)
NFC-FR: Chicago (4) vs. New Orleans (4), 1990
NFC: N.Y. Giants (6) vs. San Francisco (2), 1990
7 In many games

## SAFETIES

**Most Safeties, Game**

1 By many teams

**Most Safeties, Both Teams, Game**

1 In many games

## FIRST DOWNS

**Most First Downs, Game**

34 AFC-D: San Diego vs. Miami, 1981 (OT)
33 AFC-D: Cleveland vs. N.Y. Jets, 1986 (OT)
31 SB: San Francisco vs. Miami, 1984

**Fewest First Downs, Game**

6 NFC: N.Y. Giants vs. Green Bay, 1961
7 NFC: Green Bay vs. Boston, 1936
NFC-D: Pittsburgh vs. Philadelphia, 1947
NFC: Chi. Cardinals vs. Philadelphia, 1948
NFC: Los Angeles vs. Philadelphia, 1949
NFC-D: Cleveland vs. N.Y. Giants, 1958
AFC-D: Cincinnati vs. Baltimore, 1970
NFC-D: Detroit vs. Dallas, 1970
NFC: Tampa Bay vs. Los Angeles, 1979
8 By many teams

**Most First Downs, Both Teams, Game**

59 AFC-D: San Diego (34) vs. Miami (25), 1981 (OT)
55 AFC-FR: San Diego (29) vs. Pittsburgh (26), 1982
51 AFC: Buffalo (30) vs. L.A. Raiders (21), 1990
AFC: Buffalo (29) vs. Kansas City (22), 1993

**Fewest First Downs, Both Teams, Game**

15 NFC: Green Bay (7) vs. Boston (8), 1936
19 NFC: N.Y. Giants (9) vs. Green Bay (10), 1939
NFC: Washington (9) vs. Chi. Bears (10), 1942
20 NFC-D: Cleveland (9) vs. N.Y. Giants (11), 1950

## RUSHING

**Most First Downs, Rushing, Game**

19 NFC-FR: Dallas vs. Los Angeles, 1980
18 AFC-D: Miami vs. Cincinnati, 1973
AFC: Miami vs. Oakland, 1973
AFC-D: Pittsburgh vs. Buffalo, 1974
17 AFC-D: Cincinnati vs. Seattle, 1988
AFC: Buffalo vs. Kansas City, 1993

**Fewest First Downs, Rushing, Game**

0 NFC: Los Angeles vs. Philadelphia, 1949
AFC-D: Buffalo vs. Boston, 1963
AFC: Oakland vs. Pittsburgh, 1974
NFC-FR: New Orleans vs. Minnesota, 1987
NFC: L.A. Rams vs. San Francisco, 1989

NFC-D: Chicago vs. N.Y. Giants, 1990
1 By many teams

**Most First Downs, Rushing, Both Teams, Game**
26 AFC: Buffalo (14) vs. L.A. Raiders (12), 1990
25 NFC-FR: Dallas (19) vs. Los Angeles (6), 1980
23 NFC: Cleveland (15) vs. Detroit (8), 1952
AFC-D: Miami (18) vs. Cincinnati (5), 1973
AFC-D: Pittsburgh (18) vs. Buffalo (5), 1974

**Fewest First Downs, Rushing, Both Teams, Game**
5 AFC-D: Buffalo (0) vs. Boston (5), 1963
6 NFC: Green Bay (2) vs. Boston (4), 1936
NFC-D: Baltimore (2) vs. Minnesota (4), 1968
AFC-D: Houston (1) vs. Oakland (5), 1969
AFC-FR: N.Y. Jets (1) vs. Houston (5), 1991
7 NFC-D: Washington (2) vs. N.Y. Giants (5), 1943
NFC: Baltimore (3) vs. N.Y. Giants (4), 1959
NFC: Washington (3) vs. Dallas (4), 1972
AFC-FR: N.Y. Jets (3) vs. Buffalo (4), 1981
NFC-D: Detroit (3) vs. Dallas (4), 1991
AFC-D: Kansas City (3) vs. Houston (4), 1993

### PASSING

**Most First Downs, Passing, Game**
21 AFC-D: Miami vs. San Diego, 1981 (OT)
AFC-D: San Diego vs. Miami, 1981 (OT)
AFC-D: Cleveland vs. N.Y. Jets, 1986 (OT)
NFC-D: Philadelphia vs. Chicago, 1988
20 NFC-FR: Dallas vs. L.A. Rams, 1983
AFC-D: Buffalo vs. Cleveland, 1989
19 NFC-FR: St. Louis vs. Green Bay, 1982
NFC-FR: Dallas vs. Tampa Bay, 1982
AFC-FR: Pittsburgh vs. San Diego, 1982
AFC-FR: San Diego vs. Pittsburgh, 1982
NFC: Dallas vs. Washington, 1982
NFC-D: Detroit vs. Dallas, 1991
AFC-FR: Kansas City vs. Pittsburgh, 1993 (OT)

**Fewest First Downs, Passing, Game**
0 NFC: Philadelphia vs. Chi. Cardinals, 1948
1 NFC-D: N.Y. Giants vs. Washington, 1943
NFC: Cleveland vs. Detroit, 1953
SB: Denver vs. Dallas, 1977
2 By many teams

**Most First Downs, Passing, Both Teams, Game**
42 AFC-D: Miami (21) vs. San Diego (21), 1981 (OT)
38 AFC-FR: Pittsburgh (19) vs. San Diego (19), 1982
34 NFC-FR: Washington (18) vs. San Francisco (16), 1990
AFC-FR: Kansas City (19) vs. Pittsburgh (15), 1993 (OT)

**Fewest First Downs, Passing, Both Teams, Game**
2 NFC: Philadelphia (0) vs. Chi. Cardinals (2), 1948
4 NFC-D: Cleveland (2) vs. N.Y. Giants (2), 1950
5 NFC: Detroit (2) vs. N.Y. Giants (3), 1935
NFC: Green Bay (2) vs. N.Y. Giants (3), 1939

### PENALTY

**Most First Downs, Penalty, Game**
7 AFC-D: New England vs. Oakland, 1976
6 AFC-D: Cleveland vs. N.Y. Jets, 1986 (OT)
5 AFC-FR: Cleveland vs. L. A. Raiders, 1982

**Most First Downs, Penalty, Both Teams, Game**
9 AFC-D: New England (7) vs. Oakland (2), 1976
8 NFC-FR: Atlanta (4) vs. Minnesota (4), 1982
7 AFC-D: Baltimore (4) vs. Oakland (3), 1977 (OT)
AFC-FR: Denver (4) vs. L.A. Raiders (3), 1993

## NET YARDS GAINED RUSHING AND PASSING

**Most Yards Gained, Game**
610 AFC: San Diego vs. Boston, 1963
602 SB: Washington vs. Denver, 1987
569 AFC: Miami vs. Pittsburgh, 1984

**Fewest Yards Gained, Game**
86 NFC-D: Cleveland vs. N.Y. Giants, 1958
99 NFC: Chi. Cardinals vs. Philadelphia, 1948
114 NFC-D: N.Y. Giants vs. Washington, 1943

**Most Yards Gained, Both Teams, Game**
1,036 AFC-D: San Diego (564) vs. Miami (472), 1981 (OT)
1,024 AFC: Miami (569) vs. Pittsburgh (455), 1984
929 SB: Washington (602) vs. Denver (327), 1987

**Fewest Yards Gained, Both Teams, Game**
331 NFC: Chi. Cardinals (99) vs. Philadelphia (232), 1948
332 NFC-D: N.Y. Giants (150) vs. Cleveland (182), 1950
336 NFC: Boston (116) vs. Green Bay (220), 1936

## RUSHING

### ATTEMPTS

**Most Attempts, Game**
65 NFC: Detroit vs. N.Y. Giants, 1935
61 NFC: Philadelphia vs. Los Angeles, 1949
59 AFC: New England vs. Miami, 1985

**Fewest Attempts, Game**
9 SB: Miami vs. San Francisco, 1984
10 NFC: L.A. Rams vs. San Francisco, 1989
11 SB: New England vs. Chicago, 1985
AFC-FR: Seattle vs. Houston, 1987 (OT)
NFC: San Francisco vs. N.Y. Giants, 1990
AFC: Miami vs. Buffalo, 1992

**Most Attempts, Both Teams, Game**
109 NFC: Detroit (65) vs. N.Y. Giants (44), 1935
97 AFC-D: Baltimore (50) vs. Oakland (47), 1977 (OT)
91 NFC: Philadelphia (57) vs. Chi. Cardinals (34), 1948

**Fewest Attempts, Both Teams, Game**
32 AFC-D: Houston (14) vs. Kansas City (18), 1993
38 NFC-D: Detroit (16) vs. Dallas (22), 1991
40 NFC-D: Green Bay (13) vs. Dallas (27), 1993

### YARDS GAINED

**Most Yards Gained, Game**
382 NFC: Chi. Bears vs. Washington, 1940
338 NFC-FR: Dallas vs. Los Angeles, 1980
318 AFC: San Diego vs. Boston, 1963

**Fewest Yards Gained, Game**
7 AFC-D: Buffalo vs. Boston, 1963
SB: New England vs. Chicago, 1985
17 SB: Minnesota vs. Pittsburgh, 1974
18 AFC-D: Seattle vs. Cincinnati, 1988

**Most Yards Gained, Both Teams, Game**
430 NFC-FR: Dallas (338) vs. Los Angeles (92), 1980
426 NFC: Cleveland (227) vs. Detroit (199), 1952
404 NFC: Chi. Bears (382) vs. Washington (22), 1940

**Fewest Yards Gained, Both Teams, Game**
90 AFC-D: Buffalo (7) vs. Boston (83), 1963
106 NFC: Boston (39) vs. Green Bay (67), 1936
110 AFC-D: Houston (39) vs. Kansas City (71), 1993

### AVERAGE GAIN

**Highest Average Gain, Game**
9.94 AFC: San Diego vs. Boston, 1963 (32-318)
9.29 NFC-D: Green Bay vs. Dallas, 1982 (17-158)
7.35 NFC-FR: Dallas vs. Los Angeles, 1980 (46-338)

**Lowest Average Gain, Game**
0.58 AFC-D: Buffalo vs. Boston, 1963 (12-7)
0.64 SB: New England vs. Chicago, 1985 (11-7)
0.81 SB: Minnesota vs. Pittsburgh, 1974 (21-17)

### TOUCHDOWNS

**Most Touchdowns, Game**
7 NFC: Chi. Bears vs. Washington, 1940
6 NFC-D: San Francisco vs. N.Y. Giants, 1993
5 NFC: Cleveland vs. Detroit, 1954

**Most Touchdowns, Both Teams, Game**
7 NFC: Chi. Bears (7) vs. Washington (0), 1940
6 NFC: Cleveland (5) vs. Detroit (1), 1954
NFC-D: San Francisco (6) vs. N.Y. Giants (0), 1993
5 NFC: Chi. Cardinals (3) vs. Philadelphia (2), 1947
AFC: San Diego (4) vs. Boston (1), 1963
AFC-D: Cincinnati (3) vs. Buffalo (2), 1981

## PASSING

### ATTEMPTS

**Most Attempts, Game**
65 AFC-D: Cleveland vs. N.Y. Jets, 1986 (OT)
59 SB: Buffalo vs. Washington, 1991
55 NFC-D: Philadelphia vs. Chicago, 1988

**Fewest Attempts, Game**
5 NFC: Detroit vs. N.Y. Giants, 1935
6 AFC: Miami vs. Oakland, 1973
7 SB: Miami vs. Minnesota, 1973

**Most Attempts, Both Teams, Game**
102 AFC-D: San Diego (54) vs. Miami (48), 1981 (OT)
96 AFC: N.Y. Jets (49) vs. Oakland (47), 1968
95 AFC-D: Cleveland (65) vs. N.Y. Jets (30), 1986 (OT)

**Fewest Attempts, Both Teams, Game**
18 NFC: Detroit (5) vs. N.Y. Giants (13), 1935
23 NFC: Chi. Cardinals (11) vs. Philadelphia (12), 1948
24 NFC-D: Cleveland (9) vs. N.Y. Giants (15), 1950

# POSTSEASON GAME RECORDS

### COMPLETIONS

**Most Completions, Game**

36 AFC-FR: Houston vs. Buffalo, 1992 (OT)
34 AFC-D: Cleveland vs. N.Y. Jets, 1986 (OT)
33 AFC-D: San Diego vs. Miami, 1981 (OT)

**Fewest Completions, Game**

2 NFC: Detroit vs. N.Y. Giants, 1935
NFC: Philadelphia vs. Chi. Cardinals, 1948
3 NFC: N.Y. Giants vs. Chi. Bears, 1941
NFC: Green Bay vs. N.Y. Giants, 1944
NFC: Chi. Cardinals vs. Philadelphia, 1947
NFC: Chi. Cardinals vs. Philadelphia, 1948
NFC-D: Cleveland vs. N.Y. Giants, 1950
NFC-D: N.Y. Giants vs. Cleveland, 1950
NFC: Cleveland vs. Detroit, 1953
AFC: Miami vs. Oakland, 1973
4 NFC: N.Y. Giants vs. Detroit, 1935
NFC-D: N.Y. Giants vs. Washington, 1943
NFC-D: Pittsburgh vs. Philadelphia, 1947
NFC-D: Dallas vs. Detroit, 1970
AFC: Miami vs. Baltimore, 1971
SB: Miami vs. Washington, 1982
AFC-FR: Seattle vs. L.A. Raiders, 1984

**Most Completions, Both Teams, Game**

64 AFC-D: San Diego (33) vs. Miami (31), 1981 (OT)
57 AFC-FR: Houston (36) vs. Buffalo (21), 1992 (OT)
56 NFC-D: Dallas (28) vs. Green Bay (28), 1993

**Fewest Completions, Both Teams, Game**

5 NFC: Philadelphia (2) vs. Chi. Cardinals (3), 1948
6 NFC: Detroit (2) vs. N.Y. Giants (4), 1935
NFC-D: Cleveland (3) vs. N.Y. Giants (3), 1950
11 NFC: Green Bay (3) vs. N.Y. Giants (8), 1944
NFC-D: Dallas (4) vs. Detroit (7), 1970

### COMPLETION PERCENTAGE

**Highest Completion Percentage, Game (20 attempts)**

88.0 SB: N.Y. Giants vs. Denver, 1986 (25-22)
87.1 NFC: San Francisco vs. L.A. Rams, 1989 (31-27)
80.0 NFC-D: Washington vs. L.A. Rams, 1983 (25-20)

**Lowest Completion Percentage, Game (20 attempts)**

18.5 NFC: Tampa Bay vs. Los Angeles, 1979 (27-5)
20.0 NFC-D: N.Y. Giants vs. Washington, 1943 (20-4)
25.8 NFC: Chi. Bears vs. Washington, 1937 (31-8)

### YARDS GAINED

**Most Yards Gained, Game**

483 AFC-D: Cleveland vs. N.Y. Jets, 1986 (OT)
435 AFC: Miami vs. Pittsburgh, 1984
415 AFC-D: San Diego vs. Miami, 1981 (OT)

**Fewest Yards Gained, Game**

3 NFC: Chi. Cardinals vs. Philadelphia, 1948
7 NFC: Philadelphia vs. Chi. Cardinals, 1948
9 NFC-D: N.Y. Giants vs. Cleveland, 1950
NFC: Cleveland vs. Detroit, 1953

**Most Yards Gained, Both Teams, Game**

809 AFC-D: San Diego (415) vs. Miami (394), 1981 (OT)
747 AFC: Miami (435) vs. Pittsburgh (312), 1984
666 AFC-D: Cleveland (483) vs. N.Y. Jets (183), 1986 (OT)

**Fewest Yards Gained, Both Teams, Game**

10 NFC: Chi. Cardinals (3) vs. Philadelphia (7), 1948
38 NFC-D: N.Y. Giants (9) vs. Cleveland (29), 1950
102 NFC-D: Dallas (22) vs. Detroit (80), 1970

### TIMES SACKED

**Most Times Sacked, Game**

9 AFC: Kansas City vs. Buffalo, 1966
NFC: Chicago vs. San Francisco, 1984
AFC-D: N.Y. Jets vs. Cleveland, 1986 (OT)
AFC-D: Houston vs. Kansas City, 1993
8 NFC: Green Bay vs. Dallas, 1967
NFC: Minnesota vs. Washington, 1987
7 NFC-D: Dallas vs. Los Angeles, 1973
SB: Dallas vs. Pittsburgh, 1975
AFC-FR: Houston vs. Oakland, 1980
NFC-D: Washington vs. Chicago, 1984
SB: New England vs. Chicago, 1985
AFC-FR: Kansas City vs. San Diego, 1992
AFC-D: Pittsburgh vs. Buffalo, 1992

**Most Times Sacked, Both Teams, Game**

13 AFC: Kansas City (9) vs. Buffalo (4), 1966
AFC-D: N.Y. Jets (9) vs. Cleveland (4), 1986 (OT)
12 NFC-D: Dallas (7) vs. Los Angeles (5), 1973
NFC-D: Washington (7) vs. Chicago (5), 1984
NFC: Chicago (9) vs. San Francisco (3), 1984
AFC-FR: Kansas City (7) vs. San Diego (5), 1992
11 AFC-D: Houston (9) vs. Kansas City (2), 1993

**Fewest Times Sacked, Both Teams, Game**

0 AFC-D: Buffalo vs. Pittsburgh, 1974
AFC-FR: Pittsburgh vs. San Diego, 1982
AFC: Miami vs. Pittsburgh, 1984
AFC-D: Buffalo vs. Miami, 1990
AFC-D: Denver vs. Houston, 1991
1 In many games

### TOUCHDOWNS

**Most Touchdowns, Game**

6 AFC-D: Oakland vs. Houston, 1969
5 NFC: Chi. Bears vs. Washington, 1943
NFC: Detroit vs. Cleveland, 1957
AFC-D: Oakland vs. Kansas City, 1968
SB: San Francisco vs. Denver, 1989
4 By many teams

**Most Touchdowns, Both Teams, Game**

8 AFC-FR: Buffalo (4) vs. Houston (4), 1992 (OT)
7 NFC: Chi. Bears (5) vs. Washington (2), 1943
AFC-D: Oakland (6) vs. Houston (1), 1969
SB: Pittsburgh (4) vs. Dallas (3), 1978
AFC-D: Miami (4) vs. San Diego (3), 1981 (OT)
AFC: Miami (4) vs. Pittsburgh (3), 1984
AFC-D: Buffalo (4) vs. Cleveland (3), 1989
6 NFC-FR: Green Bay (4) vs. St. Louis (2), 1982
AFC: Cleveland (3) vs. Denver (3), 1987
AFC-D: Buffalo (3) vs. Miami (3), 1990
AFC-FR: Denver (3) vs. L.A. Raiders (3), 1993

## INTERCEPTIONS BY

**Most Interceptions By, Game**

8 NFC: Chi. Bears vs. Washington, 1940
7 NFC: Cleveland vs. Los Angeles, 1955
6 NFC: Green Bay vs. N.Y. Giants, 1939
NFC: Chi. Bears vs. N.Y. Giants, 1946
NFC: Cleveland vs. Detroit, 1954
AFC: San Diego vs. Houston, 1961
AFC: Buffalo vs. L.A. Raiders, 1990

**Most Interceptions By, Both Teams, Game**

10 NFC: Cleveland (7) vs. Los Angeles (3), 1955
AFC: San Diego (6) vs. Houston (4), 1961
9 NFC: Green Bay (6) vs. N.Y. Giants (3), 1939
8 NFC: Chi. Bears (8) vs. Washington (0), 1940
NFC: Chi. Bears (6) vs. N.Y. Giants (2), 1946
NFC: Cleveland (6) vs. Detroit (2), 1954
AFC-FR: Buffalo (4) vs. N.Y. Jets (4), 1981
AFC: Miami (5) vs. N.Y. Jets (3), 1982

### YARDS GAINED

**Most Yards Gained, Game**

138 AFC-FR: N.Y. Jets vs. Cincinnati, 1982
136 AFC: Dall. Texans vs. Houston, 1962 (OT)
130 NFC-D: Los Angeles vs. St. Louis, 1975

**Most Yards Gained, Both Teams, Game**

156 NFC: Green Bay (123) vs. N.Y. Giants (33), 1939
149 NFC: Cleveland (103) vs. Los Angeles (46), 1955
141 AFC-FR: Buffalo (79) vs. N.Y. Jets (62), 1981

### TOUCHDOWNS

**Most Touchdowns, Game**

3 NFC: Chi. Bears vs. Washington, 1940
2 NFC-D: Los Angeles vs. St. Louis, 1975
1 In many games

**Most Touchdowns, Both Teams, Game**

3 NFC: Chi. Bears (3) vs. Washington (0), 1940
2 NFC-D: Los Angeles (2) vs. St. Louis(0), 1975
NFC-D: Dallas (1) vs. Green Bay (1), 1982
NFC-D: Minnesota (1) vs. San Francisco (1), 1987
NFC-FR: Detroit (1) vs. Green Bay (1), 1993
1 In many games

## PUNTING

**Most Punts, Game**

14 AFC-D: N.Y. Jets vs. Cleveland, 1986 (OT)
13 NFC: N.Y. Giants vs. Chi. Bears, 1933
AFC-D: Baltimore vs. Oakland, 1977 (OT)
11 AFC: Houston vs. Oakland, 1967
AFC-D: Houston vs. Oakland, 1969
NFC: L.A. Rams vs. Chicago, 1985

**Fewest Punts, Game**
0 NFC-FR: St. Louis vs. Green Bay, 1982
AFC-FR: N.Y. Jets vs. Cincinnati, 1982
1 NFC-D: Cleveland vs. Dallas, 1969
AFC: Miami vs. Oakland, 1973
AFC-D: Oakland vs. Cincinnati, 1975
AFC-D: Pittsburgh vs. Baltimore, 1976
AFC: Pittsburgh vs. Houston, 1978
NFC-FR: Green Bay vs. St. Louis, 1982
AFC-FR: Miami vs. New England, 1982
AFC-FR: San Diego vs. Pittsburgh, 1982
AFC-D: Cleveland vs. Indianapolis, 1987
AFC-D: Buffalo vs. Miami, 1990
AFC-FR: L.A. Raiders vs. Kansas City, 1991
NFC-FR: Atlanta vs. New Orleans, 1991
NFC-FR: Chicago vs. Dallas, 1991
AFC-D: Houston vs. Denver, 1991
NFC: San Francisco vs. Dallas, 1992
2 In many games

**Most Punts, Both Teams, Game**
23 NFC: N.Y. Giants (13) vs. Chi. Bears (10), 1933
22 AFC-D: N.Y. Jets (14) vs. Cleveland (8), 1986 (OT)
21 AFC-D: Baltimore (13) vs. Oakland (8), 1977 (OT)
NFC: L.A. Rams (11) vs. Chicago (10), 1985

**Fewest Punts, Both Teams, Game**
1 NFC-FR: St. Louis (0) vs. Green Bay (1), 1982
2 AFC-FR: N.Y. Jets (0) vs. Cincinnati (2), 1982
3 AFC: Miami (1) vs. Oakland (2), 1973
AFC-FR: San Diego (1) vs. Pittsburgh (2), 1982
AFC-D: Buffalo (1) vs. Miami (2), 1990
AFC-FR: L.A. Raiders (1) vs. Kansas City (2), 1991
AFC-D: Houston (1) vs. Denver (2), 1991

### AVERAGE YARDAGE
**Highest Average, Punting, Game (4 punts)**
56.0 AFC: Oakland vs. San Diego, 1980
52.5 NFC: Washington vs. Chi. Bears, 1942
51.6 AFC-D: Cincinnati vs. L.A. Raiders, 1990

**Lowest Average, Punting, Game (4 punts)**
24.9 NFC: Washington vs. Chi. Bears, 1937
25.3 AFC-FR: Pittsburgh vs. Houston, 1989
25.5 NFC: Green Bay vs. N.Y. Giants, 1962

## PUNT RETURNS
**Most Punt Returns, Game**
8 NFC: Green Bay vs. N.Y. Giants, 1944
7 By eight teams

**Most Punt Returns, Both Teams, Game**
13 AFC-FR: Houston (7) vs. Oakland (6), 1980
11 NFC: Green Bay (8) vs. N.Y. Giants (3), 1944
NFC-D: Green Bay (6) vs. Baltimore (5), 1965
10 In many games

**Fewest Punt Returns, Both Teams, Game**
0 NFC: Chi. Bears vs. N.Y. Giants, 1941
AFC: Boston vs. San Diego, 1963
NFC-FR: Green Bay vs. St. Louis, 1982
AFC-FR: Houston vs. N.Y. Jets, 1991
AFC-D: Denver vs. Houston, 1991
NFC-D: San Francisco vs. Washington, 1992
1 AFC: Miami (0) vs. Pittsburgh (1), 1972
AFC: Cincinnati (0) vs. San Diego (1), 1981
AFC-FR: Cincinnati (0) vs. N.Y. Jets (1), 1982
AFC-FR: San Diego (0) vs. Pittsburgh (1), 1982
NFC-D: Minnesota (0) vs. Washington (1), 1982
AFC: Seattle (0) vs. L.A. Raiders (1), 1983
AFC-D: Pittsburgh (0) vs. Denver (1), 1989
NFC-FR: New Orleans (0) vs. Atlanta (1), 1991
AFC-FR: Buffalo (0) vs. Houston (1), 1992 (OT)
2 In many games

### YARDS GAINED
**Most Yards Gained, Game**
155 NFC-D: Dallas vs. Cleveland, 1967
150 NFC: Chi. Cardinals vs. Philadelphia, 1947
143 NFC-FR: Minnesota vs. New Orleans, 1987

**Fewest Yards Gained, Game**
–10 NFC: Green Bay vs. Cleveland, 1965
–9 NFC: Dallas vs. Green Bay, 1966
AFC-D: Kansas City vs. Oakland, 1968
–5 AFC-D: Miami vs. Oakland, 1970
NFC-D: San Francisco vs. Dallas, 1972
NFC: Dallas vs. Washington, 1972

**Most Yards Gained, Both Teams, Game**
166 NFC-D: Dallas (155) vs. Cleveland (11), 1967
160 NFC: Chi. Cardinals (150) vs. Philadelphia (10), 1947
146 NFC-D: Philadelphia (112) vs. Pittsburgh (34), 1947

**Fewest Yards Gained, Both Teams, Game**
–9 NFC: Dallas (–9) vs. Green Bay (0), 1966
–6 AFC-D: Miami (–5) vs. Oakland (–1), 1970
–3 NFC-D: San Francisco (–5) vs. Dallas (2), 1972

### TOUCHDOWNS
**Most Touchdowns, Game**
1 By 10 teams

## KICKOFF RETURNS
**Most Kickoff Returns, Game**
10 NFC-D: L.A. Rams vs. Washington, 1983
9 NFC: Chi. Bears vs. N.Y. Giants, 1956
AFC: Boston vs. San Diego, 1963
AFC: Houston vs. Oakland, 1967
SB: Denver vs. San Francisco, 1989
AFC-D: Miami vs. Buffalo, 1990
AFC: L.A. Raiders vs. Buffalo, 1990
8 By many teams

**Most Kickoff Returns, Both Teams, Game**
15 AFC-D: Miami (9) vs. Buffalo (6), 1990
13 NFC-D: Green Bay (7) vs. Dallas (6), 1982
12 In many games

**Fewest Kickoff Returns, Both Teams, Game**
1 NFC: Green Bay (0) vs. Boston (1), 1936
AFC-FR: San Diego (0) vs. Kansas City (1), 1992
2 NFC-D: Los Angeles (0) vs. Chi. Bears (2), 1950
AFC: Houston (0) vs. San Diego (2), 1961
AFC-D: Oakland (1) vs. Pittsburgh (1), 1972
AFC-D: N.Y. Jets (0) vs. L.A. Raiders (2), 1982
AFC: Miami (1) vs. N.Y. Jets (1), 1982
NFC: N.Y. Giants (0) vs. Washington (2), 1986
3 In many games

### YARDS GAINED
**Most Yards Gained, Game**
225 NFC: Washington vs. Chi. Bears, 1940
222 SB: Miami vs. Washington, 1982
215 NFC: Los Angeles vs. Cleveland, 1955
AFC: Houston vs. Oakland, 1967

**Most Yards Gained, Both Teams, Game**
379 AFC-D: Baltimore (193) vs. Oakland (186), 1977 (OT)
321 NFC-D: Dallas (173) vs. Green Bay (148), 1982
318 AFC-D: Miami (183) vs. Oakland (135), 1974

**Fewest Yards Gained, Both Teams, Game**
5 AFC-FR: San Diego (0) vs. Kansas City (5), 1992
15 NFC: N.Y. Giants (0) vs. Washington (15), 1986
31 NFC-D: Los Angeles (0) vs. Chi. Bears (31), 1950

### TOUCHDOWNS
**Most Touchdowns, Game**
1 NFC-D: San Francisco vs. Dallas, 1972
AFC-D: Miami vs. Oakland, 1974
AFC-D: Baltimore vs. Oakland, 1977 (OT)
SB: Miami vs. Washington, 1982
SB: Cincinnati vs. San Francisco, 1988
AFC-D: Cleveland vs. Buffalo, 1989

## PENALTIES
**Most Penalties, Game**
17 AFC-FR: L.A. Raiders vs. Denver, 1993
14 AFC-FR: Oakland vs. Houston, 1980
NFC-D: San Francisco vs. N.Y. Giants, 1981
13 AFC-FR: Houston vs. Cleveland, 1988
AFC-D: Houston vs. Denver, 1991

**Fewest Penalties, Game**
0 NFC: Philadelphia vs. Green Bay, 1960
NFC-D: Detroit vs. Dallas, 1970
AFC-D: Miami vs. Oakland, 1970
SB: Miami vs. Dallas, 1971
NFC-D: Washington vs. Minnesota, 1973
SB: Pittsburgh vs. Dallas, 1975
NFC: San Francisco vs. Chicago, 1988
SB: Denver vs. San Francisco, 1989
AFC-D: L.A. Raiders vs. Cincinnati, 1990
AFC-D: Miami vs. San Diego, 1992
1 By many teams

**Most Penalties, Both Teams, Game**
27 AFC-FR: L.A. Raiders (17) vs. Denver (10), 1993

22 AFC-FR: Oakland (14) vs. Houston (8), 1980
NFC-D: San Francisco (14) vs. N.Y. Giants (8), 1981
AFC-FR: Houston (13) vs. Cleveland (9), 1988
21 AFC-D: Oakland (11) vs. New England (10), 1976

**Fewest Penalties, Both Teams, Game**
1 AFC-D: L.A. Raiders (0) vs. Cincinnati (1), 1990
2 NFC: Washington (1) vs. Chi. Bears (1), 1937
NFC-D: Washington (0) vs. Minnesota (2), 1973
SB: Pittsburgh (0) vs. Dallas (2), 1975
3 AFC: Miami (1) vs. Baltimore (2), 1971
NFC: San Francisco (1) vs. Dallas (2), 1971
SB: Miami (0) vs. Dallas (3), 1971
AFC-D: Pittsburgh (1) vs. Oakland (2), 1972
AFC-D: Miami (1) vs. Cincinnati (2), 1973
SB: Miami (1) vs. San Francisco (2), 1984
NFC: San Francisco (0) vs. Chicago (3), 1988

## YARDS PENALIZED

**Most Yards Penalized, Game**
145 NFC-D: San Francisco vs. N.Y. Giants, 1981
133 SB: Dallas vs. Baltimore, 1970
130 AFC-FR: L.A. Raiders vs. Denver, 1993

**Fewest Yards Penalized, Game**
0 By 10 teams

**Most Yards Penalized, Both Teams, Game**
227 AFC-FR: L.A. Raiders (130) vs. Denver (97), 1993
206 NFC-D: San Francisco (145) vs. N.Y. Giants (61), 1981
193 AFC-FR: Houston (118) vs. Cleveland (75), 1988

**Fewest Yards Penalized, Both Teams, Game**
5 AFC-D: L.A. Raiders (0) vs. Cincinnati (5), 1990
9 NFC-D: Washington (0) vs. Minnesota (9), 1973
15 SB: Miami (0) vs. Dallas (15), 1971

## FUMBLES

**Most Fumbles, Game**
8 SB: Buffalo vs. Dallas, 1992
7 AFC-D: Houston vs. Kansas City, 1993
6 By 11 teams

**Most Fumbles, Both Teams, Game**
12 AFC: Houston (6) vs. Pittsburgh (6), 1978
SB: Buffalo (8) vs. Dallas (4), 1992
10 NFC: Chi. Bears (5) vs. N.Y. Giants (5), 1934
SB: Dallas (6) vs. Denver (4), 1977
9 NFC-D: San Francisco (6) vs. Detroit (3), 1957
NFC-D: San Francisco (5) vs. Dallas (4), 1972
NFC: Dallas (5) vs. Philadelphia (4), 1980

**Most Fumbles Lost, Game**
5 SB: Buffalo vs. Dallas, 1992
4 NFC: N.Y. Giants vs. Baltimore, 1958 (OT)
AFC: Kansas City vs. Oakland, 1969
SB: Baltimore vs. Dallas, 1970
AFC: Pittsburgh vs. Oakland, 1975
SB: Denver vs. Dallas, 1977
AFC: Houston vs. Pittsburgh, 1978
AFC: Miami vs. New England, 1985
SB: New England vs. Chicago, 1985
NFC-FR: L.A. Rams vs. Washington, 1986
3 By many teams

**Fewest Fumbles, Both Teams, Game**
0 NFC: Green Bay vs. Cleveland, 1965
AFC-D: Houston vs. San Diego, 1979
NFC-D: Dallas vs. Los Angeles, 1979
SB: Los Angeles vs. Pittsburgh, 1979
AFC-D: Buffalo vs. Cincinnati, 1981
NFC-D: San Francisco vs. Washington, 1990
1 In many games

## RECOVERIES

**Most Total Fumbles Recovered, Game**
8 SB: Dallas vs. Denver, 1977 (4 own, 4 opp)
7 NFC: Chi. Bears vs. N.Y. Giants, 1934 (5 own, 2 opp)
NFC-D: San Francisco vs. Detroit, 1957 (4 own, 3 opp)
NFC-D: San Francisco vs. Dallas, 1972 (4 own, 3 opp)
AFC: Pittsburgh vs. Houston, 1978 (3 own, 4 opp)
6 AFC: Houston vs. San Diego, 1961 (4 own, 2 opp)
AFC-D: Cleveland vs. Baltimore, 1971 (4 own, 2 opp)
AFC-D: Cleveland vs. Oakland, 1980 (5 own, 1 opp)
NFC: Philadelphia vs. Dallas, 1980 (3 own, 3 opp)
SB: Dallas vs. Buffalo, 1992 (1 own, 5 opp)

**Most Own Fumbles Recovered, Game**
5 NFC: Chi. Bears vs. N.Y. Giants, 1934
AFC-D: Cleveland vs. Oakland, 1980
4 By many teams

## TURNOVERS

(Numbers of times losing the ball on interceptions and fumbles.)

**Most Turnovers, Game**
9 NFC: Washington vs. Chi. Bears, 1940
NFC: Detroit vs. Cleveland, 1954
AFC: Houston vs. Pittsburgh, 1978
SB: Buffalo vs. Dallas, 1992
8 NFC: N.Y. Giants vs. Chi. Bears, 1946
NFC: Los Angeles vs. Cleveland, 1955
NFC: Cleveland vs. Detroit, 1957
SB: Denver vs. Dallas, 1977
NFC-D: Minnesota vs. Philadelphia, 1980
7 AFC: Houston vs. San Diego, 1961
SB: Baltimore vs. Dallas, 1970
AFC: Pittsburgh vs. Oakland, 1975
NFC-D: Chicago vs. Dallas, 1977
NFC: Los Angeles vs. Dallas, 1978
AFC-D: San Diego vs. Miami, 1982
AFC: Buffalo vs. L.A. Raiders, 1990

**Fewest Turnovers, Game**
0 By many teams

**Most Turnovers, Both Teams, Game**
14 AFC: Houston (9) vs. Pittsburgh (5), 1978
13 NFC: Detroit (9) vs. Cleveland (4), 1954
AFC: Houston (7) vs. San Diego (6), 1961
12 AFC: Pittsburgh (7) vs. Oakland (5), 1975

**Fewest Turnovers, Both Teams, Game**
0 SB: Buffalo vs. N.Y. Giants, 1990
FR: Kansas City vs Pittsburgh, 1993 (OT)
1 AFC-D: Baltimore (0) vs. Cincinnati (1), 1970
AFC-D: Pittsburgh (0) vs. Buffalo (1), 1974
AFC: Oakland (0) vs. Pittsburgh (1), 1976
NFC-D: Minnesota (0) vs. Washington (1), 1982
NFC-D: Chicago (0) vs. N.Y. Giants (1), 1985
SB: N.Y. Giants (0) vs. Denver (1), 1986
NFC: Washington (0) vs. Minnesota (1), 1987
AFC-D: Cincinnati (0) vs. L.A. Raiders (1), 1990
NFC: N.Y. Giants (0) vs. San Francisco (1), 1990
NFC-FR: N.Y. Giants (0) vs. Minnesota (1), 1993
AFC-FR: L.A. Raiders (0) vs. Denver (1), 1993
NFC: Dallas (0) vs. San Francisco (1), 1993
2 In many games

Compiled by Elias Sports Bureau

## INDIVIDUAL RECORDS

### SERVICE
**Most Games**
10 Lawrence Taylor, N.Y. Giants, 1982-91
Ronnie Lott, San Francisco, 1982-85, 1987-91; L.A. Raiders 1992
Mike Singletary, Chicago, 1984-93
9 *Ken Houston, Houston, 1971-73; Washington, 1974-79
Joe Greene, Pittsburgh, 1971-77, 1979-80
Jack Lambert, Pittsburgh, 1976-84
Walter Payton, Chicago, 1977-81, 1984-87
Harry Carson, N.Y. Giants, 1979-80, 1982-88
Mike Webster, Pittsburgh, 1979-86, 1988
**Anthony Muñoz, Cincinnati, 1982-87, 1989-90, 1992
8 Tom Mack, Los Angeles, 1971-76, 1978-79
*Franco Harris, Pittsburgh, 1973-76, 1978-81
Lemar Parrish, Cincinnati, 1971-72, 1975-77; Washington, 1978, 1980-81
Art Shell, Oakland, 1973-79, 1981
Ted Hendricks, Baltimore, 1972-74; Green Bay, 1975; Oakland, 1981-82; L.A. Raiders, 1983-84
*John Hannah, New England, 1977, 1979-83, 1985-86
*Randy White, Dallas, 1978, 1980-86
*Mike Haynes, New England, 1978-81, 1983; L.A. Raiders, 1985-87
James Lofton, Green Bay, 1979, 1981-86; Buffalo 1992
*Mike Munchak, Houston, 1985-86, 1988-93
Howie Long, L.A. Raiders, 1984-88, 1990, 1993-94
Reggie White, Philadelphia, 1987-93; Green Bay, 1994
*Also selected, but did not play, in one additional game
**Also selected, but did not play, in two additional games

### SCORING
#### POINTS
**Most Points, Career**
37 Morten Andersen, New Orleans, 1986-89, 1991, 1993 (13-pat, 8-fg)
30 Jan Stenerud, Kansas City, 1971-72, 1976; Green Bay, 1985 (6-pat, 8-fg)
26 Nick Lowery, Kansas City, 1982, 1991, 1993 (5 pat, 7 fg)
**Most Points, Game**
18 John Brockington, Green Bay, 1973 (3-td)
15 Garo Yepremian, Miami, 1974 (5-fg)
14 Jan Stenerud, Kansas City, 1972 (2-pat, 4-fg)

#### TOUCHDOWNS
**Most Touchdowns, Career**
3 John Brockington, Green Bay, 1972-74 (2-r, 1-p)
Earl Campbell, Houston, 1979-82, 1984 (3-r)
Chuck Muncie, New Orleans, 1980; San Diego, 1982-83 (3-r)
William Andrews, Atlanta, 1981-84 (1-r, 2-p)
Marcus Allen, L.A. Raiders, 1983, 1985-86, 1988; Kansas City, 1994 (2-r, 1-p)
2 By 13 players
**Most Touchdowns, Game**
3 John Brockington, Green Bay, 1973 (2-r, 1-p)
2 Mel Renfro, Dallas, 1971 (2-ret)
Earl Campbell, Houston, 1980 (2-r)
Chuck Muncie, New Orleans, 1980 (2-r)
William Andrews, Atlanta, 1984 (2-p)
Herschel Walker, Dallas, 1989 (2-r)
Johnny Johnson, Phoenix, 1991 (2-r)

#### POINTS AFTER TOUCHDOWN
**Most Points After Touchdown, Career**
13 Morten Andersen, New Orleans, 1986-89, 1991, 1993 (13 att)
6 Chester Marcol, Green Bay, 1973, 1975 (6 att)
Mark Moseley, Washington, 1980, 1983 (7 att)
Ali Haji-Sheikh, N.Y. Giants, 1984 (6 att)
Jan Stenerud, Kansas City, 1971-72, 1976; Green Bay, 1985 (6 att)
**Most Points After Touchdown, Game**
6 Ali Haji-Sheikh, N.Y. Giants, 1984 (6 att)
4 Chester Marcol, Green Bay, 1973 (4 att)
Mark Moseley, Washington, 1980 (5 att)
Morten Andersen, New Orleans, 1986 (4 att), 1989 (4 att)

#### FIELD GOALS
**Most Field Goals Attempted, Career**
15 Jan Stenerud, Kansas City, 1971-72, 1976; Green Bay, 1985
Morten Andersen, New Orleans, 1986-89, 1991, 1993
10 Nick Lowery, Kansas City, 1982, 1991, 1993
**Most Field Goals Attempted, Game**
6 Jan Stenerud, Kansas City, 1972
Eddie Murray, Detroit, 1981
Mark Moseley, Washington, 1983
5 Garo Yepremian, Miami, 1974
4 Jan Stenerud, Kansas City, 1976
Nick Lowery, Kansas City, 1991, 1993
Morten Andersen, New Orleans, 1993
**Most Field Goals, Career**
8 Jan Stenerud, Kansas City, 1971-72, 1976; Green Bay, 1985
Morten Andersen, New Orleans, 1986-89, 1991, 1993
7 Nick Lowery, Kansas City, 1982, 1991, 1993
**Most Field Goals, Game**
5 Garo Yepremian, Miami, 1974 (5 att)
4 Jan Stenerud, Kansas City, 1972 (6 att)
Eddie Murray, Detroit, 1981 (6 att)
3 Nick Lowery, Kansas City, 1991 (4 att)
Nick Lowery, Kansas City, 1993 (4 att)
**Longest Field Goal**
51 Morten Andersen, New Orleans, 1989
48 Jan Stenerud, Kansas City, 1972
Jeff Jaeger, L.A. Raiders, 1992
43 Gary Anderson, Pittsburgh, 1984
Nick Lowery, Kansas City, 1991

#### SAFETIES
**Most Safeties, Game**
1 Art Still, Kansas City, 1983
Mark Gastineau, N.Y. Jets, 1985
Greg Townsend, L.A. Raiders, 1992

### RUSHING
#### ATTEMPTS
**Most Attempts, Career**
81 Walter Payton, Chicago, 1977-81, 1984-87
68 O.J. Simpson, Buffalo, 1973-77
63 Eric Dickerson, L.A. Rams, 1984-85, 1987; Indianapolis, 1988-90
**Most Attempts, Game**
19 O.J. Simpson, Buffalo, 1974
17 Marv Hubbard, Oakland, 1974
16 O.J. Simpson, Buffalo, 1973
Marcus Allen, L.A. Raiders, 1986

#### YARDS GAINED
**Most Yards Gained, Career**
368 Walter Payton, Chicago, 1977-81, 1984-87
356 O.J. Simpson, Buffalo, 1973-77
220 Earl Campbell, Houston, 1979-82, 1984
**Most Yards Gained, Game**
112 O. J. Simpson, Buffalo, 1973
104 Marv Hubbard, Oakland, 1974
85 Neal Anderson, Chicago, 1989
**Longest Run From Scrimmage**
41 Lawrence McCutcheon, Los Angeles, 1976
39 Chris Warren, Seattle, 1994
32 Randall Cunningham, Philadelphia, 1989

#### AVERAGE GAIN
**Highest Average Gain, Career (20 attempts)**
5.81 Marv Hubbard, Oakland, 1972-74 (36-209)
5.71 Wilbert Montgomery, Philadelphia, 1979-80 (21-120)
5.36 Larry Csonka, Miami, 1971-72, 1975 (22-118)
**Highest Average Gain, Game (10 attempts)**
7.00 O.J. Simpson, Buffalo, 1973 (16-112)
Ottis Anderson, St. Louis, 1981 (10-70)
6.91 Walter Payton, Chicago, 1985 (11-76)
6.90 Earl Campbell, Houston, 1980 (10-69)

#### TOUCHDOWNS
**Most Touchdowns, Career**
3 Earl Campbell, Houston, 1979-82, 1984
Chuck Muncie, New Orleans, 1980; San Diego, 1982-83
2 John Brockington, Green Bay, 1972-74
O.J. Simpson, Buffalo, 1973-77
Walter Payton, Chicago, 1977-81, 1984-87
Marcus Allen, L.A. Raiders, 1983, 1985-86, 1988; Kansas City, 1994
Herschel Walker, Dallas, 1988-89
Johnny Johnson, Phoenix, 1991
**Most Touchdowns, Game**
2 John Brockington, Green Bay, 1973
Earl Campbell, Houston, 1980
Chuck Muncie, New Orleans, 1980
Herschel Walker, Dallas, 1989
Johnny Johnson, Phoenix, 1991

# AFC-NFC PRO BOWL RECORDS

## PASSING

### ATTEMPTS

**Most Attempts, Career**
120 Dan Fouts, San Diego, 1980-84, 1986
88 Bob Griese, Miami, 1971-72, 1974-75, 1977, 1979
68 Warren Moon, Houston, 1989-94

**Most Attempts, Game**
32 Bill Kenney, Kansas City, 1984
Steve Young, San Francisco, 1993
30 Dan Fouts, San Diego, 1983
28 Jim Hart, St. Louis, 1976

### COMPLETIONS

**Most Completions, Career**
63 Dan Fouts, San Diego, 1980-84, 1986
44 Bob Griese, Miami, 1971-72, 1974-75, 1977, 1979
34 Warren Moon, Houston, 1989-94

**Most Completions, Game**
21 Joe Theismann, Washington, 1984
18 Steve Young, San Francisco, 1993
17 Dan Fouts, San Diego, 1983

### COMPLETION PERCENTAGE

**Highest Completion Percentage, Career (40 attempts)**
68.9 Joe Theismann, Washington, 1983-84 (45-31)
64.4 Jim Kelly, Buffalo, 1988, 1991-92 (45-29)
58.9 Ken Anderson, Cincinnati, 1976-77, 1982-83 (56-33)

**Highest Completion Percentage, Game (10 attempts)**
90.0 Archie Manning, New Orleans, 1980 (10-9)
77.8 Joe Theismann, Washington, 1984 (27-21)
72.2 Jim Everett, L.A. Rams, 1991 (18-13)

### YARDS GAINED

**Most Yards Gained, Career**
890 Dan Fouts, San Diego, 1980-84, 1986
554 Bob Griese, Miami, 1971-72, 1974-75, 1977, 1979
398 Ken Anderson, Cincinnati, 1976-77, 1982-83

**Most Yards Gained, Game**
274 Dan Fouts, San Diego, 1983
242 Joe Theismann, Washington, 1984
212 Phil Simms, N.Y. Giants, 1986

**Longest Completion**
64 Dan Pastorini, Houston (to Burrough, Houston), 1976 (TD)
59 Randall Cunningham, Philadelphia (to Jackson, Philadelphia [19 yards] lateral to Byner, Washington [40 yards]), 1991
57 James Harris, Los Angeles (to Gray, St. Louis), 1975
Ken Anderson, Cincinnati (to G. Pruitt, Cleveland), 1977

### AVERAGE GAIN

**Highest Average Gain, Career (40 attempts)**
8.02 Jim Kelly, Buffalo, 1988, 1991-92 (45-361)
7.91 Randall Cunningham, Philadelphia, 1989-91 (44-348)
7.64 Joe Theismann, Washington, 1983-84 (45-344)

**Highest Average Gain, Game (10 attempts)**
15.27 Randall Cunningham, Philadelphia, 1991 (11-168)
11.40 Ken Anderson, Cincinnati, 1977 (10-114)
11.20 Archie Manning, New Orleans, 1980 (10-112)

### TOUCHDOWNS

**Most Touchdowns, Career**
3 Joe Theismann, Washington, 1983-84
Joe Montana, San Francisco, 1982, 1984-85, 1988
Phil Simms, N.Y. Giants, 1986
Jim Kelly, Buffalo, 1988, 1991-92
2 James Harris, Los Angeles, 1975
Mike Boryla, Philadelphia, 1976
Ken Anderson, Cincinnati, 1976-77, 1982-83
Mark Rypien, Washington, 1990, 1992

**Most Touchdowns, Game**
3 Joe Theismann, Washington, 1984
Phil Simms, N.Y. Giants, 1986
2 James Harris, Los Angeles, 1975
Mike Boryla, Philadelphia, 1976
Ken Anderson, Cincinnati, 1977
Jim Kelly, Buffalo, 1991
Mark Rypien, Washington, 1992

### HAD INTERCEPTED

**Most Passes Had Intercepted, Career**
8 Dan Fouts, San Diego, 1980-84, 1986
6 Jim Hart, St. Louis, 1975-78
5 Ken Stabler, Oakland, 1974-75, 1978

**Most Passes Had Intercepted, Game**
5 Jim Hart, St. Louis, 1977
4 Ken Stabler, Oakland, 1974
3 Dan Fouts, San Diego, 1986
Mark Rypien, Washington, 1990
Steve Young, San Francisco, 1993

**Most Attempts, Without Interception, Game**
27 Joe Theismann, Washington, 1984
Phil Simms, N.Y. Giants, 1986
26 John Brodie, San Francisco, 1971
Danny White, Dallas, 1983
21 Roman Gabriel, Philadelphia, 1974
Dan Marino, Miami, 1985

### PERCENTAGE, PASSES HAD INTERCEPTED

**Lowest Percentage, Passes Had Intercepted, Career (40 attempts)**
0.00 Joe Theismann, Washington, 1983-84 (45-0)
2.13 Dave Krieg, Seattle, 1985, 1989-90 (47-1)
2.22 Jim Kelly, Buffalo, 1988, 1991-92 (45-1)

## PASS RECEIVING

### RECEPTIONS

**Most Receptions, Career**
22 Jerry Rice, San Francisco, 1987-88, 1990-94
18 Walter Payton, Chicago, 1977-81, 1984-87
17 Steve Largent, Seattle, 1979, 1982, 1985-88

**Most Receptions, Game**
8 Steve Largent, Seattle, 1986
Michael Irvin, Dallas, 1992
Andre Rison, Atlanta, 1993
7 John Stallworth, Pittsburgh, 1983
Jerry Rice, San Francisco, 1992
6 John Stallworth, Pittsburgh, 1980
Kellen Winslow, San Diego, 1982
Gary Clark, Washington, 1991
Keith Byars, Miami, 1994
Andre Rison, Atlanta, 1994

### YARDS GAINED

**Most Yards Gained, Career**
317 Jerry Rice, San Francisco, 1987-88, 1990-94
236 Steve Largent, Seattle, 1979, 1982, 1985-88
226 Wes Chandler, New Orleans, 1980; San Diego, 1983-84, 1986

**Most Yards Gained, Game**
125 Michael Irvin, Dallas, 1992
114 Wes Chandler, San Diego, 1986
96 Ken Burrough, Houston, 1976

**Longest Reception**
64 Ken Burrough, Houston (from Pastorini, Houston), 1976 (TD)
59 Keith Jackson, Philadelphia (19 yards) lateral to Earnest Byner, Washington (40 yards) (from Cunningham, Philadelphia), 1991
57 Mel Gray, St. Louis (from Harris, Los Angeles), 1975
Greg Pruitt, Cleveland (from Anderson, Cincinnati), 1977

### TOUCHDOWNS

**Most Touchdowns, Career**
2 Mel Gray, St. Louis, 1975-78
Cliff Branch, Oakland, 1975-78
Terry Metcalf, St. Louis, 1975-76, 1978
Tony Hill, Dallas, 1979-80, 1986
William Andrews, Atlanta, 1981-84
James Lofton, Green Bay, 1979, 1981-86; Buffalo 1992
Jimmie Giles, Tampa Bay, 1981-83, 1986
Michael Irvin, Dallas, 1992-94

**Most Touchdowns, Game**
2 William Andrews, Atlanta, 1984

## INTERCEPTIONS BY

**Most Interceptions By, Career**
4 Everson Walls, Dallas, 1982-84, 1986
3 Ken Houston, Houston, 1971-73; Washington, 1974-79
Jack Lambert, Pittsburgh, 1976-84
Ted Hendricks, Baltimore, 1972-74; Green Bay, 1975; Oakland, 1981-82; L.A. Raiders, 1983-84
Mike Haynes, New England, 1978-81, 1983; L.A. Raiders, 1985-87
2 By nine players

**Most Interceptions By, Game**
2 Mel Blount, Pittsburgh, 1977
Everson Walls, Dallas, 1982, 1983
LeRoy Irvin, L.A. Rams, 1986
David Fulcher, Cincinnati, 1990

**YARDS GAINED**

**Most Yards Gained, Career**

77 Ted Hendricks, Baltimore, 1972-74; Green Bay, 1975; Oakland, 1981-82; L.A. Raiders, 1983-84
73 Rod Woodson, Pittsburgh, 1990-94
51 Jerry Gray, L.A. Rams, 1987-90

**Most Yards Gained, Game**

73 Rod Woodson, Pittsburgh, 1994
65 Ted Hendricks, Baltimore, 1973
51 Jerry Gray, L.A. Rams, 1990

**Longest Gain**

73 Rod Woodson, Pittsburgh, 1994 (lateral)
65 Ted Hendricks, Baltimore, 1973
51 Jerry Gray, L.A. Rams, 1990 (TD)

**TOUCHDOWNS**

**Most Touchdowns, Game**

1 Bobby Bell, Kansas City, 1973
Nolan Cromwell, L.A. Rams, 1984
Joey Browner, Minnesota, 1986
Jerry Gray, L.A. Rams, 1990
Mike Johnson, Cleveland, 1990
Junior Seau, San Diego, 1993

## PUNTING

**Most Punts, Career**

33 Ray Guy, Oakland, 1974-79, 1981
23 Rohn Stark, Indianapolis, 1986-87, 1991, 1993
19 Dave Jennings, N.Y. Giants, 1979-81, 1983

**Most Punts, Game**

10 Reggie Roby, Miami, 1985
9 Tom Wittum, San Francisco, 1974
Rohn Stark, Indianapolis, 1987
8 Jerrel Wilson, Kansas City, 1971
Tom Skladany, Detroit, 1982

**Longest Punt**

64 Tom Wittum, San Francisco, 1974
61 Reggie Roby, Miami, 1985
60 Ron Widby, Dallas, 1972

**AVERAGE YARDAGE**

**Highest Average, Career (10 punts)**

45.25 Jerrel Wilson, Kansas City, 1971-73 (16-724)
44.79 Reggie Roby, Miami, 1985, 1990 (14-627)
44.65 Rohn Stark, Indianapolis, 1986-87, 1991, 1993 (23-1,027)

**Highest Average, Game (4 punts)**

49.57 Jim Arnold, Detroit, 1988 (7-347)
49.00 Ray Guy, Oakland, 1974 (4-196)
47.75 Bob Grupp, Kansas City, 1980 (4-191)

## PUNT RETURNS

**Most Punt Returns, Career**

13 Rick Upchurch, Denver, 1977, 1979-80, 1983
11 Vai Sikahema, St. Louis, 1987-88
10 Mike Nelms, Washington, 1981-83

**Most Punt Returns, Game**

7 Vai Sikahema, St. Louis, 1987
6 Henry Ellard, L.A. Rams, 1985
Gerald McNeil, Cleveland, 1988
5 Rick Upchurch, Denver, 1980
Mike Nelms, Washington, 1981
Carl Roaches, Houston, 1982
Johnny Bailey, Phoenix, 1993

**Most Fair Catches, Game**

2 Jerry Logan, Baltimore, 1971
Dick Anderson, Miami, 1974
Henry Ellard, L.A. Rams, 1985

**YARDS GAINED**

**Most Yards Gained, Career**

183 Billy Johnson, Houston, 1976, 1978; Atlanta, 1984
138 Rick Upchurch, Denver, 1977, 1979-80, 1983
Mel Renfro, Dallas, 1971-72, 1974
119 Mike Nelms, Washington, 1981-83

**Most Yards Gained, Game**

159 Billy Johnson, Houston, 1976
138 Mel Renfro, Dallas, 1971
117 Wally Henry, Philadelphia, 1980

**Longest Punt Return**

90 Billy Johnson, Houston, 1976 (TD)
86 Wally Henry, Philadelphia, 1980 (TD)
82 Mel Renfro, Dallas, 1971 (TD)

**TOUCHDOWNS**

**Most Touchdowns, Game**

2 Mel Renfro, Dallas, 1971
1 Billy Johnson, Houston, 1976
Wally Henry, Philadelphia, 1980

## KICKOFF RETURNS

**Most Kickoff Returns, Career**

10 Rick Upchurch, Denver, 1977, 1979-80, 1983
Greg Pruitt, Cleveland, 1974-75, 1977-78; L.A. Raiders, 1984
8 Mike Nelms, Washington, 1981-83
7 Mel Gray, Detroit, 1991-92

**Most Kickoff Returns, Game**

6 Greg Pruitt, L.A. Raiders, 1984
5 Les (Speedy) Duncan, Washington, 1972
Ron Smith, Chicago, 1973
Herb Mul-Key, Washington, 1974
Mel Gray, Detroit, 1991
4 By seven players

**YARDS GAINED**

**Most Yards Gained, Career**

309 Greg Pruitt, Cleveland, 1974-75, 1977-78; L.A. Raiders, 1984
222 Rick Upchurch, Denver, 1977, 1979-80, 1983
175 Les (Speedy) Duncan, Washington, 1972

**Most Yards Gained, Game**

192 Greg Pruitt, L.A. Raiders, 1984
175 Les (Speedy) Duncan, Washington, 1972
152 Ron Smith, Chicago, 1973

**Longest Kickoff Return**

62 Greg Pruitt, L.A. Raiders, 1984
61 Eugene (Mercury) Morris, Miami, 1972
55 Ron Smith, Chicago, 1973

**TOUCHDOWNS**

**Most Touchdowns, Game**

None

## FUMBLES

**Most Fumbles, Career**

6 Dan Fouts, San Diego, 1980-84, 1986
4 Lawrence McCutcheon, Los Angeles, 1974-78
Franco Harris, Pittsburgh, 1973-76, 1978-81
Jay Schroeder, Washington, 1987
Vai Sikahema, St. Louis, 1987-88
3 O.J. Simpson, Buffalo, 1973-77
William Andrews, Atlanta, 1981-84
Joe Montana, San Francisco, 1982, 1984-85, 1988
Walter Payton, Chicago, 1977-81, 1984-87
Neil Lomax, St. Louis, 1985, 1988
Jim Kelly, Buffalo, 1988, 1991-92

**Most Fumbles, Game**

4 Jay Schroeder, Washington, 1987
3 Dan Fouts, San Diego, 1982
Vai Sikahema, St. Louis, 1987
2 By 11 players

**RECOVERIES**

**Most Fumbles Recovered, Career**

3 Harold Jackson, Philadelphia, 1973; Los Angeles, 1974, 1976, 1978 (3-own)
Dan Fouts, San Diego, 1980-84, 1986 (3-own)
Randy White, Dallas, 1978, 1980-86 (3-opp)
2 By many players

**Most Fumbles Recovered, Game**

2 Dick Anderson, Miami, 1974 (1-own, 1-opp)
Harold Jackson, Los Angeles, 1974 (2-own)
Dan Fouts, San Diego, 1982 (2-own)
Joey Browner, Minnesota, 1990 (2-opp)

**YARDAGE**

**Longest Fumble Return**

83 Art Still, Kansas City, 1985 (TD, opp)
51 Phil Villapiano, Oakland, 1974 (opp)
37 Sam Mills, New Orleans, 1988 (opp)

**TOUCHDOWNS**

**Most Touchdowns, Game**

1 Art Still, Kansas City, 1985
Keith Millard, Minnesota, 1990

# AFC-NFC PRO BOWL RECORDS

## SACKS
Sacks have been compiled since 1983.

**Most Sacks, Career**
9.5 Reggie White, Philadelphia, 1987-93; Green Bay, 1994
9 Howie Long, L.A. Raiders, 1984-88, 1990, 1993-1994
7 Mark Gastineau, N.Y. Jets, 1983-86

**Most Sacks, Game**
4 Mark Gastineau, N.Y. Jets, 1985
Reggie White, Philadelphia, 1987
3 Richard Dent, Chicago, 1985
Bruce Smith, Buffalo, 1991
2 By many players

## TEAM RECORDS

### SCORING
**Most Points, Game**
45 NFC, 1984
**Fewest Points, Game**
3 AFC, 1984, 1989, 1994
**Most Points, Both Teams, Game**
64 NFC (37) vs. AFC (27), 1980
**Fewest Points, Both Teams, Game**
16 NFC (6) vs. AFC (10), 1987

#### TOUCHDOWNS
**Most Touchdowns, Game**
6 NFC, 1984
**Fewest Touchdowns, Game**
0 AFC, 1971, 1974, 1984, 1989, 1994
NFC, 1987, 1988
**Most Touchdowns, Both Teams, Game**
8 AFC (4) vs. NFC (4), 1973
NFC (5) vs. AFC (3), 1980
**Fewest Touchdowns, Both Teams, Game**
1 AFC (0) vs. NFC (1), 1974
NFC (0) vs. AFC (1), 1987
NFC (0) vs. AFC (1), 1988

#### POINTS AFTER TOUCHDOWN
**Most Points After Touchdown, Game**
6 NFC, 1984
**Most Points After Touchdown, Both Teams, Game**
7 NFC (4) vs. AFC (3), 1973
NFC (4) vs. AFC (3), 1980
NFC (4) vs. AFC (3), 1986

#### FIELD GOALS
**Most Field Goals Attempted, Game**
6 AFC, 1972
NFC, 1981, 1983
**Most Field Goals Attempted, Both Teams, Game**
9 NFC (6) vs. AFC (3), 1983
**Most Field Goals, Game**
5 AFC, 1974
**Most Field Goals, Both Teams, Game**
7 AFC (5) vs. NFC (2), 1974

### NET YARDS GAINED RUSHING AND PASSING
**Most Yards Gained, Game**
472 NFC, 1993
**Fewest Yards Gained, Game**
114 AFC, 1993
**Most Yards Gained, Both Teams, Game**
811 AFC (466) vs. NFC (345), 1983
**Fewest Yards Gained, Both Teams, Game**
424 AFC (202) vs. NFC (222), 1987

### RUSHING
#### ATTEMPTS
**Most Attempts, Game**
50 AFC, 1974
**Fewest Attempts, Game**
14 AFC, 1994
**Most Attempts, Both Teams, Game**
80 AFC (50) vs. NFC (30), 1974
**Fewest Attempts, Both Teams, Game**
48 AFC (20) vs. NFC (28), 1991

#### YARDS GAINED
**Most Yards Gained, Game**
224 NFC, 1976
**Fewest Yards Gained, Game**
28 NFC, 1992
**Most Yards Gained, Both Teams, Game**
425 NFC (224) vs. AFC (201), 1976
**Fewest Yards Gained, Both Teams, Game**
131 NFC (28) vs. AFC (103), 1992

#### TOUCHDOWNS
**Most Touchdowns, Game**
3 NFC, 1989, 1991
**Most Touchdowns, Both Teams, Game**
4 AFC (2) vs. NFC (2), 1973
AFC (2) vs. NFC (2), 1980

### PASSING
#### ATTEMPTS
**Most Attempts, Game**
55 NFC, 1993
**Fewest Attempts, Game**
17 NFC, 1972
**Most Attempts, Both Teams, Game**
94 AFC (50) vs. NFC (44), 1983
**Fewest Attempts, Both Teams, Game**
42 NFC (17) vs. AFC (25), 1972

#### COMPLETIONS
**Most Completions, Game**
32 NFC, 1993
**Fewest Completions, Game**
7 NFC, 1972, 1982
**Most Completions, Both Teams, Game**
55 AFC (31) vs. NFC (24), 1983
**Fewest Completions, Both Teams, Game**
18 NFC (7) vs. AFC (11), 1972

#### YARDS GAINED
**Most Yards Gained, Game**
387 AFC, 1983
**Fewest Yards Gained, Game**
42 NFC, 1982
**Most Yards Gained, Both Teams, Game**
608 AFC (387) vs. NFC (221), 1983
**Fewest Yards Gained, Both Teams, Game**
215 NFC (89) vs. AFC (126), 1972

#### TIMES SACKED
**Most Times Sacked, Game**
9 NFC, 1985
**Fewest Times Sacked, Game**
0 NFC, 1971
**Most Times Sacked, Both Teams, Game**
17 NFC (9) vs. AFC (8), 1985
**Fewest Times Sacked, Both Teams, Game**
4 AFC (2) vs. NFC (2), 1978
NFC (1) vs. AFC (3), 1994

#### TOUCHDOWNS
**Most Touchdowns, Game**
4 NFC, 1984
**Most Touchdowns, Both Teams, Game**
5 NFC (3) vs. AFC (2), 1986

### INTERCEPTIONS BY
**Most Interceptions By, Game**
6 AFC, 1977
**Most Interceptions By, Both Teams, Game**
7 AFC (6) vs. NFC (1), 1977

#### YARDS GAINED
**Most Yards Gained, Game**
103 AFC, 1994
**Most Yards Gained, Both Teams, Game**
116 AFC (103) vs. NFC (13), 1994

#### TOUCHDOWNS
**Most Touchdowns, Game**
1 AFC, 1973, 1990, 1993
NFC, 1984, 1986, 1990

### PUNTING
**Most Punts, Game**
10 AFC, 1985

**Fewest Punts, Game**
0 NFC, 1989
**Most Punts, Both Teams, Game**
16 AFC (10) vs. NFC (6), 1985
**Fewest Punts, Both Teams, Game**
4 NFC (1) vs. AFC (3), 1992

**AVERAGE YARDAGE**
**Highest Average, Game**
50.50 AFC, 1991 (2-101)

## PUNT RETURNS
**Most Punt Returns, Game**
7 NFC, 1985, 1987
**Fewest Punt Returns, Game**
0 AFC, 1984, 1989
**Most Punt Returns, Both Teams, Game**
11 NFC (7) vs. AFC (4), 1985
**Fewest Punt Returns, Both Teams, Game**
3 AFC (0) vs. NFC (3), 1984
AFC (0) vs. NFC (3), 1989
NFC (1) vs. AFC (2), 1991
AFC (1) vs. NFC (2), 1992

**YARDS GAINED**
**Most Yards Gained, Game**
177 AFC, 1976
**Fewest Yards Gained, Game**
–1 NFC, 1991
**Most Yards Gained, Both Teams, Game**
263 AFC (177) vs. NFC (86), 1976
**Fewest Yards Gained, Both Teams, Game**
16 AFC (0) vs. NFC (16), 1984

**TOUCHDOWNS**
**Most Touchdowns, Game**
2 NFC, 1971

## KICKOFF RETURNS
**Most Kickoff Returns, Game**
7 AFC, 1984
**Fewest Kickoff Returns, Game**
1 NFC, 1971, 1984, 1994
AFC, 1988, 1991
**Most Kickoff Returns, Both Teams, Game**
10 AFC (5) vs. NFC (5), 1976
AFC (5) vs. NFC (5), 1986
**Fewest Kickoff Returns, Both Teams, Game**
5 NFC (2) vs. AFC (3), 1979
AFC (1) vs. NFC (4), 1988
NFC (2) vs. AFC (3), 1992
NFC (1) vs. AFC (4), 1994

**YARDS GAINED**
**Most Yards Gained, Game**
215 AFC, 1984
**Fewest Yards Gained, Game**
6 NFC, 1971
**Most Yards Gained, Both Teams, Game**
293 NFC (200) vs. AFC (93), 1972
**Fewest Yards Gained, Both Teams, Game**
99 NFC (48) vs. AFC (51), 1987

**TOUCHDOWNS**
**Most Touchdowns, Game**
None

## FUMBLES
**Most Fumbles, Game**
10 NFC, 1974
**Most Fumbles, Both Teams, Game**
15 NFC (10) vs. AFC (5), 1974

**RECOVERIES**
**Most Fumbles Recovered, Game**
10 NFC, 1974 (6 own, 4 opp)
**Most Fumbles Lost, Game**
4 AFC, 1974, 1988
NFC, 1974

**YARDS GAINED**
**Most Yards Gained, Game**
87 AFC, 1985

**TOUCHDOWNS**
**Most Touchdowns, Game**
1 AFC, 1985
NFC, 1990

## TURNOVERS
(Number of times losing the ball on interceptions and fumbles.)
**Most Turnovers, Game**
8 AFC, 1974
**Fewest Turnovers, Game**
0 AFC, 1991
NFC, 1991
**Most Turnovers, Both Teams, Game**
12 AFC (8) vs. NFC (4), 1974
**Fewest Turnovers, Both Teams, Game**
0 AFC vs. NFC, 1991

# Rules

# OFFICIALS

## 1994 NFL ROSTER OF OFFICIALS

**Jerry Seeman,** Director of Officiating
**Jack Reader,** Assistant Director of Officiating
**Leo Miles,** Supervisor of Officials
**Ron DeSouza,** Supervisor of Officials

| No. | Name | Position | College |
|---|---|---|---|
| 25 | Alderton, John | Line Judge | Portland State |
| 115 | Ancich, Hendi | Umpire | Harbor College |
| 81 | Anderson, Dave | Line Judge | Salem College |
| 34 | Austin, Gerald | Referee | Western Carolina |
| 22 | Baetz, Paul | Back Judge | Heidelberg |
| 91 | Baker, Ken | Back Judge | Eastern Illinois |
| 26 | Baltz, Mark | Head Linesman | Ohio University |
| 55 | Barnes, Tom | Line Judge | Minnesota |
| 56 | Baynes, Ron | Line Judge | Auburn |
| 32 | Bergman, Jeff | Line Judge | Robert Morris |
| 17 | Bergman, Jerry | Head Linesman | Duquesne |
| 40 | Bible, Jon | Side Judge | Texas |
| 7 | Blum, Ron | Referee | Marin College |
| 90 | Borgard, Mike | Side Judge | St. Louis |
| 110 | Botchan, Ron | Umpire | Occidental |
| 101 | Boylston, Bob | Umpire | Alabama |
| 31 | Brown, Chad | Umpire | East Texas State |
| 94 | Carey, Mike | Side Judge | Santa Clara |
| 39 | Carlsen, Don | Side Judge | Cal State-Chico |
| 63 | Carollo, Bill | Side Judge | Wisconsin |
| 43 | Cashion, Red | Referee | Texas A&M |
| 24 | Clymer, Roy | Back Judge | New Mexico State |
| 45 | Coleman, George | Back Judge | Bishop College |
| 65 | Coleman, Walt | Line Judge | Arkansas |
| 27 | Conway, Al | Umpire | Army |
| 71 | Coukart, Ed | Umpire | Northwestern |
| 61 | Creed, Dick | Side Judge | Louisville |
| 75 | Daopoulos, Jim | Back Judge | Kentucky |
| 78 | Demmas, Art | Umpire | Vanderbilt |
| 113 | Dorkowski, Don | Field Judge | Cal State-Los Angeles |
| 74 | Duke, James | Umpire | Howard |
| 57 | Fiffick, Ed | Umpire | Marquette |
| 47 | Fincken, Tom | Side Judge | Kansas State |
| 111 | Frantz, Earnie | Head Linesman | No College |
| 50 | Gereb, Neil | Umpire | California |
| 72 | Gierke, Terry | Head Linesman | Portland State |
| 15 | Glass, Bama | Line Judge | Colorado |
| 3 | Golmont, Van | Side Judge | Miami |
| 19 | Green, Scott | Field Judge | Delaware |
| 23 | Grier, Johnny | Referee | University of D.C. |
| 96 | Hakes, Don | Field Judge | Bradley |
| 104 | Hamer, Dale | Referee | California, Pa. |
| 42 | Hamilton, Dave | Umpire | Utah |
| 44 | Hampton, Donnie | Field Judge | Georgia |
| 105 | Hantak, Dick | Referee | Southeast Missouri |
| 54 | Hayward, George | Head Linesman | Missouri Western |
| 85 | Hochuli, Ed | Back Judge | Texas-El Paso |
| 114 | Johnson, Tom | Head Linesman | Miami, Ohio |
| 97 | Jones, Nate | Side Judge | Lewis & Clark |
| 106 | Jury, Al | Back Judge | San Bernardino Valley |
| 67 | Keck, John | Umpire | Cornell College |
| 14 | Knight, Jim | Back Judge | Wake Forest |
| 86 | Kukar, Bernie | Referee | St. John's |
| 120 | Lane, Gary | Referee | Missouri |
| 49 | Look, Dean | Side Judge | Michigan State |
| 98 | Lovett, Bill | Back Judge | Maryland |
| 59 | Luckett, Phil | Field Judge | Texas-El Paso |
| 82 | Mallette, Pat | Field Judge | Nebraska |
| 9 | Markbreit, Jerry | Referee | Illinois |
| 38 | Maurer, Bruce | Line Judge | Ohio State |
| 48 | McCarter, Gordon | Referee | Western Reserve |
| 95 | McElwee, Bob | Referee | Navy |
| 35 | McGrath, Bob | Head Linesman | Western Kentucky |
| 41 | McKenzie, Dick | Line Judge | Ashland |
| 64 | McPeters, Lloyd | Line Judge | Oklahoma State |
| 76 | Merrifield, Ed | Field Judge | Missouri |
| 80 | Millis, Timmie | Back Judge | Millsaps |
| 117 | Montgomery, Ben | Line Judge | Morehouse |
| 36 | Moore, Bob | Back Judge | Dayton |
| 60 | Moore, Tommy | Side Judge | Stephen F. Austin |
| 20 | Nemmers, Larry | Referee | Upper Iowa |
| 51 | Orem, Dale | Line Judge | Louisville |
| 77 | Orr, Don | Field Judge | Vanderbilt |
| 10 | Phares, Ron | Head Linesman | Virginia Tech |
| 79 | Pointer, Aaron | Head Linesman | Pacific Lutheran |
| 92 | Poole, Jim | Back Judge | San Diego State |
| 58 | Quinby, Bill | Side Judge | Iowa |
| 5 | Quirk, Jim | Line Judge | Delaware |
| 83 | Reels, Richard | Field Judge | No College |
| 53 | Reynolds, Bill | Line Judge | West Chester State |
| 68 | Richard, Louis | Back Judge | Southwest Louisiana |
| 30 | Riggs, Dennis | Umpire | Bellarmine |
| 121 | Rivers, Sanford | Head Linesman | Youngstown State |
| 46 | Robison, John | Field Judge | Utah |
| 33 | Roe, Howard | Referee | Wichita State |
| 21 | Schleyer, John | Head Linesman | Millersville |
| 122 | Schmitz, Bill | Field Judge | Colorado State |
| 109 | Semon, Sid | Head Linesman | Southern California |
| 118 | Sifferman, Tom | Back Judge | Seattle |
| 73 | Skelton, Bobby | Field Judge | Alabama |
| 29 | Slavin, Howard | Side Judge | Southern California |
| 2 | Smith, Billy | Field Judge | East Carolina |
| 119 | Spitler, Ron | Field Judge | Panhandle State |
| 88 | Steenson, Scott | Back Judge | North Texas State |
| 62 | Stewart, Charles | Line Judge | Long Beach State |
| 103 | Stuart, Rex | Umpire | Appalachian State |
| 4 | Toole, Doug | Side Judge | Utah State |
| 37 | Upson, Larry | Line Judge | Prince George C.C. |
| 93 | Vaughan, Jack | Field Judge | Mississippi State |
| 52 | Veteri, Tony | Head Linesman | Manhattan College |
| 100 | Wagner, Bob | Umpire | Penn State |
| 28 | Wedge, Don | Side Judge | Ohio Wesleyan |
| 87 | Weidner, Paul | Head Linesman | Cincinnati |
| 123 | White, Tom | Referee | Temple |
| 99 | Williams, Banks | Back Judge | Houston |
| 8 | Williams, Dale | Head Linesman | Cal State-Northridge |
| 16 | Wyant, David | Side Judge | Virginia |

## NUMERICAL ROSTER

| No. | Name | Position |
|---|---|---|
| 2 | Billy Smith | FJ |
| 3 | Van Golmont | SJ |
| 4 | Doug Toole | SJ |
| 5 | Jim Quirk | LJ |
| 7 | Ron Blum | R |
| 8 | Dale Williams | HL |
| 9 | Jerry Markbreit | R |
| 10 | Ron Phares | HL |
| 14 | Jim Knight | BJ |
| 15 | Bama Glass | LJ |
| 16 | David Wyant | SJ |
| 17 | Jerry Bergman | HL |
| 19 | Scott Green | FJ |
| 20 | Larry Nemmers | R |
| 21 | John Schleyer | HL |
| 22 | Paul Baetz | BJ |
| 23 | Johnny Grier | R |
| 24 | Roy Clymer | BJ |
| 25 | John Alderton | LJ |
| 26 | Mark Baltz | HL |
| 27 | Al Conway | U |
| 28 | Don Wedge | SJ |
| 29 | Howard Slavin | SJ |
| 30 | Dennis Riggs | U |
| 31 | Chad Brown | U |
| 32 | Jeff Bergman | LJ |
| 33 | Howard Roe | R |
| 34 | Gerry Austin | R |
| 35 | Bob McGrath | HL |
| 36 | Bob Moore | BJ |
| 37 | Larry Upson | LJ |
| 38 | Bruce Maurer | LJ |
| 39 | Don Carlsen | SJ |
| 40 | Jon Bible | SJ |
| 41 | Dick McKenzie | LJ |
| 42 | Dave Hamilton | U |
| 43 | Red Cashion | R |
| 44 | Donnie Hampton | FJ |
| 45 | George Coleman | BJ |
| 46 | John Robison | FJ |
| 47 | Tom Fincken | SJ |
| 48 | Gordon McCarter | R |
| 49 | Dean Look | SJ |
| 50 | Neil Gereb | U |
| 51 | Dale Orem | LJ |
| 52 | Tony Veteri | HL |
| 53 | Bill Reynolds | LJ |
| 54 | George Hayward | HL |
| 55 | Tom Barnes | LJ |
| 56 | Ron Baynes | LJ |
| 57 | Ed Fiffick | U |
| 58 | Bill Quinby | SJ |
| 59 | Phil Luckett | FJ |
| 60 | Tommy Moore | SJ |
| 61 | Dick Creed | SJ |
| 62 | Charles Stewart | LJ |
| 63 | Bill Carollo | SJ |
| 64 | Lloyd McPeters | LJ |
| 65 | Walt Coleman | LJ |
| 67 | John Keck | U |
| 68 | Louis Richard | BJ |
| 71 | Ed Coukart | U |
| 72 | Terry Gierke | HL |
| 73 | Bobby Skelton | FJ |
| 74 | James Duke | U |
| 75 | Jim Daopoulos | BJ |
| 76 | Ed Merrifield | FJ |
| 77 | Don Orr | FJ |
| 78 | Art Demmas | U |
| 79 | Aaron Pointer | HL |
| 80 | Timmie Millis | BJ |
| 81 | Dave Anderson | LJ |
| 82 | Pat Mallette | FJ |
| 83 | Richard Reels | FJ |
| 85 | Ed Hochuli | BJ |
| 86 | Bernie Kukar | R |
| 87 | Paul Weidner | HL |
| 88 | Scott Steenson | BJ |
| 90 | Mike Borgard | SJ |
| 91 | Ken Baker | BJ |
| 92 | Jim Poole | BJ |
| 93 | Jack Vaughan | FJ |
| 94 | Mike Carey | SJ |
| 95 | Bob McElwee | R |
| 96 | Don Hakes | FJ |
| 97 | Nate Jones | SJ |
| 98 | Bill Lovett | BJ |
| 99 | Banks Williams | BJ |
| 100 | Bob Wagner | U |
| 101 | Bob Boylston | U |
| 103 | Rex Stuart | U |
| 104 | Dale Hamer | R |
| 105 | Dick Hantak | R |
| 106 | Al Jury | BJ |
| 109 | Sid Semon | HL |
| 110 | Ron Botchan | U |
| 111 | Earnie Frantz | HL |
| 113 | Don Dorkowski | FJ |
| 114 | Tom Johnson | HL |
| 115 | Hendi Ancich | U |
| 117 | Ben Montgomery | LJ |
| 118 | Tom Sifferman | BJ |
| 119 | Ron Spitler | FJ |
| 120 | Gary Lane | R |
| 121 | Sanford Rivers | HL |
| 122 | Bill Schmitz | FJ |
| 123 | Tom White | R |

## 1994 OFFICIALS AT A GLANCE

### REFEREES
**Gerry Austin,** No. **34,** Western Carolina, president, leadership development group, 13th year.
**Ron Blum,** No. **7,** Marin College, professional golfer, 10th year.
**Red Cashion,** No. **43,** Texas A&M, chairman, insurance company, 23rd year.
**Johnny Grier,** No. **23,** University of D.C., planning engineer, 14th year.
**Dale Hamer,** No. **104,** California (Pa.) University, consultant, 17th year.
**Dick Hantak,** No. **105,** Southeast Missouri, educator, 17th year.
**Ed Hochuli,** No. **85,** Texas-El Paso, attorney, 5th year.
**Bernie Kukar,** No. **86,** St. John's, sales representative, employees benefit plan, 11th year.
**Gary Lane,** No. **120,** Missouri, vice president, medical supplies, former NFL player, 13th year.
**Jerry Markbreit,** No. **9,** Illinois, trade and barter manager, 19th year.
**Gordon McCarter,** No. **48,** Western Reserve, retired sales manager, 28th year.
**Bob McElwee,** No. **95,** Navy, owner, heavy construction firm, 19th year.
**Larry Nemmers,** No. **20,** Upper Iowa, high school principal, 10th year.
**Howard Roe,** No. **33,** Wichita State, director, administration and finance, 11th year.
**Tom White,** No. **123,** Temple, president, athletic sportswear, 6th year.

### UMPIRES
**Hendi Ancich,** No. **115,** Harbor, longshoreman, 13th year.
**Ron Botchan,** No. **110,** Occidental, college professor, former AFL player, 15th year.
**Bob Boylston,** No. **101,** Alabama, stockbroker, 17th year.
**Chad Brown,** No. **31,** East Texas State, director, intramural/sports clubs, 3rd year.
**Al Conway,** No. **27,** Army, director of manufacturing, 26th year.
**Ed Coukart,** No. **71,** Northwestern, president, commercial bank, 6th year.
**Art Demmas,** No. **78,** Vanderbilt, Southern coordinator, National Football Foundation and College Hall of Fame, 27th year.
**James Duke,** No. **74,** Howard, Ward manager, department of parks and recreation, 2nd year.
**Ed Fiffick,** No. **57,** Marquette, podiatric physician, 16th year.
**Neil Gereb,** No. **50,** California, project manager, aircraft company, 14th year.
**Dave Hamilton,** No. **42,** Utah, chief, rehabilitation therapy services, 20th year.
**John Keck,** No. **67,** Cornell, petroleum distributor, 23rd year.
**Dennis Riggs,** No. **30,** Bellarmine, president, community foundation, 7th year.
**Rex Stuart,** No. **103,** Appalachian State, insurance agent, 11th year.
**Bob Wagner,** No. **100,** Penn State, executive director, cardiovascular institute, 10th year.

### HEAD LINESMEN
**Mark Baltz,** No. **26,** Ohio University, manufacturer's representative, 6th year.
**Jerry Bergman,** No. **17,** Duquesne, executive director, pension fund, 29th year.
**Earnie Frantz,** No. **111,** no college, vice president and manager, insurance company, 14th year.
**Terry Gierke,** No. **72,** Portland State, real estate broker, 14th year.
**George Hayward,** No. **54,** Missouri Western, vice president and manager, warehouse company, 4th year.
**Tom Johnson,** No. **114,** Miami, Ohio, educator, president, security company, 13th year.
**Bob McGrath,** No. **35,** Western Kentucky, sales representative, fund raiser, 2nd year.
**Ron Phares,** No. **10,** Virginia Tech, president, construction company, 10th year.
**Aaron Pointer,** No. **79,** Pacific Lutheran, park department administrator, 8th year.
**Sanford Rivers,** No. **121,** Youngstown State, assistant vice president, school administration, 6th year.
**John Schleyer,** No. **21,** Millersville, medical sales, 5th year.
**Sid Semon,** No. **109,** Southern California, chairman, physical education department, 17th year.
**Tony Veteri,** No. **52,** Manhattan, director of athletics, 3rd year.
**Paul Weidner,** No. **87,** Cincinnati, marketing manager, 9th year.
**Dale Williams,** No. **8,** Cal State-Northridge, owner, coin-op laundromats, 15th year.

### LINE JUDGES
**John Alderton,** No. **25,** Portland State, vice president, insurance, 6th year.
**Dave Anderson,** No. **81,** Salem, insurance executive, 11th year.
**Tom Barnes,** No. **55,** Minnesota, manufacturing representative, 9th year.
**Ron Baynes,** No. **56,** Auburn, school administrator, coach, 8th year.
**Jeff Bergman,** No. **32,** Robert Morris, president and chief executive officer, medical services, 4th year.
**Walt Coleman,** No. **65,** Arkansas, president, dairy processor, 6th year.
**Bama Glass,** No. **15,** Colorado, agent, insurance/financial services, 16th year.
**Bruce Maurer,** No. **38,** Ohio State, administrator and associate director, recreational sports, 8th year.
**Dick McKenzie,** No. **41,** Ashland, financial services, 17th year.
**Lloyd McPeters,** No. **64,** Oklahoma State, business insurance sales, 2nd year.
**Ben Montgomery,** No. **117,** Morehouse, school administrator, 13th year.
**Dale Orem,** No. **51,** Louisville, executive director, community foundation, 15th year.
**Jim Quirk,** No. **5,** Delaware, vice president, government securities, 7th year.
**Bill Reynolds,** No. **53,** West Chester State, educator, 20th year.
**Charles Stewart,** No. **62,** Long Beach State, administrative deputy director, 3rd year.
**Larry Upson,** No. **37,** Prince George City College, senior personnel management specialist, 4th year.

### BACK JUDGES
**Paul Baetz,** No. **22,** Heidelberg, financial consultant, 17th year.
**Ken Baker,** No. **91,** Eastern Illinois, optician, surgical ophthalmic technician, 4th year.
**Roy Clymer,** No. **24,** New Mexico State, district marketing manager, gas company, 15th year.
**George Coleman,** No. **45,** Bishop College, executive director, YMCA, 2nd year.
**Jim Daopoulos,** No. **75,** Kentucky, mortgage broker, 6th year.
**Al Jury,** No. **106,** San Bernardino Valley, state traffic officer, 17th year.
**Jim Knight,** No. **14,** Wake Forest, manufacturer's representative, 1st year.
**Bill Lovett,** No. **98,** Maryland, managing partner, financial sales, 5th year.
**Timmie Millis,** No. **80,** Millsaps, financial investigative consultant, 6th year.
**Bob Moore,** No. **36,** Dayton, attorney, 11th year.
**Jim Poole,** No. **92,** San Diego State, college professor, 20th year.
**Louis Richard,** No. **68,** Southwestern Louisiana, sales manager, 9th year.
**Tom Sifferman,** No. **118,** Seattle, manufacturer's representative, 9th year.
**Scott Steenson,** No. **88,** North Texas State, real estate broker, 4th year.
**Banks Williams,** No. **99,** Houston, consultant, 17th year.

### SIDE JUDGES
**Jon Bible,** No. **40,** Texas, attorney/college educator, 1st year.
**Mike Borgard,** No. **90,** St. Louis, president/owner, advertising specialties, 5th year.
**Mike Carey,** No. **94,** Santa Clara, marketing manager, 5th year.
**Don Carlsen,** No. **39,** Cal State-Chico, budget analyst, comptroller, 6th year.
**Bill Carollo,** No. **63,** Wisconsin, marketing executive, 6th year.
**Richard Creed,** No. **61,** Louisville, manager, real estate, 17th year.
**Tom Fincken,** No. **47,** Emporia State, educator, 11th year.
**Van Golmont,** No. **3,** Miami, regional manager, marketing development,, 4th year.
**Nate Jones,** No. **97,** Lewis and Clark, high school principal, 18th year.
**Dean Look,** No. **49,** Michigan State, director, medical manufacturing, former AFL player, 22nd year.
**Tommy Moore,** No. **60,** Stephen F. Austin, marketing, manufacturing, representative, 3rd year.
**Bill Quinby,** No. **58,** Iowa, retired athletic director, 17th year.
**Howard Slavin,** No. **29,** Southern California, attorney, 8th year.
**Doug Toole,** No. **4,** Utah State, physical therapist, orthopedic and sports medicine, 7th year.
**Don Wedge,** No. **28,** Ohio Wesleyan, executive account manager, 23rd year.
**David Wyant,** No. **16,** Virginia, research scientist, 4th year.

### FIELD JUDGES
**Don Dorkowski,** No. **113,** Cal State-Los Angeles, department head, health and safety, 9th year.
**Scott Green,** No. **19,** Delaware, vice president, government relations, 4th year.
**Don Hakes,** No. **96,** Bradley, retired educator, 18th year.
**Donnie Hampton,** No. **44,** Georgia, mortgage banker, 7th year.
**Phil Luckett,** No. **59,** Texas-El Paso, computer program analyst, federal civil services, 4th year.
**Pat Mallette,** No. **82,** Nebraska, real estate broker, 26th year.
**Ed Merrifield,** No. **76,** Missouri, sales representative, 20th year.
**Don Orr,** No. **77,** Vanderbilt, mechanical contractor, 24th year.
**Richard Reels,** No. **83,** Chicago State, director of security, court services, 2nd year.
**John Robison,** No. **46,** Utah, high school teacher, 7th year.
**Bill Schmitz,** No. **122,** Colorado State, general sales manager, 6th year.
**Bobby Skelton,** No. **73,** Alabama, industrial representative, 10th year.
**Billy Smith,** No. **2,** East Carolina, Federal government, 1st year.
**Ron Spitler,** No. **119,** Panhandle State, owner, service center, 13th year.
**Jack Vaughan,** No. **93,** Mississippi State, financial services, 19th year.

## OFFICIAL SIGNALS

1

**TOUCHDOWN, FIELD GOAL, or SUCCESSFUL TRY**
Both arms extended above head.

2

**SAFETY**
Palms together above head.

3

**FIRST DOWN**
Arm pointed toward defensive team's goal.

4

**CROWD NOISE, DEAD BALL, or NEUTRAL ZONE ESTABLISHED**
One arm above head with an open hand.
With fist closed: **Fourth Down.**

5

**BALL ILLEGALLY TOUCHED, KICKED OR BATTED**
Fingertips tap both shoulders.

6

**TIME OUT**
Hands crisscrossed above head.

Same signal follwed by placing one hand on top of cap: **Referee's Time Out.**

Same signal followed by arm swung at side: **Touchback.**

7

**NO TIME OUT or TIME IN WITH WHISTLE**
Full arm circled to simulate moving clock.

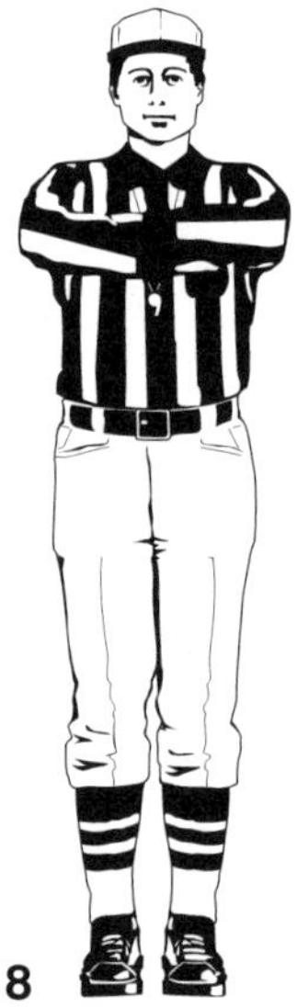

8

**DELAY OF GAME, ILLEGAL SUBSTITUTION, or EXCESS TIME OUT**
Folded arms.

9

**FALSE START, ILLEGAL SHIFT, ILLEGAL FORMATION, or KICKOFF OR SAFETY KICK OUT OF BOUNDS**
Forearms rotated over and over in front of body.

10

**PERSONAL FOUL**
One wrist striking the other above head.
Same signal followed by swinging leg: **Roughing the Kicker.**
Same signal followed by raised arm swinging forward: **Roughing the Passer.**
Same signal followed by hand striking back of calf: **Clipping.**

11

**HOLDING**
Grasping one wrist, the fist clenched, in front of chest.

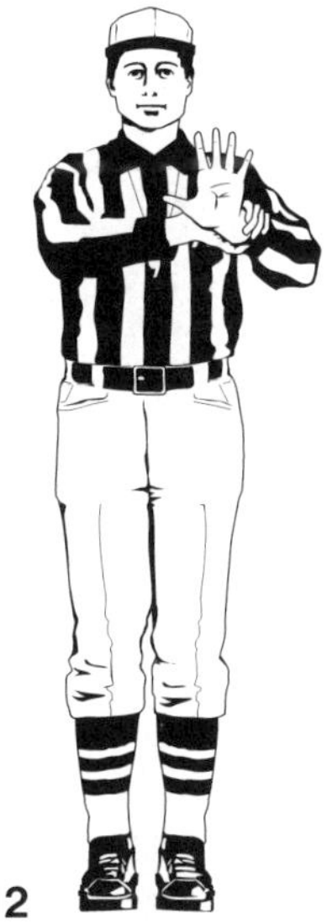

12

**ILLEGAL USE OF HANDS, ARMS, OR BODY**
Grasping one wrist, the hand open and facing forward, in front of chest.

13

**PENALTY REFUSED, INCOMPLETE PASS, PLAY OVER, or MISSED FIELD GOAL or EXTRA POINT**
Hands shifted in horizontal plane.

14

**PASS JUGGLED INBOUNDS AND CAUGHT OUT OF BOUNDS**
Hands up and down in front of chest (following incomplete pass signal).

15

**ILLEGAL FORWARD PASS**
One hand waved behind back followed by loss of down signal (23).

16

**INTENTIONAL GROUNDING OF PASS**
Parallel arms waved in a diagonal plane across body. Followed by loss of down signal (23).

## OFFICIAL SIGNALS

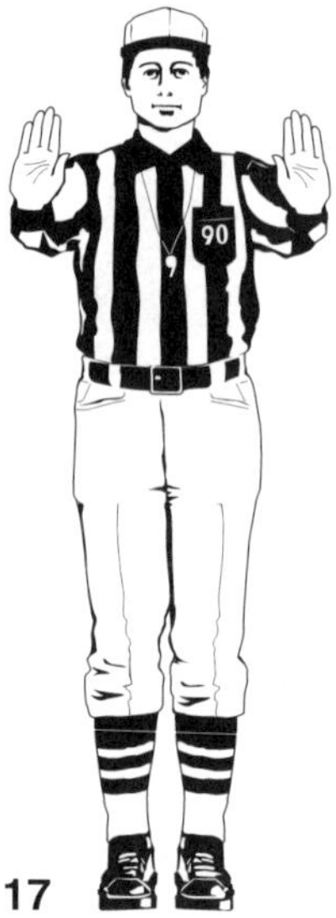

17

**INTERFERENCE WITH FORWARD PASS or FAIR CATCH**
Hands open and extended forward from shoulders with hands vertical.

18

**INVALID FAIR CATCH SIGNAL**
One hand waved above head.

19

**INELIGIBLE RECEIVER OR INELIGIBLE MEMBER OF KICKING TEAM DOWNFIELD**
Right hand touching top of cap.

20

**ILLEGAL CONTACT**
One open hand extended forward.

21

**OFFSIDE or ENCROACHING**
Hands on hips.

22

**ILLEGAL MOTION AT SNAP**
Horizontal arc with one hand.

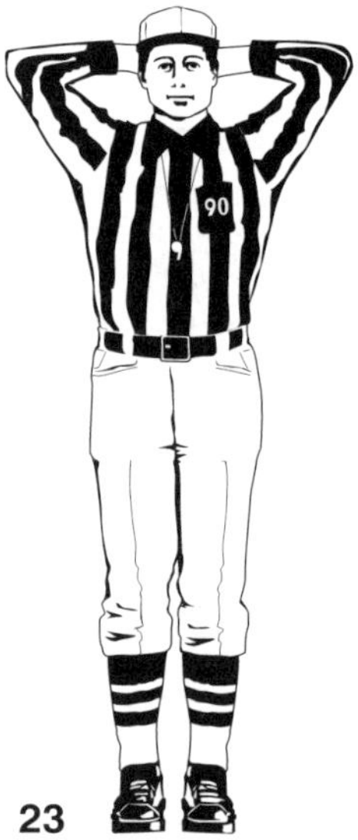

23

**LOSS OF DOWN**
Both hands held behind head.

24

**CRAWLING, INTERLOCKING INTERFERENCE, PUSHING, or HELPING RUNNER**
Pushing movement of hands to front with arms downward.

25

**TOUCHING A FORWARD PASS OR SCRIMMAGE KICK**
Diagonal motion of one hand across another.

26

**UNSPORTSMANLIKE CONDUCT**
Arms outstretched, palms down. (Same signal means continuous action fouls are disregarded.) Chop block.

27

**ILLEGAL CUT or BLOCKING BELOW THE WAIST**
Hand striking front of thigh preceded by personal foul signal (10).

28

**ILLEGAL CRACKBACK**
Strike of an open right hand against the right mid thigh preceded by personal foul signal (10).

29

**PLAYER DISQUALIFIED**
Ejection signal.

30

**TRIPPING**
Repeated action of right foot in back of left heel.

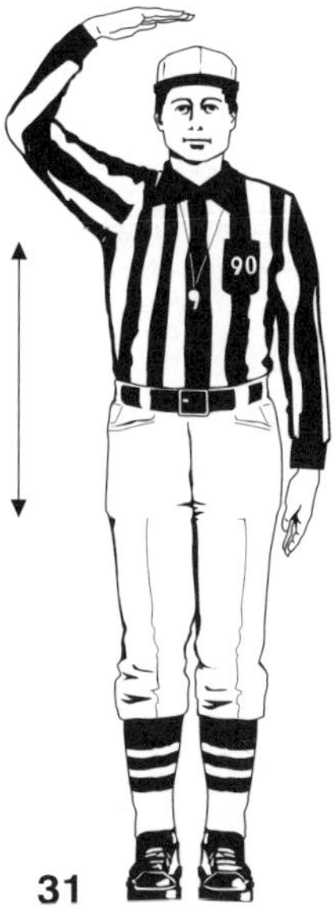

31

**UNCATCHABLE FORWARD PASS**
Palm of right hand held parallel to ground above head. and moved back and forth.

# DIGEST OF RULES

## NFL DIGEST OF RULES

**This Digest of Rules of the National Football League has been prepared to aid players, fans, and members of the press, radio, and television media in their understanding of the game.**

**It is not meant to be a substitute for the official rule book. In any case of conflict between these explanations and the official rules, the rules always have precedence.**

**In order to make it easier to coordinate the information in this digest the topics discussed generally follow the order of the rule book.**

### OFFICIALS' JURISDICTIONS, POSITIONS, AND DUTIES

**Referee**—General oversight and control of game. Gives signals for all fouls and is final authority for rule interpretations. Takes a position in backfield 10 to 12 yards behind line of scrimmage, favors right side (if quarterback is right-handed passer). Determines legality of snap, observes deep back(s) for legal motion. On running play, observes quarterback during and after handoff, remains with him until action has cleared away, then proceeds downfield, checking on runner and contact behind him. When runner is downed, Referee determines forward progress from wing official and, if necessary, adjusts final position of ball.

On pass plays, drops back as quarterback begins to fade back, picks up legality of blocks by near linemen. Changes to complete concentration on quarterback as defenders approach. Primarily responsible to rule on possible roughing action on passer and if ball becomes loose, rules whether ball is free on a fumble or dead on an incomplete pass.

During kicking situations, Referee has primary responsibility to rule on kicker's actions and whether or not any subsequent contact by a defender is legal. The Referee will announce on the microphone when each period is ended.

**Umpire**—Primary responsibility to rule on players' equipment, as well as their conduct and actions on scrimmage line. Lines up approximately four to five yards downfield, varying position from in front of weakside tackle to strongside guard. Looks for possible false start by offensive linemen. Observes legality of contact by both offensive linemen while blocking and by defensive players while they attempt to ward off blockers. Is prepared to call rule infractions if they occur on offense or defense. Moves forward to line of scrimmage when pass play develops in order to insure that interior linemen do not move illegally downfield. If offensive linemen indicate screen pass is to be attempted, Umpire shifts his attention toward screen side, picks up potential receiver in order to insure that he will legally be permitted to run his pattern and continues to rule on action of blockers. Umpire is to assist in ruling on incomplete or trapped passes when ball is thrown overhead or short.

**Head Linesman**—Primarily responsible for ruling on offside, encroachment, and actions pertaining to scrimmage line prior to or at snap. Keys on closest setback on his side of the field. On pass plays, Linesman is responsible to clear his receiver approximately seven yards downfield as he moves to a point five yards beyond the line. Linesman's secondary responsibility is to rule on any illegal action taken by defenders on any delay receiver moving downfield. Has full responsibility for ruling on sideline plays on his side, e.g., pass receiver or runner in or out of bounds. Together with Referee, Linesman is responsible for keeping track of number of downs and is in charge of mechanics of his chain crew in connection with its duties.

Linesman must be prepared to assist in determining forward progress by a runner on play directed toward middle or into his side zone. He, in turn, is to signal Referee or Umpire what forward point ball has reached. Linesman is also responsible to rule on legality of action involving any receiver who approaches his side zone. He is to call pass interference when the infraction occurs and is to rule on legality of blockers and defenders on plays involving ball carriers, whether it is entirely a running play, a combination pass and run, or a play involving a kick.

**Line Judge**—Straddles line of scrimmage on side of field opposite Linesman. Keeps time of game as a backup for clock operator. Along with Linesman is responsible for offside, encroachment, and actions pertaining to scrimmage line prior to or at snap. Line Judge keys on closest setback on his side of field. Line Judge is to observe his receiver until he moves at least seven yards downfield. He then moves toward backfield side, being especially alert to rule on any back in motion and on flight of ball when pass is made (he must rule whether forward or backward). Line Judge has primary responsibility to rule whether or not passer is behind or beyond line of scrimmage when pass is made. He also assists in observing actions by blockers and defenders who are on his side of field. After pass is thrown, Line Judge directs attention toward activities that occur in back of Umpire. During punting situations, Line Judge remains at line of scrimmage to be sure that only the end men move downfield until kick has been made. He also rules whether or not the kick crossed line and then observes action by members of the kicking team who are moving downfield to cover the kick. The Line Judge will advise the Referee when time has expired at the end of each period.

**Back Judge**—Operates on same side of field as Line Judge, 20 yards deep. Keys on wide receiver on his side. Concentrates on path of end or back, observing legality of his potential block(s) or of actions taken against him. Is prepared to rule from <u>deep</u> position on holding or illegal use of hands by end or back or on defensive infractions committed by player guarding him. Has primary responsibility to make decisions involving sideline on his side of field, e.g., pass receiver or runner in or out of bounds.

Back Judge makes decisions involving catching, recovery, or illegal touching of a loose ball beyond line of scrimmage; rules on plays involving pass receiver, including legality of catch or pass interference; assists in covering actions of runner, including blocks by teammates and that of defenders; calls clipping on punt returns; and, together with Field Judge, rules whether or not field goal attempts are successful.

**Side Judge**—Operates on same side of field as Linesman, 20 yards deep. Keys on wide receiver on his side. Concentrates on path of end or back, observing legality of his potential block(s) or of actions taken against him. Is prepared to rule from <u>deep</u> position on holding or illegal use of hands by end or back or on defensive infractions committed by player guarding him. Has primary responsibility to make decisions involving sideline on his side of field, e.g., pass receiver or runner in or out of bounds.

Side Judge makes decisions involving catching, recovery, or illegal touching of a loose ball beyond line of scrimmage; rules on plays involving pass receiver, including legality of catch or pass interference; assists in covering actions of runner, including blocks by teammates and that of defenders; and calls clipping on punt returns. On punts, field goals, and point after touchdown attempts, he becomes a double umpire.

**Field Judge**—Takes a position 25 yards downfield. In general, favors the tight end's side of field. Keys on tight end, concentrates on his path and observes legality of tight end's potential block(s) or of actions taken against him. Is prepared to rule from <u>deep</u> position on holding or illegal use of hands by end or back or on defensive infractions committed by player guarding him.

Field Judge times interval between plays on 40/25-second clock plus intermission between two periods of each half; makes decisions involving catching, recovery, or illegal touching of a loose ball beyond line of scrimmage; is responsible to rule on plays involving end line; calls pass interference, fair catch infractions, and clipping on kick returns; and, together with Back Judge, rules whether or not field goals and conversions are successful.

### DEFINITIONS

1. **Chucking:** Warding off an opponent who is in front of a defender by contacting him with a quick extension of arm or arms, followed by the return of arm(s) to a flexed position, thereby breaking the original contact.
2. **Clipping:** Throwing the body across the back of an opponent's leg or hitting him from the back below the waist while moving up from behind unless the opponent is a runner or the action is in close line play.
3. **Close Line Play:** The area between the positions normally occupied by the offensive tackles, extending three yards on each side of the line of scrimmage.
4. **Crackback:** Eligible receivers who take or move to a position more than two yards outside the tackle may not block an opponent below the waist if they then move back inside to block.
5. **Dead Ball:** Ball not in play.
6. **Double Foul:** A foul by each team during the same down.
7. **Down:** The period of action that starts when the ball is put in play and ends when it is dead.
8. **Encroachment:** When a player enters the neutral zone and makes <u>contact</u> with an opponent before the ball is snapped.
9. **Fair Catch:** An unhindered catch of a kick by a member of the receiving team who must raise one arm a full length above his head while the kick is in flight.
10. **Foul:** Any violation of a playing rule.
11. **Free Kick:** A kickoff, kick after a safety, or kick after a fair catch. It may be a placekick, dropkick, or punt, except a punt may <u>not</u> be used on a kickoff.
12. **Fumble:** The loss of possession of the ball.
13. **Game Clock:** Scoreboard game clock.
14. **Impetus:** The action of a player that gives momentum to the ball.
15. **Live Ball:** A ball legally free kicked or snapped. It continues in play until the down ends.
16. **Loose Ball:** A live ball not in possession of any player.
17. **Muff:** The touching of a loose ball by a player in an <u>unsuccessful</u> attempt to obtain possession.
18. **Neutral Zone:** The space the length of a ball between the two scrimmage lines. The offensive team and defensive team must remain behind their end of the ball.
    **Exception:** The offensive player who snaps the ball.
19. **Offside:** A player is offside when any part of his body is beyond his scrimmage or free kick line <u>when the ball is snapped.</u>
20. **Own Goal:** The goal a team is guarding.
21. **Play Clock:** 40/25 second clock.
22. **Pocket Area:** Applies from a point two yards outside of either offensive tackle and includes the tight end if he drops off the line of scrimmage to pass protect. Pocket extends longitudinally behind the line back to offensive team's own end line.
23. **Possession:** When a player controls the ball throughout the act of <u>clearly</u> touching both feet, or any other part of his body other than his hand(s), to the ground inbounds.
24. **Post-Possession Foul:** A foul by the receiving team that occurs after a ball is legally kicked from scrimmage prior to possession changing. The ball must cross the line of scrimmage and the receiving team must retain possession of the kicked ball.
25. **Punt:** A kick made when a player drops the ball and kicks it while it is in flight.
26. **Safety:** The situation in which the ball is dead on or behind a team's own goal if the <u>impetus</u> comes from a player on that team. Two points are scored for the opposing team.
27. **Shift:** The movement of two or more offensive players at the same time before the snap.
28. **Striking:** The act of swinging, clubbing, or propelling the arm or forearm in contacting an opponent.

29. **Sudden Death:** The continuation of a tied game into sudden death overtime in which the team scoring first (by safety, field goal, or touchdown) wins.
30. **Touchback:** When a ball is dead on or behind a team's own goal line, provided the impetus came from an opponent and provided it is not a touchdown or a missed field goal.
31. **Touchdown:** When any part of the ball, legally in possession of a player inbounds, is on, above, or over the opponent's goal line, provided it is not a touchback.
32. **Unsportsmanlike Conduct:** Any act contrary to the generally understood principles of sportsmanship.

**SUMMARY OF PENALTIES**

**Automatic First Down**

1. Awarded to offensive team on all defensive fouls with these exceptions:
   (a) Offside.
   (b) Encroachment.
   (c) Delay of game.
   (d) Illegal substitution.
   (e) Excessive time out(s).
   (f) Incidental grasp of facemask.
   (g) Neutral zone infraction.
   (h) Running into the kicker.

**Loss of Down** (No yardage)

1. Second forward pass behind the line.
2. Forward pass strikes ground, goal post, or crossbar.
3. Forward pass goes out of bounds.
4. Forward pass is first touched by eligible receiver who has gone out of bounds and returned.
5. Forward pass touches or is caught by an ineligible receiver on or behind line.
6. Forward pass thrown from behind line of scrimmage after ball once crossed the line.

**Five Yards**

1. Defensive holding or illegal use of hands (automatic first down).
2. Delay of game.
3. Encroachment.
4. Excessive time out(s).
5. False start.
6. Illegal formation.
7. Illegal shift.
8. Illegal motion.
9. Illegal substitution.
10. First onside kickoff out of bounds between goal lines and not touched.
11. Invalid fair catch signal.
12. More than 11 players on the field at snap for either team.
13. Less than seven men on offensive line at snap.
14. Offside.
15. Failure to pause one second after shift or huddle.
16. Running into kicker.
17. More than one man in motion at snap.
18. Grasping facemask of the ball carrier or quarterback.
19. Player out of bounds at snap.
20. Ineligible member(s) of kicking team going beyond line of scrimmage before ball is kicked.
21. Illegal return.
22. Failure to report change of eligibility.
23. Neutral zone infraction.
24. Loss of team time out(s) or five-yard penalty on the defense for excessive crowd noise.
25. Ineligible player downfield during passing down.

**10 Yards**

1. Offensive pass interference.
2. Holding, illegal use of hands, arms, or body by offense.
3. Tripping by a member of either team.
4. Helping the runner.
5. Deliberately batting or punching a loose ball.
6. Deliberately kicking a loose ball.

**15 Yards**

1. Chop block.
2. Clipping below the waist.
3. Fair catch interference.
4. Illegal crackback block by offense.
5. Piling on (automatic first down).
6. Roughing the kicker (automatic first down).
7. Roughing the passer (automatic first down).
8. Twisting, turning, or pulling an opponent by the facemask.
9. Unnecessary roughness.
10. Unsportsmanlike conduct.
11. Delay of game at start of either half.
12. Illegal low block.
13. A tackler using his helmet to butt, spear, or ram an opponent.
14. Any player who uses the top of his helmet unnecessarily.
15. A punter, placekicker, or holder who simulates being roughed by a defensive player.
16. A defender who takes a running start from beyond the line of scrimmage in an attempt to block a field goal or point after touchdown and lands on players at the line of scrimmage.

**Five Yards and Loss of Down**

1. Forward pass thrown from beyond line of scrimmage.

**10 Yards and Loss of Down**

1. Intentional grounding of forward pass (safety if passer is in own end zone). If foul occurs more than 10 yards behind line, play results in loss of down at spot of foul.

**15 Yards and Loss of Coin Toss Option**

1. Team's late arrival on the field prior to scheduled kickoff.
2. Captains not appearing for coin toss.

**15 Yards (and disqualification if flagrant)**

1. Striking opponent with fist.
2. Kicking or kneeing opponent.
3. Striking opponent on head or neck with forearm, elbow, or hands whether or not the initial contact is made below the neck area.
4. Roughing kicker.
5. Roughing passer.
6. Malicious unnecessary roughness.
7. Unsportsmanlike conduct.
8. Palpably unfair act. (Distance penalty determined by the Referee after consultation with other officials.)

**15 Yards and Automatic Disqualification**

1. Using a helmet (not worn) as a weapon.

**Suspension From Game For One Down**

1. Illegal equipment. (Player may return after one down when legally equipped.)

**Touchdown Awarded (Palpably Unfair Act)**

1. When Referee determines a palpably unfair act deprived a team of a touchdown. (Example: Player comes off bench and tackles runner apparently en route to touchdown.)

**FIELD**

1. Sidelines and end lines are out of bounds. The goal line is actually in the end zone. A player with the ball in his possession scores when the ball is on, above, or over the goal line.
2. The field is rimmed by a white border, six feet wide, along the sidelines. All of this is out of bounds.
3. The hashmarks (inbound lines) are 70 feet, 9 inches from each sideline.
4. Goal posts must be single-standard type, offset from the end line and painted bright gold. The goal posts must be 18 feet, 6 inches wide and the top face of the crossbar must be 10 feet above the ground. Vertical posts extend at least 30 feet above the crossbar. A ribbon 4 inches by 42 inches long is to be attached to the top of each post. The actual goal is the plane extending indefinitely above the crossbar and between the outer edges of the posts.
5. The field is 360 feet long and 160 feet wide. The end zones are 30 feet deep. The line used in try-for-point plays is two yards out from the goal line.
6. Chain crew members and ball boys must be uniformly identifiable.
7. All clubs must use standardized sideline markers. Pylons must be used for goal line and end line markings.
8. End zone markings and club identification at 50 yard line must be approved by the Commissioner to avoid any confusion as to delineation of goal lines, sidelines, and end lines.

**BALL**

1. Twenty-four approved footballs will be used in each game (12 each half).

**COIN TOSS**

1. The toss of coin will take place within three minutes of kickoff in center of field. The toss will be called by the visiting captain. The winner may choose one of two privileges and the loser gets the other:
   (a) Receive or kick
   (b) Goal his team will defend
2. Immediately prior to the start of the second half, the captains of both teams must inform the officials of their respective choices. The loser of the original coin toss gets first choice.

**TIMING**

1. The stadium game clock is official. In case it stops or is operating incorrectly, the Line Judge takes over the official timing on the field.
2. Each period is 15 minutes. The intermission between the periods is two minutes. Halftime is 12 minutes, unless otherwise specified.
3. On charged team time outs, the Field Judge starts watch and blows whistle after 1 minute 50 seconds, unless television does not utilize the time for commercial. In this case the length of the time out is reduced to 40 seconds.
4. The Referee will allow necessary time to attend to an injured player, or repair a legal player's equipment.
5. Each team is allowed three time outs each half.
6. Time between plays will be 40 seconds from the end of a given play until the snap of the ball for the next play, or a 25-second interval after certain administrative stoppages and game delays.
7. Clock will start running when ball is snapped following all changes of team possession.

# DIGEST OF RULES

8. With the exception of the last two minutes of the first half and the last five minutes of the second half, the game clock will be restarted following a kickoff return, a player going out of bounds on a play from scrimmage, or after declined penalties when appropriate on the referee's signal.
9. Consecutive team time outs can be taken by opposing teams but the length of the second time out will be reduced to 40 seconds.
10. When, in the judgment of the Referee, the level of crowd noise prevents the offense from hearing its signals, he can institute a series of procedures which can result in a loss of team time outs or a five-yard penalty against the defensive team.

**SUDDEN DEATH**

1. The sudden death system of determining the winner shall prevail when score is tied at the end of the regulation playing time of all NFL games. The team scoring first during overtime play shall be the winner and the game automatically ends upon any score (by safety, field goal, or touchdown) or when a score is awarded by Referee for a palpably unfair act.
2. At the end of regulation time the Referee will immediately toss coin at center of field in accordance with rules pertaining to the usual pregame toss. The captain of the visiting team will call the toss.
3. Following a three-minute intermission after the end of the regulation game, play will be continued in 15-minute periods or until there is a score. There is a two-minute intermission between subsequent periods. The teams change goals at the start of each period. Each team has three time outs per half and all general timing provisions apply as during a regular game. Disqualified players are not allowed to return.
   **Exception:** In preseason and regular season games there shall be a maximum of 15 minutes of sudden death with two time outs instead of three. General provisions that apply for the fourth quarter will prevail.

**TIMING IN FINAL TWO MINUTES OF EACH HALF**

1. On kickoff, clock does not start until the ball has been legally touched by player of either team in the field of play. (In all other cases, clock starts with kickoff.)
2. A team cannot buy an excess time out for a penalty. However, a fourth time out is allowed without penalty for an injured player, who must be removed immediately. A fifth time out or more is allowed for an injury and a five-yard penalty is assessed if the clock was running. Additionally, if the clock was running and the score is tied or the team in possession is losing, the ball cannot be put in play for at least 10 seconds on the fourth or more time out. The half or game can end while those 10 seconds are run off on the clock.
3. If the defensive team is behind in the score and commits a foul when it has no time outs left in the final 30 seconds of either half, the offensive team can decline the penalty for the foul and have the time on the clock expire.
4. Fouls that occur in the last five minutes of the fourth quarter as well as the last two minutes of the first half will result in the clock starting on the snap.

**TRY**

1. After a touchdown, the scoring team is allowed a try during one scrimmage down. The ball may be spotted anywhere between the inbounds lines, two or more yards from the goal line. The successful conversion counts one point by kick; two points for a successful conversion by touchdown; or one point for a safety.
2. The defensive team never can score on a try. As soon as defense gets possession or the kick is blocked or a touchdown is not scored, the try is over.
3. Any distance penalty for fouls committed by the defense that prevent the try from being attempted can be enforced on the succeeding try or succeeding kickoff. Any foul committed on a successful try will result in a distance penalty being assessed on the ensuing kickoff.
4. Only the fumbling player can recover and advance a fumble during a try.

**PLAYERS-SUBSTITUTIONS**

1. Each team is permitted 11 men on the field at the snap.
2. Unlimited substitution is permitted. However, players may enter the field only when the ball is dead. Players who have been substituted for are not permitted to linger on the field. Such lingering will be interpreted as unsportsmanlike conduct.
3. Players leaving the game must be out of bounds on their own side, clearing the field between the end lines, before a snap or free kick. If player crosses end line leaving field, it is delay of game (five-yard penalty).
4. Substitutes who remain in the game must move onto the field as far as the inside of the field numerals before moving to a wide position.
5. With the exception of the last two minutes of either half, the offensive team, while in the process of substitution or simulated substitution, is prohibited from rushing quickly to the line and snapping the ball with the obvious attempt to cause a defensive foul; i.e., too many men on the field.

**KICKOFF**

1. The kickoff shall be from the kicking team's 30-yard line at the start of each half and after a field goal and try-for-point. A kickoff is one type of free kick.
2. A one-inch tee may be used (no tee permitted for field goal or try attempt) on a kickoff. The ball is put in play by a placekick or dropkick.
3. If the kickoff clears the opponent's goal posts it is not a field goal.
4. A kickoff is illegal unless it travels 10 yards OR is touched by the receiving team. Once the ball is touched by the receiving team it is a free ball. Receivers may recover and advance. Kicking team may recover but NOT advance UNLESS receiver had possession and lost the ball.
5. When a kickoff goes out of bounds between the goal lines without being touched by the receiving team, the ball belongs to the receivers 30 yards from the spot of the kick or at the out-of-bounds spot unless the ball went out-of-bounds the first time an onside kick was attempted. In this case the kicking team is to be penalized five yards and the ball must be kicked again.
6. When a kickoff goes out of bounds between the goal lines and is touched last by receiving team, it is receiver's ball at out-of-bounds spot.

**FREE KICK**

1. In addition to a kickoff, the other free kicks are a kick after a safety and a kick after a fair catch. In both cases, a dropkick, placekick, or punt may be used (a punt may not be used on a kickoff).
2. On a free kick after a fair catch, captain of receiving team has the option to put ball in play by punt, dropkick, or placekick without a tee, or by snap. If the placekick or dropkick goes between the uprights a field goal is scored.
3. On a free kick after a safety, the team scored upon puts ball in play by a punt, dropkick, or placekick without tee. No score can be made on a free kick following a safety, even if a series of penalties places team in position. (A field goal can be scored only on a play from scrimmage or a free kick after a fair catch.)

**FIELD GOAL**

1. All field goals attempted (kicker) and missed from beyond the 20-yard line will result in the defensive team taking possession of the ball at the spot of the kick. On any field goal attempted and missed where the spot of the kick is on or inside the 20-yard line, ball will revert to defensive team at the 20-yard line.

**SAFETY**

1. The important factor in a safety is impetus. Two points are scored for the opposing team when the ball is dead on or behind a team's own goal line if the impetus came from a player on that team.

**Examples of Safety:**

(a) Blocked punt goes out of kicking team's end zone. Impetus was provided by punting team. The block only changes direction of ball, not impetus.
(b) Ball carrier retreats from field of play into his own end zone and is downed. Ball carrier provides impetus.
(c) Offensive team commits a foul and spot of enforcement is behind its own goal line.
(d) Player on receiving team muffs punt and, trying to get ball, forces or illegally kicks (creating new impetus) it into end zone where it goes out of the end zone or is recovered by a member of the receiving team in the end zone.

**Examples of Non-Safety:**

(a) Player intercepts a pass with both feet inbounds in the field of play and his momentum carries him into his own end zone. Ball is put in play at spot of interception.
(b) Player intercepts a pass in his own end zone and is downed in the end zone, even after recovering in the end zone. Impetus came from passing team, not from defense. (Touchback)
(c) Player passes from behind his own goal line. Opponent bats down ball in end zone. (Incomplete pass)

**MEASURING**

1. The forward point of the ball is used when measuring.

**POSITION OF PLAYERS AT SNAP**

1. Offensive team must have at least seven players on line.
2. Offensive players, not on line, must be at least one yard back at snap. **(Exception:** player who takes snap.)
3. No interior lineman may move after taking or simulating a three-point stance.
4. No player of either team may invade neutral zone before snap.
5. No player of offensive team may charge or move, after assuming set position, in such manner as to lead defense to believe snap has started.
6. If a player changes his eligibility, the Referee must alert the defensive captain after player has reported to him.
7. All players of offensive team must be stationary at snap, except one back who may be in motion parallel to scrimmage line or backward (not forward).
8. After a shift or huddle all players on offensive team must come to an absolute stop for at least one second with no movement of hands, feet, head, or swaying of body.
9. Quarterbacks can be called for a false start penalty (five yards) if their actions are judged to be an obvious attempt to draw an opponent offside.

**USE OF HANDS, ARMS, AND BODY**

1. No player on offense may assist a runner except by blocking for him. There shall be no interlocking interference.
2. A runner may ward off opponents with his hands and arms but no other player on offense may use hands or arms to obstruct an opponent by grasping with hands, pushing, or encircling any part of his body during a block. Hands (open

or closed) can be thrust forward to initially contact an opponent on or outside the opponent's frame, but the blocker must work to bring his hands on or inside the frame.

**Note:** Pass blocking: Hand(s) thrust forward that slip outside the body of the defender will be legal if blocker worked to bring them back inside. Hand(s) or arm(s) that encircle a defender—i.e., hook an opponent—are to be considered illegal and officials are to call a foul for holding.
Blocker cannot use his hands or arms to push from behind, hang onto, or encircle an opponent in a manner that restricts his movement as the play develops.

3. Hands cannot be thrust forward above the frame to contact an opponent on the neck, face or head.
   **Note:** The frame is defined as the part of the opponent's body below the neck that is presented to the blocker.
4. A defensive player may not tackle or hold an opponent other than a runner. Otherwise, he may use his hands, arms, or body only:
   (a) To defend or protect himself against an obstructing opponent.
   **Exception:** An eligible receiver is considered to be an obstructing opponent ONLY to a point five yards beyond the line of scrimmage unless the player who receives the snap clearly demonstrates no further intention to pass the ball. Within this five-yard zone, a defensive player may make contact with an eligible receiver that may be maintained as long as it is continuous and unbroken up until a point when the receiver is beyond the defender. The defensive player cannot use his hands or arms to push from behind, hang onto, or encircle an eligible receiver in a manner that restricts movement as the play develops. Beyond this five-yard limitation, a defender may use his hands or arms ONLY to defend or protect himself against impending contact caused by a receiver. In such reaction, the defender may not contact a receiver who attempts to take a path to evade him.
   (b) To push or pull opponent out of the way on line of scrimmage.
   (c) In actual attempt to get at or tackle runner.
   (d) To push or pull opponent out of the way in a legal attempt to recover a loose ball.
   (e) During a legal block on an opponent who is not an eligible pass receiver.
   (f) When legally blocking an eligible pass receiver above the waist.
   **Exception:** Eligible receivers lined up within two yards of the tackle, whether on or immediately behind the line, may be blocked below the waist at or behind the line of scrimmage. NO eligible receiver may be blocked below the waist after he goes beyond the line. (Illegal cut)
   **Note:** Once the quarterback hands off or pitches the ball to a back, or if the quarterback leaves the pocket area, the restrictions (illegal chuck, illegal cut) on the defensive team relative to the offensive receivers will end, provided the ball is not in the air.
5. A defensive player may not contact an opponent above the shoulders with the palm of his hand except to ward him off on the line. This exception is permitted only if it is not a repeated act against the same opponent during any one contact. In all other cases the palms may be used on head, neck, or face only to ward off or push an opponent in legal attempt to get at the ball.
6. Any offensive player who pretends to possess the ball or to whom a teammate pretends to give the ball may be tackled provided he is crossing his scrimmage line between the ends of a normal tight offensive line.
7. An offensive player who lines up more than two yards outside his own tackle or a player who, at the snap, is in a backfield position and subsequently takes a position more than two yards outside a tackle may not clip an opponent anywhere nor may he contact an opponent below the waist if the blocker is moving toward the ball and if contact is made within an area five yards on either side of the line.
8. A player of either team may block at any time provided it is not pass interference, fair catch interference, or unnecessary roughness.
9. A player may not bat or punch:
   (a) A loose ball (in field of play) toward his opponent's goal line or in any direction in either end zone.
   (b) A ball in player possession.
   **Note:** If there is any question as to whether a defender is stripping or batting a ball in player possession, the official(s) will rule the action as a legal act (stripping the ball).
   **Exception:** A forward or backward pass may be batted, tipped, or deflected in any direction at any time by either the offense or the defense.
   **Note:** A pass in flight that is controlled or caught may only be thrown backward, if it is thrown forward it is considered an illegal bat.
10. No player may deliberately kick any ball except as a punt, dropkick, or placekick.

### FORWARD PASS

1. A forward pass may be touched or caught by any eligible receiver. All members of the defensive team are eligible. Eligible receivers on the offensive team are players on either end of line (other than center, guard, or tackle) or players at least one yard behind the line at the snap. A T-formation quarterback is not eligible to receive a forward pass during a play from scrimmage.
   **Exception:** T-formation quarterback becomes eligible if pass is previously touched by an eligible receiver.
2. An offensive team may make only one forward pass during each play from scrimmage (Loss of down).
3. The passer must be behind his line of scrimmage (Loss of down and five yards, enforced from the spot of pass).
4. Any eligible offensive player may catch a forward pass. If a pass is touched by one offensive player and touched or caught by a second eligible offensive player, pass completion is legal. Further, all offensive players become eligible once a pass is touched by an eligible receiver or any defensive player.
5. The rules concerning a forward pass and ineligible receivers:
   (a) If ball is touched accidentally by an ineligible receiver on or behind his line: loss of down.
   (b) If ineligible receiver is illegally downfield: loss of five yards.
   (c) If touched or caught (intentionally or accidentally) by ineligible receiver beyond the line: loss of 10 yards or loss of down.
6. The player who first controls and continues to maintain control of a pass will be awarded the ball even though his opponent later establishes joint control of the ball.
7. Any forward pass becomes incomplete and ball is dead if:
   (a) Pass hits the ground or goes out of bounds.
   (b) Hits the goal post or the crossbar of either team.
   (c) Is caught by offensive player after touching ineligible receiver.
   (d) An illegal pass is caught by the passer.
8. A forward pass is complete when a receiver clearly possesses the pass and touches the ground with both feet inbounds while in possession of the ball. If a receiver would have landed inbounds with both feet but is carried or pushed out of bounds while maintaining possession of the ball, pass is complete at the out-of-bounds spot.
9. If an eligible receiver goes out of bounds accidentally or is forced out by a defender and returns to first touch and catch a pass, the play is regarded as a pass caught out of bounds. (Loss of down, no yardage.)
10. On a fourth down pass—when the offensive team is inside the opposition's 20-yard line—an incomplete pass results in a loss of down at the line of scrimmage.
11. If a personal foul is committed by the defense prior to the completion of a pass, the penalty is 15 yards from the spot where ball becomes dead.
12. If a personal foul is committed by the offense prior to the completion of a pass, the penalty is 15 yards from the previous line of scrimmage.

### INTENTIONAL GROUNDING OF FORWARD PASS

1. Intentional grounding of a forward pass is a foul: loss of down and 10 yards from previous spot if passer is in the field of play or loss of down at the spot of the foul if it occurs more than 10 yards behind the line or safety if passer is in his own end zone when ball is released.
2. Intentional grounding will be called when a passer, facing an imminent loss of yardage due to pressure from the defense, throws a forward pass without a realistic chance of completion.
3. Intentional grounding will not be called when a passer, while out of the pocket and facing an imminent loss of yardage, throws a pass that lands beyond the line of scrimmage, even if no offensive player(s) have a realistic chance to catch the ball (including if the ball lands out of bounds over the sideline or end line).

### PROTECTION OF PASSER

1. By interpretation, a pass begins when the passer—with possession of ball—starts to bring his hand forward. If ball strikes ground after this action has begun, play is ruled an incomplete pass. If passer loses control of ball prior to his bringing his hand forward, play is ruled a fumble.
2. No defensive player may run into a passer of a legal forward pass after the ball has left his hand (15 yards). The Referee must determine whether opponent had a reasonable chance to stop his momentum during an attempt to block the pass or tackle the passer while he still had the ball.
3. No defensive player who has an unrestricted path to the quarterback may hit him flagrantly in the area of the knee(s) when approaching in any direction.
4. Officials are to blow the play dead as soon as the quarterback is clearly in the grasp and control of any tackler, and his safety is in jeopardy.

### PASS INTERFERENCE

1. There shall be no interference with a forward pass thrown from behind the line. The restriction for the passing team starts with the snap. The restriction on the defensive team starts when the ball leaves the passer's hand. Both restrictions end when the ball is touched by anyone.
2. The penalty for defensive pass interference is an automatic first down at the spot of the foul. If interference is in the end zone, it is first down for the offense on the defense's 1-yard line. If previous spot was inside the defense's 1-yard line, penalty is half the distance to the goal line.
3. The penalty for offensive pass interference is 10 yards from the previous spot.
4. It is pass interference by either team when any player movement beyond the offensive line significantly hinders the progress of an eligible player or such player's opportunity to catch the ball during a legal forward pass. When players are competing for position to make a play on the ball, any contact by hands, arms or body shall be considered incidental unless prohibited. Prohibited conduct shall be when a player physically restricts or impedes the opponent in such a manner that is visually evident and materially affects the opponent's opportunity to gain position or retain his position to catch the ball. If a

player has gained position, he shall not be considered to have impeded or restricted his opponent in a prohibited manner if all of his actions are a bona fide effort to go to and catch the ball. Provided an eligible player is not interfered with in such a manner, the following exceptions to pass interference will prevail:

(a) If neither player is looking for the ball and there is incidental contact in the act of moving to the ball that does not materially affect the route of an eligible player, there is no interference. If there is any question whether the incidental contact materially affects the route, the ruling shall be no interference.
**Note:** Inadvertent tripping is not a foul in this situation.

(b) Any eligible player looking for and intent on playing the ball who initiates contact, however severe, while attempting to move to the spot of comple tion or interception will not be called for interference.

(c) Any eligible player who makes contact, however severe, with one or more eligible players while looking for and making a genuine attempt to catch or bat a reachable ball, will not be called for interference.

(d) It must be remembered that defensive players have as much right to the ball as offensive eligible receivers.

(e) Pass interference by the defense is not to be called when the forward pass is clearly uncatchable.

(f) Note: There is no defensive pass interference behind the line.

**BACKWARD PASS**

1. Any pass not forward is regarded as a backward pass or lateral. A pass parallel to the line is a backward pass. A runner may pass backward at any time. Any player on either team may catch the pass or recover the ball after it touches the ground.
2. A backward pass that strikes the ground can be recovered and advanced by either team.
3. A backward pass caught in the air can be advanced by either team.
4. A backward pass in flight may not be batted forward by an offensive player.

**FUMBLE**

1. The distinction between a fumble and a muff should be kept in mind in considering rules about fumbles. A fumble is the loss of possession of the ball. A muff is the touching of a loose ball by a player in an unsuccessful attempt to obtain possession.
2. A fumble may be advanced by any player on either team regardless of whether recovered before or after ball hits the ground.
3. A fumble that goes forward and out of bounds will return to the fumbling team at the spot of the fumble unless the ball goes out of bounds in the opponent's end zone. In this case, it is a touchback.
4. On a play from scrimmage, if an offensive player fumbles anywhere on the field during fourth down, only the fumbling player is permitted to recover and/or advance the ball. If any player fumbles after the two-minute warning in a half, only the fumbling player is permitted to recover and/or advance the ball. If recovered by any other offensive player, the ball is dead at the spot of the fumble unless it is recovered behind the spot of the fumble. In that case, the ball is dead at the spot of recovery. Any defensive player may recover and/or advance any fumble at any time.

**KICKS FROM SCRIMMAGE**

1. Any kick from scrimmage must be made from behind the line to be legal.
2. Any punt or missed field goal that touches a goal post is dead.
3. During a kick from scrimmage, only the end men, as eligible receivers on the line of scrimmage at the time of the snap, are permitted to go beyond the line before the ball is kicked.
**Exception:** An eligible receiver who, at the snap, is aligned or in motion behind the line and more than one yard outside the end man on his side of the line, clearly making him the outside receiver, replaces that end man as the player eligible to go downfield after the snap. All other members of the kicking team must remain at the line of scrimmage until the ball has been kicked.
4. Any punt that is blocked and does not cross the line of scrimmage can be recovered and advanced by either team. However, if offensive team recovers it must make the yardage necessary for its first down to retain possession if punt was on fourth down.
5. The kicking team may never advance its own kick even though legal recovery is made beyond the line of scrimmage. Possession only.
6. A member of the receiving team may not run into or rough a kicker who kicks from behind his line unless contact is:
(a) Incidental to and after he had touched ball in flight.
(b) Caused by kicker's own motions.
(c) Occurs during a quick kick, or a kick made after a run, or after kicker recovers a loose ball. Ball is loose when kicker muffs snap or snap hits ground.
(d) Defender is blocked into kicker.
The penalty for running into the kicker is 5 yards. For roughing the kicker: 15 yards, an automatic first down and disqualification if flagrant.
7. If a member of the kicking team attempting to down the ball on or inside opponent's 5-yard line carries the ball into the end zone, it is a touchback.
8. Fouls during a punt are enforced from the previous spot (line of scrimmage).
**Exception:** Illegal touching, illegal fair catch, invalid fair catch signal, and fouls by the receiving team during loose ball after ball is kicked.
9. While the ball is in the air or rolling on the ground following a punt or field goal attempt and receiving team commits a foul before gaining possession, receiving team will retain possession and will be penalized for its foul.
10. It will be illegal for a defensive player to jump or stand on any player, or be picked up by a teammate or to use a hand or hands on a teammate to gain additional height in an attempt to block a kick (Penalty: 15 yards, unsportsmanlike conduct).
11. A punted ball remains a kicked ball until it is declared dead or in possession of either team.
12. Any member of the punting team may down the ball anywhere in the field of play. However, it is illegal touching (Official's time out and receiver's ball at spot of illegal touching). This foul does not offset any foul by receivers during the down.
13. Defensive team may advance all kicks from scrimmage (including unsuccessful field goal) whether or not ball crosses defensive team's goal line. Rules pertaining to kicks from scrimmage apply until defensive team gains possession.

**FAIR CATCH**

1. The member of the receiving team must raise one arm a full length above his head and wave it from side to side while kick is in flight. (Failure to give proper sign: receivers' ball five yards behind spot of signal.) **Note:** It is legal for the receiver to shield his eyes from the sun by raising one hand no higher than the helmet.
2. No opponent may interfere with the fair catcher, the ball, or his path to the ball. Penalty: 15 yards from spot of foul and fair catch is awarded.
3. A player who signals for a fair catch is not required to catch the ball. However, if a player signals for a fair catch, he may not block or initiate contact with any player on the kicking team until the ball touches a player. Penalty: snap 15 yards behind spot of foul.
4. If ball hits ground or is touched by member of kicking team in flight, fair catch signal is off and all rules for a kicked ball apply.
5. Any undue advance by a fair catch receiver is delay of game. No specific distance is specified for undue advance as ball is dead at spot of catch. If player comes to a reasonable stop, no penalty. For violation, five yards.
6. If time expires while ball is in play and a fair catch is awarded, receiving team may choose to extend the period with one free kick down. However, placekicker may not use tee.

**FOUL ON LAST PLAY OF HALF OR GAME**

1. On a foul by defense on last play of half or game, the down is replayed if penalty is accepted.
2. On a foul by the offense on last play of half or game, the down is not replayed and the play in which the foul is committed is nullified.
**Exception:** Fair catch interference, foul following change of possession, illegal touching. No score by offense counts.
3. On double foul on last play of half or game, down is replayed.

**SPOT OF ENFORCEMENT OF FOUL**

1. There are four basic spots at which a penalty for a foul is enforced:
(a) Spot of foul: The spot where the foul is committed.
(b) Previous spot: The spot where the ball was put in play.
(c) Spot of snap, pass, fumble, return kick, or free kick: The spot where the act connected with the foul occurred.
(d) Succeeding spot: The spot where the ball next would be put in play if no distance penalty were to be enforced.
**Exception:** If foul occurs after a touchdown and before the whistle for a try-for-point, succeeding spot is spot of next kickoff.
2. All fouls committed by offensive team behind the line of scrimmage and in the field of play shall be penalized from the previous spot.
3. When spot of enforcement for fouls involving defensive holding or illegal use of hands by the defense is behind the line of scrimmage, any penalty yardage to be assessed on that play shall be measured from the line if the foul occurred beyond the line.

**DOUBLE FOUL**

1. If there is a double foul during a down in which there is a change of possession, the team last gaining possession may keep the ball unless its foul was committed prior to the change of possession.
2. If double foul occurs after a change of possession, the defensive team retains the ball at the spot of its foul or dead ball spot.
3. If one of the fouls of a double foul involves disqualification, that player must be removed, but no penalty yardage is to be assessed.
4. If the kickers foul during a kick before possession changes and the receivers foul after possession changes, the receivers will retain the ball after enforcement of its foul.

**PENALTY ENFORCED ON FOLLOWING KICKOFF**

1. When a team scores by touchdown, field goal, extra point, or safety and either team commits a personal foul, unsportsmanlike conduct, or obvious unfair act during the down, the penalty will be assessed on the following kickoff.

**PROCEDURES TO TERMINATE OR TEMPORARILY DELAY COMPLETION OF A GAME**

The National Football League holds to the position that all games should be played to their conclusion. However, if in the opinion of appropriate League authorities, it is impossible to begin or continue a game due to an emergency, or a game is deemed to be imminently threatened by any such emergency—e.g., severely inclement weather, lightning, flooding, power failure, interference by spectators, or other non-participants—then the following procedures will serve as guidelines for the Commissioner and/or his duly appointed representatives. The Commissioner will have the power to review the circumstances of each emergency and to adjust the following procedures in whatever manner he deems appropriate. If, in the Commissioner's opinion, it is reasonable to project that the resumption of an interrupted game would not change its ultimate result, he will be empowered to terminate the game.

1. The League employees vested with the authority to define emergencies under these procedures are the Commissioner, his representatives, and the game Referee. In cases where neither the Commissioner nor his representatives are present, the Referee shall have sole authority, but he must make every effort to contact the Commissioner or representative for consultation. In all cases of significant delay, the League authorities will consult with the management of the participating clubs.
2. If, due to an emergency, a regular-season or postseason game is not started at its scheduled time and cannot be played at any later time that same day, the game, nevertheless, must be played on a subsequent date to be determined by the Commissioner.
3. If there is deemed to be a threat of an emergency (e.g., incoming tropical storm) that may occur during the playing of a game, the starting time of such game will not be moved to an earlier time unless there is clearly sufficient time to make an orderly change.
4. If an interrupted regular-season or postseason game cannot be completed on the same day, such game will be rescheduled by the Commissioner and resumed at that point.
5. In instances which require the Commissioner to reschedule a regular-season game, he will make every effort to set the game for no later than two days after its originally scheduled date, and if possible, at its original site. If unable to do so, he will schedule it at the nearest available facility. If it is impossible to schedule the game within two days after its original date, the Commissioner will attempt to schedule it on the Tuesday of the next calendar week in which the two involved clubs play other clubs no earlier than Sunday.
6. If an emergency interrupts a postseason game and such game cannot be resumed on that same date, the Commissioner will make every effort to arrange for its completion as soon as possible. If unable to schedule the game at the same site, he will select an appropriate alternate site. He will terminate the game short of completion only if in his judgment the continuation of the game would not be normally expected to alter the ultimate outcome.
7. In all instances where a game is resumed after interruption, the resumption will begin at the point at which the game was interrupted. The referee will call time out when it is necessary to declare an emergency interruption, and he will make a record of the team possessing the ball, position of the ball on the field, down, distance, time remaining in the period, and any other pertinent information required for an efficient and equitable resumption of play.

**Note:** In recent history, only two games, both preseason, have been terminated. In 1976, the Chicago College All-Star game was terminated due to thunderstorms with the Steelers leading the All-Stars 24-0, and the 1980 Pro Football Hall of Fame Game at Canton, Ohio, was called with 5:29 remaining due to severe thunder and lightning with the Chargers and Packers tied 0-0.

## NOTES

## NOTES

## NOTES